THE 1987-88 JEWISH ALMANAC

THE 1987-88 JEWISH ALMANAC

Compiled and Edited by

IVAN L. TILLEM

PACIFIC PRESS
NEW YORK

ACKNOWLEDGMENTS

• *The Things They Say Behind Your Back: Stereotypes and the Myths Behind Them* by William B. Helmreich. Copyright © William B. Helmreich. Reprinted by permission of Doubleday and Co., Inc. • *Israel in Statistics.* Reprinted from *Statistical Abstract of Israel.* Copyright © 1986. The State of Israel, Central Bureau of Statistics. Reprinted by permission • *Israel Law Digest* by Yaacov Salomon, Lipschutz & Co., advocates of Haifa and Tel Aviv, excerpted from 1986 *Martindale-Hubbell Law Directory,* Volume VII. Courtesy Martindale-Hubbell, Inc., George E. Krauss, Executive Vice President • *Why Do the Jews Need a Land of Their Own?,* by Sholom Aleichem, from *Why Do the Jews Need a Land of Their Own?,* by Sholom Aleichem, translated by Joseph Leftwich and Mordecai S. Chertoff, Copyright © 1984 by Beth Shalom-Aleichem, Tel Aviv. Reprinted by permission. • *Page One* Copyright © The New York Times Company. Reprinted by permission • *Chronological Chart of Jewish History* and *Calendars 1987-2001* Copyright © Keter Publishing Company, Jerusalem. Reprinted by permission. • *Page One* Copyright © *The Jerusalem Post.* Reprinted by permission. • *Page One* Copyright © *Maariv.* Reprinted by permission • *What's it Like to Be Jewish, Black and the Law in a Southern City?* by Phil Jacobs, Copyright © *Baltimore Jewish Times.* Reprinted by permission • *"That Marvellous Movement": Early Black Views of Zionism,* excerpted from *Israel in the Black American Perspective* by Robert G. Weisbord and Richard Kazarian, Jr. Copyright © 1985 Greenwood Press. Reprinted by permission • *How* Hatikvah *Became the National Anthem of Israel* by Eliahu Ha-Cohen. Courtesy Zionist Archives, New York. • *Aliyah: "If Not Now, When?"* by Peter David Hornik, appeared originally in the May 1983 issue of *Midstream.* Copyright © World Zionist Organization. Reprinted by permission • *Jewish Religious Considerations in Artificial Insemination, In Vitro Fertilization, and Surrogate Motherhood* by Dr. Fred Rosner. Copyright © 1984 by B.C. Decker Incorporated. Reprinted by permission • *Jewish Perspectives on Issues of Death and Dying* by Dr. Fred Rosner. Copyright © 1986 *The Journal of Halacha and Contemporary Society.* Reprinted by permission • *The Babirusa: A Kosher Pig?* by J. David Bleich appeared originally in *Tradition,* 21(4), Fall 1985. Copyright © 1985 Rabbinical Council of America. Reprinted by permission • Note: Every effort has been made to locate the copyright owners of material reproduced in this book. Omissions brought to our attention will be corrected in subsequent editions.

ABOUT THE COVER

Illustration by Lynn Cutler.

Design by Sara Jaskiel of The Goldmark Group, New York, N.Y.

PHOTO CREDITS

Ethiopian Jewry: Ruth Gruber, Neal Schnall, NACOEJ mission • *What's it Like to be Jewish, Black and the Law in a Southern City?:* Craig Terkowitz, *Baltimore Jewish Times* • *The Jews of China:* Anson Laytner, Wendy Abraham, Betsy Gidwitz • *Hollywood's Image of the Jew:* Phototeque, New York, N.Y. • other photos courtesy the respective contributors.

ISBN 0-915399-04-0 Hardcover
ISBN 0-915399-03-2 Softcover

Manufactured in the United States of America

TABLE OF CONTENTS

TABLE OF CONTENTS

The Jewish Directory and Almanac
(published Spring 1984)

Copies are available @ $11.95, from:

PACIFIC PRESS
295 MADISON AVENUE, SUITE 1228
NEW YORK, N.Y. 10017
(212) 687-0500

TABLE OF CONTENTS

The 1986 Jewish Directory and Almanac

Copies are available @ $14.95 softcover, $24.95 hardcover, from:

PACIFIC PRESS
295 MADISON AVENUE, SUITE 1228
NEW YORK, N.Y. 10017
(212) 687-0500

TABLE OF CONTENTS

Preface

The job of a journalist, Mark Twain said, is to make people read something they are not interested in. I knew, when I began editing the public issues to be included in the Almanac, that many people have little interest in critical public affairs. Therefore, I included in the Almanac diverse lists, tables, charts and graphics in the areas of history, biography, filmography, sports, etc., so that the most casual reader would be attracted to the volume. The hope was that the reader would turn from the pages of this secondary material to the more substantive articles, and further, that once stirred by the stark realities presented therein, the reader would consult the Yellow Pages at the back of the volume to locate a conduit to involvement.

As Sholom Aleichem challenged, "Stop a Jew there, in the street or in the synagogue, and put the question to him—Excuse me, Mister Jew, what is your ideal?"

By what are we characterized? As people who keep the Sabbath? People who eat matzo at Passover, hamantashen at Purim and honey at the New Year? Is that all there is?

Is there a Jewish philosophy of life? Justice Louis D. Brandeis suggested such in uncommon eloquence. "Some men buy diamonds and rare works of art, others delight in automobiles and yachts. My luxury is to invest my surplus effort, beyond that required for the proper support of my family, to the pleasure of taking up a problem and solving, or helping to solve it, for the people without receiving any compensation. . . . I have only one life, and it is short enough. Why waste it on things I don't want most? I don't want money or property most. I want to be free."

What is a *mitzvah*?

The quantum of hunger, despair, homelessness, blindness, deprivation, enslavement and hopelessness exists in a relative specific quota to the tranquility, order and privilege in this world. Diminishing that quantum, anywhere in the world, in any way, is a *mitzvah*. Reduction of that ratio creates a positive benefit to the balance of the world. That is *tikkun haolam*—repairing the world, for the world can and should be different than it is.

However, *mitzvot* must never become mere physical acts, devoid of inspiration or ethical significance. *Na'aseh v'nishmah* should not be confused with instinctual obedience replacing thoughtful devotion.

Consider the bridge of Jewish history that spans the end of the Second Commonwealth to this century. For nearly 1900 years, following the destruction of Jerusalem in 70 C.E., most of the world's Jews lived in constant fear of the dominant host societies into which the *galut* had carried them. In this life of migration, poverty, persecution and statelessness, the Jews could not engage in "repairing" the world. The twentieth century, however, has afforded the greatest opportunity to the Jewish people. In 1948, Jews achieved the dream of a homeland; in subsequent battles, that dream was affirmed. In the free world, Jews enjoy unprecedented civil liberties and material comfort. Thus, we have successfully bridged that 1900-year exile. But mere survival has not been our greatest challenge. Relevance and the quality of our lives are the challenges.

Every generation, indeed every individual, has special and unique *mitzvah* opportunities. This epoch however, is the greatest opportunity of the Jewish people—the period of our national renaissance. History may not give the Jewish people another chance. What are we doing to take part in this great opportunity to contribute to *tikkun haolam* in ways that our parents, our grandparents and scores of generations before could not?

The idea of "chosenness" does not mean that Jews are good and Gentiles are evil, as the story of Jonah reminds us every Yom Kippur. Rather, chosenness signifies duty to "repair the world under the kingdom of God." Simply put, it is the responsibility of the Jew to fix what is broken, whenever crisis or need may confront him.

Perhaps Jewish responsibility can be summarized best by a single anecdote. Rabbi Israel Salanter was attending a festive occasion and was about to wash his hands preparatory to the meal. The gentleman on line ahead of him carefully washed his hands, pouring a generous jugful of water on each hand three times, then carefully dried his hands and recited the blessing. Rabbi Israel followed the procedure, using only a minute quantity of water. A curious onlooker asked the rabbi why, if washing the hands were a significant precept, he used so little water. Rabbi Israel replied that he noticed that the water supply was carried by a solitary, exhausted watercarrier. He would not be righteous on the weight of her back. "A person should be more concerned with spiritual than material matters, but another person's material welfare is *his* own spiritual concern."

Man was created *b'tzelem elokim*—in the image of God. God created the world *ex nihilo*—something from nothing, from a vacuum. What does this portend to us?

The Book of Genesis records that Joseph demonstrated to Pharaoh that impending drought need not inevitably lead to famine. Because man has the quality of *tzelem elokim*, he too can create *ex nihilo*—as Joseph discovered, in every malady the cure can be found. This principle has application not only to agriculture, but to any natural calamity; it applies to the Holocaust and to all the various social issues detailed in this volume.

Judaism cannot be summarized in any volume, nor can it be reduced to any set of volumes. This series of almanacs merely seeks to provide sample information, sample thoughts and sources to dig deeper. If this series would encourage further inquiry into Jewish affairs and communal issues, it would have done well.

I thank Falene Schuff, who coordinated the staff; I thank Solomon Swimer and his associates who typeset the text, and I thank The Goldmark Group—Eugene Markowitz and Joseph Goldbrenner—who managed and oversaw the technical aspects of production and design.

Finally, I thank my teachers, colleagues and students at Yeshiva University, whose participation and encouragement helped enable me to bring this project to its fruition.

Ivan L. Tillem
New York, N.Y.
September 1987

For my dear friend and counsel
Mrs. Esther Zuroff

1

About Jews

And Israel shall be a proverb and a by-word among all people.
1 *Kings,* 9:7.

By the rivers of Babylon, there we sat down, yea, we wept, when we remembered Zion.
We hanged our harps upon the willows in the midst thereof.
For there they that carried us away captive required of us a song; and they that wasted us required of us mirth, saying, Sing us one of the songs of Zion.
How shall we sing the Lord's song in a strange land?
If I forget thee, O Jerusalem, let my right hand forget her cunning.
If I do not remember thee, let my tongue cleave to the roof of my mouth; if I prefer not Jerusalem above my chief joy.
Remember, O Lord, the children of Edom in the day of Jerusalem; who said, Raze it, raze it, even to the foundation thereof.
O daughter of Babylon, who art to be destroyed; happy shall he be, that rewardeth thee as thou hast served us.
Happy shall he be, that taketh and dasheth thy little ones against the stones.
Psalms 137:1-9

Salvation is from the Jews.
Proverbs, 11:14. (Salus ex Judaeis.—*Vulgate.)*

Behold an Israelite indeed, in whom is no guile!
New Testament: John, 1:47. Jesus, referring to Nathanael.

The unbelieving Jews.
New Testament: Acts, 14:2

A race prone to superstition, opposed to religion.
Cornelius Tacitus, *Annals,* (c. 115 C.E.), Ch. II

The Jews have purely mental conceptions of Deity, as one in essence. They call those profane who make representations of God in human shape out of perishable materials. They believe that Being to be supreme and eternal, neither capable of representation, nor of decay. They therefore do not allow any images to stand in their cities, much less in their temples. This flattery is not paid to their kings, nor this honour to our Emperors. From the fact, however, that their priests used to chant to music of flutes and cymbals, and to wear garlands of ivy, and that a golden vine was found in the temple, some have thought that they worshipped Father Liber, the conqueror of the East, though their institutions do not by any means harmonize with the theory; for Liber established a festive and cheerful worship, while the Jewish religion is tasteless and mean.
Tacitus, *Histories,* V, 5

Without the mad rites of Mars and Bellona they [the Jews] carried on war, and while, indeed, they did not conquer without victory, yet they did not hold it to be a goddess, but the gift of their God. Without Segetia they had harvests; without Bubona, oxen; honey without Mellona; apples without Pomona; and, in a word, everything for which the Romans thought they must supplicate so great a crowd of false gods, they received much more happily from the one true God. And if they had not sinned against Him with impious curiosity, which seduced them like magic arts, and drew them to strange gods and idols, and at last led them to kill Christ, their kingdom would have remained to them and would have been, if not more spacious, yet more happy than that of Rome. And now that they are dispersed through almost all lands and nations, it is through the providence of that one true God; that whereas the images, altars, groves, and temples of the false gods are everywhere overthrown, and their sacrifices prohibited, it may be shown from their books how this has been foretold by their prophets so long before.
Augustine (354-430), *City of God,* IV, 34

Jews, like the fratricide Cain, are doomed to wander about the earth as fugitives and vagabonds, and their faces must be covered with shame. They are . . to be condemned to serfdom.
Pope Innocent, letter to Count Nevers, 1208

We decree and order that from now on, and for all time, Christians shall not eat or drink with Jews, nor admit them to feasts, nor cohabit with them, nor bathe with them.
Christians shall not allow Jews to hold civil honors over Christians, or to exercise public offices in the state.
Pope Eugenius IV, decree, 1442

We order that each and every Jew of both sexes in our temporal domain, and in all the cities, lands, places and baronies subject to them, shall depart completely out of the confines thereof within the space of three months and after these letters have been made public.
Pope Pius IV, decree, issued posthumously, 1565

Have mercy upon all Jews, Turks, Infidels, and Heretics.
Book of Common Prayer; Good Friday

A hopeless faith, a homeless race,
yet seeking the most holy place,
And owning the true bliss. . . .
Or like pale ghosts that darkling roam,
Hovering around their ancient home,
But find no refuge there.
John Keble, *The Christian Year: Fifth Sunday in Lent*

The Jews are the most miserable people on earth. They are plagued everywhere, and scattered about all countries, having no certain resting place. They sit as on a wheelbarrow, without a country, people or government . . . but they are rightly served, for seeing they refused to have Christ and his gospel, instead of freedom they must have servitude.
Martin Luther, *Table Talk,* DCCCLII (published 1569)

Either God must be unjust, or you, Jews, wicked and ungodly. You have been, about fifteen hundred years, a race rejected of God.

Martin Luther, *Table Talk,* DCCCLXI

They [the Jews] are, as it were, the first-born in the family of God.

John Calvin, *Institutes of the Christian Religion* (1536), IV, 16

Who hateth me but for my happiness?
Or who is honoured now but for his wealth?
Rather had I, a Jew, be hated thus,
Than pitied in a Christian poverty.

Christopher Marlowe, *The Jew of Malta* (1589), I, i

To undo a Jew is charity, and not sin.

Christopher Marlowe, *The Jew of Malta,* IV, vi

It is curious to see a superstition dying out. The idea of a Jew (which our pious ancestors held in horror) has nothing in it now revolting. We have found the claws of the beast, and pared its nails, and now we take it to our arms, fondle it, write plays to flatter it: it is visited by princes, affects a taste, patronizes the arts, and is the only liberal and gentleman-like thing in Christendom.

Charles Lamb (1808),
Specimens of the English Dramatic Poets: Marlowe's Rich Jew of Malta

As dear as a Jew's eye.

Gabriel Harvey, *Works,* ii, 146 (1593)

Still have I borne it with a patient shrug,
For sufferance is the badge of all our tribe.
You call me misbeliever, cut-throat dog,
And spit upon my Jewish gabardine.

William Shakespeare, *The Merchant of Venice* (1597), I, iii, 110

I'll seal to such a bond,
And say there is much kindness in the
Jew.

William Shakespeare, *The Merchant of Venice*, I, III, 153

There will come a Christian by
Will be worth a Jewess' eye.

William Shakespeare, *The Merchant of Venice,* II, v, 43

Shylock
He hath . . . laughed at my losses, mocked at my gains, scorned my nation, thwarted my bargains, cooled my friends, heated mine enemies; and what's his reason? I am a Jew.

William Shakespeare, *The Merchant of Venice,* III, i, 58

Shylock
I am a Jew. Hath not a Jew eyes? Hath not a Jew hands, organs, dimensions, senses, affection, passions? fed with the same food, hurt with the same weapons, subject to the same diseases, healed by the same means, warmed and cooled by the same winter and summer, as a Christian is? If you prick us, do we not bleed? if you tickle us, do we not laugh? if you poison us, do we not die? and if you worng us, shall we not revenge? If we are like you in the rest, we will resemble you in that. If a Jew wrong a Christian, what is his humility? Revenge. If a Christian wrong a Jew, what should his sufferance be by Christian example? Why, revenge.

William Shakespeare, *Merchant of Venice,* III, i, 60

I pray you, think you question with the
Jew:
You may as well go stand upon the beach
And bid the main flood bate his usual height;
You may as well use question with the wolf
Why he hath made the ewe bleat for the lamb;
You may as well forbid the mountain pines
To wag their high tops, and to make no noise,
When they are fretten with the gusts of heaven;
You may as well do any thing most hard,
As seek to soften that—than which what's
harder?—
His Jewish heart.

William Shakespeare, *The Merchant of Venice,* IV, i, 70

I am a Jew else, an Ebrew Jew.

William Shakespeare, *I Henry IV* (1598), II, iv, 198

I took by the throat the circumcised dog,
And smote him, thus.

William Shakespeare, *Othello* (1604), V, ii, 355

I believe there are few
But have heard of a Jew
Named Shylock, of Venice, as arrant a screw
In money transactions as ever you knew.

R.H. Barham, *The Merchant of Venice*

It is not unremarkable what *Philo* first observed, that the law of *Moses* continued two thousand years without the least alteration; whereas, we see, the Laws of other Commonweals do alter with occasions.

Sir Thomas Browne, *Reglio Medici* (1643), I, 23

The Jew is obstinate in all fortunes; the persecution of fifteen hundred years hath but confirmed them in their Errour: they have already endured whatsoever may be inflicted, and have suffered, in a bad cause, even to the condemnation of their enemies.

Sir Thomas Browne, *Religio Medici,* I, 25

The carnal Jews hold a middle place between the Christians and the pagans. The pagans do not know God, and love only the earth. The Christians know the true God, and do not love the earth.

If there is a God, He is infinitely incomprehensible, having neither parts nor limits. He has no relation to us. We are therefore incapable of knowing what He is, or whether He is. This being so, who will dare to solve the problem? Not we, who have no relation to Him.

You must wager. . . . Which will you choose? . . Let us weigh the gain and loss in calling "heads" that God is. Let us weigh the two cases: if you win, you win all; if you lose, you lose nothing. Wager then unhesitatingly that He is.

Blaise Pascal (1623-1662), *Pensees,* 289, 418

To give faith to the Messiah, it was necessary there should have been precedent prophecies, and that these should be conveyed by persons above suspicion, diligent, faithful, unusually zealous, and known to all the world.

To accomplish all this, God chose this carnal people, to whom He entrusted the prophecies which foretell the Messiah as a deliverer and as a dispenser of those carnal goods which this people loved. And thus they have had an extraordinary passion for their prophets and, in sight of the whole world, have had charge of these books which foretell their Messiah, assuring all nations that He should come and in the way foretold in the books, which they held open to the whole world. Yet this people, deceived by the poor and ignominious advent of the Messiah, have been His most cruel enemies. So that they, the people least open to suspicion in the world of favouring us, the most strict and most zealous that can be named for their law and their prophets, have kept the books incorrupt. Hence those who have rejected and crucified Jesus Christ, who has been to them an offence, are those who have charge of the books which testify of Him and state that He will be an offence and rejected. Therefore they have shown it was He by rejecting Him and He has been alike proved both by the righteous Jews who received Him and by the unrighteous who rejected Him, both facts having been foretold.

Wherefore the prophecies have a hidden and spiritual meaning to which this people were hostile, under the carnal meaning which they loved. If the spiritual meaning had been revealed, they would not have loved it, and, unable to bear it, they would not have been zealous of the preservation of their books and their ceremonies; and if they had loved these spiritual promises, and had preserved them incorrupt till the time of the Messiah, their testimony would have had no force, because they had been his friends.

Therefore it was well that the spiritual meaning should be concealed; but, on the other hand, if this meaning had been so hidden as not to appear at all, it could not have served as a proof of the Messiah. What then was done? In a crowd of passages it has been hidden under the temporal meaning, and in a few has been clearly revealed; besides that, the time and the state of the world have been so clearly foretold that it is clearer than the sun. And in some places this spiritual meaning is so clearly expressed that it would require a blindness, like that which the flesh imposes on the spirit when it is subdued by it, not to recognise it.

See, then, what has been the prudence of God. This meaning is concealed under another in an infinite number of passages, and in some, though rarely, it is revealed; but yet so that the passages in which it is concealed are equivocal and can suit both meanings; whereas the passages where it is disclosed are unequivocal and can only suit the spiritual meaning.

So that this cannot lead us into error and could only be misunderstood by so carnal a people.

For when blessings are promised in abundance, what was to prevent them from understanding the true blessings, but their covetousness, which limited the meaning to worldly goods? But those whose only good was in God referred them to God alone. For there are two principles, which divide the wills of men, covetousness and charity. Not that covetousness cannot exist along with faith in God, nor charity with worldly riches, but covetousness uses God and enjoys the world, and charity is the opposite.

Now the ultimate end gives names to things. All which prevents us from attaining it is called an enemy to us. Thus the creatures, however good, are the enemies of the righteous, when they turn them away from God, and God Himself is the enemy of those whose covetousness He confounds.

Blaise Pascal, *Pensees,* VIII, 571

The Jewish religion is wholly divine in its authority, its duration, its perpetuity, its morality, its doctrine, and its effects.

Blaise Pascal, *Pensees,* IX, 603

The religion of the Jews seemed to consist essentially in the fatherhood of Abraham, in circumcision, in sacrifices, in ceremonies, in the Ark, in the Temple, in Jerusalem, and, finally, in the law, and in the covenant with Moses.

I say that it consisted in none of those things, but only in the love of God, and that God disregarded all the other things.

Blaise Pascal, *Pensees,* IX, 610

Michael. God from the Mount of *Sinai,* whose gray top
Shall tremble, He descending, will Himself
In Thunder Lightning and loud Trumpets sound
Ordaine them Lawes; part such as appertaine
To civil Justice, part religious Rites
Of sacrifice, informing them, by types
And shadowes, of that destind seed to bruise
The Serpent, by what meanes he shall achieve
Mankind's deliverance. But the voice of God
To mortal eare is dreadful; they beseech
That *Moses* might report to them his will,
And terror cease; he grants them their desire,
Instructed that to God is no access
Without mediator, whose high Office now
Moses in figure beares, to introduce
One greater, of whose day he shall foretell,
And all the Prophets in thir Age, the times
Of great *Messiah* shall sing. Thus Laws and Rites
Establisht, such delight hath God in Men
Obedient to His will, that He vouchsafes
Among them to set up His Tabernacle,
The holy One with mortal Men to dwell:
By His prescript a Sanctuary is fram'd
Of Cedar, overlaid with Gold, therein
An Ark, and in the Ark His Testimony,
The Records of his Cov'nant, over these
A Mercie-seat of Gold between the wings
Of two bright Cherubim, before him burn
Seaven Lamps as in a Zodiac representing
The heav'nly fires; over the Tent a Cloud
Shall rest by Day, a fierie gleame by Night,
Save when they journie, and at length they come,
Conducted by his Angel to the Land
Promisd to *Abraham* and his Seed: the rest
Were long to tell, how many Battels fought,
How many Kings destroyed, and Kingdoms won,
Or how the Sun shall in mid Heav'n stand still
A day entire, and Nights due course adjourne,
Man's voice commanding, Sun in *Gibeon* stand,
And thou Moon in the vale of *Aialon,*
Till *Israel* overcome; so call the third
From *Abraham,* Son of *Issac,* and from him
His whole descent, who thus shall *Canaan* win.

John Milton, *Paradise Lost* (1667), XII, 227

The Jews, a headstrong, moody, murmuring race
As ever tried the extent and stretch of grace,
God's pampered people, whom, debauched with ease,
No king could govern nor no God could please.

John Dryden (1631-1700),
Absalom and Achitophel, pt. i, l. 45

A people still, whose common ties are gone;
Who, mixed with every race, are lost in none.

George Crabbe, *The Borough,* Letter 4

This is the Jew
That Shakespeare drew.

Attributed to Pope, after a performance of Shylock
by Charles Macklin, 14 Feb., 1741.
(*Biographica Dramatica,* Vol. i, pt. 2, p. 469.)

Even a cursory perusal will show us that the only respects in which the Hebrews surpassed other nations, are in their successful conduct of matters relating to government, and in their surmounting great perils solely by God's external aid; in other ways they were on a par with their fellows, and God was equally gracious to all.

Baruch Spinoza (1632-1677), *Theologico-Political Treatise,* III

The king of any country is the public person, or representative of all his own subjects. And God the king of Israel was the *Holy One* of Israel. The nation which is subject to one earthly sovereign is the nation of that sovereign, that is, of the public person. So the Jews, who were God's nation, were called *a holy nation.* For by *holy* is always understood either God Himself or that which is God's in propriety; as by *public* is always meant either the person of the Commonwealth itself, or something that is so the Commonwealth's as no private person can claim any propriety therein.

Therefore the Sabbath (God's day) is a *holy day;* the Temple (God's house), a *holy house;* sacrifices, tithes, and offerings (God's tribute), *holy duties;* priests, prophets, and anointed kings, under Christ (God's ministers), *holy men;* the celestial ministering spirits (God's messengers), *holy angels;* and the like; and wheresoever the word *holy* is taken properly, there is still something signified of propriety gotten by consent. In saying "Hallowed be Thy name," we do but pray to God for grace to keep the first Commandment of having no other Gods but Him. Mankind is God's nation in propriety; but the Jews only were a *holy nation.* Why, but because they became his propriety by covenant?

Thomas Hobbes, *Leviathan* (1651), III, 35

Auto de Fe: An act of faith. A dainty feast offered to the Divinity from time to time, and which consisted of roasting, in great pomp, the bodies of Jews or heretics for the salvation of their souls and the edification of the lookers-on.

Voltaire (1694-1778), *Auto de Fe*

Jews: A nation full of amenity and composed of lepers, misers, usurers, and scurvy rogues whom the God of the universe, delighted with their shining qualities, in former days fell in love with.

Voltaire, *Jews*

If the God who guided the Jews wanted to give them a good land, if these unhappy people had actually lived in Egypt, why didn't he leave them in Egypt? The only answers to this question are theological phrases.

Voltaire, *Philosophical Dictionary:* Judea

If it were permitted to reason consistently in religious matters, it is clear that we all ought to become Jews, because Jesus Christ our Saviour was born a Jew, lived a Jew, died a Jew, and that he said expressly that he was accomplishing, that he was fulfilling the Jewish religion.

Voltaire, *Philosophical Dictionary:* Tolerance

The Jews, who, under the Assyrian and Persian monarchies, had languished for many ages the most despised portion of their slaves, emerged from obscurity under the successors of Alexander; and as they multiplied to a surprising degree in the East, and afterwards in the West, they soon excited the curiosity and wonder of other nations. The sullen obstinacy with which they maintained their peculiar rites and unsocial manners seemed to mark them out a distinct species of men, who boldly professed, or who faintly disguised, their implacable hatred to the rest of humankind. Neither the violence of Antiochus, nor the arts of Herod, nor the example of the circumjacent nations, could ever persuade the Jews to associate with the institutions of Moses the elegant mythology of the Greeks. According to the maxims of universal toleration, the Romans protected a superstition which they despised. The polite Augustus condescended to give orders that sacrifices should be offered for his prosperity in the temple of Jerusalem; while the meanest of the posterity of Abraham, who should have paid the same homage to the Jupiter of the Capitol, would have been an object of abhorrence to himself and to his brethren. But the moderation of the conquerors was insufficient to appease the jealous prejudices of their subjects, who were alarmed and scandalized at the ensigns of paganism, which necessarily introduced themselves into a Roman province. The mad attempt of Caligula to place his own statue in the temple of Jerusalem was defeated by the unanimous resolution of a people who dreaded death much less than such an idolatrous profanation. Their attachment to the law of Moses was equal to their detestation of foreign religions. The current of zeal and devotion, as it was contracted into a narrow channel, ran with the strength, and sometimes with the fury, of a torrent.

Edward Gibbon, *Decline and Fall of the Roman Empire* (completed 1788), XV

The devout and even scrupulous attachment to the Mosaic religion, so conspicuous among the Jews who lived under the second temple, becomes still more surprising if it is compared with the stubborn incredulity of their forefathers. When the law was given in thunder from Mount Sinai; when the tides of the ocean and the course of the planets were suspended for the convenience of the Israelites; and when temporal rewards and punishments were the immediate consequences of their piety or disobedience, they perpetually relapsed into rebellion against the visible majesty of their Divine King, placed the idols of the nations in the sanctuary of Jehovah, and imitated every fantastic ceremony that was practised in the tents of the Arabs, or in the cities of Pheonicia.

Edward Gibbon, *Decline and Fall of the Roman Empire,* XV

It is the boast of the Jewish apologists, that, while the learned nations of antiquity were deluded by the fables of polytheism, their simple ancestors of Palestine preserved the knowledge and worship of the true God. The moral attributes of Jehovah may not easily be reconciled with the standard of *human* virtue: his metaphysical qualities are darkly expressed; but each page of the Pentateuch and the Prophets is an evidence of his power: the unity of his name is inscribed on the first table of the law; and his sanctuary was never defiled by any visible image of the invisible essence.

Edward Gibbon, *Decline and Fall of the Roman Empire,* L

Sound the loud timbrel o'er Egypt's dark sea!
Jehovah has triumph'd—His people are free.

Thomas Moore (1779-1852), *Sound the Loud Timbrel*

The God of the Jewish people is the God only of Abraham and of his seed: national individuality and a special local worship are involved in such a conception of deity. Before him all other gods are false: moreover, the distinction between "true" and "false" is quite abstract; for as regards the false gods, not a ray of the divine is supposed to shine into them. But every form of spiritual force, and *a fortiori* every religion is of such a nature, that whatever be its peculiar character, an affirmative element is necessarily contained in it. However erroneous a religion may be, it possesses truth, although in a mutilated phase. In every religion there is a divine presence, a divine relation; and a philosophy of history has to seek out the spiritual element even in the most imperfect forms. But it does not follow that because it is a religion, it is therefore *good.* We must not fall into the lax conception that the content is of no importance but only the form. This latitudinarian tolerance the Jewish religion does not admit, being absolutely exclusive.

George Wilhelm Friedrich Hegel (1770-1831),
Philosophy of History, Pt. I, III, 3

The fundamental characteristics of the Jewish religion are realism and optimism, views of the world which are closely allied; they form, in fact, the conditions of theism. For theism looks upon the material world as absolutely real, and regards life as a pleasant gift bestowed upon us.

Arthur Schopenhauer (1788-1860), *Christian System*

No Jew can ever believe in the divinity of another Jew.

Heinrich Heine (1787-1856),
Gedanken und Einfalle, Vol. 10

I see now that the Greeks were only beautiful youths; the Jews, however, were always men . . . martyrs who gave the world a God and a morality and fought and suffered on all the battlefields of thought.

Heinrich Heine, *Gestandnisse (Confessions)*

Since the Exodus, Freedom has always spoken with a Hebrew accent.

Heinrich Heine, *Germany to Luther* (1834)

When people talk about a wealthy man of my creed, they call him an Israelite; but if he is poor they call him a Jew.

Heinrich Heine, *Ms. papers*

May the children of the stock of Abraham, who dwell in this land, continue to merit and enjoy the good will of the other inhabitants, while everyone shall sit in safety under his own vine and fig tree, and there shall be none to make him afraid.

George Washington, Letter to the Hebrew Congregation,
Newport, R.I. (1790)

The Hebrews have done more to civilize men than any other nation. If I were an atheist, and believed in blind eternal fate, I should still believe that fate had ordained the Jews to be the most essential instrument for civilizing the nations.

John Adams, letter to F.A. Vanderkamp, July 13, 1815

One of the most curious of these frenzies of exclusion was that against the emancipation of the Jews. All share in the government of the world was denied for centuries to perhaps the ablest, certainly the most tenacious, race that had ever lived in it—the race to whom we owed our religion and the purest spiritual stimulus and consolation to be found in all literature.

James Russell Lowell (1819-1891), *Democracy*

The sufferance, which is the badge of the Jew, has made him, in these days, the ruler of the rulers of the earth.

Ralph Waldo Emerson, *Conduct of Life: Fate* (1860)

The Jews, instead of being stationary like other Asiatics, were, next to the Greeks, the most progressive people of antiquity, and, jointly with them, have been the starting-point and main propelling agency of modern cultivation.

John Stuart Mill, *Representative Government* (1861), II

The Jews . . . had an absolute monarchy and a hierarchy, and their organised institutions were as obviously of sacerdotal origin as those of the Hindoos. These did for them what was done for other Oriental races by their institutions—subdued them to industry and order, and gave them a national life. But neither their kings nor their priests ever obtained, as in those other countries, the exclusive moulding of their character. Their religion, which enabled persons of genius and a high religious tone to be regarded and to regard themselves as inspired from heaven, gave existence to an inestimably precious unorganised institution—the Order (if it may be so termed) of Prophets. Under the protection, generally though not always effectual, of their sacred character, the Prophets were a power in the nation, often more than a match for kings and priests, and kept up, in that little corner of the earth, the antagonism of influences which is the only real security for continued progress. Religion consequently was not there what it has been in so many other places—a consecration of all that was once established, and a barrier against further improvement.

John Stuart Mill, *Representative Government,* II

Yes, I am a Jew, and when the ancestors of the right honourable gentlemen were brutal savages in an unknown island, mine were priests in the temple of Solomon.

Benjamin Disraeli, reply, 1835,
to a racial slur by Daniel O'Connell in Parliament

You call me a damned Jew. My race was old when you were all savages. I am proud to be a Jew.

John Galsworthy, *Loyalties,* Act ii

The gentleman will please remember that when his half-civilized ancestors were hunting the wild boar in Silesia, mine were princes of the earth.

U.S. Senator Judah Benjamin (1811-1884), in reply to a taunt
by a Senator of German descent. (Moore,
Reminiscences of Sixty Years in the National Metropolis.)

When Israel, of the Lord belov'd,
Out of the land of bondage came,
Her fathers' God before her mov'd,
An awful guide in smoke and flame.

Sir Walter Scott, *Ivanhoe* (1819), Chapter 19

The Jews are among the aristocracy of every land; if a literature is called rich in possession of a few classic tragedies, what shall we say of a national tragedy lasting for fifteen hundred years, in which the poets and actors were also the heroes.

George Eliot, *Daniel Deronda* (1876)

The Jews spend at Easter.

George Herbert, *Jacula Prudentum,* No. 244

Triumphant race! and did your power decay?
Failed the bright promise of your early day?

Reginald Heber, *Palestine*

The whole problem of the *Jews* exists only in nation states, for here their energy and higher intelligence, their accumulated capital of spirit and will, gathered from generation to generation through a long schooling in suffering, must become so preponderant as to arouse mass envy and hatred. In almost all contemporary nations, therefore—in direct proportion to the degree to which they act up nationalistically—the literary obscenity is spreading of leading Jews to slaughter as scapegoats of every conceivable public and internal misfortune. As soon as it is no longer a matter of preserving nations, but of producing the strongest possible European mixed race, the Jew is just as useful and desirable an ingredient as any other national remnant. . . .

One owes to them the noblest man, the purest sage, the most powerful book, and the most effective moral law of the world. Moreover, in the darkest times of the Middle Ages, ... it was Jewish free-thinkers, scholars, and physicians who clung to the banner of enlightenment and spiritual independence. ... We owe it to their exertions, not least of all, ... that the bond of culture which now links us with the enlightenment of Greco-Roman antiquity remained unbroken.

Friedrich Nietzsche, *Human, All-too-Human* (1878)

The Jews are the most remarkable nation of world history because, faced with the question of being or not being, they preferred, with a perfectly uncanny conviction, being at any price; the price they had to pay was the radical falsification of all nature, all naturalness, all reality, the entire inner world as well as the outer. They defined themselves counter to all those conditions under which a nation was previously able to live, was permitted to live; they made of themselves an antithesis of natural conditions—they inverted religion, religious worship, morality, history, psychology, one after the other, in an irreparable way into the contradiction of their natural values.

Friedrich Nietzsche, Aphorism 24

What is Jewish, what is Christian morality? Chance robbed of its innocence; unhappiness polluted with the idea of "sin"; well-being represented as a danger, as a "temptation"; a physiological disorder produced by the canker worm of conscience.

Friedrich Nietzsche, Aphorism 25

The Christian, the *ultimo ratio* of lying, is the Jew all over again—he is threefold Jew.

Friedrich Nietzsche, Aphorism 44

The Jews are the most remarkable nation of world history because, faced with the question of being or not being, they preferred, with a perfectly uncanny conviction, being *at any price:* the price they had to pay was the radical *falsification* of all nature, all naturalness, all reality, the entire inner world as well as the outer. They defined themselves *counter* to all those conditions under which a nation was previously able to live, was *permitted* to live; they made of themselves an antithesis to *natural* conditions—they inverted religion, religious worship, morality, history, psychology one after the other in an irreparable way into the contradiction of their natural values.

Friedrich Nietzsche, *Antichrist,* XXIV

The Jewish race is "the born enemy of pure humanity and everything that is noble in it."

Richard Wagner (1813-1883)

[Democracy], the deceitful theory that the Jew would insinuate—namely, that theory that all men are created equal.

Adolf Hitler, *Mein Kampf,* 1926

I believe today that I am acting in the sense of the Almighty Creator. By warding off the Jews I am fighting for the Lord's work.

Adolf Hitler, speech, Reichstag, 1936

Antisemitism is a useful revolutionary expedient. My Jews are a valuable hostage given to me by democracy.

Adolf Hitler, quoted in Hermann Rauschning, *The Voice of Destruction: Hitler Speaks*

Christ cannot possibly have been a Jew. I don't have to prove that scientifically. It is a fact.

Paul Joseph Goebbels, quoted by John Gunther, *The Nation,* February 6, 1935

The cross between a white man and an Indian is an Indian; the cross between a white man and a Negro is a Negro; the cross between a white man and a Hindu is a Hindu; and the cross between any races and a Jew is a Jew.

When it becomes thoroughly understood that the children of mixed marriages between contrasted races belong to the lower types ... to bring half-breeds into the world will be regarded as a social and racial crime of the first magnitude.

Madison Grant, *The Passing of the Great Race* (1916)

Suavity toward the Jews! Although you have lived among them, it is evident that you little understand those enemies of the human race. Haughty and at the same time base, combining an invincible obstinacy with a spirit despicably mean, they weary alike your love and your hatred.

Anatole France (1844-1924), *The Procurator of Judea*

The emancipation of the Jews in the last significance is the emancipation of mankind from Judaism.

Karl Marx, *On the Jewish Question* (1844)

The Jewish bourgeoisie are our enemies, not as Jews but as bourgeoisie. The Jewish worker is our brother.

Lenin, speech, Council of People's Commissars, August 9, 1918

As the Vedas offer a glimpse into the antecedents of Greek mythology, so Hebrew studies open up vistas into the antecedents of Christian dogma. Christianity in its Patristic form was an adaptation of Hebrew religion to the Graeco-Roman world, and later, in the Protestant movement, a readaptation of the same to what we may call the Teutonic spirit. In the first adaptation, Hebrew positivism was wonderfully refined, transformed into a religion of redemption, and endowed with a semi-pagan mythology, a pseudo-Platonic metaphysics, and a quasi-Roman organisation. In the second adaptation, Christianity received a new basis and standard in the spontaneous faith of the individual; and, as the traditions thus undermined in principle gradually dropped away, it was reduced by the German theologians to a romantic and mystical pantheism. Throughout its transformations, however, Christianity remains indebted to the Jews not only for its founder, but for the nucleus of its dogma, cult, and ethical doctrine. If the religion of the Jews, therefore, should disclose its origin, the origin of Christianity would also be manifest.

George Santayana, *Life of Reason* (1905-06), III, 5

Who taught you tender Bible tales
Of honey-lands, of milk and wine? ...
Who gave the patient Christ? I say
Who gave your Christian creed?
  Yea, yea.
Who gave your very God to you?
Your Jew! Your Jew! Your hated Jew!

Joaquin Miller (1841-1913) (American poet), *To Russia*

Still on Israel's head forlorn,
Every nation heaps its scorn.

Emma Lazarus (1849-1887), *The World's Justice*

His cup is gall, his meat is tears,
His passion lasts a thousand years.

Emma Lazarus, *Crowing of the Red Cock*

The Jews are not hated because they have evil qualities; evil qualities are sought for them, because they are hated.

Max Nordau (1849-1923)

If my theory of relativity is proven successful, Germany will claim me as a German and France will declare that I am a citizen of the world. Should my theory prove untrue, France will say that I am a German and Germany will declare that I am a Jew.

Albert Einstein (1879-1955), *Address,* Sorbonne, Paris

The Jews generally give value. They make you pay; but they deliver the goods. In my experience the men who want something for nothing are invariably Christians.

George Bernard Shaw, *Saint Joan,* Scene 4

If Christians were Christians, there would be no antisemitism. Jesus was a Jew. There is nothing that the ordinary Christian so dislikes to remember as this awkward historical fact. But it happens, none the less, to be true.

John Haynes Holmes, *The Sensible Man's View of Religion* (1933)

To the Jewish people fate dealt a series of severe trials and painful experiences, so their God became hard, relentless, and, as it were, wrapped in gloom. He retained the character of a universal God who reigned over all lands and peoples; the fact, however, that his worship had passed from the Egyptians to the Jews found its expression in the added doctrine that the Jews were his chosen people, whose special obligations would in the end find their special reward. It might not have been easy for that people to reconcile their belief in their being preferred to all others by an all-powerful God with the dire experiences of their sad fate. But they did not let doubts assail them, they increased their own feelings of guilt to silence their mistrust and perhaps in the end they referred to "God's unfathomable will," as religious people do to this day.

Sigmund Freud, *Moses and Monotheism* (1939), Pt. III, I, 1

Of all the peoples who lived in antiquity in the basin of the Mediterranean, the Jewish people is perhaps the only one that still exists in name and probably also in nature. With an unexampled power of resistance it has defied misfortune and ill-treatment, developed special character traits, and, incidentally, earned the hearty dislike of all other peoples.

Sigmund Freud, *Moses and Monotheism,* Pt. III, II, 2

The preference which through two thousand years the Jews have given to spiritual endeavour has, of course, had its effect; it has helped to build a dike against brutality and the inclination to violence which are usually found where athletic development becomes the ideal of the people. The harmonious development of spiritual and bodily activity, as achieved by the Greeks, was denied to the Jews. In this conflict their decision was at least made in favour of what is culturally the more important.

The Christian religion did not keep to the lofty heights of spirituality to which the Jewish religion had soared. The former was no longer monotheistic; it took over from the surrounding peoples numerous symbolic rites, re-established the great mother goddess, and found room for many deities of polytheism in an easily recognizable disguise, though in subordinate positions.

Sigmund Freud, *Moses and Monotheism,* Pt. III, II, 4

The religion that began with the prohibition against making an image of its God has developed in the course of centuries more and more into a religion of instinctual renunciation.

Sigmund Freud, *Moses and Monotheism,* Pt. III, II, 5

The people met with hard times; the hopes based on the favour of God were slow in being fulfilled; it became not easy to adhere to the illusion, cherished above all else, that they were God's chosen people. If they wished to keep happiness, then the consciousness of guilt because they themselves were such sinners offered a welcome excuse for God's severity. They deserved nothing better than to be punished by him, because they did not observe the laws; the need for satisfying this feeling of guilt, which, coming from a much deeper source, was insatiable, made them render their religious precepts ever and ever more strict, more exacting, but also more petty. In a new transport of moral asceticism the Jews imposed on themselves constantly increasing instinctual renunciation, and thereby reached—at least in doctrine and precepts—ethical heights that had remained inaccessible to the other peoples of antiquity.

Sigmund Freud, *Moses and Monotheism,* Pt. III, II, 9

How odd of God to choose the Jews.

William Norman Ewer, *How Odd* (1934)

It's not so odd. The Jews chose God.

Leon Roth, *Jewish Thought* (1954)

One who belongs to the most vilified and persecuted minority in history is not likely to be insensible to the freedoms guaranteed by our Constitution.... But as judges we are neither Jew nor Gentile, neither Catholic nor agnostic.

U.S. Supreme Court Justice Felix Frankfurter,
Flag Salute Cases, 319 U.S. 624, 646 (1943)

Aryans, Jews, Italians are not races. Aryans are people who speak Indo-European, "Aryan" languages... As Hitler uses it, the term has no meaning, racial, linguistic or otherwise.

Jews are people who practice the Jewish religion. They are of all races, Negro and Mongolian. European Jews are of many different biological types; physically they resemble the populations among whom they live.

Benedict and Wiltfish, *The Races of Mankind*

I cannot be silent. I cannot live while the remnants of the Jewish population of Poland, of whom I am a representative, are perishing. My friends in the Warsaw ghetto died with weapons in their hands in the last heroic battle. It was not my destiny to die together with them but I belong to them and in their mass graves.

By my death I wish to make my final protest against the passivity with which the world is looking on and permitting the extermination of the Jewish people.

Artur Zygelboym, Bundist leader who fled Warsaw late in 1939. This was his farewell letter, as he took his life in London, on May 12, 1943, at the age of forty-eight.

There is no Jewish blood in my veins,
But I am hated with a scabby hatred
By all the antisemites,
like a Jew.
And therefore
I am a true Russian.

Yevgeny Yevtushenko, *Babi Yar* (1961)

"I'll rest," said he, "but thou shalt
walk";
So doth this wandering Jew
From place to place, but cannot rest
For seeing countries new.

The Wandering Jew (anonymous), st. 9

To be a Jew is a destiny.

Vicki Baum, *And Life Goes On,* p. 193

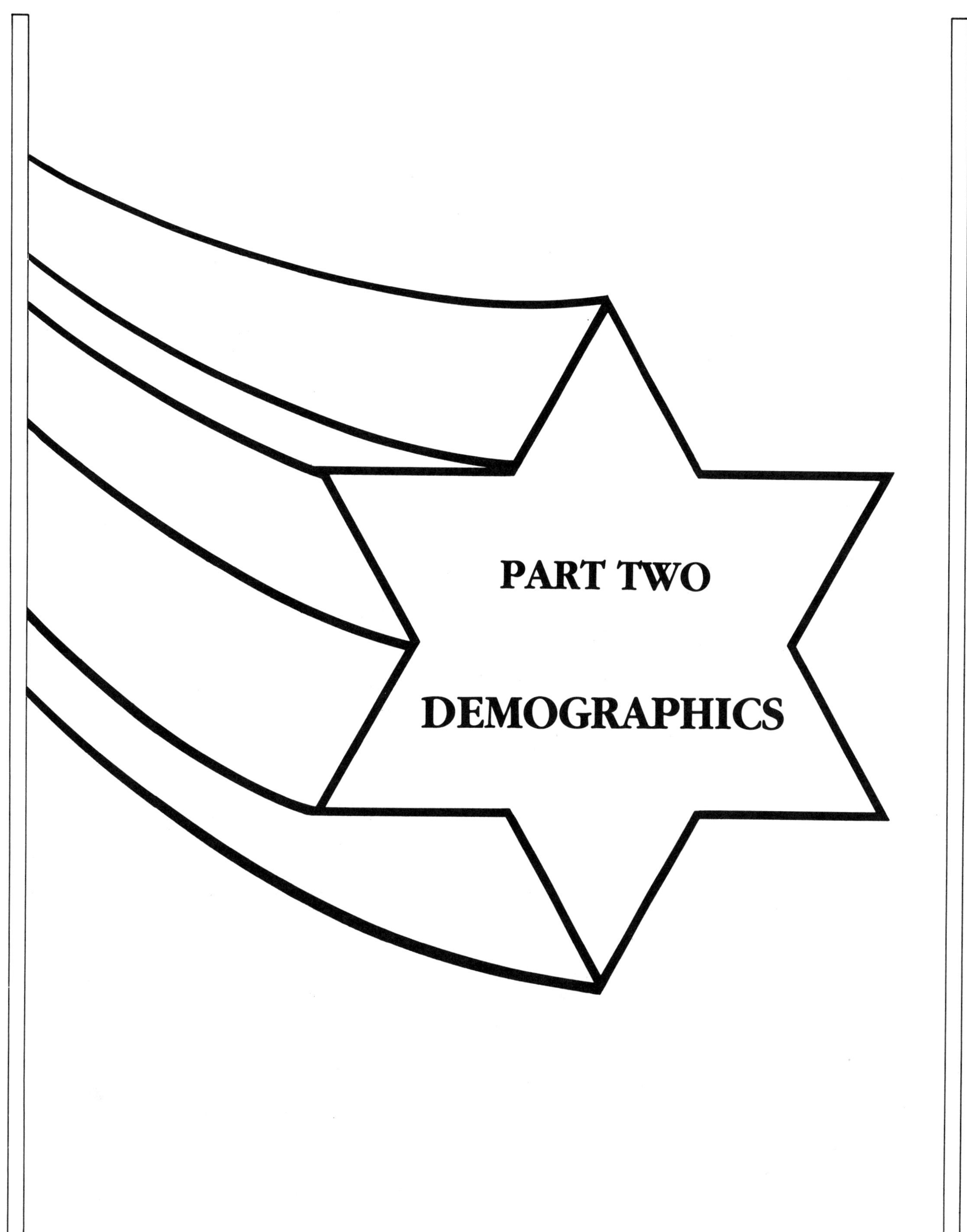
PART TWO
DEMOGRAPHICS

2

The Political Future of American Jews

Earl Raab and Seymour Martin Lipset

American Jews are a politically effective group, within certain limits, and are probably at the peak of their political influence. The question is whether that effectiveness is threatened by developing changes in American political life, in world affairs or in American Jewish circumstances. The auxiliary question is whether such changes call for adjustments in American Jewish strategy.

Preview of Factors

The factors to which Jewish political effectiveness is usually ascribed fall into several categories. There is the voting pattern of American Jews which has traditionally emphasized two factors: the Jewish *population concentration* in certain urban voting districts, compounded by the *high voting rate* of American Jews.

Those factors have been seen to give Jews a somewhat disproportionate mechanical leverage in political influence, but are usually associated with another set of factors, having to do with Jewish political activism. Such activism includes a *high level of financial contribution* to political campaigns; and a *high level of energy—involvement* in political life, in electoral campaigns, in the policy and strategy councils of aspirant politicians and of elected public officials.

A more complex and less invoked set of factors relates to the nature of that activism in the non-Jewish community. There is a *high level of integration* in business and community life in general, creating circles of access and influence which extend into the political arena; and coalition formation with other groups, which often critically multiplies the political effect of the Jews.

However, none of these factors would have sharp political point without some internal corporate factors: a certain *issue-intensiveness, a heavy communal consensus on a couple of high agenda items, and a Jewish organizational strength* through which these consensus positions are formally presented to policy makers. However, in addition to the overwhelming consensus on several prime issues of Jewish concern, there have been some other strong attitudinal tendencies among American Jews as a group—on subjects of social welfare, for example—which have shaped the strength of Jewish involvement in certain political coalitions. Partly as a result of these attitudinal patterns, American Jews have found their greatest political leverage within a coalition of the Democratic Party.

All these factors—patterns of voting, activism, integration and issue intensity—are interrelated and cumulative in effect. There is, however, one other large factor outside that system: objective conditions which affect the perceived *concordance of American values and Jewish values.* At best, Jewish political influence is marginal. There are—and have been—points beyond which a maximally effective Jewish effort could not prevail. Jewish political activity can help shape the concordance, and, to some extent, the objective conditions which affect it.

If those are the factors which have comprised American Jewish political influence, there are certain perceived changes taking place which would seem likely to affect them: Jewish demographic changes; financial and other electoral reform and changes in the American political process; changes in Jewish attitudes and institutions; and changes in objective circumstances.

Jewish Voting and Jewish Population Movement

While Jewish population statistics are inexact, there is convincing evidence that American Jews are both diminishing in proportion and dispersing outwards from inner cities and large cities.

The Jewish population percentage in America probably dropped from about 2.7 percent in 1970 to about 2.5 percent in 1980; and if median population projections hold up, that will drop further by 2000. But Jewish voting strength has never depended on sheer numbers, but rather on concentration and voting zeal. And the traditional rule of thumb has been to multiply Jewish voting-age figures by a factor of two in general elections to arrive at the percentage of Jews in the *voting* population.

That 2-1 ratio varies, of course, and may usually range a bit lower. If, for example, 85 percent of the Jewish voting-age population votes at a time when 50 percent of the general voting-age population votes, the rate is 1.7.

There are 9 states (counting the District of Columbia as a state for presidential voting purposes) in which the Jews comprise 3 percent or more of the population, from 10.6 percent in New York to 3.2 percent in California. These states have 182 of the 270 electoral votes needed to elect a president. Applying the hypothetical ratio of 1.7 percent to those estimated populations, the Jewish voting percentages range from about 18 percent in New York to about 5 percent in California (Table I).

In the 1980 and 1984 elections, at the most hypothetical, that range of Jewish voting strength did not provide the margin of Democratic victory anywhere, and could only have reversed the Republican victories in a couple of states if Jews had voted 90-10 Democratic.

Emerging from such hypothetical exercises is the reality

that the mechanical margin of Jewish votes is rarely going to make a critical difference. Sharpening that reality is the fact that the direction of Jewish voting has always corresponded to the direction of general voting (Table I), so that, for example, a massive 90-10 differential in Jewish voting is not liable to occur unless there is also an unusually large differential in general Democratic Party voting. That reduces the practical significance of the Jewish voting differential.

There are qualifications. For example, the rule of thumb is to apply a factor of at least *three* to the Jewish voting population to find the proportion of Jewish voters in the Democratic Party primaries. These can more often become significant margins. However, the fact remains that, apart from Democratic Party primaries in certain key states, and the election of a few key Congressmen from a few districts dominated by heavy Jewish population, the Jewish voting population, per se, is rarely a decisive factor in American national politics.

Of course, political candidates in close races and in Jewish-populous states cannot afford to overlook the possibility of such a rare occurrence. In 1976 the Jewish voters did provide the margin by which Carter took New York; and New York did provide the electoral margin by which he took the presidency. But that has happened only once. And in the last 7 Congressional elections, only about 5 percent of the candidates were elected in Jewish-populous states with less than 55 percent of the vote—so the Jewish vote was not critical.

In short, while the marginal Jewish voting power has occasionally some significance, it does not in itself explain the influence of American Jews in politics—and, by the same token, the diffusion of Jewish population is not by itself a seriously negative factor in that influence.

In matter of fact, while population estimates between 1955 and 1982 show a significant drop in a couple of the key states (Table I), the overall pattern does not threaten a radical collapse in state concentrations. More to the point is the estimate that the percentage of Jews in cities of a half million or more decreased from 84 percent to 72 percent during the 1980s. However, if the influence of the Jewish population depends more on political activism than on their numerical presence at the polls, then this kind of centrifugal dispersion can be a positive factor. In a sense, the spread of Jewish political activism away from the population centers follows the general spread of political power. For example, Baltimore's share of Maryland's presidential vote declined from 48 to 17 percent between 1940 and 1980. In that same period, New York City's share dropped from 51 to 31 percent. The Jewish movement from some of the major cities may actually be a productive dispersion.

Financial Contributions and Electoral Fund Reform

If the Jewish disproportion in general national elections is to be multiplied by a factor of about two, then the disproportion of Jewish financial contributions to national political campaigns must be multiplied by a factor of 15 to 20.

While there have been few reliable statistics on the subject—and some reluctance to gather any—the journalistic and anecdotal evidence is overwhelming that more than a majority of Democratic funds on a national level, and as much as a quarter of Republican funds have come from Jewish sources. In 1968, for example, 21 individuals advanced Hubert Humphrey $100,000 or more for his campaign; 15 of them were Jews.

That kind of financial participation had been typical. The disproportionate level of Jewish voting reflected a strong sense of Jewish self-interest in public affairs and a relatively high middle-class educated level of activism. The disproportionate level of political contributions reflected those factors and more. Since the end of World War II, Jews comprised a relatively affluent group and markedly included a number of individuals and families who were affluent for the first time, a famously good class of "givers."

There had long been a tradition of philanthropic giving, at least among Western Jews, dating back to the middle ages, to community needs shaped by adversity legitimated by Jewish religious tradition. And Jewish political needs in this country have been perceived as a communal need, like philanthropy. But beyond that, political involvement has been a means by which many new-rich in America have been able to gain quick community recognition and general influence.

Political campaigning has, of course, become increasingly expensive, with the growth of the population and the advent of television. In 1976, for example, winning Congressmen spent about 63 million dollars, and in 1982 about 195 million dollars, an increase roughly twice the inflation factor. There is no automatic relationship between campaign spending and political victory; in the 1980 Congressional races, half of the top ten spenders won and half lost. Of the 9 Democrats who lost in that campaign, 7 had a spending advantage. However, spending on occasion does make the difference, and it is a firm article of belief among candidates that "money is the mother's milk of politics." Thus political contributors have had, if not control and if not patronage, at least heightened "access" to their candidates.

Financial contributions are a much more certain and bankable political item than Jewish voting margins in most cases; and Jewish political effectiveness has been less closely tied to voting margins than to the access which has been gained by Jewish contributors to campaigns.

The question is whether electoral finance reform of recent years has undercut that source of effectiveness. The more-than-a-hundred-thousand-dollar contributions that were made through the early 1970s—the individual Jewish advances made to Humphrey went as high as $390,000—are no longer possible.

But so far, these restrictions on individual contributions do not seem to pose a crippling disability to Jewish political effectiveness. According to one expert on campaign financing, the role of the wealthy has not been diminished by the reforms. "The main effect," he said, "has been to exchange the big giver for the big solicitor" (Herbert Alexander, quoted in the *Wall Street Journal,* October 24, 1984, p. 1). Solicitation by the wealthy from the wealthy has been a particular Jewish tradition, and a skill sharpened in philanthropic campaigns. And such "bundling" of funds can still be raised in amounts significant enough to warrant "access." The legal limit of $1000 per individual giver per election can be multiplied by the number of one's relatives, and by the channeling of donations to funds and committees other than the candidate's direct campaign.

The Political Action Committees are simply legal and convenient fund repositories for many political groups such as industrial associations—but for groups like the Jews, they are also very useful vessels for the kind of bundling and financial negotiation which are currently called for. There are over 30 PACs which are specifically geared to supporting Congressional candidates who are favorable to Israel. In the Congressional campaign of 1982, these PACs contributed a total of $1.67 million, a little more than half going to Senatorial candidates. In the Congressional campaign of 1983-84, that amount probably doubled.

In short, while some Jewish "heavy hitters" have been hobbled insofar as their personal contributions are concerned, many Jews have maintained their "access" by dint of their fundraising activities—and the Jewish contributions have even more of a Jewish communal tinge than they had before. On that level, there is no indication that the electoral fiscal reforms have impeded Jewish effectiveness in politics.

However, there may be some clouds on the horizon, relating primarily to PACs. First of all, there is the question of whether PACs, becoming the prime contribution instrument of Jews, are so stringently one-issue in nature that they will distort or weaken the integrated position of American Jews in the political process. That question will be addressed later. More directly, there is the question of whether current methods will lead, in a kind of backlash effect, to electoral reform of a kind which could be more disabling to the Jewish pattern.

Some observers have described PACs as a scandal waiting to happen. Congressman Glickman, talking about the problem of PACs said "... study after study has shown a very high correlation between funds received and the way some key votes have been cast" (Congressional Record-House, July 8, 1981, H 4101). Most of these "high correlations" carrying the potential of scandal involve direct economic interest. Notoriously, in 1982, when the House Energy and Finance Committee voted to overturn a Federal Trade Commission regulation which the auto dealers opposed, 26 out of the 27 committee members had received contributions totalling $84,000 from the National Auto Dealers Association, and all but one voted for the auto dealers' position. That kind of situation has been repeated again and again.

Of course, the "correlation" has been frequently rationalized by the statement that funds are given not to coerce a Congressman's opinion but to strengthen Congressmen who already have the "right" opinion. But that distinction is often enough suspect, certainly in the eyes of the citizenry. When Congressman Dan Glickman of Kansas asked another Congressman to join him in an action unfavorable to the auto dealers, he was told: "I'm committed. I got a $10,000 check from the National Automobile Dealers Association. I can't change my vote now" (Brooks Jackson, *Wall Street Journal*, March 5, 1984).

Under current law, presidential candidates are eligible for substantial federal funding support and are limited in the amount they can spend. Congressional candidates do not get government funding support and are unlimited in expenditures.

Congressman Henry Reuss of Wisconsin said that "the corruption and the evil is not only in people seeming to sell access or in some cases even their vote; it lies in the preoccupation of legislators ... who have to spend a large part of their lives panhandling, going around to all of these groups saying, 'I would just love to have a check from you.' That shouldn't be."

At the moment, there seems to be little political likelihood that Congress will move towards laws which make their campaigns predominantly dependent on government funding. If, however, "the corruption and evil" to which Congressman Reuss referred broke out by way of public scandal or public outrage at escalating campaign costs, then a movement toward public funding might become more feasible. In that case, it is more likely that the possibility of "access" by the Jewish community through the means of political contributions would be reduced.

Jewish Activism and Changes in the Political Process

Disproportionate voting is, of course, an index of political activism. Disproportionate financial contribution to campaigns is an instrument as well as an index of political activism. But Jewish political activism extends beyond both phenomena and is bedded in an even larger field of social activism.

"Social activism" describes a high level of participation in the affairs of the general community. It can be measured in terms of disproportionate Jewish membership and leadership in most of the communal activities which are open to them: business and trade associations, professional associations, trade unions, student political organizations, artistic associations, general welfare associations—all of those groups which comprise the associational arena of American community life.

There are countless theories about this general Jewish activism. There is the obvious matter of educational level and middle class status and of the emerging-group syndrome, both of which may stimulate special desires for involvement and community recognition. However, there is also a theory that an additional factor exists among Jews: a prevalently high level of achievement drive, drawn presumably out of the Jewish life experience, but over and above the factors mentioned above. For example, one attempt to measure achievement drive and relate it to ethnicity found that for Protestants, for Italians, for Greeks, for Blacks, the lower socio-economic group in each group registered a significantly lower achievement drive than the middle class of that group. Only in the case of the Jews were those results reversed, the Jewish lower class registering a slightly higher score than the middle class. One social psychologist, after reviewing the evidence, wrote: "In short, there is very little doubt the average achievement (score) among Jews is higher than for the general population in the United States at this time" (McClelland).

Whatever the reasons, there is a demonstrably high level of Jewish participation in the various channels of American community life. This general social activism preceded political activism and is in aid of it. By dint of it, Jewish individuals have become "influentials" in the general community. As often as not, these influentials, as a *consequence,* have become *political* influentials. Further, this integrating process has created, by natural means, a great deal of *interfacing* between participant Jews and various other groups and circles of influence in the community.

That interfacing is the beginning of the *coalition* process.

This active integration of the Jews is at the heart of their political effectiveness. On one level, it is in itself a persuasive factor for many of the Jewish agenda items. On a top agenda item, American support of Israel, for example, this factor plays a substantial role. The basis of American support for Israel is the prevalent American perception that the support of Israel is important for American national interest.

The chief engine of that perception of Israeli importance to America is the state of objective circumstances in the Middle East, within the framework of East-West problems—but that perception is buttressed by the image of Israel as Western, politically similar to and friendly to America. And that image is strengthened by the familiar and integrated social presence of the American Jews.

But beyond that, the integrated social presence of the Jews in America, providing its own kind of access to other groups, has created the basis for coalitions of effort. Thus, it has been naturally easy to gather allies in the non-Jewish community on Jewish issues such as antisemitism, neo-Nazism, Soviet Jewry or support for Israel.

However, there has been another significance to community coalition and coalition politics for the Jews. That significance is reflected in the distinction customarily made between "faction" and "coalition" in politics. In faction politics at its most extreme, an interest group pursues its own interest only, forms its own party, runs its own candidates, does not consider compromise or negotiation. In coalition politics, negotiation and compromise among interest groups is primary. The purpose is to find a common agenda.

Coalition politics has seemed a necessity for an orderly United States because of its heterogeneity. Early in its career, the American polity learned that stronger coalition politics seemed preferable not only in the matter of issues, but in the matter of selecting public officials. In the presidential campaign of 1824, none of the five candidates received anything near a majority from the electoral college. The nominating process itself developed by the 1840s was the national party convention. The parties became coalitions for purposes of both elections and issues. Various factions struggled within each party. And factional leaders within each party, even when they gained a certain dominance, usually understood that it was necessary to pursue the party coalition process *in order to win elections* across the country. Between 1940 and 1980 the only campaigns in which one candidate received less than 40 percent of the popular vote were in 1964 and 1972 when bitter factional debates took place in the Republican and Democratic Party respectively, and clearly factional candidates were nominated.

The Jews can reasonably feel threatened by a climate of factional politics in which deadly political extremism is bred. And in somewhat narrower terms, the Jews can multiply their own effectiveness only by coalitional methods—increasing their access, helping to make it clear that their interests are the interests of a broader community and multiplying their political power.

It is a matter of history that since the 1930s, when the Jews became a cogent political force, the Democratic Party has been the national party in which the Jews have found and built their coalitional strength, because of compatibility of issue and temperment with some other Democratic Party power. And some Jews have always been engaged in Republican Party politics, with some coalition effects, especially on local and regional levels, even though the main coalitional leverage of the Jews has been within the Democratic Party.

So this active participation within the general community and coalitional effort has been the dynamic core of Jewish political effectiveness. But the circumstances within which this political effectiveness has taken place may be changing drastically. One change may be taking place within the Jewish community itself: a tendency towards some withdrawal from the integrative and coalitional process. That phenomenon will be dealt with below.

But there are apparent changes within the political process itself which, including some "electoral reform," allegedly threaten that basic dynamic of effectiveness.

The Decline of the Parties

The changes which draw most attention revolve around the weakening of the political parties. However, the American political party has never been the kind of tight mechanism which political parties represent in much of Europe and in Israel. Among the Founding Fathers, there was a monumental distaste for political parties. Jefferson once said that if he could not go to heaven except with a political party, he would prefer not to go there at all. But there was always early attraction to coalitional politics, entailing the negotiation of differences among different constituencies.

That attraction plus sheer political necessity created the networks which constitute the major American political parties. James MacGregor Burns, who wrote of these networks as four parties—two Congressional parties, Republican and Democratic, and two presidential parties—described each Congressional party in these terms:

> It is not a tight, cohesive group of men, conspiring together in a secret chamber and pushing buttons on a nation-wide machine. ... It is a loose cluster of men sharing a common concept of the public interest ... benefiting from and in turn protecting a set of rules and institutions that bolster their power. ... These men deal with one another by bargaining and accommodation rather than by direction and command.

The "presidential parties" are, of course, broader and more disciplined, but exist as a power only when a "party's" candidate is elected. The presidential networks are often different than the Congressional networks, but also often intersect.

Indeed, if there is too little intersection between the two networks, a president and his party's Congressional delegation, then it becomes more difficult for the president and the government to function. Sometimes, of course, there are inter-party coalitions, as in the frequent case of Republican conservatives and Democratic "Dixiecrats." But, by and large, the Democratic Party and the Republican Party each maintains its own identity, both because of certain prevalent ideological tendencies, and simply because individuals need the network in order to function effectively and protect their power.

These networks built their corporate strength on two foundations: patronage and control over the nomination of candidates. Both of those foundations have been crumbling as a result of electoral reform. Most recently, a party's ability to control nomination has been reduced by the growth of direct primary elections, and by reforms requiring "proportional representation" at nominating conventions. In short, an increase in direct democracy has eroded corporate party strength.

But, in reality, the weakening of the formal corporate entities known as "parties" will not mean the collapse of the political system in which the Jews flourish and exert influence, as long as the informal network arrangements known as parties continue in strength. The parties have been most important for Jewish political effectiveness because they have provided networks of "access" to policy-makers and their circles.

Jews, like others, have gained access to those networks not by connecting to a national party, or even a state party, but by connecting to the basically autonomous apparatus of a local candidate or office holder, and/or directly to the apparatus of a presidential candidate.

However, the apparatus or support system for any given political candidate does not just consist of influential and active individuals. It also includes symbolic representatives of the various constituencies which may be important to the candidate. Some constituent groups, such as trade associations, send money directly to the campaigns—and that presumably is important if they want their candidate elected—but "access" is limited if it consists only of checks in the mail and not of individuals who remain consistently close to the apparatus of the candidate and public official.

In the case of groups like Jews—a more inchoate class than dairy farmers or automobile dealers, with a more complex agenda—the role of involved individuals is even more crucial. Jewish community organizations will want some access, no matter which candidate wins. The connection is mainly through involved individuals who are also connected to those organizations. Even the pro-Israel PACs have their main impact by introducing or backing up otherwise involved individuals.

These Jewish organizations do help to organize explicit issue-coalitions which then, through symbolic individuals, become an apparent part of a support system—and agenda—of a candidate or public official.

This whole plexus of relationships, from the bottom up rather than the top down, describes political parties in America better than the image or tight national or state structures—and describes the far-flung way in which the Jewish community makes its connections. The "deterioration" of the parties refers to some further weakening of national, state and regional party entities and functions, as against the autonomy of local offices.

If this deterioration proceeds to the point where the two party networks fail to function—or if factional politics begin to operate seriously outside these networks rather than within them—the Jewish political fortunes will surely suffer in America. And if Jewish access to these networks is seriously cut off by radical electoral reform which eliminates the importance of private campaign contributions, or insists on strict proportional representation at nominating points, then Jewish political fortunes will surely suffer.

But the fact is that the two major party networks continue to function as networks, despite all the shifting permutations, because they still serve a basic purpose in the mutual protection of power, and even in the mutual expression of certain prevailing political values.

All other things being equal, as long as those networks continue to function the hyper-activism of the Jews will leave Jewish political effectiveness relatively unimpaired by current political reform and changes.

The Democratic Party and the Jews

However, there is much discussion about one specific change in the nature of these party networks which might affect the nature of Jewish political effectiveness. The fact is that the main "Jewish connection" throughout the past half century has been with the Democratic Party network. And the issue-coalitions with which the Jews have been explicitly engaged (i.e., Blacks, labor unions, liberal Christian clergy) have largely been associated with the Democratic Party. The Democratic Party network has been relatively sympathetic with the Jewish political agenda over the years.

Furthermore, the Democratic Party Congressional network, with which the Jews have been primarily associated, has dominated the political scene, having been the major political party in the House over 90 percent of the time since World War II, and in the Senate over 75 percent of the time.

If the Democratic Party loses its dominance because of some "realignment" which may be taking place . . . or if the Democratic Party network becomes less sympathetic to the basic Jewish agenda, partly because of shifting issue-coalitions . . . and if the Jews fail to find the same strength of connections in the Republican Party network, there are obvious negative implications for Jewish political influence in the future.

The 1984 voting suggests that the Jews are not leaving the Democratic Party. Table I demonstrates that, according to the best estimates, including the redistribution of third-party votes according to probable major party options, the Jews returned to a "normal" "Democratic distance" of about 25 points between their presidential voting and that of the general population. The Jewish "Democratic distance" in Congressional voting has usually been even higher than in their presidential voting. And in recent years, about 6 out of 10 American Jews have continued to indicate that their party affiliation is "Democratic"; 1 out of 10, Republican; and about 3 out of 10, Independent. Depending on the survey, there may be seen some growth of Independent affiliation at the expense of the Democratic Party, but the Republican ratio has not changed significantly.

The question, at the moment, is not whether the Jews are leaving the Democratic Party, but whether the Democratic Party network is leaving the Jews and their agenda.

As Table I suggests, Jewish voting has been affected by

the same political impulses as other Americans in voting for presidential candidates. But within those trends there has been a special dimension of loyalty to the Democratic Party. The political profile of the American Jew, statistically speaking, has something to do with that continuous loyalty.

Jews continue to score disproportionately high, among the white population, on matters of "economic liberalism;" that is, government intervention on behalf of the poor and disadvantaged. For example, the 1984 National Survey of American Jews found typically that Jews supported the goals and philosophy of such government programs as welfare and food stamps by a 75 to 17 ratio; government aid for abortions for poor women by an 81 to 13 ratio; and affirmative action without quotas by a 70 to 20 ratio. The Democratic Party is seen by the national population as the network which singly stands for such values.

There are indications that American Jewry has followed the rest of the population in becoming more "fiscally conservative." In one 1981 regional survey, where four out of five Jews called for more government spending for health care, half of them said that it is "proper to cut social spending" and two out of three supported a statutory limitation on government spending.

But, while fiscal attitudes may have shifted within the Jewish population, party loyalty has not, at least by the light of the 1984 election. There is another factor of "liberalism" which apparently has more saliency for the Jews.

That is the factor of "cultural liberalism," which might be more aptly called cultural tolerance, tolerance for differences. For the Jews these are, of course, issues of deep self-interest. Civil liberties comprise one category of such issues, but they are not really in contention in America today. Antisemitism itself is another such category. And, while American Jews never relax their foreboding about the possibility of antisemitism, it was not an issue that made an important difference in the selection of candidates in the election year.

An analysis was made of the reasons why 814 randomly selected Jewish voters in Northern California made their presidential choice (Table II). Asked to pick the one or two issues out of eight which would make the most difference to them in their selection, only about 4 percent chose antisemitism, among both Mondale and Reagan voters. The domestic issue which most concerned Mondale supporters, in twice the proportion of Reagan supporters, was "keeping church and state separate." This result was replicated in other surveys around the country. In the course of heated public discussion about religion and the state, the prominence of fundamentalists like the Rev. Jerry Falwell, and a publicized negative trend in court decisions, church-state separation became, among Jews, a code phrase for cultural tolerance.

This issue as it is embedded in the larger matter of cultural liberalism, is related also to the Democratic Party milieu in which Jews have grown up politically. Jews may have become more affluent but they still do not belong to the same social network as the middle and upper class white Protestants who form the backbone of the Republican Party. The church-state issue was not just another constitutional issue but the signal of a cultural climate important for the Jews, and it seemed clear that the Democratic Party still provided that climate better than the Republican Party.

However, while Mondale was an assurance on that score, there was still some foreboding expressed that the Democratic Party could "leave" the Jews in the future. On the matter of Israel the Jews seemed to make little distinction between the two parties (Table II). But even a majority of the Mondale voters expressed the opinion that Jesse Jackson had too much influence on the Democratic Party.

While they were concerned about antisemitism on his part, they were more concerned about his positions on Israel. There is a foreign policy faction represented by Jesse Jackson featuring non-interventionist or third world foreign policy sentiments which could prove deleterious or even openly hostile to Israel's interests if it became dominant. The dominance could change the image of the Democratic Party as the home of cultural liberalism for the Jews, hard-core opposition to Israel being translated as a form of intolerance for American Jews.

Such a reversal of foreign policy by the Democratic Party is not likely. However, contention on this issue could disrupt Jewish relationships with other elements of the Democratic Party, especially at local levels.

The main "political association" which seemed to suffer as a result of the 1984 election was that of the Black community, which voted almost 9 to 1 in favor of Mondale. It is true that the Jewish population voted almost 2 to 1 in favor of Mondale, but there are a couple of significant differences. Although the Blacks represent about 8 percent of the voters, about twice that of the Jews, they are as disproportionately low in their political activism as the Jews are disproportionately high. They have not been in a position to be as activist in terms of campaign contributions—nor in terms of other electoral involvement. And, despite the Jewish vote at the polls, there was a renaissance of organized Jewish activism among the third of the Jews who did opt for Ronald Reagan. The Republican Party generally recognized the importance of that activism, as distinct from voting, and is not likely to turn its back on the Jewish community because of the voting numbers.

Also, the *primary* "Black agenda" consists of stands on economic issues which are largely incompatible with those of the Republican Party. The *primary* "Jewish agenda" is not so incompatible with the Republican Party agenda (e.g., support for Israel, support for Soviet Jews)—except apparently in certain church-state matters about which there is division within the Republican Party.

As a result, an increasingly dominant Republican Party on the American scene would seem to leave the Black community in a greater state of political disrepair than it would the Jews. Labor leadership would also be in trouble, of course, although union members in the country came close to splitting on presidential choice (54 percent for Mondale in the ABC exit poll). Some Hispanic leadership was found on the Republican side, and 44 percent of the Hispanic voters followed suit.

But there is no evidence to support the belief that the Republican Party is about to become nationally dominant, although there may be some "realignment" in certain Southern and Southwestern regions. The presidential voters, in the *Los Angeles Times* national exit poll, indicated that they had split their congressional votes between

Democrat and Republican candidates (46-47), and the results were in accord. Also, there has already emerged sharp contention within national Republican leadership which suggests that their life after Reagan will not be as easy as the 1984 figures suggested.

However, for the Black community, there is also the question of how the contentions within the Democratic Party will be resolved. And there is the question of how the Black leadership itself will approach that political future. If, for example, the more dissident elements of the Jesse Jackson camp were to become dominant, complete with a "third world" foreign affairs approach, Democratic Party politics would become more contentious—and the Jewish community would be caught uncomfortably in that contention.

But Jesse Jackson was a spokesman for the Black community on the domestic agenda, not on the foreign policy agenda which he espoused. It would seem to be indicated for Jewish activists in the Democratic Party, in supporting the basic Black domestic agenda, to keep it separated from Jesse Jackson's foreign policy agenda. Under those conditions the Jewish/Black alliance in the Democratic Party circles could remain undisputed.

The Jewish Community and a "Narrowing" Effect

The "Jewish community" refers generally to all those Jews who are connected to or influenced by the network of organized elements in Jewish life.

There has developed a kind of "politics-intoxication" among American Jews which tends to oversimplify the political process. In doing so, they tend to overlook the fact that the Jewish community is itself a *political* force, and that politics is more than electoral or lobbying activity.

"Politics" is *all* the activity which has to do with the making and administration of public policy. Jewish political activity is all that activity on public affairs in which Jews engage in some organized and purposeful concert. When they are so engaged, American Jews comprise a *political association.* De Toqueville described a *political association* in this manner: "the public assent which a number of individuals give to certain doctrines, and the engagement which they contract to promote in a certain manner the spread of those doctrines."

The Jewish community *is* a political association at those points where there is an organized consensus on certain issues of specified interest to the Jewish community and where there is an organized Jewish community network to promote that consensus.

Most cogently, the Jewish community has established itself as a political association in matters of self-defense—i.e., American support of Israel, support for beleagured Jews abroad, international human rights generally, civil rights in its full scope, civil liberties, freedom of religion, church-state separation, protection for Jewish institutions.

The first function of that political association is to discover and shape consensual strategies on the doctrines to which there is natural assent in the bulk of the Jewish community. The second function is to promote the spread of those doctrines and strategies.

The political association represented by the Jews (and other ethnic/religious groups) differs significantly from that represented by the Automobile Dealers Association and other such business interest groups. Associations such as the automobile dealers tend to be equated with one or several specific organizations with relatively universal membership. The Jewish political association, a more complex social group with a more complex agenda, consists of a loose network of many organizations and connected individuals.

There is at least one other significant working difference. The objectives of the Jewish political association come closer to matters of redressing *citizenship* wrongs and addressing *citizenship* aspirations, as touched on directly by the Constitution, than do the profit-making objectives of a business interest group. It is largely for that reason that most of the activities of the Jewish political association are not as constrained by legal regulations as are those of a business interest group—although some of the specific lobbying and electoral activities which spin out of this Jewish political association are so regulated, especially when they relate to Israel.

But the point is that most of the combined elements of the organized Jewish community, as they address common public affairs of Jewish concern, constitute a political association and are engaged in political activity.

This Jewish political association is so defined because it is in a state of some deliberate organization directed toward common political objectives. The Jewish community is not a political association just because it has some statistically prevalent opinions on certain issues—such as those related to social welfare in general.

There are some political subjects outside the area of self-defense or of organized consensus on which there is a disproportionate weight of Jewish opinion. Jews are, for example, prevalently economic or social welfare liberals, as has been indicated above.

However, in this display of opinions on social welfare, Jews represent a disproportionate *supportive audience* rather than a political association. As a Jewish population, they are not primarily or consensually organized to promote doctrines and strategy on this subject, as they are on the subject of support for Israel or antisemitism, for example.

It is true that some of the mechanism created by the Jewish political association in America *adds* to their working agenda objectives which reflect the Jews as a supportive audience, such as social welfare liberalism. But it is also true that those objectives are most cogently and convincingly added, when they are conceived in aid of the primary agenda of the Jewish political association (e.g., poverty as a racial phenomenon related to bigotry, or lending itself to dangerous political extremism—or offering a value-compatible opportunity for coalition).

In other words, the Jewish political association in America is not a political party, meant to reflect all the prevailing political opinions of American Jews. As a *political association,* the Jews are primarily concerned with the flourishing survival of Jews and Jewish institutions, in ways that are acceptable to Jewish values. The organized network which comprises their political association is their instrument for that purpose. As a *supporting audience,* American Jews are deeply involved with many other political associations and movements, which have other primary objectives.

But this is precisely one of the strengths of the Jewish population in America—and, finally, one of the strengths of the Jewish political association itself. A political association can be better than the sum of its parts, depending on how well organized it is, but it is finally limited by the *aggregate influence* that can be wielded by its members. The aggregate influence of its members is the base on which rests the strength of the Jewish political association and Jewish political influence.

And that aggregate influence is based finally not so much on political activism relative to the "Jewish agenda," but on Jewish activism in general American public life. In the 1981 National Survey of American Jews, only 8 percent said that they had been active in some political campaign, but 39 percent said that they had been active in a professional association, 36 percent in some community cultural group, 21 percent in some neighborhood organization. In addition, as many or more Jews had been involved in a business organization, a PTA, a feminist group, an environmental group, as had been involved in a political campaign. And most of those who had been active in political campaigns had been active first in one or more of the other community activities.

In other words, Jewish influentials develop out of integrated activism in general American life. To put it another way: the influence of individual Jews is not primarily created around issues of the Jewish agenda, which emerges from the Jewish *political association;* it is more often created around issues on which the Jews represent a *supportive audience.* The result, whether in creating Jewish influentials or productive relationships with other groups, is to give the Jewish political association its base of strength as it enters the political arena on its own agenda. In turn, the organized elements of the Jewish political association give these influential Jews an organizational base, a clear Jewish agenda and a consensual message to bear.

In that formal political arena, electoral activity is a critical activity in solidifying access to public policy makers on the agenda of the Jewish political association. And "lobbying" is a critical activity as it assesses policy-making strategy, often under changing conditions, and helps to organize and inform policy-makers on the spot around that strategy.

In their various ways, the electoral activists and the lobbyists are connected to and essential to the Jewish political association, and relatively powerless without it; and the entire Jewish political association is only marginally more powerful than the aggregate influence of American Jewry and Jewish agencies, mainly gained through integrated activism on the general American public scene.

A Cautionary Note

As an antidote to intoxication, it is always worthwhile to note that the formal expressions of the Jewish political association, even if financial contributions are involved, will not be determinative if there are major countervailing factors.

There have been a few instructive signals on this matter, as it applies to American support of Israel. When the Carter Administration became party to a "Soviet-American communique" which promised to bring the Soviet Union into the forefront of Middle East negotiations, the American Jewish apparatus erupted into what was called a "firestorm" of protest. The proposal was dropped, and Abba Eban, for one, declared that the American Jewish proposal had carried the day. Subsequently, at the beginning of the Reagan Administration, the organized American Jewish apparatus again erupted in at least as rousing a "firestorm" of protest with respect to the AWACS sale to the Saudis. But the AWACS sale prevailed. All kinds of analysis can be applied, but the fact remains that it was a difference in circumstances, not a difference in Jewish effort, which distinguished the failure.

In 1983 the foreign aid bill, the largest portion of which was designated for Israel, was voted against by a significant number of Congressmen who were traditional supporters of Israel, and who had received substantial amounts of financial contribution from Jewish sources. It was not critical; the aid bill won, and the Congressmen in question who voted against it because of a Central American provision, typically said that they would have sought some other way of making sure that Israel received its funds. However, the American Jewish apparatus had fought for passage of the bill, which had a number of favorable provisions in it for Israel. And some of the larger contributors to the Congressmen in question were semi-privately outraged by the "delinquencies."

But the efforts of the Jewish political association, including its electoral and lobbying activities, will not prevail against overwhelming American tendencies in an opposite direction. The basic American commitment to Israel, for example, had its wellspring in the middle 1960s—not on the basis of a growing perception of American self-interest in the integrity of Israel. That commitment, which has not changed radically since, was based primarily on objective conditions, before the Jewish political association seemed to acquire the influence it has today.

Of course, the Jewish political association has still had a critical marginal effect on certain important policy decisions—but the marginality itself suggests that the Jewish political endeavor must not become so narrow that it does not consider some of the larger issues which will bear on the Jewish agenda. In the matter of Israel, for example, America's general foreign policy, rather than sentiment on Israel itself, may eventually determine America's policy towards Israel. And a major divisiveness between haves and have-nots in America, rather than any specific constitutional sentiment, could eventually determine the state of America's civil liberties.

The "Narrowing" Trend

Both with respect to the above cautionary note and with respect to the kind of integrated activism which has made the Jewish political association influential, observers have noted a trend of ominous "narrowing" within Jewish life.

There are two interconnected ways in which this narrowing has developed. There is a tendency towards one-issue politics. Note that the fastest-growing American Jewish organization by far has been the American Israel Public Affairs Committee (AIPAC) And there are other tendencies towards self-ghettoization on the public affairs scene. Note how often non-Jewish public officials over the age of 50 frequently complain about the narrowing agenda they have perceived in the organized Jewish community.

There is evidence that the Jewish population at large has not become as self-ghettoized in public affairs as has the Jewish organizational apparatus. Its voting patterns on issues and candidates, as noted earlier, indicate a group pattern of broader concerns. Also, the general activism of Jews continues to manifest itself through the disproportionate number of individual Jews involved in a broader range of general community activities and associations. It is suggested that there is a certain growing *discontinuity* between the American Jewish population and the dominant sector at the organized Jewish apparatus.

More and more dominantly, the center of that apparatus has been the fundraising agencies of the Jewish community: the Council of Jewish Federations and the local Federations. Their major efforts in fundraising were associated with Israel, culminating in a massive increase in 1967. These central fundraising mechanisms increasingly drew in the cream of affluent young Jewish leadership. The preoccupation of these mechanisms, and their leadership, with Israel was understandable. The leadership of AIPAC and the pro-Jewish PACs in America have been drawn from the same circles of leadership.

Of course, other developments were taking place on the American scene which promoted Jewish segregation. Much has been written about the way the interests of the Jews and some of its former group partners on the political scene seemed to separate. But the point is that the growing edge of the Jewish apparatus is becoming increasingly and markedly one-issue in its approach to political life. A smaller and smaller proportion of young Jewish influentials in the apparatus became activist in general community life.

Even so, this trend towards self-ghettoization among these Jewish elites does not create a current disability for Jewish political effectiveness *as long as there are no serious political problems for Jewish issues.* The fact is that at the end of 1986, there are no such serious problems on the surface, despite all the foreboding which Jews are wise to have. American support of Israel is more secure than it has ever been, as this is written. American politicians are publicly committed to Israel, and the American public remains highly sympathetic towards Israel.

Antisemitism is at its lowest level in the century. Even in those cities where antisemitism has traditionally been spawned, the phenomenon is muted because of the sympathy towards Israel in those circles. And there has been no break in the strength of American civil liberties.

As has been indicated, there is much concern among Jews about the "Christian" talk that has surrounded church-state issues—and the legislation and the Supreme Court have been loosening the strictures against church-state separation that existed a decade ago. While this may be a matter for serious Jewish political attention, there is no indication that the American people or politicians will stand for much more than a cyclical over-adjustment to the strict constructionists of a decade ago.

As long as these circumstances prevail, the political power of the American Jews will not be seriously tested. Within a climate of strong American partisanship towards Israel, for example, a difference can be made in this case or that with one-issue activism.

But life for American Jews can get qualitatively stickier. American support for Israel is based on perceptions of American national interest which can change. Contemplate the possibilities of diminishing Israeli power in the Middle East, especially with accompanying economic problems; diminishing American power in the Middle East; economic problems in America; a more non-interventionist American foreign policy. Under such conditions, it becomes clear that American Jewish political effectiveness will depend not on marginal political clout, nor on Israel-related activism, but on general Jewish influence in the political process. And such influence will not finally be just a matter of political mechanics; it will also be a matter of the perceptions and the values with which American Jews will impress on that process and on American policy makers.

None of this is meant to disparage one-issue organizations such as AIPAC and their efforts, which are important and effective in the present situation. But if a serious assessment is to be made of the possible needs of the future, then it must include the apparent decline within the heart of the organized Jewish community of non-ghettoized activism with which the Jews have most deeply affected the political process in America.

Summary and Remedies

Most of the developments on the American Jewish scene do not threaten Jewish political effectiveness in the foreseeable future—or at least they need not. But some of these developments may not be benign if certain characteristics of Jewish community and political life are not maintained and, in some cases, restored.

The chief remedial characteristic of Jewish public affairs activity is its *non-ghettoized activism* in American life.

Such an integrated activism can turn Jewish population dispersion into a positive factor by extending political effectiveness into new areas. As a deliberate policy, the organized Jewish community would do well to buttress this possibility by giving more support to new Jewish enclaves outside the traditional areas of Jewish concentration and fundraising.

Extreme measures of electoral reform, such as preponderant reliance on government funds for political campaigns, could certainly impede the political effectiveness of American Jews because of a direct effect on an important aspect of their activism. Such extreme measures will not be easily legislated by elected public officials. On the other hand, the Jewish community should be more actively and constructively interested in this area of public policy. Reforms that prevent abuse and scandal could also prevent the enactment of extreme measures down the road. However, the current reforms will not impede the political effectiveness of American Jews in the face of their continued activism.

The effect of mandated proportional representation in political life has already received attention, but should be included in a larger context, i.e., as not just an abstract matter of "quotas," but a matter affecting the quality of the political process. And the issue of the electoral college is not a burning one, since the electoral college vote and the popular vote have come to coincide—but the electoral college has served to dramatize the activism of Jews in certain states, and as one American Jewish Congress official once commented: "If it ain't broke, don't fix it."

The apparent weakening of those networks called political parties in America will also fail, in current circumstances, to undercut the political effectiveness of American Jews, as long as their activism is maintained and intensified. Indeed, the existence of relatively autonomous political campaign centers lends itself to more effective grass roots activism. However, there should be an active Jewish interest in strengthening the resultant networks.

Furthermore, the Jewish community should have an active interest in maintaining the strength and compatibility of that political network in which it has politically thrived: the Democratic Party, whose exact thrust and characteristics for the immediate future are problematic. But the effectiveness of Jewry on this score depends not only on general activism, but on specific emphasis on coalitional activity with other traditional constituencies of the Democratic Party network, at least in those areas where Jews are concentrated.

At the same time, it should be noted that, while the "Democratic difference" of the American Jews returned full force at the polls during the last Presidential election, there appeared to be a more organized activism by ideologically interested Jewish sectors within the Republican Party, at least at the Presidential level. The volatility of both party networks at this particular time suggests that this development could be a positive factor, as long as the common Jewish agenda, in its larger framework, is restored as a lively and fruitful dialogue within the Jewish community.

In sum, while the current developments on the American scene raise certain public policy concerns to which the organized Jewish community should give attention, the main threats to Jewish political effectiveness probably lie within the dynamics of that Jewish community itself. In ways that have been discussed, there is a tendency towards the self-ghettoization of Jewish public life. Connected to that trend is the tendency to develop "one-issue" organizations and mentalities. And connected to that trend also is the tendency to constrict—or at least not to provide the process for broadening—the kind of "Jewish discussion" of issues, relating to Israel or America, which is necessary to the complexities of this new era.

These internal factors appear to be the main threat to Jewish political effectiveness in the foreseeable future.

Table I: Jewish Population & Voting Population

	1955*		1986*		1986
	Jewish Population (1000's)	% of General Population	Jewish Population (1000's)	% of General Population	% of Voting Population (Est.)—General Election
New York	2410	15.6	1872	10.6	18.0
New Jersey	280	5.3	435	5.9	10.0
District of Columbia	40	4.6	30	4.8	8.2
Florida	84	2.4	478	4.7	8.0
Maryland	91	3.5	196	4.6	7.8
Massachusetts	205	4.1	249	4.6	7.8
Pennsylvania	355	3.3	415	3.5	6.0
Connecticut	93	4.2	102	3.3	5.6
California	430	3.4	776	3.2	5.4

*Sources: American Jewish Yearbook

Table II: The one issue or two "which makes the most important difference to me" in choosing between the two candidates*

	% Keeping Church-State Separate	% Supporting Israel	% Helping the Poor	% Helping the Economy	% Helping the Aged	% Achieving the Peace	% Strong World Defense	% Fighting U.S. Antisemitism
Reagan Voters (180)	18	26	1	54	2	32	30	4
Mondale Voters (614)	37	20	12	21	7	57	2	4

Estimated Jewish Population in 172 Cities, Towns, Suburbs and Metropolitan Areas in the United States and Canada

New York, N.Y.	1,734,500
Los Angeles, Calif.	500,870
Philadelphia, Pa.	295,000
Miami, Fla.	253,340
Chicago, Ill.	248,000
Boston, Mass.	170,000
Washington, D.C.	157,335
Toronto, Ont.	115,000
Metropolitan New Jersey	111,000
Baltimore, Md.	92,000
Montreal, Quebec	90,000
San Francisco, Calif.	80,000
Cleveland, Ohio	70,000
Detroit, Michigan	70,000
Bergen County, N.J.	69,300
South Broward, Fla.	60,000
Orange County, Calif.	60,000
St. Louis, Mo.	53,500
Fort Lauderdale, Fla.	50,000
Pittsburgh, Pa.	45,000
Palm Beach County, Fla.	45,000
Boca Raton, Fla.	40,000
Phoenix, Ariz.	35,000
Oakland, Calif.	35,000
San Diego, Calif.	34,000
Monmouth County, N.J.	33,600
Atlanta, Ga.	33,500
North Jersey, N.J.	32,500
Central New Jersey	32,000
Denver, Colo.	30,000
Southern New Jersey	28,000
Houston, Texas	28,000
Hartford, Ct.	26,000
Milwaukee, Wis.	23,900
Delaware Valley, Pa.	23,000
Minneapolis, Minn.	22,000
Rhode Island	22,000
Cincinnati, Ohio	22,000
Dallas, Texas	22,000
New Haven, Ct.	22,000
Northern Middlesex, N.J.	19,750
Raritan Valley, N.J.	19,600
Rochester, N.Y.	19,600
Seattle, Wash.	19,500
Kansas City, Mo.	19,000
North Shore, Mass.	19,000
Winnipeg, Manitoba	18,500
Buffalo, N.Y.	18,500
San Jose, Calif.	18,000
Bridgeport, Ct.	18,000
Tucson, Ariz.	18,000
Las Vegas, Nevada	17,000
Morris-Sussex Counties, N.J.	16,000
Orlando, Fla.	15,000
South County, Fla.	15,000
Columbus, Ohio	15,000
Long Beach, Calif.	13,500
Tidewater, Va.	12,100
Albany, N.Y.	12,000
Atlantic County, N.J.	12,000
Stamford, Ct.	12,000
New Orleans, La.	12,000
Springfield, Mass.	11,000
Tampa, Fla.	10,500
Indianapolis, Ind.	10,000
Worcester, Mass.	10,000
Framingham, Mass.	10,000
Delaware	9,500
Ottawa, Ontario	9,500
Pinellas County, Fla.	9,500
Englewood, N.J.	9,300
Louisville, Ky.	9,200
Memphis, Tenn.	9,000
Syracuse, N.Y.	9,000
San Antonio, Texas	9,000
Portland, Ore.	8,845
Ocean County, N.J.	8,100
Richmond, Va.	8,000
Clifton, Passaic, N.J.	7,700
St. Paul, Minn.	7,500
Sarasota, Fla.	7,500
Sacramento, Calif.	7,000
Orange County, N.Y.	7,000
Jacksonville, Fla.	6,800
Omaha, Neb.	6,500
Harrisburg, Pa.	6,500
Toledo, Ohio	6,300
Akron, Ohio	6,000
Dayton, Ohio	6,000
Portland, Me.	5,550
Schenectady, N.Y.	5,400
Youngstown, Ohio	5,230
Nashville, Tenn.	5,080
Allentown, Pa.	4,980
Palm Springs, Calif.	4,950
Albuquerque, N.M.	4,500
Calgary, Alberta	4,500
Madison, Wis.	4,500
Birmingham, Ala.	4,500
El Paso, Texas	4,500
Somerset County, N.J.	4,100
Northwest Indiana	4,000
Norwalk, Ct.	4,000
Wilkes-Barre, Pa.	4,000
Charlotte, N.C.	4,000
Greenwich, Ct.	4,000
Hamilton, Ont.	3,750
Edmonton, Alberta	3,600
Ft. Worth, Texas	3,600
Austin, Texas	3,600
Berkshire County, Mass.	3,500
Danbury, Ct.	3,500
Charleston, S.C.	3,500
Des Moines, Iowa	3,500
Eastern Connecticut	3,500
Jersey City, N.J.	3,500
Scranton, Pa.	3,400
Broome County, N.Y.	3,000
Greensboro, N.C.	3,000
Kingston, N.Y.	3,000
Manchester, N.H.	3,000
Tulsa, Okla.	2,900
Canton, Ohio	2,850
Waterbury, Ct.	2,800
Reading, Pa.	2,800
Cumberland County, N.J.	2,750
New Bedford, Mass.	2,700
Savannah, Ga.	2,600
Newport News, Va.	2,575
Ft. Myers, Fla.	2,500
London, Ontario	2,500
Salt Lake City, Utah	2,500
Oklahoma City, Okla.	2,400
Durham-Chapel Hill, N.C.	2,400
Columbia, S.C.	2,280
Flint, Mich.	2,200
Utica, N.Y.	2,100
Champaign-Urbana, Ill.	2,000
Lexington, Ky.	2,000
Chattanooga, Tenn.	2,000
Fresno, Calif.	2,000
Daytona Beach, Fla.	2,000
Windsor, Ontario	2,000
Peoria, Ill.	1,900
South Bend, Ind.	1,900
Lansing, Mich.	1,850
Quad Cities, Ill.	1,800
Lancaster, Pa.	1,800
Montgomery, Ala.	1,800
Haverhill, Mass.	1,650
Little Rock, Ark.	1,600
Augusta, Ga.	1,500
Grand Rapids, Mich.	1,500
Knoxville, Tenn.	1,350
Mobile, Ala.	1,250
Shreveport, La.	1,200
Baton Rouge, La.	1,200
Corpus Christi, Texas	1,200
Southern Illinois	1,200
Troy, N.Y.	1,200
Ft. Wayne, Ind.	1,200
Evansville, Ind.	1,200
Steubenville, Ohio	1,200
Springfield, Ill.	1,100
Elmira, N.Y.	1,100
Duluth, Mn.	1,100
Charleston, W. Va.	1,075
Roanoke, Va.	1,050
Lewiston-Auburn, Me.	1,000
Asheville, N.C.	1,000
Columbus, Ga.	1,000
Wichita, Ks.	1,000
TOTAL UNITED STATES	5,920,890
TOTAL CANADA	305,000

World Jewish Population

Rank	Country	Population
1.	United States	5,920,890
2.	Israel	3,254,000
3.	Soviet Union	2,630,000
4.	France	650,000
5.	United Kingdom	410,000
6.	Canada	305,000
7.	Argentina	300,000
8.	Brazil	150,000
9.	South Africa	118,000
10.	Hungary	80,000
11.	Iran	70,000
12.	Australia	67,000
13.	Uruguay	50,000
14.	Rumania	45,000
15.	Belgium	41,000
16.	Italy	41,000
17.	Germany	38,000
18.	Mexico	37,500
19.	Chile	30,000
20.	Netherlands	30,000
21.	Turkey	24,000
22.	Morocco	22,000
23.	Switzerland	21,000
24.	Sweden	17,000
25.	Venezuela	15,000
26.	Austria	13,000
27.	Colombia	12,000
28.	Czechoslovakia	12,000
29.	Spain	12,000
30.	Ethiopia	11,000
31.	India	8,000
32.	Denmark	7,500
33.	Bulgaria	7,000
34.	Tunisia	7,000
35.	Greece	6,000
36.	Poland	6,000
37.	Yugoslavia	5,500
38.	Peru	5,200
39.	New Zealand	5,000
40.	Syria	4,500
41.	Costa Rica	2,500
42.	Guatemala	2,000
43.	Panama	2,000
44.	Zimbabwe	1,960
45.	Ireland	1,900
46.	Cuba	1,500
47.	Paraguay	1,200
48.	Algeria	1,000
49.	Ecuador	1,000
50.	Finland	1,000
51.	Luxembourg	1,000
52.	Norway	900
53.	Bolivia	750
54.	Curacao	700
55.	Gibraltar	600
56.	Portugal	600
57.	Surinam	500
58.	Yemen Arab Republic	500
59.	Iraq	450
60.	Kenya	450
61.	Singapore	450
62.	Egypt	400
63.	Japan	400
64.	Lebanon	400
65.	Zambia	400
66.	El Salvador	350
67.	Jamaica	350
68.	Albania	300
69.	Trinidad & Tobago	300
70.	Hong Kong	250
71.	Pakistan	250
72.	Afghanistan	250
73.	Dominican Republic	200
74.	Honduras	200
75.	Nicaragua	200
76.	Philippines	200
77.	Zaire	200
78.	Haiti	150
79.	Indonesia	100
80.	Barbados	70
81.	Burma	50
82.	Malta	50
83.	China	30
84.	Cyprus	30
85.	Libya	20

Europe	4,102,350
Americas	6,839,560
Asia	3,353,810
Africa	159,340
Oceania	72,000
WORLDWIDE	14,527,150

Source: Jewish Information Center, New York, *World Zionist Handbook;* Facts on File.

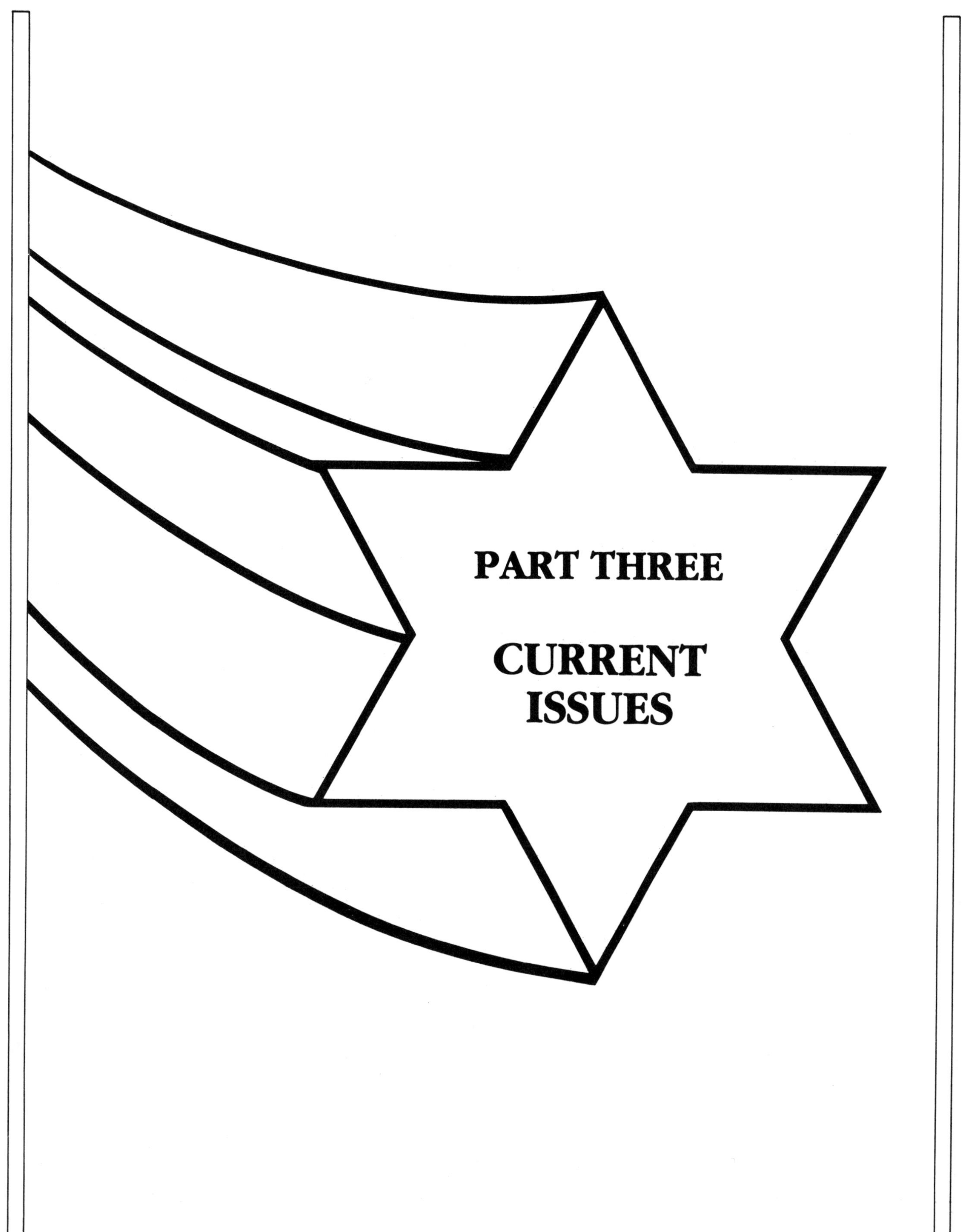

PART THREE

CURRENT ISSUES

5

Bitburg Revisited: What Is the Jewish Role In the World?

Dennis Prager

A lot happened at Bitburg.

It provided a vivid illustration of the Jews' role in forcing the world to confront evil. It demonstrated how the Jews only partially fulfill this role. And it revealed a significant difference between Christians and Jews.

I

To understand Bitburg, one must first understand the role played by Jewish suffering.

The Jews are the world's miner's canary. Canaries are taken down to mines because they quickly die upon exposure to noxious fumes. When the miner sees the canary dead, he knows there are noxious fumes to be fought. So it is with the Jews. Noxious moral forces often focus first on the Jews. But their ultimate targets are the moral values that the Jews represent. That is why non-Jews who share Jews' values have a vested interest in combating anti-Jewish forces. They make a fatal error when they dismiss antisemites as the Jews' problem.

Examples include the antisemitism or anti-Zionism of the Nazis, Idi Amin, Mouammar Qaddafi, the United Nations, and present day Islam. Each was first dismissed as the Jews' problem. By failing to understand the universal implications of antisemitism, moral non-Jews awoke too late to the threat posed by these antisemites.

Fifty-five million lives might have been saved had democracies understood the meaning of Nazi Jew-hatred. Five-hundred thousand Ugandans were eventually murdered by Idi Amin whose vicious anti-Zionism was ignored as a Jewish problem. Qaddafi, now regarded as the primary supporter of terrorism against Western democracies, first revealed his moral nature in his obsessive hatred of Israel. The transformation of the United Nations into a force inimical to democracy and human rights was rendered inevitable by its becoming an international vehicle for anti-Zionism. And the Moslem enemies of Israel are finally being perceived as the enemies as well of such Western values as individual rights, democracy, and freedom.

Antisemitism is not another hatred and it is much more than hatred of Jews. It is ultimately hatred of what the Jews, wittingly or not, willingly or not, have represented: the call to a higher moral law. Judaism and traditional Jews have always understood this. As the Talmud explains it, the Hebrew words for hatred and Sinai, *seenah* and *seenai,* are as related as they sound: the hatred of the Jews comes from Sinai. That is where the Jews received God's moral Law, and the world has never forgiven the Jews for imposing on it their ethical monotheism, their God of moral demands and moral judgment.

Non-Jewish students of antisemitism have often commented on this as well. As the Catholic historian of antisemitism, the Reverend Edward Flannery, wrote, "It was Judaism that brought the concept of a God-given universal moral law into the world; willingly or not, the Jew carries the burden of God in history, [and] for this has never been forgiven."

And Ernest van den Haag in *The Jewish Mystique* summarized the roots of antisemitism in these words: "Most unpleasant, [the Jews'] invisible God not only insisted on being the one and only and all-powerful God . . . He also developed into a moral God. . . . The Jews have suffered from their own invention ever since."

Even antisemites have acknowledged this meaning of antisemitism. The father of German racial theory, Houston Stewart Chamberlain, complained that "The Jew came into our gay world and spoiled everything with his ominous concept of sin, his law, and his cross." He was echoing Richard Wagner's words: "Emancipation from the yoke of Judaism appears to us the foremost necessity." And Hitler defined his mission as the destruction of the "tyrannical God of the Jews [and His] life-denying Ten Commandments."

The Jews have suffered for being the human representatives of God's moral demands. They have truly fulfilled Isaiah's description of them as God's "suffering servant." Whenever others reject God's moral law, Jews suffer. Of course other peoples have suffered at the hands of evil men and ideologies, but the Jews and their suffering have repeatedly focused the world on its greatest evils.

The Jews therefore have two tasks vis-a-vis evil. First, confront the world with its greatest evils—never allow it to "reconcile" itself to them, never "forgive" them (unless the evil repent, which is impossible, for example, in the case of dead Nazis). Second, explain these evils. Explain that the Jewish suffering caused by these evils is a result of the denial of Sinai, the hatred of the ethical monotheism introduced by the Jews. For this reason, and only for this reason, antisemitism has universal importance.

Bitburg helped to clarify precisely how well the Jews implement these tasks.

First Task: Confront the World With Its Evils

Most Jews, being quite human, as well as quite oblivious to their role in the world, have hardly sought to confront the world with its evils. They would just as soon let others play this role. But Bitburg showed once again that Jews are not at all willing to leave this role to others. While many nations suffered terribly at the hands of the Nazis, it was the Jews, almost alone, who screamed bloody murder at any hint of forgetting Nazi evil.

The question is, Why? Why, if they do not identify with their calling to confront the world with its evils, do Jews so consistently do precisely that?

The answer, I believe, is that their role leaves them no choice.

For even though the Jews may not want to keep reminding the world to confront evil, they do so anyway—out of what they perceive as self-interest in not allowing the world to forget *their* suffering. But since the greatest forces of evil so often focus on the Jews, the Jews' suffering and their constant talking about it serve to an unparalleled extent to focus people's attention on those evils.

It was, in fact, a Roman Catholic, William F. Buckley, Jr., who once made this point most tellingly. In a public interview with Rabbi Joseph Telushkin and myself, he pointed out that if all Soviet Jews were allowed to leave the Soviet Union, as wonderful as that may be for the Jewish people, it would not be a positive development for the world. The reason, he immediately explained, was that in the West and at the United Nations, the Jews and Israel were really the only ones constantly confronting the world with Soviet evil. And why? Because the Jews were protesting on behalf of their fellow Jews. But if there were no Jews left suffering in the Soviet Union, Western Jewry would keep silent about the Soviets, and then no one would confront the world with Soviet evil.

In other words, the Jews' screaming about their suffering, even though done for selfish ethnic, rather than religious moral, reasons, serves a universal moral purpose.

The Holocaust is the quintessential example. Had the Nazis inflicted their Holocaust upon another people, most Jews, being normal human beings and oblivious to their religious/moral role, would hardly be screaming at the world "never again"—with the result that the world would not be talking all that much about Nazi evil. The Jews do not demand that the world remember the six million Ukrainians murdered by the Soviets, or the one out of every three Cambodians killed by the Communists in Cambodia, or the genocidal destruction of Tibet by the Chinese Communists, or confront the greatest evil of this moment, the Soviet destruction of Afghanistan. *And the result is that the world ignores these evils.*

Ideally the Jews would live up to their role and scream about these other horrors. But while the Jews may be failing in this role, they can hardly be criticized for demanding only that the world confront the evils done to their own—for other groups do not even do that. The apathy of Western Christians to the horrible persecution of fellow Christians in the USSR, the silence of the Catholic Church over the virtual decimation of fellow Catholics in Lebanon, and the lack of worldwide Moslem opposition to the Soviet annihilation of Islam and Moslems in Afghanistan are simply incomprehensible to Jews.

Thus even though for most Jews it is self-interest, rather than a conscious fulfillment of their role, that motivates them to ensure that certain evils will not be ignored, it is still the Jews who most consistently demand that the world stare at evil's blinding light.

The confrontation at Bitburg was a classic reenactment of the Jewish role. Most people, including most fine, moral people who loathe what the Nazis did, and even groups that also suffered at the hands of Nazis, wanted to forgive and/or forget. The Jews said stare at evil, call it evil, remember evil. Others said "reconciliation." The Jews cried "remember."

Thus the Jews at Bitburg played their historical role.

Second task: Explain these Evils

But they played it only half way. True, almost alone, the Jews insisted on remembering Nazi evil, but because they did so primarily out of self-interest (remember *our* suffering) rather than because of their religious role, they could offer no reasons why the *world* should remember Nazi antisemitism. Consequently, the world is coming to perceive the Jews' obsession with Auschwitz as obsession with themselves rather than as obsession with evil.

The Jews are telling the world to remember Nazism, but they are giving the world no reason, other than sympathy for the Jews, to do so. Why should the world spend five more minutes on the Holocaust than on the mass murders of American Indians, Australian aborigines, Cambodians, Afghans, Ukrainians, Tartars, Armenians, or anyone else? By speaking as a suffering ethnic group rather than from our religious/moral role as spokesmen for ethical monotheism, we have little to say to the world about evil and solutions to it.

If we were to explain that Nazism is, in essence, the denial of the Jewish and Christian values of a God-based society with personal moral responsibility to that God and His moral law, then we Jews have a humanity-serving reason to keep humanity's memory focused on the Holocaust. If we would explain that the denial of God as the basis of ethics leads first to the destruction of Jews as the historical representatives of that doctrine and then to the destruction of all other decent people, then others, too, would become obsessed with the Holocaust.

Unfortunately, however, most Jews, in their alienation from Judaism and their adoption of secular values, find such notions bizarre, if not actually repugnant. That it is primarily a war on God that has led to Auschwitz, the Gulag, Cambodia; that the Jews' role is to bring mankind to ethical monotheism—to teach that God without ethics (Khomeini, Crusaders, etc.) and ethics opposed to God (Nazism, Marxism-Leninism) both lead to terrible evil; that Jewish suffering has a universal religious/moral meaning—such notions are utterly alien to most Jews whose secular worldview renders a Jewish one inscrutable.

But only such religious notions render the Holocaust meaningful—for both Jews and non-Jews. Otherwise the Holocaust is only a provincial, ethnic tragedy. Instead of teaching the world the universal meaning of Jewish suffering, we merely appear self-obsessed. We have to show how the Holocaust, as all antisemitism, threatens far more than Jews. Not because of humanist platitudes such as all suffering affects all people, or no man is an island, or so long as one people is oppressed, all are oppressed. But because the Jews, as Reverend Flannery wrote, "carry the burden of God in history." And those who wish to supplant God with a *fuhrer* or with a Party, will seek to annihilate Judaism and/or the Jews. This is what Nazi and Soviet antisemitism are all about. This is why others should never ever forget the Holocaust.

Christians, for example, should be made aware of the anti-Christian essence of Nazi antisemitism. As Robert Jay Lifton, a professor of psychiatry who studied Nazi doctors, recently wrote in a *New York Times* article explaining Dr. Josef Mengele's Jew-hatred: "According to an Auschwitz friend and fellow-SS physician, Mengele espoused the visionary SS ideology that the Nordic race ... had been weakened by Christian morality of Jewish origin." Like Hitler and many pre-Nazi German antisemites (see, for example, Uriel Tal, *Christians and Jews in Germany,* Cornell, 1975), Mengele believed that Christianity was a Jewish aberration thrust upon an unwilling German race. That plenty of despicable and foolish German Christians did not perceive the anti-God and anti-Christian components of Nazi antisemitism and actually supported Nazism tells us something about those German Christians, but nothing about Nazism.

If we showed Christians that modern antisemitism—from the Nazis to the Communists to the Moslems—is inevitably anti-Christian, we would enlist their passionate interest in the Holocaust and antisemitism generally. But instead of teaching that Auschwitz was built by an ideology that loathed the God of Judaism and of Christianity, most Jews continue to regard Christianity as if it were still calling for Crusades and inquisitions and still look to secular ideals for their salvation. Instead of teaching that Jews and Christians must fight *together* for ethical monotheism, many Jews continue to fight *against* Christianity and ethical monotheism. Instead of teaching Christians the divine role Jews and their suffering play, many Jews label Christians who do believe in the divine Jewish role fanatics and enemies.

In short, we must teach Christians and others the universal lessons of Auschwitz and the Gulag. God is necessary for a moral order, His "death" must lead to additional holocausts, and the future of mankind is either Jerusalem or Moscow, ethical monotheism or totalitarianism, because people will be morally responsible for their actions either to Almighty God or to the all mighty state.

Of course, most Jews would choke while uttering such words. Rather than teach the need for ethical monotheism, most Jews continue to preach humanism—*belief in humanity* after the Holocaust, *belief in humanity* after the Gulag, *belief in humanity* after Cambodia—and a *secular* humanism, even though the most destructive and sadistic regimes in history have been anti-religious.

If we did teach these lessons of the Holocaust, *then* non-Jews would be likely to react positively to our very appropriate obsession with it. They would understand that the Holocaust is far more than a Jewish problem.

Ironically, but as is often the case, it is the religious Jewish approach that has universal meaning, and the secular ethnic Jewish approach that means nothing to non-Jews. As of this moment, the only reason we Jews have given for a non-Jew to feel strongly about the Holocaust is human empathy. But that is hardly enough for most people, and it certainly does not answer why anyone should devote more attention to Jewish sufferings than to any other.

II

One reason, then, why Jews do not teach the lessons of the Holocaust is their ignorance of and even opposition to religion and God-based explanations for anything. There is another reason. If Jews understood their obligation to push the world to stare at its most blinding evils, and to teach that these are consequences of ideologies that are anti-God, they would have to reach a conclusion that too few Jews are willing to confront: along with Nazism (which is essentially dead), Communism has been this century's most systematic evil. If we understood what the Holocaust should teach the world and took our role seriously, we would have to confront the world with the evil that was—Nazism, and with the evil that is—Communism.

Communism has murdered far more people than did Nazism (only because Nazism was destroyed, but this fact hardly invalidates the point; it merely argues for the destruction of Communism whenever possible). It has destroyed far more national and religious cultures, subjugated more nations, ruined more lives, and tortured more innocents. And Communism, even more explicitly than Nazism, is a war against God and Judaeo-Christian Western civilization. But for reasons that are beyond the purview of this essay, Jews, while rarely (at long last) pro-Communist, still often lead opposition to anti-Communism.

Indeed, for many Jews there is a remarkable cognitive dissonance regarding Communism and the Soviet Union. On the one hand, they protest vehemently against Soviet persecution of Soviet Jews; they know that outside of Nazi Germany no regime has ever as effectively warred on Judaism; and they are aware of the methodical torture of, among others, Anatoly Shcharansky. Yet when the President of the United States calls those very same Soviets an "evil empire," they will scream that he is a war monger and cold warrior, and demand to know who we are to judge the Soviet leaders. And they will consider it *immoral* (not merely an erroneous but moral anti-Communist strategy) to fund opponents of the burgeoning Communist tyranny in Nicaragua, or for that matter to fight Communism anywhere, and they will keep silent on Afghanistan whose decimation is nearing genocidal proportions.

Western Jews' policies regarding Soviet Jewry (recalling William Buckley's point) provide a classic example of the Jews unwittingly playing their religious/moral role, and of their playing it only half way. There are far more Christians in Soviet prison camps for being Christian than there are Jews for being Jewish. Yet, by and large, Western Christians ignore, or even worse, deny, as do the National and World Councils of Churches, how terribly Christians do suffer in Communist countries. So it is often primarily thanks to the Jews screaming about the sufferings of Jews in the Soviet Union, that the West has often had to confront the evil of the Soviets. But just as we tell the world about the Holocaust but not about the meaning of Nazi evil, the Jews are telling the world about Soviet Jews, but not about Soviet evil.

So we play our role with regard to Communist evil, as we

did at Bitburg with regard to Nazi evil, provincially, and therefore only half way. But this is still half way more than Christians are doing about imprisoned Soviet Christians or Moslems are doing about Afghanistan.

I did not agree with the conservative defenders of the President's visit to Bitburg. The Jews were right, and the President and his defenders were wrong about ever having a "reconciliation" with Nazi evil, but their error emanated in part (the other part, the Christian view of forgiveness, will be discussed) from their very valid preoccupation with Communist evil. They said that because of the contemporary battle against the Soviets, doing what our strategically most important ally in Europe wanted was more important than giving in on Bitburg. If we could support Stalin in fighting the Nazis, we could stand with Kohl and his dead SS men against the Soviets.

Thus, I believe that the moral scorecard at Bitburg read: Jews right about dead evil and therefore about Bitburg, Reagan and the conservatives right about living evil, but wrong about Bitburg.

III

Some years ago Simon Wiesenthal wrote an illuminating little book entitled *The Sunflower.* In it, he recounts how one day while he was an inmate in a Nazi concentration camp, he was picked at random to go to a nearby hospital. There a young Nazi soldier who had participated in atrocities such as burning Jews alive lay dying. The Nazi had asked that a Jew, any Jew, be brought to him from the nearby camp. He wanted to ask a Jew for forgiveness before he died.

Wiesenthal was brought to the Nazi's room where he found a young man bandaged from head to toe. After recounting to Wiesenthal the atrocities he had perpetrated, he implored Wiesenthal to forgive him. Wiesenthal listened to the entire story, then left the room without forgiving the young man. Years later he sent this story to about two dozen major thinkers, and asked them to react. Was he, Wiesenthal, right or wrong?

Though Wiesenthal does not so note, there is one consistent pattern to the responses. All the Jews, whether religious or not, said Wiesenthal was right. All the non-Jews, whether religious or not, said he was wrong. I do not believe that the reason is in any way related to the fact that it was Jews who were murdered. Among other things, that would be an insult to the very fine non-Jews who responded.

Bitburg, like *The Sunflower,* illustrated one of the most significant differences between Judaism and Christianity: their attitudes to forgiveness and therefore to evil.

When Elie Wiesel implored President Reagan not to visit Bitburg, he spoke as a Jew. Virtually every Jew who heard Mr. Wiesel understood him and could barely comprehend how anyone could not see the logic and righteousness of his position. To almost every Jew, it is axiomatic that one does not, indeed one has no right to, forgive murderers and torturers on behalf of their victims.

On the other hand, almost every Christian, lapsed ones included, understood the President, and could barely comprehend how Elie Wiesel and the Jews did not see the logic and righteousness of Mr. Reagan's position. To almost every Christian, it is axiomatic that one forgives. Period.

For more than three years I have been moderating a weekly radio show featuring a Protestant minister, Catholic priest, and rabbi. With different guests each week, a broad range of opinions is assured. Yet one issue consistently united Protestants (from fundamentalist to most liberal) and Catholics and divides them from the Jews (from Reform to Orthodox)—forgiveness.

I have asked this question repeatedly to Christian clergy: "Do I understand correctly that it is the Christian position that if I hurt, even murder, another person, any person, you as a Christian are duty bound to forgive me?" Every one has said yes.

To virtually any Jew, this notion is simply immoral. Even Jews who are Jewishly ignorant hold to the basic Jewish principle that only the victim can forgive the person who has hurt him. And those who are familiar with Judaism know that according to it, God Himself does not forgive unless the victim has already done so.

It is this profoundly differing view of forgiveness—which may reflect a profoundly different view of evil—that explains more than anything else, why President Reagan and his supporters on the one hand, and Elie Wiesel and the Jews on the other, did not understand each other. President Reagan is a Christian. On this issue of forgiving evil, Jews and Christians so disagree that they simply do not understand one another.

This is not to say that for a Jew to understand the Christian position is to appreciate it any the more. One of the reasons I am so passionately committed to Judaism is precisely because of its obsession with good and evil (rather than, let us say, with love, forgiveness, and salvation). Its uncompromising attitude to the deliberate infliction of suffering on the innocent is Judaism's "light unto the nations."

At Bitburg, the Jews did not entirely fulfill their mission, while Christians who called for "reconciliation" with Nazi monsters were more consistent with theirs. But Bitburg showed once again that when it comes to having the world confront evil, it is still Judaism that leads the way.

American Jewish Disunity: An Overview

Samuel Heilman

"Split Widens on a Basic Issue: What is a Jew?" read the front page headline of the *New York Times* on February 28, 1986. The article that followed, written by Joseph Berger, went on to report that "the polemics have been marked by *uncommon* bitterness." It quoted a variety of rabbis and Jewish leaders who warned that "the dispute could result in deep and enduring divisions in the Jewish community," a schism that might ultimately lead to one group questioning the other's Jewishness, in the possibility that family pedigrees would be scrutinized by the more observant before they would allow "a son or a daughter to marry a less traditional Jew," in more restrictive and selective admission standards to Jewish day schools and summer camp, and even erosion in the general Jewish support for Israel.

While the article went on to quote some students of Jewish life, among them sociologists and rabbis, who minimized the forebodings of permanent disunity and downplayed the prospects of growing and unbridgeable divisions within the American Jewish community, the overall thrust of the report, and what made it "front-page news," was the ominous prospect that was perhaps articulated best in a quotation from Haskel Lookstein, president of the New York Board of Rabbis, who suggested: "The extremism that manifests itself on both sides threatens to isolate Jew from Jew and to rend the fabric of Jewish peoplehood so that we will no longer be one people." Or as Rabbi Irving Greenberg, a liberal Orthodox thinker, cautioned: "you have a situation ripe for schism."

To be sure, the *New York Times* article was not the first but only the latest report of such internal Jewish disunity. There have been others in practically every Jewish newspaper, periodical, and journal over the last few years, while hardly a Jewish gathering or rabbi has missed a chance to explore the matter. And, because, as writer Albert Goldman once put it, "the Jews have always been students, and their greatest study is themselves," there will undoubtedly be no early end to the discussion.

While no single document can hope to put the matter of Jewish schism and disunity to rest, an overview which goes beyond the passions or rhetoric of the moment and subjects the matter of Jewish sectarianism to study and analysis can contribute to a better understanding of the facts and help in assessing the consequences as well as suggesting what if any action can be taken to mitigate disunity. That is what these pages hope to do.

Specifically, this report will address a number of questions, the answers to which should offer some light on the vexing matter of Jewish disunity. These questions ask: What separates or threatens to divide Jew from Jew? Where, precisely, are the lines of fracture along which some argue the Jewish community is breaking apart? How deep are the divisions? Are they permanent or is there a chance that they will be bridged over time or by the changing circumstances of Jewish life?

To answer these questions, it is necessary to go beyond uncovering the current disunity that exists among Jews. We must also examine history to discover if disunity is a new phenomenon, a threat unlike any that has confronted Jews before, or whether there are parallels to it in the Jewish past. This is not simply an academic question, for if indeed the danger of schism has confronted Jews before, there is much to be learned from the way that threat was resolved. History is after all not only the great teacher; what is past can often be prologue, and a knowledge of history may sometimes offer a vision for the future.

There are sociological questions to be asked as well. If there is in fact a rift among Jews, is it growing, shrinking, or simply remaining unchanged? That numbers of Jews are expressing concern about divisions within Jewry seems obvious, but are these voices harbingers of increasing dangers or do they simply cry the loudest? Are there other voices, perhaps not as strident or histrionic, that hold out hope for unity? And beyond the voices, what are the facts? Where is the evidence of either unity or disunity?

Finally there is the question of the consequences. What will follow from the facts? If disunity is growing and schism imminent, what will that mean for the future of the Jewish community, for Jewish survival? And even if an unbridgeable rift is not likely, what might be brought about by the fears of it? Do such fears become self-fulfilling prophesies, making unity all but impossible? Is there a need to sound an alarm? If so, what action, if any, should be taken to insure a secure future for Jewry? Or, more simply, what is to be done in light of the facts?

Let us turn then to these four general questions: (1) What are the dividing lines? (2) Has there been disunity like this before? (3) What are the likely consequences of disunity? (4) What can or should be done in response and what might the future bring?

(1) What are the dividing lines?

The Issues:
A. Conversion and Patrilineal Descent

The immediate issue dividing Jews appears to focus around the question of "who or what is a Jew?" The matter of Jewish definition has undoubtedly become problematic because of a striking rise in the frequency of intermarriage between Jews and non-Jews. This increasing rate—ranging from approximately 25% on the average for American Jews to close to 40% in many communities, and in some places as high as 70%—has had several consequences. First, and most obviously, it has yielded a generation of children who have one parent that was not born a Jew, and who in only some cases (21%, as reported in a recent study of intermarriage by sociologist Egon Mayer) has been converted to Judaism. If the non-Jewish parent is the mother, then according to halacha (Jewish law), the offspring is not Jewish. Secondly, where mixed marriages do lead to conversion, these conversions are not always carried out according to the most rigorous standards of Jewish law. In such cases, the convert (either a parent or a child or both) may not be considered a Jew by those who adhere to a strict interpretation of the law.

Complicating the matter even further are several social factors. In their recent book, *The Transformation of the Jews,* Calvin Goldscheider and Alan Zuckerman, articulate these clearly: "Many intermarried Jews take part in Jewish communal life. Many, if not most, have Jewish friends and family connections. Most retain residential, occupational, and educational bonds with other Jews. Many non-Jews married to Jews develop bases of communal contacts and are part of the Jewish community." Simply stated, this means that a person raised as a Jew and tied to a network of Jewish relations and obligations, one who belongs to a synagogue or gets a Jewish education or gives to the United Jewish Appeal or identifies with the destiny of Israel may consider him or herself Jewish, *regardless of whether or not he or she meets the Jewish legal,* halachic, *demands for inclusion within the Jewish community.* Thus, for example, a child with a non-Jewish mother but a Jewish father who has been brought up in a Jewish cultural and social environment, attended the synagogue, received some sort of Jewish education, and even had a bar or bat mitzva, might consider him or herself a Jew, even though by the strict rules of the halacha, he or she is not.

Finally, someone born a non-Jew who enters the social and cultural milieu of Jewish life, either through marriage to a Jew or on his or her own, may decide to become a convert. As a neophyte to Judaism, the newcomer may often choose to enter through the path of least resistance—undergoing a conversion ritual that makes minimal demands upon him or her. Subsequently, the new convert becomes even more socially aligned and involved with the Jews. While from the social point of view, such integration appears to suggest a successful assimilation and demonstrates the capacity of the Jewish community to handle the potentially disruptive effects of intermarriage and conversion, it creates or fosters problems in other domains. Among these are the divisions between those on one side who accept the legitimacy of socially based definitions of Judaism and who seek to make entrance into Jewish communal life untroubled and those on the other side who are concerned with maintaining the integrity of the boundaries between Jews and others. Thus, the convert who has come into Judaism without undergoing the rigors of a traditional conversion under the auspices of an Orthodox Jewish court *(beit din)* may be stunned to discover that the legitimacy of his or her conversion is questioned by some segments (notably, the Orthodox and some Conservative Jews) of the community. Or the child of a mixed marriage who has been raised as a Jew, but whose mother has converted by a process other than the most stringent one, may be dismayed to find out at some point in life that his or her Jewishness is called into question by more traditionally oriented members of the Jewish community.

Complicating these divisions even further are political issues. Within America, the long-lasting and deep-seated rivalries among the various movements—Orthodox, Conservative and Reform—for the mantle of American Jewish religious and spiritual leadership has among other things led to struggles over determining the definition of who and what a Jew is. In light of the growing attachments between Jews and non-Jews, each sect of Judaism, through its rabbis and leaders, has made claims that assert its right to define and convert Jews.

On the one end are the Orthodox who point to their devotion to Jewish law and their apparent continuity with tradition as the source for their legitimacy. The fact that they still use the same criteria for defining a Jew that have been used for generations and that have been incorporated into the codes of Jewish law is presented as the basis of their claim for legitimacy. As one Orthodox rabbi put it: "Every religious group has its standards for admission, no less we Jews whose guidelines are from Sinai." (*Jewish Observer,* February 1986).

On the other extreme are the Reform who argue in favor of a definition that recognizes social realities, that confronts the fact that Jews are increasingly involved with non-Jews, and therefore calls for a definition that allows for the maximum integration possible. This means making conversion procedures less restrictive and more supportive and allowing for patrilineal as well as matrilineal lines of Jewish descent, a decision that the movement formalized in 1983.

Somewhere in the middle stand the Conservative Jews who seek to comply with the standards of the past with regard to defining Jews, to be conservative in making changes, but who have nonetheless accepted the principle that, as sociologist Marshall Sklare in his analysis of Conservative Judaism has put it, "changes in Judaism have their origin in changes in the lives of Jews." They are thus caught between an attachment to traditional Jewish law and a desire to be in tune with contemporary needs of American Jewry. While prepared to struggle with the social realities of intermarriage, they are nevertheless unwilling to make what they view as radical changes in Jewish tradition. "I think [that accepting patrilineal descent is] a fundamental rupture with the idea of a Jewish community, and communal responsibility ought to prevent us from rupturing that unity," said the newly appointed chancellor of the Jewish Theological Seminary of America, Ismar Schorsch. The Conservative dilemma is that the Jewish community to which they remain attached is not a monolith; to some of its adherents, stability and loyalty to the past are essential, while to others communal responsibility specifically encourages change.

Why the Increasing Concern?

The matter of who and what is a Jew has become of increasing concern and a matter of public debate in the last number of years because of several factors: (1) The rise in the rate of intermarriage from around 10% to 15% in the 1950s to 25% or more in the 1970s and 1980s has alarmed Jews. (2) The offspring of mixed marriages occurring during the 1950's and 1960's are now coming of age, marrying and taking their places in the Jewish community. (3) Orthodoxy, while not significantly increasing its demographic share in American Jewry (whose population of 5.6 million is reported to be about 10% Orthodox, 33% Conservative, 23% Reform, and 35% unaffiliated but still identified as Jewish) has begun to feel an increased sense of security about its position in America. It has not disappeared as many analysts a generation ago said it would; its adherents have acquired a modicum of financial and professional success, reflected in increased political power within Jewish life; its religious and educational institutions are flourishing, often encouraging a traditionalist (sometimes called "right wing") swing among many who attend or have attended them; and it can point with triumph to numbers of newly Orthodox Jews *(baaley t'shuva)* who are rejecting assimilationist trends and choosing traditional Judaism as a way of life. Accordingly, Orthodoxy is publicly challenging assimilationist and integrationist moves made by other Jews. (4) The rise of Orthodox power in the Israeli Likud government of Menachem Begin and the consequent hold this has had on defining Judaism there, coupled with greater American Jewish involvement with Israel (whereas prior to 1967 relatively few American Jews had direct contact with Israel, since that date the number has increased dramatically) has brought the Israeli parliamentary question of "who is a Jew?" to this country. (5) The 1983 decision by the Reform movement to recognize patrilineal Jewish descent stimulated debate and discussion among American Jews. (6) Finally, the recent study of intermarriage and the Jewish future sponsored by the American Jewish Committee and carried out by Egon Mayer dramatically shed light on the facts which could no longer be ignored: Jews were marrying non-Jews in greater numbers, and converts as well as offspring from mixed marriages and conversionary ones were an established part of the American Jewish community. The widespread dissemination of the findings throughout Jewish and non-Jewish media simply reinforced and focussed public awareness on the issues.

Yet if the matter of converts and offspring of intermarriage appears to divide American Jewry, they are by no means the only bones of contention. A comprehensive look at the grounds of American Jewish disunity reveals a series of other points of conflict.

B. Divorce

Among the matters dividing Jews from one another is the matter of divorce. Although Jews have enjoyed a reputation for stable marriages, there has been an increasing incidence of separation and divorce among them. In 1971, the National Jewish Population Survey found that among the 25 to 29 year old group, 15% of all the households were separated or divorced. In the last twenty-five years, the Jewish Family Service caseload of divorce has grown from 5% to 30%. And while the general American population approaches a 50% divorce rate, the Jewish one, although lagging behind, continues to grow.

Still, American Jews remain committed to marriage and the family, and they therefore tend to remarry in high numbers (indeed, more than other American religious groups). More than 50% of all divorced Jewish women remarry within five years.

While the Jewish law with regard to marriage is relatively flexible, divorce is a far more complex matter. Under the *halacha,* only a woman who has received a valid *get* (bill of divorcement), usually executed through the auspices of a Jewish court of law *(beit din),* is legally entitled to remarry. Should a Jewish woman remarry without such a valid *get,* her new marriage would, in the eyes of those who accept the authority of the *halacha,* be adulterous. Moreover, should she have a child from that new union, that child would, again in the eyes of those bound by the *halacha,* be considered illegitimate, a *mamzer.* In Jewish law, a *mamzer* may not marry a Jew. Nor may ten generations of offspring of a *mamzer* marry Jews.

To many, if not most, Orthodox Jews, civil divorces and those carried out through the aegis of non-Orthodox institutions are invalid. Consequently, all subsequent marriages and births lead to a population of people who are written out of the Jewish community as far as these Orthodox Jews are concerned. As one rabbi has expressed the problem: "Among the major tragedies of our American *golus* (exile) are the common occurrence of second marriages without benefit of a *get*. . . resulting in the proliferation of *mamzerim.* . . ." And thus divorce becomes not only a problem for the Jewish family but a source of disunity in the Jewish community.

C. The Status of Women in Judaism

While not nearly as divisive as the matters of conversion, patrilineal descent, or divorce and remarriage which, some believe, *may lead to structural rifts among Jews such that members of one group will find themselves unable to marry members of the others without compromising on their principles,* there are other lines of cleavage in the American Jewish community. Few matters have so exercised the American Jewish community as has the matter of the status of women in Judaism. Although this is not the place to review the entire debate or the course of its development, it must be pointed out that in the last century and even more during the last fifteen years, the traditional role of women in Judaism has undergone profound change. These changes have more or less paralleled the transformations in the status of women in the host societies of the West, within which most Jews reside. The keynote of that change has been the evolution of women *from a subservient to an equal* position with men.

Among the non-Orthodox, this has resulted in offering women most if not all the same rights and privileges that Judaism has accorded to men. Although the effect of change among the Orthodox has been far less comprehensive and sweeping, it can be discerned nevertheless. In Orthodox circles, including even the most uncompromising, the rising importance of women is reflected in the nearly universal acceptance of the principle that Jewish women should be provided intensive and advanced Jewish education like the men, something that in the past—

before the opening of the Sara Schnirer Beth Jacob schools for girls in this century and the expansion of day school education in post-war America—was largely unthinkable. But this change in the status of Orthodox women is symbolically far less than the non-Orthodox demand.

Accordingly, the status of women in Judaism has become a matter of dispute in the American Jewish community. The schismatic effect of this debate grows out of two symbolic issues: (1) the counting of Jewish women along with men as part of the *minyan* (quorum) for prayer, and (2) the ordination of women rabbis. Both of these options have been rejected by Orthodoxy and accepted by all other sects, although with some resistance among the traditionalist wing of Conservative Jewry. Accordingly, these two points have become part of the ideological line dividing Jews.

D. Kashrut

Without reviewing the massive and complex laws of *kashrut* (Jewish dietary laws), it is nevertheless possible to assert without doubt that American Jews are split over the matter of what they may or may not eat. In some cases, Jews will consume only foods that are certified kosher, while in others Jews will eat foods of all types. Ironically, although in their origins adherence to the dietary laws served to differentiate Jews from non-Jews, today the practice of keeping kosher has also come to separate some Jews from other Jews. Moreover, since the certification of "kosher," while subject to far greater consensus today than in the early days of the American Jewish community, is by no means universally agreed upon, even among those who keep kosher, there are divisions as to what constitutes completely kosher behavior. Such differences have also led to rifts such that one group will often not eat in the homes of another which does not share its definition of what is and is not kosher. Although not as dramatic a division as that concerning who is a Jew or whom one may marry, this separation of the kosher and the *trefe* (unkosher) represents a real and undeniable source of Jewish disunity.

E. Jewish Sectarian Affiliation

Another major split among Jews concerns the matter of Jewish affiliation. As already noted, the single largest segment of American Jewry, according to figures gleaned by Egon Mayer and supported by other surveys, notably those of sociologists Steven M. Cohen and Paul Ritterband, are the unaffiliated: those who are "just Jewish." Many, if not most, of these latter Jews are not members of Jewish organizations—including synagogues. Many have not been to Israel nor do they affiliate themselves to the community by giving to Jewish causes. This significantly differentiates them from the 65% of the remaining Jews, who are themselves divided in their affiliations.

While it is not necessary here to articulate all the nuances of difference among Orthodox, Conservative and Reform Jews, suffice it to say the differences are real. With origins in the nineteenth century communities of Germany, when some groups looked to integrate themselves wholeheartedly with society outside the Jewish one while others resisted some of the trends of this assimilation, these sectarian lines have deepened into cleavages and become part of contemporary American Jewish life. The issues of the dispute among the sects have varied since the early days, but its basic outlines remain the same: isolation and separation, with an unwillingness to adapt to change on the one extreme; integration and assimilation, with a desire to accommodate to new realities on the other—and in between a desperate search for a middle road, a synthesis.

These differences are supported by a wide array of separate organizations. There are separate rabbinical seminaries and associations, unrelated networks of synagogues and voluntary associations, camps, youth movements and the like. While there may be some ambiguities at the borders between one sect and another, with liberal or modern Orthodox Jews and traditionalist Conservative Jews or liberal Conservative and traditionalist Reform Jews being closer to one another than their formal affiliations would suggest, Jews in America have generally come to think of themselves as bound to these movements to the extent that they consider these as denominations of their Judaism. To complicate matters even further, the denominations have in some cases come into political conflict in the struggle of each to speak for all of Jewry. The results of these denominational labels has been to create intra-denominational solidarity on the one hand but inter-denominational hostility on the other.

F. Jewish Education

A final major line of cleavage among Jews concerns the matter of Jewish education. Essentially, in addition to the option of having no Jewish education (something that is true for about a third of American Jews), there are two general patterns of Jewish education in America: (1) intensive and (2) intermittent.

Those who select intensive Jewish education may send their children to day schools which combine, more or less equally, secular and religious curricula in the context of a totally Jewish environment. Or, alternatively, they may choose to send their children to a yeshiva, where the emphasis is predominantly on religious studies and particularly on Talmud, with secular education often limited only to what the state minimally requires. (Although some day schools use the term "yeshiva" in their names, yeshivas are—at least in the original meaning of the term—academies for intensive talmudical study.)

Because students in these yeshivas and day schools spend their entire school day with other Jews, and for the most part (excluding certain members of the staff) *only* with Jews, and because the Jews with whom they spend time very often come from similar denominational backgrounds, the school becomes a kind of breeding ground for perpetuating the community it serves. Thus, the modern Orthodox go to school with other modern Orthodox. In the Conservative day school, a parallel situation exists. Presumably in the newly organized Reform Jewish day schools, this pattern will be repeated. And yeshiva students spend the day with people who share their worldview. While the manifest goals of day schools and yeshivas are to provide their students with an intensive Jewish education, they at the same time inevitably foster parochialism and support sectarianism, making their graduates feel more secure and at home with others like them than with those who do not share the same religious perspectives on life. Concomitantly, they make them ill-at-ease or at the very least unfamiliar with those who are different.

In America, intermittent Jewish education is made up basically of afternoon or Sunday schools. It is supplementary Jewish education for young Jews who get their secular education and spend more of their time in a public school (or in some cases a private school under non-Jewish auspices). Although it was not always so (especially when afternoon schools provided a five-day-a-week program and day schools were few in number), students who today attend supplementary Jewish schools come mainly from families who are less involved in or committed to the idea of Jewish education than those who attend day schools or yeshivas. Because the schools offer less class time, the students receive less instruction and often know less. Moreover, their perspective on the substance of Jewish education is significantly different from and less comprehensive than the one shared by young people who have had a day school or yeshiva background. Finally, because students in supplementary Jewish schools are also in a non-Jewish school setting for their secular education and necessarily spend a large bulk of their school time with non-Jews, they would logically be likely to grow up with a less insular attitude toward those different from them. In principle, these factors will undoubtedly prepare the ground for a sense of distance in adulthood from those who received a more intensive Jewish education, and in turn from those Jews who are consequently more attached to Jewish life along with a concomitantly greater tolerance for non-Jews. Although there is no definitive evidence that these varying educational experiences lead to these effects, that intensive Jewish education leads to a greater sense of attachment to Jews than does intermittent or no education, there are strong associations that point in that direction.

Obviously those who receive no Jewish education—children of the unaffiliated—might be expected to feel even more distant both from Jews in general and from those who received a more comprehensive and intensive Jewish education. And thus one of the by-products of the patterns of Jewish education (or lack of it) in America is the perpetuation of division among Jews.

The Orthodox versus the Non-Orthodox

Considering all these divisions among Jews, one might be tempted to conclude that at bottom all the rifts are between Orthodox and non-Orthodox Jews. Undoubtedly, there are such divisions. In a recent survey, Steven M. Cohen and I found that no more than 41% of Orthodox Jews strongly agreed with the statement "an Orthodox Jew can be close friends with Jews of all degrees of religious observance." Even among those Jews who might be characterized as less parochial, "Modern Orthodox," 75% admitted that all or most of their close friends were also Orthodox (among the more traditionalist Orthodox the number jumped to 96%). And when asked how close they felt to other Orthodox Jews, over 90% said they felt either very or somewhat close, but no more than 59% had those feelings of closeness toward non-Orthodox Jews. Finally, while over 85% of Orthodox Jews overwhelmingly admitted to feeling very or somewhat similar to other Orthodox Jews, no more than 43% felt equal degrees of similarity to non-Orthodox Jews. Nor is it unusual to find statements from Orthodox rabbis and leaders such as one made last year by Rabbi Nisson Wolpin, editor of the *Jewish Observer,* that "secularists, atheists, Reform and Conservative "believers" who reject entire segments of the Torah, Written and Oral, [are] all responsible for leading away hundreds of thousands of Jews from belief, under the guise of conserving Jewish values."

On the other side, a recent Dahaf poll in Israel found that only 19% of the Jews it polled described Orthodox Jews favorably; 25% called them "opportunists, liars and charlatans." Nor is it extraordinary to read statements such as one by Rabbi Alexander Schindler of the Reform Union of American Hebrew Congregations blaming "Orthodox zealots" for establishing a divisive "selecting process" to separate Jew from Jew.

Yet to suggest that sectarianism is simply a division between the Orthodox and the non-Orthodox is less than accurate. First, as already indicated, there are Conservative Jews who are divided on some of these issues, with some leaning one way and others another. Hence, in some cases there are not two positions—pro and con—but three; for, against, and sometimes-for-and-sometimes-against.

Second, the Orthodox are not a monolith; they are often deeply divided among themselves. Some Orthodox Jews, notably those who have come to be called "Modern Orthodox," have sought rapprochement with their non-Orthodox counterparts. There are numerous examples where that has occurred: the presidents of the Conservative Rabbinical Assembly and the Orthodox Rabbinical Council of America exchanged platforms at each others' conventions; Rabbi Louis Bernstein, president of the Orthodox group, was reported by the *New York Times* to have said that cooperative ventures between the Orthodox and Conservatives in this country deserved further study. In Denver, Orthodox, Conservative and Reform rabbis cooperated in the granting of conversions to those who sought to enter Judaism. Some Orthodox have affiliated their synagogues with the interdenominational Synagogue Council of America. Increasing numbers of Orthodox Jews sit on Federation committees with non-Orthodox Jews. Many Orthodox institutions have been assisted financially with money from non-Orthodox Jews, while significant numbers of Orthodox Jews serve as teachers in non-Orthodox institutions for Jewish education.

Clearly, in some quarters of Orthodoxy there is an attitude that discourages Jewish disunity. In the words of Rabbi Reuven Bulka of Congregation Machzikei Hadas in Ottawa: "If the Orthodox stubbornly insist that Conservative and Reform Jews are out of the pale, their casting off will become a self-fullfilling prophecy, and Orthodoxy will be party to, and at least partially responsible for, a mass defection from Jewish ranks."

Indeed, the rifts *within* Orthodoxy between the Moderns and the Traditionalists are at least as wide, if not wider, than the divisions between the Orthodox and the non-

Orthodox. As one analyst of Orthodoxy, Marvin Schick, once put it: "Quite a few leaders of the Orthodox left seem more uncomfortable at meetings with belligerent right-wingers than they are when they get together with non-Orthodox leaders who eat with uncovered heads. . . ." And by now everyone is familiar with the bitter divisions among various Hasidic groups. The brawls on New York City streets between Belzer and Satmar Hasidim were widely reported in the media, while the ongoing rivalry between Lubavitcher and Satmar Hasidim have also been expressed in public and are among the bitterest divisions on the contemporary Jewish scene.

A Clash of Worldviews

Given the complexity of the picture, what then are the *real* dividing lines? A careful and objective analysis suggests that what basically divides Jews are competing worldviews which, although associated with the matter of Orthodoxy and non-Orthodoxy, go much deeper. Only by understanding the division in these terms can one explain the rifts within Orthodoxy and the ambiguities of those Jewish groups who find themselves in the middle between the extremes.

And what are those worldviews? Put most simply, *one worldview seeks to prevent all change while the other encourages or embraces change.* Both views, however, remain convinced that they will insure the survival of Judaism and the Jews—a goal that *all* appear to share.

Among Jews, the famous slogan of Rabbi Moses Sofer, the 19th century Hungarian rabbi, that "the new is prohibited by the Torah," epitomizes the view that opposes all change. From this perspective, anachronism is the first principle of order, and yesterday is more important than today or tomorrow for it is the repository of all authority, the treasury of all wisdom. In this worldview, change is suspect and ultimately threatens to erode Judaism. The new is never improved; the old is always time-honored and favored. The enemy to those who hold this point of view is anyone or anything that encourages or embraces change. And sometimes the most dangerous enemy seems to be the neighbor, even more than some distant and different Jew whose life orbit never touches mine.

On the other side is the worldview that says that those who fail to adapt and change will become fossilized and covered by the sands of time. The view from here is that reform, reconstruction, and liberalization are all necessary responses to change. In the end these adaptations are judged vital to the future of American Jewish existence. Anyone who rejects change and refuses to adapt to changing conditions is considered a threat to the progress of Judaism and in the final analysis an obstacle to Jewish survival.

(2) Has there been disunity like this before?

There is a well-known Jewish joke about the Jew on a desert island who builds two synagogues: one he goes to and one he does not. What makes this joke so familiar to Jews is the truth embedded in the humor. Disunity and the threat of schism have been companions to Jewish existence from almost the very beginning. A brief look at some of the major divisions is instructive.

The Biblical Period

Even before the Israelites had completed their wandering through the Sinai wilderness, the Bible reports that Moses' cousin, Korach, mounted an insurrection. Or, as the commentator Onkelos explains: "he separated himself from the rest of the congregation to establish dissension." After Korach's revolt, although there were uprisings against King David's rule, perhaps the best known schism of the Biblical period was the one that led to the division of Israel into two kingdoms: Judah and Benjamin on one side and the remaining ten tribes on the other.

Pharisees and Sadducees and the Talmudic Period

The opposition between the Pharisees and Sadducees in ancient Palestine is a familiar episode in Jewish history. The latter differed from the Pharisees chiefly in that they espoused a literal interpretation of the Bible, rejected the oral laws and rabbinic traditions and denied the ideas of an afterlife and the coming of a Messiah. So vituperative did the division grow that it was possible for the Talmud (*Eruvin* 68b) to quote Rabbi Yehuda who declared, "a Sadducee is nothing but a non-Jew." Although this judgment was made in a limited context, it points to the depth of division between the two groups.

In a famous Mishna in *Sanhedrin* (90a), the rabbis assert: "Every member of the congregation of Israel has a place in the world to come." And then they proceed to enumerate a list of those who do not, dissenters who could no longer be considered part of Israel: those who do not believe in the resurrection of the dead and those who deny the divine origins of the Torah. To this list, the sage Akiva added several others. Undoubtedly, this was not simply an academic discussion; there were people and groups the rabbis had in mind.

The sages argued about the acceptability of converts as well. The dispute (*Berachot* 28a) between Rabbi Joshua and Rabban Gamaliel about whether or not a certain Judah the Ammonite could in fact become a Jew is perhaps the most famous. One school of thought accepted him (and presumably his offspring) into the Jewish people; the other did not.

And there were often crucial differences between Babylonian and Palestinian Jews. Thus, for example, the scholar Joel Mueller reports that the two groups differed on whether or not a ring could effect *kiddushin* (marriage), whether or not one could carry money on the Sabbath—Babylonians did; Palestinians did not—and whether or not a widow could remarry without *halitza,* the ritual of renouncement that her husband's surviving brother customarily made.

Finally, the difference between the schools of Hillel and Shammai are well known, and while always carried on "in the name of heaven," they sometimes yielded feelings of division that were not easily stilled.

Karaites and Rabbanites

In the eighth century, beginning in the heartland of Mesopotamian Jewry, the Karaites established a sectarian challenge to what they viewed as the intolerably exclusive rabbinic hold over the process of Biblical exegesis; they too felt capable of interpreting God's law. In time, Karaites came to be characterized as a sect who replaced many rabbinical traditions with their own. Although throughout centuries they were often divided among themselves—with one ninth century Karaite elder referring to an earlier Karaite leader "as a fool and an ass" while another called him "first among the fools"—the primary division remained the one between Karaites and the rest of the Jewish community which essentially followed rabbinic doctrine. The great Jewish leader Saadia Gaon proscribed Karaites as pure heretics. And throughout the tenth century rapprochement between the two groups seemed unthinkable and impossible.

Nevertheless, for centuries, both Karaites and Rabbanites considered each other as Jews and regarded even the most violent polemics between them as an internal Jewish quarrel. In part this was because the outside world looked upon both groups as Jews. During the Chmielnicki persecutions in 1648, hardly any difference was made between the two groups. In Lithuania and Poland, state taxes payable by both groups were remitted in a lump sum. But the union between the groups was tenuous and in the eighteenth century, in Russia, a law was passed which gave each group independent status. And the policy of Karaite leaders in nineteenth and twentieth century Russia and Poland who sought to completely dissociate themselves from their Rabbanite counterparts in order to escape the crushing persecutions imposed on Jews there "led to a quiet but profound estrangement," in the words of historian Leon Nimoy.

Sephardim and Ashkenazim

While there are no differences in the basic tenets of Judaism between Sephardim, descendants of Jews who lived in the Iberian peninsula before the expulsion of 1492, and Ashkenazim, Jews of European origins, these two groups differed markedly in matters of detail and outlook. They prayed from different prayer books, worshipped in separate synagogues, and practiced diverse customs. And because they had lived in separate countries, they often spoke different Jewish dialects: the Sephardim using Ladino and the Ashkenazim more and more depending on Yiddish.

Ultimately, these differences were reinforced by a history of cultural dissimilarities and varying responses to the compulsion to abandon Judaism and convert (in fifteenth century Spain, for example, Sephardim often made public statements of conversion even as they remained secret Jews, while in Crusader Europe Ashkenazim often died rather than publicly convert). These differences led to tensions, rivalries and at times to something approaching schism at various points in Jewish history. For a long time the two groups seldom if ever intermarried, the Ashkenazim calling into question the Sephardim's Jewishness after the latter's experiences as Marranos, and the Sephardim looking upon themselves as an elite.

In nineteenth century Jerusalem, divisions between the two groups reached significant proportions because the Sephardim were recognized by the Ottoman authorities as legal residents of the city while the Ashkenazim were not. And around the same time in America, German immigrants were discovering that their Sephardic cousins who had preceded them to the New World did not always esteem the newcomers and their different ways.

Hasidim and Misnagdim

Following upon the deep rifts among Jews that were left behind by the failed messianic movements of Sabbatai Tzvi and Jacob Frank, the rise of Hasidism led to yet another division in the Jewish community. In Poland and especially in Lithuania, Hasidim were vigorously opposed by Misnagdim. The great historian Simon Dubnov reports that sectarian outbreaks between the two groups began in 1772.

At first the Misnagdim simply referred to the Hasidim as *"minim,"* a term that associated them with other divergent sects of Judaism over the ages, but in time the denunciations grew far more bitter. In 1781, as Dubnov records, the elders of the Jewish communities in Minsk, Pinsk, Brisk, Horodna and Slutsk proclaimed the Hasidim to be in *herem* (excommunication). "There are among us sects and groups which have separated themselves from the just and wider community. They make new customs for themselves and sinful laws. They take apart the yoke of Torah from their necks and encourage chaos."

Accordingly, Misnagdim prohibited any association with Hasidim, marriage with them, business contacts or any other negotiations, the burying of their dead, and just about removed them from the congregation of Israel. In Horodna in 1781, Misnagdim urged Jews neither to join with Hasidim nor "even to shake their hands." In the town of Brody, the Misnagdim warned their supporters: "Should a guest come to our community and not want to eat from the slaughter of the permanent slaughterers in the city [i.e., not accept our standards of kashrut] or want to carry on any new custom or pray in the fashion of the Sephardim . . . , the host should inform the community leader and chase that man out of town, and whoever chases him out and successfully repels him has earned the grace of Heaven." And why? "Because they deviate from all paths, and among them the truth is missing."

For their part, the Hasidim "burned the books and pamphlets which had been published against them." They continued to collect adherents and vilify the Misnagdim in their stories and homilies.

Zionists versus Anti-Zionists

Among the most distinctive of Jewish controversies is the division between the pro- and anti-Zionists. The players in this dispute have changed over the years. To some, Zionism, particularly in its secular, socialist incarnation, was tantamount to a challenge against the most deeply held beliefs in messianism. How, the anti-Zionists argued, could unbelievers like Herzl and later Ben Gurion redeem the land of their forebears? Would Heaven use these people to bring about an end to the long Jewish exile?

Other anti-Zionists, among them the early Reform Jews,

looked upon Zionism as a repudiation of the possibilities of acculturation into the host societies in which Jews found themselves. Zionists, they argued, were simply pressing the Jews into yet another ghetto.

To the Zionists, on the other hand, those who resisted the dream of a national return and renaissance in the ancient homeland—for whatever reasons—were *golus Jews,* people permanently embedded in an exile and an exile mentality. Although today most Jews are pro-Zionist supporters of Israel, there remain residual groups of anti-Zionists, like the Satmar Hasidim on the right and the American Council for Judaism on the left.

In addition to these disputes, there were of course many others. Some remained local while others went on to affect the wider Jewish world. It is neither possible nor necessary to review all of these here because the list of divisions is almost endless. One point, however, is beyond dispute: *sectarianism, division, and dissensus have been a continuing element of Jewish communal existence from the beginning and throughout the centuries.* Accordingly, in answer to our second question it is difficult to say that the current rifts and disputes represent something new. Rather, they seem to represent a contemporary incarnation of a continuing condition of Jewish life.

To be sure, the controversies over matters of patrilineal descent, halachically contested divorces (as well as the resulting offspring) and conversions represent a qualitative change over many if not all past schisms. Unlike most of the other conflicts mentioned earlier, these three are characterized not simply by a variant worldview and approach to Judaism. Although clashing worldviews and approaches to Judaism may at first account for differences in defining who and what is a Jew or how marriages should be terminated, they have as an ancillary result generated structural divisions among those who hold one viewpoint and those who hold another, for they create additional institutional barriers to unity. And unlike ideological disputes which often get washed away over the long term, structural divisions seem to deepen with the passage of time. Even those ready and willing to overlook ideological differences may find themselves divided by the halachic problems inherent in the matters of patrilineal descent, divorce and conversion. Or to put it simply: what happens to those who seem to be irrevocably defined as outside the boundaries of the Jewish community by some (the child of a Jewish father and a non-Jewish mother, the *mamzer,* and certain converts as well as their offspring)? All this leads to the next general question.

(3) What are the likely consequences of disunity?

Prophecy and prediction are always dangerous, first because the prophet places himself in jeopardy by presuming to warn his contemporaries and second because predictions have an uncanny habit of being wrong. Nevertheless, a quick review of the course that Jewish disputes in the past followed offers some hints.

The earth shattering results of Korach's revolt left the Israelites united, if somewhat chastened. The uprising subsided, with the help of God, while Moses found a way to reconcile the disaffected. In later generations, the children of Korach were the subject of many of the greatest Psalms of praise. As for the division of the Northern Kingdom from Judah and Benjamin, while both kingdoms played a part in ancient Israelite history, after the exile of the ten northern tribes by the invader, the overwhelming majority of today's Jews trace their direct roots through Judea. In truth, however, we know very little about the social and political outcomes of these divisions; they simply happened too long ago, and the documents left behind are sketchy at best and steeped in legend and religious belief.

The course which the dispute between the Pharisees and Sadducees ultimately took is likewise largely unknown. Whether the latter left the congregation of Israel or were ultimately reabsorbed into it is not clear. Nevertheless, we do know that while Rabbi Yehuda on one occasion announced that a Sadducee was equivalent to a non-Jew, Rabban Gamaliel, the head of the academy, argued in the other direction. Unquestionably, then, there was a trend toward unity and consensus that operated at the same time that disunity and dissensus were being expressed.

And the controversies between the schools of Hillel and Shammai, once at the cutting edge of Jewish disagreement, are now both part of the sacred canon of Talmud study. Even though in almost every case, Hillel's point of view predominates, the contemporary student of Talmud must master as well the opinion and reasoning of Shammai.

There are still Karaites to be found today, although their numbers have dwindled markedly. Some are in America; others may be found in Israel. Although their customs and heritage are different (they have their own synagogues, graveyards, and religious courts of law), a Karaite is these days virtually indistinguishable from a Jew. On the Israeli identity card of many, the entry reads "Karaite Jew." What was once a sect, deeply divided from the mainstream, seems these days to have evolved into one of many of the ethnic groups that make up Jewry.

There are still people who talk about social and cultural divisions between Sephardim and Ashkenazim—although for the most part the "Sephardim" to which they refer are in fact Middle-Eastern Jews, people who trace their origins from Moslem countries like Yemen, Iraq, Morocco and Tunisia. While distinctions in ritual and religious customs remain between Ashkenazim and Sephardim, the social divisions between both groups appear to be waning. In Israel where the contact between the two has been greatest in contemporary times, demographers report a growing intermarriage rate. And although there are differences, these appear to have less to do with being Ashkenazic and Sephardic than they have to do with ethnicity and economic class. As for language, both speak Hebrew; Ladino and Yiddish being languages that few any longer use.

In America, although an important Sephardic community exists, there are none of the rancorous or even subtle divisions that once characterized relations between the German Jews and the Sephardim who preceded them to these shores. One is as likely to find an Ashkenazi in the New York City Spanish-Portuguese Synagogue, Shearith Israel, as a Sephardi.

Hasidim are still clearly identifiable by their dress and many of their practices, but in many ways they have become indistinguishable from other traditionalist Orthodox Jews. The fires of the Holocaust and the winds of assimilation have made the divisions between Hasidim and Misnagdim minuscule in comparison. The day when a Misnagid would chase a Hasid out of his neighborhood is long past—anyone doubting this need only visit Boro Park in Brooklyn or Monsey in Rockland County, New York. And if the activities of the Lubavitcher Hasidim are of any significance, they point out the willingness of Hasidim to service the religious needs of all sorts of Jews. That is not to say that all is sweetness and light. As already noted, disputes and rifts still rage. But these days they are as likely to be among various sects of Hasidim as between Hasidim and non-Hasidim.

The divisions that remain between pro- and anti-Zionists, as already suggested, are now limited to fringe elements. While they play somewhat of a role in Israeli politics, their part in American Jewish sectarianism is largely nonexistent. American Jews—as indeed the world community of Jews—overwhelmingly support Israel.

As for the disputes between the champions of Orthodoxy and Reform, although they continue to flare, I have seen Rabbis Alexander Schindler, the Reform Jewish leader, and Menachem Porush, a high official of the Orthodox Agudah party in Israel, embrace like brothers at a meeting of the Memorial Foundation for Jewish Culture in Jerusalem. And, as Rabbi Alexander Shapiro, president of the Conservative Rabbinical Assembly, recently pointed out during a meeting with his Orthodox and Reform counterparts, "We are able to communicate with one another and we are talking to one another. We are not cursing at one another, God forbid. We are not saying to one another, "You are not Jews" (quoted in *Moment*, April 1986). Finally, even Lubavitcher Hasidim make their way to the enclaves of Reform Jewry.

If there is any lesson to be learned from the course that all these disputes have taken, it is that a counterforce of unity and consensus to even the most bitter disunity and dissensus emerges over time. To be sure, pressures from without play a part in all this; restrictions on Jews, persecutions, assimilatory quicksand and political change have attenuated the effects of internal divisions among Jews. **The enemies from without have always made the antagonists from within seem less menacing.**

All of which brings us back to today's divisions. They are, the *Times* writes, "marked by uncommon bitterness." In the light of history, such a characterization would be hard to support. Other disputes among Jews have also been marked by enormous bitterness.

But what of the matter of isolation of Jew from Jew, the possibility that Orthodox and some Conservative Jews will scrutinize family pedigrees before marriage, or that day schools and Jewish camps will investigate the lineage of their applicants? Does this signify a deeper rift than ever before?

To begin with, these divisions which some warn will occur and irrevocably destroy the unity of the Jewish people already exist and have since the first glimmerings of religious reform in nineteenth century Germany. For years, traditionally observant Jews (both Orthodox and Conservative) *have* scrutinized family pedigrees prior to marriage. While weddings between the observant and non-observant occur, they are in practice the exception rather than the rule. Among the various Hasidic sects, these restrictions are even more severe (although hardly anyone seems to be worried about the fragmentation of Orthodoxy in those circles). Moreover, yeshivas, day schools and Jewish camps *do* examine lineage, routinely adding questions about the religion and Jewish affiliation of parents and grandparents to application forms. Finally, not only do Jews of varying outlooks often live in different neighborhoods, but as the data reported above on the feelings of closeness and similarity to other Jews on the part of the Orthodox indicate, there are already significant barriers of estrangement. Disunity and division are facts of contemporary American Jewish life—as they have been in Jewish life throughout the ages.

The question to be asked is whether these divisions will get qualitatively worse and finally obliterate the unity of the Jewish people. Or put differently, can both ideological and structural divisions be bridged.

To answer that question, we must look first to see if there are—in addition to the undeniable division—also signs of conciliation and unity. The exchange of platforms between the leaders of the Conservative Rabbinical Assembly and the Orthodox Rabbinical Council of America is one. Not all Orthodox rabbis vilify the non-Orthodox. In a recent book on Orthodoxy, the editor, an Orthodox rabbi from Canada, argued: "Conservative and Reform Judaism, whilst having a higher assimilation rate than Orthodox Judaism, have at the same time curbed even more serious assimilation. . . . It is thus abundantly clear that burning all the bridges between Orthodoxy and Reform is not only contrary to the best interests of the total Jewish community, it also runs counter to the best interests of Orthodoxy."

Likewise, the admission by Reform Rabbi Jakob Petuchowski, in a recent issue of *Moment* magazine, that "neither the advocates of change nor its opponents may have the requisite sense of responsibility to the future and destiny of Judaism" offers hope of understanding and rapprochement between Jews of different persuasions.

Finally, the universal concern about the matter of schism is a good sign. If all Jews are worried about the same problem, this in itself suggests some light at the end of the tunnel.

But are there other matters over which American Jews of all stripes and persuasions are united besides their concern about schism? Among these are: support for Israel, concern over the plight of Soviet, Ethiopian, Syrian or other distressed Jewries, and vigilance in the struggle against antisemitism—matters of significant concern and importance and factors reinforcing solidarity. Disunity and division surely exist; but the forces and voices of unity and conciliation are still very much alive.

(4) What can or should be done in response and what might the future bring?

All this is not to say that the prophets of disunity are completely wrong and there is no cause for alarm. Current lines of fracture among Jews undermine the establishment of unity. However, it is important to keep in mind that **the American Jewish community already lives with fragmentation,** as Jews have always done.

And as for those who point to the structural divisions as a threat of a different order from any ever faced before, there is ample evidence that even the most stubborn structural and halachic problems can be overcome. The contemporary configuration of American Jewry may create very complicated and technical problems for halachic judges and those who keep track of the precise boundaries among Jews, but it is doubtful that they will create insoluble ones. Opposing those who argue that disunity will increase and that unlike ideological differences structural ones cannot be washed away by time but rather become deeper, one may place the experience of history which suggests that even the bitterest disputes get resolved in one way or another—either the various groups of Jews find that the forces that divide them are less significant than those that unite them, or some external adversary reminds them that they are one.

Yet if the long view of history gives some cause for optimism about Jewish unity and conciliation, what of the immediate future—are there steps that can be taken to mitigate the hostility and divergence that are now rife? Although there are no certain solutions, some steps would seem particularly appropriate.

First, since it is clear that the voices of gloom and disunity are making the headlines, it would be useful to give greater attention to those who demonstrate that consensus and unity are still possible, and that they exist in some quarters. This is not just a matter of telling "good news." Rather, it is a means of insuring that rifts and schism do not become self-fulfilling. Jews (and others) need to realize that there are still matters that unite them. In this regard, increased opportunities for dialogue between varying Jewish worldviews need to be encouraged, particularly under the auspices of such "neutral" organizations as the American Jewish Congress. In Israel, the Gesher program which brings together young people from observant and nonobservant backgrounds offers another example of dialogue. Projects like it are as or even more necessary in America as in the Jewish homeland. In an atmosphere of dialogue, hand-wringing and prophecies of doom often give way to hand-clasps and outlooks of optimism. People who come together to talk find they *can* work even the most complicated things out.

Second, while the immediate matter that seems to exercise the Jews is the question of who has genuinely converted or which persons may be counted as part of the congregation of Israel, *the question of who and what is a Jew goes far deeper.* It is not only important *who* gets into the Jewish fold, it is at least if not more vital *what* the content of that Jewish life is. As sociologist Egon Mayer has reminded us, *the real division in American Jewry (and indeed, among world Jewry as well) is between those who participate actively in Jewish life and those who do not.* If actions are taken to more vigorously involve Jews of all walks of Jewish life, the matters of who gets in will become less and less important. Even structural problems can be worked out in the context of active involvement in Jewish life. Has there ever been a case of an actively involved and highly committed Jew who found himself excluded from being counted in the nation?

To be sure, non-Orthodox conversions and the decision to accept patrilineal as well as matrilineal descent as criteria for inclusion in the Jewish community represent significant departures from *halacha. But they only exacerbate already existing differences among Jews; they do not create them.* Those who have fallen apart because of this issue were already deeply divided—at least, in terms of religious observance and Jewish activity.

Were these already existing divisions to begin to evaporate and were the entire Jewish community to come closer to one another, the rabbis (including the most traditional and Orthodox) would, as they always have in the past, find ways to incorporate even those Jews whose halachic legitimacy was in question. In an atmosphere of unity and active involvement in Jewish life, even long lost brothers and sisters like the Ethiopian Jews and before them the Bene Israel of India have found ways to be included in the congregation of Israel. And rabbinic courts have found means for annulling marriages where there were halachic problems with divorce. To be sure these kind of solutions have only been enlisted in extreme cases. But they set precedents, and more importantly, demonstrate the capacity for even the Orthodox point of view to show flexibility. The solution then, to the dispute over patrilineal descent and conversion, seems to be not a continued argument over the fine points of the law and procedure, but rather a program of action that will increasingly draw Jews together into a network of mutual obligations, common practices and stronger ties. And out of that unity, ideological divisions and structural rifts can be bridged.

A third step to mitigate the destructive influences of sectarianism is thus to create a Jewish community that attracts the involvement of *all* Jews. This means renewed and creative efforts at Jewish education—not just for children but for all segments of the Jewish community. Ignorance of what it means to be a Jew is the greatest of all threats, not only to the unity of the Jewish people but to its very survival. Intermittent Jewish education is simply not providing enough; it must be supplanted by more intensive instruction. If the risks of the latter are greater Jewish insularity, perhaps that will be part of the price American Jewry will have to pay to diminish its internal disunity. *Jews may have to choose between being closer to one another or to everyone else.*

A renewed emphasis on universal and intensive Jewish education will require a revitalization of the entire Jewish education apparatus, bringing our most able and brightest into the process rather than leaving the job of educating the Jewish people to those among us who have *not* taken up other professions. If all our superior and talented young people become doctors, lawyers, accountants, business people and professionals in secular fields, who will be our Jewish educators, in whose hands will the task of attracting and revitalizing Jews be left?

The matter of Jewish divorce and the divisive consequences which follow is perhaps a harder one to remedy since it stems not from a Jewish source alone but is a condition of contemporary American life. Clearly, the American Jewish community needs a policy and institutions aimed at preserving the family. These might include Jewish family life education programs whose aim is to teach Jewish families how to use Judaism as a resource for strengthening the bonds of the family. Whatever else might be said about Judaism, its practices and customs are aimed at preserving family existence; Judaism is good family practice. The problem is that American Jews do not always know how to make the best use of it; and they will have to learn formally what their forebears were able to pick up more easily by osmosis in the ghetto. Such programs and a renewed emphasis on family will not by themselves end divorce, but they will instead place the focus of Jewish energies on the positive elements of marital life rather than on the negative ones. We have of late become too concerned with how to end marriage and not enough taken up with the task of how to sustain it.

The unification of American Jewry means as well additional emphasis on Israel as the single most important consolidating element for American Jewry. As already pointed out, America's Jews overwhelmingly are supporters of Israel. Moreover, for all of its very real divisions, the Jewish state still remains the most vivid illustration of the capacity of Jews of all types to survive together. Incredibly, however, only slightly more than 35% of American Jews have ever been to Israel. More need to go and for longer periods of time. Israel can become the catalyst for Jewish unity abroad. Indeed, no young American Jew should be permitted to graduate from any Jewish educational institution without having spent a term in Israel. That way, at least the young will take their attachment to Israel into the future with them.

Conclusion

It would be nice to be able to conclude by saying that if all these steps, many of which would radically alter the face of American Jewish life, were to be taken, the divisions and disunity afflicting us would disappear. It would help, but problems would always remain. That is the nature of human existence and the character of community life.

In the Talmud when there were disputes for which there were no decisive resolutions, the rabbis concluded: "*taiku,*" an acronym that stands for "Tishbi (Elijah and his arrival in the Messianic age) will solve all problems and resolve all questions." But until that time and for the foreseeable future, variations among Jewish worldviews will remain. During the interim, if we are to survive as a people, each side will simply have to be more sensitive to the other. Jews will at last have to recognize, in the words of Jacob Petuchowski, that, in the efforts to reconcile differences among them: "Thoughtless innovation is no more helpful than heartless rigidity."

Soviet Jewry: An Update

Prepared by the Coalition to Free Soviet Jews

There are an estimated two and a half million Jews living in the Soviet Union. This number makes up the third largest Jewish community in the world; 20% of the world's Jewish population, and 1% of the population of the Soviet Union.

Of this vast number, approximately 400,000 have begun the arduous process of emigration. It is believed that up to one million would leave if they could be certain that their visa applications would be met with favorable results. Currently, there are approximately 11,000 Soviet Jews who have officially been refused permission to leave. Some of these refuseniks have been waiting over fifteen years to emigrate to their homeland—Israel. Jews applying for exit visas are usually fired from their jobs, and find subsequent employment difficult to secure. Those who cannot find even the most menial jobs, or jobs recognized as suitable means of employment by the Soviet government (Hebrew teaching is not acceptable), are arrested for "Parasitism"—unemployment is illegal in the Soviet Union.

Soviet General Secretary Mikhail Gorbachev's *glasnost* or "openness" policy has produced some positive steps in the direction of genuine human rights reform. The release of a number of Hebrew teachers from prison and labor camps—most notably Iosif Begun—and the increase in emigration during the first few months of 1987 support these moves.

However, while Gorbachev lauds *glasnost,* Jewish cultural and religious activities continue to be severely restricted. Study circles are disrupted, and Hebrew teachers harassed and threatened. In addition, Jews continue to be singled out in the Soviet media as traitors, foreign agents and anti-Soviet agitators.

Despite the fact that emigration figures for the first four months of 1987 have surpassed the entire total reached in 1986, eight families from Moscow have been issued "final refusals." Vladimir and Masha Slepak, Dr. Alexander Lerner, Natasha Khassina, Yulian Khasin, Yuli Kosharovsky, Yakov Rakhlenko and Lev and Alla Sud were informed by Soviet officials that they would never be allowed to leave the Soviet Union.

In addition, Begun's release from prison on February 20, 1987 and his dramatic return to Moscow, merely returned him—once again—to the supplicant's position. The validity of Gorbachev's claims to an "irreversible" process toward democratization can be better measured not by Begun's release from prison, but by whether the Beguns—along with their fellow refuseniks—are permitted to emigrate to Israel.

Mikhail Gorbachev has taken some important first steps, but the road to granting/guaranteeing full human rights remains very long indeed.

Anti-Semitism in the USSR: Popular Hatred/State Policy

> If the Torah is considered from the standpoint of modern civilization and communist morality, it proves to be an unsurpassed textbook of bloodthirstiness, hypocrisy, treachery, perfidy, and moral degeneracy—all the basest of human qualities.
>
> Vladimir Begun, Soviet publicist
> *Invasion Without Arms*
> Moscow (1977), p.40

To appreciate the struggle for emigration and cultural and religious freedoms, it is important to know how difficult it is to be Jewish in the Soviet Union today.

The trouble is rooted long in the past, but for many Jews today the most difficult period in history to reconcile with the present are the years of the pogroms (1881-82). According to William Korey, an American expert on Soviet Jewry, what had only begun as the ploy of Czarist emissaries to the Ukraine in the spring of 1881 (calling for the "people's wrath" to be "vented on the Jews") became the basis for hundreds of violent attacks throughout the economically depressed Russian countryside. The "peasant uprisings," as they are known to Soviet revisionists, won the approval of the Czar by mid-winter, and thus proceeded to other parts of the Empire. Property valued at $80 million was destroyed, over 120,000 Jews financially ruined, and some 20,000 left homeless.

This was not the first time in Russian history Jews were persecuted, but the physical, geographical scale was unprecedented. It was almost as though the entire country had declared war on one of its people, a civil war against Jews. Yet the most fearful aspect of the 1881-82 pogroms was the manner in which the government participated. It is unlikely that the pogroms could ever have been carried out to their conclusion without the imprimatur of the Moscow aristocracy.

It is little wonder then why the recent publication of books justifying the pogroms has caused so much fear and discomfort. Vladimir Begun, whose work speaks best for this genre, defends the peasant attacks on Jews as the classic Marxist struggle. Jews of the late 19th century were

WHY LET JEWS GO FREE WHEN YOU CAN SELL THEM?

The Soviet Union has a unique bargaining chip in international politics.

Two and a half million Jews.

When the Soviets want something from the U.S., they increase the number of Jewish emigrants.

When the Soviets don't get what they want from the U.S., they reduce the number of Jewish emigrants.

For example, when the Soviets wanted U.S. ratification of SALT II in 1979, they tried to buy it with the release of a record 51,000 Jews. And when U.S. ratification was not forthcoming, guess who paid?

Jewish emigration has dropped 98% in the past five years. And this year fewer than 950 Jews have been allowed to leave the Soviet Union.

So why should the Soviets let Jews go free when they can sell them? Because by giving the Jews their freedom, Mr. Gorbachev will be left with something far more valuable.

Credibility, as a world leader genuinely in search of world peace.

Sponsored by the Coalition to Free Soviet Jews*

Representing 85 concerned organizations in New York City, Long Island, Westchester, Rockland and Bergen Counties.

Coalition to Free Soviet Jews, 8 W. 40th St., NY, NY 10018, (212)354-1316.

*Formerly the Greater New York Conference on Soviet Jewry

"I WOULD BE GLAD TO HEAR OF JEWS ENJOYING ANYWHERE SUCH POLITICAL AND OTHER RIGHTS AS THEY HAVE IN OUR COUNTRY."

Mikhail Gorbachev,
General Secretary of the Communist Party
of the Soviet Union, October, 1985

If you tell a lie big enough, people will believe you. It worked 40 years ago. Does Soviet Leader Gorbachev honestly believe it will work today?

It's obvious that this outrageous fabrication is a Soviet ploy to sway world opinion as the Summit approaches. But Mr. Gorbachev can drop the Mr. Nice Guy act. Because his track record to date shows him for what he is: a neo-Stalinist; not a modern reformer.

In fact, since he came to power, Gorbachev has done nothing to improve conditions for Soviet Jews.

And he has the gall to insist that they enjoy all kinds of privileges, when Soviet propaganda demonstrates daily that Jews are not entitled to the most fundamental freedoms.

Does Gorbachev think he can hide behind words, when official Soviet policy is: don't employ Jews; don't promote Jews; don't let Jews into our universities?

Is there any country in the world where Jews have fewer rights? Where Jews are forbidden to study their own religion, language or culture? Where they are hounded and imprisoned for doing so?

If what Mr. Gorbachev says were true, why have 400,000 Soviet Jews requested to leave the Soviet Union? And why have only 700 this year been granted visas?

If this is how Soviet Leader Gorbachev intends to play his cards at the Summit in November, then all we have to look forward to is some fancy shuffling. After all, if Mr. Gorbachev can gloss over the human rights issue with a mere sleight of hand, how can he be trusted on issues of vital security?

Sponsored by the Coalition to Free Soviet Jews*
Representing 85 concerned organizations in New York City, Long Island, Westchester, Rockland and Bergen Counties.
Coalition to Free Soviet Jews, 8 W. 40th St., NY, NY 10018, (212) 354-1316.

*Formerly the Greater New York Conference on Soviet Jewry

ЯД
ОТРАВА
А вот эти яды действуют прежде всего на голову.

Photo credit: Richard Lobell
FROM: "Bakinsky Rabochili", June 4, 1985
INSIDE THE CARTOON: (on the bottles) Poison Venom
CAPTION: "The poisons all act on the brain."

It appears from the cartoon that all religions are poisonous but the Jewish religion has a special venom—Ed.

nothing more than the "barbarous . . . exploitive, bourgeoisie."

> One of the principal reasons for the conflicts which arose in the Ukraine and Byelorussia was economic exploitation, the personification of which were the rapacious Jewish leaseholders, moneylenders and innkeepers.
>
> *Invasion Without Arms*
> pp. 65-66

> We do not grieve today if our fathers, grandfathers, and great-grandfathers, in their distress and want, treated their brothers disrespectfully, regardless of whether they were native or alien by blood.
>
> *The Creeping Counterrevolution*
> 1974

An older person reading the works of Vladimir Begun, whose writing is generally very well received in the Soviet press, might recall *The Protocols of the Elders of Zion* (1903), which played an ideological role in the civil war of 1918-20 in the Ukraine. Some 30,000 Jews were killed, and many more homes destroyed. *The Protocols* would have served an even greater purpose had the Allied powers not intervened: they provided the philosophical basis for Hitler's Final Solution.

As long as hatred for Jews exists in the Soviet Union—in certain parts, as in the Ukraine, it is as old and stubborn as the culture itself—anti-Semitic propaganda will remain a very frightening and potentially dangerous phenomenon.

Anti-Semitism in the Soviet Union

Anti-Semitism did not die with Czarist Russia. Even government commissioned studies confirm this. In 1929, in a survey of anti-Semitism in the newly founded trade unions, one writer reported that "anti-Semitic feeling (sic) among workers is spreading chiefly in the backward sections of the working class that have close ties to the peasantry." Hatred wasn't confined to the countryside, however. In the winter of 1926, the chairman of the Central Committee wrote that white collar workers in the Soviet Union were "more anti-Semitic today than under Tsarism (sic)."

The Stalin years were especially tainted. The "black years" of 1948-53 brought the "Anti-Cosmopolitan Campaign," culminating in the well-known Doctor's Plot. False evidence was collected to implicate medical doctors (many of whom were Jewish) of attempting to murder top Soviet officials. The only hope for Jews during this period which was Stalin's Jewish Anti-Fascist Committee, founded in 1942 to whip up international support for the Soviet Union's imminent battle with Germany, was disbanded when NATO came into existence. Former members were persecuted, and its leader murdered.

The Jewish faith itself has not fared well in the Soviet Union. In part, this is the obvious result of state policy. A central commission functions to restrict the growth of all forms of religious worship, and groups that fail to register are outlawed. The decree of 1929 forbids a congregation of fewer than twenty citizens of 18 years or older—this is especially difficult for Jews living in sparsely populated areas where congregants must travel great distances to attend services. Many synagogues destroyed in the Second World War have never been rebuilt, and many others since have been shut down. Yeshivahs and Yiddish schools were closed under Stalin—leading to an unprecedented shortage of rabbis—even in the so-called Autonomous Jewish Republic of Birobidjan. There are no schools left today to train rabbis.

According to a May 1986 report by the British House of Commons Foreign Affairs Committee, Soviet authorities have recently launched a new campaign to completely eliminate Jewish religion and culture in the republics. Despite the fact that not a single prayerbook has been printed in over 30 years, nor one Bible in 70, the central target of this campaign is the Hebrew language. Jews have been frequently arrested and punished for distributing religious materials or teaching Hebrew.

In 1981 over 80 self-taught unofficial Hebrew teachers in Moscow were threatened with arrest if they did not stop their activities.

ALEKSEI MAGARIK (POC)

BORN: November 26, 1958. FROM: Moscow. OCCUPATION: Cellist. WIFE: Natalya. SON: Chaim. ARREST: March 14, 1986. CHARGES: "Drug Possession" (planted on him by the KGB in Tbilisi). SENTENCE: 3 years labor camp.

Aleksei is a very talented musician who has been denied an exit visa for 5 years. Aleksei's father Vladimir, who lives in Israel, has travelled to many countries, including the United States, to gain support for his son.

Sentence was reduced by one-half.

The Purpose of a Policy

In 1963, Nikita Khruschev, the first Soviet leader to succeed Stalin (and for a while Stalin's most severe critic) admitted that "local hatred influenced policy" in his own administration. The use of anti-Semitism as a policy of State, a practice which came into full blossom under Stalin in the early 1950s, survived well into the cold war era. It continues to serve the Soviet government as a powerful political tool today.

How does this new brand of anti-Semitism differ from the old-the traditionally popular hatred of Jews? A good case in point are the economic crimes trials of the early 1960s. In the years 1961-65, the Khruschev administration demonstrated that despite all the work it had done to correct past abuses in the judicial system, the Soviet Union had yet to rid itself of this frightening holdover from the Stalin treason trials. In an episode too well orchestrated to be believable, hundreds of Jews were rounded up throughout the Soviet Union for committing "economic crimes." Leon Shapiro, an American historian, comments:

> Anyone knowing the Soviet system finds it very hard to imagine that this kind of trial, duplicated in different cities of the Soviet Union, was not the result of a preconceived plan.
>
> *Russian Jewry, 1917-1967*
> New York: T. Yoseloff (1969)

But what was the plan, and for what purpose? What benefits can an anti-Semitic drive of this scale yield?

William Korey has a simple hypothesis worth considering. The history of anti-Semitism in the Soviet Union has been influenced by (a) the growing tendency to adopt nationalistic ideas in state policy and propaganda, and (b) the growth of a totalitarian structure in government. The totalitarian state, which cannot allow dissent, according to this view, needs safe targets for popular discontent; and since the nationalist state tends to fear its "internationalist" elements most, these elements tend to make the worthiest scapegoats. the Jews are often dubbed in the press as "internationalists," conspirators in "imperialist" or "Zionist" plots to subvert the State.

If Korey's analysis is correct, when a scapegoat is needed to shift the blame for a problem, and when it is possible to frame the problem in the context of national security, Jews are likely candidates. This seems to be what happened in the 1960s when the Soviet government became fearful that a growing number of citizens were becoming dissatisfied with the economy; hence the "economic crimes" trials. This also seems to be the case in the 1970s when the democratic movement began to gain momentum. Identifying the growing dissident movement with the politically neutral work of emigrationists, the Soviet press led a bitter campaign against Jews.

This brings us closer to the anti-Semitic milieu of the present. Despite the attacks in the media, both Jewish emigration and the dissident movement grew popular through the 1970s, forcing the Soviet government to double its efforts in the press. Every anti-Semitic slant known to the Soviet media was employed during this period (1976-79): assaults on the Jewish religion; justifications for anti-Semitism; anti-Semitic stereotypes and Jewish names (in party propaganda, emigre Alexander Solzhenitsyn was

Израильские экстремисты продолжают «вымаливать» и получать на агрессивные цели крупные пожертвования из-за океана от сионистских кругов и финансовую помощь от Пентагона.

(Из газет).

СОВРЕМЕННЫЙ ИЗРАИЛЬСКИЙ ЛАПСЕРДАК.

FROM: Vechernya Moskva, 1973
INSIDE THE CARTOON: Jewish extremists request—and receive—large donations from Zionists abroad and from the Pentagon, for their aggressive purposes.
CAPTION: "The Modern Prayercoat"

dubbed "Solzenitsker" which presumably sounds more Jewish); "evidence" of immorality and criminal activities of Jews; articles on Zionist money power, and their shameless and treasonous collaboration with reactionary forces. In the meantime, spurious charges were invented to arrest prominent Jews.

This offensive soon reached greater proportions. A magazine article in 1977 argued that Hitler conspired with Jews (even today, the Soviet press often equates Nazism with Zionism) to set up a pro-Nazi state in Israel. The irony of the comparison to Nazi Germany might not have been lost on Soviet propagandists. the Soviet revisionist view of history places an inordinate amount of importance on the Soviet Union's role in World War II, and drawing a connection between Jews and their alleged enemy only serves to portray Jews as the most inimical kind of a people—a people who would trade their own kind for freedom and financial gain.

FROM: *Sozialisticheskaya Industria, September 1982*
INSIDE THE CARTOON: A skeleton of a Nazi officer shaking hands with a Jewish soldier with a weapon "made in USA," wading in the blood of Lebanon
CAPTION: "Bloodbrothers."

ЛИВАН
Репрессии продолжаются

FROM: *Sovjetskaya Rossia, October 1982*
INSIDE THE CARTOON: Israel is shown with its roots deep in Nazism, and pointing its bloody hatchet into all directions of the world.

FROM: *Pravda Vostoka, December 15, 1971*
INSIDE THE CARTOON: Star of David is shown intertwined with the Swastika.
CAPTION: "The banner of the Zionist gang."

> Together with the Nazis, the Zionists bear responsibility for the destruction of Jews in 1941-1945 in Europe. The blood of millions of victims is on their hands and on their conscience.
>
> L. Korneyev,
> *The Sinister Secrets of Zionism* (Part II),
> Ogonyok (Moscow)
> No. 35, 1977

> Not without the help of the leaders of Zionism did hundreds of thousands of ordinary Jews meet their death in the gas chambers.
>
> I. Tsvetkov,
> *The Tool of Imperialist Aggression*
> Krasnayazvezda (Moscow)
> 1976

> To begin with, on Soviet Jews. This matter has become part of a clamorous anti-Soviet campaign, of a veritable act of psychological warfare against the USSR. Propaganda of anti-Semitism, as of other forms of racial discrimination, is prohibited by law in the Soviet Union and constitutes a crime. . . .
>
> Mikhail Gorbachev
> interview with *L'Humanite,*
> French Communist newspaper
> 1986

The most comprehensive attack on political dissent in the guise of an anti-Zionist expose appeared in the form of a government study on human rights in 1980. *The White Book* accused the human rights activists in the Soviet Union of false, treasonous motives; their "real goals" were to incite emigration and to denigrate the Soviet image. What is worse, the author claimed, human rights are almost entirely absent in the West, especially in the state of Israel, and Soviet emigres suffer the worst.

It is sometimes difficult to discern the source of disinformation in *The White Book*, for it is not always the writer's imagination which seems at fault. A good number of falsified reports seem to have crept into this study. For example, the author mentions a woman living in Nazareth who was beaten to death for living with an Arab man. Army recruits are reportedly "forced to take part in violent crimes." People *cannot leave* Israel. People *are fleeing* Israel. The lucky ones who survive the escape are starved in other countries, and many commit suicide. In America, life is worse. Emigrants cannot find work. Professors are forced to wash windows.

What makes *The White Book* a great specimen of state-sponsored anti-Semitism, however, is the specificity of its target. In a glowing appraisal, a reporter for Izvestia (a Moscow daily) commented how this "humane book . . . offered a practical implementation of the Helsinki agreements." The reference to these agreements was probably no coincidence. The Helsinki Accords (see "Conclusion") had become a major thorn on the side of the Soviet Union. In this light, *The White Book* can be seen as a rather pointed attack, a repudiation of the human misery that the monitoring of compliance with the human rights provisions in the final Act had made so popular at home and abroad. Anti-Semitic forays in the media in recent years have almost all occurred in the midst of an ideological crisis such as this. As a result, the fate of the Jews has become exceedingly dependent on the Soviet response to media events.

Over twenty years of politically useful anti-Semitic propaganda has brought about the gradual alienation of Soviet Jews. In an increasingly hostile climate, the opportunity to emigrate has met with great enthusiasm. Over 265,000 left during the years 1968-86. Many more, nearly half a million, are still waiting. Soviet officials, citing the total Jewish population at 1.8 million, are quick to note that not all Jews wish to leave the Soviet Union (hand-picked representatives have come forward in the media to tell the world that the state of Soviet Jewry is satisfactory). There is no way of knowing how many Jews are simply too frightened to begin the emigration process. Also, some would-be emigres clearly have more to lose than others. As Jerome E. Gilison, professor of political science at Baltimore Hebrew College, noted:

> . . . the Jews who remain in the Soviet Union include many high-status individuals who would leave if they had greater assurances that they would not be refused, for these people have the most to lose if they are cast in the Kafkaesque twilight world of the refuseniks.
>
> "Soviet Jewish Emigration, 1970-80: An Overview," in *Soviet Jewry in the Decisive Decade, 1971-80*, ed. Robert O. Freedman, Duke University Press, Durham (1984)

When Soviet officials need a reliable representative to speak on behalf of Soviet Jews, they invariably look to this class of fearful people.

Emigration

> Do you need to know the reasons for refusal? Well, invent them yourself!
>
> Head of Moscow Visa Office, speaking to Natan Sharansky, 1974

> I shall make you and your family rot here.
>
> Institute manager in Kiev refusing to grant a Jewish employee permission to emigrate, 1976

> If your wife does not publicly confess her "crimes," your family will remain inside the Soviet Union until the year 2000, or she will be exchanged on that bridge—the same as Sharansky.
>
> KGB agent to refusenik, 1986

In 1984, Soviet Jewish emigration came to a virtual standstill, with only 896 Jews being granted exit visas. 1985 (1140) and 1986 (914) followed suit. These low numbers were a mere trickle compared to the 51,320 Jews who were allowed to leave in 1979. While the first part of 1987 has seen an increase in Soviet Jewish emigration (1,431 through April 30th), the numbers are still far below those realized only eight years ago. Despite the fact that Jewish emigration has been by far the most successful in Soviet history, emigrating entails so many difficult steps and exposes the applicant to so many risks that there are many more Jews who are simply too frightened to attempt it.

What are the reasons for refusal? Since emigration officials are allowed such an extraordinary degree of latitude in deciding who may or may not leave, often there is no reason. However, a Jew is typically refused for working at a facility which allegedly exposes him or her to "classified information."

The bulk of the 11,000 refuseniks have been denied permission to emigrate on the basis of the alleged possession of "state secrets." In October 1985 however, Mikhail Gorbachev told reporters in Paris that there was a time limitation on refusals based on state secrecy. Gorbachev stated that after a period of five to ten years had elapsed since a person was last involved with classified or security-related information, he could no longer be refused on these grounds. In a meeting in April of 1987 with a U.S. Congressional delegation, Gorbachev reiterated this statement, adding only that in some extraordinary cases an

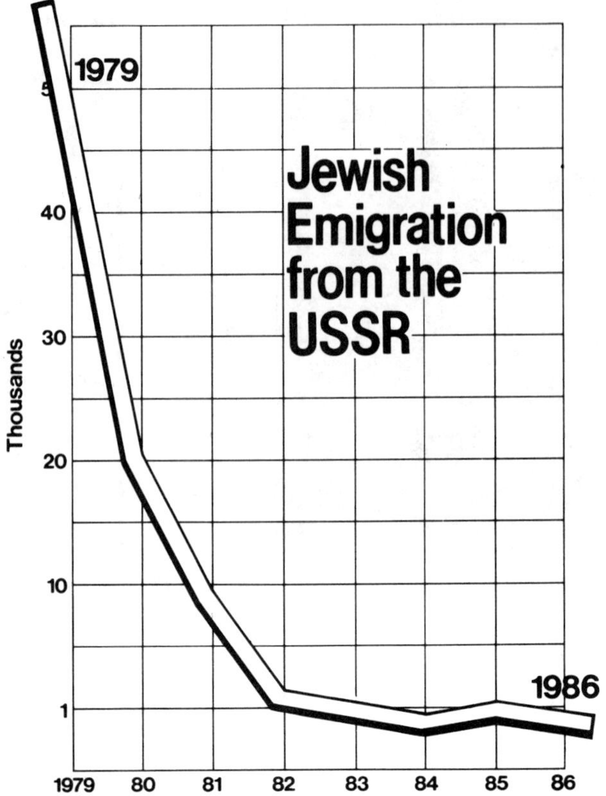

From January through April 1987, 1431 Soviet Jews received permission to emigrate.

additional one or two years might have to be added. This stated policy however, is contradicted by a plethora of examples. Professor Naum Meiman, for one, was last involved in classified work in 1955. He has been repeatedly refused on the basis of "state secrets"—32 years after he completed his work for the state. Alexander Lerner, Yuli Kosharovsky, Ida Nudel and thousands of others continue to be refused on grounds of secrecy well after a decade has passed since their work in their respective fields. Moreover, children are refused on the basis of their parents' possession of state secrets. Under the codification of emigration which took effect on January 1, 1987, applicants who had never been refused on basis of state secrecy, were now for the first time, being denied on this basis.

Clearly, in the short history of Soviet Jewish emigration, a variety of factors have affected the lives of Soviet Jews and the rate of emigration. Throughout the ebb and flow of the history of Soviet Jewish emigration, the Soviet Jewry movement has been a critical focal point and catalyst.

Jews have also been delayed by authorities demanding that they present death certificates of parents who perished in World War II concentration camps. High ranking officials have even gone so far as to reason that families should not be separated, a bizarre twist on the Helsinki Accords directive to allow emigration on the basis of family reunification. Jews living in Perm, Angorsek, and Krasnoyorsk cannot even hope to leave; emigration is forbidden to the residents of these "closed" cities.

Another common device is the "conscription trap." Young Jews applying for exit visas are routinely called up for military service and are later refused on the grounds of

EMIGRATION: PROCEDURES AND OBSTACLES

Initial steps . . .

All applicants for exit visas must submit copies of the following to the local OVIR (visa office):

- *Vysov*—invitation from relatives in Israel;
- Document of employment status—including a character reference;
- Proof of residency—including validation of housing permit;
- Birth and marriage certificates;
- Photographs;
- University diplomas (where applicable);
- Statement of Intent and autobiography;
- Parental or spousal permissions. If any are deceased, death certificates must be produced.

Obstacles . . .

While none of the following rules have been applied universally, all are sufficiently widespread to constitute serious threats to emigration.

- **Denial of visa on the basis of "access to state secrets."** This classification has been applied even to dentists and elevator operators;
- **Minimum five-year waiting period following military service**;
- **Inaccessibility of OVIR officials.** Some offices serving thousands of applicants open for only a few hours a day, two days a week;
- ***Vysovs* mailed from Israel** are often confiscated or delayed by Soviet post offices;
- **Three-year employment requirement** following completion of education;
- **Restrictions of *vysovs* to** "first degree relatives" living in Israel. Because the nuclear families of many applicants reside outside of Israel, often Israeli invitations cannot be produced. Applicants may then be turned down on the basis of "insufficient kinship;"
- **Personal and professional risks**. Applicants become vulnerable to job dismissals, school and university expulsion, conscription into the Red Army, withdrawal of residence permit, public denunciation, physical harassment, searches and arrest.

Note: If an application is refused, another cannot be filed for six months. Refuseniks must submit a completely new set of documents each time they re-apply.

"secrecy" and "access to classified information." This often means being made to leave school, but as the head of the Moscow emigration office explained to Natan Shcharansky, your right to an education is forfeited when you ask to leave the Soviet Union.

Aliyah and the Human Rights Activists

In the early stages the Soviet Aliyah movement drew considerable support from the human rights movement. The "dissidents" (or the "democrats" as they are better known in the Soviet press) were primarily involved with the rights of artists and free thinkers, but as Joshua Rubenstein, Northeast director of Amnesty International, notes: "among intellectuals, anti-Semitism has always been a personal touchstone." Andrei Sakharov, Nobel laureate physicist and human rights activist, has frequently written and spoken on behalf of Soviet Jewry (today he lives in internal exile).

FROM: Pravda, February 1971
INSIDE THE CARTOON: "Jewish Question in the USSR."
CAPTION: "Zionist Soap Bubbles."

Despite the different goals between the Moscow dissidents and the Aliyah activists, they developed a rather elaborate network. Renascent Zionist organizations in the Baltic and Georgian republics relayed the names and addresses of refuseniks into the city. Other regions reporting a growing interest in Israel (especially among younger Jews) demanded literature and information on how to emigrate. In the great tradition of Soviet dissent, letters to political leaders were drafted, and petitions were signed. The dissidents also advised Jews on the Kremlin's sensitivity to public opinion, and the importance of reliable communication. The old rumor network made way for the *samizdat* (self-published) publication.

The Chronicle of Human Events, the premier *samizdat* journal of the dissident movement, was the first modern Soviet literary forum for national Jewish expression. In 1970, *The Chronicle* gave birth to two wholly Jewish publications: *Iskod*, and the more polemical *Iton*, whose featured contributors were prominent Jews from all over the world. Also noteworthy was *Jews of the USSR*, the journal founded by former refusenik Mark Azbel. Jewish culture activist Iosif Begun and poet Felix Kandel both contributed to this special publication.

The value of the *samizdat* is inestimable. Despite the fact that circulation was severely limited (publication was so risky that a single edition of *Jews in the USSR*, for instance, never exceeded 30-40 copies), the journals passed through many hands, eventually finding a small but influential readership in the West. The Jewish *samizdat* might have been the first to bring to the attention of the world the plight of Soviet Jewry.

At least one other benefit of improved communications in the emigration movement was good leadership. Moscow, the nerve center of the emigration experiment, attracted Jews from all over to participate. Even the leaders of the Zionist strongholds of Vilnius and Riga who had kept a safe distance from the Moscow group (distrusting their association with the dissident underground) had contacts in the city. One such contact, Vitaly Rubin, scholar of ancient Chinese philosophy, organized the first refusenik meetings in his Moscow apartment. Rubin, who brought great prestige and credibility to Soviet Aliyah, was eventually succeeded by Vladimir Slepak, Ida Nudel and Anatoly (Natan) Sharansky, each a name very well known to the West. While emigration was and continues to be a largely collaborative effort, the leadership that these men and women provided and the facility each had for galvanizing international support was critical to the survival of the movement.

The Gates Open

Surprisingly, the Soviet government made the first move. In 1966, Prime Minister Alexei Kosygin announced that Jews would soon be allowed to emigrate to Israel. In the fall of 1968, word quickly spread that applications were being accepted.

The vast Jewish response was not anticipated. News of Israeli prowess in the Six-Day War had led to a resurgence of Jewish national pride everywhere. Latent desires for a better life could finally be realized. The government may have further encouraged emigration with the intense anti-Zionist propaganda campaign which immediately followed the war. Reports that the failing government of Wladyslow Gomulka had forced several thousand Jews past the Polish border in 1968 may have also contributed; and the Soviet invasion of Czechoslovakia was a terrible disappointment to the Jews who continued to believe that there was still hope for civil liberties behind the Iron Curtain (the Soviet press went one step further by blaming the Jews for what happened in Czechoslovakia: there were reports that Jews had penetrated the government, and that an internationalist coup was pending).

As greater numbers of Jews began applying for exit visas in the late 1960s, the authorities tried desperately to discourage them. News articles condemned life in Israel. In March 1970, the government organized a panel of 40 Jews (each a prominent figure in the arts, sciences and government) to extol the quality of Jewish life in the Soviet Union. The refusenik response, the "letter of 39," which was published in *The New York Times,* brought favorable publicity to the movement but it seemed to come too late. Emigration was faltering, and "the vast majority of applicants were harassed or simply ignored," Joshua Rubenstein observes.

These were desperate times. Early in 1970, a group of Jews were arrested for plotting to hijack a plane to Sweden. Under the pretense of unveiling the "conspiracy," scores of Jews were arrested and detained in many different localities. The would-be hijackers and their suspected accomplices became defendants in the infamous "Leningrad trials." As expected, the Soviet media provided the government with full coverage and ideological support but fortunately the near unanimous voice of protest from world leaders (including the leaders of West European communist parties) turned this brief but frightening episode into a giant public relations loss for the Soviet Union. Negative publicity from the trials even seems to have led to a small increase in emigration for the year 1971.

Conditions did not improve significantly, however, until the Israeli government stepped in. Although Israel had always been active on the private level, in public, perhaps fearing a military reprisal, she was exceedingly quiet. As one American political analyst observed, Israel's position was that "more Jews would be released if they avoided public criticism of the Soviet Union." However, when greater numbers of emigres began arriving in Israel in 1969, some of them claiming to know more than the Israeli experts, a more direct approach began to win appeal. People learned to talk about the "failure of Israel and Jews in the West to express vigorous commitment to Soviet Jewry." A raucous debate ensued, and pressured by the threat of the conservative faction to win popularity on the issue, the Meir government came forward. The support of American Jewry soon followed.

If the Soviet Jewish emigration movement could be summed up in a few words, "the louder, the better" seems a fitting slogan. In letters, petitions and timely appeals to the West, the movement has kept to a consistent, effective philosophy. The Jews of Moscow (as do the democrats who helped emigration in the early stages) have this much to their credit.

However, there are many victims of this strategy. There are an estimated 11,000 refuseniks in the Soviet Union. Their welfare has become a leading concern for the emigration movement, as these men, women and children demonstrated in their daily lives the extent to which Soviet citizens are made to suffer for their desire to live freely as Jews. They are a living testament to the near impossibility of Jewish life in the Soviet Union.

Prisoners of Conscience

As of May 1987, there are two Soviet Jewish Prisoners of Conscience languishing in prison. Aleksei Magarik, a twenty-seven-year-old cellist from Moscow, and Iosif Zisselis, a forty-one-year-old radio engineer from Chernovtsy, were imprisoned on trumped-up charges—Magarik for drug possession, and Zisselis for circulating anti-Soviet slander.

In the case of Magarik, he was on his way back to Moscow when he was stopped at the Tblisi Airport. The authorities there claimed to have found drugs in a suitcase that had already been placed in the plane's baggage compartment and later removed for the search. Aleksei denied ever having seen the drugs, and all evidence proves that the drugs were planted by the KGB.

Zisselis, who is also a former member of the Ukranian Helsinki Watch group, is in his second term in prison. The Soviets claim he had kept anti-Soviet literature "with the intention of distributing it."

While in prison, they have been shuttled to the most dangerous facilities and exposed to the worst elements of a correctional system badly in need of reform. However, the

Photo credit: Richard Lobell

But all these resources of a super-power are not enough towards a man who hears the voice of freedom, to an isolated Jew who hears the voice of solidarity with his people, the voice which he hears from the very chamber of his soul . . .

They sarcastically said that they will save me from the counter-influence of my religion, and tried to confiscate my psalm book, but every time they were compelled to throw it back to me.

Natan Sharansky
Solidarity Sunday, May 1986

only crimes that these men have committed was their wish to emigrate to Israel, and live their lives as Jews, free from constant persecution and harassment.

A new law went into effect in October 1983, allowing for an additional five year term for prisoners who disobey labor camp personnel. *New York Times* reporter Serge Schmemann noted that "the law apparently relieves authorities of the need to compile a new case against a dissident who is nearing the end of his or her term." A more recent development is also disturbing. In February of this year an amendment was passed which increases the penalty for first time offenders of Article 70 ("agitation") who receive material aid from foreign organizations. The new law, which seems specifically aimed at Jews, raises the penalty from 12 to 15 years.

Prison and Labor Camp Conditions

Soviet prison and labor camps suffer from mismanagement, neglect of the law and the arbitrary interference of MVD directives. The result is an appalling list of indignities. The information below was gathered from the testimony of former prisoners and independent reports compiled by the Coalition To Free Soviet Jews, and Amnesty International. The citations to articles of law in violation (the Corrective Labor Code, 1970) were first made by prominent refusenik Ida Nudel in Moscow in 1974.

Soviet Prisons and Labor Camps

> In no case known to Amnesty International has a Soviet court acquitted a defendant brought to trial either specifically or in disguised form for his political or religious activity.
>
> Amnesty International
> *Prisoners of Conscience in the USSR*

> . . . the more severe the punishment applied, the more effective will be the struggle with crime.
>
> Soviet jurist M.D. Shargorodsky
> *Punishment, Its Goals and Effectiveness*

When Soviet General Secretary Leonid Brezhnev signed the Final Act in Helsinki, Finland (August 1, 1975), the Soviet Union bound itself to several international commitments on human rights (see appendix). Unfortunately, Soviet compliance to these commitments has been unsatisfactory, on many counts.

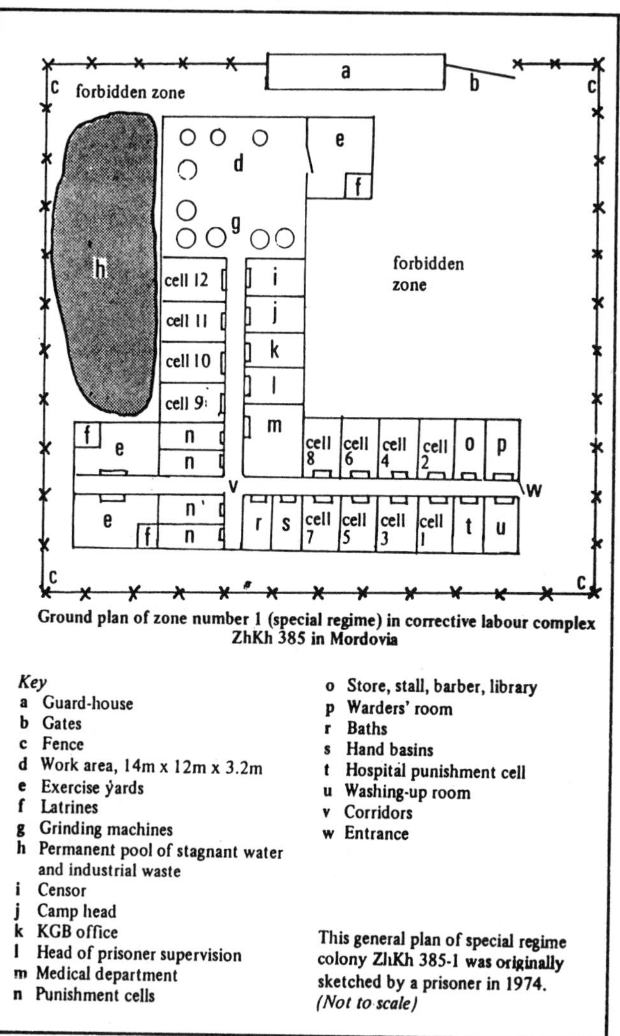

Layout of a Soviet special regime colony.

One explanation for this is that the language in these agreements (in particular, certain "escape" clauses) have made it too easy for the Soviets to renege on their promises. For example, Article 3.3 of the United Nations Declaration of 1981 reads as follows:

> Freedom to manifest one's religion or beliefs may be subject only to such limitations as are proscribed by law and are necessary to protect public safety, order, health or morals or the fundamental rights and freedoms of others.

Soviet officials have been prone to read into this article the preeminence of the Soviet Criminal Code. Since many civil liberties enjoyed in the West are subject to severe restrictions in the Soviet Union, it has not been difficult to find "limitations as are proscribed by law."

While not all agreements to which the Soviet Union is party are this vague, Soviet authorities have managed to interpret the language of almost every commitment to their liking. As Western diplomats have learned over the years, civil liberties within the Soviet Union are entirely a domestic matter, tightly circumscribed by a repressive legal code, and there is little that international agreements can do to change this.

Laws

The modern Soviet penal system rests on the cautious revision of a revolutionary code. The RSFSR (Russian Republic) Criminal Code of 1960 replaced the code of 1926 (drafted only nine years after the Bolshevik revolution).

The early code was far more repressive—for instance, it allowed imprisonment without hearing or trial—and in general it was far easier, for political purposes, to manipulate. Yet the revised code seems to have retained something of its revolutionary character, the laws for isolated detention (see "Prisoners of Conscience"), to give just one example. In other countries with poor human rights records, laws like this are sometimes invoked in a "state of siege." It is hard to think of the quiescent emigration or human rights movements in these terms. Yet in the aftermath of the Soviet Revolution, when the voice of protest

ARTICLE ONE:
Punishment Must Not Humiliate the Prisoner nor Permit Him To Suffer.

Hunger strikers are beaten in the Perm Labor Camp. In the Vladimir prison, inmates are beaten in isolation cells. Better-known prisoners are usually spared from the excesses, but there are exceptions.

ARTICLE EIGHT:
Prisoners Cannot Be Deprived of Their Civil Rights.

Nowhere in the law or in MVD directives are the religious rights of prisoners clarified. Religious articles are usually confiscated from the prisoners.

Jews are often confined with hardened criminals, and are frequently subjected to lengthy anti-Semitic harangues in the presence of other prisoners. Prison guards have been known to provoke conflicts and acts of violence against Jewish prisoners.

ARTICLE TWENTY-FOUR:
(visits from relatives)

In contradiction to the law, prisoners are regularly deprived of family visits. "Distant relatives"—grandparents, aunts and uncles—are restricted from these visits.

In Perm, visitors are undressed and searched.

ARTICLE TWENTY-SIX:
Prisoners Have the Right to Receive an Unlimited Number of Letters.

The withholding of mail and parcels is a common punishment. A prisoner in Perm reported that you cannot keep what you write. In the same facility, orders were issued by the Procurator to confiscate and destroy mail.

There are also rules on how a letter can be written, and what can be written in it. With no apparent basis in law, Natan Shcharansky was forbidden to address his wife Avital in letters to his family. Letters written in an RSFSR facility must be written in Russian, regardless of the prisoner's native language (there are many different native languages in the Soviet Union); otherwise, the prisoner must wait to have the letter translated for the censor. If the censor detects a note of criticism, a prisoner is liable to get punished.

ARTICLES THIRTY-SEVEN AND THIRTY-EIGHT:

POC Yuli Edelshtein, who suffered a very serious casualty, describes "slave-type" work conditions in Vladimir. The Vladimir and Mordavia prisons have poor ventilation in work areas. In the Urals, one worker reported that there was no rest period. Prisoners refusing to work at traditionally unpopular tasks (e.g., mending barbed wire) are severely punished.

ARTICLE TWENTY-SEVEN:
(medical care)

As a result of poor diet, most prisoners suffer from ulcers and other gastric problems; yet the legal guidelines for medical service are regularly countermanded by the MVD. Prisoners report bathing once a week to once every ten days, and prisoners with communicable diseases are seldom isolated. In very cold regions, such as the Urals, prisoners are seldom given enough warm clothing to wear. Generally, medical care is given only when there is good reason to believe that a prisoner would die without it.

ARTICLE THIRTY:
The Administration Must Carry on Educational Programs to Make the Prisoners Good Citizens of The Soviet Union.

As an example to other prisoners, POCs are treated very poorly at propaganda classes. Attendance is mandatory, and physical force is often used against the unwilling prisoner.

ARTICLE FIFTY-SIX:
Ensuring The Normal Vital Activity of the Human Organism, Convicted People Shall Receive Food.

Convicted persons who systematically and maliciously do not fulfill their output norms at work may be put on reduced food rations. There are currently 13 different diets in Soviet labor camps and prisons. Even the best—2500 to 2900 calories a day—fall short of the World Health Organization's standards for men "working very actively" (3100-3900). Ida Nudel reports that a prisoner can earn an 800 calorie-a-day diet in Perm (the caloric equivalent of 7 ounces of roasted peanuts) for poor behavior. In Vladimir, prisoners are fed on "skip days" (once every 2 days) and the water is often too dirty to drink.

was perceived as a serious threat, dissidents were dealt with very harshly and a law was devised to enable the ruling government to hold onto its new power. Twenty-four numbing years of rule under Stalin did little to advance the law, which might only have been justified under the most threatening conditions in the life of the nation. The code of 1960 marks the first attempt to move Soviet law forward in history.

Another problem is the amount of discretion that administrative bodies—central and local—are allowed in interpreting the law. This is particularly true of the Ministry of the Interior (the MVD), whose directives, from time to time, fill the wide gaps in prison and labor camp ruses. Also, the Soviet penal system seems to lack a systematic program for reviewing itself. As a result, the potential for administrative abuse is very high, and the list of violations is extraordinary.

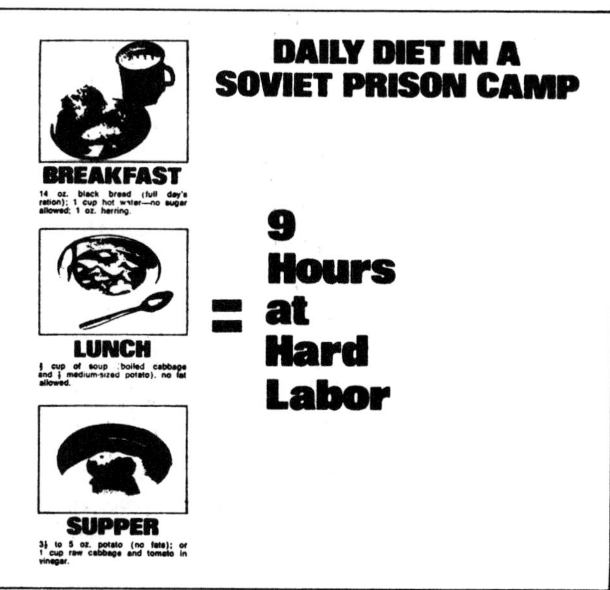

Prison Sentences

Where a prisoner goes in the Soviet Union depends upon the crime committed. Most POCs are charged with "anti-Soviet agitation and propaganda" (Article 70) or "Defamation of the Soviet State and Social System" (Article 190-1), charges which fall under the "especially dangerous crimes" category. Invariably, these charges bring imprisonment in the worst and most dangerous institutions.

Emigration activists and refuseniks are also frequently jailed on lesser charges, such as "malicious hooliganism" (Article 206) and "Parasitism" (Article 209). The language of these laws is so vague as to allow inventiveness. For instance, former POC Vladimir Slepak and his wife Maria were arrested in 1978 under Article 206 for appearing with a sign in public which read, "Let us go to our son in Israel." For this effrontery Vladimir was given five years internal exile, and Maria three years at a correctional facility.

Release

When a Prisoner of Conscience is released, he or she is immediately blacklisted and placed under administrative surveillance. They are also given conditions which they find extremely difficult to meet. Applications for residency permits, for example (*propiskas,* which are required of all Soviet citizens) are frequently rejected, forcing many former prisoners to find new homes, often in isolated areas. The former prisoner must also find acceptable work—if they cannot show visible means of support, they can readily be arrested for "parasitism."

Since Soviet Jewish POCs are former refuseniks, their re-entry into the civilian world is all the more discouraging.

Conclusion—The Heart of Detente

> The Soviet Union has undertaken some serious international obligations now, and I'm sure that the pressure you can organize from America and from international organizations will work and will help us to communicate with you and to fight for our rights. I am sure that our firm determination to continue our fight, and your continued support are two major things which help Soviet Jewry to be saved.
>
> Natan Sharansky
> September 7, 1975

> Without too much exaggeration, it could be stated that the immigration process is the single most important determinant of American policy . . . immigration policy is foreign policy.
>
> Daniel Patrick Moynihan and Nathan Glazer

Several Views

The early leaders of the Soviet emigration movement were advised by human rights activists to use the media to promote their cause. It was well known how sensitive the Soviet Union is to world opinion, how it affects their ability to perform confidently on the world stage. The advice has sometimes paid off. The Soviet Union has been at times remarkably responsive to international pressure.

For example: in 1970, a French communist newspaper—joining the chorus of criticism coming from the West in the West—denounced the outcome of the Leningrad trials, comparing the death sentences to the ones recently handed down by a Spanish court to six Basque nationalists. The comparison to Franco's Spain—the spectre of the Imperialist-Fascist hegemony which they so proudly helped to defeat—might have been too much for the Soviet Union. The death penalties were eventually commuted.

Also, in 1972 when American Jews complained about the "head tax" that emigration officials had begun to impose to recover the expenses of Soviet education, the Soviet government backed down. There are still considerable costs incurred. For example, the approximate cost of emigration for a family of four is $6000, the equivalent of two years' salary for the average Soviet white collar worker (the cost includes payment for the renunciation of Soviet citizenship). Strategically, the reversal on the head tax was a very significant gesture. As one Soviet expert observed:

> The Soviet Union's change of its position on the head tax was to be the most important example yet of Soviet sensitivity to Western concern on the emigration issue.
>
> *Soviet Jewry in the Decisive Decade, 1971-80,* ed. Robert O. Freedman (1984) p.44

Some critics suggest that it is wrong to judge Soviet behavior by Western standards. Expectations in areas such as arms control, trade and scientific exchanges have always been cautious; is it not reasonable to "expect less" for emigration too? It is conceivable that Soviet diplomacy is less evil than it is shrewd.

Looking at the emigration figures (see chart), it is worth noting the rise in 1971 from the previous year. This may have been a Soviet plea for leniency as a result of the bad publicity they received during the Leningrad trials.

The first significant leap occurred over the years 1972-73. Much happened during this time. In 1975 the Helsinki Final Act was signed, binding the Soviet Union to specific commitments in the areas of human rights and emigration (the Helsinki Accords also served to reestablish the authority of several previously ratified international agreements on human rights). In 1974 Congress adopted the Jackson-Vanik amendment (United States Trade Reform Act of 1972) linking emigration to trade credits, which were extremely important to the Soviet Union's agriculturally depressed economy. Also, in 1977 the Helsinki Final Act was reviewed in Belgrade. The diplomatic developments of the late 1970s forced the Soviet Union to perform in a way in which it had not been accustomed, and for the most part, they came through.

Two of these developments demand closer attention. The Helsinki Accords, the foremost product of detente, were invaluable to Jews emigrating in the 1970s. They were also important to the Soviets, at least in the beginning. In exchange for concessions on emigration and civil liberties, the Soviet Union won official recognition of its sovereignty over Eastern Europe. Party officials were so enthusiastic that a motion was made to incorporate the Ten Principles of the first part (or "Basket One") of the Final Act into the new constitution (1977). Since that time, however, the Soviet Union has been dogged for violating the human rights provisions, and pressured to attend international reviews (Belgrade, 1977; Madrid, 1982).

An indirect heir to detente is the Jackson-Vanik amendment, which the Kremlin has never looked favorably on. Soviet antipathy to Jackson-Vanik surfaced in the Sharansky trial (1978): the Procurator repeatedly tried to establish that Sharansky's work directly led to the adoption of the amendment. The Jackson-Vanik amendment and the Helsinki Accords were the most effective diplomatic forces in the big years for Jewish emigration and they continue to exert influence today. But taken alone they cannot explain the record figure in 1979: over 51,000 Jews emigrated that year, a 58% increase over the previous year.

In a 1984 study, Robert O. Freedman, an American expert on Soviet emigration, made an interesting discovery. Carefully charting the flow of emigration against the backdrop of Soviet-U.S. relations, he discovered that the three conditions that had contributed to the 1971-72 jump in emigration were met again in 1979.

> Soviet fear of a Sino-American alliance, the Soviet desire for a SALT treaty, and an American administration willing to provide the USSR trade benefits.
>
> Freedman, p. 62

For as long as it is necessary, the Soviet Jewry movement will continue to keep the issues alive, in public protests and in letters, hoping that someday the conditions will be right for Jews to emigrate at peak levels again.

> My KGB investigators, my prosecutors, my prison guards tried their best to convince me that I am alone, that I am powerless in their hands. But I felt, I knew what they only sensed, that I was never alone, that my wife, my people, that all of you are with me. Together we have won once. Together we will succeed again.
>
> Natan (Anatoly) Sharansky
> Solidarity Sunday, 1986

Helsinki Final Act
of the Conference on Security and Co-operation in Europe, signed August 1, 1975.

PRINCIPLE VII
(guiding relations between Participating States)

Respect for human rights and fundamental freedoms, including the freedom of thought, conscience, religion or belief

The participating States will respect human rights and fundamental freedoms, including the freedom of thought, conscience, religion or belief, for all without distinction as to race, sex, language, or religion.

They will promote and encourage the effective exercise

President Gerald R. Ford and Soviet General Secretary Leonid I. Brezhnev signing the Helsinki Final Act, in Helsinki, Finland on August 1, 1975, at the conference on security and cooperation in Europe. *Photo credit: Courtesy of the Gerald R. Ford Library*

of civil, political, economic, social, cultural and other rights and freedoms all of which derive from the inherent dignity of the human person and are essential for his free and full development.

Within this framework the participating States will recognize and respect the freedom of the individual to profess and practice, alone or in community with others, religion or belief acting in accordance with the dictates of his own conscience.

In the field of human rights and fundamental freedoms, the participating States will act in conformity with the purposes and principles of the charter of the United Nations and with the Universal Declaration of Human Rights . . . including inter alia the International Covenants on Human Rights, by which they may be bound.

SECTION (B) REUNIFICATION OF FAMILIES

The participating States will deal in a positive and humanitarian spirit with the applications of persons who wish to be reunited with members of their family, with special attention being given to requests of an urgent character such as requests submitted by persons who are ill or old. They will deal with applications in this field as expeditiously as possible.

. . . Applications for the purpose of family reunification which are not granted may be renewed at the appropriate level and will be reconsidered at reasonably short intervals by the authorities of the country of residence or destination, whichever is concerned.

SECTION (D) ADDENDUM

. . . They confirm that religious faiths, institutions and organizations, practicing within the constitutional framework of the participating States, and their representatives can, in the field of their activities, have contacts and meetings among themselves and exchange information.

Constitution of the Union of Soviet Socialist Republics

The new Constitution of the Union of Soviet Socialist Republics was adopted on October 7, 1977.

ARTICLE 29:

The USSR's relations with other states are based on observance of the following principles: . . . *respect for human rights and fundamental freedoms; the equal rights of peoples and their right to decide their own destiny. . . .*

ARTICLE 36:

Citizens of the USSR of different races and nationalities have equal rights . . . Any direct or indirect limitation of the rights of citizens, or establishment of direct or indirect privileges on grounds of race or nationality, and any advocacy of racial or national exclusiveness, hostility or contempt, are punishable by law.

ARTICLE 52:

Citizens of the USSR are guaranteed freedom of conscience, that is, the right to profess or not to profess any religion, and to conduct religious worship or atheistic propaganda. Incitement of hostility or hatred on religious grounds is prohibited.

WOMEN REFUSENIKS APPEAL

Eighty women refuseniks, many of whom have never signed a protest, wrote this special appeal.

"We are women refuseniks. We, our husbands, children, and parents have been refused emigration from the USSR to Israel—to the country which we all consider our own. Along with receiving refusals we are deprived of normal life, of a safe future, of the possibility of bringing up our children under normal conditions. **Our hearts are filled with anxiety.** We are worried about those who are close and dear to us.

"As a rule, after we apply, both our husbands and we, ourselves, lose our jobs. Then our husbands work as caretakers and watchmen, but this is not the greatest threat which our husbands and sons face. They are threatened with prison, with physical reprisals; they are thrown into prisons and camps on false accusations. **We live in an atmosphere of constant threat.**

"From the age of three, our children know that there is one world of their family and friends, and that there is another hostile world of strangers. **Our children ask us questions which we are unable to answer.** "Why are we not allowed to leave for Israel? Why are we called 'refuseniks'? Why should we never mention that we study and know Hebrew? Why did mother or father lose their job?'

"Their words bring tears of despair to our eyes. What pitiful and grown-up questions they are asking. When our homes are being searched they ask 'What are they doing in our apartment?' 'Have they lost anything here?'.

"We are afraid to pronounce the word prison in our homes with our children present. They know prisons are for criminals. **How can we explain to them that their fathers are not criminals,** that their only fault is that they want to remain Jews, and want to leave for Israel?

"We appeal to you, who struggle for women's equality, and well-being. We are the women who belong to the people who lost so many sons and daughters in the 20th century. **Help Us."**

1985

ARTICLE 56:

The privacy of citizens, and of their correspondence, telephone conversations, and telegraphic communications is protected by law.

Universal Declaration of Human Rights

The Universal Declaration of Human Rights was adopted and proclaimed by the General Assembly of the United Nations on December 10, 1948.

ARTICLE 12:

No one shall be subjected to arbitrary interference with his privacy, family, home or correspondence, nor to attacks upon his honor and reputation. Everyone has the right to the protection of the law against such interference or attacks.

ARTICLE 13:

1. Everyone has the right to freedom of movement and residence within the borders of each State.

2. *Everyone has the right to leave any country, including his own, and return to his country.*

ARTICLE 18:

Everyone has the right to freedom of thought, conscience, and religion; this right includes freedom to change his religion or belief, and freedom, either alone or in community with others and in public or private, to manifest his religion or belief in teaching, practice, worship and observance.

ARTICLE 19:

Everyone has the right to freedom of opinion and expression; this right includes freedom to hold opinions without interference and to seek, receive and impart information and ideas through any media and regardless of frontiers.

ARTICLE 20:
1. Everyone has the right to freedom of peaceful assembly and association.
2. No one may be compelled to belong to an association.

What Can You Do for Soviet Jews?

Following is a partial listing of Coalition projects:

PROJECT YACHAD—Adopt a Soviet Jew. The Coalition will provide names, biographical data and letter-writing instructions to any individual or group who wishes to "adopt" a refusenik family. Your letters provide Soviet Jews with essential support.

SPEAKERS BUREAU—Arrange for a Coalition speaker to talk to your organization, school, synagogue or youth group about Soviet Jewry.

FILMS & VIDEO—Raise awareness among members of your school, synagogue, or organization with a Soviet Jewry film or video.

BAR/BAT MITZVAH TWINNING—Dedicate your bar/-bat mitzvah to a Soviet Jewish child who is unable to publicly mark his/her entrance into Jewish adulthood.

ACTIONLINE—Call the Coalition's 24-hour hotline at (212) 391-0954 for the latest news and announcements of upcoming Soviet Jewry events.

TELEGRAM BANK—Authorize the Coalition to send a telegram to the Soviet Union when a crisis arises. You will be charged through your phone bill.

SOLIDARITY SUNDAY FOR SOVIET JEWRY—March annually in the largest Soviet Jewry rally in the world. Our combined voices send a powerful message that we will not be silent until Soviet Jews are free.

LETTER-WRITING—Tell President Reagan, Secretary of State George Shultz, other members of the administration and Soviet officials that you are concerned about Soviet Jews. Urge them to use their offices to take personal action to remedy the situation.

CONTRIBUTIONS—Send a tax-deductible donation to support the work of the Coalition to Free Soviet Jews and enable the Coalition to develop outstanding new programs.

For more information on Soviet Jewry, call the Coalition at (212) 354-1316.

Soviet Jewry Timeline: 1967—Present

1967—The Six-Day War in the Middle East arouses a new sense of national pride among Soviet Jews; on the last day of the war, the Soviet Union severs diplomatic relations with Israel.

1968—Soviet troops enter Czechoslovakia; the first government-sponsored meeting is held at Babi Yar to condemn Israel; Boris Kochubiyevsky, a young man whose father and grandfather were killed at Babi Yar, protests and is sentenced to three years in prison for "anti-Soviet slander." Kochubiyevsky is the first Soviet Jewish Prisoner of Conscience.

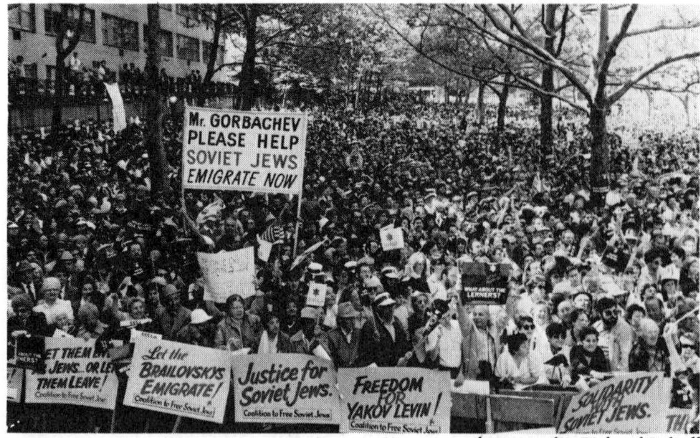

Solidarity Sunday, May 1986 photo credit: Richard Lobell

1969—Eighteen Jewish families from the Georgian Republic officially seek to emigrate to Israel.

1970—Thirty-four Soviet Jews are arrested and tried in Leningrad on the charge that they conspired to hijack a plane to Israel. Leningrad Trials spark world-wide activity on behalf of the defendants.

1971—World Jewish Conference held in Brussels, devoted to the problem of Soviet Jewry.
SOVIET JEWISH EMIGRATION: 13,022

1972—A crop failure in the Soviet Union leads to a $750 million grain deal between the USSR and the United States; an education tax is imposed on those Soviet Jews wishing to emigrate; one million Americans petition Richard Nixon to intervene on behalf of Soviet Jews during his visit to the Soviet Union; The Jackson-Vanik Amendment is passed in Congress, tying "most favored nation" status in trade to Soviet emigration policy; first annual Solidarity Sunday rally for Soviet Jewry sponsored by the Greater New York Conference on Soviet Jewry.
SOVIET JEWISH EMIGRATION: 31,681

1973—The Soviet Union backs the Arabs in the Yom Kippur War in the Middle East; Jewish emigration grows; in response to world pressure, Soviet authorities suspend collection of the education tax; twelve Jewish activists demonstrating in front of the Ministry of the Interior are arrested.
SOVIET JEWISH EMIGRATION: 34,733

1974—The Soviets begin to clamp down. Emigration drops.
SOVIET JEWISH EMIGRATION: 20,628

1975—Pledging to "respect human rights and fundamental freedoms," thirty-five nations, including the Soviet Union, sign the Helsinki Accords, guaranteeing reunification of families.
SOVIET JEWISH EMIGRATION: 13,221

1976—Brezhnev is reelected; a second World Jewish Conference is held in Brussels.
SOVIET JEWISH EMIGRATION: 14,261

1977—Anatoly Sharansky, a prominent Jewish activist, is arrested on treason charges, based on allegations that he passed secret documents to Western analysts. He is held in solitary confinement for sixteen months.
SOVIET JEWISH EMIGRATION: 16,736

1978—Sharansky is sentenced to thirteen years in prison.
SOVIET JEWISH EMIGRATION: 28,864

1979—SOVIET JEWISH EMIGRATION: a record 51,320

1980—Soviet troops invade Afghanistan; a follow-up conference to review the Helsinki Human Rights Accords convenes in Madrid; Viktor Brailovsky is arrested days before the eve of the conference.
SOVIET JEWISH EMIGRATION: 21,471

1981—Emigration continues to decline; number of arrests and visa refusals continue to rise; increase in KGB harassment of Soviet Jewish refuseniks and Prisoners of Conscience, and all those Soviet Jews who apply to emigrate. Over 80 self-taught Moscow Hebrew teachers are harassed and threatened with prosecution if they continue their activities.
SOVIET JEWISH EMIGRATION: 9,477

1982—Sharansky goes on a hunger strike lasting four months, protesting the isolation from his family; Soviets use the Israel-Lebanon war to fuel their anti-Semitic campaign.
SOVIET JEWISH EMIGRATION: 2,688

1983—Third International Conference on Soviet Jewry is held in Jerusalem; in response, Soviet authorities establish an official Anti-Zionist Committee to foster the myth that all Soviet Jews who wanted to leave have already done so; local chapters to spread libel about Soviet Jewish activists are established throughout the country.
SOVIET JEWISH EMIGRATION: 1,314

1984—Thirteen Soviet Jewish activists are arrested and brutalized. These arrests were accompanied by a series of devastating searches and threats. Jews were accused of using drugs in "religious rituals." The state-controlled Soviet media was rife with anti-Semitic articles, which culminated in a television program aired in Leningrad which attacked several refuseniks by name and called on Soviet citizens to "beware of the danger posed by Zionism."
SOVIET JEWISH EMIGRATION: 896

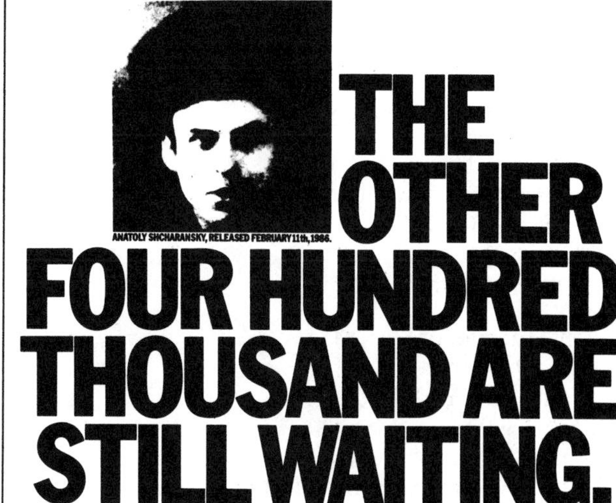

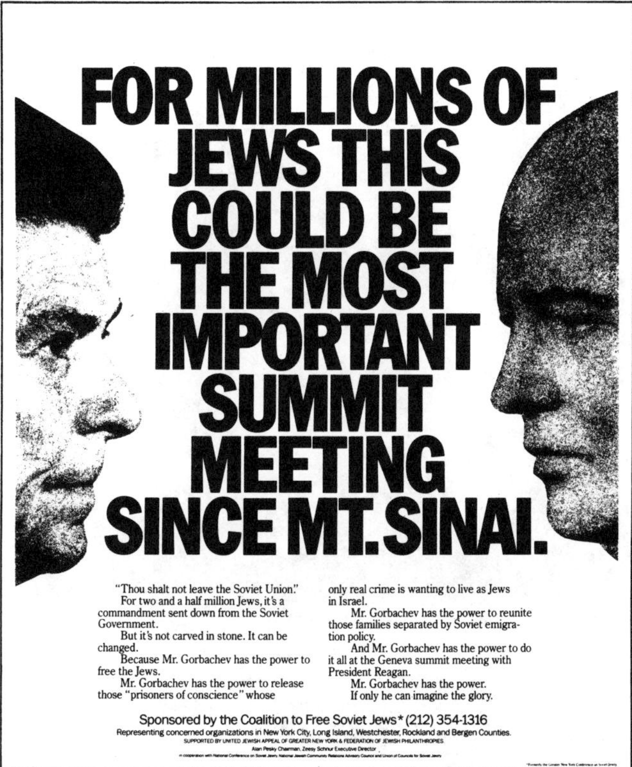

1985—Soviet General Secretary Gorbachev and President Reagan meet for the first time in Geneva; anti-Semitism continued throughout the Soviet Union as more Hebrew teachers were arrested on trumped-up charges and sentenced to labor camps.
SOVIET JEWISH EMIGRATION: 1,140

1986—Sharansky is released on February 11; a second summit meeting between Gorbachev and Reagan is held in Reykjavik, Iceland.
SOVIET JEWISH EMIGRATION: 914

1987—Soviets institute a codification of emigration; Begun is released from prison on February 15; Zunshain, Volvovsky, Levin, Nepomniashschy and Zelichonok are also released from prison; eight Moscow families are told that their cases would never be reconsidered.
SOVIET JEWISH EMIGRATION (THROUGH APRIL 30): 1,431

Additional Information . . .

If you would like to learn more about how you can help Soviet Jewry, contact one of the following organizations:

The Coalition To Free Soviet Jews
8 West 40th Street, Suite 1510
New York, New York 10018
(212) 354-1316
Chairman: Alan Pesky
Executive Director: Zeesy Schnur

National Conference on Soviet Jewry
10 East 40th Street
New York, New York 10016
(212) 679-6122
Chairman: Morris Abram, Esq.
Executive Director: Jerry Goodman

Washington Office
2027 Massachusetts Avenue, N.W.
Washington, DC 20036
(202) 265-8114
Associate Director: Mark Levin

Student Struggle for Soviet Jewry
210 West 91st Street
New York, New York 10024
(212) 799-8900
Chairman: Rabbi Avi Weiss
National Coordinator: Glenn Richter

Union of Councils for Soviet Jews
1411 K Street, N.W.
Washington, DC 20005
(202) 393-4117
President: Pamela Cohen

Or you can contact the National Jewish Community Relations Advisory Council for information on the Community Relations Council in your area. Their address is 443 Park Avenue South, New York, New York 10016. (212) 684-6950.

Compiled by Nurit Thorn Zachter, assisted by Susan Green and Michael McNamara. Written by Giovanni Rodriguez.

All graphic materials courtesy of the Coalition to Free Soviet Jews.

THERE ARE STILL 370,000 HOSTAGES IN THE SOVIET UNION.

More than 370,000 Jews are being held in the Soviet Union against their will.

The lucky ones are kept under constant surveillance, their homes are ransacked, some are even subjected to beatings.

The less fortunate are arrested on trumped up charges and sent to prisons or labor camps.

These are innocent people who have applied for emigration in order to be reunited with their families in Israel, as guaranteed them by the Soviet Union in the Helsinki Accords.

These are the people the Soviet Union has taken hostage in order to gain leverage at the international bargaining table.

Last year at Geneva, General Secretary Gorbachev promised to resolve humanitarian cases "in the spirit of co-operation." Yet more than half the Jews now in prison have been put there since Gorbachev came to power. And since Gorbachev met with President Reagan last year, fewer Jews have been allowed to emigrate than in any year since 1965.

President Reagan also made a promise last year, "to defend human rights everywhere."

When Nicholas Daniloff was arrested on trumped up charges and imprisoned in the Soviet Union, the President acted on his words. Today Daniloff is a free man, reunited with his family.

What will President Reagan do for the other 370,000 hostages?

Sponsored by
National Conference on Soviet Jewry
10 East 40th St., N.Y., N.Y. 10016
Coalition to Free Soviet Jews
8 West 40th St., N.Y., N.Y. 10018
In co-operation with American Jewish Committee, Anti-Defamation League of B'nai B'rith, B'nai B'rith International, Jewish National Fund, Simon Wiesenthal Center, Union of Councils for Soviet Jews, World Jewish Congress.
With the help of American Jewish Congress, Conference of Presidents of Major American Jewish Organizations, Council of Jewish Federations, Hadassah, National Jewish Community Relations Advisory Council, Union of American Hebrew Congregations, United Jewish Appeal, Woman's American ORT.

photo credit: Eric Kroll

"Operation Moses" Update: Two Years After

Abraham J. Bayer
Director, International Commission,
National Jewish Community Relations Advisory Council

Two years after the exhilaration in the Jewish world about the dramatic airlift rescue of Ethiopian Jews to Israel, the subject has fallen out of headline attention as the tough task of their absorption in Israel has taken over.

Current Status

Data on the exact number of Jews remaining in Ethiopia since the airlifts of November 1984 to March 1985 are not available. However, most reports seem to corroborate the estimate of approximately 10,000 Jews remaining in Ethiopia.

Aliyah: Since the airlifts concluded, refugee movement in the area has slowed. The likelihood for the resumption of November '84-March '85s developments in the near future is *bleak.* Reports from governments and foreign media monitoring events overseas point to very little movement. The long drawnout trials in Khartoum of the former Sudanese Vice President and other officials in the deposed Nimeiry government accused of involvement in Operation Moses continue. Despite the much-needed U.S. government famine aid, American influence in the Sudan and Ethiopia remains tenuous. Soviet, Libyan and other Arab-country influence in the area has grown. There have been several high-level visits to Moscow and elsewhere resulting in Soviet military aid, large outright Saudi oil grants, and Libyan and other Arab assistance.

American relations with the Marxist government of Ethiopia, headed by Col. Haile Meriam Mengistu for almost a decade, have been strained for several years. This strain is still visible despite the massive infusion of assistance during the height of the famine and at present, from both the American voluntary sector as well as from the U.S. government. Except for the very few allowed to leave for medical reasons, studies and some for compassionate reunification of families, emigration from Ethiopia also appears unlikely, but diplomatic initiatives continue.

Although the picture in the Horn appears pessimistic at this time, particularly for the *aliyah* of Ethiopian Jews, conditions there often change rapidly, and Israel and world Jewry should respond as rapidly as needed if these changes occur.

Mother and child, Wolleka. photo credit: Neal Schnall

The Famine/Life in Ethiopia

The effects of the famine have been stemmed over the peak ravages of starvation conditions we remember from the stark, terrible television images of October and November 1984. Although the famine touched the outer rim of the Gondar area, it did not reach the Jewish villages in the same scope as in northern Ethiopia. And while the general situation in the country has improved due to the massive responses of several countries, most notably the United States, life in general continues to be *grim* in Ethiopia for everyone, including Jews. The Ethiopian government's controversial resettlement programs in the north have not, to the best of our knowledge, affected Jews as a group because the north has never been a densely-populated Jewish area. Appropriate efforts are going forth for the remaining Ethiopian Jews who need help. In the Jewish tradition of concern for feeding the hungry, the Jewish community, through the NJCRAC, continues to support efforts in the U.S. Congress to increase the various aid programs to Ethiopia and other countries in Africa and elsewhere.

The children of Ambober.

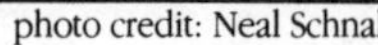

photo credit: Neal Schnall

The children of Wolleka.

Jewish home in Wolleka. photo credit: Neal Schnall

Women spend days collecting wooden branches, which they strap to their backs and carry the long trek to Gondar, the provincial capital, for sale for three birr *(about $1.47).*

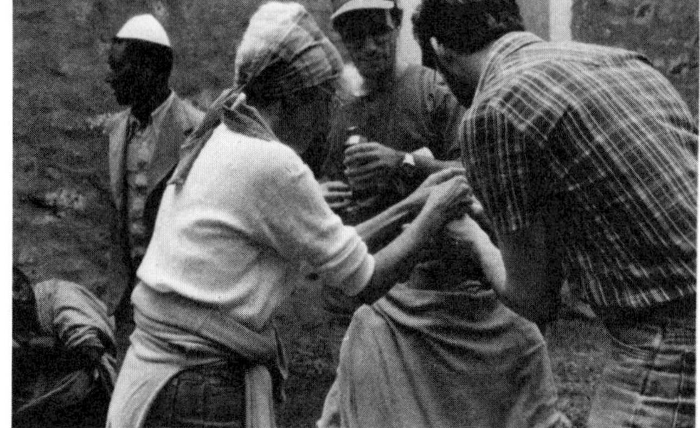

American volunteers provide medical assistance in Ambober. photo credit: Ruth Gruber

Kiddush, Wolleka. photo credit: Neal Schnall

Children of Wolleka. photo credit: Neal Schnall

Sabbath services, Wolleka.

This family asks if we know their relatives, who are now in Israel.

Elders of village of Kosheshelit affix mezuzah *to doorpost.*

In the synagogue of Abba Entonius.

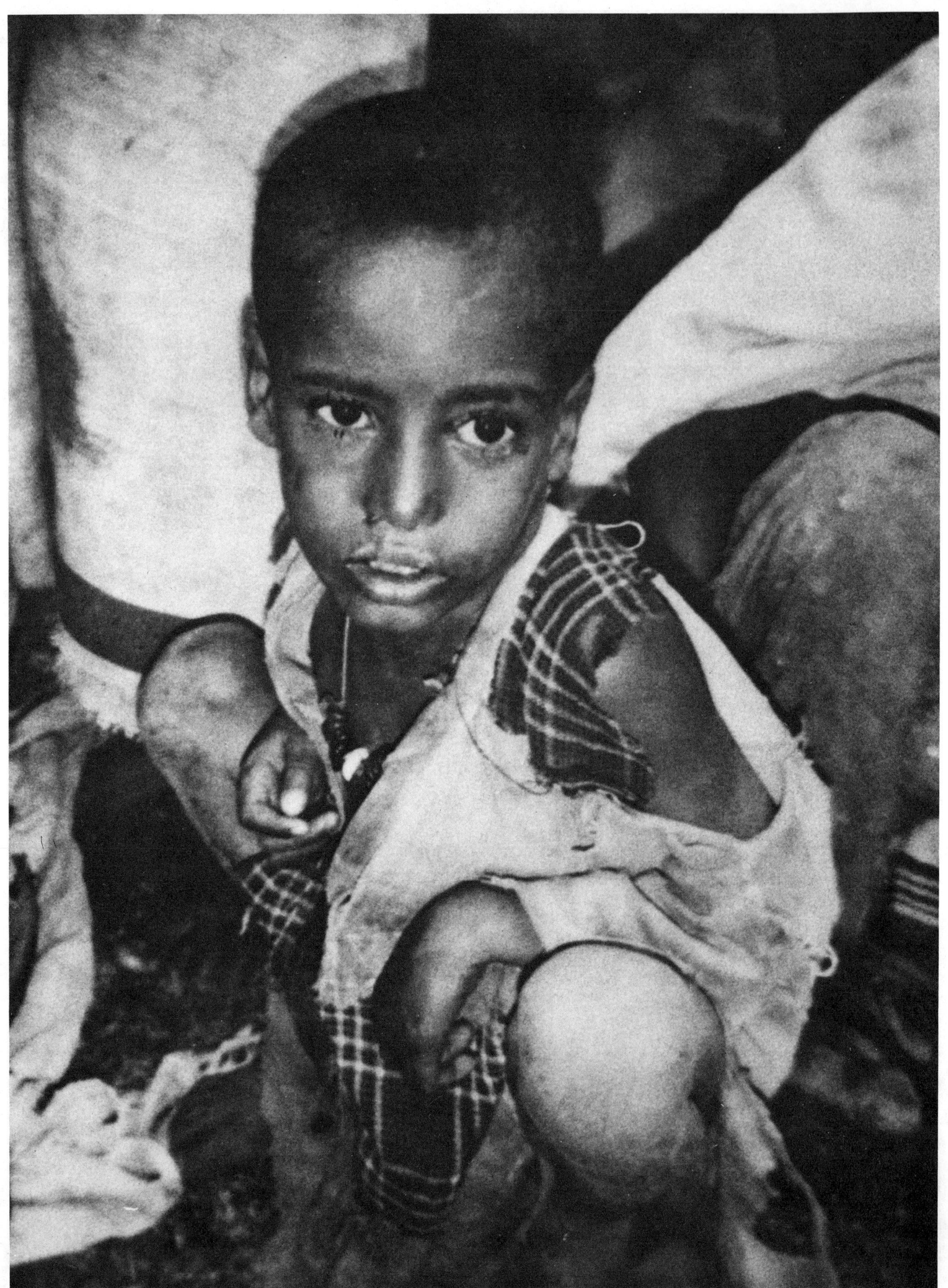

A child of Ambober.

Resettlement in Israel

Although about 7,000 Ethiopian Jews had already arrived before 1984, that number more than doubled in the short period between November 1984, when Operation Moses began, and March 1985, the concluding American airlifts. And so, it was to be expected that the infusion of such a large group needing so much assistance, and needing it quickly, would severely test the absorption process and Israeli economy. However, the heartwarming response from the people of Israel and the generous and spontaneous American Jewish community response from the Federation and UJA campaigns, together, made a difference. With all the problems of absorbing people from an underdeveloped country, the first year of resettlement went well as thousands of Americans saw when visiting absorption centers during community, UJA and organization missions to Israel.

Even though one reads about occasional negative outbursts, one still generally senses throughout Israel the warm feeling of enthusiasm about Ethiopian Jews coming home, which unfolded at the start of Operation Moses. Israelis generally continue to welcome the Ethiopian aliyah. This is shown by the very good, high level of volunteers in tutoring, clothing contributions, many special programs for Ethiopian young people conducted by yeshivot, Army volunteers who teach and lead seminars, weekend retreats, big-brother and big-sister programs for Beta Yisrael orphans, family home-hospitality programs for the Sabbath and holidays, etc.

Absorption

A large job remains to be done. In fact, the job of integration is only at the beginning since many Ethiopian Jews in Israel are still in the approximately 30 absorption centers throughout the country. They are, as a group, however, making rapid and impressive progress in being absorbed into the high-tech Israeli society. The perennial problem of immigration influxes to Israel is more complex with the Ethiopian immigration since everything has to be done all at once, sometimes making for painful choices by government officials as well as by *olim*. These are some interesting preliminary statistics from the Jewish Agency and the Ministry of Absorption:

The population of Ethiopian *olim* consists of about 3,800

families and about 2,000 singles. It is a relatively young population. 52 percent are under 18, and 30 percent are between the ages of 19 and 34. Thus, over 80 percent are under the age of 34 compared with 63 percent of the rest of the Jewish population of Israel. Those 35 and above, considered "old" in terms of Ethiopian culture and lifespan, constitute only about 20 percent of the Ethiopian Jewish emigration. The average family, including singles, numbers 3.9, but almost 30 percent are single-parent families, and of these, 83 percent are headed by women. These stunning figures underscore the ordeal of their lives in Africa and the continuing trauma of their torturous route out and the losses suffered as well as the effects on still-separated families.

About 2,000 Ethiopian Jewish youngsters are in youth aliyah villages. A tragically large number of them are orphans or became separated from their families during the perilous trek to the Sudan. Some 45 percent of the Ethiopian immigration, about 6,700 people, are between the ages of 3 and 18. These 6,700 youngsters are now part of Israel's formal education system. From a potential work force of approximately 3,400, 1,200-1,500 Ethiopian immigrants are already gainfully employed. About 100 students are in universities; about 100 are in pre-college programs.

From these preliminary figures one can see that despite the difficult economic picture in Israel, enormous efforts have been poured into ensuring a successful absorption and integration into Israeli society for Ethiopian Jews. What is needed for these *olim,* as well as for all immigrants, are the funds to ensure vocational training, education and employment, and the special care necessary for this unique group. Considering inflation and the sharp budgetary cuts into all aspects of Israel's shaky economy, the integration of Ethiopian Jews into Israeli society has been going well—or as well as can be expected.

Tensions in Israel

At the moment, there appear to be deep divisions within the Beta Yisrael community leadership due primarily to the impatience of new, younger leadership groups and the fragmentation of the leadership and diminished influence of the older generations of *Kessim,* or priests who held sway in the villages of Ethiopia but whose influence has declined in a free western society so radically different from their matrix. At present, there is only one Ethiopian-born, Amharic-speaking, Israeli-ordained rabbi to serve almost 16,000 Ethiopian *olim.* Quick quantum leaps have to be made in this direction of encouraging and training indigenous and religious community leadership. The Israelis have followed the recommendation of initiating seminars to upgrade the younger *Kessim*—priests—and *shmuglies*—non-priestly religious elders and leaders—with classes and sessions in the Hebrew language, Jewish history, Bible, and leadership development. This is a vital beginning, but the emergence of such trained leaders takes time.

Despite the problems of religious recognition, the tensions one reads about do not seem quite the same when one is in Israel. Face-to-face talks with *olim,* citizens and officials who work on the subject daily, lead one to believe that there's more reason for optimism about integration than the surface indicates.

Ivan Tillem with olim *in Mevasseret Tzion, outside Jerusalem.*

Some problems will not go away easily. Most observers in Israel feel that the issue of full religious recognition of Ethiopian Jews by the Chief Rabbinate will be resolved as it was with other immigrant groups, such as the Bene Israel of India, and with the beginning of Soviet immigration. The move from the African condition into the modern western society of Israel, made under very trying circumstances, surely had an effect on this question as well. The halacha and the Rabbinate are not likely to be changed overnight, and certainly not by confrontation although the Israeli Chief Rabbinate has been impacted by the passion of the Beta Yisrael for Jewish survival and their dream of reaching Jerusalem. Many *olim,* however, still refuse to undergo even token immersion procedures of "reunification" or conversion before marriage. Recently, however, a few rabbis have begun to perform marriages without these procedures.

The Rabbinate's requirements apply to their ruling of token immersion procedures that must be taken before a rabbi conducts a marriage ceremony, which is tantamount to a civil marriage in Israel. This is, according to the Rabbinate, so that in the future there will be no doubt about the Jewish background of Ethiopian *olim.* Beta Yisrael children born of Jewish mothers in Israel and circumcised according to traditional Jewish practice and law, as other Jewish Israelis, are unquestionably Jewish according to the Rabbinate. Ethiopian Jews, who have suffered for their Jewishness and made it to Israel despite incredible obstacles, only to meet with one more test of their faith—even if they understand it intellectually—are often left deeply hurt.

This is a painful dilemma on both sides which will only be overcome by time and good will. Even without this procedure, however, the Beta Yisrael are welcomed, considered to be Jews in all other respects, being granted burial rights, citizenship, medical aid, education, vocational training, housing and old-age assistance.

The intense will and desire to bring all Ethiopian Jews home is still felt strongly by the Israeli government and people and by the Jewish community of North America. The tragic history of Beta Yisrael's long separation from the Jewish people and their terrible suffering and languishing before their dramatic reunification with world Jewry in the last few years must be overcome. It remains the challenge and opportunity in Israel as well.

The Jews of Ethiopia in Jewish Sources

Menachem Waldman

Missive of the Forty-Three Rabbis, 1908

In response to the *cahenat's* letter of distress which Jacques Faitlovitch had brought with him after his first journey to Abyssinia, Rabbi Samuel Hirsch Margulies composed a response signed by himself and another forty-two rabbis from eighteen countries, plus the Jewish Assistance Society representative in Germany.

Dr. Jacques Faitlovitch.

Among the signatories were: Rabbi Naphtali Adler, Chief Rabbi of England, and his Sephardi colleague, Rabbi Moses Gaster; Rabbi Mordechai Horowitz, Rabbi of Frankfurt-am-Main; Rabbi Judah Leib Kowalsky, Rabbi of Wolkowysk, Poland; Rabbi Azriel Munk, Rabbi of Berlin; Rabbi Isaac Reines, Rabbi of Lida; RiDBaZ of Safed; and Rabbi Eliyahu Moshe Panigel, Sephardi Chief Rabbi of Eretz Israel.

The letter, written on parchment, was delivered to the community *cahenat* in Guraba by Jacques Faitlovitch on his second trip to Ethiopia (1908) and was translated into Amharic as part of the "Letter to the Falashas," a message of encouragement which Faitlovitch printed in Amharic in great numbers and distributed to the Abyssinian Jews, for whom it was a source of strength.

The text follows:

In the name of the L-rd, G-d of Israel:

Greetings to you, sons of Abraham, Isaac and Jacob, who dwell in the Land of Abyssinia.

We received the letter you sent us by means of the distinguished traveler, our brother Rabbi Ya'acov ben Moshe Faitlovitch, may G-d protect and redeem him. He, too, reported everything he saw and heard of your sorrows and grief of spirit over the loss of your holy books some time ago and the absence of teachers who would show you what route to pursue and what action to take.

Upon hearing our brother's message and reading your letter, our hearts pounded and our mercies waxed for you, for you are our own flesh and blood. We thank the L-rd G-d of Israel Whose kindness and truth have not forsaken you, and Who has had mercy on you before the great, pious and just King Menelik.

Be of good strength, our brethren. Neither fear nor grow soft of heart, for the G-d of our forefathers Who redeemed you and us with His great strength from the many and grievous troubles which have surrounded us thus far will neither abandon nor forsake you in the days to come.

בשם ה אלהי ישראל

שלום לכל אחינו בני אברהם יצחק ויעקב היושבים בארץ חבש

The letter of the forty-three rabbis, 1908.

Recall the holy word He sent us through His prophets, to wit: "for the mountains may depart, and the hills be removed; but My kindness shall not depart from thee, neither shall My covenant of peace be removed" (*Isaiah* 54:10). Believe in Him and trust Him at all times, and He will stand at your right hand and not allow your legs to stumble.

Do not listen, do not hunger for the voice of the inciters who speak nothingness, who lie and who seek to turn you away from the L-rd our G-d, the one, only, unique G-d, Creator of Heaven and Earth, Who took us out of the land of Egypt with a mighty hand and outstretched arm, Who performed innumerable miracles and wonders for our forefathers and for ourselves, and Who gave us His holy *Torah* through his faithful servant Moses.

We, your brethren, will do everything we can to come speedily to your assistance and to procure teachers and books for you, that your sons learn to fear the L-rd and only Him forevermore and to keep His eternal *Torah.*

May we all have the privilege of beholding the advent of the L-rd's day, when He shall cast His spirit on all the nations, and when they all become as one in doing His will with full heart; on that day He will gather us from the four ends of the earth and bring us to His city Zion in joy and to Jerusalem, His Temple, in eternal bliss.

Ethiopian Jewish Leaders Appeal to Jewish Communities, 1908

During his stay in Amba Gualit on his second trip in the fall of 1908, Jacques Faitlovitch was given many letters to bring to Europe. One of these, an appeal to the Jewish community throughout the world, was signed by thirty-three *cahenat* and community elders:

> Blessed is the L-rd, G-d of Israel, G-d of all spirit and all flesh.
>
> This letter is sent from the Jewish communities in Abyssinia to our brethren in Jewish communities the world over.
>
> Shalom. Shalom to you, Jews. How are you faring?
>
> The letter you sent us in the hand of our teacher Ya'acov Noah ben Moshe Faitlovitch has arrived and brought us satisfaction. Beforehand, we considered your very existence a legend; now, however, we are sure of the matter and are greatly delighted by it.
>
> The reports we have received from you have strengthened and consoled our hearts. We are very sorrowful. Pity us and pray for us. Thank G-d, we have clung to our faith in one G-d and the Law of Moses to this day. G-d has thus far not allowed the seed of Jacob to be exterminated in the land of Abyssinia.
>
> In past times we suffered travail and distress, and many of us were forced to convert to Christianity. Now we have a good King, thank G-d: Menelik wants each of us to live by his forefathers' faith. May G-d grant him long life. Because we have no schools and because our books have been destroyed, however, the missionaries have induced our brethren to betray [the faith] by distributing books of their faith among them.
>
> Now that we have heard your good news, we are exceedingly delighted.
>
> Abyssinian Jewry is infused with hope. Since our teacher Ya'acov arrived, all the Jews lift their eyes to you. If we get books, a school and teachers so our children may study we shall be greatly content. We cannot carry this out under our own strength.
>
> We pray that G-d give long life to us all and to our teacher Ya'acov. We also pray that G-d will allow all of us to meet. May the G-d of Abraham, Isaac, Jacob and Moses protect our teacher Ya'acov Noah ben Moshe.

An Appeal by the Chief Rabbis of Eretz Israel (Palestine), 1921

Chief Rabbi of Eretz Israel, Rabbi Abraham Isaac Hacohen Kook, became involved in efforts to establish the school in Eritrea while still serving as Rabbi of Jaffa and the Jewish pioneer settlements. In correspondence dating from 1912 with Rabbi Margulies (who had asked him to find a suitable teacher for the Ethiopian children), Rabbi Kook speaks longingly about the magnitude of the *mitzvah* involved in assisting these faraway brethren:

> . . . And it is my every desire to join with the ones involved in doing the *mitzvah* and stand at their side with their every demand, working for the eternal benefit of these faraway brethren. The Rock of Israel in His kindness has seen fit to arouse the hearts of the surviving remnant, the purest souls of our time, to labor for them, to engage in correcting them and rescuing them from the ravages of extinction.
>
> (*Letters of Rabbi A.I. Kook,* Part B, Jerusalem, 5722, Letter 432 (Heb.), see also *ibid.* 444, 620)

During a stay in Eretz Israel in 1921 before setting out on journeys throughout the Jewish world, Dr. Faitlovitch asked the Chief Rabbis, Rabbi Abraham Isaac Hacohen Kook and Rabbi Ya'acov Meir, for a letter of recommendation concerning his activities on behalf of Beta Israel.

The letter of recommendation was in fact an appeal "to our brethren, sons of Israel" to do all they could to assist and strengthen the faraway community, to make strong links between it and the rest of the Jewish world, and to fight assimilation into the gentile environment.

The full text follows:

> Dear brethren:
>
> A holy obligation has been placed upon us: to strive with all our might to restore an awareness of Judaism, the sanctity of our faith and observance of the practical commandments in purity and unity of our sacred nation, G-d's people, to Jewish communities which, because of the hardships of time and travails of exile, have grown distant from us in terms of both geography and views.
>
> In many obscure areas far from the centers of Judaism, multitudes of our brethren have remained isolated and wholly out of contact with general Judaism for centuries. Their numbers have consequently diminished; a great many have assimilated into the Gentile peoples among whom they dwell. Moreover, even those who have remained faithful to their people are in ever-present danger of assimilation in the absence of new forces in their communities which would inject a flow of Jewish life. As time passes, they will first wither and then die, no longer belonging to the eternal Jewish body and the purity of its soul.
>
> One of the faraway lands of which we speak is Abyssinia. There, far from the center of Jewish life, tens of thousands of Jews have lived for more than two thousand years, remaining loyal to their faith and people despite all the hardships and difficulties they have endured. Throughout their entire residence, however, they have had neither relations nor contact with the great Jewish world; thus their numbers are progressively falling, diminishing. The dis-

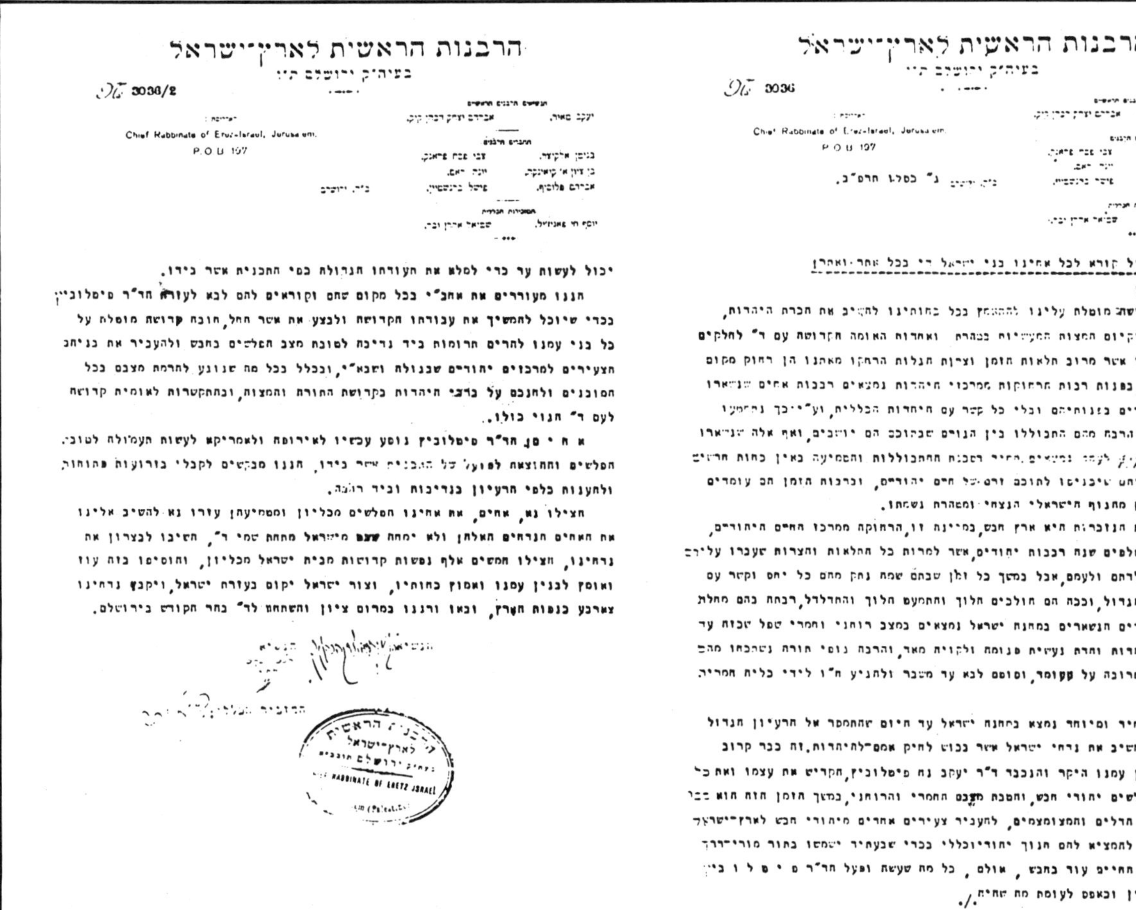

הרבנות הראשית לארץ־ישראל

Chief Rabbinate of Eretz-Israel, Jerusalem.
P.O.B. 197

הרבנות הראשית לארץ־ישראל

Chief Rabbinate of Eretz-Israel, Jerusalem.
P.O.B. 197

The appeal issued by the Chief Rabbis of Eretz Israel, 1921.

ease of forced conversion has spread grievously among them; even those Jews who remain in the Camp of Israel are in a spiritual and material state so downtrodden that their outlook on Judaism and the faith has become highly flawed and many bodies of *Torah* have utterly vanished from their memory. The shortcomings exceed the substance which remains. Their end is to reach a state of crisis leading, Heaven forbid, to material and spiritual extinction.

A single, solitary and unique man in the Jewish camp has pledged himself to the great idea of bringing the remote Jews of Abyssinia back into the lap of their mother, Judaism. For nearly twenty years this precious, distinguished Jew, Dr. Jacques Noah Faitlovitch, has devoted himself and his entire life to studying the Falashas, the Jews of Abyssinia, and to improving their material and spiritual circumstances. Over this period he has already managed with his poor, limited resources to take several young Jews out of Abyssinia to Eretz Israel and Europe and see to their Jewish and general education, so they may one day serve as guiding educators for their Falasha brethren who have remained in Abyssinia. Everything Dr. Faitlovitch has done thus far, however, is virtually nothing in comparison to what he could have done in fulfilment of his great mission according to the program he has drawn up.

Now we call upon our fellow Jews, wherever they may be, to awaken and come to Dr. Faitlovitch's aid so he may continue his holy labor and carry out that which he has begun. A holy obligation is placed upon all our fellow Jews: to contribute of themselves generously to better the Falashas' situation in Abyssinia and to bring their sons to the centers of Judaism in the Diaspora and Eretz Israel—generally speaking, to do everything possible to improve their situation in all senses and educate them in the ways of Judaism, in the sanctity of *Torah* and their commandments, and forge a holy national relationship between them and the entire Nation of G-d.

Brethren! Dr. Faitlovitch is presently traveling to Europe and America to propagandize for the Falashas and his program. Please receive him with open arms and respond to this idea with utmost generosity.

Please, fellow Jews, save our Falasha brethren from extinction and assimilation! Please help return these faraway brothers to us! May no tribe of Israel be erased from under the L-rd's skies.

Return these faraway ones to the stronghold; save fifty thousand holy souls of Israel from their end, and add thereby power and courage to the house of our people and its strength.

May the Rock of Israel rise to Israel's aid and gather our faraway ones from the four ends of the Earth: 'And they shall come and sing in the height of Zion' (Jeremiah 31:12) and bow down to G-d at the Holy Mount in Jerusalem.

(Signed)
Rabbi Abraham Isaac
Hacohen Kook

(Signed)
Rabbi Ya'acov Meir

Ruling of Sephardi Chief Rabbi of Israel, Rabbi Ovadia Yossef, 1973

For many years the Government of Israel and the Jewish Agency did little on an official level regarding the issue of Ethiopian Jewry. Individuals and small groups of Ethiopian Jews were arriving in the country, yet a general ignorance about the community and a lack of formulated policy resulted in inactivity of the major institutions on its behalf.

However, when the Sephardi Chief Rabbi of Israel, Rabbi Ovadia Yossef ruled that Beta Israel could be considered Jewish, a historic turning point was reached.

In 1973, Hezi Ovadia, a leading activist for Beta Israel, turned to Rabbi Yossef for a ruling as to whether a Jew is *halachically* obligated to help members of the Ethiopian community to settle in Israel. If a positive ruling were given, the Law of Return would have to apply in the case of Beta Israel, and the Government of Israel and the Jewish Agency would therefore be obliged to take action to bring them to Israel and to absorb them.

Rabbi Yossef responded immediately. Relying on *halachic* sources such as the rulings of RaDBaZ, Rabbi Azriel Hildesheimer and the previous Chief Rabbis, he determined that Jews are obliged to help to rescue the Falashas as Jews.

The ruling itself is as follows:

> With G-d's help, Friday, 7 Adar A 5733
>
> Dear Mr. Ovadia Hezi, precious friend and man of great action, may peace and salvation be yours:
>
> I have the following comments to make in response to your letter concerning the Falashas:
>
> Relying on the great RaDBaZ *(Responsa Divrei David, Hilchot Ishut* 8), ". . . that these Falashas are unquestionably of the Tribe of Dan and [that] only because there were no sages and masters of Oral Tradition among them were they overtaken by superficial interpretations of Written Law. Their status is one of individuals taken captive in infancy by Gentiles, and they are Jews whom we are commanded to redeem and revive. In the matter of genealogy alone is there cause for fear, because they are not knowledgeable in the nature of marriage and writs of divorce. . ."
>
> So writes RaDBaZ in brief, and so ruled his disciple, Rabbi Jacob Castro, in his commentary *'Erech Lehem (Yore Deah* 158). And so wrote a number of the greatest authorities, such as Rabbi Azriel Hildesheimer, Head of the Berlin Beit Midrash, Rabbi Abraham Isaac Hacohen Kook, head of the Chief Rabbinate of Palestine, and Rabbi Yitzhak Isaac Halevi Herzog, Chief Rabbi of Israel, may their memories be blessed: all wrote that the Falashas are Jews.
>
> I have therefore reached the conclusion that the Falashas are descendants of Israelite tribes which migrated southward to Ethiopia. The aforementioned authorities who determined that they are of the Tribe of Dan undoubtedly investigated the matter thoroughly and came to this conclusion according to the most reliable testimony and evidence.
>
> And I, too—though the humblest of authorities—have inquired and delved into their affairs after their leaders appealed to me that they be permitted to become one with our brethren the Jewish People in the spirit of *Torah* and *halacha,* Written and Oral Law, with no reservations. In short, they wish to uphold all commandments of the holy *Torah* according to instructions of our Sages of blessed memory, by whose word we live. My decision, in my humble opinion, is that the Falashas are Jews whom we are obliged to save from assimilation and whose return to Eretz Israel we must expedite. We must educate them in the spirit of our holy *Torah* and involve them in building our holy Land:
>
> And Thy children shall return to their own border" (Jeremiah 31:17).

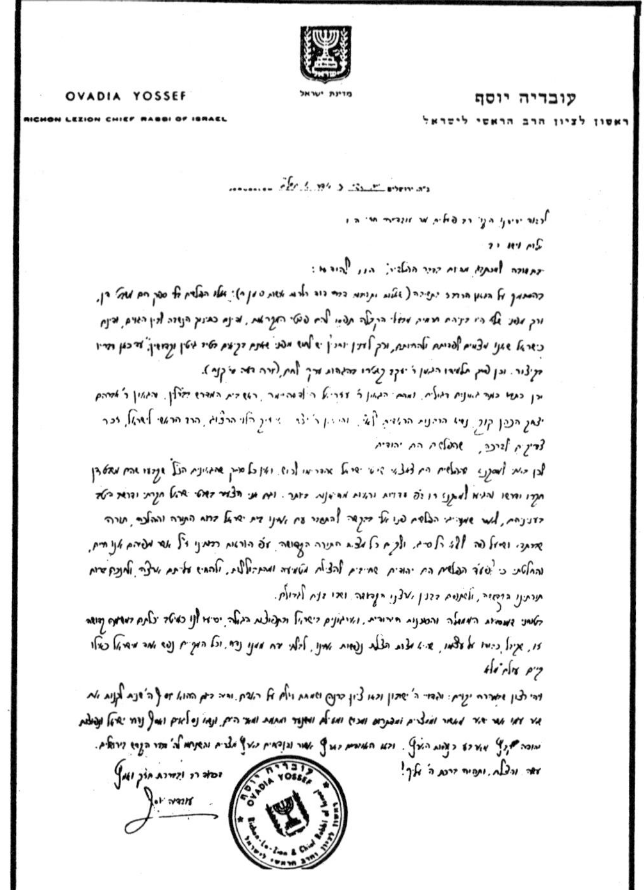

OVADIA YOSSEF
RISHON LEZION CHIEF RABBI OF ISRAEL

מדינת ישראל

עובדיה יוסף
ראשון לציון הרב הראשי לישראל

The ruling of Rabbi Ovadia Yossef, 1973.

> The institutions of the Government, the Jewish Agency and organizations in Israel and the Diaspora, I am sure, will help us to the best of their ability in this sacred mission; that each will take upon itself the honor, i.e. the *mitzvah* of saving our brethren's souls, that not a single remote soul fall along the way. To save a single Jewish soul is to save an entire world.
>
> May it be G-d's will that Isaiah's prophecy come to pass: "and the ransomed of the L-rd shall return, and come with singing unto Zion, and everlasting joy shall be upon their heads . . . And it shall come to pass in that day, that the L-rd will set His hand again the second time to recover the remnant of His people, that shall remain from Assyria and from Egypt, and from Pathros, and from Cush, and from Elam, and from Shinar, and from Hamath, and from the islands of the sea. And He shall set up an ensign for the nations, and will assemble the dispersed of Israel, and gather together the scattered of Judah from the four corners of the earth . . . And they shall come that were lost in the land of Assyria, and they that were dispersed in the land of Egypt; and they shall worship the L-rd in the holy mountain at Jerusalem."
>
> Act and succeed, and may the L-rd's blessing be upon you!
>
> With great respect and with blessings of good strength:
>
> Ovadia Yossef

Rabbi Ovadia Yossef frequently repeated this stance. He did, however, insist on a blood-letting ceremony, symbolic of the *brit mila* (circumcision), to remove any doubt that members of Beta Israel might at any time have intermarried with non-Jews or those not *halachically* converted.

The Chief Rabbi's ruling exerted influence on the Government of Israel which, several years later, ultimately resolved to apply the Law of Return to the Jews of Ethiopia and to take action to resettle them in Israel. Rabbi Ovadia ossef's ruling was strengthened when his colleague, Ashkenazic Chief Rabbi of Israel, Rabbi Shlomo Goren, ruled similarly. Additional impetus came in 1980 when the Chief Rabbinical Council of Israel called upon all rabbis, communities and organizations in the Jewish world to act on Beta Israel's behalf, in light of reports of the persecution and danger they were facing in Ethiopia.

The Letters of Rabbi Obadiah of Bertinoro

Rabbi Obadiah of Bertinoro, the famous commentator on the Mishnah, came to Jerusalem from Italy and settled there in 1488. In his letters to his family in Italy, Rabbi Obadiah described Eretz Israel, Jerusalem and the lengthy route he traveled to reach the homeland via Egypt. Among other things, he told of the Jews of Abyssinia, of their wars, and of his encounter with two members of that community in Egypt:

> . . . And in this city [Jerusalem] we always encounter travelers from all the Gentile lands—from Aram, Babel and the lands of the Faristi Yauni [Abyssinia], Arabs and Christians . . . I spoke there of the River Sabatyon; what you are about to hear is exactly as I heard it here. I have nothing clear [to report] but only world-of-mouth rumor.
>
> If so, the thing which was made clear to me, which I know beyond doubt, is that on one of the borders of the Faristi Yauni Kingdom—a land of mountains and hills and very rounded mountains: they say it is about ten days' travel—Jews have surely settled. They have five princes or kings, and they say they have been engaging the Faristi Yauni in great, tremendous warfare for more than a century.
>
> Then the hand of the Faristi Yauni overcame them and dealt them a most grievous blow. Entering their land, he destroyed and plundered and annihilated almost every Jewish male who lived there. As for the survivors, he enacted diverse edicts against their faith, similar to those instituted by Greece during Hasmonean times.
>
> In the end, G-d had mercy: other kings less harsh than the first rose to power in India [Abyssinia]. By now, they say, the old glory has nearly been restored; the Jews have multiplied exceedingly. They still pay tax to the Faristi Yauni, but are not subject as previously. The Jews have been at war with their neighbors for the past four years, plundering and looting those who hate them. These, in turn, have taken a number of prisoners—men and women—and sold them to faraway nations as slaves. Some were brought to Egypt, where the Jews redeemed them.
>
> Moreover, I saw two of them in Egypt. They are somewhat black but not as much so as the indigenous negroes. Superficially, one could not see if they adhered to Karaite or Rabbinical doctrine. In some ways they appear to uphold Karaite thinking, in that they said that no fire is found in their homes on the Sabbath; in the rest, they appear to adhere to Rabbinical doctrine. They claim descent from the tribe of Dan, and say that most of the pepper and spice which the negroes sell comes from their land.
>
> This is what I saw and heard myself, though the two men knew but a smattering of Hebrew and even their Arabic was barely understood by the locals . . .

Rabbi Obadiah again mentions the Jews of Abyssinia in a letter sent to his brothers about a year later. Jews from Aden who reached Jerusalem at the time repeatedly confirmed the reports of Jews in nearby Abyssinia who had been defeated by the Christians.

Rabbi Obadiah writes:

> These Jews from Aden said afterwards that the Jews at the farthest border of Abyssinia are the ones of whom I wrote in my first letter, who are fighting today against the Faristi Yauni and were brought by them to Egypt. I saw [two] of them with my own eyes. They are about a month's journey by desert from the Jews on the other side of the River Sabatyon.
>
> The Christians who come from the Faristi Yauni lands tell us all day long that these Jews who are fighting at the edge of their land were beaten grievously by the Faristi Yauni. We fear lest the rumor be true, Heaven forbid, for it is voiced most surely. May G-d protect His people and servants, Amen . . .
>
> (A. Ya'ari, *Igrot Eretz Yisrael,* pp. 132-133, 140-141 (Heb.))

Responsa of Rabbi David ben-Zimra (RaDBaZ)

Rabbi David ben-Zimra (the RaDBaZ) (1479-1573) is considered one of the greatest halachic authorities of all time and the supreme authority of his time in Egypt, Eretz Israel and the entire surrounding area. Among his thousands of responsa, considered to this day among the most important foundations upon which halacha is built, we find two which refer to the Jews of Abyssinia. Questions relating to them had been brought before him in his position as Chief Rabbi of Egypt, where the Ethiopians had been brought as prisoners of war.

In his responsa, RaDBaZ addresses all the substantial halachic questions concerning the community's origin and Jewish status. His decisions are regarded to this day as unquestionably the most important halachic sources with regard to Ethiopian Jewry.

The first question handled by RaDBaZ deals with a "Cushite woman from the land of Cush" who had been redeemed in Egypt by a Jew. The woman had been married in Abyssinia, but lost her husband in war and had since been considered a "deserted" wife *(aguna).* The Jew who had redeemed her in Egypt impregnated her. When the son she had borne grew and wished to marry, the question of his personal status arose.

Though RaDBaZ's response discusses the question of the woman's *aguna* status at length, a description of the "Cushite" Jews also emerges from his writings:

> *Question:* The following occurrence involves a Cushite woman from the land of Cush, or al-Habash, who was taken captive along with her two sons and was redeemed by Reuven. When we asked her of her status, she said she had been married and that these were her two sons by her husband; she mentioned [the husband's] name and also that of her son. The enemy came upon them and killed everyone in the house (or the synagogue), taking the

women and children captive and abusing them. It then became apparent that she was Jewish, a member of the tribe of Dan which dwells in the mountains of Cush; from that moment on, she has been considered *aguna.* Her master Reuven sired a son by her during this time; now an adult, the son wishes to marry into the Jewish community and be a part of it. You [the petitioner] have asked me whether he is fit to enter the community and how he can be rendered so.

RaDBaZ's response relates to the state of war in Abyssinia and the uniqueness of the Jewish community there:

> *Response:* . . . It is well-known that there is always war among the kings of Cush, where there are three kingdoms—one Arab, one Aramaic (Christian) who adhere to their faith, and one of Israelites of the tribe of Dan. The latter would appear to descend from the sect of Zadok and Beitos which is called Karaite (after Heb. *kara,* referring to Written Law) because they are ignorant of the Oral Law and do not light candles on Sabbath. They continually wage wars against each other and take one another prisoner daily . . .
>
> (*Responsa of RaDBaZ,* Part 4:219, 1290)

If the Jews of Abyssinia are identified in this responsum as descendants of Dan who resemble the Karaites in their ignorance of the Oral Law, RaDBaZ explores the matter thoroughly in the second responsum and concludes that, for halachic purposes, they are not Karaites.

The second question concerns the status of a Falasha slave, redeemed by a Jew who inquired into his workman's rights and related issues. In responding, RaDBaZ explores all the substantive questions involving the community.

Excerpts from the *Responsa of RaDBaZ,* 7:5 follow:

> *Question:* You have asked me to inform you of my stand concerning a man who bought a free slave who belongs to the Jewish community of Cush. How should one conduct himself with him? Should he be freed in six [years] or not? Furthermore, do all the laws concerning slaves apply to him, or do they not?
>
> *Response:* . . . The man who bought the free slave—now that it is clear to him that [the slave] is Jewish—has not purchased a slave but, in fact, has redeemed a captive. Every Jew is commanded to redeem [such a captive], lest he assimilate into the Gentiles . . . since this [Jew] had bought him previously, he has had the privilege of performing a great *mitzvah.*
>
> (*Erech Lehem,* Reflections on *Shulhan Aruch, Yore Deah* 158)

After asserting that it was a great *mitzvah* to have redeemed this Jew from his captivity, RaDBaZ expressed doubt over the matter: if the Ethiopian Jews were, in fact, to be regarded as Karaites, who reject Oral Law and Rabbinical tradition, Jews need not aid in their rescue:

> There is, however, another uncertainty: that all these Abyssinians in fact conduct themselves according to the Karaites, i.e. Zadok and Beitos; [if so,] we are commanded neither to redeem nor to revive them.
>
> In any event, it appears to me that these [Karaite] cases involve those who live among the rabbis and see their doings and insult and ridicule them . . . but the Cushites are undoubtedly of the tribe of Dan; because no sages who had received [Oral Law] dwelled among them, literal Written Law practices spread among them. Were they taught, they would not absolve themselves of the words of our blessed Sages. They should therefore be considered as having been taken captive in infancy by the Gentiles. Bear in mind that Zadok and Beitos were of the Second Temple [period] and the tribe of Dan had been exiled previously. Even if you should find reason to say that the matter is in doubt, we are commanded to redeem them.

At the end of his responsum, RaDBaZ expressed hesitation over the possibility of marrying members of the community, whose Jewish marriage and divorce practices had been blurred:

> But in the matter of genealogy, I fear that while their marriages are valid, their writs of divorce are not as the Sages indicated, for they are wholly ignorant of matters of divorce and marriage.

We may infer the following from RaDBaZ's responsa:

a) The Jews of Ethiopia are Jews from the tribe of Dan who reached Abyssinia before the Second Temple period.

b) They do not resemble Karaites: their ignorance of Oral Law and Rabbinical tradition stems from their lack of contact with centers of Torah and not from rejection.

Having said this, all Jews are required to "redeem and revive" them, under the dictum by which all Jews are each other's guarantors.

The implications of the second responsum are certainly consistent with RaDBaZ's conclusions. His great disciple, Rabbi Ya'acov Castro, ruled after him:

> [As for] the Abyssinian Jews, though they act as Karaites do, we are commanded to redeem and revive them; for they are of the tribe of Dan, and did not learn from Zadok and Beitos.
>
> (*Erech Lehem,* Reflections on *Shulhan Aruch, Yore Deah* 158)

c) The question of intermarriage with members of the community is problematic. RaDBaZ did not resolve the issue in favor of prohibition; his writings in several other places imply that if the question arose in practical terms concerning an entire community which wished to return to the Jewish community and its tradition, he would rule in favor. In our time, two of our greatest authorities—Sephardi Chief Rabbi Hagaon Rabbi Ovadia Yossef and Hagaon Rabbi Moshe Feinstein zt"l—have indeed rendered this ruling into practice, after performing a religious ceremony to symbolize the renewal of ties with the Jewish people and tradition.

Other rabbis and sages of the same generations made reference to the Jews of Ethiopia. One conclusion is absolutely clear: all Jewish sources of the time regarded the Jews of Ethiopia—as they did the Jews of Yemen and India—as distant brethren, Jews fighting courageously for their faith and independence.

10

Israel and the Middle East

National Jewish Community Relations Advisory Council

The American Jewish community feels a profound identification with Israel, a deep commitment to its survival and security, and an abiding concern with events and forces that affect its future. American Jews, and Americans generally, understand that the long-term national interests of the United States and Israel coincide—a premise underlined by Israel's important role as America's only politically stable and militarily effective ally in the Middle East, and reinforced by the unique cultural affinity between the two countries. Reflecting this recognition, all American administrations have been committed to Israel's security and survival. However, the vigilant involvement of the American Jewish community has been a vital factor in fostering policies toward that end.

U.S.-Israel Relations

The relationship between the United States and Israel continues to grow into one characterized by an extraordinary degree of cooperation and trust, which both parties recognize as mutually beneficial.

The United States and Israel have embarked on new ventures which enhance and deepen the degree of mutually beneficial cooperation between them, and which are evolving into a relationship of alliance as strong as any between two governments that are bound by a formal treaty. These ventures include agreements that protect the rights and security of the U.S. and its allies in the eastern Mediterranean basin. Moreover, the U.S.-Israeli relationship has expanded in a manner that promises to grow even more reciprocal in the economic, medical and military spheres.

Since the November 1983 agreement between Israel and the United States to establish a Joint Political-Military Group to put strategic cooperation into effect, tangible measures on many levels have been planned or implemented. Among the mutually beneficial measures undertaken are:

- joint medical evacuation and military exercises;
- enhanced use of Israel's port facilities by the U.S. Navy;
- joint military planning;
- U.S. financial and technological support for development of Israel's Lavi jet fighter;
- U.S. military procurement of Israeli defense industry products, including reconnaissance drones and artillery;
- enhanced intelligence sharing, particularly with respect to efforts combatting international terrorism;
- Israel's agreement to install a Voice of America transmitter to beam broadcasts to Soviet Central Asia and Afghanistan; and
- Israel's acceptance of a U.S. invitation to participate in the Strategic Defense Initiative.

Another positive dimension of the increasingly close cooperative relationship between the United States and Israel lies in the field of economic exchange. The Free Trade Area agreement, signed in 1985, provides for greater access by each nation to the other's markets. This will enable American and Israeli entrepreneurs to create joint ventures and to sell raw materials and finished products at more advantageous rates than previously. As firms become more aware of the agreement, one anticipated benefit of these trading advantages will be the stimuli to job creation and increased employment in both countries.

That the United States recognizes Israel to be not only a reliable strategic ally but also a promising trade partner with a modern technologically oriented economy and highly educated workforce is apparent. In 1985, the United States provided $1.5 billion in emergency economic assistance for distribution in 1986 and 1987 that enabled Israel to stem a drain on its foreign currency reserves, a prerequisite for mounting an effective austerity program that has brought its once rampant inflation rate under firm control. As its economy has stabilized, Israel has again shown promise of providing an attractive environment in which to conduct international trade.

The Jewish community should:

- *continue to emphasize that Israel is the United States' most reliable strategic ally and the only democracy in the Middle East, and should continue to receive American political, moral and economic support;*
- *foster programs that emphasize the nature of the strategic alliance between Israel and the United States, and the advantages gained by the U.S. from having Israel as its chief ally in the Middle East;*
- *interpret to the American public the identity of interests the United States and Israel share in making firm responses to terrorists and their sponsors;*
- *encourage increased people-to-people exchanges between Israel and the United States through tourism, leadership missions, and academic, cultural and scientific exchanges;*
- *stress the democratic process and values shared between the United States and Israel.*

U.S. Foreign Aid

The Administration and Congress continue to be favorably disposed to assist Israel in achieving economic recovery. However, enactment of the Gramm-Rudman-Hollings balanced budget legislation, even with the Supreme Court's decision invalidating certain of its key provisions, may have ramifications with regard to the amount of the foreign aid package in Fiscal Year 1987 and beyond.

Despite intense pressures on America's federal budget, Congress approved an Administration package of $1.8 billion in defense and $1.2 billion in economic grant aid to Israel for Fiscal Year 1986. Along with supplemental emergency economic grants of $750 million for both FY86 and FY87, these appropriations demonstrated the U.S. government's recognition of Israel's status as a strategic ally and of the need to provide assistance to its economic recovery plan.

Increasingly, American legislators recognize that such aid to Israel, when compared with U.S. security arrangements in other vital regions of the world, is extremely cost-effective in the value America receives for the aid it provides. Whereas the U.S. provided Israel a total of $3 billion in defense and economic grants for both FY 1986 and FY87, in 1985 alone the U.S. spent approximately $148 billion—or a little less than 40 times more—on meeting defense commitments in Europe and Asia. In meeting those commitments the U.S. currently stations 420,000 American military personnel in those areas. Israel, on the other hand, neither requires nor has it ever requested such troop deployment to defend its security and, in doing so, America's national interests overseas.

Adding to the cost-effectiveness of American aid to Israel is the fact that almost all of these grants are spent in the United States in the form of purchase orders for military equipment and other goods. Indeed, virtually all military aid to Israel is spent in the United States. Such circulation of American assistance benefits both American industry and labor by sustaining and creating employment for our nation's producers and workers.

These welcome developments have been clouded by the implementation on March 1, 1986 of the Gramm-Rudman-Hollings balanced budget act. This measure, designed to eliminate the nation's federal deficit by 1991, provided that in the event Congress and the President cannot agree on budget packages which meet predetermined ceilings, automatic across-the-board cuts must be made in appropriations according to formulas set forth in the legislation. The provision that such cuts would be determined by the Comptroller General has been invalidated by the Supreme Court. In spite of the Court's decision, however, it is likely that in the 1987 budget Congress will continue to adhere to the target goals set forth in Gramm-Rudman-Hollings. Since foreign aid is not exempt from the legislation's provisions, assistance to Israel may be affected.

An indication of Gramm-Rudman-Hollings' impact became visible in January 1986 when, three months before the legislation was due to take effect, Israel voluntarily returned $51 million of a $1.2 billion economic assistance package and $77 million in military grants for FY 86 that had been approved by Congress and forwarded to Israel in October 1985. The amount returned represented 4.3 percent of the grant, the automatic percentage reduction which the Gramm-Rudman-Hollings budget balancing law mandated for all non-exempt federal spending after Congress and the President failed to agree on a federal budget meeting the legislation's deficit reduction target figure. Indeed, Congressional budget experts conjecture that application of Gramm-Rudman-Hollings' provisions in FY87 might result in total cuts of as much as $600 million out of a total of $3 billion in combined economic and military aid for Israel should the budget deficit be more than the 1986 projected trigger level for automatic cuts.

Both House and Senate budgets for the Fiscal Year 1987, in trying to meet the Gramm-Rudman-Hollings target, have reduced the available foreign aid budget from over $14.4 billion to $14 billion. Within that framework, the Administration and key House and Senate committee heads have affirmed their commitment to maintain Israel (and Egypt) at current funding levels. This would, of necessity, require deep cuts to other U.S. foreign aid recipients.

The small but vocal constituency of American political activists that has previously lobbied (with notable lack of success or public impact) against passage of aid to Israel can be expected to resume their anti-Israel aid campaign when appropriation measures are again considered by Congress.

The Jewish community should:

- *continue to interpret to the Administration, Congress and the American people the reasons why assistance to Israel is in America's national interest;*
- *continue to monitor and develop appropriate responses to media campaigns directed against U.S. aid to Israel.*

U.S. Arms Sales to Arab Countries

Congress, by overwhelmingly opposing in 1985 and again in 1986 the sale of sophisticated American arms to Jordan and Saudi Arabia, went a long way toward establishing the principle that Arab countries must enter into direct and meaningful negotiations with Israel before such sales will be authorized. In agreeing to defer its proposed sale to Jordan, the Administration appeared to accept this position. Nevertheless, even in the face of strong Congressional opposition, the Administration sent a reduced Saudi arms package to Congress and vetoed a subsequent Congressional resolution of disapproval, thus reiterating the practice by this and previous Administrations of demonstrating support for Arab states by acquiescing to their arms requests.

Responding to President Reagan's notification to Congress of an Administration request to authorize the sale of $1.6-$1.9 billion of sophisticated arms to Jordan, overwhelming majorities in both houses of Congress adopted resolutions informing the President that they would disallow the sale if the Administration submitted it for a formal vote. In taking this stance, Congress appeared to establish the principle that it will approve future arms sales to Jordan only (in the words of the resolution postponing the sale) if Jordan is engaged in "direct and meaningful negotiations" with Israel. Indeed, a precedent for imposing such a standard was set in 1981 when, in the face of strong Senate opposition, the Administration succeeded in winning approval for sale of AWACS military reconnaissance aircraft to Saudi Arabia. A significant factor in gaining the bare majority of Senate votes needed to pass the measure was the President's assurance that before final delivery of the equipment was made, the Administration would certify to Congress that the Saudis had demonstrated support for and participation in the U.S.-sponsored Middle East peace process.

Congress's action on the Jordan arms sale proposal moves in the direction, long advocated by the Jewish community, that American arms should be sold only to Arab states that have made peace with Israel. In doing so, Congress has recognized that such sales undermine both Israel's security and economic stability by forcing her to divert already strained fiscal and manpower resources to meet the thereby-enhanced military capabilities of hostile neighbors.

The Administration persisted in efforts to sell arms to the Saudis. But it reduced the original Saudi request for $1.1 billion in F-15 fighter jets, M-1 tanks, helicopters and missiles to a package of $350 million, limited to Stinger, Sidewinder, and Harpoon missiles, and promised no more sales to the Saudis for at least a year. The Administration offered the rationale that the United States needed to make a symbolic gesture of support to the Saudis in the face of Iranian threats against Arab oil-producing states which support Iraq, and that such sales would provide leverage to secure support for American initiatives in furthering the Middle East peace process. Members of Congress—clearly disappointed in Saudi Arabia's failure to endorse the U.S.-sponsored Middle East peace process, and in Saudi Arabia's oil-pricing practices—opposed the sale with passage of resolutions of disapproval in May 1986 by margins of 73 to 22 in the Senate and 356 to 62 in the House of Representatives. Even after the President removed sale of the Stinger missiles from the package in June, he was able to sustain his veto of the Senate's resolution of disapproval by a margin of only one vote.

The Jewish community should:

- *interpret to Congress and the American people that sales of U.S. arms, such as to Saudi Arabia, have repeatedly failed to enlist its meaningful support for American policies, including participation in the Middle East peace process or curbing support for Arab states or organizations which commit or support acts of international terrorism;*
- *advocate that any sale of sophisticated American arms to any Arab state must await both its renunciation of the state of war and establishment of full normalized relations with Israel.*

The Peace Process

Greater diplomatic activity than at any time since the late 1970s has been devoted to initiating direct talks between Israel and Jordan. Israel again demonstrated its willingness to be flexible in accommodating some of the procedural preconditions set forth by Jordan in order to undertake direct peace negotiations. However, the obstacle to peace continues to be the failure of Jordan and other Arab states to come to the negotiating table.

1985 saw an intensified round of diplomatic initiatives designed to bring about direct peace talks between Jordan and Israel. However, little that was positive or substantive materialized concerning Jordan's movement toward direct peace negotiations with Israel. Similarly, despite the fact that the PLO again generated a flurry of intimations about readiness to accept UN Security Council resolutions 242 and 338, the PLO continued to reject it. Responding to this decision, King Hussein, in bitter frustration, terminated his effort with the PLO to form a joint Jordanian-Palestinian approach toward engaging in negotiations with Israel. In doing so, the King accused the PLO of reneging on commitments made to him concerning explicit acceptance of the UN resolutions, direct negotiations with Israel and renunciation of violence.

Searching for ways to gain acceptance for his proposals, Hussein reopened diplomatic relations with Egypt during 1984, hoping that the only Arab state to have a peace treaty with Israel would, in return for Jordan's gesture of restoring its status in the Arab world, lend backing to his efforts to enter the peace process. However, President Mubarak's reiteration of support for the PLO and Arafat as an essential partner in the peace process served only to stalemate further Jordan's advance toward the negotiating table, and to underscore Egypt's ambivalence about its relationship with Israel and about its role as a force for peace and moderation in the Middle East conflict.

In marked contrast to the actions of Jordan and Egypt, Israel has demonstrated increased readiness to be flexible in meeting a number of key demands set forth by Jordan as preconditions for opening direct negotiations. Reiterating his government's readiness to meet King Hussein without setting any preconditions, Prime Minister Peres used the occasion of an address before the UN General Assembly in October 1985 to respond to Hussein's call for talks under UN Security Council auspices. Israel, the Prime Minister declared, welcomed the support of the Council's five permanent members for direct Israeli-Jordanian negotiations—an indication that Israel was willing to search for a way to accommodate a key precondition of Hussein's while still preserving Israel's insistence (with respect to a Soviet or Chinese role in the peace process) that any parties that play a role in negotiations must have diplomatic relations with Israel. The critical element is that whatever international arrangement is utilized, it must immediately lead to direct negotiations between Israel and Jordan. Israel's government is also open to the direct participation of Palestinian representatives so long as those representatives are not members of the PLO. It was on this basis that Israel indicated its willingness to accept two of four Palestinian representatives proposed by Jordan (with the PLO's approval) as members of a potential joint Jordanian-Palestinian delegation for peace talks.

In sum, Israel remains ready to find grounds upon which to move the peace process forward with Jordan. For his part, however, Jordan's monarch seems as yet unable to transform his articulation of intentions to negotiate with Israel into the actual opening of negotiations.

The Jewish community should:

- *continue to support and interpret to the American public the reasons why the United States and Israel insist that any Middle East negotiations must take the form of direct, bilateral talks between Israel and each of its neighboring Arab states:*
- *continue to interpret to the American public the reasons why the United States refuses to deal with the PLO;*

• *interpret to the U.S. government and the American people that King Hussein, despite statements that he is ready to negotiate with Israel, continues to refuse to enter into negotiations without the PLO's sanction;*

• *highlight Israel's flexibility on details of preconditions demanded by King Hussein for opening negotiations, especially as demonstrated in Israel's readiness to accommodate in some fashion support by the international community and participation by Palestinians.*

The PLO

Recent events continued to expose the fractious character of the PLO. Despite increasing recognition that the PLO's use of terrorism is a fundamental and continuing element of its strategy to destroy Israel, and despite King Hussein's open questioning of its ability to represent and speak for the interests of the Palestinians, all other Arab states and a significant number of western European governments continue to invest the PLO with the status of "the legitimate representative of the Palestinians" and an essential participant in any Middle East peace negotiations. This continues to permit the PLO to exercise a veto over the peace process.

Revelations of the PLO's complicity in planning and executing the October 1985 hijacking of the Italian cruise ship *Achille Lauro* provided graphic confirmation that the PLO remains fundamentally committed to a policy of terrorism. Although the PLO attempts to portray itself as a political organization that pursues its ends through peaceful, diplomatic initiatives, this and other incidents continue to demonstrate that the PLO is duplicitous and incapable of participating in the peace process. Quite the contrary: in the absence of Arab and Palestinian leadership courageous enough to reject the PLO's nihilistic posture, the PLO can effectively veto progress toward peace in the Middle East. This has been reflected in the termination by King Hussein of his joint negotiating position with Yasir Arafat, citing Arafat's duplicity and questioning the PLO's designation as spokesman for the Palestinians. Indeed, the question of the PLO's capacity to represent the Palestinians was raised frontally by King Hussein when he terminated this joint negotiating relationship following the PLO's refusal to endorse explicitly UN Security Council resolutions 242 and 383, to agree to negotiate with Israel, and to renounce violence. Even now, the PLO is reinfiltrating men and material into southern Lebanon, hoping to regain the former base from which it once launched murderous guerrilla attacks against civilian targets in northern Israel.

When pressed by Jordan and Egypt to repair damage to the PLO's image wrought by the *Achille Lauro* incident, PLO chief Yasir Arafat issued a statement in Cairo reinvoking a pledge make in 1974—cynically and characteristically never observed—that the PLO would not conduct attacks against civilians outside of Israel and the administered territories. Apart from being a bald reassertion of the PLO's commitment to use of terror against Israelis—no Israeli civilians, including children, are innocents, according to the PLO Covenant—two days later, during a visit to Abu Dhabi, Arafat declared to the Arab press that his statement was merely intended to placate adverse Western reactions to the *Achille Lauro* affair.

Arafat's "Cairo Declaration," however, did nothing to stem the cycle of Palestinian-sponsored violence:

In November 1985 a Palestinian terrorist unit hijacked an Egyptian Boeing 737 airliner en route from Athens to Cairo and forced it to land in Malta. Of the 98 passengers held hostage aboard, 57 died in the course of a rescue attempt. A month later, 18 travelers were murdered and 158 wounded when Palestinian terrorists attacked international airports in Rome and Vienna. In early April 1986 four Americans were killed when a bomb planted by Arab terrorists blew a hole in the fuselage of a TWA airliner that had just taken off from Athens; a bomb placed by Libyan terrorists in a West Berlin discotheque killed an American army sergeant and a Turkish civilian; an Arab terrorist attempted to place a bomb in an El Al passenger jet departing from London's international airport; and French authorities thwarted an Arab terrorist attempt to bomb a U.S. government facility in Paris that processes visa applications.

This horrendous record of innocent civilians killed and wounded by Arab terrorists during 1985 and 1986 lays bare the fundamental characteristics of the PLO which undermine any contention that it is an essential element to be included as a partner in the Middle East peace process.

This perception of the PLO is shared by the American public, the American news media, and by the President of the United States.

The Jewish community should:

• *build upon recognition of the PLO's terrorist nature in interpreting to the American public the obstacles confronting the Middle East peace process;*

• *expose the duplicity of the PLO and its supporters' attempts to characterize Arafat and the PLO as "moderate";*

• *encourage America's news media to expose the PLO's practice of making different pronouncements about its policies and actions to Western and Arab reporters and news services.*

Israel's Economy

The economic news in Israel was increasingly hopeful during 1986. After experiencing significant dislocations between 1979 and 1985, when inflation steadily grew from 130 percent to monthly rates of upwards of 1000 percent per annum, an austerity program put into effect in June 1985 by the National Unity government has brought inflation to the point where it is now expected to average 20 percent a year or less. Nonetheless, this achievement has exacted a harsh human toll. To reduce its budget deficit, Israel devalued the shekel, cut subsidies for many staple consumer goods, introduced wage and price controls, and partially suspended wage indexation. Fears that these measures would add to Israel's national seven percent unemployment rate (higher in many development towns) were not borne out. But the combined effect of devaluation and subsidy cuts caused a 28 percent rise in the price level, while wage controls and wage indexation curbs combined to produce a 20 percent fall in workers' real wages. Further measures to reduce the nation's budget deficit, currently 8 percent of GNP (down from 17 percent in 1985), are paring public sector employment and government support for social service and education programs. While bringing hyperinflation under control has elicited widespread public approval for the overall effectiveness of this economic program, it has nonetheless created real and appreciable hardships for the majority of ordinary Israeli citizens.

The United States can help Israel's readjustment program in several significant ways. One is to continue economic and military aid programs, which relieve economic pressures created by Israel's security needs. Another, private-sector method, is to support Israel's export economy by encouraging American industries to take advantage of the Free Trade area agreement enacted by Congress in 1985. To this end, the Jewish community should cooperate with the U.S. Department of Commerce and other agencies interested in U.S.-Israel trade to promote better understanding among American businesspeople and the general public of the agreement and its benefts. Finally, the Jewish community should make particular efforts to encourage continued tourism to Israel, and to interpret El Al's exemplary record in providing safety and security to its passengers.

U.S. Embassy in Jerusalem

Although Congress has not acted on the question of moving the United States Embassy to Israel's capital of Jerusalem, significant support for such relocation has previously been demonstrated in the Senate and House of Representatives. The Jewish community should continue to encourage Congressional representatives to sponsor and support this measure.

11

The Kahane Debate

Falene Schuff

Rabbi Meir Kahane has gained recognition and popularity in recent years, particularly among the youth in Israel. His opponents call him "racist" and "neo-fascist" and fear his growing political constituency, built around his Kach party. Kahane claims that he is simply addressing issues that other Jewish leaders are afraid to confront.

Rabbi Marc Tanenbaum, Director of International Relations of the American Jewish Committee, says that Kahane "is using every possible means to become prime minister . . . when he can create the biblical monarchy that he has in mind." Tanenbaum claims that Kahane misrepresents figures of Arab population growth and violence in Israel in his effort to attract more followers. Kahane points to the Arab as the reason for all of Israel's problems; this is reminiscent of other fascist regimes where many times Jews were scapegoats and made to suffer. Israelis, unable or unwilling to look for the true explanation, believe Kahane.

According to Tanenbaum, when Kahane cites reports of rapid Arab population growth and a low Jewish birthrate "he is only giving us part of the truth." Actually Arabs constitute only 17% of the Israeli population—a minority still and probably to stay that way. Just as America is a Christian society because of the majority of Christians so too will Israel remain a Jewish state because of the majority of Jews. Tanenbaum does not believe that the Arabs will ever become the majority in Israel, but if they do there is every indication that they would keep Israel as the democracy that she is.

Another factor which has helped Kahane's popularity is the violence that has erupted between Jews and Arabs including recent acts of terrorism, the popularity of the PLO among West Bank Arabs and the fact that Jews have been fighting Arabs since 1948 without final success. The Israelis are becoming discouraged and Kahane's philosophy that the Arabs "are our enemies and the only way to get rid of them is to kill them, drive them out, etc. . . ." is becoming more and more appealing. But Kahane is distorting the truth; it's true that there are terrorist acts and individual killings by Arabs but the vast majority live in equality with political, economic and all other kinds of opportunities. The Arabs in Israel live under better conditions than their brethren in the other Arab nations. Another example to highlight Kahane's exaggerations is "Interns for Peace," an organization where young Arabs and Jews work together toward the quality of life for both Israelis and Arabs. Kahane selects a part of the truth, inflates it and turns it into a caricature in order to instill fear in the people and pull them after him.

The Israeli government has disappointed the Jews. The government has weakened since the resignation of Menachem Begin and Israelis have lost confidence in the major parties. Promises are made and then not fulfilled. Kahane uses this failure to his advantage. The unemployed and the working poor are following him after his party (Kach) introduced a law on July 19, 1985, in the municipalities of Hebron and Kiryat Arba, which allowed the firing of all Arabs in municipal jobs and the hiring of Jewish citizens. This law was quickly followed by a Knesset bill, July 30, passed against any party, that incites people to racism or negates Israel's democratic character, from participating in Parliamentary elections. It was designed specifically to outlaw Kahane's party. The Attorney General, Yitzchak Zamir, stated that "Racism of this accord, without shame, threatens the principle of equality before the law and threatens the entire judicial system and the social establishment of the democratic system and cultural life in Israel."

Kahane seems to feel that to establish and maintain a *Jewish* state, it must somehow be an anti-democratic state. Tanenbaum says "this is simply an unacceptable thesis for the majority of Israeli people and American Jews."

According to Tanenbaum, Jews cannot follow Kahane as a simpler solution. He is not going to prevent but rather cause more damage; Israel has come too far to go back to the biblical monarchy that he is proposing. We also have to realize that we are not going to have instant peace—ever—so we must be patient, endeavor in the peace policies that we have now and create new answers for the Arab-Israeli problem. It is unacceptable to have a Jewish State which is not democratic.

Rabbi Shalom Carmy, writing in the December 1985 *Hamevaser* (Yeshiva University) compared Kahanism and its nationalist goal of ridding Israel of all Arabs with King Saul's killing of the Gibeonites. The Talmud (*Yevamot* 78b-79a) explains that seven members of Saul's family went to their deaths as divine retribution for Saul's act. Saul's offense was *Chillul Hashem;* Rashi explains, in slaying the Gibeonites, Saul caused the Gentile nations to say: "it is not worthy to cleave unto this nation (Israel), for they took advantage of strangers in their midst to take away their support and did not avenge the injustice."

Carmy quotes Rabbi Abraham Isaac Kook on the danger of the Jewish enemy within:

> The passion for idolatry *(yetser hara d'avoda zara)* has ceased, but it was not completely vanquished . . . In the darkness it continued to exist and influence. It had to survive until the nation could overcome it. . . Then there arose nationalistic sects which had absorbed the external features of nationality and its dregs. That hatred of mankind increased, characteristic of the evil passion which does its work under the banner of nationalism. Despite the fact that this hatred is apparently intended only against the

foreign people and does not touch the nation's heritage directly, it eventually becomes an inner curse; the hatred of brothers increases and destroys all national weal. *(Derech haTechiya).*

Carmy explains Kahanism, therefore, as a disease to be withstood. The moral of the story of Saul and the Gibeonites is not only one of *Chillul Hashem,* but one of *Kiddush Hashem* as well. Jews must confront the worst in Western culture in order *not* to emulate it, as we study the best in order to benefit from it. Judaism aspires to a living, three-dimensional relationship with God, to whose *midot* Jews aspire. We refuse to countenance a religion that is no more than our basest wish fulfillments dressed up as Divine revelation.

The Contradiction Between Judaism, Zionism and Western Liberalism

Meir Kahane

It is almost impossible to fully appreciate the hysterical Jewish rejection front that has arisen in unprecedented defamation, slander, libel and smear of one Knesset member, Rabbi Meir Kahane and the supposed "Kahanism" he represents. The President, the Prime Minister of Israel, cabinet ministers and Knesset members, news media and intellectuals of the Jewish State have been joined by the American Jewish establishment in a frenzied and frenetic campaign of hysteria that has included a ban on my appearances on television and radio; a walkout from the Knesset when I speak (a la the Arabs and Israeli speakers in the UN) and a refusal by Jewish temples in America (many of whom have allowed Arabs and Black antisemites a forum) to allow me to speak.

The most fascinating thing about this phenomenon is the common denominator therein: Not one Jewish leader has had the courage, ability or willingness to debate me on the issues I raise—the painful, soul-scarring issues they cannot begin to answer and which go to the very heart of their Judaism and Zionism which I claim are on so many basic issues in utter contradiction of liberal, western democracy.

Let us consider first, Zionism—that of any ideological stripe, left or right, religious or secular. What is "Zionism," and what is its basic aim?

Why, surely, the whole purpose of Zionism, its only raison d'etre, is the establishment of a "Jewish State." And, indeed, this concept of a "Jewish State" was made the focus of the central and moving paragraph of Israel's Declaration of Independence which declares: "We hereby proclaim the establishment of a *Jewish State* in Eretz Yisrael."

Now, what does this term, a "Jewish State," mean? What is its minimal and fundamental definition, the one that *every* Zionist will agree upon? Again, it is surely a state *with a majority of Jews.* Having suffered the agonies of two millennia of Exile with its crusades, inquisitions, pogroms and holocausts, only a state with a majority of Jews could guarantee for the Jew freedom from these horrors. Only a state with a majority of Jews guarantees Jewish sovereignty and independence, promises that the Jew will be master of his own ship and fate, free from dependency and prostration before the stranger. That is Zionism: a Land of Israel with a Jewish majority—a Jewish State, at all cost.

But this being so, what is one to do with western liberal democracy? What is one to do with a concept that demands that anyone, regardless of religion or national background, has the right to quietly, peacefully and with equality have as many babies as possible and then become the majority? What does one do when, in the face of Jewish liberals who boast of a Jewish State granting equal rights and respect to the Arab minority—that minority becomes *the majority?* Simply put, the question that plants terror in the hearts of western Jews is: Do the Arabs have the elementary, democratic right in a Jewish state, to become the majority and make it an Arab one?

And since the Declaration of Independence of Israel is so selectively quoted by Jewish leaders as pledging "equal political and social rights to all its citizens regardless of religion or nationality," will they also quote the innumerable times the same document speaks of the Jewishness of the state and the fact that it declares a "Jewish State" in the Land? Which paragraph do you read? Is the schizophrenia not a mirror of those who wrote it and did not have the courage to decide whether Israel would be a Jewish state at all cost or a democratic one, albeit Arab majority? Is it not a mirror of a state which boasts liberal Jewish leaders; a state which is a "democracy," with a Law of Return that applies to Jews only and a Jewish National Fund that allows only Jews to lease national land?

One begins to see why they hate and fear Kahane for raising the issues they would so much rather bury. But the issues will never stay buried. The Arab of Israel does not want to live in a "Jewish" state. He is not a Zionist—he hates Zionism and calls *it* (not only Kahane) racist. He does not espouse the Law of Return for Jews only. He does not enjoy singing his national anthem *Hatikvah* with the words, "the soul of a Jew yearning," and he does not rush into the streets on Independence Day to celebrate his defeat. There is no need for "understanding" between Jews and Arabs because the Arab knows exactly what Jews and Zionism want. A *Jewish* state. And that is exactly what he does *not* want. And all the economic and social progress Jews give the Arab will change nothing, for not by bread alone does man (or Arab) live, and, indeed, the more educated and the more "progressive," the more dangerous and radical the Arab will be.

The problem is a real one. The Arab birthrate is among the highest in the world while Jews have many abortions but precious few babies. *Aliyah* (immigration) to Israel is at an all-time low and *yerida* (emigration) from the country, a flood. The alleged emigration of Arabs from the country has been shown to be merely workers leaving to work in the oil states and the economic crisis there finds them streaming back. The question is simply: How many Arabs will there be in Israel in 10 years? How many will sit in the Knesset? If the Galilee and the Little Triangle, today, already have a majority of Arabs, what will be tomorrow? Or should we look upon such questions as manifestations of "racism"?

And just as Jewish leaders fear to look at the contradiction between Zionism and western liberal democracy, so do they—and perhaps even more so—fear the basic inconsistency between western democracy and Judaism itself. If Judaism means the religious, Divine, non-human faith given by G-d Himself at Sinai (and if it does not, let us cease talking about Judaism but rather Cohenism or Goldbergism or any person who expounds his "Judaistic" views); if Judaism means that the Almighty sought to build a Torah society in that land, can it conceivably be supposed that He and the Judaism He gave us proposed a western democratic society in which non-Jews would have equal political rights to decide that the society would not only be a Torah one, but not even Jewish? Of course not, and Torah law clearly sets aside separate legal political status for Jews and non-Jews. The Talmudic position is succinctly stated by the great codifier of law, Maimonides, in his classic work, Mishnah Torah:

> Thou shalt not place over thyself a stranger who is not of your brethren.
>
> (Deuteronomy 17:15)
>
> Not only a king but the prohibition is for any authority in Israel. Not an officer in the armed forces . . . not even a public official in charge of the distribution of water to the fields. Any authority that you appoint shall only be from the midst of thy people.
>
> (*Hilchot Melachim* 1:4)

And again, concerning non-Jews in Israel who have agreed to give up idolatry and accept the Noahide laws of civilization: "They shall be subject under us and not be appointed to any position over Jews ever." (*Hilchot Melachim* 6:11)

It may be painful to the westernized Jew but Judaism is neither Thomas Jefferson nor Rousseau. It is Judaism. Of course, the gentile who accepts the conditions of living in the Jewish State (non-political rights and the status of a resident stranger—*ger toshav*) must then be treated properly and with justice in his social, economic and cultural affairs. Of course, we must not oppress him or persecute him. But national rights are not his in a Jewish state as conceived by Judaism.

This is the painful truth for western Jewry and their leaders. And as they condemn "Kahanism" they really know in their soul of souls that they are throwing down the gauntlet to Judaism and Zionism. As they loudly defame Kahane for his bills against intermarriage and relations between Jews and non-Jews, they know what the Torah already stated: "Neither shalt thou make marriages with them." (Deuteronomy 7) and that Ezra and Nehemiah both forceably separated Jews from their non-Jewish spouses during the return from Babylonian exile with the Bible proclaiming:

> For they have taken of their daughters . . . so that the holy seed have mingled themselves with the people of the lands."
>
> (Ezra 9)

Defamation is the last refuge of the non-thinker and of the desperate man incapable of intellectual reply. Instead of McCarthyism of the Mosaic persuasion, let there be open debate. Instead of banning free speech and people from appearing in Jewish forums, let those who differ or who have never heard the painful views, listen and refute—if they can. One thing is clear; whether Jewish leaders like it or not, time is making the problem an ever more real one and as the crisis in Israel grows the very Kahanism that is condemned so mindlessly and hysterically, will surely move to power as the only answer for the people of Israel who wonder whether, in ten years, their children will live in a Jewish state.

13

Non-Jewish Jews and Antisemitism

Dennis Prager and Joseph Telushkin

Throughout Jewish history Jews have identified with one or more of Judaism's components or converted to another religion. Beginning in the nineteenth century and through the present day, however, we encounter an entirely new group of Jews. These people do not feel rooted in anything Jewish, religious or national; their Jewish identity consists of little more than having been born Jews, and they affirm none of Judaism's components. They remain Jews by virtue of having not converted to another religion. These people are non-Jewish Jews.

Among non-Jewish Jews there have been some who, in addition to their alienation from Jewish roots, have not felt rooted in the non-Jewish society in which they lived and who in the course of the last century have helped to cause intense Jew-hatred. These are radical and revolutionary Jews. It must be understood that the reasons for the antisemitism they engender are unique. First, their challenges to non-Jews do not come from within Judaism. Second, they not only challenge the non-Jews' *values,* but the non-Jews' national and religious *identity* as well. Third, they are as opposed to Jews' values and identity as to non-Jews'. Nevertheless, and unfortunately for other Jews, the behavior of these radical non-Jewish Jews is identified as Jewish behavior.

The association of Jews with revolutionary doctrines and ideological social upheaval has not, unfortunately, been the product of antisemites' imaginations. The names Marx, Trotsky, Kamenev, Zinoviev, Luxemburg, Bela Kun, Mark Rudd, Abbie Hoffman, Jerry Rubin, Noam Chomsky, and others come immediately to mind. The phenomenon of the utterly disproportionate role played by Jews in Leftist revolutionary causes has often been commented upon. As Ernest van den Haag noted, "although very few Jews are radicals, very many radicals are Jews: out of one hundred Jews five may be radicals, but out of ten radicals five are likely to be Jewish. Thus it is incorrect to say that a very great number of Jews are radicals but quite correct to say that a disproportionate number of radicals are Jews. This was so in the past, and it has not changed."

How are these Jewish radicals made and why do they cause antisemitism?

The making of a Jewish radical is a complex social and psychological process but its essential elements can be discerned. First, these Jews have inherited a tradition of thousands of years of Jews challenging others' values—though of course in the name of Judaism and ethical monotheism rather than radical secular ideologies. Of course, non-Jewish Jews do not base their radical doctrines on the Jewish tradition, indeed they usually denigrate it, but the tradition's impact could not be avoided, only transformed.

Second, and most important, radical non-Jewish Jews are rootless. They do not feel rooted in either the Gentiles' religion or nation or the Jews' religion or nation, and they may very well have become revolutionaries in many instances precisely in order to overcome this rootlessness or alienation. Since they refuse to become like the non-Jews through identification with their traditional religious or national values, they seek to have the non-Jews become like them, alienated from traditional religious and national values. Only then will these revolutionaries cease to feel alienated.* These reflections on why non-Jewish Jews have flocked to the radical left have been made before. One of the leading sociologists in the United States, Stanford's Seymour Martin Lipset, writing in the late 1960s, when a disproportionate number of those active in the New Left were Jews—60 percent of the leadership of the Students for a Democratic Society, for example—noted that "participation in the Socialist and Communist world meant for many Jews a way of escaping their Judaism, of assimilating into a universalistic non-Jewish world."

A European historian, Peter Pulzer, has likewise noted the need for European Jews who had abandoned their Jewish roots to adopt the universalist, non-nationally rooted idea of socialism. Pulzer writes that it is mainly "those Jews who attempted to cut themselves most completely from their Jewish environment who became the Socialist leaders, such as Adler and Bauer in Austria, Singer and Kurt Eisner in Germany, Rosa Luxemburg in Poland and Germany, and Trotsky and Zinoviev in Russia."

As a consequence of their lack of rootedness many non-Jewish Jews have felt it necessary to turn radical and work to tear down traditional and national values and institutions in the name of "universalism." Feeling no kinship, hence no responsibility, to any nation (only to "mankind"), they have not felt concerned with the consequences of such destructiveness. Neither the demoralization of the non-Jewish nation nor the resultant non-Jewish antipathy to Jews concerns these people. They feel part of

*There is a related problem of Jews who do feel Jewish but who are rootless in terms of religion. These secular Jews, like non-Jewish Jews, feel much more secure, much more rooted, when non-Jews become, like them, secular. This is one major reason (the other is traditional Jewish fear of Christianity) why secular Jews have been in the vanguard of contemporary movements to secularize America. Religious Jews, on the other hand (despite the same fear of Christianity), tend to support more religious expression in the United States.

neither community, only the "community of man." Leon Trotsky, when asked whether he considered himself a Russian or a Jew, responded, "No, you are mistaken. I am a social-democrat. That's all." Fifty years later, Jerry Rubin referred to himself and other American Jewish radicals as "ex-American [*sic*] ex-Jews."

These Jews have been active in societies as diverse as the despotic and antisemitic Russia of the czars and the democracies of Weimar Germany and the United States. In Russia, non-Jewish Jews were so disproportionately represented in the less radical Menshevik wing of the Communist party that Stalin is reported to have said that with one large pogrom there would no longer be a Menshevik movement. Among the Bolsheviks there were fewer Jews than among the Mensheviks, though by 1922 they constituted 15 to 20 percent of the Bolshevik leadership. After Lenin's death in 1924, the battle to succeed him took place among five men; Stalin, Bukharin, Trotsky, Kamenev, and Zinoviev. The latter three were non-Jewish Jews.

Certainly the Russian populace identified Marxism with Jews, and since a vast number of Russians and Ukrainians did not support Communism, popular identification of Jews with Communism terribly exacerbated already deep antisemitism among those two peoples. During the 1918-20 civil war that followed the Bolshevik Revolution, the anti-Communist Ukrainian fighters murdered 50,000 innocent Ukrainian Jews. Their anti-Jewish passions were raised by General Petlura who constantly referred to the Bolshevik armies under the leadership of "the Jew Trotsky."

Russian and Ukrainian Jews found themselves in an oft-repeated modern Jewish horror story: the Jews were hated by both sides. Had the Whites won the civil war, the Jews would have suffered terribly as a result of age-old Ukrainian and Russian antisemitism as well as the new popular association of Communism with Jews. The Communists emerged victorious, and under their rule the Jews have suffered terribly, since in addition to traditional Russian (and Ukrainian, and Lithuanian, and other) antisemitism, it has been a basic tenet of Marxism and Leninism that the Jewish nation should disappear through assimilation. Thus the Russian Jewish revolutionaries helped increase antisemitism both among Communists and among anti-Communists: among Communists by their advocacy of the disappearance of the Jewish nation, and among anti-Communists by the Jew-hatred which the Jewish Communists aroused. The only Jews who did not suffer from antisemitism, at least not immediately, were the Jewish Bolsheviks. As Moscow's Chief Rabbi Mazeh is reported to have said to Trotsky in 1920 after the latter refused to help Jews suffering from the civil war pogroms, "The Trotskys make the revolutions and the Bronsteins pay the price" (Trotsky's original name was Bronstein).

A related but almost forgotten chapter of Jewish revolutionary activity is the Soviet-inspired Hungarian revolution of 1919. Bela Kun, a Jew, established the short-lived Hungarian Soviet Republic in March 1919. Of the 48 people's commissars in his government, thirty were Jewish, as were 161 of its 202 highest officials.

In Germany, until 1933 when Hitler came to power, the predominance of Jews on the revolutionary Left was as dramatic as in Russia. Unlike the radicals in Russia, however, in Germany the Left did not attain power.

But there is much to be learned from studying the German Jews of the Left prior to 1933, for while Nazi and German antisemitism was caused by factors far older and deeper than German Jewish radicalism, the radical non-Jewish Jews of the Weimar Republic greatly exacerbated German antisemitism and along with radical non-Jews helped to demoralize the Weimar democracy.

These Jewish radicals wielded a major influence over the cultural and intellectual life of Weimar Germany, an influence utterly disproportionate to their numbers. Among them were brilliant and successful satirists, writers, playwrights, artists, and orators, whose influence was seen by many Germans as destructive of German tradition, good and bad, and this perception (which is borne out in objective perspective) was a major component of Weimar German antisemitism. The great majority of German Jews voted for center parties in the Weimar Republic, but these Jews were not in the limelight; the non-Jewish Jews of the Left were, and they stood out as destroyers of everything German.

Foremost among those radicals who wielded such immense power over the intellectual and cultural life of Weimar Germany were those who convened around and published in the Berlin weekly *Die Weltbuhne.* Of the *Weltbuhne's* sixty-eight writers whose religious origins could be established, forty-two were Jews. These were of course non-Jewish Jews, so non-Jewish that "only a few of the *Weltbuhne* circle openly acknowledged that they were Jews."

A sample of *Die Weltbuhne* statements about Germany illustrates why German Jewish radicals helped to increase German antisemitism. The magazine utilized its prestige and the abundant talent of its writers and editors to *indiscriminately* attack German culture and national life. They were motivated not by an urge for reform; rather, they were attacking the very *idea* of the German nation itself. The following statements were written by its most famous satirist and critic, its onetime editor, Kurt Tucholsky, a Jew:

> This country which I am allegedly betraying is not my country; this state is not my state; this legal system is not my legal system. Its different banners are to me as meaningless as are its provincial ideals. . . .
>
> We are traitors. But we betray a state that we disavow in favor of a land that we love, for peace and for our true fatherland: Europe.

As Weimar historian Istvan Deak notes, "Tucholsky abominated the majority of his fellow citizens. Princes, barons, Junkers, officers, policemen, judges, officials, clergymen, academicians, teachers, capitalists, *Burger,* university students, peasants and all Bavarians he condemned collectively." According to Tucholsky the only thing in Germany worth loving was the countryside.

While some of the left-wing intellectuals' criticisms were specific, pointing to genuine weaknesses, their overall attacks were perceived by the overwhelming majority of Germans, including anti-Nazis, as purely destructive. And today, when one reads excerpts from old issues of *Die Weltbuhne,* it is difficult not to share the same reactions. "The left-wing intellectuals opposed the Weimar Republic all along the line," writes George Mosse, one of the foremost historians of modern Germany, "without providing what might prove to be a viable alternative method of change. Thus they tended to become critics rather than builders and in that process alienated, almost masochistically, large parts of the intellectual community from which, for all its injustices, provided an almost unprecedented freedom of expression and political action."

Indeed possibly the only nationalism that these non-Jewish Jews hated as much as the Germans' was the Jews'. As late as 1932, *Die Weltbuhne* published an article entitled "Hitler in Jerusalem," which likened Zionism to Nazism. As Mosse explains, these non-Jewish Jews "wanted to be not Jews, but part of the progressive brotherhood of all humanity. . . . [this] made them impassioned enemies of Zionism."

Tucholsky later fled to Sweden where during the war he committed suicide. But his ideological heirs live on in the United States where, again, non-Jewish Jews have played a dominant role in attacking American (and Jewish) nationalism.

While it has long been a tradition in America, as it was in Europe, for intellectuals to assume an adversary role in relation to established institutions, perhaps nowhere has the adversary role been so outspoken as among the intellectuals of the Left—as strident and garrulous a group as one could imagine. And since few of these have seemed as shrill as the Jewish intellectuals of the radical Left, it was perhaps inevitable that many of them would be received by the general public as unequivocably hostile to everything American. Since the 1930s a highly visible percentage of people on what has been perceived by many as the American-hating Left has been Jewish. While the overwhelming majority of American Jews identify themselves as politically moderate, some Jews have been as identified with destructive attacks on America as were radical Jews in Weimar Germany. And like their German and Russian predecessors, these Jews have nearly always been non-Jewish Jews, equally hostile to Jewish and American rootedness.

In the 1930s and 1940s non-Jewish Jews were among the leading pro-Soviet and anti-American agitators. During these two decades Jews constituted half of the membership of the American Communist party. Two alienated Jews, Julius and Ethel Rosenberg, were convicted of playing key roles in smuggling America's atom bomb technology to Stalin. Since the 1960s non-Jewish Jews have been among the leading radical opponents of virtually everything American. In 1970, a Harris study showed that 23 percent of Jewish college students termed themselves "Far Left" versus 4 percent of Protestants and 2 percent of Catholics. A national survey sponsored by the American Council of Education in 1966-67 revealed that the "best single predictor of campus protest was the presence of a substantial number of students from Jewish families." A study by Joseph Adelson in the early 1960s of politics and personality at the University of Michigan revealed that 90 percent of the radical students came from Jewish backgrounds.

Their similarity to the non-Jewish Jews who attacked Weimar Germany is remarkable. For example, just as the only thing about democratic Germany that Kurt Tucholsky could admit to liking was its scenery, so too, leftist philosopher Herbert Marcuse (who declared the United States to be Fascist) could find only one beautiful thing about America: its scenery. A 1971 article in *The New York Times Book Review,* reported this in an interview with Marcuse: "When Professor Marcuse, who had insisted that he loved and understood America, was pressed to specify which aspects of American life he found attractive, he fumbled for an answer, said he loved the hippies, with their long hair, and after some more fumbling, mentioned the beautiful American scenery, threatened by pollution. Despite an obvious effort, he could think of no other items."

A reader of Noam Chomsky's political writings might very well conclude that the most evil nations are the United States and Israel. They are the target of nearly all his invective, and in his recent book he denies that Israel is a democracy or that it could even become one. Every chapter in this book concerns American or Israeli evils. Typical of his statements about the evil nature of America was his statement in *The New York Review of Books* during the war in Vietnam that the U.S. Defense Department is "the most hideous institution on earth." As regards the Jews and Zionism, Chomsky has become so hostile that in 1980 he defended the publication of a book written by a French neo-Nazi professor who claimed that the Holocaust was a fiction made up by Zionists. Chomsky's defense was subsequently published as the introduction to the book. Chomsky claims that he was merely defending the French professor's academic freedom. But when Herbert Mitgang of *The New York Times* asked Chomsky to comment on the professor's views, Chomsky noted that he had no views he wished to state. As Martin Peretz, editor of *The New Republic,* has noted: "On the question, that is, as to whether or not six million Jews were murdered, Noam Chomsky apparently is an agnostic."

In the 1960s and early 1970s *The New York Review of Books* could be labeled an American *Die Weltbuhne.* It was and still is edited by Robert B. Silvers and Barbara Epstein, most of its political writers were Jews, and its tone, in the words of Irving Howe, a Democratic Socialist and identifying Jew, was a "snappish crude anti-Americanism." Journalist Richard Rovere summarized the *Review*'s attitude toward America: ". . . their American politics are Stone's and Chomsky's."

The Stone mentioned in Rovere's assessment is I. F. Stone (Isidor Feinstein Stone), contributing editor of *The New York Review of Books,* and for half a century a major American journalist. Stone has to this day devoted his considerable journalistic talents to attacking American policies, and, since 1967, Zionism and Israel. Stone's negative view of America is made evident by the overwhelming proportion of his essays that attack American policies, by the few that ever defend or praise anything American, and by the few that criticize America's adversaries. In his book *Hidden History of the Korean War,* Stone accuses the United States of equal responsibility with China for starting that war. As regards Israel, since 1967 Stone has announced that "I feel honor-bound to report the Arab side, especially since the U.S. press is so overwhelmingly pro-Zionist." This implication that Jews (or Zionists) dominate and prejudice the American press has, of course, long been a theme of antisemitism. As for Stone's honor-bound obligation to report the Arab side, Martin Peretz has written: "one would think that a writer's compulsion would be to tell the truth, regardless of whether it has been aired or not." It is worth noting that as the Arab position increasingly became the only position heard on the Left, Stone did not experience an honor-bound obligation to report the Israeli side. During the 1970s and 1980s he increased his anti-Israel rhetoric.

Jason Epstein of the *Review*'s governing board echoed the *Weltbuhne*'s view of the Weimar Republic, the German people, and its culture, in his description of the American Republic and its people and culture. Epstein found America a sick civilization. Each morning on his way to work he was oppressed by the sight, as he put it, of "so much dead culture . . . where, in the deepest winter . . . lines of New Jerseyites and others—thousands of them—stand in rows, uncomfortable, patient, grinning." So worthless is American life in Epstein's view that he sympathetically portrayed the mindset of the terrorist Weathermen. Epstein wrote that the Weathermen have been suppressed by an American "culture that has perverted and collectivized their energies and converted them to purposes of mass killing, leaving its individual members psychologically feeble and thus unable to confront their brutal culture with sufficient force."

A similar if not quite as extreme view of American culture is noted, by Ben Stein in *The View from Sunset Boulevard,* among the people who write and produce American television programs and their attitudes toward America: "A distinct majority [of the producers and writers] is Jewish. . . . TV writers and producers do not hold criminals responsible for crimes but rather place the blame on [American] society. . . . Middle-class people appear generally as either heavies or fools. . . ." These producers and writers hold that "religion is trivial and unimportant" and when depicted as significant "we see religion as sinister . . ." And echoing Tucholsky's descriptions of Weimar's respected groups, "the sum of it is that groups that have leadership or power roles—businessmen, bankers, government leaders, military men, religious figures—are treated as bad or irrelevant."

No hater of Weimar Germany described that society in more destructive terms than Norman Mailer has described America: "We kill the spirit here [in America]. . . . We use psychic bullets and kill each other cell by cell. . . . We have a tyranny here. . . . We have been fighting with sick dead hearts against the cold insidious cancer of the power that governs us. . . . our police, our secret police, our corporations, our empty politicians, our clergymen, our editors and cold frightened bullies who govern a machine made out of people they no longer understand."

There are innumerable other examples of radical non-Jewish Jews in America, particularly among journalists, writers, and professors whose basic attitude toward American society is one of hostility.*

This problem of a small number of non-Jewish Jews destroying their own and the non-Jews' roots has been recently commented upon by others. This destructive phenomenon was most clearly described by the prominent modern historian Walter Laqueur in an essay entitled "The Tucholsky Complaint." It has also been commented upon by the distinguished political scientist Leonard Schapiro: "why were there so many Jews among the intellectuals searching for utopia in Russia, China, or Cuba, *and motivated in their search by hatred of the United States?* Perhaps simply because the proportion of Jews among all intellectuals is generally high? Or is there some more profound reason?"

The problem of radical non-Jewish Jews is a painful and obvious one to Jews, so obvious that most of the writings about their harmful roles come from other Jews—Walter Laqueur, Leonard Schapiro, Nathan Glazer, Ben Stein, Stanley Rothman, and S. Robert Lichter, to cite only a few. There is, however, one other group concerned with the writings of radical non-Jewish Jews—antisemites, who attribute the destructive words and actions of these Jews to all Jews.

*Two Jewish political scientists, Stanley Rothman of Smith College and S. Robert Lichter of George Washington University, who have recently published a major study of American radicalism, *Roots of Radicalism: Jews, Christians and the New Left,* write: "The basic thrust [of a radical] is to undermine all aspects of the *culture* which contribute to his or her marginality. Thus Jews in the United States and Europe have been in the forefront of not only political radicalism but also various forms of cultural 'subversion.' The *Weltbuhne* circle played this role in the Weimar Republic. In America there was a tradition of literary criticism. Nevertheless, in the 1960s deracinated Jewish authors such as E. L. Doctorow, Joseph Heller, and Norman Mailer were disproportionately represented among those whose critical efforts, even when not overtly political, were designed to demonstrate the 'sickness' of the society. . . . Often such subversion involves an attack upon genuine inequities or irrationalities. Since all societies abound in both, there is never an absence of targets. However, the attack is generally not directed at the particular inequity or irrationality per se. Rather such inequities or irrationalities are used as a means for achieving a larger purpose: the general weakening of the social order itself."

14

International Terrorism

National Jewish Community Relations Advisory Council

The United States airstrike in April 1986 against terrorist bases in Libya, in retaliation for the death of an American soldier killed by a Libyan-conducted terrorist incident in West Berlin, demonstrated that the U.S. has implemented a policy of making measured, firm and unambiguous responses to the outrage of international terrorism. While western European nations' citizens and facilities continue to be targets for Arab terrorism, and to suffer the economic consequences of decreased business and tourist travel due to fears about air safety, these nations, with occasional and significant exceptions, have refused to join the United States or to act independently to carry out effective, coordinated action against the PLO, Libya, Syria and Iran for their sponsorship of international terrorism, or against the terrorists.

The United States, through its bold actions during the past year, demonstrated clearly that, when their sanctuaries can be identified, terrorists will no longer be allowed to act with impunity. The capture in October 1985 of the hijackers who seized the Italian liner *Achille Lauro* and the punitive bombing of Libyan military targets in April 1986, together marked a watershed in U.S. anti-terrorism policy, signaling that the U.S. is prepared, if necessary, to use its armed forces to combat international terrorism. Significantly, the American strike against Libya was the first time a nation other than Israel went to the source of state-supported terrorism in order to make the sponsoring country pay the price for conducting terrorist operations.

Many western European allies of the United States remain unwilling to undertake effective, coordinated action against Arab terrorism. Such reluctance stands out in stark contrast to these nations' policies and responses to terrorist groups operating within their own borders—such as Action Direct in France, the Red Brigades in Italy, the Baader-Meinhoff Gang in West Germany, and the ETA Basque separatists in Spain. But even the attacks carried out by Libyan-sponsored terrorist squads in Rome, Vienna and Berlin, which tragically illustrated that terrorism's victims are not confined to any single nationality, failed to evoke any significant response when the United States called for retaliatory economic sanctions against Libya. Such failures stem from these nations' calculations that appeasing those Arab states that sponsor terrorism, and the PLO and its various factions, which provide training, arms and funding to many of the major terrorist groups around the world, will provide insulation from further terrorism. Experience, however, continues to demonstrate otherwise.

Secretary of State Shultz pointed to both the problem and solution regarding effective action to counter terrorism in a speech delivered in London during December

Mike Keefe
The Denver Post
News America Syndicate

1985. Contrasting European states' recognition of the PLO with America's refusal to do so until the PLO renounces terrorism and recognizes Israel, Mr. Shultz declared: "Extremists must be resisted, not appeased. Unlike some of our European friends, we feel that gestures toward the PLO only mislead its leaders into thinking their present inadequate policy is gaining them international acceptance and stature."

It follows from these principles, long a cornerstone of U.S. Middle East policy, that a major priority of America's efforts to counter terrorism should be to continue to press our European allies to join in developing a comprehensive international strategy against terrorism, including intelligence sharing, coordinated rescue efforts, extradition treaties, and imposition of sanctions against nations offering terrorists sanctuary.

The Jewish community should:

- *support the Administration's policy that acts of terrorism must be met by determined political, economic and, if necessary, military action;*
- *support efforts by the Administration and Congress to press our Western allies and the entire community of nations to pursue an active, comprehensive anti-terrorism policy;*
- *examine the adequacy of current U.S. and international laws to enable governments, both individually and collectively, to impose sanctions upon nations that do not cooperate in apprehending and prosecuting terrorists;*
- *give higher priority to interpreting to the American public the unchanging nature of the role of violence as a fundamental instrument of terrorists around the world, for whom the PLO provides inspiration, training and financial support;*
- *urge the American and other governments, and international air carriers, to improve their nations' airport security measures in order to restore travelers' confidence in the safety of international air transportation.*

Terror Must Be Condemned, Not Condoned

J. David Bleich

Downtrodden, oppressed and persecuted for millennia, Jews practiced what others preached. When smitten, they turned the other cheek. Undoubtedly, this reaction was rooted in pragmatic considerations. Resistance would only evoke greater hostility; retribution would assuredly provoke unspeakable punishment. Eventually, reticence, timidity and fear became ingrained in the psyche of the *galut* Jew. Response in kind simply became unthinkable.

Not so in the modern-day State of Israel. Survival demanded preparedness in the form of strong defense forces and a prompt crushing response to armed aggression. Wars of attrition and endless acts of terrorism continue to sap the strength of the yet nascent state. On the governmental level the response has been a policy of swift retaliation and preventative strikes to eliminate danger.

As a result, a profound psychological metamorphosis has taken place. Fear that worse misfortune may be provoked has been eradicated. Reticence is no more. The instinctive response to violence is violence. And, now, the ultimate has arrived: terrorism against terrorism.

In formulating national policy, the State of Israel is not necessarily guided by the teachings of Jewish tradition. It has not customarily sought the prior advice of its own Chief Rabbinate with regard to the grave moral and halachic issues confronted in the defense of the State. Observant Jews have nevertheless tended to be supportive of government policy in matters pertaining to national security. They have been supportive with regard to such matters for two reasons: 1) A vague, unarticulated feeling that justification for these policies can be found in Jewish tradition. 2) A clear perception that vocal opposition to these policies could only compromise the security of the State and endanger the lives of countless thousands of its citizens. In any event, the government has not pursued policies designed to snuff out the lives of blameless persons.

Terrorists Claim Religious Justification

But, now, individuals have taken matters into their own hands and the State itself threatens them with penal sanctions. Moreover, those persons are observant Jews who, incontrovertibly, have manifested sacrificial commitment to the Land of Israel. Most significantly, those individuals plead that their actions are born of an ideological commitment to Jewish teaching. Jewish law, they contend, sanctions and even mandates the acts of terrorism which they promulgate.

Provocation, however, cannot be equated with justification. One can readily understand the mentality of those who believe that further violence can be prevented only by instilling fear of retaliation. Even were history to demonstrate that violence only serves to breed further violence, human nature is such that the evidence would be disregarded. Desire for revenge is also understandable, but to understand is not to condone. Jews dare not allow themselves to respond as others would and do; Jews dare not give free reign to feelings of anger and vengeance. Response, even to danger, must be conditioned by the teachings of the Torah.

"The Land of Their Enemies"

There is no question that the State of Israel is surrounded by enemies intent upon the annihilation of its inhabitants. The present situation is reflected in Ramban's poignant interpretation of a phrase found in the concluding section of Leviticus. "And they shall confess their iniquity, and the iniquity of their fathers, in their treachery which they committed against Me and also that they have walked contrary unto Me. I also will walk contrary unto them and bring them into the land of their enemies; if then their uncircumcised heart be humbled then the punishment of their iniquity will be accepted" (Leviticus 26:40-41). The juxtaposition of these verses is puzzling. Scripture speaks of confession of iniquity. Confession of sin is indicative of repentance. If the people of Israel are indeed repentant, such repentance should signal the close of the period of punishment and affliction foretold in the earlier versions of the *tochachah* (rebuke). And yet, the very next verse proceeds to state that, instead of responding to their confession of sin in a positive manner, God declares, "I also will walk contrary unto them and bring them into the land of their enemies." Yet a further punishment is predicted: the people of Israel are to be led into the land of their enemies. Even the nature of this further punishment is difficult to comprehend since among the earlier misfortunes which constitute the punishment for Israel's iniquity is recorded "And you will I scatter among the nations. . . ." (Leviticus 26:33).

Adversity is an Impetus to Repentance

It is obvious that it is these difficulties which prompted Ramban, in commenting upon this verse, to remark that the phrase "the land of their enemies" does not at all refer to the lands of Israel's dispersion. On the contrary, comments Ramban, the phrase refers not to the Diaspora, but rather to the Land of Israel itself. The Land of Israel is referred to as "the land of their enemies" because the verse alludes to a period during which, although Jews will reside in the land, it will be encircled on all sides by enemies. According to Ramban, "and they shall confess to their iniquity" marks the beginning of the process of repentance, but does not connote that complete repentance has taken place. God responds in kind. He allows His people to return to the land of their forefathers, but, during that stage of their spiritual rehabilitation, they do not yet live in peace and tranquility. They return to the Land of Israel, but are surrounded by "enemies." There, under such conditions, Scripture tells us, their heart will be humbled and repentance will be complete. Then, and only then, does God promise, "I will remember My covenant with Jacob and also My covenant with Isaac and also My covenant with Abraham will I remember." When repentance is complete, then will the iniquity be entirely forgiven and Israel restored to a position of favor in the eyes of God.

Whether or not merited by partial repentance, divine beneficence has permitted a partial return to our land. Encirclement by enemies, according to Ramban, is both a form of divine retribution as well as an impetus to repentance. To be sure, enemies must be recognized as such and one may respond to an enemy in an appropriate manner. Certainly, an overt act of aggression committed by an enemy need not to be accepted and suffered in silence even though the resultant suffering may well be part of the divine plan. "He who comes to slay you, arise and slay him" is a normative principle of Jewish law. Self-defense is not merely permissible but also mandatory. The "law of the pursuer" demands that any would-be murderer be summarily executed, if necessary, in order to save the life of an innocent victim.

Rodef: A Limited Concept

Settlers in newly-founded communities on the West Bank and in the Golan are assuredly entitled to the fullest measure of protection. If, indeed, governmental authorities have not provided adequate protection no one can fault settlers who engage in legitimate forms of protection.

But the "law of the pursuer" justifies only the taking of human life when it is clear that the individual is intent upon an act of aggression. Although malevolent intent may be inferred from circumstances and conduct, mere unsubstantiated suspicion of homicidal intent is not sufficient to permit the taking of a human life. Moreover, there is no dispensation to take the life of a pursuer if the danger can be obviated by less drastic measures.

The "law of the pursuer" may be invoked only when the loss of innocent life is otherwise a virtual certainty.

In analyzing the "law of the pursuer," formulated in Exodus 22:2, the Gemara, *Sanhedrin* 72a, states, ". . . if the matter is clear to you as the sun that he is not at peace with you, slay him; but if not, do not slay him." (See R. Isaac Schorr, *Teshuvot Koah Shor,* no. 20; R. Chaim Ozer Grodzinski, *Teshuvot Ahiezer,* I, no. 23, sec. 2; and R. Moshe Feinstein, *Ha-Pardes,* Nisan 5728, reprinted in *Sefer ha-Zikaron le-Maran ha-Gri Abramsky,* Jerusalem, 5738).

This is true whether the putative aggressor be a Jew or a non-Jew. While the taking of the life of a non-Jew does not occasion capital punishment at the hands of a human court, Ravan, *Baba Kamma* 111b, and Kesef Mishneh, *Hilkhot Rotzeah* 2:11 are quite clear in ruling that taking the life of a non-Jew is encompassed in the prohibition against homicide. Explicit authority for that ruling is found in *Mechilta,* Mishpatim 4:58. Indeed, there are many forms of homicide for which Jewish law does not prescribe capital punishment. The nature of the punishment administered and the absence of the severest form of punishment does not at all indicate that the act is to be condoned.

Condoning the Violence is a Transgression

Indeed, condoning the act may well be an even worse infraction than the deed itself. II Samuel 21 reports that in the time of King David there was a famine which lasted for three consecutive years. David recognized that the famine must be a punishment for some transgression. Accordingly, he approached the *urim ve-tumim* and inquired of God what the infraction might be. There came the response, "And the Lord said: 'It is for Saul and for [his] house of blood because he put the Gibeonites to death' " (II Samuel 21:1). The Gemara, *Yevamot* 78b, quite cogently poses the question: Where is it related that Saul killed the Gibeonites? In point of fact, Saul committed no untoward act against the Gibeonites. The Gemara replies that although Saul did not kill the Gibeonities, he did annihilate the priests who were the inhabitants of the city of Nob. The Gemara further indicates that the Gibeonites were servants of the priests and, in return for their labor, they received their sustenance from the priests. Subsequent to the destruction of Nob, the Gibeonites who were dependent upon the priests for food and drink, no longer had a source of sustenance and consequently a number of them perished. Since Saul was, at least indirectly, responsible for their death, Scripture regards him as culpable for the demise of the Gibeonites.

Death of Innocents Requires Atonement

King David was now apprised of the transgression for which his people were punished. He sought to make amends and called the Gibeonites and asked of them, "What shall I do for you and wherewith shall I make atonement, that you may bless the inheritance of the Lord?" (II Samuel 21:2). The Gibeonites declined to accept gold or silver in expiation for Saul's transgression or as compensation for the harm and grief that they had suffered. But Saul was no longer alive and could not be punished. Instead they demanded, ". . . let seven men of his sons be delivered unto us and we will hang them up unto the Lord in Gibeah of Saul, the chosen of the Lord" (II Samuel 21:6). David's response was immediate and forthright: "and the king said, 'I will deliver them' " (II Samuel 21:6). Scripture then proceeds to describe how David caused the grandchildren of Saul to pass before the *urim ve-tumim* and how he delivered to the Gibeonites the seven individuals selected by the *urim ve-tumim.* Assuredly, King David would not have acceded to the demands of the Gibeonites had there not been a clear indication of divine approval. Nevertheless, the Gemara questions the inherent propriety of such a course of action. "Fathers shall not be put to death for children, neither shall children be put to death for fathers" (Deuteronomy 24:16). The Gemara answers, "Rabbi Chiya the son of Abba said in the name of Rabbi Yonatan, 'Better that a letter be eradicated from the Torah than that the Divine Name be publicly profaned.' " Rashi, commenting upon the nature of the *hillul ha-Shem* (profanation of the Divine Name) which David sought to avert, explains that failure to exact punishment for the death of the Gibeonites would, in and of itself, constitute profanation of the Divine Name in the eyes of the world. Gentile nations would conclude that the Jewish people had acted unjustly in allowing strangers to be deprived of their livelihood without in any way avenging the evildoers.

Murdering a Gentile Profanes God's Name

Saul had harmed the Gibeonites only indirectly and unintentionally. Yet failure to punish the individual bearing even remote responsibility for their plight is deemed by the Gemara to constitute a *hillul ha-Shem.* It may be deduced that, *a fortiori,* any act which directly leads to loss of Gentile life would certainly be regarded as a profanation of the Divine Name and that such transgression is only compounded by failure to punish the perpetrators of such a crime.

This concern is clearly reflected in the comments of R. Meir Simchah ha-Kohen of Dvinsk in his biblical commentary, *Meshech Hokhmah,* Parshat Mishpatim. *Meshech Hokhmah* explains why it is that the Bible does not provide for capital punishment for the murder of a non-Jew. *Meshech Hokhmah* remarks that taking the life of a non-Jew is both an act of homicide and a profanation of the Divine Name. Neither Yom Kippur nor suffering atones for the transgression involved in profaning the Divine Name; expiation is possible only upon the death of the evildoer. Were the individual who takes the life of a non-Jew to receive the death penalty at the hands of a human court as punishment for the act of homicide it would serve as atonement for that crime only. As a result his death would not serve as expiation for the even graver transgression of profanation of the Name of God. Therefore punishment for the murder of a non-Jew is imposed only at the hands of Heaven. According to *Meshech Hokhmah,* the killing of a non-Jew is not a crime punishable at the hands of a human court, not because it is a less severe infraction than the murder of a Jew, but, on the contrary, because the infraction is so grave that it cannot be expiated by means of terrestrial punishment.

Terrorism Must Be Condemned

The application of these sources to acts of terrorism committed by Jews against non-Jews is clear. The question is not the guilt or the innocence of those who stand accused. That is a matter to be determined by an appropriate judicial body in accordance with due process of law. Assuredly, every person is presumed innocent until proven guilty and the rights of the accused must be vigorously safeguarded. But it is undeniable that acts of terrorism did take place and those acts were committed by some person or persons. Such actions must be condemned as violating both the letter and spirit of Jewish law. Moreover, it is clear that, if the identity of the perpetrators is known, failure to bring those individuals to justice would constititue a *hillul ha-Shem* in the eyes of all.

There is no question that the deeds committed were heinous in nature. Self-defense may be sanctionable under appropriate circumstances. Elimination of individuals who seek to spill the blood of innocent victims may also be sanctioned in some circumstances. But those considerations do not justify either collective punishment or acts of terror committed against entirely innocent persons. A hand grenade cast into a building of Beit Zair University causes indiscriminate damage and takes the lives of entirely guiltless students. A time bomb placed on a bus and designed to explode at an hour at which there are a maximum number of passengers is clearly designed to take the lives of innocent victims. Regardless of the motivation of the perpetrators, regardless of their idealism and self-sacrifice, such acts cannot be sanctioned. The only way in which the profanation of the Divine Name which has already occurred can be rectified is by resolute condemnation of such wanton acts of terrorism.

Above all, we must foster a moral climate in which acts of terrorism are anathema. The Psalmist calls out, "*Yitamu hataim min ha-aretz*—Let evil deeds cease from the earth" (Psalms 104:35). The Gemara, *Berachot* 10a, underscores the use of the word *"hataim"* in commenting, *"Mi ketiv hotim, hataim ketiv,"* i.e., we pray for the eradication of evil deeds, but not of evildoers. Even in administering punishment, the purpose is not retribution but prevention. Public condemnation and censure are essential lest silence be regarded as approval. And approval, Heaven forbid, can only lead to further violence.

16

Afghanistan: How Good People Can Ignore a Holocaust

Dennis Prager

"A whole nation is dying. People should know."
—*Afghan doctor.*

"Whole villages are bombed into oblivion, sometimes as a reprisal after a guerilla attack, sometimes for no reason at all. Soviet soldiers enter the villages, selecting non-combatant men, women and children at random to be shot, dynamited, beheaded or burned alive.

"Two men, brothers, from Mata, aged ninety and ninety-five, and blind, stayed behind when the rest of the villagers fled during last spring's offensive. Russians came, tied dynamite to their backs, and blew them up.

"Civilians are burned alive, dynamited, beheaded; bound men forced to lie down on the road to be crushed by Soviet tanks; grenades thrown into rooms where women and children have been told to wait.

"Mothers are forced to watch their infants being given electric shocks. A young woman who had been tortured in prison described how she and others had been forced to stand in water that had been treated with chemicals, which made the skin come off their feet." (Jeri Laber, Helsinki Watch, *New York Times,* November 22, 1984)

Right now there is something akin to a Holocaust taking place in Afghanistan. The systematic destruction of villages and the murder of all their inhabitants precisely parallel the infamous Nazi atrocity at Lidice. Nearly one out of every three Afghans, four to five million people, have fled Afghanistan, and approximately one million have been killed. Neutral observers are unanimous in concluding that the Soviets are literally destroying rural Afghanistan—emptying it of its population and starving those who remain.

The Soviets are, for all intents and purposes, destroying Afghanistan. Unless they are stopped, Afghanistan will cease to exist as such, and will become a Soviet republic in everything but name. Islam is being destroyed, tens of thousands of children from the major cities have been sent to the Soviet Union to be indoctrinated in Russian and Communism, and the rest of the country's population either submits to Sovietization or flees.

We Jews have always wondered how the world could basically go on during the Holocaust as if nothing were happening. Ever since Pol Pot and the Communist holocaust in Cambodia, I have understood how easy it is for people to go on with their normal lives while a nation is slaughtered. Afghanistan now provides another example.

Is the analogy to the Holocaust invalid? The Holocaust was unique, and there is no Auschwitz in Afghanistan, but on the other hand:

- The Jewish nation, religion, and culture have survived the Nazis. It is not likely that the Afghan nation, religion, and culture will comparably survive the Soviets.
- You and I know much more about Afghanistan than nearly anyone in the West knew about the Holocaust, so our silence is unforgivable.
- Once people learned of the Holocaust, no one denied how evil the Nazis were. Today, on the other hand, despite all we know about the Gulag Archipelago, Afghanistan, the systematic destruction of Judaism and Christianity in the Soviet Union, and other Soviet atrocities, to call the Soviets evil is to be considered a "cold warrior," a "reactionary."

How many Afghans will the Soviets have to burn, how many countries will they have to extinguish, how many more tens of millions will they have to murder, before Soviet cruelty becomes the primary item on the agenda of people who care about people?

We Jews must cry out on behalf of Afghanistan, and do so *davka* as Jews. Jewish organizations must speak out, take out ads and organize demonstrations to remind the world that we who endured the first Holocaust, have the duty to scream the loudest at events that approach its unique evil.

Then we will continue to be in a moral position to protest the silence that accompanied our Holocaust.

In the meantime, however, if you ever wondered how good people could ignore a holocaust, look around right now.

17

Review of Church-State Issues

Marc D. Stern
Co-Director
Commission on Law and Social Action
American Jewish Congress

Until the last day of the Term, when Justice Lewis Powell announced his retirement, it was a reasonably good Supreme Court Term for the Jewish community: three wins, all important, and one defeat.

I. Litigation

A. The most notable decision was *Edwards v. Aguilard* (1987) in which the Supreme Court struck Louisiana's equal time for scientific creationism statute, which required the public schools to teach the theory of creationism equally with the theory of evolution. The seven member majority found, based on the legislation's history, and the general history of attempts at banning evolution from the public schools, that the statute was enacted with a religious purpose, that of protecting one particular theological position from attack. Hence, said the majority, the statute was unconstitutional under the first branch of the so-called tripartite test which requires constitutional statutes to have a secular purpose, a primary secular effect, and not create excessive entanglement between religion and statutes.

The majority emphasized that ensuring a secular environment was particularly important in the public schools and that the sectarian purpose it had identified breached that requirement. Two Justices (O'Connor and Powell) concurring, agreed with the Court's reasoning, but emphasized that nothing in that opinion, or in the Court's prior decisions prohibited the public schools from teaching about religious beliefs, the role of religion in history, or its place in art and literature.

Justice Scalia (joined by Chief Justice Rehnquist), in his first opinion in an Establishment Clause case, dissented. He made two points: first, that as the case came before the Supreme Court, there was no showing either that creationism was a religious idea (the record contained numerous affidavits from 'scientists' denying that it was and no contradictory affidavits from those challenging the statute that creationism was inevitably religious; no trial had been held) or that the legislative history indicated that the legislature enacted the statute for a religious purpose. On the contrary, he wrote, all that the record showed was that the legislature intended to protect children against indoctrination in the theory of evolution.

More broadly, in a particularly powerful message, Justice Scalia challenged the entire enterprise of invalidating legislation on the basis of the motive of members of the legislature. Despite the forcefulness of the dissent, the majority found it unnecessary to respond to Justice Scalia on this latter point, perhaps relying simply on the force of precedent.

B. *Hobbie v. Unemployment Compensation Board*—What appeared to have been a case that would clarify the relationship between the Free Exercise (which appears to require certain forms of preference for religion) and Establishment (which appears to forbid such preferences) Clauses, or perhaps a rethinking of the Court's Free Exercise decisions, turned out to be a routine and uninformative reaffirmance of the Court's prior holdings. Hobbie was fired from her job because she refused to work on Friday night, which she observed as the Sabbath. The

State denied her unemployment benefits on the ground that her failure to work constituted misconduct, a decision upheld by the Florida courts without any discussion of two Supreme Court cases apparently requiring a different result.

Under the Court's prior decisions, the action by Florida courts denied Hobbie her constitutional rights, although it was not clear after *Bowen v. Roy*, (1985-86 Term), that all the Justices wanted to continue to adhere to those decisions, or that those decisions were still viable after *Estate of Thornton v. Caldor, Inc.*, (1985-86 Term), invalidating a religious accommodation statute as an establishment of religion. But it turned out that a majority adhered to the Court's prior precedents, requiring states to pay unemployment benefits to those who lose their jobs because of a conflict with religious practice. Speaking for all but Chief Justice Rehnquist, Justice Brennan largely ignored all the conflicting lines of authority and the various conceptual difficulties, and simply announced the Court's continuing adherence to its prior cases.

C. *Corporation of Presiding Bishop v. Amos* (1987) involved a challenge to a portion of the 1964 Civil Rights Act which allowed religious corporations to engage in religious discrimination in all of their hiring, not just in regard to those positions related to the furthering of the religious mission of the corporation. A building engineer, one Mayson, employed by a Mormon cross between a Jewish Community Center and a Jack La Lanne Gymnasium, was fired because he was not a member of the Mormon church in good standing. (He failed to pay a required tithe.)

Mayson sued, claiming religious discrimination, and challenging the constitutionality of the religious corporation exemption. A District Court agreed with his challenge but the Supreme Court unanimously disagreed. There were, however, two sets of opinions. The first by Justice White for five Justices and the other, for four Justices, in two largely similar opinions by Justices O'Connor and Brennan.

Justice White found it unnecessary to decide whether the Free Exercise Clause prohibited the government from regulating the affairs of religious institutions altogether. Rather, he said, the government had a significant secular purpose in exempting religious institutions from intrusive regulations which might interfere with their religious mission; and could therefore legitimately choose not to regulate these institutions as completely as it regulated non-religious ones. Moreover, since the government was not itself discriminating on the basis of religion, the fact that religious institutions could do so by virtue of the exemption could not for constitutional purposes be ascribed to government. Hence, the statute did not have the effect of advancing religion.

A group of four Justices agreed with Justice White's analysis of secular purpose, and specifically his rejection of Mayson's claim that a statute exempting religious institutions was unconstitutional as a preference for a religion, if not required by the Free Exercise Clause. On the other hand, they argued that the exemption should be seen as governmental encouragement of religious discrimination.

They nevertheless upheld the exemption on the ground that it furthered the important governmental intent in avoiding sensitive inquiries into the affairs of religious not-for-profit corporations to determine whether a particular job furthered its religious missions. All four Justices (in these opinions) suggested that a different result would be in order in the case of a for-profit religious corporations—(a point left open by the majority)—since these could not be assumed to have any religious mission.

Amos was the only one of the four cases that saw the Jewish defense agencies divided: AJCongress and COLPA filed in support of the Bishop, ADL in favor of the employee, and AJCommittee abstained.

D. *Ansonia Bd. of Education v. Philbrook* involved the application of Title VII's requirement that religious observers be accommodated in the workplace to the public school context. Philbrook was a teacher who was a member of the World-Wide Church of God. The Church observes the "Old Testament" holidays, many of which fall on weekdays.

The collective bargaining agreement provided all employees three religious absence days, in addition to three paid personal days, as well as a variety of other leave-with-pay days. These three paid personal leave days could not, by terms of the agreement, be used for religious days (or any other purpose for which the contract provided leave with pay) although it was not clear that this restriction was in fact enforced. Philbrook sought to have this restriction struck as a violation of his right to be accommodated, notwithstanding the fact that the school board allowed him to take his holidays as leave without pay and without any other penalty. He argued that allowing leave with pay for all sorts of personal business, but not religion, constituted illegal discrimination.

The Supreme Court, in an opinion by Chief Justice Rehnquist (Justice Marshall alone dissenting on this score) disagreed. It held that an employer was free to offer any accommodation which relieved an employee of the unvarnished choice between loss of employment and religious observances. The court, in the course of so holding, invalidated an Equal Employment Opportunity Commission Guideline which required employers to offer their employees the least onerous accommodation possible. On the other hand, it also held that, if the school board did not police the use of personal business days such that they were available for any purpose whatsoever, it could not ban their use for religious purposes.

*

Aside from the decision in *Philbrook*, which completed the Supreme Court efforts at draining Title VII of almost all of its vitality, the Term appeared to be a good one for the Jewish community. The three part test which has been the cornerstone of the Supreme Court's Establishment Clause jurisprudence for fifteen years was reaffirmed, despite some earlier indication that it was to be interred. Despite fear that 25 years of Free Exercise cases were about to be disavowed, those decisions were reaffirmed. Moreover, the Court in *Amos* gave religious institutions substantial freedom from state regulation.

But there are many ominous signs. At least four current Justices have expressed dissatisfaction with the entire three part test or parts of it. Three Justices have expressed doubts about the Court's approach to the Free Exercise Clause chiefly on grounds that it favors believers over non-believers. The question raised by these Justices have largely gone unanswered. These are signs of instability and weakness in a Court whose power and authority stem from its ability to rationalize its decisions.

*

II. Next Term

So far the Court has accepted three religion cases for consideration next Term (beginning in October 1987). Two involve Free Exercise claims by the Native Americans, in both of which the government seeks to ease its burden of sustaining an imposition on the religious practices of religious minorities. The other *(Karcher v. May)*, is a challenge to a New Jersey public school moment of silence statute invalidated by the lower federal courts. However, because of some unique factual circumstances, it is quite likely that the Court will not reach the issue on the merits. If it does, it appears likely, based on comments in *Wallace v. Jaffree* (1985-86 Term), to uphold it, and to distinguish moments of silence from other forms of school prayer.

The biggest question about next Term is what impact the departure of Justice Powell will have on the Court's work in this and other areas.

*

III. Other Litigation

There was relatively little legislative action in the church-state area this year. Congress is still considering legislation to overturn the Supreme Court's decision barring servicemen from wearing yarmulkas. Chances for passage are good. And an additional state (Iowa) enacted tuition tax credit legislation. There was, however, no end of litigation. Little of importance happened regarding prayer in the public schools, although several cases were brought. The major litigated question now is whether prayers may be said at graduation. The decisions are so far mixed, and several appeals are currently pending. One appellate court upheld such prayers only if they were non-denominational *(Stein v. Plainwell Community Schools)*.

The Equal Access Act has produced almost no litigation, and (as far as can be determined) almost as little activity in the public schools. The one case in which the Act's constitutionality has been raised had been tried *(Mergens v. Board of Education)* but, as of this writing, has not yet been decided.

In *Smith v. Board of Commissioners*, Judge Brevard Hand held that many of the textbooks used in the Alabama public schools were infected with the religion of "secular humanism," defined as the absence of affirmative religious teaching. The decision was widely ridiculed, immediately appealed, and quickly stayed by order of the Court of Appeals. Almost without question, it will be reversed. Nevertheless, this suit has generated a widespread interest in the treatment of religion in the public schools. A broad consensus has emerged among interest groups, educators and textbook publishers that the schools have in fact not adequately taught about religion. A related development is a growing perception that the schools have not adequately transmitted the core values of this society to their students. If the evangelical prescription for those deficiencies—teaching religion in the schools—is unacceptable, it remains true that their attacks have called attention to real problems.

A far more difficult case, often mistakenly identified with the *Smith* case, is *Mozert v. Board of Education* in which evangelical parents in Tennessee, sought not the suppression of textbooks with which they disagreed, but excusal of their elementary school children from classes in which these books were used. The school board refused on various grounds, including impracticability, and that any excusal on religious grounds would introduce religious divisiveness into the public schools and establish religion. A District Court agreed with the parents, but the School Board has appealed. The Jewish community ought to be supporting the parents, but those groups which have filed (AJCommittee and ADL) have filed friend-of-the-court briefs in support of the school board, some of whose submissions in support of reversal appear to fly in the face of the pluralism it purports to defend.

Courts are still grappling with religious symbols on public property. Creches still continue to fare badly, although one federal district judge did allow a creche to stand in Chicago City Hall, in part on the theory that America is a Christian country. (An appeal is pending.) For the first time, there was extensive litigation concerning Lubavitch's national campaign to erect menorahs on public lands. The results were mixed in the courts, but several appeals are pending.

For the first time in recent years, there have been challenges to the use of sectarian agencies to provide government funded social services. In *Kendrick v. Bowen*, a District Court invalidated at least portions of the Adolescent Family Life Act, which allowed church groups to provide sex education classes. And in *Wilder v. Sugarman*, a District Court upheld, over the objections of Jewish and Catholic child care agencies, a consent decree which in effect prohibits the City of New York from placing children with sectarian agencies who prefer children of their own faith in admissions. Appeals are either pending, or will be brought shortly, in both of these cases.

There were two important aid-to-pariochial school aid cases decided within the last year. In both, Hasidic groups sought to have constitutionally permissible forms of aid delivered to them in ways compatible with their separatist religious views. In *Parents Association v. Quinones*, the Court held that remedial services could not be provided to Hasidic girls on a sex and religious segregated basis in a functioning public school. The decision, while quite possibly correct, is marked by a tone of hostility, almost bias, toward Hasidim.

In *Bollenbach v. Board of Education*, a District Court held that a Hasidic boys school could not insist that bus drivers provided by the board of education be assigned in conformity with the school's religious beliefs about the separation of the sexes. In both cases, the court reasoned that acceding to the Hasidic requests would suggest, either to the Hasidim or outsiders, an official endorsement of Hasidic practice. They suggested as well that either accommodation would impose too great costs on affected third parties. Further litigation of this type is pending in several states as school districts grapple with the decisions in *Aguilar v. Felton* (1985-86 Term).

Continuing and Urgent Issues

National Jewish Community Relations Advisory Council

Jews in Arab and Moslem Countries

The position of the small Jewish communities remaining in the Arab and Moslem countries of the Middle East and North Africa continues to be precarious. They may at any time be threatened by a sudden change of regime, by arbitrary actions of the rulers or by violence on the part of individuals or groups who choose to scapegoat Jews when local or regional tensions erupt. During 1985 three Jews were killed and 11 others wounded while attending Simhat Torah services in Jerba, Tunisia, when a crazed security guard opened fire. The Tunisian Prime Minister attributed his action to the influence of a renewed campaign of radio broadcasts from Qadaffi's Libya calling on Tunisians to kill the Jews and overthrow the pro-Western régime, following Israel's raid on the PLO's headquarters. In Lebanon, seven prominent members of the Jewish community in Beirut were kidnapped, of whom four were murdered by Shiite fundamentalist bands; efforts to obtain release of others have thus far been unsuccessful. Rumors of a recent large-scale pogrom and mass conversion of Jews in North Yemen proved to be unfounded. However, Yemeni Jews remain largely isolated and they, like the larger Jewish community in Syria, are denied the right to emigrate. Travel from Iran is severely restricted and there are fears for the future of the Jewish community should Khomeini pass from the scene. These conditions must be closely monitored; whatever responses are required should be undertaken on the basis of interagency consultation and coordination.

Holocaust Programming

Four decades after the Holocaust even more needs to be done to convey a deeper understanding of the Holocaust's meaning. A major focus of the Jewish community should be on what programs are required to more effectively deepen the understanding of the lessons of the Holocaust, especially an awareness about the conditions that brought it about. The waning of the immediacy of the events, the aging of the generation of survivors and actual witnesses, the coming of age of post-war generations, and the troubling emergency of "historical revisionists" who seek to cloak in scholarly garb their assertions that the Holocaust did not occur, make the task of educating the public about the Holocaust's history and meaning all the more difficult but even more compelling. This vital educational effort should be undertaken on an ongoing basis, particularly in public and private schools, in the media, and in special observances on notable occasions.

Nazi War Criminals

A number of recent events have focused wide attention on the need for continued efforts to bring Nazi war criminals to justice. Perhaps the most noted development was the series of accusations that former U.N. Secretary General Kurt Waldheim had been a member of Nazi student organizations during the 1930s, and that following World War II the Yugoslav government had listed him as a war criminal in connection with German army actions taken against anti-Nazi partisans and civilians. Also notable was the conclusion to a 40-year search for Dr. Josef Mengele, Auschwitz's infamous "angel of death." Of special significance was the extradition of John Demjanjuk to Israel to stand trial for alleged war crimes. Identified by Holocaust survivors as a Treblinka guard known as "Ivan the Terrible," Demjanjuk is accused of having operated the death camp's gas chambers and crematoria. His extradition followed a successful federal prosecution and a Supreme Court ruling upholding previous federal court decisions stripping him of U.S. citizenship and ordering his extradition. Similarly, the Justice Department's Office of Special Investigations' action against Andrija Artukovic ended in extradition to Yugoslavia of the former Interior Minister of the Nazi-controlled puppet state of Croatia. Artukovic is alleged to be responsible for ordering the deaths of more than 200,000 Yugoslavs, including much of that nation's pre-war Jewish community. Additional prosecutions and appeals of prosecutions are either in progress or can be expected during the coming year. Continued education within the Jewish and general communities about the Holocaust, its perpetrators and their crimes is essential to assure effective continuation of the Justice Department's investigation, deportation, and denaturalization work and to counter the efforts of some ethnic groups to curtail the Justice Department's work.

Famine in Africa

World attention has focused on the catastrophic famine sweeping across much of sub-Saharan Africa, threatening over 150 million people. Many countries, including the United States, have responded with famine relief, which will continue to be critically needed throughout the coming year. But a long-term production crisis, reaching beyond the immediate famine into the next decade, may be anticipated. The Jewish community should continue to urge massive American famine relief for the threatened populations of Africa, and support concerted international governmental efforts to assist African countries in addressing long-term structural, agricultural and ecological problems.

Why Are So Many Young Jews Alienated from Judaism and the Jewish People?

Dennis Prager and Joseph Telushkin

> Many Jewish parents claim . . . that they gave their children everything that they did not have as children. The problem is, however, that the parents did not give what they *did* have as children—a basically Jewish environment.

Next to the survival of Israel the issue that weighs heaviest upon Jews is the loss of Jewish identity among many young Jews. "How can we bring our youth back?" is probably the most oft-posed question in American Jewish life: study groups, symposia, and commissions are constantly being organized to answer this question. Yet too often we attempt to "bring them back" without understanding why young Jews have left, or as we believe, why they were never really with us. We must first understand what has caused the alienation of many youth from the Jewish religion and community.

The essential problem underlying this rejection of Jewish identity can be summarized in a single sentence. For the great majority of young Jews who abandon Jewish identity, it is not Judaism but a caricature of Judaism that they are rejecting.

The Caricature

Instead of portraying Judaism as the all-encompassing value system and way of life which it is, most parents and institutions today treat Judaism as if it were a pastime, an adjunct to the other, really important, things in one's life. Most Jewish parents repeatedly convey the impression that Judaism is of secondary importance. This can be illustrated in a variety of ways.

Let us, for example, visit a typical Jewish home on the day when the promising young college junior or senior announces what profession he or she has chosen to pursue upon graduation. The proud Jewish parents are undoubtedly waiting to hear whether their child has decided on law, or medicine, or architecture, or one of the other professions which so many of our young Jews enter. But, alas, in this particular home, the young Jew reveals that he wishes to become a Jewish educator or enter the rabbinate or some other Jewish profession. After recuperating from their shock, the parents will probably protest loud and long against this decision which contradicts values they have been reinforcing throughout their careers as parents: viz., *what type of professional their child becomes is of far greater significance than what type of Jew he or she becomes.* And because Jewish parents have been far more interested in producing accomplished professionals than accomplished Jews, the Jewish community suffers from a surfeit of accomplished professionals who are alienated Jews. The irony is that later in life, many of these parents are saddened by the product which they so diligently molded. How often we hear of parents speaking of their "wonderful son" the lawyer, doctor or professor only to add softly "who doesn't care about being Jewish." The pursuit of a profession is, however, only one of the areas in which young Jews are taught that Judaism is of secondary importance.

The Greater Importance of Non-Jewish Values

Another reason young Jews become convinced that Judaism is of little consequence is that fearing that their children will become "too Jewish," many parents hold an attitude which may be called pseudo-universalism. This view posits that Jews must not smack of provincialism by raising their children with "too Jewish" an education, or in "too Jewish" a home, but must expose them to as many non-Jewish cultures as possible so that they may become "universal" and freely choose the lifestyle they want.

That such an approach to a Jewish child will produce an alienated Jew should be obvious. Unless deeply immersed in a minority culture, why would anyone choose to identify with that culture? There is no reason for any young Jew who is not raised in a profoundly Jewish environment to reject assimilation into the majority non-Jewish culture.

But this mode of raising a child will not only fail to produce a committed Jew, it will not produce a universalist either. The truly universal individual is first deeply rooted in a *particular* form of expression. The greatest literature, for example, is grounded in the individual, provincial, and national experience of the author. Dostoevsky knew and wrote about the Russian soul, not about everyone else's, yet individuals of every nationality read and learn from Dostoevsky's Russians.

To become a universal Jew one must first be an accomplished Jew. The attempt to be universal without roots in any particular culture does not make one universal, but merely alienated and confused. A Jew should understand and respect other religio-ethical systems,* but he must first know and live his own. If we studied everyone else's traditions and abandoned our own, we would not have increased tolerance, only fewer traditions.

As for "choosing," on what basis could a child, exposed to many differing systems of ethics, be expected to make an intelligent choice? By what standard can he measure differing religio-ethical concepts? When raised by parents who advocate universalism without particularism, a child has no standard by which to judge various lifestyles.

Many young Jews are raised in homes which communicate few clear-cut standards, and no distinctly Jewish standards. Therefore, many young Jews, lacking a strong value system, fall prey to any ideology that catches their imagination, or simply stand for nothing except self-expression.

In other crucial areas of their child's development, do parents present the child with a multiplicity of choices? Do they ask their children: "Do you want to brush your teeth, or would you prefer not to?" "Do you wish to attend school, or would you rather stay at home?" In any of these instances it would be absurd to offer choices to children, but in the words of Norman Lamm, "... a way of life that will determine whether existence has meaning, whether [the child] is rooted in history or not, whether morality is binding, whether hope and destiny are real or illusions—this any child may choose for himself."

The Greater Importance of Non-Jewish Education

Non-Jewish values are further reinforced by the manner in which we educate Jewish youth. By relegating Jewish education to a few hours per week for a few years (usually until bar mitzvah, precisely the age when a child can begin to intellectually appreciate Judaism), we eloquently tell our children that we deem math, grammar, and social studies—all of which are studied more hours per week than Judaism—of greater significance than Jewish history, philosophy, religion, and ethics. Furthermore, the unimportance of Judaism implied by the small quantity of Jewish study is confirmed by the generally low quality of Jewish education.

Most young Jews are given Jewish education equivalent to between a third- and eighth-grade level, and then are expected to compare Judaism favorably with high-school-level and later university-level secular humanism, Marxism, or other philosophical systems.

Just as a poor education in chemistry will produce poor chemists or no chemists, so a poor Jewish education will produce poor Jews or no Jews; and the chances of alienation from Jewish identity increase even more in the proportion that secular education surpasses in time and quality Jewish education.

Alienation From Strongly Jewish Homes

Less common but even sadder than the alienation of Jewish children who come from Jewishly inactive homes is the alienation of children raised in homes that are Jewishly active. Of these there are two major types: homes committed to Jewish causes but which are not religious, and homes which are also committed religiously.

Secular Homes

Many Jewish parents assume that their own deep attachments to the Jewish people should suffice to ensure that their children will retain a strong Jewish identity. Thus, one often hears parents lament something like this: "We can't understand how our child could intermarry (or follow a guru ... or join up with radical—sometimes even anti-Israel—political groups ... or care so little about being a Jew ...); we gave so much to the UJA (or devoted so much time to Hadassah ... or have such strong Jewish feelings ...)."

Unfortunately, little comfort can be offered to these parents. It is extremely difficult to undo the mistakes which parents have been making for twenty years. But in order to help prevent repetition of such problems, it is important to try to understand where these parents went wrong.

At the outset, let us acknowledge one fact unequivocally. To ensure the Jewish identity of one's children, it is not enough to work diligently for a Jewish organization, contribute to Jewish causes, cry at Jewish tragedies, or possess a "Jewish heart." For while these aspects are noble and just as essential to Jewish survival as Jewish religious observance, they do not implant a strong Jewish identity in one's children.

One reason for this insufficiency is that children often do not perceive communal service as emanating from a particularly deep and sincere commitment to Jewish life, but rather as emanating from some professional, social, or other need. Moreover, even when this work does in fact spring from a deep Jewish commitment, it may have little meaning for the child. For if the parents' entire Jewish identity is at the Federation office or at the Hadassah Luncheon, what does the child experience Jewishly himself, at home? What distinctly Jewish values have these parents taught their children? While becoming expert at *how* the Jewish people can survive, few of these parents gave thought to the basic question their children wanted answered: *Why* should the Jews survive?

At the root of this problem lies another. Many Jewish parents claim, half in pride and half in sorrow, that they gave their children everything that they did not have as children. The problem is, however, that Jewish parents did not give what many of them *did* have as children—a basically Jewish environment.

The great majority of Jewish parents who work for or contribute to Jewish causes out of a deep Jewish feeling acquired that feeling by being raised in a more or less Jewish environment. Had they given more thought to it, these parents would have realized the necessity of creating such an environment for their own children.

As a result of the materially insecure existence of their childhood, many Jewish parents concentrated on providing only for the material needs of themselves and their children. As we know now, however, affluence breeds at least as many problems as it solves. When people do not have to worry about their next meal or a roof over their heads, they have time to worry about themselves and about such abstract questions as "What is the meaning of my life?" Our generation can well appreciate the biblical observation that "not by bread alone shall man live." We are the most affluent generation in human history—and quite possibly the most troubled by being unable to find meaning in life. When the needs for food and companionship are fulfilled, the greatest human craving is for meaning.

Thus, instead of reducing the need for a meaningful and spiritual way of life, affluence and modern technology have immeasurably increased it. The sad spectacle of youths from affluent homes who are utterly lost and fall prey to peddlers of pseudo-spirituality (e.g., "revolutionary" and "underground" movements) confirms this fact.

Religious Homes

Though less frequent, the alienation of Jewish children raised in religious homes is not uncommon. This alienation rarely includes a total abandonment of Jewish identity, though it can lead to that. Alienation from religious homes often stems from, or at least includes, a strong psychological component. Rejection of the religious beliefs and practices of one's parents is often but one part of a larger rejection of parental influence or one manifestation of a general rebellion against the home. Although important, however, such psychological considerations do not fall into our present area of discussion.

We must consider the rational and religious reasons for a child's rejection of his or her parents' religious observance. There are children from observant homes who come to view their parents' religious observance as little more than meaningless rituals based upon blind belief. While it is true that some children are content to continue religious practice out of habit, others who are blessed (or cursed) with intellectual curiosity will, as soon as they are exposed to the nonobservant world, begin to radically question the religion of their upbringing; and they may eventually conclude that their parents' religion consists of habits that are not any more worthy of perpetuation than their parents' other "personal" habits.

It is, therefore, essential for observant Jewish parents who live in contemporary society to fulfill at least two requirements in order to ensure that their children will continue to be observant. First, they must exemplify the ideals that Jewish law seeks to realize. Observant parents must be able to show that Jewish practice raises their level of idealism and ethics above the average person's; otherwise, their children may regard their observance, and thus Judaism in general, as irrelevant, or even a barrier, to a moral or meaningful life.

Second, observant parents must be prepared to offer reasoned and meaningful answers to their children's questions. Certainly once a child reaches his or her teens, it is not enough to answer questions with "because that's what the Torah says." One of the uniquely impressive aspects of Judaism is that the religious Jew need not abandon reason. There are reasons to practice Judaism and there are answers to the questions which young Jews ask. It is the responsibility of parents to teach their children Judaism with reason as well as with passion.

We are living in a free society, in a huge marketplace of ideas. Young Jews are free to choose from among the many ideas and ways of life offered to them. We believe that Jews should deeply welcome this development, for Judaism is the most powerful idea in history as well as a beautiful way of life. Until a great many more Jews, young and old, articulate this appreciation, however, the problem of alienation will continue to be a crippling one.

A Note to Parents Concerning Intermarriage

A prominent rabbi told us once that he had been called about three hundred times in the last decade by frantic parents imploring him to break up the impending intermarriage of their son or daughter. He agreed every time to meet the person, yet he succeeded exactly once in dissuading the person from marrying the non-Jew.

This negligible rate of success may prompt one to dismiss this rabbi as lacking powers of persuasion. Yet, this man, Shlomo Riskin, formerly rabbi of Lincoln Square Synagogue in New York City, is one of the most dynamic and persuasive figures in Jewish religious life today. The number of young Jews he has attracted to Judaism is staggering. How then does one account for this inability to prevent prospective intermarriages?

The answer is sadly simple. Parents who approach a rabbi concerning the imminent intermarriage of their child are usually showing serious interest in their child's Judaism about twenty years too late. By this time, their son or daughter is already in love with a non-Jew, and the only obstacle to their child's complete happiness may be a guilty feeling that if he or she intermarries, "my parents would be distraught." But this will not ultimately affect their decision to intermarry, because they will refuse to sacrifice real feelings of love for vague feelings of guilt.

In most cases, the parents' approach to the rabbi, and their other efforts to prevent their child's intermarriage, constitute the first time that they have ever shown passionate interest in their child's Jewish identity. It appears quite odd to the child that all of a sudden Judaism, which until now was treated as a pastime, has become the parents' greatest passion. Had these parents shown a fraction of this Jewish commitment during the previous twenty years, their child would have taken Judaism more seriously and have become a less likely candidate for intermarriage.

Though numerous studies have confirmed the fact, one need not be a sociologist to recognize that intermarriage is rendered far more likely in homes which communicate the caricatured Judaism described in the first part of this article than in homes which live an active Judaism. Of course, one can point to the exceptional cases wherein children of actively Jewish homes have intermarried, but such pointing has no point. One can also point to instances wherein seat belts failed to save the lives of passengers in automobile accidents, but just as these instances do not negate the fact that seat belts save lives, so the exceptions do not negate the fact that actively Jewish homes save Jews.

Children from homes that constantly communicate by words and deeds that the Jewish people has a mission and that Judaism has distinctive values worthy of perpetuation are unlikely to intermarry simply because they are unlikely to find non-Jews (or, for that matter, many Jews) who share their values. If they should happen to find such a non-Jew, this is no problem, since the religion allows for conversion to Judaism.

The issue of intermarriage also reveals an interesting irony in Jewish life. When asked to characterize observant Jews, other Jews will often refer to them as "provincial," "closed minded," and "too Jewish." Yet it is most instructive to note what arguments against intermarriage these two types of Jews can offer their children. The secular "universalist" is compelled to use family or ethnic arguments—true parochialism—whereas the religious "parochialist" can offer arguments which appeal to idealism rather than ethnicity ("Does he or she share your values?").

The arguments against intermarriage of the less committed Jews are often ultimately rooted in the expressed or unexpressed opinion that Jews are superior as a people (otherwise why not intermarry, since they obviously do not consider Judaism superior). Yet no seriously committed Jew should argue (or believe) that Jews are inherently superior. He should instead argue that Judaism is a superior system, and only insofar as a Jew inculcates this system is he or she more likely to be a moral person. Thus, whereas the Jew who lives Judaism can use logical arguments by appealing to a young person to perpetuate ties rooted in ideals, other Jews can only make an emotional appeal to perpetuate ties rooted in blood.

Numerous experiences have proven to us that it is never too late to begin to study and live Judaism, and thereby eventually influence a child. If you are asking your child to make a life-changing decision, you must do the same. Otherwise your words will be as futile as they are (unintentionally) hypocritical.

Even if your son or daughter *seems* completely alienated from Judaism, or is actually planning to marry a non-Jew, or even if he or she has already intermarried, it may not be too late to influence him or her—and the non-Jewish spouse—to consider Judaism as a way of life. Of course, your ability to influence anyone depends upon your own commitment.

Conclusion

Mature people are open to new ideas, and Judaism may be characterized as a new idea for most Jews. Even many non-Jews who are married to Jews are receptive to studying Jewish philosophy, history, and theology and to begin to experiment with Judaism as a way of life, when it is presented with sophistication and warmth. We (the authors) have both met many men and women who after conversion to Judaism became leaders in their Jewish communities. We have also met a large number of people who, though born Jewish, came to take Judaism seriously only later in their lives, and who likewise developed into communal leaders.

Thus, it is never definitely too late. After seeing you infuse your life with deeper meaning, your children may also reassess their priorities and eventually realize the error of raising children without historical rootedness and without a religious-ethical way of life. We cannot, of course, promise any miracles. We can only promise you that if you show no commitment to changing your life, you will be offering little reason to your children to change theirs.

*This encouragement to study other systems does not represent a departure from Jewish tradition. Maimonides gratefully acknowledged his debt to Aristotle, while Bahya Ibn Pakudah (whose medieval *Hovot ha-Levovot,* "Duties of the Heart," is still studied in yeshivot throughout the world) not only learned from Sufi Muslim teachers but referred to them as *hasidim,* "pious men" (see Introduction to his book). Today, Rabbi Joseph Ber Soloveitchik, perhaps the greatest living Talmudist, acknowledges the influence of Soren Kierkegaard, the nineteenth-century Protestant theologian, on his own thought.

20

The Things They Say Behind Your Back: Stereotypes About Jews—Part II

William B. Helmreich

The Jewish Mother

> The story is told of a Jewish mother who went to the beach with her son and daughter-in-law. The son, a physician, swam a bit too far away from shore and began struggling in the water as he tried to make his way to safety. His mother, in an effort to attract attention to his plight, began running up and down the beach screaming at the top of her lungs, "Help! Somebody please help! My son, the Great Neck psychiatrist, he's drowning!"

Humor of this genre, depicting the Jewish mother obsessed with the status of her children, is almost passe by now. It received a great boost in popularity with the success of Philip Roth's novel *Portnoy's Complaint,* which sold several million copies. In it, Sophie Portnoy is described as overprotective, pushy, aggressive, and guilt-inducing. To some extent such adjectives could be ascribed to Italian mothers, Black mothers, and Puerto Rican mothers, all of whom share the anxieties and concerns emanating from minority status. It is, however, the Jewish mother that has been accorded the rather dubious distinction of stereotype par excellence. The answer may lie in an understanding of Jewish culture.

Judaism has always placed tremendous importance on home, family, and especially on children, who are seen as the center of family life. The task of child rearing was primarily the woman's responsibility. Although this was true of other cultures too, Judaism turned this role into a tremendous virtue. Both the Bible and the Talmud are full of references to this function. A good example is the poem "Woman of Valor" in Proverbs, attributed to King Solomon: "She looks well to the ways of her household, and never eats the bread of idleness. Her children rise up and bless her . . ." By ennobling the woman and making her feel secure as a wife and mother, Judaism ensured that she would take her responsibilities very seriously. Restricted to the home, the mother turned all her energies to the family.

In difficult economic times her role became even more important. When, as was the case with East European immigrants who came to this country around the turn of the century, the husband was forced to work long hours away from home, the mother occupied a central place in the lives of her children. It is here that the guilt factor became important. Having made a major contribution to the upbringing of her offspring, she was able to gain not only their affection but also their loyalty and dependence. Her children were often imbued with a strong sense of guilt when they failed to measure up to the expectations of their mother, who "worked so hard so that *you* should be happy." The values transmitted to the child were rooted in the strong sense of morality that permeated the culture. A mother said to her child, "Eat for the sake of your parents, who love you and want only the best for you. Study so that your parents will be proud of you." Thus the biblical notion of responsibility for others became part of the secular belief system.

If Jewish mothers (and fathers as well) pushed and fought for their children and taught them never to be satisfied ("So you got a 98. But who got the 100?"), it was in large part due to their perception of a world hostile to their kind. Since their names were not Stuart or Baker or Blake, it was necessary to give them strong egos. Only then would they have the confidence to offset the disadvantages of their religion. Unfortunately, this was sometimes carried too far, with the child brought up to think of himself or herself (the Jewish Prince and Jewish Princess syndromes) as number one.

The general view held by many non-Jews (as well as Jews who seem almost proud of it) is that Jewish parents spoil their children. In one community study, the sociologist Benjamin Ringer reported the following attitudes of Gentile parents in a Chicago suburb toward their Jewish neighbors:

> Jewish parents . . . let them [children] run wild in the stores without reprimanding them. They don't care how much trouble they cause, they don't punish them enough . . . they're always Mama's angel . . . [They] raise their children to feel superior to Gentile children either materially or else purely defensively . . . For example, my gun is better than yours. My house is better . . . My daughter came home from a Jewish home and asked why we didn't have seven telephones. (*The Edge of Friendliness,* pp. 71-72)

Such indulgence can perhaps best be understood in light of the heavy demands Jewish parents make upon their children in other areas. Because they expect so much from their children in terms of getting good grades, being admitted to the right school, marrying well, and so forth, the parents compensate in other areas, buying them what they want, letting them talk back, and generally pampering them. This often leads to overprotectiveness. The Jewish mother has therefore been immortalized in countless jokes and novels as the woman who asphyxiates her child in warm clothing, drowns him in chicken soup, and is constantly yelling at him to put on his galoshes.

No one has yet interviewed a thousand Jewish and Gentile mothers to ascertain the validity of this stereotype, though its extensive use as a focal point by many Jews in their own writings does seem to give it a stamp of authenticity. Whatever the case, it ought to be noted that being brought up in this fashion must have some positive points if one is to judge by the considerable success enjoyed by Jews as a group. If nothing else, delaying independence in the child tends to increase the education level of many children by increasing the amount of time they will spend in school. More fundamentally, the fact that the Jewish parent lets his children know how much he believes in them can often be a crucial factor in their ultimate success and confidence in themselves. Finally, the strong family structure gives the Jew a strong sense of family responsibility, thus giving rise to yet another Jewish stereotype—that Jews make good husbands. Whether or not this is true awaits further study in a more extended treatment of the subject.

The Jewish mother has also been given much of the credit for producing the whining, self-indulgent, and "I'm God's gift to the world" daughter, otherwise known as the JAP (Jewish American Princess). Since the son's fulfillment came from "the real world" where he became an attorney, a doctor, or a partner in the business with his father-in-law, all that was left for the daughter was fancy clothes, nose jobs (the excuse is usually a deviated septum, but everyone knows better), marrying well, and knowing how to "set a table" (with the help of a maid or two, of course). Unlike their own mothers, the JAPs who "married rich" no longer found it necessary to achieve fulfillment in the home, turning instead to shopping expeditions at Bloomingdale's or Bergdorf's (Rich's in Atlanta; Stix, Baer, and Fuller in St. Louis; etc.), brunches with fellow JAPs, tennis, Mah-Jongg, trips to art galleries and museums for the more intellectually inclined, and, of course, the weekly trip to the therapist and the daily call to mother.

It is, however, unlikely that the characteristics attributed to the Jewish mother, or the above caricature of the JAP, will survive beyond the present generation. In fact, they are dying out rather quickly. More and more Jewish mothers are career-oriented, and this competing interest threatens the structure of the child-centered family. Indeed, young Jewish women who become doctors and lawyers are apt to find that the self-confidence developed in a supportive environment serves them well in their chosen field. They are more likely to view the notion of "everything for the children" as archaic. Psychiatry and psychology have also contributed heavily to the demise of these stereotypes by frowning upon guilt and dependence and by encouraging their patients, Jewish or Gentile, to assert themselves and do what makes them "feel good." Finally, assimilation and intermarriage (currently estimated at over 40 percent) will result in a dilution of those attitudes toward the family that spring from Jewish culture.

The "Chosen People"

> For you are a holy people unto the Lord your God: of all the peoples that are on the face of the earth, the Lord your God has chosen you to be his treasured people. (Deut. 7:6)

The story is told of how God offered the Torah to several other nations before turning to the Jews, all of whom rejected it as too restrictive. The Jews, according to the legend, accepted it unquestioningly, agreeing to be bound by its commandments even before they knew what these commandments were. Such acceptance implied a special responsibility but did not mean superiority. Thus one can understand the response to the English writer Hilaire Belloc's quip, "How odd of God to choose the Jews," that "It was not odd—the Jews chose God."

Regardless of who chose whom, there is certainly a kernel of truth to this theory, for many Jews, especially those who are observant, believe that God has a special relationship with "His people." Many view their meticulous observance of the hundreds of biblical commandments as meriting special consideration from God. In addition, Jews have used the idea of being chosen to explain the suffering and cruelties to which they were so often subjected by other peoples. It was often only by seeing himself as destined to play a special role in the world or in the hereafter that the Jew was able to justify his suffering.

Support for the concept of chosenness comes also from Christian fundamentalists, who cite such evidence as the survival of the Jews through the ages despite the efforts of others to destroy them, their success in so many areas, and the rebirth of the State of Israel. In his book *Israel's Final Holocaust,* noted evangelist Dr. Jack Van Impe writes:

> Frederick the Great said: "No nation ever persecuted the Jew and prospered." His correct observation is proof of God's faithfulness in keeping His promise to Abraham . . . This tiny scattered people has had such a definite date with destiny that no power on earth could destroy them (pp. 56, 59).

If the Jews are "chosen," they are not unique in this sense. After all, Christianity and Islam, as well as most other religions, hold out the promise of divine grace and salvation only to believers. By contrast, Judaism believes that "all the righteous of the world have a place in the world to come." Nevertheless, it ought to be recognized that no faith or doctrine can demand the undivided loyalty of its adherents unless it believes its members occupy a special place in the scheme of life.

In modern times, as Jews have increased their contact with people outside their community, many leaders have become increasingly sensitive to this stereotype. Some have responded by asking, tongue in cheek, whether being chosen is such a great privilege when one considers that the Jews have been persecuted for so many centuries and have only recently been able to re-establish their homeland. Others have taken concrete steps to deal with the term by specifically denying its validity. The Reconstructionists, one of the denominations within the Jewish faith, have eliminated all such references from their prayer book, while Orthodox Jews have repeatedly emphasized that the concept means service and accountability, not an elite status.

Smarter

It would not be accurate to say that Jews are smarter, but it would be correct to state that they are, as a group, more educated and intellectually oriented. As a result they may appear to be more intelligent. Although a positive attribute, this stereotype is considered valid even by those who dislike Jews.

Is his book *Anti-Semite and Jew,* Jean-Paul Sartre says the following:

> The antisemite readily admits that the Jew is intelligent and hardworking; he will even confess himself inferior in these respects . . . [for] the more virtues the Jew has, the more dangerous he will be.

A number of studies have shown that Jews are believed by many to be more intelligent than most people. For example, the sociologists Charles Glock and Rodney Stark found that about half of the Christians surveyed in a sample of people from various Protestant denominations agreed that "an unusual number of the world's greatest men have been Jews."

How accurate are these views? If we take Nobel Prize winners as a form of measurement, it becomes apparent that Jews are overrepresented. Throughout the world, from 1905 to 1985, 101 Jews have been awarded this coveted honor. Close to one-third of American Nobel Prize winners have been Jews. Yet Jews make up less than 3 percent of the American population. This would seem to be more than chance occurrence. It is equally unusual that the three men with the greatest impact on the twentieth century were Jews: Karl Marx, Sigmund Freud, and Albert Einstein.

One factor is that Jews as a group are very highly educated. In 1968 less than 40 percent of the college-age population was in college. For Jews the figure was twice as high. Furthermore, among those in college, Jews were considerably more likely than non-Jews to enter professions such as law, medicine, the physical sciences, dentistry, and psychology. They were also among those least likely to go into home economics, agriculture, nursing and physical therapy. Since the fields selected by Jews include most of those in which Nobel Prizes can be won, and since Jews attend college out of proportion to their numbers, their capacity to produce outstanding scholars ought not to be so surprising.

This explanation falls short, however, in one significant respect. It does not explain *why* education is so important to the Jewish community. It only tells us that it is. To understand the reasons for this emphasis, we need to go back in history to biblical times. Even as citizens in their own independent kingdom of ancient Israel, the Jews placed great value on the written word. Their lives were lived in accordance with the precepts of the Bible or Torah, a book containing numerous references to the importance of study and the education of children in particular. Typical is the verse in Proverbs: "Train a child in the way he should go, and even when he is old, he will not depart from it." With the destruction of the Temple in C.E. 70 and the loss of their country, the Torah became even more important—in fact, crucial. It was the most concrete symbol of their glorious past. By studying it and following the commandments, the Jews created a portable homeland. Since the laws were an essential part of community life, it followed that those who understood them best, namely the rabbis, were among the most highly respected members of the community. In this way learning came to be seen as a supreme value. Through the centuries it was an important source of status. Jewish families of means took pride in being able to marry off their daughters to scholars, and Jewish communities gave financial support to Jewish institutions of learning. This was particularly true in Eastern Europe, the point of emigration for most of those who immigrated to America.

Many of those Jews who came to America abandoned their religious practices, but cultural values were much harder to shed. One of the most important was the attitude toward learning. Coincidentally, education was an avenue to success in the United States, and the Jew was able to adapt to it very well. Unlike other groups, he did not have to develop respect for education; it was already part of his culture. It only remained for him to transfer the previous emphasis on religious knowledge to one that stressed secular learning. Jewish parents reinforced the education received in school by praising their children when they did well. By saying "What a smart boy you are" instead of "Look how well he hits the ball," the parent was telling his child what he needed to do in order to gain respect, admiration, and ultimately success.

Mary Antin, a Polish immigrant who came to America just before the turn of the century, is an excellent example of the passion for education that permeated the immigrant spirit. Unusual both as a woman and even by Jewish standards, she attended Barnard, had her first book published at eighteen, and eventually married a professor. Yet the dream she saw come true was shared, in varying degrees, by countless others. Listen to the words of the grocer in Antin's neighborhood as his daughter asks him:

> "Would you send me to high school, pa? . . . Would you really?"
>
> "Sure, as I'm a Jew," Mr. Rosenblum promptly replies, a look of aspiration in his deep eyes. "Only show yourself worthy and I'll keep you in school till you get to something. In America everybody can get to something, if he only wants to. I would even send you farther than high school—to be a teacher, maybe. Why not? In America everything is possible. But you have to work hard, Goldie, like Mary Antin—study hard, put your mind to it." (*The Promised Land,* pp. 352-53)

Numbers have also played a role in the emphasis placed by Jews upon intelligence. Wherever they lived, Jews were a small minority. Unlike the Irish, who were sufficiently numerous to have rebelled against their British oppressors, Jews were forced to rely upon their wits when attacked or threatened. As a result, they came to value intelligence highly. Jewish folklore is full of stories where the Jews are saved from certain annihilation because of the cleverness of the local rabbi or community leader. Sometimes, like the biblical Joseph, the duke or king demands that the Jews interpret his dreams. On other occasions they must answer a diabolically constructed riddle. Whatever the case, the story ends with Jewish brainpower defeating the oppressor's evil intentions.

So much for the cultural argument. There is also some basis for a genetic argument, unpopular as that may be. During the Middle Ages a popular avenue of upward mobility for intellectually gifted persons was the priesthood. In fact, for the sons of peasants it was the *only* way to escape their impoverished status. It was also, as the social philosopher Ernest Van Den Haag has pointed out in *The Jewish Mystique,* an attractive calling for the intellectually oriented members of the upper classes. Unfortunately, the priesthood demanded celibacy, thus taking thousands of the brightest among the Christian population out of the gene pool. The Jews, on the other hand, had no such problem. Their shining lights, the rabbis, were encouraged to marry early, and because their education enabled them to marry wealthy girls, they were often able to afford and care for larger families. Psychologists today agree, for the most part, that genetics and culture both play a role in determining intelligence as it is usually measured. They differ primarily over how much importance to give to each. Yet even if the genetic factor is important, it must be remembered that there were married Protestant ministers hundreds of years ago and their presumably bright children should have begun making up for this supposed deficiency. Furthermore, this argument is not relevant to all the other non-Christian cultures throughout the world that have produced thousands of highly intelligent individuals.

Regardless of the merits of this argument, it no longer applies today since intellectually gifted persons can and do gravitate to many professions besides the clergy. While Jews generally do better on I.Q. tests, this fact—given their cultural emphasis on learning, reasoning ability, and the acquisition of knowledge—is probably due far more to their environment than to inherited traits. It should be noted that in addition to valuing learning, the concentration of Jews in urban areas and among the middle class are two factors long associated with respect for education and a desire to attain it.

Cheap

This stereotype can perhaps best be answered with the following statement: Jews are more likely to be in business than any other ethnic group. It is a fact of economic life that the lower the cost of producing an item and the greater the sale price, the larger the profit. Any businessman, be he Jewish or a member of another group, seeks to maximize his profit. Since more Jews, proportionately, are in business, they are more likely to be accused of what is, in fact, a basic feature of capitalism.

Another factor to consider is the image of the Jew in general. As a member of a minority group about whom economic stereotypes are common, he is more apt to be accused of fulfilling them than someone else. Thus, Abraham Lincoln is considered thrifty because he saved his money, but Abraham Goldberg is considered cheap for doing the same thing because he is a Jew. A mere choice of a descriptive adjective tells the story. Another example might be the description of a hardworking man of, shall we say, Swedish origin as an individual "who wants to get ahead and is willing to do something about it." On the other hand, the Jew works hard because "he has a sweatshop mentality." These cases portray the vicious cycle of prejudice. The person who describes Jews in this manner is already biased and is actually searching for examples to justify his opinion. He does not want to be confused by facts because his mind is already made up.

The type of businesses in which Jews have traditionally been engaged ought not to be overlooked either. Perhaps the majority of businesses in which Jews are to be found involve retail trade. Examples are clothing, food, and real estate. This means that they are likely to have greater personal contact with the public than, say, those in businesses such as utilities, oil, or steel. Consequently, they will bear the brunt of consumer antagonism even though such hostility is probably a natural by-product of customer/store or management/tenant relationships.

While there is no statistical evidence of the cheapness of Jews compared to that of other groups, it can be said that they are certainly not cheap in the area of philanthropy. Jews probably give more to both their own charities and those of nonsectarian organizations than any other nationality. In his book *Why They Give,* a study of Jewish philanthropy, Milton Goldin, a professional fund-raiser, wrote as follows:

> I often spoke with colleagues who have also worked for both Jewish and nonsectarian organizations. Again and again we agreed that goals are higher . . . in Jewish organizations. Refusal to give is an affront . . . Where else are brochures largely unnecessary because contributors will give in any case?" (p. ix)

Pushy and Aggressive

Writing about social discrimination against Jews in the *American Jewish Historical Quarterly,* the prominent historian John Higham once observed:

> The Jew [who had immigrated to America] became identified as the quintessential parvenu . . . attracting attention by clamorous behavior, and always forcing his way into society that is above him. (pp. 9-10)

While it is difficult to scientifically verify whether or not Jews are physically pushier than other people, it can be said that they are, as a group, extremely ambitious and upwardly mobile. Moreover, in his book *The Jewish Mind,* the well-known anthropologist Dr. Raphael Patai reports on numerous psychological studies—such as the Bell Adjustment Inventory and Benreuter Personality Inventory—that suggest higher aggressiveness among Jews. Looked at in terms of level of education, types of occupations, value systems, and so forth, it is clear that Jews not only want to do well but are willing to go to considerable lengths to achieve success.

To some extent prejudice against Jews may bring about such behavior. Many Jews anticipate discrimination and are not surprised when it occurs. They need only reach back one or two generations for strong evidence of its existence, be it the American context, where Jews were systematically excluded from various occupations and barred from social clubs and other organizations, or in the much harsher European context, where they were victims of mass murder. As a result, they often feel the need to "do better" than the average person. This attitude can even affect the size of their families. As one Jewish parent said to me in an interview on the effects of antisemitism, "Jack and I stopped after our second child because we wanted to provide our children with the best opportunities possible. If you're Jewish you often start out with two strikes against you." Other studies that have focused on the very low birth rate of Jews have also confirmed the presence of such concerns. Such perceptions, when transmitted to children and when supported by actual discrimination, can result in compensatory behavior such as competitiveness and aggressiveness.

In some cases the emergence of such personality traits may come about as a result of the stereotype itself. The individual *knows* that certain people will see him as pushy simply because he is Jewish. Feeling that he cannot negate this view, he decides to act in accordance with it. This is, of course, known as the "self-fulfilling prophecy." On the other hand, such stereotyping is often completely false and may be employed to explain away unpleasant truths or to rationalize failure. For example, the Jew is promoted ahead of the Gentile in a company because he is "manipulative" or "a rate-buster."

Naturally, when people are prejudiced against members of a particular group, they will be acutely sensitive toward efforts by its members to win general acceptance, as in the previously quoted statement "forcing his way into society . . ." Still, it can be speculated that Jews may sometimes deliberately test the limits of tolerance by efforts to gain admission to certain clubs or to obtain employment in firms known to have few Jews. Such attempts may be accidental, but they may also be rooted in Jewish-Christian relations. From the time most of the Jews were dispersed from their homeland in A.D. 70, they became a marginal people subject to the whims and demands of their often reluctant hosts. They could be persecuted with impunity, exiled with ease, and stripped of their rights on the slightest pretext. They had no country of their own, they had not accepted Jesus as their savior, and they were generally viewed as social outcasts. Such a legacy does not die easily, and the insecurity of this type of marginality can lead to efforts on the part of the Jew to see how far he can go and whether or not he is truly accepted. Given the continued existence of prejudice, it is not surprising that at some point he will be confronted by rejection and accusations of pushiness. Lest one blame the Jew for this, it ought to be remembered that if society were truly open, such efforts would not be necessary.

Over 95 percent of all Jews in the United States live in urban areas; some have cited the pressures of urban living, including crowds and high population density, as factors in aggressiveness. If this is true, it ought not to be applied to Jews alone. Anyone walking the streets of Port-au-Prince, Calcutta, East Berlin, or any of a hundred cities throughout the world where the Jewish population is rather low will find himself jostled, pushed, and confronted by aggressive behavior. Moreover, the cities, which are often magnets for those looking to get ahead, have opportunities for the ambitious that are pursued by members of all nations, races, and faiths. This is, therefore, not a significant factor in explaining the stereotype.

Have Big Noses

> Among the Ashkenazim [European Jews] one can pick out Palestinian types that could readily be drawn from the courts of Solomon and David; Nordics to delight the eye of Julius Streicher, if he were to see them without their passports; Alpines who could yodel in any Hofbrauhaus; and Dinarics who could be Tyrolese skiers or Parisian policemen. (p. 31)

These words were written by the noted anthropologist Dr. Carleton Coon in an essay called "Have the Jews a Racial Identity?" that appeared in 1942. Many people, however, including Jews, will swear that they can "more or less" tell who is Jewish by looking at the individual's physical features. Among those likely to be cited are: a large hooked nose; swarthy complexion; dark hair, usually curly; a weak chin and eyes; hairy body; and a shorter than average stature. In fact, Jews tend to resemble the peoples in whose countries they have lived. Thus Yemenite Jews look more like Yemenite Moslems, and German Jews more like German Christians. (One indication of this reality was the Nazi party policy requiring all Jews in Germany and elsewhere to wear a Star of David or one sewn on an armband, an obviously unnecessary procedure if Jews were readily identifiable.) The reasons for this are geography, similarities in diet, and the degree of intermarriage that has occurred over a span of hundreds or even thousands of years.

Does this mean that anyone who claims the existence of a Jewish "look" is either an antisemite or a fool? Not at all. Through a phenomenon called "selective perception" we tend at times to see what we want to see. Thus, if one thinks there is such a thing as a Jewish nose, one may take special note of it when looking at a Jew who has one while conveniently ignoring other groups, such as Arabs, who do not. One social scientist actually did a study of Jewish noses in the early part of this century. Dr. Maurice Fishberg examined over four thousand noses in New York City. To the disappointment of many antisemites, especially cartoonists, and the surprise of quite a few Jews, he found that only 14 percent of those surveyed had aquiline or hooked noses. The rest had noses that were categorized as straight, snub, flat, or broad.

To be sure, there are probably hundreds of thousands of Jews with curly hair and larger than average noses who came from countries such as Poland, Germany, Holland, and elsewhere where such features are not that representative of the general population. There are, however, *millions* of non-Jews throughout the world with identical features. Nevertheless, to deny the existence of any genetic similarities among Jews would be too extreme a statement, for there have been studies suggesting certain commonalities. For instance, Dr. Patai observes in *The Myth of the Jewish Race* that an examination of the fingerprint whorls of Yemenite, Moroccan, and other Sephardic Jews demonstrates that they are more similar to those of European Jews than to non-Jews from their own native lands. This suggests, says Patai, that while Jews today differ greatly in physical features, they do have a certain residue of Mediterranean traits. Such features, when they appear among Jews, are likely to be traceable to the fact that the Jews originated in that part of western Asia Minor where Semitic people lived. Thus, the answer to whether or not there is a Jewish race or look must be yes and no, depending on which Jew you are looking at.

21

The Relevance of Judaism

Dennis Prager

1. Doing good: "Is it right?"

I have inherited from Judaism, from my upbringing, and from personal experience, a preoccupation, perhaps even an obsession, with questions of right and wrong. Innumerable times per day, my mind hears the question, "Is it right?"—from great macro-issues like abortion and Afghanistan to relatively trivial micro-issues such as using restaurant stubs for tax write-offs or the use of canned laughter on TV comedy shows.

This may all sound trite, but the fact is that all of us have an uncanny ability to avoid asking "Is it right?"

Examples abound.

Many of us ask whether our intentions are good rather than whether the act intended will actually achieve good. The horrors of Communism bear witness to the ability of good intentions to produce holocausts.

Or we may ask "How do I feel about it?" rather than "Is it right?" This has become the operative question for many who have adopted the worldview of the Sixties. And many parents from that time continue to raise their children with "How do you feel about it?" rather than "Is it right?"

Still others will substitute "What is the law?" for "Is it right?" This substitution characterizes the ACLU and parts of the Jewish spectrum.

Some Christians, heirs of Luther's thinking in particular, and apparently most Moslems, substitute "Is my faith right?" for "Is it right?"

And, of course, most well-educated people, Jews included, ask "Do I think it is right?" rather than "Does God think it is right?" More on this below.

All of these substitutions for "Is it right?" are made by well-intentioned individuals. For others, "Is it right?" is simply not an issue. For them, "What does it do for me?" and "Can I get away with it?" are the only considerations.

Precisely because it is so easy to avoid asking "Is it right?", its paramount importance cannot be stressed too often. And once the primacy of doing good is granted, other beliefs flow logically.

2. It is more natural for people to do bad than to do good.

If we do want to do good, become good, and make a better world, we had better know with what raw material we are working. People are capable of the most beautiful acts of kindness and selflessness. But acts of goodness are not our most natural inclinations. It is more natural to be selfish than to be selfless; cheating is more tempting than honesty; it is easier to ignore evil than to fight it; adultery is more natural than fidelity.

This view of humanity is not cynical. It is simply a reality that men of wisdom have always acknowledged. What divides the cynic from the realist is the question, can people be made better? The cynic says no. Along with other non-cynics, I say yes.

Therefore, my primary question in evaluating any religion or philosophy is: how does it intend to make people better, and to what extent has it succeeded in doing so?

3. People must be taught to be good.

Since people are not basically good, the most important thing we can teach every new generation is to be good. Unfortunately, partially because our humanist culture posits that people are basically good, we rarely teach our young people to be good. We teach them everything except this, thinking that all that people need in order to be and do good are a loving upbringing and a good (value-free) education.

Our grandparents were less educated but often wiser. To them, raising a child with no moral education at school, and little discipline at home would have been unthinkable. Yet to this generation, giving our children good chemistry labs has been deemed far more important than giving them ethical, let alone religious, instruction. Thus we have produced a record-breaking number of good lawyers, good doctors, and good Ph.D.'s, but not very many good people. We will pay the consequences.

4. Ethics must be based on God.

It is not possible to prove that God exists. But we can show that if God does not exist, neither does an objective morality. If, in the ultimate analysis, it is not God who says, "Do not murder," then we have no way of knowing that murder is evil. All we can say is that we do not like it.

If good and evil do not emanate from a moral source infinitely higher than each of us, then each of us is the source of morality for himself. Right and wrong then become matters of personal, subjective taste: "What you think is good is good for you, and what I think is good is good for me." By this thinking, Hitler's morality is as valid as Mother Teresa's.

So much for the theoretical need for God. Practically speaking, the need is even more obvious. As Dostoevsky put it in *The Brothers Karamazov,* "Where there is no God, all is permitted." This statement should be placed on the doorposts of every home. People must see themselves as accountable for their actions to something higher than themselves. That something is either God or the state. Either people police themselves (by feeling answerable to God) or the state has to police them).

Of course, I am aware of atrocities committed in the name of God. Every Jew is painfully aware of centuries of horrible Jewish suffering at the hands of believing Christians, and, to a somewhat lesser extent, Moslems. But the fact that religious people have committed evil in no way negates the need for a God-based morality. Indeed, the very Jews who suffered most from other religions were the least likely to deny God and Judaism. They understood that to deny God because of what *non-Jews* had done to them would be the height of idiocy. First, it would simply render those antisemites victorious, but even more importantly, it would negate the whole purpose of Jewish survival which is to bring the world to the God who demands ethical conduct from everyone. Only modern secular Jews, who have suffered the least from religious antisemites, deny God because of what Christians have done or Moslems are doing (and despite the fact that the greatest persecutors of Jews in this century have been anti-Christian and anti-religious Nazis and Communists).

To deny the moral necessity of God because of what believers have done is logically equivalent to denying the need for laws because of what Nazi and Soviet lawyers have done. The only thing that evil done in God's name proves is that belief in God does not guarantee moral behavior—which leads to my next basic belief.

5. A belief in God that is not rooted in ethics will lead to evil.

Since religious belief does not necessarily make people moral, it is absolutely necessary for a religion to hold, and for its spokesmen to preach, that God's primary (though not exclusive) demand is that His adherents do good works.

The Ayatollah Ruhollah Khomeini is murdering communities of innocent Bahais in the name of Allah because he believes that Allah is more concerned with people having the right faith than with performing the right acts. Medieval Crusaders had a similar attitude, holding that God is more interested in humanity having one form of faith than in practicing one standard of morality. They therefore murdered, in the name of Christ, untold numbers of innocent Jews and Moslems.

For these reasons, I conclude that what matters most is not what particular faith you hold so long as you believe that (1) you are morally responsible, to God, for your actions, (2) God is more concerned with the right actions than the right form of faith, and (3) God judges those people who are not of your faith by their ethics rather than by their faith alone.

This is why I believe that ethical monotheism—the doctrine that the one universal God demands that all people live by His one universal ethic—is the moral solution to the problem of evil. God without ethics and ethics without God lead to the same thing: evil. This is the Jews' message to the world, but tragically for both the Jews and the world, the Jews have become, in Abraham Joshua Heschel's brilliantly accurate description, "a messenger who forgot his message."

6. The Jews are Chosen to spread ethical monotheism.

If I did not believe that the Jews had a divinely appointed mission, I would find remaining Jewish after the Holocaust logically absurd. We are indeed God's messenger, and indeed, Jews disproportionately believe that they have a message to convey to the world. Tragically, however, those who believe this rarely believe that Judaism is the means or that ethical monotheism is that message. Rather, they believe that secularism is the means and that some other ism—Marxism, socialism, feminism, conservatism, liberalism, humanism—is the message. And those Jews who do know and live Judaism do not believe that they have a message to convey to the world. So Jews who change the world do not do so as Jews, and those who live as Jews do not try to change the world.

Our task, in the words of a prayer in the liturgy of all Jewish denominations, is: "to repair the world under God's rule." When Jews understand Judaism and this mission, they will change the world for the better. It is this belief that guides this Jew's life.

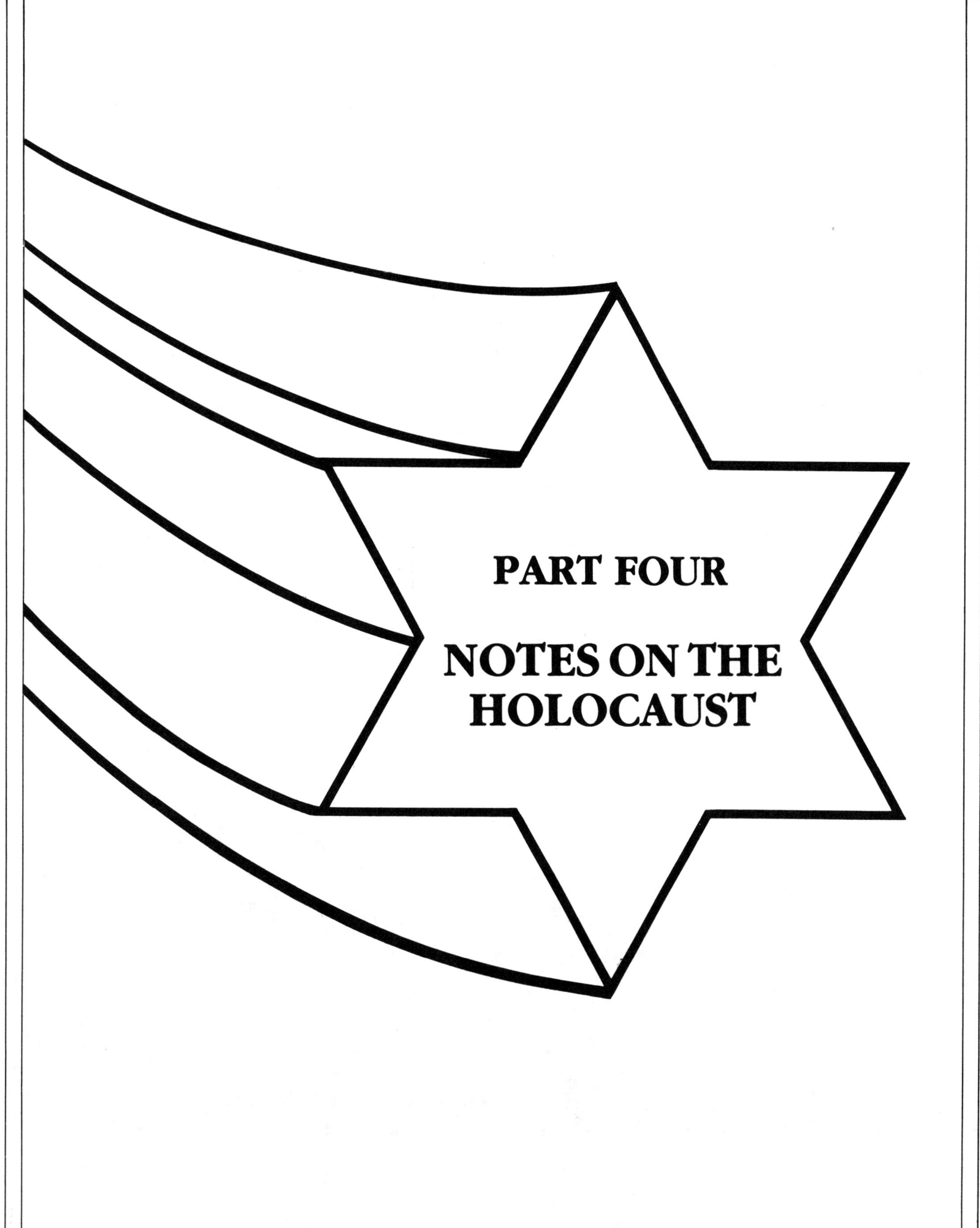

PART FOUR

NOTES ON THE HOLOCAUST

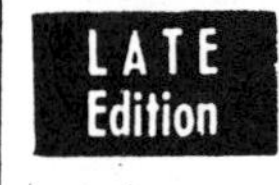

THE PALESTINE POST

JERUSALEM
SUNDAY, DEC. 16, 1945

PRICE: 15 MILS
VOL. XX, No. 5973

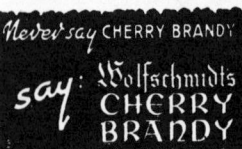

Column One

By David Courtney

WASHINGTON and Mr. Byrnes are apparently insuring against failure at Moscow. Their utterances are intended to give the impression that discussions will be informal and decisions merely provisional. They say in effect that if nothing decisive comes of Moscow no one should be surprised. Nobody will be. At the same time, despatches from London make it clear that Mr. Bevin expects something to happen, and has a pretty full dossier to draw out when he sits in front of M. Molotov. He intends to raise the central problem of Germany and, it is believed, to insist upon reaching a workable basis for the final disposal of Italian colonies and other debatable territories formerly under Italian rule. One report says that Mr. Bevin is in obstinate mood and, ready himself to lay all sorts of surprising cards on the table, is determined to force M. Molotov to display his. A Reuter message from Moscow provides further evidence to discount the American suggestion that the meeting is only to exchange views, not to unify them. It says that Persia and a settlement of the Persian problem is definitely on the agenda; and that the Russians will call for a realignment of policies in the Far East.

WHAT Moscow anticipates is indicated to a certain degree by her official and semi-official press and radio. Since the announcement of the conference of the three Foreign Secretaries, press and radio campaign have been opened affecting Persia, the Far East, Turkey, Spain, Poland and South-East Europe. The line on Persia has become much clearer. In simple terms it is this: Russia has as much right to keep her troops there as Britain to keep hers in Egypt, Palestine or Iraq, not to mention Indonesia; and since the withdrawal of all troops from Persia means virtually the political status quo, with Britain exercising supreme diplomatic influence at Teheran, the British demand that all foreign troops should clear out of the country is suspect anyway. The argument, of course, is weak; but only to those who know the facts — and even then its weakness is probably legal rather than moral. On Persia, Russia has at any rate the advantage of going to the Conference with, as it were, Azerbaijan in her pocket. Tabriz, the second town of Persia, has fallen to the Democrats and practically the whole rich province is now independent of the capital.

WHAT Russia seems to be seeking all over the world is not a balance of power on the basis of old-fashioned political and strategic values, but an equilibrium of forces designed to create stability. She regards world stability as her main defence, and probably is less avid of imperial power than anxious to diminish the imperial power of her major competitors. It is probable that she has no desire to occupy Persia; but would rather do that than submit to a frontier State under what she conceives to be the subjection of Britain. Some circles trace Russia's policy in China to the same negative source — a desire to reduce Anglo-Saxon hegemony rather than impose Soviet hegemony. If these are the facts, and there is a lot to be said for them, it looks as if there is a clear basis for international unity and collaboration; and if they are put that way to Mr. Bevin, instead of in the petulant tabulation of British troop movements appearing in Friday's "Pravda", there is some reason to hope that Britain will react. It has been said in this column before, and I repeat it now, that Britain, for all her impoverishment and financial vassalage to the United States, is still the key to world unity. She has greater flexibility than the other great powers, and her present Government has a foot in both camps. If Mr. Bevin uses the opportunity, he can raise his country's prestige and advance world progress and security. There is still a chance that he may.

WHAT, meanwhile, are we to say of the happenings in Indonesia? Not Mr. Bevin or Mr. Attlee or any other member of the Labour Government will find that easy to explain away. "Pravda" may exaggerate concerning the purpose behind the presence of British troops in Indonesia, Saigon, Egypt, Palestine and elsewhere: but nothing that can be said in malice is as bad in its effect on public opinion as such factual reports as have been published the last day or two on the burning and bombing of villages in Indo China and Java. These punitive acts cannot fail to shock progressive opinion everywhere, and to cast suspicion upon British foreign policy wherever it is applied. To be sure, far worse has been done, and is being done, by other powers; but that is not the point: the point is that far better is expected of Britain and is needful if she is to retain her voice as a moral factor in world affairs.

Jerusalem, December 16.

U.N.O. JOB FOR MRS. ROOSEVELT

WASHINGTON, Saturday (UP) Mrs. Eleanor Roosevelt is being considered by President Truman for a post with the United Nations Organization.

NAZIS ADMIT MURDERING 6 MILLION JEWS IN EUROPE

NOT ENOUGH TO SATISFY HIMMLER

By ERIC BOURNE, Reuters Special Correspondent

NUREMBERG, Saturday. — The Germans killed 6,000,000 Jews in the East, according to an S.S. Sturmbann-fuehrer (Major), Dr. Wilhelm Hoettl, whose affidavit was offered as evidence before the War Crimes Tribunal yesterday.

Hoettl's affidavit said that in August last year, he talked in Budapest with S.S. Obersturmbann-fuehrer (Lt.-Col.) Adolf Eichmann (Hebrew-speaking Nazi German born in Sarona near Tel Aviv), who "certainly had the best record of Jews who had been murdered."

Eichmann told Hoettl that he reported to Himmler that approximately 4,000,000 Jews had been killed in various extermination camps, while an additional 2,000,000 met their deaths in other ways, the majority being shot by the Security Police.

Himmler was not satisfied with this report, since in his opinion the number of Jews who had been killed must have been more than 6,000,000. "I have reasons to believe, however, that Eichmann's information was correct," Hoettl added.

Major Walsh, U.S. Deputy prosecutor, cited evidence that 1,765,000 Jews were exterminated at the Auschwitz and Birkenau death-camps, between April, 1942, and April, 1944.

According to a document from the U.S. President's War Refugee Board files, the Jews murdered were of the following nationalities:

900,000 Poles; 100,000 Dutch; 45,000 Greeks; 150,000 French; 50,000 Belgians; 60,000 Germans; 50,000 Yugoslavs, Italians and Norwegians; 50,000 Lithuanians; 30,000 Bohemians, Moravians and Austrians; 30,000 Slovaks; and 300,000 of various nationalities taken from scattered camps in Poland.

Starving of Millions

Major Walsh introduced a new series of German documents and directives clearly showing the calculated plan to starve millions of Jews to death by shutting them off from all sources of supply and certain areas, and forbidding them to participate in agriculture where they might get food.

So widespread did the executions of the Jews become that the S.S. police at Berlin wrote to Rosenberg complaining that some 5,000 Jews killed by the police and S.S. might have been used for forced labour.

The document added that it should be possible "to avoid atrocities and bury those who have been liquidated. To lock men, women and children into barns and set fire to the structures, does not appear to be a suitable method of combating these bands, even if it is desired to exterminate the population. This method is unworthy of the German cause and hurts our reputation."

S.S. Death Vans

S.S. death vans were mentioned by Major Walsh in his evidence when he produced a report on their operations at Kiev, written by S.S. officials on May 16, 1942. Another report from Riga complained that the existing three death vans were incapable of handling the Jews being brought in for execution, and requested another five vans to cope with the numbers.

Major Walsh then gave details of the German extermination camp for Jews at Treblinka, in Poland. This was part of the indictment of Hans Frank by the Polish Government for *establishing in March, 1942, an extermination camp at Treblinka intended for mass killings of Jews by suffocating them in steam-filled chambers.*

The Polish charge added: "It may be assumed that several hundreds of thousands of Jews have been exterminated at Treblinka. Exposed to the most cruel sufferings of body and soul, their death in the steam chambers must have come almost as a welcome relief.

"Their only crime consisted in fact of belonging to a race condemned by Hitler to death."

Major Walsh read an extract from a British War Office report stating that, during an interrogation, a French student deposed: "During July 1944 at the Auschwitz concentration camp, Hungarian Jews were being liquidated at the rate of 12,000 daily, and the crematoria could not deal with such numbers. Many bodies were thrown in large pits and covered with quick-lime."

"Germanizing Europe"

When Major Walsh closed the case on the murder of six million Jews, another U.S. assistant prosecutor, Mr. Sam Harris, took up the evidence on the spoliation and "Germanization" of the occupied countries.

The first document underlined the German intention to make the conquered Poles slaves of Germany and to rob the country of all its industrial assets.

Frank in a report explained how he intended to govern Poland under Hitler's directive which provided that Poland could only be administered by utilizing the country through the means of ruthless exploitation of all supplies of raw materials, machines and factory installations; making available all labour for work in Germany; and reducing Polish economy to the bare minimum for existence.

It also provided for the closing of all educational institutions lest they breed a new race of intellectuals, and for reducing Poland to "the status of a German colony, with the Poles becoming the slaves of the Great German world empire."

Poland as Test Ground

Poland was used as a testing ground, said Mr. Harris. Secret documents, introduced in Court, showed that the Nazis had plans for wholesale migrations and re-shuffling of European populations to provide a solid German race for the Reich. The Czech problem was to be solved by absorbing half of the population into Germany and stripping the other half of power and shipping it off.

This last order agreed it would take years to "Germanize" Czechoslovakia, but "any elements which resist the planned 'Germanization' are to be handled roughly and should be eliminated."

At the conclusion of yesterday's hearing, Mr. Justice Jackson, the U.S. prosecutor, announced that he proposed to seek a declaratory judgment by the Tribunal that the six Nazi organizations named in the indictment — the Reich Cabinet, the Leadership Corps of the Nazi Party, the S.S., including the Sicherheitsdienst (S.D.), the Gestapo, the S.A., and the General Staff and High Command of the German armed forces — be named in the indictment as criminal organizations.

Such findings, he pointed out, might constitute the basis for proceedings against individuals in other Courts.

The United States was anxious to present as much as possible of the evidence against these organizations before the Christmas recess, he said, in order that the defence might have an opportunity for examining it.

Court Shown Grim Exhibits of Terror

By GEORGE LICHTHEIM, Palestine Post Correspondent

NUREMBERG, Dec. 13 (delayed). — Lampshades made of the human skin of victims slain for this purpose by concentration camp guards, and shrunken human skulls used as mascots by Nazis in the same camp, figured among the exhibits when the prosecution this afternoon concluded its case against Nazi terrorism. A new chapter was then opened when the Nazi extermination of the Jewish people was detailed by Major Walsh, the American Military prosecutor, with the aid of captured evidence, including photographs of the Ghetto liquidation taken by an S.S. member.

Going back to the original Nazi programme and outlining the gradual intensification of the campaign against the Jews, the Prosecutor gradually prepared the Court for the climax of the extermination campaign in the actual liquidation of the Polish ghettoes.

Campaign of Horror

Showing the gradual development of the anti-Jewish campaign, beginning with Streicher's ritual murder ravings 20 years ago, and ending with a diary entry of Governor Frank of Poland on August 24, 1942, "that we sentenced 1,200,000 Jews to die of hunger should be noted only marginally," the prosecutor built up a case notably against Frick, who signed most of the early anti-Jewish decrees; Goering, who organized the 1938 confiscations; Streicher and Rosenberg, who supplied the ideological basis; and Frank, who directed the massacres in Poland.

Despite the somewhat sketchy and superficial presentation of the evidence, which mostly ignored the historical background of the campaign, leaving the sources of this outburst unexplained, the prosecutor succeeded in impressing upon the Court the full horror of the final extermination drive, which served the double purpose of ridding the Reich of superfluous consumers, and serving the Nazi political purpose as well as the insatiable bloodlust of Himmler's S.S.

The full S.S. report on the liquidation of the Warsaw ghetto was also issued, giving a detailed day-by-day account of the extermination, resulting in the killing of many tens of thousands of Jewish civilians, mostly unarmed.

A marked feature of this report, which was prefaced by the words, "For the Fuehrer and their Country: The following fell in the battle for the destruction of the Jews and bandits in the former ghetto of Warsaw" followed by fifteen names and then the words "They gave their utmost, their lives. We shall never forget them!" is the apparent conviction of the S.S. murderers that their "operation" with tanks, flame-throwers, and grenades against helpless humanity was a serious and dangerous military action.

Though many of the Jews were armed with primitive weapons smuggled in by Poles and others, the great majority were simply slaughtered, as evidenced by the comparison of losses on both sides.

The accused lost lots of their buoyancy during the recital but showed no sign of shame.

Truman Sees U.S. Inquiry Members

WASHINGTON, Saturday (PTA). — The six American members of the Committee of Inquiry are being received by President Truman today, the White House press secretary announces.

They are impressed with the importance of taking up their work with all possible despatch (he said) and therefore wished to talk over the whole matter with the President.

LONDON, Saturday (Reuter). —The constitution of the Joint Anglo-American Committee of Inquiry on Palestine into the Palestinian problem was the subject of an exchange of Notes between the British Ambassador, Lord Halifax, and the Secretary of State, Mr. James F. Byrnes. The text was published here yesterday.

Mr. Byrnes wrote to Lord Halifax on December 10:

"I have the honour to inform Your Excellency with reference to our conversations on the subject that the Government of the United States agrees to constitute, in co-operation with the Government of the United Kingdom, a joint Anglo-American Committee of Inquiry with the following terms of reference:

"The Committee should be composed of six nationals of the United States appointed by the Government of the United States, and six nationals of the United Kingdom appointed by the Government of the United Kingdom, and shall operate as an expedition in dealing with the subject committed to it for investigation and shall request that they may be furnished with its reports within 120 days of the inception of the inquiry.

Committee's Procedure

"The procedure of the Committee shall be determined by the Committee itself and it will be open to it, if it thinks fit, to deal simultaneously through the medium of sub-committees with any of the subjects entrusted to its consideration.

"Each Government shall be responsible for compensating its own members of the Committee and other personnel selected by it and for paying such other expenses as are not susceptible of being jointly shared by the two Governments. All other expenses of the Committee shall be borne jointly by both Governments in equal proportions."

Lord Halifax wrote to Mr. Byrnes on December 10:

"I have the honour, under instructions from the Secretary for Foreign Affairs, to inform Your Excellency that the British Government in the United Kingdom are in agreement with the terms of the Note of December 10 about the Joint Anglo-American Committee of Inquiry to report on the position of Jews in certain countries of Europe and in Palestine."

(American comment, Page 2)

LORD CHORLEY

Lord Chorley, who took part, in the debate on Palestine in the House of Lords last Monday, is

TRUMAN URGES TRUCE IN CHINA

WASHINGTON, Saturday (R). — President Truman today called for an immediate end to hostilities in China between the National Government and the Communist forces, and the summoning of a national conference of representatives of all major political elements of the Chinese nation to seek an early solution to the present internal strife.

The President issued a comprehensive statement of United States policy towards China within two hours of the departure of General George C. Marshall, new American diplomatic envoy to Chungking.

President Truman reiterated that America would continue to recognize Generalissimo Chiang Kai Shek's Government

ELEVEN BELSEN BANDITS HANGED

HAMBURG, Saturday (Reuter). — All eleven men and women of the Belsen concentration camp staff sentenced to death were hanged on Thursday, it was announced yesterday.

The executions took place in the presence of the prison governor and one British doctor. Only one scaffold was used and the executions were carried out in accordance with British practice. Witnesses from the Court at Lueneburg were present to identify the condemned persons.

German Catholic and Protestant prison chaplains were in attendance. All eleven went quietly to their death and there were no scenes outside the prison.

Chief of those executed were Josef Kramer, commandant; Irma Grese, 21 year old S.S. woman; Elisabeth Volkenrath, an S.S. guard at the camp; Fritz Klein, the camp doctor who made gas-chamber selections; and Juana Bormann, stated at the trial to have turned a dog loose on prisoners.

Five days before the executions Field-Marshal Montgomery rejected an appeal for mercy. Sentences of death were passed on November 16.

POLICE SWOOP IN LONDON

Palestine Post Cable

LONDON, Saturday. — The results of last night's police round-up was announced as follows by Scotland Yard tonight:

Total number of persons stopped — 15,161;

Deserters handed over to military escort — 32;

Arrests for alleged housebreaking — 2;

Arrests for alleged larceny — 4;

Arrests for alleged unlawful possession — 9.

In addition to these arrests, one person was detained on a charge of being found on enclosed premises, two others were R.A.F. personnel said to be wearing false decorations, and another was an escaped Italian prisoner of war. (Earlier Story, Page 3.)

U.N.O. CHOOSES U.S. FOR HEADQUARTERS

LONDON, Saturday (R). — The United Nations executive committee's recommendations that U.N.O. headquarters should be in the United States was today endorsed by the Preparatory Commission with the requisite two-thirds majority, by 30 votes to 14, with six abstentions.

The vote was later made unanimous on a motion by the Canadian delegate seconded by Mr. Philip Noel-Baker, for the United Kingdom, who had led the case for Europe.

Voting was by roll-call after a motion to vote by secret ballot had been defeated.

The Commission's decision for the United States was reached after prolonged and, in some cases, bitter debates.

BRITISH DOCKERS ACCEPT TERMS

LONDON, Saturday (Reuter). British dockers have accepted proposed terms of settlement of their wage dispute made under the Government investigation committee's report, and authorized union representatives to enter into an agreement with the employers.

Dockers' delegates from all over Britain, at a conference in London yesterday, accepted the basis of a 19/- minimum daily wage to date back to November 26, new piece rates, and a medical scheme.

The question of a 48-hour week was left in abeyance because it is being dealt with by the trade unions on a national basis.

MIDDLE EAST ACCORD HAILED IN LEVANT

French Schools in Syria to Reopen

By YEHUDA HELMAN, Palestine Post Correspondent

BEIRUT, Saturday (By Telephone). — The Syrian Government announced today its decision that all private schools, notably French schools, would reopen immediately. A French spokesman here expressed hope that normal political relations would be established between Syria and France, such as obtained between the Lebanon and France.

Commenting on the Franco-British agreements for the Middle East the spokesman told your correspondent today that it reaffirmed France's recognition of Syro-Lebanese independence proclaimed in 1941 by General Catroux. As at that time France had no constitutional government, it was highly important that the legally-elected French Government should now confirm the independence of the Levant States.

It was the aim of the signatories to help Syria and the Lebanon enter a new era of stability and development, and all progressive people would benefit by the new agreement, the spokesman went on. However, certain politicians would be disappointed that Great Britain and France were co-ordinating their policies in the Middle East which would thwart their policy of exploiting Franco-British differences for their personal ends.

Wider Implications

The agreement also had broad international implications, the spokesman continued. It had been discussed for many weeks in Paris and London, and was the subject of most serious study covering the whole area of the Middle East which actually means all territory west of India up to the Russian border.

The text of the document was communicated to Russia and the United States, and American support for it had been secured.

The agreement, said the spokesman, marked a point of departure for a common Anglo-French international policy, and it was to be hoped that other Middle East problems still unsolved might be seen in a new light.

The French press is more reserved in its comment on the Anglo-French agreement on the Middle East than official circles in Paris have been. While most papers welcome the clarification in the relations between the two Powers, they observe that the agreement does not imply a common Middle Eastern policy.

"One should remember," writes the extreme right "Epoque" (Paris) "that after the Franco-British Agreement of 1904 in North Africa a quarter of a century was needed for local agents to adopt the new state of mind indicated in their Governments' policies. It is not slandering our British friends to note that in these regions a tradition of suspicion exists towards France, and it would be unwise to expect this to disappear between one day and another".

In Beirut the agreement has been criticized as a settlement of the Levant question without the Levant States having any part. On the other hand, Sayyed Abdullah el-Yafi, Deputy for Beirut and a former Prime Minister, finds that the agreement leaves no doubt that the independence of the Levant has become secure.

In Damascus it is pointed out by a number of Deputies that under cover of organizing the withdrawal of foreign troops they might actually be concentrated in the Lebanon.

(R. and ANA)

PATTON IMPROVING

FRANKFURT, Saturday (R).— Today's bulletin on the state of health of General George Patton, Commander of the U.S. 15th Army in Germany, who was injured in a car accident last Sunday, said that his general condition was excellent.

"There has been a slight but significant improvement in sensation during the past 24 hours," the bulletin added. "The General continues alert and cheerful."

BRITISH ADVANCE IN BATAVIA

By NOEL BUCKLEY, Reuters Correspondent

BATAVIA, Saturday. —British forces have taken over the Batavian railways and telephone exchange at Buitenzorg, about 40 miles from Batavia along the Bandoeng road. The Indonesian "Resident" had left the town after declaring himself unable to maintain order.

On the whole, the present Indonesian administration is doing its utmost to end the disturbances, especially in West Java. The Indonesian Peace Preservation Corps at Bandoeng, a hill station and internee centre in Western Java, are cooperating in full military action against extremists.

Leading members of the Indonesian "Republican" Government will shortly undertake a tour of Central and Eastern Java to induce the local leaders, who wield real power, to accept its discipline.

In Eastern Java, British troops continue to fan out south and west of the Naval base of Sourabaya, and are now clearing towns about 15 miles from the port against

Batavia today for The Hague by air, on his way to confer with his home Government. He was expected to return in about three weeks to resume his talks with Indonesian leaders.

A British paratroop battalion which won fame at Arnhem and two companies of Gurkhas have arrived in Batavia. Allied military police arrested the editor of the popular Indonesian newspaper "Merdeka" and his wife, a graduate of Columbia University. The editor was later released but his wife was detained.

Restitution from Siam

At Singapore, Mr. Moberly Dening, British Foreign Office adviser, stated that it was necessary that Siam "should make restitution for the damage done to British interests, and in particular to the interests of territories bordering on Siam, for the welfare of which Britain is responsible. Siam must realize that treaties are not to be lightly broken."

Mr. Dening has resumed negotiations at Singapore to end

TALKS BEGIN IN MOSCOW

INTEREST CENTRES ON PERSIA

MOSCOW, Saturday. — Both Mr. Ernest Bevin, British Foreign Minister, and Mr. James Byrnes, U.S. Secretary of State, have arrived in Moscow after delay and some anxiety due to bad flying weather, and have already been received by the Foreign Commissar, M. Molotov.

Though official statements have specified only atomic energy as one of the subjects to be discussed, it is definite that Persia will be on the agenda. Sir Reader Bullard, the British Ambassador to Iran, and Mr. J. D. Jernegan, U.S. Embassy Representative, having left Teheran for Moscow by Soviet plane.

Another major question up for discussion appears to be Allied relations in the Far East centring round control of Japan.

The talks were "an exploratory exchange of views" and need not necessarily lead to the announcement of any major decisions, Mr. Byrnes told the press.

Meanwhile, at least as far as Persia is concerned, facts are being created which might in themselves become decisions. The latest news from Teheran is that insurgent forces have captured Tabriz, the chief town of Azerbaijan, and Ardabil, the Caspian port 20 miles from the Soviet frontier. All Persian battalions were stopped by the Red Army from moving into the "trouble province" and have returned to the capital on orders from their headquarters.

Azerbaijan Lost

"Azerbaijan seems definitely lost to Persia," said Nurteza Qualkhan Bayatt, Governor of the province, who arrived in Teheran from Tabriz on Friday and who stated that he had been advised to leave by Jafar Pishevari, president of the newly formed provincial government and leader of the Democratic Party. It appears, states one commentator, that the insurgents hope to confront the Government with a fait accompli before the Moscow Conference can make any decision.

In Teheran itself, although everything looks calm, measures have been taken to prevent disturbances, it being rumoured that several illegal groups are in existence. In spite of this, M. Hakimi, the Iranian Prime Minister, is reported to be optimistic and great hopes are placed on his coming visit to Moscow accompanied by his Foreign Minister. Whether the visit will coincide with or impinge on the talks of the three Allied Foreign Ministers remains for the latter to decide.

The actual military operations in Azerbaijan are expected to develop in intensity in the Spring.

Persian Government circles point out that the province's present rulers are neither Democrats nor Central Government, but Russian occupation authorities. Since these are pledged to evacuate Iran by March 2 at the latest the situation then is likely to develop to a grim climax.

If the Foreign Ministers in Moscow agreed that the foreign forces leave Iran appreciably in advance of that date, it is claimed that the Iran Government would be capable of restoring order, even if it involved a certain amount of fighting.

The next week or two would show to what lengths Russia is prepared to go. It is believed in Teheran that that has already been indicated by the Soviet reply of November 26 to the Iran Government's Note, when it was stated in effect that should the Iran Government despatch troops to Azerbaijan and precipitate bloodshed, it would be necessary to send additional Red Army forces from Russia to restore order.

A strong case to be consulted and represented at talks at which decisions affecting Persia are taken, was advanced by the Iranian Government two days ago. The State Department disclosed in Washington the text of a British Note expressing agreement with the American view that Persia should be able to use her own forces wherever and in whatever manner necessary to preserve its authority and security, but reiterating that British troops could not be withdrawn without similar action on the part of Russia.

U.S. Interest

The United States would prefer a solution of the Iranian question within an international frame rather than by agreement between two countries, well-informed circles in Washington state.

The Iranian crisis is part of the general situation in the Middle East, and its solution will influence public opinion in that part of the world as to the real intentions of the Big Powers in the international questions of the future. It is the United States' wish, according to these circles, that the Moscow discussion of the Iran problem should be only preliminary, and that the final solution should be left to the Security Council of the U.N.O. Although the United States did not sign the agreement fixing the date of the Anglo-Russian evacuation, American Government circles take great interest in the Persian question and also in Russian aims in the Near and Middle East.

(Reuter, U.P. and AFP)

American Securities Suffer Setback

(Reuters Economic Service)

NEW YORK, Saturday. —Wall Street this week suffered its biggest setback since mid-July. Undoubtedly, the market was discouraged by the lack of a conciliatory attitude among either labour or management. The fact that the setback was led by steels and motors was indicative of the market's temper, and the factors affecting these groups spread their depressing influence to other sections.

If the slump was technical, as some assert, the market should partly regain its equilibrium, but if it represents mounting fear about the unsolved labour and price riddle, reaction may extend.

AFTER MIDNIGHT

A Persian Cabinet reshuffle is reported from Teheran, where a former Premier, Ghavam Sultaneh, may succeed Ibrahim Hakimi.

Carlo Scorza, former Fascist Party secretary and member of the Fascist Grand Council, was arrested yesterday at his hiding-place after weeks of search.

An important religious festival at Teheran was interrupted yesterday by a secret session of the Mejlis (Parliament). This is regarded as indicating the gravity of the present situation.

RUSSIANS CLAIM RIGHTS IN PERSIA

LONDON, Saturday (R). — The presence of British troops in Palestine, Egypt, the East Indies, and several European countries was challenged today by a "Pravda" commentator, David Zaslavski, according to the Moscow radio.

M. Zaslavski stated that the U.S.S.R. had the right to station its troops in Persia under its treaty with that country, continuing:

"Just as simple is the answer concerning Soviet troops in other countries. This can arouse no doubt or perplexity.

"It may seem that the question concerning the presence of British troops in Persia, in accordance with the 1942 agreement is relatively simple. Are there not in Persia British troops who were stationed there before the 1942 agreement?

"If so, when did they appear? For what purpose? Where are they stationed? What is their number? What are they doing? Do the conditions of the 1942 agreement extend to them also? We do not hear the answers to these questions.

Other Countries

"The Egyptian press almost daily raises the same question: 'When will Great Britain at last withdraw her troops from Egypt?' Truly, ancient Oedipus encountered less difficulty in extracting a reply from the Egyptian State than contemporary Egypt has in receiving an answer from the British State," the writer added.

22

The Uniqueness of the Holocaust

Efraim Zuroff

The question of the uniqueness of the Holocaust—if so and to what degree—is one which has preoccupied numerous historians, philosophers, and theologians. While scholars acquainted with the history of the persecution and destruction of European Jewry during the Nazi era concur that the events which transpired during the years 1933-1945 —and especially during the period of the infamous "Final Solution" (1941-1945)—constituted a watershed in Jewish history, if not in the annals of Western civilization, the question remains whether the Holocaust was a unique *sui generis* event. This query is posed on two levels, initially within the framework of Jewish history, and thereafter vis-a-vis the annals of mankind. Perhaps the *Shoah* is unique in Jewish history but has its parallels in the history of other peoples.

In the course of Jewish history, Jews have often suffered persecution and oppression. Ever since Biblical times, the Jews—because of their unique tradition and culture and their determination to maintain their distinct national-religious identity—have been subjected to various forms of discrimination. There have been times when anti-Jewish sentiment determined the policy of those in power, a situation which proved particularly difficult in view of the Jews' status in the Diaspora, as a people without a homeland, a people whose existence was dependent on the goodwill of the rulers of the host countries. As such, the Jews were particularly vulnerable, and there were instances in which the persecution of the Jews assumed serious proportions and threatened Jewish existence.

In post-Biblical times there have been several cases of large-scale Jewish persecutions which preceded the Holocaust and which served as a basis for comparison with the events of World War II. Was the Holocaust significantly different from the Crusades, the persecution by the Inquisition, and the Chmielnicki pogroms or was it merely a similar tragedy on a larger scale?

When comparing events of this nature it behooves us to examine three basic criteria: the intent of the perpetrators, the implementation of the program of persecution, and the implications of the tragedy. Let us begin by delineating the distinguishing characteristics of the Holocaust in order to be able to compare it with the other cases of large-scale Jewish persecution which occurred since the destruction of the Second Temple.

The initial element, one which is crucial in determining the nature of catastrophes of this type, is the intent of the perpetrators. In the case of the Holocaust, the documents reveal that the Nazis had a clearly-defined objective: the annihilation of every Jewish man, woman, and child living in Europe. Not only were the Jews in Germany, or those in German-occupied territories, or those in the countries fighting against the Axis powers to be eliminated, but even those living in neutral countries such as Switzerland, Sweden, Spain, Portugal and Turkey. If there was any uncertainty about the all-encompassing nature of this plan, the special term coined to describe it—the "Final Solution" (*Endlosung*)—is clear proof of the designs of the perpetrators. (In this context it should perhaps be noted that Julius Streicher, for example, wrote in 1944 of campaigns which would be initiated against Jews elsewhere on the globe once the Jews of Europe had been liquidated.) Thus it is evident that the Nazis' goal was the total annihilation of the Jewish people throughout an entire continent, i.e., even beyond the borders of the Third Reich. The Nazis' goal, moreover, was not only to destroy the Jews, i.e., the physical individuals, but also to obliterate Judaism as a living faith. Time after time the Nazis attacked Judaism, waging a relentless propaganda battle against the Jewish faith. In addition, they made special efforts to destroy synagogues and Jewish institutions, as well as *sifrei Torah* and ritual objects. On many occasions the Nazis deliberately chose Jewish holidays as the dates of deportations and "selections," and holy places (cemeteries, synagogues, etc.) as the venue for mass murder. At the same time, efforts were made to collect Jewish books and ritual objects for a museum which the Nazis planned to establish once their objective had been realized, in order to educate future generations of Europeans about the great service the Nazis had performed by eliminating the Jews.

The second characteristic of the Holocaust which relates to the Nazis' intentions vis-a-vis the Jews was their application of racial determinants to distinguish between Jews and Aryans. In the infamous Nuremburg Laws of 1935, the Nazis decreed that anyone who had at least three Jewish grandparents was automatically classified as a Jew regardless of his or her religious and/or ideological beliefs. Thus the definitive criteria as far as the Nazis were concerned were racial, rather than behavioral. An individual was not judged by his or her actions or beliefs, but rather by his birth or racial origin.

The use of racial criteria by the perpetrators meant that the potential victims were, in essence, helpless as the Nazis left them no avenue of escape. They could not convert to another religion, nor could they change their ideology in order to save themselves, as their "crime" was neither religious nor political. The offense they had committed was having been born, a fact of life which no subsequent act could alter. Thus a situation was created whereby Christians were persecuted as Jews because of their Jewish ancestors, and individuals who were German patriots were ultimately murdered by the German government which viewed them as a danger to the very country they had risked their lives to defend. These phenomena emphasize the perverse logic of Nazi ideology which stressed the inherent criminality of the Jews and sought to rob them of their human status, often referring to them as "parasites" and other terms borrowed from the animal world.

This type of ideology spawned a program for mass murder which was carried out relentlessly with untold determination and zeal. So dedicated were the Nazis to their objective of murdering the Jews, that they allocated countless resources toward achieving that aim at a time when men and rolling stock were badly needed to fight against the allies. Moreover, the individuals whom the Nazis hurried to murder were in ghettos or camps under German control, in most cases working, as forced labor, on projects for the German war effort. The Nazis, however, were as determined to annihilate the Jewish people and those of Jewish origin as they were to win the war, a factor which profoundly affected the implementation of the "Final Solution."

Another factor which had a serious impact on the implementation of the Nazis' plans was the response in occupied Europe and the Free World to the persecution and destruction of European Jewry. The lack of assistance for the victims of the Nazis in no small measure contributed to the enormous scope of the tragedy. In addition, in every country in occupied Europe, as well as in the Axis satellites, the Nazis were able to enlist the assistance of collaborators who played an active role in the various phases of the annihilation process. Moreover, aid came not only from individuals, but from local governments. Lithuanians, Latvians, Ukrainians and others assisted the *Einsatzgruppen,* and Prime Minister Josef Tiso of Slovakia was willing to pay the Nazis 500 marks for every Jew deported from his country. Prime Minister Pierre Laval of Vichy agreed to employ the French gendarmes in locating Jews residing in France who were not French citizens; 8,000 Jews who were in hiding in Holland were handed over to the Gestapo by Dutch informers.

In the Allied world as well, there was a reluctance to assist the Jews of Europe. Even a relatively simple matter such as a declaration to the effect that the Allies were aware of the enormity of the crimes committed against the Jews and would hold the malefactors accountable was rarely forthcoming. Even though statements by Allied leaders noting the fate of others under Nazi rule were fairly common, only once prior to 1944 was a declaration issued, which dealt specifically with the fate of European Jewry. The failure to facilitate immigration prior to the war, the Bermuda Conference, and the refusal to bomb Auschwitz, emphasize the lack of aid from the United States, while the British policy on immigration to Palestine, the relative inaction of the International Red Cross, and the silence of Pope Pius XII indicate the indifference that was typical in the Free World.

Another characteristic of the implementation of the Holocaust was the Nazis' studied attempt to dehumanize their victims and involve them in whatever way possible in the murder process. The establishment of the *Judenraete* (Jewish councils) who were responsible for the administration of the ghettos and for implementing German decrees is one example. Another is the use of Jewish inmates as members of the *Sonderkommando* whose job was to burn the bodies of those gassed in the death camps. The abysmal and humiliating treatment accorded Jews in ghettos and concentration camps was part of the Nazis' plans to dehumanize and demoralize their victims, another manifestation of their notion of the subhuman status of the Jewish people and their inherent criminality.

Still another feature of the Holocaust was the use of the advances of modern technology, and the involvement of the intellectual and spiritual elite in the implementation of mass murder. German doctors conducted medical experiments—many designed to further Nazi political aims rather than to aid mankind—upon unwilling victims in the concentration camps. German scientists designed various devices to facilitate the murder of as many Jews as possible in as brief a period as possible at the least expense. University professors and administrators participated in the *Gleibschaltung* or coordination of academic learning and policy with the principles of the Third Reich.

In terms of the implications of the Holocaust for the Jewish people, the changes wrought as a result of the persecution and destruction of European Jewry have been profound. In demographic terms, the murder of six million Jews meant the annihilation of more than one-third of the Jewish people and the destruction of the communities with the highest birthrates in the Jewish world. To this day, the Jewish people have still not recouped the demographic losses of World War II, and in fact, remain the only people who have still not done so.

Besides the numerical losses suffered by the Jewish people, the Holocaust marked the destruction of the center of Jewish life, learning, culture, education, and politics and the end of a unique civilization developed over the course of a millennium in Eastern Europe. In the course of the war countless institutions were destroyed and religious and cultural treasures lost. Yiddish culture was dealt a deathblow as was Ladino in the course of a tragedy which for the most part marked the end of Jewish life in all of Eastern Europe except the Soviet Union.

Along with these cultural losses, the Holocaust also had an important impact on political developments which influence Jewish life the world over. The establishment of the State of Israel, while not a direct result of the Holocaust, was undoubtedly rooted in a set of circumstances which were created in no small measure by the events of World War II. The realization of the enormity of the scope of the tragedy suffered by the Jewish people, coupled with the fate of the survivors and their determination to enter Palestine and with Israel's willingness to accept every Jew, combined to create an atmosphere conducive to the establishment of a Jewish state in the Middle East.

One cannot examine the implications of the Holocaust for the Jewish people without dealing with what is perhaps the most difficult factor of all to assess—the psychological impact of these events on Jews today. Suffice it to say that throughout the Jewish world we have witnessed—and will no doubt continue to see—evidence of an increased awareness of the importance and results of the events of the Holocaust, a factor which already has had a profound effect on Jewish communities the world over. The renaissance of Jewish identity in the Soviet Union, the massive and unflinching support of Diaspora communities for the State of Israel, and the tremendous sensitivity of Jews in the Free World to the plight of their brethren in distress the world over are phenomena which can be attributed to awareness of the events of the Holocaust, which has increasingly become a dominant force in Jewish life today.

Contrasts With Other Catastrophes in Jewish History

Three major catastrophes have befallen the Jewish people in the course of the approximately nineteen centuries following their forced exile: the Crusades, the expulsion from Spain and the persecution by the Inquisition, and the Chmielnicki pogroms. The Crusades, which were launched in 1095 as a campaign by Christian Europeans to liberate the Holy Land from the Moslems, included a series of attacks by the Crusaders on the Jewish communities of Europe as they made their way to the Holy Land.

Even though the persecution of the Jews was not part of the original plan, many communities were attacked by the Crusaders who sought to take measures against the Jews living in their midst prior to going on to Palestine. During the course of the first three Crusades which took place over a period of more than two hundred years, many Jewish communities were destroyed and thousands of Jews murdered.

If, however, we compare the Crusades to the Holocaust, we see that there are several crucial differences between the two tragedies. The Crusaders gave the Jews the choice of death or apostasy, unlike the Nazis who offered them no alternative. Moreover, most of those Jews who converted to Christianity were able to return to Judaism within a very short time. During the period of the Crusades there were many instances in which bishops and even the Pope spoke out against the persecution of the Jews. Thus, for example, in the wake of the attacks on the Jews, Pope Calixtus II issued the *Sicut Judaeis* bull which specified that while Jews were not to be granted any new privileges, Christians were forbidden to take any steps to endanger Jewish lives, to force them to convert, or to desecrate Jewish cemeteries. In addition, on various occasions, secular rulers extended aid and protection to Jews in distress (often in return for bribes), a phenomenon which did not occur during the course of the Holocaust.

In terms of the number of victims, and the geographic scope of the tragedy, the results of the Crusades pale beside the results of the Holocaust. While the latter basically ended Jewish life in all of Central and Eastern Europe except in the Soviet Union, the former did not decisively alter Jewish life in Europe. Almost all the Jewish communities affected by the Crusades resumed life shortly thereafter and, in fact, the overall number of Jews in the areas in question increased. Moreover, certain parts of Europe such as Northern France, Spain and Italy, were practically untouched by the Crusades. In summation, although the Crusades left an impact on Jewish life, the victims having been immortalized in Jewish liturgy, and the concept of *Kiddush ha-Shem* having been inaugurated, they did not approach the scope of the tragedy of the Holocaust and did not radically change Jewish life as was the case with the destruction of European Jewry. Moreover, the intent of the Nazis and their systematic, unrelenting implementation of their anti-Jewish policies, which left no alternative for Jewish existence, were far more devastating than the relatively sporadic attacks carried out by the Crusaders.

The second tragedy of great magnitude in the annals of European Jewry was the expulsion from Spain and the persecution of Jewish communities by the Inquisition in Spain and Portugal. In this case, although the communities in question suffered great hardship and deprivation, their fate was different from that of European Jewry in Nazi-occupied Europe. Ferdinand and Isabella, the rulers of Spain who initiated the expulsion order, offered the Jews an alternative: conversion or expulsion—whereas the Jews in the Third Reich had no alternative whatsoever. Later, in 1497, when King Manuel I of Portugal seized the Jews and forcibly converted them, that policy offered the Jews an opportunity to remain alive, and with it the hope that subsequent developments might enable them to return to Judaism. This was indeed the case with Jews who later emigrated.

In terms of number, those affected by the decrees in Spain and Portugal were far fewer than those affected by the Holocaust. While approximately 150,000 Jews were forced to flee Spain, the number of Jews murdered by the Inquisition, even according to the highest estimate, was, until 1525, under 30,000 in Spain and under 2,000 in Portugal. While those touched by the decrees faced severe hardship, there were countries such as constituents of the Ottoman Empire, which were willing to accept them with open arms, a factor which considerably alleviated their plight.

Thus although the events of the period of the persecution by the Inquisition left an indelible impression on the Jewish consciousness and marked the end of a flourishing Jewish culture, they do not approach the Holocaust in terms of the intent of the perpetrators, the scope and nature of the implementation, and the implications for the Jewish people.

The final tragedy in Jewish history which we seek to compare with the Holocaust, is the Chmielnicki pogroms of 1648-1649, a series of attacks by Cossack hordes on the Jewish communities of Poland and the Ukraine. Led by Bogdan Chmielnicki, and spurred by religious as well as national, social, and economic motivations (Jews were often the administrators of the estates of the nobles, and were viewed as their agents and the representatives of Polish rule), the Cossacks sought to eliminate Jews from the Ukraine. As a result of their campaign, approximately 100,000 Jews were murdered and 300 communities destroyed. The brutality of the Cossacks, the barbaric nature of the atrocities, and the extent of the losses made such an impression upon Jewish leadership at the time that the Council of Lithuania decreed three consecutive years of mourning during which no fancy or ornate clothes were to be worn, and during the first year of which no music was to be played, even at weddings.

Yet despite the enormity of the tragedy, the Chmielnicki pogroms were not as severe as the measures carried out against the Jews by the Nazis. The results of the Holocaust were far more devastating in terms of the number of victims and number of Jewish communities destroyed. (In Poland alone, over 10,000 Jewish communities were destroyed during World War II.) In addition, those persecuted by the Cossacks were offered the option of conversion and could flee westward, whereas once the "Final Solution" was implemented, neither of these options was available to Jews in Nazi-occupied Europe. Following the pogroms by the Cossacks, Jewish life was renewed in the ravished areas (which a century later had one of the highest concentrations of Jewish population) and those who had been forced to convert were authorized by the Polish king to return to Judaism. The Holocaust, on the other hand, ended Jewish life in thousands of communities throughout Europe.

Contrasts With Other Tragedies in World History

Thus we see that the Holocaust is unique in the annals of the Jewish people, but is that true in terms of general history as well? During the past seventy years, there have been numerous cases of genocide (a term originally coined by Rafael Lemkin to describe the Nazis' attempt to annihilate the Jewish people). Starting with the mass murder of the Armenians by the Turks during World War I and continuing with the Nazis' persecution of Gypsies and other groups classified as "enemies of the Reich" until the recent wholesale annihilation of Cambodians by the Pol Pot regime, the world has witnessed numerous cases during the past seven decades in which ethnic and/or religious groups have been persecuted and subjected to mass murder. How does the destruction of European Jewry compare with these tragedies?

The first attempt in modern times by a nation to eliminate a people was the mass murder of the Armenians by the Turks in World War I. The Turkish documents which contain the directives for this operation are similar in content to those issued by the Nazis vis-a-vis the Jews, and it seemed clear that in terms of the intent of the perpetrators, the two tragedies do bear a close resemblance. While the Turks did not order or plan the murder of every Armenian in Europe, they did nonetheless order the death of every single Armenian man, woman and child living in Turkey. And although there seemed to be an ostensible reason for the Turks to take measures against the Armenians (their fear that the Armenians planned to cooperate with the Russians, then engaged in fighting against the Ottoman Empire), the fact remains that they—like the Nazis—issued orders for mass annihilation.

The difference between the fate of the Armenians and that of European Jewry lies in the implementation of the program of genocide rather than in the intent of the perpetrators. For, unlike the Nazis, the Turks did allow Armenian women and children the opportunity of conversion (to the consternation of officials in Istanbul). Moreover, no steps were taken against the Armenians living in Western Turkey (even in the capital of Istanbul) with the exception of approximately 200 members of the intelligentsia. Thus in terms of the realization of the program—and certainly in terms of the number of the victims (the estimates range from 800,000 to 2,000,000 Armenians murdered)—the Holocaust was a far more devastating catastrophe than the Armenian genocide. At the same time, it should be noted that the slaughter of the Armenians severely affected Armenian life and is remembered by the Armenian people in much the same way that Jews remember the Holocaust.

A critical point in our examination of the uniqueness of the Holocaust is a comparison of the fate of the Jews with that of other victims of the Third Reich. The group whose plight was closest to that of the Jews was the Gypsies. They were also considered racially inferior by the Nazis, who in some cases incarcerated them in Jewish ghettos and who in 1944 decided to have them murdered. There were, however, several important differences between the fate of both groups. First of all, the Nazi campaign against the Gypsies was not marked by the same relentless intensity as their program for the annihilation of the Jews. Thus, for example, some Gypsies were exempted from the anti-Gypsy measures such as those married to Aryans and those who had been regularly employed for five years consecutively.

The Gypsies were ordered deported to Auschwitz in late 1942, but their murder was not authorized until 1944. Moreover, Himmler for most of the war protected two tribes of Gypsies—the Sinti whom he considered pure Aryans—and the indigenous Lalleri. In addition, it should be noted that the Gypsies were classified as "asocials" (and were forced to wear the black triangle worn by the asocials in the camps) and were persecuted on those grounds rather than because of their supposed racial inferiority as was the case with the Jews. In cases in which records of lineage were not available, Gypsies were judged on such factors as: appearance, manner of life, social position and literacy. Thus we see that actions did in certain cases determine their fate. It was for this reason that individuals traveling with the Gypsies, even though not Gypsy by birth, were persecuted. On the other hand, the fate of the Jews was totally dependent on racial criteria.

Another group, many of whose members were murdered by the Nazis during the course of World War II, was the institutionalized: the mentally ill, retarded and deformed children, and those hospitalized with tuberculosis and arteriosclerosis. Shortly after the war began, Hitler issued orders to do away with these people and in the course of the next two years tens of thousands were killed, many in the first gas chambers which the Nazis built at the six special institutes they designated as the sites for the solution of the problem. Yet in this case as well, we see important differences between the fate of the Jews and that of these victims of Nazism. According to procedures established by the Nazis to deal with the institutionalized, each case was reviewed by a panel of doctors who decided whether or not to have the patient gassed. The key criterion used by the Nazis was productivity. Those who were able to do productive labor of any sort or might possibly be able to engage in such activity in the future were spared, while the others were murdered. In the case of the Jewish patients, however, all were sent to be murdered regardless of the chances of their recovery and their medical history.

An additional factor distinguishing the fate of the institutionalized from that of the Jews was the protests raised on behalf of the former by prominent German clergymen such as: Bishops Theophile Wurm, Konrad von Preysing and, most important, Clemens August of Munster. No such voices were raised to protest the persecution and destruction of European Jewry.

Still another group whose fate under Nazi rule has been compared to that of the Jews is the homosexuals. Incarcerated in concentration camps, where they were forced to wear the pink triangle, homosexuals were persecuted by the Nazis throughout the era of the Third Reich. Their fate, however, was far less severe than that of the Jews of Europe. They were never systematically murdered en masse, although thousands of homosexuals did die in the concentration and death camps. Moreover, in cases where the Nazis believed that homosexuals could be "rehabilitated," they were removed from concentration camps, i.e., they could in some way influence their own fate, a possibility denied European Jews, who were marked for annihilation regardless of their behavior and/or their ideology. Moreover, it should be pointed out that people related to homosexuals, or to the institutionalized, were never subject to persecution. This was not the case with the Jews. Whole families were decimated.

This last distinction is one of the key factors which differentiated the fate of the Jews from that of the political opponents of Nazism who, in essence, doomed themselves by their actions, rather than by their birth. It was for this reason that their kin were not persecuted and deported. Political opponents, it should be noted, could change their views. Thus, for example, in 1926 Hitler declared in a speech in Hamburg that, "We shall not rest until . . . the last Marxist [is] converted or exterminated," i.e., some element of choice did exist even for the arch-enemies, the Marxists.

The final group whose fate in Nazi-occupied Europe can be compared with that of European Jewry is the Slavs, whom the Nazis considered as racially inferior. In the course of the war, millions of Slavs (Poles, Ukrainians, Russians, etc.) were murdered by the Nazis, who took extremely harsh measures against the local population in predominately Slavic countries. Yet while the overall number of Slavs murdered is equivalent to the victims of the Final Solution, the fate suffered by the Jews was unique because of the relentlessness of the implementation of the anti-Jewish policies and because, unlike the Slavs, all Jews were marked for annihilation. While the Nazis had detailed plans for the subjugation and harsh repression of the Slavs, they had no plans to eliminate them totally. Moreover, Nazis sought to Aryanize their children with redeeming qualities, such as an Aryan appearance or lineage, by sending them to be brought up in Germany. Such a project was unthinkable as far as the Jews were concerned. In addition, the Nazis, in many instances, gave Slavs an opportunity to join the SS or other divisions of the Wehrmacht, another indication of the significant difference between the fate of the Slavs and that of the Jews in the Third Reich.

Contrasts With Recent Tragedies in World History

The above comparisons indicate the uniqueness of the Holocaust during the period from early history until the conclusion of World War II. Since then, the world has witnessed additional catastrophes which have involved the death of hundreds of thousands and in one case millions of victims. How does the Holocaust compare with Biafra and the recent tragedies in Indochina (the plight of the "boat people" and the Cambodian genocide)?

The first case pitted the Nigerian government against the secessionist state of Biafra, which was inhabited primarily by members of the Ibo tribe. In the course of the war, Nigeria, besides killing civilians in attacks and later in bombing raids, took measures which resulted in a severe famine which claimed the lives of approximately half a million women and children. The large-scale deaths made the question of the comparison with the fate of European Jewry inevitable (appropriately the Ibos were often referred to as the "Jews of Africa"), but in reality there are significant differences between the two tragedies.

First and foremost is the nature of the conflict. Although there certainly were ethnic or tribal motivations for the hostility between Nigeria and Biafra, they were not sufficient to have created a situation in which mass murder of this intensity was considered a necessary policy. The primary reason for the war was political—the secession of a part of Nigeria. This can be demonstrated by the fact that government troops not only murdered Ibos, but also members of other tribes which gave the secessionists political support. Moreover, in terms of the absolute numbers of victims, this catastrophe claimed fewer victims, and upon its completion the erstwhile victims continued to live in the contested area in relative peace with the perpetrators. It should also be pointed out that during the course of the conflict, Biafra was supported by various countries and international bodies, a factor which helped reduce the number of fatalities.

As far as the genocide in Cambodia is concerned, it is still too early to make assessments, since the entire story has still not been revealed, nor has the tragedy of the Khmer people ended. Hundreds of thousands of people still face starvation, and international relief agencies are racing against time to prevent additional deaths. What is clear is that the regime of Cambodian Communist Pol Pot launched a massive campaign to annihilate all those suspected of having different political opinions and ruthlessly carried out a forced resettlement of the entire population. In the course of the implementation of these measures, an estimated two to three million Cambodians were murdered. Self-inflicted genocide is a bizarre innovation, although it must be pointed out that the aim in Cambodia was certainly not the annihilation of an entire people, but rather the elimination of political opposition, which in this case assumed genocidal proportions (even though the term "genocide" is perhaps not accurate). These murders can best be compared to the wholesale liquidation of the Kulaks carried out by the Communist regime in the Soviet Union.

In the meantime, Pol Pot's policies and the subsequent invasion of Cambodia by the Vietnamese have created a new problem—mass starvation. Cambodia can no longer support itself. Hundreds of thousands of Cambodians have fled to Thailand and elsewhere in the hopes of finding food and shelter. Not all the fleeing Cambodians were accepted. Thailand, already full of refugees, closed its borders and in April 1979 transferred thousands of Cambodians from its refugee camps back to Cambodia, where they faced an uncertain fate. In the meantime, the number of victims of this tragedy is in the millions. Cambodia's present population is 4.8 million people out of a population which numbered between 7 and 9 million people in 1975. If we add the 300,000 Cambodians who found shelter elsewhere, we reach a figure of approximately 2,500,000 Cambodians murdered, i.e., if there were no births in the country at all during the last five years. We know, however, that children were born during this period which means that the number of those murdered was even higher. According to estimates by demographers, well over one-quarter of the Cambodian people have been murdered. However, the remaining Cambodians face starvation and thus the crisis has still not ended.

Another crisis which bears some resemblance to the plight of European Jewry (during the initial years of the Third Reich) is that of the "boat people." Forced to leave Vietnam because of ethnic hostility on the part of the Vietnamese, these refugees—most of whom are Hua people or ethnic Chinese—were forced to take to the high seas in order to escape. Expelled by the hundreds of thousands with few places of refuge available, they were preyed upon by pirates and in many cases perished at sea. While reminiscent of the plight of the German Jewish refugees during the Thirties, their fate was ultimately far better since eventually action was taken by various countries to ensure their entry.

Moreover, the Vietnamese, while ruthless in expelling people who were disloyal to their native country, never embarked upon a program of mass annihilation.

Conclusion

In terms of intent of the perpetrators, the implementation of the mass murder, and the implications of the tragedy for the victims, the destruction of European Jewry stands out as a unique event in the annals of mankind. While there have been tragedies with more victims and others which have shared certain of its features, none have been as perverse, relentless, and absolute as the Nazis' program for the elimination of the Jews. It is, therefore, particularly appropriate that a special term evolve to describe these events and that the term eventually be regarded throughout the world as the symbol of a program best-described as the epitome of evil for evil's sake. At the same time, however, we must make clear that the term "Holocaust" should only be used to describe one phenomenon—the persecution and destruction of European Jewry. And while that event has significant implications for human society as a whole, it is only via a recognition of its unique character that we can reap the benefits which accrue from its study.

Schools and Graves: The Holocaust and Jewish Education

Norman Lamm

Arbaim shanah akut be'dor. For forty years our generation struggled to understand the mystery of those fatal years of the Holocaust. Neither our speech nor our silence helped us to uncover the secrets of God or of man. Perhaps we shall have to wait another forty or another four hundred years, or perhaps we shall never be wise enough even to know how to react.

But events march on, and history does not permit us the luxury of contemplation. Hence, some reactions began to emerge fairly quickly. The first and enormously significant response to the Holocaust was the political one: the founding of the State of Israel. Powerlessness would never again be considered a Jewish trait. The desperate struggles of the heroic Jewish fighters in Warsaw and elsewhere were metamorphosed into the pride of statehood and the military confidence of the Israeli Defense Forces. Today, the future of the Jewish people is unthinkable without the State of Israel.

Another response has been a holy, compulsive drive to record and testify. We do not want to forget, and we do not want the world to forget. We have resolved to keep the memory of our *Kedoshim* alive by demonstrations and by meetings. And many of us have undertaken projects of sculpture and art and museums and exhibits to perpetuate the memory of the Six Million. As the years slip by and memory begins to fade, we desperately want to prevent their anguish and blood and cry from being swallowed up by the misty, gaping hole of eternal silence, banished from the annals of man by the Angel of Forgetfulness.

The efforts at remembering and reminding must continue. As long as so-called "revisionist historians" deny that the Holocaust occurred; as long as Babi Yar and Buchenwald behind the Iron Curtain contain almost no reference to Jews; as long as it is even conceivable that an American administration, which preaches more compassion for the victim than for the criminal on the domestic front, can see nothing wrong in its President honoring dead Waffen-SS while pointedly ignoring their Jewish victims in Dachau—there will be a need for Jews to remember and remind, even if we know in our hearts that the world will not long remember or want to be reminded. And let it be said here clearly and unequivocally: A courtesy call at a conveniently located concentration camp cannot compensate for the callous, obscene scandal of honoring dead Nazi killers. Surely the President's aides could have arranged a visit by him to the tomb of Konrad Adenauer or some of the decent German anti-Nazis who perished at Hitler's hands for their principles.

Yet—and yet . . . these responses alone are inadequate. The problem of the Jewish people today is not the State of Israel; it will survive. The problem is not the world's conscience. I have no faith in it, though we must continue to prod and prick and provoke it. The problem of the Jewish people today is—the Jewish people. With a diminishing birth rate, an intermarriage rate exceeding 40%, Jewish illiteracy gaining ascendance daily—who says that the Holocaust is over? President Herzog of Israel estimates that we are losing 250 Jews per day! From the point of view of a massive threat to Jewish continuity, the Holocaust is open-ended.

The monster has assumed a different and more benign form, a different and bloodless shape, but its evil goal remains unchanged: a *Judenrein* world.

The Holocaust is not yet ready to be "remembered"; we are still in the midst of attempting to avoid the *final* Final Solution: a world without Jews.

In the light of this sobering, ominous reality, our responses are open to serious and deep reexamination.

I deeply sympathize with the heartfelt, sincere effort of memorial-building. But is that the Jewish way? No archaeologist has yet found a statue to the memory of R. Hanina B. Tradyon or R. Ishmael. No seeker after antiquities has yet unearthed an ancient museum to preserve the story of the victims of Masada or Betar or R. Akiva and his martyred students—or, for that matter, the victims of the Crusades or the Inquisition or Kishinev.

Our people have historically chosen different forms of memorialization. They asked for the academy of Yavneh as a substitute for and in memory of the Holy Temple. They ordained days of fasting and prayer and introspection. They devised ways of expressing *zekher le'mikdash* (Reminder of the Temple) and *zekher le'churban* (Reminder of the Destruction). They created the Talmud. In other words, they remembered the past by ensuring the future.

Museums and art have their place. In the context of an overall Jewish life, they serve as powerful instruments to recall the past for the future. But without that comprehensive wholeness, all our museums are mausoleums, our statues meaningless shards, our literature so much ephemeral gibberish.

We must seek to remember our dead, but not by being obsessed with death. We must be obsessed with life. *Lo ha-metim yehallelu Yah* (Psalm 115, "The dead praise not the Lord"). The dead cannot tell their own story. Only the living can testify to them and perpetuate them: *Va'a-nachnu nevarekh Yah (Ibid.,* "But we will bless the Lord"). Their deaths make sense—even the sense of unspeakable and outrageous grief—only in the context of their lives. And their lives—their loves and hates, their faith and fears and culture and creativity and traditions and learning and literature and warmth and brightness and Yiddishkeit—are what we are called upon to redeem and to continue in our own lives and those of our children.

We know more or less how the Aztecs and Incas were butchered. But there is no one to mourn them today because there was no one to continue their ways and resume their story. That is bound to happen to our Six Million if we fail to ensure the continuity of our people. An extinct race has no memory. If there are no living Jews left, no one else will care about the Holocaust, and no one but a few cranky antiquarians will bother to view our art or read our literature or visit our museums.

Let me cite an example from the American-Jewish experience. There was a time when most American Jews memorialized their deceased parents by saying Kaddish for them for eleven months and on Yahrzeit and by reciting the Yizkor prayers four times a year; otherwise, their Jewishness became progressively more tenuous as they abandoned their parental lifestyles, values, and faith. What happened when these children died? For the most part, *their* children did not do for *them* what they had not done for their parents. For the most part, it was those who continued the whole rubric of Jewish life and living of their parents who also most fully cherished and reverenced their memories.

The reason for this is both profound and simple: Death has no staying power. Only life lives. Death is only past, it is over and done with. Who will remember a parent on Yizkor? Usually one who will be in *shul* as well on Hanukkah and Purim and Shabbat and even during the week. Those who somehow continue their parents' lives in their own lives will be there to note and recall their deaths. In a word: without life, death doesn't have a future.

At the Seder we eat a hard-boiled egg immediately before the meal as a sign of mourning. Jewish tradition teaches that since the first night of Passover always falls on the same night of the week as does Tisha B'Av, the egg is a token of grief for the victims of the destruction of Jerusalem and of pogroms throughout the ages. It occurs to me that not only do we eat an egg at the Seder because no Jewish *simchah* may be conducted or complete without remembering the tragedies of Jewish history, but equally so because there can be no enduring memorial to the fallen martyrs of our people unless it lies in the context of the Seder of Jewish life. Without a child to ask the *Mah Nishtanah,* there will be no adult to tell the story of *avadim hayyinu.* Without *seder* or order; without the holiness of *kadesh* or the purity of *rechatz*—there will be no *maggid* to tell the story of Auschwitz and relate the *marror* of Buchenwald and Belzec. And so the *churban* will remain without a *zekher.* There can be no Tisha B'Av without a Pesach. And there will be no Yom Hashoah without the rest of the Jewish calendar.

How did Jewish tradition cherish and pay homage to its heroes? We are told of the righteous King Hezekiah that upon his death he was honored greatly by the people of Judah and Jerusalem (II Chronicles 32:33), and the Talmud *(B.K.* 16b) explains that the honor that they accorded him was that *hoshivu yeshivah al kivro*—"they established a school upon his grave"!

That is what Jewish history and destiny call upon us to do now—before it is too late. The resources and energies and intellectual power of our best and brightest must be focused on making sure that there will be Jews remaining in the world lest the Holocaust prevail even while it is being denied. And that requires one thing above all else: a fierce, huge effort to expand Jewish education.

Let us resolve to build a school—a yeshiva, a day school, a Hebrew school, an elementary school, a high school, a school for adults, any genuine Jewish school—on the unmarked graves of every one of the million Jewish children done to death by the Nazi *Herrenvolk.* If not a yeshiva on every grave, then, for Heaven's sake, at the very least one more Jewish child to learn how to be a Jew for the grave of every one child martyr! A million more Jewish children learning how and what it is to be Jewish will accomplish more for the honor of the Holocaust martyrs than a million books or sculptures or buildings. Teach another million Jewish children over the globe the loveliness and meaningfulness and warmth of Jewishness, and you will have redeemed the million Jewish child-martyrs from the oblivion wished upon them by the Nazis. A million Jewish children to take the places of those million who perished—that is a celebration of their lives that will not make a mockery of their deaths and that will be worthy of our most heroic efforts.

Will we have the courage to save our and our children's future from the spiritual Holocaust that threatens us? Will we have the wisdom to reorder our priorities and "establish a yeshiva over the grave-sites" of our *Kedoshim* — before the hearts and minds of the majority of our children themselves turn into private little graves of the Jewish spirit?

That is the fateful question that we are obliged to answer. The future of our people lies in our hands. If we do nothing but utter a sigh and shrug our shoulders with palms extended as a sign of resignation and helplessness—then we will stand accused of being passive onlookers at this bloodless Holocaust, and our guilt will parallel that of the silent spectators of the 1930s. But if we resolve to live on despite all, if we stand Jewishly tall and put our shoulders to the wheel and teach and instruct a new generation in the ways of Yiddishkeit, then our hands will grasp the future firmly and surely, and we shall live and the *Kedoshim* will live through us.

Etz chayyim hi la-machazikim bah. Our Torah and our Tradition are a Tree of Life, and by holding on to them we will redeem our past and honor our people by giving them a future.

Shoah: An Oral History of the Holocaust

The result of years of research, the 9½ hour film is an oral history of the Holocaust that brings together a full range of witnesses: the SS officers who served in the death camps; the Polish villagers who tilled their fields within yards of the crematoriums; the Germans who resettled occupied Poland, moving into the houses whose Jewish owners had been sent to their death; the state employee who sold Jews half-fare excursion tickets to the camps—one way; Western scholars of the Holocaust. And then there are the survivors themselves: a Polish barber who cut the hair of women he knew were to die in the next few minutes; a thirteen-year-old boy who was to work in the death camp's "special squad"; the Pole who was taken into the Warsaw ghetto so that he could report to the outside world what he had seen; a woman who lived in hiding in Berlin for most of the war, in anguish at the fate of her people and her own escape from it.

The film shows no archival footage, and it is through the words themselves that the imagination recreates the world described in these words—a way of getting at the truth that is far more shocking than the depiction of actual images. *Shoah* is unforgettable, and it is destined to become a landmark of film and history.

Claude Lanzmann is the remarkable man behind *Shoah.* He devoted eleven years to the making of the film—tracking down survivors of the era, conducting filmed interviews in fourteen countries and bringing over 350 hours of testimony to its present form.

A native Parisian, he fought in the Resistance during World War II. Following the war, he became a close associate of Jean-Paul Sartre and contributed to and edited Sartre's monthly, *Les Temps Modernes.* As a correspondent for this and other publications, he championed such causes as Algerian independence and an end to French involvement in Indochina. In 1973, he made his first film, the documentary, "Why Israel?"

Claude Lanzmann is the remarkable man behind Shoah.

Speaking about *Shoah,* Mr. Lanzmann has said: "Making a history was not what I wanted to do. I wanted to construct something more powerful than that. And, in fact, I think that the film, using only images of the present, evokes the past with far more force than any historical document."

SOBIBOR

Motke Zaidl and Itzhak Dugin

So it was they who dug up and burned all the Jews of Vilna?

Yes. In early January 1944 we began digging up the bodies.

When the last mass grave was opened, I recognized my whole family. Mom and my sisters. Three sisters with their kids. They were all in there. They'd been in the earth four months, and it was winter. They were very well preserved. I recognized their faces, their clothes too.

They'd been killed relatively recently?

Yes.

And it was the last grave?

Yes.

The Nazi plan was for them to open the graves, starting with the oldest?

Yes. The last graves were the newest, and we started with the oldest, those of the first ghetto. In the first grave there were twenty-four thousand bodies.

The deeper you dug, the flatter the bodies were. Each was almost a flat slab. When you tried to grasp a body, it crumbled, it was impossible to pick up. We had to open the graves, but without tools. They said: "Get used to working with your hands."

With just their hands!

When we first opened the graves, we couldn't help it, we all burst out sobbing. But the Germans almost beat us to death. We had to work at a killing pace for two days, beaten all the time, and with no tools. The Germans even forbade us to use the words "corpse" or "victim." The dead were blocks of wood, with absolutely no importance. Anyone who said "corpse" or "victim" was beaten. The Germans made us refer to the bodies as *Figuren,* that is, as puppets, as dolls, or as *Schmattes,* which means "rags."

Were they told at the start how many Figuren *there were in all the graves?*

The head of the Vilna Gestapo told us: "There are ninety thousand people lying there, and absolutely no trace must be left of them."

TREBLINKA

Abraham Bomba (Tel Aviv), survivor

There was a sign, a small sign, on the station of Treblinka. I don't know if we were at the station or if we didn't go up to the station. On the line over there where we stayed there was a sign, a very small sign, which said "Treblinka." The first time in my life I heard that name "Treblinka." Nobody knew. It was not a place. There was not a city. There is not even a small village. Jewish people always dreamed, and that was part of their life, part of their messianic hope, that some day they're going to be free. That dream was mostly true in the ghetto. Every day, every single night, I dreamed about that. I think that's going to be

Simon Srebnik, survivor of Chelmno, meeting with Polish residents of Chelmno forty years later.

good. Not only the dream but the hope conserved in a dream.

The first transport from Czestochowa was sent away on the day after Yom Kippur. The day before Succoth, there was a second transport . . . I was together with them. I know in my heart that something is not good, because if they take children, if they take old people, they send them away, that means it is not good. What they said is they take them away to a place where they will be working. But on the other hand, an old woman, a little child of four weeks or five years, what is work? It was a foolish thing, but still, we had no choice—we believed in them.

Czeslaw Borowi (present-day Treblinka)

He was born here in 1923, and has been here ever since.

He lived at this very spot?

Right here.

Then he had a front-row seat for what happened?

Naturally. You could go up close or watch from a distance. They had land on the far side of the station. To work it, he had to cross the track, so he could see everything.

Does he remember the first convoy of Jews from Warsaw on July 22, 1942?

He recalls the first convoy very well, and when all those Jews were brought here, people wondered, "What's to be done with them?" Clearly, they'd be killed, but no one yet knew how. When people began to understand what was happening, they were appalled, and they commented privately that since the world began, no one had ever murdered so many people that way.

While all this was happening before their eyes, normal life went on? They worked their fields?

Certainly they worked, but not as willingly as usual. They had to work, but when they saw all this, they thought: "Our house may be surrounded. We may be arrested too!"

Were they afraid for the Jews too?

Well, he says, it's this way: if I cut my finger, it doesn't hurt him. They knew about the Jews: the convoys came in here, and then went to the camp, and the people vanished.

Villagers (present-day Treblinka)

He had a field under a hundred yards from the camp. He

Henrik Gawkowski, Polish locomotive engineer

also worked during the German occupation.

He worked his field?

Yes. He saw how they were asphyxiated; he heard them scream; he saw that. There's a small hill; he could see quite a bit.

What did this one say?

They couldn't stop and watch. It was forbidden. The Ukrainians shot at them.

But they could work a field a hundred yards from the camp?

They could. So occasionally he could steal a glance if the Ukrainians weren't looking.

He worked with his eyes lowered?

Yes.

His field was there?

Yes, right up close. It wasn't forbidden to work there.

So he worked, he farmed there?

Yes. Where the camp is now was partly his field. It was off limits, but they heard everything.

It didn't bother him to work so near those screams?

At first it was unbearable. Then you got used to it.

You get used to anything?

Yes.

Now he thinks it was impossible. Yet it was true.

Czeslaw Borowi

So he saw the convoys arriving. There were sixty to eighty cars in each convoy, and there were two locomotives that took the convoys into the camp, taking twenty cars at a time.

And the cars came back empty?

Yes. Here's how it happened: the locomotive picked up twenty cars and took them to the camp. That took maybe an hour, and the empty cars came back here. Then the next twenty cars were taken, and meanwhile, the people in the first twenty were already dead.

Henrik Gawkowski (Malkinia)

Did he hear screams behind his locomotive?

Obviously, since the locomotive was next to the cars. They screamed, asked for water. The screams from the cars closest to the locomotive could be heard very well.

Can one get used to that?

No. It was extremely distressing to him. He knew the people behind him were human, like him. The Germans gave him and the other workers vodka to drink. Without drinking, they couldn't have done it. There was a bonus—that they were paid not in money, but in liquor. Those who worked on the other trains didn't get this bonus. He drank every drop he got because without liquor he couldn't stand the stench when he got here. They even bought more liquor on their own, to get drunk on.

WARSAW

Dr. Franz Grassler

Did you think this idea of a ghetto was a good one? A sort of self-management?

That's right.

A mini-state?

Dr. Franz Grassler, deputy to Auerswald, Nazi commissioner of the Warsaw Ghetto.

It worked well.

But it was self-management for death, wasn't it?

We know that now. But at the time . . .

Even then!

No!

Czerniakow wrote: "We're puppets, we have no power."

Yes.

"No power."

Sure . . . that was . . .

You Germans were the overlords.

Yes.

The overlords. The masters.

Obviously.

Czerniakow was merely a tool.

Yes, but a good tool. Jewish self-management worked well, I can tell you.

It worked well for three years: 1941, 1942, 1943 . . . two and a half years. And in the end . . .

In the end . . .

"Worked well" for what? To what end?

For self-preservation.

No! For death!

Yes, but . . .

Self-management, self-preservation . . . for death!

That's easy to say now.

You admitted the conditions were inhuman. Atrocious . . . horrible!

Yes.

So it was clear even then . . .

No! Extermination wasn't clear. Now we see the result.

Extermination isn't so simple. One step was taken, then another, and another, and another . . .

Yes.

But to understand the process, one must . . .

I repeat: extermination did not take place in the ghetto, not at first. Only with the evacuations.

Evacuations?

The evacuations to Treblinka. The ghetto could have been wiped out with weapons, as was finally done after the rebellion. After I'd left. But at the start . . . Mr. Lanzmann, this is getting us nowhere. We're reaching no new conclusions.

I don't think we can.

I didn't know then what I know now.

You weren't a nonentity.

But I was!

You were important.

You overestimate my role.

No. You were second to the commissioner of the Warsaw "Jewish district."

But I had no power.

It was something.

You were part of the vast German power structure.

Correct. But a small part. You overestimate the authority of a deputy of twenty-eight then.

You were thirty.

Twenty-eight.

At thirty you were mature.

Yes, but for a lawyer who got his degree at twenty-seven, it's just a beginning.

You had a doctorate.

The title proves nothing.

Did Auerswald have one too?

No. But the title's irrelevant.

Doctor of Law . . . What did you do after the war?

I was with a mountaineering publishing house. I wrote and published mountain guide books. I published a mountain climbers' magazine.

Is climbing your main interest?

Yes.

The mountains, the air . . .

Yes.

The sun, the pure air . . .

Not like the ghetto air.

Gertrude Schneider and her mother (New York), survivors of the ghetto

"The words I write you
Are written with tears, not ink.
Years, the best years, are finished
And gone—never to be recovered.
It's difficult to repair what has been destroyed.
It's difficult to tie up the bonds of our love.
Ah, look, your tears,
The fault is not mine.
Because that's how it must be.
That's how it must be, that's how it must be.
We must part from one another.
That's how it must be, that's how it must be.
Love must end for both of us.
Do you remember when I
Left you on the road?
My fate told me I had to leave you,
Because I never want to stand in that road again.
Because that's how it must be."

LOHAME HAGHETTAOT KIBBUTZ MUSEUM (GHETTO FIGHTERS' KIBBUTZ), ISRAEL

The Jewish Combat Organization (JCO) in the Warsaw ghetto was officially formed on July 28, 1942. After the first mass deportation to Treblinka, which was interrupted on September 30, some sixty thousand Jews remained in the ghetto. On January 18, 1943, the deportations were resumed. Despite a severe lack of weapons, the members of the JCO called for resistance, and started fighting, to the Germans' total surprise. It lasted three days. The Nazis withdrew with losses, abandoning weapons the Jews grabbed. The deportations were stopped. The Germans now knew they had to fight to conquer the ghetto. The battle began on the evening of April 19, 1943, the eve of Pesach (Passover). It had to be a fight to the death.

Itzhak Zuckermann (known as "Antek"), second-in-command of the JCO, at the Lohame Haghettaot Kibbutz Museum (Ghetto Fighters' Kibbutz), Israel

I began drinking after the war. It was very difficult. Claude, you asked for my impression. If you could lick my heart, it would poison you.

At the request of Mordechai Anielewicz, commander-in-chief of the JCO, Antek had left the ghetto six days before the German attack. His mission: to ask Polish Resistance leaders to arm the Jews. They refused.

In fact, I left the ghetto six days before the uprising. I wanted to return on the nineteenth, the eve of Passover. I wrote to Mordechai Anielewicz and to Zivia. Zivia was my wife. I got back a very polite letter, very formal, from Anielewicz, and a very aggressive letter from Zivia that said: "You haven't done a thing so far. Nothing." I decided to go back anyway. I had no idea what was going on in the ghetto. I couldn't imagine it. But Simha's companions knew of the German encirclement before I did.

Simha Rottem (known as "Kajik")

At Passover time we felt something was going to happen in the ghetto. We could feel the pressure. On Passover eve the Germans attacked. Not just the Germans, but the Ukrainians too, along with the Lithuanians, the Polish police, and the Latvians, and this massive force entered the ghetto. We felt this was the end. On the morning the Germans went into the ghetto, the attack was concentrated on the central ghetto. We were a little away from it; we heard blasts, shots, the echo of the gunfire, and we knew the fighting was fierce in the central ghetto.

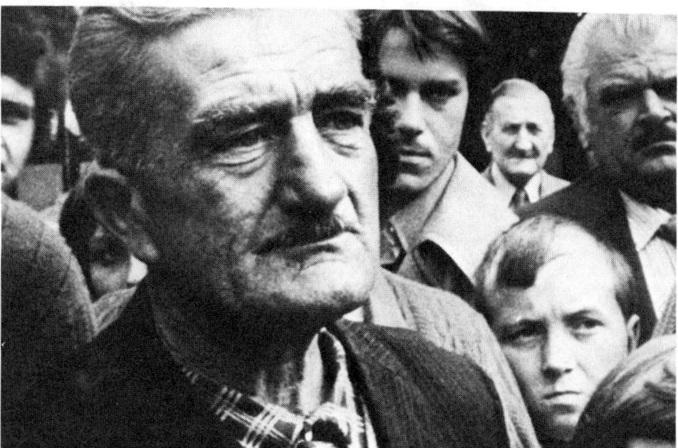

Polish residents of Auschwitz.

During the first three days of fighting, the Jews had the upper hand. The Germans retreated at once to the ghetto entrance, carrying dozens of wounded with them. From then on, their onslaught came entirely from the outside, through air attack and artillery. We couldn't resist the bombing, especially their method of setting fire to the ghetto. The whole ghetto was ablaze. All life vanished from the streets and houses. We hid in the cellars and bunkers. From there we made our sorties. We went out at night. The Germans were in the ghetto mostly by day, leaving at night. They were afraid to enter the ghetto at night.

Filip Muller, survivor of Auschwitz.

The bunkers were prepared by the residents, not by the fighters. When we could no longer stay in the streets, we fell back on the bunkers. All the bunkers were alike inside. The most striking thing was the crowding, for there were a lot of us, and the heat. It was so hot you couldn't breathe. Not even a candle could burn in those bunkers. To breathe in that intense heat, you sometimes had to lie with your face to the ground. The fact that we fighters hadn't prepared bunkers proves we didn't expect to survive our fight against the Germans.

I don't think the human tongue can describe the horror we went through in the ghetto. In the streets, if you can call them that, for nothing was left of the streets, we had to step over heaps of corpses. There was no room to get around them. Besides fighting the Germans, we fought hunger, and thirst. We had no contact with the outside world; we were completely isolated, cut off from the world. We were in such a state that we could no longer understand the very meaning of why we went on fighting. We thought of attempting a breakout to the Aryan part of Warsaw, outside the ghetto.

Just before May 1 Sigmund and I were sent to try to contact Antek in Aryan Warsaw. We found a tunnel under Bonifraterska Street that led out into Aryan Warsaw. Early in the morning we suddenly emerged into a street in broad daylight. Imagine us on that sunny May 1, stunned to find ourselves in the street, among normal people. We'd come from another planet. People immediately jumped on us, because we certainly looked exhausted, skinny, in rags. Around the ghetto there were always suspicious Poles who grabbed Jews. By a miracle, we escaped them. In Aryan Warsaw, life went on as naturally and normally as before. The cafes operated normally, the restaurants, buses, streetcars, and movies were open. The ghetto was an isolated island amid normal life.

Our job was to contact Itzhak Zuckermann to try to mount a rescue operation, to try to save the few fighters who might still be alive in the ghetto. We managed to contact Zuckermann. We found two sewer workers. On the night of May 8-9 we decided to return to the ghetto with another buddy, Rijek, and the two sewer men. After the curfew we entered the sewers. We were entirely at the mercy of the two workmen, since only they knew the ghetto's underground layout. Halfway there they decided to turn back, they tried to drop us, and we had to threaten them with our guns. We went on through the sewers until one of the workmen told us were were under the ghetto. Rijek guarded them so they couldn't escape. I raised the manhole cover to go up into the ghetto.

At bunker Mila 18,* I missed them by a day. I had returned the night of May 8-9. The Germans found the bunker on the morning of the eighth. Most of its survivors committed suicide, or succumbed to gas in the bunkers. I went to bunker Franczískanska 22. There was no answer when I yelled the password, so I had to go on through the ghetto. I suddenly heard a woman calling from the ruins. It was darkest night, no lights, you saw nothing. All the houses were in ruins, and I heard only one voice. I thought some evil spell had been cast on me, a woman's voice talking from the rubble. I circled the ruins. I didn't look at my watch, but I must have spent a half hour exploring, trying to find the woman whose voice guided me, but unfortunately I didn't find her.

Were there fires?

Strictly speaking, no, for the flames had died down, but there was still smoke, and that awful smell of charred flesh of people who had surely been burned alive. I continued on my way, going to other bunkers in search of fighting units, but it was the same everywhere. I'd give the password: "Jan."

That's a Polish first name, Jan?

Right. And I got no answer. I went from bunker to bunker, and after walking for hours in the ghetto, I went back toward the sewers.

Was he alone then?

Yes, I was alone all the time. Except for that woman's voice, and a man I met as I came out of the sewers, I was alone throughout my tour of the ghetto. I didn't meet a living soul. At one point I recall feeling a kind of peace, of serenity. I said to myself: "I'm the last Jew. I'll wait for morning, and for the Germans."

*The bunker Mila 18 was the headquarters of the Jewish Combat Organization.

Shoah

Partisans of Vilna

David G. Roskies

Imagine, if you will, a documentary on the French, the Greek, or the White Russian partisan movement during World War II. For starters, it would all be filmed on location, with the main protagonists showing us exactly where they organized their cells and fought their battles, were denounced and imprisoned, with many of these sites now turned into national shrines. All the interviews would be conducted in the same language, requiring subtitles only for export. As for the touchy political issues involved, only one version of the story would come out. In France, assuming the director were someone on the left, he (she) would play up the Communist underground over the Gaullists, and would greatly minimize the role of the British and American airforce. The "White Russian" movie, produced in Moscow, would obviously toe the party line, with not a word about the Poles, the collaborators, or the fate of the Jews. Most importantly, these hypothetical films would all have a happy end—the liberation of the country from the Fascists and the return to civility.

Not so, *Partisans of Vilna.* Except for some footage of the city (presently under Soviet rule, and officially known as Vilnius), the viewer has to go by words, drawings, scale reproductions, and a few minutes worth of valuable newsreel. The story is told in almost all the languages of the Jewish diaspora and required a veritable team of translators to decipher. Just as they speak many languages, the former partisans and participants don't weave a seamless tale: they break down and cry; they admit their mistakes; they agonize over what could have been. And when it's all over, Vilna, their beloved city, is *Judenrein,* though *they* are alive to remember.

Delving deeper, we discover that our filmmaker faced much greater obstacles than access to location, or language, or politics, or even the scope of the tragedy. For in the three hundred years that Vilna served as a center of Jewish life in eastern Europe, nothing was farther from its ethos than the idea of Jewish armed resistance. Only in its capacity as a *spiritual* center had Vilna earned the honor of being called "the Jerusalem of Lithuania." It was the unrivalled seat of learning, the source of great books and ideas, the model for a certain kind of religious discipline. Even in the modern period, which, for the Jews of eastern Europe began in the 1880s, Vilna was the seedbed of utopian solutions to "the Jewish problem"—Zionism and Socialism—while throughout most of its history, the city had been spared the scourge of pogroms. If they suffered, the Jews of Vilna suffered the plight of all Jews: discrimination, poverty and powerlessness.

Vilna, "Jerusalem of Lithuania," 1939.

No two-hour documentary could possibly fill in this background, yet without it, one can scarcely appreciate how great were the odds against there ever being an organized Jewish resistance movement. Consider what the film *does* show: How the traumatized survivors of the initial mass slaughter were rounded up into a ghetto and were slowly starved to death. How the Germans exacted collective punishment against any form of resistance. How the older generation of Jewish leaders was dedicated to maintaining a semblance of normalcy. How the head of the Jewish Police and Judenrat believed that it was safer to gamble against time, and how the vast majority of the ghetto Jews believed that, too. The fighters had no access to arms, no military training, and no hinterland (who knew anything about the woods, except as a place to picnic!). Even among themselves, there were competing strategies: some wanted a symbolic last stand in the ghetto; others wanted to regroup in the forests. And once the few survivors made it to the forests, their closest ally, Soviet General Markov, forced them to disband as a separate Jewish brigade.

Ruins of the bet medrash *of Elijah ben Solomon.*

Though *Partisans of Vilna* cannot illustrate all the historical, cultural, political, generational, and logistical factors militating against armed revolt, it does argue the opposite case very effectively—that the young fighters grew directly out of the native Jewish soil. Abba Kovner, the "star" of the film, makes this eminently clear at the outset when he describes the hub of Jewish Vilna, the synagogue courtyard, and especially the library it housed, where young and old, religious and secular, scholars and revolutionaries rubbed shoulders before the war. What he is saying, in effect, is that you have to know history to make history, and these young men and women were keenly aware of where they stood in the ongoing struggle for Jewish survival.

Thus, *Partisans of Vilna* is both the culminating chapter in a three-hundred-year saga of Jewish cultural resilience and resistance, and the story of the most radical break in that history: the decision of a few hundred young Jews to go down fighting when faced with the destruction of their entire community.

What made them do it? Not the hope of survival, since fighting back meant dying that much sooner, and death, they now understood, awaited all of Europe's Jews. Nor was it some Quixotic dream to turn the tide of war, since the ghetto was of no strategic importance to anyone. Rather, in a world where all roads led to destruction, it was a way of choosing the manner of one's death and of responding as a disciplined collective.

To act "as a disciplined collective" in the face of imminent death requires a sense of common past and common purpose; a tradition of self-reliance; a system of codes to communicate in secret; a veritable "counter-culture." And this is precisely what the members of the Jewish youth movements in the Vilna ghetto possessed—as their *natural legacy.* Armed resistance, in the wider scheme of things, was but the logical extension of the soup kitchens, schools, charities, refugee centers, hospital clinics, public health stations, laundries, orphanages, day care centers, vitamin laboratories, supply distribution centers, concert halls, libraries—in short, of the whole self-help network in the ghetto which, in turn, was based on a centuries-old tradition of Jewish autonomy in eastern Europe. Most, if not all of the partisans-to-be, were also active on these other ghetto fronts which we now identify as "spiritual resistance." Some, like Hirsh Glik, Shmerke Kaczerginski and Abraham Sutzkever, were even great poets, or were to become major poets much later—like Abba Kovner. Born of the brave new world of east European Jewry, they represented the very best that the culture had to offer. But if, at the time of the revolt, they were looked upon as rebels and madmen, it was because they alone understood that the Holocaust—a destruction so different in degree and scope from anything known before—required an equally radical response.

Jewish fighters from the Vilna ghetto. *photo credit: YIVO*

And so the point of this documentary is that not everyone becomes a hero given the worst set of circumstances; that the capacity for human survival *in extremis* is not a function of biology or chance but is largely a matter of culture. Logically, the combined force of mass murder, expulsion, ghettoization, starvation, epidemic and constant terror would have reduced any group of people to a jungle mentality. That is certainly what the Nazis had in mind. But as a people schooled in adversity, secure in its minority status and highly skilled in group behavior, the Jews of eastern Europe were able to devise a counter-strategy that defied all "normal" logic. And the heroism of those who lived to tell the tale cannot be measured in terms of how many guns they smuggled, or how many trains they blew up. Despite its name, *Partisans of Vilna* is not your run-of-the-mill war movie. Rather, it is the unknown story of how very young men and women with no hope of survival banded together; how they were united in their hopeless struggle through songs and a common set of symbols; and how, having lost their parents, their homes and their past, they clung to the collective memory until someone with a camera and a sympathetic ear relieved them—if only for a moment—of that terrible burden.

Partisan in the Vilna region.

This essay has been commissioned for Films and the Humanities, a presentation of the New York Council for the Humanities.

The partisans of Vilna. Abba Kovner stands at rear, center.

An Unusual Journey To Poland

Efraim Zuroff

After suppressing the Warsaw Ghetto revolt, Nazi general Jurgen Stroop prepared a special report for his superior Heinrich Himmler, head of the S.S. *Es gibt Keinen judischen Wohnbezirk mehr,* it began. "The Jewish residential quarter of Warsaw no longer exists." By this time, most of Polish Jewry had already been exterminated, and Stroop and his Nazi cohorts probably believed they would soon realize their objective of putting an end to hundreds of years of Jewish life in Poland.

But not all Polish Jews had been exterminated. A few had survived the camps. Others had remained in hiding all through the war. And thousands had fled to the Soviet Union or had been deported there by the Russians. And so, for a brief period after the war, there was some semblance of Jewish life in what had once been the foremost center of Jewish learning, culture and politics. This phoenix-like renaissance was ephemeral, however. Successive waves of emigration, hurried flight, and expulsion rapidly followed. Assimilation also made its inroads. Thus today General Stroop's words apply not only to Warsaw but for Poland as a whole. For all practical purposes, present-day Poland is *Judenrein*—free of Jews.

I stopped off in Poland on my way from my home in Israel to the United States to visit the sites connected with the history of the Holocaust and came away shaken—not so much by the experience of visiting the death camps at Auschwitz-Birkenau, Majdanek, Treblinka and Chelmno, but by the pain of seeing Warsaw, Cracow, Lublin and Lodz without Jews, of passing through countless villages where Jews had once lived and flourished and where today Polish children grow up without ever seeing a Jew. Had these Jews left of their own free will and moved elsewhere, one would not feel the pain of their absence so acutely. We are, however, well aware of their fate.

Warsaw

I arrived in Warsaw on a Tuesday afternoon. The main airport was surprisingly small, reminding me of Lod, outside of Tel Aviv. So did the bureaucracy. There were long lines and tough customs officials who seemed intent on blocking any Pole from getting around the local regulations on bringing things into the country. It all gave me the feeling I had stumbled upon the source of some of Israel's bureaucratic woes.

My first full day in Poland was spent in visiting the various memorials in Warsaw to the Holocaust victims—memorials which well express the ambivalent attitude of the Poles toward the Jews. There is practically no mention

Warsaw. Indigent Jew.

among them of the millions of Jews who lived and died in Poland under more or less normal circumstances over the course of generations, no mention of that they ever constituted fully a tenth of the population, no mention of their prominent role in the commercial life of the country, as well as in other spheres. Jews are never mentioned in books, exhibitions and the like, and their graves are left in utter neglect to be vandalized or laid waste by the elements.

The fate of the martyred Jews, however is an entirely different matter. Their tragic story is considered an integral part of modern Polish history and is by no means kept secret. There are many memorials to the victims of the "Hitlerite fascists" (as they are invariably referred to) and especially to the ghetto fighters. There are memorials at all the extermination camps as well as at the major concentration camps. Moreover, the fact that most of these martyrs were Jews is not concealed. Most of the time, the Jewish origin of victims is noted and even stressed.

The memorials themselves are, for the most part, not overpowering. Which is not to say they're not impressive. Nathan Rappaport's monument commemorating ghetto fighters and deportees, for example seemed a lot smaller

Sealed windows of Nozik Shul, the only surviving synagogue in Warsaw.

than I had imagined it, perhaps because the replica of it at Yad Vashem is much larger and because photographs of it are always taken at an angle which make it seem much larger. There were no visitors at the memorial, but the moment we appeared we were approached by the first of a breed of seemingly ubiquitous *schnorrers* (beggars) who infest most Jewish sites of pilgrimage in Poland and especially abound in Warsaw. This one bemoaned the plight of his mother—which strained our credulity since he looked about 70 or 80. His fancy American attire did not help his case either. A local Jew who'd accompanied me to the memorial told him I was an Israeli student, whereupon he disappeared to wait in ambush for the next American tourist.

Our next stop was the monument at 18 Mila Street, site of the bunker-headquarters of the Jewish fighting organization, where Mordechai Anielewicz, leader of the revolt, met his death. A tiny stone monument with inscriptions in Polish, Yiddish and Hebrew marked the spot. I was struck by the disparity between the drab, tiny stone and the exceptional bravery it was erected to commemorate.

These monuments, however, were a far cry from the Jewish cemetery just outside of what was once the ghetto wall. The sight which greets the visitor is appalling. The cemetery is in total disarray, with graves stuffed one on top of the other. Many of the tombstones are broken—having either been smashed by local vandals—who seem to have things their own way in most Jewish cemeteries in Poland—or been damaged by the elements.

Many famous figures from modern Jewish history are buried here: writers such as Y.L. Peretz and Ansky; historian Mayer Balaban; the chairman of the Warsaw *Judenrat,* Adam Czerniakow; as well as famous rabbis such as the Amshinover Rebbe and the Modzhetzer Rebbe. The latter's grave is a total wreck despite attempts by his followers abroad to erect a fitting tombstone and mausoleum.

Though I had been told beforehand it was in a terrible state, seeing this cemetery with my own eyes was another matter altogether. The problem seemed insoluble: the elderly remnants of Polish Jewry were obviously unable to properly maintain the Jewish cemeteries. The Poles did not seem particularly interested in doing so. I was left to conclude that until the Messiah comes, Jews interred in Poland will be denied their final resting place.

There were quite a few sites to see in Warsaw, and during the course of the day I also visited the *Umschlagplatz,* the place from which 300,000 Warsaw Jews were deported to Treblinka during the period from July 22 (Tisha B'Av) to September 13, 1942. An inconspicuous wall marks the spot and inscriptions in Polish, Yiddish and Hebrew note that, "From this place, hundreds of thousands of Jews were deported to die a martyrs' death during the years 1942-43. May their memory be blessed." How much suffering, I thought, can be squeezed into that small wall with its trilingual plaque? How can the suffering of more than half of what was once Europe's largest Jewish community be adequately expressed by this nearly invisible memorial? I thought of the famed mystic Aaron Zeitlin who came to be deported in *tallit* and *tefillin,* fully prepared to sanctify the name of G-d, and of Janusz Korczak, the noted Jewish writer, doctor, and educator, who chose to accompany the children of his orphanage to Treblinka rather than go into hiding.

From the *Umschlagplatz,* I went to the infamous Pawiak prison, now a government-run museum. Throughout the exhibition and in literature prepared by the museum, the role of the Communists in the struggle against the Nazis is emphasized out of all proportion to the reality; the theme is common to most war memorials erected in Poland. In one respect, then, the Poles and the Jews have something in common. both nations have tried hard to insure that the events of World War II will never be forgotten. Polish efforts have been truly prodigious. One cannot go far in Warsaw, for example, without seeing a monument or memorial plaque. And at the time I visited, in August, around the anniversary of the Polish revolt in Warsaw, there were fresh flowers at practically every memorial.

The Poles, unlike many other peoples, have not forgotten World War II; the problem is their selective memory. At the Jewish Historical Institute, one can see the "official" version of the history of the Warsaw Ghetto, as well as exhibitions of Jewish art and ritual objects. Most of those whose photographs are displayed are Communists. Of the Zionists, from whose ranks most of the leaders and fighters in the revolt actually came, only two or three are noted. The others apparently did not receive approval of the "big brothers" in the Kremlin. The institute is nonetheless a very important site, as it is the repository of the original Ringelblum ("Oneg Shabbat") archives, the secret archives of the Warsaw Ghetto. The milk cans in which documents were originally hidden are on display there, and seeing them was a genuine thrill, one of the few positive experiences during my visit.

I spent the rest of my day wandering around the area of the ghetto. The entire area had been razed to the ground by the Germans following the ghetto revolt, so none of the buildings were original. After the war the area was rebuilt and today it is merely another section of Warsaw. None of the sites I looked for were noted and I found myself wondering whether Poles presently living in the area had any idea about the events which had taken place on these streets. When I remarked to one young Jewish acquaintance that he lived in an area that had once been part of the ghetto he seemed surprised, as if the thought had never occurred to him.

Majdanek

The next morning I set out to visit Majdanek, an extermination camp located on the outskirts of Lublin, a city about 110 miles southeast of Warsaw. The drive afforded me my first view of rural Poland. The main highway, from the capital to Lublin, one of Poland's larger cities, has but two lanes and more than its share of horse and mule drawn carts. The latter are one of the more obvious manifestations of the backwardness of the rural areas. The cart dominates and the tractor is a rare sight. Most of the farmers grow wheat or fodder. The scenery is terribly monotonous—low, flat plains with bundles of wheat tied at the top standing in the fields. These bundles can be seen for miles on end, everywhere, and I am certain that should I ever see a bundle of that sort again I will think instantly of Poland.

On the road to Lublin we periodically saw signs indicating we were approaching the infamous death camp—"Majdanek Museum of Martyrology 43 kilometers" . . . 27 kilometers . . . 9 kilometers, etc. The Poles have not hidden the death camps. On the contrary, they have all been made official museums and/or memorials. Every effort is made to ensure that they serve as educational reminders to as many people as possible.

Majdanek is one such memorial and museum. The latter consists of the remains of the camp, which was the first of the extermination camps to be liberated. The barracks and

The city of Lublin rises over Majdanek. The Nazis felt no need to conceal the camp from the local populace and the gas chambers are clearly visible from Lublin's main highway.

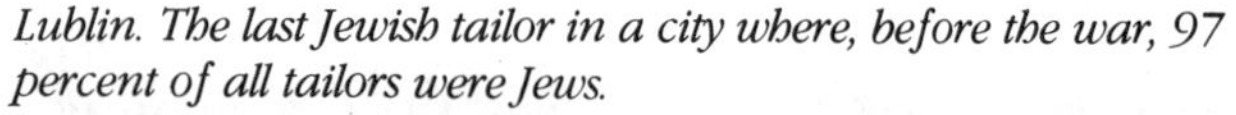

Lublin. The last Jewish tailor in a city where, before the war, 97 percent of all tailors were Jews.

camp are exactly as the Russians found them in the summer of 1944, except that several barracks house exhibitions prepared by museum staff. Wandering through the camp is an almost surrealistic experience. Despite years of studying and doing research on the Holocaust, I nonetheless found it hard to grasp that so many people had actually been murdered on these grounds. The exhibitions of the hair, clothing, and shoes of the inmates did not leave me overwhelmingly moved. I found myself wondering whether I had become immune or simply had lost my sensitivity due to my preoccupation with the subject. Even the impressive memorial failed to arouse any surge of genuine feeling. Perhaps I was expecting too much. Perhaps I was in a state of profound disbelief, having for the first time seen the sites I had read so much about. In any event, I left the camp feeling empty and headed for Lublin.

Our first stop in the city was the Jewish cemetery. Invariably, Jewish visitors to Poland end up spending much time in cemeteries. In other countries they may visit the Jewish school, a shul, a restaurant, etc. But in Poland the Jewish attractions are the cemeteries and the death camps. That fact more than any other succinctly summarizes the catastrophe of Polish Jewry.

Surrounded by a low red brick wall, the Jewish cemetery stood silent and deserted on Lubartow Street in an older section of the city. The main gate was locked, but thanks to a tip from an acquaintance who had previously visited the cemetery, my driver and I went looking for a second entrance. Eventually, we found a rusty iron door which was opened for us by a middle-aged Pole who lived inside. He told us the cemetery was "over the grassy hills" and we set out to find it. After climbing several steep inclines and making our way through jungle-thick vegetation, we found a few battered tombstones standing in the middle of nowhere. This was all that was left of the cemetery of what had once been a great center of Torah the home of such great rabbis as the Seer of Lublin and Rabbi Meir Shapiro.

We next visited the building that once was Yeshivat Chachmei Lublin, one of the most famous yeshivot in prewar Poland. Its founder, Rabbi Shapiro, had introduced a revolutionary concept into the yeshiva world by building a dormitory for his students; previously, the practice was for the students to rent rooms from local residents. The structure he built was completed in 1936 and was the largest of its kind in Europe—a beautiful six story building with a large lawn and spacious grounds. Somehow the war years left it more or less intact and it stands to this day on its original site. But it no longer houses the yeshiva. The rabbis and students were mostly killed by the Nazis and their collaborators. The yeshiva was never reopened. Today the building houses the local medical school and nary a trace remains of its original residents.

Treblinka

Next day, Friday, was set aside for the trip to Treblinka, the infamous death camp to which the Jews of Warsaw were deported. It is situated about 80 miles from Warsaw on the road to Bialystok. Unlike Majdanek (and Auschwitz) which besides being a death camp was also a labor camp and therefore held a large number of non-Jewish inmates, Treblinka was exclusively an extermination camp and hence largely Jewish.

In August of 1943, the inmates revolted, set fire to several buildings in the camp and attempted to flee to the forests. Although most of the inmates were subsequently killed or captured, Hitler shortly thereafter ordered the camp razed. Today, nothing remains of the original camp; the visitor can see only a monument.

A series of concrete trestles, symbolizing the railroad tracks upon which the inmates were brought to the camp, leads from the entrance of the camp to a large open field full of misshapen stones planted in the ground. At first glance they seem like a cross between tombstones and stalagmites. Some have names of various Polish towns engraved on them (Wyszkow, Brok, Gora, Kalawaria, etc.) but most bear no names. The field is dominated by a large mushroom-shaped monument with barely discernible figures sculpted on its crown. In front of the monument and slightly to the left is a large stone with inscriptions in Polish, Yiddish, French, English and German. All say, "Never again." There is no inscription in Hebrew and in a fit of anger I wrote *le-olam lo-oud* (never again) in very small letters in pen. Not that anyone will be able to see it—the letters were too small and all I had was a ballpoint pen—but somehow I felt I had to make some gesture to indicate the link between the Jews of Treblinka and the State of Israel. Many of those dead Jews had spoken Hebrew, many more dreamed of Israel—a fact which no amount of Polish propaganda can cover up.

The tombstone-like stones are arranged like a winding path which encircles the monument and winds its way through the field in a seemingly random manner. Standing there alone, I felt as if I had a holy obligation to walk every inch of that path, to look at each and every stone, as if with each step I too commemorated another Jew and each stone I viewed perpetuated the memory of another shtetl, another town, another Jewish community. I wandered along the path and tried to see every name inscribed on the stones. Most, however, were blank which at last I realized was perfectly appropriate; that was exactly how the Jews lived and died at Treblinka—anonymously.

On the way out, we passed the maintenance workers for the grounds lounging around on the grass. One was sprawled out under a tree while others were lying around bantering with one another. Their behavior was perfectly innocuous, of course, and yet I found it irritating. I look at the scythes they were using to cut the grass, and the thought crossed my mind that the grass had probably been cut in a similar fashion when Treblinka was in operation. In fact, a few of them looked old enough to have been aware of what was going on in the camp at that time. I wanted to ask them a few questions in this respect, but somehow could not.

We left Treblinka and passed near the village of the road of the same name. The road signs still perturbed me immensely. Wasn't even the name poison? How could anyone live in a village with that name? The old, primitive houses did not provide one with any answers, but the sign "Treblinka," which we saw as we crossed the Bug River, will forever remain engraved in my mind as a symbol of the chasm between the victims and the bystanders.

Shabbat in Warsaw

As soon as we arrived in Warsaw, I began to think about my plans for the evening. Soon it would be Shabbat and for the first time in my life I would be spending it in a city where there was no *minyan* on Friday night. Even in the smallest Jewish communities I have always been able to find a *minyan* both on Friday night and on Shabbat morning. Yet in Warsaw, in 1987, no quorum of Jewish males gathers to greet the Sabbath queen. That this could happen in a city which once probably had the largest number of synagogues in the world says perhaps much about the impact of the Holocaust as a visit to one of the death camps.

Perhaps had I known beforehand what services were like in Warsaw, I would not have been so distraught over the lack of a *minyan*. First of all, Warsaw's only remaining synagogue was in a horrible physical state. Though the Polish government claims the building is being renovated, and though a few signs of construction are visible, almost nothing seems to have actually been done. According to local observers no more than one or two people are ever at work on the building. Both exterior and interior remain in desperate need of repair. Large cracks run the length of the outside walls, and there are windows missing and the walls need paint. The interior is not much better, with several parts of the synagogue neglected and filthy. The *siddurim* came from the United States; they cannot be printed in the Polish people's democracy. The same applies for many of the other religious articles in the synagogue. They are products of the generosity and concern of American Jewry and I would not be the least bit surprised if the Polish government were not waiting for American Jews to pay for the Warsaw synagogue's renovation. Several local Jews described the Nozik synagogue's survival of the Holocaust as a miracle. Now a second miracle is badly needed.

While the synagogue edifice is in need of repairs, one gets the impression that the community itself is already beyond help. The few local Jews present spent most of the service screaming at one another. Most of those present paid little attention to the service, seemed to have little interest in the actual ritual. They had come primarily to be with other Jews. Others concentrated on accosting the American tourists, who nearly outnumbered the locals, for "donations." It was the ultimate absurdity—Jews being solicited for funds in synagogue on the Sabbath.

The Jews of Warsaw are an endangered species. Most worshippers at the Nozik synagogue were very elderly. There were only two children and one young adult among them. While these youngsters seemed to know that they—as Jews—belonged in the synagogue on the Sabbath, they did not seem aware of how to participate in the services.

I spoke to the unofficial religious leader of the synagogue and probably the only Jew in Warsaw today whose dress reminds one of the tens of thousands of Orthodox Jews who lived in the Polish capital during the years between the World Wars. Dressed in black coat and hat he attempts to provide for the religious needs of the remnants of the Jewish community. He is the *shochet,* the ritual slaughterer. He is the *ba'al koreh,* the Torah reader. He renders halachic decisions. He is also a *mohel,* but his circumcision services are practically never required these days. His most important job, however, is to educate the few Jewish youngsters still in Warsaw. This coming year he hopes to have classes for six young children and six students of college age. A learned and pious Jew—it was only logical he be asked the question I posed to practically every Jew I met in Poland—*Far vous bleibst du in Polen?* (Why do you remain in Poland?) The main reason he said, was his sense of obligation to the children he was teaching. "Soon, they will be leaving for other places and I want to teach them as much as possible before they go." Then I will be able to go too." He plans to join his daughter who lives in Israel, or as he called it, *arzeinu* (our land).

In key respects, it should be said, Polish Jews seem to be under a lot less pressure than their Soviet brethren. People speak freely of Israel, and a blessing for *Tzahal* (Israel Defense Forces) and for Israel was recited during the services I witnessed, though Israel was not mentioned by name. Of course, *Folkstimme,* the government controlled Yiddish newspaper, published by the community criticizes Israel and lauds its Peace Now movement. But all in all, the atmosphere was much more relaxed than I had anticipated.

Following the service, I was invited to eat in one of the homes where I had an opportunity to meet several members of the congregation. We conversed in Yiddish and in Hebrew, the discussion revolving around two themes—Polish Jewry and Israel. The fact that I had come from Israel naturally aroused their curiosity and they plied me with questions about life there. Each recalled his particular connection to Israel—relatives living there (Did I know so and so in Holon?), a visit one had made many years ago, etc. I, in turn, asked them the question which obsessed me throughout my stay: Why, maintaining their Jewish identity as they did, did they remain? The details differed somewhat from one individual to the next, but the basic answer was the same. "You are right, BUT—" with BUT meaning: *We are too old, too sick, too tired.* When I asked one of the younger people, a widower with two small children, how he could stay, he shrugged off the question unwilling as it were to face the dismal reality.

Auschwitz

One Sunday, I visited Auschwitz. Let me begin by saying that I was wholly unprepared for what I found there. The former concentration camp is perhaps the biggest tourist attraction in Poland. Nowhere in Poland did I see the throngs of visitors I saw at the museum. It is possible that this was because I visited on a Sunday afternoon during the summer, but the fact remains that the museum was inundated with thousands of visitors from all over Europe. Beside the ubiquitous Russians, we met tourists from Rumania; Hungarian motorcyclists outfitted in garish red jumpsuits, French and large groups of Americans; a few Germans and many Poles.

The camp is divided into two parts—a labor camp, formerly known as Auschwitz, and the extermination camp, formerly known as Birkenau. Both have been converted into museums, with major exhibitions housed in the former, probably because there were more buildings left in Auschwitz than in Birkenau. The effect of this is that because the main exhibitions are located in Auschwitz, which is situated about a mile away, few visitors ever see Birkenau. I would estimate the number of people in

Entrance to Auschwitz, a brief train-ride from Cracow.

Auschwitz that day at close to twenty thousand; those visiting Birkenau probably numbered no more than a few hundred.

The visit to Auschwitz really begins when you pass through the infamous gate with the slogan *Arbeit Macht Frei* (Work Liberates). From there you enter the section which housed the prisoners' barracks, which was found intact when the Russians liberated the camp in January 1945. We passed by the various execution sites, walked along the barbed wire fences, viewed the watchtowers—all by now familiar sites. I entered the various buildings and saw the exhibitions—the piles of hair, suitcases, shoes, and children's clothing. The exhibitions are similar to the ones in Majdanek, except that those in Auschwitz are more numerous and the artifacts are in lighted showcases rather than in dark barracks. While the visit to the camp grounds itself did not move me, the suitcases and the children's clothing did. The former, piled to the ceiling, are exhibited face-up with their owners' names prominently displayed: Hafner, Stadler, Kurz, Cohen, Freitag, etc. All Jewish names—the names of people who probably went to Auschwitz full of enough hope that they wrote their names in large letters on their suitcases to make sure they would not get lost. At the piles of children's clothing, sorrow and pain appeared on the faces of every visitor as if suddenly all national and lingual barriers were overcome and everyone shared a common grief for the young victims.

I came to Block 27, the recently reopened "Jewish pavillion" or the "Museum of Jewish Martyrology" as it is officially known. The pavillion has a long history which dates nearly two decades. Originally each of the nations whose a pavillion, the Jewish "nation" being included. However, following Poland's decision to sever diplomatic relations with Israel in the wake of the Six Day War, the Jewish pavillion was closed down by Polish authorities. This step was not considered a calamity by Jewish groups because the pavillion's historical exhibitions were no more than an attempt by the Poles to transform the story of the Holocaust into Communist propaganda. Thus, the leaders of the Judenrat were depicted as bourgeois who exploited the toiling masses of the ghettos, while the ghetto fighters rebelled due to their class consciousness.

A decade ago, however, the Poles decided—just why is not clear—to reopen the pavillion and asked for the assistance of Yad Vashem and *Beit Lohamei Hagettaot.* This put the Israeli remembrance institutions in a dilemma, one complicated by the fact that the Poles did not obligate themselves to present the material in a manner acceptable to the two groups. Following extensive deliberation, the Israeli institutions finally decided to accede to the request. Much historical material was sent to Poland, as were teams of advisors. An Israeli delegation was invited to the official opening of the pavillion, which was held in April 1978 to coincide with the 35th anniversary of the Warsaw Ghetto uprising. But would the exhibition in the new museum be historically accurate? Those present at the opening returned to Israel without a conclusive answer; they were given only a short tour of the exhibition, which had still not been completed.

It was thus with some apprehension that I approached the new pavillion. I had a sneaking suspicion that I might encounter difficulties, and I did. I went to the door of the pavillion and found it locked. A sign informed me that it was open, to groups only, from 9 a.m. to 2 p.m. daily. Those wishing to visit from 204 had to obtain written permission from camp authorities. It was 2:15 p.m. Having already experienced Polish bureaucracy on several occasions, I braced myself for what promised to be a harrowing experience. I shuddered lest some Polish official had read an article I had written in the Israeli daily *Maariv* in which I argued that the Israeli institutions should not have helped the Poles prepare the exhibition.

At that moment, the door of the pavillion swung open and several visitors emerged. I tried to enter but was politely refused by the two girls in charge. I began conversing with the tourists, Jews from New York City, when we heard the girls call out "Tourist from America?" "Of course," I answered, hoping I had hit upon an answer which might open the gates. Sure enough, I was ushered in and given a guided tour—which is apparently the only kind you can get since the pavillion has numerous audiovisual devices which have to be turned on and off. The Jewish pavillion, I should add, is the only one at Auschwitz which one cannot enter unaccompanied and to which special regulations apply.

In any event, I was ushered in by the two young smiling hostesses who brought us to the first hall and who turned on the audio-visual show. With me was a young student from New Zealand who was of Polish origin. The film showed the usual footage of Weimar, Germany, Nazi rallies, and Hitler addressing the throngs. The soundtrack was in Polish, without subtitles so my companion from New Zealand translated. The content added up to the classical Communist explanations for the rise of Nazism. We proceeded from hall to hall in the modernistic museum. The mostly black decor, the darkness of the walls, the emptiness, and the nature of the material all conspired to make me feel uneasy. So did the hostess, who seemed to be rushing us and turning on only certain monitors rather than letting us see the entire show.

The program offered a fairly extensive coverage of the Final Solution, much play to the Polish Righteous Among Nations (which leaves the impression that almost all Poles tried to help the Jews) and hardly a mention of Jewish resistance. The Hebrew titles which the Poles had promised to add are not there, save for one line which perhaps sums up the pavillion in the most appropriate manner. The one line is on the wall dedicated to the Gentiles who tried to save Jews. The inscription should read *kol hameitzil nefesh echad ke'ilu hitzil olam maleh* (He who saves one soul it is as if he saved an entire world). But the Poles confused one letter, leaving the inscription to read, *Kol ha-meitzik*... which means he who harrasses one soul.... In the case of most Poles that is certainly more accurate.

Upon leaving, I signed the visitor's log—another unique feature of the Jewish pavillion—in Hebrew, giving Jerusalem as my address. The book itself had very few entries. I sometimes wonder whether the best policy might not be to put a *herem* (a prohibition or ban) on Auschwitz. If Jews refused to set foot in Spain for hundreds of years following the expulsion, perhaps we should adopt a similar policy vis-a-vis Auschwitz. Moreover, that might be the best answer to the Poles' efforts to turn the largest Jewish graveyard in the world into a tourist attraction whose major goal is the propagation of Communist propaganda.

Birkenau

The former extermination center of Birkenau is approximately a mile from Auschwitz. To get there, you walk on a sidewalk opposite a factory and then over a small bridge which spans a railway junction. As we passed over the bridge and I looked down at the tracks, the images at the back of my mind since our arrival at the camp came flooding out—images of the trains, hurtling along the trestles to vomit out their cargos at the gates of Death. After crossing the bridge, we transversed a field and found ourselves at the entrance to Birkenau. Standing on the railway tracks which went right through the gates (the very same tracks upon which the victims had arrived), I felt as if I'd arrived at the threshhold of Hell itself, as if the entire trip had merely been a preparation for this moment. I looked up again and saw the infamous gates of Birkenau and knew that I had indeed completed the first half of my journey—from the spiritual and physical heights of Jerusalem to the Silesian lowlands and the pits of Auschwitz.

Most of Birkenau was destroyed, but there are several buildings still intact. Before entering any of them, though, we wandered along the path leading to the memorial at the far end of the camp. It is a very plain monument, almost nondescript in comparison to some of the others I had seen in Poland. In front of it, in a row, are mock graves with this inscription in some fifteen languages: "Four million men, women and children were cruelly and brutally murdered by the Nazis in this place." The languages chosen were those spoken by the inmates of the camp, and there are inscriptions in both Yiddish and Hebrew. Near the Yiddish inscription was a small *yahrzeit* candle made in Israel. We took a train back to Cracow and the thought crossed my mind that few Jews had enjoyed the privilege of being able to leave Auschwitz as free men or women. At the station, while waiting for the train along with dozens of young tourists from all over Europe, I wondered what kind of impact Auschwitz had had on these youngsters. Did they know the real truth about the Jews? Would what they saw affect them, their opinions, prejudices, and actions? What did they think of Israel? Did they understand the connection between Israel and the Holocaust?

Cracow

Cracow is a handsome city with a lot of character—stark contrast to drab Warsaw. For the most part it was spared the ravages of the war and thus the visitor comes across many very old buildings and diverse architectural styles. Cracow was also an *ir ve-aim bi-Yisrael* before the war, one of the most important Jewish communities, and the home of many great sages.

The Temple, once the synagogue of Cracow's most prosperous Jews

Most of the buildings and sites of Jewish interest one can see today are concentrated in an area of about two square miles not far from the center of the city and the central bus station. My first stop was the old Reform synagogue, which though still in use today, is closed to the public. From the synagogue I went to the cemetery. A low wall of red bricks surrounds the graveyard which is also almost anonymous. If not for the fact that I knew the address, I would never have known that this was the place I was looking for. No signs, no clues on the outside. There is a rusty iron door at the entrance which finally opened after I gave it a good shove. The scene within was depressing. Broken tombstones, terrible congestion, graves right on top of one another. No one stopped me from walking in or bothered to ask what I was doing there. I probably could have gone in with a tow truck and carted away both gravestones and corpses without arousing anyone's opposition—a fact which helps explain why Jewish cemeteries in Poland are in the condition they are.

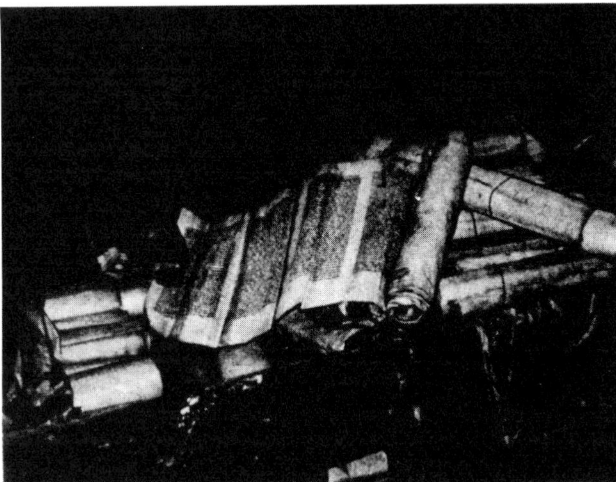

Decaying Torah scrolls in the Remah library from the Cracow synagogues that have been closed.

At my next stop, the oldest synagogue in Poland, I encountered the by now familiar "REMONTE"—closed for renovations. By a stroke of luck, however, I learned that someone was working inside and I managed to obtain entry. The individual who let me in was the museum's director and he explained that the edifice would be open to the public in one year's time. He was, however, willing to show me the shul itself and answer a few questions. Although there was still a lot of debris on the floor, from the construction work, the synagogue looked impressive. Judging from the style of the *Aron Kodesh,* I guessed the building was hundreds of years old, a conjecture confirmed by my host. The original edifice had been built in the late 14th or early 15th century, but had subsequently been destroyed by a fire and was rebuilt in the 16th century. In any event, the building was now an official state museum and the entire project was being financed by the Polish government.

Before leaving I asked the curator about his qualifications for the job. He was a language and linguistics expert, he had extensive experience translating. It was not quite clear to me how this made him qualified to run a Jewish museum, but in Poland, I knew, everything was possible.

Diagonally across the square from the museum-synagogue is a very special site—the synagogue named for one of Cracow's greatest rabbis, the Remah, Rabbi Moshe Isserles, the codifier of the *Shulchan Aruch* used to this day by Ashkenazic Jews. (As we entered, we were joined by several onlookers, one of them a young French student of Jewish origin. His name was Gottlieb and he was supposedly related to the famous Polish painter Mauricey Gottlieb, but his ancestors had converted long ago and he had been raised a Christian. Through the study of Kabbala and Jewish philosophy, he had become interested in his roots and had come to Poland to find them. Like myself, he had wandered from Jewish cemetery to closed synagogue, etc. in each of the major Polish cities.) The synagogue itself is a plain building. We were shown the small study hall where prayers are held on the Sabbath, but were not allowed into the main shul, which is currently in use. We were then taken to the small cemetery in the back of the shul where the Remah is buried. His grave sits fenced off, in splendid isolation. I could only wonder how this sage felt to be buried in the land of Jewish oblivion.

In talks with some of the Cracow Jews, the same stories are repeated. Only a few hundred Jews remain and most prefer to remain anonymous. Only on the High Holidays does the synagogue attract large numbers of Jews. On Yom Kippur, about eighty people come to the Remah synagogue and there is also a minyan in the former Reform shul—Judaism flowering compared to Warsaw! *Why do they stay?* The same reasons seem to apply—illnesses, pensions, too tired to relocate, etc. The youth are nonexistent; they have either emigrated or simply disappeared. The future is obvious—oblivion. Walking the street one finds the same situation as in Warsaw—no traces of Jews. They simply have disappeared. One notable exception is an apartment house not far from the two synagogues, one of whose walls bears the inscription *koveya etim la-Torah* (regularly setting aside time for the study of the Torah). One wonders how long it has been since anyone did just that in Poland.

Chelmno

The next day, Tuesday, was my last full day in Poland, and I wanted to use it to visit one of the lesser known camps, Chelmno. Though the first death camp to go into operation (on December 8, 1941), Chelmno is not as well publicized as Majdanek and Auschwitz. We passed only one sign informing us we were headed in the right direction and some people in the area were not exactly sure what we were talking about. When we finally arrived at the site, it was totally deserted except for a truck driver and his son who apparently had stopped for a rest and immediately hurried off. The site was quiet, unbelievably quiet. Situated near woods on a green rolling plain, the camp grounds looked beautiful. So tranquil . . . but a large stone monument brings you back to reality. On the front of it had but one word: *Piatemny* (Let us remember). On the back there was a quote in Polish by one of the survivors of the camp. Not a single word in any other language. No Yiddish. No Hebrew. Again you wonder why the powers that be in this and other countries behind the Iron Curtain do not let the Jews commemorate their martyrs in a fitting way. But by now, however, this question had already become passe. I continued to walk around, read the few small markers that tersely explain what happened and which noted the fact that most of the victims were Jews. Time goes on and you feel torn. On the one hand, you want to go as there is nothing more to see, on the other hand, you feel that you must stay longer, that every minute is a *mitzvah,* a holy obligation, because who knows when another Jew will come to this site, when another *Kaddish* will be said! But you cannot stay forever, and eventually you leave with a heavy heart.

Lodz

No visit to Poland would be complete without a stop in Lodz, once known as the Polish Manchester due to its very developed industries, and the site of the second largest Jewish community in Poland during the interwar period. As it turned out, the trip was particularly worthwhile because Lodz in several respects was quite different from the other Polish cities.

All I had with me was the address of the office of the local Jewish community, the only Jewish institution listed in the latest edition of the *Jewish Travel Guide.* I drove to the address listed, Zachodnia 7, but did not see any signs indicating where the office might be. Moreover, the building itself appeared to be an ordinary apartment building and I was beginning to get the feeling that perhaps I did not have the right information, which would have meant that we probably would be unable to locate any Jewish institutions since we were counting on obtaining the necessary information at the community offices. I decided that if I could not find them, perhaps they could find me and took off the cap I was wearing to reveal a *kippah.* Sure enough, within a split second I heard someone trying to get my attention. "Hello, *Bist du a Yid?"* (Are you Jewish?) A few elderly gentlemen were standing at the window and motioning to me to come upstairs.

I went up to their office and was ushered in and given a most cordial welcome by a group of four or five elderly Jews. Naturally the first question was where I came from, and my answer aroused their curiosity. We made the usual small talk, common when Jews from different communities meet and it seemed fairly obvious that they were happy to host a young Jew from abroad. What was a little strange, however, was their preoccupation with my American links, which they kept on referring to as if it was not exactly clear to them how an Israeli had gotten into Poland and whether I was an Israeli or an American. I assured them that I was an American citizen and that seemed to calm them down a bit. In the meantime, I related a little bit about my impressions of Poland and how I had been so disappointed with the Jews in Warsaw who apparently come to shul for three reasons only: to talk, yell at each other, and shnorr from the American tourists. This statement amused the elders of Lodz very much. "By us, there are no shnorrers, one immediately said, but the 85-year old head of the community quietly rebuked him, noting that even in Lodz, the phenomenon existed, though undoubtedly on a smaller scale. "Don't be so quick to boast that we have no shnorrers. We have a few of our own," he noted, "but not epidemic proportions."

I asked whether it would be possible to obtain information on the sites connected with the history of the Holocaust and with Jewish life in Lodz. After a short consultation among those in the office, one of the people volunteered to accompany us and we left together with him. Our host said that we had to make one stop before we could set out on our tour and took us to a cafe where we joined a relatively young man (about 55) sitting at one of the tables. He was immediately identified by our host as a Jew, a member of the community, but within a few minutes it became obvious to me that something was a bit strange about this gentleman. The first thing my guide did was repeat the conversation I had with the people at the office of the community practically word for word, with special emphasis on the question of my citizenship. Then the man whose name would best be kept secret tried to engage me in conversation. While I had not had too much difficulty understanding the Yiddish of the elderly Jews, I could barely understand what Mr. X was talking about. Moreover, his wife, who looked Polish, did not understand Yiddish at all. Mr. X questioned me about my American links and then related that he had just visited the States six months ago. He asked whether I would be willing to call a relative of his upon my arrival in New York and I gladly acceded. So he sent his wife home ostensibly to return with the phone number but all she came back with was the address which he wrote down on a napkin. When I asked him to write his name down so that I could remember who was sending the regards he balked, claiming that he just could not do so. It did not take very much to understand that hint, so the matter was dropped.

We then set out on our tour accompanied by Mr. X and his wife. According to my host, Mr. X was acquainted with the sites and should therefore come along. I did not argue as by this point what was going on was quite clear to me. My suspicions were further confirmed when I asked upon leaving one cafe whether we could possibly buy a map of the city. "No you can't get one," was the answer, which later became "No don't get one," spoken more as a command than a request.

Our first stop was the only remaining synagogue in Lodz. If you did not know exactly where it was, you would never be able to find the building, which is more or less hidden in an inner courtyard of a small street called Ulicya Revolutzyona 1905 (The Revolution of 1905 Street). You pass through a dark passageway which leads to various apartment buildings, until you reach the synagogue, which is a very small old building. There are no signs on the street to indicate the existence of the synagogue, but "those who need it, know where it is," according to my hosts. They told me, or rather my original host told me, that there is a minyan on Friday night and on the Sabbath morning and night and that on holidays they have an additional minyan at the Kehilla. Though introduced as a leading member of the community, Mr. X did not seem to know the answers to my simplest questions about these matters. I committed the address of the synagogue to memory, not wanting to write it down for fear of offending my hosts or arousing their wrath.

Next, we drove through the ghetto area. The gentleman I met at the Kehilla had lived in Lodz during the war and he pointed out various sites in what once had been the ghetto area. In the course of our tour he made a point to curse Rumkowski, the dictator, head of the Lodz Judenrat whose scheme to save some Jews at the expense of others failed and who presided over the deportation of practically every Jew in Lodz to the death camps before he himself was sent to Auschwitz. Mr. X, on the other hand, had a different story. He was in Warsaw, in hiding on the Aryan side of the city. In fact, the woman who rescued him was recognized as one of the Righteous Among the Nations by Yad Vashem and he participated in the ceremony recently held in Warsaw at which several Righteous Gentiles were honored.

Our final stop was the Jewish cemetery, which was one of the few encouraging things I saw in the course of my trip. Like the other cemeteries, it is surrounded by a low red brick wall, but the similarity ends there. The Jewish cemetery in Lodz is kept in a fitting manner, it is neat and is definitely presentable. There is a custodian who lives on the premises and he has two mean-looking dogs to ensure that no unwanted guests enter. We walked along the paths and came to the mausoleum over the grave of the known Jewish philanthropist Poznanski. He had been lucky enough to pass away in the thirties and thus was spared the horrors of the Holocaust. Surprisingly enough, the huge, lavish mausoleum he built still stands intact. It has a beautiful dome complete with scenes of Jerusalem surrounded by Biblical verses, all done in colored tile, in mosaic, and it is a sight to behold. Perhaps the only Jewish sight fit to behold in all of Poland.

The cemetery also has a special tombstone to commemorate the Lodz Jews who perished during the Holocaust. I turned to my hosts and told them I would like to say

Lukow. The tombstone monument erected by death-camp survivors following the war. No Jews remain in the village, which was 50 percent Jewish in 1939.

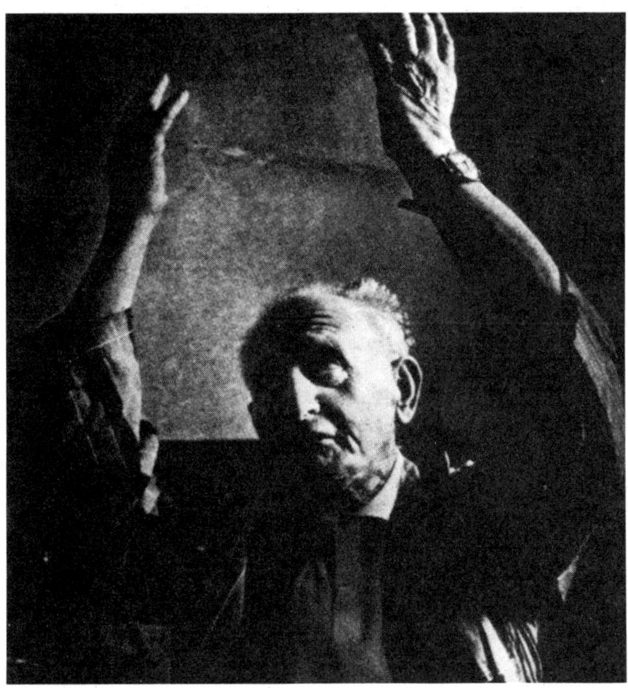

"Who will say kaddish *for us?"*

Kaddish and *El Moleh Rachamim.* Mr. X said, "no, there's no need," but my host was pleased by the thought, and inspired by his reactions I insisted on doing so.

On the way back from Lodz I wrestled with my thoughts, tempted on the one hand to try and sort them out while still on Polish soil, preferring on the other to forget about them until I had safely left the country. The cassette on the driver's tape blared out. "A good group," he told me. "Bonnie M." What did I care? At this point I was ready to listen to anything, especially if I could in the process gain some peace of mind. That, however, was apparently not destined to be. Some of the words seemed familiar so I listened a little more carefully. Sure enough, it was the words from Psalms and even if it had purposely been planned it could not have been more appropriate. The song contained the verses of the Book of Psalms, chapter 137, the song of mourning sung by the Jews exiled to Babylon. "How can we sing the songs of Zion in a strange land? If I forget thee O Jerusalem, let my right hand lose its cunning."

After an "exciting" evening reading the *Folkstimme*, I left the next morning on LOT airlines. After an unavoidable stopover in Germany I reached Amsterdam and breathed a tremendous sigh of relief. I felt as if I had finally returned to the civilized world, as if I had finally made it back to civilization. On the way in from the airport however, as I looked at quaint Dutch houses, the weight of what I had seen and the intensity of the emotions suppressed in Poland began to surface. After all, the Holocaust had happened here too. Here too, the Jews had been taken away and here too, Judaism was a shadow of its former self, even in civilized, philosemitic Holland.

I thought back to Jerusalem and thought of spending an extended stay in America. No, this was not the way to make this trip. Only in the opposite direction, ending up in Israel, in Jerusalem, could the pain of Poland be borne. And wiped the tears off that I could not help but shed.

Jewish Resistance to the Holocaust

Israel Information Center

- **Auschwitz, Poland 1940**
First successful escape 6 July 1940. Second escape on 28 October 1940.
- **Soviet Union, 1940**
Leaders of Jewish youth movements escape to **Warsaw** to organize Jewish resistance.
- **Holland, February 1941**
Jews resist Nazi attack on Jewish quarter of **Amsterdam,** killing Dutch Nazi. Jewish tavern owner, Ernst Cahn, resists German patrol, resulting in his execution by the Nazis.
- **Subotica, Hungary, April 1941**
250 Jewish youth killed for sabotage acts against German forces.
- **Yugoslavia**
Jews active in resistance from beginning of war. Over 2,000 Jews fight with Tito's partisans.
- **Croatia**
Many Croatian Jews fight with Tito's partisans.
- **Serbia, 29 July 1941**
122 Jews executed for resistance. Jewish youth join resistance, sabotage German military installations.
- **Soviet Union, September-October 1941**
First revolts against German *Einsatzgruppen* killing squads at **Tatarsk** and **Starodub.** German army, artillery, and air support used to crush growing resistance.
- **Lithuania, 26 September 1941**
Several hundred young Jews break through Lithuanian police cordon and escape eastward.
- **Bulgaria, End of 1941**
Bulgarian Jews saved from deportation as result of protest of Bulgarian king, government and people, to deportation order.
- **Eastern Galicia, February 1942**
Jews of **Tomaszow Lubelski** form partisan unit under leadership of Mendel Heler and Meir Lalimacher; 1,500 Jews killed. At **Wlodawa,** Jews escape into surrounding forests, harassing and killing German troops.
- **Ilja, Poland, March 1942**
Two Jewish partisan leaders, Josef Rodblat and David Rubin, lead Jewish resistance group; 900 Jews killed.
- **Minsk, Poland, March 1942**
Jews of **Minsk** ghetto organize resistance group under leadership of R.M. Bromberg, M.P. Malkevich and Hersh Amolar; 5,000 Jews killed.
- **White Russia, May 1942**
In **Lida** and **Stolpce** unarmed Jewish youth break out of SS police cordons, escape into woods and join partisan groups.
- **Radziwillow, Ukraine, May 1942**
Jewish resistance led by Asher Czerkaski; 1,500 Jews killed.
- **Markuszow, Poland, 9 May 1940**
Over 2,000 Jews of **Markuszow** escape into forests; resistance led by Schlomo Goldwasser, Mordechai Kirchenbaum, and the Gothelf brothers. Less than 100 Jews survive.
- **Poland, May 1942**
Jews of **Michow** and **Kamionka** resist deportations and escape into forests.
- **Berlin, Germany, 18 May 1942**
Jewish students, led by Herbert Baum, display anti-Nazi posters. Baum and 152 students shot.
- **Poland, May-October 1942**
More than 50 Jews escape **Treblinka;** several thousand escape **Warsaw;** thousands flee **Cracow, Kielce, Rarczew, Hrubieszow,** and surrounding areas. Find shelter in local forests; very few survive the war.
- **Poland, June 1942**
Jews revolt and escape death round-ups at **Druja, Braslaw, Dzisna, Glebokie, Slonim** and **Pilicia.** Most caught; a few join Russian partisan units.
- **Poland, July 1942**
Revolts take place in **Szarkowszczyzna, Nieswiez, Kleck,** and **Molczadz.** Jewish Fighters' Organization, Z.O.B. set up in **Warsaw, Bialystok, Brody** and in five other ghettos south of **Warsaw.**
- **Belgium, August 1942**
25,000 Jews hidden by local Belgian population; over 1000 Jews join Belgian partisans; 140 killed during war.
- **Poland, August 1942**
Resistance at **Mir** and **Zdziecial** leads to the escape of 500 Jews.
- **Treblinka, Poland, 26 August 1942**
Polish Jews at **Treblinka** attack Ukrainian guard with knife; entire trainload of Jewish deportees machine-gunned in retaliation.
- **Volhynia, August 1942**
15,000 Polish Jews escape German killers; less than 1000 survive war in the forests, some join Soviet partisan units.
- **Treblinka Poland, 11 September 1942**
Meir Berliner, Argentinian Jew trapped in Warsaw and deported to **Treblinka,** stabs SS officer to death with penknife.
- **Poland, September 1942**
Jews of **Dzialoszyce** led by Moshe Skoczylas and Michael Majtek, escape to forests and form partisan

units. Majtek organizes resistance in **Pinczow.**

- **Poland, September 1942**
  829 Jews of **Lachwa** fight against "liquidation;" most are killed. Armed resistance at **Stolin** and **Krzemieniec.**
- **Parczew, East Galicia, 17 September 1942**
  Several thousand Jews escape **Parczew** round-ups and flee to Parczew forest. Only 200 survive the war.
- **Brody, East Galicia, 19 September 1942**
  Mass breakout from deportation train at **Brody;** almost all would-be escapees machine-gunned.
- **Poland, 21-22 September 1942**
  Hundreds of Jews from **Wegrow** and **Sokolow** escape to nearby woods, most are shot.
- **Volhynia, 23-30 September 1942**
  Resistance organized in **Tuczyn, Korzec,** and **Serniki;** over 2,000 flee to forests, very few survive the war.
- **Zelechow, Poland, 30 September 1942**
  A few hundred young Jews of **Zelechow** manage to escape deportations and form a partisan group in the forest.
- **Opoczno, Poland, 1-14 October 1942**
  Resistance group, "The Lions," led by Julian Ajzenman, sabotages railway line near **Opoczno.**
- **Norway, October-November 1942**
  Helped by the Norwegians, 930 Norwegian Jews escape into neutral Sweden.
- **Ukraine, 15-31 October 1942**
  Hundreds of Jews escape from **Radziwillow** and **Targowica.** The resistance at **Brest-Litovsk** is led by Hana Ginsberg.
- **Bialystock, Poland, 1-6 November 1942**
  Jews of **Marcinkance** resist deportation; all are shot. At **Siemiatycze** a few dozen Jews escape to forests and form a resistance group, most are killed by Polish partisans.
- **Poland, 7-30 November 1942**
  "Amsterdam" Jewish resistance group active in **Tarnow.**
- **Buczacz, Poland, 1941, 1942, 1943**
  Following killings in August 1941 and deportations of October 1942, young Jews of **Buczacz** search for arms and train for a breakout. Some escape liquidation of ghetto in 1943, most are killed.
- **Algiers, Algeria, 8 November 1942**
  Algerian Jew, Joe Abulker leads uprising in **Algiers,** tying down German forces as Allies carry out **"Operation Torch," ending German control of Algeria.**
- **Poland, December 1942**
  Jewish resistance in Poland becomes more organized. The **Cracow** Jewish Fighters' Organization carries out acts of sabotage. Preparation for escapes and uprisings continue in other cities.
- **Poland, January 1943**
  First acts of resistance in **Warsaw** Ghetto. Uprising in Kopernic labor camp. Jews in **Czestochowa** kill 25 German soldiers; 250 Jews killed in reprisal. 1,000 Jews from Grodno attack Ukrainian guards at **Treblinka** with knives and clubs; all Jews and guards killed by SS.
- **Poland, February 1943**
  Zionist youth group, led by Eliyahu Boraks, resists deportation and kills eight SS men, are captured and sent to **Treblinka** where they attack guards with two pistols; all are killed.
- **Treblinka, Poland, February 1943**
  Young woman at **Treblinka** snatches rifle from Ukrainian, shoots dead two Nazis and wounds a third.
- **Poland, March 1943**
  Resistance plans at **Braslaw** were cut short by liquidation. 50 Jews break out of armed cordons in **Minsk** and reach the partisans.
- **Sobibor, Poland, April 1943**
  Wlodawa Jews arriving at **Sobibor** attack the SS. All Jews machine-gunned.
- **Eastern Galicia, April 1943**
  Resistance at **Skalat, Prezemysl** and **Jaworow.** Jews on transports resist German SS at **Ponary** station; only a few dozen escape.
- **Brussels, Belgium, April 1943**
  Brussels Jews derail railroad track leading to Auschwitz.
- **Warsaw, Poland, 19 April 1943**
  Warsaw Ghetto uprising, led by Mordechai Anielewicz. Jews resist German troops, tanks and artillery; drive out Germans from ghetto.
- **Warsaw, Poland, 8 May 1943**
  Jewish underground headquarters destroyed; Anielewicz and 56,000 Jews killed or deported during revolt. 15,000 manage to escape.
- **Galicia, June 1943**
  Jewish resistance in **Brody** and **Warsaw** lead to German deaths. Resistance continues at **Czestochowa, Sosnowiec, Buczacz,** and **Lvov.**
- **Treblinka, Poland, 2 July 1943**
  Two Jews escape from **Treblinka.**
- **Vilna, Poland, 24 July 1943**
  Group of 21 from Jewish underground escape Vilna and join Soviet partisans in **Narocz** forest. Nine killed in German ambush; remainder succeed in disrupting German military supplies and communications.
- **Poland, August 1943**
  Revolts in slave labor camps at **Krychow, Jaktorow, Sasow, Konin,** and **Lackie Wielkie,** and at **Sobibor** death camp. Major revolts in **Bialystok Ghetto** and **Treblinka.** Revolts brutally suppressed by German artillery and tanks; 1,000 children massacred in reprisal. At **Glebokie,** 3,000 Jews resist round-up, all are massacred.
- **Denmark, September 1943**
  Jews ferried by the Danes to safety in **Sweden.** By October 1943, only 500 out of 7,200 remain in Denmark.
- **Treblinka, Poland, 2 September 1943**
  18-year-old Seweryn Klajnman leads 12 Jewish slave laborers in break out from **Treblinka** after killing Ukrainian guard with crowbar.
- **Kiev, Russia, 30 September 1943**
  Jewish and Soviet prisoners in **Kiev,** forced to dig up and burn Babi Yar victims, revolt. SS overseers machine-gun prisoners; 14 survive and escape.
- **Sobibor, Poland, September 1943**
  Jews attack SS with stones and bottles; all attackers killed.
- **Vilna, Poland, September 1943**
  Several hundred Jews from **Vilna** escape deportation and join partisan units.

- **Miedzyrzec, Poland, 10 September 1943**
Jewish youths at **Miedzyrzec** kill two Germans; five Jews shot in retaliation.
- **Sobibor, Poland, 14 October 1943**
Alexander Pechersky, a Soviet officer and Jew, leads breakout from **Sobibor,** 12 SS men and more than 12 Ukrainian guards killed. Of 600 Jews in camp, 200 killed while escaping. 100 more captured and killed. Of remaining 300, only 30 survive the war.
- **Poland, November-December 1943**
Jews try to resist execution at **Maidanek, Janowska,** and **Poniatowa** camps.
- **Poland—Ostland—Ukraine, July-December 1943**
Jews escape from 35 towns and join partisan groups.
- **Parczew, Eastern Galicia, 1944-1945**
A Jewish Polish officer, Alexande Skonicki, leads attacks of Polish partisan units on German military installations. A Jewish partisan company under his command and led by Yehiel Grynszpan successfully acquires ammunition from German military posts.
- **France, January-June 1944**
More than 250 Jews executed for resistance and acts of sabotage.
- **Koldyczewo, Poland, 22 March 1944**
Jews kill ten SS guards at **Koldyczewo** slave labor camp. Hundreds of prisoners escape to join partisans.
- **Ponary, Galicia, 15 April 1944**
Slave laborers at **Ponary,** forced to exhume and burn mass grave, dig escape tunnel with hands and spoons; 40 escape, 15 survive.
- **Ponary, Poland, 15 April 1944**
80 Jews attempt escape from **Ponary;** only 15 survive.
- **Greece, March-April 1944**
Thousands of Jews join Greek partisan units. 40 Jewish partisans participate in sabotaging German rail communications between Greece and north. Moses Pesah, a Greek rabbi, commands main Greek national resistance in **Central Greece.**
- **Hungary, May-June 1944**
Hundreds of Jews from Eastern Hungary killed while resisting deportation at **Miskolc** and **Satoraljaujhely.**
- **Yugoslavia, July 1944**
Jews fight with partisan units liberating areas of the **Balkans.**
- **France, August 1944**
Jews active in partisan units.
- **Warsaw, Poland, 1 August-15 September 1944**
1,000 Jews take part in **Warsaw** uprising.
- **Slovakia, 26 August 1944**
Jewish battalion captures three major towns during Slovakian revolt.
- **Auschwitz, Poland, September 1944**
Anne Frank arrives on transport from Holland to Auschwitz; is gassed on arrival.
- **Auschwitz, Poland, 7 October 1944**
Polish, Hungarian, and Greek Jews, using explosives stolen by four Jewish girls, blow up one of the four crematoria at **Auschwitz.**
- **Behind German Lines, November 1944**
Jewish parachutists, recruited by the British in Palestine, drop behind German lines and contact Jewish partisan groups. Among them are Havivah Reik, Enzo Sereni, Hannah Szenes. All are captured and killed.
- **Chelmno, Germany, 17 January 1945**
Last 47 Jewish slave laborers at **Chelmno** death camp revolt against SS and take over a building. Building set on fire; only one survived.
- **Germany, 30 March 1945**
Nine women escape **Ravensbruck;** all are captured and shot.
- **Bosnia, Germany, 22 April 1945**
In the **Jasenovac** concentration camp 600 prisoners revolt and attack guards. 520 are killed; 80 escape, of whom 20 are Jews.

PART FIVE
THE STATE OF
ISRAEL

THE PALESTINE POST

JERUSALEM
SUNDAY, MAY 16, 1948

PRICE: 25 MILS
VOL. XXIII. No. 6714

STATE OF ISRAEL IS BORN

The first independent Jewish State in 19 centuries was born in Tel Aviv as the British Mandate over Palestine came to an end at midnight on Friday, and it was immediately subjected to the test of fire. As "Medinat Yisrael" (State of Israel) was proclaimed, the battle for Jerusalem raged, with most of the city falling to the Jews. At the same time, President Truman announced that the United States would accord recognition to the new State. A few hours later, Palestine was invaded by Moslem armies from the south, east and north, and Tel Aviv was raided from the air. On Friday the United Nations Special Assembly adjourned after adopting a resolution to appoint a mediator but without taking any action on the Partition Resolution of November 29.

Yesterday the battle for the Jerusalem-Tel Aviv road was still under way, and two Arab villages were taken. In the north, Acre town was captured, and the Jewish Army consolidated its positions in Western Galilee.

Most Crowded Hours in Palestine's History

Between Thursday night and this morning Palestine went through what by all standards must be among the most crowded hours in its history.

For the Jewish population there was the anguish over the fate of the few hundred Haganah men and women in the Kfar Etzion bloc of settlements near Hebron. Their surrender to a fully equipped superior foreign force desperately in need of a victory was a foregone conclusion. What could not be known, with no communications since Thursday morning, was whether and to what extent the Red Cross and the Truce Consuls would secure civilised conditions for prisoners and wounded, and proper respect for the dead. Doubts on some of these anxious questions have now been resolved.

On Friday afternoon, from Tel Aviv, came the expected announcement of the Jewish State, and its official naming at birth, "Medinat Yisrael"—State of Israel, with the swearing in of the first Council of Government. The proclamation of the State was made at midnight, coinciding with the sailing from Haifa of Britain's last High Commissioner. Within the hour, President Truman announced in Washington that the Government of the United States had decided to give *de facto* recognition to the Jewish State, with all that such recognition implied. The Assembly of the United Nations, meeting since the middle of April for "further study" of the Palestine problem was thus left, by one means or another, to ratify the Two-States decision of November last year, or dissolve with nothing concrete to its credit. The Assembly adjourned with the resolution to appoint a mediator between the Jews and Arabs, to cooperate with the Security Council's Truce Commission in Jerusalem.

Russian Recognition Awaited

Russia and her allies had given early assurance of their intention to recognize the Jewish State, whoever else did or did not. As a result of Washington's action and the Eastern Bloc's stand, other countries are expected to extend their recognition to the newly born state.

Nor did the Arab Bloc remain idle. True to their promises, or threats, the members of the Arab League completed their plans for a full-scale invasion of Palestine in what has been described as a Moslem "crusade" against the Jews. Tel Aviv was bombed twice yesterday by Egyptian war planes. One of the enemy planes was shot down by a Jewish fighter plane, and the pilot taken prisoner, showing that this move against the civilian population was not a surprise, and that the Jewish preparations include anti-aircraft defences.

A black-out has been ordered for the whole of Jewish Palestine Tel Aviv itself having blacked out on Friday.

At the same time, the air was filled with reports of two Egyptian columns on the move from the south towards Gaza and Beersheba, and of intensified shelling from across the northern border of Jewish settlements in North-Eastern Galilee.

The Security Council met yesterday in a special session to consider action on the invasion of Palestine by member states of the U.N.

In the afternoon, Jerusalem was subjected to shelling from the northwest.

Haganah forces throughout the country continued mopping up, and Jewish sources claimed most of Western Galilee safe against attack. Naharayim, near Jisr el Majamie, inside Trans-Jordan, where the Jordan River works of the Palestine Electric Corporation are, is claimed by the Arab Legion. The battle for the Tel Aviv-Jerusalem Road at Bab el Wad is still on, Haganah taking two villages — Abu Shusha and Kubab — between Ramleh and Latrun.

Converging on Old City

In Jerusalem the "cease fire" observed on both sides for six days was broken on Friday, although the more strategic buildings in Princess Mary Avenue, the Russian Compound, and Jaffa Road passed to the Jews without a shot being fired, as did the David Building commanding the road to the German Colony and Railway Station. By yesterday evening, Jewish forces were approaching some of the gates of the Old City. The Police Training School on Mt. Scopus and Sheikh Jarrah are in Jewish hands.

On Friday morning, the Truce Commission met at the French Consulate and invited Jewish and Arab representatives to confer with them. Jewish Agency delegates agreed that the "cease fire" be extended in Jerusalem for eight days. Arab representatives could not attend, they said, because of the firing in Julian's Way, and a two-hour respite was arranged from 5 to 7 in the evening. Whether they agreed or not, became academic as by that time the battle for Jerusalem had been renewed.

To Jerusalem's tension was added the aggravation of electric power failing in most parts of the city, as nearly all of the Electric Corporation's lines had been shot down. This meant, on top of the other heardships to a fuel-less city, no broadcast news yesterday, when there were no newspapers. For more than a week the city was also without piped water.

ACRE CAPTURED

Acre, the sea-coast town across the bay from Haifa, was captured by Jewish forces yesterday, the Haganah Radio reported. The surrender of the town, and subsequently two villages to the north, came after a strong Jewish attack.

Arms dumps containing enormous quantities of military equipment were captured.

The B.B.C. stated yesterday that almost all of Western Galilee was in Jewish hands, but that Naharayim, on the Jordan, had been occupied by the Legion.

Double Summer Time in Jerusalem

At midnight tonight all clocks in Jewish Jerusalem will be advanced two hours.

The Emergency Committee has instituted double summer time in order to save fuel. The measure does not apply to the rest of the country.

The Jerusalem Electric Corporation will cut off current to the Jewish Quarters from 1 to 9 p.m. as from today.

JEWS TAKE OVER SECURITY ZONES

The Battle for Jerusalem, which began when the British forces withdrew on Friday morning, continued all day Friday and yesterday. The crackle of small-arms fire and explosions of mortar shells were still being heard in the early hours of this morning as the battle entered its third day.

Repeated efforts on Friday evening and again on Saturday by the U.N. Truce Commission to bring about a "cease fire" were brought to nought when the Arab representatives failed to agree within the specified time limit.

On Friday morning, Jewish forces entered the Russian Compound and Zone C to reoccupy the buildings requisitioned from Jews last year. This operation was almost bloodless, but beyond the western edge of Zone C, Arabs engaged the Jews in Jaffa Road. The Arabs were forced back and the Barclays Bank area was taken.

In other parts of the city fighting flared up. Jews overran one after another the areas evacuated by the British. By last night, the quarters and strongpoints held by Haganah included the German Colony and part of the Baka'a Quarter in Zone A, all of Zone B except for the Red Cross area, Sheikh Jarrah (where the Jewish flag was flown from the Mufti's House), the Mea Shearim Police Station and Allenby Barracks on the Bethlehem Road. The I.Z.L. were in occupation of the Scopus Police Billet.

Yesterday afternoon eight cannon shelled Jewish Jerusalem from the Arab village of Nebi Samwil, more than 100 shells falling in the north-western quarters. Several persons were injured.

Jewish casualties in the two days of fighting were eight killed and a number of wounded. Arab casualties are not known.

EMERGENCY

A state of emergency in the Jerusalem area was declared to exist by the Haganah Area Commander as from yesterday in what is the first Order of the Day to be issued in almost 2,000 years by a Jewish Military Commander of the city.

The Order said:

With the declaration of the establishment of Medinat Israel (the State of Israel) and the setting up of its Provisional Council of Government, the Jews of Palestine have entered upon the decisive phase of the war.

In order to obviate any disturbance during the difficult time that confronts us, I hereby declare a state of emergency to exist in the Jerusalem District as from 00.01 hours on Saturday, May 15, and I hereby give the following instructions:

1. Every inhabitant must place himself at the disposal of the authorized security forces of Medinat Israel and obey their orders.
2. All property required for the needs of the Military Command may be expropriated by the security forces acting through officers carrying proper documents. Compensation for such expropriated property will be paid according to evaluation by the Jerusalem Committee and at such time as the latter shall decide.
3. The areas evacuated by the forces of the Mandatory Government and now held by the security forces are hereby declared to be Military Occupation Areas under the authority of Military Governors.
4. No person may enter any such area without permission of the Military Governor.
5. Any person found looting or committing any criminal act will be brought before a Military Court and punished with all the rigour of the law.

The Palestine Post

Despite the power failure in Jerusalem, the Electric Corporation succeeded in providing three offices with power about 10.15 last night. There was another failure about 11.15 but again the Corporation was able to restore the current.

Before the linotype machines could begin to work, however, it was 1 a.m., and in order to be able to appear this morning, The Palestine Post is published, for the third time in as many weeks, in two pages.

Egyptian Air Force Spitfires Bomb Tel Aviv; One Shot Down

Kol Israel, the Tel Aviv broadcasting station, reported at 2 o'clock yesterday afternoon that Tel Aviv had been bombed three times in the previous evening and morning, and that one plane had been shot down and its Egyptian pilot taken prisoner.

In the first raid, four planes attacked from a height of 300 feet. Two dropped bombs, while the others strafed the city. Little damage was caused. In the second attack two hours later, the airport to the north of the city was bombed, and an Air France plane parked there was damaged. The third raid was launched shortly before midday, but the planes were driven off without causing any damage.

Two settlements in the Negev had also been attacked from the air, the radio reported.

A country-wide blackout was ordered by Air Raid Precaution Headquarters in Tel Aviv.

Mr. David Ben Gurion, the Prime Minister, broadcast from Tel Aviv to the people of America yesterday morning. As he spoke, Egyptian planes were bombing the city.

In the north, the settlements of Ein Gev and Shaar Hagolan and Dan had been shelled, but no further details were available.

Kalandia airfield was taken by the Jewish army on Friday morning, shortly after the High Commissioner had left there by plane for Haifa. The field was evacuated, together with the neighbouring settlement of Ataroth, on Friday night. The settlement itself was burnt by Arabs yesterday.

2 Columns Cross Southern Border

By WALTER COLLINS
U.P. Correspondent

CAIRO, Saturday. — A communique issued today by the Egyptian Ministry of National Defence reported that two columns of Egyptian troops, including infantry and artillery, had struck across the Palestine border, preceded by aircraft.

One column was reported to have crossed the frontier 30 miles inland and to have attacked the "Jewish village of Auja on the road to Beersheba, wiping it out because its inhabitants had refused to surrender." (Auja is a police post near the frontier, about 25 miles from the nearest Jewish settlement). The column then entrenched itself on heights east of Gaza.

Meanwhile, according to this Cairo report, another column crossed the border at midnight, travelling north along the coast road towards Gaza.

Egyptian sources later reported that their forces had reached the Negev settlements of Nirim and Kfar Darom, but could give no further details.

In Cairo, at midnight, 2,000 Egyptian Police, commanded by 370 Officers, started a round-up of suspected Zionist sympathizers and arrested 600 persons within six hours.

According to Haganah sources, Jewish soldiers beat off an Egyptian "amphibious operation," an attempt to land troops near Ashdod, 20 miles north of Gaza. The ship which attempted to make the landing was forced to turn back, these sources said.

Arab Legion Cross Border

It was reported in Jerusalem last night that troops of the Arab Legion had crossed the border into Palestine in two places, over Allenby Bridge and near the Palestine Electric power station at Naharaim.

According to Reuters, the long convoy of the first route of lorry-borne troops, artillery and armoured cars, was headed by King Abdullah, who fired a symbolic pistol shot towards Palestine and wished his troops success in their campaign.

In Cairo, a group of journalists have asked the Egyptian Premier, Nokrashi Pasha, for an interview to discuss the proposed blackout of news, the Cairo Radio has reported.

A Good Thing

CAIRO, Saturday (UP). — The Egyptian Premier, Nokrashi Pasha, told the press that advance units of the Egyptian army had entered Gaza 12 hours after crossing the frontier.

"This is a very good thing," he added.

Etzion Settlers Taken P.O.W.

Fighting in the Kfar Etzion bloc continued throughout Friday, after Kfar Etzion itself had surrendered to the Arabs on the previous day. The wounded from the settlement were evacuated to Massuot Itzhak.

The fighting was broken off on Friday on the intervention of a Red Cross representative, accompanied by a Jewish Medical Officer, who went out to the settlements and supervised the transfer of the Jews from Revadim and Ein Zurim, the wounded and women being taken to Bethlehem, and the other settlers to prison.

The settlers from Massuot Itzhak, including the wounded from the first day's fighting at Kfar Etzion, were removed yesterday.

The terms of surrender agreed on by the Jews and Arabs were:

All able-bodied soldiers to be taken as prisoners of war, and kept in special camps, to be supervised by the International Red Cross.

Women, non-combatants and wounded to be brought to Jerusalem by the Red Cross.

War Office Says Legion Had Left

LAKE SUCCESS, Saturday. — Sir Alexander Cadogan, Britain's delegate to the UN, ...read in the Security Council a telegram from the War Office today, stating that ***all units of the Arab Legion had left Palestine for Trans-Jordan prior to the end of the Mandate.***

U.S. RECOGNIZES JEWISH STATE

WASHINGTON, Saturday. —Ten minutes after the termination of the British Mandate on Friday, the White House released a formal statement by President Truman that the U.S. Government intended to recognize the Provisional Jewish Government as the *de facto* authority representing the Jewish State.

The U.S. is also considering lifting the arms embargo but it is not known whether to Palestine only or the entire Middle East, and the establishment of diplomatic relations with the Jewish Provisional Government.

The White House press secretary, Mr. Charles Ross, told correspondents today that reaction so far to the recognition had been overwhelmingly favourable. He said this step had been discussed with Mr. Marshall and Mr. Lovett before action was taken, and it had their complete support.

Mr. Ross said that the President had decided several days ago to grant American recognition to the new Jewish State, but due to protocol regulations he could not announce his policy until a formal letter arrived. "We were able to move very quickly when the messenger brought the letter," he said, "because the President had already determined the course of action to be taken."

Provisional Government

A few minutes before five (midnight Palestine time), Mr. Eliyahu Epstein, of the Jewish Agency's Washington Office, handed a letter to the White House, requesting the U.S. to recognize the new Jewish State.. "With the full knowledge of the deep bond of sympathy which existed and has been strengthened over the past 30 years between the U.S. Government and the Jewish people of Palestine," the letter said, "I have been authorized by the Provisional Government of the new State to tender this message and express the hope that your Government will recognize and welcome Israel into the community of nations."

In Frankfurt, General Lucius D. Clay, the U.S. Military Commander of Germany, said today that Jews in Germany and Austria would be assisted to leave for the State of Israel as soon as official word of America's recognition was to hand.

EGYPTIAN INVASION BEFORE U.N. SECURITY COUNCIL

LAKE SUCCESS, Saturday. — Israel today appealed to an emergency meeting of the Security Council to order a halt to Arab invasions into Palestine and, if necessary, to impose economic and military sanctions.

Dr. Mordechai Eliash, representing the day-old Jewish State, appealed to the Council to act fast against the invading Arab States, because "every hour counts." He stated that King Abdullah of Trans-Jordan, through the instrument of the Arab Legion, was clearly committing an act of aggression.

At the beginning of the session, Dr. Issa Nakhleh, of the Arab Higher Committee, declared that Egyptian forces had been invited by the A.H.C. to assist in the establishment of law and order. He asked: "What right has the Jewish Agency, which represents world Jewry, to complain against this action before the Security Council?"

Mahmoud Bey Fawzi, of Egypt, declared in explanation of a cable which he had earlier read to the Council that Egyptian troops had entered Palestine by invitation and with the unequivocal consent of the Palestine people. Egyptian forces were not going to Palestine to conquer anybody, but just to restore peace.

The invasion was "not directed against the Palestine

(Continued on Page 2, Col. 7)

GROMYKO TO BE REPLACED

LAKE SUCCESS, Saturday. (UP). — M. Andrei Gromyko, the Soviet Deputy Foreign Minister and his country's representative at the U.N., will soon be replaced — probably permanently.

The 38-year-old Soviet diplomat will be replaced by M. Jacob A. Malik, Deputy Foreign Minister and a major figure in the conduct of Russian Foreign policy in the Far East. M. Malik, is already en route here by plane from Berlin.

Proclamation by Head Of Government

The creation of "Medinat Yisrael", the State of Israel, was proclaimed at midnight on Friday by Mr. David Ben Gurion, until then Chairman of the Jewish Agency Executive and now head of the State's Provisional Council of Government.

David Ben Gurion, Prime Minister

The first act of the Council of Government, as announced by its head, was to abolish all legislation of the 1939 White Paper of the late Mandatory Power, particularly the Ordinances and Orders relating to immigration and land transfer.

In the declaration of independence, Mr. Ben Gurion called on the Arabs of Palestine to restore peace, assuring them full civic rights and full representation in all governmental organs of the State.

Mr. Ben Gurion prefaced the declaration with a review of the historic connection of the Jewish people with the Land of Israel and of their efforts to return, which never ceased throughout the generations of their dispersal, until the Nazi holocaust proved anew the urgency of the need for a Jewish State.

The Balfour Declaration of 1917, confirmed by the League of Nations, had given explicit international recognition to the right of the Jewish people to reconstitute its National Home in Palestine, he said.

"On November 29, 1947," continued the declaration, "the United Nations decided on the establishment of a Jewish State and an Arab State in Palestine and called upon the inhabitants of the country to take all steps necessary for the establishment of the two States.

Historic Rights

"This decision cannot now be changed. Accordingly, we, the members of the Provisio-

(Continued on Page 2, Col. 6)

Special Assembly Adjourns

FLUSHING MEADOWS, Saturday. — The Special U.N. Assembly, called four weeks ago to discuss the U.S. proposal for a temporary Trusteeship for Palestine, adjourned yesterday until its next regular meeting in September without taking any decision to alter the resolution of November 29, which called for the setting up of two states in Palestine. The Assembly adopted only one motion — to appoint a special mediator to go to Palestine and cooperate with Truce Commission.

President Truman's announcement that the U.S. was proposing to recognize the new Jewish State reached newsmen during the session before the American delegation itself knew about it.

All the afternoon, the Assembly had been tied up in knots. After much filibustering it rejected the Franco-U.S. proposal for a special administration for Jerusalem. As the debate dragged on, correspondents sat with stop-watches to see whether a decision would be taken before the six o'clock deadline (N.Y. Summer Time) when the Mandate terminated. As zero hour was reached without a vote, they rushed to the booths, and about ten minutes later, the tickers in the local news agency offices flashed President Truman's recognition.

Gromyko and Jessup

The Assembly floor was half deserted and the American delegation had not been officially informed. The first to mention the Jewish State from the restrum was M. Gromyko, who said he saw no need for further action on the American mediator proposal, since the Jewish State had been recognized as a reality by the U.S. He asked what was being proposed for the Arab area of Palestine which was still without a government.

Shortly afterwards, Mr. Philip Jessup, the anti-Partition fighter, mounted the rostrum and officially announced U.S. recognition of the Jewish State, insisting, however, that the passage of the American mediator proposal was more necessary now than ever.

The Assembly passed it.

Between the flash from the White House and the final vote there was an eerie atmosphere in Flushing Meadows. The lights of the television cameras played on the rostrum, lighting up one Arab speaker after another who mounted the steps and expressed in a low voice frustration and anger.

To the last minute, officials of the State Department had been lobbying right on the floor against the Jewish State, even while the President's statement was already on the wires.

The Assembly did not adopt any resolution at all which altered the U.N. decision of November 29, 1947.

2 Villages Taken In Road Battle

In the battle for the Tel Aviv-Jerusalem road, the Haganah on Friday night took Kubeib and Abu Shusha villages between Latrun and Ramle. In engagements elsewhere along the route positions near Latrun and Bab el Wad changed hands.

Jewish casualties in this area in the last two days are about 40 killed. The Iraqis suffered greater losses, but their exact number is unknown.

It was reported that Iraqi troops had entered the Trappist Monastery at Latrun, and had set up strongpoints on the grounds and the building itself.

Sir Alan Sails From Palestine

The High Commissioner's departure from Palestine on Friday went according to plan — he appeared on the steps of Government House at 8 o'clock in the morning, wearing a full General's uniform. There he reviewed a guard of honour, consisting of 50 men of the Highland Light Infantry, the last British troops to leave Jerusalem.

Sir Alan Cunningham then drove to Kalandia airfield and boarded a plane for Haifa. Spitfires and Lancasters covered his short car journey.

The last British civil servants left Jerusalem together with Sir Alan: including Sir William Fitz-Gerald, the Chief Justice, and Sir Henry Gurney, the Chief Secretary.

Sir Alan's plane was piloted to Haifa by the Air Officer Commanding in Palestine, Air Commodore Dawson.

Declaration of Independence of the State of Israel

The Land of Israel was the birthplace of the Jewish people. Here their spiritual, religious and national identity was formed. Here they achieved independence and created a culture of national and universal significance. Here they wrote and gave the Bible to the world.

Exiled from the Land of Israel the Jewish people remained faithful to it in all the countries of their dispersion, never ceasing to pray and hope for their return and the restoration of their national freedom.

Impelled by this historic association, Jews strove throughout the centuries to go back to the land of their fathers and regain their statehood. In recent decades they returned in their masses. They reclaimed the wilderness, revived their language, built cities and villages, and established a vigorous and ever-growing community, with its own economic and cultural life. They sought peace, yet were prepared to defend themselves. They brought the blessings of progress to all inhabitants of the country and looked forward to sovereign independence.

In the year 1897 the First Zionist Congress, inspired by Theodor Herzl's vision of the Jewish State, proclaimed the right of the Jewish people to national revival in their own country.

This right was acknowledged by the Balfour Declaration of November 2, 1917, and reaffirmed by the Mandate of the League of Nations, which gave explicit international recognition to the historic connection of the Jewish people with Palestine and their right to reconstitute their National Home.

The recent holocaust, which engulfed millions of Jews in Europe, proved anew the need to solve the problem of the homelessness and lack of independence of the Jewish people by means of the re-establishment of the Jewish State, which would open the gates to all Jews and endow the Jewish people with equality of status among the family of nations.

The survivors of the disastrous slaughter in Europe, and also Jews from other lands, have not desisted from their efforts to reach Eretz-Yisrael, in face of difficulties, obstacles and perils; and have not ceased to urge their right to a life of dignity, freedom and honest toil in their ancestral land.

In the second World War the Jewish people in Palestine made their full contribution to the struggle of the freedom-loving nations against the Nazi evil. The sacrifices of their soldiers and their war effort gained them the right to rank with the nations which founded the United Nations.

Ben-Gurion proclaims the establishment of the State of Israel, May 14, 1948.

On November 29, 1947, the General Assembly of the United Nations adopted a Resolution requiring the establishment of a Jewish State in Palestine. The General Assembly called upon the inhabitants of the country to take all the necessary steps on their part to put the plan into effect. This recognition by the United Nations of the right of the Jewish people to establish their independent State is unassailable.

It is the natural right of the Jewish people to lead, as do all other nations, an independent existence in its sovereign State.

ACCORDINGLY WE, the members of the National Council representing the Jewish people in Palestine and the World Zionist Movement, are met together in solemn assembly today, the day of termination of the British Mandate for Palestine; and by virtue of the natural and historic right of the Jewish people and of the Resolution of the General Assembly of the United Nations.

WE HEREBY PROCLAIM the establishment of the Jewish State in Palestine, to be called Medinath Yisrael (The State of Israel).

WE HEREBY DECLARE that, as from the termination of

the Mandate at midnight, the 14th-15th May, 1948, and pending the setting up of the duly elected bodies of the State in accordance with a Constitution, to be drawn up by the Constituent Assembly not later than the 1st October, 1948, the National Council shall act as the Provisional State Council, and that the National Administration shall constitute the Provisional Government of the Jewish State, which shall be known as Israel.

THE STATE OF ISRAEL will be open to the immigration of Jews from all countries of their dispersion; will promote the development of the country for the benefit of all its inhabitants; will be based on the principles of liberty, justice and peace as conceived by the Prophets of Israel; will uphold the full social and political equality of all its citizens, without distinction of religion, race, or sex; will guarantee freedom of religion, conscience, education and culture; will safeguard the Holy Places of all religions; and will loyally uphold the principles of the United Nations Charter.

THE STATE OF ISRAEL will be ready to co-operate with the organs and representatives of the United Nations in the implementation of the Resolution of the Assembly of November 29, 1947, and will take steps to bring about the Economic Union over the whole of Palestine.

We appeal to the United Nations to assist the Jewish people in the building of its State and to admit Israel into the family of nations.

In the midst of wanton aggression, we yet call upon the Arab inhabitants of the State of Israel to preserve the ways of peace and play their part in the development of the State, on the basis of full and equal citizenship and due representation in all its bodies and institutions—provisional and permanent.

We extend our hand in peace and neighbourliness to all the neighbouring states and their peoples, and invite them to co-operate with the independent Jewish nation for the common good of all. The State of Israel is prepared to make its contribution to the progress of the Middle East as a whole.

Our call goes out to the Jewish people all over the world to rally to our side in the task of immigration and development, and to stand by us in the great struggle for the fulfillment of the dream of generations for the redemption of Israel.

With trust in the Rock of Israel, we set our hand to this Declaration, at this Session of the Provisional State Council, on the soil of the Homeland, in the city of Tel Aviv, on this Sabbath eve, the fifth of Iyar, 5708, the fourteenth of May, 1948.

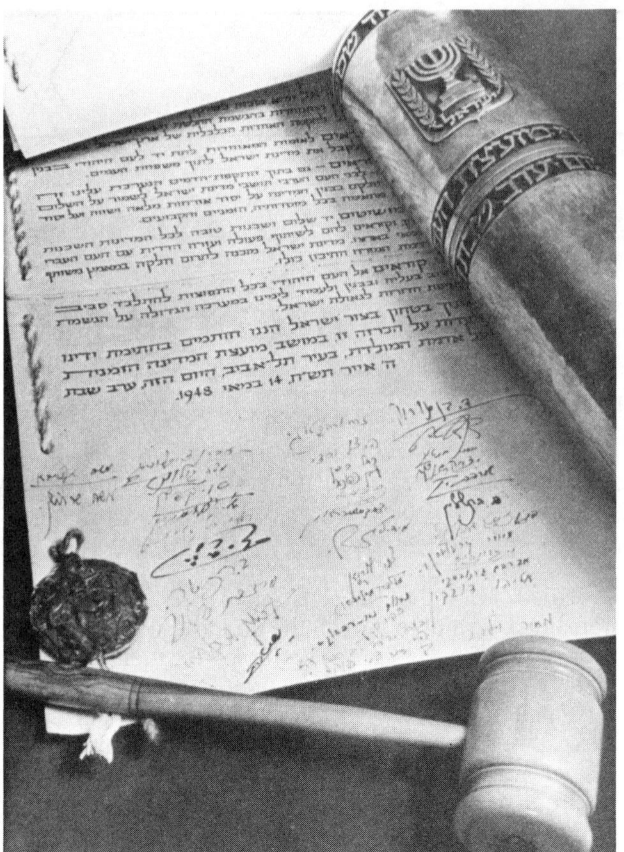

The Scroll of Independence of the State of Israel, signed May 14, 1948.

Israel's Presidents

Chaim Weizmann	(1874-1952)	President 1948-1952
Yitzhak Ben Zvi	(1884-1963)	President 1952-1963
Zalman Shazar	(1889-1974)	President 1963-1973
Ephraim Katzir	(1916-)	President 1973-1978
Yitzhak Navon	(1921-)	President 1978-1983
Chaim Herzog	(1918-)	President 1983-

Israel's Prime Ministers

David Ben-Gurion	(1886-1973)	Prime Minister 1948-1953; 1955-1963
Moshe Sharett	(1884-1965)	Prime Minister 1954-1955
Levi Eshkol	(1895-1969)	Prime Minister 1963-1969
Golda Meir	(1898-1979)	Prime Minister 1969-1974
Yitzhak Rabin	(1922-)	Prime Minister 1974-1977
Menachem Begin	(1913-)	Prime Minister 1977-1983
Yitzhak Shamir	(1915-)	Prime Minister 1983-1984
Shimon Peres	(1923-)	Prime Minister 1984-1986
Yitzhak Shamir	(1915-)	Prime Minister 1986-

Signatories of Israel's Declaration of Independence

Tova Gold

Daniel Auster (1893-1962), lawyer; born Galicia, settled in Palestine 1914. Acting mayor of Jerusalem 1936-38, 1944-45. First mayor of Jerusalem in independent Israel, 1948-51.

Mordecai Bentov (1900-), politician; Mapam leader; born Poland, settled in Palestine 1920. Leader of Ha-Shomer ha-Za'ir, editor of Mapam daily *Al ha-Mishmar* 1943-48. Member of Knesset 1949-65, minister of development 1955-61 and housing 1966-69.

Itzhak Ben Zvi (1884-1963), *yishuv* labor leader, scholar, second president of Israel (1952-63); born Poltava, Ukraine. Founded with Ber Borochov Po'alei Zion Party in Ukraine; active in self-defense organization. Settled in Palestine 1907. Among founders of Ha-Shomer 1909. Exiled during WWI; went to U.S., returning 1918 as a soldier in Jewish Legion. Chairman of Va'ad Leumi 1931, president 1945-48. Mapai member of Knesset, 1949-1952. Founded Institute for Study of Oriental Jewish Communities in the Middle East, 1948 (Ben Zvi Institute after 1952). His scholarly works devoted mainly to research on Jewish communities and sects, geography of Israel, its ancient population and antiquities.

Eliyahu Meir Berligne (1866-1959), *yishuv* leader; born Russia, settled in Palestine 1907. Among founders of Tel Aviv, member of Va'ad Leumi 1920-48.

Peretz (Fritz) Bernstein (1890-1971), Zionist leader, publicist, politician; born Germany; was president of Dutch Zionist Organization. Settled in Palestine 1936. Leader of General Zionists, later of Liberal Party. Member of Jewish Agency Executive, member of Knesset until 1965, minister of commerce and industry 1948-49, 1952-55.

Rabbi Wolf (Ze'ev) Gold (1889-1956), leader of religious Zionism; born in Poland, emigrated to U.S. 1907. Headed U.S. Mizrachi 1932-35. Settled in Palestine 1935. From 1945 member of Jewish Agency Executive and from 1951 headed Department for Torah Education and Culture. Outstanding orator who worked for religious education throughout the Diaspora.

Daniel Auster

Mordecai Bentov

Itzhak Ben Zvi

Eliyahu Meir Berligne

Peretz (Fritz) Bernstein

Rabbi Wolf (Ze'ev) Gold

Meir Grabovsky

Itzhak Grunbaum

Dr. Abraham Granovsky (Granott)

Meir David Loevenstein

Meir Grabovsky (1905-1963), Histadrut official. Born in Ukraine, settled in Palestine 1925. Representative of Mapai in Histadrut from 1931, member of Va'ad Leumi from 1930. Member of the first Knesset. In 1950, was chosen to be head of Histadrut in the U.S.

Itzhak Grunbaum (1879-1970), Polish Jewish leader. Edited weekly *Ha-Olam*. Elected to Sejm. Champion of minorities in Poland. Formed "national minorities bloc." Leader Al ha-Mishmar Zionist faction. Settled in Palestine 1933. Member of Zionist Executive, heading aliyah and labor departments. Minister of interior, 1948-49. Editor of *Encyclopaedia of the Jewish Diaspora*. Wrote 4-volume *History of Zionism*. Initially a General Zionist, later sympathized with Mapam. Spent last years at Kibbutz Gan Shemuel.

Dr. Abraham Granovsky (Granott) (1890-1962), economist; president of Jewish National Fund; born Bessarabia, settled in Jerusalem 1922. Cofounder and chairman of Progressive Party; member of first Knesset. Established principles for a progressive agrarian policy.

Meir David Loevenstein (1901-), born Copenhagen, settled in Palestine 1904. Leader of Agudat Israel and United Religious Front.

Zvi Lurie (1906-1968), Mapam labor leader; born Poland, settled in Palestine 1925. Member of Jewish Agency Executive.

Golda Meyerson (Meir) (1898-1978), prime minister, labor leader; born Kiev, emigrated to U.S. 1906, taught school in Milwaukee, settled in Palestine 1921. Secretary of Mo'ezet ha-Po'alot 1928. Joined executive committee of Histadrut 1934, becoming head of political department. Acting head of political department of Jewish Agency when leaders of the *yishuv* were arrested June 1946. Minister to Moscow 1948-49. Mapai member of Knesset 1949-74. Minister of labor, 1949-50, foreign minister 1956-65. Secretary general of Mapai and later secretary general of Israel Labor Party. Prime Minister 1969-74. Greatest legacy: strengthened relations with U.S. Ben Gurion said of her: "She is the best man in my cabinet."

Nahum Nir (Rafalkes) (1884-1968), labor leader; born Poland. Active in left wing of Po'alei Zion. Settled in Palestine 1925. A leader of Mapam, member of Knesset 1949-65, second speaker of Knesset, 1959.

Zvi Segal (Moses Hirsch) (1876-1968), Bible scholar; born Lithuania, lecturer at Oxford 1908-09. Settled in Palestine 1926, where he joined faculty of Hebrew University, teaching Semitic languages, Bible and philology. Authored popular four-volume introduction to the Bible.

Zvi Lurie

Golda Meyerson (Meir)

Nahum Nir (Rafalkes)

Zvi Segal (Moses Hirsch)

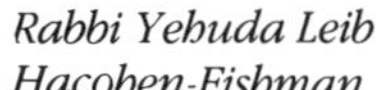
Rabbi Yehuda Leib Hacohen-Fishman

David Zvi Pinkas

Aharon Zisling

Moshe Kolodny (Kol)

Rabbi Yehuda Leib Hacohen-Fishman (Y'huda Leb Hakohen Maimon) (1875-1962), rabbi, leader of religious Zionism; born Bessarabia, settled in Palestine 1913. A founder of Mizrachi educational system. Founded Mosad Ha-Rav Kook 1936. Was among Jewish leaders arrested and interned by British 1946. Mizrachi Knesset member and minister of religion. Prolific author.

David Zvi Pinkas (1895-1952), Mizrachi leader, politician; born Hungary, settled in Palestine 1925. Member of Knesset 1949-52, minister of transportation 1951-52.

Aharon Zisling (1901-1964), labor leader; born Belorussia, settled in Palestine 1914. A founder of Ahdut ha-Avodah Party 1944 and Mapam 1948. Minister of agriculture 1948-49, member of Zionist Executive 1961-63, in charge of absorption.

Moshe Kolodny (Kol) (1911-), politician, Zionist leader; born Pinsk, settled in Palestine 1932. Head of Youth Aliyah 1948-64. Leader of Independent Liberal Party, member of Knesset, minister of tourism.

David Ben Gurion (Gruen) (1886-1973), statesman; born Plonsk, settled in Palestine 1906. Exiled by Turks 1915, formed Jewish battalion in U.S., returning in 1918, joining Jewish Legion. Among founders of Ahdut ha-Avodah 1919. Secretary-general of Histadrut 1921-33; chairman of Jewish Agency Executive 1935-48. Organized Biltmore Program 1942. Headed Va'ad Leumi, which proclaimed the rebirth of Israel. Prime Minister and minister of defense 1948-53, recalled 1955, resigned 1963. Founded Rafi party 1965, Reshimah Mamlakhtit 1969. Resigned Knesset 1970 to Kibbutz Sde Boker. Legacy: strengthened Israeli army, spearheaded settlement of Negev, encouraged assimilation of ethnic groups, advocated scientific development.

Eliyahu Dobkin (1898-1976), Labor Zionist leader; born Belorussia, settled in Palestine 1932. Member of Jewish Agency Executive.

Meir Wilner-Kovner (1919-), born Vilna, settled in Palestine 1938. Leader of Communist Party.

Zerah Wahrhaftig (1906-), Hapoel HaMizrachi leader; born Poland, settled in Palestine 1947, after serving World Jewish Congress and Hapoel HaMizrachi in New York. Member of Knesset from 1949, served as Minister of Religious Affairs from 1961.

David Ben Gurion (Gruen)

Eliyahu Dobkin

Meir Wilner-Kovner

Zerah Wahrhaftig

Herzl Vardi (Naftali Herzl Rosenblum)

Rachel Cohen (Kagan)

Rabbi Kalman Kahana

Saadia Kobashi

Herzl Vardi (Naftali Herzl Rosenblum) (1903-), born Kovno, settled in Palestine 1935. Leader of Revisionist Zionist wing.

Rachel Cohen (Kagan) (1888-1982), communal worker; born Odessa, settled in Palestine 1919; member Va'ad Leumi 1937-47; member of first and fifth Knesset; former chairman of Women's International Zionist Organization.

Rabbi Kalman Kahana (1910-), born Lvov, settled in Palestine 1938. Leader of Poalei Agudat Israel in Knesset. Co-founder of Kibbutz Chofetz Chaim. Author of numerous *seforim.*

Saadia Kobashi (1904-), born Yemen, settled in Palestine 1909. Member of Va'ad Leumi of provisional government. Leader of Yemenite community.

Rabbi Yitzhak Meir Levin (1894-1971), leader of Agudat Israel; active in Agudat Israel movement in Poland; reached Palestine in 1940; headed local branch of the movement from 1947. Member of Knesset, minister of social welfare until 1952, resigning during controversy over national service for women. Chairman of world executive of Agudat Israel from 1954.

Eliezer Kaplan (1891-1952), labor leader; born Russia, settled in Palestine 1920. Member of Jewish Agency Executive from 1933, later becoming treasurer. Member of Knesset and first minister of finance. Greatly influential in Israel's early economic and financial policy.

Avraham Katznelson (1888-1956), physician; born Bobruisk, Russia. During World War I served as a physician in the Russian Army. Served Zionist Executive in Istanbul, and Hitahdut in Vienna and Berlin. Settled in Palestine 1924. Directed Health Department of the Zionist Executive, and later, of the Va'ad Leumi. Became Director General of the Ministry of Health, 1948. Served as member of UN delegation 1949-50, Minister to the Scandinavian countries until 1956.

Felix Rosenbluth (Pinchas Rosen) (1887-1979), lawyer; chairman of Zionist Organization of Germany, 1920-23, member of Zionist Executive in London 1926-31. Settled in Palestine 1931. Member of Knesset 1949-68 and first minister of justice, 1948-61. Active in General Zionists; cofounder of Progressive Party.

Rabbi Yitzhak Meir Levin

Eliezer Kaplan

Avraham Katznelson

Felix Rosenbluth

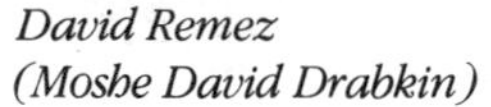

David Remez (Moshe David Drabkin)

Berl Repetur

Modekhai Shattner

Ben Zion Sternberg

David Remez (Moshe David Drabkin) (1886-1951), labor leader; born Belorussia, settled in Palestine 1913. Secretary-general of Histadrut 1935-45; chairman of Va'ad Leumi 1944-48; Mapai member of Knesset, minister of communications 1948-50, minister of education 1950-51. His son Aaron Remez was the first commander of the Israeli Air Force.

Berl Repetur (1902-   ), labor leader; secretary, Histadrut; born Ukraine; settled in Palestine 1920. Worked as a laborer in the port of Haifa for nine years. Served in Va'ad Leumi, Security Council of the Haganah and in senior positions of the Histadrut. Served in Knesset from 1949 (Mapam).

Mordekhai Shattner (1904-   ), born Hungary, settled in Palestine 1924. Member of the Executive of the Va'ad Leumi. Leader of Mapai wing.

Ben Zion Sternberg (1895-1962), lawyer; born Bukovina, managed export and appliance companies in Rumania and practiced law; settled in Palestine 1940 after serving as president of the Revisionist Party in Rumania 1925-40; member Va'ad Leumi; headed Department of Investments of Ministry of Commerce and Industry 1949-52, then returned to private law practice.

Behor Shalom Shitrit (1895-1967), Sephardi leader; commander of police in Lower Galilee, magistrate 1935-48. Mapai member of Knesset, minister of police, 1948-67.

Hayyim Moshe Shapira (1902-1970), politician; leader of National Religious Party; born Belorussia, where he was a central figure in Ze'irei HaMizrachi. Settled in Palestine 1925. Member of Zionist Executive. Founder of United Religious Front, and president of Mizrachi and HaPoel HaMizrachi.

Moshe Shertok (Sharett) (1894-1965), second prime minister of Israel; Zionist leader; born Ukraine, settled in Palestine 1906. Served Turkish army as an interpreter in World War I. Succeeded Arlosoroff as head of political department of the Jewish Agency 1933-48. Helped establish the Jewish Brigade; arrested on "Black Saturday" (June 29, 1946). Led international struggle for approval of the UNSCOP partition proposal by the UN. Israel's first foreign minister, prime minister January 1954-November 1955, again foreign minister until 1956. Elected chairman of Executive of Zionist Organization and Jewish Agency 1960.

Behor Shalom Shitrit

Hayyim Moshe Shapira

Moshe Shertok (Sharett)

Why do the Jews Need a Land of Their Own?

Sholom Aleichem (1859-1916)

> "For the Lord will have compassion on Jacob, and will yet choose Israel, and set them in their own land."
>
> —*Isaiah* 14:1

Why do Jews need a land of their own? Some question! There are people who would add another question. And they would be right. Why should Jews not want a country? If Jews are a nation, why should they be worse than all other nations? It's as though they were asking you what do you want a home for? Naturally, everyone should have a home. What else? Stay outside? If you consider it at bottom, properly, it isn't just like that. The question is, what does one want a home for, a home of his own? Does a man need a home of his own?

Jews have a saying for it—better a rich tenant than a poor landlord. But when does that apply? When there are houses galore and houses are cheap, and landlords fight each other to get you as a tenant. Everybody after you, wants you! But what if the boot is on the other foot? What if you've been a tenant all over the place, and you've got a reputation—between ourselves—as a bad tenant, so that you can't get into a house anywhere, and you have nothing left but to stay outside, under God's Heaven! What do you do then?

More than eighteen hundred years we have been dragging around as tenants from one house to another. Have we ever tried thinking seriously—how long? How much longer? What will be the end of it?

In these eighteen hundred years we have gone through all sorts of times. There was a time when houses were plentiful, and everyone was happy to have us as a tenant (Nobody, indeed, came to blows over us.). It didn't last long. They soon got fed up with us, and we were told to pack up and clear out. Go and find another lodging!

In these eighteen hundred years we have had all sorts of times. Occasions when we pulled ourselves together and recovered from our wanderings, hoping that any minute now Messiah would come, we would get over all our troubles, and be on a level with everybody else. It didn't last long. Before we could look round to see where in the world we were, we were again miles under, in the depths of despair.

That's what happened with us in the last few years, when people became wise, and the world was full of knowledge. The word *haskalah* (education) brought us a lot of new words, noble, high-sounding words, like humanity, justice, emancipation, equality, brotherhood, and suchlike words

Sholom Aleichem

that looked good and fine on paper and did your heart good to look at them.

What came of all these fine words you know by now. And if you don't know, try to read Dr. Max Nordau's speech at the Zionist Congress in Basel, and you will see that all these fine words remain no more than fine words. At bottom our position remained bitter and black. Worse than before.

That our position is bitter and black we had known before. We heard the story from our grandfathers of old, terrible, wonderful tales, of a Pharaoh in Egypt who had plagued us, a Haman who had ended up in disaster, a Titus who had collapsed in ruin, an Inquisition, and the expulsion of the Jews from Spain and Portugal and other places. And more such tales with which our history is full. We witnessed many of them ourselves. Seen them with our own eyes, read about them in the newspapers. Only those who went to the Congress opened our eyes, painted a picture of our position all over the world, and we discovered that even in those countries where we envied our brothers, thought they were living happily, it was nothing of the kind. We had been mistaken. It turned out that things are nowhere good for us; they are terribly bad. We are hated everywhere. They can't stand us anywhere. And as if to provide evidence for what we say, France came out with the notorious Dreyfus trial, and the hatred whipped up against the famous French writer Emile Zola, who wanted to put right the injustice committed against this innocent man Dreyfus. Who of you all hasn't read about that amazing trial? Who among you has been indifferent to the injustice committed before our eyes now at the end of the nineteenth century? And where? In France! "Spit on Zola!" "Death to the Jews!" That's what the antisemites shouted in Paris.

The Jewish Congress in Basel drew the right conclusions

about the position of our brothers throughout the world, and considering these conclusions we learned three things:

1. They hate us everywhere, in the whole world.
2. The situation is so bitter and black that it can't go on any longer.
3. We must find a way, but one that will work.

A. Let's consider it well, why do they hate us? We ourselves know (we don't have to pretend among ourselves) that we are no better and no worse than the rest. We have all the good qualities and the bad that all people have. And if it happens sometimes that we go a little too far, we have, to compensate, other qualities that outweigh the faults. Only what? The hatred against us is so great and so deeply ingrained that no one will consider our good qualities, and our faults are flung at us at every step, all the time.

What is the cause of this hate?

We won't go into long discussions, turning the pages of history, to get to the bottom of it. Where does this hatred come from? It is an old, persistent disease, an epidemic, (God forbid!) that goes by heritage from generation to generation. It sometimes happens that our enemies can't themselves say why they hate us. It's a real tragedy. God's own curse that has come down on us these many, many years. And going back to this question, let us make a strict account. Why should they love us? Can we demand of people that they must love us? Who are we among the nations? What are we, and what big noise do we make amongst the other nations in Europe that they should love us?

Who are we? Sons of Abraham, Isaac, and Jacob, who once had our land. We sinned and were driven out, dispersed over the whole earth, and so we wander about among strange nations for nearly two thousand years, like a lost orphan child, who is kept only for pity's sake. He is thrown a crumb, tossed a bone, and little notice is taken of him. If there is anything someone wants to say to him, it is said straight out, without mincing words. And if he doesn't catch on, he gets it in the neck.

What does the orphan do then? He hides. He pockets the blow and wipes his lips as if nothing had happened. He's a stranger! Everywhere a stranger! So as long as the native, the one who belongs, finds things going well and easy, feels comfortable, earns enough for his needs, the stranger can get by, more or less. But when the native feels cramped, crowded out, with competition growing, and his earnings going down, then the stranger assumes enormous bulk, looks gigantic. All the troubles in the land seem to stem from him. And people begin to murmur. At first under their breath, then louder and louder. "What do we want these strangers here for!"

It only needs one to say it first, and the others follow. No arguments will help. No facts and figures, to show that the stranger too is a human being, that he also has to eat, and that he can help in the common task, can be of use. Nobody will listen. Nobody wants his usefulness. Take it somewhere else, they say. We don't want it. Get out!

So what are we? We are foreigners, aliens everywhere.

Now there is a second question—who are we? Meaning, are we a People, a nation, or not? What is called a nation, and what are the signs of a People. A People should first of all have a country. A People should have an ideal. That means an idea, a thought towards which the whole People will strive, devoted to it heart and soul.

We lost our land. Where is our ideal? To have a land we must want it. That means we must all have one wish, one will, one idea, one thought. That is unity. What unity we have now we all know well enough. Our enemies accuse us from the start, saying that we have too much unity. They say about us that all Israel are brothers. All Jews are one Jew. We, of course, know how much truth there is in that. Wish it on the antisemites to have our unity. If one of us says yes, the other will say no. If one says kosher, the other will say treif. And what one finds pleasing, the other dislikes. He wants it, so I want the opposite. Two Jews have three opinions. When one says this, the other says yes, but not like that. The other man's opinion isn't worth a pinch of snuff. No need to listen when somebody else is talking. There is no elder, and surely no wiser. Because we are all wise. *Kulone Chachomim.* We are all wise men. We all know what is going on in the world. We knew it long ago, long before that other man is trying to tell us. So what's all this about an idea that will link us all together—our whole People? Take a ride, for instance, to Berditchev, a Jewish town. Stop a Jew there, in the street or in the synagogue and put the question to him—Excuse me, Mister Jew, what is your ideal? And what's going on here about Zion and Zionism?

He'll look at you as if you were mad, a man with time to think about ideals, a loafer, a drifter, a waster of time. Ideal, schmideal, Zion and Zionism. You tell me me rather how's business! Have you anything in your mind to turn an honest ruble?

I said Berditchev not as an exception, but as an example. The same sort of place. The same sort of thing will hold good in Kovno, in Riga, in Shnipishok, anywhere you like. They say the whole world is one town. And I'm not saying that all Berditchev Jews or all Shnipishok Jews are all so taken up with the chase after the ruble. Or that nobody there is interested in Zion and Zionism. I'm only saying that most Jews are miles and miles away from such things, things that don't contribute to their takings. And if there are Jews in every town who devote themselves to things like Zionism, they are no more than a few single individuals.

The argument is that Jews are poor, badly off. They must all chase after the ruble to keep going. But that argument is false. To begin with, not all Jews are poor. Thank God, we have plenty of wealthy Jews (and I am not speaking of the magnates, the really, truly rich, for where does it say that aristocrats like these, millionaires, must read little booklets written in Yiddish?) I'm talking of the middle-class Jews who have both time and the mind to devote themselves to such things as Jewish affairs. And on the other hand, the worse things are with Jews, the more and more often they have to think of these things on which their own happiness and the happiness of the entire Jewish People depend. Bad times and bad conditions getting worse every day demand that all Jews must come together, be driven together, all with one wish and one will, one purpose, one ideal. Brothers, there is something missing. The spirit is missing, the folk-spirit that we lost all this time that we have been dragging around here and there.

So what are we? Well, we have our religion. We have our

own language. And, of course, there are a few million of us, people who pray from the same prayer book, who keep the Sabbath, eat matzoth at Passover time, hamantaschen at Purim, a smear of honey at Tabernacles, and—

That's all? Nothing more? If so the world is almost right when it says we are not a nation, but just a lot of stiff-necked, stubborn people—what we are told we are, every day!

Again, what are we? How about our ideal? Where is our "Jerusalem thy city" that we repeat day by day? What of "Next year in Jerusalem" and "*Ani ma'amin*"?—Our "I believe"—our principles of Jewish faith? And our form of greeting to each other—"Live to see Messiah!"

True! Only we mustn't fool ourselves. We know well enough how a Jew speaks these words. Our question is, what has he in mind while he speaks those words—his shop, his mill, the forest where he has a lumber lease from the landowner, or his shares on the stock exchange, or far away in Yehupetz, at the Market Day Fair. As for living to see Messiah—good! Why not? If Messiah comes riding along to collect Jews and take them to *Eretz Israel* at his expense, on condition that each of us, all of us must go on that journey, and the moneyed ones go first!

Jews have such a delightful sacred ideal, and all they do is make fun of it!

No, brothers! We remember Jerusalem every day, but what we have in our minds is Yehupetz. *Eretz Israel* has till now been a place where old Jews go to die. Zion till now was a word, a fine, beautiful name that we find in our holy books, with other lovely old names, like Wailing Wall, and Mother Rachel's tomb—all names that should move our hearts, should evoke memories, conjure up pictures of our glorious past.

"Zion, how fare your wandering children?" That's a line from a poem by one our greatest Jewish singers and patriots, Rabbi Judah Halevi. That was his question to us!

But the words, alas, fly by swiftly, leave an impression with us for a moment, and vanish.

Judah Halevi was drawn to Zion all his life, till he went there and was killed there. "Where shall I find wings," he asked, "to fly there, to bring my broken heart to Zion, to the Holy Land? That I should fall with my face to the ground, embrace the holy earth, kiss the dear stones, the sacred dust, the holy graves!"

And that is where he was killed.

Unhappily, our Jewish People know little of this great Jewish poet and his intense love of Zion. Our people no longer feel what they once felt about this majestic name, "Zion." It seems that the wound must be so old that the pain is no longer felt, insensible. That is not surprising, for after all, this long *Golus,* this wandering from one land to another, suffering such things as the Spanish Inquisition, and more, much more, and still retaining some fragments of humanity, is itself an achievement, a miracle. Such a miracle as only God can work. God and his Torah, this little Pentateuch, our spiritual Fatherland, this community of soul!

This fact alone, that we hold on to our Jewishness so long, that we have not been wiped off the face of the earth like many other nations who have left no trace behind—that itself is proof that we can and with God's help will be a nation with all the signs and symbols of a nation.

That leaves us with the third question. What bonds have we with the other nations? No bonds at all!

There were times indeed when there was some talk of our being kindred, having bonds. Shem and Japhet wanted to marry into us. We were on the point of intermingling—assimilation. Both sides deluded themselves. It seemed that we were brothers, body and soul. We on our side were prepared for it, and to show how delighted we were with the match we started aping them in every way, with everything—dress, speech, behavior, manners in the house and outside. With our festivals. With our names—Abraham became Anton; Jeremiah, Jerzy; Getzel, Maxim. The women followed suit. Hannah became Gertrude; Esther, Isabel; and Dvoshe, Cleopatra! Everyone tried to outdo the other. All wanted to show that "I am not I."

What came of it? Nothing! Worse than that! It finished up with rows and scandals. What can we do if we are not really equal sides. We can't impose friendship by force. It won't work!

These are the three main reasons why they hate us, always and everywhere. They hate us because we are strangers and because we want to eat. They hate us because we are a nation without a land and without an ideal. They hate us because we do not have equal links with the nations. We only push the cart from behind, leaping and jumping and grimacing all the time to attract attention. In one word they hate us and hunt us more and more as time goes on, more and more brutally. I hope I'm wrong.

B. Because as we go on things keep getting worse, and things are becoming so dangerous that it cannot possibly continue as in the past. When they reminded us of our faults and revived all the old accusations against us, we responded by finding excuses, trying to justify ourselves, to show that we are not as bad as they made out. You will see that we are right if you give us a little more time, a little more freedom to speak. "Give us a chance to educate ourselves, give us education, and you will see that we are an entirely different people."

Now, when we see plainly that being on the defensive will not help, that self-vindication gets us nowhere, that since we are a nation like all other nations, that we will never mix and mingle with other nations, and that we are hated everywhere in the whole world, we must look for some other way to assure our existence; we must find our own remedy. Our help is in ourselves alone.

C. What is our help, what is our remedy? Our wise men have long pondered this question, have written a great deal about it, our scholars, our providers and protectors—and they have found only one way—Jews must have an ideal. And the ideal must be a land. In a word, Jews must have a land, their own land.

Only sixteen years ago a great man, Dr. Pinsker, published a little pamphlet with the name *"Auto-Emancipation."* It caused a stir in the Jewish world. "To end our troubles," Dr. Pinsker said, "we must have a land. But not to wait for someone to give us the land. We must find a land ourselves, a piece of earth, a corner, that is our own, no matter where it is, so long as it is ours."

Does a Jew realize what lies in these few simple words —"a piece of earth, a corner that is our own?" Does a Jew feel how necessary and how advantageous it is for each and every one of us, and for the whole community, for us all? Does a Jew ever think what we would have looked like among the nations of the world if we had a piece of land somewhere, our own small corner—that we would be no longer paupers, wandering gypsies, outcast and unwanted!

Dr. Pinsker had given a lot of thought to the subject, and he had concluded that only a land of our own can bring us salvation. He laid the first stone of that great structure which our people created afterwards. For he was followed by other Jewish writers who discussed and considered the matter. It started a search over the world for a land where we could settle Jews who had got stuck like a bone in the throat in the countries where they lived. One said Palestine. Another Argentina. A third Brazil. Some thought Africa would be the place. Others plumped for Cyprus. Back of Beyond! God knows where! There is an apt saying—a big world, but no room to sit down. None of the other nations came out to welcome us, to say *Sholom Aleichem,* were in no hurry to invite us in, but on the contrary fought over us like those seven towns when a synagogue cantor applied for a job, each wanting some other town to take him on. The conclusion was reached that if Jews want to live as a nation, there is no other way but to go there, to the ancient Holy Land of our forefathers, the land of the patriarchs. We were shown with all the necessary evidence that every other way was wrong, was false, that the Jewish People are too much divided already, split up, scattered, and dispersed. What we need is a *merkaz,* a center.

The question, *"Wohin?"* ("Where to?") ceased to be a question. Disappeared from the agenda. The organization "Chovevei Zion" was formed then, and it still exists. Though it is true that when the emigration started, more Jews went and still go to America, the heart of each immigrant lies over there, in the land of our Fathers, Palestine, *Eretz Israel,* Zion—those words are heard often among our people, everywhere, even in distant, free America. We already have in Palestine a good many fine colonies that Baron Edmond de Rothschild founded. We also have our own colonies there, where our brothers distinguish themselves with their work.

But time has shown that the colonizing of Palestine is proceeding too slowly. The number of Jewish people grows and their poverty grows more. Jews need, most of all, a land of their own, where they can go and settle openly, not having to sneak in as in the past. These are the words of Herzl, who convened the first Jewish Congress held in Basel.

Indeed, Dr. Herzl did nothing new by using these words. He said almost the same thing that Dr. Pinsker had said sixteen or seventeen years before. The difference was that Pinsker spoke in general terms, that Jews must have a country, and Herzl came out openly before the whole world with the demand that Jews must have a country, their own land, and pointed straight at Palestine. Dr. Pinsker poured out his bitter heart quietly, reasonably, without fuss or clamor, while Herzl demanded publicly, to the whole world, a ready-made Jewish state. I refer to Herzl's *Der Judenstadt,* which made a stir, not only among Jews, but also among other people.

"A Jewish state," Herzl said "is necessary not only for us, but for the whole world. For it is the only way to get rid of the unhappy Jewish Question. . . . Of course, as long as the idea of a Jewish state, a Jewish land remains the idea of one or a few people, it will be no more than a very fine idea, and that's that. But as soon as it becomes the idea of the whole People, it will not be difficult to carry it into effect."

"The Jewish People," Dr. Herzl proceeded, "cannot and must not be destroyed. We will not be destroyed because our enemies will not allow it. We will not be destroyed, and this is proved by our nearly two thousand years of suffering, and we are still here. We must not be destroyed, because that is not desirable. Some leaves may fall off, but the tree remains. And that we should not be destroyed, we must have a land. Our own land . . . Time now," says Herzl, "for us to reveal our mission to the world, for all we will do in our new land will be to the good not only for our people, but of everyone, all mankind."

"Palestine or Argentina?" Herzl asks, and this is how he answers his own question. "The Jewish people will say thanks for every piece of land that will be given them, to settle there freely, to develop their powers and their energies and abilities. The difference between Argentina and Palestine is that the Holy Land, Zion, is bound up with our ancient history. The very name *Eretz Israel* is enough to attract the love of the Jewish people."

Herzl went on to present his plan—how Jews should make their land purchases in *Eretz Israel,* and how in time a Jewish state would develop there, of course, with the consent of the sultan and of all the European powers.

It would take a whole book to reproduce the plan in its entirety. Yet everybody will understand that building a grand edifice like that is no easy matter. It is a work not for a year or even ten years. As the saying goes, "Things don't work as fast as we talk." Jews must first of all understand the idea properly, grow accustomed to it, get done with the question we posed before, "Why do Jews need a land of their own?"

"That means we must see to it that all Jews should feel and understand how necessary and useful it is. We must see to it that this idea should be the ideal of the entire People. We must see to it that our wives and sisters should understand it, so that our children will be brought up under our national flag, so that our children should be Jewish children, who will not be ashamed of their People . . . Jews must return to the Jewish People before they return to the Jewish land."

Professor Schapira had this to say at the Basel Congress: "If our ancestors had contributed each year the *shekel* from the time we lost our state, we could by now have enough funds to buy the whole of *Eretz Israel.*"

I think this is a mistake. With this amount of money we could have bought half of the whole world. Does it mean that because our parents didn't do it, we mustn't do it either? What a great legacy we would leave our children and our children's children. They will inherit this holy ideal from us, the ideal that will go with us, a heritage from generation to generation. A land, our own land—that will be the ideal among all Jews the world over. Our children, or our grandchildren may live to see it. We ourselves perhaps, too.

Editor's Note: This was excerpted from "Why Do the Jews Need a Land of Their Own?" *by Sholom Aleichem (written between 1888 and 1913, translated from Hebrew and Yiddish), published by Herzl Press in New York.*

Statistical Abstract of Israel

Central Bureau of Statistics, State of Israel

	1985	1980	1970	1960	1950	יחידה Unit	
POPULATION							**אוכלוסייה**
Population—total	**4,266.2**	**3,921.7**	**3,022.1**	**2,150.4**	**1,370.1**	10³	אוכלוסייה — סך הכל
Jews	82.5	83.7	85.4	88.9	87.8	%	יהודים
Non-Jews	17.5	16.3	14.6	11.1	12.2	"	לא-יהודים
Jews in Israel as % of world Jewry	27.0	25.0	20.0	. .	. .	"	היהודים בישראל כאחוז מהיהודים בעולם
Jews—total	**3,517.2**	**3,282.7**	**2,582.0**	**1,911.2**	**1,203.0**	10³	יהודים — סך הכל
Israel born	60.4	55.9	45.8	37.4	26.3	%	ילידי ישראל
Born in Asia-Africa	17.6	19.5	26.3	27.6	22.2	"	ילידי אסיה-אפריקה
Born in Europe-America	22.0	24.6	27.9	35.0	51.5	"	ילידי אירופה-אמריקה
Non-Jews—total	**749.0**	**639.0**	**440.1**	**239.1**	**167.1**	10³	לא יהודים-סך הכל
Moslems	77.1	78.0	74.7	69.6	69.5	%	מוסלמים
Christians	13.3	14.1	17.1	20.7	21.5	"	נוצרים
Druze and other	9.6	7.9	8.2	9.7	9.0	"	דרוזים ואחרים
Population by selected age groups						% מסך הכל	אוכלוסייה לפי קבוצות גיל נבחרות
Jews aged 0-14	30.0	30.4	30.1	35.1	30.0	% of total	יהודים: בגיל 0-14
65+	10.1	9.7	7.2	5.2	3.7	"	65+
Non-Jews aged 0-14	44.1	47.4	49.7	45.6	. .	"	לא-יהודים: בגיל 0-14
65+	3.2	3.1	3.9	4.5	. .	"	65+
Population density	196.3	191.8	147.7	106.2	67.7	לקמ"ר per km²	צפיפות האוכלוסייה
Population by district—total	[1]100.0	[1]100.0	100.0	100.0		%	אוכלוסייה לפי מחוזות — סך הכל
Jerusalem District	11.9	11.4	10.8	8.7	. .	"	מחוז ירושלים
Northern District	[2]16.6	15.6	15.3	15.7	. .	"	מחוז הצפון
Haifa District	13.9	14.4	15.4	17.1	. .	"	מחוז חיפה
Central District	20.8	20.1	17.9	18.9	. .	"	מחוז המרכז
Tel Aviv District	23.8	25.6	29.4	31.8	. .	"	מחוז תל אביב
Southern District	12.0	12.1	11.1	7.8	. .	"	מחוז הדרום
	31 XII 1985	4 VI 1983	20 V 1972	22 V 1961			
Population in urban localities—total	**3,815.2**	**3,616.0**	**2,789.1**	**1,837.6**		10³	אוכלוסייה ביישובים עירוניים — סך הכל
Jerusalem	457.7	428.7	313.9	167.4		10³	ירושלים
Jews	71.6	71.4	73.4	98.4		%	יהודים
Non-Jews	28.4	28.6	26.6	1.6		"	לא-יהודים

1 Including Israelis in Judea and Samaria, Gaza Area and the Golan. 2 Incl. Golan sub-district.

1 כולל ישראלים הגרים ביהודה ושומרון, בחבל עזה ובגולן. 2 כולל נפת הגולן.

	31 XII 1985	4 VI 1983	20 V 1972	22 V 1961	יחידה Unit	
POPULATION (cont.)						אוכלוסייה (המשך)
Tel Aviv conurbation[1]	1,607.8	1,555.4	1,273.2	939.6	10³	אגד ערים תל אביב[1]
Thereof: Tel Aviv-Yafo	322.8	327.3	363.8	386.1	"	מזה: תל אביב-יפו
Bene Beraq	102.4	96.1	75.7	47.0	"	בני ברק
Bat Yam	131.2	128.7	100.1	31.7	"	בת ים
Holon	138.8	133.5	98.8	49.0	"	חולון
Petah Tiqwa	129.3	123.9	93.0	54.0	"	פתח תקוה
Rishon LeZiyyon	112.3	102.2	53.0	27.9	"	ראשון לציון
Ramat Gan	116.0	117.1	118.0	90.8	"	רמת גן
Haifa conurbation[1]	392.7	387.5	339.8	263.4	"	אגד ערים חיפה[1]
Thereof: Haifa	224.6	225.8	219.6	183.0	"	מזה: חיפה
Netanya	109.6	102.3	71.1	41.3	"	נתניה
Beer Sheva	115.0	110.8	85.3	43.5	"	באר שבע
Population in rural localities—total	451.0	421.6	358.5	341.9	"	אוכלוסייה ביישובים כפריים — סך הכל
Thereof:						מזה:
Moshavim and collective moshavim	157.0	149.9	130.6	124.6	"	מושבים ומושבים שיתופיים
Qibbuzim	125.2	115.5	89.7	77.1	"	קיבוצים

	1985	1980	1970	1960	1950	יחידה Unit	
VITAL STATISTICS							תנועה טבעית
Jews							יהודים
Live births	75,267	71,372	61,209	44,981	36,359	no. מס'	לידות חי
Births per 1,000 population	21.6	22.0	24.2	23.9	33.0	Rate שיעור	לידות ל-1,000 תושבים
Deaths	[2]25,017	23,472	18,425	10,404	7,148	no. מס'	פטירות
Mortality per 1,000 population	[2]7.3	7.2	7.3	5.5	6.5	Rate שיעור	פטירות ל-1,000 תושבים
Infant mortality per 1,000 live births	[2]10.3	§12.4	18.9	27.2	46.2	"	פטירות תינוקות ל-1,000 לידות חי
Total fertility per woman	2.9	2.8	3.4	3.5	3.9	ממוצע לידות Average births	פריון כולל לאישה — סך הכל
Woman born in:							האישה ילידת:
Israel	2.9	2.8	3.1	2.8	3.9	"	ישראל
Asia-Africa	3.2	3.0	4.1	5.1	5.7	"	אסיה-אפריקה
Europe-America	2.8	2.8	2.8	2.4	3.3	"	אירופה-אמריקה
Life expectation at birth							תוחלת חיים בלידה
Males	[2]73.5	72.5	69.9	70.7	66.3	Years שנים	זכרים
Females	[2]77.1	76.2	73.3	73.5	69.5	"	נקבות
Non-Jews							לא-יהודים
Live births	23,819	22,949	16,392	11,021	7,072	no. מס'	לידות חי
Births per 1,000 population	32.3	36.5	45.7	50.3	. .	Rate שיעור	לידות ל-1,000 תושבים
Deaths	[2]2,914	2,806	1,959	1,649	1,552	no. מס'	פטירות
Mortality per 1,000 population	[2]4.1	4.5	5.5	7.5	. .	Rate שיעור	פטירות ל-1,000 תושבים
Infant mortality per 1,000 live births	[2]20.6	24.4	37.2	48.0	56.0	"	פטירות תינוקות ל-1,000 לידות חי
Total fertility per woman	4.4	5.4	7.7	8.0	. .	ממוצע לידות Average births	פריון כולל לאישה — סך הכל
Moslem	4.9	6.0	9.0	9.3	. .	"	מוסלמיות
Christian	2.1	2.7	3.6	4.6	. .	"	נוצריות
Druze	4.5	6.1	7.5	7.9	. .	"	דרוזיות

1 According to the boundaries on the date of the 1983 census. 2 1984

1 לפי גבולות מפקד 1983.

	1985	1980	1970	1960	1950	יחידה Unit	
MIGRATION							**תנועות הגירה**
Immigrants and potential immigrants	10.6	20.4	36.8	24.5	170.2	10³	עולים ועולים בכוח
Residents going abroad[1]	553.2	513.5	153.7	63.3	30.0	"	תושבים שיצאו לחו"ל[1]
Residents returning[1]	531.4	481.6	146.5	51.3	20.0	"	תושבים שחזרו מחו"ל[1]
Tourists arriving	1,436.4	1,175.8	441.3	117.7	33.1	"	תיירים נכנסים
NATIONAL ECONOMY							**המשק הלאומי**
At constant prices							במחירים קבועים
Gross national product — total	1,159.6	1,053.8	635.8	277.7	100.0	1950=100	תוצר לאומי גולמי — סך הכל
—per capita	343.8	344.3	270.8	166.2	100.0	"	— לנפש
Private consumption expenditure—total	1,100.0	925.4	544.6	256.1	100.0	"	הוצאה לצריכה פרטית — סך הכל
General government consumption expenditure	1,277.2	1,244.9	899.1	227.9	100.0	"	הוצאה לצריכה ציבורית
Gross domestic capital formation	403.1	426.4	365.0	159.3	100.0	"	השקעה גולמית מקומית
BALANCE OF PAYMENTS							**מאזן התשלומים**
Deficit in goods and services account—total	3,972	3,728	1,257	346	285	$10⁶	הגירעון בחשבון סחורות ושירותים — סך הכל
excl. direct defence imports	2,180	2,073	633	298	..	"	ללא יבוא ביטחוני ישיר
Obligations of Israel to abroad	30,187	22,184	3,323	813	..	"	חובות ישראל לחוץ לארץ
Israel's foreign assets	10,872	10,119	1,100	270	..	"	נכסים במטבע חוץ
FOREIGN TRADE							**סחר חוץ**
Net imports of goods	8,020.9	§7,845.7	1,433.5	495.7	300.3	$10⁶	יבוא סחורות נטו
Net exports of goods	6,080.4	5,291.9	733.6	211.3	35.1	"	יצוא סחורות נטו
Excess of imports over exports	1,940.5	2,553.8	699.9	284.4	265.2	"	עודף היבוא על היצוא
Exports as percent of imports	75.8	67.4	51.2	42.6	11.7	%	היצוא כאחוז מהיבוא
Index of import volume	126	100	..	..	..	1980=100	מדד נפח היבוא
Index of export volume	133	100	..	..	..	"	מדד נפח היצוא
Agricultural exports	468.5	555.7	129.6	63.1	17.0	$10⁶	יצוא חקלאי
Industrial exports (excl. diamonds) (gross)	4,355.2	3,366.7	404.5	92.6	§9.3	"	יצוא תעשייתי (פרט ליהלומים) (ברוטו)
Diamonds (gross)	1,432.7	1,615.1	244.6	60.9	8.8	"	יהלומים (ברוטו)
Imports of consumer goods (gross)	621.0	544.3	142.6	44.1	76.7	"	יבוא נכסי תצרוכת (ברוטו)
production inputs (gross)	6,284.9	§6,481.0	972.4	§353.6	169.1	"	תשומות לייצור (ברוטו)
investment goods (gross)	1,413.7	969.4	347.0	105.0	56.2	"	נכסי השקעה (ברוטו)
FINANCE							**כספים**
Total money supply (end of year)	989	7,006	338	88	..	NIS 10⁶ ש"ח	סך אמצעי התשלום (סוף שנה)
Thereof: current deposits of the public in banks	508	4,878	210	58	..	"	מזה: פיקדונות עו"ש של הציבור בבנקים
Exchange rate of the U.S. Dollar							שער החליפין של הדולר
—end of year	1,499.5	7.55	0.35	0.18	0.04		— סוף שנה
—annual average	1,178.9	5.13	0.35	0.18	0.04	IS 'ש	— ממוצע שנתי

1 Of permanent population. — 1 מהאוכלוסייה הקבועה.

	1985	1980	1970	1960	1950	יחידה Unit	
PRICES							**מחירים**
Consumer price index							מדד המחירים לצרכן
—Annual average	4,829,974.6	22,923.5	514.2	289.3	..	1951=100.0	— ממוצע שנתי
—December of each year	772,449.5	3,433.1	106.1	61.7	..	1969=100.0	— דצמבר של כל שנה
Price index of inputs in residential building	796,107.2	3,992.7	113.4	..	..	1968=100.0	מדד מחירי תשומה בבנייה למגורים
Wholesale price index of industrial output (excl. printing and publishing)	864,834.3	3,946.9	108.8	..	..	"	מדד מחירים סיטוניים של תפוקת התעשייה (ללא דפוס והוצאה לאור)
LIVING CONDITIONS							**רמת חיים**
Total annual money income per urban employee's household (at prices of beginning of 1984)	[1]1,790.0	1,441.8	1,002.0	..	..	NIS ש"ח	הכנסה כספית שנתית כוללת למשק בית של שכירים עירוניים (במחירי תחילת 1984)
Private consumption expenditure per capita (at constant prices)	326.2	302.2	231.9	153.2	100.0	1950=100.0	הוצאה לצריכה פרטית לנפש (במחירים קבועים)
Thereof:							מזה:
Food, beverages and tobacco	28.6	27.4	29.0	33.2	37.2	% מסך הכל % of total	מזון, משקאות וטבק
Clothing, footwear and personal effects	5.2	5.9	8.6	8.7	13.0	"	הנעלה, הלבשה וחפצים אישיים
Durable goods	9.9	9.5	9.6	6.9	7.6	"	מוצרים בני-קיימא
Other products, fuel and light	9.2	8.7	7.6	6.9	6.5	"	מוצרים אחרים, דלק ומאור
Services (incl. housing and non-profit institutions)	47.1	48.5	45.2	44.3	35.7	"	שירותים (כולל דיור ומלכ"ר)
Daily food consumption per capita[2]							צריכת מזון לנפש ליום[2]
Calories	3,009	2,979	2,988	2,772	2,610	Un. 'יח	קלוריות
Proteins	93.5	92.2	91.5	85.1	83.9	gr. 'גר	חלבון
Fat	118.1	111.5	104.3	86.7	73.9	"	שומן
Products:							מוצרים:
Wheat and its products	261.1	282.2	285.5	313.7	322.5	"	חיטה ומוצרי חיטה
Rice	19.5	15.9	18.1	15.6	12.1	"	אורז נקי
Sugar and its products	91.8	82.7	95.9	79.7	47.1	"	סוכר ומוצריו
Vegetables	297.8	311.2	331.2	314.0	295.9	"	ירקות
Citrus fruit	91.2	95.6	116.2	161.9	134.2	"	פרי הדר
Meat	179.2	170.4	154.3	88.2	51.8	"	בשר
Eggs	59.5	53.7	61.6	50.4	40.0	"	ביצים
Milk and dairy products	297.8	272.0	267.7	275.9	264.0	"	חלב ומוצריו
	1985	1980	1970	1960	1955		
MANPOWER, EMPLOYMENT AND WAGES							**כוח אדם, תעסוקה ושכר**
Civilian labour force	**1,466.8**	**1,318.1**	**1,001.4**	**735.8**	**631.2**	10³	כוח העבודה האזרחי
Percent civilian labour force of population aged 14+	49.9	49.5	49.3	52.9	53.6	%	אחוז כוח העבודה האזרחי מהאוכלוסייה בגיל 14 ומעלה
Percent unemployed of civilian labour force	6.7	4.8	3.8	4.6	7.2	"	אחוז הבלתי מועסקים מכוח העבודה האזרחי

2 Agricultural years. — [1]1984 — 2 שנים חקלאיות.

	1985	1980	1970	1960	1955	יחידה Unit	
MANPOWER (cont.)							**כוח אדם** (המשך)
Employed persons—total	**1,368.3**	**1,254.5**	**963.2**	**701.8**	**585.7**	10^3	מועסקים — סך הכל
Agriculture	5.7	6.4	8.8	17.3	17.6	%	חקלאות
Industry	23.1	23.7	24.3	23.2	21.5	"	תעשייה
Electricity and water	0.9	1.0	1.2	2.2	2.0	"	חשמל ומים
Construction	5.3	6.4	8.3	9.3	9.3	"	בינוי
Commerce	12.5	11.7	13.0	12.3	13.5	"	מסחר
Transport	6.4	6.9	7.5	6.2	6.6	"	תחבורה
Finance	9.7	8.2	5.2	. .	. .	"	פיננסים
Public services	29.8	29.6	24.0	22.0	21.2	"	שירותים ציבוריים
Private services	6.7	6.2	7.7	7.5	8.3	"	שירותים אישיים
Percent Jews of total employed persons	88.7	89.9	90.8	93.1	92.6	"	אחוז היהודים מסך המועסקים
Percent employees of total employed persons	79.1	77.5	73.6	67.4	63.2	"	אחוז השכירים מסך המועסקים
Percent women of total employed persons	37.8	36.0	29.4	25.6	24.4	"	אחוז הנשים מסך המועסקים
Average monthly wage per employee's post (at constant prices)	111.9	105.7	83.2	. .	. .	1978=100	שכר חודשי ממוצע למשרת שכיר (במחירים קבועים)
	1985	1980	1970	1960	1950		
AGRICULTURE[1]							**חקלאות[1]**
Cultivated area	4,370	4,386	4,105	4,075	2,480	10^3 דונם 10^3 dunam	שטח מעובד
Thereof: irrigated	2,370	2,003	1,720	1,305	375	"	מזה: בהשקייה
Net domestic product	[2]803,794	4,100.7	93.6	74.8	. .	NIS 10^3 ש״ח	תוצר מקומי נקי
Employed persons	89.4	87.7	89.8	121.1	. .	10^3	מועסקים
Net capital stock (at 1967/68 prices)	226.8	§208.8	180.6	139.7	44.1	NIS 10^3 ש״ח	מלאי ההון נטו (במחירי 1967/68)
Production: Wheat	127.7	253.2	125.0	41.3	27.0	10^3 tons 'ט	ייצור: חיטה
Vegetables	162.7	607.0	472.3	296.2	125.5	"	ירקות
Potatoes	204.4	171.7	137.1	81.8	35.3	"	תפוחי אדמה
Citrus	1,487.0	1,542.8	1,261.9	609.6	270.0	"	הדרים
Avocadoes	77.2	32.0	4.1	0.2	. .	"	אבוקדו
Poultry meat	243.6	200.0	101.7	45.7	7.4	"	בשר עוף
Beef	61.1	§55.0	35.6	25.1	1.9	"	בשר בקר
Cow's milk	788.1	670.3	440.5	277.3	92.2	l. 10^6 'ל	חלב בקר
Table eggs	1,878.5	1,614.9	1,320.0	1,114.0	330.0	10^6	ביצי מאכל
Fish	25.1	24.7	21.8	13.9	6.6	tons 10^3 'ט	דגים
Tractors	26.3	26.8	16.3	7.4	2.6	10^3	טרקטורים

1 Agricultural years. — 1 שנים חקלאיות.
2 At average prices of each year. — 2 במחירים ממוצעים של כל שנה.

	1985	1980	1970	1960	1950	יחידה Unit	
INDUSTRY							**תעשייה**
Establishments engaging 100 employees and over	447	427	375	198	. .	no. 'מס	מפעלים המעסיקים 100 שכירים ויותר
Industrial production index—total[1]	108	90	54	18	. .	1983=100.0	מדד הייצור התעשייתי-ס״ה[1]
Mining and quarrying	105	101	79	26	. .	"	כרייה וחציבה
Food, beverages and tobacco	103	82	45	28	. .	"	מזון, משקאות וטבק
Textiles, clothing and leather	99	98	62	20	. .	"	טקסטיל, הלבשה ועור
Wood and its products	100	89	78	20	. .	"	עץ ומוצריו
Paper and its products, printing and publishing	108	92	56	20	. .	"	נייר ומוצריו, דפוס והוצאה לאור
Rubber, plastic, chemical and oil products	111	85	48	12	. .	"	גומי, פלסטיק, מוצרים כימיים ומוצרי נפט
Non-metallic mineral products	90	105	83	44	. .	"	מוצרים מינרלים אל-מתכתיים
Basic metal and metal products	105	92	61	23	. .	"	מתכת בסיסית ומוצרי מתכת
Machinery, electrical & electronic equipment and vehicles	113	90	43	12	. .	"	מכונות, ציוד חשמלי ואלקטרוני וכלי הובלה
Miscellaneous	139	85	56	23	. .	"	שונות
ELECTRICITY							**חשמל**
Installed generating capacity	4,062	2,737	1,226	410	100	MWT מגו״ט	כושר ייצור מותקן
Production	15,010	12,089	6,610	2,205	543	10^6 קוט״ש 10^6 KWH	ייצור
Consumption							צריכה
Household	3,331	2,900	1,448	446		"	ביתית
Commerce	2,979	1,992	782	196	206	"	מסחר
Agricultural	602	453	195			"	חקלאות
Industrial	4,406	3,773	1,878	669	141	"	תעשייה
Water pumping	2,197	1,678	1,394	546	117	"	שאיבת מים
WATER[2]							**מים[2]**
Household consumption	422	367	254	197	. .	m^3 10^6 ^{3}מ	שימוש ביתי
Industrial	109	100	86	54	. .	"	תעשייתי
Agricultural	1,389	1,212	1,319	1,087	. .	"	חקלאי
CONSTRUCTION							**בינוי**
Building completed—total	4,450	5,140	4,478	3,485	. .	m^2 10^3 ^{2}מ	גמר בנייה — סך הכל
Building begun—total	3,705	4,930	5,910	3,433	. .	"	התחלת בנייה — סך הכל
Dwellings—building completed	24.6	30.8	31.4	31.0	. .	no. 10^3 'מס	דירות — גמר בנייה
—building begun	19.5	32.7	46.7	26.9	. .	"	— התחלת בנייה
Road construction and widening—completed	175.9	390.8	348.4	405.0	. .	km. ק״מ	סלילת כבישים חדשים והרחבות — גמר
—begun	252.3	236.2	413.2	501.4	. .	"	— התחלה
COMMERCE							**מסחר**
Index of sales value in large scale retail trade, at fixed prices	133.3	100.0	56.3	. .	. .	1980=100.0	מדד הפדיון במסחר הקמעוני המאורגן, מחירים קבועים

1 Excl. diamonds. 2 Budget years. — 1 לא כולל יהלומים. 2 שנות תקציב.

	1985	1980	1970	1960	1950	יחידה Unit	
TOURIST HOTELS[1]							**מלונות תיירות[1]**
Hotels	298	302	291	[2]190	. .	no. 'מס	בתי מלון
Rooms	30,280	25,014	15,000	[2]6,501	. .	"	חדרים
Person-nights[3]	11.4	9.6	5.1	[2]2.0	. .	10^6	לינות[3]
TRANSPORT							**תחבורה**
Private cars	614	410	148	24	[4]10	10^3	מכוניות פרטיות
Trucks and other commercial vehicles	115	89	66	22	[4]1.4	"	משאיות ורכב מסחרי
Buses	8.5	7.3	4.6	2.4	. .	"	אוטובוסים
Bus kilometrage	521	419	372	169	. .	km. 10^6 ק"מ	קילומטרז' של האוטובוסים
Railways: passengers	2,875	3,300	4,117	4,386	1,557	10^3	רכבת: נוסעים
tonnage transported	6,086	5,326	3,419	1,949	779	"	טונז' שהובל
Ships of the merchant fleet	76	100	110	50	20	no. 'מס	אוניות צי הסוחר
Gross tonnage	1,676	2,463	1,438	288	75	טונות 10^3 10^3 tons	תפוסה כוללת
Aircraft landing	10,157	10,933	9,079	2,926	2,272	no. 'מס	מטוסים שנחתו
Air transport: passengers	3,144	2,847	1,051	223	117	10^3	הובלה אוירית: נוסעים
freight	143,214	105,802	30,710	3,516	2,187	tons טונות	מטענים
Road accidents with casualties	12,761	12,716	13,355	8,356	3,132	no. 'מס	תאונות דרכים עם נפגעים
Injured	18,709	17,881	19,526	10,542	3,875	"	נפגעים
Thereof: killed	387	434	529	176	228	"	מזה: הרוגים
POSTS AND COMMUNICATION[5]							**דואר ותקשורת[5]**
Mail dispatched and received	410	425	360	165	. .	10^6	דברי דואר שנשלחו ונתקבלו
Parcels dispatched and received	2,410	2,029	2,445	1,461	730	10^3	חבילות שנשלחו ונתקבלו
Telegrams dispatched and received	746	1,112	2,208	1,570	. .	"	מברקים שנשלחו ונתקבלו
Telephones	1,780	§1,250	526	123	31	10^3	מכשירי טלפון
Applications outstanding	194	§208	70	20	13	"	בקשות ממתינות להתקנת טלפון
Public telephones	11,450	7,540	3,740	540	. .	no. 'מס	טלפונים ציבוריים
BANKS							**בנקים**
Balance sheets of banking institutions (end of year)							מאזני המוסדות הבנקאים (סוף שנה)
Assets	76,372	299	2	. .	. .	NIS 10^6 ש"ח	נכסים
Income	29,870	89	. .	. .	. .	"	הכנסות
Expenditure	29 472	86	. .	. .	. .	"	הוצאות
Operational profit	398	3	. .	. .	. .	"	רווח תפעולי

1 Annual cumulative. 3 Annual cumulative. [2]1961 [4]1951   1 סוף שנה. 3 מצטבר לשנה.

5 Budget years.   5 שנות תקציב.

	1985	1980	1970	1960	1950	יחידה Unit	
INSURANCE COMPANIES							**חברות ביטוח**
Premiums received in Israel							פרמיות שנתקבלו בישראל
Life insurance	[1]77,776	959	12	1	. .	NIS 10^3 ש"ח	ביטוח חיים
General insurance	[1]281,094	2,731	39	6	1	"	ביטוח כללי
Claims paid in Israel							תביעות ששולמו בישראל
Life insurance	[1]26,496	318	4	. .	. .	"	ביטוח חיים
General insurance	[1]123,036	1,440	19	2	. .	"	ביטוח כללי

	1985	1980	1970	1960	1949	יחידה Unit	
EDUCATION							**חינוך**
Years of schooling (aged 14+)							שנות לימוד (בני 14+)
Jews: 0 years	5.0	6.4	9.3	[2]12.6	6.3	%	יהודים: 0 שנים
13+ years	24.4	20.8	13.0	[2]9.9	. .	"	13+ שנים
Non-Jews: 0 years	13.4	18.9	36.1	[2]49.5	. .	"	לא יהודים: 0 שנים
13+ years	8.4	7.7	2.1	[2]1.5	. .	"	13+ שנים
PUPILS — TOTAL	**1,354.5**	§1,204.1	§824.3	§578.0	§140.8	10^3	תלמידים — סך הכל
Hebrew education — total	1,144.6	§1,026.9	§713.8	§531.9	§129.7	"	חינוך עברי — סך הכל
Kindergartens	248.5	246.6	107.7	75.7	25.4	"	גני ילדים
Primary	482.2	436.4	394.4	375.1	91.1	"	חינוך יסודי
Post-primary — total	279.2	216.6	137.3	55.1	10.2	"	על יסודי — סך הכל
Intermediate	103.1	72.8	7.9	—	—	"	חטיבות ביניים
Secondary — total	176.1	143.8	129.4	55.1	10.2	"	תיכון — סך הכל
General (incl. continuation classes)	86.7	68.0	72.2	40.0	8.2	"	עיוני (כולל כיתות המשך)
Vocational and agricultural	89.4	75.8	57.2	15.2	2.0	"	מקצועי וחקלאי
Teacher training colleges	12.1	11.3	§5.0	3.1	0.7	"	בתי מדרש למורים ולגננות
Post secondary and other higher institutions	18.8	14.1	6.9	2.7	0.6	"	מוסדות על־תיכונים וגבוהים אחרים
Universities	65.1	58.0	36.2	9.3	1.6		אוניברסיטאות
Other institutions	38.7	44.0	26.3	11.0	—		מוסדות אחרים
Arab education — total	209.9	§177.2	§110.5	§46.1	11.1	"	חינוך ערבי — סך הכל
Kindergartens (compulsory)	18.9	17.3	14.2	7.3	1.1	"	גני ילדים (חובה בלבד)
Primary	138.8	122.0	85.4	36.9	10.0	"	חינוך יסודי
Post-primary — total	51.5	37.3	10.6	2.0	—	"	חינוך על־יסודי — סך הכל
Intermediate	20.3	14.8	2.5	—	—	"	חטיבות ביניים
Secondary — total	31.2	22.5	8.1	2.0	—	"	תיכון — סך הכל
General	25.3	19.0	6.2	1.9	—	"	עיוני
Vocational and agricultural	5.9	3.5	1.9	0.1	—	"	מקצועי וחקלאי
Teacher training colleges	0.4	0.5	0.4	0.1	—	"	בתי מדרש למורים ולגננות
Other post-secondary and higher institutions	0.2	0.1	. .	. .	—	"	מוסדות על־תיכוניים וגבוהים אחרים

2 1961 census.   1 1984.   2 מפקד 1961.

	1985	1980	1970	1960	1949	יחידה Unit	
EDUCATION (cont.)							**חינוך** (המשך)
Field of study of university students — total	100.0	100.0	100.0	100.0	100.0	%	תחום לימוד של תלמידי אוניברסיטאות — סך הכל
Humanities	29.2	30.1	32.3	44.6	32.5	"	מדעי הרוח
Social sciences	27.4	29.0	25.8			"	מדעי החברה
Law	4.3	3.8	5.3	6.6	. .	"	משפטים
Medicine	7.0	5.7	3.9	6.9	3.2	"	רפואה
Sciences and mathematics	15.9	13.7	14.7	18.4	16.0	"	מדעי הטבע ומתמטיקה
Agriculture	2.0	2.7	1.5	3.6	4.6	"	חקלאות
Engineering	14.2	15.0	16.5	19.9	43.7	"	הנדסה
GRADUATES							מסיימים
Matriculation	22.2	14.0	11.0	3.6	0.8	10^3	בבחינות בגרות
Universities — total	11,218	9,371	5,566	1,237	193	no. .מס	באוניברסיטאות — סך הכל
First degree	8,113	6,740	4,064	779	135	"	תואר ראשון
Second degree	2,140	1,652	807	377	48	"	תואר שני
Third degree	356	378	238	81	10	"	תואר שלישי
Diploma	609	601	457	. .	. .	"	תעודה
	1985	1980	1970	1960	1950		
HEALTH							**בריאות**
Beds in hospitals	27.5	27.0	23.7	15.6	8.4	10^3	מיטות בבתי חולים
Beds per 1,000 population	6.5	6.8	7.9	7.3	6.6	Rate שיעור	מיטות ל-1,000 תושבים
Hospitalization days	9,049	8,926	8,306	5,470	2,271	10^3	ימי אשפוז
Hospitalization days per 1,000 population	2,125	2,301.9	2,878.2	2,583.8	1,792.7	Rate שיעור	ימי אשפוז ל-1,000 תושבים
Live births in hospitals						% מהלידות % of births	לידות חי בבתי חולים
Jews	[1]100.0	100.0	100.0	99.4	94.8	"	יהודיות
Non-Jews	[1]99.0	98.8	91.2	54.5	. .	"	לא-יהודיות
Mother and child health centres							תחנות לטיפול באם ובילד
Receptions: Pregnant women	[2]76.0	74.0	56.7	42.6	16.5	10^3	נתקבלו: נשים הרות
Infants	[2]93.5	89.9	72.4	48.7	28.5	"	תינוקות
	1985	1980	1970	1960	1955		
NATIONAL INSURANCE[3]							**ביטוח לאומי**[3]
Insured persons	1,797	1,636	1,060	660	535	10^3	מבוטחים
Recipients of benefits and pensions						"	מקבלי קצבאות וגמלאות
Old and survivors[4]	390.2	343.5	176.7	62.2	. .	"	זקנה ושאירים[4]
Maternity grant[5]	101.7	97.3	78.0	49.9	43.3	"	מענקי לידה[5]
Maternity allowance[5]	42.7	39.8	24.8	13.1	8.7	"	דמי לידה[5]
Children for whom allowances were paid[4]	1,287.4	1,512.9	862.3	83.1	—	"	מספר הילדים שבגינם משלמים קצבת ילדים[4]

1 1984. 2 1982. 3 Budget years. 4 Monthly average.
5 Annual cumulative.

1 1984. 2 1982. 3 שנות תקציב. 4 ממוצע לחודש.
5 מצטבר לשנה.

ב. אחוז השינוי השנתי הממוצע
B. AVERAGE ANNUAL PERCENTAGE OF CHANGE

Geometric mean — ממוצע גיאומטרי

	1985/1984	1985/1980	1980/1970	1970/1960	1960/1950	
Population—total	1.6	1.7	2.6	3.5	4.6	אוכלוסייה — סך הכל
Jews	1.3	1.4	2.4	3.1	4.7	יהודים
Non-Jews	2.9	3.2	3.7	6.3	3.6	לא-יהודים
Natural increase rate —total population	[2]0	[1]—0.6	—2.6	—1.5	[2]—2.9	שיעור ריבוי טבעי — כל האוכלוסייה
Jews	[2]—0.7	[1]—0.7	—1.3	—0.8	—3.6	יהודים
Non-Jews	[2]1.0	[1]—1.8	—1.5	—0.9	[2]1.4	לא-יהודים
Infant mortality rates —total population	[2]—13.9	[1]—4.8	—4.0	—3.2	[2]—2.9	שיעור פטירת תינוקות — כל האוכלוסייה
Jews	[2]—15.3	[1]—4.7	—4.4	—3.6	—5.2	יהודים
Non-Jews	[2]—11.1	[1]—4.7	—4.1	—2.5	[2]—0.2	לא-יהודים
Immigrants and potential immigrants	—46.7	—12.2	—5.7	4.1	—17.6	עולים ועולים בכוח
Tourists	14.1	4.1	10.3	14.1	13.5	תיירים
Gross national product per capita (at 1980 prices)	1.6	0	2.4	4.9	5.2	תוצר לאומי גולמי, לנפש (במחירי 1980)
General government consumption per capita (at 1980 prices)	1.8	—1.4	0.6	11.1	3.1	הוצאה לצריכה ציבורית לנפש (במחירי 1980)
Gross capital formation per capita (at 1980 prices)	—15.0	—3.0	—1.1	5.0	—0.5	השקעה גולמית מקומית לנפש (במחירי 1980)
Deficit in goods and services account in balance of payments	—16.7	1.3	§11.5	13.4	2.0	הגירעון בחשבון של סחורות ושירותים במאזן התשלומים
Israel's obligations to foreign countries	—0.6	6.4	§20.9	14.2	[3]12.1	חובות ישראל לחו"ל
Israel's foreign assets	2.5	1.4	§24.8	§15.1	. .	נכסים במטבע חוץ
Exports of goods (net)	8.1	2.8	21.8	13.2	19.7	יצוא סחורות (נטו)
Imports of goods (net)	—0.6	0.4	§18.5	11.2	5.1	יבוא סחורות (נטו)
Excess of imports over exports of goods	—20.8	—5.3	§13.8	9.4	0.7	עודף היבוא על היצוא של סחורות
Exchange rate of the						שער החליפין של השקל
U.S. $—end of year	134.8	188.2	35.9	6.9	16.2	לדולר — סוף שנה
U.S. $ —annual average	301.9	196.7	30.8	6.9	16.2	לדולר — ממוצע שנתי

1 1984/1980 2 1984/1983 3 1960/1955

ב. אחוז השינוי השנתי הממוצע (המשך)
B. AVERAGE ANNUAL PERCENTAGE OF CHANGE (cont.)

Geometric mean — ממוצע גיאומטרי

	1985/1984	1985/1980	1980/1970	1970/1960	1960/1950	
Consumer price index						מדד המחירים לצרכן
—December each year	304.6	195.4	41.6	5.6	12.8	—דצמבר כל שנה
—Annual average	185.2	191.6	46.2	5.9	. .	—ממוצע שנתי
Prices of input in residential building	246.0	188.4	42.8	. .	. .	מדד מחירי תשומה בבנייה למגורים
Wholesale price index of industrial output	265.7	193.9	43.2	. .	. .	מדד מחירים סיטוניים של תפוקת התעשייה
Private consumption expenditure per capita—total (at 1980 prices)	—2.4	1.5	2.7	4.1	4.4	הוצאה לצריכה פרטית לנפש — סך הכל (במחירי 1980)
Thereof:						מזה:
Food, beverages and tobacco	1.0	2.4	1.0	3.1	4.4	מזון, משקאות וטבק
Clothing, footwear and personal effects	9.3	—0.8	2.3	5.3	3.7	הנעלה, הלבשה וחפצים אישיים
Durable goods	—3.2	2.3	5.7	9.3	5.8	מוצרים בני-קיימא
Other commodities	0.6	2.7	2.2	6.4	6.1	מוצרים אחרים
Services	—1.5	0.9	3.4	3.4	4.6	שירותים
Calories per capita per day[1]	—0.9	0.2	0	0.7	0.6	קלוריות לנפש ליום[1]
Protein per capita per day[1]	—2.4	0.3	0.1	0.7	0.1	חלבון לנפש ליום[1]
Fat per capita per day[1]	—2.6	1.2	0.7	1.9	1.6	שומן לנפש ליום[1]
Civilian labour force	1.6	2.2	2.8	3.1	[2]3.1	כוח העבודה האזרחי
Employed persons	0.7	1.8	2.7	3.2	[2]3.7	מועסקים
Unemployed	15.7	9.1	5.2	1.2	[2]—5.7	בלתי מועסקים
Index of average monthly wage per employee post (at constant prices)	—9.0	1.1	2.4	. .	. .	מדד שכר חודשי ממוצע למשרת שכיר (במחירים קבועים)
Agricultural product[1] (at fixed prices)	7.5	7.0	6.4	6.3	. .	התוצר החקלאי[1] (במחירים קבועים)
Employment in agriculture[1]	4.4	0.4	—0.2	—2.9	. .	התעסוקה בחקלאות[1]
Capital stock in agriculture[1] (at fixed prices)	0.2	0.4	[2]2.1	2.6	12.2	מלאי ההון בחקלאות[1] (במחירים קבועים)
Production[1] (quantity): Wheat	—1.8	—12.8	7.3	11.7	4.3	ייצור[1] (כמות): חיטה
Cotton	17.1	4.8	8.2	13.0	. .	ייצור[1] (כמות): כותנה
Livestock for meat	—6.3	4.5	5.5	6.5	23.6	בעלי חיים לבשר
Cow's milk	—1.2	3.3	4.3	4.4	11.7	חלב בקר
Table eggs	1.6	5.3	2.0	0.7	12.9	ביצים למאכל
Citrus fruit	—3.1	—3.1	2.0	7.5	8.5	פרי הדר
Other fruit	10.3	9.9	8.4	9.8	17.5	פירות אחרים

1 Agricultural years. — 1 שנים חקלאיות.

2 1960/1955

ב. אחוז השינוי השנתי הממוצע (המשך)
B. AVERAGE ANNUAL PERCENTAGE OF CHANGE (cont.)

Geometric mean — ממוצע גיאומטרי

	1985/1984	1985/1980	1980/1970	1970/1960	1960/1950	
Industrial production index—total	2.9	3.7	5.2	11.6	. .	מדד הייצור התעשייתי — סך הכל
Thereof: Food	—1.6	4.5	6.2	4.9	. .	מזה: מזון
Textiles, clothing and footwear	2.2	0.2	4.7	12.0	. .	טקסטיל, הלבשה ועור
Rubber, plastics, chemicals and oil	2.5	5.5	5.9	14.9	. .	גומי, פלסטיק, כימיקלים ונפט
Metal and metal products	—0.3	2.8	4.2	10.2	. .	מתכת ומוצרי מתכת
Machinery, electrical equipment and transport vehicles	7.2	4.8	7.7	13.6	. .	מכונות, ציוד חשמלי וכלי הובלה
Electricity—generation	4.6	4.4	6.2	11.6	15.0	ייצור חשמל
Building completed (area)						גמר בנייה (שטח)
—total	—11.2	—2.8	1.4	2.5	10.2	—סך הכל
—dwellings (units)	—10.2	—4.4	—0.2	0.9	. .	—דירות (יחידות)
Index of sales in large scale retail trade (at fixed prices)	5.8	5.9	5.9	[1]11.6	. .	מדד המכירות במסחר הקמעוני המאורגן (במחירים קבועים)
Tourist hotels—rooms	6.5	3.9	5.2	[2]9.8	. .	מלונות תיירות — חדרים
—person-nights	21.3	3.5	6.5	[2]11.1	. .	— לינות
Motor vehicles	2.1	7.5	7.3	14.3	[3]8.3	כלי רכב מנועיים
Buses—national kilometrage	0.2	4.5	1.2	8.2	. .	אוטובוסים — קילומטרז' ארצי
Railways—passengers	—2.9	—2.7	—2.2	—0.6	10.9	רכבת — נוסעים
Freight loaded at ports	0	2.5	6.5	11.0	18.7	מטענים שנטענו בנמלים
Freight unloaded at ports	—0.8	10.9	2.5	7.7	3.5	מטענים שנפרקו בנמלים
International air passengers	—1.3	2.0	10.5	16.8	6.7	הובלה אווירית בינלאומית — נוסעים
Injured in road accidents	—2.1	0.9	—0.9	6.4	10.5	נפגעים בתאונות דרכים
Thereof: killed	—3.0	—2.3	—2.0	11.6	—2.6	מהם: הרוגים
Pupils—total	2.3	2.4	3.9	3.3	[4]13.7	תלמידים — סך הכל
Hebrew education	2.2	2.2	3.6	2.6	[4]13.6	חינוך עברי
Arabic education	2.8	3.4	4.8	9.1	[4]13.9	חינוך ערבי
Students in universities	0.7	2.5	4.7	12.3	[4]19.4	סטודנטים באוניברסיטאות
Beds in hospitals per 1,000 population	1.6	—0.9	—1.5	0.8	2.7	מיטות בבתי חולים ל-1,000 תושבים

1 1970/1964 2 1970/1961 3 1960/1951 4 1960/1949

33

Israel Law Digest

Revised for 1987 edition by Yaacov Salomon, Lipschutz & Co., Advocates & Notaries, Haifa and Tel Aviv

ABSENTEES:

Apart from Absentees' Property Law, 1950 which deals basically with local problem of care and custody of property belonging to persons who left country at time of 1948 war, there are no specific provisions regarding absentees. Power of attorney may be given for all purposes and, if executed abroad, should be authenticated. See topic Acknowledgments.

Under Protection of Deposited Property Law, 1965 where management or control of property has been committed to another, written notification thereof in form set out in Law, must be given to Administrator General if ten years have elapsed from authorisation or appointment.

ACKNOWLEDGMENTS:

Any deed, power of attorney or other instrument in writing made or executed in any place outside of Israel may be proved in any civil cause or matter in Israel if authenticated (a) before an ambassador, minister, chargé d'affaires or secretary of an embassy or legation, or any consul, vice-consul, pro-consul or consular agent of Israel, and attested by a certificate under the hand of such officer and his official seal, or (b) before a notary public and attested by a certificate under his hand and notarial seal and authenticated by any Israel officer mentioned under (a). (Evidence Ordinance [New Text] §33). Certain public documents such as court and administrative documents and notarial acts, are exempt from this requirement because Israel is party to Convention Abolishing the Requirement of Legalisation for Foreign Public Documents. See also topics Treaties; Affidavits.

ACTIONS:

Civil procedure is governed by Civil Procedure Rules, 1963. In general, courts will only exercise jurisdiction over persons within territorial limits of state and assumption of jurisdiction will depend on validity of service of process. Rules give a list of events in which courts may grant leave to serve outside jurisdiction. Foreig claims are proved in same way as local claims. Foreign law is a question of fact and is proved by evidence of an expert in law in question. See also topics Death; Limitation of Actions; and Practice.

Limitation of.—See Limitation of Actions.

Death.—See topic Death.

ADMINISTRATION:

See Executors and Administrators.

ADOPTION:

Adoption is permitted subject to an order of competent district court. Procedure to be followed is set out in The Children Adoption Law, 1981, and in Civil Procedure Rules. See topic Practice. Interest of child to be adopted is given paramount consideration. Adopted child must be under 18 years of age. Normally adoption of a child will not be allowed if adopting parents live abroad or intend to take child abroad. Secrecy is observed and neither natural parents nor adopting parents know identity of each other unless otherwise ordered by court. Religion of child and adoptive parents must be same (procedure for conversion of child in certain instances set forth in law).

See also topic Descent and Distribution.

ADVERSE POSSESSION:

Land Law 1969 has virtually abolished whole of existing Ottoman legislation and there are now no provisions relating to acquisition of title by adverse possession. See also topic Limitation of Actions.

AFFIDAVITS:

The jurat, which is a memorandum in regard to the place, time and person before whom the affidavit is made, should be without interlineation, alteration, erasure or obliteration, immediately at the foot of the document to be sworn, and towards the side of the paper, and should be signed by the person administering the oath, at the side of the date of the swearing and the place where the document or the instrument is sworn, and should state that the document or the instrument was sworn before the person administering the oath and that warning was given that document was executed under penalty of perjury. See also topic Acknowledgments.

The last paragraph of the affidavit should use words to the following effect: I swear by Almighty God (or I solemnly and sincerely declare and affirm) that this is my name and signature, and that the contents of this, my affidavit (or affirmation of declaration, as the case may be), are true.

In case of a declaration, there should be added the following words: I make this solemn declaration conscientiously believing the same to be true. Declarations may be signed before any advocate authorized to practise in Israel and have same force as an affidavit.

AGENCY: See Principal and Agent.

ALIENS:

Except in regard to elections, aliens are under no disability. Aliens wishing to enter Israel must secure a Traveller's Visa. See topic Constitution and Government, subhead Citizenship.

Corporations Owned or Controlled by Aliens.—Nonresidents may buy and sell Israeli shares provided payments made through authorised dealer, generally bank. Otherwise there are no restrictions on ownership or control of Israeli corporation by alien.

ARBITRATION:

Now governed by Arbitration Law, 1968. All disputes may be submitted to arbitration. No particular form of submission is required, except that submission must be in writing. Award may be enforced by leave of court in same manner as a judgment or order of court to same effect. Award may be set aside if it has been improperly procured, or if arbitrator has misconducted himself or award is bad on face of it. Court will usually stay an action brought in a dispute which it has been agreed should be submitted to arbitration. Where international convention to which Israel is a party, applies to arbitrators, court will stay an action, in accordance with such convention. Schedule is attached to law containing rules relating to procedure of arbitration which will apply unless a contrary intention appears in agreement.

A foreign award is enforceable as a local award and may be relied upon in any legal proceedings. In order that a foreign award may be enforceable in Israel, it must have been (a) made in pursuance of an agreement for arbitration which was valid under the law by which it was governed, (b) made by the tribunal provided for in the agreement or constituted in manner agreed upon by the parties, (c) made in conformity with the law governing arbitration procedure, and (d) has become final in the country in which it was made, and (e) is in respect of a matter which may lawfully be referred to arbitration under the law of Israel, the enforcement thereof not being contrary to the public policy or the law of Israel.

See also topic Executions.

ARCHITECTS:

Under 1958 law all architects must be entered in a register. Qualification: (a) Diploma of Technion, Technical High School; (b) registration abroad entitling to work as architect; (c) actual work for 12 years and examination.

ASSIGNMENTS:

Under Assignment of Obligations Law 1969 right of a creditor, including a conditional or a contingent right, may be assigned without consent of debtor, may be of whole or part of debt and may be conditional or by way of charge. Debtor retains same rights against assignee as he had against assignor and if he pays assignor before receiving notice he is exempt from further payment. Debtor can also assign debt in whole or in part to another with consent of creditor.

ASSOCIATIONS:

The following forms of corporate associations are recognized: (a) partnerships; (b) companies; (c) cooperative societies; (d) societies.

Partnerships.—A partnership is defined in Partnership Ordinance as relation which exists between persons carrying on a business in common with a view to profit. Partnerships are either general or limited.

A partnership formed in Israel may not consist of more than 20 persons. Every partnership formed in Israel must be registered with the Registrar of Partnerships, to whom certain particulars are to be supplied. A small registration fee is payable.

Partners of a general partnership are liable jointly and severally for all debts of the partnership. A limited partnership consists of one or more general partners who are liable for all debts, and one or more limited partners who are not liable for the debts of the firm beyond the amounts contributed by them as capital. A corporation may be a limited partner.

See also topic Business Names.

Companies.—See topic Corporations.

Cooperatives or Cooperative Societies.—A society which has as its object the promotion of thrift, self-help and mutual aid among persons with a common economic need, can be registered as a cooperative society.

No member is entitled to hold more than one-fifth of the capital. Registration fees are nominal.

Non-Profit Associations.—Association having two or more members for non-profit purposes may be registered with Registrar of Non-Profit Associations, provided regulations contain provision for annual meetings, presentation of audited accounts and proper supervision of activities. Registration fee is payable. (Non-Profit Associations Law 1980).

ATTACHMENT:

An application for an attachment may be made in all civil actions whether in contract or in tort. It must be based on a written document or other satisfactory proof as to reasonableness of claim, in which an amount of money is claimed.

An application for attachment may be made prior to or simultaneously with institution of civil proceedings. It can be granted ex parte or in presence of the respondent. It must be supported by an affidavit. A bond or other security is invariably required. Real and personal property may be attached. Property attached may include monies due or property held by third party.

Except in special circumstances such as perishables, property attached cannot be sold before final judgment in action.

Third party claims in opposition to attachment can be heard upon motion in proceedings.

Respondent may obtain release of an attachment against adequate security.

See topic Executions.

ATTORNEYS AND COUNSELLORS:

Advocates Ordinance of 1938 which regulated admission of members to Israel Bar was repealed by Chamber of Advocates Law of 1961. Israel Bar has been constituted as a recognised entity by virtue of 1961 Law, and it vested in elected bodies of members of Bar right to admit members to Bar, to regulate discipline and make other appropriate provisions affecting practice of law in Israel.

Only persons who have qualified as lawyers, are residents of Israel, and have reached age of 23 may be admitted to Israel Bar. Persons who qualify as lawyers may be graduates of Law Faculty in Israel or persons who are admitted to a foreign Bar and practiced abroad for not less than two years and/or are graduates of foreign law school. Normal period of apprenticeship prior to admission to local Bar is now 18 months from date of fulfillment of requirements for graduation with reductions for foreign lawyers related to prior experience. There are special provisions for apprenticeship preliminary to admission to local Bar.

A licence to practice as an advocate is renewable annually against the payment of an appropriate fee.

A foreign advocate or attorney may not appear even for the purposes of a particular case, unless he was nominated to defend a foreign citizen accused of a capital punishment crime, and was approved by the Ministry of Justice.

There is a special registration for pleaders before the Rabbinical courts. All advocates may be inscribed on this list upon paying a registration fee.

Under Patents Law, 1967, a patent agent has, with leave of court, right to plead in patent actions, on a nonlegal point.

BANKRUPTCY:

The principal law governing bankruptcy proceedings is Bankruptcy Ordinance (New Version) of 1980, which follows substantially English Bankruptcy Acts of 1914 and 1926.

A debtor is liable to be declared bankrupt and to have his property administered under the Bankruptcy Law upon committing any of the following acts, which are termed Acts of Bankruptcy: (1) If he makes a fraudulent gift or transfer of his property, or any part thereof; (2) if he makes any transfer of his property, or any part thereof, or creates any charge thereon which would be void as a fraudulent preference if he were adjudged bankrupt: (3) if, with intent to defeat or delay his creditors, he departs out of Israel, or being out of Israel remains out of Israel or departs from his dwelling house or absents himself from his usual place of business or abode; (4) if any of his property has been attached and sold in the execution of the decree of any court; (5) if he files in the court a declaration of his inability to pay his debts or petitions to be adjudged bankrupt (debts in such case must exceed NIS.1,000 due to at least two creditors); (6) if he gives notice to any of his creditors that he has suspended, or that he is about to suspend payment of his debts; (7) if creditor has obtained final judgment against him for any amount, and execution thereon not having been stayed, has served on him in Israel or by leave of court elsewhere bankruptcy notice requiring him to pay judgment debt, or to secure or compound for it, and he does not within seven days after service of notice (or in case service is effected out of Israel, then within time limited) either comply with requirements of notice or satisfy court that he has counterclaim, set-off or cross demand which equals or exceeds amount of judgment debt, and which he could not set up in action in which judgment was obtained.

The expression "debtor" includes any person of not less than 18 years of age of whatever nationality who at the time when any act of bankruptcy was done or suffered by him: (a) was personally present in Israel; or (b) ordinarily resided or had a place of residence in Israel; or (c) was carrying on business in Israel personally, or by means of an agent or manager; or (d) was a member of a firm or partnership which carried on business in Israel.

A creditor is unable to present a bankruptcy petition against a debtor unless: (a) the debt owing by the debtor to the petitioning creditor, or, if two or more creditors join in the petition, the aggregate amount of debts owing to the several petitioning creditors amounts to NIS.1,000, (b) debt is liquidated sum, and (c) act of bankruptcy on which petition is grounded has occurred within three months before presentation of petition. It is also required that debtor be domiciled in Israel, or within a year before date of presentation of petition that debtor (a) has ordinarily resided, or (b) had dwelling house, or (c) place of business, or (d) has carried on business personally or by means of agent or manager, or (e) is or has been member of firm or partnership of persons which has carried on business by means of partner, agent or manager in Israel.

A creditor's petition must be verified by affidavit of the creditor or of some person on his behalf having knowledge of the facts.

At the hearing the court requires proof of the debt of the petitioning creditor, of the service of the petition, and of the act of bankruptcy. A creditor's petition cannot, after presentment, be withdrawn without the leave of the court.

BANKS AND BANKING:

No banking business may be transacted in Israel except by a bank registered under provisions of Companies Ordinance. A foreign company may transact banking business if registered as a foreign company under Ordinance.

Bank may not operate in Israel unless licensed by Governor of Bank of Israel, under Banking Law (Registration) 1981, subject to compliance with Banking Ordinance 1941, as am'd. Purchase and sale of controlling rights in banks require permit of Governor. Banks Law provides for fulfilment of certain conditions preliminary to registration especially by fixing minimum of authorized and paid-up capital of banks operating in Israel. There are also provisions in regard to returns to be furnished. Under Bank of Israel Law 1954, which constituted State of Israel Bank—The Central State Bank—Bank of Israel is given certain powers in regard to control of banking institutions, especially in respect of liquidity, grant of credits, reserves, and rates of interest. 1976 amending law provides for discharge of liabilities, postponement of payments, addition of interest and linkage differences when banking services are disrupted by labour disputes. Banking Law (Service to Customer) 1981 places obligation on banks to give customers proper banking services with penalties for misleading or unfair actions.

BILLS AND NOTES:

Principal statute governing Bills and Notes is Bills of Exchange Ordinance (New Version) 1957 (as amended) which follows substantially English Bills of Exchange Act of 1882.

Inland and Foreign Bills.—An inland bill is one which is, or on its face purports to be (a) both drawn and payable within Israel, or (b) drawn within Israel on some person resident therein. Any other bill is a foreign bill.

Inland bills must be stamped before execution. Foreign bills can be stamped after execution, before presentation for payment. Bill of exchange which has been dishonoured by nonacceptance can now be executed by summary procedure whereby bill of exchange, promissory note or cheque is capable of execution like judgment of court. Amount stated in bill shall be collected in accordance with 1968 Execution Amendment Law with addition of interest so fixed therein, and if no interest is fixed therein, with addition of interest at rate fixed in Adjudication of Interest Law 1961 from date of payment of bill or from date of its presentation for payment. Person wishing to execute bill shall file application to Execution Office supported by affidavit verifying facts stated therein. Debtor may oppose application and Chief Execution Officer shall stay application and refer matter to court. For purposes of hearing in court, opposition shall be regarded as application for leave to defend in summary proceedings under Civil Procedure Regulations 1963. When a bill has been dishonoured by nonacceptance, or by nonpayment, notice of dishonour must be given to the drawer and each indorser, subject to limited exceptions. Notice of dishonour may be given either to the party himself, or to his agent in that behalf. It must be given within a reasonable time, which normally is three days after dishonour of the bill.

The provisions in regard to presentment for acceptance, acceptance, and issue of bills in a set do not apply to promissory notes.

The provisions in regard to presentment for payment apply to promissory notes, only where the promissory note is in the body of it made payable in a particular place, in which case it must be presented for payment at that place, in order to render the maker liable.

Limitation of Actions.—No action on a bill of exchange, cheque or promissory note can be maintained against any party thereto, other than an indorser, after expiration of seven years, or against an indorser after expiration of two years from time when cause of action first accrued to the then holder against such party. Where a bill is payable after sight, presentment for acceptance is necessary in order to fix maturity of instrument. When a bill payable after sight is negotiated, holder must either present it for acceptance, or negotiate it within a reasonable time, provided always that a bill payable after sight must be presented for acceptance within six months of its date, or such shorter period stipulated for either by drawer or by an indorser, or such longer period not exceeding 12 months as may be stipulated by drawer. Failure in regard to presentment discharges drawer and all indorsers prior to holder.

A bill must be presented for payment in accordance with the following rules: (a) where a bill is not payable on demand, presentment must be made on the date it falls due; (b) where a bill is payable on demand, then presentment must be within a reasonable time after its issue, in order to render the drawer liable and within a reasonable time after its endorsement, in order to render the indorser liable. Presentment must be made at a reasonable hour, on a business day, at the proper place, excluding therefore legal holidays. The legal holidays include the State holidays and certain religious days of Jewish, Moslem and Christian communities.

Conflict of Laws.—Where a bill drawn in one country is negotiated, accepted or payable in another the rights, duties and liabilities of the parties are determined as follows: (1) Validity of the bill as regards requisites of form is determined by the law of the place of issue; validity of a supervening contract (e.g., acceptance, endorsement, etc.) is determined by the law of the place where such contract was made. (2) Interpretation of the drawing, endorsement or acceptance is determined by the law where the contract was made, provided that where an inland bill is indorsed in a foreign country the endorsement must, as regards the payer, be interpreted according to the law of Israel.

BROKERS:

There is limited legislation in regard to brokers. Brokers must be licenced by the District Commissioner. Licences are renewable annually. A tariff of brokerage fees for licenced brokers is fixed by law. The usual fees range from 1% to 5%.

BUSINESS NAMES:

Under the Registration of Business Names Ordinance 1935, every individual or firm carrying on business under a business name, namely, a name which does not consist of the true surname of the individual, or of the true names of all partners, must register the name as a business name. Particulars required to be furnished under the Ordinance have to be furnished within 15 days after the person or firm commences business under the business name. A nominal fee is payable.

CHATTEL MORTGAGES:

See topics Mortgages; Pledges.

CHATTELS:

See topic Moveables.

COMMERCIAL REGISTER:

No special registration required but see topics Business Names; Corporations; Licences.

CONSTITUTION AND GOVERNMENT:

A formal Constitution of State of Israel has not yet been promulgated. Present Constitution is based on Declaration of Establishment of State of Israel, dated 14th May, 1948, on Law and Administration Ordinance, 1948, and on Transitional Law of 1949. By a resolution of 13th June, 1950, Knesset resolved to impose upon Constitution, Law and Justice Committee the task of preparing a draft constitution. Constitution would thus be built up chapter by chapter. So far, four such chapters have become law: Basic Law—The Knesset (1958), Basic Law—Israel Lands (1960), Basic Law—President of the State (1964) and Basic Law—The Government (1968). Further basic Law (1980) substituted reference to principles of Jewish Traditional Law for reference to U.K. common law and equity as prescribed by §46 of Provisional Order in Council 1922 now repealed. (Basic Law—Appointment of Judges [1984]).

The Knesset.—Basic Law—the Knesset, and Knesset Election Law, 1959 combine all previous laws in reference to sovereignty and elections of Knesset, the legislature of Israel. Knesset is elected by all Israeli citizens over age of 18 years in direct, national election by party list. Knesset consists of only one chamber, in which there are 120 members. Term of Knesset is four years. Elections take place on same day all over country and election day is a public holiday. Limits in reference to election propaganda are provided by law, and State officials, army officers, judges, etc., are not allowed to participate in election campaign. Recent amendment forbids those party lists from standing for election which call for negating of Israel's Jewish or democratic character, or which incite racism.

President of Israel is elected by Knesset for a period of five years. 1963 Law forbids holding of office of President for more than two consecutive periods of five years.

Government consists of Prime Minister and Ministers of State. Prime Minister must be a member of Knesset who enjoys confidence of Knesset. A Government which does not enjoy confidence of Knesset must resign. All powers which were formerly vested in British Crown or Mandatory Government, are now vested in Government of Israel, and are exercised through various Ministers of State.

Law and Administration.—Laws which existed on date of establishment of State of Israel on 14th May, 1948, continue to be effective insofar as they are not inconsistent with establishment of State, and insofar as they have not been abrogated or modified by laws passed since establishment of the State of Israel.

Citizenship.—Under Citizenship Law 1952 as am'd 1968, Israel nationality is acquired in one of following ways: (1) Any Jew who has emigrated or emigrates to Israel and expresses his desire to settle there, becomes an Israel citizen automatically unless (a) he ceased to reside in Israel before July 14, 1952 or (b) being a foreign citizen he makes or has made a declaration that he does not desire to be an Israel citizen and in case of an infant, his parents have made such a declaration; (2) former Palestine citizen becomes an Israel citizen if he was resident in Israel on July 14, 1952 and fulfils certain other conditions; (3) any person born in Israel is an Israel citizen if his mother or father is an Israel citizen; (4) stateless person born in Israel after setting up of State may acquire nationality by filing a request to such effect between his 18th and 21st birthdays provided he has resided in Israel five years continuously prior to application; (5) Israel citizenship may also be acquired by naturalization, conditions being (a) residence in Israel at time of and for three out of five years prior to application, (b) intention to reside permanently in Israel, (c) some knowledge of Hebrew language and (d) renunciation of any other citizenship. An infant who is a resident of Israel or one of whose parents is an Israel citizen may apply for grant of citizenship. Israel citizen living abroad may renounce his citizenship. Citizenship acquired by naturalization, may be lost in certain circumstances. Save in case of naturalization, Israel citizenship does not require giving up of any former citizenship. (Book of Laws, No. 95 of 8/4/52).

CONSUMER PROTECTION:

1981 Law forbids dealer in goods or services to mislead consumer by act or failure to act, in writing or verbally in any material matter affecting transaction, inter alia re quality, nature, quantity and type of goods and/or services, measure, weight, form, components, date of delivery of goods or supply of services.

Dealer is likewise forbidden to exploit in any way, reduced circumstances, physical or mental deficiency, ignorance, language, lack of experience or to exercise undue influence to induce transaction on unreasonable or abnormal terms.

Dealer is obliged also to disclose material defects known to him.

Misleading advertisements, or packaging are forbidden.

Detailed Regulations govern credit sales, interest calculation and marking of goods on package.

CONTRACTS:

Israel Law, broadly follows English rules of common law and equity. There are also relics of Turkish laws and there is a growing body of legislation on contracts. Contract requires consensus ad idem which is formed by offer and acceptance. To great extent Israeli legislation has either codified English Common Law or borrowed from models such as American Uniform Commercial Code. One notable departure is absence of any requirement of consideration as basis for contract. (The Gift Law 1968 however retains concept of consideration where gift is defined as ownership of property otherwise than for consideration.) What is paramount under Contracts Law 1973 is intention of parties to enter into agreement.

There are several new laws replacing existing Turkish legislation which lay down general rules in respect of various types of contract. These are Agency Law 1965, Guarantee Law 1967, Pledges Law 1967, Bailees Law 1967 and Sale Law 1968. It is always possible to contract out of these Laws.

New Law.—1973 Law of Contract Act, general part, contains a codification of general part of law of contract, which no longer follows principles of English Law of Contract which have hitherto been accepted by courts. In particular, consideration is no longer required to create enforceable contract. Law came into force on Jan. 1, 1974.

See also topics Consumer Protection; Landlord and Tenant; Mortgages; Moveables; Pledges; Principal and Agent; Restrictive Trade Practices; Sales.

Excuses for Nonperformance.—Contract is void in case of mistake going to root of contract, illegality and impossibility of performance. Impossibility must be literal impossibility. Presence of a material misrepresentation, duress or undue influence may make contract voidable by non-offending party.

Notices Required.—Notice of cancellation of contract for fundamental breach must be given within reasonable time after party becomes aware of breach. If breach is not fundamental, party in breach is given period of grace to make good breach and if necessary notice of breach is given within reasonable time of elapse of such period. Period of grace is not required to be notified in writing. (Law of Contracts [Remedies for Breach of Contract] 1970 §§7-8).

Notice is required for set-off in case of money debts owed by one party to another in same transaction whether liquidated or not, and if not in same transaction, in case of liquidated debts only. (Law of Contracts [General Part] 1973, p. 53).

Purchaser of goods must give immediate notice to vendor after inspection required to be made on delivery if goods are found not to be as ordered, or as soon as defect discovered if concealed, otherwise purchaser has no claim against vendor. (Law of Sale 1968, §14).

Vendor must give notice to purchaser of any third party claim against goods supplied which he knew of or should have known of before delivery. (Law of Sale 1968, §18).

Applicable Law.—English rules of conflict of laws apply and "proper law of the contract" is applicable law: If parties choose a law in contract, this will almost invariably be applicable law. As regards contracts for sale of goods Uniform International Commercial Code applies from Aug. 18, 1972.

Government Contracts.—There are no special forms and Government is generally liable for its contracts and can be sued on them although injunction and specific performance are not available against State.

Remedies for breach of contract have been given statutory force by Contracts (Remedies for Breach of Contract) Law 1970. Subject to provisions of Law, injured party may claim enforcement or rescission of contract and/or damages. Enforcement is similar to equitable remedy of specific performance and is granted except where contract is incapable of performance, where enforcement requires compelling carrying out of personal work, where enforcement requires unreasonable amount of supervision by court or it is inequitable in circumstances of case. Rescission is permissible in case of fundamental breach but where breach is not fundamental, reasonable time must first be given to party in breach to remedy breach. Damages are granted for injury caused by breach and its consequences and which party breaking contract foresaw or should have foreseen as a probable consequence of breach at time contract was made.

Breach of Contract.—Supreme Court has summed up 1970 Law regarding relief on breach of contract (a) that breach of contractual condition, including date of payment, agreed as being "basic" is fundamental breach; (b) on fundamental breach injured party may, and on ordinary breach, he must give an extension which other party may use to fulfil his contractual obligation within reasonable time of grant of extension; (c) right to regard contract as void and must be exercised within reasonable time after lapse of such reasonable period, in case of ordinary breach or immediately in case of fundamental breach; (d) right to regard as void, revives if extension given, even if not obligatory by law, after lapse of reasonable extension period.

Form.—In general, form of contract is immaterial but certain contracts need to be in writing in order to be enforceable, in particular contracts relating to land and to lending of money and partnerships and agreements with building contractors.

Contractors' Agreements.—1974 law regulates work undertaken by a contractor who is not an employee of person ordering work. It regulates liability of contractor to repair defects, contractor's right to refuse delivery until paid according to agreement, and liability to pay contractor.

Warranties.—§11 of Law of Sale 1968 provides that vendor fails to fulfil his obligations under sale agreement if only part of goods or larger or smaller quantity than agreed upon is delivered, if article supplied differs in kind or description from agreement, if article lacks quality or characteristics required for normal or commercial use thereof or for special purpose for which agreement implies it was purchased, or if article is not, by reference to type, description, quality or characteristics, according to sample or specimen submitted by vendor, unless so submitted without any undertaking of conformity to sample. If vendor does not within reasonable time of receiving notice from purchaser, remedy deficiency in fulfilment of his obligations, purchaser may claim specific performance, rescission or deduct from price payable value of deficiency. (§28 of Law of Sale).

CONVEYANCES: See Assignments.

COPYRIGHT:

English Copyright Act of 1911 is incorporated into Israeli Copyright Ordinance.

Nature of Copyright.—Copyright is sole right to produce or reproduce work of literature, music, drama or art or any substantial part thereof in any material form in public. Copyright in lecture exists in delivery. If work is unpublished, it is sole right to publish it wholly or partially and includes sole right to produce, reproduce, perform or publish any translation of work. Copyright exists in conversion of dramatic work into novel or vice versa; and in making of any record, perforated roll, cinematograph film or other contrivance by means of which literary, dramatic or musical work may be mechanically performed or delivered. Publication of any work means issue of copies of work to public. Any unauthorised person who performs above acts infringes copyright. According to 1953 Copyright Amendment Ordinance, copyright in unpublished work exists where author was at time of creation national or resident of Israel.

Infringement.—Copyright in work is infringed when person without copyright owner's consent does anything, sole right to do which, is conferred on owner. Thus copyright is infringed when unauthorised person sells work or lets it for hire or by way of trade exposes or offers it for hire; or where he distributes work either for trade or in manner that prejudices owner of copyright; or when he exhibits work by way of trade in public; or when he imports for hire or sale any work which to his knowledge infringes copyright; or where he for his private profit knowingly permits theatre or other place of entertainment to be used for performance of work without copyright owner's consent.

There are the following exceptions to copyright infringements: (a) Fair dealing with any work for purposes of private study, research, criticism, review or newspaper summary; (b) use by author of work of any mould, cast, sketch, plan, model or study made by him where he is not copyright owner, provided that he does not repeat or imitate main design: (c) making paintings, drawings, engravings or photographs of work of sculpture if permanently situate in public place; (d) publication of non-copyright matter for bona fide use of schools as long as not more than two passages from works by same author are published within five years and source from which passages are taken is acknowledged; (e) publication of report of lecture delivered in public unless printed notice of prohibition of publication is given; (f) reading or recitation in public by one person of any reasonable extract from any published work.

Term of copyright is for life of author and for 50 years from Jan. 1st after his death. Same position obtains in case of any anonymous or pseudonymous work.

Ownership of Copyright.—Author of work is first owner of copyright therein except: (a) In case of engraving or photograph where plate or original was ordered by some other person and was made for valuable consideration in pursuance of that order where person who orders original is first owner; (b) where author was in employ of some other person under contract of service and work was done in course of his employment, employer (in absence of any contrary agreement) is first owner. This position does not obtain where work is some contribution to newspaper, magazine or periodical where (unless there is contrary agreement) ownership of copyright remains vested in author.

Assignment.—There are no special forms for assignments or licences nor does copyright require registration.

Civil Remedies.—Where there is infringement, owner is entitled to injunction, damages or otherwise as may be conferred by law for infringement of right. Costs are in absolute discretion of court. In action for infringement plaintiff is presumed to be owner unless defendant puts existence of copyright or owner's title in issue. Even if damage resulting from infringement is not proved court may award compensation of not less than IS.500 and not more than IS.30,000 for each infringement.

Copyright Owner's Rights.—All infringing copies and plates used or intended to be used for production of such copies are deemed to be property of copyright owner who may take proceedings for recovery of possession or conversion, except as regards architectural restriction where interdict or injunction cannot be obtained or where demolition cannot be ordered. Infringing structure is not deemed to be property of copyright owner.

Prescription of Action.—According to Prescription Law of 1958 action for copyright infringement expires after seven years from date of infringement.

Protection of Foreign Works.—Where convention relating to copyright protection has been concluded between Israel and another country, or where Israel has acceded to convention, Minister of Justice may direct that works for which protection is required by such convention shall be protected. Israel is signatory of Stockholm B, Brussels and Unesco Conventions. Protection granted by Minister shall not exceed any protection were such work to have been published in Israel. Work published simultaneously in Israel and several other countries shall be considered as having been first published in Israel provided that there is no "colourless" publication.

Privacy.—By an amending Statute of Law of Civil Wrongs, use of name, connotation picture or voice of a person for commercial purposes, constitutes a civil wrong (a tort) rights to relief being given to person affected and after his death to his heirs.

Moral Right.—By 1981 Amendment, author of work has moral right in accordance with Berne Convention to have his work published without distortion, defect or alteration prejudicing its value, or his good name. Infringement of this right is compensated even if financial damage not proved.

Performer's Rights.—1984 Law grants performers, including actors, singers, musicians, dancers or other performers protection for 25 years against recording, broadcasting, televising, sale, renting, import or possession of such recording etc. for commercial purposes without consent of performer. If performance protected is given in course of performer's employment, protection is granted to employer.

CORPORATIONS:

Principal law concerning companies is Companies Ordinance based on English law. Major amendment was made to Companies Ordinance (1929) in Dec. 1980. Table B of Companies Ordinance which granted ancillary powers in addition to aims stated in memorandum has now been abolished. From day on which company has been formed in accordance with date appearing on certificate of association, company assumes all legal rights, duties and acts permitted by law. Any seven or more persons may form public company, and any two or more persons, but not more than 50, private company. Private company is exempt from certain provisions which apply to public company such as annual filing of accounts with Registrar. Both classes of companies must register memorandum and articles of association with Registrar of Companies. Objects of company are set out in memorandum which is company's charter. Any act of company not within objects set out in memorandum is ultra vires. Distinction has been drawn by new 1980 amendment between ultra vires acts and acts in which company directors act outside scope of their authority. Where servant of company acts outside scope of his authority on behalf of company, such acts have no validity vis-a-vis company, unless subsequently authorised by general meeting of company or by decision of board of directors where director has acted outside scope of his authority. According to new 1980 amendment, should company wish to change objects as determined by memorandum of association, such change may now be effected by special resolution and comes into force 21 days after adoption of resolution subject to rights of objection of minority shareholders. Articles set out internal regulations of company. Unless particular set of articles is filed, regulations contained in "Table A" of Companies Ordinance govern internal management of company. Great elasticity is possible in drafting of articles and it is common to include preemption rights and various devices for protecting interests of minority shareholders.

Companies may be: (a) Limited by shares, (b) limited by guarantee, or (c) unlimited. In a company limited by shares, liability of members is limited to amount, if any, unpaid on shares respectively held by them. In a company limited by guarantee, liability of members is limited by memorandum to such amount as members may respectively thereby undertake to contribute to assets of company in event of company being wound up. Company not having any limit on liability of its members is an unlimited company. Company limited by shares is by far most common form of company.

1980 amendment provides for split vote whereby shareholders may vote one way for portion of their shares and other way for rest of their shares at company meetings.

Registration fees are payable in form of registration fees and capital duty. Every company must file annual return with Registrar of Companies containing statutory information in regard to share capital, charges and directors. Public company must also file accounts.

Foreign Company.—1980 amendment defines foreign company as being all companies and associations, except partnerships which have been formed or registered outside Israel. Number of members is now unspecified. Foreign company which establishes place of business in Israel, has to be registered as foreign company. Registration fee is NIS. 26.40 and NIS. 13.30 for nonprofit company. NIS. 39.90 is payable annually with company's annual return.

Application for registration by foreign company has to be made within one month from establishment of place of business and has to be accompanied by following documents: (a) Certified copy of charter, statutes or memorandum and articles of company; (b) list of directors; (c) names and addresses of some one or more persons resident in Israel authorized to accept on behalf of company service of processes and any notices required to be served on company; (d) certified copy of power of attorney enabling some person ordinarily a resident in Israel to act for company in Israel. Fee of IS.13,300, plus publication fee, or in case of corporation not constituted for purposes of profit fee of IS.6,700, is payable on registration of foreign company.

New Government Companies Law 1975.—Regulates formation, management and winding-up of companies in which State has more than half voting power or right to appoint more than half directors. Law provides for compensation for minority shareholders in companies which become subject to Law, appointment of directors on behalf of State and of managing directors and appointments to government companies of accountants, legal advisers and internal comptrollers. Resolutions of government companies on certain matters require government ratification. Some of provisions of Law also apply to companies in which State has not more than half voting power or right to appoint not more than half directors.

See also topics Associations; Securities.

COURTS:

The courts of Israel consist of the following: (1) Magistrates' Courts, which deal with civil matters in which the subject matter is of NIS. 40,000 or less, and recovery of possession and partition of immovable property of any value, and in criminal matters with contraventions and misdemeanours. Claims not exceeding NIS. 3,000 where claimant appears in person may be dealt with under simplified procedure. Minister of Justice may, by Order, empower Magistrates' Court to act as Court of Local Matters and deal with defined matters, mainly municipal and local laws and offences. (2) District Courts, which have jurisdiction in all matters save as expressly vested in any other courts, e.g., magistrates' courts. There are five District Courts, one in each of following cities: Jerusalem, Tel-Aviv, Haifa, Beer Sheva and Nazareth. Admiralty jurisdiction formerly vested in Supreme Court, is now vested in district court sitting in Haifa. There is right of appeal to Supreme Court. (3) Supreme Court, which has jurisdiction as High Court of Justice to which application in nature of mandamus, petition of right, habeas corpus and any other petition against Government, or government officer or any other public authority can be made and also as Court of Appeal, i.e., appellate tribunal from decisions of district court. (4) Municipal Courts, which have jurisdiction over any offences against municipal regulations or bylaws and over certain other specified minor offences. (5) Anti-profiteering courts are attached to each magistrates' court and district court. Tribunal is composed of professional judge or magistrate, and two members of public. (6) Rent Tribunals constituted under 1954 Tenant Protection Law, consisting of magistrate and two members of public, assess rent and value of services in relation to tenancies. (7) By Labour Courts Law 1969 court was set up to deal with all matters arising from employer/employee relationships including national insurance claims. Special Juvenile Tribunals were constituted for first time in 1955. Since 1957 Chief Justice may order criminal case to be reheard either by Court of Appeal or by district court if new facts have come to light, another person has been convicted for same offence, or evidence relied on has been declared false or forged. Chief Justice can also decide to rehear any matter decided by Supreme Court if it involves question of importance, difficulty or novelty.

The religious courts of several recognized religious communities have jurisdiction in matters of marriage and divorce of residents. In other matters of personal status these courts have jurisdiction with consent of the parties concerned. The religious courts have no jurisdiction over foreigners except by consent of all parties.

Courts are empowered by Legal Aid to Foreign States Law 1977 to collect testimony, seize documents or articles, conduct searches or carry out other legal proceedings at request of legal authority of foreign country. All such proceedings are to be conducted according to Israel Law. Court is entitled to refuse request for such aid if it is convinced that proceedings are of political character. Law does not apply to extradition proceedings prior to trial or serving of sentence.

See also topic Labour Relations.

CRIMINAL LAW:

Punishments Law 1977 effected comprehensive codification of criminal law and came into force on Apr. 1, 1978. Criminal procedure is codified in Criminal Procedure Law (Consolidated Version) 1982.

Magistrates' Courts can deal with crimes for which penalty is a fine only or imprisonment up to three years. All other offences are within jurisdiction of district courts. In respect of limited offences, private complaint may be filed, otherwise Attorney-General or his representative is in charge of criminal proceedings on behalf of state.

Courts have jurisdiction to release on bail persons charged with any offence except one for which penalty is death or life imprisonment or in respect of certain offences against security of state.

Capital punishment for murder was abolished in 1954, except in respect of a limited number of offences under Nazis and Nazi Collaborators (Punishment) Law, 1950 and it is still in force under Genocide (Prevention and Punishment) Law 1950 and in respect of treason under §96 of Punishments Law.

See also topic Limitation of Actions.

CURRENCY:

Unit of currency is Israel New Shekel (NIS). Currency Law of 1985 changes old currency, Israeli Shekel (IS) to New Shekel, with banking system converting to new currency on Jan. 1, 1986. One thousand IS equals one NIS. Since 1955 the Bank of Israel is the central state bank and is the issuing bank of the Government. Dealings in foreign currency are authorized only through approved banks and there are limitations on the export of foreign currency.

Exchange Control is now governed by Currency Control Law 1978 and Currency Control Regulations 1978.

CUSTOMS:

See topic Taxation, subhead Customs Duty.

DEATH:

The Declaration of Death Law implements the United Nations Convention on the subject of declarations of death of persons who disappeared in Europe during the Nazi regime. The same law also provides for declarations of death in a case of persons dying a natural death or through accident and of whom all traces have been lost for more than two years. Application by an interested person, as defined by the Law, is to be made to the competent court, which is the Jerusalem District Court. (Book of Laws, No. 93, of 13.3.53).

A copy of death certificate of a person dying in Israel is obtainable on application to the local authorities of the area in which the death took place.

Actions.—On death of any person any cause of action in respect of a civil wrong subsisting against or vested in him survives against or, as case may be, for benefit of his estate.

Where death is caused by a civil wrong and such person would, had death not ensued, have been entitled at time of his death to recover compensation in respect of bodily injury caused to him by such civil wrong, the husband, wife, parent and child of such deceased person may recover compensation from person responsible for such civil wrong.

These laws, like all other laws, apply equally to foreigners.

See also topic Limitation of Actions.

DEEDS: See topic Real Property.

DEPOSITIONS:

See also Acknowledgments; Affidavits.

For Use Within Israel.—The court or a judge may at any time order that any particular fact or facts be proved by affidavit, or that the affidavit of any witness be read at the hearing, on such conditions as the court or judge thinks reasonable. Where it appears that either party bona fide desires the production of a witness for the court's examination and that such witness can be produced, an order will not be made authorizing evidence of the witness to be given by affidavit.

Affidavits must be in the first person, divided into paragraphs and confined to such facts as the deponent is able of his own knowledge to prove, except on interlocutory applications, in which a statement of the deponent's belief may be admitted provided that the grounds thereof are stated.

Within Israel for Use Elsewhere.—The Foreign Tribunals Evidence Act 1856 (an English Act) has been applied to Palestine and has effect in Israel. Under this Act any court or tribunal of competent jurisdiction in a foreign country before which any civil or commercial matter is pending, may obtain any testimony in Israel in relation to such matter. Application for this purpose may be made to a court or judge in Israel, and such court or judge may order the examination upon oath, upon interrogatory or otherwise, before any person or persons named, of such witness or witnesses as may be required, and the attendance of such witness or witnesses for examination or for the production of any documents may be commanded and other directions given as to time, place or manner of examination.

A certificate under the hand of an ambassador, minister or other diplomatic agent of a foreign state that any matter in relation to which an application is made is a civil or commercial matter pending before a foreign tribunal and that such tribunal is desirous of obtaining the testimony of the witness to whom the application relates, is sufficient evidence of the matter certified.

Further, under the Foreign Tribunals Evidence Rules, where any civil, criminal or commercial matter is pending before a court or tribunal of a foreign country, a district court in Israel is authorized to take the testimony of any person in relation to the matter pending before the foreign court or tribunal. The President of the District Court, if satisfied that the foreign court or tribunal is desirous of obtaining testimony within the jurisdiction, may, on an ex-parte application of any person shown to be duly authorized to make the application and on production of a commission rogatoire or letter of request, make such order as may be necessary to secure the examination of the witness or witnesses. The application should be forwarded to the court through the Israel Minister of Justice.

Under the Extradition Ordinance, depositions or statements on oath taken in a foreign state, and copies of such original depositions or statements and foreign certificates or judicial documents, stating the fact of conviction may, if duly authenticated, be received in evidence in proceedings for extradition.

Outside Israel for Use Within Israel.—On the application of any party to any civil proceedings, the court may make an order for examination upon oath before any person in any place outside jurisdiction of any witness, and court may give directions as to matters connected with examination. Person directed to take any examination may administer oath and report to court on examination, and conduct of any witness.

DESCENT AND DISTRIBUTION:

Comprehensive succession law was enacted in 1965—Inheritance Law of 1965. Former limitations on power of testamentary dispositions in respect of certain classes of immovables were abolished (see topic Wills). Subject to any testamentary dispositions, following are legal heirs entitled to succession: (1) Spouse of deceased; (2) children and their descendants and parents of deceased and their descendants.

Spouse is entitled to home contents plus automobile and: (1) One-half of rest of estate if there are surviving children of deceased either from marriage with spouse or from previous marriage, or issue of such children or surviving parent(s) of deceased if no children of deceased; (2) two-thirds of rest of estate if deceased is survived by siblings or issue of siblings, or grandparent(s). If upon death of deceased, spouse had been married to deceased for three years or more and lived with him in apartment included, wholly or partly in estate, spouse takes whole apartment or share of deceased therein and two-thirds of rest of estate. In any other case, surviving spouse is entitled to whole of estate.

State succeeds in absence of relations.

Adopted child is entitled to same share as natural child. New provisions are embodied in 1965 law entitling needy spouse, needy child or needy surviving parents to maintenance out of estate. Court is entitled to allow widow or widower a one-time grant or periodical maintenance.

Maintenance in respect of children may be granted until they reach age of 18 and in special cases up to 23 years of age, and to parents for life.

Administrator may be appointed by court to administer estate, and court may confirm as administrator an executor appointed by will.

Creditors have to be satisfied first before any distribution is made to heirs.

Spouse, children or parents who lived with deceased in his place of residence are entitled to continue to reside in same premises as lessees of legal heirs for such duration and subject to such terms as may be settled with heirs or as settled by court.

Competent court is entitled to deal with estate of any person who resided in Israel on date of his death or has left property in Israel.

Applicable law is law of residence of deceased on date of his death, except in respect of assets which devolve in accordance with lex situs. Competent court is district court (civil court) where deceased resided at time of his death, or in case of nonresident court having jurisdiction where any assets of deceased are situated in Israel.

Religious courts may exercise jurisdiction when all parties consent to such jurisdiction.

See also topic Marriage.

DESIGNS: See topic Patents.

DIVORCE:

Rabbinical Courts have exclusive jurisdiction in regard to divorce where both parties are Jews, and are either domiciled in Israel or Israeli citizens. Christian recognized Religious Courts have exclusive divorce jurisdiction in regard to Christians who are Israeli citizens. Moslem Religious Courts have exclusive divorce jurisdiction in regard to Moslems who are Israeli citizens or foreigners who, under law of their nationality, are subject in such matters to jurisdiction of Moslem Religious Courts.

Law of Jurisdiction in Dissolution of Marriage in Special Cases, 1969, authorises Chief Justice to direct that an application for divorce (which is not in jurisdiction of any Religious Court) be dealt with either by a Civil Court or a Religious Court. As a result, it is now possible in case of mixed marriages where parties belong to different religious communities, for marriage to be lawfully dissolved. Law also repealed limitation of jurisdiction in divorce cases of foreigners.

Maintenance.—By 1972 Law to ensure payment of maintenance where judgment for maintenance is given in favour of a spouse, a minor child or a parent, resident in Israel, party entitled may apply to be paid by National Insurance Institute, thereby saving himself necessity of execution proceedings. Amount payable is sum adjudged, subject to overriding maximum fixed by regulations. Rights under judgment are subrogated to Institute which may recover from defendant under judgment. Apart from right to maintenance legal separation is not recognized.

Division of Property of Spouses in Divorce.—In absence of agreement each spouse is entitled by 1973 Law of Financial Relations between Spouses to half of total property of both spouses excluding such property as either had before marriage or received as gift or by way of inheritance during marriage or non-assignable rights or property which parties agreed should not be taken into consideration.

EXCHANGE CONTROL:

See Currency; Foreign Trade Regulations; Investment Law.

EXECUTIONS:

Execution Law 1967 provides for various methods of enforcing judgments and for securing defendant's property during course of an action (see topic Attachment). Judgment debtor can be detained or prevented from leaving country if Chief Execution Officer considers he intends to impede execution. There is power to attach movable property but certain items such as foodstuffs for subsistence of debtor and family for 30 days, vital household effects and clothes, religious articles and trade implements are exempt. Attached property may be sold after seven days from date of attachment. Immovable property may also be attached and sold after 30 days. Dwelling house is exempt unless it can be shown that debtor has somewhere else to go. Agricultural land required for subsistence is also exempt. There are also provisions for attachment of property in hands of a third party which includes debts due to judgment debtor. There are certain exemptions, most important being wages up to a certain amount. In certain limited circumstances a debtor, who has not, after an inquiry into his means, paid the ordered instalments of his debt, can be arrested. Further form of execution commonly used is appointment of a receiver similar in nature to remedy of equitable execution used in Anglo-Saxon systems.

By virtue of a 1968 amendment to Law, bill of exchange may be enforced directly by execution without obtaining judgment.

Execution of Foreign Judgments.—Under Foreign Judgments Enforcement Law 1958, foreign judgment may be enforced in Israel either by action thereon before a district court or by grant of an exequatur issued by a district court. A "judgment" for this purpose means any judgment or order given by a court outside Israel in any civil proceedings, whereby a sum of money is made payable and includes an award in any arbitration, if award is, in pursuance of law enforced in place where it was made. It is enforceable in same manner as a judgment given by a court in that place. Judgment to which an exequatur has been accorded is executory in Israel. There are certain conditions required for enforcement, particularly reciprocity and that judgment was given according to rules of natural justice.

By amendment to above Law in 1977, foreign judgment will be recognized by Israel Court only if following conditions are satisfied: (a) Agreement with country where judgment was given; (b) Israel undertook by such agreement to recognize judgments of same class; (c) such undertaking applies only to judgments enforceable by Israel Law; (d) all conditions of agreement are fulfilled.

By same amendment debts in foreign currency may be paid in that currency or in Israel currency at rate of exchange in force at time of payment.

Special provisions in regard to the enforcement of foreign awards are contained in the (Arbitration) Foreign Awards Ordinance of 1934. The provisions of this ordinance apply only in respect of territories which have made reciprocal provisions. There is as yet no provision for the reciprocal enforcement of awards between Israel and the United States, but it would seem that an award issued and confirmed in the United States may be enforced in Israel under the Enforcement of Foreign Judgment Rules.

EXECUTORS AND ADMINISTRATORS:

See also topic Descent and Distribution.

An administrator may be appointed on the application of any person entitled to an interest of the estate. An administrator is personally liable at the instance of persons beneficially entitled for any wrong committed by him in the course of his administration. An administrator is required to give security, whilst an executor may be exempted from furnishing any security for the due administration of the estate. Executors or administrators are required to file returns in regard to their administration and the discharge is obtained on proper application after the conclusion of the administration or by leave of the court even before the winding up of the estate. The court will, on the application of an administrator, give such direction as may from time to time be required as to the administration of the estate.

The application for probate of a will or for the appointment of an administrator of an estate of a deceased person is made by petition to the court having jurisdiction in the area where the deceased had his last usual residence or place of business; and if the deceased had no place of residence or place of business in Israel, then the petition may be addressed to the court within whose area any part of the estate is to be found.

EXEMPTIONS:

The following are exempt from attachment: (1) a minimum income sufficient to provide the debtor with the necessities of life; (2) things necessary for the support, clothing and lodging of the family of the debtor; (3) machinery and implements used by the debtor in exercising his trade; (4) amount of salary of employees up to NIS. 280 per month for individual, NIS. 421 for married person with additions for children but not more than 80% of earnings; (5) dwelling house of debtor unless reasonable substitute dwelling is available.

FOREIGN EXCHANGE:

See topics Currency; Foreign Trade Regulations; Investment Law.

FOREIGN INVESTMENT:

See topic Investment Law.

FOREIGN TRADE REGULATIONS:

Exchange Control Regulations were imposed during World War II. Although Regulations of 1941 were substantially relaxed, dealings in foreign currency and export of foreign currency are controlled by regulations. Contracts with nonresidents required to be approved by Controller of Foreign Exchange. Tendency in recent years has steadily been a relaxation in control and the streamlining of procedures. Similarly, while for many years all imports were subject to import licences due to exchange control and for protection of local industry, present tendency is towards liberalization of imports including elimination of necessity for import licences on an ever-increasing number of goods and materials. Treaties of friendship and commerce have been concluded with many countries and are renewable annually or at other regular intervals. In Nov. 1977 necessity for import licences was virtually abolished.

Israel has concluded trade and customs agreements with European Economic Community.

See also topics Currency; Investment Law; Taxation.

Free Trade Zone.—1985 Law establishes Southern Port City of Eilat as Free Trade Zone with substantial reductions in taxes on goods and services purchased by residents and tourists. Tax benefits are also granted to employers and employees.

See also topic Taxation.

FRAUDS, STATUTE OF: See topic Contracts.

GARNISHMENT:

See topics Attachment; Executions.

GUARDIAN AND WARD:

Legal Capacity and Guardianship Law of 1962 governs appointment and duties of guardians. Legal acts of persons under 18 and other equally incapacitated persons are subject to ratification by court and where property rights are involved to consent of court. Management of affairs of and care of legally incapacitated persons is entrusted to guardian, subject to general supervision of court. Jurisdiction is vested in District Court but religious courts have jurisdiction if all parties so desire. Law of domicile applies but court has powers over incapacitated person living in Israel or over legal acts performed in Israel relating to property of incapacitated person.

HIRE:

See topic Landlord and Tenant.

HOLIDAYS:

The following are public or legal holidays for the purpose of the Bills of Exchange Ordinance: Independence Day (also day of rest); Jewish holidays (Passover, first and last days, Pentecost, New Year's, two days, Day of Atonement, and First and Eighth day of Feast of Tabernacles); Christian holidays (New Year's Day—according to both Gregorian and Julian calendar, Ascension Day, Christmas Day, and Easter Monday); Moslem holidays (Shaker Bairam, three days, Qurban Bairam, four days, and Maulid al Nabi, one day).

There are also legal rest days. The Jewish rest days are the days mentioned above under "Jewish holidays," as well as Saturdays. These need not be the rest days for non-Jews, as they may rest on their respective holidays and other religious days.

Election day is a public holiday.

HUSBAND AND WIFE:

See topics Divorce; Marriage.

IMMIGRATION:

Substantial rights are granted to new immigrants including income tax concessions, customs and purchase tax exemptions on personal and household effects, investment assistance and housing facilities.

See also topic Constitution and Government, subhead Citizenship.

INFANCY:

Age of majority of both sexes is 18. Parents of a minor (a person under 18) are natural guardians. Natural guardians or any guardians appointed by court may consent to or ratify a contract made by a minor but unless made with such consent or until ratified, contract may be repudiated by minor or by his guardians or by Attorney General. Consent or ratification need not be in writing.

Certain acts of a guardian, such as transfer of real property, charges or mortgages, gifts, donations, guarantees and transactions between a minor and his guardian or his parents, require the approval of court.

An infant is represented in court by his guardian. Court may appoint a guardian ad litem.

Adoption.—See topic Adoption.

See topic Guardian and Ward.

INSURANCE:

The 1981 Insurance Contracts Law has basically legislated much of common law position and now governs law of Commercial (as opposed to State) Insurance in Israel.

Scope.—Law regulates law pertaining to life insurance; personal accident; sickness and disability insurance; regular commercial insurance; and vehicle insurance. (However, 1970 Motor Vehicle Insurance Ordinance is still applicable.) Law does not however apply to Maritime Insurance where 1863 Ottoman Maritime Trade Law still applies (insofar as it has not been repealed). Law does not apply to air insurance, nor does it apply to re-insurance treaties.

1981 Law repeals 1976 Law dealing with rights of third parties but incorporates protection of third parties in case of insolvency of insured. 1981 Law also repeals 1904 Ottoman Insurance Law which dealt with property insurance.

1981 Law provides that should one of parties wish to cancel contract in accordance with said Law or by virtue of conditions of contract, contract is terminated 15 days after notice has been sent to other party.

Claim for insurance payment prescribes three years after occurrence of event insured against.

1981 Law applies concurrently with 1951 Insurance Business (Superintendence) Law. Latter regulates and limits carrying on of insurance business in Israel, deals with grant of licences, lodging of returns by insurance companies and payment of deposits by persons engaging in insurance business in Israel. Maximum deposit in case of Israeli Insurers is IS.580,000 in case of life insurance and IS.435,000 for other types of insurance. Maximum deposit for foreign insurers is IS.930,000. Foreign Insurance Companies licensed before 12/12/79 are liable to maximum deposit of only IS.250.000. Should such company, licensed before 12/12/79, wish to deal-in other types of insurance than stipulated in licence, further deposit of IS.30,000 is due, but total deposit shall not exceed IS.350,000.

See also topics Labour Relations; Consumer Protection.

INTEREST:

Under law of 1957, rate of interest chargeable is restricted. Minister of Finance may by order approved by Finance Committee of Knesset (Israel Legislature) fix maximum rate of interest chargeable in respect of commercial transactions of various categories. There is normally no maximum rate fixed but where repayment is limited to a currency rate of exchange or to an index, maximum permitted rate is 8%. Courts are authorized to reopen usurious transactions and penalties are provided in case of any breach of law.

INVESTMENT LAW:

Law for Encouragement of Capital Investments 1959 as am'd succeeds earlier legislation in regard to encouragement of investments in Israel. Substantial reliefs and exemptions from income tax are allowed. (See below amended benefits for approvals after July 30, 1978.) Special concessions are allowed to foreign investors whose investments are approved by Investment Centre. (See infra and topic Taxation, subhead Income Tax).

Law for Encouragement of Capital Investment in Agriculture 1980 provides special tax benefits for approved investment in agriculture.

Foreign currency invested in approved investment and profits earned thereon may be taken out in foreign currency by foreign investor.

Companies owning enterprises approved by Investment Centre are entitled to exemption from income tax and pay profits tax at 28% for five years from first year of chargeable profit (subject to overriding time limit of 12 years from commencement of production). For enterprises approved after Apr. 1, 1980 exemption period is seven years with overriding limit of 14 years. Where approval is granted after 1st Apr. 1971, profits tax is 33%; where approval is granted after Mar. 31, 1976 profits tax is 40%. Enterprises approved after July 30, 1978 pay 30%. Enterprises approved after May 31, 1981 pay 40% reducible to 30% on chargeable income equal to net investment in fixed assets in tax year. Shareholders are exempt from income tax on dividends from profits of approved enterprises on which profits tax has been paid. Dividends out of profits of enterprise approved after Mar. 31, 1976 are chargeable to income tax at 15%. Individuals and Kibbutzim owning approved enterprises pay income tax at 25% if approved before Mar. 31, 1976, 40% if approved between Mar. 31, 1976 and July 30, 1978, and 30% if approved after that date. Approved enterprises with 25% foreign investment being Industrial Companies under Encouragement of Industry (Taxes) 1969 Law are entitled to deduct provision for capital stabilisation, based on dollar exchange rate differences each year. Industrial enterprises approved 1/4/85 or later with 25% or more foreign investment enjoy ten year income tax exemption, no time limit for relief on distributions of profits for exemption period. Rate of Companies Tax is graduated from 25% if 25-49% foreign investment to 10% if 90% or more. As from tax year 1978, companies where foreign investment exceeds 49% are entitled to alternative capital stabilisation allowances based on adjustment of share capital and profits for exchange rate variation. New enterprises approved after 1/4/86 may choose alternative benefits foregoing grants and instead enjoy complete tax exemption for ten years if situated in Development Area A, six years in Development Area B, two years in any other Area, with usual exemptions for remainder of period as above. Dividends out of profits of complete exemption period are chargeable to 40% income tax.

Buildings which are assessed approved by Investment Centre completed after 1st Apr., 1968, 70% of area of which is intended for letting and two-thirds of such letting is residential, are granted relief from 80% of property tax, increased depreciation rates and reduced tax rates as for approved enterprises but without time limit.

Industrial enterprises approved between Jan. 1, 1971 and Mar. 31, 1976, and completed by Mar. 31, 1980, or approved between Apr. 1, 1976 and Mar. 31, 1981 and completed by Mar. 31, 1986 are entitled to investment grants from State, amounting to 15% or 30% of amount invested in buildings, machinery and equipment, higher rate being given where enterprise is located in less developed areas of country. Under 1976 amendment, export grants were also paid as percentage of foreign currency earned from exports of approved enterprises up to amount equal to 24% of investment in enterprise. Investments in construction of buildings intended for leasing are also entitled to certain tax exemptions and accelerated depreciation. By Amending Law of July 30, 1978, exemptions from property taxes, local taxes, purchase tax, customs and stamp duties are cancelled in relation to approvals after that date. Export grants are cancelled but investment grants and grants to cover indirect taxes are allowed.

Minister of Finance has power to exempt from income and Companies Tax, international trading concerns, otherwise liable to Israeli taxes only by reason of management and control being situate in Israel.

Investment Encouragement Law (Capital Rich Companies) (1973 Law) provides that any company, capital of which is $100,000,000 of which $20,000,000 was subscribed by signatories to memorandum and purposes of which are to acquire and maintain or enlarge industrial works, finance or agriculture, tourism, transport, land development, building, public services or advance of exports from Israel and recognized by Minister of the Treasury until Dec. 31, 1975, is entitled to extensive benefits. It is free from income tax or capital profits tax within 30 years from first year of income. It will only pay company tax not exceeding 20% and be free from any other tax upon income.

Any person receiving dividends from such a company within 15 years of year when income was obtained will be free from any income tax in addition to income tax paid by company, and any person selling shares out of a series of shares issued by company, will be free from capital profits tax. Shares owned by a nonresident will not be included in his estate for purpose of estate tax. Law contains provisions for cancellation of benefits if capital has not reached $30,000,000 within four years of issue of first series of shares and also if less than 80% of share capital was issued to nonresidents for foreign currency.

JUDGMENTS:

Enforcement of Foreign Judgments.—By a law of 1958, judgments of foreign courts are enforceable if they were given in the foreign country by a court having jurisdiction to act, and are final and not subject to appeal, and their contents are not in contradiction to the laws of Israel or public policy in Israel and they are capable of execution in the country in which they were given. The jurisdiction is based upon mutuality and special rules have been provided. See topic Executions.

LABOUR RELATIONS:

Wages.—1958 Wage Protection Law provides that wages must be paid in cash. Other modes of payment are allowed only under collective agreement; only small portion may be paid in food and lodging. Payment must be directly to labourer. Fixed amount is free from attachments. Time for payment fixed and if delayed, additional sum is payable. This rule was made applicable to compensation for dismissal by 1977 Amendment. Debts due from labourer to employer can be deducted only within limits. 1976 Sickness Pay Law provides for payment of 75% of normal wage in case of sickness for period up to 1 ½ days for each month of service, unless provided otherwise under Collective Agreement.

Employment of Children.—Employment of children and young persons is governed by Law of 1953 Relating to Employment of Youth and Apprenticeship Law of 1953. Employment of persons under age of 14 is forbidden. Minister of Labour has power to prohibit or limit employment of infants in specific occupations or to fix age for employment in certain employments. Minister may also fix work hours and conditions of employment.

The employment of women is also strictly governed by the Employment of Women Law 1954, which restricts the employment and working hours and makes provisions for the protection of women employed in the various undertakings.

Equal opportunity in Employment Law 1981 forbids discrimination in engaging employees on grounds of sex, marital or parental status unless justified by nature of employment or security considerations. 1986 Amendment empowers Minister of Labour to regulate conditions for nightwork by women.

National Insurance Law (Consolidated Version) 1968 as amended contains comprehensive code in regard to payment of old age pensions, payments in respect of compensation to workmen injured by accident, maternity payments, unemployment payments, death benefits and child allowances.

National Insurance Law provides for old age pensions to males of over 65 and females over 60 and for compensation in respect to death or injury during work both to workmen and to independent earners. It also provides certain benefits in respect to childbirth and burial expenses. Law is administered by a National Insurance Board which levies a fixed premium on all residents. The premiums vary according to income and premiums due from employed persons are deducted by employers from their salaries.

Assurance of Income Law, 1980 provides for persons resident in Israel who are unable to work or support themselves sufficiently and who are not eligible for benefits under National Insurance Law. All claims are subject to specific conditions.

National Employment Service.—By the 1959 law, employment agencies have been erected on a national basis and no labourers may be employed except through those agencies, with the exception of certain highly specialized professions or administrative employment. 1976 amending law provides youth occupational guidance and requires notification of dismissals of ten or more employees at one time.

Collective Agreements.—Collective agreements may be entered into between an employer or an organization of employers and between organized labour, regarding conditions and terms of work. Labourers rights under such agreements cannot be waived, and the Minister of Labour may extend its application.

Labour Disputes.—There is no provision in regard to compulsory settlement of disputes between employers and labourers, but the Department of Labour has power to assist the employers and labourers in the settlement of their industrial disputes and it normally intervenes in such disputes with a view of securing an amicable settlement. In case of labour disputes provision is made for settlement by mediation, the mediator possessing far-reaching powers to assemble the parties and ascertain the nature of the dispute. Certain matters are passed to compulsory arbitration, the decision of the arbitrators being binding. There is now a Labour Court which deals with labour disputes.

Under Civil Wrongs Ordinance (New Version) 1963, as amended, master is liable for acts of his servant if he authorized or ratified act or if it was committed by servant in course of his employment.

By Amendments to Law of Settlement of Labour Disputes, following limitations were introduced on right to strike: (a) By §5a of 1969 Amending Law a 15 day notice must be given of any intended strike both to Commissioner of Labour Relations and to employer; (b) by §37 b-d of 1972 Amending Law, special provisions governing public service were introduced. Term "public service" includes labour relations in service of Government, municipalities and local councils, health services, primary and higher education, aviation, oil, water and electricity. In a public service a strike declared without legal notice above-mentioned or whilst a collective agreement is in force is (with few exceptions) an "unprotected strike." Participation by individual labourer in an unprotected strike deprives him of protection granted by Collective Agreements Law to effect that a participation in a strike does not constitute a breach of personal agreement of labourer. Person causing labourers to participate in an unprotected strike is liable for procuring a breach of contract. Labour Courts are entitled to issue an injunction prohibiting individual labourers to participate in an unprotected strike. By amending law 1976, Labour Courts are empowered to order proportionate wage reduction in case of unprotected "go-slow" strike in public services. See also topic Banks and Banking.

See also subhead National Insurance Law.

Compensation for Dismissal.—By a 1963 law an employee who has worked continuously for a minimum period of one year with same employer in same job is entitled on dismissal to compensation amounting to a sum equal to one month's pay for each full year of service. No compensation is payable if employee is dismissed for dishonesty. In certain cases, such compensation may be paid even where employee resigns of his own accord, e.g., for health reasons. Female worker who leaves her employment with nine months after birth or adoption of child by her in order to attend to such child is entitled to compensation.

See also topic Wages.

Right of Dismissal.—Supreme Court, as High Court of Justice, set aside a judgment of Labour Court of Appeal ordering an employer to continue employing an employee whom he had dismissed. Rule that court does not order specific performance of a contract of personal employment, is not affected by fact that employment is governed by a collective agreement.

Labour Courts.—By a 1969 Law, special Labour Courts were created and given exclusive jurisdiction in all matters dealing with or arising from labour relations.

There are four District Labour Courts in Jerusalem, Tel-Aviv, Haifa and Beer Sheva, and a State Court in Jerusalem. In every Court there are professional judges and two members of the public, one nominated by employers' association and one by employees' association. In State Court there are three professional judges and two members of public appointed as above. District Courts have exclusive primary jurisdiction in all matters between employers and employees and in collective agreement disputes arising from a special collective agreement (i.e., one dealing with one or a limited number of employers). State Court has primary jurisdiction in disputes arising from general collective agreements (i.e., agreements covering all employers of a certain category) and an appeal jurisdiction from District Court. Both courts have criminal jurisdiction too.

There is no appeal from State Court. It is subject however to a limited "High Court jurisdiction."

Trade Unions.—Supreme Court refused to interfere with decision of Labour Association not to create a trade union consisting of workmen of one branch in certain towns. Labour Association is a voluntary body and, hence, law courts would refrain from interference with a decision, which prima facie constitutes a valid exercise of Association's discretion.

See also topic Wages.

LAND:

Under the "Basic Law—Land of Israel 1960," all the lands which belong to the State Development Authority or J.N.F. are considered as the lands of Israel, the ownership whereof cannot be assigned either by sale or by any other way. Land includes land, houses, buildings and all other appurtenances belonging thereto. Under the Land of Israel Law, 1960, several transactions in reference to these lands are exempted from the prohibition of transfer. These are mainly transactions in the nature of exchange of lands. Special authorities were created in order to manage the lands and to supervise the execution of the provisions of the law.

Land Law is now virtually codified by Land Law 1969. Existing Ottoman legislation has been abolished. Dealings with registered land not valid unless registered, and equitable rights have been abolished. Written document is required for sale or lease of land. Owner of land has right to claim possession against wrongful occupier.

Joint tenancies may only be over an undivided whole. Any joint tenant may require dissolution of joint tenancy which may be carried out by agreement or by order of court. Court may order partition or sale.

Registration.—Land registration now covers most of country except part of Galilee.

Cooperative Houses.—Cooperative Houses Law has been repealed but has been incorporated in Land Law. It facilitates registration of separate dwellings in a jointly-owned house and regulates rights between owners. Urban housing in Israel is largely based on cooperative housing.

Sale of Apartments Law 1973 came into force on 1/10/73 and provides that a sale of an apartment which has been built or is about to be built must be accompanied by a specification in a form prescribed by Minister of Housing. Any deviation from specification or from applicable town planning regulations is regarded as a noncompliance conferring upon purchaser all rights under Sales Law 1968. (See topic Sales.)

Special provisions apply to sale of an apartment in a condominium house or in a property designated to be registered as a condominium house requiring all relevant details as to management of house. Default in attaching specification is punished with a serious money penalty.

See also topic Sales, subhead Sale of Flats.

Securing Purchasers of Apartments.—By 1974-76 Law of Sale (Apartments) (securing investments of apartment purchasers) vendor or lessor by lease for more than 25 years, of an unbuilt apartment, may not receive from purchaser more than 15% of purchase price unless he gave purchaser bank guarantee securing refund of all monies paid, in event of non-delivery of apartment to purchaser as agreed, or has insured himself with an authorised insurance company against such event, with purchaser as beneficiary under policy, or has transferred ownership or long lease of apartment to purchaser or encumbered same in his favour.

Transfers.—Immovable property can only be transferred by execution of a deed which has to be signed either at competent Land Registry in Israel or before any lawyer in Israel who authenticates signatures on deed. Deed is executed before District Land Registrar, when appropriate fees must be paid. Transferee's title is entered on Register in substitution for title of transferor. All transfers of immovable property must now be reported for Betterment Tax purposes.

Recuperation Areas Authority.—By 1973 Statute this authority is set up and authorised to recommend that a certain area having qualities that would attract persons recuperating, be declared a recuperation area, of one of various categories, and any restrictions on undertakings within area. It can also encourage research, advance level of services of existing recuperation areas, encourage housing, supervise and generally regulate exploitation of area. This law contains full supplementary provisions regarding effect of such declaration, and any ensuing rights and liabilities.

Radio and Television Aerial Masts.—Local Authorities (Radio and Television Aerial Masts) Law 1975 empowers local authorities to limit number of radio and television aerial masts on buildings and to require erection of central masts on apartment buildings with compensation for persons aggrieved and financial penalties for infringements.

See topic Taxation. See also topics Adverse Possession; Landlord and Tenant; Limitation of Actions; Mortgages.

LANDLORD AND TENANT:

Land Law 1969 requires written document and registration in Land Registry to effect lease if for more than five years or with option to renew beyond five years. Registration not required for lease of dwellings or business premises unless for period exceeding in all ten years. Subject to agreement lease may be charged with mortgage or easement and tenant may transfer lease or sublet. See also subhead Hire Law 1971, infra.

Duties of landlord to provide services and effect repairs are laid down in Tenants Protection Law 1972. This Law also consolidates previous legislation regarding control of rentals and protection against eviction for tenants of residential and business premises occupying under leases prior to 1958 which have expired or who paid key-money. Protection extends to surviving spouse, children or parents who occupied premises with tenant at least six months prior to decease. Protected tenant continues to hold on terms of expired lease as varied by agreement or by Law.

Rentals of premises within Law may not be increased except within the limits fixed by Regulations issued periodically. In event of dispute between landlord and tenant, local Rent Tribunals have power to fix rental.

Outgoing tenant is entitled to share of key-money to be paid by incoming tenant, amount of which depends on whether his tenancy began before or after 1958, period of occupation and whether he himself paid key-money. Special procedure is provided to settle outgoing tenant's share if disputed.

Law ceases to apply to premises falling vacant and does not apply to buildings completed and let after 1968, nor to buildings of Approved Undertakings (see topic Investment Law).

Principal grounds for eviction of protected tenant are nonpayment of rent, breach of original lease justifying eviction, wilful damage, use of premises for unlawful purpose, molesting neighbours, premises required for own purposes or rebuilding by landlord, public body requiring premises for public purpose. In last two cases alternative accomodation must be provided.

Hire Law 1971.—Law in respect of hire applies to both moveables and immoveables where contrary intention does not appear in agreement. Object hired must comply with specifications in agreement unless lessor knew otherwise at date of agreement or lessee did not notify lessor of unsuitability within reasonable time. Lessor has liability to repair. Where object hired is a chattel, lessor may exchange defective chattel so as to comply with his obligations. Where repair not carried out, lessee may repair and debit lessor with expense or reduce rent in accordance with defect. Where object leased is land and lessee cannot use it for reasons connected with land or access thereto, he is not liable to pay rent. Lessee must give lessor facilities to inspect and repair. Lessor may assign his rights but must notify lessee. Lessee may not assign without lessor's consent, but if lessor unreasonably withholds consent, in case of land lessee may assign without lessor's consent, and in case of any object court may order transaction.

See also topic Sales, subhead Sale of Flats.

LAW REPORTS, CODES, ETC.:

There are official law reports of cases in Supreme Court and in district courts and there are also official reports of cases in rabbinical courts and certain specialised reports such as tax cases.

Certain branches of the law are codified and may be found in books of Mandatory Ordinances and Israeli Statutes. See also topic Statutes.

LEGISLATURE:

See topic Constitution and Government.

LICENCES:

Business Licencing Law of 1968, replacing pre-State legislation empowers Minister of Interior in consultation with Minister of Health to issue Orders requiring certain businesses to obtain licences in order to ensure proper environmental and health conditions, prevention of public nuisances and observation of Town Planning regulations, public safety, prevention of pollution and diseases in livestock. Special provisions are laid down for sale of intoxicating liquors and public entertainments. Comprehensive list of businesses requiring licence has been drawn up in Registration Order of 1973 covering close to 200 kinds of business. Licencing authority is local government or such authority as Minister of Interior may determine. Fine of IS.500 or six months imprisonment is imposed for noncompliance. Companies pay double fine. Court may order temporary or permanent closing of business convicted for noncompliance.

See also topic Foreign Trade Regulations.

LIENS:

There are various forms of liens which basically follow English Law. Maritime liens are provided by Shipping (Vessels) Law 1960.

LIMITATION OF ACTIONS:

Actions must be brought within following periods after respective causes of action, including civil wrongs, accrue: (a) in respect of a debt or chattels, within seven years; (b) in respect of unregistered land, 15 years. There is now no limitation period in respect of registered land. (c) parties may agree in writing to extend the period in case of land, and either to extend it or shorten it in case of movables.

Supreme Court decided in 1955 that suits for specific performance are not barred by any limitation period, but only by laches (delay causing damage).

See topics Bills and Notes; Insurance; also Adverse Possession.

In respect to crimes the following are the periods of prescription: felonies, ten years; misdemeanours, three years; contraventions, one year. Period of prescription runs from date of commission of offence or from date of last step taken in investigation or prosecution of offence in question in respect of felonies or misdemeanours; and in respect of contraventions, from date of commission of offence.

Time limits for bringing of actions under Nazis and Nazi Collaborators (Punishment) Law 1950 and under Genocide (Prevention and Punishment) Law 1950 were abolished in 1966.

Customs prosecutions must be instituted within five years.

Lost Property Law of Return.—By a new law of 1973 which came into force on Aug. 31, 1973, a person finding lost property must either return it to its owner or notify police and may keep property or deliver it to police unless police require such delivery, in which case he must comply with requirement. If owner has not been found within four months, he is presumed to have forfeited ownership, in which case it passes into finder's ownership. If, however, finder did not notify police it becomes State property. Previous owner may, however, within a year redeem lost property on paying its value at time of redemption. Goods liable to destruction or live stock may be sold after notifying police and provisions of Law apply to proceeds.

MAINTENANCE:

See topic Divorce, subhead Maintenance.

MARRIAGE:

Matters of marriage are considered as matters of personal status, which are within exclusive jurisdiction of Rabbinical religious courts in respect of all Jews and religious courts of other denominations in respect of non-foreigners who are members of respective recognized religious communities. In respect of foreigners, who are not Jews, their national law applies, and local courts will recognize as valid any marriage which is valid according to national law.

General consuls, vice-consuls and any other competent consular authority may officiate at marriages where at least one of the parties is of the consul's nationality.

No marriage of a girl under 17 is permitted unless court orders otherwise in special circumstances.

Every marriage must be registered by person performing marriage. Registration is effected by filing a copy of record with District Commissioner of district where marriage is performed. Failure to register involves considerable penalties.

Financial Relations Between Spouses.—1973 Law which came into force on Jan. 1, 1974 provides that spouses may regulate their financial relations by an agreement which requires approval by District Court or by Religious Court having jurisdiction in matters of marriage and divorce of spouses. Failing such an agreement, financial relations and ownership of property of spouses will be regulated as follows: (a) Entry into marriage or its subsistence do not affect spouse's ownership rights and do not confer upon either spouse any right in other spouse's property or any liability for other spouse's debts: (b) upon dissolution of marriage whether by divorce or by death of one spouse, each spouse is entitled to half of total property of both spouses excluding such property as either had before marriage or received as a gift or by way of inheritance during marriage or non-assignable rights or property in respect of which parties agreed that they are not to be taken into consideration. In event of death of a spouse, his heirs succeed to his rights under Law.

Law further contains provisions as to details of assessment of value, of preventing attempts of alienation in order to defeat provisions of law, and confers extensive jurisdiction upon court in application of provisions. Law does not affect such jurisdiction as is conferred upon Religious Courts but these Courts must apply provisions of Law unless both parties agreed to be judged by Religious Law. Law makes necessary amendments in Law of Succession in order to secure spouses rights according to provisions of this Law.

See also Divorce.

MINES:

Mines and minerals are the property of the state and their exploitation is governed by the Mining Ordinance of 1925, as amended. Licences for prospecting or exploring mines or for minerals may be obtained from the competent government department, and concessions are granted by the State. Mining rights or mining leases are obtainable on terms to be agreed with the State.

Oil.—The Oil Law of 1953 provides for prospecting and mining licences and regulations in regard to exploitation of mineral resources in Israel, particularly in respect of prospecting for oil and oil concessions.

National Energy Authority.—Set up by 1977 law to plan, develop and regulate sources and consumption of energy in Israel, taking over Governmental functions under Mining Ordinance and Petroleum Law.

See also topic Taxation.

MONOPOLIES AND RESTRAINT OF TRADE:

See topic Restrictive Trade Practice.

MORTGAGES:

Immovable property may be mortgaged to secure any debt or obligation. Mortgage of immovable property requires registration at District Registry in which land is situate. Mortgage fee of 1% is chargeable. Mortgage on immovable property not registered is not valid. Mortgage on land is realized by order of court or of Execution Office. Any provision denying mortgagor right to repay loan at any time is invalid.

Any mortgage pledge or charge created by company and not registered with Registrar of Companies within 21 days is void against a liquidator or any creditor.

For mortgage of chattels see topic Pledges.

Israel ships may be mortgaged by documents executed: (a) abroad, before an Israel diplomatic or consular delegate and approved by him; (b) in Israel, before Registrar of harbour of registration of ship. Mortgages must be recorded with Registrar of Ships. Mortgage on a ship is foreclosed or executed by order of Admiralty Court.

MOTOR VEHICLES:

Motor vehicles have to be licensed annually. Drivers are also licensed biennially by reference to type of vehicle driven. Age limit is $17\frac{1}{2}$, in respect of all vehicles other than motorcycles. Age limit in respect of motorcycles is 16. All vehicles must carry third party insurance. Transfers of vehicles are effected by Deed of Sale recorded with licensing authority. Identification marks are applied to various types of vehicles, by reference to registry offices. Speed limit is 50 kilometres in built-up areas, 80 kilometres in open country and 100 kilometres (at present restricted to 90 km) on fast motorways. There is detailed road-code and substantial penalties for breaches. Security belt law enacted.

Certain restrictions apply temporarily in regard to the transfer of vehicles as a result of present war conditions. Normally bona fide transactions are approved. Special provisions apply in regard to public vehicles including omnibuses and taxis, and their transfer is substantially restricted.

MOVEABLES:

Moveables Law 1971 grants to owner of moveables same rights against wrongful possession and trespass as Land Law 1969 grants in respect of immoveables. Joint ownership is over undivided whole with right to claim partition. See topic Landlord and Tenant.

NATIONAL SERVICE:

The Security Service Law, 1959, replaces all previous laws in this connection. Under the provisions of the law, every male resident of Israel from the age of 18 to 26 must serve 30 months compulsory service in the Army, and from the age of 27 to 29, 24 months.

Unmarried women from the age of 18 to 26 must serve 24 months. In the Reserves, every man up to the age of 39 years must serve one month per year and from the age of 40 to 49 years, 14 days per year. Unmarried women and married women without children up to the age of 34 years must serve one month per year. All soldiers on the reserve list are paid partly by the Army and partly by their employers.

NOTARIES PUBLIC:

All existing laws and regulations governing Notaries Public have been repealed by a 1976 Notaries Law. Notary must be Israeli citizen, member of Bar, who practises as an advocate in Israel 15 years or, if he is 65 years of age, or is a new immigrant, ten years. New law defines authority of notary, lays down procedure to be followed and code of professional ethics, confers on his confirmations status of lawfully sufficient proof of their contents; and enumerates acts which must be confirmed by him. Notary may be tried in an action before disciplinary courts of Bar, with appeal to Supreme Court. Israel diplomatic and consular representatives overseas are authorised to act as Notaries.

PARTNERSHIPS: See Associations.

PATENTS:

Patent Law was enacted in 1967.

Application.—An inventor or any person deriving title to an invention under him, whether product or process which is new, useful and susceptible of industrial or agricultural application may apply for grant of patent. Patent is granted to person who first validly applied for it in Israel, except that where owner's application for protection has already been filed in one of Convention countries, date of foreign application is deemed to be date of application filed in Israel, if application in Israel has been filed within 12 months after filing of other application.

Patent application is filed at office of Registrar of Patents in Jerusalem, and may be filed through an attorney.

Term of a patent is 20 years from date of application for patent provided that renewal fees are paid on their due dates.

Certain exploitation rights are reserved in favour of persons who prior to application date, have in good faith exploited invention in Israel.

Concept of novelty applied is that of universal novelty.

Opposition and Revocation.—Opposition to grant of a patent may be made within three months from date of publication of application in Reshumot (Government Official Gazette).

Patent may be revoked by Registrar on grounds on which opposition to grant of patent may be made, namely that invention is not patentable or that opponent and not applicant is owner of invention or if there exists another reason for which Registrar is entitled to refuse application in accordance with provisions of Law.

Licences may be granted by patentee. A licence under a patent is not effective in respect of any party other than parties to licence unless licence has been registered.

Certain rights are reserved to State in respect of use of patents which are required for security of State. Appropriate Minister may permit exploitation of patent by Government departments if it is necessary to do so in interest of defence of State or maintenance of essential supply and services. However, when such permission is given, owner of invention is entitled to compensation whether in form of royalties or otherwise, as detailed in Law. If Registrar is satisfied that owners of a patent have a monopoly which is misused he may grant a licence to exploit patent to a person who has applied for and paid prescribed fee, provided application is filed after expiration of three years from date on which patent was granted, or four years from date of filing of patent application, whichever is later.

Compulsory licence may also be ordered if it is necessary to assure public of a reasonable quantity of medical supplies. Detailed provisions are contained in Law in regard to factors to be taken into account in granting a compulsory licence, conditions of licence including payment of royalties.

Patents are assignable. Patentee may also charge patent or income thereof. Assignment and charge have to be registered.

Designs can be registered under Patents and Designs Ordinance of 1925 as am'd in respect of one or more class or classes of goods. A certificate of registration is granted by Registrar. On registration of a design proprietor of design is entitled to copyright in design for five years, and period may be renewed from time to time for five years up to three cycles of five years each.

An amendment to Ordinance brings Israel law in line with Hague International Convention for Protection of Industrial Property to which Israel has now become a signatory. A design may no longer be eliminated from Register because it is in use abroad, and not in Israel. Registration in Israel of a patent or design registered abroad receives preference over an application registered after date of foreign application, if registered in Israel within 12 or six months respectively after registration in any of signatory countries of convention. (Book of Laws, No. 99, of 12.6.52).

PLEDGES:

Law of pledges is contained in a law with effect from Oct. 1, 1967.

Pledge is a charge on chattel as security for debt and creditor may recoup from pledge if debt not discharged. Pledge is created by agreement between debtor and creditor. Pledge serves as security for interest, costs and damages due from debtor. Debtor may repledge chattel to a further creditor, but prior creditor takes precedence; if, however, prior creditor agrees, later creditor may have equal rights (pari passu).

Any profits from pledge are subject to pledge unless agreed otherwise.

In case of nonpayment, execution is obtained by court order, except in case of banks where such order is not required.

On cessation of debt, rights of pledge terminate and debtor may demand return of pledge.

PRACTICE:

Consolidated and revised Rules of Court in civil actions came into effect on Oct. 1, 1984. Actions are commenced by a statement of claim, answered by statement of defense. English procedure is closely followed with rights of request for further particulars, discovery of documents and interrogatories. New rules provide for preliminary settling of issues by court where necessary. Procedure in cases against Government is same as for other cases.

PRESCRIPTION:

See topics Adverse Possession; Limitation of Actions.

PRINCIPAL AND AGENT:

Comprehensive code covering law of principal and agent was recently promulgated as Agency Law of 1965. Law sets out duties and rights of agents. No special formality is required to establish any agency relationship, and agent may be granted unlimited or limited authority. Corporation may be appointed as agent.

Power of attorney authorising person to act as agent in respect of lands or rights in land must be in writing and in certain cases, especially if irrevocable, copy of power of attorney has to be deposited with Betterment Tax Authority and may be subject to payment of Betterment Tax.

Person entrusted with possession of assets or their management, is required, if ten years have passed since grant of authority, to advise Administrator-General of existence of the power or authority. No transaction relating to immovables may be given effect by virtue of power of attorney after expiration of ten years from date of appointment, except with authority of appointor or with leave of court.

Agents for purchase of military equipment of all kinds for Israel Army or Defence Ministry may not receive commission unless permit granted by Defence Minister.

REAL PROPERTY:

See topic Land.

RECEIVERS:

A comprehensive code in regard to liquidators is contained in the Companies Ordinance in respect of winding up of companies. Receivers may be appointed in pending proceedings by way of interlocutory remedy or by judgment. Receivers may also be appointed under a debenture according to its terms. Receivers appointed by a court are officers of the court and must submit certain periodical returns and obtain the discharge from the court. See also topic Executions.

RECORDS:

The only system of formal records is the recording at the District Land Registry of land dispositions, including sales, exchanges, leases exceeding three years and mortgages. There is a limited system of recording of documents before the Public Notary (power of attorney and pledges), and for registration of ships (transfers of ships and mortgages), registration of patents and designs, and registration of trade marks. See also Patents; Shipping; Trade Marks.

REPORTS: See topic Law Reports, Codes, Etc.

RESTRICTIVE TRADE PRACTICE:

Under Restrictive Trade Law, 1959, every "restrictive arrangement" or agreement, i.e., any arrangement or agreement which includes restrictive instructions in reference to price, profits, quality, quantity, marketing, etc., has to be registered with the competent Registrar. Restrictive arrangements which are not so registered and which are not accepted for registration by the Registrar are illegal and considered as an offence for which the offender is liable to receive a penalty. All registered arrangements are open to the public unless otherwise determined by the Registrar. Similar provisions apply in reference to monopolies. By 1963 Law of Standard Contracts, restrictive conditions in standard agreements for supply of goods or services are invalid unless approved by Council set up under Restrictive Trade Practices Law 1959. Restrictive conditions are such as limit normal contractual rights of purchaser as against supplier.

By amending 1973 Law, a monopolist, may not refuse to supply or acquire a commodity or service, in respect of which monopoly exists, except according to accepted trade usage.

SALES:

Sales Law 1968 governs sales of all assets whether movable or immovable but may be contracted out. Usage of parties or of trade may govern sale. Seller is bound to deliver property and transfer ownership therein, delivery being by putting property at disposition of purchaser. If no time is set for delivery there is an implied condition of reasonable time and delivery takes place at place of business of seller. Seller does not fulfil his duty if he does not deliver amount ordered or property of a different nature than that ordered or which does not comply with sample or to accepted usage or which in any other way does not comply with contract. Purchaser may not rely on such unsuitability if he knew of it at time of signing of contract. Purchaser has a duty to inspect property on receipt and must advise vendor immediately of unsuitability. In case of latent defects in goods, purchaser has two years within which to give notice of unsuitability.

Remedies are same as for ordinary breach of contract. In case of unsuitability, purchaser also has right of deduction from price.

International Sale of Goods.—Sale (International Sale of Goods) Law 1971 adopted, for Israel, Uniform Law on International Sale of Goods. Law is now in force.

Purchaser's Bona Fides.—Rule that a bona fide purchaser of movables in ordinary course of vendor's business, acquires clear ownership, is not affected by fact that said movable was pledged and notice was entered in Register of Pledges. Bona fides for purpose of law of sales, is not necessarily excluded by omission to examine Register of Pledges, even if such omission is negligent.

Sale of Flats.—Special 1974 Law regulates mode of securing monies paid by a purchaser of a flat to seller by providing that if purchaser pays more than 15% of price of flat, seller must either give purchaser a bank guarantee securing all sums paid if for any reason transfer cannot take place, or obtain a policy of insurance from an insurance company covering liability to repay in such a case to purchaser sums paid by him or mortgage flat or a proportional part of area on which it is to be built to secure such repayment or enter a note of sale in Land Registry books provided no mortgage is registered, or transfer ownership to purchaser.

Law provides penalties for breach of this provision.

Protection of Consumers Law 1981 provides penalties for exploitation and misleading of customers in sales and services for private purposes. Customers are to be given full and correct information, regarding goods sold and price thereof in credit and instalment sales.

Price Control.—Series of 1985 Laws establishes price freeze on most goods and services, and wage freeze for most workers. Among exemptions from price control are exports, sales and services connected with tourist industry, credit transactions, insurance, foreign currency, diamonds. Controls to remain in effect until June 30, 1986.

See also topic Contracts.

SEALS:

There is no necessity for seals on private instruments. Corporations are required to have an official seal which is to be fixed on deeds and other documents which by virtue of the statutes of the particular corporation require the corporate seal.

Municipal corporations have a corporate seal. The seal of the State of Israel is affixed to particular instruments of a very special class. The Minister of Justice is in charge of the State Seal.

SECURITIES:

Under Mutual Investment Trust Law, 1961, company, objects of which are to make as trustee mutual investment in securities, must have paid capital of not less than IS.1,000,000 and must be connected with another company which will deal with securities.

Securities Law 1968 sets up a Securities Authority to watch over interests of public investing in securities. Offer of securities to public is forbidden except by way of a prospectus permitted by Authority. Law imposes civil liability on directors and experts to purchasers in respect of contents or prospectus. Any person purchasing securities relying on an erroneous statement in prospectus has a right of rescission within a reasonable time. Provisions of law also apply to securities in Israeli companies offered abroad. Authority has power to waive provisions of law in respect of securities of a company registered abroad if satisfied that laws of country of registration adequately safeguard Israeli investors.

By 1981 Amendment "insider trading" by persons holding 10% or more in corporation where shares issued to public or dealt in on Stock Exchange, and by persons holding position in such corporation giving them access to inside information becomes criminal offence punishable by imprisonment or fine; excepted are bona fide transactions, e.g. purchase of qualifying shares, transactions by trustee, liquidator, receiver, transactions by bona fide written contract.

1984 Law protects savings invested in approved savings schemes, Government bonds, provident funds and insurance policies issued in Israel, by forbidding Government expropriation or deterioration of conditions of such savings as to amount and date of redemption, rate and due date of interest, linkage basis and rate of tax.

SHIPPING:

A substantial part of the shipping law was embodied in the Shipping (Vessels) Law 1960 dealing primarily with shipping registration and ships' mortgages. Certain parts of the (English) Merchant Shipping Act 1894 have been applied and still apply to Israel.

Ministry of Communications is in charge of maritime matters including the enforcement of the shipping laws. See also topic Mortgages.

Under Ports Authority Law of 1961, Ports Authority was constituted as a separate legal entity and, pursuant to said law, control of ports and their management is vested in Ports Authority.

Shipping (Sailors) Law 1973 regulates conditions necessary to become a sailor both of Israeli and non-Israeli citizens. It provides means of supervision and disciplinary action. Council is appointed to plan, control and supervise examinations. Law defines authority and rights of captain, and regulates his duties both on land and on high seas. It also regulates discipline, and work distribution, salary and other rights of crew and deals with offences.

STATUTES:

Statutes are published regularly in Official Gazette and there are annual volumes. There is an official translation into English of Statutes known as Laws of State of Israel which may be purchased from Government Printer.

TAXATION:

Income Tax.—Income Tax Law was codified in 1961. New Law brings up to date and incorporates in a comprehensive code the provisions of 1947 Ordinance and subsequent amendments.

Income tax is payable on income of any person arising in, derived from or received in Israel from any business, profession or employment as well as from dividends, interest and linkage differences, annuities, rents, premiums, royalties and other profits or gains. Special provisions impose tax on gains from share redemption, bond-washing, waiver of debts, stock options and fringe benefits of employees. Non-capital business expense of obtaining income is deductible, including depreciation at fixed rates on cost of business assets, interest and linkage differences on business loans. Deduction of travel and entertainment expense is restricted.

Capital and revenue expense on approved research projects in industry, agriculture, transport or energy allowed as deduction from tax year 1981. If project not approved, expense allowed in three equal annual instalments from year of outlay.

For tax year 1980, 10% of chargeable income allowed as special inflation deduction. Special inflation deduction extended to tax year 1981 with minimum 10% and maximum 50% of inventories not exceeding 15% of chargeable income. For tax years 1982, 1983, 1984, 1985 see Income Tax Law (Taxation in Inflationary Conditions) 5732–1982. *Note:* Amending legislation for tax year 1986 is under discussion.

All businesses and professions are required to keep accounts in accordance with rules. Noncompliance involves penalties and loss of tax benefits under law.

Individuals pay tax on chargeable income at progressive rates, i.e.: 25% (earned or rental income), 35%, 45%, 50%, 60%. Amounts charged at each rate are adjusted periodically for index changes. Surtax of 8.1/3% is imposed on tax due on income other than employment income for tax year 1985. Reduced rates may be charged on pay for shift work in industry. Tax credits are allowed for resident taxpayer and wife. Additional credits allowed for new immigrants and for soldiers entering industry or agriculture at end of compulsory military service. Child allowances now given as cash grants by National Insurance. These grants are exempt from tax except where taxpayer entitled to allowances for no more than three children and whose income is liable to tax at 45% rate or more (as from 1/6/85). Parent not entitled to credit as married person, but supporting child under 20 is entitled to tax credit in addition to grant. Credit of 10% of chargeable income allowed for Eilat resident from tax on income from employment in Eilat. (See topic Foreign Trade Regulations, subhead Free Trade Zone.)

Tax credit of 35% is allowed for donations to recognized charitable bodies, subject to ceiling of lower of 25% of chargeable income or NIS. 10,000, or together with Research and Research Investment deductions (see below) 45% of chargeable income before Research Investment deduction. As to companies and cooperative societies, see below.

Exemptions.—The following persons and institutions are exempt from income tax either totally or partially: municipal and local councils; public institutions for promotion of religion, charity, education and charitable trusts; pension funds: cooperative societies not deriving their income from nonmembers; blind persons in respect of earned income not exceeding NIS. 7,500 for tax year 1985, subject to three monthly index adjustments;diplomatic representatives and consular officers in regular service of foreign states in respect of salaries and emoluments payable for such services; members of Knesset (Israel Legislature) in respect of salaries and emoluments (there is no similar exemption relating to ministers); war invalids, victims of hostile action or Nazi persecution and dependents of deceased members of fighting services in respect of pensions payable by government; temporary resident in respect of income derived from property abroad, provided he did not reside in Israel for more than six months in year preceding to year of assessment and does not intend to stay permanently in country; linkage differences received by individuals on sale of assets, compensation on expropriation of land, cancellation of sale of assets, claims for damages, private loans to another individual, provided such linkage differences are not liable as trade or professional income; linkage differences on Government loans not held for trading; nonbusiness exchange differences on individual's foreign currency deposits if not business income; on loan from nonresident, in company if majority of shares in foreign currency held by nonresidents; on foreign currency deposits of payments by nonresidents on account of share purchases; income of nonresident from employment in Israel is exempt for limited period usually six months if earnings taxed in country of residence and Double Taxation Treaty so provides; new residents in respect of income received from abroad for first seven years of residence; nonresidents in respect of interest on foreign currency term deposits, income from investments in foreign currency in securities quoted on Tel-Aviv Stock Exchange provided investor receives no double taxation relief or if Double Taxation Agreement with investor's country allows "tax-sparing"; income from agriculture in certain defined development areas. See also topic Investment Law.

Regulations under Oil Law 1953 grant income tax benefits including special treatment for exploration expenses and depletion allowances.

Companies Tax.—Corporate bodies pay Company Tax at rate of 40% of chargeable income and Income Tax at rate of 35% of chargeable income after deducting amount paid by way of Company Tax. Total tax accordingly amounts to 61%. Dividends paid are deducted from income chargeable to income tax (see below as to withholding tax).

Special tax benefits are granted as from 1/4/1968 under Law for Encouragement of Industry (Taxes)-1969 to companies owning industrial undertakings. These benefits comprise deductions for accelerated depreciation, amortisation of patent rights and know-how payments, additional depreciation or revised cost base reflecting change in exchange rates 1967-1975, exchange differences on loan repayments, 10% income tax rate on profits reinvested in development. Reduced income tax rate was withdrawn as from tax year 1975 but renewed at 20% from tax year 1978. Further benefits from tax year 1978 include accelerated depreciation for leased equipment, relief for inflationary increases of inventory values, exemption from capital gains on conversion of private company to public company. Corporate groups may submit consolidated balance sheets for income tax purposes, enabling intercompany set off of losses between industrial members of group, but only for year of consolidated return. Company amalgamations, where approved by special committee, may be effected with exemption from all taxes on transfers of assets and/or shares arising out of such amalgamation, and with spread allowance of preamalgamation losses against future profits. Supreme Court has confirmed that noncompliance with accounting rules involves loss of benefits under this Law. Company, shareholders of which are all members of one family, i.e. spouse, brothers, sisters, parents, grandparents, grandchildren and their respective spouses, major shareholder may claim treatment as noncorporate taxpayer. For tax year 1980 20% of capital but not exceeding 15% and not less than 10% of chargeable income allowed as special inflation deduction. For tax year 1981 minimum 10% deduction is allowed but ceiling extended to 50% of inventories and for companies within Law for Encouragement of Industry to 75% of capital or 50% of inventories but not exceeding 25% of chargeable income. For tax years 1982, 1983, 1984 see Income Tax Law (Taxation under Inflationary Conditions) 5732–1982. For 1985 and 1986, see catchline Income Tax Law (Adjustments for Inflation) (Temporary Measure) 1985, infra. Same principles apply but with changes in methods of calculation.

All arrears of tax are charged with interest and linkage differences which are allowed as deductions from income. Interest and linkage differences are allowed on overpayments but treated as chargeable income.

Income Tax Law (Taxation in Inflationary Conditions) 5732–1982.—This complex law, applicable to tax years 1982, 1983 and 1984, provides mechanism for establishing real values of assets, liabilities and capital of business in determining their taxable income. Encouragement of Industry (Taxes) Law 1969 and Income Tax Ordinance have been amended to conform to this Law. For 1985 and 1986, see catchline Income Tax Law (Adjustments for Inflation) (Temporary Measure) 1985, infra. Same principles apply but with changes in methods of calculation.

Main elements of this Law are as follows: In order to compensate for erosion of equity caused by inflation "entitled assessees" are granted deduction from chargeable income up to 50% thereof for tax years 1982, 1983 and 1984. For 1985 and 1986, see catchline Income Tax Law (Adjustments for Inflation) (Temporary Measure) 1985, infra. Same principles apply but with changes in methods of calculation. Entitled assessee is body of persons or partnership, keeping proper double entry accounts on which income tax reports are based. Deduction is amount equal to difference adjusted for cost of living index increase during tax year, between "positive components" and "negative components" in entitled assessee's balance sheet. "Positive components" are total of equity if positive and amounts added thereto during year. "Negative components" are equity if negative, "protected assets" and amounts reducing equity during year. Detailed definitions of each of above "components" are provided in Law. "Protected assets" are generally speaking assets which are not considered to decline in value in inflationary conditions or which enjoy special tax benefits or government assistance. Further points to be noted are as follows: Special deduction of 5% for companies and 30% for individuals; index adjustment of depreciation allowances on protected assets; stocks and shares dealt in on Tel-Aviv Stock Exchange or on any other Stock Exchange approved by Minister of Finance, are "unprotected assets" but increase in their market in each tax year is treated as addition to taxable business income. This addition includes sales proceeds during year. Not applicable to shares in companies in which assessee holds 10% voting interest directly or indirectly. Such shares are regarded as "protected assets"; no inflationary amount allowed on sale of unprotected capital assets and capital assets sold in tax year in which acquired; no accelerated depreciation allowed except under Encouragement of Capital Investment Law 1959; special provisions for financial institutions, insurance companies, assessees keeping books on single entry basis or legally unacceptable double entry basis or failing to keep proper books.

Income Tax Law (Adjustments for Inflation) (Temporary Measure) 1985.— For tax year 1985 changes are introduced in methods of indexation of balance sheet figures to arrive at deduction for inflation, e.g., averaging of closing stock values, indexing of advances from customers and to suppliers, no deduction for Stock Exchange losses until 1986, restriction of deduction for inflation to 90% of index variation of balance sheet capital items and changes during year, special inflationary deduction varying with rate of inflation.

Research Investment.—1983 Law grants tax deduction to taxpayers purchasing convertible debentures or shares (participation units) issued by entitled companies with Government approval to finance scientific research on new or improved products for export. Proceeds of issue are held on dollar linked interest bearing deposit by government until required. Research expenditure out of these deposits is not deductible for income-tax but deposits are included in equity for calculation of deduction under Income Tax Law (Taxation in Inflationary Conditions)—(see above). Entitled companies must export goods produced from results of research of prescribed minimum annual value. If license to manufacture outside Israel is granted minimum royalty is payable to Government.

Sanctions are imposed for noncompliance with conditions for benefits.

Dividends.—Income Tax at the rate of 35% is withheld on payment of dividends if company is registered on Tel Aviv Stock Exchange, otherwise 45% unless lower rate fixed by special law, e.g. see topic Investment Law. 25% is withheld from dividends paid to nonresidents.

Capital Profit Tax.—By 1975 new law basis for calculating this tax has been changed. Briefly, purchase price is divided by cost of living index at time of purchase, and multiplied by cost of living index at time of resale. This is called adjusted purchase price. That part of profit on sale, equal to difference between original and adjusted purchase price is called "inflationary excess" and is taxed at 10% of such difference. Balance of profit on sale is taxed at 61% in case of corporations, and at rate of income tax applicable to an individual according to his total income. Where asset sold was acquired by inheritance after 31/3/81, cost of purchase by deceased is taken for calculating profit on sale. Amounts spent on asset sold as taxes, rates, depreciation and repairs are deductible and brought into calculation of adjusted purchase price after index adjustment. Profit on sale of assets purchased before 1948 is taxed at special rate of 12% and rate increases 1% per year for every year after 1948 and up to 1960. Sales of assets purchased after 1960 are taxed at normal rates as above. This is subject to ceiling rate of 50%. New law applies to all transactions completed after July 7, 1975.

Double Taxation.—Agreements are in force with U.K., Sweden, France, Finland, W. Germany, Denmark, Norway, Austria and Singapore, Holland, Italy, Belgium, Canada and South Africa. Mutual exemption has been agreed with many countries with regard to shipping and aviation profits. Unilateral relief may also be granted in certain circumstances.

Estate Tax.—Repealed in relation to estates of persons deceased after 31/3/81. Capital Profit Tax and Betterment Tax Laws adjusted so that profit on sale of asset inherited after 31/3/81 includes increment accrued during lifetime of deceased. See subhead Capital Profit Tax.

Property Tax.—As from 1/4/81 Property Tax is charged only on market value of land on Oct. 1, preceding year of assessment.

Purchase tax may be applied by the Minister of Finance to certain commodities. It has been applied to a large range of commodities and the usual rate is 35% of the wholesale price. Purchase tax on certain luxury items increased, as of Aug. 21, 1983.

Imports.—Importers required to deposit 15% of cost of goods imported from abroad, from June 1, 1983. On certain goods deposit of 25% or 60% required but latter has been progressively reduced now standing at 24%, and in many cases abolished.

Betterment Tax.—Imposed on sales of land, house property and rights in land. This tax is calculated on substantially same basis as Capital Profit Tax (see above). As from 10/7/78 sale of private dwellings exempted provided owner has not made exempt sale in previous four years.

Value Added Tax (VAT).—This is an entirely new tax in Israel, and is therefore treated more fully. It is imposed in Israel from July 1, 1976, is in nature of sales tax and is charged on all taxable transactions in Israel and on imports to Israel. Taxable transaction includes sale of asset or supply of services by taxable person in course of his business and also sale of asset used by taxable person in course of his business. Taxable person is person who sells asset or supplies services in course of his business. Isolated transactions of commercial nature and any sale of real estate to taxable person other than financial institution or non-profit organization are also included.

Tax is paid by taxable person as percentage of sale price of asset sold or of service supplied and amount of tax is included in invoice given to customer. Customer in his turn may if he himself is taxable person deduct tax included in invoice and paid by him from amount of any tax which he himself has to pay on sales or services supplied by him. If customer is not taxable person he cannot set off tax which he paid at time of purchase or receipt of services against any other VAT.

Rate of tax in force as from July 1, 1985 is 15%. There are number of transactions exempted from tax such as letting of living accommodation for period not exceeding ten years, letting of any property for key money, transactions of business with annual turnover of less than NIS. 2,465 and import of goods exempt from customs duty by virtue of international treaties and import of goods for diplomatic staff insofar as exempt from customs.

Certain other transactions are not charged with tax and are described as "zero-rated." These include goods imported by person entitled to purchase them free of Purchase Tax, e.g. an immigrant, hotel accommodation and services including car-hire supplied to foreign tourists, purchase of air and sea tickets, air and sea transport, sale of specified fruit and vegetables. Where taxable person has effected zero-rated transaction as distinct from an exempt transaction, he is entitled to set off any VAT paid by him in connection with any purchases made or services provided by him in connection with such zero-rated transaction.

Financial institutions such as banks and insurance companies are taxed VAT on different basis, namely on percentage of their income chargeable to tax under the Income Tax Ordinance and also on percentage of total salaries and wages as assessed to income tax. Present rate is 12%. Non-profit organizations are also liable to VAT on amount of salaries and wages paid by them unless such amount is less than NIS. 36.10 annually. Present rate is 5%.

Imported Services Levy.—As from 24/7/84 15% tax is imposed on purchase of foreign currency to pay for services, e.g. purchase of foreign currency allowance for package tours abroad by Israeli resident, payment for rights, presents, emoluments, pensions payable to nonresidents. Exemptions are granted in respect of air and sea transport and insurance of goods imported or exported, reinsurance, forward transactions, purchase of foreign currency by nonresidents provided source of currency is outside Israel. Payments liable to Imported Services Levy are exempt from Value Added Tax.

Employer's Tax.—Employer pays 7% on payroll. Exemption granted to industrial undertakings within Encouragement of Industry (Taxes) 1969 Law, farms, companies where 70% of goods sold are exports of Israel industrial or agricultural products, hotels, housing construction. Tax is paid together with income tax deducted from payroll by employer. Eilat employers exempted in respect of workers employed in Free Trade Zone. (See topic Foreign Trade Regulations, subhead Free Trade Zone.)

Municipal Rates.—Under Municipalities and Local Authorities Ordinances local governments impose tax on buildings and occupied land. Tax is based on area of chargeable assets, location, use and type of building and is payable annually by occupier. Arrears are charged with interest and linkage differences.

Stamp Duty.—A comprehensive system of taxes in the form of a stamp duty is fixed by the Stamp Duty on Documents Law, 1961, which provides for stamps to be affixed on certain classes of documents. Rates of duty are either fixed or ad valorem.

Customs Duty.—Customs are payable in respect of import of commodities subject to substantial list of exempted articles. Duty is either fixed or ad valorem. Many tariffs subject to limitation under General Agreement on Tariffs and Trade with European Economic Community.

Israel has concluded trade and customs agreements with European Economic Community and customs duties are to be progressively reduced on imports from member nations.

Eilat—Free Trade Zone.—By 1985 Law exemption from customs duty, purchase tax, excise, levies and customs deposits on imports from abroad and from Israel, also from V.A.T. except electronic equipment, dishwashers, clothes driers and deep freezers.

TRADEMARKS AND TRADENAMES:

Under Trade Marks Ordinance, trade marks are registered with Registrar of Trade Marks. A trade mark is defined as a mark used upon or in connection with goods for purpose of indicating that they are goods of proprietor of such mark by virtue of manufacture, selection, survey, or dealing with or offering for sale. Trade marks capable of registration must consist of characters, devices or marks or combinations thereof which have a distinctive character. Application for registration is advertised, and opposition may be made within three months of advertisement. Period of duration of trade mark rights is seven years from date of registration, but this period may be renewed for 14 years from expiration of original registration, or of last renewal.

Under Trade Mark Law of 1965, trade mark may be transferred even if goodwill connected therewith is not transferred. Further, licence to use trade mark may be granted by owner of mark. Such licence is subject to registration with Registrar of Trade Marks. In addition, following Lisbon Treaty of 1958, use of name of place of origin with reference to quality may be protected if product originates from such place and its qualitites are connected therewith.

Under Section 11A of Ordinance, introduced in 1965, Registrar may, subject to certain qualifications, allow registration of a mark registered in its country of origin, notwithstanding that it might not otherwise qualify for registration.

Tradenames.—See topic Business Names.

TREATIES:

Civil Procedure.—Israel is party to Convention on Service Abroad of Judicial and Extrajudicial Documents in Civil or Commercial Matters, and to Convention on Taking of Evidence Abroad in Civil or Commercial Matters. (Regulation for the execution of the Hague Convention [Civil Procedure] 1954).

Israel is party to United Nations Convention on Recognition and Enforcement of Foreign Arbitral Awards.

Extradition Treaties.—Israel has signed following bilateral Extradition Treaties: Belgium (1956), Italy (1956), Luxembourg (1956), Netherlands (1956),

France (1958), Switzerland (1958), South Africa (1959), United Kingdom (1960), Austria (1961), U.S.A. (1961), Sweden (1963), Canada (1967), Swaziland (1970).

Double Taxation.—§196 of Income Tax Ordinance empowers Minister of Finance to issue Order giving effect to Treaty made with another State for Relief of Double Taxation, regardless of anything contrary thereto in Ordinance.

Treaties are in force with following countries:

Sweden	—effective 22.12.59 by Order 20.7.61.
Great Britain & N. Ireland	—effective 1.4.61 by Order 25.4.63, revision effective 1.4.68 by Order 18.11.71.
France	—effective 1.4.61 by Order 3.3.66.
Finland	—effective 1.4.65 by Order 12.5.66.
Federal Republic of West Germany	—effective 1.4.61 by Order 19.1.67, revision effective 1.4.70 by Order 26.12.80.
Italy	—effective 1.4.62 by Order 27.6.74.
Denmark	—effective 1.4.65 by Order 20.4.67.
Norway	—effective 1.4.65 by Order 13.6.68.
Austria	—effective 1.4.68 by Order 27.1.72.
Singapore	—effective 1.4.71 by Order 28.5.72.
Holland	—effective 1.4.70 by Order 12.2.75.
Belgium	—effective 1.4.75 by Order 7.7.76.
Canada	—effective 27.7.76 by Order 14.6.77.
South Africa	—effective 27.5.80 by Order 21.5.81.

Customs Duty.—Israel is party to General Agreement on Trade and Tariffs (GATT), and to many Conventions affecting customs duties of which principal ones are Convention concerning creation of International Union for Publication of Customs Tariffs (Brussels) effective 1956, Lisbon Names of Origin Convention effective 1966, Brussels Convention on Nomenclature for Classification of Goods in Customs Tariffs effective 1970, Kyoto Convention for Simplification and Harmonisation of Customs Formalities effective 1977.

Public Documents.—Israel is party to Convention Abolishing the Requirement of Legalisation for Foreign Public Documents.

Trade Agreements.—Israel signed Agreement with European Economic Community in 1970.

Many bilateral treaties affecting aerial and maritime navigation, commerce, tourism, economic, scientific and cultural cooperation have been signed and are published in Official Treaties Gazette.

TRUSTS:

Nature of trusteeship, duties of trustees, formation of private trusts, charitable trusts and public trusts are defined in Law of Trusteeship 1979.

Trusteeship is defined as relationship to asset requiring trustee to hold such asset or act on behalf of beneficiary or for any other object. Trusteeship may be created by law, by agreement with trustee or by deed of charitable trust, which must be in writing signed in presence of notary or created by will in writing, or bequest under will. If trust is of public nature, registration (with Registrar of Trusts) and publication required. Law also provides for creation of companies for advantage of community requiring licence from Minister of Justice, approval as public institution for tax purposes, declaration by court that its objects are charitable; registration is necessary.

Duties of trustees and supervisory powers of courts are referred to in Law generally, but more detailed regulations are laid down for trusteeship in special cases, e.g. under Law of Inheritance, Law of Guardianship and Legal Capacity.

Trust (Mutual Investment Funds).—Mutual Investment Funds Law of 1961 allows establishment of mutual investment funds. It regulates constitution of the fund and its operations and, subject to compliance with provisions of the law, exempts income of the fund from company tax, and the income tax does not exceed 25%. Income derived from the realisation of securities of an approved mutual fund is free from income tax.

WAREHOUSEMEN:

There are no special provisions in regard to warehousemen, except in respect to licensed warehouses approved by the Director of Customs. There are two classes of licensed warehouses, viz., (a) general warehouses to be used for the warehousing of goods generally, and (b) private warehouses to be used only for the warehousing of goods which are the property of the licensee. Licensed warehouses are only warehouses in which dutiable goods may be warehoused prior to the payment of the duty.

General rules as to bailment are now governed by Bailees Law, 1967.

WATER:

Under the Water Law, 1959 the State acquired ownership of all the water resources in the country. The law entitles all persons to use water only in accordance with the provisions of the law. The objects of the law are to preserve water supplies, to prevent their decrease and pollution and to utilise the water resources for development purposes of the country.

WILLS:

Detailed provisions in regard to capacity to make a will and appropriate form of will are now contained in Inheritance Law 1965.

Will may be in writing or may be made verbally. Holograph will need not be attested. Any other written will must be signed by testator in presence of two witnesses at least. Witnesses must confirm execution of will by testator in their joint presence.

Will may be declared or signed before judge or registrar of civil court or before judge of religious court.

There is no limitation on right of disposition by will. Earlier limitations were abolished.

Capacity to make will is determined by law of place of residence of testator at time will is made, but will is valid in form if made in accordance wtih Israeli law or in accordance with law of place where it was made or law of residence of deceased when will was made or at time of his death. When testator is not a resident of Israel, will is valid if it is in accordance with form recognised by national law of deceased.

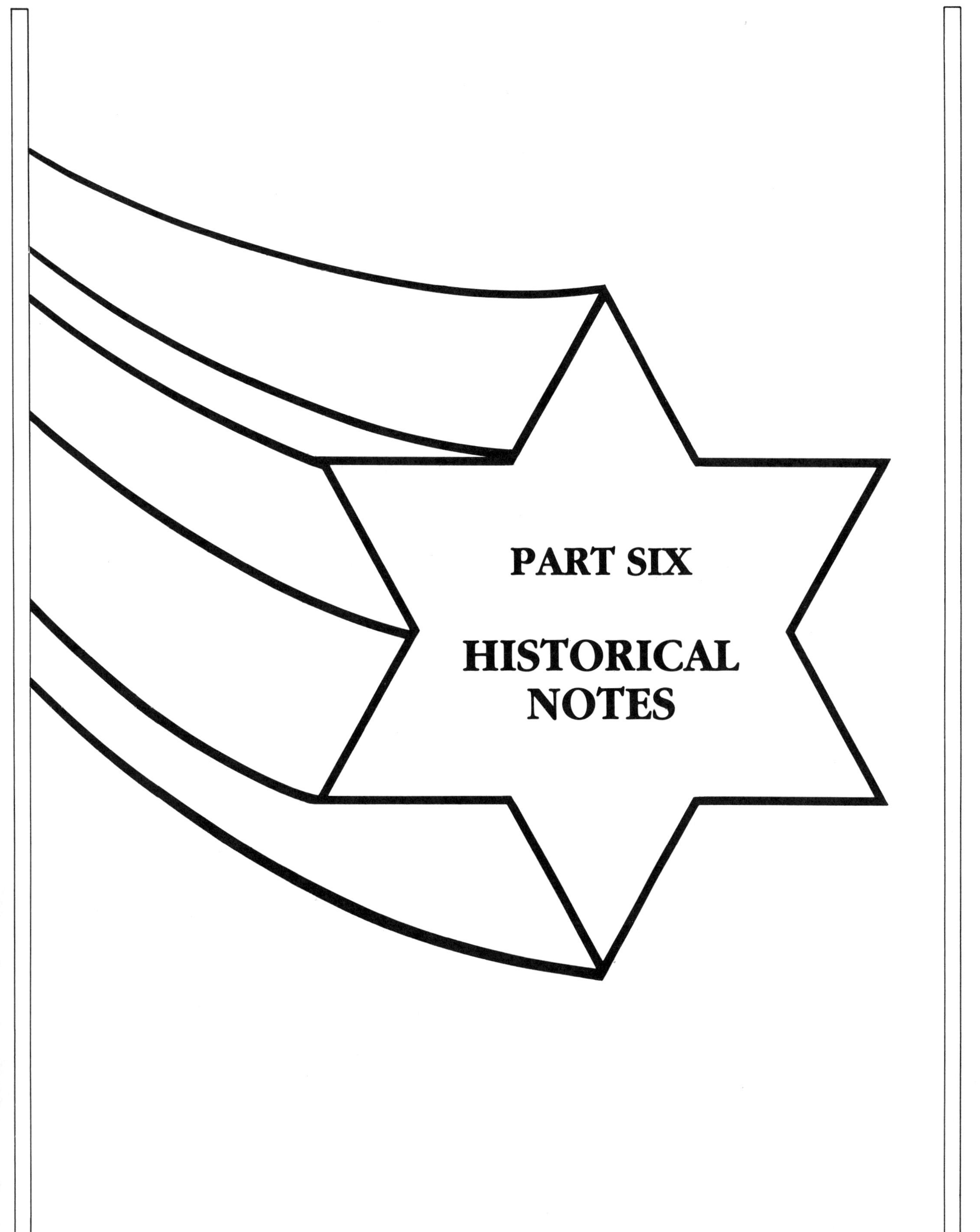
PART SIX
HISTORICAL
NOTES

34

Page One: The State of Israel as Seen in *The New York Times*

"All the News That's Fit to Print"

The New York Times.

LATE CITY EDITION

Cloudy with showers today. Partly cloudy and cooler tomorrow.

Temperatures Yesterday—Max., 64; Min., 47

Sunrise today, 5:46 A. M.; Sunset, 7:59 P. M.

VOL. XCIV..No. 31,881. Entered as Second-Class Matter. Postoffice, New York, N. Y. NEW YORK, TUESDAY, MAY 8, 1945. THREE CENTS IN NEW YORK CITY

THE WAR IN EUROPE IS ENDED! SURRENDER IS UNCONDITIONAL; V-E WILL BE PROCLAIMED TODAY; OUR TROOPS ON OKINAWA GAIN

ISLAND-WIDE DRIVE

Marines Reach Village a Mile From Naha and Army Lines Advance

7 MORE SHIPS SUNK

Search Planes Again Hit Japan's Life Line—Kyushu Bombed

By WARREN MOSCOW

By Wireless to THE NEW YORK TIMES

GUAM, Tuesday, May 8—In an island-wide American advance on Okinawa yesterday the First Marine Division drove south to the edge of Dakeshi Village, about a mile from Naha, the capital, straightening out the line on our right flank. In the center the Seventy-seventh Army Division used flame-throwing tanks for considerable advances, while the Seventh Army Division moved forward on the left flank.

[Airfields on Kyushu, southern Japan, were bombed Monday and Tuesday by Superfortresses, two of which were lost in heavy air opposition.

[Allied fliers started operating from the Tarakan airfield although fighting continued on that island off Borneo, and in the Philippines American troops made advances on Mindanao and Luzon.]

Japanese Dead at 36,535

As the United States forces on Okinawa resumed their drive, Fleet Admiral Chester W. Nimitz revealed that Japanese killed on the island had mounted to 36,535 on Monday, showing that the Americans were maintaining their rate of 1,000 a day.

The Americans have not yet taken the main Japanese artillery emplacements on Okinawa, which were the principal targets of the fleet off the island. The fleet's guns continued yesterday, along with carrier aircraft, to support the ground movements.

Meanwhile search bombers of Fleet Air Wing 1 continued to give an impressive demonstration of what the tightening air blockade of Japan will mean. Attacking at mast-head height with bombs and machine guns, these long-range aircraft, based in the Okinawa area, sank four more ships in waters off Korea and damaged five others.

The ships sunk were a large cargo ship, a medium cargo ship, a medium oiler and a large fleet tanker. Two small freighters were

Continued on Page 12, Column 2

Leopold Rescued By 7th Army Troops

By The Associated Press.

WITH THE UNITED STATES SEVENTH ARMY, Tuesday, May 8—Léopold III, King of Belgium, and his wife, Princess Rethy, have been liberated by the Seventh Army, it was announced today.

They were found near Strobl, eight miles east of Salzburg. The Americans had been told of their whereabouts by civilians.

With the King and his wife were eighteen members of their staff and four children. All were in good health.

Elements of the American 106th Cavalry Group had to overpower German Elite Guards to make the rescue. Seventh Army troops are now closely guarding the royal party.

The Pulitzer Awards For 1944 Announced

The Pulitzer Prize awards announced yesterday by the trustees of Columbia University included: For a distinguished novel, to "A Bell for Adano," by John Hersey; for an original American play of the current season, to "Harvey," by Mary Chase.

Among the newspaper awards were those to Hal Boyle, Associated Press war reporter, for distinguished correspondence; to James B. Reston of THE NEW YORK TIMES for his reporting of the Dumbarton Oaks Security Conference; to Joe Rosenthal, Associated Press photographer, for his photograph of marines raising the American flag at Iwo and to The Detroit Free Press for "distinguished and meritorious public service" in its investigation of legislative corruption at Lansing, Mich.

Further details of the awards will be found on Page 16.

MOLOTOFF HAILS BASIC 'UNANIMITY'

He Stresses Five Points in World Charter, but His View on One Is Questioned

By JAMES B. RESTON

Special to THE NEW YORK TIMES.

SAN FRANCISCO, May 7—The major allies who forced Germany's unconditional surrender have reached "unanimity" on the kind of world security organization which should be created at the United Nations conference to protect their newly won victory, Vyacheslaff M. Molotoff, Russian Foreign Commissar, said today.

While the delegates at the conference celebrated the end of the European war, and three Foreign Ministers, T. V. Soong of China, Paul Henri Spaak of Belgium and Trygve Lie of Norway left the conference to deal with urgent official business elsewhere, Mr. Molotoff told the press that the Soviet Union attached the "greatest importance" to five agreements reached by the heads of the Big Four delegations.

First, he said, these leaders agreed to support the principles of justice, international law, human rights and fundamental freedom for all.

Second, he added, the Big Four agreed not to make provision in the security charter for the revision of treaties.

His statement on this point was ambiguous and led to some speculation as to the unanimity of all four on the question.

Revision Power Called Danger

A reference in the United Nations charter to the necessity of revising treaties, Mr. Molotoff stated, "would play into the hands of enemy countries, which would certainly like to undermine and emasculate these treaties." Furthermore, he declared, to give the new League of Nations authority to consider revision of treaties would be a violation of national sovereign rights, which are guaranteed in the Dumbarton Oaks Charter.

For these reasons, he concluded, "the idea of revising treaties was rejected as untenable."

Third, Mr. Molotoff said, it was agreed among the Big Four that treaties directed against Germany, such as Russia's twenty-year alliances with Britain, France, Czechoslovakia, Yugoslavia and the Warsaw Poles, "should remain in force until such time as the Government concerned felt that the international security organization was really in a position to undertake the accomplishment of the tasks of

Continued on Page 15, Column 2

GERMANY SURRENDERS: NEW YORKERS MASSED UNDER SYMBOL OF LIBERTY

Thousands filling Times Square in spontaneous celebration yesterday

The New York Times

PRAGUE SAYS FOES ACCEPT SURRENDER

Czechoslovak Radio Reports All Fighting in Bohemia Will Be Ended Today

By The Associated Press.

LONDON, Tuesday, May 8—The Czechoslovak-controlled Prague radio announced today that the Germans in Prague and throughout Bohemia, a last major holdout pocket of German resistance, had accepted unconditional surrender.

The announcement came as the United States Third Army was reported to have advanced to the outskirts of the Czechoslovak capital, and three Russian armies hammered toward the same goal from the east and north.

"The German military plenipotentiary is negotiating with the Czechoslovak National Council on the modalities of unconditional surrender," said the broadcast, detailing what purported to be the

Continued on Page 11, Column 2

Wild Crowds Greet News In City While Others Pray

By FRANK S. ADAMS

New York City's millions reacted in two sharply contrasting ways yesterday to the news of the unconditional surrender of the German armies. A large and noisy minority greeted it with the turbulent enthusiasm of New Year's Eve and Election Night rolled into one. However, the great bulk of the city's population responded with quiet thanksgiving that the war in Europe was won, tempered by the realization that a grim and bitter struggle still was ahead in the Pacific and the fact that the nation is still in mourning for its fallen President and Commander in Chief.

Times Square, the financial section and the garment district were thronged from mid-morning on with wildly jubilant celebrators who tooted horns, staged impromptu parades and filled the canyons between the skyscrapers with fluttering scraps of paper. Elsewhere in the metropolitan area, however, war plants continued to hum, schools, offices and factories carried on their normal activities, and residential areas were calmly joyful.

One factor that helped to dampen the celebration was the bewilderment of large segments of the population at the absence of an official proclamation to back up the news contained in flaring headlines and radio bulletins. With the premature rumor of ten days ago fresh in everyone's mind, and millions still mindful of the false armistice of 1918, there was widespread skepticism over the authenticity of the news.

By mid-afternoon loudspeakers were blaring into the ears of the exulting thousands in the amusement district the news that President Truman's proclamation was being held up by the necessity of coordinating it with the announcements from London and Moscow, and that the formal celebration of the long-awaited V-E Day would be delayed until today.

This sobering note gradually

Continued on Page 7, Column 6

SHAEF BAN ON AP LIFTED IN 6 HOURS

Action Comes After Protests From Newspapers and Public—Writer Still Barred

Suspension of filing facilities of The Associated Press in the European theatre was clamped on by Supreme Headquarters, Allied Expeditionary Forces (SHAEF), yesterday in an unprecedented action and was lifted six hours and twenty minutes later.

The ban was continued, however, on all copy submitted for clearance by Edward Kennedy, chief of the press association's staff on the Western Front, who sent the momentous story announcing Germany's final surrender in a dispatch from Reims, France, which was received in New York over the AP wires at 9:35 A. M. (EWT).

It was not until seven hours and fifty-five minutes had elapsed aft-

Continued on Page 4, Column 2

Summary of News of the War and German Surrender

TUESDAY, MAY 8, 1945

The war ended in Europe yesterday after five years, eight months and six days of the bloodiest conflict in history. Grand Admiral Karl Doenitz surrendered unconditonally to the Allies in a little red schoolhouse at Reims, France. At 8:41 P. M. Sunday, New York time, Col. Gen. Gustav Jodl signed for the enemy and Lieut. Gen. Walter Bedell Smith, General Eisenhower's Chief of Staff, for the Allies. In the absence of any official announcement there was some confusion as to the compliance with the surrender. Fighting had been going on in Czechoslovakia and nothing had been heard from German pockets along the French coast. [1:7-8.]

President Truman planned a broadcast from the White House at 9 o'clock this morning. Washington, gratified that the war in Europe was over, was confused by lack of confirmation. [2:2.]

Prime Minister Churchill will also broadcast at 9 A. M. from London and Premier Stalin is expected to make a simultaneous announcement in Moscow. King George will talk over the radio six hours later. [2:8.] London will celebrate V-E Day today, but, unable to restrain its joy, staged many impromptu celebrations yesterday. [2:7.]

Most New Yorkers took the news calmly and thankfully, sobered by realization that the war in the Pacific was far from over. There were, however, noisy outbursts in such centers as Times Square and Wall Street. Scrap paper showers fluttered from roofs and windows. [1:4-5.]

German Foreign Minister Lutz Schwerin von Krosigk broke the news to his people. The future will be difficult, he warned, and then added: "We must make right the basis of our nation. In our nation justice shall be the supreme law and the guiding principle. We must also recognize law as the basis of all relations between the nations." This sudden, complete reversal in German policy was received with skepticism by the Allies. [3:1.]

Perhaps one reason for this was the announcement from Moscow that 4,000,000 men, women and children had been done to death by gas, shooting, famine, poisoning and torture in the German extermination camp at Oswiecim, Poland. [12:5.]

The actual situation in Czechoslovakia was obscure. Late last night a Patriot broadcast said the Germans were negotiating with the Czechoslovak National Council details of surrender in Prague [illegible]. Fighting had continued throughout yesterday and German planes had bombed public buildings and hospitals. [1:3; map P. 11.].

The United States Third Army continued its general advance into Czechoslovakia and the Fifth and Seventh Armies joined again in the Alps. The British Second Army moved to Denmark and Poles entered the shattered port of Wilhelmshaven. [11:1.] Breslau fell to the Red Army after an eighty-four-day siege; 40,000 Germans were captured. [11:5.]

Japan accepted the surrender of her Axis partner with a statement that she never had expected German aid and would go on to victory without the Reich. [13:1.]

Infantry and marines on Okinawa scored another general advance after naval bombardment had pulverized Japanese strong points. Pacific Fleet planes sank or damaged thirteen more ships off Korea and Japan. [1:1; map, P. 12.] B-29's maintained their assault on Kyushu airfields. Two of the big planes were shot down. [14:3-4.]

On Tarakan Allied troops were within a mile and a half of the eastern shore. Americans gained on Mindanao and Luzon in the Philippines. [13:3-4.]

Foreign Commissar Molotoff said in San Francisco that unanimity on amendments to Dumbarton Oaks assured success of the conference. He declared that the Big Four consultations had ended. [1:2.]

GERMANS CAPITULATE ON ALL FRONTS

American, Russian and French Generals Accept Surrender in Eisenhower Headquarters, a Reims School

REICH CHIEF OF STAFF ASKS FOR MERCY

Doenitz Orders All Military Forces of Germany To Drop Arms—Troops in Norway Give Up—Churchill and Truman on Radio Today

By EDWARD KENNEDY

Associated Press Correspondent

REIMS, France, May 7—Germany surrendered unconditionally to the Western Allies and the Soviet Union at 2:41 A. M. French time today. [This was at 8:41 P. M., Eastern Wartime Sunday.]

The surrender took place at a little red schoolhouse that is the headquarters of Gen. Dwight D. Eisenhower.

The surrender, which brought the war in Europe to a formal end after five years, eight months and six days of bloodshed and destruction, was signed for Germany by Col. Gen. Gustav Jodl. General Jodl is the new Chief of Staff of the German Army.

The surrender was signed for the Supreme Allied Command by Lieut. Gen. Walter Bedell Smith, Chief of Staff for General Eisenhower.

It was also signed by Gen. Ivan Susloparoff for the Soviet Union and by Gen. Francois Sevez for France.

[The official Allied announcement will be made at 9 o'clock Tuesday morning when President Truman will broadcast a statement and Prime Minister Churchill will issue a V-E Day proclamation. Gen. Charles de Gaulle also will address the French at the same time.]

General Eisenhower was not present at the signing, but immediately afterward General Jodl and his fellow delegate, Gen. Admiral Hans Georg Friedeburg, were received by the Supreme Commander.

Germans Say They Understand Terms

They were asked sternly if they understood the surrender terms imposed upon Germany and if they would be carried out by Germany.

They answered Yes.

Germany, which began the war with a ruthless attack upon Poland, followed by successive aggressions and brutality in internment camps, surrendered with an appeal to the victors for mercy toward the German people and armed forces.

After having signed the full surrender, General Jodl said he wanted to speak and received leave to do so.

"With this signature," he said in soft-spoken German, "the German people and armed forces are for better or worse delivered into the victors' hands.

"In this war, which has lasted more than five years, both have achieved and suffered more than perhaps any other people in the world."

LONDON, May 7 (AP)—Complete victory in

Continued on Page 3, Columns 2 and 3

"All the News That's Fit to Print"

The New York Times.

LATE CITY EDITION
Partly cloudy and mild today. Occasional showers tomorrow.
Temperatures Yesterday—Max., 64; Min., 41
Sunrise today, 5:54 A. M.; Sunset, 7:51 P. M.
Full U. S. Weather Bureau Report, Page 51

VOL. XCV..No. 32,239. Entered as Second-Class Matter, Postoffice, New York, N. Y. NEW YORK, WEDNESDAY, MAY 1, 1946. THREE CENTS IN NEW YORK CITY

JOINT PALESTINE BODY BARS A JEWISH STATE, BUT URGES ENTRY OF 100,000 REFUGEES

Arabs 'Outraged' by Report; Jews Are Far From Satisfied

Rival Agencies Reiterate Their Arguments —U. S., British Talks Are Forecast on Easing Burden Too Big for London

By HERBERT L. MATTHEWS

By Wireless to The New York Times.

LONDON, April 30—Now that the report of the Anglo-American Committee of Inquiry on Palestine has been published, one can safely predict tonight that the next step will be for the British to consult the United States Government about it. The British have reached the point at which they consider that Palestine is far too great a burden for them to be forced to handle alone.

No Government spokesman would say anything about the report tonight because the Cabinet and other officials have not had time to study it. One must keep in mind that the members of the committee had a mandate only to make recommendations, which do not in any sense involve Governmental responsibility.

The Arab Office in London has lost no time in issuing a scorching statement condemning the report lock, stock and barrel. The Jewish Agency for Palestine gave the report a mixed reception. It was happy about the proposal to allow 100,000 Jewish refugees to enter Palestine but asserted that without the formation of a Jewish state there could be no solution to the problem of homeless Jews.

On all sides one hears dubious comment about the fact that the committee's report makes no suggestion in terms of any sort of finality nor does it even offer any kind of long-term solution to the Palestinian problem. It is feared that even moderate elements among the Arabs will be more disturbed about that feature of the report than any other.

In their present mood of shocked disgust over the murder of seven British soldiers in Tel Aviv last Thursday the British are inclined to place the most prominence on that part of the report dealing with security and with making it clear that violence and terrorism will be resolutely repressed. The state-

Continued on Page 14, Column 5

TRUMAN FOR ACTION

Inquiry Upholds His Visa Proposal, Urges End of White Paper

WOULD GUARD ARAB RIGHTS

Report for Change in Holy Land Property Curbs—Demands a Firm Stand on Violence

The text of the report of the Anglo-American Committee of Inquiry on Palestine, Pages 15 to 21, inclusive.

By FELIX BELAIR JR.

Special to The New York Times.

WASHINGTON, April 30—The Anglo-American Committee of Inquiry on problems of Jews in Europe and Palestine, reporting to the two Governments today on its four-month investigation, urged the admission of 100,000 European Jews into the Holy Land as soon as possible, but flatly rejected the idea of a Jewish state, together with Arab claims for dominance. It asserted Christendom's own interest in the area.

Released simultaneously for publication in Washington and London, the report drew from President Truman an expression of satisfaction that his proposal for the admission of 100,000 Jews into Palestine had been recommended. He added that "the transference of these unfortunate people should now be accomplished with the greatest dispatch."

The President declared it significant that the report aimed at guarantees for Arab civil and religious rights and urged measures to improve Arab cultural, educational and economic position.

Land Changes Asked

"I am also pleased," he said, "that the committee recommends, in effect, the abrogation of the White Paper of 1939."

The report repudiated the 1939 White Paper principles, which made further Jewish immigration dependent on Arab consent and banned Jewish land purchases in a major part of Palestine.

Dependent for its final effect on adoption by both Governments, the report covered a wide range of controversial subjects on which President Truman gave no hint of his attitude except to say that he was taking them under advisement.

However, Mr. Truman seemed to have embraced the major policy statement rejecting "once and for all the exclusive claims of Jews and Arabs to Palestine," which the committee enunciated as follows:

"(I. That Jew shall not dominate Arab and Arab shall not dominate Jew in Palestine. (II) That Palestine shall be neither a Jewish state nor an Arab state. (III) That the form of government ultimately to be established shall, under international guarantees, fully protect and preserve the interests in the Holy Land of Christendom and of the Moslem and Jewish faiths."

Stress on Unique Status

With deliberate emphasis, the Committee of Inquiry declared that "Palestine is a Holy Land, sacred to Christian, to Jew and to Moslem alike; and because it is a holy land, Palestine is not, and can never become, a land which any race or religion can justly claim as its very own."

With equal emphasis, the committee said the same considerations set Palestine apart from other lands, and dedicated it to the precepts and practices of the brotherhood of man rather than to those of narrow nationalism.

The 42,000-word report was signed in Lausanne, Switzerland, by Judge Joseph C. Hutcheson, United States chairman, Sir John E. Singleton, British chairman, Frank Aydelotte, Frank W. Buxton, Bartley C. Crum, James G. McDonald and William Phillips, American members, and W. F. Crick, R. H. S. Crossman, Frederick Leggett, R. E. Manningham-Buller and M. Morrison for Britain.

For the immediate future the

Continued on Page 14, Column 2

WARSHIP BLOWS UP AT MUNITIONS PIER IN PORT, KILLING 5

60 on Escort Vessel Injured —Blasts Shake New Jersey Towns Near Big Depot

BOMBS ASHORE SET OFF

Sailor Is Only Slightly Hurt as Depth Charge Explodes as He Is Carrying It

By MEYER BERGER

Special to The New York Times.

LEONARDO, N. J., April 30—One officer and four sailors of the destroyer escort Solar's complement of fourteen officers and 136 enlisted men vanished utterly before noon today in an ammunition explosion that tore away one-third of the 306-foot ship's forward structure.

About sixty of the ship's crew were injured, but only thirty-five were hospitalized, and of them only a handful remained tonight for further treatment. The Navy withheld the names of the five missing men and the names of the injured because not all their families had been officially notified.

The explosion happened as the Solar's crew was unloading her ammunition supply in preparation for an overhaul. Normally she carries about fifteen tons of assorted ammunition, including depth bombs and smaller charges, torpedoes and shells for her cannon. Only one-third of this amount was still aboard when the blast occurred.

Tons of Explosives Near By

Near by, when the detonation shook the New Jersey coast in and around the Raritan Bay district, were a number of other vessels preparing to unload ammunition. It was unofficially estimated here that these vessels held, all told, about 25,000 tons of explosives. Tugs dragged these craft out of the danger zone.

Burning fragments from the Solar, hurled at tremendous force against freight cars on the pier, started other explosions. One car in a freight string, filled chiefly with depth charges, blew up and all but vanished in dust and smoke, scattering its parts in all directions. Three strings of cars were hauled shoreward by their locomotive crews, at great risk.

No one seemed certain tonight what had caused the explosion, but what seemed like a possible explanation came from Jack Horne, fireman second class, of Charlotte, N. C. He thought a piece of ammunition carried by Joseph Stuchinski, seaman, of Baltimore, might have done it.

"Ski," the fireman said, "was carrying a 'hedgehog' from the forward magazine. While he was holding it, it just went off. He must have bumped it against something, because those things go off when anything touches them."

Seaman Stuchinski, oddly enough, was not seriously injured. He was deafened, a few minor scratches showed on his chest when he got to the first-aid station and his dungarees were split.

"It went off. The thing just went off," he said.

The "hedgehog" Stuchinski carried was an anti-submarine depth charge. Metal-cased, weighing about sixty pounds, it is generally cylindrical, about thirty inches long and between four and five inches in diameter.

Bow Like Elephant's Trunk

The Solar lay at the northern, or bay end, of the easternmost of the three great piers that jut out from the Navy's Earle Ammunition Depot, when she blew up. She was approximately one and one-half miles from the beach end of the depot. The blast curled her bow in much the same shape as an elephant's back-bent trunk.

The concussion was felt twenty to thirty miles around. The detonation rushed across Raritan Bay to shake homes in Tottenville, Richmond Valley, Pleasant Plains, Prince's Bay, Great Kills, Oakwood and New Dorp, all on Staten Island, and shattered panes in some of those communities.

Ground tremors were felt to the west and to the southwest. There were some freakish effects. Residents in Middletown Township, including Rumson, Fair Haven, Red Bank and Little Silver, for example, felt certain the explosion was local. Several frightened housewives called the police to say, "The boiler just blew up in my cellar."

Dogs raced away from the beach

Continued on Page 3, Column 3

AFTER EXPLOSIONS RIPPED DESTROYER ESCORT

The wrecked U. S. S. Solar at the Navy Ammunition Depot in Earle, N. J., yesterday

The New York Times (U. S. Navy)

BIG FOUR RULE OUT AUSTRIA'S DEMAND FOR SOUTH TYROL

Paris Conference Rejects Any Major Frontier Revision in That Region of Italy

NO PROGRESS ON TRIESTE

Rome and Belgrade Are Asked to Send Delegates—Report of Experts Confusing

By C. L. SULZBERGER

By Cable to The New York Times.

PARIS, April 30—Italy's retention of most of the Province of Bolzano [South Tyrol], which is claimed by Austria, was virtually assured tonight after the Council of Foreign Ministers had agreed that no requests for a major frontier change would be accepted in that area so valuable in hydroelectric power.

At the same time, after examining a verbose and confused report on Trieste and Venezia Giulia, submitted at long last by the special commission sent by the Foreign Ministers' deputies to investigate the Italian-Yugoslav border area, the Ministers agreed to invite the Yugoslav and Italian Governments to send delegates here on Friday to present once again their views on this hotly disputed and vitally important region.

The report showed a complete divergence in opinion between the Soviet investigator and the three other participants on the value of a census taken in 1945 by a Yugoslav, Professor Rodlich. The Soviet member of the commission said the census was fine and the three others said it was just the opposite. Since this census is of vital importance in deciding the ethnic basis for a decision, that leaves everything up in the air.

Suggested by Molotov

The move to widen the scope of the Foreign Ministers' meeting by inviting in the Italians and Yugoslavs was suggested by Vyacheslav M. Molotov. The Soviet Foreign Minister recalled that the Potsdam decisions, the "bible" under which the peace treaties are being drafted, provided that the interested parties should be included when necessary. Thus, the doors have been opened to permit entry of those delegations—Greek, Italian, Yugoslav, Hungarian and Bulgarian—now clamoring for a

Continued on Page 4, Column 2

BAN BY MUSICIANS BLOW TO TELEVISION

Petrillo Plans to Prolong the Refusal of Union Men to the Industry Indefinitely

By JACK GOULD

The American Federation of Musicians, headed by James C. Petrillo, plans to forbid its members to work in television until some indefinite date in the future when the union can determine the effects of video's advent on present-day radio, it was learned yesterday.

Television broadcasters were agreed that Mr. Petrillo's stand would retard the immediate development of video programs, since it could be a matter of months if not years before anyone could determine to what extent television would supplant or complement sound broadcasting.

Use of "live" musicians was first denied the television industry in February, 1945, by the international executive board of the federation, but yesterday was the first time that Mr. Petrillo explained the action and indicated that the ban would be of prolonged duration.

Musical Films Already Banned

Last week Mr. Petrillo's union and the Hollywood motion picture producers entered into an agreement not to permit films containing music to be used in television, a move leaving the telecasters with only records as a possible source of music. Beginning July 1, under a rule of the Federal Communications Commission, the television stations are scheduled to offer twenty-eight hours of programs a week, but under Mr. Petrillo's edicts they will be forced to rely primarily on talks, sporting events and other non-musical fare.

Coincidentally with stating the union's position on television, Mr. Petrillo also reiterated his stand against permitting standard radio programs containing music to be presented simultaneously on frequency modulation outlets. The union is insisting on double crews of musicians in the event of such duplication.

The re-statement of the union's views on FM were regarded with

Continued on Page 28, Column 2

Stalin Warns of War Plot By 'International Reaction'

By The Associated Press.

LONDON, April 30—Generalissimo Stalin promised tonight that the Soviet Union would be true to a policy of peace and security but charged that what he described as "international reaction" was "hatching plans of a new war." In an order of the day broadcast by the Moscow radio the Russian leader also declared that it was necessary to be constantly vigilant, "to protect as the apple of one's eye the armed forces and defensive power of our country."

TEXT OF STALIN ORDER

His broadcast order, issued in connection with the Soviet Union's May Day celebration, was heard in London by the Soviet monitor, who issued the following text:

Comrades, Red Army and Red Navy men, sergeants and petty officers, comrade officers, generals and admirals, working people of the Soviet Union:

Today, for the first time since the victorious termination of the Great Patriotic War we celebrate May 1—the international holiday of working people—in conditions of peaceful life, won in a hard struggle against the enemies at the cost of heavy sacrifices and privations.

One year ago the Red Army hoisted the banner of victory over Berlin and completed the defeat of fascist Germany. Within four months after the victorious termination of the war against Germany, imperialist Japan downed her arms. The Second World War, prepared by the forces of international reaction and unleashed by the chief fascist states, ended in a full victory of the freedom-loving nations. The smashup and liquidation of the main hotbeds of fascism and world aggression resulted in changes in the political life of the nations of the world, in a wide growth of the democratic movement of the nations.

Taught by the experience of war, the popular masses realized that the destinies of states cannot be entrusted to reactionary leaders, who pursue the narrow caste and selfish anti-popular aims. It is for this reason that nations, which no longer wish to live in the old way, take destinies of their states into their own hands, establish democratic order and actively fight against the forces of reaction, against instigators of a new war. The nations of the

Continued on Page 5, Column 4

INQUIRY FINDS 'PERIL' TO SECRETS OF WAR

Senators Hear Radar Makers on Russian Buying and Urge Law Tightening

By C. P. TRUSSELL

Special to The New York Times.

WASHINGTON, April 30—Need for a tightening of the laws to provide protection for wartime secrets in the electronics and other fields was declared by Senate investigators today to be "very definite." The statement came after a closed-session inquiry into negotiations for sales of radar and similar equipment to Russia.

Members of a special Senate Judiciary subcommittee, conducting the investigation, said that there was no evidence that "classified,"

Continued on Page 3, Column 4

Truman Said to Plan Start Of Jewish Entry 'Forthwith'

By LAWRENCE RESNER

Bartley C. Crum, one of the six United States members of the Joint Anglo-American Committee of Inquiry on Palestine, predicted here yesterday, on the basis of a discussion he had with President Truman at the White House on Monday, that the directives authorizing the admission of 100,000 European Jews into Palestine would "issue forthwith."

Mr. Crum, a San Francisco lawyer, also expressed the belief that most Jewish groups would endorse the affirmative aspects of the report, although reserving their right to continue a fight for the achievement of their ideological tenets, principally a Jewish state.

An immediate endorsement of the recommendation to obtain the admission of the 100,000 European Jews came from Joseph M. Proskauer, president of the American Jewish Committee, who said the provisions for immediate action were "obviously based on the highest considerations of statesmanship and humanity."

The World Zionist Emergency Council, which speaks for some of the largest and most active Zionist groups in the United States, said a statement outlining its position probably would be issued today, after the report had been studied.

The initial negative response by a Jewish group came from the Political Action Committee for Palestine, whose executive vice chairman, Dr. Baruch Korff, said that despite "the report's few fine points, the commission had proved

Continued on Page 13, Column 4

U. N.'S SPAIN INQUIRY COMMENCES TODAY

5-Man Subcommittee to Meet Here in Secret—No Outside Witnesses at First Session

By W. H. LAWRENCE

The Franco regime in Spain goes on trial today on charges that it is a cause of international friction and a threat to world peace.

Meeting privately at 3 P. M., representatives of Australia, China, France, Poland and Brazil will set in motion the first formal investigation by the United Nations, authorized Monday by a 10-to-0 vote of the Security Council, in which Russia did not participate but refrained from exercising an asserted right to veto the inquiry.

How, where and when the Council subcommittee will function presumably will be decided in the early part of today's meeting, and the members then will turn to analyzing the evidence now before them, listing the specific charges

Continued on Page 7, Column 5

World News Summarized

WEDNESDAY, MAY 1, 1946

Palestine should become neither a Jewish state nor an Arab state, the Anglo-American Committee of Inquiry declared in its report made public simultaneously last night in Washington and London. Admission of 100,000 Jews this year and virtual abrogation of the 1939 British White Paper with its restrictions on land holdings were recommended. Other suggestions included continuation of the present mandate until establishment of a United Nations trusteeship and resolute suppression of violence and terrorism by Jews or Arabs. [1:8.]

Although President Truman expressed pleasure over certain parts of the report, it was felt in Washington that neither the Jews nor Arabs would be satisfied. [13:1.] In fact, Arab leaders threatened to combat any additional Jewish immigration [13:3] and Zionists expressed their opposition. Bartley C. Crum, a member of the committee, predicted that a directive authorizing the entry of 100,000 Jews into Palestine would "issue forthwith." [1:6-7.]

British reaction counted heavily upon American support in whatever was done, but regretted the absence of any long-term solution. [1:6-7.]

Italy will be permitted to retain most of southern Tyrol despite Austrian claims, the Foreign Ministers tentatively agreed at their conference in Paris, but they were as wide apart as ever on what to do about Trieste and the Venezia Giulia area. It was decided to invite Yugoslavia and Italy to present their cases anew. [1:5.]

Britain tried to meet French desires by suggesting internationalization of either the Ruhr or both the Ruhr and the left bank of the Rhine for fifty years. [3:1.] Secretary Byrnes' proposed four-power treaty to keep Germany disarmed was favorably received in the Senate Foreign Affairs Committee. [3:8.]

The United Nations Security Council subcommittee opens its investigation into Franco Spain this afternoon. [1:7.] Europe's ruined industries should be restored before attempts to eradicate world unemployment, the Economic and Employment Commission heard [8:5], while the Transport and Communications Commission debated the relative merits of free enterprise and government control of shipping. [7:1.] The Commission on Human Rights may seek a new international bill of rights with authority to supervise its implementation. [8:2.]

Tabriz, capital of Azerbaijan, has been formally evacuated by Russian troops, the Tabriz radio reported. [3:6.] Premier Stalin declared that, while the world must remain vigilant against reaction, it had "no reason to doubt" that Russia would remain steadfast in her devotion to international peace and security. [1:3-4.]

Japan was shocked at the plot to assassinate General MacArthur and the Government offered its apologies. No arrests have been announced. [1:6-7.]

Ammunition being unloaded from the destroyer-escort Solar in Raritan Bay exploded, killing an officer and four sailors. [1:1.]

John L. Lewis served notice that anthracite miners intended to strike on May 31 unless they obtained the same demands that led to the soft-coal strike. Negotiations will start in New York on May 10. No progress was made toward settling the bituminous dispute. [29:1.]

Further restrictions were placed on the use of grain by distillers in order to make more food available for world famine relief. [1:2-3.]

General Motors was authorized by the OPA to raise prices on its cars from $16 to $60 to cover wage increases. [27:6-7.] House members returned to Washington still opposed to extending price control without heavy restrictions. [30:5.]

Sharp Restrictions in Distilling Ordered in Food Conservation

By CHARLES E. EGAN

Special to The New York Times.

WASHINGTON, April 30—World famine is more than a short term problem, and plans to meet its reappearance next winter should be drafted immediately, Chester C. Davis, chairman of the President's Special Famine Emergency Committee, asserted today.

Mr. Davis, who conferred with President Truman, later said that emergency measures, taken to insure larger relief shipment of grains and other foods to famine-stricken areas in the next few weeks, could not be considered as final, but were merely "the first sprint" in a continuing race to avert death for millions who otherwise would starve.

Meanwhile, Secretary Anderson issued an order which operated for five days at full mashing capacity in April to three capacity days in May.

The order also limited the use of grain by the entire distilling industry to 2,500,000 bushels a month, instead of wheat in the manufacture of spirits and restricted distillers to the use of corn which is unsuitable for human consumption.

In January, distillers were permitted ten capacity mashing days, but were cut to seven and one-half in February and to five days in March and April.

Brewers, operating on a 30 per cent reduction of grain, were not included in today's order.

"Every report coming before us makes it plain that the present famine is not a short run emergency that ends on July 1," Mr. Davis' statement said, adding:

"The present food shortages have been seriously aggravated by drought in many parts of the world, but even with good weather the wartime destruction of agricultural facilities will be felt for a long time.

"Farm animals and farm machinery have been destroyed. The strength of farm workers had

MacArthur Plot Alarms Japanese; They See Possible Repercussions

By The Associated Press.

TOKYO, April 30—News of a frustrated assassination plot against General Douglas MacArthur tonight shocked the Japanese.

Their first reaction was twofold: A feeling that their country had lost face; fears that repercussions might be felt in every household.

The Government officially apologized. Katsuo Okazaki, representing Foreign Minister Shigeru Yoshida, visited General MacArthur's office two hours after Allied Headquarters had announced discovery of the plot. He did not see the general personally, but delivered a verbal message to aides.

Mr. Okazaki expressed "deep regret and concern" and said his Government was "greatly embarrassed." He asked if there was anything his Government could do.

Earlier, Premier Kijuro Shidehara, Mr. Yoshida and Home Minister Chuzo Mitsuchi conferred.

Japanese reporters speculated that they discussed tighter precautions than previously were planned for the May Day demonstrations.

Many Japanese immediately asked, "Will this create more anti-Japanese feeling in America?" They linked this with fear that adverse American reaction might complicate efforts to obtain food and might mean a longer, harsher occupation.

They also expressed regret that the incident might mar the occupation and change the attitude of General MacArthur, whom the Japanese generally respect.

Allied headquarters had previously given some details of the plot. One conspirator was seized and a nation-wide hunt was launched for a die-hard Japanese militarist named as the arch-plotter.

The accused and hunted plot leader was Hideo Tokayama, former member of the dread Kempei-tai or "thought police." In the

Continued on Page 12, Column 2

"All the News That's Fit to Print"

NEWS INDEX, PAGE 79, THIS SECTION

The New York Times.

Copyright, 1947, by The New York Times Company.

LATE CITY EDITION

Fair and continued cold today and tomorrow.

Temperature Range Today—Max.,36; Min.,26

Temperature Yesterday—Max., 45; Min., 30

U. S. Weather Bureau Report, Page 16; Sect. 1

Section 1

VOL. XCVII..No. 32,817.

Entered as Second-Class Matter, Postoffice, New York, N. Y.

NEW YORK, SUNDAY, NOVEMBER 30, 1947.

Including Magazine and Book Review.

FIFTEEN CENTS

SCHUMAN BARS DISCUSSION OF FRENCH LABOR OVERTURE; COMMUNIST PAPERS SEIZED

PREMIER ADAMANT

Strikers Must Go Back on Regime's Terms—Labor Curbs Urged

ASSEMBLY SPLIT ON CODE

324 Saboteurs Are Arrested—Paris to Expel Aliens Who Help Ruin Economy

By HAROLD CALLENDER

Special to The New York Times.

PARIS, Sunday, Nov. 30—Premier Robert Schuman refused early today to meet the leaders of the Confederation of Labor to discuss a strike settlement different from that offered by the French Government.

Meanwhile, the Premier pressed hard for immediate passage by the Assembly of a law to strengthen the Government's hand by enlarging its police force and enabling it to imprison those who sought to force men to strike or who committed or urged sabotage.

As intense activity continued throughout the night inside and outside the Assembly, it became clear that the labor leaders who had encouraged the strikes had at last taken the initiative in seeking to end them, and that the Cabinet was divided regarding the policy the Government should adopt.

Early last evening Paris police surrounded the plants of the two Communist newspapers, l'Humanité and Ce Soir, entered the buildings and seized the plates of special editions whose publication had been forbidden. No papers were allowed to leave the plants. Later the police vacated the premises.

The special edition of l'Humanité, in large headlines printed in red ink, proclaimed: "They wish to assassinate the Republic!"

Minister Begins Parley

Shortly after M. Schuman had placed his proposed law before the Assembly early yesterday, Pierre Lebrun, a Communist secretary of the labor confederation, issued a statement urging renewed negotiations and mentioning that the striking workers would have a hard time when the Dec. 1 pay day came on Monday without pay envelopes.

At the same time, Daniel Mayer, Socialist Minister of Labor, who is understood to have opposed the law that M. Schuman sought, opened negotiations with the executive committee of the confederation, which sat most of the night in his office while the Cabinet met in the Palais Bourbon. Through M. Mayer the committee asked to see M. Schuman, but the Premier refused its request and denied that the Government was negotiating with the strike leaders.

A sharp divergence of view be-

Continued on Page 46, Column 3

U. S. Troops to Stay in Italy Beyond Dec. 3 Sailing Date

Change in Plans Is Linked to Disturbances Led by Communists—Milan Is Calm Following Compromise on Prefect

By ARNALDO CORTESI

Special to The New York Times.

ROME, Nov. 29—The United States Army Department today ordered Maj. Gen. Lawrence Jaynes, commanding the Mediterranean Theatre of Operations, and his entire staff to postpone their departure from Italy. With them will remain about 2,500 officers and men who are leading specialists of the United States Army in Italy.

The order is believed to reflect the anxiety with which the Government in Washington views the Communist-fomented disturbances in Italy.

General Jaynes and his officers and men had planned to leave from Leghorn on Dec. 3 aboard the Admiral Sims. Washington ordered a postponement of departure until Dec. 14, the deadline set by the Italian peace treaty. No explanation was given for the change of plans and this strengthened the impression that it was dictated by preoccupation over Italy's political outlook.

The officers and men with General Jaynes form the skeleton organization for a large army. They include highly trained specialists, familiar with conditions in Italy. They belong to the Engineer, Signal, Ordnance, Secretariat, Quartermaster, Medical and Military Police Corps and other auxiliary services.

Washington's change of plans came after General Jaynes had said farewell to Pope Pius and President Enrico de Nicola. Ambassador James C. Dunn called on Premier Alcide de Gasperi two days ago, and it is presumed that he informed the Italian Government then of the postponement of the American troops' departure.

Though the American troops should, under present plans, leave

Continued on Page 45, Column 1

No-Parking Area Is Created From City Hall to Canal St.

After a two-hour conference with Mayor O'Dwyer at Police Headquarters, Police Commissioner Arthur W. Wallander announced yesterday two further moves in the department's efforts to ease traffic congestion in the city.

Commissioner Wallander added the section of Manhattan north of City Hall as far as Canal Street and west to but not including West Street to the restricted parking areas already established in a large part of the borough below Fifty-ninth Street.

He also said that a survey was being made throughout the city in an effort to discover additional sites for municipal parking lots like the one established at the old World's Fair parking lot in Flushing, Queens. The lot set up experimentally there "looks promising," he said, reporting that 786 motorists had used it on Friday.

Mayor Explains Needs

The Commissioner announced the moves at a press conference at the end of his talk with the Mayor. Mr. O'Dwyer sat in on the press conference and added some comments of his own after his aide had made the announcement.

About forty traffic policemen will be needed to enforce the parking regulations in the new area, the Mayor said. Commissioner Wallander has asked for 2,000 additional men for the Police Department to take care of this and other needs, which would add $8,000,000 to the department's budget, he continued.

Together with $4,000,000 for he men added to the force last July, this would amount to a total of $10,000,000 that would have to be appropriated for the Police Department next year in addition to

Continued on Page 78, Column 3

WAR PAY RACKET HUNTED BY TRUMAN

Gen. Vaughan Says President Wants Army, Navy, Air House-Cleaning on Disability Cases

Special to The New York Times.

WASHINGTON, Nov. 29—The armed services are preparing to turn over to President Truman at his request the records of 28,000 wartime Army officers who have been retired for disability on tax-free pay normally amounting to three-fourths of their active service remuneration.

This became known as an aftermath of the case against Maj. Gen. Bennett E. Meyers and was confirmed today by Maj. Gen. Harry H. Vaughan, the President's military aide, who said at Philadelphia that Mr. Truman was determined to "wipe out any possible 'racket'" in tax-free disability retirement pay.

The President has already spoken about the matter to James Forrestal, Secretary of Defense, and it is expected that a formal directive will be received soon.

Presumably the order will apply also to naval officers retired for disability so that once the President has the records in hand he

Continued on Page 27, Column 1

Major Sports Results

FOOTBALL

With Rip Rowan passing for the first touchdown and dashing ninety-two yards for the second, Army beat Navy yesterday for the fourth straight year. N.Y.U. rallied to tie Fordham. Scores of leading games:

Alabama	21	Miami, Fla.	6
Army	21	Navy	0
Florida	25	Kansas State	7
Fordham	13	N. Y. U.	13
Ga. Tech	7	Georgia	0
Holy Cross	20	Boston Coll.	6
Maryland	0	N. C. State	0
Mich. State	58	Hawaii	19
Mississippi	33	Miss. State	14
N. Carolina	40	Virginia	7
Oklahoma	21	Okla. A.&M.	13
Oregon Sta.	27	Nebraska	6
Rice	34	Baylor	6
S. M. U.	19	T. C. U.	19
Tennessee	12	Vanderbilt	7
Texas Tech	14	Hardin-Sim.	6
West Va.	17	Pittsburgh	2

CROSS COUNTRY

Curtis Stone of Philadelphia won the National A.A.U. championship at Van Cortlandt Park, but the New York A. C. took the team title for the third successive time.

HORSE RACING

Incline outran Gallorette to capture the Bryan and O'Hara Memorial Handicap at Bowie on the last day of the major Eastern season.

(Full details in Section 5.)

Congress Action Lags on Aid Bill Despite Warnings Need Is Urgent

By JOHN D. MORRIS

Special to The New York Times.

WASHINGTON, Nov. 29—Congress set aside the troublesome problems of European aid and domestic inflation today and attended the Army-Navy game practically en masse, while pressure for accelerated action on the legislative problems awaited members' return to work Monday.

Despite repeated representations of urgency in both fields, the Congressional machinery faced a slowdown in production of the authorization for winter relief to France, Italy and Austria.

Formulation of anti-inflation legislation still had hardly begun, and completion of the task was far out of sight.

The Senate was prepared to resume consideration Monday of the foreign relief bill, but earlier expectations of passage on that day had been diminished by failure yesterday to dispose of four amendments proposed by Senator James P. Kem, Republican, of Missouri.

While some of them are acceptable to the bill's managers, at least one is expected to cause considerable discussion and possible delay of a vote on the bill itself until Tuesday.

This would require detailed, written acknowledgment by every recipient of relief supplies that the goods were gifts of the United States.

Senator Kem successfully opposed action on the amendments yesterday, asserting that he wanted Thanksgiving holiday absentees to be present when the votes were taken. He thus disrupted leaders' plans for clearing the slate of all proposed amendments so that the bill itself could be disposed of Monday.

Hope for a final vote Monday

Continued on Page 26, Column 1

VAST GI HOUSING TO RISE NEAR SITE OF WORLD'S FAIR

21 14-Story Apartment Units to Form Nation's Largest Veterans' Cooperative

COST PUT AT $58,000,000

Occupancy on Tenant-Owner Basis—Work Will Start Before End of Year

By LEE E. COOPER

On a fifty-five-acre tract overlooking the site of the World's Fair of 1939, the country's largest veterans' cooperative apartment community soon will begin to take form, it became known last night.

After nearly a year of negotiations, and with the official blessing of the city and of the Veterans Administration, plans for the $58,000,000 project were revealed by Frederick Briggs, chairman of the board of the Communities Redevelopment Corporation, which is sponsoring the enterprise.

The new Queens housing center, which will occupy a large part of the former Arrowbrook Golf Club grounds, will be for occupancy exclusively by veterans of World War II and their families on a tenant-ownership basis.

Plans call for the erection of twenty-one fourteen-story apartment houses of the fireproof type, to accommodate 5,600 families. Each building will have its own garage facilities, to be rented separately, for tenants' automobiles.

Shopping Centers Will Rise

In furtherance of the plan to create a self-contained community, the builders will erect shopping centers at the edges of the property, which is bounded by Main Street, Jewel Avenue and Park Drive East, within the boundaries of Forest Hills. A promenade, with stores beneath it, will be constructed on the hillside overlooking Flushing Meadow Park. The residential buildings will be set amid winding tree-lined walks and landscaped park spaces.

The Board of Estimate gave its unanimous sanction to the over-all plan for the project at a special closed session last Wednesday, after receiving a favorable report on it from Robert Moses, City Construction Coordinator who had been in consultation with the sponsors.

The city's cooperation will be limited to street changes and zoning aids permitting stores and the erection of fourteen-story houses on the site. No municipal financial

Continued on Page 13, Column 2

ASSEMBLY VOTES PALESTINE PARTITION; MARGIN IS 33 TO 13; ARABS WALK OUT; ARANHA HAILS WORK AS SESSION ENDS

PEACE GAINS NOTED

Brazilian Says Contacts Inspired No Forecast of Imminent War

CITES ROLE OF MINORITY

Lie Regrets That Economic Issues Were Sidetracked —Others Hail Aranha

By MARSHALL E. NEWTON

It is the mission of the United Nations to achieve world peace and the General Assembly made a memorable contribution in that direction, Dr. Oswaldo Aranha of Brazil, president of the Assembly, told the delegates of the fifty-seven member nations yesterday in his speech closing the second regular session in Flushing Meadows.

When he finished his address the delegates rose and applauded Dr. Aranha, whose talents and statesmanlike handling of the difficult task of presiding at the international assembly had been lauded by several preceding speakers.

Dr. Aranha pointed out that the present post-war period had not been marked by the armed conflicts that had followed the Peace of Versailles and he said that we lived today in a different era, in which our minds must turn to the future and not the past.

Calls for Foresight

"But close contact with international political life leads to no forecast of world war in the near future," he said. "The world seeks, however, new forms of political, economic and social integration in which the contest of ideas will supersede the clash of arms. The status quo is no longer possible. A new reality is rising in our days, to which we must impart the spirit of the United Nations, the only conception capable of insuring peace, solidarity, dignity and equality for all peoples.

"Our action should not be post factum. Our task is one of foresight and of organized prevention to eliminate the elements and factors capable of disturbing world

Continued on Page 67, Column 3

Arabs See U. N. 'Murdered,' Disavow Any Partition Role

Angry Delegates Stalk From Assembly Hall Before Formal Closing—Silver Voices Gratification, Offers Friendship

By A. M. ROSENTHAL

Bitter Arab delegates walked out of the General Assembly hall at Flushing Meadow last night after the vote for the partition of Palestine and solemnly announced that in their eyes the United Nations had died.

"No, not died," said Faris el-Khouri of Syria. "Murdered."

The representatives of the Arab states swept out of the building without waiting for the formal end of the Assembly and the farewell speeches. But before they entered their limousines they announced that they would have absolutely nothing to do with the United Nations Commission for Palestine, nothing to do with the transitional period after the end of the mandate and nothing to do with partition.

There was an open thread of warning running through all the Arab delegates' comments on the Assembly's action. They spoke of bloodshed to come and said the responsibility would not be theirs, but would be on the shoulders of the countries that had pressed for partition.

On the other side of the quarter-century Arab-Zionist dispute there was jubilance and hope for the future. Dr. Abba Hillel Silver, chairman of the American section of the Jewish Agency for Palestine, expressed his gratitude to the Assembly and especially to the United States and the Soviet Union.

Dr. Silver's statement follows:

"We are deeply gratified with the action of the General Assembly of the United Nations. It marks a turning point in Jewish history. It is an impressive reaffirmation of the just claim of the Jewish people to rebuild its national life in its ancestral home.

"This noble decision to re-establish the Jewish state and restore

Continued on Page 60, Column 1

Molotov Insists on Regime Before Treaty on Germany

By DREW MIDDLETON

Special to The New York Times.

LONDON, Nov. 29—Soviet Foreign Minister Molotov urged with new fervor in the Council of Foreign Ministers today the early establishment of a central German government as a precondition of the peace treaty.

Mr. Molotov's argument was based on the futility of completing a German peace treaty with no German government to sign it or assist in its preparation. But it was obvious that the Soviet delegate was moved by fears that the Western Allies, if this Council meeting failed, would make their own arrangements for a German government and treaty.

With a stridency that disrupted an otherwise decorous meeting, Mr. Molotov declared the Soviet Union would never recognize a peace signed by Western Germany and the Western powers. No government set up in Frankfort on the Main in the United States zone and no "ersatz government for Bizonia" will be an adequate substitute for the Soviet proposal, he asserted.

Secretary of State Marshall and French Foreign Minister Bidault both flatly opposed any tendency to make the establishment of a German government a precondition of signing the German peace treaty.

A compromise proposal presented by British Foreign Secretary Bevin was as abruptly turned down by Mr. Molotov, who said it did not go far enough. Then he proceeded to add a clause that made the British proposal an echo of the Soviet suggestion.

This brisk exchange of German participation in the peace making followed an encouraging agreement by the Big Four on the ad-

Continued on Page 54, Column 3

ZIONIST AUDIENCE JOYFUL AFTER VOTE

Tears, Excited Laughter Mark Tension—Aranha Commends Public's Good Behavior

By WALTER H. SULLIVAN

The attention of the entire Arab and Jewish worlds focused on Flushing Meadow yesterday to hear the verdict of the United Nations General Assembly on the future of Palestine.

The reaction in the packed hall to the decision for partition typified that of listeners far and near. While members of the Arab delegations walked out, Zionists in the audience rejoiced.

It was a rejoicing that started with silence and grew as the meeting neared its end. In the public lobby there were kisses and tears and excited laughter. In the delegates' lounge a rabbi cried, "This is the day the Lord hath made! Let us rejoice in it and be glad!"

The initial silence resulted from a call to order by the Assembly's president, Dr. Oswaldo Aranha. A burst of applause had greeted the surprise vote of France in favor of partition, and it was this that had

Continued on Page 67, Column 2

Company Asks Rise in Gas Rate From $1.15 to $2 Sliding Scale

The Consolidated Edison Company of New York, Inc., announced yesterday it had applied to the State Public Service Commission for permission to increase the maximum charge for gas from $1.15 a thousand cubic feet to $2 with declining rates after the first thousand.

The petition said that neither Consolidated Edison nor any of its predecessor companies had increased its rates since Oct. 1, 1922, and that existing rates were confiscatory of the company's property. It was estimated that the company would lose $1,498,500 in 1947 through its gas operations.

According to the company, 57 per cent of the gas it supplies is sold at the maximum rate of $1.15 a thousand cubic feet. The company's service area includes 1,160,000 customers in Manhattan, the Bronx and the first and third wards of Queens—Astoria, Long Island City, Flushing, College Point, Whitestone, Douglaston, Bayside, Little Neck and Bellerose.

The company proposed an immediate schedule of temporary rates, which it estimated would increase its annual revenues approximately $6,290,700 on the basis of estimated gas sales for 1947.

If this increase had been in effect through 1947, the company said, it would have provided the company with a net return after taxes of $4,300,000 in connection with its gas operations.

If approved by the Public Service Commission, the new classifications would provide a minimum charge of $2 for the first thousand cubic feet or less of gas consumed in any bi-monthly billing period.

For the first 4,000 cubic feet consumed bi-monthly after the initial 1,000-foot block, residential customers would be charged 12 cents a hundred; 10 cents a hun-

Continued on Page 13, Column 1

U.N. REJECTS DELAY

Proposal Driven Through by U. S. and Soviet Will Set Up Two States

COMMISSION IS APPOINTED

Britain Holds Out Hand to It—Arabs Fail in Last-Minute Resort to Federal Plan

By THOMAS J. HAMILTON

The United Nations General Assembly approved yesterday a proposal to partition Palestine into two states, one Arab and the other Jewish, that are to become fully independent by Oct. 1. The vote was 33 to 13 with ten abstentions and one delegation, the Siamese, absent.

The decision was primarily a result of the fact that the delegations of the United States and the Soviet Union, which were at loggerheads on every other important issue before the Assembly, stood together on partition. Andrei A. Gromyko and Herschel V. Johnson both urged the Assembly yesterday not to agree to further delay but to vote for partition at once.

The Assembly disregarded last-minute Arab efforts to effect a compromise. Although the votes of a dozen or more delegations seemed to the last, supporters of partition had two votes more than the required two-thirds majority or a margin of three.

How Members Voted

The roll-call vote was as follows:

For (33)—Australia, Belgium, Bolivia, Brazil, Canada, Costa Rica, Czechoslovakia, Denmark, Dominican Republic, Ecuador, France, Guatemala, Haiti, Iceland, Liberia, Luxembourg, the Netherlands, New Zealand, Nicaragua, Norway, Panama, Paraguay, Peru, Philippines, Poland, Sweden, the Ukraine, South Africa, Uruguay, the Soviet Union, the United States, Venezuela, White Russia.

Against (13)—Afghanistan, Cuba, Egypt, Greece, India, Iran, Iraq, Lebanon, Pakistan, Saudi Arabia, Syria, Turkey, Yemen.

Abstentions (10) — Argentina, Chile, China, Colombia, El Salvador, Ethiopia, Honduras, Mexico, United Kingdom, Yugoslavia.

Absent (1)—Siam.

All other questions before the Assembly were disposed of a week ago, and it ended its second regular session at 6:57 P. M. after farewell speeches by Dr. Oswaldo Aranha, its President, and Trygve Lie, the Secretary General. The Assembly's third regular session is to open in a European capital on Sept. 21.

The vote on partition was taken at 5:35 P. M. Representatives of Iraq, Saudi Arabia, Syria and Yemen, four of the six Arab member states, announced that they would not be bound by the Assembly's decision and walked determinedly out of the Assembly Hall at Flushing Meadow. The Egyptian and Lebanese delegates were silent but walked out, too.

Britain Seeks Contact

Sir Alexander Cadogan, representative of Britain, which is to terminate the League of Nations mandate over Palestine and withdraw all British troops by Aug. 1, made a brief statement after the vote. He requested the United Nations Palestine Commission to establish contact with the British Government about the date of its arrival in Palestine and the coordination of its plans with the withdrawal of British troops.

The United Nations commission, which will be responsible to the Security Council in the event that the Arabs carry out their threat to fight rather than agree to partition, will be composed of representatives of Bolivia, Czechoslovakia, Denmark, Panama and the Philippines.

This state, which is understood to have the backing of the United States, was proposed by Dr. Aranha and approved without opposition after the Arab delegates had walked out.

The commission, as proposed by the partition subcommittee of the

Continued on Page 63, Column 2

World News Summarized

SUNDAY, NOVEMBER 30, 1947

The General Assembly of the United Nations yesterday approved the plan for the partition of Palestine by a vote of 33 to 13 with ten abstentions and one absence. After the vote there were repeated statements of bitterness and disillusion from the Arab representatives. One after another they asserted that the Charter had been violated and that their nations would not be bound by the action and would reserve "freedom of action." The Arabs then walked out of the Assembly. [1:8.]

The Arabs subsequently pronounced the United Nations "dead," and disavowed any intention of playing a part under the partition plan. They went on to say, however, that this did not mean their retirement from the United Nations. Zionist leaders were jubilant over the outcome. [1:6-7.]

Zionists attending the Assembly expressed their joy with tears and excited laughter. Dr. Oswaldo Aranha praised the public for its good behavior. [1:7.]

The Palestine debate concluded the business of the current session of the General Assembly, and Dr. Aranha of Brazil gave his closing address. He declared that this second meeting had made a notable contribution to world peace, and after the delegates had risen to applaud him the session adjourned. [1:5.]

In London, Soviet Foreign Minister Molotov demanded the early establishment of a German government to accept the peace treaty. The other Ministers, seeing this as a move to commit them against any possible partition of Germany, opposed him. [1:6-7.] Secretary Marshall plans to ask the Council of Foreign Ministers next week to achieve the economic unification of Germany through the removal of all zonal barriers in what is expected to be the most important United States proposal at the conference. [50:3.]

In the deputies' meeting the Soviet delegation continued to study the French proposals on Austria and refused to agree on principle at any point. Action was delayed, but it was felt the Russians might accept. [51:1.]

In Paris, Premier Schuman declined to discuss with leaders of the Confederation of Labor any strike settlement on terms other than the Government's. He asked for police powers to suppress Communist agitators and moved against Communist papers. They had charged that a "revolutionary coup" was planned for midnight and that "assassination of the Republic" was its objective. The editions were suppressed. [1:1.]

In Italy, the United States commander and 2,500 American troops were ordered by Washington to postpone departure, presumably because of the troubled situation. The general strike in Milan, however, was ended. [1:2-3.]

The Ronne Expedition in the Antarctic reported the exploration and mapping of a total of about 160,000 square miles of territory in the name of the United States. [35:2.]

A scientific advance that may be of importance in insect pest control was announced by the United States Army. Ultrasonic waves have been developed that are lethal to mice and small insects. [14:1.]

Defense Secretary Forrestal has been instructed by President Truman to turn over the records of 28,000 wartime Army officers who have been retired for disability on tax-free pay, in the determination to wipe out any possible "racket." [1:2.]

"All the News That's Fit to Print"

The New York Times.

LATE CITY EDITION

Fair and armer today and tomorow.

Temperature Range Today—Max., 65; Min., 46
Temperatures Yesterday—Max., 53; Min., 46
Full U. S. Weather Bureau Report, Page 31

VOL. XCVII..No. 32,984. Entered as Second-Class Matter, Postoffice, New York, N. Y. NEW YORK, SATURDAY, MAY 15, 1948. Times Square, New York 18, N. Y. Telephone Lackawanna 4-1000 THREE CENTS IN NEW YORK CITY

ZIONISTS PROCLAIM NEW STATE OF ISRAEL; TRUMAN RECOGNIZES IT AND HOPES FOR PEACE; TEL AVIV IS BOMBED, EGYPT ORDERS INVASION

AVY PUSHES PLAN 'OR CONSTRUCTION OF MISSILE VESSELS

llivan Asks House Committee Approve Halting Work on Battleship, Destroyer Types

ANTS 65,000-TON CARRIER

oating 'Submarine Killers' e Also Stressed in Plea for Diverting $300,000,000 Fund

By C. P. TRUSSELL
Special to THE NEW YORK TIMES.

WASHINGTON, May 14—The avy asked Congress today for thority to shift sharply its conruction of fighting craft from ttleship, cruiser and destroyer pes to guided missile vessels, a ,000-ton carrier able to base, far sea, planes with an operating dius of 1,700 miles, better subarines and floating "enemy subarine killers."

Such new ships, John L. Sullin, Secretary of the Navy, told e House Armed Services Comittee, must have a higher prior y "because of the more immeate need for them in the event an emergency." The immediate action of the committee apared to favor prompt action.

For such a shift in construction, cretary Sullivan brought out, e Navy wanted to halt the build- g of thirteen naval vessels, inuding the battleship Kentucky, e large cruiser Hawaii, seven stroyers, two destroyer escorts d two submarines. To date out $197,000,000 has been spent them.

However, this money was not to abandoned, Mr. Sullivan emhasized. These craft could be conrted now to the new program, explained, or be put aside for fitting-out later as new weapons ere developed.

New Aims for $300,000,000 Fund

What the Navy wanted, Secreary Sullivan asserted, was Conessional permission to divert me $300,000,000 remaining in the esent ship construction account these purposes:

Starting the 65,000-ton aircraft rrier (the biggest ones now are e two of the Midway class, at ,000 tons), which might cost round $124,000,000.

Building, for reproduction later, a "submarine killer." (Hearings the defense program have incated that Russia has made reat progress in the submarine eld.) A "killer" machine, it is dicated, is developing in new ork on the cruiser type of seaaft.

The construction of four subarines of types advanced beyond ose now building.

In addition, there was under an a conversion in an unidentied way of a carrier and two subarines.

Secretary Sullivan told the comittee that the Kentucky and the Hawaii would not have to stand by r the development of new weapns. It is planned, he disclosed, hat they be converted into guided issile ships. Apparently to allay ears in Congress that larger airaft carriers make easier targets r enemy bombers, Mr. Sullivan rew upon experience in the secnd World War and the results of tom-bomb tests at Bikini.

Speed Held Bomb Defense

"The experiments at Bikini," Mr. Sullivan said, "have proved hat a fast-moving fleet is an unrofitable target for an atomic omb."

Members of the committee interpreted this as a Navy Department conclusion that even though potential enemy might acquire he atomic bomb, the revised construction program proposed today romised a maximum of safety. Mr. Sullivan recalled that the Navy lost three large and two ight carriers in the Pacific, but one was sunk by aircraft landased. He indicated that mobility f a fleet, equipped to latest odel, would discourage the spendng of atomic bombs, even if an nemy had some.

Today, the Senate Republican

Continued on Page 7, Column 4

Heaviest Trading in 8 Years Marks Stock Market Spurt

3,840,000 Shares Change Hands as Wave of Bullish Enthusiasm Increases Securities 1 to 7 Points

The hectic days of the Nineteen Twenties were re-enacted yesterday on the floor of the New York Stock Exchange when the most turbulent session in recent years produced increases of 1 to 7 points in the share list. Accompanied by a burst of bullish enthusiasm not witnessed in almost a decade, the deluge of buying orders so taxed the facilities of the Exchange that the reporting ticker tape lagged behind floor transactions by five minutes.

The cracking of the 1947 high level at the approach of mid-day served as the signal for a buying rush. Public participation suddenly enlarged and buying orders pressed floor traders to the utmost. This condition existed for forty-five minutes in the final hour when 1,350,000 shares were traded.

Accompanied by the broadest market on record with a total of 1,151 issues dealt in, volume on the Stock Exchange spiraled to 3,840,000 shares, the largest since May 21, 1940, in contrast to the Thursday turnover of 2,030,000 shares.

Brokers termed it the "wildest" bull market in twenty years on the premise that at no time in the interval had the industrials and rails advanced with such a unity of force.

While the ground had been well laid for a movement of such scope earlier this week, it was the piercing of the 1947 resistance point that confirmed the presence of a bull market to those who act by the charts, or averages. Early in the day, telegrams were sent by several advisory services to their clients urging the purchase of securities. The response to this advice showed primarily in the late

Continued on Page 23, Column 4

Truman Sees His Election; Calls GOP 'Obstructionist'

By ANTHONY LEVIERO
Special to THE NEW YORK TIMES.

WASHINGTON, May 14—President Truman asserted tonight that there would be a Democrat in the White House during the next four years and that he would be the man. He made the statement to a cheering audience of 1,000 young Democrats at their meeting here.

The President's speech was a fighting one in the new Truman manner. He spoke extemporaneously, resorting to whimsy and irony and using forceful gestures of his arms to underscore his points.

Mr. Truman accused the Republican party of stealing Democratic platform planks. "You know," he said, "it has been their habit since 1936 of taking a few planks out of the old Democratic platforms and building a platform and then saying, 'Me, too.'"

[The text of President Truman's speech is on Page 7.]

"What have the Republicans done in the last fifteen and a half years?" Mr. Truman asked, then said:

"They have been obstructionists. They spent most of their time while I was in the Senate—and I was there for ten years—in obstructing progressive legislation that was for the welfare of the common man, and throwing bricks and mud at the greatest President that ever sat in the White House."

Mr. Truman was interrupted by applause at this obvious allusion to President Roosevelt.

"That has been their record," he continued, "and they haven't changed a bit. They were against Social Security. They were against TVA. They were against wages

Continued on Page 7, Column 2

MINNESOTA'S GUARD OUT IN MEAT STRIKE

Governor Acts After 200 Raid Cudahy Newport Plant, Attack 60 Workers and Abduct 25

Special to THE NEW YORK TIMES.

ST. PAUL, Minn., May 14—National Guard troops were ordered to South St. Paul and Newport, towns on opposite banks of the Mississippi River near here, by Governor Luther Youngdahl today following violent disorders at strike-bound packing plants in the area and the statement of the local sheriffs that their forces could not maintain law and order.

The Governor did not proclaim martial law but said the troops would take their orders from the civil authorities.

The Governor's action followed a serious outbreak at the Cudahy packing plant in Newport shortly before last midnight in which a group of about 200 men raided the plant with clubs, knives and hammers. In South St. Paul on Thursday strikers forced back police who tried to open a way through picket lines at the Swift & Co. plant in

Continued on Page 13, Column 3

Princess Elizabeth, in Paris Talk, Asks Common Effort of 2 Nations

By LANSING WARREN
Special to THE NEW YORK TIMES.

PARIS, May 14—Speaking in faultless French with just the touch of a British accent to delight French ears, Princess Elizabeth today asked France and Britain to make a common effort to lead Europe to moral and intellectual as well as economic reconstruction.

Her well-worded and discerning speech was cheered, but she went straight to the hearts of the Parisian throng when, with disarming frankness, she avowed her joy that her first foreign trip since her marriage had brought her here to Paris.

"For a long time," she said, "I have wanted to come to France. More fortunate than I, my husband already knew your admirable capital and he is all the happier to return. This trip is all the more important and agreeable for the warmth of your welcome which has touched us both."

From the time they stepped down from the train at the Gare du Nord early today, Princess Elizabeth and Prince Philip, Duke of Edinburgh, were the center of admiring attention from the throngs that lined the streets and from all the French officials who received them throughout the day.

President Vincent Auriol voiced the general feeling when in a statement issued tonight he said:

"I have been personally struck by her grace, her charm, her modesty and her nobility. I feel sure that the sentiments that she has expressed went straight to the hearts of all the French."

Elizabeth's address, broadcast to the French nation, was delivered from the top of the monumental entry to the Galliera Museum, where she came to open the British Government's exhibition of relics and souvenirs of famous Brit-

Continued on Page 6, Column 3

AIR ATTACK OPENS

Planes Cause Fires at Port—Defense Fliers Go Into Action

BORDER IS BREACHED

Cairo Vanguard Takes Colony—Trans-Jordan Reports a Movement

By The Associated Press.

TEL AVIV, Palestine, Saturday, May 15—Air raiders bombed this all-Jewish city at about dawn today.

First reports said there were "some casualties" near the power and light station.

[Cairo reported that Egyptian armed forces had been ordered to enter Palestine. Arab armies moved from Trans-Jordan at 12:01 A. M. Saturday to "liberate the Holy Land from Zionism," said a Trans-Jordan communiqué reported by The United Press from Amman.]

Tel Aviv was under complete blackout all night but no sirens were sounded during the raid. Civil guards were alerted and fifteen to twenty ships in the port area moved out to sea.

The planes swooped over Tel Aviv little more than twelve hours after Jewish leaders proclaimed the existence of a new Hebrew state of Israel.

Some bombs fell in the vicinity of the power station along the Yarkum River near Tel Aviv.

Persons at the scene said there was one hit on or near the power station, causing "some casualties."

TEL AVIV, Saturday, May 15 (UP)—Some ten bombs were dropped on Tel Aviv by two aircraft described as bombers and accompanied by two small fighters. One Jew was killed and three were hospitalized. Jewish Army aircraft took to the skies a few minutes after the enemy planes whizzed over rooftops at an estimated altitude of 300 feet.

Several fires could be seen north

Continued on Page 2, Column 3

U. S. MOVES QUICKLY

President Acknowledges de Facto Authority of Israel Immediately

TRUCE AIM STRESSED

Soviet Gesture to New Nation Anticipated—Others Due to Act

By BERTRAM D. HULEN
Special to THE NEW YORK TIMES.

WASHINGTON, May 14—President Truman announced early tonight recognition by the United States of the new Jewish State of Israel. The President acted instantly upon being informed that the new nation had been proclaimed.

"This Government," he announced, "has been informed that a Jewish state has been proclaimed in Palestine and recognition has been requested by the provisional government thereof.

"The United States recognizes the provisional government as the de facto authority of the new State of Israel."

These two paragraphs constituted the text of the President's statement.

Coupled with the announcement was an expression of hope for peace in Palestine. This was made known through a separate White House statement issued by Charles G. Ross, Presidential press secretary.

"The desire of the United States to obtain a truce in Palestine," this said, "will in no way be lessened by the proclamation of a Jewish state.

"We hope that the new Jewish state will join with the Security Council Truce Commission in redoubled efforts to bring an end to the fighting—which has been throughout the United Nations' consideration of Palestine a principal objective of this Government."

[Pending stabilization of the Palestine situation and indications that the State of Israel

Continued on Page 3, Column 2

World News Summarized

SATURDAY, MAY 15, 1948

Several hours after the state of Israel, the first Hebrew nation in 2,000 years, had been proclaimed in a Zionist declaration of independence in Tel Aviv, [1:8.], President Truman announced that the United States recognized the "provisional government" of Israel as "the de facto authority of the new state." A second White House statement expressed the hope that the new regime would cooperate with United Nations efforts to bring about peace in Palestine. [1:5.] The British High Commissioner departed from Palestine and boarded a cruiser at Haifa as Britain's rule over the Holy Land formally ended. [1:7.]

The special session of the United Nations General Assembly ended last night after it had agreed to send a mediator to Palestine to try to arrange a truce. [1:6-7.] The trusteeship plan for Jerusalem sponsored by the United States was rejected by the Assembly, with the Arab states and the Soviet opposed to the measure. [1:6-7.]

Tel Aviv was bombed at dawn. Egypt ordered her troops to invade Palestine. Trans-Jordan reported her army on the move also. [1:4.] Haganah claimed that its forces captured Acre in the north. [2:8.]

In Moscow the newspaper Pravda, in the first editorial comment on the recent exchange between Washington and Moscow, accused the United States of double-dealing. [4:8.]

Paris crowds gave an enthusiastic welcome to Princess Elizabeth and the Duke of Edinburgh when they arrived for a visit. [1:2-3.]

Congress received a request from the Navy for authority to shift the emphasis in its construction of fighting craft to guided-missile vessels. [1:1.]

President Truman predicted that he would be re-elected next November. [1:2-3.]

Minnesota National Guard troops were rushed to South St. Paul and Newport after 200 persons had raided the Cudahy meat packing plant at Newport, where a strike is in progress, attacking about sixty workers and abducting twenty-five of them. [1:2.]

The New York Stock Exchange enjoyed one of its biggest days in recent years as an avalanche of buying orders sent stocks up from 1 to 7 points. Trading reached a total of 3,840,000 shares, the largest since May 21, 1940. [1:2-3.]

Winston Churchill's War Memoirs

See Page 17 for today's installment, in which Mr. Churchill describes the invasion of Norway and the clash of the British and German fleets.

AT HELM OF THE JEWISH STATE

David Ben-Gurion
Premier

Moshe Shertok
Foreign Minister

The New York Times

U. N. Votes for a Mediator; Special Assembly Is Ended

By THOMAS J. HAMILTON

After hearing both the Soviet Union and the Arab delegates denounce the United States for its sudden recognition of the new Jewish state in Palestine, the United Nations General Assembly decided last night to send a Mediator to the Holy Land to do what he could to arrange a truce and carry on public services.

The vote was 31 to 7, with sixteen abstentions and four delegates absent, and the General Assembly, which was called into special session at Flushing Meadow on April 16 at the request of the United States, adjourned for good at 8:32 P. M.

The failure of the General Assembly either to repeal the partition resolution of last November or to provide military force to keep the peace means that the fate of Palestine will be decided by the impending war between Jews and Arabs, not by any United Nations action.

The mediation resolution conforms substantially with a United States proposal announced last Wednesday, after it had become obvious that the General Assembly would not accept the original United States plan for a temporary trusteeship.

However, the General Assembly refused to accept a United States plan for a temporary trusteeship over Jerusalem, which was rejected earlier in the evening by a vote of 20 to 15, less than the necessary two-thirds majority.

Two other proposals regarding Jerusalem were rejected, but presumably the provisions of the partition resolution on Jerusalem, which was to have been established as an international enclave under the administration of the Trusteeship Council, still stand.

In addition, the Assembly de-

Continued on Page 4, Column 4

CUNNINGHAM GOES AS MANDATE ENDS

British Commissioner Boards Cruiser Off Haifa—Jews Take Down Union Jack

By The Associated Press.

HAIFA, Palestine, Saturday, May 15—Britain ended her mandate over the Holy Land last midnight. Lieut. Gen. Sir Alan Cunningham, the last British High Commissioner, sailed from Haifa port, finishing British mandate guidance.

Sir Alan's departure from Palestine's richest port caused little excitement among the Jews, who control most of the city.

The British fired a few rockets and searchlights spotlighted the cruiser as it steamed from the harbor.

Wearing the uniform of a British Army general, Sir Alan walked down a few steps of dock into a launch that took him to the cruiser Euryalus.

Upon getting into the launch, he turned and looked soberly up across the docks. There stood an honor guard of the King's Company of Grenadier Guards and Royal Marine commandos

The launch pulled away amid the

Continued on Page 2, Column 7

U. N. Bars Jerusalem Trusteeship; Vote Follows Mandate Deadline

By MALLORY BROWNE

The United Nations General Assembly rejected yesterday the United States plan for a temporary trusteeship regime in Jerusalem.

Solidly opposed by the Arab States and the Russian bloc, the plan to set up a United Nations Commissioner authorized to protect the Holy City and its holy places failed to obtain the necessary two-thirds majority at the closing session at Flushing Meadow.

The vote, which came just after the bombshell of the United States recognition of the new Jewish State had burst in the Assembly, was 20 in favor, 15 against and 19 abstentions. The balance was turned by the hostility of Britain and most of the Dominions.

The United States fought hard all day, first in the Political and Security Committee of the Assembly, sitting at Lake Success, and then in the evening session of the Assembly, to get the trusteeship plan adopted before the end of the mandate at 6:01 P. M., New York time.

An Arab filibuster, aided by the Soviet bloc, defeated this effort. It was well past the zero hour when a roll-call vote showed that the Assembly preferred to leave Harold Evans, newly appointed Jerusalem municipal Commissioner, in sole charge of the Holy City and its treasures.

As one Arab after another filed up to the tribune and took up the maximum five-minute period allowed in repeating the arguments against a trusteeship plan, 6:01 o'clock went by.

At once Awni Khalidy of Iraq, who had led the Arab fight against the trusteeship plan, rushed up to the tribune and exultantly proclaimed that the time had passed; that the mandate was at an end, and that, since, as Francis B. Sayre of the United States had said, the measure must

Continued on Page 3, Column 5

THE JEWS REJOICE

Some Weep as Quest for Statehood Ends—White Paper Dies

HELP OF U. N. ASKED

New Regime Holds Out Hand to Arabs—U. S. Gesture Acclaimed

Text of declaration setting up new Jewish state, Page 2.

By GENE CURRIVAN
Special to THE NEW YORK TIMES.

TEL AVIV, Palestine, Saturday, May 15—The Jewish state, the world's newest sovereignty, to be known as the State of Israel, came into being in Palestine at midnight upon termination of the British mandate.

Recognition of the state by the United States, which had opposed its establishment at this time, came as a complete surprise to the people, who were tense and ready for the threatened invasion by Arab forces and appealed for help by the United Nations.

In one of the most hopeful periods of their troubled history the Jewish people here gave a sigh of relief and took a new hold on life when they learned that the greatest national power had accepted them into the international fraternity.

Ceremony Simple and Solemn

The declaration of the new state by David Ben-Gurion, chairman of the National Council and the first Premier of reborn Israel, was delivered during a simple and solemn ceremony at 4 P. M., and new life was instilled into his people, but from without there was the rumbling of guns, a flashback to other declarations of independence that had not been easily achieved.

The first action of the new Government was to revoke the Palestine White Paper of 1939, which restricted Jewish immigration and land purchase.

In the proclamation of the new state the Government appealed to the United Nations "to assist the Jewish people in the building of its state and to admit Israel into the family of nations."

The proclamation added:

"We offer peace and amity to all neighboring states and their peoples, and invite them to cooperate with the independent Jewish nation for the common good of all. The State of Israel is ready to contribute its full share to the peaceful progress and reconstitution of the Middle East."

World Jews Asked to Aid

The statement appealed to Jews throughout the world to assist in the task of immigration and development and in the "struggle for the fulfillment of the dream of generations—the redemption of Israel."

Plans for the ceremony had been laid with great secrecy. None but the hundred or more invited guests and journalists was aware of the meeting until it started, and even the guests learned of the site only ten minutes before. It was held in the Tel Aviv Museum of Art, a white, modern-design two-story building. Above it flew the Star of David, which is the state's flag, and below, on the sidewalk, was a guard of honor of the Haganah, the army of the Jewish Agency for Palestine.

As photographers' bulbs flashed and movie cameras ground out reels of the scene, great crowds gathered and cheered the Ministers and other members of the Government as they entered the building. The security arrangements were perfect. Sten guns were brandished in every direction and even the roofs bristled with them.

The setting for the reading of the proclamation was a dropped gallery whose hall held paintings by prominent Jewish artists. Many of them depicted the sufferings and joys of the people of the Diaspora, the dispersal of the Jews.

The thirteen Ministers of the

Continued on Page 2, Column 6

"All the News That's Fit to Print"

The New York Times.

LATE CITY EDITION
Partly cloudy and mild today; fair tonight and tomorrow.
Temperature Range Today—Max., 65; Min., 47
Temperature Yesterday—Max., 60; Min., 48
Full U. S. Weather Bureau Report, Page 55

Copyright, 1949, by The New York Times Company.

VOL. XCVIII..No. 33,346. Entered as Second-Class Matter, Postoffice, New York, N. Y. NEW YORK, THURSDAY, MAY 12, 1949. Times Square, New York 18, N. Y. Telephone Lackawanna 4-1000 THREE CENTS IN NEW YORK CITY

BERLIN LAND BLOCKADE IS LIFTED; FIRST TRAIN, AUTOS REACH CITY; ZONE TROOP RETIREMENT STUDIED

ISRAEL WINS A SEAT IN U. N. BY 37-12 VOTE

ARABS INDIGNANT

Quit the Assembly Hall After Poll—9 Nations Abstain in Ballot

59TH COUNTRY IN BODY

Israel's Foreign Chief Sharett Pledges Peace Effort—Debate Brings Polish Attack

By THOMAS J. HAMILTON

The General Assembly admitted Israel to membership in the United Nations at 7:28 last night by a vote of 37 to 12, with nine abstentions.

The delegations of the six Arab states—Egypt, Iraq, Lebanon, Saudi Arabia, Syria and Yemen—walked out of the Assembly Hall at Flushing Meadow in protest before the applause over the election of Israel as the fifty-ninth member of the United Nations had died away. They indignantly refused to make any statement to correspondents regarding their intentions, but drove away to New York.

The Arab delegates, who also walked out when the General Assembly adopted the resolution recommending the partition of Palestine on Nov. 29, 1947 gave no hint of their impending action in their speeches in the General Assembly in the afternoon.

Charge Israeli Violation

They protested bitterly, however, that Israel had refused to comply with the provisions of a General Assembly resolution adopted on Dec. 11, 1948, calling for an international regime in Jerusalem and the repatriation of Arab refugees. Also, they challenged the validity of a Security Council recommendation for the admission of Israel, since Britain, a permanent member of the Council, had abstained.

The Charter requires the concurring votes of the Big Five on all except procedural questions, and the Arab delegates insisted that the Assembly should first get a ruling from the International Court of Justice. This procedure was contained in a resolution presented by Iraq yesterday afternoon, but Dr. Evatt ruled it out of order on the ground that the General Assembly could not examine the decision of another United Nations body.

The Yemen delegation returned shortly after 10 o'clock for the night session of the Assembly, and an Egyptian delegate came back a few minutes later, but the other desks remained vacant.

Immediately after the vote Dr. Evatt summoned to the platform Moshe Sharett, Israeli Foreign Minister, who had arrived by plane from Tel Aviv early yesterday to hear the final speeches.

"We enter this Assembly, which represents the collective statesmanship of the world, in a spirit of humility, anxious for guidance and enlightenment," said Mr. Sharett, who re-stated the Israeli policy of "loyalty to the fundamental principles of the United Nations' Charter and friendship with all peace-loving states, especially with the United States of America and the Union of Soviet Socialist Republics."

Now a Working Member

Mr. Sharett took his seat at the desk that had previously been prepared for the Israeli delegation in the back of the Assembly hall, between the Iraqi and Lebanese delegations. United Nations officials said no additional formalities were required, and that Israel would have the right to participate in all further proceedings of the General Assembly on the same basis as the fifty-eight other members.

The vote came too late to permit the Israeli flag to be raised in the area in front of the main delegates' entrance. A flag pole, however, had been prepared in advance, and there will be a ceremony at Lake Success at 10:30 A. M. today.

The General Assembly took up the application at its afternoon session and the debate concluded at 7:30 as a result of the fact that the protests of the Arab delegates,

Continued on Page 13, Column 1

Protesters in Tripoli Tear U.S. Flag to Bits

By The United Press.

TRIPOLI, LIBYA, May 11—Demonstrators tore to shreds a United States flag in front of the United States Consulate in Tripoli today and set fire to a number of Italian establishments.

The demonstrators, demanding full independence for this former Italian colony, shouted "Long live Russia! Down with America and the United Nations!"

Special to The New York Times.

LAKE SUCCESS, May 11—A United Kingdom proposal that Eritrea, except for the western province, be incorporated into Ethiopia was approved in a subcommittee of the Political Committee this morning by a vote of ten to three with two abstentions.

A second United Kingdom proposal that the western province be incorporated in the adjacent Sudan also was approved by a vote of seven to two with six abstentions.

WAR PENSION BILL IS SHARPLY LIMITED

House Group Confines Benefit to Unemployable and Reports Measure as Rankin Protests

By JOHN D. MORRIS

Special to The New York Times

WASHINGTON, May 11—The new veterans pension bill was further watered down in committee today—to such an extent that its author, Representative John E. Rankin, Democrat, of Mississippi, voted, though in vain, against reporting it to the House.

The action was taken by the House Veterans Affairs Committee at a closed meeting that had been scheduled merely to formalize its action yesterday in approving pensions on a more liberal basis.

The committee voted, 14 to 8, to confine the $72-a-month payments to unemployable veterans. By a voice vote, it then cleared the measure formally to the House.

Approval of the limitation was prompted by Veterans Administration estimates, drawn up overnight, that without it the bill would add $65,000,000,000 to the cost of veterans' benefits over the next fifty years. Yesterday's action had been based on a $12,000,000,000 estimate.

As finally approved, the measure's fifty-year cost was estimated at $8,693,000,000 by Guy H. Birdsall, assistant veterans administrator.

Mr. Rankin was joined by Representative A. Leonard Allen, Democrat, of Louisiana, in voting against reporting the bill. Shortly afterward the Mississippi legislator arose in the House to protest the action of the committee, of which he is chairman.

The employability clause, he asserted, would bar pensions from

Continued on Page 32, Column 4

KENNY TO ASK COURT FOR ORDER TO SEIZE JERSEY CITY BOOKS

Mayor-Elect Seeks to Prevent Any Alterations of Records to Shield Old Regime

FULL INQUIRY IS PLANNED

'It's All Right With Me,' Says Hague of Defeat—Fight for State Rule Likely

By LEO EGAN

The political coalition that dethroned Frank Hague as boss of Jersey City has decided to seek a court order barring the outgoing city administration from destroying or altering official records before it leaves office next Tuesday.

John V. Kenny, who headed the coalition and who will become Mayor in the new administration, said a formal application for an order impounding city books and records would be submitted tomorrow to Judge William Brennan in Hudson County Superior Court.

One of the first acts of the new regime, Mr. Kenny added, will be to order a full-scale audit of the records and accounts of the outgoing administration, headed by Mayor Frank Hague Eggers, nephew of the 73-year-old former Mayor, who was one of the last of the old-time bosses in the United States to yield up his political power.

Drive to End State Rule Seen

While the new regime was making its plans for sifting city records for evidence of illegal acts and misuse of public funds on behalf of the Hague machine, Democrats in other parts of New Jersey were contemplating a drive to strip Mr. Hague of his control of the Democratic party in the state.

Many Democrats fear that unless Mr. Hague's connections with the state organizations are severed the fall elections will result in an overwhelming victory for the Republican State ticket, headed by Gov. Alfred E. Driscoll.

In any reorganization of the Democratic State Committee, Mr. Kenny, who was leader of the Second Ward in Jersey City for the Hague organization for many years, is expected to play a leading role. So are former Mayor Meyer C. Ellenstein of Newark, who topped all candidates for City Commissioner there in Tuesday's elections, and Mayor George Brunner of Camden.

David Wilentz, who prosecuted Bruno Richard Hauptmann for the Lindbergh kidnapping, and Mayor Michael De Vito of Paterson are also expected to play important parts in any reorganization movement.

In the interview yesterday afternoon in which he told of his plans for investigating the outgoing Administration, Mr. Kenny announced also that he would support State Senator Elmer Wene for Governor on the Democratic ticket this fall. Senator Wene won the Democratic nomination with the backing of Mr. Hague in a recent primary.

The interview was sandwiched in between posing for newsreels and making an appearance on a television program. Although he looked tired and his voice was hoarse, the Mayor-elect said he felt "fine."

With respect to his plans on taking over, Mr. Kenny said that

Continued on Page 15, Column 2

U. S. PLAN WEIGHED

Big 3 Would Withdraw to Ports in the North Under Proposal

FRENCH WOULD GO HOME

Presentation of Suggestion Will Depend on Soviet Stand in Paris Talks

By JAMES RESTON

Special to The New York Times.

WASHINGTON, May 11—The United States was reported today to have under consideration a plan under which all occupation troops in Germany would be withdrawn into restricted areas at the North German ports.

Under this plan, which is being discussed with Britain and France, Soviet troops would be situated on the West Bank of the Oder in Stettin, British troops would be restricted to the area of Hamburg, and United States troops would be concentrated in Bremen.

[Stettin was included in the Soviet zone in the Potsdam pact, but under a separate agreement reached Sept. 20, 1947, the Russians turned over control of the former German port to Poland. Bremen is a United States enclave in the British zone.]

These troops, it is understood, would be obliged, under this plan, to use only sea communications, and France, which has a common frontier with Germany, would withdraw her occupation troops into her own territory.

An understanding apparently already has been reached among the Western powers to reject any Soviet proposal at the forthcoming meeting of the Council of Foreign Ministers in Paris for the complete evacuation of all occupation troops from all of Germany.

It is felt here that total withdrawal of these troops would be detrimental to the economic recovery and sense of security of Western Europe.

However, if Soviet Foreign Minister Andrei Y. Vishinsky should demonstrate in Paris that his Government was now prepared to establish a central government in Germany along the lines laid down by the Western powers for the

Continued on Page 3, Column 2

IT'S A REAL HOLIDAY FOR THESE BERLIN YOUNGSTERS

Joyous children hold their lunch boxes over their heads as they get news that there will be no school in celebration of the end of the blockade. The sign reads "blockade free."

Associated Press Radiophoto

ACHESON STILL BARS FRANCO AS FASCIST

Says Spanish Regime Denies Basic Rights in the Pattern of Hitler and Mussolini

Secretary Acheson's remarks on Spanish regime, Page 10.

By BERTRAM D. HULEN

Special to The New York Times.

WASHINGTON, May 11—Secretary of State Dean Acheson declared today that the question of restoring full diplomatic relations with Spain turned primarily upon the attitude of Western European countries that were still opposed to bringing her back into their international family for military and economic cooperation.

This attitude, the Secretary told his weekly news conference, was conditioned by the absence of fundamental freedoms under the Franco regime which, he said, originally and still was patterned on Nazi Germany and Fascist Italy. At an-

Continued on Page 10, Column 1

Eisler Reported Stowaway; Seizure in Britain Is Asked

By WILL LISSNER

A man who has identified himself as Gerhart Eisler, native of Germany, is fleeing from the United States aboard the Gdynia-America liner Batory, it became known yesterday. The fugitive ... believed to be the former Comintern agent named by the House Un-American Activities Committee as America's No. 1 Communist, jumping $23,500 bail to escape serving a year in jail and other penalties, but his identity has not yet been definitely established.

The Federal Bureau of Investigation and the Immigration and Naturalization Service of the Department of Justice moved yesterday to fix the identity of the fugitive. If the man aboard the Batory is the German-born Communist leader Eisler, he will be placed in custody for eventual return.

The fugitive is bound for Gdynia, but the ship, which sailed last Saturday, will put into Southampton Saturday. To make sure that Polish Communists aboard the ship do not balk a return, the State Department, at the request of the Department of Justice, notified Scotland Yard of the incident and asked that top investigators meet the ship on her arrival in the English port. Scotland Yard was asked to hold the suspect.

If Eisler, the convicted Communist agent, has fled the jurisdiction of the Federal District Court, his bail would be forfeited even though the English authorities return him, it was said at the Federal Building.

The forfeiture of the $23,500 bail would be a blow to the Civil Rights Congress and the American Committee for the Protection of the Foreign Born. For a good part of

Continued on Page 4, Column 3

FIRST BERLIN TRAIN FROM WEST SEALED

Officials Lock Doors and Draw Shades to Keep Russians Out and Reporters In

By The United Press.

BERLIN, Thursday, May 12—The first western passenger train since last year arrived in Berlin at 5:11 A. M. today (11:11 P. M. Wednesday, Eastern Daylight Time)—hauled by a Soviet zone locomotive.

A combined British-American train of twelve cars, it carried approximately 140 Western nationals, including seventy-three British troops and at least a score of reporters.

Anglo-American officials ordered the doors locked and the shades drawn soon after the train left Helmstedt at 1:23 A. M., the first train to make the West-East run on the Helmstedt-Berlin road since last year.

The train officials said that the "sealing" of the cars was necessary "to keep the Russians out and to keep you newsmen in." The reporters peeked anyway but saw only a moonlit empty landscape during the eventless three hours

Continued on Page 2, Column 2

SIEGE ON 328 DAYS

Leading Car Speeds 102 Miles From the British Zone in 1½ Hours

AIRLIFT PLANES CONTINUE

West Concerned as Russians Turn Back Some Trucks—City's Lights Turned On

By DREW MIDDLETON

Special to The New York Times.

BERLIN, Thursday, May 12—Just as the morning sun rose over the jagged skyline of this broken but defiant city a Soviet zone locomotive chugged wearily into the Charlottenburg Station in the British sector hauling the first train to reach Berlin from the West in 328 days.

Arrival of the train completed the relief of the city from the iron vise of the Soviet blockade.

At one minute after midnight [6:01 P. M. Wednesday, Eastern daylight time] two jeeps and a convoy of cars, buses and trucks roared out of the city for the Western zones. An hour and three quarters later the first cars of a flotilla that simultaneously had left Helmstedt, in the British zone at the border of the Soviet zone, swept into Berlin—to re-establish the land link with the West broken since the Soviet Military administration established a complete blockade of the city last June.

By morning it was evident that the Russians had observed the letter if not the spirit of the Big-West agreement reached in New York. Traffic was flowing freely along the Autobahn.

Although there had been some difficulty over locomotives, the Russians had promised to send sixteen freight trains and one passenger train into Berlin each day. Pending settlement of the dispute the trains will be pulled by Soviet zone locomotives.

Western Officials Disturbed

To Berliners who awoke in the night to find lights burning in the streets and in their homes and intersector barriers dismantled, the blockade for the moment seemed over. Americans and British in Military Government offices, however, were distinctly disturbed by the turning back at Soviet checkpoints of trucks bound for the Western zones with Western sector exports.

This refusal to permit trucks to pass stems from a Soviet order of January, 1948. Hence it is not affected by the New York agreement on ending the blockade. But the Western Powers felt that the action indicated that the Russians would not give an inch more than called for by that agreement.

The first railroad train since June of 1948 passed through the checkpoint at Helmstedt, in the British zone at the border of the Soviet zone, at 1:23 A. M., bound for Berlin.

The first car from Helmstedt, driven by Walter G. Rundle, United Press manager for Germany, arrived at the American checkpoint outside Berlin at 1:44. Mr. Rundle had driven the distance, which the British declare is 102 miles, in an hour and thirty-seven minutes. He said that the bridge across the Elbe at Magdeburg was in good condition.

Aide's Wife Enters City

The first woman to enter Berlin after lifting of the blockade was Adelaide de Neufville, wife of Lawrence de Neufville, consultant to the civil affairs division of the United States Military Government.

The first two railroad trains to start across the Soviet zone for Berlin since June 17, 1948, left the Russian control point at Marienborn early this morning. The first of these was a passenger train carrying correspondents. It moved into the moonlit landscape of the Russian zone at 1:55 after an eleven-minute wait at the checkpoint.

Eight minutes later a freight train of forty-two cars carrying coal from the Ruhr for Berlin passed through the checkpoint en route to Berlin, symbolizing the end not only of the Russian blockade

Continued on Page 2, Column 3

Johnson Approves Air Force Plan To Distribute Negroes Among Units

Special to The New York Times.

WASHINGTON, May 11—Latest proposals by the Air Force to conform to armed service policy on racial equality were approved today by Louis Johnson, Secretary of Defense.

W. Stuart Symington, Secretary of the Air Force, wrote to Secretary Johnson on April 30 and assured the defense chief that his directive of April 6 asking equality of treatment and opportunity "without regard to race, color, religion, or national origin" would be put into effect.

One of the principal moves in this direction is an Air Force order disbanding the all-Negro 332nd Fighter Wing at Lockbourne Air Force base at Columbus, Ohio. Its 2,000 officers and men will be distributed throughout the service in non-segregated units, it was stated.

Another assurance given to Mr. Johnson, it was learned, was that "key" positions would be open to Negroes who are individually qualified to hold them.

Letters from Kenneth C. Royall, Secretary of the Army at that time, and Dan A. Kimball, Assistant Secretary of the Navy, answering the same April 6 directive, were in effect rejected by Mr. Johnson on the ground that they were too general. The Secretary of Defense asked the two officials to "clarify" the information contained in their responses. Both letters, it was learned, told Mr. Johnson that his policy was already in effect, and did not indicate that additional changes would be made.

In his reply to the Army and Navy, Mr. Johnson fixed a deadline of May 25 by which the two services are to provide more details of their plans to conform to the equality policy. The services were instructed to make their replies through Thomas R. Reid, chairman of the National Military Establishment's Personnel Policy Board.

Mr. Johnson made his April 6 directive to the armed service secretaries public on April 20, at which time he stated that he in-

Continued on Page 54, Column 1

World News Summarized

THURSDAY, MAY 12, 1949

The 328-day Soviet blockade of Berlin ended on schedule at 12:01 o'clock this morning, Berlin time, and approximately an hour and one-half later the first vehicles from the Western zones of Germany entered the city followed by the first train. [1:8; maps P. 2.]

The first Western passenger train to Berlin was sealed; a jeep led the road convoy [1:7.] Russian guards at Berlin ignored automobiles going to Helmstedt; people watched on the Autobahn. [3:1.]

Secretary of State Acheson warned that the end of the blockade did not, in itself, solve the German problem. He said Russia's willingness at the forthcoming Big Four meeting in Paris to consider proposals that would not erase the progress made in Germany by the Western powers would determine the outcome. He praised the draft constitution for a West German state. [4:2.] The United States was said to be considering a plan for withdrawal of all occupation troops to North German ports, except for French forces, which would return to France. [1:4.]

Guarded optimism was expressed by Moscow's New Times in an editorial on the Big Four meeting. The editorial said the talks could be a "turning point" in East-West relations. [4:6.]

Communists, urging at a Senate hearing in Washington that ratification of the North Atlantic treaty be deferred until after the Paris meeting, likened the pact to "Hitler's Axis." [1:6-7.]

The United States will abstain from a United Nations vote to lift the curbs on full diplomatic relations with Spain, Secretary Acheson said, because of the opposition in Western Europe to any change. Explaining this country's position, he denounced the Franco regime as still functioning along Nazi and Fascist lines. [1:5.]

Israel became the fifty-ninth member of the United Nations when the General Assembly voted, 37 to 12, to admit her. The six Arab states left the hall in protest. [1:1.] Foreign Minister Sharett, the first Israeli delegate to the United Nations, pledged his country to work for peace with its Arab neighbors and to remain friendly with both the United States and Russia. [12:3.]

Japan is not what she was ten years ago, Premier Yoshida said in appealing for proper understanding by the world. He asked access to materials and markets to enable Japan to become self-supporting. [19:1.]

Representative Rankin disowned his veterans' pension bill when a "watered-down" version was reported by a House committee. [1:2.]

Labor leaders and President Truman were said to have agreed on pressing passage of the Administration's labor bill with some amendments. [24:2.]

A man who identified himself as Gerhart Eisler, called this country's No. 1 Communist, sailed secretly on a Polish liner now at sea. [1:6-7.]

Victorious anti-Hague forces in Jersey City will seek a court order impounding all public records until an audit can be made. [1:3.]

Index to other news appears on Page 32.

U.S. Reds Liken Pact to Hitler Axis; Norman Thomas Urges Ratification

By WILLIAM S. WHITE

Special to The New York Times.

WASHINGTON, May 11—The Communist party of the United States, through a statement filed by its general secretary, Eugene Dennis, likened the North Atlantic treaty today to "Hitler's Axis," and demanded that the Senate withhold any action toward its ratification until after the Big Four Foreign Ministers' conference.

However, Norman Thomas, Socialist leader, supported ratification of the treaty before the Senate Foreign Relations Committee, but stressed that he did so with much anxiety because of the "dangers" that might lie in it.

He expressed belief that the pact should not be ratified unless the Senate made it "absolutely plain" that Spain would not be included in it, and equally plain that proposed American military aid should not be used against colonial peoples.

Senator Tom Connally, Democrat, of Texas, committee chairman, said that Spain's inclusion was "highly improbable" since it could be done only by unanimous consent of the twelve countries that signed the treaty.

Above all, Mr. Thomas recommended that before ratification this country issue "a mighty appeal for an end of the armament race under effective international controls which would make the pact unnecessary."

The Communist party proposal that the pact be held back, first advanced last week by Henry A. Wallace, was offered also by representatives of the National Council of American-Soviet Friendship and the National Council of the Arts, Sciences and Professions.

Witnesses for the three organizations appeared before the committee and further urged Soviet-United States conferences looking toward resolving differences between the two countries.

Their recommendations for de-

Continued on Page 7, Column 3

"All the News That's Fit to Print"

The New York Times.

LATE CITY EDITION
Condensation of U. S. Weather Bureau forecast: Mostly fair today and tomorrow.
Temperature range today: 65—48.
Temperature range yesterday: 62.2—48.1.
Full U. S. Weather Bureau Report, Page 71

VOL. CVI—No. 36,074. Entered as Second-Class Matter, Post Office, New York, N. Y. NEW YORK, TUESDAY, OCTOBER 30, 1956. Times Square, New York 36, N. Y. Telephone Lackawanna 4-1000 FIVE CENTS

ISRAELIS THRUST INTO EGYPT AND NEAR SUEZ; U.S. GOES TO U.N. UNDER ANTI-AGGRESSION PACT

Budapest Rebels Refuse to Yield Until Soviet Troops Leave

EISENHOWER BIDS SOUTH FIGHT BIAS ON A 'LOCAL BASIS'

In Miami He Stresses Roles of States—Hails Byrd in Speech in Virginia

Texts of Eisenhower speeches are on Pages 24 and 25.

By RUSSELL BAKER
Special to The New York Times.

RICHMOND, Va., Oct. 29—President Eisenhower, campaigning in the South today, urged that the problem of achieving racial equality be handled largely "on a local and state basis."

He told a Miami Airport audience he was convinced that progress today in equality of opportunity and equality before the law had "to be achieved finally in the hearts of men rather than in legislative halls."

The President was applauded lightly when he said that "there must be intelligent understanding of the human factors and emotions involved if we are to make steady progress in the matter rather than simply to make political promises never intended to be kept."

In the field of civil rights, he added, he had tried to bring "reason, good sense and good judgment to the performance of clear duty."

Makes 1,800-Mile Trip

Though he delivered three airport speeches in an 1,800-mile aerial campaign in Florida and Virginia, he touched on the civil rights issue only once.

That was in Miami, in the President's first speech today.

In Jacksonville, Fla., and Richmond, Va., where the southern tradition is stronger than in Miami, he did not discuss the racial theme. Nor did he refer directly in any of his speeches to the controversial school integration issue or the Supreme Court decision.

He concentrated instead on three matters: peace, prosperity and attacks on the Democratic ticket.

And at Miami General Eisenhower tried for the first time the handshaking style of campaigning developed to a high art by Senator Estes Kefauver.

Surrounded by several hundred rabid admirers on his way to his plane after speaking, he shook hands by the score with a zest rarely matched by Senator Kefauver and a folksiness as impressive as the Senator's own.

"Hi ya, folks," he said, and

Continued on Page 24, Column 4

PRESIDENT GIVEN MINNESOTA LEAD

Resurvey Finds Him Moving Ahead in a Close Contest

A Times Team Report

Teams of New York Times reporters have recently surveyed political trends in twenty-seven closely contested states. They are now rechecking the most doubtful states. Following is a resurvey report from Leonard Buder, Donald Janson and W. H. Lawrence.

By DONALD JANSON
Special to The New York Times.

MINNEAPOLIS, Oct. 28—President Eisenhower appears to hold a tenuous lead in the race for Minnesota's eleven electoral votes.

A month ago New York Times reporters found the President and Adlai E. Stevenson running neck and neck in this state. The Eisenhower victory margin of four years ago—155,000 out of 1,379,000 votes cast — had buckled under the impact of defections by farmers who were caught in a cost-price vise.

The farm revolt remains strong today in some areas.

Continued on Page 26, Column 2

Stevenson Says U.S. Gets 'Less Than Truth' on Strife

Charges President Endangered the Nation by 'Good News' From the Mideast—Boston Crowds Hail Candidate

By HARRISON E. SALISBURY
Special to The New York Times.

BOSTON, Oct. 29—Adlai E. Stevenson charged tonight that President Eisenhower had given the nation reassurances about the Middle East that had been "tragically less than the truth."

"The Government has not been telling us the whole truth," Mr. Stevenson said.

Texts of Stevenson statement and speech, Page 28.

The Presidential nominee addressed an overflow Democratic throng of more than 8,000 in Mechanics Hall in the climax of his drive for Massachusetts' sixteen electoral votes.

Mr. Stevenson's address was televised nationally by the American Broadcasting Company. After the telecast was completed, Mr. Stevenson appended one of his sharpest challenges to President Eisenhower's leadership. The Democrat declared:

"I deeply believe that we cannot afford another four years under a part-time leader of a party which will not plan, which will not create, which will not dare to see the vision of a new America and make that vision come true.

"As a campaigning politician there is none better. It is as a performing politician, as a President who knows how to control his own party, who knows how to grasp the reins of Government that he fails."

Several times Mr. Stevenson's partisan audience booed references to the President. The chorus of boos every time he mentioned Vice President Richard M. Nixon started the moment the crowd sensed that Mr.

Continued on Page 29, Column 3

POLAND'S LEADERS BACK HUNGARIANS

Support Demands for Exit of Soviet Troops—Call for End of Strife

By SYDNEY GRUSON
Special to The New York Times.

WARSAW, Oct. 29—The Polish Communist party, differing sharply once again with the Soviet Union, came out formally today in support of Hungarian demands for the withdrawal of Soviet troops from Hungary.

Yesterday the new leadership of the Polish United Workers (Communist) party rejected the Soviet allegation that foreign agents and counter-revolutionaries were responsible for the Hungarian tragedy. Today the Poles stood up again on the side of the Hungarians.

An appeal to those on both sides of the barricades in Hungary to halt fratricidal strife was issued by Wladyslaw Gomulka, the Polish party's First Secretary, and by Premier Josef Cyrankiewicz.

Emphasizing the growing insistence here for independence in foreign as well as internal affairs, the party statement ignored the Soviet charges of Western interference in Hungary.

For the Poles the statement of solidarity was a means of publicly expressing their appreciation for Hungarian help when Poland was threatened by the Soviet leaders a week ago. Poland escaped Hungary's fate

Continued on Page 22, Column 1

Russians Befriend One Hungarian City

By HOMER BIGART
Special to The New York Times.

GYOR, Hungary, Oct. 29—The small Soviet garrison of this industrial city has retired to a near-by wood, giving the townspeople free rein to rally and shout against the Nagy Government and demand democratic national elections.

The Russians here must be credited with sensible behavior. They abandoned their barracks a few days ago under no pressure and took to the wood.

There the Soviet officers are living with their wives and children in tents. They have not shot anyone. The townspeople show their gratitude by taking the Russians eggs and milk.

And although Gyor has

Continued on Page 13, Column 1

Patrols in Budapest Are Trigger-Happy From Propaganda

By JOHN MacCORMAC
Special to The New York Times.

BUDAPEST, Hungary, Oct. 29—The seventh day of the Hungarian revolution has dawned with Soviet soldiers still patrolling the Budapest streets despite a promise by Hungary's new Government that they would be withdrawn. The Government had qualified its announcement yesterday with the condition "as soon as order has been completely restored."

As far as could be learned, armed resistance in Budapest has ceased, even in the Maria Theresa barracks in Ulloi Ut, which was holding out late yesterday. But that order can ever be completely restored in Budapest as long as the Russians are here seems unlikely because of the fears and propaganda with which the Soviet troops seem to be filled.

At 10 o'clock last night, for instance, a Soviet soldier guarding an area known as Szent Istvan Ut shot and seriously wounded Noel Barber, London Daily Mail correspondent. Mr. Barber had been making a tour of inspection to get the public's reaction to Premier Imre Nagy's announcement that there would be no further firing and that the insurrection had been recognized by his Government as

Continued on Page 15, Column 1

FIGHTING PERSISTS

Russians Still Pulling Out, With Hungarian Units Taking Over

Text of editorial in Communist newspaper on Page 10.

By ELIE ABEL
Special to The New York Times.

VIENNA, Tuesday, Oct. 30—Soviet troops remained in control of Budapest this morning while the Government of Imre Nagy pleaded with the stubborn revolutionaries to lay down their arms.

But the rebels refused to give up the fight until Mr. Nagy had made good on his promise that the Soviet forces would evacuate the battered city, monitored reports from the Hungarian capital said.

This morning the Budapest radio broadcast the following communiqué:

"While Soviet forces are being withdrawn from Budapest, Hungarian police and armed youth units are maintaining order. Such armed groups as are still resisting will lay down their arms at 9 A. M. [3 A. M. New York time] and will then take part in maintaining order."

[Up to 4 A. M. New York time there had been no further reports on the situation in Hungary.]

Appeal Is Pressed

Earlier this morning the Budapest radio broadcast an appeal by Karoly Janda, Defense Minister, to the rebels to lay down their arms before 9 A. M.

In spite of the gradual Soviet withdrawal, fighting in Budapest flared up again last night. Soviet tank forces engaged in heavy combat in several parts of the city. Latest reports said artillery fire was heard in Budapest all night.

Rebels from eastern Hungary and from the region of Gyor in the west were understood to have joined the insurgents in the capital.

The rebel-held Miskolc radio in northeast Hungary, in a broadcast monitored here, urged anti-Communists in Budapest not to lay down their arms before the last Soviet soldier had left the country.

A general strike called by the rebel leaders appeared to be continuing in many parts of Hungary for the fifth day. Most factory workers, railroad men and miners stayed away from their jobs again this morning despite pressing appeals from Mr. Nagy's Government to resume work.

Nearly complete was an unofficial school strike. Instead of attending classes many teen-agers in Budapest did courier work for the rebels and even

Continued on Page 10, Column 4

1950 PLEDGE CITED

White House Recalls Promise to Assist Victim of Attack

By DANA ADAMS SCHMIDT
Special to The New York Times.

WASHINGTON, Oct. 29—The United States will take the movement of Israeli forces into Egypt to the United Nations Security Council tomorrow morning.

The planned appeal to the United Nations was announced by the White House tonight after President Eisenhower had held an emergency meeting there with Secretary of State Dulles and six other high officials.

[An emergency meeting of the Security Council was set for 11 A. M. Tuesday.]

The White House statement follows:

"At the meeting, the President recalled that the United States under this and prior Administrations has pledged itself to assist the victim of any aggression in the Middle East. We shall honor our pledge.

"The United States is in consultation with the British and French Governments, parties with us to the tripartite declaration of 1950, and the United States plans as contemplated by that declaration that the situation shall be taken to the United Nations Security Council tomorrow morning.

Special Session in Abeyance

"The question of whether and when the President will call a special session of the Congress will be decided in the light of the unfolding situation."

The statement was read by James C. Hagerty, Presidential press secretary. He said it had the full authority of the President and the other conferees.

Others at the meeting, in addition to Mr. Dulles, were Charles E. Wilson, Secretary of Defense; Admiral Arthur W. Radford, Chairman of the Joint Chiefs of Staff; Sherman Adams, Assistant to the President; Herbert Hoover Jr., Under Secretary of State, Allen W. Dulles, director of the Central Intelligence Agency, and Wilton B. Persons, deputy assistant to the President.

The one-and-a-half-hour meeting at the White House took place immediately after the President's return by air from a campaign trip in Florida and Virginia.

The State Department said Americans "not performing essential services" would be asked to leave the Middle East. Among the first to leave was a group that flew from Israel to Athens.

Earlier, Secretary of State Dulles had initiated the joint steps with Britain and France.

The State Department an-

Continued on Page 3, Column 1

The New York Times Oct. 30, 1956

ISRAELIS OPEN DRIVE: The advance into Egypt was reported made at and below Kuntilla, with a thrust near the Suez Canal. There was a flare-up in Gaza area (cross).

Cairo Says Egyptian Units Have Engaged the Israelis

By The United Press.

CAIRO, Tuesday, Oct. 30—The Egyptian Army said today it had begun "liquidating" an Israeli force that had thrust deep into Egyptian territory toward the Suez Canal. Egyptian army headquarters announced that the Israeli force had suffered "heavy casualties" in the night-long fighting. It gave no precise figures.

"The enemy's plan to penetrate deep inside Egyptian territory failed," the Egyptian communiqué said. "Egyptian armed forces early this morning started liquidating the enemy forces."

[Iraq informed Egypt early Tuesday that Iraqi troops were ready to offer immediate assistance against the Israeli thrust, The Associated Press said. The offer was announced after an urgent morning meeting of Premier Nuri as-Said's Cabinet in Baghdad.]

Leaves Are Canceled

The high command of the Egyptian armed forces recalled all officers and enlisted men on leave to meet the Israeli threat. Orders broadcast by the Cairo radio said all must "report immediately to their units." Reservists were not affected.

The Egyptian communiqué identified the three frontier checkpoints where it said the Israeli raiders had been halted at Kuntilla, Nekhet and El Mimet. All are on the eastern side of the rocky Sinai Peninsula. [No additional details on the fighting were received up to 5 A. M.]

Suez Canal authorities in Cairo said the situation along the waterway was normal. They said no blackout has been imposed and no emergency alert sounded.

Continued on Page 6, Column 2

FRANCE ACCUSES FIVE OF TREASON

Files Formal Charges Against Algerians Seized in Plane—Sends Aide to Tunisia

By ROBERT C. DOTY
Special to The New York Times.

PARIS, Oct. 29—Five leaders of the Algerian rebellion, seized a week ago, were formally charged today with treason against France. The offense is punishable by death.

The five are Mohammed ben Bella, Mohammed Khider, Mustafa Lachraf, Mohammed Boudiaf and Hossein Ait Ahmed, all members of the Algerian National Liberation Front, which has directed the two-year rebellion against France from headquarters in Cairo.

Their arrest Oct. 22, while aboard a Moroccan plane flying to a conference of North African leaders in Tunis, set off a wave of anti-French protest and violence. Arab anger was based on the theory that the five men were under the protection of Sultan Mohammed V of Morocco, with tacit French consent, at the time of their arrest.

[In the United Nations Security Council, France formally charged Egypt with gunrunning for the Algerian rebels.]

As Algerians, the five seized rebel leaders are French citizens, hence subject to a treason

Continued on Page 10, Column 2

Maria Callas Bows At Opening of 'Met'

By ROSS PARMENTER

Bellini's "Norma" has never been notably popular in this country. But last night, when it opened the Metropolitan Opera's seventy-second season, it established a compound record. Never have so many Americans tried to pay so much money to hear an opera.

The actual sum paid by those who managed to crowd into the opera house was $75,510.50. This exceeded by more than $10,000 the previous box-office record of $65,334, which was set with the opening night "Faust" in 1953. The larger sum, though, was not paid by a larger number of persons. After all, sell-outs have been customary on first nights, and fire regulations re-

Continued on Page 43, Column 4

DEEP DRIVE MADE

Tel Aviv Declares Aim Is to Smash Egyptian Commando Bases

Text of Israeli statement will be found on Page 4.

By MOSHE BRILLIANT
Special to The New York Times.

TEL AVIV, Israel, Oct. 29—An Israeli military force thrust into the Sinai Peninsula of Egypt today. It was reported to have reached within twenty miles of the Suez Canal.

Army sources said the Israelis were west of the crossroads where the road to Kuntilla branches off from the Suez-Quseima highway.

The Israelis were said to have halted there and to have dug in.

A Foreign Ministry statement said the operation had been started "to eliminate the Egyptian fedayeen [commando squad] bases in the Sinai Peninsula."

Army sources said the Israelis had smashed the Egyptian position at Kuntilla and Ras el Naqb at the southern end of the international border. The forces then advanced more than seventy-five miles.

No fighting was reported on the northern end of the border or in the Gaza Strip, which is heavily populated.

'Too Big for a Reprisal'

Reports from the Sinai area described the fighting as "too big for a reprisal and too small for a war." Details of the fighting were not available tonight, but reliable sources said there had been no aerial bombardment of Egyptian positions.

It was not clear tonight whether the Israelis proposed to push on to the Suez Canal or withdraw to Israeli territory, as they have done after reprisal raids. A high official said: "I do not know. It depends on developments."

Yesterday the Israeli Government attributed its decision to call up reserves to what it said was a renewal of commando activities, to the Egyptian-Jordanian-Syrian military alliance negotiated last Wednesday, to Arab declarations that "their principal concern is a war of destruction against Israel" and to the movement of Iraqi forces to Jordan's border.

According to information here, the Egyptians have a considerable part of their Army in the Sinai Peninsula. Their land forces are reported equipped with the

Continued on Page 5, Column 5

CITY SCHOOL AIDES SPUR INTEGRATION

District Lines Are Shifted in Some Brooklyn Areas

By BENJAMIN FINE

Without any public announcement, the Board of Education has quietly begun a program to integrate white and Negro pupils in areas where a segregation pattern has existed in the past.

A score of schools in the Bedford-Stuyvesant area of Brooklyn have become interracial since the fall term opened. Children are taken from the all-Negro schools and put into the formerly all-white schools.

At the same time, fairly large groups of children—ranging from fifty to 200—have been taken from a number of all-white schools and placed in the all-Negro schools. In doing this, the board has amended or discarded the old district and school zoning regulations.

This step is part of a "positive program" on integration, Charles H. Silver, Board of Education president, said yesterday. The board has asked its forty assistant superintendents to do everything possible to place Negro and white children in the same schools.

The superintendents are doing

Continued on Page 30, Column 3

Associated Press Radiophoto

AMERICANS LEAVE ISRAEL: Wives and children of State Department personnel boarding Air Force transport plane last night at Lydda Airport near Jerusalem. They were flown to Athens. More dependents are to follow today.

"All the News That's Fit to Print"

The New York Times.

LATE CITY EDITION
Condensation of U. S. Weather Bureau forecast: Partly cloudy, little temperature change today and tomorrow.
Temperature range today: 65—51.
Temperature range yesterday: 68.3—53.
Full U.S. Weather Bureau Report, Page 46.

VOL. CVI—No. 36,078. Entered as Second-Class Matter, Post Office, New York, N. Y. NEW YORK, SATURDAY, NOVEMBER 3, 1956. Times Square, New York 36, N. Y. Telephone Lackawanna 4-1000 FIVE CENTS

BRITISH AND FRENCH PUSH TOWARD LANDING; ISRAELIS CAPTURE GAZA AND CONTROL SINAI

Hungary Protests to Soviet Against New Troop Moves; West Urges Action by U.N.; Tension Is Rising in Poland

STEVENSON OFFERS A PROGRAM TO END STRIFE IN MIDEAST

Calls for a Cease-Fire and Israel's Security—Detroit Crowd Boos President

Speech at Detroit and remarks at Cleveland, Page 20.

By HARRISON E. SALISBURY
Special to The New York Times.

DETROIT, Nov. 2—Adlai E. Stevenson offered tonight a program to restore peace in the Middle East, based on the security of Israel and restoration of the Western Alliance.

Mr. Stevenson submitted his program to an enthusiastic overflow audience at the Fox Theatre.

He charged that President Eisenhower did not know what had been happening in the Middle East and that "someone had misled him."

Mr. Stevenson's program called for these steps:

¶A cease-fire in the Middle East.

¶Restoration of the Western grand alliance of the United States, France and Britain.

¶Security for Israel against Arab attack.

¶Establishment of the principle of international concern for the Suez Canal and an end of one-man or one-country control.

¶An all-out attack on resettlement of 900,000 Arab refugees in Middle Eastern lands.

¶A joint program for improvement of economic conditions in the Middle East.

Mr. Stevenson's address was carried on a state TV network. Several thousand persons were unable to gain admission to the theatre.

Earlier today, Mr. Stevenson spoke in Cleveland's Public Square. A huge throng heard him demand United Nations action in behalf of the new Hungarian regime.

Democratic officials put the crowd at 65,000. Newspaper reporters estimated it at closer to 30,000. There was agreement, however, that it was larger than General Eisenhower drew in the same place and time three weeks ago.

Tonight Mr. Stevenson asserted that the first task in the

Continued on Page 20, Column 5

COUNCIL HEARING ON QUINN SLATED

Mayor Backs Tenney Report on Official's Carting Job

By CHARLES G. BENNETT

The City Council will hold hearings soon to consider charges against Councilman Hugh Quinn, Queens Democrat.

In a report to Mayor Wagner on Thursday, Investigation Commissioner Charles H. Tenney found that Mr. Quinn had committed an "apparent" violation of the City Charter and had given grounds for his removal from office.

Yesterday Mayor Wagner said he agreed with the Investigation Commissioner's conclusions.

Council Majority Leader Joseph T. Sharkey, Brooklyn Democrat, said he would call the Councilmen together next week, probably Wednesday, to arrange for hearings in the Quinn case. A question for the Councilmen to determine, Mr. Sharkey said, is whether the hearings will be public or private.

The Council, under the Charter, is the judge of the qualifications of its members. It may expel a member by a two-thirds vote.

Mr. Sharkey said he thought

Continued on Page 48, Column 3

Associated Press Radiophoto

HUNGARIAN PREMIER Imre Nagy, Communist who took office during national anti-Soviet uprising, addressing nation by radio. Date when photograph was taken was not given.

Eisenhower Sees Victory, Leaves Campaign to Nixon

By RUSSELL BAKER
Special to The New York Times.

WASHINGTON, Nov. 2—President Eisenhower now is so confident of re-election Tuesday that he is treating Adlai E. Stevenson's driving campaign finish with a show of indifference. This was emphasized last night in Philadelphia when he indicated that, from his point of view, the campaign was over and that henceforth he would address the nation only in the nonpartisan role of President.

It was pointedly driven home today when the White House noted that Vice President Richard M. Nixon, rather than the President, had been selected to reply tonight to the Democratic nominee's attack on foreign policy.

James C. Hagerty, White House press secretary, said the President's discussion of the Middle Eastern and Central European crises Wednesday had been "nonpolitical." Mr. Stevenson's reply last night, he added, "was strictly political."

Mr. Hagerty's implication was that the President no longer intended to trouble with replies to Mr. Stevenson's "political" charges and that this chore now could be handled adequately by Mr. Nixon.

The President, he added, knew in advance the substance of the Vice President's speech. The White House staff had helped Mr. Nixon get "the facts to refute a lot of misstatements that Mr. Stevenson made last night," Mr. Hagerty said.

The White House also an-

Continued on Page 19, Column 6

PRESIDENT LEADS IN PENNSYLVANIA

Slim Edge Not Widened Yet by Crises Abroad—Clark's Margin for Senate Cut

A Times Team Report

Teams of New York Times reporters have now completed a survey of political trends in twenty-seven closely contested states. They have rechecked eight of those states—the most doubtful ones. Following is a final resurvey report by Leonard Buder, Donald Janson and Wayne Phillips.

By WAYNE PHILLIPS
Special to The New York Times.

PHILADELPHIA, Nov. 2—President Eisenhower is clinging to a lead in this state so insubstantial that it could be washed away by a heavy rain on election day.

Depending upon developments in the Middle East crisis, he may be able to increase that lead in the four days remaining before the election. But at the moment the world crisis has served only to create doubts in the minds of voters on both sides of the fence. Those doubts have not yet crystallized in favor of either candidate.

Two weeks ago a New York Times team found the Pennsylvania Democrats well organized and confident. They were fighting an uphill battle against the appeal of the President's personality, but the odds were on their side in a state that once was a bastion of Republicanism.

They appeared to have won the public—and some Republican newspapers, too—to their Senatorial candidate, Joseph S. Clark Jr. They had created a substantial indecision among the 1952 supporters of President Eisenhower, and had won over enough of them to give some hope of carrying the state for Adlai E. Stevenson.

For Mr. Stevenson this state is the keystone in any arch of triumph he may hope to build. Its thirty-two electoral votes, with various combinations of states, could carry him to a

Continued on Page 15, Column 2

Nixon Hails Break With Allies' Policies

By WILLIAM M. BLAIR
Special to The New York Times.

HERSHEY, Pa., Nov. 2—Vice President Richard M. Nixon hailed tonight this country's break with Anglo-French policies as a "declaration of independence that has had an electrifying effect throughout the world."

Speaking with the full backing of President Eisenhower, he assailed Adlai E. Stevenson for charging that the Administration's foreign policy was a failure and that the President should have averted the Middle East crisis.

He said that the United Nations General Assembly vote gave "the lie to [Mr. Stevenson's] preposterous charge" that the United States stood alone "in an unfriendly world."

The General Assembly early

Continued on Page 19, Column 1

TROOPS REPORTED CROSSING POLAND

Soviet Movement Is Said to Be to East Germany—Panic Buying in Warsaw

By SYDNEY GRUSON
Special to The New York Times.

WARSAW, Nov. 2—Reports reached Warsaw tonight of large-scale Soviet troop movements across Poland from Russia to East Germany. No details were available.

The purpose and the meaning of the troop movements were not disclosed. But even before they had been reported the situation in Poland had reached a point of extreme tension.

All through the day the Polish radio repeated its broadcast of an appeal by the Communist party's new leadership for "calm, discipline and a sense of responsibility" within the nation.

In Warsaw panic buying began. People bought up all the foodstuffs in the stores and then after withdrawing their money from the banks began to buy jewelry and valuables.

Word came from various parts

Continued on Page 14, Column 4

U. S. Protests Refusal by Soviet To Let Americans Quit Hungary

Special to The New York Times.

WASHINGTON, Nov. 2—The United States protested tonight to the Soviet Union against the action of Soviet troops who prevented a convoy of Americans from leaving Hungary.

A report of the incident from the United States Legation in Budapest reached the State Department in early evening. Deputy Under Secretary of State Robert Murphy called in Georgi N. Zaroubin, the Soviet Ambassador, at once.

Mr. Zaroubin told Mr. Murphy he would get in touch with his Government in Moscow about the matter.

A State Department spokesman said Mr. Murphy spoke "energetically" to the Soviet Ambassador against the "interference with American official personnel."

According to the official report, the convoy consisted of dependents—wives and children—of diplomatic personnel at the American Legation. Lincoln White, State Department press officer, said the convoy returned safely to Budapest and would attempt to leave the city again tomorrow.

"We had a report from Budapest that a convoy of our legation dependents was turned back near the Austrian border this afternoon by Soviet tank blocks," said Mr. White. "They returned to Budapest safely."

According to Mr. White, Mr. Murphy told the Soviet envoy he "assumed the incident must be due to an error on the part of the Soviet military commander, although he could not imagine why Soviet forces were in that area."

The Ambassador said he had no information on this, Mr. White told reporters, but added "he would immediately communicate with his Government and that he assumed the matter would be straightened out."

Special to The New York Times.

BUDAPEST, Hungary, Nov. 2—A diplomatic convoy carrying out the wives and children of a United State legation staff in Budapest as well as French, British and American correspondents was turned back from the Austrian border by Soviet troops at 4:30 P. M. today.

"Polemics are useless," a Soviet officer told them. "It is requested that you turn around

Continued on Page 16, Column 3

NEW PLEA BY NAGY

Premier Asks That U.N. Defend Neutrality of Hungary

By JOHN MacCORMAC
Special to The New York Times.

BUDAPEST, Hungary, Saturday, Nov. 3—The Hungarian Government made three oral protests yesterday to the Soviet Ambassador in Budapest, complaining that Russian reinforcements were still pouring across the frontier.

[Soviet tanks sealed the main crossings of the Austrian-Hungarian border Friday. This was regarded as a preliminary to dealing sternly with the insurgents.]

Premier Imre Nagy also sent a new appeal to the Secretary General of the United Nations to guarantee Hungary's neutrality and to bring her case before the General Assembly.

Similarly Joseph Cardinal Mindszenty, primate of Hungary, appealed to the West for political support of the revolutionaries and relief for the needy.

Soviet Forces Approaching

Early today, forces at the command of the Revolutionary Council of the Hungarian Army occupied the Foreign Ministry. Other Army units cordoned off the Parliament Building and took up posts on and near all bridges spanning the Danube.

These measures were prompted by information that Soviet forces were approaching the capital.

In his plea to the Secretary General of the United Nations, Premier Nagy said that Hungary's first demand for the withdrawal of Soviet troops had been received favorably by Moscow. In spite of this, he went on, fresh Soviet troops were brought in to Hungary on Tuesday and Wednesday.

The Hungarian Government then denounced the Warsaw Pact, proclaimed Hungary a neutral state and demanded the withdrawal of all Soviet troops. Budapest also proposed the appointment of two joint Hungarian-Soviet committees, one political and one military, to discuss the terms and set the timetable for this withdrawal.

The Premier said that he had protested against any further influx of Soviet soldiers, pointing out to the United Nations that new Soviet units had entered

Continued on Page 15, Column 1

Israelis Are Mopping Up; Egypt Braces for Landing

12,000 Prisoners Taken

By HOMER BIGART
Special to The New York Times.

TEL AVIV, Israel, Saturday, Nov. 3—Israel's lightning conquest of Egypt's Sinai Peninsula and the Gaza Strip is complete except for minor mopping-up operations. The ancient Philistine capital of Gaza was the last town to fall.

In its drive, Maj. Gen. Moshe Dayan's tough Army had killed, captured or put to flight 30,000 Egyptian troops east of the Suez Canal.

With Israel's southern flank secure after only four days of operations, the Government faced with calm confidence reports that Jordan was being reinforced by Syrian troops and that the Syrian-Jordanian-Egyptian defense pact was about to become operative.

Gaza collapsed after a three-hour fight yesterday morning. A United Nations truce aide,

Continued on Page 3, Column 5

Cairo Defense Held Ready

By The United Press.

CAIRO, Nov. 3—Waves of British and French bombers and fighters blasted Cairo and outlying villages today. An Egyptian communiqué said 100 persons had been killed in one town alone.

Simultaneously, President Gamal Abdel Nasser announced that Egyptian forces in the Sinai desert had "completed their withdrawal safely."

"Now we are waiting for the British and French in the delta," he said. Only "suicide commandos" had been left in Sinai to harass the advancing Israeli forces, he added.

The communiqué asserted that fourteen British and French planes had been shot down in today's raids. An earlier communiqué had claimed three kills in the last twenty-four hours in addition to six reported downed yesterday morning. This would

Continued on Page 2, Column 2

U. N. SPEAKERS ASK HELP FOR HUNGARY

Override Soviet Objections as Security Council Argues International Action

Excerpts from Security Council debate are on Page 16.

By LINDESAY PARROTT
Special to The New York Times.

UNITED NATIONS, N. Y., Nov. 2—The Western powers overrode Soviet objections today and called on the United Nations to take measures against Soviet military action in Hungary.

An emergency meeting of the Security Council heard all nations that spoke, except the Soviet Union, appeal for international action against the reinforcement of Soviet troops in Hungary, where rebel nationalists appear to have taken control. Imre Nagy, Hungarian Premier, asked the United Nations yesterday to guarantee the country's neutralism.

No decision was reached at the two-hour session of the Council tonight. The members will meet again tomorrow afternoon in an attempt to decide on a course of action.

The meeting was sparked by a new message from Mr. Nagy distributed to Council members tonight.

The letter, couched in terms similar to the one Mr. Nagy sent to the United Nations yesterday, charged that "large" Soviet military units had crossed the Hungarian border. Moving toward

Continued on Page 16, Column 5

Eisenhower Offers Relief to Hungary

Special to The New York Times.

WASHINGTON, Nov. 2—President Eisenhower late today offered $20,000,000 worth of food and medical supplies to relieve the suffering in Hungary resulting from the revolt against Soviet domination.

The White House announcement of this offer followed a conference between the President, Secretary of State Dulles, and Under Secretary of State Herbert Hoover Jr.

The aid would consist of $15,000,000 in surplus foodstuffs and $5,000,000 in specially purchased meats, oils, fats, and medical supplies.

The President urged the American people to continue sending their contributions to the American Red Cross, which is pouring relief supplies into

Continued on Page 16, Column 7

PARIS ACTS TO BAR CEASE-FIRE NOW

Fears That Immediate Halt in Military Operations Would Save Nasser

By HAROLD CALLENDER
Special to The New York Times.

PARIS, Nov. 2—The French Government moved fast today to prevent a United Nations cease-fire in the Suez Canal Zone.

It feared a halt in military operation now would save Gamal Abdel Nasser, President of Egypt, whose regime the French and British seek to liquidate. In that case the French would feel deprived of a victory they regard as already within their grasp.

This was the explanation of the hurried trip to London during the day by Christian Pineau, French Foreign Minister, that was given by high political authorities here tonight.

In London, M. Pineau, Prime Minister Eden and Selwyn Lloyd, British Foreign Secretary, were reported to have agreed they would not accept a cease-fire at least until British-French troops had landed. They were expected to land tomorrow.

Action by U. N. Noted

The United Nations General Assembly voted early today for a cease-fire in the Middle East but the question was how it could be carried out.

[Prime Minister Eden rejected a Laborite demand that he order an immediate end to British attacks on Egypt. This was in response to Laborite pressure that he comply with the resolution of the United Nations General Assembly calling for a cease-fire.]

The fear that took possession of French officials was that Prime Minister Eden might agree to a premature cease-fire. If so, he would do it, according to these officials, because he is harried by the British Labor party to call off the French-British military expedition to Egypt, and because he is pressed by Secretary of State Dulles, who is credited here with desiring a cease-fire before the United States election Tuesday.

It was even suggested that the United States Sixth Fleet, now in the Mediterranean, might be mandated by the General Assembly to occupy the Suez Canal zone, instead of the French-British forces now preparing to occupy it.

This fear arose because Lester B. Pearson, Canadian Secretary of State for External Affairs, proposed yesterday in New York that the General Assembly should authorize the immediate

Continued on Page 6, Column 4

BOMBING PRESSED

Planes Center Attacks on Army After Cairo Loses Airpower

By DREW MIDDLETON
Special to The New York Times.

LONDON, Nov. 2—The neutralization of the Egyptian Air Force, a primary condition to successful landing operations, was claimed tonight by British and French airpower.

More than a hundred Egyptian planes have been destroyed or damaged at airfields by bombers and fighters of Royal Air Force and French Air Force. A high proportion of these were Soviet-built MIG-15 jet fighter planes and Ilyushin-28 twin-jet bombers, R. A. F. sources said.

At the outset of the operations the Egyptian Air Force had ninety MIG's and fifty Ilyushins. Since not all of them were airworthy Wednesday when the attack began, the allies' claim to have neutralized Egypt's airpower appears valid.

Transit Camp Bombed

The British-French air attack is shifting away from air bases onto the Egyptian Army's central forces, now known to be moving slowly northward and northeastward away from the Cairo area.

British air reconnaissance reported the movement of tanks and infantry into the area around Port Said, one of the three sites chosen by the allies for occupation.

One target successfully attacked was a military transit camp, around which tanks and guns were concentrated, about fifteen miles northeast of Cairo in the El Khanka area.

[The British reported that the Egyptians had sunk seven ships in an effort to block the Suez Canal. It was not known in London whether the Egyptian effort had succeeded. No word of an allied landing in Egypt had been received up to 4 A. M., New York time.]

Information that the Syrian Government was placing its armed forces under the commander in chief of the Egyptian forces has not altered British or French planning for forthcoming operations.

As part of the psychological preparation for the allied landing operations the Cairo Radio, the Voice of Arabia, was silenced

Continued on Page 2, Column 3

ARABS SAID TO PUT TROOPS IN JORDAN

Syrian and Iraqi Forces Are Reported on March

By DANA ADAMS SCHMIDT
Special to The New York Times.

WASHINGTON, Nov. 2—Syrian and Iraqi troops are marching into Jordan, according to information telephoned from Cairo, the Egyptian Embassy press counselor announced tonight.

The official, Mohammed Habib, reported also that Lebanese workers had cut one of the pipelines that carry Arabian oil to the Mediterranean.

The report of the troop movements followed announcement by Syria, in a formal note to the State Department, that she had placed her armed forces under Egyptian command. This was done under terms of the Syrian-Egyptian defense pact, the Syrian Chargé d'Affaires, Mamdi Jamil, informed the State Department.

"The Syrian armed forces are now taking orders from the Egyptian Commander in Chief, Gen. Abdel Hakim Amer," Mr. Jamil said, continuing, "Syria

Continued on Page 2, Column 3

"All the News That's Fit to Print"

The New York Times.

LATE CITY EDITION

U.S. Weather Bureau Report (Page 54) forecasts: Mostly sunny, chance of showers. Clear tonight. Cloudy tomorrow. Temp. range: 88—68, yesterday: 90—69.

VOL. CXI..No. 38,114. © 1962 by The New York Times Company. Times Square, New York 36, N.Y. NEW YORK, FRIDAY, JUNE 1, 1962. 10 cents beyond 50-mile zone from New York City except on Long Island. Higher in air delivery cities. FIVE CENTS

SOVIET INCREASES MEAT PRICES 30% TO SPUR FARMING

Butter Is Also Raised 25% in Move to Obtain Funds for Livestock Needs

U.S. ARMS DRIVE BLAMED

Moscow Asserts Threat of Nuclear Attack Prevents Shift of Defense Money

By SEYMOUR TOPPING

Special to The New York Times.

MOSCOW, Friday, June 1—The Soviet Government announced early today increases of 30 per cent in the retail price of meat and 25 per cent in the price of butter.

The announcement called upon the Soviet people to support these "temporary" increases in living costs as a measure directed at stimulating lagging production of agricultural products.

It said that the collective farmers had "not been materially interested in increasing the output of livestock products" because purchase prices had been too low.

A joint statement by the Government and the Central Committee of the Communist party said that the leadership had found it impossible to divert the funds needed for adequate investment in agriculture from defense, heavy industry or housing.

Reference to Kennedy

The Soviet people were told that there was "no other way out," because the Western powers headed by the United States were engaged in an arms race and in "harboring plans for a surprise nuclear rocket attack on the Soviet Union and other Socialist countries."

As alleged proof of the United States' intention, the statement cited the remarks attributed to President Kennedy in a published interview last March that the United States in some circumstances might take the initiative in the use of nuclear weapons.

In recent weeks Soviet leaders and the press here repeatedly have cited President Kennedy's remarks without his qualifying statement that he had no intention of suggesting that the United States might take aggressive action or launch a so-called preventive war.

The President explained that his remarks had been a restate-

Continued on Page 4, Column 4

Eichmann Dies on Gallows For Role in Killing of Jews

Ben-Zvi Rejects Appeal for Mercy by Former Gestapo Officer

By LAWRENCE FELLOWS

Special to The New York Times.

RAMLE, Israel, Friday, June 1—Adolf Eichmann was hanged just before last midnight for the part he played in rounding up millions of Jews and transporting them to their deaths in Nazi camps during World War II.

President Itzhak Ben-Zvi rejected Eichmann's appeal for mercy shortly before the execution.

Eichmann's body was cremated early today, as had been requested in his will. The ashes were scattered in the Mediterranean outside Israeli waters.

Cold and unyielding to the end, Eichmann rejected an appeal by a Protestant minister that he repent. His last words, spoken in German to a small group of witnesses in the execution chamber, were:

"After a short while, gentlemen, we shall all meet again.

Associated Press

Adolf Eichmann

So is the fate of all men. I have lived believing in God and I die believing in God.

"Long live Germany. Long live Argentina. Long live Austria. These are the countries

Continued on Page 2, Column 3

U.S. AND CITY OPEN 12.6-MILLION WAR ON DELINQUENCY

3-Year Plan Aims to Reform Entire Lower East Side as Example to Nation

By MARJORIE HUNTER

Special to The New York Times

WASHINGTON, May 31—President Kennedy announced today a $12,600,000 mass social experiment on the Lower East Side of New York. It is part of a program designed to strike eventually at the roots of the national juvenile delinquency problem.

The three-year project, called Mobilization for Youth, will be financed jointly by Federal, city and private funds. It was called "the most advanced program yet devised to combat delinquency on a broad scale."

The announcement was made in the White House garden, just outside the President's office. Attending the ceremony were Attorney General Robert F. Kennedy, chairman of the President's Committee on Juvenile Delinquency; Abraham A. Ribicoff, Secretary of Health, Education and Welfare; Secretary of Labor Arthur Goldberg, Mayor Wagner and members of the New York Congressional delegation.

'Action by All' Urged

The President said juvenile delinquency was a "matter which requires action by us all in this decade."

Using the Lower East Side area as a giant laboratory, project officials will seek to reform the social patterns of an entire community as a way of guiding youth into conforming with the accepted patterns of American life.

They will cover a broad range of social activities, from organizing the play of 7-year-olds to examining the political structure and community attitudes of adults.

There will be an Urban Youth Service Corps to provide jobs for 16-to-21-year-olds, an Adventure Corps on paramilitary lines for boys 9 to 16, "cool and jazzy" coffee shops featuring art and folk music, and improved welfare services to "troubled" families.

Special Programs Set

And there will be special school programs for both youths and adults, community development programs, a narcotics demonstration project, and a program to rehabilitate juvenile offenders.

The project is based on a theory, developed by Mobilization for Youth, Inc., of 214 East Second Street, New York City, that there must be a systematic approach to the problems of juvenile delinquency.

The administrative director of the project will be James E. McCarthy, a 45-year-old graduate of the University of Notre Dame who has specialized in youth and social work.

Officials here said that the Federal and state funds for the project would be available July 1 and that the program would

Continued on Page 14, Column 1

Associated Press Wirephoto

ANNOUNCE YOUTH PROGRAM: Attorney General Robert F. Kennedy, left, Mayor Wagner, and President Kennedy discuss Mobilization for Youth project at White House.

STOCKS WIPE OUT MONDAY'S LOSSES IN NEW ADVANCE

Tuesday's Rally Is Extended—Exchange Flooded Again—Volume 10,710,000

INDEX UP 1.59 FOR WEEK

S.E.C. Chief Denies Rigging Inquiry but Says Agency Will Study Fluctuations

By BURTON CRANE

Buy orders surged into the New York Stock Exchange yesterday and erased what remained of the Monday losses.

The gain for the day was about $8,100,000,000, and for the week it was $800,000,000. At the close, aggregate values stood about 6.6 per cent below those of May 18, just before the recent six-day decline began, and 18 per cent below the high point of 1961.

It was not a unanimous advance and many leading issues did not join in it. While American Telephone was rising 4⅜ points, Corning Glass 5 and Sears, Roebuck 3⅞, Eastman Kodak was slipping 4⅞, Beckman Instruments 7¼, Pittsburgh Plate Glass 5¼ and Polaroid 4¼.

Study in Contrast

But the market's general performance yesterday was in dramatic contrast to that of Monday, when it had its widest one-day loss since "Black Tuesday," Oct. 29, 1929.

The Monday loss, based on the 500-stock index of the Standard & Poor's Corporation, was $20,800,000,000 and volume was the fifth greatest in history at 9,350,000 shares.

On Tuesday, the market rallied sharply to recover $13,500,000,000, or 60 per cent, of Monday's losses. Volume on Tuesday was 14,750,000 shares, second only to the 16,410,030 shares traded on Oct. 29, 1929.

As on Monday and Tuesday, the heavy volume yesterday again swamped the exchange, causing reporting devices to run late. At the close, the ticker was one hour and forty-six minutes late.

News yesterday dealing with economic developments appeared to have mixed implications for the stock market.

On the one hand, Washington reported a slight improvement in the nation's employment picture during May.

And the chairman of the Securities and Exchange Commis-

Continued on Page 33, Column 2

RUSK BRUSHES OFF SOVIET TRADE IDEA

Khrushchev Plan for Parley Called Attempt to Divert West From Its Goals

By MAX FRANKEL

Special to The New York Times.

WASHINGTON, May 31—Secretary of State Dean Rusk brushed aside today Premier Khrushchev's call for a world trade conference, describing it as a "diversion" that betrayed understandable concern about the economic vitality of the West.

The Secretary said at a news conference that there was no point in interrupting the "great" movement toward unity in Western Europe merely to talk about larger trade issues that were amply discussed in existing institutions.

The European Economic Community, or Common Market, he said, is flourishing and offers bright prospects not only to its members but also to its trading partners.

He Describes Commitment

Mr. Rusk cited the Common Market in rebutting charges that the Administration pursued a policy of "anything but victory."

He also said, in discussing another phase of Administration policy, that Washington expected a showdown in Laos in a few days.

The United States policy toward the Common Market, foreign aid, and the Western alliance in general, Mr. Rusk said, is evidence of the Administration's commitment "to the notion that the wave of the future lies with freedom."

He challenged Senator Barry Goldwater, Republican of Arizona, who made the "no-win" charge, to offer alternatives other than "unrealistic" ones of hydrogen war or retreat from international commitments.

The Secretary expressed disappointment over the lack of progress in negotiations with the Soviet Union both on dis-

Continued on Page 4, Column 4

Conciliation Moves Are Made in Algiers As Terrorism Ebbs

By THOMAS F. BRADY

Special to The New York Times.

ALGIERS, May 31—As terrorism here fell well below the daily level of the last two weeks, three steps were taken today in the direction of reconciling the European and Moslem communities of this violent land.

These steps, decidedly preliminary in nature, coincided with reports of contacts between some unidentified Right-Wing European leaders and Abderrahmane Fares, president of the transitional executive that is governing Algeria temporarily under an internal autonomy arrangement until the July 1 referendum on independence.

The steps appeared to be part of a concerted campaign by the Algerian nationalists and the French authorities to check the exodus of Europeans from Algeria.

Europeans at Meeting

In the Moslem section of Belcourt, a working-class district, about 200 Europeans gathered in a tiny movie theatre at 5 P. M. under "the protection of nationalist militants." They asked questions of a spokesman for the Algerian National Liberation Front and adopted a motion of confidence in the future of Algeria.

Three hours later Roger Roth, European vice president of the transitional executive, spoke on the Algiers television urging his fellow-Europeans to read the guarantees accorded them in the peace and self-determination agreements signed at Evian-les-Bains March 18 by the French Government and the Algerian Provisional Government.

He warned that there could be no question of changing or denouncing the Evian agreements, as some Europeans have demanded, but went on to say that the pact was a framework to be filled in and that the Europeans of Algeria could decide, if they would, what the content should be.

Earlier at Rocher-Noir, the fortified administrative capital, Bernard Tricot, the Delegate

Continued on Page 2, Column 2

REGENTS INCREASE TEACHER TRAINING

5th Year Added to Standard for Elementary Grades—Specialization Stressed

By FRED M. HECHINGER

A substantial tightening of teacher-training standards for New York State's elementary schools was announced by the Board of Regents yesterday.

The new regulations significantly increase the general education required of teachers. They also call for a five-year program of college education for a permanent certificate, compared with the present requirement of a four-year bachelor's degree.

At the same time, colleges and universities were warned that they must improve their teacher-training courses and the quality of their faculties.

The new regulations call for greater breadth of study in the liberal arts and for concentration in at least one selected academic subject. The reform is in line with a nation-wide trend toward greater specialization in elementary schools and toward a declining stress on courses in educational methods apart from practice teaching.

The move, made public by Dr. James E. Allen Jr., State Education Commissioner, follows the raising of academic requirements for high school teachers in September, 1960.

The rules for elementary school teachers will become effective for those seeking certification after Sept. 1, 1966. However, candidates preparing for elementary-school teaching will still be permitted to begin classroom teaching with a provisional certificate after four

Continued on Page 24, Column 4

Administration Is Hopeful Of Faster Rise in Economy

By JOHN D. MORRIS

Special to The New York Times.

WASHINGTON, May 31—The Administration held out hope today for a faster-than-expected upturn in the national economy in the last three quarters of this year.

Secretary of the Treasury Douglas Dillon and Budget Director David E. Bell cited that possibility as a factor in the Administration's decision to stand by its January forecast of a balanced Federal budget in the fiscal year that starts July 1.

They testified before the House Ways and Means Committee for an Administration bill to fix the national debt limit at $308,000,000,000 for the twelve-month period. The present limit of $300,000,000,000 automatically will drop to $285,000,000,000 July 1 in the absence of Congressional action.

The increase is being sought to cover a budget deficit of $7,000,000,000 in the current fiscal year.

Budget Balance Doubted

Questions by members indicated that the continued forecast of a balanced budget in the coming fiscal year was not wholly convincing to the committee. Words such as "unrealistic" and "highly doubtful" were used by questioners.

Actually, the unofficial position of the Administration is that a balance is now unlikely to be achieved in view of the failure of economic activity to live up to January's expectations in the first three months of the 1962 calendar year. A budget deficit of several billion dollars is now being unofficially predicted.

Secretary Dillon conceded under questioning that the official forecast was now less realistic than it had been in January and would be "much more

Continued on Page 10, Column 1

EMPLOYMENT SETS A RECORD FOR MAY

68,203,000 in Civilian Jobs for Month—Number of Idle Down by 227,000

By JOHN D. POMFRET

Special to The New York Times.

WASHINGTON, May 31—The nation's employment situation improved slightly in May.

The Labor Department announced today that unemployment fell by 227,000 in the month to 3,719,000. Civilian employment, paced by a rise in the number of nonfarm workers to a record level, rose by 1,379,000 to a record of 68,203,000 for May.

The decline in unemployment was about that expected at this time of year. The rise in employment was about 500,000 above the seasonal level.

The effect was to cut the unemployment rate, with seasonal factors eliminated, from 5.5 per cent to 5.4. The rate is the proportion of the labor force that is looking for work and cannot find it.

The last time the rate was as low as 5.4 per cent was in July, 1960. It was 7 per cent last May—its recession high—and has been dropping steadily since.

Secretary of Labor Arthur J. Goldberg, in a statement accompanying the figures, said:

"The fact that employment is at record levels and that unemployment is continuing to go down is encouraging and shows a continued improvement in the economy."

Nonfarm employment rose by 912,000 to 62,775,000 in May. The old record was 62,215,000.

Continued on Page 10, Column 5

KOREA SEIZES 41 IN PLOT ON JUNTA

Regime Says They Aimed at Restoring Civilian Rule

By The Associated Press

SEOUL, Korea, Friday, June 1—The South Korean military Government said today it had smashed a plot to overturn the ruling junta and kill its members. It said forty-one persons were under arrest.

Col. Kim Chong Pil, director of the Central Intelligence Agency, said the organizers of the plot were primarily leaders of the deposed Democratic party of former Premier John M. Chang.

He said the plan of the plotters was for a military coup d'état June 13 with restoration of the civilian Government by Aug. 15.

Colonel Kim disclosed the identity of only fifteen of the forty-one persons he said were under arrest.

If charged and convicted with counter-revolutionary activity, the forty-one could face the death penalty.

The ruling junta took over in a coup last May, ousting Dr. Chang and his party.

On July 3, Gen. Chung Hee Park took control from the officer who had become Premier, Lieut. Gen. Chang Do Young. General Chang was originally sentenced to death for counter-revolutionary activities, but his sentence was commuted to life imprisonment and he was pardoned last month.

The latest arrest list included the former Seoul Mayor, Sang Don Kim, and his wife; Cho Jung Su, Democratic party organization chief, and Kim Dai

Continued on Page 5, Column 5

Kennedy Adopts Buildings Plan To Give Capital a Modern Look

By ADA LOUISE HUXTABLE

President Kennedy directed the Government yesterday to proceed with a large Federal office-building program according to the most advanced principles of modern architectural design, and to make Pennsylvania Avenue a model of the new policy.

These plans are included in a Report to the President on Federal Office Space, approved by the President in Washington and passed on to Government departments for immediate action.

The report prepares the way for a record amount of new Federal building, calls specifically for the improvement of Federal architectural standards and endorses the use of the best modern architecture for all major new construction. Its provisions will have substantial and far-reaching effects on official building in the nation's capital and throughout the country.

The President's directive, however, does not assure smooth sailing for the program. Although his order makes it obligatory for Government departments to follow the new policy in new construction, Congress, which controls appropriations, can still be a stumbling block to its realization. Members of Congress have not been notably hospitable to modern design programs in the past, and have cut back a program of the State Department's Office of Foreign Buildings for contemporary embassies by withholding funds.

Even with these difficulties, however, two parts of the proposal will bring a sweeping new look to Government architec-

Continued on Page 12, Column 2

Associated Press Wirephoto

BEFORE HEARING ON NATIONAL DEBT: Representative Wilbur D. Mills of Arkansas, left, chairman of House Ways and Means Committee, meets with Douglas Dillon, right, Secretary of Treasury, and David E. Bell, Director of the Budget Bureau, prior to committee hearing at which Mr. Dillon and Mr. Bell testified for extension to debt limit.

School Contractors To Repay $100,000

By LEONARD BUDER

The Board of Education agreed last night to accept $100,000 in restitution from six plumbing contractors under indictment for allegedly defrauding the school system.

The payment will represent "full and final settlement of all claims by the board for damages or penalties."

Nine officials of the concerns involved were indicted last December by a Queens grand jury on charges of collusive bidding to obtain school contracts. The indictment held that the contractors had defrauded the system of $289,609 on $2,800,000 worth of school work.

A resolution adopted by the school board last night noted that the contractors had "pleaded guilty to misdemeanors with leave to withdraw such pleas and to contest the charges made in event they are unable

Continued on Page 14, Column 4

MARYLAND VOTES NEW URBAN SEATS

Adds 19 Delegates Under Order to Reapportion

By The Associated Press

ANNAPOLIS, Md., May 31—The Maryland Legislature gave metropolitan areas nineteen more seats in the House of Delegates tonight in response to a court order requiring reapportionment.

The action was completed only thirty-eight minutes before a constitutional deadline for enactment of the statute. It will replace temporarily a section of the state constitution held invalid by a Federal court.

The Senate accepted the stopgap plan by a vote of 16 to 13, one more than necessary, after it had cleared the House of Delegates, 69 to 51. This was seven more votes than necessary.

A more permanent reapportionment plan, which would take away some of the seats small counties now hold, is to be drafted at the 1963 session of the Legislature and submitted to voters as a constitutional amendment taking effect in 1966.

Legislators were deadlocked on the issue earlier today after Gov. J. Millard Tawes sent a

Continued on Page 12, Column 4

NEWS INDEX

"All the News That's Fit to Print"

The New York Times

LATE CITY EDITION

Weather: Sunny and warm today; fair tonight and tomorrow. Temp. range: today 83-61; Monday 81-62. Temp.-Hum. Index: 75; Monday 61-72. Full U.S. report on Page 93.

VOL. CXVI..No. 39,945 NEW YORK, TUESDAY, JUNE 6, 1967 10 CENTS

ISRAELI AND ARAB FORCES BATTLING; BOTH CLAIM LAND AND AIR VICTORIES; CEASE-FIRE EFFORTS STALLED IN U.N.

4 States Hit by Blackout

JERSEY HURT MOST

13 Million Affected—Power Back Quickly in Philadelphia

By PETER KIHSS

A massive electrical failure along an interconnected system shut off power at midmorning yesterday for 13 million persons in 15,000 square miles — three-fourths of New Jersey, much of eastern Pennsylvania and eastern Maryland and the northern half of Delaware.

It was more than three hours before power started to come back on in Newark. The restoration of power started in Philadelphia, the nation's fourth largest city, about a half hour after the failure occurred.

Not until 8:15 P.M. did Russell H. Williams, vice president for public relations for the Public Service Electric and Gas Company of New Jersey, report all sections served by his company had regained their electricity.

New York City escaped with only some flickering of lights in Brooklyn and Staten Island and a slight voltage drop when, according to the Consolidated Edison Company, a sensor device at 10:18 A.M. automatically cut off a tie-in to New Jersey across the Arthur Kill.

Source and Cause Sought

Last night, the Federal Power Commission said the precise source and cause—human, mechanical or just too much demand—were still being sought. But Lee C. White, its chairman, said the commission had been worrying for some time about the ability of the Pennsylvania-Jersey-Maryland grid to meet this summer's demand.

The failure — this time fortunately during sunshine, in contrast to the historic Nov. 9, 1965, blackout in New York City and the Northeast—spread with thunderbolt speed from the New Jersey-New York border and Wilkes-Barre, Pa., on the north, to south of Dover, Del., and west to Harrisburg, Pa.

Ingenuity, imagination and a gentle sense of resignation followed in the path of the blackout. Housewives sighed wearily and put away their irons. Subway riders took buses and elevator riders walked.

People sitting in front of radio and television sets listening to the news of the crisis in the Middle East felt new bewilderment as the sets faded out.

One of the last communities to have its power restored, about 7:30 P.M., was Montclair, N. J. During the day stores in the main business area closed—including a barber who finished his last haircut on the sidewalk outside his shop—and residents made thousands of calls to the police asking advice on "everything under the sun."

Continued on Page 42, Column 1

Traffic Is Snarled As Signals Go Out

By PAUL HOFMANN

Motorists blew their horns in self-defense and drove gingerly through intersections where traffic lights were out. 1,500 persons were stranded in the Philadelphia subway and railroad trains in four states rolled to a halt in yesterday's power blackout.

Air traffic over the Northeast generally suffered only little delay and disruption, but Newark Airport was severely crippled for the first hour or so after the power failure started and before emergency equipment could restore partial power.

The Newark control tower was cut off from aircraft on the ground and in the air.

Continued on Page 42, Column 7

HIGH COURT CURBS HOME INSPECTIONS

Backs Right to Deny Entry Not Supported by Warrant —Also Protects Business

By FRED P. GRAHAM
Special to The New York Times

WASHINGTON, June 5 — Property owners may refuse to open their homes or businesses to health, fire and other administrative inspectors unless they have search warrants, the Supreme Court ruled today.

In extending the search warrant requirement beyond law enforcement officials to the routine inspections of administrative authorities, the Court relaxed the traditional standards for the issuance of search warrants.

It ruled that inspectors may obtain warrants to enter premises without having cause to believe that evidence of an ordinance violation would be found inside.

The 6-to-3 opinion by Justice Byron R. White said that such warrants might be obtained for an entire city area simply by showing that a certain period of time had passed since the last inspection, or by showing that the buildings were in a rundown condition.

This provoked a strong dis-

Continued on Page 32, Column 3

The New York Times

HOSPITAL DIMMED: A nurse comforting a patient in a dark corridor of Jersey City Medical Center yesterday.

Speck Is Sentenced To Chair on Sept. 1

By DONALD JANSON
Special to The New York Times

PEORIA, Ill., June 5—Richard F. Speck was sentenced to death in the electric chair today for the murders last summer in Chicago of eight young nurses.

The 25-year-old drifter stood mute and expressionless a foot in front of the bench as Circuit Court Judge Herbert C. Paschen ordered the execution for Sept. 1.

Before sentence was passed, the public defender, Gerald W. Getty, told the judge that the lanky, itinerant seaman had nothing to say in his own behalf.

A jury of seven men and five women found Speck guilty of each of the murders last April

Continued on Page 36, Column 4

U.S. PLANES DOWN 3 MIG'S NEAR HANOI IN RAID ON BRIDGES

Foe Mounts Heavy Defense —Soviet Rejects American Denial of Ship Attack

By United Press International

SAIGON, South Vietnam, June 5—United States planes bombed North Vietnam's war industry today and shot down three MIG interceptors near Hanoi. Military spokesmen said that the North Vietnamese had put up heavy air defenses.

F-105 Thunderchiefs flew into the heart of North Vietnam's industrial triangle and bombed railroad bridges around the Thaiguyen manufacturing complex. Other United States planes bombed a manufacturing complex near the Phucyen MIG base, about 20 miles north of Hanoi.

Officials said that all three MIG's had been shot down by Phantoms flying protective cover for the Thunderchiefs. There were no reports of American air losses.

[In Moscow, the Soviet Government rejected a United States denial that American planes had attacked a Soviet merchant ship in a North Vietnamese port Friday. Page 3.]

MIG Total Reaches 77

The enemy losses brought to 77 the total number of MIG's shot down by American aircraft over North Vietnam.

The Soviet press agency, Tass, said that two United States planes were shot down over North Vietnam today, but there was no American confirmation.

Maj. Durward K. Priester, 36 years old, of Hampton, S.C., and Capt. John Pankhurst, 27, of Midland, Mich., both of the Air Force, were credited with one of the MIG's.

Pilots Fly 98 Missions

Special to The New York Times

SAIGON, June 5—Although poor weather covered most of North Vietnam yesterday, pilots flew 98 missions in the southern Panhandle, the narrow stretch of North Vietnam just north of the border.

Two United States planes were lost: an F-105 Thunder-

Continued on Page 3, Column 5

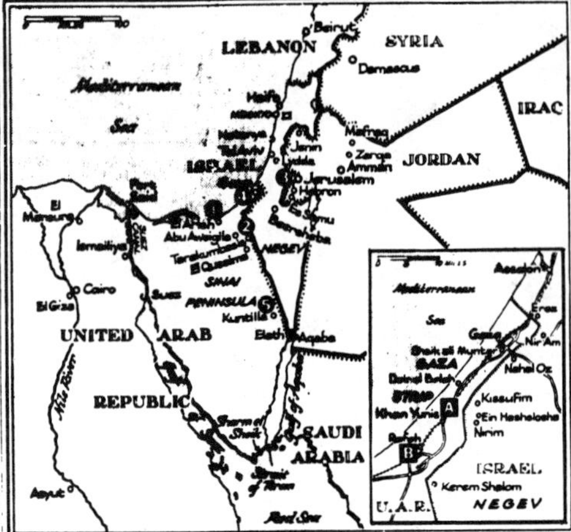

The New York Times June 6, 1967

WAR IN MIDEAST: Israelis reported they seized El Arish (1) and Tarakumbasis (2). Fighting was heavy in Jerusalem (3) and Gaza Strip (4). Cairo said it repulsed foe at Kuntilla (5) and Khan Yunis (A on inset), but Israel said she took latter and Rafah (B).

Egypt, Backed by Soviet, Blocks U.N. Call for Truce

By DREW MIDDLETON
Special to The New York Times

UNITED NATIONS, N. Y., June 5—The Security Council recessed tonight after 12 hours of futile effort to frame a resolution calling for a cease-fire and a withdrawal of forces in the Arab-Israeli war.

The refusal of the United Arab Republic to obey any resolution that demanded the withdrawal of its forces beyond the positions they occupied Sunday was the chief reason for the deadlock.

Statements in U.N. debate are printed on Page 17.

The Egyptian intransigence was strengthened, qualified sources said, by the support of the Soviet Union and India. On the other hand, there were indications Nikolai T. Fedorenko of the Soviet Union had asked his Government for further instructions.

"It is quite evident," a Western delegate said, "that the Russians do not like the prospect of another 'eyeball-to-eyeball' confrontation with the United States over what to them is a sideshow."

Denmark's representative on the 15-member Council, Hans Tabor, who is this month's President, announced the recess. He said that the consultations were still going on and would continue tomorrow, and he set 11:30 A.M. as the time for the next meeting.

Mr. Tabor asked members to be available from 10:30 A.M. He had hoped, he said, that when he recessed the first of today's meetings this morning that recess would be shorter than it was.

During the interval between the two brief meetings, the United Arab Republic, backed

Continued on Page 17, Column 3

MOSCOW DEMANDS ISRAEL QUIT EGYPT

Soviet Bids U.N. Condemn 'Aggression' and Repeats Support of Arabs

By PETER GROSE
Special to The New York Times

MOSCOW, Tuesday, June 6—The Soviet Union demanded today that Israel "immediately and unconditionally" halt military operations and pull her troops back from Egyptian territory.

A Government statement condemned "Israeli aggression," asserted the Soviet "right to take all steps that may be necessitated by the situation" and called on states, specifically including the major powers, to work for peace.

"The United Nations "must discharge its direct duty: condemn Israeli actions and promptly take steps to restore peace in the Middle East," the statement said.

It expressed the hope that other governments "will do, for their part, everything in their power to extinguish the military conflagration in the Middle East."

This was the first official reaction from the Soviet Govern-

Continued on Page 18, Column 6

U.S. SEEKS TO HOLD A NEUTRAL STANCE

Presses for a Cease-Fire—Many in Congress Oppose a Unilateral Move in Area

By JOHN W. FINNEY
Special to The New York Times

WASHINGTON, June 5—The Administration sought today to maintain a neutral role in the Middle East without formally committing itself to be neutral.

The White House, warning that "tragic consequences" would result if the fighting continued, called on both sides to accept an immediate cease-fire. The dominant Congressional reaction was that the United States should take no unilateral action in the Middle East.

In an attempt to bring about a cease-fire, the Administration deliberately refrained from fixing any blame for the outbreak of fighting.

[In London, the Foreign Secretary said that Britain's policy was "not to take sides." France suspended all deliveries of military equipment to the Middle East. Page 18.]

Confusion Develops in U.S.

The Johnson Administration, in attempting to maintain a position for mediation, became entangled in some confusion over how "neutral" it was.

The State Department spokesman, Robert J. McCloskey, started the confusion by declaring that "our position is neutral in thought, word and deed."

The Administration then spent the rest of the day attempting to tone down the McCloskey declaration by emphasizing that the United States was not neutral in terms of long-standing obligations to support the political independence and territorial integrity of Israel and of the Arab nations.

As it cast around for some way to bring the fighting to an end, the Administration announced that travel by American citizens to Israel and 13 Arab countries was being banned, unless the traveler had the specific permission of the State Department.

As of today, the State Department announced, United

Continued on Page 18, Column 1

U.S. Military Analysts Expect Short War, With Israel Winning

By WILLIAM BEECHER
Special to The New York Times

WASHINGTON, June 5 — A number of American military analysts, while admitting that the situation was still very confused in the Middle East, were of the opinion that the war would probably be short and that Israel would prevail.

Analysts at the Pentagon said that the Egyptian Army was a lot stronger today than in 1956, when Israeli forces swept through the Sinai Peninsula, but that Israel still was believed to have a better-balanced, better-trained, better-led military force.

Several experts, while conceding that predictions are treacherous, said they believed Israel should be able to "punch through" Egyptian forces in one of two directions in Sinai and elsewhere in a week to 10 days.

In 1956, Israel was able to overwhelm opposition in Sinai in 100 hours, but at that time Egypt was fighting on two fronts, with a British-French force pressing in from the north along the Suez Canal.

"Nobody, of course, knows how much better the Egyptian Army has become," said one general, "but we don't think they've had time enough to become a first-class fighting force."

Analysts speculated that Israel might want to fight hold-

Continued on Page 19, Column 1

NEWS INDEX

Fighting Is Raging In Gaza and Sinai; Action in Air Heavy

Major Mideast Developments

On the Battlefronts

Israel and the Arab nations were locked in full-scale war yesterday along the borders of Israel and in the skies.

Fighting raged from Syria, on the north, to the Sinai Desert, on the south, and on the Jordanian-Israeli border.

Israel claimed major victories in the Sinai Desert and the Gaza Strip, reporting that her troops and tanks had taken El Arish and Khan Yunis, key towns, and asserting that the fall of Gaza city was imminent. In other sectors, the Israelis reported the capture of the Jordanian town of Jenin and said that Syrian land forces had entered the conflict for the first time with an attack on a border village.

Israel also said her pilots had shattered the Egyptian, Syrian and Jordanian Air Forces. Israeli pilots were reported to have destroyed 374 enemy planes, with an additional 34 probably destroyed. Israel put her losses at 19 aircraft.

The United Arab Republic said, however, that Arab land forces had repulsed invading Israeli armor on the Gaza Strip and at two points in the Sinai Peninsula.

In Jerusalem, Jordanian and Israeli troops exchanged machine-gun and mortar fire across no man's land.

In the Capitals

In Tel Aviv, Israeli leaders declared that their goals did not include the conquest of Arab territory.

In Cairo, President Gamal Abdel Nasser said the Arabs sought to "eliminate the shadow of Zionism from Palestine."

In Washington, the Johnson Administration sought to maintain a neutral role in the conflict and, calling on both sides to accept an immediate truce, avoided placing blame.

In Moscow, the Government issued a statement denouncing "Israeli aggression" and demanding withdrawal.

Nasser Exhorts Arabs

By ERIC PACE
Special to The New York Times

CAIRO, Tuesday, June 6—The Cairo radio announced last night that the United Arab Republic's forces had invaded Israel after having "wiped out two enemy attacks" in Egyptian territory on the Sinai Peninsula.

The United Arab Republic had declared earlier that its forces had retaliated on land, sea and in the air after Israel carried out surprise ground and air attacks on Egyptian border areas and airbases this morning.

President Gamal Abdel Nasser declared in a statement relayed by the Egyptian Government news service that all Arabs were now fighting to "eliminate the shadow of Zionism from Palestine and to restore its Arabism."

Progress of Fighting Unclear

The over-all progress of the conflict was unclear from the series of military communiqués issued throughout the day by the Cairo radio. But these reported that the United Arab Republic had destroyed 86 Israeli planes by nightfall while they acknowledged only two Egyptian planes lost to the Israelis.

They said that United Arab Republic and Palestinian land forces had repulsed Israeli invaders at Khan Yunis in the Gaza Strip and at Kuntilla and El Aguila on the Sinai Peninsula. Egyptian forces were said

Continued on Page 16, Column 5

Israel Depicts Gains

By JAMES FERON
Special to The New York Times

JERUSALEM (Israel), Tuesday, June 6—The Israeli Air Force indicated early today that it had decimated the Egyptian, Syrian and Jordanian air forces in a sweeping series of air battles and ground attacks.

Israeli pilots reported that they had destroyed 374 enemy planes, and that 34 other aircraft probably had been destroyed.

The Israelis put their losses at 19 planes. Eight pilots were reported killed and 11 were reported missing, including some known to have been captured.

Movement on Sinai

Striking gains were also reported on the Sinai Peninsula where the hostilities began, according to the Israelis, with the shelling of Israeli settlements along the Gaza border at dawn yesterday.

The Israeli Chief of Staff, Maj. Gen. Itzhak Rabin, said in a statement issued at a post-midnight news conference in Tel Aviv that Israeli armor had captured El Arish and was moving rapidly along the El Arish-Abu Aweigila road.

The Gaza town of Rafah was reported captured as well as the junction of Khan Yunis in the disputed Gaza Strip. The fall of Gaza itself was considered imminent.

The Air Force chief, Mordechai Hod, said that most of the damage had been done to the Egyptians, who lost 286 air-

Continued on Page 16, Column 1

Troops and Armor Clash in Jerusalem

By TERENCE SMITH
Special to The New York Times

JERUSALEM (Israel), June 5 — War came to this divided city today at 11:20 A.M., a little more than three hours after the first announcement of the fighting at the Sinai border to the south.

Within minutes of the first shots, Arabs and Israelis were firing at each other with rifles, machine-guns, mortars, tanks and artillery from positions along an eight-mile border through the city.

The fighting continued into the night. In the darkness, the Jordanians threw up a blanket of antiaircraft fire as jets swept overhead.

In early fighting, Jordanian

Continued on Page 16, Column 7

Israeli Planes Raid Airports in Jordan

By DANA ADAMS SCHMIDT
Special to The New York Times

AMMAN, Jordan, June 5—Clouds of black smoke rose over the Amman airport today as four Israeli jet bombers circled and dived, apparently more or less at will. Only light antiaircraft and machine-gun fire appeared to be opposing them as they bombed and strafed aircraft and installations in four attacks.

The Israeli Air Force also was reported to have bombed Jordan's airport in El Mafraq. Civilians fled the streets as air-raid sirens wailed. Most residents of the leading hotel, the Intercontinental, made for an air-raid shelter in the nightclub. But some watched from

Continued on Page 16, Column 8

"All the News That's Fit to Print"

The New York Times

LATE CITY EDITION

Weather: Fair and warm today and tonight. Partly cloudy tomorrow. Temp. range: today 85-63; Wed. 81-62. Temp.-Hum. Index: mid-70's; Wed. 72. Full report on Page 93.

VOL. CXVI. No. 39,947 NEW YORK, THURSDAY, JUNE 8, 1967 — 10 CENTS

ISRAELIS ROUT THE ARABS, APPROACH SUEZ, BREAK BLOCKADE, OCCUPY OLD JERUSALEM; AGREE TO U.N. CEASE-FIRE; U.A.R. REJECTS IT

JOHNSON WILL USE CABINET TO COURT STATES' OFFICIALS

Aides Will Seek to Tighten Ties Between Governors and the White House

By WARREN WEAVER Jr.
Special to The New York Times

WASHINGTON, June 7—President Johnson has decided to use the members of his Cabinet as diplomatic agents in his campaign to improve relations between the Administration and state governments.

The President has approved a plan under which each member of the Cabinet would be assigned four or five states as his personal responsibility, with instructions to maintain personal contact between the Governors and the White House.

As part of the same effort, each of the 50 states will be given a "day" in Washington next fall and winter, when a planeload of its key officials will fly here to hold conferences all over the capital, capped by a meeting of the Governors with the President.

Bryant's Work Continued

Both projects reflect Mr. Johnson's continuing determination to build domestic as well as foreign bridges by working to sort out the tangled Federal-state relations that have been increasingly complicated by the administration of the Great Society programs.

Both are attempts to give some permanency to the contacts established during the last four months by Farris Bryant, the President's envoy to the states, on visits to 40 capitals with a squad of Federal experts.

Mr. Bryant, a former Governor of Florida who is now the director of the Office of Emergency Planning, plans to leave his White House post this summer, possibly to return to politics in his home state, and he is eager to help establish more permanent lines of communication before his departure.

As now envisioned, each Cabinet officer would visit all of

Continued on Page 29, Column 2

CONFEREES BLOCK A DRAFT LOTTERY

Compromise Bill Continues Deferment of Students

By United Press International

WASHINGTON, June 7 — Senate and House negotiators reached agreement today on a new military draft bill that rules out, for the present, any lottery-like random selection system to determine the order of induction.

The bill was a compromise of differing bills that the Senate and House had passed. It would guarantee the continuance of educational deferments for college undergraduates and students enrolled in apprentice and job training programs.

Senator Richard B. Russell, Democrat of Georgia, who is chairman of the Senate conferees, said the Senate might act on the four-year draft extension bill tomorrow. House action must await approval by the Senate.

Congressional action will clear the way for President Johnson, under current discretionary powers, to reverse the order of induction and take 19-year-olds first from the Selec-

Continued on Page 2, Column 1

NEWS INDEX

Rise in Debt Ceiling Rejected in House; Johnson Rebuffed

Special to The New York Times

WASHINGTON, June 7—The House of Representatives dealt the Johnson Administration a sharp setback today by rejecting a bill to increase the ceiling on the national debt $29-billion, to $365-billion.

The vote against passage was 210 to 197, with Republicans voting solidly to kill the bill. Enough Democrats, mostly Southerners, voted with them to turn the tide.

About six Northern Democratic "doves"—opponents of the war in Vietnam—also joined the opposition.

In all, 34 Democrats joined with 176 Republicans to defeat the measure.

Today's action raised the possibility — though a slim one—of financial chaos after June 30. At that time the debt limit reverts to its "permanent" ceiling of $285-billion, though the debt, at $330-billion, is already far above that level. The legal authority of the Treasury to pay its bills would be in doubt.

However, the Ways and

Continued on Page 30, Column 4

U.S. VOWS TO SEEK A DURABLE PEACE

Johnson Recalls Bundy for New Mideast Planning Unit —'Real Chance' Is Seen

By MAX FRANKEL
Special to The New York Times

WASHINGTON, June 7—President Johnson pledged today to do his best to help translate the new Middle Eastern situation into a more lasting settlement between Israel and her Arab neighbors.

Apparently hoping to exploit Israel's lightning military success—which has surprised but not displeased the White House—Mr. Johnson ordered the drafting of special policies for a "new peace" and set up new machinery to deal with the situation.

The President said that the United States, which had worked hard to avoid the war, felt that "there is now a real chance" to turn from "the frustrations of the past to the hopes of a peaceful future."

But Mr. Johnson said the handling of the crisis and the preparations for a lasting settlement would require the most careful consideration in the United States Government. To organize that effort he recalled McGeorge Bundy to temporary duty at the White House as executive secretary to a special subcommittee of the National Security Council.

Mr. Bundy will seek a temporary leave from the presidency of the Ford Foundation, which he assumed last year after serving as special assistant for

Continued on Page 19, Column 1

Dorothy Parker, 73, Literary Wit, Dies

By ALDEN WHITMAN

Dorothy Parker, the sardonic humorist who purveyed her wit in conversation, short stories, verse and criticism, died of a heart attack yesterday afternoon in her suite at the Volney Hotel, 23 East 74th Street. She was 73 years old and had been in frail health in recent years.

In print and in person, Miss Parker sparkled with a word or a phrase, for she honed her humor to its most economical size. Her rapier wit, much of it spontaneous, gained its early renown from her membership in the Algonquin Round Table, an informal luncheon club at the Algonquin Hotel in the nineteen-twenties, where some of

Continued on Page 38, Column 1

EBAN SEES THANT

Says Acceptance Is Based on Enemy's Reciprocal Action

Excerpts from debate at U.N. are printed on Page 18.

By DREW MIDDLETON
Special to The New York Times

UNITED NATIONS, N. Y., June 7—The Security Council unanimously adopted a Soviet resolution today calling on the combatants in the Middle East to "cease fire and all military activities" at 4 P.M., New York time today.

The Government of Israel shortly thereafter announced that she had accepted the call of the Council for a cease-fire, provided her Arab foes agreed.

In the evening, reports from the Middle East indicated rejection of the call by the United Arab Republic, Syria, Iraq, Saudi Arabia, Algeria and Kuwait. Jordan told Secretary General Thant that she would abide by the cease-fire, except in self-defense.

Says It's in Effect

Abba Eban, the Foreign Minister of Israel, told the Secretary General that a cease-fire was already in effect between Jordan and Israel.

In presenting the resolution, the Soviet delegate, Nikolai T. Fedorenko, made it clear that if Israel failed to heed the Security Council's demands, Moscow would consider severing diplomatic relations. The original Security Council resolution, adopted yesterday, simply called for a cease-fire.

But the reports from the Arab capitals indicate, diplomatic sources here said, that military operations will continue.

According to diplomats, the best hope lies in a draft resolution presented by George Ignatieff, the Canadian delegate. This proposes that the President of the Security Council and the Secretary General take measures to insure compliance with the resolutions.

Today's resolution demanded that the combatants "cease fire and all military activities on 7 June 1967 by 2000 hours Greenwich mean time." The resolution was adopted less than an hour before this time, which is 4 P.M. New York time, 10 P.M. in Jordan and Israel and 11 P.M. in the United Arab Republic and Syria.

The Council adjourned without voting on the Canadian draft largely because Milko Ta-

Continued on Page 18, Column 2

United Press International Radiophoto

OLD JERUSALEM IS NOW IN ISRAELI HANDS: Israeli soldiers in prayer at the Wailing Wall yesterday

Major Mideast Developments

On the Battlefronts

Israel claimed victory in the Sinai Desert after three days of fighting. Sharm el Sheik, guarding the entrance to the Gulf of Aqaba, fell after a paratroop attack, and the Israelis said the blockade of the gulf was broken. Other Israeli units were within 20 miles of the Suez Canal, and one Israeli report placed them in the eastern section of Ismailia, on the canal itself.

In Jerusalem, for the first time in 19 years, Israeli Jews prayed at the Wailing Wall as their troops occupied the Old City. Israeli troops captured Jericho, in Jordan, and sped northward to take Nablus, giving them control of the west bank of the Jordan.

The Egyptian High Command reported that its forces had fallen back from first-line positions in the Sinai Peninsula and were fighting fiercely from unspecified secondary positions. It announced that Egyptian troops had pulled back from Sharm el Sheik to join main defense units.

In the Capitals

In the United Nations, Israel accepted the call for a cease-fire, provided the Arabs complied. Jordan announced that she would accept and ordered her troops to fire only in self-defense. But Baghdad declared that Iraq had refused. There were indications that Syria, Algeria and Kuwait were also opposed.

In Cairo, an Egyptian official said the United Arab Republic would fight on.

In Moscow, the Soviet Union threatened to break diplomatic relations with Israel if she did not observe the cease-fire.

In Paris, the French proposed an international agreement for free passage in the Gulf of Aqaba similar to the one governing the Dardanelles in Turkey.

In Washington, President Johnson promised to seek a settlement that would assure lasting peace in the Mideast.

In London, the British urged the Israelis to halt before they aroused more turmoil in the Arab world and diminished the chances for a settlement.

Israelis Weep and Pray Beside the Wailing Wall

By TERENCE SMITH
Special to The New York Times

JERUSALEM, June 7—Israeli troops wept and prayed today at the foot of the Wailing Wall—the last remnant of Solomon's Second Temple and the object of pilgrimage by Jews through the centuries.

In battle dress and still carrying their weapons, they gathered at the base of the sand-colored wall and sang Hallel, a series of prayers reserved for occasions of great joy.

They were repeating a tradition that goes back 2,000 years but has been denied Israeli Jews since 1948, when the first of three wars with the Arabs ended in this area.

The wall is all that remains of the Second Temple, built in the 10th century before Christ and destroyed by the Romans in A.D. 70.

The Israelis, trembling with emotion, bowed vigorously from the waist as they chanted psalms in a lusty chorus. Most had submachine guns slung over their shoulders and several held bazookas as they prayed.

Among the leaders to pray at the wall was Maj. Gen. Moshe Dayan, the new Defense Minister. He told the troops:

"We have returned to the holiest of our holy places, never to depart from it again."

General Dayan, who was ap-

Continued on Page 17, Column 1

CAIRO ANNOUNCES A SINAI PULLBACK

Blames Foreign Aid to Foe, but Says Troops Fight On in Secondary Positions

By ERIC PACE
Special to The New York Times

CAIRO, June 7—An Egyptian military communiqué reported today that forces of the United Arab Republic had fallen back from some first-line positions on the Sinai Peninsula and were engaged in fierce fighting against Israeli troops from secondary positions.

Another statement of the High Command, broadcast four hours later by the Cairo radio, said Egyptian troops at Sharm el Sheik, guarding the entrance to the Gulf of Aqaba, had joined other Egyptian forces "now concentrated in the Sinai Peninsula."

There was no elaboration, but the communiqué, broadcast about 5:30 P.M., appeared to confirm Israeli reports that the Egyptians had been forced to retreat from Sharm el Sheik.

At night, the High Command reported that Israeli paratroops had dropped over the "second-line Egyptian front" but had been "completely wiped out."

The communiqué also said the Israelis had tried another drop at Sharm el Sheik after the

Continued on Page 17, Column 6

AQABA GULF OPEN

Dayan Asserts Israel Does Not Intend to Capture the Canal

By The Associated Press

TEL AVIV, June 7—Israel proclaimed victory tonight in the Sinai Peninsula campaign against the United Arab Republic. On the eastern front, both the Old City of Jerusalem and Bethlehem were captured from the Jordanians.

"The Egyptians are defeated," said Maj. Gen. Itzhak Rabin, the Israeli Chief of Staff.

"All their efforts are aimed at withdrawing behind the Suez Canal, and we are taking care of that. The whole area is in our hands. The main effort of the Egyptians is to save themselves."

Israel Losses 'Not Great'

Describing the developments through the third day of this third Arab-Israeli war in 19 years, General Rabin made these claims:

¶Sinai, the Egyptian territory between Israel's Negev Desert and the Suez Canal, is taken.

¶Most of the Jordanian territory on the west bank of the Jordan River, including Jericho, is in Israeli hands, and most of Jordan's army has been captured.

¶Relative to what was done, the number of Israelis casualties was "not great."

The Israelis were reported to have swept to the Suez Canal.

[An Israeli delegation source at the United Nations said Israeli troops had seized that part of the canal city of Ismailia that is on the eastern side of the waterway. But this was denied by an army source in Tel Aviv, who said, according to Reuters, that the Israelis had not taken any point along the canal.

[Maj. Gen. Moshe Dayan, the Israeli Defense Minister, declared that there was "no intention" of taking the canal, United Press International reported.]

'Never to Depart'

After the fall of the Old City of Jerusalem, Defense Minister Moshe Dayan said there that the Israelis had reunited their capital and would never "depart from it again."

Israel reported that paratroops aided by naval units had captured Sharm el Sheik, commanding the entrance to the Gulf of Aqaba, and said the blockade that the Egyptians had mounted from that position had been broken.

"The Strait of Tiran is now open," General Rabin said.

Israel's chief of staff said his men had taken on the United Arab Republic, Jordan, Syria and Iraq, knocked out their air forces and overrun their armor and infantry.

"All this the armed forces of Israel did alone," he declared.

The general then turned over the briefing to Brig. Mordechai Hod, commander of the air force, who announced 441 Arab

Continued on Page 16, Column 1

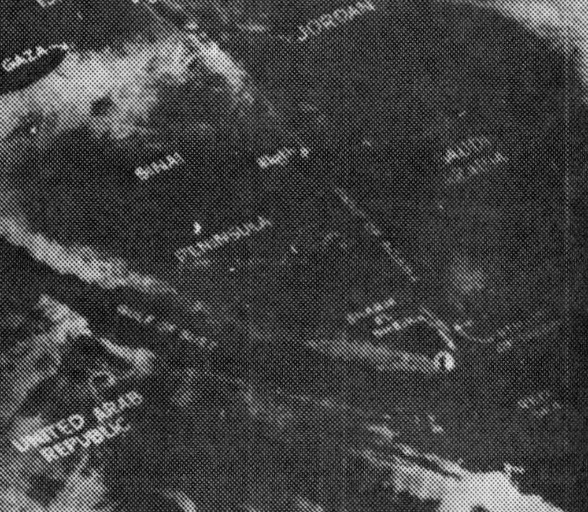

The New York Times — June 8, 1967

CONQUEST IN THE MIDEAST: Israeli troops took Sharm el Sheik (1), drove on to the Suez Canal (2) and seized control of the Old City in Jerusalem (3). Photo was taken in September, 1966, during the flight of Gemini 11.

Pentagon Believes Israeli Jets Struck From Sea, Eluded Radar

By WILLIAM BEECHER
Special to The New York Times

WASHINGTON, June 7 — At least a part of the Israeli Air Force that caught large numbers of Egyptian aircraft on the ground in the early hours of the war may have slipped through gaps in the United Arab Republic's radar net by flying in over the Mediterranean.

This possibility was raised today by Pentagon analysts. If correct, it would help to explain how Israeli pilots were able to surprise so many Egyptian jets before they could get into the air.

It might also serve to provide part of the explanation behind insistent Arab assertions that carrier-based United States and British jets participated in the raids.

The early blows to Arab, and especially Egyptian, air strength is credited by most military analysts as having been a decisive factor in the Israeli successes on land that followed.

"We know that some of the Israeli planes returned to their bases by way of the sea," one ranking officer said, "and we assume they may have approached from the seaward too."

The officer said it was obvious that Israel had excellent intelligence on weaknesses in the Egyptian radar systems and exploited them.

Shortly after the raids, he went on, the Jordanian radio charged that Jordanian radar

Continued on Page 18, Column 3

"All the News That's Fit to Print"

The New York Times

LATE CITY EDITION

Weather: Fair and warm today, tonight and tomorrow. Temp. range: today 85-63; Thurs. 85-64. Temp.-Hum. Index: today 70 to 75; Thurs. 77. Full U.S. report on Page 89.

VOL. CXVI..No. 39,948 — NEW YORK, FRIDAY, JUNE 9, 1967 — 10 CENTS

EGYPT AND SYRIA AGREE TO U.N. CEASE-FIRE; ISRAEL REPORTS TROOPS REACH SUEZ CANAL; JOHNSON, KOSYGIN USED HOT LINE IN CRISIS

SENATE APPROVES A TIGHTENED RULE ON REDISTRICTING

33 States Ordered to Bring Population Variant Down to 10% by 1968 Election

By JAMES F. CLARITY
Special to The New York Times

WASHINGTON, June 8—The Senate approved today a bill requiring that by the 1968 election no state have a population variance of more than 10 cent between its largest and smallest Congressional districts.

The approval, which came in a surprise vote of 57 to 25, was a result of a fight by Senator Edward M. Kennedy, Democrat of Massachusetts, to amend a measure that would have permitted a variance of 35 per cent until the 1972 election.

The Kennedy amendment, which was soundly defeated in committee two weeks ago, is intended, according to the Senator, to make Congressional redistricting conform with the Supreme Court's one-man, one-vote ruling of 1964. The amendment also deleted language giving the states power to determine when the compactness of a district was "practicable."

An Altered Version

The measure, before it was amended today, was an altered version of a bill already passed by the House. The House bill provided for a population variance of 30 per cent, and was amended by the Senate Judiciary Committee to cover four additional states.

The version passed today, which now goes to a Senate-House conference, would apply to 33 states having variances of more than 10 per cent. Nine of these states are under Federal court orders to redistrict. The 17 states not covered by today's Senate action either elect Representatives at large or have variances lower than 10 per cent.

Mr. Kennedy's proposal was approved, first in a crucial 44-to-39 vote as an amendment, then in the final vote on the bill as amended, 57 to 25.

"We knew it would be close.

Continued on Page 26, Column 1

Arms Cost Stress Scored by Rickover

By EVERT CLARK
Special to The New York Times

WASHINGTON, June 8—Vice Adm. Hyman G. Rickover has denounced the cost-effectiveness approach to weapons development as an "ism," a "new religion" and a "fog bomb" that is keeping the nation from gaining technology that would save lives.

In Congressional testimony released today, the head of the nuclear-powered ship program attacked present management techniques in the Pentagon.

By Presidential order, many of these techniques—including the mathematical analysis of cost vs. effectiveness—are now being spread throughout the executive branch of

Continued on Page 2, Column 4

JURY FINDS LAXITY IN BUILDINGS UNIT

Graft, Shirking and Lack of Personnel Training Are Cited—Moerdler Agrees

By JACK ROTH

A New York County grand jury criticized yesterday long-standing conditions in the Buildings Department that it said had resulted in corruption among housing inspectors and landlords.

The jury also said the situation permitted some inspectors and their supervisors to quit work as early as 10:30 A.M. and go to bars and racetracks for the rest of the day.

The jury, in a presentment handed up to Supreme Court Justice Mitchell D. Schweitzer, charged that the department suffered from lack of financial and manpower resources.

It asserted that inspectors were not properly trained for their jobs, that they were unaware of their department's rules and regulations, that there was duplication in inspections, that electronic processing equipment was failing to do its job and that unauthorized persons had access to file rooms and private departmental offices.

The Buildings Commissioner,

Continued on Page 31, Column 1

ALL SINAI IS HELD

U.A.R. Loses 50 Tanks in Actions Termed Fiercest of War

By Reuters

TEL AVIV, Friday, June 9—Israeli troops have reached the bank of the Suez Canal and have taken control of the entire Sinai Peninsula, the Israeli radio reported this morning.

The radio broadcast the text of a message from the commander in the southern front, to the Chief of Staff, Gen. Yitshak Rabin. The message said:

"Happy to inform you that our forces are stationed on the bank of the Suez Canal and the Red Sea. The Sinai Peninsula is in our hands. Greetings to you and to the whole defense forces of Israel."

Battle reports yesterday indicated that the remnants of two Egyptian armored divisions and four infantry divisions were trapped in the western part of that Sinai Desert.

50 Tanks Reported Wrecked

The news of Cairo's acceptance of the United Nations cease-fire coincided with an announcement by an Israeli spokesman that three battles in the desert yesterday had been "the fiercest in this war."

The Israelis said they had shot down eight Egyptian planes and destroyed at least 50 Egyptian tanks during the fighting.

Other tanks were wrecked and left on the road to Qantara, about 30 miles north of Ismailia, about midway along the 100-mile Suez Canal.

Among the Egyptian planes downed were a Soviet-made Ilyushin bomber and several Soviet-built Sukhoi-7's. Israeli planes also struck Soviet-made missile sites in the Suez Canal zone during daylight raids, the spokesman added.

Despite the continuation of heavy fighting, the Israeli spokesman said that all escape routes for Egyptian armored units had been closed.

He added that Israeli forces had captured oilfields at Ras Sudar, south of the port of Taufiq on the western coast of the Sinai Peninsula. Israeli soldiers said the wells were afire

Continued on Page 17, Column 6

United Press International Cablephoto

AFTER THE BATTLE: Egyptian prisoners, prone on the sand, their hands behind their heads, are guarded in a compound by Israeli troops at El Arish in the northern Sinai Peninsula. El Arish was taken by Israel Tuesday.

A SHIFT BY CAIRO

Thant Notifies Council in Middle of Debate on Resolutions

Excerpts from the U.N. debate are printed on Page 16.

By DREW MIDDLETON
Special to The New York Times

UNITED NATIONS, N. Y., June 8—The United Arab Republic, the leader of the anti-Israel coalition, today accepted the Security Council's demand for a cease-fire in the Middle East provided Israel did the same.

Yesterday, the delegate of Israel said his country accepted the cease-fire provided Israel's foes agreed to it. Reports here yesterday indicated rejection by Cairo.

Syria gave notice tonight that she would also comply, informing the Secretary General after the Security Council recessed.

This afternoon, in his dry, precise voice Secretary General Thant read to the Council a brief letter from Mohamed Awad el-Kony, the Egyptian delegate, disclosing that President Gamal Abdel Nasser's Government had "decided to accept the cease-fire" called for in the two Council resolutions "on the condition that the other party ceases fire."

He Scraps Long Speech

Mr. el-Kony wrote the letter after a long telephone conversation with Cairo shortly before the Council meeting began. After the call, he scrapped a 20-page speech he had prepared and wrote the note to Mr. Thant.

The Israeli Foreign Minister, Abba Eban, hailed "the immediate prospect" of a cease-fire as "a notable step" and called on other Arab governments to follow the Egyptian lead.

Cairo's acceptance of the Council resolutions adopted unanimously on Tuesday and Wednesday raised rather than lowered the heat of the debate between the United States and the Soviet Union over the resolutions each submitted to the Council.

Arthur J. Goldberg, the United States delegate, saying he hoped for a peace "stable and just to all concerned," submitted a draft of a resolution calling for the "withdrawal and disengagement of armed personnel," the renunciation of force, "the maintenance of vital international rights" and the establishment of a durable peace in the area.

The Administration was said

Continued on Page 17, Column 1

EGYPTIANS TOLD OF TRUCE DECISION

Cairo Broadcast Is Terse—Syrians Also Announce Approval of Cease-Fire

By ERIC PACE
Special to The New York Times

CAIRO, Friday, June 9—The Government told the Egyptian people this morning that it had conditionally accepted a cease-fire in the war with Israel.

There was no immediate popular reaction because the Cairo radio waited until early morning before announcing, more than three hours after the fact, that the United Arab Republic had told Secretary General Thant of the United Nations that it would agree to a truce if Israel did so.

[The Damascus radio announced that Syria, too, had accepted the cease-fire, Reuters reported. Page 17.]

Cairo was blacked out as protection against possible Israeli air raids when the news came, but nocturnal strollers reported that policemen were already taking down at least some of the anti-Israeli banners that have festooned the city for the last few weeks.

An early edition of a popular Cairo newspaper, Al Akhbar, put the news on the front page but made no comment. There was also no elaboration from the radio, which broadcast a military communiqué saying that the battle against Israel was continuing at all points along the Egyptian front.

The terse announcement of the cease-fire contrasted with

Continued on Page 17, Column 2

Major Mideast Developments

In the Capitals

The United Arab Republic accepted a United Nations cease-fire. Israel had previously agreed to stop hostilities if her enemies were willing to go along.

In Damascus, after a series of militant vows to fight on, the Syrians announced that they would also accept the cease-fire.

President Johnson welcomed the cease-fire agreement and urged prompt action to solve the "many more fundamental" questions in the Middle East.

An emergency declaration on oil was being considered by the Johnson Administration after major oil companies reported that a worldwide transportation problem had resulted from the war.

The hot line between Washington and Moscow was used this week for the first time during a crisis.

On the Battlefronts

Before the cease-fire went into effect, Israeli planes and torpedo boats mistakenly attacked a United States communications ship about 15 miles off Sinai. The Pentagon reported that 10 Americans had been killed and 100 wounded. Israel sent an apology.

Israel reported that her troops had reached the bank of the Suez Canal and that the entire Sinai Peninsula was under her control. Earlier Israel reported three fierce desert battles in which at least 50 Egyptian tanks had been destroyed.

The United Arab Republic announced that its air force had inflicted heavy damage on Israeli armored columns trying to advance westward from El Arish in the Sinai Peninsula.

At the Strait of Tiran, a Soviet freighter bound for the Jordanian port of Aqaba was the first ship to pass since Israel declared the waterway open to shipping on Wednesday. Two Israeli ships prepared to follow.

JOHNSON PLEASED BY GAINS ON TRUCE

Looks to a Stable Peace—White House Discloses Use of the Hot Line

Texts of the Mansfield letter and Johnson reply, Page 18.

By MAX FRANKEL
Special to The New York Times

WASHINGTON, June 8—President Johnson welcomed spreading acceptance of a cease-fire agreement in the Middle East today, but urged all parties to move promptly toward the "many more fundamental questions" bearing on a stable peace.

While thus pressing for more than merely another frail armistice, the White House also disclosed that its hot-line connection with Moscow had been used for the first time this week in an international crisis.

The United States used the teletype link this morning when it heard of an attack on an American communications ship off the Sinai Peninsula. At the time, the source of the attack was not known.

The Soviet Government, whose warships have been observing the movements of the United States Sixth Fleet in the eastern Mediterranean, was advised that the carrier-based American planes were scrambling into action for the sole purpose of assisting the distressed vessel.

It was later learned that Israeli forces had attacked the American ship in error.

The announcement of quick exchanges to prevent misunder-

Continued on Page 18, Column 1

DONATIONS POUR IN FOR ISRAELI FUND

Many Give All They Have—Some Gifts in Millions

By M. S. HANDLER

"You have got it all now," said a brief letter containing a check for $25,000.

The message was from a professor at the Jewish Theological Seminary who said he had gladly stripped himself of his worldly goods and sent the proceeds to the United Jewish Appeal for the Israel Emergency Fund.

The owner of two gas stations arrived at the appeal's offices and turned over the deeds to the stations as his contribution to the multimillion fund drive.

Other Jews walked in with the cash-surrender values of their life insurance policies. Still others, deeply moved by the Arab-Israeli war, sold real estate and securities and sent the money to the fund's headquarters, on the Avenue of the Americas at 51st street.

These were some examples of the dramas being played out in the Jewish communities across the United States, U.J.A. officials said yesterday.

The contributions, appeal of-

Continued on Page 11, Column 1

ISRAEL, IN ERROR, ATTACKS U.S. SHIP

10 Navy Men Die, 100 Hurt in Raids North of Sinai

By WILLIAM BEECHER
Special to The New York Times

WASHINGTON, June 8—An American naval vessel was mistakenly attacked by Israeli planes and torpedo boats today in international waters about 15 miles north of the Sinai Peninsula. Reports tonight listed the toll as 10 dead and 100 wounded. Twenty of the wounded were hurt critically.

The vessel, the Liberty, was on a peaceful, though war-related mission. Pentagon sources said she had been dispatched from Spain to the war zone to provide additional communications to facilitate the evacuation of American citizens from the Middle East and North Africa.

Pentagon officials said it was too early to tell whether indemnification would be asked from Israel for the loss of life and the damage to the Navy ship.

President Johnson, in a letter to the Senate majority leader, Mike Mansfield, noted that the

Continued on Page 19, Column 1

SOVIET SHIP SAILS INTO AQABA GULF

Passage Is First Since Israel Lifted Arab Blockade

By Reuters

ELATH, Israel, June 8—A Soviet freighter bound for the Jordanian port of Aqaba passed through the Strait of Tiran today, the first ship to do so since Israel declared the passage an international waterway yesterday.

Two outgoing Israeli freighters were preparing to be the first Israeli ships to pass through the strait since the Egyptians blockaded the Gulf of Aqaba on May 23.

A report from Sharm el Sheik, which dominates the strait, dis-

Continued on Page 17, Column 7

LEBANON
Damascus
SYRIA
JORDAN
El Qantara
MITLA PASS
Suez
Helwan
UNITED ARAB REPUBLIC
SINAI PENINSULA
Ras Sudar
Thamad
Elath
Aqaba
SAUDI ARABIA
Nile R.
MILES 0 75

The New York Times — June 9, 1967

CRUSHING OFFENSIVES: Israelis thrust westward across northern Sinai (1) to the Suez Canal after sharp fighting at Bir Gifgafa and Mitla Pass, and routed Egyptians at Nakhl and Thamed in drive farther south (2). Soviet ship passed through Strait of Tiran (3), now under Israeli control. Mistaken Israeli attack on U.S. ship in Mediterranean (4) killed 10 men. Israelis held west bank of the River Jordan as far north as Jenin (5).

U.S. Planes Batter MIG Base in North

Special to The New York Times

SAIGON, South Vietnam, June 8—American fighter-bombers knocked out a MIG base near Hanoi yesterday and wrecked a surface-to-air missile storage area 50 miles southwest of the capital, the United States Command reported today.

At the same time, new fighting broke out just south of the demilitarized zone at the border between North Vietnam and South Vietnam, where a fierce battle raged for control of three hills last month.

Navy carrier pilots attacked the Kep Airfield, 37 miles northeast of Hanoi, for the seventh time since April 24. A headquarters spokesman said the airfield is "closed tempo-

Continued on Page 8, Column 4

Russians Continue To Harass 6th Fleet

By NEIL SHEEHAN
Special to The New York Times

ABOARD U. S. S. AMERICA, in the Eastern Mediterranean, June 8—Two Soviet warships, a destroyer and a small, highly maneuverable patrol craft, moved into the formation of this Sixth Fleet carrier task force group this morning and began systematically harassing the American ships.

The harassment was undertaken despite a warning to another Soviet destroyer yesterday from Vice Adm. William I. Martin, the Sixth Fleet commander. Admiral Martin warned the Soviet vessel to withdraw from the area of the American formation. He said the Soviet ship, while following the carrier

Continued on Page 15, Column 1

NEWS INDEX

News Summary and Index, Page 47

"All the News That's Fit to Print"

The New York Times

LATE CITY EDITION

Weather: Mostly fair and pleasant today, tonight and tomorrow. Temp. range: today 65-84; Friday 84-67. Temp.-Hum. Index yesterday 75. Full U.S. report on Page 46.

VOL. CXIX..No. 41,104 | NEW YORK, SATURDAY, AUGUST 8, 1970 | 15 CENTS

CEASE-FIRE IN EFFECT ALONG SUEZ; ISRAEL AND EGYPT TO POLICE ZONE; INITIAL TALKS BEGINNING AT U.N.

J m Kean, San Rafael Independent-Journal, via Associated Press

BEFORE JUDGE'S SLAYING: James D. McClaine, convict holding guns against Superior Court Judge Harold J. Haley, his hostage, in San Rafael, Calif. A sawed-off shotgun was fastened to a loop of adhesive tape around the judge's neck. Both men were killed.

NIXON AIDES ISSUE 'INFLATION ALERT' CITING PRICE RISES

But the Economic Advisers Avoid Placing Any Blame on Industry or Labor

By EDWIN L. DALE Jr.

Special to The New York Times

WASHINGTON, Aug. 7—The Nixon Administration's first "inflation alert," issued today, identified several recent price increases, some accompanied by large wage increases, that it said had been important in raising the price level. It pointed no finger of blame, however.

The report attributed the rise in prices this year to a wide variety of causes. Only some of the causes were associated with "concentrated" industries, those dominated by a few large corporations, and with wage increases won by unions.

The basic conclusion of the report was that inflation in the United States always eventually responds to Government policies curbing total spending in the economy. But the longer the duration of the inflation, the slower the response, the report found.

Increases Detailed

Solely because they were important recently, the report discussed in detail price increases for coal and electric power, rubber, cigarettes and trucking.

There was no effort to say whether wage bargains won by unions, or price increases made by the industries involved, were "justified," as was done in the Kennedy and Johnson Administrations.

For 1970 to date, the report mentioned price advances in a variety of sectors of the economy, all different in their causes—steel and construction, medical care and mortgage interest rates, copper and New York City subway fares.

Smaller Union Role

It also pointed out that only 7 per cent of the labor force would have its wages determined by union negotiations this year, although it noted that wage increases in the settlements negotiated so far "have not slowed down."

The most dramatic single price increase identified in the report was that for coal, up 35 per cent in the last year. The cause was a rapid rise in demand, not higher wages, the report found.

So far, electric power rates for consumers have been slow to rise despite the coal price

Continued on Page 10, Column 1

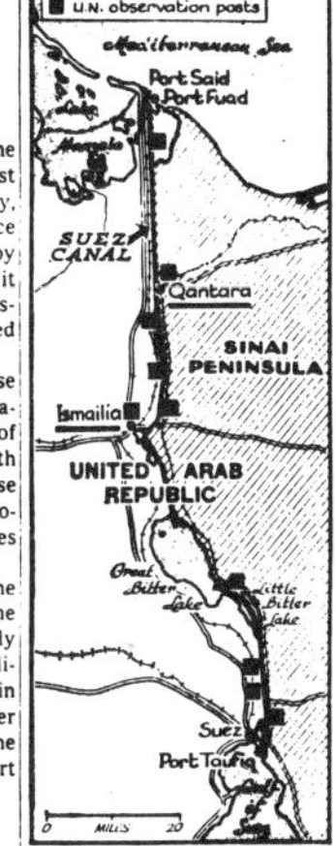

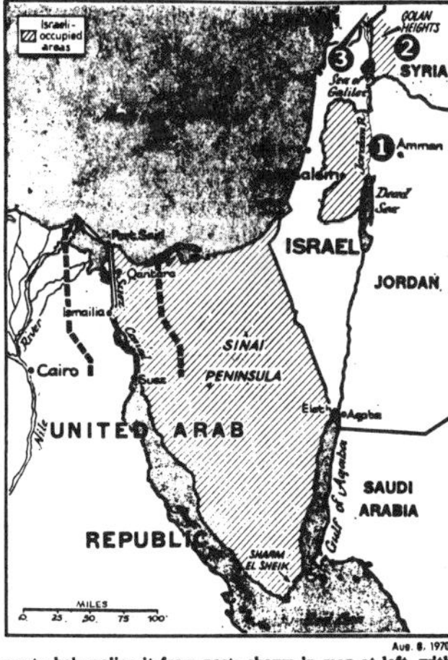

The New York Times | Aug. 8, 1970

MIDEAST TRUCE: U.N. aides are to help police it from posts shown in map at left, with command centers at Ismailia and Qantara. Dotted lines on other map indicate truce zone. U.S. sees truce applying also in area of Jordan (1), Syria (2) and Lebanon (3).

TRUCE OF 90 DAYS

U.S. Acclaims Action —Diplomats Stress Problems Ahead

Texts of related statements will be found on Page 2.

By HEDRICK SMITH

Special to The New York Times

WASHINGTON, Aug. 7—A cease-fire went into effect tonight on the Egyptian-Israeli front along the Suez Canal, and the preliminary phase of a new round of negotiations on peace in the Middle East was under way at the United Nations.

Fighting stopped on this front, where there have been frequent air and ground battles ever since the six-day war of June, 1967, when the Israelis occupied all of the Sinai Peninsula to the eastern shore of the canal. In recent months the fighting has been almost continuous.

Today's cease-fire breakthrough was hailed by President Nixon, Secretary of State William P. Rogers and Secretary General Thant of the United Nations as an important step in the drive for a "just and lasting" peace between the Arabs and Israelis.

Diplomats Are Cautious

At the same time, diplomats cautioned that major differences on the provisions of a peace settlement still divided the Israelis and Arabs, meaning that difficult negotiations lay ahead.

Mr. Rogers, who originally put forward the cease-fire proposal on June 19, was the first to announce that it had been accepted by Israel and the United Arab Republic and would take effect at midnight Israeli time (1 A.M. Saturday in Cairo and 6 P.M. Friday in New York). The 90-day cease-fire is to run until the evening of Nov. 5 in the United States. American officials hope it will lead to a permanent cease-fire.

U.N. Observers to Assist

On the Suez front, Israel and Egypt will police each other's observations of a strict standstill that rules out military build-ups or offensive action within a zone at least 32 miles wide on each side of the canal.

Informed sources said that each side would conduct aerial reconnaissance of the other's positions without actually crossing the canal or flying over the other side's lines. About 100 United Nations observers on the ground will assist in policing the cease-fire.

The depth of the cease-fire zones was described as sufficient to assure Israel that neither Egypt nor the Soviet Union would expand military positions—especially the Soviet SAM-2 and SAM-3 antiaircraft missile sites—into the 32-mile

Continued on Page 2, Column 1

SUBWAY WORKERS QUESTION SAFETY

Supervisors Predict More Serious Mishaps Because of Personnel Shortages

By FRANCIS X. CLINES

The Subway Supervisors Association said yesterday that additional serious accidents were likely on the lines because of a shortage of experienced personnel and an alleged de-emphasis of equipment maintenance by transit officials.

The association's counsel, Moss K. Schenck, said that past warnings to this effect had been ignored by transit officials and that the system, which he described as "basically sound," had deteriorated rapidly in the last two years.

As evidence of this, Mr. Schenck offered copies of Transit Authority data indicating a drop in on-time performance in recent years and listing what he termed a typically poor day of 38 trains abandoned in their runs, 185 others canceled and 953 seriously late of a total of 8,109 scheduled runs.

Personnel Problems

The personnel problems, according to Mr. Schenck, include large-scale retirements of recent years, which transit officials concede have been troublesome, and a consequent lowering, he contends, of employment standards.

The supervisors' group, which says it represents most of the system's 3,000 dispatchers, yardmasters, foremen, stationmasters and other supervisors, echoed recent criticism of subway management that was prompted by a rash of sub-

Continued on Page 34, Column 4

Judge and 3 Slain on Coast As Convicts Hold Up Court

By The Associated Press

SAN RAFAEL, Calif., Aug. 7—An armed man entered a trial court today and touched off a gun battle that took the lives of a judge, the intruder and two convicts he was trying to free.

The intruder and the convicts held the Superior Court at bay for 10 minutes but were shot to death as they fled in a small van carrying the judge and three women jurors as hostages.

Those killed were Judge Harold J. Haley, 65 years old; the convict on trial, James D. McClain, 37; a convict witness, William Arthur Christmas, 27, and the armed intruder, who was tentatively identified as Jonathan P. Jackson, 17.

Others Are Wounded

Deputy District Attorney Gary Thomas was seriously wounded in the back. Also seriously wounded was another convict witness, Ruchell Magee. A juror, Maria Graham, suffered an arm wound and three other persons were less seriously injured.

McClain, who was serving five years to life for burglary in Solano County, was on trial in the stabbing of a San Quentin Prison guard in 1969. McClain and the convict witnesses had been transferred this morning from San Quentin, about five miles away, to the Marin County Hall of Justice.

Lieut. Thomas A. Lightfoot of the Sheriff's office said that, about 11 A.M., a slender man entered the second-floor courtroom where the trial was in progress.

Opening a flight bag containing pistols and road flares taped together to look like dynamite, he tossed a pistol to McClain and covered the crowd with a carbine that he had concealed under his coat.

"This is it," the invader shouted. "Everybody line up."

McClain, with a pistol at the judge's head, forced deputies to remove shackles from himself and Magee, who was on the witness stand. He then sent Magee to the corridor to free Christmas, who was waiting with a guard.

A bailiff slipped out of the courtroom and alerted San Quentin Prison guards and Sheriff's deputies.

McClain got on a telephone, called the Sheriff's office and yelled: "Call off your dog, pigs, or we'll kill everyone in the room."

Judge Haley was put on the telephone briefly and then the four armed men herded the judge, Mr. Thomas and three women jurors to the street by elevator.

McClain had looped adhesive tape around the judge's neck and fastened it to the muzzle of a short, sawed-off shotgun, which one of the fugitives had taken from a deputy in fleeing

Continued on Page 24, Column 3

RATE OF JOBLESS AGAIN RISES TO 5%

Unemployment Among Men in 20-24 Age Group Shows Especially Big Increase

By EILEEN SHANAHAN

Special to The New York Times

WASHINGTON, Aug. 7—The nation's unemployment rate rose in July, again touching the 5 per cent mark, which it had also reached in May.

The Labor Department's monthly report on employment and unemployment, made public today, showed that the rise in unemployment had come about both because there were fewer jobs in most areas of the economy and because there were more job-seekers.

There was a particularly large increase in unemployment among young men in the 20-24 age group. This appeared to indicate, according to department experts, that discharged servicemen were having a hard time finding jobs.

The experts said that while they were not sure how many of the unemployed men in this age group were veterans, the fact that any were reported in the statistics as "re-entering the work force" rather than first-time job-seekers, indicated that many probably were veterans.

The number of men in the 20-24 age group who were looking for work in July and were unable to find it rose to 528,000 from the June level of 515,000. The unemployment rate for this group was up from 7.2 per cent in June to 9.1 per cent in July.

The other category that ex-

Continued on Page 10, Column 7

Mrs. Meir Voices Hope; U.A.R. Notes Assurances

She Looks to Other Fronts

By PETER GROSE

Special to The New York Times

JERUSALEM, Aug. 7—Premier Golda Meir expressed hope tonight that the cease-fire with the United Arab Republic would spread to other fighting fronts and that the truce would have no limit in time.

Her statement came in a message she read on national television in which she informed Israel of the cease-fire agreement.

The Premier's announcement came after a full day of consultations between the two sides—at long distance through United States intermediaries, according to Israeli sources—to work out the terms of the truce and methods of supervision.

None of the arrangements for policing the truce were announced here. Israeli sources indicated their belief, however, that each country's "national means," presumably wide-angle aerial photoreconnaissance without any crossing of the canal line, would be satisfactory assurance against military build-ups. Mrs. Meir read

Continued on Page 2, Column 6

Egypt Emphasizes Security

By RAYMOND H. ANDERSON

Special to The New York Times

CAIRO, Aug. 7—The United Arab Republic agreed today to reinstate the cease-fire along the Suez Canal. It linked the agreement to Israeli acceptance of a timetable for withdrawal from the lands seized in the war of June, 1967.

In a statement, the Foreign Ministry said that Cairo's acceptance of the cease-fire rested on assurances of security for Egypt's Suez Canal front and other Arab fronts.

The reinstatement of the 1967 cease-fire, the Foreign Ministry added, opens the way to a resumption of the mission of Dr. Gunnar V. Jarring, the special United Nations representative for the Middle East, to seek implementation of the Security Council resolution of Nov. 22, 1967.

In the past, President Gamal Abdel Nasser has repeatedly rebuffed appeals by the United States and other Western powers for a return to the 1967 cease-fire agreement, asserting that a cessation of shooting would be a "surrender" to Israeli occupation of the Sinai

Continued on Page 3, Column 1

Jarring Mission Is Reactivated For Middle East Peace Talks

By SAM POPE BREWER

Special to The New York Times

UNITED NATIONS, N. Y., Aug. 7 — Secretary General Thant announced today that the Jarring mission for peace in the Middle East "is now reactivated."

In a report to the Security Council, Mr. Thant said that Dr. Gunnar V. Jarring, his personal representative, was "already intensively at work in this new stage of his peace effort."

Dr. Jarring has been holding consultations with the heads of the three delegations directly concerned—the United Arab Republic, Jordan and Israel—with the United States and Soviet representatives and with high Secretariat officials.

But, as in all of Dr. Jarring's negotiations, almost nothing is known of his actual moves. He is in a 38th-floor office behind all the security the United Nations can muster.

None of his appointments are announced and it is only from other sources that some appointments become known.

Mr. Thant described the renewal of the mission today as "an important step forward in the search for peace in the Middle East," although he forecast a long, hard road ahead.

His report this afternoon added to a spreading feeling here that machinery for making peace might finally be in motion.

Mr. Thant's report included a letter from Dr. Jarring saying the three parties had agreed to name representatives to take part in discussions "at such places and times as I may recommend, taking into account as appropriate each side's preference as to method of procedure and previous experience."

In his earlier negotiations, Dr. Jarring had to travel from capital to capital making suggestions and trying to match positions into something useful.

Mr. Thant said that he and Dr. Jarring believed "there now is a reasonable basis on which to review immediately his contacts with the parties with a view to initiating discussions

Continued on Page 2, Column 1

Burger Finds Courts Imperiled By Breaches of Civility at Trials

By FRED P. GRAHAM

Special to The New York Times

ST. LOUIS, Aug. 7—The Chief Justice of the United States, Warren E. Burger, told the chief justices of the states today that "unseemly, outrageous episodes" in courtrooms and overly long trials were "undermining some of the public confidence in the entire system."

His remarks came during a day in which the issue of the increasing incidence of abrasive tactics by lawyers representing unpopular clients, and the means used by judges to discipline them, dominated several of the sessions at the American Bar Association meeting here.

In extemporaneous remarks to a conference of chief justices, Mr. Burger stressed the theme that he has repeated frequently during his judicial career—the need to maintain courtroom civility, as "the absolutely imperative lubricant for an inherently contentious process."

He advised the chief justices to urge the courts or legislatures in their states to adopt the series of recommendations for administering criminal justice that have been worked out by the A.B.A. during a five-year study that is in its final stages.

Specifically, he said, they should adopt the A.B.A.'s recommendations that attempt to set out the limits to which lawyers can properly go in representing their clients. These rules, including one that forbids opposing counsel to address each other directly dur-

Continued on Page 34, Column 5

Associated Press

PREPARE GAS ROCKETS FOR JOURNEY: Derrick loading concrete-encased rockets of lethal gas in Anniston, Ala. They are to be sunk in the Atlantic. Dispatch, Page 8.

Texas Sued by U.S. On Desegregation

By WILLIAM ROBBINS

Special to The New York Times

WASHINGTON, Aug. 7—The Justice Department filed suits today against the State of Texas and 26 school districts, seeking to compel desegregation for the coming school year in the last large group of holdouts not already under litigation.

The suits, announced tonight by Attorney General John N. Mitchell, named as defendants the Texas Education Agency and the State Commissioner of Education, J. W. Edgar, as well as the 26 districts. They were filed in Federal District Court in Dallas, Houston, Austin and Tyler.

The complaints charged that the school districts had continued to operate dual school systems with both student and

Continued on Page 8, Column 5

Cuba and Chileans Will Exchange TV

Special to The New York Times

MIAMI, Aug. 7 — Cuba and Chile have signed an agreement to exchange television programs. It is believed to be the first of its type between Havana and a Latin-American country since the Organization of American States imposed economic and diplomatic sanctions against the Government of Fidel Castro in 1964

The accord provides for an exchange of news programs between the Cuban Broadcasting Institute and the television channel of the Catholic University of Chile.

An announcement on the Havana radio described Chilean television executives who signed the agreement in Havana as "representatives of Chile." It said that television

Continued on Page 8, Column 4

NEWS INDEX

"All the News That's Fit to Print"

The New York Times

LATE CITY EDITION

Weather: Sunny, cool today; clear, cool tonight. Fair, mild tomorrow. Temp. range: today 60-48; Monday 66-52. Full U.S. report on Page 85.

VOL. CXX..No. 41,156

NEW YORK, TUESDAY, SEPTEMBER 29, 1970

15 CENTS

United Press International

VATICAN CITY: President Nixon with Pope Paul VI during special audience yesterday. Later, he flew by helicopter to U.S.S. Saratoga, with Sixth Fleet in the Mediterranean.

NASSER DIES OF HEART ATTACK; BLOW TO PEACE EFFORTS SEEN; NIXON CANCELS FLEET EXERCISE

A GESTURE BY U.S.

President Terms Loss Tragic—He Joins Fleet Off Italy

By Reuters

ABOARD U.S.S. SARATOGA, in the Mediterranean, Tuesday, Sept. 29—President Nixon last night ordered cancellation of today's exercises of the United States Sixth Fleet in the Mediterranean because of the death of President Gamal Abdel Nasser of Egypt.

The President, who arrived aboard this aircraft carrier last night, had planned to watch a demonstration of Sixth Fleet firepower, including the launching and recovery of aircraft.

Officials said: "Upon hearing of the death of President Nasser, the President ordered the cancellation of the firepower demonstrations, which were to be held in conjunction with his visit to the Sixth Fleet."

They said that Mr. Nixon's conferences with Sixth Fleet commanders aboard the flagship Springfield would go on as scheduled.

The President flew to this carrier off the coast of Italy by helicopter after a day in which he had conferred in Rome with the President and the Premier of Italy and with Pope Paul VI.

'Tragic Loss'

The President in a statement said that the death of President Nasser was a tragic loss of an outstanding Arab leader.

"I was shocked to hear of the sudden death of President Nasser," Mr. Nixon said. "The world has lost an outstanding leader who tirelessly and devotedly served the causes of his countrymen and the Arab world.

"This tragic loss requires that all nations, and particularly those in the Middle East, renew their efforts to calm passions, reach for mutual understanding and build lasting peace.

"On behalf of the American people I extended deep sympathy to his family and to his people."

Stresses Role of Fleet

Earlier Mr. Nixon had told the men of the Saratoga that never had American military and diplomatic power been used more effectively than in the latest Middle East crisis.

Chatting with sailors who greeted his helicopter on the flight deck, Mr. Nixon spoke of "a hard two or three weeks," which he said had been capped by success. He referred to the Jordanian truce and recovery of the hostages from the hijacked airliners.

"The fact that we were successful is the fact that you were there," he told the sailors. He mentioned their

Continued on Page 19, Column 1

United Press International

President Gamal Abdel Nasser bidding good-by to King Hussein of Jordan after meeting in Cairo yesterday. From ceremony, he returned home where he died of heart attack.

ARAB-WORLD HERO

Vice President Sadat Takes Over as the Interim Leader

Obituary article will be found on Page 16.

By RAYMOND H. ANDERSON

Special to The New York Times

CAIRO, Tuesday, Sept. 29—President Gamal Abdel Nasser, leader of Egypt for 18 years and hero of much of the Arab world, died here yesterday.

The Government radio said the 52-year-old President was the victim of a heart attack.

The death was announced on Cairo's television and radio stations shortly before 11 P.M. by Vice President Anwar Sadat. An hour earlier, regular programs on television and radio were abruptly suspended and replaced with chanting of verses from the Koran. Official mourning was proclaimed for 40 days.

The President suffered the heart attack at 3 P.M. and died three hours later.

No obvious successor to Mr. Nasser was in sight, and no Egyptian seemed in a mood tonight to speculate about the matter.

Funeral Will Be Thursday

Vice President Sadat took over as interim ruler. He reported that emergency meetings had been held by the higher executive committee of the Arab Socialist Union, the political organization created by Mr. Nasser, and the Council of Ministers.

President Nasser's funeral will be held Thursday.

The impact of Mr. Nasser's death will be felt throughout the Arab world. Despite controversies and rivalries during his long years of power, he was the strongest figure of leadership among the Arabs.

Since the battlefield defeat of three Arab armies by Israel in June, 1967, Mr. Nasser was the leader who rallied the Arabs to rebuild their forces for a war of liberation if other means to recover the lands failed.

Favored Political Solution

But he repeatedly emphasized that he favored a political solution of the conflict with Israel if one could be achieved.

Although Mr. Nasser gained a reputation in his early years in power as a fire-breathing radical, in recent years he had become a force for moderation and pragmatism.

Even on the emotional issue of Israel, he was able to swing much of the Arab world behind his acceptance in July of a United States initiative for a cease-fire and he revived efforts for a negotiated settlement. The outlook for pursuing

Continued on Page 17, Column 1

50,000 FLEE BLAZE IN SAN DIEGO AREA

Brush Fire, 30 Miles Long, Is California's Biggest Yet —5 Die in Copter Crash

By United Press International

LOS ANGELES, Sept. 28—The largest brush fire in California history raged today through mountain canyons near the Mexican border, driving thousands of persons from their homes as the flames advanced.

In the San Gabriel Mountains to the north, a helicopter being used by the United States Forest Service to fight another fire crashed late today, killing the five persons aboard.

More than 50,000 persons were evacuated from small communities in San Diego County. The 200-acre fire there erupted in the Cleveland National Forest on Saturday when a falling tree severed a power line. At least 250 structures have been destroyed.

Decreasing winds tonight and a forecast of scattered showers in mountain areas raised hopes that the blaze could be contained tomorrow.

Arson Arrests Made

The enormous blaze, 30 miles from tip to tip, eclipsed in size the Matailaja fire of 1930, which burned 125,000 acres in Kern and Los Angeles Counties.

"We've barely kept up with the situation," said Arlen B. Cartwright of the State Division of Forestry. "The problem seems to come from the fact that fire nuts run around and see flames and smoke and this makes them want to set more fires—which they do."

Arson was suspected in two other major blazes in San Diego County, and five arrests were made in Los Angeles County.

More than 5,000 men worked 36-hour shifts on the fire lines and the neighboring county of San Bernardino was stripped of all but five of its fire engines.

Continued on Page 10, Column 2

Intrepid Wins Series, 4-1, And Keeps America's Cup

By STEVE CADY

Special to The New York Times

NEWPORT, R.I., Sept. 28—The longest series in 100 years of America's Cup challenges came to a desperately dramatic close today with Intrepid completing a 4-1 conquest of Gretel II.

Once again, the defender of yachting's most famous prize had to fight off almost constant pressure by the chunky Australian challenger.

Until a wind shift put Intrepid in clover starting the final leg of the 24.3-mile race, the action had been about as close as a boat race can produce. The cynics say watching two yachts is like watching grass grow, but the grass was on fire again today, as it was so often during this controversial series.

Stage Set for Upset

When Gretel II closed to within two boat lengths at the fifth mark, the stage was set for another upset of the kind the Australian sloop brought off last Thursday. Then the wind shifted from north to east, Intrepid hit it on the right tack and the suspense evaporated.

With the final windward leg turned into a race, the redesigned 1967 defender opened up and came home safely, 1 minute 44 seconds ahead.

As Intrepid swept majestically across the line about 250 yards ahead of her dangerous rival, the familiar dream of another successful Cup defense began unfolding. Horns, whistles and sirens aboard some 150 spectator boats and Coast Guard patrol vessels cut loose with a noisy salute to the American yacht—the second ever to defend the Cup twice.

A Triumphant Allusion

Bill Ficker, the 42-year-old Californian with the bald head and the bold starting-line maneuvers, shook hands with his young crew. They, in turn, hoisted a "Ficker Is Quicker" flag to the top of Intrepid's mast, a triumphant allusion to the tactical swiftness of their skipper.

In today's race, Ficker and his young stalwarts had to be quicker. Jim Hardy gave Gretel II a slight lead at the start but Ficker took it away early on the opening windward leg. He spent the rest of a cold, overcast afternoon desperately keeping the Aussies from breaking through in the fluky

Continued on Page 53, Column 1

John Dos Passos Is Dead at 74; Acclaimed for 'U.S.A.' Trilogy

Special to The New York Times

BALTIMORE, Sept. 28—John Dos Passos, the novelist of the post-World War I generation who wrote more than 30 books, including the trilogy "U.S.A.," died today in his apartment.

Mr. Dos Passos, who was 74 years old, had been troubled by a heart ailment in recent years and was released only Saturday from Good Samaritan Hospital. When not away on his extensive travels, he divided his time between his apartment here and a home in Westmoreland, Va.

Mr. Dos Passos is survived by his widow, the former Elizabeth Hamlin Holdridge; their daughter, Lucy, and a stepson, Christopher Holdridge.

A funeral service will be held Thursday at 10 A.M. at the William Cook-Brooks Funeral Home in the nearby town of Towson, Md.

Fame From Early Books

By ALDEN WHITMAN

The life and writings of John Dos Passos were marked by a progression from left to right. "Every day I become more Red," he said in his youth. "My one ambition is to be able to sing 'The International.'" But in middle and old age, he turned against his former ideas, berating liberals, Socialists and Communists with zeal. The onetime writer for The New Masses became a contributor to The National Review; the friend of Ernest Hemingway became that of William F. Buckley Jr.; and the supporter of

Gil Friedberg-Pix

John Dos Passos

William Z. Foster turned into the backer of Barry Goldwater.

His novels, too, marched rightward. The trilogy "U.S.A.," completed in 1936 and generally recognized as one of the hinges of modern fiction, was a painstakingly detailed and angry portrait of industrial America between 1898 and 1929. It concluded with the heroine's joining the Communist party in revulsion over what she believed were the injustices of the Sacco-Vanzetti case.

His subsequent trilogy, "District of Columbia," completed in 1949, acerbically chronicled what the author clearly viewed as the failure of the New Deal,

Continued on Page 47, Column 1

Malpractice Suits Reported Soaring

By LAWRENCE K. ALTMAN

Witnesses at a State Senate public hearing testified here yesterday that a steep rise in medical malpractice suits was forcing physicians to practice "defensive medicine," shirk hazardous modes of treatment that could be of benefit to patients, and pass along the costs of skyrocketing insurance premiums to patients.

"One physician of every six has been sued for malpractice," State Senator Norman F. Lent told the hearing. And more than 10,000 Americans will initiate medical malpractice suits this year, Senator Lent, who is chairman of the Senate Committee on Health, added.

Because some insurance companies find medical malpractice insurance unprofitable, wit-

Continued on Page 32, Column 1

U.S. Officials See Period Of Instability in Mideast

By TERENCE SMITH

Special to The New York Times

WASHINGTON, Sept. 28—United States officials, startled by the death of Gamal Abdel Nasser, tended to view it today as a blow to peace-making efforts in the Middle East.

A ranking State Department official described the Egyptian President's death as a "critical loss at a decisive moment in history."

The immediate reaction of officials here was that it would bring a period of instability in the Arab world and would therefore reduce the already-thin prospects for negotiating an early resolution of the Arab-Israeli dispute.

[In Moscow, Western diplomats expected the Soviet leaders to assure the United Arab Republic that President Nasser's death would not affect Soviet support for the Arab cause. Page 17.]

An hour before the Cairo radio announcement, a cable from Donald C. Bergus, the senior United States representative in Cairo, reported a rumor that the Egyptian leader was critically ill or perhaps dead. The message was being decoded as the public announcement came.

Six hours earlier Rodger P. Davies, the Acting Assistant Secretary of State for Near Eastern and South Asian Affairs, had told a closed session of the House Foreign Affairs Committee that the Nixon Administration was "leaning toward optimism" about the prospects of getting the United States-sponsored peace initiative in the Middle East back on the track.

The Senate was informed of the news by Senator John C. Stennis, Democrat of Mississippi, who interrupted a debate on election reform. He described Mr. Nasser, the leader in Cairo since 1952, as "superior to most anyone who might have been in power."

"I hope his death does not mean upheaval and turmoil in

Continued on Page 19, Column 1

THE ARAB WORLD IS GRIEF-STRICKEN

Moslems Fire Rifles Into Air as Sign of Mourning —Koran Read on Radio

By JOHN L. HESS

Special to The New York Times

BEIRUT, Lebanon, Sept. 28—The Arab world went into mourning tonight over the loss of its major international figure. Arab distress was heightened by the fear that instability would increase in the area and diminish the already slender prospect of peace.

Television stations went off the air and radio programs were replaced by chants and readings from the Koran. In Beirut, Moslems fired thousands of shots into the air as a sign of emotion for the loss of Gamal Abdel Nasser. Men walked in the streets in impromptu procession declaiming "Allah Akbar!"—"God is great."

Security forces raced to thwart rioting of the kind that followed President Nasser's offer of resignation after the six-day war of June, 1967.

Youths started bonfires of automobile tires and a crowd began collecting outside the United States Embassy.

[A senior Cabinet minister in Israel said that the Israelis now appeared to face an indefinite stalemate on peace negotiations. Page 18.]

Observers here said that President Nasser was the only Arab

Continued on Page 17, Column 7

Arab Truce Observers Arrive In Generally Peaceful Amman

By ERIC PACE

Special to The New York Times

AMMAN, Jordan, Sept. 28—One hundred foreign Arab officers arrived here today to serve on the peace-keeping observer teams that will be deployed in Amman under the agreement reached yesterday in Cairo to end hostilities between the Jordanian Government and the Palestinian commandos.

The cease-fire instituted last Friday after nine days of civil war seemed generally effective this morning. There were no fires along the capital's skyline, although a few bursts of firing resounded in the center of Amman and on Jebel Luweibida and Jebel Amman, two of the city's seven hills.

Western diplomats also reported that shelling or shooting was continuing in part of the Palestinians' Ashrafiyeh quarter, where many of the airline hostages had been held.

There was no sign that either the army or the commandos had abandoned their positions in Amman, as the Cairo agreement called for. The guerrillas are entrenched in a populous area around the Hussein Mosque at the heart of the city, where gunfire was occasionally heard during the day.

Despite a further provision of the Cairo agreement for a release of detainees, scores were still visible this morning at the army prison camp on the way to the airport. As their women peered in through the barbed-wire fence, they were seated in orderly rows, apparently being indoctrinated by their Jordanian Army captors.

The army appeared yesterday to be trying to finish its clean-up of Ashrafiyeh, once a commando stronghold. Aside from that, no wide-scale military operations were known to be under way. The general calm this morning followed radio broadcasts of the 14-point agreement signed by King Hus-

Continued on Page 18, Column 5

Text of Cairo agreement is printed on Page 18.

Anti-Arab Jet Plot Laid to Seized Pair

By MORRIS KAPLAN

An Israeli Army veteran and his wife, accused of trying to board a London-bound plane here with a live hand grenade and four loaded gun hidden in their clothing, were reported yesterday to have planned to hijack an Arab airliner and take it to Israel.

Law-enforcement sources said that the couple reportedly had planned to board a United Arab Airlines plane bound for Cairo at the London airport and divert the flight to Israel "in retaliation" for a recent attempted hijacking of an El Al airliner in London.

The sources said that the veteran, Avraham Hershkovitz, had worked as a "manager" here for the Jewish Defense

Continued on Page 12, Column 3

Fourth Group of Hostages Here After Seeing President in Rome

By ROBERT D. McFADDEN

Thirty-three travel-weary Americans, whose ordinary lives became the focus of international concern during three harrowing weeks while they were hostages in Jordan, arrived at Kennedy International Airport last night and were met by loved ones, friends and a clamoring throng of newsmen.

The passengers—26 men, 6 women and an infant—were the fourth group of Americans brought home safely from an ordeal that began with multiple hijackings Sept. 6. All but two of the 33 were released in Amman over the weekend and were flown home through Nicosia, Cyprus, and Rome.

Their faces were haggard but smiling and their clothes rumpled after a 12-hour flight from Rome, where they met briefly with President Nixon in the morning. They stepped off a chartered flight at the Trans World Airlines terminal shortly after 6 P.M. They were ushered quickly through Customs and led into a private room for a reunion with 175 relatives.

Nearly 1,000 friends greeted them in the corridors and public waiting rooms as they emerged.

Six Americans are still being held of the original group on three hijacked planes. They are someplace in Jordan.

Contrary to the confused receptions at three previous returning flights, passengers who were not anxious to talk were not besieged by newsmen thrusting cameras and microphones into

Continued on Page 18, Column 2

NEWS INDEX

News Summary and Index, Page 45

"All the News That's Fit to Print"

The New York Times

LATE CITY EDITION

Weather: Sunny and milder today; fair and mild tonight, tomorrow. Temp. range: today 58-77; Tuesday 57-74. Temp.-Hum. Index yesterday 67. Full U.S. report on Page 90.

VOL. CXXI . . . No. 41,864 — NEW YORK, WEDNESDAY, SEPTEMBER 6, 1972 — 15 CENTS

9 ISRAELIS ON OLYMPIC TEAM KILLED WITH 4 ARAB CAPTORS AS POLICE FIGHT BAND THAT DISRUPTED MUNICH GAMES

United Press International

A copter making a test run before picking up Arabs involved in the attack on Israelis. At rear is the Olympic Tower. Sign in German says, "Olympic Village, Gate 6."

752 Air-Conditioned Cars Ordered for City Subways

By EDWARD RANZAL

Mayor Lindsay announced yesterday that 752 new air-conditioned subway cars had been ordered for $210.5-million. He said the contract was the largest ever signed in the country for the purchase of passenger railroad cars.

The first group of cars, which will be manufactured by the Pullman - Standard Company, are to be delivered by 1973.

The cars will provide a quieter ride than present equipment, according to Dr. William J. Ronan, chairman of the Metropolitan Transportation Authority.

The new equipment, which will be used on the IND and BMT lines, will enable the authority to phase out more than 1,200 pre-World War II cars, which are smaller than the new ones. A study is being made, Dr. Ronan said, to produce an air-conditioned unit that can be used in cars in the smaller tunnels of the IRT system.

20% of Fleet by '75

Each car will cost more than $273,000. The city will provide one-third of the total funds—the money has been provided in the city's 1972-73 capital budget—and the Federal Urban Mass Transportation Administration will supply the rest.

By 1975 more than 20 per cent of the city's fleet of nearly 7,000 subway cars will consist of new air-conditioned cars.

The first order under the contract will be for 454 cars at a cost of $127.4-million. Some of them will be delivered in

Continued on Page 91, Column 2

Berrigan and a Nun Get Prison Terms In Letter Smuggling

By JOHN KIFNER

Special to The New York Times

HARRISBURG, Pa., Sept. 5—The Rev. Philip F. Berrigan, cleared of charges that he led a plot to kidnap President Nixon's adviser on national security affairs, Henry A. Kissinger—was sentenced in Federal District Court here today to four concurrent two-year terms for smuggling letters out of the Lewisburg Penitentiary.

Sister Elizabeth McAlister, also cleared of the plot charges, was sentenced to one year in jail and three years' probation for smuggling letters.

Moments after the sentences were announced, Government attorneys moved to dismiss the first three substantive counts of their indictment, confirming that the Justice Department would not seek a retrial of the controversial "Harrisburg Seven" case.

The Government charged Father Berrigan, Sister Elizabeth, two other Roman Catholic priests, a former priest, a former nun and a Pakistani scholar with conspiracy to kidnap Mr. Kissinger as ransom to force a halt to the bombing in Viet-

Continued on Page 16, Column 1

MRS. MEIR SPEAKS

A Hushed Parliament Hears Her Assail 'Lunatic Acts'

By TERENCE SMITH

Special to The New York Times

JERUSALEM, Sept. 5—Her voice heavy and trembling with emotion, Premier Golda Meir today denounced "these lunatic acts of terrorism, abduction and blackmail, which tear asunder the web of international life."

Speaking to a hushed and somber parliament before the fate of the Israeli hostages held captive in Munich was known, she said, "It is inconceivable that the Olympic events should continue as long as our citizens are under the threat of being murdered in the Olympic Village."

She called on all the nations participating in the Olympics to do "whatever is necessary" to rescue the nine Israelis taken hostage by Arab guerrillas in an early-morning attack in which two other Israelis were killed.

[Official sources in Jerusalem said early Wednesday that the Cabinet would meet later in the morning and that there would be no statement on the deaths of the hostages until then.]

Cabinet Still Firm

Although she was not explicit, Mrs. Meir left the impression that Israel would continue to refuse the guerrillas' demands for the release of 200 Palestinian commandos held in this country. Cabinet sources said the Government remained committed to its hard-line policy of neither dealing with nor making concessions to the guerrillas.

Most Israelis seemed stunned by the news of the bizarre attack on the Israeli athletes, which was first reported here on a radio broadcast at 9 A.M. (3 A.M. Tuesday, New York time). Although Israeli citizens traveling abroad have been attacked by Palestinian guerrillas before, the Olympics seemed to many an unlikely setting.

"The games were going so well," one Jerusalem news dealer said, "and now this."

In parliament, where the members had gathered in an extraordinary session to confirm the Justice Minister, the attack was the sole topic of conversation.

Cabinet Ministers and members of parliament sat in the building's modern, sun-washed dining room waiting for additional news from Munich. Each hour on the hour, the large room grew silent and the ministers gathered four deep around a radio as the Israeli radio summarized the developments.

The tension was greatest at

Continued on Page 20, Column 2

West German policemen talking with a spokesman, right, for Arabs who invaded Israeli quarters at Olympic Village

Associated Press

A West German Army ambulance passing through the heavily guarded gate at the military airfield in Fürstenfeldbruck, near Munich, after the commandos and the hostages landed in three helicopters.

A 23-HOUR DRAMA

2 Others Are Slain in Their Quarters in Guerrilla Raid

By DAVID BINDER

Special to The New York Times

MUNICH, West Germany, Wednesday, Sept. 6—Eleven members of Israel's Olympic team and four Arab terrorists were killed yesterday in a 23-hour drama that began with an invasion of the Olympic Village by the Arabs. It ended in a shootout at a military airport some 15 miles away as the Arabs were preparing to fly to Cairo with their Israeli hostages.

The first two Israelis were killed early yesterday morning when Arab commandos, armed with automatic rifles, broke into the quarters of the Israeli team and seized nine others as hostages. The hostages were killed in the airport shootout between the Arabs and German policemen and soldiers.

The bloodshed brought the suspension of the Olympic Games and there was doubt if they would be resumed. Willi Daume, president of the West German Organizing Committee, announced early today that he would ask the International Olympic Committee to meet tomorrow to decide whether they should continue.

Policeman Killed

In addition to the slain Israelis and Arabs, a German policeman was killed and a helicopter pilot was critically wounded. Three Arabs were wounded.

There were some reports that two of the hostages said to have been killed might still be alive. "It is a dim hope," said Dr. Bruno Merk, the Interior Minister of Bavaria, "but I am skeptical on this point."

The bloodbath at the airport that ended at 1 A.M. today, came after long hours of negotiaton between German and Arabs at the Israeli quarters in the Olympic Village where the Arabs demanded the release of 200 Arab commandos imprisoned in Israel.

Finally the West German armed forces supplied three helicopters to transport the Arabs and their Israeli hostages to the airport at Fürstenfeldbruck. From there all were to be flown to Cairo.

A Boeing-707 provided by the Lufthansa German Airlines was waiting.

Two of the terrorists, carrying their automatic rifles, walked about 170 yards from the helicopters to the plane. And then they started back to pick up the other Arabs and the hostages.

Positions Cited

As the Arabs were returning, German sharpshooters reportedly opened fire from the darkness beyond the pools of light at the airport. The Arabs returned fire.

The torment of the entire event was heightened by confusion created in the public mind by contradictory reports from German and Olympic officials after the gunfire erupted at the airport.

Dr. Merk, in a press conference at 3 o'clock this morning said:

"In this situation our task and goal to free the hostages was made more difficult by the lack of agreement from Israel to free prisoners or to get guarantees from the Arabs not to take action against the hos-

Continued on Page 18, Column 1

PARLEY REJECTS HIJACKING TREATY

U.S.-Canadian Project for Penalizing Nations Aiding Air Pirates Rebuffed

By ROBERT LINDSEY

Special to The New York Times

WASHINGTON, Sept. 5—Delegates to a 17-nation conference here rejected today United States-Canadian efforts to negotiate an international antihijacking treaty based on a draft proposed by the two nations.

The move for nonacceptance was led by France and Britain and supported by the Soviet Union and Egypt.

Faced with what appeared to be certain defeat of the proposed treaty if it came to a vote, the two North American nations acquiesced in a French proposal to start writing a new treaty from scratch, after debates on what "principles" should be included.

The delegates have eight working days left before the conference is scheduled to end.

Today's rejection was a significant setback for the United

Continued on Page 91, Column 2

Nixon Tightens Security In U.S. Against 'Outlaws'

By TAD SZULC

Special to The New York Times

WASHINGTON, Sept. 5 — President Nixon said today that "extra security measures" would be taken in the United States to protect American citizens as well as visiting Israelis from possible attacks by Palestinian guerrillas.

Mr. Nixon, speaking to newsmen in San Francisco, left it unclear, however, whether he meant that this new protection would cover prominent American Jews or only those whom he described as "Americans of Israeli background, American citizens."

Speaking before the gunfight at a military airport in Munich, in which the Israeli hostages were killed, Mr. Nixon discussed the capture of Israeli Olympic team members by Palestinian guerrillas and the slaying of two Israelis. He said:

"Since we are dealing with international outlaws who are unpredictable, we have to take extra security measures to protect those who might be the targets of this kind of activity in the future. That might include Americans of Israeli background, American citizens."

Late tonight, after word was received in Washington of the death of the Israeli hostages and West German policemen, Secretary of State William P. Rogers issued this statement on behalf of the Administration:

"There are no words which can fully express our reaction to today's tragedy at the Olympic Games. I know I speak for all Americans in extending the deepest sympathies of the

Continued on Page 18, Column 4

Continued on Page 20, Column 1

GAMES SUSPENDED; RITES IN ARENA SET

Halt Is the First Since 1896, When the Classic Resumed —Egypt Team in Forfeit

By NEIL AMDUR

Special to The New York Times

MUNICH, West Germany, Wednesday, Sept. 6 — The Olympic Games were suspended yesterday for the first time since competition in the modern era began in 1896.

Late-afternoon and evening events were called off in the wake of an attack staged by Arab guerrillas before dawn on the Olympic Village in which two Israelis were killed and nine others taken hostage. The hostages were later killed.

After the attack, Mark Spitz, the American swimmer who won seven gold medals at the Munich Olympics and who is Jewish, flew hurriedly to London on his way back to the United States. There were fears before his departure that he too might become a victim. [Page 20.]

The announcement of the suspension, made by the International Olympic Committee, also said that a memorial service would be held for the victims

Continued on Page 18, Column 7

Reports First Said Israelis Were Safe

Contradictory reports last night about the fate of the Israeli hostages seized by Arab terrorists in the Olympic Village threw the public into confusion all over the world.

Throughout the day, as the tragedy in Munich unfolded, millions of viewers throughout the world watched on live television, which employed circuits that had been intended for the Games. But in the evening, when the events reached their climax, viewers could get no definitive word for hours on how the hostages fared.

At first the West German Government's official spokesman, Conrad Ahlers, announced

Continued on Page 20, Column 1

Elizabeth City Hall Under Investigation

By RONALD SULLIVAN

Special to The New York Times

TRENTON, Sept. 5—Law enforcement authorities reported here today that the administration of Mayor Thomas J. Dunn of Elizabeth was the target of a Union County grand jury investigation of alleged municipal corruption.

Mayor Dunn, a Democrat running for a third term, said in an interview that he had "no knowledge of any investigation involving me or my administration." But he said he volunteered last spring to go before a Union County grand jury.

According to official sources, the grand jury is investigating charges of payoffs and kickbacks involving city officials, contracts and businessmen. City license officials have already been subpoenaed, as have a number of city records and contracts.

Karl Asch, the county prosecutor, refused to comment on the nature of the reported investigation. He did say his staff had been instructed to seek indictments before the Nov. 7 elections.

Last week two of Mr. Dunn's three mayoral opponents were indicted in separate matters by a Union County grand jury.

Matthew J. Nilsen, a Republican freeholder in the county, was indicted on charges of atrocious assault in August in a case involving an alleged extortion.

In the other indictment, Michael J. DeMartino, a Democratic City Councilman in Elizabeth, was charged with misconduct in office in a case involving a $3,000 bribe in 1968.

Mayor Dunn recently endorsed President Nixon for reelection. Political observers in Union County noted that the indictments of two of his opponents were sought by a Republican prosecutor, and were seen as aiding the Mayor's re-election chances.

However, Mr. Asch, who has obtained indictments against prominent Union County political figures in recent months, contended today that his anticorruption drive was "absolutely nonpolitical" and that the investigation of the Dunn

Continued on Page 49, Column 6

NEWS INDEX

"All the News That's Fit to Print"

The New York Times

LATE CITY EDITION
Weather: Partly sunny today; fair tonight. Partly sunny tomorrow. Temp. range: today 53-75; Saturday 53-73. Additional details on Page 91.

SECTION ONE

VOL. CXXIII..No. 42,260 · NEW YORK, SUNDAY, OCTOBER 7, 1973 · 75¢ beyond 50-mile zone from New York City, except Long Island. Higher in air delivery cities. · 50 CENTS

ARABS AND ISRAELIS BATTLE ON TWO FRONTS; EGYPTIANS BRIDGE SUEZ; AIR DUELS INTENSE

Associated Press

REDS, ORIOLES WIN PLAYOFF OPENERS: Johnny Bench after his homer won National League game for Cincinnati from New York, 2-1. Sparky Anderson, manager, is at lower left. Baltimore beat Oakland, 6-0, in the American League. Details in Section 5.

U.S. ASKS A HALT

Pleas by Kissinger to Prevent the Fighting Prove Fruitless

By BERNARD GWERTZMAN
Special to The New York Times

WASHINGTON, Oct. 6—The United States appealed to Israel and Egypt today to halt the fighting.

Secretary of State Kissinger, who was in New York, was caught by surprise when the crisis developed. He made a last-minute effort by telephone with Foreign Minister Abba Eban of Israel and Foreign Minister Mohammed H. el-Zayyat of Egypt to prevent the fighting from breaking out, but it proved fruitless.

Both men had had routine talks with Mr. Kissinger in the last two days without giving any indication that fighting was about to erupt, Administration officials said.

Kissinger Urges 'Restraint'

On instructions from President Nixon, who was in Key Biscayne, Fla., for the weekend, Mr. Kissinger "urged restraint to avoid the undermining and violation of the cease-fire" in effect since August, 1970, "and to avoid any escalation and continuation of the fighting," Robert J. McCloskey, a State Department spokesman, said in New York before Mr. Kissinger returned to Washington this afternoon.

In addition, Mr. Kissinger sent cables to King Faisal of Saudi Arabia and King Hussein of Jordan, both friendly to the United States, expressing the hope that they would "use their good office to urge restraint where they have the influence to do so," Mr. McCloskey said.

Call to Waldheim

Mr. Kissinger telephoned Secretary General Waldheim of the United Nations and Sir Lawrence McIntyre of Australia, this month's President of the Security Council, to discuss possible Council action. He also called the Soviet Ambassador, Anatoly F. Dobrynin, in Washington, Mr. McCloskey said, presumably to urge Soviet restraint as well.

The crisis struck Washington without much warning. American intelligence had routinely reported signs of military build-ups in Egypt and Syria in recent weeks, but the analysts believed these were either

Continued on Page 14, Column 1

United Press International

Army boots slung over his shoulder, an Israeli reservist reports for duty in Tel Aviv

SYRIANS IN CLASH

Fighting Along Canal and Golan Heights Goes On All Night

By ROBERT D. McFADDEN

The heaviest fighting in the Middle East since the 1967 war erupted yesterday on Israel's front lines with Egypt along the Suez Canal and Syria in the Golan heights.

Official announcements by Israel and Egypt agreed that Egyptian forces had crossed the Suez Canal and established footholds in the Israeli-occupied Sinai Peninsula.

A military communiqué issued in Cairo asserted that Egyptian forces had captured most of the eastern bank of the 100-mile canal. An Israeli military communiqué said the Egyptians had attempted to cross the canal at several points by helicopters and small boats and had succeeded in laying down pontoon bridges at two points. Armored forces were pouring across them into Sinai, it said.

Fighting All Night

A communiqué issued early today in Tel Aviv said fighting had raged all night along the canal's eastern bank and along the entire cease-fire line with Syria.

Each side accused the other of having started the fighting. But military observers posted by the United Nations reported crossings by Egyptian forces at five points along the Suez, and said Syrians had attacked in the Golan heights at two points.

Israeli and Syrian artillery dueled in the Golan heights, and on both battlefronts there were air clashes. The Cairo radio said Egyptian forces had shot down 11 Israeli planes and lost 10 of their own in battles over the Sinai and the Gulf of Suez. The Israeli spokesman did not comment on losses but said Israeli planes had shot down 10 Egyptian helicopters carrying troops into the southern Sinai.

Shelling by Syrians

In Damascus, the military command said that Syrian pilots and ground fire had shot down 10 Israeli aircraft in renewed action over the Golan heights this morning.

Syrian artillery was reported by the Israelis to have shelled a number of settlements in the occupied Golan heights and the Hula Valley area.

The Damascus radio said that Syrian forces had reoccupied Mount Hermon in the Golan heights for the first time since 1967, and said Syrian troops were fighting on the ground with Israeli forces along the entire cease-fire line.

An Israeli spokesman said today that Israeli planes had sunk an Egyptian vessel and that the navy had sunk three troop-carrying Egyptian craft during the night.

Gunboats Reported Sunk

As fighting continued into the night, Syrian and Israeli gunboats clashed in the Syrian harbor of Latakia, 110 miles north of Beirut. An Israeli communiqué said that five Soviet-built Syrian vessels were sunk by Israeli sea-to-sea missiles being used for the first time.

In Damascus, however, a military spokesman said that Syrian forces had sunk four Israeli naval vessels and shot down two Israeli helicopters in the sea battle.

No military action involving Jordan or Lebanon was reported, but King Hussein of Jordan placed his armed forces on full alert and conferred by telephone with President Anwar el-Sadat of Egypt and President Hafez al-Assad of Syria. Jordan was a belligerent in the 1967 war won by Israel.

The Government radio stations in Cairo and in Damascus

Continued on Page 2, Column 3

CAB DRIVER SLAIN IN TENSE BOSTON

Found Stabbed to Death in Roxbury Area Following Two Previous Killings

By JOHN KIFNER
Special to The New York Times

BOSTON, Oct. 6—The body of a young white taxi driver who had been stabbed to death was found today in the predominantly black Roxbury neighborhood as this uneasy city tried to come to grips with its racial fears.

The police identified the driver as Kirk Miller, a student at Clarkson College, who was working for the Boston Cab Company. His body was found hidden in some bushes in a vacant lot in Roxbury.

Detectives said that he had multiple stab wounds in his back and head. They said that they "had to assume" that robbery was a possible motive although they could not discount other factors. They said that no money was found on the body.

Mr. Miller was discovered by his sister Sally and a friend, Jeffrey Carter.

Tuesday night, a young white woman was burned to death by six youths in Roxbury, and less than 48 hours later an elderly white man was slain near a housing project. There

Continued on Page 77, Column 3

Tax Agents Compile Data On Net Worth of Agnew

By MARTIN WALDRON
Special to The New York Times

BALTIMORE, Oct. 6—Agents of the Internal Revenue Service are apparently compiling a statement on Vice President Agnew's net worth as part of the continuing investigation into his financial affairs.

Although the purpose of the revenue service's investigation is not known, the service often uses the technique of the net worth audit in an attempt to show that a defendant accused of evading taxes is worth more than the amounts on which he paid taxes.

Earlier this week, the Federal grand jury investigating Mr. Agnew indicted N. Dale Anderson, who succeeded Mr. Agnew as Baltimore County Executive, on income tax charges after revenue agents compiled a net worth statement on Mr. Anderson.

By law, the revenue service is prohibited from commenting on individual income tax reports or on investigations it may have under way.

But in the last few weeks its agents have been collecting data dealing with Mr. Agnew's affairs, even minor transactions, according to sources knowledgeable about the investigations.

On Oct. 3, agents from the Charlotte, N. C., intelligence office of the service subpoenaed records in Asheville, N. C., showing a gift of four yards of homespun cloth worth $16 to Mr. Agnew in 1967 at the time of the Southern Governors Conference, the sources said.

Such gifts are sometimes considered as income for tax purposes.

In making a case charging income tax evasion against an individual, the revenue service sometimes alleges failure to pay tax on specific income items, which it then seeks to prove were received by the individual.

The revenue agents and agents of the Federal Bureau of Investigation are apparently checking every financial transaction that the Vice President

Continued on Page 33, Column 1

U.N. COUNCIL AIDES CONFER ON CRISIS

President of Body Seeks Views on Calling Meeting to Deal With Fighting

By ROBERT ALDEN
Special to The New York Times

UNITED NATIONS, N. Y., Oct. 6—The President of the Security Council, Sir Laurence McIntyre of Australia, opened formal consultations tonight with other members of the Council to seek their views on calling a Council meeting to deal with the fighting in the Middle East.

The Western powers generally favored calling such a meeting, but not prematurely. They said that a premature meeting would result in little more than invective, claim and counterclaim.

Another proposal the Council members were discussing was for the President of the Council to appeal to both sides in the Middle East to halt the fighting. While Western powers generally supported such an appeal, the Chinese and the Russians held back endorsement; the French said they would have to study the idea.

Neither the Israelis nor the Arab states called for an urgent meeting of the Council today, though the Egyptian Foreign Minister, Dr. Mohammed H. el-Zayyat, said he wanted to

Continued on Page 8, Column 1

Israelis and Egyptians Tell Of Beginnings of Conflict

Jerusalem's Report

By TERENCE SMITH
Special to The New York Times

JERUSALEM, Sunday, Oct. 7—Heavy fighting erupted yesterday between Israeli and Arab forces along the Suez Canal and Golan heights cease-fire lines, a military spokesman announced.

The forces were still fighting early this morning in what Defense Minister Moshe Dayan described as "all-out war."

Mrs. Meir's address, Page 5; Dayan excerpts, Page 6.

The fighting began at 2 P.M. yesterday, Israeli time (8 A.M. New York time). Egyptian forces managed to cross the Suez Canal during the afternoon and establish bridgeheads at several points on the Israeli-held eastern bank, but Israeli military spokesmen said last night that Israeli forces had moved into position to block them.

On the occupied Golan heights, a large-scale Syrian force including armor and artil-

Continued on Page 4, Column 1

Cairo Communiques

By HENRY TANNER
Special to The New York Times

CAIRO, Oct. 6 — The Egyptian Government announced today that Israeli ground, sea and air forces attacked Egypt and Syria early this afternoon along the entire length of their front lines with Israel.

In a succession of communiqués read on the Government-controlled Cairo radio, Egypt said that her forces had crossed the Suez Canal in several places and had placed Egyptian flags on the Israeli-held eastern bank.

The radio said that the Egyptians had crossed the canal—the cease-fire line since the 1967 war—after repelling Israeli landing attempts on the Egyptian-held western bank.

The radio interrupted its regular program just after 2 P.M., Cairo time (8 A.M., New York time) saying that the Israeli action had started at 1:30 local time with air attacks on Ain Sukhna, 30 miles south of the town of Suez on the Egyptian shore of the Red Sea, and

Continued on Page 7, Column 1

Queens Sports Center Proposed

By EMANUEL PERLMUTTER

Creation of a $275-million sports complex on air rights over the Sunnyside, Queens, railroad yards of the Penn Central was proposed yesterday by the State Racing and Wagering Board.

The project, which would be competitive with the proposed athletic complex in the New Jersey Meadows, would include two race tracks, an 80,000-seat stadium for football and other entertainments, a 1,000-room resort and convention hotel and parking for 20,000 cars.

No housing or other buildings would have to be demolished for the project since it would be built on a platform over the 300-acre yard site, which is less than a mile east of the Queensboro Bridge at the junction of Queens and Northern Boulevards and just a few minutes from Times Square by subway.

Under the proposal, the project would be financed by a bond issue and proceeds from the sale of Aqueduct Race Track. The air rights would be purchased by the Metropolitan Transportation Authority from the Penn Central and leased to the State Urban Development Corporation, which would build the necessary facilities.

Emil Mosbacher Jr., chairman of the Racing and Wager-

Continued on Page 49, Column 1

QUEENS BLVD.
NORTHERN BLVD.
SKILLMAN AVE.

Race track is flanked by Northern Boulevard at right and Skillman Avenue, left. Hotel rises at center, next to stadium. Queensboro Bridge leads to Manhattan.

Gas Pipeline Contest Develops in Alaska

By GLADWIN HILL
Special to The New York Times

PRUDHOE BAY, Alaska, Sept. 29 — Another Alaskan pipeline dispute is brewing.

While the oil companies with the big petroleum deposits here on the North Slope await a final Congressional go-ahead to build a controversial 789-mile pipeline to Alaska's south coast, a consortium of United States and Canadian concerns is pushing plans to tap the region's rich natural gas reserves via a different but equally controversial 2,000-mile route.

Current exploratory activities of the gas consortium, pointing toward a possible major incursion into the Arctic National

Continued on Page 74, Column 3

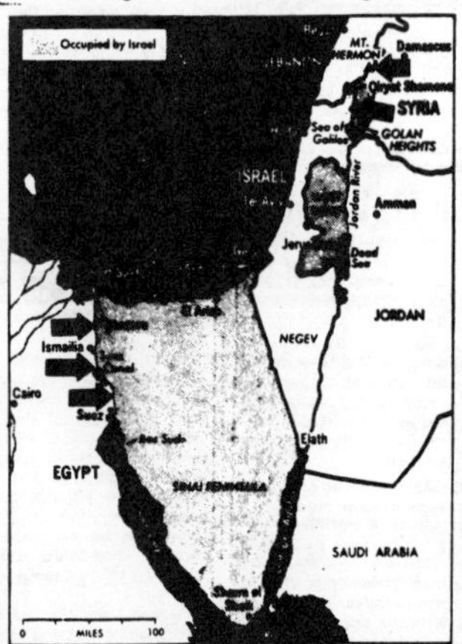

The New York Times/Oct. 7, 1973

Heavy arrows (upper right) indicate drive by Syrians and (lower left) crossing of Suez Canal by Egyptians.

Today's Sections

Index to Subjects

"All the News That's Fit to Print"

The New York Times

LATE CITY EDITION

Weather: Chance of rain today; mild tonight. Fair, mild tomorrow. Temp. range: today 53-68; Thursday 51-68. Additional details on Page 86.

VOL. CXXIII..No. 42,279 · NEW YORK, FRIDAY, OCTOBER 26, 1973 · 15 CENTS

U.S. FORCES PUT ON WORLDWIDE ALERT LEST SOVIET SEND TROOPS TO MIDEAST; CRISIS EASED AS U.N. SETS UP A PATROL

Associated Press

Members of a Texas Air National Guard group are briefed at Ellington Air Force Base

ACTION BY COUNCIL

Unit Will Be Made Up of Soldiers From Smaller Nations

By KATHLEEN TELTSCH

Special to The New York Times

UNITED NATIONS, N. Y., Oct. 25—The Security Council voted today to establish a United Nations emergency force to insure a cease-fire in the Middle East, using troops from smaller countries.

The vote was 14 to 0, with China not participating in the adoption of the resolution,

Excerpts from Malik remarks are printed on Page 19.

which asked Secretary General Waldheim to report back within 24 hours on proposals for carrying out the Council's decision.

The vote came in a meeting that was delayed as delegates watched Secretary of State Kissinger's news conference on television amid concern over a possible big-power confrontation in the Middle East.

Threat May Be Averted

The importance of the Security Council's action, as seen by some Western diplomats, was that it could head off the possibility that the Soviet Union might unilaterally send troops to the Middle East.

One Western official said that while the creation of a United Nations peace-keeping force might "be a can of worms," it might also prevent a major-power confrontation.

A quick dispatch of United Nations forces, said a European, "could get all of us off a very painful hook."

Yesterday Egypt had asked that Soviet and American forces be sent to the Middle East to compel Israel to pull back to the positions she occupied Monday when the first cease-fire was ordered. The United States rejected Cairo's appeal that American troops be sent.

Resolution Revised

During the delay this morning, at the insistence of the United States, the eight nonaligned countries sponsoring the resolution agreed to revise it to exclude the five permanent Council members—the Soviet Union, the United States, China, France and Britain—from participation in the emergency force. The original resolution, introduced in a meeting that ended at 12:35 o'clock this morning, did not exclude the major powers.

The willingness of the Soviet

Continued on Page 19, Column 7

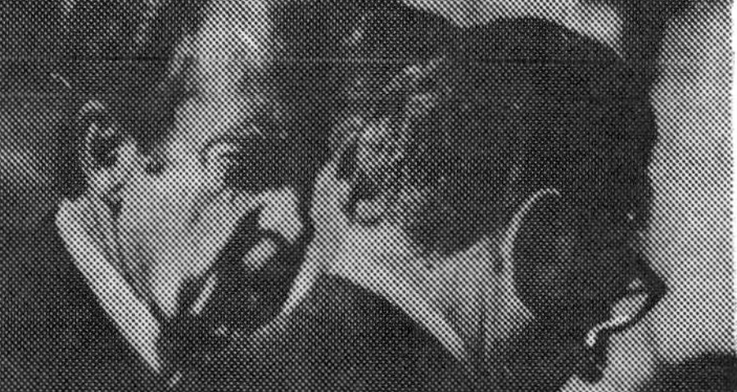

Associated Press

President Nixon sees Secretary of State Kissinger off for his Washington news session

KISSINGER SPEAKS

He Cites Ambiguous Signs by Moscow as the Cause

By BERNARD GWERTZMAN

Special to The New York Times

WASHINGTON, Friday, Oct. 26—The United States ordered its military forces on a worldwide "precautionary alert" early yesterday morning, citing concern that the Soviet Union was planning to introduce military forces into the Middle East. But the crisis seemed to abate when the Soviet Union joined later in a United Nations Security Council resolution barring big powers from participating in a Middle East peacekeeping force.

Secretary of State Kissinger said at a news conference in

Transcript of the Kissinger news conference, Page 19.

Washington that the United States was not seeking a confrontation with the Soviet Union.

And a State Department spokesman, noting that Mr. Kissinger had said that such a Security Council vote would ease tensions, termed the United Nations action "a step in the right direction." As of early today the precautionary alert was still in effect.

Other officials said that because of the Council vote some military units might be taken off alert later this morning.

Alert in Soviet Union

The alert was instituted after the Soviet Union gave what Mr. Kissinger called "ambiguous" signs that it might intervene to help out Egyptian forces caught behind Israeli lines and faced with destruction or surrender despite the cease-fire.

Military officials cited an alert of airborne troops within the Soviet Union as one cause of the American alert. [Details on Page 20.]

Intervention by the big powers, Mr. Kissinger warned, could cause major tensions in the world.

The sudden developments unforeseen yesterday when the White House was reporting that the Middle East cease-fire was taking effect, shocked the nation's capital and led President Nixon to postpone his scheduled news conference last evening in which he was expected to defend his actions in the Watergate tapes controversy.

Denial by Kissinger

The crisis, caused by uncertainty in Washington about the ability of the superpowers to avoid a direct confrontation over the Middle East, also produced some speculation that Mr. Nixon might have ordered the alert to distract domestic criticism.

Mr. Kissinger denied such allegations strongly, saying: "It is a symptom of what is happening to our country that it could even be suggested that the United States would alert its forces for domestic reasons."

He added, in his televised news conference, that "the President had no other choice as a responsible national leader" than to follow the advice

Continued on Page 19, Column 1

FORD BACKS STUDY ON IMPEACHMENT

Says He'll Support Congress if It Insists on Another Watergate Prosecutor

By JAMES M. NAUGHTON

Special to The New York Times

WASHINGTON, Oct. 25—Gerald R. Ford, President Nixon's nominee for Vice President, said today that the House of Representatives should "carry on" with an inquiry into the question of impeaching the President.

Moreover, Mr. Ford said in response to questions that he would support demands for creation of a new Watergate special prosecutor's office if a majority of the Congress insisted on it.

Mr. Ford, who is the minority leader of the House, outlined his views minutes after the House Republican Conference implored three White House officials to persuade Mr. Nixon to name a new special prosecutor and to make public the contents of the secret Watergate tape recordings.

Bryce N. Harlow, a counselor to the President, told newsmen that the Republican requests would be conveyed to Mr. Nixon and that the President would decide "very shortly" whether to name a successor to Archibald Cox, the special prosecutor who was discharged Saturday.

But Democrats in the Senate and the House pressed ahead with plans to enact legislation that would grant Chief Judge John J. Sirica of the United

Continued on Page 24, Column 5

Text of U.N. Resolution

Special to The New York Times

UNITED NATIONS, N.Y., Oct. 2[illegible]—Following is the resolution adopted by the Security Council today:

The Security Council,

Recalling its Resolutions 338 (1973) of 22 October, 1973, and 339 (1973) of 23 October, 1973,

Noting with regret the reported repeated violations of the cease-fire in noncompliance with Resolutions 338 (1973) and 339 (1973),

Noting with concern from the Secretary General's report that the United Nations military observers have not yet been enabled to place themselves on both sides of the cease-fire line,

1. Demands that immediate and complete cease-fire be observed and that the parties return to the positions occupied by them at 16:50 hours G.M.T. on 22 October, 1973;

2. Requests the Secretary General, as an immediate step, to increase the number of United Nations military observers on both sides;

3. Decides to set up immediately under its authority a United Nations emergency force to be composed of personnel drawn from states members of the United Nations except permanent members of the Security Council, and requests the Secretary General to report within 24 hours on the steps taken to this effect;

4. Requests the Secretary General to report to the Council on an urgent and continuing basis on the state of implementation of this resolution as well as Resolutions 338 (1973) and 339 (1973);

5. Requests all member states to extend their full cooperation to the United Nations in the implementation of this resolution as well as Resolutions 338 (1973) and 339 (1973).

EGYPT SAYS ISRAEL CONTINUES FIRING

Sadat's Aide Reports Road From Cairo to Suez City Was Cut During Day

By HENRY TANNER

Special to The New York Times

CAIRO, Oct. 25—Egypt accused Israel today of continuing to violate the cease-fire agreement and said Israeli troops had fired on Egyptian forces wherever they were found.

A foreign-policy adviser to President Anwar el-Sadat said at a news conference that the Israelis cut the vital road from Cairo to the city of Suez at the southern end of the canal during the day.

The adviser, Ashraf Ghorbal, expressed deep bitterness over the shipment of United States matériel to the Israeli forces, "some of it straight to the battlefield." This, he said, enables the Israelis to continue to violate the truce.

Meanwhile, United Nations truce teams took up positions on the Cairo-Suez road 63 miles from Cairo and 12 miles west of Ismailia on the Cairo-Ismailia road. Egyptian officials charged that the Israelis had prevented United Nations observers from taking up a position at the canal site at which Israeli

Continued on Page 21, Column 5

Moscow Exhibits Tension, But No Intent to Intervene

By HEDRICK SMITH

Special to The New York Times

MOSCOW, Oct. 25—The Soviet Union showed new signs of tension with the United States today, but gave no public indication that it was preparing to intervene in the Middle East.

The Soviet leader, Leonid I. Brezhnev, abruptly postponed a scheduled address to 3,000 delegates at the opening session of the World Peace Congress here, in which many had expected him to emphasize the benefits of reconciliation and of Soviet-American cooperation in defusing the Middle East conflict.

He was seen leaving his balcony box for urgent consultations during other speeches and then circulating papers to President Nikolai V. Podgorny. Afterward, Foreign Minister Andrei A. Gromyko left the box.

Moscow signaled acute concern over the fate of Egyptian forces on the east side of the Suez Canal with a string of dispatches by Tass, the official press agency, charging Israel with repeated violations of the Middle East cease-fire and with attempts to capture the city of Suez.

This was in keeping with Soviet efforts to shield Egyptian forces from further defeats along the Suez Canal. The sharpened Soviet line against Washington suggested disillusion with the American moves. It could also have been read as an effort by Moscow to convey

Continued on Page 21, Column 3

Trapped Egyptian Force Held Key Factor in Crisis

By CHARLES MOHR

Special to The New York Times

TEL AVIV, Oct. 25 — The Egyptian III Corps, estimated to number 15,000 to 30,000 men, remained trapped by the Israelis today, unable to acquire fresh supplies of water and food.

It was generally felt here that the plight of the Egyptian force was at the root of the increasingly tense international situation, in which the United States alerted its forces worldwide, citing concern that the Soviet Union was planning to introduce troops into the Middle East.

Israeli spokesmen said that there was no fighting or violation of the cease-fire by either side during the day on either the Egyptian or the Syrian fronts and that the United Nations Truce Supervision Organization's observer teams were moving into position.

Egypt's III Corps is cut off in a narrow pocket on the eastern bank of the Suez Canal south of the Great Bitter Lake and in a small enclave embracing the city of Suez at the southern end of the canal.

If the isolation of the Egyptian force is very much prolonged, the III Corps might be forced to surrender or ask for free passage through Israeli lines.

The surrender during a cease-fire of such a substantial part of the Egyptian armed forces might constitute a stinging political humiliation for the Egyptian Government.

Such a move would reduce Egypt's holdings on the eastern bank of the canal, all of which she had seized soon after the war began on Oct. 6, to a narrow strip running from Qantara to a point opposite

Continued on Page 21, Column 2

Smoke Fells 150 on IRT In Crash in South Bronx

By ROBERT D. McFADDEN

More than 150 subway riders suffered smoke inhalation and other minor injuries and hundreds more were trapped in a dark smoky tunnel in the South Bronx for an hour or more last night after an IRT express train struck the rear of another that had been stalled by a fire.

Passengers recounted scenes of confusion, crying, and even instances of hysteria as a northbound train with flames and smoke pouring from a middle car stalled just north of the Longwood Avenue station on the Pelham Bay Park line and was hit by a following train.

The impact of the collision was described by Transit Authority spokesmen as light, but riders on both trains said many had been hurled to the floor. The collision occurred on the express track — the center of three tracks—at the north end of the station, at about 7:20 P.M.

More than a dozen ambulances from hospitals in the Bronx converged on Longwood Avenue and Southern Boulevard in Hunts Point, along with Manhattan and Queens hospital disaster units, a dozen pieces of Fire Department apparatus

Continued on Page 14, Column 3

U.S. Says Mafia Informer Gave Evidence Against Rep. Brasco

By NICHOLAS GAGE

Special to The New York Times

WASHINGTON, Oct. 25—The indictment of Representative Frank J. Brasco on Tuesday came as a result of information given to the Justice Department by John A. Masiello, a Mafia captain who was involved in the case, according to Federal sources.

Masiello is the highest ranking member of the crime syndicate known to have been "turned" — converted into a Government informer or witness.

The sources told The New York Times that Mafia leaders had already learned about Masiello's cooperation with the Government and reportedly had issued a "contract" on his life. He is currently under heavy Government protection in New York.

Representative Brasco was indicted on charges of conspiring to receive $27,500 in illegal payoffs in 1968 for helping Masiello's trucking concern get contracts to haul mail for the Post Office. Masiello was named as co-conspirator with the 41-year-old Democrat and his uncle, Joseph Brasco, but not as a defendant.

Masiello was listed by the Justice Department as a captain

Continued on Page 29, Column 2

Beame Recruiting Unit

Controller Abraham D. Beame is so confident of victory in the mayoral election that he is forming a "recruiting" committee to seek out prospective top-level appointees for a Beame administration. Details, Page 31.

United Press International

U.N. observers, in vehicles towing supply trailers, moving to posts in Egypt yesterday

NEWS INDEX

"All the News That's Fit to Print"

The New York Times

LATE CITY EDITION

Weather: Fair today; rain likely tonight. Chance of rain tomorrow. Temp. range: today 61-77; Wed. 62-84. Additional details on Page 82.

VOL. CXXIII . . . No. 42,481

NEW YORK, THURSDAY, MAY 16, 1974

20c beyond 50-mile radius of New York City, except Long Island. Higher in air delivery cities.

15 CENTS

16 YOUNG ISRAELI HOSTAGES DIE AS TROOPS KILL 3 ARAB CAPTORS; KISSINGER TALKS DELAYED A DAY

Young victims being carried from school in Maalot after the clash between Arab guerrillas and Israeli troops

United Press International

A student, wounded in chest and arm, is carried from the Natia Meir school building

Associated Press

TERROR AT SCHOOL

Soldiers Rush Building as Attempt to Trade Prisoners Fails

By TERENCE SMITH

Special to The New York Times

MAALOT, Israel, May 15—A day of terror ended in this northern town this evening with a savage, 10-minute burst of gunfire and grenade explosions that killed three Arab terrorists and 16 of the high-school students they were holding hostage.

Early this morning, terrorists took command of the school, where about 90 students out on an excursion were sleeping. The three Arabs demanded the release of 20 prisoners held by Israel in return for the lives of the students.

An Israeli attempt to meet the demand failed and, as the deadline set by the guerrillas approached, soldiers rushed the school.

On 26th Independence Day

In the fighting that ensued, besides those killed 70 students were wounded, at least nine seriously. In the morning, as the day's terror began, a family of three was cut down by the Arab guerrillas as they entered the town. One soldier was also killed.

It was one of the bloodiest terrorist incidents in Israel's troubled history and it came on the 26th anniversary of the nation's independence.

After the decision to rush the school had been made, soldiers in bullet-proof vests surrounded the three-story building while snipers trained their sights on its shallow horizontal windows.

The firing broke out suddenly, while an officer with an electric megaphone was still pleading with the guerrillas in Arabic to postpone their 6 P.M. deadline.

Two of the three Arabs were hit by the opening burst of fire. One was apparently killed instantly, but the second had the strength to turn his automatic weapon on the students, spraying the second-story classroom indiscriminately.

Sought to Explode School

The third man tossed two grenades out the windows in an attempt to scatter the attacking soldiers. Then, according to one of the officers, the terrorist raced downstairs toward the entrance of the school where explosive charges had been placed. Before he could detonate them, soldiers shot him.

The screams of the terrified teen-agers could be heard a hundred yards away as the shooting erupted. One girl shrieked over and again, "Up here, he's up here," referring to the wounded terrorist who was still firing.

Even before the shooting

Continued on Page 18, Column 3

SETBACK IS SEEN IN PEACE EFFORTS

Moves for a Compromise on Israeli-Syrian Troops Are Called Impaired

Special to The New York Times

JERUSALEM, May 15—The terrorist attack at Maalot today forced Secretary of State Kissinger to suspend his Middle East peace efforts for one day.

The attack, which occupied the Israeli Cabinet through the day, was denounced by Mr. Kissinger as "this mindless and irrational action." The Secretary made it clear to his aides that he was determined not to let it undermine the progress made so far in this current Middle East negotiating trip.

But the tragic events at Maalot were viewed by both Israeli and American officials as probably having the effect of impairing his efforts to extract any last-minute compromises from either Israel or Syria on disengagement on the Syrian front before his scheduled return to Washington over the weekend.

Mr. Kissinger had been slated to meet with Israeli officials, led by Premier Golda Meir, this morning after an Israeli Cabinet meeting scheduled to discuss Israel's final ideas on disengagement to be conveyed by Mr. Kissinger to Syrian officials.

But this morning, when the dimensions of the terrorist attack became known, Mr. Kissinger put off his plans to leave Israel for Syria, preferring to wait until Mrs. Meir and other Israeli officials could deal with the disengagement problems.

Israeli officials, who spoke from time to time with Mr.

Continued on Page 19, Column 4

Mrs. Meir Pledges Steps To Protect Israeli People

By BERNARD GWERTZMAN

Special to The New York Times

JERUSALEM, May 15—Premier Golda Meir promised a numbed nation tonight that Israel would do everything possible to protect her people against terrorist attacks.

Speaking on television, Mrs. Meir went into detail about

Text of Mrs. Meir's television remarks appears on Page 18.

the "bitter day for all of us" that resulted in the death of three Arab terrorists and 16 teen-aged Israelis in the village of Maalot.

Israel, she said, will "do everything in its power to cut off the hands that want to harm a child, an adult, a settlement, a town or a village."

Mrs. Meir affirmed that Israel

reverse her long-standing policy of not negotiating with terrorists. The Government was prepared to release 23 prisoners in return for the safety of the approximately 90 teen-age hostages held by three Arab terrorists, the Premier said.

But the deal fell apart, she said, partly out of confusion, when the three terrorists insisted on a code word to begin negotiations. The code word never arrived from abroad for use by the French or Rumanian Ambassadors, who were prepared to begin discussions, she said.

Talking in a firm voice that occasionally faltered, and look-

Continued on Page 18, Column 3

Busing of Pupils Upheld In a Senate Vote of 47-46

Ban Urged by Gurney Fails After 6 Hours of Debate—Revision in Aid Formula May Cost Schools Here $23-Million

By RICHARD D. LYONS

Special to The New York Times

WASHINGTON, May 15 — The Senate in effect upheld today the busing of children to end school segregation by a vote of 47 to 46.

The victory for the Senate liberals came only seven weeks after the House of Representatives by a vote of 293 to 117 approved a provision to prohibit Federal courts from ordering long-distance busing of children.

Today's vote followed six hours of often emotional debate. The critical Senate vote tabled an antibusing amendment offered by Senator Edward J. Gurney, Republican of Florida, to the Federal aid to education bill that has been on the Senate floor all week.

The motion to table was made by Senator Jacob K. Javits, Republican of New York.

In a radio address in March, President Nixon supported the antibusing language of the House version of the Gurney amendment, which was introduced in the House by Representative Marvin L. Esch, Republican of Michigan.

After defeating the Gurney amendment, the Senate approved, by a vote of 56 to 36, a more limited provision prohibiting the busing of pupils from one school district into another unless it has been found that discrimination is practiced in both districts or that district lines in both districts were drawn for the purpose of maintaining segregation.

The amendment is aimed at situations such as that in Detroit, where a Federal court has ordered busing between city schools and those in affluent white suburbs. The Detroit case

Continued on Page 9, Column 1

HOUSE UNIT ISSUES 2 NEW SUBPOENAS TO NIXON FOR DATA

Some on the Judiciary Panel Charge Transcripts Omit Significant Material

By JAMES M. NAUGHTON

Special to The New York Times

WASHINGTON, May 15—The House Judiciary Committee issued today two new subpoenas for White House tape recordings and other documents amid charges by some committee members that significant portions of President Nixon's Watergate conversations had been omitted from edited White House transcripts.

In a series of votes on the two subpoenas, the committee

Text of two memorandums on tape subpoenas, Page 26.

demanded this morning that the President turn over to its impeachment inquiry the tape recordings of 11 Watergate-related conversations as well as diaries of Mr. Nixon's White House meetings over more than eight months in 1972 and 1973. The committee has not received any of this material, either in tape or other documentary form.

Two White House recordings previously obtained by the Judiciary Committee were played for the panel members this afternoon, prompting several Democrats to increase their resolve to obtain tapes, and not transcripts, of the relevant Watergate conversations.

Significance Disputed

Two Democratic members of the panel, Representatives Robert F. Drinan of Massachusetts and Jerome R. Waldie of California, told reporters after hearing the tape of a Sept. 15, 1972, White House conversation that material had been omitted from the White House transcripts not because it was inaudible but, as Mr. Waldie stated it, "because of the content."

Both Democrats declined to specify the nature of the missing material, however, and some Republicans on the committee said that they did not regard the omissions as serious or deliberate.

"The only thing that was deleted was the expletives, nothing of substance," Representative Delbert L. Latta, Republican of Ohio, said after the four-hour closed hearing at which recordings were played for about 40 minutes.

Renewed Effort by Panel

The new subpoenas, which "commanded" Mr. Nixon to supply the recordings and diaries by next Wednesday, were the first step in a renewed and bipartisan effort by the Judiciary Committee to obtain tapes and documents that Mr. Nixon has so far refused to yield.

John M. Doar, the committee's special counsel on impeachment, said that he would meet tomorrow with White House lawyers to get a final answer on whether Mr. Nixon would voluntarily supply recordings of 66 other conversations bearing on pledges of large political contributions to the President's re-election campaign by dairy industry groups and the International Telephone

Continued on Page 26, Column 1

Beame Asks $11.1-Billion For an 'Austerity' Budget

By GLENN FOWLER

Mayor Beame formally presented his first operating budget as the city's chief executive yesterday, labeling it an "austerity" blueprint that calls for spending $11.1-billion to run the municipal government in the fiscal year beginning July 1.

Declaring that he intended to provide "little in the way

Excerpts from Mayor Beame's budget are on Page 34.

of new money for new programs," Mr. Beame detailed in a 67-page message accompanying the basic document his financial acrobatics in overcoming a threatened $1.5-billion gap between income and outgo, enabling him finally to bring the budget into balance, as required by law.

The projected 1974-75 spending level, which is almost 8 per cent higher than the current fiscal year's actual outlay, spreads most of the available money among the areas of concern that have come to absorb much of the municipal treasury: public schools ($2.7-billion), welfare and related programs ($2.6-billion), public safety ($1.3-billion for police and fire) and health services ($1.2-billion).

One unusually large item is $1.5-billion for debt service — money to pay interest and amortization on the city's mounting debt — representing in the new budget a 63 per cent increase over the cost in the current fiscal year.

Mr. Beame placed the blame for the city's fiscal condition on his predecessor, John V. Lindsay, and he had harsh words for the

Continued on Page 34, Column 1

OIL DEPLETION AID FACES HOUSE VOTE

Democrats Mandate Action on Proposal to Repeal 22% Allowance Now

By EILEEN SHANAHAN

Special to The New York Times

WASHINGTON, May 15—Democratic members of the House of Representatives voted overwhelmingly today to force a straight yes-or-no vote in the House on immediate termination of the 22 per cent depletion allowance for the oil industry.

The action by the House Democratic Caucus, though technically only on a procedural matter, brought repeal of the depletion allowance closer than it has ever been in its 50-year history.

The vote in the caucus came about after weeks of intensive strategy planning, lobbying and nose-counting masterminded by three organizations: the American Federation of Labor and Congress of Industrial Organizations, Ralph Nader's tax reform research group and Common Cause, the citizens' lobby.

Rep. Green Is Key

The action of the caucus also brought into prominence a new leader on tax issues among the liberal Democrats in the House, Representative William J. Green of Pennsylvania.

In addition, the vote marked the first time that the new rules of the Democratic Caucus had been used to make sure that the House got to vote on a specific issue. The rules were adopted in February, 1973.

The action was deplored by Frank N. Ikard, president of the American Petroleum Institute. He said that the caucus had displayed a "lynch mob attitude" and predicted that the nation would "suffer a devastating setback in its efforts to attain a reasonable degree of energy self-sufficiency" if the ultimate victory in Congress went to those who, as he put it, "are demanding punitive tax action aimed at petroleum producers."

The caucus voted to permit

Continued on Page 17, Column 1

Police-Killing Mistrial

A mistrial was declared here yesterday in the trial of five reputed members of the Black Liberation Army who were charged with murdering two policemen. Page 45.

CHAPIN SENTENCED TO 10-30 MONTHS

Former Nixon Aide Appeals Prison Term for Lying to Watergate Grand Jury

By ANTHONY RIPLEY

Special to The New York Times

WASHINGTON, May 15 — Dwight L. Chapin, President Nixon's former appointments secretary, was sentenced today to a minimum of 10 months in prison for lying to a Watergate grand jury about political sabotage in the 1972 campaign.

Judge Gerhard A. Gesell imposed two concurrent sentences of 10 to 30 months each, calling it "a punishment sentence for a man who is not likely to repeat and needs no rehabilitation."

When Judge Gesell read the sentence, Mr. Chapin was apparently unmoved as he stood before the bench in United States District Court here. On April 5, he was convicted by a jury on two counts of lying about his dealings with Donald H. Segretti, an old college friend. Mr. Chapin was acquitted on a third count, and a fourth count was dismissed during the trial.

"It appears to the court that your resort to the convenience of swearing falsely when called before a grand jury cannot be condoned," Judge Gesell told the 33-year-old defendant. "I have therefore decided you

Threats by Nixon Reported on Tape Heard by Inquiry

By DAVID E. ROSENBAUM

Special to The New York Times

WASHINGTON, May 15—The tape recording of President Nixon's Sept. 15, 1972, conversation with H. R. Haldeman and John W. Dean 3d, which was heard today by members of the House Judiciary Committee, contains at least one long passage that does not appear in the edited White House transcript of that tape, according to a committee source.

In the passage cited by the source, President Nixon threatens to punish The Washington Post and its attorney, Edward Bennett Williams, and notes specifically that The Post owns television stations.

There is the clear implication, according to the source, that the President hoped to take Government action to deprive The Post of its television licenses.

The Post won a Pulitzer Prize last year for its many disclosures about the Watergate case and other scandals in the Nixon Administration.

Reading from a copy of the transcript prepared by the impeachment inquiry staff, the

Continued on Page 26, Column 1

Installation in Lisbon

Gen. António de Spínola took office as President of Portugal and named a left-leaning Government promising democracy at home and in Portuguese Africa. Details

SCHEEL IS ELECTED PRESIDENT IN BONN

Coalition Proves Strength in First-Ballot Victory—Bitterness Dissipates

By CRAIG R. WHITNEY

Special to The New York Times

BONN, May 15 — Walter Scheel was elected to the ceremonial office of the West German presidency today in a demonstration of solidarity between the two governing coalition parties, Mr. Scheel's Free Democrats and the Social Democrats.

The 54-year-old Mr. Scheel, who has been Vice Chancellor and Foreign Minister in the coalition Government since 1969, won a comfortable majority—530 of the 1,036 votes in the presidential electoral college on the first ballot. The fourth President since the formation of the West German Federal Republic in 1949, he is the first to be chosen so easily.

It was clear that despite bickering and fears of a revolt by some Social Democrats because of the resignation of their leader, Willy Brandt, from the chancellorship last week in the wake of a divisive spy scandal, the coalition was holding firmly together. There were only five abstentions and three absences. Mr. Scheel's opponent, Richard von Weizsäcker, received 498 votes, three fewer

Haig Said to Testify Simon Warned of Hughes Inquiry

By JOHN M. CREWDSON

Special to The New York Times

WASHINGTON, May 15 — Gen. Alexander M. Haig Jr., reportedly told a closed-door session of the Senate Watergate committee today that he was warned a year ago by William E. Simon, then Deputy Secretary of the Treasury, that a Federal investigation of a $100,000 political contribution from Howard R. Hughes had reached the point where it could eventually prove an embarrassment to President Nixon.

Sources familiar with his testimony said General Haig, the White House chief of staff, had identified Mr. Simon, who was confirmed last week as Secretary of the Treasury, as the individual who told him in the spring of 1973 that an Internal Revenue Service inquiry into the trail of the

money had led to Charles G. Rebozo, Mr. Nixon's close friend.

General Haig's testimony about his knowledge of the Hughes-Rebozo matter was given under oath during an hour-and-a-half session before the Watergate committee members and lawyers, after the President had agreed to waive a claim of executive privilege invoked earlier this month before the committee by the general.

The committee voted unanimously today to ask the full Senate to extend its mandate of the Watergate case through the end of June. Senate Resolution 60, which authorizes the select committee's investiga-

NEWS INDEX

Sid Wertsberg is President of the Jack Keller

TODAY: SPECIAL ISSUE OF THE MAGAZINE—"AMERICA AT 200"

"All the News That's Fit to Print"

The New York Times

LATE CITY EDITION

Weather: Partly cloudy, mild today and tonight. Fair, mild tomorrow. Temperature range: today 65-80; Saturday 65-86. Details on page 39.

SECTION ONE

VOL. CXXV . No. 43,261

NEW YORK, SUNDAY, JULY 4, 1976

$1.00 beyond 50-mile zone from New York City, except Long Island. Higher in air delivery cities.

75 CENTS

HOSTAGES FREED AS ISRAELIS RAID UGANDA AIRPORT

Commandos in 3 Planes Rescue 105—Casualties Unknown

By TERENCE SMITH

Special to The New York Times

JERUSALEM, Sunday, July 4—Israeli airborne commandos staged a daring night-time raid on Entebbe airport in Uganda last night, freeing the 105 mainly Israeli hostages and Air France crew members held by pro-Palestinian hijackers and flying them back to Israel aboard three Israeli planes.

The hostages and their rescuers were due back in Israel this morning after a brief stopover at Kenya's International Airport at Nairobi, where at least two persons were given medical treatment in a field hospital on the runway. No details of the extent of the casualties were available here pending notification of the families.

Only fragmentary reports of the raid were immediately available here. An unspecified number of commandos apparently flew the 2,300 miles from Israel to Entebbe Airport and surprised the hijackers on the ground.

The hijackers were spending the night with their hostages in the old passenger terminal at Entebbe where they have been confined all week. They had commandeered an Air France airliner last Sunday shortly after it had left Athens on its way to Paris.

News agency reports from Entebbe said that a number of large explosions — perhaps bombs — were set off at a distant point on the airport, apparently to divert the ring of Uganda troops that had surrounded the old terminal all week.

The commandos reportedly broke into the old terminal and fought a gun battle with the heavily armed hijackers. Reports from the scene said that the terrorists had been killed in the skirmish, but military sources here declined to confirm or deny this.

The hostages apparently were then rushed to the waiting Israeli planes and flown away before Uganda forces could intervene.

An Israeli radio report said that the raiders were infantrymen and paratroopers dressed in civilian clothes.

Government sources here said that the decision to stage the military operation was approved unanimously by a special Cabinet meeting in Tel Aviv yesterday. The decision was made, the sources said, when it became clear that the hijackers would not relent in their demands and were holding Israel responsible for the

Continued on Page 10, Column 1

The New York Times/Paul Hosefros

The cruiser Wainwright leads flotilla of ships up the Hudson for Bicentennial celebration. Following the Wainwright are the amphibious command ship Mount Whitney, the Peruvian ship Independencia, the Venezuelan destroyer Zulia, the Spanish missile frigate Asturias and the Dutch destroyer Tromp. Warships were vanguard of review.

LONG TO LET PANEL RESTUDY TAX BILL

Review to Follow Criticism of Many Provisions Put in for Special Interests

By EILEEN SHANAHAN

Special to The New York Times

WASHINGTON, July 3—Senator Russell B. Long, chairman of the Senate Finance Committee, apparently concerned by criticism of the many special-interest provisions contained in the pending tax bill, has decided to take the extraordinary step of giving the committee a chance to reconsider its earlier decisions on the bill.

Senator Long, a Louisiana Democrat, disclosed his plans in an interview just before the Senate recessed for the Fourth of July holiday and the Democratic National Convention, which begins in New York on July 12.

The exact procedures that the committee will use in its reconsideration of the measure have not yet been decided.

For example, it is not yet clear whether the panel will have hearings on the many provisions of the bill that it adopted in May and June without any hearings.

What Mr. Long said was that he was "planning, after the recess, to call the committee together and offer senators an opportunity to express their views

Continued on Page 28, Column 4

Warships of 22 Nations Arrive for Bicentennial

By FRED FERRETTI

An international flotilla of warships sailed under the Verrazano-Narrows Bridge into New York Harbor yesterday, and more than 200 high-masted sailing ships moved into temporary berths at Sandy Hook and Gravesend Bay in preparation for the city's sea and land salute to the Bicentennial celebration today.

At precisely 8 A.M., the cruiser Wainwright, her blue-tipped missiles pointing skyward, moved smartly under the bridge, leading 52 naval ships from 22 countries taking part in the International Naval Review today.

Scores of small pleasure boats scurried about as the warships began moving into New York's lower bay, and the Coast Guard reported that more than 30,000 small boats were in and around the harbor and amid the tall ships off Sandy Hook.

And as the carrier Forrestal, the review ship for today's military sea parade, moved toward its anchorage in the Narrows, the Coast Guard reported "wall-to-wall" pleasure boats around her.

Cannon salutes were exchanged between the Wainwright and Fort Hamilton in Brooklyn, fireboats sprayed arcs of water and helicopters and dirigibles dipped overhead as 17 of the international warships moved into anchorages along the Hudson River from 72d Street to the George Washington Bridge and the 35 other ships sailed into temporary overnight anchor between the Statue of Liberty and Staten Island.

At 1:46 the Forrestal moved into the Narrows.

As the military ships moved into position, the 16 tall ships

Continued on Page 22, Column 1

Oslo Crew Arrives, Bound for Manhood And Tall Adventure

By TONY KORNHEISER

Special to The New York Times

ABOARD THE CHRISTIAN RADICH, July 3—This Norwegian full-rigged ship dropped anchor off Sandy Hook, N.J., at 11:30 A.M. today, ending a six-month, 5,000-mile voyage from Oslo with a crew of boys who have sailed halfway to manhood.

They are 15, 16 and 17 years old—87 cadets in all—and they are full of briny talk and bluster, flushed with adventure and eager to see the America they have heard so much about from a variety of sources.

"The tall lady in the harbor," said 17-year-old Lorentz Kielland. "What is her name? Statue of Liberty? I see her in books ever since I am small guy. I want to see her for real."

Labor and Legends

For Lorentz and his young shipmates, the trans-Atlantic trip from Oslo to Plymouth, England; Tenerife in the Canary Islands; Bermuda; Newport, R.I., and, finally, New York for Operation Sail '76 has been a mixture of routine and the stuff that legends promise.

At sea, life on the Radich is a monotonous cycle of work and sleep—four hours on, four hours off, interrupted only by meals. A regimen to be sure, and planned that way. The cadets sleep in hammocks, in two large areas below decks that give the appearance of bat caves when the hammocks are swung. The bat caves stay quiet because sleep is a necessity and small talk and rock music are luxuries. This is an economy cruise.

"A training ship," said First Mate Fred Hegerstrom, a veter-

Continued on Page 23, Column 6

City Like a Small Town During Holiday Festival

By RICHARD SEVERO

New York was like an old-fashioned small town yesterday, presenting an image of straw hats, little girls in summer prints, unusually orderly boys in proper knee socks and air so clean and fresh you could breathe it without seeing it.

The tall ships of Operation Sail and the gray ships of the International Naval Review glided into a bright harbor where crowds were not overwhelming and where the spirit of the past somehow seemed more real than the present.

The promenade along Battery Park looked more like one of Seurat's impressions of a 19th century Sunday in France than the edge of a great city, teeming with people and the problems of the present, a day away from a gigantic maritime extravaganza.

Indeed, the idyll was challenged only by the fact that somebody forgot to unlock legions of portable toilets in Battery Park with the result that, by midday, a great many tourists and New Yorkers alike had used Beekman Downtown Hospital as a sanitary facility.

"We let them come in but we don't want the word passed around," said Beekman's president, E. Geoffrey High. But Mr. High wasn't complaining. When he got to work yesterday morning, he found that, for the first time in months, the emergency room was empty. "It's absolutely spooky," Mr. High said.

Perhaps it was the salubrious weather or perhaps it was that since everyone had feared huge crowds, the result was a more modest turnout and none of the jostling that can come with a major event in New York.

There were several thousand people at Battery Park, enjoying the passage of the ships in markedly different ways.

For Armando Marrero, a maintenance man at the Columbia Presbyterian Hospital who many years ago was in the merchant marine, it was a chance to watch ships slip by and think about the old days.

"It is so beautiful," he said, "the last time I'll be able to see anything like this."

For Roland Dahlman Jr.,

Continued on Page 22, Column 7

Italy's Major Parties Give Reds Key Legislative Post

By ALVIN SHUSTER

Special to The New York Times

ROME, July 3—The Communist Party won a victory today when the leaders of major parties agreed to give it the job of President, or Speaker, of the Chamber of Deputies.

The decision, which came at a joint meeting of Communist and non-Communist leaders, will give the Communists their most important parliamentary post in the history of the Italian Republic. The Speaker will be elected on Monday when the new Parliament, elected on June 20, assembles.

The Communist leaders had demanded the presidency of either the Chamber or the Senate. They based their demands on their increased parliamentary strength, which rose by 71 seats in both houses in the elections last month.

In the 630-seat Chamber the Communists gained 49 seats. The Christian Democrats, who retained their lead as Italy's largest party, now hold 262 seats to the Communists' 228.

The Communists are also demanding chairmanships of important committees in Parliament. But there was no word today on which they are likely to get.

The Christian Democrats, who have dominated Italian politics for 30 years, will retain the presidency of the 315-member Senate. This is symbolically the more important of the two posts because the Senate president, in effect, is the Vice President of Italy.

In the last Parliament, dis-

Continued on Page 14, Column 4

Pension Law Said to Add Costs for New York City

By FRANCIS X. CLINES

The pension revision law enacted last week in a round of legislative compromise and promises of savings actually will increase New York City's budget expenses and cut into the hopes of attrition in jobs that underlie its austerity plan, the City Actuary cautioned yesterday.

This ironic effect of a bill that the Legislature wrestled with in the name of economy was described by Jonathan Schwartz, the City Actuary, who oversees the city's pension system, as one of a number of negative aspects that make the new law an "absolute monstrosity."

"I kept calling up there to warn them, but no one in Albany seemed interested in hearing from a pension specialist when they were trying to write a pension law," Mr. Schwartz said.

The law produced by the Legislature is a compromise typical of the politically divided body's nature: a three-tiered system that includes some caveats, one of which will have a negative effect on the city budget, at least for the next several years, in Mr. Schwartz's view.

The particular caveat lets city workers enrolled in the old, pre-1973 system transfer to the new 1976 system and thereby extend their mandatory retirement age by five years, from age 65 to 70. Mr. Schwartz figures that about 1,000 city

Continued on Page 32, Column 4

Borg Wins Wimbledon

Bjorn Borg, a 20-year-old Swede, defeated Ilie Nastase of Rumania, 6-4, 6-2, 9-7, yesterday to win the Wimbledon title. Details in Section 5.

Today's Sections

Index to Subjects

U.S. Attorney Calls F.B.I. 'Out of Step'

By SELWYN RAAB

In an unusually sharp attack against the Federal Bureau of Investigation by a high Government law enforcement official, David G. Trager, the United States Attorney for the Eastern District of New York, has described the F.B.I. as "suffering from arteriosclerosis" and of being "out of step" with the major goals of Federal prosecutors.

"Most of the cases they [the F.B.I.] bring to us are insignificant," Mr. Trager said. "They are wasting resources on trivia, and I don't think they have the ability or the people to do the job in the areas we consider priorities—official corruption and white-collar crime."

Mr. Trager, who has been in charge of one of the largest Federal prosecutorial units for more than two years, accused the F.B.I. of refusing to cooperate with his office in several "sensitive areas," such as corruption inquiries. The bureau's investigative methods, he continued in an interview, were "a hangover from the Hoover days," a reference to the late J. Edgar Hoover who was the director of the F.B.I. for 48 years until his death in 1972.

"The whole organization is geared up for gangbuster crime," Mr. Trager said. "It's a hangover from the Hoover days, a mentality of the 1920's and 1930's, and the only things they are capable of investigating are bank robberies, kidnappings and interstate thefts. That may have been important, but they refuse to recognize

Continued on Page 32, Column 1

500,000 View Capital's Bicentennial Parade

By RICHARD HALLORAN

Special to The New York Times

WASHINGTON, July 3—The woman in the yellow jersey may have said it best when she clapped her hands and shouted to her friend marching by: "Everything's O.K.! Lookin' good, lookin' good!"

It was a grand day for the Bicentennial parade in the nation's capital today, and it was a grand parade celebrating the diversity that is America.

It was warm under a hazy sun but not one of Washington's blistering summer days, and 500,000 people, according to the official estimate, turned out to see more than 50 bands, 60 floats and 90 marching units.

President Ford missed the parade because he was playing golf at Burning Tree Country Club in suburban Maryland. But in a series of speeches prepared for the Bicentennial celebrations he paid tribute to the "American adventure" while saying that the blessings of liberty must still be defended. [Page 25.]

In Philadelphia, the influx of visitors to that historic city was much smaller than expected. [Page 26.]

Vice President Rockefeller and Johnny Cash, the singer, led the parade here in separate

Continued on Page 26, Column 4

The New York Times/George Tames

Vice President Rockefeller and his wife, Happy, leading the parade in Washington

"All the News That's Fit to Print"

The New York Times

LATE CITY EDITION

Weather: Cold, snow late today into tonight. Partial clearing tomorrow. Temperature range: today 27-36; yesterday 42-49. Details, page D14.

VOL. CXXVII . . No. 43,881 — NEW YORK, THURSDAY, MARCH 16, 1978 — 20 CENTS

25 cents beyond 50-mile zone from New York City. Higher in air delivery cities.

ISRAELIS SEIZE 4-TO 6-MILE 'SECURITY BELT' IN LEBANON AND SAY TROOPS WILL REMAIN; WASHINGTON SEES 'IMPEDIMENTS TO PEACE'

Senate Backers Of Canal Treaty Predict Victory

Say They Have Votes to Win Roll-Call Today

By ADAM CLYMER
Special to The New York Times

WASHINGTON, March 15—Senate supporters of the Panama Canal treaties said today that they had enough votes to win tomorrow's crucial roll-call on the first of the pacts.

On the eve of one of the most important foreign policy votes in many years, Senator Howard H. Baker Jr., Republican of Tennessee, the minority leader, told reporters he now believed that the treaty guaranteeing the neutrality of the canal after American control ends in the year 2000 would be approved. And the effective leader of the treaties' opponents, Senator Paul Laxalt, Republican of Nevada, characterized the situation as "not so good."

Tonight, Vice President Mondale told a Democratic Congressional fund-raising dinner, "Now we have 67 votes for the Panama Canal treaty tomorrow," indicating approval was insured.

Two New Votes in Favor

In a day of intense lobbying, beginning when Mr. Mondale appeared unannounced at the office of Senator Wendell H. Ford, Democrat of Kentucky, at 7:15 A.M., none of the uncommitted senators, including Mr. Ford, announced that they would vote against the treaty.

Two uncommitted senators, Edward W. Brooke, Republican of Massachusetts, and Dennis DeConcini, Democrat of Arkansas, said they would vote for the neutrality treaty. Mr. Brooke, however, said he might vote later against the treaty turning over the canal and the Canal Zone to Panama.

The backing of Mr. Brooke and Mr. DeConcini, plus the expected support of Senator Bob Packwood, Republican of Oregon, gave the treaty supporters 65 votes they could count on. They would not say where they expected to get the two other votes they needed to make up the 67 required for approval.

There were still four uncommitted senators available and at least the chance

Continued on Page A3, Column 1

CAPITAL SYMPATHETIC

U.S. Officials Relieved That Heavy Combat Activity Is Apparently Over

By BERNARD GWERTZMAN
Special to The New York Times

WASHINGTON, March 15—Israel's invasion of southern Lebanon evoked a sympathetic response from the United States today, but Secretary of State Cyrus R. Vance conceded that the Israeli attack and the Palestinian raid that inspired it had raised "impediments to the peace process."

The general mood at the highest levels of the Administration was relief this afternoon that the main fighting seemed at an end.

The evidence that the Israelis were confining their ground operations to a belt up to six miles deep along the border reduced the likelihood that the Syrians would enter the conflict and spread the warfare, one high official said.

Begin Statement Causes Worry

In Beirut, however, Syrian and Lebanese officials appealed for international help in obtaining Israeli withdrawal. [Page A17.] In Cairo, Foreign Minister Mohammed Ibrahim Kamel denounced the Israeli action as "organized genocide" and said that it harmed Egyptian peace efforts. [Page A17.]

American officials said that with Prime Minister Menachem Begin due in Washington next Monday for talks with President Carter on Tuesday and Wednesday, the chances for diplomatic progress, already dim, were now more remote.

A new problem has now arisen, officials said, over a statement by Mr. Begin today that Israeli forces would remain in the belt of Lebanese territory until an agreement was reached to prevent the Palestinians from returning to the area.

The United States, a strong backer of Lebanon's sovereignty and integrity, wants the Israelis to withdraw as soon as possible and the withdrawal issue undoubtedly will now become a major topic during Mr. Begin's talks with Mr. Carter, officials said.

Late this afternoon, Ambassador Simcha Dinitz of Israel conferred for 90 minutes with Alfred L. Atherton Jr., the Administration's top Middle East negotiator, to discuss the Israeli presence in

Continued on Page A17, Column 1

Associated Press

Israel's Prime Minister, Menachem Begin, left, arriving at the Lebanon border yesterday for a close look at the action. Defense Minister Ezer Weizman is at center, wearing flight jacket and sunglasses.

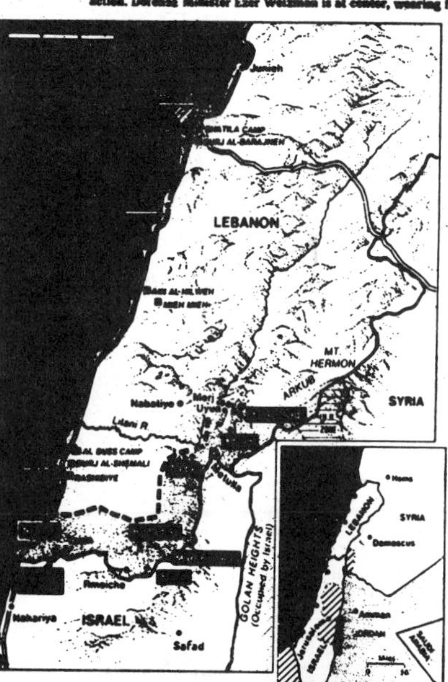

The New York Times/John Lelmong/March 16, 1978

Israelis established "security belt" in southern Lebanon after capturing Palestinian strongholds (marked by panels). Israeli gunboats attacked Tyre, and jets struck there, at Damur and also in Beirut area.

MAJOR FIGHTING ENDS

Forces Rout the Palestinians in Border Strongholds —Planes Bomb Bases

By WILLIAM E. FARRELL
Special to The New York Times

JERUSALEM, March 15—Israeli forces routed Palestinian guerrillas today from at least seven strongholds in southern Lebanon, and Prime Minister Menachem Begin said the troops would remain until an agreement was reached to insure that the area could never again be used for raids against Israel.

With land, sea and air operations conducted from the Mediterranean to the foothills of Mount Hermon, Israelis occupied what Lieut. Gen. Mordechai Gur, the Chief of Staff, called a "security belt" along the 60 or so miles of its northern border, with a depth of four and a half to six miles. Late tonight, General Gur said the major fighting was over.

[An Israeli military spokesman reported that 11 Israeli soldiers had been killed in the operation and 57 wounded, according to The Associated Press.]

Air Strikes Near Beirut

Mr. Begin's remarks about how long Israelis would remain in Lebanon were echoed by Defense Minister Ezer Weizman, who told reporters:

"We shall continue to clear the area—prevent the area from being attack positions against us as long as we find it necessary."

The ground offensive, the largest that Israel has ever carried out against Palestinians, was accompanied by air strikes against Palestinian enclaves and camps far north of the Israeli border, including at least two in the vicinity of Beirut.

The Israeli Army spokesman announced that Israeli planes had bombed a Palestinian base near Damur, about 20 miles south of Beirut, which he said had been the staging area for the Arab raiders who infiltrated into Israel on Saturday and seized a bus.

Syrians Said to Fire on Planes

The seizure touched off a wild ride on the Haifa-Tel Aviv highway, with shooting and an explosion that led to the death of 34 Israelis and an American and the injury of more than 70 persons.

The army spokesman said that Israeli planes had struck targets at the Mediterranean port of Tyre and at a site near Beirut that the spokesman described as a Palestine Liberation Organization training and supply base "for terrorist naval units and for their equipment."

In the raid at Damur, the spokesman said the Israeli planes had been fired on by a Syrian unit. The Israeli planes did not fire back at the Syrians, he said, and returned safely to base.

The Syrians have a large military

Continued on Page A16, Column 1

Guerrillas Join Civilian Retreat From Attackers

By MARVINE HOWE
Special to The New York Times

TYRE, Lebanon, March 15 — Many Palestinian and Lebanese families fled in panic today from population centers in southern Lebanon that had been bombarded by Israeli fighter-bombers, gunboats and artillery.

"We're going north, anywhere, to get away from the shelling," said Mohammed Ahmed al-Mohammed, a Lebanese farmer, as he and his family of 12 set out on foot along a road out of Tyre carrying only small bundles of blankets and clothing.

While young Lebanese and Palestinian guerrillas in the towns and villages spoke of their "fierce resistance," it was clear they were retreating in face of the heavy Israeli odds.

"We are not going to let ourselves be annihilated," said a member of the Palestine Liberation Organization's southern military command at Saida. "We cannot destroy the Israeli forces, but we can inflict as many casualties as possible and then make a tactical withdrawal."

The Palestinian military spokesman confirmed reports that the joint Palestinian-Lebanese leftist forces had lost their principal positions in the border area: Khiam, Ibl al-Saqi and Taibe in the east, Bint Jbail and Marun al-Ras in the center and Naqura and Alma al-Chaab in the southwest.

The city of Tyre was a prime target as the main port of entry for arms sup-

Continued on Page A16, Column 4

Soviet Now Termed Cool to Linking Cuban Pullout to Ethiopian Truce

By RICHARD BURT
Special to The New York Times

WASHINGTON, March 15—Contrary to what reporters were told at the State Department last week, the Soviet Union has given little sign that it is prepared to link the end of Somali-Ethiopian fighting with cuts in Cuban forces in Ethiopia, government officials said today.

They said Ambassador Anatoly F. Dobrynin, at a meeting with Secretary of State Cyrus R. Vance on Saturday, declined to commit Moscow on the future of either its own advisers or the Cuban forces in the Horn of Africa.

The previous evening, reporters were told that Moscow said the Cuban forces, estimated at 12,000, would be reduced once Somalia ended its occupation of Ogaden, an ethnic Somali region of Ethiopia. The reporters were also told that the Soviet Union had agreed to have neutral observers monitor a cease-fire. The information was supplied as "deep background," meaning that it could not be attributed.

Pullout Up to Addis Ababa

Today, a high-ranking State Department official said the information had been based on a previous "direct conversation" between Mr. Vance and Mr. Dobrynin. However, at their Saturday meeting, the Soviet envoy said the withdrawal of Cuba's forces from Ethiopia had to be taken up with those two governments, the official said..

The State Department spokesman, Hodding Carter 3d, announced that the Somali pullout, begun last week, was now complete, and he called on Moscow to facilitate the withdrawal of the Cuban troops and of the 1,000 Soviet advisers in Ethiopia.

Privately, State Department and White House officials said the Russians had been unwilling to discuss concrete plans for withdrawing the Cubans or establishing a truce-observation group.

"We have no evidence from Moscow or anywhere else that the Soviets are inclined to be cooperative on the Horn," said one White House official.

Officials expressed doubts over the likelihood of an early reduction in the

Continued on Page A9, Column 1

6 Guilty in Attack At Washington Sq.

By GREGORY JAYNES

Six of nine young men charged with taking part in a 1976 rampage in Washington Square Park that left one man dead and 13 persons injured were found guilty yesterday—three of manslaughter and three of lesser charges.

The verdict was delivered, after a nine-week trial and six days of deliberation, while a number of the defendants' parents wept in a closed courtroom in State Supreme Court in Manhattan. Parents of the three men found not guilty also cried.

Sentencing was scheduled for April 19 before Justice Robert Haft, in whose court the trial was held. Those convicted of manslaughter could be sentenced to as much as 25 years.

Calling the crime "one of great social severity," Assistant District Attorney John Moscow, the prosecutor, said that "the people will ask for imprisonment for all" those convicted.

During the trial, Mr. Moscow argued that the nine defendants had planned the attack on Washington Square to clear the park of blacks and Hispanic persons.

Of the nine defendants, one, Robert

Continued on Page B17, Column 1

United Press International

Palestinian refugees fleeing from Damur, Lebanon, following Israeli air strikes yesterday

INSIDE

Parking Rules Reinstated

Alternate-side-of-the-street parking regulations are reinstated to let sweepers get at a 62-day accumulation of slushy litter. Page B1.

Miner Council Backs Pact

The bargaining council of the United Mine Workers approved a third tentative contract that now must be voted on by the striking miners. Page D12.

Soviet Bars Rostropovich

The Soviet Union revoked the citizenship of Mstislav Rostropovich, the expatriate cellist, and his wife, Galina Vishnevskaya. Page A10.

CBS Executive Resigns

Robert J. Wussler, former president of the CBS television network and now president of CBS Sports, resigned to form a production company. Page C20.

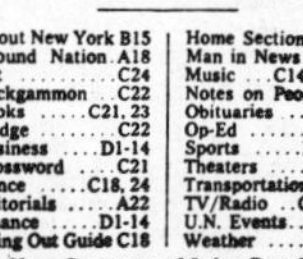

News Summary and Index, Page B1

PULLOUT SECTION ON SIGNING OF MIDEAST PEACE TREATY, PAGES A11 TO A18

"All the News That's Fit to Print"

The New York Times

LATE CITY EDITION

Weather: Mostly sunny, cool today; clear, cold tonight. Sunny tomorrow. Temperature range: today 32-48; yesterday 36-49. Details on page C12.

VOL.CXXVIII . . . No.44,169 | NEW YORK, TUESDAY, MARCH 27, 1979 | 25 cents beyond 50-mile zone from New York City. Higher in air delivery cities. | 20 CENTS

EGYPT AND ISRAEL SIGN FORMAL TREATY, ENDING A STATE OF WAR AFTER 30 YEARS; SADAT AND BEGIN PRAISE CARTER'S ROLE

OPEC PARLEY WEIGHS NEW OIL PRICE RISES AND CUTS IN OUTPUT

Saudis Say They Will Try to Resist Big Increases — Carter Puts Off Decisions on Energy

By PAUL LEWIS

Special to The New York Times

GENEVA, March 26 — Pressure for another large increase in world oil prices built up today at the opening of a meeting of oil ministers of the 13 member nations of the Organization of Petroleum Exporting Countries.

The advocates of a sharp new oil price rise, of anywhere from 20 to 35 percent from current levels on April 1, also urged other oil producers to reduce output. The aim would be to keep world markets tight as Iran resumes exports to insure that the new price levels stick.

But Saudi Arabia, the world's largest oil exporter, resisted pressure for price jumps, pointing out that they could do severe damage to the economies of both the developing and the industrialized world. "There is worry particularly about the effects of price changes on developing countries," OPEC's secretary general, René Ortise, said.

Effort to Reduce Increases

Sheik Ahmed Zaki Yamani, Saudi Arabia's oil minister, interviewed after tonight's session, said the ministers faced a "deadlock," with the Saudis feeling that the increases demanded by Iran and Libya were "too steep." Observers here interpreted his stance as an effort to cut probable increases to more moderate levels.

The ministers have not yet voted themselves the power to take any pricing action at the current two-day session but are expected to do so tomorrow. A simple majority vote would grant the meeting such authority.

On the question of possible punitive cutbacks in supplies, reflecting displeasure with some consuming nations' positions on the Palestinian question, Iraqi representatives said such moves were possible, particularly against Egypt. But they carefully noted that no such moves were planned by OPEC, although the "oil weapon" could re-emerge if conditions returned to the situation of 1973.

Carter Decisions Deferred

In Washington, meanwhile, Administration officials said that President Carter's decisions on various energy proposals, expected Thursday, would be deferred, apparently because key White House officials had not been able to devote enough time to the controversial plans. [Page D12.]

When Sheik Yamani entered the OPEC

Continued on Page D12, Column 3

United Press International

Leaders join hands after signing pact. President Anwar el-Sadat signed first, followed by Prime Minister Menachem Begin. President Carter was witness.

CEREMONY IS FESTIVE

Accord on Sinai Oil Opens Way to the First Peace in Mideast Dispute

By BERNARD GWERTZMAN

Special to The New York Times

WASHINGTON, March 26 — After confronting each other for nearly 31 years as hostile neighbors, Egypt and Israel signed a formal treaty at the White House today to establish peace and "normal and friendly relations."

On this chilly early spring day, about 1,500 invited guests and millions more watching television saw President Anwar el-Sadat of Egypt and Prime Minister

Transcripts of statements at signing are on page A11. Texts of treaty and Camp David accords are on pages A12, A13 and A14.

Menachem Begin of Israel put their signatures on the Arabic, Hebrew and English versions of the first peace treaty between Israel and an Arab country.

President Carter, who was credited by both leaders for having made the agreement possible, signed, as a witness, for the United States. In a somber speech he said, "Peace has come."

'The First Step of Peace'

"We have won, at last, the first step of peace — a first step on a long and difficult road," he added.

Later, at a state dinner, Mr. Begin suggested that Mr. Carter be given the Nobel Peace Peace, and Mr. Sadat agreed.

At the signing ceremony, all three leaders offered prayers that the treaty would bring true peace to the Middle East and end the enmity that has erupted into war four times since Israel declared its independence on May 14, 1948.

By coincidence, they all referred to the words of the Prophet Isaiah.

"Let us work together until the day comes when they beat their swords into plowshares and their spears into pruning hooks," Mr. Sadat said in his paraphrase of the biblical text.

'No More War,' Begin Says

Mr. Begin, who gave the longest and most emotional of the addresses, exclaimed: "No more war, no more bloodshed, no more bereavement, peace unto you, shalom, saalam, forever."

"Shalom" and "salaam" are the Hebrew and Arabic words for "peace."

The Israeli leader, noted for oratorical skill, provided a dash of humor when in the course of his speech he seconded Mr. Sadat's remark that Mr. Carter was "the unknown soldier of the peacemaking effort." Mr. Begin said, pausing, "I agree, but as usual with an amendment" — that Mr. Carter was not completely unknown and that his peace effort would "be

Continued on Page A10, Column 1

Mood of Peace Seems Somber And Uncertain

By BERNARD WEINRAUB

Special to The New York Times

WASHINGTON, March 26 — Shortly after 6 A.M. today, President Anwar el-Sadat arose in the residence of the Egyptian Ambassador and began wandering around the five-bedroom house.

He scanned the morning newspapers, pedaled a stationary exercise bicycle, nibbled a slice of unbuttered toast, sipped a glass of orange juice and, by 7 A.M. turned on the television to watch the morning news.

Less than one mile away, in a guarded ninth-floor suite at the Washington Hilton Hotel, Prime Minister Menachem Begin of Israel peered out the windows at the traffic moving along Connecticut Avenue.

He turned away and, carrying a cup of tea, walked to a writing desk and began working on the emotional speech that he would deliver in mid-afternoon at the White House ceremony ending 30 years of war between Israel and Egypt.

It was the start of a day marked by paradox — a triumphal day of peace that seemed curiously somber, a day of celebration blurred by protests in the heart of Washington, a bright day shadowed by uncertainty.

"There is, you know, a sense of trepi-

Continued on Page A9, Column 1

Treaty Impact Still Unknown

'Hopes and Dreams' but 'No Illusions' for Carter

By HEDRICK SMITH

Special to The New York Times

WASHINGTON, March 26 — The elusive, unprecedented peace treaty that Egypt and Israel signed today has enormous symbolic importance and the potential for fundamentally transforming the map and history of an entire region, but the agreement faces an uncertain future.

News Analysis

Israel has now won what it has sought since 1948 — formal recognition and acceptance from the most powerful Arab state and the ultimate prospect of exchanging ambassadors and entering into a full range of normal relations.

For all the violent denunciations that this historic breakthrough aroused in the Arab world, the best diplomatic estimate here is that the treaty has markedly reduced the risk of a major war in the Middle East for a considerable time by removing Egyptian strength from the active Arab arsenal.

And it has demonstrated American capacity to influence events in the Middle East despite the setbacks Washington has suffered since the overthrow of the

Continued on Page A10, Column 5

Photographs for The New York Times by TERESA ZABALA

Judge Bars Hydrogen Bomb Article After Magazine Rejects Mediation

By DOUGLAS E. KNEELAND

Special to The New York Times

MILWAUKEE, March 26 — A Federal District Court judge here, acting only after his suggestion for an attempt at out-of-court settlement was turned down, granted the Government's motion for a preliminary injunction today to keep The Progressive magazine from publishing an article about the hydrogen bomb.

In so doing, Judge Robert W. Warren became the first Federal judge ever to issue an injunction imposing prior restraint on the press in a national security case.

The magazine's attorneys said they would file an appeal shortly with the United States Court of Appeals for the Seventh Circuit in Chicago.

Court's 'Awesome Responsibility'

Before announcing his decision this afternoon, Judge Warren, a former Wisconsin Attorney General, acknowledged that he considered it an "awesome responsibility."

"Stripped to its essence, then," he said, "the question before the court is a basic confrontation between the First Amendment right to freedom of the press and national security."

The judge said "a mistake in ruling against The Progressive will seriously infringe cherished First Amendment rights." However, he added, "a mistake

Continued on Page B12, Column 3

INSIDE

Michigan State Wins

Michigan State became the National Collegiate basketball champion by defeating Indiana State, 75-64, at Salt Lake City. Page C13.

H.R.A. Administrator Quits

Blanche Bernstein, the Human Resources Administrator, resigned rather than accept Mayor Koch's offer to stay in the job without power. Page B1.

Palestinians, Reacting to the Pact, Go on Strike and Denounce Egypt

Special to The New York Times

BEIRUT, Lebanon, March 26 — Vowing revenge, staging strikes and protest marches and calling for punitive measures against Egypt, Palestinians and other Arabs reacted angrily today against the signing of the Egyptian-Israeli peace treaty in Washington.

Yasir Arafat, chairman of the Palestine Liberation Organization, vowed to chase Americans out of the Middle East and to "chop off the hands" of President Carter, President Anwar el-Sadat of Egypt and Prime Minister Menachem Begin of Israel. He spoke to a group of guerrilla recruits at the Sabra Palestinian camp here as effigies of the three signers were burned.

The inhabitants of Lebanon's 15 Palestinian camps protested the signing today by refusing to work, as did many Lebanese Moslems. Similar protests were staged in the occupied West Bank of the Jordan River and the Gaza Strip, and in the Arab Old City of Jerusalem a grenade exploded tonight, wounding five tourists.

Iran Government Condemns Pact

In Teheran, the Iranian Government condemned the treaty, and 30 Arab students took over the Egyptian Embassy there. Protesters also stormed the Egyptian Embassy in Kuwait, where 250,000 Palestinians live, forming the largest foreign community in that small country. In Damascus, Syria, demonstrators occupied the offices of the Egyptian airline, Egyptair.

Meanwhile, foreign and finance ministers of Arab League countries gathered today in Baghdad, Iraq, for a meeting tomorrow on possible economic and political measures against Egypt. The countries had vowed last November to hold such a meeting if the Egyptian-Israeli peace treaty was signed, but Saudi Arabia, Egypt's principal foreign backer, has been trying to exercise a moderating influence.

King Hussein of Jordan flew to Damascus and Baghdad during the day in what was believed to be an effort to coordinate the positions of hard-liners and moderates at tomorrow's Arab meeting.

Gromyko Comments on Treaty

In Damascus, Foreign Minister Andrei A. Gromyko of the Soviet Union ended a three-day visit to Syria today by joining with President Hafez al-Assad in denouncing the peace treaty, saying it appeared bound to increase tension in the Middle East. A joint Soviet-Syrian communiqué said the treaty was aimed at perpetuating the Israeli occupation of Arab lands, the annexation of Arab East

Continued on Page A10, Column 5

"All the News That's Fit to Print"

The New York Times

LATE CITY EDITION

Weather: Cloudy, chance of showers today and tonight. Sunny tomorrow. Temperature range: today 54-66; yesterday 62-67. Details on page 8.

VOL.CXXVIII . . . No.44,229

NEW YORK, SATURDAY, MAY 26, 1979

25 cents beyond 50-mile zone from New York City. Higher in air delivery cities.

20 CENTS

272 DIE AS JET CRASHES ON TAKEOFF IN CHICAGO AFTER LOSING ENGINE; WORST U.S. AIR DISASTER

ISRAEL LOWERS FLAG, GIVES TOWN IN SINAI BACK TO EGYPTIANS

Inhabitants of El Arish, Conquered in 1967, Cheer, Weep and Jeer at Withdrawal Ceremony

By CHRISTOPHER S. WREN

Special to The New York Times

EL ARISH, Egypt, May 25 — Egyptians cheered, prayed and wept as this town, capital of the Sinai Peninsula, was handed back to Egypt today, after 12 years under Israeli occupation.

The dusty coastal town, separated from the Mediterranean by groves of stately palms amid dunes, became the first still-inhabited Arab town conquered in the 1967 war to be relinquished.

The pullout marked the beginning of Israel's promised withdrawal from Sinai under the peace treaty signed with Egypt March 26 in Washington.

The return of El Arish and a coastal strip westward is the first step of a process that will return to Egypt nearly three-fourths of Sinai within nine months. Israel has agreed to withdraw within three years from the remainder of Sinai, to the border that prevailed before the 1967 war.

Two Sides Meet at Beersheba

As the transfer took place, Egyptian and Israeli negotiators met at Beersheba to begin negotiations on a solution to the question of autonomy for Palestinians of the West Bank and Gaza. Secretary of State Cyrus R. Vance, who attended, urged both sides, whose positions were far apart, to show "maximum restraint and farsightedness." [Page 3.]

The turnover ceremony was held in the asphalt parking lot of a former Israeli Army canteen and rest stop a mile and a half east of town. More elaborate festivities are planned tomorrow when President Anwar el-Sadat comes to El Arish.

Egyptians Whistle and Chant

As the blue and white Israeli flag was lowered to bugle accompaniment today, more than a thousand residents watching from across a road began to clap, whistle and chant.

Hundreds of young men ran toward the barbed wire of the compound where the half-hour ceremony was taking place. Armed Israeli troops in combat gear chased them back in jeeps. Four armored half-tracks sent to assist the soldiers sent up plumes of dust.

When the red, white and black Egyptian flag was run up the pole, the nearly hysterical spectators cheered wildly and surged forth again amid cries in Arabic: "God is great!" and "Long live Egypt!"

There was scuffling between some Egyptians and Israeli soldiers, who seemed unprepared for the outburst. Although the scene briefly turned ugly, violence was averted as Egyptian military policemen rushed in to calm the people.

When the Israelis got into their trucks and jeeps and began driving to their new lines a few miles east of town, some

Continued on Page 4, Column 1

Associated Press

Firemen searching through the smoldering wreckage of an American Airlines jet that crashed on takeoff yesterday at Chicago's O'Hare International Airport

NO SURVIVORS FOUND

Los Angeles-Bound DC-10 Narrowly Misses Tract of Mobile Homes

By DOUGLAS E. KNEELAND

Special to The New York Times

CHICAGO, May 25 — An American Airlines jetliner lost an engine and crashed shortly after takeoff from O'Hare International Airport this afternoon, killing all 272 persons aboard. It was the worst disaster in United States aviation history.

Flight 191, a DC-10 bound for Los Angeles at the beginning of the Memorial Day weekend, rose to the northwest from Runway 14 just after 3 P.M., central daylight time. Then, witnesses said, the plane appeared to suffer difficulties with an engine on the left wing, rolled to the left, stalled and plunged into the small abandoned Ravenswood Airport, narrowly missing a mobile home court.

Several witnesses said the engine exploded, and others reported seeing a "huge cylinder" fall from the plane to the runway and burst into flames.

No Survivors Reported

American Airlines officials said there were apparently no survivors of the crash, which scattered debris over an area about 100 by 200 yards. The crash sent up flames and black smoke that could be seen 15 miles away in Chicago's downtown Loop area, and fiery remnants struck some of the mobile homes nearby, severely damaging three of them. Two persons who were apparently working on the ground near the crash site were injured.

The plane narrowly missed a Standard Oil Company gasoline storage facility a block away.

Fire trucks, ambulances and police vehicles from the city and surrounding suburbs rushed to the area and poured water on the flames from the nearly unrecognizable wreckage of the shattered DC-10.

Late this afternoon, ambulances began removing bodies of the victims to a temporary morgue set up in an aircraft hangar. By 11 P.M., 250 bodies had been removed from the wreckage, and Douglas Dreifus, a Federal investigator, said the rest would not be removed before daylight.

Worst Previous U.S. Crash

The worst previous air disaster in the United States occurred last September, when 144 persons died in the collision of a jetliner and a small private plane over San Diego.

William Nickerson, 52 years old, of Elk Grove Village, where the plane crashed, said he saw the DC-10 take off with the left engine smoking. Almost immediately, he said, the engine fell from the plane and the massive jet lost altitude and crashed, sending flames shooting 125 feet into the air.

Danny Niemann, 25, an employee of a

Continued on Page 7, Column 1

FLORIDA EXECUTES KILLER AS PLEA FAILS

Spenkelink, Electrocuted, Is First to Die Since Gilmore in 1977

By WAYNE KING

Special to The New York Times

STARKE, Fla., May 25 — The state of Florida trussed John Arthur Spenkelink immobile in the electric chair this morning, dropped a black leather mask over his face and electrocuted him.

"He simply looked at us and he looked terrified," said Kris Rebillot, a reporter who was one of 32 persons who watched through a window from an adjoining room. "It was just a wide, wide, wide stare."

The execution was carried out a few hours after the last plea in an extended legal battle. It was the first execution in the United States since Gary Mark Gilmore faced a Utah firing squad voluntarily on Jan. 19, 1977, and the first since 1967 in which the condemned person was put to death against his will.

No Final Statement — His Wish

Mr. Spenkelink made no final statement. The prison authorities said that had been his wish.

The prisoner was given three surges of electricity. The first, 2,500 volts, was administered at 10:12 A.M. Mr. Spenkelink jerked in the chair and one hand clenched into a fist.

Then came the second, and the third, by two executioners in black hoods. A doctor stepped forward after the third surge, pulled up the prisoner's T-shirt

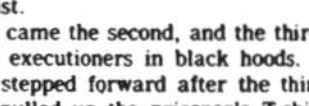

Continued on Page 6, Column 2

Flattened Debris and 'Bodies All Over'

By WILLIAM ROBBINS

Special to The New York Times

CHICAGO, May 25 — "The plane just lost power and slowly rolled over on its side," George Owens, a witness to the worst domestic air crash in history, said today shortly after the fiery disaster at O'Hare International Airport here.

Then, he said, he "saw a huge fireball."

Hours after the crash of American Airlines Flight 191, which had just taken off for Los Angeles, smoke was still pouring from the wreckage, which was too hot for removal of many of the bodies of the victims. Red and yellow stakes marked the few charred bodies that firemen could reach. It was nearly 6 P.M. before the first bodies were moved to a nearby hangar.

One of the first physicians to arrive at the scene was Dr. Robert Loguersio. "There were bodies all over," he said. "There were a lot of corpses on the scene. Obviously there was nothing I could do. Obviously there were no live injuries."

Helplessly, the police and firemen could only mill around the scene, keeping onlookers back and out of possible danger.

Wreckage Carried Off

But immediately after the crash, and before the police could cordon off the site, some small boys arrived and began to carry off bits of wreckage. One was seen walking off with what looked like a fan belt in his hand.

The wreckage of the plane was spread over part of a small abandoned airport, one of the few open areas in the populated region surrounding O'Hare. It ignited three mobile homes situated in a neatly landscaped park at the edge of the field.

A resident of one of the mobile homes, Marie Nikopoulos, had been stretched out on a couch, watching television, when she heard a "big bang."

"It threw me off the couch," she said, "and the force knocked dishes off the shelves and my chandelier fell. I ran and opened the front door and saw part of the plane burning in the street. Thick black smoke filled the neighborhood and turned it pitch black. You couldn't see a foot in front of you."

Residents Ordered Out

Soon officials arrived and ordered the residents out for fear the fires might spread.

One witness, Winnann Johnson, saw what was later determined to have been an engine fall from the wing.

"I saw this silver cylinder thing fall from the plane onto the runway," she said. "It burst into flames and then smothered real quickly."

Larry Roderick saw the flight from about the same vantage point. "The left engine was smoking badly on takeoff," he said. "Then there seemed to be an explosion. There was a burst of flame and the engine fell. The plane appeared to make a steep climb. Then it swung over to the left and plunged to the ground."

President, Angered Over Setbacks, Urges Leadership From Democrats

By TERENCE SMITH

Special to The New York Times

WASHINGTON, May 25 — President Carter, stung by a series of defeats on Capitol Hill, lashed out today at the "demagoguery and political timidity" that he said had made the American people doubt the courage and effectiveness of their political leaders.

Displaying more passion and anger than he normally allows himself on a public forum, the President lectured about 200 members of the Democratic National Committee at their spring meeting here on the need for Congress and the party to confront the difficult choices that face the nation on energy and the economy.

"The American people are looking to us for honest answers and clear leadership," Mr. Carter said. "What they see is a Government which seems incapable of action at all."

In a long answer to a question from the floor, the President also all but declared his candidacy for re-election.

"I haven't made my announcement of what I'm going to do in 1980," he said, "but I have never backed down from a fight, and I have never been afraid of public opinion polls. And if and when I decide to run, it will be in every precinct in this country, no matter who else ran, and I have no doubt it will be successful."

Excerpts from Carter remarks, page 8.

Mr. Carter also had some thinly veiled criticism for Senator Edward M. Kennedy and the five Democratic Representatives who announced their opposition to the President's re-election earlier this week. "Press conferences will not solve the serious problems we face in energy, in inflation, in maintaining peace in a troubled world," Mr. Carter said.

At a news conference on Monday, Representatives Edward P. Beard of Rhode Island, John Conyers Jr. of Michigan, Richard M. Nolan of Minnesota, Richard L. Ottinger of Westchester and Fortney H. Stark of California announced that they were organizing a campaign to dump Mr. Carter from the Democratic ticket and replace him with Senator Kennedy, who has criticized the President's domestic policies at several meetings with the press in the last fortnight.

Mr. Carter's tone ranged from anger to

Continued on Page 8, Column 5

Gas Lines Touch Off Arguments; Price Hits a Record in Manhattan

By ALAN RICHMAN

Gasoline shortages caused arguments at service stations on Long Island yesterday and forced the posting of police officers to direct a line of waiting motorists in Manhattan. Meanwhile, prices rose to record levels — 56.5 cents a half-gallon at a Getty station in lower Manhattan.

The frantic activity was expected to end soon, because many stations indicated they would run out of gas before Monday night, the end of the Memorial Day weekend.

"My particular situation is that the company is running a day behind in deliveries," said Tim Sullivan, owner of a Sunoco Station at the corner of 220th Street and Horace Harding Boulevard in Bayside, Queens. Mr. Sullivan, who usually sells 1,800 gallons a day, received a 3,000-gallon delivery yesterday morning and sold out by 3:30 yesterday afternoon.

At a Hess station in Manhattan offering regular gasoline for 82.9 cents a gallon, automobiles were lined up from the entrance on 10th Avenue down 44th Street to the corner of 11th Avenue.

Arguments started not only between drivers waiting in line and those pulling in front of the line, but also between drivers waiting in line and those attempting to leave the station. Finally, the Midtown North police precinct dispatched two officers, who spent the rest of the day asking "Leaded or unleaded?" and directing cars to appropriate pumps.

Mostly a Battle of Words

"There's been nothing worse than verbal altercations with some bumping into one another," explained Officer Tony Graffeo, who ordinarily drives a patrol car. "We call that a West Side conversation. Anything short of shooting on the West Side is a friendly discussion."

On Long Island, fist fights started at several stations and Matthew Troy, executive director of the Long Island Gasoline Retailers Association, warned that association members might close for the weekend if drivers did not "behave themselves."

Mr. Troy reported, as of midafternoon yesterday, 50 incidents of verbal abuse by motorists against gas station owners and

Continued on Page 22, Column 5

INSIDE

Inflation in Double Digits Again

The Consumer Price Index rose 1.1 percent in April, making for an annual rate of 13.9 percent. April prices were up 10.4 percent from 1978. Page 38.

E.P.A. Rules on Coal Burning

The Environmental Protection Agency introduced rules on coal emissions by power plants that will please neither industry nor environmentalists. Page 6.

An Ayatollah Shot in Teheran

An Iranian religious figure believed to be a member of the secret, ruling Revolutionary Council was shot and wounded near his home. Page 2.

Spanish Army Officers Killed

A lieutenant general in the Spanish Army, two colonels and their driver were killed by Basque terrorists who ambushed their car in Madrid. Page 5.

Associated Press

The Israeli flag being lowered and the Egyptian flag being raised yesterday in the Sinai town of El Arish

"All the News That's Fit to Print"

The New York Times

LATE CITY EDITION

Weather: Chance of drizzle today and tonight. Partly cloudy tomorrow. Temperature range: today 51-63; yesterday 59-68. Details, page D24.

VOL.CXXXI.. No. 45,094

NEW YORK, WEDNESDAY, OCTOBER 7, 1981

30 cents beyond 50-mile zone from New York City. Higher in air delivery cities.

25 CENTS

SADAT ASSASSINATED AT ARMY PARADE AS MEN AMID RANKS FIRE INTO STANDS; VICE PRESIDENT AFFIRMS 'ALL TREATIES'

Israel Stunned and Anxious; Few Arab Nations Mourning

Worry in Jerusalem

By DAVID K. SHIPLER

Special to The New York Times

JERUSALEM, Oct. 6 — Israel, which had such a high stake in the survival of President Anwar el-Sadat, reacted with stunned anxiety today to news of his assassination in Cairo.

A fear for the peace treaty between Egypt and Israel dominated all emotions. So thoroughly had the Egyptian leader come to personify that peace, and so deeply had Israelis distrusted the motives of other Egyptians, that his death today swept away confidence as swiftly as his historic visit to Jerusalem in 1977 had brought hope.

"The very fact that one bullet can cancel an agreement," said Geula Cohen, who heads the Tehiya Party in Parliament, "is a sign that not only the withdrawal, but all these procedures, must be stopped. There is no doubt that this incident confirms all that we have been saying; there is no stability in this region and one cannot make an agreement which is dependent on a nondemocratic regime and one man."

Question About Treaty

Even in the likelihood that Mr. Sadat's successor will adhere to the treaty's precepts, serious questions are bound to linger for some time, and the Government of Prime Minister Menachem Begin is certain to face rising political difficulties domestically in completing the return of Sinai to Egypt, scheduled for April 1982.

This afternoon, voices on the right were raised in demands that all prepa-

Continued on Page A9, Column 5

Jubilation in Beirut

By JOHN KIFNER

Special to The New York Times

BEIRUT, Lebanon, Oct. 6 — There was no mourning in most of the Arab world today for President Anwar el-Sadat of Egypt, whose separate peace with Israel had led to his isolation.

Public jubilation was reported in Syria, Iraq and Libya, and the streets of mostly Moslem, leftist-dominated West Beirut echoed with gunfire in celebration of the assassination. Most public statements attributed Mr. Sadat's death to discontent with the Egyptian-Israeli peace accord.

However, the Sudan, Egypt's closest friend in the Arab world, condemned the assassination and said it stood with the Egyptian Government against all forms of conspiracy and aggression.

Hope for Arab Unity Expressed

There was little public comment in Saudi Arabia. At the United Nations, Gaafar M. Allagany, the acting head of the Saudi mission, expressed sorrow "that this had to happen at a crucial stage." Noting Saudi opposition to Mr. Sadat's policies, he said, "We hope that our sister country will rejoin the Arab states."

An aide to Yasir Arafat, the leader of the Palestine Liberation Organization, said here on hearing of the shooting of Mr. Sadat, "We shake the hand that fired the bullets."

The aide, Saleh Khalef, better known by the code name Abu Iyad, said that "all attempts at dialogue" with Mr. Sadat had failed and that "it was inevi-

Continued on Page A9, Column 1

Associated Press

As President Sadat watched parade with Vice President Hosni Mubarak, left, and Defense Minister Abu Ghazala . . .

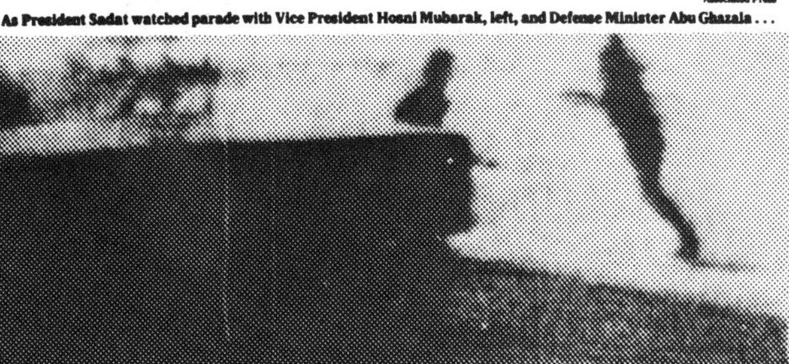

CBS News

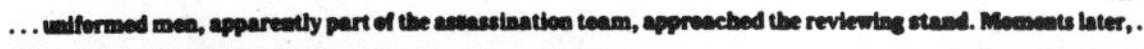

. . . uniformed men, apparently part of the assassination team, approached the reviewing stand. Moments later, . . .

CBS News

. . . after the attack, victims lay sprawled on the floor of the stand.

AT LEAST 8 KILLED

Speaker of Parliament Is Interim President — Election in 60 Days

By WILLIAM E. FARRELL

Special to The New York Times

CAIRO, Oct. 6 — President Anwar el-Sadat of Egypt was shot and killed today by a group of men in military uniforms who hurled hand grenades and fired rifles at him as he watched a military parade commemorating the 1973 war against Israel.

Vice President Hosni Mubarak, in announcing Mr. Sadat's death, said

Mubarak speech excerpted, page A9.

Egypt's treaties and international commitments would be respected. He said the Speaker of Parliament, Sufi Abu Taleb, would serve as interim President pending an election in 60 days.

The assassins' bullets ended the life of a man who earned a reputation for making bold decisions in foreign affairs, a reputation based in large part on his decision in 1977 to journey to the camp of Egypt's foe, Israel, to make peace.

Sadat Forged His Own Regime

Regarded as an interim ruler when he came to power in 1970 on the death of Gamal Abdel Nasser, Mr. Sadat forged his own regime and ran Egypt singlehandedly. He was bent on moving this impoverished country into the late 20th century, a drive that led him to abandon an alliance with the Soviet Union and embrace the West.

That rule ended abruptly and violently today. As jet fighters roared overhead, the killers sprayed the reviewing

Of humble origin, Anwar el-Sadat became a statesman known for daring actions. Obituary, pages A8 and A9.

stand with bullets while thousands of horrified people — officials, diplomats and journalists, including this correspondent — looked on.

Killers' Identity Not Disclosed

Information gathered from a number of sources indicated that eight persons had been killed and 27 wounded in the attack. Later reports, all unconfirmed, put the toll at 11 dead and 38 wounded.

The authorities did not disclose the identity of the assassins. They were being interrogated, and there were no clear indications whether the attack was to have been part of a coup attempt.

[In Washington, American officials said an army major, a lieutenant and four enlisted men had been involved in the attack. The major and two of the soldiers were killed and the others captured, the officials said.]

The assassination followed a recent crackdown by Mr. Sadat against religious extremists and other political op-

Continued on Page A8, Column 1

Egypt After Sadat

Washington's Policies Facing New Problems

By BERNARD GWERTZMAN

Special to The New York Times

WASHINGTON, Oct. 6 — The assassination of President Anwar el-Sadat of Egypt created a new series of problems for future American policy in the Middle East at a time when the Reagan Administration was already worried about the spread of disorder in the region.

Administration officials, concerned about the chaos in Lebanon, the increased subversive activity of Libya and the Soviet inroads in Afghanistan, Southern Yemen and Ethiopia, had viewed Mr. Sadat as a solid, pro-American anchor of stability in the Middle East. With his death, there is now apprehension about the situation in Egypt as well.

At the White House, President Reagan said the United States had lost "a close friend" and "a champion of peace." But the Administration refrained from any public assessment of the possible repercussions of the assassination. [Page A12.]

The mood in Washington was one of shock and sadness at the loss of a leader who had done what would have seemed impossible a decade ago. He replaced the Prime Minister of Israel as the favorite Middle East statesman in Washington.

On virtually every Middle East, African and world issue, the Reagan Administration and Mr. Sadat saw eye to eye. With the expectation that Mr. Sadat would be in control of Egypt's policies

Continued on Page A9, Column 2

Cairo Regime's Plans Now Question Marks

The following article is by William E. Farrell, who has reported on Anwar el-Sadat's diplomacy from Jerusalem as well as Cairo.

Special to The New York Times

News Analysis

CAIRO, Oct. 6 — Anwar el-Sadat's rule in Egypt was that of one man who skillfully engineered, in his 11 years in power, the means of controlling every important facet of Egyptian life.

Although he was dismissed by many as a somewhat feckless interim leader when he became President after the death of Gamal Abdel Nasser, Mr. Sadat gradually showed that he had staying power, political skill and an ability that transformed him into a world statesman when he paid his historic visit to Jerusalem in the search for peace.

Now, with his sudden, violent death, many questions about the future of Egypt and its role in the world are beginning to be raised in this saddened capital and in many other countries.

Over the years, Mr. Sadat controlled his political party, the National Democratic Party; he supervised the Egyptian press, which lauded him; he was commander of the military, a key factor in his rule, and he had a facility for taking the pulse of Egypt's masses — about 43 million people. Some 67 percent of them are illiterate, but he was able to reach them by television and radio. He often did, in long speeches that had a pedagogical tone.

Some Egyptians opposed Mr. Sadat,

Continued on Page A8, Column 5

The Scene Of the Assassination In Cairo

CAIRO

Giza

Sadat Residence

Nile

Mile

0 1

Men in military uniforms stepped from a truck and fired on President Sadat, who was in the center of the reviewing stand. The wounded president was carried to the back of the stand and flown south by helicopter to Maadi Military Hospital.

The New York Times / Oct. 7, 1981

Who Murdered President Sadat?

In the confusion swirling around the assassination of Egypt's President, Anwar el-Sadat, little information was made public in Cairo about the killers. Egyptian authorities were known to have several uniformed men in custody last night, but the Egyptians gave no details about the number or identity of the attackers or the reasons for the attack.

"Islamic fundamentalists" within the Egyptian Army was the characterization offered by Secretary of State Alexander M. Haig Jr. to a group of senators late yesterday afternoon. He also mentioned discontent among some Egyptian officers with the peace treaty that Mr. Sadat signed with Israel.

Reagan Administration officials said their information was that six uniformed men had taken part in the shooting, that three were killed and that the others were captured. They said that at least one was linked to the Takfir Wahigra Society, a radical right-wing Islamic group whose name translates as Repentance and Atonement. Its past actions include the slaying of the Egyptian Minister of Religious Affairs in 1977.

In Beirut, a handful of organizations stepped forward to claim responsibility for the killing, with representatives calling news agencies with their statements. But Reagan Administration officials said they doubted that any of them had been involved in the killing. Details are on page A12.

Other News

'Safety Net' Bill Passes

The House of Representatives approved spending $87.3 billion for social programs, despite President Reagan's threat to veto the bill. Page B10.

Ulster Prison Rule Is Eased

Britain gave inmates in Northern Ireland the right to wear their own clothing but stopped short of meeting the hunger strikers' demands. Page A3.

Runoff Due in Atlanta

Andrew Young, the former diplomat, and a State Representative, Sidney Marcus, won places in a mayoral runoff in Atlanta. Page A20.

Lindbergh Papers Unsealed

Evidence in the kidnapping-murder of the infant son of Charles A. Lindbergh 49 years ago will be opened to review by scholars and others. Page B1.

"All the News That's Fit to Print"

The New York Times

Late Edition

Weather: Rain ending today, mostly cloudy and cool; cloudy and cooler tonight. Partly cloudy and mild tomorrow. Temperatures: today 61-66, tonight 54-56; yesterday 55-60. Details, page B10.

VOL.CXXXI.. No. 45,337 NEW YORK, MONDAY, JUNE 7, 1982 — 30 CENTS

BIG ISRAELI FORCE INVADES SOUTH LEBANON; SHARP FIGHTING WITH GUERRILLAS REPORTED

Limited Summit Agreement Set on Trade and Currency

By RICHARD EDER

Special to The New York Times

VERSAILLES, France, June 6 — The eighth summit conference of the industrialized nations reached limited agreement today on two contentious subjects — East-West trade and the handling of currency fluctuations — and produced something of a breakthrough on North-South relations.

The agreements themselves were the subject of some disagreement: whether they bridged or merely papered over fundamental differences. Prime Minister Margaret Thatcher of Britain described the atmosphere as one of unanimity. Prime Minister Pierre Elliott Trudeau of Canada called it "difficult."

The conference was, in any case, shaded and sometimes interrupted by the fighting in the Falklands and Israel's invasion of Lebanon. Today's final hard bargaining on East-West trade was interrupted by the announcement by President François Mitterrand of France of the Israeli move, and the assembled leaders approved a statement expressing shock.

The accord fell short of American hopes and was seen as having little world impact. News analysis and economic analysis, with text of the communiqué, page D6.

The Falkland crisis, apart from producing an embarrassing flip-flop over the United States vote in the Security Council, caused Mrs. Thatcher to fly back to London tonight after the state dinner in the Versailles chateau's Hall of Mirrors.

She thus missed the musical masque and ballet and other festivities organized by France to make this the most glittering summit conference, whether or not it will have turned out to be the most productive.

The seven nations — the United States, Japan, Britain, France, West Germany, Italy and Canada — agreed to a compromise on the East-West trade issue. It fell short of American hopes for abolition of government-subsidized financing for such trade. Instead, it calls for "caution" in financial dealings with the Soviet bloc, and it says there is a need for "commercial prudence in limiting export credits."

The Reagan Administration had

Continued on Page D7, Column

Associated Press

President Reagan at economic meeting yesterday in Versailles.

United Press International

An armored personnel carrier, part of the Israeli invasion force, breaks through the border with southern Lebanon.

U.N. COUNCIL ASKS ISRAELI PULLBACK

But Delegate, Hinting Refusal, Notes 'Limit of Endurance'

By BERNARD D. NOSSITER

Special to The New York Times

UNITED NATIONS, N.Y., June 6 — The Security Council unanimously demanded tonight that Israel pull its invading forces out of Lebanon. There was, however, no indication that Israel would pay any more attention to this order than to the unanimous Council demand Saturday night for a cease-fire.

Instead, Yehuda Z. Blum, the Israeli delegate, taunted the Council's 15 members for "evincing not the slightest interest" in scores of terrorist acts he attributed to the Palestine Liberation Organization. "How many Israelis have to be killed by terrorists for this Council to be persuaded that the limits of our endurance have been reached?" he asked rhetorically. "Israel cannot expect this body even to deplore P.L.O. barbarism against Israel's civilian population, let alone take any steps with a view towards curbing that barbarism."

Leaders of the major industrial democracies expressed shock at Versailles over Israel's move. Page A14.

Tonight's text, a compromise drafted by Ireland after a day of discussion behind closed doors, directed Israel to withdraw its forces "forthwith and unconditionally." The Soviet Union insisted on that last phrase.

At the demand of the United States, the resolution calls on Israel and the Palestinians to halt all military action "within Lebanon and across the Lebanese-Israeli border." That language was designed to cover P.L.O. shelling into Israel as well as Israeli strikes. The document directs both sides to report

Continued on Page A14, Column 5

The New York Times / June 7, 1982

Israeli tanks and troops moved into Lebanon in three columns (arrows). The land assaults, together with air and sea attacks, were aimed at the main Palestinian strongholds — Tyre, Beaufort Castle, Nabatiye and Kawkaba. Warships destroyed the Qasmiye Bridge spanning the Litani River north of Tyre, cutting the main Palestinian supply line. Towns shown in northern Israel were among those shelled last week by Palestinian forces.

THOUSANDS ATTACK

Some Syrian Units in Area Said to Have Clashed With Raiding Force

By THOMAS L. FRIEDMAN

Special to The New York Times

BEIRUT, Lebanon, Monday, June 7 — The Israeli Army invaded southern Lebanon by land, sea and air Sunday in an attack aimed at destroying the main military bases of the Palestine Liberation Organization.

More than 250 Israeli tanks and armored personnel carriers, as well as thousands of infantrymen, rolled past the observation posts of the United Nations peacekeeping troops in southern Lebanon at 11 A.M. (5 A.M., New York time) and fanned out across the frontier, according to a United Nations spokesman in Beirut.

By late Sunday evening the Israelis had taken several P.L.O. outposts in the craggy hills of southern Lebanon and were engaged in fierce firefights with the Palestinians for control of scores of other strongholds along the 33-mile front, stretching from the port city of Tyre to the foothills of Mount Hermon, the United Nations spokesman said.

Main Targets Besieged

In the first day of the invasion the Israelis besieged all their main targets — Tyre, Beaufort Castle, Nabatiye and Kawkaba — but the Palestinians stood their ground and did not flee north. The number of casualties was not known.

Israel said this morning that Beaufort Castle, a Crusader stronghold overlooking the border that the Palestinians have used as a communications and artillery base, was captured during the night by an Israeli infantry battalion. But the Palestinians denied that the castle had fallen.

It appeared that at least a few elements of Syria's force of about 25,000 men in Lebanon had become involved in confrontations with the Israelis.

The state-run Beirut radio reported Sunday night that Syrian artillery north of Hasbeya was exchanging fire with the Israelis on the eastern route of their advance. This could not be confirmed. In Damascus, a Syrian military spokesman said Israeli forces had come into contact with Syrian troops in three places, but it was not clear whether fighting had occurred. [Page A12.]

The Israel radio broadcast a state-

Continued on Page A12, Column 1

Britain Confirms the Landing Of 3,000 Soldiers From QE2

By R.W. APPLE Jr.

Special to The New York Times

LONDON, June 6 — British troops besieging the Argentine garrison at Stanley in the Falkland Islands have been reinforced by 3,000 fresh infantrymen from the liner Queen Elizabeth 2, the Defense Ministry announced tonight.

The arrival of the Fifth Infantry Brigade, including a battalion each of Scots and Welsh Guards and Gurkha Rifles, raises British strength on East Falkland Island to about 8,000. About 5,000 paratroops and Royal Marine commandos went ashore last month, and most are drawn up opposite the 7,000 Argentine defenders of Stanley, the Falklands capital.

In Buenos Aires today, Argentina said its planes and artillery had bombarded the British positions surrounding Stanley. Senior military officers said they expected the British to launch a major assault on the Argentine garrison at any moment. [Page A8.]

There were hints in London that the long-awaited assault on Stanley had already begun in a report from Michael Nicholson of Britain's Independent Television News.

"The British push is really on," he said in a broadcast this evening. "There are under way at this moment operations which I can only describe as extraordinarily daring which cannot be revealed until they are completed, but which, almost certainly if they are successful, will surely bring the end of this war that much closer."

Mr. Nicholson reported that the Gurkhas, composed entirely of Nepalese volunteers, were operating on their own, "crisscrossing East Falkland" in a search for Argentine units lurking in the interior, between the British base at San Carlos Bay and their forward headquarters near Mount Kent.

According to unofficial sources, the Fifth Brigade transferred from the Queen Elizabeth to the assault ships In-

Continued on Page A8, Column 3

Floods Rampage in Connecticut; 8 Believed Dead

By ROBERT D. McFADDEN

Torrential weekend rains and overflowing rivers swamped wide areas of Connecticut yesterday with the state's worst floods in decades.

The state police said that eight persons were dead or missing in the storm. More than 1,300 others were removed from their homes as floodwaters invaded residential areas, washed out roads and earthen dams and disrupted electric and telephone service and public transportation for tens of thousands of residents.

The floods, accompanied by 5 to 8 inches of pounding rain, struck a wide swath of the state, from Westport and other Fairfield County communities on the west to Waterford and New London on the east. At least 38,000 homes were hit by power blackouts, and 6,000 telephones were knocked out.

Nearly all trains in the state, including those operated by Amtrak between New York and Boston, were halted as Conrail and Amtrak used buses to carry passengers. Commuters and long-distance travelers were expected to face further delays today. Many communities in flooded areas canceled school for today.

The rest of the New York metropolitan area was relatively unscathed. But on eastern Long Island, up to 9.79 inches of rain also triggered heavy weekend flooding. Many traffic accidents were reported, and a stretch of Long Island

Continued on Page B4, Column 1

The New York Times / Alan Decker

Matthew Giurintano clearing a storm drain yesterday in Higganum, Conn.

Why Israelis Invaded Now

Heavy P.L.O. Shelling Said to Tip the Scale

The following dispatch has been subjected to military censorship.

By DAVID K. SHIPLER

Special to The New York Times

JERUSALEM, June 6 — Israel's invasion of Lebanon came today as the culmination of months of military and political calculation in which Prime Minister Menachem Begin repeatedly allowed the troops to be massed and the saber to be rattled, only to pull back at what seemed like the last moment.

News Analysis

Until today the crucial factors favoring a major assault never quite lined up, and the risks seemed greater than the potential benefits.

This time, however, Mr. Begin decided to make the military gamble and to pay the political costs that he and his advisers know exist. The crucial reason was the intensive shelling of northern Israel by forces of the Palestine Liberation Organization, which began Friday afternoon after Israeli air strikes on Palestinian bases near Beirut.

P.L.O. Has Become an Army

The Israeli command described the air raids as retaliation for the shooting Thursday of Israel's Ambassador to Britain, Shlomo Argov, who was critically wounded in London. Five suspects, all traveling on passports from Arab countries, were captured. The P.L.O. denied any responsibility for the attack.

The Palestinian shelling, with artillery and rocket launchers, was the most severe ever directed against Israeli towns and kibbutzim by the P.L.O.,

Continued on Page A13, Column 1

Begin Orders Israelis to Push Palestinians 25 Miles to North

The following dispatch has been subjected to military censorship.

Special to The New York Times

JERUSALEM, Monday, June 7 — Prime Minister Menachem Begin said Sunday that the Israeli Army had been ordered to push the Palestinian forces northward to a distance of 25 miles from the Israeli border, to place their artillery beyond the range of Israeli territory.

Mr. Begin made his statement in a letter to President Reagan, excerpts of which were reported on the Israeli radio. The Cabinet, after an emergency session, issued a statement saying Israel would not attack any Syrian forces in Lebanon or Syria unless the Syrians engaged the Israelis.

The Damascus radio said the Syrian Army was battling the Israelis near Hasbeya, 10 miles north of the border. The Israeli military spokesman said there had been no verification that any such clashes with the Syrians had occurred.

Reagan Urged Restraint

Mr. Begin's letter to President Reagan, disclosing the orders to the army to push the Palestine Liberation Organizaton 25 miles north of the border, came after the President sent a letter to the Israeli leader. That letter, delivered Sunday morning, requested Israeli restraint.

In his reply, as reported by the Israeli radio, Mr. Begin said that "the terrorists aim their weapons only at the civilian population." He went on: "The aim of the enemy is to kill Jews, men, women and children. Is there any people in the world that would accept such a situation?"

The invasion operation, called "Peace for Galilee," would not be aimed at acquiring any Lebanese territory and was not being undertaken against Lebanon, according to Mr. Begin's letter. It was begun after months of sporadic terrorist attacks on Israelis here and abroad, attacks that Israel regarded as violations of the cease-fire that had been negotiated across the Lebanese-Israeli border last July.

As Israeli armored columns swept through the lines of the United Nations peacekeeping forces, a United Nations spokesman in Jerusalem reported, several United Nations units were caught in crossfire. By Sunday evening, one

Continued on Page A12, Column 3

INSIDE

Defeat for Schmidt's Party

The Social Democrats were defeated in state elections in Hamburg in what was considered a direct blow to Chancellor Helmut Schmidt. Page A9.

'Nine,' 'Nickleby' Win Tonys

"Nine," based on "8½," won the Tony award for musicals. The Royal Shakespeare Company's "Nicholas Nickleby" won for plays. Page C11.

"All the News That's Fit to Print"

The New York Times

Late Edition
Weather: Considerable sunshine early today, becoming cloudy by afternoon. Chance of rain tonight and tomorrow. Temperatures: today 77-81, tonight 55-60; yesterday 58-81. Details on page B20.

VOL.CXXXI.. No. 45,340 — NEW YORK, THURSDAY, JUNE 10, 1982 — 30 CENTS

ISRAEL REPORTS ITS AIR FORCE HAS WRECKED SYRIA'S ANTIAIRCRAFT MISSILES IN LEBANON

U.S. EASES POSITION ON RACIAL BALANCE OF CITY'S TEACHERS

Bell Bars Any Punitive Action Pending Study of Whether New York Follows Law

By JANE PERLEZ
Special to The New York Times

WASHINGTON, June 9 — The Federal Department of Education backed away today from its finding that the New York City Board of Education had failed to comply with an agreement to improve the racial balance of teachers in the city's public schools.

The Secretary of Education, T. H. Bell, promised to review the board's efforts to meet the goals of a 1977 agreement that requires the board to increase the number of minority teachers in predominantly white schools and the number of white teachers in schools attended mostly by minorities.

He also said he would review the legal grounds on which the city contends it complies with the agreement and with the Civil Rights Act of 1964.

Senator Alfonse M. D'Amato, Republican of New York, outlined the department's change of position at a news conference here after a lengthy meeting with Mr. Bell. The Secretary declined to attend the news conference or to comment on the meeting.

Mandatory Transfer Threat

Last week the Department of Education's Office for Civil Rights said that if the Board of Education could not meet the goals of the 1977 agreement by voluntary measures, the mandatory transfer of teachers would be required.

The department also indicated that the city could face the loss of $300 million a year in Federal education funds.

Mr. D'Amato said that the Secretary had indicated today that there would be "no threat of cutoff of funds until this is fully reviewed."

Discussing this threat and also that of mandatory teacher transfers, the Senator said: "This is not what the Reagan Administration is about or what I cam-

Continued on Page B6, Column 1

Reagan Suggests Limit on Troops For 2 Alliances

Expresses Sympathy for Goal of Arms Protests

By HEDRICK SMITH
Special to The New York Times

BONN, June 9 — President Reagan, expressing sympathy with the goal of the European antinuclear movement but differing with its tactics, urged today that East and West agree to a ceiling of 700,000 ground troops for each alliance as "a major step toward a safer Europe."

But with 16 leaders of the Atlantic alliance gathered here tonight, Mr. Reagan also called for the Western allies to strengthen and modernize their conventional forces as the best way of making the possibility of nuclear conflict, or any conflict, "more remote."

The formal proposal on troop ceilings, a modification of an earlier Western position at East-West talks, is to be approved by alliance leaders Thursday. The Reagan Administration considers this session especially significant for projecting alliance solidarity at a time of popular unrest and political division in Europe.

The Warmest Applause

Flying here from London on the fourth and most delicate stop of his European trip, the President drew the warmest applause when he reaffirmed American commitments to Europe's defense and specifically pledged to stand by West Germany.

To the West German Parliament he declared: "We are with you, Germany. You are not alone."

Then, indirectly addressing Moscow, he added, "Our adversaries would be foolishly mistaken should they gamble that Americans would abandon their alliance responsibilities, no matter how severe the test."

But in a carefully modulated speech that balanced firmness with sensitivity for the anxieties of hundreds of thousands of Europeans who have marched in antinuclear demonstrations, Mr. Reagan sought to calm fears that he

Continued on Page A16, Column 3

MILES 0 10
Israelis reportedly staged amphibious assault in Khalde area.
Israeli and Syrian troops battle for control of a key crossroad.
Israeli armored troops seized control of Sidon and Damur, but fighting reportedly continued.
Israel said its air force destroyed Syrian missile systems in Bekaa Valley. Syria was said to have 19 SAM batteries there.
Syrians said Israeli jets bombed Damascus suburb. Israel denied making raid.
MT. SANNIN
Junieh
Beirut
AIRPORT
Khalde
Doha
Damur
Mdeirej
Ain Dara
Ain Zhalta
Baruk
Shtaura
Beit Eddin
LEBANON
BEKAA VALLEY Where Syrian Troops Are Concentrated
Sidon
Jezzin
Meshghara
Rasheiye
Dummar
Damascus
Mediterranean Sea
Zahrani
Southernmost Limit of Syrian Presence in Lebanon
Zahrani R.
MT. HERMON
Nabatiye
Hasbeya
U.N. ZONE
BEAUFORT CASTLE
Litani R.
Metulla
SYRIA
Tyre
Ghanduriye
Qiryat Shemona
U.N. ZONE
HADDAD MILITIA AREA
GOLAN HEIGHTS (Annexed by Israel)
U.N. ZONE
Nahariya
ISRAEL
The New York Times / June 10, 1982

'A TURNING POINT'

22 MIG's Reported Shot Down in the Strikes — Troops Near Beirut

The following dispatch has been subjected to military censorship.

By HENRY KAMM
Special to The New York Times

JERUSALEM, June 9 — Israel said tonight that its air force destroyed the Syrian surface-to-air missile system in the Bekaa Valley of eastern Lebanon "in a concentrated strike" this afternoon. Twenty-two Syrian MIG's were reported shot down in the air battle that accompanied the raid, and seven more were said to have been hit.

Israel said all its planes returned safely. It did not disclose the number of planes involved. [Syria said 90 Israeli planes attacked the SAM batteries. It said 19 Israeli and 16 Syrian planes were shot down.]

An Israeli Army spokesman also said that there was no truth to a report by the official Syrian press agency that Israeli planes had bombed a suburb of Damascus too.

'Brilliant' and 'Complicated'

Defense Minister Ariel Sharon, in a broadcast interview, described the air strikes on the missile batteries as "one of the most brilliant, complicated and intricate operations" ever carried out by Israel.

Mr. Sharon called the raid "a turning point" in the conflict, which began on Sunday with Israeli forces crossing into Lebanon in force.

He said it would enable the Israeli ground forces to mop up quickly the Palestinian guerrillas who he said had sought safety in the valley "under Syrian cover." He said a withdrawal of Syria's ground forces had begun after the raid.

Israelis Seize Palestinian Town

Israeli forces along the Lebanese coast were reported to have seized control of the Palestinian town of Damur, eight miles south of Beirut, and military sources said some Israelis had pushed to a point about half way between Damur and the Lebanese capital.

The principal focus of the Israeli forces, however, appeared to be the Syrian strongholds east and southeast of Beirut.

An official source said tonight that a major "collision" between Israel and Syria was likely if the substantial Syrian ground force in the Bekaa Valley did not withdraw. He added that there was no certainty that such a confrontation would be limited in scope.

Reserves Are Called Up

The official said Israel had begun to bolster its troops in the Golan Heights by a calling up reserve units in preparation for any extended conflict with Syria.

He said Israeli troops were also poised near the Beirut-Damascus highway, the principal supply route for the Syrian troops in Lebanon, but they had so far refrained from moving to cut it. Such restraint may not last, he said, if

Continued on Page A18, Column 5

HAIG SEES A SHIFT IN AIMS OF ISRAEL

Secretary, in Bonn, Suggests Purpose Is to Fight Syrians

By STEVEN R. WEISMAN
Special to The New York Times

BONN, June 9 — Secretary of State Alexander M. Haig Jr., saying that the fighting in Lebanon had grown "somewhat more ominous" in the last 24 hours, suggested today that Israel might be shifting its originally announced objective in Lebanon and was now seeking to take on Syrian forces in combat.

With the Israelis continuing their advance, there were new reports "of the westward movement of Syrian armed forces," Mr. Haig said.

In addition, he reported that in the last 48 hours Syria added to the Soviet-supplied SAM-6 antiaircraft missiles deployed in Lebanon's Bekaa Valley, east of Beirut, by "a rather substantial number."

Israel's Defense Minister, Ariel Sharon, said today that some of the batteries attacked today were moved into Lebanon in the last 24 hours.

Mr. Haig said antiaircraft missiles were being increasingly used against the Israelis.

"If Syrian forces become engaged, then clearly there's a whole new character to the nature of this conflict," Mr. Haig said at a news conference as the leaders of the North Atlantic Treaty Organization opened their conference here.

Mr. Haig noted that Israel had origi-

Continued on Page A19, Column 1

Syrians Report Major Air Battles; Say They Downed 19 Jets, Lost 16

By HENRY TANNER
Special to The New York Times

DAMASCUS, Syria, June 9 — Israeli and Syrian jets fought two large battles this afternoon over Syrian antiaircraft missile sites in eastern Lebanon, according to communiqués made public here.

A military spokesman reported that 19 Israeli fighter-bombers — F-15's and F-16's — had been shot down. He said the Syrians had lost 16 planes.

A Damascus official said later that the missiles destroyed by the Israeli attacks had "already been replaced."

Late in the evening, a Syrian communiqué said that Israeli planes had bombed a village three miles west of Damascus. Eight civilians were killed and 47 wounded, the communiqué added. Israel denied carrying out such a raid.

A Damascus official reported that Israeli and Syrian ground forces clashed for the third consecutive day as the invaders' tanks tried to push through mountains southeast of Beirut, and up the lower Bekaa Valley toward the important Beirut-Damascus highway.

One Israeli column was said to have been halted, with heavy losses, near Beit Eddein, the principal town in the mountain region, which is known as the Shouf.

Israel's attacks on the missile sites and the push toward the Beirut-Damascus highway were seen here as evidence that Israel's main objective was not, as it had announced, to protect its people from Palestinian rockets. Rather, in the Syrian view, the Israeli aim is to drive Syrian troops from Lebanon and to surround Beirut and destroy the political and military leadership of the Palestine Liberation Organization.

Western diplomats here, who felt until Tuesday that the Israeli invasion had a limited goal, said today that the scope of the invasion clearly was much bigger than they had assumed.

Syria and the Soviet Union signed a 20-year Treaty of Friendship and Cooperation in October 1980. The treaty requires, among other terms, consulta-

Continued on Page A18, Column 1

ISRAELIS IN SIGHT OF CITY OF BEIRUT

Forces Establish a Beachhead Four Miles to the South

By THOMAS L. FRIEDMAN
Special to The New York Times

BEIRUT, Lebanon, June 9 — Israel's ground forces drove to within sight of Beirut today as its fighter-bombers struck heavily at Syrian surface-to-air missile batteries east of here.

An Israeli amphibious force established a bridgehead of five tanks and an undetermined number of infantrymen at Khalde, on the coastal highway four miles south of here near the Beirut International Airport. The bridgehead, which was spotted by reporters, came under machine-gun and mortar fire from Palestinians dug in on the beach and along the highway.

[Israeli planes bombed Beirut's airport Thursday, and fierce battles between Israelis and Palestinians raged along the Lebanese coast south of the capital, according to a Reuters report that quoted the Government radio. The radio said an Israeli attempt to land at the airport had been repulsed.]

Battle for a Key Crossroads

Earlier, Israeli forces pushed into the coastal towns of Sidon and Damur and fighting was said to be continuing. Lebanese Government sources said the Israelis had seized most of Sidon.

Israeli commanders reportedly sent raiding parties north from Damur along the coastal highway as far as Doha, a hillside village three miles south of the Khalde bridgehead.

East of Beirut, Syrian troops using tanks, artillery and truck-mounted Katyusha rocket launchers fought the Israelis for control of a key crossroads on the Beirut-Damascus highway, according to witnesses and the Beirut

Continued on Page A18, Column 3

Refugees in Lebanon Need Food Critically

The following dispatch has been subjected to military censorship.

By DAVID K. SHIPLER
Special to The New York Times

JERUSALEM, June 9 — United Nations observers said today that thousands of Lebanese civilians, uprooted from their homes by the Israeli advance, were in critical need of food and water.

Some supplies have been delivered by the army and the United Nations, but the situation is still serious, the observers said.

Since the Israeli invasion of Lebanon began Sunday, residents of several towns have been warned by Israeli leaflets and announcements over public address systems to gather on the beaches to avoid shelling attacks.

About 41,000 residents of the Tyre area did so, according to a United Nations bulletin, and were left there for two days without food or shelter. But there were apparently few civilian casualties, a United Nations official said; only nine civilians were reported wounded in Tyre.

The United Nations does not have fig-

Continued on Page A20, Column 1

City Says: No to 'Crisis Relocation'

By LESLIE BENNETTS

The City Council yesterday rejected the Reagan Administration's proposal for the development of a plan to remove New York City residents to "host" areas upstate in the event of a nuclear attack.

In a resolution adopted by a vote of 35 to 5, the Council rejected the Administration's plan to spend $4.2 billion over seven years on what is termed "crisis relocation" planning for urban areas around the United States. The proposal has yet to be approved by Congress.

Despite public antipathy and professional skepticism, the Reagan Administration is pressing its ambitious civil defense program. Page B20.

New York is not the first community to express its disapproval; crisis relocation has been rejected by officials in Marin County, Calif.; Cambridge, Mass.; Boulder, Colo.; Alexandria, Va., and Greensboro, N.C.

The resolution, sponsored by Councilwoman Susan D. Alter, Democrat-Liberal of Brooklyn, condemned the proposal as having "little or no chance of success" and asserted that "the money to develop these plans could be better used to expand health and education services in the inner cities."

Mayor Koch also expressed his opposition to the Reagan plan, saying it would be "impossible to evacuate in any timely, acceptable way."

The resolution was specifically limited to evacuation planning in the event of nuclear attack. However, Federal officials cautioned that those funds would be difficult to extricate from a larger program because as little as 10 percent of the $4.2 billion might be used for nuclear evacuation as opposed to other disaster relief efforts.

"We're not sure whether it could be

Continued on Page B21, Column 1

INSIDE

F.B.I. Reports on Donovan

The F.B.I. said a Presidential aide had discouraged it from questioning Raymond J. Donovan about his possible ties to organized crime. Page B8.

British Casualties Reported

Reports from the Falkland Islands said Britain suffered heavy losses when two ships were bombed while landing additional troops. Page A22.

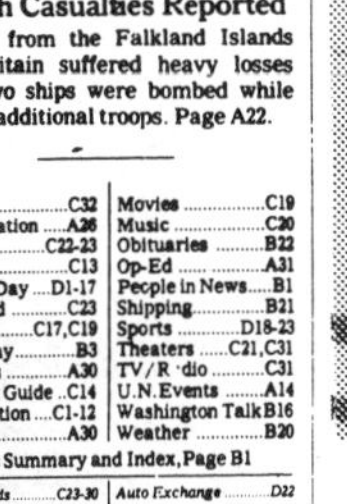

Associated Press

An Israeli soldier directing captured Palestinians yesterday near Tyre in southern Lebanon.

"All the News That's Fit to Print"

The New York Times

Late Edition

Weather: Clearing with northwesterly winds today; clear and cooler tonight. Mostly sunny and warmer tomorrow. Temperatures: today 74-76, tonight 55-60; yesterday 52-54. Details on page D7.

VOL.CXXXI . . . No. 45,344 — NEW YORK, MONDAY, JUNE 14, 1982 — 30 CENTS

NEW BATTLES SHATTER LEBANON CEASE-FIRE; ISRAEL REPORTED TO IMPERIL LAST P.L.O. EXIT

FALKLAND ADVANCE ASSURES VICTORY, BRITAIN DECLARES

Outcome Is Not Now in Doubt, London Says — Argentina Reports a New Assault

By R. W. APPLE Jr.

Special to The New York Times

LONDON, June 13 — Britain's Defense Secretary, John Nott, said tonight that his country's success in ousting Argentine troops from the Falkland Islands had been assured by fighting this weekend.

But he disclosed that the 5,400-ton light cruiser Glamorgan, carrying a crew of 471, had been hit by Argentine gunfire during the assault Friday night on enemy positions west of Stanley, the main Argentine garrison on the islands. Nine British sailors were killed and 17 injured, Mr. Nott added, but the ship remained fit for battle. Buenos Aires had claimed to have sunk a British frigate.

With British troops consolidating their positions, some less than seven miles west of Stanley, in preparation for further offensive operations, there was no news here of further infantry action today. It was not clear when the British would resume their attack, and it appeared possible they were hoping for an Argentine capitulation.

Argentina Reports New Battle

But in Argentina, the military command said that its forces repelled a British assault on Stanley in heavy fighting today and that casualties were high. [Page A8.]

Mr. Nott said: "Our successes on the ground over the weekend mark another significant step to securing the complete and final withdrawal of Argentine forces from the Falkland Islands. There is some way still to go, but the outcome is not in doubt."

He also disclosed for the first time that 50 crew members and soldiers, most of them from the Welsh Guards, had been killed in the Argentine air attacks Tuesday on the landing ships Sir Tristram and Sir Galahad off Bluff Cove and Fitzroy. At least 60 were wounded seriously, he added.

British deaths in the Falkland war have now reached at least 201, not counting those who died in this weekend's fighting. Argentina has lost more than 700 men, according to the most recent tally here.

Mr. Nott acknowledged that the Government had withheld the casualty figures from Tuesday's action in the hope of misleading the Argentines.

"It was important," he said, "that the enemy was not able to assess exactly when, where or in what strength that task force would attack. It is clear that the Argentines greatly overesti-

Continued on Page A8, Column 1

United Press International

King Fahd of Saudi Arabia

Khalid Is Dead; Fahd Succeeds In Saudi Arabia

By STEVEN RATTNER

Special to The New York Times

LONDON, June 13 — King Khalid of Saudi Arabia, ruler of the desert oil nation since 1975, died today of a heart attack in the mountain resort of Taif. The King, 60 years old, was succeeded by Crown Prince Fahd, 59, a half-brother.

Although he had been in ill health for years, the King's death was unexpected. On Saturday the ruler was shown by Saudi television arriving in Taif to spend the summer.

The change in rule came at an awkward time for Saudi Arabia. The country has been a staunch supporter of Iraq, which now appears to be losing its war against Iran. Saudi Arabia has also been active in trying to restore peace in Lebanon, where fighting continues a week after Israel's invasion.

No Immediate Changes Expected

There were differences in personality and outlook between King Khalid and his successor. But the takeover by King Fahd appeared unlikely to have any immediate effect on the country's traditional policies.

It is widely believed that in time, King Fahd, a dynamic man, could move the reclusive nation forcefully into Middle Eastern politics and international affairs.

"We will continue his path, seek to realize his hopes and complete his plan," a sobbing King Fahd said of King Khalid tonight on the Saudi radio. "We seek nothing but the glory of Arabs and Moslems."

Perhaps most immediately, the death of the King appeared likely to bring

Continued on Page A12, Column 4

INVADERS BLAME FOE

No Syria Action Reported in the Daylong Combat With Palestinians

The following dispatch has been subjected to military censorship.

By DAVID K. SHIPLER

Special to The New York Times

JERUSALEM, June 13 — The Israeli military command said today that Israeli artillery and fighter-bombers had attacked Palestinian targets in Lebanon after the Palestinians opened fire on Israeli positions at dawn. The fighting continued all day.

The Israeli truce with Syrian forces, arranged Friday, appeared to be holding, however. No clashes with Syrian forces were reported, and no Syrian planes were reported to have intervened against Israeli aircraft.

The renewed battles with Palestinian forces began just eight hours after Israel declared a cease-fire in the Beirut area. The fighting dashed prospects for a halt to the war that began with an Israeli invasion of Lebanon a week ago.

U.S. Seeks Total Pullout

In Washington, Secretary of State Alexander M. Haig Jr. said the United States would seek the withdrawal of Israeli forces from Lebanon as part of a long-term solution in which Syrian and all other foreign troops would also be pulled out. [Page A14.]

The new fighting appeared to give Israel a chance to continue inflicting damage on the Palestine Liberation Organization's military structure, which has been the principal target of the campaign. Defense Minister Ariel Sharon has said the army will continue clearing Palestinian guerrillas out of areas under Israeli control. The Israeli cease-fire with the Palestinians was intended to apply only to the Beirut area.

During Israeli "mopping up" operations today, fighting was reported in the area of the coastal city of Sidon.

Truce Began Saturday Night

Some Israeli officials had expressed regret that more damage was not done to the P.L.O. in Beirut before the cease-fire, which was firmly requested by the United States, took effect Saturday night.

Despite the devastating assault on P.L.O. forces in the south and the pounding of various P.L.O. headquarters in the Lebanese capital, there had appeared to be enough key Palestinians left in Beirut to retain and possibly rebuild the organization's presence in Lebanon. Military sources said hundreds of Palestinian guerrillas surrendered today after the heavy Israeli attacks.

On the other hand, Israel seems to have little taste for a prolongation of the

Continued on Page A15, Column 1

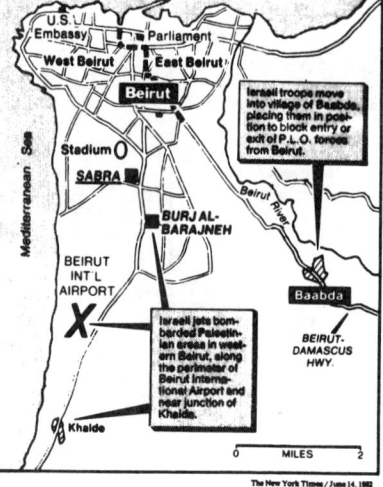

U.S. Embassy
Parliament
West Beirut
East Beirut
Beirut
Israeli troops move into village of Baabda, placing them in position to block entry or exit of P.L.O. forces from Beirut.
Mediterranean Sea
Stadium
SABRA
Beirut River
BURJ AL-BARAJNEH
BEIRUT INT'L AIRPORT
Baabda
Israeli jets bombarded Palestinian areas in western Beirut, along the perimeter of Beirut International Airport and near junction of Khalde.
BEIRUT-DAMASCUS HWY.
Khalde
0 MILES 2

The New York Times / June 14, 1982

KEY ROAD AT STAKE

Troops Land Near Home of Lebanese Leader on Beirut's Outskirts

Special to The New York Times

BEIRUT, Lebanon, June 13 — Israeli troops with tanks and armored personnel carriers reportedly moved into a village just five miles southeast of central Beirut tonight. If the troops consolidate their position, it could lead to the virtual encirclement of the capital and the Palestinian guerrilla forces there.

Earlier, a brief cease-fire between Palestinian guerrillas and Israeli forces was shattered in a day of fierce fighting south of the city between Israeli troops and Palestinian guerrillas as well as repeated Israeli air strikes against West Beirut. The cease-fire was worked out Saturday by the Lebanese and United States Governments.

If the Israelis hold their position in the village, Baabda, it would mark a major turning point in their seven-day invasion. It would put Israeli troops astride the strategic Beirut-Damascus highway at the entry of Beirut, choking off the last exit or entry route for the Palestinian guerrilla forces in the capital.

Israeli Ally Controls East Beirut

In effect, the city would be surrounded, for the Palestinians could not be expected to make their way through the area to the north of the highway controlled by Israel's ally, the heavily armed Phalangist Christian militia headed by Bashir Gemayel.

The Israeli troops were reported only a few hundred yards from the palace of Lebanon's President, Elias Sarkis. Mr. Sarkis was in the palace at the time, meeting with 10 of his ministers. The state-run Beirut radio said that the meeting had been called "to consider the formation of a strong government to save the country."

The radio, quoting official Government sources, said the Israeli force had "landed" in the village square. It added that Israeli troops were setting up positions and roadblocks inside Baabda and had commandeered several public buildings, including a police station and a Government hospital.

No Reports on Lebanese Troops

There were no immediate reports of fighting between the Israeli raiding party and Lebanese Army troops, who control Baabda and nearby Yarze, where the Ministry of Defense is situated. Reports near midnight were vague, and there was no indication that the Israelis had tried to enter the presidential palace.

The Phalangist Voice of Lebanon radio reported the Israeli entry into Baabda in the same sketchy manner as the state-run Beirut radio and gave no

Continued on Page A14, Column 4

Invasion Victims Swamp The Hospitals of Lebanon

By WILLIAM E. FARRELL

Special to The New York Times

BEIRUT, Lebanon, June 13 — The driveway was lined with stretchers. Every so often today ambulances, some of them caked with mud and camouflaged with twigs and greenery, pulled into the driveway, their sirens wailing.

Attendants and medics attached to the American University Hospital here rushed to the vehicles, removing some of the victims of Lebanon's latest bout of carnage, and rushed them to the emergency room.

Other victims straggled in on foot seeking assistance. One elderly woman, tears in her eyes, walked painfully up the driveway today and said to a stranger: "Please, I'm with the diabetes and my home is gone. Where can I get the free help?"

No one knows with any accuracy how many dead and wounded there are in this ravaged and fear-ridden country since the start of the Israeli invasion a week ago.

Regarded as Neutral Territory

The American University Hospital, so far anyway, is regarded as neutral territory and its fatigued and overworked staff have handled hundreds and hundreds of victims of bombings and strafings.

The 10-story building is filled with casualties. Some of them are lying on beds in hallways receiving fluids intravenously.

The hospital is representative of medical facilities all over this battered country where a cease-fire has been declared but the fire has not ceased.

According to the International Commitee of the Red Cross, the medical facilities in southern Lebanon, the scene of fierce exchanges between Israelis and Palestinians, are in a ruinous state. They lack space and medicines, and food hygiene is reportedly deplorable. There is a shortage of water. The wounded are lying in school buildings and hallways.

Because of fierce Israeli shelling around Beirut's International Airport, immobilized since the invasion began, a jumbo jet sitting in Geneva cannot get in to deliver medical supplies.

Private hospitals in Christian East Beirut, which has been untouched during the invasion, have offered aid to overtaxed hospitals in the city's predominantly Moslem western section, the southern outskirts of which have been the target of numerous attacks by Israeli planes and gunboats.

Palestinian Wounded Brought In

Many of West Beirut's hospitals are understaffed because technicians and medical personnel are unable to get to work through the city's dangerous streets.

The Lebanese Red Cross has issued urgent calls for doctors to help in rescue operations and have issued an international call for doctors to help them in the nearly impossible task of providing adequate medical care for the victims.

As armed Palestinian guerrillas carried in their wounded to the Ameri-

Continued on Page A13, Column 1

The New York Times / Fred R. Conrad

The Calm Restored, Sailors Return to Central Park

Sailboats, with sails and rudders that respond to radio commands, on Conservatory Pond yesterday in a model yacht competition. About 1,000 workers cleared tons of trash from hundreds of thousands of demonstrators who assembled Saturday to protest nuclear arms. Article on the cleanup is on page B1; on the yachts, on page B3.

INSIDE

France Freezes Wages

France's Socialist Government announced a four-month freeze on wages and prices to help prevent a further weakening of the franc. Page A6.

Hinckley Case Is Costly

The medical experts in the trial of John W. Hinckley Jr. have cost his parents and the taxpayers at least $350,000 to $450,000. Page D10.

Aftermath of a Murder Trial

Two children are dead and a 16-year-old boy faces the electric chair in a murder case that continues to cast a shadow over Old Forge, Pa. Page D10.

Power Shifts in Mideast

Israeli Invasion of Lebanon Alters Balance And Jumbles Relations of Friends and Foes

By THOMAS L. FRIEDMAN

Special to The New York Times

News Analysis

BEIRUT, Lebanon, June 13 — The Israeli invasion of Lebanon has recast the balance of power in this corner of the world and created a whole new set of relationships involving Israel, Syria, Lebanon and the Palestine Liberation Organization.

With Israeli forces on the fringes of Beirut and the Israeli Army in control of roughly a fourth of Lebanon's territory, the full political effect of the fighting can now begin to be assessed.

Tensions have already surfaced between the Palestine Liberation Organization and Syria. The Syrians have lost a dominant role in Lebanon. The Soviet Union's clients in the region have been weakened.

Problems for the P.L.O.

Although P.L.O. leaders have apparently not been captured or killed, damage to the organization should not be underestimated.

Southern Lebanon, the P.L.O.'s only independent base of military operations — excluding isolated pockets in Sidon, Tyre and Damur — has been occupied by the Israelis. The P.L.O. has been driven back to West Beirut, well out of striking distance to northern Israel.

This presents the P.L.O. leadership with serious problems. The guerrillas could try to continue operations out of West Beirut, harassing the Israeli occupation forces on the outskirts of the city. But that would expose Beirut's non-Palestinian Moslem and Christian populations to continuous Israeli bombardment.

Moreover, President Elias Sarkis's Government is now eager to get its fragile, but still functioning, army into West Beirut to fill the void left by a nearly total withdrawal of Syrian peacekeeping forces.

Probably the most frequent topic of conversation among the predominantly Moslem inhabitants of West Beirut today was whether the Lebanese Army would finally free the area from the six years of lawlessness presided over by the Syrians and various private militias that operated with Syria's tacit approval.

If and when the Lebanese Army does come in, there will be tremendous pressure on the P.L.O. to maintain an extremely low profile as a military force.

The alternative for the P.L.O. leader, Yasir Arafat, may be to move his military headquarters to Damascus. That appears to be one of Israel's primary objectives in its invasion.

Ever since a war of attrition in 1974 between Israel and Syria in the Golan Heights, the Government of President

Continued on Page A14, Column 1

"All the News That's Fit to Print"

The New York Times

Late Edition
Weather: Sunny today with light southeasterly winds; clear and mild tonight. Cloudy with a chance of rain tomorrow. Temperatures: today 81-83, tonight 63-67; yesterday 54-72. Details, page D24.

VOL.CXXXI . No. 45,345 — NEW YORK, TUESDAY, JUNE 15, 1982 — 30 CENTS

BRITAIN ANNOUNCES ARGENTINE SURRENDER TO END THE 10-WEEK WAR IN THE FALKLANDS

Israelis Cut Off West Beirut, Trapping P.L.O. Leaders

ACTION IN LEBANON

Tank Units Push Through the Christian Suburbs Around the Capital

By THOMAS L. FRIEDMAN
Special to The New York Times

BEIRUT, Lebanon, June 14 — Israeli tank columns completely cut off Moslem western Beirut today, trapping the military and political leadership of the Palestine Liberation Organization.

At the same time, other Israeli armored units, greeted by rice and flowers from sympathetic Lebanese Christians, began driving still deeper into Lebanon, apparently in an effort to push Syrian troops northeast of the capital into the Bekaa Valley.

There is a concentration of Syrian troops in the Khalde junction area on the coastal highway south of Beirut near the airport, and fighting was reportedly continuing there today between Israeli forces and Palestinians and Syrians.

The Israeli radio quoted Israel's Chief of Staff, Lieut. Gen. Rafael Eytan, as saying that Israeli troops had trapped guerrilla forces in Beirut and that the troops' mission was to smash the P.L.O.'s political and military nerve center there. [Page A18.]

Lebanese Leader Forms Council

The Israeli siege of guerrilla forces in Beirut came as the Lebanese Government announced the formation of a six-member Council of National Salvation to deal with the political repercussions of the Israeli invasion.

The committee, which was to contain the leading Christian and Moslem militia commanders, was formed by President Elias Sarkis and Prime Minister Shafik al-Wazzan to determine the Government's response to Israeli conditions for withdrawal.

Israel's withdrawal terms were delivered this evening to Mr. Sarkis at the presidential palace in Baabda by the special United States envoy, Philip C. Habib. Mr. Habib arrived by car from Damascus, to which he had flown earlier today from Jerusalem.

Mr. Habib declined to make any statements to the press, but Israel's conditions are reportedly the creation of a demilitarized zone stretching 25 miles north of its border to prevent attacks by Palestinian guerrillas and the withdrawal of the 30,000 Syrian peacekeeping troops from Lebanon.

Leftist Rejects Council

A meeting of the national council to consider the conditions, scheduled for this afternoon, was canceled after one proposed member, Walid Jumblat, leader of the leftist Moslem National Movement, said he would not have anything to do with the group as presently constituted.

Mr. Jumblat, who is under virtual house arrest by Israeli invasion forces occupying his mountain village of Mukhtara south of Beirut, said through a spokesman that the board should be "more comprehensive."

The other proposed council members are Bashir Gemayel, a Chrisian Phalangist militia commander; Nabim Berri, head of Lebanon's Shiite Moslem Party; Nasri Maalouf, another leading Christian political leader; Foreign

Continued on Page A18, Column 1

Associated Press

Israeli soldier atop armored vehicle in position overlooking western Beirut.

In Lebanon, White Flags Fly Amid the Misery and Rubble

By DAVID K. SHIPLER
Special to The New York Times

SIDON, Lebanon, June 14 — Along the battered Lebanese coast, in the wake of the invasion, white flags still fly.

They flutter from the antennas of cars without windows or windshields. They hang from bamboo poles stuck into the shell-pocked roofs and verandas of concrete houses. Even some pedestrians carried torn strips of white cloth to signify their neutrality, their surrender to the storm of war.

The Israeli Army warned residents of Lebanon's picturesque coast to leave their homes before the bombing and shelling began, and many followed the instructions on leaflets dropped from planes.

Battles Silently Traced

But when the fighting was over and they returned home from the beaches and the orange groves and the banana plantations where they had camped for days without food or water, what they saw took the strength out of them.

In Tyre, a stronghold and command center of the Palestine Liberation Organization, not a single building was untouched by the flying shrapnel.

Some high-rise apartments had collapsed like houses of cards, some villas were chewed into piles of dust and rubble.

Many other buildings revealed the course of battle: pits and chips around the doors and windows as Israeli troops fired at guerrillas, then a single gaping hole in a wall where a heavier weapon finished off the resistance.

The Israeli military governor of the town, Maj. Joseph Dana, who in civilian life is a lecturer in Arabic at Haifa University, estimates that 30 percent of all buildings in the town were destroyed.

In Sidon, farther up the coast toward Beirut, the damage was less ex-

Continued on Page A18, Column 4

A MIDEAST WARNING

Soviet Conveys Concern Over Military Activity Near South Border

By JOHN F. BURNS
Special to The New York Times

MOSCOW, June 14 — The Soviet Government warned Israel today not to forget that the Middle East was close to the Soviet Union's southern borders and that developments in that area "cannot help affecting the interests of the U.S.S.R."

The warning was coupled with a demand, apparently directed at the United States, for "urgent effective measures" to halt Israel's "criminal

Text of Soviet statement, page A20.

act of genocide" against Palestinians and to bring about a withdrawal of Israeli troops from Lebanon.

The statement, issued through the official press agency Tass, said in part:

"The Soviet Union takes the Arabs' side not in words but in deed and presses to get the aggressor out of Lebanon.

"The present-day Israeli policy makers should not forget that the Middle East is an area lying in close proximity to the southern borders of the Soviet Union and that developments there cannot help affecting the interests of the U.S.S.R. We warn Israel about this."

Implications of Soviet Action

The statement was evidently intended to arouse concern that American inability to arrange an early cease-fire between Israeli forces and Palestinian guerrillas could provoke direct Soviet intervention.

Theoretically, Soviet options would include an emergency airlift of arms to Palestinian guerrillas by way of Syria, which has signed a Treaty of Friendship and Cooperation with Moscow, or a new supply of weapons to the Syrian forces.

As if to underscore the Soviet warning, a Soviet general was reported to have begun talks in the Syrian capital.

Sources in Damascus identified the officer as Col. Gen. Yevgeny S. Yurasov, a first deputy commander of the air defense system. The sending of the general to Syria suggested that the

Continued on Page A20, Column 1

United Press International

Prime Minister Margaret Thatcher after addressing Parliament.

Bus-Only Lanes To Be Increased To Speed Travel

By ARI L. GOLDMAN

Mayor Koch announced yesterday the creation of a system of 10 "red zone" lanes for buses in Manhattan to help relieve traffic congestion, increase bus speeds and reduce what has long been the bane of bus travelers — bus bunching.

Along the pavement at each of the 10 thoroughfares in the program, a bright red eight-inch thermoplastic strip will remind motorists of heavy fines if they park, stand or travel in the bus lane.

"Don't Even Think of Parking Here," a sign along the routes will read. Other signs will warn that fines of at least $100 will be imposed on violators. Only cars preparing to make right turns will be permitted to travel in the lanes, and then only for short distances.

Next Tuesday, the first of the red zone lanes will go into effect, on Third Avenue from 36th to 58th Streets from 7 A.M. to 7 P.M. The others, which will be added over the course of the summer, will be in effect at various times on major thoroughfares in both midtown and lower Manhattan. Fourteen miles of city streets will be affected.

The other streets to get red zone lanes will be: Eighth Avenue from 42d to 57th Streets between 4 P.M. and 7 P.M.; Avenue of the Americas from 40th

Continued on Page B6, Column 1

TRIUMPH BY LONDON

Commander Says Enemy Troops Are Assembled 'for Repatriation'

By R. W. APPLE Jr.
Special to The New York Times

LONDON, Tuesday, June 15 — Argentine forces in the Falkland Islands have surrendered, halting the war in the South Atlantic, Prime Minister Margaret Thatcher's office announced early this morning.

A spokesman quoted Maj. Gen. Jeremy Moore, the commander of British land forces in the archipelago, as saying that enemy troops were being rounded up for eventual repatriation to Argentina. The surrender came at 1 A.M. British time, (8 P.M. Monday New York time), the official announcement said.

There was no confirmation of the surrender from Buenos Aires by early this morning, but the Argentine high command announced Monday afternoon that an unofficial cease-fire had gone into effect on the Falklands. [Page A14.]

'God Save the Queen'

General Moore radioed from his command post on Mount Kent: "Falkland Islands once more under Government desired by their inhabitants. God Save the Queen." It had taken the British three weeks and four days of fighting on the ground to retake the islands following their landings at San Carlos Bay.

The Prime Minister signaled that the end of the conflict, or at least this phase of it, was at hand in a statement to Parliament Monday night in which she said that Argentine forces in Stanley, the last major enemy stronghold in the Falklands, had begun throwing down their arms and hoisting white flags.

As the House of Commons erupted in prolonged cheers, the Prime Minister disclosed that the deputy commander of British land forces, Brig. John Waters, was negotiating surrender terms with the commander of the 6,500 Argentine defenders of the town, Brig. Gen. Mario Menéndez. The surrender terms, she added, would cover both East Falkland, the island on which Stanley is situated, and West Falkland, where two small Argentine forces are based.

Crowds Hail Victory

Within minutes of her statement to the House, crowds gathered outside Mrs. Thatcher's residence at 10 Downing Street, singing "Rule Britannia." When she returned from the House, they cheered her and she said, "What matters is that it was everyone together — we all knew what we had to do and we went out there and did it."

Although it remained possible that fighting would continue on or around

Continued on Page A15, Column 1

United Press International

Yasir Arafat, left, leader of the Palestine Liberation Organization, and an aide yesterday in Beirut.

1,600 Are Arrested In Nuclear Protests At 5 U.N. Missions

By PAUL L. MONTGOMERY

Offering daisies to policemen or chanting prayers for peace, more than 1,600 nonviolent demonstrators for disarmament were arrested in midtown Manhattan yesterday as they tried to block the entrances of the United Nations missions of five countries that have atomic weapons.

In an assembly-line operation that began at 7:30 A.M., the police carried the unresisting demonstrators to rented city buses to be booked for disorderly conduct. Some who had been arrested in the morning were back later in the day, encouraging their friends or sitting down again for another arrest.

The Police Department, which had 3,000 extra officers at the demonstration sites, said the total booked was a record for a civil disobedience campaign in the city. Patrick J. Murphy, the department's chief of operations, said, "almost everybody was very well-behaved — it was a textbook exercise."

The demonstrations, for which the participants were rehearsed and the police were briefed in advance, were a continuation of the protest that brought

Continued on Page A22, Column 1

INSIDE

Sports Pages

The New York Times today introduces Sports Pages, an expanded and redesigned sports section appearing Tuesday through Saturday. It will include added news as well as new columns and features. Today's section begins on page D25.

U.S. Enters Dollar Market

As the dollar reached new highs against the devalued French franc, the Administration intervened in trading to try to restore order. Page D1.

Ruling Due on Copying TV

The Supreme Court agreed to decide whether use of home video recorders to tape television broadcasts violates Federal copyright law. Page D1.

U.S. Challenged in Space

A lack of planning and foreign competition were reported to threaten United States leadership in nonmilitary space technology. Page C1.

17 Fakes at Met Museum

The Metropolitan Museum has discovered that 17 gold vessels it had been believed to be ancient Egyptian are modern fakes. Page C9.

U.S. Is Easing '68 Antitrust Guidelines on Mergers

By ROBERT D. HERSHEY Jr.
Special to The New York Times

WASHINGTON, June 14 — The Government, seeking to reduce uncertainty about the types of corporate mergers that it will allow, today published a new set of enforcement guidelines "more lenient" than previous antitrust policy.

Nevertheless, the Justice Department and the Federal Trade Commission, which share antitrust responsibility, said they did not believe that their long-awaited statements would lead to any significant increase in mergers, which have diminished recently.

Attorney General William French Smith described the new guidelines as an "evolutionary change — not a revolutionary change" from actual practices in recent years. William F. Baxter, the Assistant Attorney General in charge of the antitrust division, said that, "in general, the new guidelines would have to be regarded as more lenient." But he added that he did not expect them to encourage more corporate combinations than guidelines that have existed since 1968. Antitrust experts said the new guidelines were more than

Continued on Page D8, Column 4

"All the News That's Fit to Print"

The New York Times

Late Edition
Weather: Overcast and mild today with scattered rainshowers likely through tonight. Cloudy, chance of rain tomorrow. Temperatures: today 73-77, tonight 61-63; yesterday 65-81. Details on page B10.

VOL.CXXXI. No. 45,437 · NEW YORK, WEDNESDAY, SEPTEMBER 15, 1982 · 30 CENTS

GEMAYEL OF LEBANON IS KILLED IN BOMB BLAST AT PARTY OFFICES

Hussein Praises Reagan's Mideast Plan

The New York Times / Dan Miller

Grace Kelly, the actress: In "The Country Girl," 1954, for which she won an Oscar. Princess Grace of Monaco: At a tribute in Philadelphia this year.

Princess Grace Is Dead After Riviera Car Crash

By CLYDE HABERMAN

Princess Grace of Monaco, whose stately beauty and reserve gave her enduring Hollywood stardom even long after she ended her film career, died yesterday in Monte Carlo of injuries suffered when her car plunged off a mountain road Monday. She was 52 years old.

The Princess, the former Grace Kelly, died of a cerebral hemorrhage, a palace spokesman said in Monaco.

Princess Grace was driving her British Rover 3500 on a snaking road at Cap-d'Ail in the Côte d'Azur region when she lost control and plunged down a 45-foot embankment. The car burst into flames, and the Princess suffered multiple fractures, including a broken thighbone, collarbone and ribs.

Initial reports gave no sense that her life was in jeopardy. But a Monaco Government announcement yesterday said that her health had "deteriorated during the night."

"At the end of the day all therapeutic possibilities had been exceeded," the announcement said.

With her in the car was Stephanie, 17, her youngest child by Prince Rainier III of Monaco. Stephanie was under observation at a hospital where she had been treated for shock and bruises.

Reagan Praises 'Gentle Lady'

Princess Grace's death brought expressions of grief from former Hollywood colleagues and from residents of her hometown, Philadelphia. President Reagan called her "a compassionate and gentle lady." In Philadelphia, a spokesman for John Cardinal Krol said the Cardinal, who was a close friend, would offer a memorial mass for her at noon Friday.

Alfred Hitchcock, who directed Grace Kelly in three films and was certainly in a position to judge, once said she had "sexual elegance." And it was that very elegance that probably made its most lasting impression on movie audiences of the 1950's.

Whether playing the heiress in "To Catch a Thief" or the Quaker pacifist in "High Noon" or the amusedly detached career girl — a term still in vogue when "Rear Window" was made — Grace Kelly carried herself with straight back and clipped-voice self-assurance. Yet just beneath the frosty exterior lay a sensuality and warmth that cracked the formidable reserve.

It was this delicate balance of contrasts that helped give her legendary status — a remarkable achievement for an actress whose career encompassed only 11 films. She made more of that

Continued on Page C24, Column 1

KING OFFERS HELP

But Jordanian Asserts He Lacks the Authority to Enter Peace Talks

By BERNARD GWERTZMAN

Special to The New York Times

WASHINGTON, Sept. 14 — King Hussein of Jordan, in his first public comment on President Reagan's Middle East peace plan, said in an interview that it was "a very constructive and a very positive move." He added that he would play "a very active part" in trying to bring about a federation between Jordanians and the Palestinians.

But in the interview, aired by the British Broadcasting Corporation on Monday night, the King said he did not have an Arab mandate to join talks with Israel, Egypt and the United States on Palestinian self-rule.

Transcript of interview, page A10.

He said the Arab leaders who met in Fez, Morocco, last week did not alter the 1974 Arab League decision to give the Palestine Liberation Organization, not Jordan, responsibility for negotiations dealing with the Palestinians living in territories occupied by Israel.

'A Very Active Part'

Although the 1974 decision still holds, he said, "I am going to play a very active part in helping, pushing forth every possible attempt for the establishment of a just and durable peace."

King Hussein, in describing his ideas for an eventual settlement of the Palestinian issue, put forth a plan that was very similar to the one proposed by President Reagan in his address on the Middle East on Sept. 1.

In that speech, Mr. Reagan said the United States favored some kind of "association" between Jordan and the Palestinians. He said the United States rejected the idea of Israeli sovereignty over the the West Bank and the Gaza Strip, but would not support an independent Palestinian state in the occupied territories.

Israel captured the West Bank from Jordan and Gaza from Egypt in the 1967 war.

The Fez communiqué repeated the traditional Arab demand for the establishment of an independent Palestinian

Continued on Page A10, Column 1

The New York Times / George Tames

Bashir Gemayel during a visit to Washington a year ago.

8 REPORTED SLAIN

President-Elect Was 34 — No Group Reports Making the Attack

By COLIN CAMPBELL

Special to The New York Times

BEIRUT, Lebanon, Wednesday, Sept. 15 — President-elect Bashir Gemayel was killed Tuesday when a bomb shattered the headquarters of his Lebanese Christian Phalangist Party in east Beirut. The Government said he would be buried today.

Mr. Gemayel, 34 years old, who was to have been inaugurated Sept. 23, was said to have died as he was about to address 400 of his followers at a weekly meeting. The state radio said the blast left at least 8 dead, among them other Phalangist leaders, and more than 50 wounded.

Prime Minister Shafik al-Wazzan deplored the killing in a statement, describing it as "a link in a chain of criminal conspiracies against Lebanon at a time when it started to restore its strength."

New Fighting Is Feared

No one took responsibility immediately for the bombing. It raised widespread fears that it would be followed by new fighting between Lebanon's Christian and Moslem militias.

Mr. Gemayel, who had been the commander of the Christian militias, was elected President Aug. 23 at a special session of Parliament that was boycotted by many Moslem legislators. To them, many other Moslems and some Christian groups, he was an enemy and an agent of Israel, whose invading troops made his election possible. [In Israel, there was no immediate official comment on the assassination.]

Until Sept. 23, the current President, Elias Sarkis, will continue as chief of state. Government sources said he could call new elections before then or appoint a presidential council to exercise presidential power until new elections could be called. Since the President in Lebanon is by tradition a Maronite Catholic, the council would also be headed by one.

400 Pounds of Explosives

The sources said another possibility was an extension of the Sarkis term, but this would require a change in the Constitution. The Lebanese President is not allowed under current law to succeed himself.

The blast, involving the detonation of what Phalangist and Government sources estimated to be more than 400 pounds of high explosives, occurred at 4:10 P.M. Tuesday. There was no immediate explanation for how so large an amount of explosive could have been introduced into the building.

For several hours reports circulated that Mr. Gemayel had survived.

There were reports that he had said "God be praised" as he left the scene for treatment of leg bruises at the nearby French-run Hôtel Dieu hospital. Those accounts were broadcast by the Phalangist radio, which quoted wit-

Continued on Page A8, Column 4

Slaying Is Denounced by Reagan; U.S. Fears New Burst of Fighting

Special to The New York Times

WASHINGTON, Sept. 14 — President Reagan said tonight that the "cowardly assassination" of President-elect Bashir Gemayel of Lebanon was a "shock to the American people and to civilized men and women everywhere."

In an unusually sharp statement, Mr. Reagan added, "We condemn the perpetrators of this heinous crime against Lebanon and against their cause of peace in the Middle East."

The White House statement, issued late tonight, expressed deepest sympathy to the Gemayel family, and said, "The tragedy will be all the greater if men in countries friendly to Lebanon permit disorder to continue in this war-torn country."

'U.S. Stands By Lebanon'

Mr. Reagan added that the "U.S. Government stands by Lebanon with its full support in its hour of need."

American officials said earlier that the assassination raised the possibility of new fighting in that country between Mr. Gemayel's Christian Phalangist forces and Moslem leftists.

New internal strife would also raise the possibility that Syrian and Israeli forces, confronting each other in Lebanon, might enter the conflict, destroying hopes for restoring stability.

The Israelis had strongly supported Mr. Gemayel, who was an avowed enemy of Syria. Just today, the Israeli Ambassador, Moshe Arens, called on Secretary of State George P. Shultz to say Israel wanted American assistance in obtaining a peace treaty with Lebanon.

It is the American hope that Elias Sarkis, the Lebanese President, whose term of office officially ends in nine days, will remain in office pending a new consensus choice as President.

The special American Middle East envoy, Morris Draper, arrived in Israel today on his way to Lebanon to help negotiate the withdrawal of Syrian and Israeli forces and the strengthening of the Lebanese Government. His mission is even more precarious now, officials said, given the uncertain future in Lebanon.

There was no fundamental difference between Mr. Sarkis and Mr. Gemayel on the withdrawal of foreign troops from Lebanon, American officials said. They expressed hope that Mr. Sarkis

Continued on Page A9, Column 1

Primaries Won By Ex-Governor, Two Incumbents

By ADAM CLYMER

A former Massachusetts Governor trying a comeback and two important members of Congress won key tests yesterday as 12 states and the District of Columbia held primary elections.

But another incumbent, Senator Howard W. Cannon of Nevada, was locked in a tight race with Representative James D. Santini as he sought the Democratic nomination for a fifth term.

In Massachusetts, former Gov. Michael S. Dukakis, attacking his successor's administration as corrupt and too supportive of President Reagan, defeated the incumbent, Gov. Edward J. King, for the Democratic nomination for Governor, just as Mr. King did four years ago when Mr. Dukakis was the incumbent. In the heavily Democratic Bay State, Mr. Dukakis will be favored over the Republican nominee in November, John W. Sears, a former Boston City Councilor.

In Vermont, Senator Robert T. Stafford, the Republican chairman of the Committee on the Environment and Public Works, defeated two conservative foes trying to end his 11-year Senate career. The two, Stewart M. Ledbetter and John McClaughry, argued that Mr. Stafford had become more interested in Washington than in Vermont.

With 93 percent of the precincts reporting, Mr. Stafford was safely ahead with 23,815 votes, or 46 percent of the

Continued on Page B11, Column 4

I.B.M. Accuses 3 Executives Of Stealing Computer Secrets

By ANDREW POLLACK

The International Business Machines Corporation, following its second undercover investigation in recent months, said yesterday that it had dismissed three of its executives and had sued them on charges of stealing corporate secrets.

The key figure in the month-long I.B.M. investigation, conducted by the company's own security officers, was the president of a small Cleveland computer company who pretended to negotiate a business deal with the I.B.M. executives. While he negotiated, he secretly taped the conversations on recording equipment supplied by I.B.M.

One of the executives had approached the Cleveland company, Tecmar Inc., and had offered to sell designs for products that would enhance I.B.M.'s new and fast-selling personal computer, according to court papers. In some cases, they would compete with still-secret products I.B.M. itself is planning to introduce, the affidavits filed in connection with the lawsuit stated.

The president of the Cleveland company, Martin A. Alpert, reported the approach to I.B.M. and agreed to cooperate when I.B.M. suggested the tape-recording plan.

In one excerpt from the transcript quoted in the court papers, William W. Erdman, an I.B.M. product manager and one of the defendants, said to Mr. Alpert: "I guarantee you that we know more about the way I.B.M.'s going to put it [personal computer products] together than I.B.M. knows, because when the guys that we're talking about leave, a good deal of knowledge leaves with them."

The three men sued in the civil action included two high-level engineers who were heavily involved in the design of I.B.M.'s personal computer and follow-up products. Also sued was Bridge Technology Inc., a White Plains company that I.B.M. asserts was established by the three executives to market their products. The three executives were dismissed by I.B.M. on Monday.

Mr. Erdman, reached yesterday at his home in Stamford, Conn., said he

Continued on Page D7, Column 1

INSIDE

Doctor Shot to Death

A physician was fatally shot as he sat in his car near his Gramercy Park office. The victim, Dr. Philip Wald, 53, was shot once in the head. Page B6.

Tuition Credit Compromise

President Reagan, returning to the theme of social issues, backed legislative compromises aimed to advance a tuition tax credit bill. Page A20.

Thomas Victor

JOHN GARDNER IS DEAD: The novelist, killed in a motorcycle accident, was 49. Page D27.

Haig, at U.J.A., Criticizes Reagan's Mideast Plan

By BERNARD D. NOSSITER

Former Secretary of State Alexander M. Haig Jr. attacked President Reagan's Middle East plan yesterday, describing the proposal for a freeze on Israeli settlements in the occupied West Bank as "a very serious mistake."

Mr. Haig also said the Administration's plan for autonomy for the Palestinians in association with Jordan threatened a "gutting session" between Israel and the United States.

"The peace process will only move forward if there is a spirit of cooperation between Israel and the United States," Mr. Haig said. "That has been shaken in recent days."

It was the first time Mr. Haig is known to have criticized the Administration in which he served until June. He spoke without a text to 300 officials of the United Jewish Appeal at the Hilton Hotel in Manhattan.

Mr. Haig made no direct reference to the speech Sept. 1 in which Mr. Reagan announced the Middle East plan, or to his successor, George P. Shultz, who is regarded as the architect of that speech. When Mr. Haig was asked to comment on the Reagan plan, he smiled and said it would be inappropriate to "parse the pros and cons." But he added that his own remarks contained "some pertinent observations."

Ziea Oszri

Alexander M. Haig Jr. yesterday.

The United Jewish Appeal raises funds for needy Jews around the world. It has not taken a formal position on Mr. Reagan's peace plan, but the frequent applause yesterday indicated strong agreement with Mr. Haig's criticism. Mr. Haig, who reportedly received $25,000 for his 45-minute appearance, serves as a consultant for United Technologies, a leading military contractor, and is a senior fellow at the Hudson Institute, a research center.

Mr. Haig received a standing ovation by concluding, "When we are true to Israel, we are true to ourselves."

He had earlier said, "When by our policies we can't deal effectively with our friends in Israel, we are undercutting our effectiveness throughout the Arab world."

Mr. Haig also asserted that "had the credibility" of Israel's invasion of Lebanon "been left undisturbed, the Palestine Liberation Organization would have left weeks earlier, and there would have been less bloodshed."

That was apparently an allusion to

Continued on Page A12, Column 4

"All the News That's Fit to Print"

The New York Times

Late Edition

Weather: Fair and cold today with gusty winds making it feel much colder; clear tonight. Rain or snow likely tomorrow. Temperatures: today 31-33, tonight 19-23; yesterday 28-35. Details, page D20.

VOL.CXXXII . . . No. 45,584 | NEW YORK, WEDNESDAY, FEBRUARY 9, 1983 | 30 CENTS

ISRAELI INQUIRY GIVES LEADERS 'INDIRECT' BLAME IN MASSACRE; CALLS FOR SHARON'S DEPARTURE

United Press International

Defense Minister Ariel Sharon of Israel, right, and Lieut. Gen. Rafael Eytan, the Army Chief of Staff, leaving a special Cabinet meeting in Jerusalem called to discuss the release of the report on the massacre in Beirut.

REPORT STIRS FUROR

Cabinet Weighs Response — Minister of Defense Refuses to Resign

By DAVID K. SHIPLER

Special to The New York Times

JERUSALEM, Feb. 8 — A special state investigating commission said today that Israel's top civilian and military leaders bore "indirect responsibility" for the massacre of Palestinians by Lebanese Christian Phalangist militia in Beirut last September.

The panel, headed by the Chief Justice of Israel's Supreme Court, recommended the resignation or dismissal of Defense Minister Ariel Sharon.

Key excerpts from the report are printed on pages A18-A20.

Three senior generals were also found to have been seriously at fault. The commission recommended that Brig. Gen. Amos Yaron, division commander in the Beirut district, be relieved of his post as a field commander for at least three years, and that the Director of Military Intelligence, Maj. Gen. Yehoshua Saguy, no longer continue in his post. Its report noted that the Chief of Staff, Lieut. Gen. Rafael Eytan, was retiring in April and that therefore "there is no practical significance to a recommendation with regard to his continuing in office."

Inquiry Took Four Months

The commission's report, issued after a four-month investigation, also criticized Prime Minister Menachem Begin, Foreign Minister Yitzhak Shamir and other officials, and assailed inadequacies in coordination and communication within the Cabinet and the army. These inadequacies, it said, led to faulty reporting and inaction while the Phalangists were in the Sabra and Shatila refugee camps.

The 55,000-word report set off a political furor in Mr. Begin's fractious coalition Government. Key members of the National Religious Party, whose six seats are essential to maintaining the Government's slim majority in Parliament, were reported to have demanded Mr. Sharon's resignation as a condition for remaining in the coalition. Mr. Sharon refused and urged that the army officers named be praised instead of ousted. The Cabinet met in special session to discuss to the report. Most ministers were said to favor following its recommendations, but Mr. Begin was said to oppose dismissal of Mr. Sharon. [Page A21.]

The report and its political consequences could have wide-ranging effects in the Middle East, and on Israel's

Continued on Page A21, Column 1

The New York Times

Dan Rostenkowski

Key Democrat Bids Congress Halt Tax Cuts

By EDWARD COWAN

Special to The New York Times

WASHINGTON, Feb. 8 — The chief Democratic tax writer in the House of Representatives, Dan Rostenkowski, proposed today that Congress reduce future budget deficits by the repeal or delay of various tax cuts for business and individuals now scheduled to take effect after 1983.

Mr. Rostenkowski acknowledged, however, that he could not muster a majority on the House floor to repeal the 10 percent cut in individual income taxes scheduled for July 1, 1983, and he indicated that he would not try to do so.

His list of future tax cuts to be forgone included indexing, or the automatic adjustment of tax brackets for wage inflation now scheduled to start in 1985, and reductions in estate, crude oil, tobacco and telephone taxes.

Politically More Attractive

Mr. Rostenkowski, the chairman of the Ways and Means Committee, argued in a speech here to the Securities Industry Association that his "tax freeze" was a politically more attractive way for Democrats and Republicans to raise revenue than President Reagan's proposal for standby tax increases to take effect in 1985.

Because the Chicago Democrat is close to the Speaker of the House, Thomas P. O'Neill Jr., and because he is understood to be willing to negotiate with the Reagan Administration, Mr.

Continued on Page D2, Column 5

U.S. SURVEY CITES RIGHTS VIOLATIONS AROUND THE WORLD

List Ranges From Vietnam to Countries Where Improved Relations Are Sought

By BERNARD WEINRAUB

Special to The New York Times

WASHINGTON, Feb. 8 — The Reagan Administration, seeking what it terms "an active, positive human rights policy," issued an annual human rights report today. The document cited serious human rights violations in nations around the world, including some that are friendly to the United States.

The 1,300-page report to Congress contains long descriptions of human rights violations in the Soviet Union and eastern-bloc nations as well as Middle East and Asian countries with strained ties to the United States. It also lists examples of torture, brutality and violence in South Africa, Pakistan and El Salvador, where the Administration has sought to improve relations.

At a news conference in the State Department, Elliott Abrams, the Assistant Secretary for Human Rights and Humanitarian Affairs, cited improvements and "moves toward democracy" in such countries as Brazil, Uruguay, El Salvador and the Dominican Republic.

Vietnam Termed 'the Worst'

But he said in response to questions that civil liberties seemed to have worsened last year in such countries as Iran, Czechoslovakia, the Soviet Union and Lebanon. And he said the "toughest" section of the document involved Vietnam. "It seemed to me the worst country to live in," Mr. Abrams said.

The annual study draws on reports from United States missions abroad, Congressional studies and human rights groups. It includes a country-by-country examination of political and press rights, freedoms of speech and religion, arbitrary arrest and imprisonment.

In a section on Israel, the report says that although that nation is a parliamentary democracy with full "freedom of speech and the press, relations with Arabs in the occupied territories have caused "significant human rights problems." In the West Bank and Gaza, the report said, Israeli forces were observed "roughing up" individuals, freedom of expression was "restricted" and there were cases of Arabs being imprisoned for several months without formal charges or trial.

Although the Reagan Administration

Continued on Page A12, Column 1

U.S. Aides Feel if Sharon Leaves, Begin May Show More Flexibility

By LESLIE H. GELB

Special to The New York Times

WASHINGTON, Feb. 8 — Key White House and State Department officials privately expressed the hope today that the findings of the Israeli commission would lead to the departure of Defense Minister Ariel Sharon and new negotiating flexibility on the part of Prime Minister Menachem Begin.

At a meeting in the White House Friday, top Middle East advisers told President Reagan that the commission's report could help break the deadlock over Israeli withdrawal from Lebanon if it placed responsibility principally on Mr. Sharon and only indirectly on Mr. Begin. The general view was that with Mr. Sharon in the Cabinet there was no chance of movement in either the Lebanese or West Bank talks but that, without him, the Begin Government would be somewhat weakened and Mr. Begin might be more amenable to compromise.

Today, neither the White House nor the State Department would publicly comment in detail on the report. Alan Romberg, a State Department spokesman, said, however, "We don't see why the impact of this report, whatever that may be, should affect the Lebanese negotiations or the current Habib mission."

'Issues Are Urgent'

"Our view is clear: The issues being addressed are urgent, and they must be resolved as soon as possible in the interests of Lebanese stability and sovereignty, as well as in the interests of Israeli security," he said.

President Reagan told editorial writers who asked about the report today that "I just don't think we should be commenting or injecting ourselves into that internal problem." He went on to praise Israel as a "strong democracy."

Administration officials were also saying that Secretary of State George P. Shultz was becoming more disposed toward making a trip to the Middle East, perhaps soon. The officials maintained, as President Reagan said Monday, that Israel was primarily responsi-

Continued on Page A21, Column 6

REPORT HIGHLIGHTS PHALANGISTS' ROLE

Inquiry Says Israeli 'Ordered' Christians Into the Camps

By THOMAS L. FRIEDMAN

Special to The New York Times

JERUSALEM, Feb. 8 — The report of the Israeli commission of inquiry into the killings in the Palestinian camps in Beirut contains new details of the events of September and of the workings of the Christian Phalangists who carried out the operation.

For the first time, the Israeli commission officially confirmed the name of the Phalangist officer in charge of the operation in the Sabra and Shatila camps — Elie Hobeika, the head of intelligence. The report also disclosed that the Israeli Chief of Staff, Lieut. Gen. Rafael Eytan, made a personal appeal to Phalangist commanders after the massacre to admit their guilt and try to explain their behavior publicly, but they did not do so.

According to the report, when the Israeli Army entered West Beirut on Wednesday, Sept. 15, after the assassination of President-elect Bashir Gemayel — the former commander of the Phalangist militia — General Eytan went to the Phalangist military headquarters. There, it said, he "ordered the Phalangist commanders to effect a general mobilization of all their

Continued on Page A22, Column 4

The New York Times/Marilynn K. Yee

FIFTH AVENUE BUILDING TOPPED OUT: Workers placing a flag-draped girder on the addition to the Republic National Bank building. A Fifth Avenue Association official called it "the first real, meaningful construction" on the avenue below 42d Street since the Empire State Building. New York Day by Day, page B3.

Sentry Inquiry Leads to $1 Million

By SELWYN RAAB

A green plastic garbage bag stuffed with about $1 million has been found in the home of relatives of one of the suspects in the theft of $11 million from a Bronx armored-car company, the Federal Bureau of Investigation said yesterday.

F.B.I. agents came across the money after interviews Monday with Mr. and Mrs. Thomas Skiadas, the father- and mother-in-law of Demetrious Papadakos, who was arrested Saturday in Miami, law-enforcement officials said.

According to the officials, Mr. and Mrs. Skiadas said they had no idea how the bag and its 60 pounds of money in denominations of $100 and smaller had got into a closet at their home in Westport, Conn.

A spokesman for the F.B.I., Joseph Valiquette, said investigators were trying to determine whether the money was some of that stolen from the Sentry Armored Car Courier Company in December. If the money is part of the loot, it would be the first recovered from the crime.

The F.B.I. has said that the 35-year-old Mr. Papadakos, who lived in Norwalk, Conn., until two months ago, was probably the "main motivator" in the Sentry theft. Three other men were also arrested last week in the case.

As part of background checks of all the suspects, F.B.I. agents interviewed Mr. and Mrs. Skiadas in their home at 6 Fermily Lane.

A law-enforcement official said that after the interviews, the couple let the agents "look around" their home, and the bag with the money was found.

After the discovery, the F.B.I. got a search warrant from a Federal judge in Bridgeport to allow them to seize the money.

There have been no charges against

Continued on Page B7, Column 1

United Press International

Prime Minister Menachem Begin of Israel, whom report criticized.

E.P.A. Counsel Accused of Impeding Inquiry

By DAVID BURNHAM

Special to The New York Times

WASHINGTON, Feb. 8 — The general counsel to the Environmental Protection Agency was accused by a House subcommittee chairman today of violating the law by seeking to impede a Congressional investigation.

The allegation by Representative John D. Dingell, Democrat of Michigan, arose one day after President Reagan dismissed Rita M. Lavelle, a top official of the agency, and after the House of Representatives held Anne M. Gorsuch, the agency's administrator, in contempt of Congress for failure to turn over information.

In a letter to Mrs. Gorsuch, he said that his committee was being hampered in efforts to question agency employees to investigate strong evidence that waste site cleanup funds had been "manipulated for political purposes."

Representative Dingell is chairman of the Oversight and Investigations Subcommittee of the House Energy and Commerce Committee. He charges that the environmental agency's general counsel, Robert M. Perry, sought to block the subcommittee's inquiry into how the agency handled the case of the Stringfellow Acid Pits in California. That case had been supervised by Miss Lavelle, who was dismissed Monday by Mr. Reagan as assistant administrator in charge of the toxic waste cleanup program.

The Stringfellow Acid Pits site is a large toxic waste dump near Los Angeles; negotiations are under way over what steps should be taken to clean it up and who should pay for the cleanup.

A spokesman for the agency said Mrs. Gorsuch had received Mr. Dingell's letter but would have no comment

Continued on Page B13, Column 4

INSIDE

New Holocaust Report

A Jewish organization's report concludes American Jews were slow to react to the dangers Nazi Germany posed to European Jews. Page B11.

Agee Out at Bendix

William M. Agee resigned as president of the Allied Corporation and chairman of Bendix, which was acquired by Allied last year. Page D1.

"All the News That's Fit to Print"

The New York Times

Late Edition

Weather: Partly sunny and cool today, northwesterly winds; partly cloudy tonight. Partly sunny, milder tomorrow. Temperatures: today 45-50, tonight 43-47; yesterday 38-48. Details on page 25.

VOL. CXXXIII . . . No. 45,853 NEW YORK, SATURDAY, NOVEMBER 5, 1983 — 60 cents beyond 75 miles from New York City, except on Long Island — 30 CENTS

AT LEAST 39 DIE AS TRUCK BOMB RIPS ISRAELI POST IN LEBANON; JETS STRIKE PALESTINIAN SITES

The New York Times / Micha Bar-Am

An Israeli Army rabbi, left, helping to carry the body of an Israeli soldier from site of bombing in Tyre, Lebanon.

ARABS AMONG DEAD

Sentries Shot the Driver but Were Not Able to Divert the Vehicle

By TERENCE SMITH

Special to The New York Times

TYRE, Lebanon, Nov. 4 — A truck loaded with explosives crashed through the entrance to an Israeli headquarters compound here today and detonated near the main building, killing at least 39 people and wounding 32.

A few hours later, Israeli jets struck at Palestinian targets along the Beirut-Damascus Highway, knocking out a command post and a number of tanks and artillery pieces. Some reports said they also attacked Syrian positions. As many as 60 people were reported killed. [Page 8.]

In Tyre, Defense Minister Moshe Arens visited the site of the explosion and told reporters Israel would continue to "hit back" at the terrorists.

The Beirut radio reported that responsibility for the incident had been claimed by the so-called Moslem Jihad, or Moslem Holy War, one of the two groups that claimed responsibility for the Oct. 23 truck bombings in Beirut of the American Marine headquarters and a French barracks.

Sentries Opened Fire

An Israeli Army spokesman said two sentries opened fire at the green Chevrolet truck as it crashed through the main gate of the headquarters compound. The Israelis estimated that the truck was carrying 800 to 1,000 pounds of explosives.

The sentries said they believed that they had hit the driver, but the truck careered on toward the main building. One of the guards was quoted as saying the truck swerved easily around three concrete blocks set as obstacles in the driveway.

Despite the shots fired by the sentries, the truck rolled into the center of the compound to the spot where it exploded, just a few yards from the main building. Officials said it was not clear exactly what set off the explosion.

Building Collapsed

The shockwave caused the building to collapse and blew down the tents of a 35-man medical team bivouaced nearby, according to Lieut. Col. Yona Gazit, a spokesman for the Israeli Army's Northern Command. He said the blast dug a crater 15 yards deep.

The Israeli Army said at least 29 of those killed today were Israeli soldiers or security personnel. Also reported killed were 10 Arabs who were being held in detention cells in the building for interrogation as suspected Palestinian guerrillas.

As the rescue operations got under

Continued on Page 8, Column 5

'We'll Hit Back,' Israel's Defense Minister Vows

By DAVID K. SHIPLER

Special to The New York Times

JERUSALEM, Nov. 4 — Israel reacted to the bombing of its headquarters in Tyre, Lebanon, today with a series of military steps and statements designed to regain a posture of determination and resolve.

Defense Minister Moshe Arens indicated that retaliation might be taken beyond the two air strikes conducted against Palestinian factions near the Beirut-Damascus highway.

"We'll hit back against those who commit these criminal acts," he said on the army radio. "We, of course, will investigate what happened, how it happened, what must be done in order to assure that this won't happen in the future." He ordered the appointment of a commission of investigation.

Stiffer Measures Promised

The Chief of Staff, Lieut. Gen. Moshe Levy, promised stiffer measures against the local population in southern Lebanon.

"We shall have to think about additional arrangements that will surely make life in general in that region more difficult — not only for the security forces — in order that even more extreme actions can be prevented," he said.

Officials said the bridges across the Awali River, Israel's northern defense line in Lebanon, were closed to vehicles after the bombing.

In fashioning its reaction, officials here indicated that the Government was anxious to destroy illusions as well as military targets.

In recent weeks officials in Jerusalem have expressed worry that Syria and Palestinian factions in Lebanon have been seeing an irresolute Israel, weakened by domestic political objections to the involvement in Lebanon

Continued on Page 7, Column 5

Associated Press

An Israeli soldier covering the body of a comrade in demolished building.

U.S. and Israeli Interests

By BERNARD GWERTZMAN

Special to The New York Times

News Analysis

WASHINGTON, Nov. 4 — The suicide attacks on American, French and Israeli forces over the last 12 days have quickened Washington's determination to alter its policy in Lebanon by forging a closer strategic bond with the Israelis, American officials said today.

They said they hoped to create such a bond now to take advantage of what they regard as a growing convergence of American interests with Israel's.

By coincidence, Under Secretary of State Lawrence S. Eagleburger was in Israel winding up a mission aimed at reducing the misunderstandings and distrust of the last two years when the terrorist explosion occurred at an Israeli compound in Tyre. A goal of his trip was to persuade the new Prime Minister, Yitzhak Shamir, to make an early trip to Washington for discussions on how the two countries can collaborate in these tense times in Lebanon and the Middle East.

A Major Shift for U.S.

This represents a major shift in American thinking about Lebanon, a shift caused both by the diplomatic stalemate over the country's future and a major buildup of Syrian forces. Ever since Israel pulled its troops back from the Shuf Mountains against the advice of the American and Lebanese Governments in early September, the Administration has feared that the Syrians may be under the impression that they can force Israel and the United States out of Lebanon without making any concessions themselves.

In the American view, this could make it impossible to reach a diplomatic solution for the withdrawal of all foreign forces from Lebanon, and increase the risk of another Middle East war by miscalculation, a conflict that could also involve the United States and the Soviet Union.

When the American Marines and the other Western members of the multinational force were sent to the Beirut area in September 1982, after the massacres at the Palestinian camps of Sabra and Shatila, the goal was to bring about a speedy withdrawal of Israeli forces from Lebanon.

The Americans held Israel morally responsible for allowing the Christian Phalangist militiamen into the camps, and Washington wanted to distance it-

Continued on Page 8, Column 1

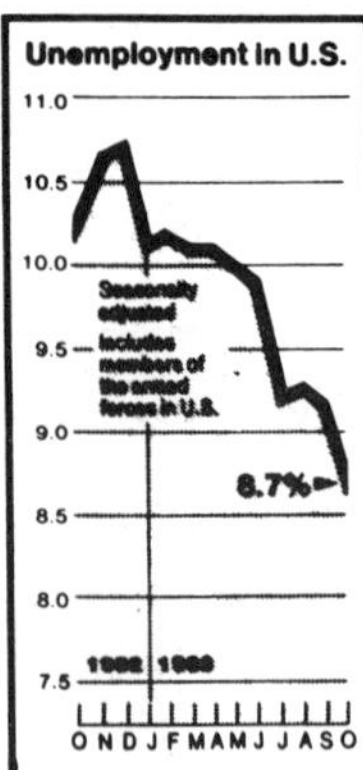

The New York Times / Nov. 5, 1983

Unemployment Drops to 8.7%; Payroll Jobs Up

By SETH S. KING

Special to The New York Times

WASHINGTON, Nov. 4 — The national unemployment rate fell four-tenths of a percentage point in October, to 8.7 percent of the labor force from 9.1 in September, the Labor Department reported today.

The Bureau of Labor Statistics said there was an increase of 320,000 payroll jobs, many of them in durable goods manufacturing and construction, two sectors hit hardest by the recession. The Government said one reason for the rise might be that employers hired more workers instead of extending work hours.

Big Decrease for Jersey

The jobless rate for civilians alone, not counting members of the armed forces in the United States, also declined, falling to 8.8 percent from the 9.3 percent recorded in September.

In New Jersey, the October unemployment rate dropped to 6.8 percent from 8.2 in September. New York City's unemployment rate dropped to 9.2 percent from 10.1 percent. The state rate declined to 8 percent from 8.6. [Page 16.]

The Bureau of Labor Statistics said 101,928,000 civilians were employed last month, down from 101,945,000 in

Continued on Page 16, Column 1

U.S. MAKES PUBLIC ARMS PACTS IT SAYS GRENADIANS MADE

Asserts Soviet, North Korea and Cuba Were to Deliver $37 Million in Weapons

By PHILIP TAUBMAN

Special to The New York Times

WASHINGTON, Nov. 4 — The Reagan Administration made public today copies of what it said were five secret military cooperation agreements concluded by the former Government of Grenada with Cuba, the Soviet Union and North Korea.

Administration officials said the documents called for the delivery of $37 million in military equipment to Grenada and the permanent basing of 27 Cuban military advisers there.

Administration officials said the documents, which were found by American forces that invaded the island last week, supported President Reagan's assertion that Cuba and the Soviet Union were turning Grenada into a military bastion.

49 Russians Leave Grenada

Early today the 126 occupants of the Soviet Embassy in Grenada, including 49 Soviet citizens, 53 Cubans and 15 North Koreans, were flown off the island and taken to Mérida, Mexico. [Page 4.]

The five treaties made public by the State Department this evening show that the Soviet Union planned to ship $25 million in military equipment to Grenada, that North Korea had agreed to provide $12 million worth of supplies and that Cuba expected to send advisers to help Grenada train and expand its armed forces.

Arms to be provided by the Soviet Union, according to the agreements, included 4,000 submachine guns, 2,500 rifles, 7,000 mines, 15,000 grenades and 60 armored-personnel carriers.

'Free Offer of Assistance'

A three-page document, dated April 14, 1983, is designated an agreement regarding "the free offer of military assistance to the People's Revolutionary Government of Grenada by the Government of the Democratic People's Republic of Korea," or North Korea. The name Maurice Bishop appears in handwriting in the signature block, alongside a signature that appears to be in Korean characters.

This agreement, which contains little detail, appears to provide for the sup-

Continued on Page 4, Column 6

U.S. Presses Salvador to Act On Men Tied to Death Squads

By LYDIA CHAVEZ

Special to The New York Times

SAN SALVADOR, Nov. 4 — The United States Embassy here is pressing the Government to take action against a number of army and security officers who are said to be "highly suspected" of involvement in assassination squads, according to high-ranking embassy officials.

The officers said to be involved include the head of security for the Constituent Assembly, two provincial commanders and the directors of intelligence for two of the country's security forces.

Héctor Antonio Regalado, the head of security for the Constituent Assembly, is said to be the "head of the thing," according to well-placed officials here.

Many Thousands Killed

Mr. Regalado is known as a close friend of Roberto d'Aubuisson, the president of the Assembly, and was hired by Mr. d'Aubuisson to direct security for the Assembly.

The death squads, which are believed to be in the pay of right-wing elements, have been blamed for many thousands of civilian deaths in El Salvador over the last four years.

Embassy officials say the death squads are believed to be responsible for the kidnapping of Amílcar Martínez, the third-highest-ranking member of the Foreign Ministry. The officials say the squads are also believed to have assassinated 10 Salvadoran labor union members and to have threatened the two highest-ranking officials in the Roman Catholic Church here, Archbishop Arturo Rivera y Damas and Msgr. Gregorio Rosa-Chávez.

Diplomats here say they believe that unless the Government takes action against these suspects it will be increasingly difficult for the United States Congress to approve further aid to El Salvador.

Some embassy officials said they had expected some of the suspects to be relieved of their duties at the beginning of this month. But the high command issued general orders concerning per-

Continued on Page 10, Column 5

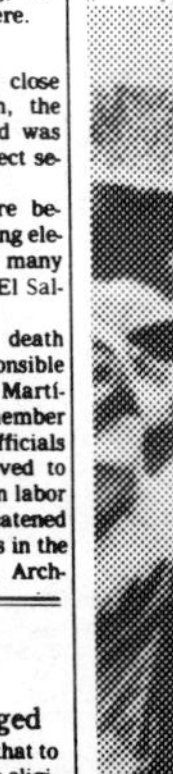

Associated Press

MARINES REMEMBERED: President Reagan and his wife, Nancy, at memorial service at Camp Lejeune, N.C., to honor marines killed in Beirut and Grenada. Gen. Paul X. Kelley, Marine commandant, is at left. Page 7.

Burma Says Agents Of North Korea Set Blast That Killed 21

By The Associated Press

RANGOON, Burma, Nov. 4 — The Burmese Government said today that it had "firmly established" that North Korean agents planted the bomb that killed 17 high-ranking officials of the South Korean Government here last month.

The state radio said that as a result Burma had cut diplomatic relations with North Korea and ordered North Korean Embassy personnel to leave within 48 hours. The two countries had previously had warm relations.

The broadcast said evidence examined by Burmese investigators "firmly established" that the explosion Oct. 9 during a state visit by President Chun Doo Hwan of South Korea was "the work of saboteurs sent by the Democratic People's Republic of Korea."

Four of President Chun's Cabinet members and 13 other presidential aides were killed, along with four Burmese reporters. Forty-six other people were injured.

The radio said the investigators had reached their conclusions from confessions by two men captured by the Burmese police shortly after the bomb attack. The broadcast said the evidence also included equipment seized from the two men and from an associate who

Continued on Page 10, Column 3

INSIDE

Medicare Overhaul Urged

A Federal advisory panel says that to avert Medicare bankruptcy, the eligibility age should go up to 67 and premiums should be raised. Page 12.

Soviet Sub Still on Surface

Officials said the submarine off South Carolina may have been forced up by a collision with a sonar device towed by a U.S. destroyer. Page 10.

"All the News That's Fit to Print"

The New York Times

Late Edition

Weather: Light rain or rain and snow today; snow likely tonight. Partly cloudy, with flurries likely tomorrow. Temperatures: today 37-42, tonight 20-23; yesterday 26-40. Details on page B9.

VOL.CXXXIV . . . No. 46,282 NEW YORK, MONDAY, JANUARY 7, 1985 — 60 cents beyond 75 miles from New York City, except on Long Island — 30 CENTS

Associated Press; United Press International

Dolphins and 49ers Win

In American Conference championship, Dolphin's William Judson, left, intercepted pass intended for Steelers' John Stallworth in first quarter. Miami won, 45-28. In National Conference game, 49ers' Wendell Tyler, with Bears' Al Harris in tow, crossed goal line for touchdown in team's 23-0 victory. The Dolphins and the 49ers will meet in Super Bowl XIX in Palo Alto, Calif., on Jan. 20. SportsMonday, page C1.

ISRAEL-RUN AIRLIFT OF ETHIOPIA'S JEWS FROM SUDAN HALTS

Spokes an Says Relief Group Hopes the End of Flights Will Be Just Temporary

By THOMAS L. FRIEDMAN

Special to The New York Times

ASHKELON, Israel, Jan. 6 — The covert airlift of Ethiopian Jews to Israel has been halted because of the publicity given the operation, a spokesman for the Jewish Agency, a semiofficial Government body, announced today.

"The flights have stopped," said Zvi Eyal, the spokesman for the Jewish Agency, the Israeli-Jewish relief organization that has been coordinating the rescue. "The last planeload arrived Saturday night. We hope this will only be temporary. We are now looking for other airlines."

On Saturday the Belgian charter carrier Trans European Airways — which had reportedly been paid to ferry some 7,000 Ethiopian Jews to Brussels by way of the Sudan since late November — announced it was ending its part in the secret airlift.

Public Disavowals

The announcement of the halt was apparently due to publication of — and fears of repercussions from — the fact that many of the flights of Ethiopian Jews to Israel reportedly began in the Sudan, an Arab country that has no diplomatic relations with Israel. Ethiopia and the Sudan have publicly disavowed the operation. There was no independent confirmation that the airlift had been halted.

News of the airlift was reported in December in two Jewish publications in New York and Washington. Later, on Dec. 11, The New York Times published an account of the increased airlift and then other news organizations around the world published their own reports. The Israeli Government officially acknowledged the airlift for the first time last Thursday.

Thousands Still Stranded

Meanwhile, Libya announced today that it would call for an emergency Arab League meeting to discuss the Israeli airlift of Ethiopian Jews, the official Libyan press agency reported.

The reported abrupt end to the rescue effort has left 6,000 to 8,000 Ethiopian Jews still inside drought-ridden Ethiopia and at least 4,000 Ethiopian Jews stranded in refugee camps outside Ethiopia, according to Mr. Eyal.

As for the 12,000 Ethiopian Jews already in to Israel, many of them re-

Continued on Page A8, Column 1

Reuters

Secretary of State George P. Shultz arriving yesterday in Geneva.

Geneva Meeting Is an Encounter On Three Fronts

By LESLIE H. GELB

Special to The New York Times

GENEVA, Jan. 6 — The superpower meeting here on arms control is taking shape in three arenas: a public propaganda battle as a backdrop to business-like private exchanges, intertwined with throngs of journalists ready to record and judge success and failure.

In the arena of public diplomacy, Moscow is trying to fan concerns about a new arms race in space, and Washington is trying to play down the issue and expectations about the results of the meeting generally.

Polite and Ritualized

In the arena of private diplomacy, the talks that begin Monday between Secretary of State George P. Shultz and Foreign Minister Andrei A. Gromyko are expected by both sides to be polite, ritualized and largely predetermined by deliberations in Washington and Moscow. Mr. Shultz is said to hope that Mr. Gromyko will invite him to visit Moscow in a few months.

The third arena emerges from the interplay between the diplomats and the journalists from around the world who are gathered here. From grimaces, nods and cryptic remarks by diplomats, the journalists pass on what they think is happening behind the closed doors. Sometimes an American official or Soviet reporter is assigned the task of disclosing a particular piece of information.

The Administration began the latest

Continued on Page A8, Column 4

SHULTZ PROMISES A 'REASONABLE' U.S. AT ARMS MEETINGS

HE MEETS GROMYKO TODAY

Secretary Is Said to Be Given New Flexibility in Talks on Antisatellite Weapons

By BERNARD GWERTZMAN

Special to The New York Times

GENEVA, Jan. 6 — Secretary of State George P. Shultz said today that he was carrying "some very interesting and reasonable positions" to present to Foreign Minister Andrei A. Gromyko when Soviet-United States arms control talks resume here on Monday.

He did not specify, in a news conference aboard his plane on his way here, what those "positions" were. But some American officials said Mr. Shultz was given additional flexibility by President Reagan two days ago in discussing possible restraints on development of an antisatellite weapons system, something that Moscow seeks to halt.

'We Have No Illusions'

In his arrival statement this morning, Mr. Shultz said he had been sent here on "a mission for peace," but he was deliberately cautious about predicting the outcome of the first important Soviet-American arms control exchange in 13 months.

"We have no illusions that progress will be easy to achieve," he said.

Mr. Gromyko, who like Mr. Shultz was wearing a fedora and a heavy overcoat against the unusually bitter Geneva weather, arrived eight hours after Mr. Shultz.

He was restrained in his remarks, which he made in English. He repeated the Soviet Union's desire for progress in the meetings and affirmed the Soviet goal, stated again on Saturday by Konstantin U. Chernenko, the Soviet leader, to have the two days of talks here Monday and Tuesday result in an agreement to orient future negotiations toward preventing "an arms race in outer space" as well as achieving "radical reduction" of nuclear arms.

Soviet Focus on Space Arms

The purpose of these talks, which have drawn hundreds of journalists to Geneva from all over the world, is to agree on a format for future negotiations covering both nuclear arsenals and space weapons. But there has already emerged what appears to be a significant difference over how to deal with the American plan for long-range research on defensive space weapons.

Mr. Shultz is working under instructions from President Reagan not to agree to negotiations that might inhibit such research, while Mr. Chernenko and Mr. Gromyko seem to be giving priority to having future negotiations focus on "the nonmilitarization" of space, as Mr. Chernenko put it on Saturday, which would mean a ban on development programs.

Washington made clear last week that it sees such weapons, known by critics as "Star Wars," as a way of enhancing stability, while Moscow re-

Continued on Page A8, Column 5

15 Years of Talks

Charts and tables summarize the negotiations between the United States and the Soviet Union. Page A9.

Zaccaro Indictment Is to Be Announced Today, Lawyers Say

By RALPH BLUMENTHAL

The Manhattan District Attorney is to announce the indictment of John A. Zaccaro today on several misdemeanor counts involving a failed real estate deal in Queens, lawyers close to the case said yesterday.

Elkan Abramowitz, a lawyer for one of three other men reported to have been indicted along with Mr. Zaccaro, said he had been notified to surrender his client, Harold Farrell, today at the office of District Attorney Robert M. Morgenthau for booking and arraignment. At that time, he said, Mr. Farrell and the three others are to be informed of the charges.

Considering Guilty Plea

A lawyer for Mr. Zaccaro, John B. Koegel, said in an interview Saturday that Mr. Zaccaro was considering pleading guilty to one of the charges in return for the dropping of the others. Mr. Koegel declined to say which charge Mr. Zaccaro might plead guilty to, and Mr. Zaccaro would not discuss the matter.

Mr. Koegel did not repond yesterday to numerous messages left at his Manhattan apartment and law office. But other lawyers familiar with the discussions said such a plea was likely today.

Jerome Blitzer, counsel to the credit union of the Port Authority of New

Continued on Page B2, Column 5

Water That Enriched Valley Becomes a Peril in California

By ROBERT LINDSEY

Special to The New York Times

FRESNO, Calif., Jan. 2 — Farmers in the Central Valley of California are facing a cruel irony: the irrigation water that transformed a desert into the nation's most bountiful agricultural area is now threatening to make much of it worthless again.

"There's already some areas of the valley where you can't grow anything," said John Pucheu, who farms 2,300 acres near the hamlet of Tranquility, 30 miles west of here.

The reason: irrigation water has picked up salt and other chemicals from the soil, and there is no natural outlet from the valley for the tainted water. A hard layer of clay concentrates the polluted water near the surface, making the soil infertile.

'We're Facing Disaster'

"If we don't solve the problem, we're facing disaster," said Mr. Pucheu, a third generation farmer in this valley. "The way it's going, it could affect half a million acres."

The Federal Bureau of Reclamation, which built the system of canals and dams that helped turn the valley into a productive farming region, acknowledges that unless the problem is solved, vast sections of the west side of the valley now farmed by more than 12,000 growers will have to be taken out of production within a few years.

Man's efforts to drain the brackish water from the valley have been snagged in politics. One plan was put into effect, with the result that some of the poisons are now being dumped into a wildlife refuge, where they are blamed for causing thousands of birds to be born with twisted wings, misshapen hearts, warped spines and other defects.

The only other option that seems feasible in the near term, building a pipeline to the Pacific Ocean, is opposed by coastal communities.

Solution May Take 20 Years

The Bureau of Reclamation says that it is looking for ways to drain the valley but that finding a solution could take as long as 20 years and cost as much as $5 billion.

Although there has been no indication that toxins in the irrigation water pose a hazard to humans, some environmentalists have warned that, in

Continued on Page A12, Column 1

Philadelphia Is 'on the Move,' Mayor Says of His First Year

By WILLIAM ROBBINS

Special to The New York Times

PHILADELPHIA, Jan. 6 — W. Wilson Goode likes to describe Philadelphia as "a city on the move," an expression that many people here would also apply to the outgoing, perpetually busy man who has now served a year as Mayor.

For both Mayor Goode and the city he leads, it was a year of highly visible successes and few setbacks, a year in which so many people found his enthusiasm for his job infectious and in which comment from the press here was so favorable that one critic complains he is being "deified."

Such criticism as the Mayor has encountered has been muted, generally involving suggestions that his assertions were overstated and he had been too quick to compromise.

Sometimes the drama of setbacks has worked in his favor. A sequence of events last month could hardly have been improved if he had written a script himself. On a single day, Dec. 15, he emerged successful in a struggle to resolve a transit crisis and in a fight to prevent the Eagles football team from moving to the Sun Belt.

Symbolic Incidents

"There were some crises that permitted me to demonstrate leadership," he acknowledged in an interview.

There was much that was symbolic of Philadelphia and its Mayor in those incidents and in his responses.

One of the year's most highly publicized events was the opening of the Center City commuter tunnel in mid-November after decades of argument over the concept and expenditures of more than $330 million.

Amid the euphoria, few people paid attention to critics who pointed out that the new tunnel connected two rundown and long-neglected commuter-rail systems. The cost of the neglect became evident a week later after an old rail

Continued on Page A15, Column 1

The New York Times

W. Wilson Goode

Associated Press

A resident of Ashkelon, Israel, befriending an Ethiopian Jew recently arrived in that city, south of Tel Aviv.

Head of Corruption Inquiry Is Slain in El Salvador

By JAMES LeMOYNE

Special to The New York Times

SAN SALVADOR, Jan. 6 — The head of a Government commission investigating official corruption was shot to death early today, and President José Napoleón Duarte said followers of a far-right party were responsible.

Two men were killed, including one of the reported assailants, and another man was seriously wounded in what was described as a fierce shootout and car chase after the slaying.

The slain Government investigator, Pedro René Yanes, was the head of the Presidential Commission on Ethics, established last year by Mr. Duarte to look into official corruption under previous governments that were controlled by conservative parties. Government officials said Mr. Yanes had found many cases of wrongdoing.

"The cause is obviously of a political character," Mr. Duarte said this evening after attending a wake for Mr. Yanes. "This was a very important person charged with investigations of corruption in all of the country."

Although several Government officials are reported to have received death threats, Mr. Yanes is the first member of Mr. Duarte's Government to be slain. Government ministers have feared such attacks amid growing tension between the Christian Democratic Party, led by Mr. Duarte, and its conservative opponents as the Government pursues peace talks with leftist rebels and prepares for legislative elections in March.

Mr. Yanes was reportedly shot by two assailants. President Duarte did not name them, but one was tentatively identified by Government officials as Reinaldo Osorto, the mayoral candidate for the far-right National Republican Alliance in the rural town of Concepción de Oriente, where the shooting occurred.

The National Republican Alliance is

Continued on Page A5, Column 1

INSIDE

Vietnam Resistance in U.S.

Groups opposed to Communist rule in Vietnam are gaining followers among refugees in the United States, but their strength is uncertain. Page A11.

Cuomo at Midterm

The Governor has made his mark on New York State, and on the nation, as much for what he has said as for what he has done. News Analysis, page B1.

Purchasers Cite Slowdown

New industrial orders fell last month, according to purchasing managers, who paint a bleaker economic picture than other recent reports. Page D1.

2 SPECIAL SECTIONS TODAY: MEN'S FASHIONS AND HIGH-TECHNOLOGY CAREERS

"All the News That's Fit to Print"

The New York Times

Late Edition

Weather: Light rain likely today; chance of light snow tonight. Partly sunny, windy and chilly tomorrow. Temperatures: today 40-42, tonight 30-32; yesterday 35-49. Details on page 37.

VOL.CXXXIV . . . No. 46,358 NEW YORK, SUNDAY, MARCH 24, 1985

$1.60 beyond 75 miles from New York City, except on Long Island. $1.25

Associated Press

Customers standing in line yesterday outside Molitor Loan and Building Company branch in suburban Cincinnati.

46 Thrift Units Reopen in Ohio; Level of Activity Is Called Normal

By GARY KLOTT

Special to The New York Times

CINCINNATI, March 23 — Forty-six more savings and loan institutions reopened in Ohio today to a steady stream of customers who had access to their accounts for the first time since Gov. Richard F. Celeste ordered 71 state-chartered, privately insured thrift units closed March 15.

State officials said a survey of thrift units open today found brisk but not unusually heavy business. They said more money was withdrawn than deposited but the level of withdrawals was not a cause for concern.

"It was excellent — beyond belief," said Robert B. McAllister, Ohio's superintendent of savings and loans. He said there were "heavy runs" on only two of the thrift institutions, which he did not name. He said, however, that these runs did not approach the magnitude of those last week when mounting concerns over insurance covering deposits at the thrift units led to a run on deposits at several of the institutions.

Only four institutions had to borrow funds today from the Federal Reserve Bank in Cleveland to meet withdrawals.

100 Customers in Line

There were reports of lines at some institutions. The longest was reported at the Molitor Loan and Building Company branch in suburban Cincinnati, where the police watched as the doors opened at 10 A.M. to about 100 customers.

There was a line of 35 to 40 depositors, some of them chanting, "We want our money," outside the Charter Oak Savings Association branch, also in suburban Cincinnati. Both institutions experienced a run on deposits before the Governor ordered the 71 thrift units closed.

At the Charter Oak Savings Association in Columbus today, two private security guards allowed 10 customers at a time into the lobby to make withdrawals limited to $750 or less, to cash checks or to make deposits. About an hour after opening about 15 people were waiting in line outside.

"This is my only bank and I've got some bills to pay," said Jim Knoblauch, a 38-year-old toolmaker who was waiting on line to replenish his checking account.

T. B. Neighbors, 29, said she planned to withdraw some of her savings from a Columbus Charter Oak branch and "put it elsewhere, so I don't have all my eggs in one basket."

Normally Closed Saturday

In downtown Cincinnati, one small thrift institution had no customers in the lobby at midday despite a large sign in the window saying, "We're Open." At another a few blocks away, only one customer was making a transaction. At the Molitor branch near the

Continued on Page 31, Column 1

INSURANCE URGED FOR NURSING CARE

Study Says Plan Can Cut Cost of Medicaid and Medicare

By ROBERT PEAR

Special to The New York Times

WASHINGTON, March 23 — Reagan Administration officials say they plan to encourage the development of private insurance for nursing home care for the elderly to help save money for Medicaid and Medicare.

The Department of Health and Human Services commissioned a study of the subject, which concluded that there was a large potential market for such insurance.

The study also said the use of private insurance could produce substantial savings for the Government.

"Long-term care insurance could have a significant impact on Medicaid expenditures" by substituting private for public financing, it said, adding, "Significant savings would occur even if only 20 percent of the elderly purchase the insurance."

The study did not give exact figures for possible savings but said Medicaid costs for a group of elderly people ranging from 67 to 69 years old could be reduced by more than 20 percent over a 35-year period.

A separate report, by the department's National Center for Health Services Research, concluded that there was "a clear need" for private insurance to protect against the costs of nursing home care.

Medicaid, the medical assistance

Continued on Page 25, Column 1

REAGAN'S MARGIN IN HOUSE MX VOTE SEEN AS SLIPPING

2 Camps Say Odds Still Favor Missile, but Backers Now Fear Chance of Defeat

By STEVEN V. ROBERTS

Special to The New York Times

WASHINGTON, March 23 — As the House prepares to vote Tuesday on President Reagan's request for 21 new MX missiles, both sides say the Administration's once-comfortable margin is slipping.

Opponents of the huge intercontinental weapon concede that the odds still favor approval, but for the first time supporters of the MX are worrying openly that it could be defeated.

Representative Les Aspin of Wisconsin, a leading Democratic proponent of the missile, assessed the fight as "very, very close."

Speaker Sees Gains

In an interview reported by The Associated Press today, House Speaker Thomas P. O'Neill Jr. said opponents of the MX had gained ground in recent days with "ones who were wavering."

"It's an uphill battle, but it's close," Mr. O'Neill said.

Another senior Democrat who backs the missile said: "There are some very ominous signs that give me concern. I think it's going to lose." He said those signs included growing opposition to the cost of the weapon at a time of budget austerity; the united efforts of the House Democratic leadership to defeat the weapon, and a backlash among some Democrats against Republican campaign tactics.

Only a Few Undecided

Opponents of the missile say they can count on a minimum of 190 Democrats and 19 Republicans, or 209 votes. Mr. O'Neill told the A.P. that a recent count by the House leadership found 196 Democratic votes solidly against the missile. Since the House has two vacancies, 217 represents a majority if all members vote.

Only 15 to 20 members still profess genuine indecision, and they have been subject to ferocious lobbying by both sides.

"This is the most intense struggle for votes I've ever seen," said David Cohen, former president of the public affairs lobby Common Cause, who is a strategist for the MX opponents. "It's one on one, member to member."

As part of that struggle, the Administration Friday night summoned home Max M. Kampelman, the chief negotia-

Continued on Page 18, Column 1

SYRIA

JORDAN

Cairo

EGYPT

SAUDI ARABIA

SUDAN

Khartoum

ETHIOPIA

Addis Ababa

Miles 0 200

The New York Times/March 24, 1985

U.S. planes picked up Ethiopian Jews near Gedaref, the Sudan.

7 Die as Unrest Flares Up Anew In South Africa

By ALAN COWELL

Special to The New York Times

JOHANNESBURG, March 23 — The police reported today that black activists had killed five fellow blacks they suspected of being Government stooges and that two other blacks were shot and killed by a black policeman.

Five of the slayings were apparently in revenge for the police killing of 19 blacks Thursday in Langa township near the southern automotive center of Uitenhage. Many blacks in South Africa feel that blacks who work with the white authorities share responsibility for the authorities' actions.

Thus, in the vengeful mood that followed the shootings Thursday, such figures would be seen as candidates for retribution. In the violence today, the homes of black policemen were set on fire.

Three of those killed today were said by the police to be friends or relatives of the township's last remaining community councilor.

In townships near Uitenhage, the focus of recent unrest that has raised the number of deaths in the last year to almost 250 across the nation, thousands of blacks massed in the streets. Witnesses said that policemen ringed the tense areas in armored vehicles and that air force helicopters were flying

Continued on Page 17, Column 1

SUDAN LETS U.S. FLY 800 ETHIOPIA JEWS TO ISRAELI REFUGE

SECRET 3-DAY OPERATION

Evacuation of Last Refugees Was Arranged by Bush in Meeting With Nimeiry

By BERNARD GWERTZMAN

Special to The New York Times

WASHINGTON, March 23 — The United States, in a secret operation, today completed the evacuation of virtually all the Ethiopian Jews who were left in the Sudan after an Israeli-sponsored airlift was halted, Administration officials said.

The operation was directed by the Central Intelligence Agency, and involved the State Department and the Air Force, the sources said. In a three-day period, 800 people were flown by C-130 Hercules transports to Israel, the officials said.

Because of the sensitivity of the issue, the United States Government would not officially comment. Israel has also refused to discuss the matter and has imposed censorship on news dispatches related to it, saying that the lives of people involved were at risk.

Reporter in the Sudan

According to United Press International, President Reagan was asked about the matter today as he and his wife, Nancy, were greeting children involved in the Special Olympics for the disabled. Mrs. Reagan looked at him and whispered, "I don't know." He then told reporters, "No comment."

Information was gained from several officials aware of the airlift who spoke on condition that there would be no attribution to them or their agency.

The operation was first disclosed by The Los Angeles Times, whose reporter was in the Sudan. As a result of that account, people who might not otherwise have spoken were willing to provide additional information.

They said the plan had been worked out when Vice President Bush met with President Gaafar al-Nimeiry of the Sudan this month. Mr. Nimeiry agreed, as long as the Jews were not evacuated by Israeli planes.

Nimeiry Coming to the U.S.

The Sudan, which has dire economic problems, has already received nearly 400,000 refugees from the famine in Ethiopia, including 8,000 Jews.

Mr. Nimeiry has relied on American military and economic aid, even though much of the aid has been held up until the Sudan carries out needed economic changes.

It was announced today that he is scheduled to come to the United States and will see President Reagan at the White House on April 1.

"It was obviously convenient for Nimeiry to win some points on the Falashas," an official said. Ethiopian Jews are sometimes called Falashas, an Amharic word for "stranger" that they find derogatory.

State Department officials said they did not believe that Mr. Nimeiry's visit was conditional on his cooperation in the airlift. They said he had been scheduled to visit earlier this month, but the date was postponed because of

Continued on Page 15, Column 1

Koreans Hold Chinese Boat on Which 6 Died

Reuters

South Korean naval vessel towing Chinese torpedo boat toward Kunsan.

By CLYDE HABERMAN

Special to The New York Times

TOKYO, March 23 — South Korea continued tonight to hold a Chinese torpedo boat that drifted into its waters with six dead crew members, killed in what some reports described as a mutiny after some crewmen tried to defect.

The South Korean Government made no direct response to a Chinese request for the return of the naval vessel and its crew "as soon as possible."

[China and South Korea were reportedly holding talks on the return of the boat and crew through officials they maintain in Hong Kong.]

2 Reportedly in Hospital

Two crew members, reportedly shot but not critically wounded, were in a hospital in the South Korean port of Kunsan, on the Yellow Sea. A total of 10 or 11 other crewmen were also believed to have been taken to Kunsan, but their whereabouts could not be determined. Their boat was apparently offshore.

It was not clear whether any of the sailors sought political asylum in South Korea or preferred to be sent home.

South Korean officials seemed to deal cautiously with the episode, which threatened to undercut recent attempts by the two countries to pursue friendly contacts even though they have no diplomatic relations.

'A Simple Scuffle'

A statement issued tonight in Seoul by the Minister of Culture and Information, Lee Won Hong, did not mention a mutiny or any deaths.

"It was determined, based on facts so far obtained, that casualties aboard the Chinese torpedo boat were due to a simple scuffle among the crewmen and that no political reason was involved," Mr. Lee said.

Officials interviewed by telephone from Seoul declined to give details. But several foreign diplomats in South Korea described the incident as a mutiny that seemed to have begun on

Continued on Page 14, Column 1

Court Weighs Suit by Parents In Birth of an Unsought Child

By DAVID MARGOLICK

For most parents, there are few events more joyous than the arrival of a healthy, normal baby. But for Brian and Susanne O'Toole of Queens, things were not so simple.

Five years ago Mr. and Mrs. O'Toole decided that for their financial and physical health, three children were enough.

Mr. O'Toole, who was 25 years old at the time, brought home barely $200 a week as a subway car cleaner for the Metropolitan Transportation Authority. His family was already jammed into a one-bedroom apartment. And Mrs. O'Toole, who was about to undergo her third Caesarian section, had been told that any more such deliveries could endanger her life.

So, in January 1980, after the birth of her third child, she was sterilized. She said the doctors at Jamaica Hospital who performed the operation, known as a tubal ligation, had assured her that she would never become pregnant again.

Child-Raising Costs Sought

But about one year later, Mrs. O'Toole became pregnant. KellyAnne Marie O'Toole was born in November 1981, two months after her parents had filed a malpractice claim against the doctors who performed the surgery and against the hospital where it was done. What distinguishes the O'Toole case from other "wrongful pregnancy" cases is the damages they seek: the costs of raising KellyAnne until she reaches adulthood.

KellyAnne and the lawsuit that revolves around her have grown together. She is now 3 years old, a pretty strawberry blonde with bright blue eyes. And the case of O'Toole v. Greenberg et al. is before the state's highest court, which has been asked, in effect,

Continued on Page 30, Column 1

The New York Times

PATRICIA R. HARRIS DIES: Former Secretary of H.E.W. and H.U.D. in the Carter Administration died in Washington. Page 36.

INSIDE

Accord in Pan Am Strike

Pan American World Airways has reached a tentative settlement with striking ground workers after a 24-day walkout. Page 23.

Zoot Sims Dies

The saxophonist, the exemplar of "swing" as he played in the bands of Benny Goodman, Woody Herman and Stan Kenton, died at 59. Page 36.

Today's Sections

Index to Subjects

"All the News That's Fit to Print"

The New York Times

Late Edition
Weather: Mixed sun and clouds today, increasing humidity; chance of showers tonight. Fair and breezy tomorrow. Temperatures: today 70-79, tonight 43-47; yesterday 57-77. Details, page C16.

VOL.CXXXIV . . . No. 46,401 NEW YORK, MONDAY, MAY 6, 1985 — 60 cents beyond 75 miles from New York City, except on Long Island. — 30 CENTS

ASTRONAUTS STOW GEAR AS THEY HEAD FOR COAST LANDING

MISSION TERMED SUCCESS

Weight of Spacelab in Cargo Bay Is a Factor in Shifting Touchdown to Mojave

By RICHARD D. LYONS
Special to The New York Times

EDWARDS AIR FORCE BASE, Calif., May 5 — The seven astronauts aboard the space shuttle Challenger ended experiments today and stowed equipment in preparation for their scheduled landing here Monday at the end of what has been hailed as a highly successful seven-day mission.

The Challenger is due to swoop in from the South Pacific, rake Los Angeles with a sonic boom from 90,000 feet and alight on the dry lake bed of the Mojave Desert here shortly after 9 A.M. (noon, Eastern daylight time).

The landing was originally scheduled to take place at Cape Canaveral, Fla., but the hard landing of the Discovery spacecraft there last month, which damaged that shuttle's brakes, blew one of its four main tires and seriously frayed the other three, led officials of the National Aeronautics and Space Administration to switch sites as a precaution.

Reason for Switching Sites

With the Spacelab scientific laboratory nestled in its cargo bay, the Challenger is 12 tons heavier than the Discovery, and the almost endless dry lake beds here provide more flexibility in case of trouble.

NASA officials have attributed problems of the last landing, at least in part, to the fact that Discovery had to make a landing bucking a stiff crosswind, which put added strain on its braking system.

The crosswind blew the Discovery 50 feet off course in the landing, which forced Col. Karol Bobko of the Air Force, the commander of that mission, to stand on the brakes much harder than had been planned.

Loss of Information

Because of the switch from Florida to California, scientists will lose some valuable information that they had hoped to obtain from the 24 white rats that are riding aboard Challenger.

The rats were to have been unloaded,

Continued on Page B11, Column 4

Demonstration For Soviet Jews Jams Fifth Ave.

Bitburg Visit Denounced as 'Denial of the Past'

By WILLIAM R. GREER

Tens of thousands of people marched down Fifth Avenue and gathered near the United Nations yesterday in a demonstration of support for Soviet Jewry that participants said was colored by anguish over President Reagan's visit to a military cemetery in Bitburg, West Germany.

"Why not admit it, today we are wounded," said Elie Wiesel, addressing the rally in Dag Hammarskjold Plaza at 47th Street and First Avenue. Mr. Wiesel is chairman of the United States Holocaust Memorial Council.

Placards and Chants

"Is there a connection between Bitburg and this rally?" he asked. "Yes, there is. What was attempted at Bitburg — a denial of the past, a disregard of Jewish agony — the same but on a larger scale has been attempted in Russia."

The organizers of the demonstration, the 14th annual Solidarity Sunday for Soviet Jewry, said it was the largest held so far in New York to protest the Soviet Union's treatment of Jews. The police estimated that 240,000 people either marched, lined the route down Fifth Avenue from 70th to 47th Street or gathered at the plaza.

Archbishop John J. O'Connor and many elected officials, including Mayor Koch, Governor Cuomo and United States Senators Alfonse M. D'Amato and Daniel Patrick Moynihan, spoke at the rally as demonstrators waved placards bearing the photographs of Soviet Jews, often behind bars, and chanted "Let my people go."

Archbishop Addresses Rally

Herbert Kornish, the chairman of the Coalition to Free Soviet Jews, which sponsored the demonstration, said that harassment of Soviet Jews had grown since 1979, when 51,320 Jews were allowed to emigrate, and that last year only 896 were allowed to emigrate.

The Archbishop, who has been designated a cardinal by Pope John Paul II, greeted the marchers as they passed St. Patrick's Cathedral and later addressed the rally.

"To all who may know or who came to learn of my presence among you," he said, "I say to destroy Jews anywhere is to destroy Christians everywhere. Let those who would write your

Continued on Page A10, Column 1

The New York Times/Paul Hosefros
President Reagan and Chancellor Helmut Kohl at ceremony at Bitburg cemetery. Accompanying them are two former Generals, Matthew B. Ridgway, right, and Johannes Steinhoff.

REAGAN JOINS KOHL IN BRIEF MEMORIAL AT BITBURG GRAVES

VISIT STIRS WIDE PROTESTS

President Voices Regret Over Continuing Controversy — Goes to Bergen-Belsen

By BERNARD WEINRAUB
Special to The New York Times

BITBURG, West Germany, May 5 — President Reagan presided over a wreath-laying today at the base of a brick cemetery tower looming over the graves of nearly 2,000 German soldiers, including 49 SS troops.

Alluding to the controversy aroused by his visit to the cemetery, Mr. Reagan voiced regret in remarks at an American air base afterward that "old wounds have been reopened."

Texts of speeches, pages A8 and A10.

Accompanied by Chancellor Helmut Kohl, Mr. Reagan walked slowly through the narrow, hilltop cemetery, ablaze with tulips and marigolds. Mr. Reagan did not glance at the graves during his eight-minute visit. Mr. Kohl brushed tears from his eyes. Neither made a speech at the cemetery.

Hours earlier, Mr. Reagan stood before an obelisk at the site of the Bergen-Belsen concentration camp, where 50,000 victims of the Nazis are buried in mass graves under mounds of heather.

"Here they lie," Mr. Reagan said in a trembling voice. "Never to hope. Never to pray. Never to love. Never to heal. Never to laugh. Never to cry."

Merging Past and Present

Mr. Reagan's visit to Bergen-Belsen, in addition to the Kolmeshöhe Cemetery at Bitburg, was designed to merge past and present — to pay homage to the millions of victims of Nazi Germany and to honor West Germany's emergence as a powerful democracy and ally of the United States.

"We who were enemies are now friends," Mr. Reagan told about 5,000 American military personnel, their families and local German residents at the Bitburg Air Base, less than one mile from the military cemetery.

"We who were bitter adversaries are now the strongest of allies," Mr. Reagan said. "In the place of fear we have sown trust, and out of the ruins of war has blossomed an enduring peace."

Jewish demonstrators from the United States, France, Britain, West Germany, Belgium, the Netherlands, Israel and other countries protested the President's visit to Bergen-Belsen as well as the stop at Bitburg. They were joined by groups of veterans and politicians, many of them weeping.

Rabbis Refuse to Attend

Although Roman Catholic and Protestant clergymen took part in the ceremonies at the Bergen-Belsen site, German rabbis refused to attend because of the Bitburg visit.

The Israeli Ambassador to West Germany, Yitzhak Ben-Ari, came to the Bergen-Belsen ceremony — despite anguish, he said, about Mr. Reagan's visit to Bitburg. "I believe the new Germany can be trusted," he said.

White House aides have acknowledged that the Bitburg visit is probably the biggest fiasco of Mr. Reagan's Presidency. The visit, which was made at the insistence of Mr. Kohl, was overwhelmingly opposed by both houses of Congress, Jewish organizations, veterans' groups and others.

Up to the last moment, White House

Continued on Page A9, Column 1

Associated Press
Mr. Reagan pays tribute to victims of Bergen-Belsen concentration camp.

For Bitburg, Day of Anger Ends Quietly

By JAMES M. MARKHAM
Special to The New York Times

BITBURG, West Germany, May 5 — It was the scene that many had feared. At the main crossroads of this small town, policemen with plastic antiriot shields confronted an advancing crowd of Jews, many of them wearing the badge that accompanied their parents and grandparents to their deaths: a six-pointed yellow star bearing the word Jude.

The Jews came from 21 countries, but many were from France, Belgium and the Netherlands. One big blue banner hoisted in their midst read in French, "Neither hate nor forgetfulness."

Another hand-painted banner, in English, said: "Don't honor SS murderers. My brother's blood cries out to me from the ground."

'They Haven't Learned'

When the protesters reached the police line they halted, some of them only inches from the policemen. Among them was Irene Quetting, 67 years old, from Traben-Trarbach, West Germany, who said she was half-Jewish.

"If you want to know my impression about the Germans," she said, nodding toward Mötscherstrasse, where Chancellor Helmut Kohl and President Reagan would shortly pass, "they haven't learned from history."

She said she was not speaking of the policemen in green uniforms who were holding back the protesters. "No," she said, "I am talking about my generation and Kohl's, who should have learned but didn't."

The policemen were correct and polite, and clearly uncomfortable. "Personally," said a dark-haired policeman, holding his white helmet to his

Continued on Page A8, Column 5

Atlanta's Years of Progress Temper New Racial Disputes

By WILLIAM E. SCHMIDT
Special to The New York Times

ATLANTA, May 5 — In the 1950's and 60's, when the civil rights movement was challenging the old order across the South, a group of white civic leaders in Atlanta began preaching a gospel of accommodation rather than confrontation.

They took to describing Atlanta as "the city too busy to hate," and with the help of local blacks like the Rev.

Race Relations: The Changing South
Last of six articles that have appeared since March 1.

Martin Luther King Sr., they set out to dismantle the legal barriers of segregation in hotels, lunch counters, jobs, schools and government, with little of the disruption and none of the violence that occurred elsewhere in the region.

"When they were putting dogs on people and beating them up in Birmingham," said Mayor Andrew Young, who plans to seek a second term this fall, "blacks and whites in Atlanta sat down together and worked out their differences around a table."

That spirit of cooperation may have had less to with racial enlightenment than it did with an abiding pragmatism among civic leaders here who argued that racial strife was bad for business. Still, over the last two decades, this cooperation has worked some powerful truths in Atlanta.

This city of 427,000 people, which is two-thirds black, has emerged not only as the booming financial capital of the Southeast, but as a national beacon of black political and economic opportunity.

However, Atlanta is not colorblind: race continues to be a constant and frequently divisive factor in the conduct of business, government and day-to-day social intercourse. And, as in the rest of the nation, there is a large economic gap between blacks and whites.

"Over the last 20 years, we have ac-

Continued on Page B8, Column 1

Rising Brutality Complaints Raise Questions About New York Police

The following article is based on reporting by Jane Perlez and Selwyn Raab and was written by Mr. Raab.

For decades, the tough methods used against criminals by a Prohibition-era detective, Johnny Broderick, were widely sanctioned in New York City's police force. Roaming the streets of Manhattan, Detective Broderick clubbed suspected gangsters and hoodlums with a lead pipe wrapped in a newspaper.

Police officials in the late 1960's tried to end that type of brutality. In response to public complaints about pervasive police misconduct, training programs were established that emphasized sensitivity and civil rights in dealing with suspects and the public in general.

But a recent string of incidents, including purported assaults with an electric stun gun, has raised questions about overall police behavior and the effectiveness of Police Department programs to prevent misconduct. Last year, 6,698 complaints were filed against city police officers for purported mistreatment and excessive force — about 600 more than in 1983.

Sociologists and police experts say policy and personnel shifts in the city's 26,000-member Police Department may have contributed to the increase in brutality allegations.

More Inexperienced Officers

Among the chief contributing factors cited by the experts are these:

¶An influx of inexperienced officers who have been assigned mainly to high-crime precincts, where conditions can be most stressful. About half of the force — 13,000 men and women — have less than five years' experience. Last year, 58 percent of the complaints filed with the Civilian Complaint Review Board were against officers on the force for three years or less.

¶A lack of adequate programs to raise morale and provide career incentives for older officers who, according to some sociologists, may become abusive after years of job frustration.

¶A failure to give periodic psychological tests to all officers and supervisors. Although precise figures are not available, sociologists say police officers generally have higher rates of suicide, alcoholism and divorce than peo-

Continued on Page B5, Column 1

Salvador Defense Lawyer Charges Cover-Up in Slaying of U.S. Nuns

By LARRY ROHTER

A lawyer who defended a Salvadoran national guardsman convicted of murdering four American churchwomen said yesterday that he had been forced to take part in a "conspiracy" aimed at preventing higher-ranking military officers from being implicated in the case.

The lawyer, Salvador Antonio Ibarra, said that another defense lawyer had pressed him not to contradict a statement that "the possibility of a cover-up had been thoroughly investigated" and rejected. Mr. Ibarra said that declaration was "an outright lie" and added that he was specifically warned not to pursue the case on his own.

After it became clear he would not cooperate fully in the plan, Mr. Ibarra said in an interview, he was abducted by Salvadoran security forces, held prisoner at National Guard headquarters and tortured. The objective, he said, was to get him off the case, either by killing him or forcing him to flee the country.

Mr. Ibarra's remarks involved one of the most controversial aspects of the murder of the three American nuns and a lay worker, who were shot by Salvadoran security forces after being stopped at a roadblock near San Salvador International Airport in December 1980.

Human rights groups and some United States diplomats have long argued that the guardsmen were not acting on their own, but carrying out orders issued by their superiors. They have also charged that the Salvadoran Government sought to hide the involvement of those high-ranking officials.

A spokesman for the United States Embassy in El Salvador, when asked yesterday about Mr. Ibarra's remarks, declined to comment on their substance, saying he did not know specifics of the statements. Speaking of the court case, the spokesman, Donald Hamilton, said, "We believe the judicial verdict was a fair and accurate one."

Maj. Salazar Brenes, a personal ad-

Continued on Page A6, Column 4

Nonpayers Hurt Long-Distance Companies

By ERIC N. BERG

Americans are paying their long-distance telephone bills later and later. And — in what communications industry experts are calling one of the seamier effects of the extraordinary competition that has broken out in long distance — many people are not paying their bills at all.

The runup in delinquent and totally uncollectible bills has already translated into higher telephone rates for consumers, according to many industry experts.

"It's adding $1 a month to phone bills in California," reports Harry Strahl, an engineer who has studied the problem for the California Public Utility Commission.

The problem in New York is difficult to gauge, because data are not readily available. Last summer, however, the New York State Public Service Commission permitted the New York Telephone Company to disconnect the telephone service of those customers who do not pay their American Telephone and Telegraph Company long-distance bills. That is cutting down on bad debt to A.T.&T., but it has been no help to the dozens of A.T.&T. rivals doing business in the state.

A.T.&T. has a similar edge in most other states, where local Bell companies handle its billing. But A.T.&T. plans to do its own bookkeeping in the future. The effect of that change, industry experts say, is that A.T.&T. will

Continued on Page D4, Column 3

INSIDE

Labor Plan Explained

The steel industry's national approach to labor bargaining eroded because of concessions at the local level, industry leaders say. Page B11.

Sikh Leadership Is Split

Prime Minister Rajiv Gandhi's attempt to soothe relations with India's Sikhs has stalled because of factionalism among the Sikhs. Page A3.

"All the News That's Fit to Print"

The New York Times

Late Edition

Weather: Partly sunny today, southerly winds; chance of showers tonight. Chance of a shower tomorrow morning. Temperatures: today 80-85, tonight 67-69; yesterday 59-79. Details on page 45.

VOL.CXXXIV.... No. 46,448 Copyright © 1985 The New York Times NEW YORK, SATURDAY, JUNE 22, 1985 50 cents beyond 75 miles from New York City, except on Long Island. 30 CENTS

SCIENTISTS DECIDE BRAZIL SKELETON IS JOSEF MENGELE'S

INQUIRY RULES OUT A HOAX

Experts From U.S. and 2 Other Countries Say They Have 'Absolutely No Doubt'

By RALPH BLUMENTHAL

Special to The New York Times

SAO PAULO, Brazil, June 21 — American, Brazilian and West German scientists announced jointly today that a skeleton recently exhumed from a graveyard near here was unquestionably that of Dr. Josef Mengele.

A separate report by American experts concluded that the bones were those of the long-sought Nazi death-

Text of Americans' report, page 8.

camp doctor "within a reasonable scientific certainty."

Under questioning, the Americans said they had "absolutely no doubt" of their findings and ruled out any possibility of a hoax.

In Washington, Attorney General Edwin Meese 3d said the Justice Department accepted the group's conclusion, while in Los Angeles, officials of the Simon Wiesenthal Center for Holocaust Studies said they were "99 percent" satisfied that the skeleton was Dr. Menegle's. [Page 8.]

There was no immediate response from the Israeli authorities, who had said last month that they would await the forensic experts' reports before drawing a conclusion on whether or not the remains were those of Dr. Mengele.

"I came here not knowing whether it was or wasn't Josef Mengele," said Dr. John J. Fitzpatrick, acting chairman of the radiology department at Cook County Hospital in Chicago and a forensic radiologist selected as an independent expert by the Wiesenthal Center. "I go home fully convinced that it was Mengele."

Brazilians Also Emphatic

Brazilian Government authorities were equally emphatic. "It is our scientific opinion that this exhumed skeleton belongs to Josef Mengele," said Romeu Tuma, the federal police chief of São Paulo, who has headed the investigation since a burst of evidence from West Germany led here three weeks ago.

Today's announcements, accompanied by considerable scientific data, appeared to mark a formal end to the 40-year mystery of the whereabouts of Dr. Mengele, whose grisly medical experiments and selections for the gas chambers at the Auschwitz death camp made him perhaps the most hunted man in history.

As unlikely as many skeptics believed the story to be when it first be-

Continued on Page 8, Column 1

N.C.A.A. APPROVES STIFFER PENALTIES

Collegiate Body Seeks to End 'Integrity Crisis' in Sports

By GORDON S. WHITE JR.

Special to The New York Times

NEW ORLEANS, June 21 — The National Collegiate Athletic Association today overwhelmingly approved the strongest sanctions it has ever enacted against colleges and coaches who violate rules governing recruiting, amateurism, academic standards and ethics.

The sanctions, approved by N.C.A.A. member institutions at a special convention here, will take effect Sept. 1.

Excerpts from speech, page 49.

They include suspension for an athletic team for as long as two seasons if it is found guilty of major infractions twice in a five-year period.

Facing what some convention delegates have described as an "integrity crisis" in collegiate athletic programs, the representatives also agreed to suspend or dismiss any coach involved in major violations and to suspend the college's right to recruit athletes in the sport. A repeat offender would also be prohibited from awarding new athletic scholarships in the sport for two years.

The special meeting — only the fifth the N.C.A.A. has held since its founding in 1906 — was called by the association's 44-member Presidents' Commission, which was concerned about a

Continued on Page 49, Column 1

Vendors of Food Face New Limit On Street Sales

Crowding in 3 Boroughs Cited in Council Vote

By ROBERT D. McFADDEN

The New York City Council voted yesterday to widen restrictions on food peddlers in the congested streets of midtown Manhattan and to extend similar limits to crowded sections of lower Manhattan, Brooklyn and Queens.

Mayor Koch said he would sign the measure, which is aimed at reducing the crush of pushcarts selling hot dogs, ice cream, knishes, pretzels and other foods during daylight hours on some of the world's busiest sidewalks and street corners.

Merchants, theater organizations and other business interests had backed the bill, contending that congestion was becoming overwhelming in some areas. Representatives of thousands of street vendors had opposed the bill, saying it would hurt peddlers and their customers. Vendors who violate the regulations face having their merchandise confiscated by the police.

'We Can't Make a Living'

"Many of the city's vending operations will go out of business, because we can't make a living if we're allowed to work only outside the prime midtown and downtown areas," said Chris Ferencsik, president of the Big Apple Food Vendors Association.

Mr. Ferencsik, in an interview, estimated that 25 percent of the city's 3,000 licensed pushcart food vendors would be forced out of business by the new law. Ripple effects, he said, would hurt the wholesalers and processors of foods sold on the carts.

Acting without debate in an unusual Friday meeting, the City Council — which usually meets on Tuesdays or Thursdays — approved the bill by a vote of 31 to 0, with 2 abstentions. Several other minor actions were taken by the council during the afternoon session.

No Vendors at Session

Vendors groups, which have staged protests and filed lawsuits against the restrictions, were caught by surprise. They had no representatives at City Hall when the vote took place, and spokesmen later said they had not expected action before next Tuesday.

"It was very strange that they acted in such a hurry," said Mr. Ferencsik. "We were under the impression the vote was going to be next week."

A spokesman for the Council said there had been no intent to pass the bill without fair notice. The Council met yesterday because action was needed

Continued on Page 33, Column 2

Associated Press

At Beirut International Airport, a masked hijacker addressed about a thousand Shiite Moslems who approached the T.W.A. airliner to express their support yesterday during a demonstration. The hijackers and Shiite clergymen denounced the United States and insisted that Israel free the Lebanese prisoners it holds.

8 Days of Mideast Terror: The Journey of Flight 847

This is the story of the hijacking of Trans World Airlines Flight 847 up to this point, as told by those who have been freed so far. Those who spoke withheld some details, and some said they were doing so because Federal authorities had warned them that the remaining hostages could be jeopardized by their remarks.

By JOSEPH BERGER

As Trans World Airlines Flight 847 waited to take off from Athens International Airport on the hot, windless morning of Friday, June 14, few passengers gave any thought to a minor commotion that had taken place at the terminal just before boarding.

A young, slender, Arabic-speaking man named Ali Atwa had gotten into an argument with T.W.A. ticket agents because they refused to let him board. The jet, they told him, was already full with 145 passengers.

Rudely Aggressive Behavior

One of those passengers, Dr. Benjamin Harris, a 62-year-old professor of education at the University of Texas, may have missed the commotion because his attention was caught by two sharply dressed men who stuck out from the mélange of tourists, military personnel, students and religious pilgrims boarding the plane.

"They were too well-dressed," he said remembering their tan Palm Beach suits, silk shirts and Italian shoes. He had also been struck by their rudely aggressive behavior. After arriving at the last minute and buying tickets at the transfer gate, they twice pushed past him, once on the line to clear security, and once at Gate 8 while waiting for buses to the jet.

As it turned out, that minor commotion and the aggressive behavior of those well-dressed men were the only signals that Flight 847 might be a troubled one. But troubled it would be. For, once the Boeing 727 had lifted off, it was taken on a flight of terror, a drama that continues nine days later. A band of Shiite Moslems commandeered the plane, forcing it to zigzag across the Mediterranean between Beirut and Algiers on a tortuous odyssey of 8,300 miles.

The passengers were compelled at gunpoint to spend up to seven hours with their arms raised and their heads

Continued on Page 7, Column 1

1,000 SHIITES RALLY AT BEIRUT AIRPORT

Supporters of the Hijackers Chant 'Death to America'

By IHSAN A. HIJAZI

Special to The New York Times

BEIRUT, Lebanon, June 21 — Hundreds of Moslem demonstrators chanting "Death to America" and "Death to Reagan" held a mass rally at the international airport here today, where they cheered the hijackers of the T.W.A. airliner.

The march was organized by the pro-Iranian Shiite group called the Party of God, whose members were believed to have commandeered the Boeing 727 last Friday.

In some ways, it was a scene reminiscent of the Iranian hostage crisis that ended in 1981. Many of the demonstrators carried huge posters of Iran's fundamentalist Shiite leader, Ayatollah Ruhollah Khomeini.

Meanwhile, the Lebanese police said they could not confirm a report by the Christian radio, the Voice of Lebanon, that the T.W.A. passengers with Jewish-sounding surnames had been transferred by the hijackers to the Shiite city of Baalbek, 50 miles east of here. The radio said those hostages, believed to number 7 to 9, were being held by the Party of God.

Eastern Lebanon, which is predomi-

Continued on Page 4, Column 1

SHULTZ AND PERES AGREE TO OPPOSE SHIITES' DEMANDS

SEEK TO EASE TENSIONS

In First High-Level Contact of Crisis, Israel Assures U.S. of Complete Support

By BERNARD GWERTZMAN

Special to The New York Times

WASHINGTON, June 21 — As the Beirut hostage crisis entered its eighth day, Prime Minister Shimon Peres of Israel and Secretary of State George P. Shultz agreed on the importance of not yielding to the demands of the hijackers holding 40 Americans hostage in Beirut, the State Department said.

Their conversation, by telephone, was said to be the first high-level Israeli-American contact since the Athens-to-Rome T.W.A. Flight 847 was hijacked by Lebanese Shiite gunmen last Friday, with 153 passengers and crew aboard. It appeared to be part of an effort to reduce the strain in relations that has developed since the hijacking.

Reagan Sees Limit to Restraint

With no visible progress in achieving the release of the hostages, Administration officials were cautioning that the crisis could continue indefinitely if Nabih Berri, the Amal Shiite leader, who has become the central intermediary, refuses to free the Americans unconditionally.

In Dallas, President Reagan said the United States would continue to show restraint in the aftermath of recent terrorist acts, but warned that "no one" should doubt America's resolve to counter such attacks. [Page 4.]

The Administration has been seeking support from many foreign governments, particularly those with possible influence on Mr. Berri. A major effort has been concentrated on persuading President Hafez al-Assad of Syria, who is currently in the Soviet Union, to support the unconditional release of the Americans.

'Support and Admiration'

State Department officials said that on Thursday, Richard R. Burt, Assistant Secretary of State for European and Canadian Affairs, met with Oleg M. Sokolov, the No. 2 diplomat at the Soviet Embassy, to discuss possible use of Soviet influence in freeing the hostages. Soviet commentaries since the hijacking have focused on the American military movements in the region, suggesting that Washington was trying to use the crisis to intimidate Arab nations.

Mr. Shultz has said publicly and told foreign governments privately that if the Americans are freed, the Israelis would return to Lebanon the 766 detainees whose release has been the princi-

Continued on Page 4, Column 4

The Quandary for Israel

Second Thoughts on Its Own Prisoner Swap Seen as Causing Strains Over U.S. Hostages

By THOMAS L. FRIEDMAN

Special to The New York Times

News Analysis

JERUSALEM, June 21 — Israel finds itself in a quandary over how to respond in the Beirut hostage crisis, and Israeli experts on terrorism say they believe it is an indirect result of the Government's decision last month to trade 1,150 prisoners, most of them Palestinians, for 3 Israeli prisoners of war.

The experts say that by giving in to the demands of a Palestinian guerrilla leader, Ahmed Jabril, last month — a move widely viewed here as a blunder — Israel helped to create the atmosphere in which the Beirut hijacking took place.

Now, the experts argue, Israel is trying to compensate for this by refusing to concede to the hijackers' demands for the release of 766 detainees unless the United States formally appeals to the Israeli Government to, in effect, "cave in" to the demands.

Friction Between Allies

This has created a great deal of strain between Jerusalem and Washington, and officials here acknowledge that coordination between the two Governments has been inconsistent.

The result, said Zeev Schiff, the military editor of the daily newspaper Haaretz, is that the hijackers have already won a major victory: Israel and America, instead of fighting the hijackers jointly, are at odds with each other.

The connection between the Beirut hijacking and the Israeli-Palestinian prisoner swap last month is multifold, the experts say.

To begin with, said Ariel Merari, Israel's leading civilian expert on terrorism, there is the price the hijackers have demanded. This is not the first time Shiites have hijacked an airplane, he noted, but it is the first time they have made such enormous demands on Israel. The hijackers requested not

Continued on Page 5, Column 1

The New York Times/Marilynn K. Yee

Guards standing at security gate in the lobby of the State Department building yesterday after shooting.

Man Kills Mother and Himself at State Dept.

By NEIL A. LEWIS

Special to The New York Times

WASHINGTON, June 21 — A young man shot and killed his mother and himself today on the seventh floor of the State Department, about 100 feet from the office of Secretary of State George P. Shultz, officials reported.

The District of Columbia police said the man, 20-year-old Edward Steven Doster, killed his mother, Carole Doster, 44, just after noon. The two lived at different addresses in Alexandria, Va. Mrs. Doster was a secretary in the office of Edward J. Derwinski, a former Republican Congressman from Illinois who is the State Department counselor.

A senior State Department official said Mr. Doster had a history of mental illness.

Mr. Shultz was in his office at the time of the shooting, speaking by telephone with Prime Minister Shimon Peres of Israel about the 40 Americans being held hostage in Lebanon by Shiite Moslems, an official said. Mr. Derwinski was traveling in Japan.

"At no time was there a threat to the Secretary of State or other senior officials," the department spokesman, Bernard Kalb, told reporters. "This was not a terrorist incident."

Nonetheless, the shooting raised questions about security at the State Department, and a senior official said procedures were being quickly reviewed. Some changes, including searches at department entrances of such hand-carried items as purses and attaché cases, were instituted within hours of the shooting.

According to a well-placed State Department official, Mr. Doster brought an unassembled rifle into the building and put it together in a men's bathroom. The official, who asked not to be identified, said Mr. Doster was able to enter the building using a card that identified him as a family member of a State Department employee.

According to one source, a witness saw Mr. Doster assembling the gun in

Continued on Page 32, Column 2

INSIDE

Test Laser Hits Shuttle

A laser beam from Hawaii hit the shuttle Discovery in what the Pentagon called a "successful test" for the proposed antimissile shield. Page 11.

Rhode Island Reprimand

Rhode Island's Chief Justice was told by an ethics panel to step down for four months because of friendships with reputed criminals. Page 10.

Officers Reported Cleared

An admiral and a captain, relieved of command because of a purchasing scandal, were later reported cleared of blame by an inquiry. Page 32.

"All the News That's Fit to Print"

The New York Times

Late Edition

Weather: Mostly cloudy today, chance of showers; cloudy, chance of showers tonight. Chance of showers tomorrow. Temperatures: today 73-77, tonight 63-67; yesterday 61-78. Details, page B2.

VOL.CXXXIV.. No. 46,458

NEW YORK, TUESDAY, JULY 2, 1985

50 cents beyond 75 miles from New York City, except on Long Island.

30 CENTS

ISRAELIS SET TO RELEASE 300; U.S. OPENS DIPLOMATIC DRIVE TO 'ISOLATE' BEIRUT AIRPORT

HIGH COURT BARS PUBLIC TEACHERS IN CHURCH SCHOOLS

REMEDIAL CLASS AT ISSUE

Strict Separation of Religion and State Affirmed, 5 to 4, in New York City Case

By LINDA GREENHOUSE

Special to The New York Times

WASHINGTON, July 1 — The Supreme Court ruled today that public school systems may not send teachers into parochial school classrooms to provide remedial or enrichment instruction.

Such programs, the Court said, forge a "symbolic union of government and religion" that is forbidden by the Constitution.

In twin cases, decided by 5-to-4 votes on most questions, the Court struck down two programs of public aid to parochial schools.

New York Program Invalidated

One was a program administered by New York City with Federal funds earmarked for "educationally deprived" children from poor neighborhoods. The

Excerpts from opinions, page A14.

other was a state-subsidized program of remedial and enrichment classes for parochial school children in Grand Rapids, Mich.

Similar remedial programs are run by hundreds of school districts across the country, especially in urban areas. Educators said that parochial school students might have to be bused to public schools for after-hours help or the remedial services might have to be delegated to contractors, in order to comply with the Supreme Court ruling as well as with their legal responsibility to provide the services to students in both public and parochial schools. [Page A14.]

Defeat for Administration

New York City's program is the largest in the country under a $3.2 billion Federal program of remedial instruction for impoverished children, which is known as Title I of the Elementary and Secondary Education Act. The New York program serves 300,000 students, about 25,000 of them in parochial schools.

The opinions, both written by Associate Justice William J. Brennan Jr., marked the third recent Supreme Court defeat for the Reagan Administration's views on the relationship between religion and government.

In its term scheduled to end Tuesday,

Continued on Page A14, Column 3

Supreme Court Historical Society

Justice William J. Brennan Jr. wrote decisions in school cases.

New York City Weighs Tapping Hudson Water

By ALEXANDER REID

Rain was plentiful in the New York City area last month. But watershed areas upstate that supply most of the city's water were abnormally dry, and the prospect for even stricter water-conservation measures has increased, officials said yesterday.

The normal level for the city's reservoirs for this time of year is 96 percent of capacity, but with the current level at 57.6 percent, environmental officials are taking steps to pump water from the Hudson River and are considering tougher restrictions on water use in homes and businesses.

In northern New Jersey, where water rationing has been imposed on 93 communities, the situation has improved. More than 11 inches of rain have fallen since April in the watershed serving that area, pushing reservoir levels close to 80 percent. [Page B2.]

Worst Since 1960's

A spokesman for New York City's Environmental Protection Department, William Andrews, said: "We haven't been this far into a drought since the 1960's. Since then, we really never had to devise measures for something this severe."

Within the next several days, he said, the City Environmental Protection Commissioner, Joseph T. McGough Jr., and Mayor Koch will discuss what measures are to be taken to handle the drought. Among the measures likely to be considered are more severe cutbacks in water use for businesses and

Continued on Page B2, Column 5

AUSTERITY IMPOSED ON ISRAEL IN PLAN TO CURB INFLATION

Labor Federation Reacts With Call for a General Strike — Shekel Devalued 18.8%

Special to The New York Times

JERUSALEM, July 1 — After a 20-hour Cabinet meeting, the Israeli Government declared an economic emergency today and imposed sweeping austerity measures intended to break the country's 260 percent inflation.

The Histadrut, Israel's labor union federation of 1.6 million members, immediately responded by calling a nationwide general strike for Tuesday. It said the Government "has gone too far."

With 90 percent of the labor force in the Histadrut, the entire country, including harbors and airports, is expected to be shut down by the strike. Services will operate on an emergency Sabbath schedule.

Plan's Principal Elements

The key elements of the 200-point economic reform package are an immediate 18.8 percent devaluation of the shekel, making it 1,500 to the dollar; price increases in Government-subsidized products such as gasoline, which will now sell for $3.44 a gallon; the dismissal of 9,000 Government employees within 30 days; a Government spending cut of $750 million, and a Government-ordered three-month wage freeze and price freeze for most goods.

Israel's economic deterioration has its roots in a decade-long combination of mismanagement by several administrations and heavy spending on the Lebanon war and the West Bank settlements and other factors.

But this is the first time an Israeli Government has used its powers of emergency decree — which do not require parliamentary approval — to take such comprehensive economic measures.

Failure of Previous Efforts

What prompted the Government to do so were mounting indications that voluntary wage-price arrangements the national unity Cabinet had worked out with the nation's manufacturers and the Histadrut in the past year had not stemmed the economic deterioration or dampened inflation.

After having slowed for a few months, inflation was projected to hit a monthly record of 30 percent for June. Meanwhile, foreign currency reserves fell to less than $2 billion in June, well below the $3 billion regarded as a safe minimum.

Having struggled with the economy for nine months and having unsuccess-

Continued on Page D9, Column 1

NONMILITARY MOVES

Washington, Responding to Hijacking, Will Bar Lebanese Carriers

By BERNARD GWERTZMAN

Special to The New York Times

WASHINGTON, July 1 — The United States announced today that in response to the hijacking of a Trans World Airlines plane last month by Lebanese Shiite extremists, it was beginning a diplomatic campaign "to isolate" Beirut International Airport.

There was no sign that immediate military action would be taken. Reagan Administration officials said they were holding in reserve several military options in response to the hijacking, but that diplomacy would be pursued first. [Page A6.]

Meeting at White House

After a meeting at the White House of President Reagan and members of the National Security Council, a senior State Department official said Mr. Reagan had decided, as a first step, to end air service to the United States by Lebanon's two air carriers, Middle East Airlines and Trans-Mediterranean Airways, a cargo carrier.

Secretary of State George P. Shultz said tonight that "the purpose is to place off limits internationally that airport until the people of Beirut place terrorists off limits."

In an interview on the Public Broadcasting Service program "The MacNeil-Lehrer Newshour," Mr. Shultz

Continued on Page A6, Column 1

Agence France-Presse

Blake Synnestvedt after being reunited with wife, Jane. Dr. Arthur W. Toga, below left, was greeted by brother, Jim.

The New York Times/Fred R. Conrad

ACTION BY CABINET

Freeing of Rest May Be Delayed to Emphasize No Deal Was Made

By THOMAS L. FRIEDMAN

Special to The New York Times

JERUSALEM, July 1 — The Israeli Cabinet decided today to release 300 of its 735 mainly Shiite Moslem detainees over the next two days, officials here said.

Freedom for the detainees, whom Israel has been holding without charges for as long as 20 months, was the principal demand of the Lebanese Shiites who hijacked a Trans World Airlines jet June 14 and held a group of Americans hostage. The Americans were freed Sunday.

There were indications that Israel would probably extend the release of the other detainees over a longer period of days, if not longer, to drive home the point that it was not responding to the hijackers' demands.

Key Cabinet Ministers Meet

The Israeli radio said key Cabinet ministers met this afternoon and decided to free the 300 detainees "in accordance with Government policy that was set out before the June 14 T.W.A. hijacking crisis."

Cabinet sources said the closed-door vote by the inner Cabinet was unanimous. The inner Cabinet is made up of five Labor Party ministers led by Prime Minister Shimon Peres and five Likud-bloc ministers led by Foreign Minister Yitzhak Shamir.

After the 300 are turned over to representatives of the International Committee of the Red Cross in southern Lebanon in the next two days, "the Cabinet will consider the release of the other detainees given the security situation in south Lebanon," the Israeli radio reported.

No Timetable From U.S. Reported

Senior officals made it clear that Israel was not involved in any deal for the release of the 39 American hostages, and that at no time did the United States either ask Israel to free the 735 prisoners in return for the hostages or suggest a timetable under which the release of the detainees should take place.

A senior official said the Americans had only sought confirmation from Israel that it would go ahead with its plans to release the 735 men on its own schedule once the hostages were free.

Israel has already prepared a list of the 300 detainees to be released, officials here said. They are the same men who were scheduled to be freed three

Continued on Page A6, Column 3

Ex-Captives Say Gunmen Planned To Kill Military Men One by One

By JOHN TAGLIABUE

Special to The New York Times

WIESBADEN, West Germany, July 1 — The hijackers of the Trans World Airlines jet separated the American servicemen from the other passengers and intended to kill them one by one, some of the former hostages said here today.

They said the decision to kill the Navy diver Robert Dean Stethem was part of an effort to force the Shiite Amal militia to cooperate in the hijacking. Mr. Stethem was beaten, then shot to death by the gunmen in the early hours of the hijacking.

The former hostages said that Mr. Stethem and the others had been brought to the first-class section of the aircraft to be killed, and that the diver was apparently chosen at random.

"We weren't told the specific reason," said Dr. Arthur W. Toga, a 33-year-old researcher in the neurology department of the Washington University School of Medicine in St. Louis. "But he was the sacrificial lamb. They weren't getting the action they needed at the airport. It seemed to me that man was picked almost at random."

Mr. Toga and others said the hijackers decided that they needed the help of the Amal militia to assure that the hijacking would not be halted.

In interviews broadcast last week on American television during their captivity, the men who had been taken hostage declined to criticize the conditions of their imprisonment. Women who had been held and were later released were also reticent, apparently fearing that they would jeopardize the safety of those remaining.

But today, freed from confinement, they laid bare details of physical and psychiatric duress.

'They Were Going to Kill Them'

"I think they had all the military guys lined up," said Blake Synnestvedt, a former hostage from Bryn Athyn, Pa. "They had them in first class. They were going to kill them off one by one."

Mr. Synnestvedt said the killing was intended to "accelerate the process" of negotiation between the hijackers and the more moderate Amal.

"They were panicked," he said of the hijackers. "They were running up and down the aisles screaming. They were panicked, and so we were panicked."

Robert Gordon Brown, a sales executive from Stow, Mass., agreed. "Hezbollah wanted to pull it off, but they could not handle it," he said, using the Arabic name for the extremist Shiite Party of God. "So they drew in the Amal by the threats."

Most of the hostages said they did not see the killing, which occurred in the cockpit, but learned of it later. The

Continued on Page A7, Column 1

New York's Rescue: The Offstage Dramas

By MARTIN GOTTLIEB

If there was one 24-hour period during New York City's long fiscal crisis when it seemed as if bankruptcy might finally be at hand, it began on the evening of Oct. 16, 1975.

The drama was played out in evening clothes, because Gov. Hugh L. Carey, Mayor Abraham D. Beame and others were called into it from the annual Alfred E. Smith political dinner at the Waldorf-Astoria Hotel.

Before it was over, the city had gone so far as to get an order from Justice Irving Saypol in State Supreme Court — an order that was never executed — allowing it to default temporarily on payment of notes that were coming due.

Deadline Approached

But as with so much else during the long crisis, the reality was different

Back From the Brink

The Enduring Legacy of New York's Fiscal Crisis

Second of five articles.

from the public's perception, because of a quiet conversation, unreported and away from center stage.

The problem of the moment was this: By 3 P.M. on Oct. 17, the city had to come up with $449 million, to pay off bondholders and a state loan and to cover a payroll. But Albert Shanker, the president of the United Federation of Teachers, was balking at investing $149 million in teacher retirement funds in Municipal Assistance Corporation bonds, something that government officials were counting on as a key part of their money-raising efforts.

State officials alerted the White House to the prospect of a bankruptcy, and millions of New Yorkers went to sleep with the prospect of the largest governmental default in American history dangling before them.

But unknown to state officials or other negotiators, not too late into the evening Mr. Beame put in a telephone call to an old friend. It was to John J. DeLury, the head of the Uniformed Sanitationmen's Association.

"John, I need this one," the Mayor said, in the recollection of Sidney J. Frigand, who was the Mayor's press secretary.

Mr. Beame recalled recently that Mr. DeLury swore him to secrecy but

Continued on Page B4, Column 1

The New York Times/Ruby Washington

Touch-Up Work Up on the George Washington Bridge

Robert Lachman painting New York tower of George Washington Bridge yesterday; in the distance across the Hudson River is Fort Lee, N.J. The touch-up, part of regular maintenance by the Port Authority of New York and New Jersey, is expected to continue until October, the 54th birthday of the 3,500-foot-long bridge.

U.S. REMAINS WARY DESPITE SYRIAN AID

Help on the Hostages Doesn't Allay Concern Over Policy

By JUDITH MILLER

American officials say that the role of Syria's President, Hafez al-Assad, in resolving the Beirut hostage crisis has improved his image in Washington for the moment and led to hopes that better relations between the two Governments might be possible.

But it has failed to allay concern within the Reagan Administration and among moderate Arab governments about Syria's foreign policy, its support for terrorism and its close ties to the Soviet Union, according to Arab officials in the Middle East and Administration officials in Washington.

A senior State Department official said yesterday that the Administration was "highly appreciative" of Syria's help in securing the release of the 39 Americans held by Lebanese Shiites.

In a subsequent State Department briefing, however, Bernard Kalb, the department spokesman, said that despite Syria's assistance, the Administration still listed Syria as a supporter of terrorism.

Citing what he called "reliable reports," Mr. Kalb said Syria had aided "a number of terrorist organizations" by permitting them to maintain headquarters or training camps in Syria or

Continued on Page A9, Column 1

INSIDE

Blasts in Madrid and Rome

A woman was killed and 29 people were wounded in attacks at airline offices in Madrid, and 12 were hurt in a Rome airport blast. Page A3.

Shake-Up in the Kremlin

Andrei A. Gromyko becomes Soviet President and Grigory V. Romanov, once a potential top leader, is out of the Politburo. Page A10.

Happy Fifth of July

Many offices will close Friday to create a four-day Fourth of July weekend. One economist called it "a ghost day." Page D20.

"All the News That's Fit to Print"

The New York Times

Late Edition

Weather: Cloudy with a chance of rain today, northwesterly winds; cloudy tonight. Partly cloudy, cool tomorrow. Temperatures: today 50-63, tonight 45-50; yesterday 62-78. Details, page D24.

VOL.CXXXV.... No. 46,550 NEW YORK, WEDNESDAY, OCTOBER 2, 1985 · 30 cents beyond 75 miles from New York City, except on Long Island. · 30 CENTS

Associated Press

President Reagan and Margaret M. Heckler yesterday at the White House.

Heckler Agrees to Leave Cabinet For Post as Ambassador to Ireland

By GERALD M. BOYD

Special to The New York Times

WASHINGTON, Oct. 1 — President Reagan said today that Margaret M. Heckler would leave her post as Secretary of Health and Human Services and become the United States Ambassador to Ireland.

With Mrs. Heckler at his side, Mr. Reagan told reporters her new position was a reward for her "fine job." He denied reports that she was being removed because he and senior White House aides were dissatisfied with her Cabinet performance.

In an appearance in the White House press room, he and the Secretary said she had been given the choice of taking the new job or staying in her post.

Opportunity Is Discerned

Mrs. Heckler, who appeared ill at ease and nervous throughout the brief session with reporters, has complained that some members of the White House staff were campaigning against her. She accepted the ambassadorship offer less than 24 hours after it was first formally made, in a private meeting Monday with Mr. Reagan.

Mrs. Heckler previously expressed a lack of interest in the Ambassador's post. But she said today that it provided her with a new opportunity for public service and a "very exciting challenge."

The announcement ended the most troublesome personnel dispute within the Administration since the start of Mr. Reagan's second term.

White House officials and members of Congress have said that Donald T. Regan, the White House chief of staff, was trying to force out Mrs. Heckler, one of the President's two Cabinet-rank appointees who are women. Conservatives in the White House and elsewhere in the Administration have criticized Mrs. Heckler as being a weak manager and as lacking ideological commitment

Continued on Page B5, Column 1

2 LEBANON GROUPS PUT OUT WARNINGS ON RUSSIAN AIDES

Organizations Threaten to Kill Prisoners Unless Attacks on Tripoli Are Halted

By IHSAN A. HIJAZI

Special to The New York Times

BEIRUT, Lebanon, Oct. 1 — Two different organizations claimed responsibility today for the abduction of four Soviet diplomats here, and both threatened to kill them all.

In anonymous calls to Western news agencies and statements distributed to the Beirut press, the professed kidnappers said the Russians would be executed unless an offensive against the northern Lebanese port of Tripoli by leftist and Communist militias backed by Syria was halted.

One caller, claiming to speak for the group Islamic Holy War, told a news agency here that two of the hostages had already been put to death, but there was no confirmation of the report from any other source.

New Group Issues Communiqué

Later, a hitherto-unknown group called the Islamic Liberation Organization issued a communiqué with photographs of three of the Soviet hostages, and said it intended to begin executing them shortly.

The pictures showed the hostages with pistols pointed at their heads. The Russians in the photograph were not positively identified.

[In Moscow, the Soviet Union issued its first public response to the kidnappings, calling the incident a "heinous crime" carried out by "bandits" from an "arch-reactionary ultra-right-wing" organization.

[The Soviet response was being closely watched by Western diplomats to see how the Kremlin deals with the kind of terrorist attack that has become a major problem for Western governments, particularly the United States. Page A17.]

[In Washington, President Reagan responded to reporters' questions about the kidnapping with a general statement condemning such acts as "the most cowardly, the most vicious thing that takes place today because

Continued on Page A17, Column 1

ISRAELI PLANES ATTACK P.L.O. IN TUNIS, KILLING AT LEAST 30; RAID 'LEGITIMATE,' U.S. SAYS

Agence France-Presse

The ruins of P.L.O. headquarters near Tunis yesterday after bombing.

ARAFAT VISITS SITE

Air Strike Is Called Reply to Killing of 3 Israelis on Yacht in Cyprus

By FRANK J. PRIAL

Special to The New York Times

TUNIS, Oct. 1 — Israeli planes flew 1,500 miles to this North African nation today and bombed the headquarters of the Palestine Liberation Organization.

Israeli officials said the attack was in retaliation for the slaying of three Israelis in Larnaca, Cyprus, six days ago. P.L.O. officials in Cyprus denied at the time that they or any group affiliated with the P.L.O. was responsible.

A P.L.O. spokesman said 60 people were killed in the attack today, "including women and children, many of them Tunisians." The Tunisian authorities said 60 people were wounded, 25 of them severely.

The Israeli military command in Tel Aviv said it believed that 30 to 50 people had been killed and "a larger number were wounded."

A Water-Filled Crater

Late today the site of the P.L.O. headquarters was a flat space of crumbled concrete, with burned-out cars and a P.L.O. bus. In the center was an enormous water-filled crater, apparently the result of a large bomb.

Yasir Arafat, the P.L.O. chairman, who arrived here this morning after meeting with King Hassan II in Morocco over the weekend, was visiting a P.L.O. installation in northern Tunis when the Israeli jets struck his offices at Borj Cedria, 21 miles south of the city. He visited the bombed-out buildings later but made no statement.

The aircraft involved in the raid were believed to be American-built F-15's or F-16's that were refueled in the air. Witnesses differed on whether there were six planes or eight.

While Israeli officials said the raid in Tunisia was in direct response to the slayings in Cyprus, the motivation appeared to run much deeper.

Affixing a 'Return Address'

In recent months there has been a dramatic increase in Palestinian attacks on Israelis in Israel and the occupied territories. Although Israeli officials contend that many of these attacks have been directly inspired by the P.L.O., they have also noted — with some frustration — that the attacks in the West Bank and the Gaza Strip have often been carried out by individual

Continued on Page A8, Column 4

As U.S. Supports Attack, Jordan And Egypt Vow to Press for Peace

By BERNARD GWERTZMAN

Special to The New York Times

WASHINGTON, Oct. 1 — The White House said today that Israel's attack on the headquarters of the Palestine Liberation Organization in Tunisia appeared to be "a legitimate response" against "terrorist attacks."

The statement, which seemed intended to justify the attack, put the United States squarely on the side of Israel in the face of a wave of protests from Arab governments, including those friendly to Washington, such as Tunisia, Egypt, Saudi Arabia and Jordan. Washington insisted, however, that it had not been consulted by the Israelis or told in advance of the attack by American-made jet fighters.

'Criminal Act,' Egypt Says

President Hosni Mubarak of Egypt and King Hussein of Jordan both condemned the attack, but at the same time vowed to continue their efforts to revive the peace process. The Egyptian Government, calling the raid "a criminal act," said it had suspended talks with Israel on the fate of Taba, a beachfront sliver of land in Sinai that has been in dispute for years. The dispute was believed to be close to resolution.

At the United Nations, Tunesia's Foreign Minster, Beji Caid Essebsi, called the raid an act of "state terrorism" intended to sabotage the Middle East peace process. [Page A10.]

In New York, Secretary of State George P. Shultz, at a luncheon with Persian Gulf Foreign Ministers, heard complaints from the Arabs about the Israeli raid.

'We Need to Be Clear'

Mr. Shultz, in a statement that notably did not include any justification for the Israeli attack, said that he was not certain what had happened but that "we need to be clear in our opposition to the acts of violence from whatever quarter they come, and without respect to the presumed rationale for them."

There seemed to be a discrepancy between the White House response and Mr. Shultz's more general condemnation of violence from all sides. But State Department officials said his comments were designed to assure the

Continued on Page A9, Column 1

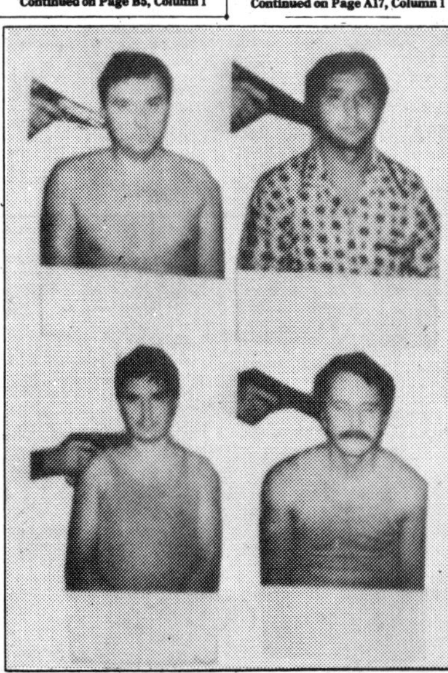

Reuters

A series of photographs delivered to a Western news agency yesterday in Beirut is said to show kidnapped Russians with pistols being held to their heads. They were identified, clockwise from top left, as Dr. Nicolai Virsky, Arkady Katakov, Valery Mirkov and Oleg Spirin.

Anger Builds As L.I. Waits For Its Power

By DIRK JOHNSON

Special to The New York Times

HAMPTON BAYS, L.I., Oct. 1 — "How are you?" asked the store clerk.

"Don't ask," snapped the customer, "or I'm liable to tell you."

After five days without hot water or electricity, pleasantries can be a bit strained. Any sense of adventure has passed, replaced by a yearning for hot showers and home-cooked meals.

Let there be light, sounds the plea. The powerless of Long Island are losing their patience.

"We are not in a good mood," said Sophie Engelberecht of Amityville. "People are starting to get testy."

In a daylong drive through the towns along the Montauk Highway on Suffolk County's South Shore, the frustrations wrought by Gloria could be sensed everywhere. On Long Island, 185,000 homes and businesses were without power today. In Connecticut, 81,000 customers still lacked power, the utilities said.

From Amityville to the Hamptons, residents stepped wearily into stores ...nd service stations in a search for ...rgency provisions — especially ...es and batteries.

... they were greeted with signs ...laimed shortages. "No ice — ..." read the sign at a 7-Eleven ...mityville. "No electricity," ... at a motel in Bay Shore. ...ead a sign at a service sta... ...hes.

...ndenhurst, a number of

...n Page B2, Column 1

Ex-C.I.A. Man Reportedly Sought in Spy Case

By STEPHEN ENGELBERG

Special to The New York Times

WASHINGTON, Oct. 1 — The Federal authorities are searching for a former Central Intelligence Agency officer who has been identified by a Soviet defector as a double agent, Administration officials said today.

The officials identified the former officer as Edward L. Howard, who, they said, had held an "operational" post with the agency.

They would not say in what country Mr. Howard had served, although an intelligence source said he had access to "significant" information that could have been damaging if provided to the Soviet Union.

According to one intelligence source, Mr. Howard worked for the agency's clandestine service under the Deputy Director for Operations.

The official said Mr. Howard was believed to have fled the country.

While it has been revealed that some former C.I.A. officers have sold classified agency documents to Soviet agents, officials said there was no record that an officer of Mr. Howard's status had been found to have worked for Moscow on a continuing basis.

The officials said Mr. Howard left the C.I.A. about two and a half years ago for a job with the Legislative Finance Committee of the New Mexico Legislature.

Philip Baca, director of the finance committee, said Mr. Howard resigned from his job effective Sept. 22 for "personal reasons." Mr. Baca would not discuss the case, but said he had been interviewed by "Federal officials" who have assured him that their investigation does not concern Mr. Howard's work for the Legislature.

Administration officials have said

Continued on Page A8, Column 5

Nigeria at 25: Misspent Past and Somber Prospects

By EDWARD A. GARGAN

Special to The New York Times

LAGOS, Nigeria, Oct. 1 — Twenty-five years ago the Oba, or tribal chief, of Lagos paid $2,800 to rainmakers to insure that a sudden downpour would not spoil the ceremony in which the British flag would be lowered for the last time and the green-and-white banner of the new country raised in independence.

Today, as the country's latest military ruler stood at attention watching precision marching by army and navy units, smartly turned out in new dress uniforms in Tafawa Balewa Stadium downtown, it poured. The ceremony was to observe the 25th anniversary of independence.

"In these economic hard times, we can't afford such things," said a newly appointed Government official squeezed under a canopy, a frail refuge from the sheets of warm rain that lashed the heavy concrete stadium.

Indeed, after two civilian Governments and six military coups — the last of which occurred in August — Nigeria, like much of Africa, has fallen on hard times. The promise of independence that surged across Africa a quarter of a century ago, a promise of economic opportunity, universal education and political freedom, has gone largely unfulfilled.

In a television address at 7 o'clock this morning, Nigeria's military leader, Maj. Gen. Ibrahim Babangida, painted the bleakest of portraits of this country's course since independence. It has been one of "social upheaval, political instability, religious intolerance and economic hardship," he said.

Then, he grimly announced a 15-month state of economic emergency for the country, a ban on imports of rice and corn and an end to the practice of

Continued on Page A6, Column 1

INSIDE

Attack on U.S. Copter

The Pentagon said a Czechoslovak military jet opened fire Saturday on an American Army helicopter on the West Germany border. Page A3.

Tax Amnesty in New York

Those who have evaded New York state or city taxes will be able to pay up and avoid penalties under a three-month amnesty program. Page B1.

A Ruling on Dr. Gross

A judge said the State Health Department could not prosecute Elliot M. Gross, the city's Medical Examiner, on charges of misconduct. Page B1.

Herbert Mitgang

E. B. WHITE IS DEAD: The essayist and stylist died yesterday at his home in North Brooklin, Me. He was 86 years old. Page B8.

"All the News That's Fit to Print"

The New York Times

Late Edition
Weather: Chance of morning showers today, sunny and cool this afternoon; clear tonight. Mostly sunny tomorrow. Temperatures: today 63-67, tonight 45-49; yesterday 60-78. Details, page C31.

VOL.CXXXV . . . . No. 46,559 | NEW YORK, FRIDAY, OCTOBER 11, 1985 | 50 cents beyond 75 miles from New York City, except on Long Island. | 30 CENTS

U.S. INTERCEPTS JET CARRYING HIJACKERS; FIGHTERS DIVERT IT TO NATO BASE IN ITALY; GUNMEN FACE TRIAL IN SLAYING OF HOSTAGE

OFFICIALS SAY C.I.A. DID NOT TELL F.B.I. OF SPY CASE MOVES

Court Papers Assert Suspect Told Colleagues He Might Give Secrets to Soviet

The following article is based on reporting by Stephen Engelberg and Joel Brinkley and was written by Mr. Brinkley.

Special to The New York Times

WASHINGTON, Oct. 10 — The Central Intelligence Agency failed to notify the Federal Bureau of Investigation after it learned more than a year ago that Edward L. Howard was considering becoming a Soviet spy, Government officials said today.

According to court records, Mr. Howard told two agency employees in September 1984 that he was thinking of disclosing classified information to the Soviet Union.

Law Calls For Reporting

The bureau has sole responsibility for domestic espionage investigations and, under Federal law, the intelligence agency and all other Government agencies are supposed to report suspected espionage to the F.B.I. It is illegal for the C.I.A. or any other Federal agency to carry out surveillance or other actions within the United States to stop potential spies.

Mr. Howard, 33 years old, a former intelligence agency officer who is now a fugitive, has been charged with espionage, accused of giving Soviet officials details of American intelligence operations in Moscow. Federal officials have called the disclosures serious and damaging.

Soviet Defector Was the Key

Federal officials said the C.I.A. told the F.B.I. nothing about Mr. Howard until after the bureau began an investigation this fall based on information from a Soviet defector, Vitaly Yurchenko, who had been a senior official of the K.G.B., the Soviet intelligence agency.

The bureau began surveillance of Mr. Howard last month, but he slipped out of his home at night and is believed to have fled the country.

Senator Patrick J. Leahy, the Vermont Democrat who is vice chairman of the Select Committee on Intelligence, said today: "If the C.I.A. did not give the F.B.I. adequate information

Continued on Page B8, Column 4

The New York Times/Oct. 11, 1985

Plane with four hijackers aboard took off from Egypt and landed at NATO airbase near Catania.

PANEL ON MILITARY TO SEEK OVERHAUL

Study Leader Cites Problems With Weapons and Delays

By BILL KELLER

Special to The New York Times

WASHINGTON, Oct. 10 — A Presidential commission has concluded that "fundamental" changes should be made in the organization of the Pentagon to correct weapon problems involving poor quality, high prices and long delays in purchasing, the panel's chairman said today.

In his first extensive public comments since he was named to head the commission in June, David R. Packard said that management reforms and new codes of conduct would not be enough to repair a system he described as "worse than it was 15 years ago."

"I think we see at this time that some structural changes are necessary," Mr. Packard said. He added that while the Reagan Administration's military buildup had improved the strength and morale of the nation's military, "I think the general conclusion is we should have gotten more for our money." The commission is to send detailed recommendations to President Reagan early next year.

Mr. Packard, a former Deputy Secretary of Defense, is the latest in a

Continued on Page A7, Column 1

P.L.O. Unit Says Ship's Hijackers Intended to Infiltrate Port in Israel

By THOMAS L. FRIEDMAN

Special to The New York Times

JERUSALEM, Oct. 10 — The four Palestinians aboard the Achille Lauro intended to stay aboard as passengers until the cruise liner reached Ashdod, Israel, and then planned either to shoot up the harbor or take Israelis hostage, according to Israeli, Palestinian and other Arab informants. The Israelis were to be held to bargain for the release of 50 Palestinians held in Israeli jails.

The leader of the faction that ordered the operation, Mohammed Abbas, also known as Abul Abbas, is a close associate of Yasir Arafat, the chairman of the Palestine Liberation Organization, and was reportedly sent by Mr. Arafat to deal with the hijackers after their original plan to infiltrate Israel at Ashdod had gone awry.

Crew Discovered Arms Cache

According to the informants, the four members of the group aborted their plans and seized the ship when their weapons were discovered by the crew after the Achille Lauro had left Alexandria on Monday. The informants say the original plan and the hijacking were part of a bungled attempt to exact revenge for Israel's raid last week on the P.L.O. headquarters near Tunis.

When relations between the P.L.O. and Italy seemed jeopardized by the seizure of the ship and an American passenger was killed by the apparently panicked hijackers, Mr. Arafat and Abul Abbas ordered the hijackers to return to Port Said and surrender.

This picture was pieced together from information provided by Israeli Foreign Ministry and military officials, Arab analysts in Beirut and a statement issued today in Nicosia, Cyprus, by a spokesman of Abul Abbas's faction in the Palestine Liberation Front, one of the guerrilla groups in the Palestine Liberation Organization.

A copy of the statement was delivered to Reuters in Nicosia and virtually all its main points have been confirmed by Israeli or Arab sources.

The statement, which apologized to the cruise passengers for the hijacking, was believed to be the first time that a Palestinian guerrilla group has expressed regret for an attack. It was apparently occasioned by widespread condemnation of the incident in Italy and in the Arab world.

Retaliation Was Aim

According to Arab and Palestinian sources in Beirut and Nicosia, the gunmen had planned the assault on Ashdod in retaliation for the Israeli attack on the P.L.O. headquarters in Tunisia, in which about 60 people were killed. The message to Israel was to have been: "If you can reach out 1,500 miles and strike at us, we can reach out 1,500 miles and strike back at you."

Israeli merchant marine and Government sources say Israel has been on the lookout for seaborne attempts at infiltration. The sources noted that Israeli naval vessels had been observed and photographed by unidentified men when they docked at Western European ports. Now that overland routes into Israel — from Lebanon, Jordan

Continued on Page A14, Column 1

U.S. Reacts: 'About Time'

After Years of Rage, A Signal to Terrorists

By BERNARD WEINRAUB

Special to The New York Times

News Analysis

WASHINGTON, Oct. 10 — In the nearly six years since Iranian revolutionaries seized the American Embassy in Teheran and provoked a crisis that undid the Carter Administration, the United States has struggled in vain to cope with Middle East terrorism and attacks against this country.

Tonight, it reacted — successfully apparently — after years of futile rage.

"This will send some signal to those who will terrorize and commit violence that they're not going to get away," said the Senate Majority Leader, Bob Dole of Kansas.

What was so unexpected this evening in a capital inured to hard-line denouncements of terrorists and no follow-up, was the swift reaction of the Reagan Administration to the latest bout with terrorism in which an elderly wheelchair-bound tourist from New York was apparently slain by Palestinians.

The Fear of Derision

Behind President Reagan's sending American aircraft to intercept a plane carrying the hijackers was a set of factors, prime among them the fear that the nation was looking like a "pitiful giant" — the term of derision used during the Carter Administration — making threatening growls but unable to stamp out a few terrorists.

Even today, as plans reached fruition for the move by the United States jets, Mr. Reagan voiced the same type of frustration that he felt four months ago when an American Navy diver was beaten to death aboard a jetliner and American passengers seized and held in Beirut for 17 days.

'You Swallow Your Gorge'

"You want to say retaliate when this is done, get even," Mr. Reagan said, "but then what do you say when you find out that you're not quite sure that a retaliation would hit the people who were responsible for the terror and that crime, and you might be killing innocent people.

"So you swallow your gorge and you don't do it."

Tonight the Administration, collectively, refused to swallow its gorge.

Most members of Congress had no official word of the United States action and heard the first accounts of the in-

Continued on Page A11, Column 4

FLOWN FROM CAIRO

4 in Custody in Sicily — Egypt Said to Refuse to Prosecute Case

By BERNARD GWERTZMAN

Special to The New York Times

WASHINGTON, Oct. 10 — An Egyptian plane carrying the hijackers of an Italian cruise ship was intercepted tonight by United States Navy F-14 fighter jets and forced to land in Italy where Italian authorities took them into custody, the White House announced.

In a late evening news conference, Larry Speakes, the White House spokesman, said President Reagan had ordered the dramatic military action after learning that Egypt had turned down repeated American pleas to prosecute the four gunmen, who apparently killed an elderly American tourist aboard the cruise ship, and was flying them to freedom.

No Shots Fired

The United States intends to seek the extradition of the hijackers from Italy, Mr. Speakes said. The extradition request was apparently meant to underscore the Administration's determination to prosecute terrorists in case the Italian legal system fails to do so.

Mr. Speakes said that the Egyptian plane, a commercial 737 airliner with armed Egyptian security men aboard, was intercepted by the F-14's from the aircraft carrier Saratoga north of Egypt in international waters. The F-14's "diverted" the plane to a joint Italian-NATO base at Sigonella in Sicily.

The incident occurred without the American planes having to fire a shot, he said.

Praise for Italians

Mr. Speakes said that the Egyptian aircraft had been headed for Tunisia but that the Tunisian Government had refused to grant it landing rights. For that, he said, the United States was grateful.

After the Egyptian plane was on the ground for several hours, Italian authorities agreed to take the four hijackers into custody, Mr. Speakes said. The Egyptian plane was flying back to Egypt, he added.

Mr. Speakes said that "the terrorists aboard were taken into custody by Italian authorities."

"We have been assured by the Government of Italy that the terrorists will

Continued on Page A10, Column 4

Orson Welles Is Dead at 70; Innovator of Film and Stage

United Press International

Orson Welles

Orson Welles, the Hollywood "boy wonder" who created the film classic "Citizen Kane," scared tens of thousands of Americans with a realistic radio report of a Martian invasion of New Jersey and changed the face of film and theater with his daring new ideas, died yesterday in Los Angeles, apparently of a heart attack. He was 70 years old and lived in Las Vegas, Nev.

An assistant coroner in Los Angeles, Donald Messerle, said Welles's death "appears to be natural in origin." He had been under treatment for diabetes as well as a heart ailment, his physician reported. Welles's body was found by his chauffeur.

An Unorthodox Style

Despite the feeling of many that his career — which evoked almost constant controversy over its 50 years — was one of largely unfulfilled promise, Welles eventually won the respect of his colleagues. He received the Lifetime Achievement Award of the American Film Institute in 1975, and last year the Directors Guild of America gave him its highest honor, the D. W. Griffith Award.

His unorthodox casting and staging for the theater gave new meaning to the classics and to contemporary works. As the "Wonder Boy" of Broadway in the 1930's, he set the stage on its ear with a "Julius Caesar" set in Fascist Italy, an all-black "Macbeth" and his presentation of Marc Blitzstein's "Cradle Will Rock." His Mercury Theater of the Air set new standards for radio drama, and in one performance panicked thousands across the nation.

In film, his innovations in deep-focus technology and his use of theater esthetics — long takes without close-ups, making the viewer's eye search the screen as if it were a stage — created a new vocabulary for the cinema.

By age 24, he was already being described by the press as a has-been — a cliché that would dog him all his life. But at that very moment Welles was creating "Citizen Kane," generally considered one of the best motion pictures ever made. This scenario was re-

Continued on Page B6, Column 1

INSIDE

40 Salvador Soldiers Killed

A leftist rebel unit killed at least 40 Salvadoran soldiers and wounded 68 in a raid on the main army training base near La Unión. Page A3.

Yul Brynner Is Dead

The actor and director, the quintessential Siamese monarch in "The King and I," died in New York at the age of 65. Page B7.

Dodgers Go 2 Games Up

The Dodgers beat the Cardinals, 8-2, in Los Angeles and lead by 2-0, in the National League playoff, which shifts to St. Louis tomorrow. Page A29.

Hostage's Death: 'A Shot to Forehead'

By E. J. DIONNE Jr.

Special to The New York Times

PORT SAID, Egypt, Oct. 10 — Passengers from the hijacked Italian cruise liner were quoted today as describing how the terrorists had dragged an elderly American tourist from his wheelchair and shot him in cold blood.

The most vivid account, based on interviews with some of the more than 400 people held hostage aboard the Achille Lauro, came from the Italian Ambassador to Egypt, Giovanni Migliudo. The Ambassador told reporters that he had put together his account of the killing after six hours of interviews.

He said the killing of the tourist, Leon Klinghoffer, had taken place on Tuesday when the ship was near Tartus, Syria.

Answer 'Slow in Coming'

"The hijackers had asked to be put in contact with the Italian and U.S. Ambassadors in Damascus to demand the liberation of 50 Palestinians held in Israel," the Italian news agency, ANSA, quoted the Ambassador as saying. "But the answer was slow in coming and to exercise further pressure, the hijackers decided to kill a first hostage."

Mr. Migliudo said that all the American and British passengers on the ship were forced to lie on the deck.

"The hijackers pushed him in his chair and dragged him to the side of the boat where — in cold blood — they fired a shot to the forehead. Then the body was dumped into the sea, together with the wheelchair," the Ambassador said.

The Ambassador's story was one of many that emerged today as the ship, the Achille Lauro, lay under a searing

Continued on Page A13, Column 1

Agence France-Presse

Marilyn Klinghoffer, whose husband, Leon, was slain, being escorted off ship in Port Said. A family friend, Neil Kantor of Metuchen, N.J., is at left.

"All the News That's Fit to Print"

The New York Times

National Edition
Midwest, variable cloudiness. South, showers scattered from Louisiana to southern Georgia. West and Southwest, valley fog. New York, mostly sunny. Details on page 7.

VOL.CXXXV.... No. 46,637 NEW YORK, SATURDAY, DECEMBER 28, 1985 50 CENTS

AIRPORT TERRORISTS KILL 12 AND WOUND 114 IN ROME AND VIENNA RAIDS ON ISRAELI LINE

REAGAN TO TRADE TELEVISION TALKS WITH GORBACHEV

New Year's Day Greetings Are to Be Broadcast at Same Time in Both Nations

By GERALD M. BOYD
Special to The New York Times

LOS ANGELES, Dec. 27 — President Reagan and Mikhail S. Gorbachev have agreed to exchange videotaped New Year's Day greetings that will be made available for broadcast in the United States and the Soviet Union, the White House announced today.

The announcement said the exchanges would give Mr. Reagan his first chance to talk to the Soviet people directly on television and would give the Soviet leader the same chance to speak to the American people.

The announcement came as Mr. Gorbachev, in Moscow, offered a cautiously upbeat assessment of relations between the Soviet Union and the United States, saying points of "potential convergence" had emerged in arms control talks. [Page 3.]

'Barbaric Methods' Assailed

Shortly before the announcement, Mr. Reagan, who flew here today to begin a weeklong vacation, issued his latest statement condemning the Soviet intervention in Afghanistan.

The statement, noting the sixth anniversary of the intervention, accused the Russians and their surrogates of resorting "to barbaric methods of waging war" to try to crush a liberation effort in Afghanistan. Mr. Reagan said the United States stood "squarely on the side of the people of Afghanistan."

The videotape exchange will achieve a longtime Administration goal of having Mr. Reagan talk on Soviet television.

Three to Five Minutes Long

The American networks have not said they would carry the Soviet leader's remarks, but White House officials expressed confidence that they would.

The speeches, both of which are to be broadcast on Wednesday, are to be three to five minutes long and will contain New Year's greetings, the officials

Continued on Page 3, Column 5

Further Growth In the Economy Forecast for '86

But Inflation and Jobless Rate Worry Analysts

By ROBERT D. HERSHEY Jr.
Special to The New York Times

WASHINGTON, Dec. 27 — The United States economy seems headed for a fourth consecutive year of expansion in 1986, but its course will be marred by gradually rising inflation and stubbornly high unemployment, according to a consensus of business and academic forecasters.

The possibility of a recession, which at various times in the last year has seemed just over the horizon, has receded and is no longer regarded as a visible threat.

One important reason is the roaring bull market in stocks and bonds. By making investors richer, it has raised both confidence and the outlook for consumer spending, which accounts for two-thirds of the economy.

'Rather Sluggish Fashion'

"The prospects for the economy in 1986 are quite good," said A. Gilbert Heebner, chief economist for the Philadelphia National Bank, in a prediction that typifies current professional thinking. "It's going to seem like more of the same, with the economy growing but in a rather sluggish fashion."

The Reagan Administration, for its part, is believed to have tentatively adopted a 4 percent growth forecast for next year, somewhat more than most private analysts.

To be sure, few economists or politicians are satisfied with the current rate of American growth, less than 3 percent for 1985 following 6.6 percent in 1984. That has been barely enough to keep unemployment from rising and it has left industry with large amounts of idle productive capacity.

Moreover, agriculture and parts of the oil, real estate and banking industries are in disarray in spite of an expansion that this month reached its third anniversary. Weak farm and crude oil prices, as well as a glut of unrented office space in some cities, could cause more problems for banks in 1986.

Yet most economists predict solid

Continued on Page 19, Column 4

VICTIMS: Bodies bearing tags affixed by police on the floor at Leonardo da Vinci Airport near Rome. Reuters

4 ATTACKERS KILLED

Gunmen Fire Into Crowds and Throw Grenades at El Al Counters

By JOHN TAGLIABUE
Special to The New York Times

ROME, Dec. 27 — Terrorists hurled grenades and fired submachine guns at crowds of holiday travelers at airports in Rome and Vienna today in attacks on check-in counters of El Al Israel Airlines.

The authorities said the gunmen had killed at least 12 people, including two Americans, and wounded 114 in the two attacks. Four terrorists were killed, and three others were wounded and captured.

While El Al appeared to be a target in both attacks, the authorities said the terrorists in Rome had also thrown grenades and fired indiscriminately with Soviet-made assault rifles into crowds of New York-bound passengers checking in at Pan American World Airways and Trans World Airlines.

Terrorists Not Identified

The assailants, who were not immediately identified, left the two airline terminals strewn with bloodied and torn bodies, luggage, overturned furniture and broken glass.

Israeli Government officials asserted that the Palestine Liberation Organization might be responsible, but P.L.O. officials here and in Tunis denied any role in the apparently coordinated attacks.

Witnesses at the airport in Vienna said panic broke out as the explosions and firing began, with passengers and airport staff throwing themselves to the ground and crawling desperately for cover. [Page 4.]

Gunmen Jumped and Shrieked

Similar accounts were given in Rome, where survivors described chaos amid thundering explosions and raking bursts of gunfire unleashed by young masked men in blue jeans who jumped up and down and shrieked as their victims fell dead or wounded and bystanders screamed and dived for cover.

"It was an inferno — they started throwing hand grenades and firing with submachines guns," said one witness who was wounded in Rome, Dora Silvestri. "We all threw ourselves to the ground. Blood spread over the floor. I fell on the body of a girl, and a grenade splinter hit me in the face."

The United States said those who carried out the attacks were "beyond the pale of civilization" and must be brought to justice. Page 5.

The authorities said seven terrorists were apparently involved — four in the attack in Rome, which began shortly after 9 A.M. (3 A.M. New York Time) and three others in the attack in Vienna, which started a few minutes later.

Security Had Been Increased

In Rome, three terrorists were slain, and one was seized after being wounded in a gun battle with the police and plainclothes Israeli security men in the terminal. Security had been increased there after recent hijackings and official warnings that airports might be attacked during the Christmas holidays.

A total of 13 people were killed in Rome, including the three terrorists, and 70 wounded. At Schwechat Airport in Vienna, 3 were killed, including one gunman, and 47 wounded, one of them critically.

Among the dead were two Americans, Natasha Simpson, the 11-year-old daughter of an Associated Press editor in Rome, and John Buonocore, 20, described only as "with the U.S. military." An Israeli security agent

Continued on Page 4, Column 5

3 Miami Policemen Charged With Murder of Drug Dealers

By United Press International

MIAMI, Dec. 27 — Three members of the Miami police force were charged today with first-degree murder in the drownings of three men thought to have been dealing in drugs, the latest in a series of scandals to hit the beleaguered department.

The drownings occurred in the course of what the authorities say was a police theft of more than 300 kilograms of cocaine. One other officer and two civilians were also arrested in the case.

"It is alleged that on July 28 six individuals dressed as police officers entered Jones Boat Yard," said a written statement from the Metro-Dade County Police, which made the arrest of the City of Miami officers.

"The individuals approached six other men guarding 300 to 400 kilos of cocaine," the statement said. "The approach caused the six guards to jump into the Miami River, causing the death of three of them."

Police spokesmen said they did not know what happened to the cocaine. That much uncut cocaine, 650 to 900 pounds, could be worth as much as $20 million on the street.

The charges followed the arrest Thursday of two former officers who were charged with stealing 150 pounds of cocaine from a 1,000-pound seizure taken last May.

In that case, bond was set today at $500,000 for Armando Lopez, 24 years old, and $250,000 for Felix A. Beruvides, 28. Neither man met bond.

Still pending is a state attorney's investigation of the theft last summer of $150,000 from a safe in the Miami Police headquarters building.

The officers charged today with first-degree murder and various cocaine trafficking charges were Armando Estrada, 26; Roman Rodriguez, 29; and Armando Garcia, 23.

Charged with armed cocaine trafficking and aggravated battery was Arturo de La Vega, 26, another Miami policeman.

Fifth Officer Is Sought

The civilians arrested were Pedro Baez, 43, charged with second-degree murder, and Ruben Ortiz, 32, charged with cocaine trafficking.

The police said they were also looking for Osvaldo Coella, who resigned from the force earlier this year. He faces cocaine and aggravated battery charges.

The four police officers arrested today were relieved of duty Dec. 10 pending the outcome of the investigation. A fifth patrolman, Rodolfo Arias, was also relieved of duty at that time. There was speculation that he was involved in plea bargaining.

According to earlier reports, Pedro Martinez, Adolfo Lopez Yanes, Juan Garcia and three other men were unloading cocaine from a 40-foot boat that docked at the boatyard a few days earlier.

Cleve Jones, the owner of the Miami

Continued on Page 7, Column 5

INSIDE

California Pact Rejected

An eight-week supermarket strike in California continued as meat cutters rejected a contract, while teamsters approved their pact. Page 8.

People Express Expands

People Express said it would buy Britt Airways, the nation's third largest commuter airline with hubs in Chicago and St. Louis. Page 17.

ARREST: A suspected terrorist being taken into custody after the attack on the Rome airport. Agence France-Presse

Israel, Blaming P.L.O., Issues a Warning

By THOMAS L. FRIEDMAN
Special to The New York Times

JERUSALEM, Dec. 27 — Although the Palestine Liberation Organization denied involvement in the attacks in Rome and Vienna, Israeli officials blamed the guerrilla group today and made it clear that Israel would respond at the appropriate time and place.

"Israel is shocked and outraged by these two new acts of senseless terror against innocent civilians," a Foreign Ministry statement said.

"The terrorist attacks come against a background of declarations by the head of the P.L.O., and those Arab states that support this organization, that these terrorists will cease terrorist operations outside of Israel. Israel will continue its struggle against terrorism in every place and at any time it sees fit."

Syrian Missiles in Lebanon

Meanwhile, Israeli analysts said Israel's ability to retaliate for the attacks had been limited by Syria's decision to move mobile surface-to-air missiles into Lebanon.

In the past, Israel has often retaliated for terrorist attacks abroad by bombing Palestinian guerrilla bases in Lebanon, regarding these as convenient "return addresses."

To do so now, however, Israeli jets would have to penetrate the new curtain of surface-to-air missiles Syria has drawn over the Bekaa region in Lebanon, which could lead to an all-out war with Syria, the analysts said.

Since Israel already destroyed the main P.L.O. compound in Tunisia last October, that too is no longer an option for retaliation. The analysts said new P.L.O. offices in Baghdad would not be easy to reach and were widely dispersed. This would seem to leave as the only option for retaliation a more surgical strike against specific individuals, the analysts said.

A Political Statement

To appreciate the full Israeli quandary, officials said, it must be understood that the Syrian decision to deploy the SAM-6 and SAM-8 mobile batteries a few miles inside Lebanon, for the second time in a month, was as much a political statement as a strategic military maneuver.

It was apparently designed, Israeli officials say, to send Israel and the United States clear signals about Damascus's intentions to change some of the rules in the Middle East.

To begin with, said Itamar Rabinovich, an authority on Syria at Tel Aviv University, the Syrians are apparently trying to establish a new relationship with Israel in Lebanon after the Israeli withdrawal.

While Israel wants to hold onto all of its old perquisites in Lebanon, particularly its freedom to fly reconnaissance missions over the Syrian-controlled Bekaa, the Syrians want to reverse once and for all this free Israeli access to their neighboring client state.

"By sending the missiles back, the

Continued on Page 5, Column 1

For Families of 2 Americans, Sudden Sorrow

By SARA RIMER

Natasha Simpson, the 11-year-old daughter of a foreign correspondent in Rome, was on her way to New York with her family for a three-week vacation among friends and relatives. John Buonocore 3d, a 20-year-old college student, was on his way home to Wilmington, Del., after a semester's study in Rome, just in time for his father's 50th birthday.

Both died at Leonardo da Vinci Airport in Rome yesterday. They were the two Americans among the 13 people killed there when terrorists hurled hand grenades and opened fire with submachine guns into crowds of holiday travelers.

Natasha Simpson was apparently killed as her father, Victor Simpson, a native New Yorker who is the news editor for the Associated Press in Rome, tried to shield her from the bullets. Mr. Simpson, 43, was wounded in the right wrist and hand.

"I think he put his arm around her to try and push her down and that's how he injured his finger," said his wife, Daniela Simpson, who was reached by telephone at her parents' home in Rome.

Mrs. Simpson, 40, had been outside the terminal walking the family terrier while her husband and two children — Natasha and 9-year-old Michael — checked in for their flight to Kennedy International Airport. Then she heard the exploding grenades.

"Suddenly there was a shattering noise as if something were collapsing," Mrs. Simpson, who is also a journalist, told the Associated Press in Rome. "And then there were machine-gun bursts. Two distinct machine-gun bursts. And then silence.

"I rushed into screams and cries, and saw my husband dripping blood from his hand and my son on the floor

Continued on Page 6, Column 1

"All the News That's Fit to Print"

The New York Times

Late Edition

Weather: Partly sunny and cold today, strong, northwesterly winds; mostly clear tonight. Mostly sunny tomorrow. Temperatures: today 28-32, tonight 15-20; yesterday 24-34. Details, page D18.

VOL.CXXXV.... No. 46,683

NEW YORK, WEDNESDAY, FEBRUARY 12, 1986

50 cents beyond 75 miles from New York City, except on Long Island. 30 CENTS

SHCHARANSKY WINS FREEDOM IN BERLIN IN PRISONER TRADE

DISSIDENT FLIES TO ISRAEL

Sees Wife for First Time Since She Emigrated in 1974 — A Walk Across Bridge

By JAMES M. MARKHAM

Special to The New York Times

WEST BERLIN, Feb. 11 — Anatoly B. Shcharansky, the Soviet human rights activist and campaigner for the right of Jews to emigrate, was freed here today after eight years in prisons and labor camps.

Wearing a fur hat, an oversize black overcoat and baggy trousers, Mr. Shcharansky, 38 years old, walked across a snow-covered stretch of bridge and threaded his way past two parked United States vans to freedom. Within hours, he had been reunited with the wife, whom he had not seen since 1974, and flown to a hero's welcome in Israel.

A Result of Summit Meeting

His release was the high point of an elaborately synchronized East-West prisoner exchange that appeared to be one of the most concrete, and dramatic, results of the meeting in November between President Reagan and Mikhail S. Gorbachev, the Soviet leader. The exchange had been secretly negotiated in the last few months by officials in Washington, Bonn and East Berlin.

Mr. Shcharansky was released along with three men accused of being North Atlantic Treaty Organization spies. In exchange, five people from Warsaw Pact countries were handed back on the Glienicke Bridge, which separates the outskirts of West Berlin from the East German town of Potsdam.

Although American officials and others confirmed last week that the exchange was set to take place today, Mr. Shcharansky learned only Monday that he would be freed from a labor camp.

Was Accused of Being a Spy

Mr. Shcharansky was sentenced in 1978 to 13 years in prison and labor camps for treason, espionage and anti-Soviet agitation. The Soviet authorities said he had been spying for the United States; he and the United States have denied it.

[In Moscow, Mr. Shcharansky's mother greeted the news of his release with sobs of joy. Page A8.]

Mr. Shcharansky was greeted on the West Berlin side of the bridge at 11:01 A.M. by the United States Ambassador to West Germany, Richard R. Burt.

According to an American diplomat who overheard him, Mr. Burt welcomed an ebullient Mr. Shcharansky "to the free world" on behalf of President Reagan and Chancellor Helmut Kohl of West Germany.

"President Reagan and others worked and prayed for many years for this." Mr. Burt was said to have told Mr. Shcharansky.

Mr. Shcharansky, who repeatedly expressed his thanks at being freed,

Continued on Page A9, Column 1

Agence France-Presse

Anatoly B. Shcharansky, in fur hat at center, crossing Glienicke Bridge into West Berlin. Flanking him were Ludwig Rehlinger, left, a West German official, and Richard R. Burt, United States Ambassador to West Germany.

SHCHARANSKY GETS WELCOME IN ISRAEL

On Arrival, He Vows to Press Human Rights Struggle

By DAVID K. SHIPLER

Special to The New York Times

JERUSALEM, Feb. 11 — Anatoly B. Shcharansky arrived in Israel today to a joyful welcome from Government leaders, friends and tumultuous crowds of supporters.

Mr. Shcharansky, who was freed from a Soviet labor camp on Monday,

Arrival statement, page A8.

pledged to continue the struggle for human rights.

His wife, Avital, who had campaigned for nine years for his freedom, stood by his side, blinking back tears as well-wishers on the tarmac sang Hebrew wedding songs.

Mr. Shcharansky looked stunned at first, but soon displayed the wit and poise for which he was known in the Soviet Union. When he spotted familiar faces of Moscow friends in the crowd, he rushed over and hugged them.

Meets His 'Criminal Contacts'

Alluding to his fellow dissidents, he quipped: "I am very glad to have an opportunity to speak to an audience in which my criminal contacts are represented so widely."

Prime Minister Shimon Peres, half the Cabinet and leading rabbis were on hand when an executive jet brought Mr. Shcharansky to Ben-Gurion Inter-

Continued on Page A8, Column 1

President Says Budget Foes Seek Tax Increase and Vows to Veto It

By GERALD M. BOYD

Special to The New York Times

WASHINGTON, Feb. 11 — President Reagan tonight accused Congressional opponents of his new budget proposal of maneuvering for a tax increase. He pledged a swift veto if they succeeded.

In a strong statement against a tax increase, Mr. Reagan began a nationally televised news conference by saying such a bill would be "vetoed on arrival."

"Let's be frank," Mr. Reagan said. "Those who say our budget is D.O.A., dead on arrival, are really saying 'Brace yourself for a tax increase.'"

'Get Its Own House in Order'

"I think taxpayers want Congress to get its own house in order. I do too. So rest assured that any tax increase Congress sends me will be V.O.A., vetoed on arrival."

In his remarks on international matters, Mr. Reagan said he was "encouraged" by the release of the Soviet dissident Anatoly B. Shcharansky and said he hoped the move by Moscow was "just a start." [Page A13.]

In response to questions about discussions in the Administration over whether to change an executive order that mandates affirmative action plans for companies doing business with the Federal Government, Mr. Reagan stuck to his position that goals and timetables for minority hiring amounted to racial quotas and were a form of illegal discrimination. He said that he would do nothing to restore "discrimination of any kind."

However, Mr. Reagan said the issue was still under review in the Administration.

In response to another question, Mr. Reagan said that he supported the affirmative action for minority group members and for women but without a "quota system." Mr. Reagan said that his goal was the same "color-blind society" that he said was sought by the Rev. Dr. Martin Luther King Jr.

Mr. Reagan was not asked a single question about the explosion of the Challenger space shuttle or the Presidential commission investigating it.

In his second news conference this year, Mr. Reagan made these other points:

¶*That he was not alarmed by the* trends in corporate mergers and that the existing laws may well be "over-

Continued on Page A13, Column 1

Manes Resigns 2 Queens Posts, Citing Problems

Quits as Borough Chief and a Leader of Party

By MICHAEL ORESKES

Donald R. Manes resigned yesterday as Borough President of Queens and county Democratic leader, saying he had to devote his attention to his ailing health and the corruption accusations against him.

"I know I will be fully vindicated," Mr. Manes said in a resignation statement. "However, I cannot ask the people I serve to wait for me while I devote whatever energies I have to my problems rather than theirs."

Mr. Manes, the city's senior borough president, made his announcement following several days in which Federal law-enforcement officials have been saying that they were considering whether to seek an indictment of Mr. Manes on charges that he solicited bribes to influence contracts at the city's Parking Violations Bureau.

A Deadline for Indictment

A longtime friend of Mr. Manes, Geoffrey G. Lindenauer, has already been arrested on charges of taking a $5,000 bribe and has been under pressure from Federal prosecutors to cooperate in their corruption investigation or face indictment.

A Federal grand jury has until tomorrow to issue such an indictment unless Mr. Lindenauer, the former deputy director of the parking bureau, agrees to waive speedy-trial rules.

Rudolph W. Giuliani, the United States Attorney in Manhattan, who is conducting an investigation into municipal corruption, said he did not know why Mr. Manes chose to resign yesterday. "It has no effect one way or the other on what we're investigating," Mr. Giuliani said.

In conjunction with his resignation, Mr. Manes, who is 52 years old, made a move to protect his city pension. He switched his pension status in a way

Continued on Page B6, Column 3

Koch Shifts Hiring Policy

The Mayor said appointments of most higher-paid city employees would need his approval. The number of jobs affected was unclear. Page B1.

PRESIDENT TO SEND AN ENVOY TO SEEK VIEWS OF FILIPINOS

HABIB WILL GO TO MANILA

Reagan Cites Reports of Fraud on Both Sides in Vote and Sees No Clear Winner

By BERNARD WEINRAUB

Special to The New York Times

WASHINGTON, Feb. 11 — President Reagan announced today that he was sending Philip C. Habib, a veteran diplomat, to the Philippines "to assess the desires and needs of the Filipino people" in the aftermath of the disputed election there.

In a written statement issued by the White House, Mr. Reagan said it was

Transcript of news session, page A12.

"a disturbing fact" that the election was marked by fraud and violence.

He also noted that no "definitive" victor had been declared in the contest between President Ferdinand E. Marcos and his challenger, Corazon C. Aquino, adding: "It is not appropriate for the United States to make such a judgment at this time."

Meeting With Observers

The statement was issued hours after Mr. Reagan, Secretary of State George P. Shultz and key Administration officials held a 35-minute meeting with Senator Richard G. Lugar, Republican of Indiana, and Representative John P. Murtha, Democrat of Pennsylvania, who headed the official 20-member American team that observed the Philippine election.

Mr. Reagan's statement reflected in large measure the conclusions reached by Mr. Lugar and Mr. Murtha, White House officials said. The two legislators urged Mr. Reagan to refrain from declaring Mr. Marcos the winner in the balloting. Instead, according to Congressional sources, they urged Mr. Reagan to use the United States' influence to spur diplomatic and political efforts to help shape a credible outcome.

Vote in Jeopardy

Senator Lugar and Representative Murtha urged Mr. Reagan not to label the election as fraudulent because it would enable Mr. Marcos to discard the results and assume dictatorial control, Congressional sources said.

In Manila, President Marcos called his opponent's protests "a childish display of petulance." He said he would abide by an official vote certification by the National Assembly, a process that Mrs. Aquino called a distortion of democracy. [Page A14.]

Fraud 'on Both Sides'

At his news conference tonight, President Reagan made carefully balanced remarks about the situation in the Philippines. He said that American observers had told him there was an "appearance of fraud" in the recent election, but he said the observers did not have hard evidence beyond that general appearance. The President added that such fraud and violence

Continued on Page A13, Column 2

Officials Say Fatal Tampering Of Tylenol Was Isolated Case

By MICHAEL NORMAN

Authorities investigating the case of a woman who died in Yonkers after taking Extra-Strength Tylenol tainted with cyanide said yesterday that they were convinced the death was an isolated case of tampering and that there was no reason to believe that other batches of the drug contained the poison.

"We don't intend to start a national scare, we don't believe the nation is smothered with tainted Tylenol," said Owen J. McClain, a deputy police chief in Yonkers, where the woman, Diane Elsroth, was found dead Saturday afternoon at the home of a friend she was visiting.

Nevertheless, supermarkets and other stores across the country removed the popular pain remedy from their shelves. And public officials in New York State, New York City and elsewhere continued to warn users of the drug not to take it in capsule form.

10 Detectives on Case

For Johnson & Johnson, the giant pharmaceutical company based in New Brunswick, N.J., whose subsidiary manufactures Tylenol, the death revived a crisis that the company hoped had ended more than three years ago. [Page B4.]

While Chief McClain described the poisoning as a case of homicide and the work of a "local perpetrator," he said little about the investigation, including what leads, if any, investigators — 10 Yonkers detectives are working on the case along with state troopers and Federal agents — had turned up or where the tampering might have taken place.

"We have to find out if the tampering occurred pre-selling or post-selling before we decide our next step," said Bruce Bendish, chief of the homicide squad at the Westchester County District Attorney's office.

Mr. Bendish said investigators "have no reason to believe" that Miss

Continued on Page B4, Column 1

NASA Acknowledges Cold Affects Booster Seals

By PHILIP M. BOFFEY

Special to The New York Times

WASHINGTON, Feb. 11 — The space agency acknowledged today that cold temperatures diminish the effectiveness of critical safety seals that are designed to prevent the escape of hot gases and flames through the joints of the space shuttle's booster rockets.

The admission came under questioning by Richard P. Feynman, a Nobel Prize-winning physicist from the California Institute of Technology, at an open hearing of the Presidential commission that is investigating the cause of the explosion that destroyed the shuttle Challenger on Jan. 28.

Key sections of testimony before presidential panel, pages B10-11.

The agency maintained that experts had judged that the seals would operate safely despite the unusually cold weather at the time of launching and the night before. But an official acknowledged, too, that on the day before, the boosters' builder had suggested cold weather might cause a problem with the seals.

Impromptu Ice-Water Test

In previous public statements on this and other issues, officials of the National Aeronautics and Space Administration have given conflicting statements about the reliability of critical shuttle equipment and the agency's preparedness for disaster. While no one has suggested the misstatements are deliberate, they have raised questions about how tightly top officials were controlling the shuttle program, and how it had been affected by pressure to keep the program on schedule and financially competitive. [News analysis, page B12.]

After a lunch break today, Dr. Feynman told the panel that he had just conducted an impromptu experiment with the rubbery material used for the giant circular rings that seal the rocket joints. He said he had immersed a piece of the material in ice water and found that it lost resiliency, a factor that space officials had said was important to the effective operation of the O ring seals.

He later asked NASA officials if it was not true that low temperatures would increase the chance of seal failure.

Lawrence B. Mulloy, the project manager for the solid-fuel booster

Continued on Page B12, Column 4

The New York Times / Marilynn K. Yee

Lawrence B. Mulloy, project manager for the solid-fuel rockets, testifying about cross section of a joint between two segments of a booster rocket.

A Leading Marcos Foe Is Chased Across Town Square and Killed

By FRANCIS X. CLINES

Special to The New York Times

SAN JOSE DE BUENAVISTA, the Philippines, Feb. 11 — A leading member of the nation's political opposition was chased by masked gunmen across the town square here this morning and shot dead after he was trapped in a backyard outhouse.

"Run! Run!" witnesses said they shouted when six gunmen leveled rifles at their target, Evelio Javier, a former Governor of Antique Province and an outspoken critic of the Government of President Ferdinand E. Marcos.

'See if They Have Proof'

The provincial Governor, Enrique Zaldivar, said he had protectively hidden witnesses who saw the gunmen flee in an jeep belonging to Arturo Pacificador, the National Assembly majority leader. Mr. Pacificador was in Manila today, leading the floor fight to certify Mr. Marcos as victor in the election vote canvass.

"That is a lie," Mr. Pacificador said in an interview, when told of Governor Zaldivar's report that his maroon jeep had been used in the killing.

"Let's see if they have proof," the assemblyman said.

"I condemn the action of whoever perpetrated this," he added, urging a "full-blown investigation to solve the case as speedily as possible."

The killing of Mr. Javier, 43 years

Continued on Page A14, Column 3

Reuters

Evelio Javier

INSIDE

No Chemical Arms Accord

The United States, at a 40-nation conference in Geneva, dismissed a Soviet proposal for an interim accord on chemical weapons. Page A3.

Liberian Offer on Duvalier

Liberia said it was prepared to offer political asylum to Jean-Claude Duvalier, the deposed Haitian leader, who is now in France. Page A27.

Arrow Air Halts Flights

Arrow Air, involved in a crash in which 248 soldiers died, halted flights and filed for reorganization under the bankruptcy law. Page A21.

Schools Backed on AIDS

A state judge ruled that children with AIDS cannot automatically be excluded from regular classes in New York City public schools. Page B1.

"All the News That's Fit to Print"

The New York Times

Weather: Mostly sunny and mild today, light, variable winds; increasing cloudiness tonight. Chance of rain tomorrow. Temperatures: today 60-63, tonight 47-50; yesterday 40-60. Details, page D14.

VOL.CXXXV. . . . No. 46,744 NEW YORK, MONDAY, APRIL 14, 1986 — 50 cents beyond 75 miles from New York City, except on Long Island. — 30 CENTS

United Press International

NICKLAUS WINS MASTERS: Jack Nicklaus at 4th green on the way to his sixth Masters championship. SportsMonday, page C1.

A Reputed Aide To Gotti Is Slain By Bomb in Car

By PETER KERR

A Staten Island man described by law-enforcement authorities as the No. 2 leader in the Gambino crime family was killed yesterday when a powerful bomb in a parked car exploded as he stood on a sidewalk in the Bensonhurst section of Brooklyn.

The victim was identified as Frank DeCicco, who became the second in command to John Gotti, reputed head of the Gambino family earlier this year.

Mr. Gotti took over the crime organization, the authorities said, less than a month after the previous head of the family, Paul Castellano, was shot to death.

Windows Broken Nearby

The blast also seriously injured a man with Mr. DeCicco who was described by the authorities as a member of the Luchese organized-crime family. He was identified as Frank Bellino, 69 years old of Staten Island.

A woman who was passing by also received minor injuries when what the authorities called an "explosive device" placed under the front part of a gray, four-door 1985 Buick Electra went off, causing the vehicle to burst into flames and shattering windows in

Continued on Page B2, Column 5

JAPAN SAID TO VOW 'HISTORIC' ACTION ON EASING TRADE

Nakasone, Meeting Reagan, Pledges Moves to Lower Barriers on U.S. Goods

By GERALD M. BOYD

Special to The New York Times

WASHINGTON, April 13 — President Reagan received assurances from Prime Minister Yasuhiro Nakasone today that Japan was determined to effect a "historic change" that could help ease the United States-Japan trade imbalance, Administration officials said.

The officials said Mr. Nakasone had expressed in a meeting with Mr. Reagan a determination to move the Japanese economy beyond its current reliance on exports for growth to greater dependence on imports and domestic consumption.

A senior Administration official said the change pledged by Mr. Nakasone amounted to a "different story" on the part of the Japanese Government in terms of previous pledges to take steps to reduce the ratio of Japanese products coming to the United States versus American products going into Japan.

'Historic Turn' Cited

"The Prime Minister expressed what he called an 'historic turn' that they're going to move their policies from export-oriented to import-oriented," said the official, who attended the 60-minute meeting, which was followed by a private lunch for the two leaders and Nancy Reagan.

The official added that the Administration believed that "there's a determination in the Government of Japan" to make such a shift.

Japanese press reports said that the United States and Japan had agreed last week to lower interest rates concurrently, but the reports differed in their accounts of how the accord had been reached. [Page D6.]

Mr. Reagan had welcomed Mr. Nakasone to a rare Sunday meeting at the Presidential retreat at Camp David, Md., to discuss a wide range of of issues, including the $49.7 billion annual trade deficit that the United States has with Japan.

A Relaxed Atmosphere

The relaxed atmosphere, for the first of two days of talks, underscored the friendship of the two leaders, who warmly embraced as they met. Mr. Reagan, like his aides and the Japanese delegation, was dressed casually for the meeting, and he chauffeured Mr. Nakasone in a golf cart after the Prime Minister had arrived by helicopter to the retreat, situated in the woods of the Catoctin Mountains.

The only other head of state to meet Mr. Reagan there has been Prime Minister Margaret Thatcher of Britain.

The Reagan-Nakasone meeting, the eighth the two leaders have held, came

Continued on Page D6, Column 3

Associated Press

Pope John Paul II being escorted by Rabbi Elio Toaff during visit to synagogue yesterday in Rome.

Pope Speaks in Rome Synagogue, Condemning All Anti-Semitism

By E. J. DIONNE Jr.

Special to The New York Times

ROME, April 13 — Pope John Paul II, embracing the world's Jews as "our elder brothers," today paid the first recorded papal visit to a synagogue and condemned persecution and displays of anti-Semitism "at any time and by anyone."

"I repeat, 'By anyone,'" John Paul declared to ringing applause at Rome's central synagogue, situated in what

Text of Pope's talk is on page A4.

was once the Rome ghetto, established by the decree of one of his predecessors.

John Paul, seeking to heal nearly 2,000 years of strife between Catholics and Jews, also expressed his "abhorrence for the genocide decreed against the Jewish people during the last war, which led to the holocaust of millions of innocent victims."

Called 'True Turning Point'

The Pope's journey to the spiritual center of what is believed to be the oldest Jewish group in the Diaspora was greeted by the Chief Rabbi, Elio Toaff, as a "gesture destined to go down in history" and a "true turning point in the policy of the church."

"The heart opens itself," Rabbi Toaff declared, "to the hope that the misfortunes of the past will be replaced by fruitful dialogue."

Rabbi Toaff embraced John Paul when he arrived on the steps of the imposing Victorian synagogue overlooking the Tiber River.

John Paul returned the embrace and then entered the synagogue to a thundering ovation from a congregation of 1,000 people, many of them descendents of Jews who had been forced to live apart from other Romans.

As a male chorus sang the 150th Psalm, "Alleluia, Praise the Lord in His Holy Place," the Pope made his way down the blue-carpeted main aisle and took his place beside Rabbi Toaff.

In a service that emphasized the equal dignity of the two faiths, the two men sat on identical gilt and brocade thrones and took turns reading from the Psalms.

'Jews Are Beloved of God'

"The Jews are beloved of God, who has called them with an irrevocable calling," John Paul said, speaking in Italian and, briefly, in Hebrew.

"The Jewish religion is not 'extrinsic' to us, but in a certain way is 'intrinsic' to our own religion," he said elsewhere in his address. "With Judaism, therefore, we have a relationship which we do not have with any other religion. You are our dearly beloved brothers, and, in a certain way, it could be said that you are our elder brothers."

At no point in his address did John Paul mention Israel. Prominent Jews around the world had expressed the hope that the visit might be the prelude to establishing formal diplomatic ties between the Vatican and Israel.

But in a series of strong attacks on

Continued on Page A4, Column 1

ISRAELI PACT ENDS CRISIS IN CABINET

Likud Ministers to Switch Jobs to Meet Premier's Demand

By THOMAS L. FRIEDMAN

Special to The New York Times

JERUSALEM, April 13 — The eight-day crisis in Israel's coalition Government was resolved late tonight when the Likud bloc agreed that two of its ministers should switch jobs to satisfy the demands of Prime Minister Shimon Peres of the Labor Party.

Although the agreement seems to have saved the 19-month-old coalition, the naked political maneuverings and name-calling between Labor Party and Likud ministers appear to have diminished all of them in the eyes of the Israeli public, judging from the mountain of commentaries and editorials in the press.

Accord Endorsed by Cabinet

Many Israelis tonight seemed to be questioning how their leaders could have become totally preoccupied for more than a week with the switching of two Cabinet portfolios.

After another day of tense negotiations, threats, proposals and counter-proposals between the coalition partners, the Likud suggested that Minister of Justice Moshe Nissim and Minister of Finance Yitzhak Modai exchange jobs, thereby satisfying Mr. Peres's demand that Mr. Modai be removed from the Treasury.

Mr. Peres and his Labor colleagues agreed to the switch and the entire 25-member Cabinet endorsed it shortly

Continued on Page A9, Column 1

REAGAN TO CONFER WITH AIDES TODAY ON LIBYA RESPONSE

DECISION EXPECTED SOON

With U.S. Fleet at the Ready, A Pentagon Official Says 'Time Is Getting Short'

By BERNARD GWERTZMAN

Special to The New York Times

WASHINGTON, April 13 — President Reagan was described by senior Administration officials today as near a decision on whether to order a military attack against Libya. A move could be ordered as early as Monday, a key Senator said.

"Prospective military action is something that only the President will decide on," Deputy Secretary of State John C. Whitehead said. "He has not yet made that decision." But Mr. Whitehead added that while there was no deadline for a decision, "time is winding down; the time is getting short."

Tension continued to build as Vernon Walters, the American representative at the United Nations, held confidential briefings in key allied capitals today about American plans [Page A6]. Two United States Navy carrier battle groups exercised in the central Mediterranean, not far from Libya.

Senator Invited to Meeting

Senator Richard G. Lugar, Republican of Indiana and chairman of the Foreign Relations Committee, said today that Secretary of State George P. Shultz had told him to go to the White House on Monday for a meeting with Mr. Reagan that is expected to discuss the possible American response. Mr. Lugar had sent a message to Mr. Shultz on Friday complaining about not being briefed on possible war plans.

"A decision will be made on that occasion, or shortly thereafter as to what our response ought to be," Mr. Lugar said in Bloomington, Ind. He also said he was assured by Mr. Shultz that the Reagan Administration would comply with the 1973 War Powers Resolution, which requires the President to inform Congress when American forces are placed in a hostile situation.

Key Advisers Return

Action would be taken against Libya for what the United States says is its support of terrorist acts, including one eight days ago in West Berlin in which an American serviceman and a Turkish woman were killed.

Vice President Bush returned to Washington from the Middle East and Defense Secretary Caspar W. Weinberger returned from a trip to East Asia and Australia today. Both are expected to meet with Mr. Reagan on Monday as well, and their advice may be crucial.

In the past, both Mr. Bush and Mr. Weinberger have been opposed to general acts of military retaliation against terrorists. They have said that military force should be limited to attacking places where the known perpetrators of

Continued on Page A6, Column 1

The New York Times/Barton Silverman

The wreckage of a car after a bomb in it exploded yesterday in Brooklyn.

Foreigners Cautioned About Staying in Libya

By EDWARD SCHUMACHER

Special to The New York Times

TRIPOLI, Libya, April 13 — As tensions continued to rise here tonight over possible United States military action against Libyan targets, a number of embassies issued advisories to their nationals to reconsider their positions in the country. None of the embassies recommended evacuation, however.

British citizens who called their consul today were given the following message: "It follows that in a period of rising tension, the British Government would expect British citizens to review very carefully the advisability of their remaining in Libya."

Evacuation Procedures Organized

The Japanese, Spanish and other embassies have been organizing emergency evacuation procedures should they be needed. Some embassies have made tentative plans with their national airlines and their national-flag cargo ships and tankers coming into Libyan ports, according to diplomats.

Almost all of the embassies are said to have worked out procedures on how to spread the word of evacuation quickly through the communities of their nationals. There has been no exodus at the airport here, however.

Colonel Qaddafi announced early this morning that a number of military bases had been evacuated and that foreign companies were being ordered to house their workers there. Western diplomats here interpreted the order as making foreign workers into virtual hostages.

The executives of two West European corporations said here tonight that a Libyan revolutionary committee had told them to begin moving their workers onto military bases immediately.

A number of European embassies reached here tonight declined to comment on the executives' assertions, but diplomats from a number of nations were at their offices trying to investigate the situation.

No coercion to move Westerners to

Continued on Page A7, Column 1

As Tuitions Rise, Colleges Adopt Banks' Role

By EDWARD B. FISKE

With the cost of tuition soaring and Federal assistance eroding, American colleges and universities are moving aggressively into the business of providing financial services to students and their parents.

College officials more accustomed to dispensing knowledge than money are finding that to assure a continued flow of students, they must play the role of banker, loan insurer, portfolio manager and family financial adviser. New plans range from revolving loan funds financed by college endowments to the academic equivalent of pork belly futures — paying today's price for a child's education years later.

School officials liken their situation to that of the automobile industry after World War I, when manufacturers began setting up such instruments as the General Motors Acceptance Corporation to make car loans.

"Most people can't pay for education out of current income any more than they can purchase a car that way," said James J. Scannell, a vice president of the University of Rochester. "We have to find ways for people to afford our product."

Among the new financial services being offered by colleges are these:

¶Dozens of schools, from the University of Miami to the University of Southern California, offer prepayment

Continued on Page A14, Column 1

INSIDE

Large Rally for Marcos

About 15,000 to 20,000 Filipinos attended the biggest pro-Marcos rally since the deposed President fled nearly seven weeks ago. Page A3.

Cities Scrutinized on Fines

Corruption inquiries have spotlighted the widespread practice of cities' hiring private companies to collect parking fines. Page A10.

Stalin Daughter Set to Leave

By PHILIP TAUBMAN

Special to The New York Times

MOSCOW, April 13 — Svetlana Alliluyeva, Stalin's daughter, said today that she had received permission from the Government to leave the Soviet Union once again and planned to do so before the end of the month.

"I requested permission to leave and I got it," she said.

She added that her daughter, Olga Peters, had also received approval to leave and expected to return to school in England in the near future.

In a brief telephone interview from her Moscow hotel, Miss Alliluyeva said she did not know whether she would ever return to the Soviet Union again.

"I can't think so far into the future," she said. She declined to answer questions about why she had decided to leave the Soviet Union again.

Miss Alliluyeva created a sensation in 1984 when, 17 years after defecting to the West, she returned to Moscow with her daughter, then 13 years old. The daughter was born in the United States while Miss Alliluyeva was married to William Wesley Peters, an American architect. They were divorced in 1973.

Any Soviet citizen must obtain permission from the Government to leave the country. Miss Alliluyeva and her daughter were granted Soviet citizenship by special decree in 1984.

Miss Alliluyeva, 59 years old, lived in the Soviet Union until 1967, when she defected to the West in India and renounced her Soviet citizenship.

An American diplomat said that the State Department still considered Miss Alliluyeva and and her daughter to be United States citizens and that they

Continued on Page A3, Column 2

"All the News That's Fit to Print"

The New York Times

Late Edition
Weather: Partly sunny, mild today, northerly winds; partly cloudy tonight. Partly cloudy and warmer tomorrow. Temperatures: today 67-70, tonight 45-50; yesterday 49-68. Details, page D10.

VOL.CXXXV . . . No. 46,772 NEW YORK, MONDAY, MAY 12, 1986 — 50 cents beyond 75 miles from New York City, except on Long Island. — 30 CENTS

The New York Times/Chester Higgins Jr.
Anatoly B. Shcharansky waving to the crowd at a rally yesterday.

300,000 AT RALLY FOR SHCHARANSKY HEAR HIS THANKS

Dissident Expresses Gratitude for 'Voice of Freedom,' at a New York Gathering

By JANE GROSS

Anatoly B. Shcharansky thanked hundreds of thousands of New Yorkers yesterday for raising the "voice of freedom" year after year in behalf of Soviet Jews who are imprisoned, persecuted or denied the right to emigrate.

Mr. Shcharansky, the human-rights activist who was freed from a Soviet prison in February, delivered his message at the annual Solidarity Sunday for Soviet Jewry, a rally at Dag Hammarskjold Plaza in Manhattan. The last nine years, his wife, Avital, had spoken for him at the rallies while he languished in labor camps and jails.

"My K.G.B. interrogators, my prison guards, they tried to convince me that I was alone, powerless in their hands," Mr. Shcharansky told the crowd, some of whom had marched to the plaza near the United Nations along a parade route that began at Fifth Avenue and 64th Street.

'All of You Were With Me'

"But I knew I was never alone," he added. "I knew my wife, my people and all of you were with me. They tried their best to find a place where I was isolated. But all the resources of a superpower cannot isolate a man who hears the voice of freedom, a voice I heard from the very chamber of my soul."

Mr. Shcharansky, who has taken the Hebrew first name Natan, did not march in the parade because of "security concerns," according to rally organizers. He arrived on the dais near the end of a two-hour program of speeches by New York officials including Mayor Koch; Governor Cuomo; Democratic Senator Daniel Patrick Moynihan; Republican Senator Alfonse M. D'Amato; State Attorney General Robert Abrams; Representative Benjamin A. Gilman, Republican of Middletown, and Representative Stephen J. Solarz, Democrat of Brooklyn.

Folk Songs and Flags

Also among the speakers were John C. Whitehead, the Deputy Secretary of State, who represented the Reagan Administration, and John Cardinal O'Connor, the Archbishop of New York.

When Mr. Shcharansky, in shirt sleeves, arrived, he seemed dazed by the reaction of the people massed in the bright spring sunshine who greeted him with lusty choruses of Hebrew folk

Continued on Page B4, Column 2

Senate Tax Bill Not as Generous As House Plan

By GARY KLOTT

Special to The New York Times

WASHINGTON, May 11 — The Senate Finance Committee's tax revision plan provides a more delicate balance between winning and losing for middle-income taxpayers than the tax bill passed by the House of Representatives, according to a detailed analysis of individual examples.

Under either bill, a majority of taxpayers are projected to receive a tax cut, while a minority will either see their tax bills little changed or increased. The Senate plan, however, would provide on average a smaller tax cut for individuals, chiefly because it curtails many more tax benefits than the House version.

An analysis of hypothetical cases, done with the help of a professional accountant, confirms this, and also shows how some middle-income taxpayers with a common mix of itemized deductions could have a tax cut under the House plan but wind up with a tax increase under the Senate version.

In one example, an upper-middle-income elderly couple would face a 1.5 percent increase in taxes under the Senate bill, largely because their charitable deduction would be lost and because of a quirk in the basic method of calculating tax liabilities.

This quirk would have the effect of

Continued on Page D3, Column 1

Associated Press
SOVIET REPORTS GAIN IN REACTOR FIGHT: The damaged reactor, center, at the Chernobyl nuclear power plant in a photograph taken Friday and released yesterday by the press agency Tass. Officials said that the plant no longer threatened a catastrophe. Western experts said this would be hard to confirm. Page A6.

U.S. Officials Denouncing Mexico For Huge Rise in Drug Trafficking

By JOEL BRINKLEY

Special to The New York Times

WASHINGTON, May 11 — American officials, normally circumspect about problems with Mexico, have begun issuing open denunciations of what they say is a huge increase in drug trafficking and related Government corruption.

United States figures show that Mexican production of heroin and marijuana are rising dramatically, while Mexican dealers have also become major traffickers in cocaine, which has gained them more than $1 billion a year.

Crop eradication has slowed, meanwhile, and American officials say they believe that even the governors of some Mexican states are now taking bribes from drug dealers.

Mexico Defends Efforts

Mexican officials do not dispute the notion that the drug problem has grown worse. But in a meeting with members of the United States Congress this year, Sergio Garcia Ramirez, the Mexican Attorney General, said drug trafficking was on the increase worldwide. Many other countries are in the same position as Mexico, he said, adding that Mexico was fighting the problem as aggressively as it could.

Other Mexican officials reject the American assertions outright and insist that their efforts against trafficking are continuing and achieving good results.

Just a few years ago the United States so admired the Mexican programs for eradicating marijuana and opium poppies that the State Department flew officials from as far away as Burma to Mexico to show them how an effective program was run. Its drug enforcement program was considered a model.

Weak Economy Is Cited

Now American officials say all that has changed, although none say with any certainty why the problem has worsened so rapidly and dramatically. The most common explanation is that Mexico's deteriorating economy has drawn poor peasants into the narcotics trade as legitimate sources of income have vanished. In addition, Mexico scholars say Government corruption traditionally increases in the last two years of a President's term, and President Miguel de la Madrid leaves office in 1988.

"The drug situation is a horror story, increasing logarithmically, and Mexico is doing nothing about it," William von Raab, the Customs Commissioner, said in an interview.

He said Mexican Government officials were "inept and corrupt," and he added, "The concern is now shared by

Continued on Page A4, Column 3

DAMASCUS EXPELS 3 BRITISH ENVOYS

London Aide Calls Retaliation a 'Quite Unjustified' Step

By IHSAN A. HIJAZI

Special to The New York Times

BEIRUT, Lebanon, May 11 — Syria said today that it had ordered the expulsion of three British diplomats in retaliation for the ouster by Britain of three Syrian envoys on Saturday.

The three members of the Syrian Embassy ordered ousted by Britain were involved in an investigation into terrorist activities in Britain. The move came after the Syrian Ambassador, Loutof Allah Haydar, refused to waive the envoys' diplomatic immunity. Britain wanted to question the three in connection with an attempt to plant explosives on an Israeli jumbo jet at Heathrow Airport last month and other terrorist acts.

Effect of Tokyo Summit

In London today, a spokesman for the Foreign Office called the Syrian expulsion order "quite unjustified and regrettable," but said Britain was not contemplating further measures.

The Foreign Office added that although the agreement on terrorism reached at the Tokyo economic summit meeting last week had played no direct role in London's decision, the move was representative of the harder line taken by the seven major industrial-

Continued on Page A5, Column 1

SHULTZ SAYS CUTS BY CONGRESS HURT ANTITERROR POLICY

IRATE OVER BUDGET MOVES

Reduction in Funds to Protect Embassies and 'Squeeze' on Foreign Aid Assailed

By BERNARD GWERTZMAN

Special to The New York Times

MOFFETT NAVAL AIR STATION, Calif., May 11 — Secretary of State George P. Shultz said today that Congress was threatening to deeply impair the Administration's foreign and counterterrorism policies by its recent budget cuts.

He said he would have "to drop everything else" to lobby for restoration of the funds.

His voice often raised in anger, he said the Administration had had to "squeeze" money to give the Philippines even an additional $150 million in aid. And he said he saw no way of finding more money for that country, or for Haiti, South Korea, Thailand and other needy nations, unless money on the verge of being cut from the budget was restored.

Mr. Shultz also said the failure of the Senate in particular to back the program for enhanced security at American embassies could cause "another tragedy" at some mission overseas.

Ends Far East Trip

He spoke as his Air Force plane headed back to Washington from a stopover in Hawaii at the end of a trip to the Far East. Mr. Shultz summoned reporters to the front of the aircraft to deliver an impassioned appeal for the foreign aid and State Department money that has been cut by the Senate and by the House Budget Committee. The House has to vote on the budget resolution, and it will then be reconciled by both the Senate and the House.

Mr. Shultz pointed out that the Administration aid request for the 1987 fiscal year was for $22.6 billion, and that the Senate had voted $17.8 billion and the House committee $17 billion. The cuts were thus severe, he said, amounting to more than 20 percent.

Warns on Embassies

Much of his concern was about the sharp reduction voted by the Senate in the Administration's $1.4 billion request for building new embassies to provide better protection against terrorist attacks for Americans serving overseas. The $1.4 billion would be the first installment in a $4.4 billion, five-year program.

The Senate voted to approve only $491 million, provoking Mr. Shultz to say angrily:

"One of these days, there'll be another tragedy at some embassy. Then they'll come around and say you're derelict in your duty because all these people got killed, and I'm going to say I'm not derelict in my duty, because you wouldn't appropriate the money to

Continued on Page A3, Column 1

The New York Times/Dith Pran
SHORT RACE FOR SHORT LEGS: Young ladies, 2 to 6 years old, starting a special quarter-mile race yesterday in Central Park. The main event was a 5-kilometer (3.1-mile) race for women, intended as a tune-up for the 15th annual L'eggs Mini Marathon May 31. Over 2,000 women and girls took part in the Mother's Day races.

Indians' Rage at Illegal Bar Fuels Upstate Fire

By ESTHER B. FEIN

Special to The New York Times

ST. REGIS INDIAN RESERVATION, N.Y., May 11 — All that remained of the rage today were the ashes of Josie's Place and the brick chimney that loomed over them.

But local residents say there are other, sadder reminders of the drinking and revelry that went on at Josie's, an unlicensed bar on this reservation in upstate New York that was burned to the ground Saturday night by a group of Mohawk Indians.

There were the fresh graves of nine Indians, all of whom died in traffic accidents in the last three weeks after drinking at Josie's and at another local speakeasy. Among those killed was a woman eight-months pregnant; her baby was stillborn after her death.

'Shut Down Speakeasies'

The most recent death occurred Saturday afternoon, as about 250 Indians from the reservation marched from their tribal headquarters down Route 37 to demonstrate outside Josie's Place. Above their chants of "shut down speakeasies," they heard a siren. Another patron of Josie's, who had just passed through their ranks to leave on a motorcycle, had joined the list of victims.

No one here seems entirely sure how a peaceful march organized by Indian mothers became a fiery protest. For months, anger and tension have been fulminating among residents of this 25,000-acre reservation, which abuts the St. Lawrence River and straddles the American-Canadian border.

"We went to three funerals one weekend and three funerals the next," said Mary Swamp, one of the mothers who organized the demonstration on Saturday and another one that was held the day before. "I was sitting in my friend Josie Back's kitchen and I said, 'Are we going to be doing this every weekend?'"

After the fatal accident Saturday, the owner of Josie's Place, an Indian woman named Josephine White, was arrested on charges of serving alcohol without a license and was taken to the local jail. To the cheers of protesters standing outside, the state police then returned to the bar and confiscated her liquor stock as evidence.

About 9 P.M. Saturday, according to local officials, a group of about 50 men pushed to the front of the crowd, which

Continued on Page D11, Column 3

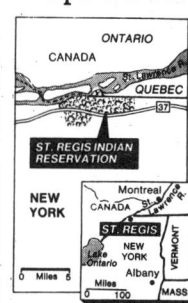

The New York Times/May 12, 1986
Reservation has 9,000 residents.

Insurance Costs Imperil Recreation Industry

By ROBERT HANLEY

Soaring costs for liability insurance are buffeting recreation facilities and businesses on the eve of the summer vacation season.

Premiums in many cases have doubled, tripled or quadrupled in recent weeks, following a year-old trend of sharply increased insurance rates for towns and cities across the New York metropolitan region and much of the nation.

Inevitably, recreation industry officials say, fun-seekers will have to help absorb the increases by paying higher prices, or will have to make do with less or, in some cases, without. The cost of insurance is already affecting a wide range of attractions and activities, from the Cyclone roller coaster at Coney Island to neighborhood ball fields, from fairs and fireworks displays to riding stables and campgrounds. The new restrictions include the following:

¶At Candlewood Lake in Connecticut, beer has been banned at park picnic areas.

¶In Queens, the Ozone Park Little League has been barred from the field it leases from the New York Racing Association until it comes up with $25 million in liability coverage.

¶In Rochester, fireworks displays have been dropped from the city's 10-day Lilac Festival, and its evening concerts have been reduced to five from eight.

¶At the Astroland amusement park at Coney Island, which is owned by New York City, the famed Cyclone has remained shut down because its operator could obtain only $1 million of the $3 million in coverage that the city demanded. City and company officials are now discussing ways to open the ride, including one proposal to pledge Astroland's assets to cover claims beyond $1 million.

The liability premium for the Rochester Lilac Festival, which usu-

Continued on Page B4, Column 5

INSIDE

Amtrak Strike Averted

Emergency negotiations put off a strike by locomotive engineers that could have crippled passenger service in the Northeast. Page A9.

Royal Fever Sweeps Japan

Nearly 100,000 people in Tokyo cheered the Prince and Princess of Wales as they drove through the streets of the city. Page A2.

Rose Gets Best of Gooden

Pete Rose, age 45, got the deciding hit off Dwight Gooden, 21, as Reds gave the Mets' ace his first loss since August. SportsMonday, page C1.

Duvalier Funds Sought

Officials believe President Jean Claude Duvalier transfered $300 million out of Haiti and that he may have hidden $900 million abroad. Page D11.

"All the News That's Fit to Print"

The New York Times

Late Edition

Weather: Partly cloudy and mild today, light winds; clear and cool tonight. Mostly sunny and seasonable tomorrow. Temperatures: today 70-75, tonight 50-55; yesterday 66-80. Details, page 43.

VOL.CXXXV . . . No. 46,890 | NEW YORK, SUNDAY, SEPTEMBER 7, 1986 | $1.25

$1.50 beyond 75 miles from New York City, except on Long Island.

2 GUNMEN KILL 21 IN SYNAGOGUE; BAR DOORS AND THEN OPEN FIRE AT SABBATH SERVICE IN ISTANBUL

The bodies of some of the victims of the attack yesterday being carried from synagogue in Istanbul, Turkey.

Associated Press

ATTACKERS DIE ALSO

7 Rabbis Among Victims — Blasts and Bullets Miss Just 4 People

By HENRY KAMM

Special to The New York Times

ISTANBUL, Turkey, Sept. 6 — Two Arab terrorists invaded a Sephardic synagogue during Sabbath services in the Jewish quarter here today and, after locking the doors with iron bars, attacked the congregation with submachine guns and hand grenades.

At least 21 worshipers, including 7 rabbis, were killed, and 4 others were wounded in the massacre, a blaze of gunfire and explosions that went on for three to five minutes and left the newly refurbished synagogue on fire. The bodies of both gunmen were found in the carnage.

Witnesses described scenes of horror as bullets from automatic weapons raked the benches, worshipers in prayer shawls screamed and fell and blasts shook the Neve Shalom Synagogue, the city's largest, in the Karakoy district near the Galata Tower. One report said the killers also poured gasoline on some victims and tried to burn the bodies.

A 'Horrifying' Scene

"It's horrifying," Hasan Ali Ozer, Istanbul's Deputy Governor, said after visiting the scene. Interior Minister Yildirim Akbulut said the killers had barred the synagogue's main doors to keep people from escaping the bullets and grenades. Only 4 of the 29 worshipers escaped unhurt.

Turkish security officials said two Czechoslovak-made submachine guns, seven unexploded Soviet-made hand grenades and more than 100 spent cartridges were found inside the synagogue after firemen put out the flames in the single-story building.

Police officials described the gunmen as Arabs in their 20's and said they were on an apparent suicide mission. A teen-aged survivor, Gabriel Shaun, said they spoke Arabic to one another. Some witnesses said the gunmen entered by posing as photographers or tourists who wanted to take pictures of the interior, but others said they wore masks and dark clothing and simply burst in and began firing.

Identification Is Difficult

Bodies and parts of bodies were strewn about the synagogue and many of the dead could not be immediately identified. The bodies were taken away in blood-spattered pine boxes. The four wounded, one seriously hurt, were taken to a hospital.

All the victims were men, most of them elderly, the authorities said. Friends of the victims said that those killed included a visiting Israeli rabbi of Iranian origin, Raphael Nesim, and Rabbi Yuda Adoni, who was leading the morning prayers.

Istanbul, Moslem Turkey's largest city with 5.5 million people, has a Jewish population of about 22,000 Turkish nationals, mostly descendents of the Sephardim who fled the Spanish Inquisition late in the 15th century and still speak an old Spanish dialect known as Ladino.

Turkey, Israel, the United States and other countries separately condemned the attack — the first in memory against a synagogue in Istanbul, where the Jewish population has lived in relative peace for years. Many Turkish Jews speak with pride of their long

Continued on Page 12, Column 1

Associated Press

An American Air Force officer helping Dirk Vorndran of West Germany to a plane.

PAKISTAN REPORTS ALL GUNMEN SEIZED IN AIRPORT ATTACK

Altering First Account, It Says the 4 Hijackers Survived — Death Toll Put at 16

By STEVEN R. WEISMAN

Special to The New York Times

KARACHI, Pakistan, Sept. 6 — The Pakistani authorities, revising the details of the capture of a hijacked Pan American jumbo jet on Friday, said tonight that all four gunmen who had seized the plane were alive and had been taken into custody by Government security forces.

Contradicting an earlier report that two of the gunmen had been killed, law enforcement officials also said one of the four was seriously wounded. They said one of the four was from Syria, one from Bahrain and one was Palestinian.

But other sources indicated that all four were from Beirut, Lebanon, and that they had entered Pakistan last month on false Bahrain passports.

Estimates Vary on Wounded

Airport security officials today put the number of dead at 16, including 14 passengers, one member of the Pan American cabin crew and one ground crew employee.

Officials said the number of critically wounded was less than 50, but others said more than 100 had been wounded or otherwise injured.

A United States official said at least two and possibly more of the dead were Americans.

The hijackers were being questioned by army and civilian investigators. But Pakistani officials had little additional information except for the disclosure that the gunmen seemed to have spent considerable time preparing for the hijacking by obtaining fake airport security uniforms and renting a van and then disguising it as an airport security vehicle.

Questions on Role of Lights

Meanwhile, there was still some confusion today about whether officials had anticipated that the airliner's lights would go off and had extinguished the tarmac lights so commandos could advance on the plane. A Pakistani official who said it had been anticipated gave a different account later.

Tonight, a United States Air Force medical evacuation plane arrived at the Karachi airport and took on 16 wounded passengers. Indian diplomats said a special Indian Government plane was on its way to Karachi to take any Indian citizens who wanted to return to Bombay, where the flight originated on Friday.

The hijacking began at 6 A.M. Friday (9 P.M. Thursday, New York time),

Continued on Page 15A, Column 1

Reagan Writes To Gorbachev About Reporter

By BERNARD GWERTZMAN

Special to The New York Times

WASHINGTON, Sept. 6 — President Reagan has sent a message to Mikhail S. Gorbachev, urging the immediate release of an American reporter held in Moscow on suspicion of espionage, Administration officials said today.

Mr. Reagan, in his first direct involvement in the case of Nicholas S. Daniloff, correspondent of the magazine U.S. News & World Report, said in the message that he could give personal assurances Mr. Daniloff was not a spy, the officials said.

The President also told Mr. Gorbachev, according to the officials, that Soviet-American relations were too important to be affected by this case.

Message Delivered on Friday

The message was reported to have been delivered Friday. It was part of a stepped-up American effort that included a public declaration by Secretary of State George P. Shultz on Friday to press for the release of Mr. Daniloff, who was arrested Aug. 30.

The K.G.B., the Soviet intelligence and internal security agency, has accused Mr. Daniloff of espionage and Moscow has rejected American demands for his release. White House and State Department officials said today that if Mr. Daniloff was not freed by Monday, they would begin taking decisions on retaliatory measures.

Officials of U.S. News and World Report said today that they were grateful

Continued on Page 17, Column 1

Religious Groups Urge a Bigger War on Terrorism

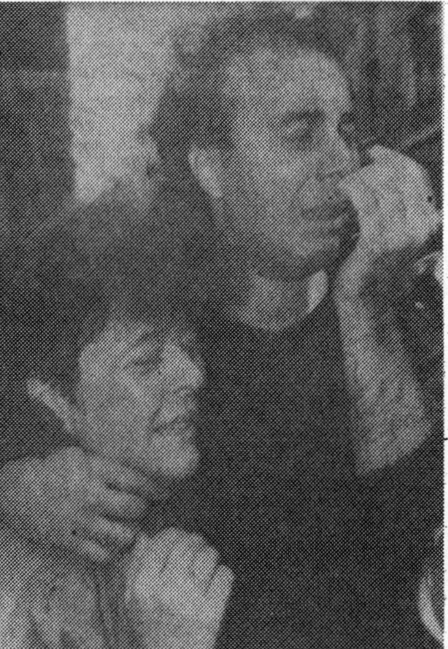

Associated Press

Relatives of victims of the attack mourning outside the synagogue.

By ROBERT O. BOORSTIN

Governments and religious groups around the world condemned the attack on a synagogue in Istanbul, Turkey, yesterday and called for increased vigilance and international cooperation to combat terrorism.

The United States and Israeli Governments, in separate statements, labeled the attack "cowardly."

In Washington, a State Department spokesman deplored the "terrible loss of life."

Peres Issues a Warning

In Tel Aviv, Prime Minister Shimon Peres said all Jews joined in praying for the souls of the 21 worshipers who were killed in the attack.

"We are also a state and we know not only to pray," he warned. "Whoever hestitates about American responses or Israeli responses can now learn a lesson."

Neither Mr. Peres, who said his Government was not clear who was responsible for the attack, nor other Israeli leaders indicated against whom or when Israel might retaliate.

In an earlier statement, Mr. Peres also called on "the free nations of the world to join in a war to the end against such disgusting deeds."

The Israeli Foreign Minister, Yitzhak Shamir, said in a radio interview that the attack "obliges the Jewish state to intensify the war against terror organizations in every place and in every way."

P.L.O. Condemns Attack

In Tunis, a spokesman for the Palestine Liberation Organization denounced the attack and said the group "condemns this form of struggle."

The spokesman, Salah Khalaf, said his group "refuses to obtain the rights of the Palestinian people by making innocent people pay the price, whether in a synagogue or in a plane." He was referring to the hijacking of a Pan American World Airways jetliner in Karachi, Pakistan, on Friday.

Clovis Maksoud, permanent ob-

Continued on Page 12, Column 3

6 Suspended at Karachi Airport

By RICHARD WITKIN

At least six members of the Karachi airport security force have been suspended for negligence in allowing the hijackers of a Pan American World Airways jumbo jet to drive onto the tarmac in a van disguised to look like an official security van, official sources at the airport disclosed yesterday.

According to reports there, three of the hijackers wore security personnel uniforms, consisting of light blue shirts and dark blue trousers. They were also apparently able to obtain security badges or stars in a marketplace in Karachi, the informants said.

In addition, officials said the Suzuki van the hijackers rented had apparently been painted the same blue color of the official van used by the airport security force. There was an unconfirmed report that they had added a light and a siren on the roof to help complete the disguise.

Systems Are Vulnerable

The hijackers' success in slipping past one or more checkpoints underscored the accepted belief of security experts that even the best screening systems are vulnerable to inventive violators.

In another development, a little more information became available on the hijackers yesterday when it was disclosed that one of them had arrived Aug. 17 with a Bahrain passport and checked in at an expensive Karachi hotel, The Taj Mahal, where he apparently made preparations for the hijacking.

Several issues are still to be resolved: What precise instructions did the checkpoint guards have for verifying the validity of plates on vans and identification documents of their occupants? Were the instructions inadequate? Did the guards fail to follow proper procedures?

Another issue raised was whether one or more of the guards might have been in collusion with the hijackers. But a senior airport security official said that the hijackers definitely had no confederates at the airport. He said

Continued on Page 15A, Column 1

Parking Unit Aide Reported Corruption in '82

By MICHAEL ORESKES

A key official in the city's Parking Violations Bureau warned the Koch administration in 1982 of corruption in the agency, four years before such corruption was discovered independently by the Federal Bureau of Investigation, according to senior investigators.

The allegations were not properly pursued by the city's Department of Investigation, the officials said, and the department's handling of the case lulled some city officials into believing that troubles at the parking bureau were the result of managerial flaws rather than wrongdoing.

The 1982 warning is cited in a report Mayor Koch requested on whether the Department of Investigation had failed to follow up signs of corruption at the parking bureau before Federal prosecutors charged that a bribery ring was operating there. The report is to be released Tuesday at City Hall.

Mr. Koch has maintained during the municipal scandal that there was no way he could have known of corruption in the Parking Violations Bureau because not even the many Federal and local investigative authorities, including the Department of Investigation, knew about it.

Last spring, for example, the Mayor said: "There are five D.A.'s; they didn't know. Two U.S. Attorneys; they didn't know. And a City Comptroller and a State Comptroller; they didn't know. And a Commissioner of the Department of Investigation; he didn't know. How the hell do you expect me to know?"

Responding to the new disclosure, Mayor Koch said yesterday, "If information was provided to the Department of Investigation that should have been followed up on, and it was not, that's a failure at D.O.I. and the decision-makers at that agency will have to be held accountable."

The head of the Department of Investigation is appointed by the Mayor. Stanley Lupkin, who served as Commissioner of Investigation until April 15, 1982, and Patrick W. McGinley, who succeeded him, each said last week he had never heard about the 1982 allegations.

One law-enforcement official said the information had been handled by Mr. McGinley's deputies, a normal procedure in an office that had to make decisions on opening or ending 20 to 30 investigations a month.

The warning of corruption came from the former comptroller of the Parking Violations Bureau, James Rose. Records of his long-forgotten interviews with Investigation Department officials were rediscovered re-

Continued on Page 40, Column 1

INSIDE

Trial of Accused Mob Chiefs

Eight men, whom prosecutors call members or associates of a "commission" that ruled the Mafia, go on trial tomorrow in New York. Page 51.

Becker Upset in U.S. Open

Miloslav Mecir beat Boris Becker and will face Ivan Lendl in the final. Martina Navratilova will face Helena Sukova in women's final. Section 5.

New Role for Universities

American higher education, founded 350 years ago, is taking a new role in the nation's economy amid doubts about academic values. Page 30.

Residential Property

A special real estate report on residential property nationwide — co-ops, condominiums, houses and rental buildings — appears today. Section 12.

Today's Sections

Index to Subjects

"All the News That's Fit to Print"

The New York Times

Late Edition

New York Today: Hazy sun, breezy and warm. High 82-87. Tonight, windy and warm. Low 66-72. Tomorrow, partly cloudy, chance of an afternoon thundershower. High 80-84. Details, page D26.

VOL.CXXXV . . . No. 46,894 | NEW YORK, THURSDAY, SEPTEMBER 11, 1986 | 50 cents beyond 75 miles from New York City, except on Long Island. | 30 CENTS

HEAD OF CBS QUITS UNDER PRESSURE; PALEY IN KEY ROLE

TENSE MEETING OF BOARD

Tisch Appointed Acting Chief — Search Committee for a Successor Is Created

By GERALDINE FABRIKANT

After a tense, lengthy board meeting yesterday, Thomas H. Wyman, the embattled chairman and chief executive of CBS Inc., resigned as head of the communications giant, the company announced last night.

Mr. Wyman will be relieved of his role immediately, CBS said. Laurence A. Tisch, the company's largest shareholder and the chairman of the Loews Corporation, will become acting chief executive and chairman of a new management committee, to serve until a new chairman and chief executive are selected, the company said in a two-page statement.

In addition, William S. Paley, the 84-year-old founder of CBS and holder of 8.1 percent of the company's stock, will become acting chairman. Harold Brown, a board member and a former Defense Secretary, will head an executive search committee.

Paley: 'I Am Delighted'

Mr. Paley said in a statement: "As founder of the company, I am delighted that Laurence Tisch will serve as acting C.E.O. during this transition. Larry has not only proven his extraordinary ability as a businessman and leader in the success of his own company, Loews, but, most important, he shares the values and principles that have guided CBS throughout the period of its growth. I respect and admire him, and look forward to working with him."

Intense speculation in the media and financial communities had surrounded the monthly board meeting, which took place amid mounting tensions among board members and heavy pressure stemming from the power struggle between Mr. Wyman and Mr. Tisch.

The management shift comes at a time when CBS's performance has been suffering, largely because of weakness in its broadcasting business, which has faced a slowdown in spending by advertisers and the rise of NBC to first place in prime-time viewership. CBS is now No. 2, ahead of ABC.

There have also been problems at CBS News. Belt-tightening measures, conflicts over the direction of the venerable news operation and uncertainty about the future of the company's top management combined to hurt morale.

Sale Helped Results

In the second quarter of this year, CBS posted $107.2 million in net income on $1.2 billion in revenues, helped by the sale of its St. Louis television station and lower tax rates. In 1985, it earned $27.4 million on revenues of $4.8 billion.

Yesterday, CBS's stock closed $3.75 a share lower, at $140, on the New York Stock Exchange.

As recently as early this week, there had been reports that Mr. Wyman, concerned about a Tisch bid for the rest of CBS, was talking to other companies about a possible merger or acquisition. It had been reported that Westinghouse

Continued on Page D6, Column 3

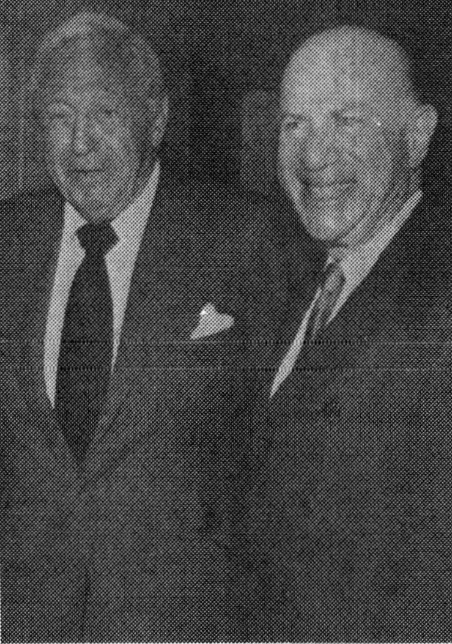

The New York Times/Susan Ferguson

William S. Paley, left, founder of CBS Inc., with Laurence A. Tisch, the company's largest shareholder, after meeting yesterday.

Primaries Show Women Emerging As Seasoned Political Contenders

By E. J. DIONNE Jr.

The outcome of primaries Tuesday in nine states and the District of Columbia marked the advancement of women who have made a career of elective office, politicians and political consultants said yesterday.

In many states, they also noted, voter turnouts were unusually low, bolstering the view of many that an unusually large number of voters will stay away from the polls in November. The analysts said the primaries also showed that voters were looking at least as much to candidates' personal histories of work on behalf of their communities as to their stands on national political issues.

This was underlined by the very nature of the women who won in Tuesday's primaries, said Peter D. Hart, a leading Democratic poll taker.

'Serious and Professional'

"The interesting thing about women running in 1986 is you don't have women aged 30 and 40," he said. "They're women aged 50 and 60. They're serious and professional candidates. They have their names at the top of the ticket because the party is looking for proven vote-getters."

This was especially true in the Democratic primary in Maryland, in which voters set up the nation's only United States Senate race between two women. It was the second such race in American history. The first was in 1960, when Senator Margaret Chase Smith, a Maine Republican, defeated Lucia Cormier, a Democrat.

Representative Barbara A. Mikulski, a social worker who started her career as a City Council member, was the overwhelming choice in the Democratic primary. The Republicans picked Linda Chavez, a former Reagan Administration aide. Although not a local activist in Ms. Mikulski's style, she built her career over many years, first as a Democratic trade unionist, then as a Republican.

In Connecticut, Republicans nominated State Representative Julie D. Belaga for Governor, while in Arizona the Democrats chose Carolyn Warner, the State Schools Superintendent, for Governor.

Maryland voters also set up a woman-against-woman House race that will be watched nationally. It will pit Kathleen Kennedy Townsend, Robert F. Kennedy's daughter, against Representative Helen Delich Bentley.

In Vermont, Gov. Madeleine M. Kunin, who was unopposed in the Democratic primary, will defend her fiscally cautious, moderately liberal record in her campaign for re-election.

With the notable exception of former

Continued on Page B13, Column 1

MAYOR COMMENDS D'AMATO AS BEING 'SUPERB SENATOR'

Koch Says the Republican Is Preferable to Mark Green — Ideology Is Cited

By FRANK LYNN

Mayor Koch said yesterday that Senator Alfonse M. D'Amato had been "a superb Senator," a better lawmaker than his newly chosen Democratic opponent, Mark Green, would be.

"I don't happen to agree with Mark Green's philosophy so I am never going to endorse him," the Mayor said at a City Hall news conference a day after Mr. Green defeated John S. Dyson in the Democratic primary.

Asked if Senator D'Amato, a Republican, was a better Senator than Mr. Green would be, the Mayor responded, "No question about it in my mind."

The Mayor, who had supported Mr. Dyson in the primary, declined to say whether he would endorse anyone in the general election. Mr. Dyson will be on the ballot, on the Liberal line.

Role of Ideology

In an election year in which political analysts said ideology was generally de-emphasized in the primaries around the country, both Senator D'Amato and Mr. Green, in separate news conferences, indicated its importance in New York. They tried to paint each other into political corners, with Senator D'Amato charging that Mr. Green was a candidate of "left-wing ideologues" and Mr. Green responding that the Senator was "a right-winger."

Mr. Dyson, who spent $6 million, almost all of it his own money, and lost by about 33,000 votes, said in a telephone interview that he intended to campaign aggressively as the Liberal Party candidate although he might divide the vote against Mr. D'Amato, who in 1980 won a three-way race with less than a majority of the votes.

"I made a commitment, and I'm a man who's known to keep his word," said Mr. Dyson, who acknowledged that he was still concerned about Mr. Green's attacks on him in the primary campaign. He added that he was prepared to spend more of his own money.

Small Impact of Commercials

The 43-year-old Mr. Dyson lost to Mr. Green, a 41-year-old lawyer, author and consumer advocate in a primary that was notable in that money, television commercials and political endorsements carried little weight. In other races in the state Tuesday, even scandals had little impact.

Mr. Green overcame the multimillion-dollar Dyson advertising campaign and the opposition of most of the state's Democratic Party establishment, including Governor Cuomo, who

Continued on Page B12, Column 5

ISRAEL AND EGYPT AGREE ON BORDER; HEAD FOR SUMMIT

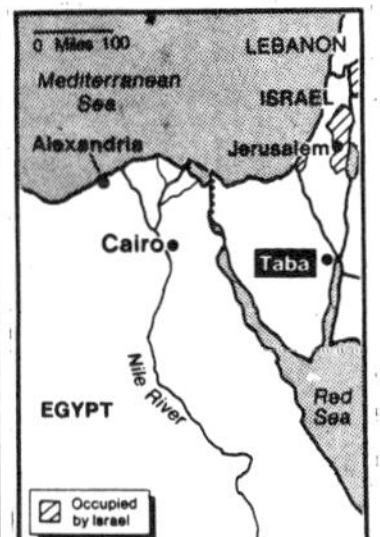

The New York Times/Sept. 11, 1986

The border dispute is over Taba, a 700-yard stretch of beach.

ARBITRATION IS DUE

Accord Clears the Way for Meeting Today by Peres and Mubarak

By JOHN KIFNER

Special to The New York Times

CAIRO, Sept. 10 — Egyptian and Israeli negotiators agreed tonight on a formula for settling a border dispute and salvaged a meeting Thursday between President Hosni Mubarak and Prime Minister Shimon Peres.

After more than 12 hours of meetings — most of them with the American special Middle East envoy, Richard W. Murphy, taking part — the two sides agreed on the terms under which their long-running border dispute over the 700-yard Sinai beach known as Taba would be sent to arbitration.

First Summit Talks Since 1981

That agreement cleared the way for the summit conference, which will be the first meeting between leaders of Egypt and Israel since 1981 and the first for Mr. Mubarak. The two-day meeting will be in Alexandria, Egypt.

[In Jerusalem, the Likud bloc demanded that a Cabinet meeting be held Thursday so strict guidelines could be laid down for the Peres-Mubarak meeting, Israeli Government sources said. Page A8.

[In Washington, officials reacted positively to the agreement on arbitration. But officials added that Secretary of State George P. Shultz would not be able to travel to the Middle East soon because of a full schedule. Page A9.]

Two-Day Meeting Planned

"We have finished everything," said Gen. Avraham Tamir, the head of Mr. Peres's office, as he emerged from the border talks shortly before 10 P.M. "The summit will start tomorrow and will go over into Friday."

The Egyptian Cabinet, sitting in a late-night session, approved the agreement.

The summit meeting has been promoted by the Reagan Administration, which is seeking a symbol of success in its Middle East policy after the collapse of the peace initiative backed by King Hussein of Jordan in February.

The United States supports the increasingly weak Egyptian economy with more than $2 billion in aid a year, and sources close to the talks said Mr. Murphy had warned Mr. Mubarak that it would be difficult to get more money from Congress if Egypt was seen as backing away from its ties with Israel.

Prime Minister Peres, who is to turn over his office to Yitzhak Shamir early next month under their power-sharing arrangement, was also eager for the summit meeting, which he sought as the cap to his term.

The more hard-line Mr. Shamir, leader of the Likud bloc, said in a

Continued on Page A6, Column 1

Soviet Is Given New U.S. Offer In Daniloff Case

By BERNARD GWERTZMAN

Special to The New York Times

WASHINGTON, Sept. 10 — The United States, in a new proposal, has suggested that an American journalist in Moscow and a Soviet employee of the United Nations in New York who are being held on espionage charges be turned over to their respective ambassadors and that the American then be allowed to return to home without trial, Administration officials said today.

Amid discussions on resolving the latest crisis in Soviet-American relations, State Department and White House officials said they could not predict whether the Soviet Union would agree to the new proposal.

Reagan Receives Reply

President Reagan said tonight that he had received a reply from the Soviet leader, Mikhail S. Gorbachev, to the American request for an early release of the journalist, Nicholas S. Daniloff, Moscow correspondent of the magazine U.S. News & World Report.

He would not give details of the response, saying, "I don't want to rock the boat." Mr. Reagan, who spoke to reporters after a state dinner for the Brazilian President, José Sarney, declined to predict when the issue might be resolved.

The arrangement would involve Mr. Daniloff and Gennadi F. Zakharov, a

Continued on Page A12, Column 1

Administration Aides Back Tests Of Federal Employees for Drugs

By BERNARD WEINRAUB

Special to The New York Times

WASHINGTON, Sept. 10 — Top Administration officials generally agreed today on widespread drug testing of Federal employees but could not agree on whether to dismiss second offenders, officials said today.

President Reagan is expected to decide Thursday on this and other details of his drive to control drug abuse. With polls showing high public concern, and with an election approaching, Congress, too, is moving rapidly toward action on the issue. The House began debate today on its bipartisan $1.5 billion plan. [Page A24.]

May Affect 1.1 Million Workers

In an extended White House meeting of the Domestic Policy Council, Cabinet officials engaged in what one Administration aide described as a "fairly strong debate" over the Government's response if a Federal employee fails a second drug test after undergoing treatment.

Officials said the Cabinet members had generally agreed to proposals that would permit drug testing of more than half of all Federal civilian workers. Under the proposed executive order, the head of almost every Federal agency would establish a drug testing program that would cover employees who have access to secret or sensitive information. The order may cover as many as 1.1 million of the 2.1 million civilian Federal employees, excluding postal workers.

The officials also generally agreed that employees found to be using drugs would be given treatment, at least the first time.

But several key Administration officials argued forcefully that a Federal employee should be dismissed if he or she failed a drug test twice. These officials included Attorney General Edwin Meese 3d, Education Secretary William J. Bennett and Constance J. Horner, director of the Office of Personnel Management.

Opposing this group, and arguing that further treatment should be provided for Federal employees who fail a second drug test, were Bill Brock, the Labor Secretary; Dr. Otis R. Bowen, the Health and Human Services Secretary, and Peter J. Wallison, the White House counsel, an official said.

The official said that at one point Mr. Wallison, arguing against dismissal,

Continued on Page A25, Column 1

The New York Times/Jose R. Lopez

BRAZILIAN LEADER VISITS WASHINGTON: President Reagan and his wife, Nancy, greeting President José Sarney and his wife, Marly, at the White House yesterday. At the welcoming ceremony, Mr. Reagan warned that a greater effort must be made by Brazil to open its markets to foreign competition. Page D3.

Death in Park: Difficult Questions for Parents

By SAMUEL G. FREEDMAN

For parents, educators and psychologists, the strangling of 18-year-old Jennifer Dawn Levin and the arrest of 19-year-old Robert E. Chambers Jr. on a charge of murder have become more than a sensational and notorious criminal case.

The events have served to illuminate a subculture of sophisticated, affluent teen-agers regularly partying and club-hopping long past midnight. And much as a suburban car accident that kills several high-school friends forces families there to confront the problem of drunken driving by teen-agers, the Levin case has raised some peculiarly urban questions:

Is it harder to rear children amid the glitter and vice of the big city? Is it inevitable to lose control of a 19-year-old? Or have some parents in demanding, high-paying professions substituted money for affection and freedom for supervision? Have they abdicated their role as parents to surrogates?

Robert E. Chambers Jr. was indicted in the death of Jennifer Dawn Levin. Page B10.

The five parents and step-parents of Miss Levin and Mr. Chambers — both of whom came from homes split by divorce — have not spoken to reporters since the Aug. 26 killing. But the questions extend far beyond the immediate families.

"The important issues in this case are the wider issues, not the specific ones," said Ronald P. Stewart, the headmaster of York Preparatory School, from which Mr. Chambers graduated. "Everyone is looking for some 'bad seed' thread in Robert Chambers, something to make us say, 'Aha, we should have known.'

"But the more worrying conclusion

Continued on Page B10, Column 2

INSIDE

Israelis Strike in Lebanon

Israeli planes struck at suspected Palestinian bases in southern Lebanon after Israel foiled an infiltration attempt by guerrillas. Page A3.

Developers Get Gimbels

The two Gimbels Manhattan stores and the chain's Queens warehouse will be sold to a group including two New York developers. Page D1.

Truman House Auctioned

A Boston developer outbid a group of Alaskan Indians in the auction of President Truman's cottage in Key West, Fla. Page A16.

Wedding Cast of Thousands

As thousands of guests watched, two young Hasidic Jews were married in Brooklyn, uniting two sects of the ultra-Orthodox movement. Page B2.

"All the News That's Fit to Print"

The New York Times

New York Today: Sunny and cool. High 57-63. Tonight, clear, chilly, low 40's in the city, 30's in the suburbs. Tomorrow, cloudy, highs in the 50's. Yesterday: High 73, low 63. Details on page C16.

VOL.CXXXVI.... No. 46,928 | NEW YORK, WEDNESDAY, OCTOBER 15, 1986 | 60 cents beyond 75 miles from New York City, except on Long Island. | 30 CENTS

CONFEREES AGREE ON VAST REVISIONS IN LAWS ON ALIENS

FINAL APPROVAL EXPECTED

Bill Would Bar Hiring of Illegal Workers and Give Several Million Legal Status

By ROBERT PEAR

Special to The New York Times

WASHINGTON, Oct. 14 — House and Senate negotiators agreed today on the terms of a landmark immigration bill that would prohibit the hiring of illegal aliens and offer legal status to several million illegal aliens already in the United States.

The agreement, reached after five hours of intense negotiations at a

Provisions of bill, page B11.

closed meeting, reconciles all differences between bills passed by the Senate last year and by the House of Representatives last week.

Biggest Changes in 20 Years

The compromise bill now goes back to the House and then the Senate for final clearance. If approved, as expected, it would then be submitted to President Reagan, who has repeatedly expressed support for such legislation.

The bill would make the biggest changes in immigration law in at least 20 years and would affect virtually every employer in the United States.

Under the bill, employers would be subject to civil penalties ranging from $250 to $10,000 for each illegal alien they hired. The bigger penalities would be imposed for a third or subsequent offense. The number of illegal aliens who might qualify for legal status under the bill is unknown; estimates range from one million to five million.

The Government would offer legal status to illegal aliens who entered the United States before Jan. 1, 1982, and had resided here continuously since then. Aliens would not be disqualified because of "brief, casual and innocent absences from the United States" in that period.

As Congress worked toward adjournment, a separate group of House and Senate negotiators agreed on a military budget of about $290 billion for the current fiscal year. [Page A20.]

'This Is Miraculous'

Approval of the immigration bill was made possible by a delicately balanced compromise on foreign agriculture workers.

"This is miraculous," Representative Peter W. Rodino Jr. said, referring to the agreement on a measure that includes many provisions he first proposed in 1972. "I feel great, but I will feel greater when the bill is on the President's desk and has been signed into law."

Mr. Rodino, a New Jersey Democrat who was the chief sponsor of the House bill, said, "This bill will regularize our immigration policy and shows the big heart of America."

Senator Alan K. Simpson, Republi-

Continued on Page B11, Column 1

The New York Times/John Sotomayor

Elie Wiesel, his wife, Marion, and their son, Shlomo-Elisha, in New York after Mr. Wiesel won Nobel Peace Prize.

Elie Wiesel Gets Nobel for Peace As 'Messenger'

By JAMES M. MARKHAM

Special to The New York Times

OSLO, Oct. 14 — Elie Wiesel, who survived Nazi death camps to become a witness against forgetfulness and violence, was awarded the Nobel Peace Prize today.

"Elie Wiesel has emerged as one of the most important spiritual leaders and guides in an age when violence, repression and racism continue to characterize the world," said Egil Aarvik, chairman of the Norwegian Nobel Committee and a former president of the Norwegian Parliament.

[Mr. Wiesel, who got the news of his award at home in Manhattan, said it would allow him to "speak louder" and "reach more people" for the causes that have driven him. Man in the News, page A10.]

In a solemn autumn ritual that each year turns the world's attention to the slumberous Norwegian capital, Mr. Aarvik announced the award of the $270,000 prize at 11 A.M. in a small room, packed with journalists, at the committee's headquarters not far from the royal palace.

"Wiesel is a messenger to mankind," Mr. Aarvik continued in Norwegian, reading from a statement. "His message is one of peace, atonement and human dignity. His belief that the forces fighting evil in the world can be victorious is a hard-won belief."

"His message is based on his own

Continued on Page A10, Column 3

Salvadoran Air Base Is Called Center for C.I.A. Operations

By LYDIA CHAVEZ

Special to The New York Times

SAN SALVADOR, Oct, 14 — Behind the high concrete-block walls that keep the Ilopango air base here from the public's view is a drab two-story building. Over the last three years, the building has served as the waiting room for agents working for the Central Intelligence Agency, leaders of the Nicaraguan rebels, mercenaries and American military advisers. according to American officials and Nicaraguan rebel sources.

Now more than ever the base is the center of C.I.A.-supported operations to supply Nicaraguan rebel forces, according to an American shot down in a supply plane over Nicaragua.

American men in civilian clothes often pass through the base's gates and American officials say privately that it is the center of C.I.A. and other clandestine operations here.

Many American visitors to the base, on the eastern edge of San Salvador, are never "officially" in the country. The honor code of silence prevails.

The base is run by the politically conservative and staunchly independent Gen. Juan Rafael Bustillo. One of the general's most recent phantom guests was the longtime C.I.A. agent, known by the alias Max Gomez, who directed the contra supply flight shot down by Nicaraguan soldiers last week, according to two highly reliable sources with close C.I.A. contracts here and Eugene Hasenfus, the American captured in Nicaragua.

Vice President Bush said this week that he had met Mr. Gomez three times. He said Mr. Gomez was an adviser in counterinsurgency who worked in El Salvador with the approval of President José Napoleón Duarte and the armed forces.

Despite Mr. Bush's statements, both Mr. Duarte and the armed forces chief, Gen. Aldolfo O. Blandón, deny knowing Mr. Gomez or approving his work.

"The air force is very jealous of its

Continued on Page A5, Column 1

GORBACHEV TERMS REAGAN TOO TIMID; U.S. IN NEW APPEAL

REAGAN CITES GAIN

He Says Accord Is Near and Asks Soviet Not to Miss Chance

By GERALD M. BOYD

Special to The New York Times

WASHINGTON, Oct. 14 — President Reagan appealed to the Soviet Union today "not to miss the opportunity" for a major breakthrough on reducing nuclear weapons, saying such an agreement was "within our grasp."

The statement by Mr. Reagan marked the second straight day he has

Talk by Reagan, page A13.

made such an appeal, and it came as he and the Soviet leader, Mikhail S. Gorbachev, engaged in a public competition to promote their own interpretations of the outcome of the meeting in Iceland.

In Washington, Mr. Reagan and other Administration officials undertook a major campaign to explain Mr. Reagan's decision to refuse to accept restraints on the development of a strategic defense system against nuclear weapons.

In Moscow, Mr. Gorbachev, in an appearance on Soviet television, challenged the Administration's description of the summit meeting and accused Mr. Reagan of missing the opportunity to achieve a historic agreement on nuclear weapons. The Soviet leader said that Moscow would be unwilling to move forward as long as Mr. Reagan's maintained his position on the missile defense system.

The White House also began an effort today to salvage something from the Iceland meeting by asserting that the

Continued on Page A13, Column 4

The Summit Aftermath

The White House has begun an extensive campaign to blame Moscow for the summit results. Page A13.

Secretary of State Shultz said he planned to meet with the Soviet Foreign Minister next month. Page A14.

Congressional leaders said there would be renewed pressure from Congress on arms control. Page A14.

RUSSIAN CRITICAL

Says President Lacked Will on Arms to Make a 'Turn in History'

By SERGE SCHMEMANN

Special to The New York Times

MOSCOW, Oct. 14 — Mikhail S. Gorbachev said today that President Reagan had proved lacking in courage and political will to take a historic step forward at their Iceland meeting.

But the Soviet leader termed the meeting a "major event" and said he was not shutting the door on the search for arms control.

Mr. Gorbachev offered his assessment in a televised speech, affirming that a Soviet proposal to scale down nuclear arsenals had foundered on Mr. Reagan's adherence to a space-based missile defense program.

Iceland Meeting 'Not in Vain'

Although Mr. Gorbachev was critical of what he said was Mr. Reagan's dependence on the "military-industrial complex," he said the meeting "was not in vain" and held out hopes for a

Excerpts from speech, page A12.

change of heart in the United States.

"We are realists," he said. "We clearly understand that questions that for many years, even decades, have not found their solution can hardly be resolved at a single sitting.

"We have sufficient experience in doing business with the United States. We know how changeable its political climate is, how strong and influential the opponents of peace are.

"That we are not losing heart and shutting the door — although there are more than enough grounds for that — is only because we are sincerely convinced about the need for fresh efforts in building normal interstate relations in the nuclear age."

Close to a 'Historic' Decision

Mr. Gorbachev gave a detailed — and at times dramatic — account of the Soviet proposals in Iceland and the bargaining that brought the two sides to the edge of agreement.

"Standing within one, or two, or three steps of a decision that could become historic for the entire nuclear-technological age, we were unable to take those steps," he said.

"A turn in world history failed to take place, although it was possible. But our conscience is clear. We did all we could. Our partners lacked the breadth of approach, an understanding of the unique character of the moment, and, ultimately, the courage, responsibility and political determination that are so necessary for resolving vital and complicated world problems. They

Continued on Page A13, Column 1

Cable Company Discussed Hiring Friedman for $10,000 Per Month

By RALPH BLUMENTHAL

The company selected to provide cable television service in the Bronx said yesterday that it had discussed hiring Stanley M. Friedman and other Bronx politicians under contracts totaling hundreds of thousands of dollars a year.

But a vice president of the company, the Cablevision Systems Corporation, said that the discussions were broken off last year, in part because of the possible appearance of improprieties, and that the contracts were not concluded.

The company official, Sheila A. Mahoney, said that Cablevision had talked with Mr. Friedman, the Bronx Democratic leader, about hiring him for $10,000 a month but that the talks lapsed amid delays in starting the cable hookups. She said that no one at the company could immediately recall whether Mr. Friedman or company officials had initiated the discussions.

Seeking Influence

Cable companies and other concerns seeking to do business with the city, have traditionally sought to hire influential politicians and former officials as lobbyists and counselors.

Current Federal and state investigations are aimed at determining, in part, whether such representatives or any other intermediaries sought to improperly influence public officials in their duties.

Two weeks ago, a Queens grand jury indictment charged John A. Zaccaro with acting in concert with the former Borough President, Donald R. Manes, in trying to extort money from Cablevision in connection with the Queens cable franchise, which the company did not get. Mr. Zaccaro has pleaded

Continued on Page B3, Column 2

INSIDE

Time Buys Text Publisher

Time agreed to buy the textbook publisher Scott, Foresman, which once supplied Dick and Jane readers, for a price of $520 million. Page D1.

Olympic Timetable Changes

The International Olympic Committee voted to alternate the summer and winter Games every two years, beginning in 1994. Page B15.

The New York Times/Barton Silverman

Mets Defeat Astros, 2-1

Gary Carter being congratulated after driving in the winning run in the 12th inning as Mets took a 3-2 lead over Houston in the National League Championship Series. His teammates were, from left, Jesse Orosco, Keith Hernandez and Howard Johnson. The series resumes in Houston this afternoon. Page B15.

Sex a Health Issue at New York School Clinics

By JANE PERLEZ

A 16-year-old student visited the health clinic at Martin Luther King Jr. High School yesterday morning for a pregnancy test. She waited 15 minutes and had her suspicions confirmed: she was pregnant.

The resident nurse practitioner, Fran Combe, called the girl's mother. "She and her mother had discussed it, and they both decided she would have an abortion," Ms. Combe said. "I recommended a clinic to her where we have been very pleased with the care."

In the first month of the school year, Ms. Combe has conducted three pregnancy tests at the school. Two were positive.

Last year, 10 girls — all except one were under 18 years old — visited the clinic and were found to be pregnant. Five were recommended to the abortion clinic in Manhattan that Ms. Combe mentioned; two others were recommended to another abortion clinic; three girls, aged 16 and 17, gave birth and dropped out of school.

The clinic at Martin Luther King, at 122 Amsterdam Avenue near 66th Street, is one of nine state-financed clinics at New York City high schools. The clinics provide general health care such as diagnosis and treatment of illnesses, physical exams and dietary advice, in addition to birth-control counseling. Two of the clinics have been dispensing contraceptives, although one has ceased; the others write prescriptions for contraceptives.

At its meeting today, the Board of Education is to have its first full discussion of the role of the health clinics since the birth-control services were revealed in a report to the board two weeks ago.

A doctor at St. Luke's-Roosevelt Hos-

Continued on Page B8, Column 4

5 RUSSIANS IN U.N. ARE OUSTED BY U.S.

Diplomats Among 25 Expelled — Soviet May Retaliate

By ELAINE SCIOLINO

Special to The New York Times

UNITED NATIONS, N.Y., Oct. 14 — The State Department announced today that the remaining Soviet diplomats ordered expelled by the Reagan Administration must leave the United States by Sunday.

According to an official at the United States Mission to the United Nations, 5 of the 25 diplomats originally named are still here but they are expected to depart by tomorrow.

A leading Soviet official, asked if his country would carry out an earlier threat to retaliate against the United States for the expulsions, said. "The retaliation will be made." He did not elaborate further.

With the departure of the remaining Russians, the Soviet Union will be in full compliance with an American order that 25 diplomats attached to the Soviet Mission leave the country. The Administration has identified the 25 as members of the K.G.B., the Soviet intelligence agency, and the G.R.U., the Soviet military intelligence agency.

It was not immediately clear why the Russians had abandoned their efforts

Continued on Page A9, Column 1

"All the News That's Fit to Print"

The New York Times

Late Edition

New York: Today, mostly sunny and mild. High 38-42. Tonight, clear and cold. Low 22-29. Tomorrow, mostly sunny, milder. High 40-44. Yesterday: High 42, low 32. Details on page C12.

VOL.CXXXVI . . No. 47,060 NEW YORK, TUESDAY, FEBRUARY 24, 1987

50 cents beyond 75 miles from New York City, except on Long Island. 30 CENTS

The New York Times/David Hutson

Gephardt Announces Presidential Bid

Representative Richard A. Gephardt of Missouri holding his 9-year-old daughter, Katherine, in St. Louis yesterday as he announced his candidacy for the Democratic Presidential nomination. Page A12.

SYRIANS ON PATROL IN EFFORT TO KEEP WEST BEIRUT PEACE

4 Lebanese Reported Killed in Clash With New Force — 60 Others Detained

By IHSAN A. HIJAZI

Special to The New York Times

BEIRUT, Feb. 23 — Syrian troops went into action today within 24 hours of their arrival in Beirut, trading gunfire with militiamen and setting up checkpoints in an attempt to stop the fighting here.

Although the Syrians were welcomed as "peacekeepers" by some Beirut residents, it was not clear that they could end the fighting in Beirut's streets, as the Americans and the Israelis had failed to do in recent years.

In the Ain Mirayseh neighborhood, where Shiite Moslem and Druse militiamen have shared influence, Syrian soldiers used rocket-propelled grenades and heavy machine guns to subdue gunmen who refused to surrender. Local radio stations said the gunmen involved were Druse.

Four Lebanese Killed

The report said four Lebanese were killed and two Syrian soldiers were wounded in the clash. The Syrians called in backup units to deal with the situation. There was no immediate report on the direct cause of the shootout.

In Hamra, where the fighting had virtually destroyed the Commodore Hotel, Syrian soldiers rounded up 60 gunmen, packed them into three trucks and took them away for questioning.

Syrian reinforcements arrived today, raising the Syrian strength in Beirut and the southern suburbs to 7,000, according to the police. The troops were requested by Lebanese leaders to help enforce a Syrian-brokered cease-fire in the latest round of factional fighting in West Beirut, which began Feb. 15. The police have said 300 people were killed and 1,300 wounded since then.

Reports of 100 Kidnappings

The gunmen had slipped out of sight Sunday night shortly after Syrian Army units began to deploy. But despite warnings from the chief of Syrian military intelligence, Brig. Gen. Ghazi Kanaan, that gunmen would be shot on sight, some reappeared today, wearing civilian clothes instead of their uni-

Continued on Page A10, Column 1

Reuters

Iosif Z. Begun being carried after his arrival yesterday in Moscow. At center is his wife, Inna, and at left is their son, Boris.

Begun, Freed Dissident, Returns To Moscow to the Sound of Cheers

By FELICITY BARRINGER

Special to The New York Times

MOSCOW, Feb. 23 — Iosif Z. Begun, the Jewish rights advocate who was freed from prison on Friday, returned home to a jubilant welcome today, pledging to devote himself to the cause of human rights in general and the rights of Jews in particular.

Mr. Begun was released from Chistopol Prison in the Tatar Autonomous Republic on Friday after a monthlong debate with authorities over what kind of statement he would sign in connection with his release. A joyous crowd greeted him on his arrival at Kazan Station in Moscow, lifting him to their shoulders, throwing flowers and chanting and singing in Hebrew.

In an interview at his apartment, Mr. Begun, who is 54 years old, said he had agreed not to engage in "anti-Soviet" activity on the condition that harassment of Soviet Jews is stopped and other rights are guaranteed. Those other rights include emigration, family reunification, and freedom to study Jewish history, language and culture.

"If all this would be realized in the process of democratization, then I am prepared to take part in it," he said.

"I won't have a reason or stimulus" to engage in any activity the state might deem anti-Soviet, he added.

Part of the New Openness

Mr. Begun's release, after more than three and a half years in prison, is the latest in a number of releases of Soviet political prisoners that began at the beginning of February as a result of the campaign by the Soviet leader, Mikhail S. Gorbachev, for greater openness in Soviet society. Since then, more than 150 have been released, according to Western monitoring groups and Soviet dissident sources.

The case of Mr. Begun, an electrical engineer who was sentenced to prison or exile three times after he first applied to emigrate to Israel in 1971, was particularly nettlesome to Soviet authorities in recent weeks.

First, small demonstrations on his behalf were permitted, then suppressed with increasing force. A series of contradictory official statements left his release in doubt for 48 hours after it had been announced by a senior

Continued on Page A10, Column 5

REAGAN REPORTED UNABLE TO RECALL IRAN ARMS DECISION

THE KEY POINT OF DISPUTE

Regan's Job Is Said to Hinge on How Issue Is Resolved by Tower Commission

By GERALD M. BOYD

Special to The New York Times

WASHINGTON, Feb. 23 — President Reagan is unable to say with certainty if he approved in advance the first American-sanctioned arms shipment to Iran in the fall of 1985 because he genuinely cannot remember, acording to a senior Administration official who is familiar with the President's testimony to the Tower Commission.

The official said Mr. Reagan's confusion on this point was responsible for the conflicting accounts he has given the commission.

The official asserted that Mr. Reagan's lack of clear recollection and the lack of documentation of what actually took place at the time of the shipment by Israel in August 1985 will make it impossible for the panel to reach anything other than a subjective judgment.

A Point of Dispute

The assertion about Mr. Reagan's recollections came as the chief counsel of the Senate committee investigating the Iran-contra affair said the Congressional committees investigating the case will begin this week the process of granting some witnesses limited immunity from prosecution to compel their testimony. [Page A6.]

How those committees and the Tower Commission — which is scheduled to issue its report Thursday — deal with the question of whether Mr. Reagan gave prior approval for the first arms shipments is expected to be an important factor in the future of Donald T. Regan, the White House chief of staff. Mr. Regan and Robert C. McFarlane, the former national security adviser and a pivotal figure in the Iran initiative, have become involved in a dispute on the question.

Regan's Ouster Sought

Congressional investigators said the question was also important because it would show whether the policy was designed in part to circumvent Congressional oversight.

Mr. Regan has reached an agreement with the President that effectively puts his future on hold until the report is made public and the President has an opportunity to assess its implications.

Such an understanding has existed for several weeks and was renewed in recent days amid new pressure from intimates of the President and allies in Congress for Mr. Regan's ouster as chief of staff.

Mr. Regan reportedly announced the

Continued on Page A5, Column 1

Files Reportedly Altered

Oliver North reportedly ordered a secretary to alter National Security Council documents. The files and motive were not specified. Page A6.

Budget Panels' Chairmen Ready To Forget the Law's Deficit Goal

By JONATHAN FUERBRINGER

Special to The New York Times

WASHINGTON, Feb. 23 — The chairmen of the House and Senate Budget Committees indicated today that they were ready to abandon the budget law's $108 billion deficit target for 1988, saying the goal cannot be met without gimmicks.

The two Democrats, Representative William H. Gray 3d of Pennsylvania and Senator Lawton Chiles of Florida, said Congress should concentrate on a package of $40 billion in spending cuts and revenue increases. That would reduce the projected deficit in the fiscal year 1988 to $130 billion, based on Congressional Budget Office estimates.

Their approach reflects a judgment that Congress will not approve much more than $40 billion in budget savings unless the plan involves a significant tax increase — which President Reagan has refused to accept as a way to more nearly balance the budget.

No 'Jimmying of Numbers'

And it would avoid the use of overoptimistic economic predictions or spending estimates, tricks they say the Administration has used in drawing up a budget to meet the $108 billion goal. "I can do real deficit reduction or I can do the same jimmying of the numbers he did," Mr. Gray said of the President's budget.

But the chairmen's strategy, if they can sell it to their party leaders and colleagues, is politically risky: It could leave them open to charges from Mr. Reagan that the Democrats are abandoning efforts to balance the budget.

James A. Miller 3d, the director of the Office of Management and Budget, said today that the Administration opposes abandoning the $108 billion target for 1988 set in the budget law.

'Credible' Plan Is Sought

House Budget Committee sources who are planning the chairman's strategy said Mr. Gray would favor a formal abandonment of the 1988 target and would push this proposal with the other committee Democrats, who begin meeting on their budget plan Tuesday. But aides said he did not yet have the support of the House Democratic leadership.

At a meeting of the United States League of Savings Institutions today, the Congressman said Congress must continue to reduce the deficit. "Let's continue the progress," he said. "Let's continue bringing it down $36 billion to $40 billion a year so that we can get these deficits solved."

Senator Chiles, at a later news conference, said, "I have never felt there was a magic in $108 billion." He said a "credible" budget reduction plan would be in the $36 billion to $40 billion range, asserting that the more than $60 billion in savings needed to reach $108 billion was not politically possible.

As originally passed, the budget-balancing law called for automatic proportional spending cuts to get the

Continued on Page A20, Column 1

Associated Press

Howser Steps Down as Royals' Manager

Dick Howser at the Kansas City Royals' training camp yesterday in Fort Myers, Fla., after telling the team of his decision to resign. Howser underwent two operations last year for brain cancer. Page B5.

Transit Authority Is Critical Of Its Newest Subway Cars

By RICHARD LEVINE

Eight months after they began to enter service, the newest subway cars in New York City's fleet — the R-68's — are performing "unacceptably," according to the Transit Authority, which is considering switching to a rival manufacturer for the final 200-car order.

The R-68's, for which the agency has already committed nearly half a billion dollars, have displayed a variety of ills, including doors that fly open when a car is moving, faulty wiring, electrical controllers that suddenly lose power, malfunctioning air brakes and what David L. Gunn, the Transit Authority president, terms "sloppy" finishing details.

'A Lot of Pressure'

The R-68's, which cost about $1 million apiece and are still under warranty, are made by Westinghouse-Amrail, a consortium that includes two French companies — ANF Industrie and Alsthom — and the Westinghouse Electric Corporation. The cars' body and undercarriage is made in France, while motors and brakes are manufactured in the United States.

"We have had some problems with the car," Mr. Gunn said. "We're putting a lot of pressure on the manufacturer."

A spokesman at the consortium's New York office, Michel De Lambert, attributed some of the car's problems to American-made components that he said are used on other city subway cars. He added that the R-68's were averaging more miles of service a month than any other car in the authority's fleet. "It means the availability of the car is very good," said Mr. De Lambert. "That is most important to the taxpayers and the riders."

So far, the authority has ordered a total of 425 R-68's from Westinghouse-Amrail, about 160 of which are in service on the D line. The car equipment report notes that the manufacturer is behind on its delivery schedule by 22 cars.

Continued on Page B3, Column 2

AIDS in the Workplace: Disruptions Growing

By THOMAS MORGAN

The number of cases of AIDS and AIDS-related diseases has caused increasing confusion and disruption in New York City's work force. Employers and employees are reacting to AIDS victims in ways ranging from support and financial assistance to ostracism and dismissal.

Last year, when Griffin Gold, a Manhattan real-estate agent, told his Greenwich Village employer that he had AIDS-related complex, a form of AIDS that may not result in death, a secretary in another office of the company threatened to quit unless Mr. Gold was dismissed.

Mr. Gold said other workers complained about using the same lavatory he used, and the fears of employees did not subside until his employer distributed literature explaining that AIDS was not transmitted by casual contact.

Tucker Ashworth's experience was somewhat better.

Mr. Ashworth, director of public affairs for the New York City Planning Department, was hospitalized several months ago with an AIDS-related illness. But the city allowed him to continue to work, answering questions about his agency from his hospital bed. Mr. Ashworth's hours are flexible and fellow workers are sympathetic to his efforts to keep working.

"I want people to know that people with AIDS can still work," said Mr. Ashworth, who has also served as deputy press secretary for the state's Urban Development Corporation. He was diagnosed about a year ago as having an illness linked to acquired immune deficiency syndrome.

"Work is so important because so many people define their lives by what they do," Mr. Ashworth said. "If you can work, you continue to have a sense of worth, and you can continue your life."

Both Mr. Ashworth and Mr. Gold say their employers have been supportive. But incidents in which AIDS patients are encouraged to quit and to apply for disability payments have been more

Continued on Page B4, Column 4

Edward Lansdale Dies at 79; Adviser on Guerrilla Warfare

By ERIC PACE

Edward G. Lansdale, an Air Force officer whose influential theories of counterinsurgent warfare proved successful in the Philippines after World War II but failed to bring victory in South Vietnam, died yesterday at his home in McLean, Va. He was 79 years old and had a heart ailment.

A dashing Californian, Mr. Lansdale is widely thought to have been the model for characters in two novels involving guerrilla warfare in Southeast Asia: "The Quiet American" by Graham Greene and "The Ugly American" by Eugene Burdick and William J. Lederer. He retired from the Air Force as a major general in 1963.

As an adviser in the newly independent Philippines in the late 1940's and early 1950's the future general came to wield great influence in operations by the Philippine leader Ramon Magsaysay against the Communist-dominated Hukbalahap rebellion. Under the leadership of Mr. Magsaysay, who was elected President while the struggle was going on, the operations succeeded.

It was in the Philippines that General Lansdale framed his basic theory, that Communist revolution was best confronted by democratic revolution. He came to advocate a four-sided campaign, with social, economic and political aspects as well as purely military operations. He put much emphasis on what came to be called civic-action programs to undermine Filipinos' backing for the Huks.

Looking back on what he learned in

Continued on Page A25, Column 1

INSIDE

Pasternak Status Restored

Boris Pasternak, best known in the West for the novel "Doctor Zhivago," has been posthumously reinstated by the Soviet writers' union. Page A10.

Moscow May Buy Grain

Washington and Moscow resumed grain talks just as reports circulated that the Russians had bought American corn at market prices. Page D6.

NEWS SUMMARY, PAGE A2

Chronological Chart of Jewish History

EGYPT	EREZ ISRAEL		MESOPOTAMIA	CULTURAL ACHIEVEMENTS
c. 1991 B.C.E.	Hebrews in Egypt	The Patriarchs		
xii Dynasty				
c. 1786 B.C.E.				
c. 1720/10 B.C.E.			*c.*1728–1686 Hammurapi	
Hyksos				
c. 1570				
c. 1550 B.C.E.				
xviii Dynasty				
c. 1400–*c.*1350 Tell el-Amarna Period				
c. 1370–*c.*53 Akhenaton				
c. 1340–*c.*10 Haremhab				
c. 1310;				
xix Dynasty				
c. 1309–*c.*1290 Seti I				
c. 1290–*c.* 24 Ramses II				
	c. 1280 Exodus			
c. 1224–*c.*16 Mer-ne-Ptah				
	c. 1250 Conquest of Canaan under Joshua			
c. 1200	*c.* 1200 Philistines settle in Erez Israel			
	The Judges			
	c. 1125 Deborah			
	c. 1100 Gideon			
	c. 1050 Fall of Shiloh			
	Samuel			
	c. 1020–1004 Saul		ARAM DAMASCUS	
	1004–965 David			
c. 935–*c.* 914 Shishak	965–928 Solomon		Rezon	
xxii Dynasty	Judah	Israel		
918/17 Shishak invades Erez Israel	928–911 Rehoboam	928–907 Jeroboam I		
	911–908 Abijah	907–906 Nadab		
	908–867 Asa	906–883 Baasha	Ben-Hadad I	
		883–882 Elah		
		882 Zimri		
		882–71 Omri	Ben Hadad II	
	867–46 Jehoshaphat	871–852 Ahab	853 Battle of Karkar	Elijah
		852–51 Ahaziah		
	846–43 Jehoram	851–42 Jehoram		
	843–42 Ahaziah	842–14 Jehu	Hazael	
	842–36 Athaliah			
	836–798 Jehoash	814–800 Jehoahaz	Ben-Hadad III	
	798–69 Amaziah	800–784 Jehoash		Amos
	769–33 Uzziah	784–48 Jeroboam II		Hosea
	758–43 Jotham (regent)	748 Zechariah	Rezin	*c.* 740–*c.* 700 Prophecies of Isaiah
		748 Shallum		
	743–33 Ahaz (regent)	747–37 Menahem		
		737–35 Pekahiah		
		735–33 Pekah	MESOPOTAMIA	
	733–27 Ahaz	733–24 Hoshea		
	727–698 Hezekiah	722 Samaria captured by Shalmaneser V		
		720 Sargon makes Samaria an Assyrian province		
		Mass deportation of Israelites		
	701 Expedition of Sennacherib against Hezekiah			
663 Sack of Thebes	698–42 Manasseh			
	641–40 Amon			
	639–09 Josiah		612 Fall of Nineveh	627–*c.* 585 Prophecies of Jeremiah
	609 Battle of Megiddo			
	609 Jehoahaz			

EGYPT	EREZ ISRAEL	BABYLONIA	CULTURAL ACHIEVEMENTS
	608–598 Jehoiakim	605 Battle of Carchemish	
	597 Jehoiachin		
	597 Expedition of Nebuchadnezzar against Judah; Jehoiachin deported to Babylonia		
	595–86 Zedekiah		
	586 Destruction of Jerusalem; mass deportation to Babylonia	Exile of Judeans in Babylonia	593–571 Prophecies of Ezekiel
	585 ? Murder of Gedaliah		
		PERSIA	6th cent., Canonization of the Pentateuch (in Babylonian Exile)
		539 Cyrus takes Babylonia	
525 Egypt conquered by Cambyses	538 First return under Sheshbazzar	538 Cyrus' edict	
	c. 522 Zerubbabel governor		
	520–15 Temple rebuilt		
460–54 Rebellion of Inaros	458? Second return under Ezra	465–24 Artaxerxes I	
		423–04 Darius II	
	445 Walls of Jerusalem reconstructed under Nehemiah; Ezra reads the Torah.		
	428? Second return under Ezra		
411 Destruction of the temple of the Jewish colony at Elephantine	*c.* 408 Bagohi governor		
404 Egypt regains freedom	398? Second return under Ezra	404–358 Artaxerxes II	
	348 Artaxerxes III deports a number of Jews to Hyrcania		4th cent., Canonization of the Prophets Section of the Bible
343 Egypt reconquered by Persia			
		333 Battle of Issus	
332 Alexander the Great conquers Egypt	332 Alexander the Great conquers Ereẓ Israel	323 d. of Alexander the Great	
323–285 Ptolemy I	301 Ptolemy I conquers Erez Israel		
		SYRIA	
285–46 Ptolemy II Philadelphus		312–280 Seleucus I	Mid-3rd cent., Pentateuch translated into Greek in Egypt (Septuagint)
246–21 Ptolemy III Euergetes		223–187 Antiochus III	
221–03 Ptolemy IV Philopator	219–17 Antiochus III conquers most of Ereẓ Israel		
	217 Ptolemy IV defeats Antiochus III in the battle of Rafah and recovers Ereẓ Israel		
203–181 Ptolemy V Epiphanes	198 Battle of Panias (Banias): Ereẓ Israel passes to the Seleucids		
181–46 Ptolemy VI Philometor		187–75 Seleucus IV	
	175 Onias III deposed by Antiochus IV	175–64 Antiochus IV Epiphanes	
	175–71 Jason high priest		
	c. 172 Jerusalem becomes a *polis* (Antiochia)		
	171–167 Menelaus high priest		*c.* 170 Book of Ben Sira written
	169 Antiochus IV plunders the Temple treasuries		
168 Antiochus IV invades Egypt	168 Antiochus IV storms Jerusalem; gentiles settled on the Acra		
	167 Antiochus IV outlaws the practice of Judaism; profanation of the Temple; the rebellion of the Hasmoneans begins		
	166–60 Judah Maccabee, leader of the rebellion, victorious over several Syrian armies		
	164 Judah Maccabee captures Jerusalem and rededicates the Temple	164–63 Antiochus V	
	162–59 Alcimus high priest	162–50 Demetrius I	

EGYPT	EREZ ISRAEL	SYRIA	CULTURAL ACHIEVEMENTS
	161 Judah Maccabee defeats Nicanor and reconquers Jerusalem; treaty between Judah and Rome		
	160 Judah Maccabee falls in battle against Bacchides Jonathan assumes the leadership; guerilla warfare		
	157 Treaty between Bacchides and Jonathan; withdrawal of Seleucid garrisons, Jonathan enters Jerusalem		
	152 Jonathan high priest	152–45 Alexander Balas	
c. 145 Onias IV builds temple in Leontopolis	142 Jonathan treacherously murdered by Tryphon	145–38 Demetrius II 145–38 Antiochus VI and Tryphon	
145–16 Ptolemy VII Physcon	Simeon assumes leadership; Demetrius II recognizes the independence of Judea; renewal of treaty with Rome		
	141 Simeon captures the Acra		
	140 Great Assembly in Jerusalem confirms Simeon as ethnarch, high priest, and commander in chief	138–29 Antiochus VII Sidetes	
	134 Simeon assassinated		
	134–104 John Hyrcanus		Latter second century. First Book of Maccabees written
	134 Treaty with Rome renewed		
	134–32 War with Antiochus VII; Jerusalem besieged; treaty between John Hyrcanus and Antiochus VII	129–25 Demetrius II 125–96 Antiochus VIII Grypus	
116—08 Ptolemy VIII Lathyrus	107 John Hyrcanus' sons capture Samaria	115–95 Antiochus IX Cyzicenus	
108–88 Ptolemy IX Alexander	104–03 Judah Aristobulus		
88–80 Ptolemy VIII Lathyrus	103–76 Alexander Yannai		
	76–67 Salome Alexandra		
	67–63 Civil war between Hyrcanus II and Aristobulus		
	63 Pompey decides in favor of Hyrcanus II. Temple Mount besieged and captured by Pompey		
	63–40 Hyrcanus II ethnarch and high priest. Judea loses its independence		
	56–55 Revolts of Alexander b. Aristobulus and Aristobulus	57–55 Gabinus governor of Syria	ITALY (ROME)
48 Hyrcanus II and Antipater help Caesar in Alexandria	48 Caesar confirms Jewish privileges		44 Assassination of Caesar
	40 Parthian invasion		43 Second Triumvirate
	40–37 Antigonus II (Mattathias)		31 Battle of Actium
	37 Jerusalem captured by Herod		27 B.C.E.–14 C.E. Augustus
	37–4 B.C.E. Herod		
	Shemaiah and Avtalion		
	19 Temple rebuilt		
	4 B.C.E.–6 C.E. Archelaus ethnarch		
	4 B.C.E.–34 C.E. Herod Philip		
	4 B.C.E.–39 C.E. Herod Antipas		
	6 C.E.–41 Judea, Samaria, and Idumea formed into a Roman province (Iudaea) under a *praefectus*		
	beginning of 1st cent., d. of Hillel		19 Tiberius expels the Jews
	26–36 Pontius Pilate *praefectus*		
	30 Jesus crucified; d. of Shammai		31 Jews allowed to return
38 Anti-Jewish riots in Alexandria	37–41 Crisis caused by Caligula's insistence on being worshiped as deity		37–41 Caligula

EGYPT	**EREZ ISRAEL**	ROMAN EMPIRE	CULTURAL ACHIEVEMENTS
40 Legation of Jews of Egypt lead by Philo to Rome	41–44 Agrippa I	41–54 Claudius 41 Claudius issues edict of toleration	until *c.*40 Philo writes in Alexandria
		54–68 Nero	
66 Massacre of the Jews at Alexandria	66 Beginning of revolt against Rome 67 Vespasian conquers Galilee; the Zealots take over in Jerusalem		
		69 Galba; Otho; Vitellius	
	*c.*70 Destruction of Qumran community 70 Siege of Jerusalem; destruction of the Temple 70 Sanhedrin established at Jabneh by Johanan b. Zakkai	69–79 Vespasian	
73 Temple in Leontopolis closed	73 Fall of Masada	79–81 Titus 81–96 Domitian	*c.* 79 Josephus completes *Jewish Wars*
115–117 Revolt of the Jews		96–98 Nerva 98–117 Trajan	93 Josephus completes *Jewish Antiquities*
	c. 115 d. of Gamaliel II *c.* 116–117 "war of Quietus"	117–38 Hadrian	
	132–35 Bar Kokhba war 135 Fall of Bethar; Aelia Capitolina established; Akiva executed		
	c. 135–38 Persecutions of Hadrian *c.* 140 Sanhedrin at Usha	138–61 Antoninus Pius 161–80 Marcus Aurelius 161–69 Lucius Aurelius Verus	2nd cent., Canonization of the *Ketuvim* (Hagiographa)
	c. 170 Sanhedrin at Bet She'arim	180–92 Commodus 193 Pertinax 193–211 Septimius Severus	
	c. 200 Sanhedrin at Sepphoris	211–17 Caracalla 212 Jews (together with most of subjects of the empire) become Roman citizens	*c.*210 Redaction of the Mishnah
BABYLONIA			
219 Arrival of Rav		217–18 Macrinus 218–22 Heliogabalus	
	c. 220 d. of Judah ha-Nasi *c.* 230 d. of Gamaliel III *c.* 235 Sanhedrin at Tiberias	222–35 Alexander Severus	
247 d. of Rav 254 d. of Samuel 259 Academy of Nehardea moves to Pumbedita		253–60 Valerian	245 Dura-Europos synagogue built
	c. 270 d. of Judah II Nesiah	270–75 Aurelian 284–305 Diocletian	
	c. 290 d. of Gamaliel IV		
c. 297 d. of Huna *c.* 299 d. of Judah b. Ezekiel			

GENERAL HISTORY	CHRISTIAN EUROPE	EREẒ ISRAEL	BABYLONIA	ARABIA	CULTURAL ACHIEVEMENTS
306–337 Constantine I 313 Edict of Milan					
325 Council of Nicaea 337–361 Constantius II	321 Jews in Cologne 325 Christian Church formulates its policy toward the Jews: the Jews must continue to exist for the sake of Christianity in seclusion and humiliation	320 d. of Judah III 351 Jews and Samaritans revolt against Gallus; destruction of Bet Sh'earim	330 d. of Rabbah b. Naḥamani 338 d. of Abbaye 352 d. of Rava		*c.* 359 Permanent calender committed to writing
361–363 Julian the Apostate	339 Constantius II prohibits marriage between Jews and Christians and possession of Christian slaves by Jews	363 Julian the Apostate allows Jews to start rebuilding the Temple *c.* 365 d. of Hillel II *c.* 385 d. of Gamaliel V *c.* 400 d. of Judah IV			*c.* 390 Jerusalem Talmud completed
379-395 Theodosius I 408–450 Theodosius II	438 Theodosius II *Novellae* against the Jews and heretics	425 Patriarchate abolished 426 d. of Gamaliel VI			
476 End of Western Roman Empire 481–511 Clovis I king of the Franks 493–526 Theodoric			427 d. of Ashi 455 Jews forbidden to keep the Sabbath *c.* 470 Persecutions by the authorities; Huna b. Mar Zutra the exilarch and others executed by the authorities 495–502 Revolt of Mar Zutra the exilarch 499 d. of Ravina II		5th cent., Yose b. Yose earliest liturgical poet known by name
527–565 Justinian I	553 Justinian interferes in the conduct of Jewish worship 590–604 Pope Gregory I	520 Mar Zutra III head of Sanhedrin at Tiberias	*c.* 500–540 *Savoraim* 589 Beginning of the period of Geonim	525 End of Jewish kingdom in southern Arabia	*c.* 499 Babylonian Talmud completed 6th–7th cent., Yannai liturgical poet *c.* 600 Eleazar Kallir liturgical poet
622 Muhammad's flight to Medina 628–38 Dagobert I 632 d. of Muhammad	612, 633, 638 Severe legal measures against the Jews in Spain 628 Dagobert I expels Jews from Frankish Kingdom	614–617 Jewish rule established in Jerusalem under the Persians 632 Heraclius decrees forced baptism		624–628 Jewish tribes of Arabia destroyed by Muhammad	
640–42 Egypt conquered by the Arabs	694–711 Jewish religion outlawed in Spain	638 Jerusalem conquered by the Arabs			

GENERAL HISTORY	MUSLIM SPAIN	CHRISTIAN EUROPE	EREẒ ISRAEL BABYLONIA	OTHERS	CULTURAL ACHIEVEMENTS
711 Spain conquered by the Arabs				*c.* 740 conversion of the Khazars	
			762–67 Anan b. David lays the foundation of Karaism		*c.* 760 *Halakhot Pesukot* (attributed to Yehudai b. Nahman)
768–814 Charlemagne		797 Charlemagne sends Isaac to Harun al-Rashid			*c.* 825 Simeon Kayyara composes *Halakhot Gedolot*
			858 d. of Natronai Gaon		*c.* 860 Amram b. Sheshna compiles order of prayers
			921–22 Dispute between Ereẓ Israel and Babylonia over the calendar		*c.* 875 Nahshon b. Zadok researches on the Jewish calendar *c.* 935 Saadiah Gaon writes *Emunot ve-De'ot*
			942 d. of Saadiah Gaon		*c.* 953 *Josippon* written
987 Rise of the Capetian dynasty	970 d. of Menahem ibn Saruq; d. of Hisdai ibn Shaprut 990 d. of Dunash b. Labrat	886 d. of Shephatiah b. Amittai of Oria	998 d. of Sherira Gaon	Beginning of 11th cent end of Khazar Kingdom	987 *Iggeret Rav Sherira Gaon*
		1012 Expulsion from Mainz	1008 Persecutions of al-Ḥakim 1013 d. of Samuel b. Hophni	*c.* 1027 d. of Hushiel b. Elhanan	
		1028 d. of Gershom b. Judah	1038 d. of Hai Gaon		
	c. 1050 d. of Jonah ibn Janaḥ			1055/56 d. of Hananel b. Hushiel	
1066 England conquered by William of Normandy	*c.* 1056 d. of Samuel ha-Nagid; d. of Solomon ibn Gabirol	*c.* 1066 Jews settle in England		1062 d. of Nissim b. Jacob	
1078 Jerusalem conquered by the Seljuks					*c.* 1080 Baḥya ibn Paquda writes *Ḥovot ha-Levavot*
1096–99 First Crusade		1096 Crusaders massacre the Jews of the Rhineland	1099 Jerusalem captured by crusaders		

GENERAL HISTORY	SPAIN & PORTUGAL	FRANCE	ENGLAND
	1103 d. of Isaac Alfasi	1105 d. of Rashi	
	c. 1135 d. of Moses ibn Ezra		
1147–49 Second Crusade	1141 d. of Judah Halevi		1144 Blood libel at Norwich
	1164 d. of Abraham ibn Ezra	1171 Destruction of the Blois community; d. of Jacob b. Meir Tam	
	1180 d. of Abraham ibn Daud		
	c. 1180 First Maimonidean controversy	1182 Expulsion	
1189–92 Third Crusade			1190 Anti-Jewish riots; massacre at York
		1198 Jews recalled	1194 *Archae* established
		1198 d. of Abraham b. David of Posquières	
1215 Magna Carta			1210 Extortions of John Lackland
			1222 Council of Oxford introduces discriminatory measures
	1230–32 Second Maimonidean controversy		1232 Domus Conversorum established in London
	1235 d. of Isaac the Blind; d. of Judah Al-Ḥarizi	*c.* 1235 d. of David Kimḥi	
		1236 Persecutions in W. France	
		1240 Disputation of Paris	
1241 Tatars reach the frontiers of Silesia		1242 Burning of Talmud at Paris	1241 "Parliament of Jews" meets at Worcester
			1255 Blood libel at Lincoln
	1263 Disputation of Barcelona		1263–64 Jews of London sacked
	1270 d. of Naḥmanides		1275 *Statutum de Judaismo*
		1288 Jews burned at Troyes	1290 Expulsion
1291 Acre captured by the Muslims; end of Latin Kingdom of Jerusalem	*c.* 1291 d. of Abraham Abulafia		
	c. 1300–06 Third Maimonidean controversy		
		1306 Expulsion	
1309–78 "Avignonese captivity" of the popes			
	c. 1310 d. of Solomon b. Abraham Adret	1315 Jews recalled (by Louis X)	
		1320 Pastoureaux persecutions	
		1321 Lepers persecutions	
	1327 d. of Asher b. Jehiel	1322 Expulsion from the Kingdom of France	
	1328 Riots in Navarre		
1337 Beginning of the Hundred Years' War			

ITALY	GERMANY & AUSTRIA	EREẒ ISRAEL	NORTH AFRICA	CULTURAL ACHIEVEMENTS
				Commentaries of Rashi
1106 d. of Nathan b. Jehiel of Rome			1106/7 d. of Jacob b. Nissim	1101 The *Arukh* of Nathan b. Jehiel of Rome completed
				1159–73 Travels of Benjamin of Tudela
1179 Third Lateran Council				1161 Abraham ibn Daud completes *Sefer ha-Kabbalah*
				1168 Maimonides completes commentary on the Mishnah
	1195–96 Anti-Jewish excesses at Speyer and Boppard	1187 Jerusalem captured by Saladin		
1198–1216 Innocent III			1204 d. of Maimonides in Fostat (Old Cairo)	1180 Maimonides completes *Mishneh Torah*
1215 Fourth Lateran Council introduces the Jewish Badge	1217 d. of Judah b. Samuel he-Hasid	1210–11 Settlement of 300 French and English rabbis		1190 Maimonides completes *Guide of the Perplexed*
1227–41 Gregory IX				
	1235 Blood libel at Fulda			
	1236 Frederick II Hohenstaufen introduces the concept of *servi camerae*			12th-13th cent., Ḥasidei Ashkenaz; *Sefer Ḥasidim* compiled.
			POLAND	12th-14th cent., *Tosafot* (France and Germany)
	1238 d. of Eleazar b. Judah of Worms			
1249 Innocent IV issues bull against blood libel	1244 Frederick II, duke of Austria, grants charter	1244 Jerusalem captured by the Khwarizms	1264 Charter of Boleslav V the Pious	
		c. 1265 d. of Jehiel b. Joseph of Paris at Acre		
		1267/70 Naḥmanides in Ereẓ Israel		
	1285 Destruction of the Munich community			*c.* 1286 *Zohar* in final form completed by Moses b. Shem Tov de Leon
	1293 d. of Meir of Rothenburg			
	1298–99 Rindfleisch persecutions			
				1310 Asher b. Jehiel compiles talmudic code.
				1329 Levi b. Gershom completes *Sefer Milḥamot Adonai*
c. 1328 d. of Immanuel b. Solomon of Rome	1336–37 Armleder massacres		1334 Casimir III extends the charter of 1264	

GENERAL HISTORY	SPAIN	FRANCE	ITALY
	1340 d. of Jacob b. Asher		
		1344 d. of Levi b. Gershom	
1348 Black Death	1348 Black Death massacres	1348–49 Black Death massacres	1348 Protective bulls of Clement VI
	1354 Council of the communities of Aragon		
		1359 Jews recalled	
	c. 1375 d. of Nissim b. Reuben Gerondi		
1386 Beginning of the union between Poland and Lithuania			
	1391 Massacres and conversions		
		1394 Expulsion from the Kingdom of France	
	1408 d. of Isaac b. Sheshet Perfet		
	1411–12 Vicente Ferrer and oppressive legislation		
	c. 1412 d. of Ḥasdai Crescas		
	1413–14 Disputation of Tortosa		
1415 Burning of John Huss			1415 Benedict XIII orders censorship of Talmud
1419–36 Hussite Wars		1420 Expulsion from Lyons	1419 Martin V against forced conversions
1431 Burning of Joan of Arc			
1431–49 Council of Basle			1427 Papal edict prohibits transportation of Jews to Ereẓ Israel in ships of Venice and Ancona
	1435 Massacre and conversion of the Jews of Majorca		
1453 Constantinople captured by the Turks; end of the Hundred Years' War	1454 d. of Abraham Benveniste		
	1473 Marranos of Valladolid and Cordoba massacred		
	1474 Marranos of Segovia massacred		1475-94 Bernardino da Feltre preaches against Jews; Jews expelled from several towns
			1475 Blood libel of Trent
1479 Castile and Aragon united	1480 Inquisition established in Spain		
	1483 Torquemada appointed inquisitor general	**EREẒ ISRAEL**	
		1488-*c.* 1515 Obadiah di Bertinoro in Jerusalem	
	1490–91 La Guardia blood libel		
1492 Conquest of Granada; discovery of America	1492 Expulsion from Castile and Aragon		1492–93 Expulsion from Sicily
	1496–97 Expulsion from Portugal; mass forced conversion		1497 d. of Elijah Delmedigo
	1506 Massacre of Marranos in Lisbon		

GERMANY & AUSTRIA	POLAND-LITHUANIA	OTTOMAN EMPIRE	CULTURAL ACHIEVEMENTS
			before 1340, Jacob b. Asher completes *Arba'ah Turim*
1342 Louis IX introduces poll tax (*Opferpfennig*)			
1348–50 Black Death massacres	1348–49 Immigration from Germany		
1356 Charles IV grants the Electors the privilege of taxing the Jews			
	1364 and 1367 Casimir III extends the charter		
	1388 Witold of Lithuania grants charter to Jews of Brest-Litovsk		
1389 Massacre of Prague community			
	1399 Blood libel in Poznan		
1421 *Wiener Gesera;* expulsion from Austria			
1424 Expulsion from Cologne			1425 Joseph Albo completes *Sefer ha-Ikkarim*
1427 d. of Jacob Moellin			
1439 Expulsion from Augsburg			
1452–53 John of Capistrano incites persecutions and expulsions	1454 Privileges revoked; riots in Cracow	1453 onward, Jews favored as a valuable trading and artisan element in the Ottoman Empire	
1460 d. of Israel Isserlein			
1473 Expulsion from Mainz			
			1475 Beginning of Hebrew printing (Rashi printed in Reggio di Calabria)
	1483 Expulsion from Warsaw		
		1492 onward, the sultans open the gates of the Ottoman Empire for the refugees from Spain	
	1495 Expulsion from Lithuania		
		1497 d. of Moses Capsali	
		1497 onward, refugees from Portugal welcomed by the sultans	
1499 Expulsion from Nuremberg			
	1503 Jews return to Lithuania		c. 1502 *Dialoghi di Amore by* Judah Abrabanel
			1504 *Sefer ha-Yuḥasin* by Abraham Zacuto

GENERAL HISTORY	PORTUGAL	ITALY (& PAPACY)	GERMANY & AUSTRIA
		1508 d. of Isaac Abrabanel	
			1510 Expulsion from Brandenburg
			1510–20 Reuchlin-Pfefferkorn controversy
1517 Luther publishes his 95 theses		1516 Venice initiates the ghetto	1519 Expulsion from Regensburg
		1523–34 Clement VII	
		1523 David Reuveni appears in Venice	
		c. 1525 d. of Abraham Farissol	
1526 Battle of Mohacs; Turks rout Hungarians	1531 Inquisition established in Portugal	1532 Solomon Molcho burned at Mantua	
1536 Calvin publishes *Institution Chrétienne*			
1540 Jesuit Order approved by the pope		1541 Expulsion from Naples	1541 Expulsion from Prague and crown cities
1545–63 Council of Trent	1542 Pseudo-Messiah (David Reuveni?) burned at Évora		1544 Luther attacks the Jews
		1549 d. of Elijah Baḥur Levita	
		1550 Expulsion from Genoa	1551 Expulsion from Bavaria
		1553 Burning of the Talmud	
		1554 Censorship of Hebrew books introduced	1554 d of Joseph b Gershom of Rosheim
1555 Peace of Augsburg		1555 Paul IV orders that Jews be confined to ghettos	
		1556 Burning of Marranos in Ancona	
		1567 Expulsion from the Republic of Genoa	
		1569 Expulsion from the Papal States	
1572 Massacre of St. Bartholomew's Day			
		c. 1575 d. of Joseph ha-Kohen	
		1578 d. of Azariah dei Rossi	
1581 The Netherlands proclaim independence from Spain		1584 Gregory XIII orders compulsory sermons to Jews	
1588 Destruction of the Spanish Armada			

POLAND-LITHUANIA	OTTOMAN EMPIRE	**EREẒ ISRAEL**	CULTURAL ACHIEVEMENTS
1514 Abraham Judaeus Bohemus appointed tax collector of the Jews of Poland		1516 Ereẓ Israel conquered by the Turks	1515–16 Jacob ibn Ḥabib's *Ein Ya'akov* published
			1520–23 First complete editions of the Talmuds printed
	1526 d. of Elijah Mizraḥi		1524–25 *Mikra'ot Gedolot* edition of the Bible
1534 Sigismund I absolves Jews from wearing the badge		1538 Jacob Berab renews *semikhah* in Safed	
			1549 Obadiah of Bertinoro's commentary on the Mishnah published
1551 Community leaders given wide juridical and administrative powers	1554 d. of Moses Hamon		1554(?) Solomon ibn Verga's *Shevet Yehudah* published
	1555 d. of Elijah Capsali		1555 Joseph Caro's *Beit Yosef* published
			1558–60 The *Zohar* printed
	1566 Joseph Nasi created duke of Naxos	*c.*1561 Joseph Nasi leases Tiberias from the sultan	1564 Joseph Caro's Shulḥan Arukh published
		1569–72 Isaac Luria in Safed	1569–71 Moses Isserles' *Mappah* published
1572 d. of Moses Isserles		1572 d. of Isaac Luria	
1574 d. of Solomon Luria		1575 d. of Joseph Caro	
1576 Stephen Bâthory issues decrees against blood libel			
	1579 d. of Joseph Nasi		
1580 First extant *takkanah* of the Council of Four Lands			
			1597 *Shalshelet ha-Kabbalah* by Gedaliah b. Joseph ibn Yaḥia published

GENERAL HISTORY	ENGLAND	FRANCE	ITALY (& PAPACY)	THE NETHERLANDS	GERMANY
			1593 Expulsion from the Papal States	*c.*1590 Marranos settle in Amsterdam	
1598 Edict of Nantes					
			1597 Expulsion from Milan		1603 *Takkanot* of the Synod of Frankfort
1613 First Romanov Czar					1614 Fettmilch's attack upon the Jews of Frankfort
					1615 Expulsion from Worms
1618 Beginning of Thirty Years' War					1616 Jews readmitted to Frankfort and Worms
1620 Mayflower arrives at Plymouth Rock; Battle of the White Mountain			1624 Ghetto established at Ferrara	1624 Excommunication of Uriel da Costa	
				1640 d. of Uriel da Costa	
1648 Treaty of Westphalia			1648 d. of Leone Modena		
1649–60 The Commonwealth in England					1649 Expulsion from Hamburg
1654 Portuguese recapture Brazil	1655 Manasseh Ben Israel in London				
	1656 Readmission of Jews			1656 Baruch Spinoza excommunicated	
			1663 d. of Simone Luzzatto	1657 d. of Manasseh Ben Israel	
1666 Great Fire of London					
		1670 Blood libel in Metz			1671 Jews permitted to settle in the Mark of Brandenburg
				1677 d. of Spinoza	
1683 Siege of Vienna by Turks	1685 Jews given religious freedom				
1689–1725 Peter the Great czar of Russia	1701 Bevis Marks Synagogue built				1711 Eisenmenger's *Entdecktes Judenthum* published
					1712 First public synagogue in Berlin
		1723 Residence of Portuguese Jews legalized by a letter patent	1723 General Council of Jews of Piedmont		1718 d. of Ẓevi Ashkenazi
	1728 d. of David Nieto			1728 d. of Solomon Ayllon	

AUSTRIA	POLAND-LITHUANIA	OTTOMAN EMPIRE	EREẒ ISRAEL	AMERICA	CULTURAL ACHIEVEMENTS
					1592 David Gans publishes *Ẓemaḥ David*
1609 d. of Judah Loew (Maharal) of Prague					
					1612–21 *Ḥiddushei Halakhot* of Samuel Edels published
	1616 d. of Meir b. Gedaliah of Lublin				
			1620 d. of Ḥayyim Vital		1617 Yom Tov Lipmann Heller completes *Tosefot Yom Tov*
	1623 Separate council for Lithuania established				
			1630 d. of Isaiah Horowitz		
	1631 d. of Samuel Edels				
	1640 d. of Joel Sirkes				
	1648–49 Chmielnicki massacres				
				1654 Jews arrive in New Amsterdam (New York) and found congregation; refugees from Brazil found communities in West Indies	1650 Manasseh Ben Israel publishes *Hope of Israel*
1654 d. of Yom Tov Lipmann Heller	1655–56 Massacres during wars of Poland against Sweden and Russia				
	1664 Riot in Lemberg (Lvov)	1665 Shabbetai Ẓevi proclaims himself the Messiah in Smyrna—fervor spreads throughout the Jewish world			
				1658 Congregation founded at Newport	
		1666 Shabbetai converts to Islam			
1670 Expulsion from Vienna		1676 d. of Shabbetai Ẓevi			
	1680 Riots in Brest-Litovsk	1680 d. of Nathan of Gaza			
	1682 Riots in Cracow				
	1687 Jews of Poznan attacked			1695 Jews settle in Charleston, S.C.	
1703 d. of Samuel Oppenheimer			1700 Judah Ḥasid and his group arrive in Jerusalem		
	1712 Jews of Sandomierz expelled after blood libel				
1724 d. of Samson Wertheimer					
1726 Familiants Laws		*c.*1730 d. of Nehemiah Ḥayon			

GENERAL HISTORY	ENGLAND	FRANCE	ITALY (& PAPACY)	GERMANY
				1738 Execution of Joseph Suess Oppenheimer
			1747 d. of Moses Ḥayyim Luzzatto	1750 Severe legislation against the Jews in Prussia 1751 Beginning of Eybeschuetz-Emden controversy
1756–63 Seven Years' War				1756 d. of Jacob Joshua Falk
	1760 Board of Deputies of British Jews estab-lished		1761 Cardinal Ganganelli's memorandum against the blood libel	1764 d. of Jonathan Eybeschuetz
1770 James Cook discovers Botany Bay	1762 d. of Samson Gideon			1769 Mendelssohn-Lavater controversy
1772 First partition of Poland 1776 American Declaration of Independence			1775 Anti-Jewish edict of Pius VI	1776 d. of Jacob Emden
1778 Deaths of Rousseau and Voltaire		1784 Body tax abolished		1781 C.W. von Dohm's *Ueber die buergerliche Verbesserung der Juden:* Christian plea for Jewish emancipation 1786 d. of Moses Mendelssohn 1787 *Leibzoll* abolished in Prussia
1789 Beginning of the French Revolution		1789 *Sur la Regeneration Physique, Morale et Politique des Juifs* by Abbé Gregoire		
1793 Second partition of Poland 1793–97 First coali-tion against France		1790 The National Assembly grants citizenship to the "Portuguese" Jews 1791 The National Assembly grants full civil rights to all the Jews	1793 Attack on the ghetto of Rome	
1795 Third partition of Poland 1797 Peace of Campo Formio 1799 Napoleon becomes First Consul 1801 Peace of Lunéville 1804 Napoleon crowned emperor	THE NETHER-LANDS 1796 Eman-cipation of the Jews of the Batavian Republic		1797–99 Temporary emancipation brought by French revolu-tionary army	1799 David Friedlaender's letter to Teller 1800 d. of Solomon Maimon

AUSTRIA-HUNGARY	POLAND-LITHUANIA	RUSSIA	EREẒ ISRAEL	AMERICA	CULTURAL ACHIEVEMENTS
				1730 First public synagogue in New York	
1736 d. of David Oppenheim	1734–36 Attacks by the Haidamacks			1733 Jews settle in Georgia	
			1742 Ḥayyim Attar and his group arrive in Jerusalem		1743 Moses Ḥayyim Luzzatto publishes *La-Yesharim Tehillah*
1745 Expulsion from Prague	1746 d. of Jehiel Heilprin			1742 Congregation founded at Philadelphia	
1748 Prague Jews allowed to return				1749 Congregation founded at Charleston	
	1757 Disputation with the Frankists at Kamenets-Podolski		*c.*1751 d. of Moses Ḥagiz		
	1759 Disputation with the Frankists at Lemberg (Lvov)				1755 First work of Moses Mendelssohn published
	1760 d. of Israel b. Eliezer Ba'al Shem Tov				1762 Isaac de Pinto's *Apologie pour la Nation Juive* in answer to Voltaire's defamation of Judaism
1764 Maria Theresa's *Judenordnung*	1764 Council of Four Lands abrogated				
	1768 Haidamack massacres				
	1772 First *ḥerem* on the Ḥasidim; d. of Dov Baer of Mezhirech	1772 Jews of eastern Poland under Russian rule			1780–83 Publication of Mendelssohn's *Biur*
			1777 Menahem Mendel of Vitebsk and his group of Ḥasidim settle in Galilee		1780 Jacob Joseph of Polonnoye's *Toledot Ya'akov Yosef* published
1782 Joseph II's *Toleranzpatent;* Naphtali Herz Wessely's *Divrei Shalom ve-Emet*	1781 Second *ḥerem* on the Ḥasidim	1783 Jews eligible for municipal councils			1783 Mendelssohn publishes *Jerusalem; Ha-Me'assef* founded
				1789 U.S. Constitution; G. Washington, first president of U.S.	
1792 "Judenamt" opened in Vienna	1791 d. of Jacob Frank	1791 Pale of Settlement established			
1793 d. of Ezekiel Landau	1794 Berek Joselewicz colonel under Kosciuszko				
	1797 d. of Elijah Gaon of Vilna		1799 Napoleon's campaign		1797 *Tanya (Likkutei Amarim)* of Shneur Zalman of Lyady published
				1803 Louisiana Purchase	

GENERAL HISTORY	FRANCE	ENGLAND	ITALY	GERMANY
1805 Battles of Trafalgar and Austerlitz				
1806 End of Holy Roman Empire	1806–07 Assembly of Jewish Notables			
1807 Treaty of Tilsit	1807 French Sanhedrin			
	1808 Napoleon's "Infamous Decree"			1808 Emancipation in Westphalia; consistory in Kassel
				1811 Emancipation in Hamburg and Frankfort
1812 Napoleon's retreat from Moscow	1812 d. of David Sintzheim			1812 Emancipation in Prussia d.of Mayer Amshel Rothschild
1813 Battle of Leipzig				1813 Bavarian Jewry edict
1814–15 Congress of Vienna				1815 Congress of Vienna permits the abolition of emancipation laws in the German states
	1816 d. of Abraham Furtado			
	1818 "Infamous Decree" abolished			1818 Hamburg Reform Temple consecrated
				1819 "Hep! Hep!" riots
1821 Greek War of Independence begins				1821 Isaac Bernays opposes the Reform Temple
1823 Monroe Doctrine				
1827 Battle of Navarino Bay	1824 Rabbinical seminary established at Metz			
1829 Emancipation of Catholics in England			1829 Instituto Rabbinico opened at Padua	1828 Wuerttemberg Jewry law
1830 July revolution in France; Uprising in Poland				
1831 Independence of Belgium recognized	1831 Judaism given equal status with other religions			
1833 Turkey recognizes independence of Egypt		1833 Beginning of parliamentary debates on the emancipation of the Jews		1833 Emancipation in Hesse-Kassel
				1834 d. of David Friedlaender
		1835 David Salomons sheriff of London		
		1836 d. of Nathan Mayer Rothschild		
		1837 Moses Montefiore knighted		
1839 Turkey invades Syria				1841 Hamburg prayer book controversy
		1842 First English Reform synagogue opened in London		1842 Bruno Bauer's *Judenfrage*
				1844 Rabbinical conference at Brunswick
		1845 Jews admitted to municipal offices		1845 Rabbinical conference at Frankfort; Reform Society formed in Berlin
1846 U.S. war with Mexico	1846 Abolition of "Jewish Oath"	1846 Minor disabilities removed		1846 Rabbinical conference in Breslau
1848 Year of Revolutions	1848 Adolphe Crémieux minister of justice	1847 Lionel de Rothschild elected to parliament but refuses to take the Christian oath	1848 Liberal constitution of Piedmont	1847 Anti-Jewish riots in Prussia 1848 Emancipation
1854–56 Crimean War				1854 Breslau Jewish Theological Seminary opened
		1855 David Salomons lord mayor of London	1855 d. of Isaac Samuel Reggio	
1856 Treaty of Paris		1856 Jews' College founded		1856 d. of Heinrich Heine
		1858 Lionel de Rothschild takes his seat in parliament after amendment of parliamentary oath	1858 Mortara case	
1859 Independence of Rumania	1859 Rabbinical seminary transferred to Paris			
1860 Sicily and Naples occupied by Garibaldi	1860 Alliance Israélite Universelle founded			1860 d. of Samuel Holdheim d. of Isaac Marcus Jost

AUSTRIA-HUNGARY	POLAND-LITHUANIA	RUSSIA	OTTOMAN EMPIRE & EREẒ ISRAEL	AMERICA	CULTURAL ACHIEVEMENTS
			1808–10 Disciples of Elijah Gaon settle in Ereẓ Israel		
1811 Jews of Vienna allowed to build a synagogue				1811 d. of Michael Gratz	
		1812 d. of Shneur Zalman of Lyady			
				1817 Jews settle in Cincinnati	1819 Verein fuer Kultur und Wissenschaft des Judentums founded
	1822 The *kahal* abolished	1824 Expulsion from the villages		1824 Reformed Society of Israelites in Charleston, S.C.; Isaac Leeser arrives in U.S.	1820 Isaac Marcus Jost begins to publish his *Geschichte der Israeliten.*
		1826–35 Velizh blood libel		1825 M.M. Noah Ararat project.	
1829 d. of Mordecai Benet		1827 Cantonist legislation introduced		1826 Maryland "Jew Bill" removes political disabilities. Jews settle in New Orleans	
	RUSSIA (& POLAND)	ASIA			
			1831 Ereẓ Israel taken by Muhammad Ali		1832 Leopold Zunz publishes his *Die gottesdienstlichen Vortraege*
1837 d. of Akiva Eger	1835 Oppressive constitution for the Jews		1837 Disastrous earthquake in Safed and Tiberias	1828 Removal of disabilities of Maryland Jews 1835 Beginning of large German-Jewish immigration	1837 *Allgemeine Zeitung des Judentums* founded in Berlin
1839 d. of Moses Sofer 1840 d. of Nachman Krochmal 1841 d. of Naphtali Herz Homberg	1842 Compulsory military service for the Jews of Russia	1839 Entire community of Meshed (Persia) forced to convert to Islam	1839 Citizenship to Turkish Jews 1840 Damascus blood libel; restoration of Turkish rule in Ereẓ Israel	1837 Jews settle in Cleveland 1841 Jews settle in Chicago 1843 B'nai B'rith founded	1841 *Jewish Chronicle* founded in London
1844 d. of Aaron Chorin	1844 Autonomy of the *kahal* abolished; government supervised schools for the Jews founded			1846 I.M. Wise arrives 1847 Jews settle in Washington, D.C. 1848 Influx of Jews from Germany	
1848 Anti-Jewish riots	1846 Montefiore visits Russia 1853 Saratov blood libel		1852 Confirmation of "Status Quo" in Holy Places	1849 Jews settle in San Francisco and Los Angeles	1853 Publication of Philippson's Bible completed; *Ahavat Ẓiyyon* by Abraham Mapu
1860 Jews allowed to own real-estate in Austria	1856 Cantonist legislation abrogated 1859 Merchants of the first class permitted to live outside the Pale			1854 First YMHA founded 1855 Cleveland Conference	1856 *Ha-Maggid,* first Hebrew weekly, founded in Lyck

GENERAL HISTORY	ENGLAND	FRANCE	ITALY (& PAPACY)	GERMANY	AUSTRIA-HUNGARY
1861–65 U.S. Civil War					
1861 Proclamation of the Kingdom of Italy					
1863–64 Polish revolution				1863 d. of Gabriel Riesser	
				1864 d. of Michael Sachs	
			1865 d. of Samuel David Luzzatto		1865 d. of Isaac Noah Mannheimer
1866 Austro-Prussian War					
		1867 d. of Solomon Munk			1867 Constitution abolishes Jewish disabilities; d. of Solomon Judah Rapoport
1869 Opening of the Suez Canal				1869 Leipzig Reform Synod; Deutsch-Israelitische Gemeindebund founded	
1870–71 Franco-German War					1868–69 General Congress of Hungarian Jews
1870 Unification of Italy	1870 United synagogue founded	1870 Adolphe Crémieux minister of justice; Jews of Algeria granted French citizenship	1870 Ghetto of Rome abolished; end of Jewish disabilities in Italy		
1871 Unification of Germany	1871 Anglo-Jewish Association founded			1871 Constitution abolishes Jewish disabilities	1871 A. Rohling publishes his anti-Semitic *Der Talmudjude*
				1872 Hochschule fuer die Wissenschaft des Judentums opened at Berlin	1872 Israelitische Allianz founded in Vienna
				1873 Rabbinical Seminary opened in Berlin	
				1874 d. of Abraham Geiger	
				1875 d. of Zacharias Frankel	
	1874–76 Publication of George Eliot's *Daniel Deronda*			1876 Orthodox Jews permitted to found independent congregation in Prussia	1877 Rabbinical seminary in Budapest opened
1878 Congress of Berlin				1878 Beginning of the political anti-Semitic movement in Berlin (A. Stoecker)	
				1879–80 Anti-Semitic articles by H. von Treitschke	
1881 Czar Alexander II assassinated	1881 d. of Benjamin Disraeli			1881 Anti-Semitic petition	
1882 British occupation of Egypt		1882 d. of Charles Netter			1882 Tiszaeszlar blood libel; Kadimah society founded at Vienna
	1885 d. of Moses Montefiore; Nathaniel de Rothschild raised to peerage			1885 Expulsion of Russian refugees	
		1886 E-A. Drumont publishes his anti-Semitic *La France Juive*		1886 d. of Leopold Zunz	
1888 Suez Canal Convention				1888 d. of Samson Raphael Hirsch	
				1889 d. of Ludwig Philippson	1890 d. of Solomon Sulzer
	1890 d. of Nathan Marcus Adler				
	1891 Jewish Colonization Association (ICA) incorporated			1891 Xanten blood libel; d. of Heinrich Graetz	1891 Thirteen anti-Semitic members enter Austrian Reichsrat
		1893 d. of Adolphe Franck		1893 Fifteen anti-Semites elected to the Reichstag; Central-Verein Deutscher Staatsbuerger Juedischen Glaubens founded	1893 d. of Adolf Jellinek
1894ff. Dreyfus Affair		1894 Dreyfus' trial			

RUMANIA	RUSSIA (& POLAND)	**EREẒ ISRAEL**	ZIONISM	AMERICA	CULTURAL ACHIEVEMENTS
	1861 Jews with academic diplomas permitted to live outside the Pale		1862 Moses Hess publishes *Rom und Jerusalem*	1862 Grant's General Order No. 11; first Jewish military chaplain.	
	1863 Society for the Promotion of Culture among the Jews of Russia founded				
	1864 Jews admitted to the bar				
	1865 Jewish craftsmen permitted to live outside the Pale			1869 Philadelphia Conference	
	1867 d. of Abraham Mapu	1870 Mikveh Israel founded			1868–85 *Ha-Shaḥar* published in Vienna
1871–72 Attacks on Jews	1871 Pogrom in Odessa				
			1874 d. of Ẓevi Hirsch Kalischer	1873 Union of American Hebrew Congregations founded	1876 Heinrich Graetz completes *Geschichte der Juden*; Goldfaden establishes Yiddish Theater in Rumania
				1875 Hebrew Union College opened in Cincinnati	
	1878 d. of Baron Yozel Guenzburg	1878 Petaḥ Tikvah founded; d. of Judah Alkalai			
1879 Citizenship granted to a number of Jews as individuals; d. of Meir Leib Malbim	1879 Kutais blood libel			1879 d. of David Einhorn	
	1881–82 Pogroms sweeps southern Russia; beginning of mass emigration	1881 Ben-Yehuda arrives in Ereẓ Israel		1881 Beginning of mass immigration from Eastern Europe	
	1882 "May Laws"	1882 Beginning of First Aliyah (Bilu); Rishon le-Zion founded	1882 Leon Pinsker publishes *Autoemanzipation;* Bilu organized in Russia	1882 Gompers a founder and president of A.F. of L.; first Yiddish play performed in N.Y.	
	1885 d. of Perez Smolenskin	1883 Beginning of Baron Edmond de Rothschild's help to Jewish settlements			
	1887 Small percentage of Jews admitted to high schools and universities	1884 Gederah founded	1884 Kattowitz conference of Ḥibbat Zion	1885 Pittsburgh Platform	
		1890–91 Large number of immigrants from Russia	1887 Druzgenik Conference of the Ḥovevei Zion	1886 Jewish Theological Seminary opened in New York	
				1888 Jewish Publication Society of America established; United Hebrew Trades founded.	
	1891 Expulsion from Moscow; d. of Leon Pinsker	1890 Reḥovot and Ḥaderah founded	1889 Vilna Conference; Benei Moshe founded by Aḥad Ha-Am	1889 Central Conference of American Rabbis established; Rabbi Jacob Joseph arrives as "Chief Rabbi" of New York City	
	1892 d. of Judah Leib Gordon				
	1893 d. of Naphtali Ẓevi Judah Berlin		1890 Odessa conference	1891 Immigration to Argentina with help of Baron Maurice de Hirsch	

GENERAL HISTORY	ENGLAND	FRANCE	ITALY	GERMANY	AUSTRIA-HUNGARY
		1896 d. of Baron Maurice de Hirsch 1898 Emile Zola's *J'accuse*			
1899–1902 Boer War		1899 Dreyfus retried and pardoned		1899 d. of Azriel Hildesheimer; H.S. Chamberlain's anti-Semitic *Die Grundlagen des neunzehnten jahrhunderts*	1899 d. of David Kaufmann; Hilsner Case
			1900 d. of Elijah Benamozegh	1900 Konitz blood libel 1901 Hilfsverein der deutschen Juden founded	
	1902 Jewish Religious Union founded			1903 d. of Moritz Lazarus	
1904–05 Russo-Japanese War				1904 Verband der deutschen Juden founded	
1905 Abortive revolution in Russia; separation of Church and State in France 1908 Young Turk revolution	1905 Aliens Act; Herbert Samuel first Jewish cabinet minister 1907 d. of Adolf Neubauer	1905 d. of Zadoc Kahn 1906 Dreyfus rehabilitated			1905 d. of Isaac Hirsch Weiss
	1911 d. of Hermann Adler; d. of Samuel Montagu		1910–11 L. Luzzatti prime minister		
1914–18 World War I				1915 d. of Abraham Berliner	1913 d. of Wilhelm Bacher
1917 U.S. enters the war; Russian Revolutions	1917 Balfour Declaration				1918 d. of Moritz Guedemann
1919 Peace of Versailles 1920 Polish-Russian War 1921 U.S. Immigration Act 3% quota by 1910 Census 1922 Advent of Fascism in Italy	1920 Britain granted Palestine mandate	1919 Comité des Délégations Juives		1921 d. of David Hoffmann 1922 Assassination of Walter Rathenau	1919 Pogroms in Hungary

RUMANIA	RUSSIA (& POLAND)	EREẒ ISRAEL	ZIONISM	AMERICA	
1895 Anti-Semitic League organized	1897 Bund founded 1898 d. of Samuel Mohilever 1903 Pogrom in Kishinev 1905 Pogroms; mass emigration 1906 Pogroms; Po'alei Zion founded 1909 d. of Baron Horace Guenzburg 1909–10 Polish boycott against Jews 1910 Expulsion from Kiev; d. of Moses Leib Lilienblum 1911–13 Beilis trial 1912 Agudat Israel founded 1915 d. of Isaac Leib Peretz; d. of Isaac Jacob Reines	1904 Beginning of Second Aliyah 1905 Joseph Vitkin's *Kol Kore*; Ha-Poel Ha-Ẓair founded 1906 Hebrew high school established in Jaffa; Bezalel founded 1909 Deganyah founded; Ha-Shomer organized; Tel Aviv founded	1896 Herzl publishes *Der Judenstaat* 1897 1st Zionist Congress convenes in Basle, Herzl president 1898 2nd Zionist Congress 1899 3rd Zionist Congress; Jewish Colonial Trust founded 1900 4th Zionist Congress 1901 5th Zionist Congress; Jewish National Fund established 1902 Mizrachi founded 1903 6th Zionist Congress Uganda project 1904 d. of Theodor Herzl 1905 7th Zionist Congress rejects Uganda project; Wolffsohn president 1906 Helsingfors program 1907 8th Zionist Congress 1911 10th Zionist Congress; Warburg president 1914 d. of David Wolffsohn	1896 Jews settle in Miami 1897 Federation of American Zionists founded; *Jewish Daily Forward* begins publication 1898 Union of Orthodox Jewish Congregations founded 1900 d. of I.M. Wise; I.L.G.W.U. founded 1901 S. Schechter goes to New York 1906–09 Peak of immigration: 642,000 Jews arrive 1906 American Jewish Committee established 1908 New York City *Kehillah* founded 1909 Dropsie College opened 1913 U.S.–Russian Treaty of 1832 abrogated because Russia does not recognize rights of American Jews under it; United Synagogue founded; Anti-Defamation League founded 1914 American Jewish Joint Distribution Committee established; Brandeis assumes Zionist leadership 1915 Menorah Journal, first Jewish literary organ; Leo Frank lynched 1916 L. Brandeis appointed to Supreme Court 1917 American Jewish Congress election 1919 Canadian Jewish Congress founded; American Jewish delegation at Versailles	1896 Cairo Genizah discovered 1904 Vaad ha-Lashon organized; Habimah Theater founded; Jewish Telegraphic agency founded 1906 *Jewish Encyclopaedia* completed 1913 *Yevreskaya Entsiklopedia* completed 1917 JPS version of the Bible
EGYPT 1915 Refugees from Ereẓ Israel form Zion Mule Corps					
1917 Anti-Jewish laws abrogated; d. of Mendele Mokher Seforim 1919 Pogroms in Ukraine and Poland; abolishment of community organization and Jewish institutions in Russia		1917 The British capture Jerusalem 1918 Zionist Commission appointed 1919–23 Third Aliyah 1920 British Mandate over Palestine; Tel Ḥai; Arabs riot in Jerusalem 1920–25 Sir Herbert Samuel High Commissioner 1920 Histadrut founded; the Haganah founded 1921 Arabs riot in Jaffa 1922 Churchill White Paper; d. of Eliezer Ben-Yehuda	1920 Keren Ha-Yesod established 1921 12th Zionist Congress; Weizmann president	1920 d. of Jacob H. Schiff; Henry Ford begins anti-Semitic *Dearborn Independent* 1921 Brandeis–Weizmann split divides American Zionism	

GENERAL HISTORY	ENGLAND	FRANCE	THE NETHERLANDS, BELGIUM ITALY, SCANDINAVIA, SWITZERLAND	GERMANY	AUSTRIA, CZECHOSLOVAKIA
1924 d. of Lenin					1923 d. of Joseph Samuel Bloch
	1925 d. of Israel Abrahams 1926 d. of Israel Zangwill			1925–27 Hitler's *Mein Kampf*	
1929–33 Wall Street crash—world depression 1931 Japanese aggression in Manchuria		1928 d. of Theodore Reinach			
1932 F.D. Roosevelt elected president of U.S.	1930 d. of Lucien Wolf		1930 Unione delle comunità israelitiche italiane formed		
1933 Hitler German chancellor	1933 Central British Fund for German refugees set up	1934 d. of Baron Edmond de Rothschild		1933 anti-Jewish economic boycott; first concentration camps	
1935 Italy invades Ethiopia 1936 Germans enter Rhineland 1936–39 Spanish Civil War		1936–37 Leon Blum heads Front Populaire government		1935 Nuremberg Laws	
1938 Austria annexed by Germany; Munich Crisis; partition of Czechoslovakia		1938 Evian Conference	1938 Racial legislation in Italy	1938 *Kristallnacht;* economic ruin of the Jews	1938 Pogroms in Vienna; anti-Jewish legislation; Deportations from Austria begun
1939 Beginning of World War II. Poland overrun	1939 d. of Moses Gaster; d. of Adolf Buechler				1939 Anti-Jewish laws in the Protectorate (Czechoslovakia)
1940 Western Europe overrun by the Germans; Churchill premier of Britain 1941 Germans invade Russia; Japan and U.S. enter war		1940 Discrimination laws of the Vichy regime 1941 Opening of concentration camp at Drancy 1941–44 83,000 Jews deported and murdered		1941 Jewish emigration prohibited	1941 Anti-Jewish laws in Slovakia
1942 Allies land in North Africa; Battle of El-Alamein			1942–44 Mass transports to Auschwitz from Belgium, Holland	1942 Wannsee Conference	

RUMANIA, HUNGARY	RUSSIA, POLAND	EREẒ ISRAEL	ZIONISM	AMERICA	CULTURAL ACHIEVEMENTS
	1924 Economic restrictions on Jews in Poland; attempt to settle Jews in Crimea 1928 Beginning of Jewish settlement in Birobidzhan 1930 Yevsektsiya abolished	1923 Mandate confirmed by League of Nations 1924 Technion opened in Haifa 1924–32 Fourth Aliyah 1925 Hebrew University in Jerusalem opened 1927 d. of Aḥad Ha-Am 1929 Arabs riot in Jerusalem Massacres in Hebron and Safed 1930 Passfield White Paper 1931 MacDonald's letter; split in the Haganah-Irgun Ẓeva'i Le'ummi (Eẓel) founded 1933–39 Fifth Aliyah; immigration from Germany 1933 Chaim Arlosoroff murdered	1923 d. of Max Nordau 1929 Jewish Agency expanded 1931 17th Zionist Congress; Nahum Sokolow president of World Zionist Organization	1923 Rabbinical Council of America founded; B'nai B'rith Hillel Foundation founded 1928 Yeshiva College opens 1929 d. of Louis Marshall	1925 YIVO founded 1925–32 *Encyclopaedia Judaica* (German) A—L
	1934 Birobidzhan—Jewish Autonomous Oblast; Poland annuls Minorities Treaties 1936 Pogrom in Przytyk (Poland)	1934 d. of Ḥayyim Naḥman Bialik (in Vienna); beginning of "illegal" immigration on a larger scale 1936 Arabs riot; Arab strike	1935 19th Zionist Congress; Weizmann reelected president of World Zionist Organization 1936 World Jewish Congress founded	1934 Jewish Labor Committee founded; H. Morgenthau Sec. of Treasury	1934 DAIA established 1936 Palestine Symphony Orchestra established
1937 Anti-Semitic legislation in Rumania	1937 Discrimination in Polish universities	1937 Peel Commission proposes partition of Palestine, Arab revolt; Haganah reunited; Stockade and watchtower settlements			
1938 Anti-Jewish economic legislation in Hungary		1938 Wingate organizes special Jewish units to fight Arab terrorism	1938 d. of Otto Warburg		
1939 Many Hungarian Jews lose citizenship 1941 Pogrom in Jassy (Rumania)	1939 Pogroms in Poland (after Nazi invasion) 1940 Formation of ghettos in Poland 1941 Pogroms in Kaunas and Lvov, massacres by Einsatzgruppen in occupied Russia; expulsions from the Reich to Poland; first death camp established (Chelmno)	1939 MacDonald White Paper. Loḥamei Ḥerut Israel (Leḥi) founded 1941 Palmaḥ organized	1939 United Jewish Appeal founded 1940 d. of Vladimir Jabotinsky	1939 Peak of Nazi refugee immigration: 43,000 arrive 1941 d. of Louis D. Brandeis	
1942 "Struma" sinks in Black Sea with 769 refugees	1942 Massacres in occupied Russia continue. death camps of Auschwitz, Maidanek and Treblinka begin to function at full capacity; transports from the ghettos to death camps		1942 American Jewish conference endorses Biltmore Program		

GENERAL HISTORY	FRANCE	THE NETHERLANDS ETC.	GERMANY	AUSTRIA CZECHOSLOVAKIA	RUMANIA HUNGARY
1943 German defeat at Stalingrad, Germans surrender in North Africa, Italy surrenders		1943 Jews of Denmark smuggled to Sweden	1943 Germany declared *Judenrein*		
1944 Allies land in Normandy; Russians advance westward. U.S. victorious in the Pacific	1944 Representative body of French Jews (CRJF)	1943–44 7,500 Italian Jews murdered			1944 Extermination of Hungarian Jewry began
1945 Germany surrenders; atomic bombs, Japan surrenders; death of Roosevelt; Truman president		1940–45 Total of Jewish victims 139,000; Jewish Brigade helps to organize survivors of death camps and send them to Palestine	1945 Total of Jewish victims 125,000	1945 Total of Jewish victims 342,000	1944–45 Total of Jewish victims (including also Greece and Yugoslavia) 557,000
1946 Communists take over in Eastern and Central Europe			1946 Major Nuremberg trial		
1947 Paris Peace Conference					
1948 Communist Coup in Czechoslovakia; State of Israel proclaimed and War of Independence					

	WESTERN EUROPE	EASTERN EUROPE
1949 NATO organized; Communist republic in China; U.S. Displaced Persons Act		
1950 Korean War	1950 Centralrat der Juden in Deutschland	
1952 Revolution in Egypt First hydrogen bomb exploded		1952 Prague Trials
1953 Eisenhower president of U.S.; Korean Armistice; d. of Stalin; Refugee Relief Act		1953 "Doctors' plot" in U.S.S.R.
1954 French defeated in Indo-China; beginning of uprising in Algeria	1954–55 Mendes-France French premier	
1955 Signing of Warsaw Pact	1954–68 Mass immigration of N. African Jews to France	
1956 Hungarian revolution; Suez Campaign		
1957 British army leaves Jordan; Russian sputnik		
1958 Fifth Republic in France; civil war in Lebanon and Iraq		
1959 Cuban revolution		
1960 Civil war in Congo	1960 Swastika daubing	
1961 Kennedy president of U.S.; Ghana independent (followed by other African states)		
1962 Independence of Algeria; Cuban crisis		
1963 Kennedy assassinated		
1964 Fall of Khrushchev		
1965 U.S. offensive in Vietnam; Immigration Act abolishes quota system	1965 Diplomatic relations between Israel and Germany established	
1967 Six-Day war	1967 De Gaulle's anti-Israel stand	1968 Fresh wave of anti-Semitism in Poland; emigration of most of remaining Jews
1968 Warsaw Pact countries invade Czechoslovakia; Paris May Riots	1968 Frankfort trials	1970 Leningrad trials Russian Jews agitate for right to emigrate
1969 First man on the moon		

RUSSIA, POLAND	EREẒ ISRAEL	AMERICA	CULTURAL ACHIEVEMENTS
1943 Transports from all over Europe to death camps. Warsaw ghetto revolt. Annihilation of most of the ghettos	1943 d. of Saul Tchernichowsky		
1944–47 Beriḥah	1944 Eẓel and Leḥi strike at the British; Jewish Brigade organized (fights in Italy)		
1945 Total of Jewish victims 4,565,000	1945 Bevin's declaration on Palestine; "Illegal" immigration intensified; Struggle against the British intensified; Cooperation between Haganah and Eẓel		
1946 Pogroms at Kielce and other places of mass emigration	1946 Anglo-American Committee publishes its conclusions; Eẓel blows up the King David Hotel; the British deport "illegal" immigrants to Cyprus	1946 Founding of Brandeis University	
	1947 U.N. General Assembly decides on partition of Palestine; Beginning of Arab attacks		1947 Discovery of Dead Sea Scrolls
1948 Jewish culture in U.S.S.R. suppressed and intellectuals shot; Golda Meir first Israel minister to Moscow	1948 Proclamation of the State of Israel; seven Arab states invade; Israel offensive; The Negev liberated	1948 U.S. recognizes Israel, May 14, 1948 1948 Peak of migration to S. California	

ISRAEL	ARAB COUNTRIES	AMERICA	CULTURAL ACHIEVEMENTS
1949 First Knesset opens; Chaim Weizmann first president of Israel; David Ben-Gurion prime minister; cease-fire agreements with Egypt, Lebanon, Transjordan, Syria; Israel member of UN; 240,000 immigrants	1949–50 Airborne transfer of c. 50,000 Jews from Yemen to Israel	1949 d. of Stephen S. Wise	
1950 Western Powers guarantee existing borders in the Middle East; Law of Return; mass immigration	1950–51 Airborne transfer of 123,000 Jews from Iraq to Israel		
1951 Second Knesset elected; Tension on borders increases; Mass immigration continues; 23rd Zionist Congress in Jerusalem adopts Jerusalem Program			
1952 d. of Chaim Weizmann; Izhak Ben-Zvi second president of Israel; Reparations agreement between W. Germany and Israel			
1953 Beginning of attacks by Arab infiltrators; first Israel reprisal action; Ben-Gurion retires to Sdeh Boker; Moshe Sharett prime minister; Kasztner trial			
	1954–55 emigration from Morocco	1954–55 Celebration of Tercentenary of Jews in U.S.	
1955 Fedayeen attacks and reprisal actions continue; Ben-Gurion prime minister; Waters of Yarkon river directed to the Negev	1955 Moshe Marzouk and Samuel Azaar executed in Cairo		
1956 Sinai Campaign	1956 Jews of Egypt expelled		
1957 Israel evacuates Sinai; U.N. observers on border with Egypt.			
1960 Eichmann kidnapped to Israel			1960 Discovery of Bar Kokhba epistles
1961 Lavon Affair; Eichmann trial; "Shavit 2" Israel missile successfully launched			
1963 d. of Izhak Ben-Zvi; Zalman Shazar third president of Israel; Levi Eshkol prime minister		1963 d. of A.H. Silver	
			1964 Memorial Foundation for Jewish Culture founded
1965 d. of Martin Buber	1965 Eli Cohen executed in Damascus		
		1966 Manifestations of Black anti-Semitism	1966 Shmuel Yosef Agnon and Nelly Sachs awarded the Nobel Prize for Literature
1967 Six-Day War, Jerusalem reunited		1967 6,000 volunteers to Israel	
		1968 New York teachers strike	1968 Excavation in Old City of Jerusalem begun
1969 War of attrition at the Suez Canal front begun; Death of Levi Eshkol; Golda Meir prime minister	1969 Jews executed in Iraq		

GENERAL HISTORY	WESTERN EUROPE	EASTERN EUROPE
1970 Allende president of Chile; Black September in Jordan; Death of Nasser; Succession of Sadat		
1971 Communist China joins UN; Bangladesh independent of Pakistan; famine in Bangladesh		
1972 Nixon visits Peking; Paris peace talks on Vietnam; Escalation of bombing of Hanoi; American withdrawal from South Vietnam; Helsinki SALT talks; Detente: Nixon to Moscow	1972 Letter bombs in London and Geneva; Massacre of Olympic team at Munich	1972 Soviet Union imposes severe fines upon academicians seeking to emigrate to Israel.
1973 Watergate scandal		
1974 Nixon resigns Presidency; Haile Selassie deposed in Ethiopia; Yassir Arafat addresses UN General Assembly		
1975 Civil War in Lebanon; Khmer Rouge regime in Cambodia; Fall of South Vietnam to Communists; Helsinki accords		
1976 Death of Mao Tse-Tung; Jimmy Carter elected president		1976 *Aliyah* protest march of Jews in Moscow
1977 Marxist Revolution in Ethiopia: Col. Mengistu takes power	1977 Attack in Rome synagogue on Rosh HaShana	1977 Drop-out rate among emigrants from USSR reaches 50%
1978 Unrest in Iran; Military coup in Afghanistan		1978 Human rights activists Ida Nudel and Vladimir Slepak sentenced by USSR; Anatoly Shcharansky tried, sentenced to 13 years
1979 US and China establish diplomatic relations; Revolution in Iran; American hostages taken in Teheran; Sandinistas take power in Nicaragua; Soviets intervene in Afghanistan		1979 Soviet emigration reaches peak of 51,320
1980 Civil war in El Salvador; U.S. grain boycott of USSR; Rise of "Solidarity" trade union in Poland; Iran-Iraq war; Ronald Reagan elected president	1980 Rue Copernic Synagogue in Paris is bombed	1980 Soviet Jews threaten hunger strikes for denial of exit visas
1981 Lebanese civil war escalates; *Columbia* space shuttle flight; Assassination attempt on Reagan and Pope John Paul II; Sadat assassinated, succeeded by Hosni Mubarak	1981 Jewish cemetery outside Paris desecrated; Aaron Lustiger, born a Jew, named Archbishop of Paris; Vienna synagogue attacked;	1981 European rabbis meet in Bucharest
1982 Falklands war; "Solidarity" outlawed in Poland; Bashir Gemayal assassinated in Lebanon; Brezhnev dies, succeeded by Andropov	1982 Jewish sites in Rome and Vienna remain terrorist targets; Attack on Central Synagogue in Rome	1982 Soviets blame Polish Jews for Poland's unrest
1983 Debate in Europe over stationing of nuclear warheads; PLO rebels battle Arafat supporters; U.S. invades Granada; dictatorship ends in Argentina	1983 Jewish restaurant in Paris bombed	1983 Iosif Begun sentenced to prison for teaching Hebrew in USSR
1984 Iran-Iraq War expands in Persian Gulf; Indira Gandhi assassinated; Andropov dies; succeeded by Chernenko; Reagan re-elected; famine in Ethiopia		1984 Only 896 Jews permitted to leave Soviet Union
1985 Chernenko dies, succeeded by Gorbachev; Geneva summit—Reagan and Gorbachev debate SDI, arms control, etc.	1985 Reagan lays wreath at Bitburg, among SS graves; *Achille Lauro* hijacking; Terrorist attacks on Rome and Vienna airports	1985 Emigration from Soviet Union continues steep decline
1986 Explosion of shuttle *Challenger;* U.S. airstrike against terrorist bases in Libya; Leak of nuclear waste in Chernobyl; Iran-Contra scandal; Lebanese hostage crisis continues	1986 Pope John Paul II visits Rome's Central Synagogue Kurt Waldheim implicated in Nazi war crimes	1986 Anatoly Shcharansky released from Soviet prison; 22 Jews slain in Istanbul synagogue 1987 Iosif Begun released from Soviet prison

ISRAEL	ARAB COUNTRIES	AMERICAS	CULTURAL ACHIEVEMENTS
1970 Pursuit of terrorists in Jordan Valley; border incidents along Suez Canal and Golan; massacre at Avivim	1970 Jewish property confiscated in Libya		
1971 Demonstrations by Israeli "Black Panthers"			1971 Sixteen Jews, of 50 Americans, are elected to the National Academy of Science
1972 Massacre at Lod Airport		1972 Reform Judaism ordains first woman	1972 *Fiddler on the Roof* closes after 3,342 Broadway performances; Mark Spitz wins seven Gold Medals in swimming at the Olympic Games
1973 Yom Kippur war; African states sever relations with Israel; Death of Ben Gurion		1973 Abraham Beame elected mayor of New York City	1973 Kissinger wins Nobel Peace Prize; Five Jews receive the Pulitzer Prize
1974 Signing of Disengagement accords with Egypt; Inquiry into government response in Yom Kippur War; Golda Meir resigns; Terrorism: Kiryat Shemona, Ma'alot; Death of Zalman Shazar; Ephraim Katzir president	1974 Rape and murder of Jewish women in Damascus	1974 Buenos Aires synagogue bombed	
1975 Agranat Commission report; UN censures Zionism; Palestinian terrorism continues; Kissinger shuttle diplomacy: withdrawal from Abu Rodeis oil fields	1975 Suez Canal reopened	1975 Argentina synagogue bombings	
		1976 Jews protest PLO participation at UN	1976 First worldwide congress on Yiddish culture and language held in Jerusalem; Saul Bellow wins Nobel Prize in Literature
1977 Rabin resigns; Menachem Begin and Likud take power; Sadat and Begin exchange visits	1977 12 young Jewish women permitted to leave Damascus for United States	1977 Edward I. Koch elected mayor of New York City	
1978 Yitzhak Navon president; Camp David talks; Death of Golda Meir; Egyptian and Israeli officials confer; Israelis seize "security belt" in Lebanon.		1978 Nazis march in Skokie, Illinois	1978 I.B. singer wins Nobel Prize for Literature; Menachem Begin shares Nobel Peace Prize with Anwar Sadat
1979 Jimmy Carter visits Israel; Camp David Accords signed at White House; Begin visits Cairo; Terrorism at Kiryat Shemona and Nahariya; Foreign Minister Moshe Dayan resigns	1979 Iranian Jews flee Iran's revolution		
1980 Israel and Egypt establish diplomatic relations; UN Security Council calls for halt in West Bank settlement; cars of West Bank mayors blown up	1980 Repression of Iranian Jews	1980 Argentine journalist Jacobo Timerman released from prison	
1981 Israelis destroy Iraqi atomic reactor; War of attrition along Lebanese border; Memorandum of Understanding signed with U.S.		1981 U.S. government and Jewish community split over AWACS sale to Saudi Arabia	1981 Elias Canetti of Bulgaria wins Nobel Prize in Literature
1982 Withdrawal from Yamit; Invasion of Lebanon; Reagan plan for autonomy talks; Sabra & Shatila massacres		1982 29 Jews elected to the House of Representatives	
1983 Negotiations between Israel and Lebanon; Kahan Commission report on Sabra & Shatila published; Chaim Herzog president; IDF redeployment along Awali River; Begin resigns, succeeded by Yitzhak Shamir	1983 Hundreds of Jews arrested in Iran; Synagogue burned in Tunisia	1983 Question of missing Argentine Jews	
1984 Lebanon abrogates agreement with Israel; Israel uncovers Jewish terrorist organization; National Unity Government under Shimon Peres; IDF begins withdrawal from Lebanon; Ethiopian Jews brought to Israel	1984 Israelis participate in Jewish conference in Rabat, Morocco	1984 Accusations of antisemitism surround presidential candidacy of Jesse Jackson; anti-semitism of Louis Farrakhan	
1985 "Operation Moses" brings Ethiopian Jews to Israel; End of Lebanon war—withdrawal of IDF forces	1985 Three Jews killed at Simchat Torah services in Jerba, Tunisia; Seven prominent Beirut Jews kidnapped, four confirmed murdered; Isolation of Yemeni Jews	1985 Skeleton of Josef Mengele found near Sao Paolo	1985 *Shoah*, a 9-hour film study of the Holocaust
1986 Shimon Peres meets King Hassan of Morocco in peace initiative; African nations renew ties with Israel; Shamir succeeds Peres	1986 21 Jews slain in synagogue in Istanbul	1986 U.S. defense analyst Jonathan Pollard convicted of spying for Israel	1986 Elie Wiesel wins Nobel Peace Prize
1987 Demjanjuk Nazi war crime trial			

Day-by-Day in Jewish History (Part II).

January

1—1837: 5,000 Jews perish in earthquake at Safed and Tiberias.
2—1782: Joseph II of Austria introduces Patent of Toleration, improving situation of Austrian Jewry.
3—1919: Agreement between Emir Feisal and Chaim Weizmann endorsing Balfour Declaration.
4—1786: Moses Mendelssohn, philosopher of the German Enlightenment, died.
5—1895: Public degradation of Dreyfus.
6—1930: Foundation of Mapai.
7—1858: Eliezer Ben Yehuda, the father of modern Hebrew, born.
8—1960: Israel presents notes to various governments expressing shock at antisemitic outrages and Swastika daubings.
9—1873: Chaim Nahman Bialik, Hebrew poet and storyteller, born.
10—1847: Jacob H. Schiff, philanthropist, born.
11—1808: Abraham Mapu, creator of the modern Hebrew novel, born.
12—1493: Jews expelled from Sicily.
13—1825: Expulsion in Russia (leading eventually to Pale of Settlement).
14—1866: Toleration in Switzerland.
15—1946: Chief Rabbi Dr. J.H. Hertz, chief rabbi of the British Commonwealth, died.
16—1921: 119 leading Americans headed by Pres. Wilson denounced antisemitic propaganda in U.S.
17—1890: Solomon Sulzer, Austrian cantor and reformer of liturgical music, died.
18—1943: Nazis' decision to liquidate Warsaw Ghetto.
19—1948: Solomon Mikhoels, Yiddish actor, murdered.
20—1942: Wannsee Conference plans implementation of the "Final Solution".
21—1306: Expulsion from France.
22—1923: Max Nordau, Zionist leader, philosopher and writer, died.
23—1639: Auto-da-Fe at Lima.
24—1893: Isaac Meir Dick, the first popular Yiddish fiction writer, died.
25—1240: Paris disputation on the Talmud.
26—1482: First edition of Hebrew Pentateuch printed at Bologna.
27—1969: Fourteen men, including nine Jews, publicly hanged in Baghdad, on charges of spying for Israel.
28—1893: Rabbi Abba Hillel Silver, Zionist leader and Reform rabbi, born.
29—1858: Nahum Sokolow, Hebrew writer and journalist, born.
30—1933: Hitler accedes to power.
31—1955: Execution of two Jews sentenced to death at Cairo trial as "Zionist spies."

February

1—1885: Peretz Smolenskin, Hebrew novelist, died.
2—1524: David Reuveni, an adventurer, began his career.
3—1807: Opening of Napoleonic Sanhedrin in Paris.
4—1738: "Jew Suess" Oppenheimer executed in Wurttemberg.
5—1840: Damascus Affair commenced.
6—1481: First Auto-da-Fe, Seville.
7—1413: Disputation of Tortosa opened.
8—1895: Maurice Samuel, U.S. author and translator, born.
9—1880: Rabbi Israel Lipkin (Salanter), founder of the Mussar movement, died.
10—1880: Issac Adolphe Cremieux, French lawyer and "defender of Jewish rights", died.
11—1868: Nachman Syrkin, the first leader of Socialist Zionism, born.
12—1886: First issue of first Hebrew daily *Hayom* in St. Petersburg.
13—1945: Henrietta Szold, Zionist leader and founder of Hadassah, died.
14—1896: "The Jewish State" by Theodor Herzl published.
15—1917: Foundation of the "Jewish Legion"
16—1870: Emancipation of Jews of Sweden.
17—1949: Weizmann elected first President of Israel.
18—1839: Zadoc Kahn, chief rabbi of France, born.
19—1939: Adolf Buechler, Jewish theologian and historian, died.
20—1959: Zalman Schneour, Hebrew and Yiddish poet and writer, died.
21—1677: Baruch Spinoza, Dutch philosopher, died.
22—1965: Justice Felix Frankfurter, U.S. Supreme Court Justice, died.
23—1913: United Synagogue of America founded.
24—1942: Sinking of *Struma.*
25—1867: Emancipation of the Jews of Hungary.
26—1969: Levi Eshkol, the third prime minister of Israel, died.
27—1670: Expulsion from Vienna.
28—1616: Vincent Fettmilch, anti-Jewish guild leader in Frankfort, executed.

March

1—1349: 4,000 Jews burned at Worms.
2—1859: Shalom Aleichem born.
3—1240: Confiscation and burning of the Talmud in France.
4—1902: Foundation of "Mizrachi".
5—1899: Cecil Roth, Jewish historian and editor-in-chief of the *Encyclopedia Judaica,* born.
6—1896: Rabbi Isaac Elchanan Spector, the rabbi of Kovno and founder of its yeshivah, died.
7—1944: Emanuel Ringelblum, historian of Warsaw Ghetto, arrested by Nazis and shot.
8—1957: Israel completes evacuation of Sinai and Gaza Strip.
9—1556: Sultan protests against papal treatment of Jews.
10—1949: Israel troops advance to Gulf of Akaba.
11—1911: The Mendel Beilis affair begins.
12—1421: Wiener Geserah; Jewish community of Vienna perished.
13—1938: Germany took over Austria (*Anschluss*).
14—1879: Albert Einstein born.
15—1939: Germans invade Czechoslovakia.
16—1190: The heroic end of the Jews of York.
17—1874: Stephen S. Wise, founder of the Free Synagogue in New York City, born.
18—1886: Leopold Zunz, German scholar, died.
19—1497: Forced baptism in Portugal.
20—1899: Jewish Colonial Trust founded in London.
21—1648: Leone Modena, Italian rabbi, scholar and writer, died.
22—1144: First ritual murder libel at Norwich.
23—1475: Blood accusation at Trent.
24—1515: Rabbi Joseph Caro died.
25—1919: Committee of Jewish Delegation formed.
26—1900: Rabbi Isaac Mayer Wise, a pioneer of Reform Judaism, died.
27—1288: Jews martyred at Troyes.
28—1038: Rav Hai Gaon died.
29—1936: Luigi Luzzatti, the first Jewish prime minister of Italy, died.
30—1135: Maimonides born.
31—1492: Edict of Ferdinand and Isabella expelling Jews from Spain.

April

1—1925: Inauguration of Hebrew University.
2—1947: Britain refers Palestine problem to U.N.
3—1953: Release of arrested Jewish doctors in Soviet Russia.
4—1918: Zionist Commission under Weizmann arrives in Palestine.
5—1872: David Pinski, Yiddish novelist, born.
6—1848: Emancipation of Jews of Prussia.
7—1957: First oil tanker reaches Eilat.
8—1915: Isaac Leib Perez, Yiddish and Hebrew author, died.
9—1506: Attacks on New Christians in Lisbon.
10—1728: Solomon Ayllon, kabbalist, died.
11—1961: Adolf Eichmann trial opened in Jerusalem.
12—1955: Dr. Jonas Salk discovers anti-poliomyelitis vaccine.
13—1948: 78 killed in Hadassah convoy to Mt. Scopus.
14—1859: Blood libel at Galatz.
15—1945: British troops enter Bergen-Belsen.
16—1795: Rabbi Zevi Hirsch Kalischer born.
17—1848: Walls of Rome ghetto removed.
18—1389: Massacre of Jews in Prague.
19—1903: Pogrom in Kishinev.
20—1344: Levi ben Gershon died.
21—1896: Baron Maurice de Hirsch, German financier and philanthropist, died.
22—1897: First issue of Yiddish *Jewish Daily Forward* in New York.
23—1720: Elijah ben Solomon Zalman, the Vilna Gaon, born.
24—1920: San Remo Conference conferred Palestine Mandate on Britain.
25—1824: Rabbi Samuel Mohilewer, an early member of Hovevei Zion in Russia, born.
26—1655: Settlement in New Amsterdam (New York) authorized.
27—1293: Rabbi Meir of Rothenburg died.
28—1881: Pogrom at Elizabethgrad spawns series of massacres throughout Eastern Europe.
29—1838: Nobel Peace Prize winner T.M.C. Asser born.
30—1492: Expulsion from Spain publicly announced.

May

1—1572: Moses Isserles died.
2—1860: Theodor Herzl born.
3—1898: Golda Meir born.
4—1915: Moshe Dayan born.
5—1818: Karl Marx born.
6—1744: Moses Hayyim Luzzatto died.
7—1945: German General Jodl signed unconditional surrender.
8—1943: Mordechai Anielewicz, commander-in-chief of the Warsaw Ghetto Uprising, fell in action.
9—1942: Extraordinary Zionist Conference at Hotel Biltmore in New York adopted "Biltmore Program" (Jewish Commonwealth).
10—1933: Burning of books in Germany.
11—1949: State of Israel becomes member of United Nations.
12—1267: Synod of Vienna orders Jews to wear pointed hats.
13—1965: Diplomatic relations between West Germany and Israel established.
14—1948: Proclamation of State of Israel.
15—1882: May Laws issued.
16— 942: Rav Saadia Gaon died.
17—1939: White Paper on Palestine published.
18—1901: Herzl meets Sultan Abdul Hamid.
19—1103; Rav Isaac Alfasi died.
20—1820: Azriel Hildesheimer, German scholar and leader of Orthodox Jewry, born.
21—1671: Jews admitted to Brandenburg.
22—1760: Rabbi Israel ben Eliezer, known as the Baal Shem Tov (Besht), founder and first leader of Hasidism in Eastern Europe, died.
23—1536: Inquisition established in Portugal.
24—1810: Abraham Geiger, leader of the Reform movement, born.

25—1096: Jews in Worms killed.
26—1895: Salo W. Baron, Jewish historian, born.
27—1096: Massacre at Mayence.
28—1948: Old City of Jerusalem surrendered to Arab Legion.
29—1839: Hermann Adler, British chief rabbi, born.
30—1972: Lydda Airport massacre.
31—1962: Adolf Eichmann executed at Ramleh Prison.

June

1—1244: Privileges to Jews in Austria.
2—1453: Martyrdom of Breslau Jews.
3—1888: Jewish Publication Society of America organized.
4—1897: First issue of *Die Welt,* founded by Herzl.
5—1967: Outbreak of Six-Day War between Israel and the Arab States.
6—1391: Massacres begun in Spain.
7—1594: Roderigo Lopez, physician to Queen Elizabeth charged with high treason and executed.
8—1818: Fanny von Arnstein, hostess of popular salon and co-founder of the Music Society of Austria, died.
9—1171: Rabbi Jacob Tam died.
10—1648: Jews of Nemirov murdered by Cossacks.
11—1948: David Marcus, retired colonel in the U.S. Army, killed in Israeli War of Independence.
12—1240: Disputation at Paris.
13—1965: Martin Buber, philosopher and theologian, died.
14—1821: Hayyim ben Issac of Volozhin died.
15—1947: Bronislav Hubermann, Polish violinist and founder of the Israeli Philharmonic Orchestra, died.
16—1933: Chaim Arlosoroff, leader of the Zionist Labor movement, murdered.
17—1242: Talmud burned in Paris.
18—1571: Rabbi Jacob Pollack, the first Polish halachic authority, died.
19—1269: Jews in France forced to wear yellow badge.
20—1757: Frankist disputation at Kameniec.
21—1943: Revolt in Treblinka extermination camp.
22—1943: *Altalena* blown up off Tel Aviv.
23—1858: Edgar Mortara of Bologna kidnaped.
24—1922: Walter Rathenau, German statesman and writer, murdered.
25—1962: U.S. Supreme Court decides against recital of prayer in public schools.
26—1570: Rabbi Moses Cordevero, kabbalist, died.
27—1939: Israel Davidson, scholar of medieval Hebrew literature, died.
28—1286: Rabbi Meir of Rothenburg imprisoned.
29—1967: Jerusalem reunified.
30—1922: U.S. Congress approves principles of Balfour Declaration.

July

1—1920: Herbert Samuel appointed High Commissioner of Palestine.
2—1808: Napoleon decreed that Jews must adopt family names.
3—1904: Death of Theodore Herzl.
4—1934: Death of Chaim Nahman Bialik.
5—1950: "Law of Return" passed by Knesset.
6—1882: First *Biluim* arrive in Palestine.
7—1887: Marc Chagall born.
8—1873: Foundation of Union of American Hebrew Congregations.
9—1885: First Lord Rothschild takes seat in House of Lords.
10—1957: Shalom Asch, Yiddish novelist and dramatist, died.
11—1739: Expulsion from Little Russia.
12—1840: Abraham Goldfaden, father of Yiddish theatre, born.
13—1096: Crusaders captured Jerusalem and killed Jews, Karaites and Moslems of the Holy City.
14—1870: United Synagogue (London) established.
15—1834: Spanish Inquisition abolished.
16—1948: Israel troops capture Nazareth.
17—1888: Samuel Joseph Agnon born.
18—1290: Edict of Expulsion of Jews from England.
19—1785: Mordecai Manuel Noah, U.S. playwright and politician, born.
20—1263: Disputation of Barcelona opened.
21—1947: *Exodus,* with 4,500 Jews from D.P. Camps arrived in Haifa; passengers transported back to Germany.
22—1306: Expulsion of Jews from France.
23—1626: Shabbetai Zevi born.
24—1861: Ernest Bloch, composer and founder of the Cleveland Institute of Music, born.
25—1670: Expulsion from Vienna.
26—1555: Ghetto in Rome established.
27—1656: Jewish community of Amsterdam pronounced decree of excommunication on Spinoza.
28—1885: Sir Moses Montefiore, Jewish leader and philanthropist, died.
29—1336: Armleder massacres began in Germany.
30—1488: Auto-da-Fe in Toledo.
31—1305: Ban on study of philosophy imposed by Rabbi Solomon ben Aderet.

August

1—1826: Last Auto-da-Fe in Valencia.
2—1492: Expulsion of Jews from Spain.
3—1960: Hadassah Medical Center dedicated in Jerusalem.
4—1922: David Frischmann, one of the first major writers in modern Hebrew literature, died.
5—1572: Death of Rabbi Isaac Luria, kabbalist.
6—1855: Sir Isaac Isaacs, Chief Justice of Australia, born.
7—1295: Jews of Silesia receive privileges.
8—1878: Foundation of Petah Tikvah.
9—1506: Pinsk community founded.
10—1794: Leopold Zunz, German scholar, born.
11—1929: First constituent meeting of the Jewish Agency opened.
12—1952: Twenty-six Soviet-Yiddish writers, among them David Bergelson, Peretz Markish, and Itzik Feffer, shot on Stalin's orders.
13—1944: Berl Katznelson, Zionist labor leader, died.
14—1874: Joseph Klausner, literary critic and historian, born.
15—1943: Resistance of Bialystok Ghetto.
16—1948: Peretz Hirschbein, Yiddish playwright and novelist, died.

17—1949: Theodor Herzl re-interred in Jerusalem.
18—1856: Ahad Ha-am, Hebrew essayist and leader of Hivvat Zion movement, born.
19—1845: Baron Edmond de Rothschild born.
20—1899: Captain Alfred Dreyfus pardoned and liberated.
21—1893: Law prohibiting Jewish ritual slaughtering passed in Switzerland.
22—1654: Jacob Barsimson arrives in New Amsterdam (New York) from Holland.
23—1929: Anti-Jewish attacks in Palestine.
24—1950: "Operation Magic Carpet" officially concluded.
25—1800: Samuel David Luzzatto, Italian scholar and philosopher, born.
26—1942: Dr. Leo Judah Landau, chief rabbi of Johannesberg, died.
27—1686: First issue of first Yiddish newspaper *Kourant* in Amsterdam.
28—1967: Arab Conference in Khartoum decided: non-recognition of Israel, no negotiations, and no peace with Israel.
29—1897: Opening of First Zionist Congress.
30—1658: Haham Zevi Ashkenazi, rabbi and halachic authority, born.
31—1864: Ferdinand Lasalle, German Socialist leader, killed.

September

1—1577: Conversionist sermons instituted in Rome.
2—1796: Emancipation of Jews in the Netherlands.
3—1189: Anti-Jewish coronation riot in London.
4—1892: Darius Milhaud, composer, born.
5—1938: First anti-Jewish decrees of Italian Fascist regime.
6—1729: Moses Mendelssohn, philosopher and spiritual leader of German Jewry, born.
7—1891: Heinrich Graetz, Jewish historian, died.
8—1962: Mane-Katz, painter, died.
9—1553: Talmud burned in Rome.
10—1952: Reparations agreement between Israel and Germany signed in Luxembourg.
11—1891: Jewish Colonization Association founded.
12—1954: U.S. Jewish tercentenary celebrations inaugurated.
13—1892: Railway from Jerusalem to Jaffa opened.
14—1427: Death of the Maharil, Rabbi Jacob ben Moses Molen, noted Talmudist.
15—1935: Nuremberg Racial Laws in Nazi Germany enacted.
16—1666: Shabbtai Zevi accepted Islam.
17—1948: Count Folke Bernadotte, Swedish statesman responsible for the release of thousands of Jews during World War II, assassinated.
18—1860: Simon Dubnow, historian, and political ideologist, born.
19—1944: Jewish Brigade founded.
20—1540: First Auto-da-Fe in Portugal.
21—1939: Nazis plan for ghettos in Poland.
22—1654: Peter Stuyvesant attempts to expel Jews from New Amsterdam (New York).
23—1941: First experiment in use of gases in Auschwitz.
24—1762: Rabbi Moses Sofer, halachic authority known as Hatam Sofer, born.
25—1920: Jacob Heinrich Schiff, U.S. financier and philanthropist, died.
26—1798: Morris Jacob Raphall, the first rabbi to give invocation before the House of Representatives, born.
27—1791: French National Assembly grants equal rights to the Jews.
28—1775: First Congregation in Stockholm.
29—1941: Babi Yar massacre.
30—1801: Zacharias Frankel, German rabbi and scholar, born.

October

1—1943: Danish Jews saved from deportation by Danish population.
2—1596: Foundation of Amsterdam community.
3—1555: Roman ghetto walled.
4—1940: Anti-Jewish Laws of Vichy government enacted.
5—1941: U.S. Supreme Court Justice Louis D. Brandeis died.
6—1973: Yom Kippur War breaks out.
7—1771: Rav Nahman of Bratislav born.
8—1918: Foundation of "Habimah".
9—1354: Casimir the Great issued a Charter to Jews of Poland.
10—1797: Vilna Gaon died.
11—1700: Jews burned in Prague.
12—1837: Rabbi Akiva Eger, famed German rabbi, died.
13—1843: First B'nai B'rith founded in New York.
14—1943: Uprising in Sobibor extermination camp.
15—1963: Edmond Fleg, French poet and essayist, died.
16—1886: David Ben-Gurion born.
17—1882: Publication of *Auto-emancipation* by Leo Pinsker.
18—1880: Vladimir Jabotinsky born.
19—1700: Judah Hasid, Shabbatean preacher, died.
20—1540: First Auto-da-Fe in Portugal.
21—1894: Arrest of Captain Dreyfus.
22—1586: Bull of Pope Sixtus V in favor of Jews.
23—1905: Abraham Geiger, a leader of the Reform movement, died.
24—1870: Emancipation in Algeria.
25—1327: Rabbi Asher ben Yehiel (the Rosh), talmudist and halakhic leader of German Jewry, died.
26—1407: Massacre of Jews in Cracow.
27—1848: Judah L. Magnes, U.S. rabbi and communal leader, died.
28—1270: Rabbi Moses Ben Nahman (Nahmanides) died.
29—1956: Israel Defense Forces advanced into Sinai Peninsula.
30—1943: Max Reinhardt, German stage producer and director, died.
31—1497: Banishment from Portugal.

November

1—1290: Expulsion of Jews from England.
2—1917: Balfour Declaration.
3—1394: Expulsion of Jews from France.
4—1571: Inquisition introduced in Mexico.
5—1573: Rabbi Solomon Luria, Polish *posek* and Talmudic commentator, died.
6—1884: Hovevei Zion Conference opens in Kattowitz.
7—1944: Hannah Senesh killed.
8—1761: Rabbi Akiva ben Moshe Eger born.

9—1952: President Chaim Weizmann died.
10—1938: Pogrom in Germany.
11—1215: Fourth Lateran Council meets and issues anti-Jewish legislation.
12—1841: First issue of *Jewish Chronicle.*
13—1757: Talmud burned in Poland.
14—1945: Mass demonstration in Palestine against British Foreign Minister Bevin's policy.
15—1940: Germans establish the Warsaw ghetto.
16—1917: Jaffa and Tel Aviv occupied by British forces.
17—1278: Order of Edward I for the imprisonment of Jews in England.
18—1874: Enzo Sereni, pioneer in Israel, labor leader and writer, died.
19—1887: Emma Lazarus died.
20—1964: The Ecumenical Council adopted a statement on the attitude of the Church toward Jews.
21—1962: Arad, new town in Negev, officially inaugurated.
22—1967: Security Council of United Nations accepted resolution concerning terms of a settlement to the Middle East conflict.
23—1510: Expulsion from Naples.
24—1962: Slansky trial in Prague.
25—1940: *Patria* with immigrants to Palestine blown up in Haifa.
26—1874: Edmond Fleg, French poet and playwright, born.
27—1874: Chaim Weizmann born; 1881: Vera Weizmann born.
28—1873: Louis Ginzberg, a scholar and *dayan* in the U.S., born.
29—1947: United Nations decides on partition of Palestine.
30—1631: Rabbi Samuel Eliezer Edels, the "Maharsha," one of the foremost Talmud commentators, died.

December

1—1909: Deganyah Aleph founded.
2—1742: Expulsion from Little Russia.
3—1823: First Yiddish weekly *Beobachter in der Weichsel* appeared in Warsaw.
4—1655: Whitehall Conference discusses Manasseh Ben Israel's petition to Cromwell.
5—1920: Foundation of Histadrut.
6—1882: Zikhron Ya'akov founded.
7—1941: Simon Dubnow, historian and idealogist, killed.
8—1941: Death camps at Chelmno begin operating.
9—1917: Jerusalem captured by the British: Allenby enters Jerusalem.
10—1966: Nobel Prize for literature presented to Samuel Joseph Agnon and Nelly Sachs.
11—321: First mention of Jews in Germany.
12—1806: Isaac Leeser, founder of the first Hebrew high school and rabbinical school in the U.S., born.
13—1797: Heinrich Heine, German poet and essayist, born.
14—1760: Board of Deputies of British Jews founded.
15—1859: Ludwik Lazar Zamenhof, Polish physician and early member of Hovevei Zion, born.
16—1922: Eliezer Ben-Yehuda, the father of modern Hebrew, died.
17—1942: Declaration of United Nations that the extermination of the Jewish people would be punished.
18—1744: Expulsion of the Jews of Bohemia.
19—1781: Poll tax abolished in Austria.
20—1835: Mendele Mocher Seforim, the founder of modern Hebrew literature, born.
21—1804: Benjamin Disraeli born.
22—1867: Emancipation in Hungary.
23—1850: Oscar Solomon Straus born.
24—1970: Leningrad trial against Jews who wished to go to Israel.
25—1886: Franz Rosenzweig, German Jewish theologian, born.
26—1495: Jews expelled from Florence.
27—1856: Naphtali Herz Imber, author of *Ha-Tikvah,* born.
28—1862: Morris Rosenfeld, pioneer of Yiddish poetry in the United States, born.
29—1901: Jewish National Fund established.
30—1942: Enrico Glicenstein, Polish sculptor and painter, died.
31—1888: Rabbi Samson Raphael Hirsch died.

Jewish Nobel Prize Winners

Peace

1911 Tobias Michael Carel Asser (Holland)
1911 Alfred H. Fried (Austria)
1968 Rene Cassin (France)
1973 Henry Kissinger (U.S.A.)
1978 Menachem Begin (Israel)
1986 Elie Wiesel (U.S.A.)

Physics

1907 Albert A. Michelson (U.S.A.)
1908 Gabriel Lippmann (France)
1921 Albert Einstein (Germany)
1922 Niels Bohr (Denmark)
1925 Gustav Hertz (Germany)
1925 James Franck (Germany)
1938 Enrico Fermi (U.S.A.)
1943 Otto Stern (U.S.A.)
1944 Isidor I. Rabi (U.S.A.)
1952 Felix Bloch (U.S.A.)
1954 Max Born (U.K.-Germany)
1958 Igor Y. Tamm (U.S.S.R.)
1959 Emilio Segre (Italy)
1960 Donald Glaser (U.S.A.)
1961 Robert Hofstadter (U.S.A.)
1962 Lev Davidovich Landau (U.S.S.R.)
1965 Richard Phillips Feynman (U.S.A.)
1965 Julian Seymour Schwinger (U.S.A.)
1967 Hans Albrecht Bethe (U.S.A.)
1969 Murray Gell-Mann (U.S.A.)
1971 Dennis Gabor (U.K.)
1973 Brian D. Josephson (U.K.)
1975 Benjamin R. Mottelson (Denmark)
1976 Burton Richter (U.S.A.)
1978 Pyotr Kapitsa (U.S.S.R.)
1978 Arno Penzias (U.S.A.)
1979 Sheldon Glashow (U.S.A.)
1979 Steven Weinberg (U.S.A.)

Literature

1910 Paul J. L. Heyse (Germany)
1927 Henri Bergson (France)
1958 Boris Pasternak (U.S.S.R.)
1966 Shmuel Yosef Agnon (Israel)
1966 Nelly Sachs (Sweden)
1976 Saul Bellow (U.S.A.)
1978 Isaac Bashevis Singer (U.S.A.)
1981 Elias Canetti (Bulgaria)

Economics

1970 Paul A. Samuelson (U.S.A.)
1971 Simon Kuznets (U.S.A.)
1972 Kenneth J. Arrow (U.S.A.)
1975 Leonid Vitalyevich Kantorovich (U.S.S.R.)
1976 Milton Friedman (U.S.A.)
1978 Herbert A. Simon (U.S.A.)
1980 Lawrence Klein (U.S.A.)
1985 Franco Modigliani (Italy-U.S.A.)

Chemistry

1905 Adolph von Baeyer (Germany)
1906 Henri Moissan (France)
1910 Otto Wallach (Germany)
1915 Richard Willstatter (Germany)
1918 Fritz Haber (Germany)
1943 George de Hevesy (Hungary/Denmark)
1961 Melvin Calvin (U.S.A.)
1962 Max Perutz (U.K.)
1971 Gerhard Herzberg (Canada)
1972 William H. Stein (U.S.A.)
1979 Herbert C. Brown (U.S.A.)
1980 Paul Berg (U.S.A.)
1980 Walter Gilbert (U.S.A.)
1981 Ronald Hoffman (U.S.A.)
1982 Aaron Klug (South Africa)
1985 Herbert Aaron Hauptman (U.S.A.)

Medicine and Physiology

1908 Paul Ehrlich (Germany)
1908 Elie Metchnikoff (Russia)
1914 Robert Barany (Austria)
1923 Otto Meyerhoff (Germany)
1930 Karl Landsteiner (Austria/U.S.A.)
1931 Otto Warburg (Germany)
1936 Otto Loewi (Austria/U.S.A.)
1944 Joseph Erlanger (U.S.A.)
1944 Herbert Gasser (U.S.A.)
1945 Sir Ernst Boris Chain (U.K.)
1946 Herman Joseph Muller (U.S.A.)
1950 Tadeus Reichstein (Switzerland)
1952 Selman Waksman (U.S.A.)
1953 Sir Hans Krebs (U.K.)
1953 Fritz Albert Lipmann (U.S.A.)
1958 Joshua Lederberg (U.S.A.)
1959 Arthur Kornberg (U.S.A.)
1964 Konrad Bloch (U.S.A.)
1965 Francois Jacob (France)
1965 Andre Lwoff (France)
1967 George Wald (U.S.A.)
1968 Marshall Nirenberg (U.S.A.)
1969 Salvador Luria (U.S.A.)
1970 Julius Axelrod (U.S.A.)
1970 Sir Bernard Katz (U.K.)
1972 Gerald Edelman (U.S.A.)
1975 David Baltimore (U.S.A.)
1975 Howard Temin (U.S.A.)
1976 Baruch Blumberg (U.S.A.)
1977 Rosalyn Yalow (U.S.A.)
1978 Daniel Nathans (U.S.A.)
1980 Baruj Benacerraf (U.S.A.)
1984 Cesar Milstein (U.K.)
1985 Michael S. Brown (U.S.A.)
1985 Joseph L. Goldstein (U.S.A.)
1986 Rita Levi-Montalcini (Italy-U.S.A.)
1986 Stanley Cohen (U.S.A.)

Elie Wiesel's Acceptance Speech, as Recipient of the 1986 Nobel Peace Prize

It is with a profound sense of humility that I accept the honor you have chosen to bestow upon me. I know: your choice transcends me. This both frightens and pleases me.

It frightens me because I wonder: do I have the right to represent the multitudes who have perished? Do I have the right to accept this great honor on their behalf? I do not. That would be presumptuous. No one may speak for the dead, no one may interpret their mutilated dreams and visions.

It pleases me because I may say that this honor belongs to all the survivors and their children, and through us, to the Jewish people with whose destiny I have always identified.

I remember: it happened yesterday or eternities ago. A young Jewish boy discovered the kingdom of night. I remember his bewilderment, I remember his anguish. It all happened so fast. The ghetto. The deportation. The sealed cattle car. The fiery altar upon which the history of our people and the future of mankind were meant to be sacrificed.

'Can This Be True?'

I remember: he asked his father: "Can this be true? This is the 20th century, not the Middle Ages. Who would allow such crimes to be committed? How could the world remain silent?"

And now the boy is turning to me: "Tell me," he asks. "What have you done with my future? What have you done with your life?"

And I tell him that I have tried. That I have tried to keep memory alive, that I have tried to fight those who would forget. Because if we forget, we are guilty, we are accomplices.

And then I explained to him how naive we were, that the world did know and remain silent. And that is why I swore never to be silent whenever and wherever human beings endure suffering and humiliation. We must always take sides. Neutrality helps the oppressor, never the victim. Silence encourages the tormentor, never the tormented.

'Sometimes We Must Interfere'

Sometimes we must interfere. When human lives are endangered, when human dignity is in jeopardy, national borders and sensitivities become irrelevant. Wherever men or women are persecuted because of their race, religion or political views, that place must—at that moment—become the center of the universe.

Of course, since I am a Jew profoundly rooted in my people's memory and tradition, my first response is to Jewish fears, Jewish needs, Jewish crises. For I belong to a traumatized generation, one that experienced the abandonment and solitude of our people. It would be unnatural for me not to make Jewish priorities my own: Israel, Soviet Jewry, Jews in Arab lands.

But there are others as important to me. Apartheid is, in my view, as abhorrent as anti-Semitism. To me, Andrei Sakharov's isolation is as much of a disgrace as Iosif Begun's imprisonment. As is the denial of Solidarity and its leader Lech Walesa's right to dissent. And Nelson Mandela's interminable imprisonment.

There is so much injustice and suffering crying out for our attention: victims of hunger, or racism and political persecution, writers and poets, prisoners in so many lands governed by the left and by the right. Human rights are being violated on every continent. More people are oppressed than free.

Palestinians and Israelis

And then, too, there are the Palestinians to whose plight I am sensitive but whose methods I deplore. Violence and terrorism are not the answer. Something must be done about their suffering, and soon. I trust Israel, for I have faith in the Jewish people. Let Israel be given a chance, let hatred and danger be removed from her horizons, and there will be peace in and around the Holy Land.

Yes, I have faith. Faith in God and even in His creation. Without it no action would be possible. And action is the only remedy to indifference: the most insidious danger of all. Isn't this the meaning of Alfred Nobel's legacy? Wasn't his fear of war a shield against war?

There is much to be done, there is much that can be done. One person—a Raoul Wallenberg, an Albert Schweitzer, one person of integrity can make a difference, a difference of life and death. As long as one dissident is in prison, our freedom will not be true. As long as one child is hungry, our lives will be filled with anguish and shame.

What all these victims need above all is to know that they are not alone; that we are not forgetting them, that when their voices are stifled we shall lend them ours, that while their freedom depends on ours, the quality of our freedom depends on theirs.

'Every Hour an Offering'

This is what I say to the young Jewish boy wondering what I have done with his years. It is in his name that I speak to you and that I express to you my deepest gratitude. No one is as capable of gratitude as one who has emerged from the kingdom of night.

We know that every moment is a moment of grace, every hour an offering; not to share them would mean to betray them. Our lives no longer belong to us alone; they belong to all those who need us desperately.

Thank you Chairman Aarvik. Thank you, members of the Nobel Committee. Thank you, people of Norway, for declaring on this singular occasion that our survival has meaning for mankind.

"That Marvellous Movement": Early Black Views of Zionism

Robert G. Weisbord
Richard Kazarian, Jr.

Even after the conclusion of the American Civil War, which brought political freedom to approximately four million bondsmen, most Blacks in the street or more commonly on the plantation had very little time to contemplate foreign affairs. Whether living in the North or the South, they were too preoccupied with the physical and emotional survival of themselves and their families in a hostile and racially prejudiced environment. Reparations in the form of forty acres and a mule for each ex-slave had been proposed but never delivered. Consequently, acquiring even the most basic necessities of life was a formidable, all-consuming task.

Yet, a few Black intellectuals and leaders were well aware of developments overseas in Africa, Europe and the Middle East, and some commented on obscure movements with what seemed to be only tenuous connections with the pressing realities of Black Americans. Zionism, which aimed at the establishment of a homeland for dispersed Jews in Palestine, their ancient homeland from which most had been expelled almost two millennia before, was one such movement. Jews drew the attention of some Black thinkers who had been raised on the Old Testament and saw a parallel between the enslavement and continuing travail of the "chosen people" and their own tragic history of thralldom and oppression. For some other Blacks the durable Jewish ethnic consciousness and Zionism's repatriationist answer to the questions of survival suggested paradigms for transplanted Africans in the Americas.

One nineteenth-century Black luminary, Edward Wilmot Blyden, fit into both categories. Born in St. Thomas in the Virgin Islands in 1832, Blyden enjoyed a remarkable multifaceted career. He was a true *uomo universale*, a Renaissance man. Blyden, who immigrated to West Africa in 1851, was an editor, a prodigious writer of books and pamphlets, an extraordinary linguist, a professor of classics, secretary of state of the newly established republic of Liberia, Liberian ambassador to the Court of St. James, and president of Liberia College. In addition, he was a Pan-Negro patriot and an apostle of diasporan Black repatriation to Africa. In the informed opinion of his biographer, Hollis Lynch, he was "easily the most learned and articulate champion of Africa and the Negro race in his own time."

Blyden's curiosity about and attraction to Jews was at least partly traceable to his boyhood in Danish St. Thomas, where a majority of the white population was Jewish at the time. It was there that he became familiar with Jewish festivals and traditions. It was also there that he was first exposed to the Hebrew tongue. One of the young Blyden's most ardent desires was to master Hebrew so that he could read the Old Testament and the Talmud in that ancient language.

In 1866 Blyden spent three months visiting Lebanon, Syria and Palestine. Peripatetic by nature, he had developed a yearning to travel to "the original home of the Jews—to see Jerusalem and Mt. Zion, the joy of the whole earth." He was deeply moved by his initial glimpse of Jerusalem and was particularly touched by the Western Wall, the holiest Jewish site in that holy city.

The sizeable Jewish population which then resided in Jerusalem and had done so for centuries was clearly a religious community bereft of political aspirations. At that period in history, political Zionism was only in embryonic form and was fated to be stillborn. In 1862, four years before Blyden's journey, Rabbi Zvi Hirsch Kalischer, who lived under Prussian rule, had published a book entitled *Derishat Zion* ("Seeking Zion"). A classic in Zionist literature, that book meticulously outlined a program that would facilitate the purchase of villages, fields and vineyards in the land of the Bible. Kalischer also envisioned the organization of self-defense units to protect colonists from hostile Bedouins and the creation of an agricultural school to teach inexperienced Jewish youth the skills of farming.

That same year Moses Hess, another pioneer Zionist, expounded his theory of Jewish nationalism in *Rome and Jerusalem*, which was also destined to become a fundamental document in Zionist annals. Influenced by the various nationalist movements which were sweeping across Europe and stung by the persistence of anti-semitism, Hess saw the Jewish future bound up with Palestine and became convinced that the political rebirth of the Jewish nation would be precipitated by the founding of Jewish colonies there. But the cries of the proto-Zionists, Kalischer and Hess, fell on deaf ears. European Jews pinned their hopes either on assimilation as a panacea or on an age-old messianic dream of divine redemption. As a general rule, Jews who travelled to Palestine in the nineteenth century went there to die, to be interred in holy soil, rather than to live and build a Jewish nation.

In point of fact, Blyden in the 1860s and 1870s was much more of a Zionist than most Jews. He advocated Jewish settlement in Palestine, a phenomenon which, in his judgment, would not have an adverse effect on the Arabs. Blyden reproved the sons of Abraham for remaining in the Diaspora and for not migrating to their ancient homeland, which the Ottoman Turks were misgoverning. His words advising Jews to repatriate themselves, which were penned in 1873, would warm the hearts of today's frustrated Jewish Agency officials as they labor, frequently in vain, to promote immigration to Israel.

By the final decades of the nineteenth century, the recrudescence of antisemitism, both in Russia following the assassination of Czar Alexander II in 1881, and in western Europe (most notably in France and Germany), had led to a rebirth of political Zionism. Zionist associations had planted colonies in Palestine, and Theodor Herzl, a Vienna-based journalist, had emerged as the prime mover, and central personality of the rejuvenated movement. In 1896 Herzl published his landmark volume, *The Jewish State*, which underlined the hopelessness of assimilation as a solution to the ubiquitous Jewish problem and offered nationhood as a viable alternative. Instead of being a vulnerable minority devoid of power and subject to the ravages of antisemitism, Jews would have a country of their own where they would constitute a power-wielding majority of the population.

The following year, 1897, 196 delegates from a score of nations and representing world Jewry gathered in Basle, Switzerland, to analyze the plight of the Jews and to forge a plan to guide Jewish destiny. One can argue that that first world Zionist Congress established the *national* character of the Jews. Without any doubt, it created a permanent international Zionist organization, the instrument which was to breathe life into a Jewish nation in Palestine in just half a century.

Blyden's response to Herzlian Zionism was set forth in *The Jewish Question*, published in 1898, the year after the Basle conclave. That twenty-four page booklet, avidly philo-Semitic and philo-Zionist, was dedicated to Louis Solomon, a Jewish acquaintance of Blyden's from his residence in West Africa. Blyden was familiar with Herzl's *The Jewish State* and predicated that it propounded ideas which "have given such an impetus to the real work of the Jews as will tell with enormous effect upon their future history." Blyden also commented on the powerful influence of the "tidal wave from Vienna—that inspiration almost Mosaic in its originality and in its tendency, which drew crowds of Israelites to Basle in August 1897 . . . and again in 1898."

Blyden, the Pan-Africanist, recognized Herzl's efforts to ingather the Jews as analogous to his own activities to effect a selective return of Afro-Americans to their fatherland. No wonder then that he described Zionism as "that marvellous movement" and indicated his backing for a Jewish nation. If conditions were propitious in Palestine, the Jewish nation could be located there. Blyden was of the opinion that "There is hardly a man in the civilized world —Christian, Mohammedan, or Jew who does not recognize the claim and right of the Jew to the Holy Land." His enthusiasm for Zionism was unbridled and he declared that there were very few "who, if the conditions were favorable would not be glad to see them return in a body and take their place in the land of their fathers as a great—a leading secular power." Zionist pioneers were no less mistaken in expecting a warm welcome from the Arab inhabitants in Zion; but, it must be recalled, that Arab nationalism was in its infancy at the turn of the century.

If conditions were not favorable in Palestine, the Jewish nation could be built somewhere else. In not limiting Zionism's field of operations exclusively to Palestine, Blyden was echoing the sentiments of "territorialists" such as the Russian-born Leo Pinsker. Pinsker, in 1882, had written a pamphlet called *Auto-Emancipation* in which he argued that "The goal of our present endeavors must not be the 'Holy Land' but a land of our own. We need nothing but a large piece of land for our poor brothers; a piece of land which shall remain our property from which no foreign master can expel us."

Geography was not crucial in Blyden's thoughts about Zionism. He was convinced that the Jewish destiny was not just to establish "a political power in one corner of the earth" but to achieve something far nobler. To the Jews had been "entrusted the spiritual hegemony of mankind." He felt that Jews, along with people of African descent, were specially qualified to be spiritual leaders of a materialistic world by virtue of their heritage of suffering and sorrow. With this in mind he invited Jews to go to Africa. "Africa appeals to the Jew . . . to come with his scientific and other culture, gathered by his exile in many lands, and with his special spiritual endowments," he wrote in 1898.

In a fascinating episode this quixotic notion was almost fulfilled in 1903 when the British government offered the Zionist Congress territory in Kenya for developing a Jewish colony. The offer came at a time of deteriorating conditions in Russia, where the largest masses of downtrodden Jews dwelled. Acquisition of a haven was imperative. If Palestine were unavailable, some other place might have to do, at least temporarily. In addition to this humanitarian consideration, Herzl also understood the diplomatic advantage of not rejecting the British offer out of hand. With an international superpower such as Britain treating the Zionists movement as the spokesman for world Jewry, Herzl's concept of Jewish nationhood stood closer than ever to realization. A Britain committed to aiding the Zionists would have to provide a substitute for East Africa if the proffered territory there proved to be unsuitable and a Zionist-sponsored commission dispatched to Kenya found it seriously deficient. Palestinocentric Jews had from the start regarded even temporary conditional acceptance of East Africa as tantamount to treason and the acrimonious dispute over East Africa which ensued made necessary a tormenting reappraisal of the Zionist movement. By 1905 the offer was finally declined, and the Zionists were resolutely determined to found a Jewish state in Palestine and only in Palestine.

Most prominent Black contemporaries of Blyden's did not share his Pan-Negro fervor or his African orientation. One who emphatically rejected back-to-Africanism in favor of a stay-at-home philosophy was Booker T. Washington. For at least twenty years, from 1895 when he delivered his famous Atlanta Exposition address until his death, Booker Taliaferro Washington was the best-known Black in white America. So great was the celebrity of Booker T. that, although he had been born a slave in western Virginia in 1856, he was asked to dine with Theodore Roosevelt in the White House (only once, however, because of the racist howls of protest) and invited to take tea with the venerable Queen Victoria. His path to fame was a torturous one. As a youngster he suffered numerous privations and often lacked the most basic necessities of life. He had to toil in saltworks but was determined to teach himself the alpha-half-truth. Virtually no *American* Jews were sailing to Palestine. In 1910 most Jewish inhabitants of the United States had just arrived from Eastern Europe during the previous two or three decades. On the other hand, the same despair born of resurgent antisemitism and chronic poverty, which had prompted in excess of a million and a half Jews to forsake the Czar's realms for western Europe and the New World, furnished the impetus for the Second Aliyah. The Second Aliyah, stimulated in part by the unsuccessful Russian revolution in 1905 and the concurrent pogroms, was well underway when Booker T. casually dismissed Zionism as a remedy for Jewish ills. It brought to Palestine many of those socialist Zionist idealists who would begin to transform the Zionist vision into reality. Those adventurous *chalutzim* (pioneers) were destined to become Israel's establishment, the power elite in the future Jewish state, and the fruits of their labor—Zionist ideology (e.g., the *kibbutzim,* the *moshavim* and the *Histadrut* [labor federation])—are still vital elements in Israel today.

Booker T. Washington died in 1915 during the carnage of World War I. It was in the midst of that global cataclysm that political Zionism won an important diplomatic victory. Britain was eager to mobilize Jewish opinion in support of the Allied cause. With the new Bolshevik regime extricating itself from the sanguinary morass of the war, Jewish influence in Russia could be beneficial, or so Britain's Prime Minister David Lloyd George thought. If properly cultivated, American Zionist sentiment could also prove useful in stimulating the war effort. Therefore, in November 1917 Foreign Minister Arthur James Balfour, who not coincidentally also had a lifelong interest in Jews and a profound admiration for their culture, issued his famous declaration. In a letter to Lord Rothschild, a member of the fabulously wealthy and prestigious international banking family and a leader of British Jewry, Balfour asserted:

> His Majesty's government views with favour the establishment in Palestine of a national home for the Jewish people, and will use their best endeavours to facilitate the achievement of this object, it being clearly understood that nothing shall be done which may prejudice the civil and religious rights of existing non-Jewish communities in Palestine, or the rights and political status enjoyed by Jews in any other country.

At that point in history, few people realized that Balfour's promise of a national home for the Jews conflicted both with the 1915 McMahon-Hussein agreement, which the British arranged to incite Arab opposition to the Ottoman empire, and with the Sykes-Picot agreement allocating Ottoman territory to France, Russia and Britain. For the Zionists the Balfour Declaration, which was subsequently incorporated in the League of Nations mandate for Palestine, was a solemn pledge to the Jewish people. For the Arabs it was treacherous, duplicitous and illegal. Thus, the seeds of future Middle Eastern conflict were sown during the Great War. Racial strife in the United States dramatically intensified during and right after the war. While Black troops were in Europe fighting to make the world safe for democracy, lynchings continued unabated in the United States; and race riots, which were actually pogroms against Black communities, occurred with unprecedented fury and frequency.

In those racially troubled times, the Black titan W.E.B. Du Bois emerged as a champion of Zionism as well as a tireless fighter for racial justice in this country. Even before the advent of World War I, Du Bois was a towering figure whose intellect and dedication to the cause of racial equality inspired hope in oppressed Black America and fear and awe in white America. Born in Great Barrington, Massachusetts in 1868, Du Bois had a legendary career as both scholar and activist that spanned almost a century of turbulent racial history. Educated at Fisk University and the University of Berlin, Du Bois later earned a Ph.D. at Harvard University. Until his death in Ghana in 1963, his scholarly output was enormous. It included historical treatises, incisive sociological studies and essays on all the important issues of his day. But Du Bois' unflagging efforts as a crusader for first-class citizenship for the Black American at least equalled and probably surpassed in importance his academic accomplishments. In pursuit of that lofty and elusive goal, he relentlessly assailed the ears of his countrymen decade after decade. He worked to end lynchings and the humiliation of Jim Crowism. Even before the dawn of the twentieth century, his militant equalitarian philosophy was offered to Black Americans as a viable alternative to Booker T. Washington's racial accommodationism, which he found demeaning and subversive of Black manhood. Du Bois deserves much of the credit for founding the National Association for the Advancement of Colored People (NAACP) in 1910, and he was a driving force behind the Pan-African movement, which concerned itself with the plight of subjugated people of African descent on the African continent and in the far-flung African dispersion.

W.E.B. DuBois

With the public disclosure of the Balfour Declaration, Du Bois recognized in the exertions of the Zionists a program and a policy that could possibly hasten the liberation of Africa. Africa's future, specifically the destiny of former German-controlled Africa, was to be determined

Booker T. Washington

bet and later managed, despite much hardship, to obtain an education at Hampton Institute. In 1881, with financial help from the Alabama state legislature, he founded Tuskegee Institute, which he headed for three and a half decades.

At a time of deteriorating conditions for Blacks, when racism was reaching its zenith, Washington, at least in public, exemplified the philosophy of accommodationism, of avoiding direct confrontations with the white power structure. In his 1895 Atlanta speech he appeared to accept the inevitability of racial segregation and described his aggrieved brethren as "the most patient, faithful, law abiding and unresentful people the world has ever seen." Rightly or wrongly, later generations of Black Americans came to view Washington's posture as a cringing and groveling one, hardly appropriate at a time when Blacks were being disfranchised, Jim Crowed and lynched.

From childhood, Washington, like countless other Blacks weaned on Scripture, had a "special and peculiar interest in the history and progress of the Jewish race." He frequently drew parallels between the tragic histories of Jews and Blacks. Speaking to a biracial audience in Little Rock, Arkansas, in 1905, he opined that ignorance and racial hatred had never solved a single problem and cautioned his Black listeners not to become discouraged or despondent because conditions for Blacks were becoming worse. "In Russia there are one-half as many Jews as there are Negroes in this country and yet I feel sure that within a month more Jews have been persecuted and killed than the whole number of our people who have been lynched during the past forty years." However, this was no excuse for lynchings, he added. Even if Booker T.'s statistics about the victims of pogroms in czarist Russia were accurate, the comparison must have provided cold comfort to Afro-Americans. For in the "land of the free and the home of the brave," 60 Blacks were lynched in the year 1905 alone and from 1889 through 1905 lynch mobs claimed no fewer than 1,707 Black victims.

Washington believed that salvation for Black Americans would be achieved through thrift and hard work. Racial solidarity would also contribute to Black progress, and Jews, Booker T. argued, could serve as a model in this respect. "There is, perhaps, no race that has suffered so much, not so much in America as in some of the countries in Europe. But these people have clung together. They have had a certain amount of unity, pride and love of race," he commented in 1899. He then prophesied, correctly as future events were to demonstrate, that Jews would become more and more influential in the United States, "a country where they were once despised and looked upon with scorn and derision." Booker T. admonished Blacks to follow the Jewish race in developing faith in themselves. Unless the Black learned to imitate Jews in this respect, he wrote, he could not expect to achieve a high degree of success.

More than a decade later, after observing the Jewish condition in diverse locales—in London's East End, in Denmark, Germany and Austria, in the Russian Pale of Settlement and in the ghettos of Poland—Washington reiterated the same theme. In a 1901 manuscript for an article, he wrote that, prejudice and persecution notwithstanding, the Jew was advancing largely by dint of education. Jews had struggled to the point where they occupied positions of power and enjoyed preeminence in civilization. Washington concluded that the "Negro has much to learn from the Jew."

Undoubtedly, Washington knew about modern political Zionism, but he apparently did not take it very seriously. Perhaps he hoped that the Jewish community, the ethnic model to be emulated, would not take it very seriously. When he was asked in 1910 if there was any back-to-Africa movement among Afro-Americans comparable to the Zionist movement, Booker T. chuckled and replied: "I think it is with the African pretty much as it is with the Jews, there is a good deal of talk about it, but nothing is done, there is certainly no sign of any exodus to Liberia." Washington was acutely aware of the repatriationist enterprises of Bishop Henry McNeal Turner, the leading apostle of back-to-Africanism in the 1890s and early 1900s, but he could "see no way out of the Negro's present condition in the South by returning to Africa." Washington, who never once visited the African homeland of his forefathers although he found ample time for several trips to Europe, preferred a future for Blacks in the United States where a satisfactory racial adjustment would have to be made. Given his staunch opposition to emigration as a solution to the "Negro problem," his disinterest in Zionism was predictable.

As far as Zionism was concerned, Washington's flippant remark about Jews paying only lip service to it was a after the armistice of November 1918. Du Bois dreamt of an independent free central African state which minimally would be carved out of German East Africa and the Belgian Congo. If the triumphant Entente powers took into account the wishes of Blacks in Africa and those elsewhere, the victors would be given an "effective weapon" militating against restoration of African colonies to the vanquished Germans. Alas, Du Bois and his Pan-African cohorts lacked the diplomatic leverage to persuade the Versailles peacemakers to sanction a Black African counterpart to the Balfour Declaration.

Du Bois' ideas about the parallel between modern political Zionism and Pan-Africanism were tersely summarized in the *Crisis*, the organ of the NAACP, which he edited. Appearing as an editorial in February 1919, when Du Bois himself was in France to organize a crucial Pan-African conference, it stated:

> The African movement means to use what the Zionist movement must mean to the Jews, the centralization of race effort and the recognition of a racial fount. To help bear the burden of Africa does not mean any lessening of efforts in our problems at home. Rather it means increased interest. For any ebullition of action and feeling that results in an amelioration of the lot of Africa tends to ameliorate the conditions of colored peoples throughout the world. And no man liveth unto himself.

Du Bois' philo-Zionism should not be seen simply as a political strategy. Nor was it an isolated, haphazard, fleeting thought. It was in keeping with his general sympathy for the liberation struggles of persecuted peoples around the globe.

As a student in Europe in 1890s, Du Bois encountered the virulent bacillus of antisemitism in Germany and Poland and came to develop a genuine appreciation of Zionism as a solution to the Jewish problem. That appreciation ripened with the passing years and fully flowered following the Holocaust. In the intervening decades Du Bois closely monitored developments in Palestine under the British mandate.

Even in the pages of *The Brownie's Book*, a monthly magazine for Afro-American children which Du Bois started in 1919-20, there were several selections dealing with the progress of Zionism. In the very first issue of that periodical, he directed the attention of young Black readers to the new Jewish state which was planned in the ancient Holy Land, "'round about Jerusalem." Eight months later he informed his juvenile readership that a "great Zionist congress of the Jews is meeting in London." Du Bois was particularly struck by proposals to "tax the Jews all over the world for the support of the new Jewish government in Palestine." In January 1921 he observed that blueprints for a Hebrew University on the biblical Mount of Olives in Jerusalem had been completed and remarked on urban planning in the "new Palestine."

For Du Bois, imperial Britain, which had plundered Africa after the unjustified partition of the "dark continent," was the bete noire, or bete blanche, to be more precise. England retained many colonies by fostering religious and national jealousies and then presiding as a benevolent arbitrator, Du Bois wrote in his "As the Crow Flies" column published in the *Crisis*. He was speculating about the reason for what he described as the "murder of Jews by Arabs in Palestine" in 1929. Tensions between Arab and Jew had smoldered for some time because of disagreement over access to the Western Wall in Jerusalem. In August defenseless Jews were massacred in Hebron and Safed by "ruthless and bloodthirsty evil-doers," as the malefactors were characterized by the British high commissioner. That violence was but a foretaste of the bloodletting to come.

Zionism's trials and tribulations had also caught the eye of another important Black leader, a bitter rival of Du Bois', the redoubtable Marcus Garvey. In 1916, the year before the Balfour Declaration was issued, Garvey arrived in the United States. Although the Jamaican-born Garvey had been inspired by Booker T. Washington's autobiography, *Up From Slavery*, his own solution to the various problems that beset Black folk was very different from that of the sage of Tuskegee. Garvey arrived, armed with a Pan-Negroist Black nationalist ideology that was to captivate millions of Blacks on the mother continent as well as in the African diaspora. In the course of a few years he was to build what the Black historian John Hope Franklin was to characterize as the "first and only really mass movement among Negroes in the United States."

The era was a favorable one for his Black nationalist crusade. It coincided with an influx of West Indians, who comprised the nucleus of Garvey's Universal Negro Improvement Association (UNIA). Moreover, Afro-Americans who had migrated by the hundreds of thousands from the rural South to the urban North expecting a dramatic improvement in their fortunes, if not a racial utopia, were sadly disillusioned. They quickly discovered that discrimination in employment and housing knew no regional boundaries, and racial violence was commonplace in the frigid North.

Garvey's philosophy of race pride could raise their hopes, lift their spirits and reinvigorate their sagging self-esteem. Long before the slogan "black is beautiful" became *de rigeur*, Garvey preached the concept that Americans of African descent need not feel ashamed, not of their pigmentation nor of their heritage.

Day in and day out Garvey advocated the cause of self-determination for Africans, both those at home in Africa and those abroad. Africa was then controlled almost entirely by European colonialists. Garvey argued that it had to be transformed into a "Negro Empire where every Black man, whether he was born in Africa or in the Western world, will have the opportunity to develop on his own lines under the protection of the most favorable democratic institutions."

In Garvey's view, which was strikingly similar to those of the political Zionists regarding Jews in the *galut* (dispersion), Blacks living as minorities in the New World faced bleak futures. Outside the confines of the land of their forefathers, "ruin and disaster" awaited Africans. Therefore, Garvey urged that Africa's dispersed and mistreated sons and daughters be restored to her. The stocky, ebony-skinned Jamaican asserted that Africa was the "legitimate, moral and righteous home of all Negroes," but he did not favor an immediate, wholesale repatriation. Even if the wherewithal were available, it would take half a century to largely depopulate the United States. Every Black was not wanted anyway. Lazy ones and those lacking self-reliance,

Marcus Garvey

for example, were not desired. Those whom Garvey wished to see immigrate to Africa were the adventurous and industrious Blacks, such as the members of his UNIA whose goal was an independent nationality. They numbered six million, Garvey claimed.

Even the stay-at-homes, those Blacks who remained outside of Africa, would benefit from the redemption of Africa. Garvey's widow, Amy Jacques Garvey, explained it this way: "Garvey saw Africa as a *nation* to which the African peoples of the world could look for help and support, moral and physical, when ill-treated or abused for being Black." Garveyite rhetoric here virtually duplicates that of the Zionists who argue to this day that a strong Jewish state enhances the security of Jews still in exile.

As a back-to-Africanist, Garvey failed. In 1924 he was conspicuously unsuccessful in his bid to establish settlements in Liberia. The next year the would-be Black Moses began to serve a prison term meted out to him following his conviction for using the U.S. mails to defraud investors in one of his Black nationalist commercial enterprises, the Black Star Steamship Line. His remaining days in this country were to be spent in a federal penitentiary in Georgia. After his sentence was commuted in 1927, he was deported to his native Jamaica as an undesirable alien, never to set foot in the United States again.

Throughout his checkered career Garvey was fond of pointing out the analogies between his brand of Black nationalism and other nationalisms, specifically those of the Irish, the East Indians, the Egyptians and the Jews. For example, in July 1920 Garvey told a UNIA meeting that Blacks in the aftermath of World War I were a new people: "A new spirit, a new courage, has come to us simultaneously as it came to other peoples of the world. It came to us at the same time it came to the Jew. When the Jew said 'We shall have Palestine!' The same sentiment came to us when we said 'We shall have Africa!' "

William H. Ferris, a leading Garveyite who was both an educator and a journalist, repeated this analogy before the same gathering:

> Our position in civilization for the last three hundred years has been the same position which the Jews have occupied during the past 2,500 years. The Jews have been scattered all over the world and been suppressed by one race and then another. But the Jews have now realized that it is necessary for them to build up an empire and a republic in their native land of Palestine. In this stage of the world's history it is necessary for the Negro to build up some sort of republic and empire in Liberia so that there will be some land which he can call his own.

Although Garvey and many of his disciples felt an affinity for Zionism, he sometimes displayed his pique over the shabby treatment accorded Black nationalism compared with other nationalist movements. Speaking in London in 1928, he lamented the fact that when the Versailles peacemakers distributed the spoils of war: "You gave to the Jew, Palestine; you gave to the Egyptians, a large modicum of self-government; you gave to the Irish Home Rule Government and Dominion status; you gave the Poles a new Government of their own." When he inquired rhetorically what he had been given to the Negro, an anonymous voice rang out from the throng gathered at London's Royal Albert Hall: "Nothing." It is clear though that Garvey's animosity was not directed at either the Zionist and the Egyptian nationalists or the Polish patriots and the Irish home rulers but at Britain and the other European powers which denied Africans the right to their continent.

Garveyite philo-Zionism was sometimes reciprocated. Louis Michael, a Jew from Los Angeles, sent the UNIA a telegram in August 1920 which read as follows: "As a Jew, a Zionist and a Socialist I join heartily and unflinchingly in your historical movement for the reclamation of Africa. There is no justice and no peace in the world until the Jew and the Negro both control side by side Palestine and Africa."

Garvey and Garveyism stirred the curiosity of much of the Yiddish press in the United States; and they received accolades from pro-Zionist Yiddish newspapers (such as the *Morgen Journal* and the *Tageblatt*), which saw the UNIA as a kindred nationalist undertaking. Those publications sometimes applied Zionist nomenclature to Garvey's movement. To cite just one illustration, his anthem, "Ethiopia—The Land of Our Fathers," which had been composed by Arnold Ford, a West Indian-born Black rabbi and Garvey apostle, was dubbed "The Negro *Hatikvah*."

Despite his support for Zionism, an example which he urged his followers to emulate, Garvey harbored ambivalent feelings about Jews. He believed that it was the Jews' obsession with money that was the root of their difficulties in Germany and later in Palestine. He subscribed to more than one unflattering stereotype of Jews and had been guilty of antisemitic utterances at his trial over which a

Jewish jurist, Judge Julian Mack, had presided. But to label him as an antisemite is to be guilty of gross over-simplification.

Initially, at least, Garvey seems not to have recognized the dangers posed by Adolf Hitler's accession to power. In this respect the Jamaican was not unique. Garvey admired the Fuhrer as a German patriot and a fervent nationalist, but he realized Hitler had outrageously mistreated the Jews and was antagonistic toward Blacks. In 1935 Garvey prophesied that it was only a matter of time before the Jews destroyed Nazi Germany as they had allegedly destroyed Russia. "Jewish finance is a powerful world factor," Garvey observed and added, "It can destroy men, organizations and nations." Yet, in the pages of *The Blackman*, his monthly journal published for a short while in Jamaica and then, beginning in the spring of 1935, in London, Garvey frequently expressed his sympathy for Jews as a despised and oppressed minority. As he had done years before in his American heyday, he lauded their efforts to rebuild their Zion in Palestine. Praise was due the Jews because they recognized the "only safe thing to do is to go after and establish racial autonomy." So wrote the Black Moses in 1936.

By 1936 Palestine was in turmoil. There was rioting and sporadic fighting, which claimed both Arab and Jewish lives. Hitlerite persecution had escalated *aliyah* from Germany and Austria, and certain Palestinian Arab leaders voiced strenuous objections. A general strike, which aimed at terminating the immigration of Jews and halting the further purchase of land by them, was called. It too was marked by bloodshed.

Faced with a rapidly worsening state of affairs, the British appointed a commission of inquiry, one of several which sought to no avail to reconcile conflicting Jewish and Arab aspirations in the Holy Land. In their report made public in July 1937, the so-called Peel Commission advocated that the country be partitioned into a British mandatory zone, an Arab state and a Jewish state. Arab opinion overwhelmingly opposed partition; but the Zionists were divided, some believing that half a loaf was better than none.

Writing from Britain, in the twilight of his career, Garvey admonished the Jews not to throw away their opportunity to establish a state of their own. What was important was not the size of a Jewish state but the chance to have an independent government that could enjoy diplomatic and economic relations with other nations. Garvey speculated that the Black man's case for a country might be strengthened by the success of the Jewish cause. In Garvey's judgment the Negro had even "more right to a free state of his own in Africa than the Jew in Palestine;" and Black unwillingness to line up behind the UNIA the way Jews supported Zionism, explained why the world did not take the Black seriously.

Territorial compromise, as recommended by the Peel Commission, did not bring peace to Palestine. Arab-Jewish frictions did not diminish in the late 1930s as ominous war clouds gathered over Europe and the plight of German Jewry was further aggravated. In May 1939, publication of the British "White Paper" dealt a cruel blow to Zionist hopes. At the very moment when the need for a refuge was most desperate, the British, in response to Arab agitation, decided to curtail Jewish immigration into Palestine. Only seventy-five thousand Jews would be admitted over a five-year period. Jewish land purchases were to be restricted as well. British policy in Palestine on the eve of World War II, which was clearly calculated to mollify the Arabs, had the tragic effect of denying sanctuary to untold numbers of Jewish refugees in flight from Nazism.

Whereas an influx of Jews into Palestine would have heightened tensions in that troubled land and added to the herculean British task of maintaining the peace, diverting a productive white population to British Guiana would have strengthened the British position there. Consequently, Prime Minister Neville Chamberlain announced in May 1939 that his government would contemplate the settlement of Jewish refugees in that South American colony. Garvey reacted with alacrity and anger. In this instance, Black rights were being subordinated to those of Jews. British Guiana was a "Negro country," Garvey exclaimed, a description with which the sizeable East Indian community would have vehemently disagreed. Jews had no claim on Guiana, and their presence there would only serve to turn Blacks and Jews into enemies. The correct goal for Jews was a Jewish nation but not in Guiana, which Garvey insisted was the property of Blacks. At that juncture Garvey was so incensed by the Guiana plan and so irritated by what he perceived as British concern with Jews that he commented that an injustice had been done the Arab in Palestine. Ostensibly, Garvey's endorsement of Zionism was predicated on the notion that Zionism's chief value was as a model for victimized diaspora Blacks to copy. When it appeared to preempt Black rights, it earned his animosity. In June 1940 Garvey died in London in relative obscurity. As for Guiana, it never materialized as a refuge for Jews. Indeed precious few havens were available at that critical juncture in the history of the Jews. After Hitler's army invaded Poland on September 1, 1939, it grew increasingly difficult for Jews to escape. The lives of millions, especially those dwelling in eastern Europe, were imperilled by the Fuhrer's mad racial schemes.

Early in 1941 W.E.B. Du Bois wrote that American Jews were proposing to raise millions of dollars for Palestine, "the only refuge that the harassed Jewry of Europe had today." Although Jews didn't really believe in segregation, they were going to make segregation in Palestine both possible and profitable and simultaneously work for an unsegregated humanity. In the process Zionism was providing Blacks who believed "someone else is going to do our fighting for us" with a constructive lesson in self-help. It is regrettable that during the war the Zionists were incapable of opening the gates of Palestine to those few harassed European Jews who managed to slip through the Nazi grip.

When the war ended in 1945, a stunned world learned the grisly truth about the Holocaust which dramatized, as no event in modern history has, the necessity of a Jewish homeland. Hitler had unwittingly convinced skeptics of the logic of Zionism. The converts included most diaspora Jews who, until then, had been lukewarm at best and downright hostile at worst towards the Zionist movement.

World War II had also dealt a serious blow to the British empire. After 1945 Britain was more favorably disposed to relinquish parts of the empire, particularly when they were costly and troublesome, owing to local agitation for independence. Palestine was a case in point. Arab-Jewish strife had not vanished miraculously. In fact, as the Jewish claim for unlimited immigration to Palestine by Holocaust survivors grew more raucous, Arabs felt still more threatened.

By 1947 Britain, caught between the conflicting claims of Arab and Jew, was not just willing to depart from Palestine. It was eager to leave and consequently presented its dilemma to the young United Nations. The plan eventually adopted by the United Nations called for the partition of Palestine into an independent sovereign Jewish state and an independent sovereign Arab state. There was to be a third entity: an international zone under United Nations trust which would encompass Jerusalem and its suburbs, including Bethlehem. Despite vociferous Arab objections to the plan, which they deemed unfair and unworkable, the General Assembly voted for it as a means of reconciling the seemingly irreconcilable national aspirations of the two peoples. Support from two-thirds of the members voting was necessary for approval. Only frantic eleventh-hour lobbying by Zionist sympathizers made possible the thirty-three for, thirteen against, ten abstention vote.

One Afro-American who was lobbied intensively and heavy-handedly by advocates of partition was Walter White, the very fair-skinned executive director of the NAACP. Zionists hoped that White could persuade two Black nations, Haiti and Liberia, to reverse their previously announced anti-partition stance. In his autobiography White recounted his doubts about both the "wisdom and practicability" of dividing the territory in dispute. But no other feasible solution had been advanced. As an unflagging believer in racial integration, White "did not like the self-segregation of Zionism, nor . . . approve of the attitude of many Jews who had made it a sacred cult." White took umbrage at some of the Zionist pressure which he found imperious and racially condescending. Nevertheless, his reluctance notwithstanding, he supported partition "because Palestine seemed the only haven anywhere in the world for nearly one million Jews of Europe." In the end, Liberia, Haiti and the Philippines, whom White had also attempted to influence, voted for the United Nations resolution. As matters turned out, their votes were crucial to the creation of Israel. After a gestation period of approximately half a century, the Jewish homeland of which Herzl had written and dreamt would become a reality. The Rubicon had been crossed, if not the Jordan.

In the months following the fateful November 1947 United Nations vote to partition Palestine, there was a resurgence of battling between Jews and Palestinian Arabs. Jews in the *Yishuv* (the Jewish community in prestate Palestine) were jubilant to learn that after two thousand years a Jewish state would reemerge in at least a portion of their ancient homeland. By contrast, Arabs were livid. They constituted a sizeable majority—two-thirds, in fact, of Palestine's entire population—and they believed that Zionist intrigue had caused the world body to forsake them. Arabs vented their spleen by attacking Jews, who then retaliated in kind. Intercommunal fighting, i.e., civil war, threatened to violently tear the country asunder. It was the very state of affairs the United Nations had sought to avoid.

Although outnumbered, the Jews were better organized and their community services operated more efficiently than those of the Arabs, many of whose leaders fled to safer Arab locales. The Jewish armies proved superior as well. Punctuating the bitter fighting were atrocities committed by both sides. Word of the notorious Deir Yassin massacre of Arabs near Jerusalem in April 1948 spread quickly and led to panic among the already anxious and often leaderless Arabs. It was this panic that touched off the exodus of terrified Palestinians and, in large measure, created the still unresolved Arab refugee problem. When the war finally ended at the beginning of 1949, approximately three-quarters of a million Palestinians found themselves in the Arab countries surrounding the triumphant "Zionist entity."

When the British withdrew and, at long last, extricated themselves from the Palestine morass, military forces of five Arab nations (Iraq, Jordan, Lebanon, Egypt and Syria) invaded the fledgling Jewish state, which David Ben-Gurion had proclaimed on May 14, 1948. What had theretofore been a civil war was broadened into an international conflict. Given their vast manpower, the Arabs prophesied a quick victory; but, as a result of poor coordination among the Arab commanders and low morale among their troops, the anticipated triumph eluded them.

It was in the midst of the sanguinary first Arab-Israeli war that Israel's fate became entwined with the career of one extraordinary Black American—Ralph Johnson Bunche. When Count Folke Bernadotte, the Swedish diplomat who was serving as the United Nations mediator, was assassinated by members of the extremist Stern Gang in September 1948, Bunche, who had been secretary of the peacekeeping Palestine Commission, was appointed acting mediator. Born in Detroit in 1904, Bunche, as a youth, was outstanding both as a scholar and an athlete. He was the first Black American to earn a doctorate in political science, which he received from Harvard in 1934. He subsequently assisted the Swedish scholar Gunnar Myrdal in researching his monumental opus on the Afro-American, *An American Dilemma*. In the early 1940s Bunche had argued that antisemitism among Blacks and the irrational fear and dislike of Blacks on the part of Jews were nonsensical examples of the pot calling the kettle black. He expressed a hope that Jewish and Black leaders and organizations would strive to improve the strained relations which existed between the two minorities. "In large measure," he maintained, "their problems—their grievances and their fears are cut to a common pattern."

It was Bunche's statesmanship which facilitated the termination of the first Arab-Israeli war. Ensconced in his headquarters on the lovely Greek island of Rhodes, Bunche mediated negotiations between King Farouk's Egypt and Israel, which resulted in an armistice agreement in February 1949. Agreements between Israel and other Arab belligerents were also concluded. For his efforts in hastening the end of hostilities, in 1950 Dr. Bunche became the first Afro-American to be awarded the Nobel Peace Prize.

On at least one occasion, the fact that Bunche was a Black American colored his outlook on the clashes between Arabs and Jews. When matters were still precarious in Palestine, Bunche thought it advisable to consult Menachem Begin, then the wanted chieftain of the Irgun, an underground "terrorist" faction. After a clandestine meeting between United Nations officials and those of the

Irgun, Begin thanked Dr. Bunche for his diligence and toil in preparing a report on their dialogue. In his personal memoir, *The Revolt*, the future prime minister characterized Dr. Bunche as the warmest of the United Nations team. As Begin remembered the conclusion of their meeting, Bunche shook his hand and exclaimed emotionally, "I can understand you. I am also a member of a persecuted minority." Begin also paid tribute to Bunche as "undoubtedly a brilliant mind."

Bunche's mediating role in nurturing Israel in its fragile infancy is also recalled by Afro-Americans, who often invoke his name to justify Black involvement in the Middle East conflict. However, in 1978 one Black columnist bewailed the fact that "although there are monuments in New York to Bunche, not one stands to his memory in Israel. Not even a tree."

In view of Bunche's contribution, it is hard to believe that as late as the fall of 1948 his work as mediator in Palestine was judged insufficiently pro-Zionist by the erudite W.E.B. Du Bois. Speaking to the American Jewish Congress on November 30 of that year, Du Bois apologized in the name of fifteen million Black Americans for "the apparent apostasy of Ralph Bunche . . . to the clear ideas of freedom and fair play, which should have guided the descendant of an American slave." Count Bernadotte, who represented the nefarious combination of European aristocracy and American money to Du Bois, could not be expected to "judge Israel justly and without bias." But from Bunche, Du Bois hoped for more than consistent adherence to State Department directives which prevented him from playing "a great role for freedom." In Du Bois' estimation the State Department was guilty of compromise, vacillation and betrayal. On the other hand, he had hoped that Bunche "would have stood fast for justice, freedom and the good faith of his nation and race."

Even before the Nazis capitulated, Du Bois, as editor of *Phylon*, wrote that millions of Jews had perished in Hitler's pogroms and millions more were in peril of extermination. America's doors had been closed to Jewish immigrants, and worse still, "Great Britain has assumed the right to limit Jewish migration to Palestine and to support the nationalism of the Arabs."

From Du Bois' prolific pen came articles and columns trumpeting the cause of the Zionists in their hour of need. In the wake of the Holocaust, Du Bois wrote that there "was one refuge, a little thing, a little corner of the world where the Jews anciently had lived." A Zionist homeland there in Palestine was a *sine qua non* for displaced and homeless Jews. There was no other place for them. Persecution was the only real alternative to migration to Zion. In a 1948 piece published as "A Case for the Jews," Du Bois depicted the objective of the Zionist movement as follows: It was a question of "young and forward thinking Jews, bringing a new civilization into an old land and building up that land out of the ignorance, disease and poverty into which it had fallen, and by democratic methods to build a new and peculiarly fateful modern state."

Du Bois excoriated British Foreign Secretary Ernest Bevin for his "half hidden dislike of Jews," for reneging on the Balfour Declaration, for using British troops against the Jews, for training Arab soldiers for future use against them and for utilizing the Royal Navy to block the immigration of displaced persons into Palestine. Uprooted Jews were being allowed to rot in Europe while the United States discussed "unworkable possibilities for the partition of Palestine," wrote Du Bois, employing words that echoed the maximalist sentiments of the Vladimir Jabotinsky-Begin Revisionists who envisioned a Jewish state on both banks of the Jordan River.

Du Bois further castigated President Harry Truman for not keeping his promise to back the establishment of a Jewish state and for not allowing weapons to be dispatched to the beleaguered Jews. Because of "sordid commercial" factors, Britain betrayed the Zionists in tandem with the United States. Under intense pressure from the State Department, which was eager to safeguard Middle East oil supplies and apprehensive about potential Soviet penetration of the Arab world, Truman had vacillated. United States repudiation of its partition position and substitution of a United Nations trusteeship was seriously contemplated for a while. "If there is one act for which President Truman and his advisors can be utterly and finally condemned and refused the support of all decent thinking people, it is this reversal of stand in the matter of Palestine," wrote Du Bois in an article to be published in the Black press. Between April 30, 1948, when Du Bois mailed the article to the *Chicago Defender* and its publication on May 15, 1948, Truman reversed himself again and came out in favor of the Zionist demands. Indeed, the United States was the first nation to extend official recognition to Israel.

Du Bois had been closely associated with Jews in the creation of the NAACP, which in June 1948 expressed its gratification that Israel had come into being. At its thirty-ninth annual conference, which was held in Kansas City, Missouri, on June 26, the NAACP adopted the following resolution: "The valiant struggle of the people of Israel for independence serves as an inspiration to all persecuted people throughout the world. We hail the establishment of the new State of Israel and welcome it into the family of nations."

By no means was Du Bois the only Black militant with a reputation for challenging tyranny against great odds who was counted among the sympathizers of Zionism. At that time there were many in the Afro-American community. Take Paul Robeson, for instance. Truly versatile, Robeson was an all-American football player at Rutgers University, an attorney, an accomplished actor and a soul-stirring vocalist. Until he openly professed his affinity for the Soviet Union and for Communism, Robeson was a national hero, venerated by millions and held up by the United States government as an example of the heights to which a talented, industrious Black could rise. During the Cold War, however, Robeson was persona non grata, and he was denied a passport.

Robeson, whose father had been a slave, was, by his own admission, especially close to the Jewish people. On many occasions he took uncompromising stands against the evil of antisemitism and the persecution of the Jews. In 1933 he had sung in Britain to aid Jewish refugee children and after the war had witnessed the horrors of Dachau first hand. Robeson saw Jews as a "race without a nation," and in a March 1948 speech in Honolulu, he said that should an all-out war start in Palestine he would travel there to sing for the Jewish troops just as he had entertained the anti-

Paul Robeson, in the 1933 version of "Emperor Jones"

Franco Loyalists during the Spanish Civil War. To Robeson this intention was in keeping with his ongoing worldwide fight for the oppressed.

When the Palestine question came before the United Nations in 1947, it received some space in the Black press. But then, as now, there was no unanimity of opinion among Black Americans. For example, columnist George Schuyler called upon Blacks to follow the model of Zionism. At the same time he took Palestinian Jews to task for their "imperialistic spirit" and "Hitler-like" methods. Jews, Schuyler argued, had "no more claim on Palestine than the Alpha Kappa Alpha." It was the "Arab aborigines" tar-brushed with Negro blood who were truly entitled to the land. The Bible, which he called the "Jewish Mein Kampf," provided no justification whatsoever for Zionism. He informed his readers that procuring the Holy Land was only the immediate objective of the Zionists. Their long-range goal was to once again build a great political state and "to become one of the richest and most powerful groups in the world today." Such strong sentiments were rarely expressed by the Black press and, as far as can be determined, virtually never by Black leaders.

Schuyler, who was something of an iconoclast and later became a leading, perhaps the preeminent, Black conservative in the United States, denied the accusation made by several "Zionist fanatics" that he was antisemitic. He added that Arabs are "far more Semitic than most of the Zionists now in Palestine or abroad." Of course, the scholarly Schuyler was playing linguistic tricks. He knew full well that the term "antisemitic" referred to animosity toward Jews and that the fact that both Hebrew and Arabic are classified as "Semitic" languages was quite irrelevant.

It is significant that in March 1948 the *Pittsburgh Courier*, which had carried Schuyler's columns, published a long editorial in which it argued strongly for the legitimacy of a Jewish state. Entitled "Persecution and Doubletalk," the editorial demanded that "the lust for Arabian oil" not be allowed to interfere with the United Nations' pledge to partition Palestine. "Not only do the Jews have the legal right to a part of Palestine based on years of international commitments," the editorial stated, "they also deserve the heartfelt sympathy and support of everyone who hates cruelty and tyranny."

* * *

Middle Eastern geography, not to mention history, was drastically altered by the 1948 Arab-Israeli war or what the Israelis have dubbed the "War of Independence." Not only did a Jewish nation emerge like a phoenix from the ashes of the Holocaust, but it was one-third larger than the political entity envisaged by the General Assembly partition plan. The projected Palestinian Arab state never came into being nor did the international zone ever materialize. King Farouk's Egypt occupied the Gaza Strip, and King Abdullah's Hashemite Kingdom of Jordan seized the West Bank, including East Jerusalem. Both areas were crowded with frustrated, disillusioned refugees. They yearned to return to their homes, fields, vineyards, shops and factories, but the envenomed politics of the Middle East made that well-nigh impossible. From the Israeli perspective they were potential fifth-columnists, and their readmission would be an act of suicide for the infant Jewish state. In a few short years their abandoned lands and other property were taken over by Jewish immigrants in dire economic straits, the bulk of whom had left Arab countries because Arab hatred toward Zionism had been directed against the local Jewish populations. That seemingly irreversible exchange of population was to enormously complicate the search for a solution to the Arab-Israeli dispute.

The whole Arab world seethed with anger over its defeat in 1948, an event they viewed as an unprecedented humiliation, an unparalleled catastrophe. Cries for justice and revenge reverberated throughout the Middle East. Even the most irrepressible optimist would not forecast peace in the area.

Note: Excerpted from *Israel in the Black American Perspective* by Robert G. Weisbord and Richard Kazarian, Jr., Greenwood Press, Westport, Ct., 1985.

The Jewish War Veterans of America

Pearl Laufer and Ronnie Shimron

"Jews are parasites, not patriots; mercenary, not military; camp followers, not combatants; a people who live on, not in, a given country." This was an often-voiced feeling in America in the late 1800s, when it was socially acceptable to be antisemitic. In polite society, there was but one consideration. Antisemitism, or any other anti, had to be dressed up or disguised, diluted by semantics and literary flourishes. The indirect slur was the order of the day. Often, in fact, no particular slight was intended to the object of the slur. Blacks, Jews, even, to a large extent, all foreigners (unless they were of noble blood), were considered inferior beings and, therefore, were talked about in belittling fashion. Blackface shows, Jewish jokes, and foreign heavy accents abounded.

There was, amongst the new Americans, a selfish, economic fear of newcomers which was exacerbated by the influx of immigrants in the 1890s. It was at the beginning of the decade, in 1891, that the *North American Review* published a letter from a Civil War veteran that read, in part, as follows: "I have served in the field about eighteen months . . . but I cannot remember meeting one Jew in uniform or hearing of any Jewish soldier . . ." This calumny was followed by more defamations and lies.

It was the publication of these ugly slanders that impelled a group of 78 aging veterans of the Civil War to form a common front and unite, determined to give the lie to these outrageous untruths. Of the 78 old soldiers who met together on March 15, 1896, they had, between them, not less than 218 medals awarded for their part in the battles of that war, and these 78 men constituted less than one-third of one percent of the Jews who were known to have served.

Within two years of the first meeting of the then fledgling forerunner of the present day JWV organization, America was at war with Spain. Some 4500 Jews voluntarily served their country with pride and honor. The first soldier to fall in Teddy Roosevelt's Rough Riders historic charge up San Juan Hill was a sixteen-year-old Jewish boy from the Bronx.

The activism that is a trademark of the Jewish War Veterans of the USA was born in the earliest years of its organizational history. In response to the bloody pogroms against the Jews of Russia (1903-1907), the Jewish Veterans conducted a campaign, throughout America, to stir up public opinion against Russia.

A concern with world-wide Jewish interests was strengthened in the camaraderie amongst the Jewish veterans in America. Following the war, more veterans joined and several new posts were set up. The close friendship of old comrades helped bind together the nucleus of a spirited and active membership. Fallen comrades were honored and the disabled were supported. Antisemitism was fought whenever and wherever possible.

Isidore Isaacs, Adjutant (Secretary), who called the first meeting of the Hebrew Union Veterans Association, held on March 15, 1896, to order.

When, in 1917, America entered WWI, many Jews who had served in 1898 went back into uniform. More than 250,000 American Jews served their nation, in numbers exceeding their proportional representation in the population at large. Jews constituted three percent of the population in 1917; yet almost five percent of those serving in the armed forces were Jews.

At the war's end, one of the first actions taken by Jewish veterans was a rally held to protest the 1919 Polish massacre of Jews. There was also continued vigilance against antisemitism at home. In 1922, at a Purim Ball, Colonel Maurice Simmons, a leader of the Jewish War Veterans,

Anti-Nazi parade, March 23, 1933.

reiterated the organization's dedication to "uphold the fair name of the Jews," when he said:

> . . . Let the hand of History tear the fangs of slander from the throat of antisemitism. No forged protocols with Old World venom, no poltroonery nor buffoonery . . . can tarnish the achievements of our Jewish boys overseas.

Jews were still being accused of not serving, and the burning desire to silence the liars was stronger than ever.

While the official name change, from Jewish Veterans of the Wars of Republic to Jewish War Veterans of the United States of America took place on April 10, 1929, goals and programs remained constant. The JWV spent the twenties and thirties fighting privation and bigotry, poverty and injustice, on every front. They were the first Jewish organization to fight Nazism, in the now famous boycott of 1933. JWV members were frequently bloodied in their clashes with the right-wing Bundist parties whose ugly, festering, antisemitic diatribes were being shouted across the nation.

The world, once again, became engulfed in war and, as throughout the history of our country, the Jewish fighter was there. 550,000 were known to have fought in the uniforms of the United States of America. Tragically, more than ten percent of them were killed or wounded. Members of the JWV who could not fight because of age or ill health worked ceaselessly for the war effort, and donated their time, their energies, and their earnings for such necessities as planes and ambulances. Always concerned about the G.I., they volunteered in hospitals and faithfully sent food parcels to soldiers on the Front Lines.

The tragedy of the war ended in triumph: triumph for the Allied fighters, and triumph for the JWV. After the war, membership rolls swelled and comrades, rather than lay down their arms and leave the fighting to others, kept up the struggle. In countless arenas, the JWV was heard from—and listened to.

They rallied, in tens of thousands, to support the birth of the State of Israel. Hundreds of war-weary veterans took up arms again and, in many tragic cases, laid down their lives, for the new Jewish homeland.

Seemingly within days, America was once again at war. Jews unhesitatingly responded to the call to service in Korea. Upon their return, they lobbied for veterans' housing, education, and health care. As Americans, concerned for the health and well-being of the country, they involved themselves in, and actively supported, the burgeoning Civil Rights movement. Always sensitive to the need to right injustice, the JWV was the only national veterans organization to join with the Reverend Dr. Martin Luther King, Jr., in his historic March on Washington.

And the fight goes on. The dream does not fade. With the help of a new generation of veterans of the Vietnam conflict to bolster our ranks, we continue to pursue our ideals. Across the land our dedication, our drive, our support of all and any fights against injustice goes on. The JWV offers advice to ALL veterans through our National Service Officers across the country. The JWV issues statements and lobbies for our members' needs as veterans and their concerns as Jews. Above all, the JWV cherishes our founders' unspoken wishes. The JWV is a comradeship of "old soldiers." We do not fade away. We are here to serve our Nation and our heritage. We remember the selflessness of our forebears, and remind the future of our contributions to this great nation.

An offshoot of the Jewish War Veterans is the National

Portable pulpits were used by rabbis ministering to the troops. A typical World War II Jewish chaplain's pulpit looks like an ordinary trunk when folded for traveling.

Memorial, which was incorporated by an Act of Congress in 1957. The NMI has purchased the new five story headquarters building in the heart of downtown Washington, D.C., at 1811 R St., N.W., where a central archives, library, and museum are dedicated to the research and display of the glorious history of the JWV members and their forebears. As we research this history, long forgotten stories of Jewish involvement in the American military come to light, constantly endorsing the slogan of the museum researchers—"We were there."

We Were There

Ronnie Shimron

The JWV archives are an "Aladdin's Cave" full of surprises and memorabilia which create interest and enrich the history of American Jewry. An example is the torn and crumpled envelope sent to the JWV by an anonymous member. Scrawled on the large buff cover, postmarked in the early fifties, was a pencilled note saying that the enclosed medals had belonged to the donor's uncle, who had served in the U.S. Army at the turn of the century. Also enclosed in the envelope was an incredible document stating that Abraham Spector of U.S. Marine Corps was appointed an Honorary Mandarin to the court of the Empress of China for his efforts and participation in the relief of the Siege of Peking. With this document and his

In a rare photograph taken after Germany's surrender in World War II, Rabbi Manuel Poliakoff, center, now spiritual leader of Beth Isaac Adath Israel Congregation, Baltimore, Maryland conducts services in ex-Nazi propaganda minister Joseph Goebbels' captured palace.

Dr. & Mrs. Chaim Weizmann arrive in the U.S. to visit President Truman in 1947. Left, foreground, Major General Julius Klein, National Commander, JWV and JWV members, background.

medals in hand, I set off with our able Historian, Al Lerner, PDC, to the National Archives here in Washington, where we were able to find the complete military record of this humble Jewish soldier.

He was indeed present during the Siege of Peking as a Corpsman in the U.S.M.C. He had participated in the forced march (217 miles) to the relief of the beleaguered city. But that was not all. He was also stationed at the site of the building of the Panama Canal and was present during the Philippine Insurrection. In a period of four years, Abraham Spector collected a chestful of medals and was present at all the major incidents and campaigns which took place during his enlistment.

Finally, the last dated letter in his military file lay on the table—a mute testament to the unadvertised courage, loyalty and dignity of our earlier comrades-in-arms. Abe Spector, some sixteen years after his last military campaign in 1901, wrote to the War Department to volunteer for service in the "war to end all wars"—World War I.

The history of this simple Jewish soldier has pride of place in our Museum. Like so very many of our comrades, both living and dead, he served willingly and bravely; and he served with dignity.

A Forgotten Hero

June weather; hot and muggy, oppressive and with that hanging, sullen sky that should promise a break in the weather but seemingly never does. Lieutenant Leighton W. Hazelhurst decided to forego more testing of the new army *Scout* plane. However, the short, dark civilian test pilot pointed out that the afternoon's tests would complete the obligatory list of trials necessary before handing over the Wright Brothers aircraft to the Army Aviation section.

The high crackling whine of the engine echoed and reverberated round the College Park, Maryland airfield. Lt. Hazelhurst, and the test pilot, Mr. Al Welsh, bumped their way across the grassy runway. The high whining pitch rose, faltered, and then gained strength as the flimsy plane and its 450 pound load took hesitantly to the sky.

On his second lap around the marked course, the pilot signalled his intention to commence the climbing tests. On the ground, the workers ignored the little biplane as it rose and plummeted.

Subsequent reports state that the plane tipped up its nose and fell some 75 feet in an abrupt dive that ended, tragically, the lives of two brave aviators. One was a tall, stately, and aristocratic graduate of the West Point Military Academy, and the other was an immigrant Jew from Kiev in Czarist Russia. This immigrant Jew was one of the first five pilots ever trained by the Wright Brothers and a man about whom "Hap" Arnold, a four-star General and commander of the Air Force, wrote in his autobiography:

". . . finished 3rd May, 10 days learning. Al Welsh signed in blanks for gasoline and oil used. He had taught me all he knew. Or rather, he had taught me all he could teach. He knew much more . . ."

Al Welsh was born Laibel Wellcher in a small town near Kiev, Russia. His family emigrated to the United States in 1890 and settled in Philadelphia. At the age of 20, he joined the Navy, giving his name as Arthur Welsh. He served as an able seaman on the U.S.S. Hancock and U.S.S. Monongahela and was honorably discharged in April 1905.

As a spectator to Orville Wright's first "cross country" flight, on July 30, 1909, he was mesmerized by this new and untried science. He applied to, and was accepted at, the Wright Flying School, under the direct instruction of Orville Wright. Upon graduation, he was persuaded to stay on at the school as an instructor.

In June 1911, at an International meeting in Belmont Park, Long Island, Al Welsh won the George Campbell Wood Cup when he established a new American two-man altitude flight record of 2,648 feet. At the same meet, he won the Aero Club of New York Cup. Two months later, in Chicago, he won $3,000—as the first aviator to fly over two hours with a passenger. Two days later, he won the Americas Duration prize for staying aloft for over three hours.

During the following year, Al Welsh became the main test pilot for the Model G Wright Brothers 6-cylinder biplane. When the army showed interest and ordered ten of these planes for military use, it was Al Welsh who was chosen to accompany Orville Wright to the College Park field to carry out the stringent tests to conform with the military standards.

At 4:30 p.m., June 11th, 1912, Al Welsh, ex-U.S. Navy able seaman and chief civilian test pilot, met his end. His passenger was afforded an honor guard and full military funeral at Arlington National Cemetery. Al Welsh was buried in Washington at the Adas Israel Congregation of Washington, D.C. cemetery under a simple stone plaque which reads Arthur L. Welsh, Father.

What's it Like to be Jewish, Black and the Law in a Southern City?

Phil Jacobs

He's tough. He's outspoken. He's Jewish, and he's black. And down in this bastion of Southern graciousness, Reuben Greenberg is the law.

In his four years as chief, crime has dropped a dramatic 21 percent. Criminals with prior records who are out on the streets are watched closely by his police department. Officers often walk the beat in more comfortable sneakers than spit-polished black shoes. Greenberg himself is well known for his swashbuckling style and contempt for repeat offenders. And he's not above putting on a pair of roller skates and directing traffic.

In his first two months in Charleston, he suspended an experienced officer for cursing at a citizen. The move was unheard of. And in this center of blue-blooded Civil War aristocracy, he doesn't care who likes or dislikes him. but based on results in this seaport and military post town, the citizens love Chief Greenberg.

And it's not just the locals who love him. He was featured on a "60 Minutes" segment, and in that segment reporter Morley Safer asked him "what's a nice Jewish boy like you doing in a place like this?" The exposure was so overwhelming that Greenberg's office received hundreds of letters of approval from citizens and police departments all over the world.

Interestingly, several of the letters targeted on the chief's religious choice. He received more than his share of Christian tracts and requests to reconsider his conversion.

On this particular spring Friday in Charleston, the magnolia trees were swaying in a warm, southern breeze. Chief Greenberg was literally running from one appointment to the next, appointments that keep him constantly occupied with government officials, police business, media interviews, and even a parade review at the Citadel.

That same evening he would attend services at a packed Synagogue Emanu-el. And after the finale of *Adon Olam,* he'd share in the joy of a bar mitzvah boy's *oneg shabbat,* surrounded by other congregants in conversation. At Emanu-el, Greenberg is a fixture. Indeed, he's a co-chairman of the adult education committee and is on the shul's board of trustees.

For Greenberg, 40, life has been a double conversion. He wasn't always Jewish, and he wasn't always a cop. His grandfather, a Jewish Russian immigrant married a black woman. While growing up in Houston's ghettos, Greenberg rarely learned about his Jewish ancestry. And it wasn't until he was 26 years old that he converted.

Chief of Police Reuben Greenberg is in charge of 235 police officers in Charleston, South Carolina.

He became interested in Judaism as an offshoot of his participation in the civil rights movement. And he noticed that during the 1960s, many of the white movement's participants were Jews, especially in the San Francisco area where he lived. Because many civil rights meetings were held in synagogues and involved rabbis, Greenberg started asking questions and doing his own religious research.

"I converted to Reform in San Francisco. I had always had some interest, but it wasn't really religious contact, but secular contacts that led to the religious part of it. When I was growing up in Houston, a black couldn't eat in restaurants owned by Jews, so one would assume you couldn't go to the synagogues as well."

"But I was interested in Judaism's philosophical approach and its questioning nature," he added. "I mean I remember people in the civil rights movement questioning and arguing with rabbis. That amazed me, because that never would have happened in the Baptist church. That kind of independence of mind is not fostered by a lot of religions in the world."

Greenberg's wife is Baptist. She does, according to the chief, respect his religious choice, and even participates with him to a degree. She is a member of Hadassah, and attends services once in a while.

It was the civil rights marches of the sixties that also led Greenberg to an interest in law enforcement. He said he started to talk to many of the police officers on the other side of the marches, and found out that they were regular family men just doing their jobs. And it was their job that interested him. Up to this point, Greenberg had a B.A. at San Francisco State University and a couple of master's degrees in city planning and public administration from U.S.C. Berkeley. He also had an academic background in anthropology.

Greenberg worked as a probation officer in Berkeley and later as an aide to San Francisco sheriff Richard Hongisto before helping administer departments in Oregon, Georgia and Florida. He was also on the faculty of the University of North Carolina at Chapel Hill for several years.

Chief Greenberg is as intense a man as you'll meet. He talks in a deep, booming voice and tends to dominate the conversation. He also loves to laugh uproariously and walks twice as fast as anyone else around. He's always in a hurry, and exudes a sense of urgency.

In addition to Chief Greenberg's easily spotted outward characteristics, there is no doubt that this man is the boss. In the police station, grown men with guns strapped onto their waists referred to him by no other form of address than "sir."

Greenberg keeps photos of redwood trees in his office. He said he loves the strength the tree symbolizes. In fact, he said, he has planted one at his house. There are also photos of his sail boat, another one of his hobbies, and a framed certificate of honor he received from Sen. Strom Thurmond.

Greenberg is usually in such a hurry that one appointment tends to blend into the next. While he was being interviewed, he began changing into his formal dress uniform. From his office, he would be going to the Citadel Military College to review the Friday parade.

Once there he sat among fellow police and military officers. Southern belles sat in stylish spring dresses on the well manicured lawn watching their boyfriends and brothers. It was an anachronism that would have been perfect, had it not been for the presence of the police chief.

On a social level, Greenberg had several groups of people to deal with directly as a newcomer to Charleston. Three of those groups were the blacks, Jews and southern aristocracy. Greenberg confirmed that the aristocracy is alive and well.

"Charleston is a place where lack of money, if coupled with the right last name, won't keep you out of society," he said. "But, if you have the wrong last name, no matter how much money you have, you can't buy your way in. This is a dress up town, a lot of parties and black tie affairs are held here. There are a lot of very poor people who are fully welcome, but there are people who are millionaires standing outside looking in at the social scene. There's a saying around here that Charlestonians are like the Chinese, they both eat a lot of rice and they both worship their ancestors. You'll find a lot of people here with the same last name, blacks and whites who are descended from plantation owners."

The chief said that he was generally accepted by the Jewish community. He said that people were curious about him. When he first attended shul, many wondered if he was a member's guest, or someone who worked for a member.

Interestingly, Greenberg seemed to catch more heat from the black community for his hard-line police stand and his openness as a Jew.

"Generally there has been a very close black and Jewish relationship in this town dating years back," he said. "It's just been more recently that a little distance has set in. And I think that's because blacks have lost the moral ground that we once had relative to civil rights and equal justice. Blacks never had to worry before about losing moral ground. We were always equal opportunity-oriented, anti-discrimination, anti-defamation and against holding anyone in bondage.

"Unfortunately," he continued, "with certain things that have been said by people like (Rev. Louis) Farrakhan and Jesse Jackson, we've been losing that moral ground. We've never had to apologize for our positions before or explain what somebody meant. But now, because of these individuals, and because blacks did little or nothing to condemn them for their statements, we lost our moral ground. I think it was the most serious loss that blacks have had since they came to this country. Even when we were slaves, we had our moral ground to stand on. Now you might say that we've adopted some of the clothing of racists that have been long active in the U.S."

Greenberg receives letters from blacks he calls "racist and antisemitic," criticizing him for being Jewish. He also receives letters from black Baptists who tell him that it's a shame he's such a nice person, because he's "going to end up in hell because of Judaism."

I've never had any problems with Southern aristocracy down here," he said. "I've never had a line of bad press since I've been here. The only problem I've had was a couple of black city councilmen who subscribed to the old line that racial discrimination is the reason for every conceivable ill in the black community. I don't believe that. I believe we blacks are capable of creating our own ills without the assistance of whites."

"Some things do point to black discrimination, but other crimes point to serious problems within the black subculture itself and would probably exist if every Caucasian disappeared from the face of the earth."

Greenberg said he is embarrassed when a black, a Jew or a police officer is convicted of a crime. He said that Charleston sees crimes among ethnic groups just like any other city does. Charleston has a population of about 85,000 with about 300,000 in the metropolitan area. And because it is a seaport and a Naval base, Charleston sees its share of embezzlement and drug trafficking. One of the vessels involved in the skirmish with Libya came to port in Charleston. The city had received two bomb threats as a result.

"You hardly see Jews involved in such crimes as homicide, rape and robbery," he said. "You'll see more blacks committing violent crimes. Jews are involved in such crimes as embezzlement; economic-related crimes. Jews commit far fewer crimes based on their population proportion. If you have a higher number of Jews in an area, you're going to have a lower number of crimes committed. The

Jewish community is probably more law-abiding than any other ethnic group, with the possible exception of the Japanese."

Part of the explanation for the drop in Charleston's crime rate since Greenberg came to town is his tough attitude toward repeat offenders. He is given credit for getting the word out that they'll be jailed, and jailed for a long time if they're caught again.

In his first year, the Charleston police made 3,100 arrests in the city. Last year, they made 8,200.

"I operate from a different perspective," said the chief. "I'm a cop. And when a guy snatches a purse, I don't care why he snatched the purse, it's just he did it. He might be broke or his family has left him or he didn't receive the right type of toilet training when he was a baby. But whatever explanation you want to come up with, psychological or sociological or genetic, I don't care, he's going to go to jail. If someone else wants to buy those explanations, let them. I don't buy nothing. You rob a bank, you get arrested."

And how does he go after repeat offenders encountered on the street?

"If you're going to provide real protection to honest citizens then you have to confront the dishonest ones. When we see a guy who has been a convicted burglar walking down the street, we know that he's not walking the same way that you or I do. He's walking the way a wolf stalks a lamb. He's looking for opportunities to commit crimes."

"So you have to say, 'Hey Jimmy! Jimmy the burglar, isn't it?' We let them know right up front that we know who they are. And if someone comes in here and files a complaint that he was told to move along by an officer on the street, we punch up his name and birth date on the computer and get a rap sheet. I ask him to sit down. I ask him how he's doing. I shake his hand. Then I pull out his rap sheet. I say, 'Mr. George Jones, arrested and convicted for armed robbery, 1980; arrested and convicted for burglary, 1983.' I read off four or five of them, and then we know where each other is at. No bull now. You'd be surprised how mellow they become. I say, 'You're George the burglar.' He says, 'Yeah, but I was harrassed on the street.' I tell him that he's not talking to one of those liberal probation officers. I tell him that he makes a living out of robbing people, and we know why he was on the street that day."

When it comes to the criminal justice system, Greenberg is down on lawyers. In fact, there are several posters in his waiting room that poke fun at attorneys. He admits to having something against lawyers, calling their profession "dishonorable."

"Any profession in which a person can go out and say anything to make enough money is bad," Greenberg said. "They'll argue anything or say anything for money. I used to be discouraged as most police officers about the court system, but to tell you the truth, I feel a lot better now than I ever have . . . now that I've given up all possible hope. You see, justice has nothing to do with the criminal justice system. Whether someone committed a crime or not is less important than the process used to prove it. Lawyers will say to me 'of course the guy committed the crime, there's no question he did it. But you've got to prove that he did it. The fact that a person is guilty is irrelevant.' "

"Criminal attorneys love me," he continued. "They say I'm the greatest thing that's ever happened here. And when you consider that 8,200 people were arrested last year, and each one needed a lawyer, no wonder they love me."

Greenberg's view on the subject of rehabilitation has been somewhat controversial. He believes in strict punishment for the offender. He also believes that when a person reaches age 35, his criminal tendencies drop to almost nothing, no matter how active a criminal he was before.

"I think he's looking at the downside of life," Greenberg said. "He says, 'I haven't accomplished anything up to this point, so now I'm going to settle down and accept life. I'm going to live a nice, peaceful life.' See, he's deciding to rehabilitate himself."

"You see, people get rehabilitation mixed up," Greenberg added. "There's a theory in sociology that says once a person is rehabilitated any punishment beyond that is worthless. My philosophy is that punishment is a good thing in and of itself regardless of whether the guy is rehabilitated. Punishment is not just revenge on the part of society, it's a means of social instruction, teaching civilized people in our culture that certain things should not be done."

Greenberg has said often in the media that real rehabilitation comes from within the self, that it is something that the criminal has to decide to do himself.

"If someone says, 'I'm never going to do it again,' that's just too convenient for me. Colson, Ehrlichman, Dean; they have all repented, but the point is they all rehabilitated after they were caught and not before, and that's too convenient for me."

The chief believes in the death sentence for a crime in which someone was killed. Greenberg doesn't consider gun control a serious issue. He said it stopped being serious about 1880, because that's when it went out of control.

"I think the disadvantages of having a gun in the home far outweigh the advantages, especially if you have kids," he said. "I've gone to hundreds of homicide scenes, and I always ask the same question, 'Is that the burglar?' And it hasn't been the burglar yet. It's always been Uncle Joe or Aunt Missy or the neighbor next door or my son or my daughter or my daddy. Then you ask why someone has a gun, and he says, 'to protect my home against burglars,' Well, he's not shooting any burglars. He's shooting the ones he supposed to love."

Away from the action of the police department, Greenberg settles down for a soft drink and a pastry at shul. It takes a while for him to go through the hugs, kisses and handshakes he gives his fellow worshippers. He gets nothing but smiles and a great deal of support.

"He's a phenomenon here," Rabbi Alan Cohen said. "This is a unique situation. but it's easy to see that he's a very important member of this Jewish community."

Rabbi Cohen said that even the old line Southern Jews, who seem to have their own brand of aristocracy, were taken by Greenberg's fierce desire to learn how to be Jewish. Around the synagogue and throughout the Jewish community, he is called simply "Reuben."

If there is any complaint by any of the congregants, it is that Greenberg often seems to be caught up in all the publicity he's receiving. Even the chief admitted he was getting weary of doing all the interviews. He said a reporter flew in from London, and he could only give him a half hour. At the same time, however, Greenberg knows he's good copy. There just aren't too many black Jewish crime-stoppers around. And because people love an underdog here, Greenberg is a natural.

Greenberg has been getting his share of requests to lecture on terrorism. He recently delivered such an address to a sisterhood-sponsored function at his synagogue. He holds no quarter for terrorism, and indicated he supported President Reagan's decision to bomb Libya.

The chief has also been to Israel. On a recent UJA trip, he consulted with Israeli police authorities on uses of computer technology to fight crime. Israel, meanwhile, will be sending officers to Charleston to see the success story up close.

A dispatcher's voice crackles over the squad car's two-way radio calling for Unit One. Greenberg is Unit One. He listens to the requests on the radio and quickly and confidently barks out commands.

He pulls through several poor black Charleston neighborhoods pointing out how street crime in the area has been cleaned up considerably. It's the street crime that he says frustrates him and his department. Police departments are often burdened by paper work and the revolving door system of justice for stolen cars, muggings and assaults. He says that the best he can do is keep a thug inconvenienced, by repeatedly bringing him into the station for processing.

"The inconvenience is the best thing I can sell with street crime," he says. "I make it difficult for them by repeatedly bringing them into the station. It used to be that if you were arrested you had a great chance to go to jail. Now about 90 percent of the cases never reach trial."

Greenberg cruises through the streets like he owns them. He waves at people he recognizes, and some people smile and wave back. The ones who don't wave probably know him all too well. This neighborhood of older wooden homes is a far cry from beautiful picturesque side of Charleston that makes it to all the postcards.

The chief must bridge the gap between the two sides of town. As a kid growing up in the ghettos of Houston, Greenberg was on the other side of the police car. His goal in life was simply to graduate from Jack Yates Senior high School.

"We were all supposed to be in the state pen by the time we were 15 years old," Greenberg says, laughing that sonic boom of a laugh.

Now he is a pillar of the community. There are those who insist that he run for public office. But the chief isn't interested.

"When you become a politician you lose your freedom of speech, and that's the only thing that's really worthwhile having. You have the right to dissent in this country. I mean "60 Minutes" was great, but that's television and that's really all fluff. It's rhinestone cowboyism, and that's not really what I'm about.

It is Saturday afternoon and Greenberg is going to take the rest of the day to relax. The next morning means a *minyan* at shul and then more afternoon police work. Maybe he and his wife will take in a movie, perhaps a police movie.

"The movies are the only place where justice is done anymore," says Greenberg, laughing that booming laugh.

Unless of course . . . you live in Charleston.

The Jews of China

Anson Laytner

The Jesuit missionaries were settled but a short time in Peking when, one summer's day in 1605, a visitor called upon Father Matteo Ricci. Entering the mission, the Chinese stranger announced himself to be an adherent of the same faith as the missionaries. In fact, he said, he had come specifically because he had heard of the arrival in the capital of foreigners who worshipped the one God of Heaven and Earth, but who were not Muslims. He had to make their acquaintance.

The two made their way to the chapel. It was St. John the Baptist Day, and over the altar was a painting of the Virgin Mary holding the infant Jesus with John the future Baptist kneeling in homage before them. When Ricci and his guest entered the chapel, Ricci bowed before the picture. Then the stranger bowed, and as he did so remarked that it was unusual to have such images present in the sanctuary. Beside the altar hung a picture of the four evangelists. "Were these four not of the twelve?" the visitor asked. Father Ricci, presuming his guest referred to the twelve disciples, acknowledged in the affirmative.

The two men returned to the reception hall for talks. The ensuing discussion led to an unexpected and surprising result. Were the two pictures in the chapel not of Rebekah with Jacob and Esau and four of the twelve sons of Jacob?" the stranger asked. "Certainly not!" Now Ricci was confused. Who was this fellow? What religion could he possibly follow? After a great deal more discussion his confusion was dispelled—his visitor was a Jew—a Chinese Jew!

The man's name was Ai Tien and he was a native of Kaifeng, the capital of Henan province, located inland, midway between Beijing and Shanghai. He was in Beijing to take the civil service examinations. He had heard of the Christian mission and, mistakenly thinking them Israelites, decided to pay them a visit.

When shown a Hebrew Bible, Ai Tien was unable to read it, but he could recognize the letters. He said that many of his people back home could still read the language, but he could not—he was pursuing a career in the imperial bureaucracy. He added that the Jews of Kaifeng constituted some ten to twelve clans, employed a rabbi and a number of teachers, possessed a very ancient Torah scroll, and owned a newly restored synagogue.

Excited by this news and driven by missionary zeal, Ricci eventually dispatched a Chinese Christian priest to Kaifeng to investigate and report back. Ai was telling the truth. But this priest also brought back less than encouraging news. When told of the existence of additional books in the Bible—the New Testament—which related the story of the Messiah already come, the rabbi and congregation adamantly insisted that the Messiah had not yet arrived. Still, they recognized the common bonds between themselves and Ricci, and graciously offered to accept Ricci as a leading member of their community if he would abandon these other books, renounce the eating of pigmeat, and undergo circumcision. For some reason the Jesuit declined the offer. But Ricci sent word of his discovery back to Europe and slowly, over several centuries, interest in the Chinese Jewish community of Kaifeng grew.

I

History does not record how or when the settlement of the Jews in China began. Some scholars think the Jews arrived as early as the destruction of the First Temple in 586 B.C.E.; other scholars, operating from a more solid basis, hold that Jewish traders, working their way eastward from Babylonia by way of Persia and Turkestan in the early centuries of the common era, were the founders of the Kaifeng community. This is paralleled in the folk recollections (i.e., the steles or memorial stones) of the Kaifeng Jewish community. According to the ancient Chinese accounts, there were enough Jews in the ninth century Chinese empire to warrant the appointment of a special officer to supervise them.

The earliest account of the Kaifeng community goes back to the year 950, and relates that 70 Jewish families were settled there. They worked as merchants, peddlers, restauranteurs, and served their own community as teachers, religious leaders, physicians, and butchers. In 1163 the first synagogue was built in Kaifeng with the express permission of the emperor. It was named the Temple of Purity and Truth—in name and design totally Chinese. The synagogue, like all institutions in China to this very day, was enclosed in a compound, in this case consisting of four courtyards.

In the first of these was a large arch dedicated to the "Creator and Preserver of all things," written in Chinese characters. The second courtyard contained the houses of the rabbi, teachers, and caretaker. The third had another marble arch on which were tablets memorializing the names of those who had helped to erect the building—a custom still in use by Jewish congregations today. In this courtyard stood the lecture and study halls, a kosher slaughterhouse and kitchen, and the *mikveh* (ritual bath). The fourth court was divided by a row of trees. In the center aisle a large incense vase was flanked by stone lions mounted on marble bases. Then came the synagogue itself. Inside, on a table, were more incense burners, candlesticks, and flower vases. A washbasin stood just inside the entrance in which worshippers could purify their hands before prayer. In the center stood a pedestal called the "Chair of Moses" on which the Torah scroll was placed for reading during the service. In the extreme rear of the hall was a section known as the "Tian Tang" or "Hall of Heaven" into which only the rabbi and his assistants were allowed to enter. The Torah scrolls were kept here in an hexagonal ark, wrapped in yellow silk and enclosed in a gilt lacquered cylindrical case topped with flame-shaped knobs. Containers on either side of this ark held other holy books. Such was their synagogue—truly a community center. The synagogue itself was destroyed four times by fires, floods, and civil war, but the community persisted and rebuilt it time and again. However, we proceed too quickly.

II

The Mongol conquest of China in the thirteenth century improved the lot of China's minorities, the Jews included, for the Mongols preferred using minority peoples to govern the country rather than entrusting the task to the ethnic (Han) Chinese. This was the time of Marco Polo's visit to China. In his journal, Polo records, with some hostility, the presence of extensive and prosperous Jewish communities. In 1279, the synagogue, which may have been damaged during the Mongol conquest, was rebuilt and enlarged.

When the Mongol, or Yuan dynasty, was overthrown, the Chinese took steps to integrate their foreign communities into Chinese society. The new Ming dynasty granted all foreign communities full Chinese citizenship including the right to own property, and the freedom of religion. On the other hand, one secondary source states that all foreign males were required by law to take Chinese wives—thus speeding, it was hoped, their assimilation into Chinese society. The Jews were no exception to the rule.

In 1421 a further barrier to assimilation came down. Until then the Jews had been legally forbidden to take Chinese surnames, but in 1421, a Jewish doctor named An San exposed local corruption and was rewarded by, among other things, being granted a Chinese surname. Soon the privilege extended to the entire Jewish community. By 1489 all the Jews had adopted Chinese surnames—and another sign of their distinctiveness vanished. But the community was prospering. Individual members, like Ai Tien, advanced into the government bureaucracy, which had both bad and good effects. Bad because the best and brightest Jews left the Kaifeng community and the direct service of their own people; good because, in the beginning, the Kaifeng Jews were able to receive state funds for their community.

In 1421 and again in 1445, funds were granted to repair the synagogue. In 1461 a flood destroyed the synagogue completely, but the emperor again provided the means to rebuild it. There was one condition, though—a plaque praising the emperor, to which the Jews had to make obeisance, was to be placed directly before the ark. Lest this appear an affront to God and their faith, the community rendered it harmless by hanging another plaque bearing the Shema (Hear, O Israel, the Lord is our God, the Lord is one (Deut. 6:4) above the imperial tablet. God was king and ruler over all—even the Emperor of the Middle Kingdom!

The fifteenth through the seventeenth centuries mark the high point of the Jewish community's life. From a commemorative stone cast in 1489, and from the records of Jesuit visitors to the community, we have a clear picture of Jewish life at that time. Prayers were offered three times a day—the customary orthodox Jewish practice—but the congregation faced westward—for that was where Jerusalem lay. On entering the synagogue the people were required to remove their shoes—a Moslem, but also an ancient Jewish custom—and to perform a ritual washing of their hands. The congregants wore blue head coverings during worship. In reading the Torah, the rabbi covered his face with a gauze veil in imitation of Moses, who brought the Torah down to the people with his face covered. No music accompanied prayers and weddings—again traditional Jewish practices. The people observed the rituals of circumcision and *kashrut* (dietary laws). They kept the Shabbat in strict traditional fashion, and observed all the holy days and fast days. Children were given a Hebrew education. Such was their life at its best. They had survived; more than that, they had prospered and persevered as Jews for over 700 years in spite of little outside contact with other Jews.

III

Then disaster struck. In 1642 civil war left Kaifeng in ruins and many thousands dead. The siege of that city ended when its defenders purposely broke the dikes that held back the waters of the Yellow River. The city was flooded. Most of Kaifeng was destroyed. The Jews lost their homes, their businesses, and their synagogue. Their Torah scrolls were swept away, as were many of their prayerbooks, and most important of all, a Chinese guide to the Hebrew pronunciation, without which the prayers could not even be recited. The community had been dealt a fatal blow.

In 1653 survivors discovered the foundations of the synagogue and obtained some funds to aid in its rebuilding. Fragments of many Torah scrolls were meticulously gathered and sewn together to form a new Torah—their only copy. But the community persevered, and by 1663 the synagogue was totally rebuilt, as were the school, ritual bath, slaughterhouse, and residences. Twelve copies of the single Torah scroll were commissioned and completed.

Had the Chinese Jews been left in peace, things might have gone well. But in 1665 the Ching court, that is the non-Chinese Manchu dynasty which had toppled the Ming dynasty, adoped an anti-foreign policy—perhaps in an effort to win support for their rule among the native Chinese. This new policy hit the Jewish community hard. Their life turned inward in an attempt to avoid trouble. While there exists no evidence of overt persecution, we do know that at this time the social and religious bonds of the community began to disintegrate. Intermarriage increased considerably; many Jews joined the larger, and hence more protective, Moslem community; many others simply disappeared into the surrounding Chinese populations.

In 1724 a renewed anti-foreign campaign broke out, leading to the banishment of the Jesuit missionaries from China. The Kaifeng Jewish community's only link with the outside world was broken, and the community was plunged into deeper isolation and despair. For the next

credit: Archives des Jesuites de Paris, Chantilly, France

A drawing made by the Jesuit Father Domenge in 1722 depicting "A Kaifeng Jew reading the Torah which is placed on the seat of Moses, with two prompters." Standing on the left is a fellow Jew holding a parasha, *a sectional book written phonetically to help the Torah reader in his pronunciation.*

century the community barely managed to survive. By 1800 the last teacher with any knowledge of Hebrew had died, and the synagogue stood neglected. By the late 1800s, when the first Protestant missionaries arrived in Kaifeng, all that remained was a handful of destitute families. Mostly British and Canadian Anglicans, these missionaries made a concerted effort to contact the Chinese Jews and to win them over to Christianity. Others, led by a nobler instinct, sought to publicize their fate. In 1849, T.H. Layton, the British consul at Amoy, wrote a letter to the Kaifeng Jews. Their reply reached him in 1870. Here is a portion of their response:

> In reply to the inquiries which you make, we have to state that during the past 40 or 50 years, our religion has been but imperfectly transmitted, and although its canonical writings are still extant, there is none who understands so much as one word of them. It happens only that there yet survives an aged female of more than 70 years, who retains in her recollection the principle tenets of the faith. Morning and night, with tears in our eyes and with offerings of incense, do we implore that our religion may again flourish. . . . But now the unexpected arrival of your letter fills us with happiness. . . . If it shall be possible again to erect our temple, it will give joy to our community. Our synagogue in this place has long been without ministers; the four walls of its principal hall are greatly dilapidated. . . . Through the whole day have tears been in our eyes, and grief at our hearts, at the sight of such things. It has been our desire to repair the synagogue, and again procure ministers to serve in it; but poverty has prevented us, and our desire was in vain. Daily with tears have we called on the Holy Name. If we could again procure a minister, and could put in order our synagogue, our religion would have a firm support for the future. . . . Day after day, and year after year, have we maintained ourselves in the belief of the vitality of our religion, and the certainty that it would again flourish. How could any other than such a desire be entertained?

A sad letter depicting a sorrowful community. But things were not to improve. Between 1854 and 1865 the Tai-ping Rebellion closed the interior of China to foreigners. At its conclusion, a Rev. Martin, the first Westerner to visit the Kaifeng Jews since 1724, reported that the synagogue no longer stood. In its place he found a large stagnant pool. Even the foundation had been sold or carried off during the rebellion. Only the memorial stones stood, still more or less intact. Other missionaries followed in Martin's footsteps—the Kaifeng Jews became a must on the missionary tourist circuit.

IV

Western interest in the Chinese Jews predates the "rediscovery" of the Chinese Jewish community of Kaifeng in the latter nineteenth century by Christian missionaries. In perhaps the first instance of attempted correspondence, in 1760, Haham Isaac Nieto, son of Haham David Nieto, sent a letter of inquiry from London to the Chinese Jews in an effort to resolve a halachic problem concerning the observance of the second day of the Jewish festivals. Another curiosity was the Hirsch-Simson letter of 1794-95, addressed to the elders and heads of the Jewish community of Kaifeng by two members of the "Portugese" synagogue Shearith Israel in New York, via a Captain Howell, bound for China. The authors asked, among other things, that the Chinese Jews relate "the number of children of Israel who are to be found there; from what tribe you are; when, after the Destruction, you migrated there; what your ritual is; if you have books of the Torah and other books; if you live in peace or are oppressed; and what you do for a living." A third letter of note was sent by a group of English Jews via a Dr. Morrison through Canton in 1815. None of these letters apparently reached their destination; at any rate, none was answered.

Action of various sorts was also contemplated. Two visits were proposed, one by Henri Hirsch in 1842, which was postponed because of Hirsch's ill-health, and another by that remarkable traveler, I.J. Benjamin II in 1864, which was cancelled upon his sudden death. In 1852 an American Jewish organization dedicated itself to the task of serving the needs of far-flung Jewish communities, including presumably, the Chinese Jews, but this plan was thwarted by the outbreak of the Civil War in America and the Tai-ping Rebellion in China. An exchange of letters between the chief rabbi of London, Nathan Adler, and S.J. Solomon of Shanghai, led to a plan of action, according to which young Chinese Jews would be brought to Shanghai, educated, and sent back home to serve as teachers and leaders. This was undertaken in 1864, and two young Chinese Jews were

Photograph of Scroll of Esther, *Oriental Script, illuminated in China. 18th century (?); ink on vellum, paint and gold; partially backed by Chinese silk. Cecil Roth Collection, Beth Tzedec Museum, Toronto. Photograph courtesy of Beth Hatefutsoth.*

brought to Shanghai, only to soon grow homesick and return home.

In the latter half of the eighteenth century, the Kaifeng Jewish community was host to a growing number of Christian missionary-visitors, whose reports on the Kaifeng Jews, coupled with the books on the subject published by Mr. James Finn, stirred further Jewish interest and concern in these "lost" Jews. On May 14, 1900, the Occidental Jewish community of Shanghai formed the "Society for the Rescue of Chinese Jews." During its four years of activity a promising beginning was made toward saving the Kaifeng Jews. Letters were exchanged, and two Kaifeng Jews came for an extended visit to Shanghai, followed by six others in 1902. They reported that the Jewish community of Kaifeng consisted of fifty families, numbering some 250 individuals; Jewish ritual observance was minimal. It was the hope of the Kaifeng Jews that their Western brethren could raise enough money to rebuild their ruined synagogue, for only the synagogue could rally the sickly community together once again. But this was not to be—the task proved too large and financially impossible for the Shanghai Jewish community to undertake alone, and Western Jewry was preoccupied with caring for Russia's Jews, who had just been hard hit by the pogroms, and who were seeking to emigrate en masse. Disappointed, six of the Chinese Jews returned home to Kaifeng. The project ended in failure.

Beginning in 1910 and continuing until 1935, the Anglican Church of Canada, through its mission in Kaifeng headed by Bishop William Charles White (author of *Chinese Jews,* University of Toronto Press, 1942), played an active role in the affairs of the Chinese Jewish community. White attempted to halt the rapid disintegration of the Jewish community first by preserving their historic steles and by partially rehabilitating the synagogue site, by this time a stagnant cesspool. Then in 1919, White convened a conference of Chinese Jews in Kaifeng with the intention of educating them in their Jewish heritage. Actually there is doubt about White's intentions, since in a Christian missionary journal he wrote that his aims were:

1. of making them mutually acquainted and organizing them;
2. of making them acquainted with their own history;
3. of making them acquainted with the religion of their forefathers and the Scriptures;
4. of making them realize their connections with their co-religionists throughout the world; and
5. of teaching them that Jesus Christ was a Jew, and that he came to save the world.

Perhaps the Chinese Jews distrusted White even if they were unaware of his ultimate intentions—perhaps they simply distrusted the foreigner as did other Chinese—perhaps they had no interest in a communal revival. At any rate, this "mission" also ended in a failure.

In 1924 the "Shanghai Society for the Rescue of Chinese Jews" was revived for a brief period of time (two years), but no action was undertaken save several meetings and the dispatch of a visitor to Kaifeng.

Several American Jews journeyed to Kaifeng prior to, and during, the Second World War, chief among these being a physician, David A. Brown, in 1932. His detailed and moving account of his encounter with the Kaifeng Jews graced the pages of the *American Hebrew and Jewish Tribune* from January to March 1933. There, Brown recorded the Jewish community's urgent pleas for aid, as expressed by the community spokesman, Mr. Ali:

> We need a school for our children, that they may learn who they are and in what respects they are different from the other Chinese. We know we are Jews, and that our people came here many centuries ago; that we once had a synagogue and a rabbi, but we have lost all knowledge of this; and we are anxious that our children shall walk in the footsteps of those ancient people from whom we have sprung.

Brown left promising Bishop White to take the case of the Kaifeng Jewish community to America's Jews, with the hope that a Jewish school might be established and the synagogue rebuilt. But once again these well-intentioned plans came to naught. The Western world was sliding rapidly into the chaos that preceded the Second World War, and the need to defend and protect European Jewry from the onslaught of Nazism directed the energies of Western Jewry along more concrete and immediate lines.

Following World War II, access to the Kaifeng Jewish community was impeded by the renewal of the Chinese Civil War. However, Dr. Josef Preuss, then a resident of Shanghai and a student of the Kaifeng Jews (he is the author of an essay on the subject entitled *The Chinese Jews of Kaifeng-fu,* published posthumously by Museum Haaretz in Tel Aviv in 1961), received several reports from two other Western physicians who had visited Kaifeng in 1948-49. These doctors estimated that only five families remained there. We also know that the Japanese conducted field studies on the Kaifeng Jews during the Second World War.

With the victory of Communist forces in 1949, almost all contact between Westerner and the Kaifeng Jews came to an end. Until recently, one of the last accounts published was penned by the Czech sinologue, Timoteus Pokora, who visited in 1957. According to a summary of Pokora's account by Donald Leslie in his definitive work, *The Survival of the Chinese Jews* (Leiden: E.J. Brill, 1972, p. 74), Pokora was told that 100 families with a total of 200 dependents still classed themselves as Jews. Primarily businessmen and tradesmen, they resided no longer in the Jewish quarter, but rather had dispersed throughout the city. Most saw their Jewishness as a nationality. This has generally been considered as the last word on the subject, the concluding chapter in the long and tragic history of the Chinese Jews of Kaifeng. Donald Leslie has observed in conclusion, "one can hardly say that a community still exists. Though individuals may still trace Jewish descent, they are no longer Jews by race, nor by religion, nor by culture, merely by name," and further, "The hope of finding Chinese Jews elsewhere with any real knowledge of Judaism is nil. We may perhaps find some who trace descent, but that is all."

Leslie's conclusions are indisputable in all but one respect: numbers. Recent evidence suggests that the Chinese Jews total anywhere from several dozen to possibly several hundred and that they maintain a sense of identity that goes beyond that of merely tracing Jewish descent.

In the summer of 1973, during the course of my interview for approval to take part on the first Canada-China student exchange program, I was told a most unusual story. One of my interviewers, a Jewish French-Canadian professor of Chinese Studies named Rene Goldman, related to me the story of his visit to Kaifeng in 1957, when he was a student at Peking University. Later, he wrote his story for inclusion in a recent book on the Chinese Jews by Michael Pollack, *Mandarins, Jews, and Missionaries: The Jewish Experience in the Chinese Empire* (Philadelphia: Jewish Publication Society of America, 1980). Here is Goldman's recollection of his experience:

> In the course of this visit, two of us had to be quite persistent in our entreaties with the city cadres, before they acknowledged that indeed the Kaifeng Jews existed. They informed us that there were some 2000 persons in Kaifeng of Jewish ancestry. How they came to that figure is a mystery, considering the history of the Kaifeng Jewish community.
>
> One afternoon they drove several of us who were interested in the question to visit one such family, which still lived in the ancient lane of the Chinese Jews, *Tiao Chin Chiao Hutung.* We were received by an elderly gentleman surnamed Lee, and his wife; unfortunately, because of the presence of the cadre, the discussion was formal and reserved. Nevertheless, when upon leaving the house, I discreetly whispered to the old gentleman that two of us were Jewish, he beamed effusively and shook our hands. Later in the day, I saw the two old Jewish steles, still standing in front of the former Canadian Anglican church.

Goldman's testimony is remarkable because the number he gives—a figure provided him by the Party cadres themselves—far exceeds those given by previous visitors. Given the source of his information the figure should be believed or at least seriously considered—there would have been no reason for the cadres to err on the side of exaggeration! But at least Goldman met a Chinese Jewish family and was able to inform them that he too was Jewish—that they had not been forgotten by other Jews. Later would-be visitors, myself included, were not so fortunate. The official reticence Goldman experienced in 1957 later hardened into a stance of subtle but outright refusal.

In my own case, despite the fact that the Chinese knew that I was Jewish, and despite my repeated request to visit Kaifeng made over the period of my eight-month stay in China in 1973-74, I was not permitted to travel there. Nor did I receive any information about the Chinese Jews. Similarly, Party cadres in Shanghai were singularly uncooperative about my contacting the few remaining Western Jews still living there. In both cases there was never an outright refusal, only evasiveness—all the more telling because the Chinese officials were generally efficient and well-organized.

Later Jewish visitors to China have told much the same story.

In 1976, Rabbi Bernard Raskas visited Shanghai, made inquiries about Chinese Jews, and was told that two elderly Jewish women (no doubt Western Jews) had recently died in one of the city's homes for the aged. There remained one elderly Jewish man (again probably Western) at the home, and arrangements were purportedly made for Rabbi Raskas to visit him. At the last moment, however, "difficulties" arose and the meeting had to be cancelled. Other than the fact that the Chinese officials did not want the meeting to transpire, what could account for this? Rabbi Raskas was being given the run-around.

In the summer of 1978, a group of American historians and archeologists visited Kaifeng. Two members of the delegation, American Jews by the name of Mr. and Mrs. Weill, asked if a visit to the ancient synagogue site could be arranged. The Party officials declared that it would be impossible because a workers' apartment (actually a hospital) had been built on the site. After requesting permission to view the steles, the Weills were told that they were "under repair" and could not be seen. (The phrase "under repair" has frequently been used as a euphemism to mean "closed to the public for political reasons.")

The experiences of foreign visitors, from Goldman in

1957 through the Weills in 1978, all seem to point to one conclusion—that Party officials considered the subject of Chinese Jews to be politically sensitive and therefore "closed" them off from foreign visitors. And, although it must be assumed that the number of Chinese Jews has indeed declined in the 23 years since Goldman's visit, the fact that the Chinese authorities acted continually in an obstructionist manner does suggest that a significant number of Chinese Jews must remain—enough to warrant, at least until recently, their isolation.

The obstructionist practices described here characterized the period when China was under the dominance of the "Gang of Four." Since the purging of the gang, China has blossomed forth with initiatives in all major fields of endeavor. These changes have affected both information about, and access to, the Chinese Jews as well.

In 1978, the renowned sociologist Fei Xiaotong told a group of American tourists that academic and archeological research was being conducted by the Chinese on the Kaifeng Jews. Fragments of a Torah scroll and other artifacts had been discovered at the site of the ancient synagogue, and Professor Fei also reported that he had a student doing Ph.D. level work on the Chinese Jews. Still more recently, word has come out that an associate of Fei's, Pan Guongdan, now deceased, has written a book-length study on the Chinese Jews. A digest of the book recently appeared in article form in the prestigious journal of the Chinese Academy of the Social Sciences, and soon after in an official English translation.

Another professor, Jin Xiaojing, recently wrote of her discovery of her Jewish roots during the course of a colleague's lecture at a conference on national minorities in China. Prior to this conference she had always thought her family to be Moslems (Huis). Following the publication of this article entitled "I am a Chinese Jew," which appeared in the Beijing monthly *Encyclopedic Knowledge,* Professor Jin wrote a brief history of her people for the fourth issue of the 1981 edition of *Social Sciences Battlefront.* All this shows the degree to which China has altered its former attitudes regarding the Chinese Jews.

But even more significant events occurred just last year. The Chinese Jews were visited on at least two occasions: once by the United Press International correspondent, Aline Mosby, at the start of 1980, and a second time by Arthur Rosen, president of the National Committee on U.S.-China Relations, towards the end of the year. These were the first two major Western encounters with the Chinese Jews since 1957!

In her UPI news feature dated February 18, 1980, Ms. Mosby reports that only several dozen members of each of the seven family clans remain. Mr. Rosen was told that there are over 70 families in Kaifeng who still trace their Jewish ancestry, but he reports that, primarily as a result of the Cultural Revolution, many of the younger generation has been dispersed to other areas. (In terms of the preservation of their group identity, this latter bit of information bodes ill for the Chinese Jews.) Mosby apparently met with members of two families: Ai and Shi (Shih); Rosen interviewed five individuals of three clans: Zhao (Chao), Jin (Chin), and Shi (Shih). Members of the Ai and Zhao clans still live in the vicinity of the site of the ancient synagogue.

How have the Chinese Jews fared these many years?

Chinese Jews today:
(Left to right) Shi Hong Yu, Zhao Ping Yu, Shi Yu Liang
photo credit: Betsy Gidwitz

How Jewish are they? Mosby reports that during World War II the Japanese, at the instigation of their Nazi allies, came to Kaifeng to search for Jews. The Chinese Jews did not identify themselves as Jews to the soldiers. Ai Fen Ming, the same man who told this to Mosby, also said: "Some people used to be afraid to say they were Jews because minority groups were oppressed before the revolution. But not now." (Apparently, Mr. Ai refers here to the Cultural Revolution. Otherwise, we must ask: Why then in 1957 did only 700 of the 2,000 Chinese Jews acknowledge their Jewish ancestry?) Another Kaifeng Jew, a much younger man surnamed Shi (Shih), stated: "I have five sisters and brothers and we all graduated from university and the government gave us all jobs, so this means equal treatment for Jews and Hans." Rosen reports that the Zhao (Chao) children (who are workers) know little about Judaism, but do know that they were the offspring of Jews. None of Rosen's contacts tell of having suffered any discrimination either.

It is clear that a residual sense of Jewish identity remains. Both old Mr. Ai and young Mr. Shi equate the terms "Jew" and "Han" (the dominant ethnic group in China), implying that being Jewish in China means belonging to an ethnic minority rather than denoting a religious affiliation. This confirms Pokora's report that in 1957 the Chinese Jews identified *themselves* as being of Jewish nationality. However, this does not mean that the Chinese Jews hold any special status as a recognized national minority. Shi Zhengyu comes from a Jewish landlord family and studied at the Institute of Minorities after Liberation. As one who works in the field of national minorities (he has worked with the Hui nationality in their autonomous region), he told Mr. Rosen that the Chinese Jews are no longer entitled to be classified as a national minority, the Chinese characteristics of which are: special customs, living in a compact area, and maintaining a separate language, and a sense of national identity. (Actually the terms of definition are Stalin's.) While it is true that the Chinese Jews can no longer claim three of these characteristics as their own, the fact that these families in Kaifeng still consider themselves Jewish after all religious observance has ceased, despite the long break in contact with other Jews, the many years of communal decline, and the lack of any Jewish materials or Jewish leadership, is proof of the tenacity and continued strength of their residual Jewish identity—this at a time when identity has been all they have had to transmit to the next generation.

Both Ms. Mosby and Mr. Rosen report some curious adaptations and transformations of traditional Jewish customs. Mr. Shi told Mr. Rosen that he remembered his grandfather telling him of their custom of smearing the blood of a lamb or chicken on the doorposts of their house at the time of the Spring Festival (i.e., to fulfill the biblical injunction regarding Passover). In a similar attempt to fulfill a biblical commandment, Mr. Shi to this day still extracts the sinew from the hindquarters of the animals he and his family eat—even pigs! (The families all know that in the past their ancestors did not eat pork. Mosby tells of Shih Shiao Yu, who according to Jewish tradition neither smokes nor drinks alcohol but who, unlike his parents, does eat pork. The former customs are obviously a borrowing from the Moslem community, who constitute some ten percent of Henan province's population, and with whom the Chinese Jews are often linked by the Han Chinese. As Professor Jin's account confirms, Jews joined the larger Moslem community for better security during recent centuries. Furthermore, the mosque in Kaifeng is reputed to contain many artifacts that once belonged to the synagogue.) In this regard, the experience of another visitor to Kaifeng is worth recounting.

In the spring of 1981, an American Jewish physician, Dr. Ronald Kaye, was lecturing in Kaifeng. After several requests and repeated denials, he was permitted to meet some Chinese Jews. He held a Passover *seder* for himself and them. Later, Kaye visited the Dong Da (Great East) Mosque and met with the local mullahs. One mullah apparently told Kaye that the mosque held many artifacts from the synagogue. This earned him a sharp and immediate reprimand from the other mullah. The first mullah then reversed his earlier statement and told Kaye that he had been mistaken, the mosque had no artifacts from the old synagogue.

To return to Rosen and Mosby, both were able to view the steles which are still in storage awaiting display in a new museum to be opened some time in the future in Kaifeng.

Mosby and Rosen are the first visitors to contact the Chinese Jews in over twenty years. Until recently, Kaifeng was closed to foreign visitors. Now, however, under the new leadership, China has once again opened Kaifeng to tourists and has set about restoring its ancient Buddhist temples and Sung dynasty palaces. Today, tour groups can visit Kaifeng on a regular and routine basis. The interest we display and the contacts we make are important in and of themselves.

The opportunity to visit the Kaifeng Jewish community, extended first to Ms. Mosby and Mr. Rosen and now to others, and the disclosures of recent Chinese interest in the study of the Kaifeng Jewish community appear to indicate a shift in policy on the part of the Chinese government. Their interest in their Jewish minority seems to parallel a renewed interest in, and appreciation for, the traditional cultures and histories of their other minorities, even though, by the Chinese definition, the Jews are not a full-fledged national minority. In the cases of the recognized national minorities, the Chinese have already made efforts to study and preserve these minority cultures. Perhaps they may be inclined to do the same for the Jewish community as well.

China also grants its Christians and Moslems freedom of religion, and both religions have witnessed a reflowering in recent years. Perhaps this too might benefit the Chinese Jews, for should any Jews wish to learn more about their Jewish heritage, then conceivably they may now have more of an opportunity than before for doing so. In the final analysis, however, everything depends upon the wishes of the Chinese Jews themselves, and, of course, on the Chinese government. Unfortunately, we do not know what the wishes or needs of the Chinese Jews are. They have not had the opportunity to really communicate their desires to World Jewry since Dr. Brown's visit back in 1932. Nonetheless, there remains much for those interested to do—whether or not the Chinese Jews survive; whether or not they have any interest in regaining a portion of their Jewish heritage.

On her recent visit to the United States, Shirley Wood, long-time professor of English at Henan University in Kaifeng, attended a meeting in New York City with a number of us interested in the Kaifeng Jews. Referring to the interest in the Chinese Jews both here and in China, she outlined a number of projects that cannot long be postponed. These included: photographing and/or preserving the remnants of tombstones from the soon-to-be, or already destroyed, Jewish cemetery on the outskirts of Kaifeng; photographing and/or preserving (repairing) the ancient Jewish homes on the Street of Scriptures; identifying and photographing the timbers, stones, and relics of the ancient synagogue which were sold to, and are now found in, the Great East Mosque of Kaifeng; and recording the oral histories of the most elderly Jews before they and their stories vanish altogether. This work is the most important of all.

China has opened up tremendously since the purging of the "Gang of Four," but we have no idea how long the opportunity will remain for us to visit the Chinese Jews. China has currently established good relations with many Western countries, so whether on business or tourist trips, we in the West are now in a unique position to express an interest in, and a concern for, the Chinese Jews. Given the Chinese initiatives in studying the Kaifeng community, we must encourage them to study and preserve what little remains of that community. I cannot stress enough that this work must be undertaken together in a cooperative effort. Permit me to give one illustration. My current work consists of piecing together the reports of the most recent visitors to Kaifeng—whom they met, what was discussed, etc. A Chinese scholar—perhaps a Chinese Jew like Professor Jin—could do a much more complete survey of indi-

Li Jin ("Moshe Leah") with Isaiah scroll written in Hebrew. Chapters 38 and 40 (both incomplete) are shown here.

Li Jin ("Moshe Leah") with scroll written in Hebrew characters but in an as-yet unidentified language.

viduals involved and record their oral histories much more effectively and without all the difficulties that a foreigner would have. By the same token the Chinese need our knowledge of Judaism to balance their work. Professor Pan's article on the Chinese Jews is marred by an insufficient knowledge of Jewish history and an almost nonexistent understanding of Judaism. He concludes his article by suggesting that the Jews came to China from Bombay, India. Why? Because only the Chinese Jews, like the Jews of Bombay, have the saying "Shema Yisrael." In fact, as every Jew knows, this prayer is the cardinal statement of the Jewish faith.

Chinese chair with Torah case and scroll.

Back in 1933, Dr. Brown attempted to stir the conscience of Western Jewry into action with these words:

> The excuses of the past hold no longer, and these ancient Jews of China are both a challenge and a responsibility to the Jews of the world. . . . They know they are Jews, but know nothing of Judaism. They realize they are Chinese, completely assimilated, yet there is pride in the knowledge that they sprang from an ancient people who are different from the other Chinese in Kaifeng.

Dr. Brown's appeal is no less urgent in our own day. Without an effort on everyone's part, it will not be long before the few surviving Jews, their history, and their relics could become lost forever. We may well be the last generation able to do any work on, or for, the Chinese Jewish community of Kaifeng. The opportunity and the obligation are too great to ignore.

The Jewish Community of Nairobi

Ivor Davis

Miles away from home, American tourists on safari in Kenya—you are allowed to "shoot" elephants, lions and rhinos only with cameras nowadays—make a beeline to the Nairobi synagogue for the Friday night Shabbat service.

Generally reformniks, they are not necessarily regular synagogue-goers, but as Pliny said, "there's always something new out of Africa," and a visit to Kenya's very lovely synagogue, alongside the Nairobi University campus, is a "must" for Jewish tourists.

Though somewhat put off by the *mechitsa* (the partition separating men and women), the visitors seem to enjoy the Orthodox-style chanting and format.

The Jews of Nairobi—immortalized in a book by Julius Carlebach, one of their former ministers, who has become a Sussex University don—started to arrive at the turn of the century when the so-called "lunatic express" railway was being laid from Mombasa on the coast to Uganda in the hinterland.

Cold Water Spot

The construction stopped at a railhead in Masai-land where there was plenty of cold water for the tribe's cattle: Nairobi.

Young British aristocrats were sent to try their luck in Kenya, and took a distinctly hostile antisemitic line when a ranching area in Uasin Gishu, some 200 miles north of Nairobi, was offered in 1903 by the British Colonial Secretary, Mr. Joseph Chamberlain, to Theodor Herzl as a Jewish homeland.

Called the Uganda Plan (the area was then part of the Uganda Protectorate), it was a non-starter because the Zionists meeting in Basle rejected it. But some of the British settlers were already screaming in the local press about the need to keep out "Jewish peddlers" and "aliens who will not fit in."

Kenyan caretaker Wellington by the Nairobi Synagogue.

The British offer was well-meaning enough; it followed a dreadful pogrom in Kishinev. Mr. Herzl favored acceptance of the Uganda Plan as a halfway house to Palestine.

The argument about the correctness of the decision goes on; some claim the Jews would have found themselves like the Rhodesian whites in recent times. Others say that it might have been a haven during the Nazi Holocaust.

Whatever the case, as a result of the controversy, Jews started to trickle to East Africa to find out for themselves what the Uganda Plan was all about.

Among them was Abraham Block, from the Ukraine, who travelled from South Africa, pioneered Kenya's hotel industry—and helped to found the *kehila* in the African bush.

With his wife, appropriately named Sarah, and his sister, "Auntie" Lilly, together with other Kenyan Jewish pioneers, they built the first Nairobi synagogue in 1912. The present building was opened in 1956.

The community was always a tiny one. There was an influx of Second World War refugees from the Nazis which reached a peak of some 165 families in 1957. Among the *kehila's* alumni is Mr. Issy Somen, a past president who was mayor of Nairobi in 1957 to 1959. He was also Honorary Israeli Consul until Kenya gained independence in 1963, and played an important role in creating good Kenyan-Israeli relations.

These ties still exist today, although Kenya and most other African States severed diplomatic relations with Israel during the 1973 Yom Kippur War.

Now an octogenarian, Mr. Somen represents Kenyan Jewry on the Board of Deputies in London. The late Mr. Arthur Levinson, active in recent years in the campaign to help the Falashas—the Black Jews of Ethiopia—was a past president of the *kehila*.

Another group of Jews who arrived in Kenya were Irgun prisoners brought from Mandatory Palestine by the British in 1947 to a detention camp at Gilgil, 75 miles north of Nairobi—and they escaped. By the time they found their way across Africa back to Palestine, the State of Israel had been born. Their story has been recorded by one of these Irgun prisoners, Mr. Yaacov Meridor, who is now Israeli Minister for Economic Affairs.

Today, the *kehila*'s 112 families keep the Jewish flag flying in East Africa although at the time of independence, wiseacres were convinced that given five to ten years, they would disappear like many a small community in Zambia to the south.

Hotelier in control

Viability is difficult with such small numbers, but under the leadership of Mr. Charles Szlapak, who, like Abraham Block, is a hotelier, the *kehila* has no intention of lying down to die.

Shabbat and *Yomtov* services are held throughout the year, and burials are conducted. A tourist not only has a synagogue to attend, but if he finds himself in a hospital, he'll get a Jewish visitor.

Matzot and wine are imported from Israel, and no Jew goes short over Passover.

The community has been revitalized by the Rev. Zeev Amit, an Israeli, who was formerly minister of Glasgow's Garnethill Synagogue and northern region students' chaplain.

With his wife, Yaffa, the Rev. Amit is "uniting" the local families with some 180 Israeli families, mostly engaged in construction. An active community center is being created in the synagogue's Vermont social hall with classes in Judaica, Hebrew, English, fitness, handicrafts, and bridge as well as youth activities.

There have been few signs of antisemitism in Kenya apart from the difficulty which Jews have experienced over the years in joining exclusive clubs. However, since the country came under black rule 25 years ago, Africans and Indians are blackballed no longer—nor are Jews.

Bible Readers, English Speakers

Isaac Mozeson

If a vote in the Continental Congress had gone the other way, Americans would all be speaking Hebrew. Many "new Israelites," the American Puritans, came to this promised land reading the Hebrew Bible, writing Hebrew diaries and peppering their English poetry with bilingual Hebrew puns. Today, it is hard to find any descendants of our colonials who can read the Hebrew motto of Yale College—even if they teach classical language and literature at Ivy League schools.

As testimony to the state of Bible illiteracy in our dictionaries, let me call to the stand the word TESTIS. The American Heritage Dictionary (Dell, 1982) correctly gives the Latin meaning "witness," but goes on to add "to virility." Yes, testicles are related to the verb TESTIFY, "to make a declaration of fact under oath," but testicles do not testify to anyone's virility. The scholars behind this fine dictionary were not aware that declarations of fact under oath were made while holding the second party's testicles. Eliezer does this for Abraham in Genesis 24:2-3, as cupping the family jewels predated our hand-on-the-Bible oath in biblical days.

This was merely an example of an English word clarified by familiarity with biblical text. I want to go on and propose that several English words of problematic origin have come to us from names of biblical characters or places.

The word BLAME is one of these etymological suspects. Beyond the English term *blamen,* we are supposed to accept the Greek word *blasphemein* as the source of BLAME. But a leap of faith is required to accept the radical differences between these two terms. Moreover, the original meaning of blame, a condemnation or expletive like damned, doesn't quite match the profanation of the sacred inferred by BLASPHEMY.

Now the Hebrew Bible records a long and humorous episode of a professional damner or curse monger named Balaam (pronounced Bill-UM in Hebrew). If fictional and real people can give us words like malapropisms and spoonerisms, surely this memorable character in Numbers 22-24 can offer us a more satisfactory etymon for BLAME than the Greek source of blasphemy.

The adjective COLOSSAL dates back to the *Kolossus* statue of Apollo which spanned the harbor of Rhodes. Without insisting that the statue commemorates an actual giant who stood on that same spot, I'd suggest that the most famous giant of the Bible might have originally been involved. (There must be a reason why the statue wasn't simply named Apollo.) Goliath pronounced correctly is GOLL-yos. The Greek of the Hebrew of I Samuel 17:4 would sound much like COLL-ios. (Ya'akov was heard as *Iakobos,* and the *gamal* became camel.) I don't want the Statue of Liberty to be renamed the Goliath of New York Harbor, but the poor big guy had suffered enough from the slings and arrows of smaller men.

Sodom is the acknowledged source of the word sodomy. Its twin city Gomorrah (Genesis 19:24) was also nuked to oblivion. In Joseph T. Shipley's book, *The Origin of English Words* (Johns Hopkins Univ. Press, 1984), it is noted that GONORRHEA was spelled *gomoria* in the 16th century in the belief that the disease was an affliction of Sodom and Gomorrah. The etymon offered in most dictionaries, and the one which influences our current spelling of the term, is *gon* (semen) + *rhoia* (flow). These Greek words represent the mistaken notion that discharges of semen are involved, but the etymon may be an attempt to Hellenize an elusive, foreign term. Aware of the current Bible Belt attitude towards sodomizers who get AIDS, I'd bet on the biblical source for the word GONORRHEA.

There are forty words related to the name Jack. Everything from jackasses to jockstraps has been attributed to the many variants of the Greek name *Iakobos.* Whether a word is linked to the Latin *Jacobus* or to the Old French *Jacques,* a dictionary might remind you that the granddaddy of them all was the patriarch Jacob (*Ya'akov* in Hebrew) but it will never attempt to link the word to this major biblical figure.

The JACK for your car, for instance, is the device which supplants the need for an assistant and which heels or lifts it up. In *Genesis* Jacob is named the Hebrew term which means heel, to supplant, to overreach, and deceitful. His career begins as a younger twin baby who grabs Esau by the heel and who, using deceit, supplants his brother as the privileged firstborn. To JOCKEY, not surprisingly, means to cheat, swindle, and maneuver for position or advantage. An unrefined Bible reader (and everyone read or heard Bible stories before novels and movies) would consider Jacob a JACK (knave) or a JACKAL who jewed his brother (not a true Hebrew) out of his inheritance or JACKPOT with his JOCULAR brand of JUGGLING. And why would this maligned patriarch be the inspiration for JACKDAWS, JACKRABBITS and a dozen other male birds, beasts and fish? It might be because, after much jockeying and financial juggling with Laban, he hits the jackpot with some magical tricks of animal breeding. In addition, after some juggling and jockeying of wives, Jacob ended up with four wives and a minimum of thirteen kids.

Nobody knows where the word JINX came from. But this hoodoo person or thing that is supposed to bring bad luck sounds exactly like what we all call a Jonah. Jonah caused a near shipwreck until he was tossed overboard. There are several ways to explain the *X* at the end of JINX, but perhaps no better way to explain the term.

Jacob's son Judah may provide one example of an ending *H* in Hebrew becoming an *X. Judex* means JUDGE in Latin, and Judah, Judea and Judaism have always been synonymous with things JUDICIAL. All the "jud" words in English involve JUDICIOUS things or Judean ones. Judah happens to be the first judge in recorded history. The courtroom drama of Judah judging his own daughter-in-law for adultery is striking. It is so striking, in fact, that Genesis 38 gave American literature one of its greatest moments. Arthur Dimmesdale publicly condemns the adulterous mother of his own child in Hawthorne's *The Scarlet Letter.* Tamar, too, stands trial for adultery as the guilty but innocent mother of Judah's own twin boys. Judah's progeny take up their dad's law practice as Solomonic judges and kings, and Judean legal principles are noted by the early Greeks and Romans before anyone coins the term *judex* or JUDGE.

If you thought Goliath was colossal, you should have met that OGRE named OG (pronounced "oag" in English). Mighty OG, king of Bashan (Numbers 21:33) was the Wilt Chamberlain in the All-Canaan league where Goliath would later be the Tiny Archibald. In Deuteronomy 3:11 we read that Og, King of Bashan, had an iron bedstead nine cubits long and four cubits wide that was kept on display by the Ammonites. Gigantic artifacts and legends were circulating in antiquity long before the OGRE (a hideous monster or giant) appeared in print. French fairy tale writer Charles Perrault (d. 1703) did not claim to have coined the word OGRE; we who forgot our Bible merely guess that he did.

The Greeks and Vikings more correctly pronounced the Hebrew *ayin* as a *G.* Thus the Old Norse term for OGRESS is *gygr,* and the etymon for GIGANTIC is *gigas.* Just as the giant Gigas looms large in Greek legends of the Titans battling the gods, old Og (or Gog) battles God's army in the biblical conquest of Canaan.

Eight generations after Judah, we come to King Solomon's great-grandfather and Ruth's son. The story and character of Ruth are marked by sorrow, grief, pity and, above all, compassion. These terms are all listed as definitions of the archaic word RUTH. The latter two are antonyms of our surviving term RUTHLESS. The best your dictionary can do is to connect *reuthe* (Middle English) to rue. Look up rue and you'll see words like raw, crude, crust and gore. That modest phrase "origin uncertain" might have been in place here.

I conclude with another even saltier reference to Sodom. The entire region was to have been nuked into a wasteland of "sulphur and salt" (Deut. 29:22). The Dead Sea near Sodom is so saline that it makes Utah's Great Salt Lake look like a watering hole for animals on a low SODIUM diet. Lot's wife, perhaps forgetting her American Express card, turns back toward the city and becomes a pillar of salt. The Arabs have named a shapely mound of salt *Jebel Usdum,* so Lot's wife remains well-preserved.

To further spice my SODIUM/Sodom equation, I'll add that "salt of Sodom" was common table fare in the Near East according to first century talmudic literature.

So SODIUM need not be a Modern Latin derivative of Soda. SODIUM is more literally connected to Sodom than the word *sodomy,* as there are no actual sex crimes in that horrific episode where everyone gets it in the end.

This was a brief sampling of English words whose source may lie with biblical names. English has many words like *spartan* and *odyssey* which were borrowed from Greek history and lore, and the Hellenic influences on our culture has been less wide and less deep than the Bible's. It is time for our language historians to refrain from BABBLE (which they feel is imitative of children's prattle and *not* from the tower of Babel) and to dust off their Bibles.

850th Anniversary of the Birth of Maimonides

Atlas Stamp Company, New York City

The 850th anniversary of the birth of Maimonides (Rabbi Moshe ben Maimon, 1135-1204) was marked by the release of commemorative stamps by nine nations.

The first to issue a series of stamps for Maimonides was Antigua & Barbuda, a former British colony in the Leeward chain of the West Indies. The Caribbean nation issued a $2 stamp and $5 souvenir sheet featuring Maimonides' portrait on June 17, 1985.

The Republic of Guinea, a former French colony in West Africa released an interesting 7 Syli stamp and 7 Syli souvenir sheet. They pictured Maimonides when a young man of 13, beng forced to flee with the other Jews of Cordoba in the aftermath of the town's conquest by a band of fanatical Moslems.

In the foreground of the stamp is another portrait of the famed Jewish philosopher as he appeared in later life. At the bottom of the souvenir sheet is an illustration of a rabbi reading from a Torah scroll to a group of young Jewish orphans in the State of Israel today.

Bolivia

Antigua and Barbuda

Antigua and Barbuda

Lesotho

The artwork on the Guinea souvenir sheet would appear to serve as an effective contrast by showing the enduring strength of the Jewish faith over the centuries despite the outbreak of major persecutions against the Jews in various Gentile-dominated lands.

Five other nations—Dominica, Grenada, the Grenada Grenadines, Lesotho and Sierra Leone—have issued single stamps bearing a portrait of Maimonides and highlighting his important contributions in the field of medicine.

Two countries to recently honor the legacy of Maimonides on the occasion of his 850th birth anniversary are the South American republics of Paraguay and Bolivia. Both issued special souvenir sheets in rather limited editions of only 5,000 copies.

Grenada (1971)

Paraguay

Guinea

Spain (1967)

Israel (1953)

Grenada

Dominica

Sierra Leone

Grenada Grenadines

ידיעות מעריב

יום ו' ה' אייר 14.5.48

8 עמודים | המערכת: תל־אביב רחוב צ'לנוב 2 טלפון 3452 4920 המנהלה: ת"א דרך פ"ת 13, קומה א' תיבת דאר 4198 | סניף בחיפה רח' ביאליק 5 | סודר בדפוס „ספר" צ'לנוב 2 נדפס בדפוס החדש בע"מ תל־אביב רחוב רענן 22 | העורך ד"ר. עזריאל קרליבך | מחיר הגליון 25 מא"י

המנדט מת! תחי - מדינתנו!

הנציב הבריטי האחרון עזב את יבשת הארץ

הנציב העליון הבריטי — אחרון הנציבים הזרים בארצנו — והפקידים הבריטיים עזבו אמש — זמן קצר אחר שידורו של קנינגהם ברדיו — את ירושלים בדרכם לחיפה.

הדגל הבריטי הורד מארמון הממשלה במעמד משמר כבוד ונערך מסדר לפני מלון המלך דוד.

מגו דרקסן, סופר „יונייטד פרס" מודיע מחיפה:

המנדט הבריטי יסתיים היום בשורה של טקסים. בשעה 9.30 עמד הנציב העליון הבריטי, ה־גנרל סיר אלן גורדון קנינגהם לרדת בסירה שתביא אותו באניית הסיור „יוריאלוס". ברגע זה יופסק כל קשר רשמי בין הממשלה הבריטית לבין ארץ ישראל. במשך כל היום ישאר הנציב העליון על סיפון אנית המלחמה ובדקה אחת אחר חצות היא תרים את העוגן תוך הפעלת זיקוקין די נור, ניגון תזמורת ושריקת הצופרים של האניה. הערב עם חשכה ימריאו מטוסים מהאניה „אושין" העוגנת בנמל חיפה בתור הפגנה אחרונה של העצמה הצבאית הבריטית לפני היציאה מארץ־ישראל.

ממשלת מדינת ישראל מקבלת לידה את השלטון

את יום ההכרזה קידמה תל אביב בדריכות ובמתח עילאי של נכונות, שהעיר העברית עוד לא ראתה דוגמתה. אין התכונה מתבטאת בהתקהלויות של רוב עם, אך פניה של העיר נשתנו באופן הנראה לעין. המוני התושבים, קטן וגדול, איש ואשה, כל אחד במקומו ועל מכונו.

על עמודי המודעות — הכרוז של הרבנות הראשית הקוראת לתפלה והודייה ומעודדת: „אל מורך, אלקי ישראל יהיה בעזרכם". והעיריה קוראת לנקוט באמצעים להתגוננות מפני התקפות אויר, הידועים מימי ה־מלחמה — הדבקת חלונות, אי־פול, צפירות אזעקה וארגעה. על בנינים רבים התנוססו כבר בבקר, הדגלים הלאומיים. אישי ההנהגה יושבים בהתיעצויות מאז הבוקר. מירושלים הגיעו גם יתר חברי מנהלת העם, כדי להיות נוכח במעמד הכרזת העצמאות. לאולם בו תהיה ההכרזה, יורשו להיכנס רק המוזמנים — חברי מנהלת ומועצת העם, כמה מראשוני חלוצי הישוב, עורכים ונציגי העתונות המקומית והזרה.

בן־גוריון יקרא את ההכרזה

הטקס יהיה קצר מאד וההכרזה שנוסחה אתמול על ידי ועדה מיוחדת ושתיקרא על ידי מר ד. בן־גוריון, יכללו הנקודות היסודיות של הקונסטיטוציה ויינתן בו ביטוי לתיקון העוול ההיסטורי בשיבת עם ישראל לארצו ובכינון עצמאותו ומדינתו. אחרי ההכרזה תהיה ברכה קצרה מפי אחד מחלוציה הישישים של תנועת התחיה והגאולה.

עבדאללה מתלונן בפני טריגווה לי

טריגווה לי קיבל מברק מ־עבדאללה: „הריני מוחה נגד ה־התקפות היהודיות על הטריטוריה הערבית בקרבת תול־כרם ונגד התוקפנות האיומה על העיר בית שאן. פרובוקציות אלה אם יימשכו, יכניסו סיבוכים נוספים למצב".

הודעת ה„הגנה" על סכנת־הפלישה

היום לפנה"צ פורסמה ה־הודעה הבאה מטעם מטה ה„הגנה":

האויב מאיים בפלישה. אי־סור להתעלם מסכנה זו. ייתכן שהיא קרובה. כוחות הב־טחון אוחזים באמצעים הד־רושים. הצבור כולו צריך לתת כל עזרה הדרושה מצ־דו.

א) יש לחפור מקלטים בכל הישובים ולמלא אחר כל ההו־ראות של הג"א (התגונה ח־אנטי אוירית).

ב) יש להמנע מהתקהלו־יות המוניות במגרשים וברחובות.

ג) יש לתת כל עזרה למ־פקדי כחות הבטחון בהקמת מחסומים, בצורים וכיוצא בזה.

אל בהלה, אל שאננות. דריכות ומשמעת.

חתום: ההגנה

7 נפלו בכיבוש כפר־סבא הערבית

רדיו ירושלים בשידור העברי הודיע הבוקר כי בכיבוש כפר סבא הערבית נפלו 7 יהודים.

משלחת הצלב האדום הגיעה לגוש־עציון

רדיו ירושלים מודיע, כי עוד אמש יצאה משלחת הצלב האדום הבינלאומי לגוש עציון.

הידיעה מוסיפה, כי הקרבות בגוש נמשכים. מאנשי עין־צורים ורבדים לא נפגע איש.

הוצאו פצועים

אותו מקור מוסר כי קבוצה יהודית הצליחה אתמול להב־קיע דרכה לכפר עציון הנצור ולהוציא משם פצועים ותשושים.

נידם קולו של הכזבן

רדיו ירושלים לא שידר כבר הבוקר בשפה האנגלית. נראה שהכזבן הראשי, ג'חי כבר עזב את העיר.

נמשכים הקרבות בכביש ירושלים

רדיו ירושלים הודיע הבוקר כי הקרבות בכביש ירושלים נמשכים, זה היום הששי. כחות ה„הגנה" מוסיפים להחזיק ב־משלטים שכבשו. הפעולות נמ־שכות בהתאם לתכנית.

מוסף מצוייר מיוחד ליום עצמאותנו וסיום המנדט

מצורף לגליון זה במקום התוספת הרגילה לערב שבת.

המוסף המיוחד מורכב כולו מתמונות, שבהן משתקפות תולדות המנדט הבריטי מתחלתו ועד סופו. רבים מבין הצילומים מתפרסמים כאן בפעם הראשונה. הם הועמדו לרשותנו מאלבומים ואוספים שונים, ביניהם של א. סוסקין, יוסף פעמוני, י. קלוגר, „העולם הזה" ודוד תדהר.

התיעצות אחרונה ברבת עמון לפני הפלישה

רדיו לונדון מודיע כי אמש נתכנסה ברבת־עמון הועדה ה־פוליטית של הליגה הערבית ל־התיעצות אחרונה ערב פלישת צבאות ערב לא"י. בהתיעצות משתתפים עזאם פחה, עבדאל־לה, עוצר עירק, הגנרל נור־א־דין מוחמד פחה — המצביא ה־חדש של צבאות ערב וקצינים גבוהים אחרים.

מחכים להודעת בווין על הלגיון - היום

לונדון (טלגראפית מאת סו־פרנו) — מיניסטר החוץ בווין ויתכן כי גם קריץ' ג'ונס ישיבו היום בפרלמנט על מספר שא־לות בכתב שהוגשו לממשלה ב־קשר למצב בארץ ישראל — אחר סיום המנדט הבריטי.

מניחים כי בווין ימסור „הס־בר" על מעמדו של הלגיון ה־ערבי.

ה„הגנה" תפסה בנינים רבים בירושלים

בניני ג'נרלי ואפ"ק וכן חלק גדול מאזור הבטחון הבריטי ב־ירושלים, עברו אתמול לידי ה־„הגנה".

אתמול לפנות ערב הודיעו הבריטים על פנוי אזורי הבטחון ברחביה ורחוב המלך ג'ורג' ו־שוטרים צבאיים יהודיים נכנסו לבנינים. גם בית הספר לשוטרים שעל הר הצופים עבר לידי יהודים.

הערב מתחיל לכהן מפקד המשטרה העברית

הערב נכנסים לתפקידיהם מר יחזקאל סחרוב, מפקד המשטרה העברית בארץ וסגנו מר יוסף נחמיאס.

בפגישה עם העתונאים מסר מר סחרוב שעם כניסתו לתפקיד ימונו עשרות קצינים לתפקידים מנהלתיים ואפרטיביים במשטרה. לעת עתה הוא יקים את ה־משטרות של שני מחוזות בלבד, אולם המשטרה תקיף אח"כ את ארבעת המחוזות האדמיניסטרטיביים של הארץ. עתה גומרים בכל שבועיים 150 שוטרים את הקורסים בהם הם מתאמנים.

לשאלת עתונאי אמר שאת כניסתו לתפקיד התנה בתנאי מפורש של הטבת משכורתם של אנשי המשטרה כדי שיוכלו למלא את תפקידם בנאמנות וביושר לב.

כמו כן הודיע שהתואר שלו הוא „מפקח ראשי של המשטרה ובתי הסוהר במדינת ישראל". לע"ע נתמנו שני סגני מפקדים — למחוז ת"א וחיפה. ברוך גרפר, לשעבר קצין משטרה בת"א יהיה סגן המפקד למחוז חיפה. וי. ברטר — לת"א.

הקצין ר. לוסטיג העומד ב־ראש המחלקה לחקירת הפשעים. הסמל של המשטרה העברית טרם נקבע.

עתון אחיד „ביום המדינה"

הטקס יסתיים עוד לפני כניסת השבת. נוסח ההכרזה חדר"ח מהטקס יימסר בעתון בשם „ב־יום המדינה", שיצא במשותף על ידי כל העתונים בסיום טקס ההכרזה.

ידיעות מעריב

יום א' ז' אייר 16.5.48

4 עמודים | המערכת: תל-אביב רחוב צ'לנוב 2 טלפון 4920 3452 המנהלה: ת"א דרך פ"ת 13, קופה, א' תיבת דאר 4198 | סניף בחיפה רח' ביאליק 5 | יודר בדפוס ספר' צ'לנוב 2 ידפס בדפוס החדש בע"מ תל-אביב רחוב רוונו 22 | העורך: דר. עזריאל קרליבר | מחיר הגליון 10 מא"י

המערכה לשחרור ירושלים נמשכת

קרבות עזים בעיר העתיקה

עבדאללה דורש הוצאת צבאותינו ואז יואיל להסכים לשביתת-נשק בבירה...

קשר הידיעות עם ירושלים רופף מאד. גם קשרי האלחוט בין הסופרים הזרים והעולם החיצוני אינם פועלים עוד מאחר שרוב הסופרים האלה שהשתכנו באזור ה"ניטראלי" נמצאים אחרי הכיבושים האחרונים היהודיים באזור היהודי ואין להם מגע עם הערבים.

היחידי המתיימר לעמוד במגע מתמיד עם הערבים הוא — ובודאי לא במקרה — ריצ'רד וויליאמס, סופר רדיו לונדון בירושלים.

הוא שידר היום תאור דרמטי על הקרב שהתלקח לדבריו על העיר העתיקה. הוא מספר כי היהודים מתקרבים לשער ציון, לאחר שערכו התקפת נגד חזקה על הערבים. וויליאמס מודיע, כי התפוצצויות חזקות נשמעו בכוון הרובע היהודי של העיר העתיקה וסבורים כי אלה היו התפוצציות של פגזי מרגמות.

סופר בי. בי. סי. מציין, כי תחנת השידור הקטנה שהוא משתמש בה היא אמצעי הקשר היחידי עם העולם החיצוני. לדבריו נפגעו מקורות הכוח החשמלי ורוב הטלפונים בעיר.

המו"מ עם עבדאללה

רדיו קהיר מודיע, כי הצלב האדום הבינלאומי פתח במו"מ עם עבדאללה, בקשר לשביתת-נשק בירושלים. עבדאללה בתור המפקד העליון של צבאות ערב מוכן להסכים לשביתת-נשק ל־8 ימים בתנאי שהיהודים יוציאו את כחותיהם המזויינים מן העיר, יסגירו את נשקם ויפנו את השכונות הערביות.

מטוסים מצריים הרעישו שיירה בריטית

מטוסים מצריים הרעישו שדה תעופה באזור באר־שבע ו־ פגעו בכמה מתקנים ומטוסים. כן הרעישו מטוסים מצריים שיירה בריטית שנעה בדרכי הדרום וכ־6 חיילים נפגעו. מספר מכוניות בריטיות נפגעו.

מחכים להכרת מדינות נוספות בממשלתנו

ניו יורק (טלגרפית מאת סופרנו ד"ר י. הררי)

בגלל סוף השבוע לא נתקבלו עוד ההודעות הרשמיות בדבר הכרה במדינתנו, שלהן חיכו. אמנם מסתבר שהחל ממחר יתחילו להתקבל התשובות החיוביות הראשונות לבקשת ההכרה הרשמית שהוגשה על ידי ממשלתנו לכל מדינות או"מ.

עתוני ניו יורק מוספרים כי נוסף לאמריקה וגואטמלה הכירו במדינת ישראל גם ניו זילנד ושוודיה.

הקבינט הקאנאדי עומד להחליט עוד השבוע בענין ההכרה, אולם פרשנים מציינים כי ההחלטה תלויה גם ב"עצה" שתקבל קאנאדה מממשלת בריטניה.

רדיו שטוקהולם מודיע: מיניסטר החוץ השוודי מכחיש כי שוודיה הכירה במדינת ישראל.

פאקיסטן תסייע לערבים

מיניסטר החוץ של פאקיסטן, זפרולה חאן, הודיע שארצו תתמוך בערבים במלחמה נגד הציונים.

המופתי בישיבת ועדת הליגה

המופתי השתתף הבוקר בישיבת הועדה הפוליטית של הליגה הערבית.

פארוק — לעבדאללה

פארוק שלח אגרת ברכה אישית לעבדאללה לרגל כניסת הצבאות הערביים לא"י.

שוב התנכל אוירון ערבי לתל-אביב

בשעה 2.30 התקרב אוירון ערבי לתל אביב והטיל פצצות בצפון העיר. האוירון נתקל באש חזקה של מגיני העיר והונס.

דגל עברי על בניני-המכס

דגל מדינת ישראל הונף הבוקר על בניני המכס בת"א. מר הדס, מנהל המכס, נאם במסיבה חגיגית, שבה נוכחו נציגי שלטונות הנמל, עמילי המכס ופקידי המכס. מר ייאב כ"ץ דיבר בשם העמילים. וזקן עמילי המכס, מר שמרלינג, קיבל את הטופס הראשון של שלטונות המכס העבריים.

המכס בת"א עבד, בבל חדשי "התוהו ובוהו" ובהשתדלותו של מר הדס הוחזרו לסוחרים יהודים למעלה ממאה אלף לא"י שהממשלה היתה חייבת להם.

עתוני לונדון חוזים אפשרות של שלום עם עבה"י

נדון (סי"צ) — המצב בא־ שראל משמש נושא לתגר־ ברבים מעתוני לונדון הבר־ בעל המאמר הראשי ב"סנ־ גראפיק" מותח בקורת קשה היזמה הנחפזת של ארצות־ ית. "הכרה במדינת ישראל ידי טרומן הנחיתה מכת־ כנראה לכל התקוות בד־ שביתת נשק או הסכם בין דים" אומר העתון. ושואל: התמיכה האמריקנית בי־ ים לא תעורר את הסובייטים יע ציוד ונשק לערבים, לא־ שהדיפלומטיה הסובייטית מאד גמישה והסכוי לקבל הנפט המזרח התיכוני עושה קולציה פוליטית ממין זה עסק מכניס ביותר". העתון מרני מסיים ואומר: "בינ־ ים אם אפילו אפשר יהיה לק־ את המדינה העברית נוכח בתם של מדינות ערב הרי שגשוגה של מדינת ישראל לא תיתכן בלי רצונם הטוב של הערבים".

"פיפל" עתון יום א' של הציבור מצדו כותב כי "בחוגים יודעי דבר בלונדון אשרו אמש, כי המלך עבדאללה כבר פתח בשיחות שלום סודיות. המלך עבדאללה הוא די פקח כדי להבין כי במוקדם או במאוחר תפתחנה שיחות לשלום אך הוא לא יג־ע לידי הסכם לפני שלא יוכל לרשום לזכותו כמה נצחונות, כדי לספק את האמביציות הערביות ולשפר את מצבו הוא".

סופרו של "סנדיי טיימס" ברבת עמון מדגיש את חולשתם הצבאות הערביים ומציין כי אין להם כל סכוי להשיג נצחונות אלא על ידי טכסיסי גרילה".

הפרשן הדיפלומטי של "סנדי דיספאטש" סבור כי "לא היהודים וגם לא הערבים אין בכוחם להשיג נצחון שלם". בהדגישו בין השאר כי רק ה"הגנה" ו־צבא עבר הירדן מהווים את הצבאות הממשיים הרי גם בן־גוריון וגם עבדאללה יהיו בסרפן של דבר נוטים לפשרה.

עתון איטלקי רואה את רוסיה מאחורי היהודים

רומא (סי"צ) המאורעות בארץ ישראל הם הנושא העיקרי בעתוני רומא הבוקר. "מסג'רו" הבלתי תלוי כותב כי "הבעיה נעשתה חמורה יותר מעבר לכל ההשערות עקב ההתחויות בין המעצמות הגדולות הלוחמות במזרח הקרוב כדי לקדם את האינטרסים הכלכליים והאסטרטגיים שלהם. מאחורי היהודים — אומר "מסג'רו" עומדת כפי הנראה רוסיה הסובייטית, שאינה מחמיצה כל הזדמנות כדי לגרום קשיים לבריטניה ולארצות הברית. ואילו אחרי הערבים עומד כל העולם המושלמי. אשר כפי הנראה יצא מתרדמתו וקרא מתוך יאוש ל"מלחמת קודש". "אי מומנטו" אומר שבמאבק המתנהל עכשיו בארץ ישראל נראה כי המנצח היחידי לפי שעה הוא הנשיא טרומאן, שרכש לעצמו חזרה את אהדת הצבור היהודי על ידי הכרתו במדינת ישראל אך "החידה הארצישראלית עוד רחוקה מפתרונה הסופי".

העתון הקומוניסטי "אוניטה" תוקף את האמריקנים, שעל ידי פרצופיותם עוררו את חמת חברי האומות המאוחדות ואשר לרגל זה סבלה קשות הפרסטיג'ה האמריקנית.

הממשלה תשכון ב־75 בנינים

עדיין לא הוחלט אם תל־אביב תהיה עיר בירה

75 בנינים נמסרו כבר כדי לשכן בתוכם את משרדי הממשלה של "מדינת ישראל".

עד עתה כבר הועברו לבנינים אלה: מיניסטריון לכספים, הנהלת הדאר, משרדו של ראש הממשלה, מיניסטריון החוץ, המיניסטריון למשפטים, אולפן הרדיו המרכזי, מפקדת המשטרה, המיניסטריון לעניני ערבים, מיניסטריון לעניני פנים, המחלקות לעניני תחבורה יבשתית, ימית ואוירית. המחלקות המלחמתיות (המפקח על המזונות, הפיקוח על המלאי וכו') מחלקת הימיה, הנמלים והרכבת, בית הדפוס הממשלתי וכו'.

יתכן שמיניסטריונים אחדים עוד ימשיכו לשכן במחלקות הקודמות כגון המיניסטריון לעליה, מסחר ותעשיה, המחלקה לעניני סים ואוצר העם ועוד.

למעשה, כל המשרדים והכלים לכינון המנגנון הממשלתי, מועברים על ידי העיריה לידי הממשלה. ד"ר ב. קרוגליאקוב המנהל את המחלקה לעניני הנכסים העירוניים — שמו יירשם בהיסטוריה של יום הקמת מדינתנו. הוא שקיבל לידיו את מאות חדרי המשרדים וכל האינוונטר שיש בהם, הוא שחתם בחתימת ידו ואישר את "העברת השלטון" ומידיו הנאמנות תקבל המדינה העברית את כל הרכוש הגדול הזה המגיע למאות אלפי לירות.

בעצמו לא ידע, שיש כל כך הרבה מחלקות ממשלתיות בתל אביב. נמסרו לו: בתי המכס, מחלקת העליה, הטאבו, מחלקת העבודה, מחלקת החינוך, מחלקה וטרינרית והמעבדה שבצדה, היחידה במינה במזרח התיכון כולו. עבודות ציבוריות עם ציוד עצום, סילות הברזל, כוניות רבות, מחלקת המסחר והתעשיה, מחלקת בנין ערים, משרדי המחוז לת"א המושבות מס ההכנסה ועוד.

כל זה עובר היום לידי הממשלה העברית. העיריה שימשה בתפקיד של "שבת גוי" — הבריטים לא רצו למסור את המשרדים לידי שלטון מרכזי יהודי ומסרום לידי העיריה שתהיה "קונה המץ"...

עדיין לא הוחלט שת"א תהיה בירתה של מדינת ישראל. הממשלה היא זמנית והבירה היא זמנית.

עוד היום והערב תשאנה תעודות־המלוה את החותמת «ביום העצמאות לישראל»

המוני תושבי ת"א התרכזו אמש ליד ששת האהלים שהוקמו במקומות מרכזיים של העיר וליד סניפי כל הבנקים כדי לחתום על המילוה הלאומי ולזכות בתעודות נושאות החותמת ההיסטורית "ביום העצמאות לישראל".

למעלה מ־5 אלפים איש עמדו בטורים ארוכים, ולמרות ההאפלה חיכו לתורם והתמו על סכום של עשרות אלפי לירות. אולם לא כולם הספיקו לחתום מפאת סגירת האהלים. לכן החליטו הנהלת המלוה והבנקים להמשיך בהחתמה עממית גם היום והערב בכל סניפי הבנקים ואהליהם מ־4 אחה"צ עד 12 בלילה. כל התעודות אשר יוצאו בשעות אלו תשאנה גם הן את החותמת "ביום העצמאות לישראל".

אהל מיוחד בשכ' התקוה

על פי בקשת תושבי שכ' התקוה והסביבה הוקם אהל מיוחד במרכז השכונה. מול בית המרקחת. עסקני השכונות קבלו על עצמם את היזמה לשתף את כל תושביהן בהחתמה העממית על המלוה הלאומי.

"MAAR… [illegible] כ[…]ז בחשון תשי"ז ★ 30 […]

המערכת, המנהלה והדפוס: ת"א רח' בני־ברק 20, טל. 9—67776. מחלקת המודעות: מזאה 52, טל. 67218, ת. ד. 1491; ירושלים: בית גדית, טל. 2352, 5895; חיפה: רח' הנביאים 32, טל. 3254, 66468. תאחראי: א. דיסנצ'יק. הסו"ל: הוצאת מודיעין בע"מ

המיסד [illegible] ר"ד עזריאל קרליבך ז"ל

70 פר'

דובר ירדני: בגבולנו שקט

דובר ירדני ציין ברבת עמון הבוקר, כי בגבול ישראל־ירדן שורר שקט. הדובר אמר, כי יחידות ירדניות "נכונות לכל" ונקטו בכל אמצעי הזהירות הדרושים, כדי לקדם התקפה ישראלית.

"ערכנו את כוחותינו" — אמר. "שיתקיפו הישראלים, אם הם רוצים בכך. הם ימצאו הפתעה בלתי נשימה מחכה להם, אם יעשו כן".

מעבר מנדלבאום נפתח הבוקר כרגיל בשעה שמונה, ללא כל שינוי. המכונית הראשונה שעברה בשער היתה ג'יפ של או"ם שהגיע למשרדי ועדת שביתת הנשק הישראלית־ירדנית.

התנועה בשער שכם ושער הורדוס הגיעו עשרות אוטובוסים מסביבות ירושלים. התנועה לרמאללה בצפון ולבית לחם בדרום נמשכת כרגיל.

לפי ידיעות מהימנות אינה מורגשת כל תכונה בסביבות ירושלים הערבית.

צה"ל מתבסס בחצי־האי סיני

הצבא המצרי הופתע — לא היה מוכן

צחות צה"ל, שפתחו אתמול במיבצע לחיסול התוקפנות המצרית, מתבססים בחצי האי סיני, לפי הידיעות שהגיעו לפני הצהרים.

עד עתה לא נודע על התנגדות רצינית מצד המצרים, שהופתעו הפתעה מוחלטת מן המיבצע הזה, אשר בוצע הרחק מן הריכוזי[illegible]ריים של הצבא המצרי [illegible] הכוחות המצריים מרוכזים [illegible] באזור רפיח – אל־עריש – אבו־עגילה ואיל־קוסימה. הם נאמדים בשלש דיביזיות של חיל־רגלים ודיביזיה אחת של שריון.

המפקד המצרי עמד הבוקר בפני בעייה קשה, כשצריך היה להחליט אם להשאיר את הריכוזים הגדולים האלה במקומם, אף על פי שהם מאוגפים ע"י הזרוע הארוכה ששלח צה"ל לתוך חצי האי סיני מדרום מערב לאזור חנייתם, או להזרים כוחות מצריים דרומה־מערבה לשם התמודדות עם כוחות צה"ל, ולהחליש בזה את המערך המצרי העיקרי מדרום־מערב לרצועת עזה ומול ניצנה.

לפי שעה אין סימנים לתזוזה מצרית בלב חצי האי סיני. מאידך מרוכזים כוחות מצריים נוספים באזור תעלת סואץ. ייתכן שאלה יתיצבו בדרכם של הכוחות הישראליים.

בהודעה שפורסמה היום לפנות בוקר ע"י מפקדת הכוחות המזויינים המצרים נקראו כל הקצינים והחיילים לחזור מיד לבסיסיהם. מפקדת חיל־התרבה והאספקה המצרית הודיעה, כי תדאג להסעת החיילים ליחידות שבאיזור הקרבות.

עד כה לא גילו המצרים שום פרטים על ממדי ההתנגשות ועל עומק החדירה הישראלית. גם בהודעתם ששודרה הבוקר מטעם מפקדת הצבא המצרי, חזרו על הגירסה, כי כוחות צה"ל פשטו לאיזור מדברי וריק **וכי עד שעות הבוקר המוקדמות לא היתה כל התנגשות בין הכוחות המצריים והישראליים.**

נאצר מתייעץ

מיד בהיוודע דבר ההתקפה הישראלית הזעיק אליו הרודן המצרי את מפקדי צבאו. סמוך לחצות הוא קיים עדיין התייעצויות עם מיניסטר המלחמה, הגנראל עאמר אשר חזר אתמול מדמשק לאחר דיונים פוליטיים צבאיים עם מפקדי צבאות ירדן וסוריה.

בניגוד לנימת התוקפנות והבטחון העצמי, שהפגינה העתונות המצרית ביחס לישראל עד כה, נשמע הבוקר קול ענות חלושה מבין טוריה של עתונות קאהיר.

המהדורות הראשונות של העתונות המצרית, שהופיעו בקאהיר בשעות הבוקר המוקדמות הכתירו את הפעולה הישראלית בכותרות אדומות ולרוחב כל העמודים.

בסאון הכת הצבאית השלטת, "אל־גומהורייה", כתב הבוקר במאמר ראשי, כי ישראל פתחה במלחמה בהיקף מלא וכי הדבר היה צפוי לאחר שהוכרזה פעולת הגיוס בצה"ל ולאחר שנדחתה פנייתו של נשיא ארצות הברית למר דוד בן גוריון. העתון טוען, כי מטרת הפעולה הישראלית היא פגיעה בכבוד מצרים ושבירת הגאווה הערבית וכי בחירת הזמן מעידה על "מזימה אימפריאליסטית" גדולה שישראל נוטלת בה חלק. "זוהי מלחמת חיים ומוות למצרים וכשם שנכשלו כל המזימות הקודמות תיכשל גם זו, כי לנו הנצחון". מסיים "אל־גומהורייה" את מאמרו הראשי.

העתון הבלתי תלוי והנפוץ ביותר במצרים, "אל־אהרם", נוקט נימה של התנצלות וטוען, כי הפיקוד המצרי־סורי־ירדני המשותף, ששימש עילה להתקפה הישראלית, לא נועד אלא לצרכי הגנה ולא הוקם אלא לאחר שהתוקפנות הישראלית הגיעה לשיאה. העתון מכנה את בן גוריון "בן דמים" ומנמק כינויו בספור הבא: "בשעה שבא מזכיר או"ם, מר דג האמרשילד, לביקורו האחרון בישראל, קיבל אותו מר דוד בן־גוריון כשהוא לבוש במדים צבאיים. כשהשתומם על כך מר האמרשילד, השיב בן גוריון: "אני תמיד מוכן למלחמה ולשפיכות דמים".

"אל־אהרם" מלמד סניגוריה על כוונות עיראק להיכנס לירדן ומבליט את רתיעתן של בריטניה ועיראק מפני צעד זה **עקב הלחץ הישראלי ולנוכח האיומים בפעולה ישראלית.**

העתון המצרי "אל אחבאר" קורא לשלוש מעצמות המערב להוכיח את ערכה של הצהרת

(סוף בעמוד 4)

ממשלת צרפת נועדה לישיבת־חרום

— מאת א. מאיסי, סופר "מעריב" בפאריס —

כניסת הכוחות הישראליים למצרים השפיעה בפאריס כפצצה.

הודעה על ישיבה מיוחדת של מועצת המיניסטרים הצרפתית הבוקר ב־9.30 לשם דיון בעניני המזרח התיכון, מוכיחה את החשיבות החיונית, שמייחסת הממשלה הצרפתית להתפתחות באזור הים התיכון המזרחי.

מקורות ישראליים מדגישים כי תכלית הפעולה הישראלית היא לשים קץ לחדירות הפדאיון.

אמש עם חצות נערכה התייעצות בין ראש הממשלה מר מולה מיניסטר החוץ כריסטיאן פינו, מיניסטר ההגנה מר מוריס בורז'ס־מונורי וסגן המיניסטר לעניני הצבא מר מאכס לזן.

הפגישה הדחופה נמשכה 40 דקה. בצאת המיניסטרים מארמון ראש הממשלה, בשעה 12.45 סירבו להשיב על שאלות העתונאים.

מקורות רשמיים למחצה הבהירו, כי צרפת איננה מרוצה מעמדתו של הנשיא אייזנהאואר, שציין מראש את ישראל כתוקפנית באזהרתו לראש הממשלה מר ד. בן־גוריון. צרפת, אומרים מקורות אלה, מבינה בהחלט שיש הכרח להביא בחשבון את התנהגותן הפרובוקטיבית של מדינות ערב.

ארה"ב הזעיקה את מועצת הבטחון

ידונו הערב במבצע צה"ל. – נציגי צרפת ובריטניה מחכים להוראות

— מאת ה. יוסטוס, סופר "מעריב" בארה"ב —

וואשינגטון נטלה בידיה את היזמה לפעולה נגד "ההתקפה" הישראלית, ולפי בקשתה תתכנס מועצת הבטחון היום אחר הצהרים (בשעה 6 בערב לפי שעון ישראל) לשם דיון במיבצע של צה"ל במדבר סיני.

הנשיא אייזנהאואר הפסיק את מסע מערכת הבחירות שלו, כדי להיפגש עם מיניסטר החוץ מר ג'ון פוסטר דאלס. אחר כך יצא בגילוי דעת, כי מנוי וגמור עם ארה"ב לקיים את הבטחתה לבוא לעזרת כל קרבן של תוקפנות במזרח התיכון, בהתאם להכרזת שלוש המעצמות משנת 1950. כן דיבר על האפשרות של כינוס מושב מיוחד של הקונגרס.

בריטניה וצרפת מגלות הסתייגות מסויימת לגבי צעדי וואשינגטון. מקורות בריטיים וצרפתיים בוואשינגטון אמרו, שיבקשו הוראות מאת ממשלותיהם.

נשיא מועצת הבטחון, מר קורני־ז'אנסי מצרפת, אמר לאחר פגישה עם מזכיר האו"ם, מר דאג האמרשילד, ועם נציגי בריטניה וארה"ב כי הוא "מחכה לידיעות נוספות". הוא הוסיף, ש"אפשר" להעלות את ענין ישראל ומצרים בהתכנס מועצת הבטחון היום לחידוש הדיון בתלונות ישראל וירדן.

דיפלומאט בריטי בוואשינגטון אמר, כי תגובת הישראלים על התקפות ה"פראיון" איננה מפתיעה לגמרי.

פקידי מיניסטריון החוץ האמריקני אומרים, שקרוב לודאי כי שלושת הגדולים יביאו לפני מועצת הבטחון הצעת־החלטה, שתציין את התוקפן. במקרה זה, תדרוש הפסקת האש מיד ותעיין בעונש על אי־ציות.

"ניו יורק טיימס" מודיע ממרכז האו"ם, כי אחדות מן המשלחות נוטות לראות את פעולתה של ישראל כפעילת תגמול ולא כמבצע מלחמתי.

פגישות הנשיא

בראשונה עמד הנשיא אייזנהאור להיפגש רק עם מר דאלס לדיון במשבר החדש, אך ברגע האחרון הוחלט להרחיב את הפגישה והשתתפו בה רוב חברי מועצת הבטחון הלאומי של ארה"ב: מיניסטר ההגנה מר צ'ארלס ווילסון, סגן מיניסטר החוץ מר הרברט הובר הבן, יושב־ראש המטות המאוחדים אדמיראל רדפורד, מנהל סוכנות המודיעין המרכזית מר אלן דאלס, ומר שרמן אדאמס, שרי המיוחד של הנשיא.

מזכיר העתונות של הנשיא, מר ג'יימס האגרטי, שמסר לעתונאים את הודעתו של אייזנהאור לאחר הפגישה עם מועצת הבטחון הלאומי, סירב להשיב על שאלות, וביחוד נמנע מלומר, אם הנשיא ועוזריו כבר החליטו בדעתם, שישראל היא התוקפנית

סנקציות — מה פירושן

לפי סעיפי מגילת האו"ם, הדנים באיומים על השלום, יכולה מועצת הבטחון לקרוא למדינות חברות האו"ם לנתק את היחסים הדיפלומאטיים עם מדינה שהוכרזה כתוקפנית, ולהטיל סאנקציות כלכליות, כגון הפסקת התחבורה בים, ביבשה ובאוויר, הפסקת קשר הראדיו והטלגראף והטלפון וכו'. אם פעולות אלה אינן מספיקות, אפשר "לנקוט פעולות של כוחות ים, יבשה או אוויר לפי הצורך לשם קיום או חידוש של השלום והבטחון הבינלאומיים".

„יותר מדי בשביל פעולת תגמול פחות מדי בשביל מלחמה ממש"

— מאת סופר מיוחד —

„הפעולה בחצי האי סיני היא גדולה מדי משתהיה פעולת־תגמול וקטנה מדי משיראו בה מלחמה" — במלים אלו הגדיר אמש אחר חצות מקור ממשלתי גבוה את מהות החדירה הישראלית לאדמת מצרים.

המקור, שתיאר כך את המצב בשעה שכוחות ישראל כבר היו במרחק כ־30 ק"מ מהסואץ הוסיף ואמר:

מה שמציין פעולה זו ומבדיל אותה ממלחמה היא העובדה, שלא הופעלו בה כוחות אויר, ומה שמבדיל אותה מפעולת־תגמול הוא בזה, שכוחות ישראל אינם חוזרים לבסיסיהם עם תום פעולת חיסול קני הפדאיון, אלא מתבססים במקומותיהם".

כשנשאל מקור רשמי אחר חצות אם הפעולות קשורות **עם המצב בסואץ**, אמר הדובר "זאת איני יודע!"

מקור ממשלתי הדגיש, כי הפעולה בחצי־האי סיני בוצעה לאחר ששם היה מרכז המפקדה והאימונים של חוליות הפדאיון אשר פעלו בישראל מרצועת עזה, מירדן, מסוריה ומלבנון.

הפעולה היתה הכרח — אמר המקור — כיון שהפדאיון הסכו באחרונה כוח צבאי גדול.

אמנם שרר במשך כמה שבועות שקט יחסי בגבולות מצרים, היות שנאצר היה טרוד במשבר סואץ. אך לאחר שמועצת הבטחון סיימה את דיוני סואץ, נתחדשו בשבוע האחרון פעולות־הדמים של ה"פדאיון".

הפעולות לסיכון ישראל הגיעו לשיאן אתמול כאשר יחידות צי־המלחמה המצרי — משחתת אחת, שתי מטילות־מוקשים ואניה רביעית שלא זוהתה — יצא מבסיסן באלכסנדריה לעבר חופי ישראל.

כשנשאל המקור על כוונות הפעולה וכיוונה אמר: **עמדת צבאנו והיקף פעולתו תלויים במצב.**

בתשובה לשאלה, אם עיראק הוזהרה לפני התחלת הפעולה במצרים, שלא לחדור לירדן, אמר המקור: "אזהרת שרת החוץ, הגב' גולדה מאיר, ששודרה בשבת ב"קול ישראל", יש לפרשה כאזהרה אחרונה".

ברנס מבקש הפסקת אש

ראש משקיפי האו"ם, הגנרל ברנס, פנה אמש אחרי חצות באגרת דחופה לשרת החוץ מרת גולדה מאיר ודרש מישראל הפסקת־אש מידית והתחלת פו"מ על הוצאת כוחות ישראל מחצי האי סיני.

הגנרל ברנס ביקש פגישה דחופה עם שרת החוץ. ייתכן שלמרות טרדותיה הרבות במשך היום יתקבל הגנרל ברנס על ידה, אולם השעה המדוייקת טרם נקבעה.

קנדה דנה בענין ה"סייברים"

ממשלת קאנאדה החליטה לעיין מחדש בהחלטתה כדבר היתר מכירת 24 מטוסי קרב סילוניים "סייבר ג'ט" לישראל, — על זאת נמסרה הודעה באוטאווה אמש.

מיניסטר החוץ, מר לסטר פירסון אמר אמש, כי אף אחד מן המטוסים לא יצא עדיין מקאנאדה, ולאור ההתפתחות החדשה במזרח התיכון מעיינת הממשלה בשאלה, אם היא יכולה להרשות את משלוח המטוסים.

אזרחים אמריקניים באים להיפרד מהקונסול ולקבל את דרכוניהם — לפני צאתם מן הארץ

שגרירים "בתור" – לפגישה עם ג. מאיר

— מאת סופר מיוחד —

שרת החוץ גב' גולדה מאיר עמדה הלילה והבוקר תחת "מצור" של שגרירים וצירי מדינות חוץ בישראל, שביקשו להיפגש עמה, כדי לקבל הסברים על המצב.

ראשון נתקבל על ידי שרת־החוץ השגריר הבריטי, סיר ג'ון ניקולס. הוא נפגש עמו עוד לפני שנתפרסם דבר החדירה הישראלית למצרים. שרת החוץ הסתפקה בהסברת המניעים לגיוס.

עתונאי, שביקש לדעת, אם שופרו היחסים בין ישראל ובין בריטניה מאז המתיחות לפני כ־10 ימים, קיבל את התשובה הבאה מדובר ממשלתי: "מספיק להאזין לרדיו המזרח הקרוב הבריטי בקפריסין ולדברי הסתתו, כדי להיווכח שלא חל כל שיפור ביחסים".

מיד לאחר שנודע דבר הפעולה הישראלית בחצי־האי סיני נתקבל לשיחה ע"י שרת החוץ השגריר הצרפתי, מר פייר ז'ילבר.

השגרירים הסובייטי, האיטלקי והתורכי אף הם היו בתור להתקבל במשך הלילה והבוקר. בינתים נרשמו לשיחות גם רבים אחרים מהקורפוס הדיפלומטי.

שני פקידים בכירים של משרד החוץ צורפו הלילה מאתמול למפקדת הפעולה, כדי לעמוד לצד ראש הממשלה ושר הבטחון בעצה.

דחיית שרות פעיל

ניתנת בזה לפירסום רשימת הכתובות של הועדות האזוריות לדחיית שרות פעיל:

ירושלים — קצין העיר ירושלים, רח' החבצלת 2. תל־אביב — קצין העיר תל־אביב, רח' הירקון 71. חיפה — רח' פרץ 10. פתח־תקוה — לשכת הגיוס פתח־תקוה, שכון פג'ה. צפת — משטרת הר כנען. טבריה — רח' הכנרת. עפולה — רח' יהושע 37. חדרה — שד"ר. רמלה — קצין העיר רמלה, רח' הרצל. רחובות — רח' הרצל 187. נתניה — רח' סמילנסקי.

מעריב

שנה תשיעית גליון מס. 2692 | יום ו' ★ כ"ח בחשון תשי"ז ★ 2 בנובמבר 1956

150 פר'

המערכת, המנהלה והדפוס: ת"א רח' בני־ברק 20, טל. 9—67776, מחלקת המודעות: מזאה 52, טל. 67218, ת. ד. 1491; ירושלים: בית גזית, טל. 2352, 5895; חיפה: רח' הנביאים 32, טל. 3254, 66468, תאחראי: א. דיסנצ'יק; המו"ל: הוצאת מודיעין בע"מ

המיסד והעורך הראשון ד"ר עזריאל קרליבך ז"ל

הוצאה מיוחדת

עם תוספת – 150 פרוטה

בלי תוספת – 70 פרוטה

עזה נכנעה

העיר עזה נכנעה בפני כוחות צה"ל. בשורה זו נמסרה סמוך לשעה עשר בבוקר ע"י דובר הצבא

מטה משטרת באר־שבע יצא לעזה, כדי להבטיח סדר ברצועה.

רצועת עזה, שהוחזקה בידי הפולש המצרי מאז מלחמת השחרור, שימשה בסיס למעשי רצח ותוקפנות נגד מדינת ישראל. במשך שמונה שנים המרידו אנשי „פדאיון" מה־רצועה, את תושבי ישראל.

לאחר שצה"ל השלים אתמול את ניתוק רצועת עזה, עם כי־בוש רפיח, החל כוח צבאי ל־התקרב למבואות העיר. חיל ה־מצב בעזה, המורכב בעיקר מ־פלשתינאים שאומנו ע"י הצבא המצרי, הניח את נשקו לפני כוחות צה"ל שעלו על העיר.

עוד בשעה 9 בבוקר הודיע רדיו לונדון, כי קרבות רחוב מתנהלים בעיר.

מרצחי ה„פדאיון" ניסו ב־24 השעות האחרונות לפרוץ את טבעת הניתוק ולברוח לירדן. תוך כדי מנוסתם ביצעו מעשי רצח בארץ. עתה הגיעה שעת החשבון אתם.

„רצועת עזה" שנוצרה על פי הסכמי שביתת הנשק משנת 1949, אורכה 40 ק"מ ורוחבה הממוצע 8 ק"מ. מספר תושביה נאמד אומדנות שונים מ־250 עד 310 אלף. רק 95 אלף הם תושבי קבע של הרצועה.

אל-עריש נכבשה

אל־עריש, העיר היחידה בחצי האי סיני נכ־בשה ע"י כוחות צה"ל.

על כיבוש העיר הודיע דובר צה"ל הבוקר.

אל־עריש מונה כעשרת אל־פים תושבים ומשמשת מרכז אדמיניסטרטיבי לחצי האי. על אף קירבתה לים התיכון אין יורדים בה גשמים יותר מאשר בחוף אילת. מפעלי השקאה, ש־נעשו ביוזמת הבריטים, איפשרו פיתוח חקלאות. חורשות דקלים וציד השלוים מהווים מקורות פרנסה לתושבים. מקור־הכנסות אחר של תושבי העיר הוא מתן הלוואות ברבית לבדווי חצי ה־אי, הנזקקים להלוואות, כדי ל־התקיים בשנות בצורת. אל־עריש אף משמשת שוק לבדווים בצפון חצי האי.

הושמדו 50 מטוסים מצריים ו־40 נפגעו

בהפצצות בריטיות־צרפתיות. – הוצתה משחתת מצרית „סקורי"

למעלה מחמשים מטוסים מצריים הושמדו על ה־קרקע ולפחות ארבעים מטוסים נפגעו קשה – נמסר בהודעה של מיניסטריון ההגנה הבריטי.

בהודעה שפורסמה אחת ה־צות הלילה, נאמר, כי פעולות חילות האוויר של בריטניה ו־צרפת, שתכליתן לשתק את חיל האוויר המצרי, עברו את־מול מהפצצת ..דות תעופה צ־באיים להתקפות על מטוסים בודדים ועל מיתקני שדות ה־תעופה. עד כה אין ידיעות על אבידות של חילות האוויר של הברית.

ההודעה אומרת, שלפי אומ־דן הושמדו למעלה מחמישים מטוסים מצריים על הקרקע, ו־לכל הפחות 40 ניזוקו נזקים רציניים.

ההודעה מוסיפה, כי שדה ה־תעופה הצבאי המערבי של ה־עיר קאהיר הופצץ אתמול ב־פעם הראשונה. עד כה לא פע־לו נגד שדה תעופה זה, עד ש־שיירת המטוסים, המוציאים א־זרחי אמריקה מבירת מצרים, התרחקו מן הסביבה.

גם „אילושינים" הושמדו

בין המטוסים המצריים, ש־הושמדו או שניזוקו היו כנראה מפציצים סילוניים מתוצרת סובייטית, מדגם „איליושין 28". מטוסים אלה חנו בשדה ה־תעופה הצבאי המערבי של קאהיר.

משחתת מצרית, מדגם „סקורי" הסובייטי, הות־קפה והוצתה באש את־מול בבוקר בחוף אלכסנ־דריה ע"י מטוסי חיל הים הצרפתי. המשחתות מ־סוג זה חן בנות 3000 טונה.

ש. לוי – למנוחות

שבתי לוי, שכיהן שנים רבות כראש עיריית חיפה, נפטר את־מול אחה"צ בגיל 82. הלויתו תצא היום ב־12 בצהרים מרח־בת העיריה בחיפה.

הניח בן ושלש בנות.

אהרון שורצמן מקוריץ, נפטר הלילה. ההלויה תצא מ־בי"ח הדסה היום בשעה 12.

7 יהודים נהרגו בהתקפות „פדאיון"

6 נספו במיקוש טנדר.– אחד נהרג בתקומה.– ה„מתאבדים" בורחים לירדן

מספר ניכר של חוליות „פדאיון" פעלו הלילה ב־מרכזי הנגב. הותקפו מספר מכוניות ופוצצו צנורות ומעבירי מים – מוסר דובר הצבא. עד כה נודע על 7 הרוגים.

6 יהודים נהרגו אתמול אחר הצהרים כאשר טנדר עלה על מוקש בסביבות קבוץ ארז שליד רצועת עזה.

2 מההרוגים הם שמחה קוריכמן, מנהל „מקורות" ב־דרום, ושלמה קליגשטיין, מרא־שוני אשקלון.

שמחה קוריכמן, בן 46, עמד בראש מפעל המים בכל רחבי הדרום והנגב, ובתוקף תפקידו היה נמצא בדרכים בכל עת. אף בימי המתיחות הגדולה ביר־תר. עשרות פעמים, ממלחמת השחרור ואילך ובעת כל מסעי ה„פדאיך", חירף את נפשו כדי להבטיח אספקת מים סדירה ל־ישובי הנגב. יד ה„פדאיך" השי־גתו בשעה שמשמש ובא קצין של כנופיות המרצחים.

הוא הניח אחריו אשה, בן ובת נשואה.

שלמה גליקשטיין, בן 31, מותיקי אשקלון, הניח אחריו אשה וילדה. אחיו של גליק־שטיין נסע במכונית מאחורי הטנדר וראה את ההתפוצצות בה מצא אחיו את מותו.

עוד אזרח אחד שהיה בטנדר נפצע.

קבוצה גדולה של אנשי פד־אין, כשתי עשרות במספר, הת־קיפה אמש את מושב תלמים בנגב הצפוני. איש לא נפגע.

בהתקפה על מושב תקומה נהרג תושב אחד.

כן פעלו אנשי פדאין בכביש באר שבע. צרורות מנשק אר־טומטי נורו אמש בשעה 6.30 על שתי מוניות שנסעו בין בית קמה ואחוזם. באותו קטע פר־צץ גשר אירי.

בשעה יותר מאוחרת עלה קו־מנדקאר על מוקש בסביבות שעה 9.00. לפי ידיעה ראשונה נפגעו כמה אזרחים שבו.

כוחות הבטחון סבורים, כי חוליות ה„פדאיך" אשר פעלו ב־לילה האחרון בנגב ובדרום שמו פעמיהם לגבול ירדן, כיוון ש־נשמט מהם בסיסם ברצועת עזה.

ארבעה אנשי „פדאיך" נהרגו ואחד נתפס כשהוא מצוע בקרב שהיה ביום שני לפנות ערב בין יחידת בטחון ישראלית לבין חולית האויב בגזרת נצנים, מצ־פון לאשקלון.

„הגיע יום הדין של הפדאיון"

„חוי ה„פדאיון" ברצועת עזה, סוף סוף בא יום הדין! – אזהרה זו שודרה ב„קול ישר־אל" ברציפות בשידוריו הער־ביים החל מחצות אמש.

„עם ניתוקה המוחלט של ר־צועת עזה ממצרים" – נאמר בתחילת דברי האזהרה – „בא השלטון המצרי ברצועה לקצו. ועתה נשארו ה„פידאיון" בעזה לבדם מול כוחות צה"ל המש־תלטים וההולכים על הרצועה.

„שמונה שנים השתוללו ה„פידאיון" ברצועת עזה, הסת־ננו לישראל, חבלו ברכוש ד־רצחו תושבים שוחרי־שלום, אולם עתה הגיעה שעת החש־בון. שמותיהם של ה„פידאיון" ידועים".

„מטוסים בריטיים וצרפתיים בישראל"

נציגות מצרים באו"ם פירסמה הודעה האומרת, כי מטוסים בריטיים וצרפתיים משתמשים בשדות תעופה ישראליים.

נציגי ארה"ב ובריטניה מכריזים בעצרת או"ם:

„לא די בהסכמי שביתת נשק"

— מאת ה. יוסטוס, סופר „מעריב" בארה"ב —

נציגי ארה"ב ובריטניה הדגישו שניהם, במושב המיוחד של עצרת האו"ם, אשר נתכנסה הלילה, כי הסכמי שביתת הנשק אינם מספיקים לקיים את ה־שלום. שניהם עמדו על הצורך, שהמושב הרגיל הבא של העצרת ידון דיון יסודי בכל הבעיה הארצישרא־לית.

הבוקר חידשה העצרת את דיוניה. הנואם הראשון הוא שגריר ישראל מר א. אבן.

6 תמציתם של תכנית דאלס

(יו. פ.). מר דאלס הציע לפני העצרת תכנית של שש נקודות:

● העצרת רואה כדחוף ביותר שכל הצדדים המעורבים עתה במעשי איבה באזור המז־רח התיכון, יסכימו להפסקת ה־אש מיד, ויפסיקו כניסת כוחות צבאיים ונשק בתוך האזור.

● היא קוראת לצדדים התחר־מים על הסכמי שביתת הנשק להחזיר מיד את כוחותיהם אל מאחורי קוי שביתת הנשק, ל־המנע מפשיטות אל הטריטוריות השכנות, ולקיים בדייקנות את הוראות הסכמי שביתת הנשק.

● העצרת ממליצה שכל חברי האו"ם יימנעו מלשלוח צרכי צבא לאזור מעשה האיבה, יי־מנעו מכל פעולה העלולה ל־השהות ביצוע החלטה זו.

● העצרת תובעת שעם הפס־קת האש ייעשו צעדים לפתוח שוב את תעלת סואץ ולחדש את חופש השיט.

● היא מבקשת מן המזכיר ה־כללי לעקוב אחר ביצוע החלטה זו ולהודיע מיד למועצת הבט־חון ולעצרת על פעולות נוספות הנחוצות לדעתו בהתאם למגי־לה.

● העצרת מחליטה להמשיך את מושב החירום עד שתבוצע החלטה זו.

תים במיבצעם, בוזאת שלל את סוכנות־היסוד הבריטית.

בעת שהעצרת דנה בפרשת מצרים נודע, כי איטליה אומרת להביא לפני העצרת מיד את קריאתה של הונגאריה. ביחוד נוכח הידיעות כי בודאפשט הו־פצצה על ידי מטוסים סובייטיים.

עצרת האו"ם הסכימה לש־מוע שלושה נציגים בעד הה־צעה האמריקנית ושלושה נג־דה, לפני שתיערך הצבעה. כן יישמעו דבריהם של הנואמים שנרשמו לויכוח. רשימת הנו־אמים היא: ישראל, אקוואדור, אוסטראליה, יוגוסלאביה, צר־פת, הודו, סעודיה וניו־זילאנד.

ההצבעה על הצעת ההחלטה האמריקנית תיערך כנראה עוד היום לפני הצהרים.

ברגע האחרון

עצרת האו"ם קיבלה היום ב־רוב מכריע את הצעת ההחלטה האמריקנית הקוראת להפסקת אש מידית במצרים, והמביעה דאגה חמורה על הפעולות ה־צבאיות של ישראל בסיני, ושל בריטניה ושל צרפת באזור סו־אץ.

בעד ההצעה האמריקנית הצ־ביעו 64 מדינות, ונגדה – יש־ראל, בריטניה, צרפת, ניו־זי־לאנד ואוסטראליה.

נמנעו מהצבעה בלגיה, קא־נאדה, לאוס, הולאנד, פורטו־גאל ודרום אפריקה.

עם זה נודע, כי ארה"ב מת־כוונת להציע – כנראה ביום ד', בהתכנס מועצת הבטחון ל־דיון בתלונות ישראל וירדן – לחזק מיד את ארגון המשקיפים של האו"ם ואת הוועדה המשותפת לשביתת הנשק ישראל־ירדן פ־ויוס לארץ־ישראל.

הצעת ההחלטה האמ־ריקנית שהוגשה לעצרת־ממליצה על הפסקת אש גמורה והוצאת הכוחות הישראליים מגבולות מצ־רים. ההחלטה איננה קוראת ליציאת כוחות בריטניה וצרפת, אם כי עלו בינתים על אדמת מצרים.

רק בריטניה וצרפת הצביעו נגד העלאת הצעת ההחלטה ה־אמריקנית על סדר היום. שבעה נציגים, ובתוכם ישראל, נמנעו מהצבעה. האחרים שנמנעו הם: אוסטרליה, דרום־אפריקה, קנ־דה, ניו־זילנד, תור יה והולנד.

הנציג הבריטי, סיר פירסון, הדגיש את חומר המצב שהצ־ריך התערבות בריטית־צרפ־תית, ואלו מר דאלס טען כי „תהליכים של שלום" התנהלו בעת שפתחו הבריטים והצרפ־

צבא סובייטי חודר להונגריה

טנקים רוסיים מקיפים את בודפשט

— מאת דוד גלעדי, שליח „מעריב" בהונגריה —

יצאתי מבודפשט המנותקת בשעה שטנקים רו־סיים התחילו לסגור את העיר בטבעת של פלדה.

עיר־הבירה ההונגרית היתה שרויה באוירה של חופש. כל המפלגות הישנות קמו לתחיה ו־גם חדשות נוסדו. בעיר פועלות שבע מפלגות, שכל אחת מהן התחילה להוציא עתון משלה ופתחה משרדיה וכוננה הנהגתה. בכל משרד ומפעל החל איתור של אלמנטים סטאליניסטיים ו־מצוד כללי על חברי המשטרה הפוליטית. כמה מבצרים של משטרה זו נכבשו בכוח הנשק וכל יושביהם נקטלו או שנל־חמו עד סופם המר.

מאז שככו הקרבות ביום ג' התנהל מו"מ קדחתנית לכי־נון ממשלה קואליציונית. ממ־שלת מעבר עד הבחירות. לנאג' היו סכויים טובים לגמור משא־ומתן זה בהצלחה. לאחר שהשיג הסכמת מיקויאן להוצאת הכר־חות הרוסיים מבודפשט ובהד־רגה מכל הונגריה. אך במוסק־בה החליטו, כנראה, בינתיים אחרת, ונתנו פקודה לשריונים לעלות על הבירה ההונגרית, ה־שיכורה משמחת הדרור והעצמ־אות.

לפני כן נמסר, כי הונגריה עזבה את ברית ורשה ופנתה בקריאה לארבעת הגדולים ל־ערוב לנייטרליותה.

ליהודי בודפשט שלום ולא היו שום פגיעות ב־הם.

(רויטר) כוחות סובייט־יים חדשים נכנסים להונ־גאריה מרומניה ומברית המועצות, – מודיע כתב „פוליטיקה" הבלגראדי בבודא־פשט.

הכתב מוסיף, כי ריכוזי צבא גדולים בצד ארוסי של הגבול ההונגארי היו מוכנים אמש ל־היכנס להונגאריה. כל הדרכים בהונגאריה המזרחית מוצפות חיילים וטאנקים סובייטיים.

בבודאפשט התחדשו חילופי יריות כבדים, לפי ידיעה שהגי־עה מן העיר בהשכמת הבוקר מבלגראד.

ברחובות מקימים מחסומים ונשמעים מטחי מקלעים.

(יו. פי.) רדיו בודפשט הו־דיע, כי חיל האויר ההונגארי מוכן להתנגדות לכניסת הרו־סים, אולם הממשלה נתנה לה הוראה שלא לפתוח באש.

נוסעים שחזרו אמש בשעה מאוחרת מבודאפשט לוינה, סיפרו, כי שמעו וראו הפצצה כבדה של שדה התעופה סאסא באזור דיור.

עם זה נפוצו בוינה שמועות על קרבות בין כוחות סובייט־יים והונגארים, אך לא היה אי־שור לכך.

לדברי ראדיו בודאפשט הו־דיעה השגרירות הסובייטית ל־ממשלה ההונגארית, כי הכוחות הסובייטיים הקיפו את שדות־התעופה, כדי להבטיח הוצאת החיילים והפצועים הסובייטים.

סין תומכת בפולין ובהונגריה

בהודעה של סין העממית, א־שר שודרה ברדיו פקין, נאמר כי סין מביעה תמיכתה בדרי־שות של ממשלת הונגריה ופו־לין לדמוקרטיה, עצמאות יש־וין ולצמצים הקשרים עם ב־רית המועצות.

מעריב

יום א' * ל' בחשון תשי"ז * 4 בנובמבר — גליון מס' 2093

70 פרי

המערכת, המנהלה והדפוס: ת"א רח' בני־ברק 20 טל. 9—67776 מחלקת המודעות: מזאה 52, טל. 67218; ת. ד. 1491; ירושלים: בית גזית, טל 2352, 5895; חיפה: רח' הנביאים 32, טל. 3254, 66468; האחראי: א. דיסנצ'יק; המו"ל: הוצאת מודיעין בע"מ

המיסד והעורך הראשי: ד"ר עזריאל קרליבך ז"ל

הוצאה אחרונה

נפרץ הסגר אילת

חוסל הכוח המצרי אשר קיים את המצור ומיע כניסת אניות ישראל

ייתכן שכבר הערב אפשר יהיה לפרסם הודעה האומרת, שהחוף המזרחי של חצי האי סיני נוקה מכוחות האויב. פירוש הדבר, כי ההסגר, אשר המצרים הטילו על נמל אילת — נפרץ.

ההסגר קוים על ידי פריגאטה מצרית, שהיתה משוטטת בים סוף, ועל ידי סוללת תותחים, שהציב הצבא המצרי באי טיראן, בכניסה למפרץ אילת. לאחר שחיל הים המצרי הוכה מכה ניצחת על ידי חיל הים הישראלי, וכן על ידי הפעולות האויריות של כוחות צרפת ובריטניה, שוב אין בכוחו לקיים הסגר על החוף הישראלי. ואילו סוללת התותחים המצרית באי שבמבוא מפרץ אילת — אפילו עדיין לא נלכדה על ידי כוחות צה"ל, העוסקים בביעור קני ההתנגדות האחרונים בחצי האי סיני, שוב אין לה כל קשר עם מצרים. אין ביכלתה של סוללת־תותחים זו להחזיק מעמד בלי אספקה ואפשרות חילוף.

כל התכניות שנרקמו בקשר לפיתוחו של נמל גדול באילת, אשר ישמש שערה של ישראל למזרח הרחוק, נכנסו עתה לשלב של התגשמות.

מאות אנשי „פדאיון" נתפסו בעזה

העוצר בעיר הוסר זמנית. — אנשי או"ם חזרו ומחלקים מזון לפליטים

נודע, כי עד־כה נעצרו ברצועת כמה מאות אנשי „פדאיון".

העוצר בעזה הופר הבוקר זמנית, כדי שהתושבים יוכלו להצטייד במיצרכי מזון. ואמנם מיד עם הסרת העוצר הסתערו התושבים על חנויות המכולת שבעיר.

עם שוך הקרבות והשלטת סדר בעיר, חזרו לעזה אנשי אונרוו"א, מוסד הסעד של האו"ם, הדואג לכלכלת הפליטים באזור עזה. הם פתחו מחדש את משרדיהם והתחילו בחלוקת מזון לפליטים. אך חיש מהר נתברר, כי חלק ממחסני המזון נשדד ע"י ערבים בין שעת יציאתם מהעיר בעת הקרבות לבין שעת כניסתם של חיילי צה"ל.

חולית משטרת ישראל, שנכנסה לעיר כדי לפקח על הסדר האזרחי, הגבירה שרותיה ע"י גיוסם למשטרה של שוטרים ערביים פלשתינאיים ממשטרת פלשתינה־א"י לשעבר.

הוקלה ההאפלה

מותר להאיר הבתים

הערב מותר יהיה להאיר את בתי המגורים.

הודעה של מפקדת הג"א, שנתפרסמה היום אחר הצהרים, מכילה הקלות רבות בתקנות האיפול.

מותר יהיה להאיר לא רק בתי מגורים, אלא גם בתי עסק כל זמן שהם פתוחים, רק יוארו מחדש רחובות הערים. גם כלי רכב יוכלו לנסוע באור מלא.

אולם כל ההקלות יבוטלו ברגע שינתן אות אזעקה.

ראה המודעה בעמוד ד'

ב. ג. ימסור הודעה בכנסת ביום ד'

ראש הממשלה מר ד. בן־גוריון עומד למסור ביום ד' הודעה בכנסת על המצב הצבאי והמדיני.

החלטה על מועד שמיעת ההודעה הממשלתית נתקבלה הבוקר בישיבה של נשיאות הכנסת.

ההצעה של מק"י להביע אי־אמון לממשלה תועלה על סדר־היום של הכנסת בישיבתה ביום ד'.

קהיר: אין לנו מלחמה בישראל אלא באנגליה ובצרפת

„אידן מנסה לשוא לגולל את אשמת המלחמה התוקפנית על ישראל, אך המלחמה איננה מתנהלת בין ישראל לבין מצרים, אלא בין בריטניה וצרפת לבין מצרים" — זאת נאמר הבוקר בהודעה של ממשלת מצרים, אשר באה כתגובה על נאומו של אידן בפרלמנט הבריטי.

ההודעה מדגישה מספר פעמים, כי בין מצרים לישראל אינו קיים מצב של מלחמה.

הממשלה: אנו מוכנים לשלוח מיד נציגים למו"מ עם נציגי מצרים על שלום

ישראל מסכימה להפסקת אש מידית תוך הנחה, כי הסכמה דומה ניתנת על ידי מצרים.

ישראל רואה את המוצא היחיד מן המצב בכריתת שלום עם מצרים בדרך של מו"מ ישיר בין שני העמים. הממשלה מוכנה לשגר מיד את נציגיה לפגישה עם נציגי מצרים.

על עמדה זו החליטה הממשלה בישיבה מיוחדת שנערכה אמש בראשותו של ראש הממשלה.

בישיבה זו דנה הממשלה במצב ועיינה בהמלצת כנס החרום של עצרת האו"ם מה־2 בנובמבר. הממשלה הורתה את נציגות ישראל באו"ם להעביר לנשיא כנס החרום של העצרת את ההודעה הבאה:

„לדגל החלטת כנס החרום המיוחד של עצרת או"ם מיום 2 בנובמבר 1956 מתכבדת ממשלת ישראל להודיע את הדברים הבאים:

1. ישראל מסכימה להפסקת אש מידית תוך הנחה, כי הסכמה דומה ניתנת על ידי מצרים.

2. מצרים שטענה הזור ושנון במשך שנים, כי מצב מלחמה שורר בינה לבין ישראל. על ידי כך סילפה מצרים את עצם טעמו ותכליתו של הסכם שביתת הנשק, המבקש כמפורש להשיב את השלום על כנו, ואילו מצרים ניצלה הסכם זה לשם חיפוי על התקפות רצחניות נגד תושבי ישראל ועל מצור אכזרי על המדינה ביבשה, בים ובאויר. שבוע־שבוע וחודש־חודש חדרו לשטח ישראל חוליות הצבא המצרי המכונות „פדאיון" המאומנות אימון מיוחד למטרה

(הסוף בעמוד ד')

העצרת מתכנסת לדיון על הונגריה

אולטימטום סובייטי: נפציץ את בודפשט אם לא תיכנע

מושב מיוחד של עצרת או"ם עומד להתכנס היום, לאחר שברית המועצות הטילה וטו במועצת הבטחון על הצעת ההחלטה של המערב, הקוראת למוסקבה להפסיק את התערבותה הצבאית בהונגריה.

◆ בינתיים מגיעות ידיעות מבירת הונגריה, כי הכוחות הסובייטיים השתלטו אחרי קרבות כבדים על בנין הפארלמנט בבודאפשט ואסרו את ראש הממשלה אימרה נג' וחברים אחרים של ממשלתו.

◆ עם סגירת הגליון נמסר: ברית המועצות הגישה אולטימאטום לממשלת הונגריה בתביעה לכניעה עד שעה 2 בצהרים.

באולטימאטום נאמר, שאם עד אז לא ייכנעו ההונגרים, תופצץ בודפשט מן האויר.

צירות בריטניה בבירה ההונגרית העבירה ידיעה על כך למשרד החוץ הבריטי.

בידיעות קודמות נמסר: אש תותחים כבדה ומפציצים הרעידו את העיר. בעת שהודיע ראש הממשלה, מר אימרה נג' על ההתקפה הסובייטית בשידור מיוחד, רבע שעה לפני פתיחת השידורים הרגילים של ראדיו בודאפשט.

בשעה 9 הודיע הב.ב.ס., כי נקלט שידור אחרון של ראדיו בודאפשט, בו אמר הקריין שיש הכרח להפסיק את השידורים. לפני הפסקת השידורים אמר ראדיו בודאפשט, כי הקרבות מתפשטים בכל רחבי הונגריה.

נג' פונה ל„מצפון העולם"

„הצבא הסובייטי פתח בהתקפות על בודאפשט הבוקר, כדי להרוס את הדמוקראטיה החדשה שלנו. המערכה נטושה כעת. הממשלה מחזיקה במעמדה. רצוני להודיע על כך לאומה ולעורר את מצפון העולם", אמר מר נג', ראש ממשלת הונגריה, בשידור מיוחד ברדיו בודפשט.

מר נג' אמר, כי כוחות הונגריים עורכים התקפות־נגד.

מר נג' שידר קריאה אל חברי משלחת הונגריה, שנפגשה עם המפקדים הסובייטיים לשם משא ומתן על יציאת הכוחות הרוסיים, ולא חזרה עדיין. נראה כי הרוסים עצרו את המשלחת, וכך שללו מן ההונגרים את גדול מצביאיהם כיום, גנראל פאל מאלטר.

אתמול דחתה מועצת הבטחון את דיונה על המצב בהונגריה לאחר שנתקבלה הדעה ההונגרית, כי רוסיה הסכימה שלא להוסיף ולשלוח תגבורת צבא לתוך הונגריה עד תום השיחות עם שתי המדינות.

ארה"ב עלולה להתערב בהונגריה

(סי"צ) ממשלת ארה"ב מעיינת בהתערבות צבאית בהונגריה, לאחר שהרוסים שלחו כרתות צבא לדכא את מרד ההונגארים בים של דם — זאת נרמז לפיליפ דין, כתב „אובזרור" בוואשינגטון, ע"י פקיד ממשלה אמריקני גבוה.

הפקיד אמר, שאם המערכה בהונגריה תימשך עד ביום ד' „נהיה קרובים למלחמה יותר משהיינו ימעולם למן אבגוסט 1939".

או"ם החליט לשגר כוח־משטרה למצרים

העצרת דורשת תשובה תוך 12 שעות להחלטה על הפסקת־אש

— מאת ה. יוסטוס, סופר „מעריב" באו"ם —

עצרת האו"ם אישרה הבוקר הצעה קאנאדית לשלוח כוח משטרה של האו"ם למצרים.

ההצעה אושרה ב־57 קולות ללא התנגדות, ו־19 נמנעים.

העצרת החליטה לבקש מן המזכיר הכללי מר דאג האמרשילד להכין תוך 48 שעות תכניות להקמת כוח משטרה של האו"ם שיישלח למזרח התיכון.

גם נגד הצעה זו לא הצביע איש.

בהצבעה הראשונה נמנעו ישראל, מצרים, בריטניה וצרפת (ארבע מדינות המשתתפות בקרבות). והצטרפו אליהן הגוש הסובייטי, רוב ארצות חבר העמים הבריטי, אוסטריה, פורטוגאל ולאוס.

לבסוף אישרה העצרת ב־59 קולות ו־5 נמנעים הצעת החלטה הודית בשם 19 ממדינות הגוש האפריקני האסיאתי, המחדשת את דרישת העצרת להפסקת אש מידית, ודורשת תשובה תוך 12 שעות.

העצרת הפסיקה את דיוניה בצהריב (לפי שעון ישראל), אך לא קבעה מועד חדש לישיבתה הבאה. סבורים, שהישיבה תיערך בעוד יומיים. בהתאם להצעת ההחלטה הקאנאדית — למשלוח כוח בינלאומי למצרים — חייב המזכיר הכללי להגיש לאו"ם תכנית תוך 48 שעות.

לפני ההצבעה הודיע נציג ישראל מר א. אבן על נכונותה של ישראל להפסיק את האש מיד ולפתוח במו"מ ישיר עם מצרים על הסכם שלום.

דבריו של אבא אבן, על הסכמת ישראל להפסקת־אש, נתקבלו בתשואות על ידי חברי העצרת.

בסיימו את נאומו נשמעו שוב מחיאות־כפים מצד חברי העצרת.

הנציג הסובייטי, מר סובולב, טען, כי בריטניה וצרפת הנחיתו מהלומה כבדה לארגון הבינלאומי. „תעלת סואץ פעלה יפה לפני ההתקפה על מצרים. עתה, כתוצאה מן ההפצצות, היא הוצאה מכלל פעולה למשך זמן רב. עמי אירופה ואסיה — שכלכלתן תלויה בתעלה — נאלצים לשלם מחיר יקר בעבור כך".

נציג ירדן באו"ם, עבד אל־מונעים ריפאעי, האשים את צרפת, שהיא מעורבת במישרין בהתקפת ישראל על הכוחות המצריים.

ריפאעי אמר, כי נוסעת שהגיעה אתמול לשדה התעופה הבינלאומי של ניו־יורק סיפרה, שביום א' ראתה חיילים צרפתיים בשדה התעופה של לוד.

ריפאעי ציטט ידיעה מתוך העתון „דיילי־מירור". אדבר

(הסוף בעמוד ד')

חברי המשלחת הצבאית המצרית בעזה — בשבי צה"ל

שיחה עם 2 הגנרלים המצריים שנשבו

— מאת מ. מייזלס, סופר „מעריב" —

הגנרל המצרי אשר דן למוות, לפני כשנה וחצי, את ד"ר משה מרזוק ושמואל עזר, על סיוע לישראל, — ישב לפני עתונאים ישראליים היום בצהרים כשבוי מלחמה.

בקול נמוך, כשאצבעותיו מתופפות בעצבנות על גבי השולחן, טען המיור־גנראל מרחמד פאוד אל דיגואי בערבית (הוא סירב לדבר באנגלית), כי כקצין גבוה בצבא המצרי, וכשבוי מלחמה, אינו רשאי להשיב על שאלות עתונאים. הוא היה מוכן לומר רק זאת, שלא עסק בעזה בענינים צבאיים והיה הממונה מטעם מיניסטריון המלחמה המצרי על אזור הרצועה.

◆ על אף מטר השאלות, שניתכו על הגנראל, הוא עמד בסירובו להשיב על שאלות. כאשר הוצגה לו השאלה, אם הוא האיש שדן את שני היהודים למיתה בקאהיר, העמיד פנים כאילו הוא שומע רק ערבית והזדקק כל הזמן למתורגמן. הוא נראה כבן ששים, היה חבוש כובע צבאי עם סרט אדום ובדש בגדו שלש שורות של אותות הצטיינות.

הגנראל המצרי השני שנשבה ע"י כוחות צה"ל, — במפקדתו בחאן־יוניס — המיור גנראל יוסף עבדאללה אל־אגורדי — נתגלה כאיש־שיחה מלבב. הוא השיב ברצון בשפה אנגלית רהוטה לשאלות העתונאים. הוא חבש כומתה צבאית והרכיב משקפיים שחורים. פניו גרמיים ושפמו מטופח. לשאלות העתונאים מסר, כי היה מפקד הדיביזיה השמינית שהיתה מורכבת מחיילים פלשתינאיים ומצרים ומפקדתה בחאן־יוניס.

הגנראל, שדיבר בקול תקיף ובטוח, הצביע על אחד מאותות ההצטיינות שלו ואמר שקיבל אותו על שרותו במלחמה המצרית־ישראלית ב־1948, כששימש כמפקד של בטליון בעזה. הוא סיפר, כי הופתע במפקדתו ע"י הסתערות כוחות צה"ל, שהגיעו למרחק של 100 מטר מהמטה שלו. מכיוון שהוא איש צבא ותפקידו להילחם עד הסוף, לא ברח מהמקום. „בעצם לא היתה לי כל אפשרות לברוח, כי כל הדרכים, לרבות, דרך הים, היו חסומות. לא קיבלתי סעד מחיל האוויר המצרי והייתי נתון להפצצה כבדה של חיל־האויר הישראלי. טווח התותחים שלי היה קצר מכדי למנוע את ההסתערות".

הגנרל המצרי שדן למוות את מרזוק ועזר

הגנראל טען, כי אינו נמנה עם הכת הצבאית, אך הוא מכיר את עבדול נאצר. הוא חניך האקדמיה הצבאית הנודעת סנדהורסט באנגליה.

מעריב
יום ג' כ"ז באייר תשכ"ז 6.6.67 גליון 6955 שנה 20
20 אג'
העתון הנפוץ ביותר במדינה • MAARIV
המייסד והעורך הראשון ד"ר ע. קרליבך ז"ל

הסורים פתחו בהתקפה על שאר־ישוב בהשתתפות חי"ר, שריון וארטילריה

דובר צה"ל מודיע: הבוקר בשעה 7 בערך החלו כוחות רגלים סוריים, בסיוע שריון וארטילריה, בהתקפה על שאר ישוב בגליל המזרחי.

מוצבים סוריים פתחו הבוקר השכם בהפגזת ישובים לאורך הגיזרה הצפונית.

כפי שנודע, ההתקפה תחילה גדות ואיזור משמר הירדן, ואחרי כן מעיין ברוך, כפר סולד, ויישובים אחרים בגיזרה זו.

אותה שעה נשמעו הדי התפוצצויות בצד הסורי מהפגזת תותחינו על העמדות התוקפות.

מטבריה אפשר היה לראות היטב עשן שחור העולה ממוצבי תואפיק, וכן מהגדה המזרחית והצפונית של הכינרת. בשפך הירדן יש עשן. נראה, כי הסורים מתקפים גם את אלמגור וישובים אחרים.

אתמול נורו כמה רקטות לעבר טבריה.

בעמק הירדן פתחו איתם מטוסים באש מקלעים, ובאש זו נהרג סמל משטרת הדייגים, ארנולד רוזנטל, בן 50.

לטרון, ג'נין ושייך ג'אראח - בידי צה"ל

בסיני הושלם כיבוש אום כתאף, אחת מנקודות ההיערכות המרכזיות של הצבא המצרי

ממקורות זרים נודע הבוקר כי כוחות צה"ל בחזיתות מצרים וירדן ביצעו הלילה שורה של כיבושים חדשים העשויים לקדם במידה ניכרת את התוכניות האופראטיביות ביממה הקרובה.

בחזית ירדן — אומרים מקורות אלה — נכבשה שכונת שייך ג'אראח בירושלים ובכך יצרו קשר בלתי אמצעי עם הר הצופים. שכונת שייך ג'אראח היתה מוקד לקרבות דמים בימי מלחמת השיחרור ב־1948 ועברה אז כמה פעמים מיד ליד.

כן כבשו כוחות צה"ל בשעות הלילה את ג'נין, אחת משלוש הערים החשובות במשולש הירדני, שאף היא היתה זירת מאבק בין כוחות צה"ל לבין יחידות הצבא העיראקי בשנת 1948. העיר עצמה נכבשה אז על ידי חיילי ישראל, אולם הם נאלצו לסגת ממנה בעקבות התקפת נגד של צבא עיראקי.

לבסוף נמסר כי כוחות ישראליים כבשו הלילה את מובלעת לטרון ובכך נוצר למעשה רצף־קו בין השפלה לבין ירושלים, ללא הצורך לבצע את האיגוף שנוצר מאז מלחמת השיחרור. כוחות ישראליים, אמרו המקורות הזרים, נעים עתה בכביש ירושלים—רמאללה, לאחר שנבי סמואל, הכפר החולש על מבואות ירושלים ושממנו הופגזה העיר בתותחי הלגיון בשנת 1948, נפלה בידי צה"ל.

בחזית הדרום הושלם כיבושה של אום כתף, אחת מנקודות ההערכות המרכזיות של הצבא המצרי בסיני. מטוסי חיל האוויר הישראלי המשיכו עם שחר בביצוע התקפות על יעדים בתוך סיני ובין היתר נפגע גדוד שריון מצרי והושמדו 3 מטוסים נוספים מדגם „סוחי 7".

ניתוח קרבות האוויר שהתחוללו במשך יום אתמול בין חיל האוויר הישראלי לבין חילות האוויר הערביים מוכיח כי כל 19 המטוסים הישראלים הופלו באש תותחים ולא באש סוללות טילים נגד מטוסים. דבר זה מאשר את אשר גילו האמריקנים לפני כן בוייטנאם, כאשר מרבית מטוסיהם הופלו על ידי צפון־וייטנאם באש תותחים נ. מ. 57 מ"מ ו־85 מ"מ ולאו דווקא בטילים. תותחי נ. מ. מסוגים אלה נופקו למצרים על ידי בריה"מ.

בינתיים מסר דובר צה"ל כי לראשונה מזה מספר שנים חידשו המצרים את פעולות הפדאיון מרצועת עזה. בשעה 22.15 פתחה חוליה מרצועת עזה באש לעבר מכונית ליד צומת ניר עם ופוצצה שם צינור מים. בשעה 23.15 בוצעה חבלה בעמוד חשמל ליד חלץ, ובאותה שעה נפתחה אש לעבר אמבולנס שנסע מניר־עם ליד־מרדכי. לא נמסר על נפגעים. עזה עצמה טרם נפלה בידי כוחות צה"ל.

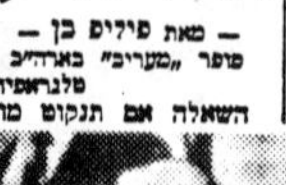

דובר צה"ל הודיע, כי במשך הלילה נכבשו ג'נין, נבי סמואל ובית איקסא בגיזרה הירדנית ואום כתאף בחזית סיני.

אפשרות של פעולה במועצת הבטחון תלויה עתה במו"מ סובייטי־אמריקני

— מאת פידים בן — סופר „מעריב" בארה"ב טלגראפית.

השאלה אם תנקוט מועצת הבטחון פעולה כלשהי ביחס למלחמה בין ישראל לבין ארצות ערב תלוייה במו"מ הסובייטי—אמריקני.

אתמול אחר הצהריים כבר נתקיימה ישיבה ממושכת בין הנציג הסובייטי, ניקולאי פדורנקו, לבין נציג ארה"ב, ארתור גולדברג. השניים עומדים להיפגש מחדש היום, שעה לפני כינוס מועצת הבטחון (ב־5.30 אחה"צ לפי שעון ישראל).

מאז פרוץ המשבר במזרח התיכון לא נפגשו עדיין הסובייטים והאמריקנים לשום ישיבה. במרוצת ישיבת מועצת הבטחון הסתבכו שני הצדדים בחילופי דברים קשים ביותר, בהם כמעט ונשכח המזרח הקרוב, ובמקום זאת דיברו על וייטנאם, על קובה ועל סיכסוכים אחרים בין ברה"מ וארה"ב.

הסובייטים רמזו אתמול, כי תמיכתם בדרישת הערבים להפסקת אש, שאחריה יהיו כל הכוחות חייבים לחזור לעמדותיהם שלפני ה־4 ביוני, הוחלשה, וכי בעניין זה יהיו מוכנים למו"מ.

דעת האמריקנים היא, שהנסיגה חייבת להיות נרחבת הרבה יותר, וכי היא חייבת לכלול את פינוי שארם אל שייך על ידי המצרים, דבר שיפתור את בעיית ההסגר על מפרץ אילת.

האמריקנים רוצים גם הבטחות בדבר דמוביליזציה של הכוחות הצבאיים העומדים עתה זה מול זה לאורך גבולות ישראל וארצות ערב.

[illegible] — בשעת [illegible] של מועצת הבטחון, [illegible] ומשמאל — נציג סין הלאומית, ליאו צ'יה, שהיה הנשיא התורן בחודש שעבר (צילום ראדיו־טלגראפי, מיוחד ל„מעריב")

נאצר וסגנו עבדול חכים עאמר ביקרו ב־22 במאי בסיני וברצועת עזה. בפגישה עם טייסי סילון מצריים בבסיסי סיני אמר נאצר: „אם ישראל רוצה מלחמה, אנחנו מוכנים — אהלן וסהלן"...

אבא אבן המריא לארה"ב
בריה"מ דורשת מישראל „לפנות שטחים שכבשה"

השגריר צ'ובאחין הביא שדר למשרד החוץ ✶ קודם לכן ביקש אשכול מקוסיגין להצטרף למאמצים למען השלום

— מאת יוסף חריף —

שגריר בריה"מ בישראל מסר אתמול למשרד החוץ שדר ממוסקבה, שבו נתבקשה ישראל „להפסיק את הקרבות ולפנות את השטחים אשר כבשה".

את השדר מסר השגריר צ'ובאחין לסגן המנכ"ל של משרד החוץ, מר יוסף תקוע.

קודם־לכן שלח ראש הממשלה, מר לוי אשכול, איגרת לראש ממשלת בריה"מ, מר אלכסיי קוסיגין, ובה ביקש, שגם בריה"מ תצטרף למאמץ להבטיח שלום המבוסס על כיבוד הריבונות של כל עם ועם. איגרות דומות נשלחו לכל שאר ראשי המעצמות.

[illegible] מציינים, כי בשדר שהביא [illegible] ראל לא בא כתגובה על איגרתו של ראש הממשלה. הדברים הכלולים בשדר חופפים בעיקרם את הדברים שהשמיע נציג בריה"מ באו"ם, שגם הוא תבע את הפסקת הקרבות ואת פינוי השטחים הכבושים בידי ישראל.

יודעי דבר מציינים, כי אף על־פי שהנימה של השדר הסובייטי, שלא כאיגרת האחרונה של מר קוסיגין, אינה יכולה להיחשב כמתונה במיוחד, אין גם להעריך בחומרה. משרד החוץ נמנע לפי שעה [illegible] הסובייטית.

שר החוץ, מר אבא אבן, יצא לפנות בוקר בלווית מזכירו המדיני, מר משה רביב, לניו־יורק, כדי לעמוד בראש המשלחת הישראלית בדיוני מועצת הבטחון בימים הבאים. כן ייפגש מר אבן עם שר החוץ האמריקני מר דין ראסק.

האמבארגו החלקי על נשק מצרפת – מיום ד' אחה"צ

— מאת סופר „מעריב" בפאריס — טלגראפית

האמבארגו החלקי על משלוחי הנשק למדינות הלוחמות במזרח התיכון — כלומר, הפסקתם עד להודעה חדשה — ייכנס לתוקפו רק ביום ד' אחר הצהרים. כך מסרו בפאריס אמש מקורות צרפתיים נאמנים.

ביום ד' ימסור מיניסטר החוץ, מר מוריס קוב דה מירוויל, הודעה באסיפה הלאומית על המצב במזרח התיכון ועל עמדת צרפת לאור המלחמה שפרצה אתמול, ובמסגרת נאום זה יודיע גם על האמבארגו.

פרשנים צבאיים אמריקניים: ישראל לא תפנה את כל סיני

מאת סופר „מעריב" בארה"ב טלגראפית

פרשנים צבאיים אמריקניים התחילו כבר מתנבאים ביחס לכיוון התנועה הצבאית הישראלית בסיני.

„כמובן אין להניח, שישראל תסכים לפנות את כל חצי האי סיני, כפי שעשתה ב־1956, באמרה, כי דבר זה יאפשר לנאצר להטיל מחדש הסגר על המפרץ". אומר פרשן אחד: „מתקבל יותר על הדעת, שישראל תדרוש לפקח על הגישה לנמל אילת".

המתכננים הצבאיים ב„פנטאגון" ביטלו כלאחר יד ידיעות האומרות, כי יועצים צבאיים סובייטיים הגיעו לשטח יחד עם יחידות הצבא המצרי. פקידי מיניסטריון ההגנה האמריקני אמרו, שאין כל הוכחות לכך.

ראסק מבהיר: הנייטראליות של ארה"ב איננה שוויון־נפש

מיניסטר החוץ האמריקני, מר דין ראסק, אמר אמש, כי „הנייטראליות של ארה"ב אין פירושה שיוויון נפש". ראסק אמר את הדברים הללו בנסותו להבהיר את העמדה של וואשינגטון.

מיניסטר החוץ האמריקני ציטט את הודעתו של הנשיא ג'ונסון, החוזרת ומאשרת את השלמות הטריטוריאלית של כל ארצות המזרח התיכון.

„אנו נתונים במצב שבו הכריזו כמה מדינות מלחמה. אנו איננו צד להם ושום כוח מכוחותינו אינו מעורב בקרבות".

ראסק הוסיף: „ברצוני להדגיש שהנייטראליות שלנו לא יכולה להיות ביטוי של שוויון־נפש, משום שמוטלת עלינו אחריות כבדה כחברת מועצת הבטחון."

כאשר נשאל בדבר פתיחת מעשי האיבה, אמר ראסק: „כנראה שיעבור זמן מה, בטרם אפשר יהיה להבהיר את העובדות לאמיתן. ייתכן שנזדקק אפילו לזמן רב". (סט"א).

המצאה של מצרים וירדן: ישראל קיבלה „מטריה אווירית" מאניות של ארה"ב ובריטניה

— מאת סופר „מעריב" לענינים ערביים — [illegible] הונחתה עליהן אתמול על ידי כוחות צה"ל, [illegible] „מטריה אווירית".

רדיו קאהיר מסר הבוקר, כי „נושאות מטוסים של ארה"ב ובריטניה מקיימות פעילות נרחבת ונותנות לישראל הגנה מפני חילות האוויר הערביים". לדברי אותו מקור, התקשר המלך חוסיין עם קולונל נאצר הבוקר והודיע לו, כי מסכי הראדאר הירדניים גילו בבירור את סימני הזיהוי של המטוסים האמריקניים והבריטיים.

הבוקר הודיע רדיו בגדאד, כי דובר צבאי ירדני טען, שכוחות אוויר ירדניים ועיראקיים תקפו במשותף שדה תעופה בישראל והסבו לו נזקים כבדים. שם שדה התעופה שהופצץ כביכול — לא נמסר.

דובר ירדני הודה הבוקר, כי כוחות צה"ל כבשו הלילה את שייך ג'אראח בקרבת ירושלים ואת ג'נין בצפון המשולש.

הדובר הירדני טען, כי ההתקפה על ג'נין בוצעה בעוצמה של דיוויזיות חיל רגלים ובסיוע שריון. לדברי אותו מקור, היה גם סיוע אווירי ישראלי, וכתוצאה מהפעולות הללו הופלו 3 מטוסים ישראליים ו־3 טייסיהם נישבו.

נוכח התבוסה שסבלו את מול כוחות מצרים, ירדן וסוריה, הודיעו הבוקר אלג'יריה ומארוקו על שיגור כוחות צבא למצרים. האלג'ירים הודיעו על שיגור 48 מטוסים מדגם „מיג 21" למצרים, ואילו המארוקנים הודיעו על כוונתם לשלוח כוחות יבשה. גם סודאן מתכוונת לשלוח כוחות למצרים.

בון לא תתערב

מאת סופר „מעריב" בבון

שר־החוץ המערב גרמני, וילי בראנדט, עמד אמש על העקרון המערב־גרמני של אי־התערבות בסכסוך במזרח־התיכון, אך הוסיף, כי אין פירושו של העקרון „נייטראליות מוסרית".

מר בראנדט אמר, כי אינו רואה סיבה לסרב לשלוח לישראל משאיות.

כ־600 אזרחים גרמניים טילפנו או באו אישית לשגרירות ישראל בבון, כדי להיוודע כיצד אפשר לסייע לישראל. מאז תחילת המשבר הולך וגדל מספר המבקשים לעזור והפניות גברו עוד אתמול בבוקר כשהתחילו להגיע הידיעות על פרוץ הקרבות.

מטוסו של אייבי נתן — התקלקל בקפריסין

אייבי נתן, שהתכוון עד אתמול בבוקר לחזור על „מבצע השלום" שלו ולטוס בשניה לקאהיר, נראה מדוכא מפרוץ הקרבות, אבל החליט מיד לטוס לישראל כדי להתייצב לשרות. אלא שגם דבר זה נמנע ממנו, משום שמנוע מטוסו הקטן התקלקל והוא הוכרח לשוב ולנחות בניקוסיה. (יו. פי.)

✶ ירדן ביקשה ממערב גרמניה למכור לה 20 אלף מסכות גאז, — מוסר משרד החוץ בבון.

מיצעד למען ישראל באמסטרדם – לאורך 2 ק"מ

באמסטרדם השתתפו אמש 6000 איש במצעד למען ישראל, לאורך 2 ק"מ. בין הכרזות שנישאו: „שלום לישראל", „לא תהיה מינכן שניה".

● בממפיס, במדינת טנסי בארה"ב, החליטה קבוצת ניצולי רדיפות הנאצים להקדיש את הכסף שנאסף להקמת אנדרטה לזכר הקרבנות — למען ישראל. „הגיע הזמן לחשוב על החיים", — אמר נשיא הקהילה היהודית.

● בשטוקהולם קראה ממשלת שוודיה אמש לאו"ם להתערב במהירות וביעילות במלחמה במזרח התיכון, אחר שהתקיימה אחה"צ ישיבת הממשלה.

● ממשלת דרום אפריקה נוקטת מדיניות של „נייטראליות אוהדת לישראל", — מסרו מקורות ממשלתיים בקייפטאון. אותם מקורות הוסיפו, כי אין להניח שדרום אפריקה תתמוך בגלוי בישראל, בגלל עמדתה בעבר כלפי מדינה זו, אך „מנהיגי דרום אפריקה מעריכים את עמדתה המסובכת של ישראל באפריקה ואינם רוגזים עליה על כך" (יו.פ. וא.פ.).

קצין סורי ביקש מיקלט בתורכיה

קצין סורי ביקש מיקלט מדיני בתירכיה. לפי ידיעה של סוכנות „רויטר" מאיסטאמבול, חצה הקצין, כהאלד ג'אבר, את הגבול התירכי, הסגיר עצמו למשמר תירכי וביקש מיקלט. (רויטר).

[illegible] של צבא מצרי ברפיח — נטוש, אחר שחיילי נאצר ברחו מול כוחות צה"ל המתקדמים.

האפיפיור מקווה שירושלים תוכרז כ„עיר פרזות"

— מאת עדה לוצ'אני —

[illegible] שאם יורע ה[illegible] תוכרז ירושלים כעיר־פרזות שאין לפגוע בה, בשל קדושתה המיוחדת — הביע האפיפיור פאולוס הששי במכתב אל מזכיר האו"ם מר תאנט. כן ביקש ממר תאנט „לעשות כל מאמץ למען יצליח [illegible] לשים קץ לסכסוך".

האפיפיור שלח איגרות גם לנאצר, לממשלות ישראל, לבנון, סוריה, עיראק וירדן. באיגרת אל נאצר הוא „פונה אל [illegible] ההומאניות שלו, אל [illegible] האחריות ואל יוקרתו ב[illegible] עמי ערב".

[illegible] „בהילים" ואגרות [illegible] שיגרו לירושלים [illegible] וכן אל ממשלות ואשינגטון, לונדון, מוסקבה [illegible] ובהם קריאת ממשלת [illegible] לפעול למען הפסקת [illegible]

[illegible] הראשי של רומא, הרב אליה טואף, פירסם אתמול כרוז, כי „עתה, שהעולם יודע מי התוקפן, צריכה גם ממשלת איטליה, שעד כה התייחסה בחיוב לשיטתו של דה־גול, לקבוע עמדה ברורה.

סרן יורם הרפז
יקירנו אהוב נפשנו
נפל במילוי תפקידו
אנו מבכים אותו מרה
אשתו
ומשפחות קטן וזנדברג

תודתנו
נתונה לאישים, מוסדות וארגונים, לידידים, מכרים ומוקירי זכרה של אמנו וסבתנו היקרה
לאה שמושקוביץ ז"ל
בהביעם לנו תנחומים ובהשתתפותם באבלנו על אבדתנו הכבדה
בנה — ד"ר יעקב שנון וב"ב
בתה — אידה זידלר וב"ב
בתה — אולה לוינסון וב"ב

לחברי בית הלל ל„בני־ברית" בישראל
ברכות שלום לכולכם
אנו עומדים לרשותכם גם בהיותכם בחזית.
התקשרו אתנו אם אתם זקוקים לספרים, כתבי עת, בגדים ואוכל.
כן מוכנים אנו להגיש עזרה למשפחותיכם או למסור אינפורמציה עליהן לכם.
נא לכתוב אלינו — רח' בלפור 4, ירושלים, או לרב ברנד אוך, שדרות הצבי 32, חיפה.
ד"ר יעקב, י. כהן, מנהל בית הלל ירושלים, מר דוד ברסלאו, סגן מנהל.
הרב ברנד אוך, מנהל בית הלל, ע"י הטכניון חיפה.

מודעה דחופה
השוטרים מתל־אביב והסביבה, ששירתו במשטרה, בשרותי בתי הסוהר וחיל הספר ואשר אינם מוצבים ליחידה או מועסקים בתפקידים בטחוניים, יתייצבו בת"א, רח' אחד העם 13, קומה ד' חדר 408 בין השעות 8 עד 17.00 וייפנו אל שגאי.
איגוד השוטרים היהודים לשעבר

לעודד ארז
תהיה בריא
מאחיך

ארגון ארצי של אסירי הנאצים לשעבר
שולח בזה את מיטב ברכותיו לחברי הארגון, שלחמו נגד הנאצים במחנות הריכוז וכעת עומדים על המשמר למען שלמותה וקיומה של מדינתנו. אנו פונים לכל החברים שטרם השתלבו במאמץ הבטחוני לפנות לסניפי הארגון.
הועד המרכזי

רמאללה בידי כוחותינו

רמאללה נכבשה אתמול ע״י כוחות צה״ל. הידיעה על כך לא פורסמה עדיין רשמית על ידי דובר צה״ל, אך היא נתאשרה על ידי מקורות אחרים.

עם כיבוש עיר זו, חדרו כוחות צה״ל חדירה עמוקה לתוך השטח שהיה מוחזק בידי ירדן בגדה המערבית.

רמאללה שוכנת בקילומטר ה־16 בדרך מירושלים לשכם, על פסגת הרים, בגובה של 870 מטר מעל פני הים. לפיכך הקימו בה הבריטים בשנות השלושים את מיתקן השידור לארץ ישראל. שעד לאחרונה שירת את שרותי השידור של הממלכה הירדנית. פירוש שם העיר רמאללה הוא רמת ה־אלהים; יש סוברים, כי רמאללה מצויה על גבעת האלהים, הנזכרת במקרא צמוד לכפר ערבי גדול הנקרא בירה. סמוך לעיר נמצא שדה התעופה קלנדיה.

מועצת הבטחון החליטה פה אחד על הפסקת־אש

רוסיה השלימה עם המציאות – ויתרה על תביעת הנסיגה

אבא אבן: ביצוע ההחלטה תלוי בקבלתה על ידי הערבים בכנות ובשלמות

— מאת פיליפ בן —
סופר „מעריב״ בארה״ב
טלגראפית

בדיוק בשעה 7.10 בערב בניו־יורק — 1.10 אחר חצות לפי שעון ישראל, — נתפרץ מאורע גדול סביב השלחן הגדול בצורת פר־סת־ברזל של מועצת הבטחון: כל 15 הנציגים הרימו ידיהם בהצבעה פה־אחד. הם הצביעו לאשר הצעה, השוברת כנראה את כל שיאי הקיצור של הודעות האו״ם. ההחלטה ממליצה רק, שתיעשה מיד הפסקת אש.

אך לפני ההצבעה המהירה פה־אחד על הנוסח הקצר כל כך התנהל משא־ומתן דיפלומטי שיוצא בהיסטוריה כדוגמה ומופת לפיתולים המעניינים, לוויתורים קיצוניים הנעשים שעות ספורות אחרי נקיפות עמדות נוקשות ביותר ופירוב גמור לגלות גמישות מינימאלית.

כבר אור ליום ג׳, בפגישת נציגי ארה״ב וברית המועצות,

מר ארתור גולדברג וניקולאי פדרנקו, הוצע על ידי הצד האמריקני נוסח, שאחרי הפסקת־האש יחזרו כל הכוחות הצבאיים כשני הצדדים אל מ־אחורי שביתת הנשק מ־1949. נוסח זה התנה גם, שחופש השיט במפרץ עקבה יובטח ל־כל המדינות, בלא יוצא מן הכלל.

רצו לחכות

והנה, אתמול בבוקר הודיע הנציג הסובייטי לעמיתו ה־אמריקני ולשאר כל חברי מועצת הבטחון, כי לדעת ה־ממשלה הסובייטית אין הצעה זו יכולה להתקבל, כיוון ש־נאצר כשרב מכל וכל לבטל את הדפנר. אשר לנציגי ארצות ערב — הללו הכריזו, כי ממשלותיהן לא יסכימו ל־הפסקת אש כלל, בשעה שה־מצב הצבאי הוא לרעתן כל כך. הם הביעו את התקווה, שתוך

(הסוף בעמוד 7)

שר החוץ, מר אבא אבן, אמר אמש באו״ם — לפי שידור של „קול ישראל״ — כי ביצוע החלטת מועצת הבטחון בדבר הפסקת האש תהיה בכך שהצד השני יקבל־הו בכנות ובשלימות והוא שיתוף פעולה.

בעת שימסור לממשלה על החלטת המועצה — אמר מר אבן — יהיה עליו לציין, כי הצד השני טרם נענה לפניית מועצת הבטחון.

מיתקני נפט של המערב חובלו בלבנון – טוענת קהיר

מיתקני נפט אמריקניים ו־בריטיים בלבנון חובלו ה־לילה בקרבת ביירות — מו־סרת „סוכנות הידיעות המזרחית״ (המצרית).

הסוכנות מוסרת, כפי שדיווח רדיו דמשק, שהמיתקנים שייכים פלט לארה״ב ובריטניה.

כן נמסר, כי תמרות אש ענקיות והתפוצצו במיתקני הנפט, מצפון לעיר. והאירו את השטח המואפל. מצבורי הנפט של חברת „של״ ושל חברת „סוקוני־ואקום״ פוצצו בזה אחר זה.

בוואשינגטון הוציקה הממשלת את האחראי של חברות הנפט האמריקניות, שיכין תוכניות חרום וידאג לאספקת נפט אפשרית לארה״ב מאירופה, מיפאן וממקומות אחרים בעולם.

ג׳ונסון: הקריאה להפסקת אש – צעד ראשון אל עידן של שלום

נשיא ארה״ב, לינדון ג׳ונסון, אמר אמש, כי קריאתה של מועצת הבטחון ל־הפסקת אש בקרבות בין ישראלים לערבים פותחת „נתיב של תקוה מסכנות ה־מזרח התיכון״.

„אנו מקווים, שהצדדים ה־נוגעים ישירות יפעלו בהתאם ללא דיחוי״, אמר מר ג׳ונסון והוסיף, כי הקריאה היא „צעד ראשון לקראת עידן חדש של שלום רגוע ושל קידמה לכל עמי המזרח התיכון. מעתה נש־אף למטרה זו״, — הכריז.

מר ג׳ונסון הופיע בשידור טלוויזיה, ששודר מן האולפן בבית הלבן מיד לאחר שמועצת הבטחון הצביעה פה אחד על הפסקת האש. ובשעה שה־נציג הסובייטי במועצה עדיין סיכם את הודעתו.

„רק צעד ראשון״

מיניסטר החוץ הקנדי, מר פול מארטין, הזהיר אמש, כי הפסקת אש במלחמה בין ישראל לבין הערבים חייבת ל־היות רק צעד ראשון להשכנת שלום באיזור. מר מארטין קידם בברכה את החלטת מועצת הבטחון, בהדגישו, כי ישראל הוקמה על־ידי האו״ם והיא ה־ייבת להמשיך לחיות בשלום, ועל הכל להכיר בזכותה לשיט חופשי במפרץ אילת.

סינאטור סקוט: אל יינתן לגזול מישראל בדרך מו״מ זכויות שכבשו בכוח צבא

„אני תקווה, כי ארה״ב לא תיתן יד לגזילה בדרך המו״מ של הזכויות שרכשו הישראלים בכוח מאמציהם הצבאיים״ — אמר אתמול הסינאטור האמריקני, יו סקוט, בנאום שנשא בסינאט.

מר סקוט דרש ממשלת ארה״ב לפרסם הצהרת מדיניות חד־משמעית, שלא תשאיר ספק בלב איש, כי אהדתה של ארה״ב נתונה לישראל.

סנאטור יעקב יעבץ אמר בנאום בסנאט, כי על מועצת הבטחון לתבוע לא רק את [illegible]

לארה״ב לספק לישראל נשק בכמות הדרושה לה. הוא הדגיש כי ארה״ב חייבת להעמיד לרשות ישראל אספקה וציוד בנשק לא פחות מן הכמות ש־העמידה ארה״ב לרשותם של אויבי ישראל. עוד קרא סנאטור מורס להצבתו מחדש של חיל החירום של או״ם במזרח התיכון כדי להבטיח את ישראל אחרי נסיגת כוחותיה.

סנאטור צ׳ארלס פרסי קרא לארה״ב להגביר את סיועה ה־כלכלי לישראל. הוא הזהיר, כי המלחמה „עלולה להמיט עד מהרה חורבן על כלכלת ישראל [illegible]

ישראל הגשימה מחצית תכניתה

ג׳יימס רסטון, הפרשן הנודע של „ניו יורק טיימס״

— שירות „מעריב״ —

כתב הבוקר ג׳יימס רסטון, [illegible]

ירושלים העתיקה, על כל אוצרותיה ההיסטוריים והרוחניים, נתונה לאש מנשק קל למן פרוץ המלחמה.

ברגע האחרון

סיכומי דובר צה״ל

דובר צה״ל מודיע: אתמול נמשכה התקדמות מהירה של כוחותינו בסיני, בכל הצירים. כוחות שריון ניהלו במשך יום אתמול בהתקדמות קרבות שריון עם האויב המצרי. כאשר ממוסי חיל־האויר משתתפים בהיקף רב בלוחמה היבשתית ותוקפים טנקים וכוחות אויב. בציר הצפוני בסיני מתקדם הכוח שלנו מערבה לעבר אל־עריש עד רומאני. בציר המרכזי התקדמו כוחותינו מערבה לג׳אבל ליבני ובדרכם כבשו את דיר חאמה. בציר הדרומי נמצאו כוחותינו בהתקדמותם לעבר דיר חאסנה. בגיזרה הירדנית נמשכו קרבות ארטילריה לעבר ירושלים וישובים ישראלים אחרים. רמאללה וסובאס נכבשו אתמול על־ידי כוחותינו. ארטילריה ירדנית ממשיכה הביקר בהפגזות העיר ירושלים. בגיזרה הסורית נהדפו אתמול נסיונות התקפה של כוחות רגלים ושריון בסיוע ארטילריה לעבר שאר־ישוב ותל־דן. הארטילריה הסורית הפגיזה ישובים לאורך הגבול כולו. מטוסי חיל־האויר והארטילריה שלנו הופעלו לשתק ארטילריה סורית.

„השבועות המסוכנים״

מחוץ הם חוששים, כי ה־כוחות המדיניים בוואשינגטון ובאו״ם, שלא נחלצו לעזרה כאשר התרכזו הערבים על גבולות ישראל, ינסו לכפות הפסקת־אש על הצדדים, לפני שיספיקו להשמיד את הכוחות הערביים המאיימים על בטחונה. אתמול נתרתחה תל־אביב בשל טענות קאהיר ומוסקבה, כי האמריקנים והבריטים התערבו שלשום בקרבות האוויר והם גרמו לנצחון הישראלים.

לא זו בלבד שזהו שקר, אלא לדעת הישראלים זה גרוע עוד יותר. כי בישראל רווחת ההרגשה, שהישראלים ניצחו לא בגלל האמריקנים והבריטים, אלא על אפם ועל חמתם. לכן אין ממשלת ישראל נוטה לכרות ארון לקריאת־שלום מציבור שלמי, ש־

שני השבועות המסוכנים ביותר בתולדות ארצנו״, אמר לי ביום ג׳ שר העבודה מר יגאל אלון. שר ההגנה החדש משה דיין אף הוא דעתו כך; ועוד לפני הקרבות רמזה ה־עתונות הישראלית. כי ממשלה הלוקה במורך־לב מסכנת את בטחון המדינה.

גיבורי השעה בממשלה זו אינם איפוא האנשים שרצו לחכות. אלא האנשים שרצו להלחם; ובעוד ראש הממשלה ושר החוץ אומרים שאינם רוצים ברווחים טריטוריאליים, אולי לא יצליחו להתגבר על הצעירים שבקאבינט ועל ה־חיילים הצעירים שהוצרכו ל־הלחם על הגבולות הישנים.

הגבול הירדני קרוב כל כך אל ירושלים הישראלית. עד שביום ב׳ צעדו חיילים ירד־נים ארבעה רחובות במעלה

חיילי צה״ל נופשים שעה קלה — בחוצות עזה

כל שכיר ירכוש מלווה־בטחון בסכום של חצי משכורת חודשית

האיגרות ישולמו בארבעה תשלומים חודשיים ✱ העצמאים יקנו איגרות בשווי של לפחות 5 אחוזים מהתכנסה השנתית

כל שכיר במדינה ירכוש מיפשו הקרובים איגרות מלווה הבטחון החדש, בסכום מחצית משכורת חודשית, בתשלומים שישולמו תוך ארבעת חדשים.

צרכי שעת־חירום יישמרו מ־לוא הזכויות הסוציאליות. ה־עבודה במפעל, שאליו הוצב העובד, תיחשב כזמנית באותו מפעל, בלי לנתק את קשריו עם מפעלו הקבוע.

ערביי העיר העתיקה מבקשים מחסה במוסדות הצרפתיים והארמניים

— מאת ג. צפריני —

רבים־רבים נשארו בוודאי ב־תוך הבתים ובבתי־כנסים העתיקים. הבוקר כאשר נפסקה ה־הפגזה הכללית, נשמע מהיך חצר הכנזר סו־סביאר הפרנציסקאני הנמצא סמוך לשער החדש, קריאות רבות של אנשים שלא ראו אוהם, ש־ביקשו כחסה. בבית־ספר ה־

גם שם הגיעו הושבים לכוס־דות הנוצרים כמו בית חסדא (סנט אנה) שהוא בחסות דגל צרפת.

עד כמה שניתן לבחון את התנועה בעיר העתיקה גדולה הנהירה אל המוסדות הצרפתיים.

מבצעים על רכבת מאשקלון לעזה

הוצאה מיוחדת

מהדורת שעה 13.30

ירושלים העתיקה ושכם נכבשו על ידי צה"ל

ישראל כבשה את ירושלים העתיקה בין החומות היום. במהלומה כבדה אחרת לירדן השתלטו כוחות צה"ל על שכם, החולשת על סביבתה, 48 ק"מ מצפון לירושלים. ידיעה זו מסרה סוכנות „אסושיאייטד פרס" בשעה 12.20 ומיד אחריה גם כל שאר סוכנויות הידיעות.

סוכנות א.פ. מוסיפה:

הקרב על החלק האחרון של ירושלים החל הבוקר בשעה 5 כאשר אחרי שלוש שעות של דומיה גמורה כמעט נפתחה אש מרגמות רצופה ובחלל ניסרו טרטור שריון כבד ותקתוק אש מנשק קל. נראה שאותו רגע התקדמו הטאנקים הישראליים בדרכים ההיסטוריות יריחו וים המלח העוברים בקרבת החלק הדרומי של הגזרה הערבית באזור המפוזר על הר הצופים.

מטוסים ישראלים חגו מעל והטילו פצצות ומדרום נשמעה אש של תותחי נ.מ. — קלושה והססנית.

ראדיו רבת־עמון שידר היום סמוך לשעות הצהרים קריאה נרגשת לכל המוסלמים להחלץ לעזרתה של ירושלים העתיקה.

קריין הראדיו אמר, כי „האויב העמוני תקף את ירושלים בתותחים ופצצות. צבאנו האמיץ לחם והקיז דם יקר בהגנה על האוצרות הקדושים. ערבים ומוסלמים קומו לעזרתה של ירושלים. הגנו על קדושתה".

קריין הראדיו המשיך ותקף את ישראל על שאינה פועלת לפי החלטת מועצת־הבטחון, ולא הפסיקה את האש.

ראדיו רבת־עמון הוסיף, כי הצבא הירדני „נלחם על כל שעל אדמה של חזיתנו הארוכה" והוא נשבע „להקריב עצמו" למען האומה — מודיעה סוכנות „רויטר".

הראדיו קרא לתושבים שלא לשים לב לשמועות שמפיץ האויב בתורת נשק של החרשת המוראל. „הצד דימיננו בדיגננו על עגין נעדר", קרא ראדיו רבת־עמון.

שעה קלה אחרי כיבוש העיר העתיקה זרם כוח ישראלי גדול פנימה דרך שער האריות ואחר כך גם דרך שערים אחרים — מוסרת סוכנות „איי.פי.".

שירת „התקווה"

בשירת „התקווה" פרצו חברי מועצת עירית תל אביב היום, בעת שנתקבלה, תוך כדי ישיבה, הידיעה על כיבוש העיר העתיקה על ידי כוחות צה"ל. הידיעה הועברה לראש העיריה, מר מרדכי נמיר, בעת שחברי המועצה קיימו ישיבה במקלט בית העיריה.

ראש העיריה מסר את הידיעה לנוכחים שפתחו באופן ספונטאני בשירת „התקווה".

(א.פ.) הישראלים המנצחים הזמינו את הרב הצבאי הראשי, הרב שלמה גורן אל הכותל המערבי לתקוע שם תקיעת שופר.

כמעט באותו זמן הודיעו על נפילת שכם שעה קלה לפני צהרי היום.

ברגע האחרון

ראדיו קאהיר הודיע היום בשעה 12.30 בצהרים כי ד' כוחות הצבא של מצרים נ... תנה הוראה „לסגת לקו ה... שני".

הדמיון הסורי: כבשו החולה, עולים לנצרת...

ראדיו דמשק הודיע הבוקר, כי הכוחות הסוריים, הנלחמים בצפון ישראל, שטפו את עמק החולה ורודפים אחר הכוחות הישראליים לצד נצרת. „האויב מובס עתה בכל החזיתות בגליל, על הקרקע ובאוויר", מספר ראדיו דמשק את בדותותיו. (רויטר).

ובני ירושלים עיר הקודש במהרה בימנו

„שאלו שלום ירושלים"... — בימים האחרונה התענינו הכל בשלומה של ירושלים העיר, הניצבת בגבורה נוכח פני האוייב.

רבה הראשי של צה"ל, אלוף הרב שלמה גורן, הגיע אל הבירה בשעות הלילה המאוחרות, כדי לעודד את החיילים בעמדות הקדמיות ואת תושבי שכונות הספר — שרבים מהם מילמלו חרישית „שייבנה בית המקדש"...

בלוותו את הלוחמים במערכה הגדולה של עיר הקודש בברכה ובתפילות, כשספר תורה בידו, נזכר הרב גורן בשעות הקשות של ימי תש"ח, בהן לחם בעמדות העיר ופעל כצלף. עם הנץ החמה ערך הרב תפילה, בפנותו לעבר הכותל המערבי, וסביב הידהדה התפילה „ובנה ירושלים עיר הקודש במהרה בימינו".

סוכנות „רויטר": בית הנשיא נפגע בהפגזה

סוכנות „רויטר" מודיעה מתל אביב, כי ביתו של נשיא ישראל, מר זלמן שזר, נפגע הבוקר בהפגזה מן העמדות הירדניות באזור ירושלים תיזוק במידת מה.

בשעת מסירת הידיעה — כותבת סוכנות „רויטר" — עדיין לא נודע אם הנשיא שזר שהה באותה עת בבנין. אך נמסר, שאף אם שהה בו, אין כל ספק שהיה במקלט שבבנין.

כן מודיעה סוכנות הידיעות כי הוויטראז'ים של האמן מארק שאגאל בבית הכנסת של בית החולים „הדסה" בירושלים התנפצו מפגז ירדני.

קהיר: אנו נמשיך במלחמה

ידיעה מוושינגטון: חוסיין פתח בגישושי שלום

ראדיו קאהיר הודיע היום לתושבי מצרים, כי נגמר עם ארצות ערב להמשיך במלחמה, למרות קריאת מועצת הבטחון להפסקת האש.

ראדיו קאהיר שידר את הקריאה למלחמה טוטאלית, נופח דאגה מבבירה והולכת על התקדמות הכוחות הישראליים.

„למדו את הישראלים לקח — גרשו אותם מארץ הקודש", הכריז ראדיו קאהיר.

ירדן, שדרכתה קשות בחזית הקרב, החלה בגישושים ביחס להפסקת אש, — מוסרת סוכנות „אסושיאייטד פרס" מוואשינגטון, ומוסיפה, כי משרד החוץ האמריקני ושגרירות ירדן בוואשינגטון סירבו לאשר או להכחיש ידיעות אלה ממקורות דיפלומאטיים.

כפי שנמסר, החלו גישושים אלה עוד לפני החלטת מועצת הבטחון.

בינתיים ניסו דיפלומאטים אמריקניים להשיג היענות ישראלית מהירה, בעקבות פנייתו הפומבית של הנשיא ג'ונסון, להצעת הפסקת האש של מועצת הבטחון, שנתקבלה הלילה. הנשיא ג'ונסון הביע תקווה להסכמת הערביים ולהסכמת ישראל כאחת.

„טיימס" הלונדוני מביא הבוקר ידיעה מאת כתבו בירושלים, האומר אף הוא, כי לישראל נודע, שירדן תהיה מוכנה לפתוח במשא־ומתן על הפסקת אש.

בידיעת „טיימס" נאמר, כי „גישושי השלום של ירדן עדיין מעורפלים וחששאיים ביותר". בידיעה נאמר עוד, כי „משלחת שלום מטעם האו"ם נוטלת חלק בגישושים חששאיים אלה". „טיימס" מודיע: „החלטת ירדן (לפתוח במשא־ומתן עם ישראל להפסקת אש) עשויה להיות גורלית ביותר לתוצאות המלחמה".

כרבת־עמון אמר היום דובר רשמי, כי נמשך המגע בין רבת־עמון, קאהיר ובגדאד, על שיתוף פעולה בין החזית הירדנית והמצרית.

ראדיו רבת־עמון אמר, כי המלך חוסיין שיגר מברק אל נאצר, בו הסביר את המצב הצבאי. הדובר הירדני הוסיף, כי מלך ירדן קיבל גם מברק מנשיא מצרים, המסביר את המצב בחזית המצרית. הדובר הוסיף, כי ההסבר לווה „דברים על ההתלהבות וההחלטה הנחושה של מצרים וצבאה לפעול למען מטרות הערביים ולהגנת המולדת".

כן החליף המלך חוסיין איגרות על המצב הצבאי עם סגן נשיא מצרים, עבד אל חכים עאמר. מברקים ישלחו גם לנשיא עיראק, עבד אל רחמן עארף. (א.פ., יו.פ. ורויטר).

בטאון המפלגה הקומוניסטית הסובייטית „פראוודה" נמנע מכל תגובה על המשבר במזרח התיכון או על החלטת מועצת הבטחון, שהגיעה למוסקבה מאוחר מכדי לפרסמה.

בעמוד הראשון מביא „פראוודה" סקירת התגובות בעולם על ההכרזה הסובייטית. בכותרת „תמיכה נלהבת בעמדה צודקת".

בעמוד פנימי, בכותרת גדר לה „לבלום את התוקפנות, להחזיר את השלום על כנו", מביא העתון שורה של מברקים של סוכנות „טאס" על הפעולות בחזיתות.

העתון עדיין אינו מביא אף מלה כי הטענות שהעצמות הערביים אתמול נגד ארה"ב ובריטניה בדבר הגשת עזרה צבאית לישראל. אבל העתון מביא מברק קצר מקאהיר על ניתוק היחסים הדיפלומאטיים בין קאהיר לארה"ב.

החוד של כוחות צה"ל 30 ק"מ מתעלת סואץ

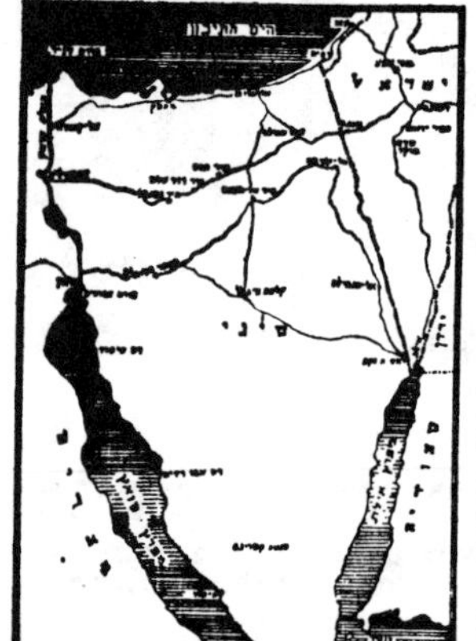

סוכנות „רויטר" מוסרת (בשעה 11.42), כי החוד הצפוני הישראלי מרוחק עכשיו כ־32 ק"מ מקנטרה. הטור מתקדם יותר מ־80 ק"מ מאל־עריש שעל כיבושה הודיעו אתמול.

קנטרה יושבת על תעלת הסואץ, ארבעים קילומטרים דרומית־מזרחית לפורט־סעיד בקו ישר. המרחק בכביש מקנטרה לפורט־סעיד הוא 80 ק"מ.

אחרי כיבוש הצומת החשוב אבו־עגילה, שהודיעו עליו הלילה, מסתער הכוח הישראלי בציר איסמעיליה על תעלת סואץ, מרחק 204 ק"מ מאבו־עגילה. לביר־חסנה הגיע צה"ל כנראה מכוציימה, מרחק 69 ק"מ, שנכבשה אתמול. ביר־חסנה היא 140 ק"מ מפורט־תאופיק ממזרח לסואץ על הצוואר של מפרץ סואץ.

ג'ונסון וקוסיגין החליפו איגרות על מניעת התנגשות במזרח התיכון

הנשיא ג'ונסון וראש ממשלת ברית־המועצות מר אלכסיי קוסיגין החליפו ביניהם איגרות על רצונם ההדדי למנוע עימות במזרח־התיכון — כך מודיע „וואשינגטון פוסט".

בכותרת ראשית אומר העתון, כי שתי המדינות הגיעו לכלל „הסכמה" ביניהן, וכי חילופי־האיגרות הסודיים בין הבית הלבן לבין הקרמל נערכו גם לפני פרוץ הקרבות בין ישראל לערביים, וגם בעת הקרבות.

בימים האחרונים היו ידיעות אחרות על חילופים כאלה. מקורות דיפלומאטיים מוסמכים אמרו, שהנשיא ג'ונסון ומר קוסיגין „החליפו דעות" על המזרח התיכון.

הבית הלבן ומיניסטריון החוץ בוואשינגטון עדיין לא הגיבו על הידיעה ב„וואשינגטון פוסט". אך בחוגים דיפלומאטיים בבירת ארה"ב רווחת הדעה, שחילופי הדעות בין ראשי שתי המדינות היה להם חלק בהכשרת הקרקע להסכם האמריקני־הסובייטי, שהוליד את החלטת מועצת הבטחון מאמש, הקוראת להפסקת־האש. (יו.פ.)

כוחות ישראל ימשיכו להתקדם בחצי־אי סיני – מודיעה „טאס" מניו־יורק

סוכנות טא"ס אומרת הבוקר במברק על דיוני הישיבה האחרונה של מועצת הבטחון כי „המשלחות המערביות, העומדות במגע הדוק עם המשלחת הישראלית, רמזו כי כוחות ישראל יוסיפו להתקדם בחצי האי סיני, כיוון שנציגי מדינות ערב במועצה לא הודיעו בבירור שהם מקבלים את החלטת הפסקת־האש".

לדברי הסוכנות הסובייטית, נתבררה גישה זו של המשלחות המערביות אחרי נאומו הקצר של הנציג הסובייטי, מר ניקולאי פדרנקו, שדרש להגשים מיד את החלטת מועצת הבטחון בדבר הפסקת האש. (סי"צ)

שר הבטחון מ. דיין ביקר אתמול על הר הצופים

שר הבטחון, מר משה דיין, ביקר אתמול אחרי הצהרים על הר הצופים. נילווה אליו אלוף פיקוד המרכז, אלוף עוזי נרקיס.

„גוף לא־מזוהה" גרם אזעקה בת"א

גוף זר בלתי מזוהה שנראה באיזור תל־אביב מעמדות תצפית גרם אזעקה הבוקר.

מועצת הבטחון החליטה פה אחד על הפסקת־אש

רוסיה השלימה עם המציאות – ויתרה על תביעת הנסיגה

אבא אבן: ביצוע ההחלטה תלוי בקבלתה על ידי הערבים בכנות ובשלמות

— מאת סיליס בן — ספר „מעריב" בארה"ב טלגראפית

ניו־יורק, בשעה 7.10 בערב בניו־יורק — 1.10 אחר חצות לפי שעון ישראל, — ... מאריך ... סביב שולחן ... בעצרת פה־אחד של מועצת הבטחון: כל 15 הנציגים הרימו ידיהם בהצבעה פה־אחד. הם הצביעו לאשר הצעה, השוברת כנראה את כל שיאי הקיצור של הודעות האו"ם. ההחלטה ממליצה ... שתיעשה מיד הפסקת אש.

אך לפני ההצבעה ... פה־אחד על ...

30 טנקים מצריים „ט־54" הושמדו אמש בג'בל לבני

הודעה לתושבי ירושלים: אפשר לצאת מהמקלטים

„קול ישראל" מסר בחדשות של שעה 11, בשם מפקדת הג"א כי תושבי ירושלים יכולים כבר לצאת מן המקלט.

שר החוץ, מר אבא אבן, אמר אמש באו"ם — לפי שידור של „קול ישראל" — כי ביצוע החלטת מועצת הבטחון בדבר הפסקת האש תלוי בכך שהצד השני יקבל ...

ג'ונסון: הקריאה להפסקת אש - צעד ראשון אל עידן של שלום

מר ג'ונסון הופיע בשידור טלוויזיה, ששודר מן האולפן בבית הלבן מיד לאחר שמועצת הבטחון הצביעה פה אחד על הפסקת האש. ובשעה שהנציג הסובייטי במועצה עדיין סיכם את הודעתו.

„אני מקווה, שהצדדים הנוגעים ישירות יפעלו בהתאם לכך", אמר מר ג'ונסון והוסיף, כי הקריאה היא „צעד ראשון לקראת עידן חדש של שלום רגוע של קידמה לכל עמי המזרח התיכון. מעתה נשאף למטרה זו", — הכריז.

נשיא ארה"ב, לינדון ג'ונסון, אמר אמש, כי קריאתה של מועצת הבטחון להפסקת אש בקרבות בין ישראלים לערבים פותחת „נתיב של תקוה בספינות המזרח התיכון".

מעריב ים
יום ד' כ"ט באייר תשכ"ז 7.6.67 גליון 6956 שנה 20
המייסד והעורך הראשון ד"ר ע. קרליבך ז"ל
העתון הנפוץ ביותר במדינה • MAARIV

הוצאה מיוחדת

מהדורת שעה 17.30

שארם־א־שייך בידי צה"ל

שארם א־שייך בידינו הודעה משמחת זו מסר היום אחר הצהריים דובר צה"ל. תפיסתה של נקודה זו כניסה למצרי טיראן על־ידי נאצר היא שהיוותה את נקודת המפנה ביחסי ישראל־מצרים בחודש האחרון. לאחר שגירש נאצר את חיל האו"ם משארם א־שייך, הודיע על ההסגר על מפרץ אילת. הודעה זו על ההסגר המצרי במצרי טיראן שהיה בה משום תוקפנות גלויה כלפי ישראל היא שגרמה להתלקחות באזור ועם כיבושה של שארם א־שייך ע"י צה"ל השיגה למעשה ישראל עוד אחת משלש מטרותיה שהציבה לעצמה.

א) פתיחת המעבר החפשי במפרץ אילת.

ב) הזזת הכוחות המצריים המאיימים מקדמת סיני.

ג) ביטול האיום של פעולות הסתננויות וחבלה מעבר לגבול.

בד בבד עם כיבושה של שארם א־שייך בוטל למעשה ההסגר במיצרי טיראן ועם התקדמותו של צה"ל עד ל־30 ק"מ לפיתחה של תעלת סואץ נהרס בחלקו הגדול הצבא המצרי המאיים בקדמת סיני. כיבושה של הרצועה ע"י צה"ל שחרר גם את האיום של ההסתננויות והחבלה מצד אנשי צבא השחרור הפלשתינאי שהתמקמו ברצועת עזה ובימים האחרונים גם בגדה המערבית של ירדן.

שכם נכבשה הבוקר

צה"ל כבש את שכם הבוקר. עם כיבושה של עיר זו התמוטטה למעשה כל מערכת ההגנה הירדנית בגדה המערבית.

דה־גול מקיים מגע עם קוסיגין

הנשיא דה־גול עמד במגע הדוק עם ראש הממשלה הסובייטית מר אלכסיי קוסיגין שלשום ואתמול, באמצעות „הטלפון הירוק" הישיר בין פאריס למוסקבה. כך אמר היום מיניסטר האינפורמציה הצרפתי מר ז'ורז' גורס, בתום ישיבת הממשלה. (סי"צ).

צ'ו אן־לאי שלח איגרת לנאצר

שגריר סין העממית בקאהיר נתקבל הבוקר על ידי נאצר ומסר לו איגרת מאת מר צ'ו אן לאי, ראש ממשלת סין. זאת מודיע ראדיו קאהיר.

עתונאי ארה"ב גורשו ממצרים

כל כתבי העתונים האמריקניים השוהים בקאהיר גורשו היום על ידי השלטונות. לשכת העתונות הודיעה להם שעליהם להתקשר עם השגרירות האמריקנית ולדאוג לכך שיצאו את גבולות המדינה יחד עם הדיפלומטים האמריקנים. (רויטר).

ואשינגטון: אם לא תסכים מצרים להפסקת־אש תשתלט ישראל על תעלת סואץ

חוסיין הסכים לשיחות על הפסקת־אש

יונייטד פרס מודיעה: מקורות ממשלתיים בוואשינגטון אמרו היום, כי המסע הישראלי בדרום ובמערב יכריח כנראה את מצרים לקבל את הפסקת האש במהירות או לעמוד לפני האפשרות של השתלטות ישראלית על תעלת סואץ.

המקורות מסרו כי ירדן הסכימה להפסיק את הקרבות וכי הדבר מוכיח שהמלך חוסיין [illegible] והישראלים עומדים להשתלט על נהר הירדן.

בינתיים פעלו הדיפלומאטים מאחורי הקלעים בנסיון להביא את המדינות הקשורות לסכסוך לקבלת הסכם הפסקת אש לפני שישראל תרחיב את הצלחתה עד כדי כך, שיהיה קשה בכלל להגיע להסדר במזרח התיכון.

דגל ציון על הר־הבית

תיאורים ראשונים של הכיבוש ומעמד התקיעה

החיילים הקשוחים מיררו בבכי

— מאת אלי לנדאו —
שנכנס עם הכוחות לעיר העתיקה

„הר הבית בידי. אני חוזר: הר הבית בידי". מספר יחידות צה"ל עמד ברחבת הכותל כשסביבו כמה חיילים שדמעות שטפו את פניהם המאובקים.

שלושה ימים של קרבות קשים נשכחו ברגע זה תחושה עמוקה של היפעמות שרתה על המעמד. כל מי שזכה להשתתף בו ידע שזה הרגע האחד אשר לא יימחה מזכרו כל ימי חייו.

אחרי שפרץ כוח החוד ונכנס דרך שער האריות לירושלים העתיקה, פתחו החיילים במרוצה אל הכותל — בלי לדעת בדיוק היאך מגיעים אליו. שום יעד אחר לא עמד ברגע ההוא לנגד עיניהם. בתוך סבך הסימטאות והמבואות התקשו למצוא את דרכם, ואחד מתושבי ירושלים העתיקה שימש להם — ולי — כמורה דרך.

זעקתו של צנחן

לפתע שמעתי קריאה, חייל שראה ראשון את הכותל, השמיע צעקה פראית: „אני רואה את הכותל המערבי". כולנו פרצנו אחריו דרך פשפש, ומיששנו את האבנים באהבה גדולה שנתלהטה פתאום בכל לב. חיילים נצמדו אל הכותל והחלו למרר בבכי. אינני זוכר במשך שלושת ימי הקרב על ירושלים העתיקה חיילים בוכים. למרות העובדה שראו את טובי רעיהם נפגעים. ואילו עתה כרעו ליד הכותל ומיררו בבכי כילדים קטנים. חיילים שפניהם מכוסים זיפי זקן ועיניהם אדומות מעייפות של קרב, התחבקו והתנשקו כשהם צועקים „ירושלים שלנו". סגן מפקד היחידה העלה כיתת משמר אל קיר הכותל המערבי. דגלן, קצין חבוש כיפה, עמד ב[illegible] הכותל והניף על תורן מאולתר את דגל ישראל. יחידת צה"ל ירתה מטחי כבוד [illegible] ידים.

השופר של הר סיני

רגעי התדהמה וההתפעלות הראשונים חלפו. עתה החילונו באמת מאמינים כי אמנם צה"ל על הר הבית. קצין צה"ל עלה אל מסגד עומר והניף שם את הדגל הישראלי. לפתע נשמעו תקיעות שופר בזו אחר זו. הרב הראשי לצה"ל, האלוף שלמה גורן, התקרב בריצה להר הבית כשבידיו ספר תורה ושופר — איתו שופר בו תקע על הר סיני ב־1956. הרב קרא דברי ברכה מרחבת הר הבית ואחרי כן המשיך במירוצו אל הכותל המערבי. במקום נערכה תפילה וכן קריאת „יזכור" לזכרם של החיילים שנפלו במערכה על כיבוש הר הבית.

עם הרב היו אותה שעה סגן הרמטכ"ל, האלוף חיים בר־לב, אלוף פיקוד המרכז עוזי נרקיס וכן קצינים בכירים אחרים, ביניהם אלוף משנה אברהם תמיר, יליד ירושלים, אשר היה בשבי הלגיון כאשר גוש עציון נפל במלחמת השחרור. כולם יחד החלו ספונטנית לשיר את „התקווה". קצינים ישראליים עמדו והצדיעו לכותל הקדוש.

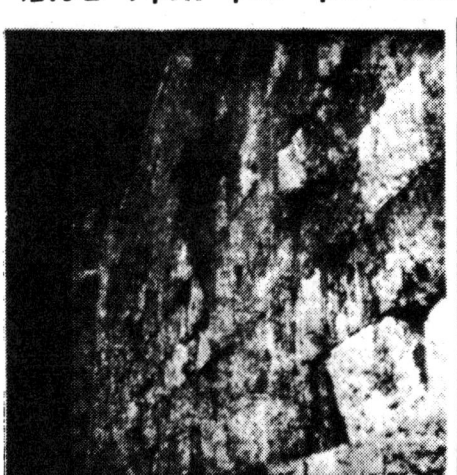

„אנחנו עולים על הר הבית"

לעולם לא אשכח את הדקות בהן רצתי ברחבה הנפלאה של הר הבית. לעולם לא אשכח את אלה אשר עשו את המלאכה כשהם חשים כי אמנם משימה היסטורית היא. בפקודה שנתן המפקד דקות אחדות לפני שפרצו היחידות אל העיר העתיקה. בעמדו עם פקודיו על גבעה החולשת על העיר העתיקה, תחת אש צלפים ומטר פצצות מרגמה, אמר: „מפקדים וחיילים, אנחנו עולים עתה על הר הבית. זוהי משימה היסטורית, העם היהודי מתפלל לנצחוננו. ישראל כולה מחכה עתה לדברכם. עלו והצליחו". באותו רגע החלו היחידות פורצות את חומת העיר העתיקה.

כאשר עמדו החיילים את השער, החלו רצים כולם בכיוון אחד. הפיקוד עבר מידי מפקדיהם לידי כוח אחר. פנימי, שבעמקי הלב. כולם רצו להיות ראשונים ליד הכותל המערבי. כולם רצו לזכות בחוויה הגדולה ולהיות כאלה המגישים לעם היהודי ולישראל את ההר הקדוש. השעה הוכשרה, והמשימה בוצעה.

דגל ישראלי מתנוסס בשעה זו בגאון מעל הכותל המערבי. על האבנים הכבדות הניצבות ומצפות לשעות היסטוריות אלה שנים ארוכות. חיילים ישראליים מתפללים בשעה זו ליד הכותל המערבי כשעיניהם זולגות דמעות.

הבחורים שנפלו בדרך

כשעמדתי הבוקר ליד אבן [illegible] בפינת הכותל המערבי והסבתי פני מזרחה, ידעתי כי אמנם שעה היסטורית היא. גם אני בכיתי ללא בושה. באותן דקות בהן עמדתי כחולם ליד הכותל הקדוש. כשמשמאלי מתנופף דגל ישראל ולידי חיילים קצתם מתפללים, קצתם בוכים. [illegible] עוצמים עיניהם כחולמים. זכרתי את החבורה הנפלאה שבמחיצתה הייתי בימים האחרונים. זכרתי את הבחורים שנפלו בדרך, ליד הגדרות של בית הספר לשוטרים של שייך ג'ראח. במעלה הגבעה הצרפתית וגבעת התחמושת בהסתערות על אותם מוצבים שנדמה היה כי לא ניתן לכבשם. הם עשו את הבלתי אפשרי. הלפתי בדרכי עם הכוחות ששטפו אל המוצבים שנכבשו בזה אחר זה.

בבוקר, בשעה 6.30 לערך, הגעתי בג'יפ־סיור עם שני לוחמים אגדיים להר הצופים. עמדתי על ההר תוהה ומשתומם. ירושלים של זהב סבלה בערפילי בוקר, ומתוך הערפילים התאבכו ענני עשן מפגיעות פגזים. דומה היה כאילו השכינה פורשת כנפיה על העיר. בשעה זו עדיין נמשכו חילופי היריות. זמן קצר אחרי כן החלו היחידות לנוע לכיוון „ויקטוריה אוגוסטה" ומלון „הילטון". שם התבצרו כוחות הלגיון. בשעה 8.30 החלו מטוסים ישראליים לרדת על המוצבים הירדניים ובמקביל החלו טנקים ויחידות רגלים לשטוף את הגבעות החולשות על העיר העתיקה. לפני שעה 10 היו הגבעות החולשות על ירושלים בידי כוחותינו ואחרי כן החל המסע ההיסטורי לכיבוש הר הבית. „אריות" החיילים החלו לצעוד אל שער האריות.

במסגד עומר

לא עבר זמן רב ועמדתי לפני מסגד עומר. הייתי בין ראשוני הבאים בשעריו. הלכתי על בהונות רגלי על השטיחים הרכים והגעתי ל„אבן השתיה". המקום שלפי המסורת המוסלמית קשר בו הנביא מוחמד את סוסו. גם כאן היתה לי הרגשה, כי אמנם משק כנפי ההיסטוריה מרחף מעלי. ניתנה הוראה על ידי סגן הרמטכ"ל לא להרשות לאיש להיכנס אל המקום הזה. הוראה זו נמסרה גם לגבי מקומות קדושים של דתות אחרות.

סיירתי ברחובות העיר העתיקה. בין בתיה הנמוכים והצפופים: פגשתי אזרחים, הזוכרים עוד את הישוב היהודי מלפני מלחמת השחרור. היו ביניהם ששוחחו עמי בעברית. רובם ידעו כי איש לא יפגע בהם לרעה. סיבבתי בין הבתים הצפופים. נכנסתי למספר חצרות עתיקות יומין וידעתי כי אמנם בירושלים דורכות רגלי. — ירושלים של דוד ושלמה. בעודני משוטט בעיר. המשיכו צלפים מנקודות שונות, מחלונות ומפתחי בתים לירות ביחידות. אך עד מהרה גילו שצליפה בשעה זו אינה סגולה לאריכות־ימים.

כוחות צה"ל מצאו עתה מנוחה קלה בין הבתים וליד החומות. מן העיר העתיקה יצאתי שוב דרך שער האריות לרמאללה. לכל אורך כביש האספלט רחב הידיים, היו פזורים כוחות ישראליים, שריון ורגלים. נסענו במהירות, כשאנו חולפים בדרכנו על פני מהמורות שנחרשו בפגזים והגענו אל מרכז רמאללה. בעיר החל הסדר לשוב על כנו. אזרחים תושבי העיר בעלי יוזמה, הפעילו כבר אוטובוס וביקשו להמשיך את חיי העיר כאילו לא קרה דבר. ערביה יצאה מפתח בית כשכד מים קרים בידה, מזגה לתוך כוס ואמרה לי בערבית: „שתה, חייל, שתה. איננו רוצים עוד מלחמה". גברים שחששו בתחילה לצאת, עמדו בפתח הבית ואחרי כן, כשראו שלא יאונה להם כל רע, יצאו ולחצו ידי. „איננו רוצים יותר במלחמה". חזרו הגברים הירדנים על דבריה של האשה.

עפולה
בית שאן
ג'נין
טול־כרם
שכם
יריחו
ראמאללה
ירושלים
חברון
ים המלח
הירדן

הגדה המערבית: היום נכבשה שכם. אתמול: רמאללה

„זה היום קיווינו לו, נגילה ונשמחה" - קרא הרב אלוף גורן ותקע בשופר

— מאת ג. צפרוני —

ב־12.05 בצהריים, כחצי שעה אחר שסגן הרמטכ"ל, אלוף חיים בר־לב, נכנס עם כוח צה"ל לעיר העתיקה דרך שער האריות, עמדתי מול מסגד עומר. חייל הניף את הדגל הלאומי על [illegible] המוזהב בראש כיפת מסגד עומר.

מסביב לרחבה ניצבו חיילים, ואשר לפניהם נכנעו מאות חיילים וקצינים שהרימו ידיהם.

המשכתי את דרכי לעבר מסגד אל אקצה, ומשם לשער מארוקו, יחד עם הרב הראשי של צה"ל, אלוף הרב גורן, הנושא בידיו ספר תורה ושופר.

ירדנו לרחבת הכותל. חיילים עברו דרך הרחבה לעבר שער יפו, תוך חילופי יריות עם קיני צלפים שטרם נכנעו. תושבי שכונת המוגרבים, שנהגו בערב להתנכל לבאים אל הכותל, מניפים עתה דגלים לבנים. מפנים הבתים נשמע בכי נשים ויללת תינוקות. בעוד חיילינו זורמים לתוך הסימטאות ועולים לישיבת פורת יוסף ליד בית הכנסת יהודה החסיד ותפארת ישראל. פשטו יתר החיילים לשער יפו, תוך יריות.

תקיעות שופר

אין לתאר את ההרגשה של כל אחד שהגיע לרחבה. את החיילים קידם הרב גורן בתפילה ובקריאת „מזל טוב". לידו בנו של הרב הקוק, הרב צבי יהודה קוק, ולידם „הנזיר" רבי דוד כהן, חמו של הרב הראשי הרב גורן. ולידו בנו. סגן ראש עיריית ירושלים הרב שאר ישוב כהן, שלפני 19 שנה היה אסיר בשבי הירדני, אחר שנשבה בעיר העתיקה.

כאשר הרב גורן עלה עם שופרו לרחבת המסגד — עולה במעלות השיש ותוקע בשופר. הוא קרא את ההכרזה לגאולת העיר העתיקה, הכותל המערבי והר הבית מידי [illegible] האויב.

בעת הקריאה התקבצו סביבו יחידות, שזרמו ברגל וברכב לתוך העיר העתיקה, דרך „ויא דולורוזה" לעבר שער שכם. הוא קרא: „חיילי ישראל, אהובי העם, עטורי הגבורה והנצחון, ה' עמכם, גבורי החיל". בהגיעו לרחבה, קרא לעבר החיילים: „אם אשכחך ירושלים תשכח ימיני". וכולו משולהב, קרא: „אני מדבר אליכם מרחבת הכותל המערבי, נחמו נחמו עמי, יאמר אלוהיכם, זה היום קיווינו לו, נגילה ונשמחה בישועתו".

תפילת מנחה

בעוד הרב גורן עורך תפילת מנחה כשהרחבה מתמלאת חיילים, פשטו חיילים אחרים לעבר קיני צלפים, שהמשיכו להתנגד.

מחוץ לחומות של מה שנקרא ירושלים העתיקה הירדנית, פוחתים והולכים הצלפים. הם מסגירים את עצמם, כשהם לבושים פיג'אמות וטוענים שאינם אנשי צבא. אולם רבים מופיעים בבגדי צבא ומסגירים את עצמם. נערכים חיפושים קיצוניים ושבויים רבים מוצאים [illegible].

החדירה החלה משער האריות. כאשר הגעתי לשם, קרוב לשעה 12.15, ראיתי את השער, שיירות הג'יפים עם הבאזוקות עברו לאורך „ויא דולורוזה".

הספקתי להיכנס למינזר בנות ציון ה„אקו הומו"; אמרו לי, שכמה יתומות יהודיות, מנישואין מעורבים, נמצאות במקום. ביקרתי במנזר הצרפתי של סנט אנה וראיתי במרתפיו. במבט חטוף, מאות נשים וילדים וגם גברים.

דגלים לבנים

משם עברתי לשער הורדוס. בשעה שיחידותיו ביערו קיני צלפים. ראיתי רובים וחגורות כדורים מושלכים מהחלונות. נושאי דגלים לבנים בידיהם התרבו, ככל שהיחידות התקדמו לעבר שער שכם ושער יפו ולמגדל דוד.

מגג בית הספר „מערופת אל דפטר" — אחד מבתי הספר התיכוניים העתיקים בעיר העתיקה — הסתכלתי לעבר השוק החדש. יחד עם יחידת חיילים התקדמתי לעבר שוק הבשמים ומשם לפרשת הדרכים לרחוב דוד.

בכניסה למסגד הייתי בחברת הלוחם הירושלמי הוותיק מחברת החשמל, משה הילמן, שלפני עשרים שנה היה ממונה על כמה רובעים בעיר העתיקה לזרם החשמל. במכונית האזרחית שלו נכנסתי לרחבת המסגד ומשם הקפנו את כל הרחבה, לאורך החומות, והגענו לשער הזהב, שלפי האמונה המוסלמית הוא שער סגור. הפתח להר הצופים, ויישאר סגור, כיוון שאם יפתח באחד הימים — יחזרו היהודים ויכבשו את הר הבית... הוא נקרא בפיהם „שער הזהב". השער נשאר סגור, אבל שער האריות ושער השבטים — או כפי שהוא ידוע בעולם הנוצרי, „שער סטפאן הקדוש" — נפתח לרווחה לפני לוחמינו.

סביב המיסגד השאיר הצבא הירדני מחסני נשק ותחמושת עצומים, אם כי לא לחמו במסגד כי הוא מקום קדוש. את התחמושת החלו להעביר במשאיות.

מרימים ידיים

בדרך מונחים [illegible]. השבויים בידיים מורמות מופנים למחסנים.

בג'יפ של גד עציון, ממושב ניר בנים, הגענו למחסן גדול, חבוי ליד באב אל סילסלה, הוא שער השושלת, הפתח אל רחוב דוד ושער יפו. בשער זה עברו גדולי מנצחי המוסלמים בכל הדורות, מאז קיים מיסגד עומר, שנבנה על ידי הכליף עבדול מאלק. ליד באב אל סילסלה היו עדיין צליפות. לפני 15 שנה נרצח בשער זה המלך עבדאללה, סבו של חוסיין.

המיסגד נשאר סגור, ויחידות הצבא לא נכנסו לתוכו. השערים נשברו על ידי חיילינו,

מעריב

יום ה׳ כ״ט באייר תשכ״ז 8.6.67 גליון 6957 שנה 20

20 אג׳

המייסד והעורך הראשון ד״ר ע. קרליבך ז״ל

העתון הנפוץ ביותר במדינה

ישראל שינתה את מאזן הכוחות במזה״ת לזמן רב – כותב „טיימס״ הלונדוני

„דיילי טלגראף״: ישראל רשמה פרק מופלא בהיסטוריה הצבאית. תחזיק בהישגים עד שיהיה הסכם־שלום ממשי

„טיימס״ הלונדוני במאמר ראשי.

הוא מוסיף, כי אין לזלזל באחדות הדעים הנדירה שנתגלתה באו״ם, שבדרך כלל מפגר תמיד אחרי המאורעות.

יתכן כי זהו סימן ראשון שרוסיה רואה נכוחה את העובדות של המצב החדש. רק אם הרוסים יחד עם האמריקנים, ובעצם שאר כל המדינות, יגיעו לכלל מסקנה שפשטו את

והרגל במדיניותן המזרח תיכונית, יהיה סיכוי גם לאו״ם.

„דיילי טלגראף״ אומר, כי ישראל לא נהנתה מיתרון של הפתעה, ותגובתה היתה דראמאטית וסבירה, והיא הצילה את העולם מן הסכנה של מכה במזרח התיכון. המעצמות הגדולות רעדו מפני התוצאות, אך ישראל פעלה לבדה ורשמה פרק מופלא בהיסטוריה הצבאית.

(הסוף בעמוד 8)

הופסקה האש בחזית הירדנית
המצרים והסורים ממשיכים להלחם

כל מעברות הירדן בידי כוחותינו * חיל האוויר מוסיף לתקוף את הצבא המצרי הנסוג לתעלה * הצבא הסורי נסוג לעבר דמשק

— מאת שמואל שגב —

משרד ההגנה האמריקני מסביר:
מטוסי ישראל תקפו את מצרים מצד הים – בפירצה של המכ״ם
לכן חשבו המצרים שהם באים מנושאות־מטוסים

חיילי או״ם הודיים שלחמו לצד המצרים בעזה – עצורים בקסרקטין

— מאת שמואל שגב —

(הסוף בעמוד 7)

שתי אניות של „צים״ יפליגו מאילת למיצרים

— מאת י. שרמי —

שתי האוניות „אנג׳ירד״ ו„עמליח״, המופעלות על ידי חברת צי״ם, יהיו הראשונות שיפליגו מנמל אילת לכיוון שארם א־שייך ויהיו בכך האוניות הראשונות העוברות את מיצרי טיראן אחרי פרי־

שתי האוניות שמכינים אותן להפלגה, מועמסות סחורות יצוא שונות, בין היתר שימורים, מיצי פרי הדר וכו׳, מתוצרת חברת „עסיס״, שהוכנו במחסני הנמל עוד לפני פרוץ הקרבות. הסחורות היו מיוע־

ג׳ונסון ומנהיגי ארה״ב מרוצים מנצחון ישראל

הקובאני ב־1962.

ההתלהבות ששררה אתמול בבית הלבן, במשרד החוץ האמריקני ובקונגרס — עמדה בניגוד חריף להלך הרוח הקודר שהילך שם ביום ב׳. נראה, כי הנשיא ג׳ונסון אסיר תודה במיוחד לישראל, משום שנצחונה שחרר אותו מן הצורך לשבור בכוח את ההסגר המצרי בטיראן, דבר שלא התלהב ממנו כלל וכלל.

התמוטטה החזית המצרית בתימן

החזית המצרית בתימן התמוטטה וכוחות המלוכנים החלו לזנב אחרי הצבא המצרי שם.

נאצר השאיר בתימן רק 10 אלפים חיילים, ואת היתר העביר לסיני, שם נשבו או הושמדו על ידי צה״ל.

באגרת חדשה לראש הממשלה
בריה״מ מאיימת בניתוק יחסים אם ישראל לא תפסיק את האש

— מאת יוסף חריף —

ישראל. עתידת מוסקווה לשקול גם „צעדים נוספים״. לא נאמר לאילו צעדים מתכוונת מוסקבה.

נודע, כי איגרת זו לא גרמה הפעם לעצבנות בירושלים.

ההודעה שמסר שר־החוץ במרכז האו״ם — על הפסקת אש עם ירדן — באה בעקבות דיון שקיימה אתמול ועדת השרים לעניני בטחון — בסמכות הממשלה — אשר הסמיכה את מר אבן להודיע באו״ם על הסכמת ממשלת ישראל להפסיק את האש, בתנאי שהמדינות הנוגעות בדבר תודענה גם הן על הסכמתן להפסיק את האש.

תציית ישראל להחלטת האו״ם בדבר הפסקת אש, תנתק בריה״מ את יחסיה הדיפלומאטיים עם ישראל. כן נאמר באיגרת, כי במקרה של אי הפסקת האש מצד

מימין לשמאל: הרמטכ״ל רב אלוף יצחק רבין, שר הבטחון, רב־אלוף משה דיין, והאלוף פיקוד המרכז אלוף עוזי נרקיס — בהיכנסם אתמול דרך „שער האריות״ לעיר העתיקה.

צרפת יירטה מטוס תובלה צבאי ישראלי שעבר בשמיה

— מאת אורי דן —

סופר „מעריב״ בפאריס

טלגראפית.

שלטונות התעופה של צרפת יירטו אתמול מטוס תובלה ישראלי צבאי, ש־

על כך חריפות באוזני השלטונות הצרפתיים.

מטוס ישראלי אחר מטוס הורשה על ידי הצרפתים לנחות אתמול — רק אחר שאול לו תדלק.

ידי הדין, האחבר „הצפתון בצרפת נתכנסה ... לדיון, ... והתעשיינים הצרפתיים, כדי לבדוק את שאלת אמברגו הנשק על ישראל.

הפסקה בבריטניה

הוחל בהקמת מנגנון למינהל בגדה המערבית

— מאת נ. צפריני —

נאצר ממרה פי מוסקבה

— מאת אורי דן —

גנראל למניצר: „הצבא הישראלי — הטוב בעולם״

מאת סופר „מעריב״ בפאריס טלגראפית

יקירנו

סרן אלכסנדר ערמון
(קסטנבאום)

נפל במילוי תפקידו

מתאבלים: אשתו ובתו, הוריו, אחיו ואחיותיו וכל המשפחה

הננו מודיעים בצער רב על פטירתה של

חנה (ראודנסקי) בן־אברהם

מקובנה, ליטא

הלויה תצא היום יום חמישי 8.6.67 מבית הלויות העירוני רח׳ דפנה 5, ת״א בשעה 1.00 בצהריים.

אוטובוס יעמוד לרשות המלווים בביתה רח׳ גורדון 5 ת״א, בשעה 12.15.

המתאבלים: בעלה צבי

בתה רבקה שפיר ובני ביתה

בנה עמי ובני ביתו

משפחות: ראודנסקי, איינשטיין

יד״ר בקשט

הועד האולימפי הבינלאומי דן באפשרות הפסקת התחרויות

מאת ישראל רוזנבלט
שליח „מעריב" במינכן

הבוקר בשעה 10, עמד הועד האולימפי הבינלאומי להתכנס לישיבה נוספת, כדי להחליט אם להמשיך את המשחקים האולימפיים או־לימפיקה. נשיא הועדה ה־מארגנת ווילי דאומה, שמסר על כך לפנות בוקר במסי־בת עתונאים, אמר כי לאור מותם של 11 הישראלים, יהיה לו קשה להמליץ על המשך המשחקים.

דאומה ציין, כי לאור ש־בתחילה נתקבלה הידיעה ה־מוטעית בשלו הצלחת הפעו־לה, החליט אמש הועד האו־לימפי הבינלאומי לחדש את המשחקים. אולם עתה, ייתכן שההחלטה תשונה.

שר הפנים של ממשלת בא־ואריה ד"ר מארק, הודה, כי אחדים מן המחבלים הערביים הועסקו בעבודות שונות בכפר האולימפי ! בלי לשים לב ל־ציניות שבדבר, מסר, כי תוך כדי המו"מ עם המחבלים, אי־

שר המפקדים כי לפחות אחד מאנשיו עבד בכפר האולימפי.

מסיבת העתונאים שהתקיימה לפני קהל רוגש של מאות עתו־נאים, שרגזו על התנהגות ה־

(סוף בעמ' 3, טורים 3, 4)

9 בני הערובה הישראליים במינכן נרצחו
בקרב עם הצלפים הגרמניים נהרגו גם 4 מחבלים

3 מחבלים נתפסו פצועים;— נהרג שוטר גרמני וטייס הליקופטר נפצע קשה בנסיון החילוץ שנעשה בשדה־תעופה צבאי ליד מינכן

אמבולנסים נכנסים בשערו של בסיס חיל האוויר הצבאי, הנתון במשמר כבד (משמאל). שוטרים ומכונית משוריינת מפקחים על התנועה במבואות שדה התעופה ליד מינכן (מימין).

מאת ישעיהו פורת וישראל רוזנבלט, שליחי „מעריב" במינכן

כל בני הערובה הישראליים שנישבו אור ליום אתמול בכפר האו־לימפי במינכן — 9 במספר — נהרגו הלילה לאחר חצות. בכך הגיע מספר ההרוגים הישראליים מבין חברי המשלחת האולימפית הישראלית ל־11. ההרוגים הם: מרימי המשקולות דוד ברגר, זאב פרידמן ויוסף רומנו; המתאבקים מארק סלאווין ואליעזר חלפין; המאמנים עמיצור שפירא, קהת שור, אנדריי שפיצר, משה ויינברג והשופטים יעקב שפרינ־גר ויוסף גוטפרוינד.

משה וויינברג ויוסף רומנו נרצחו אתמול לפנות בוקר בכפר האולימפי. שאר התשעה מצאו מותם בשעת הנסיון לחלצם בנמל התעופה הצבאי „פירסטנפלדברוק" ליד מינכן. ארבעה מבין שבעת המחבלים שתקפו את הישראלים מצאו מותם בנמל התעופה, שוטר גרמני קיפח את חייו וטייס ההליקופטר הגרמני נפצע קשה בתקרית. 3 מחבלים נתפסו כשהם פצועים.

הנהלת משלחת ישראל למשחקים האולימפיים התכנסה הבוקר לישיבה דחופה ותוך התייעצות עם גורמים ממשלתיים בירושלים הוחלט לחזור מחר לישראל.

הבוקר תשתתף משלחת ישראל בטקס אזכרה לנרצחים שייערך באיצטדיון האו־לימפי במינכן, בהשתתפות נציגי כל המשלחות המשתתפות במשחקים.

בדם קר ירו הערבים בישראלים שישבו כבולים בתוך המסוקים

מאת ישעיהו פורת
שליח „מעריב" במינכן

„עמדנו והסתכלנו עליהם מן החלון. אנו בקומה השניה, הם למטה כפותים בידיהם, אחדים גם ברגליהם. חלקם היו לבושים במדי הייצוג, אחרים בבגדים אזרחיים. השעה היתה 22.05 לפי ה־שעון המקומי. ארבעה מבין המחבלים ניצבו בצד אחד, מחבל נוסף ישב בחלקו האחורי של האוטובוס. לא יכו־לים היו להיות מטרה נוחה יותר. אבל הגרמנים החליטו ללכת בדרך משלהם. הם הלכו — ועמם הלכו תשעה אחים

יקרים" — במלים אלה ניתח קצין צה"ל את מה שאירע אתמול במינכן, מה שתואר בשעות המוקדמות של ה־לילה כהישג לכוחות הבטחון הגרמניים ונעשה תוך שעתיים אחד הכשלונות המחפירים.

קשה להבין כיצד ספח דוברה הרשמי של ממשלת גרמניה קונראד אלרס על שכמו, כאשר בשעה מוקדמת אמר לאחד מראשי המשלחת הישראלית: „זו היתה הצלחה גדולה".

„ממרחק של 50 מטרים לא הצליחו הצלפים לחסל את הרוצחים" — סיפר עד ראיה.

בפעולה ברברית, רצחו אתמול 8 ערבים בדם קר 11 ספורטאים, מאמנים ושופטים חסרי ישע — חברי משלחת ישראל לאו־לימפיאדה.

וזה קרה דווקא כאן במינכן, נוכח אי־יכולתם של כוחות הבטחון המקומיים לקיים את התוכנית שהיתה בדייקנות.

* * *

המיבצע כולו החל סמוך לשעה 10 בערב. אחרי 14 שעות של מיקוחים, אולטימטום חוזר ונדחה, דרישות שהלכו ונצטמצמו — וכאשר מדינה ערבית ראשונה, טוני־סיה, הביעה נכונותה לקבל את הרוצחים

וקרבנותיהם — השמידו הערבים משום אורחי מדגם בואינג 727 לרשות המסוקים. כדי למנוע מהומה בנמל־התעופה ור

(סוף בעמוד 8)

11 קרבנות
האסון הכבד
במינכן

ראה עמוד 12

מזועזעים מהאסון המחריד אנו מבכים מרה את מותם של בחירי הספורט הישראלי:

ברגר דוד
גוטפרוינד יוסף
ויינברג משה
חלפין אליעזר
סלאווין מארק
פרידמן זאב
רומנו יוסף
שור קהת
שפיצר אנדריי
שפירא עמיצור
שפרינגר יעקב

קרבנות הפשע המתועב במינכן

הועד האולימפי בישראל	מרכז א.ס.א.
מרכז הפועל	ההתאחדות לספורט
מרכז מכבי	ההתאחדות לכדורגל
מרכז בית"ר	אגוד הכדורסל
מרכז אליצור	אגוד הטניס

הממשלה מתכנסת לישיבה מיוחדת

יימסר דו"ח על המגעים עם גרמניה * נשלחו תנחומים למשפחות ההרוגים

מאת יוסף חריף

ראש הממשלה, גב' גול־דה מאיר, קראה להבוקר בשעה 9 לישיבת ממשלה מיוחדת. בישיבה זו יימסר דו"ח מלא על המגעים ש־נתקיימו בין ירושלים לבין מינכן משך כל הלילה עד למבצע החילוץ של בני ה־ערובה הישראליים מידי המחבלים הערביים.

משעה 5 לפנות בוקר נמ־סרו הודעות למשפחות מצד המטה המיוחד של רשות ה־ספורט במשרד החינוך והתר־בות ירושלים.

הודעה לראש הממשלה

סמוך לשעה 4.00 לפנות בו־קר נודע לראש הממשלה ו־לקבוצת השרים שהיתה בבי־תה, דבר האסון. מביתה של ראש הממשלה נתקיים כל ה־עת הקשר עם מינכן וכמנו ניתנו ההוראות מטעם ממש־לת ישראל לגורמים שהיו מעורבים במשא ומתן ובפעו־לות לקראת חילוץ בני הע־רובה הישראליים בידי ה־מחבלים הערביים.

השמחה ששררה לרגעים ב־ירושלים לשמע הבשורה כי כל הישראלים נחלצו נמוגה בהדרגה, ככל שידיעות אשר זרמו ממינכן לביתה של ראש הממשלה, באמצעות קו ה־טלפון הישיר שהותקן בין שתי הערים, היה בהן כדי לעורר ספקות אם אמנם הצליח ה־מבצע (ראה עמוד 3).

נתחזקו הספקות

סמוך לשעה 4.00 נתחזקו הספקות והתמונה שנצטיירה באותם רגעים היתה קודרת. זמן קצר לאחר מכן נמסרו לידיעת ראש הממשלה כל פר־טי האסון. מועקה ותדהמה יר־דו על הבית והנוכחים במקום לא יכלו להוציא הגה מפיהם לרגעים ארוכים, מגודל הכאב והתדהמה.

הפעולות שקדמו למבצע ו־פרטי המשא־ומתן עם המחב־לים נמסרו באורח שוטף ל־ירושלים. בביתה של ראש ה־ממשלה היה כל העת מזכיר הממשלה, מיכאל ארנון, אשר דאג להביא לידיעת השרים שלא היו בביתה של ראש הממשלה, את ההתפתחויות ה־חשובות. באותם רגעים שנד־רשו תגובות משמעותיות לג־בי התפתחות זו או אחרת, או במקרה שהיה צורך להחליט על מהלך מסויים — קיימה ראש הממשלה התייעצות טל־לית, כעין ישיבה טלפונית עם כל חברי הממשלה.

זמן קצר לאחר שנודע דבר האסון נוסחה הודעה מטעם הממשלה, שפרסומה נקבע ב־שעה, שבה יהיה ברור כי כבר נמסר למשפחות על אשר אי־רע ליקיריהם.

עד ראייה בנמל הצבאי פירסטנפלדברוק:

„זה היה דבר נורא ביותר"

„זה היה הדבר הנורא ביותר שראיתי מימי" — אמר אמש פקיד של חברת תעופה מערב־גרמנית לסופר „רויטר", לאחר שעזב את נמל התעופה הצבאי פירסטנפלדברוק, המקום שם נהרגו אמש תשעה אנשי המשלחת הישראלית לאו־לימפיאדה.

בנסיעה חזרה למינכן, לאחר שהיה לכוד בנמל התעופה ב־משך רוב הלילה, בעוד שה־מחבלים מארגון „ספטמבר ה־שחור" ערכו את התמודדות הרצח שלהם עם המשטרה ה־מערב־גרמנית, אמר האיש, כי שש גופות האנשים שהיו עדיין לבושים בבגדי איכון ספור־טיביים, הונחו בשורה על כס־לול ההמראה. „בטנם של כמה מהם היתה מרוטשת, מכדורי ה„מיקלעים" — סיפר.

עדי ראיה אחרים סיפרו: לאחר שהמסוקים נחתו, יצאו שני מחבלים מן המסוק ה־ראשון וצעדו אל כיוון „לופט־האנזה", כדי לבידקו. בעת ש־היו בדרכם חזרה למסוק, פת־חו צלפי המשטרה באש.

הפיישים המערב גרמ־ניים של שני המסוקים קפצו מן המסוקים. אחד מהם הצליח לחמוק, אך השני נפל לארץ, לאחר שספג כדורים של המח־בלים והמשטרה כאחד פגע בו.

לאחר שניות התפוצץ המסוק השני ועלה בלהבות. המש־טרה ניסתה לכבות את ה־שריפה — אך התיאשה.

לאחר שנסתיימה הפעולה והאש הופסקה, נראו ארבע גופות שרועות על המסלול.

זמן קצר לפני השעה 2 אחר חצות הובא אחד מן המחבלים לנמל התעופה במכונית שי־טור. השוטרים, שישבו בספ־סל האחורי של כלי הרכב, החזיקו במחבל בשערותיו ו־בידיו ורגליו. האיש נראה כ־אדם בגיל 20, כהה־שיער ו־בעל גוון פנים שחום. פניו היו מכוסים בוץ ודם.

שורה ארוכה של מכוניות משטרה החלה יוצאת מנמל התעופה בשעה 2.30 כיוון הדים נסתיים.

(רויטר)

לשאר חברי המשלחת שלום

אלה הם: הספורטאים: ה־סייפים דן אלון ויהודה וינ־שטיין; הקלעים הנרי הרש־קוביץ וזליג שטרוך; האתל־טים ד"ר שאול לדני ואסתר שחמורוב; המתאבק גד צברי; השחיינית שלומית ניר וכן ה־שייטים יאיר מיכאלי ויצחק ניר והאכנם אלי פרידלנדר, שהיו בקיל.

חברי הנהלת המשלחת: יו־סף ענבר, יצחק פוקס, יצחק כספי, שמואל ללקין, חיים גלוד־בינסקי, צבי פינקלשטיין, ד"ר סיוס ויינל.

כוננות בצבא הסורי מחשש לגמול ישראלי

מאת עודד זרעי
סופר „מעריב"
לעניינים ערביים

כוננות מיוחדת הוכרזה לפנות בוקר ביחידות הצבא הסורי ויחידות שריון הוזזו צבאות מסביב לדמשק נצטוו לתפוס עמדות הגנה מחשש לפעולת גמול ישראלית נגד המחבלים ובצבא הסורי ב־עקבות הרצח במינכן — כך מוסר הכתב ג'ין בידוק ביפר „דיילי טלגראף" ב־ביירות.

עם זאת, מעריכים דיפלו־מאטים ערביים, כי דווקא ב־של העובדה שישראל הדגישה שסוריה משמשת מרכז לפעי־לות התארגנות מחבלים, עלו־לה ישראל להלום גם ביעדים אחרים ובראשם ביירות, שם נמצאים המטות של ארגוני ה־מחבלים השונים לרבות האר־גון שביצע את פעולת הרצח במינכן.

משום כך סבורים דיפ־לומאטים אלו, כי יש ל־צפות לפעולת תגמול דר־מאטית ישראלית נגד ה־מחבלים בלבנון בדיוק כ־

צהלה בקהיר

בהיוודע דבר מותם של בני הערובה, לא הסתירה הבוקר קהיר את צהלות הנצחון על כשלון הנסיון לחילוץ הישרא־לים. עתוני קאהיר יצאו ה־בוקר בכותרות ראשיות המב־ליטות את „פעולתם ההירו־אית" של המחבלים והדגישו, כי ישראל חייבת להסיק שני לקחים עיקריים מתקרית מי־נכן:

צילה על הפעולה של פי־צוץ 14 המטוסים בשדה־התעופה של ביירות על־ידי כוחות צה"ל.

* פעולות הפידאיונים

(סוף בעמ' 2, טורים 3, 4, 5, 6, 7)

מעריב
היום 16 עמודים
יום א' י"ב תשרי תשל"ד 7.10.73
40 אג'
העתון הנפוץ ביותר במדינה • MAARIV
מייסד והעורך הראשון ד"ר ע. קרליבך ז"ל

הממשלה החליטה בישיבתה בלילה: מאבק – עד הדיפת אחרון הפולשים

הממשלה עומדת להתכנס שוב, לפנה"צ, כדי לשמוע דיווח מדיין

הממשלה נחושה בדעתה להמשיך את המאבק עד הדיפת אחרון הפולשים — כך סוכם בלילה בישיבה מיוחדת של הממשלה בתל-אביב.

ישראל עומדת במגע עם גורמים בינלאומיים ועם מדינות ידידותיות, כדי להבהיר עמדתה.

הממשלה שמרה להתכנס לישיבה בשעה 10. תהא זו הישיבה השניה תוך מהלך הקרבות והשלישית ביממה האחרונה מאז נפתחה התקפת ה... אפשרות של התפתחות איש. בישיבה זו ימסור שר הבטחון, משה דיין, על המצב בחזיתות המלחמה.

קרבות בלימה כבדים בסיני ובגולן
מצרים לא הצליחו להעביר שריון בלילה

...ידות קשות לאויב * טובעו 9 כלי שייט סוריים ומצריים
...שמדו 150 טנקים סוריים * כוחות קומנדו מצריים הושמדו

מאת יעקב ארז, סופרו הצבאי של „מעריב"
וכן סופרי „מעריב" מאיר הראובני ויוסף וקסמן

...בות שריון בשריון וחילופי אש ארטילריים נמשכו הלילה ...ם בגזרות הלחימה בסיני וברמת-הגולן. מטוסי חיל-האוויר ...כלילה ספינת מלחמה מצרית צפונית-מזרחית לפורט סעיד ...של חיל-הים הישראלי פשטו על ריכוז סירות מצרי בים ...טיבעו שלוש מהן שהיו מלאות כוחות פשיטה מצריים ...התארגנות לקראת תקיפה בחופנו. בסיני לוחצים הטנקים ...ל על הכוחות המצריים שצלחו את התעלה בשני ראשי-...קריים, שבהם הוקמו גשרים למעבר טנקים וחיילים. רק

כוחות קטנים של שריון מצרי הצליחו לחצות את התעלה נקודות מעטות מאד לאורך תעלת סואץ נמצאות בידי המצריב ומרבית השליטה על קו המים — בידי כוחות צה"ל. הקרב המכריע בסיני עדיין לא החל וכוחות צה"ל מכינים את המהלומה המכרעת על כוחות הפלישה.

ברמת-הגולן התנהלו בלילה קרבות שריון כבדים לאורך קו המוצבים — בעיקר באזור קונייטרה ובאזור חושנייה שבמרכז הגולן, שם בולמים כוחותינו את השריון הסורי ומסבים לו אבידות. הבוקר החלו מטוסי חיל האוויר בתקיפה גדולה על הכוחות הסוריים.

לא השיגו הישג בעל משמעות

יחידות שריון וארטילריה — לסיני

(סוף בעמ' 2 טור 5, 6, 7, 8, 9)

דמשק: קרב אויר חדש בשמי הגולן

הפיקוד הסורי טען הבוקר בדמשק כי טייסים ותותחני נ.מ. סורים הפילו מטוסים ישראלים, בקרב חדש בשמי רמת הגולן הבוקר. (ע"ר)

ארה"ב עדיין לא החליטה על דרך פעולתה
ישראל מסכימה לטאקטיקה האמריקנית

מאת שמואל שגב, סופר „מעריב" בוואשינגטון

אף שארה"ב רוצה לעשות כל מה שביכולתה לשם הפסקת הקרבות על גבולות ישראל עם מצרים וסוריה, עדיין לא החליטה על דרך פעולתה, באמצעות או"ם או בדרכים דיפלומטיות אחרות.

ישיבת חרום של צוות המשימה המיוחד בוושינגטון, שבראשו ישב שר החוץ ד"ר הנרי קיסינג'ר נסתיימה בהשכמת הבוקר (לפי שעון ישראל)...

כפרות תשל"ד

מצרים

סוריה

בטליתות של תאקי

את תפילות יום הכיפורים אמרו אתמול המונים מגבריה של ישראל בטליתות-של-תאקי.

וכל מי שנפרד מהם כאשר יצאו לדרך — האבות והאמהות והרעיות והילדים הרכים — התפלל שתפילתם תירצה.

המלים העתיקות שבמחזור לבשו משמעות חדשה, נוראה ומלאת הוד. כל מה שנאמר בהן על החיים ועל המוות, על הדין ועל הרחמים, נעשה קרוב מאד, ממשי מאד, אישי מאד.

כאשר יצאו המוני המתפללים מבתי הכנסיות והלכו אל מקומות האיסוף של יחידותיהם, ראשיהם עדיין עטורים בכיפות ולבם כבד עליהם מחמת הפרידה הפתאומית ומחמת משא האחריות שהועמס על כתפיהם, לא נפסקו הפיוטים והיוצרות וסדר העבודה. הם הוסיפו להתרונן, בלבות היוצאים, ונהימת המנועים וטרטור הגלגלים לא יכלו להחריש את לחנם. הכבישים המוליכים אל מרחבי סיני ואל הרי הגולן נהפכו לבתי תפילה, ומן האוטובוסים והמשאיות נישאה תחינה חרישית אל השמים הכחולים והבקיעה את שעריהם ועלתה ובאה לפני כסא הכבוד.

לא אומה זכה ממנה שכל תפילות עולם, ולא נאמרה שמנה במנה בשום בית של לך ...

האויב שביקש להשבית את קדושת יום הכיפורים, שאמר להפתיע אומה חשרויה בצום ועמודת בתפילה, טעה גם הפעם בחישוביו. הקדושה לא נפגמה. היא נתעלתה למעלות חדשות.

שליטי קאהיר ודמשק, שדימו בנפשם כי הנה באה להם שעת כושר לפגוע במפתיע, לקטול באין מגן, ולזכות בנצחון קל, יודעים מעט מאד על טיבה ופגולותיה של האומה היהודית. אם סבורים היו שיום אחד בשנה נעשית מדינת ישראל חסרת-ישע, הם טעו טעות מרה. אם האמינו כי התענית והתפילה יפריעו בגיוס האומה למלחמת הקיום, הם השלו את עצמם עד מאד.

שעה שהמטירו את פגזיהם ואת פצצותיהם על המעונים ועל המחנות, סגרו המוני בית ישראל את מחזוריהם וכיוונו את לבותיהם ואת ידיהם אל המשימה החדשה שהוטלה עליהם. והמעבר היה טבעי ומובן כאליו. היד ששמטה את המחזור אחזה ברובה.

האומה נתלכדה מאמוניה, בחרדה ובאמונה. התפילה לא נפסקה; היא נמשכת בכלים אחרים ובמקומות אחרים.

אבל באותה קדושה, באותה טהרה.

המלחמה בגבולות בטוחים

המלחמה, שנגזרה עלינו המצרים והסורים — היא המלחמה הראשונה, שישראל מנהלת אותה בגבולות בטוחים.

זו המלחמה הראשונה, שצבאות האויב מזנקים לקרב כשגבולות המדינה רחוקים מלבה של המדינה וכשקרבות מתנהלים בשטחים נרחבים והרחק מריכוזי האוכלוסיה, כשלצבא ...

רוסיה לא רצתה להיות מעורבת בהרפתקה הצבאית המצרית-סורית — אולי גם בגלל הערכתה מה יהיה סופה, וגם — או בעיקר — בגלל הסכם ברז'נייב-ניכסון על אי-התערבות ובגלל שאיפתה של מוסקווה, לשמור את אוירת ההפוגה ביחסי-המעצמות וגם למנוע התערבות פעילה אמריקנית.

חטנקים יוצאים לקרב, אי שם בצפון (תצלום: נרי גביש, ישראל סאן)

חוסיין העמיד צבאו במצב הכן: משקיפים: מלך ירדן עלול להתערב

סאדאת קורא להתערבותן של כל חברות הליגה הערבית

אתמול קיים חוסיין, מלך ירדן, התייעצויות דחופות עם מפקדי צבאו, והורה להעמיד את צבא ירדן במצב כוננות נוכח ההתפתחויות בחזית המצרית והסורית.

מלך ירדן שוחח אתמול טלפונית עם נשיאי מצרים וסוריה, אשר הבטיחו להעמידו באופן שוטף על השתלשלות הקרבית.

משקיפים בערביים, ציינו הבוקר כי אם יימשכו הקרבות עלול המלך חוסיין להצטרף למלחמה אך לא מתוך תקווה להצלחה, אלא מתוך „אבירות ערבית".

נשיא מצרים, אנוואר סאדאת, שלח מברק למזכיר הכללי של הליגה הערבית, מחמוד ריאד, הנמצא עתה במטה או"ם בניו-יורק, ובו הוא מפנה את תשומת לבן של כל המדינות הערביות החברות בליגה הערבית לסעיף באמנת הליגה, הקובע כי כל פעולה תוקפנית נגד מדינה ערבית אחרת, תיחשב לפעולה תוקפנית נגד כל מדינות הליגה.

רדיו לוב יצא אתמול בקריאות חוזרות ונישנות למלך חוסיין להצטרף למלחמה.

עדות טייס מצרי שבוי: המצרים יזמו המלחמה

מאת יעקב ארז, סופרו הצבאי של „מעריב"

טייס מצרי, שנשבה אתמול בצהריים בידי כוחות צה"ל באזור רפידים, כשמטוסו מטיפוס „סוחוי" שתקף את הבסיס, הופל באש כוחותינו, מסר בחקירתו עדות המוכיחה, כי המצרים הם אשר יזמו את המלחמה.

הטייס סיפר, כי הוא השתייך לרביעית מטוסי „סוחוי" שמשימתה היתה לתקוף בשעה 2 בצהרים את שדה התעופה ברפידים. הוא אמר, כי את פקודת המשימה קיבל המבנה, שאליו השתייך, עוד בשעה 11 בבוקר.

לרגל מצב החירום והגיוסים הנרחבים מופיע גליון זה — גליון ראשון ל„מלחמת יום כיפור" — ב-16 עמודים בלבד. „מעריב" וויתר לרגל מצב החרום על עמודי-פרסום רבים ו התרכז בתיאור המערכה בלבד.

„אהרם": ברז'נייב שלח איגרת לסאדאת

עוד יומיים לפני פרוץ הקרבות, עשתה בריה"מ מאמצים להניא את מצרים וסוריה מלפתוח במלחמה, ורק משנכשלו מאמצים אלה הורתה, כי כל הנראה, על פינוי היועצים הסובייטיים ובני משפחותיהם ברכבת אוירית.

הבוקר נודע, כי מנהיג בריה"מ ברז'נייב שלח איגרת לנשיא סאדאת, אחרי פריץ הקרבות. אשר תוכנה לא נמסר לפירסום.

יומיים בלבד לפני שפתחה מצרים בהתקפה, נפגש שגריר בריה"מ בקאהיר, ולאדימיר וינוגראדוב עם הנשיא סאדאת בפעם השניה תוך עשרה ימים. בפגישות הובהרו לשגריר הסובייטי, בקווים כלליים, פרטי המיתקפה המצרית. פגישה דומה היתה בין נשיא סוריה, חאפז אל-אסד, לבין השגריר הסובייטי בדמשק, נור א-דין מוחידינוב.

מגיהים, כי בפגישות אלו הבהירו השגרירים הסובייטיים את הסתייגות ממשלתם מחידוש הלוחמה באיזור. כשהעלו חרס בידם החליטה בריה"מ לפנות את כרבית היועצים הסובייטיים בסוריה ובמצרים ובני משפחותיהם ברכבת אוירית.

ממקורות מהימנים נודע, כי הפיגני הסובייטי כלל את היועצים ובני משפחותיהם החלק מן הסגל הדיפלומטי, שהוטסו ברכבת אוירית.

לא היה זה מקרה, כי השגריר הסובייטי בקאהיר, ולאדימיר וינוגראדוב, היה אתמול השגריר הזר הראשון עמו נפגש מנכ"ל משרד החוץ המצרי בקאהיר, כדי לדווח לו על מהלך הקרבות.

השגריר מיהר לדווח לממשלתו ובתגובה שלחה בריה"מ איגרת לנשיא סאדאת, כפי שדווח הבוקר ב„אל-אהראם" הקאהירי.

...כום יום ראשון למלחמה

צה"ל שיחרר את החטופים

אחרי קרב עם טרוריסטים וחיילי אוגנדה באנטבה

מעריב

יום א'
ו' תמוז תשל"ו
4.7.76
גליון 9727
שנה כ"ט

1.10 ל"י

MAARIV • העתון הנפוץ ביותר במדינה

מייסד והעורך הראשון ד"ר ע. קרליבך ז"ל

המטוסים והמשוחררים בדרך לארץ

מאת דן אביקו

צה"ל שילח הלילה את זרועו הארוכה ל־מרחק של 3600 ק"מ. במבצע נועז ומהיר, שנמשך זמן קצר ביותר חילצה אחת היחידות המובחרות בצה"ל את כל חטופי מטוס „אייר פראנס" ואת הצוות הצרפתי של המטוס, משדה התעופה של אנטבה. החטופים ומ־חלציהן נמצאים — ב־שעת כתיבת שורות אלו (05.00) בדרכם ארצה.

„השמידו מיגים של חיל־האויר האוגנדי"

רדיו פאריס הודיע הבוקר, בבסגרת הדיווח מ־אוגנדה, כי בעת הפעולה הושמדו כספר מטוסי מיג של חיל־האויר האוגנדי, שחנו בנמל התעופה של אנטבה.

הטרמינל בנמל התעופה באנטבה שבו פעלו כוחות צה"ל הלילה

אחרי הפשיטה באנטבה תודלקו המטוסים בנמל התעופה בניירובי

מטוס אחד נשאר עוד שעה אחת כדי „לקבל עזרה כירורגית לפצועים ואחר כך המריא"

(סוף בעמ' 11, טורי 5, 6, 7)

„מיבצע הרקולס" של ישראל מעורר תדהמה והערצה בעולם

בארה"ב: גלי שמחה והערכה ✶ בצרפת: התלהבות בכלי־התקשורת — הפתעה ורוגז בממשלה

(סוף בעמ' 2, טורי 1, 2)

האוגנדים סיפקו נשק נוסף לחוטפים

„המחבלים הלכו לישון וחיילי־אידי החליפום בשמירה על החטופים"

פעולת קומנדו ללא תקדים מבחינת התעוזה והטווח

הבעייה המרכזית: להגיע, להפתיע ולנטרל את הטרוריסטים והחיילים

מאת אורי דן

מיבצע הקומנדו של צה"ל באוגנדה היה הנועז ביותר כסוגו שבוצע עד כה וה־מרחק הגדול ביותר. היה זה מיבצע משולב של חיל ה־

המשימה היתה קשה לביצוע ונועזת לא רק בגלל הבריחה אשר צה"ל לא התנסה בו עד היום, אלא בגלל הצורך לשמור על כך שבני הערובה לא יפגעו

(סוף בעמ' 11, טורי 3, 4, 5)

עתוני קהיר: הקומאנדו הישראלי שיחרר

מאת עידוד נרנות

תחנת השידור של לוב היתה התחנה הערבית הראשונה שדיווחה הלילה, בשעה 2.30 אחר חצות על פעולת צה"ל באנטבה, בהסתמך על דיווח סוכנויות הידיעות.

כמה מעתוני קאהיר יצאו הבוקר בכותרת: „הקומאנדו הישראלי חילץ את בני הערובה משדה התעופה של אנטבה". „מטוסים ישראליים הטסו את ניסיוני המטוס החטוף לניירובי".

בשיחה טלפונית עם סופר „מעריב" אורי דן

אידי אמין: אני סופר את הגופות של חיילי

טוען: אני מאמין שגרמתם לי רעה תחת טובה

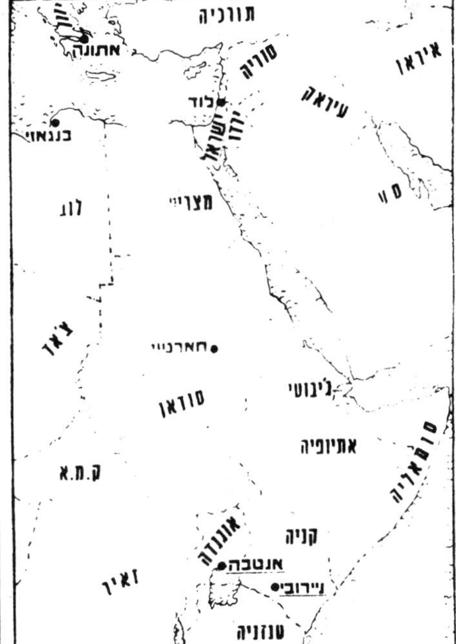

מפה הממחישה את המסלול שנאלצו לעשות מטוסי החילוץ של צה"ל.

„בוקר טוב אדוני הנשיא"

מעריב

יום א'
ו' תמוז תשל"ו
4.7.76
גליון 9727
שנה כ"ט

1.10 ל"י
כולל מס ערך מוסף

המייסד והעורך הראשון ד"ר ע. קרליבך ז"ל

העתון הנפוץ ביותר במדינה • MAARIV

הוצאה מיוחדת

גליון מיוחד מוקדש לשחרור חטופי אוגנדה

המשוחררים שהוחזרו לארץ במטוסי הרקולס מספרים:

שמענו קול בעברית: „שכבו על הארץ" אז ידענו שצה"ל בא להצילנו

„אילו רצו האוגנדים, הם היו יכולים לחסל את הטרוריסטים בקלות" ✶ „אידי שיחק – פעם היה בעדנו, פעם בעד המחבלים" ✶ „חיילי אוגנדה ברחו כמו פחדנים בהישמע היריות" ✶ „ראינו את הגרמני והגרמניה הרוגים" ✶ רבין ופרס קיבלו הלוחמים בשובם ✶ שגריר צרפת: „נתתם שיעור לעולם כולו"

כתבי „מעריב" שכיסו שובם של החטופים וחיילי צה"ל: דן ארקין, אורי דן, רוני אשל, ישעיהו אביעם, מרדכי אלקן, אבי בטלהיים, יהושע כהנא, גיל קיסרי, מנחם שמואל, שרגא הרגיל.

„כששמעתי את פרץ היריות הראשון, לא ידעתי מה בדיוק קורה, שכן כולנו כבר היינו במיטותינו. האינסטינקט הראשון שלי היה לתחוב את הראש נמוך ככל האפשר, כדי לא להוות מטרה. כעבור כמה שניות הרמתי את ראשי כדי להציץ סביבי וראיתי אחד המחבלים יורה. תחבתי את ראשי שוב עמוק לתוך המזרון. כעבור דקות אחדות שמעתי משפטים בעברית: „חבר'ה, שכבו על הארץ עד שהיריות יסתיימו". הבנתי תיכף ש,כוחותינו' הגיעו" — כך סיפר הבוקר איתן אהרונוביץ מרמת גן, מחטופי המטוס, שהגיע למרכז הרפואי על-שם שיבא בתל-השומר, לשם הובאה אשתו. מרים, שנפצעה

(סוף בעמ' 2, טור' 3, 4, 5)

ביצעו „בז" שימחה בשמי אילת

מאת יצחק בן-חורין

טייסי ה„הרקולסים" שהחזירו את החטופים מנמל אנטבה, לא יכלו להסתיר את שמחתם.

שני מטוסים שהובילו חטופים לנמל התעופה בן-גוריון ביצעו סיבוב נצחון בשמי העיר אילת וסיימו ב„בז" — הנמכה עד לגובה של מטרים ספורים מעל למסלול שדה התעופה האילתי — לפני שהמשיכו בדרכם צפונה.

3 מהחטופים נהרגו במבצע החילוץ — 2 פצועים מאושפזים בניירובי

שניים מההרוגים: אידה בורוביץ מבת-ים וז'אן ז'אק מימוני מנתניה

שניים מבני הערובה — אידה בורוביץ מבת-ים, וז'אן ממוני, בן 19, מנתניה, נהרגו הלילה בפעולת החילוץ באנטבה.

מימוני עלה לארץ לפני חמש שנים מצרפת, יחד עם בני משפחתו. אביו, ויקטור, עובד בקונסוליה הצרפתית בישראל.

ז'אן ז'אק מימוני יצא בשבוע שעבר בדרכו לפאריס, כדי לסיים שם את לימודיו. לפי בקשת חברו, בנו של הקנסול הצרפתי, דחה את נסיעתו בכמה ימים ויצא במטוס „אייר פראנס", שהגיע בסופו של דבר לאוגנדה.

אביו של ז'אן ז'אק מימוני היה הבוקר בין הראשונים שהגיע לבסיס חיל האוויר, והשתתף יחד עם האחרים בשמחה. מאוחר יותר נקרא מימוני לאחד המיתקנים של הבסיס, ואז בישרו לו את הבשורה המרה, שבנו נהרג. מימוני הנדהם יצא החוצה, קרע את חולצתו וקרא קריאות גנאי נגד ממשלת צרפת, שלא ידעה לדאוג לנוסעי מטוס „אייר פראנס". הוא ניגש אל דגל הלאום, שהניף אחד האנשים ב-

(סוף בעמ' 2, טור' 6, 7, 8, 9)

דורה בלוך נשארה בקמפלה

הגב' דורה בלוך, ישישה בת 80, אמו של העתונאי דניאל בלוך, היא היחידה שנשארה באוגנדה. היא אושפזה לפני ימים אחדים בבית החולים בקאמפאלה, בגלל מחלה ותשישות.

בנה, אילן, אחיו של דניאל בלוך — שהיה אף הוא בין החטופים — חזר היום במטוס של צה"ל ללוד. הוא סיפר, כי לפני ימים אחדים חשה אמו חולשה, והחוטפים נענו לבקשת הרופאים והעבירוה לבית החולים.

אחד מהרוגי הפעולה באנטבה

ז'אן ז'אק מימוני

דני דוידסון בן 13, מהחטופים ששוחררו, מספר:

שיחקנו תופסת וקראנו ספר מצחיק: גברים במלכודת

מאת עפרה אדיגין

„היו 20 ילדים חטופים, מהם 10 ישראליים" — מספר דני דוידסון, בן 13, מתל-אביב, אשר היה בין החטופים, עם אימו ואחיו הגדול בן 16, ששמו רון.

„מה אכלתם?" — שאלו את דני, והוא מספר שכל הזמן אכלו אורז ובננות.

„לא איבדנו אף לרגע אחד את הביטחון; ידענו שיוציאו אותנו איך-שהוא. אני פחדתי מאוד. בשביל להעביר את הזמן שיחקנו בקלפים שהיו לנו, עם ההורים ועם חברים אחרים. בין המחבלים אשר חטפו אותנו היתה בחורה גרמניה, כנראה מבאדר-מיינהוף. היא היתה שחורה. ואיתה גבר צעיר בלונדיני. הם היו גסי-רוח והתנהגו איתנו לא יפה. הם נהרגו וכבר אינם. אני לא ראיתי כיצד נהרגו. אני ראיתי אותם רק אחרי-כן".

„האם פגשת את אידי אמין?"

„כן, הוא היה אצלנו ודיבר איתנו ומישהו תירגם. כל יום נתנו לנו לצאת לשחק בחוץ ולטייל; היינו יוצאים עם ההורים. שיחקנו גם קצת בתופסת".

„האם היו לכם ספרים?"

„לי היה ספר מצחיק מאוד, ,גברים במלכודת'. ביום האחרון הפסיקו לנו את המים והיינו צמאים מאוד. רבים מאיתנו קילקלו את הקיבה. היתה הרעלה כללית, ומסיבה זאת כנראה הפסיקו את המים. כל אלה שבאו הגיעו בצורה מסודרת, וזה פלא. משום שמאז שנחטפנו לא החלפנו בגד. ישנו באותם הבגדים. ישנו עם מזרנים על ריצפה".

„האם שוחחתם עם המחבלים?"

„כן, הם דיברו איתנו. הם אמרו לנו שהם לא יהרגו אותנו. אנחנו שיחקנו בחוץ ,אחת שתיים שלוש דג מלוח'. היה צוות הצרפתי. צוות המטוס היה נה-

(סוף בעמ' 2, טור' 7, 8, 9)

יום ג' 27.3.79 | כ"ח אדר תשל"ט

גליון מס' 9559 — שנה ל"ב

המחיר —.4 ל"י כולל מע"מ

המייסד והעורך הראשון ע. קרליבך ז"ל

היום 60 עמוד

מזג האוויר להיום: מעונן חלקית עד מעונן. ירדו גשמים בודדים במשך היום וייעשה בהדרגה מעונן חלקית.
טמפרטורות: רמת הגולן: 12—8; חיפה: 19—13; ירושלים: 13—6; תל־אביב: 19—12; הר שומרון: 13—7; מישור עזה: 19—11; אילת: 24—13; כפרץ שלמה: 25—16; באר־שבע: 18—9.

שלום

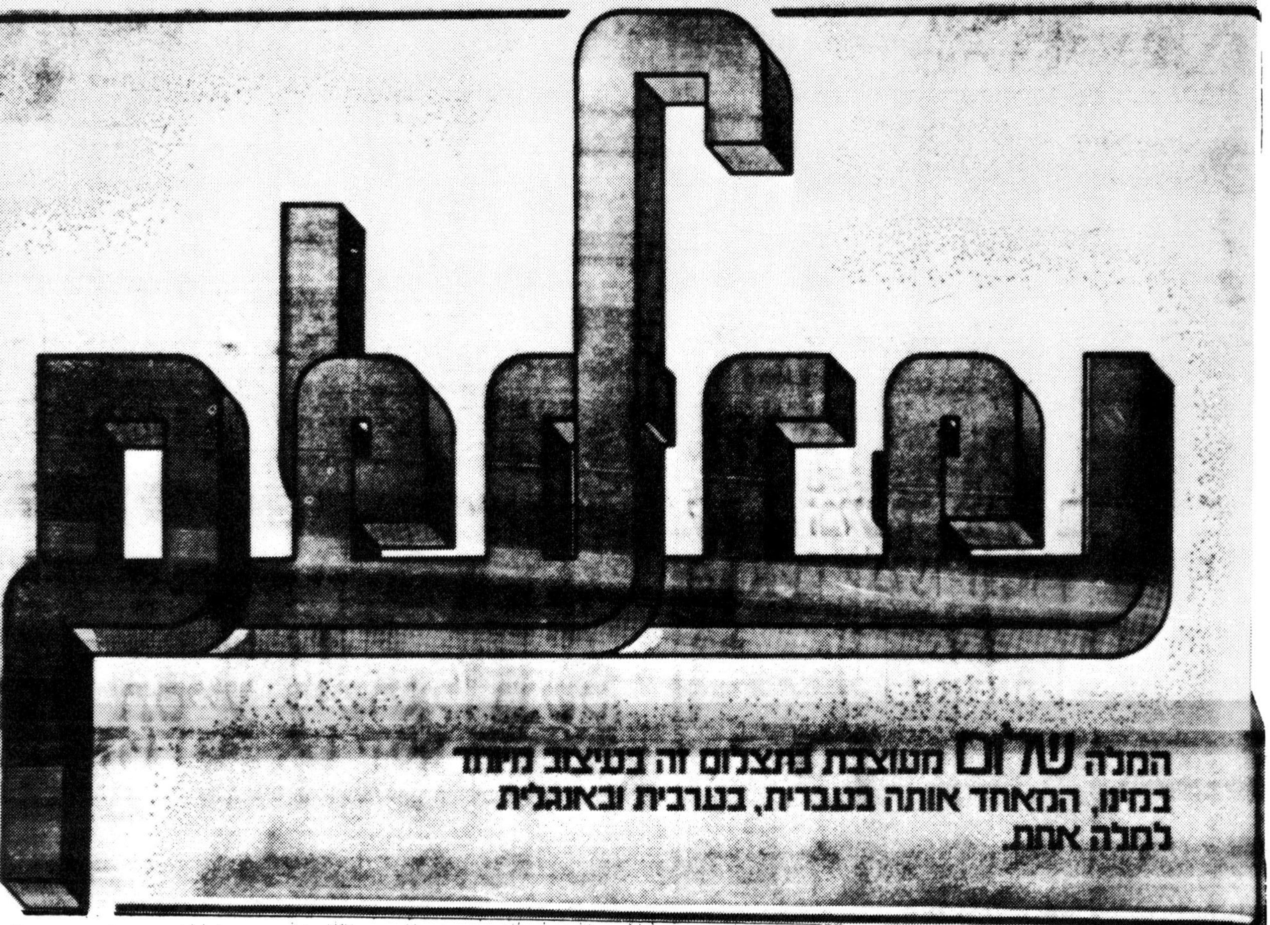

המלה **שלום** מעוצבת בתצלום זה בעיצוב מיוחד במינו, המאחד אותה בעברית, בערבית ובאנגלית למעלה אתם.

ישבתי, רשמתי שלום

קארטר סאדאת ובגין חתמו על התדפיס

מאת עידו דיסנצ'יק
וושינגטון

נשיאי ארה"ב ומצרים וראש ממשלת ישראל חתמו לפנות בוקר על תדפיס הכרזה „שלום" המופיעה בראש עמוד זה בשלוש שפות.

בחתמו על התדפיס אמר הנשיא סאדאת:

„הרי אתם רואים, תמיד אמרתי שיהיה שלום, תמיד אמרתי שיג חוזה, תמיד הייתי אופטימי ואמרתי לכם לא להתייאש".

ראש הממשלה מנחם בגין בחותמו על התדפיס, אמר: „הרי זה יוצא מן הכלל" — והציג זאת מיד לפני הנשיא קארטר שישב

(ס"ף בעמוד 11)

מאת שלום רוזנפלד,
עורכו הראשי של „מעריב"
וושינגטון

על המידשאה הצפונית של הבית הלבן נסתיימה זה עתה נגינת שלושת ההימנונים — כשחלק מן הקהל מצטרף לשירת „התקווה" — ולנשיא הריפובליקה המצרית אנואר סאדאת הוגש צרור דפים כרוך בכריכת עור כחולה מפוארת, שזורה בפסי זהב לאורכה ולרוחבה.

נשיא מצרים — הבעה פניו רצינית כמעט קפואה — חותם על החוזה [illegible] הראשון בהיסטוריה בין מדינה ערבית לבין מדינת ישראל. ראש ממשלת ישראל, מנחם בגין — בארשת חגיגית — חותם אחריו, כל אחר טופס, בערבית, עבריה ואנגלית, ונשיא ארה"ב חותם ומשלים.

השעה שתים ושמונה דקות. כ"ז באדר תשל"ט. 26 במרס 1979.

[illegible] כאלף וחמש מאות אנשים מישראל, מצרים ומכל קצווי ארה"ב, [illegible] בשערי הכניסה כדי להתהכך [illegible] בהיסטוריה.

[illegible] מצמיד מבטו אל שלושת האישים בחליפות הכהות, היושבים ליד [illegible] העץ העתיק, כשבגבם מתנופפים ברוח שלושת הדגלים של מדינותיהם, ומנסה לקרוא בפני השחורים [illegible] והמהורהרים של נשיא מצרים, [illegible] מימינו של קארטר, מה מתרחש בלבו של מנהיג ערבי שרק לפני [illegible] שנים היה אלילם של כמאה [illegible] מאחז בכל המרחב הערבי — [illegible] עד [illegible]

(ס"ף בעמוד 11)

נחתם הסכם השלום בין ישראל למצרים

ברצותן לשים קץ למצב המלחמה ביניהן ולכונן שלום

Desiring to bring to an end the state of war between them and to establish a peace

ورغبة منهما في إنهاء حالة الحرب بينهما وإقامة سلام تستطيع فيه كل دولة في المنطقة أن تعيش في أمن

ראומה מזגה יין מצרי

בארוחת צהריים שנערכה את־מול בבלייר האוז, מעון האורחים הרישמי של ארה״ב אירח שר ה־חוץ של ארה״ב, סיירוס ואנס, את ראשי המשלחת מישראל, מצרים וארה״ב לסעודה של נוסטלגיה.

לשולחן אחד הסבו המארח, ואנס, שר ההגנה בראון, שר ההגנה של מצ־רים, עלי, שר הבטחון, וייצמן, וראש ממשלת מצרים, ד״ר מוצטאפה חליל. כולם באו יחד עם רעיותיהם. בארו־חה שלפה ראומה וייצמן מארנקה בקבוק יין מצרי, שקנתה בעת ביקורה הראשון במצרים בחברת בעלה בשנה שעברה.

היא ביקשה רשות מן המארח, ואנס, לפתוח את הבקבוק ולמזוג לכוסות כל המסובים לשולחן. ואנס התלהב מאוד, ואף עזר לה למזוג את היין.

הם הרימו כוסות „לחיים״, וראומה וייצמן ביקשה מכל הנוכחים לחתום את שמם על תווית הבקבוק, וכולם עשו זאת ברצון רב. עתה יש בידה בקבוק יין מצרי ועליו חתימות ב־אנגלית, ערבית ועברית של כל מש־תתפי הסעודה שהסבו לאותו שולחן.

שר ההגנה כמאל חסן עלי אמר לראומה, כי מעולם לא באה טיפת יין לפיו. אולם לרגל גודל המאורע, הוא עבר על איסור זה וטבל את קצה לשונו ביין שהיה מזוג בכוסו.

עלי אמר לראומה: „הרבה אירו־עים היסטוריים התחוללו היום, והפחות שבהם הוא שבפעם הראשונה בחיי טעמתי יין״.

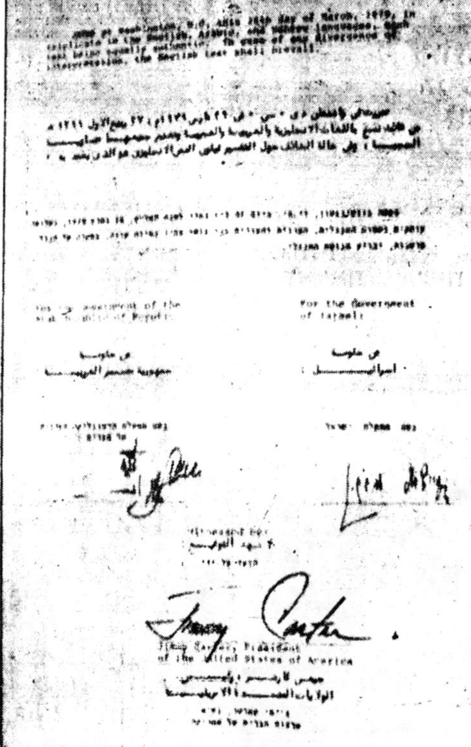

...the English text shall prevail.

For the Government of Israel:

عن حكومة
إسرائيل

عن حكومة
جمهورية مصر العربية

Jimmy Carter, President of the United States of America

תצלומים אלה ממעמד חתימת ההסכם בין ישראל למצרים, נעשו על־ידי צלמי סוכנות איי.פי. בוושינגטון. למעלה משמאל: בעת הסעודה אמש; למעלה מימין: בעת נגינת ההמנונים; משמאל: החתימות ומימין: קריאת פסוקי תהילים מפי ראש הממשלה.

הקהל הריע לבגין בהציעו נובל לקארטר

הברכות שנשאו שלושת המנהיגים בארוחת הערב החגיגית באוהל הענקי שהוקם במדשאה הדרומית של הבית הלבן, שינו לגמרי את אווירת יום חתימת הסכם השלום.

במקום הקרירות והריחוק שאיפיינו את תחילתו של היום אפפה לפתע אווירה חמה, ידידותית, ואפילו הומו־ריסטית במקצת, את סיומו של היום.

ג׳ימי קארטר עדיין נשא נאום די ענייני, דיבר על הפלשתינים ועל הדרך שהם ישתתפו בתהליך השלום. הוא חילק שבחים לבגין ולסאדאת אבל הזהיר, כי זוהי ההתחלה של תהליך ממושך, ולא סיומו.

אחריו דיבר אנואר סאדאת, ובדבריו גרם מיד את הפשרת הקרח. ראשית, הזכיר את בגין בשמו ואפילו את אשתו. הוא הדגיש, כי הוא שותף לתקוותו של קארטר, ואף כי דיבר די בתקיפות על מצוקת הפלשתינים ועל הצורך לייסד אוטונומיה מלאה, היתה נימת דבריו ידידו־תית ובעיקר הודגשה הבקשה להפגין אמון הדדי.

סאדאת חילק שבחים לא רק לאמריקנים ולנשיאם, אלא גם לישראלים ולראש ממשלתם, ובסוף הרים כוסית לחיי קארטר, העם האמריקני, העם בישראל, בגין ואשתו.

שלישי דיבר מנחם בגין, ובפעם הראשונה מאז החל תהליך השלום, לא שירבב בדבריו שום אלמנט מדיני. כל דבריו הוקדשו להבעת הערכה וידידות לאלה שתרמו חלקם לתהליך השלום.

כאשר הציע בגין להציג את מועמדותו של קארטר לפרס נובל לשלום לשנת 1979, פרץ הקהל בתרועות סוערות. הוא גם חילק שבחים רבים לשר החוץ סיירוס ואנס ולאשתו אליזה, ואף שיכתב מעט את התנ״ך בציינו, כי הלכה אחריו בארץ „זרועת מוקשים״ בעוד שבתנ״ך כתוב „בארץ לא זרועה״.

הופעתם הלבבית של השלושה גרמה שהנשיא סאדאת חזר לדוכן הנואמים ואמר, כי זו הפעם הראשונה בכל מגעיו עם ראש הממשלה בגין, שהוא תמים־דעים עמו. היא הצטרף להצעה שקארטר יהיה מועמד לפרס נובל.

גם הנשיא קארטר עצמו חזר לדוכן והוסיף נימת צחוק משלו בהזהירו את שני האחרים, כי רק אם תשעת החודשים הבאים עלינו במשא־ומתן קשה יעלו יפה, יקבל את הצעתם להיות מועמד לפרס נובל.

שעות אחדות אחרי רצח הנשיא סאדאת בעת המצעד

החל טיהור בצבא מצרים

...ים בודדים של מחתרת דתית הוחדרו לצבא ✶ הוכרז מצב חירום ✶ ייערך משאל־עם לבחירת מובאראך כמועמד לנשיא ✶ מובאראך: „נמשיך בדרך השלום"

...ים מן המתנקשים בדרכם מהרכב ... אל עבר בימת ... ליצב, מחייך הנשיא אנואר סאדאת. זהו התצלום האחרון של נשיא מצרים
(צילומי רדיו אי.פי.)

עודד גרנות, סופר „מעריב" לענינים ערביים

...נערך עתה, טיהור נרחב במגמה לאתר את גורמי ...ים, שהצליחו להסתנן לשורותיו. הטיהור החל שעות ... הנשיא אנואר סאדאת בידי קבוצת מתנקשים, בעת ...

מהלך זה הוא — להערכת משקיפים — חלק ממדיניות כוללת של יד חזקה, שינקוט הנשיא המיועד גנראל חוסני מובארך, כלפי מתנגדי המשטר, בעיקר מקרב האגודות המוסלמיות הקיצוניות.

ההערכה הרווחת בשלב זה היא, כי לשורות הצבא חדרו תאים בודדים של תנועות המחתרת הדתיות, שמטרתן להפיל את המשטר במצרים. הצבא המצרי כגוף ממשיך לגלות תאמנות למשטר ולממשיכי דרכו של אנואר סאדאת.

(ב„קול ישראל" נמסר הבוקר כי גם הרמטכ"ל המצרי, הגנראל ... אלע... נהרג ... [illegible])

...

...בארץ כי מצרים תכבד את כל המסמכים, החוזים וההתחייבויות הבינלאומיות, וכי „ידינו לא יחדלו מלדחוף את עגלת השלום, כדי למבצע עד תום את שליחותו של הנשיא סאדאת עד שיתנפו דגלינו בכל רחבי סיני ...

...י השאלה

... מורא, ועל סימני־השאלה ... הקודמים ... מה שנראה לנו ...

...שלים ערבי ... כך מסתבר ... אינו יכול לעשות שלום עם ישראל בלי לשים את נפשו בכף הקלע. ר... המוות יכול לא... רוב לו במשך ... הבלתי־משוערים ...

שליח „מעריב" מתאר את שהתרחש אמש בבירה המצרית

קהיר מתכוננת ללוויית ה„ראיס"; התושבים מוכי־תדהמה הסתגרו בבתים

מאת שעיה סגל
שליח „מעריב" בקאהיר

קאהיר מתכוננת ללווית הנשיא אנואר סאדאת בשבת הקרובה. גורמים רשמיים חיוו דעתם, כי ללוויה יבואו ראשי מדינות ואישים בכירים מרחבי תבל. נעשות הכנות לאירוחם ולאבטחתם.

במצרים הוכרז אתמול על 40 ימי אבל על מותו של סאדאת. בימי האבל לא ייערכו שום אירועים רשמיים והדגלים ברחבי המדינה יורדו לחצי התורן. כל הטקסים שתוכננו לציון יום השנה למלחמת יום הכיפורים בוטלו

פקיד מצרי רשמי אמר אמש ל„מעריב": „זוהי מכה קשה למצרים — בעיקר למימשל. בשלושה באוקטובר, לפני שמונה שנים, עשה סאדאה
(סוף בעמוד 2)

נבון ובגין רוצים להשתתף בלווייה

בגלל קביעת מועד הלווייה לשבת יווצרו בעיות בטחוניות מיוחדות, כיוון שהאישים הישראלים יאלצו ללכת ברגל ✶ היום דיון בממשלה

מאת יהוף תריף

ראש הממשלה, מנחם בגין, מתכוון לצאת ללווייתו של נשיא מצרים, אנואר סאדאת, שתיערך ביום השבת. הנושא יידון בישיבה המיוחדת של הממשלה שנקבעה להבוקר בירושלים.

נודע שגם נשיא המדינה, מר יצחק נבון, הביע רצון להשתתף בלווייה. לפי שעה לא ברור אם גם אישים אחרים ייצאו לקהיר. ההשתתפות תחייב את הישראלים ללכת ברגל ביום השבת הן בעת מסע הלוויה והן אל מקום הקבורה וממנו. דבר זה כרוך, כמובן, בבעיות בטחוניות מורכבות שגורמי הבטחון כבר החלו לתת דעתם על כך.

הוכרזה כוננות בצי הששי

אניות הצי הפסיקו תרגיל ימי, הפליגו לעבר אלכסנדריה וכנראה למפרץ סידרה, מול חופי לוב

מאת מ. מאיר ורפי מן
סופרי „מעריב"
באתונה ובוושינגטון

אניות מלחמה וצוללות של הצי השישי האמריקני ביטלו תרגיל ימי שערכו מדרום לאי כרתים והפליגו ל־ כיוון לא ידוע — ככל הנראה לעבר מפרץ סידרה. ספינות אחרות של הצי השישי עשו דרכן לאלכסנדריה — נודע אתמול ממקורות יווניים.

ארה"ב הודיעה אתמול כי חלקים מכוח הפרישה המהירה ומהצי השישי בים התיכון „הועמדו במצב של כוננות מוגברת" בעקבות ההתנקשות בנשיא מצרים אנואר סאדאת. פקידים במשרד ההגנה בוושינגטון מסרו באורח בלתי רשמי כי מצב הכוננות נועד להרתיע את שליט לוב קדאפי, „או כל גורם אחר" מלנסות ולנצל „סיטואציה אפשרית של חוסר יציבות במצרים".

בוושינגטון נודע, כי ארה"ב עשויה לשלוח בקרוב משלחת רשמית רמת דרג לקהיר ולהחיש משלוחי נשק לצבא המצרי, כדי לתת ביטוי פומבי לתמיכה האמריקנית המלאה במשטרו של חוסני מובאראק. צעדים אלה, הנשקלים עתה בצמרת המימשל בוושינגטון, מיועדים לשמש איתות אזהרה לגורמים חיצוניים ופנימיים העלולים לאיים על המימשל החדש לאחר הירצחו של אנואר סאדאת אתמול — כך מסרה אמש רשת הטלוויזיה „איי.בי.סי.

הארוחה המפסקת עד 16.40

מהרבנות הראשית נמסר הבוקר כי יש לסיים היום את הסעודה המפסקת עד לשעה 16.40. זמן הדלקת הנרות הוא 16.59 ותפילת „כל נדרי" מתחילה ב־17.15. מחר יסתיים הצום בשעה 17.54.

ה„אוקטובר" של סאדאת
דיוקנו של נשיא
מאת עודד גרנות
בעמוד 15

היום 58 עמוד
יום ב' 7.6.82 | ט"ז בסיון תשמ"ב
גליון מס' 10529 — שנה ל"ה
המחיר — 6.- שקלים (כולל מע"מ)
העורך הראשון ע. קרליבך ז"ל

צה"ל כבש מבצר הבופור

מבצר הופגזו ישובי הצפון; „צה"ל נחת מהים, צור מכותרת, קרבות רחוב בנבטייה"

מאת יעקב ארז ועודד גרנות

...ים של דרום לב־ מבצר הבופור, ה־ ...גובה של 717 מטר ...הים על המובלעת הנוצרית ו„אצבע הגליל", נכבש הלילה בקרב עז בידי חיל הרגלים. דגל יש־ראל מתנוסס מאז שעות הבוקר המוקדמות מעל ה־מבצר האימתני, החולש מ־מצוקו של הליטאני על ה־איזור כולו.

עם חשיכה החל הקרב על המבצר, שהופצץ קשות ב־ימים האחרונים ונפגע גם ב־כל הקרבות שניטשו בדרום־לבנון. למרות כל זאת, המ־שיכו המחבלים להחזיק ב־מקום. המחילות העמוקות של הבופור, הבנוי על חורבות מבצר צלבני עתיק, מאפש־רות מיסתור ומחסה מפגיעה.

במחילות הבופור התנהל קרב פנים־אל־פנים. בדרך זהירה התקדמו לוחמי חיל הרגלים בתוך מדורי המבצר וטיהרוהו ממחבלים. פרטי ה־קרב עדיין לא נתפרסמו ב־מלואם, אך היה זה קרב קשה, שבו מיצו החיילים את יכולתם הצבאית והאישית. המחבלים לא נסוגו מן ה־מקום. הם נאחזו בבופור, עד שהוכרעו.

ממבצר הבופור הפגיזו ה־מחבלים בימים האחרונים את הגיזרה המזרחית של לבנון ואת אצבע הגליל. המבצר, המצוי בשיפולים המזרחיים של רמת־ארנון, היה השטח החיוני של המחבלים בגיזרה זו. הלילה, סמוך לחצות, הו־עברה התשדורת: „הבופור ב־ידיי".

כוחות צה"ל בדרום לבנון חידשו הבוקר את התקדמותם. מטוסי חיל־האוויר הופעלו ב־גיזרה רחבה לשיתוק מקורות ירי של מחבלים ולריכוך יע־דים.

על־פי ידיעות מלבנון, נחת

(סוף בעמוד 7)

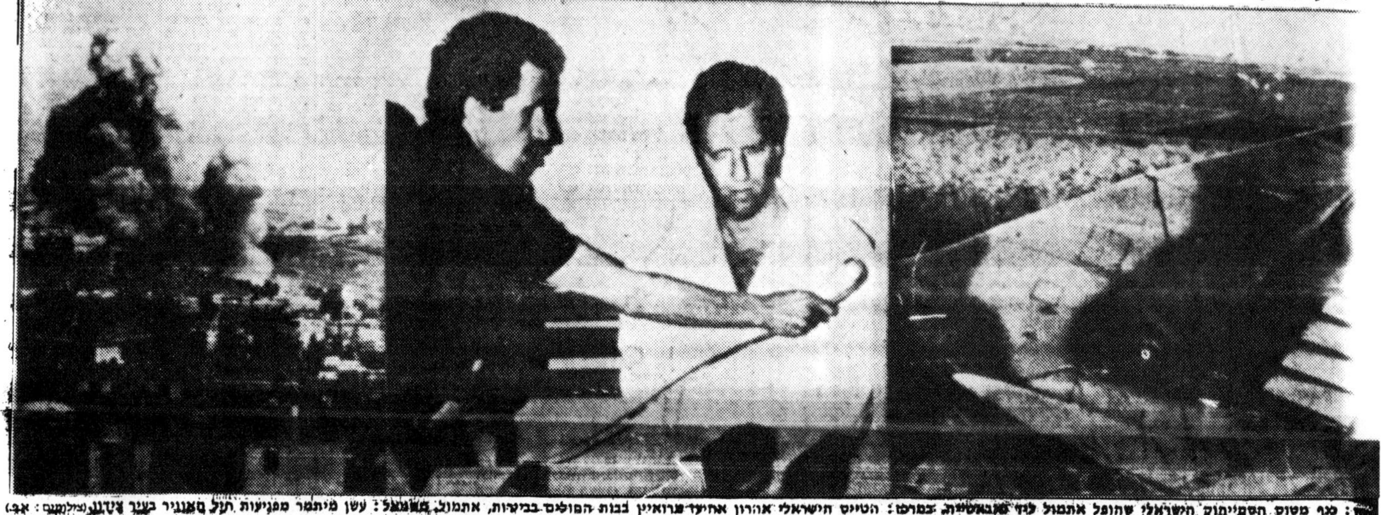

...: כנף מטוס הסקייהוק הישראלי שהופל אתמול ליד נבאטיה. במרכז: הטייס הישראלי אהרון אחיעד פרואיין בבית הפולים בביירות, אתמול. משמאל: עשן מיתמר מפגיעות על ...

הסורים החישו תגבורת - נמנעו מקרב

מאת עודד גרנות, סופר „מעריב" לעניינים ערביים

ביום הראשון לפעולת צה"ל בלבנון החישו הסו־רים תגבורות משטחם אל השטח הלבנוני והניעו כו־ננות שריון דרומה, אולם נמנעו ממגע ישיר עם כו־חות צה"ל — כך מדווחים מקורות ערביים.

הדיווח היחיד, מפי דובר צבאי סורי, שצוטט ברדיו ה־פאלאנגות, הוא על ירי ארטילרי של הכוחות הסוריים על כוחות צה"ל באיזור ג'ר־מק ובאיזור חצבייה.

האיפוק הסורי ביום הרא־שון ללחימת כוחות צה"ל ב־לבנון עומד עד כה בסתירה להכרזות שנשמעו אתמול מ־דמשק, על נכונות סורית „ל־היחלץ נגד האויב הישראלי". נשיא סוריה חאפז אסד שו־חח הלילה בטלפון עם מנהיג המחבלים יאסר ערפאת ועם נשיא לבנון, אליאס סארכיס, והבטיח, כי „סוריה לא תאפ־שר לאיש לחסל את המהפכה הפלשתינית".

על פי הדיווחים המגיעים ממקורות ערביים שונים, נכ־נסו תגבורות סוריות אל ה־שטח הלבנוני בבקעת הלב־נון אתמול בשעות אחרי ה־צהריים והתקדמו לאיזור ה־עיירות ג'זין וראשייה אל־ואדי. רדיו הפאלאנגות מסר, כי שתי חטיבות שריון סור־יות החלו לנוע לכיוון העיי־רה אשייה בדרום לבנון. כן מוסר רדיו הפאלאנגות על ה־הוראה שניתנה לחטיבה 85 הסורית, לנוע מאיזור ביירות לכיוון ג'זין.

עד כה נתנו הסורים הס־בר רק להימנעות חיל האוויר שלהם, ביום הראשון לפעולת צה"ל בלבנון, מכניסה לק־רבות אוויר עם המטוסים ה־ישראליים. ההסבר הסורי ה־דחוק טוען, כי פעולת חיל־האוויר הסורי נמנעה בגלל „ריבוי המטוסים הישראליים באוויר".

האיפוק הסורי בלבנון ב־יום הראשון ללחימת צה"ל הביא על דמשק כבר עתה התקפות חריפות מצד הלו־בים. רדיו לוב שאל הלילה: „מדוע לא הופנו טילים סו־ריים לעבר המטוסים הישר־אליים? מדוע לא קיבל צבא

(סוף בעמוד 15)

השטח המקווקו מציין את היערכות הסורים (עפ"י מקורות זרים) בדרום מזרח לבנון.

פריסת הסורים בלבנון

מאת עודד גרנות

הכוחות הסוריים בלבנון מונים כ־ דיוויזיית חי"ר ממוכן, נוסף לכוחות שריון, קומנדו, ארטילריה, נ.ט. ונ.מ. — לפי הפירוט הבא: שלוש חטיבות טנקים (אחת מהן ערוכה בשטח סוריה, סמוך לגבול לבנון), שתי חטיבות חי"ר ממוכן, שתי חטיבות צבא השחרור הפלשתיני (הכפופות לפיקוד הסורים בביירות), כ־15 גדודי קומנדו (מחציתם באיזור זחלה־סנין) ויחידות ארטילריה.

(סוף בעמוד 15)

שר ההגנה האמריקני תובע „להפסיק היחסים המיוחדים עם ישראל"

מאת רפאל מן, סופר „מעריב" בוושינגטון

שר ההגנה האמריקני, קאספר וויינברגר, תובע „להפסיק את היחסים ה־מיוחדים" בין ארה"ב ויש־ראל בשל פעולת צה"ל ב־לבנון — מסרו הבוקר מקו־רות יודעי־דבר בוושינגטון.

וויינברגר אמר את הדברים בדיונים פנימיים שנערכו את־מול בבירה האמריקנית, ו־מעריכים, כי בימים הקרובים יתבע מן הנשיא רייגן לנהוג יד תקיפה כלפי ישראל ולנ־קוט צעדי־עונשין, חריפים יותר מאלה שהופנו כלפי ישראל בעבר.

עמדה ביקורתית ביותר נגד פעולת צה"ל השמיע בהתייע־צויות פנימיות גם סגן הנשיא ג'ורג' בוש.

עמדתו של שר־החוץ אלכ־סנדר הייג, כפי שגם הובעה בפומבי, היא, כי בשלב רא־שון על ארה"ב לפעול להפ־סקת הלחימה בלבנון ונסיגת כוחות צה"ל. ורק אחר כך יש להתפנות לטפל בהיבטים ה־אחרים של הפעולה.

כתבים הנלווים לנשיא ריי־גן ולשר החוץ הייג באירופה מוסרים, כי בפמליית הנשיא נמתחת בעיקר ביקורת על כך, שהתגובה הישראלית ל־התקפה על שגריר ישראל ב־לונדון היא מוגזמת בממדיה ובעוצמתה.

הם גם טוענים, כי פעולת צה"ל עלולה להביא להידרד־רות חמורה במצב ולמעורבות צבאית של גורמים אחרים ב־אזור ומחוצה לו. עמדה זו יביע היום השליח פיליפ חביב, אשר יגיע ארצה על פי הנחייתו של הנשיא רייגן, עימו נפגש אתמול בוורסאי.

ביקורת על פעולת צה"ל השמיעו אתמול בשיחות פר־טיות חברי קונגרס ויועצים בגבעת הקפיטול.

היום תתחיל ישראל בפעו־לת הסברה נרחבת בקרב חב־רי הקונגרס, באמצעי התק־שורת ובתחומים נוספים ב־ארה"ב.

לפי התכנית

מאת יעקב ארז, סופר הצבאי של „מעריב"

רשימת היעדים שכבר הושגו ביממת הלחימה ה־ראשונה של מבצע „שלום הגליל" עדיין חסויה. „ער־פל הקרב" טרם התפוגג, ו־הרבה מן המהלכים אינם לפרסום.

אבל הבוקר החל דובר צה"ל לפרסם פרטים ראשונים, ה־מסירים את מעטה האיפול מעל הישג אחד שהושג הלילה, ואשר משמעותו גדולה לתוש־בי אצבע הגליל ודרום לבנון: מבצר הבופור נפל, דגל ישר־אל מתנופף מעל השרידים ה־מצולקים של המבצר האימתני שחלש על צפון הגליל וגיזרת מארג' עיון.

היעד הזה שנפל בידי צה"ל במלחמה בלבנון מעיד, כי ב־כוונת הכוחות אשר חדרו ל־לבנון, לפי הסיכנויות הזרות, בכמה טורי שריון וחיל רגלי־מוסע להשתלט על גיזרה רח־בה, ממורדות החרמון ועד חוף הים התיכון, ואחר־כך „לנקות את השטח" ממאחזי המחבלים.

על־פי ההתרשמות הראשונה מתבצע מבצע „שלום הגליל" בהתאם ללוח הזמנים, ולשל־בים שתוכננו עוד לפני זמן. יש להדגיש כי הם עשו זאת למרות הקשיים בשטח, התנג־דות המחבלים ופני הקרקע ו־הנוף.

המבצע הנרחב של ישראל

(סוף בעמוד 7)

12

יום ג' 8.2.83 | כ"ה בשבט תשמ"ג

גליון מס' 10736 — שנה ל"ה

המחיר — 12 שקלים (כולל מע"מ)

המייסד והעורך הראשון ע. קרליבך ז"ל

לגליון זה מצורף **עסקים** שבועון לכלכלה ולכספים

מעריב

העתון הנפוץ ביותר במדינה · MAARIV ·

הוצאה מיוחדת

הערכה בירושלים: שרון צריך להתפטר מתפקידו עוד היום

אריאל שרון · אבי דודאי · רפאל איתן · אמיר דרורי · ראש המוסד · עמוס ירון · יהושע שגיא · יצחק שמיר · מנחם בגין

ההתפטרות עשויה להימסר בישיבת הממשלה ★ הוועדה ממליצה ששר הבטחון יסיק מסקנות ולא – שראש הממשלה יביא לפיטוריו ★ הוועדה ממליצה עוד: להפסיק כהונתו של אלוף שגיא כראש אמ"ן ולמנוע מתת־אלוף ירון מילוי תפקיד פיקוד בצה"ל ל־3 שנים ★ לגבי הרמטכ"ל ביקורת קשה אך אין המלצה משום שהוא מסיים תפקידו באפריל 1983 ★ גם ביחס לאלוף דרורי אין המלצה בענין עתידו ★ באשר לבגין, שמיר וראש המוסד מסתפקת הוועדה בקביעת אחריות ללא מסקנות מעשיות

מאת יוסף חריף

„מצאנו שעל שר הבטחון אריאל שרון מוטלת אחריות אישית, כפי שפורט בדין וחשבון זה. לדעתנו מן הראוי ששר הבטחון יסיק מסקנות אישיות נאותות מן הפגם שנתגלו במילוי תפקידו ואם יהיה צורך בכך שראש הממשלה ישקול האם עליו להשתמש בסמכותו לפי סעיף 21 א' (א') של חוק יסוד הממשלה, לפיו „ראש הממשלה רשאי, לאחר שהודיע לממשלה על כוונתו לעשות כן, להעביר שר מכהונתו". זוהי ההמלצה מרחיקת הלכת ביותר הכלולה בדו"ח הוועדה שחקרה את הארועים במחנות הפליטים בביירות. המלצות הוועדה פורסמו הבוקר בירושלים.

בפרק המוקדש לניתוח עדותו של שר הבטחון בפני הוועדה נאמר בין השאר „לולא היה מתברר לשר הבטחון שלא ניתן להפעיל פיקוח של ממש על כוח הפאלאנגות שנכנס בהסכמת צה"ל למחנות, חובתו היתה למנוע כניסה כזו. התועלת שבכניסת הפאלאנגה למחנות לא היתה שקילה כלל כנגד הנזק של כניסה כזו, כשהיא בלתי מבוקרת", אומרת הוועדה.

לאור המלצה זו רווחה בירושלים הבוקר הערכה כי שר הבטחון צריך להתפטר עוד היום. ישיבת הממשלה המיוחדת לדיון בדו"ח ועדת החקירה עמדה להתחיל בשעה 3 אחר הצהריים. בינתיים מעיינים השרים ואחרים הנוגעים בדבר בדו"ח הוועדה.

להלן המלצות הוועדה במלואן:

● בהחלטותינו דלהלן המתייחסות לשורה של אנשים בעלי תפקידים בכירים בשלטון ובצה"ל הבאנו בחשבון שלכל אחד מהאנשים האלה זכויות רבות בפעילות ציבורית או צבאית לטובת מדינת ישראל, מתוך הקרבה ומסירות. אם אף על פי כן הגענו לכלל דעה שחובתנו להמליץ על צעדים מסויימים נגד כמה מאותם אנשים, הרי זה מתוך הכרה שחומרת הענין והשלכתו על אושיות המוסר הציבורי במדינת ישראל מחייבות צעדים כאלה.

ראש הממשלה, שר החוץ, ראש המוסד

● קבענו לעיל את העובדות והמסקנות לגבי אחריות ראש הממשלה, שר החוץ וראש המוסד. לאור מה שקבענו על מידת האחריות של כל אחד מהם, סבורים אנו שניתן להסתפק בקביעת האחריות ואין צורך בהמלצות כלשהן.

אלוף פיקוד הצפון, אלוף אמיר דרורי

● פרטנו לעיל את מסקנותינו לגבי אחריותו של אלוף פיקוד הצפון אמיר דרורי. על אלוף דרורי היו מוטלים בשבוע של כניסת צה"ל למערב ביירות תפקידים רבים, סבוכים וקשים שאותם היה עליו למלא אחרי תקופה ארוכה של מלחמה לא קלה. הוא נקט באמצעים מסויימים להפסקת פעולות הפלנגות, ה[...] חש בכך שלא תתמיד בדרך זו. בהתחשב עם נסיבות אלה נראה לנו כי ניתן להסתפק לגבי אלוף דרורי בקביעה לגבי אחריותו ללא כל המלצה נוספת.

שר הבטחון, מר אריאל שרון

לדעתנו מן הראוי, ששר הבטחון יוציא מסקנות אישיות נאותות מהפגמים שנתגלו במילוי

● מצאנו שמוטלת אחריות אישית על שר הבטחון, כפי שפורט בדין וחשבון זה. תפקידו ואם יהיה צורך בכך שראש הממשלה ישקול, האם עליו להשתמש בסמכותו לפי סעיף 21א(א) של חוק יסוד הממשלה, לפיו „ראש הממשלה רשאי, לאחר שהודיע לממשלה על כוונתו לעשות כן, להעביר שר מכהונתו."

ראש המטה הכללי, רב אלוף רפאל איתן

● הגענו למסקנות חמורות לגבי פעולותיו ומחדליו של הרמטכ"ל רב אלוף רפאל איתן. הרמטכ"ל עומד לסיים את תפקידו בחודש אפריל 1983. בהתחשב בעובדה שלא נשקלת הארכה תקופת כהונתו אין משמעות בהמלצה לגבי המשך כהונתו כרמטכ"ל, ועל כן החלטנו להסתפק בקביעת האחריות מבלי המלצה נוספת.

ראש אגף המודיעין, אלוף יהושע שגיא

● פרטנו את המחדלים השונים החמורים למדי של ראש אמ"ן אלוף יהושע שגיא במילוי תפקידו. אנו ממליצים שאלוף יהושע שגיא לא ימשיך בתפקידו כראש אמ"ן.

מפקד האוגדה, תת אלוף עמוס ירון

את מידת אחריותו של תת אלוף עמוס ירון קבענו לעיל. בהביאנו בחשבון את כל הנסיבות אנו ממליצים שתת אלוף עמוס ירון לא ימלא תפקיד פיקודי בצה"ל, ושביטול הגבלה זו לא יישקל לפני תום שלוש שנים.

● במהלך החקירה נתגלה שהיו ליקויים בתיפקוד מערכות כמפורט בפרק הדן בנושא זה. מהליקויים האלה יש להפיק לקח מתאים ואנו ממליצים שבנוסף לביקורת פנימית בענין זה, תערך בדיקת הליקויים והדרך לתיקונם על ידי מומחה או מומחים, שיתמנו על ידי ועדת שרים לעניני בטחון. אם תוך כדי בדיקה זו יימצא כי אנשים מסויימים נושאים באחריות לליקויים אלה, מן הראוי שיוסקו לגביהם מסקנות מתאימות, בין על פי ההוראות המתאימות של חוק השיפוט הצבאי, ובין בדרך אחרת.

הערות סיום

בדברי עדים ובמסמכים שונים הודגש ההבדל בין מוסר הלחימה הנהוג בצה"ל לבין מוסר הלחימה בהתנגשויות הדמים ובפעולות מלחמה בין העדות, המיליציות והכוחות הלוחמים השונים בלבנון. ההבדל הוא ניכר. במלחמה שניהל צה"ל בלבנון נפגעו אזרחים לא מעטים ואבידות לא מעטות בנפש נגרמו, על אף המאמץ שנעשה על ידי צה"ל וחייליו שלא לפגוע באזרחים. מאמץ זה גרם לא פעם לאבידות נוספות לכוחות צה"ל. חיילי צה"ל, במשך המלחמה, חזו לא פעם במראות של הרג, הרס וחורבן. מתגובותיהם, שעליהן שמענו, למעשי התעללות באזרחים, נראה שעל אף המראות והנסיונות הקשים במלחמה ועל אף חובתו של חייל לנהוג כלוחם בקשיחות מסויימת, לא נעלמה רגישות אצל חיילי צה"ל למעשי זוועה המבוצעים באנשים שאינם לוחמים, מתוך אכזריות או פורקן לרגשות נקמה. יש להצטער שלא תמיד תגובת חיילי צה"ל למעשים כאלה היתה נמרצת למדי ולא הביאה להפסקת המעשים הנלוזים. נראה לנו כי מן הראוי להמשיך לטפח בצה"ל את חובות המוסר היסודיות, שאותן יש לקיים גם בתנאי מלחמה, מבלי לפגוע בכושר הלחימה של כוחות צה"ל.

תנאי הלחימה מחייבים את הלוחמים בקשיחות שמשמעותה להעמיד בעדיפות את הדבקות במטרה ואת הנכונות להקרב, וזאת כדי להשיג את היעדים המוטלים עליהם, אפילו בתנאים קשים ביותר, אך המטרה לעולם אינה מקדשת את האמצעים וצריך להפעיל את העשק תוך שמירה על ערכים מוסריים ואנושיים יסודיים.

בין הפניות מן הציבור אל הועדה היו כאלה שהביעו תרעומת על עריכת חקירה בנושא שאינו קשור ישירות לאחריותה של ישראל. נשמעו טענות שבמקרים קודמים של טבח בלבנון, שבהם קופחו חייהם של אנשים במספר רב בהרבה מהקורבנות שנפלו בסברה ושתילה, לא גרם הדבר לזעזוע בדעת הקהל העולמית ולא הוקמו כל ועדות חקירה. גישה זו לענין עריכת החקירה אין ביכולתנו להצדיק ולא רק מן הטעם הפורמלי, שלא אנו החלטנו על עריכת החקירה, אלא החליטה על כך ממשלת ישראל. המטרה העיקרית של החקירה היתה להוציא לאור את כל העובדות החשובות המתייחסות לביצוע מעשי הזוועה ולכך יש חשיבות מבחינת חוסנה המוסרי של ישראל ותפקודה כמדינה דמוקרטית, המקפידה על שמירת עקרונות היסוד של העולם התרבותי. אין אנו משלים את עצמנו שתוצאות חקירה זו ישכנעו או יניחו את דעתם של בעלי הדעות הקדומות ובעלי המצפון הסלקטיבי אך לא עבור סוג של של אנשים נועדה חקירה זו. השתדלנו ולא חסכנו במאמצים להגיע לחקר האמת ואנו מקווים, שכל אלה המונחים על ידי רצון טוב שיבחנו את הענין ללא דעות קדומות, ישתכנעו שהחקירה נערכה ללא כל משוא פנים.

שמירה הופקדה על חברי הוועדה

מאת אילן כפיר, אילן בכר וברוך מאירי

שמירה הופקדה אמש על בתיהם של כל חברי ועדת החקירה הממלכתית, מחשש שגב פרסום הממצאים והמסקנות ינסו חמומי־מוח להתנכל לחברי הוועדה או רכושם.

ליד בתיהם של יו"ר הוועדה השופט יצחק כהן, והשופט אהרן ברק, בירושלים, ואלוף (מיל.) יונה אפרת ברמת־השרון הוצב שוטר חמוש. המשטרה תחליט הבוקר אם להג־

סוף בעמוד 15 תחת הכותרת „הממשלה לדיון מיוחד"

ניחושים בממשל ארה"ב

מאת רפאל מן,

סופר „מעריב" בוושינגטון

פקידי ממשל אמריקניים מצפים בדריכות לפרסום מסקנות ועדת החקירה היום, על רקע ההערכה, כי תהיה להן השפעה על מעמדה של ממשלת בגין, ובעיקר על מעמדו האישי של שר הבטחון אריאל שרון, הנחשב בוושינגטון לאחראי לעיכובים בנסיגת הכוחות הזרים מלבנון. האמריקנים גם מעריכים, כי לתוצאות תהיה השפעה על קצב המשא ומתן בלבנון.

אמצעי התקשורת האמריקניים דיווחו אמש בהרחבה על הגשת המסקנות לראש הממשלה, ורשתות הטלוויזיה נערכות לסיקור נרחב של הפרסום היום. מגיש חדשות החוץ של רשת „אי.בי.סי.", פיטר ג'אנינגס, יגיע היום ארצה, כדי ל־

סוף בעמוד 2 תחת הכותרת הדו"ח ישפיע על

בבית ראש הממשלה

מאת אילן בכר

לראש־הממשלה, שרים וקצינים בצה"ל. האורות במעונו של מר בגין בשכונת רחביה בירושלים לא כבו אלא רק לפנות בוקר.

ראש הממשלה עיין שעות ארוכות במסקנות הוועדה הממלכתית לבדיקת נסיבות הטבח במחנות הפליטים סאברה ושתילה, ואם לנחש את משמעותן על־פי מבט פניהם של האישים אשר כינס ראש־הממשלה במעונו — שר המשפטים משה נסים, מזכיר הממשלה דן מרידור ויועץ ראש־הממשלה לענייני תקשורת אורי פורת — הרי שמסקנות הוועדה חמורות וקשות מאד.

רק בשעה 1.30 אחר־חצות הסתיים הדיון הראשוני שקיים ראש־הממשלה עם יועציו. בחוץ, בקור עז, המתינו עתונאים וצוותי־טלוויזיה רבים מהארץ ומהעולם, אשר

סוף בעמוד 2 תחת הכותרת הדחות והקדמת הבחירות

ציפיה בפיקוד הצבאי

מאת יעקב ארז,

סופר הצבאי של „מעריב"

אלה מקציני צה"ל, שקיבלו בזמנו מכתבי־אזהרה מטעם ועדת החקירה, או נציגיהם, הוזמנו להבוקר כ־8.30 לבניין פאפיק בירושלים כדי לקבל שם את מסקנות הוועדה.

אמש והלילה לא הוזמנו הרמטכ"ל, רב־אלוף רפאל איתן, ראש אמ"ן, אלוף יהושע שגיא, אלוף פיקוד הצפון, אלוף אמיר דרורי, ותא"ל עמוס ירון, שהיה מפקד כוחות צה"ל בביירות לישיבת הממשלה שתיערך היום.

א.ש, עד לשעות המאוחרות של הלילה, דנו שר הבטחון, אריאל שרון, הרמטכ"ל איתן, והאלופים שגיא ודרורי וכן קצינים ומומחים אחרים, ב־

סוף בעמוד 2 תחת הכותרת עסקים כרגיל

משכן הכנסת כמרקחה

מאת יוסף צוריאל

„שקט, אף לא מלה" עד לפירסום המסקנות. זאת תבע יו"ר מפלגת העבודה, ח"כ שמעון פרס, וחבריו לסיעה הבטיחו לציית.

„אחדות" — ביקש ראש הממשלה, מנחם בגין, שעה קלה לאחר שנמסר לו על פרסום מימצאי ועדת החקירה, ואנשי הקואליציה אמרו „אמן".

במליאת הכנסת דיברו אחרוני הנואמים על המלחמה בלבנון, במסגרת הדיון על תקציב משרד ראש הממשלה. בחוץ — רחשו שמועות על אפשרות של פירסום דו"ח ועדת החקירה. ח"כ יעקב גיל מהמערך אמר: „אני מריח משהו". וח"כ פנחס גולדשטיין מהליכוד העיר: „זה כנראה קרוב. קרוב מאוד, פירסום המסקנות".

בתום הדיון בתקציב משרד ראש הממשלה פנה מר בגין ללשכתו במשכן, שם נועד עם ראש המפד"ל. אלה באו אליו כדי לתבוע את המגיע להם על־פי ההסכם הקואליציוני, עבור „ישיבות ההסדר" ומוסדות חינוך שונים. בדיון נכחו: שר האוצר, יורם ארידור, וראש אגף התקציבים באוצר, יעקב גדיש. אלה הציגו תביעות ומר גדיש השיב ב„אין תקציב", עד שהשר בורג העיר בבדיחות דעת:

סוף בעמוד 15 תחת הכותרת „שקט אף לא מלה"

המצב מהיבט משפטי

מימצאי ועדת החקירה, שחקרה את ארועי סברה ושאתילה, אינם מחייבים את הממשלה מבחינה משפטית, אף כי אין לפקפק בחשיבותם המדינית.

בניגוד לפסק־דין של בית־משפט אין לתוצאות החקירה משמעות של הוצאה אל הפועל, למשל. החוק איפשר לממשלה להחליט על הקמת ועדה, שתחקור „ענין שהוא בעל חשיבות ציבורית חיונית אותה שעה". כל שהועדה חייבת לעשות בתום עבודתה הוא למסור לממשלה דו"ח.

החוק בענין זה מרחיק־לכת וחד־משמעי ונאמר בו, שדו"ח ועדת חקירה לא ישמש ראיה בכל הליך משפטי. נמצא, שאפילו יעלו מדו"ח הוועדה עובדות, שישתמע מהן כאילו פעלו אנשים ברשלנות ויהיה מקום להעמידם לדין, צריך יהיה להוכיח את אשמתם במערכת ראיות חדשה ובבית־משפט.

אין לדעת בשלב זה אם תסכים הועדה לפרסם גם חלקים מהפרוטוקול של דיוניה, אך היא רשאית לעשות כן. בדו"ח יהיו מסקנות וייתכן, שיתלוו אליו גם המלצות, אך לא בהכרח.

מתח בצמרת הפוליטית

מאת אילן כפיר

מתח וחרדה ליוו הלילה את ראשי המערכת הפוליטית בישראל. הכל היו דרוכים לקראת הבוקר, שעשוי להיות גורלי לעתידה של ממשלת ישראל.

מן הרגע שקול־ישראל שידר לראשונה, על הפרסום הקרוב של דו"ח ועדת החקירה והגשתו לראש־הממשלה, היתה המערכת הפוליטית כמרקחה: ממשלה, קואליציה ואופוזיציה כאחת.

חרושת השמועות פרחה מראשיתו של הלילה, אולם בלילה שכזה היתה ציפייה לידיעות בדוקות. לעובדות כפי שהן מופיעות שחור על גבי לבן בדו"ח הסופי של הוועדה.

האורות דלקו הלילה עד לשעות הקטנות בביתו

סוף בעמוד 15 תחת הכותרת — „ציפיה לביקור"

החקירה הלבנונית משתהה ספק אם תשלים עבודתה

אין רמז כלשהו להתקדמות החקירה של ממשלת לבנון בפרשת הטבח במחנות סברה ושתילה. על כך נמסר הבוקר מביירות בשעה שהגיעו הידיעות הראשונות ממסקנות הועדה הישראלית.

האחראי לחקירה מטעם מבשלת לבנון, התובע הצבאי אסד ג'רמנוס, הבטיח בשעתו להשלים את מלאכת החקירה במארס או באפריל, אך פקידים אחרים אמרו בשיחות פרטיות, כי ספק אם תוצאות החקירה יבואו אי־פעם לידי פירסום.

ג'רמנוס נשבע, כי לא יהיה חיפוי כלשהו על מי שימצאו אשמים, אולם מקורביו וכן דיפלומטים זרים מתנבאים, כי הדו"ח הסופי ייגנז אי־שם בגנזך הממשלה.

„אם יצביע הדו"ח של ג'רמנוס על קבוצה מסויימת כאחראית להרג, והממשלה תפרסם דו"ח זה, עלול ג'רמנוס ליהרג למחרת היום", אמר באחרונה לבנוני המקורב לחקירה.

בחודש שעבר טען התובע ג'רמנוס בראיון, כי תיקריו העלו עדויות סותרות מפיהם של קומץ ניצולים שהיו כיכבים להעיד. (א.פ.)

מזג אוויר

בהיר עד מעונן חלקית.

הטמפרטורות: ירושלים 4—14; תל־אביב 8—18; חיפה 11—18; אילת 6—21. הטמפרטורות בארץ ובעולם בעמוד 11.

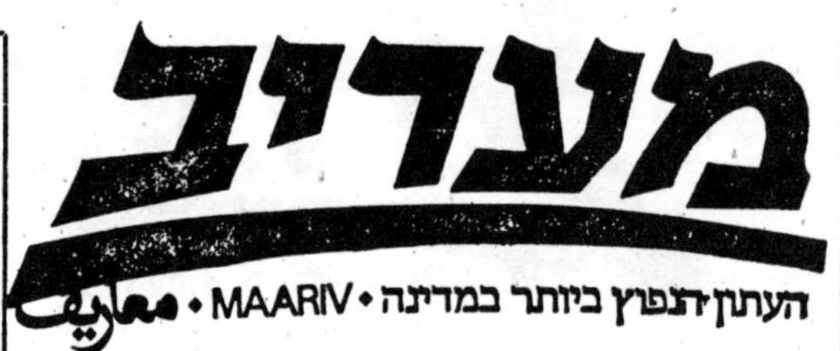

לגליון זה מצורף **ספורט** בצבעים לספורטאים ולמתעניינים בספורט

150 | היום 28 עמוד

יום א' 6.1.1985 | י"ג בטבת תשמ"ה

גליון מס' 11316 — שנה ל"ז

המחיר — 150 שקלים (כולל מע"מ)

המייסד והעורך הראשון ע. קרליבך ז"ל

חשש לגורל „השבט היהודי האבוד"

וושינגטון: אילו שתקו בישראל עוד חודש אחד אפשר היה להציל את כל יהודי אתיופיה ● אתמול הגיע המטוס האחרון; לא נקבעו מועדים לטיסות נוספות ● ראשי העולים מאתיופיה מאשימים: יש בארץ כאלה שישמחו על הפסקת העלייה; זה אסון וטרגדיה נוראה

● העיניים אומרות הכל — בתחילת הדרך בארץ החדשה (צילם: עזרא ינוב)

סודאן: הפסקנו שיתוף הפעולה במיבצע צבא אתיופיה מפציץ את שיירות הפליטים

שתי המדינות מאשימות זו את זו בשיתוף פעולה עם ישראל; „'מבצע משה' — שיאו של מבצע הצלה סודי שנמשך כבר עשר שנים"; זעם בעולם הערבי על סודאן

מאת סופרי „מעריב" בוושינגטון, דורית לנדס, יעקב ארז, שמי גבאי, שרי רוזנר, מאיר בליקוף, צדוק סורני

ממשלת סודאן הודיעה לארה"ב כי היא מפסיקה את שיתוף הפעולה בנושא הצלת הפליטים היהודיים מאתיופיה — מוסר הביקר „וושינגטון פוסט" מפי פקידי רשות אמריקניים. במקביל הודיע דובר של חברת השכר הבלגית „טראנס יורופיאן איירווייס" שהטיסה, לדברי מקורות זרים, את פליטי הרעב לישראל, כי אתמול נפסקו הטיסות.

לדברי „בי.בי.סי." יצאה אתמול לארץ הטיסה האחרונה ולא נקבעו מועדים לשום טיסות נוספות, אף על פי שקודם־לכן תוכננו טיסות למשך השבועיים הבאים. כתב „רויטר" בתל־אביב מוסר, כי מטוס „בואינג 707" אכן הביא אמש לישראל עוד פליטים־יהודים מאתיופיה.

הפקידים האמריקניים בוושינגטון ציינו, לדברי „וושינגטון פוסט" כי הודעת ממשלת סודאן, על הפסקת שיתוף הפעולה בנושא הצלת הפליטים האתיופיים, באה לאחר שממשלת ישראל מסרה הודעה רשמית בנושא זה. הפקידים האמריקניים ציינו, כי לו היו הפקידים האחראים בישראל ממשיכים לשתוק עוד כחודש ימים, אפשר היה להציל את כל היהודים האתיופיים.

כתבי בי.בי.סי. מוסרים, כי אלפים מיהודי אתיופיה נמצאים במחנות פליטים בסודאן וממתינים למטוסים. על פי הערכות באדיס אבבה, המצוטטות ב„ניו־יורק טיימס" נותרו באתיופיה בין 6,000 ל־10,000 יהודים. במחנות פליטים בסודאן נותרו בין 5,000 ל־7,000 יהודים.

כתב בי.בי.סי. בירושלים שוחח עם אישיות בכירה בליכוד, שאמרה לו אמש, כי מדליפי הידיעה „ראויים להירות" בגלל התוצאות הטרגיות של דברגותם.

פרסום הידיעות על יהודי אתיופיה יועלה כנראה היום בישיבת הממשלה. כמה שרים מתכוננים למתוח ביקורת על פרסום המבצע

(סוף בעמוד 8)

סופר „מעריב" מתאר נחיתת מטוס עם אתיופים ביום ו'

[illegible] הם יורדים מהמטוס ומנשקים את הקרקע

חלקם מובלים מיד לשורת האמבולנסים הממתינים [illegible]

קבלת פנים חמה לעולים חדשים מאתיופיה בהגיעם אתמול לארץ (צילם: עזרא ינוב)

מאת דן ארקין

אף הציניקנים, שבקומץ מקבלי־הפנים, היו אחוזי התרגשות ותדהמה. הנה פותח הדייל הבלגי את דלת המטוס ושולי „מרבד הקסמים 1985" יוצאים־רוחפים החוצה אל הכבש. קהל גדול של זקנים, גברים, נשים וטף. ממהרים לרדת במדרגות כדי לנשק את עפר הארץ. מתעלמים מ־

(סוף בעמוד 11)

חילוקי־דעות מערך—ליכוד על סמכויות ועדת החקירה

להתחיל מרבינוביץ — או מיורם ארידור?

הממשלה תחליט היום עקרונית על הקמת הוועדה

מאת כתבי „מעריב"

הממשלה תחליט היום עקרונית על הצורך להקים ועדת חקירה, שתבדוק את פרשת מניות הבנקים בעקבות דו"ח מבקר המדינה. ההחלטה על הקמתה כפועל של הוועדה תעוכב, לפי שעה, כדי לאפשר לוועדת הכנסת לביקורת המדינה לקבל החלטה מקבילה. מקורות ממשלתיים העריכו אמש, כי

(סוף בעמוד 11)

רמב"ם הפחיד: רק מעטים באו ל„מיון"

הנהלת משרד הבריאות דרשה ממנו להכחיש ההודעה ששידר ברדיו, לפיה יש חשש שלא יוכל לטפל כראוי בחולים

מאת ראובן בן צבי, מנחם רהט ודליה מזורי

הנהלת משרד הבריאות תבקש בסוף השבוע מהנהלת המרכז הרפואי רמב"ם בחיפה להכחיש את הידיעה, ששודרה בקול־ישראל, ושהופנתה לתושבי חיפה והצפון, להימנע מלבוא לבית־החולים, בשל החשש שלא יוכלו לטפל בהם כראוי. הודעה זו שודרה בעקבות ישי־

(סוף בעמוד 11)

חיילת נרצחה ליד ביתה בב"ש

הרוצח המתין לדינה ברוק ששבה מבילוי ביום ו' ב־4 לפנות בוקר; האדם שהמשטרה מחפשת כחשוד ברצח — הכיר את דינה

● דינה ברוק ז"ל

מאת אירי בינדר

ציוד יריות מרובה צבאי החריד בשבת, סמוך לשעה 4 לפנות בוקר את דיירי רחוב בני אור בבאר־שבע. אלה שהציצו

(סוף בעמוד 11)

דולצין — הראשון שחשף ברבים סוד הצלתם של יהודי אתיופיה

שבועות ארוכים היו הפיות חתומים ואפילו אמצעי תקשורת זרים הסכימו לשמור על הסוד; עד שבא דולצין וחשף הס יפור בהודעה לעיתונות שפירסם בניו־יורק

מאת יעקב ארז, סופר „מעריב" בניו־יורק וסופר „מעריב" בת"א

פניו המיוסרים והתחינה שבצבצה מקולו של אחד האתיופים הוותיקים בארץ, שדיבר בטלוויזיה בערב־שבת, ביטאה היטב את החרדה האמיתית שתקפה את יהודי אתיופיה בישראל ואת העוסקים בהצלתם, למראה סכר הסודיות שנפרץ בצורה כה בלתי־מובנת. נוצר הרושם שמישהו רוצה לחבל במבצע ההצלה המופלא הזה, אולם האמת היא עצובה יותר ולא כל־כך דראמאטית. כמו במקרים רבים אחרים, הסוד נעשה נחלת יותר מדי אנשים, ודווקא אלה שלא עוסקים ישירות במעשה — כלומר עסקנים ועיתונאים — אצו לחשוף אותו מתוך תאוות פרסום או רדיפת תהילה.

במשך שבועות ארוכים היו הפיות חתומים. יתרה מזאת, אמצעי התקשורת בישראל קיבלו על עצמם בהבנה ולפנים משורת הדין מגבלות פרסום שלא היו כמותם לחומרה. ועדת העורכים הסכימה לא לפרסם בארץ אפילו דברים שראו אור בחו"ל.

(סוף בעמוד 11)

150 | היום 36 עמוד

יום ב' 7.1.1985 | י"ד בטבת תשמ"ה

גליון מס' 11317 — שנה ל"ז

המחיר — 150 שקלים (כולל מע"מ)

המייסד והעורך הראשון ע. קרליבך ז"ל

לגליון זה מצורף **קריאת ביניים** שבועון מעריב לאנשים צעירים

מזג אוויר

בהיר עד מעונן חלקית

● **הטמפרטורות:** — ירושלים 7—13; תל־אביב 10—21; חיפה 12—18; אילת 8—22. הטמפרטורות בארץ ובעולם בעמוד מודיעין.

רוב בוועדת הביקורת של הכנסת תומך במתן סמכויות רחבות לוועדת החקירה ב„מפולת הבנקאיות"

ה„ויסות" ייחקר מראשיתו; תיבדק גם מעורבות המערכת הפוליטית

הקמת הוועדה — שדיוניה יהיו פתוחים — מסיימת שבוע של מאמצים קדחתניים מצד גורמים פוליטיים שניסו למצוא פתרון אחר; מנהלי הבנקים טענו: לא יתכן שגם נתפטר וגם נועמד לדין פלילי; ארידור חייב לשאת באחריות; בהיעדר יכולת לפטר „בכירים", כולל הנגיד, הוחלט לבחור בחקירה

מאת גבי קסלר, דוד ליפקין וגיל קיפרי

ההחלטה הצפוייה היום כי ועדת הכנסת לביקורת המדינה על הקמתה של ועדת חקירה משפטית בפרשת מפולת מניות הבנקים — באה כתום שבוע של דיונים קדחתניים שבהם ניסו הגורמים במשק ובמערכת הפוליטית־שלטונית למצוא פתרון אחר; אך בהיעדר יכולת חוקית־משפטית לפטר מנהלים בכירים, הוחלט על הקמת ועדת חקירה.

סמכויותיה של ועדת החקירה יהיו רחבות ביותר והיא תוסמך לחקור את הפרשה מראשיתה (בשנת 1972), ולכלול בה את כל [illegible] ה[illegible] הפוליטית. דיוני הועדה יהיו גלויים.

[illegible] סמכויותיה של הוועדה שוכנן אתמול בהתייעצות שקיימו חברים ביסים ורשקבי, שהוסמכו לטפל בהקמת ועדת החקירה.

אתמול התברר סופית כי בוועדת הביקורת של הכנסת יש עתה רוב התומך בהקמת ועדת החקירה. בשבוע שעבר נוצר בוועדה תיקו 5—5 בנושא זה. אתמול הודיע ח"כ יהושע מצא (ליכוד), כי גם הוא יצטרף לתומכים בהקמת ועדת החקירה.

בעת הבירורים לפני ההחלטה הביעו שרים, חברי־כנסת ואישי משק התנגדות להקמת ועדת חקירה משפטית שדיוניה יהיו ממושכים, ישתקו את פעילותה של המערכת הפיננסית, יחשפו נושאים המוגדרים כסודיים ובבנקים ויגרמו הדים שליליים בחו"ל. הרקע חשש שמינויה של ועדת חקירה ירתיע בנקים בחו"ל מהמשך הקשרים עם הבנקים הישראליים. הועלתה תביעה שיש לפעול על פי מימצאי דו"ח מבקר המדינה ולהסיק מסקנות אישיות נגד ראשי בנק ישראל.

אבל, על פי חוות דעת משפטית שהוגשה לראש הממשלה, התברר כי על פי החוק הקיים ספק אם הממשלה יכולה לפטר את נגיד בנק ישראל והמפקחת של הבנקים. מתברר כי החוק מסורבל, ובמצב החוקי הקיים עלול היה נגיד בנק ישראל לפנות לבג"ץ כדי למנוע הדחתו.

הנוטים בדבר בממשלה ובמערכת הפוליטית העלו גם תביעה עד שראשי הבנקים לא ישוחררו מאחריות לפרשה ויסיקו מסקנות אישיות. אך במגעים לא־רשמיים שהיו עם אחדים מראשי הבנקים, הם הבהירו כי לא ייתכן לדרוש מהם גם להסיק מסקנות אישיות וגם שוקלים להעמידם לדין פלילי

(סוף בעמוד 11)

הצעת פשרה ל„חבילה ב'"

כל מצרכי היסוד והדלק יתייקרו בעשרות אחוזים

עם סיומה של החבילה הנוכחית; אחר־כך יתייקרו מדי 6 שבועות

* התעשיינים דוחים הצעת ההסתדרות להאריך תוקף העיסקה הראשונה
* עליה מתונה יחסית במספר המובטלים במשק בגלל תחילת עונת הקטיף

מאת שרגא מקל, ע. פליישר, גיל קיפרי וברוך מאירי

מצרכי היסוד והדלק יתייקרו בתום עיסקת החבילה הנוכחית ולאחר מכן יתייקרו מדי 6 שבועות — זו הצעת הפשרה שהועלתה על־ידי האוצר בדיונים הי[illegible] [illegible] ההסתדרות. [illegible] לייקר את מצרכי היסוד, הדלק והחשמל בעשרות אחוזים — כדי להתקרב ליעד של צמצום עומק הסובסידיות ל־25% בלבד מהמחיר לצרכן — עד סוף שנת התקציב.

בצמרת האוצר חלוקות הדעות [illegible] שר האוצר יצחק מודעי מצדד בייקור גבוה. לעומת זאת גורס סגן שר האוצר עדי אמוראי כי די בייקור מתון של המצרכים והדלק בשיעור של — 15%. כדי לשמור על הרגיעה במשק.

משרד האוצר אינו מוכן להתפשר על הוצאת המוצרים המסובסדים [illegible]

המירוץ על תפקיד המפכ"ל נכנס ל„הילוך גבוה"

בר־לב מציע לניצב בר לפקד על המחוז הצפוני

מקורבי בר: „סטירת לחי למי שקיווה לראות את המשטרה מתנערת ממצוקת היעדר מנהיגות"

מאת אילן בכר

שר המשטרה, חיים בר־לב, הציע בימים אלה לראש אגף המבצעים במשטרת ישראל, ניצב צבי בר, והציע לו ליטול לידיו את הפיקוד על המחוז הצפוני של המשטרה במקומו של ניצב רחמים חדד העומד לפרוש.

מקורות בכירים אומרים, כי ניצב בר דחה בזעף את ההצעה, שכן הוא רואה עצמו מועמד לתפקיד מפכ"ל המשטרה. אותם מקורות הדגישו, כי הצעה זאת פירושה הרחקת ניצב בר מהמירוץ על כס המפכ"ל.

מקורביו של ניצב בר, בתוך

(סוף בעמוד 11)

פרס ורבין תומכים בנסיגה של צה"ל לקו חדש בלבנון

שיחות נאקורה מתחדשות היום באווירה פסימית; ג'מאייל דורש מישראל לוח־זמנים מפורט לנסיגה מוחלטת

מאת יוסף ולטר, רפאל מן ושפי גבאי

ראש־הממשלה, שמעון פרס, ושר הבטחון, יצחק רבין, תומכים בהיערכות בקו חדש בלבנון, כשלב ראשון לנסיגה הדרגתית של צה"ל, זאת אם לא תהיה תזוזה בשיחות נאקורה.

אתמול נפגש שר הבטחון עם ראש־הממשלה פרס, והציג בפניו את האפשרויות השונות לפריסה חדשה של צה"ל בלבנון. תוכניות אלה גובשו בשבועות שעברו במטה־הכללי. רבין סייר במשך השבוע בלבנון ועמד מקרוב אתר אפשרויות הפריסה השונות.

האפשרות העיקרית, העומדת בפני ישראל, היא של נסיגה אל קו חדש מצפון לליטאני, שיצא מצור, יכלול את רמת נבטיה ויגמר בחצביה.

גורמים בדרג המדיני־בטחוני מדגישים, כי בשיחות נאקורה לא תציע היום משלחת ישראל הצעות חדשות, ותנקוט ב„טקטיקה של האזנה". בישראל מצפים כי

(סוף בעמוד 11)

ישראלית שחזרה מ„התופת האתיופית":

,העצים נעלמו, נהרות יבשו והארץ חרבה'

תרצה אתגר, חברת קיבוץ נצר סירני שביקרה בארץ הולדתה מספרת: השמועה על מבצע ההצלה פשטה בקרב יהודי אתיופיה כאש בשדה קוצים; רבים את החלו לתלות לצווארם תכשיטי מגן דוד

מאת גיל ידידלוביץ

הבטתי למטה מחלון המטוס, זמן קצר לפני הנחיתה בבירה[illegible]; הגע[illegible] גלים הסבוכים, הנהרות שעלו על גדותיהם והצמחייה הדשעבותה נעלמו כלא היו. הארץ שהיתה פעם קשורה — חרבה. כך מספרת תרצה אתגר, חברת קיבוץ נצר סירני, יוצאת אתיופיה, ש

(סוף בעמוד 2)

● תרצה אתגר מתארת שבתה אמנהו הגיהו ברקלו — בעת הביקור באתיופיה.

המריבה סביב חשיפת „מבצע משה"

הליכוד: לשכת פרס אשמה; המערך: מנצלים המצב לניגוח פוליטי

מאת רפאל מן ויוסף צוריאל

שרים בליכוד מתחו אתמול ביקורת על לשכת ראש הממשלה, בטענה כי התדרוך לכתבים, שערכה לשכת העיתונות הממשלתית — מהנהלת לשכת ראש־הממשלה — היא שגרמה להחלטת סודאן להפסיק את השיפוט של יהודי אתיופיה.

(סוף בעמוד 2)

שלושה לא־יהודים נמצאו בין האתיופים

בגל העליה הגדול של השבועות שעברו

מאת אברהם תירוש

מספרים של האתיופים הלא־יהודים, שהצליחו להסתנן אל שירות היהודים שעלו מאתיופיה לישראל, הוא אפסי. בגל העליה של השבועות שעברו התגלו שלושה מקרים כאלה בלבד.

המדובר בזוג נשוי ובגבר נוסף, שנתברר כי אינם יהודים כלל וניצלו את ההזדמנות לה

(סוף בעמוד 11)

רמטכ"ל ירדן:

טילי סאם־6 יוצבו בירדן בתחילת 1985

כתבה — בעמ' 5

ראש־ישיבה פיתה אשת אברך; הסכימה להתגרש וילדה לו ילד

— כך טוען פרקליט חיפני בתביעה אזרחית נגד הרב אביגדור יוניוב ראש ישיבת „הפקדתי שומרים", נשוי ואב ל־5 ילדים

מאת דוד זוהר

הרב אביגדור יוניוב, ראש ישיבת „הפקדתי שומרים", נשוי ואב ל־5 ילדים, פיתה אשתו של אברך צעיר, תלמיד בישיבה, להתגרש מבעלה תהלל עימה פרשת אהבים שנסתיימה בלידת ילד מחוץ לנישואין — כך מסופר בתביעה משפטית שהוגשה אתמול לבית־המשפט המחוזי בחיפה.

מגיש התביעה הוא עורך־דין חיפני. בתביעתו, שסיבתה סיכסוך בעלות על שתי חנויות, טוען הפרקליט, כי ההיכרות בין הרב החלה לפני כשנה במשרדו בחיפה, כאשר הרב הופיע שם בלווית אשה צעירה, אשת האברך לשעבר, וחתם בפני

(סוף בעמוד 11)

מזג אוויר

בהיר עד מעונן חלקית. עליה במעלות החום.

● הטמפרטורות: — ירושלים 15—28; תל אביב 18—26; חיפה 16—24; אילת 20—35. הטמפרטורות בארץ ובעולם בעמ' 20.

235 | היום 44 עמוד

יום ב' 6.5.85 | ט"ו באייר תשמ"ה

גליון מס' 11416 — שנה ל"ח

המחיר —235. שקלים (כולל מע"מ)

המייסד והעורך הראשון ע. קרליבך ז"ל

לגליון זה מצורף

קריאת ביניים

שבועון מעריב לאנשים צעירים

המורים מקיימים היום "כנסי הסברה" ברחבי הארץ; השיבושים בבחינות הבגרות נמשכים

היום מ־11 מושבתים כל בתי־הספר התיכונים וחלק מחטיבות הביניים

בבתי־ספר אחדים החליטו מנהלים להתעלם מהנחיות ארגונם וקיימו את בחינות הבגרות ו"המגן מתוך התחשבות ו"כדי למנוע נזק לתלמידים" ✶ סיכוי להפסקה זמנית של העיצומים התגבש בפגישה עם שר החינוך נבון

מאת נורית דברת

הלימודים בבתי הספר העל יסודיים ובחלק ניכר מחטיבות הביניים ישבתו היום משעה 11 בבוקר. מחר יתקיימו הלימודים כסדרם. ארגון המורים העל יסודיים שהחליט על השביתה במחאה על פיטורי מורים, יצא בקריאה גם לחברי הסתדרות המורים להצטרף לשביתה וככל הנראה יצטרפו לשביתה גם חברי הסתדרות המורים.

המורים העל־יסודיים זומנו היום לכנסי הסברה במקומות שונים בארץ. השיבושים בבחינות הבגרות (בחינות בעל־פה, מתכונת ומגן) נמשכים זה היום השני.

מפח־נפש נגרם אתמול לתלמידים ולמורים בבתי הספר בהם ביטלו את הבחינות. במקומות שונים בארץ החליטו מנהלים להתעלם מהנחיות ארגון העל־יסודיים וקיימו את הבחינות במועד. אחד המנהלים אמר ל"מעריב": "כל מורה עושה את חשבון הנפש שלו ומבין איזה נזק עלול להיגרם לתלמידיו אם לא יקיים את הבחינות ואיזה מאמץ שהשקיע ללמוד ייהרד לטמיון".

סיכוי להפסקה, לפחות זמנית, של העיצומים, הועלה אתמול בפגישת שר החינוך, יצחק נבון עם יו"ר ארגון המורים שושנה בייר. הגברת בייר תביא הערב לפני הנהלת ארגונה את הצעת השר לדיון בהצעות פשרה חדשות, בתמורה לאי־החרפת השיבושים בימים הקרובים. גם מזכ"ל הסתדרות המורים יצחק ולבר, נענה אתמול לפניית נבון, והודיע כי לא יחדש השבוע את העיצומים בבתי הספר היסודיים. מחר ייפגש ולבר עם נבון להמשך המו"מ.

צו משפטי שהוצא ב־1 אחר חצות:

עובדי בתיה"ח חייבים לחזור לעבודה תקינה

החל מהבוקר בשעה 06.00 ✶ ארבלי־אלמוזנינו: השר מרדכי גור לא היה צריך לנסוע לחו"ל

מאת דליה מזורי

שופט בית הדין האיזורי לעבודה בירושלים, השופט נחמיה גוטמן, הוציא הלילה צו המורה על עובדי המינהל והמשק והאחיות בבתי החולים הממשלתיים לשוב הבוקר לעבודה

(סוף בעמוד 11)

האוצר דורש ביטול עצמאות בנק ישראל

תובע לקבוע בחוק שפעולות הבנק בשוק הפתוח ייעשו רק בהסכמת שר האוצר

מאת שרגא מקל

משרד האוצר הכניס במפתיע סעיף חדש ל"הצעת חוק בנק ישראל" שמשמעותו ביטול העצמאות של בנק ישראל בתחום מרכזי של פעילותו — הסעיף קובע, ש"הפעולות בשוק הפתוח של בנק ישראל ייעשו בהסכמת האוצר".

מדובר בפעילות של הבנק במסחר בניירות־ערך בבורסה. ל־

(סוף בעמוד 11)

● נשיא ארה"ב, רונלד רייגן, נושא את זר שאותו הניח באתר ההנצחה של מחנה הריכוז ברגן בלזן, אתמול. כתבה — בעמ' 3. (צילום אי.פי.)

שגריר ישראל בגרמניה יצחק בן־ארי משיב לתוקפים אותו:

החרמת הטקס בברגן־בלזן היתה מתקבלת כפגיעה בנשיא ארה"ב

מצדיק בואו למרות החרם שהטילה על הארוע היהדות העולמית; אומר על הביקור בביטבורג: לא סמל גולגלות המוות של ה־ס.ס. צריך לסמל הפיוס עם גרמניה

מאת עפרה ישועה־ליית, יעקב ארז ועודד גרנות

הופעתו של שגריר ישראל, יצחק בן־ארי, בטקס שנערך אתמול במחנה הריכוז בברגן־בלזן, זכתה למירב תשומת־הלב. אמצעי התקשורת הדגישו, שמר בן ארי הוא הנציג היהודי הרשמי היחיד שהגיע לטקס. (כתבה — בעמ' ד').

לדעת השגריר, החלטתו להגיע לטקס היתה נכונה. החרמה רשמית של הטקס מצד מדינת ישראל היתה מתפרשת, לדעתו, כפגיעה בנשיא ארצות־הברית ו־

(סוף בעמוד 11)

פרס ושמיר מסכימים על "שיחות קהיר"

מאת רפאל מן

סופרו המדיני של "מעריב"

ראש הממשלה שמעון פרס, העביר אתמול מסר קצר לנשיא מצרים חוסני מובארך. המסר הועבר למזכיר הכוח המצרי מוחמד בסיוני, בפגישה שהתקיימה אתמול אתר הצהריים

(סוף בעמוד 8)

קונצרן "כלל" המועמד הכמעט־יחיד לרכוש את תשלובת "אתא"

מאת דוד ליפקין

מאמצי הגורמים הממשלתיים הבכירים וההסתדרותיים למציאת קונה לתשלובת "אתא" יתמקדו בימים הקרובים בנסיון לשכנע את קונצרן "כלל" לרכוש את המפעל. היום צפויים מגעים בנושא זה בין נציגי הממשלה לראשי "כלל". (כתבה — בעמוד 23).

בבירורים שהתנהלו בימים אלה התברר כי "כלל" הפכה כמעט למועמדת היחידה לרכישת "אתא". אולם ל"כלל" יש שורה של תנאים, במיוחד לגבי התובות שיש ל"אתא" בהיקף של כ־20 מיליון דולר לבנק לאומי ולבנק דיסקונט.

לעומת זאת, התברר, כי הסיכויים שקבוצת ז'אק נאסר או התעשיין היהודי־אנגלי דוד אליאנס ירכשו את "אתא" הם מעטים.

צ'רני: לא עזר ויצמן דיווח לי מהממשלה אלא איש ליכוד אחר

"וייצמן מעולם לא הדליף לי מישיבות ממשלה; שמיר ומילוא מקנאים בעזר בגלל הצלחותיו"

מאת יעקב ארז,

סופר "מעריב" בניו־יורק

"המקור שדיווח לי מישיבות הממשלה לא היה עזר ויצמן. המקור היה איש־ליכוד אחר שאיננו ויצמן", אמר אמש איש העסקים היהודי־אמריקני ליאון צ'רני, אשר ספרו "יועץ מיוחד" גורם לסערה פוליטית בארץ.

הכל יודעים שאני חבר של עזר ויצמן, אבל הייתי מקורב לאנשים רבים בליכוד ובממשלה, כמו חיים לנדאו המנוח, מנחם בגין, יצחק מודעי, איתן לבני וגם אישים במערך כמו יצחק רבין חיים בר־לב ושמעון פרס. ויצמן מעולם לא הדליף לי מישיבות ממשלה. הוא לא דיבר איתי על כך. יצחק שמיר ורוני מילוא מבקשים להפוך את הכתוב בספרי לפרשה פוליטית כדי לנגח את עזר ויצמן, שכן הם מקנאים בגלל הצלחותיו בתהליך השלום עם מצרים", אמר צ'רני ל"מעריב".

"בעמוד 109 של ספרי אין שום התייחסות לעזר ויצמן. אני מודיע לך: עזר איננו המקור לקטע הזה. אני העברתי פעמים רבות התרשמויות ממה שקורה

(סוף בעמוד 11)

גם בגין השתמש בשרותיו של צ'רני

גילוי זה נכלל אף הוא בספרו של עורך־הדין האמריקני

מאת סופר "מעריב"

בשנת 1979 ישב יהודי, אורח ארה"ב, ליד שולחן הכתיבה של שגריר ארה"ב בישראל סם לואיס. שמו עו"ד ליאון צ'רני. לדעתו הוא האורח היחיד שהותר לו להשתמש בטלפון־המעורבל כדי לשוחח ישירות מרחוב הירקון בתל־אביב עם הבית־הלבן בשדרות פנסילווניה. השיחות היו דחופות ועסקו בדיונים בתוך ממשלת ישראל. ה.ט. שהשיחות התנהלו בטלפון "בטוח", נזקקו צ'רני ובן שיחו מעבר

(סוף בעמוד 8)

חרדים מבני־ברק מפיצים בישיבות תיכוניות תעמולה נגד השרות בצה"ל

הפעילות נעשית מטעם אגודת "ערכים" שממומנת בחלקה מתקציב משרד החינוך ✶ יו"ר תנועת "נאמני תורה ועבודה" מתלונן: "שטיפת־מוח היונקת מהשקפת עולם אנטי־ציונית" ✶ משרד החינוך בודק

מאת נורית דברת

חוברות הסברה שמהן נקראים תלמידי כיתות י"ב שלא להתגייס לשרות בצה"ל, מופצות בימים אלה בין תלמידים בישיבות תיכוניות, הנתונות לפיקוח משרד החינוך. החוברות, המגנות את האידיאולוגיה המוצהרת של הישיבות התיכוניות ושל החינוך הממלכתי־דתי, מופצות במסגרת פעולות הסברה מטעם האגודה החרדית "ערכים", המקבלת חלק מתקציבה ממשרד החינוך.

בספר התקציב של משרד החינוך מוקצבים לאגודה, שמרכזה בבני־ברק, עשרות מיליוני שקלים לשנה.

(סוף בעמוד 11)

גרנות — עשות אשקלון

אל מגדלי הכותנה

הנכם מוזמנים

ליום שדה של עבודת המרחב

שיתקיים מחר, יום שלישי (7.5.85), משעה 09.00—14.00, בקיבוץ מבוא חמה, רמת הגולן.

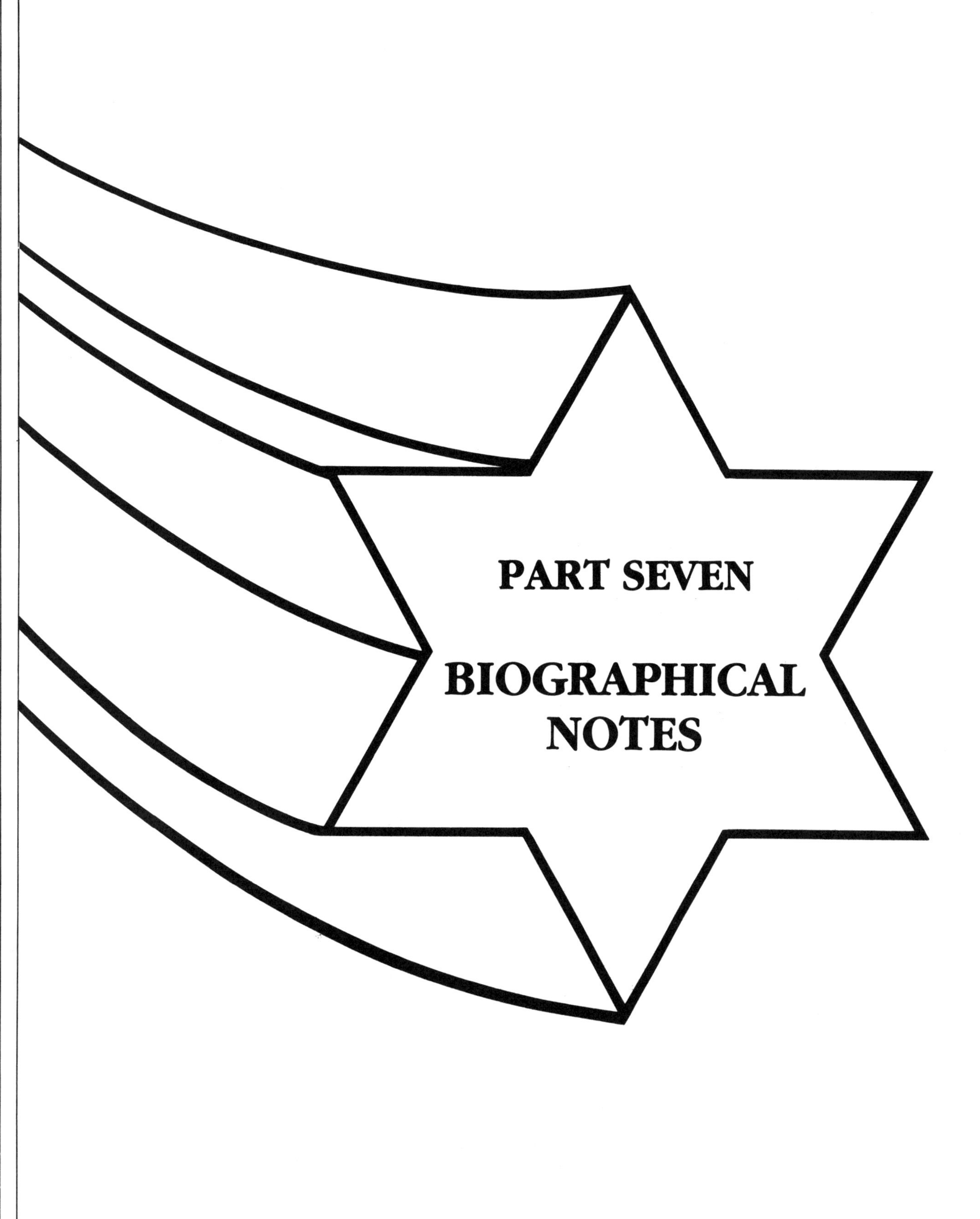

PART SEVEN

BIOGRAPHICAL NOTES

Current Biography

Academics; Historians; Scholars; Educators

Alter, Robert B.; b. 1935; professor of Hebrew and comparative literature at Berkeley; critic of Judaica and modern Jewish fiction

Baron, Salo W.; b. 1895; professor of Jewish studies at Columbia; prolific scholar of Jewish social history

Boorstin, Daniel J.; b. 1914; historian; educator; author; Librarian of Congress, 1975-present; recipient of 1974 Pulitzer Prize for History

Botstein, Leon; b. 1946; Zurich-born educator, historian, musician; former president of Franconia (New Hampshire) College; president of Bard College, New York

Chomsky, Noam; b. 1928; linguist; political writer; revisionist historian; early opponent of Vietnam War; professor of linguistics at MIT

Elazar, Daniel J.; b. 1934; political scientist; professor at Bar-Ilan University and Temple University; author of *Community and Polity: The Organizational Dynamics of American Jewry*

Chyet, Stanley Franklin; b. 1931; historian; Reform rabbi; editor; professor of American Jewish history at HUC-LA.

Cohen, Arthur A.; b. 1928; novelist; publisher; scholar of fiction, nonfiction, theological, philosophical and spiritual issues.

Cohen, Gerson David; b. 1924; historian; Conservative rabbi; chancellor of the Jewish Theological Seminary of America, 1972-85

Cohen, Naomi W. (Naomi Weiner); b. 1927; specialist of 20th century American and American Jewish history; professor at Hunter College; author of *Not Free to Desist*

Cremin, Lawrence; b. 1925; educator; historian; president of Teachers College, Columbia University since 1974; winner of 1981 Pulitzer Prize for History

Dawidowicz, Lucy (Lucy Schildkret); b. 1915; historian; author; professor at Yeshiva University; major scholar of the Holocaust era

Edel, Leon (Joseph Leon Edel); b. 1907; biographer of Henry James, James Joyce, Henry David Thoreau and Willa Cather; winner of 1963 Pulitzer Prize for biography

Ehrlich, Paul R.; b. 1932; geologist; biologist; evolutionist; leader in the international crusade for population control; professor of biology at Stanford U.; author of *The Population Bomb* (1968)

Falk, Richard Anderson; b. 1930; professor of international law at Princeton University; questioned legality of U.S. role in Vietnam; spokesman for international human rights

Feingold, Henry L.; b. 1931; German-born historian; authored *Politics of Rescue: The Roosevelt Administration and the Holocaust 1938-1945,* which questioned official efforts to save European Jewry; editor of *American Jewish History* (American Jewish Historical Society)

Finkelstein, Louis; b. 1895; rabbi; former chancellor of Jewish Theological Seminary of America; authored *The Jews: Their History, Culture and Religion*

Friedberg, Maurice; b. 1929; Polish-born professor of Russian literature and Slavic languages at University of Illinois (Urbana-Champaign); expert on role of Jews in Russian literature

Gay, Peter; b. 1923; Berlin-born professor of history at Yale University; expert on the Enlightenment and on pre-war German cultural life

Gershman, Carl; b. 1943; author; lecturer; counselor to the United States representative to the United Nations since 1981

Glatzer, Nahum N.; b. 1903; Austrian-born historian; professor of Judaic studies and religion at Boston University (previously at Brandeis)

Goldman, Eric; b. 1915; historian; professor at Princeton University; former special consultant to President Lyndon Johnson; scholar of 20th century American liberalism and reform

Gordon, Cyrus H.; b. 1908; historian; Semitic scholar and archaeologist; authored *Before Columbus: Links Between the Old World and Ancient America*

Gottschalk, Alfred; b. 1930; Reform rabbi; president of Hebrew Union College—Jewish Institute of Religion; ordained first woman rabbi; member of the United States Holocaust Memorial Council; Cincinnati

Gutman, Herbert; b. 1928; historian; professor at the Graduate School of the City University of New York; specialist in social history and Afro-American history

Halpern, Ben; b. 1912; scholar; activist; Zionist thinker; professor of Near Eastern and Judaic Studies at Brandeis University

Handlin, Oscar; b. 1915; historian; scholar of the emotional and social impact of immigration, especially of Jews in America; professor at Harvard; winner of 1952 Pulitzer Prize for History

Jakobson, Roman; b. 1896; Moscow-born linguist; taught in Czechoslovakia in the 1930's, Scandinavia and Colombia in the 1940's, Harvard from 1949 until retirement; studied culture and language of Jewish communities in Slavic countries.

Katsh, Abraham I.; b. 1908; educator, scholar; pioneered the teaching of Hebrew in American colleges; former president of Dropsie University

Kohl, Herbert; b. 1937; educational reformer; author of *36 Children;* advocate of the "open classroom"

Kozol, Jonathan; b. 1936; educational writer and critic, especially of inner-city school practices

Lachman, Seymour P.; b. 1933; educator; former president of the New York City Board of Education; leading advocate for Soviet Jewry

Lamm, Norman; b. 1927; rabbi; philosopher; prolific writer; president of Yeshiva University; founder of *Tradition* quarterly

Lander, Bernard; b. 1915; sociologist; founder and president, Touro College; former dean, Bernard Revel Graduate School of Yeshiva University

Luttwak, Edward; b. 1942; Rumanian-born military scholar and writer; associate of Georgetown University's Center for Strategic and International Studies; wrote *A Dictionary of Modern War, The Israeli Army* (with Dan Horowitz), *Coup d'Etat: A Practical Handbook;* frequent contributor to Commentary

Marcus, Jacob Rader; b. 1896; historian; rabbi; founder and director of the American Jewish Archives in Cincinnati; professor at Hebrew Union College; former president of the Central Conference of American Rabbis

Marcus, Steven; b. 1928; scholar of 19th century English literature; professor at Columbia University

Miller, Israel; b. 1919; rabbi; vice-president of Yeshiva University; former chairman of the Conference of Presidents of Major American Jewish Organizations

Nagel, Ernest; b. 1901; Hungarian-born scholar of philosophy; professor at Columbia University since 1931; known for his application of systematization to knowledge

Neusner, Jacob; b. 1932; scholar of ancient Jewish history; professor at Brown University; prolific author, particularly of Mishnaic law; outspoken advocate of *aliyah*

Nozick, Robert; b. 1938; philosopher; professor at Harvard University; authored *Anarchy, State and Utopia,* in which he argues for limitation of governmental functions and authority

Patai, Raphael; b. 1910; Budapest-born anthropologist; authored *The Jewish Mind;* in *The Myth of the Jewish Race,* he argued that Jews are not a single race, but take on characteristics of their host peoples

Rackman, Emanuel; b. 1910; rabbi; attorney; president of Bar-Ilan University since 1977; former professor of political philosophy and jurisprudence at Yeshiva University

Redlich, Norman; b. 1925; dean of the New York University School of Law

Rivkin, Ellis; b. 1918; historian; scholar of Pharisaic Judaism; professor at Hebrew Union College

Rubenstein, Richard L; b. 1924; theologian; rabbi; leading thinker and writer on the Holocaust; leading designer of Holocaust curricula; professor at Florida State University

Sachar, Abram; b. 1899; historian; first president of Brandeis University; leading architect of the growth of the Hillel Foundation; author of *A History of the Jews* and *The Course of Our Times*

Sarna, Nahum; b. 1923; London-born scholar of Biblical history; professor at Brandeis University; authored *Understanding Genesis;* leading translator of the simplified JPS version of *The Writings*

Schapiro, Meyer; b. 1904; Lithuanian-born art historian; professor emeritus at Columbia University; author of *Romanesque Art; Modern Art*

Schappes, Morris Urman; b. 1907; Ukrainian-born historian and editor; professor of American Jewish history at Queens College; author of *A Documentary History of Jews in the U.S.A.: 1654-1875;* editor of *Jewish Currents*

Schiff, Alvin; b. 1926; educator; executive vice-president of the Board of Jewish Education of Greater New York; author of *The Jewish Day School in America;* editor of quarterly *Jewish Education*

Schorsch, Ismar; b. 1935; chancellor of the Jewish Theological Seminary of America since 1985

Schrag, Peter; b. 1931; writer; education system critic; author of *Decline of the WASP*

Shapiro, Harold T.; b. 1935; economist; president of Princeton University former president, University of Michigan

Silverman, Ira; b. 1945; president of the Rabbinical Reconstructionist College

Sovern, Michael I.; b. 1931; president of Columbia University; former professor and dean of the Columbia University School of Law; specialist in civil rights and labor law

Tuchman, Barbara; b. 1912; historian; journalist; won Pulitzer Prizes for *The Guns of August* and *Stilwell and the American Experience in China, 1911-1945*

Urofsky, Melvin; b. 1939; historian; professor at Virginia Commonwealth University; authored *American Zionism from Herzl to the Holocaust; A Voice that Spoke for Justice: The Life and Times of Stephen S. Wise*

Weiss-Rosmarin, Trude; b. 1908; Frankfurt-born scholar; writer; Hebraist; founder and editor of *The Jewish Spectator;* leading Jewish feminist

Zinn, Howard; b. 1922; historian; professor at Boston University; stresses experiences of neglected groups—women, blacks, manual laborers; author of *A People's History of the United States*

Art; Architecture

Amen, Irving; b. 1918; woodcut artist

Baskin, Leonard; b. 1922; anti-abstractionist; sculptor and graphic artist

Glaser, Milton; b. 1929; graphic designer; illustrator

Goodman, Percival; b. 1904; architect; major designer of synagogues and Jewish community centers

Gross, Chaim; b. 1904; sculptor and graphic artist, especially of Judaic and Hasidic themes

Hirschfeld, Al (Albert); b. 1903; caricaturist

Levine, David; b. 1926; caricaturist; painter

Nevelson, Louise (Louise Berliawsky); b. 1899; Kiev-born abstract tor; has used her art to make significant political statements

Segal, George; b. 1924; sculptor of neo-realist school

Sendak, Maurice; b. 1928; illustrator; set designer

Steinberg, Saul; b. 1914; Rumanian-born artist, who created *The New Yorker* view of New York and beyond

Commerce and Industry

Annenberg, Walter; b. 1908; communications; Triangle Publications; former ambassador to Great Britain; philanthropist

Bernstein, Robert; b. 1923; publisher; president of Random House; leading human rights activist

Bronfman, Edgar; b. 1929; Montreal-born industrialist; president of Distillers Corporation; president of World Jewish Congress; naturalized American; philanthropist

Davis, Marvin; b. 1925; industrialist; America's most successful independent oil wildcatter; co-owner of 20th Century Fox; philanthropist

Fisher, Max M.; b. 1908; industrialist; former board chairman of United Brands and Aurora Gasoline; the leading Jewish Republican during the Nixon and Ford Administrations; philanthropist; former chairman of the Jewish Agency, and of the Council of Jewish Federations

Goldenson, Leonard; b. 1905; chairman and chief executive officer of ABC

Hammer, Armand; b. 1898; industrialist; art collector; president of Occidental Petroleum; pioneer (since 1921) in Soviet trade

Hess, Leon; b. 1914; industrialist; chairman of Amerada Hess Corporation; principal owner and chairman of the New York Jets football team

Icahn, Carl; b. 1936; financier; chairman of TWA; philanthropist

Klein, Calvin; b. 1942; fashion designer

Krim, Arthur B.; b. 1910; former president of United Artists, former chairman of Transam Corporation; attorney (Phillips, Nizer, Benjamin, Krim and Ballon); active in Democratic party fund-raising and policy-making

Lefrak, Samuel J.; b. 1918; realtor; developer of middle-class communities in New York; philanthropist

Marcus, Stanley; b. 1905; chairman emeritus of Neiman-Marcus Company

Paley, William; b. 1901; founder and chairman of CBS, Inc.; trustee of the Federation of Jewish Philanthropies

Pritzker, Jay; b. 1922; industrialist; attorney; leading figure in Chicago-based Pritzker family, owners of Hyatt International Corp.; chairman of the family corporation, the Marmon Group

Sarnoff, Robert W.; b. 1918; chairman of RCA; helped develop use of color broadcasting

Shapiro, Irving S.; b. 1916; attorney; former chairman of E. I. du Pont de Nemours & Company; head of the Business Roundtable

Stern, Leonard; b. 1940; industrialist; head of Hartz Mountain Industries

Straus, Roger; b. 1917; publisher; founder and president of Farrar, Straus and Giroux, Inc.

Sulzberger, Arthur Ochs; b. 1926; publisher of *The New York Times*

Tisch, Laurence A.; b. 1923; financier; chief executive of CBS, Inc.; chairman of the Loew's Corporation; past president of the United Jewish Appeal of New York

Tisch, Preston Robert; b. 1926; formerly president of the Loew's Corporation, presently U.S. Postmaster General

Werblin, David "Sonny"; b. 1910; entertainment and sports entrepreneur; former owner of the New York Jets; developer of the Meadowlands Sports Complex

Wexner, Leslie H.; b. 1937; chairman, The Limited, Inc.; philanthropist

Winter, Elmer Louis; b. 1912; attorney; co-founder of Manpower, Inc.; former president of the American Jewish Committee

Communal Affairs

Bayer, Abraham J.; b. 1932; director of International Commission, NJCRAC; vice chairman, board of advisors, United States Holocaust Memorial Council; former coordinator, American Jewish Conference on Soviet Jewry; community relations and international affairs activist

Berger, Graenum; b. 1908; communal executive and planner; defender of Ethiopian Jewry; founding president of AAEJ

Berman, Julius; b. 1936; attorney; former president of the Union of Orthodox Jewish Congregations of America; chairman of the Conference of Presidents of Major American Jewish Organizations, 1982-84

Bialkin, Kenneth; b. 1929; attorney; national chairman of the Anti-Defamation League of B'nai B'rith; chairman of the Conference of Presidents of Major American Jewish Organizations, 1984-

Bookbinder, Hyman; b. 1916; Washington director of American Jewish Committee; longtime associate of Hubert H. Humphrey; former official of HUD

Chernin, Albert D.; b. 1928; executive vice-chairman of National Jewish Community Relations Advisory Council (NJCRAC) since 1975

Commoner, Barry; b. 1917; biologist; ecologist; educator; 1980 Presidential candidate on Citizens Party ticket

Decter, Midge; b. 1927; writer; editor; leader of neo-conservative movement; a founder of the Committee for the Free World

Evans, Eli N.; b. 1936; president of the Charles H. Revson Foundation; attorney; student of the Jewish experience in the South

Foxman, Abraham H.; b. 1939; associate director and director of international affairs, Anti-Defamation League of B'nai B'rith; Holocaust survivor

Friedan, Betty; b. 1921; feminist leader; authored *The Feminine Mystique* (1963), which helped create the women's movement; former president, National Organization for Women

Glasser, Ira; b. 1937; executive director of ACLU since 1978

Gold, Bertram H.; b. 1916; Canadian-born former executive vice-president of the American Jewish Committee; reversed AJC's policy of non-Zionism and assimilationism

Goodman, Jerry; b. 1933; executive director, National Conference on Soviet Jewry since 1971; long-time advocate for Soviet Jewry

Goodman, Naomi (Naomi Ascher); b. 1920; leading pacifist and feminist historian; president since 1972 of the Jewish Peace Fellowship

Gordis, David; b. 1940; former executive vice-president, American Jewish Committee; former vice-chancellor, University of Judaism in Los Angeles

Haddad, Heskel; b. 1928; Baghdad-born physician; Sephardic leader; clinical professor of ophthalmology at New York Medical College; founder (1968) and president of the American Committee for the Rescue and Resettlement of Iraqi Jews; president since 1978 of the World Organization of Jews from Arab Countries

Hier, Marvin; b. 1939; rabbi; founder and dean of Yeshiva University of Los Angeles; founder and dean of the Simon Wiesenthal Center; leading spokesman for Holocaust and genocide-related issues

Hoenlein, Malcolm; b. 1944; executive director, Conference of Presidents of Major American Jewish Organizations; founding director of the JCRC of New York and the Greater New York Conference on Soviet Jewry

Jacobson, Charlotte; b. 1914; Zionist leader; president of the Jewish National Fund; former president of the World Zionist Organization; former president of Hadassah; critic of those (especially HIAS) who aid Soviet Jewish emigres who refuse to move to Israel

Kahane, Meir; b. 1932; rabbi; founder and leader of the militant Jewish Defense League; holds degrees in law and international relations from New York University; critic of the Jewish establishment; founder of Israeli Kach party in 1976; member of Knesset

Klutznick, Philip M.; b. 1907; businessman; former secretary of commerce under Jimmy Carter; former president of the World Jewish Congress

Korey, William; b. 1922; scholar; director of policy research for the B'nai B'rith International Council; leading expert on Soviet Jewry and related human rights issues; prolific journalist; authored *The Soviet Cage: Anti-Semitism in Russia*

Kreutzer, Franklin D.; b. 1940; attorney; president, United Synagogue of America, 1985-present

Levine, Irving M.; b. 1929; communal executive; founder of the Institute of Pluralism and Group Identity of the American Jewish Committee; urban affairs specialist

Levine, Jacqueline K.; b. 1926; long-time civil rights advocate; former chairperson, NJCRAC; founding chair, Women's Plea for Soviet Jewry; chair, Washington Mobilization for Summit II

Levine, Naomi (Naomi Bronheim); b. 1923; attorney; former executive director of the American Jewish Congress; currently vice-president for external affairs at New York University

Lowell, Stanley H. (Stanley H. Lowenbraun); b. 1919; attorney; a founder of the New York City Commission on Human Rights; former chairman of the National Conference on Soviet Jewry

Neier, Aryeh; b. 1937; Berlin-born civil libertarian; vice-chairman of Americas Watch; former executive director of the NYCLU and ACLU; defended right of American Nazi Party to march in Skokie, Illinois in 1978; later wrote *Defending My Enemy* regarding that experience

Novick, Ivan J.; b. 1927; former president of the Zionist Organization of America; leading advocate of defense buildup by the United States

Pollack, Allen; b. 1938; leading Labor Zionist; former professor of Russian history at Yeshiva University; former president of the Labor Zionist Alliance; helped create American Professors for Peace in the Middle East

Regenstein, Lewis; b. 1943; conservationist; heads the Fund for Animals; lobbied for the Marine Mammal Act and the Endangered Species Act; helped save the bowhead whale from extinction

Rudin, A. James; b. 1934; rabbi; national director for interreligious affairs at the American Jewish Committee; expert on effect of cults on Jewish youth

Schindler, Alexander M.; b. 1925; rabbi; president of the Union of American Hebrew Congregations; former chairman of the Conference of Presidents of Major American Jewish Organizations

Sherer, Morris; b. 1921; rabbi; president of Agudath Israel of America; first Jewish leader to support federal aid to parochial schools

Squadron, Howard; b. 1926; attorney; former president of the American Jewish Congress; former chairman of the Conference of Presidents of Major American Jewish Organizations

Taub, Henry; b. 1927; co-founder of Automatic Data Processing; former president of the American Jewish Joint Distribution Committee

Vorspan, Albert; b. 1924; writer; vice-president of the Union of American Hebrew Congregations

Wishner, Maynard I.; b. 1923; attorney; former president of the American Jewish Committee

Economics

Arrow, Kenneth J.; b. 1921; economist; professor at Stanford University; equilibrium and welfare theorist; winner of 1972 Nobel Prize

Bergson, Abram; b. 1914; economist; professor at Columbia and Harvard; expert on the Soviet economy

Cherne, Leo M.; b. 1912; management specialist; attorney; sculptor

Drucker, Peter; b. 1909; Vienna-born management consultant; former professor of political science and philosophy

Friedman, Milton; b. 1912; economist; proponent of free enterprise; opponent of state intervention in business and trade; winner of Nobel Prize, 1976

Ginzberg, Eli; b. 1911; economist; professor of economics at Columbia; manpower advisor to seven U.S. presidents

Goldman, Marshall; b. 1930; economist; professor at Wellesley College; expert in Russian studies as well as the economics of pollution

Greenspan, Alan; b. 1926; economist; chairman of the Federal Reserve Board, 1987-present; confidant of Presidents Nixon, Ford and Reagan; supporter of fiscal restraint and a balanced budget; chairman of the Council of Economic Advisors, 1974-77

Heilbroner, Robert; b. 1919; economist; best-selling author of economics texts; professor of economics at the New School for Social Research in New York

Klein, Lawrence R.; b. 1920; economist; developer of econometrics; 1980 Nobel Prize winner

Kuznets, Simon S.; b. 1901; Russian-born economist; theorist of the gross national product; professor emeritus at Harvard University; 1971 Nobel Prize winner

Lekachman, Robert; b. 1920; economist; professor at Lehman College and at the Graduate Center of the City University of New York; prolific writer, especially regarding the social aspects of economics

Samuelson, Paul; b. 1915; economist; leading Keynesian theorist; consultant to the Rand Corporation and the Eisenhower, Kennedy and Johnson Administrations; professor at MIT; author of the all-time best-selling economics textbook; winner of 1970 Nobel Prize

Silk, Leonard; b. 1918; economics editor for *The New York Times;* author of *The American Establishment*

Stein, Herbert; b. 1916; economist; leading policy maker in the Nixon Administration as chairman of the Council of Economic Advisers; professor at the University of Virginia

Weidenbaum, Murray; b. 1927; economist; chief economic advisor to President Reagan; professor at Washington University in St. Louis; specialist on government regulation

Williams, Harold; b. 1928; managerial specialist; former head of the Securities and Exchange Commission; former dean of the Graduate School of Business and Management at UCLA; former attorney and executive with Hunt-Wesson Inc. and Norton Simon Inc.; president of the J. Paul Getty Museum

Journalism and Media

Abel, Elie; b. 1920; professor of journalism at Stanford University; former dean, Columbia School of Journalism; former NBC correspondent

Agronsky, Martin; b. 1915; PBS commentator

Alexander, Shana (Shana Ager); b. 1925; formerly commentator for *60 Minutes, Newsweek*

Bernstein, Carl; b. 1944; ABC news commentator; formerly reporter for the *Washington Post;* broke Watergate story; winner 1973 Pulitzer Prize

Block, Herbert L. (Herblock); b. 1909; editorial cartoonist for the *Washington Post;* three-time Pulitzer Prize winner

Broder, David; b. 1929; columnist for the *Washington Post;* winner of 1973 Pulitzer Prize

Buchwald, Art; b. 1925; nationally syndicated social and political satirist; winner of 1982 Pulitzer Prize

Cosell, Howard (William Howard Cohen); b. 1920; ABC radio and television sportscaster

Cowan, Paul; b. 1940; journalist and author; former staff writer for the *Village Voice;* authored *An Orphan in History;* active in Havurah movement in New York

Drew, Elizabeth; b. 1935; writer and television commentator; analyst of the human element within the national political scene

Epstein, Jason; b. 1928; editor and publisher; co-founder of *The New York Review of Books;* vice-president of Random House; supporter of individual rights in America and abroad

Feiffer, Jules; b. 1929; political cartoonist; playwright; *Village Voice* regular; authored *Little Murders* and *Carnal Knowledge*

Fein, Leonard; b. 1934; writer; political activist; founder and former editor of *Moment;* critic of Menachem Begin's government; Reform theorist and planner

Frankel, Max; b. 1930; German-born *New York Times* executive editor; promoted 1971 publication of the Pentagon Papers

Friendly, Fred (Frederick Wachenheim); b. 1915; former executive producer of CBS, president of CBS News; professor of journalism at Columbia University; proponent of honesty and ethics in broadcast journalism

Gelb, Arthur; b. 1924; deputy managing editor of *The New York Times*

Goodman, Ellen (Ellen Holtz); b. 1941; syndicated (over 700 newspapers) columnist (*At Large*); 1980 Pulitzer Prize winner

Goodman, Walter; b. 1927; former *New York Times* editor; directed humanities programming for public television (WNET in New York City); authored *The Committee,* a study of HUAC

Grunwald, Henry Anatole; b. 1922; Vienna-born editor-in-chief of Time Inc.

Halberstam, David; b. 1934; journalist; author; former *New York Times* reporter; authored *The Best and the Brightest* and *The Powers That Be;* 1964 Pulitzer Prize winner

Hechinger, Fred Michael; b. 1920; president of The New York Times Company Foundation; former education editor of *The New York Times*

Hentoff, Nat; b. 1925; journalist; commentator; jazz expert; *Village Voice* columnist since 1957, especially focusing on civil liberties issues

Hersh, Seymour; b. 1937; Pulitzer Prize-winning journalist who broke the My Lai massacre story; also noted for reportage regarding Henry Kissinger, secret B-52 bombings in Cambodia and domestic spying operations of the C.I.A.

Himmelfarb, Milton; b. 1918; researcher; director of information for the American Jewish Committee; editor of the American Jewish Yearbook; advocate of traditional Jewish values, conservatism, preservation of Jewish population

Isaac, Rael Jean (Isaacs); b. 1933; journalist and writer; leading factor in disintegration of Breira movement; fierce defender of conservative Israeli policies

Kael, Pauline; b. 1919; film critic for *The New Yorker* magazine

Kalb, Bernard; b. 1922; news correspondent; author; former State Department correspondent for NBC; co-author of *Kissinger* with brother Marvin; Assistant Secretary of State for Public Affairs, 1984-86

Kalb, Marvin; b. 1930; television journalist; chief diplomatic correspondent for NBC News; author; leading chronicler of events in Eastern Europe; leading reporter of events of Iranian revolution

Kauffman, Stanley Jules; b. 1916; theater and film critic

Koppel, Ted (Edward James Koppel); b. 1940; host of ABC's *Nightline* since 1979

Kraft, Joseph; b. 1924; widely syndicated columnist; writer for the *Washington Post;* specialist on foreign affairs and on the executive branch of American government

Landers, Ann (Esther Friedman); b. 1918; advice columnist

Lerner, Max; b. 1902; Minsk-born journalist; long-time *New York Post* columnist

Lewis, Anthony; b. 1927; editorial columnist for *The New York Times;* winner of 1955 Pulitzer Prize for articles on a McCarthy era victim; severe critic of Menachem Begin's government

Lewis, Flora; b. 1920; journalist; editorial columnist for *The New York Times*

Lukas, J. Anthony; b. 1933; journalist; won 1968 Pulitzer Prize for coverage of the trials of the Chicago Seven; former *New York Times* reporter; professor of journalism at the Kennedy School of Government at Harvard

Mankiewicz, Frank; b. 1924; journalist; attorney; president of National Public Radio; former press secretary to Robert F. Kennedy; leading critic of television programming

Mitgang, Herbert; b. 1920; journalist; cultural correspondent for *The New York Times;* biographer of Abraham Lincoln; playwright (*Mr. Lincoln,* 1980)

Navasky, Victor; b. 1932; journalist; editor of *The Nation;* leading liberal and advocate of freedom of expression in America; author of *Naming Names,* a study of the 1947 HUAC investigation

Newfield, Jack; b. 1939; investigative reporter for the *Village Voice,* with focus on New York City corruption

Newman, Edwin; b. 1919; television commentator for NBC; author of two books on language art, *Strictly Speaking* and *A Civil Tongue*

Peretz, Martin; b. 1939; editor and publisher of *The New Republic,* lecturer in political science at Harvard University; active spokesman for liberal causes and Israel

Podhoretz, Norman; b. 1930; editor of *Commentary* since 1960; leading neo-conservative voice; authored *The Present Danger, Why We Were In Vietnam*

Pogrebin, Letty Cottin; b. 1939; founding editor of *Ms.* magazine; *Ladies Home Journal* columnist

Polner, Murray; b. 1928; journalist; editor of *Present Tense;* prolific writer; author of *Branch Rickey: A Biography, Rabbi: The American Experience,* editor of *American Jewish Biographies*

Porter, Sylvia (Sylvia Feldman); b. 1913; syndicated financial columnist

Raskin, A. H. (Abraham Henry Raskin); b. 1911; long-time labor correspondent and editor for *The New York Times*

Rosenthal, A. M. (Abraham Michael Rosenthal); b. 1922; former managing editor of *The New York Times;* responsible for publication of the Pentagon Papers; winner of Pulitzer Prize in 1960; presently editorial columnist for *The New York Times*

Safire, William; b. 1929; columnist; formerly speechwriter for President Nixon and Vice-President Agnew; leading conservative voice at *The New York Times;* humorous analyst of spoken English; won Pulitzer Prize in 1978 for his probe into the financial affairs of Bert Lance

Schanberg, Sydney; b. 1934; journalist; winner of 1976 Pulitzer Prize for his reportage of Cambodian atrocities for *The New York Times;* currently op-ed page columnist for the *The New York Times*

Schoenbrun, David; b. 1915; television correspondent

Schorr, Daniel; b. 1916; journalist; known for Watergate and CIA investigation coverage in the 1970's

Shanks, Hershel; b. 1929; attorney; editor and publisher of *Biblical Archaeology Review, Biblical Review* and *Moment;* author of seven books on Jewish and legal issues

Shapiro, Harvey; b. 1924; poet; editor of *The New York Times Book Review*

Shawn, William (William Chon); b. 1907; former editor-in-chief of *The New Yorker*

Silvers, Robert B.; b. 1929; editor and founder of *The New York Review of Books*

Stone, I. F. (Isidor Feinstein); b. 1907; prototypical investigative journalist; publisher of *I. F. Stone's Weekly,* which attacked Defense Department corruption and waste

Syrkin, Marie; b. 1899; Swiss-born journalist and writer; leading Labor Zionist; former editor of the *Jewish Frontier;* former professor of humanities at Brandeis University

Szulc, Tad; b. 1926; Warsaw-born journalist; specialist in Latin American affairs and known for coverage of Czechoslovakia in 1968; former foreign affairs reporter for *The New York Times*

Van Buren, Abigail (Pauline Friedman); b. 1918; advice columnist

Wallace, Mike (Myron Leon Wallace); b. 1918; television journalist; host of *60 Minutes;* formerly narrator of *Biography*

Walters, Barbara; b. 1931; television journalist

Wattenberg, Ben; b. 1933; editor; author; former aide to Lyndon Johnson; former Democratic party official

Weber, Simon; b. 1911; Polish-born editor-in-chief of the *Jewish Daily Forward*

Labor

Chaikin, Sol "Chick"; b. 1918; attorney; former president of ILGWU; member of Trilateral Commission and the Council on Foreign Relations

Finley, Murray Howard; b. 1922; attorney; president of the Amalgamated Clothing and Textile Workers Union of America; leading labor organizer in the Sunbelt

Gotbaum, Victor; b. 1921; former leader of New York City's District Council 37, the largest union of public employees; liberal, reformer; powerful influence in municipal government

Kheel, Theodore; b. 1914; mediator; attorney; helped settle New York newspaper strike (1962-63), transit strike (1966), sanitation strike (1968), etc.

Mazur, Jay; b. 1932; president, ILGWU

Miller, Marvin; b. 1917; executive director of the Major League Baseball Players Association; spearheaded the 1972 and 1981 baseball players strikes

Shanker, Albert; b. 1928; president of the American Federation of Teachers; AFL-CIO vice president; leader of the 1968 teachers strike against the Ocean Hill-Brownsville Governing Board in Brooklyn

Tyler, Gus (Gus Tilve); b. 1911; ILGWU official; writer on labor history and on the conflict between business and labor

Law

Abram, Morris B.; b. 1918; attorney; chairman, Conference of Presidents of Major American Jewish Organizations; former American Jewish Committee president; chairman, National Conference on Soviet Jewry

Amsterdam, Anthony G.; b. 1935; professor (N.Y.U.) of constitutional law

Bazelon, David; b. 1909; judge, U.S. Court of Appeals, District of Columbia Circuit; pioneer of insanity defense (*Durham Rule*)

Dershowitz, Alan M.; b. 1938; attorney; civil libertarian; Harvard Law School professor; author

Dorsen, Norman; b. 1930; attorney; civil libertarian; author; past general counsel, chairperson of the ACLU

Freedman, Monroe H.; b. 1928; attorney; former dean, Hofstra University School of Law; former director of the United States Holocaust Memorial Council

Garment, Leonard; b. 1924; attorney; special counsel to President Nixon, 1969-1974; prepared defense of Watergate

Ginsburg, Ruth Bader; b. 1933; judge, U.S. Court of Appeals, District of Columbia Circuit; professor at Columbia University Law School; specialist in constitutional law, civil procedure, sex discrimination

Goldberg, Arthur J.; b. 1908; attorney; former U.S. Secretary of Labor, Supreme Court Justice, U.S. representative to the United Nations

Hauser, Rita E. (Abrams); b. 1934; international lawyer; former U.S. representative to the United Nations

Kampelman, Max; b. 1920; attorney; State Department counselor; chairman of the U.S. delegation to the Conference on Security and Cooperation in Europe (Madrid 1980, 1982); former protege of Hubert Humphrey; leading advocate for Soviet Jewry; chief U.S. negotiator, arms control talks, Geneva since 1985

Kaufman, Irving; b. 1910; judge, U.S. Court of Appeals, Second Circuit; chiefly known for presiding over the controversial 1951 Rosenberg spy case

Kozinski, Alex; b. 1950, Romania; judge, U.S. Court of Appeals, Ninth Circuit; formerly Chief Judge, U.S. Court of Claims; youngest federal appellate judge in 20th century

Kunstler, William; b. 1919; attorney; defender of civil liberties and civil rights cases; defender of the Chicago Seven, Rev. Philip Berrigan, the Black Panthers, etc.

Levi, Edward H.; b. 1911; scholar; U.S. attorney general, 1975-77 under Gerald Ford; president of the University of Chicago 1968-75; integrated social sciences into curriculum while dean at University of Chicago Law School

Lewin, Nathan; b. 1936; Washington, D.C.-based constitutional lawyer, particularly regarding rights of Orthodox Jews

Liman, Arthur L.; b. 1932; attorney; chief counsel to the Senate Select Committee investigating Iran-contra; specialist in white-collar crime and securities law

Nizer, Louis; b. 1902; London-born attorney; leading trial counsel; general counsel for the Motion Picture Association of America; author of *My Life in Court, What To Do With Germany* (1944) and *The Implosion Conspiracy,* in which he argued the guilt of Ethel and Julius Rosenberg

Pfeffer, Leo; b. 1910; Hungarian-born attorney; leading supporter of the separation of church and state; authored *Church, State and Freedom;* professor of constitutional law at Long Island University

Pilpel, Harriet (Harriet Fleishl); b. 1911; attorney; civil libertarian; general counsel for Planned Parenthood and the ACLU; successfully litigated *New York Times v. Sullivan,* in which the scope of protection for the press against libel suits was significantly enlarged

Rapps, Dennis; b. 1942; attorney; executive director, National Jewish Commission on Law and Public Affairs (COLPA); leading advocate for the protection of civil rights for practicing Jews

Rauh, Joseph L., Jr.; b. 1911; attorney; helped move Democratic party into field of civil rights in 1948; defended many 1950's loyalty and HUAC-related cases; early opponent of U.S. policy regarding Vietnam; defended University of California in Bakke case (1978)

Rifkind, Simon H.; b. 1901; Russian-born attorney and former federal judge; leading civil libertarian and devotee to Jewish causes

Shestak, Jerome; b. 1925; attorney; helped found Legal Services Corporation; founder of the Lawyers Committee for International Human Rights

Tenzer, Herbert; b. 1905; senior partner, Tenzer, Greenblatt, Fallon & Kaplan; congressman from New York, 1965-69; chairman, board of trustees of Yeshiva University, 1977-present; chairman, Rescue the Children, post WW II

Literature

Bellow, Saul (Solomon Bellows); b. 1915; novelist; Nobel laureate, 1976; *Mr. Sammler's Planet, Humboldt's Gift, To Jerusalem and Back* and others

Caras, Roger; b. 1928; naturalist; author of books on wildlife, conservation and humane treatment of animals

Charyn, Jerome; b. 1937; novelist; educator

Colwin, Laurie; b. 1944; short story writer and novelist

Doctorow, E.L. (Edgar Lawrence Doctorow); b. 1931; novelist; editor; *The Book of Daniel, Ragtime,* etc.

Elkin, Stanley; b. 1930; novelist and short-story writer, particularly of Jewish-American black humor

Fast, Howard; b. 1914; widely-translated writer, formerly blacklisted following non-compliance with HUAC; authored *Spartacus, The Jews, The Immigrants* and several novels of the American Revolutionary period

Frank, Gerold; b. 1907; biographer of Dr. Martin Luther King, Jr., Sheila Graham, Lillian Roth, etc.; authored *The Deed* (1963), which examined Jewish terrorist groups in Palestine

Ginsberg, Allen; b. 1926; poet; 1960's activist; best known for *Howl* and *Kaddish*

Gold, Herbert; b. 1924; novelist; essayist; visiting professor at various universities; themes include racial discrimination, violence, alienation

Gottlieb, Robert A.; b. 1931; editor of *The New Yorker;* former president and editor-in-chief of Alfred A. Knopf, Inc.; responsible for developing works of Joseph Heller, John Updike, Chaim Potok and others

Green, Gerald; b. 1922; writer; novelist; author of *The Last Angry Man* and the screenplay of *Holocaust*

Greenberg, Joanne; b. 1932; novelist; author of *I Never Promised You a Rose Garden, A Season of Delight*

Harris, Mark (Mark Finkelstein); b. 1922; prolific author; *Bang The Drum Slowly, The Goy,* as well as theater, television and films

Heller, Joseph; b. 1923; novelist; *Catch-22, Something Happened, Good As Gold, God Knows*

Hellman, Lillian; b. 1907; playwright; author of *The Children's Hour, The Little Foxes, Toys in the Attic;* outspoken anti-Fascist, opponent of HUAC

Howe, Irving; b. 1920; editor; critic; author of *World of Our Fathers, How We Lived, We Lived There Too,* and editor (with Yiddish poet Eliezer Greenberg) of a series of translated Yiddish works; professor of English at the Graduate Center of the City University of New York

Jong, Erica (Erica Mann); b. 1942; novelist; poet; author of *Fear of Flying, How to Save Your Own Life*

Kahn, Roger; b. 1927; sportswriter; author of *The Boys of Summer*

Kaplan, Justin; b. 1925; biographer; won 1966 Pulitzer Prize for *Mr. Clemens and Mark Twain*

Kazin, Alfred; b. 1915; literary critic; literary historian; professor of English at Hunter College and the Graduate Center of the City University of New York; authored *New York Jew* and other memoirs

Koch, Kenneth; b. 1925; poet; playwright; professor of English at Columbia; has taught poetry to nursing home residents as well as to children

Kosinski, Jerzy Nikodem; b. 1933; Polish-born author of *The Painted Bird, Being There* and other novels; has taught English at Princeton and Yale

Kotlowitz, Robert; b. 1924; author of *Somewhere Else* and *The Boardwalk;* programming executive in public television

Kumin, Maxine (Maxine Winokur); b. 1925; Pulitzer Prize-winning poet and writer

Kunitz, Stanley; b. 1905; Pulitzer Prize-winning poet; professor of English at numerous universities

Lash, Joseph P.; b. 1909; biographer of Helen Keller, Eleanor Roosevelt and Dag Hammarskjold; former editorial page writer for *The New York Post;* Pulitzer Prize winner

Levin, Ira; b. 1929; author of *Rosemary's Baby, The Boys from Brazil;* playwright, *No Time for Sergeants, Critics Choice, Deathtrap*

Levine, Philip; b. 1928; poet; professor at California State University (Fresno)

Lurie, Alison; b. 1926; novelist; authored *The War Between the Tates; The Language of Clothes,* and others; professor of English at Cornell University

Mailer, Norman; b. 1923; novelist; essayist; helped found the *Village Voice;* writings include *The Naked and the Dead, Barbary Shore, Miami and the Siege of Chicago; The Executioner's Song;* a leader of the anti-Vietnam War movement; winner of 1969 Pulitzer Prize

Mamet, David; b. 1947; playwright; created *American Buffalo* and *The Water Engine*

Michaels, Leonard; b. 1933; novelist; authored *The Men's Club;* professor of English at Berkeley

Miller, Arthur; b. 1915; playwright; won Pulitzer Prize for *Death of a Salesman,* 1949; also *The Crucible, A View From the Bridge, After the Fall, Playing for Time*

Nemerov, Howard; b. 1920; Pulitzer Prize-winning poet (*Collected Poems,* 1977); professor of English at Washington University

Nissenson, Hugh; b. 1933; author of short stories and a novel, *My Own Ground,* on the Jewish condition

Olsen, Tillie (Tillie Lerner); b. 1913; authored *Tell Me a Riddle;* focuses on problems of working people and on women trying to cope with their pre-determined roles

Ozick, Cynthia; b. 1928; novelist; authored *The Pagan Rabbi, The Cannibal Galaxy, The Messiah of Stockholm*

Paley, Grace; b. 1922; author of short stories; peace activist

Potok, Chaim; b. 1929; novelist of Hasidic life; authored *The Chosen, The Promise, My Name Is Asher Lev, Wandering—Chaim Potok's History of the Jews;* special projects editor for the Jewish Publication Society

Rosenthal, M.L. (Macha Louis Rosenthal); b. 1917; poet; critic; professor of English at New York University

Rosten, Leo; b. 1908; Polish-born author of *The Education of H*Y*M*A*N K*A*P*L*A*N, The Joys of Yiddish, Captain Newman, M.D.*

Roth, Philip; b. 1933; novelist; author of *Goodbye, Columbus, Portnoy's Complaint, Our Gang, Zuckerman Unbound, Zuckerman Bound* and others

Salinger, J.D. (Jerome); b. 1919; author of *The Catcher in the Rye* and *Franny and Zooey*

Schulberg, Budd; b. 1914; screenwriter; novelist; author of *What Makes Sammy Run?, On the Waterfront, The Harder They Fall*

Segal, Erich; b. 1937; novelist; author of *Love Story, Oliver's Story,* screenplay for film *Yellow Submarine;* professor of classics at Yale University

Shaw, Irwin; b. 1913; novelist; playwright; author of *The Young Lions, Rich Man, Poor Man, Beggarman, Thief* and others

Singer, Isaac Bashevis; b. 1904; Polish-born writer; author of *In My Father's House, Crown of Feathers, Gimpel the Fool* and others; winner of 1978 Nobel Prize for Literature

Sontag, Susan; b. 1933; writer; critic; essayist; author of *Against Interpretation;* early opponent of the Vietnam War

Stone, Irving (Irving Tennenbaum); b. 1903; biographical novelist; author of *Lust for Life, The Agony and the Ecstasy, The Origin* and others

Uris, Leon; b. 1924; novelist; author of *Exodus, Battle Cry, Mila 18, QB VII* and others

Wallace, Irving (Irving Wallechinsky); b. 1916; novelist; authored *The Chapman Report, The Prize, The Man, The Seven Minutes;* co-authored *The People's Almanac* series

Wiesel, Elie; b. 1928; Transylvanian-born writer and philosopher of the Holocaust as well as Hasidic and Kabbalistic themes; titles include *Night, Dawn,* and *The Fifth Son;* chairman of the United States Holocaust Memorial Council; winner of 1986 Nobel Peace Prize

Wouk, Herman; b. 1915; writer; won Pulitzer Prize in 1952 for *The Caine Mutiny;* also—the *Winds of War, War and Remembrance, This Is My God* and in 1985, *Inside, Outside*

Performing Arts

Allen, Mel (Melvin Israel); b. 1911; sportscaster

Allen, Woody (Allen Konigsberg); b. 1935; actor; director; writer

Alpert, Herb; b. 1935; composer

Arkin, Alan; b. 1934; actor; director; writer

Asner, Ed; b. 1929; actor

Bacall, Lauren (Betty Joan Perske); b. 1924; actress

Bacharach, Burt; b. 1929; composer; pianist

Bakshi, Ralph; b. 1938; Palestinian-born film animator; director

Balsam, Martin; b. 1919; actor

Barry, Gene (Eugene Klass); b. 1922; actor

Benjamin, Richard; b. 1938; actor

Berle, Milton (Milton Berlinger); b. 1908; comedian; actor
Berlin, Irving (Israel Baline); b. 1888; songwriter
Bernstein, Leonard; b. 1918; conductor; composer; pianist
Bikel, Theodore; b. 1924; Vienna-born actor; folk singer
Bishop, Joey (Joseph Gottlieb); b. 1919; comedian
Borge, Victor (Borge Rosenbaum); b. 1909; Danish-born entertainer
Brooks, Mel (Melvyn Kaminsky); b. 1926; comedian; actor; film director
Burns, George (Nathan Birnbaum); b. 1896; comedian; actor
Buttons, Red (Aaron Chwatt); b. 1919; actor; comedian
Caan, James; b. 1940; actor
Cahn, Sammy; b. 1913; lyricist
Clayburgh, Jill; b. 1944; actress
Cohen, Alexander; b. 1920; theatrical producer
Comden, Betty; b. 1919; actress; songwriter
Copland, Aaron; b. 1900; composer; conductor; critic; performer
Cosell, Howard (William Howard Cohen); b. 1920; sportscaster
Curtis, Tony (Bernard Schwartz); b. 1925; actor
Dangerfield, Rodney; b. 1921; comedian
Diamond, Neil; b. 1941; singer; songwriter
Douglas, Kirk (Issur Danielovitch); b. 1918; actor; producer
Dreyfuss, Richard; b. 1947; actor
Dylan, Bob (Robert Zimmerman); b. 1941; folk singer; composer
Falk, Peter; b. 1927; actor
Farber, Barry; b. 1930; radio commentator
Feld, Eliot; b. 1942; dancer; choreographer (ballet)
Fisher, Eddie (Edwin); b. 1928; singer
Friedkin, William; b. 1939; film director
Garfunkel, Art; b. 1941; singer; actor
Gould, Elliot (Elliot Goldstein); b. 1938; actor
Gray, Barry (Bernard Yaroslaw); b. 1916; radio commentator
Green, Adolph; b. 1915; lyricist
Greene, Lorne; b. 1915; actor
Grey, Joel (Joel Katz); b. 1932; actor; singer; dancer
Hackett, Buddy (Leonard Hacker); b. 1924; comedian
Hall, Monty; b. 1923; television personality
Hamlisch, Marvin; b. 1944; composer
Heifetz, Jascha; b. 1901; Vilna-born violinist
Hodes, Art; b. 1904; Russian-born blues pianist
Hoffman, Dustin; b. 1937; actor
Horowitz, Vladimir; b. 1904; pianist
Kahn, Madeline; b. 1942; actress
Kaplan, Gabe (Gabriel); b. 1945; comedian
Kidd, Michael (Michael Greenwald); b. 1917; choreographer
King, Alan (Irwin Alan Kniberg); b. 1927; comedian
King, Carole (Carole Klein); b. 1941; singer; songwriter
Klugman, Jack; b. 1922; actor
Korman, Harvey; b. 1927; comedian
Kramer, Stanley; b. 1913; film producer
Kubrick, Stanley; b. 1928; film director
Landon, Michael (Eugene Maurice Orowitz); b. 1936; actor
Lawrence, Steve (Sidney Leibowitz); b. 1935; singer
Lear, Norman; b. 1922; producer; writer; director
Leinsdorf, Erich; b. 1912; conductor
Leonard, Sheldon (Sheldon Bershad); b. 1907; actor; director
Levine, James; b. 1943; conductor
Levine, Joseph E.; b. 1905; film producer
Lewis, Jerry (Joseph Levich); b. 1926; comedian; actor; director
Lewis, Shari (Shari Hurwitz); b. 1934; puppeteer
Linden, Hal (Harold Lipshitz); b. 1931; actor
Lumet, Sidney; b. 1924; film director
Manilow, Barry; b. 1946; singer; composer
Mankiewicz, Joseph L.; b. 1909; film writer and director
Mann, Herbie (Herbert Solomon); b. 1930; jazz flutist
Matlin, Marlee; b. 1965; actress
Matthau, Walter; b. 1920; actor
May, Elaine (Elaine Berlin); b. 1932; actress; playwright; director
Mazursky, Paul (Irwin Mazursky); b. 1930; director; screenwriter
Menuhin, Yehudi; b. 1916; violinist
Merrill, Robert (Moishe Miller); b. 1919; opera singer
Midler, Bette; b. 1945; singer; actress
Milstein, Nathan; b. 1904; Odessa-born violinist
Nichols, Mike (Michael Igor Peshkowsky); b. 1931; Berlin-born director and producer
Nimoy, Leonard; b. 1931; actor
Papp, Joseph (Joseph Papirofsky); b. 1921; theatrical producer and director
Penn, Arthur; b. 1922; director
Perahia, Murray; b. 1947; pianist; conductor
Perlman, Itzhak; b. 1945; violinist
Peters, Roberta (Roberta Peterman); b. 1930; opera singer
Picon, Molly; b. 1898; actress
Polanski, Roman; b. 1933; film director
Polonsky, Abraham; b. 1910; film director; screenwriter
Previn, Andre; b. 1929; conductor
Prince, Harold; b. 1928; producer; director
Radner, Gilda; b. 1946; comedienne
Randall, Tony (Leonard Rosenberg); b. 1920; actor
Raskin, Judith; b. 1928; opera singer
Reiner, Carl; b. 1922; actor; writer; producer; director
Rickles, Don; b. 1926; comedian
Ritt, Martin; b. 1920; film director; producer
Rivers, Joan (Joan Molinsky); b. 1935; comedienne
Robbins, Jerome (Jerome Rabinowitz); b. 1918; choreographer
Sahl, Mort; b. 1927; satirist
St. John, Jill (Jill Oppenheim); b. 1940; actress
Schneider, Alexander; b. 1908; Vilna-born violinist; conductor
Sedaka, Neil; b. 1939; singer
Segal, George; b. 1934; actor
Shatner, William; b. 1931; actor
Shore, Dinah (Frances Rose Shore); b. 1917; singer
Sills, Beverly (Belle Silverman); b. 1929; opera singer; opera company director
Silver, Joan Micklin; b. 1935; director; producer
Silverman, Fred; b. 1937; television executive
Simon, Neil; b. 1927; playwright
Simon, Paul; b. 1941; songwriter; singer
Sondheim, Stephen; b. 1930; composer
Spielberg, Steven; b. 1947; film director; producer
Steinberg, David; b. 1942; comedian
Stern, Isaac; b. 1920; Russian-born violinist
Streisand, Barbra; b. 1942; singer; actress
Tureck, Rosalyn; b. 1914; pianist; symphony director
Wallach, Eli; b. 1915; actor
Wilder, Billy; b. 1906; Vienna-born film producer; director
Wilder, Gene (Jerome Silberman); b. 1935; actor; director; producer; scriptwriter
Winger, Debra; b. 1955; actress
Winkler, Henry; b. 1945; actor
Winters, Shelly (Shirley Schrift); b. 1923; actress
Wolper, David; b. 1928; film producer
Youngman, Henny; b. 1906; comedian
Zukerman, Eugenia; b. 1944; flutist
Zukerman, Pinchas; b. 1948; Tel-Aviv born violinist

Photography

Avedon, Richard; b. 1923; preeminent fashion photographer
Capa, Cornell (Cornell Friedmann); b. 1918; photojournalist; creator of "Concerned Photography"
Newman, Arnold; b. 1918; official photographer to several U.S. presidents; specialist of environmental portraiture
Penn, Irving; b. 1917; leading portraitist
Vishniac, Roman; b. 1897; Russian-born photographer; photomicrographer; scientist; author of *A Vanished World*, 180 photographs of pre-war Polish Jewry

Politics and Government

Abrams, Elliot; b. 1948; attorney; head of State Department's Latin American bureau; formerly Assistant Secretary of State for Human Rights and Humanitarian Affairs

Abzug, Bella (Bella Savitzky); b. 1920; attorney; congresswoman from New York, 1970-76

Ackerman, Gary L.; b. 1942; newspaper publisher; Democratic congressman from New York, 1983-present

Beilenson, Anthony C.; b. 1932; attorney; Democratic congressman from California, 1977-present

Berman, Howard L.; b. 1941; attorney; Democratic congressman from California, 1983-present

Boschwitz, Rudy; b. 1930; Berlin-born businessman (retail lumber); Republican U.S. Senator from Minnesota, 1978-present

Boxer, Barbara; b. 1940; journalist; stockbroker; Democratic congresswoman from California, 1983-present

Cardin, Benjamin; b. 1943; attorney; Democratic congressman from Maryland, 1987-present

Eizenstat, Stuart E.; b. 1943; attorney; presidential adviser for domestic affairs during the Carter Administration

Erdreich, Ben; b. 1938; attorney; Democratic congressman from Alabama, 1983-present

Feinstein, Dianne; b. 1933; mayor of San Francisco, 1978-present

Frank, Barney; b. 1940; attorney; Democratic congressman from Massachusetts, 1981-present

Frost, Martin; b. 1942; attorney; Democratic congressman from Texas, 1979-present

Garth, David (David Goldberg); b. 1930; media consultant for politicians; foreign clients include Menachem Begin

Gejdenson, Sam; b. 1948, Eschwege, Germany; dairy farmer; Democratic congressman from Connecticut, 1981-present

Gilman, Benjamin A.; b. 1922; attorney; Republican congressman from New York, 1973-present

Glickman, Dan; b. 1944; attorney; Democratic congressman from Kansas, 1977-present

Goldschmidt, Neil; b. 1939; governor of Oregon; former mayor of Portland, Secretary of Transportation in Carter Administration

Gradison, Willis D.; b. 1928; investment broker; Republican congressman from Ohio, 1975-present

Green, Bill; b. 1929; attorney; Republican congressman from New York, 1978-present

Harris, Louis; b. 1921; pollster

Hecht, Chic; b. 1928; Republican U.S. Senator from Nevada, 1983-present

Hoffman, Abbie (Abbott); b. 1936; political activist; writer; 1960's civil rights and anti-war movement figure; founder of the Youth International Party, the Yippies

Holtzman, Elizabeth; b. 1941; attorney; former U.S. Congresswoman from Brooklyn; currently Kings County District Attorney (Brooklyn)

Kissinger, Henry (Heinz Alfred Kissinger); b. 1923; Bavarian-born former U.S. Secretary of State; 1973 Nobel Prize winner (with North Vietnamese negotiator Le Duc Tho); currently heads U.S. Commission on Central America

Koch, Edward I.; b. 1924; attorney; mayor of New York City, 1978-present; former congressman

Kunin, Madeleine M.; b. 1933; governor of Vermont, 1985-present

Lantos, Tom; b. 1928; Budapest-born former economics professor, San Francisco State University; Democratic congressman from California, 1981-present

Lautenberg, Frank; b. 1924; businessman, Democratic U.S. Senator from New Jersey, 1982-present; founder and former chairman of Automatic Data Processing; former chairman of the United Jewish Appeal

Lehman, William; b. 1913; auto distributor; Democratic congressman from Florida, 1973-present

Levin, Carl; b. 1934; attorney; Democratic U.S. Senator from Michigan, 1978-present; leading human rights activist

Levin, Sander M.; b. 1931; attorney; Democratic congressman from Michigan, 1983-present

Levine, Mel; b. 1943; attorney; Democratic congressman from California, 1983-present

Linowitz, Sol M.; b. 1913; attorney; roving ambassador; former chairman of Xerox Corporation; former U.S. representative to the Organization of American States; President Carter's representative on Middle East negotiations, 1979-1981; leading communal leader

Metzenbaum, Howard; b. 1917; businessman; attorney; Democratic U.S. Senator from Ohio, 1976-present

Miller, John; b. 1938; attorney; Republican congressman from Washington, 1985-present

Minow, Newton; b. 1926; attorney; former chairman of the Federal Communications Commission; media critic

Myerson, Bess; b. 1924; consumer consultant; political aspirant; television personality; former New York City Commissioner of Consumer Affairs; Commissioner of Cultural Affairs

Ottinger, Richard; b. 1929; attorney; congressman from New York, 1965-1971, 1975-1984; leading advocate of liberal and Jewish causes

Ravitch, Richard; b. 1933; businessman; attorney; former chairman of the Metropolitan Transportation Authority (MTA) of New York

Ribicoff, Abraham A.; b. 1910; attorney; former congressman, governor and senator from Connecticut; former Secretary of HEW; leading liberal; staunch defender of Israel

Rohatyn, Felix; b. 1928; Vienna-born financial consultant; corporate merger specialist; as chairman of the Municipal Assistance Corporation (MAC), helped avert New York City's bankruptcy during the mid-1970's fiscal crisis

Rostow, Eugene; b. 1913; legal scholar; former undersecretary of state for political affairs under President Johnson; former director of the Arms Control and Disarmament Agency under President Reagan; former dean of Yale Law School; leading supporter of Israel's West Bank policy

Rostow, Walt Whitman; b. 1916; economist; historian; special assistant for national security affairs under President Johnson; considered the most significant influence on Vietnam policy, 1961-1969

Rudman, Warren; b. 1930; attorney; Republican U.S. Senator from New Hampshire, 1980-present; former New Hampshire attorney general

Scheuer, James H.; b. 1920; attorney; Democratic congressman from New York, 1965-73, 75-present

Schumer, Charles E.; b. 1950; attorney; Democratic congressman from New York, 1981-present

Sisisky, Norman; b. 1927; businessman; Democratic congressman from Virginia, 1983-present

Smith, Larry; b. 1941; attorney; Democratic congressman from Florida, 1983-present

Sofaer, Abraham; b. 1938, Bombay; legal advisor, U.S. Department of State; former federal judge

Solarz, Stephen; b. 1940; Democratic congressman from New York, 1975-present; Israel's most outspoken supporter in Congress

Sonnenfeldt, Helmut; b. 1926; Berlin-born senior aide to Henry Kissinger; chief planner of the detente policy toward the Soviet Union in the Nixon Administration

Specter, Arlen; b. 1930; attorney; Republican U.S. Senator from Pennsylvania, 1981-present; assistant counsel to Warren Commission, 1964

Strauss, Annette; b. 1923; mayor of Dallas, 1987-present

Strauss, Robert S.; b. 1918; attorney; former chairman of the Democratic National Committee; former U.S. ambassador to the Egyptian-Israeli talks on Palestinian autonomy; recipient of the Medal of Freedom

Waxman, Henry A.; b. 1939; attorney; Democratic congressman from California, 1975-present

Weiss, Ted; b. 1927; attorney; Democratic congressman from New York, 1977-present

Wolpe, Howard; b. 1939; former political science professor, Western Michigan University; Democratic congressman from Michigan, 1979-present

Wyden, Ron; b. 1949; attorney; Democratic congressman from Oregon, 1981-present

Yarmolinsky, Adam; b. 1922; attorney; leading figure in the formation of domestic policy in the Kennedy and Johnson Administrations; professor at University of Massachusetts; author of *The Military Establishment: Its Impact on American Society*

Yates, Sidney R.; b. 1909; attorney; Democratic congressman from Illinois, 1949-63, 65-present

Rabbinate

Angel, Marc; b. 1945; Orthodox; leader of Sephardic Jewish community; New York

Axelrad, Albert S.; b. 1938; Reform; Hillel, civil-rights leader; Boston

Beerman, Leonard I.; b. 1921; Reform; civil rights and anti-nuclear activist; Los Angeles

Berkowitz, William; b. 1924; Conservative; pioneer in adult Jewish education, prayer-service innovation; New York

Bleich, J. David; b. 1936; Orthodox; theorist on bioethics issues; professor at Yeshiva University; New York

Borowitz, Eugene B.; b. 1924; Reform; theologian; editor of *Sh'ma;* New York (HUC-JIR)

Brickner, Balfour; b. 1926; Reform; social activist; New York

Carlebach, Shlomo; b. 1926; Orthodox (Hasidic); "singing Rabbi"; New York

Cohen, Gerson David; b. 1924; Conservative; fifth chancellor of Jewish Theological Seminary of America, 1972-85; professor of history; New York

Eisenstein, Ira; b. 1906; Reconstructionist; past president of the Reconstructionist Rabbinical College in Philadelphia

Finkelstein, Louis; b. 1895; Conservative; former professor, president and chancellor of the Jewish Theological Seminary of America; pioneer in interreligious dialogue

Freifeld, Shlomo; b. 1926; Orthodox; dean of Shor Yoshuv Institute in Far Rockaway, New York; leader in *kirov rechokim* movement

Gordis, Robert; b. 1908; Conservative; professor of biblical studies at Jewish Theological Seminary; founder and editor of *Judaism* magazine

Gottlieb, Lynn; b. 1949; Conservative (privately ordained) minister in sign language to deaf congregations; leader in efforts for ordination of women; New York

Gottschalk, Alfred; b. 1930; Reform; president of Hebrew Union College—Jewish Institute of Religion; ordained first woman rabbi; member of the United States Holocaust Memorial Council; Cincinnati

Greenberg, Irving; b. 1933; Orthodox; director of CLAL; a founder of Yavneh; a founder of the Center for Russian Jewry; president of the United States Holocaust Memorial Council; leading proponent of interdenominational dialogue; New York

Hertzberg, Arthur; b. 1921; Conservative; former president of the World Jewish Congress, former president of the American Jewish Congress; professor of history at Columbia University since 1961; leading Zionist spokesman

Horowitz, Levi Isaac; b. 1921; Orthodox; the *Bostoner Rebbe;* head of the New England Hassidic Center; developed significant outreach program to assimilated Jews; Boston

Jung, Leo; b. 1892; Orthodox; long-time rabbi of the Jewish Center in Manhattan's Upper West Side; professor emeritus at Yeshiva University; prolific writer, was sole American contributor to Soncino translation of the Talmud; wrote on ethics, against intermarriage; New York

Kelman, Wolfe; b. 1923; Conservative; executive vice-president of the Rabbinical Assembly; formerly director of the United Synagogue of America; New York

Klaperman, Gilbert; b. 1921; Orthodox; vice-president of the Rabbinical Council of America; spiritual leader of Cong. Beth Sholom, Lawrence, New York

Lifshutz, Dovid; b. 1907; Orthodox; the *Suvalker Rav; rosh yeshiva* at Rabbi Isaac Elchanan Theological Seminary of Yeshiva University since 1945; active in guiding Orthodox Jewry in its relationship to the State of Israel; New York

Priesand, Sally; b. 1946; Reform; first woman to be ordained by Hebrew Union College (1972); first woman to head a congregation (Congregation Beth El, Elizabeth, New Jersey, 1979)

Riskin, Shlomo; b. 1940; Orthodox; founded Lincoln Square Synagogue; leader in return to active participation in Jewish life by thousands of Jews; founder of two Hebrew high schools and New York's most extensive adult education courses; New York and Israel

Schachter, Zalman; b. 1924; Polish-born mystic; a founder of the Havurah movement; professor of religion at Temple University; founder of B'nai Or; Philadelphia

Schneerson, Menahem Mendel; b. 1902; Orthodox; seventh *Lubavitcher Rebbe;* New York

Schulweis, Harold; b. 1925; Conservative; leader of Havurah movement; Encino, California

Serotta, Gerold; b. 1946; Reform; president of the New Jewish Agenda; former leader of Breira and Dorot; New York

Sherer, Morris; b. 1921; Orthodox; president of Agudath Israel of America; leading promoter of safeguards to Jewish religious life; New York

Siegel, Seymour; b. 1927; Conservative; professor of ethics and theology at the Jewish Theological Seminary; chairman of the Committee on Jewish Law of the Rabbinical Assembly; favors opening of rabbinate to women; New York

Soloveitchik, Joseph Dov; b. 1903; Orthodox; *rosh yeshiva* of Rabbi Isaac Elchanan Theological Seminary of Yeshiva University; leading Jewish philosopher and thinker; New York

Tanenbaum, Marc; b. 1925; Conservative; director of international affairs of the American Jewish Committee; leading advocate of Christian-Jewish dialogue; co-founder of the National Conference on Race and Religion; New York

Tendler, Moses D.; b. 1926; Orthodox; *rosh yeshiva* at Rabbi Isaac Elchanan Theological Seminary; professor of biology at Yeshiva University, leading authority on Jewish medical ethics; New York

Wurzburger, Walter S.; b. 1920; Orthodox; theologian; president of the Synagogue Council of America; former president of the Rabbinical Council of America; professor at Yeshiva University; editor of *Tradition;* New York

Science; Medicine

Asimov, Isaac; b. 1920; chemist; popular science fiction writer

Benacerraf, Baruj; b. 1920; physician; Harvard professor; Nobel laureate, 1980, in physiology for research in immunology

Berg, Paul; b. 1926; chemist; Stanford professor; 1980 Nobel laureate

Blumberg, Baruch; b. 1925; physician, anthropologist; U. of Pennsylvania professor; 1976 Nobel laureate in physiology

Brown, Michael S.; b. 1942; molecular geneticist at University of Texas Health Center; co-recipient of 1985 Nobel Prize in medicine; leader in cholesterol metabolism research

Cohen, Bernard L.; b. 1924; physicist; U. of Pittsburgh professor; leading force in the development of safe nuclear energy

Djerassi, Isaac; b. 1925; Bulgarian-born physician, cancer researcher, especially of leukemia

Feld, Bernard T.; b. 1919; physicist; leading spokesman for nuclear arms control, pacifism and civilian control of atomic energy

Gell-Man, Murray; b. 1929; theoretical physicist; professor at California Institute of Technology; leader in classification of subatomic particles

Goldstein, Joseph L.; b. 1941; molecular geneticist at University of Texas Health Center; co-recipient of 1985 Nobel Prize in medicine; leader in cholesterol metabolism research

Hiatt, Howard H.; b. 1925; physician; dean of the Harvard School of Public Health; proponent of nuclear freeze and disarmament

Hoffman, Jeffrey A.; b. 1945; astronaut; astrophysicist; member of crew of space shuttle Discovery, April 1985

Hofstadter, Robert; b. 1915; physicist; professor at Stanford, won 1961 Nobel Prize for designing a device that enabled physicists to measure the size and shape of protons and neutrons

Kline, Nathan S.; b. 1916; psychiatrist; introduced use of modern tranquilizers in the early 1950's; was the first to test anti-depressant drugs on mental patients

Lederberg, Joshua; b. 1925; geneticist; demonstrated sexual reproduction in microorganisms; president of Rockefeller University; co-recipient of 1958 Nobel Prize in physiology

Mandelbrot, Benoit; b. 1924; Warsaw-born innovative geometrist for IBM

Rabi, Isidor; b. 1898; physicist; winner of 1944 Nobel Prize; was active in development of the atomic bomb, and later was active in seeking its peaceful uses

Rosenberg, Steven A.; b. 1940; physician; leading researcher at National Cancer Institute

Rosner, Fred; b. 1935; physician; leading scholar and lecturer on Jewish medical ethics and Jewish medical history; professor of medicine, State University of New York at Stony Brook

Sabin, Albert B.; b. 1905; physician; developer of oral vaccine against polio; developed lesser-known vaccine against dengue fever in the Pacific during World War II; former professor of research pediatrics at University of Cincinnati

Salk, Jonas; b. 1914; physician; developed first effective polio vaccine in 1954; founded the Salk Institute of Biological Studies in La Jolla, California, where he currently is researching a cure for multiple sclerosis

Teller, Edward; b. 1908; Budapest-born nuclear physicist; "father" of the hydrogen bomb; helped create Manhattan Project; senior research fellow at Stanford University

Wald, George; b. 1906; biologist; humanist; professor at Harvard University; recipient of 1967 Nobel Prize in physiology; leading opponent of the Vietnam War and nuclear weaponry

Weisskopf, Victor; b. 1908; Vienna-born physicist; leading opponent of nuclear arms proliferation; formerly professor at MIT

Wiesner, Jerome; b. 1915; electrical engineer; early developer of radar; former president of MIT; adviser to Presidents Kennedy and Johnson; early proponent of nuclear disarmament

Yalow, Rosalyn S.; b. 1921; medical physicist; pioneer in radioimmunoassay; second woman to win a Nobel Prize, in Medicine in 1977

Sociology; Public Policy; Psychology; Political Science; Public Affairs

Aronowitz, Stanley; b. 1933; activist; labor organizer; leader of anti-war movement in the 1960's

Barnet, Richard J.; b. 1929; political analyst; critic of American foreign policy

Bell, Daniel (Daniel Bolotsky); b. 1919; professor at Columbia and Harvard; leading social critic

Bettelheim, Bruno; b. 1903; child psychologist; scrutinizer of social behavior under stress; professor of education at University of Chicago

Chesler, Phyllis; b. 1940; psychologist; author; feminist theorist

Epstein, Edward Jay; b. 1935; political scientist and critic of the Warren Commission and network media

Erikson, Erik H.; b. 1902; German-born pyschoanalyst; pioneer in child development; biographer of Luther and Gandhi (Pulitzer Prize winner); coined phrase "identity crisis"

Gaylin, Willard; b. 1925; psychoanalyst; clinical professor of psychiatry at Columbia; expert in bioethics

Glazer, Nathan; b. 1923; sociologist; professor at Harvard; authored *The Lonely Crowd,* co-authored *Beyond the Melting Pot;* leading student of ethnicity in America

Goodwin, Richard N.; b. 1931; author; attorney; speechwriter for JFK, confidant of LBJ, for whom he helped create "The Great Society"

Harris, Louis; b. 1921; pollster

Hess, Stephen; b. 1933; political scientist; prolific political writer; former White House staff member under Eisenhower and Nixon; senior fellow at the Brookings Institution

Hoffman, Stanley; b. 1928; Vienna-born political scientist; chairman of the Western European studies department at Harvard

Horowitz, Irving Louis; b. 1929; sociologist; professor at Rutgers University; prolific writer, especially in areas of Latin American development, militarism and upheaval and Jewish-Israeli relations

Hurewitz, Jacob C.; b. 1914; political scientist; Middle East specialist; professor at Columbia University

Janowitz, Morris; b. 1919; sociologist; professor at University of Chicago; analyst of effect of technology on society

Karpatkin, Rhoda; b. 1930; attorney and civil rights advocate; executive director of the Consumers Union of the United States

Kristol, Irving; b. 1920; writer; prolific journalist; leading neo-conservative; professor at New York University; highly influential advocate of capitalist theory

Lifton, Robert Jay; b. 1926; psychiatrist; psychohistorian; his *Death in Life, Survivors of Hiroshima* studied the impact of war and barbarism on survivors

Lipset, Seymour; b. 1922; sociologist; political scientist; professor of political science at Stanford University; national president of American Professors for Peace in the Middle East

Mayer, Egon; b. 1944; Swiss-born sociologist; student of Jewish family life in America, particularly education and intermarriage; associate professor at Brooklyn College; author of *From Suburb to Shtetl* and numerous monographs

Mayer, Martin; b. 1928; writer; critic of the American school system and the American economy

Melman, Seymour; b. 1917; industrial engineer; peace activist; co-chairman of SANE: A Citizen's Organization for a Sane World; professor at Columbia University

Pipes, Richard; b. 1923; Polish-born Russian expert; serves on National Security Council; professor of history at Harvard; influenced mid-1970's reevaluation of the Soviet Union as a far greater threat than previously believed

Raskin, Marcus; b. 1934; political scientist; co-founder of the Institute for Policy Studies; early critic of U.S. policy in Vietnam

Riesman, David; b. 1909; sociologist; attorney; authored *The Lonely Crowd* (1950); professor of social sciences at Harvard University

Rothenberg, David; b. 1933; prison reformer; founder and executive director of the Fortune Society in New York; teacher of criminology and of prisoners themselves, as well

Shulman, Marshall D.; b. 1916; Sovietologist; special advisor to Secretary of State Cyrus Vance in the Carter Administration; leading supporter of SALT II; director of the Russian Institute at Columbia University

Silberman, Charles Eliot; b. 1925; social analyst; lecturer; journalist; author of *Crisis in the Classroom: The Remaking of American Education* and *The Open Classroom Reader*

Sklare, Marshall; b. 1921; sociologist; professor at Brandeis University; commentator on the condition of American Jewry; author of *Not Quite at Home: How an American Jewish Community Lives with Itself and its Neighbors* and others

Steel, Ronald; b. 1931; author; political and foreign policy analyst; author of *Walter Lippman and the American Century*

Steinem, Gloria; b. 1935; feminist advocate; editor, *Ms.* magazine

Szasz, Thomas; b. 1920; Budapest-born psychiatrist; writer; defender of the civil rights of the mentally ill; professor of psychiatry at Upstate Medical Center in Syracuse

Toffler, Alvin; b. 1928; writer; futurist; author of *Future Shock, The Third Wave*

Walzer, Michael; b. 1935; social scientist; professor at the Institute for Advanced Study in Princeton; author of *Just and Unjust Wars*

Waskow, Arthur; b. 1933; writer; theologian; organizer of Trees for Vietnam, the Farbrangen Community; author of *Godwrestling*

Wildavsky, Aaron; b. 1930; political scientist; head of the Survey Research Center at Berkeley; scholar on the power of the American presidency and of public policy

Yankelovich, Daniel; b. 1924; pollster; sociologist; research professor of psychology; co-founder of the Public Agenda Foundation

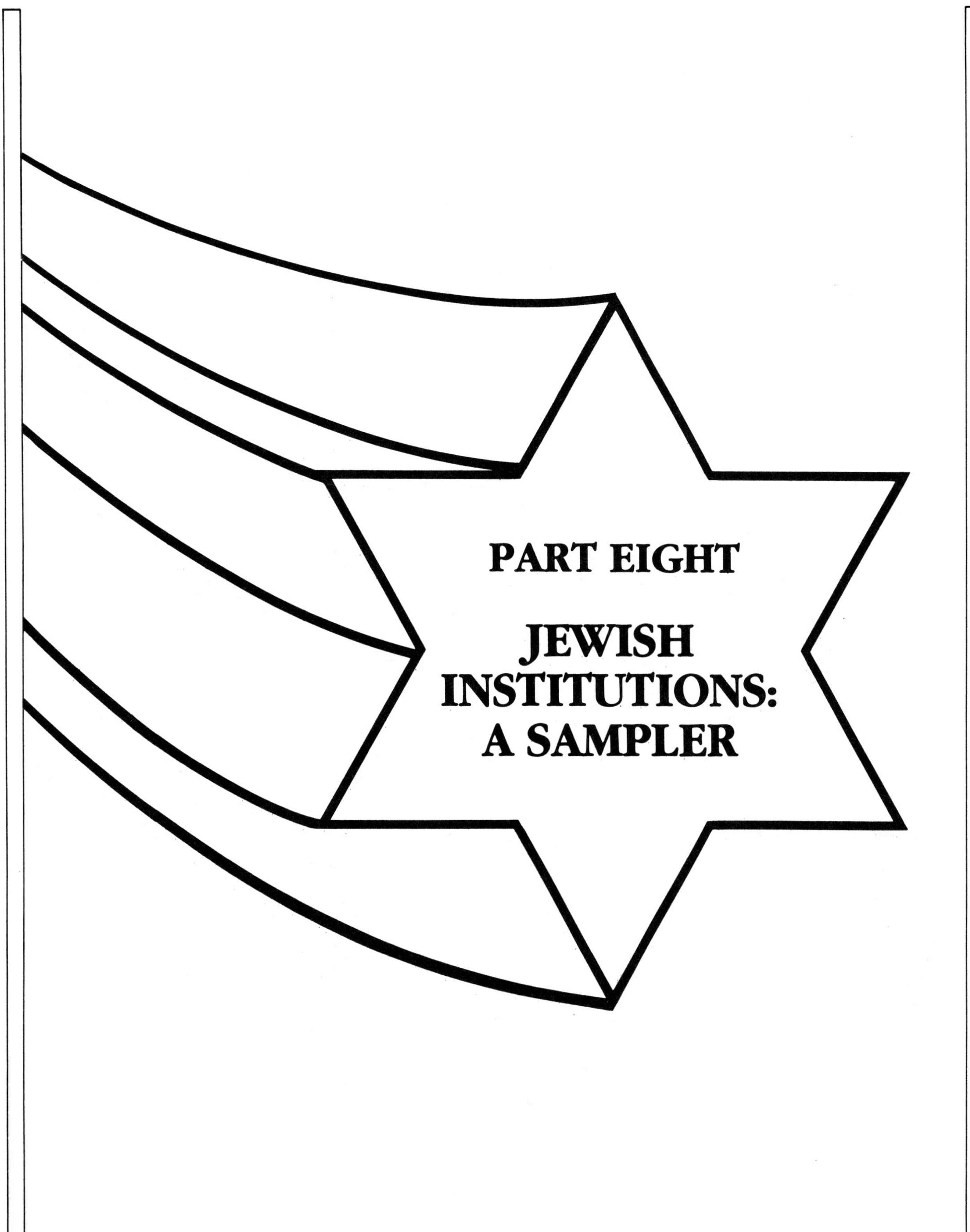

PART EIGHT

JEWISH INSTITUTIONS: A SAMPLER

48

Jewish Organizations at a Glance

	RECONSTRUCTIONIST	REFORM	CONSERVATIVE	ORTHODOX "Modern Orthodox"	ORTHODOX "Strictly Orthodox"	ORTHODOX "Hasidic"
CONGREGATIONAL ORGANIZATIONS	—Federation of Reconstructionist Congregations —Jewish Reconstructionist Foundation	—Union of American Hebrew Congregations	Synagogue Council of America (umbrella) —United Synagogue of America —Union for Traditional Conservative Judaism	—Union of Orthodox Jewish Congregations of America —National Council of Young Israel (not a member of Synagogue Council)	—Agudath Israel of America	—Hasidic groups: —Lubavitch —Satmar —Stolin —Bobov —Skverer —Pupa —Ger —Munkatch —Bostoner —Sigeter —Skulener —Viznitz —Belz
RABBINIC ARM		—Central Conference of American Rabbis	—Rabbinical Assembly	—Rabbinical Council of America —Council of Young Israel Rabbis	—Agudath Harabbonim —Igud Harabbonim	—Hisachdus Horabbonim
RABBINICAL SEMINARIES	—Reconstructionist Rabbinical College—Wyncote, Pa.	—Hebrew Union College— Cincinnati New York Los Angeles Jerusalem	—Jewish Theological Seminary—New York —University of Judaism—Los Angeles	—Yeshiva University (RIETS)—New York —Hebrew Theological College—Skokie, Ill.	—Beth Medrash Govoha—Lakewood, N.J. —Mesivta Rabbi Chaim Berlin—Brooklyn, N.Y. —Ner Israel—Baltimore, MD. —Torah Vodaath—Brooklyn, N.Y. —Mirrer Yeshiva—Brooklyn, N.Y. —Telshe—Wickliffe, Ohio —Mesivta Tifereth Jerusalem—New York, N.Y. —Chofetz Chaim—Forest Hills, N.Y. —Yeshivas Brisk—Skokie, Ill.	—Lubavitch—Brooklyn, N.Y. —Satmar—Brooklyn, N.Y.
PUBLICATIONS	—Reconstructionist	—Reform Judaism —CCAR Journal	—United Synagogue Review —Conservative Judaism	—Tradition —Young Israel Viewpoint	—Jewish Observer —Jewish Press—Brooklyn, N.Y. —Algemeine Journal	
YOUTH ORGANIZATIONS		—National Federation of Temple Youth	—United Synagogue Youth	—National Conference of Synagogue Youth —Bnai Akiva	—Pirchei Agudath Israel —Bnos Agudath Israel	—Pirchai Chabad —Bnos Chabad
CANTORIAL ORGANIZATIONS		—American Conference of Cantors	—Cantors Assembly	—Cantorial Council of America		
COMMUNITY RELATIONS, SOCIAL, POLITICAL AND LEGAL ORGANIZATIONS			National Jewish Community Relations Advisory Council (umbrella) Conference of Presidents of Major American Jewish Organizations (umbrella) —American Jewish Congress —American Jewish Committee —B'nai B'rith —Anti-Defamation League of B'nai B'rith —Jewish Labor Committee —Jewish War Veterans of the U.S.A. —National Council of Jewish Women —Women's American ORT —Hadassah		—National Jewish Commission on Law and Public Affairs (COLPA) —Commission on Legislation and Civic Action of Agudath Israel —Association of Orthodox Jewish Scientists	
ZIONIST ORGANIZATIONS		—ARZA—Association of Reform Zionists of America	American Zionist Federation (umbrella) —Mercaz —Bnai Zion —Pioneer Women —Labor Zionist Alliance	—Mizrachi —Hapoel Hamizrachi —AMIT Women —Emunah Women —Religious Zionists of America		

49

How *Hatikvah* Became The National Anthem of Israel

Eliyahu Ha-Cohen

"To potential printers, lovers of Zion! I have a book I called *Barkaii* which contains different poems written in the Holyland about *Eretz Israel* and its settlements—all written with a national spirit. I can be found at the following address: Naftali Hertz Imber, Jerusalem."

Naftali Hertz Imber, author of Hatikvah.

This announcement, which appeared in the newspaper *Hatz'vi* in 1886, heralded the first publication of the poem that would later become the national anthem of the Jewish people and the State of Israel. Not long after this announcement, the book of poetry entitled *Barkaii,* written by Imber, a pioneer of the first Aliyah, was published in Jerusalem. The book contained the song *Tikvateinu* (Our Hope).

It is easy to imagine the impact that this collection of Hebrew poems had on the Jewish people—poems written by a "new immigrant" and published in Jerusalem. All the *Chovevei Zion* groups in the diaspora celebrated this event—the publication of a book of reports and live greetings, the sounds of *Eretz Israel* and the settlements of Judea and Galilee. In *Hamelitz,* the most widely circulated Hebrew newspaper in the diaspora, *Hatikvah* was quoted in articles from Israel. The poet himself was not named—only his description: *Baal Barkaii* (the "master of *Barkaii*") as befitting an eminent person.

Only four years after the development of new settlements, the settlers were equipped with a repertoire of *Moshavot* songs. Imber wrote a poem for each settlement in *Barkaii,* as yet without melody. The poem *Tikvateinu* was written, according to the author's comment: "at the request of one of the nations."

From that time on, the poem did not cease to arouse controversy and stimulate various opinions. The veterans of the *Yishuv* and its researchers were divided on almost every detail of the history of the poem: When was it written? How? Under the influence of what other composition? How and when was the melody fitted to the lyrics? When did it become the anthem of the Jewish people? Who made the changes in the words and melody? When were these changes made? Scores of versions, which include a mixture of legend and mystery, accompany the history of this song. These are the distinguishing marks of a folksong.

The first draft of *Hatikvah* was written by Imber in the house of a Jewish scholar in Jasi, Romania in 1877. This was confirmed by the poet himself in a dedication on his photograph and in other documents. When Imber emigrated to Israel in 1882, he went around to the settlements with his poems in hand. From time to time he was invited to stay as a guest at the settlements. He would first accept a drink, then take out his papers and read enthusiastically certain verses of the *Hatikvah.* Under these circumstances, the "creative forces" would often come upon him. Imber began to add extra verses to his poem, until it reached a total of nine verses. The settlements started competing among themselves for the honor of hosting the birth of the anthem. Imber finished the poem in his room in Jerusalem where the walls were covered with bits of verses and writings. Eyewitnesses recount that each time a rhyme would flash through his mind, he would hurriedly set it down in pencil on the walls, as high as his hand could reach.

Was Imber influenced by foreign poetry? It seems that there was a possible outside influence. The poetic structure of *Hatikvah,* with its repetition of *"Kol Od,"* at the beginning of each verse, is reminiscent of a song published in the annual *Bikurei Haitim Hachadashim* (1845). This was a poem by Mendel Stern entitled *Maaneh,* a translation of the *Poems of the Rhine* by Nicholas Becker. It is also fair to assume, that as a native of Galicia, Imber was well acquainted with the opening line of the Polish National Anthem—"We have still not lost Poland." These structural influences, however, suggest the intentions of Imber to create an anthem and do not relate to the content of *Hatikvah* which is original and typical of Imber's style.

The first attempt at composing a melody for the *Hatikvah* was not successful. Israel Belkind, a member of the "Bilu" organization from Rishon Le-Zion, received a letter from his friend, Leon Igli of Zichron Yaacov. The letter contained a request for help. Igli wanted to be discharged from physical labor work that would allow him to concentrate on composing songs. It seems that Igli was a professional singer with a musical education. He was one of six young men sent to Israel by Baron de Rothschild to prepare for agricultural work. In Zichron Yaacov he was employed as a porter and was engaged in difficult physical labor that he was unused to. The local clerk of the Baron was convinced that this was a musical talent gone to waste. Soon after, Igli was asked to compose the music to Imber's poems, and an original melody to *Hatikvah* was conceived. Igli composed a different melody for each of the nine verses of the song. This long and complicated melody was not easily learned by the settlers. Belkind would give a piece of chocolate, a rare delicacy at that time, to every child who could sing the song in its entirety.

One year later, a new melody of *Hatikvah* was heard in Rishon LeZion—"A pleasant and easy melody." No one asked where it came from or how. In the Levontin House, the youth center of the settlement, the song was learned from mouth to mouth. It is the same melody known to us today.

The Prohibited *Moldava*

In the Yishuv, the impression existed that the *Hatikvah* melody was loaned from the symphonic poem *Moldava* ("Vlatava") by the composer Smetana.

Actually, the previous version of the melody of *Hatikvah* was a Romanian folksong from the district of Moldavia. Shmuel Cohen, of the first Aliyah, testified to the circumstances surrounding its adaptation to Imber's poem in his memoirs: "In the year 5347 (1887) my older brother Zvi attempted to plant wheat in Yesod HaMaalah. In those days, Naftali Hertz Imber was residing in Rosh Pina. He gave my brother a copy of his collection of songs *Barkaii* with a warm inscription as a souvenir. My brother sent me this pamphlet. I liked *Hatikvah* best of all the poems. A short time afterwards, I too, emigrated to Israel. In my native country we used to sing the Romanian song *Oys-Tzi* in choir. When I came to Rishon Le-Zion they did not sing *Hatikvah* or any other songs from *Barkaii.* I was the first to sing the *Hatikvah* with a melody known to me, the melody sung today in all of Israel and the diaspora . . . and may I say that everytime I participate in conferences and gatherings and *Hatikvah* is officially sung, I feel I was privileged to be the first to have sung *Hatikvah.*"

There is no mention of the singing of the anthem at the first Zionist Congresses. Before the fourth Zionist Congress in London in 1900, a Zionist Conference was held with the participation of Herzl, Nordau, Zangwill (the English translator of *Hatikvah)* and others. At its conclusion, the audience sang the English anthem. A spontaneous singing of the *Hatikvah* soon followed. The higher echelon of the Zionist leadership thus learned that *Hatikvah* was becoming the anthem. At the fourth Zionist Congress, therefore, a motion was brought to the floor to declare a competition for the composition of the anthem. It was emphasized that the anthem be in Hebrew with a melody. The competition did not come about. But the facts speak for themselves: In Germany, the association "Ezra" held a conference, demonstrating for the settlement of Israel. At its conclusion, the song "We have not lost our hope" was greeted enthusiastically. In Vilna that same year, a conference of many delegates assembled. At its conclusion the delegates held hands and in one voice and great feeling sang the national song *Hatikvah.* Itzi Fernhoff, a poet and writer from the same city as Agnon, published a "Utopia" entitled *Two Visions.* In it he foresees that the "State of the Jews" by Herzl is called "The State of Israel," its flag is embroidered with a Star of David and its National Anthem is the *Hatikvah.* Fernhoff inserted verses of the *Hatikvah* in his work.

In anticipation of official recognition of the *Hatikvah* by the fifth Zionist Congress, Imber reminded the delegates that *Hatikvah* was already 25 years old. "I am happy to see my dream come true" he writes. But official recognition was delayed. Between the fifth and sixth Zionist Congresses, a minor Congress was convened by the Russian Zionists. It concluded with a "burst of one thousand voices singing *Hatikvah.* The words "the eye looks toward Zion" took on special meaning at this Congress which was called the "Uganda Congress." From then on, each of the Congresses ended with the singing of *Hatikvah.* This was the unofficial decision of the people, as yet without proclamation, referendum or the sanction of the Zionist Organization.

During that same year in Israel, a songbook entitled *The Violin of Zion* was published by Lorintz. *Hatikvah* appeared as the opening song to the thirty-one songs included. The newspapers recounted stories of school parties concluding with the "National Song."

The final change in the words of *Hatikvah* took place in 1905. Dr. I.L. Matman Cohen, a school teacher in Rishon Le-Zion, changed the sentence "to return to the land of our fathers; to the city that David encamped" to "to be free in our land; the land of Zion and Jerusalem." In place of the "old hope," he wrote: "to the hope of two thousand years." This change was only accepted in Israel. The Jews of the diaspora continued to sing the original version of *Hatikvah* for over fifty years.

The layman loved *Hatikvah* but many leaders and musicians fought it. Usishkin complained of its "musical sluggishness." Yoel Engel contended that it was a "loathsome anthem."

The second Aliyah brought with it a song of Bialik entitled *Blessing of the Nation (Techezakna).* It seemed for awhile that this song would be heir to the *Hatikvah.* Bialik himself did not take a stand but refused to rise at the singing of *Techezakna.* Every workers' meeting ended with *Techezakna.* Berel Katznelson was alarmed at this and pleaded not to abandon the *Hatikvah.* The newspapers were full of discussions; *Hatikvah or Techezakna?*"

The Failure of Additional Attempts

Attempts have been made to propose other anthems. One of the defenders of the *Hatikvah,* Y.L. Motzkin, brought before the "Jewish Parliament," the eighteenth congress in 1933, the following proposal: "The Congress establishes that according to a long-standing tradition, the blue and white flag is the flag of the World Zionist Organization and the anthem *Hatikvah* is the national anthem of the Jewish people."

The debate continued, however. In 1947, Moshe Halevi, director of the theatre "Ohel" suggested to David Ben Gurion that a new anthem be chosen. Religious organizations wanted to establish *Shir Hamaalot*—"When the Lord brought back the exiles to Zion" as the state anthem. When the State of Israel was established the *Hatikvah* did not gain official status as the national anthem. But the *Hatikvah* is still sung by the authority of tradition if not law.

כָּל עוֹד בַּלֵּבָב פְּנִימָה	*Kol od balevav p'nima*	So long as still within our breasts
נֶפֶשׁ יְהוּדִי הוֹמִיָּה,	*Nefesh yehudi homee'ya*	The Jewish heart beats true,
וּלְפַאֲתֵי מִזְרָח קָדִימָה	*U'lefa-atei mizrach kadima*	So long as still towards the East,
עַיִן לְצִיּוֹן צוֹפִיָּה,	*Ayin le-Zion tzofee'ya*	To Zion, looks the Jew,
עוֹד לֹא אָבְדָה תִּקְוָתֵנוּ	*Od lo avda tikvateynu*	So long our hopes are not yet lost—
הַתִּקְוָה מִשְּׁנוֹת אַלְפַּיִם,	*Hatikva bat shnot alpayim*	Two thousands years we cherished them—
לִהְיוֹת עַם חָפְשִׁי בְּאַרְצֵנוּ,	*Leehiyot am chofshi b'artzeinu*	To live in freedom in the land
בְּאֶרֶץ צִיּוֹן וִירוּשָׁלַיִם.	*Eretz Zion v'Yerushalayim*	Of Zion and Jerusalem.

Kol od ba - le - vav pe - ni - mah
ne - fesh ye - hu - di ho - mi - yah, U - le -
fa - a - tey miz - rah ka - di - mah
a - yin le - Tzi - yon tzo - fi - yah,
Od lo av' - dah tik - va - te - nu,
Ha - tik - vah sh'not al - pa - yim,
Li - h'yot am hof - shi be - ar - tze - nu,
E - retz Tzi - yon vi - ru - sha - la - yim.
Li - h'yot am hof - shi be - ar - tze - nu,
E - retz Tzi - yon vi - ru - sha - la - yim.

The Jewish Braille Institute of America

Dedicated to equality of Jewish participation for the blind, partially-sighted and reading disabled.

For more than half a century, the Jewish Braille Institute of America has pioneered in developing programs to insure that blind and partially-sighted Jewish children and adults may participate fully and equally in Jewish religious, educational and communal life. All of JBI's material and services are free.

Headquartered in New York, JBI has adapted its programs over the years to the changing needs of its client population. When the agency was founded in 1931, many of its clients were youngsters—blind from birth or early childhood—who needed prayer books and texts in braille in order to become bar-mitzvah and participate in synagogue services. Today the causes of visual impairment have their greatest effect on older people. Thus, most of JBI's clients today are senior citizens who have become blind or visually-handicapped in their later years but who wish to take part in Jewish community activities and continue their reading of Jewish literary material. For JBI, this means creating whole new libraries of large-print reading matter and "Talking Books"—novels, histories, biographies, liturgy and scholarly material of Jewish interest on audio tape.

Visual impairment affects an estimated 150,000 American Jews today. Of these, 20,000 are legally blind, 50,000 have severe visual impairment, and the remainder cannot read standard size print easily even with the strongest prescription glasses or contact lenses. For these blind and partially-sighted persons, JBI offers a full array of programmatic services and works toward erasing age-old negative stereotypes about blindness and blind persons.

A gathering of the Jewish blind to celebrate Sukkot.

Blind children making preparations for the Passover seder.

In keeping with its philosophy of positive integration of the visually disabled into the life of the Jewish community, JBI offers a wide variety of free materials and services. There are religious publications and general reading in braille, "Talking Books" and books in large print. There are programs for blind boys and girls training for bar and bat mitzvah. There are special counseling programs for blind college students and the elderly. All are designed to help the blind and partially-sighted lead full Jewish lives. In addition, JBI is making available its audiocassettes of Judaic interest to learning disabled children who are particularly apt to benefit from such materials.

JBI began 55 years ago as the dream of a young man who had become blind at the age of six—the late Leopold Dubov. He envisioned a world in which the blind and visually impaired would have equal opportunity to learn and to work along with sighted persons.

Because his father, a rabbi, had gone to great lengths to instruct him in Jewish learning, Mr. Dubov readily understood what other blind Jews were missing. He joined forces with Rabbi Michael Aaronson, a determined young man who had lost his sight in combat during World War I but returned to the Hebrew Union College to complete his rabbinical training. In 1931, in response to Rabbi Aaronson's plea at the convention of the National Federation of

Temple Sisterhoods, the women's arm of the Reform movement agreed to assume sponsorship of a new organization that was named the Jewish Braille Institute of America. Leopold Dubov became the Institute's first director. In short order, NFTS was joined in sponsoring JBI by the Women's League for Conservative Judaism and the woman's branch of the Union of Orthodox Jewish Congregations of America, thus uniting all streams of Judaism in support of this historic effort.

One of the new agency's first tasks was to publish the *Jewish Braille Review,* the first magazine in braille to deal with topics of Jewish interest. Shortly thereafter, the JBI established a braille lending library to make volumes of Judaica in braille available to the blind. The library now numbers 65,000 volumes in Hebrew and English. In 1935, the *Children's Supplement of the Jewish Braille Review* was launched.

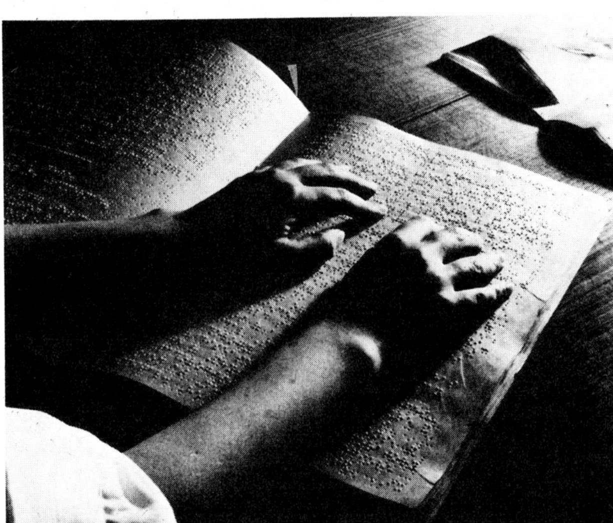

Reading braille.

JBI opened the world of Hebrew literature to the Jewish blind by developing the Hebrew braille code. Other steps taken by the Institute to provide the blind with greater access to the world of music and letters were the publication of *The Braille Musician,* launched in 1942, and the establishment of the First International Literary Competition for the Blind in 1949.

A giant stride toward equality of opportunity for the blind in worship and religious study took place when the Institute published a 20-volume edition of the Bible in braille. This was followed in 1952 by the publication of the first braille edition of the primer, *Hebrew Self-Taught.* These braille materials assured every blind child the opportunity for a complete Jewish education.

As the number of blind children declined and the proportion rose of visually-handicapped persons who were elderly and who found it difficult to master braille, JBI established its "Talking Book" library of audiocassette recordings and its Large-Print Judaica Library to enable the elderly to continue to enjoy reading matter of Jewish interest in comfort. During this period, the Institute published Conservative, Orthodox and Reform Jewish prayerbooks in braille, followed by the publication of high holy day *mahzorim* and prayerbooks for festivals and other occasions.

THE HEBREW ALPHABET

(הָאָלֶף־בֵּית)

CONSONANTS (אוֹתִיּוֹת):

א	בּ	ב	ג
ד	ה	ו	ז
ח	ט	י	כּ
כ	ך	ל	מ
ם	נ	ן	ס
ע	פּ	פ	ף
צ	ץ	ק	ר
שׁ	שׂ	תּ	ת

VOWELS (תְּנוּעוֹת):

The Hebrew alphabet in braille.

These were developed not only in braille, but also in large print and on audiocassette tapes, as were musical recordings.

In 1965, JBI opened a professional sound studio in its national headquarters for recording Jewish materials to be duplicated on cassettes for distribution to the blind and visually-impaired throughout the world. Among the Institute's most noteworthy transcriptions is the English and Hebrew recording of the entire Soncino *Chumash* (the

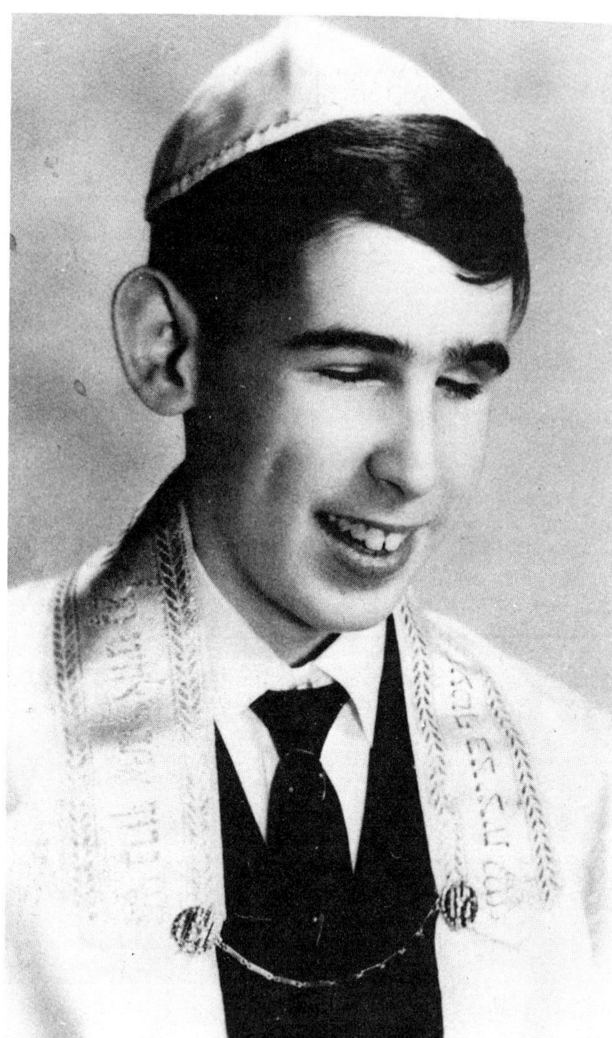

A blind Jewish boy celebrating his bar mitzvah.

Five Books of Moses)—117 hours of listening on 78 cassettes. Today JBI's "Talking Book" library contains nearly 100,000 audiocassette recordings of novels, plays, poems, biographies and historical works on Jewish themes, as well as religious material. For more than 25 years, the studio and the JBI libraries have been under the direction of Richard Borgersen.

As the life span of American Jews increases—and, with it, the infirmities associated with aging—JBI is developing innovative programs to serve growing numbers of Jewish clients who wish to remain actively involved in Jewish religious, communal and cultural life.

In 1969, the Institute issued a conversation course in Hebrew for the blind and partially-sighted. A major highlight of JBI activity in the mid-1970s was the historic First World Conference of the Jewish Blind in Jerusalem. More than 500 persons attended the daily sessions of the gathering, which was aimed at gaining improved understanding of and status for the blind and visually-impaired. Among the blind alumni of JBI bar and bat mitzvah training who had made aliyah to Israel were Lea Levavi, staff member of the *Jerusalem Post;* Ari Gamliel, honor graduate student of Hebrew University; and Ellen Rubin, rehabilitation counselor in Be'er Sheva.

The *JBI Voice,* a "Talking Book" magazine on Jewish topics, began circulating in 1978, bringing a reservoir of relevant Jewish articles and discussion pieces to blind persons unable to read braille.

Under the direction of Gerald M. Kass, the agency's current executive vice president, JBI has launched a nationwide program of seminars to sensitize professional and lay leaders of Jewish communal agencies to the needs of the blind and visually-impaired. Seminars have been conducted in most major centers of Jewish population in the United States.

In the 1980s, JBI has expanded its programmatic activities on several fronts to assist the blind and severely visually-impaired in Israel. To inform blind persons in Israel of new developments relating to their concerns, JBI began publishing *Or Chadash,* a magazine in Hebrew relating to the blind in 1982. JBI has also equipped Israel's first recording studio for preparing talking books for the blind.

Rabbi Rami Rabby, blind since birth, teaching other blind Jewish children.

In 1983 JBI established a Low Vision Clinic at the Tel Aviv Medical Center for Israelis with severe ophthalmological problems. The clinic serves some 1,500 patients a year, including children, adults and wounded veterans of the

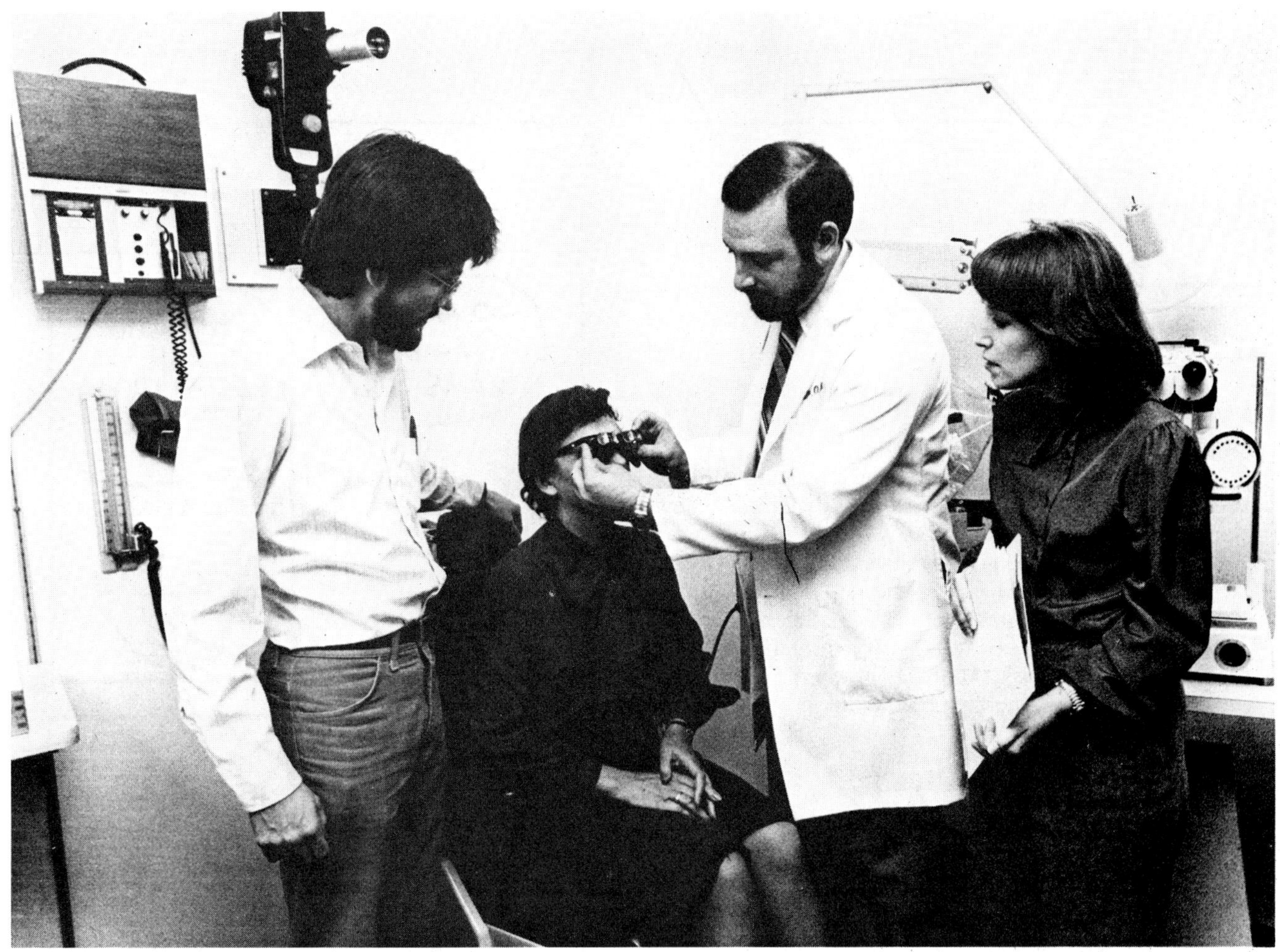

PRECIOUS GIFT OF SIGHT—Optometrists and low vision care specialists at Israel's newest medical facility—the Jewish Braille Institute's Low Vision Clinic—help Israelis with severe visual impairment achieve maximum sight. The Clinic uses ultramodern optical aids and special enlarging devices to restore functional eyesight to severely visually handicapped adults and children and to war-wounded members of the Israel Defense Forces. The Clinic is located at the Tel Aviv Medical Center.

Israel Defense Forces. In 1986, both the Jane Evans Talking Book Library for Children, named in honor of JBI's president, and the Naomi Adir Large Print Library were established by the JBI at the Central Library for the Blind in Netanya, Israel.

Under the leadership of its longtime president, Dr. Jane Evans, JBI continues toward its goal of full and equal participation of the Jewish blind in all aspects of Jewish communal life and in the life of the larger community.

Persons seeking information on how to obtain JBI's free services and materials, or who wish to volunteer as readers of "Talking Books" or as "braillers" (turning printed matter into braille) may contact the Jewish Braille Institute of America at 110 East 30th Street, New York, NY 10016; telephone (212) 889-2525.

Aliyah: "If Not Now, When?"

"If I am not for myself, who is for me?
If I am only for myself, what am I?
If not now, when?"

The above quotation was formulated by Rabbi Hillel in the first century, but these are questions that thinking Jews have pondered through the ages.

Never have they been more relevant than now, with the return of Jews to our Land. And with the establishment of Israel, the first Jewish state on the face of the earth in 1900 years, the moment has come for you, a thinking Jew living in the Diaspora, to ask, "If not now, when?" and to play your part in the ingathering of the Exile.

Ten Arguments for Aliyah

Peter David Hornik

I decided to make aliyah on September 19, 1982. The immediate catalyst was the world reaction to the Sabra and Shatila massacres. It would not be quite accurate to say that my decision was the culmination of a long process, one side finally winning out after a protracted internal debate; I had kept the idea of aliyah at some distance for years, when suddenly it overwhelmed me.

Since then relatives, friends, and sundry aliyah people have been asking me why I made this decision. If I have trouble responding, it is not because I do not know the answer but because it is so complex. In the following attempt to work out this complexity the different facets inevitably overlap and intertwine.

1. *Aliyah offers the only reasonable assurance that one will have Jewish descendants.* It is by conscious choice that I put this "argument" first. The intermarriage problem in America is well known, the figures appalling—35 percent here, 50 percent there. All of us know vestigial Jews for whom the intermarriage of their children poses no crisis, perhaps eliciting a certain mild regret. Far stranger are the "committed" Jews who may be active in their synagogues, advocates or fundraisers for Israel, involved with Jewish learning and culture, whose attitudes toward intermarriage range from painful acquiescence to outright proscription and yet who refuse to face squarely the simple truth: there is no way to prevent intermarriage in America, nor does one have the right to expect one's children to shun it *if one has chosen to live in the Diaspora rather than in Israel.*

Seen in this light, the widespread acceptance of conversion as a sort of compromise bespeaks weakness, self-deception, or desperation. Yes, one may meet a convincing

convert here or there; but most converts are *not* convincing (no surprise, since they did not convert out of any prior interest whatsoever in Jews or Judaism), their own parents and relatives are not Jews (and are certain to include, by

sheer statistical probability, antisemites), and the Jewish status of the children of these marriages is all too often both questionable and fragile.

The lamentations one hears about this situation are becoming tiresome. Judaism cannot take root in alien American soil, nor can it be kept separate and pure like a secret baggage. And there is after all an alternative.

2. *Antisemitism is endemic in America, and is unforgivable.* The word "endemic" will jar only those who have spent little time around blue-collar people. Having grown up in a predominantly non-Jewish upstate New York town, having worked in restaurants and supermarkets, I can assure Jews whose experience in America has been more restricted to the professional class that antisemitism—and, to be sure, racism in general, but particularly against Jews and blacks—is simply part of the casual, assumed ambience of working-class life in America today.

In professional circles, an anti-racism etiquette has prevailed since at least the sixties. How deep it runs is another matter. From our white-collar friends, too, we have heard antisemitic innuendos, cracks, outright insults—even if delivered a little less often or unabashedly. And then there is the political expression of antisemitism. By now a small literature has grown up around the war in Lebanon and the wild anti-Israel reactions it provoked from the American and world media and political establishment; a prime example is Norman Podhoretz's "J'Accuse" in the September 1982 *Commentary*.

Most discussions of American antisemitism focus on statistics about swastika daubings and the like. Of more immediate concern to most American Jews is the question how tolerant one should be toward more everyday manifestations of antisemitism. I submit that at this late date one can be tolerant only by betraying oneself and much else besides.

3. *Life in America, in general, is getting worse, not better.* One can hope for an improvement in the economy or in the crime situation, but there is little to foster optimism. The quality of life in America declines with the erosion of values, the triumph of commercialism and pornography. National pride, purpose, and cohesiveness have vanished so completely that one has to jog one's memory to realize that a scant 20 years ago they still (seemingly) ran high. Every man is an island unto himself, functioning mainly as an economic unit; while the political process degenerates into a cacophony of competing interest groups.

4. *Aliyah will not weaken pro-Israel advocacy in America.* Convincing arguments can be offered on both sides of the question whether American Jewish activism helps to strengthen the U.S.-Israel alliance. There are now record numbers of Jews in the Senate as well as the House, most of them strongly pro-Israel; most legislators from states or districts with large Jewish communities continue to support Israel to varying degrees.

At any rate, individuals contemplating aliyah need not trouble themselves with this question. It is not pro-Israel American Jews who are in short supply.

5. *Unlike Jews in Russia or Syria or Ethiopia, American Jews are free to make aliyah.*

6. *Israel has suffered too much.* Here too I need not expound at length. One war was not enough to spark the mass American aliyah of Zionist dreams, nor a second, nor a third, a fourth, a fifth. Nor terrorism, blockades and boycotts, economic struggle, *yeridah,* international slander.

7. *Israel needs aliyah.* Israel is the only country in the world that offers special privileges to (Jewish) immigrants. *Olim* can live free of charge for six months at absorption centers where they are given free intensive Hebrew courses; after that they can stay up to two years for nominal charges. When they look for housing, handsome mortgage or rent subsidies are available from the government; if they have trouble finding work, subsidized job retraining courses abound. They get tax breaks, six months of free medical insurance, special funds if they run out of them; *full Israeli citizenship is granted automatically as soon as the oleh requests it.*

In Israel's first decade, a massive ingathering did indeed occur; these *olim* were mostly refugees from displaced persons camps or hostile Arab societies. There has been no comparable wave of aliyah since. For a while in the seventies Soviet Jews came in considerable numbers; but now even that has all but stopped as the Soviet Union takes hostage an entire internal nationality. Now, as everyone knows and appears to regret, *yeridah* exceeds aliyah.

Whether or not one supports the present government's policies in the administered territories, and whether or not one is persuaded that Israel faces a full-blown demographic crisis, there is no question that aliyah is badly needed economically, demographically, psychologically, and morally and that it is the highest contribution one can make to this valiant, abnormally burdened state.

8. *To reject life in Israel because it is economically harder is to acquiesce in the strategy of the Arabs.* Everyone who knows what he is talking about will tell you that *klitah* (absorption into Israeli society) is difficult. *Olim* face the

typical problems of immigrants: the language barrier (in most cases), adjusting and being accepted in a very different culture, dealing with the bureaucracy (in Israel's case especially notorious). For most American *olim*, however, these problems are transitional; more critical and long-term is learning to cope with Israel's sterner lifestyle.

Many American Jews are shocked to find that most Israelis still hang their laundry on clothes-lines; that families considered middle-class live in small, plain apartments; that some Israeli couples work three or more jobs between them to make ends meet. Although it must be pointed out that Israel's unemployment rate is less than half the rate in the United States and that to a large extent Israeli life is geared to the inflation rate (e.g., there is less pressure to meet payment deadlines), there is no question that Israel's standard of living cannot compare to America's.

This situation is one intended result of Arab aggression and orchestrated pressure. Because Israel must put an abnormally high proportion of gross national product into defense, because it must struggle to find and keep trading partners, its economy suffers. Arafat has succeeded in making Israel a less attractive place to live. Israelis (the vast majority of whom still do not emigrate) must cope with the fear and violence, *and* the economic hardship, *and* the knowledge that their brothers and sisters from pleasanter climes regard their little country as a nice place for a spiritual holiday but wouldn't—sans microwave ovens and posh houses in the suburbs—want to live there.

9. *The accumulated moral infamy of the 20th century requires response.* It goes on—the Pope's audience with Arafat, the equating of the Israelis with Nazis, the terrorist attacks in France and elsewhere, the persecution of Soviet and other Jewries. Anybody can add to the list. Jews are not the only sufferers; but they are most sensitized to the outrages against Jews.

For several years I read and argued, contributed and then solicited money, wrote letters to the editor and to columnists. As the Lebanese war raged on, the feeling grew in me that it was not enough.

10. *Israel is the eternal home of the Jewish people.*

The Yarmulke

Sara Stein

The yarmulke lost a legal battle in 1986 in the United States Supreme Court case of Goldman v. Weinberger. On March 25, the Supreme Court ruled by a 5-4 margin that the Air Force had the right not to permit an Orthodox Jewish officer to wear a yarmulke on duty. The court ruling denied the claim of Rabbi Simcha Goldman, a captain and psychologist in the U.S. Air Force, under the free exercise clause of the First Amendment to the United States Constitution, and contended that to wear a yarmulke is an impermissible variation of the military dress code.

The yarmulke in the "yarmulke case" has long been a part of the Jewish dress code. Nearly all Orthodox and some Conservative Jewish men cover their heads as a sign of humility and reverence before G-d. Even some less traditional Jews wear a yarmulke when praying or quoting the Bible. The yarmulke is a symbol of the recognition that there is always Someone above man. The term "yarmulke," a word of Slavic derivation, may be attributed to the Hebrew words meaning "awe of the King" (*yirah Melech*).

The practice of covering one's head is a relatively recent custom in Jewish history. It is not a commandment explicitly written in the Torah, nor is it collectively required by talmudic law. However, biblical references to covering one's head do exist. The high priests kept their heads covered while working in the sanctuary. (Exodus 28: 4, 37, 40.) In biblical times, covering one's head was also a sign of mourning. (II Samuel 15:30, 19:5; Jeremiah 13:3, 4; Esther 6:12.)

During the period of the Talmud, the custom was mainly restricted to dignified personages. Several reasons for covering one's head are given in the Talmud:

1. As an expression of awe before G-d, especially during prayer and the study of Torah (*Hagigah* 14b, *Rosh Hashana* 17b, *Ta'anit* 20a).

2. As an indication of elevated position among scholars (*Pesachim* 11b).

3. To ensure the piety of a child and prevent his becoming a thief (*Shabbat* 156b).

Some sages did not walk even four steps with an uncovered head (*Shabbat* 118b, *Kiddushin* 31a). However, a talmudic statement still maintained that head coverings were optional and a matter of custom (*Nedarim* 30b).

The opinions as to the obligation of covering one's head vary. While the Palestinian custom did not require the head to be covered during the priestly benediction, the Babylonian custom upheld the covering of the priest's head while performing this function. (Joel Mueller, *Hilluf Minhagim*, No. 44.) The practice of covering one's head while performing a religious duty was thus originally introduced in Babylonia. This *minhag* was ultimately transferred to Western European Jewish communities when the Babylonian Jews moved there during the eighth century. There was widespread acceptance of the custom among the Sephardic communities, particularly those situated in Spain. In the twelfth century, Maimonides wrote in the *Guide to the Perplexed*, "One should not bare his head for even four steps or within his home." In *Hilchot Dei'ot* 85:6, he wrote, "The great sages conducted themselves with an extra measure of modesty by not baring their heads." In the sixteenth century, the *Shulchan Aruch*, also a product of Sephardic Jewry, Rabbi Yosef Karo cites certain authorities that forbade mentioning the name of G-d or entering a synagogue with an uncovered head. He recommends that one should cover his head at all times as an act of piety. (*Orach Hachayim* 8:282.)

This *minhag* did not spread as quickly among the Ashkenazic communities of Eastern Europe. These Jewish communities were influenced by the Palestinian tradition. In the thirteenth century, Rabbi Meir of Rothenburg said that "bareheadedness was not forbidden," and in the sixteenth century, Solomon Luria was quoted as saying that "praying with one's head uncovered was not prohibited." It was not until the seventeenth century that covering one's head gained a significant foothold among Ashkenazim. David HaLevy of Ostrog quoted the sixteenth century Rav Moshe Isserles and claimed a biblical basis for head coverings because of *hukkat hagoyim*, the prohibition of following the practices of other nations. Since Christians usually prayed with bare heads, it is the Jewish obligation not to imitate them and therefore to accept the custom of covering the head. Despite this affirmation, there were still those who dissented. In the eighteenth century, the Vilna Gaon denied the precedent that praying or entering a synagogue with one's head covered is rooted in Jewish law, but maintained that since the *minhag* is "a matter of propriety . . . it would seem to be good manners to cover one's head when standing in the presence of great men and also during the religious service."

In the nineteenth century, the *minhag* finally gained the rigidity of law throughout the Orthodox Jewish world. One of the divisive factors between Reform and Orthodox Jewry now exists over the issue of covering one's head. The Reform Jews argue that since the Western world calls for the uncovered head as proper decorum and good manners, the custom of covering one's head should be abolished. The Orthodox maintain that the covered head shows allegiance to Jewish tradition. Not only is it a symbol of humility before G-d, but it also serves to immediately identify the Jew both to his fellow Jew and to strangers.

Nowadays, Orthodox Jewish men and boys wear many

different forms of attire to cover their heads, from a *streimel* to a baseball cap. The original priestly headgear was the *mitznefet*, which Rashi describes as "a kind of tall, arched cap." Very little is known about the headdress of the ancient Israelites. The turbans and hats they wore most probably resembled those worn by the Assyrians and Babylonians of the time, which in turn influenced the styles of the East and the Orient. Since the Moslems wore turbans in Spain, the eighth century Jews retained the Babylonian-style hats to remain different. The dress of later Ashkenazic communities became more distinct. The garb of Polish and Russian upper classes was adopted by the Jews. By the eighteenth century, their costume included a skullcap (yarmulke), a cap with ear flaps (*lappenmutze* or *klapove bitl*), a high fur hat trimmed with plush fur (*spodik*), or one made of sable (*kolpak*). A silk skullcap (*mosalka*) and a fur cap (*dichowny*) were common among Hasidim. In Galicia, the *streimel* was popularly worn on the Sabbath. The *streimel* is a saucer shaped hat with a flat fur brim. Many Hasidim continue to wear the *streimel* on the Sabbath, although plainer hats are more prevalent. It is the yarmulke, however, which is the most common of head-coverings among the Orthodox.

The yarmulke gained national attention in the Goldman suit. The case began in April 1981 on the Pease Air Force Base in California, where Rabbi Simcha Goldman had served as a clinical psychologist. Rabbi Goldman served as a Navy chaplain for two years until 1979, when he completed a doctorate in psychology under the Armed Forces Health Professions Scholarship Program.

He then entered the Air Force as a clinical psychologist, where he consistently received outstanding performance ratings. For three years he wore a yarmulke on duty without objection. In 1981, after Captain Goldman testified as a defense witness in a military trial, he was ordered to remove his yarmulke while on duty or face a court-martial. The Base commander claimed that wearing a yarmulke was a violation of the Air Force dress code (regulation AFR 35-10 states that "headgear will not be worn . . . while indoors"). Goldman claimed that the First Amendment secured his right to wear a yarmulke as a "free exercise of religion." Captain Goldman, represented by COLPA (National Jewish Commission on Law and Public Affairs) attorneys Nathan Lewin and David Butler, took the case to federal district court. District Judge Aubrey E. Robinson, Jr. concluded in Goldman's favor that the Captain's wearing of a yarmulke did not adversely affect his performance and was protected by the Constitution. The Air Force appealed to the Court of Appeals, D.C. Circuit, which reversed the district court's ruling on the grounds that the "Air Force's interest in uniformity renders the strict enforcement of its regulation permissible" even against free exercise rights. The decision stated that the military had absolute power to determine the uniform of its personnel, because it encourages a sense of unity and necessary subordination.

The case was then taken to the U.S. Supreme Court. In a 5-4 decision, the Supreme Court upheld the Court of Appeals ruling. The majority opinion, written by then-Associate Justice William H. Rehnquist, maintained that the "desirability of dress regulations in the military is decided by the appropriate constitutional mandate to abandon their considered professional judgment . . . The First Amendment therefore does not prohibit them from being applied to petitioner even though the effect is to restrict the wearing of the headgear required by his religious beliefs."

Associate Justice John Paul Stevens concurred with the majority opinion and expressed the fear that "the very strength of Captain Goldman's claim creates the danger that a similar claim on behalf of a Sikh or a Rastafarian might readily be dismissed. For the difference between a turban or a dreadlock on the one hand, and a yarmulke on the other . . . is also the difference between a Sikh or a Rastafarian, on the one hand, and an Orthodox Jew on the other." It would be hard, Justice Stevens reasoned, for the Air Force to deny more obvious exceptions to the dress code, such as a turban, without seeming to play favoritism among religions.

Dissenting from the majority were Associate Justices William J. Brennan, Jr., Thurgood Marshall, Harry A. Blackmun, and Sandra Day O'Connor. Justice Brennan led a forcible dissent in favor of the yarmulke and wrote, "The Court's response to Goldman's request is to abdicate its role as principal expositor of the Constitution and protector of individual liberties . . . It is the lack of any reasoned basis for prohibiting yarmulkes that is so striking here." Justice Brennan concluded with the realization that "The Court and the military services have presented patriotic Orthodox Jews with a painful dilemma—the choice between fulfilling a religious obligation and serving their country. . . . The Court and the military have refused these servicemen their constitutional rights; we must hope that Congress will correct this wrong."

Though Justice Brennan did suggest the possibility of congressional intervention, the "yarmulke case" will always remain as a reminder of the "painful dilemma" that Jews are often confronted with. As the yarmulke itself serves only as a reminder of man's position before G-d, it is that position itself which must ultimately be resolved.

Final Note: In August 1986, the U.S. Senate defeated, by a vote of 51-49, an amendment that would have allowed Jewish members of the military to wear yarmulkes if it did not interfere with the performance of their military duty. The bill had been introduced by Senators Frank Lautenberg (D., N.J.) and Alphonse D'Amato (R., N.Y.).

The Brandeis-Bardin Institute: Teaching Jews to Ask *Why* to Be Jewish

For over forty-five years, the Brandeis-Bardin Institute has been dedicated to the perpetuation of the Jewish people. It has stimulated and inspired tens of thousands of Jews of all ages and from all religious backgrounds to rediscover their Judaism. Thousands have been motivated to return to their community as Jewish leaders.

The Brandeis-Bardin Institute has a rich history and a promising future. Founder Dr. Shlomo Bardin met Justice Louis D. Brandeis in the 1930s while he was pursuing his doctorate in education at Columbia University. Justice Brandeis passionately voiced his concern over the assimilation of young American Jews. Dr. Bardin became his ally and the end result was an innovative attempt to blend American summer camps (which emphasized recreation in a nature setting), the Danish Folke schule (which stresses cultural activities like dance, music, art and drama) and the kibbutz (which utilized group living and physical work on the land). Dr. Bardin tightly tied the three together with a dedication to living Judaism.

The first camp was started in Amherst, New Hampshire with subsequent locations in Winterdale, Pennsylvania and Hendersonville, North Carolina. Motivated by their daughters' impressive Brandeis experience, Molly and Julius Fligelman brought Dr. Bardin to Southern California. In 1947, the Institute found its permanent home covering 3200 acres in the lush, secluded countryside of Simi Valley.

BCI, the Institute's college program, is still the only program of its kind in the world. BCI provides the opportunity for college-aged men and women to enjoy an intensive month-long experience in Jewish living. Between fifty-five and seventy-five specially selected, outstanding young people from the United States and around the world attend one of the two month-long leadership building sessions.

This experience has a tremendous impact on a young person's life. Studies conducted by the Department of Sociology at the University of California at Los Angeles confirm the programs life-long effect. Of 8,000 alumni, many of them are Jewish leaders in communities throughout the world.

Also, during the summer months, the Institute is filled with energy and excitement. Hundreds of impressionable youngsters are exploring Judaism through art, dance, music, study and prayer at Camp Alonim. Camp Alonim (the Hebrew word for "Oaks") provide these young people with a unique opportunity to experience Judaism in an eye-opening, senses-awakening atmosphere.

U.S. Supreme Court Justice Louis D. Brandeis.

From September through June, individuals age 25 and older are welcomed to attend one of the many introductory weekends. These weekends are specially designed for single and married adults who are interested in an inspirational and experiential introduction or reintroduction to Judaism. The weekends are conducted by leading Jewish scholars who utilize study, music, dance, art, lecture and prayer to address the question "Why be Jewish?" Over 12,000 people have attended introductory weekends since their beginning.

Attendance at an introductory weekend enables an individual or couple to join the Institute and participate in the "House of the Book" weekends. Fifteen hundred people

Dr. Shlomo Bardin.

belong to HOB and participate in the weekend and Shabbat afternoon lectures which are led by internationally renowned scholars, theologians, artists and performers such as Rabbi Shlomo Riskin, Prof. Alan Dershowitz and Theodore Bikel.

Brandeis-Bardin, also has special Rikud dance weekends led by some of the world's greatest dancers and choreographers and family Shabbat Weekends with innovative programming for parents and children.

The uniqueness of Brandeis-Bardin

• Brandeis-Bardin emphasizes *why* to be Jewish over *how* to be Jewish. Nearly every Jewish institution teaches the hows of Jewish life, how to fund Jewish causes, how to combat antisemitism, how to support Israel, how to read Hebrew, how to pray, etc. But Jews today are not alienated from Judaism primarily because they lack the knowledge of how to be Jewish. They are alienated because they have little reason why to be Jewish. Why bother to be different? Why bother with a commitment to ethical monotheism? Brandeis-Bardin offers answers to these questions.

• Brandeis-Bardin does not merely explain Judaism. It advocates Judaism.

• The goal of Brandeis-Bardin is not to fund Jewish causes, or to defend Jewish interests, but to make committed Jews out of the uncommitted and Jewish leaders out of the committed. People who come to Brandeis-Bardin move on—in startling numbers—to become the leaders, defenders, and supporters of Jewry and society at large.

• Brandeis-Bardin teaches Jews to live with themselves and with others as Jews. The Institute's goal is to create Jews whose lives manifest Jewish values in relating to the non-Jewish as well as to the Jewish world.

• Brandeis-Bardin addresses its message to all of society and not only to Jews. Judaism and the Jewish mission to improve the world through ethical monotheism are the primary concerns. Only when Jews take Judaism seriously will non-Jews take the Jewish people seriously.

• Brandeis-Bardin does not dismember Judaism. At the Institute, Judaism in its totality is advocated and experienced.

• A Jew is a member of a people and of a religion—not just one or the other. Both are emphasized.

• Brandeis-Bardin neither affiliates with nor advocates any particular Jewish denomination. It is not Reform, nor Conservative, nor Orthodox. Nor is it secular. It is Jewish.

• Brandeis-Bardin is a passionate place; love, warmth, and human support pervade all its activities. "Love thy neighbor" is not a biblical cliche; it is the core operating principle of Judaism and the Brandeis-Bardin Institute.

The Brandeis-Bardin Institute in Simi Valley, California.

Toward a Jewish Lingua Franca

Irwin Shaw

It was just a hundred years ago that Eliezer Ben Yehuda began his efforts to make spoken Hebrew the official language of the Jewish settlers in Eretz Israel.

While great Zionist leaders like Smolenskin and Herzl could envision a Jewish homeland without Hebrew as its mother tongue, and while Orthodox Jews objected to any secular use of Hebrew, Ben Yehuda made spoken Hebrew a national goal. It was not an easy campaign. As late as 1913 there was still serious debate whether German or Hebrew should be the language of instruction at the Technion. A milestone was reached in 1919 when Ben Yehuda and Menachem Ussishkin prevailed upon Herbert Samuel, the British High Commissioner, to declare Hebrew one of the official languages of the country.

Ben Yehuda did not limit his vision of a national language only to the Jews of Palestine. As early as 1879, he spoke of the establishment of a community in Eretz Israel that would be a focal point for all Jews, so that even those who would remain in the Diaspora would know that "they belonged to a people that dwells in its own land and has its own language and culture."

Ben Yehuda's dream of spoken Hebrew as the language of Eretz Israel has now of course been realized. But his broader goal to make Hebrew the lingua franca of the Jewish people has not been—nor does seem likely to be—in the foreseeable future.

If there *is* a lingua franca of the Jews of the world today, it is English—the lingua franca of most of the world. As the writer Cynthia Ozick has noted, English has become for most Jews the "new Yiddish," and for perhaps 60 percent of all Jews, English is their *first* language. She recognizes the powerful connection between language and culture, between language and cultural identity:

> . . . although we address ourselves inwardly, by virtue of the language, we also address ourselves outwardly. We have ears that are not Jewish, listening; and . . . we inevitably, unconsciously, address ourselves to those ears too. And that's not because we are looking to please them, but because we are assimilated. Because insofar as we use the language of their culture, we also belong to it. (Quoted in *Present Tense,* Summer 1982)

The continuing secularization of Jews throughout the world, and the Jews' increasing use of English as their primary language for everyday communication, means that neither religion nor language is any longer the principal instrument of identification it once was. Today, Jewish identity for a majority of Jews is expressed principally through their support of the State of Israel.

Noble as this expression may be, there is in the long run something fundamentally unhealthy about a relationship that is based largely on a sense of either fear or dependency. If, God willing, peace would come "quickly and in our day" to Israel, what will be left to bind together the Jews of the Diaspora and the Jews of Israel?

It is doubtful whether, in the near future, the Jewish religion by itself will to any great extent serve this purpose. In fact, religious sectarianism has already resulted in a good deal of conflict and divisiveness. Language on the other hand, because it is politically and religiously neutral, *could* serve as a binding force between the Jews of Israel and the Jews of the Diaspora, just as it now unifies the great variety of Jews within Israel itself.

But why hasn't spoken Hebrew become the lingua franca of world Jewry, even though many efforts have been made since the establishment of the State to encourage the learning of Hebrew in the Diaspora? While there are a number of obvious barriers to the achievement of this goal, it is perhaps that *the single most serious obstacle is the orthography of modern Israeli Hebrew.*

Early Attempts at Reform

When the use of written Hebrew was limited solely to the Bible and the Siddur (books that hardly ever changed and were more "memorized" than read), the language was printed with Tiberian "pointing." In this system, vowels are indicated by dots and other marks located above, in front of, and underneath the consonants (the only "real" letters). This system not only requires expertise in "pointing," but it is also terribly cumbersome to typeset.

With the advent of modern spoken Hebrew and the concomitant publication of daily newspapers, magazines and books in Hebrew, the cost of printing with Tiberian "points" became prohibitive. The Israelis found a simple (if procrustean) solution to this problem: They simply dropped all the vowel signs. In solving the problem of printing, however, they created a more serious problem in reading, which moved Beryl Katzenelson to write:

> How pathetic is a language which requires that a person must first know it perfectly before he can try to read it—something which does not obtain for any other language. (*Hatsefirah,* Sept. 2, 1913)

If one must first have command of a language in order to read it, how then can one use *reading* to gain this command? Ze'ev Jabotinsky complained about this "catch-22" more than fifty years ago when he wrote:

> Take a man who studies French: After he has acquired his first 500 or 600 words from his textbooks or from his lessons, he takes an easy and interesting book or a daily

> paper and tries to enrich his knowledge by reading. . . . But where self-study of another language is easy, in Hebrew it is exceedingly difficult. . . . As long as we have this difference between "letters" and "pointing," we shall have stenography. That, however, is for stenographers, not for the masses of a nation. (*Ha'arets,* June 28, 1925)

Jabotinsky's reference to the "Stenographic" nature of Hebrew orthography can be illustrated with the (English) shorthand system known as "Speedwriting." In this system, only the consonants are written; thus (for example) the "st" notation might stand for sit, sat, seat, suite, soot, set, etc., depending on the context. Obviously, since the writer—who is also the transcriber—is aware of the context, the reconstruction is not very difficult. But it *would* be difficult for any *other* reader/transcriber who did not record the original text. The fact is that one does not in any case actually 'read" Speedwriting, one "decodes" it.

This is the problem with modern printed Hebrew. And this problem was recognized as such quite early on by official and semi-official language organizations. They tried to mitigate the problem by introducing a few modifications. For example, they doubled the vowel "yod" to represent the consonant "y"; and they doubled the vowel "vav" to represent the consonant "v" (and also, for transliteration, the letter "w").

These and similar modifications have proved to be only moderately helpful, and over the years many other suggestions were put forth for the adoption of a comprehensive, "one symbol/one sound" system.

One such system would have replaced the Hebrew alphabet entirely, in favor of the Roman alphabet. This was proposed in the 1920s and '30s by men like Ze'ev Jabotinsky and Ittamar ben Avi (the son of Eliezer ben Yehuda). This approach had the great practicality that it could take advantage of existing printing and typing equipment, and that it articulated well with the presentation of scientific and technical data. But the emotional opposition to discarding the Hebrew script was (and remains) too great to overcome, and the approach met with no success.

Most of the other suggestions for orthographic reform involved totally new designs for the Hebrew letters or the addition of new symbols to the existing alphabet. While these proposals were (from the printer's and typesetter's viewpoint) an improvement over the Tiberian "pointing" system, their adoption would have in every case required tremendous investment in new printing equipment. More important, however, these systems would have required everyone to learn a totally new alphabet. There was thus never any real possibility that any of them could be widely accepted.

Because each of these systems had its own drawback, no agreement could be reached on any of them. The situation exemplified Voltaire's observation of how often "the best is the enemy of the good." The result is that the reform of Hebrew orthography has remained in a state of arrested development for decades.

A Modern Approach to Reform

Hebrew language experts had long been aware of the language's problems. But it is precisely because they *are* experts that most of them never experience the kind of trauma felt by most non-Israelis, by most *olim* (immigrants) and by less well-educated Israelis in trying to read "unpointed" Hebrew. (There is the story of the new *oleh* who asked his boss for a day off to read the newspaper—because it took him all day to do so!) As a result, the experts aren't highly motivated to champion even those improvements in the present orthography that *would* be feasible and would not involve the wholesale transmutation of the alphabet.

What are some of these "painlessly correctable" problems? Among them we would single out three in particular as perhaps the first to be addressed. All three have been identified by intermediate level Hebrew students as their main sources of wasted effort and frustration.

1. Foreign Words or Words of Foreign Derivation. It is most frustrating to try to read (i.e., decipher) an unrecognized Hebrew word—applying all the analytical rules for Hebrew grammar—only to find after much wasted effort that it is not a Hebrew word at all, but a foreign word rendered in Hebrew transliteration. There is nothing to alert the reader that the usual translation clues and paradigms will be of no help.

2. Proper Names and Adjectives Derived from Them. In English (as in most languages using the Roman alphabet), proper names are immediately distinguishable because they are capitalized. Since there are no capital letters in Hebrew, the reader/decoder is, again, thrown off track.

3. Prefixes. To find the meaning of a word in the dictionary, you must first know how the word is spelled. In Hebrew this can sometimes be very difficult because of Hebrew's frequent use of prefixes. Hebrew employs prefixes to express the conjunction "and," the definite article "the," the interrogative indicator "hey," and a number of prepositions, such as "in," "to," "from," and so on. There can be three or four such prefixed letters in front of the root word—as in, for example, the word "oo-mey-ha-bayit," meaning "and from the house." This often makes it difficult for the reader to determine where the prefixes end and the root word—the one he can find in the dictionary—begins.

What can be done to help the beginning-to-intermediate reader of unpointed Hebrew overcome these three hurdles? Actually, a quite practical answer has existed for some time. It simply hasn't been recognized for the powerful, reading-simplification tool that it is.

In 1922, the forerunner agency of the present Academy of the Hebrew Language solved the problem of transliterating consonant sounds that do not exist in Hebrew simply by adding an apostrophe (the "geresh" in Hebrew) to an approximate Hebrew letter. Thus, to express the English "j" sound, an apostrophe is added to the Hebrew "gimmel"; to express the English "ch" sound (as in "lunch"), an apostrophe is added to the Hebrew "tzadi." What was so delightful about this solution was that it was so easy and clear, and made use of an already existing and readily available typographic symbol.

The same approach could be applied to the solution of the three problems we have outlined here, and it could ultimately be systematized into an easily implemented "Augmented Hebrew Orthography" (AHO) that applies some of the ideas of the early reformers.

It would be a simple intervention, for example, to precede every foreigh word in a Hebrew text with the solidus

(/). Every proper noun and the adjectives derived from proper nouns could be preceded by a left-parenthesis—"(". And prefixes could be indicated simply by inserting a comma (,) between the prefix letter(s) and the main word (a semicolon would be used for a prefix normally "pointed" with the "sheva" and located immediately before the main word).

All three of these "solutions" would employ symbols already available on present-day typesetting equipment. None would involve any special line-spacing, word-spacing or letter-spacing. None would entail any confusion with the conventional uses of the chosen symbols. And all could be readily and easily assimilated by Hebrew readers at any level of competency.

An additional element of an Augmented Hebrew Orthography would be the use of the colon (:) to indicate certain syllabication. For example, the colon could be used after every non-final letter which (if it were "pointed") would have a "sheva" under it. While this would add somewhat to the word length, it would be a small price to pay for the increased clarity that would result.

An even further extention of the AHO would be the use of the apostrophe after each of the four Hebrew letters whose pronunciation in regular "pointing" would be determined by the "dagesh" (dot) within the body of the letter—i.e., the "bet," the "kaf," the "pay" and the "shuruk." The apostrophe could similarly be used to distinguish the "sin" from the "shin," and—in conjunction with the double "vav"—to designate the English "w" sound (as distinguished from the "v" sound in Hebrew).

Can It Work?

Samples of newspaper articles that have been re-written at various levels of orthographic augmentation have been tested with groups of students at the intermediate level of Hebrew instruction. The additional functions assigned to the six punctuation marks were easily assimilated. The students found that their reading time was reduced significantly by the addition of these symbols.

There remained the question of what effect augmentation would have on those who already can read standard unpointed Hebrew with facility. In November of 1982, a sample of material prepared according to AHO was presented to a group of thirty Israeli *shelichim*. No explanation was given for the presence of the additional punctuation marks. The subjects were asked simply to disregard the marks as they read the material. The unanimous reaction of the *shelichim* was that they experienced no palpable difficulty whatever—although a few indicated some slight irritation until they got used to "not seeing" the additional marks.

The simplicity and the logic of the AHO system was further confirmed when a number of the *shelichim* deduced on their own the nature and function of the added marks. Several subjects expressed the idea that the use of AHO would prove helpful even for those who can read unpointed Hebrew well.

It is, finally, immaterial whether the particular augmentation system we have described here is adopted—or whether a modification of it or some wholly different system is used. But while an augmented Hebrew orthography won't guarantee Hebrew's evolution into a Jewish lingua franca, the absence of an improved orthography *virtually guarantees that this will never happen.*

For centuries, Yiddish was the lingua franca of most of the Jews of the world. As recently as fifty years ago, more than 10 million Jews spoke Yiddish. Could it be that one of the important reasons for the universality of Yiddish was that its orthography was so simple that even five-year-olds were able to read it?

There will be those who will feel that the case for Hebrew as the lingua franca of the Jewish people is either impractical or impossible. I would only remind these critics of Rabbi Solomon Schechter's admonition that "the Jews of America cannot live without English but will not survive without Hebrew"—a truism that applies, *mutatis mutandis,* to all the Jews of the Diaspora.

Augmented Hebrew Orthography (AHO) (A Proposal)

The purpose of AHO is to improve the readability of "unpointed" Hebrew orthography, i.e., Hebrew printed without vowel signs. AHO augments regular "unpointed" material with seven standard punctuation marks, each of which has been assigned an additional function. They cannot be confused with their standard functions because of their location in the augmented word.

While AHO does not provide the specificity of full vocalization, it does improve readability so that people with less than a full command of Hebrew can more effectively use AHO material for self-study and language improvement. The punctuation marks' new "signals" can quickly be learned and immediately understood by intermediate level students. (The accomplished reader can easily learn to disregard these marks if he or she wishes to.)

AUGMENTED HEBREW ORTHOGRAPHY (AHO)

Stage I

1. The comma—(,)

A comma is inserted between a word and its prefixes* if the prefix immediately before the word would *not* have a "sh'va" under it in "pointed" printing.

Example: from the roof—מה,גג

2. The semicolon—(;)

A semicolon is inserted between a word and its prefixes* if the prefix immediately before the word *would* have a "sh'va" under it in "pointed" printing.

Example: to a child—ל;ילד

3. The Left Parenthesis—(( )

The left parenthesis immediately precedes any *proper* noun and any adjective derived from a proper noun. (It replaces the comma or semicolon if a prefix precedes the noun; see #1 and #2 above.)

Example: Arabia—(ערב

4. The Solidus—(/)

The solidus immediately precedes all foreign words, including those which have been Hebraized. (It replaces the comma or the semicolon when a prefix precedes the word; see #1 and #2 above.)

Example: symptom—סימפטום/

5. The Colon—(:)

The colon is placed *after* each letter which, in "pointed" printing, has a "sh'va" under it. (It is not used after the final letter of a verb or when a semi-colon is used as in #2 above.)

Example: desert—מד:בר

Stage II

6. The Apostrophe—(')

The apostrophe is placed *after*

a. a "vav" to indicate the vowel "oo" ("shuruk" or "kooboots").

Example: stable—או'ר;וה

b. a double "vav" in transliterated words to express the English "w".

Example: walker—וו'יקר/

c. the letter "sin" to distinguish it from "shin."

Example: language—ש'פה

d. the three letters in which a "dagesh" would indicate that they are pronounced "bet," "kaf" and "pey" respectively.

Example: purity—זכ'ו'ת privilege—ז:כו'ת

Stage III

7. The Right Parenthesis—( ))

The right parenthesis is used only with verbs. It is used to separate the prefixes from the root (except for the prefix "lamed" which indicates the infinitive). The following examples illustrate how it may be used in various "binyonim" (conjugations):

he will learn—י)ל:מד
he will teach—י)למד
to enter—ל;ה)כ'נס
he entered—נ)כ:נס
he lights—מ)ד:ליק
he lit—ה)ד:ליק
he was invited—הו')ז:מן
he opposes—מת)נגד
to use—ל;הש)תמש
he uses—מש)תמש

*This does not apply to those prefixes which represent the personal pronouns in the future tense of verbs or those which indicate the verb's conjugational category ("binyon").

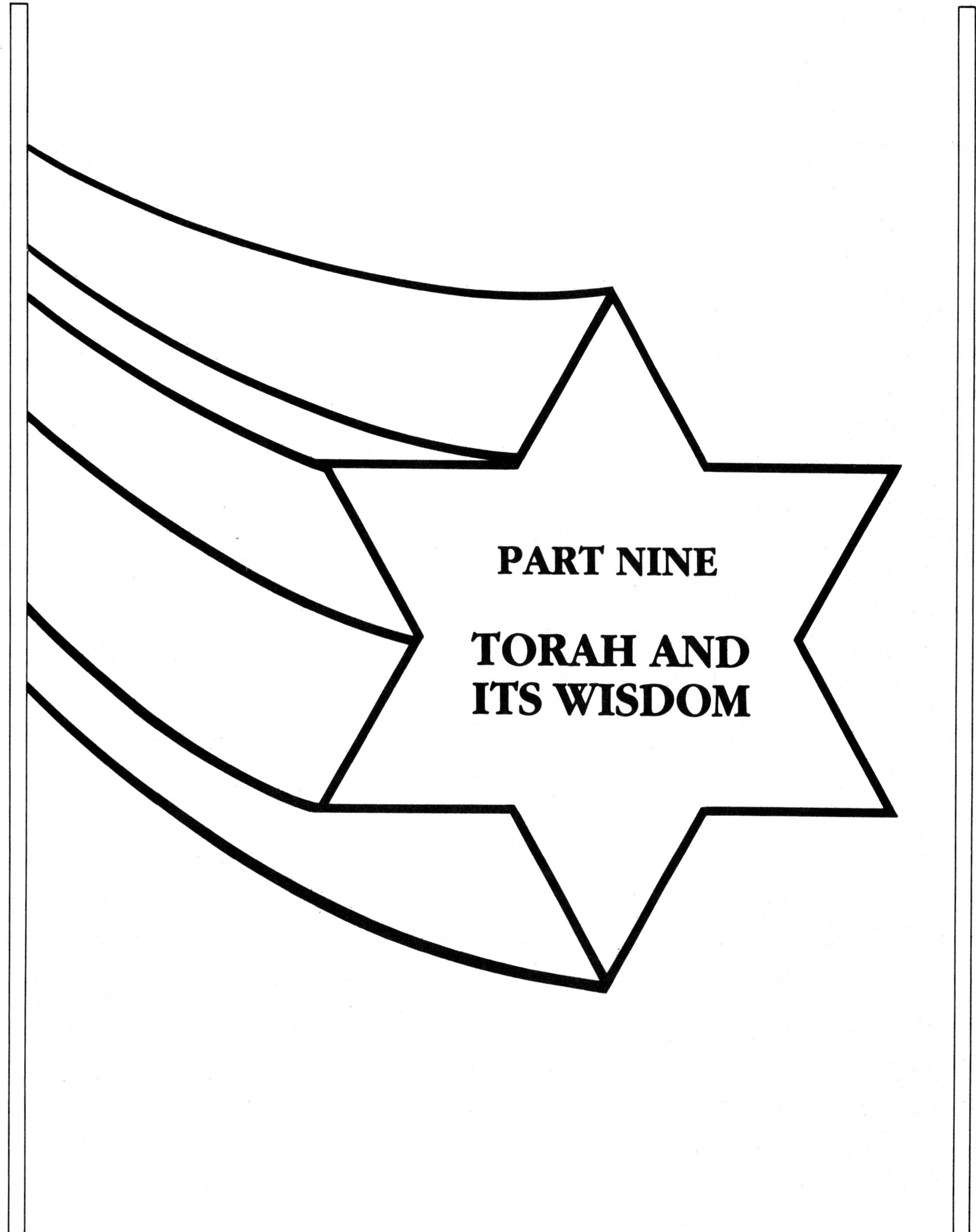

PART NINE

TORAH AND ITS WISDOM

Tanakh: The 24 Books of the Bible

The Law *(Torah)*—Pentateuch

	Chapters	Verses	Letters
Genesis	50	1534	78,064
Exodus	40	1209	63,529
Leviticus	27	859	44,790
Numbers	36	1288	63,530
Deuteronomy	34	955	54,892
	187	5845	304,805

The Prophets *(Nevi'im)*

Former Prophets

Joshua	24
Judges	21
I Samuel	31
II Samuel	24
I Kings	22
II Kings	25

Latter Prophets

	Chapters
Isaiah	66
Jeremiah	52
Ezekiel	48
The Twelve Prophets	
Hosea	14
Joel	4
Amos	9
Obadiah	1
Jonah	4
Micah	7
Nahum	3
Habakkuk	3
Zephaniah	3
Haggai	2
Zechariah	14
Malachi	3

The Writings *(Ketuvim)*—Hagiographa

Psalms	150
Proverbs	31
Job	42
Five Scrolls *(Megillot)*	
Song of Songs	8
Ruth	4
Lamentations	5
Ecclesiastes	12
Esther	10
Daniel	12
Ezra	10
Nehemiah	13
I Chronicles	29
II Chronicles	36

GENESIS

Chs. 1:1—11:32 Universal History

1—6 Creation. From Adam to Noah.

1:1—2:4a The story of Creation; the Sabbath.
2:4b—3:24 Adam and Eve in the Garden of Eden.
4:1—16 Cain and Abel.
4:17—26 The genealogy of Cain; the rise of civilization.
5:1—32 The line of Adam to Noah.
6:1—4 The "sons of God" and the daughters of men.

6—11 From Noah to Abraham.

6:5—8:32 The Flood.
9:1—17 The blessing and the covenant with man.
9:18—29 Noah's drunkenness.
10:1—32 The table of nations.
11:1—9 The Tower of Babel.
11:10—32 The line of Shem to Abraham.

12:1—50:26 Patriarchal History.

12—25 Abraham.

12:1—9 The call of Abraham; the migration to Canaan.
12:10—20 Abraham and Sarah in Egypt.
13:1—18 Abraham and Lot.
14:1—24 The battle of the kings; Abraham blessed by Melchizedek.
15.1—21 The covenant with Abraham.
16:1—16 Abraham, Sarah and Hagar; Divine promises regarding Ishmael.
17.1—27 The covenant concerning circumcision.
18:1—33 Abraham and the three messengers; the intercession for Sodom.
19:1—29 The destruction of Sodom and Gomorrah.
19:30—38 Lot and his daughters; the birth of Moab and Ammon.
20:1—18 Abraham and Sarah at Gerar.
21:1—8 The birth of Isaac.
21:9—21 The expulsion of Hagar and Ishmael
21:22—34 Abraham and Abimelech at Beer-Sheba.
22:1—19 The binding of Isaac *(Akedah).*
22:20—24 The line of Nahor.

Chs.	
23:1—20	The purchase of Machpelah and the burial of Sarah.
24:1—67	The marriage of Isaac to Rebekah.
25:1—6	The line of Keturah.
25:7—18	The death and burial of Abraham; the line of Ishmael.
25—36	**Isaac and Jacob.**
25:19—34	The birth of Jacob and Esau; the sale of the birthright.
26:1—33	Isaac, Rebekah and Abimelech at Gerar.
26:34—35	Esau's Hittite wives.
27:1—28:5	Jacob's deception of Isaac.
28:6—9	Esau's Ishmaelite wife.
28:10—22	Jacob at Bethel.
29:1—30:43	Jacob with Laban.
31:1—54	Jacob's flight from Laban.
32:1—32	Jacob at Mahanaim and Penuel; Jacob wrestles with the angel.
33:1—20	Jacob meets Esau; his purchase of land at Shechem.
34:1—31	The rape of Dinah.
35:1—15	Jacob revisits Bethel.
35:16—29	Family affairs in Canaan.
36:1—43	The lines of Esau and Seir the Horite; early kings of Edom.
37—50	**Joseph and his brothers.**
37:1—36	Joseph and his brothers.
38:1—30	Judah and Tamar
39:1—23	Joseph in Potiphar's house.
40:1—23	Joseph in prison.
41:1—57	Pharaoh's dreams; Joseph's rise to power; the years of abundance and the start of the famine.
42:1—44:34	Joseph encounters his brothers.
45:1—28	Joseph discloses his identity.
46:1—47:10	The migration of the Israelites to Egypt.
47:11—27	Joseph's agrarian policy.
48:1—50:21	Jacob's farewell blessings; his death and burial.
50:22—26	The death of Joseph.

EXODUS

1:1—18:27	**The Liberation**
1:1—2:25	The enslavement of Israel and the advent of Moses.
3:1—7:13	The call and commissioning of Moses.
7:14—11:10	The plagues.
12:1—13:16	Firstborn plague and Passover rite.
13:17—15:21	The miracle at the sea.
15:22—17:16	Trouble and deliverance on the way to Sinai.
18:1—27	Jethro's visit and the organization of the people.
19:1—24:18	**The Covenant**
19:1—20:21	The theophany at Mt. Sinai and the Decalogue.
20:22—23:33	Rules and admonitions.
24:1—18	The Covenant ceremony
25:1—40:38	**The Tabernacle and the Golden Calf**
25:1—27:19	Orders to build the Tabernacle.
27:20—31:18	Activities and actors in the Sanctuary.
32:1—34:35	The Golden Calf.
35:1—40:38	Building the Tabernacle.

LEVITICUS

Chs.	
1:1—7:38	**The sacrificial system.**
1:1—2	General introduction.
1:3—17	The whole offering *(Olah).*
2:1—16	The tribute (cereal) offering *(minhah).*
3:1—17	The well-being offering *(shelamim).*
4:1—35	The purification offering *(hatta'at).*
5:1—13	Borderline cases requiring the purification offering.
5:14—26	The reparation offering *(asham).*
6:1—7:38	Supplementary instructions on sacrifices.
8:1—10:20	**The inaugural service at the sanctuary.**
8:1—36	The installation of the priests.
9:1—24	The priests assume office.
10:1—11	The sin of Nadab and Abihu.
10:12—20	The consumption of the initiatory offerings.
11:1—16:34	**The laws of impurities.**
11:1—47	Animal impurities.
12:1—8	The impurity of childbirth.
13:1—14:57	The impurity of skin diseases (leprosy).
15:1—33	The impurity of genital discharges.
16:1—34	The impurities of the sanctuary and the nation.
17:1—26:46	**The holiness source.**
17:1—16	Killing for food.
18:1—20:27	On being holy.
21:1—22:33	The disqualifications of priests and sacrifices.
23:1—44	The festivals.
24:1—23	Miscellanea.
25:1—26:46	The Sabbatical and Jubilee Years.
27:1—34	Communtation of gifts to the sanctuary.

NUMBERS

1:1—4:20	**The organization of the camp.**
1:1—54	The census of the tribes.
2:1—34	The position of the tribes in the camp.
3:1—20	The Levites taken to assist the priests.
5:1—6:27	Various laws.
7:1—89	The consecration of the altar.
8:1—10:10	Various laws.
10:11—22:1	From Mt. Sinai to the border of Canaan.
10:11—11:35	Setting out for Canaan.
12:1—16	Miriam's leprosy.
13:1—14:45	The 12 spies sent to Canaan.
15:1—41	Regulations concerning offerings.
16:1—17:28	The rebellion of Korah, Dathan, and Abiram.
18:1—19:22	Regulations concerning priests and Levites.
20:1—22:1	Israel at Kadesh.
22:2—24:25	Various events at the border of Canaan, and various laws.
22:2—24:25	The story of Balaam.
25:1—19	Israel at Shittim.
26:1—65	The second census.
27:1—11	The law of inheritance of daughters of Zelophehad.
27:12—14	Moses commanded to view Canaan before his death.
27:15—23	Joshua selected as Moses' successor.
28:1—29:39	A priestly calendar of sacrifices for each season.
30:1—17	The law of vows.
31:1—54	The war of vengeance against Midian.

Chs. 32:1—42	Allotment of Transjordanian region.
33:1—49	The journey from Raamses to the steppes of Moab.
33:50-56	Directions concerning the occupation of Canaan.
34:1—15	The borders of Israel's territory west of the Jordan.
34:16—29	A list of Joshua's assistants for the allotment of the territory.
35:1—34	Levitical cities and cities of refuge.
36:1—13	Laws for female heirs.

DEUTERONOMY

1—32	**The Covenant before entering Canaan.**
1—11	Prologue and exhortation.
1:1—5	Historical Introduction.
1:6—4:43	Moses' Introductory discourse.
4:44—11:32	The second discourse.
12—28	**The Deuteronomic code of laws.**
12:1—31	Ceremonial laws.
13:1—19	Injunction against idolatry.
14:1—2	Pagan mourning rites.
14:3—21	Clean and unclean food.
14:22—29	Tithes.
15:1—18	Year of release.
15:19—23	Firstling offerings.
16:1—17	Holy seasons.
16:18—17:13	Appointment of judges and supreme tribunal.
17:14—20	Election of a king.
18:1—18	Rights and revenues of priests and Levites.
19:1—13	Homicide.
19:14	Encroachment on property.
19:15—21	False testimony.
20:1—26:15	Various laws.
26:16—19	Epilogue.
27:1—28:69	Ceremonial blessing and cursing.
29—32	Appendices.
29:1—30:20	Moses' third discourse.
31:1—50	The appointment of Joshua.
32:1—52	The song of Moses.
33—34	**Moses' blessing and his death.**
33:1—29	Moses; blessing.
34:1—12	Moses' death.

JOSHUA

1:1—12:24	**The Conquest of Canaan.**
1:1—5:12	Crossing the Jordan.
5:13—8:35	First conquests (Jericho, Ai).
9:1—10:27	Success in south-central Canaan.
10:28—43	Southern campaign.
11:1—15	Northern campaign.
11:16—12:24	Summary of conquest.
13:1—21:43	**Allotment of the land.**
13:1—7	Land still unconquered.
13:8—33	Inheritance of Transjordanian tribes.
14:1—19:51	Allotment of Canaan.
20:1—9	Cities of refuge.
21:1—43	Levitical cities.
Chs. 22:1—34	**Departure of Transjordanian tribes.**
23:1—24:33	**Joshua's last days.**
23:1—16	Joshua's farewell address.
24:1—28	Covenant at Shechem.
24:29—31	Death and burial of Joshua.
24:32—33	Two burial traditions. Joseph's at Shechem. Eleazar's at Gibeah.

JUDGES

1:1—2:5	**Completion of the conquest.**
2:6—3:6	Introduction to the careers of the judges.
3:7—11	Othniel.
3:12—30	Ehud.
3:31	Shamgar.
4:1—5:31	Deborah and Barak (and Jael).
6:1—8:35	Gideon (Jerubbaal).
9:1—57	Abimelech.
10:1—5	Tola and Jair.
10:6—16	Introduction to later judges.
10:17—12:7	Jephthah.
12:8—15	Ibzan, Elon and Abdon.
13:1—16:31	Samson.
17:1—21:25	Migration of Dan to the North and war against the Benjamites.

I & II SAMUEL

I Samuel

1:1—7:17	**Samuel.**
1:1—2:10	Samuel's birth and dedication to the Lord.
2:11—3:21	Announcement of doom of the priestly family of Eli.
4:1—22	Samuel's war against the Philistines at Aphek; the death of Eli and his sons.
5:1—6:21	The Ark in Philistia and its return.
7:1—17	Samuel's miraculous deliverance from the hands of the Philistines at Mizpah.
8:1—15:35	**Samuel and Saul.**
8:1—22	The people's demand for a king.
9:1—10:21	Saul in search of the lost asses; his anointment as king.
11:1—15	The battle of Jabesh-Gilead.
12:1—25	The "last words" of Samuel.
13:1—14:52	Saul's military campaigns against the Philistines.
15:1—35	The war against the Amalekites; the rejection of Saul.
16:1—31:13	**Saul and David.**
16:1—23	The anointment of David.
17:1—58	David and Goliath.
18:1—30	Saul's jealousy and his plan to kill David.
19:1—27:12	David as refugee.
28:1—31:13	The battle of Gilboa; the death of Saul and his sons.

II Samuel

Chs. 1:1—8:18	**David's rise to power.**
1:1—27	David sings a dirge over Saul and Jonathan.
2:1—32	David anointed in Hebron; Ish-Bosheth king of Israel.
3:1—5	David and his family in Hebron.
3:6—39	Abner, David, and Joab.
4:1—12	The death of Ish-Bosheth.
5:1—25	David becomes king of Israel; Jerusalem becomes the capital.
6:1—23	The Ark brought to Jerusalem.
7:1—29	Nathan's prophecy concerning the Temple.
8:1—18	Summary of David's wars; a list of his chief officials.
9:1—20:26	**Court history of David.**
9:1—13	David and Mephibosheth.
10:1—19	David's wars against the Ammonites.
11:1—27	David, Uriah, and Bath-Sheba.
12:1—24	Nathan denounces David concerning Uriah and Bath-Sheba; the birth of Solomon.
12:25—31	The end of the war against the Ammonites.
13:1—39	Amnon, Tamar, and Absalom.
14:1—33	Absalom's return to Jerusalem.
15:1—19:44	The rebellion of Absalom.
20:1—22	The rebellion of Sheba.
20:23—26	David's chief officials.
21:1—24:25	**Appendix concerning David's reign.**
21:1—14	The burial of Saul and his descendants.
21:15—22	David's heroes.
22:1—51	A psalm attributed to David (= Ps. 18).
23.1—7	The "last words" of David.
23.8—39	Summary of the feats of David's heroes.
24:1—25	The census of Israel.

I & II KINGS

1:1—11:43	**The Monarchy under David and Solomon.**
1:1—2:46	The end of David's reign and Solomon's accession.
3:1—10:29	The reign of Solomon.
11:1—43	The troubles of Solomon's reign and its end.
12:1-17:41	**The Divided Kingdom.**
12:1—24	The disruption of the Kingdom.
12:25—32	Significant events of the reign of Jeroboam I of Israel.
12:33—14:18	A prophetic tradition of the reign of Jeroboam.
14:19—16:34	Synchronistic history of Israel and Judah.
17:1—II Kings 10:31	The reign of Ahab and the fall of the House of Omri.
10:32—17:41	Synchronistic history of Judah and Israel.
Chs. 18:1—25:21	**Judah alone.**
18:1—20:21	The reign of Hezekiah.
21:1—26	The reigns of Manasseh and Amon.
22:1—23:30	The reign and reformation of Josiah.
23:31—35	The reign and removal of Jehoahaz.
23:36—25:21	The end of the Kingdom of Judah.
25:22—30	**Appendixes.**
25:22—26	The Mizpah incident.
25:27—30	The captive King Jehoiachin.

ISAIAH

1—12	Prophecies of reproof and consolation on Judah and Israel.
13—27	Oracles against the nations.
13:1—23:18	Oracles on the neighbors of Judah, on Babylonia, and on Egypt.
24:1—27:13	Universalistic prophecies and "apocalypses."
28—35	Prophecies of consolation and reproof on Judah.
36—39	Miracle stories of the Prophet.
40—66	A collection of consolation prophecies assigned to an anonymous exilic prophet (40—48, 49—57, 58—66).

JEREMIAH

1—6	Baruch's scroll.
1:1—19	The call of Jeremiah.
2:1—4:4	Indictment of the nation's sin.
4:5—6:30	The coming disaster "from the North."
7—10	First editorial addition to Baruch's scroll.
7:1—8:3	Temple sermons and appended sayings.
8:4—9:21	An incorrigible people and their tragic ruin.
9:22—10:16	Miscellaneous sayings.
10:17—25	An incorrigible people and their tragic ruin.
11—20	Second editorial addition to Baruch's scroll.
11:1—17	Preaching on the broken covenant.
11:18—12:6	Jeremiah's persecution by his relatives and fellow townsmen.
12:7—17	God expresses His sorrow for the dereliction of his people.
13:1—27	Parabolic vision of the linen waistcloth and attached sayings.
14:1—15:4	The time of drought and national emergency.
15:5—16:21	Oracles and confessions in poetry and prose.
17:1—27	Miscellany.
18:1—23	Jeremiah at the potter's house with attached sayings.
19:1—20:18	Prophetic symbolism and persecutions: further confessions.
21—24	Oracles concerning the House of David and the prophets.

Chs. 25	Oracles against foreign nations.
26—29	The biography of Jeremiah.
26:1—24	The "Temple sermon"; Jeremiah narrowly escapes death.
27:1—28:17	Events of 594 B.C.E.; The incident of the ox-yoke.
29:1—32	594 B.C.E.: Jeremiah and the exile in Babylon.
30—31	The "Book of Consolation."
32—44	The biography of Jeremiah.
32:1—33:26	Restoration of Judah and Jerusalem.
34:1—7	Words of Jeremiah as the Babylonian blockade tightens.
34:8-22	Incidents during lifting of siege.
35:1—19	Jeremiah and the Rechabites.
36:1—32	Incident of the scroll.
37:1—10	Incident during lifting of siege.
37:11—38:28	Jeremiah in prison.
39:1—40:6	Jeremiah's release from prison.
40:7—43:7	Assassination of Gedaliah and the flight to Egypt.
43:8—44:30	Jeremiah in Egypt.
45	Baruch.
46—51	Oracles against foreign nations.
52	The fall of Jerusalem.

EZEKIEL

1:1—3:21	The call of the prophet.
3:22—24:27	The doom of Judah and Jerusalem.
3:22—5:17	House arrest and dramatic representation of siege and punishment.
6:1—7:27	Prophecies against the mountains of Israel and the populations of the land.
8:1—11:25	A visionary transportation to Jerusalem.
12:1—20	Dramatic representation of the exile of Judah and its king.
12:21—14:11	On false prophets and the popular attitude toward prophecy.
14:12—23	No salvation through vicarious merit.
15:1—8	Parable of the vine wood.
16:1—63	Parable of the nymphomaniacal adulteress.
17:1—24	Parable of the two eagles.
18:1—32	God's absolute justice.
19:1—14	A dirge over the monarchy.
20:1—44	The compulsory new exodus.
21:1—37	The punishing sword: three oracles.
22:1—31	Unclean Jerusalem: three oracles.
23:1—49	The dissolute sisters. Oholah and Oholibah.
24:1—14	The filthy pot: a parable of Jerusalem.
24:15—27	Death of the prophet's wife.
25:1—32:32	Dooms against foreign nations.
25:1—17	Brief dooms against Ammon, Moab, Edom, and Philistia.
26:1—28:26	Doom against Phoenicia.
29:1—32:32	Seven oracles against Egypt.
33:1—33	A miscellany from the time of the fall.
34:1—39:29	Prophecies of Israel's restoration.
34:1—31	Replacement of the leadership of Israel.
35:1—36:15	Fate of Edom; redemption and repopulation of Israel.
36:16—38	A new heart and spirit; the condition of lasting possession of the land.
37:1—28	The revival of the dead bones of Israel and the unification of its two scepters.
38:1—39:29	The invasion of Gog and his fall.
40:1—48:35	A messianic priestly code.
40:1—43:12	A visionary transportation to the future temple.
43:13—46:24	Ordinances of the cult and its personnel.
Chs. 47:1—12	The life-giving stream issuing from the temple.
47:13—48:35	Allocation of the land.

THE TWELVE PROPHETS

Hosea	Israel's infidelity and future repentance.
Joel	Retribution and Israel's restoration at the end of days.
Amos	Prophecies against the nations; reproof; visions.
Obadiah	Oracle of doom on Edom.
Jonah	Message of repentance to Nineveh.
Micah	Moral rebukes; vision of the universal reign of peace.
Nahum	Prophecy of the downfall of Nineveh.
Habakkuk	The problem of injustice; prayer for compassion.
Zephaniah	Condemnation of idolatry; vision of restored Zion.
Haggai	Encouragement to build Second Temple; its role.
Zechariah	Visions of rebuilt Jerusalem and Divine rule of the universe.
Malachi	Moral exhortations; condemnation of intermarriage.

FIVE SCROLLS—*(Megillot)*

Song of Songs	Metaphoric love poetry.
Ruth	Narrative of period of the Judges.
Lamentations	Descriptive dirge of the Babylonian destruction of Jerusalem.
Ecclesiastes	Wisdom literature on worldly vanities.
Esther	The Purim story: the salvation of Jews in ancient Persia.

PSALMS

1:1—41:14	The first collection.
42:1—72:20	The second collection.
44:1—49:21	Korahite psalms.
56:1—60:14	"Michtam" psalms.
73:1—89:53	The third collection.
73:1—83:19	Asaphite psalms.
90:1—106:48	The fourth collection.
107:1—150:6	The fifth collection.
111:1—113:9	Hallelujah psalms.
114:1—118:29	Hallel psalms.
120:7—134:3	Songs of ascent.

PROVERBS

1-9	Didactic discourses and "wisdom poems."
10-22:16	First collection of "Solomonic Proverbs."
22:17-24:22	The "Thirty Precepts" of the Sages; other Sayings of the Sages.
25-29	Second collection of "Solomonic Proverbs," transmitted by Hezekiah's scribes.

Chs.	30:1-9	The skepticism of Agur, and a believer's reply.
	30:10-13	Warnings and numerical proverbs.
	31:1-9	A queen mother's diatribe.
	31:10-31	Acrostic poem on the capable housewife.

JOB

1:1—2:13	Prologue (in prose).
3:1—31:40	The dialogue or symposium.
32:1—37:24	The Elihu speeches.
38:1—42:6	The theophany and speeches of the Lord.
42:7—17	Epilogue (in prose).

DANIEL

1—6	Stories.
1:1—21	Daniel and His Friends.
2:1—49	Nebuchadnezzar's Dream.
3:1—30	The Furnace.
4:1—34	Nebuchadnezzar's Madness.
5:1—30	The Writing on the Wall.
6:1—29	Daniel in the Lion's Den.
7—12	Visions
7:1—28	The Four Beasts.
8:1—27	The Ram and the He-Goat.
9:1—27	The Seventy Weeks.
10:1—12:13	The Revelation of the Angel.

EZRA

1—6	The beginning of the return from Babylon and the reconstruction of the Temple.
1:1—11	The decree of Cyrus and the response of the Exile.
2:1—70	A list of those who returned under Zerubbabel.
3:1—13	Reestablishment of worship.
4:1—24	Building operations interrupted by Samaritan opposition.
5:1—6:22	Reconstruction of the temple carried out after clearance with Persian authorities.
7—10	Character and Achievements of Ezra.
7:1—10	Identification and journey to Jerusalem.
7:11—26	Ezra and Artaxerxes.
7:27—28	Ezra's praise of the Lord for his goodness.
8:1—14	List of the *golah* (repatriated exiles) who returned with Ezra.
8:15—20	Solicitation of Temple personnel.
8:21—23	Services of intercession before departure.
8:24—30	Selection of bearers for the sacred vessels and treasures.
8:31—36	Trip to and deliverance of vessels at Jerusalem.
9:1—10:44	The sin of the new community—marriage with outsiders.

NEHEMIAH

Chs.	1:1—13:3	Nehemiah's governorship of Judah.
	1:1—2:10	Nehemiah's concern about affairs in Judah.
	2:11—20	Nehemiah resolves to rebuild the walls of Jerusalem.
	3:1—4:17	Restoration of the walls.
	5:1—19	Community problems.
	6:1—7:3	Despite designs against Nehemiah the walls are finally completed.
	7:4—73	A list of those who returned with Zerubbabel.
	8:1—9:37	The Torah reading and worship services.
	10:1—40	Execution of a written and officially sealed covenant.
	11:1—36	Redistribution of Jews in Jerusalem and Judah.
	12:1—26	Clerical lists.
	12:27—43	Dedication of the newly reconstructed wall.
	12:44—13:3	Further religious concerns.
	13:4—31	Second period of Nehemiah's governorship of Judah.
	13:4—9	Events leading to the expulsion of Tobiah from the Temple.
	13:10—31	Further reforms of Nehemiah.

CHRONICLES—I & II

I Chron.		
	1:1—9:44	An introduction
	1:1—54	A collection of genealogical lists.
	2:1—9:1	Various lists of the Israelite tribes.
	9:2—18	A list of the inhabitants of Jerusalem.
	9:19—34	Detailed list of the Levitical functionaries.
	9:19—44	A list of the inhabitants of Gibeon.
	10:1— II 9:31	The monarchy under David and Solomon.
	10:1—29:30	David.
II Chron.		
	1:1—9:31	Solomon.
	10:1—36:23	History of the kings of Judah.
	10:1—12:16	The reign of Rehoboam.
	13:1—23	The reign of Abijah.
	14:1—16:14	The reign of Asa.
	17:1—20:37	The reign of Jehoshaphat.
	21:1—20	The reign of Jehoram.
	22:1—9	The reign of Ahaziah.
	22:10—23:21	The reign of Athaliah.
	24:1—27	The reign of Joash.
	25:1—28	The reign of Amaziah.
	26:1—23	The reign of Uzziah.
	27:1—9	The reign of Jotham.
	28:1—27	The reign of Ahaz.
	29:1—32:33	The reign of Hezekiah.
	33:1—20	The reign of Manasseh.
	33:21—25	The reign of Amon.
	34:1—35:27	The reign of Josiah.
	36:1—4	The reign of Jehoahaz.
	36:5—8	The reign of Jehoiakim.
	36:9—10	The reign of Jehoiachin.
	36:11—21	The reign of Zedekiah.
	36:22—23	The decree of Cyrus.

בתולה נישאת פרק ראשון כתובות

בתולה

א *נישאת ביום הרביעי ואלמנה ביום החמישי שפעמים בשבת בתי דינין יושבין בעיירות ביום השני וביום החמישי שאם היה לו טענת בתולים היה משכים לבית דין : גמ׳ בר קפרא אמר מפני שכתיב כם ברכה *והלא אין כתיב ברכה אלא בחמישי ובששי בלבד בחמישי בעופות ובדגים בששי באדם וחוה אמר רבי יוסי טעמא דבר קפרא רביעי ג׳ אור חמישי אור ששי והלא כתיב ברכה בשביעי אין כתיב ברכה בבריות אלא ביום מפני שאין כתיב ברכה בבריות הא אילו הוה כתיב ברכה בבריות היתה נישאת בשבת לא כן תני לא יבעול אדם בעילה בתחילה

1 2 3 4 5

A Guide to Torah Texts

Esther Zeffren-Schnaidman

THE JERUSALEM TALMUD

1. **The Jerusalem Talmud**—Compiled in Eretz Israel, by Rabbi Yohanan and succeeding disciples, as distinguished from the Babylonian Talmud which was authored by Babylonian scholars. The texts of the Mishnayot found in the two Talmuds are not always identical, though many disagree as to the explanation of the discrepancies. Halacha is determined from the Babylonian Talmud, but not from the Jerusalem Talmud.

2. **P'nai Moshe**—***Rabbi Moshe Margoliot***
The P'nai Moshe (d. 1781, Lithuania) was the teacher of the Vilna Gaon. His commentary serves as a simple explanation to the Talmud text. Although he commented on many orders of the Mishnah, only two were published during his lifetime.

3. **Mareh HaPanim**—***Rabbi Moshe Margoliot***
This commentary indicates corresponding passages between the Babylonian Talmud and the Jerusalem Talmud. Additionally, it explains each specific topic with an emphasis on the text's deeper meaning.

4. **Korban HaAidah**—***Rabbi David ben Naphtali Fraenkel of Berlin, 1707-1762.***
Also known as Dovid Mireles. Like the P'nai Moshe, it gives a simple explanation of the Talmud. This commentary covers only Moed, Nashim and Nezikin.

5. **Shirei Korban**— ***Rabbi David ben Naphtali Fraenkel***
In his second commentary, Fraenkel provides additional insight to understanding the Talmud. He also reconciles various contradictions in the Talmud.

6. **Ridbaz**—***Rabbi Yaakov David ben Ze'ev, 1845-1913.***
Lithuanian scholar and *rosh yeshiva* in Israel. Initially he gives a simple Rashi-type explanation. In the second part of his commentary, he delves into a particular subject to gain a deeper explanation for the Talmudic passage.

RIF

1. Rif—*Rabbi Isaac ben Jacob Alfasi, 1013-1103.*
Born late Gaonic period, in Fez. Authored much responsa literature, but is known best for his Sefer haHalachot, which he wrote on three orders, Moed, Nashim and Nezekin (those orders which contain practical application in contemporary times). The Rif collects all the legal conclusions, adding his own decision. The Rif omits the Talmudic discussions, leaving an abridgement of the final outcome.

2. Rabbeinu Nissim—*Rabbi Nissim ben Reuwen Gerondi (Ran), 1310-1375.*
Served as a rabbi and judge in Barcelona. Because of his medical knowledge, he also served as a physician in the palace of Barcelona. In his commentary, the Ran provides the simple meaning of the Rif, as Rashi does in his commentary on the Talmud. In addition, he records the arguments of the scholars, while reconciling contradictory decisions, concluding with his own legal decisions.

3. Sefer HaMaor—*Rabbi Zechariah ben Isaac haLevi.*
This commentary on the Rif includes an analysis of both earlier and contemporary scholarly discussions. This author disputes the rulings of the Rif.

4. Reivid—*Rabbi Abraham ben David of Posquieres, c. 1125-1198.*
The Reivid is best known for his attacks on many of Maimonides' rulings in the Mishnah Torah. In his commentary to the Rif, the Reivid critiques the Rif, and finds exceptions to the Rif's halachic conclusions.

5. Ramban — *Rabbi Moses ben Nachman, 1194-1270, Spain.*
Defends Rif against the Ba'al Ha Maor, although Nachmanides himself does not always agree with the Rif. He argues objectively as he states in his introduction. It was now a style among Rishonim to bring down interpretations of the Talmud. He wrote the Sefer HaZechut in defense of the Rif to the Reivid.

6. Nemukai Yosef—*Rabbi Yosef ibn Haviva*
Like the Ran, he lists all the previous opinions and discussions of Rishonim, concluding with his own opinions.

7. Sheltai Geborim—*Rabbi Joshua Boaz ben Shimon Baruch of Spain, 16th century.*
He brings down various legal decisions from rabbis who have commented on the Rif.

כ׳ אבן העזר הלכות פריה ורביה א כח ב

יתברך

שמו של הקב"ה שהוא חפץ בטוב בריותיו (א) שידע שאין טוב לאדם להיות לבדו ועל כן עשה לו עזר כנגדו [א] ועוד כי כוונת הבריאה באדם כדי לפרות ולרבות (א) וזה אי אפשר בלא העזר ועל כן צוהו לדבק בעזר שעשה לו לכך חייב כל אדם לישא אשה כדי לפרות ולרבות (ב) [ב] שכל מי שאינו עוסק בפריה ורביה א כאילו שופך דמים דכתיב שופך דם האדם וסמיך ליה ואתם פרו ורבו וכאילו ממעט הדמות דכתיב כי בצלם אלהים עשה את האדם ואתם פרו ורבו (ג) [ג] וגורם לשכינה שתסתלק מישראל וכל מי ששרוי בלא אשה (ד) שרוי בלא טובה בלא ברכה [ד] בלא דירה בלא תורה בלא חומה בלא שלום ואמר ר"א כל מי שאין לו אשה (ה) אינו אדם וכיון

1

2

3

4

5

THE TUR (ARBAH TURIM)

1. The Tur—*Rabbi Yaakov ben Asher, 1270-1340*
Son of the Rosh. In this code of laws, the Tur includes proofs and footnotes to give his work credibility, differing from the style of the Rambam. Included in this original work are other scholar's opinions, to enable his readers to have all other opinions on the topic. His work is concerned solely with practical halacha (bearing relevance from the destruction of the Temple). His code of law is divided into four parts: Orach Hayyim, Yoreh Deah, Even haEzer, Choshen Mishpat.

2. Bait Chadosh—*Rabbi Joel ben Samuel Sirkes, 1561-1640.* Polish scholar. Among the various functions of this commentary are 1) to list the Tur's sources; 2) to record opinions from those who argue in the Tur, particularly the Bait Yosef and Darchai Moshe; 3) to give legal decisions.

3. Darchai Moshe—*Rabbi Moshe Isserles, 1525-1572.*
Polish codifier. In this commentary, he provides his *psak* and the customs which reflect the Ashkenazic tradition. He represents a school of thinkers, operating under the principle of *hilkheta ke'vatraei*—meaning the law is decided by the latter period rabbis and not the earlier ones. (This concept is not in accord with Rabbi Yosef Karo.) The commentary is also a collection of all the relevant halachic material to date, in a more concise style.

4. Bait Yosef—*Rabbi Yosef ben Efraim Karo, 1488-1575, Chief Rabbi of Safed.*
Rabbi Karo was a Spanish Jew who moved to Turkey and later to Safed. Well known for his code of laws which represent the Sephardic tradition. In the Bait Yosef, he primarily achieves two objectives: First, he traces all laws from the period of the Talmud and includes the Talmudic sources. Second, he records his *psak*. He developed a rule by which to determine the correct law. In certain circumstances, this task is based on majority opinion. Other times, he will record the opinion of two leading scholars.

5. Prisha and Drisha
Both commentaries were written by Rabbi Yehoshua Falk Katz, 1555-1614, a student of Rabbi Moshe Isserles in Poland. The Prisha explains the decisions of the Tur. The Drisha deals with various opinions of other halachic scholars.

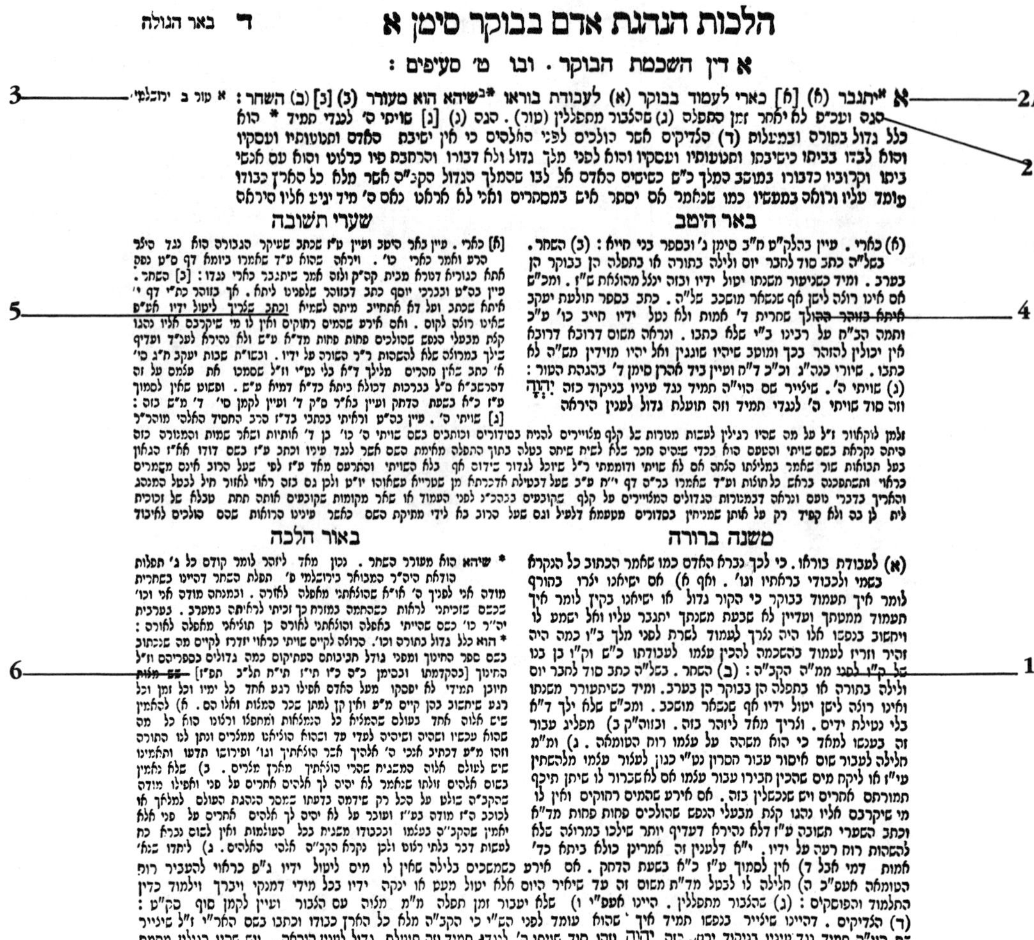

ד באר הגולה

הלכות הנהגת אדם בבוקר סימן א

א דין השכמת הבוקר · ובו ט׳ סעיפים :

א יתגבר (א) [א] כארי לעמוד בבוקר (א) לעבודת בוראו *שיהא הוא מעורר (ב) [ב] (ב) השחר : הגה ועכ״פ לא יאחר זמן התפלה (ג) שהצבור מתפללין (טור) . הגה (ג) [ג] שויתי ה׳ לנגדי תמיד * הוא כלל גדול בתורה ובמעלות (ד) הצדיקים אשר הולכים לפני האלהים כי אין ישיבת האדם ותנועותיו ועסקיו והוא לבדו בביתו כישיבתו ותנועותיו ועסקיו והוא לפני מלך גדול ולא דבורו והרחבת פיו כרצונו והוא עם אנשי ביתו וקרוביו כדבורו במושב המלך כ״ש כשישים האדם אל לבו שהמלך הגדול הקב״ה אשר מלא כל הארץ כבודו עומד עליו ורואה במעשיו כמו שנאמר אם יסתר איש במסתרים ואני לא אראנו נאם ה׳ מיד יגיע אליו היראה

א טור ב ירושלמי

באר היטב

שערי תשובה

משנה ברורה

באור הלכה

שער הציון

MISHNAH BRURAH

1. Mishnah Brurah—The Mishnah Brurah is an in-depth commentary on the Orach Chaim section of the Shulchan Aruch dealing with laws of prayer, blessings, Sabbath and holidays. Written by Rabbi Yisroel Meir Kagen (the Chofetz Chaim, 1838-1933), the Mishnah Brurah looks at former and contemporary views and indicates which to follow.

2. Shulchan Aruch & Rema

A. The Shulchan Aruch—(Lit. 'Set Table')
This is the code of Jewish law written by Rabbi Yosef ben Efraim Karo, 1488-1575. Divided into four parts, it deals with every aspect of Jewish law which is applicable today. Rabbi Karo was a Spanish Jew who moved to Turkey and later to Safed, where he served as Chief Rabbi. The Shulchan Aruch was basically wirtten with a Sephardic orientation. He was also the author of the Bait Yosef on the Tur.

B. Hagah ('Note' or 'Comment') of the Rema.
Acronym for Rabbi Moses Isserles, 1525-1572, Rabbi of Cracow, Poland. The Rema wrote his comments with an Ashkenazic orientation and they were subsequently included in the text of the Shuichan Aruch as an addendum. The work is often referred to as the 'Mapah' (Lit. 'Tablecloth') as it complemented the 'Set Table'.

3. Be'er Hagolah—***Rabbi Moshe Rivkis, mid-17th century.***
Gaon from Vilna, who lived (together with Rabbi Shabtai Cohen ('Shoch') through the upheavals of the Hetman Chmielnitzki massacre of Vilna Jewry. This sourcework that shows enormous erudition, traces every law in the Shulchan Aruch to its origin in the Talmudic corpus.

4. Be'er Hetev—***Rabbi Yehuda ben Shimon Ashkenazi, Dayan, Tiktin, Poland.***
A more basic commentary devoted to an understanding of the text and its immediate ramifications.

5. The Shaarei Tshuvah — ***Rabbi Chaim Mordechai Margolies.***
Rav of Dubnow, Poland in the 18th-19th century, this halachic authority makes mention of this brother, Rabbi Efraim Zalman Margolies. His comments are very valuable, among other things, as a summing up of the opinions of the later authorities in responsa literature (*achronim*) as well as some of the newer problems which were resolved by them.

6. Be'or Halacha—***Rabbi Yisroel Meir Kagen.***
In the Be'er Halacha, the Chofetz Chaim gives a more thorough explanation of the laws discussed by the Shulchan Aruch.

7. Shaar Ha Zion—***Rabbi Yisroel Meir Kagen.***
The Chofetz Chaim cites his sources in this commentary and includes footnotes for some additional points not mentioned previously.

Jewish Religious Considerations in Artificial Insemination, in Vitro Fertilization, and Surrogate Motherhood

Fred Rosner, M.D.

> There are three partners in man, the Holy One, blessed be He, his father and his mother. His father supplies the semen of the white substance out of which are formed the child's bones, sinews, nails, the brain in his head and the white of his eye. His mother supplies the semen of the red substance out of which is formed his skin, flesh, hair, blood and the black of his eye. And the Holy One, blessed be He, gives him the spirit and the breath, beauty of features, eyesight, the power of hearing and the ability to speak and walk, understanding and discernment.
>
> Talmud, Tractate Niddah 31a

The efforts of Drs. Patrick S. Steptoe and Robert G. Edwards in England culminated in the birth of Louise Brown on July 25, 1978, as a result of in vitro fertilization and reimplantation of the human embryo in the mother's womb. The same investigators later reported the birth of a boy by this technique. In brief, the procedures developed by Steptoe and Edwards consist of three steps: recovery of an ovum that has completed meiotic maturation, fertilization of the mature ovum in vitro and subsequent culture of the embryo through part of its preimplantation development, and replacement of the embryo in the uterus of the patient from whom the ovum was obtained. This procedure differs from that usually performed in laboratory and domestic animals in that the embryo is placed in the uterus of the patient, rather than in the uterus of a surrogate mother.

Moral Issues

The reimplantation of a human embryo in the mother for the cure of infertility seems to need no moral or religious justification if no other method can be used. Although the underlying infertility is not cured, the desire of (and biblical command to) the parents to have children is fulfilled. The situation is perhaps analogous to a diabetic whose clinical signs and symptoms are treated by insulin but whose underlying disorder is not cured thereby. However, conflicting claims might be made on the child by an embryo donor and the uterine mother, resulting in divided loyalty of the child. Furthermore, the surrogate mother might request an abortion or refuse to hand over the child; the donor might reject the child at birth; or the child might suffer psychologically on learning of the circumstances of its birth.

Does one tell the child born of a surrogate mother and/or following in vitro fertilization of the circumstances surrounding its birth? What does the surrogate mother tell her own children or friends and neighbors or colleagues at work about the "loss" of the baby if she surrenders it to the adoptive parents? Should she lie and say the baby died? What if the adoptive parents die or get divorced before the birth of the child, or decide they do not want the baby after all? What if the child is born defective?

The discussions about the morality and ethics of in vitro fertilization and surrogate motherhood relate to similar discussions in regard to abortion, contraception, artificial insemination, genetic engineering, cloning, and the like and are clearly beyond the scope of this essay.

Jewish Religious Issues

It is a cardinal principle in Judaism that life is of infinite value and that each moment of life is equal to seventy years thereof. In Jewish law, all biblical and rabbinic commandments are set aside for the overriding consideration of saving a life. It is therefore permitted and even mandated to desecrate the Sabbath to save the life of someone who may only live for a short while and certainly for a patient who may recover from illness or traumatic injuries.

A second fundamental principle of Judaism concerns the sanctity of human life. Man was created in the image of G-d, and hence human beings are holy and must be treated with dignity and respect, in life and after death. Our bodies are G-d given, and we are commanded to care for our physical and mental well-being and to preserve and hallow our health and our lives. Only G-d gives and takes life.

Are we tampering with life itself when we perform artificial insemination or in vitro fertilization? Are we interfering with the divine plan for humanity? If G-d's will is for a man or woman to be infertile, who are we to undertake artificial insemination or test-tube fertilization and embryo reimplantation into the natural or genetic mother, or into a host or surrogate mother, to overcome the infertility problem?

Judaism teaches that nature was created by G-d for man to use to his advantage and benefit. Animal experimentation is certainly permissible provided one minimizes the pain or discomfort to the animal. The production of hormones such as insulin from bacteria or in tissue culture or in animals by recombinant DNA technology for man's benefit is also permissible. Gene therapy, such as the replacement of the missing or defective gene in Tay-Sachs disease or hemophilia, if and when it becomes medically possible, may also be sanctioned in Jewish law. But is man permitted to alter humanity by in vitro fertilization, by transfer of the embryo from a woman inseminated with her husband's (or other) sperm into another woman's womb or by artificial gestation in a test tube or glass womb, and the like?

The following questions are important to the Jewish couple contemplating artificial insemination or in vitro fertilization: the legal relationship of the offspring to the sperm donor; the possible fulfillment of the commandment of procreation by the sperm donor; the legality of procurement of sperm from the husband for artificial insemination and the preferred methods for its procurement; the insemination of the husband's sperm into his wife during or shortly after her menstrual cycle when she is *niddah* (ritually unclean); the possibility of the insemination itself rendering her ritually unclean by "opening the mouth of the womb"; the question of the woman becoming ritually unclean following birth after artificial insemination; whether such a male child may be circumcised on the Sabbath; whether such a child absolves the obligation of Levirate marriage; whether or not a woman who is inseminated with donor sperm becomes prohibited to her husband; the legitimacy or bastardy of the offspring of artificial insemination using donor sperm; the circumstance in which sperm of the husband was mixed with donor sperm prior to insemination; whether or not a woman who claims she became pregnant in a bathhouse is believed; whether or not a husband can divorce his wife if she underwent artificial insemination without his knowledge; the obligation of the father to support his child born after artificial insemination; the status of the child if the sperm donor was a bastard; the case of insemination of semen from a priest into a profaned woman; whether Levirate marriage can be consummated through artificial insemination; and the legality of using sperm from a gentile donor for artificial insemination into a Jewish woman.

Artificial Insemination and Judaism

There is near unanimity of rabbinic opinion that the use of semen from the husband is permissible if no other method is possible for the wife to become pregnant. However, certain qualifications exist. There must have been a reasonable period of waiting since marriage (two, five or ten years or until medical proof of the absolute necessity for artificial insemination), and, according to many authorities, the insemination may not be performed during the wife's period of ritual impurity. Rabbinic opinion generally holds that artificial insemination using the semen of a donor other than the husband is an abomination and strictly prohibited for a variety of reasons, including the possibility of incest (the child born of such insemination may later marry a sibling, unknowingly), lack of genealogy (father's identity is unknown), and the problems of inheritance (does the child inherit from the real father, the adopted father, or both). A few rabbis regard such insemination as adultery, requiring the husband to divorce his wife and the wife to forfeit her marriage settlement *(ketubbah)*. Most rabbinic opinion, however, holds that without a sexual act involved, the woman is not guilty of adultery and is not prohibited from cohabiting with her husband.

Regarding the status of the child, rabbinic opinion is divided. Most consider the offspring to be legitimate, as was Ben Sira, the product of conception *sine concubito;* a small minority of rabbis consider the child illegitimate, and at least two authorities take a middle view. A considerable body of rabbinic opinion regards the child (legitimate or illegitimate) to be the son of the donor in all respects (that is, inheritance, support, custody, incest, Levirate marriage, and the like). Some regard the child to be the donor's son in some respects but not in others. Some rabbis state that although the child is considered the donor's son in all respects, the donor has not fulfilled the commandment of procreation. A minority of rabbinic opinion asserts that the child is not considered the donor's son at all.

It is permitted by most rabbis to obtain sperm from the husband both for analysis and for insemination, but a difference of opinion exists as to the method to be used to obtain it. Masturbation should be avoided if at all possible, and *coitus interruptus,* retrieval of sperm from the vagina, and the use of a condom seem to be the preferred methods.

In Vitro Fertilization and Judaism

In a situation in which the husband produces far too few sperm with each ejaculation to impregnate his wife or in which a woman is unable to move the egg from the ovary into the uterus because of blocked fallopian tubes, qualified approval can be given to the in vitro fertilization of the woman's egg with the husband's sperm and the reimplantation of the fertilized zygote in the same woman's womb. This situation represents a type of barrenness akin to physical illness and therefore justifies acts that entail a small amount of risk, such as the procurement of eggs from the mother's ovary by laparoscopy, a minor surgical procedure.

There is certainly no question of adultery involved, since the sperm used is that of the husband. Sperm and egg procurement for this procedure is permissible because the aim is to fulfill the biblical commandment of procreation. The offspring is legitimate, and the parents thereby fulfill their obligation of having children. However, certain serious moral and Jewish legal problems relate to this type of test-tube baby. If one uses sperm other than that of the husband, objections as discussed above under artificial insemination can be made. Furthermore, if one obtains several eggs from the mother's ovary at one time and fertilizes all of them so as to select the best embryo for reimplantation, is one permitted to destroy the other fertilized eggs? Do they not constitute human seed and therefore should not be "cast away for naught?" Is one permitted to perform medical research on the unused fertilized eggs? What is the status of the other fertilized ova in the Petri dish? Is the destruction of such fertilized ova tantamount to abortion? Is such a fertilized ovum regarded as "mere water" during the first 40 days of its development?

There is no concept in Judaism of waste applied to tens of millions of superfluous sperm that are lost following normal coitus. Perhaps excess fertilized eggs might be implanted into nonovulating women. What, then, should be the approach if no woman is available for an additional implant and there has been more than one successful fertilization? If a fertilized ovum is "more than nothing," would Jewish law mandate in vitro procedures with only one ovum at a time? There may well be a Jewish legal and ethical distinction between a fertilized egg in a Petri dish and a fertilized egg in a uterus. If there is no human fetal life outside the uterus, a superfluous fertilized ovum could be disposed of by any means, such as flushing down the drain. An alternative course of action would be to refrain from supplying nutrients to the ovum, thereby allowing it to perish. One can redefine the question in terms of whether or not an unfertilized egg may be deemed to be of ethical import as potential life. Since the vast majority of unfertilized sperm and eggs are never fertilized and do not constitute a new life, only a fertilized ovum might be considered as potential life. If a fertilized ovum was equated with human life, Jewish law would even require the expenditure of substantial sums of money to transport a superfluous fertilized ovum great distances, if necessary, for implantation into a nonovulating woman.

The question of the possible independent existence of a zygote has legal import. Jewish law requires the desecration of the Sabbath to preserve the existence of an embryo in the mother's womb even less than 40 days old. Is there a Jewish legal distinction between a fertilized ovum reposing within the mother and a similar ovum lying in a Petri dish? The Committee on Medical Ethics of the Federation of Jewish Philanthropies of New York, chaired by Rabbi Moshe D. Tendler, concluded that a fertilized egg not in the womb but in an environment—the Petri dish or test tube—in which it can never attain viability does not have humanhood and may be discarded or used for the advancement of scientific knowledge.

Even in the absence of Jewish legal or moral objections to in vitro fertilization using the husband's sperm, no woman is required to submit to this procedure. The obligations of women, whether by reason of the scriptural exhortation to populate the universe or by virtue of marital contract, are limited to bearing children by means of natural intercourse.

If and when medical science develops more advanced techniques of test-tube gestation, it may be necessary to re-examine these moral and legal questions. How does one address the issue of a fetus incubated for its full gestation in a totally artificial womb or incubator without using either the natural mother or a surrogate mother's uterus? Is such a child human when it is "born"? Although this creature may have the hereditary characteristics of its biologic parents, humanhood is usually assumed to occur following natural conception, pregnancy, and birth through a woman's womb. Does the interruption of this natural process even for a short period, such as for in vitro fertilization, negate the humanhood of such an infant? Is such an infant to be considered as a *golem* (artificially created "human" being) or as an angel, neither of whom is conceived and born from a woman's womb and neither of whom is included in the human race? If so, destroying it might not be considered an act of murder. Would the destruction of a baby "born" in an artificial womb or incubator without ever having been in a human uterus be an act of murder?

Finally, in regard to in vitro fertilization, it may soon be possible to separate male-from female-producing sperm and thereby to predetermine the sex of one's baby, either by artificial insemination of male- or female-producing sperm or by the use of the appropriate sperm to fertilize an egg in the test tube for reimplantation in the mother. Is such sex predetermination permissible in Jewish law? The freezing of human sperm and eggs for later use is another subject not yet adequately addressed by Jewish authorities.

Surrogate Motherhood and Judaism

The case of host motherhood in Jewish law concerns the implantation of a fertilized egg or tiny embryo in the womb of a woman other than the donor of the egg, perhaps because the true mother is unable to carry a fetus to term. The host mother thus serves as a surrogate and "incubates" the fetus for the true mother. The fetus can either be transplanted from one mother to another or the egg and sperm can be united in vitro in a test tube or Petri dish and directly implanted in the host mother. There is a serious question in Jewish law of whether or not the biological mother is allowed to give up her child for transplantation into another womb and whether or not the host mother is allowed to accept it. What is the legal parenthood of the child? If a married woman becomes a host mother, would Jewish law require her to abstain from sexual relations with her husband for ninety days, in order to ensure that the child is not his, that is to say, that she did not miscarry the implanted fetus and become pregnant by her husband? The husband would certainly not have to divorce his wife for serving as a host mother, since no act of adultery was committed.

Regarding the permissibility of host motherhood in Judaism, the Federation's Committee on Medical Ethics states that such procedures are permissible only in the absence of an alternative and may not be resorted to by fertile parents who prefer the services of a host mother. The "using" of a fellow human being "is in violation of the principle that man is not in man's service, destroys the natural family bond for convenience, with unknown psychological and spiritual consequences, and poses the risk of inviting improper commerce in babies, donor organs and the like." While the use of surrogate mothers for the convenience of couples able to have children cannot be condoned, continues the committee statement, an infertile couple may have recourse to a surrogate mother in the absence of alternatives "to save a marriage or bring happiness to the depressed." There should, of course, be absolute assurance that the surrogate is participating without coercion and with fully informed consent, and that the arrangement is protected by all necessary legal and social safeguards.

Summary

The explosion of medical knowledge and technology in the past decade has made in vitro fertilization, host mothers, sex organ transplants, genetic engineering, and their like a reality of the present and not a dream for the future. The potential risks, potential benefits, and ethical considerations of such advances in biomedical technology must be carefully considered. Tampering with the very essence of life and encroaching upon the Creator's domain are considerations worthy of extensive discussion from the Jewish standpoint. In the meantime, Britain's Chief Rabbi Jakobovits has expressed sentiments that one might take to heart:

> Man, as the delicately balanced fusion of body, mind, and soul, can never be the mere product of laboratory conditions and scientific ingenuity. To fulfill his destiny as a creative creature in the image of his Creator, he must be generated and reared out of the intimate love joining husband and wife together, out of identifiable parents who care for the development of their offspring, and out of a home which provides affectionate warmth and compassion.

Philosophical Perspectives of the Dietary Code

Judith Bleich

The basic corpus of the biblical laws of forbidden foods constitutes the concluding section of *Parshat Shemini* (Leviticus 1:1-23 and 41-47). The dietary laws are reiterated and amplified in *Parshat Re'eh* (Deuteronomy 14:3-21). These passages deal primarily with identification of permissible and forbidden species of animals, fish and fowl. In addition, there are specific prohibitions regarding a limb torn from an animal while the animal is yet alive (Genesis 9:4), against eating the sciatic sinew (Genesis 32:33), the laws of *trefah* (literally, "torn") (Exodus 22:3) and *nevelah* (Deuteronomy 14:21), as well as the thrice reiterated proscription, "Thou shalt not seethe a kid in its mother's milk" (Exodus 33:19; Exodus 34:26; and Deuteronomy 25:21). The eating of blood "for the life of the flesh is in the blood" is also repeatedly prohibited (Leviticus 3:17; Leviticus 17:10-12; and Deuteronomy 12:16), as is *"helev,"* the fat covering certain portions of an ox, sheep or goat (Leviticus 7:23).

There are various other categories of foods proscribed under specific circumstances, such as *orlah, hadash, kilei hakerem, hametz* on Passover, sacrificial offerings, foods consecrated to idol-worship and several foods prohibited by the rabbis such as life-endangering substances or foods prepared by gentiles. Moreover, to be permitted as meat, Jewish dietary law prescribes that animals must be slaughtered in accordance with the rites of *shehitah* and prepared according to the manifold prescriptions and regulations of the *Shulhan Arukh.*

Divine Regulation

The Sages of the Talmud classify the dietary laws among the *hukkim,* divinely ordained statutes which the Jew must observe if for no other reason than divine fiat. Thus in the classic talmudic discussion *(Yoma* 67b) in which the *mitzvot* are divided into two major categories, laws whose rational basis is perceived readily and those which must be accepted as a divine imperative, the laws of forbidden foods figure prominently in the latter group:

> "My judgments shall ye do," such matters which if they were not written [in Scripture] they should by right have been written and these are they: [the laws concerning] idolatry, immorality and bloodshed, robbery and blasphemy. "And my statutes shall ye keep," such commandments to which Satan [other versions: and the nations of the world] object[s] and they are the eating of swine, the wearing of *sha'atnez,* the *halitzah* performed by a sister-in-law, the purification of the leper, and the he-goat to be sent away. And perhaps you might think those are vain things, therefore Scripture says "I am the Lord," I the Lord have made it a statute and you have no right to criticize it.

As expressed in the *Midrash (Tanhuma, Shemini* 11), the source of these commandments is divine sanction, "and God showed Moses the different species of animals and said, 'These ye may eat, and these not,' " and their purpose is "to test and purify Israel." Their observance should be based not on the personal predilection of the individual but simply on obedience to the divine decree. As stated by R. Eleazar ben Azariah, "I would indeed like them [forbidden foods] but what can I do since my Father in heaven has imposed these decrees upon me?

In fact, the seemingly arbitrary nature of divine command is emphasized by the Sages precisely in connection with the dietary laws: "What difference does it make to God whether a beast is killed by cutting the neck in the front or in the back? Surely, the commandments are only a means of trying man in accordance with the verse, 'The word of God is tried' " *(Bereshit Rabbah,* 44:1). Establishing the intent of this dictum is crucial with regard to the entire question of whether or not it is possible to offer *ta'amei ha-mitzvot* (reasons for precepts). Do the individual *mitzvot* have no specific inherent purpose other than as dictates of God's will or, as products of divine wisdom, does each of them have a definite intrinsic value and aim, albeit one that may be unknown to man and beyond the limited scope of his comprehension?

Saadia Gaon classified a significant portion of the *mitzvot* as rational precepts *(sikhliyot)* and regarded even the remaining laws, those he termed traditional *(shimiyot),* as incidentally having "a slight justification from the point of view of reason." He believed that although the chief importance of the latter category is that they "represent the command of our Lord and enable us to reap a special advantage, yet . . . most of them have as their basis partially useful purposes."

Maimonides goes even further, asserting that there is most assuredly an intrinsic reason for every single precept. To assume that *hukkim* have no inherent objective whatsoever would be to brand God's actions as purposeless. Hence the difference, in his view, between *mishpatim* and *hukkim* is that whereas the purpose of the *mishpat* is self-evident, the reason underlying the *hok* is merely not readily apparent. In line with this rationalistic approach Maimonides interprets the perplexing midrashic passage cited above as follows. Each commandment has a distinct objective. However, the details of the commands are arbitrary. It is thus permissible to kill animals for the purpose of obtaining sustenance, but the particular details of ritual slaughter are tests of man's obedience.

Throughout the years numerous rabbinic authorities have sought to uncover the reasons and purposes underlying the *mitzvot.* Since the Middle Ages scholars have striven to demonstrate the truth of Maimonides' proposition that all laws of the Torah reflect the divine wisdom which ordained them and have endeavored to show that these laws can be made intelligible even "to a non-Jew and even to Jews who conceive of religion as involving only metaphysical principles and ethical commandments."

Turning in particular to the question of *ma'akhalot assurot* (forbidden foods), one may ask what are the reasons underlying this complex body of law? Are there central motifs which recur in the varied literature regarding this subject? How are the concepts *"tamei"* (unclean) and *"tahor"* (clean) to be understood within the context of the dietary laws?

Hygiene

One of the most popular explanations of the dietary laws is that they are related to our physical well-being and health. This concept is expressed as early as the Pseudepigrapha and alluded to in the works of Philo. Although these writings are not authoritative and did not directly affect the mainstream of rabbinic thought, it is of interest to include them in our discussion as illustrative of a very early approach to *ta'amei ha-mitzvot* and, as shall be noted, as important examples of the allegorical method of interpretation. The relationship of forbidden foods to bodily welfare is referred to in IV Maccabees 5:25-27: "Therefore, do we eat no unclean meat; for believing our Law to be given by God, we know also the Creator of the world, as a lawgiver, feels for us according to our nature. He has commanded us to eat the things that will be convenient for our souls, and he has forbidden us to eat meats that would be contrary." Philo, whose emphasis is on the moral and ethical intent of these laws, does note the hygienic factor with regard to the eating of *nevelah* which he presumes was forbidden because "eating such food is a noxious and insanitary practice since the body contains the dead serum as well as blood."

Maimonides, *Guide,* III, chap. 48, maintains that the forbidden foods are unwholesome and injurious to the body. He believes that blood and the flesh of *nevelah* and *trefah* are harmful and cause digestive difficulties and that *helev* likewise has an adverse effect on the body, producing cold and thick blood and being more fit for fuel than for human consumption. A host of other philosophers and commentators follow this line of reasoning. Citing medical authorities who assert that the milk of swine may cause leprosy, Nahmanides (Commentary on the Bible, Leviticus 11:13) concludes that doubtless all other forbidden foods are possessed of debilitating properties. He dwells on the physical characteristics of forbidden animals which may be dangerous from the standpoint of health and suggests that some of the forbidden foods may even have a deleterious effect on a person's reproductive system and future progeny. A similar statement is cited by Abraham Ibn Ezra, Commentary on the Bible (Exodus 22:30), with regard to *trefah;* namely, that in the opinion of a certain R. Moshe haKohen, flesh of an animal that is *trefah* contains a type of dangerous poison which may harm a person's offspring. Accordingly, *trefah,* unlike *nevelah,* may neither be given to the "stranger in your gates" nor sold to a non-Jew.

Similarly, Gersonides maintains that, apart from their spiritual value, the laws of the Torah result in "wondrous physical benefits." In his opinion, the permitted animals are those most suited nutritively to the composition of the human body. Rashbam, Commentary on the Bible, Leviticus 11:3, also declares that those animals forbidden by God are termed "unclean-*tamei*" because they are repugnant and destructive to the body. This interpretation he considers most consistent with the literal meaning of Scripture and most useful as a rebuttal to heretics. Hygienic reasons are also included by R. Aaron haLevi of Barcelona, author of the *Sefer ha-Hinnukh,* in his analysis of these *mitzvot.* Blood and helev produce especially bad physical after-effects, he avers (no. 147), and in the case of *trefah* there is some indication of sickness in the animal likely to harm anyone who would partake of its flesh (no. 72). Thus, the general principle applicable to the dietary laws, declares *Sefer ha-Hinnukh,* is that God, in his infinite kindness, has removed from us all harmful foods. Elaborating on this theme, he notes that often the adverse physical effect is unknown to man but for him therefore to deny its existence would be folly. For "the true physician who has warned us against them [these foods] is wiser than you . . . and how foolish and confounded is he who believes there is no harm or value to him in these things other than that which he [himself] can determine."

In modern times scientific studies and statistical surveys have been undertaken in an attempt to prove that the dietary laws have contributed to the endurance and physical health of the Jew. Specifically, sturgeon, shellfish, scaleless fish and the flesh of the pig have been singled out as causing various diseases. Certainly, however, no comprehensive analysis can be cited to warrant conclusions of a sweeping nature regarding the hygienic value of the dietary laws. This hypothesis has, indeed, often been challenged on purely scientific grounds. With the rapid advances of medicine and technology, any possible hygienic value of *kashrut* is commonly believed to have been superseded, and those who base their observance on this rationale alone consider the dietary laws obsolete.

Bearing in mind these current criticisms of the hygienic rationale, it is most significant to note the opinions of those rabbis who took sharp issue with the hygienic interpretation of the laws of forbidden foods. Striking to the root of the problem, Isaac Abravanel comments:

> Heaven forfend that I should believe so [that the reasons for the forbidden foods are hygienic]. For if this were so, the Book of God's Law would be in the category of a brief work among medical books . . . This is not the way of God's Law and the depth of its intentions.

In the first place, he notes, people who eat the forbidden foods appear to be quite healthy and robust, Secondly, the Torah fails to enumerate poisonous herbs among the prohibitions. All this points to the conclusion that the divine law

> did not come to heal bodies and promote their physical health but to seek the health of the soul and to heal its sickness . . . Scripture terms them [these forbidden animals] neither harmful nor inductive of sickness but rather *temeim,* unclean, and *toevah,* an abomination, indicating

to us that the reason for their having been forbidden is on account of the soul, not on account of the body and its well-being.

In almost identical language, Isaac Arama *(Akedat Yitzhak, Parshat Shemini, sha'ar* 60) criticizes that view which would "lower the status of the divine law to the status of any brief medical composition." He foresees the dangers of offering a purely hygienic rationale, noting that if medical methods to combat the alleged physical ills should be discovered, "the prohibition would not remain in force and the Torah would be made a fraud." The *Kle Yakor* commentary, Leviticus 11:1, and Menahem ha-Bavli, *Ta'amei ha-Mitzvot,* negative commandments, no. 84, make essentially the same point.

In modern times, this approach is found in the writings of R. Samson Raphael Hirsch and R. David Zevi Hoffman. Although Hirsch, in specific instances, did recognize an incidental hygienic value, as in the case of the concrete physical components of blood, he rejects medical considerations as a general underlying motif. Remarking on the use of the term *"tamei,"* Hirsch declares that this expression denotes "that dietary health considerations are not what lies at the root of the prohibition, but rather that the reasons are to be sought in that sphere in which the idea *tumah* has its meaning."

Contravention of Idolatry

Opposition to idolatry has also been considered a motivating factor of the dietary laws. As early as the beginning of the third century, Origen, one of the early Church Fathers, wrote that the sacrificial code and the designation of certain animals as unclean had as its aim contravention of the Egyptian cult of animal worship. Saadia Gaon, in his explanation of the rational aspect of what he considers to be essentially a *mitzvah shimi'it,* also sees abstention from forbidden foods as a deterrent to idol worship. These laws should prevent man from comparing the Creator to animals, either those he eats or those forbidden to him. Similarly, one is not likely to worship either that animal which one eats or that which has been declared unclean.

In Maimonides' analysis of the forbidden foods, eradication of idolatrous practices is seen as an important motif. With regard to the prohibitions against eating a limb severed from a living animal and meat boiled in milk, he notes that these actions were probably part of pagan rituals which, in all likelihood, took place in conjunction with heathen festivals. The biblical injunction which twice appears following the laws concerning Jewish festivals is understood as emphasizing that festivals should not be marred by heathen practices. More particularly, with regard to the prohibition of blood, he emphasizes the need to oppose and discredit idolatry, in this instance worship of spirits which was intimately bound up with blood rituals. Some heathens drank blood; a Jew is enjoined to abstain from blood. Another heathen practice was to collect the blood in a vessel for spirits to partake of; a Jew is told to sprinkle and pour out the blood of sacrifices. One ritual involved feasting in a circle around the blood; a Jew is commanded, "You shall not eat around the blood." Similarly, the blood of a *hayah* or of birds must be covered with earth to preclude gatherings around the blood. Maimonides notes that the admonition against eating blood concludes with the words, "I will set My face against the soul that eateth blood" (Leviticus 17:10), an expression used elsewhere in reference to idolatrous practices and a further indication of the close connection of the prohibition of blood with the idea of pagan rites.

At the conclusion of his analysis of the spiritual importance of the dietary prohibitions, Abravanel also cites Maimonides' view regarding the identification of forbidden foods with idolatry and indicates his agreement with this general principle, noting that the word *"toevah"* used both in connection with idol-worship and with certain "unclean" foods is indicative of their intrinsic relationship.

Moral and Ethical Lessons

Temperance

A primary objective of the *mitzvot* is to teach man to control and sanctify his natural desires. One of the most powerful physical drives is the craving for food. Teaching self-control in the gratification of instincts, the dietary laws remind man that he does not live by bread alone.

Philo emphasizes the fundamental importance of these laws in teaching restraint and in curbing gluttony and ultimately other physical excesses. He considers the forbidden animals to be those whose flesh is "finest and fattest . . . none is so delicious as pig, nor among the aquatic animals as the scaleless." The laws aim to train man to live in accordance with the mean. For the divine Lawgiver approved "neither of rigorous austerity like the Spartan legislator nor of dainty living like he who introduced the Donians and Sybarites to luxurious and voluptuous practices. Instead, he opened up a path midway between the two. He relaxed the overstrained and tightened the lax. Consequently, he neglected nothing and drew up very careful rules as to what they should or should not take as food."

Maimonides, as well, sees virtue in seeking the mean and avoiding either extreme. Divine law aims at teaching man to conquer his desires, for sensuality impedes man's ultimate perfection. Man must not think of food and drink as the goals of existence. Rather should temperance and self-control pave the way for the attainment of holiness.

Similarly, in *Hovot ha-Levavot,* Bahya ibn Paquda underscores the necessity to restrict physical desire lest untrammeled lust undermine man's intellect. The intellect is preserved by Torah: "The Torah is the remedy for such spiritual maladies and moral diseases. The Torah therefore prohibits many kinds of food, apparel, sexual relations, and certain acquisitions and practices all of which strengthen sensual lust." This interpretation is in the same vein as the concept expressed in the Talmud, *Kiddushin* 30b:

> The Torah is like a life-giving drug. It is as if a man had severely wounded his son and placed a poultice upon the wound, saying, "My son, so long as this poultice is on your wound, you can eat and drink and bathe as you please and you need not fear. If you remove it, however, the wound will become ulcerous." Thus spoke God unto Israel, "My son, I have created the evil instinct but I have also created Torah as an antidote. Study and observe the Torah and you will not be delivered into its hand . . . If you wish you can even become its master."

Cruelty

One of the moral lessons inculcated by the dietary laws is abhorrence of violence and cruelty. This message underlies the laws of *shehitah* as well as many of the specific prohibitions. The most obvious example is the ban against eating a limb cut from a living animal. Many of the commentators also see an ethical lesson in the prohibition of mingling meat and milk. Philo comments on the impropriety of using the milk which sustained an animal to flavor it after death and views the person who partakes in such fare as cruelly brutal in character and utterly devoid of compassion. For man to eat the flesh of an animal torn by wild beasts is to descend to their level of cruelty and savagery. The laws of the Torah are designed to foster precisely the opposite character traits: "With such instructions he [Moses] tamed and softened the minds of the citizens [of Israel]."

Maimonides, too, *Guide* III, chaps. 26 and 48, notes the ethical lessons implicit in many of these laws. If man must not cause grief to animals, must he not be all the more careful with his fellow man? Abraham ibn Ezra, Commentary on the Bible, Exodus 23:19; Rashbam, *ad loc;* and Nahmanides, Commentary on the Bible, Deuteronomy 14:21, all view the prohibition against mingling meat and milk as the admonition against cruel and heartless behavior.

Some of the commentators view the eating of certain animals as having an actual, concrete physical effect on personality. Hence, ingestion of cruel predatory animals, they assert, may literally produce these cruel traits in the one who partakes of them. We find this approach in the Commentary of Nahmanides, Leviticus 11:13, who mentions that the Torah prohibits predatory fowl because the individual who consumes the flesh of such birds is affected thereby and acquires a cruel nature. In like manner, *Sefer ha-Hinnukh,* no. 148, notes that partaking of the blood of an animal is detrimental to character for thereby a person may acquire animal-like traits. In a rather novel interpretation, *Kle Yokor,* Leviticus 11:1, illustrates this approach with regard to different character traits. Thus, for example, the behavior of a swine, who deceivingly stretches out a split hoof, although lacking the second prerequisite of permitted animals, epitomizes hypocrisy. This interpretation is not intended as symbolic but rather as describing a very real occurrence, viz., the effect of what is eaten in transforming the nature of the eater. This approach is echoed in the works of a much later commentator, Malbim, Commentary on the Bible, Genesis 32:33, who observes that "the flesh of the animal eaten becomes part of the person who is fed and therefore [does the Torah] forbid unclean foods and abominations for in partaking of them one acquires the nature and cruelty of a predatory animal."

Moral Order

One explanation offered for some of the dietary laws is that they teach man to preserve the moral order of the universe. Thus Philo deemed it contrary to nature for men to eat blood, the essence of the soul which sustains the life which both man and animal possess in common. Similarly, the prohibition of *nevelah* teaches us that "the fitness of things bids us to keep untouched what we find deceased and respect the fate which the compulsion of nature has already imposed." In discussing the prohibition of mingling meat and milk, *Sefer ha-Hinnukh,* no. 62, suggests that this would be contrary to the divinely ordained laws of nature, creating a mingling of various systems of natural laws which are intended to dominate different spheres. These forces are incompatible and their merging is harmful and destructive. Similarly, *Kle Yokor,* Exodus 23:19, remarks that the mingling of contrary elements is a distortion of nature.

Symbolism of the *Simanei Taharah*

A recurrent theme explaining dietary laws is that they are designed to advance moral lessons by means of symbolism. Maimonides, *Guide,* III, chap. 48, writes that the presence of *simanei taharah* (the distinguishing characteristics of permitted species) is not the intrinsic reason that the particular animal is or is not to be permitted but is merely a sign whereby one can differentiate between what is forbidden and what is permitted. Without necessarily departing from this premise, many of the other commentators did see secondary reasons or symbolic lessons which could be drawn from the physical characteristics of the various types of animals described in the Torah. These lessons were not to be construed as the underlying purpose of the dietary laws but were ethical teachings woven into the wondrous fabric of divine law.

This allegorical method of interpretation was prevalent in the Hellenistic period of the Pseudepigrapha. In particular the writings of Philo present striking examples of the symbolic approach. In the *Letter of Aristeas* the ordinances concerning forbidden foods are presented as an important vehicle for the transmission of moral precepts. Unlike those commentators who espoused what might be termed a "psychophysical" approach, i.e., that partaking of forbidden foods actually transforms the physical composition of the eater's body and soul, the *Letter of Aristeas* presents a purely symbolic approach. Wild and carnivorous birds are proscribed "as a sign ... that those for whom the legislation was ordained must practice righteousness in their hearts and not tyrannize over anyone ... nor rob them of anything but steer their course of life in accordance with justice ... It is by such methods as these that indications were given to the wise...." In like manner, it is asserted that the prohibition against touching the carcass of an unclean animal is a precaution against association with that which may destroy character. The division of the hoof and the separation of the claws is symbolic of the necessity to discriminate between different modes of conduct. Chewing the cud is representative of that gift of memory so necessary to a people who must continually be mindful of the God of the Universe and the purpose of whose entire life is "to practice righteousness before all men being mindful of the Almighty God. And so concerning meats and things unclean, creeping things and wild beasts, the whole system aims at righteousness and righteous relationships between man and man."

Philo (*De Specialibus Legibus,* IV, 103-131) also remarks on the moral lessons implicit in the physical characteristics of forbidden animals. He interprets the signs of the cloven hoof and the chewing of the cud as symbols of the method whereby knowledge should be acquired. The cud-chewing process symbolizes the manner in which a pupil should prolong the learning process. Wisdom cannot be apprehended immediately; the student must recall facts by searching his memory and through constant rethinking arrive at firm conceptions. The cloven hoof symbolizes the discrimination and discretion needed in distinguishing concepts. With a different allegorical twist, Philo sees the cloven hoof as indicative of the twin paths of virtue and vice and the clear choice between them. Unclean animals represent either a single hoof implying that good and bad are identical or a multiform hoof indicating a variety of roads among which it is difficult to select the best path. The fins and scales on permitted fish illustrate their ability to resist the force of the stream; those lacking such characteristics are swept away by the current. Reptiles which crawl on their stomachs are symbolic of the lowliness of those who devote themselves to gratification of the stomach. Four-footed and many-footed reptiles signify subjugation to a multitude of passions. On the other hand, creeping creatures such as grass-hoppers, with legs above their feet enabling them to leap up from the ground, are classified as *tahor* for here too "by symbols he [Moses] searches into temperaments and ways of a reasonable soul.... Blessed are they who have the strength to leap upward from earth-bound things into the ether and the revolving heavens."

Centuries later other commentators described the characteristics of permitted animals as embodying moral lessons. These interpretations are, of course, presented by them in a homiletic vein, not as the literal meaning. Thus one interpretation notes that the fins and scales of permitted fish express symbolically the need for a person to cover his body with the protective armor of *mitzvot*. Another sees the emphasis on the nonpredatory nature of permitted animals as teaching the need to identify with the underdog. An unusual example is the comment of R. Shabetai ha-Kohen (Shakh) who discerns moral connotations in the very names of the animals. *"Paras"* symbolizes an individual whose effort is directed solely to the acquisition of reward (*paras*); *"nesher"* may be etymologically derived from the root *"nashor"*—one who falls away, symbolizing a person who discards the *mitzvot*. Conversely, the names of permitted animals represents traits worthy of emulation as, for example, *"arbeh"*, symbolic of one who increases (*marbeh*) Torah and good deeds.

Symbolism of the Sciatic Sinew

Many symbolic lessons are derived from the prohibition of the sciatic sinew. Tradition teaches that the angel who fought with Jacob was the guardian spirit of Esau. The Midrash interprets the incident of the *gid ha-nasheh* symbolically to the effect that the angel of Esau "touched all the righteous that were to be born from Jacob; he hinted to him the generation of apostasy." Nahmanides understands the Midrash as relating that the angel indicated the destiny of Jacob's descendants and the coming of the time of overpowering persecution as in the days of R. Judah ben Baba. The prohibition may thus serve as a reminder of Israel's historic destiny. Gersonides, who explains the struggle as a prophetic vision, sees the prohibition not only as a symbol of Israel's history and the salvation wrought by faith but as a deep religious affirmation of the fundamental importance and veracity of prophecy.

A slightly different explanation of the same theme is to be found in Menahem ha-Bavli, *Ta'amei ha-Mitzvot,* neg. comm., no. 1. The negative precepts parallel the 365 days of the year. Appropriately, the *gid ha-nasheh*, representative of the ascendancy of Edom, of Esau's guardian angel, is parallel to the ninth of Av. For a Jew to eat this part of the animal would be tantamount to incorporating into his body his bitterest adversary.

Finally, note should be taken of the comments of the author of the *Sefer ha-Hinnukh* in his beautiful and moving portrayal of this *mitzvah*. Just as Esau's angel strove to destroy Jacob but succeeded only in inflicting pain upon him, so too, declares *Sefer ha-Hinnukh,* the descendants of Esau may afflict Jacob's children but can never annihilate them. This *mitzvah* is an allusion to Israel's ultimate redemption and is a spur to greater faith and trust: "Remembering this whole matter by means of the *mitzvah* may serve as a reminder that they [Israel] remain firm in their faith and their righteousness..." assured that just as Scripture relates that "the sun shone for him [Jacob] to heal him and he was released from his agony, so too shall the sun of the Messiah shine forth for us and heal us from our affliction...."

Preservation of Identity

Particularly in the writings of modern-day scholars there is emphasis on the role of *mitzvot* in preserving the Jewish people as a distinctive nation. In this frame of reference, the dietary laws can be seen as an obvious deterrent to carefree intermingling and assimilation. Assuredly, the rabbinic prohibitions against gentile wines and foods cooked by gentiles, which were enacted for the specific purpose of forestalling the intimacy which may lead to intermarriage, proved effective in guarding the separatism of the Jew.

The *Letter of Aristeas* takes note of this function of the *mitzvot* and states that lest Israel assimilate "God hedged us round on all sides by rules of purity affecting alike what we eat or drink or touch or hear or see... (142); the laws must teach discrimination ... because we have been distinctly separated from the rest of mankind (151)." This theme is stressed by Abraham ibn Ezra in his comments on *"stam yenam"* and in particular in his interpretation of the prohibition of *gid ha-nasheh.* Of the Patriarchs it was only Jacob whose progeny were all committed to the service of the true God; Abraham and Isaac both sired offspring who were not destined to become Jews. It is most fitting, therefore, commencing with the *gid ha-nasheh,* to recall God's kindness to Jacob and to continue to preserve the ethnic purity of the Jewish people by separating from the food and drink of non-Jews and thus erecting barriers against assimilation. This motif is also suggested by Isaac Arama in his *Akedat Yitzhak, Shemini, sha'ar* 60. The laws governing food restrict the contact of Jews and non-Jews. These social barriers create a distance between them similar to that which exists "between the peasant or provincial and the prince" who feasts on the bread and wine of the king. Just as they are separate in their foods so are they to be different from others in their thoughts and deeds.

A Chosen People

Many of the biblical commentators formulate the concept that the laws are intended to separate Israel from other nations in a manner which does not reflect nationalistic sentiments but religious ones. The goal is expressed in terms of Israel's role as a holy people. This concept can be found in the words of the Bible itself: "For you are a holy people unto the Lord your God, and the Lord has chosen you to be His treasured people from among all the peoples on the face of the earth. Ye shall eat nothing abominable" (Deuteronomy 14:2-3).

Adherence to these laws indicates recognition of the unique nature of Israel's redemption from Egypt. God commands Israel (Leviticus 11:44-45) to differentiate between clean and unclean foods and demands such behavior because "I am the Lord who has brought you up from the land of Egypt to be your God." The Midrash comments that the Exodus occurred for the express purpose that Israel accept the laws: "Whosoever takes upon himself the yoke of *mitzvot* attests to the Exodus from Egypt." But more is involved than the special nature of Israel's deliverance. The sages view the dietary code in particular as indicative of the peculiar status of the Jewish people, i.e., of their having been selected from among the nations of the world in order to maintain a singular standard of holiness. Observance of the laws is portrayed by the Midrash as the unique privilege of the Jewish people, marking the great distinction between them and the other nations. *Midrash Tanhuma* expresses a similar concept. Explaining the word *"hayah"* as an expression denoting "life," the Midrash observes that Israel alone among the nations was given the dietary laws, for Israel alone is destined for eternal life. The case is analogous to that of a physician who imposes no restrictions on an incurable patient but gives detailed prescriptions to the patient who may recover.

The special nature of Israel's destiny is basic to the discussion of dietary laws in the *Zohar.* Israelites may not defile themselves with unclean animals in which the spirit of impurity dwells. To partake of such foods is to imbibe the impurity of idolatrous nations. The role of Israel is different:

> Happy is the portion of Israel in that the Holy King delights in them and desires to sanctify and purify them above all others because they cling to Him. It is written "Israel in whom I am glorified." If the Holy One, blessed be He, takes pride in Israel, how can they go and defile themselves and cling to the *sitra ahara?* . . . Whoever eats of those unclean foods cleaves to the *sitra ahara* and defiles himself.

In a very similar vein, R. Hayyim ibn Atar, *Or ha-Hayyim* (Commentary on Leviticus 11:1), envisions these laws as a special sign of privilege and honor. He emphasizes the notion of Israel's separatism in terms of their singular mission. Commenting on the Scriptural reference "For I am the Lord your God and ye shall be holy," (Leviticus 11:44), *Or ha-Hayyim* states, "the Israelite people is unique in its propensity for holiness and purity." Only with regard to Israel did God allow Himself to be referred to in the genitive case and therefore, indeed, must they separate themselves from impurity.

Attainment of Holiness

Among later thinkers, emphasis on these laws as a symbol of Israel's separateness and unique destiny is found in the writings of the noted Enlightenment figure, Samuel David Luzzatto. In his opinion, the various prohibitions of *trefah* and *nevelah,* for example, serve to eliminate that which might possibly be degrading and to present a way of life suitable for a holy people. The dietary laws serve to isolate Israel from the surrounding heathen peoples and to impress upon them their high station. However, many of the commentators further develop this concept. They see these laws not merely as creating a separate *modus vivendi* for a holy nation, but in a metaphysical sense, as necessary for a spiritual elevation of the people and their attainment of holiness. Thus, R. David Zevi Hoffman (whose approach is modelled on that of Hirsch which we shall discuss below) observes pointedly that he accepts Luzzatto's above analysis only in part; namely, that dietary laws are binding on Israel in their role as holy people. However, their purpose is not merely to serve as an external means of distinguishing between Jew and non-Jew. Rather, he argues, forbidden foods concretely affect the degree of holiness the Jew attains. If a Jew partakes of them he defiles his body, and his ability to perform his divine mission is impaired.

The concrete effect of forbidden foods is portrayed graphically by Nahmanides. In his Commentary on the Bible, Deuteronomy 14:3, he writes, "Forbidden foods are an 'abomination' to the pure soul . . . for forbidden foods are gross and breed coarseness and impurity in the soul." The food ingested becomes part of the body and soul of the individual who partakes thereof. By imbibing the blood of an animal one incorporates into one's soul the "animal soul" and becomes imbued with the animal's nature.

The manner in which mind and body interact is discussed by Menachem Recanati, a thirteenth-century Kabbalist, who in the *Ta'amei ha-Mitzvot* illustrates how the forbidden foods influence a person's spiritual well-being. The body is the instrument of the soul, serving as the intermediary between the physical world and the spiritual soul. Just as a craftsman requires fine tools for his work, so too, to fulfill its task, the soul requires a cooperative body. Thus, ultimately the body affects the degree of holiness the soul attains. Forbidden food coarsens the body, awakening the animal in man. By demeaning the quality of the body as an instrument of the soul and deadening its finer qualities, such food literally clogs the heart, is *metamtem et ha-lev.*

A common way of expressing the baleful effect of prohibited foods is that they breed spiritual malaise. Thus, *Sefer ha-Hinnukh,* no. 159, declares, "This *'tumah'* damages the soul, causing it to become somewhat sick . . . The fount of the mind, the soul, becomes defective through *'tumah.'* " Abravanel, Commentary on the Bible, Leviticus 11:13, also speaks of forbidden foods as detrimental to spiritual well-being, stupefying the heart and deadening the spirit. *Akedat Yitzhak (Shemini, sha'ar* 60), again in language almost identical to that of Abravanel, discusses the grave effect of *ma'akhalot assurot* which "harm the souls to heal which this entire [body of laws] was designed." So powerful is the effect of forbidden food on the soul that it can sever the special bond between Israel and God. *Or ha-Hayyim* (Leviticus 17:10) explains the punishment of *"karet"* in connection with the prohibition of blood as a manifestation of a cause and effect relationship. Blood so degrades the person who partakes of it that the special tie which binds his soul to the Creator is severed. Conversely, by eating permitted foods, a Jew maintains a high degree of holiness; his eternal soul is preserved and he is enabled to emulate the ways of God: "Ye shall therefore sanctify yourselves for I am holy."

These thoughts form the basis upon which R. Samson Raphael Hirsch constructs his comprehensive exposition of the forbidden foods and the laws of *"tumah"* and *"taharah"* as fundamental to the destiny of Israel as a kingdom of priests and a holy nation.

The priestly ideal of the nation is symbolized in the sanctuary; it becomes a reality only in the lives of the community of the faithful. Hirsch views *tumat maga,* uncleanliness of touch, referring to the carcasses of dead animals, as symbolic purity, paralleling the symbol of the Sanctuary. Concrete *tumah,* in which category he classifies the dietary laws, parallels and influences the actual moral holiness, the essential *kedushah,* of the people. To Hirsch *tumah* represents the absence of moral freedom. The purpose of both symbolic and concrete *tumah* is that man be ever conscious of his moral freedom:

> The free moral energy which should oppose the immoral paths into which the demands of our desires have been driven, is weakened by eating *ma'akhalot assurot.* And so such eating has a baneful influence on . . . our spiritual lives . . . it effects *tumah,* a laming of that sense of Godlike mastery of ourselves and certainty of being free of will and not bound slaves to our passions . . . I have made you participate in My nature, have given you the power of moral self-determination, so that you reign in the little world of forces which I have made part of your material sensuous nature for you to master as a small god, accomplishing My will of your own free will and determination, even as I, as the absolute free-willed God, reign over all the great forces in the great cosmos. The completely free personal God is the warranty of free personal man. "Because I am holy, you are to be holy, and can become holy!"

Whereas *tumah* makes a person unfit for holiness, *"sheketz"* (abomination) stands in total opposition to spirituality. Both these qualities, inherent in forbidden foods, contaminate the body. Only the permitted foods are suitable to preserve the body as the ready instrument of the soul.

Turning to some of the details of the laws, Hirsch explains *nevelah* and *trefah* as unsuited to a holy person for moral considerations. Blood, the essence of the animal, and *helev,* the quintessence of selfish animal purpose, are completely heterogeneous to man. If man partakes of such food "the influences of the animal soul which still adhere to it enter with it into the human . . . body . . . [It] is prone to bring about . . . such a depravement of human nature that could be capable of robbing the aptness for the moral heights which God's Torah has set for the vocation of a Jew."

Beyond Reason

The nature of the various rational bases for the dietary laws are thematically correlative with diverse intellectual climates. During the Hellenistic period, the allegorical method predominates, and humanistic and ethical reasons are proposed. Centuries later, rationalists such as Maimonides and Rashbam favor logical explanation of the laws on hygienic grounds. In the religious sphere they emphasize the role of Judaism as the one purely monotheistic religion of antiquity and, in this framework, explain the significance of some of the specific prohibitions in discouraging idolatrous practices. Mystics and Kabbalists such as Nahmanides and *Or ha-Hayyim* portray the subtle psychophysical effect of forbidden foods on body and soul. Toward the modern era we find increasing emphasis on the sociological and psychological role of *mitzvot* in preserving the identity of Israel as a nation and in refining the character and enhancing the morality of its individual members.

It must, however, be underscored that at no time did rabbinic commentators consider any particular rationale as exhausting the implications of the *mitzvah.* The reason offered is but one aspect of the *mitzvah;* the *mitzvah* as divine command has a singular importance above and beyond its rationale. The *mitzvah qua mitzvah* has a significance which is *sui generis.* In fact, in his elucidation of *mitzvot,* Rabbi Joseph Ber Soloveitchik, author of the *Bet ha-Levi,* goes much further. Speaking particularly of those *mitzvot* which are commemorative of historical events, in light of the talmudic dictum "He [God] looked into the law and created the world," he postulates that God ordained history to provide a rationale for the *mitzvot.* In order to satisfy man's natural inclination to seek an understanding of the *mitzvot,* God created historical events to give meaning, in human terms, to *mitzvot* which intrinsically are beyond human comprehension. Thus, in effect, "the *mitzvah*" was not created on account of the reason; rather, the reverse took place, on account of the *mitzvah* was the reason created."

Accordingly, the dietary laws and all other *mitzvot* of the Torah, quite apart from any specific rationalistic base, are seen as constituting the unique expression of the relationship between God and Israel. Alluding to the verse, "That ye may remember and do all my commandments and be holy unto your God" (Numbers 15:40), the sages declare in the Midrash:

> Heart and eyes are two middlemen of sin to the body, leading him astray . . . The matter is to be compared to a man drowning in water, to whom the shipmaster threw out a cord, saying unto him, "Hold fast to this cord, for if thou permit it to escape thee there is no life for thee." Likewise the Holy One, Blessed be He, said to Israel, "As long as you cling to my laws, you cleave unto the Lord your God [which means life] . . ." Be holy, for as long as you fulfill my commandments you are sanctified . . . but if you neglect them you will become profaned."

CLEAN	UNCLEAN
MAMMALS	
RUMINANTS WITH WHOLLY CLOVEN HOOVES (Deut. 14:16), e.g., buffalo, cattle, goat, sheep, ibex, gazelle, deer, antelope, wild ox, wild goat, giraffe (?).	a. **CLOVEN-HOOFED BUT NON-RUMINANTS,** e.g., pig, bear, hippopotamus. b. **RUMINANTS BUT NOT CLOVEN HOOFED,** e.g., camel, llama. c. **SOLID-HOOFED,** e.g., horse, ass, mule, onager, zebra.

d. **CARNIVOROUS,** e.g., cat, lion, leopard, dog, wolf, jackal, fox, hyena, bear.
e. **OTHER MAMMALS; NEITHER RUMINANTS NOR CLOVEN-HOOFED,** e.g., hare, mouse, hyrax, bat, rat, elephant, ape, whale.

BIRDS

a. COLUMBIFORMES, e.g., pigeon, turtle dove, palm dove.
b. **GALLIFORMES,** e.g., hen, quail, partridge, peacock, pheasant.
c. **PASSERINAE,** e.g., house sparrow.
d. **ANSERIFORMES,** e.g., domestic duck, domestic goose.

a. **DIURNAL BIRDS OF PREY**
(i) falconidae, e.g., kestrel, hawk, eagle, kite, buzzard.
(ii) Vulturidae, e.g., griffon vulture, black vulture, Egyptian vulture, bearded vulture.
b. **NOCTURNAL BIRDS OF PREY** (Strigiformes), e.g., owl.
c. **WATER AND MARSH FOWLS.** With the exception of the goose and the duck, they are all regarded as unclean, e.g., stork, bittern, heron, crane, gull.
d. **VARIOUS OTHER BIRDS** which either have no characteristics of a clean bird, or about which there is no tradition that they are permitted, e.g., warbler, crow, swift, hoopoe, ostrich.

REPTILES AND AMPHIBIANS

All reptiles and amphibians are unclean (see Lev. 11:41-42). Regarding the crocodile, see Lev. 11:12.

FISH

According to the Bible those fish are permitted which have "fins and scales, in the waters, in the seas and in the rivers" (Lev. 11:9; Deut. 14:9). In this category only Bony-Skeletons are included, since they alone possess fins and scales. Those fish which have scales only early or late in life are clean (Av. Zar. 39a). Examples: carp, trout, salmon, herring.

a. **CARTILAGINOUS** (Chondrichthytes). These fish either have no scales or have thick scales like teeth, which are not, however, true scales as they do not overlap, e.g., shark, ray.
b. **CARTILAGINOUS-BONY** (Chondrostei). They also lack true scales. It is from these fish that much caviar (mainly black in color) is derived, e.g., sturgeon.
c. **BONY SKELETONS** (Holostei). Fish which have no scales visible to the eye, or which have no fins, e.g., catfish, eel.

INVERTEBRATES

Of all the invertebrates, only a group of four species belonging to the order of locusts (Orthoptera) are permitted by the Bible. The Rabbis enumerate eight species of permitted Orthoptera (Hul. 65a-b, cf. Maim. Yad, Ma'akhalot Asurot 1:21-22). The Mishnah gives four signs whereby permitted insects may be recognized: four jointed legs, and four wings covering the greater part of the body (Hul. 3:7). If the wings develop only at a certain stage, the species is nonetheless permitted.

The invertebrates which live on land and in water are forbidden. The main group of forbidden invertebrates are: leeches, mollusks, e.g., (snail, oyster, squid), segmented worms, flatworms, jellyfish, sponges, protozoa.

Jewish Perspectives on Issues of Death and Dying

Fred Rosner, M.D.

Because of advances in medical technology, some people who in an earlier era would have died are today alive and well. Others who would have died are now alive but in a coma or a vegetative state. Medical technology has created as many problems as it has solved.

The new technology denies the physician a simple physiological end point for death. When is a donor dead (*vide infra*) so that his organs can be removed for organ transplantation? Is it ethical to infuse mannitol into a patient dying of a head injury to preserve his kidneys for grafting? Dare we remove kidneys from a donor whose heart is still beating? Is it "cruel" in the presence of a fatal disease, in the agonal hours, to prolong life (or death) by the use of machines?

What should be done and what should not be done for a terminally ill patient? Is an eighty-year old man with terminal prostatic cancer to be treated differently from a child dying of leukemia? Who is to weigh the value of a few more days of life? Who is to decide when the end should come? The physician? The patient? Should the decision be put upon the family? Should the patient have the option to choose a peaceful death without exposure to the seemingly relentless application of medical technology? Should one discuss this option with the patient? One basic question seems to be the extent to which any individual owns his own death. Does a person have the right to select how and when he will die? Is such a decision by the patient akin to suicide? We believe that only G-d gives life and hence only G-d can take it away. Individual responsibility for the preservation of one's life and health is apart from the duty of one person (including a physician) toward another's life and health, and society's responsibility concerning the life and health of its citizens.

The doctor-patient relationship is no longer what it used to be because of a variety of factors. There are legal forces, such as the medical malpractice issue, that may interfere with the physician's best clinical and ethical judgment. There are psychological forces pushing the physician to "do something." There are professional forces that may force a physician to act to protect himself from peer review. Patients are better informed and becoming more vocal. The physician's own religious and ethical values, his own experiences, his teaching by preceptor all play a role in deciding how he approaches a dying patient.

This essay discusses Jewish perspectives on death and dying and focuses on the subjects of euthanasia, hazardous medical or surgical therapy for the terminally ill, when not to use heroic or extraordinary measures to prolong life, the definition of death in Jewish law, and Living Wills.

Euthanasia

Arguments in favor and against euthanasia are numerous, have and continue to be heatedly debated in many circles, and will be only briefly summarized here.

Opponents of euthanasia say that if voluntary, it is suicide. Jewish religious teachings certainly outlaw suicide. The answer offered to this argument is that martyrdom, a form of suicide, is condoned under certain conditions. However, the martyr seeks primarily not to end his life but to accomplish a goal, death being an undesired side product. Thus, martyrdom and suicide do not seem comparable.

It is also said that euthanasia, if voluntary, is murder. Murder, however, usually connotes premeditated evil. The motives of the person administering euthanasia are far from evil. On the contrary, such motives are commendable and praiseworthy, although the methods may be unacceptable.

I would like to present the classic Jewish sources which relate to this subject.

In Genesis 9:6, we find: "Whoso sheddeth man's blood, by man shall his blood be shed." In Exodus 20:13, it is stated: "And if a man come presumptuously upon his neighbor, to slay him with guile; thou shalt take him from Mine altar, that he may die." In Leviticus 24:17, there is the phrase "And he that smiteth any man mortally shall surely be put to death," and four sentences later we find, again, . . . "And he that killeth a man shall be put to death." In Numbers 35:30, it is stated, "Whoso killeth any person, the murderer shall be slain at the mouth of witnesses." . . . Finally, in Deuteronomy 5:17, the sixth commandment of the decalogue is repeated: "Thou shalt not kill." Thus, in every book of the Pentateuch, we find at least one reference to murder or killing. These citations, however, all relate to intentional homicide and not to mercy killing.

Probably the first recorded instance of euthanasia concerns the death of King Saul. At the end of the first book of Samuel 31:1-6, we find the following:

> Now the Philistines fought against Israel, and the men of Israel fled from before the Philistines and fell down slain in Mount Gilboa. And the Philistines pursued hard upon Saul and upon his sons; and the Philistines slew Jonathan and Abinadab and Malchishua, the sons of Saul. And the battle went sore against Saul and the archers overtook him and he was greatly afraid by reason of the archers. Then said Saul to his armor-bearer: "Draw thy sword, and thrust me through therewith, lest these uncircumcised come and thrust me through and make a mock of me." But his armor-bearer would not; for he was sore afraid. Therefore,

> Saul took his sword and fell upon it. And when the armor-bearer saw that Saul was dead, he likewise fell upon his sword and died with him. So Saul died and his three sons, and his armor-bearer, and all his men, that same day together.

From this passage it would appear as if Saul committed suicide. However, at the beginning of the second book of Samuel 1:5-10, when David is informed of Saul's death, we find the following:

> And David said unto the young man that told him: "How knowest thou that Saul and Jonathan his son are dead?" And the young man that told him said: "As I happened by chance upon Mount Gilboa, behold Saul leaned upon his spear; and lo, the chariots and the horsemen pressed hard upon him. And when he looked behind him, he saw me, and called unto me. And I answered: 'Here am I.' And he said unto me: 'Who art thou?' And I answered him: 'I am an Amalekite.' And he said unto me: 'Stand, I pray thee, beside me, and slay me, for the agony hath taken hold of me; because my life is just yet in me.' So I stood beside him, and slew him, because I was sure that he would not live after that he was fallen."

Many commentators consider this a case of euthanasia. Radak specifically states that Saul did not die immediately on falling on his sword but was mortally wounded and, in his death throes, asked the Amalekite to hasten his death. Ralbag and Rashi also support this viewpoint, as does *Metzudat David.*

The Mishnah states as follows (*Semachot* 1:1): "One who is in a dying condition *(gosses)* is regarded as a living person in all respects." This rule is reiterated by later codifiers of Jewish law including Rambam and the *Shulchan Aruch* as described below. The Mishnah continues (*Semachot* 1:2 to 4):

> One may not bind his jaws, nor stop up his openings, nor place a metallic vessel or any cooling object on his navel until such time that he dies as it is written (Ecclesiastes 12:6): "Before the silver cord [Midrash interprets this as the spinal cord] is snapped asunder."
>
> One may not move him nor may one place him on sand nor on salt until he dies.
>
> One may not close the eyes of the dying person. He who touches them or moves them is shedding blood because Rabbi Meir used to say: "This can be compared to a flickering flame. As soon as a person touches it, it becomes extinguished. So, too, whosoever closes the eyes of the dying is considered to have taken his soul."

The fifth century Babylonian Talmud (*Shabbat* 151b) mentions as follows: "He who closes the eyes of a dying person while the soul is departing is a murderer (literally, he sheds blood). This may be compared to a lamp that is going out. If a man places his finger upon it, it is immediately extinguished." Rashi explains that this small effort of closing the eyes may slightly hasten death.

The twelfth century Code of Maimonides (Book of Judges, laws of Mourning, chapter 4:5) treats our subject matter as follows:

> One who is in a dying condition is regarded as a living person in all respects. It is not permitted to bind his jaws, to stop up the organs of the lower extremities, or to place metallic or cooling vessels upon his navel in order to prevent swelling. He is not to be rubbed or washed, nor is sand or salt to be put upon him until he expires. He who touches him is guilty of shedding blood. To what may he be compared? To a flickering flame, which is extinguished as soon as one touches it. Whoever closes the eyes of the dying while the soul is about to depart is shedding blood. One should wait a while; perhaps he is only in a swoon. . . .

Thus, we again note the prohibition of doing anything that might hasten death. Maimonides does not specifically forbid moving such a patient as does the Mishnah but such a prohibition is implied in Maimonides' text. Maimonides also forbids rubbing and washing a dying person, acts which are not mentioned in the Mishnah. Finally, Maimonides raises the problem of the recognition of death. This problem is becoming more pronounced as scientific medicine improves the methods for supporting respiration and heart function.

The sixteenth century Code of Jewish Law, the *Shulchan Aruch,* compiled in 1564 by Rabbi Joseph Karo, devotes an entire chapter (*Yoreh Deah,* chapter 339) to the laws of the dying patient. The individual in whom death is imminent is referred to as a *gosses.* Rabbi Karo's code begins, as do Maimonides, and the Mishnah, with the phrase: "A *gosses* is considered as a living person in all respects," and then enumerates various acts that are prohibited. All the commentaries explain these prohibitions "lest they hasten the patient's death." One of the forbidden acts not mentioned by Maimonides or the Mishnah is the removal of the pillow from beneath the patient's head. This act had already been prohibited two centuries earlier by *Tur* (Rabbi Jacob ben Asher) in his code (*Tur Yoreh Deah,* chapter 339). The text of the *Shulchan Aruch* is nearly identical to that of *Tur. Tur,* however, has the additional general explanation: "The rule in this matter is that any act performed in relation to death should not be carried out until the soul has departed." Thus, not only are physical acts on the patient such as those described above forbidden, but one should also not provide a coffin or prepare a grave or make other funeral or related arrangements lest the patient hear of this and his death be hastened. Even psychological stress is prohibited.

On the other hand, Rabbi Judah the *Chasid,* author of the thirteenth century work *Sefer Chasidim,* states in section 723, "If a person is dying and someone near his house is chopping wood so that the soul cannot depart, one should remove the [wood] chopper from there. . . ."

Based on the *Sefer Chasidim,* the *Ramo* (Rabbi Moses Isserles), in his glosses on *Shulchan Aruch,* section *Yoreh Deah,* chapter 339:1, states that

> If there is anything which causes a hindrance to the departure of the soul such as the presence near the patient's house of a knocking noise such as wood chopping or if there is salt on the patient's tongue; and these hinder the soul's departure, then it is permissible to remove them from there because there is no act involved in this at all but only the removal of the impediment.

Examples of such removal of impediments are cited in the Talmud. In a famous passage (*Avodah Zarah* 18a), a distinction is implied between the deliberate termination of life and the removal of means which artificially prolong the painful process of death. The passage describes the martyrdom of Rabbi Hananya Ben Teradyon, who was a victim of the Romans during the Hadrianic persecutions of the second century. The martyr was wrapped in the Scroll of the Torah from which he had been teaching, and placed on a pyre of green brushwood. His chest was covered with woolen sponges, drenched with water, to prolong the agony of dying. His disciples advised him to open his mouth so that he might be asphyxiated and have a quicker end to his suffering. He refused to do so saying: "It is best that He who has given life should take it away; no one may hasten his death." He did, however, allow the executioner to remove the wet sponges; the fire could then consume at its natural, unimpeded pace. This act of removing hindrances to natural death was deemed meritorious.

Another talmudic reference is to be found in *Ketubot* 104a: When Rabbi Judah the Prince was dying, the rabbis decreed a public fast and offered prayers for the prolongation of his life. When Rabbi Judah's maid, renowned in legend for her sagacity, discerned that he was approaching death and suffering great pain, she threw a jar from the roof to distract the rabbis and interrupt their incessant prayers. This, the Talmud relates approvingly, enabled his soul to depart in peace.

While this latter passage and later rabbinic statements based on it suggest that it is proper that a life in mortal suffering be ended (or at least to cease praying that it be prolonged), the first passage teaches clearly that it is proper actively to remove an artificial impediment to the process of dying. Various rabbinic responsa on this subject are summarized by Rabbi J.D. Bleich in the recent book, *Judaism and Healing.*

The sum total of this discussion of the Jewish attitude toward euthanasia seems to indicate, as expressed by Rabbi Jacobovits, that "Any form of active euthanasia is strictly prohibited and condemned as plain murder . . . anyone who kills a dying person is liable to the death penalty as a common murderer. At the same time, Jewish law sanctions the withdrawal of any factor—whether extraneous to the patient himself or not—which may artificially delay his demise in the final phase."

Rabbi Jacobovits is quick to point out, however, that all the Jewish sources refer to an individual in whom death is expected to be imminent, three days or less in rabbinic references. Thus, passive euthanasia in a patient who may yet live for weeks or months may not necessarily be condoned. Furthermore, in the case of an incurably ill person in severe pain, agony, or distress, the removal of an impediment which hinders his soul's departure, although permitted by Jewish law (as described by Ramo), may not be analogous to the withholding of medical therapy that is perhaps sustaining the patient's life, albeit unnaturally. The impediments spoken of in the codes of Jewish law, whether far removed from the patient as exemplified by the noise of wood chopping, or in physical contact with him such as the case of salt on the patient's tongue, do not constitute any part of the therapeutic armamentarium employed in the medical management of this patient. For this reason, these impediments may be removed. However, the discontinuation of instrumentation and machinery which is specifically designed and utilized in the treatment of incurably ill patients might only be permissible if one is certain that in doing so one is shortening the act of dying and not interrupting life. Yet who can make the fine distinction between prolonging life and prolonging the act of dying? Certainly only a scholar of Jewish law is qualified to offer an opinion.

Hazardous or Experimental Therapy for the Terminally Ill

A cardinal principle in Judaism is that human life is of infinite value. The preservation of human life takes precedence over all biblical commandments, with three exceptions: idolatry, murder and incest or adultery. Life's value is absolute and supreme. Thus, an old man or woman, a mentally retarded person, a defective baby, a dying cancer patient and their like all have the same right to life as you or I. In Jewish law, a young patient does not have preference over an old one. In order to preserve a human life, even the Sabbath or the Day of Atonement may be desecrated and all other rules and laws, save the above three, are suspended for the overriding consideration of saving a human life. The corollary of this principle is that one is prohibited from doing anything that might shorten a life even for a very short time since every moment of human life is of infinite value.

How are these basic principles applied when a physician is confronted with the following dilemma? His extremely ill patient will, under normal circumstances, die shortly, perhaps in a few days or weeks. His patient's only chance for survival is dangerous experimental surgery or therapy. However, if the surgery or therapy fails to heal, the patient will die immediately. What should the physician do? Should he risk the definite short period of life remaining for the patient by administering the drastic remedy in the hope that the patient may be cured and live a prolonged period? In other words, should the physician abandon the *definite* short life span of the patient in favor of the *possible* significant prolongation of his life?

In his famous early responsa, Rabbi Moshe Feinstein states that one is permitted to submit to dangerous surgery even though it may hasten death if unsuccessful, because of the potential, however small, of the operation being successful and effecting a cure. In his most recent collection of responsa, however, Rav Feinstein rules that if the surgery might hasten his death if it does not heal him, the patient should not be subjected to it. Only when there is at least a fifty-fifty chance of success must the sick person undergo the treatment. He cautions that forcing a person to undergo this treatment may arouse such anxiety as to cause his death, which would render it an act of murder. However, he does not cite the reasoning or precedent on which he relies. Israel's former Chief Rabbi, Shlomo Goren, writes that one should use hazardous experimental therapy not only in a case where the patient will certainly die without the medical or surgical therapy but also where the possibility exists of prolonging the patient's life by the therapy. Britain's Chief Rabbi, Immanuel Jakobovits, agrees that hazardous therapy may be applied to patients if it may be potentially helpful to the patient, however remote the chances of success.

Two earlier rabbinic sources also clearly enunciate the Jewish legal view concerning hazardous therapy for the dying. Rabbi Chaim Ozer Grodzinski was asked about the permissibility of performing a dangerous surgical procedure on a seriously ill patient. He answered that if all the attending physicians, without exception, recommend such an operation, it should be performed, even if the chances for success are smaller than those for failure (Responsa

Achiezer, Yoreh Deah #16:6). A similar pronouncement is made by Rabbi Jacob Reischer with regard to dangerous medical therapy for a seriously ill patient. He permits such therapy since it may cure the patient although it may hasten the patient's death (Responsa *Shevut Yaakov,* Section 3 #75). Rabbi Reischer also requires a group of physicians to concur in the decision.

Do heroic or extraordinary measures constitute impediments to dying? How does one define heroic measures? What may be considered heroic for Karen Ann Quinlan (e.g., use of antibiotics to treat pneumonia) may be standard therapy for an otherwise healthy person. When, if ever, may treatment be withheld? May a terminally ill patient request that his agony not be prolonged? Must a patient in a deep coma but breathing without mechanical assistance be afforded all the care and concern due any ill person including hydration via intravenous infusion, antibiotics to treat infections, and optimum care to maintain good kidney, liver and cardiac function? Jewish tradition answers the latter question in the affirmative in view of the supreme value of human life whose preservation takes precedence over virtually all other considerations. Human life is not regarded as a goal to be preserved as a condition of other values but as an absolute basic good.

A basic tenet of Judaism is the supreme value of human life. This principle is based in part upon our belief that man was created in the image of G-d. Therefore, when a person's life is in danger, even when there is no hope for survival for a prolonged period but only for a very short time, all commandments of the Torah are set aside. Any act which can prolong life supersedes all the biblical comdandments, except the three cardinal ones. However, Rav Feinstein has recently ruled that if a person is in great pain, he does not have to undergo treatment that will extend his life but not alleviate the pain. Also, he cannot be forced to accept intravenous feeding. For the patient who has difficulty breathing, Rav Feinstein counsels giving only enough oxygen to alleviate pain for a short while, then removing the equipment to see if the patient is still alive. Apparently, he does not consider it necessary to keep the patient artificially breathing and thus prolong his dying—but enough should be given to prevent pain to him.

The Living Will

The living will is a recently-adopted method, in some jurisdictions of the United States, that would recognize the right of an adult person to prepare a written directive instructing his physician to withhold life-sustaining procedures in the event of the patient's incompetence to do so while in a terminal condition. The living will is designed to promote patient autonomy while removing onerous decision-making from physicians and the patients' families. Experience with the living will indicates that it can either help or hinder clinical decision-making.

If the patient changes his mind during the period when the living will is in effect, yet fails to formally rescind the declaration, it may be activated without proper "informed consent." Moreover, since intractable pain is often a major cause for activating the living will, medical science may by then have developed better methods to deal with such pain. A patient who signs a living will thinks that he is opting for a painless, conscious, dignified, decent, comfortable, peaceful, natural death. In fact, what the patient perceives as his "right to die" may backfire. The living will only protects refusal of treatment but does not guarantee a peaceful easy death.

In essence, Judaism is opposed to the concept of the living will in that the patient may not have the "right to die." Only G-d gives and takes life. Man does not have full title over his life or body. He is charged with preserving, dignifying and hallowing that life. However, we have noted that in certain cases it is not required to prolong the suffering, and the patient may refuse treatment under certain circumstances.

The complexities of the issues relating to death and dying, mercy killing, withholding treatment, heroic measures, discontinuation of life support systems, and the living will, among others, are such that it is difficult to specify the halacha in general terms, and each situation must be studied individually. Jewish law requires the physician to do everything in his power to prolong life, but does not mandate the use of measures that prolong the act of dying. In Jewish law and moral teaching, "the value of human life is infinite and beyond measure, so that any part of life—even if only an hour or a second—is of precisely the same worth as seventy years of it, just as any fraction of infinity, being indivisible, remains infinite. Accordingly, to kill a decrepit patient approaching death constitutes exactly the same crime of murder as to kill a young, healthy person who may still have many decades to live. . . ."

Euthanasia is opposed without qualification in Jewish law, which condemns as sheer murder any active or deliberate hastening of death, whether the physician acts with or without the patient's consent. Some rabbinic views do not allow any relaxation of efforts, however artificial and ultimately hopeless, to prolong life. Others, however, do not require the physician to resort to "heroic" methods, but sanction the omission of machines and artificial life support systems that only serve to draw out the dying patient's agony, provided, however, that basic care such as food and good nursing is provided. An organ may not be removed for transplantation until the patient has been pronounced dead, defined in Judaism as the cessation of spontanous respiration and heartbeat in a patient where resuscitation is deemed impossible. Specifically questioned about the Karen Ann Quinlan case, most rabbis offered the opinion that in Jewish law we are not required to utilize heroic measures to prolong the life of hopelessly sick patients, but we are forbidden to terminate the use of such measures once they have been begun.

The modern phrase "quality of life" or "quality of existence" embodies within it a concept of worthiness with connotations of personal character and social status. Emotional and financial burdens are frequently cited as justification for decisions about "heroic" measures; suffering of the family is another reason offered for allowing a patient to die by removing artificial life supports. On this basis, the sanctity of life as a pre-eminent value is being threatened. Evil has small beginnings. When the quality of life replaces the sanctity of life, society has done itself irreparable harm.

The Babirusa: A Kosher Pig?

J. David Bleich

An Associated Press news bulletin dated November 13, 1984, reported that a species of swine closely related to the domestic pig is a kosher animal. The author alleged that the babirusa, whose native habitat is Indonesia, is an animal possessing two stomachs and suggested that it also chews the cud. Since, in common with all swine, the babirusa also has split hoofs, the animal was alleged to possess the physical characteristics of a kosher species. The news item appeared in many American newspapers and was featured on television newscasts.

The Associated Press bulletin was based upon a report published by the National Research Council (NRC). In an article appearing in the Fall 1984 issue of *Horizons,* a publication of the U.S. Agency for International Development, John Daly writes:

> The babirusa stands out among pig-like animals because of its unique stomach, similar to a ruminant's.... This may make the babirusa a more efficient meat producer in some environments. In addition, cultures that do not eat swine might accept the babirusa. (p. 28)

In Israel, the report of the existence of an animal whose meat is allegedly indistinguishable from that of a pig in taste and appearance, but which is nevertheless kosher, created somewhat of a sensation. Newspaper accounts indicate that a number of prominent rabbinic authorities whose views were solicited were understandably incredulous and reserved decision. In particular, some scholars expressed concern with regard to whether the configuration of the animal's toes manifests the criteria of split hoofs which are the hallmark of a kosher species. *Gilyon Maharsha, Yoreh De'ah* 79:1, citing earlier authorities, states that the hoofs must be split along their entire length. The London *Jewish Chronicle,* November 16, 1984, p. 1, quoted an anonymous Anglo-Jewish scholar who expressed concern that the animal may have been the product of crossbreeding between a kosher animal and the non-kosher pig.

The phenomenon of a kosher pig is not entirely unknown in rabbinic literature. R. Hayyim ibn Attar, *Or ha-Hayyim,* Leviticus 11:3, quotes an unidentified aggadic source which comments: "Why is it named *'hazir'?* Because it will one day 'return' to become permissible," i.e, the pig will return to its pre-Sinaitic status as a permitted source of meat. In his commentary on Leviticus 11:7, *Or ha-Hayyim* questions the meaning of this statement. It is a fundamental principle of Judaism that the Torah is immutable; hence a pig which does not chew its cud cannot at any time be declared kosher. Accordingly, *Or ha-Hayyim* comments that the phrase "but it does not chew its cud" which occurs in Leviticus 11:7 is conditional in nature, i.e, the pig is forbidden only so long as it does not chew its cud, "but in the eschatological era it will chew its cud and will 'return' to become permissible." Indeed, the etymological analysis presented by *Or ha-Hayyim* would lead to acceptance of a cud-chewing pig not only as a kosher animal but as a harbinger of the eschatological era as well. A similar statement is made by Rema of Panu, *Asarah Ma'amarot, Ma'amar Hikur Din,* II, chapter 17.

The comments of *Or ha-Hayyim* are, however, sharply challenged by R. Baruch ha-Levi Epstein, *Torah Temimah,* Leviticus 11:7, sec. 21. *Torah Temimah* asserts that the only rabbinic statement even vaguely resembling that which is quoted by *Or ha-Hayyim* is an etymological comment on the word *"hazir"* was found in *Vayikra Rabbah* 13:5 and repeated in *Kohelet Rabbah* 1:28. In context, the midrashic statement is clearly an allegorical reference to the eschatological role of Gentile nations in causing the return of Israel to her original state of grandeur. A similar interpretation was presented much earlier by Rabbenu Bahya in his commentary on Leviticus 11:7.

Whether or not there is a specific midrashic reference to a pig which chews the cud, it would appear that an animal which has split hoofs and which also chews its cud is *ipso facto* kosher. Indeed, Jewish law does not even deem it essential to examine an animal for the manifestation of both split hoofs and the chewing of the cud. Leviticus 11:4-6 enumerates three species of ruminants which chew the cud but which do not have split hoofs: the camel, the rock-badger and the hare. Deuteronomy 14:7 names a fourth animal, the *shesu'ah,* which is described as chewing the cud but as not having cloven hoofs. This animal is described by the Gemara, *Hullin* 60b, as a creature which has two backs and two spinal columns. The Gemara, *Niddah* 24a, further explains that the *shesu'ah* is the progeny of a permitted species. In effect, the birth of a *shesu'ah* is an anomaly. Both Leviticus 11:7 and Deuteronomy 14:8 name only one animal, the swine, which has split hoofs but does not chew its cud. The Gemara, *Hullin* 59a, on the basis of a pleonasm, regards these enumerated species not as paradigmatic, but as exhaustive. Thus the Gemara comments, "The Ruler of the universe knows that there is no other beast that chews the cud and is unclean except the camel [and the other species enumerated by Scripture]" and similarly comments, "The Ruler of the universe knows that there is no other beast that parts the hoofs and is unclean except the swine." These dicta pave the way for a determination that an animal may be declared kosher even without examination for the presence of both split hoofs and the chewing of the cud. The Gemara, *Hullin* 59a, notes that the absence of upper incisors and canines is a characteristic of all ruminants with the exception of the camel which has canines in both jaws. Accordingly, declares the Gemara, "If a man was walking in the desert and found an animal with its hoofs cut off, he should examine the mouth; if it has no upper teeth, he may be certain that it is clean; otherwise he may be certain that it is unclean; provided, however, . . . he recognizes the young camel." The possibility that the animal may be a young camel must be excluded since, even though the young camel has no teeth, it will eventually develop canines. The Gemara explicitly negates the possibility that there may exist some other animal that lacks teeth, i.e., a ruminant that chews the cud is non-kosher by virtue of its non-cloven hoofs. Thus, if it were to be shown that the babirusa lacks incisors and canines on its upper jaw it may be declared a kosher species on that basis alone. Absence of incisors and canines is itself evidence that the animal is a cud-chewing ruminant.

The Gemara continues with the description of another criterion by means of which an animal may be recognized as a member of a permitted species: "If a man was walking in a desert and found an animal with its hoofs cut off and its mouth mutilated, he should examine its flank; if it runs crosswise he may be certain that it is clean, but if not he may be certain that it is unclean; provided, however, he recognizes the *arod*. . . . Where should he examine the flesh?. . . Under the rump." In kosher species the flesh under the tail in the vicinity of the rump runs in a criss-cross fashion; one series of muscles run downward so that that portion of the meat is readily torn vertically and another series of muscles runs transversely so that that portion of the meat is readily torn horizontally. The Gemara explicitly states that we are the recipients of a tradition received by Moses at Mount Sinai to the effect that the *arod* is the sole non-kosher animal manifesting this characteristic. Thus, if the babirusa indeed manifests this characteristic there would be yet additional grounds for assuming that it is a kosher species.

There is yet another means of recognizing a kosher species. The Mishnah, *Niddah* 51b, declares, "Every [species] which has horns has [split] hoofs," i.e., is a kosher species. According to Rabbenu Tam, cited by *Tosafot, Hullin* 59a, that dictum is accepted as a unanimous pronouncement and hence, as Maharshah, *ad locum,* explains, the presence of any type of horn is a sufficient criterion of *kashrut.* However, Ravan, also cited by *Tosafot, Hullin* 59a, maintains that this dictum reflects the opinion of R. Dosa who is reported to have declared, "Those that have horns need not be examined as to their hoofs" (*Hullin* 59b). According to Ravan, the Sages disagree with R. Dosa and require the presence of both horns and split hoofs. However, even according to Ravan, the Sages accept the presence of any type of horn as a sufficient criterion of the *kashrut* of the species provided that the animal also manifests split hoofs. Thus, if an animal possesses split hoofs, the presence of horns is sufficient to guarantee that it is not a forbidden swine. Accordingly, *Shulhan Arukh, Yoreh De'ah* 79:1, rules ". . . if its hoofs are split it is certain that it is clean, provided he recognizes a pig; if it has horns there is no possibility that it might be a pig and it is clean."

The Gemara, *Hullin* 59b, does indeed state that, in order to qualify as a distinguishing criterion of an animal whose *helev* is permitted, the horn must be forked (according to Rashi: branched, like antlers; according to *Tosafot:* bent or hooked at the end) or, if not forked, the horn must be rounded (i.e., composed of tubes or scales, one over the other), pointed (or, according to one interpretation advanced by Rashi, rounded and narrow) and notched (i.e., rough), and the notches must run one into the other. However, such distinctive horns are required only in order to determine that the animal is a *hayyah* or "wild beast" whose *helev* is permitted; the presence of any type of horn is indicative of the fact that the animal is a member of a kosher species. Thus *Shulhan Arukh* omits reference to the presence of a distinctive horn in declaring that the presence of horns is sufficient to exclude the possibility that an animal may be a pig.

In discussing the status of the babirusa, the *Jewish Chronicle* quotes the Sephardic Chief Rabbi of Israel, Rabbi Mordecai Eliyahu, as stating, *inter alia,* ". . . the question of its tusks is also relevant." The question of the babirusa's tusks, which are virtually perpendicular and point upwards in the manners of horns, is indeed relevant in the sense that the presence of horns would also, in and of itself, be sufficient to distinguish the babirusa from forbidden forms of swine. Coupled with split hoofs, the presence of horns would be sufficient evidence of the animal's *kashrut.* Horns, however, by definition, emerge from the head. Pictures of the babirusa show upwardly curved projections emanating from the area of the snout. Presumably, those tusk-like projections are rooted in the jaw or in the cheek, rather than in the head or skull, and, halakhically, would not be categorized as horns. Accordingly, the presence or absence of such tusks would be of no halakhic significance.

Assuming that the babirusa manifests the requisite criteria of a kosher animal, the fact that it resembles a pig in appearance and taste is not sufficient grounds for banning its consumption as kosher meat. The Sages of the Talmud did indeed promulgate numerous edicts in order to prevent inadvertent transgression of biblical laws as the result of possible confusion between that which is permitted and that which is forbidden in situations in which the permitted and the prohibited closely resemble one another. Yet, absent specific rabbinic legislation, there are no grounds to forbid any matter which has not been expressly prohibited.

The earliest formulation of this principle occurs in a responsum of Rav Sar Shalom Ga'on, *Teshuvot ha-Ge'onim: Hemdah Genuzah,* no. 77. Sandwiches were apparently known and enjoyed as early as the geonic period since the interlocutor asks whether it is permissible "to make a bun and to place in it [a piece of] tail or fat meat." His concern was that the bread might crumble and the particles of bread which break off from the bun might later be eaten with cheese. It is because of such concern that rabbinic law declares bread containing either dairy or meat products to be non-kosher, unless the bread is baked in a distinctive manner. However, with regard to placing meat in the already baked bun, Rav Sar Shalom Ga'on answers unequivocally that there is no reason for concern since there is no decree of "our early teachers" prohibiting the eating of meat sandwiches.

There are, however, two logical possibilities that must be discussed which would have the effect of negating the conclusion that, upon manifesting the physical criteria of a permitted species, the babirusa may be considered a kosher animal. The possibility must be considered that the animal may have originated either as the result of crossbreeding between a kosher species and a swine or as the result of a genetic mutation. The contention that the babirusa may perhaps be the result of crossbreeding may be dismissed quite readily. The possibility of the emergence of an interspecies of this nature, particularly of one which is not sterile and can reproduce, is extremely unlikely, to say the least. From the halakhic vantage point it is regarded as impossible. Although the Gemara, *Bekhorot* 7a, accepts the possibility of animals of different species mating and producing offspring, it rejects the opinion which asserts that progeny may be born of a union between members of kosher and non-kosher species.

The possibility of a genetic mutation which is transmitted to future generations is much more within the realm of both scientific and halakhic possibility. The halakhah to be applied in the event of the occurrence of such a contingency is clear. Codifying a principle laid down in the Mishnah, *Bekhorot* 5b, *Shulhan Arukh, Yoreh De'ah* 79:2, rules that the offspring of an unclean mother is non-kosher even if the animal itself manifests all the characteristics of a kosher animal. The comments of many authorities, particularly Shakh, *Yoreh De'ah* 79:4, and *Pri Megadim, Siftei Da'at* 79:1, indicate that the principle involved is that of *yotse,* i.e., anything which "emerges" from, or is produced by, an unclean animal is itself not kosher. It is on the basis of this principle that, for example, the milk of non-kosher animals is forbidden.

R. Hayyim ha-Levi Soloveitchik, in his commentary on the Rambam, *Hilkhot Ma'akhalot Asurot* 3:11, explains this halakhic provision in an entirely different manner. R. Hayyim states that, in effect, an animal is a member of a given species, not because it possesses the distinctive characteristics of that species, but because it was born to a mother who is a member of that species. It is, then, maternal identity which is transmitted to progeny and which determines the species to which the offspring belong for purposes of halakhic classification. On the basis of either analysis, the offspring of a non-kosher animal is not kosher even if, as the result of genetic mutation, it manifests the criteria of a kosher animal.

The two theories do, however, yield a halakhic difference with regard to the punishment to be administered for consuming the meat of an ostensibly "kosher" animal born to a non-kosher mother. If the animal is regarded as intrinsically non-kosher, the punishment is lashes; if the offspring is only the "product" of a non-kosher species, no lashes are administered for eating its flesh. There are also other halakhic ramifications which are contingent upon acceptance of one or the other of these theories. If the offspring is intrinsically non-kosher there is no punishment of *karet* for partaking of the animal's *helev,* since the prohibition against partaking of *helev* does not extend to the fat of non-kosher species which cannot be offered as sacrifices. Furthermore, if the animal is itself kosher, but forbidden as the "product" of a non-kosher animal, upon *shehitah* its flesh would not defile as carrion; if the animal is intrinsically not kosher, it would defile as carrion even if killed by means of *shehitah.*

Although a clean animal born of an unclean animal is not kosher, absent evidence that such a phenomenon has occurred, there is no halakhic basis for suspecting that an animal manifesting the characteristics of a kosher species is in reality the offspring of a non-kosher animal. Were this not the case, no animal could be definitively accepted as kosher unless a witness was present at its birth to observe that, in actuality, it is the offspring of a kosher mother. The general halakhic principle is that such unlikely contingencies need not be contemplated.

Thus it might appear that there are no halakhic grounds for a suspicion that the babirusa is a genetic mutation of a forbidden species of swine and hence itself non-kosher. There are, however, grounds for skepticism with regard to the permissibility of the babirusa. The Gemara, *Hullin* 109b, declares:

> For everything God has forbidden us He has permitted us an equivalent: He has forbidden us blood but has permitted us liver; He has forbidden us intercourse during menstruation but has permitted us the blood of purification; He has forbidden us the fat of cattle but has permitted us the fat of a wild beast; He has forbidden us swine's flesh but has permitted us the brain of the *shibbuta*. . . .

If the babirusa is indeed a "kosher pig" it is a much more obvious example of a kosher counterpart to the non-kosher swine than is the brain of the fish known as the *shibbuta.* Moreover, the Gemara, *Hullin* 80a, states that the only animals which are kosher are the ten species specifically enumerated in Deuteronomy 14:4-5. This dictum is recorded as a normative ruling by Rambam, *Hilkhot Ma'akhalot Asurot* 1:8. There are, of course, other kosher animals which one might regard as distinct species, including perhaps the *kevi,* which according to one talmudic opinion is an "independent species." Those animals, for purposes of halakhic classification, are subsumed under one or another of the species enumerated by Scripture.

Thus, assuming that the babirsua manifests the criteria of a clean animal, to be regarded as kosher it must be classified, not as a"kosher pig," or even as an independent species, but as a subspecies of one of the ten kosher animals enumerated by Scripture. Given its biological and anatomical similarity to the swine, the possibility that it is a mutation of a swine appears more cogent. Since, in this case, there are grounds for suspecting that the babirusa is "a clean animal which has been born of an unclean animal" it would appear to this writer that its status would be if not definitively non-kosher, *de minimus,* that of a *safek,* i.e., an animal of doubtful *kashrut.*

In any event, it would not be permitted to eat the babirusa for an entirely different consideration. According to a number of latter-day authorities, it is forbidden to eat the meat of any hitherto unknown species even if it possesses the characteristics of a kosher animal and does not in any way resemble a non-kosher species. *Hokhmat Adam* 36:1 declares, ". . . we eat only [those animals] with regard to which we have received a tradition from our fathers." Therefore, "it is forbidden for us to eat of the 'wild beasts' *[hayyot]* except the deer which is recognized by us." This rule is stated by Rema, *Yoreh De'ah* 82:3, with regard to birds and is extended by *Hokhmat Adam* to encompass animal species as well. *Hokhmat Adam's* position appears to be based upon a comment of Shakh, *Yoreh De'ah* 80:1, although the thrust of Shakh's comment is understood in a different manner by *Pri Megadim, Siftei Da'at* 80:1. *Hokhmat Adam's* ruling is endorsed by *Hazon Ish, Yoreh De'ah* 11:4-5, as an established practice.

In point of fact, the entire discussion is only of academic interest. *Science News,* vol. 126, no. 2 (November 24, 1984), p. 327, reveals that babirusas are to be found in this country in the Los Angeles Zoo. A zoo official, Dr. Warren Thomas, is reported as stating that the babirusa is not a ruminant and does not chew its cud.

In actuality, it has been known for some time that the babirusa is not a true ruminant. With the exception of an early investigation conducted by Willem Vrolik, *Recherches d'anatomie comparee sur le Babyrussa* (Amsterdam, 1844) and a brief discussion by a noted nineteenth-century English anatomist and paleontologist, Sir Robert Owen, *On the Anatomy of Vertebrates* (London, 1868), III, 465, the sole scientific study of the babirusa is the 1940 report of D. Dwight Davis, "Notes on the Anatomy of the Babirusa," *Field Museum of Natural History,* XXII, 363-411. That study was based upon post-mortem dissection of a babirusa that had died in the Chicago Zoo. Davis, p. 388, reports that, although the animal's stomach, except for the absence of an omasum, is strikingly similar to that of the domestic sheep, the arrangement of the stomach "is scarcely such that true rumination could take place . . . and it is certain that the similarity is due to convergence, and consequently is without such phylogenetic significance." Moreover, the non-ruminating character of the babirusa was recognized well over a hundred years ago by Sir Robert Owen, in his previously cited discussion.

Moreover, a report issued by the National Research Council, *Little-Known Asian Animals with a Promising Economic Future* (Washington, 1983), p. 89, states, "The male has large upper canines that grow upwards, piercing right through the flesh of the snout and curving back and downwards toward the forehead without even entering the mouth." Thus the tusks of the babirusa are not horns, but are described as canines. As has been indicated earlier, the Gemara, *Hullin* 59a, declares that the presence of incisors or canines is a conclusive indication that the animal does not chew the cud. As stated by Rabbi Eliyahu, the "question of [the babirusa's] tusks" is certainly "relevant." Indeed, it is more than relevant; it is dispositive.

It is of interest to note that R. Meir Leibush Malbim, in his commentary on Leviticus 11:7, describes an animal remarkably similar to the babirusa. Malbim reports that the animal, which he calls a "tai'asu," is found in the tropical areas of South America and possesses four stomachs. Although Malbim is unclear, and perhaps even contradictory, with regard to whether this animal chews the cud, he reports that it has incisors in the upper jaw. As has been noted earlier, absence of incisors is regarded by the Gemara, *Hullin* 59a, as proof that the animal chews its cud and the converse is regarded as proof that it is unclean, i.e., the presence of incisors is incompatible with chewing the cud. Accordingly, it must be assumed that Malbim intends us to understand that the tai'asu does not chew its cud. Malbim declares the animal to be non-kosher and points to its physical characteristics in order to illustrate the use of the future tense in the phrase *"ve-hu gera lo yigar*—it will not chew the cud." According to Malbim, the verse alludes to this particular species of swine and declares that, although it has developed some characteristics of a ruminant, viz., four stomachs, it remains non-kosher because "it will not chew the cud."

The animals described by Malbim are peccaries originally known as dicotyles and now usually referred to as tayassu. Their anatomical characteristics are described in some detail by Georges Cuvier, *Regne Animal* (Paris, 1817), I, 237, and W. H. Flower and R. Lydekker, *An Introduction to the Study of Mammals Living and Extinct* (London, 1891), p. 289.

61

Ethics of the Fathers *(Pirkei Avot)*

A new linear translation, by the Editor

Chapter 1:	פרק א׳
All Israel	כָּל־יִשְׂרָאֵל
has for them a portion	יֵשׁ לָהֶם חֵלֶק
in the world to come.	לָעוֹלָם הַבָּא.
As it is said,	שֶׁנֶּאֱמַר,
"and your nation are all righteous,	וְעַמֵּךְ כֻּלָּם צַדִּיקִים,
Forever they will inherit the land —	לְעוֹלָם יִירְשׁוּ אָרֶץ —
a seed that I planted,	נֵצֶר מַטָּעַי,
the work of My hands (in order) to glorify (Me)" (Isaiah 60:21).	מַעֲשֵׂה יָדַי לְהִתְפָּאֵר (ישעיה ס, כא).
1: Moses received the Torah from Sinai	1. מֹשֶׁה קִבֵּל תּוֹרָה מִסִּינַי
and he passed it to Joshua;	וּמְסָרָהּ לִיהוֹשֻׁעַ;
and Joshua to the elders;	וִיהוֹשֻׁעַ לִזְקֵנִים;
and the elders to the prophets;	וּזְקֵנִים לִנְבִיאִים;
and the prophets passed it to the men of the Great Assembly.	וּנְבִיאִים מְסָרוּהָ לְאַנְשֵׁי כְנֶסֶת הַגְּדוֹלָה.
They said three things:	הֵם אָמְרוּ שְׁלשָׁה דְבָרִים:
Be fair in judging,	הֱווּ מְתוּנִים בַּדִּין,
and raise many students,	וְהַעֲמִידוּ תַּלְמִידִים הַרְבֵּה,
and make a fence around the Torah.	וַעֲשׂוּ סְיָג לַתּוֹרָה.
2: Simon, the Righteous, was	2. שִׁמְעוֹן הַצַּדִּיק הָיָה
from the remaining members of the Great Assembly.	מִשְּׁיָרֵי כְּנֶסֶת הַגְּדוֹלָה.
He used to say:	הוּא הָיָה אוֹמֵר:
On three things the world stands —	עַל־שְׁלשָׁה דְבָרִים הָעוֹלָם עוֹמֵד —
on the Torah,	עַל הַתּוֹרָה,
on the work (of the Temple),	וְעַל הָעֲבוֹדָה,
and on acts of kindness.	וְעַל גְּמִילוּת חֲסָדִים.
3: Antignos, a man from Socho,	3. אַנְטִיגְנוֹס אִישׁ שׂוֹכוֹ,
received (the Tradition) from Simon, the Righteous.	קִבֵּל מִשִּׁמְעוֹן הַצַּדִּיק.
He used to say:	הוּא הָיָה אוֹמֵר:
Do not be like servants	אַל־תִּהְיוּ כַּעֲבָדִים
who serve their master	הַמְשַׁמְּשִׁים אֶת־הָרַב
in order to receive a reward.	עַל־מְנָת לְקַבֵּל פְּרָס.

Rather, be like servants	אֶלָּא, הֱיוּ כַּעֲבָדִים
who serve their master	הַמְשַׁמְּשִׁים אֶת־הָרַב
not in order	שֶׁלֹּא עַל־מְנָת
to receive a reward.	לְקַבֵּל פְּרָס.
And the fear of Heaven should be upon you.	וִיהִי מוֹרָא שָׁמַיִם עֲלֵיכֶם.
4: Yose, the son of Yo'ezer, a man from Zrada,	4. יוֹסֵי בֶּן־יוֹעֶזֶר אִישׁ צְרֵדָה,
and Yose, the son of Yochanan, a man from Jerusalem,	וְיוֹסֵי בֶּן־יוֹחָנָן אִישׁ יְרוּשָׁלַיִם,
received from them.	קִבְּלוּ מֵהֶם.
Yose, the son of Yo'ezer, a man from Zrada, says:	יוֹסֵי בֶּן־יוֹעֶזֶר אִישׁ צְרֵדָה אוֹמֵר:
Your house should be a meeting place for wise men;	יְהִי בֵיתְךָ בֵּית וַעַד לַחֲכָמִים;
and you should cling to the dust of their feet;	וֶהֱוֵה מִתְאַבֵּק בַּעֲפַר רַגְלֵיהֶם;
and you should drink thirstily of their words.	וֶהֱוֵה שׁוֹתֶה בַצָּמָא אֶת־דִּבְרֵיהֶם.
5: Yose, the son of Yochanan, a man from Jerusalem, says:	5. יוֹסֵי בֶּן־יוֹחָנָן אִישׁ יְרוּשָׁלַיִם אוֹמֵר:
Your house should be open wide,	יְהִי בֵיתְךָ פָּתוּחַ לִרְוָחָה,
and poor people should be (like) the members of your house.	וְיִהְיוּ עֲנִיִּים בְּנֵי בֵיתֶךָ.
And do not have excessive conversations with women —	וְאַל תַּרְבֶּה שִׂיחָה עִם הָאִשָּׁה —
regarding one's wife, it was said,	בְּאִשְׁתּוֹ אָמְרוּ,
how much more so with the wife of one's friend.	קַל וָחֹמֶר בְּאֵשֶׁת חֲבֵרוֹ.
From here the Sages said,	מִכָּאן אָמְרוּ חֲכָמִים,
All who speak excessively with women	כָּל־הַמַּרְבֶּה שִׂיחָה עִם הָאִשָּׁה
bring evil to one's self,	גּוֹרֵם רָעָה לְעַצְמוֹ,
and is wasting (time) from learning Torah,	וּבוֹטֵל מִדִּבְרֵי תוֹרָה,
and in the end will inherit Gehenna.	וְסוֹפוֹ יוֹרֵשׁ גֵּיהִנֹּם.
6: Joshua, the son of Prachya	6. יְהוֹשֻׁעַ בֶּן־פְּרַחְיָה
and Nitai, the Arabelite,	וְנִתַּאי הָאַרְבֵּלִי,
received from them.	קִבְּלוּ מֵהֶם.
Joshua, the son of Prachya, says:	יְהוֹשֻׁעַ בֶּן־פְּרַחְיָה אוֹמֵר:
Establish for yourself a teacher;	עֲשֵׂה לְךָ רַב;
and acquire for yourself a friend;	וּקְנֵה לְךָ חָבֵר;
and judge each man	וֶהֱוֵי דָן אֶת־כָּל־הָאָדָם
in his own merit.	לְכַף זְכוּת.
7: Nitai, the Arabelite, says,	7. נִתַּאי הָאַרְבֵּלִי אוֹמֵר,
Keep distance from a bad neighbor,	הַרְחֵק מִשָּׁכֵן רָע,
and do not be friends with a wicked person;	וְאַל־תִּתְחַבֵּר לָרָשָׁע;
and do not despair	וְאַל־תִּתְיָאֵשׁ
from the troubles (retribution).	מִן־הַפֻּרְעָנוּת.
8: Judah, the son of Tabbai, and Simon, the son of Shatach	8. יְהוּדָה בֶּן טַבַּי וְשִׁמְעוֹן בֶּן־שָׁטַח
received from them.	קִבְּלוּ מֵהֶם.
Judah, the son of Tabbai, says:	יְהוּדָה בֶּן־טַבַּי אוֹמֵר:
Do not make yourself like the lawyers;	אַל־תַּעַשׂ עַצְמְךָ כְּעוֹרְכֵי הַדַּיָּנִים;
and when the litigants are standing before you,	וּכְשֶׁיִּהְיוּ בַּעֲלֵי הַדִּין עוֹמְדִים לְפָנֶיךָ,

they should appear culpable.	יִהְיוּ בְעֵינֶיךָ כִּרְשָׁעִים.
And when they leave you	וּכְשֶׁנִּפְטָרִים מִלְּפָנֶיךָ
they should appear innocent	יִהְיוּ בְעֵינֶיךָ כְּזַכָּאִים
when they accepted upon themselves the judgment.	כְּשֶׁקִּבְּלוּ עֲלֵיהֶם אֶת־הַדִּין.
9: Simon, the son of Shatach, says:	9. שִׁמְעוֹן בֶּן־שָׁטַח אוֹמֵר:
Be careful to examine the witnesses carefully,	הֱוֵה מַרְבֶּה לַחֲקוֹר אֶת־הָעֵדִים,
and be careful with your words	וֶהֱוֵה זָהִיר בִּדְבָרֶיךָ
lest, from them they will learn to lie.	שֶׁמָּא מִתּוֹכָם יִלְמְדוּ לְשַׁקֵּר.
10: Shmaya and Avtalyon received (the Tradition) from them.	10. שְׁמַעְיָה וְאַבְטַלְיוֹן קִבְּלוּ מֵהֶם.
Shmaya says:	שְׁמַעְיָה אוֹמֵר:
Love the work and hate lordship,	אֱהַב אֶת־הַמְּלָאכָה וּשְׂנָא אֶת־הָרַבָּנוּת,
and do not become involved with those in authority.	וְאַל־תִּתְוַדַּע לָרָשׁוּת.
11: Avtalyon says:	11. אַבְטַלְיוֹן אוֹמֵר:
Sages — Be careful with your words,	חֲכָמִים — הִזָּהֲרוּ בְּדִבְרֵיכֶם,
lest they should bring about an exile	שֶׁמָּא תָחוּבוּ חוֹבַת גָּלוּת
and you will become exiled to a place of evil waters,	וְתִגְלוּ לִמְקוֹם מַיִם הָרָעִים,
and the disciples who come after you will drink	וְיִשְׁתּוּ הַתַּלְמִידִים הַבָּאִים אַחֲרֵיכֶם
and they will die,	וְיָמוּתוּ,
and it will be found that the name of Heaven is profaned.	וְנִמְצָא שֵׁם שָׁמַיִם מִתְחַלֵּל.
12: Hillel and Shammai received from them.	12. הִלֵּל וְשַׁמַּאי קִבְּלוּ מֵהֶם.
Hillel says:	הִלֵּל אוֹמֵר:
Be of the students of Aaron;	הֱוֵה מִתַּלְמִידָיו שֶׁל אַהֲרֹן;
love peace and chase after peace;	אוֹהֵב שָׁלוֹם וְרוֹדֵף שָׁלוֹם;
love humanity	אוֹהֵב אֶת־הַבְּרִיּוֹת
and bring them closer to the Torah.	וּמְקָרְבָן לַתּוֹרָה.
13: He used to say:	13. הוּא הָיָה אוֹמֵר:
He who advances his name, loses his name;	נְגַד שְׁמָא אֲבַד שְׁמָא;
if he does not increase (knowledge), he decreases (knowledge);	וּדְלָא מוֹסִיף יָסֵיף;
he who does not study deserves to die;	וּדְלָא יָלֵיף קְטָלָא חַיָּב;
And if he uses (to his material advantage) the crown (of Torah)	וּדְאִשְׁתַּמֵּשׁ בְּתָגָא
he will perish.	חֳלָף.
14: He used to say:	14. הוּא הָיָה אוֹמֵר:
If I am not for myself,	אִם אֵין אֲנִי לִי,
who will be for me?	מִי לִי?
And if I am only for myself,	וּכְשֶׁאֲנִי לְעַצְמִי,
what am I?	מָה אֲנִי?
And if not now, when?	וְאִם לֹא עַכְשָׁיו אֵימָתָי?
15: Shammai says:	15. שַׁמַּאי אוֹמֵר:
Make your Torah (learning) set;	עֲשֵׂה תוֹרָתְךָ קֶבַע;
say little and do much;	אֱמוֹר מְעַט וַעֲשֵׂה הַרְבֵּה;
and greet each person	וֶהֱוֵה מְקַבֵּל אֶת־כָּל־הָאָדָם

with a pleasant countenance.	בְּסֵבֶר פָּנִים יָפוֹת.
16: Rabban Gamliel says:	16. רַבָּן גַּמְלִיאֵל אוֹמֵר:
Establish for yourself a teacher;	עֲשֵׂה לְךָ רַב;
and stay away from doubt;	וְהִסְתַּלֵּק מִן הַסָּפֵק;
and do not exceed the tithe by estimate.	וְאַל־תַּרְבֶּה לְעַשֵּׂר אוּמָדוֹת.
17: Simon, his son, says:	17. שִׁמְעוֹן בְּנוֹ אוֹמֵר:
All my days I was raised amongst sages,	כָּל־יָמַי גָּדַלְתִּי בֵּין הַחֲכָמִים,
and I did not find anything for the body (person)	וְלֹא מָצָאתִי לַגּוּף
better than silence;	טוֹב מִשְּׁתִיקָה;
and study is not the main aspect	וְלֹא הַמִּדְרָשׁ עִקָּר
rather the action is;	אֶלָּא הַמַּעֲשֶׂה;
and all who speak excessively	וְכָל־הַמַּרְבֶּה דְּבָרִים
bring upon themselves sin.	מֵבִיא חֵטְא.
18: Rabban Simon, the son of Gamliel, says:	18. רַבָּן שִׁמְעוֹן בֶּן־גַּמְלִיאֵל אוֹמֵר:
On three things the world is sustained —	עַל שְׁלשָׁה דְבָרִים הָעוֹלָם קַיָּם —
On truth, and on judgment and on peace,	עַל הָאֱמֶת וְעַל הַדִּין וְעַל הַשָּׁלוֹם,
as it says,	שֶׁנֶּאֱמַר,
"truth, justice and peace	אֱמֶת וּמִשְׁפַּט שָׁלוֹם
you shall judge in your gates" (Zechariah 8:16).	שִׁפְטוּ בְּשַׁעֲרֵיכֶם (זכריה ח, טז).

Chapter 2: / פרק ב׳

1: Rabbi says:	1. רַבִּי אוֹמֵר:
Which is the straight path	אֵיזוֹ הִיא דֶרֶךְ יְשָׁרָה
that man should choose?	שֶׁיָּבוֹר לוֹ הָאָדָם?
All that is (brings) glory to the doer,	כָּל־שֶׁהִיא תִּפְאֶרֶת לְעוֹשֶׂיהָ,
and (brings) glory to him from mankind.	וְתִפְאֶרֶת לוֹ מִן הָאָדָם.
And be careful in (performing) an easy commandment, as in (performing) a hard one,	וֶהֱוֵי זָהִיר בְּמִצְוָה קַלָּה כְּבַחֲמוּרָה,
for you do not know the reward given for commandments,	שֶׁאֵין אַתָּה יוֹדֵעַ מַתַּן שְׂכָרָן שֶׁל מִצְוֹת,
and one should calculate the loss	וֶהֱוֵי מְחַשֵּׁב הֶפְסֵד
(incurred through performance) of a commandment against its reward,	מִצְוָה כְּנֶגֶד שְׂכָרָהּ,
and the reward of a sin against its loss.	וּשְׂכַר עֲבֵרָה כְּנֶגֶד הֶפְסֵדָהּ.
Look at three things,	הִסְתַּכֵּל בִּשְׁלשָׁה דְבָרִים,
and you will not come to sin —	וְאֵין אַתָּה בָא לִידֵי עֲבֵרָה —
know what is above you:	דַּע מַה־לְּמַעְלָה מִמְּךָ:
an eye that sees and an ear that hears,	עַיִן רוֹאָה וְאֹזֶן שׁוֹמַעַת,
and all your actions are written in The Book.	וְכָל־מַעֲשֶׂיךָ בַּסֵּפֶר נִכְתָּבִים.
2: Rabban Gamliel, the son of Rabbi Judah HaNasi, says:	2. רַבָּן גַּמְלִיאֵל בְּנוֹ שֶׁל רַבִּי יְהוּדָה הַנָּשִׂיא אוֹמֵר:
Optimal is the learning of Torah (together) with worldly endeavor,	יָפֶה תַּלְמוּד תּוֹרָה עִם דֶּרֶךְ אֶרֶץ,

the efforts of both	שֶׁיְּגִיעַת שְׁנֵיהֶם
make sin to be forgotten.	מְשַׁכַּחַת עָוֹן.
And all Torah that does not have with it (worldly) endeavor	וְכָל־תּוֹרָה שֶׁאֵין עִמָּהּ מְלָאכָה
its end is void and brings sin.	סוֹפָהּ בְּטֵלָה וְגוֹרֶרֶת עָוֹן.
And all who involve themselves with the community	וְכָל־הָעוֹסְקִים עִם הַצִּבּוּר
shall be involved with them for the name of Heaven,	יִהְיוּ עוֹסְקִים עִמָּהֶם לְשֵׁם שָׁמַיִם,
because the merit of their fathers sustains them	שֶׁזְּכוּת אֲבוֹתָם מְסַיַּעְתָּן
and their righteousness stands forever.	וְצִדְקָתָם עוֹמֶדֶת לָעַד.
"And as for you, (says G-d) — I place upon you much reward	וְאַתֶּם — מַעֲלֶה אֲנִי עֲלֵיכֶם שָׂכָר הַרְבֵּה
as if you had done it alone."	כְּאִלּוּ עֲשִׂיתֶם.
3: Be careful with the government authorities	3. הֱווּ זְהִירִים בָּרָשׁוּת
as (they) do not come close to a person	שֶׁאֵין מְקָרְבִים לוֹ לְאָדָם
but for their own need.	אֶלָּא לְצֹרֶךְ עַצְמָם.
They seem like loved ones in the time of their benefit,	נִרְאִים כְּאוֹהֲבִים בִּשְׁעַת הֲנָאָתָם,
but (they) do not stand behind a person in the hour of his need.	וְאֵין עוֹמְדִים לוֹ לְאָדָם בִּשְׁעַת דָּחְקוֹ.
4: He used to say:	4. הוּא הָיָה אוֹמֵר:
Make His will like your will	עֲשֵׂה רְצוֹנוֹ כִּרְצוֹנֶךָ
in order that He make your will like His will.	כְּדֵי שֶׁיַּעֲשֶׂה רְצוֹנְךָ כִּרְצוֹנוֹ.
Nullify your will before His will	בַּטֵּל רְצוֹנְךָ מִפְּנֵי רְצוֹנוֹ
in order that he nullify the will of others against your will.	כְּדֵי שֶׁיְּבַטֵּל רְצוֹן אֲחֵרִים מִפְּנֵי רְצוֹנֶךָ.
5: Hillel says:	5. הִלֵּל אוֹמֵר:
Do not separate yourself from the community;	אַל תִּפְרוֹשׁ מִן הַצִּבּוּר;
and do not believe in yourself (i.e., have confidence) until the day of your death;	וְאַל תַּאֲמֵן בְּעַצְמְךָ עַד יוֹם מוֹתְךָ;
and do not judge your friend	וְאַל תָּדִין אֶת־חֲבֵרְךָ
until you reach his place;	עַד שֶׁתַּגִּיעַ לִמְקוֹמוֹ;
and do not say something	וְאַל תֹּאמַר דָּבָר
that is impossible to hear (i.e. should not be heard)	שֶׁאִי אֶפְשַׁר לִשְׁמוֹעַ
because in the end it will be heard;	שֶׁסּוֹפוֹ לְהִשָּׁמַע;
and do not say "When I have a chance I will learn,"	וְאַל תֹּאמַר לִכְשֶׁאֶפָּנֶה אֶשְׁנֶה,
lest, you will not have a chance.	שֶׁמָּא לֹא תִפָּנֶה.
6: He used to say:	6. הוּא הָיָה אוֹמֵר:
A boorish person does not fear sin;	אֵין בּוֹר יְרֵא חֵטְא;
and an ignorant person cannot be pious;	וְלֹא עַם הָאָרֶץ חָסִיד;
and a shy person cannot learn;	וְלֹא הַבַּיְשָׁן לָמֵד;
and an overly strict person cannot teach;	וְלֹא הַקַּפְּדָן מְלַמֵּד;
and all who engage in too much business cannot become wise.	וְלֹא כָּל־הַמַּרְבֶּה בִסְחוֹרָה מַחְכִּים.
And in a place where there are no men	וּבְמָקוֹם שֶׁאֵין אֲנָשִׁים
endeavor to be a man.	הִשְׁתַּדֵּל לִהְיוֹת אִישׁ.
7: Once he saw a skull	7. אַף הוּא רָאָה גֻּלְגֹּלֶת אַחַת
that was floating on the surface of the water.	שֶׁצָּפָה עַל פְּנֵי הַמָּיִם.

He said to it,	אָמַר לָהּ,
"Because you drowned others they drowned you,	עַל דַּאֲטֵפְתְּ אַטְפוּךְ,
and the end of those who drowned you	וְסוֹף מְטַיְּפָיִךְ
will be their drowning."	יְטוּפוּן.
8: He used to say:	8. הוּא הָיָה אוֹמֵר:
The more flesh, the more worms;	מַרְבֶּה בָשָׂר מַרְבֶּה רִמָּה;
the more riches, the more worries;	מַרְבֶּה נְכָסִים מַרְבֶּה דְאָגָה;
the more women, the more witchcraft;	מַרְבֶּה נָשִׁים מַרְבֶּה כְשָׁפִים;
the more maidservants, the more lewdness;	מַרְבֶּה שְׁפָחוֹת מַרְבֶּה זִמָּה;
the more slaves, the more theft;	מַרְבֶּה עֲבָדִים מַרְבֶּה גָזֵל;
the more Torah, the more life;	מַרְבֶּה תוֹרָה מַרְבֶּה חַיִּים;
the more schooling, the more wisdom;	מַרְבֶּה יְשִׁיבָה מַרְבֶּה חָכְמָה;
the more counsel, the more understanding;	מַרְבֶּה עֵצָה מַרְבֶּה תְבוּנָה;
the more charity, the more peace.	מַרְבֶּה צְדָקָה מַרְבֶּה שָׁלוֹם.
One who has acquired a good name has acquired it for himself.	קָנָה שֵׁם טוֹב קָנָה לְעַצְמוֹ.
One who has acquired for himself words of Torah	קָנָה לוֹ דִּבְרֵי תוֹרָה
has then acquired life in the world to come.	קָנָה לוֹ חַיֵּי הָעוֹלָם הַבָּא.
9: Rabbi Yochanan, the son of Zakkai,	9. רַבָּן יוֹחָנָן בֶּן־זַכַּאי,
received from Hillel and Shammai.	קִבֵּל מֵהִלֵּל וּמִשַּׁמַּאי.
He used to say:	הוּא הָיָה אוֹמֵר:
If you learned a lot of Torah	אִם לָמַדְתָּ תּוֹרָה הַרְבֵּה
do not take credit for yourself,	אַל תַּחֲזֵק טוֹבָה לְעַצְמְךָ,
because for this you were created.	כִּי לְכָךְ נוֹצָרְתָּ.
10: Five students were (disciples) to Rabbi Yochanan, the son of Zakkai,	10. חֲמִשָּׁה תַלְמִידִים הָיוּ לוֹ לְרַבָּן יוֹחָנָן בֶּן־זַכַּאי,
and these are them —	וְאֵלּוּ הֵן —
Rabbi Eliezer, the son of Hyrkanus;	רַבִּי אֱלִיעֶזֶר בֶּן־הוֹרְקְנוֹס;
Rabbi Joshua, the son of Chanania;	רַבִּי יְהוֹשֻׁעַ בֶּן־חֲנַנְיָה;
Rabbi Yose, the priest;	רַבִּי יוֹסֵי הַכֹּהֵן;
Rabbi Simon, the son of Natanel;	רַבִּי שִׁמְעוֹן בֶּן־נְתַנְאֵל;
and Rabbi Elazer, the son of Arach.	וְרַבִּי אֶלְעָזָר בֶּן־עֲרָךְ.
11: He used to recite their praise.	11. הוּא הָיָה מוֹנֶה שִׁבְחָן.
Eliezer, the son of Hyrkanus:	אֱלִיעֶזֶר בֶּן־הוֹרְקְנוֹס:
a cement well that does not lose a drop;	בּוֹר סוּד שֶׁאֵינוֹ מְאַבֵּד טִפָּה;
Joshua, the son of Chanania:	יְהוֹשֻׁעַ בֶּן־חֲנַנְיָה:
fortunate is she who bore him;	אַשְׁרֵי יוֹלַדְתּוֹ;
Yose, the priest: the pious one;	יוֹסֵי הַכֹּהֵן: חָסִיד;
Simon, the son of Natanel: the one feared sin;	שִׁמְעוֹן בֶּן־נְתַנְאֵל: יְרֵא חֵטְא;
Elazer, the son of Arach:	אֶלְעָזָר בֶּן־עֲרָךְ:
like an expanding spring.	כְּמַעְיָן הַמִּתְגַּבֵּר.
12: He used to say:	12. הוּא הָיָה אוֹמֵר:

If there were all the sages of Israel on one side of a scale	אִם יִהְיוּ כָּל־חַכְמֵי יִשְׂרָאֵל בְּכַף מֹאזְנַיִם
and Rabbi Eliezer, the son of Hyrkanus, on the second side,	וֶאֱלִיעֶזֶר בֶּן־הוֹרְקְנוֹס בְּכַף שְׁנִיָּה,
it (the second) would outweigh them all.	מַכְרִיעַ אֶת־כֻּלָּם.
Abba Shaul said, in his name:	אַבָּא שָׁאוּל אוֹמֵר מִשְּׁמוֹ:
If all the sages of Israel were in one scale	אִם יִהְיוּ כָּל־חַכְמֵי יִשְׂרָאֵל בְּכַף מֹאזְנַיִם
and even if Rabbi Eliezer, the son of Hyrkanus, was with them,	וֶאֱלִיעֶזֶר בֶּן־הוֹרְקְנוֹס אַף עִמָּהֶם,
and Rabbi Elazer, the son of Arach, in the second side,	וְאֶלְעָזָר בֶּן־עֲרָךְ בְּכַף שְׁנִיָּה,
it (the second) would outweigh them all.	מַכְרִיעַ אֶת־כֻּלָּם.
13: He said to them:	13. אָמַר לָהֶם:
Go out and see which is the correct path	צְאוּ וּרְאוּ אֵיזוֹ הִיא דֶּרֶךְ טוֹבָה
that man should cleave unto.	שֶׁיִּדְבַּק בָּהּ הָאָדָם.
Rabbi Eliezer says a good eye;	רַבִּי אֱלִיעֶזֶר אוֹמֵר עַיִן טוֹבָה;
Rabbi Joshua says a good friend;	רַבִּי יְהוֹשֻׁעַ אוֹמֵר חָבֵר טוֹב;
Rabbi Yose says a good neighbor;	רַבִּי יוֹסֵי אוֹמֵר שָׁכֵן טוֹב;
Rabbi Simon says one who looks into the future (i.e., is aware of the consequences of his actions);	רַבִּי שִׁמְעוֹן אוֹמֵר הָרוֹאֶה אֶת־הַנּוֹלָד;
Rabbi Elazer says a good heart.	רַבִּי אֶלְעָזָר אוֹמֵר לֵב טוֹב.
He (Rabbi Yochanan) said to them:	אָמַר לָהֶם:
I prefer the words of Rabbi Elazer, the son of Arach, to your words,	רוֹאֶה אֲנִי אֶת־דִּבְרֵי אֶלְעָזָר בֶּן־עֲרָךְ מִדִּבְרֵיכֶם,
because in his words are your words.	שֶׁבִּכְלָל דְּבָרָיו דִּבְרֵיכֶם.
14: He said to them:	14. אָמַר לָהֶם:
Go out and see which is a bad path	צְאוּ וּרְאוּ אֵיזוֹ הִיא דֶּרֶךְ רָעָה
from which man should distance himself.	שֶׁיִּתְרַחֵק מִמֶּנָּה הָאָדָם.
Rabbi Eliezer says an evil eye;	רַבִּי אֱלִיעֶזֶר אוֹמֵר עַיִן רָעָה;
Rabbi Joshua says a bad friend;	רַבִּי יְהוֹשֻׁעַ אוֹמֵר חָבֵר רָע;
Rabbi Yose says a bad neighbor;	רַבִּי יוֹסֵי אוֹמֵר שָׁכֵן רָע;
Rabbi Simon says one who borrows and does not repay.	רַבִּי שִׁמְעוֹן אוֹמֵר הַלֹּוֶה וְאֵינוֹ מְשַׁלֵּם.
The same whether one borrows from man	אֶחָד הַלֹּוֶה מִן הָאָדָם
or whether one borrows from G-d,	כְּלֹוֶה מִן הַמָּקוֹם,
as it is said,	שֶׁנֶּאֱמַר,
"a wicked person borrows and does not repay,	לֹוֶה רָשָׁע וְלֹא יְשַׁלֵּם,
and a righteous person finds favor and gives" (Psalms 37:21).	וְצַדִּיק חוֹנֵן וְנוֹתֵן (תהלים לז, כא).
Rabbi Elazer says a bad heart.	רַבִּי אֶלְעָזָר אוֹמֵר לֵב רָע.
He (Rabbi Yochanan) said to them:	אָמַר לָהֶם:
I prefer the words of Elazer, the son of Arach, to your words,	רוֹאֶה אֲנִי אֶת־דִּבְרֵי אֶלְעָזָר בֶּן־עֲרָךְ מִדִּבְרֵיכֶם,
because in his words are your words.	שֶׁבִּכְלָל דְּבָרָיו דִּבְרֵיכֶם.
15: They said three things:	15. הֵם אָמְרוּ שְׁלֹשָׁה דְבָרִים:
Rabbi Eliezer says:	רַבִּי אֱלִיעֶזֶר אוֹמֵר:
Your friend's honor should be dear to you like your own;	יְהִי כְבוֹד חֲבֵרְךָ חָבִיב עָלֶיךָ כְּשֶׁלָּךְ;
and do not be quick to anger,	וְאַל תְּהִי נוֹחַ לִכְעוֹס,
and repent one day before your death;	וְשׁוּב יוֹם אֶחָד לִפְנֵי מִיתָתְךָ;

warm yourself by the light of sages	וֶהֱוֵה מִתְחַמֵּם כְּנֶגֶד אוּרָן שֶׁל חֲכָמִים
and be careful by the coals so you should not burn.	וֶהֱוֵה זָהִיר בְּגַחַלְתָּן שֶׁלֹּא תִכָּוֶה.
Their bite is like that of a fox,	שֶׁנְּשִׁיכָתָן נְשִׁיכַת שׁוּעָל,
and their sting is like that of a scorpion,	וַעֲקִיצָתָן עֲקִיצַת עַקְרָב,
and their hiss is like that of a fiery serpent,	וּלְחִישָׁתָן לְחִישַׁת שָׂרָף,
and all of their words are like burning coals.	וְכָל־דִּבְרֵיהֶם כְּגַחֲלֵי אֵשׁ.
16: Rabbi Joshua says:	16. רַבִּי יְהוֹשֻׁעַ אוֹמֵר:
An evil eye and the evil inclination	עַיִן הָרַע וְיֵצֶר הָרַע
and hatred of mankind	וְשִׂנְאַת הַבְּרִיּוֹת
remove man from the world.	מוֹצִיאִים אֶת־הָאָדָם מִן הָעוֹלָם.
17: Rabbi Yose says:	17. רַבִּי יוֹסֵי אוֹמֵר:
The property of your friend should be special to you as your own;	יְהִי מָמוֹן חֲבֵרְךָ חָבִיב עָלֶיךָ כְּשֶׁלָּךְ;
and prepare yourself to learn Torah	וְהַתְקֵן עַצְמְךָ לִלְמוֹד תּוֹרָה
because it is not an inheritance to you;	שֶׁאֵינָהּ יְרֻשָּׁה לָךְ;
and all your deeds should be for the name of Heaven.	וְכָל־מַעֲשֶׂיךָ יִהְיוּ לְשֵׁם שָׁמָיִם.
18: Rabbi Simon says:	18. רַבִּי שִׁמְעוֹן אוֹמֵר:
Be careful in the saying of Shema and in prayer,	הֱוֵה זָהִיר בִּקְרִיאַת שְׁמַע וּבִתְפִלָּה,
and when you pray	וּכְשֶׁאַתָּה מִתְפַּלֵּל
do not make your prayer routine,	אַל־תַּעַשׂ תְּפִלָּתְךָ קֶבַע,
rather (an appeal for) mercy and grace before G-d,	אֶלָּא רַחֲמִים וְתַחֲנוּנִים לִפְנֵי הַמָּקוֹם,
as it is said,	שֶׁנֶּאֱמַר,
"Because He is merciful and forgiving,	כִּי־חַנּוּן וְרַחוּם,
He is slow to anger and One of abundant kindness	הוּא אֶרֶךְ אַפַּיִם וְרַב־חֶסֶד
and He is forgiving of bad" (Joel 2:13).	וְנִחָם עַל־הָרָעָה (יואל ב, יג).
And do not consider yourself wicked.	וְאַל תְּהִי רָשָׁע בִּפְנֵי עַצְמֶךָ.
19: Rabbi Elazer says:	19. רַבִּי אֶלְעָזָר אוֹמֵר:
Be diligent in learning Torah;	הֱוֵה שָׁקוּד לִלְמוֹד תּוֹרָה;
and know how to reply to a non-believer;	וְדַע מַה שֶּׁתָּשִׁיב לְאַפִּיקוֹרוֹס;
and know before Whom you toil	וְדַע לִפְנֵי מִי אַתָּה עָמֵל
and Who is the master of your work,	וּמִי הוּא בַּעַל מְלַאכְתְּךָ,
that will pay you the reward of your labor.	שֶׁיְּשַׁלֶּם־לְךָ שְׂכַר פְּעֻלָּתֶךָ.
20: Rabbi Tarfon says:	20. רַבִּי טַרְפוֹן אוֹמֵר:
The day is short and work is great;	הַיּוֹם קָצֵר וְהַמְּלָאכָה מְרֻבָּה;
and the workers are lazy and the reward is much;	וְהַפּוֹעֲלִים עֲצֵלִים וְהַשָּׂכָר הַרְבֵּה;
and the Master of the house is persistent.	וּבַעַל הַבַּיִת דּוֹחֵק.
21: He used to say:	21. הוּא הָיָה אוֹמֵר:
It is not upon you to finish the work	לֹא עָלֶיךָ הַמְּלָאכָה לִגְמוֹר
yet you are not a free man	וְלֹא־אַתָּה בֶן־חוֹרִין
to desist from it.	לְהִבָּטֵל מִמֶּנָּה.
If you learn a lot of Torah	אִם לָמַדְתָּ תּוֹרָה הַרְבֵּה
much reward is given to you;	נוֹתְנִים לְךָ שָׂכָר הַרְבֵּה;

and faithful is He, the Master of your work,	וְנֶאֱמָן הוּא בַּעַל מְלַאכְתְּךָ,
that He will pay you the reward of your labor.	שֶׁיְּשַׁלֶּם לְךָ שְׂכַר פְּעֻלָּתֶךָ.
And know that the giving of reward tc the righteous	וְדַע שֶׁמַּתַּן שְׂכָרָם שֶׁל צַדִּיקִים
is in the world to come.	לֶעָתִיד לָבוֹא.

Chapter 3	פרק ג׳
1: Akavya, the son of Mahalalel, says:	1. עֲקַבְיָא בֶּן־מַהֲלַלְאֵל אוֹמֵר:
Look at three things	הִסְתַּכֵּל בִּשְׁלֹשָׁה דְבָרִים
and you will not come to sin —	וְאֵין אַתָּה בָא לִידֵי עֲבֵרָה —
know from what you came,	דַּע מֵאַיִן בָּאתָ,
and to where you are going,	וּלְאָן אַתָּה הוֹלֵךְ,
and before whom you will stand	וְלִפְנֵי מִי אַתָּה עָתִיד
to give an account and reckoning.	לִתֵּן דִּין וְחֶשְׁבּוֹן.
From what do you come?	מֵאַיִן בָּאתָ?
From an odorous drop;	מִטִּפָּה סְרוּחָה;
And to where are you going?	וּלְאָן אַתָּה הוֹלֵךְ?
To a place of dust, worms and decay;	לִמְקוֹם עָפָר רִמָּה וְתוֹלֵעָה;
And before whom will you stand to give your account?	וְלִפְנֵי מִי אַתָּה עָתִיד לִתֵּן דִּין וְחֶשְׁבּוֹן?
Before the King of kings, the Holy One, blessed be He.	לִפְנֵי מֶלֶךְ מַלְכֵי הַמְּלָכִים הַקָּדוֹשׁ בָּרוּךְ הוּא.
2: Rabbi Chanina, the deputy high priest, says:	2. רַבִּי חֲנִינָא סְגַן הַכֹּהֲנִים אוֹמֵר:
You should pray for the peace of the government,	הֱוֵי מִתְפַּלֵּל בִּשְׁלוֹמָהּ שֶׁל מַלְכוּת,
because but for that fear	שֶׁאִלְמָלֵא מוֹרָאָהּ
each man would swallow his neighbor alive.	אִישׁ אֶת־רֵעֵהוּ חַיִּים בְּלָעוֹ.
3: Rabbi Chanina, the son of Tradyon, says:	3. רַבִּי חֲנַנְיָה בֶּן־תְּרַדְיוֹן אוֹמֵר:
(When) two people are sitting and there are no words of Torah between them,	שְׁנַיִם שֶׁיּוֹשְׁבִים וְאֵין בֵּינֵיהֶם דִּבְרֵי תוֹרָה,
this is a dwelling of scorners.	הֲרֵי זֶה מוֹשַׁב לֵצִים.
As it is said,	שֶׁנֶּאֱמַר,
"And in a house of scorners he never sat" (Psalms 1:1).	וּבְמוֹשַׁב לֵצִים לֹא יָשָׁב (תהלים א, א).
But (when) two are sitting	אֲבָל שְׁנַיִם שֶׁיּוֹשְׁבִים
and there are words of Torah between them,	וְיֵשׁ בֵּינֵיהֶם דִּבְרֵי תוֹרָה,
The Divine Presence rests with them.	שְׁכִינָה שְׁרוּיָה בֵינֵיהֶם.
As it is said,	שֶׁנֶּאֱמַר,
"Then those who fear G-d spoke,	אָז נִדְבְּרוּ יִרְאֵי ה׳,
each to his friend,	אִישׁ אֶל־רֵעֵהוּ,
and G-d listened and He heard,	וַיַּקְשֵׁב ה׳ וַיִּשְׁמָע,
and He wrote in the Book of Remembrance before Him	וַיִּכָּתֵב סֵפֶר זִכָּרוֹן לְפָנָיו
those who fear G-d	לְיִרְאֵי ה׳
and those who think about His name" (Malachi 3:16).	וּלְחֹשְׁבֵי שְׁמוֹ (מלאכי ג, טז).

It is not (i.e., does not apply) except for two people.	אֵין לִי אֶלָּא שְׁנַיִם.
From where (do we learn) that even one who sits and busies himself with Torah	מִנַּיִן אֲפִילוּ אֶחָד שֶׁיּוֹשֵׁב וְעוֹסֵק בַּתּוֹרָה
that the Holy One, blessed be He, sets for him a reward?	שֶׁהַקָּדוֹשׁ בָּרוּךְ הוּא קוֹבֵעַ לוֹ שָׂכָר?
As it is said,	שֶׁנֶּאֱמַר,
"He sits alone and keeps silent	יֵשֵׁב בָּדָד וְיִדֹּם
and he receives what was set for him" (Lamentations 3:28)	כִּי נָטַל עָלָיו (איכה ג, כח).
4: Rabbi Simon says:	4. רַבִּי שִׁמְעוֹן אוֹמֵר:
Three that eat at one table,	שְׁלשָׁה שֶׁאָכְלוּ עַל שֻׁלְחָן אֶחָד,
and words of Torah are not spoken between them,	וְלֹא אָמְרוּ עָלָיו דִּבְרֵי תוֹרָה,
it is as if they ate from the sacrifices of the dead.	כְּאִלּוּ אָכְלוּ מִזִּבְחֵי מֵתִים.
As it is said,	שֶׁנֶּאֱמַר,
"Because all their tables are filled with filth	כִּי כָּל־שֻׁלְחָנוֹת מָלְאוּ קִיא צֹאָה
without room (for anything else, i.e., G-d)" (Isaiah 28:8).	בְּלִי מָקוֹם (ישעיה כח, ח).
But three that eat at one table,	אֲבָל שְׁלשָׁה שֶׁאָכְלוּ עַל שֻׁלְחָן אֶחָד,
and do speak words of Torah,	וְאָמְרוּ עָלָיו דִּבְרֵי תוֹרָה,
it is like they ate from the table of G-d.	כְּאִלּוּ אָכְלוּ מִשֻּׁלְחָנוֹ שֶׁל מָקוֹם.
As it is said,	שֶׁנֶּאֱמַר,
"And he said to me this is the table that is before G-d" (Ezekiel 41:22).	וַיְדַבֵּר אֵלַי זֶה הַשֻּׁלְחָן אֲשֶׁר לִפְנֵי ה' (יחזקאל מא, כב).
5: Rabbi Chanina, the son of Chachinai, says:	5. רַבִּי חֲנִינָא בֶּן־חֲכִינַי אוֹמֵר:
One who is awake at night,	הַנֵּעוֹר בַּלַּיְלָה,
and one who goes along a path alone,	וְהַמְהַלֵּךְ בַּדֶּרֶךְ יְחִידִי,
and finds room in his heart for wastefulness —	וּמְפַנֶּה לִבּוֹ לְבַטָּלָה —
this is forfeiture of life.	הֲרֵי זֶה מִתְחַיֵּב בְּנַפְשׁוֹ.
6: Rabbi Nechunya, the son of Hakana, says:	6. רַבִּי נְחוּנְיָא בֶּן־הַקָּנָה אוֹמֵר:
Everyone who accepts the yoke of the Torah	כָּל־הַמְקַבֵּל עָלָיו עֹל תּוֹרָה
will be relieved of the yoke of the kingdom and the yoke of worldly care.	מַעֲבִירִים מִמֶּנּוּ עֹל מַלְכוּת וְעֹל דֶּרֶךְ אֶרֶץ.
And anyone who throws away the yoke of Torah	וְכָל־הַפּוֹרֵק מִמֶּנּוּ עֹל תּוֹרָה
will be burdened by the yoke of the kingdom and the yoke of worldly care.	נוֹתְנִים עָלָיו עֹל מַלְכוּת וְעֹל דֶּרֶךְ אֶרֶץ.
7: Rabbi Chalafta, the son of Dosa, a man from the village of Chananya, says:	7. רַבִּי חֲלַפְתָּא בֶּן־דּוֹסָא אִישׁ כְּפַר חֲנַנְיָא אוֹמֵר:
When ten people are sitting and are busy with Torah,	עֲשָׂרָה שֶׁיּוֹשְׁבִים ועוֹסְקִים בַּתּוֹרָה,
G-d rests with them.	שְׁכִינָה שְׁרוּיָה בֵינֵיהֶם.
As it is said,	שֶׁנֶּאֱמַר,
"G-d stands in a congregation of the Almighty" (Psalms 82:1).	אֱלֹקִים נִצָּב בַּעֲדַת־אֵ'ל (תהלים פב, א).
And from where (do we learn) even if five people?	וּמִנַּיִן אֲפִילוּ חֲמִשָּׁה?
As it is said,	שֶׁנֶּאֱמַר,
"And His band on the earth	וַאֲגֻדָּתוֹ עַל־אֶרֶץ
He has founded" (Amos 9:6).	יְסָדָהּ (עמוס ט, ו).
And from where (do we learn) even if three people?	וּמִנַּיִן אֲפִילוּ שְׁלשָׁה?

As it is said,	שֶׁנֶּאֱמַר,
"Amongst judges He judges" (Psalms 82:1).	בְּקֶרֶב אֱלֹהִים יִשְׁפֹּט (תהלים פב, א).
And from where (do we learn) even if two people?	וּמִנַּיִן אֲפִלּוּ שְׁנַיִם?
As it is said,	שֶׁנֶּאֱמַר,
"Then those who fear G-d spoke to each other,	אָז נִדְבְּרוּ יִרְאֵי ה׳ אִישׁ אֶל־רֵעֵהוּ,
G-d listened and He heard" (Malachi 3:16).	וַיַּקְשֵׁב ה׳ וַיִּשְׁמָע (מלאכי ג, טז).
And from where (do we learn) even if one person?	וּמִנַּיִן אֲפִלּוּ אֶחָד?
As it is said,	שֶׁנֶּאֱמַר,
"In every place that I have My name remembered	בְּכָל־הַמָּקוֹם אֲשֶׁר אַזְכִּיר אֶת־שְׁמִי
I will come to you and I will bless you" (Exodus 20:24).	אָבוֹא אֵלֶיךָ וּבֵרַכְתִּיךָ (שמות כ, כד).
8: Rabbi Elazar, a man from Bartosa, says:	8. רַבִּי אֶלְעָזָר אִישׁ בַּרְתּוֹתָא אוֹמֵר:
Give to Him from (what) is His	תֶּן־לוֹ מִשֶּׁלּוֹ
because you and what is yours is His,	שֶׁאַתָּה וְשֶׁלְּךָ שֶׁלּוֹ,
and so with David, he says,	וְכֵן בְּדָוִד הוּא אוֹמֵר,
"Because from You, is everything,	כִּי־מִמְּךָ הַכֹּל,
and from Your hand we give to You" (1 Chronicles 29:14).	וּמִיָּדְךָ נָתַנּוּ לָךְ (דברי הימים א׳ כט, יד).
9: Rabbi Jacob says:	9. רַבִּי יַעֲקֹב אוֹמֵר:
One who is walking on a path and studying (Torah)	הַמְהַלֵּךְ בַּדֶּרֶךְ וְשׁוֹנֶה
and he stops from studying and says,	וּמַפְסִיק מִמִּשְׁנָתוֹ וְאוֹמֵר,
"How nice is this tree, how nice is this field,"	מַה־נָּאֶה אִילָן זֶה מַה־נָּאֶה נִיר זֶה
the Torah regards him	מַעֲלֶה עָלָיו הַכָּתוּב
as one who forfeited his life.	כְּאִלּוּ מִתְחַיֵּב בְּנַפְשׁוֹ.
10: Rabbi Dostai, the son of Yannai, in the name of Rabbi Meir, says:	10. רַבִּי דוֹסְתַּאי בַּר יַנַּאי מִשּׁוּם רַבִּי מֵאִיר אוֹמֵר:
Anyone who forgets one word from his studying,	כָּל־הַשּׁוֹכֵחַ דָּבָר אֶחָד מִמִּשְׁנָתוֹ,
the Torah regards him	מַעֲלֶה עָלָיו הַכָּתוּב
as one who forfeited his life.	כְּאִלּוּ מִתְחַיֵּב בְּנַפְשׁוֹ.
As it is said,	שֶׁנֶּאֱמַר,
"Only be careful and guard your soul diligently,	רַק הִשָּׁמֶר לְךָ וּשְׁמֹר נַפְשְׁךָ מְאֹד,
lest, you forget the words that your eye sees" (Deuteronomy 4:9).	פֶּן־תִּשְׁכַּח אֶת־הַדְּבָרִים אֲשֶׁר רָאוּ עֵינֶיךָ (דברים ד, ט).
You may (think) even one who forgot because it was too hard,	יָכוֹל אֲפִילוּ תָּקְפָה עָלָיו מִשְׁנָתוֹ,
(therefore) the Torah says,	תַּלְמוּד לוֹמַר,
"And lest they will be turned away from your heart all the days of your life" (Deuteronomy 4:9);	וּפֶן־יָסוּרוּ מִלְּבָבְךָ כֹּל יְמֵי חַיֶּיךָ (שם);
so he is not guilty	הָא אֵינוֹ מִתְחַיֵּב בְּנַפְשׁוֹ
until he purposely turns them away from his heart.	עַד שֶׁיֵּשֵׁב וִיסִירֵם מִלִּבּוֹ.
11: Chanina, the son of Dosa, says:	11. רַבִּי חֲנִינָא בֶּן־דּוֹסָא אוֹמֵר:
Anyone whose fear of sin comes before his wisdom,	כֹּל שֶׁיִּרְאַת חֶטְאוֹ קוֹדֶמֶת לְחָכְמָתוֹ,
his wisdom will endure;	חָכְמָתוֹ מִתְקַיֶּמֶת;
and anyone whose wisdom comes before his fear of sin,	וְכֹל שֶׁחָכְמָתוֹ קוֹדֶמֶת לְיִרְאַת חֶטְאוֹ,
his wisdom will not endure.	אֵין חָכְמָתוֹ מִתְקַיֶּמֶת.
12: He used to say:	12. הוּא הָיָה אוֹמֵר:

Anyone whose actions are greater than his wisdom,	כֹּל שֶׁמַּעֲשָׂיו מְרֻבִּים מֵחָכְמָתוֹ,
his wisdom will endure;	חָכְמָתוֹ מִתְקַיֶּמֶת;
and anyone whose wisdom is greater than his actions,	וְכֹל שֶׁחָכְמָתוֹ מְרֻבָּה מִמַּעֲשָׂיו,
his wisdom will not endure.	אֵין חָכְמָתוֹ מִתְקַיֶּמֶת.
13: He used to say:	13. הוּא הָיָה אוֹמֵר:
Anyone who is pleasant to people	כֹּל שֶׁרוּחַ הַבְּרִיּוֹת נוֹחָה הֵימֶנּוּ
is pleasant to G-d,	רוּחַ הַמָּקוֹם נוֹחָה הֵימֶנּוּ,
and anyone who is not pleasant to people	וְכֹל שֶׁאֵין רוּחַ הַבְּרִיּוֹת נוֹחָה הֵימֶנּוּ
is not pleasant to G-d.	אֵין רוּחַ הַמָּקוֹם נוֹחָה הֵימֶנּוּ.
14: Rabbi Dosa, the son of Hyrkanos, says:	14. רַבִּי דוֹסָא בֶּן־הַרְכִּינָס אוֹמֵר:
Sleep in the morning, wine in the afternoon,	שֵׁנָה שֶׁל שַׁחֲרִית וְיַיִן שֶׁל צָהֳרַיִם,
childish conversations and sitting in the gathering places of the ignorant	וְשִׂיחַת הַיְלָדִים וִישִׁיבַת בָּתֵּי כְנֵסִיּוֹת שֶׁל עַמֵּי הָאָרֶץ
remove man from the world.	מוֹצִיאִים אֶת־הָאָדָם מִן־הָעוֹלָם.
15: Rabbi Elazar, from Modin, says:	15. רַבִּי אֶלְעָזָר הַמּוֹדָעִי אוֹמֵר:
One who desecrates holy things,	הַמְחַלֵּל אֶת־הַקֳּדָשִׁים,
and degrades the holidays,	וְהַמְבַזֶּה אֶת־הַמּוֹעֲדוֹת,
and embarrasses the face of his friend in public,	וְהַמַּלְבִּין פְּנֵי חֲבֵרוֹ בָּרַבִּים,
and violates the covenant of Abraham, our father,	וְהַמֵּפֵר בְּרִיתוֹ שֶׁל אַבְרָהָם אָבִינוּ,
and reveals the inners of the Torah not according to the law,	וְהַמְגַלֶּה פָנִים בַּתּוֹרָה שֶׁלֹּא כַהֲלָכָה,
even though he has in his hand (knows) Torah and good deeds,	אַף עַל פִּי שֶׁיֵּשׁ בְּיָדוֹ תּוֹרָה וּמַעֲשִׂים טוֹבִים,
there is no portion for him in the world to come.	אֵין לוֹ חֵלֶק לָעוֹלָם הַבָּא.
16: Rabbi Ishmael says:	16. רַבִּי יִשְׁמָעֵאל אוֹמֵר:
Yield to elders,	הֱוֵה קַל לְרֹאשׁ,
and be pleasant to the suppliant,	וְנוֹחַ לְתִשְׁחֹרֶת,
and receive each person with happiness.	וֶהֱוֵה מְקַבֵּל אֶת־כָּל־הָאָדָם בְּשִׂמְחָה.
17: Rabbi Akiva says:	17. רַבִּי עֲקִיבָא אוֹמֵר:
Laughter and lightheadedness	שְׂחוֹק וְקַלּוּת רֹאשׁ
accustom man to abominations.	מַרְגִּילִים אֶת־הָאָדָם לְעֶרְוָה.
Tradition (i.e., Oral Law) is a fence for the Torah;	מַסֹּרֶת סְיָג לַתּוֹרָה;
the tithes are a fence for riches;	מַעַשְׂרוֹת סְיָג לָעֹשֶׁר;
vows are a fence for voluntary abstinance;	נְדָרִים סְיָג לַפְּרִישׁוּת;
the fence for wisdom is silence.	סְיָג לַחָכְמָה שְׁתִיקָה.
18: He used to say:	18. הוּא הָיָה אוֹמֵר:
Beloved is man, for he was created in the form (of G-d),	חָבִיב אָדָם שֶׁנִּבְרָא בְּצֶלֶם,
it was with an even greater love that it was made known to man	חִבָּה יְתֵרָה נוֹדַעַת לוֹ
that he was created in the form (of G-d).	שֶׁנִּבְרָא בְּצֶלֶם אֱלֹקִים.
As it is said,	שֶׁנֶּאֱמַר,
"Because in the image of G-d	כִּי בְּצֶלֶם אֱלֹקִים
He made man" (Genesis 9:6).	עָשָׂה אֶת־הָאָדָם (בראשית ט, ו).
Beloved is Israel, for they are called children of G-d;	חֲבִיבִים יִשְׂרָאֵל שֶׁנִּקְרְאוּ בָנִים לַמָּקוֹם;

it was with an even greater love that it was made known to them	חִבָּה יְתֵרָה נוֹדַעַת לָהֶם
that they are called children of G-d.	שֶׁנִּקְרְאוּ בָנִים לַמָּקוֹם.
As it is said,	שֶׁנֶּאֱמַר,
"You are the children of the Lord, your G-d" (Deuteronomy 14:1).	בָּנִים אַתֶּם לַה׳ אֱלֹקֵיכֶם (דברים יד, א).
Beloved is Israel, for they were given a coveted instrument;	חֲבִיבִים יִשְׂרָאֵל שֶׁנִּתַּן לָהֶם כְּלִי חֶמְדָּה;
it was with an even greater love that it was made known to them	חִבָּה יְתֵרָה נוֹדַעַת לָהֶם
that they were given a coveted instrument,	שֶׁנִּתַּן לָהֶם כְּלִי חֶמְדָּה,
through which was the creation of the world,	שֶׁבּוֹ נִבְרָא הָעוֹלָם,
As it is said,	שֶׁנֶּאֱמַר,
"For I have given to you a good doctrine,	כִּי לֶקַח טוֹב נָתַתִּי לָכֶם,
My Torah, do not forsake" (Proverbs 4:2).	תּוֹרָתִי אַל תַּעֲזֹבוּ (משלי ד, ב).
19: Everything is foreseen,	19. הַכֹּל צָפוּי,
yet freedom of choice is given;	וְהָרְשׁוּת נְתוּנָה;
in goodness the world is judged,	וּבְטוּב הָעוֹלָם נָדוֹן,
and everything is according to the greatness of one's actions.	וְהַכֹּל לְפִי רֹב הַמַּעֲשֶׂה.
20: He used to say:	20. הוּא הָיָה אוֹמֵר:
Everything is given on a pledge,	הַכֹּל נָתוּן בְּעֵרָבוֹן,
and a net is spread on all the living.	וּמְצוּדָה פְּרוּסָה עַל כָּל־הַחַיִּים.
The store is open and the storeowner gives credit;	הֶחָנוּת פְּתוּחָה וְהַחֶנְוָנִי מַקִּיף;
and the ledger is open and the Hand writes in it;	וְהַפִּנְקָס פָּתוּחַ וְהַיָּד כּוֹתֶבֶת;
and anyone who wants to borrow,	וְכָל־הָרוֹצֶה לִלְווֹת,
he should come and borrow;	יָבֹא וְיִלְוֶה;
and the collectors return each day,	וְהַגַּבָּאִים מַחֲזִירִים תָּדִיר בְּכָל־יוֹם,
and take payment from the man	וְנִפְרָעִים מִן הָאָדָם
with his knowledge or without his knowledge;	מִדַּעְתּוֹ וְשֶׁלֹּא מִדַּעְתּוֹ;
and there is to them on what to rely;	וְיֵשׁ לָהֶם עַל מַה־שֶּׁיִּסְמֹכוּ;
and the judgment is a true (i.e., correct) one;	וְהַדִּין דִּין אֱמֶת;
and everything is prepared for the feast.	וְהַכֹּל מְתֻקָּן לִסְעוּדָה.
21: Rabbi Elazar, the son of Azariah, says:	21. רַבִּי אֶלְעָזָר בֶּן־עֲזַרְיָה אוֹמֵר:
If there is no Torah,	אִם אֵין תּוֹרָה,
there is no respect;	אֵין דֶּרֶךְ אֶרֶץ;
if there is no respect,	אִם אֵין דֶּרֶךְ אֶרֶץ,
there is no Torah;	אֵין תּוֹרָה;
if there is no wisdom,	אִם אֵין חָכְמָה,
there is no fear;	אֵין יִרְאָה;
if there is no fear,	אִם אֵין יִרְאָה,
there is no wisdom;	אֵין חָכְמָה;
if there is no knowledge,	אִם אֵין דַּעַת,
there is no understanding;	אֵין בִּינָה;
if there is no understanding,	אִם אֵין בִּינָה,
there is no knowledge;	אֵין דַּעַת;

if there is no flour (i.e., food),	אִם אֵין קֶמַח,
there is no Torah;	אֵין תּוֹרָה;
if there is no Torah,	אִם אֵין תּוֹרָה,
there is no flour (i.e., food).	אֵין קֶמַח.
22: He used to say:	22. הוּא הָיָה אוֹמֵר:
One whose wisdom is greater than his actions,	כֹּל שֶׁחָכְמָתוֹ מְרֻבָּה מִמַּעֲשָׂיו,
to what is he compared?	לְמָה הוּא דוֹמֶה?
To a tree that has many branches and few roots,	לְאִילָן שֶׁעֲנָפָיו מְרֻבִּים וְשָׁרָשָׁיו מֻעָטִים,
and a wind comes and uproots it	וְהָרוּחַ בָּאָה וְעוֹקַרְתּוֹ
and turns it upon its face.	וְהוֹפַכְתּוֹ עַל פָּנָיו.
As it is said,	שֶׁנֶּאֱמַר,
"And he will be like a juniper tree in a desert,	וְהָיָה כְּעַרְעָר בָּעֲרָבָה,
and he will not be able to see when the good will come,	וְלֹא יִרְאֶה כִּי־יָבֹא טוֹב,
and he will dwell in the parched places of the desert —	וְשָׁכַן חֲרֵרִים בַּמִּדְבָּר —
a salty land, uninhabitable" (Jeremiah 17:6).	אֶרֶץ מְלֵחָה וְלֹא תֵשֵׁב (ירמיה יז, ו).
But one whose actions are greater than his wisdom,	אֲבָל כֹּל שֶׁמַּעֲשָׂיו מְרֻבִּים מֵחָכְמָתוֹ,
to what is he compared?	לְמָה הוּא דוֹמֶה?
To a tree that has less branches and many roots,	לְאִילָן שֶׁעֲנָפָיו מֻעָטִים וְשָׁרָשָׁיו מְרֻבִּים,
that even if all the winds of the earth come and blow on it	שֶׁאֲפִילוּ כָּל־הָרוּחוֹת שֶׁבָּעוֹלָם בָּאוֹת וְנוֹשְׁבוֹת בּוֹ
they will not be able to move it from its place.	אֵין מְזִיזוֹת אוֹתוֹ מִמְּקוֹמוֹ.
As it is said,	שֶׁנֶּאֱמַר,
"For he will be like a tree planted by the waters	וְהָיָה כְּעֵץ שָׁתוּל עַל־מַיִם
that spreads out its roots by the river,	וְעַל־יוּבַל יְשַׁלַּח שָׁרָשָׁיו,
and it will not see the coming of heat,	וְלֹא יִרְאֶה כִּי יָבֹא חֹם,
and it will be vibrant,	וְהָיָה עָלֵהוּ רַעֲנָן,
and in a drought year it will not travail,	וּבִשְׁנַת בַּצֹּרֶת לֹא יִדְאָג,
and it will not cease from yielding fruit" (Jeremiah 17:8).	וְלֹא יָמִישׁ מֵעֲשׂוֹת פֶּרִי (ירמיה יז, ח).
23: Rabbi Elazer, the son of Chisma, says:	23. רַבִּי אֶלְעָזָר חִסְמָא אוֹמֵר:
The laws concerning sacrificial birds and the laws of purification of women	קִנִּין וּפִתְחֵי נִדָּה
are main laws;	הֵן הֵן גּוּפֵי הֲלָכוֹת;
astronomy and numerical values	תְּקוּפוֹת וְגֵמַטְרִיָּאוֹת
are the desserts to wisdom.	פַּרְפְּרָאוֹת לַחָכְמָה.

Chapter 4 — פרק ד׳

1: Ben Zoma says:	1. בֶּן זוֹמָא אוֹמֵר:
Who is wise?	אֵיזֶהוּ חָכָם?
He who learns from every man.	הַלּוֹמֵד מִכָּל־אָדָם.
As it is said,	שֶׁנֶּאֱמַר,
"From all my teachers I gained understanding" (Psalms 119:99.)	מִכָּל־מְלַמְּדַי הִשְׂכַּלְתִּי (תהלים קיט, צט).

Who is mighty?	אֵיזֶהוּ גִּבּוֹר?
He who subdues his passions.	הַכּוֹבֵשׁ אֶת־יִצְרוֹ.
As it is said,	שֶׁנֶּאֱמַר,
"He who is slow to anger is greater than the mighty,	טוֹב אֶרֶךְ אַפַּיִם מִגִּבּוֹר,
and he who controls his spirit is greater than one who conquers a city" (Proverbs 16:32).	וּמשֵׁל בְּרוּחוֹ מִלֹּכֵד עִיר (משלי טז, לב).
Who is rich?	אֵיזֶהוּ עָשִׁיר?
He who rejoices in his portion.	הַשָּׂמֵחַ בְּחֶלְקוֹ.
As it is said,	שֶׁנֶּאֱמַר,
"When you enjoy the fruits of your labor,	יְגִיעַ כַּפֶּיךָ כִּי תֹאכֵל,
happy are you and it shall be well with you" (Psalms 128:2).	אַשְׁרֶיךָ וְטוֹב לָךְ (תהלים קכח, ב).
You will be happy in this world,	אַשְׁרֶיךָ בָּעוֹלָם הַזֶּה,
and it shall be well with you in the world to come.	וְטוֹב לָךְ לָעוֹלָם הַבָּא.
Who is honored?	אֵיזֶהוּ מְכֻבָּד?
He who honors his fellow man.	הַמְכַבֵּד אֶת־הַבְּרִיּוֹת.
As it is said,	שֶׁנֶּאֱמַר,
"Those who honor Me, I will honor,	כִּי מְכַבְּדַי אֲכַבֵּד,
and those who despise Me shall be lightly esteemed" (1 Samuel 2:30).	וּבֹזַי יֵקָלּוּ (שמואל א, ב, ל).
2: Ben Azzai says:	2. בֶּן־עַזַּי אוֹמֵר:
Run to perform an easy commandment	הֱוֵה רָץ לְמִצְוָה קַלָּה
and flee from transgression,	וּבוֹרֵחַ מִן הָעֲבֵרָה,
for (fulfillment of) a commandment leads to (fulfillment of) a commandment	שֶׁמִּצְוָה גּוֹרֶרֶת מִצְוָה
and (commission of) a transgression leads to (commission of) a transgression.	וַעֲבֵרָה גּוֹרֶרֶת עֲבֵרָה.
For the reward of a commandment is a commandment	שֶׁשְּׂכַר מִצְוָה מִצְוָה
and the reward of a transgression is a transgression.	וּשְׂכַר עֲבֵרָה עֲבֵרָה.
3: He used to say:	3. הוּא הָיָה אוֹמֵר:
Do not despise any man,	אַל תְּהִי בָז לְכָל־אָדָם,
and do not consider anything impossible,	וְאַל תְּהִי מַפְלִיג לְכָל־דָּבָר,
for there is no man that does not have his time	שֶׁאֵין לְךָ אָדָם שֶׁאֵין לוֹ שָׁעָה
and there is no thing that does not have its place.	וְאֵין לְךָ דָבָר שֶׁאֵין לוֹ מָקוֹם.
4: Rabbi Levitas of Yavneh says:	4. רַבִּי לְוִיטַס אִישׁ יַבְנֶה אוֹמֵר:
Be extremely humble	מְאֹד מְאֹד הֱוֵה שְׁפַל רוּחַ
for the hope of the man is but the worm.	שֶׁתִּקְוַת אֱנוֹשׁ רִמָּה.
5: Rabbi Yochanan, the son of Berokah, says:	5. רַבִּי יוֹחָנָן בֶּן־בְּרוֹקָה אוֹמֵר:
All who profane the name of G-d in private	כָּל־הַמְחַלֵּל שֵׁם שָׁמַיִם בַּסֵּתֶר
will be punished in public,	נִפְרָעִים מִמֶּנּוּ בְּגָלוּי,
whether the profanity is unintentional or intentional.	אֶחָד בְּשׁוֹגֵג וְאֶחָד בְּמֵזִיד בְּחִלּוּל הַשֵּׁם.
6: Rabbi Ishmael, his son, says:	6. רַבִּי יִשְׁמָעֵאל בְּנוֹ אוֹמֵר:
He who learns in order to teach	הַלּוֹמֵד עַל מְנָת לְלַמֵּד

will be given the means both to learn and to teach;	מַסְפִּיקִים בְּיָדוֹ לִלְמוֹד וּלְלַמֵּד;
and one who learns in order to practice	וְהַלּוֹמֵד עַל מְנָת לַעֲשׂוֹת
will be given the means to learn, teach, observe and practice.	מַסְפִּיקִים בְּיָדוֹ לִלְמוֹד וּלְלַמֵּד לִשְׁמוֹר וְלַעֲשׂוֹת.
7: Rabbi Tzadok says:	7. רַבִּי צָדוֹק אוֹמֵר:
Do not separate yourself from the community,	אַל תִּפְרוֹשׁ מִן הַצִּבּוּר,
do not make yourself as the lawyers,	וְאַל תַּעַשׂ עַצְמְךָ כְּעוֹרְכֵי הַדַּיָּנִים,
do not make (Torah knowledge) a crown to elevate yourself	וְאַל תַּעֲשֶׂם עֲטָרָה לְהִתְגַּדֵּל בָּהּ
nor a spade to dig with.	וְלֹא קַרְדֹּם לַחְפֹּר בָּהּ.
This is what Hillel used to say:	וְכָךְ הָיָה הִלֵּל אוֹמֵר:
One who uses the Torah for worldly use shall die;	וּדְאִשְׁתַּמֵּשׁ בְּתָגָא, חֲלָף;
Thus, one learns,	הָא לָמַדְתָּ,
one who profits from the Torah	כָּל־הַנֶּהֱנֶה מִדִּבְרֵי תוֹרָה
removes his own life from this world.	נוֹטֵל חַיָּיו מִן הָעוֹלָם.
8: Rabbi Yose says:	8. רַבִּי יוֹסֵי אוֹמֵר:
All who honor the Torah	כָּל־הַמְכַבֵּד אֶת־הַתּוֹרָה
will himself be honored by mankind,	גּוּפוֹ מְכֻבָּד עַל־הַבְּרִיּוֹת,
and all who dishonor the Torah	וְכָל הַמְחַלֵּל אֶת־הַתּוֹרָה
will be dishonored by mankind.	גּוּפוֹ מְחֻלָּל עַל הַבְּרִיּוֹת.
9: Rabbi Ishmael, his son, says:	9. רַבִּי יִשְׁמָעֵאל בְּנוֹ אוֹמֵר:
One who avoids judgment	הַחוֹשֵׂךְ עַצְמוֹ מִן הַדִּין
rids himself of hatred, robbery and false swearing;	פּוֹרֵק מִמֶּנּוּ אֵיבָה וְגָזֵל וּשְׁבוּעַת שָׁוְא;
and one who is haughty in his own decisions	וְהַגַּס לִבּוֹ בְּהוֹרָאָה
is foolish, wicked and arrogant.	שׁוֹטֶה רָשָׁע וְגַס רוּחַ.
10: He used to say:	10. הוּא הָיָה אוֹמֵר:
Do not judge alone,	אַל תְּהִי דָן יְחִידִי,
for there is no single judge except One,	שֶׁאֵין דָּן יְחִידִי אֶלָּא אֶחָד,
and do not say (to colleagues), "Accept my view,"	וְאַל תֹּאמַר קַבְּלוּ דַעְתִּי,
for they are the authority — not you.	שֶׁהֵם רַשָּׁאִים וְלֹא אַתָּה.
11: Rabbi Jonathan says:	11. רַבִּי יוֹנָתָן אוֹמֵר:
One who fulfills the Torah despite poverty,	כָּל־הַמְקַיֵּם אֶת־הַתּוֹרָה מֵעֹנִי,
shall ultimately fulfill it in wealth;	סוֹפוֹ לְקַיְּמָהּ מֵעֹשֶׁר;
and one who neglects the Torah in the midst of wealth	וְכָל־הַמְבַטֵּל אֶת־הַתּוֹרָה מֵעֹשֶׁר,
shall ultimately neglect it due to poverty.	סוֹפוֹ לְבַטְּלָהּ מֵעֹנִי.
12: Rabbi Meir says:	12. רַבִּי מֵאִיר אוֹמֵר:
Be less occupied with work and occupy yourself with Torah,	הֱוֵה מְמַעֵט בְּעֵסֶק וַעֲסֹק בַּתּוֹרָה,
and be humble before all men.	וֶהֱוֵה שְׁפַל־רוּחַ בִּפְנֵי כָל־אָדָם.
If you neglect the Torah (deliberately),	וְאִם בָּטַלְתָּ מִן הַתּוֹרָה,
many causes for neglect will come your way;	יֶשׁ לְךָ בְּטֵלִים הַרְבֵּה כְּנֶגְדְּךָ;
yet if you toil in the Torah,	וְאִם עָמַלְתָּ בַּתּוֹרָה,
He has great reward to give you.	יֶשׁ לוֹ שָׂכָר הַרְבֵּה לִתֶּן לָךְ.
13: Rabbi Eliezer, the son of Jacob, says:	13. רַבִּי אֱלִיעֶזֶר בֶּן־יַעֲקֹב אוֹמֵר:

One who performs one commandment	הָעוֹשֶׂה מִצְוָה אַחַת
gains for himself an advocate,	קוֹנֶה לוֹ פְּרַקְלִיט אֶחָד,
and one who transgresses with one sin	וְהָעוֹבֵר עֲבֵרָה אַחַת
acquires for himself an accuser.	קוֹנֶה לוֹ קַטֵּגוֹר אֶחָד.
Repentence and good deeds	תְּשׁוּבָה וּמַעֲשִׂים טוֹבִים
are a shield against punishment.	כִּתְרִיס בִּפְנֵי הַפֻּרְעָנוּת.
14: Rabbi Yochanan HaSandlar says:	14. רַבִּי יוֹחָנָן הַסַּנְדְּלָר אוֹמֵר:
Every assembly congregated in the name of Heaven	כָּל־כְּנֵסִיָּה שֶׁהִיא לְשֵׁם שָׁמַיִם
will endure,	סוֹפָהּ לְהִתְקַיֵּם,
and one not in the name of Heaven	וְשֶׁאֵינָהּ לְשֵׁם שָׁמַיִם
will not endure.	אֵין סוֹפָהּ לְהִתְקַיֵּם.
15: Rabbi Elazer, the son of Shamua, says:	15. רַבִּי אֶלְעָזָר בֶּן־שַׁמּוּעַ אוֹמֵר:
Let the honor of your student be as dear as your own;	יְהִי כְבוֹד תַּלְמִידְךָ חָבִיב עָלֶיךָ כְּשֶׁלְּךָ;
let the honor due your friend be like the reverence due your teacher;	וּכְבוֹד חֲבֵרְךָ כְּמוֹרָא רַבְּךָ;
and the reverence accorded your teacher be like the reverence due G-d.	וּמוֹרָא רַבְּךָ כְּמוֹרָא שָׁמָיִם.
16: Rabbi Judah says:	16. רַבִּי יְהוּדָה אוֹמֵר:
Be cautious in teaching,	הֱוֵי זָהִיר בְּתַלְמוּד,
for an error in teaching amounts to intentional sin.	שֶׁשִּׁגְגַת תַּלְמוּד עוֹלָה זָדוֹן.
17: Rabbi Simon says:	17. רַבִּי שִׁמְעוֹן אוֹמֵר:
There are three crowns:	שְׁלשָׁה כְתָרִים הֵן:
the crown of Torah, the crown of priesthood and the crown of kingdom,	כֶּתֶר תּוֹרָה וְכֶתֶר כְּהֻנָּה וְכֶתֶר מַלְכוּת,
yet the crown of a good name overrides them all.	וְכֶתֶר שֵׁם טוֹב עוֹלֶה עַל גַּבֵּיהֶן.
18: Rabbi Nehorai says:	18. רַבִּי נְהוֹרַי אוֹמֵר:
Move to a place of Torah,	הֱוֵי גוֹלֶה לִמְקוֹם תּוֹרָה,
and do not say that it will follow you,	וְאַל תֹּאמַר שֶׁהִיא תָבוֹא אַחֲרֶיךָ,
for your associates will confirm it to you;	שֶׁחֲבֵרֶיךָ יְקַיְּמוּהָ בְיָדֶךָ;
and on your (own) understanding do not depend.	וְאֶל בִּינָתְךָ אַל תִּשָּׁעֵן.
19: Rabbi Yannai says:	19. רַבִּי יַנַּי אוֹמֵר:
It is not in our power to explain the prosperity of the wicked,	אֵין בְּיָדֵינוּ לֹא מִשַּׁלְוַת הָרְשָׁעִים,
or the afflictions of the righteous.	וְאַף לֹא מִיִּסּוּרֵי הַצַּדִּיקִים.
20: Rabbi Matitya, the son of Cheresh, says:	20. רַבִּי מַתְיָה בֶּן־חָרָשׁ אוֹמֵר:
Be first in greeting every man;	הֱוֵי מַקְדִּים בִּשְׁלוֹם כָּל־אָדָם;
and be a tail among lions,	וֶהֱוֵה זָנָב לָאֲרָיוֹת,
and do not be a head among foxes.	וְאַל תְּהִי רֹאשׁ לַשְּׁעָלִים.
21: Rabbi Jacob says:	21. רַבִּי יַעֲקֹב אוֹמֵר:
This world is like a hallway	הָעוֹלָם הַזֶּה דּוֹמֶה לִפְרוֹזְדוֹר
before the world to come:	בִּפְנֵי הָעוֹלָם הַבָּא:
prepare yourself in the hallway,	הַתְקֵן עַצְמְךָ בִּפְרוֹזְדוֹר,
so that you may enter the banquet hall.	כְּדֵי שֶׁתִּכָּנֵס לַטְּרַקְלִין.

22: He used to say:	22. הוּא הָיָה אוֹמֵר:
Better is one hour (spent)	יָפָה שָׁעָה אַחַת
in repentence and good deeds in this world	בִּתְשׁוּבָה וּמַעֲשִׂים טוֹבִים בָּעוֹלָם הַזֶּה
than the whole life of the world to come;	מִכָּל־חַיֵּי הָעוֹלָם הַבָּא;
and better is one hour	וְיָפָה שָׁעָה אַחַת
of spiritual satisfaction in the world to come	שֶׁל קֹרַת רוּחַ בָּעוֹלָם הַבָּא
than all the life of this world.	מִכָּל־חַיֵּי הָעוֹלָם הַזֶּה.
23: Rabbi Simon, the son of Elazer, says:	23. רַבִּי שִׁמְעוֹן בֶּן־אֶלְעָזָר אוֹמֵר:
Do not pacify your friend	אַל תְּרַצֶּה אֶת־חֲבֵרְךָ
in the moment of his anger;	בִּשְׁעַת כַּעְסוֹ;
and do not comfort him	וְאַל תְּנַחֲמֶנּוּ
during the moment that his dead lies before him;	בְּשָׁעָה שֶׁמֵּתוֹ מוּטָל לְפָנָיו;
and do not question him	וְאַל תִּשְׁאַל לוֹ
at the time he makes a vow;	בִּשְׁעַת נִדְרוֹ;
and seek not to see him	וְאַל תִּשְׁתַּדֵּל לִרְאוֹתוֹ
in the hour of his degradation.	בִּשְׁעַת קַלְקָלָתוֹ.
24: Shmuel HaKatan says:	24. שְׁמוּאֵל הַקָּטָן אוֹמֵר:
With your enemy's fall do not rejoice,	בִּנְפֹל אוֹיִבְךָ אַל־תִּשְׂמָח,
and when he stumbles do not let your heart be glad,	וּבִכָּשְׁלוֹ אַל־יָגֵל לִבֶּךָ,
lest G-d witness it and it will be bad in His eyes	פֶּן־יִרְאֶה ה׳ וְרַע בְּעֵינָיו
and He will turn away His wrath from him. (Proverbs 24:17-18)	וְהֵשִׁיב מֵעָלָיו אַפּוֹ (משלי כד, יז־יח).
25: Elisha, the son of Abuya, says:	25. אֱלִישָׁע בֶּן־אֲבוּיָה אוֹמֵר:
If one learns when he is young,	הַלּוֹמֵד יֶלֶד,
to what is it compared?	לְמָה הוּא דוֹמֶה?
To ink written on clean paper.	לִדְיוֹ כְּתוּבָה עַל נְיָר חָדָשׁ.
If one learns when he is old,	וְהַלּוֹמֵד זָקֵן,
to what is it compared?	לְמָה הוּא דוֹמֶה?
To ink written on smudged paper.	לִדְיוֹ כְּתוּבָה עַל נְיָר מָחוּק.
26: Rabbi Yossi, the son of Judah, of the village of HaBavli, says:	26. רַבִּי יוֹסֵי בַּר יְהוּדָה אִישׁ כְּפַר הַבַּבְלִי אוֹמֵר:
He who learns from the young,	הַלּוֹמֵד מִן הַקְּטַנִּים,
to what is he compared?	לְמָה הוּא דוֹמֶה?
To one who eats unripe grapes,	לְאוֹכֵל עֲנָבִים קֵהוֹת,
and drinks wine from the wine press.	וְשׁוֹתֶה יַיִן מִגִּתּוֹ;
He who learns from the old,	וְהַלּוֹמֵד מִן הַזְּקֵנִים,
to what is he compared?	לְמָה הוּא דוֹמֶה?
To one who eats ripe grapes,	לְאוֹכֵל עֲנָבִים בְּשׁוּלוֹת,
and drinks old wine.	וְשׁוֹתֶה יַיִן יָשָׁן.
27: Rabbi Meir says:	27. רַבִּי מֵאִיר אוֹמֵר:
Do not look at the bottle,	אַל תִּסְתַּכֵּל בְּקַנְקַן,
but at what it has in it;	אֶלָּא בְּמַה שֶּׁיֵּשׁ בּוֹ;
a new bottle may be filled with old (wine),	יֵשׁ קַנְקַן חָדָשׁ מָלֵא יָשָׁן,

and an old bottle may not even have new wine.	וְיָשָׁן שֶׁאֲפִלּוּ חָדָשׁ אֵין בּוֹ.
28: Rabbi Elazer HaKappar says:	28. רַבִּי אֶלְעָזָר הַקַּפָּר אוֹמֵר:
Envy, lust and ambition	הַקִּנְאָה וְהַתַּאֲוָה וְהַכָּבוֹד
remove man from the world.	מוֹצִיאִים אֶת־הָאָדָם מִן הָעוֹלָם.
29: He used to say:	29. הוּא הָיָה אוֹמֵר:
Those who are born are destined to die,	הַיִּלּוֹדִים לָמוּת,
and those who die are destined to be brought back to life again;	וְהַמֵּתִים לְהֵחָיוֹת;
the living are destined to be judged,	וְהַחַיִּים לִדּוֹן,
to know, teach and proclaim that G-d is.	לֵידַע וּלְהוֹדִיעַ וּלְהִוָּדַע שֶׁהוּא אֵ׳ל.
He is the Maker, the Creator;	הוּא הַיּוֹצֵר, הוּא הַבּוֹרֵא;
He understands everything, He is the Judge,	הוּא הַמֵּבִין, הוּא הַדַּיָּן,
the Witness, the Plaintiff.	הוּא הָעֵד, הוּא בַּעַל דִּין.
In the future He will judge; blessed be He,	הוּא עָתִיד לָדוּן, בָּרוּךְ הוּא,
in whose presence there is no wrong,	שֶׁאֵין לְפָנָיו לֹא עַוְלָה,
no forgetfulness, no partiality,	וְלֹא שִׁכְחָה, וְלֹא מַשּׂוֹא פָנִים,
nor taking of bribes.	וְלֹא מִקַּח שֹׁחַד.
Know that all is subject to reckoning,	וְדַע שֶׁהַכֹּל לְפִי הַחֶשְׁבּוֹן,
and do not imagine	וְאַל יַבְטִיחֲךָ יִצְרְךָ
that the grave will provide a place of escape for you.	שֶׁהַשְּׁאוֹל בֵּית מָנוֹס לָךְ.
For against your will you were formed	שֶׁעַל כָּרְחֲךָ אַתָּה נוֹצָר
and against your will you were born;	וְעַל כָּרְחֲךָ אַתָּה נוֹלָד;
and against your will you live	וְעַל כָּרְחֲךָ אַתָּה חַי
and against your will you will die;	וְעַל כָּרְחֲךָ אַתָּה מֵת;
and against your will you shall, in the future,	וְעַל כָּרְחֲךָ אַתָּה עָתִיד
give a strict account	לִתֵּן דִּין וְחֶשְׁבּוֹן
before the Supreme King of kings,	לִפְנֵי מֶלֶךְ מַלְכֵי הַמְּלָכִים,
the Holy One, blessed be He.	הַקָּדוֹשׁ בָּרוּךְ הוּא.

Chapter 5 — פרק ה׳

1: By ten sayings the world was created.	1. בַּעֲשָׂרָה מַאֲמָרוֹת נִבְרָא הָעוֹלָם.
and what does this teach us?	וּמַה־תַּלְמוּד לוֹמַר?
Certainly with just one saying the world could have been created.	וַהֲלֹא בְּמַאֲמָר אֶחָד יָכוֹל לְהִבָּרְאוֹת.
But (it teaches us that G-d) will punish the wicked	אֶלָּא לְהִפָּרַע מִן הָרְשָׁעִים
who destroy the world,	שֶׁמְּאַבְּדִים אֶת־הָעוֹלָם,
which was created by ten sayings,	שֶׁנִּבְרָא בַּעֲשָׂרָה מַאֲמָרוֹת,
and (that He will) reward the righteous	וְלִתֵּן שָׂכָר טוֹב לַצַּדִּיקִים
who uphold the world,	שֶׁמְּקַיְּמִים אֶת־הָעוֹלָם,
which was created by ten sayings.	שֶׁנִּבְרָא בַּעֲשָׂרָה מַאֲמָרוֹת.
2: There were ten generations from Adam to Noah,	2. עֲשָׂרָה דוֹרוֹת מֵאָדָם וְעַד נֹחַ,

to show how great is G-d's patience,	לְהוֹדִיעַ כַּמָּה אֶרֶךְ אַפַּיִם לְפָנָיו,
for all those generations provoked Him	שֶׁכָּל־הַדּוֹרוֹת הָיוּ מַכְעִיסִים לְפָנָיו
until he brought upon them the waters of the Flood.	עַד שֶׁהֵבִיא עֲלֵיהֶם אֶת־מֵי הַמַּבּוּל.
3: There were ten generations from Noah to Abraham,	3. עֲשָׂרָה דוֹרוֹת מִנֹּחַ וְעַד אַבְרָהָם,
to show how great is G-d's patience,	לְהוֹדִיעַ כַּמָּה אֶרֶךְ אַפַּיִם לְפָנָיו,
for all those generations provoked Him,	שֶׁכָּל־הַדּוֹרוֹת הָיוּ מַכְעִיסִים לְפָנָיו,
until our forefather Abraham came	עַד שֶׁבָּא אַבְרָהָם אָבִינוּ
and received the reward of them all.	וְקִבֵּל שְׂכַר כֻּלָּם.
4: With ten trials	4. עֲשָׂרָה נִסְיוֹנוֹת
was our forefather Abraham tried	נִתְנַסָּה אַבְרָהָם אָבִינוּ
and he withstood them all,	וְעָמַד בְּכֻלָּם,
to show how great was the love of our forefather Abraham.	לְהוֹדִיעַ כַּמָּה חִבָּתוֹ שֶׁל אַבְרָהָם אָבִינוּ.
5: Ten miracles were performed for our forefathers in Egypt	5. עֲשָׂרָה נִסִּים נַעֲשׂוּ לַאֲבוֹתֵינוּ בְּמִצְרַיִם
and ten by the sea.	וַעֲשָׂרָה עַל הַיָּם.
6: Ten plagues the Holy One, blessed be He, brought	6. עֶשֶׂר מַכּוֹת הֵבִיא הַקָּדוֹשׁ בָּרוּךְ הוּא,
on the Egyptians in Egypt	עַל הַמִּצְרִיִּים בְּמִצְרַיִם
and ten by the sea.	וְעֶשֶׂר עַל הַיָּם.
7: Ten times our ancestors tried	7. עֲשָׂרָה נִסְיוֹנוֹת נִסּוּ אֲבוֹתֵינוּ
the Holy One, blessed be He, in the desert;	אֶת־הַקָּדוֹשׁ בָּרוּךְ הוּא בַּמִּדְבָּר;
as it is said,	שֶׁנֶּאֱמַר,
"They have tested Me now ten times	וַיְנַסּוּ אֹתִי זֶה עֶשֶׂר פְּעָמִים
and did not listen to My voice" (Numbers 14:22).	וְלֹא שָׁמְעוּ בְּקוֹלִי (במדבר יד, כב).
8: Ten miracles were performed for our ancestors in the Temple;	8. עֲשָׂרָה נִסִּים נַעֲשׂוּ לַאֲבוֹתֵינוּ בְּבֵית הַמִּקְדָּשׁ;
no woman miscarried from the scent of the sacrificial meat;	לֹא הִפִּילָה אִשָּׁה מֵרֵיחַ בְּשַׂר הַקֹּדֶשׁ;
the sacrificial meat never spoiled;	וְלֹא הִסְרִיחַ בְּשַׂר הַקֹּדֶשׁ מֵעוֹלָם;
no fly was seen in the slaughterhouse;	וְלֹא נִרְאָה זְבוּב בְּבֵית הַמִּטְבְּחַיִם;
no unclean accident ever occurred on the Day of Atonement to the High Priest;	וְלֹא אֵרַע קֶרִי לְכֹהֵן גָּדוֹל בְּיוֹם הַכִּפֻּרִים;
the rain never extinguished the fire on the wood-pile;	וְלֹא כִבּוּ הַגְּשָׁמִים אֵשׁ שֶׁל עֲצֵי הַמַּעֲרָכָה;
the wind never prevailed over the column of smoke;	וְלֹא נָצְחָה הָרוּחַ אֶת־עַמּוּד הֶעָשָׁן;
never was a defect found in the Omer,	וְלֹא נִמְצָא פְסוּל בָּעֹמֶר,
or in the two loaves or the showbread;	וּבִשְׁתֵּי הַלֶּחֶם וּבְלֶחֶם הַפָּנִים;
the people stood, pressed close together, yet were able to bow down;	עוֹמְדִים צְפוּפִים וּמִשְׁתַּחֲוִים רְוָחִים;
never did a snake or scorpion cause harm to anyone in Jerusalem;	וְלֹא הִזִּיק נָחָשׁ וְעַקְרָב בִּירוּשָׁלַיִם מֵעוֹלָם;
and no man ever said to his friend,	וְלֹא אָמַר אָדָם לַחֲבֵרוֹ,
"There is no room for me to sleep in Jerusalem."	צַר לִי הַמָּקוֹם שֶׁאָלִין בִּירוּשָׁלַיִם.
9: Ten things were created	9. עֲשָׂרָה דְבָרִים נִבְרְאוּ
on the Sabbath eve at dusk,	בְּעֶרֶב שַׁבָּת בֵּין הַשְּׁמָשׁוֹת,
and these are them:	וְאֵלּוּ הֵן:
the mouth of the earth;	פִּי הָאָרֶץ;

the mouth of the well;	פִּי הַבְּאֵר;
the mouth of the ass;	פִּי הָאָתוֹן;
and the rainbow, and the manna, and the rod, and the shamir-worm;	הַקֶּשֶׁת וְהַמָּן וְהַמַּטֶּה וְהַשָּׁמִיר;
the form of the written characters;	הַכְּתָב;
and the writing;	וְהַמַּכְתֵּב;
and the tablets of the Law.	וְהַלּוּחוֹת.
And there are those who say,	וְיֵשׁ אוֹמְרִים,
even the demons, and the grave of Moses,	אַף הַמַּזִּיקִין, וּקְבוּרָתוֹ שֶׁל מֹשֶׁה,
and the ram of our forefather Abraham;	וְאֵילוֹ שֶׁל אַבְרָהָם אָבִינוּ;
and there are those who say	וְיֵשׁ אוֹמְרִים
even the original fashioning tool.	אַף צְבָת בִּצְבָת עֲשׂוּיָה.
10: There are seven characteristics of a boor	10. שִׁבְעָה דְבָרִים בְּגֹלֶם
and seven of a wise man.	וְשִׁבְעָה בְּחָכָם.
A wise man does not speak	חָכָם אֵינוֹ מְדַבֵּר
in the presence of one who is greater than him in wisdom;	לִפְנֵי מִי שֶׁגָּדוֹל מִמֶּנּוּ בְּחָכְמָה;
and he does not interrupt the words of his friend;	וְאֵינוֹ נִכְנָס לְתוֹךְ דִּבְרֵי חֲבֵרוֹ;
he is not hasty to respond;	וְאֵינוֹ נִבְהָל לְהָשִׁיב;
he asks what is pertinent	שׁוֹאֵל כְּעִנְיָן
and answers according to the law;	וּמֵשִׁיב כַּהֲלָכָה;
and he speaks on the first issue first	וְאוֹמֵר עַל רִאשׁוֹן רִאשׁוֹן
and the final issue last;	וְעַל אַחֲרוֹן אַחֲרוֹן;
and in regard to that which he has not heard	וְעַל מַה־שֶּׁלֹּא שָׁמַע
he says, "I have not heard,"	אוֹמֵר לֹא שָׁמָעְתִּי,
and he acknowledges the truth.	וּמוֹדֶה עַל הָאֱמֶת.
And the opposite of these are found in a boor.	וְחִלּוּפֵיהֶם בְּגֹלֶם.
11: Seven types of punishment come upon the world	11. שִׁבְעָה מִינֵי פֻרְעָנִיּוֹת בָּאִים לָעוֹלָם
for seven principal transgressions:	עַל שִׁבְעָה גוּפֵי עֲבֵרָה:
If some tithe	מִקְצָתָם מְעַשְּׂרִים
and others do not tithe,	וּמִקְצָתָם אֵינָם מְעַשְּׂרִים,
famine as a result of drought comes,	רָעָב שֶׁל בַּצֹּרֶת בָּא,
some will go hungry and some will have plenty.	מִקְצָתָם רְעֵבִים וּמִקְצָתָם שְׂבֵעִים.
If all resolve not to tithe,	גָּמְרוּ שֶׁלֹּא לְעַשֵּׂר,
then famine resulting from panic and drought comes.	רָעָב שֶׁל מְהוּמָה וְשֶׁל בַּצֹּרֶת בָּא.
If they resolve not to separate bread from their dough,	וְשֶׁלֹּא לִטּוֹל אֶת־הַחַלָּה,
a famine of extermination comes.	רָעָב שֶׁל כְּלָיָה בָּא.
Pestilence comes to the world	דֶּבֶר בָּא לָעוֹלָם
to fulfill those death penalties mentioned in the Torah	עַל מִיתוֹת הָאֲמוּרוֹת בַּתּוֹרָה
which are not within the jurisdiction of the civil court,	שֶׁלֹּא נִמְסְרוּ לְבֵית דִּין,
and for (using the forbidden) harvest of the Sabbatical year.	וְעַל פֵּרוֹת שְׁבִיעִית.
The sword comes upon the world	חֶרֶב בָּא לָעוֹלָם

because of the delay of justice,	עַל עִנּוּי הַדִּין,
and for the perversion of justice,	וְעַל עִוּוּת הַדִּין,
and for those that teach the Torah not according to the law.	וְעַל הַמּוֹרִים בַּתּוֹרָה שֶׁלֹּא כַהֲלָכָה.
Wild beasts come upon the world	חַיָּה רָעָה בָּא לָעוֹלָם
because of perjury and profaning G-d's name.	עַל שְׁבוּעַת שָׁוְא וְעַל חִלּוּל הַשֵּׁם.
Exile comes upon the world	גָּלוּת בָּאָה לָעוֹלָם
because of idolatry, and sexual immorality,	עַל עֲבוֹדַת אֱלִילִים וְעַל גִּלּוּי עֲרָיוֹת,
and bloodshed,	וְעַל שְׁפִיכוּת דָּמִים,
and for not allowing the soil to rest in the Sabbatical year.	וְעַל שְׁמִטַּת הָאָרֶץ.
12: At four periods pestilence increases:	12. בְּאַרְבָּעָה פְרָקִים הַדֶּבֶר מִתְרַבֶּה:
In the fourth year, in the seventh year, in the year following the seventh year	בָּרְבִיעִית וּבַשְּׁבִיעִית וּבְמוֹצָאֵי שְׁבִיעִית
and following the festival in every year.	וּבְמוֹצָאֵי הֶחָג שֶׁבְּכָל שָׁנָה וְשָׁנָה.
In the fourth year for not giving the tithe to the poor in the third year;	בָּרְבִיעִית מִפְּנֵי מַעְשַׂר עָנִי שֶׁבַּשְּׁלִישִׁית;
in the seventh year for not giving the tithe to the poor in the sixth year;	בַּשְּׁבִיעִית מִפְּנֵי מַעְשַׂר עָנִי שֶׁבַּשִּׁשִּׁית;
in the year following the Sabbatical year for using the forbidden harvest;	בְּמוֹצָאֵי שְׁבִיעִית מִפְּנֵי פֵּרוֹת שְׁבִיעִית;
and following the festival every year	בְּמוֹצָאֵי הֶחָג שֶׁבְּכָל־שָׁנָה וְשָׁנָה
for stealing the gifts of the poor.	מִפְּנֵי גֶזֶל מַתְּנוֹת עֲנִיִּים.
13: There are four characters of men:	13. אַרְבַּע מִדּוֹת בָּאָדָם:
He who says, "What is mine is mine and what is yours is yours,"	הָאוֹמֵר שֶׁלִּי שֶׁלִּי וְשֶׁלְּךָ שֶׁלָּךְ,
is the average type;	זוֹ מִדָּה בֵינוֹנִית;
and there are those who say that this is the type of Sodom;	וְיֵשׁ אוֹמְרִים זוֹ מִדַּת סְדוֹם;
"What is mine is yours and what is yours is mine," is ignorant;	שֶׁלִּי שֶׁלָּךְ וְשֶׁלְּךָ שֶׁלִּי, עַם הָאָרֶץ;
"What is mine is yours and what is yours is yours," is pious;	שֶׁלִּי שֶׁלָּךְ וְשֶׁלְּךָ שֶׁלָּךְ חָסִיד;
"What is yours is mine and what is mine is mine," is wicked.	שֶׁלְּךָ שֶׁלִּי וְשֶׁלִּי שֶׁלִּי רָשָׁע.
14: There are four types of disposition:	14. אַרְבַּע מִדּוֹת בְּדֵעוֹת:
Quick to anger and quick to assuage,	נוֹחַ לִכְעוֹס וְנוֹחַ לִרְצוֹת,
his loss is cancelled by his gain;	יָצָא הֶפְסֵדוֹ בִּשְׂכָרוֹ;
hard to anger and hard to assuage,	קָשֶׁה לִכְעוֹס וְקָשֶׁה לִרְצוֹת,
his gain is cancelled by his loss;	יָצָא שְׂכָרוֹ בְּהֶפְסֵדוֹ;
hard to anger and easy to assuage is pious;	קָשֶׁה לִכְעוֹס וְנוֹחַ לִרְצוֹת חָסִיד;
easy to anger and hard to assuage is wicked.	נוֹחַ לִכְעוֹס וְקָשֶׁה לִרְצוֹת רָשָׁע.
15: There are four types of students:	15. אַרְבַּע מִדּוֹת בְּתַלְמִידִים:
Quick to learn and quick to forget,	מַהִיר לִשְׁמוֹעַ וּמַהִיר לְאַבֵּד,
his gain is cancelled by his loss;	יָצָא שְׂכָרוֹ בְּהֶפְסֵדוֹ;
slow to learn and slow to forget,	קָשֶׁה לִשְׁמוֹעַ וְקָשֶׁה לְאַבֵּד,
his loss is cancelled by his gain;	יָצָא הֶפְסֵדוֹ בִּשְׂכָרוֹ;
quick to learn and slow to forget	מַהִיר לִשְׁמוֹעַ וְקָשֶׁה לְאַבֵּד
is the finest quality;	זוֹ חֵלֶק טוֹב;

slow to learn and quick to forget	קָשֶׁה לִשְׁמוֹעַ וּמָהִיר לְאַבֵּד
is the worst quality.	זוֹ חֵלֶק רָע.
16: There are four types of donors to charity:	16. אַרְבַּע מִדּוֹת בְּנוֹתְנֵי צְדָקָה:
He who gives but does not want others to give	הָרוֹצֶה שֶׁיִּתֵּן וְלֹא יִתְּנוּ אֲחֵרִים
begrudges others;	עֵינוֹ רָעָה בְּשֶׁל אֲחֵרִים;
he who wants others to give but will not give himself,	יִתְּנוּ אֲחֵרִים וְהוּא לֹא יִתֵּן,
begrudges himself;	עֵינוֹ רָעָה בְּשֶׁלּוֹ;
he who gives and wants others to give is pious;	יִתֵּן וְיִתְּנוּ אֲחֵרִים חָסִיד;
he who will not give and does not want others to give is wicked.	לֹא יִתֵּן וְלֹא יִתְּנוּ אֲחֵרִים רָשָׁע.
17: There are four types of those who go to the house of study:	17. אַרְבַּע מִדּוֹת בְּהוֹלְכֵי בֵית הַמִּדְרָשׁ:
He who goes but does not practice,	הוֹלֵךְ וְאֵינוֹ עוֹשֶׂה,
the reward for his going is in his hand;	שְׂכַר הֲלִיכָה בְּיָדוֹ;
he who practices but does not go,	עֹשֶׂה וְאֵינוֹ הוֹלֵךְ,
the reward for practicing is in his hand;	שְׂכַר מַעֲשֶׂה בְּיָדוֹ;
he who goes and practices is pious;	הוֹלֵךְ וְעוֹשֶׂה חָסִיד;
he who neither goes nor practices is wicked.	לֹא הוֹלֵךְ וְלֹא עוֹשֶׂה רָשָׁע.
18: There are four types that sit in the presence of wise men:	18. אַרְבַּע מִדּוֹת בְּיוֹשְׁבִים לִפְנֵי חֲכָמִים:
A sponge, a funnel, a strainer and a sieve.	סְפוֹג וּמַשְׁפֵּךְ מְשַׁמֶּרֶת וְנָפָה.
The sponge absorbs all;	סְפוֹג שֶׁהוּא סוֹפֵג אֶת־הַכֹּל;
the funnel accepts at one end and releases at the other;	וּמַשְׁפֵּךְ שֶׁמַּכְנִיס בְּזוֹ וּמוֹצִיא בְזוֹ;
the strainer allows the wine to flow through	מְשַׁמֶּרֶת שֶׁמּוֹצִיאָה אֶת־הַיַּיִן
and retains the sediment;	וְקוֹלֶטֶת אֶת־הַשְּׁמָרִים;
and the sieve which releases the coarse flour	וְנָפָה שֶׁמּוֹצִיאָה אֶת־הַקֶּמַח
and retains the fine flour.	וְקוֹלֶטֶת אֶת־הַסֹּלֶת.
19: All love which relies on a specific aspect	19. כָּל־אַהֲבָה שֶׁהִיא תְלוּיָה בְדָבָר
will fail once that aspect no longer exists;	בָּטֵל דָּבָר בְּטֵלָה אַהֲבָה;
if it does not rely on a specific aspect	וְשֶׁאֵינָהּ תְּלוּיָה בְדָבָר
it will never fail, forever.	אֵינָהּ בְּטֵלָה לְעוֹלָם.
Which love relied on a specific aspect?	אֵיזוֹ הִיא אַהֲבָה שֶׁהִיא תְלוּיָה בְדָבָר?
The love of Amnon for Tamar.	זוֹ אַהֲבַת אַמְנוֹן וְתָמָר.
And which love did not rely on a specific aspect?	וְשֶׁאֵינָהּ תְּלוּיָה בְדָבָר?
The love of David and Jonathan.	זוֹ אַהֲבַת דָּוִד וִיהוֹנָתָן.
20: An argument which is for the name of Heaven	20. כָּל־מַחֲלֹקֶת שֶׁהִיא לְשֵׁם שָׁמַיִם
its end will be established,	סוֹפָהּ לְהִתְקַיֵּם,
and when it is not for the name of Heaven	וְשֶׁאֵינָהּ לְשֵׁם שָׁמַיִם
its end will never be established.	אֵין סוֹפָהּ לְהִתְקַיֵּם.
Which argument was for the name of Heaven?	אֵיזוֹ הִיא מַחֲלֹקֶת שֶׁהִיא לְשֵׁם שָׁמַיִם?
The argument between Hillel and Shammai.	זוֹ מַחֲלֹקֶת הִלֵּל וְשַׁמַּאי.
And which was not for the name of Heaven?	וְשֶׁאֵינָהּ לְשֵׁם שָׁמַיִם?
That of Korach and his followers.	זוֹ מַחֲלֹקֶת קֹרַח וְכָל־עֲדָתוֹ.
21: All who lead the people to righteousness,	21. כָּל־הַמְזַכֶּה אֶת־הָרַבִּים,

no sin will ever be on his hand;	אֵין חֵטְא בָּא עַל יָדוֹ;
and all who lead people to sin	וְכָל־הַמַּחֲטִיא אֶת־הָרַבִּים
will be unable to repent.	אֵין מַסְפִּיקִים בְּיָדוֹ לַעֲשׂוֹת תְּשׁוּבָה.
Moses was righteous and led the people to righteousness,	מֹשֶׁה זָכָה וְזִכָּה אֶת־הָרַבִּים,
the people's righteousness is ascribable to him,	זְכוּת הָרַבִּים תָּלוּי בּוֹ,
as it is said,	שֶׁנֶּאֱמַר,
"The righteousness of G-d he performed	צִדְקַת ה׳ עָשָׂה
and His ordinances with Israel" (Deuteronomy 33:21).	וּמִשְׁפָּטָיו עִם יִשְׂרָאֵל (דברים לג, כא).
Jeroboam, the son of Nevat, sinned and brought the people to sin,	יָרָבְעָם בֶּן־נְבָט חָטָא, וְהֶחֱטִיא אֶת־הָרַבִּים,
the sin of the people is ascribable to him,	חֵטְא הָרַבִּים תָּלוּי בּוֹ,
as it is said,	שֶׁנֶּאֱמַר,
"Because of the sins of Jeroboam which he committed	עַל חַטֹּאות יָרָבְעָם אֲשֶׁר חָטָא
and caused Israel to sin" (1 Kings 15:30).	וַאֲשֶׁר הֶחֱטִיא אֶת־יִשְׂרָאֵל (מלכים א, טו, ל).
22: Anyone who possesses these three attributes	22. כָּל־מִי שֶׁיֵּשׁ בּוֹ שְׁלֹשָׁה דְבָרִים
is of the students of our forefather Abraham;	הַלָּלוּ הוּא מִתַּלְמִידָיו שֶׁל אַבְרָהָם אָבִינוּ;
and anyone who possesses another three qualities	וּשְׁלֹשָׁה דְבָרִים אֲחֵרִים
is of the students of Balaam, the wicked.	הוּא מִתַּלְמִידָיו שֶׁל בִּלְעָם הָרָשָׁע.
A good eye, a humble spirit and a quiet soul	עַיִן טוֹבָה וְרוּחַ נְמוּכָה וְנֶפֶשׁ שְׁפָלָה
are from the students of our forefather Abraham.	מִתַּלְמִידָיו שֶׁל אַבְרָהָם אָבִינוּ.
An evil eye, a haughty spirit and a proud soul	עַיִן רָעָה וְרוּחַ גְּבוֹהָה וְנֶפֶשׁ רְחָבָה
are from the students of Balaam, the wicked.	מִתַּלְמִידָיו שֶׁל בִּלְעָם הָרָשָׁע.
What is the difference between the students of our forefather Abraham	מַה בֵּין תַּלְמִידָיו שֶׁל אַבְרָהָם אָבִינוּ
and those of the wicked Balaam?	לְתַלְמִידָיו שֶׁל בִּלְעָם הָרָשָׁע?
The disciples of Abraham enjoy this world	תַּלְמִידָיו שֶׁל אַבְרָהָם אָבִינוּ אוֹכְלִים בָּעוֹלָם הַזֶּה
and inherit the world to come,	וְנוֹחֲלִים הָעוֹלָם הַבָּא,
as it is said,	שֶׁנֶּאֱמַר,
"That I may cause those who love Me to inherit wealth	לְהַנְחִיל אֹהֲבַי יֵשׁ
and their treasuries I will fill" (Proverbs 8:21).	וְאֹצְרֹתֵיהֶם אֲמַלֵּא (משלי ח, כא).
Those who follow Balaam inherit Gehenna	תַּלְמִידָיו שֶׁל בִּלְעָם הָרָשָׁע יוֹרְשִׁים גֵּיהִנֹּם
and descend into a pit of destruction,	וְיוֹרְדִים לִבְאֵר שַׁחַת,
as it is said,	שֶׁנֶּאֱמַר,
"You, G-d, will bring them down into the pit of destruction;	וְאַתָּה אֱלֹקִים תּוֹרִדֵם לִבְאֵר שַׁחַת;
men of murder and deceit will not live out half their days,	אַנְשֵׁי דָמִים וּמִרְמָה לֹא־יֶחֱצוּ יְמֵיהֶם,
and I trust in you" (Psalms 55:24).	וַאֲנִי אֶבְטַח־בָּךְ (תהלים נה, כד).
23: Judah, the son of Tema, says:	23. יְהוּדָה בֶּן־תֵּימָא אוֹמֵר:
Be bold as a leopard and light as an eagle,	הֱוֵה עַז כַּנָּמֵר וְקַל כַּנֶּשֶׁר,
swift as a deer and strong as a lion	רָץ כַּצְּבִי וְגִבּוֹר כָּאֲרִי
to do the will of our Father in heaven.	לַעֲשׂוֹת רְצוֹן אָבִיךָ שֶׁבַּשָּׁמָיִם.
He used to say:	הוּא הָיָה אוֹמֵר:
The boldfaced are (destined) for Gehenna	עַז פָּנִים לְגֵיהִנֹּם

but the shamefaced are (destined) for the Garden of Eden.	וּבוֹשׁ פָּנִים לְגַן־עֵדֶן.
May it be Your will,	יְהִי רָצוֹן מִלְּפָנֶיךָ,
Lord our G-d and G-d of our fathers,	ה׳ אֱלֹקֵינוּ וֵאלֹקֵי אֲבוֹתֵינוּ,
that the Temple be rebuilt speedily in our days,	שֶׁיִּבָּנֶה בֵּית הַמִּקְדָּשׁ בִּמְהֵרָה בְיָמֵינוּ,
and give us a portion in Your Torah.	וְתֵן חֶלְקֵנוּ בְּתוֹרָתֶךָ.
24: He used to say:	24. הוּא הָיָה אוֹמֵר:
At five years is (the time) for the study of the Bible;	בֶּן־חָמֵשׁ שָׁנִים לַמִּקְרָא;
at ten, the study of the Mishna;	בֶּן־עֶשֶׂר שָׁנִים לַמִּשְׁנָה;
at thirteen, fulfilling commandments;	בֶּן־שְׁלֹשׁ עֶשְׂרֵה לַמִּצְוֹת;
at fifteen, the study of Talmud;	בֶּן־חֲמֵשׁ עֶשְׂרֵה לַתַּלְמוּד;
at eighteen, marriage;	בֶּן־שְׁמֹנֶה עֶשְׂרֵה לַחֻפָּה;
at twenty, pursuing (a livelihood);	בֶּן־עֶשְׂרִים לִרְדּוֹף;
at thirty, physical strength;	בֶּן־שְׁלֹשִׁים לַכֹּחַ;
at forty, understanding;	בֶּן־אַרְבָּעִים לַבִּינָה;
at fifty, giving advice;	בֶּן־חֲמִשִּׁים לָעֵצָה;
at sixty, attainment of old age;	בֶּן־שִׁשִּׁים לְזִקְנָה;
at seventy, fullness (of years);	בֶּן־שִׁבְעִים לְשֵׂיבָה;
at eighty, (spiritual) strength;	בֶּן־שְׁמוֹנִים לִגְבוּרָה;
at ninety, decrepitude;	בֶּן־תִּשְׁעִים לָשׁוּחַ;
at one hundred he is as if he is already dead	בֶּן־מֵאָה כְּאִלּוּ מֵת
and is departed and nullified from the world.	וְעָבַר וּבָטֵל מִן הָעוֹלָם.
25: Ben Bag-Bag says:	25. בֶּן־בַּג בַּג אוֹמֵר:
Study the Torah again and again	הֲפֹךְ בָּהּ וַהֲפֹךְ בָּהּ
for everything is contained therein;	דְּכֹלָּה בָהּ;
through it you will see the truth	וּבָהּ תֶּחֱזֵא
wax old and aged while examining it,	וְסִיב וּבְלֵה בַהּ,
and from it do not desist,	וּמִנַּהּ לָא תְזוּעַ,
for there is no quality more excellent than it.	שֶׁאֵין לְךָ מִדָּה טוֹבָה הֵימֶנָּה.
26: Ben Hai-Hai says:	26. בֶּן־הֵא הֵא אוֹמֵר:
According to the suffering is the reward.	לְפוּם צַעֲרָא אַגְרָא.

Chapter 6 — פרק ו׳

The Sages taught in the manner of the Mishnah:	שָׁנוּ חֲכָמִים בִּלְשׁוֹן הַמִּשְׁנָה:
Blessed be He who chose them and their teaching.	בָּרוּךְ שֶׁבָּחַר בָּהֶם וּבְמִשְׁנָתָם.
1: Rabbi Meir says:	1. רַבִּי מֵאִיר אוֹמֵר:
One who occupies himself with the Torah for its own sake	כָּל־הָעוֹסֵק בַּתּוֹרָה לִשְׁמָהּ
merits numerous things	זוֹכֶה לִדְבָרִים הַרְבֵּה
and even more so he alone is sufficient cause for the existence of the world.	וְלֹא עוֹד אֶלָּא שֶׁכָּל־הָעוֹלָם כֻּלּוֹ כְּדַאי הוּא לוֹ.

נִקְרָא רֵעַ, אָהוּב;
He is called friend, beloved;

אוֹהֵב אֶת־הַמָּקוֹם אוֹהֵב אֶת־הַבְּרִיּוֹת;
he loves G-d, he loves mankind;

מְשַׂמֵּחַ אֶת־הַמָּקוֹם מְשַׂמֵּחַ אֶת־הַבְּרִיּוֹת;
he pleases G-d and pleases mankind;

וּמַלְבַּשְׁתּוֹ עֲנָוָה וְיִרְאָה
It (the Torah) cloaks him in humility and reverence

וּמַכְשַׁרְתּוֹ לִהְיוֹת
and enables him to be

צַדִּיק חָסִיד יָשָׁר וְנֶאֱמָן.
righteous, pious, upright and faithful.

וּמְרַחַקְתּוֹ מִן הַחֵטְא
It keeps him from sin

וּמְקָרַבְתּוֹ לִידֵי זְכוּת.
and brings him closer to merit.

וְנֶהֱנִים מִמֶּנּוּ עֵצָה,
Through him men enjoy counsel,

וְתוּשִׁיָּה בִּינָה וּגְבוּרָה.
wisdom, understanding and strength.

שֶׁנֶּאֱמַר,
As it is said,

לִי עֵצָה וְתוּשִׁיָּה,
"Counsel and wisdom are Mine,

אֲנִי בִינָה לִי גְבוּרָה (משלי ח, יד).
I am understanding, might is Mine" (Proverbs 8:14).

וְנוֹתֶנֶת לוֹ מַלְכוּת וּמֶמְשָׁלָה
It gives him royalty and dominion

וְחִקּוּר דִּין.
and the ability to judge.

וּמְגַלִּים לוֹ רָזֵי תוֹרָה,
The secrets of the Torah are revealed to him,

וְנַעֲשֶׂה כְּמַעְיָן שֶׁאֵינוֹ פּוֹסֵק
and he is like a well that does not stop

וּכְנָהָר שֶׁמִּתְגַּבֵּר וְהוֹלֵךְ וְהֹוֶה;
and like a river that grows stronger;

צָנוּעַ וְאֶרֶךְ רוּחַ וּמוֹחֵל עַל עֶלְבּוֹנוֹ;
he is modest, patient and forgives insults;

וּמְגַדַּלְתּוֹ וּמְרוֹמַמְתּוֹ
and it magnifies him and exalts him

עַל כָּל־הַמַּעֲשִׂים.
above all things.

2. אָמַר רַבִּי יְהוֹשֻׁעַ בֶּן־לֵוִי:
2: Rabbi Joshua, the son of Levi, said:

בְּכָל־יוֹם וָיוֹם בַּת־קוֹל יוֹצֵאת מֵהַר חוֹרֵב,
each day a heavenly voice goes out from Mount Horeb,

וּמַכְרֶזֶת וְאוֹמֶרֶת אוֹי לָהֶם —
making a proclamation and saying, "Woe to them —

לַבְּרִיּוֹת מֵעֶלְבּוֹנָהּ שֶׁל תּוֹרָה.
to mankind for their contempt of the Torah."

שֶׁכָּל־מִי שֶׁאֵינוֹ עוֹסֵק בַּתּוֹרָה
For anyone who does not occupy himself with Torah

נִקְרָא נָזוּף,
is called "rebuked,"

שֶׁנֶּאֱמַר,
as it is said,

נֶזֶם זָהָב בְּאַף חֲזִיר,
"As a golden ring in a swine's snout,

אִשָּׁה יָפָה וְסָרַת טָעַם (משלי יא, כב).
so is a fair woman that turns away from discretion" (Proverbs 11:22).

וְאוֹמֵר, וְהַלֻּחֹת מַעֲשֵׂה אֱלֹקִים הֵמָּה,
And it says, "The tablets are the work of G-d,

וְהַמִּכְתָּב מִכְתַּב אֱלֹקִים
and the writing is the writing of G-d

הוּא חָרוּת עַל־הַלֻּחֹת (שמות לב, טז).
graven upon the tablets" (Exodus 32:16).

אַל תִּקְרָא חָרוּת,
Do not read "charuth" — (engraved),

אֶלָּה חֵרוּת,
rather "cheruth" — (freedom),

שֶׁאֵין לְךָ בֶּן־חוֹרִין
because there is not a free man

אֶלָּא מִי שֶׁעוֹסֵק בְּתַלְמוּד תּוֹרָה.
except one who occupies himself in the study of Torah.

וְכָל־מִי שֶׁעוֹסֵק בְּתַלְמוּד תּוֹרָה,
And anyone who occupies himself in the study of Torah,

הֲרֵי זֶה מִתְעַלֶּה,
behold, he is exalted,

שֶׁנֶּאֱמַר,
as it is said,

"From the gift (one attains) G-d's inheritance,	וּמִמַּתָּנָה נַחֲלִיאֵל
and from G-d's inheritance (one is raised to) high places" (Numbers 21:19).	וּמִנַּחֲלִיאֵל בָּמוֹת (במדבר כא, יט).
3: He who learns from his friend	3. הַלּוֹמֵד מֵחֲבֵרוֹ
one chapter, or one law,	פֶּרֶק אֶחָד אוֹ הֲלָכָה אַחַת,
or one verse or one word,	אוֹ פָּסוּק אֶחָד אוֹ דִּבּוּר אֶחָד,
or even one letter	אוֹ אֲפִלּוּ אוֹת אַחַת
must treat him with respect;	צָרִיךְ לִנְהָג בּוֹ כָּבוֹד;
for so we find this with David, king of Israel,	שֶׁכֵּן מָצִינוּ בְּדָוִד מֶלֶךְ יִשְׂרָאֵל,
who did not learn from Achitophel	שֶׁלֹּא לָמַד מֵאֲחִיתֹפֶל
except two things only	אֶלָּא שְׁנֵי דְבָרִים בִּלְבָד
yet called him his master, teacher and familiar friend,	קְרָאוֹ רַבּוֹ אַלּוּפוֹ וּמְיֻדָּעוֹ,
as it is said,	שֶׁנֶּאֱמַר,
"And you, a man my equal, are my teacher and special friend" (Psalms 55:14).	וְאַתָּה אֱנוֹשׁ כְּעֶרְכִּי אַלּוּפִי וּמְיֻדָּעִי (תהלים נה, יד).
Is this not an "a fortiori" argument?	וַהֲלֹא דְבָרִים קַל וָחֹמֶר?
If David, king of Israel	וּמַה דָּוִד מֶלֶךְ יִשְׂרָאֵל
who did not learn from Achitophel	שֶׁלֹּא לָמַד מֵאֲחִיתֹפֶל
except two things only	אֶלָּא שְׁנֵי דְבָרִים בִּלְבָד
called him his master, teacher and familiar friend,	קְרָאוֹ רַבּוֹ אַלּוּפוֹ וּמְיֻדָּעוֹ,
one who learns from his friend	הַלּוֹמֵד מֵחֲבֵרוֹ
one chapter or one law,	פֶּרֶק אֶחָד אוֹ הֲלָכָה אַחַת,
or one verse or one word,	אוֹ פָּסוּק אֶחָד אוֹ דִּבּוּר אֶחָד,
or even one letter,	אוֹ אֲפִלּוּ אוֹת אַחַת,
how much more so	עַל אַחַת כַּמָּה וְכַמָּה
he needs to treat him with honor;	שֶׁצָּרִיךְ לִנְהָג בּוֹ כָּבוֹד;
and there is no honor except with the Torah.	וְאֵין כָּבוֹד אֶלָּא תוֹרָה.
As it is said,	שֶׁנֶּאֱמַר,
"Honor, the wise shall inherit" (Proverbs 3:35),	כָּבוֹד חֲכָמִים יִנְחָלוּ (משלי ג, לה),
"and the perfect shall inherit good" (Proverbs 28:10).	וּתְמִימִים יִנְחֲלוּ טוֹב (שם כח, י).
And there is no good except with the Torah.	וְאֵין טוֹב אֶלָּא תוֹרָה.
As it is said,	שֶׁנֶּאֱמַר,
"For I have given you a good doctrine,	כִּי לֶקַח טוֹב נָתַתִּי לָכֶם,
My Torah do not forsake" (Proverbs 4:2).	תּוֹרָתִי אַל־תַּעֲזֹבוּ (שם ד, ב).
4: This is the path of the Torah:	4. כָּךְ הִיא דַּרְכָּהּ שֶׁל תּוֹרָה:
(a morsel of) bread with salt you shall eat,	פַּת בְּמֶלַח תֹּאכֵל,
and water by measure you should drink,	וּמַיִם בִּמְשׂוּרָה תִּשְׁתֶּה,
you should sleep on the ground,	וְעַל הָאָרֶץ תִּישָׁן,
a life of hardship you should live,	וְחַיֵּי צַעַר תִּחְיֶה,
and in the Torah you should toil;	וּבַתּוֹרָה אַתָּה עָמֵל;
if you do this	אִם אַתָּה עֹשֶׂה כֵּן

you will be happy and it will be well with you.	אַשְׁרֶיךָ וְטוֹב לָךְ.
You will be happy in this world,	אַשְׁרֶיךָ בָּעוֹלָם הַזֶּה,
and it will be well with you in the world to come.	וְטוֹב לָךְ לָעוֹלָם הַבָּא.
5: Do not seek greatness for yourself	5. אַל תְּבַקֵּשׁ גְּדֻלָּה לְעַצְמְךָ
and do not covet honor;	וְאַל תַּחְמֹד כָּבוֹד;
let your actions surpass your learning	יוֹתֵר מִלִּמּוּדְךָ עֲשֵׂה
and do not crave for the tables of kings;	וְאַל תִּתְאַוֶּה לְשֻׁלְחָנָם שֶׁל מְלָכִים;
because your own table is greater that theirs	שֶׁשֻּׁלְחָנְךָ גָּדוֹל מִשֻּׁלְחָנָם
and your crown is bigger than their crown;	וְכִתְרְךָ גָּדוֹל מִכִּתְרָם;
and faithful is the Master of your work	וְנֶאֱמָן הוּא בַּעַל מְלַאכְתְּךָ
for He pays you the reward of your actions.	שֶׁיְּשַׁלֶּם לְךָ שְׂכַר פְּעֻלָּתֶךָ.
6: The Torah is greater than	6. גְּדוֹלָה תּוֹרָה יוֹתֵר מִן
the priesthood and royalty.	הַכְּהֻנָּה וּמִן הַמַּלְכוּת.
Royalty is acquired by thirty qualifications,	שֶׁהַמַּלְכוּת נִקְנֵית בִּשְׁלֹשִׁים מַעֲלוֹת,
and priesthood by twenty-four	וְהַכְּהֻנָּה בְּעֶשְׂרִים וְאַרְבַּע
and the Torah is acquired by forty-eight qualifications,	וְהַתּוֹרָה נִקְנֵית בְּאַרְבָּעִים וּשְׁמוֹנָה דְּבָרִים,
and these are them:	וְאֵלּוּ הֵן:
Study, a listening ear,	בְּתַלְמוּד, בִּשְׁמִיעַת הָאֹזֶן,
orderly speech, understanding and intuitive insight,	בַּעֲרִיכַת שְׂפָתַיִם, בְּבִינַת הַלֵּב, בְּשִׂכְלוּת הַלֵּב,
awe, reverence, humility, joy,	בְּאֵימָה, בְּיִרְאָה, בַּעֲנָוָה, בְּשִׂמְחָה,
attendance to sages, attaching oneself to friends,	בְּשִׁמּוּשׁ חֲכָמִים, בְּדִבּוּק חֲבֵרִים,
discussion with students, deliberation,	בְּפִלְפּוּל הַתַּלְמִידִים, בְּיִשּׁוּב,
knowledge of the Scriptures and the Mishnah,	בְּמִקְרָא וּבְמִשְׁנָה,
moderation in business matters,	בְּמִעוּט סְחוֹרָה,
moderation in worldly ways,	בְּמִעוּט דֶּרֶךְ אֶרֶץ,
moderation in pleasure,	בְּמִעוּט תַּעֲנוּג,
moderation in sleep,	בְּמִעוּט שֵׁנָה,
moderation in conversation,	בְּמִעוּט שִׂיחָה,
moderation in laughter,	בְּמִעוּט שְׂחוֹק,
patience,	בְּאֹרֶךְ אַפַּיִם,
good naturedness, trust in the sages,	בְּלֵב טוֹב, בֶּאֱמוּנַת חֲכָמִים,
acceptance of suffering,	בְּקַבָּלַת הַיִּסּוּרִים,
knowing one's place,	הַמַּכִּיר אֶת־מְקוֹמוֹ,
rejoicing in one's portion,	וְהַשָּׂמֵחַ בְּחֶלְקוֹ,
and making a fence to one's words,	וְהָעוֹשֶׂה סְיָג לִדְבָרָיו,
claiming no merit for one's self,	וְאֵינוֹ מַחֲזִיק טוֹבָה לְעַצְמוֹ,
by being beloved, loving G-d,	אָהוּב, אוֹהֵב אֶת־הַמָּקוֹם,
loving mankind,	אוֹהֵב אֶת־הַבְּרִיּוֹת,
loving righteousness,	אוֹהֵב אֶת־הַצְּדָקוֹת,
loving straightforwardness,	אוֹהֵב אֶת־הַמֵּישָׁרִים,
loving rebuke and distancing oneself from honor,	אוֹהֵב אֶת־הַתּוֹכָחוֹת, וּמִתְרַחֵק מִן הַכָּבוֹד,

by not being arrogant with one's learning,	וְלֹא מֵגִיס לִבּוֹ בְּתַלְמוּדוֹ,
not delighting in giving decision,	וְאֵינוֹ שָׂמֵחַ בְּהוֹרָאָה,
sharing the burden of one's friend,	נוֹשֵׂא בְעֹל עִם חֲבֵרוֹ,
and judging him according to his merit,	וּמַכְרִיעוֹ לְכַף זְכוּת,
and establishing him to the truth,	וּמַעֲמִידוֹ עַל הָאֱמֶת,
and establishing him to peace,	וּמַעֲמִידוֹ עַל הַשָּׁלוֹם,
by being organized in one's learning,	וּמִתְיַשֵּׁב בְּתַלְמוּדוֹ,
by asking and answering,	שׁוֹאֵל וּמֵשִׁיב,
listening and adding thereto,	שׁוֹמֵעַ וּמוֹסִיף,
studying in order to teach,	הַלּוֹמֵד עַל מְנָת לְלַמֵּד,
and studying in order to practice,	וְהַלּוֹמֵד עַל מְנָת לַעֲשׂוֹת,
adding to one's teacher's wisdom,	הַמַּחְכִּים אֶת־רַבּוֹ,
paying deliberate consideration to what one has learned,	וְהַמְכַוֵּן אֶת־שְׁמוּעָתוֹ,
attributing something to the name of the one who said it (originally).	וְהָאוֹמֵר דָּבָר בְּשֵׁם אוֹמְרוֹ.
So you learned that anyone who attributes a thing to the name of the person who said it (originally)	הָא לָמַדְתָּ כָּל־הָאוֹמֵר דָּבָר בְּשֵׁם אוֹמְרוֹ
brings deliverance to the world.	מֵבִיא גְאֻלָּה לָעוֹלָם.
As it is said,	שֶׁנֶּאֱמַר,
"And Esther said to the king in the name of Mordechai" (Esther 2:22).	וַתֹּאמֶר אֶסְתֵּר לַמֶּלֶךְ בְּשֵׁם מָרְדֳּכָי (אסתר ב, כב).
7: Great is the Torah	7. גְּדוֹלָה תוֹרָה
for it is life-giving to those who fulfill it	שֶׁהִיא נוֹתֶנֶת חַיִּים לְעוֹשֶׂיהָ
in this world and in the world to come.	בָּעוֹלָם הַזֶּה וּבָעוֹלָם הַבָּא.
As it is said,	שֶׁנֶּאֱמַר,
"For they are life to those who find them	כִּי חַיִּים הֵם לְמֹצְאֵיהֶם
and health to all their flesh" (Proverbs 4:22).	וּלְכָל־בְּשָׂרוֹ מַרְפֵּא (משלי ד, כב).
And it says, "It will be health to your navel	וְאוֹמֵר, רִפְאוּת תְּהִי לְשָׁרֶּךָ
and marrow to your bones" (Proverbs 3:8).	וְשִׁקּוּי לְעַצְמוֹתֶיךָ (שם ג, ח).
And it says, "It is a tree of life to those who lay hold on it.	וְאוֹמֵר, עֵץ חַיִּים הִיא לַמַּחֲזִיקִים בָּהּ
And happy are those that hold her fast" (Proverbs 3:18).	וְתֹמְכֶיהָ מְאֻשָּׁר (שם ג, יח).
And it says, "They shall be a graceful garland for your head	וְאוֹמֵר, כִּי לִוְיַת חֵן הֵם לְרֹאשֶׁךָ
and necklaces about your neck" (Proverbs 1:9).	וַעֲנָקִים לְגַרְגְּרֹתֶיךָ (שם א, ט).
And it says, "It gives to your head an ornament of grace,	וְאוֹמֵר, תִּתֵּן לְרֹאשְׁךָ לִוְיַת־חֵן
a crown of glory it will bestow on you" (Proverbs 4:9).	עֲטֶרֶת תִּפְאֶרֶת תְּמַגְּנֶךָּ (שם ד, ט).
And it says, "Through Me your days will be multiplied,	וְאוֹמֵר, כִּי־בִי יִרְבּוּ יָמֶיךָ
and the years of your life will be increased" (Proverbs 9:11).	וְיוֹסִיפוּ לְךָ שְׁנוֹת חַיִּים (שם ט, יא).
And it says, "Length of days are in its right hand,	וְאוֹמֵר, אֹרֶךְ יָמִים בִּימִינָהּ
wealth and honor are in its left hand" (Proverbs 3:16).	בִּשְׂמֹאולָהּ עֹשֶׁר וְכָבוֹד (שם ג, טז).
And it says, "Length of days	וְאוֹמֵר, כִּי אֹרֶךְ יָמִים
and years of life and peace will be added to you" (Proverbs 3:12).	וּשְׁנוֹת חַיִּים וְשָׁלוֹם יוֹסִיפוּ לָךְ (שם ג, ב).

8: Rabbi Simon, the son of Judah, in the name of Rabbi Simon, the son of Yochai, says:	8. רַבִּי שִׁמְעוֹן בֶּן־יְהוּדָה מִשּׁוּם רַבִּי שִׁמְעוֹן בֶּן־יוֹחַי אוֹמֵר:
Beauty and strength and riches and honor,	הַנּוֹי וְהַכֹּחַ וְהָעֹשֶׁר וְהַכָּבוֹד,
and wisdom, old age and a gray head,	וְהַחָכְמָה הַזִּקְנָה וְהַשֵּׂיבָה,
and children are pleasant to the righteous	וְהַבָּנִים נָאֶה לַצַּדִּיקִים,
and pleasant to the world.	וְנָאֶה לָעוֹלָם.
As it is said,	שֶׁנֶּאֱמַר,
"A gray head is a crown of glory	עֲטֶרֶת תִּפְאֶרֶת שֵׂיבָה
it is found in the way of righteousness" (Proverbs 16:31).	בְּדֶרֶךְ צְדָקָה תִּמָּצֵא (שם טז, לא).
And it says, "The glory of young men is their strength,	וְאוֹמֵר, תִּפְאֶרֶת בַּחוּרִים כֹּחָם,
and the beauty of old men is the gray head.	וַהֲדַר זְקֵנִים שֵׂיבָה (שם כ, כט).
And it says, "The crown of the wise are their riches" (Proverbs 14:24).	וְאוֹמֵר, עֲטֶרֶת חֲכָמִים עָשְׁרָם (שם יד, כד).
And it says, "Grandchildren are the crown of the old,	וְאוֹמֵר, עֲטֶרֶת זְקֵנִים בְּנֵי בָנִים,
and the glory of children are their fathers" (Proverbs 17:6).	וְתִפְאֶרֶת בָּנִים אֲבוֹתָם (שם יז, ו).
And it says, "The moon will be confounded	וְאוֹמֵר, וְחָפְרָה הַלְּבָנָה
and the sun ashamed	וּבוֹשָׁה הַחַמָּה
for the Lord of hosts will reign in Mount Zion and in Jerusalem	כִּי־מָלַךְ ה׳ צְבָאוֹת בְּהַר צִיּוֹן וּבִירוּשָׁלַיִם
and before His elders will be His glory" (Isaiah 24:23).	וְנֶגֶד זְקֵנָיו כָּבוֹד (ישעיה כד, כג).
Rabbi Simon, the son of Menasya, says:	רַבִּי שִׁמְעוֹן בֶּן־מְנַסְיָא אוֹמֵר:
These seven characteristics	אֵלּוּ שֶׁבַע מִדּוֹת
which the Sages enumerated for the righteous	שֶׁמָּנוּ חֲכָמִים לַצַּדִּיקִים
were all realized in Rabbi (Judah Ha-Nasi) and his sons.	כֻּלָּם נִתְקַיְּמוּ בְּרַבִּי וּבְבָנָיו.
9: Said Rabbi Yose, the son of Kisma:	9. אָמַר רַבִּי יוֹסֵי בֶּן־קִסְמָא:
I was once walking by the way	פַּעַם אַחַת הָיִיתִי מְהַלֵּךְ בַּדֶּרֶךְ
when a man met me	וּפָגַע בִּי אָדָם אֶחָד
and he greeted me	וְנָתַן לִי שָׁלוֹם
and I greeted him in return.	וְהֶחֱזַרְתִּי לוֹ שָׁלוֹם.
He said to me,	אָמַר לִי,
"Rabbi, from which place are you?"	רַבִּי מֵאֵיזֶה מָקוֹם אָתָּה?
I said to him,	אָמַרְתִּי לוֹ,
"From a great city of sages and scribes I come."	מֵעִיר גְּדוֹלָה שֶׁל חֲכָמִים וְשֶׁל סוֹפְרִים אָנִי.
He said to me,	אָמַר לִי,
"Rabbi if you would be willing to live with us in our place	רַבִּי, רְצוֹנְךְ שֶׁתָּדוּר עִמָּנוּ בִּמְקוֹמֵנוּ
I would give you a thousand thousand golden dinars,	וַאֲנִי אֶתֵּן לְךָ אֶלֶף אֲלָפִים דִּינְרֵי זָהָב,
precious stones and pearls."	וַאֲבָנִים טוֹבוֹת וּמַרְגָּלִיּוֹת.
I said to him, "My son,	אָמַרְתִּי לוֹ, בְּנִי,
If you were to give to me all the silver and gold	אִם אַתָּה נוֹתֵן לִי כָּל כֶּסֶף וְזָהָב
and precious stones and pearls in the world	וַאֲבָנִים טוֹבוֹת וּמַרְגָּלִיּוֹת שֶׁבָּעוֹלָם
I would not live (anywhere) other than a place of Torah."	אֵינִי דָר אֶלָּא בִּמְקוֹם תּוֹרָה.
And it is also written in the book of Psalms,	וְכֵן כָּתוּב בְּסֵפֶר תְּהִלִּים,

by David, king of Israel —	עַל יְדֵי דָוִד מֶלֶךְ יִשְׂרָאֵל —
"Preferred by me is the law of your mouth	טוֹב־לִי תוֹרַת־פִּיךָ
than thousands of gold and silver" (Psalms 119:72).	מֵאַלְפֵי זָהָב וָכָסֶף (תהלים קיט, עב).
Moreover, in the time of a man's death,	וְלֹא עוֹד אֶלָּא שֶׁבִּשְׁעַת פְּטִירָתוֹ שֶׁל אָדָם,
nothing follows him;	אֵין מְלַוִּים לוֹ לְאָדָם;
not silver, nor gold,	לֹא כֶסֶף וְלֹא זָהָב,
nor precious stones nor pearls;	וְלֹא אֲבָנִים טוֹבוֹת וּמַרְגָּלִיּוֹת;
rather Torah and good deeds alone.	אֶלָּא תּוֹרָה וּמַעֲשִׂים טוֹבִים בִּלְבָד.
As it is said,	שֶׁנֶּאֱמַר,
"When you walk, it shall lead you;	בְּהִתְהַלֶּכְךָ תַּנְחֶה אֹתָךְ;
when you lie down, it shall watch over you;	בְּשָׁכְבְּךָ תִּשְׁמֹר עָלֶיךָ;
when you awaken, it shall talk to you" (Proverbs 6:22).	וַהֲקִיצוֹתָ הִיא תְשִׂיחֶךָ (משלי ו, כב).
When you walk — it shall lead in this world;	בְּהִתְהַלֶּכְךָ תַּנְחֶה אֹתָךְ בָּעוֹלָם הַזֶּה;
when you lie down — it shall watch over you in the grave;	בְּשָׁכְבְּךָ תִּשְׁמֹר עָלֶיךָ בַּקֶּבֶר;
when you awaken — it shall talk to you in the world to come.	וַהֲקִיצוֹתָ הִיא תְשִׂיחֶךָ לָעוֹלָם הַבָּא.
And it says, "The silver is Mine and the gold is Mine, says the Lord of hosts" (Haggai 2:8).	וְאוֹמֵר, לִי הַכֶּסֶף וְלִי הַזָּהָב נְאֻם ה׳ צְבָאוֹת (חגי ב, ח).
10: Five possessions	10. חֲמִשָּׁה קִנְיָנִים
has the Holy One, blessed be He commanded as His own in His world,	קָנָה לוֹ הַקָּדוֹשׁ בָּרוּךְ הוּא בְּעוֹלָמוֹ,
and these are them:	וְאֵלּוּ הֵן:
Torah is one possession,	תּוֹרָה קִנְיָן אֶחָד,
Heaven and Earth is one possession,	שָׁמַיִם וָאָרֶץ קִנְיָן אֶחָד,
Abraham is one possession,	אַבְרָהָם קִנְיָן אֶחָד,
Israel is one possession,	יִשְׂרָאֵל קִנְיָן אֶחָד,
and the Temple is one possession.	בֵּית הַמִּקְדָּשׁ קִנְיָן אֶחָד.
From where (do we learn this of) the Torah?	תּוֹרָה מִנַּיִן?
Because it is written, "The Lord possessed me as the beginning of His way	דִּכְתִיב, ה׳ קָנָנִי רֵאשִׁית דַּרְכּוֹ
before His works of old" (Proverbs 8:22).	קֶדֶם מִפְעָלָיו מֵאָז (משלי ח, כב).
From where (do we learn this of) Heaven and Earth?	שָׁמַיִם וָאָרֶץ מִנַּיִן?
Because it is written, "Thus said the Lord —	דִּכְתִיב, כֹּה אָמַר ה׳ —
'The heaven is My throne,	הַשָּׁמַיִם כִּסְאִי,
the earth is my footstool.	וְהָאָרֶץ הֲדֹם רַגְלָי.
Where is the house that you would build for me?	אֵי־זֶה בַיִת אֲשֶׁר תִּבְנוּ־לִי?
and where is the place of my rest?' " (Isaiah 66:1)	וְאֵי־זֶה מָקוֹם מְנוּחָתִי (ישעיה סו, א).
And it says, "How numerous are Your works, O G-d,	וְאוֹמֵר, מָה־רַבּוּ מַעֲשֶׂיךָ ה׳,
You have made them all with wisdom;	כֻּלָּם בְּחָכְמָה עָשִׂיתָ;
the earth is filled with Your possession" (Psalms 104:24).	מָלְאָה הָאָרֶץ קִנְיָנֶךָ (תהלים קד, כד).
From where (do we learn this of) Abraham?	אַבְרָהָם מִנַּיִן?
Because it is written, "He blessed him and said	דִּכְתִיב, וַיְבָרְכֵהוּ וַיֹּאמַר
'Blessed is Abram of the most High G-d,	בָּרוּךְ אַבְרָם לְאֵ־ל עֶלְיוֹן,

the Possessor of heaven and earth' " (Genesis 14:19).	קֹנֵה שָׁמַיִם וָאָרֶץ (בראשית יד, יט).
From where (do we learn this of) Israel?	יִשְׂרָאֵל מִנַּיִן?
Because it is written, "Until Your nation passes over, O Lord,	דִּכְתִיב, עַד־יַעֲבֹר עַמְּךָ ה׳,
until the nation you have acquired pass over" (Exodus 15:16).	עַד־יַעֲבֹר עַם־זוּ קָנִיתָ (שמות טו, טז).
And it says, "The holy ones that are in this land —	וְאוֹמֵר, לִקְדוֹשִׁים אֲשֶׁר־בָּאָרֶץ —
they are excellent, all of My desires in them" (Psalms 16:3).	הֵמָּה וְאַדִּירֵי כָּל־חֶפְצִי־בָם (תהלים טז, ג).
From where (do we learn this of) the Temple?	בֵּית הַמִּקְדָּשׁ מִנַּיִן?
Because it is written, "The dwelling place that You, O Lord, made,	דִּכְתִיב, מָכוֹן לְשִׁבְתְּךָ פָּעַלְתָּ ה׳,
the holy place of the Lord,	מִקְּדָשׁ ה׳,
which Your hands established" (Exodus 15:17).	כּוֹנְנוּ יָדֶיךָ (שמות טו, יז).
And it says, "He brought them to the border of His holy place,	וְאוֹמֵר, וַיְבִיאֵם אֶל־גְּבוּל קָדְשׁוֹ,
this mountain which His right hand possessed" (Psalms 78:54).	הַר־זֶה קָנְתָה יְמִינוֹ (תהלים עח, נד).
11: All that the Holy One, blessed be He, created in His world	11. כֹּל מַה־שֶּׁבָּרָא הַקָּדוֹשׁ בָּרוּךְ הוּא בְּעוֹלָמוֹ
He did not create except for His honor.	לֹא בְרָאוֹ אֶלָּא לִכְבוֹדוֹ.
As it is said,	שֶׁנֶּאֱמַר,
"Everything that is called by My name	כֹּל הַנִּקְרָא בִשְׁמִי
for My honor it was created;	וְלִכְבוֹדִי בְּרָאתִיו;
I have formed it and even made it" (Isaiah 43:7).	יְצַרְתִּיו אַף־עֲשִׂיתִיו (ישעיה מג, ז).
And it says, "The Lord will reign	וְאוֹמֵר. ה׳ יִמְלֹךְ
for ever and ever" (Exodus 15:18).	לְעוֹלָם וָעֶד (שמות טו, יח).
Rabbi Chananya, the son of Akashya, says:	רַבִּי חֲנַנְיָא בֶּן עֲקַשְׁיָא אוֹמֵר:
The Holy One, blessed be He wanted	רָצָה הַקָּדוֹשׁ בָּרוּךְ הוּא
to (give) merit to Israel	לְזַכּוֹת אֶת־יִשְׂרָאֵל
therefore multiplied for them the Torah and commandments,	לְפִיכָךְ הִרְבָּה לָהֶם תּוֹרָה וּמִצְווֹת,
as it is said,	שֶׁנֶּאֱמַר,
"The Lord was pleased for His righteousness' sake,	ה׳ חָפֵץ לְמַעַן צִדְקוֹ
to magnify Torah and elevate it" (Isaiah 42:21).	יַגְדִּיל תּוֹרָה וְיַאְדִּיר (ישעיה מב, כא).

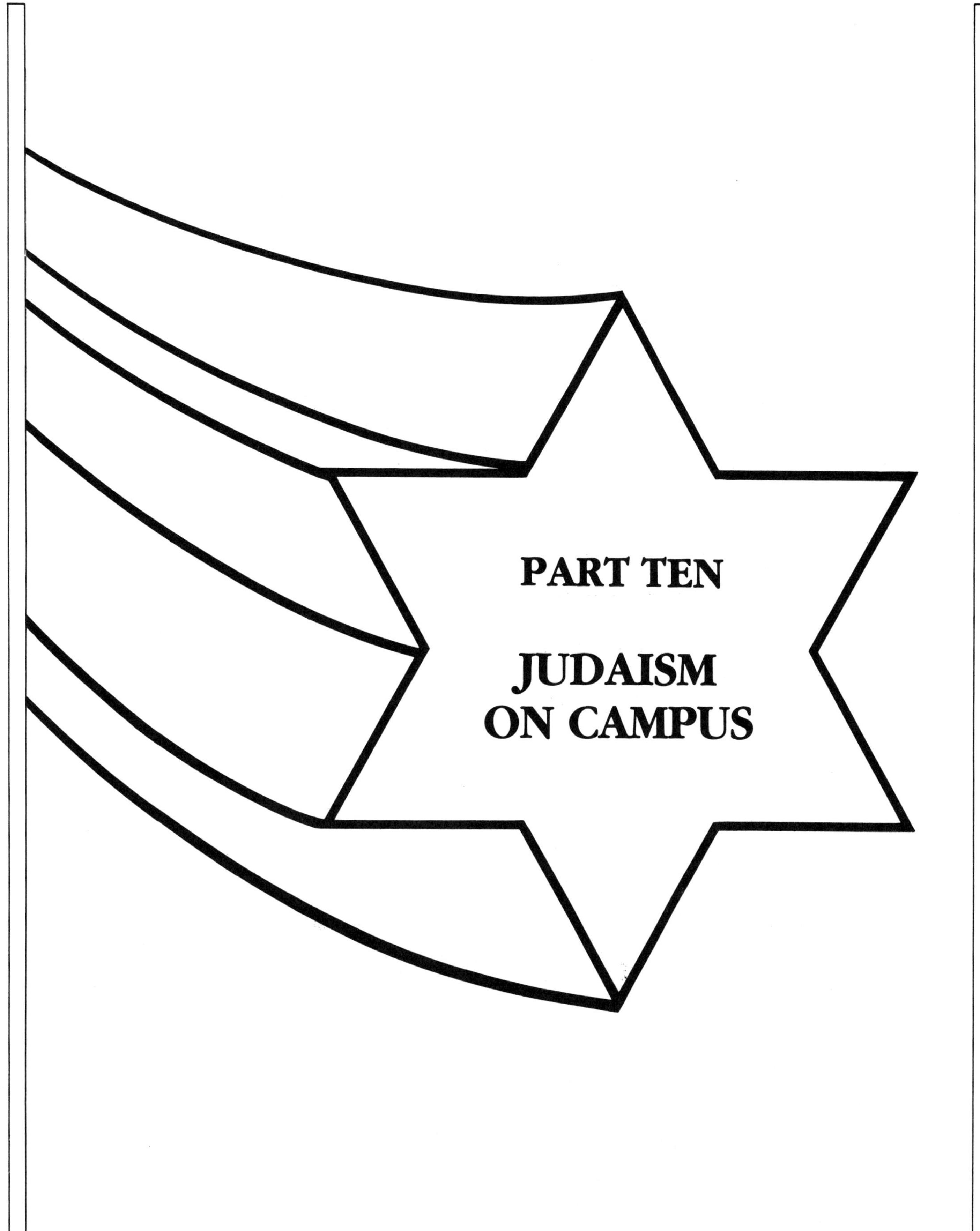

PART TEN

JUDAISM ON CAMPUS

Judaism on Campus

	Enrollment (1987)	Estimated Jewish Enrollment	Judaica Courses; Major	Kosher Food
ALABAMA				
Auburn University Auburn, Alabama	18,000	70	—	—
University of Alabama Tuscaloosa, Alabama	17,000	400	5	Vegetarian Dining
University of Alabama in Birmingham Birmingham, Alabama	12,000	125	—	Dormitory Cooking
ARIZONA				
Arizona State University Tempe, Arizona	38,000	2,200	15; BA	Vegetarian Dining
Northern Arizona University Flagstaff, Arizona	13,000	150	1	Dormitory Cooking
Phoenix College Tempe, Arizona	7,700	100	1; BA	Kosher Meals by: ASU Hillel
University of Arizona Tucson, Arizona	30,000	2,500	13; BA, MA	Kosher Meals—Hillel Vegetarian Dining Dormitory Cooking
ARKANSAS				
University of Arkansas Fayetteville, Arkansas	16,000	60	—	Vegetarian Dining
CALIFORNIA				
California Institute of Technology Pasadena, California	1,500	250	—	Dormitory Cooking
California State University—Chico Chico, California	14,000	250	4	Dormitory Cooking Vegetarian Dining
California State Univ.—Dominguez Hills Los Angeles, California	8,700	150	—	—
California State Univ.—Fresno Fresno, California	15,000	70	2	—
California State Univ.—Fullerton Fullerton, California	25,000	1,250	5	Locally available
California State Univ.—Hayward Hayward, California	11,000	250	—	—
California State Univ.—Long Beach Long Beach, California	33,000	3,000	9; BA	Local; Chabad; Vegetarian Dining
California State Univ.—Los Angeles Los Angeles, California	25,000	500	1	—
California State Univ.—Northridge Northridge, California	28,000	8,000	10	—
California State Univ.—San Bernardino San Bernardino, California	—	—	—	—
Cerritos Community College Long Beach, California	20,000	100	—	—
Chapman College Orange, California	1,200	100	—	—
Claremont Colleges Claremont, California	5,500	800	12, BA, MA	Kosher Meals by Bayit Project Vegetarian Dining Dormitory Cooking

	Enrollment (1987)	Estimated Jewish Enrollment	Judaica Courses; Major	Kosher Food
El Camino College Los Angeles, California	28,000	1,000	—	—
Hastings College of Law San Francisco, California	—	400	—	—
Long Beach City College Long Beach, California	26,000	750	—	—
Los Angeles Harbor College Los Angeles, California	11,000	450	—	—
Los Angeles Pierce College Los Angeles, California	18,000	2,000	1	—
Los Angeles Valley College Van Nuys, California	17,000	3,000	5	—
Loyola Marymount University Los Angeles, California	5,500	100	5	—
Loyola University Law School Los Angeles, California	1,400	600	1	—
Mills College Oakland, California	930	50	—	—
Occidental College Los Angeles, California	1,500	120	2	Vegetarian Dining Dormitory Cooking
Pasadena City College Pasadena, California	—	—	—	—
San Diego State University San Diego, California	30,000	4,500	15; BA	Vegetarian Dining
San Francisco State University San Francisco, California	28,000	3,000	2	—
San Jose State University San Jose, California	29,000	1,000	5	Hillel; Vegetarian Dining Dormitory Cooking
Santa Monica College Los Angeles, California	25,000	1,500	1	—
Southwestern Law School Los Angeles, California	1,700	—	—	—
Stanford University Stanford, California	12,000	1,500	4; BA	Hillel (occasional) Vegetarian Dining; Local
University of California Medical School San Francisco, California	—	500	—	—
University of California—Berkeley Berkeley, California	30,000	5,500	25; BA, MA, PhD	Kosher Meals by Hillel Vegetarian Dining Dormitory Cooking
University of California—Davis Davis, California	19,000	2,200	8; BA	Hillel
University of California—Irvine Tustin, California	13,000	1,000	—	Locally available
University of California—Los Angeles Los Angeles, California	32,000	6,500	18; BA, MA, PhD	Vegetarian Dining Kosher Meals-Hillel Dormitory Cooking
University of California—Riverside Riverside, California	3,500	300	1	—
University of California—San Diego San Diego, California	10,000	2,000	15; BA	Vegetarian Dining Dormitory Cooking
University of California—Santa Barbara Goleta, California	16,000	1,600	3; BA	—
University of California—Santa Cruz Santa Cruz, California	7,000	1,500	6	Vegetarian Dining Hillel (occasional)
University of Judaism Los Angeles, California	160	160	35; BA, MA	Kosher Dining
University of Redlands Redlands, California	1,150	25	2	Vegetarian Dining
University of San Francisco San Francisco, California	—	300	—	—
University of Santa Clara San Jose, California	3,300	—	2	—
University of Southern California Los Angeles, California	25,000	2,000	25; BA, MA, PhD	Hillel (Friday eves) Dormitory Cooking

	Enrollment (1987)	Estimated Jewish Enrollment	Judaica Courses; Major	Kosher Food
Whittier College Whittier, California	1,500	50	—	Dormitory Cooking
COLORADO				
Colorado State University Ft. Collins, Colorado	16,000	275	—	Hillel
United States Air Force Academy Colorado Springs, Colorado	4,500	38	—	Holidays; occasional
University of Colorado Boulder, Colorado	22,500	1,500	6	Vegetarian Dining Kosher Gourmet Club
University of Denver Denver, Colorado	9,000	3,300	16; BA	Hillel Co-op
University of Northern Colorado Greeley, Colorado	10,500	150	—	Vegetarian Dining
CONNECTICUT				
Central Connecticut State College New Britain, Connecticut	3,000	200	4	Frozen, on request
Connecticut College New London, Connecticut	2,000	500	3	Vegetarian Dining
Quinnipiac College New Haven, Connecticut	2,000	100	—	—
Trinity College Hartford, Connecticut	1,700	150	8; BA	Vegetarian Dining Dormitory Cooking
U.S. Coast Guard Academy New London, Connecticut	300	12	—	—
University of Bridgeport Bridgeport, Connecticut	6,500	1,000	4	Kosher Meals by: Dining Hall (Frozen) Dormitory Cooking
University of Connecticut Storrs, Connecticut	15,750	2,000	8; BA	Kosher Meals by: Hillel Kosher Co-Op Vegetarian Dining
University of Hartford West Hartford, Connecticut	10,000	1,500	6	Vegetarian Dining
Wesleyan University Middletown, Connecticut	2,600	900	11; BA	Kosher Meals by: Co-Op at Bayit Vegetarian Dining
Yale University New Haven, Connecticut	10,000	3,000	20; BA, MA, PhD	Kosher Meals by Young Israel Vegetarian Dining
DELAWARE				
University of Delaware Newark, Delaware	12,000	1,200	1	Hillel (dinner) Vegetarian Dining
DISTRICT OF COLUMBIA				
American University Washington, D.C.	9,100	2,700	24; BA; MA	Hillel; Vegetarian Dining Dormitory Cooking
Antioch Law School Washington, D.C.	400	100	—	—
Catholic University Washington, D.C.	7,000	300	8; MA, PhD	—
Gallaudet College Washington, D.C.	1,400	100	1	Frozen, on request
George Washington Univ. Washington, D.C.	18,000	5,000	15; BA, MA	Kosher Meals by: Hillel Vegetarian Dining
Georgetown University Washington, D.C.	10,500	1,500	12; BA	Kosher Meals by: Jewish Student House Vegetarian Dining Dormitory Cooking
Howard University Washington, D.C.	13,000	150	—	—
Mt. Vernon College Washington, D.C.	460	30	—	—

	Enrollment (1987)	Estimated Jewish Enrollment	Judaica Courses; Major	Kosher Food
FLORIDA				
Barry University Miami Shores, Florida	2,150	150	BA, MA	Vegetarian Dining
Broward Community College (3 campuses) Fort Lauderdale, Florida	22,000	4,000	1	—
College of Boca Raton Pembroke Pines, Florida	450	56	—	—
Eckerd College St. Petersburg, Florida	1,300	65	—	Vegetarian Dining Dormitory Cooking
Florida Atlantic Univ. Boca Raton, Florida	6,000	600	1	—
Florida International Univ. Miami, Florida	12,300	1,000	2	Hillel; Vegetarian Dining
Florida International Univ. North Pembroke Pines, Florida	3,300	280	1	Vegetarian Dining
Florida Southern College Lakeland, Florida	2,000	15	—	—
Florida State University Tallahassee, Florida	22,000	2,000	4	Kosher Meals by: Hillel & FSU Vegetarian Dining
Jacksonville University Jacksonville, Florida	2,600	120	—	Vegetarian Dining Dormitory Cooking
Miami-Dade Community College, North Miami, Florida	24,000	1,000	1	—
Miami-Dade Community College, South Miami, Florida	12,000	1,000	2, BA	Vegetarian Dining
Palm Beach Junior College Pembroke Pines, Florida	2,000	300	1	—
Rollins College Winter Park, Florida	1,400	100	6	Vegetarian Dining
Southeastern College of Osteopathic Medicine North Miami Beach, Florida	180	100		
University of Central Florida Orlando, Florida	15,000	400	9	—
University of Florida Gainesville, Florida	35,000	3,800	12; BA	Kosher Meals by: Hillel
University of Miami Coral Gables, Florida	14,000	2,300	12; BA	Kosher Meals by: Hillel Vegetarian Dining Dormitory Cooking
University of North Florida Jacksonville, Florida	4,500	150	1	—
University of South Florida Tampa, Florida	30,000	3,000	7; BA; MA; PhD	Kosher Meals by : Hillel Vegetarian Dining
University of South Florida—New College Sarasota, Florida	500	50	—	Vegetarian Dining
University of Tampa Tampa, Florida	2,000	225	2	Vegetarian Dining Dormitory Cooking
GEORGIA				
Emory University Atlanta, Georgia	7,500	3,000	8; BA, MA	Dormitory Cooking
Georgia State University Atlanta, Georgia	23,000	1,000	1	—
Georgia Institute of Technology Atlanta, Georgia	11,000	700	—	Dormitory Cooking
Oglethorpe University Atlanta, Georgia	700	125	—	—
University of Georgia Athens, Georgia	25,000	1,200	2	Kosher Meals by: Hillel
ILLINOIS				
Bradley University Peoria, Illinois	5,100	400	1	—
Chicago Kent School of Law Chicago, Illinois	1,200	900	—	—

	Enrollment (1987)	Estimated Jewish Enrollment	Judaica Courses; Major	Kosher Food
De Paul University Chicago, Illinois	1,000	100	BA (Spertus)	—
De Paul University School of Law Chicago, Illinois	800	100	—	—
Illinois State University Normal, Illinois	20,000	400	—	Dormitory Cooking
John Marshall Law School Chicago, Illinois	1,000	800	—	—
Loyola University Chicago, Illinois	11,750	600	BA, MA (Spertus)	Kosher Meals by: Food Service (frozen) Vegetarian Dining
Loyola University Law School Chicago, Illinois	600	60	—	—
Northeastern Illinois Univ. Evanston, Illinois	10,000	500	BA (Spertus)	—
Northern Illinois University DeKalb, Illinois	25,000	700	2 (Spertus)	Kosher Meals by: Hillel
Northwestern University Evanston, Illinois	10,000	2,000	15; BA, MA, PhD	Kosher Meals by: Hillel Vegetarian Dining Dormitory Cooking
Northwestern Univ. Dental School Chicago, Illinois	600	300	—	—
Nortwestern Univ. Medical School Chicago, Illinois	600	300	—	—
Oakton Community College Des Plaines, Illinois	8,600	2,000	1	—
Southern Illinois Univ. Carbondale, Illinois	23,000	750	2	—
University of Chicago Chicago, Illinois	8,000	1,500	8; BA, MA, PhD	Hillel; Vegetarian Dining Dormitory Cooking
University of Illinois at Champaign Champaign, Illinois	35,000	4,000	10; BA	Kosher Meals by: Hillel
Univ. of Illinois at Chicago Health Sciences Chicago, Illinois	4,700	400	—	—
University of Illinois at Chicago Chicago, Illinois	21,000	3,000	BA (Spertus)	—
Western Illinois University Macomb, Illinois	11,000	200	1	—
William S. Scholl School of Podiatry Chicago, Illinois	800	500	—	—
INDIANA				
Indiana University Bloomington, Indiana	32,000	1,800	30; BA, MA, PhD	Vegetarian Dining Dormitory Cooking
Purdue University West Lafayette, Indiana	31.500	600	15	Kosher Meals by: Hillel
IOWA				
Briar Cliff College Sioux City, Iowa	700	40	—	Vegetarian Dining
Drake University Des Moines, Iowa	4,500	400	3	Vegetarian Dining
Grinnell College Grinnell, Iowa	1,200	350	7; BA	Vegetarian Dining
Iowa State University Ames Iowa	26,000	75	—	Vegetarian Dining
Morningside College Sioux City, Iowa	2,000	60	2	—
University of Iowa Iowa City, Iowa	30,000	1,200	10	Hillel (occasional) Vegetarian Dining
KANSAS				
Kansas State Univ. Manhattan, Kansas	19.000	230	5	—
University of Kansas Lawrence, Kansas	22,000	1,200	5; BA	Hillel (occasional) Dormitory Cooking

	Enrollment (1987)	Estimated Jewish Enrollment	Judaica Courses; Major	Kosher Food
KENTUCKY				
University of Kentucky Lexington, Kentucky	22,000	200	3	Dormitory Cooking
University of Louisville Louisville, Kentucky	20,000	300	10; BA	Dormitory Cooking
LOUISIANA				
Louisiana State Univ. Baton Rouge, Louisiana	30,000	200	2	—
Louisiana Technical Univ. Ruston, Louisiana	10,000	12	—	Dormitory Cooking
Loyola University New Orleans, Louisiana	4,500	125	2	Kosher Meals by: Hillel at Tulane
Tulane Univ. & Newcomb College New Orleans, Louisiana	9,000	3,000	12; BA	Kosher Meals by: Hillel
University of New Orleans New Orleans, Louisiana	14,000	200	2	Kosher Meals by: Hillel at Tulane
MAINE				
Bates College Auburn, Maine	1,400	250	3	Vegetarian Dining Dormitory Cooking
Bowdoin College Brunswick, Maine	1,400	120	2	Vegetarian Dining Dormitory Cooking
Colby College Waterville, Maine	1,650	200	6	Vegetarian Dining
University of Maine Orono, Maine	10,000	200	1	Vegetarian Dining
MARYLAND				
Catonsville Community College Catonsville, Maryland	3,000	360	—	Vegetarian Dining
Goucher College Towson, Maryland	1,000	300	5	Young Israel
Hood College Frederick, Maryland	1,850	80	—	Vegetarian
Johns Hopkins University Baltimore, Maryland	3,000	600	15; BA, MA, PhD	Kosher Meals by Young Israel Dormitory Cooking
Loyola College Baltimore, Maryland	5,000	35	1	—
Montgomery College Rockville, Maryland	17,000	2,000	2	—
Towson State University Towson, Maryland	15,000	1,0000	3	Vegetarian Dining Dormitory Cooking
U.S. Naval Academy Annapolis, Maryland	4,200	40	—	Holidays; occasional
Univ. of Maryland—Baltimore County Baltimore, Maryland	6,000	1,500	1	Dormitory Cooking
University of Maryland at Baltimore Baltimore, Maryland	6,000	1,500	—	Vegetarian Dining Dormitory Cooking
University of Maryland—College Park College Park, Maryland	35,000	6,500	20; BA, MA	Kosher Meals by Hillel, Young Israel Vegetarian Dining
Western Maryland College Westminster, Maryland	1,800	50	—	Vegetarian Dining
MASSACHUSETTS				
Amherst College Amherst, Massachusetts	1,600	300	4; BA	Kosher Meals by: Food Services Vegetarian Dining
Babson College Wellesley, Massachusetts	2,950	800	—	—
Bentley College Waltham, Massachusetts	5,000	200	—	Kosher Meals by: Food Services Dormitory Cooking

	Enrollment (1987)	Estimated Jewish Enrollment	Judaica Courses; Major	Kosher Food
Berkeley College of Music Boston, Massachusetts	850	100	—	—
Boston College Newton, Massachusetts	12,000	500	8; BA	—
Boston University Boston, Massachusetts	25,000	6,000	25; BA, MA, PhD	Kosher Meals by: YBU and Hillel
Brandeis University Waltham, Massachusetts	3,350	2,150	60; BA, MA, PhD	Kosher Meals by: Univ. Food Services Vegetarian Dining Dormitory Cooking
Clark University Worcester, Massachusetts	2,000	1,000	20; BA	Kosher Meals by: Clark Vegetarian Dining Dormitory Cooking
Curry College Boston, Massachusetts	850	325	—	Holidays; occasional
Emerson College Boston, Massachusetts	1,600	500	—	Vegetarian Dining Dormitory Cooking
Harvard University and Radcliffe College Cambridge, Massachusetts	12,000	3,000	30; BA, MA, PhD	Kosher Meals by: Hillel Vegetarian Dining
Lesley College Cambridge, Massachusetts	1,640	300	1	Vegetarian Dining
Massachusetts Bay Community College Wellesley, Massachusetts	4,000	150	—	Dormitory Cooking
Massachusetts College of Art Boston, Massachusetts	1,200	200	—	—
Massachusetts College of Pharmacy Boston, Massachusetts	1,118	50	—	—
Massachusetts Institute of Technology Cambridge, Massachusetts	8,000	2,000	—	Kosher Meals by: MIT & Hillel Vegetarian Dining Dormitory Cooking
Mount Holyoke College South Hadley, Massachusetts	1,850	130	4	Vegetarian Dining Dormitory Cooking
New England Conservatory of Music Boston, Massachusetts	750	150	1	—
Northeastern University Boston, Massachusetts	28,000	3,000	4	Hillel; Vegetarian Dining Dormitory Cooking
Salem State College Salem, Massachusetts	5,800	150	—	—
Simmons College Boston, Massachusetts	2,800	1,000	—	Kosher Meals by: Coop Kitchen
Smith College Northampton, Massachusetts	2,500	250	5, BA	Kosher Meals by: Food Service Vegetarian Dining
Southeastern Massachusetts University New Bedford, Massachusetts	5,000	200	—	Vegetarian Dining
Suffolk University Boston, Massachusetts	4,600	250	—	—
Tufts University Medford, Massachusetts	6,000	2,100	10; BA	Kosher Meals by: Hillel Co-op Vegetarian Dining
University of Lowell Lowell, Massachusetts	8,800	350	1	—
University of Massachusetts Amherst, Massachusetts	24,000	3,700	16; BA	Kosher Meals by: Food Service Vegetarian Dining
University of Massachusetts—Boston Harbor Boston, Massachusetts	2,220	90	1	—
Wellesley College Wellesley, Massachusetts	2,500	250	4; BA	Kosher Meals by: College Vegetarian Dining
Western New England College Springfield, Massachusetts	5,140	—	4	University (frozen)
Westfield State College Westfield, Massachusetts	3,000	50	—	Kosher Meals by: Seiler Food Services Vegetarian Dining Dormitory Cooking

	Enrollment (1987)	Estimated Jewish Enrollment	Judaica Courses; Major	Kosher Food
Wheelock College Boston, Massachusetts	700	70	—	Kosher Meals by: Simmons College Vegetarian Dining Dormitory Cooking
Williams College Williamstown, Massachusetts	1,900	170	5; BA	Kosher Meals by: College Jewish Assn. Vegetarian Dining
MICHIGAN				
Central Michigan University Mt. Pleasant, Michigan	16,000	150	4	Vegetarian Dining
Michigan State Univ. E. Lansing, Michigan	39,000	2,500	4	Kosher Meals by: Hillel Co-op Vegetarian Dining Dormitory Cooking
Oakland University Rochester, Michigan	12,000	300	1	Vegetarian Dining
University of Michigan Ann Arbor, Michigan	32,700	6,000	15; BA, MA, PhD	Kosher Meals by: Hillel Vegetarian Dining Dormitory Cooking
Wayne State University Detroit, Michigan	30,000	1,500	3	Kosher Meals by: Public Restaurant
Western Michigan University Kalamazoo, Michigan	20,000	350	3	—
MINNESOTA				
Carleton College Northfield, Minnesota	1,500	125	5	Kosher Meals by: JSC
Macalester College St. Paul, Minnesota	1,500	150	3	Kosher Meals by: Hebrew House
University of Minnesota Minneapolis, Minnesota	47,000	2,000	12; BA	Kosher Meals by: Hillel Vegetarian Dining
MISSISSIPPI				
University of Mississippi University, Mississippi	9,000	45	—	—
MISSOURI				
St. Louis University St. Louis, Missouri	8,200	200	1	—
Stephens College Columbia, Missouri	990	100	1	Vegetarian Dining
University of Missouri—Columbia Columbia, Missouri	22,600	1,000	1	Kosher Meals by: Hillel
University of Missouri—St. Louis Clayton, Missouri	11,400	150	1	Vegetarian Dining
Washington University Clayton, Missouri	8,200	2,400	10; BA	Kosher Meals by: University Vegetarian Dining
Webster College St. Louis, Missouri	1,800	150	1	Dormitory Cooking
NEBRASKA				
Creighton University Omaha, Nebraska	4,100	150	2	Vegetarian Dining
University of Nebraska—Lincoln Lincoln, Nebraska	20,000	60	—	—
University of Nebraska—Omaha Omaha, Nebraska	15,500	150	5; BA	Vegetarian Dining
NEVADA				
University of Nevada—Las Vegas Las Vegas, Nevada	12,000	400	—	Hillel
University of Nevada—Reno Reno, Nevada	9,900	225	3	—

	Enrollment (1987)	Estimated Jewish Enrollment	Judaica Courses; Major	Kosher Food
NEW HAMPSHIRE				
Dartmouth College Hanover, New Hampshire	4,600	450	6; BA	Kosher Meals by: Hillel Vegetarian Dining
University of New Hampshire Durham, New Hampshire	10,000	400	—	Vegetarian Dining
NEW JERSEY				
Atlantic Community College Mays Landing, New Jersey	1,500	150	—	—
Drew University Madison, New Jersey	1,850	160	2	—
Fairleigh Dickinson University Newark, New Jersey	3,100	150	—	—
Fairleigh Dickinson University Teaneck, New Jersey	8,500	1,700	6	Kosher Meals by: University
Glassboro State College Glassboro, New Jersey	10,000	1,000	1	Frozen meals on request Vegetarian Dining
Kean College of New Jersey Union, New Jersey	2,000	—	—	—
Montclair State College Upper Montclair, New Jersey	13,900	900	3	—
Princeton University Princeton, New Jersey	5,700	1,000	12; BA	Kosher Meals by: Univ. and Young Israel Vegetarian Dining Dormitory Cooking
Ramapo College Mahwah, New Jersey	4,000	100	4	Vegetarian Dining Dormitory Cooking
Rider College Trenton, New Jersey	4,000	500	—	—
Rutgers U. (incl. Douglass, Cook, Lvgstn.) New Brunswick, New Jersey	21,000	3,000	12; BA	Kosher Meals by: Hillel Vegetarian Dining
Rutgers University—Newark Newark, New Jersey	7,000	300	12; BA	—
Stevens Institute of Technology Hoboken , New Jersey	3,100	400	—	Kosher Meals by: Institute
Stockton State College Pomona, New Jersey	4,000	400	3	Vegetarian Dining Dormitory Cooking
Trenton State College Trenton, New Jersey	10,000	200	—	—
William Patterson College Wayne, New Jersey	10,000	900	1	JSA and University
NEW MEXICO				
New Mexico State University University Park, New Mexico	12,000	100	3	Dormitory Cooking
University of New Mexico Albuquerque, New Mexico	23,000	150	—	—
NEW YORK				
Adelphi University Garden City, New York	4,000	500	3	Kosher Meals by: University
Alfred University Alfred, New York	2,000	300	1	Vegetarian Dining Dormitory Cooking
Bramson Ort Technical Institute New York, New York	150	100	—	Locally available
C. W. Post Center of Long Island U. New York, New York	13,000	3,000	15; BA	—
Colgate University Hamilton, New York	2,600	450	5; BA	Kosher Meals By: Colgate Jewish Union Vegetarian Dining Dormitory Cooking
Columbia University and Barnard College New York, New York	18,000	7,000	35; BA, MA, PhD	Kosher Meals by: Barnard and Residences Vegetarian Dining

	Enrollment (1987)	Estimated Jewish Enrollment	Judaica Courses; Major	Kosher Food
Cornell University Ithaca, New York	17,000	3,200	14; BA, MA, PhD	Kosher Meals by: Young Israel Vegetarian Dining Dormitory Cooking
CUNY—Baruch College New York, New York	15,000	2,000	10; BA	—
CUNY—Brooklyn College Brooklyn, New York	25,000	15,000	50; BA, MA	Kosher Meals by: Public Facility
CUNY—City College New York, New York	13,000	1,000	30	Kosher Meals by: Hillel
CUNY—Hunter College New York, New York	17,800	3,000	17; BA	—
CUNY—Queens College Flushing, New York	16,000	8,000	25; BA	Kosher Meals by: Campus Restaurants
Hamilton College Clinton, New York	1,600	160	2; BA	Univ. (on request) Vegetarian Dining
Hobart & William Smith Colleges Geneva, New York	1,850	350	10; BA	Vegetarian Dining Dormitory Cooking
Hofstra University Hempstead, New York	9,500	2,500	7; BA	Kosher Meals by: ARA
Ithaca College Ithaca, New York	5,000	1,200	—	Vegetarian Dining Dormitory Cooking
New York Institute of Technology New York, New York	10,000	—	1	—
New York University New York, New York	40,000	15,000	30; BA, MA, PhD	Kosher Meals by: Kosher Kitchen Dormitory Cooking
Pace University—Downtown New York, New York	13,000	350	2	Local restaurants
Pace University—Westchester Pleasantville, New York	3,700	250	—	Dormitory Cooking
Rensselaer Polytechnic Institute Troy, New York	6,000	800	Joint Program, SUNY, Albany	Vegetarian Dining
Rochester Inst. of Tech./NTID Rochester, New York	16,000	1,125	—	Kosher Meals by: Co-op
Russell Sage College Troy, New York	1,500	300	Joint Program, SUNY, Albany	—
Saint Lawrence Univ. Canton, New York	2,100	50	3	Kosher Meals by: Food Service Vegetarian Dining
Sarah Lawrence College Bronxville, New York	850	250	1	Vegetarian Dining
Skidmore College Saratoga Springs, New York	2,100	450	2	Vegetarian Dining
SUNY at Albany Albany, New York	16,000	5,000	41; BA	Kosher Meals by: Young Israel Vegetarian Dining
SUNY at Binghamton Binghamton, New York	12,000	6,000	10; BA	Kosher Meals by: Campus Enterprises Vegetarian Dining Dormitory Cooking
SUNY at Buffalo Buffalo, New York	28,000	3,500	20; BA, MA	Vegetarian Dining Dormitory Cooking
SUNY at Cortland Cortland, New York	6,000	400	2; BA	Vegetarian Dining
SUNY at New Paltz New Paltz, New York	7,000	1,000	5	Vegetarian Dining Dormitory Cooking
SUNY at Oswego Oswego, New York	6,500	1,000	2	Frozen on request
SUNY at Stony Brook Stony Brook, New York	16,000	3,000	7; BA	Kosher Meals by: Hillel, Young Israel Vegetarian Dining Dormitory Cooking
SUNY College at Brockport Brockport, New York	7,400	600	5	Kosher Meals by: Food Service Vegetarian Dining Dormitory Cooking
SUNY College at Buffalo Buffalo, New York	15,000	1,000	10; BA	Kosher Meals by: Hillel/JSU Vegetarian Dining

	Enrollment (1987)	Estimated Jewish Enrollment	Judaica Courses; Major	Kosher Food
SUNY College at Purchase Purchase, New York	1,500	270	4	—
Syracuse University Syracuse, New York	16,000	2,000	6	Kosher Meals by: Hillel
Union College Schenectady, New York	2,000	650	10	Kosher Meals by: Kosher Co-op
United States Military Academy West Point, New York	4,400	50	—	Jewish Congregation
University of Rochester Rochester, New York	7,500	1,400	10; BA	Kosher Meals by: Food Service Vegetarian Dining Dormitory Cooking
Vassar College Poughkeepsie, New York	2,250	800	10	Vegetarian Dining Dormitory Cooking
Yeshiva University New York, New York	7,000	4,800	200; BA, MA, PhD.	Univ. Cafeterias
NORTH CAROLINA				
Appalachian State University Boone, North Carolina	10,300	26	2	—
Duke University Durham, North Carolina	8,800	1,500	10; BA, MA, PhD	University/Frozen Vegetarian Dining Dormitory Cooking
East Carolina Univ. Greenville, North Carolina	14,000	125	—	—
Guilford College Chapel Hill, North Carolina	1,675	40	—	—
North Carolina State University—Raleigh Raleigh, North Carolina	22,000	130	—	Dormitory Cooking
Univ. of North Carolina—Chapel Hill Chapel Hill, North Carolina	21,500	700	10; BA, MA, PhD	Dormitory Cooking
Univ. of North Carolina—Charlotte Chapel Hill, North Carolina	10,000	75	—	Dormitory Cooking
Univ. of North Carolina—Greensboro Greensboro, North Carolina	10,000	100	—	—
OHIO				
Baldwin Wallace University Cleveland, Ohio	3,400	20	1	—
Bowling Green State University Bowling Green, Ohio	16,000	250	—	—
Case Western Reserve University Cleveland, Ohio	7,500	1,100	3; BA	Kosher Meals by: Hillel Co-op/Chabad
Cleveland State University Cleveland, Ohio	19,000	800	—	—
College of Wooster Wooster, Ohio	1,750	35	1	Vegetarian Dining
Cuyahoga Community College Cleveland, Ohio	23,000	300	—	—
Denison University Granville, Ohio	2,200	100	4	Vegetarian Dining Dormitory Cooking
Hiram College Cleveland, Ohio	1,000	20	1	—
John Carroll University Cleveland, Ohio	4,000	200	4	—
Kent State University Kent, Ohio	20,000	900	10; BA	Hillel
Kenyon College Gambier, Ohio	1,450	150	3	Vegetarian Dining
Miami University Oxford, Ohio	14,700	700	3	Kosher Meals by: Hillel Kosher Co-op
Oberlin College Oberlin, Ohio	2,800	1,200	4; BA	Kosher Meals by: Student Co-op Vegetarian Dining
Ohio State University Columbus, Ohio	53,000	2,700	25; BA, MA, PhD	Kosher Meals by: Hillel

	Enrollment (1987)	Estimated Jewish Enrollment	Judaica Courses; Major	Kosher Food
Ohio University Athens, Ohio	14,500	900	—	Kosher Meals by: Hillel Co-op
Ohio Wesleyan University Delaware, Ohio	1,350	100	4	Vegetarian Dining Dormitory Cooking
University of Cincinnati Cincinnati, Ohio	35,000	2,500	10; BA	Kosher Meals by: Hillel Dining Co-op
University of Toledo Toledo, Ohio	19,000	450	1	—
OKLAHOMA				
University of Oklahoma Norman, Oklahoma	24,000	250	2; BA	Kosher Meals by: Hillel Co-op
OREGON				
Oregon State University Corvallis, Oregon	16,500	300	—	—
University of Oregon Eugene, Oregon	15,000	2,000	5	Community Co-op Vegetarian Dining
PENNSYLVANIA				
Albright College Reading, Pennsylvania	1,300	110	—	Vegetarian Dining Dormitory Cooking
Allegheny College Meadville, Pennsylvania	1,900	50	1	—
Beaver College Jenkintown, Pennsylvania	800	100	—	—
Bloomsburg University Bloomsburg, Pennsylvania	6,000	20	—	Vegetarian Dining
Bryn Mawr College Haverford, Pennsylvania	1,100	300	4; BA	Frozen, on request
Bucknell University Lewisburg, Pennsylvania	3,400	240	6	—
Carnegie-Mellon Univ. Pittsburgh, Pennsylvania	5,000	1,500	3	Kosher Meals by: Hillel at Pitt.
Cedar Crest College Allentown, Pennsylvania	700	20	—	—
Chatham College Pittsburgh, Pennsylvania	600	50	—	Kosher Meals by: Hillel at Pitt.
Community College of Philadelphia Philadelphia, Pennsylvania	11,000	500	2	—
Delaware Valley College of Science and Agriculture Doylestown, Pennsylvania	1,300	30	1	Vegetarian Dining
Dickinson College Carlisle, Pennsylvania	1,800	265	6; BA	University
Drexel University Philadelphia, Pennsylvania	11,000	2,000	1	Kosher Meals by: Hillel at Penn. Dormitory Cooking
Duquesne University Pittsburgh, Pennsylvania	7,700	800	2	Kosher Meals by: Hillel at Pitt.
Elizabethtown College Elizabethtown, Pennsylvania	1,450	20	1	Vegetarian Dining
Franklin & Marshall College Lancaster, Pennsylvania	2,000	500	3	Hillel; Dormitory Cooking
Gettysburg College Gettysburg, Pennsylvania	1,950	30	—	Frozen, Vegetarian Dormitory Cooking
Harcum Junior College Philadelphia, Pennsylvania	850	200	—	—
Haverford College Haverford, Pennsylvania	1,100	300	4; BA	Kosher Meals by: Hillel Co-op
Indiana University of Pa. Indiana, Pennsylvania	12,000	80	—	Vegetarian Dining
Kutztown State College Kutztown, Pennsylvania	5,500	50	2	Vegetarian Dining Dormitory Cooking
La Salle College Philadelphia, Pennsylvania	3,200	200	1	University/Frozen on request

	Enrollment (1987)	Estimated Jewish Enrollment	Judaica Courses; Major	Kosher Food
Lafayette College Easton, Pennsylvania	2,000	250	14; BA	Kosher Meals by: Hillel Co-op
Lehigh University Bethlehem, Pennsylvania	6,200	660	6	Kosher Meals by: Hillel Dormitory Cooking
Millersville University Millersville, Pennsylvania	6,000	50	—	—
Moravian College Bethlehem, Pennsylvania	1,275	30	2	Hillel at Lehigh
Muhlenberg College Allentown, Pennsylvania	1,500	300	6	Vegetarian Dining Dormitory Cooking
Pennsylvania State Univ. State College, Pennsylvania	33,000	3,200	8; BA	Dormitory Cooking
Pennsylvania State Univ.—Ogontz Philadelphia, Pennsylvania	1,500	600	—	—
Philadelphia College of Pharmacy & Science Philadelphia, Pennsylvania	1,100	100	—	Vegetarian Dining
Philadelphia College of Textiles & Science Philadelphia, Pennsylvania	1,600	200	—	Vegetarian Dining
Point Park College Pittsburgh, Pennsylvania	1,650	150	—	Kosher Meals by: Hillel at Pitt.
St. Joseph's College Philadelphia, Pennsylvania	?	200	—	—
Swarthmore College Philadelphia, Pennsylvania	1,200	200	2	Kosher Meals by: Co-op
Temple University—Main & Ambler Campus Philadelphia, Pennsylvania	33,000	6,000	25; BA, MA, PhD	Kosher Meals by: Hillel Vegetarian Dining
University of Pennsylvania Philadelphia, Pennsylvania	16,875	6,000	25; BA, MA	Kosher Meals by: Hillel Vegetarian Dining Dormitory Cooking
University of Pittsburgh Pittsburgh, Pennsylvania	31,600	4,000	12; BA, MA	Kosher Meals by: Hillel
Ursinus College Collegeville, Pennsylvania	1,100	60	—	Vegetarian Dining Dormitory Cooking
Villanova University Philadelphia, Pennsylvania	?	200	—	—
Washington & Jefferson College Washington, Pennsylvania	1,300	100	—	Vegetarian Dining Dormitory Cooking
West Chester University West Chester, Pennsylvania	9,300	500	5	Locally available Vegetarian Dining
Widener College Chester, Pennsylvania	4,200	80	—	Vegetarian Dining
York College York, Pennsylvania	2,500	200	—	Vegetarian Dining
RHODE ISLAND				
Brown University Providence, Rhode Island	6,400	1,600	12; BA, MA, PhD	Kosher Meals by: Hillel & Young Israel Vegetarian Dining Dormitory Cooking
Bryant College Smithfield, Rhode Island	4,000	150	—	Locally Available
Rhode Island School of Design Providence, Rhode Island	—	—	2	Kosher Meals by: Brown Hillel Vegetarian Dining
University of Rhode Island Kingston, Rhode Island	8,000	800	4	Kosher Meals by: Hillel Vegetarian Dining
SOUTH CAROLINA				
Clemson University Clemson, South Carolina	12,000	120	2	Locally available
The Citadel-Military College of S.C. Charleston, South Carolina	1,900	20	—	—
University of South Carolina Columbia, South Carolina	20,000	650	12	Vegetarian Dining

	Enrollment (1987)	Estimated Jewish Enrollment	Judaica Courses; Major	Kosher Food
TENNESSEE				
George Peabody College for Teachers Nashville, Tennessee	1,500	100	—	—
Memphis State University Memphis, Tennessee	26,000	300	1	Kosher Meals by : JSU Dormitory Cooking
Rhodes College Memphis, Tennessee	1,000	?	—	JSU at Memphis State Univ.
Southern College of Optometry Memphis, Tennessee	600	?	—	Kosher Meals by: JSU
Southwestern University Memphis, Tennessee	1,000	—	—	Kosher Meals by: JSU
U. of Tenn.—Medical & Nursing Memphis, Tennessee	2,000	?	—	Kosher Meals by: JSU
University of Tennessee—Chattanooga Chattanooga, Tennessee	8,200	100	1	Cong. Beth Shalom
University of Tennessee—Knoxville Knoxville, Tennessee	25,000	500	4	Vegetarian Dining
University of Tennessee—Memphis Memphis, Tennessee	2,000	—	—	Kosher Meals by: JSU
Vanderbilt University Nashville, Tennessee	7,000	350	3	Kosher Meals by: JSU
TEXAS				
Austin College Sherman, Texas	1,200	25	—	Vegetarian Dining
Brookhaven College Dallas, Texas	7,500	90	—	—
North Texas State Univ. Denton, Texas	18,800	250	—	—
Rice University Houston, Texas	3,600	250	2	Hillel
Richland College Dallas, Texas	14,000	90	—	—
Southern Methodist Univ. Dallas, Texas	9,200	400	2	—
Texas A & M University College Station, Texas	40,000	500	—	Hillel
Texas Medical Center (Baylor & V. T.) Houston, Texas	2,500	700	—	Hillel
Texas Tech University Lubbock, Texas	23,000	150	4	—
University of Houston Houston, Texas	32,000	2,000	3	Hillel
University of Texas—Austin Austin, Texas	49,000	3,200	15; BA, MA, PhD	Dormitory Cooking
University of Texas—Arlington Arlington, Texas	23,000	300	—	—
University of Texas—Dallas Dallas, Texas	10,000	75	—	—
UTAH				
University of Utah Salt Lake City, Utah	25,000	200	10	Vegetarian Dining
VERMONT				
Middlebury College Middlebury, Vermont	1,900	190	1	Vegetarian Dining Dormitory Cooking
University of Vermont Burlington, Vermont	10,000	800	5	Hillel
VIRGINIA				
College of William & Mary Williamsburg, Virginia	6,000	200	5	Vegetarian Dining
Ferrum College Martinsville, Virginia	1,300	13	—	—

	Enrollment (1987)	Estimated Jewish Enrollment	Judaica Courses; Major	Kosher Food
George Mason University Fairfax, Virginia	8,000	150	1	Vegetarian Dining
James Madison University Harrisonburg, Virginia	9,000	200	3	—
Mary Washington College Fredericksburg, Virginia	3,030	15	—	—
Northern Virginia Community College Annandale, Virginia	20,000	100	—	Vegetarian Dining
Old Dominion University Norfolk, Virginia	15,000	300	—	Vegetarian Dining
Radford University Radford, Virginia	7,000	50	—	—
University of Richmond Richmond, Virginia	2,900	50	2	Kosher Meals by: VCU Kosher Kitchen
University of Virginia Charlottesville, Virginia	16,000	1,200	4; BA, MA, PhD	Kosher Meals by: Hillel Kitchen Vegetarian Dining Dormitory Cooking
Virginia Commonwealth Univ. Richmond, Virginia	19,000	800	7	Kosher Meals by: Hillel Kitchen . Vegetarian Dining Dormitory Cooking
Virginia Polytechnic Inst. & State U. Blacksburg, Virginia	21,000	550	—	Community Co-op
Washington and Lee Univ. Lexington, Virginia	1,750	40	3	—
WASHINGTON				
University of Puget Sound Tacoma, Washington	4,000	50	—	—
University of Washington Seattle, Washington	35,000	1,700	26; BA	Hillel
Washington State University Pullman, Washington	17,000	200	—	Vegetarian Dining
WEST VIRGINIA				
West Virginia University Morgantown, West Virginia	20,000	350	1	Vegetarian Dining Dormitory Cooking
WISCONSIN				
Beloit College Beloit, Wisconsin	1,100	100	6; BA	Vegetarian Dining
University of Wis.—Milwaukee/Marquette Milwaukee, Wisconsin	27,000	650	6	Kosher Meals by: Hillel Kitchen Available
University of Wisconsin Madison, Wisconsin	42,000	3,600	13; BA, MA, PhD	Kosher Meals by: Kibbutz Langdon Vegetarian Dining
CANADA				
Carleton University Ottawa, Ontario K1N 7Y2	10,000	750	9	Vegetarian Dining
Concordia University—Sir George & Loyola Montreal, Que. H3A 1R8	10,000	600	20; BA, MA, PhD	Kosher Meals by: McGill Hillel
Dalhousie University Halifax, Nova Scotia	9,000	200	—	Locally available
Dawson Cegep Montreal, Que. H3A 1R8	8.000	600	—	—
Marianopolis Cegep Montreal, Que. H3A IR8	1,300	250	—	—
McGill University Montreal, Que. H3A 1R8	18,000	4,000	50; BA, MA, PhD	Kosher Meals by : Hillel Vegetarian Dining Dormitory Cooking
McMaster University Toronto, Ontario	?	300	—	—
Queen's University Kingston, Ontario	10,000	400	2	Hillel

	Enrollment (1987)	Estimated Jewish Enrollment	Judaica Courses; Major	Kosher Food
University of Alberta Edmonton, Al. T6G 2E0	25,000	300	3	Kosher Meals by: Hillel
University of British Columbia Vancouver, B.C. V6T 1W5	23,000	400	1	Kosher Meals by: Hillel
University of Calgary Calgary, Alberta	20,000	400	—	JCC
University of Guelph Guelph, Ontario	?	300	—	—
University of Manitoba Winnipeg, Man. R3T 2N2	20,000	800	14; BA	—
University of Montreal Montreal, Que. H3A 1K8	—	500	10	—
University of Ottawa Ottawa, Ont. K1N 7Y2	17,000	750	2	Vegetarian Dining
University of Quebec/Cegep St. Laurent Montreal, Que. H3A 1K8	—	300	—	—
University of Toronto Toronto, Ont. M5S 2H4	37,000	3,000	50; BA	Kosher Meals by: Hillel and University Residents
University of Waterloo Waterloo, Ontario	?	300	—	—
University of Western Ontario London, Ontario	20,000	800	4	Hillel
University of Windsor Windsor, Ontario	?	300	—	WJCC
University of Winnipeg Winnipeg, Manitoba	2,000	100	3	—
Vanier Cegep (St. Croix & Snowdown) Montreal, Que.	6,000	1,500	—	—
York University Downsview, Ont. M6C 1S3	20,000	3,500	8; BA	Kosher Meals by: Public Restaurant Vegetarian Dining

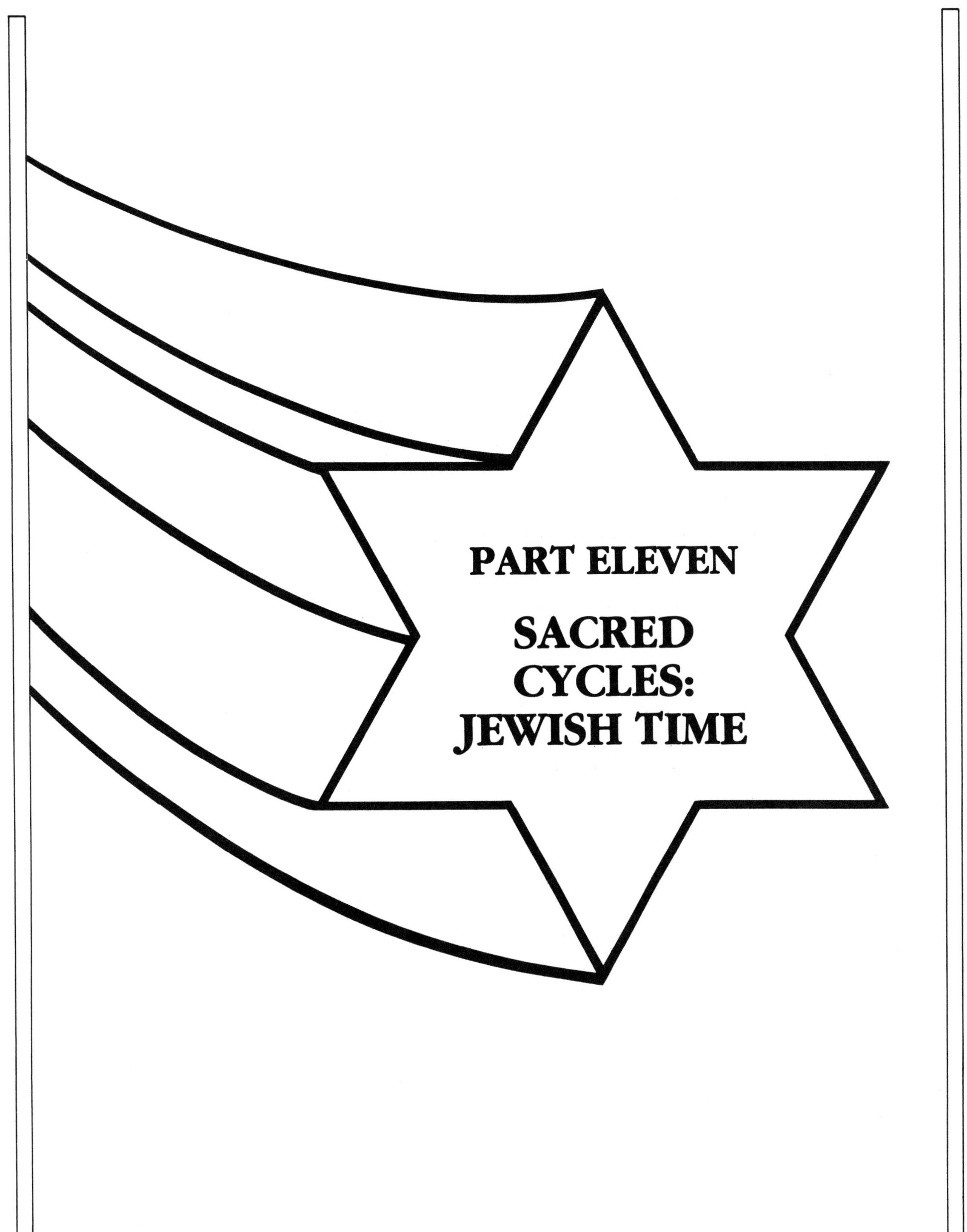

PART ELEVEN

SACRED CYCLES: JEWISH TIME

1987

5747/48 — תשמ״ז / תשמ״ח

	January	February	March	April	May	June	July	August	September	October	November	December
1	30 Kislev Hanukkah R. Ḥ. 6	2	30 R. Ḥ.	2	2	4	4	6 Devarim	7	8	9	10
2	1 Tevet R. Ḥ. 7	3	1 Adar R. Ḥ.	3	3 Tazri'a Meẓora	5	5	7	8	9	10	11
3	2 Mi-Keẓ 8	4	2	4	4	6 Shavuot	6	8	9	10 Yom Kippur	11	12
4	3	5	3	5 Va-Yikra	5 Yom ha-Aẓma'ut	7	7 Ḥukkat	9 Tishah be-Av	10	11	12	13
5	4	6	4	6	6	8	8	10	11 Ki Teẓe	12	13	14 Va-Yishlaḥ
6	5	7	5	7	7	9 Naso	9	11	12	13	14	15
7	6	8 Bo	6 Terumah	8	8	10	10	12	13	14	15 Va-Yera	16
8	7	9	7	9	9	11	11	13 Va-Etḥannan	14	15 Sukkot	16	17
9	8	10	8	10	10 Aḥarei Mot Kedoshim	12	12	14	15	16	17	18
10	9 Va-Yiggash	11	9	11	11	13	13	15	16	17	18	19
11	10 Fast	12	10	12 Ẓav Shabbat ha-Gadol	12	14	14 Balak	16	17	18 Ḥol ha-Mo'ed	19	20
12	11	13	11 Ta'anit Esther	13	13	15	15	17	18 Ki Tavo	19	20	21 Va-Yeshev
13	12	14	12	14	14	16 Be-Ha'alotkha	16	18	19	20	21	22
14	13	15 Be-Shallaḥ	13 Teẓavveh Zakhor	15 Pesaḥ	15	17	17 Fast	19	20	21 Hoshana Rabba	22 Ḥayyei Sarah	23
15	14	16	14 Purim	16 Omer	16	18	18	20 Ekev	21	22 Shemini Aẓeret	23	24
16	15	17	15 Shushan Purim	17	17 Emor	19	19	21	22	23 Simḥat Torah Va-Zot Ha-Berakhah	24	25 Ḥanukkah 1
17	16 Va-Yeḥi	18	16	18 Ḥol ha-Mo'ed	18 Lag ba-Omer	20	20	22	23	24 Bereshit	25	26 2
18	17	19	17	19	19	21	21 Pinḥas	23	24	25	26	27 3
19	18	20	18	20	20	22	22	24	25 Niẓẓavim Va-Yelekh	26	27	28 Mi-Keẓ 4
20	19	21	19	21 Pesaḥ	21	23 Shelaḥ	23	25	26	27	28	29 5
21	20	22 Yitro	20 Ki Tissa Parah	22	22	24	24	26	27	28	29 Toledot	30 R. Ḥ. 6
22	21	23	21	23	23	25	25	27 Re'eh	28	29	1 Kislev R. Ḥ.	1 Tevet R. Ḥ. 7
23	22	24	22	24	24 Be-Har Be-Ḥukkotai	26	26	28	29	30 R. Ḥ.	2	2 8
24	23 Shemot	25	23	25	25	27	27	29	1 Tishri Rosh Ha-Shanah	1 Ḥeshvan R. Ḥ. No'aḥ	3	3
25	24	26	24	26 Shemini	26	28	28 Mattot Masei	30 R. Ḥ.	2	2	4	4
26	25	27	25	27	27	29	29	1 Elul R. Ḥ.	3 Ha'azinu Shabbat Shuvah	3	5	5 Va-Yiggash
27	26	28	26	28	28	30 R. Ḥ. Koraḥ	1 Av R. Ḥ.	2	4 ↓ Fast	4	6	6
28	27	29 Mishpatim Shekalim	27 Va-Yakhel Pekudei Ha-Ḥodesh	29	29	1 Tammuz R. Ḥ.	2	3	5	5	7 Va-Yeẓe	7
29	28		28	30 R. Ḥ.	1 Sivan R. Ḥ.	2	3	4 Shofetim	6	6	8	8
30	29		29	1 Iyyar R. Ḥ.	2 Be-Midbar	3	4	5	7	7	9	9
31	1 Shevat R. Ḥ. Va-Era		1 Nisan R. Ḥ.		3		5	6		8 Lekh Lekha		10 Fast

1988

5748/49 תשמ״ח / תשמ״ט

	January	February	March	April	May	June	July	August	September	October	November	December
1	11 **Tevet**	13	12	14	14	16	16	18	19	**20** Ḥol ha-Mo'ed	21	22
2	**12** *Va-Yeḥi*	14	13 Ta'anit Esther	**15** Pesaḥ	15	17	**17** *Balak*	19	20	21 Hoshana Rabba	22	23
3	13	15	14 Purim	**16** Omer	16	18	18 Fast	20	**21** *Ki Tavo*	22 Shemini Aẓeret	23	**24** *Va-Yeshev*
4	14	16	15 Shushan Purim	17 Ḥol ha-Mo'ed	17	**19** *Be-Ha'alotkha*	19	21	22	23 Simḥat Torah *Ve-Zot Ha-Berakhah*	24	25 Ḥanukkah 1
5	15	17	**16** *Ki Tissa*	18	18 Lag ba-Omer	20	20	22	23	24	**25** *Ḥayyei Sarah*	26 2
6	16	**18** *Yitro*	17	19	19	21	21	**23** *Ekev*	24	25	26	27 3
7	17	19	18	20	**20** *Emor*	22	22	24	25	26	27	28 4
8	18	20	19	**21** Pesaḥ	21	23	23	25	26	**27** *Bereshit*	28	29 5
9	**19** *Shemot*	21	20	**22**	22	24	**24** *Pinḥas*	26	27	28	29	1 **Tevet** R. Ḥ. 6
10	20	22	21	23	23	25	25	27	**28** *Niẓẓavim*	29	1 **Kislev** R. Ḥ.	**2** *Mi-Keẓ* 7
11	21	23	22	24	24	**26** *Shelaḥ*	26	28	29	30 R. Ḥ.	2	3 8
12	22	24	**23** *Va-Yakhel Pekudei* Parah	25	25	27	27	29	1 **Tishri** Rosh Ha-Shanah	1 **Ḥeshvan** R. Ḥ.	**3** *Toledot*	4
13	23	**25** *Mishpatim* Shekalim	24	26	26	28	28	**30** R. Ḥ. *Re'eh*	2	2	4	5
14	24	26	25	27	**27** *Be-Har Be-Ḥukkotai*	29	29	1 **Elul** R. Ḥ.	3 Fast	3	5	6
15	25	27	26	28	28	30 R. Ḥ.	1 **Av** R. Ḥ.	2	4	**4** *No'aḥ*	6	7
16	**26** *Va-Era*	28	27	**29** *Shemini*	29	1 **Tammuz** R. Ḥ.	**2** *Mattot Masei*	3	5	5	7	8
17	27	29	28	30 R. Ḥ.	1 **Sivan** R. Ḥ.	2	3	4	**6** *Va-Yelekh* Shabbat Shuvah	6	8	**9** *Va-Yiggash*
18	28	30 R. Ḥ.	29	1 **Iyyar** R. Ḥ.	2	**3** *Koraḥ*	4	5	7	7	9	10 Fast
19	29	1 **Adar** R. Ḥ.	1 **Nisan** R. Ḥ. *Va-Yikra* Ha-Ḥodesh	2	3	4	5	6	8	8	**10** *Va-Yeẓe*	11
20	1 **Shevat** R. Ḥ.	**2** *Terumah*	2	3	4	5	6	**7** *Shofetim*	9	9	11	12
21	2	3	3	4 Yom ha-Aẓma'ut	**5** *Be-Midbar*	6	7	8	**10** Yom Kippur	10	12	13
22	3	4	4	5	**6** Shavuot	7	8	9	11	**11** *Lekh Lekha*	13	14
23	**4** *Bo*	5	5	**6** *Tazri'a Meẓora*	7	8	**9** Tishah be-Av *Devarim*	10	12	12	14	15
24	5	6	6	7	8	9	10 Fast	11	**13** *Ha'azinu*	13	15	**16** *Va-Yeḥi*
25	6	7	7	8	9	**10** *Ḥukkat*	11	12	14	14	16	17
26	7	8	**8** *Ẓav* Shabbat ha-Gadol	9	10	11	12	13	**15** Sukkot	15	**17** *Va-Yishlaḥ*	18
27	8	**9** *Teẓavveh* Zakhor	9	10	11	12	13	**14** *Ki Teẓe*	**16**	16	18	19
28	9	10	10	11	**12** *Naso*	13	14	15	17 Ḥol ha-Mo'ed	17	19	20
29	10	11	11	12	13	14	15	16	18	**18** *Va-Yera*	20	21
30	**11** *Be-Shallaḥ*		12	**13** *Aḥarei Mot Kedoshim*	14	15	**16** *Va-Etḥannan*	17	19	19	21	22
31	12		13		15		17	18		20		**23** *Shemot*

1989

5749/50 תשמ״ט / תש״ן

	January	February	March	April	May	June	July	August	September	October	November	December
1	24 **Tevet**	26	24	**25** *Shemini* Ha-Ḥodesh	26	27	**28** *Shelaḥ*	29	1 **Elul** R. Ḥ.	2 Rosh Ha-Shanah	3	3
2	25	27	25	26	27	28	29	1 **Av** R. Ḥ.	**2** *Shofetim*	3 Fast	4	**4** *Toledot*
3	26	28	26	27	28	**29** *Be-Midbar*	30 R. Ḥ.	2	3	4	5	5
4	27	**29** *Mishpatim*	**27** *Va-Yakhel* Shekalim	28	29	1 **Sivan** R. Ḥ.	1 **Tammuz** R. Ḥ.	3	4	5	**6** *No'aḥ*	6
5	28	30 R. Ḥ.	28	29	30 R. Ḥ.	2	2	**4** *Devarim*	5	6	7	7
6	29	1 **Adar I** R. Ḥ.	29	1 **Nisan** R. Ḥ.	**1 Iyyar** R. Ḥ. *Kedoshim*	3	3	5	6	7	8	8
7	**1 Shevat** R. Ḥ. *Va-Era*	2	30 R. Ḥ.	2	2	4	4	6	7	**8** *Ha'azinu* Shabbat Shuvah	9	9
8	2	3	1 **Adar II** R. Ḥ.	**3** *Tazri'a*	3	5	**5** *Koraḥ*	7	8	9	10	10
9	3	4	2	4	4	**6 Shavuot**	6	8	**9** *Ki Teẓe*	**10 Yom Kippur**	11	**11** *Va-Yeẓe*
10	4	5	3	5	5 Yom ha-Aẓma'ut	**7**	7	9 Tishah be-Av	10	11	12	12
11	5	**6** *Terumah*	**4** *Pekudei*	6	6	8	8	10	11	12	**13** *Lekh Lekha*	13
12	6	7	5	7	7	9	9	**11** *Va-Etḥannan*	12	13	14	14
13	7	8	6	8	**8** *Emor*	10	10	12	13	14	15	15
14	**8** *Bo*	9	7	9	9	11	11	13	14	**15 Sukkot**	16	16
15	9	10	8	**10** *Meẓora* Shabbat ha-Gadol	10	12	**12** *Ḥukkat Balak*	14	15	16	17	17
16	10	11	9	11	11	13	13	15	**16** *Ki Tavo*	17 Ḥol ha-Mo'ed	18	**18** *Va-Yishlaḥ*
17	11	12	10	12	12	**14** *Naso*	14	16	17	18	19	19
18	12	**13** *Teẓavveh*	**11** *Va-Yikra* Zakhor	13	13	15	15	17	18	19	**20** *Va-Yera*	20
19	13	14	12	14	14	16	16	**18** *Ekev*	19	20	21	21
20	14	15	13 Ta'anit Esther	**15 Pesaḥ**	**15** *Be-Har*	17	17 Fast	19	20	21 Hoshana Rabba	22	22
21	**15** *Be-Shallaḥ*	16	14 Purim	16 Omer	16	18	18	20	21	**22 Shemini Aẓeret**	23	23
22	16	17	15 Shushan Purim	**17** Ḥol ha-Mo'ed	17	19	**19** *Pinḥas*	21	22	23 Simḥat Torah *Ve-Zot Ha-Berakhah*	24	24
23	17	18	16	18	18 Lag ba-Omer	20	20	22	**23** *Niẓẓavim Va-Yelekh*	24	25	**25** Ḥanukkah *Va-Yeshev* 1
24	18	19	17	19	19	**21** *Be-Ha'alotkha*	21	23	24	25	26	26 2
25	19	**20** *Ki Tissa*	**18** *Ẓav* Parah	20	20	22	22	24	25	26	**27** *Ḥayyei Sarah*	27 3
26	20	21	19	**21 Pesaḥ**	21	23	23	**25** *Re'eh*	26	27	28	28 4
27	21	22	20	22	**22** *Be-Ḥukkotai*	24	24	26	27	28	29	29 5
28	**22** *Yitro*	23	21	23	23	25	25	27	28	**29** *Bereshit*	30 R. Ḥ.	30 R. Ḥ. 6
29	23		22	**24** *Aḥarei Mot*	24	26	**26** *Mattot Masei*	28	29	30 R. Ḥ.	1 **Kislev** R. Ḥ.	1 **Tevet** R. Ḥ. 7
30	24		23	25	25	27	27	29	**1 Tishri** Rosh Ha-Shanah	1 **Ḥeshvan** R. Ḥ.	2	**2** *Mi-Keẓ* 8
31	25		24		26		28	30 R. Ḥ.		2		3

1990

5750/51 — תש״ן / תשנ״א

	January	February	March	April	May	June	July	August	September	October	November	December
1	4 Tevet	6	4	6	6	8	8	10	11 Ki Teẓe	12	13	14 Va-Yishlaḥ
2	5	7	5	7	7	9 Naso	9	11	12	13	14	15
3	6	8 Bo	6 Terumah	8	8	10	10	12	13	14	15 Va-Yera	16
4	7	9	7	9	9	11	11	13 Va-Etḥannan	14	15 Sukkot	16	17
5	8	10	8	10	10 Aḥarei Mot Kedoshim	12	12	14	15	16	17	18
6	9 Va-Yiggash	11	9	11	11	13	13	15	16	17 Ḥol ha-Mo'ed	18	19
7	10 Fast	12	10	12 Zav Shabbat ha-Gadol	12	14	14 Balak	16	17	18	19	20
8	11	13	11 Ta'anit Esther	13	13	15	15	17	18 Ki Tavo	19	20	21 Va-Yeshev
9	12	14	12	14	14	16 Be-Ha'alotkha	16	18	19	20	21	22
10	13	15 Be-Shallaḥ	13 Teẓavveh Zakhor	15 Pesaḥ	15	17	17 Fast	19	20	21 Hoshana Rabba	22 Ḥayyei Sarah	23
11	14	16	14 Purim	16 Omer	16	18	18	20 Ekev	21	22 Shemini Aẓeret	23	24
12	15	17	15 Shushan Purim	17 Ḥol ha-Mo'ed	17 Emor	19	19	21	22	23 Simḥat Torah Ve-Zot Ha-Berakhah	24	25 Ḥanukkah 1
13	16 Va-Yeḥi	18	16	18	18 Lag ba-Omer	20	20	22	23	24 Bereshit	25	26 2
14	17	19	17	19	19	21	21 Pinḥas	23	24	25	26	27 3
15	18	20	18	20	20	22	22	24	25 Niẓẓavim Va-Yelekh	26	27	28 Mi-Keẓ 4
16	19	21	19	21 Pesaḥ	21	23 Shelaḥ	23	25	26	27	28	29 5
17	20	22 Yitro	20 Ki Tissa Parah	22	22	24	24	26	27	28	29 Toledot	30 R. Ḥ. 6
18	21	23	21	23	23	25	25	27 Re'eh	28	29	1 Kislev R. Ḥ.	1 Tevet R. Ḥ. 7
19	22	24	22	24	24 Be-Har Be-Ḥukkotai	26	26	28	29	30 R. Ḥ.	2	2 8
20	23 Shemot	25	23	25	25	27	27	29	1 Tishri Rosh Ha-Shanah	1 Ḥeshvan R. Ḥ. No'aḥ	3	3
21	24	26	24	26 Shemini	26	28	28 Mattot Masei	30 R. Ḥ.	2	2	4	4
22	25	27	25	27	27	29	29	1 Elul R. Ḥ.	3 Ha'azinu Shabbat Shuvah	3	5	5 Va-Yiggash
23	26	28	26	28	28	30 R. Ḥ. Koraḥ	1 Av R. Ḥ.	2	4 Fast	4	6	6
24	27	29 Mishpatim Shekalim	27 Va-Yakhel Pekudei Ha-Ḥodesh	29	29	1 Tammuz R. Ḥ.	2	3	5	5	7 Va-Yeẓe	7
25	28	30 R. Ḥ.	28	30 R. Ḥ.	1 Sivan R. Ḥ.	2	3	4 Shofetim	6	6	8	8
26	29	1 Adar R. Ḥ.	29	1 Iyyar R. Ḥ.	2 Be-Midbar	3	4	5	7	7	9	9
27	1 Shevat R. Ḥ. Va-Era	2	1 Nisan R. Ḥ.	2	3	4	5	6	8	8 Lekh Lekha	10	10 Fast
28	2	3	2	3 Tazri'a Meẓora	4	5	6 Devarim	7	9	9	11	11
29	3		3	4	5	6	7	8	10 Yom Kippur	10	12	12 Va-Yeḥi
30	4		4	5 Yom ha-Aẓma'ut	6 Shavuot	7 Ḥukkat	8	9	11	11	13	13
31	5		5 Va-Yikra		7		9 Tishah be-Av	10		12		14

1991

5751/52 — תשנ״א / תשנ״ב

	January	February	March	April	May	June	July	August	September	October	November	December
1	15 Tevet	17	15 Shushan Purim	17	17	**19** Be-Ha'alotkha	19	21	22	**23** Simḥat Torah Ve-Zot Ha-Berakhah	24	24
2	16	**18** Yitro	**16** Ki Tissa	18 Ḥol ha-Mo'ed	18 Lag ba-Omer	20	20	22	23	24	**25** Ḥayyei Sarah	25 Ḥanukkah 1
3	17	19	17	19	19	21	21	**23** Ekev	24	25	26	26 2
4	18	20	18	20	**20** Emor	22	22	24	25	26	27	27 3
5	**19** Shemot	21	19	**21** Pesaḥ	21	23	23	25	26	**27** Bereshit	28	28 4
6	20	22	20	**22**	22	24	**24** Pinḥas	26	27	28	29	29 5
7	21	23	21	23	23	25	25	27	**28** Niẓẓavim	29	30 R. Ḥ.	**30** R. Ḥ. Mi-Keẓ 6
8	22	24	22	24	24	**26** Shelaḥ	26	28	29	30 R. Ḥ.	1 Kislev R. Ḥ.	1 Tevet R. Ḥ. 7
9	23	**25** Mishpatim Shekalim	Va-Yakhel Pekudei **23** Parah	25	25	27	27	29	1 Tishri Rosh Ha-Shanah	1 Ḥeshvan R. Ḥ.	**2** Toledot	2 8
10	24	26	24	26	26	28	28	**30** R. Ḥ. Re'eh	2	2	3	3
11	25	27	25	27	**27** Be-Har Be-Ḥukkotai	29	29	1 Elul R. Ḥ.	3 Fast	3	4	4
12	**26** Va-Era	28	26	28	28	30 R. Ḥ.	1 Av R. Ḥ.	2	4	**4** No'aḥ	5	5
13	27	29	27	**29** Shemini	29	1 Tammuz R. Ḥ.	**2** Mattot Masei	3	5	5	6	6
14	28	30 R. Ḥ.	28	30 R. Ḥ.	1 Sivan R. Ḥ.	2	3	4	**6** Va-Yelekh Shabbat Shuvah	6	7	**7** Va-Yiggash
15	29	1 Adar R. Ḥ.	29	1 Iyyar R. Ḥ.	2	**3** Koraḥ	4	5	7	7	8	8
16	1 Shevat R. Ḥ.	**2** Terumah	**1** Nisan R. Ḥ. Va-Yikra Ha-Ḥodesh	2	3	4	5	6	8	8	**9** Va-Yeẓe	9
17	2	3	2	3	4	5	6	**7** Shofetim	9	9	10	10 Fast
18	3	4	3	4 Yom ha-Aẓma'ut	**5** Be-Midbar	6	7	8	**10** Yom Kippur	10	11	11
19	**4** Bo	5	4	5	**6** Shavuot	7	8	9	11	**11** Lekh Lekha	12	12
20	5	6	5	**6** Tazri'a Meẓora	7	8	**9** Devarim Tishah be-Av	10	12	12	13	13
21	6	7	6	7	8	9	10 Fast	11	**13** Ha'azinu	13	14	**14** Va-Yeḥi
22	7	8	7	8	9	**10** Ḥukkat	11	12	14	14	15	15
23	8	**9** Teẓavveh Zakhor	**8** Ẓav Shabbat ha-Gadol	9	10	11	12	13	15 Sukkot	15	**16** Va-Yishlaḥ	16
24	9	10	9	10	11	12	13	**14** Ki Teẓe	16	16	17	17
25	10	11	10	11	**12** Naso	13	14	15	17	17	18	18
26	**11** Be-Shallaḥ	12	11	12	13	14	15	16	18 Ḥol ha-Mo'ed	**18** Va-Yera	19	19
27	12	13 Ta'anit Esther	12	**13** Aḥarei Mot Kedoshim	14	15	**16** Va-Etḥannan	17	19	19	20	20
28	13	14 Purim	13	14	15	16	17	18	**20**	20	21	**21** Shemot
29	14		14	15	16	**17** Balak	18	19	21 Hoshana Rabba	21	22	22
30	15		**15** Pesaḥ	16	17	18 Fast	19	20	22 Shemini Aẓeret	22	**23** Va-Yeshev	23
31	16		16 Omer		18		20	**21** Ki Tavo		23		24

1992

5752/53 תשנ״ב / תשנ״ג

	January	February	March	April	May	June	July	August	September	October	November	December
1	25 **Tevet**	**27** *Mishpatim*	26	27	28	29	30 R. Ḥ.	**2** *Mattot Masei*	3	4	5	6
2	26	28	27	28	**29** *Aḥarei Mot*	1 **Sivan** R. Ḥ.	1 **Tammuz** R. Ḥ.	3	4	5	6	7
3	27	29	28	29	30 R. Ḥ.	2	2	4	5	**6** *Va-Yelekh* Shabbat Shuvah	7	8
4	**28** *Va-Era*	30 R. Ḥ.	29	**1** **Nisan** *Tazri'a* R. Ḥ. Ha-Hodesh	1 **Iyyar** R. Ḥ.	3	**3** *Koraḥ*	5	6	7	8	9
5	29	1 **Adar I** R. Ḥ.	30 R. Ḥ.	2	2	4	4	6	**7** *Shofetim*	8	9	**10** *Va-Yeẓe*
6	1 **Shevat** R. Ḥ.	2	1 **Adar II** R. Ḥ.	3	3	**5** *Be-Midbar*	5	7	8	9	10	11
7	2	3	**2** *Pekudei*	4	4 Yom ha-Aẓma'ut	**6** Shavuot	6	8	9	10 Yom Kippur	**11** *Lekh Lekha*	12
8	3	**4** *Terumah*	3	5	5	7	7	**9** *Devarim* Tishah be-Av	10	11	12	13
9	4	5	4	6	**6** *Kedoshim*	8	8	10 Fast	11	12	13	14
10	5	6	5	7	7	9	9	11	12	**13** *Ha'azinu*	14	15
11	**6** *Bo*	7	6	**8** *Meẓora* Shabbat ha-Gadol	8	10	**10** *Ḥukkat*	12	13	14	15	16
12	7	8	7	9	9	11	11	13	**14** *Ki Teẓe*	15 Sukkot	16	**17** *Va-Yishlaḥ*
13	8	9	8	10	10	**12** *Naso*	12	14	15	16	17	18
14	9	10	**9** *Va-Yikra* Zakhor	11	11	13	13	15	16	17	**18** *Va-Yera*	19
15	10	**11** *Teẓavveh*	10	12	12	14	14	**16** *Va-Etḥannan*	17	18 Ḥol ha-Mo'ed	19	20
16	11	12	11	13	**13** *Emor*	15	15	17	18	19	20	21
17	12	13	12	14	14	16	16	18	19	**20**	21	22
18	**13** *Be-Shallaḥ*	14	13 Ta'anit Esther	**15** Pesaḥ	15	17	**17** *Balak*	19	20	21 Hoshana Rabba	22	23
19	14	15	14 Purim	16 Omer	16	18	18 Fast	20	**21** *Ki Tavo*	22 Shemini Aẓeret	23	**24** *Va-Yeshev*
20	15	16	15 Shushan Purim	17	17	**19** *Be-Ha'alotkha*	19	21	22	23 Simḥat Torah Ve-Zot Ha-Berakhah	24	25 Ḥanukkah 1
21	16	17	**16** *Ẓav*	18 Ḥol ha-Mo'ed	18 Lag ba-Omer	20	20	22	23	24	**25** *Ḥayyei Sarah*	26 2
22	17	**18** *Ki Tissa*	17	19	19	21	21	**23** *Ekev*	24	25	26	27 3
23	18	19	18	20	**20** *Be-Har*	22	22	24	25	26	27	28 4
24	19	20	19	21 Pesaḥ	21	23	23	25	26	**27** *Bereshit*	28	29 5
25	**20** *Yitro*	21	20	**22**	22	24	**24** *Pinḥas*	26	27	28	29	1 **Tevet** R. Ḥ. 6
26	21	22	21	23	23	25	25	27	**28** *Niẓẓavim*	29	1 **Kislev** R. Ḥ.	**2** *Mi-Keẓ* 7
27	22	23	22	24	24	**26** *Shelaḥ*	26	28	29	30 R. Ḥ.	2	3 8
28	23	24	**23** *Shemini* Parah	25	25	27	27	29	1 **Tishri** Rosh Ha-Shanah	1 **Heshvan** R. Ḥ.	**3** *Toledot*	4
29	24	**25** *Va-Yakhel* Shekalim	24	26	26	28	28	**30** R. Ḥ. *Re'eh*	2	2	4	5
30	25		25	27	**27** *Be-Ḥukkotai*	29	29	1 **Elul** R. Ḥ.	3 Fast	3	5	6
31	26		26		28		1 **Av** R. Ḥ.	2		**4** *No'aḥ*		7

1993

5753/54 תשנ״ג / תשנ״ד

	January	February	March	April	May	June	July	August	September	October	November	December
1	8 **Tevet**	10	8	10	**10** *Aḥarei Mot Kedoshim*	12	12	14	15	**16**	17	17
2	**9** *Va-Yiggash*	11	9	11	11	13	13	15	16	**17** Ḥol ha-Mo'ed	18	18
3	10 Fast	12	10	**12** *Ẓav* Shabbat ha-Gadol	12	14	**14** *Balak*	16	17	18	19	19
4	11	13	11 Ta'anit Esther	13	13	15	15	17	**18** *Ki Tavo*	19	20	**20** *Va-Yeshev*
5	12	14	12	14	14	**16** *Be-Ha'alotkha*	16	18	19	20	21	21
6	13	**15** *Be-Shallaḥ*	**13** *Teẓavveh* Zakhor	15 Pesaḥ	15	17	17 Fast	19	20	21 Hoshana Rabba	**22** *Ḥayyei Sarah*	22
7	14	16	14 Purim	16 Omer	16	18	18	**20** *Ekev*	21	22 Shemini Aẓeret	23	23
8	15	17	15 Shushan Purim	17	**17** *Emor*	19	19	21	22	23 Simḥat Torah Ve-Zot Ha-Berakhah	24	24
9	**16** *Va-Yeḥi*	18	16	18 Ḥol ha-Mo'ed	18 Lag ba-Omer	20	20	22	23	**24** *Bereshit*	25	25 Ḥanukkah 1
10	17	19	17	**19**	19	21	**21** *Pinḥas*	23	24	25	26	26 2
11	18	20	18	20	20	22	22	24	**25** *Niẓẓavim Va-Yelekh*	26	27	**27** *Mi-Keẓ* 3
12	19	21	19	21 Pesaḥ	21	**23** *Shelaḥ*	23	25	26	27	28	28 4
13	20	**22** *Yitro*	**20** *Ki Tissa* Parah	22	22	24	24	26	27	28	**29** *Toledot*	29 5
14	21	23	21	23	23	25	25	**27** *Re'eh*	28	29	30 R. Ḥ.	30 R. Ḥ. 6
15	22	24	22	24	**24** *Be-Har Be-Ḥukkotai*	26	26	28	29	30 R. Ḥ.	1 **Kislev** R. Ḥ.	1 **Tevet** R. Ḥ. 7
16	**23** *Shemot*	25	23	25	25	27	27	29	1 **Tishri** Rosh Ha-Shanah	**1** R. Ḥ. **Ḥeshvan** *No'aḥ*	2	2 8
17	24	26	24	**26** *Shemini*	26	28	**28** *Mattot Masei*	30 R. Ḥ.	2	2	3	3
18	25	27	25	27	27	29	29	1 **Elul** R. Ḥ.	**3** *Ha'azinu* Shabbat Shuvah	3	4	**4** *Va-Yiggash*
19	26	28	26	28	28	**30** R. Ḥ. *Koraḥ*	1 **Av** R. Ḥ.	2	4 ↓ Fast	4	5	5
20	27	**29** *Mishpatim* Shekalim	**27** *Va-Yakhel Pekudei* Ha-Ḥodesh	29	29	1 **Tammuz** R. Ḥ.	2	3	5	5	**6** *Va-Yeẓe*	6
21	28	30 R. Ḥ.	28	30 R. Ḥ.	1 **Sivan** R. Ḥ.	2	3	**4** *Shofetim*	6	6	7	7
22	29	1 **Adar** R. Ḥ.	29	1 **Iyyar** R. Ḥ.	**2** *Be-Midbar*	3	4	5	7	7	8	8
23	**1** **Shevat** R. Ḥ. *Va-Era*	2	1 **Nisan** R. Ḥ.	2	3	4	5	6	8	**8** *Lekh Lekha*	9	9
24	2	3	2	**3** *Tazri'a Meẓora*	4	5	**6** *Devarim*	7	9	9	10	10 Fast
25	3	4	3	4	5	6	7	8	**10** Yom Kippur	10	11	**11** *Va-Yeḥi*
26	4	5	4	5 Yom ha-Aẓma'ut	**6** Shavuot	**7** *Ḥukkat*	8	9	11	11	12	12
27	5	**6** *Terumah*	**5** *Va-Yikra*	6	7	8	9 Tishah be-Av	10	12	12	**13** *Va-Yishlaḥ*	13
28	6	7	6	7	8	9	10	**11** *Ki Teẓe*	13	13	14	14
29	7		7	8	**9** *Naso*	10	11	12	14	14	15	15
30	**8** *Bo*		8	9	10	11	12	13	**15** Sukkot	**15** *Va-Yera*	16	16
31	9		9		11		**13** *Va-Etḥannan*	14		16		17

1994

5754/55 תשנ״ד / תשנ״ה

	January	February	March	April	May	June	July	August	September	October	November	December
1	18 Tevet Shemot	20	18	20 Ḥol ha-Mo'ed	20	22	22	24	25	26 Bereshit	27	28 4
2	19	21	19	21 Pesaḥ	21	23	23 Pinḥas	25	26	27	28	29 5
3	20	22	20	22	22	24	24	26	27 Niẓẓavim	28	29	30 R. Ḥ. Mi-Keẓ 6
4	21	23	21	23	23	25 Shelaḥ	25	27	28	29	1 Kislev R. Ḥ.	1 Tevet R. Ḥ. 7
5	22	24 Mishpatim	22 Va-Yakhel Parah	24	24	26	26	28	29	30 R. Ḥ.	2 Toledot	2 8
6	23	25	23	25	25	27	27	29 Re'eh	1 Tishri Rosh Ha-Shanah	1 Ḥeshvan R. Ḥ.	3	3
7	24	26	24	26	26 Be Har Be-Ḥukkotai	28	28	30 R. Ḥ.	2	2	4	4
8	25 Va-Era	27	25	27	27	29	29	1 Elul R. Ḥ.	3 Fast	3 No'aḥ	5	5
9	26	28	26	28 Shemini	28	30 R. Ḥ.	1 Av R. Ḥ. Mattot Masei	2	4	4	6	6
10	27	29	27	29	29	1 Tammuz R. Ḥ.	2	3	5 Va-Yelekh Shabbat Shuvah	5	7	7 Va-Yiggash
11	28	30 R. Ḥ.	28	30 R. Ḥ.	1 Sivan R. Ḥ.	2 Koraḥ	3	4	6	6	8	8
12	29	1 Adar R. Ḥ. Terumah Shekalim	29 Pekudei Ha-Ḥodesh	1 Iyyar R. Ḥ.	2	3	4	5	7	7	9 Va-Yeẓe	9
13	1 Shevat R. Ḥ.	2	1 Nisan R. Ḥ.	2	3	4	5	6 Shofetim	8	8	10	10 Fast
14	2	3	2	Yom ha-Aẓma'ut	4 Be-Midbar	5	6	7	9	9	11	11
15	3 Bo	4	3	4	5	6	7	8	10 Yom Kippur	10 Lekh Lekha	12	12
16	4	5	4	5 Tazri'a Meẓora	6 Shavuot	7	8 Devarim	9	11	11	13	13
17	5	6	5	6	7	8	9 Tishah be-Av	10	12 Ha'azinu	12	14	14 Va-Yeḥi
18	6	7	6	7	8	9 Ḥukkat	10	11	13	13	15	15
19	7	8 Teẓavveh Zakhor	7 Va-Yikra	8	9	10	11	12	14	14	16 Va-Yishlaḥ	16
20	8	9	8	9	10	11	12	13 Ki-Teẓe	15 Sukkot	15	17	17
21	9	10	9	10	11 Naso	12	13	14	16	16	18	18
22	10 Be-Shallaḥ	11	10	11	12	13	14	15	17 Ḥol ha-Moed	17 Va-Yera	19	19
23	11	12	11	12 Aḥarei Mot Kedoshim	13	14	15 Va-Etḥannan	16	18	18	20	20
24	12	13 Ta'anit Esther	12	13	14	15	16	17	19	19	21	21 Shemot
25	13	14 Purim	13	14	15	16 Balak	17	18	20	20	22	22
26	14	15 Ki Tissa Shushan Purim	14 Ẓav Shabbat ha-Gadol	15	16	17 Fast	18	19	21 Hoshana Rabba	21	23 Va-Yeshev	23
27	15	16	15 Pesaḥ	16	17	18	19	20 Ki-Tavo	22 Shemini Aẓeret	22	24	24
28	16	17	16 Omer	17	18 Be-Ha'alotkha	19	20	21	23 Simḥat Torah Ve-Zot Ha-Berakhah	23	25 Ḥanukkah 1	25
29	17 Yitro		17 Ḥol ha-Mo'ed	18 Lag ba-Omer	19	20	21	22	24	24 Ḥayyei Sarah	26 2	26
30	18		18	19 Emor	20	21	22 Ekev	23	25	25	27 3	27
31	19		19		21		23	24		26		28 Va-Era

1995

5755/56 תשנ״ה / תשנ״ו

	January	February	March	April	May	June	July	August	September	October	November	December
1	29 **Tevet**	1 **Adar I** R. Ḥ.	29	**1** R. Ḥ. **Nisan** *Tazri'a* Ha-Hodesh	1 **Iyyar** R. Ḥ.	3	**3** *Koraḥ*	5	6	7	8	8
2	1 **Shevat** R. Ḥ.	2	30 R. Ḥ.	2	2	4	4	6	**7** *Shofetim*	8	9	**9** *Va-Yeẓe*
3	2	3	1 **Adar II** R. Ḥ.	3	3	**5** *Be-Midbar*	5	7	8	9	10	10
4	3	**4** *Terumah*	**2** *Pekudei*	4	4 Yom ha-Aẓma'ut	**6** **Shavuot**	6	8	9	**10** **Yom Kippur**	**11** *Lekh Lekha*	11
5	4	5	3	5	5	**7**	7	**9** *Devarim* Tishah be-Av	10	11	12	12
6	5	6	4	6	**6** *Kedoshim*	8	8	10 Fast	11	12	13	13
7	**6** *Bo*	7	5	7	7	9	9	11	12	**13** *Ha'azinu*	14	14
8	7	8	6	**8** *Meẓora* Shabbat ha-Gadol	8	10	**10** *Ḥukkat*	12	13	14	15	15
9	8	9	7	9	9	11	11	13	**14** *Ki Teẓe*	**15** **Sukkot**	16	**16** *Va-Yishlaḥ*
10	9	10	8	10	10	**12** *Naso*	12	14	15	**16**	17	17
11	10	**11** *Teẓavveh*	**9** *Va-Yikra* Zakhor	11	11	13	13	15	16	17	**18** *Va-Yera*	18
12	11	12	10	12	12	14	14	**16** *Va-Etḥannan*	17	18 Ḥol ha-Mo'ed	19	19
13	12	13	11	13	**13** *Emor*	15	15	17	18	19	20	20
14	**13** *Be-Shallaḥ*	14	12	14	14	16	16	18	19	**20**	21	21
15	14	15	13 Ta'anit Esther	**15** **Pesaḥ**	15	17	**17** *Balak*	19	20	21 Hoshana Rabba	22	22
16	15	16	14 Purim	**16** Omer	16	18	18 Fast	20	**21** *Ki Tavo*	**22** **Shemini Aẓeret**	23	**23** *Va-Yeshev*
17	16	17	15 Shushan Purim	17	17	**19** *Be-Ha'alotkha*	19	21	22	**23** **Simḥat Torah** *Ve-Zot Ha-Berakhah*	24	24
18	17	**18** *Ki Tissa*	**16** *Ẓav*	18 Ḥol ha-Mo'ed	18 Lag ba-Omer	20	20	22	23	24	**25** *Ḥayyei Sarah*	25 Hanukkah 1
19	18	19	17	19	19	21	21	**23** *Ekev*	24	25	26	26 2
20	19	20	18	20	**20** *Be-Har*	22	22	24	25	26	27	27 3
21	**20** *Yitro*	21	19	21 **Pesaḥ**	21	23	23	25	26	**27** *Bereshit*	28	28 4
22	21	22	20	**22**	22	24	**24** *Pinḥas*	26	27	28	29	29 5
23	22	23	21	23	23	25	25	27	**28** *Nizzavim*	29	30 R. Ḥ.	**30** R. Ḥ. *Mi-Keẓ* 6
24	23	24	22	24	24	**26** *Shelaḥ*	26	28	29	30 R. Ḥ.	1 **Kislev** R. Ḥ.	1 **Tevet** R. Ḥ. 7
25	24	**25** *Va-Yakhel* Shekalim	**23** *Shemini* Parah	25	25	27	27	29	**1 Tishri** **Rosh Ha-Shanah**	1 **Heshvan** R. Ḥ.	**2** *Toledot*	2 8
26	25	26	24	26	26	28	28	**30** R. Ḥ. *Re'eh*	**2**	2	3	3
27	26	27	25	27	**27** *Be-Ḥukkotai*	29	29	1 **Elul** R. Ḥ.	3 Fast	3	4	4
28	**27** *Mishpatim*	28	26	28	28	30 R. Ḥ.	1 **Av** R. Ḥ.	2	4	**4** *No'aḥ*	5	5
29	28		27	**29** *Aḥarei Mot*	29	1 **Tammuz** R. Ḥ.	**2** *Mattot Masei*	3	5	5	6	6
30	29		28	30 R. Ḥ.	1 **Sivan** R. Ḥ.	2	3	4	**6** *Va-Yelekh* Shabbat Shuvah	6	7	**7** *Va-Yiggash*
31	30 R. Ḥ.		29		2		4	5		7		8

1996

5756/57 תשנ״ו / תשנ״ז

	January	February	March	April	May	June	July	August	September	October	November	December
1	9 **Tevet**	11	10	12	12	**14** *Naso*	14	16	17	18	19	20
2	10 Fast	12	**11** *Teẓavveh Zakhor*	13	13	15	15	17	18	19 Ḥol ha-Mo'ed	**20** *Va-Yera*	21
3	11	**13** *Be-Shallaḥ*	12	14	14	16	16	**18** *Ekev*	19	20	21	22
4	12	14	13 Ta'anit Esther	**15 Pesaḥ**	**15** *Emor*	17	17 Fast	19	20	21 Hoshana Rabba	22	23
5	13	15	14 Purim	**16 Omer**	16	18	18	20	21	**22 Shemini Aẓeret**	23	24
6	**14** *Va-Yeḥi*	16	15 Shushan Purim	**17** Ḥol ha-Mo'ed	17	19	**19** *Pinḥas*	21	22	**23 Simḥat Torah** *Ve-Zot ha-Berakhah*	24	25 Ḥanukkah 1
7	15	17	16	18	18 Lag ba-Omer	20	20	22	**23** *Niẓẓavim Va-Yelekh*	24	25	**26** *Va-Yeshev* 2
8	16	18	17	19	19	**21** *Be-Ha'alotkha*	21	23	24	25	26	27 3
9	17	19	**18** *Ki Tissa Parah*	20	20	22	22	24	25	26	**27** *Ḥayyei Sarah*	28 4
10	18	**20** *Yitro*	19	**21 Pesaḥ**	21	23	23	**25** *Re'eh*	26	27	28	29 5
11	19	21	20	**22**	**22** *Be-Har Be-Ḥukkotai*	24	24	26	27	28	29	1 **Tevet** R. Ḥ. 6
12	20	22	21	23	23	25	25	27	28	**29** *Bereshit*	1 **Kislev** R. Ḥ.	2 7
13	**21** *Shemot*	23	22	**24** *Shemini*	24	26	**26** *Mattot Masei*	28	29	30 R. Ḥ.	2	3 8
14	22	24	23	25	25	27	27	29	**1 Tishri Rosh Ha-Shanah**	1 **Ḥeshvan** R. Ḥ.	3	**4** *Mi-Keẓ*
15	23	25	24	26	26	**28** *Shelaḥ*	28	30 R. Ḥ.	**2**	2	4	5
16	24	26	**25** *Va-Yakhel-Pekudei* Ha-Ḥodesh	27	27	29	29	1 **Elul** R. Ḥ.	3 Fast	3	**5** *Toledot*	6
17	25	**27** *Mishpatim* Shekalim	26	28	28	30 R. Ḥ.	1 **Av** R. Ḥ.	**2** *Shofetim*	4	4	6	7
18	26	28	27	29	**29** *Be-Midbar*	1 **Tammuz** R. Ḥ.	2	3	5	5	7	8
19	27	29	28	30 R. Ḥ.	1 **Sivan** R. Ḥ.	2	3	4	6	**6** *No'aḥ*	8	9
20	**28** *Va-Era*	30 R. Ḥ.	29	**1 Iyyar** R. Ḥ. *Tazri'a Meẓora*	2	3	**4** *Devarim*	5	7	7	9	10 Fast
21	29	1 **Adar** R. Ḥ.	1 **Nisan** R. Ḥ.	2	3	4	5	6	**8** *Ha'azinu* Shabbat Shuvah	8	10	**11** *Va-Yiggash*
22	1 **Shevat** R. Ḥ.	2	2	3	4	**5** *Koraḥ*	6	7	9	9	11	12
23	2	3	**3** *Va-Yikra*	4	5	6	7	8	**10 Yom Kippur**	10	**12** *Va-Yeẓe*	13
24	3	**4** *Terumah*	4	5 Yom ha-Aẓma'ut	**6 Shavuot**	7	8	**9** *Ki Teẓe*	11	11	13	14
25	4	5	5	6	**7**	8	9 Tishah be-Av	10	12	12	14	15
26	5	6	6	7	8	9	10	11	13	**13** *Lekh Lekha*	15	16
27	**6** *Bo*	7	7	**8** *Aḥarei Mot Kedoshim*	9	10	**11** *Va-Etḥannan*	12	14	14	16	17
28	7	8	8	9	10	11	12	13	**15 Sukkot**	15	17	**18** *Va-Yeḥi*
29	8	9	9	10	11	**12** *Ḥukkat Balak*	13	14	**16**	16	18	19
30	9		**10** *Ẓav* Shabbat ha-Gadol	11	12	13	14	15	17 Ḥol ha-Mo'ed	17	**19** *Va-Yishlaḥ*	20
31	10		11		13		15	**16** *Ki Tavo*		18		21

1997

5757/58 תשנ״ז / תשנ״ח

	January	February	March	April	May	June	July	August	September	October	November	December
1	22 **Tevet**	**24** *Yitro*	**22** *Ki Tissa*	23	24	25	26	27	29	29	**1 Ḥeshvan** R. Ḥ. *No'aḥ*	2
2	23	25	23	24	25	26	27	**28** *Mattot Masei*	30 R. Ḥ.	**1 Tishri** Rosh Ha-Shanah	2	3
3	24	26	24	25	**26** *Aḥarei Mot*	27	28	29	1 **Elul** R. Ḥ.	2	3	4
4	**25** *Shemot*	27	25	26	27	28	29	1 **Av** R. Ḥ.	2	**3** *Ha'azinu* Shabbat Shuvah	4	5
5	26	28	26	**27** *Shemini* Ha-Ḥodesh	28	29	**30** R. Ḥ. *Koraḥ*	2	3	4 Fast	5	6
6	27	29	27	28	29	1 **Sivan** R. Ḥ.	1 **Tammuz** R. Ḥ.	3	**4** *Shofetim*	5	6	**7** *Va-Yeẓe*
7	28	30 R. Ḥ.	28	29	30 R. Ḥ.	**2** *Be-Midbar*	2	4	5	6	7	8
8	29	**1 Adar I** R. Ḥ. *Mishpatim*	**29** *Va-Yakhel* Shekalim	1 **Nisan** R. Ḥ.	1 **Iyyar** R. Ḥ.	3	3	5	6	7	**8** *Lekh Lekha*	9
9	1 **Shevat** R. Ḥ.	2	30 R. Ḥ.	2	2	4	4	**6** *Devarim*	7	8	9	10
10	2	3	1 **Adar II** R. Ḥ.	3	**3** *Kedoshim*	5	5	7	8	9	10	11
11	**3** *Va-Era*	4	2	4	4	6 Shavuot	6	8	9	**10** Yom Kippur	11	12
12	4	5	3	**5** *Tazri'a*	5 Yom ha-Aẓma'ut	**7**	**7** *Ḥukkat*	9 Tishah be-Av	10	11	12	13
13	5	6	4	6	6	8	8	10	**11** *Ki Teẓe*	12	13	**14** *Va-Yishlaḥ*
14	6	7	5	7	7	**9** *Naso*	9	11	12	13	14	15
15	7	**8** *Terumah*	**6** *Pekudei*	8	8	10	10	12	13	14	**15** *Va-Yera*	16
16	8	9	7	9	9	11	11	**13** *Va-Etḥannan*	14	15 Sukkot	16	17
17	9	10	8	10	**10** *Emor*	12	12	14	15	16	17	18
18	**10** *Bo*	11	9	11	11	13	13	15	16	**17**	18	19
19	11	12	10	**12** *Meẓora* Shabbat ha-Gadol	12	14	**14** *Balak*	16	17	18 Ḥol ha-Mo'ed	19	20
20	12	13	11 Ta'anit Esther	13	13	15	15	17	**18** *Ki Tavo*	19	20	**21** *Va-Yeshev*
21	13	14	12	14	14	**16** *Be-Ha'alotkha*	16	18	19	20	21	22
22	14	**15** *Teẓavveh*	**13** *Va-Yikra* Zakhor	15 Pesaḥ	15	17	17 Fast	19	20	21 Hoshana Rabba	**22** *Ḥayyei Sarah*	23
23	15	16	14 Purim	16 Omer	16	18	18	**20** *Ekev*	21	22 Shemini Aẓeret	23	24
24	16	17	15 Shushan Purim	17	**17** *Be-Har*	19	19	21	22	23 Simḥat Torah *Ve-Zot Ha-Berakhah*	24	25 Ḥanukkah 1
25	**17** *Be-Shallaḥ*	18	16	18 Ḥol ha-Mo'ed	18 Lag ba-Omer	20	20	22	23	**24** *Bereshit*	25	26 2
26	18	19	17	**19**	19	21	**21** *Pinḥas*	23	24	25	26	27 3
27	19	20	18	20	20	22	22	24	25 *Niẓẓavim Va-Yelekh*	26	27	**28** *Mi-Keẓ* 4
28	20	21	19	21 Pesaḥ	21	**23** *Shelaḥ*	23	25	26	27	28	29 5
29	21		**20** *Ẓav* Parah	22	22	24	24	26	27	28	**29** *Toledot*	30 R. Ḥ. 6
30	22		21	23	23	25	25	**27** *Re'eh*	28	29	1 **Kislev** R. Ḥ.	1 **Tevet** R. Ḥ. 7
31	23		22		**24** *Be-Ḥukkotai*		26	28		30 R. Ḥ.		2 8

1998

5758/59 תשנ"ח / תשנ"ט

	January	February	March	April	May	June	July	August	September	October	November	December
1	3 **Tevet**	5	3	5	5	7	7	**9** Tishah be-Av *Devarim*	10	11	12	12
2	4	6	4	6	**6** *Tazri'a Meẓora*	8	8	10 Fast	11	12	13	13
3	**5** *Va-Yiggash*	7	5	7	7	9	9	11	12	**13** *Ha'azinu*	14	14
4	6	8	6	**8** *Ẓav* Shabbat ha-Gadol	8	10	**10** *Ḥukkat*	12	13	14	15	15
5	7	9	7	9	9	11	11	13	**14** *Ki Teẓe*	15 Sukkot	16	**16** *Va-Yishlaḥ*
6	8	10	8	10	10	**12** *Naso*	12	14	15	16	17	17
7	9	**11** *Be-Shallaḥ*	**9** *Teẓavveh* Zakhor	11	11	13	13	15	16	17	**18** *Va-Yera*	18
8	10 Fast	12	10	12	12	14	14	**16** *Va-Etḥannan*	17	18	19	19
9	11	13	11	13	**13** *Aḥarei Mot Kedoshim*	15	15	17	18	19	20	20
10	**12** *Va-Yeḥi*	14	12	14	14	16	16	18	19	**20** Ḥol ha-Mo'ed	21	21
11	13	15	13 Ta'anit Esther	**15** Pesaḥ	15	17	**17** *Balak*	19	20	21 Hoshana Rabba	22	22
12	14	16	14 Purim	16 Omer	16	18	18 Fast	20	**21** *Ki Tavo*	22 Shemini Aẓeret	23	**23** *Va-Yeshev*
13	15	17	15 Shushan Purim	17	17	**19** *Be-Ha'alotkha*	19	21	22	23 Simḥat Torah *Ve-Zot Ha-Berakhah*	24	24
14	16	**18** *Yitro*	**16** *Ki Tissa*	18 Ḥol ha-Mo'ed	18 Lag ba-Omer	20	20	22	23	24	**25** *Ḥayyei Sarah*	25 Ḥanukkah 1
15	17	19	17	19	19	21	21	**23** *Ekev*	24	25	26	26 2
16	18	20	18	20	**20** *Emor*	22	22	24	25	26	27	27 3
17	**19** *Shemot*	21	19	21 Pesaḥ	21	23	23	25	26	**27** *Bereshit*	28	28 4
18	20	22	20	**22**	22	24	**24** *Pinḥas*	26	27	28	29	29 5
19	21	23	21	23	23	25	25	27	**28** *Niẓẓavim*	29	30 R. H.	**30** R. H. *Mi-Keẓ* 6
20	22	24	22	24	24	**26** *Shelaḥ*	26	28	29	30 R. H.	1 **Kislev** R. H.	1 **Tevet** R. H. 7
21	23	**25** *Mishpatim* Shekalim	**23** *Va-Yakhel Pekudei* Parah	25	25	27	27	29	1 **Tishri** Rosh Ha-Shanah	1 **Heshvan** R. H.	**2** *Toledot*	2 8
22	24	26	24	26	26	28	28	**30** R. H. *Re'eh*	2	2	3	3
23	25	27	25	27	**27** *Be-Har Be-Ḥukkotai*	29	29	1 **Elul** R. H.	3 Fast	3	4	4
24	**26** *Va-Era*	28	26	28	28	30 R. H.	1 **Av** R. H.	2	4	**4** *No'aḥ*	5	5
25	27	29	27	**29** *Shemini*	29	1 **Tammuz** R. H.	**2** *Mattot Masei*	3	5	5	6	6
26	28	30 R. H.	28	30 R. H.	1 **Sivan** R. H.	2	3	4	**6** *Va-Yelekh* Shabbat Shuvah	6	7	**7** *Va-Yiggash*
27	29	1 **Adar** R. H.	29	1 **Iyyar** R. H.	2	**3** *Koraḥ*	4	5	7	7	8	8
28	1 **Shevat** R. H.	**2** *Terumah*	**1** R. H. *Va-Yikra* **Nisan** Ha-Hodesh	2	3	4	5	6	8	8	**9** *Va-Yeẓe*	9
29	2		2	3	4	5	6	**7** *Shofetim*	9	9	10	10 Fast
30	3		3	4 Yom ha-Aẓma'ut	**5** *Be-Midbar*	6	7	8	**10** Yom Kippur	10	11	11
31	**4** *Bo*		4		**6** Shavuot		8	9		**11** *Lekh Lekha*		12

1999

5759/60 תשנ״ט / תש״ס

	January	February	March	April	May	June	July	August	September	October	November	December
1	13 **Tevet**	15	13 Ta'anit Esther	**15** Pesaḥ	**15** *Emor*	17	17 Fast	19	20	21 Hoshana Rabba	22	22
2	**14** *Va-Yeḥi*	16	14 Purim	**16** Omer	16	18	18	20	21	**22** Shemini Aẓeret	23	23
3	15	17	15 Shushan Purim	**17** Ḥol ha-Mo'ed	17	19	**19** *Pinḥas*	21	22	23 Simḥat Torah *Ve-Zot Ha-Berakhah*	24	24
4	16	18	16	18	18 Lag ba-Omer	20	20	22	**23** *Niẓẓavim Va-Yelekh*	24	25	**25** *Va-Yeshev* Hanukkah 1
5	17	19	17	19	19	**21** *Be-Ha'alotkha*	21	23	24	25	26	26 2
6	18	**20** *Yitro*	**18** *Ki Tissa* Parah	20	20	22	22	24	25	26	**27** *Ḥayyei Sarah*	27 3
7	19	21	19	**21** Pesaḥ	21	23	23	**25** *Re'eh*	26	27	28	28 4
8	20	22	20	**22**	**22** *Be-Har Be-Ḥukkotai*	24	24	26	27	28	29	29 5
9	**21** *Shemot*	23	21	23	23	25	25	27	28	**29** *Bereshit*	30 R. H.	30 R. H. 6
10	22	24	22	**24** *Shemini*	24	26	**26** *Mattot Masei*	28	29	30 R. H.	1 **Kislev** R. H.	1 **Tevet** R. H. 7
11	23	25	23	25	25	27	27	29	**1 Tishri** Rosh Ha-Shanah	1 **Ḥeshvan** R. H.	2	**2** *Mi-Keẓ* 8
12	24	26	24	26	26	**28** *Shelaḥ*	28	30 R. H.	2	2	3	3
13	25	**27** *Mishpatim* Shekalim	**25** *Va-Yakhel Pekudei* Ha-Ḥodesh	27	27	29	29	1 **Elul** R. H.	3 Fast	3	**4** *Toledot*	4
14	26	28	26	28	28	30 R. H.	1 **Av** R. H.	**2** *Shofetim*	4	4	5	5
15	27	29	27	29	**29** *Be-Midbar*	1 **Tammuz** R. H.	2	3	5	5	6	6
16	**28** *Va-Era*	30 R. H.	28	30 R. H.	1 **Sivan** R. H.	2	3	4	6	**6** *No'aḥ*	7	7
17	29	1 **Adar** R. H.	29	**1 Iyyar** R. H. *Tazri'a Meẓora*	2	3	**4** *Devarim*	5	7	7	8	8
18	1 **Shevat** R. H.	2	1 **Nisan** R. H.	2	3	4	5	6	**8** *Ha'azinu* Shabbat Shuvah	8	9	**9** *Va-Yiggash*
19	2	3	2	3	4	**5** *Koraḥ*	6	7	9	9	10	10 Fast
20	3	**4** *Terumah*	**3** *Va-Yikra*	4	5	6	7	8	**10** Yom Kippur	10	**11** *Va-Yeẓe*	11
21	4	5	4	5 Yom ha-Aẓma'ut	**6** Shavuot	7	8	**9** *Ki Teẓe*	11	11	12	12
22	5	6	5	6	**7**	8	9 Tishah be-Av	10	12	12	13	13
23	**6** *Bo*	7	6	7	8	9	10	11	13	**13** *Lekh Lekha*	14	14
24	7	8	7	**8** *Aḥarei Mot Kedoshim*	9	10	**11** *Va-Etḥannan*	12	14	14	15	15
25	8	9	8	9	10	11	12	13	**15** Sukkot	15	16	**16** *Va-Yeḥi*
26	9	10	9	10	11	**12** *Ḥukkat Balak*	13	14	**16**	16	17	17
27	10	**11** *Teẓavveh* Zakhor	**10** *Ẓav* Shabbat ha-Gadol	11	12	13	14	15	17 Ḥol ha-Mo'ed	17	**18** *Va-Yishlaḥ*	18
28	11	12	11	12	13	14	15	**16** *Ki Tavo*	18	18	19	19
29	12		12	13	**14** *Naso*	15	16	17	19	19	20	20
30	**13** *Be-Shallaḥ*		13	14	15	16	17	18	20	**20** *Va-Yera*	21	21
31	14		14		16		**18** *Ekev*	19		21		22

2000

5760/61 תש״ס / תשס״א

	January	February	March	April	May	June	July	August	September	October	November	December
1	**23** Tevet *Shemot*	25	24	**25** *Shemini* Ha-Ḥodesh	26	27	**28** *Shelaḥ*	29	1 Elul R. Ḥ.	2 Rosh Ha-Shanah	3	4
2	24	26	25	26	27	28	29	1 Av R. Ḥ.	**2** *Shofetim*	3 Fast	4	**5** *Toledot*
3	25	27	26	27	28	**29** *Be-Midbar*	30 R. Ḥ.	2	3	4	5	6
4	26	28	**27** *Va-Yakhel* Shekalim	28	29	1 Sivan R. Ḥ.	1 Tammuz R. Ḥ.	3	4	5	**6** *No'aḥ*	7
5	27	**29** *Mishpatim*	28	29	30 R. Ḥ.	2	2	**4** *Devarim*	5	6	7	8
6	28	30 R. Ḥ.	29	1 Nisan R. Ḥ.	**1** Iyyar R. Ḥ. *Kedoshim*	3	3	5	6	7	8	9
7	29	1 Adar I R. Ḥ.	30 R. Ḥ.	2	2	4	4	6	7	**8** *Ha'azinu* Shabbat Shuvah	9	10
8	**1** Shevat R. Ḥ. *Va-Era*	2	1 Adar II R. Ḥ.	**3** *Tazri'a*	3	5	**5** *Koraḥ*	7	8	9	10	11
9	2	3	2	4	4	6 Shavuot	6	8	**9** *Ki Teẓe*	10 Yom Kippur	11	**12** *Va-Yeẓe*
10	3	4	3	5	5 Yom ha-Aẓma'ut	7	7	9 Tishah be-Av	10	11	12	13
11	4	5	**4** *Pekudei*	6	6	8	8	10	11	12	**13** *Lekh Lekha*	14
12	5	**6** *Terumah*	5	7	7	9	9	**11** *Va-Etḥannan*	12	13	14	15
13	6	7	6	8	**8** *Emor*	10	10	12	13	14	15	16
14	7	8	7	9	9	11	11	13	14	15 Sukkot	16	17
15	**8** *Bo*	9	8	**10** *Meẓora* Shabbat ha-Gadol	10	12	**12** *Ḥukkat Balak*	14	15	16	17	18
16	9	10	9	11	11	13	13	15	**16** *Ki Tavo*	17	18	**19** *Va-Yishlaḥ*
17	10	11	10	12	12	**14** *Naso*	14	16	17	18	19	20
18	11	12	**11** *Va-Yikra* Zakhor	13	13	15	15	17	18	19 Ḥol ha-Mo'ed	**20** *Va-Yera*	21
19	12	**13** *Teẓavveh*	12	14	14	16	16	**18** *Ekev*	19	20	21	22
20	13	14	13 Ta'anit Esther	15 Pesaḥ	**15** *Be-Har*	17	17 Fast	19	20	21 Hoshana Rabba	22	23
21	14	15	14 Purim	16 Omer	16	18	18	20	21	22 Shemini Aẓeret	23	24
22	**15** *Be-Shallaḥ*	16	15 Shushan Purim	17	17	19	**19** *Pinḥas*	21	22	23 Simḥat Torah Ve-Zot Ha-Berakhah	24	25 Ḥanukkah 1
23	16	17	16	18 Ḥol ha-Mo'ed	18 Lag ba-Omer	20	20	22	**23** *Niẓẓavim Va-Yelekh*	24	25	**26** *Va-Yeshev* 2
24	17	18	17	19	19	**21** *Be-Ha'alotkha*	21	23	24	25	26	27 3
25	18	19	**18** *Ẓav* Parah	20	20	22	22	24	25	26	**27** *Ḥayyei Sarah*	28 4
26	19	**20** *Ki Tissa*	19	21 Pesaḥ	21	23	23	**25** *Re'eh*	26	27	28	29 5
27	20	21	20	22	**22** *Be-Ḥukkotai*	24	24	26	27	28	29	1 Tevet R. Ḥ. 6
28	21	22	21	23	23	25	25	27	28	**29** *Bereshit*	1 Kislev R. Ḥ.	2 7
29	**22** *Yitro*	23	22	**24** *Aḥarei Mot*	24	26	**26** *Mattot Masei*	28	29	30 R. Ḥ.	2	3 8
30	23		23	25	25	27	27	29	1 Tishri Rosh Ha-Shanah	1 Ḥeshvan R. Ḥ.	3	**4** *Mi-Keẓ*
31	24		24		26		28	30 R. Ḥ.		2		5

2001

5761/62 תשס״א / תשס״ב

	January	February	March	April	May	June	July	August	September	October	November	December
1	6 **Tevet**	8	6	8	8	10	10	12	**13** *Ki Teẓe*	14	15	**16** *Va-Yishlaḥ*
2	7	9	7	9	9	**11** *Naso*	11	13	14	**15** Sukkot	16	17
3	8	**10** *Bo*	**8** *Terumah* Zakhor	10	10	12	12	14	15	**16**	**17** *Va-Yera*	18
4	9	11	9	11	11	13	13	**15** *Va-Etḥannan*	16	17 Ḥol ha-Mo'ed	18	19
5	10 Fast	12	10	12	**12** *Aḥarei Mot Kedoshim*	14	14	16	17	18	19	20
6	**11** *Va-Yiggash*	13	11	13	13	15	15	17	18	**19**	20	21
7	12	14	12	**14** *Ẓav* Shabbat ha-Gadol	14	16	**16** *Balak*	18	19	20	21	22
8	13	15	13 Ta'anit Esther	**15** Pesaḥ	15	17	17 Fast	19	**20** *Ki Tavo*	21 Hoshana Rabba	22	**23** *Va-Yeshev*
9	14	16	14 Purim	**16** Omer	16	**18** *Be-Ha'alotkha*	18	20	21	**22** Shemini Aẓeret	23	24
10	15	**17** *Be-Shallaḥ*	**15** *Teẓavveh* Shushan Purim	17	17	19	19	21	22	**23** Simḥat Torah *Ve-Zot Ha-Berakhah*	**24** *Ḥayyei Sarah*	25 1
11	16	18	16	18 Ḥol ha-Mo'ed	18 Lag ba-Omer	20	20	**22** *Ekev*	23	24	25	26 2
12	17	19	17	19	**19** *Emor*	21	21	23	24	25	26	27 3
13	**18** *Va-Yeḥi*	20	18	20	20	22	22	24	25	**26** *Bereshit*	27	28 4
14	19	21	19	**21** Pesaḥ	21	23	**23** *Pinḥas*	25	26	27	28	29 5
15	20	22	20	**22**	22	24	24	26	**27** *Niẓẓavim*	28	29	**30** R. H. *Mi-Keẓ* 6
16	21	23	21	23	23	**25** *Shelaḥ*	25	27	28	29	1 **Kislev** R. H.	1 **Tevet** R. H. 7
17	22	**24** *Yitro*	**22** *Ki Tissa* Parah	24	24	26	26	28	29	30 R. H.	**2** *Toledot*	2 8
18	23	25	23	25	25	27	27	**29** *Re'eh*	**1 Tishri** **Rosh Ha-Shanah**	1 **Ḥeshvan** R. H.	3	3
19	24	26	24	26	**26** *Be-Har Be-Ḥukkotai*	28	28	30 R. H.	**2**	2	4	4
20	**25** *Shemot*	27	25	27	27	29	29	1 **Elul** R. H.	3 Fast	**3** *No'aḥ*	5	5
21	26	28	26	**28** *Shemini*	28	30 R. H.	**1 Av** R. H. *Mattot Masei*	2	4	4	6	6
22	27	29	27	29	29	1 **Tammuz** R. H.	2	3	**5** *Va-Yelekh* Shabbat Shuvah	5	7	**7** *Va-Yiggash*
23	28	30 R. H.	28	30 R. H.	1 **Sivan** R. H.	**2** *Koraḥ*	3	4	6	6	8	8
24	29	**1 Adar** R. H. *Mishpatim* Shekalim	**29** *Va-Yakhel Pekudei* Ha-Ḥodesh	1 **Iyyar** R. H.	2	3	4	5	7	7	**9** *Va-Yeẓe*	9
25	1 **Shevat** R. H.	2	1 **Nisan** R. H.	2	3	4	5	**6** *Shofetim*	8	8	10	10 Fast
26	2	3	2	3 Yom ha-Aẓma'ut	**4** *Be-Midbar*	5	6	7	9	9	11	11
27	**3** *Va-Era*	4	3	4	5	6	7	8	**10** Yom Kippur	**10** *Lekh Lekha*	12	12
28	4	5	4	**5** *Tazri'a Meẓora*	**6** Shavuot	7	**8** *Devarim*	9	11	11	13	13
29	5		5	6	**7**	8	9 Tishah be-Av	10	**12** *Ha'azinu*	12	14	**14** *Va-Yeḥi*
30	6		6	7	8	**9** *Ḥukkat*	10	11	13	13	15	15
31	7		**7** *Va-Yikra*		9		11	12		14		16

Candle Lighting Times

ATLANTA, GEORGIA

DAY	JAN.	FEB.	MAR.	APR.	MAY	JUNE	JULY	AUG.	SEPT.	OCT.	NOV.	DEC.
1	5:22 P.M.	5:51	6:16	6:40	7:03	7:25	7:34	7:20	6:46	6:04	5:28	5:11
2	5:23	5:52	6:17	6:41	7:03	7:25	7:34	7:19	6:44	6:03	5:27	5:11
3	5:24	5:53	6:18	6:42	7:04	7:26	7:34	7:18	6:43	6:02	5:26	5:11
4	5:25	5:54	6:19	6:42	7:05	7:26	7:34	7:17	6:42	6:00	5:25	5:11
5	5:25	5:55	6:19	6:43	7:06	7:27	7:34	7:16	6:40	5:59	5:24	5:11
6	5:26	5:55	6:20	6:44	7:06	7:27	7:33	7:16	6:39	5:58	5:23	5:11
7	5:27	5:56	6:21	6:44	7:07	7:28	7:33	7:15	6:38	5:56	5:23	5:11
8	5:28	5:57	6:22	6:45	7:08	7:28	7:33	7:14	6:36	5:55	5:22	5:11
9	5:29	5:58	6:23	6:46	7:09	7:29	7:33	7:13	6:35	5:54	5:21	5:11
10	5:30	5:59	6:23	6:47	7:09	7:29	7:32	7:12	6:33	5:53	5:20	5:12
11	5:31	6:00	6:24	6:47	7:10	7:30	7:32	7:11	6:32	5:51	5:20	5:12
12	5:31	6:01	6:25	6:48	7:11	7:30	7:32	7:10	6:31	5:50	5:19	5:12
13	5:32	6:02	6:26	6:49	7:12	7:31	7:32	7:08	6:29	5:49	5:18	5:12
14	5:33	6:03	6:27	6:50	7:12	7:31	7:31	7:07	6:28	5:48	5:18	5:13
15	5:34	6:04	6:27	6:50	7:13	7:31	7:31	7:06	6:27	5:46	5:17	5:13
16	5:35	6:05	6:28	6:51	7:14	7:32	7:30	7:05	6:25	5:45	5:16	5:13
17	5:36	6:06	6:29	6:52	7:15	7:32	7:30	7:04	6:24	5:44	5:16	5:14
18	5:37	6:07	6:30	6:53	7:15	7:32	7:29	7:03	6:22	5:43	5:15	5:14
19	5:38	6:08	6:30	6:53	7:16	7:33	7:29	7:02	6:21	5:42	5:15	5:14
20	5:39	6:08	6:31	6:54	7:17	7:33	7:28	7:01	6:20	5:40	5:14	5:15
21	5:40	6:09	6:32	6:55	7:17	7:33	7:28	6:59	6:18	5:39	5:14	5:15
22	5:41	6:10	6:33	6:56	7:18	7:33	7:27	6:58	6:17	5:38	5:14	5:16
23	5:42	6:11	6:33	6:56	7:19	7:33	7:27	6:57	6:15	5:37	5:13	5:16
24	5:43	6:12	6:34	6:57	7:20	7:34	7:26	6:56	6:14	5:36	5:13	5:17
25	5:44	6:13	6:35	6:58	7:20	7:34	7:25	6:54	6:13	5:35	5:13	5:17
26	5:45	6:14	6:36	6:59	7:21	7:34	7:25	6:53	6:11	5:34	5:12	5:18
27	5:46	6:14	6:36	7:00	7:22	7:34	7:24	6:52	6:10	5:33	5:12	5:19
28	5:47	6:15	6:37	7:00	7:22	7:34	7:23	6:51	6:09	5:32	5:12	5:19
29	5:48	6:16	6:38	7:01	7:23	7:34	7:22	6:49	6:07	5:31	5:12	5:20
30	5:49		6:39	7:02	7:23	7:34	7:22	6:48	6:06	5:30	5:11	5:21
31	5:50		6:39		7:24		7:21	6:47		5:29		5:21

BALTIMORE, MARYLAND

DAY	JAN.	FEB.	MAR.	APR.	MAY	JUNE	JULY	AUG.	SEPT.	OCT.	NOV.	DEC.
1	4:36 P.M.	5:09	5:41	6:12	6:41	7:09	7:19	7:01	6:20	5:32	4:48	4:26
2	4:37	5:10	5:42	6:13	6:42	7:09	7:19	7:00	6:18	5:30	4:47	4:26
3	4:38	5:12	5:43	6:14	6:43	7:10	7:19	6:59	6:17	5:29	4:46	4:26
4	4:39	5:13	5:44	6:15	6:44	7:11	7:18	6:58	6:15	5:27	4:45	4:26
5	4:40	5:14	5:45	6:16	6:45	7:11	7:18	6:56	6:14	5:25	4:44	4:26
6	4:41	5:15	5:46	6:17	6:46	7:12	7:18	6:55	6:12	5:24	4:43	4:26
7	4:42	5:16	5:47	6:18	6:47	7:13	7:18	6:54	6:10	5:22	4:42	4:26
8	4:43	5:17	5:48	6:19	6:48	7:13	7:17	6:53	6:09	5:21	4:41	4:26
9	4:44	5:19	5:49	6:20	6:49	7:14	7:17	6:52	6:07	5:19	4:40	4:26
10	4:45	5:20	5:50	6:21	6:50	7:14	7:17	6:51	6:06	5:18	4:39	4:26
11	4:46	5:21	5:51	6:22	6:51	7:15	7:16	6:49	6:04	5:16	4:38	4:26
12	4:47	5:22	5:52	6:23	6:52	7:15	7:16	6:48	6:02	5:15	4:37	4:26
13	4:48	5:23	5:53	6:24	6:53	7:16	7:15	6:47	6:01	5:13	4:36	4:26
14	4:49	5:24	5:54	6:25	6:54	7:16	7:15	6:46	5:59	5:12	4:35	4:26
15	4:50	5:26	5:55	6:26	6:55	7:16	7:14	6:44	5:58	5:10	4:34	4:27
16	4:51	5:27	5:56	6:27	6:56	7:17	7:14	6:43	5:56	5:09	4:34	4:27
17	4:52	5:28	5:57	6:28	6:57	7:17	7:13	6:42	5:54	5:07	4:33	4:27
18	4:53	5:29	5:58	6:29	6:57	7:17	7:12	6:40	5:53	5:06	4:32	4:28
19	4:54	5:30	5:59	6:30	6:58	7:18	7:12	6:39	5:51	5:05	4:32	4:28
20	4:55	5:31	6:00	6:31	6:59	7:18	7:11	6:37	5:49	5:03	4:31	4:29
21	4:57	5:32	6:01	6:32	7:00	7:18	7:10	6:36	5:48	5:02	4:30	4:29
22	4:58	5:33	6:02	6:33	7:01	7:18	7:10	6:35	5:46	5:01	4:30	4:30
23	4:59	5:34	6:03	6:34	7:02	7:19	7:09	6:33	5:45	4:59	4:29	4:30
24	5:00	5:36	6:04	6:35	7:03	7:19	7:08	6:32	5:43	4:58	4:29	4:31
25	5:01	5:37	6:05	6:36	7:03	7:19	7:07	6:30	5:41	4:57	4:28	4:31
26	5:02	5:38	6:06	6:37	7:04	7:19	7:06	6:29	5:40	4:55	4:28	4:32
27	5:03	5:39	6:07	6:38	7:05	7:19	7:06	6:27	5:38	4:54	4:28	4:33
28	5:05	5:40	6:08	6:39	7:06	7:19	7:05	6:26	5:37	4:53	4:27	4:33
29	5:06	5:41	6:09	6:40	7:07	7:19	7:04	6:24	5:35	4:52	4:27	4:34
30	5:07		6:10	6:40	7:07	7:19	7:03	6:23	5:33	4:50	4:27	4:35
31	5:08		6:11		7:08		7:02	6:21		4:49		4:35

BOSTON, MASSACHUSETTS

DAY	JAN.	FEB.	MAR.	APR.	MAY	JUNE	JULY	AUG.	SEPT.	OCT.	NOV.	DEC.
1	4:04 P.M.	4:40	5:16	5:52	6:26	6:56	7:07	6:46	6:01	5:08	4:20	3:55
2	4:05	4:41	5:17	5:53	6:27	6:57	7:07	6:45	5:59	5:07	4:19	3:55
3	4:06	4:43	5:18	5:54	6:28	6:58	7:06	6:44	5:57	5:05	4:17	3:54
4	4:07	4:44	5:20	5:55	6:29	6:58	7:06	6:42	5:56	5:03	4:16	3:54
5	4:08	4:45	5:21	5:56	6:30	6:59	7:06	6:41	5:54	5:01	4:15	3:54
6	4:09	4:47	5:22	5:57	6:31	7:00	7:06	6:40	5:52	5:00	4:14	3:54
7	4:10	4:48	5:23	5:59	6:32	7:00	7:05	6:39	5:50	4:58	4:13	3:54
8	4:11	4:49	5:24	6:00	6:33	7:01	7:05	6:37	5:49	4:56	4:12	3:54
9	4:12	4:51	5:25	6:01	6:34	7:02	7:05	6:36	5:47	4:55	4:10	3:54
10	4:13	4:52	5:27	6:02	6:35	7:02	7:04	6:35	5:45	4:53	4:09	3:54
11	4:14	4:53	5:28	6:03	6:36	7:03	7:04	6:33	5:43	4:51	4:08	3:54
12	4:15	4:54	5:29	6:04	6:37	7:03	7:03	6:32	5:42	4:50	4:07	3:54
13	4:16	4:56	5:30	6:05	6:39	7:04	7:03	6:31	5:40	4:48	4:06	3:54
14	4:18	4:57	5:31	6:06	6:40	7:04	7:02	6:29	5:38	4:46	4:05	3:54
15	4:19	4:58	5:32	6:08	6:41	7:05	7:01	6:28	5:36	4:45	4:05	3:54
16	4:20	5:00	5:34	6:09	6:42	7:05	7:01	6:26	5:35	4:43	4:04	3:55
17	4:21	5:01	5:35	6:10	6:43	7:05	7:00	6:25	5:33	4:42	4:03	3:55
18	4:22	5:02	5:36	6:11	6:44	7:06	6:59	6:23	5:31	4:40	4:02	3:55
19	4:24	5:03	5:37	6:12	6:45	7:06	6:59	6:22	5:29	4:38	4:01	3:56
20	4:25	5:05	5:38	6:13	6:46	7:06	6:58	6:20	5:28	4:37	4:01	3:56
21	4:26	5:06	5:39	6:14	6:47	7:06	6:57	6:19	5:26	4:35	4:00	3:57
22	4:27	5:07	5:41	6:15	6:48	7:07	6:56	6:17	5:24	4:34	3:59	3:57
23	4:29	5:08	5:42	6:17	6:49	7:07	6:55	6:15	5:22	4:32	3:59	3:58
24	4:30	5:10	5:43	6:18	6:49	7:07	6:54	6:14	5:21	4:31	3:58	3:58
25	4:31	5:11	5:44	6:19	6:50	7:07	6:53	6:12	5:19	4:30	3:57	3:59
26	4:32	5:12	5:45	6:20	6:51	7:07	6:52	6:11	5:17	4:28	3:57	4:00
27	4:34	5:13	5:46	6:21	6:52	7:07	6:51	6:09	5:15	4:27	3:56	4:00
28	4:35	5:15	5:47	6:22	6:53	7:07	6:50	6:07	5:13	4:25	3:56	4:01
29	4:36	5:16	5:48	6:23	6:54	7:07	6:49	6:06	5:12	4:24	3:56	4:02
30	4:38		5:50	6:24	6:55	7:07	6:48	6:04	5:10	4:23	3:55	4:02
31	4:39		5:51		6:55		6:47	6:02		4:21		4:03

CHICAGO, ILLINOIS

DAY	JAN.	FEB.	MAR.	APR.	MAY	JUNE	JULY	AUG.	SEPT.	OCT.	NOV.	DEC.
1	4:13 P.M.	4:48	5:23	5:58	6:30	7:00	7:11	6:51	6:06	5:15	4:27	4:03
2	4:13	4:49	5:24	5:59	6:31	7:01	7:11	6:50	6:05	5:13	4:26	4:03
3	4:14	4:50	5:25	6:00	6:33	7:02	7:11	6:48	6:03	5:11	4:25	4:02
4	4:15	4:52	5:26	6:01	6:34	7:03	7:10	6:47	6:01	5:10	4:24	4:02
5	4:16	4:53	5:27	6:02	6:35	7:03	7:10	6:46	6:00	5:08	4:23	4:02
6	4:17	4:54	5:29	6:03	6:36	7:04	7:10	6:45	5:58	5:06	4:21	4:02
7	4:18	4:55	5:30	6:04	6:37	7:05	7:09	6:44	5:56	5:05	4:20	4:02
8	4:19	4:57	5:31	6:05	6:38	7:05	7:09	6:42	5:55	5:03	4:19	4:02
9	4:20	4:58	5:32	6:06	6:39	7:06	7:09	6:41	5:53	5:01	4:18	4:02
10	4:21	4:59	5:33	6:07	6:40	7:06	7:08	6:40	5:51	5:00	4:17	4:02
11	4:22	5:01	5:34	6:09	6:41	7:07	7:08	6:38	5:49	4:58	4:16	4:02
12	4:23	5:02	5:35	6:10	6:42	7:07	7:07	6:37	5:48	4:57	4:15	4:02
13	4:25	5:03	5:37	6:11	6:43	7:08	7:07	6:36	5:46	4:55	4:14	4:02
14	4:26	5:04	5:38	6:12	6:44	7:08	7:06	6:34	5:44	4:53	4:13	4:03
15	4:27	5:06	5:39	6:13	6:45	7:09	7:06	6:33	5:42	4:52	4:12	4:03
16	4:28	5:07	5:40	6:14	6:46	7:09	7:05	6:31	5:41	4:50	4:12	4:03
17	4:29	5:08	5:41	6:15	6:47	7:09	7:04	6:30	5:39	4:49	4:11	4:03
18	4:30	5:09	5:42	6:16	6:48	7:10	7:04	6:28	5:37	4:47	4:10	4:04
19	4:32	5:11	5:43	6:17	6:49	7:10	7:03	6:27	5:36	4:46	4:09	4:04
20	4:33	5:12	5:44	6:18	6:50	7:10	7:02	6:25	5:34	4:44	4:09	4:05
21	4:34	5:13	5:46	6:19	6:51	7:11	7:01	6:24	5:32	4:43	4:08	4:05
22	4:35	5:14	5:47	6:21	6:52	7:11	7:01	6:22	5:30	4:41	4:07	4:06
23	4:36	5:15	5:48	6:22	6:53	7:11	7:00	6:21	5:29	4:40	4:07	4:06
24	4:38	5:17	5:49	6:23	6:54	7:11	6:59	6:19	5:27	4:38	4:06	4:07
25	4:39	5:18	5:50	6:24	6:55	7:11	6:58	6:18	5:25	4:37	4:05	4:07
26	4:40	5:19	5:51	6:25	6:56	7:11	6:57	6:16	5:23	4:35	4:05	4:08
27	4:41	5:20	5:52	6:26	6:56	7:11	6:56	6:15	5:22	4:34	4:04	4:09
28	4:43	5:21	5:53	6:27	6:57	7:11	6:55	6:13	5:20	4:33	4:04	4:09
29	4:44	5:22	5:54	6:28	6:58	7:11	6:54	6:11	5:18	4:31	4:04	4:10
30	4:45		5:55	6:29	6:59	7:11	6:53	6:10	5:17	4:30	4:03	4:11
31	4:46		5:57		7:00		6:52	6:08		4:29		4:12

CINCINNATI, OHIO

DAY	JAN.	FEB.	MAR.	APR.	MAY	JUNE	JULY	AUG.	SEPT.	OCT.	NOV.	DEC.
1	5:08 P.M.	5:41	6:12	6:43	7:13	7:40	7:50	7:32	6:51	6:03	5:20	4:58
2	5:09	5:42	6:13	6:44	7:14	7:41	7:50	7:31	6:50	6:02	5:18	4:58
3	5:10	5:43	6:14	6:45	7:15	7:41	7:50	7:30	6:48	6:00	5:17	4:58
4	5:11	5:44	6:16	6:46	7:16	7:42	7:49	7:29	6:46	5:58	5:16	4:57
5	5:12	5:45	6:17	6:47	7:17	7:43	7:49	7:28	6:45	5:57	5:15	4:57
6	5:12	5:47	6:18	6:48	7:17	7:43	7:49	7:27	6:43	5:55	5:14	4:57
7	5:13	5:48	6:19	6:49	7:18	7:44	7:49	7:25	6:42	5:54	5:13	4:57
8	5:14	5:49	6:20	6:50	7:19	7:44	7:48	7:24	6:40	5:52	5:12	4:57
9	5:15	5:50	6:21	6:51	7:20	7:45	7:48	7:23	6:39	5:51	5:11	4:57
10	5:16	5:51	6:22	6:52	7:21	7:45	7:48	7:22	6:39	5:49	5:10	4:57
11	5:17	5:52	6:23	6:53	7:22	7:46	7:47	7:21	6:35	5:48	5:09	4:58
12	5:18	5:54	6:24	6:54	7:23	7:46	7:47	7:19	6:34	5:46	5:09	4:58
13	5:19	5:55	6:25	6:55	7:24	7:47	7:46	7:18	6:32	5:45	5:08	4:58
14	5:20	5:56	6:26	6:56	7:25	7:47	7:46	7:17	6:31	5:43	5:07	4:58
15	5:21	5:57	6:27	6:57	7:26	7:48	7:45	7:16	6:29	5:42	5:06	4:58
16	5:23	5:58	6:28	6:58	7:27	7:48	7:45	7:14	6:27	5:40	5:05	4:59
17	5:24	5:59	6:29	6:59	7:28	7:48	7:44	7:13	6:26	5:39	5:05	4:59
18	5:25	6:00	6:30	7:00	7:29	7:49	7:44	7:12	6:24	5:38	5:04	4:59
19	5:26	6:01	6:31	7:01	7:30	7:49	7:43	7:10	6:22	5:36	5:03	5:00
20	5:27	6:03	6:32	7:02	7:30	7:49	7:42	7:09	6:21	5:35	5:03	5:00
21	5:28	6:04	6:33	7:03	7:31	7:49	7:42	7:07	6:19	5:33	5:02	5:01
22	5:29	6:05	6:34	7:04	7:32	7:50	7:41	7:06	6:18	5:32	5:01	5:01
23	5:30	6:06	6:35	7:05	7:33	7:50	7:40	7:04	6:16	5:31	5:01	5:02
24	5:32	6:07	6:36	7:06	7:34	7:50	7:39	7:03	6:14	5:29	5:00	5:02
25	5:33	6:08	6:37	7:07	7:35	7:50	7:38	7:02	6:13	5:28	5:00	5:03
26	5:34	6:09	6:38	7:08	7:35	7:50	7:38	7:00	6:11	5:27	5:00	5:04
27	5:35	6:10	6:39	7:09	7:36	7:50	7:37	6:59	6:10	5:26	4:59	5:04
28	5:36	6:11	6:40	7:10	7:37	7:50	7:36	6:57	6:08	5:24	4:59	5:05
29	5:37	6:12	6:41	7:11	7:38	7:50	7:35	6:56	6:06	5:23	4:59	5:06
30	5:38		6:42	7:12	7:38	7:50	7:34	6:54	6:05	5:22	4:58	5:06
31	5:40		6:43		7:39		7:33	6:53		5:21		5:07

CLEVELAND, OHIO

DAY	JAN.	FEB.	MAR.	APR.	MAY	JUNE	JULY	AUG.	SEPT.	OCT.	NOV.	DEC.
1	4:50 P.M.	5:25	6:00	6:34	7:07	7:36	7:47	7:27	6:43	5:52	5:05	4:41
2	4:51	5:27	6:01	6:35	7:08	7:37	7:47	7:26	6:41	5:50	5:04	4:41
3	4:52	5:28	6:02	6:36	7:09	7:38	7:46	7:25	6:40	5:48	5:02	4:40
4	4:53	5:29	6:03	6:38	7:10	7:38	7:46	7:23	6:38	5:47	5:01	4:40
5	4:54	5:30	6:04	6:39	7:11	7:39	7:46	7:22	6:36	5:45	5:00	4:40
6	4:55	5:32	6:06	6:40	7:12	7:40	7:46	7:21	6:35	5:43	4:59	4:40
7	4:56	5:33	6:07	6:41	7:13	7:40	7:45	7:20	6:33	5:42	4:58	4:40
8	4:57	5:34	6:08	6:42	7:14	7:41	7:45	7:18	6:31	5:40	4:57	4:40
9	4:58	5:35	6:09	6:43	7:15	7:42	7:45	7:17	6:29	5:38	4:56	4:40
10	4:59	5:37	6:10	6:44	7:16	7:42	7:44	7:16	6:28	5:35	4:55	4:40
11	5:00	5:38	6:11	6:45	7:17	7:43	7:44	7:15	6:26	5:34	4:54	4:40
12	5:01	5:39	6:12	6:46	7:18	7:43	7:43	7:13	6:24	5:32	4:53	4:40
13	5:02	5:40	6:14	6:47	7:19	7:44	7:43	7:12	6:23	5:30	4:52	4:40
14	5:03	5:42	6:15	6:48	7:20	7:44	7:42	7:10	6:21	5:29	4:51	4:40
15	5:05	5:43	6:16	6:49	7:21	7:44	7:42	7:09	6:19	5:27	4:50	4:41
16	5:06	5:44	6:17	6:50	7:22	7:45	7:41	7:08	6:17	5:26	4:49	4:41
17	5:07	5:45	6:18	6:52	7:23	7:45	7:40	7:06	6:16	5:24	4:48	4:41
18	5:08	5:47	6:19	6:53	7:24	7:46	7:40	7:05	6:14	5:23	4:48	4:42
19	5:09	5:48	6:20	6:54	7:25	7:46	7:39	7:03	6:12	5:21	4:47	4:42
20	5:10	5:49	6:21	6:55	7:26	7:46	7:38	7:02	6:11	5:20	4:46	4:42
21	5:12	5:50	6:22	6:56	7:27	7:46	7:37	7:00	6:09	5:18	4:46	4:43
22	5:13	5:51	6:23	6:57	7:28	7:46	7:36	6:59	6:07	5:17	4:45	4:43
23	5:14	5:53	6:25	6:58	7:29	7:47	7:36	6:57	6:05	5:16	4:44	4:44
24	5:15	5:54	6:26	6:59	7:30	7:47	7:35	6:56	6:04	5:14	4:44	4:45
25	5:17	5:55	6:27	7:00	7:31	7:47	7:34	6:54	6:02	5:13	4:43	4:45
26	5:18	5:56	6:28	7:01	7:31	7:47	7:33	6:53	6:00	5:11	4:43	4:46
27	5:19	5:57	6:29	7:02	7:32	7:47	7:32	6:51	5:59	5:10	4:42	4:46
28	5:20	5:59	6:30	7:03	7:33	7:47	7:31	6:49	5:57	5:09	4:42	4:47
29	5:22	6:00	6:31	7:04	7:34	7:47	7:30	6:48	5:55	5:07	4:41	4:48
30	5:23		6:32	7:06	7:35	7:47	7:29	6:46	5:53	5:06	4:41	4:49
31	5:24		6:33		7:36		7:28	6:44		5:06		4:49

DENVER, COLORADO

DAY	JAN.	FEB.	MAR.	APR.	MAY	JUNE	JULY	AUG.	SEPT.	OCT.	NOV.	DEC.
1	4:28 P.M.	5:01	5:34	6:06	6:36	7:04	7:14	6:55	6:14	5:25	4:40	4:18
2	4:29	5:03	5:35	6:07	6:37	7:04	7:14	6:54	6:12	5:23	4:39	4:18
3	4:30	5:04	5:36	6:08	6:38	7:05	7:14	6:53	6:11	5:22	4:38	4:18
4	4:31	5:05	5:37	6:09	6:39	7:06	7:13	6:52	6:09	5:20	4:37	4:18
5	4:32	5:06	5:38	6:10	6:40	7:06	7:13	6:51	6:07	5:19	4:36	4:17
6	4:32	5:07	5:39	6:11	6:41	7:07	7:13	6:50	6:06	5:17	4:35	4:17
7	4:33	5:09	5:40	6:12	6:42	7:08	7:13	6:49	6:04	5:15	4:34	4:17
8	4:34	5:10	5:41	6:13	6:43	7:08	7:12	6:48	6:03	5:14	4:33	4:17
9	4:35	5:11	5:42	6:14	6:44	7:09	7:12	6:46	6:01	5:12	4:32	4:17
10	4:36	5:12	5:43	6:15	6:45	7:09	7:12	6:45	5:59	5:11	4:31	4:17
11	4:37	5:13	5:44	6:16	6:46	7:10	7:11	6:44	5:58	5:09	4:30	4:18
12	4:38	5:14	5:45	6:17	6:47	7:10	7:11	6:43	5:56	5:08	4:29	4:18
13	4:39	5:16	5:46	6:18	6:48	7:11	7:10	6:41	5:54	5:06	4:28	4:18
14	4:41	5:17	5:48	6:19	6:48	7:11	7:10	6:40	5:53	5:05	4:27	4:18
15	4:42	5:18	5:49	6:20	6:49	7:12	7:09	6:39	5:51	5:03	4:27	4:18
16	4:43	5:19	5:50	6:21	6:50	7:12	7:09	6:37	5:50	5:02	4:26	4:19
17	4:44	5:20	5:51	6:22	6:51	7:12	7:08	6:36	5:48	5:00	4:25	4:19
18	4:45	5:21	5:52	6:23	6:52	7:13	7:07	6:35	5:46	4:59	4:24	4:19
19	4:46	5:23	5:53	6:24	6:53	7:13	7:07	6:33	5:45	4:57	4:24	4:20
20	4:47	5:24	5:54	6:25	6:54	7:13	7:06	6:32	5:43	4:56	4:23	4:20
21	4:48	5:25	5:55	6:26	6:55	7:13	7:05	6:30	5:41	4:55	4:22	4:21
22	4:50	5:26	5:56	6:27	6:56	7:14	7:05	6:29	5:40	4:53	4:22	4:21
23	4:51	5:27	5:57	6:28	6:57	7:14	7:04	6:27	5:38	4:52	4:21	4:22
24	4:52	5:28	5:58	6:29	6:57	7:14	7:03	6:26	5:36	4:51	4:21	4:22
25	4:53	5:29	5:59	6:30	6:58	7:14	7:02	6:24	5:35	4:49	4:20	4:23
26	4:54	5:30	6:00	6:31	6:59	7:14	7:01	6:23	5:33	4:48	4:20	4:23
27	4:55	5:32	6:01	6:32	7:00	7:14	7:00	6:21	5:32	4:47	4:19	4:24
28	4:57	5:33	6:02	6:33	7:01	7:14	6:59	6:20	5:30	4:45	4:19	4:25
29	4:58	5:34	6:03	6:34	7:01	7:14	6:58	6:18	5:28	4:44	4:19	4:26
30	4:59		6:04	6:35	7:02	7:14	6:57	6:17	5:27	4:43	4:18	4:26
31	5:00		6:05		7:03		6:56	6:15		4:42		4:27

DETROIT, MICHIGAN

DAY	JAN.	FEB.	MAR.	APR.	MAY	JUNE	JULY	AUG.	SEPT.	OCT.	NOV.	DEC.
1	4:54 P.M.	5:30	6:05	6:41	7:14	7:45	7:56	7:35	6:50	5:57	5:09	4:44
2	4:55	5:31	6:06	6:42	7:15	7:46	7:55	7:34	6:48	5:56	5:08	4:44
3	4:56	5:32	6:07	6:43	7:17	7:46	7:55	7:33	6:46	5:54	5:07	4:44
4	4:57	5:33	6:09	6:44	7:18	7:47	7:55	7:31	6:45	5:52	5:06	4:44
5	4:58	5:35	6:10	6:45	7:19	7:48	7:55	7:30	6:43	5:51	5:04	4:43
6	4:59	5:36	6:11	6:46	7:20	7:48	7:54	7:29	6:41	5:49	5:03	4:43
7	5:00	5:37	6:12	6:48	7:21	7:49	7:54	7:28	6:40	5:47	5:02	4:43
8	5:01	5:39	6:13	6:49	7:22	7:50	7:54	7:26	6:38	5:46	5:01	4:43
9	5:02	5:40	6:15	6:50	7:23	7:50	7:53	7:25	6:36	5:44	5:00	4:43
10	5:03	5:41	6:16	6:51	7:24	7:51	7:53	7:24	6:34	5:42	4:59	4:43
11	5:04	5:43	6:17	6:52	7:25	7:51	7:52	7:22	6:33	5:41	4:58	4:43
12	5:05	5:44	6:18	6:53	7:26	7:52	7:52	7:21	6:31	5:39	4:57	4:43
13	5:05	5:45	6:19	6:54	7:27	7:52	7:51	7:19	6:29	5:37	4:56	4:44
14	5:07	5:46	6:20	6:55	7:28	7:53	7:51	7:18	6:27	5:36	4:55	4:44
15	5:08	5:48	6:22	6:56	7:29	7:53	7:50	7:17	6:26	5:34	4:54	4:44
16	5:09	5:49	6:23	6:58	7:30	7:54	7:49	7:15	6:24	5:32	4:53	4:44
17	5:11	5:50	6:24	6:59	7:31	7:54	7:49	7:14	6:22	5:31	4:52	4:45
18	5:12	5:51	6:25	7:00	7:32	7:54	7:48	7:12	6:20	5:29	4:52	4:45
19	5:13	5:53	6:26	7:01	7:33	7:55	7:47	7:11	6:19	5:28	4:51	4:45
20	5:14	5:54	6:27	7:02	7:34	7:55	7:47	7:09	6:17	5:26	4:50	4:46
21	5:15	5:55	6:28	7:03	7:35	7:55	7:46	7:08	6:15	5:25	4:49	4:46
22	5:17	5:56	6:30	7:04	7:36	7:55	7:45	7:06	6:13	5:23	4:49	4:47
23	5:18	5:58	6:31	7:05	7:37	7:55	7:44	7:04	6:11	5:22	4:48	4:47
24	5:19	5:59	6:32	7:07	7:38	7:56	7:43	7:03	6:10	5:20	4:47	4:48
25	5:21	6:00	6:33	7:08	7:39	7:56	7:42	7:01	6:08	5:19	4:47	4:48
26	5:22	6:01	6:34	7:09	7:40	7:56	7:41	7:00	6:06	5:17	4:46	4:49
27	5:23	6:03	6:35	7:10	7:41	7:56	7:40	6:58	6:04	5:16	4:46	4:50
28	5:24	6:04	6:36	7:11	7:42	7:56	7:39	6:56	6:03	5:15	4:45	4:51
29	5:26	6:05	6:37	7:12	7:43	7:56	7:38	6:55	6:01	5:13	4:45	4:51
30	5:27		6:39	7:13	7:43	7:56	7:37	6:53	5:59	5:12	4:45	4:52
31	5:28		6:40		7:44		7:36	6:51		5:11		4:53

HOUSTON, TEXAS

DAY	JAN.	FEB.	MAR.	APR.	MAY	JUNE	JULY	AUG.	SEPT.	OCT.	NOV.	DEC.
1	5:15 P.M.	5:41	6:03	6:22	6:40	6:59	7:08	6:56	6:26	5:49	5:17	5:04
2	5:16	5:42	6:03	6:23	6:41	7:00	7:08	6:56	6:25	5:48	5:16	5:04
3	5:17	5:43	6:04	6:23	6:42	7:00	7:08	6:55	6:24	5:47	5:15	5:04
4	5:18	5:43	6:05	6:24	6:42	7:01	7:08	6:54	6:23	5:46	5:15	5:04
5	5:18	5:44	6:05	6:24	6:43	7:01	7:08	6:53	6:21	5:45	5:14	5:04
6	5:19	5:45	6:06	6:25	6:43	7:02	7:08	6:53	6:20	5:43	5:13	5:04
7	5:20	5:46	6:07	6:25	6:44	7:02	7:08	6:52	6:19	5:42	5:13	5:04
8	5:21	5:47	6:07	6:26	6:45	7:03	7:07	6:51	6:18	5:41	5:12	5:04
9	5:21	5:48	6:08	6:27	6:45	7:03	7:07	6:50	6:16	5:40	5:11	5:04
10	5:22	5:48	6:09	6:27	6:46	7:03	7:07	6:49	6:15	5:39	5:11	5:05
11	5:23	5:49	6:09	6:28	6:47	7:04	7:07	6:48	6:14	5:38	5:10	5:05
12	5:24	5:50	6:10	6:28	6:47	7:04	7:07	6:47	6:13	5:36	5:09	5:05
13	5:25	5:51	6:10	6:29	6:48	7:05	7:06	6:46	6:12	5:35	5:09	5:05
14	5:25	5:52	6:11	6:30	6:49	7:05	7:06	6:45	6:10	5:34	5:08	5:06
15	5:26	5:52	6:12	6:30	6:49	7:05	7:06	6:44	6:09	5:33	5:08	5:06
16	5:27	5:53	6:12	6:31	6:50	7:06	7:05	6:44	6:08	5:32	5:07	5:06
17	5:28	5:54	6:13	6:32	6:50	7:06	7:05	6:43	6:07	5:31	5:07	5:07
18	5:29	5:55	6:14	6:32	6:51	7:06	7:04	6:42	6:05	5:30	5:07	5:07
19	5:30	5:55	6:14	6:33	6:52	7:06	7:04	6:40	6:04	5:29	5:06	5:08
20	5:31	5:56	6:15	6:33	6:52	7:07	7:04	6:39	6:03	5:28	5:06	5:08
21	5:31	5:57	6:15	6:34	6:53	7:07	7:03	6:38	6:02	5:27	5:06	5:09
22	5:32	5:58	6:16	6:35	6:54	7:07	7:03	6:37	6:00	5:26	5:05	5:09
23	5:33	5:58	6:17	6:35	6:54	7:07	7:02	6:36	5:59	5:25	5:05	5:10
24	5:34	5:59	6:17	6:36	6:55	7:07	7:02	6:35	5:58	5:24	5:05	5:10
25	5:35	6:00	6:18	6:36	6:55	7:08	7:01	6:34	5:57	5:23	5:05	5:11
26	5:36	6:00	6:18	6:37	6:56	7:08	7:00	6:33	5:55	5:22	5:04	5:11
27	5:37	6:01	6:19	6:38	6:56	7:08	7:00	6:32	5:54	5:21	5:04	5:12
28	5:38	6:02	6:20	6:38	6:57	7:08	6:59	6:31	5:53	5:20	5:04	5:12
29	5:38	6:03	6:20	6:39	6:58	7:08	6:59	6:30	5:52	5:19	5:04	5:13
30	5:39		6:21	6:40	6:58	7:08	6:58	6:28	5:51	5:19	5:04	5:14
31	5:40		6:21		6:59		6:57	6:27		5:18		5:14

LOS ANGELES, CALIFORNIA

DAY	JAN.	FEB.	MAR.	APR.	MAY	JUNE	JULY	AUG.	SEPT.	OCT.	NOV.	DEC.
1	4:37 P.M.	5:05	5:31	5:56	6:19	6:41	6:50	6:36	6:01	5:20	4:42	4:26
2	4:37	5:06	5:32	5:56	6:19	6:42	6:50	6:35	6:00	5:18	4:41	4:26
3	4:38	5:07	5:33	5:57	6:20	6:42	6:50	6:34	5:58	5:17	4:41	4:25
4	4:39	5:08	5:34	5:58	6:21	6:43	6:50	6:33	5:57	5:15	4:40	4:25
5	4:40	5:09	5:34	5:59	6:22	6:43	6:50	6:32	5:56	5:14	4:39	4:25
6	4:41	5:10	5:35	5:59	6:22	6:44	6:50	6:31	5:54	5:13	4:38	4:25
7	4:41	5:11	5:36	6:00	6:23	6:44	6:49	6:30	5:53	5:11	4:37	4:26
8	4:42	5:12	5:37	6:01	6:24	6:45	6:49	6:29	5:52	5:10	4:36	4:26
9	4:43	5:13	5:38	6:02	6:25	6:45	6:49	6:28	5:50	5:09	4:36	4:26
10	4:44	5:14	5:39	6:02	6:26	6:46	6:49	6:27	5:49	5:07	4:35	4:26
11	4:45	5:15	5:39	6:03	6:26	6:46	6:48	6:26	5:47	5:06	4:34	4:26
12	4:46	5:16	5:40	6:04	6:27	6:47	6:48	6:25	5:46	5:05	4:33	4:26
13	4:47	5:17	5:41	6:05	6:28	6:47	6:48	6:24	5:45	5:04	4:33	4:27
14	4:48	5:18	5:42	6:05	6:29	6:47	6:47	6:23	5:43	5:02	4:32	4:27
15	4:49	5:19	5:43	6:06	6:29	6:48	6:47	6:22	5:42	5:01	4:31	4:27
16	4:50	5:20	5:43	6:07	6:30	6:48	6:46	6:21	5:40	5:00	4:31	4:27
17	4:51	5:21	5:44	6:08	6:31	6:48	6:46	6:20	5:39	4:59	4:30	4:28
18	4:52	5:21	5:45	6:08	6:32	6:49	6:46	6:19	5:38	4:57	4:30	4:28
19	4:52	5:22	5:46	6:09	6:32	6:49	6:45	6:17	5:36	4:56	4:29	4:29
20	4:53	5:23	5:46	6:10	6:33	6:49	6:44	6:16	5:35	4:55	4:29	4:29
21	4:54	5:24	5:47	6:11	6:34	6:49	6:44	6:15	5:33	4:54	4:28	4:30
22	4:55	5:25	5:48	6:12	6:34	6:50	6:43	6:14	5:32	4:53	4:28	4:30
23	4:56	5:26	5:49	6:12	6:35	6:50	6:43	6:13	5:31	4:52	4:28	4:31
24	4:57	5:27	5:49	6:13	6:36	6:50	6:42	6:11	5:29	4:51	4:27	4:31
25	4:58	5:28	5:50	6:14	6:37	6:50	6:41	6:10	5:28	4:49	4:27	4:32
26	4:59	5:29	5:51	6:15	6:37	6:50	6:41	6:09	5:26	4:48	4:27	4:32
27	5:00	5:29	5:52	6:15	6:38	6:50	6:40	6:08	5:25	4:47	4:26	4:33
28	5:01	5:30	5:53	6:16	6:38	6:50	6:39	6:06	5:24	4:46	4:26	4:34
29	5:02	5:31	5:53	6:17	6:39	6:50	6:38	6:05	5:22	4:45	4:26	4:34
30	5:03		5:54	6:18	6:40	6:50	6:38	6:04	5:21	4:44	4:26	4:35
31	5:04		5:55		6:40		6:37	6:02		4:43		4:36

MIAMI, FLORIDA

DAY	JAN.	FEB.	MAR.	APR.	MAY	JUNE	JULY	AUG.	SEPT.	OCT.	NOV.	DEC.
1	5:23 P.M.	5:46	6:04	6:19	6:34	6:50	6:58	6:49	6:22	5:50	5:21	5:11
2	5:24	5:47	6:05	6:20	6:34	6:50	6:58	6:48	6:21	5:49	5:21	5:11
3	5:25	5:48	6:05	6:20	6:35	6:51	6:58	6:48	6:20	5:48	5:20	5:11
4	5:25	5:49	6:06	6:21	6:35	6:51	6:58	6:47	6:19	5:46	5:19	5:11
5	5:26	5:49	6:07	6:21	6:36	6:52	6:58	6:46	6:18	5:45	5:19	5:12
6	5:27	5:50	6:07	6:22	6:36	6:52	6:58	6:46	6:17	5:44	5:18	5:12
7	5:27	5:51	6:08	6:22	6:37	6:52	6:58	6:45	6:16	5:43	5:18	5:12
8	5:28	5:51	6:08	6:23	6:37	6:53	6:58	6:44	6:15	5:42	5:17	5:12
9	5:29	5:52	6:09	6:23	6:38	6:53	6:58	6:43	6:14	5:41	5:17	5:12
10	5:30	5:53	6:09	6:23	6:39	6:54	6:58	6:43	6:13	5:40	5:16	5:13
11	5:30	5:53	6:10	6:24	6:39	6:54	6:57	6:42	6:12	5:39	5:16	5:13
12	5:31	5:54	6:10	6:24	6:40	6:54	6:57	6:41	6:10	5:38	5:15	5:13
13	5:32	5:55	6:11	6:25	6:40	6:55	6:57	6:40	6:09	5:37	5:15	5:13
14	5:33	5:55	6:11	6:25	6:41	6:55	6:57	6:39	6:08	5:36	5:14	5:14
15	5:33	5:56	6:12	6:26	6:41	6:55	6:56	6:38	6:07	5:35	5:14	5:14
16	5:34	5:57	6:12	6:26	6:42	6:56	6:56	6:38	6:06	5:34	5:14	5:14
17	5:35	5:57	6:12	6:27	6:42	6:56	6:56	6:37	6:05	5:34	5:13	5:15
18	5:36	5:58	6:13	6:27	6:43	6:56	6:56	6:36	6:04	5:33	5:13	5:15
19	5:37	5:59	6:13	6:28	6:43	6:56	6:55	6:35	6:03	5:32	5:13	5:16
20	5:37	5:59	6:14	6:28	6:44	6:57	6:55	6:34	6:02	5:31	5:12	5:16
21	5:38	6:00	6:14	6:29	6:44	6:57	6:54	6:33	6:01	5:30	5:12	5:17
22	5:39	6:00	6:15	6:29	6:45	6:57	6:54	6:32	5:59	5:29	5:12	5:17
23	5:40	6:01	6:15	6:30	6:45	6:57	6:54	6:31	5:58	5:28	5:12	5:18
24	5:40	6:02	6:16	6:30	6:46	6:57	6:53	6:30	5:57	5:27	5:12	5:18
25	5:41	6:02	6:16	6:31	6:46	6:58	6:53	6:29	5:56	5:27	5:12	5:19
26	5:42	6:03	6:17	6:31	6:47	6:58	6:52	6:28	5:55	5:26	5:11	5:19
27	5:43	6:03	6:17	6:32	6:47	6:58	6:52	6:27	5:54	5:25	5:11	5:20
28	5:43	6:04	6:18	6:32	6:48	6:58	6:51	6:26	5:53	5:24	5:11	5:21
29	5:44	6:04	6:18	6:33	6:48	6:58	6:51	6:25	5:52	5:24	5:11	5:21
30	5:45		6:18	6:33	6:49	6:58	6:50	6:24	5:51	5:23	5:11	5:22
31	5:46		6:19		6:49		6:49	6:23		5:22		5:22

NEW YORK, NEW YORK

DAY	JAN.	FEB.	MAR.	APR.	MAY	JUNE	JULY	AUG.	SEPT.	OCT.	NOV.	DEC.
1	4:21 P.M.	4:56	5:29	6:03	6:34	7:03	7:13	6:54	6:11	5:21	4:35	4:11
2	4:22	4:57	5:30	6:04	6:35	7:03	7:13	6:53	6:09	5:19	4:34	4:11
3	4:23	4:58	5:31	6:05	6:36	7:04	7:13	6:51	6:07	5:17	4:32	4:11
4	4:24	4:59	5:32	6:06	6:37	7:05	7:13	6:50	6:06	5:16	4:31	4:11
5	4:25	5:00	5:34	6:07	6:38	7:06	7:12	6:49	6:04	5:14	4:30	4:11
6	4:26	5:02	5:35	6:08	6:39	7:06	7:12	6:48	6:03	5:12	4:29	4:11
7	4:27	5:03	5:36	6:09	6:40	7:07	7:12	6:47	6:01	5:11	4:28	4:11
8	4:28	5:04	5:37	6:10	6:41	7:07	7:11	6:46	5:59	5:09	4:27	4:11
9	4:29	5:05	5:38	6:11	6:42	7:08	7:11	6:44	5:58	5:08	4:26	4:11
10	4:30	5:07	5:39	6:12	6:43	7:08	7:11	6:43	5:56	5:06	4:25	4:11
11	4:31	5:08	5:40	6:13	6:44	7:09	7:10	6:42	5:54	5:04	4:24	4:11
12	4:32	5:09	5:41	6:14	6:45	7:09	7:10	6:40	5:53	5:03	4:23	4:11
13	4:33	5:10	5:42	6:15	6:46	7:10	7:09	6:39	5:51	5:01	4:22	4:11
14	4:34	5:11	5:43	6:16	6:47	7:10	7:09	6:38	5:49	5:00	4:21	4:11
15	4:35	5:13	5:45	6:17	6:48	7:11	7:08	6:36	5:48	4:58	4:20	4:12
16	4:36	5:14	5:46	6:18	6:49	7:11	7:07	6:35	5:46	4:57	4:20	4:12
17	4:37	5:15	5:47	6:19	6:50	7:11	7:07	6:34	5:44	4:55	4:19	4:12
18	4:39	5:16	5:48	6:20	6:51	7:12	7:06	6:32	5:42	4:54	4:18	4:13
19	4:40	5:17	5:49	6:21	6:52	7:12	7:05	6:31	5:41	4:52	4:17	4:13
20	4:41	5:19	5:50	6:22	6:53	7:12	7:05	6:29	5:39	4:51	4:17	4:13
21	4:42	5:20	5:51	6:23	6:54	7:13	7:04	6:28	5:37	4:49	4:16	4:14
22	4:43	5:21	5:52	6:24	6:55	7:13	7:03	6:26	5:36	4:48	4:15	4:14
23	4:45	5:22	5:53	6:26	6:55	7:13	7:02	6:25	5:34	4:47	4:15	4:15
24	4:46	5:23	5:54	6:27	6:56	7:13	7:01	6:23	5:32	4:45	4:14	4:15
25	4:47	5:25	5:55	6:28	6:57	7:13	7:01	6:22	5:31	4:44	4:14	4:16
26	4:48	5:26	5:56	6:29	6:58	7:13	7:00	6:20	5:29	4:42	4:13	4:17
27	4:49	5:27	5:57	6:30	6:59	7:13	6:59	6:19	5:27	4:41	4:13	4:17
28	4:51	5:28	5:58	6:31	7:00	7:13	6:58	6:17	5:26	4:40	4:12	4:18
29	4:52	5:29	5:59	6:32	7:00	7:13	6:57	6:16	5:24	4:39	4:12	4:19
30	4:53		6:00	6:33	7:01	7:13	6:56	6:14	5:22	4:37	4:12	4:20
31	4:54		6:01		7:02		6:55	6:12		4:36		4:20

PHILADELPHIA, PENNSYLVANIA

DAY	JAN.	FEB.	MAR.	APR.	MAY	JUNE	JULY	AUG.	SEPT.	OCT.	NOV.	DEC.
1	4:29 P.M.	5:02	5:35	6:07	6:37	7:05	7:15	6:57	6:15	5:26	4:41	4:19
2	4:30	5:03	5:36	6:08	6:38	7:06	7:15	6:56	6:13	5:24	4:40	4:19
3	4:30	5:04	5:37	6:09	6:39	7:06	7:15	6:55	6:12	5:23	4:39	4:18
4	4:31	5:06	5:38	6:10	6:40	7:07	7:15	6:54	6:10	5:21	4:38	4:18
5	4:32	5:07	5:39	6:11	6:41	7:08	7:15	6:52	6:09	5:20	4:37	4:18
6	4:33	5:08	5:40	6:12	6:42	7:08	7:14	6:51	6:07	5:18	4:36	4:18
7	4:34	5:09	5:41	6:13	6:43	7:09	7:14	6:50	6:05	5:16	4:35	4:18
8	4:35	5:10	5:42	6:14	6:44	7:10	7:14	6:49	6:04	5:15	4:34	4:18
9	4:36	5:12	5:43	6:15	6:45	7:10	7:13	6:48	6:02	5:13	4:33	4:18
10	4:37	5:13	5:44	6:16	6:46	7:11	7:13	6:46	6:00	5:12	4:32	4:18
11	4:38	5:14	5:45	6:17	6:47	7:11	7:13	6:45	5:59	5:10	4:31	4:18
12	4:39	5:15	5:46	6:18	6:48	7:12	7:12	6:44	5:57	5:09	4:30	4:18
13	4:40	5:16	5:47	6:19	6:49	7:12	7:12	6:43	5:56	5:07	4:29	4:18
14	4:41	5:18	5:49	6:20	6:50	7:13	7:11	6:41	5:54	5:06	4:28	4:19
15	4:42	5:19	5:50	6:21	6:51	7:13	7:11	6:40	5:52	5:04	4:27	4:19
16	4:43	5:20	5:51	6:22	6:52	7:13	7:10	6:39	5:51	5:03	4:26	4:19
17	4:44	5:21	5:52	6:23	6:53	7:14	7:09	6:37	5:49	5:01	4:26	4:20
18	4:46	5:22	5:53	6:24	6:54	7:14	7:09	6:36	5:47	5:00	4:25	4:20
19	4:47	5:23	5:54	6:25	6:54	7:14	7:08	6:34	5:46	4:58	4:24	4:20
20	4:48	5:25	5:55	6:26	6:55	7:15	7:07	6:33	5:44	4:57	4:24	4:21
21	4:49	5:26	5:56	6:27	6:56	7:15	7:07	6:32	5:42	4:55	4:23	4:21
22	4:50	5:27	5:57	6:28	6:57	7:15	7:06	6:30	5:41	4:54	4:22	4:22
23	4:51	5:28	5:58	6:29	6:58	7:15	7:05	6:29	5:39	4:53	4:22	4:22
24	4:53	5:29	5:59	6:30	6:59	7:15	7:04	6:27	5:37	4:51	4:21	4:23
25	4:54	5:30	6:00	6:31	7:00	7:15	7:03	6:26	5:36	4:50	4:21	4:23
26	4:55	5:31	6:01	6:32	7:00	7:15	7:03	6:24	5:34	4:49	4:20	4:24
27	4:56	5:32	6:02	6:33	7:01	7:15	7:02	6:23	5:32	4:47	4:20	4:25
28	4:57	5:34	6:03	6:34	7:02	7:15	7:01	6:21	5:31	4:46	4:20	4:25
29	4:58	5:35	6:04	6:35	7:03	7:15	7:00	6:20	5:29	4:45	4:19	4:26
30	5:00		6:05	6:36	7:04	7:15	6:59	6:18	5:28	4:44	4:19	4:27
31	5:01		6:06		7:04		6:58	6:16		4:42		4:28

PHOENIX, ARIZONA

DAY	JAN.	FEB.	MAR.	APR.	MAY	JUNE	JULY	AUG.	SEPT.	OCT.	NOV.	DEC.
1	5:13 P.M.	5:41	6:07	6:30	6:53	7:14	7:24	7:10	6:36	5:55	5:19	5:02
2	5:14	5:42	6:07	6:31	6:53	7:15	7:24	7:09	6:35	5:54	5:18	5:02
3	5:15	5:43	6:08	6:32	6:54	7:16	7:24	7:08	6:33	5:52	5:17	5:02
4	5:16	5:44	6:09	6:32	6:55	7:16	7:24	7:07	6:32	5:51	5:16	5:02
5	5:16	5:45	6:10	6:33	6:56	7:17	7:23	7:07	6:31	5:50	5:15	5:02
6	5:17	5:46	6:11	6:34	6:56	7:17	7:23	7:06	6:29	5:48	5:14	5:02
7	5:18	5:47	6:11	6:35	6:57	7:18	7:23	7:05	6:28	5:47	5:13	5:02
8	5:19	5:48	6:12	6:35	6:58	7:18	7:23	7:04	6:27	5:46	5:13	5:02
9	5:20	5:49	6:13	6:36	6:59	7:19	7:23	7:03	6:25	5:44	5:12	5:02
10	5:21	5:50	6:14	6:37	6:59	7:19	7:22	7:02	6:24	5:43	5:11	5:03
11	5:21	5:51	6:15	6:38	7:00	7:20	7:22	7:01	6:22	5:42	5:10	5:03
12	5:22	5:52	6:15	6:38	7:01	7:20	7:22	7:00	6:21	5:41	5:10	5:03
13	5:23	5:53	6:16	6:39	7:02	7:20	7:21	6:59	6:20	5:39	5:09	5:03
14	5:24	5:54	6:17	6:40	7:02	7:21	7:21	6:58	6:18	5:38	5:08	5:03
15	5:25	5:54	6:18	6:41	7:03	7:21	7:21	6:56	6:17	5:37	5:08	5:04
16	5:26	5:55	6:18	6:41	7:04	7:21	7:20	6:55	6:16	5:36	5:07	5:04
17	5:27	5:56	6:19	6:42	7:05	7:22	7:20	6:54	6:14	5:35	5:07	5:04
18	5:28	5:57	6:20	6:43	7:05	7:22	7:19	6:53	6:13	5:33	5:06	5:05
19	5:29	5:58	6:21	6:44	7:06	7:22	7:19	6:52	6:11	5:32	5:06	5:05
20	5:30	5:59	6:21	6:44	7:07	7:23	7:18	6:51	6:10	5:31	5:05	5:06
21	5:31	6:00	6:22	6:45	7:07	7:23	7:18	6:50	6:09	5:30	5:05	5:06
22	5:32	6:01	6:23	6:46	7:08	7:23	7:17	6:48	6:07	5:29	5:04	5:07
23	5:33	6:02	6:24	6:47	7:09	7:23	7:17	6:47	6:06	5:28	5:04	5:07
24	5:34	6:02	6:24	6:47	7:09	7:23	7:16	6:46	6:05	5:27	5:04	5:08
25	5:35	6:03	6:25	6:48	7:10	7:24	7:15	6:45	6:03	5:26	5:03	5:08
26	5:36	6:04	6:26	6:49	7:11	7:24	7:15	6:44	6:02	5:24	5:03	5:09
27	5:37	6:05	6:27	6:50	7:11	7:24	7:14	6:42	6:00	5:23	5:03	5:10
28	5:37	6:06	6:27	6:50	7:12	7:24	7:13	6:41	5:59	5:22	5:03	5:10
29	5:38	6:07	6:28	6:51	7:13	7:24	7:12	6:40	5:58	5:21	5:03	5:11
30	5:39		6:29	6:52	7:13	7:24	7:12	6:38	5:56	5:20	5:02	5:12
31	5:40		6:30		7:14		7:11	6:37		5:19		5:12

PITTSBURGH, PENNSYLVANIA

DAY	JAN.	FEB.	MAR.	APR.	MAY	JUNE	JULY	AUG.	SEPT.	OCT.	NOV.	DEC.
1	4:46 P.M.	5:20	5:53	6:26	6:57	7:26	7:36	7:17	6:34	5:45	4:59	4:36
2	4:47	5:21	5:54	6:27	6:58	7:27	7:36	7:16	6:33	5:43	4:58	4:36
3	4:48	5:22	5:55	6:28	6:59	7:27	7:36	7:15	6:31	5:41	4:57	4:36
4	4:49	5:24	5:57	6:29	7:00	7:28	7:36	7:14	6:30	5:40	4:56	4:36
5	4:50	5:25	5:58	6:30	7:01	7:29	7:35	7:13	6:28	5:38	4:55	4:35
6	4:50	5:26	5:59	6:31	7:02	7:29	7:35	7:11	6:26	5:37	4:53	4:35
7	4:51	5:27	6:00	6:32	7:03	7:30	7:35	7:10	6:25	5:35	4:52	4:35
8	4:52	5:29	6:01	6:34	7:04	7:30	7:35	7:09	6:23	5:33	4:51	4:35
9	4:53	5:30	6:02	6:35	7:05	7:31	7:34	7:08	6:21	5:32	4:50	4:35
10	4:54	5:31	6:03	6:36	7:06	7:32	7:34	7:06	6:20	5:30	4:49	4:35
11	4:56	5:32	6:04	6:37	7:07	7:32	7:33	7:05	6:18	5:29	4:48	4:35
12	4:57	5:33	6:05	6:38	7:08	7:33	7:33	7:04	6:16	5:27	4:48	4:36
13	4:58	5:35	6:06	6:39	7:09	7:33	7:32	7:03	6:15	5:26	4:47	4:36
14	4:59	5:36	6:07	6:40	7:10	7:33	7:32	7:01	6:13	5:24	4:46	4:36
15	5:00	5:37	6:09	6:41	7:11	7:34	7:31	7:00	6:11	5:22	4:45	4:36
16	5:01	5:38	6:10	6:42	7:12	7:34	7:31	6:58	6:10	5:21	4:44	4:37
17	5:02	5:39	6:11	6:43	7:13	7:35	7:30	6:57	6:08	5:19	4:43	4:37
18	5:03	5:41	6:12	6:44	7:14	7:35	7:29	6:56	6:06	5:18	4:43	4:37
19	5:04	5:42	6:13	6:45	7:15	7:35	7:29	6:54	6:05	5:17	4:42	4:38
20	5:06	5:43	6:14	6:46	7:16	7:35	7:28	6:53	6:03	5:15	4:41	4:38
21	5:07	5:44	6:15	6:47	7:17	7:36	7:27	6:51	6:01	5:14	4:41	4:39
22	5:08	5:45	6:16	6:48	7:18	7:36	7:26	6:50	6:00	5:12	4:40	4:39
23	5:09	5:46	6:17	6:49	7:19	7:36	7:26	6:48	5:58	5:11	4:39	4:40
24	5:10	5:48	6:18	6:50	7:19	7:36	7:25	6:47	5:56	5:09	4:39	4:40
25	5:11	5:49	6:19	6:51	7:20	7:36	7:24	6:45	5:55	5:08	4:38	4:41
26	5:13	5:50	6:20	6:52	7:21	7:36	7:23	6:44	5:53	5:07	4:38	4:41
27	5:14	5:51	6:21	6:53	7:22	7:36	7:22	6:42	5:51	5:05	4:37	4:42
28	5:15	5:52	6:22	6:54	7:23	7:36	7:21	6:41	5:50	5:04	4:37	4:43
29	5:16	5:53	6:23	6:55	7:24	7:36	7:20	6:39	5:48	5:03	4:37	4:43
30	5:18		6:24	6:56	7:24	7:36	7:19	6:38	5:46	5:02	4:36	4:44
31	5:19		6:25		7:25		7:18	6:36		5:00		4:45

ST. LOUIS, MISSOURI

DAY	JAN.	FEB.	MAR.	APR.	MAY	JUNE	JULY	AUG.	SEPT.	OCT.	NOV.	DEC.
1	4:32 P.M.	5:04	5:35	6:06	6:34	7:01	7:11	6:54	6:13	5:26	4:43	4:22
2	4:33	5:06	5:37	6:07	6:35	7:02	7:11	6:53	6:12	5:25	4:42	4:22
3	4:34	5:07	5:38	6:08	6:36	7:03	7:11	6:52	6:10	5:23	4:41	4:22
4	4:35	5:08	5:39	6:09	6:37	7:03	7:11	6:51	6:09	5:21	4:40	4:21
5	4:36	5:09	5:40	6:10	6:38	7:04	7:11	6:49	6:07	5:20	4:39	4:21
6	4:36	5:10	5:41	6:11	6:39	7:04	7:10	6:48	6:06	5:18	4:38	4:21
7	4:37	5:11	5:42	6:12	6:40	7:05	7:10	6:47	6:04	5:17	4:37	4:21
8	4:38	5:12	5:43	6:13	6:41	7:06	7:10	6:46	6:03	5:15	4:36	4:21
9	4:39	5:14	5:44	6:14	6:42	7:06	7:09	6:45	6:01	5:14	4:35	4:21
10	4:40	5:15	5:45	6:14	6:43	7:07	7:09	6:44	5:59	5:12	4:34	4:22
11	4:41	5:16	5:46	6:15	6:44	7:07	7:09	6:42	5:58	5:11	4:33	4:22
12	4:42	5:17	5:47	6:16	6:45	7:08	7:08	6:41	5:56	5:09	4:32	4:22
13	4:43	5:18	5:48	6:17	6:46	7:08	7:08	6:40	5:55	5:08	4:31	4:22
14	4:44	5:19	5:49	6:18	6:47	7:08	7:07	6:39	5:53	5:06	4:31	4:22
15	4:45	5:20	5:50	6:19	6:48	7:09	7:07	6:37	5:52	5:05	4:30	4:22
16	4:46	5:21	5:51	6:20	6:48	7:09	7:06	6:36	5:50	5:04	4:29	4:23
17	4:48	5:23	5:52	6:21	6:49	7:10	7:06	6:35	5:48	5:02	4:28	4:23
18	4:49	5:24	5:53	6:22	6:50	7:10	7:05	6:34	5:47	5:01	4:28	4:24
19	4:50	5:25	5:54	6:23	6:51	7:10	7:04	6:32	5:45	4:59	4:27	4:24
20	4:51	5:26	5:54	6:24	6:52	7:10	7:04	6:31	5:44	4:58	4:26	4:24
21	4:52	5:27	5:55	6:25	6:53	7:11	7:03	6:29	5:42	4:57	4:26	4:25
22	4:53	5:28	5:56	6:26	6:54	7:11	7:02	6:28	5:40	4:55	4:25	4:25
23	4:54	5:29	5:57	6:27	6:54	7:11	7:02	6:27	5:39	4:54	4:25	4:26
24	4:55	5:30	5:58	6:28	6:55	7:11	7:01	6:25	5:37	4:53	4:24	4:26
25	4:56	5:31	5:59	6:29	6:56	7:11	7:00	6:24	5:36	4:52	4:24	4:27
26	4:58	5:32	6:00	6:30	6:57	7:11	6:59	6:22	5:34	4:50	4:24	4:28
27	4:59	5:33	6:01	6:31	6:58	7:11	6:58	6:21	5:32	4:49	4:23	4:28
28	5:00	5:34	6:02	6:32	6:58	7:11	6:57	6:19	5:31	4:48	4:23	4:29
29	5:01	5:35	6:03	6:33	6:59	7:11	6:57	6:18	5:29	4:47	4:22	4:30
30	5:02		6:04	6:34	7:00	7:11	6:56	6:16	5:28	4:45	4:22	4:30
31	5:03		6:05		7:01		6:55	6:15		4:44		4:31

SAN FRANCISCO, CALIFORNIA

DAY	JAN.	FEB.	MAR.	APR.	MAY	JUNE	JULY	AUG.	SEPT.	OCT.	NOV.	DEC.
1	4:44 P.M.	5:15	5:45	6:14	6:42	7:08	7:17	7:01	6:21	5:35	4:53	4:33
2	4:44	5:16	5:46	6:15	6:43	7:08	7:17	7:00	6:20	5:34	4:52	4:33
3	4:45	5:17	5:47	6:16	6:44	7:09	7:17	6:59	6:18	5:32	4:51	4:33
4	4:46	5:18	5:48	6:17	6:45	7:10	7:17	6:57	6:17	5:31	4:50	4:33
5	4:47	5:20	5:49	6:18	6:46	7:10	7:17	6:56	6:15	5:29	4:49	4:33
6	4:48	5:21	5:50	6:19	6:46	7:11	7:17	6:55	6:14	5:28	4:48	4:33
7	4:49	5:22	5:51	6:20	6:47	7:11	7:16	6:54	6:12	5:26	4:47	4:33
8	4:50	5:23	5:52	6:21	6:48	7:12	7:16	6:53	6:11	5:25	4:46	4:33
9	4:51	5:24	5:53	6:22	6:49	7:12	7:16	6:52	6:09	5:23	4:45	4:33
10	4:52	5:25	5:54	6:23	6:50	7:13	7:15	6:51	6:08	5:22	4:44	4:33
11	4:52	5:26	5:55	6:23	6:51	7:13	7:15	6:50	6:06	5:20	4:44	4:33
12	4:53	5:27	5:56	6:24	6:52	7:14	7:15	6:48	6:05	5:19	4:43	4:33
13	4:54	5:28	5:57	6:25	6:53	7:14	7:14	6:47	6:03	5:17	4:42	4:33
14	4:55	5:29	5:58	6:26	6:54	7:15	7:14	6:46	6:01	5:16	4:41	4:34
15	4:57	5:31	5:59	6:27	6:54	7:15	7:13	6:45	6:00	5:15	4:41	4:34
16	4:58	5:32	6:00	6:28	6:55	7:15	7:13	6:43	5:58	5:13	4:40	4:34
17	4:59	5:33	6:01	6:29	6:56	7:16	7:12	6:42	5:57	5:12	4:39	4:34
18	5:00	5:34	6:02	6:30	6:57	7:16	7:12	6:41	5:55	5:10	4:38	4:35
19	5:01	5:35	6:02	6:31	6:58	7:16	7:11	6:40	5:54	5:09	4:38	4:35
20	5:02	5:36	6:03	6:32	6:59	7:17	7:10	6:38	5:52	5:08	4:37	4:36
21	5:03	5:37	6:04	6:33	6:59	7:17	7:10	6:37	5:51	5:06	4:37	4:36
22	5:04	5:38	6:05	6:34	7:00	7:17	7:09	6:36	5:49	5:05	4:36	4:37
23	5:05	5:39	6:06	6:34	7:01	7:17	7:08	6:34	5:47	5:04	4:36	4:37
24	5:06	5:40	6:07	6:35	7:02	7:17	7:07	6:33	5:46	5:03	4:35	4:38
25	5:07	5:41	6:08	6:36	7:03	7:17	7:07	6:31	5:44	5:01	4:35	4:38
26	5:08	5:42	6:09	6:37	7:03	7:18	7:06	6:30	5:43	5:00	4:34	4:39
27	5:10	5:43	6:10	6:38	7:04	7:18	7:05	6:29	5:41	4:59	4:34	4:40
28	5:11	5:44	6:11	6:39	7:05	7:18	7:04	6:27	5:40	4:58	4:34	4:40
29	5:12	5:45	6:12	6:40	7:06	7:18	7:03	6:26	5:38	4:57	4:34	4:41
30	5:13		6:13	6:41	7:06	7:18	7:02	6:24	5:37	4:56	4:33	4:42
31	5:14		6:13		7:07		7:01	6:23		4:54		4:43

WASHINGTON, DISTRICT OF COLUMBIA

DAY	JAN.	FEB.	MAR.	APR.	MAY	JUNE	JULY	AUG.	SEPT.	OCT.	NOV.	DEC.
1	4:39 P.M.	5:11	5:43	6:13	6:42	7:09	7:19	7:01	6:21	5:33	4:50	4:29
2	4:40	5:13	5:44	6:14	6:43	7:10	7:19	7:00	6:19	5:32	4:49	4:29
3	4:41	5:14	5:45	6:15	6:44	7:11	7:19	6:59	6:18	5:30	4:48	4:28
4	4:41	5:15	5:46	6:16	6:45	7:11	7:19	6:58	6:16	5:29	4:47	4:28
5	4:42	5:16	5:47	6:17	6:46	7:12	7:19	6:57	6:15	5:27	4:46	4:28
6	4:43	5:17	5:48	6:18	6:47	7:12	7:18	6:56	6:13	5:26	4:45	4:28
7	4:44	5:18	5:49	6:19	6:48	7:13	7:18	6:55	6:12	5:24	4:44	4:28
8	4:45	5:19	5:50	6:20	6:49	7:14	7:18	6:54	6:10	5:22	4:43	4:28
9	4:46	5:21	5:51	6:21	6:50	7:14	7:17	6:53	6:08	5:21	4:42	4:28
10	4:47	5:22	5:52	6:22	6:51	7:15	7:17	6:51	6:07	5:19	4:41	4:28
11	4:48	5:23	5:53	6:23	6:52	7:15	7:17	6:50	6:05	5:18	4:40	4:28
12	4:49	5:24	5:54	6:24	6:53	7:16	7:16	6:49	6:04	5:17	4:39	4:29
13	4:50	5:25	5:55	6:25	6:54	7:16	7:16	6:48	6:02	5:15	4:38	4:29
14	4:51	5:26	5:56	6:26	6:54	7:16	7:15	6:46	6:00	5:14	4:37	4:29
15	4:52	5:27	5:57	6:27	6:55	7:17	7:15	6:45	5:59	5:12	4:37	4:29
16	4:53	5:29	5:58	6:28	6:56	7:17	7:14	6:44	5:57	5:11	4:36	4:30
17	4:54	5:30	5:59	6:29	6:57	7:18	7:14	6:42	5:56	5:09	4:35	4:30
18	4:55	5:31	6:00	6:30	6:58	7:18	7:13	6:41	5:54	5:08	4:35	4:30
19	4:57	5:32	6:01	6:31	6:59	7:18	7:12	6:40	5:52	5:06	4:34	4:31
20	4:58	5:33	6:02	6:32	7:00	7:18	7:12	6:38	5:51	5:05	4:33	4:31
21	4:59	5:34	6:03	6:33	7:01	7:19	7:11	6:37	5:49	5:04	4:33	4:32
22	5:00	5:35	6:04	6:34	7:02	7:19	7:10	6:36	5:48	5:02	4:32	4:32
23	5:01	5:36	6:05	6:35	7:02	7:19	7:09	6:34	5:46	5:01	4:32	4:33
24	5:02	5:37	6:06	6:36	7:03	7:19	7:09	6:33	5:44	5:00	4:31	4:33
25	5:03	5:38	6:07	6:36	7:04	7:19	7:08	6:31	5:43	4:59	4:31	4:34
26	5:04	5:39	6:08	6:37	7:05	7:19	7:07	6:30	5:41	4:57	4:30	4:34
27	5:06	5:41	6:09	6:38	7:06	7:19	7:06	6:28	5:40	4:56	4:30	4:35
28	5:07	5:42	6:10	6:39	7:06	7:19	7:05	6:27	5:38	4:55	4:30	4:36
29	5:08	5:43	6:11	6:40	7:07	7:19	7:04	6:25	5:36	4:54	4:29	4:36
30	5:09		6:12	6:41	7:08	7:19	7:03	6:24	5:35	4:52	4:29	4:37
31	5:10		6:12		7:09		7:02	6:22		4:51		4:38

ISRAEL

BE'ER SHEVA

Jan.	1	4:32
	4	4:34
	7	4:36
	10	4:39
	13	4:41
	16	4:44
	19	4:46
	22	4:49
	25	4:52
	28	4:55
	31	4:57
Feb.	3	5:00
	6	5:03
	9	5:05
	12	5:08
	15	5:10
	18	5:13
	21	5:15
	24	5:18
	27	5:20
Mar.	2	5:22
	5	5:24
	8	5:26
	11	5:28
	14	5:31
	17	5:33
	20	5:35
	23	5:37
	26	5:39
	29	5:40
Apr.	1	5:42
	4	5:44
	7	5:46
	10	5:48
	13	5:50
	16	5:52
	19	5:54
	22	5:56
	25	5:58
	28	6:00
May	1	6:02
	4	6:04
	7	6:06
	10	6:08
	13	6:10
	16	6:13
	19	6:14
	22	6:16
	25	6:18
	28	6:20
	31	6:22
June	3	6:24
	6	6:25
	9	6:27
	12	6:28
	15	6:29
	18	6:30
	21	6:31
	24	6:31
	27	6:32
	30	6:32
July	3	6:32
	6	6:31
	9	6:31
	12	6:30
	15	6:29
	18	6:28
	21	6:27
	24	6:25
	27	6:23
	30	6:21
Aug.	2	6:19
	5	6:17
	8	6:14
	11	6:11
	14	6:08
	17	6:05
	20	6:02
	23	5:59
	26	5:55
	29	5:52
Sept.	1	5:48
	4	5:44
	7	5:41
	10	5:37
	13	5:33
	16	5:29
	19	5:25
	22	5:21
	25	5:17
	28	5:14
Oct.	1	5:10
	4	5:06
	7	5:02
	10	4:59
	13	4:55
	16	4:52
	19	4:48
	22	4:45
	25	4:42
	28	4:39
	31	4:36
Nov.	3	4:34
	6	4:32
	9	4:29
	12	4:29
	15	4:26
	18	4:24
	21	4:23
	24	4:22
	27	4:21
	30	4:21
Dec.	3	4:21
	6	4:21
	9	4:21
	12	4:22
	15	4:23
	18	4:24
	21	4:25
	24	4:26
	27	4:28
	30	4:30

HAIFA

Jan.	1	4:27
	4	4:29
	7	4:31
	10	4:34
	13	4:36
	16	4:39
	19	4:42
	22	4:45
	25	4:47
	28	4:50
	31	4:53
Feb.	3	4:56
	6	4:59
	9	5:02
	12	5:04
	15	5:07
	18	5:10
	21	5:12
	24	5:15
	27	5:17
Mar.	2	5:20
	5	5:22
	8	5:24
	11	5:26
	14	5:29
	17	5:31
	20	5:33
	23	5:35
	26	5:37
	29	5:40
Apr.	1	5:42
	4	5:44
	7	5:46
	10	5:48
	13	5:50
	16	5:52
	19	5:54
	22	5:57
	25	5:59
	28	6:01
May	1	6:03
	4	6:05
	7	6:08
	10	6:10
	13	6:12
	16	6:14
	19	6:16
	22	6:18
	25	6:20
	28	6:22
	31	6:24
June	3	6:26
	6	6:27
	9	6:29
	12	6:30
	15	6:31
	18	6:32
	21	6:33
	24	6:34
	27	6:34
	30	6:34
July	3	6:34
	6	6:34
	9	6:33
	12	6:32
	15	6:31
	18	6:30
	21	6:29
	24	6:27
	27	6:25
	30	6:23
Aug.	2	6:20
	5	6:18
	8	6:15
	11	6:12
	14	6:09
	17	6:06
	20	6:03
	23	5:59
	26	5:55
	29	5:52
Sept.	1	5:48
	4	5:44
	7	5:40
	10	5:36
	13	5:32
	16	5:28
	19	5:24
	22	5:20
	25	5:16
	28	5:12
Oct.	1	5:08
	4	5:04
	7	5:00
	10	4:56
	13	4:53
	16	4:49
	19	4:45
	22	4:42
	25	4:39
	28	4:36
	31	4:33
Nov.	3	4:30
	6	4:28
	9	4:25
	12	4:23
	15	4:21
	18	4:20
	21	4:18
	24	4:17
	27	4:16
	30	4:16
Dec.	3	4:16
	6	4:16
	9	4:16
	12	4:16
	15	4:17
	18	4:18
	21	4:20
	24	4:21
	27	4:23
	30	4:25

JERUSALEM

Jan.	1	4:28
	4	4:30
	7	4:32
	10	4:35
	13	4:38
	16	4:40
	19	4:43
	22	4:46
	25	4:48
	28	4:51
	31	4:54
Feb.	3	4:57
	6	4:59
	9	5:02
	12	5:05
	15	5:07
	18	5:10
	21	5:12
	24	5:15
	27	5:17
Mar.	2	5:19
	5	5:21
	8	5:24
	11	5:26
	14	5:28
	17	5:30
	20	5:32
	23	5:34
	26	5:36
	29	5:38
Apr.	1	5:40
	4	5:42
	7	5:44
	10	5:46
	13	5:48
	16	5:50
	19	5:52
	22	5:54
	25	5:56
	28	5:59
May	1	6:01
	4	6:03
	7	6:05
	10	6:07
	13	6:09
	16	6:11
	19	6:13
	22	6:15
	25	6:17
	28	6:19
	31	6:21
June	3	6:22
	6	6:24
	9	6:25
	12	6:27
	15	6:28
	18	6:29
	21	6:30
	24	6:30
	27	6:30
	30	6:31
July	3	6:31
	6	6:30
	9	6:30
	12	6:29
	15	6:28
	18	6:27
	21	6:25
	24	6:24
	27	6:22
	30	6:20
Aug.	2	6:18
	5	6:15
	8	6:12
	11	6:10
	14	6:07
	17	6:03
	20	6:00
	23	5:57
	26	5:53
	29	5:50
Sept.	1	5:46
	4	5:42
	7	5:39
	10	5:35
	13	5:31
	16	5:27
	19	5:23
	22	5:19
	25	5:15
	28	5:11
Oct.	1	5:07
	4	5:03
	7	5:00
	10	4:56
	13	4:52
	16	4:49
	19	4:45
	22	4:42
	25	4:39
	28	4:36
	31	4:33
Nov.	3	4:31
	6	4:28
	9	4:26
	12	4:24
	15	4:22
	18	4:21
	21	4:19
	24	4:18
	27	4:18
	30	4:17
Dec.	3	4:17
	6	4:17
	9	4:17
	12	4:18
	15	4:19
	18	4:20
	21	4:21
	24	4:23
	27	4:24
	30	4:26

TEL AVIV

Jan.	1	4:29		17	5:32		31	6:23		14	6:09		28	4:38
	4	4:31		20	5:34	June	3	6:25		17	6:06		31	4:35
	7	4:34		23	5:36		6	6:27		20	6:03	Nov.	3	4:32
	10	4:36		26	5:38		9	6:28		23	5:59		6	4:30
	13	4:39		29	5:40		12	6:29		26	5:56		9	4:27
	16	4:42	Apr.	1	5:42		15	6:31		29	5:52		12	4:25
	19	4:44		4	5:44		18	6:32	Sept.	1	5:48		15	4:24
	22	4:47		7	5:46		21	6:32		4	5:45		18	4:22
	25	4:50		10	5:48		24	6:33		7	5:41		21	4:21
	28	4:53		13	5:50		27	6:33		10	5:37		24	4:20
	31	4:55		16	5:53		30	6:33		13	5:33		27	4:19
Feb.	3	4:58		19	5:55	July	3	6:33		16	5:29		30	4:18
	6	5:01		22	5:57		6	6:33		19	5:25	Dec.	3	4:18
	9	5:04		25	5:59		9	6:32		22	5:21		6	4:18
	12	5:06		28	6:01		12	6:32		25	5:17		9	4:19
	15	5:09	May	1	6:03		15	6:31		28	5:13		12	4:19
	18	5:11		4	6:05		18	6:29	Oct.	1	5:09		15	4:20
	21	5:14		7	6:07		21	6:28		4	5:05		18	4:21
	24	5:16		10	6:10		24	6:26		7	5:01		21	4:22
	27	5:19		13	6:12		27	6:24		10	4:58		24	4:24
Mar.	2	5:21		16	6:14		30	6:22		13	4:54		27	4:26
	5	5:23		19	6:16	Aug.	2	6:20		16	4:50		30	4:28
	8	5:26		22	6:18		5	6:18		19	4:47			
	11	5:28		25	6:20		8	6:15		22	4:44			
	14	5:30		28	6:22		11	6:12		25	4:41			

CANADA

MONTREAL, QUEBEC

Jan.	1	4:04		17	5:45		31	7:17		14	6:48		28	4:31
	4	4:07		20	5:49	June	3	7:19		17	6:43		31	4:27
	7	4:10		23	5:52		6	7:22		20	6:38	Nov.	3	4:23
	10	4:13		26	5:56		9	7:24		23	6:33		6	4:18
	13	4:17		29	6:00		12	7:26		26	6:27		9	4:15
	16	4:21	Apr.	1	6:04		15	7:27		29	6:22		12	4:11
	19	4:24		4	6:08		18	7:28	Sept.	1	6:16		15	4:08
	22	4:29		7	6:12		21	7:29		4	6:11		18	4:05
	25	4:33		10	6:16		24	7:30		7	6:05		21	4:02
	28	4:37		13	6:20		27	7:30		10	6:00		24	4:00
	31	4:41		16	6:24		30	7:30		13	5:54		27	3:58
Feb.	3	4:46		19	6:27	July	3	7:29		16	5:48		30	3:56
	6	4:50		22	6:31		6	7:28		19	5:42	Dec.	3	3:55
	9	4:54		25	6:35		9	7:27		22	5:36		6	3:54
	12	4:59		28	6:39		12	7:25		25	5:31		9	3:54
	15	5:03	May	1	6:43		15	7:23		28	5:25		12	3:54
	18	5:07		4	6:47		18	7:21	Oct.	1	5:19		15	3:54
	21	5:12		7	6:50		21	7:18		4	5:13		18	3:55
	24	5:16		10	6:54		24	7:16		7	5:08		21	3:56
	27	5:20		13	6:58		27	7:12		10	5:02		24	3:58
Mar.	2	5:24		16	7:01		30	7:09		13	4:57		27	4:00
	5	5:28		19	7:05	Aug.	2	7:05		16	4:51		30	4:02
	8	5:33		22	7:08		5	7:01		19	4:46			
	11	5:37		25	7:11		8	6:57		22	4:41			
	14	5:41		28	7:14		11	6:52		25	4:36			

TORONTO, ONTARIO

Jan.	1	4:34		17	6:08		31	7:33		14	7:06		28	4:58
	4	4:36		20	6:11	June	3	7:35		17	7:02		31	4:54
	7	4:39		23	6:15		6	7:38		20	6:57	Nov.	3	4:50
	10	4:43		26	6:19		9	7:40		23	6:52		6	4:46
	13	4:46		29	6:22		12	7:41		26	6:47		9	4:42
	16	4:50	Apr.	1	6:26		15	7:43		29	6:42		12	4:39
	19	4:53		4	6:29		18	7:44	Sept.	1	6:37		15	4:36
	22	4:57		7	6:33		21	7:45		4	6:32		18	4:33
	25	5:01		10	6:37		24	7:45		7	6:26		21	4:31
	28	5:05		13	6:40		27	7:46		10	6:21		24	4:29
	31	5:09		16	6:44		30	7:45		13	6:16		27	4:27
Feb.	3	5:13		19	6:47	July	3	7:45		16	6:10		30	4:25
	6	5:17		22	6:51		6	7:44		19	6:05	Dec.	3	4:24
	9	5:21		25	6:54		9	7:43		22	5:59		6	4:24
	12	5:25		28	6:58		12	7:42		25	5:54		9	4:23
	15	5:29	May	1	7:01		15	7:40		28	5:48		12	4:23
	18	5:33		4	7:05		18	7:38	Oct.	1	5:43		15	4:24
	21	5:37		7	7:08		21	7:35		4	5:37		18	4:25
	24	5:41		10	7:12		24	7:32		7	5:32		21	4:26
	27	5:45		13	7:15		27	7:30		10	5:27		24	4:28
Mar.	2	5:49		16	7:18		30	7:26		13	5:22		27	4:30
	5	5:53		19	7:22	Aug.	2	7:23		16	5:17		30	4:32
	8	5:57		22	7:25		5	7:19		19	5:12			
	11	6:00		25	7:28		8	7:15		22	5:07			
	14	6:04		28	7:30		11	7:11		25	5:02			

VANCOUVER, BRITISH COLUMBIA

Jan.	1	4:07
	4	4:10
	7	4:13
	10	4:17
	13	4:21
	16	4:25
	19	4:30
	22	4:34
	25	4:39
	28	4:44
	31	4:49
Feb.	3	4:54
	6	4:59
	9	5:04
	12	5:08
	15	5:13
	18	5:18
	21	5:23
	24	5:28
	27	5:33
Mar.	2	5:38
	5	5:43
	8	5:47
	11	5:52
	14	5:57
	17	6:01
	20	6:06
	23	6:10
	26	6:15
	29	6:19
Apr.	1	6:24
	4	6:28
	7	6:33
	10	6:37
	13	6:42
	16	6:46
	19	6:51
	22	6:55
	25	7:00
	28	7:04
May	1	7:09
	4	7:13
	7	7:17
	10	7:22
	13	7:26
	16	7:30
	19	7:33
	22	7:38
	25	7:41
	28	7:45
	31	7:48
June	3	7:51
	6	7:54
	9	7:56
	12	7:58
	15	8:00
	18	8:01
	21	8:02
	24	8:02
	27	8:02
	30	8:02
July	3	8:01
	6	8:00
	9	7:59
	12	7:57
	15	7:54
	18	7:52
	21	7:48
	24	7:45
	27	7:41
	30	7:37
Aug.	2	7:33
	5	7:28
	8	7:24
	11	7:18
	14	7:13
	17	7:08
	20	7:02
	23	6:56
	26	6:51
	29	6:44
Sept.	1	6:38
	4	6:32
	7	6:26
	10	6:20
	13	6:13
	16	6:07
	19	6:00
	22	5:54
	25	5:47
	28	5:41
Oct.	1	5:35
	4	5:28
	7	5:22
	10	5:16
	13	5:10
	16	5:04
	19	4:58
	22	4:52
	25	4:47
	28	4:42
	31	4:36
Nov.	3	4:31
	6	4:27
	9	4:22
	12	4:18
	15	4:14
	18	4:11
	21	4:08
	24	4:05
	27	4:02
	30	4:00
Dec.	3	3:59
	6	3:58
	9	3:57
	12	3:57
	15	3:57
	18	3:58
	21	3:59
	24	4:00
	27	4:02
	30	4:05

WINNIPEG, MANITOBA

Jan.	1	4:19
	4	4:23
	7	4:26
	10	4:30
	13	4:34
	16	4:38
	19	4:43
	22	4:48
	25	4:53
	28	4:57
	31	5:03
Feb.	3	5:08
	6	5:13
	9	5:18
	12	5:23
	15	5:28
	18	5:33
	21	5:39
	24	5:44
	27	5:49
Mar.	2	5:53
	5	5:59
	8	6:04
	11	6:08
	14	6:13
	17	6:18
	20	6:23
	23	6:28
	26	6:32
	29	6:37
Apr.	1	6:42
	4	6:46
	7	6:51
	10	6:56
	13	7:01
	16	7:05
	19	7:10
	22	7:15
	25	7:19
	28	7:24
May	1	7:29
	4	7:33
	7	7:38
	10	7:42
	13	7:46
	16	7:51
	19	7:55
	22	7:59
	25	8:03
	28	8:06
	31	8:10
June	3	8:13
	6	8:15
	9	8:18
	12	8:20
	15	8:22
	18	8:23
	21	8:24
	24	8:24
	27	8:24
	30	8:24
July	3	8:23
	6	8:22
	9	8:20
	12	8:18
	15	8:16
	18	8:13
	21	8:10
	24	8:06
	27	8:02
	30	7:58
Aug.	2	7:53
	5	7:49
	8	7:44
	11	7:38
	14	7:33
	17	7:27
	20	7:21
	23	7:16
	26	7:09
	29	7:03
Sept.	1	6:57
	4	6:51
	7	6:44
	10	6:38
	13	6:31
	16	6:24
	19	6:18
	22	6:11
	25	6:04
	28	5:58
Oct.	1	5:51
	4	5:45
	7	5:38
	10	5:32
	13	5:26
	16	5:20
	19	5:14
	22	5:08
	25	5:02
	28	4:56
	31	4:51
Nov.	3	4:46
	6	4:41
	9	4:36
	12	4:32
	15	4:28
	18	4:24
	21	4:21
	24	4:18
	27	4:15
	30	4:13
Dec.	3	4:12
	6	4:10
	9	4:10
	12	4:09
	15	4:09
	18	4:10
	21	4:11
	24	4:13
	27	4:15
	30	4:17

INTERNATIONAL CITIES WITH LARGE JEWISH POPULATIONS

AMSTERDAM, THE NETHERLANDS

Jan.	1	4:19
	4	4:23
	7	4:26
	10	4:31
	13	4:35
	16	4:40
	19	4:45
	22	4:50
	25	4:55
	28	5:01
	31	5:06
Feb.	3	5:12
	6	5:17
	9	5:23
	12	5:29
	15	5:34
	18	5:40
	21	5:46
	24	5:51
	27	5:57
Mar.	2	6:02
	5	6:08
	8	6:13
	11	6:19
	14	6:24
	17	6:29
	20	6:35
	23	6:40
	26	6:45
	29	6:50
Apr.	1	6:55
	4	7:01
	7	7:06
	10	7:11
	13	7:16
	16	7:21
	19	7:27
	22	7:32
	25	7:37
	28	7:42
May	1	7:47
	4	7:52
	7	7:57
	10	8:02
	13	8:07
	16	8:12
	19	8:17
	22	8:21
	25	8:25
	28	8:29
	31	8:33
June	3	8:36
	6	8:39
	9	8:42
	12	8:44
	15	8:46
	18	8:48
	21	8:49
	24	8:49
	27	8:49
	30	8:49
July	3	8:48
	6	8:46
	9	8:44
	12	8:42
	15	8:39
	18	8:36
	21	8:32
	24	8:28
	27	8:24
	30	8:19
Aug.	2	8:14
	5	8:09
	8	8:03
	11	7:57
	14	7:51
	17	7:45
	20	7:39
	23	7:33
	26	7:26
	29	7:19
Sept.	1	7:12
	4	7:05
	7	6:59
	10	6:51
	13	6:44
	16	6:37
	19	6:30
	22	6:23
	25	6:16
	28	6:09
Oct.	1	6:02
	4	5:55
	7	5:48
	10	5:41
	13	5:34
	16	5:28
	19	5:21
	22	5:15
	25	5:08
	28	5:02
	31	4:56
Nov.	3	4:51
	6	4:45
	9	4:40
	12	4:36
	15	4:31
	18	4:27
	21	4:23
	24	4:20
	27	4:17
	30	4:14
Dec.	3	4:12
	6	4:11
	9	4:10
	12	4:09
	15	4:09
	18	4:10
	21	4:11
	24	4:12
	27	4:14
	30	4:17

BUENOS AIRES, ARGENTINA

Month	Day	Time	Month	Day	Time	Month	Day	Time	Month	Day	Time	Month	Day	Time
Jan.	1	6:52		17	5:52		31	4:33		14	5:04		28	6:01
	4	6:52		20	5:48	June	3	4:32		17	5:06		31	6:03
	7	6:52		23	5:44		6	4:32		20	5:08	Nov.	3	6:06
	10	6:52		26	5:40		9	4:31		23	5:10		6	6:09
	13	6:52		29	5:35		12	4:31		26	5:12		9	6:12
	16	6:51	Apr.	1	5:31		15	4:31		29	5:14		12	6:15
	19	6:50		4	5:27		18	4:32	Sept.	1	5:17		15	6:18
	22	6:49		7	5:23		21	4:32		4	5:19		18	6:21
	25	6:47		10	5:19		24	4:33		7	5:21		21	6:24
	28	6:46		13	5:15		27	4:34		10	5:23		24	6:27
	31	6:43		16	5:12		30	4:35		13	5:25		27	6:29
Feb.	3	6:41		19	5:08	July	3	4:36		16	5:27		30	6:32
	6	6:39		22	5:04		6	4:38		19	5:29	Dec.	3	6:35
	9	6:36		25	5:01		9	4:39		22	5:31		6	6:37
	12	6:33		28	4:57		12	4:41		25	5:34		9	6:40
	15	6:30	May	1	4:54		15	4:43		28	5:36		12	6:42
	18	6:27		4	4:51		18	4:45	Oct.	1	5:38		15	6:44
	21	6:23		7	4:49		21	4:47		4	5:40		18	6:46
	24	6:20		10	4:46		24	4:49		7	5:43		21	6:48
	27	6:16		13	4:43		27	4:51		10	5:45		24	6:49
Mar.	2	6:12		16	4:41		30	4:53		13	5:47		27	6:50
	5	6:08		19	4:39	Aug.	2	4:55		16	5:50		30	6:51
	8	6:04		22	4:37		5	4:57		19	5:53			
	11	6:00		25	4:36		8	4:59		22	5:55			
	14	5:56		28	4:34		11	5:01		25	5:58			

JOHANNESBURG, SOUTH AFRICA

Month	Day	Time	Month	Day	Time	Month	Day	Time	Month	Day	Time	Month	Day	Time
Jan.	1	6:46		17	6:05		31	5:06		14	5:30		28	6:04
	4	6:47		20	6:02	June	3	5:06		17	5:31		31	6:06
	7	6:47		23	5:59		6	5:05		20	5:32	Nov.	3	6:08
	10	6:48		26	5:55		9	5:05		23	5:34		6	6:10
	13	6:48		29	5:52		12	5:05		26	5:35		9	6:12
	16	6:47	Apr.	1	5:49		15	5:06		29	5:36		12	6:14
	19	6:47		4	5:46		18	5:06	Sept.	1	5:37		15	6:16
	22	6:46		7	5:43		21	5:07		4	5:39		18	6:19
	25	6:45		10	5:40		24	5:07		7	5:40		21	6:21
	28	6:44		13	5:37		27	5:08		10	5:41		24	6:23
	31	6:43		16	5:34		30	5:09		13	5:42		27	6:25
Feb.	3	6:42		19	5:31	July	3	5:10		16	5:43		30	6:28
	6	6:40		22	5:28		6	5:11		19	5:45	Dec.	3	6:30
	9	6:38		25	5:26		9	5:12		22	5:46		6	6:32
	12	6:36		28	5:23		12	5:14		25	5:47		9	6:34
	15	6:34	May	1	5:21		15	5:15		28	5:48		12	6:36
	18	6:31		4	5:19		18	5:17	Oct.	1	5:50		15	6:38
	21	6:29		7	5:16		21	5:18		4	5:51		18	6:40
	24	6:26		10	5:15		24	5:19		7	5:53		21	6:41
	27	6:23		13	5:13		27	5:21		10	5:54		24	6:43
Mar.	2	6:21		16	5:11		30	5:22		13	5:55		27	6:44
	5	6:18		19	5:10	Aug.	2	5:24		16	5:57		30	6:45
	8	6:15		22	5:09		5	5:25		19	5:59			
	11	6:11		25	5:08		8	5:27		22	6:00			
	14	6:08		28	5:07		11	5:28		25	6:02			

KIEV, U.S.S.R.

Month	Day	Time	Month	Day	Time	Month	Day	Time	Month	Day	Time	Month	Day	Time
Jan.	1	4:44		17	6:47		31	8:43		14	8:05		22	5:35
	4	4:47		20	6:52	June	3	8:46		17	7:59		25	5:29
	7	4:51		23	6:57		6	8:49		20	7:53		28	5:23
	10	4:55		26	7:02		9	8:52		23	7:47		31	5:18
	13	4:59		29	7:07		12	8:54		26	7:40	Nov.	3	5:12
	16	5:03	Apr.	1	7:12		15	8:56		29	7:34		6	5:07
	19	5:08		4	7:17		18	8:57	Sept.	1	7:28		9	5:02
	22	5:13		7	7:21		21	8:58		4	7:21		12	4:58
	25	5:18		10	7:26		24	8:59		7	7:14		15	4:54
	28	5:23		13	7:31		27	8:59		10	7:08		18	4:50
	31	5:28		16	7:36		30	8:58		13	7:01		21	4:46
Feb.	3	5:34		19	7:41	July	3	8:57		16	6:54		24	4:43
	6	5:39		22	7:46		6	8:56		19	6:47		27	4:40
	9	5:44		25	7:51		9	8:54		22	6:40		30	4:38
	12	5:50		28	7:56		12	8:52		25	6:33	Dec.	3	4:36
	15	5:55	May	1	8:00		15	8:49		28	6:27		6	4:35
	18	6:01		4	8:05		18	8:46	Oct.	1	6:20		9	4:34
	21	6:06		7	8:10		21	8:43		4	6:13		12	4:34
	24	6:11		10	8:15		24	8:39		7	6:07		15	4:34
	27	6:16		13	8:19		27	8:35		10	6:00		18	4:34
Mar.	2	6:22		16	8:24		30	8:31		13	5:53		21	4:35
	5	6:27		19	8:28	Aug.	2	8:26		16	5:47		24	4:37
	8	6:32		22	8:32		5	8:21		19	5:41		27	4:39
	11	6:37		25	8:36		8	8:16					30	4:42
	14	6:42		28	8:40		11	8:10						

LENINGRAD, U.S.S.R.

Jan.	1	3:45
	4	3:49
	7	3:54
	10	4:00
	13	4:06
	16	4:13
	19	4:20
	22	4:27
	25	4:35
	28	4:42
	31	4:50
Feb.	3	4:58
	6	5:06
	9	5:14
	12	5:22
	15	5:30
	18	5:37
	21	5:45
	24	5:53
	27	6:01
Mar.	2	6:08
	5	6:16
	8	6:23
	11	6:31
	14	6:38
	17	6:41
	20	6:53
	23	7:00
	26	7:07
	29	7:15
Apr.	1	7:22
	4	7:29
	7	7:37
	10	7:44
	13	7:51
	16	7:59
	19	8:06
	22	8:14
	25	8:21
	28	8:25
May	1	8:36
	4	8:43
	7	8:51
	10	8:58
	13	9:05
	16	9:12
	19	9:19
	22	9:26
	25	9:32
	28	9:39
	31	9:44
June	3	9:50
	6	9:54
	9	9:59
	12	10:02
	15	10:05
	18	10:08
	21	10:08
	24	10:08
	27	10:08
	30	10:06
July	3	10:04
	6	10:02
	9	9:58
	12	9:54
	15	9:49
	18	9:44
	21	9:38
	24	9:31
	27	9:26
	30	9:18
Aug.	2	9:10
	5	9:03
	8	8:55
	11	8:47
	14	8:39
	17	8:30
	20	8:22
	23	8:13
	26	8:04
	29	7:55
Sept.	1	7:46
	4	7:32
	7	7:28
	10	7:19
	13	7:10
	16	7:01
	19	6:52
	22	6:42
	25	6:33
	28	6:29
Oct.	1	6:15
	4	6:06
	7	5:46
	10	5:43
	13	5:39
	16	5:31
	19	5:22
	22	5:13
	25	5:05
	28	4:57
	31	4:49
Nov.	3	4:41
	6	4:33
	9	4:26
	12	4:19
	15	4:12
	18	4:06
	21	4:00
	24	3:55
	27	3:50
	30	3:45
Dec.	3	3:41
	6	3:38
	9	3:36
	12	3:34
	15	3:33
	18	3:33
	21	3:34
	24	3:36
	27	3:38
	30	3:42

LONDON, ENGLAND

Jan.	1	3:43
	4	3:47
	7	3:50
	10	3:54
	13	3:59
	16	4:03
	19	4:08
	22	4:13
	25	4:18
	28	4:23
	31	4:29
Feb.	3	4:34
	6	4:40
	9	4:45
	12	4:51
	15	4:56
	18	5:01
	21	5:07
	24	5:12
	27	5:18
Mar.	2	5:23
	5	5:28
	8	5:33
	11	5:39
	14	5:44
	17	5:49
	20	5:54
	23	5:59
	26	6:04
	29	6:09
Apr.	1	6:14
	4	6:19
	7	6:24
	10	6:29
	13	6:34
	16	6:39
	19	6:44
	22	6:49
	25	6:54
	28	6:59
May	1	7:04
	4	7:09
	7	7:14
	10	7:18
	13	7:23
	16	7:28
	19	7:32
	22	7:36
	25	7:40
	28	7:44
	31	7:48
June	3	7:51
	6	7:54
	9	7:57
	12	7:59
	15	8:01
	18	8:02
	21	8:03
	24	8:03
	27	8:03
	30	8:03
July	3	8:02
	6	8:01
	9	7:59
	12	7:57
	15	7:54
	18	7:51
	21	7:47
	24	7:43
	27	7:39
	30	7:35
Aug.	2	7:30
	5	7:25
	8	7:20
	11	7:14
	14	7:08
	17	7:02
	20	6:56
	23	6:50
	26	6:43
	29	6:37
Sept.	1	6:30
	4	6:24
	7	6:17
	10	6:10
	13	6:03
	16	5:56
	19	5:49
	22	5:42
	25	5:35
	28	5:29
Oct.	1	5:22
	4	5:15
	7	5:08
	10	5:01
	13	4:55
	16	4:48
	19	4:42
	22	4:36
	25	4:30
	28	4:24
	31	4:18
Nov.	3	4:13
	6	4:08
	9	4:03
	12	3:58
	15	3:54
	18	3:50
	21	3:46
	24	3:43
	27	3:40
	30	3:38
Dec.	3	3:36
	6	3:35
	9	3:34
	12	3:33
	15	3:33
	18	3:34
	21	3:35
	24	3:37
	27	3:39
	30	3:41

MELBOURNE, AUSTRALIA

Jan.	1	7:28
	4	7:28
	7	7:28
	10	7:28
	13	7:27
	16	7:26
	19	7:25
	22	7:23
	25	7:22
	28	7:19
	31	7:17
Feb.	3	7:14
	6	7:12
	9	7:08
	12	7:05
	15	7:02
	18	6:58
	21	6:54
	24	6:50
	27	6:46
Mar.	2	6:42
	5	6:38
	8	6:33
	11	6:29
	14	6:24
	17	6:20
	20	6:15
	23	6:11
	26	6:06
	29	6:02
Apr.	1	5:57
	4	5:52
	7	5:48
	10	5:44
	13	5:39
	16	5:35
	19	5:31
	22	5:27
	25	5:23
	28	5:20
May	1	5:16
	4	5:13
	7	5:10
	10	5:07
	13	5:04
	16	5:01
	19	4:59
	22	4:57
	25	4:55
	28	4:54
	31	4:52
June	3	4:51
	6	4:50
	9	4:50
	12	4:50
	15	4:50
	18	4:50
	21	4:50
	24	4:51
	27	4:52
	30	4:53
July	3	4:55
	6	4:56
	9	4:58
	12	5:00
	15	5:02
	18	5:05
	21	5:06
	24	5:08
	27	5:11
	30	5:13
Aug.	2	5:16
	5	5:18
	8	5:21
	11	5:23
	14	5:26
	17	5:28
	20	5:31
	23	5:33
	26	5:36
	29	5:38
Sept.	1	5:41
	4	5:43
	7	5:46
	10	5:48
	13	5:51
	16	5:53
	19	5:56
	22	5:58
	25	6:00
	28	6:04
Oct.	1	6:06
	4	6:09
	7	6:12
	10	6:14
	13	6:17
	16	6:20
	19	6:23
	22	6:26
	25	6:29
	28	6:32
	31	6:35
Nov.	3	6:39
	6	6:42
	9	6:45
	12	6:48
	15	6:52
	18	6:55
	21	6:58
	24	7:01
	27	7:05
	30	7:08
Dec.	3	7:10
	6	7:13
	9	7:16
	12	7:18
	15	7:20
	18	7:22
	21	7:24
	24	7:26
	27	7:27
	30	7:28

MEXICO CITY, MEXICO

Jan.	1	5:51
	4	5:53
	7	5:55
	10	5:57
	13	5:58
	16	6:00
	19	6:02
	22	6:04
	25	6:06
	28	6:08
	31	6:10
Feb.	3	6:11
	6	6:13
	9	6:15
	12	6:16
	15	6:18
	18	6:19
	21	6:20
	24	6:22
	27	6:22
Mar.	2	6:24
	5	6:24
	8	6:25
	11	6:27
	14	6:27
	17	6:28
	20	6:29
	23	6:30
	26	6:30
	29	6:31
Apr.	1	6:32
	4	6:33
	7	6:34
	10	6:34
	13	6:35
	16	6:36
	19	6:37
	22	6:38
	25	6:39
	28	6:40
May	1	6:41
	4	6:41
	7	6:43
	10	6:44
	13	6:45
	16	6:47
	19	6:47
	22	6:49
	25	6:50
	28	6:51
	31	6:52
June	3	6:53
	6	6:54
	9	6:54
	12	6:57
	15	6:58
	18	6:58
	21	6:59
	24	7:00
	27	7:00
	30	7:01
July	3	7:01
	6	7:01
	9	7:01
	12	7:00
	15	7:00
	18	7:00
	21	6:59
	24	6:58
	27	6:57
	30	6:56
Aug.	2	6:55
	5	6:53
	8	6:51
	11	6:50
	14	6:47
	17	6:45
	20	6:43
	23	6:41
	26	6:39
	29	6:36
Sept.	1	6:33
	4	6:31
	7	6:29
	10	6:26
	13	6:24
	16	6:21
	19	6:18
	22	6:15
	25	6:12
	28	6:10
Oct.	1	6:06
	4	6:05
	7	6:02
	10	5:59
	13	5:57
	16	5:55
	19	5:53
	22	5:51
	25	5:49
	28	5:46
	31	5:45
Nov.	3	5:43
	6	5:42
	9	5:41
	12	5:41
	15	5:39
	18	5:39
	21	5:38
	24	5:38
	27	5:38
	30	5:38
Dec.	3	5:39
	6	5:39
	9	5:40
	12	5:41
	15	5:42
	18	5:43
	21	5:45
	24	5:46
	27	5:48
	30	5:50

MOSCOW, U.S.S.R.

Jan.	1	3:48
	4	3:57
	7	4:01
	10	4:06
	13	4:11
	16	4:16
	19	4:22
	22	4:28
	25	4:34
	28	4:40
	31	4:47
Feb.	3	4:53
	6	5:00
	9	5:06
	12	5:13
	15	5:20
	18	5:26
	21	5:33
	24	5:39
	27	5:45
Mar.	2	5:52
	5	5:58
	8	6:05
	11	6:11
	14	6:17
	17	6:23
	20	6:29
	23	6:35
	26	6:42
	29	6:48
Apr.	1	6:55
	4	7:00
	7	7:06
	10	7:12
	13	7:18
	16	7:24
	19	7:30
	22	7:37
	25	7:43
	28	7:49
May	1	7:55
	4	8:01
	7	8:07
	10	8:13
	13	8:18
	16	8:24
	19	8:30
	22	8:35
	25	8:40
	28	8:45
	31	8:49
June	3	8:53
	6	8:57
	9	9:00
	12	9:03
	15	9:05
	18	9:06
	21	9:07
	24	9:08
	27	9:08
	30	9:07
July	3	9:06
	6	9:04
	9	9:01
	12	8:58
	15	8:54
	18	8:50
	21	8:46
	24	8:41
	27	8:36
	30	8:30
Aug.	2	8:24
	5	8:18
	8	8:12
	11	8:02
	14	7:58
	17	7:51
	20	7:44
	23	7:37
	26	7:29
	29	7:21
Sept.	1	7:14
	4	7:06
	7	6:58
	10	6:50
	13	6:42
	16	6:34
	19	6:26
	22	6:18
	25	6:10
	28	6:02
Oct.	1	5:54
	4	5:47
	7	5:39
	10	5:31
	13	5:23
	16	5:16
	19	5:08
	22	5:01
	25	4:54
	28	4:47
	31	4:40
Nov.	3	4:34
	6	4:28
	9	4:22
	12	4:16
	15	4:10
	18	4:05
	21	4:01
	24	3:57
	27	3:53
	30	3:50
Dec.	3	3:47
	6	3:45
	9	3:43
	12	3:42
	15	3:42
	18	3:43
	21	3:44
	24	3:45
	27	3:47
	30	3:50

PARIS, FRANCE

Jan.	1	4:47
	4	4:50
	7	4:53
	10	4:57
	13	5:01
	16	5:05
	19	5:09
	22	5:14
	25	5:19
	28	5:23
	31	5:28
Feb.	3	5:33
	6	5:38
	9	5:43
	12	5:48
	15	5:53
	18	5:58
	21	6:03
	24	6:07
	27	6:12
Mar.	2	6:17
	5	6:22
	8	6:26
	11	6:31
	14	6:36
	17	6:40
	20	6:45
	23	6:49
	26	6:54
	29	6:58
Apr.	1	7:03
	4	7:07
	7	7:12
	10	7:16
	13	7:21
	16	7:25
	19	7:29
	22	7:34
	25	7:38
	28	7:43
May	1	7:47
	4	7:51
	7	7:56
	10	8:00
	13	8:04
	16	8:08
	19	8:12
	22	8:16
	25	8:20
	28	8:23
	31	8:26
June	3	8:29
	6	8:32
	9	8:34
	12	8:36
	15	8:38
	18	8:39
	21	8:40
	24	8:40
	27	8:40
	30	8:40
July	3	8:39
	6	8:38
	9	8:37
	12	8:35
	15	8:32
	18	8:30
	21	8:27
	24	8:23
	27	8:20
	30	8:16
Aug.	2	8:11
	5	8:07
	8	8:02
	11	7:57
	14	7:52
	17	7:46
	20	7:41
	23	7:35
	26	7:29
	29	7:23
Sept.	1	7:17
	4	7:11
	7	7:05
	10	6:58
	13	6:52
	16	6:46
	19	6:39
	22	6:33
	25	6:26
	28	6:20
Oct.	1	6:14
	4	6:08
	7	6:01
	10	5:55
	13	5:49
	16	5:43
	19	5:37
	22	5:32
	25	5:26
	28	5:21
	31	5:16
Nov.	3	5:11
	6	5:06
	9	5:02
	12	4:58
	15	4:54
	18	4:50
	21	4:47
	24	4:45
	27	4:42
	30	4:40
Dec.	3	4:39
	6	4:37
	9	4:37
	12	4:37
	15	4:37
	18	4:38
	21	4:39
	24	4:40
	27	4:42
	30	4:45

RIO DE JANEIRO, BRAZIL

Jan.	1	6:26		17	5:52		31	5:00		14	5:20		28	5:47
	4	6:27		20	5:48	June	3	4:59		17	5:22		31	5:48
	7	6:27		23	5:46		6	4:59		20	5:23	Nov.	3	5:50
	10	6:28		26	5:43		9	4:59		23	5:24		6	5:52
	13	6:28		29	5:40		12	4:59		26	5:25		9	5:53
	16	6:28	Apr.	1	5:37		15	5:00		29	5:26		12	5:56
	19	6:27		4	5:34		18	5:00	Sept.	1	5:26		15	5:58
	22	6:27		7	5:32		21	5:01		4	5:27		18	6:00
	25	6:27		10	5:29		24	5:02		7	5:28		21	6:01
	28	6:26		13	5:26		27	5:02		10	5:29		24	6:04
	31	6:25		16	5:24		30	5:03		13	5:31		27	6:05
Feb.	3	6:23		19	5:21	July	3	5:04		16	5:31		30	6:08
	6	6:22		22	5:18		6	5:05		19	5:32	Dec.	3	6:10
	9	6:21		25	5:17		9	5:06		22	5:33		6	6:12
	12	6:19		28	5:14		12	5:07		25	5:33		9	6:14
	15	6:17	May	1	5:12		15	5:08		28	5:35		12	6:16
	18	6:15		4	5:10		18	5:10	Oct.	1	5:35		15	6:18
	21	6:13		7	5:08		21	5:11		4	5:37		18	6:19
	24	6:11		10	5:07		24	5:12		7	5:38		21	6:21
	27	6:07		13	5:05		27	5:14		10	5:39		24	6:22
Mar.	2	6:05		16	5:05		30	5:15		13	5:40		27	6:24
	5	6:02		19	5:02	Aug.	2	5:17		16	5:41		30	6:25
	8	6:00		22	5:02		5	5:17		19	5:43			
	11	5:57		25	5:01		8	5:19		22	5:44			
	14	5:55		28	5:01		11	5:20		25	5:46			

ROME, ITALY

Jan.	1	4:31		17	6:00		31	7:19		14	6:55		28	4:53
	4	4:34		20	6:03	June	3	7:22		17	6:51		31	4:49
	7	4:37		23	6:07		6	7:24		20	6:46	Nov.	3	4:45
	10	4:40		26	6:10		9	7:26		23	6:42		6	4:41
	13	4:43		29	6:13		12	7:26		26	6:37		9	4:38
	16	4:47	Apr.	1	6:17		15	7:29		29	6:32		12	4:35
	19	4:50		4	6:20		18	7:30	Sept.	1	6:27		15	4:32
	22	4:54		7	6:23		21	7:31		4	6:22		18	4:30
	25	4:57		10	6:27		24	7:31		7	6:17		21	4:27
	28	5:01		13	6:30		27	7:31		10	6:12		24	4:25
	31	5:05		16	6:33		30	7:31		13	6:07		27	4:24
Feb.	3	5:09		19	6:37	July	3	7:31		16	6:01		30	4:23
	6	5:13		22	6:40		6	7:30		19	5:56	Dec.	3	4:22
	9	5:17		25	6:43		9	7:29		22	5:51		6	4:21
	12	5:20		28	6:46		12	7:28		25	5:46		9	4:21
	15	5:24	May	1	6:50		15	7:26		28	5:40		12	4:21
	18	5:28		4	6:53		18	7:24	Oct.	1	5:35		15	4:22
	21	5:32		7	6:56		21	7:21		4	5:30		18	4:23
	24	5:35		10	6:59		24	7:19		7	5:25		21	4:24
	27	5:39		13	7:03		27	7:17		10	5:20		24	4:25
Mar.	2	5:43		16	7:06		30	7:14		13	5:15		27	4:27
	5	5:46		19	7:09	Aug.	2	7:10		16	5:10		30	4:29
	8	5:50		22	7:11		5	7:07		19	5:06			
	11	5:53		25	7:14		8	7:03		22	5:01			
	14	5:57		28	7:17		11	6:59		25	4:57			

SAO PAULO, BRAZIL

Jan.	1	6:39		17	6:03		31	5:09		14	5:30		28	5:59
	4	6:40		20	5:59	June	3	5:08		17	5:32		31	6:01
	7	6:40		23	5:57		6	5:08		20	5:33	Nov.	3	6:03
	10	6:41		26	5:54		9	5:08		23	5:34		6	6:05
	13	6:41		29	5:51		12	5:08		26	5:35		9	6:06
	16	6:41	Apr.	1	5:48		15	5:09		29	5:36		12	6:09
	19	6:40		4	5:45		18	5:09	Sept.	1	5:37		15	6:10
	22	6:40		7	5:42		21	5:10		4	5:38		18	6:13
	25	6:39		10	5:39		24	5:11		7	5:39		21	6:14
	28	6:39		13	5:36		27	5:11		10	5:40		24	6:17
	31	6:37		16	5:34		30	5:12		13	5:41		27	6:18
Feb.	3	6:36		19	5:31	July	3	5:13		16	5:42		30	6:21
	6	6:35		22	5:28		6	5:14		19	5:43	Dec.	3	6:23
	9	6:33		25	5:26		9	5:15		22	5:44		6	6:25
	12	6:31		28	5:24		12	5:16		25	5:44		9	6:27
	15	6:29	May	1	5:22		15	5:18		28	5:46		12	6:29
	18	6:27		4	5:19		18	5:19	Oct.	1	5:46		15	6:31
	21	6:24		7	5:18		21	5:21		4	5:48		18	6:33
	24	6:23		10	5:16		24	5:22		7	5:49		21	6:34
	27	6:19		13	5:15		27	5:23		10	5:51		24	6:35
Mar.	2	6:17		16	5:14		30	5:24		13	5:52		27	6:37
	5	6:14		19	5:12	Aug.	2	5:26		16	5:53		30	6:39
	8	6:11		22	5:11		5	5:27		19	5:55			
	11	6:09		25	5:10		8	5:28		22	5:56			
	14	6:06		28	5:10		11	5:30		25	5:58			

STOCKHOLM, SWEDEN

Jan.	1	2:40		17	5:35		31	8:27		14	7:25		28	3:49
	4	2:45		20	5:42	June	3	8:32		17	7:17		31	3:41
	7	2:50		23	5:49		6	8:37		20	7:08	Nov.	3	3:34
	10	2:55		26	5:56		9	8:41		23	7:00		6	3:26
	13	3:01		29	6:03		12	8:44		26	6:51		9	3:19
	16	3:08	Apr.	1	6:11		15	8:47		29	6:43		12	3:12
	19	3:14		4	6:18		18	8:49	Sept.	1	6:34		15	3:06
	22	3:21		7	6:25		21	8:50		4	6:25		18	3:00
	25	3:29		10	6:32		24	8:50		7	6:16		21	2:54
	28	3:36		13	6:39		27	8:50		10	6:07		24	2:49
	31	3:43		16	6:46		30	8:48		13	5:59		27	2:44
Feb.	3	3:51		19	6:53	July	3	8:47		16	5:50		30	2:40
	6	3:59		22	7:00		6	8:44		19	5:41	Dec.	3	2:37
	9	4:06		25	7:08		9	8:41		22	5:32		6	2:34
	12	4:14		28	7:15		12	8:37		25	5:23		9	2:32
	15	4:22	May	1	7:22		15	8:32		28	5:14		12	2:30
	18	4:29		4	7:29		18	8:27	Oct.	1	5:05		15	2:29
	21	4:37		7	7:36		21	8:21		4	4:56		18	2:29
	24	4:44		10	7:43		24	8:15		7	4:47		21	2:30
	27	4:52		13	7:50		27	8:09		10	4:39		24	2:32
Mar.	2	4:59		16	7:57		30	8:02		13	4:30		27	2:34
	5	5:05		19	8:03	Aug.	2	7:55		16	4:22		30	2:38
	8	5:14		22	8:10		5	7:48		19	4:13			
	11	5:21		25	8:16		8	7:40		22	4:05			
	14	5:28		28	8:22		11	7:33		25	3:57			

TOKYO, JAPAN

Jan.	1	4:20		17	5:32		31	6:32		14	6:15		28	4:33
	4	4:23		20	5:34	June	3	6:34		17	6:11		31	4:30
	7	4:25		23	5:37		6	6:36		20	6:07	Nov.	3	4:27
	10	4:28		26	5:39		9	6:37		23	6:04		6	4:24
	13	4:31		29	5:42		12	6:39		26	6:00		9	4:21
	16	4:34	Apr.	1	5:44		15	6:40		29	5:56		12	4:19
	19	4:37		4	5:47		18	6:41	Sept.	1	5:52		15	4:17
	22	4:40		7	5:49		21	6:42		4	5:47		18	4:15
	25	4:43		10	5:51		24	6:42		7	5:43		21	4:13
	28	4:46		13	5:54		27	6:43		10	5:39		24	4:12
	31	4:49		16	5:56		30	6:43		13	5:34		27	4:11
Feb.	3	4:52		19	5:59	July	3	6:43		16	5:30		30	4:10
	6	4:55		22	6:01		6	6:42		19	5:26	Dec.	3	4:10
	9	4:58		25	6:04		9	6:41		22	5:21		6	4:10
	12	5:01		28	6:06		12	6:40		25	5:17		9	4:10
	15	5:04	May	1	6:09		15	6:39		28	5:12		12	4:10
	18	5:07		4	6:11		18	6:38	Oct.	1	5:08		15	4:11
	21	5:10		7	6:14		21	6:36		4	5:04		18	4:12
	24	5:13		10	6:16		24	6:34		7	5:00		21	4:13
	27	5:16		13	6:19		27	6:32		10	4:55		24	4:15
Mar.	2	5:19		16	6:21		30	6:30		13	4:51		27	4:17
	5	5:21		19	6:23	Aug.	2	6:27		16	4:47		30	4:19
	8	5:24		22	6:26		5	6:24		19	4:44			
	11	5:27		25	6:28		8	6:21		22	4:40			
	14	5:29		28	6:30		11	6:18		25	4:36			

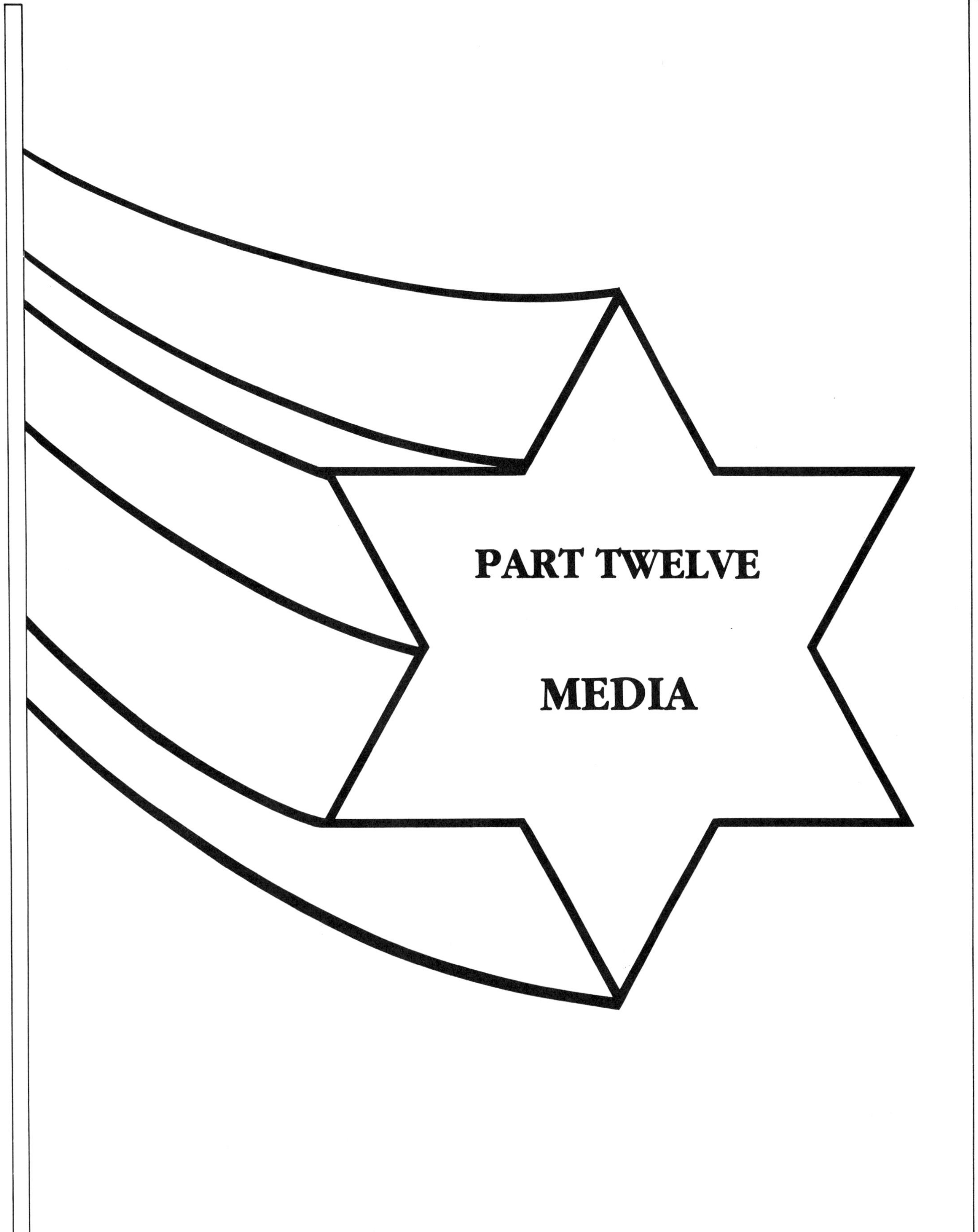

PART TWELVE

MEDIA

Jewish Books in Review

THE HOLOCAUST: A History of the Jews of Europe During the Second World War

Martin Gilbert. Henry Holt, Inc., New York. 1986. 959 pages (including notes and index; photographs and maps), $24.95.

Reviewed by David M. Szony

More than any other major history of the Holocaust, this massive new work (828 pages of text) has a graphic immediacy to it. The main reason for this is that Martin Gilbert, the prolific British-Jewish historian, relies far more extensively than other chroniclers of the Holocaust such as Lucy Dawidowicz or Raul Hilberg on eyewitness accounts related at the Nuremberg and Eichmann trials, and found in dozens of survivor memoirs.

The central paradox of the Holocaust is that the overwhelming, ungraspable horror became routinized. In one of his numerous lengthy citations—an extraordinary account of a deportation to and gassing at the Belzec death camp by Rudolf Reder, one of two survivors of the death camp, Gilbert helps us to at least begin to feel, intellectually and viscerally, the nature of "rational" mass murder.

Another great strength of this history is that it compels us to understand how the Holocaust, while centrally directed, was implemented—and resisted—in thousands of local actions. In particular, *The Holocaust* does an excellent job in recording the activities of the *Einsatzgruppen* (SS mobile mass murder units) who killed 1½ million Jews in the USSR and Baltic countries, as well as in recounting feats of partisans and rescuers. Gilbert offers details on a number of partisan groups which are little-known because all their members were eventually killed.

Using the skills that went into his *Atlas of the Holocaust,* Gilbert also provides many new maps that help the reader place the events he discusses. In addition, he, almost alone among general historians of the Holocaust, discusses the Polish pogroms which claimed several thousand Jewish lives *after* the German final surrender in May 1945.

The Holocaust's graphic immediacy is also its primary weakness. For me, reading account after account of deportations, tortures (including the most gruesome "medical" experiments) and massacres began to have a numbing effect. The intellect, and the psyche, may simply have a limited capacity to encounter mass horror.

If Gilbert is "long" on description, he is short on analysis. There is almost nothing on the ideological and political roots of Nazi ideology, on Protestant versus Catholic versus Greek and Russian Orthodox responses to the killing of Jews, and on what factors influenced Jewish responses to the spreading Nazi juggernaut of murder.

A more serious flaw is the book's omissions. Surprisingly, for the author of a fine work on *Auschwitz and the Allies,* Gilbert has included almost nothing on how the actions and non-actions of Great Britain and the U.S., as well as of their and other Jewish communities, affected the fate of European Jewry. No mention is even made, for example, of the August 1942 Riegner telegram, by which the governments in London and Washington, as well as British and American Jewish leaders, were given detailed information concerning the Final Solution.

Finally, the author's strict adherence to a chronological format—as opposed to a geographical (country-by-country) or thematic one—may make for more confusion on the part of the general reader. Because of the "simultaneous" nature of the Holocaust in over fifteen countries, Gilbert sometimes is forced to "cut" abruptly from event to event.

At times, too, Gilbert's choice of emphasis seems questionable. For example, the deportation of the Jews from the island of Rhodes is accorded five pages, but the equally improbable rescue of Danish Jewry is dispensed with in three short paragraphs—and none of the key German, Danish, Christian, or Jewish figures is mentioned.

Despite these flaws, *The Holocaust* is an impressive achievement of reconstructing the details of the darkest, as well as the most elusive event in modern Jewish history. The product of seven years of research, *The Holocaust* is such an intense history that it can best be read and absorbed slowly, in short sections at a time.

THE DESTRUCTION OF THE JEWS.

Raul Hilberg. Holmes and Meier, New York. 1985. 1274 pages. Three-volume set, $105.00.

Reviewed by Monty Noam Penkower

Rare are the works which dominate an area of scholarship like Raul Hilberg's *The Destruction of the European Jews.* Ever since that volume's appearance in 1961, specialists in Holocaust studies have come to rely on its exhaustive research and methodical analysis of the German bureaucratic process which ultimately achieved the murder of European Jewry during World War II. Publication now of a revised and definitive edition, in three handsome volumes, bears testimony to one man's singular achievement.

Step by step, Hilberg unfolds the manner in which four Nazi hierarchies—civil service, military, business, and party—fused into "a machinery of destruction." Relentlessly, administrative gears separated Jews from the rest of society through legal definition, expropriation, and concentration, pursuing all the while an emigration policy to make the Third Reich *Judenrein.* Irrevocable annihilation commenced in mid-1941 with mobile killing operations in occupied Soviet Russia, proceeded to deportations across Nazi-held Europe, and reached its climax in the unprecedented establishment of six death centers in Poland.

These sober volumes indict an entire nation, which overcame any considerations of morality or cost to the war effort. Expulsion and exclusion, regularly practiced heretofore against Jews by Christian and secular rulers, gave way to murder for the one people guilty in German ideology of birth itself. This momentous shift in history, Hilberg reveals, perforce drew upon every sector of German life; fresh documentation here on railroad transport buttresses his earlier conclusion. Collaborators played their part—Rumania's government excelling on occasion—but efficient, even zealous, Nazi bureaucrats proved most instrumental in implementing their *Fuehrer's* demonic obsession.

More could be said about opportunistic administrators eager for power, as in the Foreign Office's *Abteilung Deutschland.* Readers will have to look elsewhere for information on, among other things, Nazi educational propaganda, the post-January 1945 death marches to the German interior, and the reasons why Himmler halted the gassing apparatus at Auschwitz-Birkenau. Hilberg's low estimate of 5.1 million Holocaust victims is open to debate, as well.

Those who stood by without intervening are discussed in the chapter on rescue, an expanded account enhanced by new archival material about U.S. wartime intelligence and the possibility of bombing Auschwitz. Important outside forces like the International Red Cross, the Vatican, and the neutral states are given scant attention, but the focus on Washington and London demonstrates their complicity in Jewry's destruction. Indeed, a discussion of heroic activities by Raoul Wallenberg and Charles Lutz in Hungary, by young Jewish Palestinians operating out of Turkey, or by Jewish individuals in Switzerland and Sweden, for example, would have highlighted the fact that definite possibilities for checking the tempo of slaughter did exist. Absent was an Allied will to save. Confronted by indifference and political expediency in the Western councils of war, Jewish free world organizations (the criticism of them levelled here notwithstanding) remained fundamentally powerless.

Most problematical is Hilberg's conclusion that "the Jewish victims—caught in the straitjacket of their history—plunged themselves physically and psychologically into catastrophe." Reliance on German sources and limited attention to Jewish history led to the charge that European Jewry, which had "unlearned the art of revolt" while in the Diaspora, complied in the end with Nazi directives.

Aside from a human tendency to deny imminent danger and to remain passive when devoid of hope—witness the quiescent behavior of Polish and Russian prisoners-of-war or of millions of foreign laborers on German soil—Jews faced a hostile environment in and outside Axis-held Europe. German deception, unavailable havens, the real threat of collective responsibility, and a natural inability to comprehend the irrationality of the hitherto inconceivable—all compounded the Jewish tragedy. Remarkably (a few instances receive mention here), people hid and sought escape, various Jewish Councils and youth movements defied the "Final Solution," and uprisings took place in ghettos and three killing centers. And in several ways other than armed revolt, many Jews resisted the Nazi attempt at dehumanization and adhered to their basic values *de profundis.*

It is the domain of the perpetrators which this classic brilliantly illuminates. The fruits of a scholar's dedicated commitment force a deeper appreciation of Justice Robert Jackson's opening theme at the postwar Nuremberg trials: "The wrongs which we seek to condemn and punish have been so calculated, so malignant and so devastating, that civilization cannot tolerate their being ignored because it cannot survive their being repeated." A world witness since then to genocides and nuclear threat, as well as sensational treatment, and even denial, of the Holocaust, ignores this wisdom at gravest peril. For Raul Hilberg's seminal contribution, all pledged to the standard of human decency will be forever in his debt.

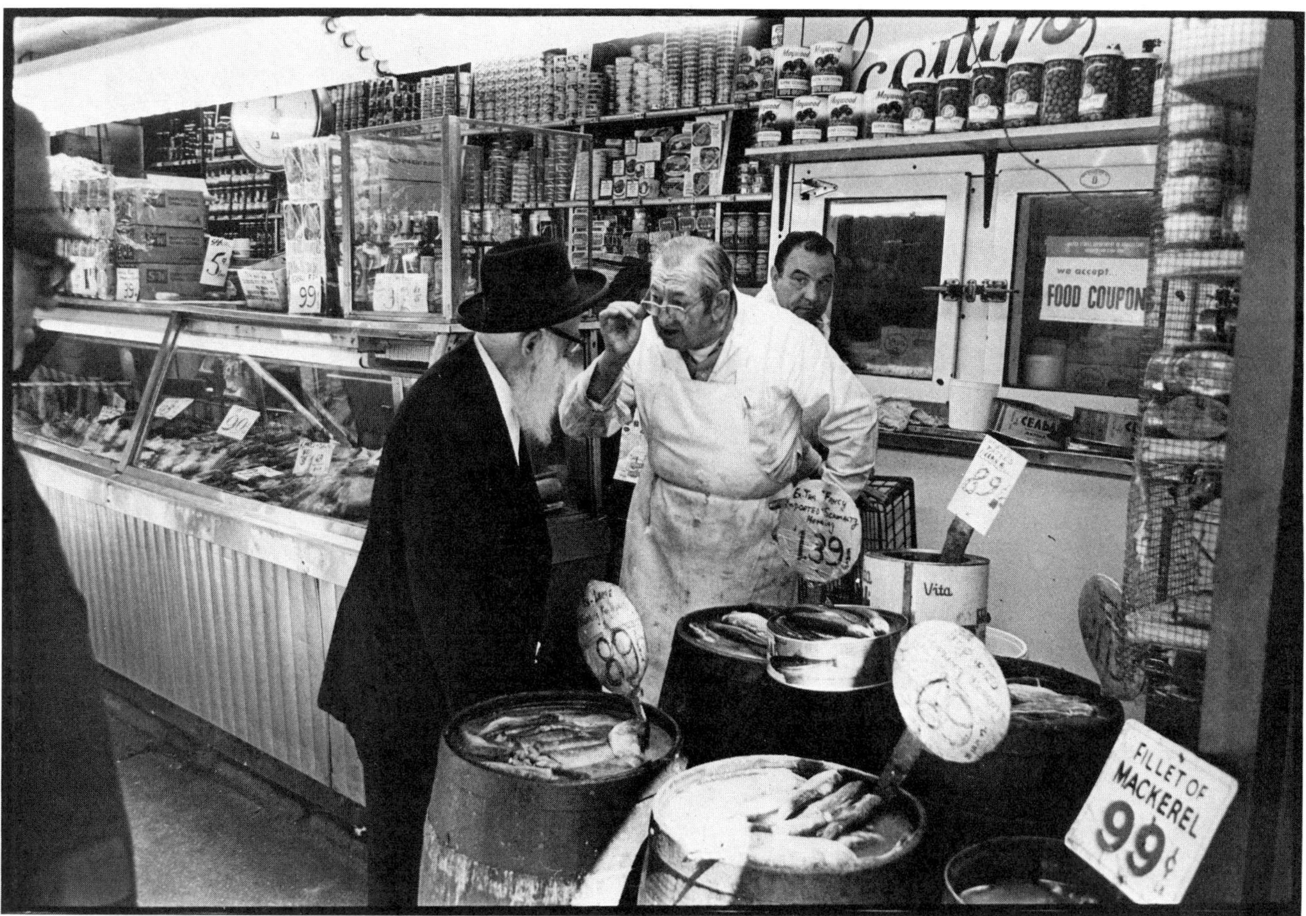

Bargaining for fish, 1976. There are no fixed prices on the Lower East Side; that is, if you know how to bargain.

FROM THE CORNERS OF THE EARTH: Contemporary Photographs of The Jewish World.

Bill Aron, Introduction by Chaim Potok. The Jewish Publication Society, Philadelphia. 1985. 143 pages. $35.00 paper.

Reviewed by Evelyn M. Cohen

The Jewish world as experienced by Aron is revealed to us through 122 black-and-white photographs. What is presented is the artist's personal vision of contemporary Jewry, rather than an all-encompassing survey of Jews around the world.

The book is divided into five main sections: New York, Los Angeles, Cuba, the Soviet Union and Jerusalem. Each is introduced by a text that explains the significance of the subject for the artist, and his experience while photographing it. Many of the individual images are accompanied by a few sentences that recount the specific circumstances under which the photographs were taken.

The myriad aspects of Jewish life in New York are conveyed by scenes of the divergent worlds of the Lower East Side, which Aron frequented, and the Upper West Side and the New York Havurah, to which he belonged.

In addition to the hustle and bustle of daily life on the Lower East Side, the first part records religious scenes like the writing of the Torah and the wedding of a young Hasidic woman. A powerfully romantic photograph records the interior shambles of the oldest synagogue in New York, which closed in 1974.

The section on the Havurah shows the group's observance of various Jewish rituals, like *Tashlich,* circumcision and services for different holidays. The sunrise recitation of *Hallel* for *Shavuot* is captured in a spiritually infused, grainy, gray-toned photograph.

A double focus is utilized for Los Angeles. Aron begins with scenes of Fairfax, the area in which he resides; and he records the various shops and community members. More moving are his portraits of elderly Jews from Venice, California. The photographs capture an inner life and hint at the uniqueness of the sitters' personal experiences.

The section on Cuba concentrates on the Sephardic synagogue of Chevet Ahim, its congregants and customs. The text accompanying the photographs contributes to our understanding of the religious experiences of Cuban Jews.

Various aspects of the life of Soviet Jews are represented in the photographs that Aron guilefully smuggled out of the Soviet Union. Many of the images are of interest as historical records of the synagogues of Leningrad, Minsk, and Moscow, and the observance of holidays there. They provide insight into the repressed but still undefeated

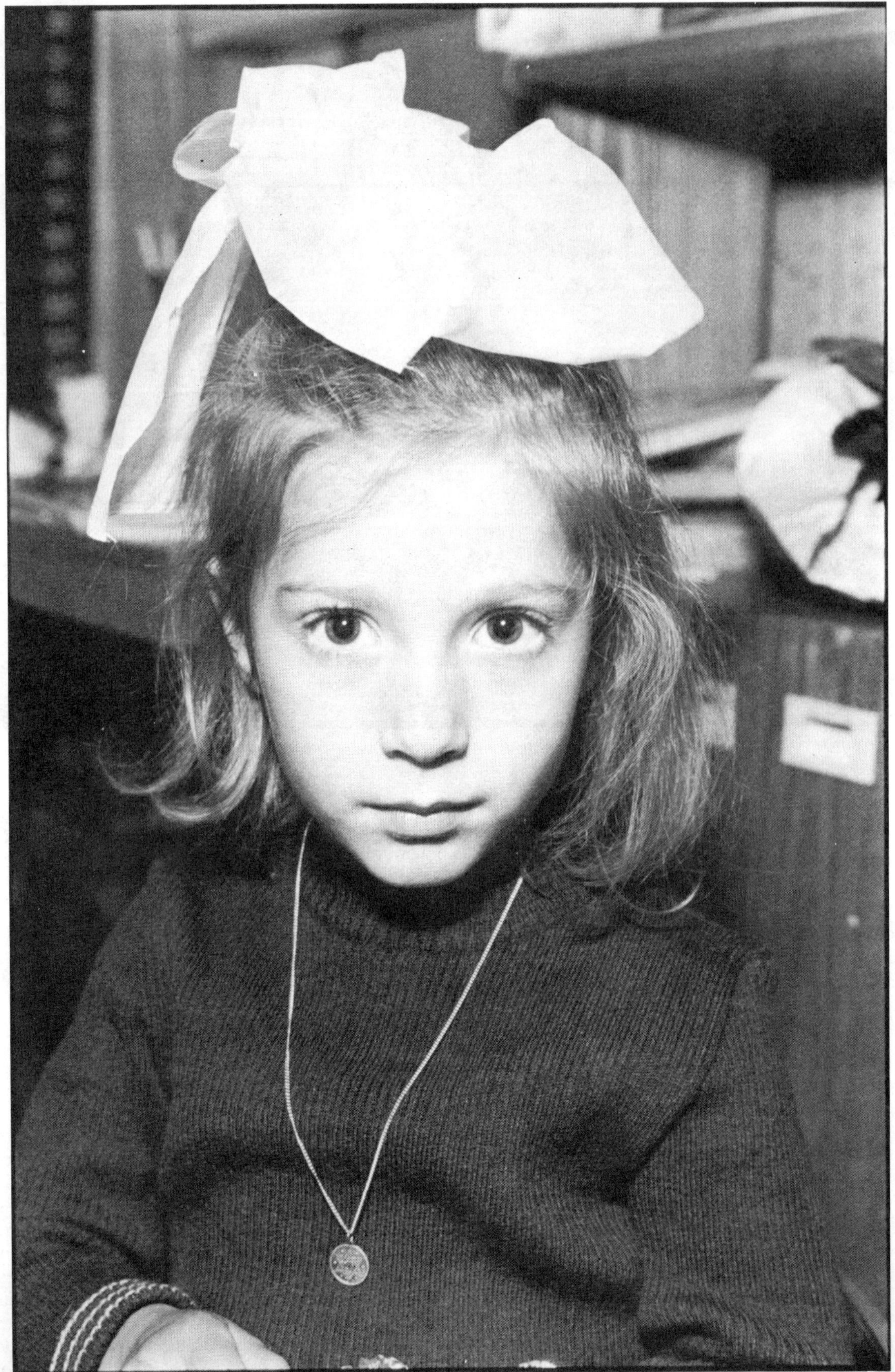

Alla Zeliger, child of Soviet refuseniks.
"Being a child refusenik is to suffer disappointment at second hand. They are the barometers of how things are with us. When our hopes are high, we see it in their faces, and when things are particularly difficult, we see our own anxiety reflected in them" (refusenik parent).

Isaac Kogan, Leningrad. Electronics Engineer. First applied: 1974. His passion about Judaism, about the Torah and about Israel has inspired scores of younger refuseniks in Leningrad.

Talis Steps

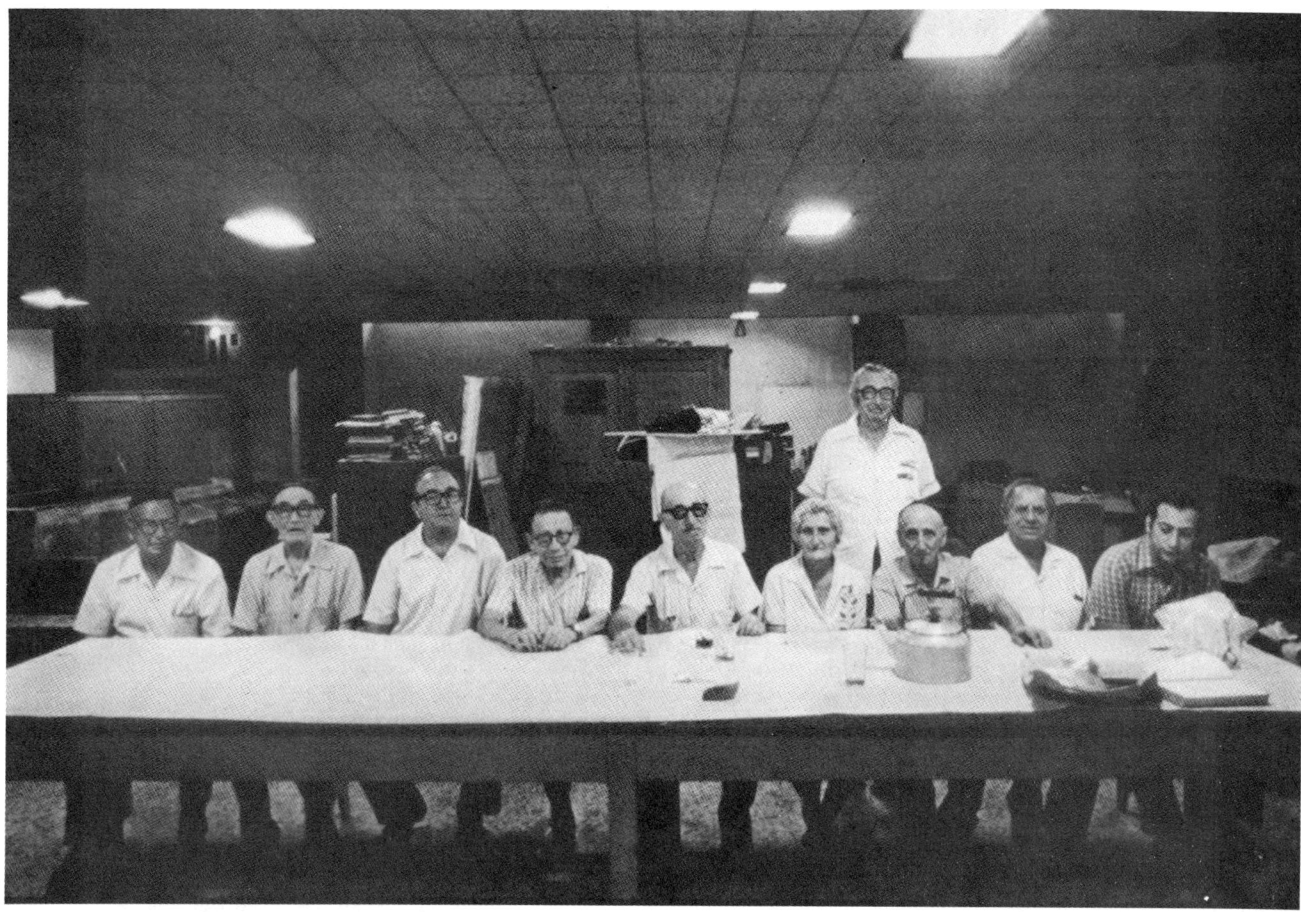

Adath Israel's minyan. *Adath Israel is the Orthodox Ashkenazic synagogue in Havana, Cuba.*

Jewish spirit. The accompanying text in this section is moving and enlightening, and the photographs of the refuseniks are the most penetrating in the book.

The most original and striking images are in the section on Jerusalem. Aron was concerned that it would be difficult to discover something new in a city that has been photographed so frequently, but the way he captured the pervasive contrast of light and shadow creates surprising and lasting images.

From the Corners of the Earth is an interesting record of Jewish life as seen through the eyes of Bill Aron. The photographs sensitively record Jewish circumstances, customs, and monuments. The book functions as a visual historical record, and as a work of art.

SYNAGOGUES OF EUROPE: Architecture, History, Meaning.

Carol Herselle Krinsky. The Architectural History Foundation and The MIT Press, Cambridge, MA. 1985. 457 pages. $50.00.

Reviewed by Vivian B. Mann

More than twenty years have passed since the publication of the last serious survey of European synagogue architecture (*The Architecture of the European Synagogue* by Rachel Wischnitzer). New archaeological discoveries, restorations, and research in the intervening years demanded a book like Carol Herselle Krinsky's *Synagogues of Europe.*

The scope of the topic obviously presented problems of presentation, even within the confines of a 457-page book. The diverse potential audiences, scholarly or public, Jewish or Gentile, must have also been a factor in determining the organization of the material and the contents. Professor Krinsky has chosen an unusual format as an answer to these questions. The first 138 pages are devoted to three essays: an introduction on the origin and definition of the synagogue, which also includes a comparison to other religious buildings and to secular ones; "Ritual Arrangements," which discusses the perennial problem of synagogue architecture—the relative arrangement of the Torah ark and the reader's desk, as well as lighting, spaces for women, auxiliary spaces, and the placement of pulpit, choir and organ; and thirdly, an essay on the history of the synagogue from antiquity to modern times. These essays are annotated, but accompanied by very few illustrations, so that readers who are unfamiliar with the monuments mentioned in the text must turn to the second half of the book, "Selected Examples," both for illustrations and for examples which deepen their knowledge of the general points being made.

The organization of the second half is entirely different. The selected synagogues discussed are arranged geographically under nine headings: Austria-Hungary and the Balkans (there are no Greek synagogues in this section or elsewhere), Eastern Europe and the U.S.S.R., France and Belgium, Germany and Switzerland, Iberian Peninsula, Italy, The Netherlands, Scandinavia, and the United Kingdom. Within areas, the synagogues are listed by city, from the oldest to the most recent. Each monument is treated in a concise essay accompanied by a helpful bibliography and illustrations. One has the impression that this part of the book is intended as a ready reference for those planning a trip to a particular area of Europe, an impression which is reinforced by the "Notes for the Visitor" at the back of the book, a peculiar inclusion if the book were intended only for a scholarly audience. Yet, if the book is also aimed for the lay public, as it clearly is, then it is unfortunate that there is no glossary of architectural terms to explain *artesonado,* pendentives, Tuscan columns, and the like. There is a glossary of Hebrew terms, an extensive bibliography, and two appendices, a list of selected architects subdivided into Christian and Jewish, and a list of extant Polish synagogues and their present uses (but no listing of extant Greek or Italian synagogues or of any other country whose Jewish population was decimated by the war).

Turin, Mole Antonelliana, built 1862-89.

Synagogues of Europe is a very well-written book. Carol Krinsky's sprightly prose carries the reader along, and her text includes lively comments not usually found in works by academics. The book is also beautifully designed and printed. Professor Krinsky is fortunate to have as publishers the Architectural History Foundation and the MIT Press.

Still, this is in some ways an annoying book, particularly the introductory essays of the first section. The author often presents sweeping generalizations based on incomplete evidence. In explaining why her book focuses on Central and Western European synagogues instead of including more material on Eastern Europe, Ms. Krinsky writes: "Adherents of the ultraorthodox, mystically-oriented Hasidic sect, which was prominent especially in Eastern Europe from the late eighteenth century onward, profess indifference to their surroundings during prayer and

Florence Synagogue, built 1874-82.

Essen, Steelerstrasse. Today the shell stands as a memorial to the victims of the Holocaust.

Lutsk, fortified synagogue, built 1626-28.

Stockholm Synagogue, built 1869-70.

Moscow Synagogue, Arkhipova Street, built 1891.

Vienna, Tempelgasse, built 1853-58.

devote more attention to rooms where they study," as if all Hasidim were indifferent to architecture, an implication disproved elsewhere in the book, or that all East European Jews were Hasidim. (For some inexplicable reason, Ms. Krinsky keeps referring to the plural as Hasids.) Equally disconcerting in a book on synagogues is the constant use of the terms "Holy Land," a name with distinct Christological references, and "ultra-orthodox," an adjective which is indiscriminately used, even for Judaism of Rabbi Samson Raphael Hirsch (1808-1888) who advocated a union of traditional Jewish life with modernism. Despite shortcomings such as these, *Synagogues of Europe* is a significant work which will remain an important reference.

JEWS IN AN ARAB LAND:
Libya, 1835-1970.
Renzo De Felice. University of Texas Press, Austin. 1985. 406 pages. $22.50.

THE JEWS OF MOSLEM SPAIN:
Volume 3.
Eliyahu Ashtor. Jewish Publication Society, Philadelphia. 1984. 310 pages. $19.95

THE LAST ARAB JEWS:
The Communities of Jerba, Tunisia.
Abraham L. Udovitch and Lucette Valensi. Harwood Academic Publishers, New York. 1985. 178 pages. $36.00.

THE DHIMMI:
Jews and Christians Under Islam.
Bat Ye'or. Fairleigh Dickinson University Press, Madison, NJ. 1985. 444 pages. $25.00 (cloth), $9.95 (paper).

THE JEWS OF ISLAM.
Bernard Lewis. Princeton University Press, Princeton, NJ. 1984. 245 pages. $17.50.

Reviewed by Arnold Ages

There is a marvelous dictum in French which comes to mind in scrutinizing the vast literature which deals with Jews and Arab-Islamic civilization. "Tout peut etre prouve contre quelqu'un. La culpabilite est une notion elastique. Cela depend de l'eclairage." (Anything can be proved against an individual, guilt being an elastic concept. It all depends on the lighting.).

This tendency to focus the lighting for polemical effects has been all too common in recent years in the arena of the Arab-Jewish encounter. Arab sources have been portraying the historical aspect of that meeting as a congenial condominium rent asunder only by the unhappy emergence of political Zionism and its step-sister, Israel. The obverse side of that coin is the depiction of Jewish life under Islam as uniformly oppressive and dark.

The truth about this phenomenon is, of course, much

Forty-five unmarked graves of unidentifiable Jews killed in the 1945 pogrom. From Jews in an Arab Land.

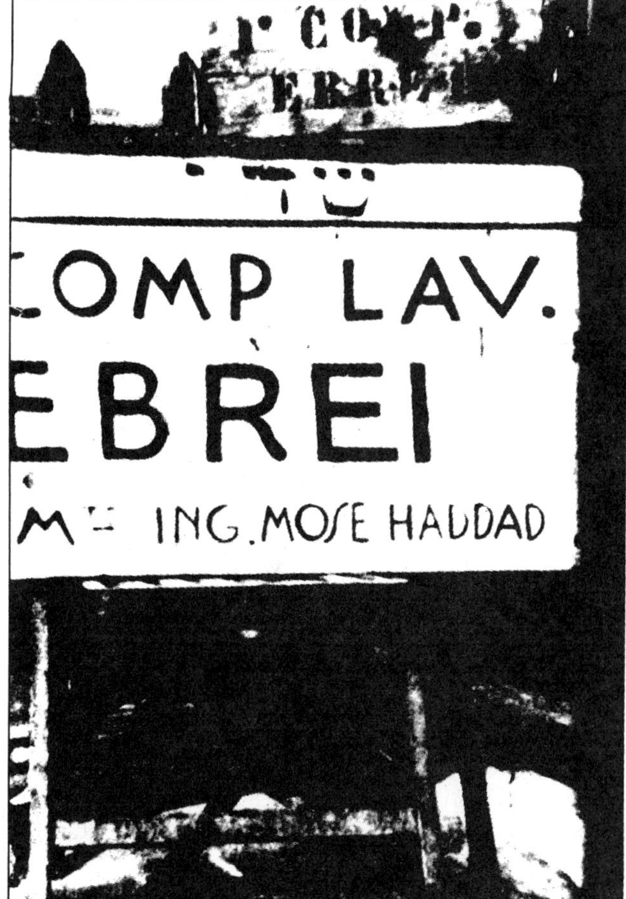

Entrance to a labor camp for Jews in Libya during the Second World War. From Jews in an Arab Land.

more complex, as a host of new books on the subject shows. A consensus elicited from a selection of these studies suggests even more pointedly that both versions of Jewish-Islamic civilization have elements of truth in them.

Renzo De Felice's study of Libyan Jewry and Bat Ye'or's survey of the concept of the *dhimmi* concentrate on the infelicitous experience of Jews (and, in the latter case, of Christians as well) under Islamic hegemony. The term itself means the "protected one," but it shows merely that the Arabs had a gift for euphemism.

The *dhimmi* represented non-Muslim groups in conquered lands who were required to submit themselves to various incivilities as part of Islam's colonization efforts. In the early stages, the *dhimmi* sometimes outnumbered the followers of Allah and restrictions against them were administered with circumspection. When the Muslims became the dominant population, the rigors of *dhimmi* status became more pronounced.

Dhimmi status conveyed inferiority and in the case of Jews promoted contempt by Arabs, the magnitude of that sentiment being dictated by the era in question, the form of Islam, and the political status of the Arab population. The Jews of Libya seem to have gone through various stages of negative stereotyping and treatment during the Ottoman period, the epoch of Italian rule, and the current Quadaffi regime.

The harsh conditions under which Jews lived in Islamic society were often mitigated, however, by accommoda-

ANNO III. N. 7 PREZZO M.A.L. 10

HAIENU

ORGANO BENÉ AKIVA E BACHAD DELLA LIBIA · VIA ARBAA ARSAAT 99 · P.O.B. 210 TRIPOLI

A tutti gli Ebrei di Libia

BERACHA' VESHALOM

Masthead of the last Jewish newspaper published in Libya (1951). From Jews in an Arab Land.

tions through which the Jewish spirit endured and often flourished.

The Jews of Moslem Spain, so ably described in Ashtor's third volume on the subject, reached great cultural and religious heights under Islamic civilization. Spurred in part by Arab intellectual and artistic energies, Jews in that society produced poetry of great technical brilliance and made significant advances in philosophy, Biblical criticism, and other pursuits.

In tracing the daily life style of a Jew in eleventh-century Spain, Ashtor shows that despite discriminatory taxes, housing regulations, and commercial restrictions, it was possible to maintain one's Jewish equilibrium in the synagogue and the home.

The equilibrium was perpetuated right into the twentieth century. The Udovitch-Valensi volume on the Jews of Jerba demonstrates the astonishing resilience which Jews under Islamic rule manifested. Jerban Jews, the descendants of one of the oldest Jewish collectives to populate an Islamic area, are shown in striking photographs and essays to have been a strikingly vital community.

The Hebrew of Jerban Jews is said to be pure and pristine and they still retain characteristic Jewish dress, body language, occupations and trades. The religious traditions and rites which the community observes to this day are poignant reminders of an authentic Jewish ritual.

Bernard Lewis, the dean of orientalists today, feels that the current Arab antisemitism and the consequent embitterment of Arab-Jewish relations is strictly the product of political turmoil related to Palestine and the emergence of the State of Israel.

In his magisterial survey of several centuries of contact between Jews and Islam he also discourses on the question of the *dhimmi,* pointing out that the issue of tolerance is really an irrelevant one. No societies before the Age of Enlightenment (and not many after) entertained the concept of tolerance, and it would have been unthinkable for Muslim civilization to have invoked it.

What is remarkable, as Lewis suggests, is that in the face of Islamic restrictions, Jews achieved important symbioses with Arab cultures and borrowed heavily from them in many areas. He also shows that in many instances there was

Every Sabbath eve, and every eve of the New Moon, women light candles in memory of the dead. From The Last Arab Jews.

reciprocity. In Turkey, for example, Jews made contributions to medicine, the performing arts, and printing.

"There have been many chapters in the long history of the Jewish people," writes Lewis. "The Judeao-Islamic symbiosis was another great period of Jewish life and creativity, a long, rich, and vital chapter. . . . It has now come to an end."

The experience has ended but the composition of books and monographs on the theme is just beginning. The fine studies represented in this survey of recent texts show that the intellectual task of reconstruction and criticism is an exciting and important exercise.

Friday afternoon fever: every family carries its Sabbath meal to the communal oven. From The Last Arab Jews.

ISRAEL IN THE BLACK AMERICAN PERSPECTIVE

Robert G. Weisbord and Richard Kazarian, Jr. Greenwood Press, Westport, CT. 1985. 213 pages. $29.95

Reviewed by Alan M. Schwartz

If a Jewish Rip Van Winkle were to wake up today after a 20-year nap, one change he would find most startling is the nature of the relationship between America's Black and Jewish communities.

Having seen the growth of close Black-Jewish ties during the period of the great civil rights marches and other acts of social conscience led by Dr. Martin Luther King, Jr.—supported in disproportionate numbers by Jews as compared to other non-Black Americans—the sleeper might be shocked by the strained state of the current U.S. Black-Jewish relationship. "What happened?" he would ask, blinking awake.

Quite a lot. For he had slumbered through several crucial developments:

- The 1967 Six Day War, which deceptively transformed Israel's image in some quarters from underdog David to aggressive Goliath;
- The extremism and Jew-baiting of Black radical groups such as the Black Panthers and the formerly integrationist Student Non-Violent Coordinating Committee;
- The hostile Black-Jewish polarization generated by the New York City teachers' strike of 1968;
- The increasingly anti-American, anti-Israel and even antisemitic attitudes of many younger, university-educated Blacks who identify with Third World "liberation movements," including the PLO;
- Growing propaganda efforts to link Israel to South Africa and its oppressive apartheid policy;
- The contentious policy dispute over quotas and "affirmative action";
- The controversial resignation of Andrew Young, the first Black U.S. ambassador to the U.N., and its bitter consequences;
- And the highly publicized antisemitism of charismatic Black figures Jesse Jackson and Louis Farrakhan.

Robert G. Weisbord, professor of history at the University of Rhode Island, and Richard Kazarian, Jr., a history instructor there, have intelligently described all these events and much more in their recent useful book, *Israel in the Black American Perspective.*

In fact, the authors go considerably beyond the title's central theme, analyzing a broad range of issues affecting the relationship between America's Black and Jewish minorities. It must be noted that in their analysis of these broader themes, the authors occasionally allow their own political views to color, and thereby weaken, their otherwise more objective and well-rounded analysis.

Yet there is much to compliment in the book. Of particular interest is the enlightening and little-known historical perspective of significant Black sympathy for the early Zionist movement, which was viewed as an example of self-help and effective political activism for other oppressed minorities.

The authors provide richly documented background data on the increasingly divergent views and priorities that have evolved between Blacks and Jews over the last two decades, while not ignoring more positive signs of a continuing mutuality of concern—including the generally solid pro-Israel voting record of the Congressional Black Caucus, and strong Jewish electoral support for Black candidates in several important races.

In addition, the book contains a helpful and extensive bibliography of books, articles, reports, interviews and other sources, reflecting the authors' feel for well-rounded detail and genuine scholarship.

Commendably, Weisbord and Kazarian often seek to clarify the underlying reasons for painfully clashing opinions, and to set the record straight with respect to unfair accusations by all sides. At times, however, this effort is strained. The authors go beyond the requirements of fairness in offering rationales for Jesse Jackson's insensitive and unacceptable 1979 comments about the Holocaust; in suggesting that Menachem Begin, having "snubbed" Jackson, bore some blame for the latter's hostile anti-Zionism; and in proclaiming that recent backing for Israel by Christian Fundamentalists "is not based on a love for Jews." The book's reference to that last issue is contentious and distorted.

All in all, however, *Israel in the Black American Perspective* is a significant and worthwhile contribution to a troubled subject area in need of such broad and thoughtful exploration. The authors conclude on the positive note that Blacks and Jews, still confronting a common enemy in bigotry, "share a fundamental vision of a just society devoid of racial or religious hatred," in which both groups have much at stake.

At the same time, the very events catalogued in the book give the informed realist pause. As Professor Glenn C. Loury of Harvard observed recently in *Commentary* magazine ("Behind the Black-Jewish Split," January 1985):

> There is something inexorable about Black-Jewish conflict over the Middle East. For much of Black elite opinion . . . rejects the very civilization of which the Jewish state is the sole representative in that part of the world. . .(O)ur reflective and influential elites have come to order their experience, as Americans and as citizens of the world, in profoundly different ways."

(An excerpt appears earlier in this volume.)

ANTI-SEMITISM IN THE SOVIET UNION: Its Roots and Consequences.

Edited by Theodore Freedman. Freedom Library Press of the Anti-Defamation League of B'nai B'rith, New York. 1984. 664 pages. $35.00 (cloth), $16.95 (paper).

THE JEWS OF HOPE

Martin Gilbert. Elizabeth Sifton Books/Viking Penguin, New York. 1985. 237 pages. $15.95.

THE SOVIET GOVERNMENT AND THE JEWS 1948-1967: A Documented Study.

Benjamin Pinkus. Cambridge University Press, New York. 612 pages. $59.50.

Reviewed by Mark Friedman

These three books represent important, yet very different, contributions to the large body of literature on Soviet Jewry.

In his foreward to *Anti-Semitism in the Soviet Union,* Kenneth Bialkin, president of the ADL and chairman of the Presidents' Conference, writes that "Simply put, there is no way that a fair-minded person can avoid drawing anything but the most ominous conclusions after reading these essays." Mr. Bialkin seems to be describing both the purpose and the effect of this first book to bear the imprint of the Freedom Library Press of the ADL.

It is curious that no mention is made anywhere in the book that much of its content was published in 1983 in Jerusalem under the same title by the Hebrew University and its Centre for Research and Documentation of East European Jewry. The book is nonetheless effective. It offers many first-rate essays by Soviet Jewish emigres, Western Jewish scholars, and other prominent individuals, including a founder of the Italian Communist Party. The essays examine the political anti-Semitism of the Soviet government, the anti-Semitism of the people, and even the anti-Semitism of the dissidents, as evidenced in the underground samizdat publications reproduced in the book.

The usefulness of the book is limited by its index, which is restricted to names and titles. Even so, when this reviewer searched for an entry on Freemasons and their alleged connections to the Jews, a theme of the notorious anti-Semitic work, *Protocols of the Elders of Zion,* there was no listing at all, although the subject was raised in several places in the book.

Martin Gilbert, the noted British historian and cartographer, and the biographer of Winston Churchill, has written a short, very readable account of his trip to the Soviet Union in 1983. *The Jews of Hope* comes a generation after Eli Wiesel's *The Jews of Silence* and indeed describes a new generation of Soviet Jews—that of the refuseniks—those Jews who have been refused the right to emigrate, but who have not lost hope.

This is a work of advocacy, relating the stories of the refuseniks such as Vladimir Slepak, Yosif Begun, Ilya Essas, Anatoly Scharansky, and others in a personal, moving style. Gilbert stresses repeatedly that the refuseniks are not anti-Soviet, although their requests to leave the Soviet Union represent a most serious challenge to the communist system. While Gilbert tells his story well, it is an oft-told tale, and one that has been told well in the first person by Mark Azbel in his *Refusenik* (Boston, 1981).

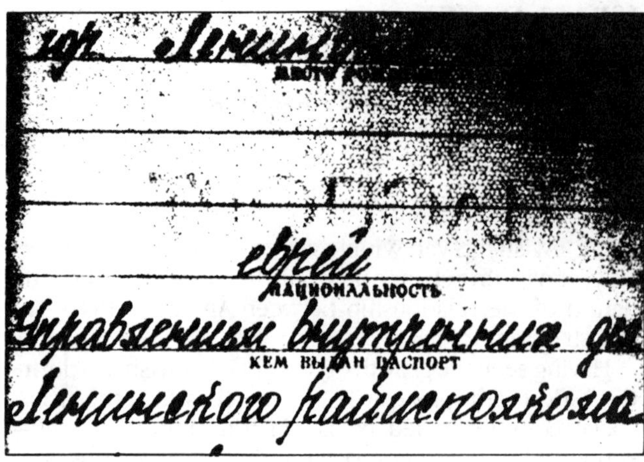

The word Evrei *(Jew) as it appears in the "nationality" section of a Soviet identity card.*

Benjamin Pinkus has produced an important work of scholarship in his *The Soviet Government and the Jews 1948-1967.* This book is the culmination of ten years of work by Professor Pinkus, who for several years headed the Centre for Documentation and Research of East European Jewry in Jerusalem. He compiled and edited the seven-volume Russian language collection of documents, *Jews and the Jewish People 1948-1953.*

It is not surprising that Pinkus should prepare "A documented study," replete with 172 documents, which support and elaborate his text, and are of great value in themselves. It is also not surprising that the study seeks roots before 1948 and implications for after 1967. However, the price of the book, $59.50, is more than surprising, it is shocking.

The Soviet Government and the Jews is the product of immense labor by a good scholar and will be cited for many years to come. *The Jews of Hope* and *Anti-Semitism in the Soviet Union,* on the other hand, will be more useful books for informing and motivating the public on the plight of Soviet Jewry.

JOINING THE CLUB: A History of Jews and Yale.

Dan A. Oren. Yale University Press, New Haven. 1986. 440 pages. $19.95.

Reviewed by Joseph Aaron

Just because you're paranoid, goes the old saying, doesn't mean that someone's not following you.

Don't judge a university, goes the variation on another old saying, by the Hebrew on its seal.

What prompts this wallowing in old sayings is the publication of *Joining the Club,* which documents, for the first time, what many have suspected for a long time. Namely, that Ivy League schools, for a good part of this century, had quotas to limit the number of Jewish students they would let in.

The book deals specifically with the policies of one of those Ivy League schools, Yale, but, says author Dan Oren, what took place at Yale almost certainly took place also at

Harvard, Columbia, Princeton and others of the prestigious Eastern universities.

What took place, as Oren shows in this thoroughly researched work, is that for almost four decades, Jews were officially kept out of Yale while those who were let in were unofficially kept down. This at a school which features Hebrew words on its official seal and that was founded on the principles of "Enlightenment and Truth."

And the truth, notes Oren, is that the philosophy pretty much held from Yale's founding in 1707 through the end of the 19th century. Yale was known for its tradition of open enrollment and tolerance, with Jews receiving equal access to clubs and classrooms. That, however, was simply because there weren't very many Jews at Yale. But with the mass immigration of Eastern European Jews at the end of the 19th and beginning of the 20th centuries, far greater numbers of Jews applied to, and were accepted into Yale.

And that proved to be too much for members of the elite that made up much of Yale's alumni. They felt threatened by the rise of the "alien and unwashed element," were concerned about Yale maintaining itself as "one of the links in the national chain protecting the WASP establishment." They insisted that something had to be done.

The book, in fascinating detail and in an appealingly anecdotal style, describes how members of the Yale alumni got their message across about what that something should be. Equally gripping are specifics of how members of the Yale administration devised ways of keeping Jews out, without anyone knowing that that was what they were doing.

What they did, beginning in 1923, was set up a Limitation of Numbers Policy which, while announced publicly as a measure aimed at paring total enrollment, sought, specifically and privately, to reduce the number of Jewish Students. Under the policy, which would remain in effect until 1960, Jewish enrollment at Yale was deliberately limited to about 10 percent of the student body.

Just as riveting is Oren's account of how those Jews who were let into the student body were kept out of fraternities, clubs, publications and secret societies that made up Yale's campus elite and that did much to determine campus policy.

Citing example after example, Oren shows convincingly that the only way for a Jew to make it at Yale was to give up all signs of his Jewishness. Perhaps the saddest example of that is Dr. Milton Winternitz, a Jew who transformed the Yale Medical School from a fourth-rate institution to one of the nation's best, yet did much to hide his own Jewish background and did much to harass those students who didn't do the same.

Oren provides many such intriguing and telling behind-the-scenes peeks at the personalities and inner workings of this major university. Workings it was able to hide until Oren began snooping around while working on a sophomore term paper for the Jewish history class he was taking at Yale.

That's right, Yale. Oren researched and wrote the book beginning while he was an undergraduate at Yale and continuing as a student in Yale's Medical School. Which shows not only that he's an excellent investigative reporter and a surprisingly good writer for a chemistry major, but that he's not short on guts either. Happily, Oren suffered no ill effects from airing his alma mater's dirty linen. On the contrary, he received nothing but help and support from Yale officials.

That fact, along with the facts that Jews now make up more than 30 percent of Yale's student body and that the book was published by Yale University Press, shows the truth of yet another variation on yet another old saying: You *can* teach an old university new tricks.

A CERTAIN PEOPLE: American Jews and Their Lives Today.

Charles E. Silberman. Summit Books, New York. 1985. 458 pages. $19.95

Reviewed by Mark Friedman

There is a joke that goes, "Just because you are paranoid, it does not mean that you are not being chased." The Jewish people is unquestionably paranoid, but Charles Silberman has written an important book telling us that we are not being chased.

Spurred by the pessimism clouding the Jewish horizon during the time of the energy shortage, the Andrew Young affair, and Billy Carter, the noted journalist and social observer Charles Silberman undertook to study the state of American Jewry. His findings are optimistic: Jews are secure; antisemitism is not a significant factor in American Jewish life; all the doors to American society are now open to Jews; the Jewish establishment is becoming more Jewish; Judaism is being renewed in America; intermarriage is lower than we feared; American Jewry may be strengthened by Gentiles by birth who become Jews by choice.

The United States is indeed different. It has no history of medieval antisemitism to overcome. But it is a very small world, and attacks on Jews in Rome, Paris, Copenhagen, London, and many other places in recent years make it difficult for Jews anywhere to feel too secure.

There is no question that antisemitism is not respectable in America. It is unfashionable on the suburban commuter lines, but it is alive on the subways. There is a difference between the lower class in America and the middle and upper classes in how they relate to the Jews. Neither all the Gentiles nor all the Jews have moved to the civil society of uptown.

Silberman does not write about the Jews of downtown—the Jews who are today of the first or second generations. He is not kind to the Orthodox. The text, notes, and acknowledgements show that he did not listen to the Orthodox, much less to the different groups among them.

America is the ultimate laboratory for the experiment of modernity. The community of Jews is dissolving as today's Jews no longer share common roots. Even the lowest common denominator of Jewish identity and unity—caring for other Jews—is deteriorating as the basis for tying American Jews together. It is more difficult now for Jews of different types to speak to each other and there are no signs on the horizon that this will change.

This makes it all the more difficult to write about American Jews. Silberman might well have paid more attention to the economic factor as it affects Judaism. He might also have done well to compare America's Jews to Jews elsewhere. But Silberman has done a marvelous job of presenting a certain view of a certain people, one that will certainly enliven the debate on Jewish life in America.

WHY DO THE JEWS NEED A LAND OF THEIR OWN?

Sholom Aleichem; translated by Joseph Leftwich and Mordecai S. Chertoff. Herzl Press/Cornwall Books, Cranbury, NJ. 1984. 242 pages. $19.95

Reviewed by Jacob Kabakoff

Upon the initiative of the Shalom Aleichem House in Tel-Aviv, where the writer's archives are housed, a collection of his scattered Zionist writings in Yiddish was published some seven years ago. It was followed in 1981 by a Hebrew translation, and now has been made available in English translation.

At a time when Yiddish writers paid obeisance to a variety of ideologies regarding the Jewish problem, Sholom Aleichem identified completely with the Zionist cause. He gave expression to his warm feelings for Zion in various literary genres—stories, dramatizations, a short novel, political essays, and Menachem Mendel letters. His deep attachment to Zion is clearly evident in words such as those he had his well-known character Menachem Mendel dispatch in 1913 to his wife Sheine Sheindel:

> When I hear the word Zion or the word Jerusalem, I am transported! Something catches fire in me, and I am filled with longing for our ancient home and for our state. My soul faints in me for something that is our own. . . .

Already a quarter of a century earlier, in 1888, Sholom Aleichem wrote to Leon Pinsker, chairman of the Lovers of Zion in Russia, asking to be enrolled as a member. He sent along his dues and signed his letter, "One of the Lovers of Zion, not on paper, but with all my heart as it should be."

Sholom Aleichem remained active in the movement and with the advent of Herzl became an enthusiastic follower of the Zionist leader. He put his pen at the service of the Zionist cause and devoted a brochure to the first Zionist Congress in Basel in which he vividly depicted its leaders and deliberations. When Herzl died, Sholom Aleichem published a pamphlet extolling Herzl as a legendary figure who was not fully appreciated during his lifetime.

But it was not only in his brochures that were circulated in thousands of copies that the celebrated writer reached out to the masses. In a number of his short stories he depicted the longings of East European Jews for a homeland of their own. He has Selig Mechanic, in a story by this name, undertake a long journey in order to share in the mitzvah of contributing to Palestine. In his story, "Homesick," the Jews of Kasrilevky subscribe to a share of the Jewish Bank established by Herzl. When it finally arrives, Rabbi Yosifl recites a blessing over it and sighs tearfully, "I am homesick."

Sholom Aleichem did not merely play upon the emotions of his readers. He exposed the foibles of his contemporaries and castigated them for their assimilatory views, their divisiveness and their inability to agree on a program of action. In his satire, "The First Republic," for example, thirteen Jews who are shipwrecked on an island decide to build a Jewish state, but they end up with thirteen different constitutions.

The title essay, "Why Do Jews Need a Land of Their Own?" was also originally published in brochure form for propaganda purposes. Here Sholom Aleichem bemoaned lost opportunities to acquire Palestine, and in his concluding remarks exhorted his fellow-Jews to continue to strive for Zion as follows:

> What a great legacy we would leave our children and our children's children. They will inherit the holy ideal from us. . . . A land, our own land—that will be the ideal among all Jews the world over. Our children, or our grandchildren, may live to see it. We ourselves perhaps, too.

Sholom Aleichem died in New York in 1916, at the age of fifty-nine. Like everything he touched, his Zionist writings are imbued with a freshness and a vitality that have not been diminished over the years.

(An excerpt appears earlier in this volume.)

THE MAVERICK RABBI: Rabbi Herbert S. Goldstein and the Institutional Synagogue—A New Organizational Form.

Rabbi Aaron I. Reichel, J.D. Foreword by Sir Immanuel Jakobovits, Chief Rabbi of England; Preface by former U.S. District Court Chief Judge Hon. David N. Edelstein. Donning Publishers, Norfolk, Va. Second Edition, 1986. 362 pages. $12.95 (cloth), $7.95 (paper).

Reviewed by Matthew L. Zizmor, D.D.S.

Let us go back in time to the era of the immigrant Jew in America. Even though most immigrants were at least nominally Orthodox, their children did not appreciate their parents' synagogue. What had suited the fathers was not compatible to the children, the first generation of American-born Jews. This was the problem that confronted Rabbi Herbert S. Goldstein (1890-1970), a born leader. Even though he graduated from the Jewish Theological Seminary (the Conservative rabbinic school), he obtained a private Orthodox *semicha* (ordination) conferred by the president of the leading Orthodox rabbinic national organization of the day, and occupied the pulpit of the prestigious Kehilath Jeshurun of Manhattan's Upper East Side. Just a few years later, he left a very comfortable position and life style to embark on an ambitious project. He accepted, in 1917, an invitation from a group of young men and women in Harlem to become their rabbi and founded The Institutional Synagogue. Here under one roof he merged a synagogue, a Hebrew school, and a community center with activities for young and old. His community centered around that building seven days a week. Why should a community have to support three institutions—a synagogue, a Talmud Torah (Hebrew school), and a YM-YWHA—when that community could build one "super-institution" and let everyone be exposed to all three facets of Jewish life?

His synagogue placed its emphasis on the youth, with

The Maverick Rabbi
Rabbi Herbert S. Goldstein.

young adults having full participation in the services. This was markedly different from the "Golden Age of Chazzanim" when congregants sat back and listened to the best cantors, when each Shabbat the davening (prayer service) became a concert and a show. The youth were encouraged to take over the services at The Institutional Synagogue.

The Hebrew school was educationally sound, with pleasant modern classrooms and facilities, in contrast to most synagogues of the day, which had their Hebrew schools in the basement. It had an up-to-date curriculum for both boys and girls, meeting five days a week.

The social programs that The Institutional Synagogue offered ran the gamut from religious to secular, from Scouts to gymnastics, from swimming to theater, from civic instruction to journalism, from Hebrew study to political lectures. All clubs and organizations had some form of Jewish content to them. In this context it was much easier for the children to be actively involved in Jewish culture and tradition. Many clubs would have a Bible lesson at the beginning of their meetings, or they would stop for a few minutes to join the worshippers in the synagogue for an afternoon or evening service. Since all the religious and social activities were in the same building, one did not feel strange about combining a club meeting with a quick *Minchah* or *Maariv* (afternoon or evening service).

This was the time when the Young Israel movement was in its infancy and the Jewish Center concept was just getting off the ground. Rabbi Goldstein was one of the architects of the modern American Orthodox synagogue as we have come to know it. Today we are blessed with countless charismatic rabbis and communities where Jewish life is characterized as being "dynamic." Yet Rabbi Herbert Goldstein was a pioneer in the American rabbinate and synagogue. To understand and appreciate today's situation, one must go back 70 years, which is just what Aaron Reichel did in his research for this fine book. He has performed a valuable service by telling the story of this farsighted rabbi and his trail-blazing efforts.

There is so much to learn from this book, not only from a historical perspective but from the contexts of leadership, organization, and programming. It is very relevant for our community today when we are trying to reach out to the unaffiliated Jews to attract them into the synagogue to teach them what Judaism has to offer. Rabbi Goldstein faced the same problems 70 years ago and found some solutions, paving the way for us. My only regrets after reading Aaron Reichel's book are that I did not live in that era and that Herbert Goldstein was not my rabbi.

THE JEWISH WOMAN IN RABBINIC LITERATURE:

Psychological and Psychohistorical Perspective

Rabbi Dr. Menachem Brayer. Ktav Publishing House, Hoboken, N.J., 1986. Two volumes, 637 pp. $40.00 (cloth), $23.90 (paper).

Orthodox Judaism, which may not see the need for such radical change of the traditional sex roles, has nonetheless shown understanding of and flexibility to the general needs for sexual equality and nondiscrimination in the domestic and career areas, as long as woman's important role in shaping the family and Jewish community remains primary. In all such considerations, halakhic guidelines are based on human concerns. The Orthodox woman, by and large, seems satisfied with her role within the Jewish community, particularly in the higher educational sphere, where she is becoming more and more actively engaged as teacher, administrator and guide in the secondary-education system and on campuses for women.

Judaism is well aware of the fact that some individual women would not be able to find total fulfillment in the mother-wife-homemaker role alone. It leaves open to them the opportunity to seek additional fulfillment elsewhere, as in the pursuit of their intellectual and social interests. But the fact that the Torah has encouraged the woman to assume the role of devoted wife and mother may signify more than a desire to protect the interests of her family and the community at large. For is there anything more fulfilling than the investment of one's talents and energies in the shaping of Jewish souls?

The Orthodox Jewish woman has found the identity

crisis less threatening and mysterious than that experienced by women in general. In fact, the Jewish woman has always thought of herself as person, a viable entity, and Jewish thought, law and literature recognized woman as possessing a free will, fulfilling a significant function in life, granted rights and charged with duties. She is not a man's subordinate but his other self. At the great moments of Jewish history, she is found side by side with man—from the Theophany at Sinai till modern times. The biblical word for woman—*isha,* from the Hebrew *ish* (man) signifies phonetically and symbolically the identity of man and woman as companions.

It is imperative that understanding of the social change affecting the woman be shown by contemporary halakhic authorities to enable her to develop new self-actualizing roles and models, in accordance with her intellectual and emotional capacity and spiritual needs. Open-mindedness and true appreciation of the social, psychological and cultural changes which the woman has undergone will enable her to share more fully in the *mitzvot* and in the Torah, within the framework of halakhic Judaism. Responsive concern for the woman, and continuous faith in the viability of halakhah, will open the gates of active participation of the Torah-observant daughter in the meaningful and creative spiritual drama of Jewish realization and in the daily traditional life of the community.

These thoughts as well as chapters on love, marriage, motherhood, singlehood, woman and sex, and sex education are found in the two volumes. Written in a brisk, scholarly style, illustrated by rabbinic idiom and anecdote, with sources well documented and with complete bibliography and appendixes, *The Jewish Woman in Rabbinic Literature* is an invaluable contribution to Jewish and women's studies.

Dr. Menachem Brayer, who is Stone-Sapirstein Professor of Jewish Education at Yeshiva University, worked on this study for more than 18 years. He is also a professor of Biblical literature and consulting psychologist at the University.

A TREASURY OF SEPHARDIC LAWS AND CUSTOMS:
The Ritual Practices of Syrian, Moroccan, Judeo-Spanish, and Spanish and Portuguese Jews of North America

Rabbi Dr. Herbert C. Dobrinsky, Yeshiva University Press, New York and Ktav Publishing House, Hoboken, N.J., 520 pp. $25.00 (cloth), $16.95 (paper).

This long-awaited publication provides a comprehensive overview of the traditions of four major Sephardic communities who are among the most dominant groups of Sephardim in North America. The author, Yeshiva University's vice president for university affairs, has been a pioneer of the renaissance and revitalization of Sephardic Jewry on these shores since 1964, when he helped to organize Yeshiva University's Sephardic Studies Program and Sephardic Community Activities Program. Dr. Dobrinsky later co-founded the American Society of Sephardic Studies.

This unique volume has the approbation of the Rishon Lezion and Chief Rabbi of Israel Rabbi Mordechai Eliahu, and of Rabbi Ovadia Yossef, who formerly held those posts, as well Rabbi Shalom Messas, Chief Rabbi and head of the religious courts of Jerusalem. Other rabbinic leaders and Jewish educators attest to its importance. This book, the first of its kind, provides a compendium of laws and customs covering all the holiday observances, special family occasions such as birth, bar-mitzvah, engagement and marriage, divorce and *halitzah,* death, burial, mourning and memorial observances. It describes the distinctive practices relating to *tefillin, mezuzah, tzitzit* and *tallit,* and the full gamut of distinctive dietary observances. Especially meaningful is its treatment of family life through sections on honor to parents and elders, husband-wife relationships, Jewish family purity, modesty, and education of children. The section on communal life and views regarding the State of Israel and attitudes to proselytes, provide an unprecedented insight into the infrastructure of the Sephardic Jewish community, their multiple organizations, and their past and present participation in the upbuilding of the Jewish state.

The detailed presentation on worship in public and private, as well as the distinguishing characteristics of the organizational structure of the synagogue, its religious personnel, volunteers and activities, is fascinating. The specific information on divergent practices in daily, Sabbath, festival and holiday worship services, stresses the importance of the synagogue as a central force which has preserved the life of the Sephardim throughout the world.

The appendix provides detailed explanations of divorce *halitzah* proceedings, and the order of washing the dead. These detailed ceremonies give the reader a fuller understanding of unusual rituals which are generally unknown.

Here in one volume we have a virtual handbook of the rituals and liturgy, as well as a Jewish historic and religious sociological presentation of the development of Sephardic Judaism in North America.

The volume includes treatment of current issues such as Jewish education, the State of Israel, the problem of intermarriage, and others which affect the future of the Jewish community. The outlook described is an authentic reflection of the distinctive views of the rabbinic scholars of each of the communities, which provides a positive contribution to the future growth and preservation of the rich and vital Sephardic heritage.

A separate book entitled "A Teacher's Guide for *A Treasury of Sephardic Laws and Customs*" is being prepared for educators who will wish to use the volume as a textbook in classrooms. It has wide application for day schools, afternoon schools, adult education programs and in the field of higher education.

The National Jewish Book Awards

National Jewish Book Award—Biography

Dr. Moses Leo Gitelson Award

1984—DAN KURZMAN, for *Ben Gurion: Prophet of Fire,* Simon & Schuster.

1985—MAURICE FRIEDMAN, for *Martin Buber's Life and Work: The Later Years, 1945-1965,* E.P. Dutton, Inc.

1986—JEHUDA REINHARZ, for *Chaim Weizmann: The Making of a Zionist Leader,* Oxford University Press

National Jewish Book Award—Children's Literature

Isaac Siegel Memorial Award

1952—SYDNEY TAYLOR, for *All-Of-A-Kind Family,* Wilcox and Follett.

1953—LILLIAN S. FREEHOF, for *Stories of King David,* Jewish Publication Society; and *Star Light Stories,* Bloch Publishing Co.

1954—DEBORAH PESSIN, for *The Jewish People: Book Three,* United Synagogue Commission on Jewish Education.

1955—NORA BENJAMIN KUBIE, for *King Solomon's Navy,* Harper and Brothers.

1956—SADIE ROSE WEILERSTEIN, for her cumulative contributions to Jewish juvenile literature.

Temple B'nai Jeshurun Award, Newark, N.J.

1957—ELMA E. LEVINGER, for her cumulative contributions to Jewish juvenile literature.

Pioneer Women's Hayim Greenberg Memorial Award

1958—NAOMI BEN ASHER and HAYIM LEAF, for *Jewish Junior Encyclopedia,* Shengold Publishers.

Isaac Siegel Memorial Award

1959—LLOYD ALEXANDER, for *Border Hawk: August Bondi,* Farrar, Straus and Cudahy; Jewish Publication Society

1960—SYLVIA ROTHCHILD, for *Keys to a Magic Door: Isaac Leib Peretz,* Farrar, Straus and Cudahy; Jewish Publication Society

1961—REGINA TOR, for *Discovering Israel,* Random House.

1962—SADIE ROSE WEILERSTEIN, for *Ten and a Kid,* Doubleday & Co.

1963—JOSEPHINE KAMM, for *Return to Freedom,* Abelard-Schuman.

1964—SULAMITH ISH-KISHOR, for *A Boy of Old Prague,* Pantheon Books.

1965—DOV PERETZ ELKINS and AZRIEL EISENBERG, for *Worlds Lost and Found,* Abelard-Schuman.

1966—BETTY SCHECHTER, for *The Dreyfus Affair,* Houghton-Mifflin.

1967—MEYER LEVIN, for *The Story of Israel,* G.P. Putnam's Sons.

Charles and Bertie G. Schwartz Juvenile Award

1970—CHARLIE MAY SIMON, for *Martin Buber: Widsom in Our Time,* E.P. Dutton.

—GERALD GOTTLIEB, for *The Story of Masada by Yigael Yadin: Retold for Young Readers,* Random House.

1971—SONIA LEVITIN, for *Journey to America,* Atheneum.

1972—SULAMITH ISH-KISHOR, for *The Master of Miracle: A New Novel of the Golem,* Harper & Row.

1973—JOHANNA REISS, for *The Upstairs Room,* Thomas Y. Crowell.

1974—YURI SUHL, for *Uncle Misha's Partisans,* Four Winds Press.

1975—BEA STADTLER, for *The Holocaust: A History of Courage and Resistance,* Behrman House.

1976—SHIRLEY MILGRIM, for *Haym Salomon: Liberty's Son,* Jewish Publication Society.

1977—CHAYA BURSTEIN, for *Rifka Grows Up,* Bonim Books/Hebrew Publishing Co.

1978—MILTON MELTZER, for *Never to Forget: The Jews of the Holocaust,* Harper & Row.

1979—IRENE NARELL, for *Joshua: Fighter for Bar Kochba,* Akiba Press.

1980—ARNOST LUSTIG, for *Dita Saxova,* Harper & Row.

William (Zev) Frank Memorial Award

Presented by Ellen and David Scheinfeld

1981—LEONARD EVERETT FISHER, for *A Russian Farewell,* Four Winds Press.

1982—KATHRYN LASKY, for *The Night Journey,* Frederick Warne & Co. Inc.

1983—BARBARA COHEN, for *King of the Seventh Grade,* Lothrop, Lee & Shepard Books.

1984—CHAYA M. BURSTEIN, for *The Jewish Kids Catalog,* Jewish Publication Society.

1985—GARY PROVOST and GAIL LEVINE-FREIDUS, for *Good If It Goes,* Bradbury Press.

1986—LINDA ATKINSON, for *In Kindling Flame: The Story of Hannah Senesh, 1921-1944,* Lothrop, Lee & Shepard

1987—EILEEN BLUESTONE SHERMAN, for *Monday in Odessa,* Jewish Publication Society.

National Jewish Book Award—Children's Picture Book

Marcia and Louis Posner Award

1983—BARBARA COHEN and MITCHELL J. DERANEY (illustrator), for *Yussel's Prayer: A Yom Kippur Story,* Lothrop, Lee & Shepard.

1985—AMY SCHWARTZ, for *Mrs. Moskowitz and the Sabbath Candlesticks,* Jewish Publication Society.

1986—FLORENCE B. FREEDMAN, for *Brothers,* illustrated by Robert Andrew Parker, Harper & Row

1987—MYRA C. LIVINGSTON and LLOYD BLOOM (illustrator), for *Poems for Jewish Holidays,* Holiday House

National Jewish Book Award—Fiction

Harry and Ethel Daroff Award

1949—HOWARD FAST, for *My Glorious Brothers,* Little, Brown.

1950—JOHN HERSEY, for *The Wall,* Alfred A. Knopf.

1951—SOMA MORGENSTERN, for *The Testament of the Lost Son,* Jewish Publication Society.

1952—ZELDA POPKIN, for *Quiet Street,* J.B. Lippincott.

1953—MICHAEL BLANKFORT, for *The Juggler,* Little, Brown.

1954—CHARLES ANGOFF, for *In the Morning Light,* Beechurst Press.

1955—LOUIS ZARA, for *Blessed is the Land,* Crown Publishers.

1956—JO SINCLAIR, for *The Changelings,* McGraw-Hill.

1957—LEON FEUCHTWANGER, for *Raquel: The Jewess of Toledo,* Julian Messner.
1958—BERNARD MALAMUD, for *The Assistant,* Farrar, Straus & Cudahy.
1959—LEON URIS, for *Exodus,* Doubleday & Co.
1960—PHILIP ROTH, for *Goodbye, Columbus,* Houghton Mifflin Co.
1961—EDWARD L. WALLANT, for *The Human Season,* Harcourt, Brace & Co.
1962—SAMUEL YELLEN, for *Wedding Band,* Atheneum Publishers.
1963—ISAAC BASHEVIS SINGER, for *The Slave,* Farrar, Straus & Cudahy.
1964—JOANNE GREENBERG, for *The King's Persons,* Holt, Rinehart and Winston.
1965—ELIE WIESEL, for *The Town Beyond the Wall,* Atheneum.
1966—MEYER LEVIN, for *The Stronghold,* Simon and Schuster.
1967—CHAIM GRADE, for *The Well,* Jewish Publication Society of America.
1969—DR. CHARLES ANGOFF, for *Memory of Autumn,* Thomas Yoseloff.
1970—DR. LEO LITWAK, for *Waiting for the News,* Doubleday & Co.
1972—CYNTHIA OZICK, for *The Pagan Rabbi and Other Stories,* Alfred A. Knopf.

William and Janice Epstein Award
1973—ROBERT KOTLOWITZ, for *Somewhere Else,* Charterhouse.
1974—FRANCINE PROSE, for *Judah the Pious,* Atheneum.
1975—JEAN KARSAVINA, for *White Eagle, Dark Skies,* Charles Scribner's Sons.
1976—JOHANNA KAPLAN, for *Other People's Lives,* Alfred A. Knopf.
1977—CYNTHIA OZICK, for *Bloodshed and Three Novellas,* Alfred A. Knopf.
1978—CHAIM GRADE, for *The Yeshiva, Vols. I and II,* Bobbs-Merrill Co.
1979—GLORIA GOLDREICH, for *Leah's Journey,* Harcourt Brace Jovanovich.
1980—DANIEL FUCHS, for *Apathetic Bookie Joint,* Methuen, Inc.
1981—JOHANNA KAPLAN, for *O, My America!,* Harper & Row.
1982—MARK HELPRIN, for *Ellis Island and Other Stories,* Delacorte Press.
1983—ROBERT GREENFIELD, for *Temple,* Summit Books.
1984—ARTHUR A. COHEN, for *An Admirable Woman,* David R. Godine.
1985—FREDERICK BUSCH, for *Invisible Mending,* David R. Godine.
1986—ARNOST LUSTIG, for *The Unloved: From the Diary of Perla S.,* translated by Vera Kalina-Levine, Arbor House

National Jewish Book Award—Holocaust

Leon Jolson Award
1966—ZOSA SZAJKOWSKI, for *Analytical Franco-Jewish Gazetteer 1939-1945.*
1967—ABRAHAM KIN, MORDECAI KOSOVER and ISAIAH TRUNK, for their editorship of *Alqemeyne Entsiklopedye: Yidn VII (General Encyclopedia: Jews VII),* Dubnow Fund and Encyclopedia Committee.
1968—DR. JACOB ROBINSON, for *And The Crooked Shall be Made Straight: The Eichmann Trial, Jewish Catastrophe and Hannah Ahrendt's Narrative,* Macmillan.
1969—DR. JUDAH PILON, for *The Jewish Catastrophe in Europe,* American Association for Jewish Education.
—NORA LEVIN, for *The Holocaust: The Destruction of European Jewry,* Thomas Y. Crowell.
1970—ZALMAN AYLBERCWEIG, for *Lexicon of the Yiddish Theater: Martyrs Volume,* Hebrew Actors Union of America.
1971—RABBI EPHRAIM OSHRY, for *Sheelot u-Teshuvot: Mi-Maamakim.*
1972—DR. HENRY L. FEINGOLD, for *The Politics of Rescue: The Roosevelt Administration and the Holocaust, 1938-1945,* Rutgers University Press.
1973—DR. AARON ZEITLIN, for *Veiterdike Lider Fun Hurban un Lider Fun Gloiben un Yanish Korshaks Letzte Gang* (More Poems of the Holocaust and Poems of Faith and Yanish Kortshak's Last Walk), New York, Bergen-Belsen Memorial Press.
1975—DR. ISAIAH TRUNK, for *Judenrat: The Jewish Councils in Eastern Europe Under Nazi Occupation,* Macmillan Co.
1976—LEYZER RAN, for *Yerushalayim de Lite: Jerusalem of Lithuania.*
1977—RABBI EPHRAIM OSHRY, for *Sefer Sheelot u-Teshuvot Mi-Maamakim: Part 4: Book of Questions and Answers from the Depths.*
1978—TERRENCE DES PRES, for *The Survivor: An Anatomy of Life in the Death Camp,* Oxford University Press.
1979—MICHAEL SELZER, for *Deliverance Day: The Last Hours at Dachau,* J.B. Lippincott Company.
1980—BENJAMIN B. FERENCZ, for *Less Than Slaves: Jewish Forced Labor and the Quest for Compensation,* Harvard University Press.
1981—RANDOLPH L. BRAHAM, for *The Politics of Genocide—The Holocaust in Hungary, 2 Vols.,* Columbia University Press.
1982—MICHAEL MARRUS AND ROBERT O. PAXTON, for *Vichy France and the Jews,* Basic Books Inc.
1983—IRVING ABELLA and HAROLD TROPER, for *None is Too Many: Canada and the Jews of Europe 1933-1948,* Lester & Orpen Dennys, Publishers.
1984—MARGUERITE DORIAN, for *The Quality of Witness: A Rumainian Diary 1937-44,* Jewish Publication Society.
1985—DAVID S. WYMAN, for *The Abandonment of the Jews: America and the Holocaust 1941-1945,* Pantheon.
1986—RAUL HILBERG, for *The Destruction of the European Jews: Revised and Definitive Edition,* Holmes & Meier.
1987—ROBERT J. LIFTON, for *Nazi Doctors: Medical Killing and the Psychology of Genocide,* Basic Books

National Jewish Book Award—Israel

Morris J. Kaplun Award
1974—ISAIAH FRIEDMAN, for *The Question of Palestine, 1914-1918: British-Jewish-Arab Relations,* Schocken Books.
1975—ARNOLD KRAMMER, for *The Forgotten Friendship: Israel and the Soviet Bloc, 1947-1953,* University of Illinois Press.
1976—MELVIN I. UROFSKY, for *American Zionism from Herzl to the Holocaust,* Doubleday & Co.
1977—HOWARD M. SACHAR, for *A History of Israel,* Alfred A. Knopf.
1978—HILLEL HALKIN, for *Letters to an American Jewish Friend,* Jewish Publication Society.
1979—RUTH GRUBER, for *Raquela: A Woman of Israel,* Coward, McCann & Geoghegan.
1980—EMANUEL LEVY, for *The Habima-Israel's National Theater 1917-1977: A Study of Cultural Nationalism,* Columbia University Press.
1981—No Award given.
1982—HOWARD M. SACHAR, for *Egypt and Israel,* Richard Marek Publishers.
1983—J. ROBERT MOSKIN, for *Among Lions: The Battle for Jerusalem June 5-7, 1967,* Arbor House Publishing Co.
1984—PETER GROSE, for *Israel in the Mind of America,* Alfred A. Knopf.
1985—JOAN PETERS, for *From Time Immemorial: The Origins of the Arab-Jewish Conflict Over Palestine,* Harper & Row.
1986—STEVEN L. SPIEGEL, for *The Other Arab-Israeli Conflict: Making America's Middle East Policy from Truman to Reagan,* University of Chicago Press.
1987—SAMUEL HEILMAN, for *A Walker in Jerusalem,* Summit Books

National Jewish Book Award—Jewish History

Bernard H. Marks Award
1973—ARTHUR J. ZUCKERMAN, for *A Jewish Princedom in Feudal France, 768-900,* Columbia University Press.
1974—BERNARD D. WEINRYB, for *The Jews of Poland: A Social and Economic History, 1100 to 1800,* Jewish Publication Society.
1975—SOLOMON ZEITLIN, for his cumulative contribution to Jewish history.
1976—RAPHAEL PATAI and JENNIFER PATAI WING, for *The Myth of the Jewish Race,* Charles Scribner's Sons.
1977—IRVING HOWE, for *World of Our Fathers,* Harcourt Brace Jovanovich.

Gerrard and Ella Berman Award

1978—CELIA S. HELLER, for *On the Edge of Destruction,* Columbia University Press.

1979—SALO W. BARON, for his cumulative contribution to Jewish historic research and thought. Columbia University Press and Jewish Publication Society.

1980—TODD M. ENDELMAN, for *The Jews of Georgian England, 1714-1830,* Jewish Publication Society.

1981—MARK R. COHEN, for *Jewish Self-Government in Medieval Egypt: The Origins of the Office of Head of the Jews, ca. 1065-1126,* Princeton University Press.

1982—PROF. DAVID RUDERMAN, for *The World of a Renaissance Jew,* Hebrew Union College.

1983—YOSEF HAYIM YERUSHALMI, for *Zakhor: Jewish History and Jewish Memory,* University of Washington Press.

1984—MICHAEL STANISLAWSKI, for *Tsar Nicholas I and the Jews: The Transformation of Jewish Society in Russia, 1825-1855,* Jewish Publication Society.

1985—NAOMI W. COHEN, for *Encounter with Emancipation: The German Jews in the United States, 1830-1914,* Jewish Publication Society.

1986—ROBERT LIBERLES, for *Religious Conflict in Social Context: The Resurgence of Orthodox Judaism in Frankfort Am Main, 1838-1877,* Leo Baeck Institute/Greenwood Press.

1987—DAVID BIALE, for *Power and Powerlessness in Jewish History,* Schocken Books

National Jewish Book Award—Jewish Thought

Jewish Community Council of Washington, D.C. Award

1949—HARRY A. WOLFSON, for *Philo: Foundations of Religious Philosophy in Judaism, Christianity and Islam,* Harvard University Press.

Isadore Hershfield Memorial Award for Non-Fiction

1950—GUIDO KISCH, for *The Jews in Medieval Germany: A Study of Their Legal and Social Status.*

Frank and Ethel S. Cohen Non-Fiction Award

1963—MOSES RISCHIN, for *The Promised City: New York's Jews, 1870-1914,* Harvard University Press.

Frank and Ethel S. Cohen Award For A Book On Jewish Thought

1964—BEN ZION BOKSER, for *Judaism: Profile of a Faith,* Burning Bush Press and Alfred A. Knopf.

1965—ISRAEL EFROS, for *Ancient Jewish Philosophy,* Wayne State University Press.

1966—DAVID POLISH, for *The Higher Freedom: A New Turning Point in Jewish History,* Quadrangle Press.

1967—NAHUM M. SARNA, for *Understanding Genesis: The Heritage of Biblical Israel,* Jewish Theological Seminary of America.

1968—DR. MICHAEL A. MEYER, for *Origins of the Modern Jews,* Wayne State University Press.

1969—DR. EMIL L. FACKENHEIM, for *Quest for Past and Future: Essays in Jewish Theology,* University of Indiana Press.

1970—DR. ABRAHAM JOSHUA HESCHEL, for *Israel: An Echo of Eternity,* Farrar, Straus & Giroux, and for his cumulative contributions to Jewish thought.

1971—DR. MORDECAI M. KAPLAN, for *The Religion of Ethical Nationhood: Judaism's Contribution to World Peace,* Macmillan, and for his cumulative contributions to Jewish thought.

1972—DR. ABRAHAM E. MILLGRAM, for *Jewish Worship,* Jewish Publication Society.

1973—SAMUEL SANDMEL, for *Two Living Traditions: Essays on Religion and The Bible,* Wayne State University Press; and

—ELIE WIESEL, for *Souls on Fire: Portraits and Legends of Hasidic Masters,* Random House.

1974—EUGENE BOROWITZ, for *The Masks Jews Wear: The Self-Deception of American Jewry,* Simon & Schuster.

1975—ELIEZER BERKOVITS, for *Major Themes in Modern Philosophies of Judaism,* Ktav Publishing.

1976—SOLOMON B. FREEHOF, for *Contemporary Reform Responsa,* Hebrew Union College Press.

1977—DAVID HARTMAN, for *Maimonides: Torah and Philosophic Quest,* Jewish Publication Society.

1978—RAPHAEL PATAI, for *The Jewish Mind,* Charles Scribner's Sons.

1979—ROBERT GORDIS, for *Love and Sex: A Modern Jewish Perspective,* Women's League for Conservative Judaism/Farrar, Straus & Giroux.

1980—DAVID BIALE, for *Gershom Scholem: Kabbalah and Counter-History,* Harvard University Press.

1981—ISADORE TWERSKY, for *Introduction to the Code of Maimonides (Mishneh Torah),* Yale University Press.

1982—ROBERT ALTER, for *The Art of Biblical Narrative,* Basic Books Inc.

1983—BERNARD SEPTIMUS, for *Hispano-Jewish Culture in Transition: The Career and Controversies of Ramah,* Harvard University Press.

1984—STEVEN T. KATZ, for *Post Holocaust Dialogues: Critical Studies in Modern Jewish Thought,* New York University Press.

1985—JOSEPH B. SOLOVEITCHIK, for *Halakhic Man,* Jewish Publication Society.

1986—DAVID HARTMAN, for *A Living Covenant: The Innovative Spirit in Traditional Judaism,* The Free Press

1987—ARNOLD M. EISEN, for *Galut: Modern Jewish Reflection on Homelessness and Homecoming,* Indiana University

National Jewish Book Award—Poetry

Florence Kovner Memorial Poetry Awards English Poetry

1951—JUDAH STAMPFER, for *Jerusalem Has Many Faces,* Farrar, Straus & Giroux.

1952—A.M. KLEIN, for cumulative contributions to English-Jewish poetry.

1953—ISIDORE GOLDSTICK, for translation of *Poems of Yehoash.*

1954—HARRY H. FEIN, for cumulative contributions to English-Jewish poetry.

Harry and Florence Kovner Memorial Poetry Award

1959—GRACE GOLDIN, for *Come Under the Wings: A Midrash on Ruth,* Jewish Publication Society.

1960—AMY K. BLANK, for *The Spoken Choice,* Hebrew College Press.

1962—IRVING FELDMAN, for *Work and Days and Other Poems,* Little Brown & Co.

1963—CHARLES REZNIKOFF, for *By the Waters of Manhattan,* New Directions; San Francisco Review.

1966—RUTH FINER MINTZ, for *The Darkening Green,* Big Mountain Press.

1969—RUTH WHITMAN, for *The Marriage Wig and Other Poems,* Harcourt, Brace and World.

1971—RUTH FINER MINTZ, for *Traveler Through Time,* Jonathan David.

1974—HAROLD SCHIMMEL, for translation of Yehuda Amichai's *Songs of Jerusalem and Myself,* Harper & Row.

1977—MYRA SKLAREW, for *From the Backyard of the Diaspora,* Dryad Press.

National Jewish Book Award—Hebrew Poetry

1951—AARON ZEITLIN, for *Shirim u'Poemot* (Songs and Poems), Mossad Bialik.

1952—HILLEL BAVLI, for cumulative contributions to Hebrew poetry.

1953—A.S. SCHWARTZ, for cumulative contributions to Hebrew poetry.

1954—EPHRAIM E. LISITZKY, for *Be-Ohalei Kush* (In Negro Tents), Mossad Bialik.

1955—GABRIEL PREIL, for *Ner Mul Kochavim* (Candle Under the Stars) Mossad Bialik.

1956—HILLEL BAVLI, for *Aderet Ha-Shanim* (Mantle of Years), Mossad Bialik.

1957—MOSHE FEINSTEIN, for *Avraham Abulafia,* Mossad Bialik.

1958—AARON ZEITLIN, for *Bein ha-Esh veha-Esha* (Between the Man and The Woman), Yavneh.

1959—MOSHE BEN-MEIR, for *Tzil va-Tzel* (Sound and Shadow), Ogen Publishing House.
1960—EISIG SILBERSCHLAG, for *Kimron Yamai* (Arch of My Days), Kiryat Sefer.
1961—EPHRAIM E. LISITZKY, for *K'Mo Hayom Rad* (As the Day Wanes), Mahbarot Lesifrut.
1962—GABRIEL PREIL, for *Mapat Erev,* Dvir Publishing Co.
1964—ARNOLD BAND, for *Ha-Rei Boer ba-Esh* (The Mirror Burns in Fire), Jerusalem, Ogdan; New York, Ogen.
1966—SIMON HALKIN, for *Ma'avar Yabok* (Crossing the Yabok), Am Oved.
1967—LEONARD D. FRIEDLAND, for *Shirim be-Sulam Miner* (Poems in a Minor Key), M. Newman.
1969—REUVEN BEN YOSEF, for *Derech Eretz* (Respect), Hakebutz Hameuchad Publishing House.
1972—DR. EISIG SILBERSCHLAG, for *Igrotai El Dorot Aherim* (Letters to Other Generations), Kiryat Sefer.
1975—REUVEN BEN-YOSEF, for *Metim ve-Ohavim* (The Dead and Lovers), Masada Publishing Co.
1978—T. CARMI, for *El Eretz Aheret* (To Another Land), Dvir Publishing Co.

National Jewish Book Award—Yiddish Poetry

1951—BER LAPIN, for *Der Fuller Krug,* (The Brimming Jug), Ykuf.
1952—MORDECAI JAFFE, for editing and translation of *Antologia fun Der Hebraishe Poesie* (Anthology of Hebrew Poetry), CYCO (2 volumes)
1953—MARK SCHWEID, for *Collected Poems.*
1954—ELIEZER GREENBERG, for *Banachtiger Dialog* (Night Dialogue), Gezelten.
1955—ALTER ESSELIN, for *Lider Fun a Midbarnik* (Poems of a Hermit), Culture Club of the Peretz Hirschbein Folk Theater.
1956—NAFTALI GROSS, for cumulative contributions to Yiddish poetry.
1957—JACOB GLATSTEIN, for *Fun Mein Gantzer Mei: 1919-1956* (Of All My Toil: Collected Poems: 1919-1956).
1958—I.J. SCHWARTZ, for his cumulative contributions to Yiddish poetry.
1959—BENJAMIN I. BIALOSTOTZKY, for *Lid Tzu Lid* (Poem to Poem), CYCO.
1960—EPHRAIM AUERBACH, for *Gildene Shekia* (Golden Sunset), Kium.
1961—JOSEPH RUBINSTEIN, for *Megilath Russland* (Scroll of Russia), CYCO.
1962—ISRAEL EMIOT, for *In Nigun Eingehert* (In Melody Absorbed), Rochester Culture Council.
1963—CHAIM GRADE, for *Der Mentsh Fun Fier* (The Man of Fire), CYCO.
1964—AARON GLANZ-LEYELES, for *Amerike un Ich* (America and I), Der Kval.
1965—ALEPH KATZ, for *Di Emesse Hasunah* (Some Wedding), CYCO.
1966—KADIA MOLODOWSKY, for *Light fun Dorenboim* (Light from the Thornbush), Kium.
1967—JACOB GLATSTEIN, for *A Yid fun Lublin* (A Jew from Lublin), CYCO.
1968—AARON ZEITLIN, for *Liderfun Hurban un Lider fun Gloiben* (Poems of the Holocaust and Poems of Faith), World Federation of Bergen-Belsen.
1969—RACHEL H. KORN, for *Di Gnod fun Vort,* Hemenora Publishing House.
1970—ELIEZER GREENBERG, for *Eibiker Dorsht* (Eternal Thirst).
1973—MEIR STICKER, for *Yidishe Landshaft* (Jewish Landscape), Peretz Farlag.
1976—M. HUSID, for *A Shotn Trogt Main Kroin* (A Shadow Wears My Crown).
1979—MOISHE STEINGART, for *In Droisen fun der Velt* (Outside of the World), Shulsinger Brothers.

JWB Jewish Book Council Award for Poetry
1980—CHARLES REZNIKOFF, for the totality of his poetic achievement, (posthumously awarded).
1981—LOUIS SIMPSON, for *Caviare at the Funeral,* Franklin Watts, Inc.

National Jewish Book Award—Scholarship

Sarah H. Kushner Memorial Award
1983—JEREMY COHEN, for *The Friars and the Jews: The Evolution of Medieval Anti-Judaism,* Cornell University Press.
1984—S.D. GOITEN, for *A Mediterranean Society: The Jewish Community of the Arab World, As Portrayed in the Documents of the Cairo Geniza—Daily Life,* University of California Press.
1985—SEYMOUR FELDMAN, translator, for *The Wars of the Lord: Book One, Immortality of the Soul,* by Levi Ben Gershom (Gersonides), Jewish Publication Society.
1986—MICHAEL FISHBANE, for *Biblical Interpretation in Ancient Israel,* Oxford University Press.
1987—REUVEN HAMMER, for *Sifre: A Tannaitic Commentary on the Book of Deuteronomy,* Yale University Press

National Jewish Book Award—Translation of a Jewish Classic

Rabbi Jacob Freedman Award
1975—MAX ARZT, BERNARD J. BAMBERGER, HARRY FREEDMAN, H.L. GINSBERG, SOLOMON GRAYZEL, and HARRY M. ORLINSKY, for *The Book of Isaiah,* Jewish Publication Society.
1976—WILLIAM G. BRAUDE and ISRAEL J. KAPSTEIN, for *Pesikta de-Rab Kahana: R. Kahana's Compilation of Discourses for Sabbaths and Festival Days,* Jewish Publication Society.
1977—ZVI L. LAMPEL, for *Maimonides' Introduction to the Talmud,* Judaica Press.
1979—WILLIAM M. BRINNER, for Nissim Ben Jacob ibn Shahin's *An Elegant Composition Concerning Relief After Adversity,* Yale University Press.

National Jewish Book Award—Visual Arts

Leon L. Gildesgame Award
1981—YESHIVA UNIVERSITY MUSEUM, for *Purim: The Face and the Mask.*
1982—JANET BLATTER and DR. SYBIL MILTON, for *Art of the Holocaust,* The Rutledge Press.
1983—ANDREW S. ACKERMAN and SUSAN L. BRAUNSTEIN, *Israel in Antiquity: From David to Herod,* The Jewish Museum.
1984—ROMAN VISHNIAC, for *A Vanished World,* Farrar, Straus & Giroux.
1985—EVELYN M. COHEN, *The Rotschild Mahzor: Florence, 1492,* The Library/The Jewish Theological Seminary of America.
1986—CAROL HERSELLE KRINSKY, for *Synagogues of Europe: Architecture, History, Meaning,* The Architectural History Foundation/MIT Press.
1987—JOY UNGERLEIDER-MAYERSON, for *Jewish Folk Art: From Biblical Days to Modern Times,* Summit Books

National Jewish Book Award—Yiddish Literature

The Workmen's Circle Award
1980—PERETZ MIRANSKY, for *Tzwishn Shmeichl Un Trern* (Between Smiles and Tears).
1981—HYMAN BASS, for *Pathways in Yiddish Literature,* I.L. Peretz Publishing.
1982—JOSHUA A. FISHMAN, for *Never Say Die!,* Mouton Publishers.
1983—CHAIM SPILBERG and YAACOV ZIPPER, for *Kanader Yidisher Zamlbukh* (Canadian Jewish Anthology), National Committee for Yiddish at the Canadian Jewish Congress.
1984—CHAIM LEIB FOX, for *Tsu Di Himlen Arof* (To The Heavens Above), CYCO Publishing Company.
1985—SHEA TENENBAUM, for *Fun Ash Un Fayer Iz Dayn Kroyn* (From Ash and Fire Is Your Crown), CYCO Publishing Company.

Hollywood's Image of the Jew

Lester Friedman

Three recent films demonstrate that Jewish stereotypes continue to thrive in contemporary Hollywood: *Goonies, Cocoon,* and *St. Elmo's Fire.*

Goonies includes Chunk (Jeff Cohen) as the Jewish representative in an ethnically mixed bunch of kids known as "the Goonies." Chunk does several things which typify him, and in fact, paint a portrait of Jews common since the early days of silent pictures. His language is sprinkled with references to Jewish elements in his culture. While exploring his friend's attic, where they find a treasure map, Chunk exclaims that all he has in his house are "left over Hanukkah decorations." Later, he describes bullet holes as "the size of matzah balls." When confronted with the film's villain, the cowardly Chunk is reduced to mumbling some Hebrew prayers, which provide him with scant protection.

Chunk's most typical actions revolve around his relationship with Sloth (John Matuszuk), a misshapen and ill-treated creature who ultimately saves the Goonies from the clutches of some hoods. For a good part of the film, Chunk is tied up with Sloth; in fact, he misses much of the action segments. Finally, he takes pity on the monster kept chained and locked up by members of his own family. It is his act of compassion which convinces Sloth to turn against his family and help the Goonies. At the end of the movie, Chunk declares he will take Sloth home to live with him and his own family, an appropriately fat and constantly eating crew. So, once again, the Jewish outsider shows compassion for other outsiders, this time a hideous looking but tender hearted monster.

Chunk is both a physically and emotionally familiar figure. In fact, he represents an uncomfortable reincarnation of an earlier age's archetypal Jew, George Sidney. Like Sidney's Nathan Cohen, Chunk is fat, emotional, funny, volatile, compassionate, and very Jewish. For much of the story, Chunk functions as the butt of the film's humor though he is given an incongruous heroism at its climax when he becomes "Captain Chunk." Yet no small moment of bravery can counteract the portrait of the scarred, obese figure who screams and eats his way through most of the film. Director Richard Donner and Executive Producer Steven Spielberg do endow Chunk with a sense of personal kindness and private compassion, traits which allow him to rise at least a bit above the ethnic stereotypes which threaten to overwhelm him.

If Chunk is a throwback to male stereotypes, Wendy Beamish (Mare Winningham) and her parents (Martin Balsam/Joyce Van Patten) in *St. Elmo's Fire* represent a return to the Jewish family struggles depicted in the films of the sixties. First of all, Wendy is an almost totally assimilated Jewish woman, even to the point of attending Catholic Georgetown University. Like Jewish girls of the past, Wendy's wealthy parents cannot understand why she wastes her life working in the Department of Human Services, worry about her weight, and criticize her loaning money to a married Christian musician (Rob Lowe).

The Goonies. *Our subject is seen far left.*

Mainly, they want her to settle down with a nice Jewish boy like Howie Krantz (Jon Culter) and give them a few grandchildren.

The most overtly Jewish scene occurs when Wendy goes home for dinner with Billy the musician. Her father, a wealthy greeting card manufacturer, constantly brings up news of their Jewish friends. Her mother whispers certain words like "cancer," "drugs," and "money," words that should not be said too loudly in public. To Mr. and Mrs. Beamish, "family business is important," whereas for Wendy her college friends have become more important than her mother and father. In fact, she is part of an extended family where ethnicity, relatives, and religion are simply of passing interest. Finally, Wendy must leave the stifling environment of her parents' house, though she expresses a strong love for them. Like so many Jewish men and women of the past, Wendy finds freedom away from her childhood home, her given religion, and her cultural identity.

Finally, there is *Cocoon,* director Ron Howard and screenwriter Tom Benedek turned a story by David Saperstein into the surprise summer hit of 1985. The story of a group of retired Florida residents who meet some altruistic aliens who offer them immortality struck a responsible chord in a gradually aging American population. Viewed from one perspective, therefore, *Cocoon* is the baby boomer generation's first response to their own mortality. The reaction from a generation accustomed to getting its own way is, as one might expect, rather optimistic: Death won't get us. At the last moment some supernatural happening will save us from the fate of others who went before us. Yet one dissenting vote is cast in this film, the Jewish Bernie Lefkowitz (Jack Gilford).

The film opens with Bernie cast as the grouch. Unhappy with his life, unwilling to be flexible, he complains about most everything. Eventually, these traits result in tragedy. When his friends tell Bernie about the life-restoring powers of the aliens' pool, he refuses to believe them or to use the miraculous water to help his wife. Finally it is too late for the gentle Rose (Herta Ware). In one of the film's most emotional moments, Bernie brings Rose's lifeless body to the pool and begs the extraterrestrial to give her back to him. His inability to believe anything beyond his five senses has doomed the person most precious to Bernie.

Yet perhaps even more crucial is Bernie's refusal to accompany his friends to the aliens' home planet. This is not done out of fear. Instead, Bernie articulates a philosophical position: "I'll play out the hand I was dealt." Though the film never explores his ethnic identity, Bernie's plain response echoes many Jews over the centuries. He accepts what God has given him. He knows you cannot really cheat death by leaving on a spaceship, even if that is what an audience wishes to believe. Bernie does not ignore the possibility of supernatural intervention, in fact he has witnessed it first hand. But he plants himself firmly on the side of those who do not seek it. By rejecting this possibility of immortality, Bernie simply accepts the human condition, a state characterized by our movement toward death from the moment we are born. For Bernie, surviving is a matter of living life, not avoiding death.

Woody Allen's recent movie, *Hannah and Her Sisters* (1986), is also about living life. It starts at a family Thanksgiving dinner and ends at a similar meal two years later. In between these symbolic meetings, Allen introduces us to a cast of urban neurotics: Hannah (Mia Farrow), an ex-actress who gives up her career for her family; Elliot (Michael Caine), her husband, who is sexually obsessed with her sister Lee (Barbara Hershey), who lives with an overbearing mentor (Max von Sydow); Holly (Diane Wiest), a middle-class druggie who failed as an actress and now runs the Stanislavski Catering Company. For the first time in one of his movies, Allen casts himself in a supporting role as Mickey Sachs, a chronic worrier about everything from his health to profound philosophical questions. Mickey Sachs, Hannah's ex-husband, becomes another of Allen's death-obsessed characters who wander the streets claiming life has no meaning as they continue to search for it.

In one of the film's most hilarious segments, the very Jewish Mickey, who cannot believe in God, attempts to convert to Roman Catholicism. Of course, his parents go crazy, his mother (Helen Miller) locking herself in the bedroom and his father (Leo Postrel) not understanding his son's actions. "If there is a God, why does he allow evil? Why were there Nazis?" Mickey questions his father. "How should I know," responds the puzzled old man, "I can't even understand how the can opener works." Mickey cannot comprehend that his father is not worried about death and what happens afterwards. "Why should I worry? If I'm unconscious I won't know it and if I'm not I'll worry about it then," his down-to-earth father responds. Mickey even buys the outer symbols of Catholicism, a crucifix and some statues, as well as a loaf of Wonder bread and some mayonnaise. By the end of the film, however, Mickey realizes he cannot be anything other than what he is, a skeptical Jewish intellectual. He finally rejects Catholicism, calling it a "die now, pay later" religion.

Woody Allen in Hannah and Her Sisters.

In a recent interview with Caryn James, Allen talked about *Hannah and Her Sisters* as "an ensemble story about the intersecting lives of groups of characters," a methodology that struck him after rereading *Anna Karenina.* Indeed, Allen once again demonstrates, his incredible ability to weave diverse characters into a stunning cinematic tapestry of intriguing complexity, this time following each of Hannah's sisters through an affair with one of Hannah's men. The movie, with its hopeful happy ending, shows Allen affirming life, though in a slightly reluctant manner. The key scene depicts Mickey watching a Marx Brothers movie. "He realizes," says Allen, "he'll never know whether life has meaning, but maybe it's worth living after all. Maybe life isn't meaningless, and that's the best you can do . . . Be part of the experience . . . Enjoy it while it lasts." For Allen, the thinking man must eventually give way to the feeling man, an attitude which marks a new phase and significant change for Woody Allen.

Film critic Vincent Canby claims that "There is no one else in American films who comes anywhere near Woody Allen in originality and interest. One has to go back to Chaplin and Keaton . . . to find anybody comparable." Like those revered early masters of the medium, Allen totally controls his pictures, from story idea, to shooting, to advertising. He wouldn't have it any other way: "If I had to make films without complete control from start to finish, I definitely would not do it." Allen, like Chaplin and Keaton, continually treads the thin line between sentimentality and sweetness. In *Hannah and Her Sisters,* he fashions another stunning film about life and death, love and honesty, alienation and interaction.

Conspicuous consumption meets reality in Down and Out In Beverly Hills.

The other pre-eminent Jewish-American director, Paul Mazursky, was as busy as Woody Allen in 1986. In Mazursky's newest film, *Down and Out in Beverly Hills*, the Whitemans seem not only pursue to happiness and the American Dream but to grasp them in a headlock and squeeze. Dave (Richard Dreyfuss) is a coat hanger king who lives in a mansion, drives a Rolls-Royce, and provides his family with everything they need. So why is his medicine cabinet filled with Pepto-Bismol? Why is his wife Barbara (Bette Midler) unable to relax? Why is his daughter (Tracy Nelson), who goes to posh Sarah Lawrence, unwilling to eat? Why is his son (Evan Richards) unsure of his sexual preferences? Why does his dog, Matisse, need a shrink for his pre-anorexic condition? The tentative answers are provided when Dave saves a down-and-out bum, Jerry Baskin (Nick Nolte), from drowning in his pool. (Mazursky based his film on Jean Renoir's classic, *Boudu Saved From Drowning.*) Jerry is a kind of emotional Santa Claus bringing each character what he/she needs, from manly bonding, to sexual fulfillment, to personal confidence, to mature understanding.

The Whitemans are clearly Jewish. Dave sprinkles his conversations with Yiddish expressions like "putz," "nudge," and "schmuck." Jerry and Dave share a Brooklyn background, and they cement their friendship over bagel, cream cheese, and lox sandwiches. Yet Mazursky's portrait of these financially successful Jews remains quite disturbing. What is missing, he implies, is the family strength so evident in many earlier Jewish-American pictures. The wife and husband have an unsatisfying sexual relationship. The parents are so alienated from the son that, in order to communicate with them, the boy makes vitriolic videos that show his mother and father yelling at him. The daughter shares little of herself with her parents, refusing even to introduce them to her boyfriend. The Whitemans are less a family than a series of related neuroses. Each feeds off the other in a sick and sickening manner. Externally, this family is a picture of Jewish success; internally, they represent the destruction of the Jewish family structure.

The Whitemans represent almost total Jewish assimilation into American society. One can rather easily overlook that they are Jewish, since the film is devoid of religious and cultural overtones. In fact, the Jews are not the film's outsiders; instead, their Black neighbor, Orvis (Little Richard), functions as the picture's minority figure. The Whitemans have made the long journey from bleak ghetto to golden suburb. They have attained prominence and wealth, but something is missing from their lives. Something has gone wrong. They have gained material wealth but sacrificed emotional stability and their ethnic identity.

Two major Jewish-American movies appeared in the late Fall of 1986: *Brighton Beach Memoirs* and *An American Tail.* The former is the best version of any Neil Simon play yet brought to the screen. Directed by Eugene Saks, who won a 1983 Tony award for his Broadway production of the comic drama, *Brighton Beach Memoirs* follows the adventures of Eugene Jerome (Jonathan Silverman), a fifteen-year-old intent on uncovering life's mysteries and making personal value judgments. "Actually," he confesses at one point, "I'd give up writing if I could see a naked girl while I was eating ice cream." Eugene lives at home with his parents (Bob Dishy/Blythe Danner), his older brother (Brian Drillinger), his widowed aunt (Judith Ivey), and her two daughters (Lisa Waltz/Stacey Glick). The story of these seven people trapped under one roof unfolds through the eyes of Eugene who keeps a journal "so that if I grow up warped or crazy, the world will know why."

Brighton Beach Memoirs, set in Brooklyn in 1937, is the first in Simon's autobiographical trilogy, and he adapted it

Brian Drillinger and Jonathan Silverman in Brighton Beach Memoirs.

for the screen himself. (Can movie adaptations of *Biloxi Blues* and *Broadway Bound* be far behind?) In it, he traces the activities of this extended Jewish family, never allowing Eugene's sardonic commentary to obscure the inner strength and moral toughness of his characters. "I don't write a lot of one-liners anymore," says Simon in a recent interview, "now I just need the right situation." Perhaps the most daring aspect of the production is casting Blythe Danner and Judith Ivey, two very WASP-looking performers, as Jewish sisters; yet the gamble pays off and both actresses manage their roles with very few Molly Goldberg-like stereotypes. In Eugene, the precocious adolescent whose love of baseball is exceeded only by his pubescent desires, Simon fashions a worthy alter ego who both participates in and yet stands outside the events in the picture. *Brighton Beach Memoirs* presents a richly evocative portrait of Jews in the 1930s struggling and ultimately making it in America.

Fievel Mousekewitz and family in An American Tail.

An American Tail lists Don Bluth as its director, but with Steven Spielberg credited as executive producer one can never be sure whose vision dominates the completed movie. This animated feature presents one more version of the old-world Jewish immigrant confronted with the new-world values of America. Fievel Mousekewitz, the central figure, and his family flee the oppression and prejudice of Russia in 1885. "There are no cats (cossacks) in America," says his father. Unfortunately, he is wrong, and the recent arrivals must stand together to defeat different foes in this new land. Separated from his family by accident, Fievel must face the perils and pleasures of America alone, ever searching for his lost mother, father, and sister. Bluth/Spielberg allow the mice's adventures to parallel the human experiences of that time. Many of the Jewish elements in the Mousekewitz's homelife disappear after they leave Russia. Though they celebrate Hanukkah in their homeland, no such Jewish rituals appear in the American segment, an apt representation of how these religious events played a smaller and smaller part in the lives of most immigrants.

The most controversial aspect of *An American Tail,* however, occurred offscreen. Giant MacDonald's Corporation purchased the merchandising rights to Fievel and put his image on Christmas stockings given away in their local fast-food restaurants. To many, this seemed an insensitive marketing strategy: grafting a Jewish mouse onto a Christian tradition. Others saw little harm in this incident, noting the secular tone of the picture and the seeming innocence of MacDonald's gesture. But the most telling aspect of the incident was the lack of any organized protests, boycotts, or letter campaigns. That the American Jewish community felt it could simply let this one go by is, in and of itself, a statement of how comfortable Jews in 1986 felt about their American homeland. In any case, *An American Tail* stands as the first Jewish-American Christmas film, an event which would have probably been unthinkable twenty-five years ago.

Chariots of Fire: A Reconsideration

At the time of its initial release *Chariots of Fire* (1982) stirred up few controversies, though perhaps it should have. The surprise winner of the 1982 Oscar for best picture, its stylish production, invigorating musical score (by Vangelis), stirring story, and uplifting ending caused many viewers to cherish this tale of two runners competing in the 1924 Olympics. Unfortunately, often missed or at least tactfully ignored, was the film's implicit anti-Jewish sentiments. An objective treatment is implied from the beginning of the film when the title, "A true story" appears. A closer look at this particular movie, however, shows how its creators subtly infuse it with a particularly Christian bias, one that makes Judaism far less acceptable than Christianity.

Chariots of Fire.

Director Hugh Hudson constructs the film via a series of cuts back and forth between the lives of the two athletes, an editing structure that invites comparisons between the two men. Eric Liddell (Ian Charleson) is a Christian missionary and the national hero of Scotland. He runs to honor God; he even refuses to race on Sunday, though it may mean forfeiting his chance for an Olympic medal. In fact, in one scene after he wins a race in the rain, Eric talks about loving Christ as the best way to run a straight race. Miraculously, the downpour suddenly stops and it becomes sunny. Eric, the perfect Christian, sees running as a form of worship, of showing God he appreciates the gifts bestowed upon him.

Harold Abrahams' (Ben Cross) motives for running are quite different from Eric Liddell's. Harold seems to run in order to get back at a Christian world that has denied him access to its upper levels of power. "They may lead me to water," he says early in the film, "but they won't let me drink." But, except for some snobby comments by the Master of Trinity College, Harold is never seen as the victim of antisemitism. His classmates respect and even envy him. He wins the most sought-after girl (Alice Krige) in the picture, a beautiful non-Jewish actress to whom his religion is a matter of indifference. He triumphs in the Olympics. So when Harold claims "I'm going to take them on one at a time and beat them," a viewer can only wonder who he is talking about and what experiences have made him so bitterly obsessed with winning. Finally, one must question why, given these feelings, Harold eventually converts to Christianity, since it is obviously a Christian funeral that frames the film. Does he, as Pat Erens suggests, place ambition and assimilation above personal and religious commitment?

A small scene clearly points up the emotional distinctions between these two men. Harold's trainer, Sam Mussabini (Ian Holm), shows him a slide of Eric running. He says that Liddell is not a sprinter, but a "true runner" because he has "heart." Sam then tells Harold that he is a sprinter and that sprinters run on "nerves." Mussabini's speech implies that running on heart is superior to running on nerves; one is natural and the other neurotic. In fact, Sam's very presence goes to the center of the matter. To win the Jew must hire a professional coach, while the Christian can simply train with his friends. Eric can switch events at a moment's notice and still triumph. Harold chokes and loses a race he should have won. When Eric refuses to run on Sunday, another runner gives him a note which reads, "He that honors me, I will honor." Therefore, when he wins God seems to be behind the victory. Conversely, when Harold wins it is because he had the money to hire a professional coach. Throughout the picture, the Christian wins for God, while the Jew competes for nothing higher than personal glory.

68

A Chronological Listing of Jewish-American Films

Title	Year	Director	Distributor/ Production Company
Features till 1919			
Absalom	1912		Pathe
Accused by Darkest Russia	1913		Liberty
The Airship, or One Hundred Years Hence	1908		Vitagraph
Arabian Jewish Dance	1903		Edison
Athaliah	1911		Pathe
A Bad Day for Levinsky	1909		Precision
Bar Kochba-The Hero of a Nation	1913		Fox
The Barrier of Faith	1915	V. Brooke	Vitagraph
Becky Gets a Husband	1912		Lubin Films
The Bells	1913		Reliance
The Bells	1914		Sawyer's
Belshazar's Feast	1913		Gaumont
Ben Hur	1907	F. O. Rose	Kalem
Bizzy Izzy	1915		Gaumont
The Black 107	1913	S. Golden	Ruby Features
Bleeding Hearts or Jewish Freedom Under King Casimir of Poland	1913	S. Golden	Imperial
Blood of the Poor	1912		Champion
The Blood Red Tape of Charity	1913	E. August	Powers
The Broker's Daughter	1910		Yankee
Business and Love	1914		Lubin
Business Is Business	1915		United Film Svc.
Cain and Abel	1910		Gaumont
Cast into the Flame	1910		Gaumont
A Child of the Ghetto	1910	D. W. Griffith	Biograph
The Children of the Ghetto	1915	F. Powell	Fox
Children of the Tenements	1913		Kalem
A Citizen in the Making	1912		Selig Polyscope
Cohen and Murphy	1910		Powers
Cohen at Coney Island	1909		Vitagraph
Cohen Collects a Debt	1912	M. Sennett	Keystone
Cohen Saves the Flag	1913	F. Powell	Keystone
Cohen's Advertising Scheme	1904		Edison
Cohen's Dream of Coney Island	1909		Vitagraph
Cohen's Fire Sale	1907		Edison
Cohen's Generosity	1910		Defender
Cohen's Luck	1915	J. H. Collins	T. Edison
Cohen's Outing	1913		Keystone
The Copper & the Crook	1910		Yankee
Cupid at Cohen's	1916	A. McMackin	Beauty
Cupid Puts One Over on the Shadchen	1915		Vitagraph
Daniel	1913		Vitagraph
A Daughter of Israel	1914	V. D. Brooke	Vitagraph
David and Goliath	1908		Kalem
David's War with Absalom	1912		N.Y. Film Co.
The Death of Saul	1912		Pathe
Deborah or The Jewish Maiden's Wrong	1914		Thanhouser
The Deluge	1911		Vitagraph
Disraeli	1917		Paul Cromelin
The Embodied Thought	1916	E. Sloman	Lubin
Escape From Siberia	1914		Great Players Feature Film Co.
Esther	1914		Eclectic
Esther and Mordecai	1910		Gaumont
The Fable of How Weisenstein Did Not Lose Out to Buttinsky	1916	R. F. Baker	Essanay
The Faith of Her Fathers	1914	E. Lewis	Reliance
Faith of Her Fathers	1915		Universal
The Fall of Babylon	1919	D. W. Griffith	Wark
Father and Son or The Curse of the Golden Land	1913		Vitagraph
A Female Fagin	1913		Kalem
Fighting is No Business	1914		Universal
The Firebug	1913		Keystone
A Flurry in Diamonds	1913		Essanay
For Sale, A Baby	1916	P. N. Vekroff	C. K. Harris
For the Love of Mike and Rosie	1916		Universal
Foxy Izzy	1911		Lubin
The Fur Coat	1916		Vitagraph
Gesture Fight in Hester Street	1903		Pathe
Get Rich Quick Billington	1913		Pathe
The Ghetto Seamstress	1910		Yankee
The Girl of the Ghetto	1910		Thanhouser
Guaranteed Rainproof	1914		Lubin
Gwendolyn	1914		Biograph
The Heart of a Jewess	1913		Universal
Her Condoned Sin	1917	D. W. Griffith	Biograph
His First Long Trousers	1911		Selig Polyscope
How Izzy Stuck to His Post	1914		Reliance

Title	Year	Director	Distributor/ Production Company
How Izzy Was Saved	1914		Reliance
How Mosha Came Back	1912		Chrystal-Universal
How the Jews Take Care of Their Poor	1913	S. Golden	Imperial
In the Czar's Name	1910		Yankee
In the Days of King Solomon	1913		Feature Film Co.
Intolerance	1916	D. W. Griffith	Wark
Ireland and Israel	1912		Champion
Isabella of Aragon	1910		Itala
Ivanhoe	1913	H. Brenon	Universal
Izzy and His Rival	1914		Reliance
Izzy and the Diamond	1914		Reliance
Izzy's Night Out	1914		Reliance
Izzy the Detective	1914		Reliance
Jephthah's Daughter	1909		Vitagraph
Jephthah's Daughter	1913	J.F. McDonald	Warner's Features
Jerusalem in the Time of Christ	1908		Kalem
The Jewess	1913		Nesster
A Jewish Dance at Jerusalem	1903		Edison
The Jewish Maiden's Wrong	1913		
The Jew's Christmas	1913	P. Smalley/L. Weber	Universal
The Jew's Gratitude	1910		Yankee Film Co.
Joseph and His Brethren	1915		Dormet
Joseph and His Coat of Many Colors	1914		Sawyer
Joseph in Egypt	1912		Cines
Joseph in the Land of Egypt	1914		Thanhouser
Joseph Sold by His Brethren	1910		Pathe
Joseph's Trials in Egypt	1914		Eclectic
The Judgment of Solomon	1909		Vitagraph
Judith and Holofernes	1910		Gaumont
Judith of Bethulia	1914	D. W. Griffith	Biograph
The Kiss of Hate	1916	W. Nigh	Columbia
L'Chayim (Good Luck)	1911		Pathe
Leah, the Forsaken	1908		Vitagraph
Leah, the Forsaken	1912	H. Brenon	Universal
Legally Dead	1910		Powers
Legend of the Erring Jew	1911		Eclair
Levi and Cohen, The Irish Comedians	1903		American Mutoscope
Levi and Family at Coney Island	1910		Atlas
Levi and McGuiness Running for Office	1913		Imperial
Levi the Cop	1910		Atlas
Levinsky's Gold Mine	1914		Imperial
Levinsky's Holiday	1913		Majestic
Levi's Dilemma	1910		Essanay
Levi's Luck	1914		Komic
Levitsky Sees the Parade	1909		Independent
Levy's Seven Daughters	1915	W. Van Nostrand	Vitagraph
Life of Moses (5 parts)	1909-10	J. S. Blackton	Vitagraph
The Lily of Poverty Flat	1915		
The Little Jewess	1914		Kinetophoto
Little Old New York	1912		Champion
Love in the Ghetto	1913	O. Eagle	Selig-Polyscope
Lucky Cohen	1914		Lubin
The Maccabees	1911		Pathe
The Man's A Man	1912		
The Marriage of Esther	1910		Gaumont
The Melting Pot	1915	O. D. Bailey	Cort Film Corp.
The Merchant of Venice	1908		Vitagraph
The Merchant of Venice	1912		Champion
The Merchant of Venice	1912		Thanhouser
The Merchant of Venice	1914	P. Smalley	Universal
Michael Strogoff	1914		Popular Plays & Players
Mike and Jake as Heroes	1913		Joker
Mike and Jake as Pugilists	1913		Joker
Mike and Jake in Mexico	1913		Joker
Mike and Jake in Society	1913		Universal
Mike and Jake in the Wild West	1913		Joker
The Miser's Heart	1911	D. W. Griffith	Biograph
The Missing Diamond	1914		Lubin
The Money Lender	1914		Eclectic
The Moneylender's Son	1910		Lux
The Monster of Fate or The Golem	1917		Hawk Film Co.
Mr. Isaacs and the Sporting Mice	1909		Cricks & Martin
Murphy and the Mermaids	1914		Biograph
The New Baby	1913		Keystone
The New Fire Chief	1912		Universal
Nihilist Vengeance	1913		Victor
Oh, Sammy	1913		Biograph
The Old Chess Players	1912		Lubin
The Old Cobbler	1914		Bison
Old Isaacs the Pawnbroker	1908	W.McCotchen	Biograph
The Old Peddler	1911		Universal
Old Women on the Streets of New York	1913		Kalem
Oliver Twist	1909		Vitagraph
Oliver Twist	1910		Pathe
Oliver Twist	1912		General
Oliver Twist	1916		
The Pawnbroker's Daughter	1913		Kalem
A Passover Miracle	1914		Kalem
The Pawnshop	1910		Solaz
The Pawnshop	1916	C. Chaplin	Mutual
The Peddler's Find	1912		Reliance
Pharaoh or Israel in Egypt	1910		Gaumont
The Question	1911		Power's Picture Plays
Rebecca the Jewess	1914		World's Leader Features
Regeneration	1915	R. Walsh	Fox
The Riot	1913		Keystone
The Romance of the Jewess	1908	D. W. Griffith	Griffith

Title	Year	Director	Distributor/ Production Company
Russia, the Land of Oppression	1910		Defender
Samson	1914		Universal
Samson's Betrayal	1910		Gaumont
Samuel of Posen	1910		Selig Polyscope
Sandy and Shorty Work Together	1913		Vitagraph
Saul and David	1911		Gaumont
Saul and David	1909		Vitagraph
Shylock	1913		Eclipse
Solomon's Son	1912		Reliance
The Son of the Shunammite	1911		Gaumont
The Song of Solomon	1914	E. Boulder	Edison
The Sorrows of Israel	1913	S. Golden	Imperial
A Stage Door Flirtation	1914		Lubin
The Stone Heart	1915		Edison
Such a Business	1914		Royal
Threads of Destiny	1914	J. W. Smiley	Lubin
Toplitsky and Co.	1913		Keystone
Tough Guy Levi	1912		Lubin
Traffickers on Souls	1914		Universal
Two Overcoats	1911		Vitagraph
The Ungrateful Daughter-in-Law	1910		Yankee
Unto the Third Generation	1913	H. Salter	Universal
Uriel Acosta	1914		Great Players
Vengeance of the Oppressed	1916		Lubin
The Vow	1910		Gaumont
When Tony Pawned Louisa	1913		Lubin
The Wife of Cain	1913	C. L. Gaskill	Charles Fuller
A Woodland Christmas in California	1912		Melies
The Yellow Passport	1916		World Films
The Yellow Ticket	1918	W. Parke	Pathe
The Yiddisher Cowboy	1909		N.Y. Motion Picture Co. Bison
The Yiddisher Cowboy	1911		American Bank Flor

Features 1920-1929

Title	Year	Director	Distributor/ Production Company
Abie's Imported Bride	1925	R. Calneck	Temple
Abie's Irish Rose	1928	V. Fleming	Paramount
Adam and Eve	1920	R. Vignola	John Franklin Meyer
Auction of Souls	1922	O. Apfel	Associated First
The Auctioneer	1927		National
The Bells	1925	J. Young	Universal
Ben Hur	1927	F. Niblo	MGM
Blind Prejudice	1921	L. M. Allaire	Regal
Breaking Home Ties	1922	F. Seltzer/G. Rolands	Manheimer
Broadway Broke	1923	J. S. Dawley	Murray Garsson
Broken Hearts	1926	M. Schwartz	Jaffe Art Film Corp.
Cheated Love	1921	K. Baggot	Universal
Children of Fate	1926		Ivan Abramson
Clancy's Kosher Wedding	1927	A. E. Gilstrom	R-C Pictures
Cohen on the Telephone	1929	R. Bloss	Universal
The Cohens and Kellys	1926	H. Pollard	Universal
The Cohens and Kellys in Atlantic City	1929	W. J. Craft	Universal
The Cohens and Kellys in Paris	1928	W. Beaudine	Universal
A Daughter of Israel	1929	E. Jose	Bell
The Delicatessen Kid	1929	W. Fabian	Universal
Disraeli	1921	H. Kolker	Distinctive Artists
Disraeli	1929	A. Green	Warner Bros.
East Side Sadie	1929	H. Beaumont	Metro Pictures
Fanny Lear	1920		Delac, Vandal & Co.
The Five Dollar Baby	1922	H. Beaumont	Metro
Flying Romeo	1928	M. LeRoy	E. M. Asher
Fool's Highway	1924	I. Cummings	Universal
For the Love of Mike	1927	F. Capra	First National
Frisco Sally Levy	1927	W. Beaudine	MGM
George Washington Cohen	1928	G.Archinbaud	Tiffany-Stahl
The Ghetto	1928	N. Laurog	Tiffany-Stahl
A Harp in Hock	1927	R. Hoffman	Pathe
His People	1925	E. Sloman	Universal
Humoresque	1920	F. Borzage	Paramount
Hungry Hearts	1922	E. M. Hopper	Goldwyn
In Hollywood with Potash and Perlmutter	1924	A. Green	Goldwyn
Izzy and Lizzy	1926		
The Jazz Singer	1927	A. Crosland	Warner Brothers
Jewish Prudence	1927	H. Roach	Pathe
Just Around the Corner	1921	M. Frances	Cosmopolitan
Kosher Kitty Kelly	1926	J. Horn	R-C Pictures
Little Miss Smiles	1922	J. Ford	Fox Films Corp.
Little Old New York	1923	S. Olcott	
Love's Blindness	1926	J. Dillon	MGM
The Magic Cup	1921	J. Robertson	Realart
Mazel-Tov	1924		Listo-Picon
Millionaires	1926	H. Raymaker	Warner Brothers
My Man	1929	A. Mayo	Warner Brothers
New York	1927	L. Reed	Famous Players Lasky
Noah's Ark	1929	M. Curtiz	Warner Brothers
None So Blind	1923	B. King	Arrow
The Oath	1921	R. Walsh	Mayflower Photoplay
Old Clothes	1925	E. Cline	MGM
Oliver Twist	1922	F. Lloyd	Jackie Coogan Prod.
Oliver Twist, Jr.	1921	W. Webb	Fox
One of the Bravest	1925	F. O'Conner	Lumas
Orphans of the Ghetto	1922		Arista Film Corp.
Partners Again	1926	H. King	U.A.
Pass the Gravy	1928	F. Guidol	MGM
Pawn Ticket 210	1922	S. Dunlap	Fox
Potash and Perlmutter	1923	C. Badger	Goldwyn
Prejudice	1922	J. Belmont	Arista
Princess from Hoboken	1927		

Title	Year	Director	Distributor/ Production Company
Private Izzy Murphy	1926	L. Bacon	Warner Brothers
The Queen of Sheba	1921	J. G. Edwards	Fox
The Rag Man	1925	E. Kline	MGM
Raggedy Rose	1926	H. Roach	Pathe
The Rawhide Kid	1927		Universal
Rose of the Tenements	1926	P. Rosen	R-C Pictures
Sailor Izzy Murphy	1927	H. Lehrman	Warner Bros.
Sally in Our Alley	1927	W. Lang	Columbia
Salome of the Tenements	1925	S. Olcott	Famous Players
Second Hand Rose	1922	L. Ingraham	Universal
Shamrock and the Rose	1927	J. Nelson	Chadwick Prod.
The Shepherd King	1923	J. G. Edwards	Fox
Surrender	1927	E. Sloman	Universal
Sweet Daddies	1926	A. Santell	First National
A Tailor Made Man	1922	J. DeGrasse	Charles Ray
Talk of Hollywood	1929	M. Sandrick	Sono Art World Wide Pictures
Temperamental Tillie	1928		Warner Brothers
The Ten Commandments	1923	C. DeMille	Paramount
The Way of a Man	1922	C. C. Calvert	Gaumont
We Americans	1928	E. Sloman	Universal
Welcome Stranger	1924	J. Young	Belasco
The Women He Loved	1927	E. Sloman	J. L. Frothingham
The Younger Generation	1928	F. Capra	Columbia

Features 1930-1939

Title	Year	Director	Distributor/ Production Company
Around the Corner	1930	B. Glennon	Columbia
Be Yourself	1930	T. Freeland	United Artists
The Big Butter and Yegg Man	1931	Henry Lehrman	Universal
The Bowery	1933	R. Walsh	20th Century-Fox
Caught Cheating	1931	F. Strayer	Tiffany
The Cohens and Kellys in Africa	1930	V. Moore	Universal
The Cohens and Kellys in Hollywood	1932	J. F. Dillon	Universal
The Cohens and Kellys in Scotland	1930	W. J. Craft	Universal
The Cohens and Kellys in Trouble	1933	G. Stevens	Universal
Confessions of a Nazi Spy	1939	A. Litvak	First National Warner
Counsellor-at-Law	1933	W. Wyler	Universal
The Dreyfus Case	1934	F. Kraemer and M. Rosmer	Columbia
East of Fifth Avenue	1933	A. Rogell	Columbia
Gunboat Ginsburg	1930	M. Sandrich	RCA Photophone
The Heart of New York	1932	M. LeRoy	Warner Brothers
High Pressure	1932	M. LeRoy	Warner Brothers
Hitler's Reign of Terror	1934	M. Mindlin	Jewel Prod.
House of Rothschild	1934	A. Werker	20th Century Fox
The Kibitzer	1930	E. Sloman	Paramount-Famous Players-Lasky
Life of Emile Zola	1937	W. Dieterle	Warner Brothers
Light of Western Stars	1930	O. Brewer/E. Knopf	Paramount
Manhattan Melodrama	1934	Van Dyke	MGM
Manhattan Parade	1932	L. Bacon	Warner Brothers
Models and Wives	1931	C. Lamont	Universal
Night Class	1931	H. Fraser	RKO
No Greater Love	1932	L. Seiler	Columbia
Oliver Twist	1933	W. Cowen	Monogram
Power	1934	L. Mendez	Gaumont
Professor Mamlock	1938	A. Minkin/H. Rappaport	Brandon
Side Streets	1934	A. Green	First National
The S.S. Malaria	1931	H. Bretherton	Paramount
The Strange Case of Clara Deane	1932	L. Gasnier/M. Marcin	Paramount
Street Scene	1931	K. Vidor	United Artists
Subway Express	1931	F. Newmeyer	Columbia
Svengali	1931	A. Mayo	Warner Brothers
Symphony of Six Million	1932	G. La Cava	RKO
Taxi	1932	R. DelRuth	Warner Brothers
This Day and Age	1933	C. DeMille	Paramount
The Vice Squad	1931	J. Cromwell	Paramount
The Yellow Ticket	1931	R. Walsh	20th Century-Fox

Features 1940-1949

Title	Year	Director	Distributor/ Production Company
Abie's Irish Rose	1946	E. Sutherland	Bing Crosby
Action in the North Atlantic	1943	L. Bacon	Warner Brothers
Address Unknown	1944	W. C. Menzies	Columbia
Air Force	1943	H. Hawks	Warner Brothers
Bataan	1943	T. Garnett	MGM
Big City	1948	N. Taurog	MGM
Body & Soul	1947	R. Rossen	Somerset
Burning Cross	1947	W. Colmes	Screen Guild
Crossfire	1947	E. Dmytryk	RKO
The Dolly Sisters	1945	I. Cummings	20th Century-Fox
East Side, West Side	1949	M. LeRoy	MGM
Escape	1940	M. LeRoy	MGM
Gentleman's Agreement	1947	E. Kazan	20th Century-Fox
The Great Dictator	1940	C. Chaplin	Chaplin
Hitler's Children	1942	E. Dmytryk	RKO
The Hitler Gang	1944	J. Farrow	Paramount
Humoresque	1947	J. Negulesco	Warner Brothers
Jolson Sings Again	1949	H. Levin	Columbia
The Jolson Story	1946	A. E. Green	Columbia
Margin for Error	1943	O. Preminger	20th Century-Fox
Men of Boys Town	1941	N. Taurog	MGM
The Mortal Storm	1940	F. Borzage	MGM

Title	Year	Director	Distributor/ Production Company
Mr. Skeffington	1945	V. Sherman	Warner Brothers
Night Train	1940	C. Reed	20th Century-Fox
None Shall Escape	1944	W. DeToth	Columbia
Objective-Burma	1945	R. Walsh	Warner Brothers
Oliver Twist	1948	D. Lean	Rank
Once Upon a Honeymoon	1942	L. McCarey	RKO
Open Secret	1948	J. Reinhardt	Marathon Pictures
Pride of the Marines	1945	D. Daves	Warner Brothers
The Purple Heart	1944	L. Milestone	20th Century-Fox
The Red Menace	1949	R. G. Springsteen	Republic
Rhapsody in Blue	1945	I. Rapper	Warner Brothers
Samson and Delilah	1949	C. DeMille	Paramount
Sands of Iwo Jima	1949	A. Dwan	Republic
Sealed Verdict	1948	L. Allen	Paramount
The Search	1947	F. Zinneman	MGM
The Seventh Cross	1944	F. Zinneman	MGM
The Sword in the Desert	1949	G. Sherman	Universal
Three Faces West	1940	B. Vorhaus	Republic
Till the Clouds Roll By	1947	R. Whorf	MGM
To Be or Not To Be	1942	E. Lubitsch	United Artists
Tomorrow the World	1944	L. Fenton	Lester Cowan
Winged Victory	1944	G. Cukor	20th Century-Fox

Features 1950-1959

Title	Year	Director	Distributor/ Production Company
Attack	1956	R. Aldrich	United Artists
Battle Hymn	1957	D. Sirk	Universal
The Benny Goodman Story	1956	V. Davies	Universal
The Big Knife	1955	R. Aldrich	United Artists
A Bucket of Blood	1959	R. Corman	American International Pictures
Caine Mutiny	1954	E. Dmytryk	Columbia
Compulsion	1959	R. Fleischer	Zanuck
David and Bathsheba	1951	H. King	20th Century-Fox
The Deep Sea	1958	R. Mate	Jaguar
Detective Story	1951	W. Wyler	Paramount
Diary of Anne Frank	1959	G. Stevens	20th Century-Fox
The Eddie Cantor Story	1953	A. Green	Warner Brothers
Espresso Bongo	1959	V. Guest	Conquest
Garment Jungle	1957	V. Sherman	Columbia
Good Morning, Miss Dove	1955	H. Koster	20th Century-Fox
Home Before Dark	1958	M. LeRoy	Warner Brothers
I Accuse	1958	J. Ferrar	MGM
I Can Get It For You Wholesale or Only the Best	1951	M. Gordon	20th Century-Fox
It's a Big Country	1951	D. Schary	MGM
Ivanhoe	1952	R. Thorpe	MGM
The Jazz Singer	1953	M. Curtiz	Warner Brothers
The Juggler	1953	E. Dmytryk	Columbia
The Last Angry Man	1959	D. Mann	Columbia
The Last Ten Days	1956	G. B. Pabst	Columbia
The Magnificent Yankee	1951	J. Sturges	MGM
Marjorie Morningstar	1958	I. Rapper	Beechwald
Me and the Colonel	1958	P. Glenville	Court Goetz
Middle of the Night	1959	D. Mann	Columbia
Molly	1951	Hart	Paramount
The Naked and the Dead	1958	R. Walsh	RKO
Never Love a Stranger	1958	R. Stevens	Allied Artists
Not as a Stranger	1955	S. Kramer	United Artists
The Prodigal	1955	R. Thorpe	MGM
The Proud Rebel	1958	M. Curtiz	Buena Vista
Say One For Me	1958	F. Tashlin	20th Century-Fox
Singing in the Dark	1956	M. Nosseck	A.N.O.
Solomon and Sheba	1959	K. Vidor	United Artists
Somebody Up There Likes Me	1956	R. Wise	MGM
Stalag 17	1953	W. Wilder	Paramount
The Sun Also Rises	1957	H. King	20th Century-Fox
The Sword in the Desert	1952	G. Sherman	Universal
The Ten Commandments	1956	C. DeMille	Paramount
Three Brave Men	1957	P. Dunne	20th Century-Fox
Titanic	1953	G. Negulesco	20th Century-Fox
The Young Lions	1958	E. Dmytryk	20th Century-Fox

Features 1960-1969

Title	Year	Director	Distributor/ Production Company
Act One	1963	D. Schary	Warner Brothers
The Bible . . . In the Beginning	1966	J. Huston	20th Century-Fox
Bye Bye Braverman	1968	S. Lumet	Warner Brothers
Captain Newman, M.D.	1963	D. Miller	Universal
Cast a Giant Shadow	1966	M. Shavelson	Mirish-Llenroc-Batjac
Come Blow Your Horn	1963	B. Yorkin	Paramount
Dark at the Top of the Stairs	1960	D. Mann	Warner Brothers
The Detective	1968	Gordon Douglas	20th Century-Fox
Enter Laughing	1967	C. Reiner	Acre-Sajo Prod.
Esther and the King	1960	R. Walsh	20th Century-Fox
Exodus	1960	O. Preminger	Otto Preminger
The Fearless Vampire Killers	1967	R. Polanski	MGM
The Fixer	1968	J. Frankenheimer	MGM
The Fortune Cookie	1966	W. Wilder	United Artists
Freud	1962	J. Huston	Universal
Funny Girl	1968	W. Wyler	Columbia
Goldstein	1965	P. Kaufman/ B. Monaster	Montrose

Title	Year	Director	Distributor/ Production Company
Goodbye, Columbus	1969	L. Peerce	Willow Tree Prod.
Hello, Dolly!	1969	G. Kelly	20th Century-Fox
The Hoodlum Priest	1961	I. Kershner	Murr Woods
A House Is Not a Home	1964	R. Rouse	Embassy
I Love You, Alice B. Toklas!	1968	H. Averback	Warner Brothers
John Goldfarb, Please Come Home	1964	J. L. Thompson	20th Century-Fox
Judgment at Nuremberg	1961	S. Kramer	Roxlam
Judith	1965	D. Mann	Paramount
King of the Roaring Twenties: The Story of Arnold Rothstein	1961	J. Newman	Allied Artists
Lisa	1962	P. Dunne	20th Century-Fox
The Little Shop of Horrors	1960	R. Corman	Film Group
Luv	1967	C. Donner	Columbia
A Majority of One	1961	M. LeRoy	Warner Brothers
Me, Natalie	1969	F. Loe	National General Pictures
Night of the Generals	1967	A. Litvak	Columbia
The Night They Raided Minsky's	1968	W. Freidkin	Norman Lear
No Way to Treat a Lady	1968	J. Smight	Paramount
Oliver!	1968	C. Reed	Columbia
Operation Eichmann	1961	R. G. Springsteen	Allied Artists
The Out-of-Towners	1969	A. Hiller	Paramount
The Pawnbroker	1965	S. Lumet	Eli Landau
The Producers	1968	M. Brooks	Embassy Pictures
The Saboteur: Code Name Mori	1965	B. Wicki	20th Century-Fox
Ship of Fools	1965	S. Kramer	Columbia
The Spy Who Came In From the Cold	1965	Martin Ritt	Paramount
The Story of Ruth	1960	H. Kostler	Fox
Thoroughly Modern Millie	1967	G. R. Hill	Universal
Tobruk	1966	A. Hiller	Universal
Ulysses	1967	J. Strick	Continental
Walk in the Shadow	1962	B. Dearden	Allied Film Makers

Features 1970-1979

Title	Year	Director	Distributor/ Production Company
Alex in Wonderland	1970	P. Mazursky	MGM
The All American Boy	1973	C. Eastman	Warner Bros.
All the President's Men	1976	A. Pakula	Warner Bros.
Americathon	1979	N. Israel	United Artists
The Angel Levine	1970	J. Kadar	United Artists
Annie Hall	1977	W. Allen	United Artists
The Apprenticeship of Duddy Kravitz	1974	T. Kotcheff	Paramount
The Assassination of Trotsky	1973	J. Losey	Cinerama
Bananas	1971	W. Allen	United Artists
The Big Fix	1978	J. P. Kagan	Universal
Black Sunday	1977	J. Frankenheimer	Paramount
Blazing Saddles	1974	M. Brooks	Warner Bros.
Bloodline	1979	T. Young	Paramount
Blume in Love	1973	P. Mazursky	Warner Bros.
Boardwalk	1979	S. Verona	Atlantic Releasing Co.
The Boys from Brazil	1979	F. Schaffner	20th Century-Fox
Cabaret	1972	R. Fosse	Allied Artists
California Suite	1978	H. Ross	Columbia
Children of Rage	1975	A. Seidelman	Emessee
The Devil and Sam Silverstein	1975		
The Diary of a Mad Housewife	1970	F. Perry	Universal
The Duchess and The Dirtwater Fox	1976	M. Frank	20th Century-Fox
The Eagle Has Landed	1977	J. Sturges	Columbia
Everything You Always Wanted to Know About Sex But Were Afraid to Ask	1972	W. Allen	United Artists
Fiddler on the Roof	1971	N. Jewison	United Artists
For Pete's Sake	1974	P. Yates	Columbia
The Frisco Kid	1979	R. Aldrich	Warner Bros.
Fritz The Cat	1972	R. Bakshi	Cinemation Industries
The Front	1976	M. Ritt	Columbia
Funny Lady	1975	H. Ross	Columbia
The Gambler	1974	K. Reisz	Paramount
The Godfather, Pt. II	1974	F. F. Coppola	Paramount
Godspell	1973	D. Green	Columbia
Going in Style	1979	M. Brest	Warner Bros.
The Great Gatsby	1974	J. Clayton	Paramount
Harry and Tonto	1974	P. Mazursky	20th Century-Fox
The Heartbreak Kid	1972	E. May	20th Century-Fox
Hearts of the West	1975	H. Zieff	United Artists
Hester Street	1975	J. M. Silver	Midwest Film
Hit	1973	S. Furie	Paramount
House Calls	1978	Howard Zeiff	Universal
I Never Sang for My Father	1970	G. Cates	Columbia
I Will . . . I Will . . . For Now	1975	N. Panama	20th Century-Fox
The In-Laws	1979	A. Hiller	Warner Bros.
Interiors	1978	W. Allen	United Artists
The Jerusalem File	1971	J. Flynn	MGM
Jesus Christ Superstar	1973	N. Jewison	Universal
Julia	1977	F. Zinneman	20th Century-Fox
Kelly's Heroes	1970	B. Hutton	MGM
Kotch	1971	J. Lemmon	Cinerama
The Last Embrace	1979	J. Demme	United Artists
Lenny	1974	R. Fosse	United Artists
Lepke	1975	M. Golan	Warner Bros.
Lies My Father Told Me	1975	J. Kadar	Columbia
Little Murders	1971	A. Arkin	20th Century-Fox
The Long Goodbye	1973	R. Altman	United Artists
Love and Death	1975	W. Allen	United Artists

Title	Year	Director	Distributor/ Production Company
Love at First Bite	1979	S. Dragoti	American International
Made for Each Other	1971	R. Bean	20th Century-Fox
The Main Event	1979	H. Zieff	Warner Bros.
Making It	1971	A. Jacobs	20th Century-Fox
The Man in the Glass Booth	1975	A. Hiller	American Film Theater
Manhattan	1979	W. Allen	United Artists
Marathon Man	1976	J. Schlesinger	Paramount
Meatballs	1979	I. Reitman	Paramount
Mikey and Nicky	1976	E. May	Paramount
Minnie and Moskowitz	1971	J. Cassavetes	Universal
A New Leaf	1970	E. May	Paramount
Next Stop, Greenwich Village	1976	P. Mazursky	20th Century-Fox
Norma Rae	1979	M. Ritt	20th Century-Fox
The Owl and the Pussycat	1970	H. Ross	Columbia
Play It Again Sam	1972	H. Ross	Paramount
Play It As It Lays	1972	F. Perry	Universal
Plaza Suite	1970	A. Hiller	Paramount
Portnoy's Complaint	1972	E. Lehman	Warner Bros.
The Poseidon Adventure	1972	R. Neame	20th Century-Fox
Prisoner of Second Avenue	1975	M. Frank	Warner Bros.
Romance of a Horsethief	1971	A. Polonsky	Allied Artists
Running	1979	S. H. Stern	Universal
The Salzburg Connection	1972	L. Katzin	Fox
Save the Tiger	1973	J. Avildsen	Paramount
Shampoo	1975	H. Ashby	Universal
Sheila Levine is Alive and Well	1975	S. Furie	Paramount
Sleeper	1973	W. Allen	United Artists
Some of My Best Friends Are	1971	M. Nelson	American International
A Star is Born	1976	F. Pierson	Warner Bros.
Such Good Friends	1971	O. Preminger	Paramount
The Sunshine Boys	1975	H. Ross	MGM
An Unmarried Woman	1978	P. Mazursky	20th Century-Fox
Voyage of the Damned	1979	S. Rosenberg	Auco Embessy
Voices	1979	R. Markowitz	MGM
The Way We Were	1973	S. Pollack	Columbia
Where's Poppa?	1970	C. Reiner	United Artists
Who Is Harry Kellerman and Why Is He Saying Those Terrible Things About Me?	1971	U. Grosbard	National Gen. Pictures

Features 1980 to Present

Title	Year	Director	Distributor/ Production Company
Altered States	1981	K. Russell	Warner Bros.
The Amateur	1982	C. Jarrott	20th Century-Fox
American Pop	1981	R. Bakshi	Columbia
An American Tail	1986	D. Bluth	Universal
An American Werewolf in London	1981	J. Landis	Universal
The Assisi Underground	1985		
Baby, It's You	1983	J. Sayles	Paramount
Bad Boys	1983	R. Rosenthal	EMI/ Universal
The Big Chill	1983	L. Kasdan	Columbia
Brighton Beach Memoirs	1986	G. Saks	Universal
Broadway Danny Rose	1984	Woody Allen	United Artists
The Cannonball Run	1981	H. Needham	20th Century-Fox
Chariots of Fire	1982	H. Hudson	Warner Bros./ Ladd Co.
A Chorus Line	1985	R. Atten borough	Columbia
The Chosen	1982	J. Kagan	20th Century-Fox
Cocoon	1985	Ron Howard	20th Century-Fox
Compromising Positions	1985	Frank Perry	Paramount
The Cotton Club	1984	F.F. Coppola	Orion
Daniel	1984	S. Lumet	20th Century-Fox
Diner	1982	B. Levinson	MGM
Down and Out in Beverly Hills	1986	Paul Mazursky	Touchstone
Endless Love	1981	F. Zefferelli	Universal
Every Time We Say Goodbye	1986	Moshe Mizrachi	Tri-Star
Eyewitness	1981	P. Yates	20th Century-Fox
Falling in Love Again	1980	Steven Paul	International
Fame	1980	A. Parker	MGM
Flash Gordon	1980	M. Hodges	Universal
Fort Apache, The Bronx	1981	D. Petrie	20th Century-Fox
Four Friends	1981	A. Penn	Filmways Pictures
Frances	1982	G. Clifford	EMI
Garbo Talks	1984	S. Lumet	
Gilda Live	1980	M. Nichols	Warner Bros.
The Goodbye People	1986	Herb Gardner	
The Goonies	1985	Richard Donner	Warner Bros.
Hannah and Her Sisters	1986	Woody Allen	Orion
Hanna K	1983	C. Costa-Gavras	Universal
Heavy Metal	1981	G. Potterton	Columbia
History of the World, Part I	1981	M. Brooks	20th Century-Fox
The Hotel New Hampshire	1984	T. Richardson	Orion
The Hunter	1980	B. Kulik	Paramount
It's My Turn	1980	C. Weill	Columbia
The Jazz Singer	1981	R. Fleischer	Associated Film Development
Just Tell Me What You Want	1980	S. Lumet	Warner Bros.
The Keep	1983	Michael Mann	Paramount
King David	1985	B. Beresford	Paramount
The King of Comedy	1983	M. Scorcese	20th Century-Fox
Kiss of the Spider Woman	1985	Hector Babenco	Warner Bros.
The Last Winter	1983	Riki Nissimoff	Tri-Star

Title	Year	Director	Distributor/ Production Company
The Little Drummer Girl	1984	G.R. Hill	Warner Bros.
Lovesick	1983	M. Brickman	Warner Bros.
Mommie Dearest	1981	Frank Perry	Paramount
The Morning After	1986	S. Lumet	Lorimar
Moscow on the Hudson	1984	P. Mazursky	Columbia
My Favorite Year	1982	R. Benjamin	MGM
1984	1985	M. Radford	
Once Upon a Time in America	1984	S. Leone	Ladd Co.
Ordinary People	1980	R. Redford	Paramount
Over the Brooklyn Bridge	1984	M. Golan	MGM
Popeye	1980	R. Altman	Paramount
Porky's	1982	Bob Clark	20th Century-Fox
Porky's II	1984	Bob Clark	20th Century-Fox
Prince of The City	1981	S. Lumet	Warner Bros.
Private Benjamin	1980	H. Zieff	Warner Bros.
Prizzi's Honor	1985	John Huston	20th Century-Fox
Quicksilver	1986	Tom Donnelly	Columbia
Radio Days	1987	W. Allen	Orion
Ragtime	1981	M. Forman	Paramount
Reds	1981	W. Beatty	Paramount
Rocky III	1982	S. Stallone	United Artists
Sharkey's Machine	1981	B. Reynolds	Orion
Simon	1980	M. Brickman	Orion

Title	Year	Director	Distributor/ Production Company
A Small Circle of Friends	1980	R. Cohen	United Artists
S.O.B.	1981	B. Edwards	Paramount
So Fine	1982	A. Bergman	Warner Bros.
Sophie's Choice	1983	A. Pakula	Universal
Soup for One	1981	John Kaufer	Warner Bros.
Stardust Memories	1980	W. Allen	United Artists
St. Elmo's Fire	1985	Joel Schumacker	Columbia
Streets of Gold	1986		
Tell Me A Riddle	1980	L. Grant	Filmways Pictures
Tempest	1982	Paul Mazursky	Columbia
Those Lips, Those Eyes	1980	M. Pressman	United Artists
Ticket to Heaven	1982	R. L. Thomas	United Artist Classics
To Be or Not To Be	1983	A. Johnson	Brooksfilm
The Twilight Zone, The Movie (Pt. 1)	1983	J. Landis	Warner Bros.
The Twilight Zone, The Movie (Pt. 2)	1983	S. Speilberg	Warner Bros.
Up the Creek	1983	Robert Butler	Orion
Volunteers	1985	Nicholas Meyer	Orion
Wholly Moses	1980	G. Weiss	Columbia
Willy and Phil	1980	P. Mazursky	20th Century Fox
Yentl	1983	B. Streisand	MGM
Zelig	1983	W. Allen	Warner Bros.

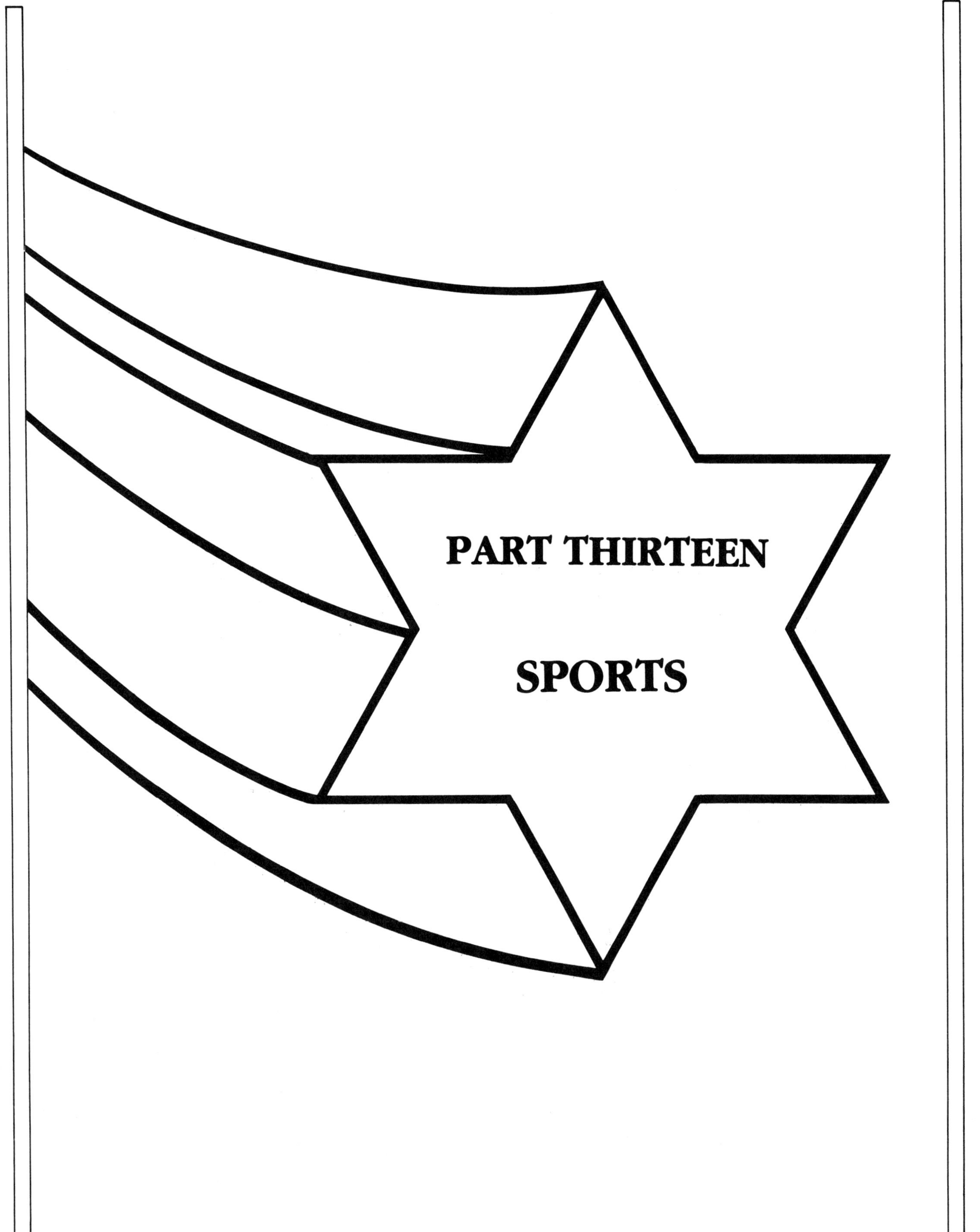
PART THIRTEEN
SPORTS

The Jewish Sports Hall of Fame

The Jewish Sports Hall of Fame was founded in 1979 to recognize Jewish men and women who achieve distinction in sports.

The Hall of Fame is located at the Wingate Institute for Physical Education and Sport, in Netanya, Israel. To be eligible, a candidate must have retired from sports.

Harold Abrahams, *Great Britain*—Track & Field 1981
Dr. Joseph Alexander, *USA*—Football 1984
Mel Allen, *USA*—Sportscaster 1980
Abe Attell, *USA*—Boxing 1982
Red Auerbach, *USA*—Basketball 1979
Victor Barna, *Hungary/Great Britain*—Table Tennis 1981
Senda Berenson, *USA*—Basketball 1986
Isaac Berger, *USA*—Weightlifting 1980
Samuel Berger, *USA*—Boxing 1984
Richard Bergmann, *Austria*—Table Tennis 1982
Gyorgy Brody, *Hungary*—Water Polo 1982
Angela Buxton, *Great Britain*—Tennis 1981
Alain Calmat, *France*—Figure Skating 1986
Zephania Carmel/Lydia Lazarov, *Israel*—Yachting 1982
Lillian Copeland, *USA*—Track & Field 1980
Barney Dreyfuss, *USA*—Baseball 1980
Charlotte Epstein, *USA*—Swimming 1982
Jackie Fields, *USA*—Boxing 1979
Alfred Flatow, *Germany*—Gymnastics 1981
Benny Friedman, *USA*—Football 1979
Jeno Fuchs, *Hungary*—Fencing 1982
Sir Arthur Abraham Gold, *Great Britain*—Official 1986
Marshall Goldberg, *USA*—Football 1980
Alexander Gomelsky, *USSR*—Basketball 1981
Eddie Gottlieb, *USA*—Basketball 1980
Hank Greenberg, *USA*—Baseball 1979
George Gulak, *USA*—Gymnastics 1983
Boris Gurevich, *USSR*—Wrestling 1982
Bela Guttmann, *Hungary*—Soccer 1981
Sir Ludwig Guttmann, *Germany/Great Britain*—Sports Medicine 1981
Alfred Hajos-Guttmann, *Hungary*—Swimming 1981
Hakoah-Vienna, *Austria*—Soccer 1982
Nat Holman, *USA*—Basketball 1979
Hirsch Jacobs, *USA*—Horse Racing 1979
Jim Jacobs, *USA*—Handball 1979
Irving Jaffe, *USA*—Ice Skating 1979
Alan Jay, *Great Britain*—Fencing 1984
Endre Kabos, *Hungary*—Fencing 1985
Louis "Kid" Kaplan, *USA*—Boxing 1985
Elias Katz, *Finland*—Track & Field 1981
Agnes Keleti, *Hungary*—Gymnastics 1981
Irena Kirszenstein, *Poland*—Track & Field 1981
Abel Kiviat, *USA*—Track & Field 1983
Sandy Koufax, *USA*—Baseball 1979
Lily Kronberger, *Hungary*—Figure Skating 1982
Benny Leonard, *USA*—Boxing 1979
Battling Levinsky, *USA*—Boxing 1982
Ted "Kid" Lewis, *Great Britain*—Boxing 1982
Alexandre Lippmann, *France*—Fencing 1983
Harry Litwack, *USA*—Basketball 1980
Sid Luckman, *USA*—Football 1979
Gyula Mandy, *Hungary*—Soccer 1982
Walentin Mankin, *USSR*—Yachting 1986
Hugo Meisl, *Austria*—Soccer 1981
Faina Melnik, *USSR*—Track & Field 1983
Daniel Mendoza, *Great Britain*—Boxing 1981
Ferenc Mezo, *Tunisia*—Olympic Historian 1985
Mark Midler, *USSR*—Fencing 1982
Szabados Miklos, *Hungary*—Table Tennis 1986
Walter Miller, *USA*—Horse Racing 1982
Ron Mix, *USA*—Football 1980
Sir Ivor Goldsmid Montagu, *England*—Table Tennis 1983
Lady Swathling, Gladys Goldsmid Montagu, *England*—Table Tennis 1984
Samuel Mosberg, *USA*—Boxing 1984
Lon Myers, *USA*—Track & Field 1980
Paul Neumann, *Austria*—Swimming 1983
Zvi Nishri, *Israel*—Physical Education 1981
Grigori Novak, *USSR*—Weightlifting 1984
Ivan Osiier, *Denmark*—Fencing 1985
Victor Perez, *Tunisia*—Boxing 1985
Attila Petschauer, *Hungary*—Fencing 1984
Lipman Pike, *USA*—Baseball 1984
Myer Prinstein, *USA*—Track & Field 1982
Al Rosen, *USA*—Baseball 1980
Maxie Rosenbloom, *USA*—Boxing 1983
Fanny Rosenfeld, *Canada*—Track & Field 1981
Barney Ross, *USA*—Boxing 1979
Angelica Adelstein-Rozeanu, *Romania/Israel*—Table Tennis ... 1981
Louis Rubenstein, *Canada*—Ice Skating 1981
Yakov Rylsky, *USSR*—Fencing 1985
Abe Saperstein, *USA*—Basketball 1979
Dick Savitt, *USA*—Tennis 1979
Dolph Schayes, *USA*—Basketball 1979
Jody Scheckter, *South Africa*—Auto Racing 1982
Frank Spellman, *USA*—Weightlifting 1982
Mark Spitz, *USA*—Swimming 1979
Eva Szekely, *Hungary*—Swimming 1981
Richard Weisz, *Hungary*—Wrestling 1982
Sylvia Wene Martin, *USA*—Bowling 1979
Henry Wittenberg, *USA*—Wrestling 1979
Max Zaslovsky, *USA*—Basketball 1982

Jewish Olympic Medalists

George Eisen

1896 (ATHENS)

Gold

Alfred Hajos-Guttman, Hungary, 100-meter freestyle swimming
Alfred Hajos-Guttman, Hungary, 1,500-meter freestyle swimming
Paul Neumann, Austria, 400-meter freestyle swimming
Alfred Flatow, Germany, gymnastics, parallel bars
Alfred Flatow, Germany, gymnastics, team parallel bars
Alfred Flatow, Germany, gymnastics, team horizontal bar
Gustav Felix Flatow, Germany, gymnastics, team parallel bars
Gustav Felix Flatow, Germany, gymnastics, team horizontal bar

Silver

Alfred Flatow, Germany, gymnastics, horizontal bar

Bronze

Otto Herschmann, Austria, 100-meter freestyle swimming

1900 (PARIS)

Gold

Myer Prinstein, USA, athletics, triple jump

Silver

Myer Prinstein, USA, athletics, long jump
Otto Wahle, Austria, 1000-meter freestyle swimming
Otto Wahle, Austria, 200-meter swimming obstacle race
Henri Cohen, Belgium, water polo
Jean Bloch, France, soccer

Bronze

Siegfried Flesch, Austria, fencing, individual saber

1904 (ST. LOUIS)

Gold

Myer Prinstein, USA, athletics, long jump
Myer Prinstein, USA, athletics, triple jump
Samuel Berger, USA, heavyweight boxing

Silver

Albert Lehman, USA, lacrosse
Philip Hess, USA, lacrosse
Daniel Frank, USA, athletics, long jump

Bronze

Otto Wahle, Austria, 400-meter freestyle swimming

1906 (ATHENS/unofficial)

Gold

Myer Prinstein, USA, athletics, long jump
Otto Scheff, Austria, 400-meter freestyle swimming
Henrik Hajos-Guttman, Hungary, 800-meter freestyle swimming relay

Silver

Edgar Seligman, Great Britain, fencing, team epee

Bronze

Hugo Friend, USA, athletics, long jump
Otto Scheff, Austria, 1,500-meter freestyle swimming

1908 (LONDON)

Gold

Richard Weisz, Hungary, Greco-Roman heavyweight wrestling
Jean Stern, France, fencing, team epee
Alexandre Lippmann, France, fencing, team epee
Dr. Jeno Fuchs, Hungary, fencing, individual saber
Dr. Jeno Fuchs, Hungary, fencing, team saber
Lajos Werkner, Hungary, fencing, team saber
Dr. Oszkar Gerde, Hungary, fencing, team saber

Silver

Edwin "Barney" Solomon, Great Britain (Ireland), rugby
Bethel "Bert" Solomon, Great Britain (Ireland), rugby
Harry Simon, USA, free rifle
Edgar Seligman, Great Britain, fencing, team epee
Alexandre Lippmann, France, fencing, individual epee

Bronze

Odon Bodor, Hungary, athletics, 1,600-meter relay
Charles "Clair" Jacobs, USA, athletics, pole vault
Otto Scheff, Austria, 400-meter freestyle swimming

1912 (STOCKHOLM)

Gold

Jacques Ochs, Belgium, fencing, team epee
Gaston Salmon, Belgium, fencing, team epee
Dr. Jeno Fuchs, Hungary, fencing, team saber
Dr. Oszkar Gerde, Hungary, fencing, team saber
Lajor Werkner, Hungary, fencing, team saber
Dr. Jeno Fuchs, Hungary, fencing, individual saber

Silver

Alvah T. Meyer, USA, athletics, 100-meter dash
Abel Kiviat, USA, athletics, 1,500-meter run
Imre Gellert, Hungary, gymnastics, team combined exercises
Ivan Osiier, Denmark, fencing, individual epee
Edgar Seligman, Great Britain, fencing, team epee
Dr. Otto Herschmann, Austria, fencing, team saber
Samu Fodi, Hungary, team gymnastics
Joszef Szalai, Hungary, team gymnastics

1920 (ANTWERP)

Gold

Samuel Mosberg, USA, lightweight boxing
Albert Schneider, Canada (USA citizen), welterweight boxing
Morris Fisher, USA, free rifle
Morris Fisher, USA, 300-meter team shooting
Morris Fisher, USA, prone team shooting

Silver

Gerard Blitz, Belgium, water polo
Maurice Blitz, Belgium, water polo
Samuel Gerson, USA, freestyle featherweight wrestling
Alexandre Lippmann, France, fencing, individual epee

Bronze

Gerard Blitz, Belgium, 100-meter backstroke swimming
Frederick Meyer, USA, freestyle heavyweight wrestling
Montgomery "Moe" Herscovitch, Canada, middleweight boxing
Alexandre Lippmann, France, fencing, team epee

1924 (Chamonix/PARIS)

Gold

Elias Katz, Finland, athletics, 3,000-meter steeplechase
Harold Abrahams, Great Britain, athletics, 100-meter dash
Louis Clarke, USA, athletics, 400-meter relay
Elias Katz, Finland, athletics, 3,000-meter team cross-country
John "Jackie" Fields, USA, featherweight boxing
Alexandre Lippmann, France, fencing, team epee
Morris Fisher, USA, free-rifle
Morris Fisher, USA, 300-meter team shooting

Silver

Harold Abrahams, Great Britain, athletics, 400-meter relay
Maurice Blitz, Belgium, water polo
Gerard Blitz, Belgium, water polo
Janos Garay, Hungary, fencing, team saber
Elias Katz. Finland, individual steeplechase

Bronze

Baron Umberto Luigi de Morpurgo, Italy, tennis singles
Janos Garay, Hungary, fencing, individual saber
Sidney Jelinek, USA, rowing, coxed-fours

1928 (St. Moritz/AMSTERDAM)

Gold

Fanny Rosenfeld, Canada, athletics, 400-meter relay
Dr. Sandor Gombos, Hungary, fencing, team saber
Attila Petschauer, Hungary, fencing, team saber
Janos Garay, Hungary, fencing, team saber

Silver

Fanny Rosenfeld, Canada, athletics, 100-meter dash
Lillian Copeland, USA, athletics, discus throw
Istvan Barta, Hungary, water polo
Attila Petschauer, Hungary, fencing, individual saber

Bronze

Ellis Smouha, Great Britain, athletics, 400-meter relay
Harry Isaacs, South Africa, bantamweight boxing
Harold Devine, USA, featherweight boxing
Samuel Rabin, Great Britain, freestyle middleweight wrestling

1932 (Lake Placid/LOS ANGELES)

Gold

Lillian Copeland, USA, athletics, discus throw
Irving Jaffee, USA, 5,000-meter speed skating
Irving Jaffee, USA, 10,000-meter speed skating
George Gulack, USA, gymnastics, rings
Gyorgy Brody, Hungary, water polo
Istvan Barta, Hungary, water polo
Miklos Sarkany, Hungary, water polo
Endre Kabos, Hungary, fencing, team saber
Attila Petschauer, Hungary, fencing, team saber

Silver

Karoly Karpati, Hungary, freestyle lightweight wrestling
Abraham Kurland, Denmark, Greco-Roman lightweight wrestling
Peter Jaffe, Great Britain, Star-class yachting
Phillip Erenberg, USA, gymnastics, club swinging

Bronze

Albert Schwartz, USA, 100-meter freestyle swimming
Nickolaus Herschl, Austria, freestyle heavyweight wrestling
Nickolaus Herschl, Austria, Greco-Roman heavyweight wrestling
Nathan Bor, USA, lightweight boxing
Endre Kabos, Hungary, fencing, individual saber
Rudolf Ball, Germany, ice hockey

1936 (Garmisch-Partenkirchen/BERLIN)

Gold

Samuel Balter, USA, basketball
Gyorgy Brody, Hungary, water polo
Miklos Sarkany, Hungary, water polo
Karoly Karpati, Hungary, lightweight freestyle wrestling
Endre Kabos, Hungary, fencing, individual saber
Endre Kabos, Hungary, fencing, team saber

Silver

Irving Maretzky, Canada, basketball

Bronze

Gerard Blitz, Belgium, water polo
Rudi Ball, Germany, ice hockey
Laszlo Szollas, Hungary, pair figure skating
Emilia Rotter, Hungary, pair figure skating

1948 (St. Moritz/LONDON)

Gold

Frank Spellman, USA, middleweight weightlifting
Henry Wittenberg, USA, freestyle light-heavyweight wrestling

Silver

Steve Seymour, USA, athletics, javelin throw

Bronze

James Fuchs, USA, athletics, shot put

1952 (Oslo/HELSINKI)

Gold

Eva Szekely, Hungary, 200-meter breaststroke swimming
Robert Antal, Hungary, water polo
Boris Gurevitsch, USSR, Greco-Roman flyweight wrestling
Claude Netter, France, fencing, team foil
Mikhail Perelman, USSR, gymnastics, team combined exercises
Agnes Keleti, Hungary, gymnastics, floor exercises
Sandor Geller, Hungary, soccer
Valeria Gyenge, Hungary, 400-meter freestyle swimming

Silver

Aleksandr Moiseyev, USSR, basketball
Grigoriy Novak, USSR, middle-heavyweight weightlifting
Henry Wittenberg, USA, light-heavyweight freestyle wrestling
Agnes Keleti, Hungary, gymnastics, team combined exercises

Bronze

James Fuchs, USA, athletics, shot put
Lev Vainschtein, USSR, free rifle
Agnes Keleti, Hungary, gymnastics, team exercise with portable apparatus
Agnes Keleti, Hungary, gymnastics, asymmetrical bars

1956 (Cortina d'Ampezzo/MELBOURNE)

Gold

Leon Rotman, Rumania, canoe, 1,000-meter Canadian singles
Leon Rotman, Rumania, canoe, 10,000-meter Canadian singles
Isaac Berger, USA, featherweight weightlifting
Agnes Keleti, Hungary, gymnastics, asymmetrical bars
Agnes Keleti, Hungary, gymnastics, floor exercises
Agnes Keleti, Hungary, gymnastics, balance beam
Agnes Keleti, Hungary, gymnastics, team exercise with portable apparatus
Aliz Kertesz, Hungary, gymnastics, team exercise with portable apparatus
Boris Rasinsky, USSR, soccer

Silver

Eva Szekely, Hungary, 200-meter breaststroke swimming
Claude Netter, France, fencing, team foil
Agnes Keleti, Hungary, gymnastics; individual combined exercises
Agnes Keleti, Hungary, gymnastics, team combined exercises
Aliz Kertesz, Hungary, gymnastics, team combined exercises
Rafael Gratsch, USSR, 500-meter speed skating

Bronze

Imre Farkas, Hungary, canoe, 10,000-meter Canadian pairs
Boris Goikhman, USSR, water polo
Yves Dreyfus, France, fencing, team epee
Armand Mouyal, France, fencing, team epee
Yakov Rylsky, USSR, fencing, team saber
David Tyschler, USSR, fencing, team saber

1960 (Squaw Valley/ROME)

Gold

Mark Midler, USSR, fencing, team foil

Silver
Boris Goikhman, USSR, water polo
Isaac Berger, USA, featherweight weightlifting
Allan Jay, Great Britain, fencing, individual epee
Allan Jay, Great Britain, fencing, team epee
Guy Nosbaum, France, rowing, coxed-fours
Jean Klein, France, rowing, coxed-fours
Vladimir Portnoi, USSR, gymnastics, team combined exercises

Bronze
Leon Rotman, Rumania, canoe, 1,000-meter Canadian singles
Imre Farkas, Hungary, canoe, 1,000-meter Canadian pairs.
Klara Fried-Banfalvi, Hungary, kayak, 500-meter pairs
Moyses Blas, Brazil, basketball
David Segal, Great Britain, athletics, 400-meter relay
Albert Axelrod, USA, fencing, individual foil
Robert Halperin, USA, Star-class yachting
Vladimir Portnoi, USSR, gymnastics, long horse vault
Rafael Gratsch, USSR, 500-meter speed skating

1964 (Innsbruck/TOKYO)

Gold
Lawrence Brown, USA, basketball
Gerald Ashworth, USA, athletics, 400-meter relay
Irena Kirszenstein, Poland, athletics, 400-meter relay
Mark Midler, USSR, fencing, team foil
Yakov Rylsky, USSR, fencing, team saber
Tamas Gabor, Hungary, team epee

Silver
Irena Kirszenstein, Poland, athletics, 200-meter dash
Irena Kirszenstein, Poland, athletics, long jump
Marilyn Ramenofsky, USA, 400-meter freestyle swimming
Nelly Abramova, USSR, volleyball
Isaac Berger, USA, featherweight weightlifting

Bronze
Yves Dreyfus, France, fencing, team epee
James Bregman, USA, middleweight judo

1968 (Grenoble/MEXICO CITY)

Gold
Irena Szewinska-Kirszenstein, Poland, athletics, 200-meter dash
Mark Spitz, USA, 400-meter freestyle swimming relay
Mark Spitz, USA, 800-meter freestyle swimming relay
Boris Gurevitsch, USSR, freestyle middleweight wrestling

Silver
Mark Spitz, USA, 100-meter butterfly swimming
Semyon Belits-Geiman, USSR, 400-meter freestyle swimming relay
Alain Calmat, France, figure skating

Bronze
Irena Szewinska-Kirszenstein, Poland, athletics, 100-meter dash
Mark Spitz, USA, 100-meter freestyle swimming
Semyon Belits-Geiman, USSR, 800-meter freestyle swimming relay

1972 (Sapporo/MUNICH)

Gold
Mark Spitz, USA, 100-meter freestyle swimming
Mark Spitz, USA, 200-meter freestyle swimming
Mark Spitz, USA, 100-meter butterfly swimming
Mark Spitz, USA, 200-meter butterfly swimming
Mark Spitz, USA, 400-meter freestyle swimming relay
Mark Spitz, USA, 400-meter medley swimming relay
Mark Spitz, USA, 800-meter freestyle swimming relay
Faina Melnik, USSR, athletics, discus throw
Sandor Erdoes, Hungary, fencing team epee

Silver
Andrea Gyarmati, Hungary, 100-meter backstroke swimming
Neal Shapiro, USA, equestrian team jumping

Bronze
Irena Szewinska, Poland, athletics, 200-meter dash
Andrea Gyarmati, Hungary, 100-meter butterfly swimming
Peter Asch, USA, water polo
Neal Shapiro, USA, equestrian individual jumping
Don Cohan, USA, Dragon-class yachting
Barry Weitzenberg, USA, water polo

1976 (Innsbruck/MONTREAL)

Gold
Ernest Grunfeld, USA, basketball
Irena Szewinska, Poland, athletics, 400-meter run

Silver
Nancy Lieberman, USA, basketball
Natalia Kushnir, USSR, volleyball

Bronze
Wendy Weinberg, USA, 800-meter freestyle swimming
Victor Zilbermann, Rumania, welterweight boxing
Edith Master, USA, equestrian team dressage

1980 (Lake Placid/MOSCOW)

Gold
Shamir Sabyrov, USSR, boxing
Svetlana Krachevskaja, USSR, track and field
John Harmanberg, Sweden, fencing

Silver
Vladimir Myshkin, USSR, ice hockey

1984 (Sarajevo/LOS ANGELES)

Gold
Mitch Gaylord, USA, team gymnastics

Silver
Mitch Gaylord, USA, vaulting
Bob Berland, USA, middleweight judo

Bronze
Mitch Gaylord, USA, rings
Mitch Gaylord, USA, parallel bars

Jews in Major League Baseball

PLAYER REGISTER

	Position	Years	Teams	Games	HR	RBI	BA
CAL ABRAMS / *Calvin Ross Abrams* (1924-)	OF	1949-56	BKN, CIN, PIT, BAL, CHI (A)	567	32	138	.269
MORRIE ADERHOLT / *Morris Woodrow Aderholt* (1915-1955)	OF, 2B	1939-41, 44-45	WASH, BKN, BOS (N)	106	3	32	.267
MORRIE ARNOVICH / *Morris Arnovich* (1910-1959)	OF	1936-41, 46	PHI (N)	590	22	261	.287
JAKE ATZ / *Jacob Henry Zimmerman* (1879-1945)	2B, SS	1902, 07-09	WASH, CHI (A)	208	0	49	.219
RICK AUERBACH / *Frederick Steven Auerbach* (1950-)	SS, 2B, 3B	1971-81	MIL, LA(N), CIN, SEA	624	9	86	.220
STEVE BEHEL / *Stephen Arnold Douglas Behel*	OF	1884, 86	MIL (U), NY (AA)	68	0	?	.210
JOE BENNETT / *Joseph Rosenblum Bennett* (1900-)	3B	1923	PHI (N)	1	0	0	—
MOE BERG / *Morris Berg* (1902-1972)	C, SS	1923, 26-39	BKN, CHI (A), CLE, WASH, CLE, BOS (A)	662	6	206	.243
BOB BERMAN / *Robert Leon Berman* (1899-)	C	1918	WASH	2	0	0	—
CY BLOCK / *Seymour Block* (1919-)	3B, 2B	1942, 45-46	CHI (N)	17	0	5	.302
RON BLOMBERG / *Ronald Mark Blomberg* (1948-)	IB, OF, DH	1969, 71-76, 78	NY (A), CHI (A)	461	52	224	.293
SAMMY BOHNE / *Sammy Arthur Cohen* (1896-1977)	2B, SS, 3B	1916, 21-26	STL (N), CIN, BKN	663	16	228	.261
LOU BROWER / *Louis Lester Brower* (1900-)	SS	1931	DET	21	0	6	.161
HARRY CHOZEN / *Harry Kenneth Chozen* (1915-)	C	1937	CIN	1	0	0	.250
ALTA COHEN / *Albert Cohen* (1908-)	OF	1931-33	BKN, PHI (N)	29	0	2	.194
ANDY COHEN / *Andrew Howard Cohen* (1904-)	2B	1926, 28-29	NY (N)	262	14	114	.281
PHIL COONEY / *Phillip Cohn* (1886-?)	3B	1905	NY (A)	1	0	0	.000
HARRY DANNING / *(Harry the Horse)* (1911-)	C	1933-42	NY (N)	890	57	397	.285
IKE DANNING (1905-)	C	1928	STL (A)	2	0	1	.500

Moe Berg *Ron Blomberg* *Mike Epstein*

Sidney Gordon

Hank Greenberg

Benny Kauff

	Position	Years	Teams	Games	HR	RBI	BA
MIKE EPSTEIN / *Michael Peter Epstein* (1943-)	1B	1966-74	BAL, WASH, OAK, TEX, CAL	907	130	380	.244
REUBEN EWING / *Reuben Cohen* (1899-1970)	SS	1921	STL (N)	3	0	0	.000
AL FEDEROFF / *Alfred Federoff* (1924-)	2B	1951-52	DET	76	0	14	.238
EDDIE FEINBERG / *Edward (Itzy) Feinberg* (1918-)	SS, 2B, OF	1938-39	PHI (N)	16	0	0	.184
MURRAY FRANKLIN (1914-1978)	SS, 2B	1941-42	DET	61	2	16	.262
MILT GALATZER / *Milton Galatzer* (1907-1976)	OF	1933-36, 39	CLE, CIN	251	1	57	.268
JOE GINSBERG / *Myron Nathan Ginsberg* (1926-)	C	1948, 50-54, 56-62	DET, CLE, KC, BAL, CHI (A), BOS (A), NY (N)	695	20	182	.241
JONAH GOLDMAN / *Jonah John Goldman* (1906-1980)	SS, 3B	1928, 30-31	CLE	148	1	49	.224
LONNIE GOLDSTEIN / *Leslie Elmer Goldstein* (1918-)	1B	1943, 46	CIN	11	0	0	.100
JAKE GOODMAN / *Jacob Goodman* (1853-1890)	1B	1878, 82	MIL (N), PIT (AA)	70	1	27	.256
SID GORDON / *Sidney Gordon* (1917-1975)	OF, 3B	1941-43, 46-55	NY (N), BOS (N), MIL (N), PIT (N), NY (N)	1475	202	805	.283
HERB GORMAN / *Herbert Allen Gorman* (1924-1953)	—	1952	STL (N)	1	0	0	.000
HANK GREENBERG / *Henry Benjamin Greenberg* (1911-1987). Hall of Fame, 1956	1B, OF	1930, 33-41, 45-47	DET, PIT	1394	331	1276	.313
STEVE HERTZ / *Stephen Allan Hertz* (1945-)	3B	1964	HOU	5	0	0	.000
IZZY HOFFMAN / *Harry C. Hoffman* (1875-1942)	OF	1904, 07	WASH, BOS (N)	29	0	4	.233
MERWIN JACOBSON (1894-1978)	OF	1915-16, 26-27	NY (N), CHI (N), BKN	133	0	24	.230
BENNY KAUFF / *Benjamin Michael Kauff* (1890-1961)	OF	1912, 14-20	NY (A), IND (F), BKN (F), NY (N)	859	49	454	.311
JOHNNY KLING / *John Gradwohl Kling* (1875-1947)	C	1900-08, 10-13	CHI (N), BOS (N), CIN	1260	20	513	.271
JIM LEVEY / *James Julius Levey* (1906- 1970)	SS	1930-33	STL (A)	440	11	140	.230
LOU LIMMER / *Louis Limmer* (1925-)	1B	1951, 54	PHI (A)	209	19	62	.202
ELLIOTT MADDOX (1948-)	OF, 3B	1970-80	DET, WASH, TEX, NY (A), BAL, NY (N)	1029	18	234	.261
SAM MAYER / *Samuel Frankel Erskine* (1893-1962)	OF	1915	WASH	11	1	4	.241
LEVI MEYERLE / *Levi Samuel Meyerle* (1849-1921)	IF	1876-77, 84	PHI (N), CIN, PHI (U)	85	0	49	.329
NORM MILLER / *Norman Calvin Miller* (1946-)	OF	1965-74	HOU, ATL	540	24	159	.238
BUDDY MYER / *Charles Solomon Myer* (1904-1974)	2B, SS, 3B	1925-41	WASH, BOS (A), WASH	1923	38	850	.303
BILLY NASH / *William Mitchell Nash* (1865-1929)	3B	1884-98	RICH (AA), BOS (N), BOS (P), BOS (N), PHI (N)	1549	61	977	.275

	Position	Years	Teams	Games	HR	RBI	BA
JEFF NEWMAN / *Jeffrey Lynn Newman* (1948-) (record through 1984)	C, 1B	1976-	OAK, BOS (A)	735	63	233	.224
JAY PIKE	OF	1877	HART (N)	1	0	0	.250
LIP PIKE / *Lipman Emanuel Pike* (1845-1893) Generallv acknowledged to be the first paid professional baseball player, 1866.	OF, 2B	1876-78, 81, 87	STL (N), CIN, PRO (N), WOR (N), NY (AA)	163-	5	88	.304
JAKE PITLER / *Jacob Albert Pitler* (1894-1968)	2B	1917-18	PIT	111	0	23	.232
JIMMY REESE / *James Hymie Soloman* (1904-)	2B	1930-32	NY (A), STL (N)	232	8	70	.278
AL RICHTER / *Allen Gordon Richter* (1927-)	SS	1951, 53	BOS (A)	6	0	0	.091
CHIEF ROSEMAN / *James J. Roseman* (1856-?)	OF	1882-87, 90	TROY (N), NY (AA), PHI (AA), NY (AA), BKN (AA), STL (AA), LOU (AA)	681	15	43	.263
AL ROSEN / *Albert Leonard Rosen* (1924-)	3B, 1B	1947-56	CLE	1044	192	717	.285
GOODY ROSEN / *Goodwin George Rosen* (1912-)	OF	1937-39, 44-46	BKN, NY (N)	551	22	197	.291
HARRY ROSENBERG (1909-)	OF	1930	NY (N)	9	0	0	.000
LOU ROSENBERG / *Louis C. Rosenberg* (1903-)	2B	1923	CHI (A)	3	0	0	.250
MAX ROSENFELD (1902-1969)	OF	1931-33	BKN	42	2	7	.298
SI ROSENTHAL (1903-1969)	OF	1925-26	BOS (A)	123	4	42	.266
MICKEY RUTNER / *Milton Rutner* (1920-)	3B	1947	PHI (A)	12	1	4	.250
IKE SAMUELS / *Samuel Earl Samuels* (1876-?)	3B	1895	STL (N)	24	0	5	.230
HEINIE SCHEER / *Henry William Scheer* (1900-1976)	2B, 3B	1922-23	PHI (A)	120	6	33	.212
RICHIE SCHEINBLUM / *Richard Alan Scheinblum* (1942-)	OF	1965, 67-69, 71-74	CLE, WASH, KC, CIN, CAL, KC, STL (N)	462	13	127	.263
MIKE SCHEMER / *Michael Schemer* (1917-)	1B	1945-46	NY (N)	32	1	10	.330
ART SHAMSKY / *Arthur Lewis Shamsky* (1941-)	OF, 1B	1965-72	CIN, NY (N), CHI (N), OAK	665	68	233	.253
DICK SHARON / *Richard Louis Sharon* (1950-)	OF	1973-75	DET, SD	242	13	46	.218
NORM SHERRY / *Norman Burt Sherry* (1931-)	C	1959-63	LA (N), NY (N)	194	18	69	.215
AL SILVERA / *Aaron Albert Silvera* (1935-)	OF	1955-56	CIN	14	0	2	.143
MIKE SIMON / *Michael Edward Simon* (1883-1963)	C	1909-15	PIT, STL (F), BKN (F)	378	1	90	.225
FRED SINGTON / *Frederick William Sington* (1910-)	OF	1934-39	WASH, BKN	181	7	85	.271
BROADWAY ALECK SMITH / *Alexander Benjamin Smith* (1871-1919)	C, OF	1897-1904, 06	BKN, BAL (N), BKN, NY (N), BAL (A), BOS (A), CHI (N), NY (N)	290	1	130	.263
MOE SOLOMON / *Moses H. Solomon* (1900-1966)	OF	1923	NY (N)	2	0	1	.375
CHICK STARR / *William Starr* (1911-)	C	1935-36	WASH	13	0	1	.208

Jeff Newman (Topps, 1978)

Al Rosen.

Art Shamsky

George Stone

Ken Holtzman

Sandy Koufax

	Position	Years	Teams	Games	HR	RBI	BA
DAN STEARNS / *William Eckford Stearns* (1861-1944)	1B	1880-85, 89	BUF (N), DET (N), CIN (AA), BAL (AA), BUF (N), KC (AA)	509	7	109	.242
BEN STEINER / *Benjamin Saunders Steiner* (1921-)	2B	1945-47	BOS (A), DET	82	3	20	.256
GEORGE STONE (1876-1945)	OF	1903, 05-10	BOS (A), STL (A)	848	23	268	.301
JOE STRAUSS / *Joseph Strauss* (?-?)	OF	1884-86	KC (U), LOU (AA), BKN (AA)	101	1	?	.216
DON TAUSSIG / *Donald Franklin Taussig* (1932-)	OF	1958, 61-62	SF, STL (N), HOU	153	4	30	.262
EDDIE TURCHIN / *Edward Lawrence Turchin* (1917-)	3B, SS	1943	CLE	11	0	1	.231
PHIL WEINTRAUB / *Philip (Mickey) Weintraub* (1907-)	1B, OF	1933-35, 37-38, 44-45	NY (N), CIN, NY (N), PHI (N), NY (N)	444	32	207	.295

PITCHER REGISTER

	Years	Teams	Games	W	L	Pct.	ERA
LLOYD ALLEN / *Lloyd Cecil Allen* (1950-)	1969-75	CAL, TEX, CHI (A)	159	8	25	.242	4.70
ROSS BAUMGARTEN (1955-)	1978-82	CHI (A), PIT	90	22	36	.379	3.99
BO BELINSKY / *Robert Belinsky* (1936-)	1962-67, 69-70	LA (A), PHI (N), HOU, PIT, CIN	146	28	51	.354	4.10
CONRAD CARDINAL / *Conrad Seth Cardinal* (1942-)	1963	HOU	6	0	1	.000	6.08
HY COHEN / *Hyman Cohen* (1931-)	1955	CHI (N)	7	0	0	—	7.94
SID COHEN / *Sydney Harry Cohen* (1908-)	1934, 36-37	WASH	55	3	7	.300	4.54
DICK CONGER / *Richard Conger* (1921-1970)	1940-43	DET, PIT, PHI (N)	19	3	7	.300	5.14
MOE DRABOWSKY / *Myron Walter Drabowsky* (1935-)	1956-72	CHI (N), MIL, CIN, KC, BAL, KC, BAL, STL, CHI (A)	589	88	105	.456	3.71
HARRY EISENSTAT (1915-)	1935-42	BKN, DET, CLE	165	25	27	.481	3.84
HARRY FELDMAN (1919-1962)	1941-46	NY (N)	143	35	35	.500	3.80
JULIE FREEMAN / *Julius B. Freeman* (1869-?)	1888	STL (AA)	1	0	1	.000	4.26
IZZY GOLDSTEIN / *Isadore Goldstein* (1908-)	1932	DET	16	3	2	.600	4.47
KEN HOLTZMAN / *Kenneth Dale Holtzman* (1945-)	1965-79	CHI (N), OAK, BAL, NY (A), CHI (N)	451	174	150	.537	3.49
HAM IBURG / *Herman Edward Iburg* (1878-1945)	1902	PHI (N)	30	11	18	.379	3.89
HARRY KANE / *Harry Cohen "Klondike"* (1883-1932)	1902-03, 05-06	STL (A), DET, PHI (N)	15	2	7	.222	4.81
HERB KARPEL / *Herbert Karpel "Lefty"* (1917-)	1946	NY (A)	2	0	0	—	10.80
BOB KATZ / *Robert Clyde Katz* (1911-1962)	1944	CIN	6	0	1	.000	3.93

	Years	Teams	Games	W	L	Pct.	ERA
BILL KLING / *William Kling* (1867-1934)	1891-92, 95	PHI (N), BAL (N), LOU	15	4	4	.500	5.17
ALAN KOCH / *Alan Goodman Koch* (1938-)	1963-64	DET, WASH	42	4	11	.267	5.41
HOWIE KOPLITZ / *Howard Dean Koplitz* (1938-)	1961-62, 64-66	DET, WASH	54	9	7	.563	4.21
SANDY KOUFAX / *Sanford (Braun) Koufax* (1935-) Hall of Fame, 1971	1955-1966	BKN, LA (N)	397	165	87	.655	2.76
BARRY LATMAN / *Arnold Barry Latman* (1936-)	1957-67	CHI (A), CLE, LA (A), CAL, HOU	344	59	68	.465	3.91
DUKE MARKELL / *Harry Duquesne Makowsky* (1923-1984)	1951	STL (A)	5	1	1	.500	6.33
ED MAYER / *Edwin David Mayer* (1931-)	1957-58	CHI (N)	22	2	2	.500	4.31
ERSKINE MAYER / *James Erskine* (1891-1957)	1912-19	PHI (N), PIT, CHI (A)	245	91	70	.565	2.96
SAM MAYER / *Samuel Frankel Erskine* (1893-1962)	1915	WASH	1	0	0	—	0.00
SAM NAHEM / *Samuel Ralph Nahem* (1915-)	1938, 41-42, 48	BKN, STL (N), PHI (N)	90	10	8	.556	4.69
BARNEY PELTY (1880-1939)	1903-12	STL (A), WASH	266	91	117	.438	2.62
STEVE RATZER / *Stephen Wayne Ratzer* (1953-)	1980-81	MON	13	1	1	.500	7.29
ED REULBACH / *Edward Marvin Reulbach* (1882-1961)	1905-17	CHI (N), BKN, NWK (F), BOS (N)	399	185	104	.640	2.28
DAVE ROBERTS / *David Arthur Roberts* (1944-)	1969-81	SD, HOU, DET, CHI (N), SF, PIT, SEA, NY (N)	445	103	125	.452	3.78
SAUL ROGOVIN / *Saul Walter Rogovin* (1922-)	1949-57	DET, CHI (A), BAL, PHI (N)	150	48	48	.500	4.06
CHIEF ROSEMAN / *James J. Roseman* (1856-?)	1885-87	NY (AA), BKN (AA)	4	0	1	.000	7.88
MARV ROTBLATT / *Marvin Joseph Rotblatt* (1927-)	1948, 50-51	CHI (A)	35	4	3	.571	4.82
LARRY ROTHSCHILD / *Lawrence Lee Rothschild* (1954-)	1981-82	DET	7	0	0	—	5.19
MOE SAVRANSKY / *Morris Savransky* (1929-)	1954	CIN	16	0	2	.000	4.88
AL SCHACHT / *Alexander Schacht* (1892-1984)	1919-21	WASH	53	14	10	.583	4.48
SID SCHACHT / *Sidney Schacht* (1918-)	1950-51	STL (A), BOS (N)	19	0	2	.000	14.34
LARRY SHERRY / *Lawrence Sherry* (1935-)	1958-1968	LA (N), DET, HOU, CAL	416	53	44	.546	3.67
HARRY SHUMAN (1916-)	1942-44	PIT, PHI (N)	30	0	0	—	4.44
STEVE STONE / *Steven Michael Stone* (1947-)	1971-81	SF, CHI (A), CHI (N), CHI (A), BAL	320	107	93	.535	3.97
BUD SWARTZ / *Sherwin Merle Swartz* (1929-)	1947	STL (A)	5	0	0	—	6.75
ED WINEAPPLE / *Edward Wineapple "Lefty"* (1906-)	1929	WASH	1	0	0	—	4.50
RALPH WINEGARNER (1909-)	1932, 34-36, 49	CLE, STL (A)	70	8	6	.571	5.33
MELLIE WOLFGANG / *Meldon John Wolfgang* (1890-1947)	1914-18	CHI (A)	77	14	14	.500	2.18
LARRY YELLEN / *Lawrence Alan Yellen* (1943-)	1963-64	HOU	14	0	0	—	6.23

Erskine Mayer

Ed Reulbach

Al Schacht

MANAGERS

	Team/League	Years	Games	W	L	Pct.	Standing
ANDY COHEN / *Andrew Howard Cohen* (1904-)	Philadelphia (N)	1960	1	1	0	1.000	8
BENJAMIN J. FINE	St. Louis (N)	1885					last
JUDGE FUCHS / *Emil Edwin Fuchs* (1878-1961)	Boston (N)	1929	154	56	98	.364	8
LOUIE HEILBRONER (1861-1933)	St. Louis (N)	1900	38	17	20	.459	5
JOHNNY KLING / *John Gradwohl Kling* (1875-1947)	Boston (N)	1912	153	52	101	.340	8
JAKE MORSE (1860-1937)	Boston (U)	1884	75	46	28	.622	5
BILLY NASH / *William Mitchell Nash* (1865-1929)	Philadelphia (N)	1896	131	62	68	.477	8
LEFTY PHILLIPS / *Harold Ross Phillips* (1919-1972)	California (A)	1969	124	60	63	.488	6
		1970	162	86	76	.531	3
		1971	162	76	86	.469	4
			448	222	225	.497	
LIP PIKE / *Lipman Emanuel Pike* (1845-1893)	Cincinnati (N)	1877	14	3	11	.214	6
CHIEF ROSEMAN / *James J. Roseman* (1856- ?)	St. Louis (AA)	1890	51	32	19	.627	4
NORM SHERRY / *Norman Burt Sherry* (1931-)	California (A)	1976	66	37	29	.561	4
		1977	81	39	42	.481	5
			147	76	71	.517	

Jews in Basketball

Haskell Cohen

ALL-AMERICA JEWISH COLLEGE BASKETBALL PLAYERS

Year	Player	College	Year	Player	College
1908	Ira Streusand	CCNY	1936	William Fleishman	Western Reserve
1909	Samuel Melitzer	Columbia	1937	Jules Bender	LIU
1916-17	Cyril Haas	Princeton	1937	Marvin Colen	Loyola (Ill.)
1918-19	Leon (Bob) Marcus	Syracuse	1938	Meyer (Mike) Bloom	Temple
1920-21	Maclyn (Mac) Baker	NYU	1938	Bernard Fliegel	CCNY
1922	Louis Farer	CCNY	1938-39	Irving Torgoff	LIU
1923	Samuel Pite	Yale	1939	Bernard Opper	Kentucky
1925-26	Emanuel (Menchy) Goldblatt	Pennsylvania	1939	Robert Lewis	NYU
1925	Pincus (Pinky) Match	CCNY	1939	John Bromberg	LIU
1926	Carl Loeb	Princeton	1939	Daniel Kaplowitz	LIU
1926	William (Red) Laub	Columbia	1939	Jack (Dutch) Garfinkel	St. John's (NY)
1929	Edward Wineapple	Providence	1940	Louis Possner	De Paul
1930	Max (Mac) Kinsbrunner	St. John's (NY)	1941	Oscar (Ossie) Schectman	LIU
1930, 32	Louis Bender	Columbia	1941	Moe Becker	Duquesne
1931	Max (Mack) Posnack	St. John's (NY)	1942	William (Red) Holzman	CCNY
1931	Louis Hayman	Syracuse	1943, 46	Harry Boykoff	St. John's (NY)
1932	Moe Spahn	CCNY	1943	Jerry Fleishman	NYU
1933	Jerry Nemer	Southern California	1944-45	Hyman (Hy) Gotkin	St. John's (NY)
1933	Nathan Lazar	St. John's (NY)	1946-47	Sid Tanenbaum	NYU
1934	Moe Goldman	CCNY	1946	Jackie Goldsmith	LIU
1936	Herbert Bonn	Duquesne	1948	Don Forman	NYU
1936	Milton Schulman	NYU	1948	Adolph Schayes	NYU
1936	Ben Kramer	LIU	1950	Irwin Dambrot	CCNY

Red Auerbach

Max Friedman

Eddie Gottlieb

Art Heyman

Nat Holman

Maurice Podoloff

Year	Player	College
1953	Irving Bemoras	Illinois
1955-57	Leonard Rosenbluth	North Carolina
1957	Larry Friend	California
1958-59	Alan Seiden	St. John's (NY)
1959	Don Goldstein	Louisville
1960-61	Jeff Cohen	William & Mary
1961	Howard Carl	De Paul
1961-63	Art Heyman	Duke
1963-64	Barry Kramer	NYU
1964	Robert (Rick) Kaminsky	Yale
1965	Talbot (Tal) Brody	Illinois
1966	Dave Newmark	Columbia
1968-69	Neal Walk	Florida
1976-77	Ernest (Ernie) Grunfeld	Tennessee
1978-80	Nancy Lieberman	Old Dominion
1981	Danny Schayes	Syracuse

JEWS IN PROFESSIONAL BASKETBALL

Player	Teams
RED AUERBACH (1917-)	Boston Celtics (headcoach, gm)
HERSHEL BALTIMORE	St. Louis Bombers
DAVID "PRETZEL" BANKS (1901-1952)	Original Celtics
MOE BECKER (1917-)	Baltimore, Pittsburgh, Boston, Detroit, etc.
IRV BEMORAS	Milwaukee Hawks
JULES BENDER (1914-)	Baltimore, etc.
LOUIS BENDER (1910-)	
BEN BERGER	Minneapolis Lakers (president)
MARK BINSTEIN	coach
MIKE BLOOM	Baltimore Bullets
NELSON BOBB	Philadelphia Warriors
HARRY BOYKOFF (1922-)	Boston Celtics, etc.
TALBERT "TAL" BRODY (1943-)	Baltimore (draft only)
LARRY BROWN (1940-)	New Orleans, Oakland, Washington, Virginia, Denver, Carolina, Denver, New Jersey (as headcoach)
PHIL BROWNSTEIN	Chicago Stags (coach)
NORMAN DRUCKER	NBA referee
LOU EISENSTEIN	NBA referee
PHIL FARBMAN	Philadelphia Warriors
GEORGE FEIGENBAUM (1929-)	Baltimore, Milwaukee
LEO FISCHER (1897-1970)	President, National Basketball League
JEROME FLEISHMAN (1922-)	Philadelphia Warriors
DONALD J. FORMAN (1926-)	Minneapolis Lakers
PHIL FOX	NBA referee
NAT FRANKEL	Pittsburgh Ironmen
MAX "MARTY" FRIEDMAN (1889-?)	New York Whirlwinds
LAWRENCE FRIEND (1935-)	New York Knicks
JACK GARFINKEL (1920-)	Rochester Royals, Boston Celtics
EMANUEL GOLDBLATT (1904-)	
BEN GOLDFADEN	Washington Capitols
MOE GOLDMAN (1913-)	Philadelphia Sphas
EDWARD B. GOTTLIEB (1898-1979)	Founder, NBA Philadelphia Warriors (owner and headcoach)
LEO GOTTLIEB	New York Knicks
NORMAN GREKIN (1930-)	Philadelphia Warriors
ERNIE GRUNFELD (1955-)	Milwaukee, Kansas City, New York
LES HARRISON	Rochester Royals (coach)
ARNOLD HEFT	NBA referee; part owner Baltimore Bullets
SONNY HERTZBERG (1922-)	New York, Washington, Boston

Player	Teams
ARTHUR HEYMAN (1941-)	New York, San Francisco, New Jersey, Pittsburgh, Minnesota, Miami
MEL HIRSCH (1921-)	Boston Celtics
NAT HOLMAN (1896-)	New York Whirlwinds, Original Celtics
RED HOLZMAN (1920-)	Rochester Royals, Milwaukee, St. Louis, New York (headcoach)
RALPH KAPLOWITZ (1920-)	Philadelphia, New York
BEN KERNER (1917-)	owner, St. Louis Hawks
HERMAN KLOTZ (1921-)	Baltimore Bullets
BARRY KRAMER (1942-)	New York (NBA & ABA), San Francisco
BENJAMIN KRAMER (1913-)	various teams; Baltimore (headcoach)
JOEL KRAMER (1955-)	Phoenix Suns
HERB KRAUTBLATT	Baltimore Bullets
RUDY LARUSSO (1937-)	Minneapolis, Los Angeles Lakers
HENRY LEFKOWITZ	Cleveland Rebels
BARRY LEIBOWITZ	New Jersey, Pittsburgh
HARRY LITWACK (1907-)	Philadelphia (coach)
LIONEL MALAMED (1924-)	Indianapolis Jets
JULIE MEYER	NBA referee
NATHAN MILITZOK	New York Knicks
BORIS NACHAMKIN	Rochester Royals
DAVE NEWMARK (1946-)	Atlanta Hawks
BERNARD OPPER (1918-)	Detroit, etc.

Player	Teams
MAURICE PODOLOFF (1890-1985)	NBA Commissioner
IRWIN RAIKEN	New York Knicks
ALEXANDER ROSENBERG	Philadelphia Warriors
LEONARD ROSENBLUTH (1933-)	Philadelphia Warriors
HENRY ROSENSTEIN	New York Knicks
IRVING ROTHENBERG	Cleveland Rebels, Baltimore Bullets
MARVIN ROTTNER	Chicago Stags
MENDY RUDOLPH (1928-1979)	NBA referee
ABE SAPERSTEIN (1901-1966)	creator and coach, Harlem Globetrotters
MARVIN SCHATZMAN	Syracuse Nationals
ADOLPH SCHAYES (1928-)	Syracuse, Philadelphia; Philadelphia, Buffalo (headcoach)
DAN SCHAYES (1959-)	Utah, Denver
OSSIE SCHECTMAN	New York Knicks
BARNEY SEDRAN (1891-1969)	New York Whirlwinds
ARTHUR SPECTOR (1920-)	Boston Celtics
LOUIS L. SUGARMAN (1890-1951)	
SIDNEY H. TANENBAUM (1925-)	New York, Baltimore
DAVID TOBEY (1898-)	
IRVING TORGOFF	Washington Capitols, Baltimore, Philadelphia
NEAL WALK (1948-)	Phoenix, New York
RON WATTS	Boston Celtics
GEORGE WOLFE (1905-1970)	Philadelphia Sphas
MAX ZASLOFSKY (1925-1985)	Chicago, New York, Baltimore, Milwaukee, Ft. Wayne

Abe Saperstein

Dolph Schayes

Barney Sedran

73

Jews in Football

Haskell Cohen

ALL-AMERICA JEWISH COLLEGE FOOTBALL PLAYERS

Year	Player	College
1891-93	Phil King—Quarterback	Princeton
1903-4	Sig Harris—Quarterback	Minnesota
1905-6	Israel Levene—End	Pennsylvania
1909-10	Joe Magidsohn—Halfback	Michigan
1911-12	Arthur Bluethenthal—Center	Princeton
1911	Leonard Frank—Tackle	Minnesota
1911	Harry Kallet—End	Syracuse
1918-20	Joe Alexander—Guard, Center	Syracuse
1918	Victor Frank—Guard	Pennsylvania
1920	Arnold Horween—Fullback	Harvard
1922	Max Kadesky—End	Iowa
1924	George Abramson—Guard	Minnesota
1925-26	Benny Friedman—Quarterback	Michigan
1925	Milton Levy—Guard	Tulane
1927	Ray Baer—Guard	Michigan
1927-29	Benny Lom—Halfback	California
1929	Louis Gordon—Tackle	Illinois
1929	Louis Gordon—Lineman	Illinois
1929-30	Fred Sington—Tackle	Alabama
1930	Gabe Bromberg—Guard	Dartmouth
1931	John Grossman—Backfield	Rutgers
1932	Harry Newman—Quarterback	Michigan
1932	Franklin Meadow—End	Brown
1932-33	Aaron Rosenberg—Guard	USC
1934	Isadore Weinstock—Fullback	Pittsburgh
1934	Dave Smukler—Fullback	Temple
1937-38	Marshall Goldberg—Halfback, Fullback	Pittsburgh
1937	Leroy Monsky—Guard	Alabama
1937-38	Sid Luckman—Halfback	Columbia
1938	Sid Roth—Guard	Cornell
1943	Mervin Pregulman—Tackle, Guard	Michigan
1943	William Stein—Quarterback	Georgia Tech
1944	Maurice Furchgott—Guard	Georgia Tech
1946	Hyman Harris—End	Oregon
1947	Dan Dworsky—Center, Linebacker	Michigan
1950	Bernard Lemonick—Guard	Pennsylvania
1952	Myron Berliner—End	UCLA
1958	Alan Goldstein—End	No. Carolina
1959	Ron Mix—Tackle	USC
1967	Richard Stotter—Guard	Houston
1967-68	Bob Stein—Defensive End	Minnesota
1971	Gary Wichard—Quarterback	C.W. Post
1973	Randy Grossman—Tight End	Temple
1978	Dave Jacobs—Placekicker	Syracuse
1984	John Frank—Tight End	Ohio

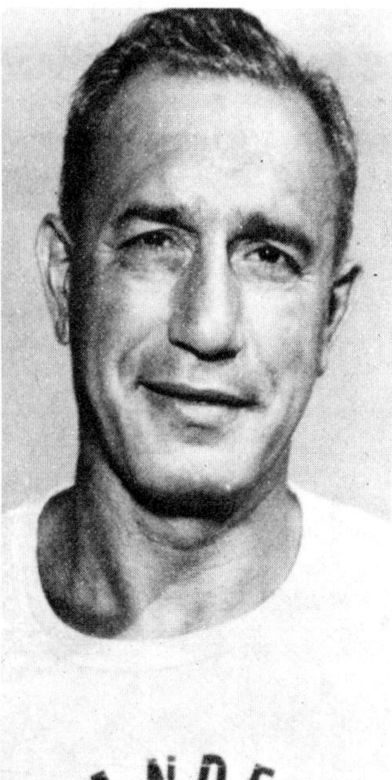

Benny Friedman

Aaron Rosenberg

Randy Grossman

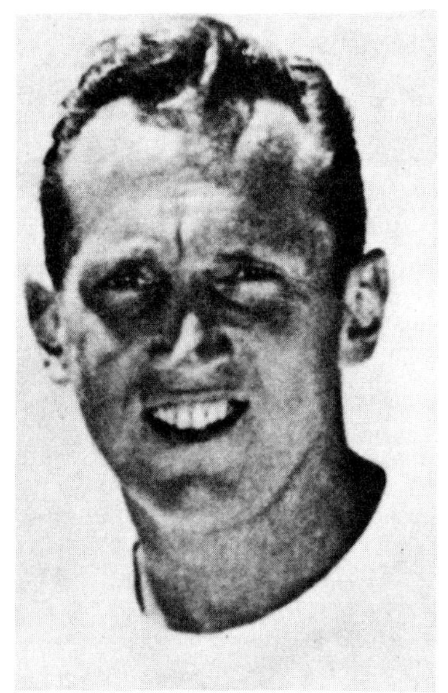

Al Davis

Sid Gillman

Marshall Goldberg

JEWS IN PROFESSIONAL FOOTBALL

	Position	Teams
GEORGE ABRAMSON (1903-)	guard	Green Bay Packers
JOSEPH A. ALEXANDER (1898-1975)	lineman, guard	New York Giants
	headcoach	New York Giants
LYLE ALZADO (1949-)	end	Denver Broncos
JOHN BARSHA (1900-)		
MORRIS BODENGER (1909-)	guard	Detroit Lions
NORMAN CAHN (1892-1965)	referee	NFL
AL DAVIS (1929-)	coach, gm	Oakland, L.A. Raiders
	commissioner	AFL, 1966
SAM FOX (1924-)	end	New York Giants
BENNY FRIEDMAN (1905-1982)	quarterback	Cleveland Bulldogs, Detroit Wolverines, New York Giants, Brooklyn Dodgers
	headcoach	Brooklyn Dodgers
SIDNEY GILLMAN (1911-)	headcoach	L.A. Rams, San Diego Chargers, Houston Oilers
MARSHALL GOLDBERG (1917-)	running back	Chicago Cardinals
CHARLES R. "BUCKETS" GOLDENBERG (1911-)	lineman	Green Bay Packers
LOUIS J. GORDON (1908-)	tackle	Green Bay Packers, Chicago Cardinals, Brooklyn Dodgers, Chicago Bears
JEROME GREEN (1936-)	end	Boston Patriots
RANDY GROSSMAN (1952-)	tight end	Pittsburgh Steelers
PHILIP J. "MOTSY" HANDLER (1908-1968)	lineman	Chicago Cardinals
	coach	Chicago Cardinals, Chicago Bears
ARNOLD HORWEEN (1898-)	back	Chicago Cardinals
	headcoach	Chicago Cardinals
RALPH HORWEEN (1896-)	running back	Chicago Cardinals
EDWIN B. "KING KONG" KAHN (1911-1945)	guard	Boston Patriots, Wash. Redskins
MIKE KATZ (1939-)	guard	New York Jets
IRVING KUPCINET (1912-)	back	Philadelphia Eagles
MARVIN D. LEVY (1928-)	headcoach	Kansas City Chiefs
BENJAMIN F. LINDHEIMER (1890- 1960)	commissioner	All-America Conference 1946-47
SAMUEL J. LIPP (1889-1958)	referee	NFL
SIDNEY LUCKMAN (1916-)	quarterback	Chicago Bears
JOSEPH MAGIDSOHN (1888-?)	referee	NFL
RONALD J. MIX (1938-)	offensive lineman	San Diego Chargers
SAUL MIELZINER (1905-)		
ARTHUR B. MODELL (1925-)	owner	Cleveland Browns
	president	NFL 1967-70
ED NEWMAN (1953-)	guard	Miami Dolphins
HARRY NEWMAN (1909-)	quarterback	New York Giants
RED PEARLMAN (1898-)		Steubenville, others
MERVIN PREGULMAN (1922-)	lineman, guard	Green Bay Packers, Detroit Lions, Canton Bulldogs
HERBERT RICH (1928-)		
DONALD ROGERS (1936-)	center	San Diego Chargers
CARROLL ROSENBLOOM (1908-1978)	owner	Baltimore Colts, Los Angeles Rams
LEONARD SACHS (1897-1942)		
JACK SACK (1902-)	guard	
HERMAN "BIFF" SCHNEIDMAN (1913-)	halfback	Green Bay Packers, Chicago Cardinals
ALEXANDER "ALLIE" SHERMAN (1923-)	quarterback	Philadelphia Eagles
	headcoach	New York Giants
DAVID SMUKLER (1914-)	fullback	Philadelphia Eagles, Detroit Lions, Boston Yankees
MICHAEL SOMMER (1936-)		
SAMUEL STEIN (1906-1966)		
WILLIAM STEIN (1924-)	referee	NFL
PAUL "TWISTER" STEINBERG (1880-?)	running back	Phildelphia, Syracuse,
ABRAHAM B. WATNER (1891-1961)	executive	Baltimore Colts
SAMUEL A. WEISS (1902-)	referee	NFL
SIDNEY YOUNGELMAN (1933-)	tackle	S.F. 49ers, Phila. Eagles, Cleveland Browns, N.Y. Titans, Buffalo Bills

74

Jews in Boxing

Irving Rudd

RAY ARCEL (1899-)	trainer of 20 world champions
BOB ARUM (1931-)	promoter
ABRAHAM ATTELL/*Albert Knoehr* (1884-1969)	Featherweight, World Champion, 1901-12
MONTE ATTELL/*M. Knoehr* (1885-1960)	Bantamweight, U.S. Champion, 1909-10
JACOB "SOLDIER" BARTFIELD (1892-1970)	Middleweight
BENNY BASS (1904-1975)	Featherweight, World Champion, 1927-28; Junior Lightweight, World Champion, 1929-31
JOE BENJAMIN (1899-1985)	Lightweight
JACKIE BERG/*Judah Bergman* (1909-)	Junior Welterweight, World Champion, 1930-31
SAMUEL BERGER (1884-1925)	Olympic Heavyweight, Gold Medal 1904 (U.S.)
JACK BERNSTEIN/*John Dodick* (1899-1945)	Junior Lightweight, World Champion, 1923
JOE BERNSTEIN (1877-1931)	Featherweight
HARRY BLITMAN (1908-)	Bantamweight
PHIL BLOOM (1894-)	Lightweight
NATHAN BOR (1913-1972)	Olympic Lightweight, Bronze Medal 1932 (U.S.)
NEWSBOY BROWN/*David Montrose* (1904-1977)	Bantamweight, Flyweight
MUSHY CALLAHAN/*Vincente M. Scheer* (1905-1986)	Junior Welterweight, World Champion, 1926-30
JOE CHOYNSKI (1869-1943)	Heavyweight
GILBERT COHEN (1948-)	Light-Middleweight, European Champion, 1978
ROBERT COHEN (1930-)	Bantamweight, World Champion, 1954-56
LEACH CROSS/*Louis C. Wallach* (1886-1957)	Lightweight
HARRY DEVINE (1909-)	Olympic Featherweight, Bronze Medal 1928 (U.S.)
SAMUEL "DUTCH SAM" ELIAS (1776-1816)	English champion; credited with invention of the uppercut
JACKIE FIELDS/*Jacob Finkelstein* (1908-)	Olympic Featherweight, Gold Medal 1924 (U.S.)
	Welterweight, World Champion, 1929-30, 32-33
NAT FLEISCHER (1887-1972)	Boxing historian; Founder and Editor of *Ring* magazine; initiated boxing's rating system
CHARLEY GOLDMAN (1887-1968)	Flyweight; Bantamweight
ABE GOLDSTEIN (1900-1976)	Bantamweight, World Champion, 1924
RUBY GOLDSTEIN (1907-1984)	Lightweight, later a championship referee
ALPHONSE HALIMI (1932-)	Bantamweight, World Champion, 1957-59

Abe Attell

Jackie Fields

Nat Fleischer

Benny Leonard

Daniel Mendoza

Maxie Rosenbloom

HARRY HARRIS (1880-1959)	Bantamweight, World Champion, 1901-02
SIG HART (1872-1963)	Bantamweight, later a leading manager
MONTGOMERY HERSCOVITZ	Olympic Middleweight, Gold Medal 1920 (Canada)
ABE "THE NEWSBOY" HOLLANDERSKY (1888-)	Welterweight
HARRY ISAACS	Olympic Bantamweight, Bronze Medal 1928 (S. Africa)
WILLIE JACKSON/*Oscar Tobler* (1897-1961)	Lightweight
JOE JACOBS (1896-1940)	manager of Max Schmeling, others
MIKE JACOBS (1880-1953)	promoter
BEN JEBY/*Morris B. Jebaltowsky* (1907-1985)	Middleweight, World Champion, 1932-33
LOUIS "KID" KAPLAN (1902-1970)	Featherweight, World Champion, 1925-27
DANNY KRAMER (1900-)	Featherweight
SOLLY KRIEGER (1909-1965)	Middleweight, World Champion, 1938-39
BENNY LEONARD/*Benjamin Leiner* (1896-1947)	Lightweight, World Champion, 1917-25
BATTLING LEVINSKY/*Barney Lebrowitz* (1891-1949)	Light-Heavyweight, World Champion, 1916-20
HARRY LEWIS/*Henry Besterman* (1886-1956)	Welterweight
TED LEWIS/*Gershon Mendeloff* (1894-1970)	Welterweight, World Champion, 1915, 1917-19
AL McCOY/*Al Rudolph* (1894-1966)	Middleweight, World Champion, 1914-17
HARRY MARKSON (1906-)	promoter
DANIEL MENDOZA (1764-1836)	Heavyweight, World Champion (unofficial), 1792-95
RAY MILLER (1908-1987)	Lightweight; Welterweight
SAMUEL MOSBERG (1896-1967)	Olympic Lightweight, Gold Medal 1920 (U.S.)
HENRY NISSEN (1948-)	Flyweight, British Commonwealth Champion, 1971-74
BOB OLIN/*Robert Olinsky* (1908-1956)	Light-Heavyweight, World Champion, 1934-35
YOUNG PEREZ/*Victor Perez* (1911-1942)	Flyweight, World Champion, 1931-32
CHARLEY PHIL ROSENBERG/*Charles Green* (1902-1976)	Bantamweight, World Champion, 1925-27
DAVE ROSENBERG (1901-1974)	Welterweight, National AAU Champion, 1919
"SLAPSIE" MAXIE ROSENBLOOM (1904-1976)	Light-Heavyweight, World Champion, 1930-34
JOHNNY ROSNER (1895-)	Flyweight
BARNEY ROSS/*Barnet Rasofsky* (1909-1967)	Lightweight, World Champion, 1933-35; Junior Welterweight, World Champion, 1933-35; Welterweight, World Champion, 1934-38
MIKE ROSSMAN (1947-)	Light Heavyweight, World Champion, 1978-79
CORPORAL IZZY SCHWARTZ (1902-)	Flyweight, World Champion, 1927-29
AL SINGER (1907-1961)	Lightweight, World Champion, 1930
JACK SOLOMONS (1900-)	British promoter
LEW TENDLER (1898-1970)	Lightweight, welterweight
SID TERRIS (1904-1974)	Lightweight
MATT WELLS (1886-1953)	Lightweight and Welterweight Champion of Great Britain; Welterweight Champion of the British Empire
CHARLEY WHITE/*Charles Anschowitz* (1891-)	Lightweight
YOUNG OTTO/*Arthur Susskind* (1886-1967)	Lightweight
YOUNG MONTREAL/*Morris Billingkoff* (1898-)	Flyweight

Ivan L. Tillem, Esq. is an assistant professor at Stern College of Yeshiva University. Formerly associate general counsel of COLPA, the National Jewish Commission on Law and Public Affairs, he has authored and/or edited several volumes, including *The Jewish Directory and Almanac* (1984), *The 1986 Jewish Directory and Almanac, The 1987-88 Jewish Almanac* and *Issue Analysis and Conflict Resolution.* An alumnus of Yeshiva University, the Israel Torah Research Institute (ITRI), and Sh'or Yoshuv Institute, he is a founder and the chairman of the board of American Friends of Yeshivat Ner Moshe of Jerusalem. In 1987, he became a member of the board of Yeshiva University, the youngest individual ever to serve in that capacity. A native of Far Rockaway, he practices law in New York and Boston.

Contributors

Sholom Aleichem (1859-1916).

Charles R. Allen, Jr. is a prolific writer on the subject of anti-fascism. Formerly senior editor of *The Nation,* he is the author of *Heusinger of the Fourth Reich: The Step-by-Step Resurgence of the German General Staff.* His latest book is *From Hitler to Uncle Sam: How American Intelligence Used Accused Nazi War Criminals.*

American Jewish Congress.

American Zionist Federation.

Anti-Defamation League of B'nai B'rith.

Abraham J. Bayer is Director, International Commission, of the National Jewish Community Relations Advisory Council (NJCRAC).

Rabbi Dr. J. David Bleich is *Rosh Yeshiva* (Professor of Talmud) at Yeshiva University, and Professor of Law at the Benjamin N. Cardozo School of Law of Yeshiva University. He has written extensively on Jewish law and ethics.

Judith Bleich, Ph.D., is an associate professor of Judaic studies at Touro College in New York.

B'nai B'rith International.

Central Bureau of Statistics, State of Israel.

The Coalition to Free Soviet Jews.

Haskell Cohen was public relations director of the National Basketball Association for 20 years. A two-term president of the U.S. Committee for Sports in Israel, two-term president of New York B'nai B'rith Sports Lodge and member of the Board of Trustees, U.S. Basketball Hall of Fame, he ghostwrote Joe Louis' *My Life Story.*

Ivor Davis is a journalist, writing for British newspapers, including the *Financial Times,* the *Guardian* and London-based pan-African magazines. A past president of the Nairobi Hebrew Congregation, this Londoner of east European parentage has resided in Kenya for almost 30 years. He entertains Jewish visitors to Kenya at his lovely Nairobi home.

Dr. George Eisen received his Ph.D. degree from the University of Maryland, and serves presently as a professor at the California State Polytechnic University at Pomona.

Encyclopaedia Judaica.

Lester D. Friedman, Ph.D. lectures frequently on the cinematic view of Jews. He teaches film at Syracuse University and the humanities at SUNY Upstate Medical Center in Syracuse.

Murray Frost, Ph.D. is Research Coordinator at the Center for Applied Urban Research at the University of Nebraska at Omaha. He contributed "Judaica in U.S. Postage Stamps" to *The 1986 Jewish Directory and Almanac.*

Tova Gold is a member of the Class of 1987, Stern College of Yeshiva University, majoring in Jewish history and music. Tova is pursuing a career in Jewish historical research.

Eliyahu Ha-Cohen.

Samuel Heilman is a professor of sociology at Queens College of the City University of New York and the author of *Synagogue Life* and *The People of the Book.* Born in Germany and raised in Brookline, Massachusetts, he lives in New Rochelle, New York.

William B. Helmreich, Ph.D. is a professor of sociology at The City College and the Graduate School and University Center of The City University of New York. He has written five books and is a frequent contributor to both popular magazines and scholarly journals.

Peter David Hornik is an executive editor at the Davis Institute at Hebrew University on Mount Scopus in Jerusalem.

Israel Information Center.

Phil Jacobs has been assistant editor of the *Baltimore Jewish Times* for five years, covering government and politics. A native of Baltimore, he is married to Lisa and is father to Diana and is active in the Baltimore Jewish community.

The *Jerusalem Post.*

Jewish Telegraphic Agency.

JWB Jewish Book Council.

Meir Kahane, a rabbi, is a member of the Knesset.

Richard Kazarian, Jr., is History Department Coordinator and Instructor of American History at the College of Continuing Education at the University of Rhode Island.

Dr. Norman Lamm, President of Yeshiva University, is a rabbi, philosopher, teacher, author and member of the United States Holocaust Memorial Council.

Pearl Laufer holds a Ph.D. in English from the University of Maryland. She is the national director of public relations for the Jewish War Veterans of the United States of America.

Rabbi Anson Laytner, a native of Toronto, Canada, majored in Chinese studies and studied in the People's Republic of China in 1973-74 on the first Canada-China Student Exchange Program. A graduate of York University and Hebrew Union College, Rabbi Laytner is currently director of the Community Relations Council of the Jewish Federation of Greater Seattle, secretary of the Sino-Judaic Institute and editor of its newsletter *Points East.*

Chaim J. Leibtag earned his M.S.W. from Wurzweiler School of Social Work and was formerly assistant executive director of the Hartman YMHA in Far Rockaway, New York. He and his wife Sheila are parents of three children.

Israel E. Levine is Director of Communications for the American Jewish Congress.

Seymour Martin Lipset, a political sociologist, is a senior fellow at the Hoover Institution at Stanford University.

Maariv.

Martindale-Hubbell, Inc., George E. Krauss, Executive Vice-President.

Isaac Elchanan Mozeson has taught at Yeshiva University and at Bramson ORT. He is the author of *The Watcher,* a collection of poetry, and *The Word,* an analysis of the Hebrew origin of English words.

National Jewish Community Relations Advisory Council (NJCRAC).

The *New York Times.*

North American Conference on Ethiopian Jewry (NACOEJ)

Dennis Prager was Director of the Brandeis-Bardin Institute in California from 1976 to 1983. He does political and social commentary nightly for KABC Radio in Los Angeles, and publishes his own national newsletter, *Ultimate Issues.*

Earl Raab, a communal relations specialist, is Executive Director of the Jewish Community Relations Council of San Francisco.

Aaron I. Reichel, Esq. is a rabbi, lawyer and editor. He serves as Attorney Editor for Prentice-Hall, Inc. He is the author of *The Maverick Rabbi,* the biography of Rabbi Herbert S. Goldstein.

Joseph L. Reichler, the preeminent baseball archivist, is a special assistant to the commissioner of baseball and is chairman of baseball's official records committee. His books include *The Baseball Encyclopedia* and *The Great All-Time Baseball Record Book.*

David G. Roskies is Associate Professor of Jewish Literature at the Jewish Theological Seminary of America. His book, *Against the Apocalypse: Responses to Catastrophe in Modern Jewish Culture* (1984), was awarded the Ralph Waldo Emerson Award by Phi Beta Kappa, and contains a detailed discussion of the Vilna ghetto. He currently holds a Guggenheim Fellowship to research the art of modern Jewish storytelling.

Fred Rosner, M.D. is Director, Department of Medicine, Long Island Jewish-Hillside Medical Center, and Professor of Medicine, School of Medicine, Health Services Center, State University of New York at Stony Brook. He is one of the world's leading authorities on Jewish bioethics.

Irving Rudd is Director of Publicity for Top Rank, Inc., the leading promoter of championship boxing matches.

Esther Zeffren-Schnaidman, a native St. Louisan, received her BA in English/Communications with a Marketing minor from Stern College of Yeshiva University.

Neal Schnall is the principal of Valley Beth Shalom Hebrew School in Encino, California. He and his wife Yael have been active members of NACOEJ for several years.

Falene Schuff, a member of the class of 1986 at Stern College of Yeshiva University, is the general manager of Pacific Press.

Joseph Seigman is vice-president, West Coast region of the United States Committee Sports for Israel.

Irwin Shaw is Executive Vice-President Emeritus of the Jewish Community Center of Metropolitan Detroit.

Ronald Shimron, a historian, is consulting curator of the JWV National Memorial Museum in Washington, D.C.

Sara Stein, a native Detroiter, spent two years at Michlalah Jerusalem College and is a member of the Stern College Class of 1987. An English major, she has held many positions as a writer and editor.

Marc D. Stern, Esq. is associate director, legal department of the American Jewish Congress.

Joseph Telushkin is an ordained rabbi and holds a Ph.D. in Jewish history from Columbia University. He is the former Education Director of the Brandeis-Bardin Institute. He now lives in Jerusalem, where he is a Jerusalem Fellow.

Nurit Thorn-Zachter is a freelance artist and is director of publicity for the Coalition to Free Soviet Jews.

Menachem Waldman edited *Anthology of Rabbinical Opinions Concerning the Falashas.*

Robert G. Weisbord is Professor of History at the University of Rhode Island. He is the author of several books on Jewish and Afro-American historical themes including *Bittersweet Encounter: The Afro-American and the American Jew,* and *African Zion: The Attempt to Establish a Jewish Colony in the East Africa Protectorate 1903-1905.*

Elie Wiesel, winner of the 1986 Nobel Peace Prize, is Andrew W. Mellon Professor in the Humanities at Boston University. Among his many acclaimed books are *The Gates of the Forest* and most recently, *The Fifth Son.*

World Zionist Organization, American Section.

Yaacov Salomon, Lipschutz & Co. are advocates and notaries with offices in Haifa and Tel Aviv.

Zionist Archives and Library, Esther Togman, director.

Efraim Zuroff was Director of the Department for Overseas Activities at Yad Vashem and Assistant Editor of *Yad Vashem Studies* Vols. 10 and 11 (Hebrew and English editions). From 1978 to 1980, he was the first Director of the Simon Wiesenthal Center and a lecturer at Yeshiva University of Los Angeles. Subsequently, he was Israel Liaison to U.S. Department of Justice, Office of Special Investigations. Currently, he is Director of the Jerusalem office of the Simon Wiesenthal Center and correspondent for *Page One,* the Wiesenthal Center's national radio news program.

INDEX

THE JEWISH ALMANAC YELLOW PAGES

Corrections and additions are welcome for The 1989 Jewish Directory and Almanac. Rates for display advertising are described in our rate card. For a copy, write:
PACIFIC PRESS, DEPT. JD & A
295 MADISON AVENUE, SUITE 1228
NEW YORK, NEW YORK 10017

The Jewish Directory and Almanac has attempted to verify the kashrut of all food products, manufacturers, and retailers listed herein; however, we cannot guarantee the kashrut of any listing.

TABLE OF CONTENTS

AL	Alabama	HA	Hawaii	MN	Minnesota	NC	North Carolina	SK	Saskatchewan
AK	Alaska	IA	Iowa	MO	Missouri	ND	North Dakota	TN	Tennessee
AR	Arkansas	ID	Idaho	MS	Mississippi	OH	Ohio	TX	Texas
AT	Alberta	IL	Illinois	MT	Montana	OK	Oklahoma	UT	Utah
AZ	Arizona	IN	Indiana	NB	New Brunswick	ON	Ontario	VA	Virginia
BC	British Columbia	KS	Kansas	NE	Nebraska	OR	Oregon	VI	Virgin Islands
CA	California	KY	Kentucky	NF	Newfoundland	PA	Pennsylvania	VT	Vermont
CO	Colorado	LA	Louisiana	NH	New Hampshire	PR	Puerto Rico	WA	Washington
CT	Connecticut	MA	Massachusetts	NJ	New Jersey	PZ	Panama Canal Zone	WI	Wisconsin
DC	District of Columbia	MB	Manitoba	NM	New Mexico	QU	Quebec	WV	West Virginia
DE	Delaware	MD	Maryland	NS	Nova Scotia	RI	Rhode Island	WY	Wyoming
FL	Florida	ME	Maine	NV	Nevada	SC	South Carolina		
GA	Georgia	MI	Michigan	NY	New York	SD	South Dakota	IS	Israel

ADVERTISING AGENCIES

CIS GRAPHICS 674 8TH STREET	LAKEWOOD	NJ	08701	(201) 364-1629
CIS GRAPHICS 674 8TH STREET	LAKEWOOD	NJ	08701	(201) 367-7858
ALEF BES MEDIA GROUP P.O. BOX 96	BROOKLYN	NY	11204	(718) 998-3201
BRENNER TRADE CONSULTATION & MEDIA SERVICE P.O. BOX 10	BROOKLYN	NY	11230	(718) 339-4256
G & G SALES 1856 EAST 27TH STREET	BROOKLYN	NY	11229	(718) 376-0443
JUDAH H. KLEIN ASSOCIATES, PUBLIC RELATIONS 433 BARNARD AVENUE, SUITE 100	CEDARHURST	NY	11516	(516) 295-5646
GOLDMARK GROUP, THE 6 WEST 18TH STREET	NEW YORK	NY	10011	(212) 691-7111
ISRAEL COMMUNICATIONS 350 FIFTH AVENUE	NEW YORK	NY	10118	(212) 695-2998
J.J. GROSS & CO. 11 WEST 25TH STREET	NEW YORK	NY	10010	(212) 989-9600
JERUSALEM POST ADVERTISING AGENCY, THE 120 E. 56TH STREET	NEW YORK	NY	10022	(212) 355-4440
JOSEPH JACOBS ORGANIZATION, INC. 60 EAST 42ND STREET	NEW YORK	NY	10165	(212) 687-6234
LUBICOM 21 W. 38TH ST.	NEW YORK	NY	10018	(212) 302-6677
LUBINSKY COMMUNICATIONS 21 W. 38TH STREET	NEW YORK	NY	10018	(212) 302-6677
MARK WEISZ CORP. 175 FIFTH AVENUE	NEW YORK	NY	10010	(212) 254-5170
NORMARK/NORTHEAST MARKETS INC. - JEWISH DIVISION 110 WEST 34TH STREET	NEW YORK	NY	10001	(212) 714-2935
SCHILLER DIRECT RESPONSE 137 WEST 25TH STREET	NEW YORK	NY	10001	(212) 645-0333
DAUPHIN HARRIS ADVERTISING BOX 142	PORT ROYAL	PA	17082	(717) 436-8916
ALL MAIL DIRECT MARKETING 2500 MOUNT MORIAH ROAD, SUITE 110	MEMPHIS	TN	38115	(901) 794-4445
A.B. DATA LTD. 8050 NORTH PORT WASHINGTON ROAD	MILWAUKEE	WI	53217	(414) 352-4404

AIRLINES TO ISRAEL

EL AL 1225 CONNECTICUT AVENUE N.W.	WASHINGTON	DC	20036	(202) 296-5440
EL AL 407 LINCOLN ROAD, SUITE 4B	MIAMI BEACH	FL	33139	(305) 532-5441
EL AL 174 NORTH MICHIGAN AVENUE, RM. 310	CHICAGO	IL	60601	(312) 236-7264
EL AL 20 PARK PLAZA	BOSTON	MA	02116	(617) 267-9220
EL AL:CARGO EXPORT JFK INT'L AIRPORT	JAMAICA	NY	11430	(718) 656-2931
EL AL:CARGO IMPORT JFK INT'L AIRPORT	JAMAICA	NY	11430	(718) 656-2921
EL AL:FLIGHT ARRIVAL INFORMATION JFK INT'L AIRPORT	JAMAICA	NY	11430	(718) 656-7750
EL AL:PASSENGER SERVICE JFK INT'L AIRPORT	JAMAICA	NY	11430	(718) 656-2900
EL AL JFK INTERNATIONAL AIRPORT	JAMAICA	NY	11430	(718) 656-2900
TOWER AIR JFK INTERNATIONAL AIRPORT, HANGAR 8	JAMAICA	NY	11430	(718) 917-8500
TOWER AIR JFK INTERNATIONAL AIRPORT, HANGAR 8	JAMAICA	NY	11430	(800) 221-2500
AIR FRANCE 666 FIFTH AVENUE	NEW YORK	NY	10019	(212) 247-0100
ALITALIA 666 FIFTH AVENUE	NEW YORK	NY	10019	(212) 582-8900
ARKIA ISRAELI AIRLINES 350 FIFTH AVENUE	NEW YORK	NY	10118	(212) 695-2998
AUSTRIAN AIRLINES 608 FIFTH AVENUE	NEW YORK	NY	10019	(212) 307-6226
BRITISH AIRWAYS 245 PARK AVENUE	NEW YORK	NY	10167	(212) 878-4500
EL AL:CARGO SALES 850 3RD AVENUE	NEW YORK	NY	10010	(212) 940-0703
EL AL:INSURANCE & CLAIMS 850 3RD AVENUE	NEW YORK	NY	10010	(212) 940-0634
EL AL RESERVATIONS & INFORMATION	NEW YORK	NY		(212) 486-2600
EL AL TOLL FREE RESERVATIONS	NEW YORK	NY		(800) 223-6700
EL AL ISRAEL AIRLINES 850 THIRD AVENUE	NEW YORK	NY	10022	(212) 486-2600
EL AL - MAIN OFFICE 850 3RD AVENUE	NEW YORK	NY	10022	(212) 486-2600
EL AL:N.Y. DISTRICT SALES OFFICES 850 3RD AVENUE	NEW YORK	NY	10022	(212) 940-0708
IBERIAN AIRLINES OF SPAIN 565 FIFTH AVENUE	NEW YORK	NY	11130	(212) 793-3300
KLM 437 MADISON AVENUE	NEW YORK	NY	10022	(212) 759-3600
LUFTHANSA GERMAN AIRLINES 680 FIFTH AVENUE	NEW YORK	NY	10022	(212) 397-9250
OLYMPIC AIRWAYS 647 FIFTH AVENUE	NEW YORK	NY	10022	(212) 838-3600
SAS SCANDINAVIAN AIRLINES 630 FIFTH AVENUE	NEW YORK	NY	10111	(212) 841-0100
SABENA BELGIAN WORLD AIRLINES 720 FIFTH AVENUE	NEW YORK	NY	10019	(212) 961-6200
SWISSAIR 608 FIFTH AVENUE	NEW YORK	NY	10019	(212) 995-8400
TWA 605 THIRD AVENUE	NEW YORK	NY	10016	(212) 290-2121
TAROM ROMANIAN AIR 200 EAST 38TH STREET	NEW YORK	NY	10016	(212) 687-6013
EL AL 3 PENN CENTER, SUITE 922	PHILADELPHIA	PA	19102	(215) 563-8011
EL AL 555 DORCHESTER BOULEVARD WEST	MONTREAL	QU		(514) 875-8900
EL AL AVENIA DE LOS PALMAS	MEXICO CITY	MX		(05) 202-2243
EL AL 151 BLOOR STREET WEST, SUITE 860	TORONTO	ON	M5S 1S4	(416) 864-9779

ALIYAH ORGANIZATIONS

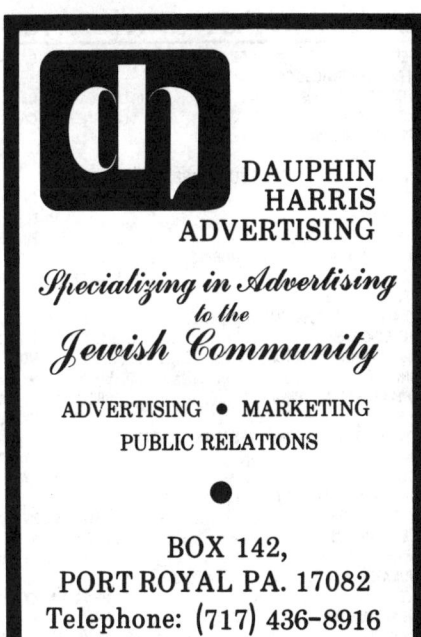

ISRAEL ALIYAH CENTER 950 WEST 41ST AVENUE	VANCOUVER	BC	V5Z 2N7	(604) 266-5366
ISRAEL ALIYAH CENTER 6505 WILSHIRE BLVD	LOS ANGELES	CA	90048	(213) 655-7881
ISRAEL ALIYAH CENTER 870 MARKET STREET, SUITE 1083	SAN FRANCISCO	CA	94102	(415) 392-8998
JEWISH COMMUNITY CENTER 4800 ALAMEDA AVE. P.O. BOX 6196	DENVER	CO	80206	(303) 399-2660
ISRAEL ALIYAH CENTER 4200 BISCAYNE BLVD	MIAMI	FL	33137	(305) 573-2556
HADASSAH ZIONIST YOUTH COMMITTEE 1655 PEACHTREE STREET NORTHEAST, SUITE 904	ATLANTA	GA	30309	(404) 876-1554
ISRAEL ALIYAH CENTER 205 WEST WACKER DRIVE, ROOM 516	CHICAGO	IL	60606	(312) 332-2709
ISRAEL ALIYAH CENTER 31 ST. JAMES AVENUE, PARK SQUARE BLDG., SUITE 450	BOSTON	MA	02116	(617) 423-0868
ISRAEL ALIYAH CENTER 8730 GEORGIA AVENUE	SILVER SPRING	MD	20910	(301) 589-6136
JEWISH COMMUNITY CENTER 6600 WEST MAPLE	WEST BLOOMFIELD	MI	48033	(313) 661-1084
JEWISH COMMUNITY CENTER 4330 CEDAR LAKE ROAD SOUTH	MINNEAPOLIS	MN	55416	(612) 377-8330
ISRAEL PROGRAM CENTER 760 NORTHFIELD AVENUE	WEST ORANGE	NJ	07052	(201) 736-3200
ISRAEL ALIYAH CENTER 1416 AVENUE M	BROOKLYN	NY	11230	(718) 336-1215
ISRAEL ALIYAH CENTER 118-21 QUEENS BOULEVARD	FOREST HILLS	NY	11375	(718) 793-3557
ISRAEL ALIYAH CENTER, MAIN OFFICE 515 PARK AVENUE	NEW YORK	NY	10022	(212) 752-0600
KIBBUTZ ALIYAH DESK 27 WEST 20TH STREET	NEW YORK	NY	10011	(212) 255-1338
NORTH AMERICAN ALIYAH MOVEMENT 515 PARK AVENUE	NEW YORK	NY	10022	(212) 752-0600
ORTHODOX UNION ALIYAH DEPT., RABBI SHMUEL HIMELSTEIN 45 W. 36TH STREET	NEW YORK	NY	10018	(212) 563-4000
JEWISH COMMUNITY CENTER 1200 EDGEWOOD AVENUE	ROCHESTER	NY	14618	(716) 461-2000
ISRAEL ALIYAH CENTER 13967 CEDAR ROAD, SUITE 201	CLEVELAND	OH	44118	(216) 321-0757
ISRAEL ALIYAH CENTER 1111 FINCH AVENUE WEST, SUITE 355	DOWNSVIEW	ON	M3J 2E5	(416) 665-7772
ISRAEL ALIYAH CENTER 225 S. 15TH STREET, SUITE 2528	PHILADELPHIA	PA	19102	(215) 546-2088
ISRAEL ALIYAH CENTER 1310 GREENE AVENUE	MONTREAL	QU	H3Z 2B2	(514) 934-0804
JEWISH COMMUNITY CENTER 6560 POPLAR AVENUE	MEMPHIS	TN	38138	(901) 761-0810
ISRAEL ALIYAH CENTER 6420 HILLCROFT, SUITE 403	HOUSTON	TX	77081	(713) 778-0643
JEWISH COMMUNITY CENTER 1400 NORTH PROSPECT AVENUE	MILWAUKEE	WI	53202	(414) 276-0716

ANTI-MISSIONARY ORGANIZATIONS

SPIRITUAL COUNTERFEITS PROJECT P.O. BOX 4308	BERKELEY	**CA**	94704	(415) 540-0300
CULT CLINIC—JEWISH FAMILY SERVICES OF LOS ANGELES 6505 WILSHIRE BOULEVARD, SUITE 608	LOS ANGELES	**CA**	90048	(213) 852-1234
JEWS FOR JUDAISM P.O. BOX 24903	LOS ANGELES	**CA**	90024	(213) 557-2566
TASK FORCE ON CULTS AND MISSIONARY EFFORTS COMMUNITY RELATIONS COMMITTEE JEWISH FEDERATION COUNCIL 6505 WILSHIRE BOULEVARD, SUITE 802	LOS ANGELES	**CA**	90048	(213) 852-1234
HINENI OF FLORIDA P.O. BOX 763	MIAMI	**FL**		
JEWS FOR JEWS 17720 NORTH BAY ROAD, #8D	MIAMI BEACH	**FL**	33160	
JEWS FOR JEWS ORGANIZATION—RABBI RUBIN R. DOBIN P.O. BOX 6194	MIAMI BEACH	**FL**	33154	(305) 931-0001
CULT AWARENESS NETWORK P.O. BOX 608370	CHICAGO	**IL**	60626	(312) 267-7777
RESPONSE CENTER 9304 N. SKOKIE BOULEVARD	SKOKIE	**IL**	60077	(312) 676-0078
JEWS FOR JUDAISM P.O. BOX 15059	BALTIMORE	**MD**	21208	(301) 764-7788
PROJECT YEDID 5700 PARK HEIGHTS AVENUE	BALTIMORE	**MD**	21215	(301) 542-4900
BETH SHIFRA 3044 CONEY ISLAND AVENUE	BROOKLYN	**NY**	11235	(718) 449-1397
N.C.J.F.E. ANTI-SHMAD 824 EASTERN PARKWAY	BROOKLYN	**NY**	11213	(718) 735-0200
E.M.E.S. P.O. BOX 122	MONSEY	**NY**	10952	(914) 352-0630
CULT AWARENESS NETWORK OF THE CITIZEN'S FREEDOM FOUNDATION 67 IRVING PLACE	NEW YORK	**NY**	10003	(212) 777-7137
CULT HOT-LINE AND CLINIC	NEW YORK	**NY**		(212) 860-8533
INTERFAITH COALITION OF CONCERN ABOUT CULTS 711 THIRD AVENUE, 12TH FLOOR	NEW YORK	**NY**	10017	(212) 983-4977
JBFCS CULT HOTLINE & CLINIC 1651 THIRD AVENUE	NEW YORK	**NY**	10028	(212) 860-8533
P'EYLIM 3 WEST 16TH STREET	NEW YORK	**NY**	10011	(212) YU9-2500
TASK FORCE ON MISSIONARIES AND CULTS 711 THIRD AVENUE, 12TH FLOOR	NEW YORK	**NY**	10017	(212) 983-4800
YAD L'ACHIM 156 FIFTH AVENUE, ROOM 226	NEW YORK	**NY**	10010	(212) 620-6133
EMES 14 EAST CHURCH STREET	SPRING VALLEY	**NY**	10977	(914) 352-0630
LONDON CULT AWARENESS CENTRE INC. BOX 1838, STATION A	LONDON	**ON**	N6A 5H9	
JEWISH RESOURCE CENTER OF OVERBROOK PARK 7331 BRENTWOOD ROAD	PHILADELPHIA	**PA**	19151	(215) 477-5390
S. JACOBS P.O. BOX 15892	PHILADELPHIA	**PA**	19103	
TASK FORCE ON MISSIONARY ACTIVITY OF THE JEWISH CAMPUS ACTIVITIES BOARD 202 SOUTH 36TH STREET	PHILADELPHIA	**PA**	19104	(215) 763-1186
TASK FORCE ON MISSIONARY ACTIVITY OF THE JEWISH CAMPUS ACTIVITIES BOARD 202 SOUTH 36TH STREET	PHILADELPHIA	**PA**	19104	(215) 898-8265
CULT PROJECT 3460 STANLEY STREET	MONTREAL	**QU**	H3A 1R8	(514) 845-9171

ANTIQUES & ANTIQUE JUDAICA

HERMAN BERMAN COMPANY 6510 VAN NUYS BOULEVARD	VAN NUYS	**CA**	91401	(818) 873-3503
LEWIS A. SHEPARD 2 CONGRESS STREET	WORCESTER	**MA**	01609	(617) 756-0172
ADIR GALLERY 22 SOLHILL	EDISON	**NJ**	08817	(201) 572-1751
HA'ATIKOS 1258 43RD STREET	BROOKLYN	**NY**	11219	(718) 851-6833
MANHATTAN SILVER CO. 4922 16TH AVENUE	BROOKLYN	**NY**	11204	(718) 436-2800
ALEXANDER OLAND 120 WEST 44TH STREET	NEW YORK	**NY**	10036	(212) 730-7900
ATIKOTH, INC. 16 EAST 71ST STREET	NEW YORK	**NY**	10021	(212) 570-2591
BEN ARI ARTS LTD. 11 AVENUE A	NEW YORK	**NY**	10009	(212) 677-4730
EMANUEL WEISBERG ANTIQUE JUDAICA 45 ESSEX STREET	NEW YORK	**NY**	10002	(212) 674-1770
GRAND STERLING SILVER COMPANY 345 GRAND STREET	NEW YORK	**NY**	10002	(212) 674-6450
IN THE SPIRIT 460 EAST 79TH STREET	NEW YORK	**NY**	10021	(212) 662-6693
JEWISH FOLKLORE AND ETHNOLOGY NEWSLETTER, YIVO JEWISH RESEARCH 1048 FIFTH AVENUE	NEW YORK	**NY**	10028	(212) 535-6700
MORIAH ARTCRAFT 699 MADISON AVENUE	NEW YORK	**NY**	10021	(212) 751-7090
THE JEWISH MUSEUM SHOP 1109 FIFTH AVENUE	NEW YORK	**NY**	10028	(212) 860-1888
PRESTIGE ANTIQUES 9931 65TH ROAD	REGO PARK	**NY**	11374	(718) 897-9503
R. ITTELSON 9931 65TH ROAD	REGO PARK	**NY**	11374	(718) 897-9503
CHARLES SESSLER, INC. 1308 WALNUT STREET	PHILADELPHIA	**PA**	19107	(215) 735-1086
BROBURY HOUSE GALLERY BROBURY	HEREFORDSHIRE	**UK**		
GALLERIES VERSAILLES DEKEYZERLEI 58	ANTWERP	**BG**	2018	(03) 2343736

ARCHITECTS

SANFORD WERFEL STUDIOS 133 AVENEL STREET	AVENEL	**NJ**	07001	(201) 636-2320
ASCALON STUDIOS 115 ATLANTIC AVENUE	BERLIN	**NJ**	08009	(609) 768-3779
EMANUEL MILSTEIN 29 WYNCREST ROAD	MARLBORO	**NJ**	07746	(201) 946-8604
ERNA WEILL 886 ALPINE DRIVE	TEANECK	**NJ**	07666	(201) 837-1627
ARCHITECTS ADVISORY PANEL, UNION OF AMERICAN HEBREW CONG. 838 FIFTH AVENUE	NEW YORK	**NY**	10021	(212) 249-0100
TOBE PASCHER WORKSHOP, THE JEWISH MUSEUM 1109 FIFTH AVENUE	NEW YORK	**NY**	10028	(212) 860-1864
ALBERT WOOD AND FIVE SONS, INC. ONE PLEASANT AVENUE	PORT WASHINGTON	**NY**	11050	(516) 767-0794
SHAMIR STUDIO 609 KAPPOCK STREET	RIVERDALE	**NY**	10463	(212) 695-5378

ARCHIVES & ARCHIVAL INSTITUTIONS

WESTERN JEWISH HISTORY CENTER OF THE JUDAH L. MAGNES MUSEUM 2911 RUSSELL STREET	BERKELEY	**CA**	94705	(415) 849-2710
ROCKY MTN. JEWISH HIST. SOCIETY - IRA. M. BECK MEM. ARCHIVES UNIVERSITY OF DENVER	DENVER	**CO**	80208	(303) 753-1964
JEWISH HISTORICAL SOCIETY OF GREATER HARTFORD 335 BLOOMFIELD AVENUE	WEST HARTFORD	**CT**	06117	(203) 236-4571
JEWISH HISTORICAL SOCIETY OF DELAWARE 101 GARDEN OF EDEN ROAD	WILMINGTON	**DE**	19803	(302) 656-8558
CHICAGO JEWISH ARCHIVES - SPERTUS COLLEGE OF JUDAICA 618 SOUTH MICHIGAN AVENUE	CHICAGO	**IL**	60605	(312) 922-9012
INDIANA JEWISH HISTORICAL SOCIETY, THE 215 EAST BERRY STREET	FORT WAYNE	**IN**	46802	(219) 422-3862
HEBREW COLLEGE LIBRARY 43 HAWES STREET	BROOKLINE	**MA**	02146	(617) 232-8710
AMERICAN JEWISH HISTORICAL SOCIETY 2 THORNTON ROAD	WALTHAM	**MA**	02154	(617) 891-8110
BRANDEIS UNIVERSITY LIBRARY 215 SOUTH STREET	WALTHAM	**MA**	02254	(617) 647-2000
THE JEWISH HISTORICAL SOCIETY OF WESTERN CANADA 402-365 BARGRAVE STREET	WINNIPEG	**MB**	3B 2K3	(204) 942-4822
CENTER FOR HOLOCAUST STUDIES - DOCUMENTATION & RESEARCH 1610 AVENUE J	BROOKLYN	**NY**	11230	(718) 338-6494
CHABAD RESEARCH CENTER 770 EASTERN PARKWAY	BROOKLYN	**NY**	11213	(718) 774-4001
AGUDATH ISRAEL OF AMERICA ARCHIVES 84 WILLIAM STREET	NEW YORK	**NY**	10038	(212) 797-9000
AMERICAN JEWISH ARCHIVES 300 EAST 71ST STREET, APT. 5-R	NEW YORK	**NY**	10021	
BUND ARCHIVES OF THE JEWISH LABOR MOVEMENT 25 EAST 78TH STREET	NEW YORK	**NY**	10021	(212) 535-1209
HADASSAH, THE WOMEN'S ZIONIST ORGANIZATION OF AMERICA 50 WEST 58TH STREET	NEW YORK	**NY**	10019	(212) 355-7900
JEWISH THEOLOGICAL SEMINARY ARCHIVES 3080 BROADWAY	NEW YORK	**NY**	10027	(212) 678-8080
LEO BAECK INSTITUTE 129 EAST 73RD STREET	NEW YORK	**NY**	10021	(212) 744-6400
YESHIVA UNIVERSITY LIBRARY 500 WEST 185 STREET, ROOM 405	NEW YORK	**NY**	10033	(212) 960-5400
YIVO ARCHIVES 1048 FIFTH AVENUE	NEW YORK	**NY**	10028	(212) 535-6700
ZIONIST ARCHIVES & LIBRARY/WORLD ZIONIST ORG.-AMER. SECTION 515 PARK AVENUE	NEW YORK	**NY**	10022	(212) 753-2167
AMERICAN JEWISH ARCHIVES 3101 CLIFTON AVENUE	CINCINNATI	**OH**	45220	(513) 221-1875
AMERICAN JEWISH PERIODICAL CENTER 3101 CLIFTON AVENUE	CINCINNATI	**OH**	45220	(513) 221-1875
HEBREW UNION COLLEGE-JEWISH INST. OF RELIGION, KLAU LIBRARY 3101 CLIFTON AVENUE	CINCINNATI	**OH**	45220	(513) 221-1875
CLEVELAND JEWISH ARCHIVES-WESTERN RESERVE HISTORICAL SOCIETY 10825 EAST BLVD	CLEVELAND	**OH**	44026	(216) 721-5722
OTTAWA JEWISH HISTORICAL SOCIETY 151 CHAPEL STREET	OTTAWA	**ON**	K1N 7Y2	(613) 232-7306
CANADIAN JEWISH CONGRESS CENTRAL REGION ARCHIVES 4600 BATHURST	WILLOWDALE	**ON**	M2R 3V2	(416) 635-2883
PHILADELPHIA JEWISH ARCHIVES CENTER BALCH INSTITUTE, 18 S. SEVENTH STREET	PHILADELPHIA	**PA**	19106	(215) 923-2729
RECONSTRUCTIONIST RABBINICAL COLLEGE CHURCH ROAD & GREENWOOD AVENUE	WYNCOTE	**PA**	19095	(215) 576-0800
JEWISH PUBLIC LIBRARY 5151 COTE ST. CATHERINE ROAD	MONTREAL	**QU**	H3W 1M6	(514) 735-6535
RHODE ISLAND JEWISH HISTORICAL ASSOCIATION 130 SESSIONS STREET	PROVIDENCE	**RI**	02906	(401) 421-4111
SEATTLE JEWISH ARCHIVES UNIVERSITY OF WASHINGTON LIBRARY	SEATTLE	**WA**	98195	(206) 543-9158
WISCONSIN JEWISH ARCHIVES 816 STATE STREET	MADISON	**WI**	53706	(608) 262-3266
'MASSUA'-MEM. TO MEMBERS OF ZIONIST YOUTH MOVEMENTS KIBBUTZ TEL ITZHAK, 45805		**IS**		
GHETTO FIGHTERS' HOUSE IN MEMORY OF YIZHAK KATZNELSON AKKO POST OFFICE, KIBBUTZ LOHAMEI HAGHETAOT	AKKO	**IS**		
ISRAEL LABOUR PARTY ARCHIVES KFAR SABA 44905	BEIT BERL	**IS**		
MILITARY (I.D.F.) & DEFENSE ESTABLISHMENT ARCHIVES JABOTINSKY STREET 50	GIVATAYIM	**IS**		
HAIFA CITY ARCHIVES HAGEFEN STREET 4	HAIFA	**IS**		
CENTRAL ARCHIVES FOR THE HISTORY OF THE JEWISH PEOPLE, THE HEBREW UNIV. CAMPUS GIVAT RAM. SPRINZAK BLDG. POB 1149	JERUSALEM	**IS**		
CENTRAL ZIONIST ARCHIVES, THE BLDG. OF THE NATIONAL INSTITUTIONS, P.O. BOX 92	JERUSALEM	**IS**		
ISRAEL STATE ARCHIVES - GANSAKH HAMEDINAH PRIME MINISTER'S OFFICE, QIRYAT BEN-GURION, BUILDING 3	JERUSALEM	**IS**		
JERUSALEM MUNICIPALITY HISTORICAL ARCHIVES 28 AGRON STREET	JERUSALEM	**IS**		
JEWISH NATL. & UNIV. LIB.-DEPT. OF MANUSCRIPTS & ARCHIVES, THE GIVAT RAM, P.O.B. 503	JERUSALEM	**IS**		
YAD VASHEM CENTRAL ARCHIVES HAR HAZIKARON, P.O. BOX 3477	JERUSALEM	**IS**		
ARCHIVES OF THE KIBBUTZ ARTZI HASHOMER HATZAIR POST OFFICE MERHAVIYA	KIBBUTZ MERHAVIYA	**IS**		
WEIZMANN INSTITUTE ARCHIVES, THE THE WEIZMANN INSTITUTE OF SCIENCE, P.O. BOX 26	REHOVOT	**IS**		
ARCHIVES & MUSEUM OF THE ISRAEL LABOUR MOVEMENT 34 WEIZMANN STREET, P.O.B. 21010	TEL AVIV	**IS**		
ARCHIVES OF THE ISRAEL TEACHERS' UNION, THE BEN SARUQ STREET 8	TEL AVIV	**IS**		
DIASPORA RESEARCH INSTITUTE, TEL AVIV UNIVERSITY RAMAT AVIV	TEL AVIV	**IS**		
JABOTINSKY INSTITUTE IN ISRAEL 38 KING GEORGE STREET, P.O. BOX 23110	TEL AVIV	**IS**		
TEL AVIV-YAFO MUNICIPALITY HISTORICAL ARCHIVES 27 BIALIK ST., TEL AVIV-YAFO MUN., KIKAR MALKHEI ISRAEL	TEL AVIV	**IS**		
ZVI NISHRI ARCHIVES ON PHYSICAL EDUCATION & SPORT, THE WINGATE INSTITUTE FOR PHYSICAL EDUCATION & SPORT	WINGATE POST OFFICE	**IS**		
CENTRO DI DOCUMENTAZIONE EBRAICA CONTEMPORANEA 6 VIA EUPILI, JEWISH CONTEMPORARY DOCUMENTATION CENTER	MILANO	**IT**		
CENTRE DE DOCUMENTATION JUIVE CONTEMPORAINE 17 RUE GEOFFROY L'ASNIER	PARIS	**FR**		
CONSISTOIRE CENTRALE ISRAELITE DE FRANCE ET D'ALGERIE 17 RUE SAINT GEORGES	PARIS	**FR**		
CONSISTOIRE DE PARIS (ASSOCIATION CONSISTORIAL DE PARIS) 17 RUE SAINT GEORGES	PARIS	**FR**		
BIBLIOTHEQUE ET ARCHIVES DE L'ALLIANCE ISRAELITE UNIVERSELLE 4K RUE BRUYERE, F 75425	PARIS CEDEX09	**FR**		
JEVREJSKI ISTORIJSKI MUSEJ - JEWISH HISTORICAL MUSEUM 7 JUL 71A/L, P.O. BOX 841	BELGRADE			
MAGYAR ZSIDO LEVELTAR - HUNGARIAN JEWISH ARCHIVES 27 JOZSEF KRT	BUDAPEST			
STATNI ZIDOWSKE MUZEUM-STATE JEWISH MUSEUM 3 JACHYMOVA	PRAGUE 1			
AUSTRALIAN JEWISH HISTORICAL SOCIETY 166 CASTLEREAGH STREET	SYDNEY, N.S.W. 2000			
ZYDOWSKI INSTYTUT HISTORYCZNY W POLSCE AL. SWIECZEWSKIEGO 79, JEWISH HISTORICAL INSTITUTE	WARSZAWA			
ANGLO-JEWISH ARCHIVES MOCATTA LIBRARY, UNIVERSITY COLLEGE, GOWER STREET	LONDON	**UK**		

ART GALLERIES & ART

BAT SHEVA IMPORTS P.O. BOX 4866	AHAHEIM	**CA**	92803	(714) 520-0334
GALLERY JUDAICA	LOS ANGELES	**CA**		(213) 459-2657
MICHAEL HITTLEMAN GALLERY 8797 BEVERLY BOULEVARD	LOS ANGELES	**CA**	90048	(213) 655-5364
SKIRBALL MUSEUM, HEBREW UNION COLLEGE 3077 UNIVERSITY MALL	LOS ANGELES	**CA**	90007	(213) 749-3424
ALON GALLERY 1407 MONTANA AVENUE	SANTA MONICA	**CA**	90403	(213) 394-6545
M & M GALLERIES 6125 WEATHERLY DRIVE	ATLANTA	**GA**	30328	(404) 252-1060
THE JEWISH DEVELOPMENT COMPANY 18331-C IRVINE BOULEVARD	TUSTIN	**CA**	92680	(714) 730-1419
ALPERT AND CARTER MERCHANDISE MART	CHICAGO	**IL**	60654	
GOLDMAN-KRAFT GALLERY 233 EAST ONTARIO	CHICAGO	**IL**	60611	(312) 943-9088
PUCKER/SAFRAI GALLERY 171 NEWBURY STREET	BOSTON	**MA**	02116	(617) 267-9474
KOLBO 435 HARVARD STREET	BROOKLINE	**MA**	02146	(617) 731-8743
ARTUOSO 22 CHURCH	LENOX	**MA**	01240	(413) 637-0668
LIPMAN'S ART SHOP 300 E. DIAMOND AVENUE	GATHERSBURG	**MD**	20760	
LIPMAN'S ART SHOP 8209 GEORGIA AVENUE	SILVER SPRING	**MD**	20910	(301) 587-5581
MR. B'S ART & FRAMING 7913 SANTA FE DRIVE	KANSAS CITY	**MO**	64100	(913) 649-3676
ADIR GALLERY 22 SOLHILL	EDISON	**NJ**	08817	(201) 572-1751
RAYE LANDIS ART CENTER 1050 GEORGE STREET	NEW BRUNSWICK	**NJ**	08901	(201) 249-7776
HERITAGE GRAPHICS P.O. BOX 139	BLAUVELT	**NY**	10913	
ENGEL GALLERY 1533 52ND STREET	BROOKLYN	**NY**	11219	(718) 438-6339
THE CHASSIDIC ART INSTITUTE (CHAI) 375 KINGSTON AVENUE	BROOKLYN	**NY**	11213	(718) 774-9149
VISUAL DIMENSIONS-PAINTINGS AND LITHOGRAPHS 1661 MCDONALD AVENUE	BROOKLYN	**NY**	11230	(718) 627-0903
NATIONAL ART AUCTION GALLERY 85F SOUTH HOFFMAN LANE	CENTRAL ISLIP	**NY**	11722	(516) 582-4666
MARLIN ART INCORPORATED 920 GRAND BOULEVARD	DEER PARK	**NY**	11729	(516) 242-3344
WILLIAM HABER GALLERY 139-11 QUEENS BOULEVARD	JAMAICA	**NY**	11435	(718) 739-1000
YUSSEL'S PLACE 59 MERRICK AVENUE	MERRICK	**NY**	11566	(516) 223-7050
BLD, LIMITED, ART PUBLISHERS 118 EAST 25TH STREET	NEW YORK	**NY**	10010	(212) 460-8700
BEN ARI ARTS 11 AVENUE A	NEW YORK	**NY**	10009	(212) 677-4730
BEZALEL JEWISH ART GALLERY 11 ESSEX STREET	NEW YORK	**NY**	10002	(212) 228-5982
CARIMOR GALLERIES 20 E. 76TH STREET	NEW YORK	**NY**	10021	(212) 772-1701
EDELWEISS CO. - GLASS STUDIO 65 MERCER STREET	NEW YORK	**NY**	10012	(212) 431-5022
HA-ATIKOT-JUDAICA ANTIQUES 17 ESSEX STREET	NEW YORK	**NY**	10002	(212) 254-8395
IN THE SPIRIT 460 EAST 79TH STREET	NEW YORK	**NY**	10021	(212) 662-6693
ISRA-ART PRODUCTIONS, INC. 157 WEST 57TH STREET	NEW YORK	**NY**	10019	(212) 246-3363
ISRAEL ARTS CENTER/AMERICAN-ISRAEL CULTURAL FOUNDATION 4 EAST 54TH STREET	NEW YORK	**NY**	10022	
ISRAEL CREATIONS 212 5TH AVENUE	NEW YORK	**NY**	10010	(212) 686-7005
ISRAELI GIFTS 575 7TH AVENUE	NEW YORK	**NY**	10018	(212) 391-4928
J. LEVINE CO. - LOWER EAST SIDE 58 ELDRIDGE STREET	NEW YORK	**NY**	10002	(212) 966-4460
J. LEVINE CO. - MIDTOWN STORE 5 WEST 30TH STREET	NEW YORK	**NY**	10001	(212) 695-6888
JEWISH ART GALLERY 11 ESSEX STREET	NEW YORK	**NY**	10002	
MORIAH ARTCRAFT 699 MADISON AVENUE	NEW YORK	**NY**	10021	(212) PL1-7090
MORRIS KATZ STUDIO 406 SIXTH AVENUE	NEW YORK	**NY**	10011	(212) 673-4660
MURRAY S. GREENFIELD 21 WEST 39TH STREET	NEW YORK	**NY**	10018	(212) 391-8350
NECHEMIA GLEZER GALLERY 760 WEST END AVENUE	NEW YORK	**NY**	10025	(212) 684-0160
SHAPOLSKY'S GREAT JUDAICA GALLERY 56 EAST 11TH STREET	NEW YORK	**NY**	10003	(212) 505-2505
THE EAGLE'S NEST 142 11TH AVENUE	NEW YORK	**NY**	10011	(212) 929-9304
TRADITIONS-ART JUDAICA 24700 CHAGRIN BOULEVARD, SUITE 103	CLEVELAND	**OH**	44122	(216) 831-3451
ARI EDITIONS BOX 921	SOUTHAMPTON	**PA**	18966	(215) 364-3571
ELIJAH'S CUP 12306 MEADOW LAKE DR.	HOUSTON	**TX**	77077	(713) 497-2243
MILLIOUD INTERNATIONAL GALLERY WEST ALABAMA & BUFFALO	HOUSTON	**TX**	77027	(713) 621-3330
RACHEL DAVID GALLERY 2402 ADDISON	HOUSTON	**TX**	77030	(713) 664-4130

ARTISTS

JOANNE ABENSOUR 1500 S. WOOSTER ST.	LOS ANGELES	**CA**	90035	(213) 854-5921
JOE HARNIK 8110 LONGRIDGE AVENUE	NORTH HOLLYWOOD	**CA**	91605	(818) 782-2548
NEEMAN'S ORIGINAL ART 296 CREEKSIDE DRIVE	PALO ALTO	**CA**	94306	(415) 493-3740
BOSTON JEWISH ARTS COALITION 113 COLLEGE AVENUE	SOMERVILLE	**MA**	02144	(617) 623-3376
JANIS PEROMSIK 28 HADWEN ROAD	WORCESTER	**MA**	01602	(617) 753-6781
YANNAI ART 1046 MEDICAL ARTS BUILDING	MINNEAPOLIS	**MN**	55402	(612) 332-1336
ASCALON STUDIOS 115 ATLANTIC AVENUE	BERLIN	**NJ**	08009	(609) 768-3779
EMANUEL MILSTEIN 29 WYNCREST ROAD	MARLBORO	**NJ**	07746	(201) 946-8604

ROSLYN HOLLANDA 5 DOGWOOD DRIVE	NEWTON	NJ	07860	(201) 383-4966
BASSYA EIN 1534 53RD STREET	BROOKLYN	NY	11219	
ALBERT HAKAKIAN 1460 58TH STREET	BROOKLYN	NY	11219	(718) 436-8590
SHARON LEVINSON 5649 KINGS HIGHWAY	BROOKLYN	NY	11203	(718) 541-1151
SHARON GELLER METAL 144-15 78TH AVENUE	FLUSHING	NY	11367	(718) 969-0417
ZAMY STEYNOVITZ 67-12 YELLOWSTONE BOULEVARD	FOREST HILLS	NY	11375	(718) 275-3058
JONATHAN CRAIG 1 SWALLOW LANE	HAPPAUGE	NY	11787	(516) 724-7250
LORRAINE ROSENBAUM 250-14 GASKILL ROAD	LITTLE NECK	NY	11363	(718) 428-3658
KAREN KAUFMAN 1918 GEORGE COURT	MERRICK	NY	11566	(516) 546-3843
HUGH MESIBOV 377 SADDLE RIVER ROAD	MONSEY	NY	10952	(914) 356-2610
BONNIE SROLOVITZ DESIGNS - CONTEMPORARY JUDAICA 155 EAST 88TH STREET, SUITE GG	NEW YORK	NY	10128	(212) 348-0879
CHARLES J. STANLEY PO BOX 1132, PETER STUYVESANT STATION	NEW YORK	NY	10009	(212) 673-2705
THE CUTTING EDGE 270 WEST 89TH STREET	NEW YORK	NY	10024	(212) 496-5399
EFREM WEITZMAN - SYNAGOGUE ARTIST 334 WEST 86TH STREET	NEW YORK	NY	10024	(212) 877-6590
DR. MARK PODWAL 999 FIFTH AVENUE	NEW YORK	NY	10028	(212) 288-7488
NATIONAL COUNCIL ON ART IN JEWISH LIFE 15 E. 84TH STREET	NEW YORK	NY	10028	(212) 879-4500
NEIL H. YERMAN 17 EAST 67TH STREET	NEW YORK	NY	10021	(212) 744-4355
ART & DESIGN STUDIO OF SARA SHAPIRO 13 DR. FRANK ROAD	SPRING VALLEY	NY	10977	(914) 352-3988
LAUREL PRESS 26 WEST FENIMORE STREET	VALLEY STREAM	NY	11580	
TRADITIONS, ART FOR JEWISH LIVING 24700 CHAGRIN BOULEVARD, SUITE 103	CLEVELAND	OH	44122	(216) 831-3451
BEVERLY A. MOSLER 8629 ALGON AVENUE	PHILADELPHIA	PA	19152	
EMES EDITIONS 2001 LEVICK STREET	PHILADELPHIA	PA	19149	(215) 288-8787

BAKERIES - RETAIL

GOLD STAR BAKERY 3219 EAST CAMELBACK ROAD	PHOENIX	AZ	85018	(602) 955-7670
KARSH'S BAKERY 5539 NORTH 7TH STREET	PHOENIX	AZ	85016	(602) 264-4874
KARSH'S BAKERY 10893 NORTH SCOTTSDALE ROAD	SCOTTSDALE	AZ	85016	(602) 951-0202
CARMEL BAKERY 3885 OAK STREET	VANCOUVER	BC		(604) 733-6815
LEON'S KOSHER BAKERY 3710 OAK STREET	VANCOUVER	BC	V6H 2M3	(604) 736-5888
HANSEN CAKES 193 SOUTH BEVERLY DRIVE	BEVERLY HILLS	CA	90212	(213) 272-0474
MICKEY'S KOSHER BAKERY 2298 SOUTH BASKIN AVENUE	CAMPBELL	CA	95008	(408) 371-5151
BEVERLY HILLS PATISSERIE 9100 W. PICO BLVD.	LOS ANGELES	CA	90035	(213) 275-6873
DOVE'S BAKERY 8924 W. PICO BLVD.	LOS ANGELES	CA	90035	(213) 276-6150
EILAT BAKERY 515 N. FAIRFAX	LOS ANGELES	CA	90036	(213) 653-5553
FAMOUS BAKERY 350-354 N. FAIRFAX AVENUE	LOS ANGELES	CA	90036	(213) 939-8367
HAIMISH BAKERY 9100 WEST PICO BOULEVARD	LOS ANGELES	CA	90035	(213) 276-3116
HANSEN'S CAKES 1060 SOUTH FAIRFAX AVENUE	LOS ANGELES	CA	90019	(213) 936-5527
KING DAVID BAKERY 357 N. FAIRFAX AVENUE	LOS ANGELES	CA	90036	(213) 655-3021
LITTLE JERUSALEM 8971 WEST PICO BOULEVARD	LOS ANGELES	CA	90035	(213) 858-8361
MODEL 8377 WEST THIRD	LOS ANGELES	CA	90036	(213) 651-3938
SCHWARTZ BAKERY 441 N. FAIRFAX AVENUE	LOS ANGELES	CA	90036	(213) 653-1683
SCHWARTZ BAKERY 8616 W. PICO BOULEVARD	LOS ANGELES	CA	90035	(213) 854-0592
SCHWARTZ PASSOVER BAKERY 431 N. FAIRFAX AVENUE	LOS ANGELES	CA	90036	(213) 653-2106
REUBENS CONTINENTAL BAKERY, INC. 12419 BURBANK BLVD	NORTH HOLLYWOOD	CA	91607	(818) 762-5005
ERNIE'S INTERNATIONAL PASTRIES 3264 GRAND AVENUE	OAKLAND	CA	94610	(415) 444-8226
WEDEMEYER'S BAKERY 314 HARBOR WAY	SOUTH SAN FRANCISCO	CA	94080	(415) 873-1000
HANSEN'S CAKES 18466 VENTURA BLVD.	TARZANA	CA	91356	(818) 708-1208
THE BAGEL STORE 942 SOUTH MONACO PARKWAY	DENVER	CO	80224	(303) 388-2648
MOISHE'S 2081 BLACK ROCK TURNPIKE	FAIRFIELD	CT	06430	(203) 333-3059
LEON'S BAKERIES 1359 DIXWELL AVENUE	HAMDEN	CT	06514	(203) 281-6560
REYMOND BAKING COMPANY 2457 EAST MAIN STREET	WATERBURY	CT	06702	(203) 756-7871
CREATIVE COOKIE CO. 3900 16TH STREET NORTHWEST	WASHINGTON	DC	20011	(202) 722-1048
OTTENBERG'S BREAD 655 TAYLOR N.E.	WASHINGTON	DC	20019	(202) 529-5800
POSIN'S BAKERY-DELICATESSEN 5756 GEORGIA AVENUE N.W.	WASHINGTON	DC	20011	(202) 726-4424
ABRAHAM'S BAKERY 7423 COLLINS AVENUE	MIAMI BEACH	FL	33141	(305) 861-0291
BUTTERFLAKE NEW YORK BAKERY 1349 WASHINGTON AVENUE	MIAMI BEACH	FL	33139	(305) 532-4445
CARMEL HUNGARIAN BAKERY 847 WASHINGTON AVENUE	MIAMI BEACH	FL	33139	(305) 538-7592
FRIEDMAN'S BAKERY 685 WASHINGTON AVENUE	MIAMI BEACH	FL	33139	(305) 531-6173
PARAMOUNT BAKERY 1407 WASHINGTON AVENUE	MIAMI BEACH	FL	33139	(305) 534-2683
ABRAHAM'S BAKERY 757 N.E. 167 STREET	N. MIAMI BEACH	FL	33162	(395) 652-3343
BEN ZION BAKERY 1360 N.E. 163 STREET	N. MIAMI BEACH	FL	33162	(305) 947-4092
GORDON'S OF NEW YORK 781 NORTH MIAMI BEACH BLVD.	N. MIAMI BEACH	FL	33162	(305) 674-9107
PARAMOUNT BAKERY 757 NORTH MIAMI BEACH BLVD	N. MIAMI BEACH	FL	33162	(305) 652-9176
PASTRY LANE, INC. 1692 N.E. 164TH STREET	N. MIAMI BEACH	FL	33162	(305) 944-5934
BAKE MASTERS OF ATLANTA 3818 OAKCLIFF INDUSTRIAL COURT	ATLANTA	GA	30340	(404) 447-6823
GOLDBERG & SON 4383 ROSWELL ROAD N.E.	ATLANTA	GA	30329	(404) 256-3751
SUNSHINE BAKERY 1209 BROAD STREET	AUGUSTA	GA	30900	(404) 724-2302
DUNKIN' DONUTS (DAIRY/CRC) 3132 WEST DEVON	CHICAGO	IL	60659	(312) 262-4560
GITEL'S BAKERY 2745 W. DEVON AVENUE	CHICAGO	IL	60659	(312) 262-3701
NORTH SHORE KOSHER BAKERY 2919 W. TOUHY	CHICAGO	IL	60645	(312) 262-0600
TAMTOV KOSHER BAKERY 3909 W. LAWRENCE AVENUE	CHICAGO	IL	60625	(312) 267-3383
TEL AVIV KOSHER BAKERY 2944 WEST DEVON	CHICAGO	IL	60645	(312) 764-8877
DUNKIN' DONUTS (DAIRY/CRC) 3900 WEST DEMPSTER	SKOKIE	IL	60076	(312) 673-7099
KING DAVID'S KOSHER BAKERY 3309 WEST DEMPSTER	SKOKIE	IL	60076	(312) 677-4355
TEL AVIV 4956-60 WEST DEMPSTER	SKOKIE	IL	60077	(312) 675-1005
HANS PASTRIES, INC. 3089 BRECKINRIDGE LANE	LOUISVILLE	KY	40220	(502) 452-9164
MONTILLO'S BAKERY SHOP 33-35 FANEUIL HALL MARKET	BOSTON	MA	02115	(617) 267-4700
DUBIN'S BAKERY 1010 WEST ROXBURY PKWY	BROOKLINE	MA	02167	(617) 469-9241
KUPEL'S BAKE & BAGEL 421 HARVARD STREET	BROOKLINE	MA	02146	(617) 566-9528
PASTRYLANE PRODUCTS 305 HARVARD STREET	BROOKLINE	MA	02146	(617) 566-8136
TAAM TOV BAKERY 305A HARVARD	BROOKLINE	MA	02146	(617) 566-8136
TOWNE LYNNE BAKERY 12 WASHINGTON STREET	CANTON	MA	02021	(617) 828-2260
BREAD BASKET 151 COCHITUATE ROAD	FRAMINGHAM	MA	01701	(617) 875-9441
MONTILIO'S BAKERY SHOP 70 WATER STREET	HINGHAM	MA	02025	(617) 749-9851
M&M CAKE BOX 237 FERRY STREET	MALDEN	MA	02148	(617) 322-4447
EAGERMAN'S BAKERY 810 WORCESTER ROAD	NATICK	MA	01760	(617) 653-9474
NEEDHAM BAKERY 117 CHAPEL STREET	NEEDHAM	MA	02192	(617) 444-9619
DIAMOND'S BAKERY 1136 BEACON STREET	NEWTON	MA	02158	(617) 527-5100
HANNA'S BAKERY 551 COMMONWEALTH AVENUE	NEWTON	MA	02158	(617) 527-9503
LEDERMAN'S 1223 CENTRE STREET	NEWTON	MA	02158	(617) 527-7896
MONTILIO'S BAKERY SHOP 29 CHESTNUT STREET	QUINCY	MA	02169	(617) 773-2300
ZEPPY'S BAKERY 937 NORTH MAIN STREET	RANDOLPH	MA	02368	(617) 963-9837
LIBERMAN'S BAKERY 107 SHIRLEY AVENUE	REVERE	MA	02151	(617) 289-0041
RAIN'S BAKERY 55 NICHOLAS ROAD	SAXONVILLE	MA	01701	(617) 877-3927
GREEN & FREEDMAN BAKERY 75 OLD COLONY AVENUE	SOUTH BOSTON	MA	02127	(617) 269-4700
RUTH'S BAKE SHOP 987 CENTRAL STREET	STOUGHTON	MA	02072	(617) 344-8993
NEWMAN'S BAKERY 248 HUMPHREY STREET	SWAMPSCOTT	MA	01907	(617) 592-1550
CHARLES GILBERT AND DAVIS 1580 VFW PARKWAY	WEST ROXBURY	MA	02132	(617) 325-7750
CITY BREAD 238 DUFFERIN AVENUE	WINNIPEG	MB		(204) 586-8409
GUNN'S 247 SELKIRK AVENUE	WINNIPEG	MB		(204) 582-2364
MIRACLE 1385 MAIN STREET	WINNIPEG	MB		(204) 586-6140
TASTY 419 SELKIRK AVENUE	WINNIPEG	MB		(204) 589-5033
TASTY 1419 MAIN STREET	WINNIPEG	MB		(204) 586-7263
GOLDMAN'S KOSHER FANCY BAKERY 6848 REISTERSTOWN ROAD	BALTIMORE	MD	21215	(301) 358-9625
PARISER'S, INC. 6711 REISTERSTOWN ROAD	BALTIMORE	MD	21215	(301) 764-1700
SCHMELL & AZMAN KOSHER BAKERY 104 REISTERSTOWN ROAD	PIKESVILLE	MD	21208	(301) 484-7343
SHAPIRO'S SUPERMARKET 1504 REISTERSTOWN ROAD	PIKESVILLE	MD	21208	(301) 484-2400
KATZ'S KOSHER SUPERMARKET 4860 BOILING BROOK PKWY	ROCKVILLE	MD	20852	(301) 468-0400
DELUXE BAKE SHOP WHITE OAK SHOPPING PLAZA	SILVER SPRING	MD	20910	(301) 593-6607
WOODEN SHOE BAKERY 11301 GEORGIA AVENUE	WHEATON	MD	20902	(301) 942-9330
INTERBAKE FOODS 19TH STREET AT AVENUE C	BATTLE CREEK	MI	49016	(616) 963-5575
NEW MODERN BAKERY 12533 LINWOOD	DETROIT	MI	48206	(313) 868-3313
HOLLAND HONEY CAKES 420 WEST 17TH STREET	HOLLAND	MI	49423	(616) 396-6311
BROADWAY BAGEL CO. 23334 WEST 7 MILE ROAD	NORTHVILLE	MI	48167	(313) 349-2444
DUNKIN' DONUTS 25170 GREENFIELD	OAK PARK	MI	48237	(313) 967-3975
MERTZ BAKE SHOPPE 24770 COOLIDGE	OAK PARK	MI	48237	(313) 548-4835
MERTZ BAKE SHOPPE 23005 COOLIDGE	OAK PARK	MI	48237	(313) 547-3581
ZEMAN'S NEW YORK BAKERY 25258 GREENFIELD RD.	OAK PARK	MI	48237	(313) 967-3905
DAWN'S DONUT SHOP 15526 WEST 12 MILE ROAD	SOUTHFIELD	MI	48075	(313) 552-9127
ZEMAN'S NEW YORK BAKERY 30760 SOUTHFIELD RD.	SOUTHFIELD	MI	48076	(313) 646-7159
DESSERTS BY SYLVIA LEE 24370 WEST 10 MILE ROAD	SOUTHFIELD	MI	48034	(313) 355-0088
GELPE'S OLD WORLD BAKERY 2447 HENNEPIN AVENUE SOUTH	MINNEAPOLIS	MN	55405	(612) 377-1870
CECIL'S KOSHER DELICATESSEN RESTAURANT & BAKERY 651 CLEVELAND SOUTH	ST. LOUIS PARK	MN	55416	(612) 698-6276
EPSTEIN KOSHER FOODS 403 WEST 79TH STREET	KANSAS CITY	MO	64119	(816) 361-0200
PETROFSKY'S BAKERY 7649 DELMAR STREET	ST. LOUIS	MO	63130	(314) 725-1882
PRATZEL'S BAKERY 928 NORTH MCKNIGHT	ST. LOUIS	MO	63132	(314) 991-0708
PRATZEL'S BAKERY 727 NORTH NEW BALLAS	ST. LOUIS	MO	63141	(314) 567-9197
BAGEL BIN 1215 SOUTH 119 STREET	OMAHA	NE	68144	(402) 334-2744
SPINDLER'S 247 BOULEVARD	HASBROUCK HEIGHTS	NJ	07604	(201) 288-1348
FISCHL BAKERY 156 ROCHELLE AVENUE	ROCHELLE PARK	NJ	07662	(201) 843-2462
GOLD BELL BAKERY 1133 ST. GEORGE AVENUE	ROSSELLE	NJ	07203	(201) 245-2172
GRATZEL'S BAKERY 474 CEDAR LANE	TEANECK	NJ	07666	(201) 836-4049
HOT BAGELS 573 CEDAR LANE	TEANECK	NJ	07666	(201) 836-9705
BAGEL BOX 642 EAGLE ROCK ROAD	WEST ORANGE	NJ	07052	(201) 731-4985
BAGEL DEN 212-47 26TH AVENUE	BAYSIDE	NY	11360	(718) 224-3579
WAGNER'S 46 SEMINARY AVENUE	BINGHAMTON	NY	13905	(607) 722-9200
BAGEL CORNER 581 WEST 235TH STREET	BRONX	NY	10463	(212) 549-9709
GRUENEBAUM'S BAKERY 741 LYDIG AVENUE	BRONX	NY	10461	(212) 822-9874
HEISLER FOOD ENTERPRISES INC. 5760-A BROADWAY	BRONX	NY	10463	(212) 543-0855
13TH AVENUE BAGEL BAKERY CORP. 4807 13TH AVENUE	BROOKLYN	NY	11219	(718) 633-4009
AVENUE M KOSHER BAKERY 1218 AVENUE M	BROOKLYN	NY	11230	(718) 998-7819
BAGEL HOLE 1431 CONEY ISLAND AVENUE	BROOKLYN	NY	11230	(718) 377-9700
BAGEL WHEEL 734 FLATBUSH AVENUE	BROOKLYN	NY	11226	(718) 284-9726
B-H BAGELS 1431 CONEY ISLAND AVENUE	BROOKLYN	NY	11230	(718) 377-9700
CAKE CENTER 430 AVENUE P	BROOKLYN	NY	11230	(718) 998-7530
CHIFFON'S BAKE SHOP 1373 CONEY ISLAND AVENUE	BROOKLYN	NY	11230	(718) 258-8822
C.P.C. BAKERY CORP. 1506 ELM AVENUE	BROOKLYN	NY	11230	(718) 339-8138
CONGREGATION BETH ABRAHAM 210 CORTELYOU ROAD	BROOKLYN	NY	11218	(718) 438-9869
CONGREGATION SATMAR MATZOH BAKERY 427 BROADWAY	BROOKLYN	NY	11211	(718) 388-4008
DESSERTFULLY YOURS 1587 EAST 8TH STREET	BROOKLYN	NY	11230	(718) 376-2263
FLATBUSH KOSHER HOMEMADE BAKERY 412 AVENUE M	BROOKLYN	NY	11230	(718) 375-5010
FRANCZOZ BAKERY 4623 13TH AVENUE	BROOKLYN	NY	11219	(718) 438-8978
FRANKEL'S 18TH AVENUE BAKE SHOP 4616 18TH AVENUE	BROOKLYN	NY	11204	(718) 436-6777
FREUND BAKERY 5014 12TH AVENUE	BROOKLYN	NY	11219	(718) 854-9582
FRIEDMAN, DOV 422 BEDFORD AVENUE	BROOKLYN	NY	11211	(718) 388-4044

GOLDEN BAGELS 1119 KINGS HIGHWAY ... BROOKLYN **NY** 11223 (718) 336-4750
HIRSCH BROS. BAKERY 1079 CLARKSON AVENUE ... BROOKLYN **NY** 11212 (718) 498-7614
ISAAC'S BAKE SHOP 1419 AVENUE J ... BROOKLYN **NY** 11230 (718) 377-9291
J.E.R.O.D. HOT BAGELS 3913 13TH AVENUE ... BROOKLYN **NY** 11219 (718) 851-1716
KAFF'S BAKERY 4518 FORT HAMILTON PARKWAY ... BROOKLYN **NY** 11219 (718) 633-2600
KORF'S MATZOS BAKERY 460 ALBANY AVENUE ... BROOKLYN **NY** 11213 (718) 778-7914
KORN'S BAKERY 4322 15TH AVENUE ... BROOKLYN **NY** 11219 (718) 435-9522
KORN'S BAKERY 5004 16TH AVENUE ... BROOKLYN **NY** 11204 (718) 851-0268
LA BRIOCHE INTERNATIONAL BAKERY 440 AVENUE U ... BROOKLYN **NY** 11223 (718) 376-5800
LECHEM BAKE SHOPS INC. 4814 13TH AVENUE ... BROOKLYN **NY** 11219 (718) 438-9752
LEE AVENUE KOSHER BAKERY 73 LEE AVENUE ... BROOKLYN **NY** 11211 (718) 387-4736
LIBBY'S DELIGHTS INC. 8205 FLATLANDS AVENUE ... BROOKLYN **NY** 11236 (718) 241-6666
LOWEN'S BAKE SHOP 311 ROGERS AVENUE ... BROOKLYN **NY** 11225 (718) 467-3500
LOWEN'S BAKE SHOP 1419 CONEY ISLAND AVENUE ... BROOKLYN **NY** 11230 (718) 253-0462
MANDELBAUM BAKERY 4410 14TH AVENUE ... BROOKLYN **NY** 11219 (718) 853-7089
MOISHE'S BAKERY 902 CORTELYOU ROAD ... BROOKLYN **NY** 11218 (718) 941-4264
NOSHIN' GOOD DONUTS 1217 AVENUE J ... BROOKLYN **NY** 11230 (718) 252-3731
PARKWAY BAKERY 2213 65TH STREET ... BROOKLYN **NY** 11214 (718) 837-0782
PRESSER'S KOSHER BAKERY 1720 AVENUE M ... BROOKLYN **NY** 11230 (718) 375-5067
REISMAN'S 110 AVENUE O ... BROOKLYN **NY** 11204 (718) 331-2012
SCHICK'S BAKERY 4710 16TH AVENUE ... BROOKLYN **NY** 11204 (718) 436-8020
SHMURAH MATZOH BAKERY 1285 36TH STREET ... BROOKLYN **NY** 11218 (718) 438-9764
SHOMER SHABBOS BAKE SHOP 425 KINGSTON AVENUE ... BROOKLYN **NY** 11225 (718) 493-2627
SOVA BAKERY OUTLET 1267 CONEY ISLAND AVENUE ... BROOKLYN **NY** 11230 (718) 692-2234
SOVA BAKERY OUTLET 182 WILSON STREET ... BROOKLYN **NY** 11211 (718) 387-5843
SPITZER'S KOSHER BAKERY 657 BEDFORD AVENUE ... BROOKLYN **NY** 11211 (718) 875-0668
STRAUSS KOSHER BAKERY 5209 13TH AVENUE ... BROOKLYN **NY** 11219 (718) 851-7728
SZABO KOSHER BAKERY 702 AVENUE U ... BROOKLYN **NY** 11223 (718) 376-8003
TEMPTATIONS 7406 13TH AVENUE ... BROOKLYN **NY** 11228 (718) 680-5959
WEISS BAKERY 5011 13TH AVENUE ... BROOKLYN **NY** 11219 (718) 436-3864
WEISS HEIMISHE BAKERY 123 LEE AVENUE ... BROOKLYN **NY** 11211 (718) 387-7708
WERZBERGER KOSHER BAKERY & CANDY SHOP 5502 13TH AVENUE ... BROOKLYN **NY** 11219 (718) 435-2490
WILLIAMSBURG KOSHER BAKE SHOP 159 LEE AVENUE ... BROOKLYN **NY** 11211 (718) 387-7411
SCHROEDER'S COSMOPOLITAN BAKERY 2971 DELAWARE ... BUFFALO **NY** 14217 (716) 874-2253
FIVE TOWNS BAGELS & CATERERS 584 CENTRAL AVENUE ... CEDARHURST **NY** 11516 (516) 569-7070
G & I KOSHER BAKERY 536 CENTRAL AVENUE ... CEDARHURST **NY** 11516 (516) 374-2525
BROADWAY BAGELS 1627 DUTCH BROADWAY ... ELMONT **NY** 11003 (516) 825-9696
DAVID'S BAGELS & BIALIES 67-11 MAIN STREET ... FLUSHING **NY** 11367 (718) 520-8892
G & I KOSHER BAKERY 72-22 MAIN STREET ... FLUSHING **NY** 11367 (718) 544-8736
G & I KOSHER BAKERY 69-72 MAIN STREET ... FLUSHING **NY** 11367 (718) 261-1155
KOSHER BAKERY 69-30 JEWEL AVENUE ... FLUSHING **NY** 11367 (718) 544-0225
MENORAH BAKERY 189-09 UNION TURNPIKE ... FLUSHING **NY** 11366 (718) 468-1243
ABRAHAM'S KOSHER CAKELAND 64-17 108TH STREET ... FOREST HILLS **NY** 11375 (718) 897-7744
BAGEL HUT 485 MIDDLE NECK ROAD ... GREAT NECK **NY** 11023 (516) 482-8939
CLEVER HANS BAKERY 102 ADAMS STREET ... ITHACA **NY** 14850
EL BAKERY 8120 LEFFERTS BOULEVARD ... KEW GARDENS **NY** 11415 (718) 441-3471
BAGELS AROUND THE CLOCK 72-02 MAIN STREET ... KEW GARDENS HILLS **NY** 11367 (718) 520-8499
G&I KOSHER BAKERIES 141-11 70TH ROAD ... KEW GARDENS HILLS **NY** 11367 (718) 544-9433
NOT JUST DONUTS 72-04 MAIN STREET ... KEW GARDENS HILLS **NY** 11367 (718) 268-7830
ZOMICK'S '2' 392 CENTRAL AVENUE ... LAWRENCE **NY** 11559 (516) 569-5520
ELSAHA BAKERY 100 FAIRGROUNDS DRIVE ... MANLIUS **NY** 13104 (315) 682-2780
EUROPEAN HOMEMADE FOODS 82 ROUTE 59 ... MONSEY **NY** 10952 (914) 356-9555
KOSHER TOWN 46 MAIN STREET ... MONSEY **NY** 10952 (914) 352-8696
MONSEY KOSHER BAKE SHOP 51 MAIN STREET ... MONSEY **NY** 10952 (914) 352-6435
MONTICELLO SHOMER SHABBOS BAKERY 292 BROADWAY ... MONTICELLO **NY** 12701 (914) 794-1911
BIALYSTOKER KUCHEN BAKERY 367 GRAND STREET ... NEW YORK **NY** 10002 (212) 674-9747
B-J'S BAGELS 130 WEST 72ND STREET ... NEW YORK **NY** 10023 (212) 769-3350
GERTEL'S BAKE SHOP 53 HESTER STREET ... NEW YORK **NY** 10002 (212) 982-3250
GRANDMA'S COOKIE JAR 2543 AMSTERDAM AVENUE ... NEW YORK **NY** 10033 (212) 568-4855
GRUENEBAUM BAKERIES 725 W. 181ST STREET ... NEW YORK **NY** 10033 (212) 567-4500
H & H BAGELS 2239 BROADWAY ... NEW YORK **NY** 10024 (212) 799-9680
ISRAEL BAGELS EAST BROADWAY KOSHER BAKERY
181 EAST BROADWAY ... NEW YORK **NY** 10002 (212) 228-1110
JERUSALEM II 1375 BROADWAY ... NEW YORK **NY** 10018 (212) 398-1475
MOISHE'S BAKERY 181 EAST HOUSTON STREET ... NEW YORK **NY** 10002 (212) 475-9624
MOISHE'S SECOND AVENUE HOME MADE KOSHER BAKE SHOP
115 SECOND AVENUE ... NEW YORK **NY** 10003 (212) 505-8555
ROYALE PASTRY SHOP 237 WEST 72ND STREET ... NEW YORK **NY** 10023 (212) 874-5642
YONAH SCHIMMEL KNISHERY 137 EAST HOUSTON ... NEW YORK **NY** 10002 (212) 477-2858
YONAH SCHIMMEL KNISHERY 1275 LEXINGTON AVENUE ... NEW YORK **NY** 10028 (212) 722-4049
ZARO'S BREAD BASKET 625 8TH AVENUE ... NEW YORK **NY** 10018 (212) 279-7663
ZARO'S BREAD BASKET GRAND CENTRAL TERMINAL ... NEW YORK **NY** 10017 (212) 599-1515
ZARO'S BREAD BASKET 32ND AND BROADWAY ... NEW YORK **NY** 10001 (212) 564-7968
PEARL'S BAKERY 26 MANETTO HILL MALL ... PLAINVIEW **NY** 11803 (516) 935-5225
BRIGHTON DONUTS 1760 MONROE ... ROCHESTER **NY** 14618 (716) 271-6940
DANKER'S QUALITY BAKERY 687 JOSEPH AVENUE ... ROCHESTER **NY** 14614 (714) 544-2100
ISRAEL BAKERY 1248 CLINTON AVENUE NORTH ... ROCHESTER **NY** 14612 (716) 342-6060
LEA MALEK'S 1795 MONROE AVENUE ... ROCHESTER **NY** 14618 (716) 461-1720
MADNICK'S BAKERY BOX 445, LAKE STREET ... SOUTH FALLSBURG **NY** 12779 (914) 434-7272
NOVELTY KOSHER PASTRY SHOP, INC. 10 HOFFMAN STREET ... SPRING VALLEY **NY** 10977 (914) 356-0428
FAMOUS KOSHER BAKERY 2208 VICTORY BOULEVARD ... STATEN ISLAND **NY** 10314 (718) 494-1411
WASSERMAN'S KOSHER BAKERY 460 BRADLEY AVENUE ... STATEN ISLAND **NY** 10314 (718) 698-6489
DEWITT BAGELRY 4451 EAST GENESEE STREET ... SYRACUSE **NY** 13214 (315) 445-0959
HARRISON BAKERY 1306 WEST GENESSEE STREET ... SYRACUSE **NY** 13204 (315) 422-1468
SNOWFLAKE BAKERY 2012 EAST FAYATTE STREET ... SYRACUSE **NY** 13210 (315) 472-3041
BAGEL POLE, INC. 1075 OLD COUNTRY ROAD ... WESTBURY **NY** 11590 (516) 334-9466
BAGEL PLACE 964 MAPLE ROAD ... WILLIAMSVILLE **NY** 14221 (716) 688-4255
WOODBOURNE BAKE MASTERS MAIN STREET ... WOODBOURNE **NY** 12788 (914) 434-6310
LAX & MANDEL KOSHER BAKERY 2070 SOUTH TAYLOR ROAD ... CLEVELAND **OH** 44118 (216) 932-6445
UNGAR'S BAKERY & FOOD SHOP 1831 S. TAYLOR ROAD ... CLEVELAND **OH** 44118 (216) 321-7176
VROMAN FOOD INC. 4117 FITCH ROAD ... TOLEDO **OH** 43613 (800) 537-1996
ANITA BENGIO PATISSERIE 870 STEEPROCK DRIVE ... DOWNSVIEW **ON** M2J 2X2 (416) 638-3051
DAIRY TREATS 7241 BATHURST ... THORNHILL **ON** L3T 3M9 (416) 764-0582
CARMEL BAKERY 3856 BATHURST STREET ... TORONTO **ON** M3H 3N3 (416) 633-5315
DAIRY TREATS 3522 BATHURST ... TORONTO **ON** M3H 1S8 (416) 782-5334
FOOD CITY (THE OSHAWA GROUP LTD.) ... TORONTO **ON** (416) 764-3770
HERMES 2885 BATHURST STREET ... TORONTO **ON** M6B 3A4 (416) 787-1234
HERMES 3543 BATHURST STREET ... TORONTO **ON** M6A 2C7 (416) 787-2611
HERMES 924 ST. CLAIR AVENUE WEST ... TORONTO **ON** M6C 1C6 (416) 654-4456
HERMES 652 SHEPPARD AVENUE WEST ... TORONTO **ON** M2K 1B8 (416) 635-1932
ISACC'S 3390 BATHURST STREET ... TORONTO **ON** M6A 2B9 (416) 789-7587
ISACC'S 221 WILMINGTON AVENUE ... TORONTO **ON** M3H 5J9 (416) 630-1678
MY ZAIDY'S BAGEL 3456 BATHURST STREET ... TORONTO **ON** M6A 2C4 (416) 789-0785
RICHMAN'S BAKERY 4119 BATHURST STREET ... TORONTO **ON** M3H 3P4 (416) 636-9710
SILVERMAN'S 2839 BATHURST STREET ... TORONTO **ON** M6B 3A4 (416) 787-6791
ALL SPICE BAKERY 1530 WADSWORTH ... PHILADELPHIA **PA** 19150 (215) 248-0178
GREENBERG'S BAKERY 7594 HAVERFORD AVENUE ... PHILADELPHIA **PA** 19151 (215) 878-1127
LISS BAKERY 1921 NORTH 54TH STREET ... PHILADELPHIA **PA** 19131 (215) 477-6100
ROLINGS FINE BAKING—"THE BAKERY" 6773 NORTH 5TH STREET ... PHILADELPHIA **PA** 19126 (215) 635-0377
HOME-MADE KOSHER BAKERY 5638 WESTMINSTER ... COTE ST. LUC **QU** H4W 2J4 (514) 486-2024
EUROPEAN BAKERIES 206 ST. VIATEUR WEST ... MONTREAL **QU** H2T 2L5 (514) 274-4633
EUROPEAN BAKERIES 1587 VAN HORNE ... MONTREAL **QU** H2V 2L6 (514) 272-3003
EUROPEAN BAKERIES 125 LAURIER WEST ... MONTREAL **QU** H2T 2N6 (514) 277-5893
EUROPEAN BAKERIES 4595 CHRISTOPHER COLUMBUS ... MONTREAL **QU** H2J 3G7 (514) 527-1249
HOME-MADE KOSHER BAKERY 5483 VICTORIA AVENUE ... MONTREAL **QU** H3W 2P9 (514) 737-1751
HOME-MADE KOSHER BAKERY 1085 BERNARD WEST ... MONTREAL **QU** H2V 1V1 (514) 276-2105
HOME-MADE KOSHER BAKERY 1465 VAN HORNE ... MONTREAL **QU** H2V 1L3 (514) 279-2827
HOME-MADE KOSHER BAKERY 6685 VICTORIA AVENUE ... MONTREAL **QU** H3W 2T2 (514) 733-4141
HOME-MADE KOSHER BAKERY 925 BEAUMONT ... MONTREAL **QU** H2N 1W3 (514) 270-5567
HOME-MADE KOSHER BAKERY 6795 DARLINGTON ... MONTREAL **QU** H3S 2J7 (514) 342-1991
KOSHER QUALITY BAKERY 5855 VICTORIA AVENUE ... MONTREAL **QU** H3W 2R6 (514) 731-7883
KOSHER QUALITY BAKERY 2865 VAN HORNE ... MONTREAL **QU** H3S 1P6 (514) 737-0393
MAISON KADOSH 6690 DARLINGTON ... MONTREAL **QU**
MONTREAL KOSHER 7005 VICTORIA AVENUE ... MONTREAL **QU** H4P 2N9 (514) 739-3651
KORB BAKING COMPANY 508 ARMISTICE BOULEVARD ... PAWTUCKET **RI** 02800 (401) 726-8983
KORB BAKING COMPANY 540 PAWTUCKET AVENUE ... PAWTUCKET **RI** 02800 (401) 421-9273
GUTTIN'S BAKERY 1095 BROAD STREET ... PROVIDENCE **RI** 02906 (401) 781-8929
KORB BAKING COMPANY 1617 WARWICK AVENUE ... WARWICK **RI** 02886 (401) 737-9625
MARI ANGE BAKERY 9790 FONDREN ... HOUSTON **TX** 77096 (713) 988-3079
ORIGINAL NY BAGELS 9724 HILLCROFT ... HOUSTON **TX** 77096 (713) 723-5879
BRENNER BAKERY 1200 E. BELLEVUE-REDMOND ROAD ... BELLEVUE **WA** 98110 (206) 454-0600

BAKERIES - WHOLESALE

IVERSON BAKING CO. P.O. BOX B ... ROGERS **AR** 72756 (501) 636-5904
LENDER'S BAGELS P.O. BOX 869 ... ORANGE **CT** 06477
PARAMOUNT BAKERY 1407 WASHINGTON AVENUE ... MIAMI BEACH **FL** 33139 (305) 534-2683
CRESCENT BAKING CORP. 427 IOWA STREET ... DAVENPORT **IA** 52801 (319) 322-3539
PITA BAKING CO. 6540 W. DIVERSEY AVENUE ... CHICAGO **IL** 60635 (312) 635-0556
RUBSCHLAGER BAKING CORPORATION 3220 WEST GRAND AVENUE ... CHICAGO **IL** 60651 (312) 826-1245
INTERNATIONAL BAKERS SERVICES, INC. 3839 PROGRESS DRIVE ... SOUTH BEND **IN** 46628
ORIGINAL FREEDMAN BAKING CO. 406 HARVARD STREET ... BROOKLINE **MA** 02146 (617) 566-8798
ORIGINAL FREEDMAN BAKING CO. 1655A BEACON STREET ... BROOKLINE **MA** 02146 (617) 734-9250
H & S BAKERY 603 SOUTH BOND ... BALTIMORE **MD** 21231 (301) 276-7254
NATURAL WAY MILLS, INC. ROUTE 2, BOX 37 ... MIDDLE RIVER **MN** 56737 (218) 222-3677
DEER PARK BAKING CO. P.O. BOX 500, S. EGG HARBOR ... HAMMONTOWN **NJ** 08037 (609) 561-2900
PECHTER'S BAGEL CO. 227 MANOR AVENUE ... HARRISON **NJ** 07029 (201) 483-3374
CHRISTINA'S STRUDEL, INC. 322 COMMERCIAL AVENUE ... PALISADES PARK **NJ** 07650 (201) 461-4064
ENTENMANN'S BAKERY INC. 1724 FIFTH AVENUE ... BAY SHORE **NY** 11706 (718) 273-6000
STELLO D'ORO BISCUIT COMPANY 184 WEST 237TH STREET ... BRONX **NY** 10463 (212) 549-3700
BLUE BAKING COMPANY 1003 METROPOLITAN AVENUE ... BROOKLYN **NY** 11232 (718) 782-4245
DAMASCUS BAKERY INC. - MIDDLE EASTERN BREADS & PASTRIES
56 GOLD STREET ... BROOKLYN **NY** 11201 (718) 855-1457
EAST COAST PITA BAKERS 243 26TH STREET ... BROOKLYN **NY** 11232 (718) 499-1818
GREEN & ACKERMAN BAKING CO. 216 ROSS STREET ... BROOKLYN **NY** 11211 (718) 384-2540
J.M.P. BAKERY COMPANY, INC. 508 JUNIUS ... BROOKLYN **NY** 11212 (718) 272-5400
JASON DAIRY PRODUCTS COMPANY 2350 LINDEN BOULEVARD ... BROOKLYN **NY** 11208 (718) 498-1881
KOSHER BAKERS INC. 814 BERGEN STREET ... BROOKLYN **NY** 11238 (718) 857-6464
MOSHA'S PUMPERNICKEL BAKERY 170 WYETH AVENUE ... BROOKLYN **NY** 11211 (718) 638-6100
PALAGONIA ITALIAN BREAD 508 JUNIUS STREET ... BROOKLYN **NY** 11218 (718) 272-5400
PECHTER-FIELD BAKING CORPORATION 800 PACIFIC STREET ... BROOKLYN **NY** 11238 (718) 638-6100
PITA HOUSE BAKERY, INC. 2610 AVENUE U ... BROOKLYN **NY** 11229 (718) 934-4717
POLLACK'S KOSHER COOKIE BAKERY INC. 5007 18TH AVENUE ... BROOKLYN **NY** 11204 (718) 435-3700
REISMAN BROTHERS BAKERY INC. 110 AVENUE O ... BROOKLYN **NY** 11204 (718) 331-1975
SAM'S FAMOUS KOSHER KNISHES 504 BRIGHTON BEACH AVENUE ... BROOKLYN **NY** 11235 (718) 646-5450
NATIONAL BAGEL CO., INC. 3100 N. TRIPHAMMER ... LANSING **NY** 14882 (607) 533-4265
FINK BAKING CORPORATION 5-35 54TH AVENUE ... LONG ISLAND CITY **NY** 11106 (718) 392-8300
ELSAHA BAKERY 100 FAIRGROUNDS DRIVE ... MANLIUS **NY** 13104 (315) 682-2780
THE CAKE STYLISTS, INC. 56-64 58TH PLACE ... MASPETH **NY** 11378 (718) 894-3494
SOVA BAKING CORP. 290 DYCKMAN STREET ... NEW YORK **NY** 10034 (212) 567-4500
BELLACICCO & SONS INC. 217-44 98TH AVENUE ... QUEENS VILLAGE **NY** 11429 (718) 479-5100
RESTIVO BROTHERS BAKERIES 1633 CENTRE STREET ... RIDGEWOOD **NY** 11385 (718) 456-0454
PHILADELPHIA BAKING CO. P.O. BOX 6914 ... PHILADELPHIA **PA** 11915 (215) 464-4242

BANKS

BANK LEUMI LE-ISRAEL B.M. 9731 WILSHIRE BOULEVARD ... BEVERLY HILLS **CA** 90212 (213) 278-7001
ISRAEL DISCOUNT BANK, LTD. 9465 WILSHIRE BOULEVARD ... BEVERLY HILLS **CA** 90212 (213) 275-1411
BANK HAPOALIM B.M. 6501 WILSHIRE BOULEVARD ... LOS ANGELES **CA** 90048 (213) 658-7350
UNITED MIZRAHI BANK 727 WEST SEVENTH STREET ... LOS ANGELES **CA** 90017 (213) 623-7345
ISRAEL DISCOUNT BANK, LTD. 14 N.E. FIRST AVENUE ... MIAMI **FL** 33132 (305) 579-9200
BANK HAPOALIM/MIAMI BRANCH 407 LINCOLN ROAD ... MIAMI BEACH **FL** 33139 (305) 532-4476
BANK LEUMI LE-ISRAEL B.M. 407 LINCOLN ROAD MALL ... MIAMI BEACH **FL** 33139 (305) 531-3378
ISRAEL DISCOUNT BANK, LTD. 420 LINCOLN ROAD ... MIAMI BEACH **FL** 33139 (305) 579-9260

Name / Address	City	State	Zip	Phone
BANK HAPOALIM/CHICAGO BRANCH 174 NORTH MICHIGAN AVENUE	CHICAGO	IL	60601	(312) 621-0800
BANK LEUMI LE-ISRAEL B.M. 100 NORTH LASALLE STREET	CHICAGO	IL	60602	(312) 781-1800
BANK HAPOALIM/BOSTON BRANCH 70 FEDERAL STREET	BOSTON	MA	02110	(617) 482-7440
BANK LEUMI TRUST COMPANY OF NEW YORK 301 EAST FORDHAM ROAD	BRONX	NY	10458	(212) 220-5777
BANK LEUMI TRUST COMPANY OF NEW YORK 1321 KINGS HIGHWAY	BROOKLYN	NY	11229	(718) 998-6500
BANK LEUMI TRUST COMPANY OF NEW YORK 3851 NOSTRAND AVENUE AT AVENUE Z	BROOKLYN	NY	11235	(718) 891-6700
BANK LEUMI TRUST COMPANY OF NEW YORK 4410 13TH AVENUE	BROOKLYN	NY	11219	(718) 854-1800
BANK LEUMI TRUST COMPANY OF NEW YORK 2095 RALPH AVENUE	BROOKLYN	NY	11234	(718) 968-7174
BANK LEUMI TRUST COMPANY OF NEW YORK 188 MONTAGUE STREET	BROOKLYN	NY	11201	(718) 834-4800
BANK LEUMI TRUST COMPANY OF NEW YORK 104-70 QUEENS BOULEVARD	FOREST HILLS	NY	11375	(718) 896-9200
BANK LEUMI TRUST COMPANY OF NEW YORK 121 MIDDLE NECK ROAD	GREAT NECK	NY	11020	(516) 466-6270
BANK LEUMI TRUST COMPANY OF NEW YORK 1280 BROADWAY	HEWLETT	NY	11557	(516) 569-5400
BANK LEUMI TRUST COMPANY OF NEW YORK KENNEDY AIRPORT-EL AL TERMINAL	JAMAICA	NY	11430	(718) 656-4560
BANK HAPOALIM/HUNTINGTON BRANCH 445 BROAD HOLLOW ROAD	MELVILLE	NY	11747	(516) 752-7979
BANK DISCOUNT LE-ISRAEL 511 FIFTH AVENUE	NEW YORK	NY	10017	(212) 551-8500
BANK HAPOALIM B.M. - NEW YORK BRANCH 10 ROCKEFELLER PLAZA	NEW YORK	NY	10020	(212) 397-9650
BANK HAPOALIM B.M., INTERNATIONAL DEPARTMENT 10 ROCKEFELLER PLAZA	NEW YORK	NY	10020	(212) 397-7244
BANK HAPOALIM B.M., LETTERS OF CREDIT 10 ROCKEFELLER PLAZA	NEW YORK	NY	10020	(212) 397-9670
BANK HAPOALIM B.M., MONEY MARKET - OPERATIONS 10 ROCKEFELLER PLAZA	NEW YORK	NY	10020	(212) 397-9602
BANK HAPOALIM B.M., MONEY MARKET - TRADERS 10 ROCKEFELLER PLAZA	NEW YORK	NY	10020	(212) 397-9490
BANK HAPOALIM B.M., MONEY TRANSFER 10 ROCKEFELLER PLAZA	NEW YORK	NY	10020	(212) 397-8354
BANK HAPOALIM B.M., SECURITIES DEPARTMENT 10 ROCKEFELLER PLAZA	NEW YORK	NY	10020	(212) 397-8352
BANK HAPOALIM/ROCKEFELLER CENTER BRANCH 10 ROCKEFELLER PLAZA	NEW YORK	NY	10020	(212) 397-9650
BANK LEUMI LE-ISRAEL B.M. NEW YORK AGENCY 342 MADISON AVENUE	NEW YORK	NY	10017	(212) 850-9500
BANK LEUMI LE-ISRAEL REGIONAL MANAGEMENT 342 MADISON AVENUE	NEW YORK	NY	10017	(212) 850-9500
BANK LEUMI TRUST COMPANY 111 BROADWAY	NEW YORK	NY	10006	(212) 669-0333
BANK LEUMI TRUST COMPANY 1960 BROADWAY	NEW YORK	NY	10023	(212) 362-1443
BANK LEUMI TRUST COMPANY 605 THIRD AVENUE	NEW YORK	NY	10016	(212) 286-0860
BANK LEUMI TRUST COMPANY OF NEW YORK 1660 SECOND AVENUE AT 86TH STREET	NEW YORK	NY	10028	(212) 534-8800
BANK LEUMI TRUST COMPANY OF NEW YORK 1148 THIRD AVENUE AT 67TH STREET	NEW YORK	NY	10021	(212) 570-2800
BANK LEUMI TRUST COMPANY OF NEW YORK 120 BROADWAY	NEW YORK	NY	10006	(212) 602-9320
BANK LEUMI TRUST COMPANY OF NEW YORK 1960 BROADWAY AT LINCOLN SQUARE	NEW YORK	NY	10023	(212) 580-4000
BANK LEUMI TRUST COMPANY OF NEW YORK 845 THIRD AVENUE AT 52ND STREET	NEW YORK	NY	10022	(212) 935-7561
BANK LEUMI TRUST COMPANY OF NEW YORK 579 FIFTH AVENUE AT 47TH STREET	NEW YORK	NY	10017	(212) 382-4407
BANK LEUMI TRUST COMPANY OF NEW YORK 535 SEVENTH AVENUE AT 39TH STREET	NEW YORK	NY	10018	(212) 382-4606
BANK LEUMI TRUST COMPANY OF NEW YORK 605 THIRD AVENUE AT 39TH STREET	NEW YORK	NY	10158	(212) 687-9666
BANK LEUMI TRUST COMPANY OF NEW YORK 301 THIRD AVENUE AT 23RD STREET	NEW YORK	NY	10010	(212) 679-5305
BANK LEUMI TRUST COMPANY OF NEW YORK 85 DELANCEY AT ORCHARD	NEW YORK	NY	10002	(212) 477-1150
BANK LEUMI TRUST COMPANY OF NEW YORK 177 EAST BROADWAY	NEW YORK	NY	10002	(212) 477-1201
BANK LEUMI TRUST COMPANY OF NEW YORK 25 BROAD STREET	NEW YORK	NY	10004	(212) 943-3400
BANK LEUMI TRUST COMPANY OF NEW YORK 111 BROADWAY (NEAR WALL STREET)	NEW YORK	NY	10006	(212) 669-0333
BANK LEUMI TRUST COMPANY OF NEW YORK - BROKERS LOAN 579 FIFTH AVENUE	NEW YORK	NY	10017	(212) 669-0327
BANK LEUMI TRUST COMPANY OF NEW YORK - COMMERCIAL FINANCE 579 FIFTH AVENUE	NEW YORK	NY	10017	(212) 382-4576
BANK LEUMI TRUST COMPANY OF NEW YORK-COMMERCIAL SERVICES 579 FIFTH AVENUE	NEW YORK	NY	10017	(212) 669-0257
BANK LEUMI TRUST COMPANY OF NEW YORK-EXECUTIVE OFFICES 579 FIFTH AVENUE	NEW YORK	NY	10017	(212) 382-4000
BANK LEUMI TRUST COMPANY OF NEW YORK-FOREIGN COLL. DEPT. 579 FIFTH AVENUE	NEW YORK	NY	10017	(212) 382-4070
BANK LEUMI TRUST COMPANY OF NEW YORK-INSTALLMENT LOANS 579 FIFTH AVENUE	NEW YORK	NY	10017	(212) 669-0219
BANK LEUMI TRUST COMPANY OF NEW YORK-LETTERS OF CR-ISSUE 579 FIFTH AVENUE	NEW YORK	NY	10017	(212) 382-4057
BANK LEUMI TRUST COMPANY OF NEW YORK-LETTERS OF CR-PAYMENT 579 FIFTH AVENUE	NEW YORK	NY	10017	(212) 382-4064
BANK LEUMI TRUST COMPANY OF NEW YORK-MONEY MARKET DEPT. 579 FIFTH AVENUE	NEW YORK	NY	10017	(212) 382-4503
BANK LEUMI TRUST COMPANY OF NEW YORK-PERSONNEL DEPT. 579 FIFTH AVENUE	NEW YORK	NY	10017	(212) 382-4451
BANK LEUMI TRUST COMPANY OF NEW YORK-PUBLIC RELATIONS 579 FIFTH AVENUE	NEW YORK	NY	10017	(212) 382-4494
BANK LEUMI TRUST COMPANY OF NEW YORK-TRUST DEPARTMENT 579 FIFTH AVENUE	NEW YORK	NY	10017	(212) 943-3613
BANK LEUMI TRUST COMPANY, COLLECTION DEPARTMENT 111 BROADWAY	NEW YORK	NY	10006	(212) 669-0200
ISRAEL DISCOUNT BANK OF N.Y. (MAIN OFFICE-COLLECTIONS) 511 FIFTH AVENUE	NEW YORK	NY	10017	(212) 551-8598

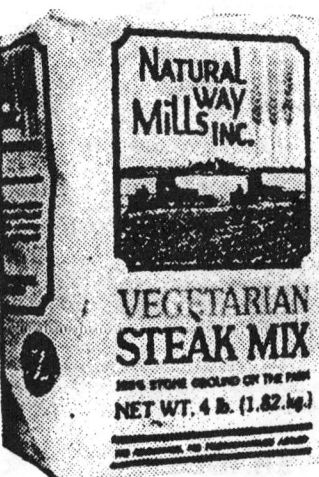

ISRAEL DISCOUNT BANK OF N.Y. (MAIN OFFICE-CREDIT INQUIRIES)
511 FIFTH AVENUE ... NEW YORK **NY** 10017 (212) 551-8573
ISRAEL DISCOUNT BANK OF N.Y. (MAIN OFFICE-ISRAEL INFO.)
511 FIFTH AVENUE ... NEW YORK **NY** 10017 (212) 551-8702
ISRAEL DISCOUNT BANK OF N.Y. (MAIN OFFICE-MONEY DESK)
511 FIFTH AVENUE ... NEW YORK **NY** 10017 (212) 551-8648
ISRAEL DISCOUNT BANK OF N.Y. (MAIN OFFICE-PERSONNEL)
511 FIFTH AVENUE ... NEW YORK **NY** 10017 (212) 551-8664
ISRAEL DISCOUNT BANK OF N.Y. (MAIN OFFICE-COMMERCIAL LOANS)
511 FIFTH AVENUE ... NEW YORK **NY** 10017 (212) 551-8532
ISRAEL DISCOUNT BANK OF N.Y. (MAIN OFFICE-INSTALLMENT LOANS)
511 FIFTH AVENUE ... NEW YORK **NY** 10017 (212) 551-8728
ISRAEL DISCOUNT BANK OF N.Y. (MAIN OFFICE-LETTERS OF CREDIT)
511 FIFTH AVENUE ... NEW YORK **NY** 10017 (212) 551-8590
ISRAEL DISCOUNT BANK OF N.Y. (MAIN OFFICE-MONEY TRANSFERS)
511 FIFTH AVENUE ... NEW YORK **NY** 10017 (212) 551-8617
ISRAEL DISCOUNT BANK OF N.Y. (MAIN OFFICE-NEW ACCOUNTS)
511 FIFTH AVENUE ... NEW YORK **NY** 10017 (212) 551-8709
ISRAEL DISCOUNT BANK OF NEW YORK 511 FIFTH AVENUE ... NEW YORK **NY** 10017 (212) 551-8500
ISRAEL DISCOUNT BANK OF NEW YORK 1350 BROADWAY ... NEW YORK **NY** 10018 (212) 551-8750
ISRAEL DISCOUNT BANK OF NEW YORK (MAIN OFFICE)
511 FIFTH AVENUE ... NEW YORK **NY** 10017 (212) 551-8500
NORTH AMERICAN BANK (TEL AVIV) 608 FIFTH AVENUE SUITE 403 ... NEW YORK **NY** 10020 (212) 245-2430
UMB BANK & TRUST COMPANY 630 FIFTH AVENUE ... NEW YORK **NY** 10020 (212) 541-8070
UMB BANK & TRUST COMPANY ONE WORLD TRADE CENTER ... NEW YORK **NY** 10048 (212) 466-1114
UMB BANK & TRUST COMPANY 350 FIFTH AVENUE ... NEW YORK **NY** 10118 (212) 947-3611
BANK LEUMI TRUST COMPANY OF NEW YORK
1105 OLD COUNTRY ROAD ... PLAINVIEW **NY** 11803 (516) 935-4800
BANK HAPOALIM B M - QUEENS BRANCH 97-77 QUEENS BOULEVARD .. REGO PARK **NY** 11374 (718) 544-7900
BANK HAPOALIM/QUEENS BRANCH 97-77 QUEENS BOULEVARD ... REGO PARK **NY** 11374 (718) 544-7900
BANK LEUMI TRUST COMPANY OF NEW YORK
97-03 QUEENS BOULEVARD ... REGO PARK **NY** 11374 (718) 896-7300
BANK HAPOALIM B.M. 1 FIRST CANADIAN PLACE, SUITE 2575,
P.O. BOX 35 ... TORONTO **ON** M5X 1A9 (416) 362-1441
BANK LEUMI LE-ISRAEL 3055 BATHURST STREET ... TORONTO **ON** M6B 3B7 (416) 789-7981
BANK LEUMI TRUST CO. OF N.Y. 2 FIRST CANADIAN PLACE, SUITE 842 ... TORONTO **ON** M5X 1E3 (416) 869-0875
ISRAEL DISCOUNT BANK OF CANADA 150 BLOOR STREET WEST,
SUITE M100 ... TORONTO **ON** M5S 2Y5 (416) 926-7200
UNITED MIZRACHI BANK 330 BAY STREET, SUITE 708 ... TORONTO **ON** M5H 2S8 (416) 947-0510
BANK HAPOALIM B.M. 3 PENN CENTER PLAZA ... PHILADELPHIA **PA** 19102 (215) 665-2200
BANK HAPOALIM/PHILADELPHIA BRANCH 3 PENN CENTER PLAZA .. PHILADELPHIA **PA** 19102 (215) 665-2200
BANK LEUMI LE-ISRAEL B.M. 1511 WALNUT STREET ... PHILADELPHIA **PA** 19102 (215) 299-4400

BET DIN - JEWISH COURT

RABBINICAL ASSEMBLY-WESTERN STATES REGION
C/O UNIVERSITY OF JUDAISM, 15600 MULHOLLAND DRIVE ... LOS ANGELES **CA** 90077 (213) 476-9777
JEWISH CONCILIATION BOARD 163 SOUTH FAIRFAX AVENUE ... LOS ANGELES **CA** 90036 (213) 938-6271
BETH DIN, JEWISH COURT & ARBITRATION COMMITTEE
1850 ORTEGA STREET ... SAN FRANCISCO **CA** 94122 (415) 661-4055
BET DIN - RABBI DR. TIBOR H. STERN 1532 WASHINGTON AVENUE ... MIAMI BEACH **FL** 33139 (305) 534-1004
BET DIN C/O RABBI DAVID LEHRFIELD 1400 LENOX AVENUE ... MIAMI BEACH **FL** 33139 (305) 672-0894
BET DIN 5718 N. DRAKE AVENUE ... CHICAGO **IL** 60659 (312) 588-4252
BET DIN ZEDEK 2735 WEST DEVON ... CHICAGO **IL** 60659 (312) 764-0259
SYNAGOGUE COUNCIL OF MASSACHUSETTS 177 TREMONT STREET ... BOSTON **MA** 02115 (617) 426-1832
JEWISH BOARD OF ARBITRATION 319 WEST MONUMENT ... BALTIMORE **MD** 21201 (301) 752-2630
SUPREME RABBINIC COURT OF AMERICA 1401 ARCOLA AVENUE ... SILVER SPRING **MD** 20902 (301) 649-2799
RABBINIC COURT OF EAST FLATBUSH 333 EAST 52ND STREET ... BROOKLYN **NY** 11203 (718) 498-2801
RABBINICAL COURT OF BROOKLYN 1447 56TH STREET ... BROOKLYN **NY** 11219 (718) 851-2626
RABBINICAL COURT OF BROOKLYN 5424 16TH AVENUE ... BROOKLYN **NY** 11204 (718) 633-6378
BETH DIN OF AMERICA 275 SEVENTH AVENUE ... NEW YORK **NY** 10001 (212) 807-9042
BETH DIN OF THE U.S.A. 220 PARK AVENUE S. ... NEW YORK **NY** 10003 (212) 677-4030
JEWISH CONCILIATION BOARD OF AMERICA
120 W. 57TH STREET, SUITE 2600 ... NEW YORK **NY** 10019 (212) 582-3577
RABBINICAL ASSEMBLY 3080 BROADWAY ... NEW YORK **NY** 10027 (212) 678-8000
RABBINICAL COURT OF THE RABBINICAL ALLIANCE OF AMERICA
156 FIFTH AVENUE, ROOM 810 ... NEW YORK **NY** 10011 (212) 242-6420
BET DIN C/O RABBI PELBERG 904 WEST DUNCANNON STREET ... PHILADELPHIA **PA** 19140 (215) 745-4292
BETH DIN-RABBINICAL COURT 7926 ALGON AVENUE ... PHILADELPHIA **PA** 19111 (215) 722-6161
BET DIN C/O RABBI JOSEPH RADINSKY - UNITED ORTHODOX SYNAGOGUES
9001 GREENWILLOW ... HOUSTON **TX** 77096 (713) 723-3850

BEVERAGES

MAYIM CHAIM BEVERAGE CORP. 626 WITTIER AVENUE ... BRONX **NY** 10450 (212) 378-2525
CORNELL BEVERAGES INC. 105 HARRISON PLACE ... BROOKLYN **NY** 11237 (718) 381-3000
CROWN BEVERAGE CORP. 458 COZINE AVENUE ... BROOKLYN **NY** 11208 (718) 257-2320

BIG BROTHER/BIG SISTER ORGANIZATIONS

JEWISH BIG BROTHERS ASSOCIATION 6505 WILSHIRE BOULEVARD,
#417 ... LOS ANGELES **CA** 90048 (213) 653-3630
JEWISH BIG BROTHERS ASSOCIATION 6851 LENNOX AVENUE ... VAN NUYS **CA** 91405 (818) 785-8861
JEWISH BIG SISTERS 2451 NORTH SACRAMENTO ... CHICAGO **IL** 60647
JEWISH BIG BROTHER ASSOCIATION OF BOSTON
31 NEW CHARDON STREET ... BOSTON **MA** 02110 (617) 367-5818
BIG BROTHER LEAGUE OF BALTIMORE 5750 PARK HEIGHTS AVENUE .. BALTIMORE **MD** 21215 (301) 542-6300
JEWISH BIG BROTHER & BIG SISTER LEAGUE
5750 PARK HEIGHTS AVENUE ... BALTIMORE **MD** 21215 (301) 466-4242
BIG BROTHER OF JEWISH FAMILY SERVICE 20 BANTA PLACE ... HACKENSACK **NJ** 07601 (201) 488-8340
JEWISH BIG BROTHERS OF THE JEWISH BOARD OF GUARDIANS
120 WEST 57TH STREET ... NEW YORK **NY** 10019 (212) 582-9100
BIG BROTHER ASSOCIATION OF CINCINNATI 1580 SUMMIT ROAD ... CINCINNATI **OH** 45237 (513) 761-3200
THE JEWISH BIG BROTHERS AND BIG SISTERS ASSOCIATION
22001 FAIRMONT BOULEVARD ... CLEVELAND **OH** 44118 (216) 932-2800

BIKUR CHOLIM SOCIETIES

BIKUR CHOLIM SHEVET ACHIM 278 WINTHROP AVENUE ... NEW HAVEN **CT** 06502 (203) 776-4997
BIKUR CHOLIM LODGE 1400 S. DES PLAINES AVENUE ... FOREST PARK **IL** 60130 (312) 366-4541
BIKUR CHOLIM 22 MARKET STREET ... PASSAIC **NJ** 07055
BIKUR CHOLIM MEDICAL OFFICE 566 BEDFORD AVENUE ... BROOKLYN **NY** 11211
BIKUR CHOLIM MEDICAL OFFICE 281 MARCY AVENUE ... BROOKLYN **NY** 11211
BIKUR CHOLIM OF BORO PARK 1102 52ND STREET ... BROOKLYN **NY** 11219 (718) 438-2020
BIKUR CHOLIM OF REMSEN VILLAGE 9202 AVENUE A ... BROOKLYN **NY** 11236 (718) 338-6230
BIKUR CHOLIM VISITING SICK SOCIETY OF BROOKLYN
8656 21ST AVENUE ... BROOKLYN **NY** 11230 (718) 372-8848
BIKUR CHOLIM OF THE STATE OF NEW YORK 260 BROADWAY ... BROOKLYN **NY** 11211 (718) 387-3876
KUPATH CHOLIM 372 KINGSTON AVENUE ... BROOKLYN **NY** 11213 (718) 604-0900
KUPATH CHOLIM 1277 55TH STREET ... BROOKLYN **NY** 11210 (718) 438-2367
TZIVOS HASHEM HOSPITAL VISITATIONS 770 EASTERN PARKWAY ... BROOKLYN **NY** 11213 (718) 467-6991
UNITED BIKUR CHOLIM OF WILLIAMSBURG 260 BROADWAY ... BROOKLYN **NY** 11211 (718) 387-4517
UNITED BIKUR CHOLIM OF WILLIAMSBURG 260 BROADWAY ... BROOKLYN **NY** 11211 (718) 387-4517
UNITED BIKUR CHOLIM OF WILLIAMSBURG 80 LEE AVENUE ... BROOKLYN **NY** 11211 (718) 387-4517
BIALYSTOKER CENTER & BIKUR CHOLIM 228 EAST BROADWAY ... NEW YORK **NY** 10002 (212) 475-7755
BIKUR CHOLIM 12 REDDICK COURT ... TORONTO **ON** M6B 2S5 (416) 787-9538
BIKUR HOLIM DAVID & JEROME ROADS ... TREVOSE **PA** 19047 (215) 357-7131
BIKUR CHOLIM 5145 S. MORGAN STREET ... SEATTLE **WA** 98102 (206) 723-0970
SEPHARDIC BIKUR CHOLIM 6500 52ND STREET ... SEATTLE **WA** 98118 (206) 723-9661

BLIND, HOMES & ORGANIZATIONS FOR THE

CHICAGO RABBINICAL COUNCIL 3525 PETERSON AVENUE ... CHICAGO **IL** 60659 (312) 588-1600
HOME OF THE ASSOCIATION OF JEWISH BLIND 3525 WEST FOSTER ... CHICAGO **IL** 60625 (312) 478-7040
NEW YORK INSTITUTE FOR THE EDUCATION OF THE BLIND
999 PELHAM PARKWAY ... BRONX **NY** 10469 (212) 547-1234
AMERICAN-ISRAELI LIGHTHOUSE 30 EAST 60TH STREET ... NEW YORK **NY** 10023 (212) 838-5322
JEWISH BRAILLE INSTITUTE OF AMERICA 110 EAST 30TH STREET ... NEW YORK **NY** 10016 (212) 889-2525
JEWISH BRAILLE REVIEW (PUBLICATION) 110 EAST 30TH STREET ... NEW YORK **NY** 10016 (212) 889-2525
JEWISH GUILD FOR THE BLIND 15 W. 65TH STREET ... NEW YORK **NY** 10023 (212) 595-2000
KEREN-OR JERUSALEM INSTITUTE FOR THE BLIND, INC.
1133 BROADWAY ... NEW YORK **NY** 10010 (212) 255-1180
JEWISH GUILD FOR THE BLIND HOME 75 STRATTON STREET ... YONKERS **NY** 10701 (914) 963-4661

B'NAI B'RITH HILLEL FOUNDATIONS

AUBURN UNIVERSITY-B'NAI B'RITH HILLEL COUNSELORSHIP
442 CARY DRIVE ... AUBURN **AL** 36830 (205) 887-9550
UNIVERSITY OF ALABAMA IN BIRMINGHAM, HILLEL AFFILIATE
C/O HESSE, 3824 HALBROOK LANE ... BIRMINGHAM **AL** 35243 (205) 969-2801
UNIVERSITY OF ALABAMA-B'NAI B'RITH HILLEL FOUNDATION
728 10TH AVENUE ... TUSCALOOSA **AL** 35401 (205) 758-3280
UNIVERSITY OF ARKANSAS FOREIGN LANGUAGE DEPARTMENT ... FAYETTEVILLE **AR** 72701 (501) 575-2951
UNIVERSITY OF ALBERTA 11036 88TH AVENUE ... EDMONTON **AT** T6G 0Z2 (403) 432-5166
NORTHERN ARIZONA UNIVERSITY-HILLEL C.U. BOX 15036 ... FLAGSTAFF **AZ** 86011 (602) 523-3163
ARIZONA STATE UNIVERSITY-B'NAI B'RITH HILLEL FOUNDATION
1012 SOUTH MILL ... TEMPE **AZ** 85281 (602) 967-7563
PHOENIX COLLEGE-B'NAI B'RITH HILLEL COUNSELORSHIP
1012 SOUTH MILL ... TEMPE **AZ** 85281 (602) 967-7563
UNIVERSITY OF ARIZONA-B'NAI B'RITH HILLEL FOUNDATION
1245 E. 2ND STREET, BOX 40523 ... TUCSON **AZ** 85719 (602) 624-6561
UNIV. OF BRIT. COL.-VANCOUVER B'NAI B'RITH HILLEL FOUNDATION
BOX 43 SUB, UBC ... VANCOUVER **BC** V6T 1W5 (604) 224-4748
UNIV. OF CALIFORNIA-BERKELEY-B'NAI B'RITH HILLEL FOUNDATION
2736 BANCROFT WAY ... BERKELEY **CA** 94704 (415) 845-7793
CALIFORNIA STATE UNIV./CHICO-JEWISH STUDENT UNION
BMU CHICO STATE ... CHICO **CA** 95929 (916) 895-6774
CLAREMONT COLLEGES-HILLEL AT THE CLAREMONT COLLEGES
MCALISTER, 919 N. COLUMBIA ... CLAREMONT **CA** 91711 (714) 621-8000
UNIV. OF CALIFORNIA-DAVIS-B'NAI B'RITH HILLEL COUNSELORSHIP
328 A STREET ... DAVIS **CA** 95616 (916) 756-3708
CALIFORNIA STATE UNIVER./FRESNO-B'NAI B'RITH HILLEL COUNSEL.
POST OFFICE BOX 1328 ... FRESNO **CA** 93710 (209) 264-2929
UNIV. OF CALIF.-SANTA BARBARA-B'NAI B'RITH HILLEL FOUNDATION
URC. 770 CAMINO PESCADERO ... GOLETA **CA** 93117 (805) 968-1555
CALIFORNIA STATE UNIV./HAYWARD-HILLEL EXTENSION CSU ... HAYWARD **CA** 94542 (415) 845-7793
CALIFORNIA STATE UNIV./LONG BEACH-JEWISH STUDENT SERVICES
JCC 3801 E. WILLOW ... LONG BEACH **CA** 90815 (213) 426-7601
CERRITOS COMMUNITY COLLEGE-JEWISH COLLEGE STUDENT SERVICE
JCC 3801 E. WILLOW ... LONG BEACH **CA** 90815 (213) 426-7601
CYPRESS COLLEGE-JEWISH COLLEGE STUDENT SERVICES
JCC 3801 E. WILLOW ... LONG BEACH **CA** 90815 (213) 426-7601
LONG BEACH CITY COLLEGE-JEWISH COLLEGE STUDENT SERVICES
JCC 3801 E. WILLOW ... LONG BEACH **CA** 90815 (213) 426-7601
CALIFORNIA STATE UNIV./DOMINGUEZ HILLS-SOUTH BAY HILLEL
C/O LAHC 900 HILGARD AVENUE ... LOS ANGELES **CA** 90024 (213) 208-4427
CALIFORNIA STATE UNIV./LOS ANGELES-HILLEL EXTENSION
5151 STATE COLLEGE DRIVE ... LOS ANGELES **CA** 90032 (213) 224-0111
EL CAMINO COLLEGE-SOUTH BAY HILLEL
C/O LAHC, 900 HILGARD AVENUE ... LOS ANGELES **CA** 90024 (213) 208-4427

LOS ANGELES HARBOR COLLEGE-SOUTH BAY HILLEL
C/O LAHC, 900 HILGARD AVENUE ... LOS ANGELES **CA** 90024 (213) 208-4427

LOS ANGELES HILLEL COUNCIL 900 HILGARD AVENUE ... LOS ANGELES **CA** 90024 (213) 208-6639

LOS ANGELES PIERCE COLLEGE-HILLEL EXTENSION
C/O LAHC, 900 HILGARD AVENUE ... LOS ANGELES **CA** 90024 (213) 208-4427

LOYOLA MARYMOUNT U.-S. BAY HILLEL/JEWISH LAW STUDENT ASSOC.
C/O LAHC, 900 HILGARD AVENUE ... LOS ANGELES **CA** 90024 (213) 208-4427

OCCIDENTAL COLLEGE-HILLEL EXTENSION 1600 CAMPUS ROAD ... LOS ANGELES **CA** 90041 (213) 259-2621

SANTA MONICA COLLEGE-HILLEL EXTENSION
C/O LAHC, 900 HILGARD AVENUE ... LOS ANGELES **CA** 90024 (213) 208-4427

SOUTHWESTERN LAW SCHOOL-JEWISH LAW STUDENTS ASSOCIATION
C/O LAHC, 900 HILGARD AVENUE ... LOS ANGELES **CA** 90024 (213) 208-4427

UCLA-B'NAI B'RITH HILLEL FOUNDATION 900 HILGARD AVENUE ... LOS ANGELES **CA** 90024 (213) 208-3081

UNIV. OF CALIFORNIA-L.A.-B'NAI B'RITH HILLEL FOUNDATION
900 HILGARD AVENUE ... LOS ANGELES **CA** 90024 (213) 208-3081

UNIV. OF SOUTHERN. CAL.-B'NAI B'RITH HILLEL FOUNDATION
3300 S. HOOVER BLVD ... LOS ANGELES **CA** 90035 (213) 747-9135

WHITTIER SCHOOL OF LAW-JEWISH LAW STUDENTS ASSOCIATION
C/O LAHC, 900 HILGARD AVENUE ... LOS ANGELES **CA** 90024 (213) 208-4427

CALIFORNIA STATE UNIV./NORTHRIDGE-B'NAI B'RITH HILLEL FOUND.
17729 PLUMMER STREET ... NORTHRIDGE **CA** 91325 (818) 886-5101

MILLS COLLEGE-HILLEL EXTENSION 5000 MACARTHUR BLVD ... OAKLAND **CA** 94613 (415) 845-7793

CALIFORNIA INSTITUTE OF TECHNOLOGY-HILLEL EXTENSION
1201 E. CALIFORNIA ... PASADENA **CA** 91109 (818) 356-6811

PASADENA CITY COLLEGE-HILLEL EXTENSION 1570 E. COLORADO ... PASADENA **CA** 91106 (818) 578-7391

UNIVERSITY OF REDLANDS-JEWISH STUDENT GROUP
COUNTY CENTER, 1200 E. COLTON AVENUE ... REDLANDS **CA** 92373 (714) 793-2121

UNIV. OF CALIF.-RIVERSIDE-B'NAI B'RITH HILLEL COUNSELORSHIP
2532 GONZAGA LANE ... RIVERSIDE **CA** 92507 (714) 682-6341

CALIFORNIA STATE UNIV./SAN BERNARDINO-HILLEL
6000 STATE COLLEGE PARKWAY ... SAN BERNARDINO **CA** 92404

SAN DIEGO STATE UNIVERSITY-JEWISH CAMPUS CENTERS
5742 MONTEZUMA ROAD ... SAN DIEGO **CA** 92115 (619) 583-6080

UNIV. OF CALIFORNIA-SAN DIEGO-JEWISH CAMPUS CENTERS
OFFICE OF RELIGIOUS AFFAIRS, UCSD ... SAN DIEGO **CA** 92037 (619) 452-2521

SAN FRANCISCO STATE UNIV.-B'NAI B'RITH HILLEL FOUNDATION
33 BANBURY DRIVE ... SAN FRANCISCO **CA** 94132 (415) 333-4922

SAN JOSE STATE UNIV.-B'NAI B'RITH HILLEL COUNSELORSHIP
300 S. 10TH STREET ... SAN JOSE **CA** 95112 (408) 294-8311

UNIVERSITY OF SANTA CLARA-HILLEL EXTENSION 300 S. 10TH STREET .. SAN JOSE **CA** 95112 (408) 267-2770

UNIV. OF CALIFORNIA-SANTA CRUZ-JEWISH STUDENT COALITION
TEMPLE BETH-EL, 920 BAY STREET ... SANTA CRUZ **CA** 95060 (408) 423-3012

STANFORD UNIVERSITY-B'NAI B'RITH HILLEL FOUNDATION
OLD UNION CLUBHOUSE, BOX Y ... STANFORD **CA** 94305 (415) 723-1602

CALIFORNIA STATE UNIV./FULLERTON-JEWISH STUDENT PROGRAM
13411 CROMWELL DRIVE ... TUSTIN **CA** 92680 (714) 838-2825

UNIV. OF CALIFORNIA-IRVINE-JEWISH STUDENT PROGRAM
13411 CROMWELL DRIVE ... TUSTIN **CA** 92680 (714) 838-2825

LOS ANGELES VALLEY COLLEGE-B'NAI B'RITH HILLEL FOUNDATION
13162 BURBANK BLVD ... VAN NUYS **CA** 91401 (818) 994-7443

WHITTIER COLLEGE-HILLEL EXTENSION 13500 PHILADELPHIA STREET ... WHITTIER **CA** 90608 (213) 693-0771

UNIV. OF COLORADO-B'NAI B'RITH HILLEL FOUNDATION
2795 COLORADO AVENUE ... BOULDER **CO** 80302 (303) 442-6571

UNIVERSITY OF DENVER 1959 SOUTH COLUMBINE ... DENVER **CO** 80210 (303) 777-2773

COLORADO STATE UNIVERSITY 406 WEST LAUREL AVENUE ... FORT COLLINS **CO** 80521 (303) 493-7052

UNIV. OF NORTH. COLORADO-B'NAI B'RITH HILLEL COUNSELORSHIP
STUDENT CENTER ... GREELEY **CO** 80639 (303) 394-2001

UNIV. OF BRIDGEPORT-B'NAI B'RITH HILLEL COUNSELORSHIP
174 UNIVERSITY AVENUE ... BRIDGEPORT **CT** 06601 (203) 576-4532

TRINITY COLLEGE-B'NAI B'RITH HILLEL COUNSELORSHIP
30 CRESCENT STREET ... HARTFORD **CT** 06106 (213) 527-3151

UNIVERSITY OF HARTFORD-JEWISH STUDENT UNION
BOX 3027 TRINITY COLLEGE ... HARTFORD **CT** 06106 (213) 527-3151

WESLEYAN UNIVERSITY-HAVURAH
C/O DEPARTMENT OF RELIGION ... MIDDLETOWN **CT** 06457 (203) 347-9411

CENTRAL CONNECTICUT STATE COLLEGE JCC OF HARTFORD ... NEW BRITAIN **CT** 06053 (203) 236-4571

YALE UNIVERSITY-B'NAI B'RITH HILLEL FOUNDATION
1904A YALE STATION ... NEW HAVEN **CT** 06520 (203) 432-4174

CONNECTICUT COLLEGE-CONNECTICUT COLLEGE CHAVURAH
C/O JEWISH FEDERATION, 300 STATE STREET ... NEW LONDON **CT** 06320 (203) 432-0667

U.S. COAST GUARD ACADEMY-CONNECTICUT COLLEGE CHAVURAH
C/O JEWISH FEDERATION, 300 STATE STREET ... NEW LONDON **CT** 06320 (203) 432-0667

UNIV. OF CONNECTICUT-B'NAI B'RITH HILLEL FOUNDATION
54 N. EAGLEVILLE ROAD ... STORRS **CT** 06268 (203) 429-9007

AMERICAN UNIVERSITY-B'NAI B'RITH HILLEL FOUNDATION
KAY SPIRITUAL LIFE CENTER/AU ... WASHINGTON **DC** 20016 (202) 885-3322

ANTIOCH LAW SCHOOL-JEWISH COMMUNITY CAUCUS
2633 16TH STREET N.W. BOX 159 ... WASHINGTON **DC** 20009 (202) 468-3422

CATHOLIC UNIVERSITY-HILLEL COMMUNITY CAMPUS MINISTRY ... WASHINGTON **DC** 20064 (202) 483-3422

GALLAUDET COLLEGE-B'NAI B'RITH HILLEL COUNSELORSHIP
CAMPUS MINISTRIES/GALLAUDET 125 ELY CENTER ... WASHINGTON **DC** 20002 (202) 651-5347

GEORGE WASHINGTON UNIVERSITY 2025 EYE STREET NORTHWEST,
SUITE 1002 ... WASHINGTON **DC** 20006 (202) 296-8873

GEORGETOWN UNIVERSITY-HILLEL-JSA
CAMPUS MINISTRIES-ONE HEALY ... WASHINGTON **DC** 20057 (202) 625-2694

INTERNATIONAL OFFICE 1640 RHODE ISLAND AVENUE, N.W. ... WASHINGTON **DC** 20036 (202) 857-6560

WASHINGTON, D.C.-JEWISH CAMPUS ACTIVITIES BOARD
2129 F STREET, N.W. ... WASHINGTON **DC** 20037 (202) 333-5923

UNIV. OF DELAWARE 64 EAST MAIN STREET, 2ND FLOOR ... NEWARK **DE** 19711 (302) 453-0479

FLORIDA ATLANTIC UNIVERSITY-HILLEL EXTENSION
UNITED CAMPUS MINISTRY SSB212 ... BOCA RATON **FL** 33431 (305) 393-3510

MIAMI/FLORIDA-B'NAI B'RITH HILLEL FOUNDATIONS OF GR. MIAMI
1100 STANFORD DRIVE ... CORAL GABLES **FL** 33146 (305) 661-8549

UNIVERSITY OF MIAMI-B'NAI B'RITH HILLEL FOUNDATION
1100 STANFORD DRIVE ... CORAL GABLES **FL** 33146 (305) 665-6948

BROWARD COMMUNITY COLLEGE-B'NAI B'RITH HILLEL EXTENSION
(3 CAMPUSES) ... FORT LAUDERDALE **FL** 33301

UNIVERSITY OF FLORIDA-B'NAI B'RITH HILLEL FOUNDATION
16 NW 18TH STREET ... GAINESVILLE **FL** 32603 (904) 372-2900

JACKSONVILLE UNIVERSITY 1415 LASALLE STREET ... JACKSONVILLE **FL** 32207 (904) 396-2941

FLORIDA SOUTHERN COLLEGE-HILLEL ... LAKELAND **FL** 33803

UNIVERSITY OF NORTH FLORIDA-B'NAI B'RITH HILLEL EXTENSION
11136 RIVER CK.DR.W ... MANDARIN **FL** 32217 (904) 268-7649

FLORIDA INT'L UNIVERSITY-B'NAI B'RITH HILLEL FOUNDATION
F.I.U. TAMIAMI TRAIL ... MIAMI **FL** 33199 (305) 554-2215

MIAMI-DADE COMMUNITY COLLEGE, NO.
11380 NORTHWEST 27TH AVENUE ... MIAMI **FL** 33167 (305) 685-4477

MIAMI-DADE COMMUNITY COLLEGE, SO.
11011 SOUTHWEST 104TH STREET ... MIAMI **FL** 33176 (305) 554-2215

BARRY UNIVERSITY-HILLEL JEWISH STUDENT UNION
11300 N.E. SECOND AVENUE ... MIAMI SHORES **FL** 33161 (305) 758-3392

UNIVERSITY OF CENTRAL FLORIDA-B'NAI B'RITH HILLEL EXTENSION
P.O. BOX 26, 279 ... ORLANDO **FL** 32816 (305) 275-2233

COLLEGE OF BOCA RATON-HILLEL: JSU 10371 FAIRWAY ROAD ... PEMBROKE PINES **FL** 33026 (305) 432-6281

FLORIDA INT'L UNIVERSITY NORTH-HILLEL JSU
10371 FAIRWAY ROAD ... PEMBROKE PINES **FL** 33026 (305) 432-6287

PALM BEACH JUNIOR COLLEGE-HILLEL JSU
10371 FAIRWAY ROAD ... PEMBROKE PINES **FL** 33026 (305) 432-6281

UNIVERSITY OF S. FLORIDA/NEW COLLEGE-HILLEL EXTENSION
5700 N. TAMIAMI TRAIL, BOX 526 ... SARASOTA **FL** 33580 (813) 355-7671

ECKERD COLLEGE-HILLEL JEWISH STUDENT UNION
ECKERD COLLEGE-BOX J ... ST. PETERSBURG **FL** 33733 (813) 867-1166

FLORIDA STATE UNIVERSITY-B'NAI B'RITH HILLEL FOUNDATION
843 W. PENSACOLA STREET ... TALLAHASSEE **FL** 32304 (904) 222-5454

UNIVERSITY OF SOUTH FLORIDA USF CENTER, BOX 2382 ... TAMPA **FL** 33620 (813) 988-7076

UNIVERSITY OF TAMPA U. OF TAMPA. BOX 2794 ... TAMPA **FL** 33606 (813) 988-7076

ROLLINS COLLEGE-JEWISH STUDENT LEAGUE
PO BOX 2666 ROLLINS COLLEGE ... WINTER PARK **FL** 32789 (305) 646-2000

UNIVERSITY OF GEORGIA-B'NAI B'RITH HILLEL FOUNDATION
1155 S. MILLEDGE AVENUE ... ATHENS **GA** 30605 (404) 543-6393

EMORY UNIVERSITY-B'NAI B'RITH HILLEL FOUNDATION
DRAWER A. EMORY UNIVERSITY ... ATLANTA **GA** 30329 (404) 727-6490

GEORGIA STATE UNIVERSITY-B'NAI B'RITH HILLEL EXTENSION
DRAWER A. EMORY UNIVERSITY ... ATLANTA **GA** 30329 (404) 727-6490

GEORGIA TECHNICAL INSTITUTE-B'NAI B'RITH HILLEL EXTENSION
DRAWER A. EMORY UNIVERSITY ... ATLANTA **GA** 30329 (404) 727-6490

OGLETHORPE UNIVERSITY-B'NAI B'RITH HILLEL EXTENSION
DRAWER A. EMORY UNIVERSITY ... ATLANTA **GA** 30329 (404) 727-6490

IOWA STATE UNIVERSITY-B'NAI B'RITH HILLEL COUNSELORSHIP
C/O DEPT. OF ZOOLOGY-601 SCI 2 ... AMES **IA** 50011 (515) 294-1309

DRAKE UNIVERSITY-B'NAI B'RITH HILLEL COUNSELORSHIP
3303 UNIVERSITY ... DES MOINES **IA** 50311 (515) 274-5769

GRINNELL COLLEGE GRINNELL COLLEGE FORUM ... GRINNELL **IA** 50112 (515) 236-2552

UNIVERSITY OF IOWA-B'NAI B'RITH HILLEL FOUNDATION
122 E. MARKET STREET ... IOWA CITY **IA** 52240 (319) 338-0778

SOUTHERN ILLINOIS UNIVERSITY 913 SOUTH ILLINOIS,
P.O. BOX 3336 ... CARBONDALE **IL** 62902 (618) 529-1306

UNIV. OF ILLINOIS AT CHAMPAIGN-B'NAI B'RITH HILLEL FOUND.
503 E. JOHN STREET ... CHAMPAIGN **IL** 61820 (217) 344-1328

CHICAGO/ILLINOIS-B'NAI B'RITH HILLEL FOUNDATIONS, JEWISH FD.
ONE SOUTH FRANKLIN ST., COLLEGE AGE YOUTH SERVICES OF IL ... CHICAGO **IL** 60606 (312) 346-6700

LOYOLA UNIVERSITY-LOYOLA JEWISH STUDENT ORGANIZATION
ASSISI CENTER, 1132 W. LOYOLA ... CHICAGO **IL** 60626 (312) 274-3000

UNIV. OF ILLINOIS AT CHICAGO-B'NAI B'RITH HILLEL FOUNDATION
516 CCC UNIV. OF ILLINOIS CIRCLE CAMPUS ... CHICAGO **IL** 60680 (312) 996-3385

UNIVERSITY OF CHICAGO-B'NAI B'RITH HILLEL FOUNDATION
5715 S. WOODLAWN AVENUE ... CHICAGO **IL** 60637 (312) 752-1127

NORTHERN ILLINOIS UNIVERSITY-B'NAI B'RITH HILLEL FOUNDATION
JCC 820 RUSSELL ROAD ... DEKALB **IL** 60115 (815) 758-4582

OAKTON COMMUNITY COLLEGE-GESHER 1600 EAST GOLF ROAD ... DES PLAINES **IL** 60016 (312) 635-1600

NORTHWESTERN UNIVERSITY-B'NAI B'RITH HILLEL FOUNDATION
1935 SHERMAN AVENUE ... EVANSTON **IL** 60201 (312) 328-0650

WESTERN ILLINOIS UNIVERSITY 349 SEAL HALL ... MACOMB **IL** 61455 (309) 295-2917

ILLINOIS STATE UNIVERSITY-B'NAI B'RITH HILLEL COUNSELORSHIP
225 N. UNIVERSITY STREET ... NORMAL **IL** 61761

BRADLEY UNIVERSITY-B'NAI B'RITH HILLEL COUNSELORSHIP
HILLEL HOUSE 1410 W. FREDONIA ... PEORIA **IL** 61606 (309) 676-7611

INDIANA UNIVERSITY-B'NAI B'RITH HILLEL FOUNDATION
730 EAST 3RD STREET ... BLOOMINGTON **IN** 47401 (812) 336-3824

PURDUE UNIVERSITY-B'NAI B'RITH HILLEL FOUNDATION
912 W. STATE STREET ... WEST LAFAYETTE **IN** 47906 (317) 743-1293

UNIVERSITY OF KANSAS-B'NAI B'RITH HILLEL COUNSELORSHIP
B-117 KANSAS UNION ... LAWRENCE **KS** 66045 (913) 864-3948

KANSAS STATE UNIVERSITY-B'NAI B'RITH HILLEL COUNSELORSHIP
1509 WREATH AVENUE ... MANHATTAN **KS** 66502 (913) 539-2836

UNIVERSITY OF LOUISVILLE-B'NAI B'RITH HILLEL COUNSELORSHIP
ECUMENICAL CENTER ... LOUISVILLE **KY** 40292 (502) 588-6598

LOUISIANA STATE UNIVERSITY-B'NAI B'RITH HILLEL COUNSELORSHIP
PO BOX 116420A ... BATON ROUGE **LA** 70893 (504) 383-1495

LOYOLA UNIVERSITY-B'NAI B'RITH HILLEL EXTENSION
912 BROADWAY ... NEW ORLEANS **LA** 70118 (504) 866-7060

TULANE-NEWCOMB UNIVERSITIES-B'NAI B'RITH HILLEL FOUNDATION
912 BROADWAY ... NEW ORLEANS **LA** 70118 (504) 866-7060

UNIVERSITY OF NEW ORLEANS-B'NAI B'RITH HILLEL EXTENSION 912 BROADWAY ... NEW ORLEANS **LA** 70118 (504) 866-7060
LOUISIANA TECHNICAL UNIVERSITY-JEWISH STUDENT ORGANIZATION C/O DEPT. OF PHYSICS-LTU ... RUSTON **LA** 71272 (318) 257-4670
AMHERST COLLEGE-B'NAI B'RITH HILLEL COUNSELORSHIP 108 CHAPIN HALL ... AMHERST **MA** 01003 (413) 542-2181
UNIVERSITY OF MASSACHUSETTS-B'NAI B'RITH HILLEL FOUNDATION 302 STUDENT UNION ... AMHERST **MA** 01003 (413) 545-2526
BOSTON UNIVERSITY-B'NAI B'RITH HILLEL FOUNDATION 233 BAY STATE ROAD ... BOSTON **MA** 02215 (617) 266-3880
BOSTON-B'NAI B'RITH HILLEL COUNCIL OF METROPOLITAN BOSTON 233 BAY STATE ROAD ... BOSTON **MA** 02215 (617) 266-3882
EMERSON COLLEGE-HILLEL EXTENSION 130 BEACON STREET ... BOSTON **MA** 02216 (617) 266-3882
MASSACHUSETTS COLLEGE OF PHARMACY 233 BAY STATE ROAD ... BOSTON **MA** 02115 (617) 732-2855
NEW ENGLAND CONSERVATORY OF MUSIC-HILLEL EXTENSION 290 HUNTINGTON AVENUE ... BOSTON **MA** 02115 (617) 262-1120
NORTHEASTERN UNIVERSITY-B'NAI B'RITH HILLEL FOUNDATION 456 PARKER STREET ... BOSTON **MA** 02115 (617) 437-3937
SIMMONS COLLEGE-HILLEL EXTENSION 300 FENWAY ... BOSTON **MA** 02115 (617) 738-2000
SUFFOLK UNIVERSITY 233 BAY STATE ROAD ... BOSTON **MA** 02115 (617) 266-3882
UNIVERSITY OF MASS./BOSTON HARBOR-HILLEL EXTENSION UNIV. OF MASSACHUSETTS, HARBOR CAMPUS ... BOSTON **MA** (617) 287-1900
WHEELOCK COLLEGE-B'NAI B'RITH HILLEL EXTENSION 200 THE RIVERWAY ... BOSTON **MA** 02215 (617) 734-5200
HARVARD UNIV./RADCLIFFE COLLEGE-B'NAI B'RITH HILLEL FOUND. 74 MT. AUBURN STREET ... CAMBRIDGE **MA** 02138 (617) 495-4696
LESLEY COLLEGE-HILLEL EXTENSION 29 EVERETT STREET ... CAMBRIDGE **MA** 02238 (617) 868-9600
MASS. INSTITUTE OF TECHNOLOGY-B'NAI B'RITH HILLEL FOUNDATION 312 MEMORIAL DRIVE ... CAMBRIDGE **MA** 02139 (617) 253-2982
TUFTS UNIVERSITY-B'NAI B'RITH HILLEL FOUNDATION CURTIS HALL, 474 BOSTON AVENUE ... MEDFORD **MA** 02155 (617) 381-3242
BOSTON COLLEGE-HILLEL EXTENSION BOSTON COLLEGE CAMPUS ... NEWTON **MA** 02167 (617) 969-0100
SMITH COLLEGE-B'NAI B'RITH HILLEL FOUNDATION HELEN HILLS CHAPEL ... NORTHAMPTON **MA** 01063 (413) 584-2700
MOUNT HOLYOKE COLLEGE-JEWISH STUDENT UNION ELIOT HOUSE-MHC ... SOUTH HADLEY **MA** 01075 (413) 538-2054
BENTLEY COLLEGE-B'NAI B'RITH HILLEL EXTENSION STUDENT CENTER ... WALTHAM **MA** 02254 (617) 891-2194
BRANDEIS UNIVERSITY-B'NAI B'RITH HILLEL FOUNDATION 133 USDAN STUDENT CENTER ... WALTHAM **MA** 02254 (617) 647-2177
BABSON COLLEGE-HILLEL EXTENSION BABSON PARK ... WELLESLEY **MA** 02157 (617) 235-1200
MASSACHUSETTS BAY COMMUNITY COLLEGE-HILLEL EXTENSION ROUTE 9 ... WELLESLEY **MA** 02157 (617) 237-1100
WELLESLEY COLLEGE-B'NAI B'RITH HILLEL COUNSELORSHIP ... WELLESLEY **MA** 02181 (617) 235-0320
WESTFIELD STATE COLLEGE-JEWISH STUDENT ORGANIZATION C/O DEPT. OF HISTORY, WSC ... WESTFIELD **MA** 01086 (413) 568-3311
WILLIAMS COLLEGE-JEWISH ASSOCIATION S.U. BOX 3195 ... WILLIAMSTOWN **MA** 01267 (413) 597-2184
CLARK UNIVERSITY-JEWISH STUDENT COALITION BOX A-84, CLARK UNIVERSITY ... WORCESTER **MA** 01610 (617) 793-7296
UNIVERSITY OF MANITOBA - JEWISH STUDENT ASSOCIATION ROOM 149, UNIVERSITY CENTER ... WINNIPEG **MB** R3T 1X1 (204) 474-9325
UNIVERSITY OF WINNIPEG - JEWISH STUDENT ASSOCIATION 515 PORTAGE AVENUE ... WINNIPEG **MB** (204) 786-7811
U.S. NAVAL ACADEMY-L'CHAIM, 25TH COMPANY CHAPLAIN'S CENTER, MITSCHER ... ANNAPOLIS **MD** 21402 (301) 267-2881
JOHNS HOPKINS UNIVERSITY-JEWISH STUDENT ASSOCIATION CHARLES STREET & 34TH STREET ... BALTIMORE **MD** 21218 (301) 338-8349
LOYOLA COLLEGE-JEWISH STUDENT ASSOCIATION CHARLES STREET & 34TH STREET ... BALTIMORE **MD** 21218 (301) 356-5200
UNIV. OF MARYLAND AT BALTIMORE-JEWISH STUDENT ASSOCIATION C/O 5700 PARK HEIGHTS AVENUE ... BALTIMORE **MD** 21215 (301) 542-4900
UNIV. OF MARYLAND/BALTIMORE COUNTY-JEWISH STUDENTS ASSC. 5401 WILKEN AVENUE ... BALTIMORE **MD** 21228 (301) 455-3611
CATONSVILLE COMMUNITY COLLEGE-JEWISH STUDENT ASSOCIATION ... CATONSVILLE **MD** 21228 (301) 455-4506
UNIV. OF MARYLAND/COLLEGE PARK-B'NAI B'RITH HILLEL FOUND. 7612 MOWATT LANE, BOX 187 ... COLLEGE PARK **MD** 20740 (301) 422-6200
MONTGOMERY COLLEGE-HILLEL DEPARTMENT OF SOCIOLOGY ... ROCKVILLE **MD** 20850 (301) 279-5247
GOUCHER COLLEGE-JSA OFFICE 109 PEARLSTONE UNION ... TOWSON **MD** 21204 (301) 337-6415
TOWSON STATE UNIVERSITY-JEWISH STUDENT ASSOCIATION PO BOX 1953 ... TOWSON **MD** 21204 (301) 321-2270
WESTERN MARYLAND COLLEGE-JEWISH STUDENT UNION ... WESTMINSTER **MD** 21157 (301) 848-7000
BATES COLLEGE-B'NAI B'RITH HILLEL COUNSELORSHIP TEMPLE SHALOM, 74 BRADMAN STREET ... AUBURN **ME** 04210 (207) 786-4201
BOWDOIN COLLEGE-BOWDOIN JEWISH ORGANIZATION- ENGLISH DEPARTMENT ... BRUNSWICK **ME** 04011 (207) 725-8731
UNIVERSITY OF MAINE-B'NAI B'RITH HILLEL COUNSELORSHIP MEMORIAL UNION, UNIVERSITY OF MAINE ... ORONO **ME** 04473 (207) 581-3157
COLBY COLLEGE-B'NAI B'RITH HILLEL COUNSELORSHIP ... WATERVILLE **ME** 04901 (207) 872-3523
UNIVERSITY OF MICHIGAN-B'NAI B'RITH HILLEL FOUNDATION 1429 HILL STREET ... ANN ARBOR **MI** 48104 (313) 663-3336
WAYNE STATE UNIVERSITY-B'NAI B'RITH HILLEL FOUNDATION 667 STUDENT CENTER ... DETROIT **MI** 48202 (313) 577-3459
MICHIGAN STATE UNIVERSITY-B'NAI B'RITH HILLEL FOUNDATION 402 LINDEN STREET ... EAST LANSING **MI** 48823 (517) 332-1916
WESTERN MICHIGAN UNIVERSITY P.O. BOX 1538 ... KALAMAZOO **MI** 49007 (616) 323-9341
OAKLAND UNIVERSITY-JEWISH STUDENTS ORGANIZATION 34 OAKLAND CENTER ... ROCHESTER **MI** 48063 (313) 370-2020
UNIVERSITY OF MINNESOTA-B'NAI B'RITH HILLEL FOUNDATION 1521 UNIVERSITY AVENUE, S.E. ... MINNEAPOLIS **MN** 55414 (612) 379-4026
CARLETON COLLEGE-JEWISH STUDENT CENTER JSC 100 NORTH UNION STREET ... NORTHFIELD **MN** 55057 (507) 663-4589
MACALESTER COLLEGE-MACALESTER HEBREW HOUSE GRAND & MACALESTER AVENUES ... ST. PAUL **MN** 55105 (612) 696-6464
UNIV. OF MISSOURI 6300 FORSYTH BOULEVARD ... CLAYTON **MO** 63105 (314) 726-6177
WASHINGTON UNIVERSITY-B'NAI B'RITH HILLEL FOUNDATION 6300 FORSYTH BOULEVARD ... CLAYTON **MO** 63105 (314) 726-6177
STEPHENS COLLEGE-B'NAI B'RITH HILLEL EXTENSION BOX 2003 ... COLUMBIA **MO** 65215 (314) 876-7139
UNIV. OF MISSOURI/COLUMBIA-B'NAI B'RITH HILLEL FOUNDATION 1107 UNIVERSITY AVENUE ... COLUMBIA **MO** 65201 (314) 443-7460
ST. LOUIS UNIVERSITY-JEWISH STUDENTS ORGANIZATION BUSCH CENTER, ROOM 310 ... ST. LOUIS **MO** 63103 (314) 658-2425
WEBSTER UNIVERSITY-B'NAI B'RITH HILLEL EXTENSION 470 EAST LOCKWOOD AVENUE, C/O RELIGIOUS DEPARTMENT ... ST. LOUIS **MO** 63119 (314) 968-7047
UNIVERSITY OF MISSISSIPPI-B'NAI B'RITH HILLEL COUNSELORSHIP ... UNIVERSITY **MS** 38677 (601) 232-7076
GUILFORD COLLEGE-B'NAI B'RITH HILLEL COUNSELORSHIP 210 WEST CAMERON AVENUE ... CHAPEL HILL **NC** 27514 (919) 942-4057
UNIV. OF NORTH CAROLINA/CHAPEL HILL-B'NAI B'RITH HILL FOUND. 210 W. CAMERON AVENUE ... CHAPEL HILL **NC** 27514 (919) 942-4057
UNIV. OF NORTH CAROLINA/CHARLOTTE-B'NAI B'RITH HILLEL COUN. 210 W. CAMERON AVENUE ... CHAPEL HILL **NC** 27514 (919) 942-4057
DUKE UNIVERSITY-B'NAI B'RITH HILLEL FOUNDATION DUKE CHAPEL ... DURHAM **NC** 27706 (919) 684-5955
UNIV. OF NORTH CAROLINA 711 MUIRS CHAPEL ROAD ... GREENSBORO **NC** 27410 (919) 299-6460
EAST CAROLINA UNIVERSITY-B'NAI B'RITH HILLEL COUNSELORSHIP DEPT. OF FOREIGN LANGUAGES ... GREENVILLE **NC** 27834 (919) 757-6232
NORTH CAROLINA STATE UNIVERSITY 2704 BARMETTLER STREET ... RALEIGH **NC** 27607 (919) 737-2481
CREIGHTON UNIVERSITY-JEWISH STUDENT ORGANIZATION 333 S. 132 STREET ... OMAHA **NE** 68154 (402) 334-8200
UNIVERSITY OF NEBRASKA-B'NAI B'RITH HILLEL COUNSELORSHIP 333 S. 132ND STREET ... OMAHA **NE** 68154 (402) 334-8200
UNIVERSITY OF NEW HAMPSHIRE-HILLEL/JEWISH STUDENT ORG. MEMORIAL UNION, UNH ... DURHAM **NH** 03824 (603) 862-1524
DARTMOUTH COLLEGE-B'NAI B'RITH HILLEL FOUNDATION COLLEGE HALL ... HANOVER **NH** 03755 (603) 646-3441
RUTGERS UNIVERSITY-B'NAI B'RITH HILLEL FOUNDATION CLIFTON AVENUE & RYDERS LANE ... NEW BRUNSWICK **NJ** 08901 (201) 545-2407
PRINCETON UNIVERSITY-B'NAI B'RITH HILLEL FOUNDATION MURRAY-DODGE HALL ... PRINCETON **NJ** 08544 (609) 452-3635
RIDER COLLEGE-B'NAI B'RITH HILLEL COUNSELORSHIP 499 GREENWOOD AVENUE ... TRENTON **NJ** 08609 (609) 695-3479
TRENTON STATE COLLEGE-B'NAI B'RITH HILLEL COUNSELORSHIP 499 GREENWOOD AVENUE ... TRENTON **NJ** 08609 (609) 695-3479
KEAN COLLEGE OF NEW JERSEY-JEWISH STUDENT UNION GREEN LANE ... UNION **NJ** 07083 (201) 351-5060
UNIVERSITY OF NEVADA-B'NAI B'RITH HILLEL COUNSELORSHIP 4765 BRUSSELS AVENUE, CRL ... LAS VEGAS **NV** 89109 (702) 736-0887
SUNY AT ALBANY-JEWISH STUDENTS COALITION-HILLEL PO BOX 22249, 1400 WASHINGTON AVENUE ... ALBANY **NY** 12222 (518) 489-8573
ALFRED UNIVERSITY-B'NAI B'RITH HILLEL COUNSELORSHIP BOX 1217 ... ALFRED **NY** 14802 (607) 871-2215
SUNY AT BINGHAMTON-JEWISH STUDENT UNION ... BINGHAMTON **NY** 13901 (607) 777-4980
SUNY COLLEGE AT BROCKPORT-B'NAI B'RITH HILLEL EXTENSION HAVURAH/HILLEL, 212 SEYMOUR UNION ... BROCKPORT **NY** 14420 (716) 637-2310
SARAH LAWRENCE COLLEGE-JEWISH STUDENT UNION/JACY ... BRONXVILLE **NY** 10708 (212) 696-1590
CUNY/BROOKLYN COLLEGE-B'NAI B'RITH HILLEL FOUNDATION 2901 CAMPUS ROAD ... BROOKLYN **NY** 11210 (718) 859-1151
SUNY COLLEGE AT BUFFALO-B'NAI B'RITH HILLEL COUNSELORSHIP B6 CASSITY HALL SUCB ... BUFFALO **NY** 14222 (716) 835-3832
SUNY AT BUFFALO-B'NAI B'RITH HILLEL OF BUFFALO 40 CAPEN BOULEVARD ... BUFFALO **NY** 14214 (716) 835-3832
SAINT LAWRENCE UNIVERSITY-JEWISH STUDENTS ORGANIZATION CHAPLAIN'S OFFICE ... CANTON **NY** 13617 (315) 379-5211
SUNY AT CORTLAND-JEWISH STUDENT SOCIETY C/O DEPARTMENT OF HISTORY ... CORTLAND **NY** 13045 (607) 753-7381
CUNY/QUEENS COLLEGE-B'NAI B'RITH HILLEL FOUNDATION PO BOX 446 ... FLUSHING **NY** 11367 (718) 793-2222
CUNY/QUEENS COLLEGE-B'NAI B'RITH HILLEL FOUNDATION PO BOX 446 ... FLUSHING **NY** 11367 (718) 793-2222
ADELPHI UNIVERSITY-B'NAI B'RITH HILLEL FOUNDATION RELIGIOUS CENTER-EARLE HALL ... GARDEN CITY **NY** 11530 (516) 294-8700
HOBARD & WILLIAM SMITH COLLEGES - ATID - JEWISH STUDENTS ORG. CHAPLAIN'S OFFICE ... GENEVA **NY** 14456 (212) 789-5500
HOBART & WILLIAM SMITH COLLEGES-ATID-JEWISH STUDENTS ORG. CHAPLAIN'S OFFICE ... GENEVA **NY** 14620 (315) 789-5500
COLGATE UNIVERSITY-B'NAI B'RITH HILLEL COUNSELORSHIP COLGATE JEWISH UNION ... HAMILTON **NY** 13346 (315) 824-1000
HOFSTRA UNIVERSITY 224 STUDENT CENTER ... HEMPSTEAD **NY** 11550 (516) 560-6922
CORNELL UNIVERSITY-B'NAI B'RITH HILLEL FOUNDATION G-34 ANABEL TAYLOR HALL ... ITHACA **NY** 14853 (607) 255-4227
ITHACA COLLEGE-B'NAI B'RITH HILLEL COUNSELORSHIP MULLER CHAPEL, ITHACA COLLEGE ... ITHACA **NY** 14850 (607) 274-3323
SUNY AT NEW PALTZ-J.S.O. HILLEL S. U. B. BUILDING 427 ... NEW PALTZ **NY** 12561 (914) 257-2121
C.W. POST CENTER OF LONG ISLAND UNIVERSITY-JACY 130 E. 59TH STREET ... NEW YORK **NY** 10022 (212) 688-0808
CUNY/BARUCH COLLEGE-HILLEL JEWISH STUDENT COUNCIL 17 LEXINGTON AVENUE ... NEW YORK **NY** 10010 (212) 734-2600
CUNY/CITY COLLEGE-B'NAI B'RITH HILLEL FOUNDATION 475 W. 140TH STREET ... NEW YORK **NY** 10031 (212) 234-7317
CUNY/HUNTER 47 EAST 65TH STREET ... NEW YORK **NY** 10021 (212) 734-2600
COLUMBIA UNIVERSITY/BARNARD COLLEGE-COUNCIL FOR JEWISH ORGS. 105 EARL HALL, COLUMBIA UNIVERSITY ... NEW YORK **NY** 10027 (212) 280-5111
NEW YORK CITY-JEWISH ASSOCIATION FOR COLLEGE YOUTH 130 EAST 59TH STREET ... NEW YORK **NY** 10022 (212) 688-0808

NEW YORK INSTITUTE OF TECHNOLOGY 95 MADISON AVENUE — NEW YORK **NY** 10016 (212) 696-1590

NEW YORK UNIVERSITY-JEWISH CULTURAL FOUNDATION, JACY 715 LOEB CENTER-566 LA GUARDIA — NEW YORK **NY** 10012 (212) 598-5284

PACE UNIVERSITY 41 PARK ROW — NEW YORK **NY** 10038 (212) 488-1590

SUNY AT OSWEGO-B'NAI B'RITH HILLEL COUNSELORSHIP HEWITT UNION — OSWEGO **NY** 13126 (315) 341-2350

PACE UNIVERSITY - WESTCHESTER, JEWISH STUDENT ASSOC. - JACY CAMPUS CENTER — PLEASANTVILLE **NY** 10570 (914) 769-3200

VASSAR COLLEGE-JEWISH STUDENT UNION BOX 180, VASSAR — POUGHKEEPSIE **NY** 12601 (914) 452-7000

SUNY COLLEGE AT PURCHASE-RUACH/JACY SUNY-PURCHASE — PURCHASE **NY** 10577 (914) 761-1230

ROCHESTER INST. OF TECH/NTID-B'NAI B'RITH HILLEL EXTENSION 1 LOMB MEMORIAL DRIVE, CHAPLAIN'S OFFICE — ROCHESTER **NY** 14623 (716) 475-5171

UNIVERSITY OF ROCHESTER-B'NAI B'RITH HILLEL FOUNDATION INTERFAITH CHAPEL, WILSON BOULEVARD — ROCHESTER **NY** 14627 (716) 275-4323

SKIDMORE COLLEGE-JEWISH STUDENT UNION — SARATOGA SPRINGS **NY** 12866 (518) 584-5000

UNION COLLEGE-B'NAI B'RITH HILLEL COUNSELORSHIP DEPARTMENT OF HISTORY — SCHENECTADY **NY** 12308 (518) 370-6075

SUNY AT STONY BROOK INTERFAITH CENTER — STONY BROOK **NY** 11794 (516) 246-6842

SYRACUSE UNIVERSITY-B'NAI B'RITH HILLEL FOUNDATION HENDRICKS MEMORIAL CHAPEL — SYRACUSE **NY** 13210 (315) 423-2904

RENSSELAER POLYTECH. INST.-B'NAI B'RITH HILLEL COUNSELORSHIP RPI STUDENT UNION, CHAPLAIN'S OFFICE, ROOM 217 — TROY **NY** 12180 (518) 266-8621

RUSSELL SAGE COLLEGE-B'NAI B'RITH HILLEL COUNSELORSHIP STUDENT UNION, RPI — TROY **NY** 12180 (518) 270-2000

OHIO UNIVERSITY-B'NAI B'RITH HILLEL FOUNDATION 21 MILL STREET — ATHENS **OH** 45701 (614) 592-1173

BOWLING GREEN STATE UNIVERSITY-JEWISH STUDENT GROUP DEPT. OF HISTORY — BOWLING GREEN **OH** 43403 (419) 372-2940

UNIVERSITY OF CINCINNATI-B'NAI B'RITH HILLEL FOUNDATION 2615 CLIFTON AVENUE — CINCINNATI **OH** 45220 (513) 221-6728

BALDWIN WALLACE UNIVERSITY-B'NAI B'RITH HILLEL EXTENSION 11291 EUCLID AVENUE — CLEVELAND **OH** 44106 (216) 231-0040

CASE WESTERN RESERVE UNIVERSITY-B'NAI B'RITH HILLEL FOUND. 11291 EUCLID AVENUE — CLEVELAND **OH** 44106 (216) 231-0040

CLEVELAND STATE UNIVERSITY-B'NAI B'RITH HILLEL EXTENSION 11291 EUCLID AVENUE — CLEVELAND **OH** 44106 (216) 231-0040

CUYAHOGA COMMUNITY COLLEGE-B'NAI B'RITH HILLEL EXTENSION 11291 EUCLID AVENUE — CLEVELAND **OH** 44106 (216) 231-0040

HIRAM COLLEGE-B'NAI B'RITH HILLEL EXTENSION 11291 EUCLID AVENUE — CLEVELAND **OH** 44106 (216) 231-0040

JOHN CARROLL UNIVERSITY-B'NAI B'RITH HILLEL EXTENSION 11291 EUCLID AVENUE — CLEVELAND **OH** 44106 (216) 231-0040

NORTHEASTERN OHIO-B'NAI B'RITH HILLEL FOUNDATIONS OF NE OHIO 11291 EUCLID AVENUE — CLEVELAND **OH** 44106 (216) 231-0040

OHIO STATE UNIVERSITY-B'NAI B'RITH HILLEL FOUNDATION 46 EAST 16TH AVENUE — COLUMBUS **OH** 43201 (614) 294-4797

OHIO WESLEYAN UNIVERSITY-JEWISH STUDENT GROUP, OWU CHAPLAIN'S OFFICE — DELAWARE **OH** 43015 (614) 369-4431

DENISON UNIVERSITY-DENISON JEWISH COMMUNITY — GRANVILLE **OH** 43023 (614) 587-0810

KENT STATE UNIVERSITY-B'NAI B'RITH HILLEL FOUNDATION 202 NORTH LINCOLN — KENT **OH** 44240 (216) 678-0397

OBERLIN COLLEGE, B'NAI B'RITH HILLEL FOUNDATION, WILDER HALL — OBERLIN **OH** 44074 (216) 775-8128

MIAMI UNIVERSITY-B'NAI B'RITH HILLEL COUNSELORSHIP 11-15 E. WALNUT STREET, BERMAN CENTER — OXFORD **OH** 45056 (513) 523-5190

UNIVERSITY OF TOLEDO-B'NAI B'RITH HILLEL COUNSELORSHIP 3436 GODDARD ROAD — TOLEDO **OH** 43606 (419) 472-7238

COLLEGE OF WOOSTER-JEWISH STUDENTS ASSOCIATION COLLEGE OF WOOSTER — WOOSTER **OH** 44691 (216) 263-2405

UNIVERSITY OF OKLAHOMA-B'NAI B'RITH HILLEL FOUNDATION 494 ELM AVENUE — NORMAN **OK** 73069 (405) 321-3703

YORK UNIVERSITY - JEWISH STUDENT FEDERATION CS140B ROSS, 4700 KEALE STREET — DOWNSVIEW **ON** M3J 1P3 (416) 667-3647

CARLETON UNIVERSITY - JEWISH STUDENT UNION 151 CHAPEL STREET — OTTAWA **ON** K1N 7Y2 (613) 232-7306

UNIVERSITY OF OTTAWA - JEWISH STUDENTS UNION-HILLEL 151 CHAPEL STREET — OTTAWA **ON** K1N 7Y2 (613) 232-7306

UNIVERSITY OF TORONTO - B'NAI B'RITH HILLEL FOUNDATION 604 SPADINA AVENUE — TORONTO **ON** M5S 2H4 (416) 923-9861

OREGON STATE UNIVERSITY-B'NAI B'RITH HILLEL COUNSELORSHIP DEPARTMENT OF HISTORY, OSU — CORVALLIS **OR** 97331 (503) 754-3421

UNIVERSITY OF OREGON KONIONIA CENTER, 1414 KINKAID — EUGENE **OR** 97401 (503) 484-1707

CEDAR CREST COLLEGE-B'NAI B'RITH HILLEL COUNSELORSHIP — ALLENTOWN **PA** 18104 (215) 433-3191

MUHLENBERG COLLEGE-B'NAI B'RITH HILLEL COUNSELORSHIP — ALLENTOWN **PA** 18104 (215) 433-3191

LEHIGH UNIVERSITY 214-16 SUMMIT STREET — BETHLEHEM **PA** 18105 (215) 861-3368

MORAVIAN COLLEGE-B'NAI B'RITH HILLEL COUNSELORSHIP DEPARTMENT OF ENGLISH, MORAVIAN — BETHLEHEM **PA** 18018 (215) 861-1391

DICKINSON COLLEGE-B'NAI B'RITH HILLEL COUNSELORSHIP BOX 135 — CARLISLE **PA** 17013 (717) 245-1267

WIDENER UNIVERSITY - HILLEL CLUB P. O. BOX 1184 - WIDENER UNIVERSITY — CHESTER **PA** 19013 (215) 449-4375

URSINUS COLLEGE - ORGANIZATION OF JEWISH STUDENTS — COLLEGEVILLE **PA** 19426 (215) 489-4111

LAFAYETTE COLLEGE-B'NAI B'RITH HILLEL COUNSELORSHIP 329 MCCARTNEY — EASTON **PA** 18042 (215) 250-5174

BRYN MAWR COLLEGE-BRYN MAWR-HAVERFORD HILLEL YARNALL HOUSE, ROOM 113 — HAVERFORD **PA** 19041 (215) 642-9356

HAVERFORD COLLEGE - BRYN MAWR-HAVERFORD HILLEL YARNALL HOUSE, ROOM 113 — HAVERFORD **PA** 19041 (215) 642-9356

BEAVER COLLEGE-HILLEL EXTENSION 1096 SPARROW ROAD — JENKINTOWN **PA** 19046 (215) 886-1297

KUTZTOWN STATE COLLEGE-B'NAI B'RITH HILLEL COUNSELORSHIP — KUTZTOWN **PA** 19530 (215) 683-4397

FRANKLIN & MARSHALL COLL. P.O. BOX 3003, 645 COLLEGE AVENUE — LANCASTER **PA** 17604 (717) 291-4290

BUCKNELL UNIVERSITY-B'NAI B'RITH HILLEL COUNSELORSHIP MARTIN HOUSE, 532 ST. GEORGE — LEWISBURG **PA** 17837 (717) 286-1127

ALLEGHENY COLLEGE-B'NAI B'RITH HILLEL COUNSELORSHIP BOX 14, ALLEGHENY COLLEGE — MEADVILLE **PA** 16335 (814) 724-2368

COMM. COLLEGE OF PHILADELPHIA 202 SOUTH 36TH STREET — PHILADELPHIA **PA** 19104 (215) 898-8265

DREXEL UNIVERSITY-DREXEL HILLEL 224 CREESE ACTIVITY CENTER — PHILADELPHIA **PA** 19104 (215) 895-2531

LA SALLE COLLEGE-HILLEL EXTENSION, CAMPUS MINISTRY CENTER 6809 EMLEN — PHILADELPHIA **PA** 19104 (215) 848-2115

PENNSYLVANIA STATE UNIVERSITY 202 SOUTH 36TH STREET — PHILADELPHIA **PA** 19104 (215) 898-8265

PHILADELPHIA COLLEGE OF PHARMACY 202 SOUTH 36TH STREET — PHILADELPHIA **PA** 19104 (215) 898-8265

PHILADELPHIA COLL. OF TEXTILES 202 SOUTH 36TH STREET — PHILADELPHIA **PA** 19104 (215) 898-8265

PHILADELPHIA-JEWISH CAMPUS ACTIVITIES BOARD 202 SOUTH 36TH STREET — PHILADELPHIA **PA** 19104 (215) 898-8265

SWARTHMORE COLLEGE 202 SOUTH 36TH STREET — PHILADELPHIA **PA** 19104 (215) 898-8265

TEMPLE UNIV.-MAIN & AMBLER CAMPUS-B'NAI B'RITH HILLEL FOUND. 2014 N. BROAD STREET — PHILADELPHIA **PA** 19121 (215) 769-1174

UNIVERSITY OF PENNSYLVANIA-B'NAI B'RITH HILLEL FOUNDATION 202 SOUTH 36TH STREET — PHILADELPHIA **PA** 19104 (215) 898-7391

CARNEGIE MELLON UNIVERSITY-B'NAI B'RITH HILLEL FOUNDATION 315 SOUTH BELLEFIELD AVENUE — PITTSBURGH **PA** 15213 (412) 621-8875

CHATHAM COLLEGE-B'NAI B'RITH HILLEL EXTENSION 315 SOUTH BELLEFIELD AVENUE — PITTSBURGH **PA** 15213 (412) 621-8875

DUQUESNE UNIVERSITY-B'NAI B'RITH HILLEL FOUNDATION 315 SOUTH BELLEFIELD AVENUE — PITTSBURGH **PA** 15213 (412) 621-8875

POINT PARK COLLEGE-B'NAI B'RITH HILLEL EXTENSION 315 SOUTH BELLEFIELD AVENUE — PITTSBURGH **PA** 15213 (412) 621-8875

UNIVERSITY OF PITTSBURGH-B'NAI B'RITH HILLEL FOUNDATION 315 SOUTH BELLEFIELD AVENUE — PITTSBURGH **PA** 15213 (412) 621-8875

ALBRIGHT COLLEGE-B'NAI B'RITH HILLEL COUNSELORSHIP P.O. BOX 516 — READING **PA** 19603 (215) 921-2381

PENNSYLVANIA STATE UNIV.-B'NAI B'RITH HILLEL FOUNDATION 224 LOCUST LANE — STATE COLLEGE **PA** 16801 (814) 237-2408

WASHINGTON & JEFFERSON COLLEGE - HILLEL SOCIETY — WASHINGTON **PA** 15301 (412) 222-4400

CONCORDIA UNIV.-SIR GEORGE & LOYOLA-B'NAI B'RITH HILLEL EXT. 2070 MCKAY STREET NORTH 401 — MONTREAL **QU** H3A 1R8 (514) 845-9171

DAWSON CEGEP 350 SELBY STREET — MONTREAL **QU** H3X 2H8 (514) 845-9171

MARIANOPOLIS CEGEP - MCGILL HILLEL 3460 STANLEY STREET — MONTREAL **QU** H3A 1R8 (514) 845-9171

MCGILL UNIVERSITY - B'NAI B'RITH HILLEL FOUNDATION 3460 STANLEY STREET — MONTREAL **QU** H3X 2H8 (514) 845-9171

MONTREAL-B'NAI B'RITH HILLEL FOUNDATIONS OF MONTREAL, INC. 3460 STANLEY STREET — MONTREAL **QU** H3A 1R8 (514) 845-9171

UNIVERSITY OF MONTREAL 5325 GATINEAU AVENUE — MONTREAL **QU** H3T 1X1 (514) 738-2655

UNIVERSITY OF QUEBEC 5325 GATINEAU AVENUE — MONTREAL **QU** H3T 1X1 (514) 738-2655

VANIER CEGEP (ST. CROIX & SNOWDON)-B'NAI B'RITH HILLEL EXT. 5160 DECAIRE BLVD — MONTREAL **QU** H3X 2H9 (514) 845-9171

UNIVERSITY OF RHODE ISLAND-B'NAI B'RITH HILLEL FOUNDATION 34 LOWER COLLEGE ROAD — KINGSTON **RI** 02881 (401) 792-2740

BROWN UNIVERSITY - B'NAI B'RITH HILLEL FOUNDATION 80 BROWN STREET — PROVIDENCE **RI** 02906 (401) 863-2805

RHODE ISLAND SCHOOL OF DESIGN-B'NAI B'RITH HILLEL EXTENSION 80 BROWN STREET — PROVIDENCE **RI** 02906 (401) 863-2805

BRYANT COLLEGE - JEWISH STUDENTS ORGANIZATION BRYANT COLLEGE — SMITHFIELD **RI** 02917 (401) 232-6045

THE CITADEL-MILITARY COLL. OF SC-B'NAI B'RITH HILLEL COUNSL. 182 RUTLEDGE AVENUE — CHARLESTON **SC** 29403 (803) 722-7261

CLEMSON UNIVERSITY - HILLEL-BRANDEIS STUDENT ORGANIZATION CLEMSON UNIVERSITY — CLEMSON **SC** 29631 (803) 656-3746

UNIV. OF SOUTH CAROLINA-B'NAI B'RITH HILLEL COUNSELORSHIP USC BOX 80128 — COLUMBIA **SC** 29208 (803) 799-9132

UNIV. OF TENN.-KNOXVILLE-B'NAI B'RITH HILLEL COUNSELORSHIP BOX 16204, 2100 TERRACE AVENUE — KNOXVILLE **TN** 37996 (615) 637-0502

MEMPHIS STATE UNIVERSITY - JEWISH STUDENT UNION 3581 MIDLAND — MEMPHIS **TN** 38111 (901) 452-2453

SOUTHERN COLLEGE OF OPTOMETRY-JEWISH STUDENT UNION 3581 MIDLAND MSU — MEMPHIS **TN** 38111 (901) 452-2453

SOUTHWESTERN UNIVERSITY - JEWISH STUDENT UNION 3581 MIDLAND — MEMPHIS **TN** 38111 (901) 452-2453

UNIV. OF TENN.-MEMPHIS 3581 MIDLAND-MSU — MEMPHIS **TN** 38111 (901) 452-2453

GEORGE PEABODY COLLEGE FOR TEACHERS-JEWISH STUDENT UNION BOX 6311-STA B — NASHVILLE **TN** 37235 (615) 322-2457

VANDERBILT UNIVERSITY-JEWISH STUDENT UNION BOX 6311, STA B — NASHVILLE **TN** 37235 (615) 322-2457

UNIV. OF TEXAS AT ARLINGTON - JEWISH STUDENT ORGANIZATION C/O UNIV. OF TEXAS BOX 19348, #160 — ARLINGTON **TX** 76019 (817) 273-3701

UNIV. OF TEXAS - AUSTIN - B'NAI B'RITH HILLEL FOUNDATION 2105 SAN ANTONIO, P.O. BOX H — AUSTIN **TX** 78705 (512) 476-0125

TEXAS A & M UNIVERSITY-B'NAI B'RITH HILLEL FOUNDATION 800 JERSEY — COLLEGE STATION **TX** 77840 (409) 696-7313

RICE UNIVERSITY - B'NAI B'RITH HILLEL EXTENSION 3801 CULLEN BOULEVARD — HOUSTON **TX** 77004 (713) 749-2271

TEXAS MEDICAL CENTER (BAYLOR & U.T.) - HILLEL EXTENSION RELIGION CENTER, U. OF HOUSTON — HOUSTON **TX** 77004 (713) 749-2271

UNIVERSITY OF HOUSTON-B'NAI B'RITH HILLEL FOUNDATION RELIGION CENTER — HOUSTON **TX** 77004 (713) 749-2271

TEXAS TECH. UNIVERSITY-B'NAI B'RITH HILLEL COUNSELORSHIP MATHEMATICS DEPARTMENT TEXAS TECH — LUBBOCK **TX** 79409 (806) 742-2566

UNIVERSITY OF UTAH - B'NAI B'RITH HILLEL COUNSELORSHIP C/O FREEDMAN, MIDEAST CENTER — SALT LAKE CITY **UT** 84112 (801) 581-7843

NORTHERN VIRGINIA COMMUNITY COLLEGE-JEWISH STUDENT CLUB — ANNANDALE **VA** 22003 (301) 468-3422

VA. POLYTECHNIC INST. & STATE U.-B'NAI B'RITH HILLEL COUNSL. PHYSICS DEPARTMENT, VPI & SU — BLACKSBURG **VA** 24061 (703) 961-5109

UNIVERSITY OF VIRGINIA-B'NAI B'RITH HILLEL FOUNDATION 1824 UNIVERSITY CIRCLE — CHARLOTTESVILLE **VA** 22903 (804) 295-4963

GEORGE MASON UNIVERSITY - JEWISH STUDENT GROUP — FAIRFAX **VA** 22030 (301) 468-3422

MARY WASHINGTON COLLEGE-B'NAI B'RITH HILLEL COUNSELORSHIP
COMBS HALL .... FREDERICKSBURG VA 22401 (703) 899-4018
JAMES MADISON UNIVERSITY-B'NAI B'RITH HILLEL COUNSELORSHIP
DEPARTMENT OF ECONOMICS, JMU .... HARRISONBURG VA 22807 (703) 568-6451
FERRUM COLLEGE - HILLEL C/O OHEV ZION 801 PARKVIEW .... MARTINSVILLE VA 24112 (703) 638-3704
OLD DOMINION UNIVERSITY-B'NAI B'RITH HILLEL COUNSELORSHIP
DEPARTMENT OF SOCIOLOGY, ODU .... NORFOLK VA 23508 (804) 440-3961
UNIVERSITY OF RICHMOND-B'NAI B'RITH HILLEL COUNSELORSHIP
1103 WEST FRANKLIN STREET .... RICHMOND VA 23220 (804) 353-6477
VIRGINIA COMMONWEALTH UNIV.-B'NAI B'RITH HILLEL FOUNDATION
1103 WEST FRANKLIN STREET .... RICHMOND VA 23220 (804) 353-6477
COLLEGE OF WILLIAM & MARY-B'NAI B'RITH HILLEL COUNSELORSHIP
DEPARTMENT OF ENGLISH, CWM .... WILLIAMSBURG VA 23185 (804) 229-8795
UNIVERSITY OF VERMONT-B'NAI B'RITH HILLEL COUNSELORSHIP
349 WATERMAN .... BURLINGTON VT 05405 (802) 656-3212
MIDDLEBURY COLLEGE - B'NAI B'RITH HILLEL COUNSELORSHIP
BOX 2242 MIDDLEBURY COLLEGE .... MIDDLEBURY VT 05753 (802) 388-3711
WASHINGTON STATE UNIV.-B'NAI B'RITH HILLEL COUNSELORSHIP
JSO, COMPTON UNION BUILDING .... PULLMAN WA 99164 (509)335-5139
UNIVERSITY OF WASHINGTON-B'NAI B'RITH HILLEL FOUNDATION
4745 17TH AVENUE .... SEATTLE WA 98105 (206) 522-1060
UNIVERSITY OF PUGET SOUND - JEWISH STUDENT ASSOCIATION
C/O TEMPLE BETHEL 5975 S 12 STREET .... TACOMA WA 98465 (206) 564-7101
INTERNATIONAL ASSOCIATION OF HILLEL DIRECTORS
611 LANGDON STREET .... MADISON WI 53703 (608) 256-8361
UNIVERSITY OF WISCONSIN - B'NAI B'RITH HILLEL FOUNDATION
611 LANGDON STREET .... MADISON WI 53703 (608) 256-8361
U. OF WISC.-MILWAUKEE/MARQUETTE-B'NAI B'RITH HILLEL FOUND.
3035 N. STOWELL AVENUE .... MILWAUKEE WI 53211 (414) 961-2010
WEST VIRGINIA UNIVERSITY - B'NAI B'RITH HILLEL FOUNDATION
1420 UNIVERSITY AVENUE .... MORGANTOWN WV 26505 (304) 296-2660

BOARDS OF JEWISH EDUCATION

JEWISH EDUCATION COUNCIL 3310 N. TENTH AVENUE .... PHOENIX AZ 85013 (602) 279-7005
JEWISH EDUCATION SERVICE OF ORANGE COUNTY
12181 BUARO .... GARDEN GROVE CA 92640 (714) 537-2424
BUREAU OF JEWISH EDUCATION
6505 WILSHIRE BOULEVARD, SUITE 710 .... LOS ANGELES CA 90048 (213) 852-1234
AGENCY FOR JEWISH EDUCATION 3245 SHEFFIELD AVENUE .... OAKLAND CA 94602 (415) 533-7032
BUREAU OF JEWISH EDUCATION 2351 WYDA WAY .... SACRAMENTO CA 95825 (916) 485-4151
SAN DIEGO BUREAU OF JEWISH EDUCATION 5511 EL CAJON BLVD .... SAN DIEGO CA 92115 (619) 583-8532
BUREAU OF JEWISH ED. OF SAN FRANCISCO, MARIN CTY & PENINSULA
639 14 AVENUE .... SAN FRANCISCO CA 94118 (415) 751-6983
CENTRAL AGENCY FOR JEWISH EDUCATION
300 SOUTH DAHLIA STREET (#207) .... DENVER CO 80222 (303) 321-3191
DEPT. OF JEWISH ED. OF THE NEW HAVEN JEWISH FEDERATION
1162 CHAPEL STREET .... NEW HAVEN CT 06511 (203) 562-3163
COMMITTEE ON JEWISH ED. OF GREATER HARTFORD JEWISH EDUCATION
333 BLOOMFIELD AVENUE .... WEST HARTFORD CT 06117 (203) 232-4483
CENTRAL AGENCY FOR JEWISH EDUCATION 4200 BISCAYNE BOULEVARD .... MIAMI FL 33137 (305) 576-4030
JEWISH FEDERATION OF PALM BEACH COUNTY
501 SOUTH FLAGLER DRIVE (SUITE 305) .... WEST PALM BEACH FL 33401 (305) 832-2120
ATLANTA BUREAU OF JEWISH EDUCATION
1745 PEACHTREE ROAD, NORTH EAST .... ATLANTA GA 30309 (404) 873-1248
BUREAU FOR JEWISH LIVING 924 POLK BOULEVARD .... DES MOINES IA 50312 (515) 277-5566
ASSOCIATED TALMUD TORAHS OF CHICAGO
2828 WEST PRATT BOULEVARD .... CHICAGO IL 60645 (312) 973-2828
BOARD OF JEWISH EDUCATION OF METROPOLITAN CHICAGO
618 SOUTH MICHIGAN AVENUE .... CHICAGO IL 60605 (312) 427-5570
BUREAU OF JEWISH EDUCATION 6711 HOOVER ROAD .... INDIANAPOLIS IN 46260 (317) 255-3124
JEWISH EDUCATION COUNCIL OF GREATER KANSAS CITY
2210 WEST 75 STREET (SUITE 12) .... SHAWNEE MISSION KS 66208 (913) 722-2922
JEWISH EDUCATION ASSOCIATION OF LOUISVILLE
3600 DUTCHMANS LANE .... LOUISVILLE KY 40205 (502) 459-0798
JEWISH ED. COMMITTEE-JEWISH FED. OF GREATER NEW ORLEANS
3625 HOUMA BOULEVARD (#B) .... METAIRIE LA 70002 (504) 455-6434
BUREAU OF JEWISH EDUCATION OF GREATER BOSTON
333 NOHANTUM STREET .... NEWTON MA 02159 (617) 965-7350
UNITED HEBREW SCHOOL 979 DICKINSON STREET .... SPRINGFIELD MA 01108 (413) 734-8215
WINNIPEG BOARD OF JEWISH EDUCATION 365 HARGRAVE STREET .... WINNIPEG MB R3B 2K3 (204) 949-1482
BOARD OF JEWISH EDUCATION 5800 PARK HEIGHTS AVENUE .... BALTIMORE MD 21215 (301) 367-8300
BOARD OF JEWISH EDUCATION OF GREATER WASHINGTON
11710 HUNTER'S LANE .... ROCKVILLE MD 20852 (301) 984-4455
BOARD OF JEWISH EDUCATION OF GREATER WASHINGTON
9325 BROOKVILLE ROAD .... SILVER SPRING MD 20910 (301) 589-3180
UNITED HEBREW SCHOOLS OF METROPOLITAN DETROIT
21550 WEST TWELVE MILE ROAD .... SOUTHFIELD MI 48076 (313) 354-1050
TALMUD TORAH OF MINNEAPOLIS 8200 WEST 33 STREET .... MINNEAPOLIS MN 55426 (612) 935-0316
CENTRAL AGENCY FOR JEWISH EDUCATION
12 MILLSTONE CAMPUS DRIVE .... ST. LOUIS MO 63146 (314) 432-0020
BUREAU OF JEWISH EDUCATION 333 SOUTH 123 STREET .... OMAHA NE 68154 (402) 334-8200
BUREAU OF JEWISH EDUCATION OF SOUTHERN NEW JERSEY
2393 WEST MARLTON PIKE .... CHERRY HILL NJ 08002 (609) 662-6300
JEWISH ED. SERVICES OF THE JEWISH COMMUNITY OF BERGEN COUNTY
111 KINDERMACK ROAD P.O. BOX 4176
NORTH HACKENSACK STATION .... RIVER EDGE NJ 07661 (201) 488-6800
BUREAU OF JEWISH EDUCATION OF NORTH JERSEY 1 PIKE DRIVE .... WAYNE NJ 07470 (201) 595-0560
JEWISH EDUCATION ASSOCIATION 1 HENDERSON DRIVE .... WEST CALDWELL NJ 07006 (201) 575-6050
BUREAU OF JEWISH EDUCATION OF GREATER BUFFALO, INC.
2640 NORTH FOREST ROAD .... GETZVILLE NY 14068 (716) 689-8844

BOARD OF JEWISH EDUCATION OF GREATER NEW YORK
426 WEST 58TH STREET .... NEW YORK NY 10019 (212) 245-8200
DEPARTMENT OF EDUCATION, UNION OF AMERICAN HEBREW CONGS.
838 FIFTH AVENUE .... NEW YORK NY 10021 (212) 249-0100
DEPARTMENT OF EDUCATION, UNITED SYNAGOGUE OF AMERICA
155 FIFTH AVENUE .... NEW YORK NY 10010 (212) 260-8450
NATIONAL COMMISSION ON TORAH EDUCATION, YESHIVA UNIVERSITY
500 WEST 185TH STREET .... NEW YORK NY 10033 (212) 960-5266
BUREAU OF JEWISH EDUCATION OF ROCHESTER, NEW YORK, INC.
441 EAST AVENUE .... ROCHESTER NY 14607 (716) 461-0290
CAROLINA AGENCY FOR JEWISH EDUCATION
1727 PROVIDENCE ROAD .... CHARLOTTE NC 28207 (704) 366-5560
BUREAU OF JEWISH EDUCATION 1580 SUMMIT ROAD .... CINCINNATI OH 45237 (513) 761-0203
BUREAU OF JEWISH EDUCATION OF CLEVELAND
2030 SOUTH TAYLOR ROAD .... CLEVELAND OH 44118 (216) 371-0446
THE COLUMBUS HEBREW SCHOOL 1125 COLLEGE AVENUE .... COLUMBUS OH 43209 (614) 231-7764
BUREAU OF JEWISH EDUCATION OF GREATER DAYTON
4501 DENLINGER ROAD .... DAYTON OH 45426 (513) 854-2021
TOLEDO BOARD OF JEWISH EDUCATION 2727 KENWOOD BOULEVARD .... TOLEDO OH 43606 (419) 531-8969
COMMISSION FOR JEWISH EDUCATION
P.O. BOX 8021 3970 LOGAN WAY .... YOUNGSTOWN OH 44505 (216) 759-0452
BOARD OF JEWISH EDUCATION 4600 BATHURST STREET .... WILLOWDALE ON M2R 3V3 (416) 633-7770
DEPT. OF EDUCATION & CULTURE CANADIAN JEWISH CONGRESS
4600 BATHURST STREET (SUITE 232) .... WILLOWDALE ON M2R 3V2 (416) 635-2883
JEWISH EDUCATION ASSOCIATION
6651 SOUTH WEST CAPITOL HIGHWAY .... PORTLAND OR 97219 (503) 244-0126
DIVISION OF COMMUNITY SERVICES OF GRATZ COLLEGE
TENTH STREET AND TABOR ROAD .... PHILADELPHIA PA 19141 (215) 329-3363
HEBREW INSTITUTE OF PITTSBURGH 6401-07 FORBES AVENUE .... PITTSBURGH PA 15217 (412) 521-1100
SCHOOL OF ADVANCED JEWISH STUDIES
315 SOUTH BELLEFIELD AVENUE .... PITTSBURGH PA 15213 (412) 681-1630
HILLEL ACADEMY 900 GIBSON STREET .... SCRANTON PA 18510 (717) 343-7837
JEWISH EDUCATION COUNCIL OF GREATER MONTREAL
5151 COTE STREET CATHERINE ROAD (ROOM 201) .... MONTREAL QU H3W 1M6 (514) 735-3541
BUREAU OF JEWISH EDUCATION OF RHODE ISLAND
130 SESSIONS STREET .... PROVIDENCE RI 02906 (401) 331-0956
COMMISSION FOR JEWISH EDUCATION
5603 SOUTH BRAESWOOD BOULEVARD .... HOUSTON TX 77096 (713) 729-7000
JEWISH EDUCATION COUNCIL 516 SECURITIES BUILDING .... SEATTLE WA 98101 (206) 625-0665
MILWAUKEE ASSOCIATION FOR JEWISH EDUCATION
4560 NORTH PORT WASHINGTON ROAD .... MILWAUKEE WI 53212 (414) 962-8860

BOOK CLUBS & SERVICES

ZIONIST BOOK CLUB 788 MARLEE AVENUE .... TORONTO ON
PERCHIK'S - REUBEN CANNON 345 S. MC DOWELL BLVD .... PETALUMA CA 94952 (707) 763-2482
B'NAI B'RITH PAPERBACK SERVICE
1640 RHODE ISLAND AVENUE, N.W. .... WASHINGTON DC 20036 (202) 857-6600
NATIONAL YIDDISH BOOK CENTER OLD E. ST. SCHOOL, P.O. BOX 969 .... AMHERST MA 01004 (413) 253-9201
MA'AYAN: A WELLSPRING OF JEWISH BOOKS P.O. BOX 246 .... SUDBURY MA 01776 (617) 877-5128
MA'AYAN: A WELLSPRING OF JEWISH BOOKS P.O. BOX 246 .... SUDBURY MA 01776 (800) 292-2629
B'NAI B'RITH JEWISH BOOK CLUB
C/O DAVID MYERS, 230 LIVINGSTON STREET .... NORTHVALE NJ 07647 (201) 767-4093
JEWISH BOOKSHELF, THE PO BOX 434 .... TEANECK NJ 07666

CHEMED BOOKS, INC. 915 EAST 17TH STREET	BROOKLYN	**NY**	11230	(718) 253-2112
TZIVOS HASHEM BOOK CLUB 332 KINGSTON AVENUE	BROOKLYN	**NY**	11213	(718) 467-6630
JUDAICA BOOK CLUB C/O THE JONATHAN DAVID CO. 68-22 ELIOT AVENUE	MIDDLE VILLAGE	**NY**	11379	(718) 456-8611
BOOKAZINE CO., INC. 303 W. 10 STREET	NEW YORK	**NY**	10014	(212) 675-8877
ISAIAH BOOK CLUBS, INC. P.O. BOX 692, COOPER STATION	NEW YORK	**NY**	10276	
JEWISH BOOK COUNCIL OF THE JEWISH WELFARE BOARD 15 EAST 26TH STREET	NEW YORK	**NY**	10010	(212) 532-4949
PHILIPP FELDHEIM, INC. 96 EAST BROADWAY	NEW YORK	**NY**	10002	(212) 925-3180
UNITED SYNAGOGUE OF AMERICA BOOK SERVICE 155 FIFTH AVENUE	NEW YORK	**NY**	10010	(212) 533-7800
ENJOY-A-BOOK CLUB 1 STATION PLAZA	WOODMERE	**NY**	11598	(516) 569-0830
ENJOY-A-BOOK CLUB P.O. BOX 101	WOODMERE	**NY**	11598	(516) 569-0324
JEWISH PUBLICATION SOCIETY 1930 CHESTNUT STREET	PHILADELPHIA	**PA**	19103	(215) 564-5925
NOAH'S ARK BOOKS c/o L.F. BLOCK 5514 RUTHERGLEN	HOUSTON	**TX**	77096	(713) 729-6221
THE HEBREW BOOK CLUB 78A SHENKIN STREET, P.O. BOX 14235	TEL AVIV	**IS**	64112	
YIDDISH BOOK CLUB COMMITTEE FOR JEWISH CULTURE IN ISRAEL BNEI EPHRAIM STREET	MAOZ AVIV, TEL AVIV	**IS**		

BOOK DEALERS

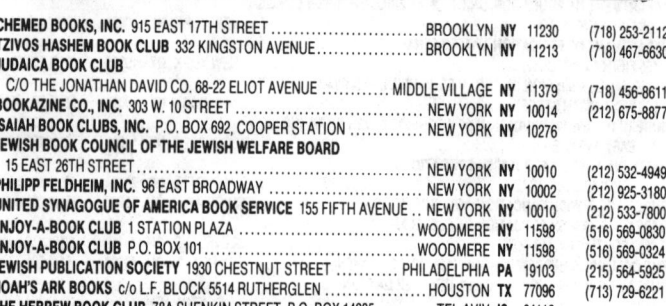

CENTERSTORE JUDAIC BOOKS AND GIFTS 1718 W. MARYLAND	PHOENIX	**AZ**	85015	(602) 249-9090
CENTERSTORE JUDAIC BOOKS AND GIFTS 7119 E. SHEA BLVD.	SCOTTSDALE	**AZ**	85253	(602) 998-4206
CENTERSTORE JUDAIC BOOKS AND GIFTS 1965 EAST HERMOSA	TEMPE	**AZ**	85282	(602) 894-0588
SHALOM BOOKS AND GIFTS GALORE 3712 OAK STREET	VANCOUVER	**BC**	V6H 2M3	(604) 734-1106
ATARA'S 450 NORTH FAIRFAX AVENUE	LOS ANGELES	**CA**	90036	(213) 655-3050
CALIFORNIA HOUSE OF ISRAEL BOX 48425	LOS ANGELES	**CA**	90048	(213) 653-6757
CHABAD MID-CITY CENTER 420 NORTH FAIRFAX AVENUE	LOS ANGELES	**CA**	90036	(213) 655-9282
HERSKOVITZ HEBREW BOOKSTORE 428 NORTH FAIRFAX AVENUE	LOS ANGELES	**CA**	90036	(213) 852-9310
J. ROTH BOOKSELLER 9427 WEST PICO BOULEVARD	LOS ANGELES	**CA**	90035	(213) 557-1848
JEWISH AMERICAN BOOKSTORE 9427 WEST PICO BOULEVARD	LOS ANGELES	**CA**	90035	(213) 557-1848
JOSEPH HERSKOVITZ HEBREW BOOK STORE 428 NORTH FAIRFAX AVENUE	LOS ANGELES	**CA**	90036	(213) 852-9310
SKIRBALL MUSEUM GIFT SHOP, HEBREW UNION COLLEGE 3077 UNIVERSITY MALL	LOS ANGELES	**CA**	90007	(213) 749-3424
SOLOMON'S BOOKS & GIFTS 447 N. FAIRFAX AVENUE	LOS ANGELES	**CA**	90036	(213) 653-9045
BOB & BOB BOOKS 151 FOREST AVENUE	PALO ALTO	**CA**	94301	(415) 329-9050
PERCHIKS JUDAICA 345 S. MCDOWELL #115	PETALUMA	**CA**	94952	(707) 763-2482
CHABAD HOUSE - LUBAVITCH 6115 MONTEZUMA ROAD	SAN DIEGO	**CA**	92115	(619) 265-7700
JERUSALEM WEST 6515 UNIVERSITY AVENUE	SAN DIEGO	**CA**	92115	(619) 582-2013
LIEBER'S BOOK STORE 3240 GEARY BOULEVARD	SAN FRANCISCO	**CA**	94115	(415) 387-3077
GOLDSTEIN'S GIFTS 6803 ROYALWOOD WAY	SAN JOSE	**CA**	95120	
JERUSALEM FAIR 14537 VENTURA BOULEVARD	SHERMAN OAKS	**CA**	91403	(818) 995-0116
THE JEWISH DEVELOPMENT COMPANY 18331-C IRVINE BOULEVARD	TUSTIN	**CA**	92680	(714) 730-1419
SELIGMAN / BENCHMARKS 307 ROSE AVENUE	VENICE	**CA**	90291	(213) 392-1010
YTC SEFORIM STORE 1400 QUITMAN ST #4067	DENVER	**CO**	80204	
MEDIA JUDAICA 1363 FAIRFIELD AVENUE	BRIDGEPORT	**CT**	06605	(203) 384-2284
ISRAEL GIFT SHOP & HEBREW BOOK SHOP 262 S. WHITNEY STREET	HARTFORD	**CT**	06105	(203) 232-3984
JEWISH BOOK SHOP 570 WHALLEY AVENUE	NEW HAVEN	**CT**	06511	(203) 387-1818
B'NAI B'RITH MUSEUM SHOP 1640 RHODE ISLAND AVENUE, NW	WASHINGTON	**DC**	20036	(202) 857-6600
THE SOURCE 751 ORIENTA PLAZA	ALTAMONTE SPRINGS	**FL**	32701	(305) 830-1948
JUDAICA OF BROWARD 1295 EAST HALLANDALE BEACH BOULEVARD	HALLANDALE	**FL**	33009	(305) 454-9050
THE CHOSEN GIFT 7146 SOUTHWEST 117TH AVENUE	MIAMI	**FL**	33183	(305) 596-3639
AMERICAN-ISRAELI SHOP 1357 WASHINGTON AVENUE	MIAMI BEACH	**FL**	33139	(305) 531-7722
NATIONAL HEBREW ISRAELI GIFT CENTER 1507 WASHINGTON AVENUE	MIAMI BEACH	**FL**	33139	(305) 532-2210
TORAH TREASURES 1309 WASHINGTON AVENUE	MIAMI BEACH	**FL**	33139	(305) 673-6095
JUDAICA ENTERPRISES, INC. 1074 N.E. 163RD ST.	NORTH MIAMI BEACH	**FL**	33162	(305) 945-5091
NER TAMID BOOK DISTRIBUTORS PO BOX 10401	RIVIERA BEACH	**FL**	33404	(305) 686-9095
ANSLEY MALL BOOK STORE 1544 PIEDMONT AVENUE N.E.	ATLANTA	**GA**	30320	(404) 875-6492
CHICAGO HEBREW BOOK STORE 2942 WEST DEVON AVENUE	CHICAGO	**IL**	60659	(312) 973-6636
HAMAKOR JUDAICA BOOK STORE 6112 N. LINCOLN AVENUE	CHICAGO	**IL**	60659	(312) 463-6186
MUSEUM STORE SPERTUS COLLEGE OF JUDAICA 618 SOUTH MICHIGAN AVENUE	CHICAGO	**IL**	60605	(312) 922-9012
ROSENBLUM HEBREW BOOK STORE 2906 WEST DEVON AVENUE	CHICAGO	**IL**	60659	(312) 262-1700
CHABAD BOOKS 7037 FRERET ST	NEW ORLEANS	**LA**	70118	(504) 866-5164
NEW ENGLAND JUDAICA & GIFT 154 CHESTNUTHILL AVENUE	BRIGHTON	**MA**	02135	(617) 783-9254
ISRAEL BOOKSHOP INC. 410 HARVARD STREET	BROOKLINE	**MA**	02146	(617) 566-7113
DAVIDSON'S HEBREW BOOK STORE 1106 N. MAIN STREET	NORTH RANDOLPH	**MA**	02368	(617) 961-4989
JEWISH BOOK FINDER 30 WESTERN VIEW	SPRINGFIELD	**MA**	01108	
EPHRAIM'S BOOK STORE 72 FRANKLIN STREET	WORCESTER	**MA**	01608	(617) 755-9505
CENTRAL HEBREW BOOK STORE 228 REISTERSTOWN ROAD	BALTIMORE	**MD**	21208	(301) 653-0550
PERN'S HEBREW BOOK & GIFT SHOP 7012 REISTERSTOWN ROAD	BALTIMORE	**MD**	21215	(301) 653-2450
ABE'S JEWISH BOOKSTORE 11250 GEORGIA AVENUE	WHEATON	**MD**	20902	(301) 942-2237
LISBON'S HEBREW BOOKS AND GIFTS 2305 UNIVERSITY BOULEVARD WEST	WHEATON	**MD**	20902	(301) 933-1800
JEWISH BOOK STORE OF GREATER WASHINGTON 11250 GEORGIA AVENUE	WHEATON	**MD**	20902	(301) 942-2237
BORENSTEIN'S BOOK STORE 25242 GREENFIELD ROAD	OAK PARK	**MI**	48237	(313) 967-3920
SPITZER'S HEBREW BOOK AND GIFT CENTER 21770 ELEVEN MILE ROAD	SOUTHFIELD	**MI**	48076	(313) 356-6080
BROCHIN'S JEWISH BOOK & GIFT SHOP 4813 MINNETONKA BOULEVARD	MINNEAPOLIS	**MN**	54416	(612) 926-2011
MIDWEST JEWISH BOOK & GIFT CENTER 8318 OLIVE STREET ROAD	ST. LOUIS	**MO**	63132	(314) 993-6300
SOURCE UNLIMITED 11044 OLIVE ST. RD	ST. LOUIS	**MO**	63141	(314) 567-1925
JUDAIC SPECIALTIES 45 BROAD STREET	CARLSTADT	**NJ**	07002	(201) 939-4522
THE JUDAICA HOUSE, LTD. 19 GRAND AVENUE	ENGLEWOOD	**NJ**	07631	(201) 567-1199
HIGHLAND PARK JUDAICA 227 RARITAN AVENUE	HIGHLAND PARK	**NJ**	08904	(201) 246-1690
KTAV 900 JEFFERSON STREET	HOBOKEN	**NJ**	07030	(201) 963-9524
CIS DISTRIBUTORS 674 8TH STREET	LAKEWOOD	**NJ**	08701	(201) 364-1629
CIS DISTRIBUTORS 674 8TH STREET	LAKEWOOD	**NJ**	08701	(201) 367-7858
LAKEWOOD JUDAICA & GIFT CENTER 428 CLIFTON AVENUE	LAKEWOOD	**NJ**	08701	(201) 364-8860
LAKEWOOD JUDAICA & GIFT CENTER 428 CLIFTON AVENUE	LAKEWOOD	**NJ**	08701	(201) 364-8716
SKY HEBREW BOOKSTORE 1923 SPRINGFIELD AVENUE	MAPLEWOOD	**NJ**	07040	(201) 763-4244
BEHRMAN HOUSE INC. 235 WATCHUNG AVENUE	WEST ORANGE	**NJ**	07052	(201) 669-0447
PELHAM PARKWAY HEBREW BOOKSTORE 781 LYDIG AVENUE	BRONX	**NY**	10462	(212) 892-2522
BIEGELEISEN SFORIM STORE 4409 16TH AVENUE	BROOKLYN	**NY**	11204	(718) 436-1165
BLUM'S HEBREW BOOK STORE 75 LEE AVENUE	BROOKLYN	**NY**	11211	(718) 963-1234
COHEN'S RELIGIOUS ARTICLES 5302 16TH AVENUE	BROOKLYN	**NY**	11204	(718) 851-4877
CROWN HEIGHTS JUDAICA 329 KINGSTON AVENUE	BROOKLYN	**NY**	11213	(718) 774-0198
EICHLER'S RELIGIOUS ARTICLES & GIFTS 1429 CONEY ISLAND AVENUE	BROOKLYN	**NY**	11230	(718) 258-7643
EICHLER'S RELIGIOUS ARTICLES & GIFTS 5004 13TH AVENUE	BROOKLYN	**NY**	11219	(718) 633-1505
THE 18TH AVENUE SEFORIM CENTER 4607 18TH AVENUE	BROOKLYN	**NY**	11204	(718) 633-9225
FLOHR'S GIFTS & RELIGIOUS ARTICLES 4603 13TH AVENUE	BROOKLYN	**NY**	11219	(718) 854-0865
FLUSBERG'S HEBREW BOOK STORE 1276 47TH STREET	BROOKLYN	**NY**	11219	(718) 853-7302
FRANKEL'S BOOK STORE 4904 16TH AVENUE	BROOKLYN	**NY**	11204	(718) 851-7766
GRUNFELD HEBREW BOOK STORE 4624 16TH AVENUE	BROOKLYN	**NY**	11204	(718) 871-8885
HAICHAL HASEFORIM 4401 16TH AVENUE	BROOKLYN	**NY**	11204	(718) 438-8414
HEBREW PUBLISHING COMPANY 100 WATER STREET	BROOKLYN	**NY**	11201	(718) 858-6928
HECHT HEBREW BOOKS & RELIGIOUS SUPPLIES 1265 CONEY ISLAND AVENUE	BROOKLYN	**NY**	11230	(718) 258-9696
KEHOT BOOKSTORE 291 KINGSTON AVENUE	BROOKLYN	**NY**	11213	(718) 778-0226
KODESH RELIGIOUS ARTICLES 5205 13TH AVENUE	BROOKLYN	**NY**	11219	(718) 633-8080
LEVITZ SEFORIM CENTER 1470 CONEY ISLAND AVENUE	BROOKLYN	**NY**	11230	
MATZLIACH SEFORIM CENTER 5114 12TH AVENUE	BROOKLYN	**NY**	11219	(718) 438-9523

MEKOR HASEFORIM	1989 CONEY ISLAND AVENUE	BROOKLYN	**NY**	11223	(718) 627-4385
MERCAZ STAM	309 KINGSTON AVENUE	BROOKLYN	**NY**	11213	(718) 773-0090
MISHOR, LTD. - WHOLESALE & RETAIL	43 LEE AVENUE	BROOKLYN	**NY**	11211	(718) 384-0397
PINTER'S HEBREW BOOKS	4408 14TH AVENUE	BROOKLYN	**NY**	11219	(718) 871-2260
REBECCA BENNET PUBLICATIONS	5409 18TH AVENUE	BROOKLYN	**NY**	11204	(718) 256-1954
RIGLER'S SEFORIM	1206 AVENUE M	BROOKLYN	**NY**	11230	(718) 627-3818
SEFORIM WORLD	4401 16TH AVENUE	BROOKLYN	**NY**	11204	(718) 633-5500
SEPHER-HERMON PRESS, INC.	1265 46TH STREET	BROOKLYN	**NY**	11219	(718) 972-9010
Z. BERMAN BOOKS	1340 53RD STREET	BROOKLYN	**NY**	11219	(718) 851-5372
ELBAUM JUDAICA	694 CENTRAL AVENUE	CEDARHURST	**NY**	11516	(516) 569-4577
KI-TOV/HEBREW BOOK & GIFT CENTER	1847 MOTT AVENUE	FAR ROCKAWAY	**NY**	11691	(718) 471-0963
BOOK NOOK PUBLICATIONS	1525 CENTRAL AVENUE	FAR ROCKAWAY	**NY**	11691	(718) 327-0163
HOUSE OF ISRAEL	100-23 QUEENS BLVD	FOREST HILLS	**NY**	11375	(718) 459-4556
JEWISH BOOK SHOP	2640 NORTH FOREST ROAD	GETZVILLE	**NY**	14068	(716) 689-8844
NEFESH AMI	107 BROADWAY, SUITE #3	HICKSVILLE	**NY**	11801	(516) 933-2660
THEODORE S. CINNAMON LIMITED	420 JERUSALEM AVENUE	HICKSVILLE	**NY**	11801	(516) 935-7480
HEBREW BOOK AND GIFT WORLD	72-20 MAIN STREET	KEW GARDENS HILLS	**NY**	11367	(718) 261-0233
YUSSEL'S PLACE	59 MERRICK AVENUE	MERRICK	**NY**	11566	(516) 223-7050
JONATHAN DAVID COMPANY	68-22 ELIOT AVENUE	MIDDLE VILLAGE	**NY**	11379	(718) 456-8611
HEBREW BOOK STORE (CONGREGATION VAYOEL MOSHE)	214 MAPLE AVENUE	MONSEY	**NY**	10952	(914) 356-9807
MONSEY BOOK & RELIGIOUS ARTICLES	42 MAIN STREET	MONSEY	**NY**	10952	(914) 425-8530
SIMCHA SHOPPE, THE	18 HILLTOP LANE	MONSEY	**NY**	10952	(914) 352-4543

ZIEGELHEIM HEBREW BOOKS & RELIGIOUS ARTICLES 68 MAIN STREET	MONSEY	NY	10952	(914) 354-5842
TIFERES BOOKS 9 LINCOLN AVENUE	NEW SQUARE	NY	10952	(914) 362-0881
BLOCH PUBLISHING COMPANY 19 WEST 21ST STREET	NEW YORK	NY	10010	(212) 989-9104
CENTRAL YIDDISH CULTURE ORGANIZATION - CYCO 25 EAST 78TH STREET	NEW YORK	NY	10024	(212) 535-4320
GOLDMAN'S OTZAR HASEFARIM, INC. 33 CANAL STREET	NEW YORK	NY	10002	(212) 674-1707
GURARY ISRAELI TRADING CORP. 49 CANAL STREET	NEW YORK	NY	10002	(212) 226-0820
HANAUER, CARLA, CO. 195 BENNETT AVENUE	NEW YORK	NY	10040	(212) 942-6454
H & M SKULLCAP CO. 46 HESTER STREET	NEW YORK	NY	10002	(212) 475-1910
ISRAELI GIFTS 23 ESSEX	NEW YORK	NY	10002	(212) 475-6075
ISRAELI GIFTS & BOOKSTORES 575 SEVENTH AVENUE	NEW YORK	NY	10018	(212) 391-4928
ISRAEL TRADE BOOKS 49 CANAL ST	NEW YORK	NY	10002	(212) 226-8020
ISRAEL WHOLESALE 21 ESSEX STREET	NEW YORK	NY	10002	(212) 477-2310
J. LEVINE CO. - LOWER EAST SIDE 58 ELDRIDGE STREET	NEW YORK	NY	10002	(212) 966-4460
J. LEVINE CO. - MIDTOWN STORE 5 WEST 30TH STREET	NEW YORK	NY	10001	(212) 695-6888
JEWISH GIFT SHOP 2404 BROADWAY	NEW YORK	NY	10024	(212) 362-7846
JEWISH MUSEUM BOOKSHOP, THE 1109 FIFTH AVENUE	NEW YORK	NY	10028	(212) 860-1860
JUDAICA EMPORIUM 3070 BROADWAY	NEW YORK	NY	10027	(212) 864-6501
LOUIS STAVSKY COMPANY, INC. 147 ESSEX STREET	NEW YORK	NY	10002	(212) 674-1289
M. LANDY FINE JUDAICA P.O. BOX 801	NEW YORK	NY	10002	(212) 925-3180
OTZER SEFORIM 33 CANAL STREET	NEW YORK	NY	10002	(212) 674-1707
PHILIPP FELDHEIM 96 E. BROADWAY	NEW YORK	NY	10002	(212) 925-3180
RABBI MOSES EISENBACH BOOKSTORE 49 ESSEX STREET	NEW YORK	NY	10002	(212) 674-8840
SEFER ISRAEL, INC. 156 FIFTH AVENUE	NEW YORK	NY	10010	(212) 929-6411
SHALLER'S BOOKSTORE 2555 AMSTERDAM AVENUE	NEW YORK	NY	10033	(212) 928-2140
SHAPOLSKY'S GREAT JUDAICA BOOKSTORE/ART GALLERY 56 EAST 11TH STREET	NEW YORK	NY	10003	(212) 505-2505
SHILO PUBLISHING COMPANY 73 CANAL STREET	NEW YORK	NY	10002	(212) 925-3468
STAVSKY'S HEBREW BOOK STORE 147 ESSEX STREET	NEW YORK	NY	10002	(212) 674-1289
THE JEWISH MUSEUM BOOKSHOP 1104 FIFTH AVENUE	NEW YORK	NY	10028	(212) 860-1888
WEST SIDE JUDAICA 2404 BROADWAY	NEW YORK	NY	10024	(212) 362-7846
ZIONTALIS/BOOK DIVISION 48 ELDRIDGE STREET	NEW YORK	NY	10002	(212) 925-8558
SFARIM MEHABAYIT LTD. 98-38 QUEENS BLVD.	REGO PARK	NY	11374	(718) 275-2000
ORGEL'S JEWISH RELIGIOUS ARTICLES & ISRAEL GIFTWARE 984 MONROE AVENUE	ROCHESTER	NY	14609	(716) 271-2310
INSPIRATION GALLERY	SCARSDALE	NY		(914) 636-6776
HAKOL B'SEFER MAIN STREET	SOUTH FALLSBURG	NY	12779	(914) 434-2294
PHILIPP FELDHEIM, INC. 200 AIRPORT EXECUTIVE PARK SMITH ROAD	SPRING VALLEY	NY	10977	(914) 356-2282
CARMEL JUDAICA 10 CARMEL AVENUE	STATEN ISLAND	NY	10314	(718) 761-8480
JUDAICA UNLIMITED, INC. 433 HEMPSTEAD AVENUE	WEST HEMPSTEAD	NY	11552	(516) 486-3636
LONG ISLAND TEMPLE SUPPLIES 433 HEMPSTEAD AVENUE	WEST HEMPSTEAD	NY	11552	(516) 486-3636
HAKOL B'SEFER JUDAICA MAIN STREET	WOODBOURNE	NY	12788	(914) 434-2626
ENJOY-A-BOOK CLUB P.O. BOX 101	WOODMERE	NY	11598	(516) 569-0324
K'TONTON BOOK STORE 1 STATION PLAZA	WOODMERE	NY	11598	(516) 569-0830
HEBREW UNION COLLEGE BOOKSTORE 3101 CLIFTON AVENUE	CINCINNATI	OH	45220	(513) 221-1875
FRANK'S HEBREW BOOK STORE 1647 LEE ROAD	CLEVELAND	OH	44118	(216) 321-6850
FRIEDMAN'S GIFTS & BOOK STORE 14077 CEDAR ROAD, #101	SOUTH EUCLID	OH	44118	(216) 321-7499
PAUL'S JUDAIC BOOK & GIFT CENTER 13962 CEDAR ROAD	UNIVERSITY HEIGHTS	OH	44118	(216) 321-7200
ISRAEL'S... THE JUDAICA CENTRE 830 STEEPROCK DRIVE	DOWNSVIEW	ON	M3J 2X2	(416) 630-9261
ISRAEL'S... THE JUDAICA CENTRE 243 WILMINGTON AVENUE	DOWNSVIEW	ON	M3H 5J9	(416) 636-0371
ISRAEL'S... THE JUDAICA CENTRE 973 EGLINTON AVENUE WEST	TORONTO	ON	M6C 2C4	(416) 789-2169
MATOV JEWISH BOOKS 3173A BATHURST STREET	TORONTO	ON	M6A 2B1	
MIRIAM'S GIFT GALLERY 3007 BATHURST STREET	TORONTO	ON	M6B 3B3	(416) 781-8261
NEGEV BOOK & GIFT STORE 3509 BATHURST STREET	TORONTO	ON	M6A 2C5	(416) 781-0071
ZUCKER'S JEWISH BOOKS AND ART 3453 BATHURST STREET	TORONTO	ON	M5A 2C5	(416) 781-2133
RABBI PIOTRKOWSKI'S JUDAICA CENTER 289 MONTGOMERY AVENUE	BALA CYNWYD	PA	19004	(215) 664-1303
ROSENBERG HEBREW BOOK STORE 409 OLD YORK ROAD	JENKINTOWN	PA	19046	(215) 884-1728
ROSENBERG HEBREW BOOK STORE 6408 CASTOR AVENUE	PHILADELPHIA	PA	19149	(215) 744-5205
PINSKER'S HEBREW BOOKS 2028 MURRAY AVENUE	PITTSBURGH	PA	15217	(412) 421-3033
BOOK CENTER, INC. 1140 BEAULAC STREET	MONTREAL	QU		(514) 332-4154
BOOK CENTRE 5168 QUEEN MARY ROAD	MONTREAL	QU	H3W 1X5	(514) 481-5609
CAPLANSKY BOOK STORE 39-20 ST. KEVIN STREET	MONTREAL	QU		(514) 737-6237
RODAL'S HEBREW BOOK STORE 4689 VAN HORNE STREET	MONTREAL	QU		(514) 733-1876
THE KOTEL BOOKS 6414 VICTORIA AVENUE	MONTREAL	QU	H3W Z56	
VICTORIA GIFT SHOP & BOOK CENTRE 5869 VICTORIA AVENUE	MONTREAL	QU		(514) 738-1414
MELZER'S HEBREW BOOK STORE 742 HOPE STREET	PROVIDENCE	RI	02906	(401) 831-1710
MRS. FRED GLATZER 6630 NORTHPORT DRIVE	DALLAS	TX	75230	(214) 368-2479
HOUSE OF BOOKS 9215 STELLA LINK ROAD	HOUSTON	TX	77025	(713) 667-9434
SOURCE OF HOUSTON 9760 HILLCROFT	HOUSTON	TX	77096	(713) 721-4624
JUDAICA EXPRESS 5401 WEST KEEFE AVENUE	MILWAUKEE	WI	53216	(414) 449-3403
CHEVRAT SEFORIM 92 HOTHAM ST.	BALACLAVA	AU		
AMZALAH BOOKS 10 CASTLEFIELD STREET	BOND, NEW SOUTH WALES	AU	2026	
J. LEHMAN 20 CAMBRIDGE TERRACE	GATESHEAD	GB	NE8 1RP	
BLUE & WHITE SHOP 6 BEEHIVE LANE	ILFORD ESSEX	GB	1G1 3RD	(01) 518-1982
JEWISH BOOK CENTER 25 ASHBOURNE GROVE	MANCHESTER	GB	M70 DB	
CARMEL GIFTS 62 EDGWARE WAY	MIDDLESEX	GB		(01) 958-7632
MESORAH MAFITZIM/J. GROSSMAN RECHOV HARAV UZIEL 117	JERUSALEM	IS		
STEIMATZKY, LTD. CITRUS HOUSE, 22 HARAKEVET STREET, P.O. BOX 628	TEL AVIV	IS	61006	(03) 622537
LUBAVITCH PUBLICATIONS P.O. BOX 39276	BRAMLEY	SA	2018	
KOLLEL BOOKSHOP P.O. BOX 27784 YEOVILLE 2143	JOHANNESBURG	SA		
RUBIN BOOKSELLERS 34 GLENEAGLES RD., GREENSIDE 2193	JOHANNESBURG	SA		

BOOK DEALERS - YIDDISH

YIDDISH BOOK CLUB COMMITTEE FOR JEWISH CULTURE IN ISRAEL BNEI EPHRAIM STREET	MAOS AVIV, TEL AVIV	IS		
NATIONAL YIDDISH BOOK EXCHANGE P.O. BOX 969	AMHERST	MA	01004	(413) 256-1241
CYCO - YIDDISH BOOK DISTRIBUTORS 25 EAST 78TH STREET	NEW YORK	NY	10021	(212) 535-4320

BURIAL SOCIETIES - CHEVRA KADISHA

CHEVRA KADISHA CHAPEL 12313 105TH AVENUE	EDMONTON	AT		(403) 482-3065
SCHARA TZEDECK CHAPEL-CHEVRA KADISHA 3642 WEST BROADWAY	VANCOUVER	BC	V6R 2B7	(604) 733-2277
JEWISH BURIAL SOCIETY 7832 SANTA MONICA BOULEVARD	LOS ANGELES	CA	90046	(213) 656-9783
JEWISH COMMUNITY BURIAL COMMITTEE 599 NORTH VERMONT	LOS ANGELES	CA	90004	
JEWISH COMMUNITY BURIAL PROGRAM, JEWISH FAMILY SERVICE 6505 WILSHIRE BOULEVARD	LOS ANGELES	CA	90048	(213) 852-1234
MOUNT ZION CEMETERY FUND, JEWISH FEDERATION COUNCIL 6505 WILSHIRE BOULEVARD	LOS ANGELES	CA	90048	(213) 852-1234
THE JEWISH SACRED SOCIETY 415 NORTH STANLEY AVENUE	LOS ANGELES	CA	90036	
JEWISH FAMILY SERVICE - FREE BURIAL & LOAN SERVICE 3245 SHEFFIELD AVENUE	OAKLAND	CA	94602	(415) 532-6314
JEWISH FAMILY SERVICE - FREE BURIAL SERVICE 3355 FOURTH AVENUE	SAN DIEGO	CA	92103	(619) 291-0473
SHALOM GARDENS 2255 LOS GATOS-ALMADEN ROAD	SAN JOSE	CA	95124	(408) 356-4151
JEWISH BURIAL SOCIETY OF SOUTHERN COUNTIES 13031 JUSTIN STREET	SANTA ANA	CA	92703	(714) 530-6636
DENVER RABBINICAL COUNCIL FREE BURIAL SERVICES C/O RODEF SHALOM SYNAGOGUE, 450 SOUTH KEARNEY	DENVER	CO	80222	
INDEPENDENT TRUE BIKUR CHOLIM 726 CAPITAL AVENUE	BRIDGEPORT	CT	06606	
HEBREW FUNERAL HOME - CHESED SHEL EMES 1061 ALBANY AVENUE	HARTFORD	CT	06114	
HEBREW FUNERAL ASSOCIATION 906 FARMINGTON AVENUE	WEST HARTFORD	CT	06119	(203) 527-3890
FREE BURIAL SOCIETY - CHEVRA KADISHA 31 WILLIAMSON DRIVE	WATERBURY	CT	06705	
JEWISH FEDERATION OF DELAWARE-FREE BURIAL SERVICE 101 GARDEN OF EDEN ROAD	WILMINGTON	DE	19801	(302) 478-6200
MOUNT SINAI CEMETERY - FREE BURIAL SERVICE 1125 N.W. 137TH STREET AND 11TH AVENUE	MIAMI	FL	33124	(305) 681-4432
CHEVRA KADISHO MACHZIKAI HADAS 2040 W. DEVON AVENUE	CHICAGO	IL	60645	(312) 764-8760
JEWISH BURIAL SOCIETY 221 N. LASALLE	CHICAGO	IL	60659	(312) 346-7950
JEWISH FREE BURIAL SOCIETY 1300 WEST DEVON	CHICAGO	IL	60660	(312) 761-2400
JEWISH SACRED SOCIETY-CHEVRA KADISHA 6633 NORTH SACRAMENTO	CHICAGO	IL	60645	(312) 743-0074
HEBREW CEMETERY ASSOCIATION - FREE BURIAL SERVICE 3127 SHERIDAN ROAD	PEORIA	IL	61604	
ORTHODOX JEWISH CEMETERY ASSOCIATION C/O FORT WAYNE JEWISH FEDERATION, 227 E. WASHINGTON BLVD	FORT WAYNE	IN	46802	(219) 422-8566
JEWISH FAMILY & CHILDREN'S SERVICE - FREE BURIAL SERVICE 2026 ST. CHARLES AVENUE	NEW ORLEANS	LA	70130	(504) 524-8475
CHEVRA KADISHA - FREE BURIAL SOCIETY 27 DICK DRIVE	WORCESTER	MA	01608	
JEWISH CHILD & FAMILY SERVICE - FREE BURIAL SERVICE 956 MAIN STREET	WINNIPEG	MB		(204) 943-6425
HEBREW BURIAL & SOCIAL SERVICE SOCIETY 5750 PARK HEIGHTS AVENUE	BALTIMORE	MD	21215	(301) 466-9200
HEBREW BURIAL & SOCIAL SERVICE SOCIETY OF BALTIMORE 319 W. MONUMENT STREET	BALTIMORE	MD	21201	(301) 727-4828
HEBREW ORTHODOX FREE BURIAL SOCIETY P.O. BOX 5778	BALTIMORE	MD	21208	
HEBREW ORTHODOX MEMORIAL SOCIETY 6820 GERMAN HILL ROAD	BALTIMORE	MD	21216	(301) 633-5806
HEBREW BENEVOLENT SOCIETY (CHESED SHEL EMES) 26640 GREENFIELD ROAD	OAK PARK	MI	48237	(313) 543-1622
JEWISH FAMILY & CHILDREN'S SERVICES - FREE BURIAL SERVICE 1115 EAST 65TH STREET	KANSAS CITY	MO	64110	(816) 333-1172
CHEVRA KADISHA 1601 NORTH AND SOUTH ROAD	ST LOUIS	MO	63123	(314) 427-0160
HEBREW FREE BURIAL SOCIETY C/O PHILIP APTER & SON 1600 SPRINGFIELD AVENUE	MAPLEWOOD	NJ	07040	
BOROUGH PARK HEBREW BURIAL ASSOCIATION 9322 AVENUE L	BROOKLYN	NY	11230	
HEBREW BURIAL SOCIETY 1283 CONEY ISLAND AVENUE	BROOKLYN	NY	11230	(718) 776-8100
MAALIN BAKODESH SOCIETY 4511 FORT HAMILTON PARKWAY	BROOKLYN	NY	11219	(718) 435-6100
PINCUS MANDEL-CEMETERY CONSULTANT 1569 47TH STREET	BROOKLYN	NY	11219	(718) 855-5121
JEWISH FAMILY SERVICE OF ERIE COUNTY - FREE BURIAL ASSOC. 2600 NORTH FOREST ROAD	GETZVILLE	NY	14068	(716) 668-2321

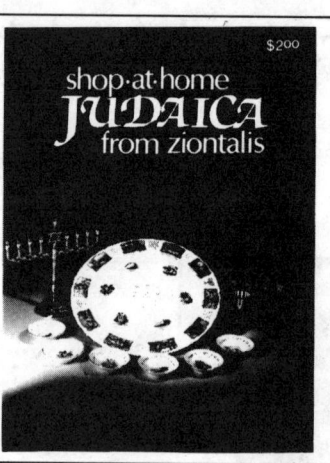

ADATH ISRAEL OF NEW YORK, UNITED HEBREW COMMUNITY OF NEW YORK				
201 EAST BROADWAY	NEW YORK	NY	10002	(212) 674-3580
AUSTRO-HUNGARIAN HEBREW FREE BURIAL 245 EAST 63RD STREET	NEW YORK	NY	10021	(212) 838-1187
HEBREW FREE BURIAL ASSOCIATION INC. (EXECUTIVE OFFICES)				
1170 BROADWAY	NEW YORK	NY	10001	(212) 686-2433
KUPATH RAMBAN COLEL POLEN 1133 BROADWAY, SUITE 416	NEW YORK	NY	10010	(212) 255-7800
UNITED HEBREW COMMUNITY OF N.Y., ADATH ISRAEL OF N.Y.				
201 EAST BROADWAY	NEW YORK	NY	10002	(212) 674-3580
WEIL FUNERAL HOME-FREE BURIAL SERVICE 3901 READING ROAD	CINCINNATI	OH	45229	(513) 281-0178
CHESED SHEL EMETH FREE BURIAL ASSOCIATION-FREE BURIAL SERVC.				
3740 RIDGE ROAD	CLEVELAND	OH	44114	(216) 631-4493
JEWISH SACRED SOCIETY 3555 BENDEMEER ROAD	CLEVELAND	OH	44118	(216) 371-5717
JEWISH FAMILY SERVICE - FREE BURIAL SERVICE 4501 DENLINGER	DAYTON	OH	45406	(513) 854-2944
JEWISH FAMILY SERVICE - FREE BURIAL SERVICE				
6525 SYLVANIA AVENUE	SYLVANIA	OH	43560	(419) 885-2561
JEWISH CHILD & FAMILY SERVICE - FREE BURIAL SERVICE				
4600 BATHURST STREET	TORONTO	ON		(416) 638-7800
HEBREW BURIAL ASSOCIATION - FREE BURIAL SERVICE				
234 MCKEE PLACE	PITTSBURGH	PA	15213	(412) 683-4900
CHEVRA KADISHA-HOLY SOCIETY OF BUCKS COUNTY				
400 DAVID DRIVE	TREVOSE	PA	19047	(215) 357-7130
JEWISH FAMILY SERVICES OF THE BARON DE HIRSCH INSTITUTE				
FREE BURIAL SERVICES, 3600 VAN HORNE AVENUE	MONTREAL	QU		(514) 731-3881
CHARLESTON JEWISH SOCIAL SERVICE - FREE BURIAL SERVICE				
1645 WALLENBERG BOULEVARD	CHARLESTON	SC	29407	(803) 571-6565
JEWISH SOCIAL SERVICE FEDERATION - FREE BURIAL SERVICE				
8434 AHERN STREET	SAN ANTONIO	TX	78216	(512) 341-8234
HEBREW BURIAL SOCIETY - FREE BURIAL SERVICE				
814 RIVERSIDE DRIVE	NEWPORT NEWS	VA	23606	
HEBREW LADIES CHARITY SOCIETY - FREE BURIAL SERVICE				
8065 BUFFALO AVENUE	NORFOLK	VA	23518	
JEWISH FAMILY SERVICES - FREE BURIAL SERVICES				
7027-3 CHOPT ROAD	RICHMOND	VA	23200	(804) 282-5644
SEATTLE JEWISH CHAPEL - FREE BURIAL SERVICE				
104 12TH STREET (CONGREGATION BIKUR CHOLIM)	SEATTLE	WA	98144	(206) 323-7321

CALENDARS

ADVERTISING CORPORATION OF AMERICA 110 LYMAN STREET	HOLYOKE	MA	01040	(413) 533-7151
HEBREW PUBLISHING COMPANY 100 WATER STREET	BROOKLYN	NY	11201	(718) 858-6928
VAAD L'CHIZUK KIYUM HAMITZVOTH 4911 - 16TH AVENUE	BROOKLYN	NY	11204	(718) 851-1314
ADATH ISRAEL OF NEW YORK, UNITED HEBREW COMMUNITY OF NEW YORK				
201 EAST BROADWAY	NEW YORK	NY	10002	(212) 674-3580
ISRAEL DISCOUNT BANK 511 FIFTH AVENUE	NEW YORK	NY	10017	(212) 551-8500
JEWISH NATIONAL FUND STUDENT CALENDAR 42 EAST 69TH STREET	NEW YORK	NY	10021	(212) 879-9300
UNITED HEBREW COMMUNITY OF N.Y.-ADATH ISRAEL OF N.Y.				
201 EAST BROADWAY	NEW YORK	NY	10002	(212) 674-3580
UNITED SYNAGOGUE OF AMERICA - PROGRAM SUGGESTIONS				
155 FIFTH AVENUE	NEW YORK	NY	10010	(212) 533-7800
UNIVERSE BOOKS 381 PARK AVENUE SOUTH	NEW YORK	NY	10016	(212) 685-7400
YAD L'ACHIM CALENDAR 156 FIFTH AVENUE	NEW YORK	NY	10010	(212) 624-2003
ZIONTALIS MANUFACTURING COMPANY 48 ELDRIDGE STREET	NEW YORK	NY	10002	(212) 925-8558

CALLIGRAPHERS

CALLIGRAPHERS II,- TAMARA GREENSTEIN				
1101 SOUTH ROBERTSON BOULEVARD, SUITE 210	LOS ANGELES	CA	90035	(213) 278-5370
DAVID WILLNER, TOBY S. WILLNER	LOS ANGELES	CA		(213) 931-6298
GUY-PAUL BISMUTH, LINDA BISMUTH				
1432 SOUTH CRESCENT HEIGHTS BOULEVARD	LOS ANGELES	CA	90035	(213) 939-4713
JOANNE ABENSOUR 1500 S. WOOSTER STREET	LOS ANGELES	CA	90035	(213) 854-5921
JODY MYERS	LOS ANGELES	CA		(213) 397-4248
ORA COOPER 412 WEST SIXTH STREET, SUITE 615	LOS ANGELES	CA	90014	(213) 622-2823
ROBIN MUER 612 NORTH KINGS ROAD, APT 306	LOS ANGELES	CA	90048	(213) 653-0019
SUSAN SREBO 9215 ALCOTT STREET	LOS ANGELES	CA	90035	(213) 550-7752
HEDY M. HARRIS 6325 BEN AVENUE	NORTH HOLLYWOOD	CA	91606	(818) 763-4339
ROBIN HALL/RICH SIGBERMAN 600 SECOND AVENUE	SAN FRANCISCO	CA	94118	(415) 668-8832
CHARLES H. BAUM 72 CALHOUN AVENUE	TRUMBULL	CT	06611	(203) 268-2512
NANCY GREENBERG DESIGNS 7045 S.W. 110TH TERRACE	MIAMI	FL	33156	(305) 667-1324
SHELLEY EPSTEIN-DESIGNERS CONNECTION				
1822-A NORTH UNIVERSITY DRIVE	PLANTATION	FL	33322	(305) 473-1040
THE KETUBAH-MIRIAM KARP 880 SOMERSET DRIVE N.W.	ATLANTA	GA	30327	(404) 237-5882
GERSHON YUDKOWSKY 2927 WEST TOUHY AVENUE	CHICAGO	IL	60645	(312) 262-5700
HANNAH DRESNER 920 EAST 61ST STREET	CHICAGO	IL	60637	(312) 955-2882
JUDITH KANIN 833 WEST BUCKINGHAM	CHICAGO	IL	60657	(312) 348-8432
KADISH GAIBEL				
C/O JOSARAH ENTERPRISES 523 SOUTH PLYMOUTH COURT	CHICAGO	IL	60605	(312) 922-6897
ROSE ANN CHASMAN 6147 NORTH RICHMOND	CHICAGO	IL	60659	(312) 764-4169
NESSIE FRANK 1642 LINDEN AVENUE	HIGHLAND PARK	IL	60035	(312) 432-6668
YOCHANAN CENTER C/O NAJARIAN 22 SOUTH CHASE	LOMBARD	IL	60148	
SHARON SAVITSKY 20 PARK AVENUE	NEWTON	MA	02158	(617) 965-1940
MIRIAM KARP 17 BIGELOW STREET	BRIGHTON	MA	02135	
A.N. GOLDSTEIN C/O J.C.C. OF GREATER MINNEAPOLIS				
4330 CEDAR LAKE ROAD SOUTH	MINNEAPOLIS	MN	55416	(612) 698-0751
AVCO GRAPHICS 3313 SHELBURNE ROAD	BALTIMORE	MD	21208	
ANN ZAIMAN 7912 WINTERSET AVENUE	BALTIMORE	MD	21208	(301) 484-4377
MARSHA GOLDFINE 8486 SNOWDEN OAKS PLACE	LAUREL	MD	20708	(301) 953-9260
PEGGY H. DAVIS CALLIGRAPHY 3249 HENNEPIN AVE. SO. SUITE 144	MINNEAPOLIS	MN	55408	(612) 929-3362
ADIR GALLERY	EDISON	NJ	08817	(201) 572-1751
BRENDA STOCHEL 14 OLDEN ROAD	EDISON	NJ	08817	(201) 572-2488
SIMCHA BACK STUDIOS 325 11TH STREET	LAKEWOOD	NJ	08701	(201) 363-4702
SIMCHA STUDIOS 325 11TH STREET	LAKEWOOD	NJ	08701	(201) 363-4702
EMANUEL MILSTEIN 29 WYNCREST ROAD	MARLBORO	NJ	07746	(201) 946-8604
ABIGAIL CHAPMAN 529 LAUREL ROAD	RIDGEWOOD	NJ	07450	(201) 652-7535

SANDY WEINER 104 GRIGGS AVENUE .... TEANECK **NJ** 07666 (201) 836-3989
CHAIM J. BERNATH .... BROOKLYN **NY** (718) 435-1753
DOV BER SCHWARTZ .... BROOKLYN **NY** (718) 387-1363
KALI-GRAPHICS 3801 MAPLE AVENUE .... BROOKLYN **NY** 11224 (718) 372-4573
KATZ & COHEN, CALLIGRAPHICALLY YOURS 638 EAST 2ND STREET ..... BROOKLYN **NY** 11218 (718) 854-3159
LIPOT FRIEDMAN 5501 15TH AVENUE .... BROOKLYN **NY** 11219 (718) 436-0901
NORMAN SAPOZNIK 2321 EAST 24TH STREET .... BROOKLYN **NY** 11229 (718) 769-2566
NUSACH 195 LEE AVENUE .... BROOKLYN **NY** 11211
RAPHAEL POSNER 993 EAST 18TH STREET .... BROOKLYN **NY** 11230 (718) 253-7922
RENEE SANDRA GREENBERG 18 BRIGHTON 10 PATH .... BROOKLYN **NY** 11235 (718) 891-8846
SHIMON KATZMAN 1468 51ST STREET .... BROOKLYN **NY** 11219 (718) 853-3014
SIMCHA ARTWORK 199 ROTH STREET .... BROOKLYN **NY** 11211 (718) 387-0739
WAXMAN'S CALLIGRAPHY STUDIOS 4713 13TH AVENUE .... BROOKLYN **NY** 11219 (718) 851-9595
YONAH WEINRIB/JUDAICRAFT 713 AVENUE D .... BROOKLYN **NY** 11223 (718) 375-8167
YEHUDAH CLAPMAN 719 MONTGOMERY STREET .... BROOKLYN **NY** 11213 (718) 774-9313
YEKUSIEL YEHUDA LAX .... BROOKLYN **NY** (718) 946-2934
GALAXY GRAPHICS 113 BROOK AVENUE .... DEER PARK **NY** 11729 (516) 242-5726
IRWIN RAPPAPORT .... FAR ROCKAWAY **NY** 11691 (718) 474-7300
NECHAMA FELLER 740 MADOR COURT .... FAR ROCKAWAY **NY** 11691 (718) 337-5295
LILI WRONKER 144-44 VILLAGE ROAD .... JAMAICA **NY** 11435 (718) 380-3990
CARA GOLDBERG MARKS 388 KENRIDGE ROAD .... LAWRENCE **NY** 11559 (516) 374-5574
NOAMI NADATA 39 STEVENS PLACE .... LAWRENCE **NY** 11559 (516) 239-0292
CALLIGRAPHER'S INK
KETUBOT & CALLIGRAPHY BY JOANNE FINK, 1734 GORMLEY AVENUE ... MERRICK **NY** 11566 (516) 378-1515

FRED SPINOWITZ KETUBOT 5 OVERLOOK ROAD .... NEW ROCHELLE **NY** 10804 (914) 632-9794
BETSY PLATKIN TEUTSCH 789 WEST END AVENUE, APT. 9C .... NEW YORK **NY** 10025 (212) 866-5448
JAY GREENSPAN PO BOX 914 .... NEW YORK **NY** 10025 (212) 737-2444
JEWISH ART & CALLIGRAPHY STUDIO 17 EAST 67TH STREET .... NEW YORK **NY** 10021 (212) 744-4355
KETUBOT ETC. .... NEW YORK **NY** (212) 598-0393
CLAIRE MENDELSON 499 FORT WASHINGTON AVENUE, #6H .... NEW YORK **NY** 10033 (212) 928-2732
NISSIM HIZME 82 CANAL STREET .... NEW YORK **NY** 10002 (212) 925-2922
PAMELA WEIMAN 543 EAST 6TH STREET .... NEW YORK **NY** 10009 (212) 473-7019
SHEL BASSEL 305 PALMWOOD DRIVE .... TROTWOOD **OH** 45426 (513) 837-3439
SHARON BINDER, BETH TZEDEC CONGREGATION
1700 BATHURST STREET .... TORONTO **ON** M5P 3K3 (416) 781-3511
CLAIRE MENDELSON 446 LAWRENCE AVENUE WEST .... TORONTO **ON** M5M 1C2 (416) 534-5268
REEVA KIMBLE 2352 VAN NESS .... EUGENE **OR** 97439 (503) 345-8129
EMES EDITIONS 2001 LEVICK STREET .... PHILADELPHIA **PA** 19149 (215) 268-8787
MARCIA KAUNTER 50 SARGENT AVENUE .... PROVIDENCE **RI** 02906 (401) 331-0219

CAMPS

AMERICAN JEWISH SOCIETY FOR SERVICE
15 EAST 26TH STREET ROOM 1304 .... NEW YORK **NY** 10010 (212) 683-6178
ASSOCIATION OF JEWISH SPONSORED CAMPS, INC.
130 EAST 59TH STREET .... NEW YORK **NY** 10022 (212) 751-0477
DIVISION OF COMMUNITY SERVICES, YESHIVA UNIVERSITY
185TH STREET & AMSTERDAM AVENUE .... NEW YORK **NY** 10033 (212) 960-5400
UNION OF AMERICAN HEBREW CONGREGATIONS 838 FIFTH AVENUE ... NEW YORK **NY** 10021 (212) 249-0100

CAMPS - CHILDREN & TEENS

B'NAI B'RITH PINE LAKE, CAMP - ALBERTA 7200-156TH STREET .... EDMONTON **AT** T5R IX3 (403) 487-0899
CAMP CHARLES PERLSTEIN
C/O TEMPLE BETH ISRAEL, 3310 N. 10TH AVENUE .... PHOENIX **AZ** 85013 (602) 264-4428
CAMP TEVA
C/O PHOENIX JEWISH COMMUNITY CENTER, 1718 W. MARYLAND .... PHOENIX **AZ** 85015 (602) 249-1832
CAMP HATIKVAH C/O CAMP HATIKVAH FOUNDATION,
950 WEST 41ST AVENUE .... VANCOUVER **BC** V5Z 2N7 (604) 327-9072
CAMP MIRIAM C/O HABONIM ZIONIST SOCIETY,
950 WEST 41ST AVENUE .... VANCOUVER **BC** V5Z 2N7 (604) 266-5333
CAMP SOLOMON SCHECHTER C/O CONG. BETH ISRAEL,
4350 OAK STREET .... VANCOUVER **BC** V6H 2N4 (604) 731-4161
CAMP SWIG C/O TEMPLE SHOLOM, 4426 WEST 10TH AVENUE .... VANCOUVER **BC** V6R 2H9 (604) 224-1381
GAN ISRAEL DAY CAMP 5750 OAK STREET .... VANCOUVER **BC** V6M 2V7 (604) 266-1313
JEWISH COMMUNITY CENTRE DAY CAMP 950 WEST 41ST AVENUE ..... VANCOUVER **BC** V5Z 2N7 (604) 266-9111
CAMP ALONIM, BRANDEIS-BARDIN INSTITUTE
1101 PEPPERTREE LANE .... BRANDEIS **CA** 93064 (213) 348-7201
CAMP KOMAROFF 3801 EAST WILLOW AVENUE .... LONG BEACH **CA** 90815 (213) 424-8159
CAMP KOMAROFF
C/O LONG BEACH JEWISH COMMUNITY CENTER, 3801 E. WILLOW ... LONG BEACH **CA** 90815 (213) 426-7601
CAMP GILBOA, HABONIM 8339 WEST THIRD STREET .... LOS ANGELES **CA** 90048 (213) 655-1858
CAMP HESS KRAMER
C/O WILSHIRE BOULEVARD TEMPLE, 3663 WILSHIRE BOULEVARD .. LOS ANGELES **CA** 90010 (213) 388-2401
CAMP JCA OF THE JCCA 5870 WEST OLMPIC BOULEVARD .... LOS ANGELES **CA** 90036 (213) 938-2531
CAMP JCA - MALIBU 8455 BEVERLY BOULEVARD .... LOS ANGELES **CA** 90048
CAMP MAOZ 10400 WILSHIRE BOULEVARD .... LOS ANGELES **CA** 90024 (213) 474-1518
CAMP MAX STRAUS C/O JEWISH BIG BROTHERS ASSOCIATION,
6505 WILSHIRE BOULEVARD .... LOS ANGELES **CA** 90048 (213) 852-1234
CAMP MOSHAVA, B'NEI AKIVA 7269 BEVERLY BOULEVARD .... LOS ANGELES **CA** 90036 (213) 934-1854
CAMP NCSY C/O NATIONAL CONFERENCE OF SYNAGOGUE YOUTH,
7269 BEVERLY BOULEVARD .... LOS ANGELES **CA** 90048 (213) 938-6576
CAMP RAMAH IN CALIFORNIA 15600 MULHOLLAND DRIVE .... LOS ANGELES **CA** 90077 (213) 879-4114
CAMP SHOMRIA, HASHOMER HATZAIR
1070 SOUTH CRESCENT HEIGHTS .... LOS ANGELES **CA** 90035 (213) 935-3758
CAMP USY, UNITED SYNAGOGUE YOUTH
15600 MULHOLLAND DRIVE .... LOS ANGELES **CA** 90077 (213) 879-4114
CAMP YOUNG JUDAEA C/O HADASSAH ZIONIST YOUTH COMMISSION,
6505 WILSHIRE BOULEVARD .... LOS ANGELES **CA** 90048 (213) 653-4771

CAMP YOUNG JUDEA, HASHACHAR 6505 WILSHIRE BOULEVARD ...... LOS ANGELES **CA** 90048 (213) 653-4771
CHABAD SUMMER YESHIVA 7215 WARING AVENUE ...... LOS ANGELES **CA** 90036 (213) 937-3763
GINDLING HILLTOP CAMP
C/O WILSHIRE BOULEVARD TEMPLE, 3663 WILSHIRE BOULEVARD .. LOS ANGELES **CA** 90010 (213) 388-2401
HABONIM - CAMP GILBOA 8339 WEST 3RD STREET ...... LOS ANGELES **CA** 90048 (213) 655-1868
YOUNG JUDEA-CAMP JUDEA 6505 WILSHIRE BLVD., #201 ...... LOS ANGELES **CA** 90048 (213) 653-4771
CAMP ARAZIM 1419 BROADWAY, SUITE 612 ...... OAKLAND **CA** 94612 (415) 839-6044
CAMP YOUNG JUDEA 1419 BROADWAY, SUITE 308 ...... OAKLAND **CA** 94612 (415) 832-8448
CAMP RAMAH IN CALIFORNIA 385 FAIRVIEW ROAD ...... OJAI **CA** 93023 (805) 646-4301
CAMP ARAZIM
C/O UNITED SYNAGOGUE OF AMERICA, PO BOX 9154 ...... SACRAMENTO **CA** 95816
CAMP TAWONGA 3272 CALIFORNIA STREET ...... SAN FRANCISCO **CA** 94118 (415) 929-1996
CAMP TAWONGA C/O UNITED JEWISH COMMUNITY CENTERS-BAY AREA,
3200 CALIFORNIA STREET ...... SAN FRANCISCO **CA** 94118 (415) 346-6040
UAHC SWIG CAMP INST. C/O UNION OF AMERICAN HEBREW CONGS.,
703 MARKET STREET ...... SAN FRANCISCO **CA** 94103 (415) 392-7080
UAHC SWIG CAMP INSTITUTE 24500 BIG BASIN WAY ...... SARATOGA **CA** 95070 (415) 392-7080
J BAR DOUBLE C RANCH C/O JEWISH COMMUNITY CENTER,
P.O. BOX 6196, CHERRY CREEK STATION ...... DENVER **CO** 80206 (303) 399-2660
RANCH CAMP, THE P. O. BOX 6196 ...... DENVER **CO** 80206 (303) 399-2660
CAMP HADAR CARTER HILL ...... CLINTON **CT** 06413 (203) 669-8312
CAMP HADAR 435 BROOKLAWN AVENUE ...... FAIRFIELD **CT** 06432 (203) 333-0343
CAMP LAURELWOOD ...... MADISON **CT** 06443 (203) 421-3736
INT'L TORAH CAMPS-RABBI GERALD BRIEGER AT TEMPLE EMANUEL
150 DERBY AVENUE ...... ORANGE **CT** 06477
CAMP SHALOM C/O JCC OF GREATER HARTFORD
335 WEST BLOOMFIELD AVENUE ...... WEST HARTFORD **CT** 06117 (203) 236-4571
B'NAI B'RITH BEBER CAMP (NAT'L OFFICE)
1640 RHODE ISLAND AVENUE N.W. ...... WASHINGTON **DC** 20036 (202) 857-6600
B'NAI B'RITH PERLMAN CAMP 1640 RHODE ISLAND N.W. ...... WASHINGTON **DC** 20036 (202) 857-6600
CAMP TEL SHALOM
C/O ADAS ISRAEL CONGREGATION, 2850 QUEBEC STREET N.W. .... WASHINGTON **DC** 20008 (202) 362-4433
CAMP COLEMAN C/O UNION OF AMERICAN HEBREW CONGREGATIONS,
3785 NW 82 AVENUE ...... MIAMI **FL** 33131 (305) 592-4792
CAMP SHALOM OF CENTRAL FLORIDA BOX 160306 ...... MIAMI **FL** 33116 (305) 271-8377
UAHC COLEMAN CAMP INSTITUTE 119 E. FLAGLER STREET ...... MIAMI **FL** 33131 (305) 379-4553
GAN ISRAEL DAY CAMP 1140 ALTON ROAD ...... MIAMI BEACH **FL** 33139 (305) 673-5664
SAVAGE'S MT. LAKE (NORTH CAROLINA)
PO BOX 4450, NORMANDY DRIVE ...... MIAMI BEACH **FL** 33141 (305) 866-3045
CAMP BARNEY MEDINTZ
C/O JEWISH COMMUNITY CENTER, 1745 PEACHTREE STREET, N.E. ...... ATLANTA **GA** 30309 (404) 875-7881
CAMP JUDAEA 1655 PEACHTREE STREET N.W. ROOM 405 ...... ATLANTA **GA** 30309 (404) 876-1526
UAHC COLEMAN CAMP INSTITUTE ROUTE #3 ...... CLEVELAND **GA** 30528 (404) 865-3521
CAMP CHI 1 SOUTH FRANKLIN ...... CHICAGO **IL** 60606 (312) 346-6700
CAMP MOSHAVA
C/O BNEI AKIVA, 6500 N. CALIFORNIA AVENUE ...... CHICAGO **IL** 60645 (312) 338-2871
CAMP RAMAH (WISCONSIN) 59 EAST VAN BUREN ...... CHICAGO **IL** 60605 (312) 939-2393
HARAND CAMP 708 CHURCH STREET ...... CHICAGO **IL** 60201 (312) 864-1500
HENRY HORNER, CAMP 30 W. WASHINGTON STREET ...... CHICAGO **IL** 60602 (312) 726-8891
RAMAH, CAMP 72ND E. 11TH STREET ...... CHICAGO **IL** 60605 (312) 939-2393
UAHC OLIN-SANG-RUBY CAMP C/O UNION OF AMERICAN HEBREW CONG.,
100 WEST MONROE STREET ...... CHICAGO **IL** 60603 (312) 782-1477
YEHUDAH, CAMP 6328 NORTH CALIFORNIA ...... CHICAGO **IL** 60659 (312) 973-3232
CAMP GAN ISRAEL 2014 ORRINGTON ...... EVANSTON **IL** 60201 (312) 869-8060
CAMP MENORAH 8 BLACKHAWK HILLS DRIVE ...... ROCK ISLAND **IL** 61201 (309) 786-1866
HABONIM LABOR ZIONIST YOUTH
HABONIM CAMP TAVOR, 3740 DEMPSTER ...... SKOKIE **IL** 60076 (312) 676-9790
YOUNG JUDEA, CAMP 4155 W. MAIN STREET ...... SKOKIE **IL** 60076 (312) 676-9790
UAHC MYRON S. GOLDMAN CAMP INSTITUTE 9349 MOORE ROAD ...... ZIONSVILLE **IN** 46077 (317) 873-3361
CAMP BEN F. WASHER C/O JEWISH COMMUNITY CENTER
3600 DUTCHMANS LANE ...... LOUISVILLE **KY** 40205 (502) 459-0660
CAMP PEMBROKE 30 MAIN STREET, ROOM 16 ...... ASHLAND **MA** 01721 (617) 881-1002
CAMP KINGSWOOD-BRIDGTON, ME C/O COMBINED JEWISH PHILANTHROPIES
72 FRANKLIN STREET ...... BOSTON **MA** 02110 (617) 542-8080
GROSSMAN CAMP
C/O ASSOC. JEWISH COMMUNITY CENTERS, 72 FRANKLIN STREET ...... BOSTON **MA** 02110 (617) 329-9300
CAMP RAMAH IN NEW ENGLAND 233 HARVARD STREET, SUITE 200 ...... BROOKLINE **MA** 02146 (617) 232-7400
CAMP YAVNEH C/O HEBREW COLLEGE 43 HAWES STREET ...... BROOKLINE **MA** 02146 (617) 232-8710
INT'L TORAH CAMPS RABBI DOV TAYLOR AT TEMPLE OHABEI SHALOM,
1187 BEACON STREET ...... BROOKLINE **MA** 02147 (617) 277-6610
PIRCHAI DAY CAMP/BAIS SARAH DAY CAMP
C/O NEW ENGLAND CHASSIDIC CENTER, 1710 BEACON STREET ...... BROOKLINE **MA** 02146
YAVNEH, CAMP
C/O HEBREW COLLEGE 43 HAWES STREET ...... BROOKLINE **MA** 01907 (617) 232-8710
CAMP BAUERCREST 10 PERKINS ROAD ...... CHELSEA **MA** 02150
UAHC EISNER CAMP INSTITUTE BROOKSIDE ROAD ...... GREAT BARRINGTON **MA** 01230 (413) 528-1652
CAMP AVODA 11 ESSEX STREET ...... LYNNFIELD **MA** 01940
CAMP JOSEPH
C/O JEWISH COMMUNITY CENTER CAMPS, 50 HUNT STREET ...... WATERTOWN **MA** 02172 (617) 924-2030
CAMP NAOMI
C/O JEWISH COMMUNITY CENTER CAMPS, 50 HUNT STREET ...... WATERTOWN **MA** 02172 (617) 924-2030
CAMP YOUNG JUDAEA 81 KINGSBURY STREET ...... WELLESLEY **MA** 02181
JEWISH COMMUNITY CENTER DAY CAMP MANNING HOLD STREET ... WORCESTER **MA** 01602 (617) 756-7109
B'NAI B'RITH CAMPS 370 HARGRAVE STREET ...... WINNIPEG **MB** (204) 947-0601
CAMP MASSAD 388 DONALD STREET, #110 ...... WINNIPEG **MB** (204) 943-2815
GAN ISRAEL 2095 SINCLAIR STREET ...... WINNIPEG **MB** R2V 3K2 (204) 339-8737
CAMP AIRY C/O STRAUS FOUNDATION, 5750 PARK HEIGHTS AVENUE .. BALTIMORE **MD** 21215 (301) 466-9010
CAMP LOUISE
C/O STRAUS FOUNDATION, 5750 PARK HEIGHTS AVENUE ...... BALTIMORE **MD** 21215 (301) 466-9010
MILLDALE CAMPS ...... BALTIMORE **MD** (301) 356-5200

CAMP MOSHAVA
C/O ICHUD HABONIM, 920 SLIGO AVENUE ...... SILVER SPRING **MD** 20910
CAMP TAMARACK
C/O FRESH AIR SOCIETY, 6600 WEST MAPLE ROAD ...... WEST BLOOMFIELD **MI** 48033 (313) 661-0600
CAMP TAVOR
C/O HABONIM CAMP TAVOR, 2005 MERRIL #5 ...... YPSILANTI **MI** 48197
CAMP TIKVAH C/O JEWISH COMMUNITY CENTER OF GREATER MINN.,
4330 CEDAR LAKE ROAD SOUTH ...... MINNEAPOLIS **MN** 55416 (612) 377-8330
CAMP HERZL 790 S. CLEVELAND #202 ...... ST. PAUL **MN** 55116 (612) 827-2108
GAN ISRAEL DAY CAMP 15 MONTCALM COURT ...... ST. PAUL **MN** 55116 (612) 698-3858
HERZL CAMP 1698 GRAND AVENUE ...... ST. PAUL **MN** 55116 (612) 698-3895
JEWISH COMMUNITY CENTER DAY CAMPS 1375 ST. PAUL AVENUE ...... ST. PAUL **MN** 55116 (612) 698-0751
CAMP SABRA C/O JEWISH COMMUNITY CENTERS ASSOCIATION,
2 MILLSTONE CAMPUS DRIVE ...... ST. LOUIS **MO** 63146 (314) 432-5700
UAHC JACOBS CAMP INSTITUTE BOX C ...... UTICA **MS** 39175 (601) 885-6042
BLUE STAR CAMPS KANUGA ROAD, PO BOX 1029 ...... HENDERSONVILLE **NC** 28739 (704) 692-3591
CAMP ESTHER F. NEWMAN
C/O JEWISH FEDERATION OF OMAHA, 333 SOUTH 132ND STREET ...... OMAHA **NE** 68154 (402) 334-8200
INTERLOCKEN/ISRAEL FRIENDSHIP CAMP RFD 2, BOX 165A ...... HILLSBORO **NH** 03244 (603) 478-3166
CAMP PEMBROKE
C/O COHEN FOUNDATION CAMPS, 250 BEDFORD ...... MANCHESTER **NH** 03101 (603) 627-1100
CAMP TEL NOAR
C/O COHEN FOUNDATION CAMPS, 250 BEDFORD ...... MANCHESTER **NH** 03101 (603) 627-1100
CAMP TEVYA
C/O COHEN FOUNDATION CAMPS, 250 BEDFORD ...... MANCHESTER **NH** 03101 (603) 627-1100
YM/YMHA OF PASSAIC SCOLES AVENUE ...... CLIFTON **NJ** 07012 (201) 779-2980
NEW JERSEY YMHA/YWHA CAMPS
C/O NEW JERSEY FEDERATION OF YS, 21 PLYMOUTH STREET ...... FAIRFIELD **NJ** 07006 (201) 575-3333
YAC DAY CAMP WEST ST. GEORGES AVENUE AND ORCHARD TERRACE ..... LINDEN **NJ** 07036 (201) 486-2866
CAMP-BY-THE-SEA OF THE JEWISH COMM. CENTER OF ATLANTIC CTY.
501 N. JEROME AVENUE ...... MARGATE **NJ** 08402 (609) 822-1167
CAMP KADIMAH C/O ATLANTIC JEWISH COUNCIL,
1515 SOUTH PARK STREET, SUITE 304 ...... HALIFAX **NS** B3J 2L2 (902) 422-7491
AKIVA DAY CAMP 420 WHITEHALL ROAD ...... ALBANY **NY** 12208 (518) 458-9329
JEWISH COMMUNITY CENTER DAY CAMP 340 WHITEHALL ROAD ...... ALBANY **NY** 12208 (518) 438-6651
LOUEMMA - R.D.2-SUSSEX, N.J.(55 MILES FROM NYC) 41-25 BELL BLVD .... BAYSIDE **NY** 11361 (718) 631-3747
BRONX HOUSE-EMANUEL-COPAKE, N.Y. (110 MILES FROM NYC)
990 PELHAM PARKWAY SOUTH ...... BRONX **NY** 10461 (212) 828-8952
BEER MORDECHAI SCHOOL & DAY CAMP 1670 OCEAN AVENUE ...... BROOKLYN **NY** 11230 (718) 377-1838
BROAD CHANNEL DAY CAMP, YESHIVA OF FLATBUSH
919 EAST 10TH STREET ...... BROOKLYN **NY** 11230 (718) 377-4466
CAMP ACHVAH (BOYS) 3495 NOSTRAND AVENUE ...... BROOKLYN **NY** 11219 (718) 648-7703
CAMP EMUNAH TINY TOTS
C/O LUBAVITCH, 824 EASTERN PKWY ...... BROOKLYN **NY** 11213 (718) 735-0200
CAMP GAN ISRAEL 770 EASTERN PARKWAY ...... BROOKLYN **NY** 11213 (718) 756-8007
CAMP GILA 1533 48TH STREET ...... BROOKLYN **NY** 11219
CAMP HASC C/O HEBREW ACADEMY FOR SPECIAL CHILDREN,
1311 55TH STREET ...... BROOKLYN **NY** 11219
CAMP HATIKVAH-PUTNAM VALLEY(65 MILES FROM NYC)
1305 CONEY ISLAND AVENUE ...... BROOKLYN **NY** 11230 (718) 338-3534
CAMP H.E.S. 9502 SEAVIEW AVENUE ...... BROOKLYN **NY** 11236 (718) 241-3000
CAMP NAARIM 1726 45TH STREET ...... BROOKLYN **NY** 11204
CAMP NA-IM C/O KINGS HIGHWAY JEWISH CENTER,
2810 NOSTRAND AVENUE ...... BROOKLYN **NY** 11229 (718) 376-7195
CAMP NISSIAH
C/O YM/YWHA OF WILLIAMSBURG, 575 BEDFORD AVENUE ...... BROOKLYN **NY** 11211
CAMP NU-YU (NUTRITION & DIET) 1561 EAST 12TH STREET ...... BROOKLYN **NY** 11230 (718) 998-4477
CAMP RAIYUS (GIRLS) 3495 NOSTRAND AVENUE ...... BROOKLYN **NY** 11219 (718) 648-7703
CAMP SDEI CHEMED INTERNATIONAL 1618 43RD STREET ...... BROOKLYN **NY** 11204 (718) 633-1909
CAMP SPATT
C/O YM/YWHA, 575 BEDFORD AVENUE ...... BROOKLYN **NY** 11211
CAMP TORAH VODAATH 425 EAST 9TH STREET ...... BROOKLYN **NY** 11218 (718) 941-8000
DORA GOLDING - P.O.B. 531, R.D. #2 E. STROUDSBURG, PA(100MI FROM NYC)
27 WEST END AVENUE ...... BROOKLYN **NY** 11235 (718) 891-4800
HEBREW EDUCATIONAL SOCIETY - SUFFERN, N.Y. (45 MILES FROM NYC)
9502 SEAVIEW AVENUE ...... BROOKLYN **NY** 11236 (718) 241-3000
KINGS BAY DAY CAMP 2611 AVENUE Z ...... BROOKLYN **NY** 11235 (718) 646-3447
MACHNE YISRAEL DAY CAMPS C/O NCFJE, 824 EASTERN PARKWAY ...... BROOKLYN **NY** 11213 (718) 735-0200
MENUCHA DAY CAMP 841-853 OCEAN PKWY ...... BROOKLYN **NY** 11230 (718) 434-5421
MIKAN-RECRO-ARDEN, N.Y. (50 MILES FROM NYC)
1201 PENNSYLVANIA AVENUE (SUITE 1C) ...... BROOKLYN **NY** 11239 (718) 642-1700
MORASHA - LAKE COMO, PA. (135 MILES FROM NYC)
1364 CONEY ISLAND AVENUE ...... BROOKLYN **NY** 11230 (718) 252-9696
MORASHA, CAMP 1277 EAST 14TH STREET ...... BROOKLYN **NY** 11215 (718) 253-5742
NOAM DAY CAMP
C/O YESHIVA CHSAN SOFER, 1705 49TH STREET ...... BROOKLYN **NY** 11204 (718) 853-8100
OCEAN PRIMARY SCHOOL & DAY CAMP 904 EAST 98TH STREET ...... BROOKLYN **NY** 11236 (718) 649-1567
SHEVES ACHIM DAY CAMP 1818 54TH STREET ...... BROOKLYN **NY** 11204 (718) 232-7800
YESHIVA ATERES YISROEL 8101 AVENUE K ...... BROOKLYN **NY** 11236 (718) 258-3585
ELLA FOHS - NEW MILFORD, CONN. (80 MILES FROM NYC)
257 B. 17 STREET ...... FAR ROCKAWAY **NY** 11691 (718) 327-5500
AGUDAH, CAMP ...... FERNDALE **NY** 12734 (914) 292-8830
CAMP COEUR D'ALENE
C/O YM/YMHA OF GREATER FLUSHING, 4535 KISSENA BOULEVARD ...... FLUSHING **NY** 11355 (718) 461-3030
CAMP N'VEI ASHDOD 6861 SELFRIDGE STREET ...... FOREST HILLS **NY** 11375 (718) 434-2258
EDWARD ISAACS-HOLMES, NY (65 MILES FROM NYC)
67-09 108TH STREET ...... FOREST HILLS **NY** 11375 (718) 268-5011
FOREST HILLS SUMMER PLAY PROGRAM 71-02 113TH STREET ...... FOREST HILLS **NY** 11375 (718) 261-9624
FOREST PARK DAY CAMP 102-35 63RD ROAD ...... FOREST HILLS **NY** 11375 (718) 896-4444
SIMCHA DAY CAMP 1170 WILLIAM STREET ...... HEWLETT **NY** 11557

BETAR, CAMP 85-40 149TH STREET KEW GARDENS **NY** 11415
CAMP HILLEL 33 WASHINGTON AVENUE LAWRENCE **NY** 11559 (516) 569-3370
CAMP SHALOM
C/O ARONSKIND, 60-29 264TH STREET LITTLE NECK **NY** 11363
AVNET, CAMP 530 WEST BROADWAY, P. O. BOX 329 LONG BEACH **NY** 11561
SENECA LAKE CAMP 31-53 CRESCENT STREET LONG ISLAND CITY **NY** 11106 (718) 726-6094
CAMP KFAR MASADA
C/O LONG ISLAND ZIONIST FOUNDATION, 381 SUNRISE HIGHWAY LYNBROOK **NY** 11563 (516) 593-9222
AGUDAH, CAMP (BOYS) 84 WILLIAM STREET NEW YORK **NY** 10038 (212) 797-9000
AMERICAN ZIONIST YOUTH FOUNDATION 515 PARK AVENUE NEW YORK **NY** 10022 (212) 751-6070
ANNA HELLER - NARROWSBURG, N.Y. (100 MILES FROM NYC)
1123 BROADWAY NEW YORK **NY** 10010 (212) 691-5548
ASSOCIATION OF JEWISH SPONSORED CAMPS, INC.
130 EAST 59TH STREET NEW YORK **NY** 10022 (212) 751-0477
B'NAI B'RITH PERLMAN - STARLIGHT, PA.18461 (150 MI FROM NYC)
823 UNITED NATIONS PLAZA NEW YORK **NY** 10017 (212) 490-3327
CAMP BNOS 84 WILLIAM STREET NEW YORK **NY** 10038 (212) 797-9000
CAMP WILDWOOD
C/O RECREATION ROOMS AND SETTLEMENT, 12 AVENUE D NEW YORK **NY** 10009 (212) 865-0925
CEJWIN CAMPS, INC.- PORT JERVIS, N.Y. (80 MILES FROM NYC)
15 E. 26TH STREET NEW YORK **NY** 10010 (212) 696-1024
CHAVATZELETH - WOODBOURNE, N.Y.(100 MILES FROM NYC)
142 BROOME STREET NEW YORK **NY** 10002 (212) 473-4500
EISNER CAMP INSTITUTE - GREAT BARRINGTON, MASS. (120 MILES FROM NYC)
838 FIFTH AVENUE NEW YORK **NY** 10021 (212) 249-0100
GALIL-OTTSVILLE, PA (80 MILES FROM NYC)
HABONIM CAMPING ASSOCIATION, 27 WEST 20TH STREET NEW YORK **NY** 10011 (212) 255-1796
KINDER RING - HOPEWELL JUNCTION, N.Y. (70 MILES FROM NYC)
45 E. 33RD STREET NEW YORK **NY** 10016 (212) 889-6800
KINDERLAND - TOLLAND, MASS. (130 MILES FROM NYC)
1 UNION SQUARE WEST NEW YORK **NY** 10003 (212) 255-6283
LEAH - BEAR MOUNTAIN, N.Y. (45 MILES FROM NYC)
197 EAST BROADWAY NEW YORK **NY** 10002 (212) 475-6061
MASSAD HEBREW CAMPS 426 WEST 58TH STREET NEW YORK **NY** 10019
MOGEN AVRAHAM/AVRAHAM CHAIM HELLER
1123 BROADWAY, ROOM 1019 NEW YORK **NY** 10010 (212) 691-5548
MOGEN AVRAHAM-STERNBERG-SPATT, INC.
1123 BROADWAY, ROOM 1019 NEW YORK **NY** 10010 (212) 691-5548
MORASHA, CAMP 2540 AMSTERDAM AVENUE NEW YORK **NY** 10033 (718) 252-9696
MOSHAVA - INDIAN ORCHARD, PA. (110 MILES FROM NYC)
25 W. 26TH STREET NEW YORK **NY** 10010 (212) 683-4484
MOSHAVA OF BNAI AKIVA OF NORTH AMERICA, CAMP
25 W. 26TH STREET NEW YORK **NY** 10010 (212) 683-4484
NATIONAL JEWISH WELFARE BOARD, DIRECTOR CAMPING SERVICES
15 EAST 26TH STREET NEW YORK **NY** 10010 (212) 532-4949
NATIONAL RAMAH 3080 BROADWAY NEW YORK **NY** 10027 (212) 749-8000
POYNTELLE-RAY HILL & LEWIS VILL. TEEN CAMP-POYNTELLE,PA
(135 MILES FROM NYC) 253 W. 72ND STREET NEW YORK **NY** 10023 (212) 787-7974
RAMAH IN THE BERKSHIRES, INC.-WINGDALE, N.Y. (80 MILES FROM NYC)
3080 BROADWAY NEW YORK **NY** 10027 (212) 749-0754
RAMAH, CAMP BROADWAY & 122ND STREET NEW YORK **NY** 10027 (212) 749-8000
RECEIVE-A-GUEST OF LONDON - DEPT T 200 PINEHURST AVENUE NEW YORK **NY** 10033 (212) 568-0270
SENECA LAKE, CAMP 510 EAST 86TH STREET NEW YORK **NY** 10028 (212) 794-0105
SHOMRIA - LIBERTY, N.Y. (90 MILES FROM NYC)
150 FIFTH AVENUE (SUITE 911) NEW YORK **NY** 10011 (212) 929-4955
STERNBERG-NARROWSBURG, N.Y. (100 MILES FROM NYC)
1123 BROADWAY, ROOM 1019 NEW YORK **NY** 10010 (212) 691-5548
SURPRISE LAKE CAMP - COLD SPRING, N.Y. (60 MILES FROM NYC)
80 FIFTH AVENUE NEW YORK **NY** 10011 (212) 924-3131
SUSSEX LAKE CAMP - R.D.#5, SUSSEX, N.J. (55 MILES FROM NYC)
1140 BROADWAY NEW YORK **NY** 10001 (212) 683-8528
TEL YEHUDAH - BARRYVILLE, N.Y. (100 MILES FROM NYC)
50 W. 58TH STREET NEW YORK **NY** 10019 (212) 355-7900
TEL YEHUDAH, CAMP 50 WEST 58TH STREET NEW YORK **NY** 10019 (212) 303-8247
THE AMERICAN JEWISH SOCIETY FOR SERVICE
15 EAST 26TH STREET, ROOM 1302 NEW YORK **NY** 10010 (212) 683-6178
TORAH VAAVODAH INSTITUTE
C/O BNEI AKIVA, 25 WEST 26TH STREET NEW YORK **NY** 10010
UAHC EISNER CAMP INSTITUTE 838 FIFTH AVENUE NEW YORK **NY** 10021 (212) 249-0100
UAHC HENRY S. JACOBS CAMP INST.
C/O UNION OF AMER HEB CONGS., 838 FIFTH AVENUE NEW YORK **NY** 10021 (212) 249-0100
UAHC KUTZ CAMP INSTITUTE 838 FIFTH AVENUE NEW YORK **NY** 10021 (212) 249-0100
UNION CAMP INSTITUTE
C/O UNION OF AMERICAN HEBREW CONGS., 838 FIFTH AVENUE NEW YORK **NY** 10021 (212) 249-0100
YOUNG JUDEA-SPROUT LAKE - VERBANK, N.Y. (75 MILES FROM NYC)
50 W. 58TH STREET NEW YORK **NY** 10019 (212) 303-8247
CAMP EAGLE COVE 164 LONGACRE ROAD ROCHESTER **NY** 14621 (716) 544-0600
CAMP MODIN FOR BOYS/GIRLS (CANAAN, ME)
791-T CENTRAL AVENUE SCARSDALE **NY** 10583 (914) 472-7713
CAMP TA-GO-LA 1 DOVER LANE SYOSSET **NY** 11791 (516) 921-5644
UAHC KUTZ CAMP INSTITUTE BOWEN ROAD WARWICK **NY** 10990 (914) 986-1174
CAMP LAKELAND C/O JEWISH CENTER OF GREATER BUFFALO,
2600 N. FOREST ROAD WEST AMHERST **NY** 14228 (716) 688-4033
CAMP BETH JACOB WOODBOURNE **NY** 12788 (914) 434-4440
LAVI, CAMP 301 JORDAN AVENUE WOODMERE **NY** 11598 (718) 327-6565
MORRIS, CAMP WOODRIDGE **NY** 12789 (914) 434-7480
CAMP LIVINGSTON
C/O JEWISH COMMUNITY CENTER, 1580 SUMMIT ROAD CINCINNATI **OH** 45237 (513) 761-7500
JEWISH COMMUNITY CENTER 3505 MAYFIELD ROAD CLEVELAND **OH** 44118 (216) 382-4000
YOUNG ISRAEL - B'NEI AKIVA 14141 CEDAR ROAD CLEVELAND **OH** 44121 (216) 382-5740
CAMP WISE
C/O JEWISH COMMUNITY CENTER, 3505 MAYFIELD ROAD CLEVELAND HEIGHTS **OH** 44118 (216) 382-4000
JEWISH CENTER 125 COLLEGE AVENUE COLUMBUS **OH** 43209 (614) 231-2731
YOUNG ISRAEL MOSHEVET STONE 14141 CEDAR ROAD SOUTH EUCLID **OH** 44121 (216) 382-5740
CAMP KOL TORAH 28400 EUCLID AVENUE WICKLIFFE **OH** 44092 (216) 943-5300
CAMP MOSHAVA 159 ALMORE AVENUE DOWNSVIEW **ON** (416) 630-7578
CAMP REENA 100 ELDER STREET DOWNSVIEW **ON**
CAMP KADIMA 57 DELAWARE AVENUE HAMILTON **ON**
CAMP B'NAI B'RITH OF OTTAWA 34 ELM BANK CRESCENT OTTAWA **ON** (613) 825-3067
CAMP BILUIM
C/O CANADIAN YOUNG JUDAEA, 788 MARLEE AVENUE TORONTO **ON** (416) 787-5350
CAMP MACHAR C/O YOUNG JUDAEA AND ZIONIST ORG. OF CANADA,
788 MARLEE AVENUE TORONTO **ON** (416) 787-5350
CAMP MASSAD 4140 BATHURST STREET TORONTO **ON**
CAMP MOSHAVA
C/O BNEI AKIVA, 86 VAUGHAN ROAD TORONTO **ON** (416) 630-7578
CAMP RAMAH IN CANADA
C/O JEWISH THEOLOGICAL SOCIETY, 3101 BATHURST STREET TORONTO **ON** (416) 789-2193
CAMP SHALOM
C/O CANADIAN YOUNG JUDAEA, 788 MARLEE AVENUE TORONTO **ON** (416) 787-5350
CAMP SOLELIM
C/O CANADIAN YOUNG JUDAEA, 788 MARLEE AVENUE TORONTO **ON** (416) 787-5350
CAMPS NORTHLAND, BNAI BRITH
C/O JEWISH CAMP COUNCIL OF TOR., 750 SPADINA AVENUE TORONTO **ON** (416) 924-6211
GOOD FELLOWSHIP
C/O JEWISH CAMP COUNCIL OF TORONTO, 750 SPADINA AVENUE TORONTO **ON** (416) 924-6211
CAMP GALIL BUCKS COUNTY **PA** 18942 (717) 469-4423
CAMP KVUTZA GALIL
C/O MID-STATES HABONIM, PO BOX 64 MERION **PA** 19066
CAMP SAGINAW OXFORD **PA** 19363 (215) 932-8467
ASSOCIATED CAMPING SERVICES 401 S. BROAD STREET PHILADELPHIA **PA** 19147 (215) 546-6600
CAMP JOSEPH & BETTY HARLAM
C/O UNION OF AMER. HEB. CONGS., 117 S. 17TH STREET PHILADELPHIA **PA** 19103 (215) 563-8183
CAMP RAMAH IN THE POCONOS 1701 WALNUT STREET PHILADELPHIA **PA** 19103 (717) 798-2504
JYC CAMPS
C/O JEWISH YS & CENTERS, 401 S. BROAD STREET PHILADELPHIA **PA** 19147 (215) 545-4400
PINEMERE CAMP OF THE MIDDLE ATLANTIC REGION OF J.W.B.
438 W. TABOR ROAD (WINTER ADDRESS) PHILADELPHIA **PA** 19120 (215) 924-0402
S.G.F. VACATION CAMP
C/O FEDERATION OF JEWISH AGENCIES, 1511 WALNUT STREET PHILADELPHIA **PA** 19102 (215) 893-5600
EMMA KAUFMANN CAMP
C/O JEWISH COMMUNITY CENTER, 5738 FORBES AVENUE PITTSBURGH **PA** 15217 (412) 521-8010
B'NAI B'RITH PERLMAN CAMP STARLIGHT **PA** 18461
CAMP PINEMERE RD #8, BOX 8001 STROUDSBURG **PA** 18360
JYC CAMPS ZIEGLERVILLE **PA** 19492 (215) 545-4400
B'NAI B'RITH, CAMP 5151 COTE ST. CATHERINE ROAD MONTREAL **QU** H3W 1M6 (514) 735-3669
CAMP MASSAD 1310 GREENE AVENUE, 8TH FLOOR MONTREAL **QU** H3Z 2B2 (514) 488-6610
CAMP WOODEN ACRES C/O JEWISH COMMUNITY CAMPS,
5170 COTE STE. CATHERINE ROAD #203 MONTREAL **QU** (514) 739-2301
JEWISH LAURENTIAN FRESH AIR CAMP
C/O GOLDEN AGE ASSOCIATION, 5700 WESTBURY MONTREAL **QU** (514) 739-4731
Y COUNTRY CAMP
C/O YM/YWHA OF MONTREAL, 5500 WESTBURY AVENUE MONTREAL **QU** (514) 737-6551
CAMP SHALOM
C/O TEMPLE OHAVE SHALOM, 305 HIGH STREET PAWTUCKET **RI** 02864
CAMP JORI C/O JEWISH FAMILY & CHILDREN'S SERVICE,
229 WAYLAND AVENUE PROVIDENCE **RI** 02906 (401) 783-7000
UAHC GREENE FAMILY CAMP BRUCEVILLE **TX** 76630 (817) 859-5411
CAMP BENBOW C/O SEATTLE JEWISH COMMUNITY CENTER,
3801 E. MERCER WAY, PO BOX 779 MERCER ISLAND **WA** 98040 (206) 232-7115
GAN ISRAEL CAMP 4541 19TH AVENUE N.E. SEATTLE **WA** 98118
CAMP INTERLAKEN C/O JEWISH COMMUNITY CENTER,
1400 NORTH PROSPECT AVENUE MILWAUKEE **WI** 53202 (414) 276-0716
B'NAI B'RITH BEBER CAMP MUKWONAGO **WI** 53149
UAHC OLIN-SANG-RUBY CAMP INSTITUTE
600 LAC LA BELLE DRIVE OCONOMOWOC **WI** 53066 (414) 567-6277

CAMPS - HANDICAPPED

MAX STRAUS C/O JEWISH BIG BROTHERS ASSOCIATION,
6505 WILSHIRE BOULEVARD LOS ANGELES **CA** 90048 (213) 852-1234
CAMP HENRY HORNER
C/O YOUNG MEN'S JEWISH COUNCIL, 30 WEST WASHINGTON STREET CHICAGO **IL** 60602 (312) 276-8891
CAMP RAMAH IN WISCONSIN 59 EAST VAN BUREN CHICAGO **IL** 60605 (312) 939-7400
CAMP RAMAH IN NEW ENGLAND 233 HARVARD BROOKLINE **MA** 02146 (617) 232-7400
CAMP TAMARACK
C/O FRESH AIR SOCIETY, 6600 WEST MAPLE ROAD WEST BLOOMFIELD **MI** 48033 (313) 627-2821
NEW JERSEY YM-YWHA CAMPS (ROUND LAKE CAMP, LAKE COMO, PA.)
21 PLYMOUTH STREET FAIRFIELD **NJ** 07006 (201) 575-3333
HEBREW ACADEMY FOR SPECIAL CHILDREN-PARKSVILLE NY (110 MILES FROM NYC)
1311 55TH STREET BROOKLYN **NY** 11219 (718) 851-6100
CAMP RAINBOW CROTON-ON-HUDSON **NY** 10520 (914) 949-6761
CUMMINGS CAMPGROUNDS - BREWSTER, N.Y. (65 MILES FROM NYC)
197 EAST BROADWAY NEW YORK **NY** 10002 (212) 475-6061
OAKHURST - OAKHURST, N.J. (61 MILES FROM NYC)
853 BROADWAY NEW YORK **NY** 10003 (212) 533-4020
RAINBOW - CROTON-ON-HUDSON, N.Y. 235 PARK AVENUE SOUTH NEW YORK **NY** 10003 (212) 460-0900
RAMAPO ANCHORAGE - RHINEBECK, N.Y.(95 MILES FROM NYC) RHINEBECK **NY** 12572 (914) 876-4273
SUMMIT CAMP & TRAVEL PROGRAMS 339 NORTH BROADWAY UPPER NYACK **NY** 10960 (914) 358-7772
CAMP EMMA KAUFMANN C/O JEWISH COMMUNITY CENTER,
315 SOUTH BELLEFIELD AVENUE PITTSBURGH **PA** 15213 (412) 521-8010

CAMPS - ISRAEL

Name & Address	City	State	Zip	Phone
CAMP N'VEI ASHDOD 6861 SELFRIDGE STREET	FOREST HILLS	NY	11375	(718) 434-2258
AMERICAN ZIONIST YOUTH FOUNDATION 515 PARK AVENUE	NEW YORK	NY	10022	(212) 750-7773
BETAR SUMMER PROGRAMS 9 EAST 38TH STREET	NEW YORK	NY	10016	(212) 696-0080
MASADA/ZOA ISRAEL SUMMER PROGRAM ZOA HOUSE, 4 EAST 34TH STREET	NEW YORK	NY	10016	(212) 481-1500
CAMP NCSY 45 W. 36TH STREET	NEW YORK	NY	10018	(212) 563-4000
KIBBUTZ ALIYA DESK BOX 30 27 W 20 STREET	NEW YORK	NY	10011	(212) 255-1338

CAMPS - SENIOR CITIZENS

Name & Address	City	State	Zip	Phone
BRONX HOUSE-EMANUEL - COPAKE, N.Y. (110 MILES) 990 PELHAM PARKWAY SOUTH	BRONX	NY	10461	(212) 828-8952
BORO PARK Y - OLDER ADULT DAY CAMP 4912 14TH AVENUE	BROOKLYN	NY	11219	(718) 438-5921
ELLA FOHS - NEW MILFORD, CONN. 257 BEACH 17TH STREET	FAR ROCKAWAY	NY	11691	(718) 327-5500
BLOCK & HEXTER VACATION CENTER - POYNTELLE, PA. (160 MILES FROM NYC) 130 E. 59TH STREET	NEW YORK	NY	10022	(212) 751-8580
ISABELLA FREEDMAN - FALLS VILLAGE, CONN. 80 FIFTH AVENUE	NEW YORK	NY	10011	(212) 242-5586
KINDER RING - HOPEWELL JUNCTION, N.Y. (70 MILES FROM NYC) 45 E. 33RD STREET	NEW YORK	NY	10016	(212) 889-6800
SALOMON VACATION CENTER - BREWSTER, N.Y. (65 MILES FROM NYC) 197 EAST BROADWAY	NEW YORK	NY	10002	(212) 475-6061

CAMPS - TOURS

Name & Address	City	State	Zip	Phone
USY ON WHEELS 72 EAST 11TH STREET	CHICAGO	IL	60605	(312) 939-2353
92ND STREET Y BICYCLE TOURS YM/YWHA 92ND STREET & LEXINGTON AVENUE	NEW YORK	NY	10028	(212) 427-6000
NAOM 25 W. 26TH STREET	NEW YORK	NY	10010	(212) 684-6091
USY ON WHEELS 155 FIFTH AVENUE	NEW YORK	NY	10010	(212) 533-7800

CANDY

Name & Address	City	State	Zip	Phone
BEN MYERSON CANDY CO. 928 TOWNE AVENUE	LOS ANGELES	CA	90021	(213) 623-6266
SETTON'S PISTACHIO CORP. 2901 FALCON DRIVE	MADERA	CA	93637	(209) 673-4949
BLUM'S 635 MARKET STREET	SAN FRANCISCO	CA	94105	(415) 777-9251
LE CHOCOLATIER 1836 NORTHEAST 164TH STREET	NORTH MIAMI BEACH	FL	33162	(305) 944-3020
BARTON'S KOSHER CANDIES 2816 WEST DEVON AVENUE	CHICAGO	IL	60645	(312) 274-1273
KOSHER CHOCOLATE FACTORY 1827 WILLOW ROAD	NORTHFIELD	IL	60093	(312) 441-7110
HILLS OF WESTCHESTER 3400 WINDOM ROAD	BRENTWOOD	MD	20722	(301) 864-4421
PLANTER'S NUT HOUSE 11419 GEORGIA AVENUE	WHEATON	MD	20902	(301) 942-6886
BOGDON CANDY CO. 3034 HOLMES STREET	KANSAS CITY	MO	64109	(816) 561-4402
BIERMANN MARZIPAN CO. 5418 TONNELLE AVENUE	NORTH BERGEN	NJ	07047	(201) 863-2928
BARRY CHOCOLATE, INC. 1500 SUCKLE HIGHWAY	PENNSAUKEN	NJ	08110	(609) 665-4940
BANNER CANDY CORP. 700 LIBERTY AVENUE	BROOKLYN	NY	11208	(718) 647-4747
BLOOM PACKING CO. 4222 10TH AVENUE	BROOKLYN	NY	11219	(718) 853-2800
CANDY LAND 4819 16TH AVENUE	BROOKLYN	NY	11204	(718) 436-9308
CANDY MAN (KOSHER CANDY, DRIED FRUITS, NUTS, ETC.) 4702 13TH AVENUE	BROOKLYN	NY	11219	(718) 438-5419
JOYVA CORP. 53 VARIK AVENUE	BROOKLYN	NY	11212	(718) 497-0170
LIEBER CHOCOLATE COMPANY 100 19TH STREET	BROOKLYN	NY	11232	(718) 499-0888
MADANIM CHOCOLATE 513 FLUSHING AVENUE	BROOKLYN	NY	11205	(718) 855-7876
THE NUT CASE 4417 18TH AVENUE	BROOKLYN	NY	11204	(718) 438-1508
PASKESZ CANDY CO. 125 51ST STREET	BROOKLYN	NY	11232	(718) 439-6222
PASKESZ KOSHER CANDIES 5315 13TH AVENUE	BROOKLYN	NY	11219	(718) 851-4657
SHUFRA 585 MANHATTAN AVENUE	BROOKLYN	NY	11222	(718) 383-5760
CROWN KOSHER CANDIES 10 RASON ROAD	CEDARHURST	NY	11516	(516) 239-0800
ASTOR CHOCOLATE CORP. 48-25 METROPOLITAN AVENUE	GLENDALE	NY	11385	(718) 386-7400
BARRICINI CANDIES 82-02 37TH	JACKSON HEIGHTS	NY	11372	(718) 429-8335
KRUM'S CHOCOLATIERS CLARKSTOWN SHOPPING CENTER	NEW CITY	NY	10956	(914) 634-6676
KRUM'S CHOCOLATIERS 4 DEXTER PLAZA, P.O. BOX 1020	PEARL RIVER	NY	10965	(914) 735-5100
SETTON'S INTERNATIONAL FOODS 150 DUPONT STREET	PLAINVIEW	NY	11803	(516) 349-8090
THE NUT CASE MAIN STREET	WOODBOURNE	NY	12788	
THE PARTY NASH 2821 BATHURST STREET	TORONTO	ON	M6B 3A4	(416) 781-9779
GOLDENBERG CANDY CO. 161 W. WYOMING AVENUE	PHILADELPHIA	PA	19140	(215) 455-7505
AMBROSIA CHOCOLATE CO. 1133 N. 5TH STREET	MILWAUKEE	WI	53203	(414) 271-2089

CANDY - ISRAELI

Name & Address	City	State	Zip	Phone
R.L. ALBERT & SON, INC., ALTRAY COMPANY 19 WEST ELM STREET	GREENWICH	CT	06830	(203) 622-8655
HAMAKOR JUDAICA, INC. 6112 N. LINCOLN AVENUE	CHICAGO	IL	60659	(312) 463-6186
KOSHER PRODUCTS OF LOUISVILLE 3723 STANTON BLVD.	LOUISVILLE	KY	40220	(502) 452-6519
EXPO-EL INC. 3000 TOWN CENTER	SOUTHFIELD	MI	48075	(313) 358-1560
THE KELLER FOOD CO. 2917 BROOKLYN AVENUE, P.O. BOX 4824	KANSAS CITY	MO	64109	(816) 921-3500
I. ROKEACH & SONS, INC. 560 SYLVAN AVENUE	ENGLEWOOD CLIFFS	NJ	07632	(201) 568-7550
I. ROKEACH & SONS, INC. WATER & CHESTNUT STREETS	FARMINGDALE	NJ	07727	(201) 938-6131
SPITZER DISTRIBUTOR CO., INC. 320 MANIDA STREET	BRONX	NY	10474	(212) 378-1470
ATALANTA CORPORATION 17 VARICK STREET	NEW YORK	NY	10013	(212) 431-9000
ISRAEL ASSORTED COMMODITIES, INC. 350 FIFTH AVENUE, SUITE 5315	NEW YORK	NY	10118	(212) 563-4895
MIDLAND MARINE FOODS, INC. 4540 COMMERCE AVENUE	CLEVELAND	OH	44103	(216) 391-1005
REISER KOSHER WINE CO. 4834 NORTH BROAD STREET	PHILADELPHIA	PA	19141	(215) 329-3350

CANTORIAL INSTITUTIONS & SCHOOLS

Name & Address	City	State	Zip	Phone
NEW CANTORIAL STUDIO 275 WEBSTER AVENUE	BROOKLYN	NY	11230	(718) 871-9520
JEWISH THEOLOGICAL SEMINARY CANTORIAL INSTITUTE 3080 BROADWAY	NEW YORK	NY	10027	(212) 678-8000
SCHOOL OF SACRED MUSIC, HUC-JIR 1 W. 4TH STREET	NEW YORK	NY	10012	(212) 873-0388
YESHIVA UNIVERSITY CANTORIAL INSTITUTE 500 W. 185TH STREET	NEW YORK	NY	10033	(212) 960-5400

CANTORIAL ORGANIZATIONS

Name & Address	City	State	Zip	Phone
AMERICAN CONFERENCE OF CANTORS, THE 838 FIFTH AVENUE	NEW YORK	NY	10021	(212) 249-0100
CANTORIAL COUNCIL OF AMERICA 2540 AMSTERDAM AVENUE, ROOM 166	NEW YORK	NY	10033	(212) 960-5353
CANTORS ASSEMBLY-JEWISH THEOLOGICAL SEMINARY OF AMERICA 155 FIFTH AVENUE	NEW YORK	NY	10010	(212) 691-8020
JEWISH MINISTERS CANTORS ASSOCIATION OF AMERICA, INC. 3 W. 16TH STREET	NEW YORK	NY	10011	(212) 675-6601

CATERERS & CATERING HALLS

Name & Address	City	State	Zip	Phone
FEIG'S KOSHER FOODS 35071 E. 5TH STREET	TUCSON	AZ	85711	(602) 325-2255
JOSH LAX CATERING 9030 OLYMPIC BOULEVARD	BEVERLY HILLS	CA	90211	(213) 278-1911
BALEBOSTE CATERERS 5180 YARMOUTH	ENCINO	CA	91316	(818) 344-3417
JOSH LAX CATERING 7269 BEVERLY BOULEVARD	LOS ANGELES	CA	90036	(213) 935-2532
JOSH LAX CATERERS 8056 BEVERLY BOULEVARD	LOS ANGELES	CA	90048	(213) 938-7147
JOSH LAX CATERERS 6505 WILSHIRE BOULEVARD	LOS ANGELES	CA	90048	(213) 938-7147
LA DIFFERENCE CATERERS SEPHARDIC TEMPLE, 10500 WILSHIRE BLVD.	LOS ANGELES	CA	90024	(213) 475-7311
CUSNER'S KOSHER CUSTOM CATERING 11744 VICTORY BOULEVARD	NORTH HOLLYWOOD	CA	91606	(818) 766-5131
HARTFORD KOSHER CATERERS HARTFORD HILTON-FORD & PEARL STREETS	HARTFORD	CT	06103	(203) 527-7770
GUTKIN CATERERS 363 WHALLEY AVENUE	NEW HAVEN	CT	06511	(203) 562-6184
M&T APPETIZERS & DELICATESSEN 1150 WHALLEY AVENUE	NEW HAVEN	CT	06515	(203) 389-5603
MAISON DE JULES 131 RICHARD COURT	NEWINGTON	CT	06111	(203) 666-4610
GAMIEL BROTHERS DELICATESSEN & RESTAURANT 13 E. 7TH STREET	WILMINGTON	DE	19801	(302) 655-2748
MADAN KOSHER CATERING 130 SOUTHWEST 3RD AVENUE	DANIA	FL	33004	(305) 944-6644
MAZEL KOSHER CATERING 107 S. 20TH AVENUE	HOLLYWOOD	FL	33020	(305) 922-6666
MASTER HOST DINNER SERVICE 3095 N.W. 40TH STREET	MIAMI	FL	33142	(305) 635-5201
CLAUDINE UZAN 1425 LENOX AVENUE	MIAMI BEACH	FL	33139	(305) 532-2201
EMBASSY KOSHER STEAK HOUSE 1417 WASHINGTON AVENUE	MIAMI BEACH	FL	33139	(305) 538-7550
ROYAL HUNGARIAN KOSHER RESTAURANT & CATERERS SASSON HOTEL	MIAMI BEACH	FL	33139	(305) 538-5401
ISAAC'S KOSHER KITCHEN & CATERING 16460 NORTHEAST 16TH AVENUE	NORTH MIAMI BEACH	FL	33162	(305) 944-5222
KOSHER TREATS 1678 N.E. 164TH STREET	NORTH MIAMI BEACH	FL	33162	(305) 947-1800
DANZIGER 2932 WEST GREENLEAF	CHICAGO	IL	60645	(312) 743-4325
KOSHER KARRY 2828 WEST DEVON	CHICAGO	IL	60659	(312) 973-4355
POLSKI KOSHER CATERING	CHICAGO	IL		(312) 539-2288
SHELAT KOSHER FOODS 711 WEST GRAND AVENUE	CHICAGO	IL	60610	(312) 243-3473
TURNER KOSHER CATERERS 7771 S. EXCHANGE AVENUE	CHICAGO	IL	60649	(312) 721-8017
GOLDMAN-SEGAL KOSHER CATERERS 3411 WEST CHURCH	SKOKIE	IL	60076	(312) 338-4060
KOSHER GOURMET 3552 DEMPSTER	SKOKIE	IL	60077	(312) 679-0432
MAYER STIEBEL CATERERS 9599 SKOKIE BLVD	SKOKIE	IL	60076	(312) 679-7000
SIMCHAS' SIMCHAS 3552 W. DEMPSTER	SKOKIE	IL	60077	(312) 679-0432
TWO'S COMPANY 301-2 COUNTRY ACRES	LOUISVILLE	KY	40218	(502) 491-0499
BOSTON MARRIOTT-COPLEY PLACE, KOSHER DEPT. 110 HUNTINGTON AVENUE	BOSTON	MA	02116	(617) 578-0607
FOUR SEASONS HOTEL, KOSHER DEPT. 200 BOYLSTON STREET	BOSTON	MA	02116	(617) 338-4400
THE WESTIN HOTEL, KOSHER DEPT. COPLEY PLACE	BOSTON	MA	02116	(617) 262-9600
CATERING BY ANDREW 404A HARVARD STREET	BROOKLINE	MA	02146	(617) 731-6585
CHATEAU GAROD 1581 BEACON STREET	BROOKLINE	MA	02146	(617) 232-8444
CATERING BY RUBIN 1500 WORCESTER	FRAMINGHAM	MA	01701	(617) 527-6045
WALD'S FOODS 561 WARD STREET	NEWTON	MA	02159	(617) 969-1317
TRADITIONALLY YOURS 709 WASHINGTON STREET	NEWTONVILLE	MA	02160	(617) 969-0439
MYER'S KOSHER KITCHEN 168 SHIRLEY AVENUE	REVERE	MA	02151	(617) 289-2063
BELL HOUSE 162 NORTH MAIN STREET	SHARON	MA	02067	(617) 784-6000
GREEN MANOR 80 MASSAPOAG AVENUE	SHARON	MA	02067	(617) 784-6000
GREEN MANOR 31 TOSCA DRIVE	STOUGHTON	MA	02072	(617) 341-1600
CHARLES GILBERT AND DAVIS 1580 VFW PARKWAY	WEST ROXBURY	MA	02132	(617) 325-7750
MOONI'S 1597 MAIN STREET	WINNIPEG	MB	R2V 1Y2	(204) 339-5949
BLUEFIELD CATERERS 401 REISTERSTOWN ROAD	BALTIMORE	MD	21208	(301) 486-2100
GOLDMAN'S FANCY KOSHER BAKERY 6848 REISTERSTOWN ROAD	BALTIMORE	MD	21202	(301) 358-9625
SCHLEIDER CATERERS 5805 OAKLEAF AVENUE	BALTIMORE	MD	21215	(301) 881-3787
MARION'S CUSTOM CATERING 2702 NAVARE DRIVE	CHEVY CHASE	MD	20815	(301) 587-5820
MR. OMELETTE 5020 LAGUNA ROAD	COLLEGE PARK	MD	20740	(202) 441-2695
KNISH SHOP 508 REISTERSTOWN ROAD	PIKESVILLE	MD	21208	(301) 484-5850
BLUEFIELD CATERERS 6011 EXECUTIVE BOULEVARD, SUITE 110	ROCKVILLE	MD	20852	(301) 468-1313
CORNED BEEF STATION OCEAN PLAZA MALL, OCEAN HWY & 94TH STREET	SILVER SPRING	MD		(301) 723-3222
HALLMARK KOSHER CATERERS	SILVER SPRING	MD		(301) 622-2239
SHABAT, CATERING BY	SILVER SPRING	MD		(301) 621-5577
ROSENBERG KOSHER CATERERS 29901 MIDDLEBELT ROAD	FARMINGTON	MN	48024	(313) 626-5702
JEWEL KOSHER CATERING 28555 MIDDLEBELT ROAD	FARMINGTON HILLS	MN	48024	(313) 661-4050
BLOOM'S KOSHER CATERING & CARRY OUT 24711 COOLIDGE	OAK PARK	MI	48237	(313) 546-5444
JEWEL KOSHER CATERING 14800 WEST LINCOLN	OAK PARK	MI	48237	(313) 968-9784
SPERBER KOSHER CATERERS 24601 COOLIDGE	OAK PARK	MI	48237	(313) 398-1177
SPERBER KOSHER CATERERS 14309 WEST 10 MILE ROAD	OAK PARK	MI	48237	(313) 548-9000
GOLDSHLAG CATERING 27705 LAHSER ROAD	SOUTHFIELD	MI	48034	(313) 358-0154
QUALITY KOSHER CATERING 27375 BELL ROAD	SOUTHFIELD	MI	48034	(313) 352-7758
QUALITY KOSHER CATERING 24350 SOUTHFIELD ROAD	SOUTHFIELD	MI	48075	(313) 559-4610
SPERBER KOSHER CATERERS 21100 WEST 12 MILE ROAD	SOUTHFIELD	MI	48076	(313) 357-2910
QUALITY KOSHER CATERING 5075 WEST MAPLE ROAD	WEST BLOOMFIELD	MI	48033	(313) 851-6880
KOHN SIMON KOSHER MEAT MARKET 10424 OLD OLIVE STREET ROAD	ST. LOUIS	MO	64131	(314) 569-0727
SOL & ELY'S KOSHER MEAT MARKET 8627 OLIVE STREET ROAD	ST. LOUIS	MO	64132	(314) 993-9977
KEN'S DELICATESSEN STATE HIGHWAY 34	ABERDEEN TOWNSHIP	NJ		(201) 583-1111

GOODWILL PANTRY CATERING 815 BROADWAY	BAYONNE	**NJ**	07002	(201) 339-2392
KOSHER KITCHEN 5901 BROADWAY	BAYONNE	**NJ**	07002	(201) 437-1594
FOSTER VILLAGE KOSHER CATERING 469 SOUTH WASHINGTON	BERGENFIELD	**NJ**	07621	(201) 384-7100
MERION CATERERS U.S. HIGHWAY 130 & WYNWOOD DRIVE	CINNAMINSON	**NJ**	08077	(609) 829-2111
VICTOR MAYER & SONS 100 HEPBURN ROAD	CLIFTON	**NJ**	07012	(201) 471-5096
VILLAGE KOSHER CATERERS 389 PIAGET AVENUE	CLIFTON	**NJ**	07011	(201) 772-5387
MIN GOLDBLATT & SONS 211 ELIZABETH AVENUE	EAST LINDEN	**NJ**	07052	(201) 925-3869
KOSHER PARADISE 155 ELMORA AVENUE	ELIZABETH	**NJ**	07202	(201) 354-0448
SUPERIOR DELI & APPETIZER COMPANY 150 ELMORE AVENUE	ELIZABETH	**NJ**	07202	(201) 352-0355
ENGLEWOOD KOSHER DELI 95 WEST PALISADE AVENUE	ENGLEWOOD	**NJ**	07631	(201) 567-0732
PETAK BROS. KOSHER DELICATESSEN 19-03 FAIR LAWN AVENUE	FAIR LAWN	**NJ**	07410	(201) 797-5010
SQUIRE KOSHER RESTAURANT & DELI 209 MAIN STREET	FT. LEE	**NJ**	07024	(201) 461-7410
ZELLY'S 1347 16TH STREET	FT. LEE	**NJ**	07024	(201) 224-4848
SHERATON HEIGHTS 650 HARRIS AVENUE	HASBROUCK HEIGHTS	**NJ**	07604	(201) 288-6100
IMPERIAL KOSHER CATERERS 1170 STUYVESANT AVENUE	IRVINGTON	**NJ**	07111	(201) 373-7464
FOX LIEBERMAN HOTEL 814 MADISON AVENUE	LAKEWOOD	**NJ**	08701	(201) 367-9199
DELI KING 628 ST. GEORGES AVENUE	LINDEN	**NJ**	07036	(201) 925-3909
EPPES ESSEN OF LIVINGSTON 105 MT PLEASANT AVENUE	LIVINGSTON	**NJ**	07039	(201) 994-1120
KEN'S DELICATESSEN STATE HIGHWAY 34	MATAWAN	**NJ**	07747	(201) 583-1111
GOVERNOR MORRIS INN, THE 2 WHIPPANY ROAD	MORRISTOWN	**NJ**	07960	(201) 539-7300
MIDDLEBROOK KOSHER DELICATESSEN ROUTE 35 & DEAL, MIDDLEBROOK SHOPPING MALL	OAKHURST	**NJ**	07755	(201) 493-8300
PATERSON CATERERS 12 MORTON STREET	PATERSON	**NJ**	07501	(201) 279-1941
LARRY'S KOSHER DELI RESTAURANT APPETIZERS & CATERERS 1353 SOUTH AVENUE	PLAINFIELD	**NJ**	07062	(201) 755-8013
SHORT HILLS CATERERS 610 MORRIS TURNPIKE	SHORT HILLS	**NJ**	07078	(201) 379-6950
TOMS RIVER KOSHER CATERERS 1065 MULBERRY PLACE	TOMS RIVER	**NJ**	08753	(201) 349-7914
LILY BARON KOSHER CATERERS 1363 BURNETT AVENUE	UNION	**NJ**	07083	(201) 688-4911
QUALITY DELI & APPETIZERS 638 OCEAN AVENUE	WEST END	**NJ**	07740	(201) 222-9753
GOLDMAN CATERERS 350 PLEASANT VALLEY WAY	WEST ORANGE	**NJ**	07052	(201) 731-4408
WEST MONT COUNTRY CLUB RIFLE CAMP ROAD	WEST PATERSON	**NJ**	07424	(201) 256-2700
FOREMOST KOSHER CATERERS 58 JEFFERSON AVENUE	WESTWOOD	**NJ**	07090	(201) 664-2465
TABATCHNICK OF WESTWOOD KOSHER DELICATESSEN & APPETIZERS 226 FAIRVIEW AVENUE	WESTWOOD	**NJ**	07090	(201) 666-1051
BIRCHWOOD MANOR 111 NORTH JEFFERSON ROAD	WHIPPANY	**NJ**	07981	(201) 887-1414
GOLDENBERG CATERERS, INC.		**NY**		(516) 239-5652
D & D CATERERS 8 MAGNOLIA TERRACE	ALBANY	**NY**	12209	(518) 462-2510
KAYE'S CATERERS 22 WILLOW STREET	ALBANY	**NY**	12206	(518) 538-5275
SANDS AT ATLANTIC BEACH 1395 BEACH BLVD	ATLANTIC BEACH	**NY**	11509	(516) 239-0660
SCHARF CATERERS, INC. 1395 BEECH BLVD	ATLANTIC BEACH	**NY**	11509	(516) 239-0900
BEN'S KOSHER GOURMET RESTAURANTS & CATERERS 933 ATLANTIC AVENUE	BALDWIN	**NY**	11510	(516) 868-2072
BAYSIDE JEWISH CENTER 203-05 32ND AVENUE	BAYSIDE	**NY**	11361	(718) 352-7900
LEDERMAN CATERERS LIMITED, BAYSIDE JEWISH CENTER 203-05 32ND AVENUE	BAYSIDE	**NY**	11363	(718) 461-6998
PRESTIGE CATERERS 61-35 220TH STREET	BAYSIDE	**NY**	11364	(718) 631-4217
SHORE TERRACE CATERERS, BAY TERRACE JEWISH CENTER 209TH STREET & CROSS ISLAND PARKWAY	BAYSIDE	**NY**	11364	(718) 224-5577
BELLE HARBOR JEWISH CENTER 134-01 ROCKAWAY BEACH BLVD	BELLE HARBOR	**NY**	11694	(718) 474-3300
LEVINE'S WASHINGTON HOTEL BEACH 125TH STREET & ROCKAWAY BEACH BLVD	BELLE HARBOR	**NY**	11694	(718) 634-4244
ZORN'S POULTRY FARMS 4321 HEMPSTEAD TURNPIKE	BETHPAGE	**NY**	11714	(516) 731-5500
CAL-TUV CATERERS 3483 JEROME AVENUE	BRONX	**NY**	10467	(212) 881-5770
KOL-TUV CATERERS 3483 JEROME AVENUE	BRONX	**NY**	10467	(212) 881-5770
LOESER'S KOSHER DELICATESSEN & CATERER 214 WEST 231ST STREET	BRONX	**NY**	10463	(212) 548-9735
MARINA DEL REY 2894 SCHURZ AVENUE	BRONX	**NY**	10465	(212) 931-6500
MEAL MART 798 LYDIG AVENUE	BRONX	**NY**	10462	(212) 931-2900
RIVERDALE CATERERS 27-40 JOHNSON AVENUE	BRONX	**NY**	10463	(212) 543-6750
SAMUEL ADLER & SONS 54 WEST KINGSBRIDGE ROAD	BRONX	**NY**	10463	(212) 367-3888
SCHWELLER'S KOSHER CATERERS 3411 JEROME AVENUE	BRONX	**NY**	10467	(212) 655-8649
SIMON'S KOSHER TAKE HOME FOODS 3532 JOHNSON AVENUE	BRONX	**NY**	10463	(212) 796-7530
ZION KOSHER DELICATESSEN & RESTAURANT 750 LYDIG AVENUE	BRONX	**NY**	10462	(212) 597-6360
ACH TOV KOSHER DAIRY RESTAURANT 5001 13TH AVENUE	BROOKLYN	**NY**	11219	(718) 438-8494
ADAM CATERERS 111 WEST END AVENUE	BROOKLYN	**NY**	11235	(718) 646-3400
ADELMAN'S 4514 13TH AVENUE	BROOKLYN	**NY**	11219	(718) 853-5680
AHI EZER CONGREGATION 1885 OCEAN PARKWAY	BROOKLYN	**NY**	11223	(718) 376-8600
ALEX KLEIN/LA MER 1060 OCEAN PARKWAY	BROOKLYN	**NY**	11230	(718) 692-2111
APERION MANOR 815 KINGS HIGHWAY	BROOKLYN	**NY**	11223	(718) 339-4466
ARMON TERRACE CATERERS 5120 NEW UTRECHT AVENUE	BROOKLYN	**NY**	11219	(718) 438-5700
AVENUE O JEWISH CENTER CATERERS 54 AVENUE O	BROOKLYN	**NY**	11204	(718) 232-3443
AVON CATERERS 17 EASTERN PARKWAY	BROOKLYN	**NY**	11238	(718) 836-6868
BAIS ROCHEL HALL 125 HEYWARD STREET	BROOKLYN	**NY**	11206	(718) 387-9022
BANQUETS BY LOCKER C/O YOUNG ISRAEL OF AVENUE K, 2818 AVENUE K	BROOKLYN	**NY**	11229	(718) 258-7088
BANQUETS BY LOCKER C/O KEVELSON JEWISH CENTER, 1387 EAST 96TH STREET	BROOKLYN	**NY**	11236	(718) 209-1006
CAROUSEL SMOKED FISH COMPANY 1504 ALBANY AVENUE	BROOKLYN	**NY**	11210	(718) 434-0700
CHAP-A-NOSH 1426 ELM AVENUE	BROOKLYN	**NY**	11230	(718) 627-0072
CHEESE'N THINGS 1117 AVENUE J	BROOKLYN	**NY**	11230	(718) 377-4911
CHEEZE D'LOX 4912 NEW UTRECHT AVENUE	BROOKLYN	**NY**	11219	(718) 436-7833
CONTINENTAL GLATT KOSHER CATERERS 75 RUTLEDGE STREET	BROOKLYN	**NY**	11211	(718) 875-0400
CONTINENTAL HOUSE OF GOURMET FOODS 2123 NOSTRAND AVENUE	BROOKLYN	**NY**	11210	(718) 859-9090
COTILLION TERRACE 7307 18TH AVENUE	BROOKLYN	**NY**	11204	(718) 436-2112
COUSINS KOSHER DELICATESSEN 5014 AVENUE D	BROOKLYN	**NY**	11203	(718) 629-0830
CROWN GLATT KOSHER CATERERS & RESTAURANT 4909 13TH AVENUE	BROOKLYN	**NY**	11219	(718) 853-9000
DEE & JAY KOSHER CATERERS 1902 UTICA AVENUE	BROOKLYN	**NY**	11234	(718) 968-8908
EDEN CATERING 5124 NINTH AVENUE	BROOKLYN	**NY**	11220	(718) 438-9523
ELM CATERERS 1213 ELM AVENUE	BROOKLYN	**NY**	11230	(718) 851-5444
EMBASSY TERRACE 401 AVENUE U	BROOKLYN	**NY**	11223	(718) 449-4040
EMPRESS KOSHER DELICATESSEN 2210 86TH STREET	BROOKLYN	**NY**	11214	(718) 266-7679
FLATBUSH KOSHER TAKE HOME FOODS 1383 CONEY ISLAND AVENUE	BROOKLYN	**NY**	11230	(718) 252-8888
GERSON CATERERS 1387 EAST 96TH STREET	BROOKLYN	**NY**	11236	(718) 251-1060
GLUCK'S TAKE HOME FOODS 2271 65TH STREET	BROOKLYN	**NY**	11204	(718) 232-1444
GOLDEN CATERERS 1416 AVENUE J	BROOKLYN	**NY**	11230	(718) 338-9865
GRABSTEIN BROS. 1845 ROCKAWAY PARKWAY	BROOKLYN	**NY**	11236	(718) 251-2280
GRUNWALD GOURMET 4901 16TH AVENUE	BROOKLYN	**NY**	11204	(718) 851-1162
GUTTMAN'S CATERING 5602 11TH AVENUE	BROOKLYN	**NY**	11219	(718) 851-7179
GUTTMAN'S GLATT KOSHER TAKE HOME & CATERING 5120 13TH AVENUE	BROOKLYN	**NY**	11219	(718) 436-4830
IRWIN JAY'S DELICATESSEN 1121 AVENUE J	BROOKLYN	**NY**	11230	(718) 258-9363
JAARON GLATT KOSHER CATERERS 1500 SHEEPSHEAD BAY ROAD	BROOKLYN	**NY**	11235	(718) 891-2442
JAFFA RESTAURANT 4210 18TH AVENUE	BROOKLYN	**NY**	11218	(718) 435-9661
JUDEA CATERERS CONGREGATION BETH SHOLOM, 2710 AVENUE X	BROOKLYN	**NY**	11235	(718) 891-7878
KENERETH GLATT KOSHER CATERERS 1920 AVENUE U	BROOKLYN	**NY**	11229	(718) 743-2473
KINGSBAY STRICTLY KOSHER CATERERS 3692 NOSTRAND AVENUE	BROOKLYN	**NY**	11229	(718) 891-7178
KINGSWAY JEWISH CENTER 2902 KINGS HIGHWAY	BROOKLYN	**NY**	11229	(718) 338-5000
KOEGEL & JACOBS KOSHER CATERERS 4305 15TH AVENUE	BROOKLYN	**NY**	11219	(718) 871-4727
KOSHER DELIGHT 1223 AVENUE I	BROOKLYN	**NY**	11230	(718) 377-6873
KOSHER DELIGHT 13TH AVENUE, CORNER OF 46TH STREET	BROOKLYN	**NY**	11219	(718) 435-8500
KOTIMSKY & TUCHMAN 111 WEST END AVENUE	BROOKLYN	**NY**	11235	(718) 939-9000
L & E CATERERS, INC. 1710 AVENUE M	BROOKLYN	**NY**	11230	(718) 375-7919
LA PERVILLE CATERERS 1815 65TH AVENUE	BROOKLYN	**NY**	11204	(718) 236-4600
LANDAU'S DELICATESSEN 65 LEE AVENUE	BROOKLYN	**NY**	11211	(718) 782-3700
LE GOURMET 1210 KINGS HIGHWAY	BROOKLYN	**NY**	11213	(718) 778-3999
LE PALAIS ISRAELI-GREEK RESTAURANT 923 KINGS HIGHWAY	BROOKLYN	**NY**	11223	(718) 336-2500
LEVENSTEIN & SARNOFF, KINGSWAY JEWISH CENTER 2902 KINGS HIGHWAY	BROOKLYN	**NY**	11229	(718) 338-5000
LOWINGER & JACOB CATERERS 1982 53RD STREET	BROOKLYN	**NY**	11204	(718) 258-1175
MANN NATT HOLLYWOOD CATERERS 3311 AVENUE S	BROOKLYN	**NY**	11234	(718) 375-8433
MANSOURA'S 515 KINGS HIGHWAY	BROOKLYN	**NY**	11223	(718) 645-7977
MARARD CATERERS 1387 EAST 96TH STREET	BROOKLYN	**NY**	11236	(718) 251-1060
MATAMIM GLATT KOSHER CATERERS 5815 20TH AVENUE	BROOKLYN	**NY**	11204	(718) 232-3701
MAZEL TOV CATERERS 114 WEBSTER AVENUE	BROOKLYN	**NY**	11230	(718) 871-1607
MEAL MART 1412 AVENUE J	BROOKLYN	**NY**	11230	(718) 338-8100
MEAL MART 1920 AVENUE M	BROOKLYN	**NY**	11230	(718) 998-0800
MEAL MART 5417 NEW UTRECHT AVENUE	BROOKLYN	**NY**	11219	(718) 851-8800
MEAL MART 510 BRIGHTON BEACH AVENUE	BROOKLYN	**NY**	11235	(718) 769-6800
MEAL MART 4722 16TH AVENUE	BROOKLYN	**NY**	11219	(718) 871-5335
MEAL MART 54 LEE AVENUE	BROOKLYN	**NY**	11211	(718) 387-8900
MEAL MART 4621 13TH AVENUE	BROOKLYN	**NY**	11219	(718) 854-7800
MEAL MART 54 LEE AVENUE	BROOKLYN	**NY**	11211	(718) 387-1445
MEAL MART 502 FLUSHING AVENUE	BROOKLYN	**NY**	11205	(718) 855-9600
MEAL MART 206 DIVISION AVENUE	BROOKLYN	**NY**	11211	(718) 963-3450
MEISNER'S 1312 55TH STREET	BROOKLYN	**NY**	11219	(718) 436-5592
MELROSE CATERING 268 BRIGHTON BEACH AVENUE	BROOKLYN	**NY**	11235	(718) 646-6460
MENASHE HIRSCH CATERERS 222 OCEAN PARKWAY	BROOKLYN	**NY**	11218	
MENDELES & ABRAHAM 942 MCDONALD AVENUE	BROOKLYN	**NY**	11218	(718) 436-1702
MENORAH BALLROOM 5000 14TH AVENUE	BROOKLYN	**NY**	11219	(718) 438-6490
MENROSE CATERERS 1114 52ND STREET	BROOKLYN	**NY**	11219	(718) 438-5977
MERMELSTEIN CATERERS 351 KINGSTON AVENUE	BROOKLYN	**NY**	11213	(718) 778-3100
MOISHE'S TAKE HOME FOODS 1706 EAST 16TH STREET	BROOKLYN	**NY**	11229	(718) 627-9438
NEGEV HOME MADE FOODS INC. 1211 AVENUE J	BROOKLYN	**NY**	11230	(718) 258-8440
NEWMAN & LEVENTHAL KOSHER CATERERS 1625 OCEAN AVENUE	BROOKLYN	**NY**	11230	(718) 338-3800
OCEAN BREEZE HOTEL 3811 SURF AVENUE	BROOKLYN	**NY**	11224	(718) 372-9813
OCEAN PARKWAY JEWISH CENTER 550 OCEAN PARKWAY	BROOKLYN	**NY**	11218	(718) 436-4900
PALACE, THE 4910 13TH AVENUE	BROOKLYN	**NY**	11219	
PARADISE GLATT KOSHER CATERERS 1426 ELM AVENUE	BROOKLYN	**NY**	11230	(718) 627-0072
PARKSIDE GARDEN CATERERS 83 DIVISION AVENUE	BROOKLYN	**NY**	11211	(718) 388-4204
RIMONIM CATERERS EMBASSY TERRACE, 401 AVENUE U	BROOKLYN	**NY**		(212) 684-5694
ROYALE, THE 770 MCDONALD AVENUE	BROOKLYN	**NY**	11218	(718) 435-1047
RUTHIE'S RESTAURANT 1427 CONEY ISLAND AVENUE	BROOKLYN	**NY**	11230	(718) 252-5308
S & D MAYER CATERERS INC. 2030 OCEAN PARKWAY	BROOKLYN	**NY**	11223	(718) 376-1300
SAMMY'S BAGEL NOSH 533 KINGS HIGHWAY	BROOKLYN	**NY**	11223	(718) 266-5920
SARNOFF CATERERS 2902 KINGS HIGHWAY	BROOKLYN	**NY**	11228	(718) 338-5000
SCHICK'S MANOR 4901 12TH AVENUE	BROOKLYN	**NY**	11219	(718) 853-6329
SCHREIBER CATERERS,INC. 9024 FOSTER AVENUE	BROOKLYN	**NY**	11236	(718) 272-9184
SEAVIEW JEWISH CENTER 1440 EAST 99TH STREET	BROOKLYN	**NY**	11236	(718) 763-5600
SHANG CHAI RESTAURANT 2189 FLATBUSH AVENUE	BROOKLYN	**NY**	11234	(718) 377-6100
SILBER GLATT KOSHER CATERERS 135 ROSS STREET	BROOKLYN	**NY**	11211	(718) 384-8085
SIMCHA CATERERS - COTILLION TERRACE 7307 18TH AVENUE	BROOKLYN	**NY**	11204	(718) 436-2112
SIMON'S KOSHER CATERERS 391 CROWN STREET	BROOKLYN	**NY**	11211	(718) 773-1480
TAM-GAN EDEN 2363 RALPH AVENUE	BROOKLYN	**NY**	11234	(718) 241-6102
TORAS EMES KAMENITZ 1650 56TH STREET	BROOKLYN	**NY**	11204	(718) 851-4735
TORATH MOSHE JEWISH CENTER 4314 10TH AVENUE	BROOKLYN	**NY**	11219	(718) 438-9578
TREE OF LIFE 1643 EAST 13TH STREET	BROOKLYN	**NY**	11223	(718) 375-5511
TUVIA'S GLATT KOSHER TAKE OUT 1813 KINGS HIGHWAY	BROOKLYN	**NY**	11219	(718) 627-8626
TWO FRIENDS CATERERS (CHOLOV YISROEL) 1017 EAST 29TH STREET	BROOKLYN	**NY**	11210	(718) 258-6018
YOUNG ISRAEL OF AVENUE K 2818 AVENUE K	BROOKLYN	**NY**	11229	(718) 258-8550
YUN KEE RESTAURANT & CATERERS 1416 ELM AVENUE	BROOKLYN	**NY**	11230	(718) 627-0072
ROSENTHAL CATERERS 283 TACOMA AVENUE	BUFFALO	**NY**	14216	(716) 876-8888
FIVE TOWNS BAGELS & CATERERS 584 CENTRAL AVENUE	CEDARHURST	**NY**	11516	(516) 569-7070
PRESTIGE CATERERS 555 VANDERBILT PARKWAY	DIX HILLS	**NY**	11746	(516) 499-4515
BRODIE'S KOSHER DELICATESSEN 1518 FRONT	EAST MEADOW	**NY**	11545	(516) 483-5382
DELRAY CATERERS 354 LARKFIELD ROAD	EAST NORTHPORT	**NY**	11731	(516) 266-9801
KOTIMSKY & TUCHMAN 295 MAIN STREET	EAST ROCKAWAY	**NY**	11518	(516) 599-1330
BAYSWATER JEWISH CENTER CATERERS 23-55 HEALY AVENUE	FAR ROCKAWAY	**NY**	11691	(718) 471-5252
CONGREGATION KNESETH ISRAEL 728 EMPIRE AVENUE	FAR ROCKAWAY	**NY**	11691	(718) 327-7545

Name / Address	City	State	Zip	Phone
KARMEL'S TAKE HOME FOODS INC. 19-03 CORNAGA AVENUE	FAR ROCKAWAY	**NY**	11691	(718) 327-7317
CONTINENTAL HOSTS LTD. FLUSHING MEADOW PARK	FLUSHING	**NY**	11368	(718) 592-5000
ELECTRIC INDUSTRY,THE 158-11 JEWEL AVENUE	FLUSHING	**NY**	11365	(718) 591-2000
JOY CATERERS INC.-UTOPIA JEWISH CENTER 64-41 UTOPIA PARKWAY	FLUSHING	**NY**	11365	(718) 461-9510
LINDEN HILL KOSHER DELICATESSEN & CATERERS 29-20 UNION STREET	FLUSHING	**NY**	11355	(718) 762-1515
MAUZONE TAKE HOME FOOD 69-60 MAIN STREET	FLUSHING	**NY**	11367	(718) 261-7723
MEAL MART 72-10 MAIN STREET	FLUSHING	**NY**	11367	(718) 261-3300
MEHL CATERERS,TERRACE ON THE PARK FLUSHING MEADOW PARK	FLUSHING	**NY**	11368	(718) 592-7373
NOT JUST DONUTS 72-04 MAIN STREET	FLUSHING	**NY**	11367	(718) 268-7830
TERRACE ON THE PARK FLUSHING MEADOW PARK	FLUSHING	**NY**	11368	(718) 592-5000
KNISH NOSH CATERERS 101-02 QUEENS BLVD	FOREST HILLS	**NY**	11374	(718) 897-5554
KOTIMSKY & TUCHMAN 106-06 QUEENS BLVD	FOREST HILLS	**NY**	11375	(718) 939-9000
PATRICIAN CATERERS 106-06 QUEENS BLVD	FOREST HILLS	**NY**	11375	(718) 939-9000
ROYALTY CATERERS C/O YOUNG ISRAEL OF FOREST HILLS 71-00 YELLOWSTONE BOULEVARD	FOREST HILLS	**NY**	11375	(718) 263-0489
SHARMEL CATERERS 71-00 YELLOWSTONE BLVD	FOREST HILLS	**NY**	11375	(718) 793-1130
ROSEBROOKE KOSHER CATERERS 366 DOGWOOD AVENUE	FRANKLIN SQUARE	**NY**	10010	(516) 483-3361
ALLISON KOSHER CATERERS GREAT NECK ROAD	GREAT NECK	**NY**	11021	(516) 466-5263
JEM CATERERS OF GREAT NECK, INC. 26 OLD MILL ROAD	GREAT NECK	**NY**	11023	(516) 482-2100
LEONARD'S OF GREAT NECK 555 NORTHERN BLVD	GREAT NECK	**NY**	11021	(516) 487-7900
MENORAH RESTAURANT 75 NORTH STATION PLAZA	GREAT NECK	**NY**	11021	(516) 466-8181
PRUZANSKY FAMILY CATERERS-LEONARD'S OF GREAT NECK 555 NORTHERN BLVD	GREAT NECK	**NY**	11021	(516) 851-5272
TEMPLE ISRAEL OF GREAT NECK 108 OLD MILL ROAD	GREAT NECK	**NY**	11023	(516) 487-2230
BEN'S KOSHER GOURMET RESTAURANTS & CATERERS 140 WHEATLEY PLAZA	GREENVALE	**NY**	11548	(516) 621-3340
EPSTEIN'S KOSHER DELICATESSEN & RESTAURANT 387 CENTRAL AVENUE	HARTSDALE	**NY**	10712	(914) 428-5320
VICTOR MAYER & SON CATERERS 1255 HEWLETT PLAZA	HEWLETT	**NY**	11557	(516) 374-6300
FELDWOOD KOSHER CATERING 428 SOUTH OYSTER BAY ROAD	HICKSVILLE	**NY**	11801	(516) 681-7766
HUNTINGTON TOWN HOUSE 124 EAST JERICHO TURNPIKE	HUNTINGTON STATION	**NY**	11743	(516) 427-8485
HUNTINGTON TOWN HOUSE 124 EAST JERICHO TURNPIKE	HUNTINGTON STATION	**NY**	11743	(516) 895-5855
A & B CATERING 182-69 WEXFORD TERRACE	JAMAICA	**NY**	11423	(718) 658-8900
BORENSTEIN CATERERS 179-29 150TH ROAD	JAMAICA	**NY**	11434	(718) 656-3600
FOUNTAINBLEU CATERERS JERICHO TURNPIKE	JERICHO	**NY**	11753	(516) 333-8585
COLONIAL CATERERS ROUTE 209	KERHONKSON	**NY**	12446	(914) 647-7575
NOT JUST DONUTS 72-04 MAIN STREET	KEW GARDENS HILLS	**NY**	11367	(718) 268-7830
TAIN LEE CHOW 72-24 MAIN STREET	KEW GARDENS HILLS	**NY**	11367	(718) 268-0960
BETH SHALOM OF LAWRENCE BROADWAY & WASHINGTON AVENUE	LAWRENCE	**NY**	11559	(516) 569-1880
LEVENSTEIN & SARNOFF CATERERS 390 BROADWAY	LAWRENCE	**NY**	11559	(516) 569-1880
TEMPLE TORAH CATERERS 54-27 LITTLE NECK PARKWAY	LITTLE NECK	**NY**	11362	(718) 423-2100
JACKSON HOTEL 10 WEST BROADWAY	LONG BEACH	**NY**	11561	(516) 431-3700
MICHELE CATERERS PARK AVENUE AT ROOSEVELT BLVD	LONG BEACH	**NY**	11561	(516) 334-7681
TEMPLE ISRAEL OF LONG BEACH RIVERSIDE BLVD	LONG BEACH	**NY**	11561	(516) 432-1410
BETH DAVID OF LYNBROOK 185 DENTON AVENUE	LYNBROOK	**NY**	11563	(516) 887-9595
CLASSIC CATERERS 185 DENTON AVENUE	LYNBROOK	**NY**	11563	(516) 887-9595
JERRAND CATERERS 153 BROADWAY	LYNBROOK	**NY**	11563	(516) 887-1533
LEVENSTEIN & SARNOFF CATERERS 185 DENTON AVENUE	LYNBROOK	**NY**	11563	(516) 887-9595
MALVERNE KOSHER CATERERS 370 HEMPSTEAD AVENUE	MALVERNE	**NY**	11565	(516) 599-1070
NEWMAN & LEVENTHAL CATERERS 333 SEARINGTON ROAD	MANHASSET	**NY**	11030	(516) 621-8049
MILJAY KOSHER CATERERS 1282 HICKSVILLE ROAD	MASSAPEQUA	**NY**	11758	(516) 541-0402
BAIS YAAKOV OF SPRING VALLEY 11 SMOLLEY DRIVE	MONSEY	**NY**	10952	(914) 356-3113
BETH ROCHEL SADDLE RIVER ROAD	MONSEY	**NY**	10952	(914) 356-7985
EUROPEAN HOMEMADE FOODS,INC. 82 ROUTE 59	MONSEY	**NY**	10952	(914) 356-9555
LANDAU CATERERS 9 JEFFREY PLACE	MONSEY	**NY**	10952	(914) 425-2837
MEAL MART 41 C MAIN STREET	MONSEY	**NY**	10952	(914) 352-9008
RAM CATERERS,INC. 20B ROBERT PITT DRIVE	MONSEY	**NY**	10952	(914) 352-0733
YESHIVA OF SPRING VALLEY ROUTE 306 & MAPLE AVENUE	MONSEY	**NY**	10952	(914) 352-1247
MARC AARON CATERERS 261 EAST LINCOLN AVENUE	MOUNT VERNON	**NY**	10552	(914) 668-7100
PELHAM CATERERS 675 EAST LINCOLN AVENUE	MOUNT VERNON	**NY**	10552	(914) 667-1116
DORNSTEIN'S BIG THREE CATERERS C/O TEMPLE EMANUEL,3315 HILLSIDE AVENUE	NEW HYDE PARK	**NY**	11040	(516) 747-8484
ROBBINS & ROBBINS 15 DRAKE AVENUE	NEW ROCHELLE	**NY**	10805	(914) 632-9115
BERNSTEIN'S ON ESSEX STREET 135 ESSEX STREET	NEW YORK	**NY**	10002	(212) 473-3900
DELI ART KOSHER DELICATESSEN 333 7TH AVENUE	NEW YORK	**NY**	10001	(212) 564-5994
DELI-GLATT KOSHER 150 FULTON STREET	NEW YORK	**NY**	10038	(212) 349-3622
FIFTH AVENUE SYNAGOGUE 5 EAST 62ND STREET	NEW YORK	**NY**	10021	(212) 838-2122
FINE & SCHAPIRO'S RESTAURANT 138 WEST 72ND STREET	NEW YORK	**NY**	10023	(212) 877-2874
G & M KOSHER CATERERS CO. 41 ESSEX STREET	NEW YORK	**NY**	10002	(212) 254-5370
HIRSCHFELD CATERERS 809 WEST 177TH STREET	NEW YORK	**NY**	10033	(212) 923-2148
KAY CATERERS 200 AMSTERDAM AVENUE	NEW YORK	**NY**	10023	(212) 362-5555
KOSHER CATALOGUE 41 MADISON AVENUE, 29TH FLOOR	NEW YORK	**NY**	10010	(212) 879-9300
KOSHER CATALOGUE 41 MADISON AVENUE, 29TH FLOOR	NEW YORK	**NY**	10010	(800) 5-KOSHER
LEVANA'S CAFE & RESTAURANT 148 WEST 67TH STREET	NEW YORK	**NY**	10021	(212) 877-8457
LINCOLN SQUARE SYNAGOGUE CATERERS 200 AMSTERDAM AVENUE	NEW YORK	**NY**	10023	(212) 362-5555
LOU G. SIEGEL'S RESTAURANT 209 WEST 38TH STREET	NEW YORK	**NY**	10018	(212) 921-4433
MACCABEEM RESTAURANT 147 WEST 47TH STREET	NEW YORK	**NY**	10036	(212) 575-0226
MARCY KOSHER DELICATESSEN 2511 BROADWAY	NEW YORK	**NY**	10025	(212) 222-0700
MEAL MART 4403 BROADWAY	NEW YORK	**NY**	10040	(212) 568-7401
MEAL MART 2189 BROADWAY	NEW YORK	**NY**	10024	(212) 787-4720
MERMELSTEIN CATERERS, INC.	NEW YORK	**NY**		(212) 778-3100
MICHELE & JOEL KARMAZIN-COMET CATERING (DAIRY OR MEAT)	NEW YORK	**NY**		(212) 362-0412
MT. SINAI JEWISH CENTER 135 BENNETT AVENUE	NEW YORK	**NY**	10040	(212) 928-9870
NEW YORK HILTON, THE AVENUE OF THE AMERICAS & 53RD STREET	NEW YORK	**NY**	10019	(212) 586-7000
NEW YORK PENTA 33RD STREET & 7TH AVENUE	NEW YORK	**NY**	10001	(212) 736-5000
NEW YORK UNIVERSITY-ARA 22 WASHINGTON SQUARE NORTH	NEW YORK	**NY**	10011	(212) 598-3396
NEWMAN & LEVENTHAL KOSHER CATERERS 45 WEST 81ST STREET	NEW YORK	**NY**	10024	(212) 362-9400
PAPILSKY CATERERS 305 WEST END AVENUE	NEW YORK	**NY**	10023	(212) 724-3761

Name / Address	City	State	Zip	Phone
PARAMOUNT GLATT CATERERS 23 WEST 73RD STREET	NEW YORK	**NY**	10023	(212) 362-8404
RATNER'S DAIRY RESTAURANT 138 DELANCEY STREET	NEW YORK	**NY**	10002	(212) 677-5588
SCHUSTER HALL 85-93 BENNETT AVENUE	NEW YORK	**NY**	10033	(212) 923-3582
SHAARE HATIKVAH AHAVATH TORAH,CONGREGATION 711 WEST 179TH STREET	NEW YORK	**NY**	10033	(212) 927-2720
SOMEPLACE SPECIAL 401 GRAND STREET	NEW YORK	**NY**	10002	(212) 473-7630
TEMPLE ISRAEL 112 EAST 75TH STREET	NEW YORK	**NY**	10021	(212) 249-5000
ZISKIN CATERERS 23 WEST 73RD STREET	NEW YORK	**NY**	10023	(212) 362-8404
CHATEAU CATERERS,LTD. 1373 BELLMORE ROAD	NORTH BELLMORE	**NY**	11710	(516) 569-4447
CATERERS OF WOODMERE,INC. 410 HUNGRY HARBOR ROAD	NORTH WOODMERE	**NY**	11581	(516) 791-1414
JEM CATERERS OF NORTH WOODMERE 1000 ROSEDALE ROAD	NORTH WOODMERE	**NY**	11598	(516) 791-3100
TAPPAN ZEE TOWNE HOUSE MOUNTAIN VIEW AVENUE	NYACK	**NY**	10960	(914) 358-8400
MR. OMELETTE 3445 LAWSON BLVD	OCEANSIDE	**NY**	11572	(516) 766-1884
GALAXIE CATERERS 1600 ROUND SWAMP ROAD	PLAINVIEW	**NY**	11803	(516) 694-6200
RICHMAN CATERERS (AT PLAINVIEW JEWISH CENTER)	PLAINVIEW	**NY**	11803	(516) 938-1310
RYE TOWN HILTON 699 WESTCHESTER AVENUE	PORT CHESTER	**NY**	10573	(914) 939-6300
NORTH SHORE JEWISH CENTER NORWOOD AVENUE & OLD TOWN ROAD	PT.JEFFERSON STATION	**NY**	11776	(516) 473-5525
FOREST PARK JEWISH CENTER 90-45 MYRTLE AVENUE	QUEENS	**NY**	11419	(718) 849-8817
CAFE BABA OF ISRAEL 91-33 63RD DRIVE	REGO PARK	**NY**	11374	(718) 275-2660
TOV CATERERS 97-22 63RD ROAD	REGO PARK	**NY**	11374	(718) 896-7788
PARKSIDE CATERERS 117-15 MYRTLE AVENUE	RICHMOND HILLS	**NY**	11419	(718) 849-8817
ALL-KOSHER CATERING 80 GUILDHALL ROAD	ROCHESTER	**NY**	14623	(716) 334-1614
BARDY KOSHER CATERERS 339 RUTGERS STREET	ROCHESTER	**NY**	14609	(716) 271-6948
BITTKER CATERERS 1700 EAST AVENUE	ROCHESTER	**NY**	14609	(716) 473-7635
BON APETIT CATERERS 444 WILLIS AVENUE	ROSLYN HEIGHTS	**NY**	11577	(516) 621-0402
ROSLYN COUNTRY CLUB CLUB DRIVE	ROSLYN HEIGHTS	**NY**	11577	(516) 621-0333
DUNOWITZ & LESSER CATERERS, TEMPLE ISRAEL 2655 CLUBHOUSE ROAD	S. MERRICK	**NY**	11566	(516) 379-7436
TEMPLE ISRAEL 2655 CLUBHOUSE ROAD	S.MERRICK	**NY**	11566	(516) 379-7436
CHEF-AH KOSHER CATERERS 33 MAPLE AVENUE	SPRING VALLEY	**NY**	10977	(914) 356-4410
GARTNER'S INN HUNGRY HOLLOW ROAD	SPRING VALLEY	**NY**	10977	(914) 356-0875
MAZEL GLATT CATERERS-SINGER'S HOTEL CENTRAL AVENUE	SPRING VALLEY	**NY**	10977	(914) 356-2306
ROYALE GOURMET CATERERS 23 ROOSEVELT AVENUE	SPRING VALLEY	**NY**	10977	(914) 354-3237
SINGER'S HOTEL CENTRAL AVENUE	SPRING VALLEY	**NY**	10977	(914) 356-2300
THE ISLAND/KOSHER ISLAND 2206 VICTORY BOULEVARD	STATEN ISLAND	**NY**	10314	(718) 698-5800
KAPLAN'S KOSHER CATERING 20 TOWNLY AVENUE	STATEN ISLAND	**NY**	10314	(718) 442-3877
SHALIMAR 2380 HYLAN BLVD	STATEN ISLAND	**NY**	10306	(718) 987-4800
SIMCHA BY THE SEA 1111 CAPODANNO BLVD	STATEN ISLAND	**NY**	10306	(718) 979-7400
YOUNG ISRAEL OF STATEN ISLAND WILLOWBROOK AT WOOLLEY	STATEN ISLAND	**NY**	10314	(718) 494-6700
HOLIDAY INN 3 EXECUTIVE BLVD	SUFFERN	**NY**	10901	(914) 357-4800
MEAL MART	SWAN LAKE	**NY**	12783	(914) 292-9439
NOAM CATERERS 310A SOUTH OYSTER BAY ROAD	SYOSSET	**NY**	11791	(516) 921-1800
RICHMAN CATERERS (AT EAST NASSAU JEWISH CENTER), 310 OYSTER BAY ROAD	SYOSSET	**NY**	11791	(516) 496-3390
RICHMAN CATERERS (AT MIDWAY JEWISH CENTER)	SYOSSET	**NY**	11791	(516) 433-6563
PICKLES UNLIMITED 4469 EAST GENESSEE	SYRACUSE	**NY**	13214	(315) 445-1294
HILTON INN 455 SOUTH BROADWAY	TARRYTOWN	**NY**	10591	(914) 631-5700
GINSBURG CATERERS 23 HORTON AVENUE	TROY	**NY**	12180	(518) 272-4828
CONGREGATION TREE OF LIFE 502 NO. CENTRAL AVENUE	VALLEY STREAM	**NY**	11580	(516) 825-2090
JEM CATERERS OF NASSAU,INC. 1000 ROSEDALE ROAD	VALLEY STREAM	**NY**	11581	(212) 297-1240
RIMONIM CATERERS EMBASSY EAST-FRANKLIN AVENUE	VALLEY STREAM	**NY**	11581	(212) 684-5694
CONCORD CATERERS 3710 WOODBINE AVENUE	WANTAGH	**NY**	11793	(516) 781-5577
GILARI CATERING 710 DOGWOOD AVENUE	WEST HEMPSTEAD	**NY**	11552	(516) 481-2060
JOY CATERERS, INC.-JCC OF WEST HEMPSTEAD 711 DOGWOOD AVENUE	WEST HEMPSTEAD	**NY**	11552	(516) 292-0111
WOLLOWICK CATERING OF WHITESTONE 12-25 CLINTON STREET	WHITESTONE	**NY**	11378	(718) 767-7000
CREST HOLLOW COUNTRY CLUB JERICHO TURNPIKE	WOODBURY	**NY**	11797	(516) 692-8000
LE CORDON BLEU 96-01 JAMAICA AVENUE	WOODHAVEN	**NY**	11421	(718) 441-8800
SONS OF ISRAEL,CONGREGATION 111 IRVING PLACE	WOODMERE	**NY**	11598	(516) 379-7436
BATTERMAN & HIRSCHEL CATERERS 311 CENTRAL PARK DRIVE	YONKERS	**NY**	10704	(914) 963-0602
EPSTEIN'S KOSHER DELICATESSEN & RESTAURANT 2369 CENTRAL PARK AVENUE	YONKERS	**NY**	10710	(914) 793-3131

ACADEMY PARTY CENTER CATERING 4182 MAYFIELD STREET ... CLEVELAND **OH** 44116 (216) 381-2066

DAVIS KOSHER CATERERS 1805 SOUTH TAYLOR STREET ... CLEVELAND **OH** 44116 (216) 321-7945

DISTINCTIVE CATERING CORPORATION/WORLD OF MOUTH C/O THE CIVIC, 3130 MAYFIELD ROAD ... CLEVELAND **OH** 44118 (216) 371-1112

EXECUTIVE CATERERS 27629 CHAGRIN BOULEVARD ... CLEVELAND **OH** 44122 (216) 831-1714

FISHMAN CATERING CORPORATION 3300 MAYFIELD STREET ... CLEVELAND **OH** 44118 (216) 291-1220

FISHMAN CATERING CORPORATION 2437 SOUTH GREEN ROAD ... CLEVELAND **OH** 44122 (216) 291-1220

PERSONAL TOUCH CATERING BY EVA 1926 SOUTH TAYLOR ROAD ... CLEVELAND **OH** 44118 (216) 932-7411

SIEGLE'S DELICATESSEN & FOOD MART 15 WEST BANCROFT ... TOLEDO **OH** 43620 (419) 243-6261

SIEGLE'S DELICATESSEN & FOOD MART 2636 WEST CENTRAL ... TOLEDO **OH** 43606 (419) 473-2791

LE'CHAIM CATERERS 2150 STEELES AVENUE WEST, UNIT 19 ... CONCORD **ON** L4K 2Y7 (416) 669-4831

ADATH SHOLOM SYNAGOGUE 864 SHEPPARD AVENUE WEST ... DOWNSVIEW **ON** (416) 635-0131

BETH DAVID B'NAI ISRAEL BETH AM 55 YEOMANS ROAD ... DOWNSVIEW **ON** M3H 3J7 (416) 633-5500

BETH EMETH BAIS YEHUDA SYNAGOGUE 100 ELDER STREET ... DOWNSVIEW **ON** M3H 5G7 (416) 633-3838

BETH JACOB SYNAGOGUE 147 OVERBROOK PLACE ... DOWNSVIEW **ON** M3H 4R1 (416) 638-5955

BETH RADOM SYNAGOGUE 18 REINER ROAD ... DOWNSVIEW **ON** (416) 636-3451

BOROCHOV CENTRE 272 CODSELL AVENUE ... DOWNSVIEW **ON** (416) 636-4021

CLANTON PARK SYNAGOGUE CLANTON & LOWESMOOR ... DOWNSVIEW **ON** M3H 2B5 (416) 633-4193

PETACH TIKVAH ANSHE CASTILLA 20 DANBY AVENUE ... DOWNSVIEW **ON** M3H 2J3 (416) 636-4719

SHAAR SHALOM SYNAGOGUE 2 SIMONSTON BOULEVARD ... THORNHILL **ON** (416) 889-4975

TASTEFULLY YOURS 2300 JOHN STREET ... THORNHILL **ON** L3T 6G6 (416) 731-1735

ASSOCIATED HEBREW SCHOOLS 3630 BATHURST ... TORONTO **ON** M6A 2E3 (416) 789-7471

BETH TORAH SYNAGOGUE 47 GLENBROOK AVENUE ... TORONTO **ON** M6B 2L7 (416) 782-4495

BETH TZEDEC SYNAGOGUE 1700 BATHURST ... TORONTO **ON** M5P 3K3 (416) 781-3511

CATERERS YORK LTD. 1700 BATHURST ... TORONTO **ON** M5P 3K3 (416) 783-4293

MALMAR CATERERS C/O BETH SHOLOM SYNAGOGUE 1445 EGLINTON AVENUE WEST ... TORONTO **ON** (416) 663-6203

MAX ZUCHTER CATERER LTD. 3995 BATHURST, SUITE 204 ... TORONTO **ON** (416) 638-FOOD

MONTECASSINO PALACE 3710 CHESSWOOD DRIVE ... TORONTO **ON** (416) 630-8100

SHAAREI SHOMAYIM SYNAGOGUE 470 GLENCAIRN AVENUE ... TORONTO **ON** M5N 1V8 (416) 789-3213

SHAAREI TEFILLAH SYNAGOGUE 3600 BATHURST ... TORONTO **ON** M6A 2C9 (416) 787-1631

SWEET YORK DESERTS 1700 BATHURST ... TORONTO **ON** M5P 3K3 (416) 782-1798

YITZ'S CATERING SERVICE 346 EGLINTON AVENUE WEST ... TORONTO **ON** (416) 487-4506

BETH TIKVAH SYNAGOGUE 3080 BAYVIEW AVENUE ... WILLOWDALE **ON** M2N 5L3 (416) 221-3433

B'NAI TORAH SYNAGOGUE 465 PATRICIA AVENUE ... WILLOWDALE **ON** M2R 2N1 (416) 226-3700

PRIDE OF ISRAEL SYNAGOGUE 59 LISSOM CRESCENT ... WILLOWDALE **ON** M2R 2P2 (416) 226-0111

BOLOTIN CATERING SERVICE YORK & ASBOURNE ROADS ... ELKINS PARK **PA** 19117 (215) 782-8660

ROSENTHAL & KAUFMAN OLD LANCASTER ROAD AND HIGHLAND AVENUE ... MERION **PA** 19066 (215) 667-4050

BETTY THE CATERER 25 EAST WALNUT LANE ... PHILADELPHIA **PA** 19144 (215) 844-6798

NORM THE CATERER 5163 KERSHAW ... PHILADELPHIA **PA** 19131 (215) 878-6300

R.PRESSMAN KOSHER CATERING 4027 WEST GIRARD AVENUE ... PHILADELPHIA **PA** 19104 (215) 382-4971

ROTHSCHILD CATERING 610 STRATHAVEN AVENUE ... SWARTHMORE **PA** 19081 (215) 544-5915

ADAM THE CATERER 9800 MEILLEUR ... MONTREAL **QU** (514) 381-2909

CATERED BY ERNIE 9775 TOLLHURST ... MONTREAL **QU** H3L 2Z7 (514) 385-0000

EDELSTEIN CATERING 285 QUERBES ... MONTREAL **QU** H2V 3W1 (514) 272-6979

GOLDEN CATERERS 5500 WESTBURY ... MONTREAL **QU** (514) 737-1182

MAUZONE CATERER 7005 VICTORIA ... MONTREAL **QU** (514) 739-3651

PERLMAN'S KOSHER CATERERS 4655 COURTRAI ... MONTREAL **QU** (514) 733-7141

SHALOM KOSHER CATERING 4693 VAN HORNE ... MONTREAL **QU** (514) 342-0087

CHARITABLE ORGANIZATIONS

UNITED ORTHODOX SERVICES 202 E. BENRIDGE LANE ... PHOENIX **AZ** 85012 (602) 277-7479

HEBREW ASSISTANCE ASSOCIATION C/O JEWISH FAMILY SERVICE AGENCY, 2025 WEST 42ND AVENUE, #305 ... VANCOUVER **BC** V6M 2B5 (604) 266-2396

JEWISH IMMIGRANT AID SERVICES (JIAS) 2025 WEST 42ND AVENUE, #305 ... VANCOUVER **BC** V6M 2B5 (604) 266-2396

ASSOCIATION FOR ETHIOPIAN JEWS 304 ROBIN HOOD LANE ... COSTA MESA **CA** 92627 (714) 642-8613

AMERICAN ASSOCIATION FOR ETHIOPIAN JEWS, NAT'L MATERIALS CTR. 6505 WILSHIRE BLVD., ROOM 802 ... LOS ANGELES **CA** 90048 (213) 852-1234

JEWISH NATIONAL HOSPITAL AT DENVER 440 NORTH LA BREA ... LOS ANGELES **CA** 90036 (213) 938-7273

NATIONAL INSTITUTE FOR JEWISH HOSPICE 8700 BEVERLY BOULEVARD, SHUMAN BUILDING, ROOM 310 ... LOS ANGELES **CA** 90048 (213) 467-7423

UNITED ORTHODOX SERVICES 150 NORTH GARDENER ... LOS ANGELES **CA** 90036 (213) 934-0849

UNITED ORTHODOX SERVICES 441 NORTH GENESSEE ... LOS ANGELES **CA** 90036 (213) 655-8373

UNITED ORTHODOX SERVICES 1850 ORTEGA STREET ... SAN FRANCISCO **CA** 94122 (415) 661-4055

STOCKTON JEWISH WELFARE FUND 5105 N. EL DORADO STREET ... STOCKTON **CA** 95204

UNITED ORTHODOX SERVICES, INC. 175 MAPLE STREET ... NEW HAVEN **CT** 06511 (203) 865-0923

UNITED ORTHODOX SERVICES, INC. 18 PEARL STREET ... NORWICH **CT** 06360 (203) 889-1900

UNITED ORTHODOX SERVICES 876 FARMINGTON AVENUE ... WEST HARTFORD **CT** 06119

DAVENPORT JEWISH WELFARE FUND 1115 MISSISSIPPI AVENUE ... DAVENPORT **IA** 52803 (319) 326-4419

JEWISH WELFARE FUND 1712 W. SUNSET DRIVE ... CARBONDALE **IL** 62901

HIAS 130 NORTH WELLS ... CHICAGO **IL** 60606 (312) 263-6880

JEWISH STUDENTS SCHOLARSHIP FUND 10 S. LASALLE STREET, SUITE 1100 ... CHICAGO **IL** 60603 (312) 346-4537

JEWISH UNITED FUND 1 S. FRANKLIN STREET ... CHICAGO **IL** 60606 (312) 346-6700

NATIONAL JEWISH WELFARE BOARD 127 NORTH DEARBORN, SUITE 510 ... CHICAGO **IL** 60602 (312) 332-3302

UNITED ORTHODOX SERVICES, INC. 6342 NORTH TROY ... CHICAGO **IL** 60645 (312) 973-5161

DANVILLE JEWISH COMMUNITY CHEST 1655 NORTH VERMILION ... DANVILLE **IL** 61832 (217) 443-2063

UNITED JEWISH CHARITIES OF ROCK ISLAND COUNTY 1804 7TH AVENUE ... ROCK ISLAND **IL** 61201

UNITED ORTHODOX SERVICES 7334 BERYL STREET ... NEW ORLEANS **LA** 70124 (504) 283-5840

NOAM SHABBOS ASSOCIATION 192 KELTON STREET ... ALLSTON **MA** 02134

COMBINED JEWISH PHILANTHROPIES OF GREATER BOSTON 72 FRANKLIN STREET ... BOSTON **MA** 02110 (617) 542-8080

OHEL CHESED CHARITY FUND 26 PRISCILLA ROAD ... BRIGHTON **MA** 02135 (617) 254-5067

UNITED ORTHODOX SERVICES 119 SUTHERLAND ROAD, SUITE A ... BRIGHTON **MA** 02146 (617) 731-8316

HEBREW IMMIGRANT AID SOCIETY (HIAS) C/O H. ALPERT, 9 SEWALL AVENUE #115 ... BROOKLINE **MA** 02146

JEWISH PHILANTHROPIES CENTER 233 HARVARD STREET ... BROOKLINE **MA** 02140

UNITED ORTHODOX SERVICES, INC. 1710 BEACON STREET ... BROOKLINE **MA** 02146 (617) 734-5101

COMBINED JEWISH PHILANTHROPIES 1793 MASSACHUSETTS AVENUE ... LEXINGTON **MA** 02173 (617) 861-1560

UNION OF COUNCILS FOR SOVIET JEWS 24 CRESCENT STREET, SUITE 3A ... WALTHAM **MA** 02154

UNITED ORTHODOX SERVICES 69 S. FLAGG STREET ... WORCESTER **MA** 01602 (617) 754-3681

HIAS OF BALTIMORE, INC. 5750 PARK HEIGHTS AVENUE ... BALTIMORE **MD** 21215 (301) 466-9200

NATIONAL JEWISH HOSPITAL AT DENVER 6301 LINCOLN AVENUE ... BALTIMORE **MD** 21202 (301) 752-7207

UNITED ORTHODOX SERVICES 3800 LABYRINTH ROAD ... BALTIMORE **MD** 21215 (301) 764-6122

UNITED ORTHODOX SERVICES 1201 BALLARD STREET ... SILVER SPRING **MD** 20910 (301) 585-1720

UNITED ORTHODOX SERVICES, INC. 14 HOLWELL STREET ... PORTLAND **ME** 04103 (207) 773-1022

BETH ISRAEL SYNAGOGUE C 291 MAIN STREET ... WATERVILLE **ME** 04901 (207) 773-4453

SHABBOS-YOM TOV FUND 14000 WEST NINE MILE ROAD ... OAK PARK **MI** 48237

UNITED ORTHODOX SERVICES 15030 SUTHERLAND ... OAK PARK **MI** 48237 (313) 967-3728

UNITED ORTHODOX SERVICES, INC. 24031 BEVERLY ... OAK PARK **MI** 48237 (313) 967-3728

ST. PAUL UNITED JEWISH FUND & COUNCIL 790 S. CLEVELAND, SUITE 201 ... MINNEAPOLIS **MN** 55116 (612) 690-1707

UNITED ORTHODOX SERVICES 439 E. 80TH STREET ... KANSAS CITY **MO** 64131 (816) 363-6272

JEWISH FOUNDATION FOR RETARDED CHILDREN 6271 DELMAR ... UNIVERSITY CITY **MO** 63130 (314) 863-3913

UNITED JEWISH CHARITIES-HIGH POINT HEBREW CONGREGATION KENSINGTON DRIVE ... HIGH POINT **NC** 27260

UNITED ORTHODOX SERVICES, INC. 225 HIGHLAND AVENUE ... EDISON **NJ** 08817 (201) 572-1936

UNITED ORTHODOX SERVICES 375 BROOK AVENUE ... PASSAIC **NJ** 07055 (201) 472-3203

UNITED ORTHODOX SERVICES 22 BENNETT AVENUE ... BINGHAMTON **NY** 13905 (607) 724-3900

ACADEMY FOR JEWISH RELIGION 250 STREET & HENRY HUDSON PARKWAY ... BRONX **NY** 10471 (212) 543-8400

AMERICAN JEWISH REFUGEE AID SOCIETY 2632 UNIVERSITY AVENUE ... BRONX **NY** 10468 (212) 364-9680

SHOLOM ALEICHEM FOLK INSTITUTE 3301 BAINBRIDGE AVENUE ... BRONX **NY** 10467 (212) 881-6555

BETH SHIFRA, INC. 3044 CONEY ISLAND AVENUE ... BROOKLYN **NY** 11235 (718) 449-1397

CHESED L'ABRAHAM, INC. 118 HOOPER STREET ... BROOKLYN **NY** 11211

FRIENDS OF REFUGEES OF EASTERN EUROPE 1383 PRESIDENT STREET ... BROOKLYN **NY** 11213 (718) 467-0860

HACHNOSAS KALLAH FUND 879 44TH STREET ... BROOKLYN **NY** 11220 (718) 633-0998

HACHNOSAS ORCHIM L'ANASHIM D'BORO PARK 1554 49TH STREET ... BROOKLYN **NY** 11219 (718) 851-6178

LISHKAS EZRAS ACHIM 688 LEFFERTS AVENUE ... BROOKLYN **NY** 11203

OHR JOSEPH RABBINICAL SEMINARY IN FRANCE 1362 46TH STREET ... BROOKLYN **NY** 11219 (718) 871-4861

PROJECT ARI: ACTION FOR RUSSIAN IMMIGRANTS 3300 CONEY ISLAND AVENUE ... BROOKLYN **NY** 11235 (718) 934-3500

RAV TOV - NATIONAL COMMITTEE TO AID NEW IMMIGRANTS 125 HAYWARD STREET ... BROOKLYN **NY** 11206 (718) 875-8300

TOMCHE CHOLIM ASSOCIATION 543 BEDFORD AVENUE ... BROOKLYN **NY** 11211

TOMCHE SHABBOS OF BORO PARK & FLATBUSH 4712 FORT HAMILTON PARKWAY ... BROOKLYN **NY** 11219

UNITED HEBREW COMMUNITY 1381 CONEY ISLAND AVENUE ... BROOKLYN **NY** 11230 (718) 377-2566

UNITED ORTHODOX SERVICES 1178 44TH STREET ... BROOKLYN **NY** 11219 (718) 854-1620

UNITED ORTHODOX SERVICES 1674 47TH STREET ... BROOKLYN **NY** 11204 (718) 854-1620

YAD L'ACHIM 4820 16TH AVENUE ... BROOKLYN **NY** 11204 (718) 633-0776

ZALMAN ARYEH HILSENRAD KEREN HACHESED 1746 E. 13TH STREET ... BROOKLYN **NY** 11229

UNITED ORTHODOX SERVICES, INC. 129 COMMONWEALTH AVENUE ... BUFFALO **NY** 14216 (716) 876-9344

UNITED ORTHODOX SERVICES 14 WEST MAPLE AVENUE ... MONSEY **NY** 10952 (914) 356-9523

ADATH ISRAEL OF NEW YORK, UNITED HEBREW COMMUNITY OF NEW YORK 201 EAST BROADWAY ... NEW YORK **NY** 10002 (212) 674-3580

AMERICAN COUNCIL FOR JUDAISM PHILANTHROPIC FUND 386 PARK AVENUE SOUTH ... NEW YORK **NY** 10016 (212) 684-1525

AMERICAN FRIENDS OF THE ALLIANCE ISRAELITE UNIVERSELLE INC. 135 WILLIAM STREET ... NEW YORK **NY** 10038 (212) 349-0537

AMERICAN FRIENDS OF SHVUT AMI 1025 FIFTH AVENUE, APT. 3ES ... NEW YORK **NY** 10028 (212) 628-0390

AMERICAN JEWISH JOINT DISTRIBUTION COMMITTEE 60 EAST 42ND STREET ... NEW YORK **NY** 10017 (212) 687-6200

AMERICAN JEWISH SOCIETY FOR SERVICE 15 EAST 26TH STREET ... NEW YORK **NY** 10010 (212) 683-6178

CENTRAL COMMITTEE KNESSETH ISRAEL 245 EAST BROADWAY ... NEW YORK **NY** 10002 (212) 267-6969

DOROT 251 WEST 100TH STREET ... NEW YORK **NY** 10025 (212) 864-7410

FRIENDS OF BELLEVUE HOSPITAL SYNAGOGUE FIRST & 27TH STREET ... NEW YORK **NY** 10016 (212) 685-1376

JEWISH BOARD OF GUARDIANS 120 W. 57TH STREET ... NEW YORK **NY** 10019 (212) 582-9100

JEWISH COMMUNAL FUND OF NEW YORK 745 FIFTH AVENUE ... NEW YORK **NY** 10151 (212) 752-8277

JEWISH PHILANTHROPIC FUND OF 1933 INC. 570 SEVENTH AVENUE ... NEW YORK **NY** 10018 (212) 921-3860

JEWISH UNMARRIED MOTHERS SERVICE 12 E. 94TH STREET ... NEW YORK **NY** 10028 (212) 876-3050

JOINT DISTRIBUTION COMMITTEE 60 EAST 42ND STREET ... NEW YORK **NY** 10165 (212) 687-6200

NATIONAL ASSOCIATION FOR THE JEWISH POOR, THE 234 FIFTH AVENUE, RM. 301 ... NEW YORK **NY** 10001 (212) 687-2570

OZAR HATORAH 411 FIFTH AVENUE ... NEW YORK **NY** 10016 (212) 684-4733

P'EYLIM 3 WEST 16TH STREET ... NEW YORK **NY** 10011 (212) 989-2500

REFORM JEWISH APPEAL 838 FIFTH AVENUE ... NEW YORK **NY** 10021 (212) 249-0100

RE'UTH WOMEN'S SOCIAL SERVICE 240 WEST 98TH STREET ... NEW YORK **NY** 10025

THE JEWISH BRAILLE INSTITUTE OF AMERICA, INC. 110 EAST 30TH STREET ... NEW YORK **NY** 10016 (212) 889-2525

UNITED HIAS SERVICE 200 PARK AVENUE S ... NEW YORK **NY** 10003 (212) 674-6800

UNITED HEBREW COMMUNITY OF NEW YORK, ADATH ISRAEL OF NEW YORK 201 EAST BROADWAY ... NEW YORK **NY** 10002 (212) 674-3580

UNITED JEWISH APPEAL 1290 AVENUE OF THE AMERICAS ... NEW YORK **NY** 10019 (212) 757-1500

UNITED JEWISH APPEAL OF GREATER NEW YORK, INC. 130 EAST 59TH STREET ... NEW YORK **NY** 10019 (212) 980-1000

UNITED RESTITUTION ORGANIZATION 570 SEVENTH AVENUE, 16TH FLOOR ... NEW YORK **NY** 10018 (212) 921-3860

WEST POINT JEWISH CHAPEL FUND 342 MADISON AVENUE, #625 ... NEW YORK **NY** 10017 (212) 986-4086

UNITED JEWISH CHARITIES P.O. BOX 168 ... NEWBURGH **NY** 12550

UNITED JEWISH WELFARE FUND 440 MAIN STREET EAST ... ROCHESTER **NY** 14604 (716) 325-3393

UNITED ORTHODOX SERVICES, INC. 107 UNIVERSITY PARK ... ROCHESTER **NY** 14620 (716) 275-0489

UNITED ORTHODOX SERVICES, INC. 7866 GREENLAND ... CINCINNATI **OH** 45237 (513) 761-2212

RUSSIAN IMMIGRANT AID SOCIETY 1924 LEE ROAD ... CLEVELAND **OH** 44118

UNITED ORTHODOX SERVICES 3575 HARVEY ROAD ... CLEVELAND **OH** 44118 (216) 321-5002
UNITED JEWISH CAMPAIGN (JESSE PHILLIPS BLDG.)
4501 DENLINGER ROAD ... DAYTON **OH** 45426 (513) 854-4150
CANADIAN FRIENDS OF YESHIVA UNIVERSITY
2788 BATHURST STREET, SUITE 300 ... TORONTO **ON** M6B 3A3 (416) 785-5011
UNITED ORTHODOX SERVICES 1130 NORTH MAIN STREET ... ALLENTOWN **PA** 18104 (215) 776-1935
UNITED ORTHODOX SERVICES 103 EDGE HILL ROAD ... BALA CYNWYD **PA** 19004 (215) 664-4680
UNITED ORTHODOX SERVICES 1545 OHIO AVENUE ... MCKEESPORT **PA** 15131 (412) 678-2725
AMERICAN FRIENDS OF LUBAVITCH 7622 CASTOR AVENUE ... PHILADELPHIA **PA** 19152 (215) 725-2030
UNITED ORTHODOX SERVICES 5534 RALEIGH STREET ... PITTSBURGH **PA** 15217 (412) 421-4943
UNITED JEWISH CHARITIES 2300 MAHANTONGO STREET ... POTTSVILLE **PA** 17901 (412) 622-5890
UNITED ORTHODOX SERVICES 441 MONROE STREET ... SCRANTON **PA** 18510 (412) 846-8222
CANADIAN FRIENDS OF YESHIVA UNIVERSITY
4950 QUEEN MARY ROAD, SUITE 365 ... MONTREAL **QU** H3W 1X3 (514) 738-0011
JEWISH IMMIGRANT AID SERVICES OF CANADA
5151 COTE ST. CATHERINE ROAD ... MONTREAL **QU** H3W 1M6 (514) 342-9351
JEWISH IMMIGRANT AID SOCIETY 1590 DOCTEUR PENFIELD AVENUE ... MONTREAL **QU** H3G 1C5 (514) 931-7531
UNITED JEWISH RELIEF AGENCIES OF CANADA
1590 DOCTEUR PENFIELD AVENUE ... MONTREAL **QU** H3G 1C5 (514) 931-7531
SOCIETY OF FRIENDS OF TOURO SYNAGOGUE 85 TOURO STREET ... NEWPORT **RI** 02840 (401) 847-4794
UNITED ORTHODOX SERVICES 249 ROCHAMBEAU AVENUE ... PROVIDENCE **RI** 02906 (401) 751-0192
UNITED ORTHODOX SERVICES 9602 GREENWILLOW ... HOUSTON **TX** 77096 (713) 721-1594
UNITED ORTHODOX SERVICES 4404 A WEST FRANKLIN STREET ... RICHMOND **VA** 23221 (804) 358-6895
UNITED ORTHODOX SERVICES 5218 S. HOLLY STREET ... SEATTLE **WA** 98118 (206) 722-5574
UNITED ORTHODOX SERVICES 5237 57TH AVENUE SOUTH ... SEATTLE **WA** 98118
UNITED ORTHODOX SERVICES 3259 NORTH 51ST BLVD ... MILWAUKEE **WI** 53216 (414) 442-6983
FEDERATED JEWISH CHARITIES 1576 VIRGINIA STREET EAST ... CHARLESTON **WV** 25311

CHARITABLE ORGANIZATIONS - ISRAEL

JEWISH NATIONAL FUND 1323 ANNAPOLIS AVENUE ... ANCHORAGE **AK** 99504 (907) 278-2777
JEWISH NATIONAL FUND 2100 S. CUSHMAN STREET ... FAIRBANKS **AK** 99701 (907) 452-1981
JEWISH NATIONAL FUND 3070 RIVERWOOD DRIVE ... JUNEAU **AK** 99801 (907) 789-4638
JEWISH NATIONAL FUND 5039 N. 19TH AVENUE #5 ... PHOENIX **AZ** 85015 (602) 246-7676
CANADIAN SOCIETY FOR WEIZMANN INSTITUTE OF SCIENCE
P.O. BOX 80886 ... BURNABY **BC** V5H 3Y1 (604) 522-1432
CANADIAN ASSOCIATES OF THE BEN-GURION UNIVERSITY OF THE NEGEV
5763 OAK STREET, SUITE 14 ... VANCOUVER **BC** V6H 2V7 (604) 263-1522
CANADIAN FRIENDS OF AMAL 950 WEST 41ST AVENUE ... VANCOUVER **BC** V5Z 2N7 (604) 266-8308
CANADIAN FRIENDS OF BOYS TOWN, JERUSALEM
5976 TISDALL STREET, #405 ... VANCOUVER **BC** V5Z 3N2 (604) 261-1610
CANADIAN FRIENDS OF HEBREW UNIVERSITY 5763 OAK STREET ... VANCOUVER **BC** V6M 2V7 (604) 263-0093
AMERICAN COMMITTEE FOR SHAARE ZEDEK HOSPITAL IN JERUSALEM
265 SOUTH ROBERTSON BOULEVARD, SUITE 5 ... BEVERLY HILLS **CA** 90212 (213) 278-6050
AMERICAN FRIENDS OF ASSAF HAROFEH HOSPITAL OF ISRAEL
9701 WILSHIRE BOULEVARD, SUITE 800 ... BEVERLY HILLS **CA** 90212 (213) 273-2402
AMERICAN FRIENDS OF HAIFA UNIVERSITY
9301 WILSHIRE BOULEVARD ... BEVERLY HILLS **CA** 90210 (213) 273-4707
AMERICAN FRIENDS OF HEBREW UNIVERSITY
8665 WILSHIRE BLVD ... BEVERLY HILLS **CA** 90221 (213) 657-6511
SHELTERS FOR ISRAEL 603 NORTH CAMDEN DRIVE ... BEVERLY HILLS **CA** 90210 (213) 936-6321
TEL HASHOMER HOSPITAL-CHAIM SHEBA MEDICAL CENTER
9100 WILSHIRE BOULEVARD, SUITE 333 ... BEVERLY HILLS **CA** 90212 (213) 278-6050
AMERICAN COMMITTEE FOR THE WEIZMANN INSTITUTE OF SCIENCE
1801 MURCHISON DRIVE ... BURLINGAME **CA** 94010 (415) 697-3253
JEWISH NATIONAL COUNCIL 17337 VENTURA BOULEVARD ... ENCINO **CA** 91316 (213) 990-0511
JEWISH NATIONAL FUND 17337 VENTURA BLVD. #216 ... ENCINO **CA** 91316 (213) 990-0511
JEWISH NATIONAL FUND 12181 BUARO STREET ... GARDEN GROVE **CA** 92640 (213) 638-4483
AMERICAN FRIENDS OF AISH HATORAH
10100 SANTA MONICA BOULEVARD, SUITE 550 ... LOS ANGELES **CA** 90067 (213) 556-3054
AMERICAN FRIENDS OF BOYS TOWN JERUSALEM ... LOS ANGELES **CA** (213) 203-0300
AMERICAN FRIENDS OF HAIFA UNIVERSITY
9301 WILSHIRE BOULEVARD ... LOS ANGELES **CA** 90210 (213) 273-4707
AMERICAN FRIENDS OF HEBREW UNIVERSITY
8665 WILSHIRE BOULEVARD ... LOS ANGELES **CA** 90211 (213) 657-6511
AMERICAN FRIENDS OF KIRYAT SANZ-LANIADO HOSPITAL ... LOS ANGELES **CA** (213) 825-5075
AMERICAN FRIENDS OF TEL AVIV UNIVERSITY
1900 AVENUE OF THE STARS ... LOS ANGELES **CA** 90067 (213) 556-3141
AMERICAN RED MAGEN DAVID FOR ISRAEL
8230 BEVERLY BOULEVARD ... LOS ANGELES **CA** 90048 (213) 655-1582
AMERICAN TECHNION SOCIETY 8170 BEVERLY BLVD ... LOS ANGELES **CA** 90048 (213) 651-3321
BEN-GURION UNIVERSITY OF THE NEGEV
1801 AVENUE OF THE STARS, SUITE 701 ... LOS ANGELES **CA** 90067 (213) 277-9787
BONDS FOR ISRAEL-DEVELOPMENT CORPORATION FOR ISRAEL
6380 WILSHIRE BOULEVARD ... LOS ANGELES **CA** 90048 (213) 653-8400
FRIENDS OF THE ISRAEL DEFENSE FORCES
9911 WEST PICO BOULEVARD, SUITE 560 ... LOS ANGELES **CA** 90035 (213) 551-3011
FRIENDS OF PORYIAH HOSPITAL ... LOS ANGELES **CA** (213) 858-8354
FUND FOR HIGHER EDUCATION IN ISRAEL
6404 WILSHIRE BOULEVARD ... LOS ANGELES **CA** 90048 (213) 655-7850
ISRAEL HISTADRUT CAMPAIGN
8455 BEVERLY BOULEVARD, SUITE 308 ... LOS ANGELES **CA** 90048 (213) 651-4892
JEWISH NATIONAL FUND 6420 WILSHIRE BLVD. #430 ... LOS ANGELES **CA** 90048 (213) 655-8100
KEREN-OR CENTER FOR MULTI-HANDICAPPED BLIND CHILDREN
1317 NORTH CRESCENT HEIGHTS BOULEVARD ... LOS ANGELES **CA** 90046 (213) 654-3109
WEST COAST FRIENDS OF BAR ILAN UNIVERSITY
6505 WILSHIRE BOULEVARD, SUITE 404 ... LOS ANGELES **CA** 90048 (213) 658-6688
WEST COAST FRIENDS OF PONEVEZ YESHIVA & ISRAEL BOYS TOWN
... LOS ANGELES **CA** (213) 655-2073
JEWISH NATIONAL FUND 262 GRAND AVENUE #101 ... OAKLAND **CA** 94610 (415) 465-0740
JEWISH NATIONAL FUND 6363 EL CAJON BLVD. #200 ... SAN DIEGO **CA** 92115 (619) 287-3447
AMERICAN COMMITTEE FOR SHAARE ZEDEK IN JERUSALEM-NW REGION
1654 33RD AVENUE ... SAN FRANCISCO **CA** 94122 (415) 661-2160
AMERICAN FRIENDS OF THE HEBREW UNIVERSITY OF JERUSALEM
717 MARKET STREET, SUITE 323 ... SAN FRANCISCO **CA** 94103 (415) 391-9056
AMERICAN TECHNION SOCIETY 870 MARKET STREET, SUITE 542 ... SAN FRANCISCO **CA** 94102 (415) 392-1032
JEWISH NATIONAL FUND 2266 GEARY BLVD ... SAN FRANCISCO **CA** 94115 (415) 567-3440
LOS ANGELES COMMITTEE FOR THE WEIZMANN INSTITUTE OF SCIENCE
3235 BARRY DRIVE ... STUDIO CITY **CA** 91604 (213) 654-0540
B.M.H. SYNAGOGUE 560 S. MONACO PARKWAY ... DENVER **CO** 89224 (303) 333-0213
JEWISH NATIONAL FUND 65 COOPER PLACE ... NEW HAVEN **CT** 06525 (203) 397-3767
JEWISH NATIONAL FUND 1430 'K' STREET, N.W. #701 ... WASHINGTON **DC** 20005 (202) 783-8700
JEWISH NATIONAL FUND 800 W. OAKLAND PARK BLVD. #201 ... FORT LAUDERDALE **FL** 33311 (305) 561-4812
AMERICAN COMMITTEE FOR SHAARE ZEDEK IN JERUSALEM-S.E. REGION
605 LINCOLN ROAD, SUITE 211 ... MIAMI BEACH **FL** 33139 (305) 531-8329
AMERICAN FRIENDS OF HAIFA UNIVERSITY, THE
420 LINCOLN ROAD ... MIAMI BEACH **FL** 33139 (305) 531-1174
JEWISH NATIONAL FUND 420 LINCOLN ROAD, #335 ... MIAMI BEACH **FL** 33139 (305) 538-6464
JEWISH NATIONAL FUND 730 S. STERLING AVENUE #213 ... TAMPA **FL** 33609 (813) 876-9327
JEWISH NATIONAL FUND 3 PIEDMONT CENTER, #416 ... ATLANTA **GA** 30305 (404) 237-1132
AMERICAN COMMITTEE FOR SHAARE ZEDEK IN JERUSALEM-MIDWEST RGN
79 MONROE STREET ... CHICAGO **IL** 60603 (312) 236-5778
AMERICAN FRIENDS OF HEBREW UNIVERSITY
4001 W. DEVON AVENUE, SUITE 208 ... CHICAGO **IL** 60646 (312) 236-6395
AMERICAN SOCIETY FOR TECHNION-ISRAEL 59 E. VAN BUREN ... CHICAGO **IL** 60605
EZRA CHAPTER OF MAGEN DAVID ADOM
1212 N. LAKE SHORE DRIVE, SUITE 23 ... CHICAGO **IL** 60610 (312) 649-1583
HISTADRUT CAMPAIGN OF CHICAGO 320 SOUTH STATE ... CHICAGO **IL** 60604 (312) 427-4086
JEWISH NATIONAL FUND 230 N. MICHIGAN AVENUE #420 ... CHICAGO **IL** 60601 (312) 236-9100
MAGEN DAVID ADOM 6952 N. CALIFORNIA AVENUE ... CHICAGO **IL** 60645 (312) 465-0664
MIZRACHI-HAPOEL HAMIZRACHI 6500 N. CALIFORNIA AVENUE ... CHICAGO **IL** 60645 (312) 338-2871
JEWISH NATIONAL FUND 1265 W. 86TH STREET ... INDIANAPOLIS **IN** 46260 (317) 253-5577
GUARDIANS OF THE WESTERN WALL, THE 18 AMOS STREET ... JERUSALEM **IS**
JEWISH NATIONAL FUND 2210 W. 75TH STREET #18 ... SHAWNEE MISSION **KS** 66208 (913) 432-9330
AMERICAN RED MAGEN DAVID FOR ISRAEL-DAVID BEN-GURION CHAPTER
1701 DRYADES STREET ... NEW ORLEANS **LA** 70113 (504) 525-2971
JEWISH NATIONAL FUND 6227 ST. CHARLES AVENUE ... NEW ORLEANS **LA** 70118 (504) 861-3693
AMERICAN PHYSICIANS FELLOWSHIP, INC. 2001 BEACON STREET ... BROOKLINE **MA** 02146 (617) 232-5382
JERUSALEM DENTAL CENTER FOR CHILDREN 268 MASON TERRACE ... BROOKLINE **MA** 02146 (617) 566-4420
JEWISH NATIONAL FUND 1330 BEACON STREET, #202 ... BROOKLINE **MA** 02146 (617) 731-6850
CANADIAN FRIENDS OF BEN GURION UNIVERSITY
211 PORTAGE AVENUE, #407 ... WINNIPEG **MB** (204) 942-7347
CANADIAN FRIENDS OF HEBREW UNIVERSITY
259 PORTAGE AVENUE, #407 ... WINNIPEG **MB** R3B 2A9 (204) 942-3085
JEWISH NATIONAL FUND 14 OLD COURT ROAD ... BALTIMORE **MD** 21208 (301) 486-3317
AMERICAN COMMITTEE FOR SHAARE ZEDEK IN JERUSALEM-DETROIT
13128 WALES ... HUNTINGTON WOODS **MI** 48070 (313) 544-8412
JEWISH NATIONAL FUND 18877 W. TEN MILE ROAD ... SOUTHFIELD **MI** 48075 (313) 557-6644
AMERICAN FRIENDS OF HAIFA UNIVERSITY, THE
8701 E. EIGHT MILE ROAD ... WARREN **MI** 48089 (313) 758-1048
JEWISH NATIONAL FUND 425 HENNEPIN AVENUE, #210 ... MINNEAPOLIS **MN** 55401 (612) 339-0862
AMERICAN SOCIETY FOR TECHNION-ST. LOUIS CHAPTER
111 SOUTH BEMISTON, SUITE 518 ... ST. LOUIS **MO** 63105 (314) 725-7330
ISRAEL HISTADRUT CAMPAIGN 8029 CLAYTON ROAD ... ST. LOUIS **MO** 63117 (314) 727-9019
JEWISH NATIONAL FUND 8420 DELMAR ROAD, SUITE 5031-504 ... ST. LOUIS **MO** 63124 (314) 991-0451
AMERICAN FRIENDS OF HAIFA UNIVERSITY, THE P.O. BOX 18137 ... RALEIGH **NC** 27619 (919) 876-7270
JEWISH NATIONAL FUND 545 CEDAR LANE ... TEANECK **NJ** 07666 (201) 836-6888
AMERICAN FRIENDS OF YESHIVA ZVI HATZADIK
3100 BRIGHTON 3RD STREET ... BROOKLYN **NY** 11235
COLEL CHABAD 784 EASTERN PARKWAY ... BROOKLYN **NY** 11213 (718) 774-5446
COLEL HIBATH JERUSALEM 1282 49TH STREET ... BROOKLYN **NY** 11219 (718) 633-7112
DISKIN ORPHAN HOME OF ISRAEL 4305 18TH AVENUE ... BROOKLYN **NY** 11218 (718) 851-2598
DONATE USED CLOTHING TO ISRAEL ... BROOKLYN **NY** (718) 435-1041
FEDERATED COUNCIL OF ISRAEL INSTITUTIONS - FCLL
1475 47TH STREET ... BROOKLYN **NY** 11219 (718) 462-0603
FRIENDS OF LUBAVITCH FOR SEFAD 625 MONTGOMERY STREET ... BROOKLYN **NY** 11225 (718) 778-3962
GIDULEI YAAKOV KOLLEL IN JERUSALEM 1530 53RD STREET ... BROOKLYN **NY** 11219 (718) 851-7676
HAMAAYAN 1119 EAST 24TH STREET ... BROOKLYN **NY** 11210 (718) 377-8172
ISRAELI WAR HEROES FUND 667 EASTERN PARKWAY ... BROOKLYN **NY** 11213 (718) 773-4960
JERUSALEM INSTITUTE OF TALMUDIC RESEARCH 1481 44TH STREET ... BROOKLYN **NY** 11219 (718) 435-8877
JERUSALEM RABBINICAL ACADEMY, THE 1260 59TH STREET ... BROOKLYN **NY** 11219 (718) 853-3273
JEWISH NATIONAL FUND 1369 CONEY ISLAND AVENUE ... BROOKLYN **NY** 11230 (718) 338-4555
KOLLEL GIDULEI YAAKOV IN JERUSALEM 1530 53RD STREET ... BROOKLYN **NY** 11219 (718) 851-7676
MIFAL HASHAS 4606 16TH AVENUE ... BROOKLYN **NY** 11204 (718) 436-7790
NACHAL NOVEA MEKOR CHOCHMA 1514 40TH STREET ... BROOKLYN **NY** 11218 (718) 435-0087
TSHECHENOV INSTITUTIONS IN ISRAEL 4533 16TH AVENUE ... BROOKLYN **NY** 11204 (718) 438-2100
TSHEBINER YESHIVA KOHAV MIYAACOV OF JERUSALEM
1434 57TH STREET ... BROOKLYN **NY** 11219 (718) 851-5474
YAD ELIEZER 1102 EAST 26TH STREET ... BROOKLYN **NY** 11210 (718) 258-1580
YAD L'ACHIM-BORO PARK-FLATBUSH 4702 16TH AVENUE ... BROOKLYN **NY** 11204 (718) 633-0776
AMERICAN RED MAGEN DAVID FOR ISRAEL 888 SEVENTH AVENUE ... HEMPSTEAD **NY** 11552 (516) 757-1627
DEBORAH HOSPITAL FOUNDATION 135-25 NORTHERN BOULEVARD ... LINDEN HILL **NY** 11354 (718) 762-1400
ALEH INSTITUTION FOR BRAIN INJURED CHILDREN
1180 AVENUE OF THE AMERICAS, SUITE 1910-A ... NEW YORK **NY** 10036 (212) 730-2088
AM. FRIENDS/JERUSALEM MENTAL HEALTH CTR.-EZRATH NASHIM, INC.
10 E. 40TH STREET ... NEW YORK **NY** 10016 (212) 725-8175
AM. FRIENDS/YAD BENJAMIN-ED. CTR. OF POALE AGUDATH ISRAEL
147 W. 42ND STREET ... NEW YORK **NY** 10036 (212) 279-0816
AMERICAN ASSOCIATES BEN-GURION UNIVERSITY OF THE NEGEV
342 MADISON AVENUE, SUITE 1923 ... NEW YORK **NY** 10173 (212) 687-7721
AMERICAN ASSOCIATION FOR BIKUR CHOLIM HOSPITAL
119 FIFTH AVENUE ... NEW YORK **NY** 10021 (212) 260-4260
AMERICAN COLLEGE IN JERUSALEM 342 MADISON AVENUE ... NEW YORK **NY** 10017

AMERICAN COMM. FOR SHAARE ZEDEK HOSPITAL IN JERUSALEM, INC.
49 WEST 45TH STREET .... NEW YORK **NY** 10036 (212) 354-8801
AMERICAN COMMITTEE FOR THE ISRAEL FASHION COLLEGE INC.
855 AVENUE OF THE AMERICAS .... NEW YORK **NY** 10001 (212) 947-1597
AMERICAN COMMITTEE FOR THE NATIONAL SICK FUND OF ISRAEL
60 E. 42ND STREET, SUITE 1144 .... NEW YORK **NY** 10165 (212) 599-3670
AMERICAN COMMITTEE FOR THE WEIZMANN INST. OF SCIENCE, INC.
515 PARK AVENUE .... NEW YORK **NY** 10022 (212) 752-1300
AMERICAN FRIENDS OF ATERET COHANIM 475 FIFTH AVENUE, #1810 .... NEW YORK **NY** 10017 (212) 725-0598
AMERICAN FRIENDS OF BAR ILAN UNIVERSITY
853 SEVENTH AVENUE, SUITE 1018 .... NEW YORK **NY** 10019 (212) 315-1990
AMERICAN FRIENDS OF BEIT HALOCHEM BNAI ZION FOUNDATION
136 EAST 39TH STREET .... NEW YORK **NY** 10157 (212) 725-1211
AMERICAN FRIENDS OF BETH HATEFUTSOTH 515 PARK AVENUE .... NEW YORK **NY** 10022 (212) 752-0246
AMERICAN FRIENDS OF BOYS TOWN JERUSALEM 22 W. 38TH STREET ... NEW YORK **NY** 10018 (212) 921-1380
AMERICAN FRIENDS OF HAIFA UNIVERSITY 206 FIFTH AVENUE .... NEW YORK **NY** 10010 (212) 696-4022
AMERICAN FRIENDS OF HEBRON YESHIVA IN JERUSALEM
1220 BROADWAY .... NEW YORK **NY** 10001 (212) 695-2230
AMERICAN FRIENDS OF JERUSALEM MENTAL HEALTH CENTER-EZ.NASHIM
10 EAST 40TH STREET .... NEW YORK **NY** 10016 (212) 725-8175
AMERICAN FRIENDS OF KIRYAT SANZ LANIADO HOSPITAL
18 WEST 45TH STREET .... NEW YORK **NY** 10036 (212) 944-2690
AMERICAN FRIENDS OF LANIADO KIRYAT SANZ HOSPITAL
580 FIFTH AVENUE .... NEW YORK **NY** 10017 (212) 944-2690
AMERICAN FRIENDS OF MICHLALAH 10 COLUMBUS CIRCLE .... NEW YORK **NY** 10019 (212) 586-1232
AMERICAN FRIENDS OF MIDRASHA AND UNITED ISRAEL INSTITUTIONS LTD.
310 MADISON AVENUE, SUITE 1711 .... NEW YORK **NY** 10017 (212) 370-1470
AMERICAN FRIENDS OF MIGDAL OHR (ISRAEL)
11 WEST 36TH STREET .... NEW YORK **NY** 10018 (212) 947-8740
AMERICAN FRIENDS OF NEVEH YEHOSHUA 3 WEST 16TH STREET .... NEW YORK **NY** 10011 (212) 929-1836
AMERICAN FRIENDS OF OHR SOMAYACH 39 BROADWAY .... NEW YORK **NY** 10006 (212) 344-2000
AMERICAN FRIENDS OF YESHIVAT KEREM B'YAVNEH
6 EAST 45TH STREET .... NEW YORK **NY** 10017 (212) 687-0805
AMERICAN FRIENDS OF YESHIVAT NER MOSHE OF JERUSALEM
295 MADISON AVENUE, SUITE 1228 .... NEW YORK **NY** 10017 (212) 687-0500
AMERICAN FRIENDS OF YESHIVAT SHALAVIM
156 FIFTH AVENUE, SUITE 811 .... NEW YORK **NY** 10010 (212) 989-1695
AMERICAN FRIENDS OF YESHIVOT BNEI AKIVA IN ISRAEL
50 WEST 34TH STREET .... NEW YORK **NY** 10001 (212) 947-6787
AMERICAN FRIENDS OF THE ALLIANCE ISRAELITE UNIVERSELLE
61 BROADWAY, ROOM 811 .... NEW YORK **NY** 10006 (212) 425-5171
AMERICAN FRIENDS OF THE HAIFÁ MARITIME MUSEUM, INC.
18 E. 74TH STREET, P.O. BOX 616 .... NEW YORK **NY** 10021 (212) 776-4509
AMERICAN FRIENDS OF THE HAIFA MEDICAL CENTER
136 EAST 39TH STREET .... NEW YORK **NY** 10016 (212) 725-1211
AMERICAN FRIENDS OF THE HEBREW UNIVERSITY
11 EAST 69TH STREET .... NEW YORK **NY** 10021 (212) 472-9800
AMERICAN FRIENDS OF THE HEBREW UNIVERSITY
1140 AVENUE OF THE AMERICAS .... NEW YORK **NY** 10036 (212) 840-5820
AMERICAN FRIENDS OF THE ISRAEL MUSEUM
10 E. 40TH STREET, SUITE 1208 .... NEW YORK **NY** 10016 (212) 683-5190
AMERICAN FRIENDS OF THE ISRAEL PHILHARMONIC ORCHESTRA INC.
1715 BROADWAY .... NEW YORK **NY** 10019 (212) 581-4374
AMERICAN FRIENDS OF THE JERUSALEM ACADEMY & CONFERENCE CTR.
75 EAST 55TH STREET .... NEW YORK **NY** 10022 (212) 688-7979
AMERICAN FRIENDS OF THE JERUSALEM MENTAL HEALTH CENTER-
EZRATH NASHIM, 10 EAST 40TH STREET .... NEW YORK **NY** 10016 (212) 725-8175
AMERICAN FRIENDS OF THE KIBBUTZIM IN ISRAEL INC.
150 FIFTH AVENUE .... NEW YORK **NY** 10003 (212) 255-8760
AMERICAN FRIENDS OF THE MIRRER YESHIVA IN JERUSALEM
1133 BROADWAY .... NEW YORK **NY** 10010 (212) 243-3987
AMERICAN FRIENDS OF THE TEL AVIV UNIVERSITY INC.
342 MADISON AVENUE .... NEW YORK **NY** 10017 (212) 687-5651
AMERICAN HECHAL SHLOMO 358 FIFTH AVENUE .... NEW YORK **NY** 10016 (212) 736-4698
AMERICAN ISRAELI LIGHTHOUSE 30 E. 60TH STREET .... NEW YORK **NY** 10022 (212) 838-5322
AMERICAN MIZRACHI WOMEN 817 BROADWAY .... NEW YORK **NY** 10003 (212) 477-4720
AMERICAN RED MAGEN DAVID FOR ISRAEL 888 SEVENTH AVENUE .... NEW YORK **NY** 10019 (212) 757-1627
AMERICAN SOCIETY FOR CRIPPLED CHILDREN IN ISRAEL
19 WEST 44TH STREET .... NEW YORK **NY** 10036 (212) 869-0369
AMERICAN SOCIETY FOR TECHNION-ISRAEL INSTITUTE OF TECHNOLOGY
271 MADISON AVENUE .... NEW YORK **NY** 10016 (212) 889-2050
BIKUR CHOLIM HOSPITAL, JERUSALEM 119 FIFTH AVENUE .... NEW YORK **NY** 10011 (212) 989-2525
COLEL POLEN-RABBI MEIR BAAL HANESS JERUSALEM
373 FIFTH AVENUE .... NEW YORK **NY** 10016 (212) 689-4500
DISKIN ORPHAN HOME OF ISRAEL 156 FIFTH AVENUE .... NEW YORK **NY** 10010 (212) 924-0494
EMET-RABBI HERZOG WORLD ACADEMY 122 WEST 76TH STREET .... NEW YORK **NY** 10023 (212) 787-1051
ETZ CHAIM TORAH CENTER OF JERUSALEM 1141 BROADWAY .... NEW YORK **NY** 10001 (212) 683-3221
EZRAS TORAH FUND-TORAH RELIEF SOCIETY, INC.
235 EAST BROADWAY .... NEW YORK **NY** 10002 (212) 227-8960
EZRATH NASHIM JERUSALEM MENTAL HEALTH CENTER
10 EAST 40TH STREET .... NEW YORK **NY** 10016 (212) 725-8175
FEDERATED COUNCIL OF ISRAEL INSTITUTIONS, INC.
15 BEEKMAN STREET .... NEW YORK **NY** 10038 (212) 962-0603
FRIENDS OF DAVID YELLIN TEACHERS COLLEGE, INC.
1501 BROADWAY, SUITE 1715 .... NEW YORK **NY** 10036 (212) 391-8686
FRIENDS OF THE ISRAEL DEFENSE FORCES 15 EAST 26TH STREET .... NEW YORK **NY** 10010 (212) 684-0669
FRIENDS OF JERUSALEM 545 FIFTH AVENUE .... NEW YORK **NY** 10017 (212) 687-4187
FRIENDS OF JUDEA & SAMARIA/AMERICANS FOR A SAFE ISRAEL/
GUSH EMUNIM, LTD./TEHIYA, USA 207 WEST 86TH STREET .... NEW YORK **NY** 10024 (212) 724-1642
FRIENDS OF MEVAKSHEI DERECH
225 PARK AVENUE SOUTH, 17TH FLOOR .... NEW YORK **NY** 10003
FRIENDS OF NEVE SHALOM 225 WEST 34TH STREET, ROOM 918 .... NEW YORK **NY** 10122
FRIENDS OF YESHIVA SHALAVIM, INC. 156 FIFTH AVENUE .... NEW YORK **NY** 10010 (212) 989-1695
FUND FOR HIGHER EDUCATION IN ISRAEL, INC. 1500 BROADWAY .... NEW YORK **NY** 10036 (212) 354-4660
GENERAL ISRAEL ORPHANS HOME FOR GIRLS IN JERUSALEM
132 NASSAU STREET .... NEW YORK **NY** 10038 (212) 267-7222
GESHER FOUNDATION, THE 421 SEVENTH AVENUE .... NEW YORK **NY** 10001 (212) 564-0338
GREAT CHARITY CHAYE OLAM INSTITUTION OF JERUSALEM
5 BEEKMAN STREET .... NEW YORK **NY** 10038 (212) 962-0224
HADASSAH MEDICAL RELIEF ASSOCIATION INC.
50 WEST 58TH STREET .... NEW YORK **NY** 10019 (212) 355-7900
HADASSAH, THE WOMEN'S ZIONIST ORG. OF AMERICA
50 WEST 58TH STREET .... NEW YORK **NY** 10019 (212) 355-7900
HASHOMER HATZAIR, INC. 150 FIFTH AVENUE .... NEW YORK **NY** 10011 (212) 255-8760
HEBREW UNIVERSITY-TECHNION JOINT MAINTENANCE APPEAL
11 E. 69TH STREET .... NEW YORK **NY** 10021 (212) 472-9800
HEBRON YESHIVA IN JERUSALEM 1220 BROADWAY .... NEW YORK **NY** 10001 (212) 695-2230
HEICHAL HATALMUD OF TEL AVIV 247 EAST BROADWAY .... NEW YORK **NY** 10002 (212) 608-3301
HISTADRUT ISRAEL CAMPAIGN 33 EAST 67TH STREET .... NEW YORK **NY** 10021 (212) 628-1000
ISRAEL CANCER RESEARCH FUND
1290 AVENUE OF THE AMERICAS, SUITE 270 .... NEW YORK **NY** 10104 (212) 969-9800
ISRAEL EDUCATION FUND 51 WEST 51ST STREET .... NEW YORK **NY** 10019 (212) 757-1500
ISRAEL EDUCATIONAL & BENEVOLENT RELIEF SOCIETY
203 EAST BROADWAY .... NEW YORK **NY** 10002 (212) 233-9275
ISRAEL EDUCATIONAL & BENEVOLENT RELIEF SOCIETY
126 EAST BROADWAY .... NEW YORK **NY** 10002 (212) 233-9275
ISRAEL FOUNDATION FUND (KEREN HAYESOD), INC.
515 PARK AVENUE .... NEW YORK **NY** 10022 (212) 688-0800
ISRAEL HISTADRUT CAMPAIGN, INC. 33 EAST 67TH STREET .... NEW YORK **NY** 10021 (212) 628-1000
ISRAEL INSTITUTIONS FOR THE BLIND-KEREN-OR, INC.
1133 BROADWAY .... NEW YORK **NY** 10010 (212) 255-1180
JABOTINSKY FOUNDATION, INC., THE 261 FIFTH AVENUE .... NEW YORK **NY** 10016 (212) 679-6868
JERUSALEM ACADEMY FOR GIRLS 225 BROADWAY .... NEW YORK **NY** 10007 (212) 233-1500
JERUSALEM FOUNDATION, THE 500 FIFTH AVENUE .... NEW YORK **NY** 10110 (212) 840-1101
JERUSALEM INSTITUTION FOR THE BLIND-KEREN OR, INC.
1133 BROADWAY .... NEW YORK **NY** 10010 (212) 255-1180
JEWISH NATIONAL FUND 42 E. 69TH STREET .... NEW YORK **NY** 10021 (212) 879-9300
KEREN KAYEMETH LE-ISRAEL, INC. (JEWISH NATIONAL FUND)
42 E. 69TH STREET .... NEW YORK **NY** 10021 (212) 879-9300
KEREN OR, INC. 1133 BROADWAY .... NEW YORK **NY** 10010 (212) 255-1180
KEREN YALDENU 51 EAST 42ND STREET .... NEW YORK **NY** 10017 (212) 490-2340
KEREN-OR JERUSALEM INSTITUTE FOR THE BLIND, INC.
1133 BROADWAY .... NEW YORK **NY** 10010 (212) 255-1180
KOLEL AMERICA 132 NASSAU STREET .... NEW YORK **NY** 10038 (718) 871-4111
KOLEL AMERICA TIFERETH JERUSALEM 132 NASSAU STREET .... NEW YORK **NY** 10038 (212) 349-3078
KOLEL SHOMRE HACHOMOS 5 BEEKMAN STREET .... NEW YORK **NY** 10038 (212) 732-0300
KUPATH RABBI MEIR HANESS JERUSALEM 373 FIFTH AVENUE .... NEW YORK **NY** 10016 (212) 691-1330
KUPATH RAMBAN COLEL POLEN JERUSALEM 373 FIFTH AVENUE .... NEW YORK **NY** 10016 (212) 691-1330
MIGDAL OHR 11 WEST 36TH STREET .... NEW YORK **NY** 10018 (212) 947-8740
MIZRACHI PALESTINE FUND 200 PARK AVENUE S .... NEW YORK **NY** 10003 (212) 673-8100
NAT'L COMMITTEE FOR LABOR ISRAEL (ISRAEL HISTADRUT CAMPAIGN)
33 EAST 67TH STREET .... NEW YORK **NY** 10021 (212) 628-1000
NAT'L JEWISH HOSPITAL AT DENVER 49 WEST 45TH STREET .... NEW YORK **NY** 10036 (212) 382-0711
NEW ISRAEL FUND 111 WEST 40TH STREET, SUITE 2600 .... NEW YORK **NY** 10018 (212) 302-0066
OHR TORAH INSTITUTIONS OF ISRAEL
1 WEST 85TH STREET, SUITE 2F .... NEW YORK **NY** 10024 (212) 496-1618
POALE AGUDATH ISRAEL OF AMERICA 156 FIFTH AVENUE .... NEW YORK **NY** 10010 (212) 924-9475
POALE AGUDATH ISRAEL OF AMERICA - WOMEN'S DIVISION
156 FIFTH AVENUE, SUITE 881 .... NEW YORK **NY** 10010 (212) 924-9475
RELIGIOUS ZIONISTS OF AMERICA 25 W. 26TH STREET .... NEW YORK **NY** 10010
TEL-HAI FUND, INC. 47 W. 34TH STREET .... NEW YORK **NY** 10001 (212) 594-2879
TORAH SCHOOLS FOR ISRAEL-CHINUCH ATZMAI
167 MADISON AVENUE .... NEW YORK **NY** 10016 (212) 889-0606
UNITED CHARITY INSTITUTIONS OF JERUSALEM 1141 BROADWAY .... NEW YORK **NY** 10001 (212) 683-3221
UNITED ISRAEL APPEAL, INC. 515 PARK AVENUE .... NEW YORK **NY** 10022 (212) 688-0800
UNITED JEWISH APPEAL 1290 AVENUE OF THE AMERICAS .... NEW YORK **NY** 10104 (212) 757-1500
UNITED TIBERIAS INSTITUTIONS RELIEF SOCIETY 195 HENRY STREET .. NEW YORK **NY** 10002 (212) 349-8755
WOMEN'S LEAGUE FOR ISRAEL, INC. 1860 BROADWAY .... NEW YORK **NY** 10023 (212) 245-8742
YESHIVA BETH ABRAHAM OF JERUSALEM 73 WEST 47TH STREET .... NEW YORK **NY** 10036 (212) 819-0355
YESHIVA LOMZA-PETACH TIKVA ISRAEL 249 EAST BROADWAY .... NEW YORK **NY** 10002 (212) 349-1934
YESHIVA PONEVEZ 1133 BROADWAY .... NEW YORK **NY** 10010 (212) 675-9260
YESHIVA SFATH EMETH OF JERUSALEM 145 EAST BROADWAY .... NEW YORK **NY** 10002 (212) 964-2830
YESHIVA WOLOZIN 210 WEST 91ST STREET .... NEW YORK **NY** 10024 (212) 787-3820
YESHIVAT HAR ETZION 310 MADISON AVENUE .... NEW YORK **NY** 10017 (212) 883-0883
YESHIVATH CHATAM SOFER TORAH CENTER 119 NASSAU STREET .... NEW YORK **NY** 10038 (212) 732-0301
YESHIVATH HANEGEV 860 WEST 181ST STREET .... NEW YORK **NY** 10033 (212) 568-1647
YESHIVATH SFATH EMETH OF JERUSALEM 150 FIFTH AVENUE .... NEW YORK **NY** 10011 (212) 929-3899
FEDERATED COUNCIL OF ISRAEL INSTITUTIONS, INC.
15 BEEKMAN STREET .... NEW YORK **NY** 10038 (212) 227-3152
P.E.F.ISRAEL ENDOWMENT FUNDS, INC. 342 MADISON AVENUE .... NEW YORK **NY** 10173 (212) 599-1260
JEWISH NATIONAL FUND 1400 WANTAGH AVENUE, SUITE L2 .... WANTAGH **NY** 11793 (516) 826-8700
JEWISH NATIONAL FUND 1720 SECTION ROAD .... CINCINNATI **OH** 45237 (513) 631-1796
AM. COMMITTEE FOR SHAARE ZEDEK IN JERUSALEM-MID-CENTRAL REG.
3507 WARRENSVILLE CENTER ROAD .... CLEVELAND **OH** 44122 (216) 283-9222
AMERICAN RED MAGEN DAVID ADOM FOR ISRAEL (ISRAEL RED CROSS)
3645 WARRENSVILLE CENTER ROAD, NO. 330 .... CLEVELAND **OH** 44122 (216) 752-6884
AMERICAN TECHNION SOCIETY - WOMEN'S DIVISION
2992 LINCOLN BLVD .... CLEVELAND **OH** 44118 (216) 321-4320
ANSHE GRODNO LADIES AUXILIARY 3351 DESOTA AVENUE .... CLEVELAND **OH** 44118 (216) 932-4138
CLEVELAND CHAPTER OF BEN-GURION UNIVERSITY .... CLEVELAND **OH** (216) 283-2400
CLEVELAND COMMITTEE FOR WEIZMANN INSTITUTE
23 PEPPER CREEK DRIVE .... CLEVELAND **OH** 44124 (216) 464-1103

CLEVELAND FRIENDS OF THE JERUSALEM BOTANICAL GARDENS
28950 GATES MILLS BLVD ... CLEVELAND **OH** 44124 (216) 464-3084

ISRAEL HISTADRUT CAMPAIGN 13969 CEDAR ROAD ... CLEVELAND **OH** 44118 (216) 321-4900

JEWISH NATIONAL FUND 14055 CEDAR ROAD, #304 ... CLEVELAND **OH** 44118 (216) 371-8733

JEWISH NATIONAL FUND 2700 E. MAIN STREET ... COLUMBUS **OH** 43209 (614) 231-1397

CANADIAN FRIENDS OF BAR-ILAN UNIVERSITY
333 WILSON AVENUE ... DOWNSVIEW **ON** M3H 1T2 (416) 635-1966

CANADIAN SOCIETY FOR THE WEIZMANN INSTITUTE OF SCIENCE
345 WILSON AVENUE, SUITE 403 ... DOWNSVIEW **ON** M3H 5W1

CANADIAN FRIENDS OF BAR-ILAN UNIVERSITY
825 EGLINTON AVENUE WEST, SUITE 314 ... TORONTO **ON** M5N 1E7 (416) 783-8546

CANADIAN FRIENDS OF OHR SOMAYACH
2939 BATHURST ... TORONTO **ON** M6B 2B2 (416) 785-5899

CANADIAN FRIENDS OF THE HEBREW UNIVERSITY
2081 YORKDALE ROAD ... TORONTO **ON** M6A 3A1 (416) 789-2633

CANADIAN FRIENDS OF THE SHALOM HARTMAN INSTITUTE
3300 BLOOR STREET WEST, 16TH FLOOR, EAST TOWER ... TORONTO **ON** M8X 2X3 (416) 237-0446

CANADIAN TECHNION SOCIETY 2828 BATHURST STREET, SUITE 502 ... TORONTO **ON** M6B 3A7

NEW ISRAEL FUND OF CANADA
P.O. BOX 114, SUITE 1500, COMMERCE COURT WEST ... TORONTO **ON** M5L 1E2 (416) 922-6343

JEWISH NATIONAL FUND 5765 S.W. GLENBROOK ROAD ... BEAVERTON **OR** 97005 (503) 644-0944

AM. COMMITTEE FOR SHAARE ZEDEK IN JERUSALEM-MID-ATLANTIC RGN
1518 WALNUT STREET, SUITE 900 ... PHILADELPHIA **PA** 19102 (215) 735-3306

AMERICAN FRIENDS OF HAIFA UNIVERSITY
226 W. RITTENHOUSE SQUARE, SUITE 2301 ... PHILADELPHIA **PA** 19103 (215) 735-8074

AMERICAN FRIENDS OF HEBREW UNIVERSITY
2400 LEWIS TOWER BLDG ... PHILADELPHIA **PA** 19102

JEWISH NATIONAL FUND 1405 LOCUST STREET, #1621 ... PHILADELPHIA **PA** 19102 (215) 545-6660

JEWISH NATIONAL FUND 6315 FORBES AVENUE ... PITTSBURGH **PA** 15217 (412) 521-6866

CANADIAN ASSOCIATION FOR LABOR ISRAEL 4770 KENT AVENUE ... MONTREAL **QU** H3W 1H2 (514) 735-1593

CANADIAN FRIENDS OF THE ALLIANCE ISRAELITE UNIVERSELLE
5711 EDGEMORE AVENUE ... MONTREAL **QU** H4W 1V8 (514) 487-1243

CANADIAN SOCIETY FOR THE WEIZMANN INSTITUTE OF SCIENCE
5180 QUEEN MARY ROAD, SUITE 360 ... MONTREAL **QU**

CANPAL-CANADIAN ISRAEL CORP. LTD.
1550 MAISONNEUVE BOULEVARD WEST, SUITE 1030 ... MONTREAL **QU** H3G 1N2 (514) 935-6577

UNITED ISRAEL APPEAL OF CANADA, INC. 1310 GREENE AVENUE ... WESTMOUNT **QU** H3Z 2B2 (514) 932-1431

JEWISH NATIONAL FUND 6584 POPLAR AVENUE #310 ... MEMPHIS **TN** 38138 (901) 682-2414

JEWISH NATIONAL FUND 11333 N. CENTRAL EXPRESSWAY ... DALLAS **TX** 75243 (214) 363-1498

JEWISH NATIONAL FUND 6006 BELLAIRE BLVD. #106 ... HOUSTON **TX** 77081 (713) 432-7070

AMERICAN FRIENDS OF THE SHALOM HARTMAN INSTITUTE
1735 JEFFERSON DAVIS HIGHWAY, CRYSTAL CITY ... ARLINGTON **VA** 22202 (703) 769-1240

JEWISH NATIONAL FUND 629 SECURITIES BUILDING ... SEATTLE **WA** 98101 (206) 624-8625

JEWISH NATIONAL FUND 1119 WEST KILBOURN ... MILWAUKEE **WI** 53233 (414) 276-0630

BRITISH FRIENDS OF OHR SOMAYACH 12 HALLSWELLE ROAD ... LONDON **GB** NW11 (1) 458-5231

CHILDREN'S HOMES & SERVICES

CALIFORNIA HAMBURGER HOME 7357 HOLLYWOOD BOULEVARD ... LOS ANGELES **CA** 90046 (213) 876-0550

VISTA DEL MAR CHILD-CARE SERVICES 3200 MOTOR AVENUE ... LOS ANGELES **CA** 90034 (213) 836-1223

EMANU-EL RESIDENCE 300 PAGE STREET ... SAN FRANCISCO **CA** 94102

HOMEWOOD TERRACE 160 SCOTT STREET ... SAN FRANCISCO **CA** 94102 (415) 562-2788

JEWISH HOME FOR CHILDREN 152 TEMPLE STREET ... NEW HAVEN **CT** 06500 (203) 776-5130

JEWISH FOSTER HOME 1341 G STREET, N.W. ... WASHINGTON **DC** 20026

JEWISH FAMILY & CHILDREN'S SERVICE 1790 S.W. 27TH AVENUE ... MIAMI **FL** 33145 (305) 445-0555

JEWISH CHILDREN'S BUREAU 1 SOUTH FRANKLIN STREET ... CHICAGO **IL** 60606 (312) 346-6700

NICHOLAS J. PRITZKER CENTER-JEWISH CHILDREN'S BUREAU
800 E. 55TH STREET ... CHICAGO **IL** 60615 (312) 643-7300

VIRGINIA FRANK CHILD DEVELOPMENT CENTER 3033 WEST TOUHY ... CHICAGO **IL** 60645 (312) 761-4550

JEWISH CHILDREN'S HOME SERVICE
5342 ST. CHARLES AVENUE, PO BOX 15225 ... NEW ORLEANS **LA** 70115 (504) 897-0143

JEWISH CHILDREN'S REGIONAL SERVICE OF JEWISH CHILDREN'S HOME
5342 CHARLES AVENUE, P.O. BOX 15225 ... NEW ORLEANS **LA** 70175 (504) 889-1595

JEWISH FAMILY & CHILDREN'S SERVICE 107 CAMP STREET ... NEW ORLEANS **LA** 70130 (504) 524-8476

SHREVEPORT JEWISH FAMILY & CHILDREN'S SERVICES
2030 LINE AVENUE ... SHREVEPORT **LA** 71104 (318) 221-4129

JEWISH CHILD AND FAMILY SERVICE
228 NOTRE DAME STREET/SUITE 1001 ... WINNIPEG **MB** R3B 1N7 (204) 943-6425

JEWISH SOCIAL SERVICE AGENCY 6123 MONTROSE ROAD ... ROCKVILLE **MD** 20852 (301) 881-3700

JEWISH CHILDREN'S HOME 9385 OLIVE STREET ROAD ... ST. LOUIS **MO** 63100 (314) 993-0100

HEBREW BENEVOLENT & ORPHAN ASYLUM 161 MILLBURN AVENUE ... MILLBURN **NJ** 07041 (201) 467-3300

BROOKLYN HEBREW ORPHAN ASYLUM
(CALL JEWISH CHILD CARE ASSOCIATION OF N.Y.) ... **NY** (718) 490-9160

HEBREW CHILDREN'S HOME 1682 MONROE AVENUE ... BRONX **NY** 10457

CONEY ISLAND COMMUNITY SUPPORT SYSTEMS PROJECT
3312-30 SURF AVENUE ... BROOKLYN **NY** 11224 (718) 372-3300

FAMILY COURT LIAISON OFFICE - BROOKLYN
283 ADAMS STREET, ROOM 304 ... BROOKLYN **NY** 11201 (718) 875-1841

IHB DAY TREATMENT CENTER AND RESIDENCE 1358 56TH STREET ... BROOKLYN **NY** 11219 (718) 851-8000

INFANTS HOME OF BROOKLYN JEWISH BOARD OF FAMILY SERVICES
1358 56TH STREET ... BROOKLYN **NY** 11219 (718) 851-8000

IRANIAN JEWISH PROGRAM 1113 AVENUE J ... BROOKLYN **NY** 11230 (718) 258-7700

JEWISH BOARD OF GUARDIANS 283 ADAMS STREET ... BROOKLYN **NY** 11201 (718) 875-5951

JEWISH BOARD OF GUARDIANS 1484 FLATBUSH AVENUE ... BROOKLYN **NY** 11210 (718) 434-4158

JEWISH BOARD OF GUARDIANS MENTAL HEALTH CENTER
1301 SURF AVENUE ... BROOKLYN **NY** 11224 (718) 226-5300

JEWISH BOARD OF GUARDIANS MIDWOOD ADOLESCENT PROJECT
1484 FLATBUSH AVENUE ... BROOKLYN **NY** 11210 (718) 434-6200

JEWISH CHILD CARE ASSOC. OF N.Y.-KINGSBROOK RESIDENCE
150 E. 49TH STREET ... BROOKLYN **NY** 11203 (718) 756-1900

JEWISH CHILD CARE ASSOCIATION OF NEW YORK 663 RUGBY ROAD ... BROOKLYN **NY** 11230 (718) 859-7809

JEWISH CHILD CARE ASSOCIATION OF NEW YORK 1810 AVENUE H ... BROOKLYN **NY** 11230 (718) 859-0503

MADELEINE BORG COUNSEL. SVCS. - THOMAS ASKIN YOUTH PROJECT
307 BRIGHTON BEACH AVENUE ... BROOKLYN **NY** 11235 (718) 934-8025

MADELEINE BORG COUNSEL. SVCS.-CAREY GARDENS EARLY CHILDHOOD
2964 WEST 23RD STREET ... BROOKLYN **NY** 11224 (718) 372-4044

MADELEINE BORG COUNSELING SERVICES - BORO PARK OFFICE
1276 47TH STREET ... BROOKLYN **NY** 11219 (718) 435-5700

MADELEINE BORG COUNSELING SERVICES - CANARSIE OFFICE
164 CONKLIN AVENUE ... BROOKLYN **NY** 11236 (718) 257-0002

MADELEINE BORG COUNSELING SERVICES - CONEY ISLAND OFFICE
2857 WEST 8TH STREET ... BROOKLYN **NY** 11224 (718) 266-5300

MADELEINE BORG COUNSELING SERVICES - MID-BROOKLYN OFFICE
1113 AVENUE J ... BROOKLYN **NY** 11230 (718) 258-7700

MADELEINE BORG COUNSELING SERVICES - MONTAGUE STREET OFFICE
186 MONTAGUE STREET ... BROOKLYN **NY** 11201 (718) 855-6900

MADELEINE BORG COUNSELING SERVICES - STARRETT CITY OFFICE
1201 PENNSYLVANIA AVENUE ... BROOKLYN **NY** 11239 (718) 642-8955

MIDWOOD ADOLESCENT PROJECT 1484 FLATBUSH AVENUE ... BROOKLYN **NY** 11210 (718) 434-4158

MISHKON B'NAI YISROEL 4105 16TH AVENUE ... BROOKLYN **NY** 11219 (718) 851-6570

MONTAGUE SCHOOL 180 MONTAGUE STREET ... BROOKLYN **NY** 11201 (718) 858-0886

OHEL CHILDREN'S HOME & FAMILY SERVICES 4423 16TH AVENUE ... BROOKLYN **NY** 11204 (718) 851-6300

PROGRAM FOR RUSSIAN JEWISH IMMIGRANTS 2857 WEST 8TH ... BROOKLYN **NY** 11224 (718) 266-5300

TIFERETH SHLOMO BOYS INSTITUTIONS 5121 17TH AVENUE ... BROOKLYN **NY** 11204 (718) 435-0206

JEWISH CH. CARE ASSOC. OF N.Y.-LEFRAK RESIDENCE
98-25 HORACE HARDING EXPRESSWAY ... CORONA **NY** 11368 (718) 592-0190

PRIDE OF JUDEA CHILDREN'S SERVICES 243-02 NORTHERN BLVD ... DOUGLASTON **NY** 11363

JEWISH CH. CARE ASSOC. OF N.Y.-REGO PARK RESIDENCE FOR BOYS
94-30 60TH AVENUE ... ELMHURST **NY** 11380 (718) 271-4555

JEWISH CH. CARE ASSOC. OF N.Y.-REGO PARK RESIDENCE FOR GIRLS
94-31 60TH AVENUE ... ELMHURST **NY** 11380 (718) 271-2199

JEWISH CH. CARE ASSOC. OF N.Y.-WOODHAVEN RESIDENCE
94-30 59TH AVENUE ... ELMHURST **NY** 11380 (718) 271-0228

HEBREW KINDERGARTEN AND INFANTS HOME
310 BEACH 20TH STREET ... FAR ROCKAWAY **NY** 11691 (718) 327-1140

JEWISH CH. CARE ASSOC./N.Y.-HARTMAN HOMECREST FAR ROCK. RES.
25-32 BEACH CHANNEL DRIVE ... FAR ROCKAWAY **NY** 11691 (718) 327-3300

JEWISH CH. CARE ASSOC. OF N.Y.-PROGRESS HOUSE FOR BOYS
162-19 76TH AVENUE ... FLUSHING **NY** 11366 (718) 591-2552

JEWISH CH. CARE ASSOC. OF N.Y.-PROGRESS HOUSE FOR GIRLS
162-08 77TH AVENUE ... FLUSHING **NY** 11366 (718) 591-9339

JEWISH CH. CARE ASSOC. OF N.Y.-VERNONDALE RESIDENCE
111 N. 3RD AVENUE ... MT. VERNON **NY** 10550 (914) 699-7324

JEWISH CH. CARE ASSOC./N.Y.-HARTMAN HOMECREST MT.VERNON RES.
165 ESPLANADE AVENUE ... MT. VERNON **NY** 10553 (914) 699-4083

ASSOCIATION OF JEWISH FAMILY & CHILDREN'S AGENCIES
200 PARK AVENUE SOUTH ... NEW YORK **NY** 10003 (212) 674-6659

COMMUNITY HOMEMAKER SERVICE 120 WEST 57TH STREET ... NEW YORK **NY** 10019 (212) 582-9100

FAMILY LOCATION & LEGAL SERVICE 120 WEST 57TH STREET ... NEW YORK **NY** 10019 (212) 582-9100

JEWISH BOARD OF FAMILY & CHILDREN'S SERVICES
120 WEST 57TH STREET ... NEW YORK **NY** 10019 (212) 582-9100

JEWISH BOARD OF GUARDIANS 120 WEST 57TH STREET ... NEW YORK **NY** 10019 (212) 582-9100

JEWISH BOARD OF GUARDIANS CHILD GUIDANCE INSTITUTE
120 WEST 57TH STREET ... NEW YORK **NY** 10019 (212) 582-9100

JEWISH CH. CARE ASSOC. OF N.Y.-CHILDVILLE DIVISION
440 E. 88TH STREET ... NEW YORK **NY** 10028 (212) 490-9160

JEWISH CH. CARE ASSOC. OF N.Y.-CNTRL. INTAKE & REFERRAL SERV
345 MADISON AVENUE ... NEW YORK **NY** 10017 (212) 490-9161

JEWISH CH. CARE ASSOC. OF N.Y.-DIV./DEVELOPMENTALLY DISABLED
345 MADISON AVENUE ... NEW YORK **NY** 10017 (212) 490-9161

JEWISH CH. CARE ASSOC. OF N.Y.-EXECUTIVE & ADMIN. OFFICES
345 MADISON AVENUE ... NEW YORK **NY** 10017 (212) 490-9160

JEWISH CH. CARE ASSOC. OF N.Y.-FAMILY DAY CARE SERVICE
345 MADISON AVENUE ... NEW YORK **NY** 10017 (212) 490-9160

JEWISH CH. CARE ASSOC. OF N.Y.-FOSTER HOME DIVISION
345 MADISON AVENUE ... NEW YORK **NY** 10017 (212) 490-9160

JEWISH CH. CARE ASSOC. OF N.Y.-FRIENDLY HOME
465 WEST END AVENUE ... NEW YORK **NY** 10024 (212) 874-2522

JEWISH CH. CARE ASSOC. OF N.Y.-FRIENDLY HOME
320 WEST END AVENUE ... NEW YORK **NY** 10023 (212) 595-2620

JEWISH CH. CARE ASSOC. OF N.Y.-FRIENDLY HOME
465 WEST END AVENUE ... NEW YORK **NY** 10023 (212) 595-2620

JEWISH CH. CARE ASSOC. OF N.Y.-GROUP RESIDENCE DIVISION
345 MADISON AVENUE ... NEW YORK **NY** 10017 (212) 490-9160

JEWISH CH. CARE ASSOC. OF N.Y.-PREVENTIVE SERVICES
2521 BROADWAY ... NEW YORK **NY** 10025 (212) 864-5600

JEWISH CH. CARE ASSOC. OF N.Y.-TWO TOGETHER PROGRAM
345 MADISON AVENUE ... NEW YORK **NY** 10017 (212) 490-9160

JEWISH CH. CARE ASSOC. OF N.Y.-YOUTH RESIDENCE CENTER
217 E. 87TH STREET ... NEW YORK **NY** 10028 (212) 427-6655

JEWISH CHILD CARE ASSOCIATION OF NEW YORK
345 MADISON AVENUE ... NEW YORK **NY** 10017 (212) 490-9160

JEWISH YOUTH SERVICES OF BROOKLYN
CALL JEWISH CHILD CARE ASSOCIATION OF N.Y. ... NEW YORK **NY** (212) 490-9160

LOUISE WISE SERVICES 12 EAST 94TH STREET ... NEW YORK **NY** 10028 (212) 876-3050

SERVICES TO THE WIDOWED 33 WEST 60TH STREET ... NEW YORK **NY** 10023 (212) 586-2900

JEWISH CH. CARE ASSOC. OF N.Y.-COTTAGE 4 BROADWAY ... PLEASANTVILLE **NY** 10570 (914) 769-0164

JEWISH CH. CARE ASSOC. OF N.Y.-EDENWALD CENTER
ROUTE 141 ... PLEASANTVILLE **NY** 10570 (914) 769-7150

JEWISH CH. CARE ASSOC. OF N.Y.-PLEASANTVILLE COTTAGE SCHOOL
BROADWAY ... PLEASANTVILLE **NY** 10570 (914) 769-0164

JEWISH CH. CARE ASSOC. OF N.Y.-ELMHURST RESIDENCE FOR BOYS
94-30 58TH AVENUE ... REGO PARK **NY** 11374 (718) 592-8417
JEWISH CH. CARE ASSOC. OF N.Y.-ELMHURST RESIDENCE FOR GIRL
94-30 60TH AVENUE ... REGO PARK **NY** 11374 (718) 592-8316
JEWISH CH. CARE ASSOC. OF N.Y.-FAMILY DAY CARE SERVICE
97-45 QUEENS BLVD. ... REGO PARK **NY** 11374 (718) 268-8870
GELLER HOUSE - JEWISH BOARD OF GUARDIANS
77 CHICAGO AVENUE ... STATEN ISLAND **NY** 10305 (718) 442-7828
JEWISH CHILDREN'S BUREAU 21811 FAIRMOUNT ... CLEVELAND **OH** 44118 (216) 932-2800
JEWISH CHILDREN'S BUREAU 22001 FAIRMOUNT BLVD. ... CLEVELAND **OH** 44118 (216) 932-2800
JEWISH FAMILY AND CHILD SERVICE 4600 BATHURST STREET ... WILLOWDALE **ON** M2R-3V3 (416) 638-7800
ASSOCIATION FOR JEWISH CHILDREN 1301 SPENCER STREET ... PHILADELPHIA **PA** 19141 (215) 549-9000
JEWISH HOME FOR BABIES AND CHILDREN 5808 FORBES AVENUE ... PITTSBURGH **PA** 15200 (412) 441-0174
LUBAVITCH NURSERY SCHOOL 3109 NORTH LAKE DRIVE ... MILWAUKEE **WI** 53211 (414) 962-2444
MILWAUKEE JEWISH CHILDREN'S HOME 1360 NORTH PROSPECT ... MILWAUKEE **WI** 53202 (414) 273-6515

COINS & MEDALS

JEWISH-AMERICAN HALL OF FAME-JUDAH L. MAGNES MEMORIAL MUSEUM
2911 RUSSEL STREET ... BERKELEY **CA** 94705 (415) 849-2710
JOSEPH J. GOLDBERG, INC. 9454 WILSHIRE BOULEVARD ... BEVERLY HILLS **CA** 90212 (213) 273-4452
BICK INTERNATIONAL P.O.BOX 854 ... VAN NUYS **CA** 91408 (818) 997-6496
ISRAEL STAMP COLLECTORS SOCIETY P.O. BOX 854 ... VAN NUYS **CA** 91408 (818) 997-6496
ISRAEL NUMISMATIC SOCIETY OF ILLINOIS P.O. BOX 427 ... SKOKIE **IL** 60076 (312) 673-8514
HY GOLDBERG, CALHOUN COLLECTOR'S SOCIETY
CALHOUN CENTER ... MINNEAPOLIS **MN** 55435 (612) 835-0300
AARON C. OPPENHEIM, INC.
P.O. BOX 709 ROCKEFELLER CENTER STATION ... NEW YORK **NY** 10185 (212) 568-0342
ABRAHAM NACHMANY COINS PO BOX 1193/ANSONIA STATION ... NEW YORK **NY** 10023 (212) 246-6233
ISRAEL GOVERNMENT COINS & MEDALS CORP., LTD.
350 FIFTH AVENUE ... NEW YORK **NY** 10118 (212) 560-0690
JUDAICA SALES REG'D P.O. BOX 276, YOUVILLE STATION ... MONTREAL **QU** H2P 2V5 (514) 687-0632

COLLEGES & UNIVERSITIES

HEBREW UNION COLLEGE - JEWISH INSTITUTE OF RELIGION
3077 UNIVERSITY AVENUE ... LOS ANGELES **CA** 90007 (213) 749-3424
JEWISH THEOLOGICAL SEMINARY OF AMERICA
15600 MULHOLLAND DRIVE ... LOS ANGELES **CA** 90077 (213) 879-4114
UNIVERSITY OF JUDAISM 15600 MULHOLLAND DRIVE ... LOS ANGELES **CA** 90077 (213) 476-9777
YESHIVA UNIVERSITY OF LOS ANGELES
9760 WEST PICO BOULEVARD ... LOS ANGELES **CA** 90035 (213) 553-4478
SAN FRANCISCO COLLEGE OF JUDAIC STUDIES
639 14TH AVENUE ... SAN FRANCISCO **CA** 94118 (415) 751-2225
CENTER FOR JUDAIC STUDIES UNIVERSITY OF DENVER ... DENVER **CO** 80208 (303) 753-2068
CENTER FOR JUDAIC STUDIES, THE - UNIVERSITY OF DENVER
UNIVERSITY PARK ... DENVER **CO** 80208 (303) 753-1964
YESHIVA UNIVERSITY, SOUTHEAST REGION
2301 COLLINS AVENUE, SUITE M-25 ... MIAMI BEACH **FL** 33139 (305) 538-5558
SPERTUS COLLEGE OF JUDAICA 618 S. MICHIGAN AVENUE ... CHICAGO **IL** 60605 (312) 922-9012
HEBREW THEOLOGICAL COLLEGE 7135 N. CARPENTER ROAD ... SKOKIE **IL** 60077 (312) 267-9800
HEBREW COLLEGE 43 HAWES STREET ... BROOKLINE **MA** 02146 (617) 232-8710
BRANDEIS UNIVERSITY ... WALTHAM **MA** 02254 (617) 647-2177
BALTIMORE HEBREW COLLEGE & LIBRARY
5800 PARK HEIGHTS AVENUE ... BALTIMORE **MD** 21215 (301) 466-7900
COLLEGE OF JEWISH STUDIES OF GREATER WASHINGTON
9325 BROOKVILLE ROAD ... SILVER SPRING **MD** 20910 (301) 589-3180
MIDRASHA COLLEGE OF JEWISH STUDIES
21550 W. TWELVE MILE ROAD ... SOUTHFIELD **MI** 48076 (313) 352-7117
PHILIP & FLORENCE DWORSKY CTR./JEWISH STUDIES, UNIV. OF MINN
178 KLABER CT., 320 16TH AVENUE S.E. ... MINNEAPOLIS **MN** 55455 (612) 373-2851
ALBERT EINSTEIN COLLEGE OF MEDICINE-YESHIVA UNIV. BRONX CTR.
EASTCHESTER ROAD & MORRIS PARK AVENUE ... BRONX **NY** 10461 (212) 430-2000
JACK & PEARL RESNICK GERONTOLOGY CTR. ALBERT EINSTEIN COLLEGE OF MED
BRONX CENTER, EASTCHESTER RD. & MORRIS PARK AVENUE ... BRONX **NY** 10461 (212) 430-2900
YESHIVA UNIVERSITY-ALBERT EINSTEIN COLLEGE HOSPITAL
1825 EASTCHESTER ROAD ... BRONX **NY** 10461 (212) 430-2000
YESHIVA UNIVERSITY-ALBERT EINSTEIN COLLEGE OF MEDICINE
1300 MORRIS PARK AVENUE ... BRONX **NY** 10461 (212) 430-2000
YESHIVA UNIVERSITY-BELFER INST. FOR ADV. BIOMEDICAL STUDIES
1300 MORRIS PARK AVENUE ... BRONX **NY** 10461 (212) 430-2801
YESHIVA UNIVERSITY-FERKAUF GRAD. SCHOOL OF PSYCHOLOGY
1165 MORRIS PARK AVENUE ... BRONX **NY** 10461 (212) 430-4204
YESHIVA UNIVERSITY-FERKAUF GRAD. SCHOOL/PSYCH. (ADMIN.)
1165 MORRIS PARK AVENUE ... BRONX **NY** 10461 (212) 430-4207
YESHIVA UNIVERSITY-FERKAUF GRAD. SCHOOL/PSYCH. (REGISTRAR)
1165 MORRIS PARK AVENUE ... BRONX **NY** 10461 (212) 430-4206
YESHIVA UNIVERSITY-FERKAUF GRAD. SCHOOL/PSYCH: (FACULTY & OFF.)
1165 MORRIS PARK AVENUE ... BRONX **NY** 10461 (212) 430-4201
YESHIVA UNIVERSITY-FERKAUF GRAD.SCHOOL/PSYCH: (STUDENT FINANCE)
1165 MORRIS PARK AVENUE ... BRONX **NY** 10461 (212) 430-4208
YESHIVA UNIVERSITY-SUE GOLDING GRAD. DIV. OF MEDICAL SCIENCE
1300 MORRIS PARK AVENUE ... BRONX **NY** 10461 (212) 430-2107
BETH JACOB TEACHERS SEMINARY OF AMERICA 132 S. 8TH STREET ... BROOKLYN **NY** 11211 (718) 388-2701
TOURO COLLEGE - LAW SCHOOL 300 NASSAU ROAD ... HUNTINGTON **NY** 11743 (516) 421-2244
TOURO COLLEGE - TECHNION MEDICAL EDUCATION PROGRAM
300 NASSAU ROAD ... HUNTINGTON **NY** 11743 (516) 421-2246
TOURO COLLEGE - PHYSICAL THERAPY PROGRAM
300 NASSAU ROAD ... HUNTINGTON **NY** 11743 (516) 421-2244

YESHIVA UNIVERSITY

Undergraduate Schools

YESHIVA COLLEGE (YC)[1]

ISAAC BREUER COLLEGE OF HEBRAIC STUDIES (IBC)
JAMES STRIAR SCHOOL OF GENERAL JEWISH STUDIES (JSS)
YESHIVA PROGRAM/MAZER SCHOOL OF TALMUDIC STUDIES (YP)

STERN COLLEGE FOR WOMEN (SCW)[2]

Teachers Institute for Women (TIW)

SY SYMS SCHOOL OF BUSINESS (SSSB)[1]

Graduate and Professional Schools

BERNARD REVEL GRADUATE SCHOOL (BRGS)[1]

Harry Fischel School for Higher Jewish Studies (HFS)

DAVID J. AZRIELI GRADUATE INSTITUTE OF JEWISH EDUCATION AND ADMINISTRATION (AGI)[2]

ALBERT EINSTEIN COLLEGE OF MEDICINE (AECOM)[3]

SUE GOLDING GRADUATE DIVISION OF MEDICAL SCIENCES (SGG)
BELFER INSTITUTE FOR ADVANCED BIOMEDICAL STUDIES

Camp David Institute for International Health
Jack D. Weiler Hospital of Albert Einstein College of Medicine
Irwin S. and Sylvia Chanin Institute for Cancer Research
Rose F. Kennedy Center for Research in Mental Retardation and Human Development
Florence and Theodore Baumritter Kidney Dialysis and Research Center
Marion Bessin Liver Cancer Research Center
Cardiovascular Center
Center for Research in Neuropsychopharmacology
Children's Evaluation and Rehabilitation Center
Einstein-Montefiore Diabetes Research and Training Center
Genetic Counseling Program
Institute for Human Communication Disorders
Institute of Neurotoxicology
Jack and Pearl Resnick Gerontology Center
Meshulam Riklis/Rapid American Center for the Study of Brain Aging and Alzheimer's Disease

WURZWEILER SCHOOL OF SOCIAL WORK (WSSW)[1]

Brookdale Institute for the Study of Gerontology (BISG)[2]
Irving and Hanni Rosenbaum Israel Institute

FERKAUF GRADUATE SCHOOL OF PSYCHOLOGY (FGS)[3]

Yeshiva University Center for Psychological and Psychoeducational Services
Marcus Family Project for the Study of the Disturbed Adolescent

BENJAMIN N. CARDOZO SCHOOL OF LAW (CSL)[4]

Bet Tzedek Legal Services Clinic
Center for Professional Development
Leonard and Bea Diener Institute of Jewish Law

Yeshiva University Centers

[1] **Main Center**
500 West 185th Street
New York, N.Y. 10033
(212) 960-5400

[2] **Midtown Center**
245 Lexington Avenue
New York, N.Y. 10016

[3] **Bronx Center**
Eastchester Road and Morris Park Avenue
Bronx, N.Y. 10461
(212) 430-2000

[4] **Brookdale Center**
55 Fifth Avenue
New York, N.Y. 10003

Affiliates

RABBI ISAAC ELCHANAN THEOLOGICAL SEMINARY (RIETS)[1]

Rabbi Joseph B. Soloveitchik Center of Rabbinic Studies
Caroline and Joseph S. Gruss Institute in Jerusalem[5]
Caroline and Joseph S. Gruss Kollel Elyon (Post-Graduate Kollel Program)
Marcos and Adina Katz Kollel (Institute for Advanced Research in Rabbinics)
Kollel l'Horaah (Yadin Yadin)
External Yadin Yadin/Continuing Rabbinic Education
Chaver Program
Brookdale Chaplaincy Internship Program
Maybaum Sephardic Fellowship Program
Morris and Nellie L. Kawaler Rabbinic Training Program
Gindi Program for the Enhancement of Professional Rabbinics
Philip and Sarah Belz School of Jewish Music (BSJM)
Max Stern Division of Communal Services (MSDCS)
• Cantorial Services (Cantorial Council of America) • Educational Services (Educators Council of America) • New Communities—Synagogue Services • Pre-Rabbinics • Rabbinic Services • Rabbinic Alumni • Camp Morasha • Youth Services • Community Outreach Programs
Stone-Sapirstein Center for Jewish Education
National Commission on Torah Education (NACOTE)
Sephardic Community Activities Programs
Dr. Joseph and Rachel Ades Sephardic Community Outreach Program

YESHIVA UNIVERSITY HIGH SCHOOLS

The Marsha Stern Talmudical Academy—Yeshiva University High School for Boys (TMSTA)[1]
Alexander P. Hirsch Computer Center
Joseph Alexander Foundation Library
Tonya Soloveitchik Yeshiva University High School for Girls at the Olga Gruss Lewin Educational Center (TSHSG)[7]
Mary E. Hirsch Computer Center
Leo and Beatrix Kern Library
Samuel H. Wang Yeshiva University High School for Girls (SWHSG)[8]
Mr. and Mrs. Fred Horowitz Computer Room
Rabbi Jacob Bobrowsky Hebrew Library
Dr. Hyman Zahtz English Library

YESHIVA UNIVERSITY OF LOS ANGELES[6]

University-Wide Services to the Community and the Nation[1]

Holocaust Studies Program
Interdisciplinary Conference on Bereavement and Grief
Jacob E. Safra Institute of Sephardic Studies
Institute of Yemenite Studies
Yeshiva University Gerontological Institute (YUGI)
Yeshiva University Museum (YUM)
Yeshiva University Press

Libraries

Mendel Gottesman Library[1]
Pollack Library
Mendel Gottesman Library of Hebraica-Judaica
Landowne-Bloom Library
Hedi Steinberg Library[2]
Dr. Lillian and Dr. Rebecca Chutick Law Library[4]
D. Samuel Gottesman Library[3]

Affiliated Centers

[5]**Israel:**
Gruss Institute
Rehov HaVaad Haleumi
Givat Mordechai
Jerusalem, Israel 93721
(02) 430-326

[6]**Los Angeles:**
9760 West Pico Boulevard
Los Angeles, Calif. 90035
(213) 553-4478

[7]**Midtown:**
425 Fifth Avenue
New York, N.Y. 10016
(212) 340-7800

[8]**Queens:**
86-86 Palo Alto Street
Holliswood, N.Y. 11423
(718) 479-8550

ACADEMY FOR JEWISH RELIGION C/O TEMPLE ANSCHE CHESED 251 WEST 100TH STREET	NEW YORK	NY	10025	(212) 995-8387
BAR-ILAN UNIVERSITY IN ISRAEL 853 SEVENTH AVENUE	NEW YORK	NY	10019	(212) 315-1990
BEIT MIDRASH L'TORAH, JERUSALEM TORAH COLLEGE FOR MEN TORAH DEPT., WORLD ZIONIST ORGANIZATION, 515 PARK AVENUE	NEW YORK	NY	10022	(212) 752-0600
BENJAMIN N. CARDOZO SCHOOL OF LAW - YESHIVA UNIVERSITY 55 FIFTH AVENUE	NEW YORK	NY	10003	(212) 790-0310
BERNARD REVEL GRADUATE SCHOOL-YESHIVA UNIVERSITY 500 W. 185TH STREET	NEW YORK	NY	10033	(212) 960-5253
BRAMSON ORT 304 PARK AVENUE SOUTH	NEW YORK	NY	10010	(212) 677-7420
BRANDEIS UNIVERSITY 12 EAST 77TH STREET	NEW YORK	NY	10021	(212) 472-1501
HEBREW UNION COLLEGE - JEWISH INSTITUTE OF RELIGION 1 WEST FOURTH STREET	NEW YORK	NY	10003	(212) 674-5300
HERZLIAH - JEWISH TEACHERS SEMINARY 69 BANK STREET	NEW YORK	NY	10014	(212) 575-1819
HORACE M. KALLEN CENTER FOR JEWISH STUDIES 69 BANK STREET	NEW YORK	NY	10014	(212) 575-1819
JEWISH THEOLOGICAL SEMINARY OF AMERICA, THE 3080 BROADWAY	NEW YORK	NY	10027	(212) 678-8000
MACHON GOLD COLLEGE FOR WOMEN TORAH DEPT. WORLD ZIONIST ORGANIZATION, 515 PARK AVENUE	NEW YORK	NY	10022	(212) 752-0600
MOUNT SINAI SCHOOL OF MEDICINE OF CUNY, THE 100TH STREET & FIFTH AVENUE	NEW YORK	NY	10029	(212) 650-6500
MT. SINAI SCHOOL OF MEDICINE OF CUNY, THE (FUND DEVELOPMENT) 100TH STREET & FIFTH AVENUE	NEW YORK	NY	10029	(212) 650-6976
RABBI ISAAC ELCHANAN THEOLOGICAL SEMINARY 2540 AMSTERDAM AVENUE	NEW YORK	NY	10033	(212) 960-5346
RECONSTRUCTIONIST RABBINICAL COLLEGE 432 PARK AVENUE SOUTH	NEW YORK	NY	10016	(212) 889-9080
STERN COLLEGE FOR WOMEN 245 LEXINGTON AVENUE	NEW YORK	NY	10016	(212) 340-7700
STONE-SAPIRSTEIN CENTER FOR JEWISH EDUCATION-YESHIVA UNIV. 500 W. 185TH STREET	NEW YORK	NY	10033	(212) 960-5400
TEACHERS INSTITUTE - SEMINARY COLLEGE OF JEWISH STUDIES 3080 BROADWAY	NEW YORK	NY	10027	(212) 678-8000
TOURO COLLEGE 30 WEST 44TH STREET	NEW YORK	NY	10036	(212) 575-0190
TOURO COLLEGE - DEAN OF FACULTIES 30 WEST 44TH STREET	NEW YORK	NY	10036	(212) 575-0190
TOURO COLLEGE - DEAN OF STUDENTS 30 WEST 44TH STREET	NEW YORK	NY	10036	(212) 221-2296
TOURO COLLEGE - FINANCIAL AID 30 WEST 44TH STREET	NEW YORK	NY	10036	(212) 575-0190
TOURO COLLEGE - GRADUATE PROGRAM - JEWISH STUDIES 30 WEST 44TH STREET	NEW YORK	NY	10036	(212) 575-0190
TOURO COLLEGE - JEWISH PEOPLE'S UNIVERSITY OF THE AIR 30 WEST 44TH STREET	NEW YORK	NY	10036	(212) 575-0190
TOURO COLLEGE - OFFICE OF ADMISSIONS 30 WEST 44TH STREET	NEW YORK	NY	10036	(212) 719-9865
TOURO COLLEGE - PHYSICIAN'S ASSISTANT PROGRAM 30 WEST 44TH STREET	NEW YORK	NY	10036	(212) 575-0190
TOURO COLLEGE - REGISTRAR 30 WEST 44TH STREET	NEW YORK	NY	10036	(212) 575-0190
WURZWEILER SCHOOL OF SOCIAL WORK-YESHIVA UNIVERSITY 500 W. 185TH STREET	NEW YORK	NY	10033	(212) 960-0800
YESHIVA UNIVERSITY 500 WEST 185TH STREET	NEW YORK	NY	10033	(212) 960-5400
YESHIVA UNIVERSITY - ADMISSIONS OFFICE 500 WEST 185TH STREET	NEW YORK	NY	10033	(212) 960-5277
YESHIVA UNIVERSITY - BENJAMIN N. CARDOZO SCHOOL OF LAW 55 FIFTH AVENUE	NEW YORK	NY	10003	(212) 790-0310
YESHIVA UNIVERSITY - BEQUESTS 55 FIFTH AVENUE	NEW YORK	NY	10003	(212) 790-0200
YESHIVA UNIVERSITY - BERNARD REVEL GRADUATE SCHOOL 500 W. 185TH STREET	NEW YORK	NY	10033	(212) 960-5253
YESHIVA UNIVERSITY - BROOKDALE CENTER 55 FIFTH AVENUE	NEW YORK	NY	10003	(212) 790-0200
YESHIVA UNIVERSITY - BROOKDALE RESIDENCE HALL 50 E. 34TH STREET	NEW YORK	NY	10016	(212) 686-5900
YESHIVA UNIVERSITY - BUSINESS AFFAIRS 500 WEST 185TH STREET	NEW YORK	NY	10033	(212) 960-5396
YESHIVA UNIVERSITY - COMMENTATOR (YESHIVA COLLEGE NEWSPAPER) 2525 AMSTERDAM AVENUE	NEW YORK	NY	10033	(212) 923-1879
YESHIVA UNIVERSITY - DEVELOPMENT 500 WEST 185TH STREET	NEW YORK	NY	10033	(212) 960-0863
YESHIVA UNIVERSITY - DINING HALLS 2501 AMSTERDAM AVENUE	NEW YORK	NY	10033	(212) 568-2440
YESHIVA UNIVERSITY - DIVISION OF COMMUNAL SERVICES 500 W. 185TH STREET	NEW YORK	NY	10033	(212) 960-5265
YESHIVA UNIVERSITY - ERNA MICHAEL COLLEGE OF HEBRAIC STUDIES 500 W. 185TH STREET	NEW YORK	NY	10033	(212) 960-5347
YESHIVA UNIVERSITY - FURMAN DINING HALL 2501 AMSTERDAM AVENUE	NEW YORK	NY	10033	(212) 960-5248
YESHIVA UNIVERSITY - GUARD EMERGENCY 55 FIFTH AVENUE	NEW YORK	NY	10003	(212) 790-0303
YESHIVA UNIVERSITY - HAMEVASER 2501 AMSTERDAM AVENUE	NEW YORK	NY	10033	(212) 927-8571
YESHIVA UNIVERSITY - HARRY FISCHEL SCHOOL OF HIGHER JEWISH STUDIES 500 W. 185TH STREET	NEW YORK	NY	10033	(212) 960-5253
YESHIVA UNIVERSITY - HIGH SCHOOL FOR BOYS 2540 AMSTERDAM AVENUE	NEW YORK	NY	10033	(212) 960-5337
YESHIVA UNIVERSITY - HIGH SCHOOL FOR GIRLS 425 FIFTH AVENUE	NEW YORK	NY	10016	(212) 340-7800
YESHIVA UNIVERSITY - J. STRIAR SCHOOL FOR GEN. JEWISH STUDIES 500 W. 185TH STREET	NEW YORK	NY	10033	(212) 960-5225
YESHIVA UNIVERSITY - MAIN CENTER 500 WEST 185TH STREET	NEW YORK	NY	10033	(212) 960-5400
YESHIVA UNIVERSITY - MIDTOWN CENTER 245 LEXINGTON AVENUE	NEW YORK	NY	10016	(212) 340-7700
YESHIVA UNIVERSITY - MORGENSTERN RESIDENÇE 2525 AMSTERDAM AVENUE	NEW YORK	NY	10033	(212) 960-5249
YESHIVA UNIVERSITY - MUSEUM 2520 AMSTERDAM AVENUE	NEW YORK	NY	10033	(212) 960-5390
YESHIVA UNIVERSITY - OBSERVER (STERN COLLEGE NEWSPAPER) 50 EAST 34TH STREET	NEW YORK	NY	10016	(212) 340-7700
YESHIVA UNIVERSITY - 185TH ST. EMERGENCY GUARD 500 WEST 185TH STREET	NEW YORK	NY	10033	(212) 960-5200
YESHIVA UNIVERSITY - PUBLIC RELATIONS 500 WEST 185TH STREET	NEW YORK	NY	10033	(212) 960-5285
YESHIVA UNIVERSITY - RABBI ISAAC ELCHANAN THEOLOGICAL SEMINARY 2540 AMSTERDAM AVENUE	NEW YORK	NY	10033	(212) 960-5346
YESHIVA UNIVERSITY - REGISTRAR 500 WEST 185TH STREET	NEW YORK	NY	10033	(212) 960-5274
YESHIVA UNIVERSITY - RIETS HALL RESIDENCE 526 W. 187TH STREET	NEW YORK	NY	10033	(212) 960-5249
YESHIVA UNIVERSITY - RUBIN RESIDENCE 2501 AMSTERDAM AVENUE	NEW YORK	NY	10033	(212) 960-5249
YESHIVA UNIVERSITY - STERN COLLEGE FOR WOMEN 245 LEXINGTON AVENUE	NEW YORK	NY	10016	(212) 340-7700
YESHIVA UNIVERSITY - STUDENT FINANCE 500 WEST 185TH STREET	NEW YORK	NY	10033	(212) 960-5269
YESHIVA UNIVERSITY - 34TH STREET GUARD EMERGENCY 245 LEXINGTON AVENUE	NEW YORK	NY	10016	(212) 340-7709
YESHIVA UNIVERSITY - UNIVERSITY AFFAIRS 500 WEST 185TH STREET	NEW YORK	NY	10033	(212) 960-0850
YESHIVA UNIVERSITY - WOMEN'S ORGANIZATION 2495 AMSTERDAM	NEW YORK	NY	10033	(212) 960-0855
YESHIVA UNIVERSITY - WURZWEILER SCHOOL OF SOCIAL WORK 2495 AMSTERDAM AVENUE	NEW YORK	NY	10033	(212) 960-0800
YESHIVA UNIVERSITY - YESHIVA COLLEGE 500 W. 185TH STREET	NEW YORK	NY	10033	(212) 960-5124
CLEVELAND COLLEGE OF JEWISH STUDIES 26500 SHAKER BLVD.	BEACHWOOD	OH	44122	(216) 464-4050
HEBREW UNION COLLEGE-JEWISH INSTITUTE OF RELIGION 3101 CLIFTON AVENUE	CINCINNATI	OH	45220	(513) 221-1875
CLEVELAND COLLEGE OF JEWISH STUDIES 26500 SHAKER BLVD.	CLEVELAND	OH	44122	(216) 464-4050
TELSHE YESHIVA COLLEGE 28400 EUCLID AVENUE	CLEVELAND	OH	44092	(216) 943-5300
CLEVELAND COLLEGE OF JEWISH STUDIES 26500 SHAKER BLVD.	CLEVELAND HEIGHTS	OH	44122	(216) 464-4370
YAVNE TEACHER'S COLLEGE FOR WOMEN 1970 S. TAYLOR ROAD	CLEVELAND HEIGHTS	OH	44118	(216) 943-5300
MAIMONIDES COLLEGE P.O. BOX 6510, STATION A	TORONTO	ON	M5W 1X4	(416) 961-1527
DROPSIE COLLEGE 250 N. HIGHLAND AVENUE	MERION	PA	19066	(215) 667-1830
GRATZ COLLEGE 10TH STREET & TABOR ROAD	PHILADELPHIA	PA	19141	(215) 329-3363
RECONSTRUCTIONIST RABBINICAL COLLEGE CHURCH ROAD AT GREENWOOD	WYNCOTE	PA	19095	(215) 576-0800
TOURO COLLEGE - ISRAEL OFFICE 3 RECHOV HASHAYIS	JERUSALEM	IS		(02) 761-427

COMEDY

MARC WEINER'S KOSHER COMEDY 104 GRIGGS AVENUE	TEANECK	NJ	07666	(201) 836-3989
MENDY ENTERPRISES-THE KOSHER COMIC BOOK 450 SEVENTH AVENUE	NEW YORK	NY	10001	(718) 774-4660

COMMUNITY RELATIONS ORGANIZATIONS

JEWISH COMMUNITY COUNCIL P.O. BOX 9157 3960 MONTCLAIR ROAD	BIRMINGHAM	AL	36213	(205) 849-0416
AMERICAN JEWISH COMMITTEE-PHOENIX AREA 3550 NORTH CENTRAL AVENUE, SUITE 420	PHOENIX	AZ	85012	(602) 279-9695
COMMUNITY RELATIONS COMMITTEE OF GREATER PHOENIX JEWISH FED. 1718 WEST MARYLAND AVENUE	PHOENIX	AZ	95015	(602) 249-1845
COMMUNITY RELATIONS COMMITTEE OF THE TUCSON J.C.C. 102 NORTH PLUMER	TUCSON	AZ	85719	(602) 884-8921
CANADIAN JEWISH CONGRESS-PACIFIC REGION 950 WEST 41ST AVENUE	VANCOUVER	BC	V5Z 2N7	(604) 261-8101
JEWISH FEDERATION OF ORANGE COUNTY 12181 BUARO	GARDEN GROVE	CA	92640	(714) 530-6636
JEWISH COMMUNITY FED. OF GREATER LONG BEACH & W. ORANGE CTY 3801 EAST WILLOW STREET	LONG BEACH	CA	90815	(213) 426-7601
AMERICAN JEWISH COMMITTEE-WESTERN REGION 6505 WILSHIRE BOULEVARD SUITE 315	LOS ANGELES	CA	90048	(213) 655-7071
AMERICAN JEWISH CONGRESS-SOUTHERN CALIFORNIA REGION 6505 WILSHIRE BOULEVARD SUITE 1103	LOS ANGELES	CA	90048	(213) 651-4601
ANTI-DEFAMATION LEAGUE OF B'NAI B'RITH-PACIFIC SOUTHWEST 6505 WILSHIRE BLVD., SUITE 814	LOS ANGELES	CA	90048	(213) 655-8205
BEVERLY FAIRFAX NEIGHBORHOOD ORGANIZATIONS 163 SOUTH FAIRFAX AVENUE	LOS ANGELES	CA	90036	(213) 931-1511
COMMUNITY RELATIONS COMMITTEE OF THE JEWISH FED. COUNCIL 6505 WILSHIRE BOULEVARD, SUITE 802	LOS ANGELES	CA	90048	(213) 852-1234
JEWISH COMMITTEE FOR PERSONAL SERVICE 1891 EFFIE STREET	LOS ANGELES	CA	90026	(213) 666-0171
JEWISH COMMUNITY FOUNDATION 6505 WILSHIRE BLVD.	LOS ANGELES	CA	90048	(213) 852-1234
JEWISH LABOR COMMITTEE-CALIFORNIA 6505 WILSHIRE BOULEVARD, SUITE 403	LOS ANGELES	CA	90048	(213) 653-350T
AMERICAN JEWISH COMMITTEE-ORANGE COUNTY AREA 4500 CAMPUS DRIVE SUITE 420	NEWPORT BEACH	CA	92660	(714) 546-2914
JEWISH COMMUNITY RELATIONS COUNCIL OF THE GREATER EAST BAY 3245 SHEFFIELD AVENUE	OAKLAND	CA	94602	(415) 533-7462
SACRAMENTO JEWISH COMMUNITY RELATIONS COUNCIL P.O. BOX 254589	SACRAMENTO	CA	95865	(916) 486-0906
AMERICAN JEWISH COMMITTEE - SAN DIEGO AREA 1551 CAMINO DEL RIO SOUTH	SAN DIEGO	CA	92108	(619) 284-0487
ANTI-DEFAMATION LEAGUE OF B'NAI B'RITH-SAN DIEGO-ARIZONA 7850 MISSION CENTER COURT STREET	SAN DIEGO	CA	92108	(619) 293-3370
JEWISH COMMUNITY RELATIONS COUNCIL OF THE UNITED JEWISH FED. 5511 EL CAJON BOULEVARD	SAN DIEGO	CA	92115	(619) 582-2483
JEWISH PUBLIC AFFAIRS COMMITTEE 5511 EL CAJON BLVD.	SAN DIEGO	CA	92115	(619) 582-2483
AMERICAN JEWISH COMMITTEE-NORTHWEST PACIFIC AND BAY AREA 703 MARKET STREET, SUITE 1500	SAN FRANCISCO	CA	94103	(415) 392-1892
AMERICAN JEWISH CONGRESS-NORTHERN CALIFORNIA REGION 942 MARKET STREET SUITE 501	SAN FRANCISCO	CA	94102	(415) 391-6590
JEWISH COMMUNITY RELATIONS COUNCIL 920 FLOOD BUILDING 870 MARKET STREET	SAN FRANCISCO	CA	94102	(415) 391-4655
JEWISH COMMUNITY RELATIONS COUNCIL OF S.F., MARIN & PENIN. 870 MARKET STREET, SUITE 920	SAN FRANCISCO	CA	94102	(415) 391-4655
JEWISH COMMUNITY RELATIONS COMMITTEE OF GREATER SAN JOSE 1777 HAMILTON AVENUE, SUITE 210	SAN JOSE	CA	95125	(408) 267-2770
AMERICAN JEWISH COMMITTEE-DENVER AREA 609 EAST SPEER BUILDING	DENVER	CO	80203	(303) 320-1742
ANTI-DEFAMATION LEAGUE OF B'NAI B'RITH-MOUNTAIN STATES 300 SOUTH DAHLIA STREET, SUITE 202	DENVER	CO	80222	(303) 321-7177

JEWISH LABOR COMMITTEE-COLORADO 346 ACOMA	DENVER	**CO**	80223	(303) 759-3439
JEWISH FEDERATION OF GREATER BRIDGEPORT 4200 PARK AVENUE	BRIDGEPORT	**CT**	06604	(203) 372-6504
JEWISH FEDERATION OF GREATER DANBURY 5 MAIN STREET, SUITE E	DANBURY	**CT**	06810	(203) 792-6353
JEWISH FEDERATION OF GREATER NORWALK SHOREHAVEN ROAD	EAST NORWALK	**CT**	06885	(203) 853-3440
ANTI-DEFAMATION LEAGUE OF B'NAI B'RITH-CONNECTICUT 1162 CHAPEL STREET	NEW HAVEN	**CT**	06511	(203) 787-4281
CONNECTICUT JEWISH COMMUNITY RELATIONS COUNCIL 1162 CHAPEL STREET	NEW HAVEN	**CT**	06511	(203) 562-2137
NEW HAVEN JEWISH FEDERATION 1162 CHAPEL STREET	NEW HAVEN	**CT**	06511	(203) 562-2137
JEWISH FEDERATION OF EASTERN CONNECTICUT, INC. 302 STATE STREET, ROOM 221	NEW LONDON	**CT**	06320	(203) 442-8062
UNITED JEWISH FEDERATION P.O. BOX 3038	STAMFORD	**CT**	06905	(203) 322-6935
JEWISH FEDERATION 1020 COUNTY CLUB ROAD	WATERBURY	**CT**	06708	(203) 758-2441
JEWISH FED. COMMUNITY RELATIONS COMM. OF GREATER HARTFORD 333 BLOOMFIELD AVENUE	WEST HARTFORD	**CT**	06117	(203) 232-4483
AMERICAN JEWISH COMMITTEE-CENTRAL ATLANTIC AREA 2027 MASSACHUSETTS AVENUE, NW	WASHINGTON	**DC**	20036	(202) 387-8641
AMERICAN JEWISH CONGRESS-NATIONAL CAPITAL CHAPTER 2027 MASSACHUSETTS AVENUE, NW	WASHINGTON	**DC**	20036	(202) 332-3888
ANTI-DEFAMATION LEAGUE OF B'NAI B'RITH-D.C.-MARYLAND 1640 RHODE ISLAND AVENUE, NW	WASHINGTON	**DC**	20036	(202) 960-0342
COORDINATING BOARD OF JEWISH ORGANIZATIONS 1640 RHODE ISLAND AVENUE N.W.	WASHINGTON	**DC**	20036	(202) 857-6545
JEWISH COMMUNITY COUNCIL OF GREATER WASHINGTON 1522 K STREET, N.W., SUITE 920	WASHINGTON	**DC**	20005	(202) 347-4628
JEWISH WAR VETERANS OF THE UNITED STATES OF AMERICA 1811 R STREET, N.W.	WASHINGTON	**DC**	20009	(202) 265-6280
JEWISH FEDERATION OF DELAWARE 101 GARDEN OF EDEN ROAD	WILMINGTON	**DE**	19803	(302) 478-6200
JEWISH FEDERATION OF PINELLAS COUNTY 302 S. JUPITER AVENUE	CLEARWATER	**FL**	33515	(813) 446-1033
JEWISH FEDERATION OF GREATER FORT LAUDERDALE 8358 WEST OAKLAND PARK BOULEVARD	FORT LAUDERDALE	**FL**	33321	(305) 748-8200
JEWISH FEDERATION OF SOUTH BROWARD 2719 HOLLYWOOD BOULEVARD	HOLLYWOOD	**FL**	33020	(305) 921-8810
JACKSONVILLE JEWISH FEDERATION 10829-1 OLD STREET, AUGUSTINE ROAD	JACKSONVILLE	**FL**	32223	(904) 262-2800
JEWISH FEDERATION OF GREATER ORLANDO P.O. BOX 1508 851 N. MAITLAND AVENUE	MAITLAND	**FL**	32751	(305) 645-5933
AMERICAN JEWISH COMMITTEE-SOUTHEAST REGION 3000 BISCAYNE BLVD.	MIAMI	**FL**	33137	(305) 576-4240
AMERICAN JEWISH CONGRESS-SOUTHWEST REGION 4200 BISCAYNE BOULEVARD	MIAMI	**FL**	33137	(305) 673-9100
ANTI-DEFAMATION LEAGUE OF B'NAI B'RITH-FLORIDA 1520 S.E. 2ND AVENUE, SUITE 800	MIAMI	**FL**	33131	(305) 373-6306
GREATER MIAMI JEWISH FEDERATION 4200 BISCAYNE BOULEVARD	MIAMI	**FL**	33137	(305) 576-4000
AMERICAN JEWISH COMMITTEE-PALM BEACH AREA 120 SOUTH OLIVE AVENUE, SUITE 614	PALM BEACH	**FL**	33480	(305) 655-5118
ANTI-DEFAMATION LEAGUE OF B'NAI B'RITH-PALM BEACH COUNTY 120 S. OLIVE AVENUE, SUITE 614	PALM BEACH	**FL**	33401	(305) 832-7144
SARASOTA-MANATEE JEWISH FEDERATION 2197 RINGLING BOULEVARD	SARASOTA	**FL**	33577	(813) 365-4410
JEWISH FEDERATION OF PALM BEACH SUITE 305 501 SOUTH FLAGLER DRIVE	WEST PALM BEACH	**FL**	33401	(305) 832-2120
AMERICAN JEWISH COMMITTEE-ATLANTA AREA 1649 TULLY CIRCLE, N.E.	ATLANTA	**GA**	30329	(404) 233-5501
ANTI-DEFAMATION LEAGUE OF B'NAI B'RITH-SOUTHEAST 805 PEACHTREE STREET, NE SUITE 633	ATLANTA	**GA**	30308	(404) 523-3391
ATLANTA JEWISH FEDERATION, INC. 1753 PEACHTREE ROAD, N.E.	ATLANTA	**GA**	30309	(404) 873-1661
JEWISH LABOR COMMITTEE-GEORGIA 1000 RHODES HAVERTY BLDG. 134 PEACHTREE STREET, NW	ATLANTA	**GA**	30303	
SAVANNAH JEWISH COUNCIL 5111 ABERCORN STREET	SAVANNAH	**GA**	31499	(912) 355-8111
JEWISH FEDERATION OF GREATER IOWA 910 POLK BOULEVARD	DES MOINES	**IA**	50312	(515) 277-6321
AMERICAN JEWISH COMMITTEE-MIDWESTERN REGION 55 JACKSON BOULEVARD SUITE 1870	CHICAGO	**IL**	60604	(312) 663-5500
AMERICAN JEWISH CONGRESS-CHICAGO COUNCIL, MIDWEST REGION 22 WEST MONROE STREET SUITE 2101	CHICAGO	**IL**	60603	(312) 332-7355
ANTI-DEFAMATION LEAGUE OF B'NAI B'RITH-MIDWEST 222 WEST ADAMS STREET	CHICAGO	**IL**	60606	(312) 782-5080
JEWISH LABOR COMMITTEE-ILLINOIS JEWELRY WORKERS LOCAL 4A 1640 N. WELLS STREET	CHICAGO	**IL**	60603	(312) 642-3151
JEWISH LABOR COMMITTEE-ILLINOIS 54 WEST RANDOLPH STREET, ROOM 703	CHICAGO	**IL**	60602	(312) 641-5086
PUBLIC AFFAIRS COMM. OF JEWISH UNITED FUND OF METRO CHICAGO ONE SOUTH FRANKLIN STREET	CHICAGO	**IL**	60606	(312) 346-6700
JEWISH FEDERATION OF PEORIA 3100 N. KNOXVILLE, SUITE 17	PEORIA	**IL**	61603	(309) 686-0611
SPRINGFIELD JEWISH FEDERATION 730 EAST VEIN STREET	SPRINGFIELD	**IL**	62703	(217) 528-3446
INDIANA JEWISH COMMUNITY RELATIONS COUNCIL 1100 WEST 42ND STREET	INDIANAPOLIS	**IN**	46208	(317) 926-2935
INDIANAPOLIS JEWISH COMMUNITY RELATIONS COUNCIL 1100 WEST 42ND STREET	INDIANAPOLIS	**IN**	46208	(317) 926-2935
JEWISH FEDERATION OF ST. JOSEPH VALLEY, INC. 804 SHERLAND BUILDING	SOUTH BEND	**IN**	46601	(219) 233-1164
JEWISH COMMUNITY FEDERATION P.O. BOX 33035	LOUISVILLE	**KY**	40232	(502) 451-8840
ANTI-DEFAMATION LEAGUE OF B'NAI B'RITH-SOUTH CENTRAL 535 GRAVIER STREET SUITE 806	NEW ORLEANS	**LA**	70130	(504) 522-9534
JEWISH FEDERATION OF GREATER NEW ORLEANS 1539 JACKSON AVENUE	NEW ORLEANS	**LA**	70130	(504) 525-0673
SHREVEPORT JEWISH FEDERATION 2030 LINE AVENUE	SHREVEPORT	**LA**	71104	(318) 221-4129
AMERICAN JEWISH COMMITTEE-NEW ENGLAND REGION 72 FRANKLIN STREET ROOM 403	BOSTON	**MA**	02110	(617) 426-7415
AMERICAN JEWISH CONGRESS-NEW ENGLAND REGION 72 FRANKLIN STREET	BOSTON	**MA**	02110	(617) 542-0265
ANTI-DEFAMATION LEAGUE OF B'NAI B'RITH-NEW ENGLAND 72 FRANKLIN STREET, SUITE 504	BOSTON	**MA**	02110	(617) 542-4977
JEWISH COMMUNITY COUNCIL OF METROPOLITAN BOSTON 72 FRANKLIN STREET, SUITE 406	BOSTON	**MA**	02110	(617) 542-7525
JEWISH FEDERATION OF NORTH SHORE,INC. 4 COMMUNITY ROAD	MARBLEHEAD	**MA**	01945	(617) 745-4222
JEWISH FEDERATION OF GREATER NEW BEDFORD, INC. 467 HAWTHORN STREET	N. DARTMOUTH	**MA**	02747	(617) 997-7417
SPRINGFIELD JEWISH FEDERATION 1160 DICKINSON STREET	SPRINGFIELD	**MA**	01108	(413) 737-4313
WORCESTER JEWISH FEDERATION 633 SALISBURY STREET	WORCESTER	**MA**	01609	(617) 756-1543
CANADIAN JEWISH CONGRESS-MANITOBA REGION 370 HARGRAVE STREET	WINNIPEG	**MB**	R3B 2K1	(204) 943-0406
AMERICAN JEWISH COMMITTEE-BALTIMORE AREA 829 MONSEY BUILDING FAYETTE & CALVERT STREETS	BALTIMORE	**MD**	21201	(301) 539-4777
AMERICAN JEWISH CONGRESS-MARYLAND REGION 7504 SEVEN MILE LANE	BALTIMORE	**MD**	21208	(301) 484-8863
ANTI-DEFAMATION LEAGUE OF B'NAI B'RITH 3 GREENWOOD PLACE	BALTIMORE	**MD**	21208	(301) 484-6200
BALTIMORE JEWISH COUNCIL 101 WEST MOUNT ROYAL, SUITE 208	BALTIMORE	**MD**	21201	(301) 752-2630
JEWISH LABOR COMMITTEE-WASHINGTON, D.C. 7106 WILSON LANE	BETHESDA	**MD**	22034	(301) 229-0683
JEWISH FEDERATION-COMMUNITY COUNCIL OF SOUTHERN MAINE 57 ASHMONT STREET	PORTLAND	**ME**	04103	(207) 773-7254
AMERICAN JEWISH COMMITTEE-MICHIGAN-INDIANA AREA 163 MADISON AVENUE	DETROIT	**MI**	48226	(313) 965-3353
ANTI-DEFAMATION LEAGUE OF B'NAI B'RITH-MICHIGAN 163 MADISON AVENUE, SUITE 120	DETROIT	**MI**	48226	(313) 962-9686
JEWISH COMMUNITY COUNCIL OF METROPOLITAN DETROIT 163 MADISON AVENUE	DETROIT	**MI**	48226	(313) 962-1880
JEWISH LABOR COMMITTEE-MICHIGAN 163 MADISON AVENUE	DETROIT	**MI**	48226	(313) 965-3939
FLINT JEWISH FEDERATION 120 WEST KEARSLEY	FLINT	**MI**	48502	(313) 767-5922
AMERICAN JEWISH CONGRESS-MICHIGAN REGION 21550 WEST 12 MILE ROAD	SOUTHFIELD	**MI**	48076	(313) 357-2766
ANTI-DEFAMATION LEAGUE OF B'NAI B'RITH-MINNESOTA-DAKOTAS 15 SOUTH 9TH STREET BUILDING	MINNEAPOLIS	**MN**	55402	(612) 338-7816
JEWISH COMMUNITY RELATIONS COUNCIL 15 SOUTH 9TH STREET BLDG., SUITE 400	MINNEAPOLIS	**MN**	55402	(612) 338-7816
JEWISH COMMUNITY RELATIONS COUNCIL, ADL OF MINN. & DAKOTAS 15 S. 9TH STREET BUILDING, SUITE 400	MINNEAPOLIS	**MN**	55402	(612) 338-7816
ANTI-DEFAMATION LEAGUE OF B'NAI B'RITH-MISSOURI-S. ILLINOIS 225 SOUTH MERAMEC	CLAYTON	**MO**	63105	(314) 726-3303
AMERICAN JEWISH COMMITTEE-KANSAS CITY AREA C/O JEWISH FAMILY & CHILDREN'S SERVICES 1115 EAST 65 ST	KANSAS CITY	**MO**	64114	(816) 333-1172
JEWISH COMMUNITY RELATIONS BUREAU OF GREATER KANSAS CITY 25 EAST 12TH STREET, 10TH FLOOR	KANSAS CITY	**MO**	64106	(816) 421-5808
AMERICAN JEWISH COMMITTEE-WEST CENTRAL AREA 7750 CLAYTON ROAD	ST. LOUIS	**MO**	63117	(314) 647-2519
AMERICAN JEWISH CONGRESS-SOUTHWEST REGION 8420 DELMAR, SUITE 201	ST. LOUIS	**MO**	63124	(314) 993-5505
ANTI-DEFAMATION LEAGUE OF B'NAI B'RITH - MISSOURI REGION 225 SOUTH MERAMEC, SUITE 414	ST. LOUIS	**MO**	63105	(314) 726-3303
JEWISH COMMUNITY RELATIONS COUNCIL 722 CHESTNUT STREET, SUITE 1019	ST. LOUIS	**MO**	63101	(314) 241-2584
JEWISH COMMUNITY RELATIONS COUNCIL 12 MILLSTONE CAMPUS DRIVE	ST. LOUIS	**MO**	63146	(314) 432-0020
JEWISH LABOR COMMITTEE-MISSOURI 10353 CORBELL	ST. LOUIS	**MO**	63141	
ADL/COMMUNITY RELATIONS COMMITTEE OF THE JEW. FED. OF OMAHA 333 SOUTH 132ND STREET	OMAHA	**NE**	68154	(402) 333-1303
ANTI-DEFAMATION LEAGUE OF B'NAI B'RITH-PLAIN STATES 333 S. 132ND STREET	OMAHA	**NE**	68154	(402) 392-2274
JEWISH COMMUNITY RELATIONS COUNCIL OF THE JEW FED OF S. N.J. 2393 W. MARLTON PIKE	CHERRY HILL	**NJ**	08002	(609) 665-6100
UNITED JEWISH FEDERATION OF METROWEST 60 GLENWOOD AVENUE	EAST ORANGE	**NJ**	07017	(201) 673-6800
JEWISH FEDERATION OF NORTHERN MIDDLESEX COUNTY, NEW JERSEY 100 MENLO PARK, SUITE 101-102	EDISON	**NJ**	08837	(201) 494-3920
JEWISH FEDERATION OF RARITAN VALLEY 2 SOUTH ADELAIDE AVENUE	HIGHLAND PARK	**NJ**	09804	(201) 246-1905
ANTI-DEFAMATION LEAGUE OF B'NAI B'RITH-NEW JERSEY 513 WEST MOUNT PLEASANT AVENUE	LIVINGSTON	**NJ**	07039	(201) 994-4546
JEWISH LABOR COMMITTEE-NEW JERSEY 63 OAKWOOD AVENUE	LIVINGSTON	**NJ**	07039	(201) 992-4709
AMERICAN JEWISH COMMITTEE-NEW JERSEY AREA 303 MILBURN AVENUE	MILBURN	**NJ**	07041	(201) 379-7844
AMERICAN JEWISH CONGRESS-NEW JERSEY REGION 24 COMMERCE STREET	NEWARK	**NJ**	02110	(201) 623-4754
JEWISH COMMUNITY RELATIONS COMM. OF UNITED JEWISH COMMUNITY 111 KINDERKAMACK ROAD (BERGEN)	RIVER EDGE	**NJ**	07661	(201) 488-6800
JEWISH FEDERATION OF CENTRAL NEW JERSEY GREEN LANE	UNION	**NJ**	07083	(201) 351-5060
FEDERATION OF JEWISH AGENCIES OF ATLANTIC COUNTY 5321 ATLANTIC AVENUE	VENTNOR CITY	**NJ**	08406	(609) 822-7122
JEWISH FEDERATION OF NORTH JERSEY 1 PIKE DRIVE	WAYNE	**NJ**	07470	(201) 595-0555
COMMUNITY RELATIONS COMMITTEE OF ALBUQUERQUE 12800 LOMAS, N.E. SUITE F	ALBUQUERQUE	**NM**	87112	(505) 292-1061
CANADIAN JEWISH CONGRESS-ATLANTIC REGION 1515 SOUTH PARK STREET	HALIFAX	**NS**	B3J 2L2	(902) 422-7491
GREATER ALBANY JEWISH FEDERATION 350 WHITE HALL ROAD	ALBANY	**NY**	12208	(518) 459-8000
JEWISH FEDERATION OF BROOME COUNTY 500 CLUB HOUSE ROAD	BINGHAMTON	**NY**	13903	(607) 724-2332
AMERICAN JEWISH CONGRESS-BRONX REGION 2510 VALENTINE AVENUE	BRONX	**NY**	10458	(212) 367-1500

BROOKLYN JEWISH COMMUNITY COUNCIL 16 COURT STREET	BROOKLYN	**NY**	11201	(718) 332-4459
COUNCIL OF JEWISH ORGANIZATIONS OF BORO PARK 4616 13TH AVENUE	BROOKLYN	**NY**	11219	(718) 436-5800
CROWN HEIGHTS JEWISH COMMUNITY COUNCIL 1695 PRESIDENT STREET	BROOKLYN	**NY**	11213	(718) 467-0166
CROWN HEIGHTS JEWISH COMMUNITY COUNCIL 387 KINGSTON AVENUE	BROOKLYN	**NY**	11225	(718) 778-8808
NATIONAL COMMITTEE ORTHODOX JEWISH COMMUNITIES 260 BROADWAY	BROOKLYN	**NY**	11211	(718) 936-1911
UNITED JEWISH ORGANIZATIONS OF WILLIAMSBURG 454 BEDFORD AVENUE	BROOKLYN	**NY**	11211	(718) 387-1888
JEWISH FEDERATION OF GREATER BUFFALO 787 DELAWARE AVENUE	BUFFALO	**NY**	14209	(716) 886-7750
ANTI-DEFAMATION LEAGUE OF B'NAI B'RITH-LONG ISLAND 2310 HEMPSTEAD TURNPIKE	EAST MEADOW	**NY**	11554	(516) 731-3400
ELMIRA JEWISH WELFARE FUND P.O. BOX 3087	ELMIRA	**NY**	14905	(607) 734-8122
AMERICAN JEWISH COMMITTEE-LONG ISLAND AREA 5 BOND STREET	GREAT NECK	**NY**	11201	(516) 466-2980
AMERICAN JEWISH CONGRESS-NORTH & SOUTH SHORE REGION 33 GREAT NECK ROAD	GREAT NECK	**NY**	11021	(516) 466-4650
JEWISH FEDERATION OF GREATER KINGSTON 159 GREEN STREET	KINGSTON	**NY**	12401	(914) 338-8131
AGUDATH ISRAEL WORLD ORGANIZATION 84 WILLIAM STREET	NEW YORK	**NY**	10038	(212) 797-9000
AGUDATH ISRAEL OF AMERICA 84 WILLIAM STREET	NEW YORK	**NY**	10038	(212) 797-9000
AMERICAN COUNCIL FOR JUDAISM 298 FIFTH AVENUE	NEW YORK	**NY**	10001	(212) 947-8878
AMERICAN JEWISH COMMITTEE 165 EAST 56TH STREET	NEW YORK	**NY**	10022	(212) 751-4000
AMERICAN JEWISH COMMITTEE-METROPOLITAN NEW YORK REGION 165 EAST 56TH STREET	NEW YORK	**NY**	10022	(212) 751-4000
AMERICAN JEWISH CONGRESS 15 EAST 84TH STREET	NEW YORK	**NY**	10028	(212) 879-4500
AMERICAN JEWISH CONGRESS-NEW YORK METROPOLITAN COUNCIL 15 EAST 84TH STREET	NEW YORK	**NY**	10028	(212) 879-4500
AMERICAN JEWISH PUBLIC RELATIONS SOCIETY 234 FIFTH AVENUE	NEW YORK	**NY**	10016	(212) 697-5895
ANTI-DEFAMATION LEAGUE OF B'NAI B'RITH 823 UNITED NATIONS PLAZA	NEW YORK	**NY**	10017	(212) 490-2525
COMMISSION ON SOCIAL ACTION OF REFORM JUDAISM 838 FIFTH AVENUE	NEW YORK	**NY**	10021	(212) 249-0100
COMMITTEE TO BRING NAZI WAR CRIMINALS TO JUSTICE IN USA, INC. 135 WEST 106TH STREET	NEW YORK	**NY**	10025	(212) 866-0692
CONFERENCE OF JEWISH COMMUNAL SERVICE, THE 15 E. 26TH STREET	NEW YORK	**NY**	10010	(212) 683-8056
CONFERENCE OF PRESIDENTS OF MAJOR AMERICAN JEWISH ORGANIZATIONS 515 PARK AVENUE	NEW YORK	**NY**	10022	(212) 752-1616
CONSULTATIVE COUNCIL OF JEWISH ORGANIZATIONS 135 WILLIAM STREET	NEW YORK	**NY**	10038	(212) 349-0537
COUNCIL OF JEWISH ORGANIZATIONS IN CIVIL SERVICE, INC. 45 E. 33RD STREET	NEW YORK	**NY**	10016	(212) 689-2015
INTERNATIONAL CENTER OF THE ANTI-DEFAMATION LEAGUE FOUND. 823 UNITED NATIONS PLAZA	NEW YORK	**NY**	10017	(212) 986-8371
INTERNATIONAL CONFERENCE OF JEWISH COMMUNAL SERVICE 15 E. 26TH STREET	NEW YORK	**NY**	10010	(212) 683-8056
INTERNATIONAL COUNCIL OF B'NAI B'RITH 823 UNITED NATIONS PLAZA	NEW YORK	**NY**	10017	(212) 557-0018
JEWISH COMMUNITY COUNCIL SERVICES COMMISSION, INC. 15 PARK ROW	NEW YORK	**NY**	10038	(212) 233-2500
JEWISH COMMUNITY COUNCIL OF WASHINGTON HEIGHTS IN INWOOD 121 BENNETT AVENUE	NEW YORK	**NY**	10033	(212) 568-5450
JEWISH COMMUNITY RELATIONS COUNCIL OF NEW YORK 111 WEST 40TH STREET, SUITE 2600	NEW YORK	**NY**	10018	(212) 221-1535
JEWISH DEFENSE LEAGUE (EXEC. & ADMN. OFFICES) 34 WEST 38TH STREET, 6TH FLOOR	NEW YORK	**NY**	10018	(212) 382-3333
JEWISH LABOR COMMITTEE 25 EAST 21ST STREET	NEW YORK	**NY**	10010	(212) 477-0707
JEWISH LABOR COMMITTEE-NEW YORK (NATIONAL OFFICE) 25 EAST 21ST STREET	NEW YORK	**NY**	10010	(212) 477-0707
JEWISH MOBILIZATION COMMITTEE 3 W. 16TH STREET	NEW YORK	**NY**	10011	(212) 929-1525
JEWISH POVERTY COORDINATING COUNCIL 15 PARK ROW	NEW YORK	**NY**	10038	(212) 267-9500
JEWISH RIGHTS COUNCIL 501 W. 123RD STREET	NEW YORK	**NY**	10027	(212) 362-3353
JOINT COMM. ON SOC. ACTION/COMM. ON JEW. COMMUNITY & PUB. POL 155 FIFTH AVENUE	NEW YORK	**NY**	10010	(212) 533-7800
NATIONAL JEWISH COMMUNITY RELATIONS ADVISORY COUNCIL 443 PARK AVENUE SOUTH	NEW YORK	**NY**	10016	(212) 684-6950
NEW JEWISH AGENDA 64 FULTON STREET, SUITE 1100	NEW YORK	**NY**	10038	(212) 227-5885
SOUTHERN BKLYN COMMUNITY ORG. (SBCO) C/O AGUDATH ISRAEL OF AMERICA, 84 WILLIAM STREET	NEW YORK	**NY**	10038	(212) 797-9000
UNITED JEWISH COUNCIL OF THE EAST SIDE 235 EAST BROADWAY	NEW YORK	**NY**	10002	(212) 233-6037
WORLD CONFERENCE OF JEWISH COMMUNAL SERVICE 15 EAST 26TH STREET	NEW YORK	**NY**	10010	(212) 532-2526
WORLD JEWISH CONGRESS ONE PARK AVENUE, SUITE 418	NEW YORK	**NY**	10016	(212) 679-0600
WORLD JEWISH CONGRESS 15 EAST 84TH STREET	NEW YORK	**NY**	10028	(212) 879-4500
JEWISH COMMUNITY FEDERATION OF ROCHESTER, N.Y., INC. 50 CHESTNUT STREET 1200 CHESTNUT PLAZA	ROCHESTER	**NY**	14604	(716) 325-3393
JEWISH FEDERATION OF GREATER SCHENECTADY 2565 BALLTOWN ROAD	SCHENECTADY	**NY**	12309	(518) 393-1136
SYRACUSE JEWISH FEDERATION 2223 E. GENESSEE STREET P.O. BOX 5004	SYRACUSE	**NY**	13250	(315) 422-4104
ANTI-DEFAMATION LEAGUE OF B'NAI B'RITH-NY STATE REGIONAL 65 SOUTH BROADWAY	TARRYTOWN	**NY**	10591	(914) 332-1166
JEWISH COMMUNITY COUNCIL 2310 ONEIDA STREET	UTICA	**NY**	13501	(315) 733-2343
AMERICAN JEWISH COMMITTEE-NEW JERSEY-NEW YORK REGION 48 MAMARONECK AVENUE	WHITE PLAINS	**NY**	10601	(914) 948-5585
JEWISH COUNCIL OF YONKERS 122 SOUTH BROADWAY	YONKERS	**NY**	10701	(914) 423-5009
AKRON JEWISH COMMUNITY FEDERATION 750 WHITE POND DRIVE	AKRON	**OH**	44320	(216) 867-7850
AMERICAN JEWISH CONGRESS-NORTHERN OHIO REGION 23715 MERCANTILE ROAD	BEACHWOOD	**OH**	44122	(216) 464-5244
JEWISH COMMUNITY FEDERATION 2631 HARVARD AVENUE, N.W.	CANTON	**OH**	44709	(216) 452-6444
AMERICAN JEWISH COMMITTEE-CINCINNATI AREA 105 WEST FOURTH STREET SUITE 818	CINCINNATI	**OH**	45202	(513) 621-4020
JEWISH COMMUNITY RELATIONS COUNCIL 105 WEST FOURTH STREET, SUITE 614	CINCINNATI	**OH**	45202	(513) 241-5620
AMERICAN JEWISH COMMITTEE-OHIO-KENTUCKY AREA 1220 EAST HURON ROAD, SUITE 703	CLEVELAND	**OH**	44115	(216) 781-6035
JEWISH COMMUNITY FEDERATION 1750 EUCLID AVENUE	CLEVELAND	**OH**	44115	(216) 566-9200
JEWISH LABOR COMMITTEE-OHIO 1980 S. GREEN ROAD	CLEVELAND	**OH**	44121	(216) 381-4515
ANTI-DEFAMATION LEAGUE OF B'NAI B'RITH-OHIO-KENTUCKY 1175 COLLEGE AVENUE	COLUMBUS	**OH**	43209	(614) 239-8414
COMMUNITY RELATIONS COMMITTEE OF THE COLUMBUS JEWISH FED. 1175 COLLEGE AVENUE	COLUMBUS	**OH**	42209	(614) 237-7686
COMMUNITY RELATIONS COUNCIL (JESSE PHILIPS BLDG.) 4501 DENLINGER ROAD	DAYTON	**OH**	45426	(513) 854-4150
JEWISH FEDERATION OF GREATER DAYTON 4501 DENLINGER ROAD	DAYTON	**OH**	45426	(513) 854-4150
JEWISH WELFARE FEDERATION OF TOLEDO 6505 SYLVANIA AVENUE	SYLVANIA	**OH**	43560	(419) 885-4461
YOUNGSTOWN AREA JEWISH FEDERATION 505 GYPSY LANE, P.O. BOX 449	YOUNGSTOWN	**OH**	44501	(216) 746-3251
JEWISH COMMUNITY COUNCIL 3022 N.W. EXPRESSWAY, SUITE 116	OKLAHOMA CITY	**OK**	73112	(405) 949-0111
JEWISH FEDERATION OF TULSA 2021 E. 71ST STREET	TULSA	**OK**	74136	(918) 495-1100
CANADIAN JEWISH CONGRESS-ONTARIO REGION 4600 BATHURST STREET	TORONTO	**ON**	M2R 3V2	(416) 635-2883
NATIONAL JOINT COMMUNITY RELATIONS COMMITTEE 150 BEVERLEY STREET	TORONTO	**ON**	M5T 1Y6	(416) 869-3811
AMERICAN JEWISH COMMITTEE-PORTLAND AREA 1220 S.W. MORRISON, SUITE 930	PORTLAND	**OR**	97205	(503) 295-6761
JEWISH FEDERATION OF PORTLAND 4850 S.W. SCHOLLS FERRY ROAD, SUITE 304	PORTLAND	**OR**	97225	(503) 297-8104
JEWISH FEDERATION OF ALLENTOWN 702 N. 22ND STREET	ALLENTOWN	**PA**	18104	(215) 821-5500
JEWISH COMMUNITY COUNCIL 702 G. DANIEL BALDWIN BUILDING, 1001 STATE STREET	ERIE	**PA**	16501	(814) 455-5575
JEWISH FEDERATION OF THE DELAWARE VALLEY 28 N. PENNSYLVANIA AVENUE	MORRISVILLE	**PA**	19067	(215) 736-8022
AMERICAN JEWISH COMMITTEE-MIDDLE ATLANTIC REGION 1616 WALNUT STREET, SUITE 42106	PHILADELPHIA	**PA**	19103	(215) 735-6182
AMERICAN JEWISH CONGRESS-PENNSYLVANIA REGION 255 SOUTH 16TH STREET	PHILADELPHIA	**PA**	19102	(215) 546-4366
ANTI-DEFAMATION LEAGUE OF B'NAI B'RITH-PA.-WEST VA.-DEL. 225 S. 15TH STREET, SUITE 614	PHILADELPHIA	**PA**	19102	(215) 735-4267
JEWISH COMMUNITY RELATIONS COUNCIL OF GREATER PHILADELPHIA 1520 LOCUST STREET, 5TH FLOOR	PHILADELPHIA	**PA**	19102	(215) 545-8430
JEWISH LABOR COMMITTEE-PENNSYLVANIA 1211 CHESTNUT STREET	PHILADELPHIA	**PA**	19107	(215) 568-4770
AMERICAN JEWISH COMMITTEE-WESTERN PENNSYLVANIA AREA 128 NORTH CRAIG STREET SUITE 215	PITTSBURGH	**PA**	15213	(412) 683-7927
JEWISH LABOR COMMITTEE-PENNSYLVANIA 5260 CENTRE AVENUE, SUITE 312	PITTSBURGH	**PA**	15232	(412) 687-6857
UNITED JEWISH FEDERATION OF PITTSBURGH 234 MCKEE PLACE	PITTSBURGH	**PA**	15213	(412) 681-8000
SCRANTON-LACKAWANNA JEWISH FEDERATION, THE 601 JEFFERSON AVENUE	SCRANTON	**PA**	18510	(717) 961-2300
JEWISH FEDERATION OF GREATER WILKES-BARRE 60 S. RIVER STREET	WILKES-BARRE	**PA**	18702	(717) 822-4146
CANADIAN JEWISH CONGRESS 1590 AVENUE DOCTEUR PENFIELD	MONTREAL	**QU**	H3G 1C5	(514) 931-7531
COMBINED JEWISH ORGANIZATIONS OF MONTREAL 4180 DE COURTRAI, SUITE 218	MONTREAL	**QU**	H3S 1C3	(514) 735-6577
JEWISH FEDERATION OF RHODE ISLAND 130 SESSIONS STREET	PROVIDENCE	**RI**	02906	(401) 421-4111
CHARLESTON JEWISH FEDERATION 1645 RAOUL WALLENBERG BLVD., P.O. BOX 31298	CHARLESTON	**SC**	29206	(803) 787-2023
JEWISH COMMUNITY RELATIONS COUNCIL 6560 POPLAR AVENUE	MEMPHIS	**TN**	38183	(901) 767-5161
MEMPHIS JEWISH FEDERATION 6505 POPLAR AVENUE, P.O. BOX 38268	MEMPHIS	**TN**	38138	(901) 767-7100
JEWISH FEDERATION OF NASHVILLE & MIDDLE TENNESSEE 3500 WEST END AVENUE	NASHVILLE	**TN**	37205	(615) 269-0729
JEWISH COMMUNITY COUNCIL OF AUSTIN 5758 BALCONES DRIVE, SUITE 104	AUSTIN	**TX**	78731	(512) 451-6435
AMERICAN JEWISH COMMITTEE-SOUTHWEST REGION 1809 TOWER PETROLEUM BUILDING	DALLAS	**TX**	75201	(214) 387-2943
AMERICAN JEWISH CONGRESS-DALLAS CHAPTER P.O. BOX 12826	DALLAS	**TX**	75225	(214) 368-2731
ANTI-DEFAMATION LEAGUE OF B'NAI B'RITH-DALLAS 12800 HILLCREST ROAD SUITE 219	DALLAS	**TX**	75230	(214) 960-0342
JEWISH FEDERATION OF GREATER DALLAS 7800 NORTHAVEN, SUITE 104	DALLAS	**TX**	75203	(214) 369-3313
JEWISH COMMUNITY RELATIONS COMMITTEE 405 MARDI GRAS DRIVE, P.O. BOX 12097	EL PASO	**TX**	79912	(915) 584-4437
JEWISH FEDERATION OF FORT WORTH & TARRANT COUNTY 6801 DAN DANCIGER ROAD	FORT WORTH	**TX**	76133	(817) 292-3081
AMERICAN JEWISH COMMITTEE-HOUSTON AREA 2600 SOUTHWEST FREEWAY, SUITE 1030	HOUSTON	**TX**	77098	(713) 524-4789
ANTI-DEFAMATION LEAGUE OF B'NAI B'RITH-SOUTHWEST-HOUSTON 4211 SOUTHWEST FREEWAY SUITE 209	HOUSTON	**TX**	77027	(713) 627-3490
JEWISH FEDERATION OF GREATER HOUSTON 5603 SOUTH BRAESWOOD	HOUSTON	**TX**	77096	(713) 729-7000
JEWISH FEDERATION OF SAN ANTONIO 8434 AHERN DRIVE	SAN ANTONIO	**TX**	78216	(512) 341-8234
UNITED JEWISH COMMUNITY 2700 SPRING ROAD, P.O. BOX 6680	NEWPORT NEWS	**VA**	23606	(804) 595-5544
UNITED JEWISH FEDERATION OF TIDEWATER, THE 7300 NEWPORT AVENUE, P.O. BOX 9776	NORFOLK	**VA**	23505	(804) 489-8040
ANTI-DEFAMATION LEAGUE OF B'NAI B'RITH-N. CAROLINA-VIRGINIA 3311 W. BROAD STREET	RICHMOND	**VA**	23230	(804) 355-2884
JEWISH COMMUNITY FEDERATION OF RICHMOND P.O. BOX 8237, 5403 MONUMENT AVENUE	RICHMOND	**VA**	23226	(804) 288-0045

AMERICAN JEWISH COMMITTEE-SEATTLE AREA
729 JOSEPH VANCE BLDG ... SEATTLE **WA** 98101 (206) 622-6315
ANTI-DEFAMATION LEAGUE OF B'NAI B'RITH-PACIFIC NORTHWEST
1809 7TH AVENUE, SUITE 1609 ... SEATTLE **WA** 98101 (206) 624-5750
JEWISH FEDERATION OF GREATER SEATTLE
510 SECURITIES BUILDING, 1904 THIRD AVENUE ... SEATTLE **WA** 98101 (206) 622-8211
MADISON JEWISH COMMUNITY COUNCIL 310 N. MIDVALE BLVD ... MADISON **WI** 53705 (608) 231-3426
AMERICAN JEWISH COMMITTEE-MILWAUKEE AREA
759 NORTH MILWAUKEE STREET ... MILWAUKEE **WI** 53202 (414) 273-6833
ANTI-DEFAMATION LEAGUE OF B'NAI B'RITH-WISC.-UPPER MIDWEST
1360 N. PROSPECT AVENUE ... MILWAUKEE **WI** 53202 (414) 276-7920
MILWAUKEE JEWISH COUNCIL 1360 N. PROSPECT AVENUE ... MILWAUKEE **WI** 53202 (414) 276-7920

COMPUTER SERVICES

DAVKA CORPORATION 845 NORTH MICHIGAN AVENUE, SUITE 843 ... CHICAGO **IL** 60611 (312) 944-4070
ANTHRO-DIGITAL, INC. P.O. BOX 1385 ... PITTSFIELD **MA** 01202 (413) 448-8278
ESF COMPUTER SERVICES, INC. 70-50 AUSTIN STREET ... FOREST HILLS **NY** 11375 (718) 261-9797
BRAMSON ORT 304 PARK AVENUE SOUTH ... NEW YORK **NY** 10010 (212) 677-7420
CLAL TRADING (N.Y.) INC. 440 PARK AVENUE SOUTH ... NEW YORK **NY** 10016 (212) 889-7750
ARLINGTON ASSOCIATES, INC. 195 ARLINGTON AVENUE ... PROVIDENCE **RI** 02906 (401) 273-1341

CONVERSION ORGANIZATIONS

NAT'L JEWISH INFO. SERVICE FOR THE PROPAGATION OF JUDAISM
5174 WEST 8TH STREET ... LOS ANGELES **CA** 90036
RABBI SAMUEL KATZ, RABBINICAL COUNCIL OF CALIFORNIA 525 SOUTH FAIRFAX
AVENUE, C/O CONGREGATION OHEV SHALOM ... LOS ANGELES **CA** 90036 (213) 653-7190
CHICAGO BOARD OF RABBIS 1 SOUTH FRANKLIN ... CHICAGO **IL** 60606 (312) 427-5863
CHICAGO RABBINICAL COUNCIL 3525 WEST PETERSON ... CHICAGO **IL** 60659 (312) 588-1600
JEWISH CONVERSION CENTER 752 STELTON STREET ... TEANECK **NJ** 07666 (201) 837-7552
CONVERSION CLASSES-NEW YORK FEDERATION OF REFORM SYNAGOGUES
838 FIFTH AVENUE ... NEW YORK **NY** 10021 (212) 249-0100
JEWISH NEWCOMER SERVICE 6651 S.W. CAPITAL HIGHWAY ... PORTLAND **OR** 97201 (503) 244-0111

CORRESPONDENCE COURSES

ALTERNATIVES IN RELIGIOUS EDUCATION 3945 ONEIDA STREET ... DENVER **CO** 80237 (303) 363-7779
HEINLE & HEINLE ENTERPRISES 29 LEXINGTON ROAD ... CONCORD **MA** 01742 (617) 369-7525
THE JEWISH CENTER FOR SPECIAL EDUCATION 430 KENT AVENUE ... BROOKLYN **NY** 11211 (718) 782-0064
ACADEMY FOR JEWISH STUDIES WITHOUT WALLS, THE
165 E. 56TH STREET ... NEW YORK **NY** 10022 (212) 751-4000
AMERICAN ASSOCIATION FOR JEWISH EDUCATION
114 FIFTH AVENUE ... NEW YORK **NY** 10011 (212) 675-5656
COMMISSION ON JEWISH AFFAIRS, AMERICAN JEWISH CONGRESS
15 EAST 84TH STREET ... NEW YORK **NY** 10028 (212) 879-4500
WORLD ZIONIST ORGANIZATION, PUBLICATIONS DEPARTMENT
515 PARK AVENUE ... NEW YORK **NY** 10022 (212) 752-0600

COUNSELING

VALLEY BETH SHALOM COUNSELING CENTER
15739 VENTURA BOULEVARD ... ENCINO **CA** 91436 (213) 788-6000
ALCOHOLISM PROGRAM, JEWISH FAMILY SERVICE
6505 WILSHIRE BOULEVARD ... LOS ANGELES **CA** 90048 (213) 852-1234
CHABAD DRUG REHABILITATION AND MENTAL HEALTH PROGRAMS
6333 WILSHIRE BOULEVARD ... LOS ANGELES **CA** 90048 (213) 653-9230
CHABAD DRUG TREATMENT CENTER 1952 S. ROBERTSON BLVD ... LOS ANGELES **CA** 90035 (213) 204-3196
CHAPLAINCY SERVICE, BOARD OF RABBIS OF SOUTHERN CALIFORNIA
6505 WILSHIRE BOULEVARD ... LOS ANGELES **CA** 90048 (213) 852-1234
JULIA SINGER PRE-SCHOOL PSYCHIATRIC CENTER
8730 ALDEN DRIVE ... LOS ANGELES **CA** 90048 (213) 855-5000
ONE PARENT INFORMATION NETWORK 8857 SATURN STREET ... LOS ANGELES **CA** 90035 (213) 556-1687
THE CULT CLINIC, JEWISH FAMILY SERVICE
6505 WILSHIRE BOULEVARD ... LOS ANGELES **CA** 90048 (213) 852-1234
THE WIDOWS CENTER ... LOS ANGELES **CA** 90064 (213) 933-5411
JEWISH CAREER COUNSELING & EMPLOYMENT SERVICE
703 MARKET STREET, ROOM 2007 ... SAN FRANCISCO **CA** 94103 (415) 777-2022
TEMPLE JUDEA COMMUNITY OUTREACH CENTER
5429 LINDLEY AVENUE ... TARZANA **CA** 91356 (213) 780-4994
B'NAI B'RITH CAREER & COUNSELING SERVICES
1640 RHODE ISLAND AVENUE N.W. ... WASHINGTON **DC** 20036 (202) 857-6600
TAMPA JEWISH SOCIAL SERVICE 2808 HORATIO ... TAMPA **FL** 33609 (813) 872-4451
THE ARK 3509 W. LAWRENCE AVENUE ... CHICAGO **IL** 60625 (312) 478-9600
ROFEH 1710 BEACON STREET ... BROOKLINE **MA** 02146 (617) 566-9182
ASSOCIATED PLACEMENT & GUIDANCE SERVICE
5750 PARK HEIGHTS AVENUE ... BALTIMORE **MD** 21215 (301) 466-9200
CENTER FOR COUNSELING REFERRAL, THE 6 WYNKOOP COURT ... BETHESDA **MD** 20034
JEWISH SOCIAL SERVICE AGENCY & JEWISH FOSTER HOME
6123 MONTROSE ROAD ... ROCKVILLE **MD** 20852 (301) 881-3700
CHAPLAINCY SERVICE TO STATE INSTITUTIONS
2640 QUENTIN AVENUE S ... ST. LOUIS PARK **MN** 55426 (612) 922-0322
JEWISH COUNSELING SERVICE 161 MILLBURN AVENUE ... MILLBURN **NJ** 07041 (201) 467-3300
RABBINIC CENTER FOR RESEARCH & COUNSELING
128 E. DUDLEY AVENUE ... WESTFIELD **NJ** 07090 (201) 233-0419
INTERBOROUGH CONSULTATION CENTER 1402 AVENUE N ... BROOKLYN **NY** 11230 (718) 375-1200
OHEL CHILDREN'S HOME & FAMILY SERVICES 4423 16TH AVENUE ... BROOKLYN **NY** 11204 (718) 851-6300
SHALVA COUNSELING CENTER 1402 AVENUE N ... BROOKLYN **NY** 11230 (718) 375-1200
SHALVA COUNSELING CENTER 823 FRANKLIN AVENUE ... BROOKLYN **NY** 11238 (718) 774-4605
KAYAMA P.O. BOX 4007 ... COLLEGE POINT **NY** 11356 (718) 544-0357
JEWISH COMMUNITY SERVICES OF LONG ISLAND
1600 CENTRAL AVENUE ... FAR ROCKAWAY **NY** 11691 (718) 327-1600
SUMMIT INSTITUTE IN ISRAEL, LTD. 71-11 112TH STREET ... FOREST HILLS **NY** 11375 (718) 268-0020
JEWISH COMMUNITY SERVICES OF LONG ISLAND
50 CLINTON STREET ... HEMPSTEAD **NY** 11550 (516) 485-5710
WESTCHESTER JEWISH COMMUNITY SERVICES, INC.
9 W. PROSPECT AVENUE ... MT. VERNON **NY** 10550 (914) 668-8938
B'NAI B'RITH - CAREER & COUNSELING SERVICES
823 UNITED NATIONS PLAZA ... NEW YORK **NY** 10017 (212) 490-0677
COUNSELING CENTER OF N.Y. FEDERATION OF REFORM SYNAGOGUES
838 FIFTH AVENUE ... NEW YORK **NY** 10021 (212) 249-7700
JACS FOUNDATION (JEWISH ALCOHOLICS) 10 EAST 73RD STREET ... NEW YORK **NY** 10021 (212) 737-6261
JEWISH CONCILIATION BOARD OF AMERICA
235 PARK AVENUE SOUTH ... NEW YORK **NY** 10003 (212) 777-9034
JEWISH CONSULTATION SERVICE ... NEW YORK **NY** (212) 752-2406
JEWISH UNMARRIED MOTHERS SERVICE 12 E. 94TH STREET ... NEW YORK **NY** 10028 (212) 876-3050
LOSS & BEREAVEMENT CENTER OF N.Y. 170 EAST 83RD STREET ... NEW YORK **NY** 10028 (212) 879-5655
MID-WAY COUNSELING CENTER 27 E. 20TH STREET ... NEW YORK **NY** 10003 (212) 475-7081
JEWISH COMMUNITY SERVICES OF LONG ISLAND
97-45 QUEENS BLVD ... REGO PARK **NY** 11374 (718) 896-9090
JEWISH COMMUNITY SERVICES OF LONG ISLAND
22 LAWRENCE AVENUE ... SMITHTOWN **NY** 11787 (516) 724-6300
JEWISH COMMUNITY SERVICES OF LONG ISLAND
175 JERICHO TURNPIKE ... SYOSSET **NY** 11791 (516) 364-8040

CULTURAL ORGANIZATIONS

BRANDEIS-BARDIN INSTITUTE, THE 1101 PEPPERTREE LANE ... BRANDEIS **CA** 93064 (213) 348-7201
PATRONS ART SOCIETY 4455 LOS FELIZ BLVD., SUITE 804 ... LOS ANGELES **CA** 90027 (213) 664-7703
SEPHARDIC HEBREW CENTER 4911 W. 59TH STREET ... LOS ANGELES **CA** 90056 (213) 295-5541
B'NAI B'RITH INTERNATIONAL 1640 RHODE ISLAND AVENUE N.W. ... WASHINGTON **DC** 20036 (202) 857-6600
JEWISH CULTURAL ORGANIZATION 429 LENOX AVENUE ... MIAMI BEACH **FL** 33139 (305) 673-9079
AMERICA-ISRAEL CULTURAL FOUNDATION 79 WEST MONROE ... CHICAGO **IL** 60611 (312) 726-4672
JEWISH CULTURAL CLUBS OF CHICAGO 1740 WEST GREENLEAF ... CHICAGO **IL** 60626 (312) 338-9283
VLADECK EDUCATIONAL CENTER WORKMEN'S CIRCLE
6500 NORTH CALIFORNIA ... CHICAGO **IL** 60645 (312) 274-5400
NATIONAL CENTER FOR UNDERSTANDING JUDAISM
BOX 651, WOODMOOR ... SILVER SPRING **MD** 20901
ARTHUR SIDNEY MENDEL EDUCATIONAL CENTER
BROADWAY & DELAWARE ... BENTON HARBOR **MI** 49022 (616) 925-8021
JEWISH EDUCATIONAL CENTER 1602 E. 2ND STREET ... DULUTH **MN** 55812 (218) 724-8857
KOLLEL ZECHER NAFTALI, THE 1550 SUMMIT AVENUE ... HILLSIDE **NJ** 07205 (201) 923-6191
JEWISH ACADEMY OF ARTS & SCIENCES, INC.
123 GREGORY AVENUE ... WEST ORANGE **NJ** 07052 (201) 731-1137
SHOLEM ALEICHEM FOLK INSTITUTE, INC. 3301 BAINBRIDGE AVENUE ... BRONX **NY** 10467 (212) 881-6555
AKIVA JEWISH CULTURE CLUBS OF THE N.Y.C. PUBLIC HIGH SCHOOLS
1577 CONEY ISLAND AVENUE ... BROOKLYN **NY** 11230 (718) 258-3585
ASSOCIATION FOR THE SOCIOLOGICAL STUDY OF JEWRY
DEPARTMENT OF SOCIOLOGY - BROOKLYN COLLEGE ... BROOKLYN **NY** 11210 (718) 780-5315
HEBREW EDUCATIONAL SOCIETY 9502 SEAVIEW AVENUE ... BROOKLYN **NY** 11236 (718) 241-3000
CENTER FOR RETURN 85-35 117TH STREET ... KEW GARDENS **NY** 11418 (718) 849-6787
AMERICAN BIBLICAL ENCYCLOPEDIA SOCIETY 24 W. MAPLE AVENUE ... MONSEY **NY** 10952 (914) 352-4609
JEWISH COMMUNITY CENTER OF MONTICELLO
PARK AVENUE, BOX 208 ... MONTICELLO **NY** 12701 (914) 794-4560
ABRAHAM GOODMAN HOUSE 129 WEST 67TH STREET ... NEW YORK **NY** 10023 (212) 362-8060
AMERICAN ACADEMY FOR JEWISH RESEARCH 3080 BROADWAY ... NEW YORK **NY** 10027 (212) 678-8864
AMERICAN HISTADRUT CULTURAL EXCHANGE INSTITUTE
33 E. 67TH STREET ... NEW YORK **NY** 10021 (212) 628-1000
AMERICAN JEWISH INSTITUTE 250 W. 57TH STREET ... NEW YORK **NY** 10019 (212) 582-5318
ASSOC. OF JEWISH LIBRARIES, C/O NAT'L FOUND. JEWISH CULTURE
122 E. 42ND STREET, ROOM 1512 ... NEW YORK **NY** 10168 (212) 490-2280
CENTRAL YIDDISH CULTURE ORGANIZATION 25 EAST 78TH STREET ... NEW YORK **NY** 10021 (212) 535-4320
CLAL—THE NATIONAL JEWISH CENTER FOR LEARNING AND LEADERSHIP
421 SEVENTH AVENUE ... NEW YORK **NY** 10001 (212) 714-9500

CLAL's Am Echad (One People) Programs: Building Bridges

CLAL has undertaken a major new challenge—dealing with the dissolving bonds of Jewish unity. To strengthen the forces committed to Clal Yisrael, CLAL has created Am Echad (One People), a new programming division devoted to promoting intermovement understanding and interaction.

The common objective of all of CLAL's Am Echad (One People) programs is to reduce polarization and increase cooperation between movements by creating the occasions and the voices which will spread the message of Clal Yisrael.

CLAL's Am Echad (One People) activities will include:

1) **Chevra**: A community based program, currently in 8 cities, designed to bring together local rabbis and scholars from the four movements for learning and regular discussions of religious, theological, and halakhic issues.

2) **Lay and Rabbinic Communal Programming**: Am Echad seeks to advance dialogue in all forms at the local and national levels.

3) **Symposia for Unity**: In January 1986, CLAL with the cosponsorship of the Jewish Federation, Washington Jewish Week, and the JCRC, held the first national "Symposium for Unity" in Washington, D.C. Four distinguished rabbis, all past presidents of their respective rabbinical associations, appeared together on a panel and publicly discussed the positions of their movements and their relationship with each other. A second symposium has been scheduled for November in Chicago.

4) **Advanced Theological/Halakhic Dialogue**: A theological thinktank, designed to allow scholars time and resources to explore unifying approaches to divisive issues as well as potential cooperation in areas like outreach, liturgy, ritual, and increasing lay observance.

5) **Modern Orthodox Forum**: It is the centrist position which offers the best hope for creating intermovement respect. By identifying today's young Orthodox scholars, engaging them in study, discussion and communal experiences, CLAL hopes to quicken the pulse of Jewish unity.

6) **International Activities**: The Jewish community is worldwide and interrelated. Recognizing this reality, CLAL is in touch with groups in Israel, England and Holland.

Ziegelmans Pledge $1 Million for Keren Am Echad

CLAL Associate Chairman, Aaron Ziegelman and his wife Marjorie, both powerful advocates of Jewish unity, have established a challenge grant of $1,000,000 to fund CLAL's efforts toward promoting the vision and reality of a unified Jewish people.

This second grant from the Ziegelman family comes just six months after their first grant to CLAL, a $500,000 matching fund gift used to initiate a fund to endow CLAL's ongoing educational programs.

The new $1,000,000 gift will be put into a special fund called Keren Am Echad (One People Fund). Herschel Blumberg, Chairman of CLAL, said "we plan to match this gift over the next fifteen months and go on to create an endowment worthy of the challenge of Jewish unity."

Aaron Ziegelman explained the need for this additional gift. "This endowment will allow us to take the long term approach toward solving a problem of historic proportion. It will allow CLAL staff more time to focus on the structure and programs they are building rather than on the scaffolds that are necessary to build it."

Aaron Ziegelman, in addition to being CLAL's Associate Chairman, is General Chairman of the Reconstructionist Rabbinical College and founder of the West End Synagogue in New York.

Critical Issues Conference: A First Step Toward Jewish Togetherness

Rabbi Gerson Cohen

Rabbi Norman Lamm

Rabbi Alexander Schindler

Ira Silverman

Charles Silberman

More than 250 people gathered at CLAL's first Critical Issues Conference to focus on the disturbing question, "Will There Be One Jewish People by the Year 2000?"

The conference demonstrated the commitment of Jewish leaders, lay and rabbinic, from each movement, to spend two days dealing head-on with issues of profound religious significance.

Through informal discussions, problem solving workshops, and addresses by leading Jewish thinkers—including Rabbi Gerson Cohen (then Chancellor of the Conservative movement's Jewish Theological Seminary), Rabbi Norman Lamm (President of the Orthodox movement's Yeshiva University), Rabbi Alexander Schindler (President of Reform Jewry's Union of American Hebrew Congregations), Ira Silverman (then President of the Reconstructionist Rabbinical College), writers Elie Wiesel and Charles Silberman, and Rabbi Irving Greenberg (President of CLAL)—conference participants witnessed the power and promise of dialogue as a means of closing the gap between the movements and establishing a foundation for cooperation and mutual respect.

In their call to renew Jewish unity, participants urged:

1. Jews must recognize that intermovement dialogue is at least as vital and fundamental as the dialogue between Jews and Christians.
2. Jews must make a conscious effort to establish friendships, relationships, and alliances, across all lines.
3. Intermovement criticism is not nearly as effective as self-criticism and assessment.
4. Each group should strive to avoid making generalizations about other groups and learn to recognize the differences and various viewpoints within each movement.
5. The test of a true Clal Yisrael orientation is a willingness to sacrifice to at least the same degree that one expects from others.

Another important accomplishment of the Critical Issues Conference was the offering of policy suggestions by the four movement leaders in effort to soften the disputes:

Rabbi Gerson Cohen called for a longstanding, joint committee to study problems, data and possible solutions; and for the establishment of a joint, permanent commission to collect information on the Jewish condition.

Rabbi Norman Lamm asked for the establishment of a national Bet Din (Rabbinic Court) to deal with Jewish divorce issues.

Rabbi Alexander Schindler called for the establishment of an informal forum to explore issues and air differences; joint study by seminary faculties; and the assessment of textbooks to ensure that presentations of other movements are not prejudicial or stereotypical.

Ira Silverman suggested the establishment of a joint committee to set standards for marriage and divorce.

CLAL's Am Echad (One People) programs, designed to bring the Jewish people together, do not have an easy task. However, CLAL's Critical Issues Conference has already had far-reaching effects and an historical impact toward reaching the ultimate goal of Clal Yisrael.

Rabbi Irving Greenberg

Elie Wiesel

CLAL: The National Jewish Center for Learning and Leadership

WHO WE ARE

CLAL is a national Jewish organization whose goal is to promote Jewish learning and dialogue, especially among lay leaders, in the spirit of Clal Yisrael—The Unity and Totality of the Jewish People.

CLAL (formerly the National Jewish Resource Center) was founded in 1973 by Rabbi Irving (Yitz) Greenberg, Elie Wiesel and Rabbi Steven Shaw.

WHAT WE DO

CLAL offers special programming to Jewish communities and organizations throughout North America in the form of retreats, classes, seminars, dialogues, study groups, conferences, and publications.

Shamor (guard/preserve), the educational division of CLAL, identifies, educates and motivates individuals who assume the obligations and responsibilities of leadership in the Jewish community. **Zachor** (Remember!), the first Holocaust Resource Center in the United States, was founded by CLAL to commemorate and explore the fundamental challenge of the Holocaust and the emergence of Israel as turning points. **Am Echad** (One People), the newest CLAL division, is designed to promote and sponsor intermovement programming and dialogue, to protect and strengthen the spirit of Clal Yisrael.

Organization / Address	City	State	Zip	Phone
CONFERENCE ON JEWISH SOCIAL STUDIES 250 W. 57TH STREET, ROOM 904	NEW YORK	NY	10019	(212) 247-4718
CONFERENCE ON JEWISH SOCIAL STUDIES, INC. 2112 BROADWAY	NEW YORK	NY	10023	(212) 724-5336
CONGRESS FOR JEWISH CULTURE 25 E. 21ST STREET	NEW YORK	NY	10010	(212) 505-8040
DEPARTMENT OF EDUCATION & CULTURE-WORLD ZIONIST ORGANIZATION 515 PARK AVENUE	NEW YORK	NY	10022	(212) 752-0600
EDUCATIONAL ALLIANCE 197 EAST BROADWAY	NEW YORK	NY	10002	(212) 475-6200
ELIAS A. COHEN INSTITUTE 251 W. 100 STREET	NEW YORK	NY	10025	
HEBREW ARTS SCHOOL FOR MUSIC & DANCE 129 WEST 67TH STREET	NEW YORK	NY	10023	(212) 362-8060
HEBREW CULTURE FOUNDATION 1776 BROADWAY	NEW YORK	NY	10019	(212) 247-0741
HEBREW CULTURE FOUNDATION 515 PARK AVENUE	NEW YORK	NY	10022	(212) 752-0600
HEBREW CULTURE SERV. COMM. FOR AM. HIGH SCHOOLS & COLLEGES 1776 BROADWAY	NEW YORK	NY	10019	(212) 247-0741
HEBREW LANGUAGE & CULTURE ASSOCIATION 1841 BROADWAY	NEW YORK	NY	10023	(212) 581-5151
HINENI 155 E 38TH STREET	NEW YORK	NY	10016	(212) 557-1190
HISTADRUT IVRITH OF AMERICA 1841 BROADWAY	NEW YORK	NY	10023	(212) 581-5151
INSTITUTE FOR JEWISH EXPERIENCE, THE 157 W. 57TH STREET	NEW YORK	NY	10019	(212) 265-0370
INSTITUTE OF ADULT JEWISH STUDIES 270 W. 89TH STREET	NEW YORK	NY	10024	(212) 787-7600
INSTITUTE OF JEWISH HUMANITIES 47 BEEKMAN STREET	NEW YORK	NY	10038	(212) 227-7800
ISRAEL-IBEROAMERICAN CULTURAL INSTITUTE 515 PARK AVENUE	NEW YORK	NY	10022	(212) 752-0600
JEWISH ACADEMY OF ARTS & SCIENCES 136 WEST 39TH STREET	NEW YORK	NY	10016	(212) 725-1211
JEWISH BOOK COUNCIL OF JWB 15 E. 26TH STREET	NEW YORK	NY	10010	(212) 532-4949
JEWISH CULTURAL CLUBS & SOCIETIES 1133 BROADWAY	NEW YORK	NY	10010	(212) 675-8854
JEWISH HISTORICAL SOCIETY OF NEW YORK 8 W. 70TH STREET	NEW YORK	NY	10023	(212) 873-0300
JEWISH MINORITIES RESEARCH 16 E. 85TH STREET	NEW YORK	NY	10028	
JEWISH MUSIC COUNCIL 15 E. 26TH STREET	NEW YORK	NY	10010	(212) 532-4949
JEWISH PROGRAM SERVICE COMMITTEE 1133 BROADWAY	NEW YORK	NY	10010	(212) 675-8854
JEWISH STORYTELLING CENTER - PENINAH SCHRAMM 92ND STREET Y LIBRARY - 92ND STREET YM-YWHA, 1392 LEXINGTON AVENUE	NEW YORK	NY	10128	(212) 427-6000
JEWISH WELFARE BOARD 15 E. 26TH STREET	NEW YORK	NY	10011	(212) 532-4949
JEWISH WELFARE BOARD-ARMED FORCES & VETERANS SERVICE 15 E. 26TH STREET	NEW YORK	NY	10010	(212) 532-4949
JEWISH WELFARE BOARD-COMMISSION ON JEWISH CHAPLAINCY 15 E. 26TH STREET	NEW YORK	NY	10010	(212) 532-4949
JEWISH WELFARE BOARD-JEWISH BOOK COUNCIL 15 E. 26TH STREET	NEW YORK	NY	10010	(212) 532-4949
JEWISH WELFARE BOARD-JEWISH LECTURE BUREAU 15 E. 26TH STREET	NEW YORK	NY	10010	(212) 532-4949
JEWISH WELFARE BOARD-JEWISH MEDIA SERVICE 15 E. 26TH STREET	NEW YORK	NY	10010	(212) 532-4949
JEWISH WELFARE BOARD-JEWISH MUSIC COUNCIL 15 E. 26TH STREET	NEW YORK	NY	10010	(212) 532-4949
JEWISH WELFARE BOARD-NATIONAL OFFICE 15 E. 26TH STREET	NEW YORK	NY	10010	(212) 532-4949
JEWISH WELFARE BOARD-WOMEN'S ORGANIZATIONS SERVICE 15 E. 26TH STREET	NEW YORK	NY	10010	(212) 532-4949
LEO BAECK INSTITUTE, INC. 129 E. 73RD STREET	NEW YORK	NY	10021	(212) 744-6400
MAX WEINREICH CENTER FOR ADVANCED STUDIES 1048 FIFTH AVENUE	NEW YORK	NY	10028	(212) 535-6700
MEMORIAL FOUNDATION FOR JEWISH CULTURE 15 E. 26TH STREET	NEW YORK	NY	10010	(212) 679-4074
MESORAH INSTITUTE 111 EIGHTH AVENUE	NEW YORK	NY	10011	(212) 691-0894
NATIONAL FOUNDATION FOR JEWISH CULTURE 408 CHANIN BUILDING, 122 EAST 42ND STREET	NEW YORK	NY	10017	(212) 490-2280
NATIONAL HEBREW CULTURE COUNCIL 14 E. 4TH STREET	NEW YORK	NY	10012	(212) 674-8412
NATIONAL JEWISH MUSIC COUNCIL 15 E. 26TH STREET	NEW YORK	NY	10010	(212) 532-4949
NATIONAL JEWISH WELFARE BOARD 15 EAST 26TH STREET	NEW YORK	NY	10010	(212) 532-4949
NEW YORK UNIVERSITY JEWISH CULTURAL FOUNDATION LOEB STUDENT CENTER ROOM 715, 566 LA GUARDIA PLACE	NEW YORK	NY	10012	(212) 598-3584
RESEARCH CENTER OF KABBALAH 200 PARK AVENUE, SUITE 303 EAST	NEW YORK	NY	10017	(212) 986-2515
RESEARCH FOUNDATION FOR JEWISH IMMIGRATION 570 SEVENTH AVENUE	NEW YORK	NY	10018	(212) 921-3871
RESEARCH INSTITUTE OF RELIGIOUS JEWRY 471 WEST END AVENUE	NEW YORK	NY	10024	
SAM & ESTHER MINSKOFF CULTURAL CENTER 164 E. 68TH STREET	NEW YORK	NY	10021	(212) 737-1196
SINAI HERITAGE CENTER 350 5TH AVENUE SUITE 6809	NEW YORK	NY	10118	(212) 967-8060
USDAN CENTER FOR CREATIVE & PERFORMING ARTS 315 WEST 57TH STREET	NEW YORK	NY	10019	(212) 757-5015
WORKMEN'S CIRCLE 175 EAST BROADWAY	NEW YORK	NY	10002	(212) 674-3400
WORKMEN'S CIRCLE COMMUNITY CENTER 45 EAST 33RD STREET	NEW YORK	NY	10016	(212) 889-6800
YIVO INSTITUTE FOR JEWISH RESEARCH 1048 FIFTH AVENUE	NEW YORK	NY	10028	(212) 535-6700
YIDDISHER KULTUR FARBAND - YKUF 1123 BROADWAY	NEW YORK	NY	10019	(212) 692-0708
JEWISH PEACE FELLOWSHIP BOX 271	NYACK	NY	10960	(914) 358-4601
CANADA-ISRAEL CULTURAL FOUNDATION 980 YONGE STREET, SUITE 402	TORONTO	ON	M4W 2J5	(416) 921-2103
CANADIAN FOUNDATION FOR JEWISH CULTURE 4600 BATHURST STREET	TORONTO	ON	M2R 3V2	(416) 635-2883
CENTER FOR JEWISH COMMUNITY STUDIES 1017 GLADFELTER HALL, TEMPLE UNIVERSITY	PHILADELPHIA	PA	19122	(215) 787-1459
SOCIETY FOR THE SOCIOLOGICAL STUDY OF JEWRY, THE 3718 LOCUST WALK	PHILADELPHIA	PA	19104	

DAIRY PRODUCTS

Business / Address	City	State	Zip	Phone
MOSER FARMS DAIRY 58 WEST ROAD	ROCKVILLE	CT	06066	(203) 872-8346
BLINTZES 'N THINGS 16460 NORTHEAST 16TH AVENUE	NORTH MIAMI BEACH	FL	33162	(305) 944-5222
SHELAT KOSHER FOODS 711 WEST GRAND AVENUE	CHICAGO	IL	60610	(312) 243-3473
RASKAS DAIRY 25 NORTH BRENTWOOD	ST. LOUIS	MO	63105	(800) 325-0071
CHEESE'N THINGS 1117 AVENUE J	BROOKLYN	NY	11230	(718) 377-4911
CHEESE WORLD 1734 CONEY ISLAND AVENUE	BROOKLYN	NY	11230	(718) 339-1755
GOLD STAR ICE CREAM COMPANY, INC. 921 EAST NEW YORK AVENUE	BROOKLYN	NY	11203	(718) 756-1500
GOLDEN FLOW DAIRY FARMS 166 BERRY STREET	BROOKLYN	NY	11211	(718) 963-2000
J & J DAIRY PRODUCTS, INC 72 STEUBEN STREET	BROOKLYN	NY	11205	(718) 636-1888
JASON DAIRY PRODUCTS CO., INC. 9204 DITMAS AVENUE	BROOKLYN	NY	11236	(718) 498-1881
LA GVINA CHEESE CORP. 379 KINGSTON AVENUE	BROOKLYN	NY	11213	(718) 604-0200
MEHADRIN DAIRY 30 MORGAN AVENUE	BROOKLYN	NY	11237	(718) 456-9494
METRO KOSHER ICES 147 METROPOLITAN AVENUE	BROOKLYN	NY	11212	(718) 388-1323
MILLER'S CHEESE CORP. 196 28TH STREET	BROOKLYN	NY	11232	(718) 965-1840
MILLER'S FAMOUS CHEESE 5214 13TH AVENUE	BROOKLYN	NY	11219	(718) 633-1600
TAAM-TOV FOODS, INC. 344 AVENUE Y	BROOKLYN	NY	11223	(718) 376-5400
WORLD CHEESE CO., INC. 178 28TH STREET	BROOKLYN	NY	11232	(718) 965-1700
BISON FOODS COMPANY 196 SCOTT STREET	BUFFALO	NY	14204	(716) 854-8400
KIRYAS JOEL KOSHER P.O. BOX 728	MONROE	NY	10950	(914) 783-4414
LEIBEL'S KOSHER SPECIALTIES 39 ESSEX STREET	NEW YORK	NY	10002	(212) 254-0335
MILLER'S CHEESE 643 AMSTERDAM AVENUE	NEW YORK	NY	10025	(212) 496-8143
MILLER'S CHEESE 2192 BROADWAY	NEW YORK	NY	10024	(212) 496-8855
MILLER'S CHEESE MAIN STREET	SOUTH FALLSBURG	NY	12779	(914) 434-8081
BALLAS EGG PRODUCTS CORPORATION 40 NORTH 2ND STREET	ZANESVILLE	OH	43701	(614) 453-0386
ZAUSNER FOODS CORP. 254 S. CUSTARD AVENUE	NEW HOLLAND	PA	17557	(717) 354-4411

DANCE

Name / Address	City	State	Zip	Phone
SHLOMO BACHAR 3638 GREEN VISTA DRIVE	ENCINO	CA	91436	(213) 907-0147
SHOMREL TARBUT DANCERS C/O SHALOM CONCERT BUREAU PO BOX 35092	LOS ANGELES	CA	90036	(213) 931-6125
ANN BARZEL 3950 LAKE SHORE DRIVE	CHICAGO	IL	60613	(312) 935-7458
DR MAYER GRUBER 618 S. MICHIGAN AVENUE	CHICAGO	IL	60605	(312) 922-9012
SHLOMO BARCHECHAT 4522 NORTH ASHLAND	CHICAGO	IL	60640	(312) 769-4529
PHIL MOSS 2341 MEADOW LANE SOUTH	WILMETTE	IL	60091	(312) 251-2676
JEFFREY MARC ROCKLAND 106 FRANCIS STREET	BROOKLINE	MA	02146	(617) 735-9050
MIRIAM ROSENBLUM 73 COOLIDGE STREET	BROOKLINE	MA	02146	(617) 739-1826
KEREN SHEMESH ISRAELI DANCE GROUP C/O MIT HILLEL 312 MEMORIAL DRIVE	CAMBRIDGE	MA	02139	(617) 253-2982
GERRY KAPLAN 73 MORAN AVENUE	PRINCETON	NJ	98540	(609) 924-6370
ADINA KAUFMAN 3755 HENRY HUDSON PARKWAY	BRONX	NY	10463	
FELIX FIBICH 50 WEST 97TH STREET	NEW YORK	NY	10025	(212) 865-3935
ISRAEL FOLK DANCE INST.-AMERICAN ZIONIST YOUTH FOUNDATION 515 PARK AVENUE	NEW YORK	NY	10022	(212) 751-6070
ISRAEL FOLK DANCE INSTITUTE 515 PARK AVENUE	NEW YORK	NY	10022	(212) 888-1770
MOSHE ESKAYO 99 HILLSIDE AVENUE	NEW YORK	NY	10040	(212) 942-0274
NATIONAL JEWISH WELFARE BOARD 15 EAST 26TH STREET	NEW YORK	NY	10010	(212) 532-4949
RAKDANEEM, ROBERTA KAPLAN 100 EAST END AVENUE, #7E	NEW YORK	NY	10028	(212) 734-5062

WORLDTONE MUSIC, INC., RECORD LOFT INTERNATIONAL
230 SEVENTH AVENUE .... NEW YORK **NY** 10011 (212) 691-1934

ADINA KAUFMAN 64 ELDERWOOD DRIVE .... TORONTO **ON** M5P 1X4 (416) 549-0529

RAKDANEEM, ROBERTA KAPLAN 552 NORTH NEVILLE STREET .... PITTSBURGH **PA** 15213

JEFFREY MARC ROCKLAND
PO BOX 488, VIRGINIA INTERMONT COLLEGE .... BRISTOL **VA** 24201

DAY CARE CENTERS & NURSERIES

TEMPLE BETH ISRAEL NURSERY & DAY SCHOOL
3310 NORTH 10TH AVENUE .... PHOENIX **AZ** 85103 (602) 264-4429

JEWISH COMMUNITY CENTER DAY CARE PRE-SCHOOL
38-22 EAST RIVER ROAD .... TUCSON **AZ** 85718

RICHMOND PRE-SCHOOL-CONSERVATIVE 9711 GEAL ROAD .... RICHMOND **BC** V7E 1R4 (604) 271-6262

RICHMOND PRE-SCHOOL-ORTHODOX 9711 GEAL ROAD .... RICHMOND **BC** V7E 1R4 (604) 274-0090

JEWISH COMMUNITY CENTRE NURSERY 950 WEST 41ST AVENUE .... VANCOUVER **BC** V5Z 2N7 (604) 266-9111

LUBAVITCH CENTRE 5750 OAK STREET .... VANCOUVER **BC** V6M 2V7 (604) 266-1313

TEMPLE BETH EMET PRESCHOOL 1770 WEST CERRITOS STREET .... ANAHEIM **CA** 92804 (714) 772-2770

BETH EL NURSERY SCHOOL 2301 VINE STREET .... BERKELEY **CA** 94708 (415) 848-3988

TEMPLE BETH TIKVAH OF NORTH ORANGE COUNTY TEMPLE SCHOOL
1600 NORTH ACACIA .... FULLERTON **CA** 92634 (714) 871-9555

GAN BRACHA 927 NORTH FAIRFAX .... LOS ANGELES **CA** 90046 (213) 656-0213

VISTA DEL MAR CHILD CARE SERVICE 3200 MOTOR AVENUE .... LOS ANGELES **CA** 90034 (213) 836-1223

BRANDEIS HILLEL NURSERY 655 BROTHERHOOD WAY .... SAN FRANCISCO **CA** 94132 (415) 344-9841

HEBREW ACADEMY OF SAN FRANCISCO NURSERY
763 25TH AVENUE .... SAN FRANCISCO **CA** 94121 (415) 752-9583

JEWISH COMMUNITY CENTER NURSERY
655 BROTHERHOOD WAY .... SAN FRANCISCO **CA** 94132 (415) 334-7474

JEWISH COMMUNITY CENTER NURSERY
3200 CALIFORNIA STREET .... SAN FRANCISCO **CA** 94118 (415) 346-6040

TEMPLE BETH SHALOM COMMUNITY NURSERY SCHOOL
13031 TUSTIN .... SANTA ANA **CA** 92705 (714) 633-1984

EZRA TORAH INSTITUTE 1525 CLEARVIEW ROAD .... SANTA BARBARA **CA** 93101 (805) 968-0515

HEBREW ACADEMY OF GREATER HARTFORD 53 GABB ROAD .... BLOOMFIELD **CT** 06002 (203) 243-8333

HILLEL ACADEMY 4200 PARK ROAD .... BRIDGEPORT **CT** 06601 (203) 374-6147

NORWALK JEWISH CENTER SHORE HAVEN ROAD .... NORWALK **CT** 06851 (203) 838-7504

EMANUEL SYNAGOGUE NURSERY SCHOOL
160 MEHEGAN DRIVE .... WEST HARTFORD **CT** 06117 (203) 233-2774

TEMPLE ISRAEL NURSERY SCHOOL 14 COLEYTOWN ROAD .... WESTPORT **CT** 06880 (203) 227-1293

BETH SHOLEM NURSERY 13TH AND EASTERN AVENUE N.W. .... WASHINGTON **DC** 20012 (202) 723-9202

GAN YELADIM PRE-SCHOOL 13TH & EASTERN AVENUES, NW .... WASHINGTON **DC** 20012 (202) 723-3466

JEWISH COMMUNITY CENTER 101 GARDEN OF EDEN ROAD .... WILMINGTON **DE** 19802 (302) 478-5660

TEMPLE BETH SHALOM KINDERGARTEN & NURSERY SCHOOL
4601 ARTHUR .... HOLLYWOOD **FL** 33020 (305) 966-2200

TEMPLE SINAI JEWISH COMMUNITY CENTER
1201 JOHNSON STREET .... HOLLYWOOD **FL** 33020 (305) 920-1577

ETZ CHAIM EARLY EDUCATION CENTER
5846 UNIVERSITY BOULEVARD WEST .... JACKSONVILLE **FL** 32216 (904) 733-0720

JACKSONVILLE JEWISH CENTER 3662 CROWN POINT ROAD .... JACKSONVILLE **FL** 32217 (904) 268-6736

THE JEWISH COMMUNITY PRE-SCHOOL/GAN YELADIM, INC.
4131 SUNBEAM ROAD .... JACKSONVILLE **FL** 32217 (904) 737-0564

TEMPLE ISRAEL OF MIRAMAR 6920 S.W. 35TH STREET .... MIRAMAR **FL** 33023 (305) 961-1700

AKIBA-SOUTHSIDE SCHOOL 5200 HYDE PARK BOULEVARD .... CHICAGO **IL** 60615 (312) 493-8880

HILLEL TORAH NORTH SUBURBAN DAY SCHOOL
3003 WEST TOUHY AVENUE .... CHICAGO **IL** 60645 (312) 262-2010

ROGERS PARK JEWISH COMMUNITY CENTER 7101 NORTH GREENVIEW .. CHICAGO **IL** 60626 (312) 274-0920

TRI-CON CHILD CARE CENTER 425 LAUREL AVENUE .... HIGHLAND PARK **IL** 60635 (312) 433-1450

MAYER KAPLAN JEWISH COMMUNITY CENTER 5050 CHURCH STREET .... SKOKIE **IL** 60077 (312) 675-2200

SOUTH BEND HEBREW DAY SCHOOL 206 WEST 8TH STREET .... MISHAWAKAU **IN** 46544 (219) 255-3351

ADATH JESHURUN PRESCHOOL NURSERY
2401 WOODBOURNE AVENUE .... LOUISVILLE **KY** 40205 (502) 458-5359

SOUTH SHORE HEBREW ACADEMY 144 BELMONT AVENUE .... BROCKTON **MA** 02401 (617) 583-0717

YAL-DAY-NEW 62 GREEN STREET .... BROOKLINE **MA** 02146 (617) 232-6019

ASSOCIATED JEWISH COMMUNITY CENTERS (PRESCHOOL)
1 BLUE HILL AVENUE .... CANTON **MA** 02021 (617) 828-3507

TEMPLE BETH AM KINDERGARTEN & NURSERY
300 PLEASANT STREET .... FRAMINGHAM **MA** 01701 (617) 872-3622

TEMPLE BETH SHALOM NURSERY SCHOOL PAMELA ROAD .... SAXONVILLE **MA** 01701 (617) 877-2540

BAIS YAAKOV SCHOOL FOR GIRLS SEVEN MILE LANE .... BALTIMORE **MD** 21209 (301) 363-3300

BETH TFILOH CONGREGATION 3300 OLD COURT ROAD .... BALTIMORE **MD** 21208 (301) 486-1900

GAN YELADIM 6300 PARK HEIGHTS AVENUE .... BALTIMORE **MD** 21215 (301) 764-7640

JEWISH COMMUNITY CENTER 5750 PARK HEIGHTS AVENUE .... BALTIMORE **MD** 21215 (301) 542-4900

SHAAREI ZION 6602 PARK HEIGHTS AVENUE .... BALTIMORE **MD** 21215 (301) 764-6812

BET YELADEM P.O. BOX 2189 .... COLUMBIA **MD** 21045 (301) 997-7378

BAIS YAAKOV SCHOOL FOR GIRLS 11111 PARK HEIGHTS AVENUE ... OWINGS MILLS **MD** 21117 (301) 363-3300

JEWISH COMMUNITY CENTER-OWINGS MILLS
3506 GWYNNBROOK AVENUE .... OWINGS MILLS **MD** 21117 (301) 356-5200

LIBERTY JEWISH CENTER 8615 CHURCH LANE .... RANDALLSTOWN **MD** 21133 (301) 922-1333

SOUTHEAST HEBREW CONGREGATION NURSERY SCHOOL
C/O TEITELBAUM, 11556 LOCKWOOD DRIVE .... SILVER SPRING **MD** 20904 (301) 593-2120

UNITED HEBREW SCHOOLS NURSERY SCHOOL
21550 WEST 12 MILE ROAD .... SOUTHFIELD **MI** 48076 (313) 356-7378

JEWISH COMMUNITY CENTER ASSOC. DAY CARE CENTER
7400 OLIVE STREET ROAD .... ST. LOUIS **MO** 63132 (314) 432-5700

GOLDBERG CHILD CARE CENTER 410 CENTER AVENUE .... WESTWOOD **NJ** 07675 (201) 664-4013

KINNERET DAY SCHOOL 2510 VALENTINE AVENUE .... BRONX **NY** 10453 (212) 548-0900

YESHIVA KINDERGARTEN & NURSERY 1925 GRAND CONCOURSE .... BRONX **NY** 10453 (212) 588-5800

BAIS ISAAC ZVI 1019 46TH STREET .... BROOKLYN **NY** 11219 (718) 854-7777

BEER MORDECHAI 1670 OCEAN AVENUE .... BROOKLYN **NY** 11230 (718) 377-1838

BETH AM-LABOR ZIONIST CENTER & DAY SCHOOL
1182 BRIGHTON BEACH AVENUE .... BROOKLYN **NY** 11235 (718) 743-4442

BETH JACOB DAY SCHOOL FOR GIRLS 550 OCEAN PARKWAY .... BROOKLYN **NY** 11218 (718) 375-7771

BETH KIRSCH PRE-SCHOOL & DAY CAMP 1014 E. 15TH STREET .... BROOKLYN **NY** 11230 (718) 377-8426

DAY CARE NURSERY OF THE INSTITUTE OF ADAS ISRAEL
1454 OCEAN PARKWAY .... BROOKLYN **NY** 11230 (718) 375-9292

OCEAN PRIMARY SCHOOL & DAY CAMP 904 EAST 98TH STREET .... BROOKLYN **NY** 11212 (718) 649-1567

OHOLEI TORAH 1267 EASTERN PARKWAY .... BROOKLYN **NY** 11213 (718) 778-3340

REISHIS CHOCHMAH PRE-SCHOOL 1937 OCEAN AVENUE .... BROOKLYN **NY** 11230 (718) 951-6559

YESHIVA IMREI YOSEF SPINKA 1460 56TH STREET .... BROOKLYN **NY** 11219 (718) 851-1600

YESHIVA MAHARYATS MARGARETEN 7902 15TH AVENUE .... BROOKLYN **NY** 11228 (718) 259-0423

YESHIVA TORAH UMIDOS (BETH MORDECHAI NURSERY)
1358 EAST 13TH STREET .... BROOKLYN **NY** 11230 (718) 339-7672

YESHIVA TORAS EMES KAMENITZ 53RD STREET AND 14TH AVENUE .... BROOKLYN **NY** 11219 (718) 435-3973

YESHIVA TORAS EMES KAMENITZ 1167 EAST 13TH STREET .... BROOKLYN **NY** 11230 (718) 851-4735

BNOS ISRAEL INSTITUTE 612 BEACH 9TH STREET .... FAR ROCKAWAY **NY** 11691 (718) 327-0196

HEBREW KINDERGARTEN & INFANTS HOME
210 BEACH 20TH STREET .... FAR ROCKAWAY **NY** 11691 (718) 327-1140

YESHIVA DARCHEI TORAH 257 BEACH 17TH STREET .... FAR ROCKAWAY **NY** 11691 (718) 337-5880

YOUNG ISRAEL OF KEW GARDEN HILLS PRIMARY SCHOOL
150-05 70TH ROAD .... FLUSHING **NY** 11367 (718) 261-9723

TEMPLE SINAI NURSERY SCHOOL 70-35 112TH STREET .... FOREST HILLS **NY** 11375 (718) 261-2900

YESHIVA DOV REVEL OF FOREST HILLS 71-02 113TH STREET .... FOREST HILLS **NY** 11375 (718) 261-9624

HEBREW ACADEMY OF WEST QUEENS 34-25 82ND STREET .... JACKSON HEIGHTS **NY** 11372 (718) 899-9193

JEWISH NURSERY SCHOOL 82-17 LEFFERTS BOULEVARD .... KEW GARDENS **NY** 11415 (718) 849-7988

YESHIVA BAIS YITZCHOK 184 MAPLE AVENUE .... MONSEY **NY** 10952 (914) 356-3113

CENTRAL SYNAGOGUE NURSERY 123 EAST 55TH STREET .... NEW YORK **NY** 10022 (212) 838-5122

FRIENDLY HOME JEWISH CHILD CARE ASSOC. OF NEW YORK
465 WEST END AVENUE .... NEW YORK **NY** 10024 (212) 874-2522

FRIENDLY HOME JEWISH CHILD CARE ASSOC. OF NEW YORK
320 WEST END AVENUE .... NEW YORK **NY** 10023 (212) 595-2620

JEWISH CHILD CARE ASSOCIATION OF NEW YORK
345 MADISON AVENUE .... NEW YORK **NY** 10017 (212) 490-9160

LINCOLN SQUARE SYNAGOGUE NURSERY AND KINDERGARTEN
200 AMSTERDAM AVENUE .... NEW YORK **NY** 10023 (212) 874-6100

THE NATIONAL COUNCIL OF JEWISH WOMEN, NEW YORK SECTION
CHILDCARE CENTER, 9 EAST 69TH STREET .... NEW YORK **NY** 10021 (212) 535-5900

THE 92ND STREET YM-YWHA-FAMILY DAY CARE NETWORK
1395 LEXINGTON AVENUE .... NEW YORK **NY** 10023 (212) 427-6000

THE STEPHEN WISE FREE SYNAGOGUE-EARLY CHILDHOOD & DAY CARE CENTER
30 WEST 68TH STREET .... NEW YORK **NY** 10023 (212) 877-4050

TINOK BABY CENTER C/O PARK AVENUE SYNAGOGUE
50 EAST 87TH STREET .... NEW YORK **NY** 10028 (212) 369-2600

WEST SIDE JEWISH COMMUNITY NURSERY SCHOOL
131 WEST 86TH STREET .... NEW YORK **NY** 10025 (212) 873-6464

YESHIVA DAY SCHOOL OF SOUTH QUEENS
115-70 LEFFERTS BOULEVARD .... OZONE PARK **NY** 11420 (718) 641-0100

JEWISH FOUNDATION SCHOOL NURSERY
835 FOREST HILL ROAD .... STATEN ISLAND **NY** 10314 (718) 494-7477

YESHIVA OF WILLOWBROOK 61 RUPERT AVENUE .... STATEN ISLAND **NY** 10314 (718) 494-7477

JEWISH COMMUNITY CENTER OF WEST HEMPSTEAD-NURSERY SCHOOL
711 DOGWOOD AVENUE .... WEST HEMPSTEAD **NY** 11552 (516) 481-7448

ADATH ISRAEL-JARSON EDUCATIONAL CENTER
3201 EAST GALBRAITH ROAD .... CINCINNATI **OH** 45236 (513) 793-1805

YAVNEH DAY SCHOOL 1636 SUMMIT ROAD .... CINCINNATI **OH** 45237 (513) 984-3770

AGNON PRESCHOOL/PREKINDERGARTEN 26500 SHAKER BLVD .... CLEVELAND **OH** 44122 (216) 464-4055

FAIRMOUNT TEMPLE PRESCHOOL 23737 FAIRMOUNT BLVD .... CLEVELAND **OH** 44122 (216) 464-1330

FAMILY PLACE JEWISH COMMUNITY CENTER,3505 MAYFIELD ROAD .... CLEVELAND **OH** 44118 (216) 382-4000

GANON GIL PRESCHOOL 25400 FAIRMOUNT BLVD .... CLEVELAND **OH** 44122 (216) 464-0536

GANON GIL PRESCHOOL 1960 LANDER ROAD .... CLEVELAND **OH** 44124 (216) 442-6414

HEBREW ACADEMY OF CLEVELAND 1860 SOUTH TAYLOR ROAD .... CLEVELAND **OH** 44118 (216) 321-5838

JEWISH COMMUNITY CENTER PRESCHOOL 3505 MAYFIELD ROAD .... CLEVELAND **OH** 44118 (216) 382-4000

JEWISH DAY NURSERY DAY CARE CENTER 22201 FAIRMOUNT BLVD .... CLEVELAND **OH** 44118 (216) 932-2802

KINDER RING WORKMEN'S CIRCLE PRESCHOOL
1980 SOUTH GREEN ROAD .... CLEVELAND **OH** 44121 (216) 381-4515

LILLIAN RATNER MONTESSORI PRESCHOOL 4900 ANDERSON ROAD ... CLEVELAND **OH** 44124 (216) 291-0033

PARK SYNAGOGUE NURSERY SCHOOL 3300 MAYFIELD ROAD .... CLEVELAND **OH** 44118 (216) 371-4177

TAYLOR ROAD SYNAGOGUE NURSERY 1970 SOUTH TAYLOR ROAD .... CLEVELAND **OH** 44118 (216) 321-4875

TORAH NURSERY (CHABAD) 1825 SOUTH GREEN ROAD .... CLEVELAND **OH** 44121 (216) 381-9178

YOUNG ISRAEL SHULAMITH NURSERY 14141 CEDAR ROAD .... CLEVELAND **OH** 44121 (216) 381-7526

JEWISH CENTER NURSERY 1821 EMERSON STREET .... DAYTON **OH** 45406 (513) 854-4014

GAN YELADIM 100 ELDER ST .... DOWNSVIEW **ON** (416) 638-1796

KENESETH ISRAEL NURSERY SCHOOL
YORK ROAD AND TOWNSHIP LINE .... ELKINS PARK **PA** 19117 (215) 855-2425

BETH DAVID NURSERY SCHOOL 5220 WYNNEFIELD AVENUE .... PHILADELPHIA **PA** 19131

DOWNTOWN CHILDREN'S CENTER 366 SNYDER AVENUE .... PHILADELPHIA **PA** 19148 (215) 389-1018

FEDERATION DAY CARE SERVICES
JAMISON AVENUE & GARTH ROAD .... PHILADELPHIA **PA** 19116 (215) 676-7550

NORTHEAST FAMILY DAY CARE
JAMISON AVENUE & GARTH ROAD .... PHILADELPHIA **PA** 19116

NORTHERN HEBREW DAY NURSERY 10800 JAMISON AVENUE .... PHILADELPHIA **PA** 19116

NORTHERN HEBREW DAY SCHOOL NURSERY
10TH AND RUSCOMB .... PHILADELPHIA **PA** 19141 (215) 677-7191

SAMUEL PALEY DAY CARE CENTER
STRABLE & HORROCKS STREETS .... PHILADELPHIA **PA** 19152 (215) 725-8930

TEMPLE SINAI NURSERY SCHOOL 30 HAGAN AVENUE .... CRANSTON **RI** 02920 (401) 942-8350

DAY SCHOOLS

BIRMINGHAM JEWISH DAY SCHOOL 3960-A MONTCLAIR ROAD - P.O. BOX 9206	BIRMINGHAM	AL	35213	(205) 879-1068
HEBREW INSTITUTE OF ARIZONA AT MESA 104 WEST FIRST STREET	MESA	AZ	85201	(602) 249-6338
ARIZONA TORAH HIGH SCHOOL-BOYS 1123 W.GEORGIA	PHOENIX	AZ	85013	(602) 266-2586
ARIZONA TORAH HIGH SCHOOL-GIRLS 1123 W.GEORGIA	PHOENIX	AZ	85013	(602) 277-3389
HEBREW INSTITUTE OF ARIZONA 935 WEST MARYLAND AVENUE	PHOENIX	AZ	85013	(602) 249-6338
PHOENIX HEBREW ACADEMY 515 EAST BETHANY HOME ROAD	PHOENIX	AZ	85012	(602) 277-7479
TUCSON HEBREW ACADEMY 5550 EAST 5TH STREET	TUCSON	AZ	85711	(602) 745-5592
TUCSON HIGH SCHOOL FOR JEWISH STUDIES 225 NORTH COUNTRY CLUB	TUCSON	AZ	85716	(602) 795-7221
EMANUEL COMMUNITY DAY SCHOOL 8844 BURTON WAY	BEVERLY HILLS	CA	90211	(213) 274-6388
HILLEL HEBREW ACADEMY 9120 WEST OLYMPIC BLVD	BEVERLY HILLS	CA	90212	(213) 276-6135
KADIMA HEBREW ACADEMY 22600 SHERMAN WAY	CANOGA PARK	CA	91307	(818) 346-0849
VALLEY BETH SHALOM DAY SCHOOL 15739 VENTURA BOULEVARD	ENCINO	CA	91436	(818) 788-6000
EZRA TORAH INSTITUTE 7631 EVERGREEN DRIVE	GOLETA	CA	93117	(805) 968-3768
LONG BEACH HEBREW ACADEMY 3981 ATLANTIC AVENUE	LONG BEACH	CA	90807	(213) 424-9787
AKIBA ACADEMY 10400 WILSHIRE BOULEVARD	LOS ANGELES	CA	90024	(213) 475-6401
BAIS YAAKOV SCHOOL FOR GIRLS 461 NORTH LA BREA AVENUE	LOS ANGELES	CA	90036	(213) 938-3231
HERZL SCHOOLS 1039 SOUTH LA CIENEGA BOULEVARD	LOS ANGELES	CA	90035	(213) 652-1854
JEWISH ACADEMY OF LOS ANGELES, NEW JEWISH HIGH SCHOOL 1317 NORTH CRESCENT HEIGHTS BOULEVARD	LOS ANGELES	CA	90046	(213) 656-5020
NEW JEWISH HIGH SCHOOL 1317 N.CRESCENT HEIGHTS BLVD	LOS ANGELES	CA	90046	
SAMUEL A.FRYER YAVNEH ACADEMY 7353 BEVERLY BLVD	LOS ANGELES	CA	90036	(213) 938-2636
SEPHARDIC HEBREW ACADEMY 310 NORTH HUNTLEY DRIVE	LOS ANGELES	CA	90048	(213) 659-2456
SHALOM HEBREW ACADEMY 1419 SOUTH BEVERLY DRIVE	LOS ANGELES	CA	90035	(213) 275-2457
SHAPELL-FEINTECH JUNIOR HIGH SCHOOL,STEPHEN S.WISE TEMPLE 1550 STEPHEN S.WISE DRIVE	LOS ANGELES	CA	90077	(213) 788-7554
STEPHEN S.WISE DAY SCHOOL 15500 STEPHEN S.WISE DRIVE	LOS ANGELES	CA	90077	(213) 788-7554
TEMPLE BETH AM DAY SCHOOL 1039 SOUTH LA CIENEGA BOULEVARD	LOS ANGELES	CA	90035	(213) 655-6401
WEST COAST TALMUDICAL SEMINARY-YESHIVA OHR ELCHONON CHABAD 7215 WARING AVENUE	LOS ANGELES	CA	90046	(213) 937-3763
YAVNEH HEBREW ACADEMY 7353 BEVERLY BOULEVARD	LOS ANGELES	CA	90036	(213) 938-2636
YESHIVA GEDOLA OF LOS ANGELES 5822 WEST THIRD	LOS ANGELES	CA	90036	(213) 938-2071
YESHIVA OHR ELCHONON 7215 WARING AVENUE	LOS ANGELES	CA	90046	(213) 937-3763
YESHIVA OHR ELCHONON CHABAD/WEST COAST TALMUDICAL SEMINARY 7215 WARING AVENUE	LOS ANGELES	CA	90046	(213) 937-3763
YESHIVA RAV ISACSOHN/YESHIVATH TORATH EMETH 540 NORTH LA BREA AVENUE	LOS ANGELES	CA	90036	(213) 938-8147
YESHIVA RAV ISACSON-TORATH EMETH ACADEMY 540 NORTH LA BREA AVENUE	LOS ANGELES	CA	90036	(213) 939-1148
YESHIVA UNIVERSITY OF LOS ANGELES, BOY'S DIVISION 9760 WEST PICO BOULEVARD	LOS ANGELES	CA	90035	(213) 553-4478
YESHIVA UNIVERSITY OF LOS ANGELES HIGH SCHOOLS 9760 WEST PICO BLVD	LOS ANGELES	CA	90035	(213) 553-1574
YESHIVA UNIVERSITY OF LOS ANGELES, GIRL'S DIVISION 10345 WEST PICO BOULEVARD	LOS ANGELES	CA	90035	(213) 552-0513
ADAT ARI EL DAY SCHOOL 5540 LAUREL CANYON BOULEVARD	NORTH HOLLYWOOD	CA	91607	(818) 766-3506
EMEK HEBREW ACADEMY 12732 CHANDLER BLVD	NORTH HOLLYWOOD	CA	91607	(818) 980-0155
EMEK HIGH SCHOOL, BOY'S DIVISION 12326 RIVERSIDE DRIVE	NORTH HOLLYWOOD	CA	91607	(818) 980-0155
EMEK HIGH SCHOOL, GIRL'S DIVISION 12422 CHANDLER BOULEVARD	NORTH HOLLYWOOD	CA	91607	(818) 980-0155
UNION HEBREW HIGH SCHOOL 13107 VENTURA BLVD	NORTH HOLLYWOOD	CA	91604	(818) 872-3550
VALLEY TORAH CENTER-STANLEY M.LINTZ HIGH SCHOOL-BOY'S DIV 12003 RIVERSIDE DRIVE	NORTH HOLLYWOOD	CA	91607	(818) 984-1805
VALLEY TORAH CENTER-STANLEY M.LINTZ HIGH SCHOOL-GIRL'S DIV 12326 RIVERSIDE DRIVE	NORTH HOLLYWOOD	CA	91607	(818) 985-8682
ABRAHAM J. HESCHEL DAY SCHOOL 17701 DEVONSHIRE STREET	NORTHRIDGE	CA	91325	(818) 368-5781
HILLEL ACADEMY OF EAST BAY 3778 PARK BLVD	OAKLAND	CA	94610	(415) 482-3470
CHAIM WEIZMANN COMMUNITY DAY SCHOOL 1434 NORTH ALTADENA DRIVE	PASADENA	CA	91107	(818) 797-0204
ETZ CHAIM HEBREW INSTITUTE OF CALIFORNIA 13609 TWIN PEAKS RD	SAN DIEGO	CA	90264	(619) 748-7750
SAN DIEGO HEBREW DAY SCHOOL 6880 MOHAWK STREET	SAN DIEGO	CA	92115	(619) 460-3300
BEN YEHUDA SCHOOL 639 14TH AVENUE	SAN FRANCISCO	CA	94118	(415) 751-6983
BRANDEIS HILLEL DAY SCHOOL 2266 CALIFORNIA STREET	SAN FRANCISCO	CA	94115	(415) 346-2244
HEBREW ACADEMY OF SAN FRANCISCO 763 25TH AVENUE	SAN FRANCISCO	CA	94121	(415) 752-9583
PACIFIC JEWISH CENTER DAY SCHOOL 1515 MAPLE STREET	SANTA MONICA	CA	91405	(213) 396-8780
MIDRASHA KEREM 1030 ASTORIA DRIVE	SUNNYVALE	CA	94087	(408) 735-0921
SOUTH PENINSULA HEBREW DAY SCHOOL 1030 ASTORIA DRIVE	SUNNYVALE	CA	94087	(408) 738-3060
EMANUEL STREISAND JEWISH DAY SCHOOL 720 ROSE AVENUE	VENICE	CA	90291	(213) 399-0303
SAN GABRIEL/POMONA VALLEYS JEWISH DAY SCHOOL 3508 EAST TEMPLE WAY	WEST COVINA	CA	91791	(818) 967-3881
HEBREW ACADEMY, THE (LUBAVITCH) 1401 WILLOW LANE	WESTMINSTER	CA	92683	(714) 898-0051
BETH JACOB HIGH SCHOOL OF DENVER 5100 WEST 14TH AVENUE	DENVER	CO	80204	(303) 893-1333
HILLEL ACADEMY OF DENVER 450 SOUTH HUDSON STREET	DENVER	CO	80222	(303) 333-1511
ROCKY MOUNTAIN HEBREW ACADEMY 560 S.MONACO PARKWAY	DENVER	CO	80224	(303) 355-7642
YESHIVA TORAS CHAIM 1400 QUITMAN STREET	DENVER	CO	80204	(303) 629-8200
THE BESS AND PAUL SIGEL HEBREW ACADEMY OF GREATER HARTFORD 53 GABB ROAD	BLOOMFIELD	CT	06002	(203) 243-8333
HILLEL ACADEMY 4200 PARK AVENUE	BRIDGEPORT	CT	06604	(203) 347-6147
HILLEL ACADEMY 1571 STRATFIELD ROAD	FAIRFIELD	CT	06432	(203) 347-6147
NEW ENGLAND ACADEMY FOR JEWISH STUDIES 155 PENDLETON ST	NEW HAVEN	CT	06511	(203) 397-2791
THE GAN SCHOOL 765 ELM STREET	NEW HAVEN	CT	06511	(203) 777-2200
TORAH ACADEMY HIGH SCHOOL FOR GIRLS 570 WHALLEY AVE	NEW HAVEN	CT	06515	(203) 397-1808
TORAH ACADEMY OF CONNECTICUT-YESHIVA MAOR HATORAH 330 BLAKE STREET	NEW HAVEN	CT	06515	(203) 397-3243
HEBREW DAY SCHOOL OF EASTERN CONNECTICUT 2 BROAD STREET	NORWICH	CT	06360	(203) 889-9169
BETH CHANA ACADEMY H.S. FOR GIRLS AND BOYS H.S. OF CONN. 261 DERBY AVENUE	ORANGE	CT	06477	(203) 795-5261
LUBAVITCH YESHIVAH 261 DERBY AVENUE	ORANGE	CT	06477	(203) 795-5261
YESHIVA ACHEI TMIMIM LUBAVITCH NEW HAVEN HEBREW DAY SCHOOL 261 DERBY AVENUE	ORANGE	CT	06477	(203) 795-5261
BI-CULTURAL DAY SCHOOL 2186 HIGH RIDGE ROAD	STAMFORD	CT	06903	(203) 329-2186
BI-CULTURAL DAY SCHOOL BRANCH 2186 HIGH RIDGE ROAD	STAMFORD	CT	06903	(203) 329-1761
YESHIVA BAIS BINYOMIN 132 PROSPECT STREET	STAMFORD	CT	06710	(212) 582-1540
EZRA ACADEMY RIMMON ROAD	WOODBRIDGE	CT	06525	(203) 389-5500
ALBERT EINSTEIN HEBREW ACADEMY 300 LEA BLVD	WILMINGTON	DE	19802	
BETH SHOLOM ACADEMY 1400 N 46 AVENUE	HOLLYWOOD	FL	33021	(305) 966-2000
ARTHUR & ANNA GOLDSTEIN HEBREW ACADEMY OF SOUTH DADE 12401 SOUTHWEST 102ND AVENUE	MIAMI	FL	33156	(305) 253-2300
SOUTH DADE HEBREW ACADEMY 5950 N.KENDALL DRIVE	MIAMI	FL	33156	(305) 667-6667
TORAS EMES ACADEMY 16020 N.W. 2ND AVENUE	MIAMI	FL	33169	(305) 947-8074
AGUDATH ISRAEL HEBREW INSTITUTE-YESHIVA TORAS CHAIM 7801 CARLYLE AVENUE, P.O. BOX 4443	MIAMI BEACH	FL	33141	(305) 865-0243
BAIS YAAKOV OF MIAMI 7055 BONITA DRIVE	MIAMI BEACH	FL	33141	(305) 865-0763
HEBREW ACADEMY 2400 PINETREE DRIVE	MIAMI BEACH	FL	33140	(305) 532-6421
LUBAVITCH YESHIVA-CHEDER OF GREATER MIAMI 1140 ALTON ROAD	MIAMI BEACH	FL	33139	(305) 673-5664
MESIVTA HIGH SCHOOL 1965 ALTON ROAD	MIAMI BEACH	FL	33139	(305) 538-5543
RABBI ALEXANDER S. GROSS HEBREW ACADEMY OF GREATER MIAMI 2400 PINETREE DRIVE	MIAMI BEACH	FL	33140	(305) 532-6421
RABBI ALEXANDER S. GROSS JUNIOR AND SENIOR HIGH SCHOOL 2425 PINETREE DRIVE	MIAMI BEACH	FL	33140	(305) 532-6421
TORAS EMES ACADEMY 7902 CARLYLE AVENUE	MIAMI BEACH	FL	33141	(305) 868-1388
THE JEWISH HIGH SCHOOL OF SOUTH FLORIDA 18900 NORTHEAST 25TH AVENUE	NORTH MIAMI BEACH	FL	33180	(305) 935-5620
SAMUEL SCHECK HILLEL COMMUNITY DAY SCHOOL 19000 N.E. 25 AVENUE	NORTH MIAMI BEACH	FL	33180	(305) 931-2831
HEBREW DAY SCHOOL OF CENTRAL FLORIDA 4917 ELI STREET	ORLANDO	FL	32804	(305) 647-0713
HILLEL SCHOOL OF TAMPA 2801 BAYSHORE BLVD	TAMPA	FL	33609	(813) 839-7047
HEBREW ACADEMY OF ATLANTA 1892 NORTH DRUID HILLS ROAD	ATLANTA	GA	30319	(404) 634-7388
YESHIVA HIGH SCHOOL OF ATLANTA 1745 PEACHTREE ROAD, N.E.	ATLANTA	GA	30309	(404) 873-1492
SAVANNAH HEBREW DAY SCHOOL 5111 ABERCORN STREET	SAVANNAH	GA	31499	(912) 355-8111
DES MOINES JEWISH ACADEMY 954 CUMMINS PARKWAY	DES MOINES	IA	50312	(515) 274-0453
AKIBA JEWISH DAY SCHOOL 5200 SOUTH HYDE PARK BLVD	CHICAGO	IL	60615	(312) 493-8880
BAIS YAAKOV HEBREW PAROCHIAL SCHOOL 2447 WEST GRANVILLE AVENUE	CHICAGO	IL	60659	(312) 465-3770
BAIS YAAKOV OF CHICAGO-BOYS DIVISION 6122 NORTH CALIFORNIA	CHICAGO	IL	60659	(312) 465-9878
BIAS YAAKOV OF CHICAGO - BOYS DIVISION 6526 NORTH CALIFORNIA AVENUE	CHICAGO	IL	60659	(312) 465-5761
HANNA SACKS GIRLS HIGH SCHOOL/IDA CROWN JEWISH ACADEMY 3021 WEST DEVON AVENUE	CHICAGO	IL	60659	(312) 338-9222
HILLEL TORAH NORTH SUBURBAN DAY SCHOOL 3021 WEST DEVON AVENUE	CHICAGO	IL	60659	(312) 262-2010
IDA CROWN JEWISH ACADEMY 2828 W PRATT AVENUE	CHICAGO	IL	60645	(312) 973-1450
TELSHE YESHIVA OF CHICAGO 3535 WEST FOSTER AVENUE	CHICAGO	IL	60625	(312) 463-7738
YESHIVAS BRISK 2956 WEST PETERSON AVENUE	CHICAGO	IL	60659	(312) 275-5166
YESHIVAS TIFERES TZVI 6122 NORTH CALIFORNIA AVE	CHICAGO	IL	60659	(312) 764-1170
PEORIA HEBREW DAY SCHOOL 3616 NORTH SHERIDAN ROAD	PEORIA	IL	61604	(309) 688-2821
ARIE CROWN HEBREW DAY SCHOOL 8150 NORTH TRIPP AVENUE	SKOKIE	IL	60076	(312) 982-9192
HILLEL TORAH NORTH SUBURBAN DAY SCHOOL 8825 EAST PRAIRIE	SKOKIE	IL	60076	(312) 677-1021
HILLEL TORAH NORTH SUBURBAN DAY SCHOOL 7120 NORTH LARAMIE AVENUE	SKOKIE	IL	60077	(312) 674-6533
YESHIVA H.S.-PREP. DIV. OF THE HEBREW THEOLOGICAL COLLEGE 7135 NORTH CARPENTER ROAD	SKOKIE	IL	60077	(312) 674-7750
YESHIVAS BRISK 9000 FORESTVIEW ROAD	SKOKIE	IL	60203	(312) 674-4652
HEBREW ACADEMY OF INDIANAPOLIS 6602 HOOVER ROAD	INDIANAPOLIS	IN	46260	(317) 251-1261
SOUTH BEND HEBREW DAY SCHOOL 206 WEST 8TH STREET	MISHAWAKA	IN	46544	(219) 255-3351
HYMAN BRAND HEBREW ACADEMY 5901 COLLEGE BLVD	OVERLAND PARK	KS	66211	(913) 649-1993
ELIAHU ACADEMY 3819 BARDSTOWN ROAD	LOUISVILLE	KY	40218	(502) 459-0927
LAKESHORE HEBREW DAY SCHOOL 5210 WEST ESPLANADE AVENUE	METAIRIE	LA	70002	(504) 885-4532
NEW ENGLAND HEBREW ACADEMY-LUBAVITCH YESHIVA 1845 COMMONWEALTH AVENUE	BRIGHTON	MA	02135	(617) 787-0020
SOUTH SHORE HEBREW ACADEMY 144 BELMONT AVENUE	BROCKTON	MA	02401	(617) 583-0717
BROOKLINE I.L. PERETZ SCHOOL OF THE WORKMEN'S CIRCLE 1762 BEACON STREET	BROOKLINE	MA	02146	
GAN TORAH 1611 BEACON STREET	BROOKLINE	MA	02146	(800) 343-0470
MAIMONIDES SCHOOL PHILBRICK ROAD	BROOKLINE	MA	02146	(617) 232-4452
NEW ENGLAND HEBREW ACADEMY-LUBAVITCH YESHIVA 9 PRESCOTT STREET	BROOKLINE	MA	02146	(617) 731-5330
SOUTH AREA JEWISH COMMUNITY CENTER MASORET PROGRAM 1 BLUE HILL RIVER ROAD	CANTON	MA	02021	(617) 773-3000
HERITAGE ACADEMY 594 CONGRESS STREET	LONGMEADOW	MA	01106	(413) 567-1517
LUBAVITCHER YESHIVA ACADEMY 1148 CONVERSE STREET	LONGMEADOW	MA	01106	(413) 736-9420
MERRIMACK VALLEY HEBREW ACADEMY 460 WESTFORD STREET	LOWELL	MA	01851	(617) 459-9400
SHALOH HOUSE OHOLEI TORAH 68 SMITH ROAD	MILTON	MA	02186	(617) 333-0477
LUBAVITCHER YESHIVA ACADEMY 15 ELWOOD DRIVE	SPRINGFIELD	MA	01108	(413) 373-7998
SHALOH HOUSE OHOLEI TORAH 50 ETHYL WAY	STOUGHTON	MA	02072	(617) 333-0477
HILLEL ACADEMY OF THE NORTH SHORE 837 HUMPHREY STREET	SWAMPSCOTT	MA	01907	(617) 599-3837
BAIS CHANA JUNIOR AND SENIOR H.S. AND DORMITORY FOR GIRLS 9 MIDLAND STREET	WORCESTER	MA	01602	(617) 752-0904
YESHIVA ACHEI TMIMIM ACADEMY 22 NEWTON AVENUE	WORCESTER	MA	01602	(617) 752-0904

HERZLIA-TORAH ACADEMY	620 BROCK STREET	WINNIPEG	**MB**	R3N 0Z4	(204) 489-6668
I.L. PERETZ FOLK SCHOOL	600 JEFFERSON AVENUE	WINNIPEG	**MB**	R2V 0P2	(204) 338-7828
RAMAH HEBREW SCHOOL	LANARK STREET & GRANT AVENUE	WINNIPEG	**MB**	R3N 1M4	(204) 453-4136
BETH TFILOH COMMUNITY DAY SCHOOL	3300 OLD COURT ROAD	BALTIMORE	**MD**	21208	(301) 486-1905
NER ISRAEL HIGH SCHOOL	400 MT WILSON LANE	BALTIMORE	**MD**	21208	(301) 484-7200
TALMUDICAL ACADEMY	4445 OLD COURT ROAD	BALTIMORE	**MD**	21208	(301) 484-6600
TORAH INSTITUTE OF BALTIMORE	4300 BEDFORD ROAD	BALTIMORE	**MD**	21207	(301) 484-1104
YESHIVA KOCHAV YITZCHAK	4300 BEDFORD AVENUE	BALTIMORE	**MD**	21208	(301) 484-2340
YESHIVAS CHOFETZ CHAIM	4445 OLD COURT ROAD	BALTIMORE	**MD**	21208	(301) 484-6600
BAIS YAAKOV SCHOOL FOR GIRLS	11111 PARK HEIGHTS AVENUE	OWINGS MILLS	**MD**	21117	(301) 363-3300
SILVER SPRING HEBREW DAY INSTITUTE	4511 BESTOR DRIVE	ROCKVILLE	**MD**	20853	(301) 460-7070
HEBREW ACADEMY OF GREATER WASHINGTON	2010 LINDEN LANE	SILVER SPRING	**MD**	20910	(301) 587-4100
HEBREW DAY SCHOOL OF MONTGOMERY COUNTY	1401 ARCOLA AVENUE	SILVER SPRING	**MD**	20902	(301) 649-5400
YESHIVA HIGH SCHOOL OF GREATER WASHINGTON INC.-GIRLS DIV.	8915 COLESVILLE RD.	SILVER SPRING	**MD**	20910	(301) 587-6187
YESHIVA HIGH SCHOOL OF GREATER WASHINGTON, INC.-BOYS DIV.	1216 ARCOLA AVENUE	SILVER SPRING	**MD**	20902	(301) 649-7077
HEBREW ACADEMY OF BANGOR	28 SOMERSET STREET	BANGOR	**ME**	04401	(207) 945-5631
THE ABRAHAM S. AND FANNIE B. LEVEY HEBREW DAY SCHOOL	76 NOYES STREET	PORTLAND	**ME**	04103	(207) 773-0693
SALLY ALLAN ALEXANDER BETH JACOB SCHOOL FOR GIRLS	32605 BELLVINE TRAIL	BIRMINGHAM	**MI**	48010	(313) 644-3113
YESHIVAT AKIVA-THE AKIVA HEBREW DAY SCHOOL	27700 SOUTHFIELD ROAD	LATHRUP VILLAGE	**MI**	48076	(313) 552-9690
YESHIVA GEDOLAH OF METROPOLITAN DETROIT-DIV. OF BETH YEHUDA	24600 GREENFIELD ROAD	OAK PARK	**MI**	48237	(313) 968-4270
YESHIVA BETH YEHUDA	15751 WEST LINCOLN DRIVE	SOUTHFIELD	**MI**	48076	(313) 557-6750
TORAH ACADEMY	2800 JOPPA AVENUE, SOUTH	MINNEAPOLIS	**MN**	55416	(612) 920-6630
LUBAVITCH HOUSE CHEDER	1758 FORD PKWY	ST. PAUL	**MN**	55116	(612) 698-0556
RABBI H.F. EPSTEIN HEBREW ACADEMY	1138 NORTH WARSON ROAD	ST. LOUIS	**MO**	63132	(314) 994-7856
YESHIVA HIGH SCHOOL OF ST. LOUIS	9723 GRANDVIEW DRIVE	ST. LOUIS	**MO**	63132	(314) 997-3940
YESHIVA OF ST. LOUIS RABBINICAL COLLEGE	7400 OLIVE ST	ST. LOUIS	**MO**	63130	(314) 727-1379
B'NAI ISRAEL SYNAGOGUE, DAY SCHOOL	P.O. BOX 10214	GREENSBORO	**NC**	27404	(919) 855-5091
HILLEL SCHOOL	7400 FALLS OF THE NEUSE ROAD	RALEIGH	**NC**	27609	(919) 847-8986
TALMUDICAL ACADEMY OF NEW JERSEY	ROUTE 524	ADELPHIA	**NJ**	07710	(201) 431-1600
YESHIVA OF HUDSON COUNTY	5 BERGEN COURT	BAYONNE	**NJ**	07002	(201) 865-2484
BAIS KALLA TORAH PREPARATORY HIGH SCHOOL	503 - 11TH AVENUE	BELMAR	**NJ**	07719	(201) 681-9400
HEBREW ACADEMY OF MORRIS COUNTY	219 HILL STREET	BOONTON	**NJ**	07005	(201) 335-9009
HILLEL HIGH SCHOOL	100 GRANT AVE	DEAL PARK	**NJ**	07723	(201) 531-9300
MORRIS NAMIAS SHALOM TORAH ACADEMY	639 ABBINGTON DRIVE-TWIN RIVERS TOWN CENTER	EAST WINDSOR	**NJ**	08520	(609) 443-4877
RABBI PESACH RAYMON YESHIVA ACADEMY	2 HARRISON STREET	EDISON	**NJ**	08817	(201) 572-5052
BRURIAH HIGH SCHOOL FOR GIRLS	35 NORTH AVENUE	ELIZABETH	**NJ**	07208	(201) 351-6315
JEWISH EDUCATIONAL CENTER	330 ELMORA AVENUE	ELIZABETH	**NJ**	07208	(201) 353-4446
MORIAH SCHOOL OF ENGLEWOOD	53 S. WOODLAND STREET	ENGLEWOOD	**NJ**	07631	(201) 567-0208
ROGOSIN YESHIVA HIGH SCHOOL	25 COTTAGE STREET	JERSEY CITY	**NJ**	07306	(201) 798-0055
BEZALEL HEBREW DAY SCHOOL	419 5TH STREET	LAKEWOOD	**NJ**	08701	(201) 363-1748
LAKEWOOD CHEDER SCHOOL	901 MADISON AVENUE	LAKEWOOD	**NJ**	08701	(201) 364-1552
LAKEWOOD CHEDER SCHOOL-BAIS YAAKOV OF LAKEWOOD	602 7TH STREET	LAKEWOOD	**NJ**	08701	(201) 363-5070
LIMUD LEARNING CENTER	414 YESHIVA PLAZA, APT 4A	LAKEWOOD	**NJ**	08701	(201) 364-1877
MESIVTA OF LAKEWOOD	215 PRIVATE WAY	LAKEWOOD	**NJ**	08701	(201) 367-7345
YESHIVA YETEV LEV SATMAR	405 FOREST AVENUE	LAKEWOOD	**NJ**	08701	(201) 363-9746
THE HEBREW ACADEMY	C/O CONGREGATION SONS OF ISRAEL-GORDONS CORNER ROAD	MANALAPAN	**NJ**	07726	
HEBREW ACADEMY OF ATLANTIC COUNTY	601 NORTH JEROME AVENUE, PO BOX 3163	MARGATE	**NJ**	08402	(609) 823-6681
HILLEL ACADEMY	P.O. BOX 287	METUCHEN	**NJ**	08840	
TORAH ACADEMY OF TEANECK	435 RIVER ROAD	NEW MILFORD	**NJ**	07646	(201) 265-0600
HILLEL YESHIVA	1025 DEAL ROAD	OCEAN	**NJ**	07712	(201) 493-9300
THE FRISCH SCHOOL-YESHIVA H.S. OF NORTHERN NEW JERSEY	EAST 243 FRISCH COURT	PARAMUS	**NJ**	07652	(201) 845-0555
YAVNEH ACADEMY	155 FAIRVIEW AVENUE	PARAMUS	**NJ**	07652	(201) 262-8494
HILLEL ACADEMY	565 BROADWAY	PASSAIC	**NJ**	07055	(201) 777-0735
HEBREW FREE SCHOOLS	660 14TH AVENUE	PATERSON	**NJ**	07504	(201) 742-9345
REGIONAL HIGH SCHOOL OF JEWISH STUDIES	152 VAN HOUTEN STREET	PATERSON	**NJ**	07505	
YAVNEH ACADEMY	413 12TH AVENUE	PATERSON	**NJ**	07514	(201) 274-7005
TORAH ACADEMY OF TEANECK	NORTH STREET AND ELM	TEANECK	**NJ**	07666	(201) 836-8005
YESHIVA OF HUDSON COUNTY/BERGEN BRANCH	800 BROAD STREET	TEANECK	**NJ**	07666	(201) 833-0203
MESIVTA SANZ OF HUDSON COUNTY	3400 NEW YORK AVENUE	UNION CITY	**NJ**	07087	(201) 867-8690
YESHIVA OF HUDSON COUNTY	2501 NEW YORK AVENUE	UNION CITY	**NJ**	07087	(201) 865-2484
JEWISH DAY SCHOOL	ORCHARD ROAD	VINELAND	**NJ**	08360	
KADIMAH TORAH SCHOOL OF SOUTH NEW JERSEY	321 GRAPE STREET	VINELAND	**NJ**	08360	
HILLEL SCHOOL OF THE SHORE AREA	LOGAN ROAD AND PARK BLVD	WANAMASSA	**NJ**	07712	(201) 531-1220
REGIONAL H.S. OF JEWISH STUDIES	1 PIKE DRIVE	WAYNE	**NJ**	07470	(201) 595-0560
HEBREW YOUTH ACADEMY OF ESSEX COUNTY	1 HENDERSON DRIVE	WEST CALDWELL	**NJ**	07006	(201) 575-1194
YESHIVA TALMIDEI TELSHE	111 WASHINGTON	WESTWOOD	**NJ**	07675	(201) 358-0900
NEW MEXICO HEBREW ACADEMY	4800 EUBANK N.E.	ALBUQUERQUE	**NM**	87111	(505) 296-5553
MAIMONIDES HEBREW DAY SCHOOL OF THE CAPITAL DISTRICT	420 WHITEHALL ROAD	ALBANY	**NY**	12208	(518) 482-5889
OHAEL SHMUEL, YESHIVA	165 HAINES ROAD	BEDFORD HILLS	**NY**	10507	(914) 241-2700
YESHIVAH OF BELLE HARBOR	134-01 ROCKAWAY BEACH BLVD	BELLE HARBOR	**NY**	11694	(718) 945-0309
HILLEL ACADEMY OF BROOME COUNTY	DEERFIELD PLACE	BINGHAMTON	**NY**	13903	(607) 722-9274
BETH JACOB HIGH SCHOOL OF THE BRONX	2058 WALLACE AVENUE	BRONX	**NY**	10462	(212) 547-7860
BETH JACOB-BETH MIRIAM	2126 BARNES AVENUE	BRONX	**NY**	10462	(212) 892-1476
BETH JACOB-BETH MIRIAM HIGH SCHOOL OF THE BRONX	3006 WILLIAMSBRIDGE ROAD	BRONX	**NY**	10467	(212) 583-8993
BRONX YESHIVA HIGH SCHOOL	1328 ALLERTON AVENUE	BRONX	**NY**	10469	(212) 653-1363
BRONX YESHIVA HIGH SCHOOL	1524 PARKER STREET	BRONX	**NY**	10462	(212) 829-4570
HEBREW DAY NURSERY	5720 MOSHOLU AVENUE	BRONX	**NY**	10471	(212) 884-1101
KINNERET DAY SCHOOL	2600 NETHERLAND AVENUE	BRONX	**NY**	10463	(212) 548-0900
LUBAVITCHER YESHIVA ACHEI TMIMIM	3415 OLINVILLE AVENUE	BRONX	**NY**	10467	(212) 654-5318
SALANTER AKIBA RIVERDALE ACADEMY	655 WEST 254 STREET	BRONX	**NY**	10471	(212) 549-5160
TORAH V'EMUNAH YESHIVA	1778 EAST 172 STREET	BRONX	**NY**	10472	(212) 829-4701
ACHPRI TEVUAH, YESHIVA	1449 50TH STREET	BROOKLYN	**NY**	11219	(718) 436-5555
AHAVAS ISRAEL, YESHIVA	6 LEE AVENUE	BROOKLYN	**NY**	11211	(718) 388-0848
AHI EZER YESHIVA	2433 OCEAN PARKWAY	BROOKLYN	**NY**	11223	(718) 648-6100
AHI EZER YESHIVA ANNEX	293 NEPTUNE AVENUE	BROOKLYN	**NY**	11235	(718) 332-7000
ALTERNATIVE SCHOOL-BAIS SHOLOM, YESHIVA	555 REMSEN AVENUE	BROOKLYN	**NY**	11236	(718) 495-2100
ARUGATH HABOSEM, YESHIVA	171 HOOPER STREET	BROOKLYN	**NY**	11211	(718) 388-7534
ASSOCIATED BETH RIVKAH SCHOOLS	310 CROWN STREET	BROOKLYN	**NY**	11225	(718) 735-0400
ATERES YISRAEL, YESHIVA	8101 AVENUE K	BROOKLYN	**NY**	11236	(718) 763-6777
BAIS ISAAC ZVI	1019 46 STREET	BROOKLYN	**NY**	11219	(718) 854-7887
BAIS ROCHEL SCHOOL FOR GIRLS	225 PATCHEN AVENUE	BROOKLYN	**NY**	11233	(718) 453-0250
BAIS YAACOV D'KHAL ADAS YEREIM	563 BEDFORD AVENUE	BROOKLYN	**NY**	11211	(718) 782-2486
BAIS YAAKOV D'CHASIDEI GER	1681 49TH STREET	BROOKLYN	**NY**	11204	(718) 435-0077
BAIS YAAKOV KHAL ADAS YEREIM KINDERGARTEN	574 BEDFORD AVENUE	BROOKLYN	**NY**	11211	(718) 384-7187
BAIS YAAKOV OF 18TH AVENUE	4419 18TH AVENUE	BROOKLYN	**NY**	11204	(718) 633-6050
BAIS YAAKOV OF BROOKLYN	1362 49 STREET	BROOKLYN	**NY**	11219	(718) 435-7776
BAIS YAAKOV OF BROOKLYN ANNEX	4910 14TH AVENUE	BROOKLYN	**NY**	11219	(718) 854-1219
BAIS YAAKOV OF FERNDALE	1676 52TH STREET	BROOKLYN	**NY**	11204	(718) 851-5180
BAIS YITZCHAK FOR BOYS	1413 45TH AVENUE	BROOKLYN	**NY**	11219	(718) 851-6959
BAIS YITZCHAK FOR BOYS	4722 18TH AVENUE	BROOKLYN	**NY**	11204	(718) 854-0800
BE'ER HAGOLAH INST.-ADMINISTRATIVE OFFICES AND GIRLS H.S.	1709 KINGS HIGHWAY	BROOKLYN	**NY**	11229	(718) 627-7800
BE'ER HAGOLAH INSTITUTE	1709 KINGS HIGHWAY	BROOKLYN	**NY**	11229	(718) 627-7800
BE'ER HAGOLAH INSTITUTES	2810 NOSTRAND AVENUE	BROOKLYN	**NY**	11229	(718) 377-8423
BE'ER HAGOLAH INSTITUTES	2114 BROWN STREET	BROOKLYN	**NY**	11229	(718) 934-9247
BE'ER HAGOLAH INSTITUTES HIGH SCHOOL	1542 CONEY ISLAND AVENUE	BROOKLYN	**NY**	11230	(718) 338-0724
BE'ER MORDECAI	1670 OCEAN AVENUE	BROOKLYN	**NY**	11230	(718) 338-6064
BE'ER SHMUEL MESIVTA	4407 12TH AVENUE	BROOKLYN	**NY**	11219	(718) 853-1376
BE'ER SHMUEL, YESHIVA & MESIVTA	1363 50TH STREET	BROOKLYN	**NY**	11219	(718) 438-6100
BEN YEHUDA SCHOOL	111 WEST END AVENUE	BROOKLYN	**NY**	11235	(718) 769-6601
BETH AM-LABOR ZIONIST CENTER & DAY SCHOOL	1182 BRIGHTON BEACH AVENUE	BROOKLYN	**NY**	11235	(718) 743-4442
BETH CHANA ELEMENTARY AND HIGH SCHOOL	620 BEDFORD AVENUE	BROOKLYN	**NY**	11211	(718) 552-7422
BETH CHANA ELEMENTARY AND HIGH SCHOOL	204 KEAP STREET	BROOKLYN	**NY**	11211	(718) 338-5491
BETH CHANA SCHOOL FOR GIRLS	204 KEAP STREET	BROOKLYN	**NY**	11211	(718) 522-7422
BETH EL ELEMENTARY SCHOOL	457 GRAND AVENUE	BROOKLYN	**NY**	11238	(718) 789-1259
BETH EL TALMUDIC INSTITUTE	1981 HOMECREST AVENUE	BROOKLYN	**NY**	11229	(718) 339-9117
BETH HAMEDRASH SHAAREI YOSHER	4102 16TH AVENUE	BROOKLYN	**NY**	11204	(718) 854-2290
BETH HATALMUD	2127 82ND STREET	BROOKLYN	**NY**	11219	(718) 259-2525
BETH HILLEL OF KRASNA, YESHIVA	1364 66 42ND STREET	BROOKLYN	**NY**	11219	(718) 871-0210
BETH JACOB ACADEMY HIGH SCHOOL OF BROOKLYN	4419 18TH AVENUE	BROOKLYN	**NY**	11204	(718) 435-8478
BETH JACOB DAY SCHOOL FOR GIRLS	85 PARKVILLE	BROOKLYN	**NY**	11230	(718) 633-6555
BETH JACOB DAY SCHOOL FOR GIRLS	550 OCEAN PARKWAY	BROOKLYN	**NY**	11218	(718) 633-6555
BETH JACOB ELEMENTARY SCHOOL	4412 15TH STREET	BROOKLYN	**NY**	11219	(718) 851-2900
BETH JACOB ELEMENTARY SCHOOL	616 BEDFORD AVENUE	BROOKLYN	**NY**	11211	(718) 782-7117
BETH JACOB HIGH SCHOOL	4421 15TH AVENUE	BROOKLYN	**NY**	11219	(718) 851-2255
BETH JACOB PAROCHIAL HIGH SCHOOL	4121 CROWN STREET	BROOKLYN	**NY**	11219	(718) 851-2900
BETH JACOB SCHOOL	616 BEDFORD AVENUE	BROOKLYN	**NY**	11211	(718) 625-8390
BETH JACOB OF BORO PARK	1371 46TH STREET	BROOKLYN	**NY**	11219	(718) 436-7300
BETH JACOB OF BORO PARK	1413 45TH STREET	BROOKLYN	**NY**	11219	(718) 853-7197
BETH JACOB OF FLATBUSH	1823 OCEAN PARKWAY	BROOKLYN	**NY**	11223	(718) 375-7771
BETH JACOB OF FLATBUSH	1823 OCEAN PARKWAY	BROOKLYN	**NY**	11223	(718) 645-2009
BETH JACOB OF MIDWOOD-OCEAN PRIMARY SCHOOL	904 EAST 98TH STREET	BROOKLYN	**NY**	11236	(718) 649-1567
BETH KIRSH NURSERY	1014 EAST 15TH STREET	BROOKLYN	**NY**	11230	(718) 377-8426
BETH MOSHE COMMUNITY SCHOOL	910 48TH STREET	BROOKLYN	**NY**	11219	(718) 633-1591
BETH RACHEL SCHOOL FOR GIRLS	62 HARRISON AVENUE	BROOKLYN	**NY**	11211	(718) 963-9593
BETH RACHEL SCHOOL FOR GIRLS	277 MARCY AVENUE	BROOKLYN	**NY**	11211	(718) 384-4923
BETH RACHEL SCHOOL FOR GIRLS	165 CLYMER STREET	BROOKLYN	**NY**	11211	(718) 782-8811
BETH RACHEL SCHOOL FOR GIRLS-PRE-SCHOOL	960 49TH STREET	BROOKLYN	**NY**	11219	(718) 438-7822
BETH RACHEL SCHOOL OF BORO PARK	5301 14TH AVENUE	BROOKLYN	**NY**	11219	(718) 438-7822
BETH RIVKA ELEMENTARY SCHOOL	2270 CHURCH AVENUE	BROOKLYN	**NY**	11226	(718) 856-4451
BETH RIVKA SCHOOLS	2270 CHURCH AVENUE	BROOKLYN	**NY**	11226	(718) 856-4457
BETH RIVKAH HIGH SCHOOL	310 CROWN STREET	BROOKLYN	**NY**	11225	(718) 735-0400
BETH RIVKAH SCHOOLS	310 CROWN STREET	BROOKLYN	**NY**	11225	(718) 735-0400
BETH SARAH SCHOOL	5801 16TH AVENUE	BROOKLYN	**NY**	11204	(718) 851-5198
BETH SHEARIM YESHIVA	5306 16TH AVENUE	BROOKLYN	**NY**	11204	(718) 851-0089
BETH YEHUDA V'CHAIM D'BETLAN YESHIVA	52-62 KEAP STREET	BROOKLYN	**NY**	11211	(718) 855-3546
BETH YITZCHOK D'SPINKA, YESHIVA	192 KEAP STREET	BROOKLYN	**NY**	11211	(718) 387-4597
BIALIK SCHOOL, THE	500 CHURCH AVENUE	BROOKLYN	**NY**	11218	(718) 853-7100
BNOS ISRAEL OF EAST FLATBUSH	9214 AVENUE B	BROOKLYN	**NY**	11236	(718) 498-1991
BNOS ISRAEL OF EAST FLATBUSH	2818 AVENUE K	BROOKLYN	**NY**	11210	(718) 338-4833
BNOS JERUSALEM-BELZ GIRLS SCHOOL	12 FRANKLIN AVENUE	BROOKLYN	**NY**	11211	(718) 852-5551
BNOS YAAKOV EDUCATIONAL CENTER FOR GIRLS	62 HARRISON STREET	BROOKLYN	**NY**	11211	(718) 855-8275
BNOS YAAKOV EDUCATIONAL CENTER FOR GIRLS	95 PENN STREET	BROOKLYN	**NY**	11211	(718) 387-6880
BNOS YAAKOV EDUCATIONAL CENTER FOR GIRLS	5000 14TH AVENUE	BROOKLYN	**NY**	11219	(718) 438-3080

Name / Address	City	State	Zip	Phone
BNOS YAKOV SCHOOL FOR GIRLS 174 PACIFIC STREET	BROOKLYN	NY	11201	(718) 963-3940
BNOS YISROEL SCHOOL FOR GIRLS 2 LEE AVENUE	BROOKLYN	NY	11211	(718) 388-0848
BNOS ZION OF BOBOV 5000 14TH AVENUE	BROOKLYN	NY	11219	(718) 438-3080
BNOS ZION OF BOBOV 5220 13TH AVENUE	BROOKLYN	NY	11219	(718) 853-7182
BOBOVER YESHIVA 1533 48TH STREET	BROOKLYN	NY	11219	(718) 438-8411
BOBOVER YESHIVA BNEI ZION 1533 48TH STREET	BROOKLYN	NY	11219	(718) 871-0300
BOBOVER YESHIVA BNEI ZION 4715 15TH AVENUE	BROOKLYN	NY	11219	(718) 436-3479
BORO PARK TORAH INSTITUTE 1417 49TH STREET	BROOKLYN	NY	11219	(718) 438-7633
BRIGHTON YESHIVA 293 NEPTUNE AVENUE	BROOKLYN	NY	11235	(718) 332-7000
BROOKLYN SCHOOL FOR SPECIAL CHILDREN 376 BAY 44TH STREET	BROOKLYN	NY	11234	(718) 946-9700
BROOKLYN, YESHIVA OF 1462-66 OCEAN PARKWAY	BROOKLYN	NY	11230	(718) 376-3775
BROOKLYN, YESHIVA OF (BOYS) 1210 OCEAN PARKWAY	BROOKLYN	NY	11230	(718) 376-3775
BROOKLYN, YESHIVA OF (GIRLS) 1470 OCEAN PARKWAY	BROOKLYN	NY	11230	(718) 376-3775
CENTRAL YESHIVA TOMCHEI TMIMIM LUBAVITCH 841-853 OCEAN PARKWAY	BROOKLYN	NY	11230	(718) 859-7600
CH'SAN SOFER YESHIVA-RABBI SOLOMON KLUGER 1876 50TH STREET	BROOKLYN	NY	11204	(718) 236-1171
CHANOCH LENAAR, YESHIVA 876 EASTERN PARKWAY	BROOKLYN	NY	11213	(718) 774-8456
CHATZAR HAKODESH, YESHIVA 1450 50TH STREET	BROOKLYN	NY	11219	(718) 436-1234
CHESED YISRAEL, YESHIVA 2422 AVENUE K	BROOKLYN	NY	11210	(718) 338-8300
COMMUNITY SCHOOL BETH MOSHE 910 48TH STREET	BROOKLYN	NY	11219	(718) 633-1591
CROWN HEIGHTS, YESHIVA OF 6363 AVENUE U	BROOKLYN	NY	11234	(718) 444-5800
CROWN OF ISRAEL TALMUD TORAH 1769 56TH STREET	BROOKLYN	NY	11204	(718) 232-4827
DARKEI TSHUVA OF MUNKATSCH, YESHIVA 240 KEAP STREET	BROOKLYN	NY	11211	
DEJESHER YESHIVA, MAGLE ZEDEK 1223 35TH STREET	BROOKLYN	NY	11219	(718) 436-0239
DERECH EMUNOH 1554 49TH STREET	BROOKLYN	NY	11219	(718) 851-6774
EDUCATIONAL INSTITUTE OHOLEI TORAH 667 EASTERN PARKWAY	BROOKLYN	NY	11213	(718) 778-3340
EITZ CHAIM OF BOBOV-BOBOVER YESHIVA 1533 48TH STREET	BROOKLYN	NY	11219	(718) 871-0300
EZRA ACADEMY C/O RABBI GREENWALD, 20 AMHERST STREET	BROOKLYN	NY	11235	
FLATBUSH, YESHIVA OF 919 EAST 10TH STREET	BROOKLYN	NY	11230	(718) 377-4466
FLATBUSH, YESHIVA OF-JOEL BRAVERMAN HIGH SCHOOL 1609 AVENUE J	BROOKLYN	NY	11230	(718) 377-4466
FREE SCHOOL 1383 PRESIDENT STREET	BROOKLYN	NY	11213	(718) 467-0860
GERER YESHIVA & MESIFTA-MACHZEIKI HADATH 5407 16TH AVENUE	BROOKLYN	NY	11204	(718) 438-7700
HARAMA, YESHIVA 2600 OCEAN AVENUE	BROOKLYN	NY	11229	(718) 743-3141
HADAR HATORAH 824 EASTERN PARKWAY	BROOKLYN	NY	11213	(718) 735-0200
HAICHEL HATORAH, MESIVTA 2449 OCEAN AVENUE	BROOKLYN	NY	11229	(718) 648-1150
HARMA INSTITUTE SEPHARDIC COMMUNITY HIGH SCHOOL 2600 OCEAN AVENUE	BROOKLYN	NY	11229	(718) 743-3141
HARMA RELIGIOUS INST. OF SEC EDUC-YESHIVA H.S. FOR GIRLS 2600 OCEAN AVENUE	BROOKLYN	NY	11229	(718) 743-3141
HEBREW ACADEMY FOR SPECIAL CHILDREN 1311 55TH STREET	BROOKLYN	NY	11219	(718) 851-6100
HEBREW INSTITUTE FOR THE DEAF & EXCEPTIONAL CHILDREN 2025 67TH STREET	BROOKLYN	NY	11204	(718) 259-2626
HEBREW INSTITUTE OF BORO PARK 4702 15TH AVENUE	BROOKLYN	NY	11219	(718) 853-1600
HEBREW MIDRASHA OF BROOKLYN 1609 AVENUE J	BROOKLYN	NY	11230	
IMREI YOSEF SPINKA, YESHIVA 1460 56TH STREET	BROOKLYN	NY	11219	(718) 851-1600
INSTITUTE FOR OLEI RUSSYA 4901 11TH AVENUE	BROOKLYN	NY	11219	(718) 633-6244
INSTITUTE OF ADAS ISRAEL 1454 OCEAN PARKWAY	BROOKLYN	NY	11230	
JESODE HATORAH NACHLAS YAKOV, YESHIVA 1350 50TH STREET	BROOKLYN	NY	11219	(718) 851-6462
JESODE HATORAH OF ADAS YEREIM, YESHIVA 505 BEDFORD AVENUE	BROOKLYN	NY	11211	(718) 384-6393
JEWISH CENTER FOR SPECIAL EDUCATION 430 KENT AVENUE	BROOKLYN	NY	11211	(718) 782-0064
JOSEPH S. GRUSS HIGH SCHOOL-TORAS EMES OF KAMINETZ 1650 56TH STREET	BROOKLYN	NY	11204	(718) 851-4735
KARLIN STOLIN, YESHIVA 1818 54TH STREET	BROOKLYN	NY	11204	(718) 232-7800
KEHILATH YAKOV, YESHIVA 206 WILSON STREET	BROOKLYN	NY	11211	(718) 963-3940
KESSER MALKA 1315 43RD STREET	BROOKLYN	NY	11219	(718) 854-2528
KESSER MALKA 1315 43RD STREET	BROOKLYN	NY	11219	(718) 854-7777
KHAL ADAS PAYE, YESHIVA 296 MARCY AVENUE	BROOKLYN	NY	11211	(718) 387-2231
KINGS BAY, YESHIVA OF 2611 AVENUE Z	BROOKLYN	NY	11235	(718) 646-8500
KINGSWAY ACADEMY 2810 NOSTRAND AVENUE	BROOKLYN	NY	11229	(718) 258-3344
LEV SOMEACH, YESHIVA 674 EAST 2ND STREET	BROOKLYN	NY	11218	(718) 338-3929
M'KOR CHAIM, MESIFTA 1571 55TH STREET	BROOKLYN	NY	11219	(718) 851-0183
MACHON BAIS YAAKOV-HILDA BIRN HIGH SCHOOL 1037 46TH STREET	BROOKLYN	NY	11219	(718) 972-7900
MACHZIKE TALMUD TORAH OF BORO PARK 4622 14TH AVENUE	BROOKLYN	NY	11219	(718) 436-8690
MACHZIKEI HADAS, YESHIVA 1601 42ND STREET	BROOKLYN	NY	11204	(718) 436-4445
MACHZIKEI TORAH, YESHIVA 630 BEDFORD AVENUE	BROOKLYN	NY	11211	(718) 875-2164
MAGEN DAVID YESHIVA 50 AVENUE P	BROOKLYN	NY	11204	(718) 236-5905
MANHATTAN BEACH, YESHIVA OF 60 WEST END AVENUE	BROOKLYN	NY	11235	(718) 743-5511
MESIVTA EITZ CHAIM OF BOBOV 1573 48TH STREET	BROOKLYN	NY	11219	(718) 438-2018
MESIVTA HAICHEL HATORAH 2449 OCEAN AVENUE	BROOKLYN	NY	11229	(718) 648-1150
MESIVTA M'KOR CHAIM 1571 55TH STREET	BROOKLYN	NY	11219	(718) 851-0197
MESIVTA NACHLAS YAKOV 185 WILSON STREET	BROOKLYN	NY	11211	(718) 388-1751
MESIVTA RABBI CHAIM BERLIN 1593 CONEY ISLAND AVENUE	BROOKLYN	NY	11230	(718) 377-0777
MESIVTA SHAAREI EMUNAH 1631 42ND STREET	BROOKLYN	NY	11204	(718) 853-1898
MESIVTA TORAH VODAATH 425 EAST 9TH STREET	BROOKLYN	NY	11218	(718) 941-8000
MIDWOOD INSTITUTE OF TORAH 1286 E 10TH STREET	BROOKLYN	NY	11230	(718) 252-6168
MINCHAS ELUZAR D'MUNKACS, YESHIVA 1377 42ND STREET	BROOKLYN	NY	11219	(718) 438-5246
MIRRER YESHIVA 1791 OCEAN PARKWAY	BROOKLYN	NY	11223	(718) 645-0536
MIRRER YESHIVA CENTRAL INST.-MORRIS MORGENSTERN HIGH SCHOOL 1795 OCEAN PARKWAY	BROOKLYN	NY	11223	(718) 645-0536
MIZRACHI L'BONIM 2114 BROWN STREET	BROOKLYN	NY	11229	(718) 934-3663
NACHLAS YAAKOV OF ADAS YEREIM, MESIFTA 185 WILSON STREET	BROOKLYN	NY	11211	(718) 388-1751
NODAH B'YEHUDA, INC. 750 REMSEN AVENUE	BROOKLYN	NY	11236	
OHEL MOSHE, YESHIVA 7914 BAY PARKWAY	BROOKLYN	NY	11214	(718) 236-4003
OHEL SOROH SCHOOL 771 CROWN STREET	BROOKLYN	NY	11213	(718) 756-8300
OHOLEI TORAH 706 EASTERN PARKWAY	BROOKLYN	NY	11213	(718) 778-3340
OHOLEI TORAH 667 EASTERN PARKWAY	BROOKLYN	NY	11213	(718) 778-3340
OHOLEI TORAH 417 TROY AVENUE	BROOKLYN	NY	11213	(718) 773-9658
PHILIP HIRTH ACADEMY 4419 18TH STREET	BROOKLYN	NY	11204	(718) 435-8478
PHILIP HIRTH ACADEMY OF BROOKLYN 1213-1223 ELM STREET	BROOKLYN	NY	11230	(718) 339-4747
PROSPECT PARK YESHIVA 1202 AVENUE P	BROOKLYN	NY	11229	(718) 645-7800
PROSPECT PARK YESHIVA 1609 AVENUE R	BROOKLYN	NY	11229	(718) 376-0004
RABBI CHAIM BERLIN, MESIVTA 1302 AVENUE I	BROOKLYN	NY	11230	(718) 277-0777
RABBI CHAIM BERLIN, YESHIVA 1302 AVENUE I	BROOKLYN	NY	11230	(718) 253-1000
RABBI HARRY HALPERN DAY SCHOOL/EAST MIDWOOD JEWISH CENTER 1625 OCEAN AVENUE	BROOKLYN	NY	11230	(718) 338-3800
RABBI HIRSH DACHOWITZ SCHOOL R'TZAHD YESHIVA 1800 UTICA AVENUE	BROOKLYN	NY	11234	(718) 763-5500
RABBINICAL SEMINARY OF MUNKACS 1377 42ND STREET	BROOKLYN	NY	11219	(718) 438-5246
RAMBAM, YESHIVA 3300 KINGS HIGHWAY	BROOKLYN	NY	11234	(718) 338-6918
SARA SCHENIRER HIGH SCHOOL AND TEACHERS SEMINARY 4622 14TH AVENUE	BROOKLYN	NY	11219	(718) 633-8557
SAVE RUSSIAN JEWRY 2324 WEST 13TH STREET	BROOKLYN	NY	11223	(718) 449-6741
SEPHARDIC HIGH SCHOOL 511 AVENUE R	BROOKLYN	NY	11223	(718) 998-8171
SEPHARDIC INSTITUTE 511 AVENUE R	BROOKLYN	NY	11223	(718) 998-8171
SHAAREI EMUNAH, MESIVTA 153 OCEAN AVENUE	BROOKLYN	NY	11225	(718) 287-4700
SHAAREI YOSHER, YESHIVA 4104 16TH AVENUE	BROOKLYN	NY	11204	(718) 854-2290
SHAREI ZEDEK, YESHIVA 3701 SURF AVENUE	BROOKLYN	NY	11224	(718) 266-4604
SHEVET YEHUDA, YESHIVA 5220 13TH AVENUE	BROOKLYN	NY	11219	(718) 342-6878
SHEVET YEHUDAH RESNICK INSTITUTE OF TECHNOLOGY 5220 13TH AVENUE	BROOKLYN	NY	11219	(718) 853-1212
SHULAMITH SCHOOL FOR GIRLS 1350-1353 50TH STREET	BROOKLYN	NY	11219	(718) 853-7070
SHULAMITH SCHOOL FOR GIRLS 1277 EAST 14TH STREET	BROOKLYN	NY	11230	(718) 338-4000
SHULAMITH SCHOOL FOR GIRLS 60 WEST END AVENUE	BROOKLYN	NY	11235	(718) 338-4000
SOLOMON SCHECHTER HIGH SCHOOL OF BROOKLYN 500 CHURCH AVENUE	BROOKLYN	NY	11218	(718) 854-3500
TALMUD TORAH TIFERES BUNIM 5202 13TH AVENUE	BROOKLYN	NY	11219	(718) 436-6868
TALMUD TORAH TOLDOS YAKOV YOSEF 1383 44TH STREET	BROOKLYN	NY	11219	(718) 436-2550
TALMUD TORAH TOLDOS YAKOV YOSEF 105 HEYWARD ST (MAIL:GPO BOX 1721, BKLN 11206)	BROOKLYN	NY	11211	(718) 852-0502
TALMUD TORAH TOLDOS YAKOV YOSEF 94 WILSON	BROOKLYN	NY	11237	(718) 387-1130
TALMUD TORAH TOMCHAI TORAH 1722 AVENUE N	BROOKLYN	NY	11230	(718) 336-8072
TALMUDICAL HIGH SCHOOL OF BROOKLYN 1182 BRIGHTON BEACH AVENUE	BROOKLYN	NY	11235	(718) 796-4646
THE JEWISH CENTER FOR SPECIAL EDUC-YESHIVA LIMUDEI HASHEM 430 KENT AVENUE	BROOKLYN	NY	11211	(718) 782-0064
TIFERES BUNIM 5202 13TH AVENUE	BROOKLYN	NY	11219	(718) 436-6870
TIFERES ELIMELICH, YESHIVA 54 AVENUE O	BROOKLYN	NY	11204	(718) 236-1001
TINOK SCHOOL 1440 E 99TH STREET	BROOKLYN	NY	11236	(718) 436-5555
TOMER D'VORA SCHOOL FOR GIRLS 1413 45TH STREET	BROOKLYN	NY	11219	(718) 853-9400
TOMER DVORA HIGH SCHOOL 1462 50TH STREET	BROOKLYN	NY	11219	(718) 438-4600
TOMER DVORA SCHOOL FOR GIRLS 4500 9TH AVENUE	BROOKLYN	NY	11219	(718) 853-9400
TORAH ACADEMY OF BROOKLYN 1540 CONEY ISLAND AVENUE	BROOKLYN	NY	11230	(718) 998-0110
TORAH TEMIMAH, YESHIVA 555 OCEAN PARKWAY	BROOKLYN	NY	11218	(718) 853-8500
TORAH UMESORAH HEADSTART PROGRAM 1315 43RD STREET	BROOKLYN	NY	11219	(718) 851-0402
TORAH V'YIRAH FOR GIRLS, YESHIVA 5301 14TH STREET	BROOKLYN	NY	11219	(718) 438-7822
TORAH VODAATH, YESHIVA 425 EAST 9TH STREET	BROOKLYN	NY	11218	(718) 941-8000
TORAS EMES OF KAMINETZ, YESHIVA 1650 56TH STREET	BROOKLYN	NY	11204	(718) 851-4735
TZE ULMAD 1725 E. 27TH STREET	BROOKLYN	NY	11229	
UNGVARER YESHIVA 5306 16TH AVENUE	BROOKLYN	NY	11219	(718) 851-0806
UNITED LUBAVITCHER YESHIVAH HIGH SCHOOL 841 OCEAN PARKWAY	BROOKLYN	NY	11230	(718) 434-0795
UNITED LUBAVITCHER YESHIVOTH 841 OCEAN PARKWAY	BROOKLYN	NY	11230	(718) 434-0795
UNITED LUBAVITCHER YESHIVOTH 841 OCEAN PARKWAY	BROOKLYN	NY	11230	(718) 859-7600
UNITED TALMUDICAL ACADEMY/BETH RACHEL SCHOOL FOR GIRLS 62 HARRISON AVENUE	BROOKLYN	NY	11211	(718) 963-9260
UNITED TALMUDICAL ACADEMY HIGH SCHOOL 227 MARCY AVENUE	BROOKLYN	NY	11211	(718) 963-9260
UNITED TALMUDICAL ACADEMY TORAH V'YIRAH 5301 14TH AVENUE	BROOKLYN	NY	11219	(718) 438-7822
UNITED TALMUDICAL ACADEMY TORAH V'YIRAH 94 THROOP AVENUE	BROOKLYN	NY	11206	(718) 963-9290
UNITED TALMUDICAL ACADEMY TORAH V'YIRAH 236-238 MARCY AVENUE	BROOKLYN	NY	11211	(718) 563-0658
UNITED TALMUDICAL ACADEMY TORAH V'YIRAH 212 WILLIAMSBURG STREET EAST	BROOKLYN	NY	11211	(718) 963-9288
UNITED TALMUDICAL ACADEMY TORAH V'YIRAH 165 CLYMER STREET	BROOKLYN	NY	11211	(718) 384-9585
UNITED TALMUDICAL ACADEMY/TORAH V'YIRAH FOR BOYS, YESHIVA 82 LEE AVENUE	BROOKLYN	NY	11211	(718) 963-9260
YAGDIL TORAH, YESHIVA 5110 18TH AVENUE	BROOKLYN	NY	11204	(718) 871-9100
YESHIVA & BETH JACOB OF CANARSIE 904 E. 98TH STREET	BROOKLYN	NY	11234	(718) 649-1567
YESHIVA & MESIFTA BEER SHMUEL 4407 12TH AVENUE	BROOKLYN	NY	11219	(718) 853-1376
YESHIVA & MESIVTA BAIS YITZCHOCK D'CHASIDEI SKWERE 4722 18TH AVENUE	BROOKLYN	NY	11204	(718) 436-9434
YESHIVA ACH PRI TEVUAH 1449 50 STREET	BROOKLYN	NY	11219	
YESHIVA AHAVAS YISROEL 6 LEE AVENUE	BROOKLYN	NY	11211	(718) 388-0848
YESHIVA ATERES YISROEL 8101 AVENUE K	BROOKLYN	NY	11236	(718) 763-6777
YESHIVA ATERET TORAH 1020 OCEAN PARKWAY	BROOKLYN	NY	11230	(718) 258-1776
YESHIVA BAIS EPHRAIM 2802 AVENUE J	BROOKLYN	NY	11210	(718) 377-8448
YESHIVA BAIS HILLEL MOSES 229 NEPTUNE AVENUE	BROOKLYN	NY	11235	
YESHIVA BAIS JEHUDO OF BORO PARK 1383 44TH STREET	BROOKLYN	NY	11219	
YESHIVA BAIS YITZCHOK 1334 47TH AVENUE	BROOKLYN	NY	11219	
YESHIVA BAIS YITZCHOK D'SPINKA 182 KEAP STREET	BROOKLYN	NY	11211	(718) 387-4597
YESHIVA BAIS YITZCHOK D'SPINKA 191 RODNEY STREET	BROOKLYN	NY	11211	(718) 387-4597
YESHIVA BETH HATALMUD 2127 82ND STREET	BROOKLYN	NY	11214	(718) 259-2525
YESHIVA BETH HILLEL OF KRASNE 1364 42ND STREET	BROOKLYN	NY	11219	(718) 871-0210
YESHIVA BETH REUVEN 1111 55TH STREET	BROOKLYN	NY	11219	(718) 435-2535
YESHIVA BETH YITZCHAK SPINK 205 HOOPER STREET	BROOKLYN	NY	11211	
YESHIVA CHANOCH LENAAR 876 EASTERN PARKWAY	BROOKLYN	NY	11213	(718) 774-8456
YESHIVA CHASDEI TORAH 2025 67TH STREET	BROOKLYN	NY	11204	(718) 256-1132
YESHIVA CHATZAR HAKODESH SANZ-KLAUSENBERG 1420 50TH STREET	BROOKLYN	NY	11219	(718) 436-1234

School / Address	City	State	ZIP	Phone
YESHIVA CHESSED YISROEL 2422 AVENUE K	BROOKLYN	NY	11210	(718) 338-8300
YESHIVA DARKEI TSHIVO OF MUNKATSH 240 KEAP STREET	BROOKLYN	NY	11211	
YESHIVA FARM SETTLEMENT 194 DIVISION AVENUE	BROOKLYN	NY	11211	(718) 387-0422
YESHIVA HAICHEL HATORAH 2449 OCEAN AVENUE	BROOKLYN	NY	11229	
YESHIVA HARAMA HIGH SCHOOL FOR GIRLS 2600 OCEAN AVENUE	BROOKLYN	NY	11223	(718) 743-3142
YESHIVA HARAMA TIFERETH ZVI 319 CROWN STREET	BROOKLYN	NY	11225	(718) 773-5530
YESHIVA HARBOTZAS TORAH 203 AVENUE F	BROOKLYN	NY	11218	(718) 853-1376
YESHIVA IMREI YOSEF SPINKA 5801 15TH AVENUE	BROOKLYN	NY	11219	(718) 851-1600
YESHIVA IMREI YOSEF SPINKA 1460 56TH STREET	BROOKLYN	NY	11219	(718) 851-1600
YESHIVA INSTITUTE 6414 BAY PARKWAY	BROOKLYN	NY	11204	(718) 259-1432
YESHIVA JESODE HATORAH OF BORO PARK 1350 50TH STREET	BROOKLYN	NY	11219	(718) 851-6462
YESHIVA JESODE HATORAH OF BORO PARK 5402 14TH AVENUE	BROOKLYN	NY	11219	
YESHIVA KAHAL MAGLEI ZEDEK DEJ 1223 45TH STREET	BROOKLYN	NY	11219	
YESHIVA KEHILATH YAAKOV 206 WILSON STREET	BROOKLYN	NY	11211	(718) 963-3940
YESHIVA KETANA OF OCEAN AVENUE 2449 OCEAN AVENUE	BROOKLYN	NY	11229	(718) 648-1152
YESHIVA KOL TORAH 2449 OCEAN AVENUE	BROOKLYN	NY	11229	(718) 646-8900
YESHIVA M'KOR CHAIM 1571 55TH STREET	BROOKLYN	NY	11219	(718) 851-0183
YESHIVA MACHZIKEI HADAS BELZ 1601 42ND STREET	BROOKLYN	NY	11204	(718) 436-4445
YESHIVA MACHZIKEI TORAH D'CHASSIDEI BELZ 630 BEDFORD AVENUE	BROOKLYN	NY	11211	(718) 237-1818
YESHIVA MEOR HATORAH 2221 OCEAN AVENUE	BROOKLYN	NY	11229	
YESHIVA NACHLAS HALEVYIM 544 E. 92ND STREET	BROOKLYN	NY	11236	
YESHIVA NESEVOS OLUM 205 HEWES STREET	BROOKLYN	NY	11211	
YESHIVA OHR MOLEH KOSON 1645 53RD STREET	BROOKLYN	NY	11204	
YESHIVA R'TZAHD - THE RABBI HIRSH DACHOWITZ DAY SCHOOL 1800 UTICA AVENUE	BROOKLYN	NY	11234	(718) 763-5500
YESHIVA RABBI CHAIM BERLIN 1302 AVENUE I	BROOKLYN	NY	11230	(718) 253-1000
YESHIVA RABBI CHAIM BERLIN 1569 CONEY ISLAND AVENUE	BROOKLYN	NY	11230	(718) 252-7190
YESHIVA RABBI DAVID LEIBOWITZ 9102 CHURCH AVENUE	BROOKLYN	NY	11236	
YESHIVA RABBI HACOHEN 289 EAST 53RD STREET	BROOKLYN	NY	11203	
YESHIVA RABBI SOLOMON KLUGER-MESIVTA CHASAN SOFER 1876 50TH STREET	BROOKLYN	NY	11204	(718) 236-1171
YESHIVA RAMBAM 3300 KINGS HIGHWAY	BROOKLYN	NY	11234	(718) 338-6918
YESHIVA SHAAREI SIMCHA 4619 13TH AVENUE	BROOKLYN	NY	11219	
YESHIVA SHAAREI TORAH 1326 OCEAN PARKWAY	BROOKLYN	NY	11230	(718) 998-3883
YESHIVA SHAAREI YOSHER 4102 16TH AVENUE	BROOKLYN	NY	11204	(718) 854-2290
YESHIVA SHAREI ZEDEK IN SEA GATE 3701 SURF AVENUE	BROOKLYN	NY	11224	(718) 266-4604
YESHIVA SHARIE HAYOSHER 1440 E. 99TH STREET	BROOKLYN	NY	11236	(718) 436-5555
YESHIVA TIFERES ELIMELECH 54 AVENUE O	BROOKLYN	NY	11204	(718) 236-1001
YESHIVA TIFERETH AVROHOM 2997 OCEAN PARKWAY	BROOKLYN	NY	11235	
YESHIVA TOLDOS YAKOV YOSEF CHASIDEI SQVERE 1383 44TH STREET	BROOKLYN	NY	11219	(718) 436-2550
YESHIVA TORAH 5114 18TH AVENUE	BROOKLYN	NY	11204	
YESHIVA TORAH M'ZION 1440 E. 99TH STREET	BROOKLYN	NY	11236	
YESHIVA TORAH V'YIRAH OF BORO PARK 1356 53RD STREET	BROOKLYN	NY	11219	
YESHIVA TORAH VODAATH 425 EAST 9TH STREET	BROOKLYN	NY	11218	(718) 941-8000
YESHIVA TORAS EMES KAMENITZ 1650 56TH STREET	BROOKLYN	NY	11204	(718) 851-4735
YESHIVA TORAS EMES KAMENITZ-JOSEPH S. GRUSS HIGH SCHOOL 1650 56TH STREET	BROOKLYN	NY	11204	(718) 851-4735
YESHIVA TORAS EMES KAMENITZ-JOSEPH S. GRUSS HIGH SCHOOL 1310 53RD STREET	BROOKLYN	NY	11219	(718) 851-4735
YESHIVA TORAS EMES KAMENITZ-JOSEPH S. GRUSS HIGH SCHOOL 321 AVENUE N	BROOKLYN	NY	11230	(718) 851-4735
YESHIVA YAGDIL TORAH 5110 18TH AVENUE	BROOKLYN	NY	11204	(718) 871-9100
YESHIVA YESODE HATORAH 187 HOOPER STREET	BROOKLYN	NY	11211	(718) 387-6242
YESHIVA YESODE HATORAH 131 LEE AVENUE	BROOKLYN	NY	11211	(718) 384-1611
YESHIVA YESODE HATORAH SHEARITH HAPLETA 131 LEE AVENUE	BROOKLYN	NY	11211	
YESHIVA YESODE HATORAH OF ADAS YEREIM 505 BEDFORD AVENUE	BROOKLYN	NY	11211	(718) 384-6393
YESHIVA YESODEI HACHAIM HIGH SCHOOL 4514 11TH AVENUE	BROOKLYN	NY	11219	(718) 851-5755
YESHIVA YESODEI HATORAH (WEINER YESHIVA) 1350 50TH STREET	BROOKLYN	NY	11219	(718) 851-6462
YESHIVA ZICHRON ELIEZER MESKIN 725 CROWN STREET	BROOKLYN	NY	11213	(718) 773-1298
YESHIVA ZICHRON YOSEF ARYEH 4911 16TH AVENUE	BROOKLYN	NY	11204	
YESHIVA AND MESIVTA ARUGATH HABOSEM 171-173 HOOPER STREET	BROOKLYN	NY	11211	(718) 388-7534
YESHIVA AND MESIVTA BAIS SHOLOM ALTERNATIVE SCHOOL 555 REMSEN AVENUE	BROOKLYN	NY	11236	(718) 494-2100
YESHIVA AND MESIVTA BAIS YITZCHOK 4314 10TH AVENUE	BROOKLYN	NY	11220	(718) 851-6959
YESHIVA AND MESIVTA BE'ER SCHMUEL 4407 12TH AVENUE	BROOKLYN	NY	11219	(718) 853-1376
YESHIVA AND MESIVTA BE'ER SCHMUEL 1363 50TH STREET	BROOKLYN	NY	11219	(718) 438-6100
YESHIVA AND MESIVTA KARLIN STOLIN 1818 54TH STREET	BROOKLYN	NY	11204	(718) 232-7800
YESHIVA AND MESIVTA MAHARYATS MARGARETEN 7902 15TH AVENUE	BROOKLYN	NY	11228	(718) 259-0423
YESHIVA AND MESIVTA TORAH TEMIMAH 555 OCEAN PARKWAY	BROOKLYN	NY	11218	(718) 853-8500
YESHIVA OF BENSONHURST, INC. 2025 79TH STREET	BROOKLYN	NY	11214	(718) 232-7400
YESHIVA OF BRIGHTON 293 NEPTUNE AVENUE	BROOKLYN	NY	11235	
YESHIVA OF BROOKLYN 1470-1476 OCEAN PARKWAY	BROOKLYN	NY	11230	(718) 376-3775
YESHIVA OF BROOKLYN-BOYS DIVISION 1210 OCEAN PARKWAY	BROOKLYN	NY	11230	(718) 376-3775
YESHIVA OF BROOKLYN-GIRLS HIGH SCHOOL DIVISION 1470-1476 OCEAN PARKWAY	BROOKLYN	NY	11230	(718) 376-3775
YESHIVA OF CANARSIE 904 EAST 98TH STREET	BROOKLYN	NY	11236	(718) 649-1567
YESHIVA OF CROWN HEIGHTS 6363 AVENUE U	BROOKLYN	NY	11234	(718) 444-5800
YESHIVA OF FLATBUSH 919 E. 10TH STREET	BROOKLYN	NY	11230	(718) 377-4466
YESHIVA OF FLATBUSH ELEMENTARY SCHOOL 919 EAST 10TH STREET	BROOKLYN	NY	11230	(718) 377-4466
YESHIVA OF FLATBUSH HIGH SCHOOL 1609 AVENUE J	BROOKLYN	NY	11230	(718) 377-4466
YESHIVA OF FLATBUSH-JOEL BRAVERMAN HIGH SCHOOL & ELEMENTARY 1609 AVENUE J	BROOKLYN	NY	11230	(718) 377-4466
YESHIVA OF KINGS BAY 2611 AVENUE Z	BROOKLYN	NY	11235	(718) 646-8500
YESHIVA OF MANHATTAN BEACH 60 WEST END AVENUE	BROOKLYN	NY	11235	(718) 743-5511
YESHIVA OF MIDWOOD 904 EAST 98TH STREET	BROOKLYN	NY	11203	
YESHIVAH MAGEN DAVID 50 AVENUE P	BROOKLYN	NY	11204	
YESHIVAH OHEL MOSHE 7914 BAY PARKWAY	BROOKLYN	NY	11214	(718) 236-4003
YESHIVAS CH'SAN SOFER 1876 50TH STREET	BROOKLYN	NY	11204	(718) 236-1171
YESHIVAT MIKDASH MELECH 1616 OCEAN PARKWAY	BROOKLYN	NY	11223	(718) 339-1090
YESHIVAT MIZRACHI L'BANIM 2114 BROWN STREET	BROOKLYN	NY	11229	(718) 252-3579
YESHIVATH CHACHMEY LUBLIN 1404 E. 7TH STREET	BROOKLYN	NY	11230	
YESOD HACHAIM YESHIVA 4514 11TH AVENUE	BROOKLYN	NY	11219	(718) 851-5755
YESODE HATORAH, YESHIVA SHEARITH HAPLETAH 204 KEAP STREET	BROOKLYN	NY	11211	(718) 384-1611
ZICHRON MEILECH OF EASTERN PARKWAY, YESHIVA 3121 KINGS HIGHWAY	BROOKLYN	NY	11234	(718) 338-6100
HEBREW ACADEMY OF BUFFALO-YESHIVA LUBAVITZ 85 SARANAC AVENUE	BUFFALO	NY	14216	
HEBREW ACADEMY OF FIVE TOWNS AND ROCKAWAYS CEDARHURST AND LOCUST AVENUE	CEDARHURST	NY	11516	(516) 569-3807
HEBREW ACADEMY OF THE FIVE TOWNS AND THE ROCKAWAYS CENTRAL & LOCUST AVENUES	CEDARHURST	NY	11516	(516) 569-3370
SOLOMON SCHECHTER DAY SCHOOL OF SUFFOLK COUNTY 74 HAUPPAUGE ROAD	COMMACK	NY	11725	(516) 462-5999
L.I. PERETZ JEWISH SCHOOL 574 NEWBRIDGE AVENUE	EAST MEADOW	NY	11554	(516) 542-9640
BNOS ISRAEL INSTITUTE 612 BEACH 9TH STREET	FAR ROCKAWAY	NY	11691	(718) 327-8007
MAIMONIDES INSTITUTE 3401 MOTT AVENUE	FAR ROCKAWAY	NY	11691	(718) 471-0100
SH'OR YOSHUV INSTITUTE 1526 CENTRAL AVENUE	FAR ROCKAWAY	NY	11691	(718) 327-2048
SIACH YITZCHOK (BOYS) 1513-17 CENTRAL AVENUE	FAR ROCKAWAY	NY	11691	(718) 327-2048
TAPEINU ELEMENTARY SCHOOL 1284 CENTRAL AVENUE	FAR ROCKAWAY	NY	11691	(718) 327-9273
TAPEINU ELEMENTARY SCHOOL (GIRLS) 1284 CENTRAL AVENUE	FAR ROCKAWAY	NY	11691	(718) 327-8305
TORAH ACADEMY FOR GIRLS 444 BEACH 6TH STREET	FAR ROCKAWAY	NY	11691	(718) 471-8444
YESHIVA DARCHEI TORAH 257 BEACH 17TH STREET	FAR ROCKAWAY	NY	11691	(718) 337-5880
YESHIVA OF FAR ROCKAWAY-DERECH AYSON 802 HICKSVILLE ROAD	FAR ROCKAWAY	NY	11691	(718) 327-7600
BETH SHOSHANA ACADEMY OF QUEENS 75-09 MAIN STREET	FLUSHING	NY	11367	(718) 268-2626
CENTRAL QUEENS, YESHIVA OF 147-37 70TH ROAD	FLUSHING	NY	11367	(718) 793-8500
EZRA ACADEMY OF QUEENS 71-25 MAIN STREET	FLUSHING	NY	11367	(718) 263-5500
SOLOMON SCHECHTER DAY SCHOOL 76-16 PARSONS BOULEVARD	FLUSHING	NY	11366	(718) 591-9800
YESHIVA OF CENTRAL QUEENS (INCORP. MAX & ROSE HELLER ACADEMY) 147-37 70TH ROAD	FLUSHING	NY	11367	(718) 793-8500
YOUNG ISRAEL OF KEW GARDEN HILLS PRIMARY SCHOOL 150-05 70TH ROAD	FLUSHING	NY	11367	(718) 261-9723
FOREST HILLS, MESIVTA OF 108-55 69TH AVENUE	FOREST HILLS	NY	11375	(718) 263-1445
FOREST PARK SCHOOL-BETH JACOB EDUCATIONAL CENTER 102-35 63RD RD	FOREST HILLS	NY	11375	(718) 896-4444
MAX & DOROTHY COHN HIGH SCHOOL FOR GIRLS-OHR TORAH 66-35 108TH STREET	FOREST HILLS	NY	11375	(718) 268-3444
MESIVTA OF FOREST HILLS 68-54 KESSEL STREET	FOREST HILLS	NY	11375	(718) 263-1445
OHR TORAH INSTITUTE 66-35 108TH STREET	FOREST HILLS	NY	11375	(718) 268-3444
OHR YISROEL, MESIFTA 66-20 THORNTON PLACE	FOREST HILLS	NY	11374	(718) 263-6242
OHR YISROEL, YESHIVA 66-20 THORNTON PLACE	FOREST HILLS	NY	11375	(718) 263-6242
RABBI DOV REVEL YESHIVA OF FOREST HILLS 71-02 113TH STREET	FOREST HILLS	NY	11375	(718) 261-9624
YESHIVA CHOFETZ CHAIM 68-54 KESSEL STREET	FOREST HILLS	NY	11375	(718) 263-1445
YESHIVA CHOFETZ CHAIM-MESIVTA OF FOREST HILLS 92-15 69TH AVENUE	FOREST HILLS	NY	11375	(718) 263-1445
YESHIVA SHUVAY YISROEL 100-09 METROPOLITAN AVENUE	FOREST HILLS	NY	11375	(718) 544-7960
YESHIVA AND MESIVTA OHR YISROEL 66-20 THORNTON PLACE	FOREST HILLS	NY	11374	(718) 263-6242
BUREAU OF JEWISH ED./INSTITUTE & H.S. OF JEWISH STUDIES 2640 NORTH FOREST ROAD	GETZVILLE	NY	14068	(716) 689-8844
TORAH TEMIMAH SCHOOL 2501 NORTH FOREST ROAD	GETZVILLE	NY	14068	(716) 688-6524
NORTH SHORE HEBREW ACADEMY 26 OLD MILL ROAD	GREAT NECK	NY	11023	(516) 487-9163
NORTH SHORE HEBREW ACADEMY 16 CHERRY LANE	GREAT NECK	NY	11024	(516) 487-8687
NORTH SHORE HEBREW ACADEMY 26 OLD MILL ROAD	GREAT NECK	NY	11023	(516) 487-8694
BETH SHRAGA HEBREW ACADEMY 2211-A WESTERN AVENUE	GUILDERLAND	NY	12084	(914) 456-6816
TORAS CHAIM OF SOUTH SHORE, YESHIVA 1170 WILLIAM STREET	HEWLETT	NY	11557	(516) 374-7363
YESHIVA AND MESIVTA TORAS CHAIM AT SOUTH SHORE 1170 WILLIAM STREET	HEWLETT	NY	11557	(516) 374-7363
SAMUEL H. WANG YESHIVA HIGH SCHOOL OF QUEENS 86-86 PALO ALTO STREET	HOLLISWOOD	NY	11423	(718) 479-8550
YESHIVA HIGH SCHOOL OF QUEENS, OHR TORAH 86-86 PALO ALTO STREET	HOLLISWOOD	NY	11423	(718) 479-8550
HEBREW ACADEMY OF WEST QUEENS 34-25 82ND STREET	JACKSON HEIGHTS	NY	11372	(718) 899-9193
SOLOMON SCHECHTER DAY SCHOOL OF NASSAU COUNTY BARBARA LANE	JERICHO	NY	11753	(516) 935-1441
BAIS YAAKOV ACADEMY OF QUEENS 124-50 METROPOLITAN AVENUE	KEW GARDENS	NY	11415	(718) 847-5352
SHAAREY BNOS CHAYIL-SHEVACH HIGH SCHOOL 124-27 85TH AVENUE	KEW GARDENS	NY	11415	(718) 847-4402
SHEVACH HIGH SCHOOL 124-27 85TH STREET	KEW GARDENS	NY	11415	(718) 847-4402
TIFERETH MOSHE, YESHIVA 83-06 ABINGDON ROAD	KEW GARDENS	NY	11415	(718) 846-7300
YESHIVA SHAAR HATORAH 83-96 117 STREET	KEW GARDENS	NY	11418	(718) 846-1940
YESHIVA TIFERETH MOSHE 83-06 ABINGDON ROAD	KEW GARDENS	NY	11415	(718) 846-7300
HEBREW DAY SCHOOL OF SULLIVAN AND ULSTER COUNTY ROUTE 42	KIAMESHA LAKE	NY	12751	(914) 794-7890
BRANDEIS SCHOOL 25 FROST LANE	LAWRENCE	NY	11559	(516) 371-4747
HEBREW ACADEMY OF FIVE TOWNS AND ROCKAWAY 44 FROST LANE	LAWRENCE	NY	11559	(516) 569-3488
HEBREW ACADEMY OF FIVE TOWNS AND ROCKAWAY 33 WASHINGTON AVENUE	LAWRENCE	NY	11559	(516) 569-3370
HEBREW ACADEMY OF LONG BEACH 530 WEST BROADWAY	LONG BEACH	NY	11561	(516) 432-8285
MESIVTA OF LONG BEACH 205 WEST BEECH STREET	LONG BEACH	NY	11561	(516) 431-7414
TORAH HIGH SCHOOL OF LONG BEACH 205 W. BEECH STREET	LONG BEACH	NY	11561	(516) 431-7414
KEHILATH YAAKOV, MESIFTA 33-23 GREENPOINT AVENUE	LONG ISLAND CITY	NY	11101	(718) 963-3940
YESHIVA KEHILATH YAAKOV 33-23 GREENPOINT AVENUE	LONG ISLAND CITY	NY	11101	(718) 729-9857
WESTCHESTER DAY SCHOOL 856 ORIENTA AVENUE	MAMARONECK	NY	10543	(914) 698-8900
WESTCHESTER HEBREW HIGH SCHOOL 856 ORIENTA AVENUE	MAMARONECK	NY	10543	(914) 698-0806

School / Address	City	State	Zip	Phone
HEBREW DAY SCHOOL OF ORANGE COUNTY 195 WATKINS AVENUE	MIDDLETOWN	NY	10940	(914) 343-8588
BAIS ROCHEL SCHOOL BAKERTOWN ROAD	MONROE	NY	10950	(914) 782-5889
YESHIVA TORAH V'YIRAH D'RABBEINU YOEL D'SATMAR SCHUNEMUNK ROAD	MONROE	NY	10950	(914) 782-0844
ADOLPH H. SCHREIBER HEBREW ACADEMY OF ROCKLAND COUNTY 70 HIGHVIEW ROAD	MONSEY	NY	10952	(914) 357-1515
BAIS MIKRA 23 WEST MAPLE AVENUE	MONSEY	NY	10952	(914) 356-1239
BAIS YAAKOV H.S. 11 SMOLLEY DRIVE-P.O. BOX 116	MONSEY	NY	10952	(914) 356-3113
BAIS YITZCHOK, YESHIVA 184 MAPLE AVENUE	MONSEY	NY	10952	(914) 352-9635
BETH DAVID, YESHIVA 20 WEST MAPLE AVENUE, P.O. BOX 136	MONSEY	NY	10952	(914) 352-2111
BETH JACOB HIGH SCHOOL FOR GIRLS 11 SMOLLEY DRIVE, P.O. BOX 116	MONSEY	NY	10952	(914) 356-3113
BETH ROCHEL SCHOOL FOR GIRLS P.O. BOX 302, 145 SADDLE RIVER ROAD	MONSEY	NY	10952	(914) 352-5000
BETH ROCHEL SCHOOL FOR GIRLS 145 SADDLE RIVER ROAD - P.O. BOX 302	MONSEY	NY	10952	(914) 352-7654
BETH SHRAGA, MESIVTA 28 SADDLE RIVER ROAD, P.O. BOX 412	MONSEY	NY	10952	(914) 356-1980
BNOS YISROEL GIRLS SCHOOL OF VIZNITZ 73 MAIN STREET	MONSEY	NY	10952	(914) 356-1010
BNOS YISROEL GIRLS SCHOOL OF VIZNITZ 73 MAIN STREET	MONSEY	NY	10952	(914) 356-2322
HADAR, YESHIVAT 70 HIGHVIEW ROAD	MONSEY	NY	10952	
MESIVTA BETH SHRAGA 145 SADDLE RIVER ROAD - P.O. BOX 412	MONSEY	NY	10952	(914) 356-1980
MESIVTA HIGH SCHOOL 207 MAPLE AVENUE	MONSEY	NY	10952	(914) 356-5929
ROCKLAND HEBREW DAY SCHOOL 101 ROUTE 306	MONSEY	NY	10952	(914) 352-6629
SHAAREI TORAH OF ROCKLAND COUNTY 1 SCHOOL TERRACE	MONSEY	NY	10952	(914) 356-4773
SPRING VALLEY, YESHIVA OF 229-230 MAPLE AVENUE	MONSEY	NY	10952	(914) 356-1400
UNITED TALMUDICAL ACADEMY 89 SOUTH MAIN STREET - P.O. BOX 188	MONSEY	NY	10952	(914) 425-0392
VIZNITZ, YESHIVA P.O. BOX 446	MONSEY	NY	10952	(914) 356-1010
YESHIVA BETH DAVID 20 WEST MAPLE AVENUE - P.O. BOX 136	MONSEY	NY	10952	(914) 352-2111
YESHIVA VIZNITZ 20 ASHEL LANE	MONSEY	NY	10952	(914) 356-1010
YESHIVA OF SPRING VALLEY - BAIS SARAH 230 MAPLE AVENUE	MONSEY	NY	10952	(914) 356-1400
YESHIVA K'TANA OF MOUNTAINDALE P.O. BOX 118	MOUNTAINDALE	NY	12763	(914) 434-3612
BETH MIRIAM-LEAH PINESBRIDGE ROAD	MT KISCO	NY	10549	(914) 387-0422
FARM SETTLEMENT OF NITRA, YESHIVA PINESBRIDGE ROAD	MT KISCO	NY	10549	(914) 666-8746
TALMUD TORAH BAIS YECHIEL-YESHIVA OF NITRA PINESBRIDGE ROAD	MT KISCO	NY	10549	(914) 387-0422
YESHIVA FARM SETTLEMENT SCHOOL R.D. 4 BOX 428	MT KISCO	NY	10549	(914) 387-0422
SOLOMON SCHECHTER DAY SCHOOL OF ROCKLAND COUNTY ROUTE 45	NEW CITY	NY	10956	(914) 354-5500
OHR HAMEIR HIGH SCHOOL 3 BOULEVARD	NEW ROCHELLE	NY	10801	(914) 632-6192
OHR HAMEIR THEOLOGICAL SEMINARY AND H.S. 3 BOULEVARD	NEW ROCHELLE	NY	10801	(914) 828-6520
GRUSS GIRLS SCHOOL OF NEW SQUARE 15 ROOSEVELT AVENUE	NEW SQUARE	NY	10977	(914) 354-5778
YESHIVA OF NEW SQUARE 91 WASHINGTON AVENUE	NEW SQUARE	NY	10977	(914) 354-5591
ABRAHAM HESCHEL SCHOOL 270 WEST 89TH STREET	NEW YORK	NY	10024	(212) 595-7087
BETH JACOB SCHOOL 142 BROOME STREET	NEW YORK	NY	10002	(212) 473-4500
BNAI JESHURUN DAY SCHOOL 270 WEST 89TH STREET	NEW YORK	NY	10024	(212) 787-7600
CHOFETZ CHAIM, MESIVTA 346 WEST 89TH STREET	NEW YORK	NY	10024	(212) 362-1435
LINCOLN SQUARE SYNAGOGUE NURSERY SCHOOL 200 AMSTERDAM AVENUE	NEW YORK	NY	10023	(212) 874-6100
MANHATTAN DAY SCHOOL-YESHIVA OHR TORAH 310 WEST 75TH STREET	NEW YORK	NY	10023	(212) 595-6800
MESIVTA RABBI SAMSON RAPHAEL HIRSCH 220 BENNETT AVENUE	NEW YORK	NY	10040	(212) 568-6200
MESIVTA TIFERETH JERUSALEM 141-7 EAST BROADWAY	NEW YORK	NY	10002	(212) 964-2830
PARK EAST DAY SCHOOL-EAST SIDE HEBREW INSTITUTE 164 EAST 68TH STREET	NEW YORK	NY	10021	(212) 737-6900
PARK EAST-ESHI DAY SCHOOL 164 EAST 68TH STREET	NEW YORK	NY	10021	(212) 737-6900
RABBI JOSEPH KONVITZ, YESHIVA 313 HENRY STREET	NEW YORK	NY	10002	(212) 473-5078
RABBI MOSES SOLOVEICHIK, YESHIVA 560 WEST 185TH STREET	NEW YORK	NY	10033	(212) 923-2900
RABBI SAMSON RAPHAEL HIRSCH, MESIVTA 91 BENNETT AVENUE	NEW YORK	NY	10033	(212) 568-6200
RABBI SAMSON RAPHAEL HIRSCH, YESHIVA 85-91 BENNETT AVENUE	NEW YORK	NY	10033	(212) 568-6200
RAMAZ-UPPER SCHOOL 60 EAST 78TH STREET	NEW YORK	NY	10028	(212) 427-1000
RAMAZ-LOWER SCHOOL 125 EAST 85TH STREET	NEW YORK	NY	10028	(212) 427-1000
RODEPH SHOLOM DAY SCHOOL 10 WEST 84TH STREET	NEW YORK	NY	10024	(212) 362-8800
RODEPH SHOLOM DAY SCHOOL 10 WEST 84TH STREET	NEW YORK	NY	10024	(212) 362-8769
SOLOMON SCHECHTER DAY SCHOOL ASSOCIATION 155 FIFTH AVENUE	NEW YORK	NY	10010	(212) 533-7800
THE RABBI JOSEPH H.LOOKSTEIN UPPER SCHOOL OF RAMAZ 60 EAST 78TH STREET	NEW YORK	NY	10021	(212) 427-1000
TIFERETH JERUSALEM, MESIVTA 147 EAST BROADWAY	NEW YORK	NY	10002	(212) 964-2830
TIFERETH JERUSALEM, YESHIVA 145 EAST BROADWAY	NEW YORK	NY	10002	(212) 964-2830
TONYA SOLOVEITCHIK-YESHIVA UNIVERSITY H.S. FOR GIRLS 425 5TH AVENUE	NEW YORK	NY	10016	(212) 481-3746
YESHIVA CHOFETZ CHAIM 346 WEST 89TH STREET	NEW YORK	NY	10024	(212) 363-1435
YESHIVA HECHAL MOSHE-BETH JACOB SCHOOL 303 WEST 91ST STREET	NEW YORK	NY	10024	(212) 877-8709
YESHIVA RABBI JOSEPH KONVITZ 313 HENRY STREET	NEW YORK	NY	10002	(212) 473-1000
YESHIVA RABBI MOSES SOLOVEITCHIK 560 WEST 185TH STREET	NEW YORK	NY	10033	(212) 923-2900
YESHIVA RABBI SAMSON RAPHAEL HIRSCH 85-93 BENNETT AVENUE	NEW YORK	NY	10033	(212) 568-6200
YESHIVA RABBI SAMSON RAPHAEL HIRSCH-BETH JACOB HIGH SCHOOL 85-93 BENNETT AVENUE	NEW YORK	NY	10033	(212) 568-6200
YESHIVA UNIVERSITY HIGH SCHOOL FOR BOYS 2540 AMSTERDAM AVENUE	NEW YORK	NY	10033	(212) 960-5345
YESHIVA UNIVERSITY HIGH SCHOOL FOR GIRLS 425 FIFTH AVENUE	NEW YORK	NY	10016	(212) 481-3746
HEBREW DAY SCHOOL OF ORANGE COUNTY 290 NORTH STREET	NEWBURGH	NY	12550	(914) 343-8588
YESHIVA DAY SCHOOL OF QUEENS 107-01 CROSS BAY BLVD	OZONE PARK	NY	11417	
YESHIVA DAY SCHOOL OF SOUTH QUEENS 115-70 LEFFERTS BLVD	OZONE PARK	NY	11420	(718) 641-0100
HANC MID-ISLAND HEBREW DAY SCHOOL JOYCE ROAD	PLAINVIEW	NY	11803	(516) 681-5922
HEBREW ACADEMY OF NASSAU COUNTY-MID-ISLAND SCHOOL JOYCE ROAD	PLAINVIEW	NY	11803	(516) 681-5922
MESORAT YISRAEL ACADEMY 98-12 66TH AVENUE	REGO PARK	NY	11374	(718) 459-1274
KINNERET DAY SCHOOL 2600 NETHERLAND AVENUE	RIVERDALE	NY	10463	(212) 584-0900
SAR ACADEMY 655 W. 254TH STREET	RIVERDALE	NY	10471	(212) 549-5160
SALANTER AKIBA RIVERDALE ACADEMY 655 WEST 254 STREET	RIVERDALE	NY	10471	(212) 549-5160
HILLEL SCHOOL OF ROCHESTER 191 FAIRFIELD DRIVE	ROCHESTER	NY	14620	(716) 271-6877
TALMUDICAL INSTITUTE OF UPSTATE NEW YORK 769 PARK AVENUE	ROCHESTER	NY	14607	(716) 473-2810
ROBERT GORDIS DAY SCHOOL OF TEMPLE BETH EL 445 BEACH 135TH STREET	ROCKAWAY PARK	NY	11694	(718) 634-7711
HEBREW ACADEMY OF SUFFOLK COUNTY 525 VETERANS HIGHWAY	SMITHTOWN	NY	11787	(516) 543-3377
YESHIVA GEDOLAH ZICHRON MOSHE ELEMENTARY AND HIGH SCHOOL LAUREL PARK ROAD	SOUTH FALLSBURG	NY	12779	(914) 434-5240
BETH ESTHER D'SATMAR 89 SOUTH MAIN STREET, P.O. BOX 188	SPRING VALLEY	NY	10977	(914) 425-6758
BETH ESTHER D'SATMAR 5502 COMMERCE STREET	SPRING VALLEY	NY	10977	(914) 425-6758
UNITED TALMUDICAL ACADEMY 89 SOUTH MAIN STREET, P.O. BOX 188	SPRING VALLEY	NY	10977	(914) 425-0392
UNITED TALMUDICAL BOYS ACADEMY 89 SOUTH MAIN	SPRING VALLEY	NY	10977	(914) 356-4480
UNITED TALMUDICAL GIRLS ACADEMY 206 VIOLA ROAD	SPRING VALLEY	NY	10977	(914) 425-6758
JEWISH FOUNDATION SCHOOL 20 PARK HILL CIRCLE	STATEN ISLAND	NY	10304	(718) 981-6700
MESIVTA OF STATEN ISLAND 1870 DRUMGOOLE ROAD, E	STATEN ISLAND	NY	10309	(718) 356-2101
RABBI JACOB JOSEPH SCHOOL 3495 RICHMOND ROAD	STATEN ISLAND	NY	10306	(718) 979-6333
YESHIVA TIFERET SHMUEL EZRA JEWISH FOUNDATION SCHOOL OF S.I. 20 PARK HILL CIRCLE	STATEN ISLAND	NY	10304	(718) 981-6700
YESHIVA TIFERETH SHMUEL EZRA 20 PARK HILL CIRCLE	STATEN ISLAND	NY	10304	(718) 981-6700
YESHIVA OF STATEN ISLAND 1870 DRUMGOOLE ROAD EAST	STATEN ISLAND	NY	10309	(718) 356-4323
BAS TORAH ACADEMY 4 CAMPBELL AVENUE	SUFFERN	NY	10901	(914) 357-0774
CHOFETZ CHAIM, YESHIVA 24 HIGHVIEW ROAD	SUFFERN	NY	10901	(914) 357-9821
MAX GILBERT HEBREW ACADEMY 5655 THOMPSON ROAD - P.O. BOX 189	SYRACUSE	NY	13214	(315) 446-1900
KADIMAH SCHOOL OF BUFFALO 300 FRIES ROAD	TONAWANDA	NY	14150	(716) 836-6903
HEBREW ACADEMY 215 OAK STREET	UNIONDALE	NY	11553	(516) 538-8161
HEBREW ACADEMY OF NASSAU COUNTY 215 OAK STREET	UNIONDALE	NY	11553	(516) 538-8161
HEBREW ACADEMY OF NASSAU COUNTY - BROOKDALE HIGH SCHOOL 215 OAK STREET	UNIONDALE	NY	11553	(516) 538-8161
HEBREW ACADEMY OF NASSAU COUNTY - MOSES HORNSTEIN JR. H.S. 215 OAK STREET	UNIONDALE	NY	11553	(516) 538-8161
HILLEL DAY SCHOOL 2310 ONEIDA STREET	UTICA	NY	13501	(315) 724-7317
HEBREW ACADEMY OF NASSAU COUNTY 609 HEMPSTEAD AVENUE	WEST HEMPSTEAD	NY	11552	(516) 485-7786
HEBREW DAY SCHOOL OF WESTCHESTER 311 CENTRAL PARK AVENUE	YONKERS	NY	10704	(914) 965-7082
MESIVTA OF YONKERS 63 HAMILTON AVENUE	YONKERS	NY	10705	(914) 963-1951
HILLEL ACADEMY OF AKRON 750 WHITE POND DRIVE	AKRON	OH	44320	(216) 836-0419
AGNON SCHOOL, THE 26500 SHAKER BLVD	BEACHWOOD	OH	44122	(216) 464-4055
CINCINNATI HEBREW DAY SCHOOL 7855 DAWN ROAD	CINCINNATI	OH	45237	(513) 761-1614
YAVNEH DAY SCHOOL 1636 SUMMIT ROAD	CINCINNATI	OH	45237	(513) 984-3770
AGNON SCHOOL 26500 SHAKER BLVD	CLEVELAND	OH	44122	(216) 464-4055
AKIVA HIGH SCHOOL 26500 SHAKER BLVD	CLEVELAND	OH	44122	(216) 464-4370
BET SEFER MIZRACHI 1970 SOUTH TAYLOR ROAD	CLEVELAND	OH	44118	(216) 932-8633
HEBREW ACADEMY OF CLEVELAND 1860 SOUTH TAYLOR ROAD	CLEVELAND	OH	44118	(216) 382-6495
MOSDOS OHR HATORAH - BOYS DIVISION 1508 WARRENSVILLE CENTER ROAD	CLEVELAND	OH	44121	(216) 382-6248
MOSDOS OHR HATORAH - GIRLS DIVISION 3246 DESOTA AVENUE	CLEVELAND	OH	44118	(216) 321-1547
RATNER DAY SCHOOL 4900 ANDERSON ROAD	CLEVELAND	OH	44124	(216) 291-0034
TELSHE HIGH SCHOOL 28400 EUCLID AVENUE	CLEVELAND	OH	44092	(216) 944-0299
YESHIVATH ADATH BNAI ISRAEL 2308 WARRENSVILLE CENTER ROAD	CLEVELAND	OH	44118	(216) 932-7664
HEBREW ACADEMY OF CLEVELAND 1860 SOUTH TAYLOR ROAD	CLEVELAND HEIGHTS	OH	44118	(216) 321-5838
HEBREW ACADEMY OF CLEVELAND-FOREIGN DIVISION (RUSSIAN STUDENTS) 1970 SOUTH TAYLOR ROAD	CLEVELAND HEIGHTS	OH	44118	(216) 321-2941
MOSDOS OR HATORAH 1508 WARRENSVILLE CENTER ROAD	CLEVELAND HEIGHTS	OH	44121	(216) 382-6248
YAVNE HIGH SCHOOL FOR GIRLS 1860 SOUTH TAYLOR ROAD	CLEVELAND HEIGHTS	OH	44118	(216) 321-5838
COLUMBUS TORAH ACADEMY 181 NOE-BIXBY ROAD	COLUMBUS	OH	43213	(614) 864-0299
HILLEL ACADEMY OF DAYTON 100 EAST WOODBURY DRIVE	DAYTON	OH	45415	(513) 277-8966
MESIVTA HIGH SCHOOL OF HEBREW ACADEMY OF CLEVELAND 1975 LYNDWAY	LYNDHURST	OH	44121	(216) 382-6495
HEBREW ACADEMY OF TOLEDO 2727 KENWOOD BLVD	TOLEDO	OH	43606	(419) 531-8960
TELSHE HIGH SCHOOL 28400 EUCLID AVENUE	WYCKLIFFE	OH	44092	(216) 943-5300
HERITAGE ACADEMY 1719 SOUTH OWASSO	TULSA	OK	74120	(918) 584-2596
HILLEL ACADEMY OF PORTLAND 920 N.W. 25TH AVENUE	PORTLAND	OR	97210	(503) 223-0155
JEWISH DAY SCHOOL OF ALLENTOWN 2313 PENNSYLVANIA STREET	ALLENTOWN	PA	18104	(215) 437-0721
TORAH ACADEMY OF GREATER PHILADELPHIA WYNNEWOOD AND ARGYLE ROADS	ARDMORE	PA	19003	(215) 642-7870
BETH JACOB SCHOOLS OF PHILADELPHIA HIGH SCHOOL ROAD AND MONTGOMERY AVENUE	ELKINS PARK	PA	19117	(215) 635-6805
YESHIVA ACADEMY OF HARRISBURG 100 VAUGHN STREET	HARRISBURG	PA	17110	(717) 238-2074
ISRAEL BEN ZION ACADEMY THIRD AVENUE AND INSTITUTE LANE	KINGSTON	PA	18704	(717) 287-9608
LANCASTER JEWISH DAY SCHOOL 2120 OREGON PIKE	LANCASTER	PA	17602	(717) 560-1904
AKIBA HEBREW ACADEMY 223 N. HIGHLAND AVENUE	MERION STATION	PA	19066	(215) 839-3540
BETH JACOB - LOWER GIRLS SCHOOL PENWAY & FRIENDSHIP STREETS	PHILADELPHIA	PA	19111	
BETH JACOB SCHOOL HIGHSCHOOL ROAD & MONTGOMERY AVENUE	PHILADELPHIA	PA	19124	(215) 635-6805
HEBREW ACADEMY OF N.E. PHILADELPHIA 97-68 VERREE ROAD	PHILADELPHIA	PA	19115	(215) 969-3956
TALMUDICAL YESHIVA OF PHILADELPHIA 6063 DREXEL ROAD	PHILADELPHIA	PA	19131	(215) 477-1000
COMMUNITY DAY SCHOOL 6401 FORBES AVENUE	PITTSBURGH	PA	15217	(412) 521-5127
HILLEL ACADEMY OF PITTSBURGH 5685 BEACON STREET	PITTSBURGH	PA	15217	(412) 521-8131
NECHAMA MINSKY SCHOOL FOR GIRLS 2100 WIGHTMAN STREET	PITTSBURGH	PA	15217	(412) 422-7779
YESHIVA ACHEI TMIMIM FOR BOYS 2408 5TH AVENUE	PITTSBURGH	PA	15213	(412) 681-2446
BAIS YAAKOV INSTITUTE 901 OLIVE STREET	SCRANTON	PA	18510	(717) 342-4247

HILLEL ACADEMY 900 GIBSON STREET ... SCRANTON **PA** 18510 (717) 343-7837
SCRANTON HEBREW DAY SCHOOL 540 MONROE AVENUE ... SCRANTON **PA** 18510 (717) 346-1576
YESHIVA BETH MOSHE 930 HICKORY STREET - P.O. BOX 1141 ... SCRANTON **PA** 18505 (717) 346-1747
ABRAMS HEBREW ACADEMY 31 WEST COLLEGE AVENUE ... YARDLEY **PA** 19067
NEW ENGLAND ACADEMY OF TORAH 450 ELMGROVE AVENUE ... PROVIDENCE **RI** 02906 (401) 331-5327
PROVIDENCE HEBREW DAY SCHOOL 450 ELMGROVE AVENUE ... PROVIDENCE **RI** 02906 (401) 331-5327
ADDLESTONE HEBREW ACADEMY 182 RUTLEDGE AVENUE ... CHARLESTON **SC** 29403 (803) 577-6597
CHATTANOOGA JEWISH DAY SCHOOL
5326 LYNNLAND TERRACE ... CHATTANOOGA **TN** 37411 (615) 892-2337
BAIS YAACOV 392 CONWELL ROAD ... MEMPHIS **TN** 38117 (901) 685-7451
MEMPHIS HEBREW ACADEMY
390 SOUTH WHITE STATION ROAD - P.O. BOX 171154 ... MEMPHIS **TN** 38117 (901) 682-2409
YESHIVA OF THE SOUTH 5255 MEADOWCREST COVE ... MEMPHIS **TN** 38117 (901) 767-4140
AKIVA SCHOOL 3600 WEST END AVENUE ... NASHVILLE **TN** 37205 (615) 292-6614
AKIBA ACADEMY OF DALLAS 6210 CHURCHILL WAY ... DALLAS **TX** 75230 (214) 239-7248
TORAH ACADEMY HIGH SCHOOL OF TEXAS 7120 SPRING VALLEY ROAD ... DALLAS **TX** 75240 (214) 386-9213
TORAH HIGH SCHOOL OF TEXAS 7120 SPRING VALLEY ROAD ... DALLAS **TX** 75240 (214) 233-6766
EL PASO HEBREW DAY SCHOOL 220 EAST CLIFF STREET ... EL PASO **TX** 79902 (915) 532-4484
FORT WORTH HEBREW DAY SCHOOL 4050 SOUTH HULEN ... FORT WORTH **TX** 76109 (817) 731-9179
HEBREW ACADEMY 5435 SOUTH BRAESWOOD ... HOUSTON **TX** 77096 (713) 723-7170
TORAH DAY SCHOOL OF HOUSTON-LUBAVITCH
10900 FONDREN ROAD ... HOUSTON **TX** 77096 (713) 777-2000
THE JEWISH DAY SCHOOL OF SAN ANTONIO
703 TRAFALGAR ROAD ... SAN ANTONIO **TX** 78216 (512) 341-0735
GESHER JEWISH DAY SCHOOL 2908 VALLEY DRIVE ... ALEXANDRIA **VA** 22302 (703) 998-6733
HENRIETTA KURZER HEBREW ACADEMY
1815 CHESTNUT AVENUE ... NEWPORT NEWS **VA** 23607
THE JOSEPH AND FANNIE RUDLIN TORAH ACADEMY
6801 PATTERSON AVENUE ... RICHMOND **VA** 23226 (804) 288-7610
HEBREW ACADEMY OF TIDEWATER 1244 THOMPKINS LANE ... VIRGINIA BEACH **VA** 23464 (804) 424-4327
SEATTLE HEBREW ACADEMY 1617 INTERLAKEN DRIVE EAST ... SEATTLE **WA** 98112 (206) 323-5750
YESHIVAT OR HAZAFON 1617 INTERLAKEN DRIVE EAST ... SEATTLE **WA** 98112 (206) 323-5750
HILLEL ACADEMY 4650 NORTH PORT WASHINGTON ROAD ... MILWAUKEE **WI** 53212 (414) 962-9545
TORAH ACADEMY OF MILWAUKEE 1144 EAST HENRY CLAY ... MILWAUKEE **WI** 53217 (414) 963-0621
WISCONSIN INSTITUTE FOR TORAH STUDY 3288 NORTH LAKE DRIVE ... MILWAUKEE **WI** 53211 (414) 963-9317
AKIVA ACADEMY 19-2323 OAKMOOR DRIVE ... CALGARY **AT** T2V HT2 (403) 252-0339
EDMONTON TALMUD TORAH 1312 106TH AVENUE ... EDMONTON **AT** T5N 1A3 (403) 455-9114
VANCOUVER TALMUD TORAH 998 WEST 26TH AVENUE ... VANCOUVER **BC** V5Z 2G1 (604) 736-7307
JOSEPH WOLINSKY COLLEGIATE 437 MATHESON AVENUE ... WINNIPEG **MB** R2W 0E1 (204) 589-4311
RAMAH HEBREW SCHOOL 705 LANKARK STREET ... WINNIPEG **MB** R3N 1M4 (204) 453-4136
TORAH ACADEMY 620 BROCK STREET ... WINNIPEG **MB** R3N 0Z4 (204) 489-6262
WINNIPEG HEBREW SCHOOLS 427-437 MATHESON AVENUE ... WINNIPEG **MB** R2W 0E1 (204) 586-5822
WINNIPEG HEBREW SCHOOLS TALMUD TORAH
427 MATHESON AVENUE ... WINNIPEG **MB** R2W 0E1 (204) 586-5822
BETH ISRAEL RELIGIOUS SCHOOL 1480 OXFORD STREET ... HALIFAX **NS** (902) 422-1301
ASSOCIATED HEBREW SCHOOLS OF TORONTO - BETH DAVID BRANCH
55 YEOMANS ROAD ... DOWNSVIEW **ON** M3H 3J7 (416) 630-4162
ASSOCIATED HEBREW SCHOOLS OF TORONTO - BETH EMETH BRANCH
100 ELDER STREET ... DOWNSVIEW **ON** M3H 5G7 (416) 223-4845
COMMUNITY HEBREW ACADEMY 200 WILMINGTON AVENUE ... DOWNSVIEW **ON** M3H 5J8 (416) 636-5984
NETIVOT HATORAH DAY SCHOOL 55 YEOMANS ROAD ... DOWNSVIEW **ON** M3H 3J7 (416) 636-4050
OHR CHAIM BNAI AKIVA YESHIVA HIGH SCHOOL
159 ALMORE AVENUE ... DOWNSVIEW **ON** M3H 2H9 (416) 630-6772
OR HAEMET DAY SCHOOL 37 SOUTHBOURNE AVENUE ... DOWNSVIEW **ON** M3H 1A4 (416) 635-9881
OR HAEMET SEFARDIC SCHOOL 210 WILSON STREET ... DOWNSVIEW **ON** M5M 3B1 (416) 630-3216
SHE'ARIM HEBREW DAY SCHOOL 100 ELDERS STREET ... DOWNSVIEW **ON** M3H 5G7 (416) 630-8247
ULPANAT OROT 45 CANYON AVENUE ... DOWNSVIEW **ON** M3H 3S4 (416) 638-5434
ULPANAT OROT GIRL'S SCHOOL-NACHMAN SOKOL TORAH CENTRE
45 CANYON AVENUE ... DOWNSVIEW **ON** M3H 3S4 (416) 638-5434
YESHIVA OR CHAIM-ISRAEL & GOLDA KOSCHITZKY TORAH CENTER
159 ALMORE AVENUE ... DOWNSVIEW **ON** M3H 2H9 (416) 630-6772
HAMILTON HEBREW ACADEMY 60 DOW AVENUE ... HAMILTON **ON** L8S 1W4 (416) 528-0330
LONDON COMMUNITY HEBREW DAY SCHOOL 247 EPWORTH AVENUE ... LONDON **ON** N6A 2M2 (519) 439-8419
HILLEL ACADEMY 1400 COLDREY AVENUE ... OTTAWA **ON** K1Z 7P9 (613) 728-1759
HILLEL ACADEMY-OTTAWA TALMUD TORAH BOARD
453 RIDEAY STREET ... OTTAWA **ON** K1N 5Z3 (613) 235-1841
OTTAWA TORAH INSTITUTE 2310 VIRGINIA DRIVE ... OTTAWA **ON** K1H 6S2 (613) 521-9700
ASSOCIATED HEBREW SCHOOLS OF TORONTO
3630 BATHURST STREET ... TORONTO **ON** M6A 2E3 (416) 789-7471
BAIS YAAKOV OF TORONTO 85 STORMONT AVENUE ... TORONTO **ON** M5N 2C3 (416) 783-6181
BETH JACOB HIGH SCHOOL FOR GIRLS 410 LAWRENCE AVENUE WEST ... TORONTO **ON** M5M 1C2 (416) 787-4949
BIALIK HEBREW DAY SCHOOL 12 VIEWMOUNT AVENUE ... TORONTO **ON** M6C 1S6 (416) 783-3346
EITZ CHAIM YESHIVA 1 VIEWMOUNT AVENUE ... TORONTO **ON** M6B 1T2 (416) 789-4366
TALMUD TORAH OF BOBOV 250 CARMICHAEL AVENUE ... TORONTO **ON** M5M 2X4 (416) 781-3056
YESHIVA YESODEI HATORAH 567 LAWRENCE AVENUE WEST ... TORONTO **ON** M6A 1A5 (416) 789-1891
ASSOCIATED HEBREW SCHOOLS OF TORONTO-HURWICH EDUCATION CNTR.
252 FINCH AVENUE WEST ... WILLOWDALE **ON** M2R 1M9 (416) 223-4845
ASSOCIATED HEBREW SCHOOLS OF TORONTO - LESLIE BRANCH
6100 LESLIE STREET ... WILLOWDALE **ON** M2H 3J1 (416) 494-7666
EITZ CHAIM YESHIVA-WILLOWDALE 475 PATRICIA AVENUE ... WILLOWDALE **ON** M2R 2N1 (416) 225-1187
LEO BAECK DAY SCHOOL 34 KENTON DRIVE ... WILLOWDALE **ON** M2R 2H8 (416) 222-9220
NER ISRAEL YESHIVA COLLEGE OF TORONTO
625 FINCH AVENUE WEST ... WILLOWDALE **ON** M2R 1N8 (416) 636-2360
UNITED TALMUD TORAHS OF MONTREAL
931 EMERSON DRIVE ... CHOMEDEY, LAVAL **QU** H7W 3Y5 (514) 681-9146
HEBREW ACADEMY OF MONTREAL 8205 MACKLE ROAD ... COTE ST. LUC **QU** H4W 1B1 (514) 489-8289
UNITED TALMUD TORAHS OF MONTREAL 5554 ROBINSON AVENUE ... COTE ST. LUC **QU** H4W 2P8 (514) 484-1151
HEBREW FOUNDATION SCHOOL OF CONGREGATION BETH TIKVAH
2 HOPE DRIVE ... DOLLARD DES ORMEAUX **QU** H9A 2V5 (514) 684-6270
BETH ESTHER SCHOOL 5402 PARK AVENUE ... MONTREAL **QU** H2V 3G7 (514) 272-4998
BETH JACOB SCHOOL OF MONTREAL 1750 GLENDALE AVENUE ... MONTREAL **QU** H2V 1B3 (514) 739-3614
BETH RIVKAH ACADEMY FOR GIRLS 5001 VEZINA AVENUE ... MONTREAL **QU** H3W 1C2 (514) 731-3681
BETH ZION HEBREW ACADEMY 5740 HUDSON AVENUE ... MONTREAL **QU** H4W 2K5 (514) 489-8411
BIALIK H.S. OF THE JEWISH PEOPLE'S SCHOOL & PERETZ SCHOOLS
7946 WAVELL ROAD ... MONTREAL **QU** (514) 489-8291
FIRST MESIVTA OF CANADA 2325 EKERS AVENUE ... MONTREAL **QU** (514) 342-0977
HERZLIAH HIGH SCHOOL 805 DORAIS ... MONTREAL **QU** H4M 2A2 (514) 336-7490
HERZLIAH HIGH SCHOOL 4840 ST. KEVIN AVENUE ... MONTREAL **QU** H3W 1P2 (514) 739-2291
JEWISH PEOPLE'S SCHOOLS & PERETZ SCHOOLS
570 VAN HORNE AVENUE ... MONTREAL **QU** H3W 1J6 (514) 731-7741
MEOR HAGOLA RABBINICAL COLLEGE OF CANADA
5815 JEANNE MANCE AVENUE ... MONTREAL **QU** H2V 4K9 (514) 274-8467
RABBINICAL COLLEGE OF CANADA - TOMCHE TMIMIM LUBAVITCH
6405 WESTBURY AVENUE ... MONTREAL **QU** H3W 2X5 (514) 735-2201
UNITED TALMUD TORAHS OF MONTREAL 4850 ST. KEVIN AVENUE ... MONTREAL **QU** H3W 1P2 (514) 739-2291
UNITED TALMUD TORAHS OF MONTREAL 4894 ST. KEVIN AVENUE ... MONTREAL **QU** H3W 1P2 (514) 739-2291
UNITED TALMUD TORAHS OF MONTREAL 2250 RUE DE L'EGLISE ... MONTREAL **QU** H3M 1G5 (514) 337-4566
YESHIVA CHASIDEI BELZ 5340 JEANNE MANCE STREET ... MONTREAL **QU** H2V 4K4 (514) 270-5086
YESHIVA GEDOLA MERKAZ HATORAH 6155 DEACON ROAD ... MONTREAL **QU** H3S 2P4 (514) 735-6611
YESHIVA TORAS MOSHE 5214 ST. URBAIN ... MONTREAL **QU** (514) 273-1698
BAIS MALKA 1495 DUCHARME AVENUE ... OUTREMENT **QU** H2V 1E8 (514) 279-8033
BNOS YERUSHALAYIM 1495 DUCHARME AVENUE ... OUTREMENT **QU** H2V 1E8 (514) 271-9464
HEBREW ACADEMY OF MONTREAL 1500 DUCHARME AVENUE ... OUTREMENT **QU** H2V 1G1 (514) 274-3573
UNITED ORTHODOX JEWISH SCHOOL 1495 DUCHARME AVENUE ... OUTREMENT **QU** H2V 1E8 (514) 273-1698
THE AKIVA SCHOOL 1000 LUCERNE ROAD ... TOWN OF MT. ROYAL **QU** H3R 2H9 (514) 731-3491
SEPHARDIC ACADEMY OF MONTREAL (ECOLE SEPHARDE)
805 TASSE ... VILLE ST. LAURENT **QU** 4HL 1N8 (514) 744-2861

DAY SCHOOLS - SOLOMON SCHECHTER

SOLOMON SCHECHTER DAY SCHOOL OF TUCSON 8016 E. 7TH STREET ... TUCSON **AZ** 85710 (704) 366-6390
JEWISH STUDIES INSTITUTE DAY SCHOOL 1770 W. CERRITOS AVENUE ... ANAHEIM **CA** 92804 (714) 535-3665
KADIMA HEBREW ACADEMY (K-7) 22600 SHERMAN WAY ... CANOGA PARK **CA** 91307 (213) 346-0849
JEWISH STUDIES INSTITUTE DAY SCHOOL (N-7)
12181 BUARO STREET ... GARDEN GROVE **CA** 92640 (714) 636-3361
AKIBA ACADEMY (K-7) 10400 WILSHIRE BLVD ... LOS ANGELES **CA** 90024 (213) 475-6401
GOLDA MEIR ACADEMY NEW JEWISH HIGH SCHOOL
1317 N. CRESCENT HTS. ... LOS ANGELES **CA** 90046 (213) 656-3060
HERZL SCHOOLS (7-9) 1039 S. LA CIENEGA BLVD ... LOS ANGELES **CA** 90035 (213) 652-1854
ADAT ARI-EL DAY SCHOOL (K-6) 5540 LAUREL CANYON BLVD ... N. HOLLYWOOD **CA** 91607 (818) 766-3506
YAVNEH DAY SCHOOL 19700 PROSPECT RD. ... SARATOGA **CA** 95070 (408) 446-2956
ETZ CHAIM DAY SCHOOL PO BOX 246 ... WALNUT CREEK **CA** 94596 (415) 934-9449
SOLOMON SCHECHTER ACADEMY OF NEW LONDON COUNTY (K-6)
660 OCEAN AVENUE ... NEW LONDON **CT** 06320 (203) 443-5589
SOLOMON SCHECHTER DAY SCHOOL OF GREATER HARTFORD (K-6)
160 MOHEGAN DRIVE ... WEST HARTFORD **CT** 06117 (203) 233-1418
EZRA ACADEMY (K-8) 75 RIMMON ROAD ... WOODBRIDGE **CT** 06525 (203) 389-5500
SOLOMON SCHECHTER DAY SCHOOL - JACKSONVILLE JEWISH CTR. (N-7)
3662 CROWN POINT ROAD ... JACKSONVILLE **FL** 32217 (904) 268-6736
BETH DAVID SOLOMON SCHECHTER DAY SCHOOL (N-6)
7500 S.W. 120TH STREET ... MIAMI **FL** 33156 (305) 238-2601
LEHRMAN DAY SCHOOL OF TEMPLE EMANU-EL (N-9)
727 77TH STREET ... MIAMI BEACH **FL** 33141 (305) 866-2771
SARASOTA HEBREW DAY SCHOOL (K-6) 1050 S. TUTTLE AVENUE ... SARASOTA **FL** 33577 (813) 955-8121
PINELLAS COUNTY JEWISH DAY SCHOOL (K-3)
301 59TH STREET N. ... ST. PETERSBURG **FL** 33710 (813) 381-8111
HARRY EPSTEIN SCHOOL (1-8) 600 PEACHTREE BATTLE AVENUE N.W. ... ATLANTA **GA** 30327 (404) 351-7623
AKIBA-SCHECHTER JEWISH DAY SCHOOL (1-3)
5200 S. HYDE PARK BLVD ... CHICAGO **IL** 60615 (312) 493-8880
SAGER SOLOMON SCHECHTER DAY SCHOOL (K-6) 350 LEE ROAD ... NORTHBROOK **IL** 60062 (312) 498-2100
SOLOMON SCHECHTER DAY SCHOOL OF SKOKIE (K-6)
9301 GROSS POINT ROAD ... SKOKIE **IL** 60076 (312) 679-6270
SOLOMON SCHECHTER SECONDARY EDUCATION DEPARTMENT (7-12)
9301 GROSS POINT ROAD ... SKOKIE **IL** 60076 (312) 679-6270
SOLOMON SCHECHTER DAY SCHOOL OF THE MERRIMACK VALLEY
514 MAIN STREET ... HAVERHILL **MA** 01830 (617) 887-9790
SOLOMON SCHECHTER DAY SCHOOL 60 STEIN CIRCLE ... NEWTON CENTRE **MA** 02159 (617) 964-7765
HILLEL ACADEMY OF THE NORTH SHORE (K-9)
837 HUMPHREY STREET ... SWAMPSCOTT **MA** 01907 (617) 599-3837
SOLOMON SCHECHTER DAY SCHOOL OF WORCESTER (K-6)
633 SALISBURY STREET ... WORCESTER **MA** 01609 (617) 799-7888
SOLOMON SCHECHTER DAY SCHOOL (K-2) 8100 STEVENSON ROAD ... BALTIMORE **MD** 21208 (301) 486-6400
CHARLES E. SMITH JEWISH DAY SCHOOL (9-12)
1901 E. JEFFERSON STREET ... ROCKVILLE **MD** 20852 (301) 881-1408
CHARLES E. SMITH JEWISH DAY SCHOOL (K-6)
1901 E. JEFFERSON STREET ... ROCKVILLE **MD** 20852 (301) 881-1403
HEBREW DAY SCHOOL OF ANN ARBOR (K-6) 1920 AUSTIN ... ANN ARBOR **MI** 48104 (313) 668-6770
HILLEL DAY SCHOOL (K-9) 32200 MIDDLEBELT ROAD ... FARMINGTON **MI** 48018 (313) 851-2394
SOLOMON SCHECHTER DAY SCHOOL OF ST. LOUIS (K-2)
324 S. MASON ROAD ... ST. LOUIS **MO** 63141 (314) 576-6177
JEWISH DAY SCHOOL OF OMAHA 12604 PACIFIC ST. ... OMAHA **NE** 68154 (402) 334-0517
NORTH CAROLINA HEBREW DAY ACADEMY (K-6) P.O.B. 220176 ... CHARLOTTE **NC** 28222 (704) 366-6390
B'NAI SHALOM SYNAGOGUE DAY SCHOOL (K-6)
904 WINVIEW DRIVE ... GREENSBORO **NC** 27410 (919) 855-5091
SOLOMON SCHECHTER DAY SCHOOL OF CENTRAL NEW JERSEY (K-1)
NORTH BRIDGE STREET, P.O. BOX 6007 ... BRIDGEWATER **NJ** 08807 (201) 722-2089
HARRY B. KELLMAN ACADEMY (N-8) 2901 WEST CHAPEL AVENUE ... CHERRY HILL **NJ** 08002 (609) 667-1300

Name / Address	City	State	Zip	Phone
SOLOMON SCHECHTER DAY SCHOOL OF ESSEX & UNION (K-8) 721 ORANGE AVENUE	CRANFORD	NJ	07016	(201) 272-3400
SOLOMON SCHECHTER HIGH SCHOOL OF ESSEX & UNION (9-12) 721 ORANGE AVENUE	CRANFORD	NJ	07016	(201) 272-3400
SOLOMON SCHECHTER DAY SCHOOL OF EAST BRUNSWICK (N-6) 511 RYDERS LANE	EAST BRUNSWICK	NJ	08816	(201) 238-7971
SOLOMON SCHECHTER DAY SCHOOL OF BERGEN COUNTY (K-7) 153 TENAFLY ROAD	ENGLEWOOD	NJ	07631	(201) 879-1152
SOLOMON SCHECHTER ACADEMY OF OCEAN & MONMOUTH COUNTIES (K-8) 101 KENT ROAD	HOWELL	NJ	07731	(201) 370-1767
SOLOMON SCHECHTER DAY SCHOOL OF MARLBORO PO BOX 203	MARLBORO	NJ	07746	(201) 431-5525
SOLOMON SCHECHTER DAY SCHOOL OF MARLBORO (N-2) P.O. BOX 94	MORGANVILLE	NJ	07751	
THE HEBREW ACADEMY OF THE SHORE AREA PO BOX 324 301 MONMOUTH ROAD	OAKHURST	NJ	07755	(201) 531-0300
HEBREW ACADEMY OF MORRIS COUNTY (N-8) 146 DOVER-CHESTER ROAD	RANDOLPH	NJ	07869	(201) 584-5530
BIALIK SCHOOL (N-8) 500 CHURCH AVENUE	BROOKLYN	NY	11218	(718) 853-7100
RABBI HARRY HALPERN DAY SCHOOL (N-8) 1625 OCEAN AVENUE	BROOKLYN	NY	11230	(718) 338-3800
SOLOMON SCHECHTER HIGH SCHOOL (9-12) 500 CHURCH AVENUE	BROOKLYN	NY	11218	(718) 854-3500
SOLOMON SCHECHTER SCHOOL OF SUFFOLK COUNTY 74 HAUPPAUGE RD.	COMMACK	NY	11725	(516) 462-5999
SOLOMON SCHECHTER DAY SCHOOL OF QUEENS (K-9) 76-16 PARSONS BLVD	FLUSHING	NY	11366	(718) 591-9800
HEBREW ACADEMY OF THE CAPITAL DISTRICT (K-8) 2211A WESTERN AVENUE	GUILDERLAND	NY	12084	(518) 456-6816
SOLOMON SCHECHTER DAY SCHOOL OF NASSAU COUNTY (K-8) BARBARA LANE	JERICHO	NY	11753	(516) 935-1441
THE BRANDEIS SCHOOL (N-8) 25 FROST LANE	LAWRENCE	NY	11559	(516) 371-4747
THE BRANDEIS SCHOOL-LAWRENCE EVAN SLOATE HIGH SCHOOL (9-12) 25 FROST LANE	LAWRENCE	NY	11559	(516) 371-4747
THE REUBEN GITTELMAN HEBREW DAY SCHOOL ROUTE 45	NEW CITY	NY	10956	(914) 354-5500
B'NAI JESHURUN DAY SCHOOL (N-8) 270 WEST 89TH STREET	NEW YORK	NY	10024	
THE PROZDOR 3080 BROADWAY	NEW YORK	NY	10027	(212) 678-8824
MID-HUDSON HEBREW DAY SCHOOL (K-6) 110 GRAND AVENUE	POUGHKEEPSIE	NY	12603	(914) 454-0474
RBERT GORDIS DAY SCHOOL (N-8) 445 BEACH 135TH STREET	ROCKAWAY PARK	NY	11694	(718) 634-7711
SOLOMON SCHECHTER DAY SCHOOL OF WESTCHESTER (N-8) 30 DELLWOOD ROAD	WHITE PLAINS	NY	10605	(914) 948-3111
SOLOMON SCHECHTER DAY SCHOOL OF CLEVELAND (K-3) 3557 WASHINGTON BLVD	CLEVELAND HEIGHTS	OH	44118	(216) 371-1364
SOLOMON SCHECHTER DAY SCHOOL OF CLEVELAND 1825 GREEN RD.	SOUTH EUCLID	OH	44121	(216) 381-3282
UNITED SYNAGOGUE DAY SCHOOL (N-9) 1700 BATHURST STREET	TORONTO	ON	M5P 3K3	(416) 781-5658
UNITED SYNAGOGUE DAY SCHOOL BAYVIEW BRANCH (N-6) 3080 BAYVIEW AVENUE	WILLOWDALE	ON	M2N 5L3	(416) 225-1143
SOLOMON SCHECHTER DAY SCHOOL OF PHILADELPHIA (K-6) 971 OLD YORK ROAD	ABINGTON	PA	19001	(215) 886-2355
SOLOMON SCHECHTER DAY SCHOOL OLD LANCASTER & HIGHLAND RDS.	BALA CYNWYD	PA	19004	(215) 664-5480
FORMAN HEBREW DAY SCHOOL (K-6) OLD YORK & FOXCROFT ROADS	ELKINS PARK	PA	19117	(215) 887-6981
SOLOMON SCHECHTER DAY SCHOOL OF GREATER PITTSBURGH (K-1) 1900 COCHRAN RD	PITTSBURGH	PA	15220	(412) 344-5877
SOLOMON SCHECHTER ACADEMY (N-7) 5555 COTE ST. LUC ROAD	MONTREAL	QU	H3X 2C9	(514) 481-7719
SOLOMON SCHECHTER DAY SCHOOL OF RHODE ISLAND (K-4) 99 TAFT AVENUE	PROVIDENCE	RI	02906	(401) 751-2470
I. WEINER SECONDARY SCHOOL (6-10) 4610 BELLAIRE AVENUE	BELLAIRE	TX	77401	(713) 668-0393
SOLOMON SCHECHTER ACADEMY OF DALLAS (K-3) 9401 DOUGLAS AVENUE	DALLAS	TX	75225	(214) 369-8237
I. WEINER SECONDARY SCHOOL 12583 S. GESSNER	HOUSTON	TX	77071	(713) 668-0393
WILLIAM S. MALEV SCHOOL OF RELIGIOUS STUDIES (N-6) 4525 BEECHNUT BLVD	HOUSTON	TX	77096	(713) 666-1884

DEAF, ORGANIZATIONS FOR THE

Name / Address	City	State	Zip	Phone
TEMPLE BETH SOLOMON OF THE DEAF 13580 OSBOURNE STREET	ARLETA	CA	91331	(213) 899-2202
CHABAD HOUSE-WEST COAST 741 GAYLEY AVE	LOS ANGELES	CA	90024	
LOS ANGELES HAD 458 N. DETROIT AVENUE	LOS ANGELES	CA	90036	
TEMPLE BETH SOLOMON OF THE DEAF 8936 LANGDON	SAN FERNANDO	CA	91343	
GALLAUDET COLLEGE HILLEL CLUB, THE HILLEL CLUB, C/O OFF OF CAMPUS MINISTRIES, GALLAUDET COLLEGE	WASHINGTON	DC	20002	(202) 651-5106
JEWISH COMM CTR ASSN J FERSHLEISER CENT VILL V D79	DEERFIELD	FL	33441	
CONGREGATION BENE SHALOM OF THE HEBREW ASSOC. OF THE DEAF 5920 NORTH KENMORE	CHICAGO	IL	60660	
BENE SHOLOM, CONGREGATION - HEBREW ASSOCIATION FOR THE DEAF 4435 WEST OAKTON	SKOKIE	IL	60076	(312) 677-3330
BOSTON HAD 154 SALISBURY ROAD	BROOKLINE	MA	02146	
"OUR WAY"-NCSY 236 RAWSON ROAD	BROOKLINE	MA	02146	(617) 731-8554
BALTIMORE JSD 5709 GREENSPRING	BALTIMORE	MD	21209	
"OUR WAY" 4001 CLARKS LANE	BALTIMORE	MD	21215	(301) 358-6279
"OUR WAY"-NCSY 6108 GIST AVENUE	BALTIMORE	MD	21215	(301) 358-7060
NATIONAL CONGRESS OF JEWISH DEAF 9102 EDMONSTON CT. #302	GREENBELT	MD	20770	
WASHINGTON SOCIETY OF THE JEWISH DEAF 6610 23 AVENUE	WEST HYATTS	MD	20782	
"OUR WAY"-NCSY 4001 WEST 31ST STREET	MINNEAPOLIS	MN	55416	(612) 929-7899
"OUR WAY"-NCSY 769 RINGWOOD AVENUE	POMPTON LAKES	NJ	07442	(201) 835-9030
TEMPLE BETH OR OF THE DEAF 195 PRINCETON DRIVE	RIVER EDGE	NJ	07661	
BETH TORAH OF THE DEAF 1949 E 21ST ST	BROOKLYN	NY	11229	
B'KLYN HSD/SISTERHOOD 1230 AVENUE Y	BROOKLYN	NY	11235	
HEBREW INSTITUTE FOR THE DEAF AND EXCEPTIONAL CHILDREN 1401 AVENUE I	BROOKLYN	NY	11230	(718) 377-7507
"OUR WAY"-NCSY 759 EAST 10TH STREET, #3C	BROOKLYN	NY	11230	(718) 434-2446
TEMPLE BETH OR OF THE DEAF R GEFFEN-TREAS 582 BENTON RD	EAST MEADOW	NY	11554	
NEW YORK SOCIETY FOR THE DEAF (PHONE FOR THE HEARING PERSON) 344 E. 14TH STREET	NEW YORK	NY	10003	(212) 673-6500
NEW YORK SOCIETY FOR THE DEAF (TELETYPEWRITER PHONE FOR DEAF) 344 E. 14TH STREET	NEW YORK	NY	10003	(212) 673-6974
"OUR WAY"-NCSY 45 WEST 36TH STREET	NEW YORK	NY	10018	(212) 244-2011
"OUR WAY"-NCSY 30 STRATFORD COURT	NORTH BELLMORE	NY	11710	(516) 826-3556
HEARING IMPAIRED CHAVURA 199 DORKING RD	ROCHESTER	NY	14610	
RIT/NTID HILLEL C/O CHAPLAIN'S OFFICE, 1 LOMB MEMORIAL DRIVE	ROCHESTER	NY	14623	(716) 475-2135
HEBREW ASSOCIATION OF THE DEAF - JEWISH COMMUNITY CENTER 3505 MAYFIELD ROAD	CLEVELAND	OH	44118	(216) 382-4000
HAD - CLEVELAND P.O. BOX 29114	PARMA	OH	44129	
HAD - PHILADELPHIA 7005 CALVERT STREET	PHILADELPHIA	PA	19149	
PHILADELPHIA HAD 9801 HALDEMAN AVENUE APT. D204	PHILADELPHIA	PA	19115	
TORONTO JEWISH DEAF SOCIETY-JACK OSTEN 58 SUMERSIDE CR	WILLOWDALE	ON	M2H 1X1	

DRIVER EDUCATION

Name / Address	City	State	Zip	Phone
PROSPECT PARK YESHIVAH HIGH SCHOOL 1609 AVENUE R	BROOKLYN	NY	11229	(718) 376-0006
YESHIVAH OF FLATBUSH 1609 AVENUE J	BROOKLYN	NY	11230	(718) 377-4466
HEBREW ACADEMY OF FIVE TOWNS & ROCKAWAY 33 WASHINGTON AVENUE	LAWRENCE	NY	11559	(516) 569-3370
RAMAZ DAY SCHOOL 60 EAST 78TH STREET	NEW YORK	NY	10021	(212) 427-1000
HEBREW ACADEMY OF NASSAU COUNTY 215 OAK STREET	UNIONDALE	NY	11553	(516) 538-8161

EDUCATIONAL ORGANIZATIONS

Name / Address	City	State	Zip	Phone
COMMUNITY HEBREW EDUCATION COUNCIL 950 WEST 41ST AVENUE	VANCOUVER	BC	V5Z 2N7	(604) 266-9111
BRANDEIS-BARDIN INSTITUTE, THE 1101 PEPPERTREE LANE	BRANDEIS	CA	93064	(805) 348-7201
EDUCATIONAL HORIZONS 126 SOUTH GLENDALE AVENUE	GLENDALE	CA	91316	(213) 500-4828
BUREAU OF JEWISH EDUCATION 6505 WILSHIRE BLVD	LOS ANGELES	CA	90048	(213) 852-1234
THE SEPHARDIC EDUCATIONAL CENTER IN JERUSALEM 6505 WILSHIRE BOULEVARD, #208	LOS ANGELES	CA	90048	(213) 653-7365
AMERICAN FRIENDS OF THE HEBREW UNIVERSITY OF JERUSALEM 717 MARKET STREET, SUITE 323	SAN FRANCISCO	CA	94103	(415) 391-9056
BRANDEIS-BARDIN INSTITUTE 1101 PEPPERTREE LANE	SIMI VALLEY	CA	93064	(805) 523-1131
ASSOCIATED TALMUD TORAH 2828 W. PRATT BLVD	CHICAGO	IL	60645	(312) 973-2828
TEACHER CENTER 415 GREEN BAY ROAD	WILMETTE	IL	60091	(312) 256-6056
JEWISH EDUCATIONAL ASSOCIATION 6711 HOOVER ROAD	INDIANAPOLIS	IN	46260	(317) 255-3124
JEWISH EDUCATION ASSOCIATION 3600 DUTCHMANS LANE	LOUISVILLE	KY	40205	(502) 459-0798
JEWISH EDUCATIONAL VENTURES, THE 462 BOYLSTON STREET	BOSTON	MA	02116	(617) 536-6252
ASSOCIATION FOR JEWISH STUDIES WIDENER LIBRARY, HARVARD UNIVERSITY	CAMBRIDGE	MA	02138	(617) 495-2985
UNITED HEBREW SCHOOLS 15110 W. TEN MILE ROAD	OAK PARK	MI	48237	(313) 548-4747
UNITED HEBREW SCHOOLS OF DETROIT 21550 W. TWELVE MILE ROAD	SOUTHFIELD	MI	48076	(313) 354-1050
CENTRAL AGENCY FOR JEWISH EDUCATION 12 MILLSTONE CAMPUS DRIVE	ST. LOUIS	MO	63146	(314) 432-0020
ASSOCIATION OF ORTHODOX JEWISH TEACHERS 1577 CONEY ISLAND AVENUE	BROOKLYN	NY	11230	(718) 258-3585
EDUCATIONAL INSTITUTE OHOLEI TORAH 667 EASTERN PARKWAY	BROOKLYN	NY	11213	(718) 778-3340
JEWISH EDUCATION PROGRAM 425 E. 9TH STREET	BROOKLYN	NY	11218	(718) 941-2600
MERKOS L'INYONEI CHINUCH, CENTRAL ORG. FOR JEWISH EDUCATION 770 EASTERN PARKWAY	BROOKLYN	NY	11213	(718) 493-9250
MIFAL HASHAS 4606 16TH AVENUE	BROOKLYN	NY	11204	(718) 436-7790
NATIONAL COMMITTEE FOR THE FURTHERANCE OF JEWISH EDUCATION 824 EASTERN PARKWAY	BROOKLYN	NY	11213	(718) 735-0200
NATIONAL COUNCIL OF BETH JACOB SCHOOLS 1415 EAST 7TH STREET	BROOKLYN	NY	11230	(718) 375-3533
NATIONAL COUNCIL OF BETH JACOB SCHOOLS, INC. 1415 E. 7TH STREET	BROOKLYN	NY	11230	(718) 979-7400
P'TACH - PARENTS FOR TORAH FOR ALL CHILDREN 4612 13TH AVENUE	BROOKLYN	NY	11219	(718) 436-5125
JEWISH ADULT ENRICHMENT - J.A.D.E. 85-35 117TH STREET	KEW GARDENS	NY	11418	(718) 849-1473
JEWISH ADULT ENRICHMENT - J.A.D.E. 85-35 117TH STREET	KEW GARDENS	NY	11418	(914) 997-8085
AMERICAN BIBLICAL ENCYCLOPEDIA SOCIETY 24 WEST MAPLE AVENUE	MONSEY	NY	10952	(914) 352-4609
AGUDAS ISRAEL WORLD ORGANIZATION 471 WEST END AVENUE	NEW YORK	NY	10024	(212) 874-7979
AMERICAN ASSOCIATION FOR JEWISH EDUCATION 114 FIFTH AVENUE	NEW YORK	NY	10011	(212) 675-5656
AMERICAN COUNCIL FOR JUDAISM 307 FIFTH AVENUE	NEW YORK	NY	10001	(212) 889-1313
AMERICAN ORT FEDERATION 817 BROADWAY	NEW YORK	NY	10003	(212) 677-4400
ASSOCIATION OF ADVANCED RABBINICAL & TALMUDIC SCHOOLS 175 FIFTH AVENUE	NEW YORK	NY	10010	(212) 477-0950
COALITION FOR ALTERNATIVES IN JEWISH EDUCATION 468 PARK AVENUE SOUTH SUITE 904	NEW YORK	NY	10016	(212) 696-0740
COMMISSION ON JEWISH EDUCATION OF U.S.A. 427 WEST 58TH STREET	NEW YORK	NY	10019	(212) 245-8200
DAF YOMI COMMISSION C/O AGUDATH ISRAEL OF AMERICA 84 WILLIAM STREET	NEW YORK	NY	10038	(212) 797-9000
DEPARTMENT OF EDUCATION & CULTURE-WORLD ZIONIST ORGANIZATION 515 PARK AVENUE	NEW YORK	NY	10022	(212) 752-0600

FEDERATED COUNCIL OF BETH JACOB SCHOOLS
142 BROOME STREET .... NEW YORK **NY** 10002 (212) 473-4500
FUND FOR HIGHER EDUCATION 1500 BROADWAY, SUITE 1900 .... NEW YORK **NY** 10036 (212) 354-4660
INTERNATIONAL SEPHARDIC EDUCATION FOUNDATION
1345 AVENUE OF THE AMERICAS .... NEW YORK **NY** 10105 (212) 841-6073
ISRAEL EDUCATION FUND 51 WEST 51ST STREET .... NEW YORK **NY** 10019 (212) 757-1500
THE JERUSALEM FELLOWS 515 PARK AVENUE .... NEW YORK **NY** 10022 (212) 752-0600
JEWISH CHAUTAUQUA SOCIETY 838 FIFTH AVENUE .... NEW YORK **NY** 10021 (212) 570-0707
JEWISH EDUCATION SERVICE OF NORTH AMERICA, INC.
730 BROADWAY .... NEW YORK **NY** 10003 (212) 529-2000
JEWISH FOLK SCHOOLS 575 AVENUE OF AMERICAS .... NEW YORK **NY** 10011
JEWISH FOUNDATION FOR EDUCATION OF GIRLS
120 W. 57TH STREET .... NEW YORK **NY** 10019 (212) 265-2565
JEWISH FOUNDATION FOR EDUCATION OF WOMEN
120 W. 57TH STREET .... NEW YORK **NY** 10019 (212) 265-2565
JEWISH NATIONAL FUND - YOUTH & EDUCATION DEPARTMENT
42 EAST 69TH STREET .... NEW YORK **NY** 10021 (212) 879-9300
JEWISH RECONSTRUCTIONIST FOUNDATION, EDUCATION DEPARTMENT
270 WEST 89TH STREET .... NEW YORK **NY** 10024 (212) 496-2960
NAT'L COUNCIL FOR JEWISH EDUCATION 114 FIFTH AVENUE .... NEW YORK **NY** 10011 (212) 675-5656
NATIONAL ACADEMY FOR ADULT JEWISH STUDIES 155 FIFTH AVENUE.. NEW YORK **NY** 10010 (212) 260-8450
NATIONAL COMMISSION ON TORAH EDUCATION
2540 AMSTERDAM AVENUE .... NEW YORK **NY** 10033 (212) 960-5400
NATIONAL COMMITTEE OF JEWISH FOLK SCHOOLS 575 6TH AVENUE ... NEW YORK **NY** 10011
NATIONAL CONFERENCE OF YESHIVA PRINCIPALS 160 BROADWAY ..... NEW YORK **NY** 10038 (212) 406-4190
NATIONAL COUNCIL FOR JEWISH EDUCATION 114 FIFTH AVENUE ...... NEW YORK **NY** 10011 (212) 675-5656
NATIONAL COUNCIL FOR TORAH EDUCATION
C/O RELIGIOUS ZIONISTS OF AMERICA, 25 W. 26TH STREET .... NEW YORK **NY** 10011 (212) 289-1414
OZAR HATORAH 411 FIFTH AVENUE .... NEW YORK **NY** 10016 (212) 684-4733
P'EYLIM - AMERICAN YESHIVA STUDENT UNION 3 WEST 16TH STREET .. NEW YORK **NY** 10011 (212) 989-2500
PROJECT ACHY (ACHDUT CHEVRAT YISRAEL) 25 WEST 26TH STREET ... NEW YORK **NY** 10010 (212) 684-6091
RESEARCH INSTITUTE OF RELIGIOUS JEWRY, INC.
471 WEST END AVENUE .... NEW YORK **NY** 10024 (212) 874-7979
RESHET - TORAH EDUCATION NETWORK
84 WILLIAM STREET .... NEW YORK **NY** 10038 (212) 797-9000
STONE-SAPIRSTEIN CENTER FOR JEWISH EDUCATION-YESHIVA UNIV.
500 W. 185TH STREET .... NEW YORK **NY** 10033 (212) 960-5400
TORAH UMESORAH 160 BROADWAY, 4TH FLOOR-EAST BUILDING .... NEW YORK **NY** 10038 (212) 406-4190
UNITED PARENT-TEACHERS ASSOCIATION OF JEWISH SCHOOLS
426 W. 58TH STREET .... NEW YORK **NY** 10019 (212) 245-8200
UNITED SYNAGOGUE DEPT. OF EDUCATION/COMMISSION OF JEWISH ED.
155 FIFTH AVENUE .... NEW YORK **NY** 10010 (212) 533-7800
UNITED HEBREW SCHOOLS & YESHIVOS OF PHILADELPHIA
701 BYBERRY ROAD .... PHILADELPHIA **PA** 19116 (215) 677-7261
PITTSBURGH JEWISH PUBLICATION & EDUCATION FOUNDATION
315 S. BELLEFIELD AVENUE .... PITTSBURGH **PA** 15213 (412) 687-1000
UNITED TALMUD TORAHS OF MONTREAL, INC.
4894 ST. KEVIN AVENUE .... MONTREAL **QU** H3W 1P2 (514) 739-2291

EDUCATIONAL RESOURCES

EKS PUBLISHING 5336 COLLEGE AVENUE .... OAKLAND **CA** 94618 (415) 653-5183
EDUCATIONAL RESOURCES 24010 OXNARD STREET .... WOODLAND HILLS **CA** 91367 (213) 992-6330
ALTERNATIVES IN RELIGIOUS EDUCATION, INC. 3945 SOUTH ONEIDA ...... DENVER **CO** 80237 (303) 363-7779
AUDIO-FORUM 96 BROAD STREET .... GUILFORD **CT** 06437 (203) 453-9794
THE LEARNING PLANT 6950 COUNTRY PLACE ROAD .... WEST PALM BEACH **FL** 33411
KOHL JEWISH TEACHER CENTER 161 GREEN BAY ROAD .... WILMETTE **IL** 60091 (312) 256-6056
HEINLE & HEINLE ENTERPRISES 29 LEXINGTON ROAD .... CONCORD **MA** 01742 (617) 369-7525
TZIVOS HASHEM EDUCATIONAL RESOURCES 332 KINGSTON AVENUE .. BROOKLYN **NY** 11213 (718) 467-6991
TORAH MICROFICHE LIBRARY - THE RUDMAN FOUNDATION
1051 BAY 25TH STREET .... FAR ROCKAWAY **NY** 11691 (718) 634-8000
ARTA FILMS, INC. 2130 BROADWAY, SUITE 1602 .... NEW YORK **NY** 10023 (212) 362-8535
BOARD OF JEWISH EDUCATION 426 WEST 58TH STREET .... NEW YORK **NY** 10019 (212) 245-8200
JEWISH STORYTELLING CENTER-PENINAH SCHRAM
92ND STREET YM-YWHA LIBRARY,
92ND STREET YM-YWHA, 1392 LEXINGTON AVENUE .... NEW YORK **NY** 10128 (212) 427-6000
UNION OF AMERICAN HEBREW CONGREGATIONS 838 FIFTH AVENUE ... NEW YORK **NY** 10021 (212) 249-0100
UNITED SYNAGOGUE OF AMERICA 155 FIFTH AVENUE .... NEW YORK **NY** 10010 (212) 533-7800
HEBREW ACADEMY PUBLICATIONS DEPARTMENT
1860 SOUTH TAYLOR ROAD .... CLEVELAND HEIGHTS **OH** 44118 (216) 321-5838
B. ARBIT BOOKS 8050 NORTH PORT WASHINGTON ROAD .... MILWAUKEE **WI** 53217 (414) 352-4404

EDUCATORS ORGANIZATIONS

JEWISH EDUCATORS ASSOCIATION 6505 WILSHIRE BOULEVARD..... LOS ANGELES **CA** 90048 (213) 852-1234
HEBREW TEACHERS FEDERATION PO BOX 824 .... VAN NUYS **CA** 91408 (818) 980-2191
COALITION FOR ALTERNATIVES IN JEWISH EDUCATION
468 PARK AVENUE SOUTH, SUITE 904 .... NEW YORK **NY** 10016 (212) 696-0740
JEWISH EDUCATORS ASSEMBLY OF AMERICA 155 FIFTH AVENUE .... NEW YORK **NY** 10010 (212) 533-7800
JEWISH TEACHERS ASSOCIATION - MORIM 45 E. 33RD STREET .... NEW YORK **NY** 10016 (212) 684-0556
NATIONAL ASSOCIATION OF HEBREW DAY SCHOOL ADMINISTRATORS
160 BROADWAY .... NEW YORK **NY** 10038 (212) 406-4190
NATIONAL ASSOCIATION OF TEMPLE ADMINISTRATORS
838 FIFTH AVENUE .... NEW YORK **NY** 10021 (212) 249-0100
NATIONAL ASSOCIATION OF TEMPLE EDUCATORS 838 FIFTH AVENUE .. NEW YORK **NY** 10021 (212) 249-0100
NATIONAL CONFERENCE OF YESHIVA PRINCIPALS 160 BROADWAY ..... NEW YORK **NY** 10038 (212) 406-4190
NATIONAL COUNCIL FOR JEWISH EDUCATION 114 FIFTH AVENUE ...... NEW YORK **NY** 10011 (212) 675-5656

EMERGENCY SERVICES

Name / Address	City	State	ZIP	Phone
HATZOLOH GENERAL P.O. BOX 3500	BROOKLYN	**NY**	11202	(718) 387-1750

EMPLOYMENT AGENCIES

Name / Address	City	State	ZIP	Phone
AIDES TO THE ELDERLY 330 NORTH FAIRFAX AVENUE	LOS ANGELES	**CA**	90048	(213) 760-1423
PROJECT GELT 128 LA BREA STREET	LOS ANGELES	**CA**	90036	(213) 658-5111
YOUNG ISRAEL EMPLOYMENT SERVICE	LOS ANGELES	**CA**	90007	(213) 936-6101
BUREAU OF JEWISH EMPLOYMENT PROBLEMS 220 SOUTH STATE STREET, SUITE 1703	CHICAGO	**IL**	60603	(312) 663-9470
BUREAU OF JEWISH EMPLOYMENT PROBLEMS 220 S. STATE STREET	CHICAGO	**IL**	60604	(312) 663-9470
FEDERATION EMPLOYMENT & GUIDANCE SERVICE 1 THORNTON STREET	BROOKLYN	**NY**	11206	(718) 782-6060
FEDERATION EMPLOYMENT & GUIDANCE SERVICE 3312-30 SURF AVENUE	BROOKLYN	**NY**	11224	(718) 449-4000
FEDERATION EMPLOYMENT & GUIDANCE SERVICE 1622 MERMAID AVENUE	BROOKLYN	**NY**	11224	(718) 449-7900
KOLLEL EMPLOYMENT SERVICE P.O. BOX 255, 125 HEYWARD STREET	BROOKLYN	**NY**	11211	(718) 388-7118
REMBRANDT PERSONNEL AGENCY 1422 AVENUE J	BROOKLYN	**NY**	11230	(718) 258-9202
COUNCIL OF JEWISH MANPOWER ASSOCIATION 299 BROADWAY	NEW YORK	**NY**	10013	(212) 233-8333
TRADITION PERSONNEL-"THE SHOMER SHABAT AGENCY" 6 EAST 45TH STREET	NEW YORK	**NY**	10017	(212) 972-4740
YOUNG ISRAEL EMPLOYMENT BUREAU 3 WEST 16TH STREET	NEW YORK	**NY**	10011	(212) 929-1525

ENCYCLOPAEDIA JUDAICA

Name / Address	City	State	ZIP	Phone
AMER. COMMITTEE FOR SHAARE ZEDEK HOSPITAL IN JERUSALEM, INC. 49 WEST 45TH STREET	NEW YORK	**NY**	10036	(212) 354-8801
KETER, INC. 475 FIFTH AVENUE	NEW YORK	**NY**	10017	(212) 889-7750

ENDOWMENTS & FOUNDATIONS

Name / Address	City	State	ZIP	Phone
JEWISH FUND FOR JUSTICE 1334 G STREET, NORTHWEST, 6TH FLOOR	WASHINGTON	**DC**	20005	(205) 638-0550
JEWISH ENDOWMENT FOUNDATION 211 CAMP STREET	NEW ORLEANS	**LA**	70130	(504) 525-0673
JEWISH FOUNDATION 370 HARGRAVE STREET	WINNIPEG	**MB**	R3B 2K1	(204) 943-0406
AMERICA CHAI TRUST 350 FIFTH AVENUE	NEW YORK	**NY**	10118	(212) 736-3633
AMERICAN COUNCIL FOR JUDAISM PHILANTHROPIC FUND 386 PARK AVENUE SOUTH	NEW YORK	**NY**	10016	(212) 684-1525
AMERICAN HISTADRUT DEVELOPMENT FOUNDATION 33 EAST 67TH STREET	NEW YORK	**NY**	10021	(212) 628-1000
BARON DE HIRSCH FUND 386 PARK AVENUE SOUTH	NEW YORK	**NY**	10016	(212) 532-7088
HARRY AND JANE FISCHEL FOUNDATION 310 MADISON, SUITE 1711	NEW YORK	**NY**	10017	(212) 599-2828
ISRAEL ENDOWMENT FUNDS 342 MADISON AVENUE	NEW YORK	**NY**	10173	(212) 599-1260
ISRAEL ENDOWMENT FUNDS, INC. 511 FIFTH AVENUE	NEW YORK	**NY**	10017	(212) 687-2400
JEWISH PHILANTHROPIC FUND OF 1933 570 SEVENTH AVENUE	NEW YORK	**NY**	10018	
MEMORIAL FOUNDATION FOR JEWISH CULTURE 15 EAST 26TH STREET	NEW YORK	**NY**	10010	(212) 679-4074
NATIONAL FOUNDATION FOR JEWISH CULTURE, INC. 122 EAST 42ND STREET	NEW YORK	**NY**	10017	(212) 490-2280

ERUV

Name / Address	City	State	ZIP	Phone
ERUV	BEVERLY HILLS-WEST LOS ANGELES	**CA**		(213) 275-ERUV
ERUV	NORTH HOLLYWOOD	**CA**		(818) 763-4395
ERUV	FAIRFAX-LA BREA	**CA**		(213) 938-1142
ERUV	NORTH MIAMI BEACH-SKYLAKES	**FL**		(305) 945-8712
ERUV	SILVER SPRINGS	**MD**		(301) 593-4465
ERUV	BROOKLYN	**NY**		(718) 377-4242
ERUV HOTLINE-NYC	NEW YORK	**NY**		(212) 362-2602
ERUV CONSTRUCTION 2589 RICHMOND TERRACE	STATEN ISLAND	**NY**	10303	(718) 448-2744
ERUV	CLEVELAND	**OH**		(216) 321-ARUV

FEDERATIONS, WELFARE FUNDS & COMMUNITY COUNCILS

Name / Address	City	State	ZIP	Phone
BIRMINGHAM JEWISH FEDERATION, THE PO BOX 9157	BIRMINGHAM	**AL**	35213	(205) 879-3438
MOBILE JEWISH WELFARE FUND, INC. 407 ONE OFFICE PARK	MOBILE	**AL**	36609	(205) 343-7197
JEWISH FEDERATION OF MONTGOMERY, INC. PO BOX 1150	MONTGOMERY	**AL**	36101	(205) 263-7674
JEWISH FEDERATION OF LITTLE ROCK 4942 WEST MARKHAM, SUITE 5	LITTLE ROCK	**AR**	72205	(501) 663-3571
JEWISH FEDERATION OF GREATER PHOENIX 1718 WEST MARYLAND AVENUE	PHOENIX	**AZ**	85015	(602) 249-1845
JEWISH COMMUNITY COUNCIL 102 N. PLUMER	TUCSON	**AZ**	85719	(602) 884-8921
CALGARY JEWISH COMMUNITY COUNCIL 1607 90TH AVENUE S.W.	CALGARY	**AT**	T2V 4V7	(403) 253-8600
EDMONTON JEWISH COMMUNITY COUNCIL, INC. 7200-156TH STREET	EDMONTON	**AT**	T5R 1X3	(403) 487-5120
COMBINED JEWISH APPEAL/JEWISH COMMUNITY FUND & COUNCIL 950 WEST 41ST AVENUE	VANCOUVER	**BC**	V5Z 2N7	(604) 266-8371
JFC EASTERN REGION OFFICE 801 WEST SAN BERNARDINO ROAD	COVINA	**CA**	91822	(213) 686-0631
JEWISH FEDERATION COUNCIL-EASTERN REGION 801 WEST SAN BERNARDINO ROAD	COVINA	**CA**	91722	(213) 444-4584
JEWISH FEDERATION OF FRESNO 5094 NORTH WEST AVENUE	FRESNO	**CA**	93711	(209) 432-2162
JEWISH FED. OF ORANGE COUNTY-UNITED JEWISH WELFARE FUND 12181 BUARO	GARDEN GROVE	**CA**	92640	(714) 530-6636
JEWISH COMMUNITY FED. OF GREATER LONG BEACH & W. ORANGE CO. 3801 EAST WILLOW STREET	LONG BEACH	**CA**	90815	(213) 426-7601
JFC METROPOLITAN REGION OFFICE 6505 WILSHIRE BOULEVARD	LOS ANGELES	**CA**	90048	(213) 852-1234
JEWISH FEDERATION COUNCIL OF GREATER LOS ANGELES 6505 WILSHIRE BLVD	LOS ANGELES	**CA**	90048	(213) 852-1234
JEWISH FEDERATION OF GREATER SAN JOSE 14855 OKA ROAD	LOS GATOS	**CA**	95030	(408) 358-3033
JEWISH FEDERATION OF THE GREATER EAST BAY 3245 SHEFFIELD AVENUE	OAKLAND	**CA**	94602	(415) 533-7462
JEWISH FEDERATION OF PALM SPRINGS - DESERT AREA 611 SOUTH PALM CANYON DRIVE, SUITE 215	PALM SPRINGS	**CA**	92264	(619) 325-7281
JEWISH FEDERATION OF SACRAMENTO PO BOX 254589	SACRAMENTO	**CA**	95865	(916) 486-0906
SAN BERNARDINO UNITED JEWISH WELFARE FUND, INC. 3512 NO. 'E' STREET, CONGREGATION EMANU-EL	SAN BERNARDINO	**CA**	92405	(714) 886-4818
CJF WESTERN AREA OFFICE 2831 CAMINO DEL RIO SOUTH, SUITE 217	SAN DIEGO	**CA**	92108	(619) 296-2949
UNITED JEWISH FEDERATION OF SAN DIEGO COUNTY 4797 MERCURY STREET	SAN DIEGO	**CA**	92111	(619) 571-3444
JEWISH COMMUNITY FEDERATION OF SAN FRANCISCO, THE PENINSULA, MARIN AND SONOMA COUNTIES 121 STEUART STREET	SAN FRANCISCO	**CA**	94105	(415) 777-0411
SANTA BARBARA JEWISH FEDERATION, THE PO BOX 6782	SANTA BARBARA	**CA**	93111	
JFC WESTERN REGION OFFICE 2811 WILSHIRE BOULEVARD	SANTA MONICA	**CA**	90403	(213) 828-9521
JFC SAN FERNANDO VALLEY REGION OFFICE 15477 VENTURA BOULEVARD, SUITE 300	SHERMAN OAKS	**CA**	91403	(818) 986-7900
STOCKTON JEWISH WELFARE FUND 5105 NORTH EL DORADO STREET	STOCKTON	**CA**	95207	(209) 477-9306
JFC SOUTHERN REGION OFFICE 3848 CARSON STREET, SUITE 101	TORRANCE	**CA**	90503	(213) 772-9186
VENTURA COUNTY JEWISH COUNCIL, TEMPLE BETH TORAH 7620 FOOTHILL ROAD	VENTURA	**CA**	93004	(805) 647-4181
ALLIED JEWISH FEDERATION OF DENVER-ALLIED JEWISH CAMPAIGN 300 SOUTH DAHLIA STREET	DENVER	**CO**	80222	(303) 321-3399
JEWISH FEDERATION OF GREATER BRIDGEPORT, INC., UJ CAMPAIGN 4200 PARK AVENUE	BRIDGEPORT	**CT**	06604	(203) 372-6504
JEWISH FEDERATION OF GREATER DANBURY 54 MAIN STREET, SUITE E	DANBURY	**CT**	06810	(203) 792-6353
JEWISH FEDERATION OF GREATER NORWALK, INC. SHOREHAVEN ROAD	EAST NORWALK	**CT**	06855	(203) 853-3440
GREENWICH JEWISH FEDERATION 22 WEST PUTNAM AVENUE, SUITE 18	GREENWICH	**CT**	06830	(203) 622-1434
JEWISH FED. OF MERIDEN/MERIDEN JEWISH WELFARE FUND, INC. 127 EAST MAIN STREET	MERIDEN	**CT**	06450	(203) 235-2581
NEW HAVEN JEWISH FEDERATION 419 WHALLEY AVENUE	NEW HAVEN	**CT**	06511	(203) 562-2137
JEWISH FEDERATION OF EASTERN CONNECTICUT, INC. 1 BULKELEY PLACE	NEW LONDON	**CT**	06320	(203) 442-8062
UNITED JEWISH FEDERATION 1035 NEWFIELD AVENUE, PO BOX 3038	STAMFORD	**CT**	06905	(203) 322-6935
JEWISH FEDERATION OF WATERBURY, INC. 1020 COUNTRY CLUB ROAD	WATERBURY	**CT**	06708	(203) 758-2441
GREATER HARTFORD JEWISH FEDERATION 333 BLOOMFIELD AVENUE	WEST HARTFORD	**CT**	06117	(203) 232-4483
CJF WASHINGTON ACTION OFFICE 227 MASSACHUSETTS AVE. N.E. SUITE 220	WASHINGTON	**DC**	20002	(301) 652-6480
JEWISH FEDERATION OF DELAWARE, INC. 101 GARDEN OF EDEN ROAD	WILMINGTON	**DE**	19803	(302) 478-6200

SOUTH COUNTY JEWISH FEDERATION
336 NORTHWEST SPANISH RIVER BOULEVARD ... BOCA RATON **FL** 33431 (305) 368-2737
JEWISH FEDERATION OF PINELLAS COUNTY, INC.
301 SOUTH JUPITER AVENUE ... CLEARWATER **FL** 33515 (813) 446-1033
BREVARD COUNTY JEWISH COMMUNITY COUNCIL PO BOX 1816 .. MERRITT ISLAND **FL** 32952 (305) 453-4695
JEWISH FEDERATION OF VOLUSIA & FLAGLER COUNTIES, INC.
533 SEABREEZE BOULEVARD ... DAYTONA BEACH **FL** 32018 (904) 255-6260
JEWISH FEDERATION OF GREATER FORT LAUDERDALE
8360 WEST OAKLAND PARK BLVD ... FORT LAUDERDALE **FL** 33321 (305) 748-8400
JEWISH FEDERATION OF LEE COUNTY 3628 EVANS AVENUE ... FORT MYERS **FL** 33901 (813) 275-3554
JEWISH FEDERATION OF SOUTH BROWARD, INC.
2719 HOLLYWOOD BLVD ... HOLLYWOOD **FL** 33020 (305) 921-8810
JACKSONVILLE JEWISH FEDERATION, THE
10829 OLD ST. AUGUSTINE ROAD ... JACKSONVILLE **FL** 32223 (904) 262-2800
THE JEWISH FEDERATION OF GREATER ORLANDO
851 NORTH MAITLAND AVENUE, P.O. BOX 1508 ... MAITLAND **FL** 32751 (305) 645-5933
GREATER MIAMI JEWISH FEDERATION, INC. 4200 BISCAYNE BLVD ... MIAMI **FL** 33137 (305) 576-4000
PENSACOLA FEDERATED JEWISH CHARITIES 1320 EAST LEE STREET .. PENSACOLA **FL** 32503 (904) 474-1449
SARASOTA-MANATEE JEWISH FEDERATION 2197 RINGLING BLVD ... SARASOTA **FL** 33577 (813) 371-4546
TAMPA JEWISH FEDERATION 2808 HORATIO ... TAMPA **FL** 33609 (813) 875-1618
JEWISH FEDERATION OF PALM BEACH COUNTY, INC.
501 SOUTH FLAGLER DRIVE, SUITE 305 ... WEST PALM BEACH **FL** 33401 (305) 832-2120
ATLANTA JEWISH FEDERATION 1753 PEACHTREE ROAD N.E. ... ATLANTA **GA** 30309 (404) 873-1661
FEDERATION OF JEWISH CHARITIES P.O. BOX 3251, SIBLEY ROAD ... AUGUSTA **GA** 30904 (404) 736-1818
JEWISH WELFARE FEDERATION OF COLUMBUS, INC. P.O. BOX 6313 ... COLUMBUS **GA** 31907 (404) 563-4766
SAVANNAH JEWISH COUNCIL-UJA FEDERATION CAMPAIGN
P.O. BOX 23527 ... SAVANNAH **GA** 31403 (912) 355-8111
JEWISH FEDERATION OF HAWAII 817 COOKE STREET ... HONOLULU **HI** 96813 (808) 531-4634
JEWISH FEDERATION OF GREATER DES MOINES 910 POLK BLVD ... DES MOINES **IA** 50312 (515) 277-6321
JEWISH FEDERATION 525 14TH STREET ... SIOUX CITY **IA** 51105 (712) 258-0618
JEWISH FEDERATION OF SOUTHERN ILLINOIS
6464 WEST MAIN, SUITE 7A ... BELLEVILLE **IL** 62223 (618) 398-6100
CHAMPAIGN-URBANA JEWISH FEDERATION 503 EAST JOHN STREET ... CHAMPAIGN **IL** 61820 (217) 367-9872
JEWISH FEDERATION OF METROPOLITAN CHICAGO
ONE SOUTH FRANKLIN STREET ... CHICAGO **IL** 60606 (312) 346-6700
DECATUR JEWISH FEDERATION, C/O TEMPLE B'NAI ABRAHAM
1326 WEST ELDORADO ... DECATUR **IL** 62522 (217) 429-5740
ELGIN AREA JEWISH WELFARE CHEST 330 DIVISION STREET ... ELGIN **IL** 60120 (312) 741-5656
JOLIET JEWISH WELFARE CHEST 250 NORTH MIDLAND AVENUE ... JOLIET **IL** 60435 (815) 741-4600
JEWISH FEDERATION OF PEORIA 3100 NORTH KNOXVILLE, SUITE 17 ... PEORIA **IL** 61603 (309) 686-0611
JEWISH FEDERATION OF THE QUAD CITIES
224 18TH STREET, SUITE 511 ... ROCK ISLAND **IL** 61201 (309) 793-1300
ROCKFORD JEWISH COMMUNITY COUNCIL 1500 PARKVIEW AVENUE ... ROCKFORD **IL** 61107 (815) 399-5497
SPRINGFIELD JEWISH FEDERATION 730 EAST VINE STREET ... SPRINGFIELD **IL** 62703 (217) 528-3446
EVANSVILLE JEWISH COMMUNITY COUNCIL, INC. P.O. BOX 5026 ... EVANSVILLE **IN** 47715 (812) 477-7050
FORT WAYNE JEWISH FEDERATION 227 E. WASHINGTON BLVD ... FORT WAYNE **IN** 46802 (219) 422-8566
THE JEWISH FEDERATION, INC. 2939 JEWETT STREET ... HIGHLAND **IN** 46322 (219) 972-2251
JEWISH WELFARE FEDERATION, INC.
615 NORTH ALABAMA STREET ... INDIANAPOLIS **IN** 46204 (317) 637-2473
FEDERATED JEWISH CHARITIES P.O. BOX 708 ... LAFAYETTE **IN** 47902 (317) 742-9081
MICHIGAN CITY UNITED JEWISH WELFARE FUND
2800 FRANKLIN STREET ... MICHIGAN CITY **IN** 46360 (219) 874-4477
JEWISH FEDERATION OF ST. JOSEPH VALLEY 804 SHERLAND BLDG ... SOUTH BEND **IN** 46601 (219) 233-1164
TOPEKA-LAWRENCE JEWISH FEDERATION
3237 SOUTHWEST WESTOVER ROAD ... TOPEKA **KS** 66604 (913) 357-4244
MID-KANSAS JEWISH FEDERATION, INC.
400 NORTH WOODLAWN, SUITE 8 ... WICHITA **KS** 67208 (316) 686-4741
CENTRAL KENTUCKY JEWISH ASSOCIATION
333 WALLER, SUITE 5 ... LEXINGTON **KY** 40504 (606) 252-7622
JEWISH COMMUNITY FEDERATION OF LOUISVILLE, INC., UJ CAMPAIGN
P.O. BOX 33035, 3630 DUTCHMANS LANE ... LOUISVILLE **KY** 40232 (502) 451-8840
THE JEWISH WELFARE FEDERATION & COMMUNITY COUNCIL OF CENTRAL LA
1227 SOUTHHAMPTON ... ALEXANDRIA **LA** 71303 (318) 445-4785
JEWISH FEDERATION OF GREATER BATON ROUGE
11744 HAYMARKET AVENUE, SUITE B ... BATON ROUGE **LA** 70898 (504) 291-5895
UNITED JEWISH CHARITIES OF NORTHEAST LOUISIANA
2400 ORREL PLACE ... MONROE **LA** 71201 (318) 387-0730
JEWISH FEDERATION OF GREATER NEW ORLEANS
1539 JACKSON AVENUE ... NEW ORLEANS **LA** 70130 (504) 525-0673
SHREVEPORT JEWISH FEDERATION 2032 LINE AVENUE ... SHREVEPORT **LA** 71104 (318) 221-4129
COMBINED JEWISH PHILANTHROPIES OF GREATER BOSTON, INC.
72 FRANKLIN STREET ... BOSTON **MA** 02110 (617) 542-8080
JEWISH FEDERATION OF FITCHBURG 40 BOUTELLE STREET ... FITCHBURG **MA** 01420 (617) 342-2227
GREATER FRAMINGHAM JEWISH FEDERATION
76 SALEM END ROAD ... FRAMINGHAM **MA** 01701 (617) 879-3301
HAVERHILL UNITED JEWISH APPEAL, INC. 514 MAIN STREET ... HAVERHILL **MA** 01830 (617) 372-4481
JEWISH COMMUNITY COUNCIL OF GREATER LAWRENCE
580 HAVERHILL STREET ... LAWRENCE **MA** 01841 (617) 686-4157
LEOMINSTER JEWISH COMMUNITY COUNCIL, INC.
268 WASHINGTON STREET ... LEOMINSTER **MA** 01453 (617) 534-6121
JEWISH FEDERATION OF THE NORTH SHORE, INC.
4 COMMUNITY ROAD ... MARBLEHEAD **MA** 01945 (617) 598-1810
JEWISH FEDERATION OF GREATER NEW BEDFORD, INC.
467 HAWTHORN STREET ... NEW BEDFORD **MA** 02747 (617) 997-7471
JEWISH FEDERATION OF THE BERKSHIRES 235 EAST STREET ... PITTSFIELD **MA** 01201 (413) 442-4360
SPRINGFIELD JEWISH FEDERATION, INC., UJ WELFARE FUND
1160 DICKINSON ... SPRINGFIELD **MA** 01108 (413) 737-4313
WORCESTER JEWISH FEDERATION, INC., JEWISH WELFARE FUND
633 SALISBURY STREET ... WORCESTER **MA** 01609 (617) 756-1543
WINNIPEG JEWISH COMMUNITY COUNCIL 370 HARGRAVE STREET ... WINNIPEG **MB** R3B 2K1 (204) 943-0406
ANNAPOLIS JEWISH WELFARE FUND 601 RIDGLEY AVENUE ... ANNAPOLIS **MD** 21401

ASSOCIATED JEWISH CHARITIES & WELFARE FUND
101 W. MOUNT ROYAL AVENUE ... BALTIMORE **MD** 21201 (301) 727-4828
UNITED JEWISH APPEAL FEDERATION OF GREATER WASHINGTON, INC.
7900 WISCONSIN AVENUE ... BETHESDA **MD** 20814 (301) 652-6480
LEWISTON-AUBURN JEWISH FEDERATION, UJA
74 BRADMAN STREET, P.O. BOX 259 ... AUBURN **ME** 04210 (207) 786-4201
JEWISH COMMUNITY COUNCIL & JEWISH FEDERATION OF BANGOR
28 SOMERSET STREET ... BANGOR **ME** 04401 (207) 945-5631
JEWISH FEDERATION COMMUNITY COUNCIL OF SOUTHERN MAINE, UJA
57 ASHMONT STREET ... PORTLAND **ME** 04103 (207) 773-7254
JEWISH WELFARE FEDERATION OF DETROIT, ALLIED JEWISH CAMPAIGN
163 MADISON, FRED M. BUTZEL MEMORIAL BLDG ... DETROIT **MI** 48226 (313) 965-3939
GREATER LANSING JEWISH WELFARE FEDERATION PO BOX 975 ... EAST LANSING **MI** 48823 (517) 351-3197
FLINT JEWISH FEDERATION 619 CLIFFORD STREET ... FLINT **MI** 48502 (313) 767-5922
JEWISH COMMUNITY FUND OF GRAND RAPIDS
1410 PONTIAC SOUTHEAST ... GRAND RAPIDS **MI** 49506 (616) 452-6619
KALAMAZOO JEWISH FEDERATION C/O CONGREGATION OF MOSES
2501 STADIUM DRIVE ... KALAMAZOO **MI** 49008 (616) 349-8396
SAGINAW JEWISH WELFARE FEDERATION
1424 SOUTH WASHINGTON AVENUE ... SAGINAW **MI** 48601 (517) 753-5230
JEWISH FEDERATION AND COMMUNITY COUNCIL
1602 EAST SECOND STREET ... DULUTH **MN** 55812 (218) 724-8857
MINNEAPOLIS FEDERATION FOR JEWISH SERVICES
811 LASALLE AVENUE ... MINNEAPOLIS **MN** 55402 (612) 339-7491
UNITED JEWISH FUND & COUNCIL 790 SOUTH CLEVELAND ... ST. PAUL **MN** 55116 (612) 690-1707
JEWISH FEDERATION OF GREATER KANSAS CITY
25 EAST 12TH STREET, 10TH FLOOR ... KANSAS CITY **MO** 64106 (816) 421-5808
UNITED JEWISH FUND OF ST. JOSEPH 509 WOODCREST DRIVE ... ST. JOSEPH **MO** 64506 (816) 279-7154
JEWISH FEDERATION OF ST. LOUIS 10957 SCHUETZ ROAD ... ST. LOUIS **MO** 63141 (314) 432-0200
JACKSON JEWISH WELFARE FUND, INC. P.O. BOX 12329 ... JACKSON **MS** 39211 (601) 944-0607
FEDERATED JEWISH CHARITIES OF ASHEVILLE, INC.
236 CHARLOTTE STREET ... ASHEVILLE **NC** 28801 (704) 253-0701
DURHAM-CHAPEL HILL JEWISH FEDERATION & COMMUNITY COUNCIL
205 MT. BOLUS ROAD ... CHAPEL HILL **NC** 27514 (919) 967-6916
CHARLOTTE JEWISH FEDERATION P.O. BOX 13369 ... CHARLOTTE **NC** 28211 (704) 366-5007
GREENSBORO JEWISH FEDERATION
713-A NORTH GREENE STREET ... GREENSBORO **NC** 27401 (919) 272-3189
HIGH POINT JEWISH FEDERATION P.O. BOX 2063 ... HIGH POINT **NC** 27261 (919) 431-7101
WINSTON-SALEM JEWISH COMMUNITY COUNCIL
980 BRYANS PLACE ... WINSTON-SALEM **NC** 27104 (919) 768-3358
LINCOLN JEWISH WELFARE FEDERATIONS, INC., THE P.O. BOX 80014 ... LINCOLN **NE** 68501 (402) 477-6987
JEWISH FEDERATION OF OMAHA 333 SOUTH 132ND STREET ... OMAHA **NE** 68154 (402) 334-8200
JEWISH FEDERATION OF GREATER MANCHESTER
698 BEECH STREET ... MANCHESTER **NH** 03104 (603) 627-7679
BAYONNE JEWISH COMMUNITY COUNCIL 1050 KENNEDY BLVD ... BAYONNE **NJ** 07002 (201) 436-6900
JEWISH FEDERATION OF SOMERSET COUNTY
120 FINDERNE AVENUE ... BRIDGWATER **NJ** 08807 (201) 725-6994
JEWISH FEDERATION OF SOUTHERN NEW JERSEY
2393 WEST MARLTON PIKE ... CHERRY HILL **NJ** 08002 (609) 665-6100
JEWISH FEDERATION OF GREATER CLIFTON-PASSAIC, UJ CAMPAIGN
199 SCOLES AVENUE ... CLIFTON **NJ** 07012 (201) 777-7031
JEWISH FEDERATION OF GREATER MONMOUTH COUNTY
100 GRANT AVENUE, P.O.BOX 210 ... DEAL **NJ** 07723 (201) 531-6200
JEWISH COMMUNITY FEDERATION OF METROPOLITAN NEW JERSEY-UJA
60 GLENWOOD AVENUE ... EAST ORANGE **NJ** 07017 (201) 673-6800
JEWISH FEDERATION OF GREATER MIDDLESEX COUNTY
100 METROPLEX DRIVE, SUITE 101 ... EDISON **NJ** 08817 (201) 985-1234
JEWISH FEDERATION OF NORTHERN MIDDLESEX COUNTY-UJA
1775 OAK TREE ROAD ... EDISON **NJ** 08820 (201) 494-3920
JEWISH FEDERATION OF RARITAN VALLEY
2 SOUTH ADELAIDE AVENUE ... HIGHLAND PARK **NJ** 08904 (201) 246-1905
UNITED JEWISH APPEAL 71 BENTLEY AVENUE ... JERSEY CITY **NJ** 07304 (201) 332-6644
OCEAN COUNTY JEWISH FEDERATION 301 MADISON AVENUE ... LAKEWOOD **NJ** 08701 (201) 363-0530
UNITED JEWISH COMMUNITY OF BERGEN COUNTY 111 KINDERKAMACK ROAD,
P. O. BOX 4176, NORTH HACKENSACK STATION ... RIVER EDGE **NJ** 07661 (201) 488-6800
JEWISH FEDERATION OF DELAWARE VALLEY
999 LOWER FERRY ROAD ... TRENTON **NJ** 08628 (609) 883-5000
JEWISH FEDERATION OF CENTRAL NEW JERSEY, UJ CAMPAIGN
GREEN LANE ... UNION **NJ** 07083 (201) 351-5060
FEDERATION OF JEWISH AGENCIES OF ATLANTIC COUNTY
5321 ATLANTIC AVENUE ... VENTNOR CITY **NJ** 08406 (609) 822-7122
THE JEWISH FEDERATION OF CUMBERLAND COUNTY
629 WOOD STREET, SUITE 204 ... VINELAND **NJ** 08360 (609) 696-4445
JEWISH FEDERATION OF NORTH JERSEY- UJA DRIVE ONE PIKE DRIVE ... WAYNE **NJ** 07470 (201) 595-0555
JEWISH FEDERATION OF GREATER ALBUQUERQUE
12800 LOMAS NORTHEAST, SUITE F ... ALBUQUERQUE **NM** 87112 (505) 292-1064
ATLANTIC JEWISH COUNCIL
LORD NELSON HOTEL, 1515 SOUTH PARK STREET, SUITE 304 ... HALIFAX **NS** B3J 2L2 (902) 422-7491
JEWISH FEDERATION OF LAS VEGAS 1030 EAST TWAIN AVENUE ... LAS VEGAS **NV** 89109 (702) 732-0556
GREATER ALBANY JEWISH FEDERATION 350 WHITEHALL ROAD ... ALBANY **NY** 12208 (518) 459-8000
THE JEWISH FEDERATION OF BROOME COUNTY
500 CLUBHOUSE ROAD ... BINGHAMTON **NY** 13903 (607) 724-2332
CROWN HEIGHTS JEWISH COMMUNITY COUNCIL
387 KINGSTON AVENUE ... BROOKLYN **NY** 11225 (718) 778-8808
JEWISH FEDERATION OF GREATER BUFFALO, INC
787 DELAWARE AVENUE ... BUFFALO **NY** 14209 (716) 886-7750
ELMIRA JEWISH WELFARE FUND, INC.
P.O. BOX 3087, GRANDVIEW ROAD EXT ... ELMIRA **NY** 14905 (607) 734-8122
QUEENS JEWISH COMMUNITY COUNCIL
114-18 QUEENS BOULEVARD ... FOREST HILLS **NY** 11375 (718) 544-9033
GREATER GLEN FALLS JEWISH WELFARE FUND P.O. BOX 177 ... GLEN FALLS **NY** 12801 (518) 792-6438

JEWISH WELFARE FUND OF HUDSON, N.Y. JOSLEN BLVD ... HUDSON **NY** 12354 (518) 828-6848
JEWISH FEDERATION OF GREATER KINGSTON, INC. 159 GREEN STREET ... KINGSTON **NY** 12401 (914) 338-8131
COUNCIL OF JEWISH FEDERATIONS & WELFARE FUNDS, INC. 730 BROADWAY ... NEW YORK **NY** 10003 (212) 475-5000
FEDERATION OF JEWISH PHILANTHROPIES OF NEW YORK 130 EAST 59TH STREET ... NEW YORK **NY** 10022 (212) 980-1000
INTERNATIONAL COUNCIL ON JEWISH SOCIAL & WELFARE SERVICES 200 PARK AVENUE S ... NEW YORK **NY** 10003 (212) 674-6800
UNITED JEWISH APPEAL OF GREATER NEW YORK, INC. 130 EAST 59TH STREET ... NEW YORK **NY** 10022 (212) 980-1000
UNITED JEWISH COUNCIL OF THE EAST SIDE, INC. 235 EAST BROADWAY ... NEW YORK **NY** 10002 (212) 233-6037
JEWISH FEDERATION OF GREATER ORANGE COUNTY 360 POWELL AVENUE ... NEWBURGH **NY** 12550 (914) 562-7860
JEWISH FEDERATION OF NIAGARA FALLS, NEW YORK, INC. TEMPLE BETH ISRAEL, ROOM #5, COLLEGE & MADISON AVENUES ... NIAGARA FALLS **NY** 14305 (716) 284-4575
JEWISH WELFARE FUND OF DUTCHESS COUNTY 110 GRAND AVENUE ... POUGHKEEPSIE **NY** 12603 (914) 471-9811
JEWISH COMMUNITY FEDERATION OF ROCHESTER, NY 441 EAST AVENUE ... ROCHESTER **NY** 14607 (716) 325-3393
JEWISH FEDERATION OF GREATER SCHENECTADY 2565 BALLTOWN ROAD ... SCHENECTADY **NY** 12309 (518) 393-1136
UNITED JEWISH COMMUNITY OF ROCKLAND COUNTY 300 NORTH MAIN STREET, #311 ... SPRING VALLEY **NY** 10977 (914) 352-7100
SYRACUSE JEWISH FEDERATION, INC 2223 EAST GENESEE STREET, PO BOX 5004 ... SYRACUSE **NY** 13214 (315) 422-4104
TROY JEWISH COMMUNITY COUNCIL, INC. 2430 21ST STREET ... TROY **NY** 12180 (518) 274-0700
JEWISH FEDERATION OF UTICA, NEW YORK, INC. 2310 ONEIDA STREET ... UTICA **NY** 13501 (315) 733-2343
AKRON JEWISH COMMUNITY FEDERATION 750 WHITE POND DRIVE ... AKRON **OH** 44320 (216) 867-7850
CANTON JEWISH COMMUNITY FEDERATION 2631 HARVARD AVENUE N.W. ... CANTON **OH** 44709 (216) 452-6444
JEWISH FEDERATION OF CINCINNATI 1811 LOSANTIVILLE, SUITE 320 ... CINCINNATI **OH** 45237 (513) 351-3800
JEWISH COMMUNITY FEDERATION OF CLEVELAND 1750 EUCLID AVENUE ... CLEVELAND **OH** 44115 (216) 566-9200
COLUMBUS JEWISH FEDERATION 1175 COLLEGE AVENUE ... COLUMBUS **OH** 43209 (614) 237-7686
JEWISH FEDERATION OF GREATER DAYTON 4501 DENLINGER ROAD ... DAYTON **OH** 45426 (513) 854-4150
FEDERATED JEWISH CHARITIES OF LIMA DISTRICT 2417 WEST MARKET STREET ... LIMA **OH** 45805 (419) 224-8941
JEWISH COMMUNITY COUNCIL P.O. BOX 472 ... STEUBENVILLE **OH** 43952 (614) 282-9031
JEWISH WELFARE FEDERATION OF GREATER TOLEDO 6505 SYLVANIA AVENUE, P.O. BOX 587 ... SYLVANIA **OH** 43560 (419) 885-4461
YOUNGSTOWN AREA JEWISH FEDERATION P.O. BOX 449, 505 GYPSY LANE ... YOUNGSTOWN **OH** 44501 (216) 746-3251
JEWISH FEDERATION OF GREATER OKLAHOMA CITY 3022 NORTHWEST EXPRESSWAY, #116 ... OKLAHOMA CITY **OK** 73112 (405) 949-0111
JEWISH COMMUNITY COUNCIL 11032 QUAIL CREEK ROAD #201 ... OKLAHOMA CITY **OK** 73120 (405) 755-6030
JEWISH FEDERATION OF TULSA 2021 EAST 71ST STREET ... TULSA **OK** 74136 (918) 495-1100
HAMILTON JEWISH FEDERATION 57 DELAWARE AVENUE ... HAMILTON **ON** L8M 1T6 (416) 528-8570
LONDON JEWISH COMMUNITY COUNCIL 532 HURON STREET ... LONDON **ON** N5Y 4J5 (519) 673-3310
JEWISH COMMUNITY COUNCIL OF OTTAWA 151 CHAPEL STREET ... OTTAWA **ON** K1N 7Y2 (613) 232-7306
TORONTO JEWISH CONGRESS 150 BEVERLY STREET ... TORONTO **ON** M5T 1Y6 (416) 635-2883
CJF CANADIAN OFFICE 4600 BATHURST STREET SUITE 251 ... WILLOWDALE **ON** M2R 3V3 (416) 635-9567
JEWISH COMMUNITY COUNCIL 1641 OUELLETTE AVENUE ... WINDSOR **ON** N8X 1K9 (519) 973-1772
JEWISH FEDERATION OF PORTLAND 6651 SOUTHWEST CAPITAL HIGHWAY ... PORTLAND **OR** 97219 (503) 245-6219
JEWISH FEDERATION OF ALLENTOWN, INC. 702 NORTH 22ND STREET ... ALLENTOWN **PA** 18104 (215) 821-5500
FEDERATION OF JEWISH PHILANTHROPIES 1308 17TH STREET ... ALTOONA **PA** 16601 (814) 944-4072
BUTLER JEWISH WELFARE FUND 148 HAVERFORD DRIVE ... BUTLER **PA** 16001 (412) 287-3814
JEWISH COMMUNITY COUNCIL OF ERIE 701 G. DANIEL BALDWIN BLDG., 1001 STATE STREET ... ERIE **PA** 16501 (814) 455-4474
UNITED JEWISH FEDERATION OF GREATER HARRISBURG 100 VAUGHN STREET ... HARRISBURG **PA** 17110 (717) 236-9555
JEWISH COMMUNITY COUNCIL LAUREL & HEMLOCK STREETS ... HAZELTON **PA** 18201 (717) 454-3528
UNITED JEWISH FEDERATION OF JOHNSTOWN 922 WINDAN LANE ... JOHNSTOWN **PA** 15905 (814) 535-6756
LANCASTER JEWISH FEDERATION 2120 OREGON PIKE ... LANCASTER **PA** 17601 (717) 569-7352
JEWISH FEDERATION OF DELAWARE VALLEY 20-28 NORTH PENNSYLVANIA AVENUE ... MORRISVILLE **PA** 19067 (215) 736-8022
UNITED JEWISH APPEAL OF NEW CASTLE, PENNSYLVANIA P.O. BOX 5050 ... NEW CASTLE **PA** 16105 (412) 658-8389
TIFERES ISRAEL JEWISH CENTER 1541 POWELL STREET ... NORRISTOWN **PA** 19401 (215) 275-8797
FEDERATION OF JEWISH AGENCIES OF GREATER PHILADELPHIA 226 SOUTH 16TH STREET ... PHILADELPHIA **PA** 19102 (215) 893-5600
UNITED JEWISH FEDERATION OF GREATER PITTSBURGH 234 MCKEE PLACE ... PITTSBURGH **PA** 15213 (412) 681-8000
UNITED JEWISH CHARITIES 2300 MAHANTONGO STREET ... POTTSVILLE **PA** 17901 (717) 622-5890
JEWISH FEDERATION OF READING, PENNSYLVANIA, INC. 1700 CITY LINE STREET ... READING **PA** 19604 (215) 921-2766
SCRANTON-LACKAWANNA JEWISH FEDERATION 601 JEFFERSON AVENUE ... SCRANTON **PA** 18510 (717) 961-2300
JEWISH FEDERATION OF GREATER WILKES-BARRE 60 SOUTH RIVER STREET ... WILKES-BARRE **PA** 18702 (717) 822-4146
YORK COUNCIL OF JEWISH CHARITIES, INC. 120 EAST MARKET STREET ... YORK **PA** 17401 (717) 843-0918
ALLIED JEWISH COMMUNITY SERVICES 5151 COTE ST. CATHERINE ROAD ... MONTREAL **QU** H3W 1M6 (514) 735-3541
JEWISH FEDERATION OF RHODE ISLAND 130 SESSIONS STREET ... PROVIDENCE **RI** 02906 (401) 421-4111
CHARLESTON JEWISH FEDERATION 1645 RAOUL WALLENBERG BLVD., P.O. BOX 31298 ... CHARLESTON **SC** 29407 (803) 571-6565

COLUMBIA UNITED JEWISH WELFARE FEDERATION 4540 TRENHOLM ROAD ... COLUMBIA **SC** 29206 (803) 787-2023
JEWISH WELFARE FUND NATIONAL RESERVE BUILDING, ROOM 513 ... SIOUX FALLS **SD** 57102 (605) 336-2880
CHATTANOOGA JEWISH FEDERATION 5326 LYNNLAND TERRACE, P.O. BOX 8947 ... CHATTANOOGA **TN** 37411 (615) 894-1317
JEWISH WELFARE FUND, INC. 6800 DEANE HILL DRIVE, P.O. BOX 10882 ... KNOXVILLE **TN** 37919 (615) 693-5837
MEMPHIS JEWISH FEDERATION 6560 POPLAR AVENUE, P.O. BOX 38268 ... MEMPHIS **TN** 38138 (901) 767-7100
JEWISH FEDERATION OF NASHVILLE & MIDDLE TENNESSEE 801 PERRY WARNER BOULEVARD ... NASHVILLE **TN** 37205 (615) 356-3242
JEWISH COMMUNITY COUNCIL OF AUSTIN 11713 JOLLYVILLE ROAD ... AUSTIN **TX** 78759 (512) 331-1144
BEAUMONT JEWISH FEDERATION OF TEXAS, INC. P.O. BOX 1981 ... BEAUMONT **TX** 77704 (713) 833-5427
CORPUS CHRISTI JEWISH COMMUNITY COUNCIL 750 EVERHART ROAD ... CORPUS CHRISTI **TX** 78411 (512) 855-6239
JEWISH FEDERATION OF GREATER DALLAS 7800 NORTHHAVEN ROAD, SUITE A ... DALLAS **TX** 75230 (214) 369-3313
JEWISH FEDERATION OF EL PASO, INC. 405 MARDI GRAS, P.O. BOX 12097 ... EL PASO **TX** 79913 (915) 584-4437
JEWISH FEDERATION OF FORT WORTH & TARRANT COUNTY 6801 DAN DANCIGER ROAD ... FORT WORTH **TX** 76133 (817) 292-3081
GALVESTON COUNTY JEWISH WELFARE ASSOCIATION P.O. BOX 146 ... GALVESTON **TX** 77553 (409) 744-8295
JEWISH FEDERATION OF GREATER HOUSTON 5603 SOUTH BRAESWOOD BLVD ... HOUSTON **TX** 77096 (713) 729-7000
JEWISH FEDERATION OF SAN ANTONIO 8434 AHERN DRIVE ... SAN ANTONIO **TX** 78216 (512) 341-8234
FEDERATION OF JEWISH WELFARE FUND P.O. BOX 8601 ... TYLER **TX** 75711
JEWISH WELFARE COUNCIL OF WACO P.O. BOX 8031 ... WACO **TX** 76714 (817) 776-3740
UNITED JEWISH COUNCIL & SALT LAKE JEWISH WELFARE FUND 2416 EAST 1700 SOUTH ... SALT LAKE CITY **UT** 84108 (801) 581-0098
JEWISH FEDERATION OF THE VIRGINIA PENINSULA, INC. 2700 SPRING ROAD, P.O. BOX 6680 ... NEWPORT NEWS **VA** 23606 (804) 595-5544
UNITED JEWISH FEDERATION OF TIDEWATER 7300 NEWPORT AVENUE, P.O. BOX 9776 ... NORFOLK **VA** 23505 (804) 489-8040
JEWISH COMMUNITY FEDERATION OF RICHMOND P.O. BOX 8237, 5403 MONUMENT AVENUE ... RICHMOND **VA** 23226 (804) 288-0045
JEWISH COMMUNITY COUNCIL P.O. BOX 1074 ... ROANOKE **VA** 24005 (703) 774-2828
JEWISH FEDERATION OF GREATER SEATTLE 510 SECURITIES BLDG., 1904 THIRD AVENUE ... SEATTLE **WA** 98101 (206) 622-8211
JEWISH COMMUNITY COUNCIL OF SPOKANE 521 PARKADE PLAZA ... SPOKANE **WA** 99201 (509) 838-4261
UNITED JEWISH CHARITIES OF APPLETON 3131 NORTH MEADE STREET ... APPLETON **WI** 54911 (414) 733-1848
GREEN BAY JEWISH WELFARE FUND P.O. BOX 335 ... GREEN BAY **WI** 54305 (414) 432-9347
KENOSHA JEWISH WELFARE FUND 6537 7TH AVENUE ... KENOSHA **WI** 53140 (414) 658-8635
MADISON JEWISH COMMUNITY COUNCIL, INC. 310 NORTH MIDVALE BLVD., SUITE 325 ... MADISON **WI** 53705 (608) 231-3426
MILWAUKEE JEWISH FEDERATION, INC. 1360 N. PROSPECT AVENUE ... MILWAUKEE **WI** 53202 (414) 271-8338
RACINE JEWISH WELFARE COUNCIL 944 SOUTH MAIN STREET ... RACINE **WI** 53403 (414) 633-7093
JEWISH WELFARE COUNCIL OF SHEBOYGAN 1404 NORTH AVENUE ... SHEBOYGAN **WI** 53081
FEDERATED JEWISH CHARITIES OF CHARLESTON, INC. P.O. BOX 1613 ... CHARLESTON **WV** 25326 (304) 346-7500
FEDERATED JEWISH CHARITIES P.O. BOX 947 ... HUNTINGTON **WV** 25713 (304) 523-9326
FEDERACION DE COMUNIDADES ISRAELITAS ARGENTINAS PASTEUR 633 ... BUENOS AIRES **AR** 479096
AUSTRALIAN JEWISH WELFARE & RELIEF SOCIETY 466 PUNT ROAD, SOUTH YARRA ... MELBOURNE **AU** 26-3727
EXECUTIVE COUNCIL OF AUSTRALIAN JEWRY 343 LITTLE COLLINS STREET ... MELBOURNE **AU** 67-5341
CJF ISRAEL OFFICE 11 PINSKER STREET ... JERUSALEM **IS** 92228 (02) 636-850

FILMS & FILM STRIPS

BUREAU OF JEWISH EDUCATION 590 NORTH VERMONT AVENUE ... LOS ANGELES **CA** 90004
BUREAU OF JEWISH EDUCATION 6505 WILSHIRE BOULEVARD ... LOS ANGELES **CA** 90048 (213) 852-1234
HEBREW UNION COLLEGE-JEWISH INSTITUTE OF RELIGION 3077 UNIV. MALL, EDUCATION LABORATORY & LEARNING CNTR. ... LOS ANGELES **CA** 90007 (213) 749-2434
DEPT. OF ANTHROPOLOGY, UNIV. OF S. CALIF. UNIVERSITY PARK ... LOS ANGELES **CA** 90007 (213) 743-7100
UNIVERSITY OF SOUTHERN CALIFORNIA-FILM & VIDEO DISTRIBUTION CENTER SCHOOL OF CINEMA & TELEVISION, UNIVERSITY PARK, MC 2212 ... LOS ANGELES **CA** 90089 (213) 743-2238
CONTEMPORARY FILMS 1714 STOCKTON STREET ... SAN FRANCISCO **CA** 94133

TELEVISUALS 4224 ELLENITA AVENUE ... TARZANA **CA** 91356
LIVING ARCHIVES LIMITED PO BOX 86 ... BARRINGTON **IL** 60010 (312) 381-3736
BOARD OF JEWISH EDUCATION 618 SOUTH MICHIGAN AVENUE ... CHICAGO **IL** 60605 (312) 427-5570
CHICAGO BOARD OF RABBIS 1 SOUTH FRANKLIN ... CHICAGO **IL** 60605 (312) 444-2896
FILMS INC./PMI 5547 NORTH RAVENSWOOD ... CHICAGO **IL** 60640 (800) 323-4222
TEXTURE FILMS/PMI 5547 NORTH RAVENSWOOD ... CHICAGO **IL** 60640 (800) 323-4222
SIMON & SCHUSTER 108 WILMOT ROAD ... DEERFIELD **IL** 60015 (800) 323-5343
MIDWEST FILM CONFERENCE 800 CUSTER AVENUE ... EVANSTON **IL** 60602 (312) 869-0600
NATIONAL EDUCATIONAL TELEVISION FILM LIBRARY
INDIANA UNIVERSITY ... BLOOMINGTON **IN** 47401 (812) 332-0211
RAPHAEL FILMS 23 IRVING STREET ... CAMBRIDGE **MA** 02138 (617) 547-2865
MIRIAM WEINSTEIN 36 SHEPARD STREET ... CAMBRIDGE **MA** 02138
MIRAMAR FILM LIBRARY 19 CORNELL STREET ... NEWTON **MA** 02162
MODI'IN PRODUCTIONS 415 SOUTH STREET ... WALTHAM **MA** 02254
RUTTENBERG & EVERETT YIDDISH FILM LIBRARY
BRANDEIS UNIVERSITY ... WALTHAM **MA** 02254 (617) 899-7044
JEWISH MEDIA SERVICE OF THE INSTITUTE FOR JEWISH LIFE
65 WILLIAM STREET ... WELLESLEY **MA** 02181
JUDAICA CAPTIONED FILM CENTER P.O. BOX 21439 ... BALTIMORE **MD** 21208 (301) 922-4642
MEDIA RESOURCES CNTR. UNIV. OF MICHIGAN, EDUC. FILM LIBRARY
416 FOURTH STREET ... ANN ARBOR **MI** 48104 (313) 764-1817
MICHIGAN STATE UNIVERSITY AUDIO-VISUAL DEPARTMENT ... EAST LANSING **MI** 48824 (517) 355-6532
DIRECT CINEMA, LTD. P.O. BOX 315 ... FRANKLIN LAKES **NJ** 07417 (201) 891-8240
CONTEMPORARY FILMS PRINCETON ROAD ... HIGHTSTOWN **NJ** 08520 (609) 488-1700
SOSUA-SOL PRODUCTIONS 84 BOORAEM AVENUE ... JERSEY CITY **NY** 07307 (201) 963-7859
KOL REE ASSOCIATES 1923 SPRINGFIELD AVENUE ... MAPLEWOOD **NJ** 07040 (201) 763-4244
LEWIS SCHOENBRUN FILMS 95 REDMONT ROAD ... WATCHUNG **NJ** 07060 (201) 757-5602
NEW DAY FILMS 22 RIVERVIEW DRIVE ... WAYNE **NJ** 07470 (201) 633-0212
BEHRMAN HOUSE 235 WATCHUNG AVENUE ... WEST ORANGE **NJ** 07052 (201) 669-0447
ALDEN FILMS 7820 20TH AVENUE ... BROOKLYN **NY** 11214 (718) 331-1045
JEWISH EDUCATIONAL MEDIA 784 EASTERN PARKWAY ... BROOKLYN **NY** 11213 (718) 774-6000
LEV-ARI COMMUNICATIONS 16 COURT STREET, SUITE 1501 ... BROOKLYN **NY** 11241 (718) 768-5591
MIRIAM/LILLIAN FILMS 6416 STRICKLAND AVENUE ... BROOKLYN **NY** 11234 (718) 763-5950
SPHINX PRODUCTIONS 151 JORALEMON STREET, SUITE 10 ... BROOKLYN **NY** 11201 (718) 858-4898
TARYAG MEDIA INC. 719 CROWN STREET ... BROOKLYN **NY** 11213 (718) 467-3077
ZELMAN STUDIOS, LTD. 623 CORTELYOU ROAD ... BROOKLYN **NY** 11218 (718) 941-5500
TORAH MICROFICHE LIBRARY-THE RUDMAN FOUNDATION
1051 BAY 25TH STREET ... FAR ROCKAWAY **NY** 11691 (718) 634-8000
MACMILLAN AUDIO-BRANDON FILMS
34 MACQUESTEN PARKWAY SOUTH ... MT. VERNON **NY** 10550
AMERICAN ASSOCIATION FOR JEWISH EDUCATION
114 FIFTH AVENUE ... NEW YORK **NY** 10011 (212) 675-5656
AMERICAN FRIENDS OF THE ALLIANCE ISRAELITE UNIVERSELLE
61 BROADWAY ... NEW YORK **NY** 10006 (212) 349-0537
AMERICAN JEWISH CONGRESS, COMMISSION ON JEWISH AFFAIRS
15 EAST 84TH STREET ... NEW YORK **NY** 10028 (212) 879-4500
AMERICAN LIBRARY COLOR SLIDE COMPANY 222 WEST 23RD STREET ... NEW YORK **NY** 10011 (212) 255-5356
AMERICAN ZIONIST YOUTH FOUNDATION 515 PARK AVENUE ... NEW YORK **NY** 10022 (212) 751-6070
AMRAM NOWAK ASSOCIATES 15 WEST 26TH STREET, 9TH FLOOR ... NEW YORK **NY** 10010 (212) 686-1660
ANTI-DEFAMATION LEAGUE OF B'NAI B'RITH
823 UNITED NATIONS PLAZA ... NEW YORK **NY** 10017 (212) 490-2525
ARTA FILMS, INC. 2130 BROADWAY, SUITE 1602 ... NEW YORK **NY** 10023 (212) 362-8535
ARTHUR CANTOR, INC. 33 WEST 60TH STREET ... NEW YORK **NY** 10023 (212) 664-1290
B. LONDIN VOICE-N-VISION 1365 YORK AVENUE ... NEW YORK **NY** 10021
BEN-LAR PRODUCTIONS 311 WEST 24TH STREET ... NEW YORK **NY** 10011 (212) 255-5553
CAROUSEL FILMS, INC. 241 EAST 34TH STREET ... NEW YORK **NY** 10016 (212) 683-1660

CHILDREN'S TELEVISION WORKSHOP ISRAELI SESAME STREET PROJECT
1 LINCOLN PLACE ... NEW YORK **NY** 10023 (212) 595-3456
THE CINEMA GUILD 1697 BROADWAY, SUITE 802 ... NEW YORK **NY** 10019 (212) 246-5522
CITY LIGHTS PRODUCTIONS 505 EIGHTH AVENUE, SUITE 2502 ... NEW YORK **NY** 10018 (212) 564-9106
CONTEMPORARY FILMS - MCGRAW HILL
1221 AVENUE OF THE AMERICAS ... NEW YORK **NY** 10020 (212) 997-4100
ETERNAL LIGHT C/O UNITED SYNAGOGUE OF AMERICA
155 FIFTH AVENUE ... NEW YORK **NY** 10010 (212) 533-7800
FIRST RUN FEATURES 153 WAVERLY PLACE ... NEW YORK **NY** 10014 (212) 243-0600
FRIENDSHIP PRESS 475 RIVERSIDE DRIVE ... NEW YORK **NY** 10027 (212) 870-2586
HADASSAH FILM LIBRARY 50 W. 58TH STREET ... NEW YORK **NY** 10016 (212) 355-7900
INTERNATIONAL FILM EXCHANGE LIMITED 159 WEST 53RD STREET ... NEW YORK **NY** 10019 (212) 582-4318
ISRA-ART 157 WEST 57TH STREET ... NEW YORK **NY** 10019 (212) 246-4500
ISRAEL EDUCATIONAL MATERIALS & GAMES, C/O ISRAEL TRADE CNTR.
111 WEST 40TH STREET ... NEW YORK **NY** 10018
ISRAEL FILM CENTER 515 PARK AVENUE ... NEW YORK **NY** 10022 (212) 688-0800
ISRAEL GOVERNMENT TOURIST OFFICE 350 FIFTH AVENUE ... NEW YORK **NY** 10001 (212) 560-0600
ISRAEL GOVERNMENT TRADE OFFICE 350 FIFTH AVENUE ... NEW YORK **NY** 10001 (212) 560-0600
ISRAEL PHILATELIC AGENCY IN AMERICA 116 WEST 32ND STREET ... NEW YORK **NY** 10001 (212) 695-0008
J. LEVINE CO. - LOWER EAST SIDE 58 ELDRIDGE STREET ... NEW YORK **NY** 10002 (212) 966-4460
J. LEVINE CO. - MIDTOWN STORE 5 WEST 30TH STREET ... NEW YORK **NY** 10001 (212) 695-6888
JWB LECTURE BUREAU, THE NATIONAL JEWISH WELFARE BOARD
15 EAST 26TH STREET ... NEW YORK **NY** 10010 (212) 532-4949
JEWISH AGENCY 515 PARK AVENUE ... NEW YORK **NY** 10022 (212) 752-0600
JEWISH BOOK COUNCIL, THE NATIONAL JEWISH WELFARE BOARD
15 EAST 26TH STREET ... NEW YORK **NY** 10010 (212) 532-4949
JEWISH CHAUTAUQUA SOCIETY, FILM DISTRIBUTION CENTER
838 FIFTH AVENUE ... NEW YORK **NY** 10021 (212) 249-0100
JEWISH EDUCATION COMMITTEE 426 WEST 58TH STREET ... NEW YORK **NY** 10019 (212) 245-8200
JEWISH EDUCATION PRESS 426 WEST 58TH STREET ... NEW YORK **NY** 10019 (212) 245-8200
JEWISH EDUCATIONAL SERVICE 489 THIRD AVENUE ... NEW YORK **NY** 10016 (212) 683-1522
JEWISH MEDIA SERVICE, THE NATIONAL JEWISH WELFARE BOARD
15 EAST 26TH STREET ... NEW YORK **NY** 10010 (212) 532-4949
JEWISH NATIONAL FUND - DEPT. OF YOUTH & EDUCATION
42 EAST 69TH STREET ... NEW YORK **NY** 10021 (212) 879-9300
JEWISH THEOLOGICAL SEMINARY OF AMERICA, DEPT. OF RADIO & TV
3080 BROADWAY ... NEW YORK **NY** 10027 (212) 678-8000
MARQUIS FILM DISTRIBUTOR 416 WEST 45TH STREET ... NEW YORK **NY** 10036 (212) 245-8900
MAXI COHEN 31 GREEN STREET ... NEW YORK **NY** 10013 (212) 966-6326
MIZRACHI 817 BROADWAY ... NEW YORK **NY** 10003 (212) 477-4720
NAT'L ACADEMY FOR ADULT JEWISH STUDIES OF THE U. SYN. OF AM.
155 FIFTH AVENUE ... NEW YORK **NY** 10010 (212) 260-8450
NATIONAL COMMITTEE FOR LABOR ISRAEL 33 EAST 67TH STREET ... NEW YORK **NY** 10021 (212) 628-1000
NATIONAL JEWISH WELFARE BOARD 15 EAST 26TH STREET ... NEW YORK **NY** 10010 (212) 532-4949
NEW JEWISH MEDIA PROJECT C/O NORTH AMERICAN JEWISH STUDENTS
36 WEST 37TH STREET ... NEW YORK **NY** 10017
NEW YORK BOARD OF RABBIS 10 EAST 73RD STREET ... NEW YORK **NY** 10021 (212) 879-8415
PHOENIX FILMS, INC. 468 PARK AVENUE SOUTH, SUITE 802 ... NEW YORK **NY** 10016 (212) 684-5910
PIONEER WOMEN 200 MADISON AVENUE ... NEW YORK **NY** 10016 (212) 725-8010
STUDENT STRUGGLE FOR SOVIET JEWRY 210 WEST 91ST STREET ... NEW YORK **NY** 10024 (212) 799-8900
TARBUTH FOUNDATION 129 WEST 67TH STREET ... NEW YORK **NY** 10023 (212) 874-7837
TELECULTURE, INC. 1457 BROADWAY, SUITE 802 ... NEW YORK **NY** 10036 (212) 719-3833
TORAH UMESORAH 160 BROADWAY ... NEW YORK **NY** 10038 (212) 406-4190
UNION OF AMERICAN HEBREW CONGREGATIONS 838 FIFTH AVENUE ... NEW YORK **NY** 10021 (212) 249-0100
UNITED JEWISH APPEAL 1290 AVENUE OF THE AMERICAS ... NEW YORK **NY** 10019 (212) 757-1500
UNITED SYNAGOGUE OF AMERICA 155 FIFTH AVENUE ... NEW YORK **NY** 10010 (212) 260-8450

THE WELL PRODUCTIONS 108 WEST 15TH STREET, #6D .... NEW YORK **NY** 10011 (212) 242-3307
WNET/THIRTEEN-DISTRIBUTION AND SALES 356 WEST 58TH STREET ... NEW YORK **NY** 10019 (212) 560-3045
WOMEN'S AMERICAN ORT 1250 BROADWAY .... NEW YORK **NY** 10001 (212) 594-8500
YIVO SLIDE BANK, MAX WEINREICH CENTER 1048 FIFTH AVENUE .... NEW YORK **NY** 10028 (212) 535-6700
THE CENTER FOR JEWISH MEDIA LIMITED 48 URBAN AVENUE .... WESTBURY **NY** 11590 (516) 333-5300
ROBERT BINDER - B'YAD HAYOTZER 24 WARWICK AVENUE .... TORONTO **ON** M6C 1T6 (416) 979-3393
AMIN PRODUCTIONS 425 ASHBOURNE ROAD .... ELKINS PARK **PA** 11917
GRATZ COLLEGE, DIVISION OF COMMUNITY SERVICES
1000 WEST TABOR ROAD .... PHILADELPHIA **PA** 19141 (215) 329-3363
LAURENCE SALZMANN 3607 BARING STREET .... PHILADELPHIA **PA** 19104 (215) 382-1410
FAGEL FILMS 6510 BARTLETT STREET .... PITTSBURGH **PA** 15217 (412) 422-8223
FELIX LAZARUS 441 DUFFERIN ROAD .... MONTREAL **QU**
MEDIA PROJECTS, INC. 5215 HOMER .... DALLAS **TX** 75206 (214) 826-3863
RARIG'S FILM SERVICE 1941 AURORA NORTH .... SEATTLE **WA** 98109 (206) 282-1941

FISH

SAX FISH AVENUE 370 NORTH FAIRFAX AVENUE .... LOS ANGELES **CA** 90036 (213) 936-3445
FLORIDA SMOKED FISH CO. 111 NW 159TH DRIVE .... MIAMI **FL** 33169 (305) 625-5112
REG'S KOSHER FISH MARKET
1676 NORTHEAST 164TH STREET .... NORTH MIAMI BEACH **FL** 33162 (305) 940-1718
STOLLER FISHERIES, INC. BOX B .... SPIRIT LAKE **IA** 51360 (712) 336-1750
VITA FOOD PRODUCTS INC. 2222 WEST LAKE .... CHICAGO **IL** 60612 (312) 738-4500
LAKEWOOD GEFILTE FISH 32 CLIFTON AVENUE .... LAKEWOOD **NJ** 08701 (800) 433-4583
BLUE RIBBON SMOKED FISH CO. 5901 FOSTER AVENUE .... BROOKLYN **NY** 11234 (718) 251-9100
DAGIM TAHORIM CO., INC. 1644 52ND STREET .... BROOKLYN **NY** 11204 (718) 851-1006
DANY'S KOSHER FISH MARKET 4104 18TH AVENUE .... BROOKLYN **NY** 11218 (718) 853-7816
DELICIOUS KOSHER FISH CO. 211 HOOPER STREET .... BROOKLYN **NY** 11211 (718) 851-9860
MUNCHICK'S FISH MARKET, INC. 68 BELMONT AVENUE .... BROOKLYN **NY** 11212 (718) 345-0400
NOVA SCOTIA FOOD PRODUCTS CORP. 77 LOMBARDY STREET .... BROOKLYN **NY** 11222 (718) 388-2876
KINERET FOOD CORP. 24 JERICHO TPKE .... JERICHO **NY** 11753 (516) 333-2626
BELNORD FISH MARKET 544 AMSTERDAM AVENUE .... NEW YORK **NY** 10024 (212) 724-4214
MIDWEST LIVE FISH 88-90 LAIGHT STREET .... NEW YORK **NY** 10013 (212) 349-1430
UNGAR'S P.O. BOX 490 .... SPRING VALLEY **NY** 10977 (914) 354-8067
PUREPAK FOODS, INC. 47-39 49TH STREET .... WOODSIDE **NY** 11377 (718) 784-3344
NEWMARK'S KOSHER FISH MARKET 13897 CEDAR ROAD .... CLEVELAND **OH** 44118 (216) 321-1048
MONTROSE FOOD PRODUCTS 3650 SOUTH GALLOWAY STREET ..... PHILADELPHIA **PA** 19148 (215) 336-5800

FLOWERS

KENNICOTT BROTHERS COMPANY 2660 NORTH CLYBOURN .... CHICAGO **IL** 60614 (312) 549-0465
AGREXCO U.S.A. LTD. 149-32 132ND STREET .... JAMAICA **NY** 11430 (718) 529-4411
N'SHEI AHAVAS CHESED 1549 46TH STREET .... NEW YORK **NY** 11219 (212) 438-0211
MILWAUKEE FLORIST EXCHANGE 123 EAST KNAPP .... MILWAUKEE **WI** 53202 (414) 273-4903

FOOD PRODUCTS

M. SQUARE CORP./IMAGINE FOODS
BOX 35513, #475 FIFTH AVENUE .... LOS ANGELES **CA** 90035 (213) 852-0094
KING SALMON, INC. 171 N. GREEN STREET .... CHICAGO **IL** 60607 (312) 666-3226
TOMSON FOODS INTERNATIONAL 305 WELLS STREET .... GREENFIELD **MA** 01301 (413) 774-6501
TULKOFF'S HORSERADISH PRODUCTS CO., INC. 1101 S. CONKLIN ...... BALTIMORE **MD** 21224 (301) 327-6585
GREENFIELD NOODLE & SPECIALTY CO. 600 CUSTER AVENUE .... DETROIT **MI** 48202 (313) 873-2212
KELLER FOOD CO. 2917 BROOKLYN AVENUE, P.O. BOX 4824 .... KANSAS CITY **MO** 64109 (816) 921-3500
INTERNATIONAL MASTERPIECES LTD.
ABA MGT., 38 COMMERCE DRIVE .... CRANBURY **NJ** 08512 (609) 395-8810
CARMEL KOSHER FOOD PRODUCTS BOUMAR PLACE .... ELMWOOD PARK **NJ** 07407 (201) 791-9170
I. ROKEACH & SONS, INC. 560 SYLVAN AVENUE .... ENGLEWOOD CLIFFS **NJ** 07632 (201) 568-7550
MACABEE FOODS, INC. 107 PINK STREET .... HACKENSACK **NJ** 07601 (201) 489-4343
SEASON PRODUCTS CORPORATION 34 LORETTO STREET .... IRVINGTON **NJ** 07111 (201) 923-1818
B. MANISCHEWITZ CO. ONE MANISCHEWITZ PLAZA .... JERSEY CITY **NJ** 07302 (212) 333-3700

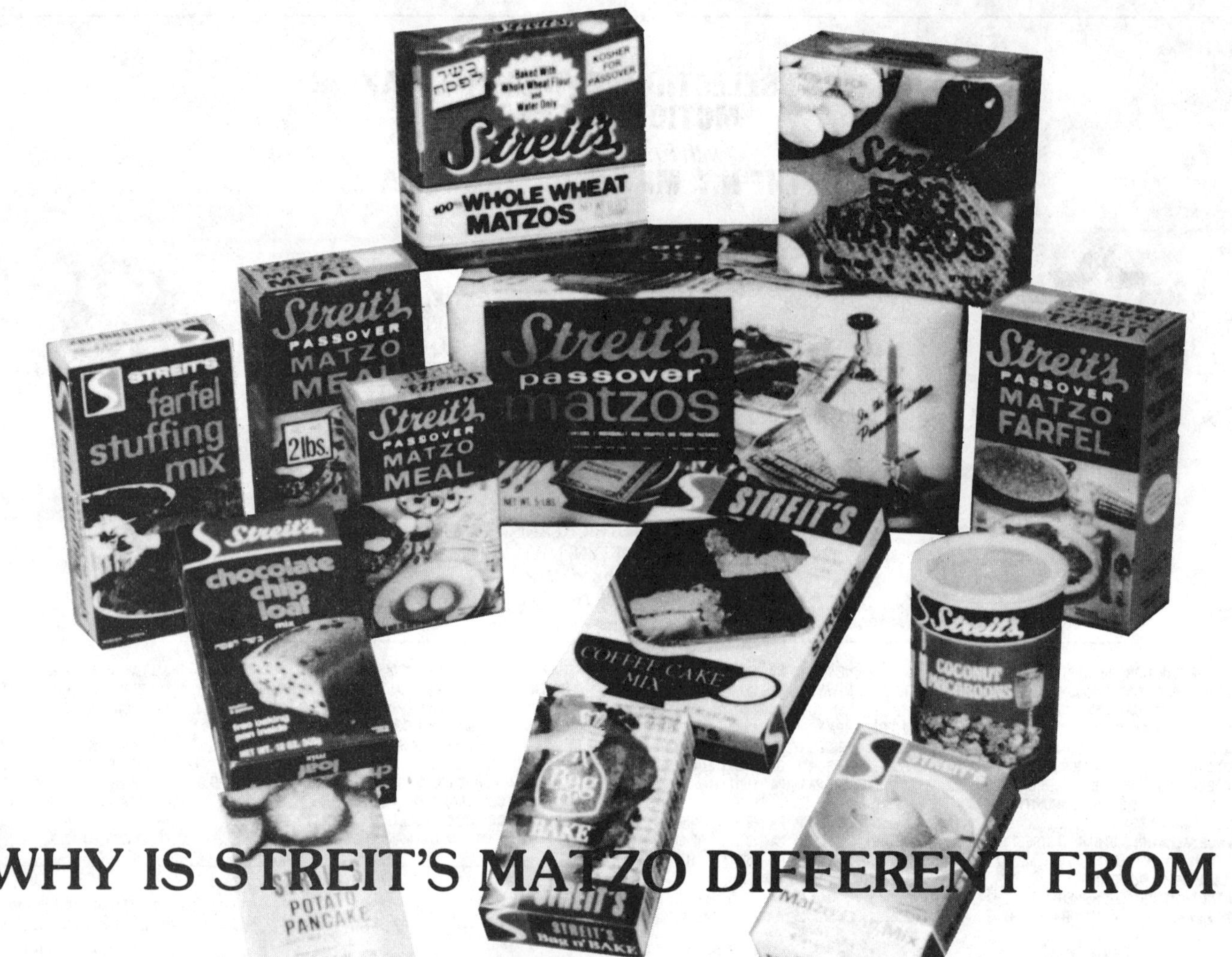
Streit's
KOSHER FOR PASSOVER
Baked With Whole Wheat Flour and Water Only
100 WHOLE WHEAT MATZOS
EGG MATZOS
Streit's PASSOVER MATZO MEAL
2lbs.
STREIT'S farfel stuffing mix
Streit's passover matzos
Streit's PASSOVER MATZO FARFEL
Streit's chocolate chip loaf
STREIT'S
COFFEE CAKE MIX
Streit's COCONUT MACAROONS
STREIT'S POTATO PANCAKE
STREIT'S Bag n' BAKE

Name / Address	City	State	Zip	Phone
FAMIGLIA INDUSTRIES INC. 75 AMITY STREET	JERSEY CITY	NJ	07304	(201) 451-2222
BENAN FOODS, INC. 30 JABEZ STREET	NEWARK	NJ	07105	(201) 589-0323
MOTHER'S FOOD PRODUCTS INC. 80 AVENUE K	NEWARK	NJ	07105	(201) 589-5297
GLYNGORE PRODUCTS, INC. 28 CHARLEMAGNE PLACE	PINE BROOK	NJ	07058	(201) 575-6299
TABATCHNICK SOUPS 2951 VAUXHALL ROAD	VAUXHALL	NJ	07088	(201) 687-6447
MALLMAR KOSHER FOODS 1303 HERSCHEL STREET	BRONX	NY	10461	(212) 824-5040
MRS. WEINBERG'S FOOD PRODUCTS INC. 1303 HERSCHEL STREET	BRONX	NY	10461	(212) 824-6940
STELLA D'ORO BISCUIT CO, INC. 184 WEST 237TH STREET	BRONX	NY	10463	(212) 549-3700
ADLER'S FOOD CORP. 902 ESSEX STREET	BROOKLYN	NY	11208	(718) 649-9121
BATAMPTE PICKLE PRODUCTS INC. 77 BROOKLYN TERMINAL MARKET	BROOKLYN	NY	11236	(718) 251-2100
BOUREKA NOSH 5914 20TH AVENUE	BROOKLYN	NY	11204	(718) 236-1232
GOLD PURE FOOD PRODUCTS CO., INC. 895 MCDONALD AVENUE	BROOKLYN	NY	11218	(718) 435-1910
GWB IMPORTS LTD. 5405 13TH AVENUE	BROOKLYN	NY	11219	(718) 972-5596
KEMACH FOOD PRODUCTS CORP. 778 ROCKAWAY PARKWAY	BROOKLYN	NY	11236	(718) 385-1544
LANDAU COMPANY 19 HEYWARD STREET	BROOKLYN	NY	11211	(718) 875-5702
LEIBOWITZ DIVISION-VLASIC FOODS, INC. 9301 DITMAS AVENUE	BROOKLYN	NY	11236	(718) 342-4886
LIEBER'S KOSHER FOOD SPECIALTIES 100 19 STREET	BROOKLYN	NY	11232	(718) 499-0888
METRO KOSHER FROZEN DESSERTS, INC. 147 METROPOLITAN AVENUE	BROOKLYN	NY	11211	(718) 388-1323
OLD DUTCH MUSTARD CO., INC. 80 METROPOLITAN AVENUE	BROOKLYN	NY	11211	(718) 387-9155
PALETA/FROZFRUIT 38 HALL STREET	BROOKLYN	NY	11205	(718) 934-7751
QUALITY FROZEN FOODS, INC. 1663 62ND STREET	BROOKLYN	NY	11204	(718) 256-9100
VICTOR VICTOR CORP. 401 MARCY AVENUE	BROOKLYN	NY	11206	(718) 384-1777
WINSTON NATIONAL FOOD CORP. 3 NORTH OAK STREET	COPIAGUE	NY	11726	(516) 842-6600
PARVE FROZEN DELIGHTS INC. 15-20 CENTRAL AVENUE	FAR ROCKAWAY	NY	11691	(718) 327-9808
KINERET FOOD CORP. 24 JERICHO TPKE	JERICHO	NY	11753	(516) 333-2626
KOSHERIFIC FOODS 24 JERICHO TPKE.	JERICHO	NY	11753	(516) 333-2626
HOROWITZ-MARGARETEN KOSHER FOODS 29-00 REVIEW AVENUE	LONG ISLAND CITY	NY	11101	(718) 729-5420
HEBREW NATIONAL FOODS 58-80 MAURICE AVENUE	MASPETH	NY	11378	(718) 894-4300
J. ITZKOWITZ, INC. 56-75 49TH STREET	MASPETH	NY	11378	(718) 497-4480
CANTON NOODLE MANUFACTURING COMPANY, INC. 101 MOTT STREET	NEW YORK	NY	10013	(212) 226-3276
SOLCOOR INC.-ISRAELI FOOD PRODUCTS 2 PARK AVENUE	NEW YORK	NY	10016	(212) 561-7230
STREIT MATZO COMPANY 150 RIVINGTON STREET	NEW YORK	NY	10002	(212) 475-7000
BARRICINI FOODS INC. 123 SOUTH STREET	OYSTER BAY	NY	11771	(516) 922-6212
SETTON INTERNATIONAL FOODS 150 DUPONT STREET	PLAINVIEW	NY	11803	(516) 349-8090
FRIDAY'S IMPORTING BREAD CRUMB 211-10 HILLSIDE AVENUE	QUEENS VILLAGE	NY	11427	(718) 776-2929
WILTON FOODS, INC./WILTON CATERERS, INC. 710 SOUTH MAIN STREET	SPRING VALLEY	NY	10977	(914) 352-4800
CANNOLI FACTORY 1250 SHAMES DRIVE	WESTBURY	NY	11590	(516) 334-4394
EMPIRE KOSHER FOODS, INC. R.D. #3 P.O. BOX 165	MIFFLINTOWN	PA	17059	(717) 436-2131
HERR FOODS INC. INTERSECTION OF ROUTES 272 & 131, P.O. BOX 300	NOTTINGHAM	PA	19362	(215) 932-9330
CANTOR & SMOLAR, INC. 1816 BEDFORD AVENUE	PITTSBURGH	PA	15219	(412) 281-5239

FREE CLOTHES

Name / Address	City	State	Zip	Phone
JEWISH SALVAGE BUREAU 130 NORTH WELLS	CHICAGO	IL	60606	(312) 346-5883
JEWISH FREE STORE - MALBISH ARUMIM 306 WEST 37TH STREET	NEW YORK	NY	10018	

FREE LOAN SOCIETIES

Name / Address	City	State	Zip	Phone
PHOENIX JEWISH FREE LOAN ASSOCIATION 1718 WEST MARYLAND AVENUE	PHOENIX	AZ	85015	(602) 249-1832
HEBREW FREE LOAN ASSOCIATION 4032 EAST WHITTIER	TUCSON	AZ	85712	
HEBREW ASSISTANCE ASSOCIATION C/O JEWISH FAMILY SERVICE AGENCY 2025 WEST 42ND AVENUE, #305	VANCOUVER	BC	V6M 2B5	(604) 266-2396
FEDERATION FREE LOAN ASSOCIATION 2601 GRAND AVENUE	LONG BEACH	CA	90815	
JEWISH FREE LOAN ASSOCIATION 6505 WILSHIRE BLVD., SUITE 614	LOS ANGELES	CA	90048	(213) 655-6922
JEWISH FAMILY SERVICE 3245 SHEFFIELD AVENUE	OAKLAND	CA	94602	(415) 532-6314
HEBREW FREE LOAN ASSOCIATION 703 MARKET STREET, SUITE 445	SAN FRANCISCO	CA	94103	(415) 982-3177
MAX GORDON MEMORIAL LOAN FUND OF THE JEWISH COMMUNITY COUNCIL 1024 EMORY STREET	SAN JOSE	CA	95126	
HEBREW FREE LOAN ASSOCIATION 187 EATON STREET	BRIDGEPORT	CT	06604	
HEBREW FREE LOAN ASSOCIATION 34 GILBERT AVENUE	NEW HAVEN	CT	06511	(203) 562-0584
HEBREW FREE LOAN ASSOCIATION 19 AVALON CIRCLE	WATERBURY	CT	06710	
JEWISH FAMILY SERVICE 2105 WASHINGTON STREET	WILMINGTON	DE	19802	(302) 478-9411
HEBREW FREE LOAN 500 S.W. 17TH AVENUE	MIAMI	FL	33160	
GREATER MIAMI HEBREW FREE LOAN ASSOCIATION, THE 1545 ALTON ROAD	MIAMI BEACH	FL	33139	(305) 532-1392
HEBREW GEMILATH CHESED SOCIETY PO BOX 6546	SAVANNAH	GA	31408	
FREE LOAN FUND 525 14TH STREET	SIOUX CITY	IA	51105	(712) 258-0618
GEMILAS CHESED - FREE LOAN FUND 3453 WEST FOSTER	CHICAGO	IL	60625	
HEBREW FREE LOAN ASSOCIATION 262 WASHINGTON STREET	BOSTON	MA	02108	
HEBREW FREE LOAN ASSOCIATION 2 ATWATER STREET	WORCESTER	MA	01602	
HEBREW FREE LOAN ASSOCIATION 5752 PARK HEIGHTS AVENUE	BALTIMORE	MD	21215	(301) 466-9206
HEBREW FREE LOAN ASSOCIATION 341 CUMBERLAND ROAD	PORTLAND	ME	04101	
HEBREW FREE LOAN ASSOCIATION 18100 MEYERS ROAD	DETROIT	MI	48235	
HEBREW FREE LOAN ASSOCIATION 457 CENTER STREET	ORANGE	NJ	07079	
HEBREW FREE LOAN ASSOCIATION 152 VAN HOUTEN	PATERSON	NJ	07505	(201) 742-8395
HEBREW FREE LOAN ASSOCIATION 457 CENTER	SOUTH ORANGE	NJ	07079	
HEBREW FREE LOAN ASSOCIATION 1418 WEST STATE STREET	TRENTON	NJ	08618	
HEBREW BENEVOLENT LOAN ASSOCIATION 787 DELAWARE AVENUE	BUFFALO	NY	14209	(716) 886-7750
GEMILUTH CHESSED OF GREATER NEW YORK, INC. 717 W. 177TH STREET	NEW YORK	NY	10033	(212) 923-8701
HEBREW FREE LOAN SOCIETY INC. (MAIN OFFICE) 205 EAST 42ND STREET	NEW YORK	NY	10017	(212) 687-0188
HEBREW FREE LOAN ASSOCIATION 1220 HURON ROAD, #709	CLEVELAND	OH	44115	(216) 771-7349
HEBREW FREE LOAN ASSOCIATION ARCADE BUILDING, 338 THE ARCADE	CLEVELAND	OH	44143	(216) 771-7349
LADIES FREE LOAN ASSOCIATION 3351 DESOTA AVENUE	CLEVELAND	OH	44118	(216) 932-4138
JEWISH FAMILY SERVICE 184 SALEM AVENUE	DAYTON	OH	45406	
JEWISH FAMILY SERVICE 2247 COLLINGWOOD BOULEVARD	TOLEDO	OH	43620	
FREE LOAN COMMITTEE JEWISH COMMUNITY COUNCIL, 200 MCBIRNEY BUILDING	TULSA	OK	74103	
HEBREW RE-ESTABLISHMENT SERVICES 150 BEVERLY STREET	TORONTO	ON		
TORONTO HEB. RE-ESTABLISHMENT SERVICE-GMILATH CHASODIM ASSOC 3199 BATHURST STREET, ROOM 205	TORONTO	ON	M6A 2B2	(416) 789-1844
TORONTO JEWISH ASSISTANCE SERVICE 4600 BATHURST STREET	WILLOWDALE	ON	M2R 3V2	(416) 635-1217
HEBREW FREE LOAN ASSOCIATION 234 MCKEE PLACE	PITTSBURGH	PA	15213	(412) 683-4900
A.B. COHEN HEBREW FREE LOAN SOCIETY 601 JEFFERSON AVENUE	SCRANTON	PA	18510	(717) 961-2300
HEBREW FREE LOAN ASSOCIATION 5775 VICTORIA AVENUE	MONTREAL	QU		
HEBREW FREE LOAN ASSOCIATION 128 NORTH MAIN STREET	PROVIDENCE	RI	02906	
SOUTH PROVIDENCE HEBREW FREE LOAN 1027 BROAD STREET	PROVIDENCE	RI	02905	
HEBREW BENEVOLENT SOCIETY 105 BROAD STREET	CHARLESTON	SC	29402	
HEBREW FREE LOAN ASSOCIATION 701 NORTH CHAPARRAL	CORPUS CHRISTI	TX	78401	
HEBREW FREE LOAN ASSOCIATION 2821 CANAL	HOUSTON	TX	77003	
HEBREW FREE LOAN ASSOCIATION 107 SOUTH PECOS STREET	SAN ANTONIO	TX	78207	

Women's League of Sh'or Yoshuv

EVERY BALABOOSTA WANTS TO ENTERTAIN EASILY AND GRACIOUSLY, AND SHE CAN.

The Women's League of Yeshiva Sh'or Yoshuv has prepared a most unique and valuable cookbook. We have combined our talent and culinary experience, and have stirred together our favorite recipes, dividing them into 11 food categories. (Shabbos and Yom Tov, Fish, Soup and Accompaniments, Fleishigs, Kugels and Side Dishes, Salads and Vegetables, International Cuisine, Nature's Best, Cakes, Pies and Frostings, The Sweet Tooth and Misc.) We have flavored them with that unique "Yiddisher Taam" and whipped them up into a culinary delight of 600 mouth watering dishes for every meal or occasion.

In addition to all the recipes, "A Yiddisher Taam" will contain a complete section of select cooking information. All the basic cooking information one could ask for is collected and bound together, with our favorite recipes, into one book.

The Price of "A Yiddisher Taam" will be $9.95 plus $1.50 postage and handling for each cookbook. Please make checks payable to Sh'or Yoshuv Cookbook. Remember, it makes the perfect gift for special occasions. In order to be assured that the number of books you would like to purchase will be reserved for you, please fill out the form at the bottom of the page and return in with your check.

Sincerely yours,

Chaya Bracha Goldfein

Chaya Bracha Goldfein
Cookbook Chairperson

"A YIDDISHER TAAM"
WOMEN'S LEAGUE OF SH'OR YOSHUV
1526 Central Avenue • Far Rockaway, New York 11691

— MY ORDER FOR COOKBOOKS —

Please send me _______ cookbooks at $9.95 plus $1.50 postage and handling each.

Amount Enclosed ____________________

Name ____________________

Address ____________________

City ____________ State ____________ Zip ____________

1526 Central Avenue • Far Rockaway, N.Y. 11691 • (718) 327-2048

HEBREW FREE LOAN ASSOCIATION P.O. BOX 12131 .... SAN ANTONIO **TX** 78212
FREE LOAN SOCIETY 113 LONGWOOD DRIVE .... NEWPORT NEWS **VA** 23606
HEBREW LADIES CHARITY SOCIETY 1416 WEST PRINCESS ANNE ROAD .. NORFOLK **VA** 23507
HEBREW LADIES FREE LOAN SOCIETY 1110 HARVARD STREET .... SEATTLE **WA** 89115
SEATTLE HEBREW FREE LOAN 1501 17TH AVENUE .... SEATTLE **WA** 89104

FREE SHELTER

HEBREW SHELTERING HOME 699 WEST JACKSON AVENUE .... BRIDGEPORT **CT** 06605
HEBREW LADIES SHELTERING HOME-INDEPENDENT TRANSIENT SERVICE
922 ALBANY AVENUE .... HARTFORD **CT** 06614
JEWISH SHELTER HOUSE 5050 N. KIMBALL AVENUE .... CHICAGO **IL** 60625 (312) 539-6956
KANSAS CITY KANSAS RELIEF - INDEPENDENT TRANSIENT SERVICE
726 MINNESOTA AVENUE .... KANSAS CITY **KS** 66101
HEBREW SHELTERING HOME 53 WHEELER STREET .... LYNN **MA** 01908
HEBREW SHELTERING SOCIETY 744 SILVER SPRING AVENUE .... SILVER SPRING **MD** 20910 (301) 585-5108
JEWISH SHELTERING HOME 1231 N. & S. ROADS .... ST. LOUIS **MO** 63123
HEBREW FREE SHELTERING HOME 65 QUINCY .... PASSAIC **NJ** 07055
HEBREW SHELTERING HOME-INDEPENDENT TRANSIENT SERVICE
138 NORTH PARK AVENUE .... BUFFALO **NY** 14216
HEBREW SHELTER HOME 1775 SOUTH TAYLOR ROAD .... CLEVELAND **OH** 44105 (216) 321-3650
JEWISH RELIEF & BENEVOLENT SOCIETY-INDEPENDENT TRANSIENT SVC
6651 S.W. CAPITOL HIGHWAY .... PORTLAND **OR** 97218
HEBREW SHELTERING LADIES AID SOCIETY - IND. TRANSIENT SVC.
C/O 540 WESTMORELAND AVENUE .... KINGSTON **PA** 18704
HEBREW FRIENDLY INN - INDEPENDENT TRANSIENT SERVICE
2126 OAK AVENUE .... NEWPORT NEWS **VA** 23607

FROCKS

BROADWAY CLOTHING CORP. 234 KEAP STREET .... BROOKLYN **NY** 11211 (718) 387-1915
FRANKFURTER QUALITY CLOTHING 4203 13TH AVENUE .... BROOKLYN **NY** 11219 (718) 435-7223
FRANKFURTER QUALITY CLOTHING 314 ROEBLING STREET .... BROOKLYN **NY** 11211 (718) 387-2977
LEE AVENUE CLOTHING 122 LEE AVENUE .... BROOKLYN **NY** 11211 (718) 522-6792
REINHOLD CLOTHIERS 4421 14TH AVENUE .... BROOKLYN **NY** 11219 (718) 438-9342
ROTH CLOTHING 300 PENN STREET .... BROOKLYN **NY** 11211 (718) 384-4927
SINGER'S CLOTHING 116 LEE AVENUE .... BROOKLYN **NY** 11211 (718) 384-6200
STUHL CLOTHING 59 LEE AVENUE .... BROOKLYN **NY** 11211 (718) 387-3213

FUND RAISING

CELEBRITY ART AUCTIONS
10511 ANDORA AVENUE, DEPARTMENT N .... CHATSWORTH **CA** 91311 (818) 341-7373
FEDERAL MARKETING COMPANY, INC./MARCUS J. COHEN
1246 MIDLAND, P.O. BOX 3208 .... ST. LOUIS **MO** 63130 (314) 725-0211
ART AUCTION, J. RICHARDS GALLERY 64 EAST PALISADE AVENUE .... ENGLEWOOD **NJ** 07631 (201) 871-1050
AGENTS CARD & GIFT COMPANY 4543 THIRD AVENUE .... BRONX **NY** 10458 (212) 933-1080
FLARE 2884 NOSTRAND AVENUE .... BROOKLYN **NY** 11229 (718) 258-8860
JUDAH H. KLEIN ASSOCIATES 433 BARNARD AVENUE, SUITE 100 ..... CEDARHURST **NY** 11516 (516) 295-5646
DEVELOPMENT CONSULTANTS OF AMERICA, INC. 1776 BROADWAY ..... NEW YORK **NY** 10019 (212) 265-8333
ISRAEL AMERICAN FUND RAISING CORP. 315 FIFTH AVENUE .... NEW YORK **NY** 10016 (212) 532-2757
ARI EDITIONS BOX 921 .... SOUTHAMPTON **PA** 18966 (215) 364-3571

FUNERAL DIRECTORS

SINAI MORTUARY OF ARIZONA 4538 N. 16TH STREET .... PHOENIX **AZ** 85016 (602) 248-0030
ARIZONA MORTUARY, UNIVERSITY CHAPEL
7 EAST UNIVERSITY BOULEVARD .... TUCSON **AZ** 85705 (602) 624-8685
EAST LAWN MORTUARY & CEMETERY 580 EAST GRANT ROAD .... TUCSON **AZ** 85712 (602) 885-6741
CHEVRA KADISHA MORTUARY 7209 ALABAMA .... CANOGA PARK **CA** 91303 (818) 884-4008
GLASBAND-WILLEN LONG BEACH MORTUARY
638 ATLANTIC AVENUE .... LONG BEACH **CA** 90810 (213) 436-1273
CHEVRA KADISHA MORTUARY 7832 SANTA MONICA BLVD. .... LOS ANGELES **CA** 90046 (213) 653-8886
GLASBAND-WILLEN MEMORIAL CHAPELS
7700 SANTA MONICA BLVD .... LOS ANGELES **CA** 90046 (213) 656-6260
GROMAN EDEN MORTUARY 11500 NORTH SEPULVEDA BLVD .... LOS ANGELES **CA** 91345 (213) 877-0335
GROMAN MORTUARY 830 WEST WASHINGTON BLVD .... LOS ANGELES **CA** 90015 (213) 748-2201
MALINOW & SILVERMAN MORTUARY 1500 SOUTH SEPULVEDA .... LOS ANGELES **CA** 90025 (213) 479-4600
MT. SINAI MEMORIAL PARK & MORTUARY
5950 FOREST LAWN DRIVE .... LOS ANGELES **CA** 90028 (213) 469-6000
AM ISRAEL MORTUARY 6316 EL CAJON BLVD .... SAN DIEGO **CA** 92115 (619) 583-8850
HOME OF PEACE SANCTUARIES 3668 IMPERIAL .... SAN DIEGO **CA** 92115 (619) 264-0832
SINAI MEMORIAL CHAPEL 1501 DIVISADERO STREET .... SAN FRANCISCO **CA** 94115 (415) 921-3636
CHEVRA KADISHA MORTUARY 1218 SANTA MONICA MALL #3 .... SANTA MONICA **CA** 90401 (213) 393-7942
FELDMAN FUNERAL HOME 1673 YORK STREET .... DENVER **CO** 80206 (303) 322-7764
ABRAHAM L. GREEN & SONS 927 GRAND STREET .... BRIDGEPORT **CT** 06604 (203) 334-8893
HEBREW FUNERAL ASSOCIATION 906 FARMINGTON WEST .... HARTFORD **CT** 06091 (203) 527-3890
WEINSTEIN MORTUARY 640 FARMINGTON AVENUE .... HARTFORD **CT** 06105 (203) 233-2675
ROBERT E. SHURE FUNERAL HOME, INC. 543 GEORGE STREET .... NEW HAVEN **CT** 06511 (203) 562-8244
WELLER FUNERAL HOME, INC. 425 GEORGE STREET .... NEW HAVEN **CT** 06511 (203) 624-6912
DONALD M. STEIN HEBREW MEMORIAL FUNERAL HOME, INC.
232 CARROLL STREET, N.W. .... WASHINGTON **DC** 20012 (202) 726-4222
SCHOENBERG MEMORIAL CHAPEL, INC. 519 PHILADELPHIA PIKE ..... WILMINGTON **DE** 19809 (302) 762-0334
BELKOFF JEWISH MEMORIAL CHAPEL .... **FL** (305) 865-0638
MAX SUGARMAN MEMORIAL CHAPEL .... **FL** (305) 861-9066
SCHWARTZ BROTHERS MEMORIAL CHAPEL, INC. .... **FL** (305) 949-1656
STANETSKY MEMORIAL CHAPELS (REPRESENTED BY MENORAH CHAPELS) .... **FL** (305) 742-6000
GARLICK FUNERAL HOMES, INC. .... BROWARD COUNTY **FL** (305) 925-2209
GARLICK FUNERAL HOMES, INC. .... DADE COUNTY **FL** (305) 947-2229
MENORAH CHAPELS 2305 WEST HILLSBORO BLVD .... DEERFIELD BEACH **FL** 33442 (800) 327-9192
PISER MENORAH CHAPELS 2305 W. HILLSBORO BLVD .... DEERFIELD BEACH **FL** 33442 (305) 427-4700
BETH ISRAEL - RUBIN MEMORIAL CHAPEL
5808 WEST ATLANTIC AVENUE .... DELRAY BEACH **FL** 33445 (305) 499-8000
MENORAH CHAPELS 6800 WEST OAKLAND PARK BLVD .... FT. LAUDERDALE **FL** 33313 (800) 327-9192
PISER MENORAH CHAPELS 6800 W. OAKLAND PARK BLVD .... FT. LAUDERDALE **FL** 33313 (305) 742-6000
RUBIN-ZILBERT MEMORIAL CHAPEL 100 S. DIXIE HWY .... HALLANDALE **FL** 33009 (305) 456-4011
BERNHEIM-GOLDSTICKER 5801 HOLLYWOOD BOULEVARD .... HOLLYWOOD **FL** 33020 (305) 922-2101
JEFFER FUNERAL HOMES, INC.-FLORIDA 1921 PEMBROKE ROAD ...... HOLLYWOOD **FL** 33020 (305) 925-2743
LEVITT-WEINSTEIN MEMORIAL CHAPELS 1921 PEMBROKE ROAD ...... HOLLYWOOD **FL** 33020 (305) 921-7200
RIVERSIDE MEMORIAL CHAPEL, INC. 2230 HOLLYWOOD BLVD .... HOLLYWOOD **FL** 33020 (305) 523-5801
MENORAH CHAPELS 5915 PARK DRIVE AT U.S. 441 .... MARGATE **FL** 33063 (800) 327-9192
BERNHEIM-GOLDSTICKER 1717 S.W. 37TH AVENUE .... MIAMI **FL** 33145 (305) 922-2101
BERNHEIM-GOLDSTICKER 16480 N.E. 19TH AVENUE .... MIAMI **FL** 33162 (305) 922-2101
ETERNAL LIGHT LAKESIDE MEMORIAL PARK
10301 NORTHWEST 25TH STREET .... MIAMI **FL** 33172 (305) 592-0690
GORDON FUNERAL HOME 710 S.W. 12TH AVENUE .... MIAMI **FL** 33130 (305) 858-5566
JEFFER FUNERAL HOMES, INC.-FLORIDA 13385 W. DIXIE HWY .... MIAMI **FL** 33161 (305) 947-1185
RIVERSIDE MEMORIAL CHAPEL, INC.
DOUGLAS ROAD AT S.W. 17TH AVENUE .... MIAMI **FL** (305) 531-1151
BERNHEIM-GOLDSTICKER 1920 ALTON ROAD .... MIAMI BEACH **FL** 33139 (305) 531-1151
BERNHEIM-GOLDSTICKER 1250 NORMANDY DRIVE .... MIAMI BEACH **FL** 33139 (305) 531-1151
BLASBERG FUNERAL CHAPEL 720 71ST STREET .... MIAMI BEACH **FL** 33141 (305) 865-2353
NEWMAN FUNERAL HOME 1333 DADE BLVD .... MIAMI BEACH **FL** 33139 (305) 531-7677
PARKSIDE MEMORIAL CHAPELS, INC. .... MIAMI BEACH **FL** (212) 896-9000
RIVERSIDE MEMORIAL CHAPEL, INC. 1920 ALTON ROAD .... MIAMI BEACH **FL** 33139 (305) 531-1151
RIVERSIDE MEMORIAL CHAPEL, INC. 1250 NORMANY DRIVE .... MIAMI BEACH **FL** 33139 (305) 531-1151
RUBIN-ZILBERT MEMORIAL CHAPEL 1701 ALTON ROAD .... MIAMI BEACH **FL** 33139 (305) 538-6371
GARLICK FUNERAL HOMES 18840 WEST DIXIE HIGHWAY ..... NORTH MIAMI BEACH **FL** 33180 (305) 947-2229
JEFFER FUNERAL HOMES 18840 WEST DIXIE HIGHWAY .... NORTH MIAMI BEACH **FL** 33180 (305) 947-1185
LEVITT-WEINSTEIN MEMORIAL CHAPELS
18840 WEST DIXIE HIGHWAY .... NORTH MIAMI BEACH **FL** 33180 (305) 949-6315
MENORAH CHAPELS 20955 BISCAYNE BLVD .... NORTH MIAMI BEACH **FL** 33180 (800) 327-9192
PISER MENORAH CHAPELS
BISCAYNE BLVD. AND 209TH STREET .... NORTH MIAMI BEACH **FL** 33180 (305) 945-3939
RIVERSIDE MEMORIAL CHAPEL, INC.
16480 N.E. 19TH AVENUE .... NORTH MIAMI BEACH **FL** 33162 (305) 531-1151
LEVITT-WEINSTEIN MEMORIAL CHAPELS
7500 NORTH STATE ROAD 7 .... POMPANO BEACH **FL** 33067 (305) 427-6500
MENORAH CHAPELS 5915 PARK DRIVE AT U.S. 441 .... POMPANO BEACH **FL** 33063 (800) 327-9192
ARNOLD & GRUNDWAG, INC. 4100 16TH STREET NORTH .... ST. PETERSBURG **FL** 33703 (813) 521-2444
BETH DAVID CHAPEL, JEWISH FUNERAL DIRECTORS
4100 16TH STREET NORTH .... ST. PETERSBURG **FL** 33703 (813) 521-2444
DAVID C. GROSS FUNERAL HOME, INC. 6366 CENTRAL AVENUE ... ST. PETERSBURG **FL** 33707 (813) 381-4911
RIVERSIDE MEMORIAL CHAPEL, INC. 1171 NORTHWEST 61ST AVENUE ..... SUNRISE **FL** 33313 (305) 531-1151
RIVERSIDE MEMORIAL CHAPEL 6701 COMMERCIAL BLVD .... TAMARAC **FL** 33319 (305) 523-5801
LEVITT-WEINSTEIN MEMORIAL CHAPELS
3201 NORTH 72ND AVENUE .... WEST HOLLYWOOD **FL** 33024 (305) 963-2400
LEVITT-WEINSTEIN MEMORIAL CHAPELS
5411 OKEECHOBEE BLVD .... WEST PALM BEACH **FL** 33409 (305) 689-8700
MENORAH GARDENS AND FUNERAL CHAPEL
9321 MEMORIAL PARK ROAD .... WEST PALM BEACH **FL** 33412 (800) 327-9192
RIVERSIDE MEMORIAL CHAPEL 4714 OKEECHOBEE BLVD ...... WEST PALM BEACH **FL** 33409 (305) 683-8676
FURTH & CO. 5206 NORTH BROADWAY .... CHICAGO **IL** 60640 (312) 784-4300
HARTMAN-MILLER, INC. 6130 NORTH CALIFORNIA AVENUE .... CHICAGO **IL** 60659 (312) 463-5000
KATZ-LEVE MEMORIALS 4350 NORTH HARLEM AVENUE .... CHICAGO **IL** 60634 (312) 761-3334
ORIGINAL WEINSTEIN MENORAH CHAPELS
3019 WEST PETERSON ROAD .... CHICAGO **IL** 60659 (312) 561-1890
ORIGINAL WEINSTEIN MENORAH CHAPELS 5206 BROADWAY .... CHICAGO **IL** 60640 (312) 561-1890
PAUL BRENNER 6450 W. CORTLAND .... CHICAGO **IL** 60635 (312) 666-8811
PISER WEINSTEIN MENORAH CHAPELS 5206 BROADWAY .... CHICAGO **IL** 60640 (312) 561-4740
PISER WEINSTEIN MENORAH CHAPELS
6130 NORTH CALIFORNIA AVENUE .... CHICAGO **IL** 60659 (312) 338-2300
PISER WEINSTEIN MENORAH CHAPELS 3019 WEST PETERSON ROAD ..... CHICAGO **IL** 60659 (312) 561-1890
WEINSTEIN BROS., INC. 1300 WEST DEVON AVENUE .... CHICAGO **IL** 60660 (312) 761-2400
PISER WEINSTEIN MENORAH CHAPELS 9200 SKOKIE BLVD .... SKOKIE **IL** 60077 (312) 679-4740
WEINSTEIN BROS., INC. 111 SKOKIE BLVD .... WILMETTE **IL** 60091 (312) 256-5700
AARON-RUBEN-NELSON MERIDIAN HILLS MORTUARY
1328 WEST 86TH STREET .... INDIANAPOLIS **IN** 46260 (317) 846-6501
HERMAN MEYER & SON, INC. 1338 ELLISON AVENUE .... LOUISVILLE **KY** 40204 (502) 458-9569
THARP-SONTHEIMER-THARP, INC.
4127 SOUTH CLAIBORNE AVENUE .... NEW ORLEANS **LA** 70125 (504) 821-8411
STANETSKY MEMORIAL CHAPELS .... BOSTON **MA** (617) 232-9300
LEVINE CHAPEL, INC. 470 HARVARD STREET .... BROOKLINE **MA** 02146 (617) 277-8300
STANETSKY MEMORIAL CHAPELS 1668 BEACON STREET .... BROOKLINE **MA** 02146 (617) 232-9300
SCHLOSSBERG-GOLDMAN-FISHER MEMORIAL CHAPELS
824 WASHINGTON STREET .... CANTON **MA** 02021 (617) 828-6990
TORF FUNERAL SERVICE, INC. 151 WASHINGTON AVENUE .... CHELSEA **MA** 02150 (617) 889-2900
LEVINE CHAPELS 394 WASHINGTON STREET .... DORCHESTER **MA** 02146 (617) 436-1550
FISHER MEMORIAL CHAPEL 422 NORTH MAIN STREET .... FALL RIVER **MA** 02723 (617) 678-6300
IRVING FISHER MEMORIAL CHAPEL, INC.
LOWELL AT WARREN STREET .... LAWRENCE **MA** 01841 (617) 683-2411
SCHLOSSBERG-GOLDMAN-FISHER MEMORIAL CHAPELS
174 FERRY STREET .... MALDEN **MA** 02148 (617) 324-1122
LEVINE-BRISS FUNERAL HOME, INC. 84 MAZZEO DRIVE .... RANDOLPH **MA** 02368 (617) 963-2900
STANETSKY-HYMANSON MEMORIAL CHAPELS 10 VINNIN STREET .... SALEM **MA** 01970 (617) 581-2300

Name / Address	City	State	Zip	Phone
HAROLD R. ASCHER & SON MEMORIAL CHAPEL, INC. 44 SUMNER AVENUE	SPRINGFIELD	MA	01108	(413) 734-5229
PERLMAN FUNERAL HOME, INC. 1026 MAIN STREET	WORCESTER	MA	01603	(617) 756-2200
CHESED SHEL EMES CHAPEL 1023 MAIN STREET	WINNIPEG	MB		(204) 582-5088
SOL LEVINSON & BROS., INC. 6010 REISTERSTOWN ROAD	BALTIMORE	MD	21215	(301) 358-1700
DANZANSKY-GOLDBERG MEMORIAL CHAPELS, INC. 1170 ROCKVILLE PIKE	ROCKVILLE	MD	20852	(301) 340-1400
JEWISH FUNERAL DIRECTORS OF AMERICA 1170 ROCKVILLE PIKE	ROCKVILLE	MD	20852	(301) 340-1400
HEBREW MEMORIAL CHAPEL 26640 GREENFIELD ROAD	OAK PARK	MI	48237	(313) 543-1622
IRA KAUFMAN CHAPEL, INC., THE 18325 W. NINE MILE ROAD	SOUTHFIELD	MI	48075	(313) 569-0020
AARON HODROFF & SONS FUNERAL CHAPEL 126 EAST FRANKLIN	MINNEAPOLIS	MN	55404	(612) 871-1234
DUBE FUNERAL HOME 2730 HENNEPIN AVENUE SOUTH	MINNEAPOLIS	MN	55408	(612) 872-1600
AARON HODROFF & SONS FUNERAL CHAPEL 671 SOUTH SNELLING AVENUE	ST. PAUL	MN	55116	(612) 698-8311
LOUIS MEMORIAL CHAPEL 6830 TROOST AVENUE	KANSAS CITY	MO	64131	(816) 361-5211
BERGER MEMORIAL CHAPEL 4715 MCPHERSON AVENUE	ST. LOUIS	MO	63108	(314) 361-0622
HERMAN RINDSKOPF, INC. 5216 DELMAR BLVD	ST. LOUIS	MO	63108	(314) 367-0438
MAYER FUNERAL HOME 4356 LINDELL STREET	ST. LOUIS	MO	63108	(314) 371-9067
JEWISH FUNERAL CHAPEL 1912 CUMING STREET	OMAHA	NE	68104	(402) 346-1184
ROTH MEMORIAL CHAPEL 116 PACIFIC AVENUE	ATLANTIC CITY	NJ	08401	(609) 344-9004
PLATT MEMORIAL CHAPELS, INC. 2001 HADDONFIELD-BERLIN ROAD	CHERRY HILL	NJ	08003	(609) 428-9442
HIGGINS & BONNER 414 WESTMINSTER AVENUE	ELIZABETH	NJ	07208	(201) 352-5414
KREITZMAN'S MEMORIAL HOME 1055 EAST JERSEY STREET	ELIZABETH	NJ	07201	(201) 351-4414
WIEN & WIEN 129 ENGLE STREET	ENGLEWOOD	NJ	07631	(201) 569-2404
LOUIS SUBURBAN CHAPELS 13-01 BROADWAY	FAIR LAWN	NJ	07410	(201) 278-4126
GUTTERMAN-MUSICANT 402 PARK STREET	HACKENSACK	NJ	07602	(201) 489-3800
BERNHEIM-GOLDSTICKER MEMORIAL HOME 1200 CLINTON AVENUE	IRVINGTON	NJ	07111	(201) 375-2400
EPSTEIN & SONS, INC. 34 LORETTO STREET	IRVINGTON	NJ	07111	(201) 923-1818
GUTTERMAN-MUSICANT 2030 KENNEDY BOULEVARD	JERSEY CITY	NJ	07304	(201) 433-6500
WIEN & WIEN 2030 KENNEDY BLVD	JERSEY CITY	NJ	07305	(201) 333-8360
BELKOFF JEWISH MEMORIAL CHAPEL 313 SECOND STREET	LAKEWOOD	NJ	08701	(201) 364-0900
PHILIP APTER & SON 1600 SPRINGFIELD AVENUE	MAPLEWOOD	NJ	07040	(201) 763-3505
BLOOMFIELD-COOPER FUNERAL CHAPEL 2130 STATE HIGHWAY 35	OCEAN TOWNSHIP	NJ	07712	(201) 493-4343
ROBERT SCHOEM'S MENORAH CHAPEL W-150, ROUTE 4	PARAMUS	NJ	07652	(201) 843-9090
JEWISH MEMORIAL CHAPEL 66 HOWE AVENUE	PASSAIC	NJ	07056	(201) 779-3048
DAVID A. BERSCHLER FUNERAL CHAPELS 5341 STATE HIGHWAY NO. 38	PENNSAUKEN	NJ	08110	(609) 665-5401
ORLAND'S EWING MEMORIAL CHAPEL, INC. 1534 PENNINGTON ROAD	TRENTON	NJ	08618	(609) 883-1400
RIVERSIDE MEMORIAL CHAPELS, INC. 1009 WHITEHEAD ROAD EXT	TRENTON	NJ	08638	(609) 771-9109
MENORAH CHAPELS AT MILLBURN 2950 VAUXHALL ROAD	UNION	NJ	07083	(201) 964-1500
LEVINE MEMORIAL CHAPEL, INC. 649 WASHINGTON AVENUE	ALBANY	NY	12206	(518) 438-1002
SWARTZ MEMORIAL CHAPEL, INC. 864 MADISON AVENUE	ALBANY	NY	12208	(518) 482-5355
GARLICK FUNERAL HOMES, INC. 1439 UNIONPORT ROAD	BRONX	NY	10462	(212) 892-9400
GUTTERMAN'S, INC. 1345 JEROME AVENUE	BRONX	NY	10452	(212) 681-2033
HIRSEN & SONS 1225 JEROME AVENUE	BRONX	NY	10452	(212) 473-2050
PARKSIDE MEMORIAL CHAPELS 1219 JEROME AVENUE	BRONX	NY	10452	(212) 588-7970
RIVERSIDE MEMORIAL CHAPEL, INC. 1963 GRAND CONCOURSE	BRONX	NY	10453	(212) 362-6600
BOULEVARD-PARK WEST CHAPELS, INC. 1901 FLATBUSH AVENUE	BROOKLYN	NY	11210	(718) 633-0400
GARLICK FUNERAL HOMES, INC. 1700 CONEY ISLAND AVENUE	BROOKLYN	NY	11230	(718) 377-4848
I.J. MORRIS, INC. 1895 FLATBUSH AVENUE	BROOKLYN	NY	11210	(718) 377-8610
JACK YABLOKOFF KINGSWAY MEMORIAL CHAPEL, INC. 1978 CONEY ISLAND AVENUE	BROOKLYN	NY	11223	(718) 645-9800
JEFFER COMMUNITY CHAPELS 4620 FT. HAMILTON PKWY	BROOKLYN	NY	11219	(718) 853-4000
JEFFER FUNERAL HOMES 1283 CONEY ISLAND AVENUE	BROOKLYN	NY	11230	(718) 716-8100
JEFFER NORMAN L. COMMUNITY CHAPELS, INC. 4620 FORT HAMILTON PARKWAY	BROOKLYN	NY	11219	(718) 853-4000
KIRSCHENBAUM BROS., INC., WESTMINSTER CHAPELS 1153 CONEY ISLAND AVENUE	BROOKLYN	NY	11230	(718) 859-2020
MAALIN BAKODESH SOCIETY 4511 FT. HAMILTON PARKWAY	BROOKLYN	NY	11219	(718) 435-6100
MIDWOOD MEMORIAL CHAPEL 1625 CONEY ISLAND AVENUE	BROOKLYN	NY	11230	(718) 377-2700
NIEBERG MIDWOOD CHAPEL, INC. 1625 CONEY ISLAND AVENUE	BROOKLYN	NY	11230	(718) 377-2700
PARKSIDE MEMORIAL CHAPELS, INC. 2576 FLATBUSH AVENUE	BROOKLYN	NY	11234	(718) 338-1500
PINCUS B. MANDEL 1569 47TH STREET	BROOKLYN	NY	11219	(718) 436-6088
RIVERSIDE MEMORIAL CHAPEL, INC. 310 CONEY ISLAND AVENUE	BROOKLYN	NY	11218	(718) 854-2000
SHERMAN'S FLATBUSH MEMORIAL CHAPEL, INC. 1283 CONEY ISLAND AVENUE	BROOKLYN	NY	11230	(718) 377-7300
SHOMREI HADAS CHAPELS, INC. 4511 FT. HAMILTON PKWY	BROOKLYN	NY	11219	(718) 436-8700
WEST END FUNERAL CHAPEL 1283 CONEY ISLAND AVENUE	BROOKLYN	NY	11230	(718) 854-6900
YEREIM ORTHODOX CHAPEL 93 BROADWAY	BROOKLYN	NY	11211	(718) 384-6784
DELAWARE PARK MEMORIAL CHAPEL, INC. 2141 DELAWARE AVENUE	BUFFALO	NY	14216	(716) 873-2141
I.J. MORRIS, INC. 21 EAST DEER PARK ROAD	DIX HILLS	NY	11746	(516) 499-6060
RIVERSIDE MEMORIAL CHAPEL 1250 CENTRAL AVENUE	FAR ROCKAWAY	NY	11691	(718) 327-7100
RIVERSIDE MEMORIAL CHAPEL, INC. 1250 CENTRAL AVENUE	FAR ROCKAWAY	NY	11691	(718) 362-6600
TEMPLE MEMORIAL 134-35 NORTHERN BOULEVARD	FLUSHING	NY	11354	(718) 359-1010
GUTTERMAN'S, INC. QUEENS BLVD. AT 66TH AVENUE	FOREST HILLS	NY	11374	(718) 896-5252
PARKSIDE MEMORIAL CHAPELS, INC. 98-60 QUEENS BLVD	FOREST HILLS	NY	11374	(718) 896-9000
SCHWARTZ BROS. MEMORIAL CHAPEL, INC. 114-03 QUEENS BLVD	FOREST HILLS	NY	11375	(718) 263-7600
SINAI CHAPELS (RESNICK & BUCHBINDER) 162-05 HORACE HARDING EXPRESSWAY	FRESH MEADOWS	NY	11365	(718) 445-0300
PARKSIDE MEMORIAL CHAPELS, INC. 14 CALVERT STREET	HARRISON	NY	10528	(212) 896-9000
I.J. MORRIS, INC. 46 GREENWICH STREET	HEMPSTEAD	NY	11550	(516) 486-2500
BOULEVARD-PARK WEST CHAPELS, INC. 1450 BROADWAY	HEWLETT	NY	11557	(516) 295-3100
JEFFER FUNERAL HOMES 188-11 HILLSIDE AVENUE	HOLLIS	NY	11423	(718) 776-8100
SUNSET CHAPELS, INC. 1285 NORTHERN BLVD	MANHASSET	NY	11030	(516) 482-3600
GARLICK FUNERAL HOMES, INC. 186 BROADWAY	MONTICELLO	NY	12701	(914) 794-7474
PARKSIDE MEMORIAL CHAPELS 195 BROADWAY	MONTICELLO	NY	12701	(914) 794-1141
THE WESTCHESTER RIVERSIDE MEMORIAL CHAPEL, INC. 21 WEST BROAD STREET	MT. VERNON	NY	10502	(914) 664-6800
ABRAHAM BLAU MEMORIAL CHAPELS, INC. 153 EAST BROADWAY	NEW YORK	NY	10002	(212) 226-1617
BOULEVARD-PARK WEST CHAPELS, INC. 115 WEST 79TH STREET	NEW YORK	NY	10024	(212) 362-3600
BROADWAY MEMORIAL CHAPEL, INC. 4120 BROADWAY	NEW YORK	NY	10033	(212) 927-2250
HARRY NEIBERG & SONS	NEW YORK	NY		(212) 674-3600
JEWISH FUNERAL DIRECTORS OF AMERICA 122 E. 42ND STREET	NEW YORK	NY	10017	(212) 370-0024
MIDWOOD MEMORIAL CHAPELS 141 LUDLOW STREET	NEW YORK	NY	10002	(212) 674-3600
NAGEL ISADOR & SONS 152 SECOND AVENUE	NEW YORK	NY	10003	(212) 674-3200
PARK WEST CHAPELS 333 AMSTERDAM AT 76TH STREET	NEW YORK	NY	10023	(212) 362-3600
PARK WEST CHAPELS 115 WEST 79TH STREET	NEW YORK	NY	10024	(212) 362-3600
PARKSIDE MEMORIAL CHAPELS, INC. 400 COLUMBUS AVENUE (AT WEST 79TH STREET)	NEW YORK	NY	10024	(212) 896-9000
PLAZA MEMORIAL CHAPEL 924 AMSTERDAM AVENUE	NEW YORK	NY	10024	(212) 769-4400
RESNICK FUNERAL HOME 156 EAST BROADWAY	NEW YORK	NY	10002	(212) 349-1166
RIVERSIDE MEMORIAL CHAPEL, INC. 180 WEST 76TH STREET	NEW YORK	NY	10023	(212) 362-6600
WIEN & WIEN 152 SECOND AVENUE	NEW YORK	NY	10003	(212) 285-9659
GARLICK FUNERAL HOMES, INC. 38-08 DITMARS BLVD	QUEENS	NY		(718) 274-1050
PARSKY FUNERAL HOME, INC. 1125 ST. PAUL STREET	ROCHESTER	NY	14621	(716) 423-0220
PARKSIDE MEMORIAL CHAPELS, INC. 175 LONG BEACH ROAD	ROCKVILLE CENTRE	NY	11570	(212) 896-9000
HELLMAN MEMORIAL CHAPELS, INC. 15 STATE STREET	SPRING VALLEY	NY	10977	(914) 356-8600
MENORAH CHAPELS, INC. 2145 RICHMOND AVENUE	STATEN ISLAND	NY	10314	(718) 494-7700
BIRNBAUM FUNERAL SERVICE, INC. 1909 E. FAYETTE STREET	SYRACUSE	NY	13210	(315) 472-5291
SURRIDGE & JACOBSON MEMORIAL HOME, INC. 2212 GENESEE STREET	UTICA	NY	13502	(315) 797-9121
GUTTERMAN'S, INC. 8000 JERICHO TURNPIKE	WOODBURY	NY	11797	(516) 921-5757
GARLICK FUNERAL HOMES, INC. 1091 YONKERS AVENUE	YONKERS	NY	10704	(914) 237-3300
HELLMAN MEMORIAL CHAPELS 1652 CENTRAL PARK AVENUE	YONKERS	NY	10710	(914) 779-7333
GORDON MEMORIAL HOME, INC. 1260 COLLIER ROAD	AKRON	OH	44320	(216) 836-7989
WEIL FUNERAL HOME 3901 READING ROAD	CINCINNATI	OH	45229	(513) 281-0178
CLEVELAND TEMPLE MEMORIAL HOME 1985 SOUTH TAYLOR ROAD	CLEVELAND	OH	44118	(216) 421-8484
JEWISH SACRED SOCIETY 3492 SEVERN ROAD	CLEVELAND	OH	44118	(216) 371-5717
MILLER-DEUTSCH MEMORIAL CHAPEL 27570 CHAGRIN BOULEVARD	CLEVELAND	OH	44118	(216) 831-1303
PLYMOUTH MEMORIAL COMPANY 1936 SOUTH TAYLOR ROAD	CLEVELAND	OH	44118	(216) 321-1800
BARNETT BOOKATZ CLEVELAND TEMPLE MEMORIAL 1985 SOUTH TAYLOR ROAD	CLEVELAND HEIGHTS	OH	44118	(216) 421-8484
BERKOWITZ-KUMIN, INC. 1985 SOUTH TAYLOR ROAD	CLEVELAND HEIGHTS	OH	44118	(216) 932-7900
EPSTEIN MEMORIAL CHAPELS 3232 EAST MAIN STREET	COLUMBUS	OH	43213	(614) 235-3232
BRADFORD-CONNELLY & GLICKLER FUNERAL HOME 1849 SALEM AVENUE	DAYTON	OH	45406	(513) 278-4287
ZIMMERMAN-WICK MEMORIAL CHAPEL, INC. 2221 JEFFERSON AVENUE	TOLEDO	OH	43624	(419) 535-5840
STEELES-COLLEGE MEMORIAL CHAPEL 350 STEELES AVENUE WEST	THORNHILL	ON	L4J 1A1	(416) 881-6003
BENJAMIN'S PARK MEMORIAL CHAPEL 2401 STEELES AVENUE WEST	TORONTO	ON	M3J 2P1	(416) 663-9060
THE PARK MEMORIAL CHAPEL 2401 STEELES AVENUE WEST	TORONTO	ON		(416) 663-9060
IRWIN M. JUDD FUNERAL HOME 1314 HAMILTON STREET	ALLENTOWN	PA	18102	(215) 434-5555
BERSCHLER FUNERAL CHAPELS 4300 NORTH BROAD STREET	PHILADELPHIA	PA	19140	(215) 329-2900
GOLDSTEIN'S FUNERAL DIRECTORS, INC. 6410 NORTH BROAD STREET	PHILADELPHIA	PA	19126	(215) 927-5800
J. LEVINE & SONS MEMORIAL CHAPEL 7112 NORTH BROAD STREET	PHILADELPHIA	PA	19126	(215) 927-2700
RAPHAEL SACKS MEMORIAL CHAPEL, INC 4720 NORTH BROAD STREET	PHILADELPHIA	PA	19141	(215) 455-0100
REISMAN-GOLD FUNERAL CHAPEL, INC. 2315-17 NORTH BROAD STREET	PHILADELPHIA	PA	19132	(215) 223-5100
ROSENBERG'S CHAPEL 4720 NORTH BROAD STREET	PHILADELPHIA	PA	19141	(215) 455-0100
STILLMAN'S MEMORIAL CHAPEL 4324 NORTH BROAD STREET	PHILADELPHIA	PA	19140	(215) 324-8800
BLANK BROTHERS 3222 FORBES AVENUE	PITTSBURGH	PA	15213	(412) 682-4000
BURTON L. HIRSCH FUNERAL HOME, INC. 2704 MURRAY AVENUE	PITTSBURGH	PA	15217	(412) 521-2600
RALPH SCHUGAR, INC. 5509 CENTRE AVENUE	PITTSBURGH	PA	15232	(412) 621-8282
ZIMAN FUNERAL HOME 612 GIBSON STREET	SCRANTON	PA	18510	(717) 344-1716
ROSENBERG FUNERAL CHAPEL 348 SOUTH RIVER STREET	WILKES BARRE	PA	18702	(717) 822-1210
CHESED SHEL EMES FUNERAL HOME 935 BEAUMONG	MONTREAL	QU		(514) 273-3211
PAPERMAN & SONS, INC. 5605 COTE DES NEIGES ROAD	MONTREAL	QU	H3T 1Y8	(514) 733-7101
MAX SUGARMAN FUNERAL HOME, INC. 458 HOPE STREET	PROVIDENCE	RI	02906	(401) 331-8094
SINAI MEMORIAL CHAPEL 825 HOPE STREET	PROVIDENCE	RI	02906	(401) 331-3337
FISHER MEMORIAL CHAPELS 972 WEST SHORE ROAD	WARWICK	RI	02888	(401) 738-5300
LEVY FUNERAL DIRECTORS, INC. 1402 CLEBURNE AT AUSTIN STREET	HOUSTON	TX	77004	(713) 529-6179
H.D. OLIVER FUNERAL APARTMENTS COLONIAL AND SHIRLEY AVENUE	NORFOLK	VA	23523	(804) 622-7353
HEBREW CEMETERY 4TH AND HOSPITAL	RICHMOND	VA	23221	(804) 648-2289
JEWISH FUNERAL CHAPEL 162 12TH STREET	SEATTLE	WA	98101	(206) 323-7321
GOODMAN-BENSMAN FUNERAL HOME 5831 WEST BURLEIGH STREET	MILWAUKEE	WI	53210	(414) 964-3111
GOODMAN-BENSMAN WHITEFISH BAY FUNERAL HOME 4750 NORTH SANTA MONICA BLVD	MILWAUKEE	WI	53211	(414) 964-3111

FUNERAL SUPPLIES - SHROUDS

Name / Address	City	State	Zip	Phone
A & G MFRS., INC. 183 LORRAINE STREET	BROOKLYN	NY	11231	(718) 875-6297
KLEIN BROS. FUNERAL SUPPLIES 4104 14TH AVENUE	BROOKLYN	NY	11219	(718) 633-4490
GEMILAS CHESED ZICHRON YESHIVA ZVI P.O. BOX 95	MONROE	NY	10950	(914) 783-1680
MIRIAM FUNERAL SUPPLIES, INC. 48 CANAL STREET	NEW YORK	NY	10002	(212) 925-9272
ROSE SOLOMON, INC. 6 EAST 2ND STREET	NEW YORK	NY	10003	(212) 473-0404

GAMES & TOYS - IMPORTERS (ISRAEL)

Name / Address	City	State	Zip	Phone
EXECUTIVE SPORTS PROMOTERS 2029 CENTURY PARK EAST, 2029 CENTURY PLAZA, SUITE 600	LOS ANGELES	CA	90067	(213) 924-5788
SHARON PRODUCTS P.O. BOX 55-7579	MIAMI	FL	33155	(305) 266-4595
HAMAKOR JUDAICA, INC. 6112 NORTH LINCOLN AVENUE	CHICAGO	IL	60659	(312) 463-6186
SCHWARTZ-ROSENBLUM INC. 2906 WEST DEVON AVENUE	CHICAGO	IL	60659	(312) 338-3919
TIC & TUC 1 O'NEIL PLACE, P.O. BOX 51	BRIGHTON	MA		(617) 782-4423

Name / Address	City	State	Zip	Phone
EXPO-EL, INC. 3000 TOWN CENTER	SOUTHFIELD	MI	48075	(313) 358-1560
CHILDCRAFT EDUCATION CORP. 20 KILMER ROAD	EDISON	NJ	08817	(201) 572-6118
DRYBRANCH INC. P.O. BOX 83	ALBERTSON	NY	11507	(516) 681-7000
PUPPET LOVERS COMPANY 406 SEVENTH STREET	BROOKLYN	NY	11215	(718) 965-2765
NATHAN NEUMANN-ISRAEL NOVELTIES 75-71 UTOPIA PARKWAY	FLUSHING	NY	11366	(718) 969-7740
GLENOIT MILLS INC. 111 WEST 40TH STREET	NEW YORK	NY	10018	(212) 391-3915
ISRAEL CREATIONS INC. 350 FIFTH AVE	NEW YORK	NY	10118	(212) 213-2200
MARVEL EDUCATION CORP. 212 FIFTH AVENUE, SUITE 1303	NEW YORK	NY	10010	(212) 662-7005
HOKUS POKUS AMERICA, INC. P.O.BOX 376	SOUTHAMPTON	PA	18966	(215) 947-6175

GAMES & TOYS - PRODUCERS

Name / Address	City	State	Zip	Phone
THE DREIDEL FACTORY 2445 PRINCE STREET	BERKELEY	CA	94705	
JUDAICA UNLIMITED P.O.BOX 6394	ORANGE	CA	92667	(714) 630-9064
ALTERNATIVES IN RELIGIOUS EDUCATION, INC. 3945 S. ONEIDA	DENVER	CO	80237	(303) 363-7779
LUCKEY EDUCATIONAL PUBLICATIONS 89 ABBOTSFORD ROAD	BROOKLINE	MA	02146	
PEOPLE PENCILS & GOODIES NOVELTIES 12825 EPPING TERRACE	SILVER SPRING	MD	20906	(301) 949-3629
FEDERAL MARKETING COMPANY, INC./MARCUS J. COHEN 1246 MIDLAND, P.O. BOX 3208	ST. LOUIS	MO	63130	(314) 725-0211
KTAV PUBLISHING HOUSE INC. 900 JEFFERSON ST	HOBOKEN	NJ	07030	(201) 963-9524
BEHRMAN HOUSE 235 WATCHUNG AVENUE	WEST ORANGE	NJ	07052	(201) 669-0447
SELCHOW & RIGHTER COMPANY, (SCRABBLE IN HEBREW)	BAY SHORE	NY	11706	(516) 666-7390
A TOUCH OF TORAH 579 CROWN STREET	BROOKLYN	NY	11213	(718) 774-3076
ABC HEBREW NOVELTY CO. 1115 52ND STREET	BROOKLYN	NY	11219	(718) 436-0862
IT'S FUN TO BE JEWISH - TOYS & GIFTS 1903 AVENUE J	BROOKLYN	NY	11230	
JEWISH EDUCATIONAL TOYS P.O. BOX 469	BROOKLYN	NY	11225	(718) 778-0226
AMCOR GROUP, LTD., THE 350 FIFTH AVENUE, SUITE 1907	NEW YORK	NY	10118	(212) 736-7711
BOARD OF JEWISH EDUCATION 426 WEST 58TH STREET	NEW YORK	NY	10019	(212) 245-8200
CHILDREN'S TELEVISION WORKSHOP - ISRAELI SESAME STREET PROJECT 1 LINCOLN PLACE	NEW YORK	NY	10023	(212) 595-3456
TORAH TOYS, J. LEVINE COMPANY 58 ELDRIDGE STREET	NEW YORK	NY	10002	(212) 966-4460
MITZVAH TOYS, INC. P.O. BOX 5765	AKRON	OH	44372	(216) 867-1818
JULIA SHERMAN/TOYS RT. 1, 235B MCGHEE ROAD	NEWMARKET	TN	37820	(615) 475-4311
ARBIT BOOKS 8050 NORTH PORT WASHINGTON ROAD	MILWAUKEE	WI	53217	(414) 352-4404

GENEALOGY

Name / Address	City	State	Zip	Phone
JEWISH GENEALOGICAL SOCIETY OF LOS ANGELES P.O. BOX 25245	LOS ANGELES	CA	90025	
JEWISH FAMILY RESEARCH INSTITUTE 1368 44TH STREET	BROOKLYN	NY	11219	(718) 851-4748
WORLD JEWISH GENEALOGY ORGANIZATION: THE YOCHSIN INSTITUTE P.O. BOX FF	BROOKLYN	NY	11219	(718) 435-0700
JEWISH GENEALOGY RESEARCH SERVICE P.O. BOX 126	FLUSHING	NY	11367	(718) 261-0525
GENEALOGY SERVICE 190 WEST NECK ROAD	HUNTINGTON	NY	11743	(516) 673-5430
THE JEWISH GENEALOGY SOCIETY OF GREATER WASHINGTON P.O. BOX 412	VIENNA	VA	22180	(703) 938-2840
CHARLES TUCKER 111A NETHER STREET	FINCHLEY, LONDON	UK	N.12	

GENETIC DISEASES

Name / Address	City	State	Zip	Phone
TAY SACHS DISEASE PREVENTION PROGRAM, UNIV. OF CAL. MED CTR., HEALTH SCIENCE WEST, HSW 1475	SAN FRANCISCO	CA	94143	(415) 666-4157
TAY-SACHS DISEASE SCREENING-HARBOR GENERAL HOSPITAL, E 4 1124 WEST CARSON STREET, PROFESSIONAL STAFF ASSOCIATES	TORRANCE	CA	90502	(213) 775-7333
NATIONAL TAY-SACHS & ALLIED DISEASES ASSOCIATION 92 WASHINGTON AVENUE	CEDARHURST	NY	11516	(516) 569-4300
TAY-SACHS TESTING CENTER - LONG ISLAND JEWISH MEDICAL CENTER 271-16 76TH AVENUE	NEW HYDE PARK	NY	11042	(718) 470-3010
DYSAUTONOMIA FOUNDATION 370 LEXINGTON AVENUE	NEW YORK	NY	10028	(212) 889-0370
NATIONAL FOUNDATION FOR JEWISH GENETIC DISEASES 250 PARK AVENUE	NEW YORK	NY	10017	(212) 682-5550

GIFT SERVICES & MAIL ORDER

Name / Address	City	State	Zip	Phone
THE JEWISH DEVELOPMENT COMPANY 18331-C IRVINE BOULEVARD	TUSTIN	CA	92680	(714) 730-1419
YEHUDIT ISRAELI IMPORTS 33 CROSSROADS PLAZA, P.O. BOX 17091	WEST HARTFORD	CT	06117	(203) 236-6069
POTPOURRI OF GIFTS INC. 12356 S.W. 117 CT.	MIAMI	FL	33186	(305) 252-2094
JULIE SILVERMAN/KOSHERWARE DIVISION - FLEXIWARE, INC. 407 YESHIVA LANE	BALTIMORE	MD	21208	(301) 653-1840
HAPPY HOLIDAY 7629 FONTAINE STREET	POTOMAC	MD	20854	(301) 762-9339
FEDERAL MARKETING COMPANY, INC./MARCUS J. COHEN 1246 MIDLAND, P.O. BOX 3208	ST. LOUIS	MO	63130	(314) 725-0211
AMERICAN JEWISH HOME... GIFTS BY MAIL 26 BROOKDALE DRIVE	CHERRY HILL	NJ	08034	(609) 667-8098
TO ISRAEL WITH LOVE 61-08 218TH STREET	BAYSIDE	NY	11364	(718) 261-4850
CANDYLAND 4819 16TH AVENUE	BROOKLYN	NY	11204	(718) 436-9308
CHADISH MEDIA 453 EAST 9 STREET	BROOKLYN	NY	11218	(718) 856-3882
SPECIAL BASKETS	LONG BEACH	NY		(516) 889-6809
TORAH TECHNICS - "WHERE TORAH & TECHNOLOGY MEET" 1603 CARROLL STREET	BROOKLYN	NY	11213	(718) 953-7028
BEN ARI ARTS LTD. 11 AVENUE A	NEW YORK	NY	10009	(212) 677-4730

Name / Address	City	State	Zip	Phone
BEN-EZER (CITRUS) 440 PARK AVENUE	NEW YORK	NY	10016	(212) 532-7097
GAN EDEN GIFTBASKETS 1587 SECOND AVENUE, SUITE #3	NEW YORK	NY	10028	(212) 517-6385
JEWISH NATIONAL FUND (TREES) 42 EAST 69TH STREET	NEW YORK	NY	10021	(212) 879-9300
SHOP-AT-HOME JUDAICA/ZIONTALIS 48 ELDRIDGE STREET	NEW YORK	NY	10002	(212) 925-8558
MEAT SERVICE C/O MRS. IRVING FREISTAT (TO ISRAEL) 1 NORTH DAWES AVENUE	KINGSTON	PA	18704	(717) 288-4002
TEMPO DESIGNS (JUDAICA) 42 LADD STREET	EAST GREENWICH	RI	02818	(401) 884-2443

GLASSWORK

Name / Address	City	State	Zip	Phone
GIANNI TOSO, MAESTRO VETRAIO D'ARTE 26 PITNEY STREET	WEST ORANGE	NJ	07052	(201) 731-5422
EAGLE WINDOW CORP. 96 SPRUCE STREET	CEDARHURST	NY	11516	(516) 569-7101
STAINED GLASS JUDAICA 144-25 JEWEL AVENUE	KEW GARDENS HILLS	NY	11367	(718) 263-8017
EDELWEISS CO. - GLASS STUDIO 65 MERCER STREET	NEW YORK	NY	10012	(212) 431-5022

GREETING CARDS

Name / Address	City	State	Zip	Phone
MARCEL SCHURMAN COMPANY, INC. 954 60TH STREET	OAKLAND	CA	94608	(415) 428-0200
HANUCRAFT 8271 N.W. 56TH STREET	MIAMI	FL	33166	(305) 592-1552
CHICAGO CHAPTER MDA OFFICES 6952 N. CALIFORNIA AVENUE	CHICAGO	IL	60645	(312) 465-0664
ROSE ANN CHASMAN 6147 NORTH RICHMOND	CHICAGO	IL	60659	(312) 764-4169
ARTFORMS CARD CORPORATION 1207 GLENCOE AVENUE	HIGHLAND PARK	IL	60035	(312) 433-0532
PUCKER/SAFRAI GALLERY 171 NEWBURY STREET	BOSTON	MA	02116	
TIC & TUC 1 O'NEIL PLACE, P.O. BOX 51	BRIGHTON	MA		(617) 782-4423
AMERICAN JEWISH HISTORICAL SOCIETY 2 THORNTON ROAD	WALTHAM	MA	02154	(617) 891-8110

RUTTENBERG & EVERETT YIDDISH FILM LIBRARY
LOWN BUILDING, 415 SOUTH STREET ... WALTHAM **MA** 02154 (617) 647-2000
AVCO GRAPHICS 3313 SHELBURNE ROAD ... BALTIMORE **MD** 21208
PEGGY H. DAVIS CALLIGRAPHY
3249 HENNEPIN AVENUE SOUTH, SUITE 144 ... MINNEAPOLIS **MN** 55408 (612) 929-3362
BINAH BINDELL, 'SILENT STORIES ART CREATIONS'
19 OAKWOOD STREET ... ALBANY **NY** 12208 (518) 438-1889
AGENTS CARD & GIFT 4543 THIRD AVENUE ... BRONX **NY** 10458 (212) 933-1080
SHULSINGER BROTHERS 50 WASHINGTON STREET ... BROOKLYN **NY** 11205 (718) 852-0042
NATHAN NEUMANN-ISRAEL NOVELTIES 75-71 UTOPIA PARKWAY ... FLUSHING **NY** 11366 (718) 969-7740
KING DAVID PUBLISHERS INC. 109-05 72ND AVENUE ... FOREST HILLS **NY** 11375 (718) 969-1772
KOSHER CARDS 125 EAST 93RD STREET ... NEW YORK **NY** 10128 (212) 860-4422
WORKMEN'S CIRCLE EDUCATION DEPARTMENT
45 EAST 33RD STREET ... NEW YORK **NY** 10016 (212) 889-6600
YIVO INSTITUTE FOR JEWISH RESEARCH 1048 FIFTH AVENUE ... NEW YORK **NY** 10028 (212) 535-6700
REJOICERS 2795 LOSANTIRIDGE AVE. ... CINCINNATI **OH** 45213 (513) 631-5478

HASIDIC CENTERS

CONGREGATION OHEL DAVID, RABBI ELIEZER ADLER
7067 BEVERLY BOULEVARD ... LOS ANGELES **CA** 90007
GERER BET MEDRASH 7575 MELROSE AVENUE ... LOS ANGELES **CA** 90024
RABBI LEVI HOROWITZ; RABBI MEIER HOROWITZ
NEW ENGLAND CHASSIDIC CENTER, 1710 BEACON STREET ... BROOKLINE **MA** 02146
TALNER BETH DAVID 64 COREY ROAD ... BROOKLINE **MA** 02146
BELZER BET MIDRASH 662 EASTERN PARKWAY ... BROOKLYN **NY** 11213
BELZER BET MIDRASH 4814 16TH AVENUE ... BROOKLYN **NY** 11219
BRESLOV RESEARCH INSTITUTE 3100 BRIGHTON 3 STREET ... BROOKLYN **NY** 11235 (718) 769-0086
GERER SHTIBEL 1327 49TH STREET ... BROOKLYN **NY** 11219
KAPISHNITZER BET MEDRASH 1415 55TH STREET ... BROOKLYN **NY** 11219
LUBAVITCHER REBBE, RABBI MENACHEM M. SCHNEERSON
770 EASTERN PARKWAY ... BROOKLYN **NY** 11213 (718) 493-9250
MUNKATCHER BET MEDRASH 1377 42ND STREET ... BROOKLYN **NY** 11219
PUPOVER CHASSIDIM 656 BEDFORD AVENUE ... BROOKLYN **NY** 11211
RABBI L.Y. GRUNWALD 559 BEDFORD AVENUE ... BROOKLYN **NY** 11211
RABBI LEO ROSENFELD; RABBI GEDALIA FLEER 864 44TH STREET ... BROOKLYN **NY** 11219
RABBI SHEINGARTEN'S SHTIBEL 1520 49TH STREET ... BROOKLYN **NY** 11219
SIGETER CHASSIDIM 152 HEWES STREET ... BROOKLYN **NY** 11211
SKULENER REBBE - RABBI PORTUGAL 420 CROWN STREET ... BROOKLYN **NY** 11213
SKVERER CHASSIDIM 571 BEDFORD AVENUE ... BROOKLYN **NY** 11211
STOLINER BET MEDRASH 1818 54TH STREET ... BROOKLYN **NY** 11219
THE BOBOVER REBBE-RABBI HALBERSTAM-YESHIVA BNAI ZION
1501 48TH STREET ... BROOKLYN **NY** 11219 (718) 853-0086
SKVERER TOWN ... NEW SQUARE **NY** 10977

HATS

MODERN HATTERS 313 THIRD STREET ... JERSEY CITY **NJ** 07302 (201) 659-9300
BENCRAFT HATTERS 236 BROADWAY ... BROOKLYN **NY** 11211 (718) 384-8956
HAT RACK, THE 5416 16TH AVENUE ... BROOKLYN **NY** 11204 (718) 871-2278
KOVA QUALITY HATTERS 4311 13TH AVENUE ... BROOKLYN **NY** 11219 (718) 871-2944
M. HIRSHFELD 225 DIVISION AVENUE ... BROOKLYN **NY** 11211 (718) 387-3265
SELCO HATTERS 228 BROADWAY ... BROOKLYN **NY** 11211 (718) 388-6848
THE HAT RACK 5416 16TH AVENUE ... BROOKLYN **NY** 11204 (718) 871-2278
FELTY HATS 97 ORCHARD STREET ... NEW YORK **NY** 10002 (212) 226-0322
MOE PENN HATS 395 GRAND STREET ... NEW YORK **NY** 10002 (212) 475-4156

HEBREW SOFTWARE

DAVKA CORPORATION 845 NORTH MICHIGAN AVENUE, SUITE 843 ... CHICAGO **IL** 60611 (800) 621-8227
ANTHRO-DIGITAL, INC. P.O. BOX 1385 ... PITTSFIELD **MA** 01202 (413) 448-8278
THE SOFT WAREHOUSE - JUDAIC COMPUTER SOFTWARE
DEPARTMENT H, BOX 1983 ... WINNIPEG **MB** R3C 3R3
ISRACOMP P.O. BOX 1091 ... KING OF PRUSSIA **PA** 19406
MICRO-MELAMED SOFTWARE CO. 6130 CORALRIDGE ... CORPUS CHRISTI **TX** 78413

HISTORICAL SOCIETIES

JEWISH HISTORICAL SOCIETY OF BRITISH COLUMBIA C/O CANADIAN
JEWISH CONGRESS, 950 WEST 41ST AVENUE ... VANCOUVER **BC** V5Z 2N7 (604) 261-8101
WESTERN JEWISH HISTORY CTR. OF THE JUDAH I. MAGNES MEM. MUS.
2911 RUSSELL AVENUE ... BERKELEY **CA** 94705 (415) 849-2710
SOUTHERN CALIFORNIA JEWISH HISTORICAL SOCIETY
590 NORTH VERMONT AVENUE ... LOS ANGELES **CA** 90004
JEWISH HISTORICAL SOCIETY OF NEW HAVEN, INC., THE
169 DAVENPORT AVENUE ... NEW HAVEN **CT** 06519 (203) 787-3183
JEWISH HISTORICAL SOCIETY OF GREATER HARTFORD, THE
24 CLIFFMORE ROAD ... WEST HARTFORD **CT** 06117 (203) 236-4571
JEWISH HISTORICAL SOCIETY OF GREATER WASHINGTON
701 3RD STREET ... WASHINGTON **DC** (202) 789-0900
JEWISH HISTORICAL SOCIETY OF DELAWARE
101 GARDEN OF EDEN ROAD ... WILMINGTON **DE** 19803 (302) 656-8558
SOUTH FLORIDA JEWISH HISTORICAL SOCIETY
C/O A.S. ROSICHAN, 50 SHORE DRIVE W. ... MIAMI **FL** 33133 (305) 854-0450
JEWISH HISTORICAL SOCIETY OF SOUTH FLORIDA
605 LINCOLN ROAD ... MIAMI BEACH **FL** 33139 (305) 538-6213
CHICAGO JEWISH HISTORICAL SOCIETY, THE
618 S. MICHIGAN AVENUE ... CHICAGO **IL** 60635 (312) 663-5634
ISRAEL HISTORICAL SOCIETY 1 S. WACKER DRIVE ... CHICAGO **IL** 60606 (312) 782-8920
INDIANA JEWISH HISTORICAL SOCIETY
215 E. BERRY STREET, ROOM 303 ... FORT WAYNE **IN** 46802 (219) 422-3862
AMERICAN JEWISH HISTORICAL SOCIETY 21 BLAKE ROAD ... BROOKLINE **MA** 02146
AMERICAN JEWISH HISTORICAL SOCIETY 2 THORNTON ROAD ... WALTHAM **MA** 02154 (617) 891-8110
GREATER BOSTON JEWISH HISTORICAL SOCIETY
TWO THORNTON ROAD ... WALTHAM **MA** 02154 (617) 891-8110
JEWISH HISTORICAL SOCIETY OF WESTERN CANADA
365 HARGRAVE STREET, SUITE 404 ... WINNIPEG **MB** R3B 2K3 (204) 942-4822
JEWISH HISTORICAL SOCIETY OF ANNAPOLIS 24 ROMAR STREET ... ANNAPOLIS **MD** 21403
JEWISH HISTORICAL SOCIETY OF MARYLAND 15 LLOYD STREET ... BALTIMORE **MD** 21202 (301) 732-6400
JEWISH HISTORICAL SOCIETY OF MICHIGAN 163 MADISON STREET ... DETROIT **MI** 48226
JEWISH HISTORICAL SOCIETY OF MICHIGAN 24680 RENSSELAER ... OAK PARK **MI** 48237 (313) 548-9176
JEWISH HISTORICAL SOCIETY OF RARITAN VALLEY
1050 GEORGE STREET ... NEW BRUNSWICK **NJ** 08901 (201) 247-0288
JEWISH HISTORICAL SOCIETY OF RARITAN VALLEY
185 WESTWOOD AVENUE ... RIVER VALE **NJ** 07675 (201) 666-2370
JEWISH HISTORICAL SOCIETY OF TRENTON
999 LOWER FERRY ROAD/PO BOX 7249 ... TRENTON **NJ** 08628
SOCIETY FOR THE HISTORY OF CZECHOSLOVAK JEWS
C/O LEWIS WEINER, 87-08 SANTIAGO STREET ... HOLLISWOOD **NY** 11423 (718) 468-6844
SOCIETY FOR THE HISTORY OF CZECHOSLOVAK JEWS
25 MAYHEW AVENUE ... LARCHMONT **NY** 10538 (914) 834-4333
AM. JEWISH HISTORY CENTER OF THE JEWISH THEOLOGICAL SEMINARY
3080 BROADWAY ... NEW YORK **NY** 10027 (212) 749-8000
JEWISH HISTORICAL SOCIETY OF NEW YORK 8 WEST 70TH STREET ... NEW YORK **NY** 10023 (212) 873-0300
CANADIAN JEWISH CONGRESS 150 BEVERLY STREET ... TORONTO **ON** (416) 977-3811
TORONTO JEWISH HISTORICAL SOCIETIES 2 SHELBORNE AVENUE ... TORONTO **ON** M5N 1Y7 (416) 781-1214
OREGON JEWISH HISTORICAL SOCIETY 6651 S.W. CAPITOL HIGHWAY .. PORTLAND **OR** 97219 (503) 246-9844
PHILADELPHIA JEWISH ARCHIVES CENTER
BALCH INSTITUTE, 18 SOUTH SEVENTH STREET ... PHILADELPHIA **PA** 19106 (215) 925-8090
RHODE ISLAND JEWISH HISTORICAL SOCIETY
130 SESSIONS STREET ... PROVIDENCE **RI** 02926
SOUTHERN JEWISH HISTORICAL SOCIETY
C/O CONG. BETH AHABAH, 1111 WEST FRANKLIN STREET ... RICHMOND **VA** 23220 (401) 358-6757

HOLOCAUST RESOURCES

MARTYRS MEMORIAL AND MUSEUM OF THE HOLOCAUST
6505 WILSHIRE BLVD ... LOS ANGELES **CA** 90048 (213) 852-1234
SIMON WIESENTHAL CENTER NATIONAL HEADQUARTERS
9760 WEST PICO BOULEVARD ... LOS ANGELES **CA** 90035 (213) 553-9036
SIMON WIESENTHAL CENTER FOR HOLOCAUST STUDIES
9760 W. PICO BLVD ... LOS ANGELES **CA** 90035 (213) 553-9035
THE 1939 CLUB CHAIR IN HOLOCAUST STUDIES UNIVERSITY OF CALIFORNIA
AT LOS ANGELES, DEPT OF HISTORY ... LOS ANGELES **CA** 90024 (213) 825-4601

HOLOCAUST LIBRARY & RESEARCH CENTER 601-14TH AVENUE ... SAN FRANCISCO **CA** 94118 (415) 751-6040
ALTERNATIVES IN RELIGIOUS EDUCATION, INC.
3945 SOUTH ONEIDA STREET ... DENVER **CO** 80237 (303) 363-7779
VIDEO ARCHIVE FOR HOLOCAUST TESTIMONIES AT YALE
STERLING MEMORIAL LIBRARY, ROOM 331C, YU ... NEW HAVEN **CT** 06520 (203) 432-1879
HOLOCAUST RESOURCE & EDUCATION CENTER
851 NORTH MAITLAND AVENUE ... MAITLAND **FL** 32751 (305) 628-0555
SOUTHEAST FLORIDA HOLOCAUST MEMORIAL CENTER
NORTHEAST 151ST STREET & BISCAYNE BOULEVARD ... MIAMI **FL** 33181 (305) 940-5690
YAD V'KIDUSH HASHEM, HOUSE OF MARTYRS
4200 SHERIDAN AVENUE ... MIAMI BEACH **FL** 33140 (305) 532-0363
ROSENBUSH PRODUCTIONS 6033 NORTH SHERIDAN ROAD, SUITE 43D .. CHICAGO **IL** 60660
SIMON WIESENTHAL CENTER 5715 NORTH LINCOLN AVE. ... CHICAGO **IL** 60659 (312) 989-0022
SPERTUS COLLEGE OF JUDAICA 618 SOUTH MICHIGAN AVENUE ... CHICAGO **IL** 60605 (312) 922-9012
HOLOCAUST MEMORIAL FOUNDATION OF ILLINOIS P.O. BOX 574 ... NORTHBROOK **IL** 60062 (312) 595-2025
FACING HISTORY AND OURSELVES RESOURCE CENTER
25 KENNARD ROAD ... BROOKLINE **MA** 02146 (617) 232-1595
DAVID BERGMAN 23011 PARKLAWN ... OAK PARK **MI** 48237 (313) 557-2440
REMEMBRANCE EDUCATION MEDIA P.O. BOX 37111 ... OAK PARK **MI** 48237 (313) 557-2440
HOLOCAUST MEMORIAL CENTER 6602 WEST MAPLE ROAD ... WEST BLOOMFIELD **MI** 48033 (313) 661-0840
ST. LOUIS CENTER FOR HOLOCAUST STUDIES
12 MILLSTONE CAMPUS DRIVE ... ST. LOUIS **MO** 63146 (314) 432-0020
JUDAIC RESEARCH INSTITUTE 747 LIVINGSTON ROAD ... ELIZABETH **NJ** 07208
SECOND GENERATION OF NORTH JERSEY P.O. BOX 141 ... FAIR LAWN **NJ** 07410
RESOURCE CTR./HOLOCAUST & GENOCIDE STUDIES-RAMAPO COLLEGE
505 RAMAPO VALLEY ROAD ... MAHWAH **NJ** 07430 (201) 825-2800
CENTER FOR HOLOCAUST STUDIES 1609 AVENUE J ... BROOKLYN **NY** 11230 (718) 338-6494
INTERNATIONAL BOOKS AND RECORDS 40-11 24TH STREET ... LONG ISLAND CITY **NY** 11101 (718) 786-2966
AMERICAN SOCIETY FOR YAD VASHEM, INC.
48 WEST 37TH STREET, 9TH FLOOR ... NEW YORK **NY** 10018 (212) 564-1865
BOARD OF JEWISH EDUCATION 426 WEST 58TH STREET ... NEW YORK **NY** 10019 (212) 245-8200
THE FOUNDATION FOR FUTURE GENERATIONS, INC.
393 WEST END AVENUE, SUITE 4D ... NEW YORK **NY** 10024
HOLOCAUST PUBLICATIONS 216 WEST 18TH STREET ... NEW YORK **NY** 10011 (212) 691-9220
HOLOCAUST SURVIVORS MEMORIAL FOUNDATION
350 FIFTH AVENUE ... NEW YORK **NY** 10118 (212) 594-8765
JEWISH DOCUMENTATION CENTER, INC. 666 FIFTH AVENUE ... NEW YORK **NY** 10103 (212) 581-1100
JEWISH MEDIA SERVICE OF J.W.B. 15 EAST 26TH STREET ... NEW YORK **NY** 10010 (212) 532-4949
JEWISH PEOPLE'S UNIVERSITY OF THE AIR 30 WEST 44TH STREET ... NEW YORK **NY** 10036
NEW YORK CITY HOLOCAUST MEMORIAL COMMISSION
111 WEST 40TH STREET ... NEW YORK **NY** 10018 (212) 221-1574
PHOENIX FILMS 470 PARK AVENUE SOUTH ... NEW YORK **NY** 10016 (212) 684-5910
THE RAOUL WALLENBERG COMMITTEE OF THE UNITED STATES
127 EAST 73RD STREET ... NEW YORK **NY** 10021 (212) 737-7790
SIMON WIESENTHAL CENTER-N.Y. OFFICE
342 MADISON AVENUE SUITE 437 ... NEW YORK **NY** 10017 (212) 370-0320
WORLD FEDERATION OF BERGEN-BELSEN ASSOCIATES P.O. BOX 333 ... NEW YORK **NY** 10021 (212) 752-0600
ZACHOR, HOLOCAUST STUDY/COMMEMORATION-NATL JEW. RESOURCE CTR
421 SEVENTH AVENUE ... NEW YORK **NY** 10001 (212) 714-9500
LIFE CENTER FOR HOLOCAUST STUDIES 884 CENTRAL AVENUE ... WOODMERE **NY** 11598 (516) 374-6465
SIMON WIESENTHAL CENTER 8 KING STREET EAST, SUITE 204 ... TORONTO **ON** M5C 1B5 (416) 864-9735
JEWISH IDENTITY CENTER 1453 LEVICK STREET ... PHILADELPHIA **PA** 19149
HOLOCAUST CENTER OF GREATER PITTSBURGH
234 MCKEE PLACE ... PITTSBURGH **PA** 15213 (412) 682-7111
CANADIAN JEWISH CONGRESS 1590 AVENUE DR. PENFIELD ... MONTREAL **QU** H3G 1C5 (514) 931-7531

HOLOCAUST SURVIVOR ORGANIZATIONS

1939 CLUB 435 SOUTH PALM DRIVE, SUITE 6 ... BEVERLY HILLS **CA** 90212
SHELTERS FOR ISRAEL 603 NORTH CAMDEN DRIVE ... BEVERLY HILLS **CA** 90210
UNITED NOWY-DWOR SOCIETY 422 SOUTH MAPLE DRIVE, #4 ... BEVERLY HILLS **CA** 90212
WOLYNER SOCIETY OF LOS ANGELES
329 SOUTH REXFORD DRIVE, SUITE 8 ... BEVERLY HILLS **CA** 90212
AMER. CONGRESS/JEWS FROM POLAND & SURV./CONCENTRATION CAMPS
6534 MOORE DRIVE ... LOS ANGELES **CA** 90048 (213) 938-7881
AMERICAN ROMANIAN JEWISH AID SOCIETY ... LOS ANGELES **CA** (213) 653-2109
BELGIAN JEWISH SOCIETY 715 NORTH SPAULDING AVENUE ... LOS ANGELES **CA** 90048
COUNCIL OF POSTWAR JEWISH ORG'S.-SURVIVORS OF THE NAZI HOLOCAUST
6205 ORANGE STREET ... LOS ANGELES **CA** 90048
JEWISH CLUB OF 1933
112 SOUTH ROBERTSON BOULEVARD, SUITE 6 ... LOS ANGELES **CA** 90035 (213) 271-6873
LODZER ORGANIZATION OF AMERICA 1241 SOUTH HOLT AVENUE ... LOS ANGELES **CA** 90035
LUBLINER ORGANIZATION 1136 SOUTH ORLANDO AVENUE ... LOS ANGELES **CA** 90035
LUKVOR MEZRICHER SOCIETY
337½ NORTH HAYWORTH AVENUE ... LOS ANGELES **CA** 90048
NASHELSKER SOCIETY 418 NORTH DETROIT STREET ... LOS ANGELES **CA** 90036
SECOND GENERATION-MARTYRS MEMORIAL & MUSEUM OF THE HOLOCAUST
6505 WILSHIRE BOULEVARD ... LOS ANGELES **CA** 90048 (213) 852-1234
SEPHARDIC ASSOC. MAX NORDAU, C/O AMERICAN SEPHARDIC FED.
6505 WILSHIRE BOULEVARD ... LOS ANGELES **CA** 90048
THE GENERATION AFTER, JEWISH FAMILY SERVICE
11646 WEST PICO BOULEVARD ... LOS ANGELES **CA** 90064 (213) 478-8241
WILNO VICINITY AND FRIENDS 6310 ORANGE STREET ... LOS ANGELES **CA** 90048
LOS ANGELES CHILD DEVELOPMENT CENTER
225 26TH STREET, ROOM 2 ... SANTA MONICA **CA** 90402 (213) 394-4069
JEWISH LITHUANIAN ORGANIZATION 4631 CEDROS AVENUE ... SHERMAN OAKS **CA** 91403
SECOND GENERATION OF NORTH JERSEY P.O. BOX 141 ... FAIR LAWN **NJ** 07410
SECOND GENERATION COUNCIL OF NEW JERSEY P.O. BOX 259 ... ROCKAWAY **NJ** 07866
HOLOCAUST SURVIVORS AND FRIENDS IN PURSUIT OF JUSTICE
TEMPLE ISRAEL, 600 NEW SCOTLAND AVENUE ... ALBANY **NY** 12208 (518) 438-7858
SURVIVORS OF NAZI CAMPS & RESISTANCE FIGHTERS
2747 THROOP AVENUE ... BRONX **NY** 10469 (212) 231-5456
AMERICAN FEDERATION FOR POLISH JEWS 1 UNION SQUARE ... NEW YORK **NY** 10003 (212) 691-7415
AMERICAN FEDERATION OF JEWISH FIGHTERS, CAMP INMATES, & NAZI VICTIMS
823 UNITED NATIONS PLAZA ... NEW YORK **NY** 10017 (212) 697-5670
AMERICAN FEDERATION OF JEWS FROM CENTRAL EUROPE INC.
570 SEVENTH AVENUE ... NEW YORK **NY** 10036 (212) 921-3860
AMERICAN GATHERING OF JEWISH HOLOCAUST SURVIVORS
122 WEST 30TH STREET ... NEW YORK **NY** 10001 (212) 239-4230
ASSOCIATION OF YUGOSLAV JEWS IN THE U.S., INC.
247 WEST 99TH STREET ... NEW YORK **NY** 10025 (212) 865-2211
COMMISSION ON STATUS OF JEWISH WAR ORPHANS IN EUROPE
47 BEEKMAN STREET ... NEW YORK **NY** 10038 (212) 227-7800
CONFERENCE ON JEWISH MATERIAL CLAIMS AGAINST GERMANY
15 E. 26TH STREET ... NEW YORK **NY** 10010 (212) 679-4704
FEDERATION OF POLISH JEWS, INC. 342 MADISON AVENUE ... NEW YORK **NY** 10017 (212) 986-3693
THE GENERATION AFTER BOX 364, BAYCHESTER STATION ... NEW YORK **NY** 10469 (212) 231-1196
HERITAGE OF POLISH JEWS FOUNDATION 12 WEST 44TH STREET ... NEW YORK **NY** 10036 (212) 921-8011
INTERNATIONAL NETWORK OF CHILDREN OF JEWISH HOLOCAUST SURVIVORS, INC.
1 PARK AVENUE ... NEW YORK **NY** 10016
SECOND GENERATION OF NY 350 FIFTH AVENUE, ROOM 3508 ... NEW YORK **NY** 10118 (212) 594-8765
SELFHELP COMMUNITY SERVICES 300 PARK AVENUE SOUTH ... NEW YORK **NY** 10010 (212) 533-7100
THANKS TO SCANDINAVIA 745 FIFTH AVENUE ... NEW YORK **NY** 10151 (212) 486-8600
SECOND GENERATION OF STATEN ISLAND 32 BAGOR STREET ... STATEN ISLAND **NY** 10314 (718) 698-1232
KOL ISRAEL FOUNDATION 14462 E. CARROLL BLVD ... CLEVELAND **OH** 44122 (216) 382-7597

HOSPITALS & MEDICAL CENTERS

LEO N. LEVI NATIONAL ARTHRITIS HOSPITAL 300 PROSPECT ... HOT SPRINGS PARK **AR** 71901 (501) 321-9496
SUN AIR FEDERATION AND HOME FOR ASTHMATIC CHILDREN
221 N. ROBERTSON BLVD ... BEVERLY HILLS **CA** 90212 (213) 272-4371
CEDARS-SINAI MEDICAL CENTER 8700 BEVERLY BOULEVARD ... LOS ANGELES **CA** 90048 (213) 855-5000
JEWISH NATIONAL HOSPITAL AT DENVER 4929 WILSHIRE BLVD ... LOS ANGELES **CA** 90010 (213) 938-7263
SINAI MEDICAL CENTER 8720 BEVERLY BLVD ... LOS ANGELES **CA** 90048 (213) 652-5000
MOUNT ZION HOSPITAL & MEDICAL CENTER
1600 DIVISADERO STREET ... SAN FRANCISCO **CA** 94115 (415) 567-6600
HOPE CENTER FOR THE RETARDED 3601 E. 32ND AVENUE ... DENVER **CO** 80205 (303) 388-4801
JEWISH NATIONAL HOME - HOME FOR ASTHMATIC CHILDREN
1989 JULIAN STREET ... DENVER **CO** 80204 (303) 458-1999
NATIONAL JEWISH CENTER FOR IMMUNOLOGY AND RESPIRATORY MEDICINE
1400 JACKSON STREET ... DENVER **CO** 80206 (303) 388-4461
NAT'L JEWISH HOSPITAL & RESEARCH CTR.-NATIONAL ASTHMA CENTER
3800 E. COLFAX AVENUE ... DENVER **CO** 80206 (303) 388-4461
NATIONAL JEWISH HOSPITAL/NATIONAL ASTHMA CENTER
3800 E. COLFAX AVENUE ... DENVER **CO** 80206 (800) 222-5864
CANCER RESEARCH CENTER & HOSPITAL 6401 W. COLFAX AVENUE ... LAKEWOOD **CO** 80214 (303) 233-6501
MOUNT SINAI HOSPITAL 500 BLUE HILLS AVENUE ... HARTFORD **CT** 06112 (203) 243-1441
MICHAEL REESE HOSPITAL & MEDICAL CENTER 2929 S. ELLIS AVENUE ... CHICAGO **IL** 60616 (312) 791-2330
SCHWAB REHABILITATION HOSPITAL 1401 S. CALIFORNIA BLVD ... CHICAGO **IL** 60608 (312) 522-2010
THE ARK 2341 W. DEVON ... CHICAGO **IL** 60659 (312) 973-1000
JEWISH HOSPITAL 217 EAST CHESTNUT STREET ... LOUISVILLE **KY** 40202 (502) 587-4308
TOURO INFIRMARY 1401 FOUCHER STREET ... NEW ORLEANS **LA** 70115 (504) 897-3311
BETH ISRAEL HOSPITAL 330 BROOKLINE AVENUE ... BOSTON **MA** 02215 (617) 735-2000
LEVINDALE HEBREW GERIATRIC CENTER & HOSPITAL
BELVEDERE & GREENSPRING AVENUE ... BALTIMORE **MD** 21215 (301) 466-8700
SINAI HOSPITAL OF BALTIMORE
2401 WEST BELVEDERE AVENUE ... BALTIMORE **MD** 21215 (301) 578-5678
SINAI HOSPITAL OF DETROIT 6767 W. OUTER DRIVE ... DETROIT **MI** 48235 (313) 493-5500
MOUNT SINAI HOSPITAL OF MINNEAPOLIS 2215 PARK AVENUE ... MINNEAPOLIS **MN** 55404 (612) 339-1692
MENORAH MEDICAL CENTER 4949 ROCKHILL ROAD ... KANSAS CITY **MO** 64110 (816) 276-8000
JEWISH HOSPITAL P.O. BOX 14109 ... ST. LOUIS **MO** 63178 (314) 454-7000
JEWISH HOSPITAL AND REHABILITATION CENTER OF NEW JERSEY
HUDSON CITY COMPLEX, 198 STEVENS AVENUE ... JERSEY CITY **NJ** 07305 (201) 451-9000
NEWARK BETH ISRAEL MEDICAL CENTER 201 LYONS AVENUE ... NEWARK **NJ** 07112 (201) 926-7175
ALBERT EINSTEIN COLLEGE HOSPITAL 1825 EASTCHESTER ROAD ... BRONX **NY** 10461 (212) 430-2000
ALBERT EINSTEIN COLLEGE OF MEDICINE OF YESHIVA UNIVERSITY
1300 MORRIS PARK AVENUE ... BRONX **NY** 10461 (212) 430-2000
BETH ABRAHAM HOSPITAL 612 ALLERTON AVENUE ... BRONX **NY** 10467 (212) 920-5881
HEBREW HOSPITAL FOR CHRONIC SICK, INC. 2200 GIVAN AVENUE ... BRONX **NY** 10475 (212) 379-5020
BROOKDALE HOSPITAL MEDICAL CENTER
1275 LINDEN BOULEVARD & ROCKAWAY PARKWAY ... BROOKLYN **NY** 11212 (718) 240-5000
KINGSBROOK JEWISH MEDICAL CENTER
RUTLAND ROAD & E. 49TH STREET ... BROOKLYN **NY** 11203 (718) 756-9700
KINGSBROOK JEWISH MEDICAL CENTER 585 SCHENECTADY AVENUE ... BROOKLYN **NY** 11203 (718) 756-9700
MAIMONIDES MEDICAL CENTER 4802 TENTH AVENUE ... BROOKLYN **NY** 11219 (718) 270-7679
MOUNT SINAI HOSPITAL - CITY HOSPITAL AT ELMHURST AFFILIATE
79-01 BROADWAY ... ELMHURST **NY** 11380 (718) 830-1515
L.I. JEWISH-HILLSIDE MEDICAL CENTER
1554 NORTHERN BOULEVARD ... MANHASSET **NY** 11030 (212) 539-9800
LONG ISLAND JEWISH-HILLSIDE MEDICAL CENTER
270-05 76TH AVENUE ... NEW HYDE PARK **NY** 11040 (212) 343-6700
ALBERT EINSTEIN COLLEGE OF MEDICINE OF YESHIVA UNIVERSITY
55 FIFTH AVENUE ... NEW YORK **NY** 10003 (212) 790-0200
AMERICAN ASSOCIATION FOR BIKUR CHOLIM HOSPITAL
119 FIFTH AVENUE ... NEW YORK **NY** 10021 (212) 260-4260
AMERICAN COMM. FOR SHAARE ZEDEK HOSPITAL IN JERUSALEM, INC.
49 WEST 45TH STREET ... NEW YORK **NY** 10036 (212) 354-8801
BETH ISRAEL MEDICAL CENTER 10 NATHAN D. PERLMAN PLACE ... NEW YORK **NY** 10003 (212) 420-2000
BETH ISRAEL MEDICAL CENTER-ALCOHOLISM TREATMENT PROGRAM
50 COOPER SQUARE ... NEW YORK **NY** 10003 (212) 420-4300
JEWISH MEMORIAL HOSPITAL BROADWAY & 196TH STREET ... NEW YORK **NY** 10040 (212) 569-4700

MOUNT SINAI MEDICAL CENTER, THE
FIFTH AVENUE & 100TH STREET, ONE GUSTAVE L. LEVY PLACE .... NEW YORK **NY** 10029 (212) 650-6500
JEWISH HOSPITAL OF CINCINNATI, THE 3212 BURNET AVENUE......... CINCINNATI **OH** 45229 (513) 872-3220
MOUNT SINAI MEDICAL CENTER, THE UNIVERSITY CIRCLE............ CLEVELAND **OH** 44106 (216) 795-6000
THE MOUNT SINAI HOSPITAL 600 UNIVERSITY AVENUE.................. TORONTO **ON** M5G 1X5 (416) 596-4200
EAGLEVILLE HOSPITAL & REHABILITATION CENTER
100 EAGLEVILLE ROAD, P.O. BOX 45 .... EAGLEVILLE **PA** 19408 (215) 539-6000
MONTEFIORE HOSPITAL 3459 FIFTH AVENUE .... PITTSBURGH **PA** 15213 (412) 648-6000
HERZL FAM. PRACTICE CTR.-SIR MORTIMER DAVIS JEWISH GEN. HOS.
5750 COTE DES NEIGES .... MONTREAL **QU** H3T 1E2 (514) 739-6371
JEWISH HOSPITAL OF HOPE CENTRE
7745 EST RUE SHERBROOKE STREET EAST................................ MONTREAL **QU** H1L 1A3 (514) 352-3120
MAIMONIDES HOSPITAL & HOME FOR THE AGED
5795 CALDWELL AVENUE.. MONTREAL **QU** H4W 1W3 (514) 488-2301
MIRIAM HOSPITAL, THE 164 SUMMIT AVENUE.......................... PROVIDENCE **RI** 02906 (401) 274-3700
MT. SINAI MEDICAL CENTER 950 NORTH 12TH STREET .... MILWAUKEE **WI** 53233 (414) 289-8200

HOTELS & MOTELS

BEVERLY GRAND 7257 BEVERLY BOULEVARD.......................... LOS ANGELES **CA** 90036 (213) 939-1653
SHALOM KOSHER HOTEL 330 NORTH HAYWORTH .... LOS ANGELES **CA** 90024 (213) 655-1500
GRAND LAKE LODGE .... LEBANON **CT** 06249 (203) 642-6512
VOYAGER GLATT KOSHER HOTEL
2424 NORTH ATLANTIC AVENUE................................ DAYTONA BEACH **FL** 32018 (800) 874-1824
ASTOR HOTEL 956 WASHINGTON AVENUE............................ MIAMI BEACH **FL** 33139 (305) 534-8536
BARCELONA HOTEL COLLINS AT 43RD STREET .... MIAMI BEACH **FL** 33140 (305) 532-3311
BLACKSTONE HOTEL 8TH STREET AT WASHINGTON AVENUE....... MIAMI BEACH **FL** 33139 (305) 538-1811
CARIBBEAN HOTEL 3737 COLLINS AVENUE............................ MIAMI BEACH **FL** 33140 (305) 531-0061
CROWN HOTEL 4041 COLLINS AVENUE................................. MIAMI BEACH **FL** 33140 (305) 531-5771
KENMORE HOTEL 1040 WASHINGTON AVENUE .... MIAMI BEACH **FL** 33139 (305) 531-6621
MARSEILLES HOTEL 1741 COLLINS AVENUE .... MIAMI BEACH **FL** 33139 (305) 538-5711
RALEIGH HOTEL OCEANFRONT AT 18TH STREET...................... MIAMI BEACH **FL** 33139 (305) 534-7025
ROYAL PALM HOTEL 1545 COLLINS AVENUE........................... MIAMI BEACH **FL** 33139 (800) 327-3195
SASSON HOTEL ON THE OCEAN AT 20TH STREET .... MIAMI BEACH **FL** 33139 (212) 436-8820
SAXONY HOTEL 3201 COLLINS AVENUE................................ MIAMI BEACH **FL** 33140 (305) 538-6811
SEA ISLE HOTEL OF MIAMI BEACH 3001 COLLINS AVENUE........... MIAMI BEACH **FL** 33140 (305) 538-7841
SEAGULL HOTEL OCEAN AND 21ST STREET .... MIAMI BEACH **FL** 33139 (305) 538-6631
SHELBORNE HOTEL OCEANFRONT AT 18TH STREET .... MIAMI BEACH **FL** 33139 (800) 327-8757
SHORE CLUB 19TH STREET AND COLLINS AVENUE..................... MIAMI BEACH **FL** 33139 (305) 538-7811
SOVEREIGN HOTEL ON THE OCEAN AT 44TH STREET .... MIAMI BEACH **FL** 33140 (800) 327-4733
SURREY HOTEL 4390 COLLINS AVENUE................................ MIAMI BEACH **FL** 33140 (305) 534-2227
TARLETON HOTEL 25TH STREET AND COLLINS AVENUE .... MIAMI BEACH **FL** 33140 (305) 538-5721
TIDES HOTEL 1222 OCEAN DRIVE...................................... MIAMI BEACH **FL** 33139 (305) 531-6701
VERSAILLES HOTEL 34TH STREET AND COLLINS AVENUE .... MIAMI BEACH **FL** 33140 (305) 531-4213
WALDMAN'S HOTEL 4299 COLLINS AVENUE............................ MIAMI BEACH **FL** 33140 (305) 538-5731
KOSHER WORLD TOWER HOTEL
109 S. NORTH CAROLINA AVENUE...................................... ATLANTIC CITY **NJ** 08404 (718) 377-1170
TEPLITZKY'S INTERNATIONAL MOTEL
BOARDWALK-END OF CHELSEA AVENUE............................... ATLANTIC CITY **NJ** 08401 (609) 344-7071
FOX & LIEBERMAN HOTEL 814 MADISON AVENUE...................... LAKEWOOD **NJ** 08701 (201) 367-9199
HARBOR ISLAND SPA 701 OCEAN AVENUE............................. LONG BRANCH **NJ** 07740 (201) 222-2600
PARK HOTEL 123 WEST 7TH STREET.................................... PLAINFIELD **NJ** 07060 (201) 754-2211
LEVINE'S WASHINGTON HOTEL
124-19 ROCKAWAY BEACH BOULEVARD.............................. BELLE HARBOR **NY** 11694 (718) 634-4244
OCEAN BREEZE HOTEL 3811 SURF AVENUE............................ BROOKLYN **NY** 11224 (718) 266-1456
PARK HOUSE HOTEL 1206 48TH STREET............................... BROOKLYN **NY** 11219 (718) 871-8100
FALLSVIEW .... ELLENVILLE **NY** 12428 (914) 647-5100
NEVELE COUNTRY CLUB NEVELE ROAD .... ELLENVILLE **NY** 12428 (914) 647-6000
REGAL HOTEL BOX C.. FALLSBURG **NY** 12733 (914) 434-7788
HY-SA-NA LODGE .... FERNDALE **NY** 12734 (914) 292-7330
PEAR HOTEL (FORMERLY HOTEL SHALOM) .... FERNDALE **NY** 12734 (914) 272-4464
OPPENHEIMER'S REGIS HOTEL .... FLEISCHMANNS **NY** 12430 (914) 254-5080
ZUCKER'S GLEN WILD HOTEL .... GLEN WILD **NY** 12738 (914) 434-7470
TAMARACK LODGE .... GREENFIELD PARK **NY** 12435 (914) 647-7000
GROSSINGER'S HOTEL AND COUNTRY CLUB .... GROSSINGER **NY** 12734 (914) 292-5000
BROOKSIDE HOTEL .... KERHONKSON **NY** 12446 (914) 626-7311
CONCORD HOTEL .... KIAMESHA LAKE **NY** 12751 (914) 794-4000
HOTEL GIBBER P.O. BOX G .... KIAMESHA LAKE **NY** 12751 (914) 794-6900
BROWN'S HOTEL ROUTE 52 EAST.................................. LOCH SHELDRAKE **NY** 12759 (914) 434-5151
DELMAR HOTEL .... LOCH SHELDRAKE **NY** 12759 (914) 292-5234
JACKSON HOTEL 10 WEST BROADWAY .... LONG BEACH **NY** 11561 (516) 431-3700
LINCOLN HOTEL 405 EAST BROADWAY .... LONG BEACH **NY** 11561 (516) 889-7100
KUTSHER'S COUNTRY CLUB .... MONTICELLO **NY** 12701 (914) 794-6000
CAMBRIDGE HOUSE 333 WEST 86TH STREET .... NEW YORK **NY** 10024 (212) 873-8800
DAN HOTELS GROUP 120 EAST 56TH STREET........................... NEW YORK **NY** 10022 (212) 752-6120
ESPLANADE HOTEL 305 WEST END AVENUE .... NEW YORK **NY** 10023 (212) 874-5000
H. SHIFF ISRAEL LEADING HOTELS, INC. 420 LEXINGTON AVENUE....... NEW YORK **NY** 10170 (212) 986-5782
HAIFA DAN CARMEL HOTEL 120 EAST 56TH STREET .... NEW YORK **NY** 10022 (212) 752-6120
HERZLIA ACCADIA GRAND HOTEL 120 EAST 56TH STREET .... NEW YORK **NY** 10022 (212) 752-6120
ISRAEL HOTEL REPRESENTATIVES, INC. 120 EAST 56TH STREET......... NEW YORK **NY** 10022 (212) 752-6120
ISRAEL LEADING HOTELS, INC. 420 LEXINGTON AVENUE .... NEW YORK **NY** 10017 (212) 986-5782
JERUSALEM KING DAVID HOTEL 120 EAST 56TH STREET .... NEW YORK **NY** 10022 (212) 752-6120
MORIAH HOTELS, LTD. 10 ROCKEFELLER PLAZA........................ NEW YORK **NY** 10020 (212) 541-5009
RAMADA SHALOM HOTEL JERUSALEM 370 EAST 76TH STREET .... NEW YORK **NY** 10021 (212) 570-0606
HOTEL MOUNTAINAIRE .... PARKSVILLE **NY** 12768
PARAMOUNT HOTEL .... PARKSVILLE **NY** 12768 (914) 252-6700
HOTEL COLUMBIA .... SHARON SPRINGS **NY** 13459 (518) 284-2220
YARKONY'S ADLER HOTEL .... SHARON SPRINGS **NY** 13459 (518) 284-2285
AVON LODGE .... SOUTH FALLSBURG **NY** 12779 (914) 434-9110
BRICKMAN HOTEL BRICKMAN ROAD .... SOUTH FALLSBURG **NY** 12779 (914) 434-5000
LA VISTA COUNTRY HOTEL P.O. BOX 1080 .... SOUTH FALLSBURG **NY** 12779 (914) 434-3090
PINES HOTEL .... SOUTH FALLSBURG **NY** 12779 (914) 434-6000
RALEIGH HOTEL .... SOUTH FALLSBURG **NY** 12779 (914) 434-7000
HOMOWACK LODGE .... SPRING GLEN **NY** 12483 (914) 647-6800
BADER'S LAKE STREET .... SPRING VALLEY **NY** 10977 (914) 356-7700
GARTNER'S INN HUNGRY HOLLOW ROAD .... SPRING VALLEY **NY** 10977 (914) 356-0875
SINGER'S HOTEL CENTRAL AVENUE................................ SPRING VALLEY **NY** 10977 (914) 356-2300
WEISMAN'S HOTEL 42 CLINTON STREET............................ SPRING VALLEY **NY** 10977 (914) 356-2131
WHITE HOUSE 180 NORTH PASCAK ROAD .... SPRING VALLEY **NY** 10977 (914) 356-0964
STEVENSVILLE HOTEL & COUNTRY CLUB .... SWAN LAKE **NY** 12783 (914) 292-8000
ALADDIN HOTEL .... WOODBOURNE **NY** 12788 (914) 434-7700
CHALET VIM CHESTER ROAD... WOODBOURNE **NY** 12788 (914) 434-5786
LAKE HOUSE HOTEL LAKE HOUSE ROAD .... WOODRIDGE **NY** 12789 (914) 434-7800
SUNNY OAKS HOTEL .... WOODRIDGE **NY** 12789 (914) 434-7580
VEGETARIAN HOTEL BOX 566.. WOODRIDGE **NY** 12789 (914) 434-4455
POCMONT LODGE HOTEL .... BUSHKILL **PA** 18324 (800) 762-6668
GLENCAIRN MOTOR HOTEL MANOR ROAD .... BOURNEMOUTH **GB** 0202 27636
NEW AMBASSADOR BOURNEMOUTH EAST CLIFF..................... BOURNEMOUTH **GB** BH1 3DP 0202 25453
HOTEL SILBERHORN .... GRINDELWALD **SW** 036/52 28 22
LEVIN'S GLATT HOTEL METROPOL .... AROSA **SW** 01141-81
BERMANN'S HOTEL EDELWEISS ST. MORITZ .... ST. MORITZ **SW** (082) 355-33

HOTLINES

VALLEY BETH SHALOM COUNSELING CENTER
14739 VENTURA BOULEVARD.. ENCINO **CA** 91436 (818) 788-6000
ALCOHOLICS ANONYMOUS .... LOS ANGELES **CA** (213) 387-8316
CEDARS-SINAI MEDICAL EMERGENCY .... LOS ANGELES **CA** (213) 855-6517
CEDARS-SINAI PSYCHIATRY EMERGENCY .... LOS ANGELES **CA** (213) 855-6527
ISRAEL HOTLINE .... SAN FRANCISCO **CA** (415) 392-6397
EZRA HOTLINE OF THE JEWISH FEDERATION
1 SOUTH FRANKLIN STREET .... CHICAGO **IL** 60606 (312) 346-6700
MEZUZAH HOTLINE 305 KINGSTON AVENUE........................... BROOKLYN **NY** 11213 (718) 774-1780
CULT CLINIC HOTLINE (JBFCS) 1651 THIRD AVENUE .... NEW YORK **NY** 10028 (212) 860-8533
JEWISH CENTER HOT LINE 1125 COLLEGE STREET .... COLUMBUS **OH** 43209 (614) 231-2731

IMPORT & EXPORT - AMERICAN - ISRAELI TRADE

AMERICAN-ISRAEL CHAMBER OF COMMERCE
6505 WILSHIRE BOULEVARD, SUITE 201 .... LOS ANGELES **CA** 90048 (213) 658-7910
I AM EXPORTING C/O LBB ASSOCIATES, 88 BRADLEY ROAD .... WOODBRIDGE **CT** 06525 (203) 397-3977
AMERICAN-ISRAEL CHAMBER OF COMMERCE & INDUSTRY, INC.
180 NORTH MICHIGAN AVENUE .... CHICAGO **IL** 60601 (312) 641-2937
NEW ENGLAND-ISRAEL CHAMBER OF COMMERCE & INDUSTRY, INC.
471 STATLER OFFICE BUILDING.. BOSTON **MA** 02116 (617) 423-9510
SEABOARD AMERICA-ISRAEL CHAMBER OF COMMERCE
1000 HAVERHILL ROAD .... BALTIMORE **MD** 21229 (301) 525-2110
AMERICAN-ISRAEL CHAMBER OF COMMERCE & INDUSTRY, INC.
6600 WEST MAPLE ROAD .... WEST BLOOMFIELD **MI** 48033 (313) 661-1948
AMERICAN-ISRAEL CHAMBER OF COMMERCE & INDUSTRY OF MINNESOTA, INC.
LASALLE COURT BUILDINGS, 811 LASALLE AVENUE, ROOM 301 ..... MINNEAPOLIS **MN** 55402 (612) 332-1284
TORAH TECHNICS - "WHERE TORAH & TECHNOLOGY MEET"
1603 CARROLL STREET.. BROOKLYN **NY** 11213 (718) 953-7028
HOD LAVAN TURKEY PRODUCTS, LIMITED 149-32 132ND STREET .... JAMAICA **NY** 11430 (718) 529-4411
AMERICAN-ISRAEL CHAMBER OF COMMERCE & INDUSTRY, INC.
500 FIFTH AVENUE .... NEW YORK **NY** 10110 (212) 354-6510
AMERICAN-ISRAELI SHIPPING COMPANY, INC.
1 WORLD TRADE CENTER .... NEW YORK **NY** 10048 (212) 432-0300
ATALANTA CORPORATION 17 VARICK STREET .... NEW YORK **NY** 10013 (212) 431-9000
DISTRIBUTOR'S CENTER FOR ISRAELI BOOKS LTD. 350 FIFTH AVENUE .. NEW YORK **NY** 10118 (212) 736-9888
GOVT. OF ISRAEL TRADE CENTER, S. BEN-TOVIM, CONSUL & COMM.
350 FIFTH AVENUE .... NEW YORK **NY** 10118 (212) 560-0660
ISRAEL AIRCRAFT INDUSTRIES INTERNATIONAL, INC.
50 WEST 23 STREET .... NEW YORK **NY** 10011 (212) 620-4400
ISRAEL WHOLESALERS IMPORT CO., INC. 21 1/2 ESSEX STREET .... NEW YORK **NY** 10002 (212) 228-1661
ISRAELI COAT CORP. OF AMERICA 512 SEVENTH AVENUE .... NEW YORK **NY** 10018 (212) 354-7110
ISRAELI HANDICRAFT IMPORTING CO. 168 FIFTH AVENUE................. NEW YORK **NY** 10003 (212) 929-4928
OVERSEAS PUBLIC UTILITIES & GAS CORP. 310 MADISON AVENUE ...... NEW YORK **NY** 10017 (212) 687-6377
AMERICAN-ISRAEL CHAMBER OF COMMERCE & INDUSTRY, INC.
10800 BROOKPARK ROAD .... CLEVELAND **OH** 44130 (216) 267-1200
AMERICAN-ISRAEL CHAMBER OF COMMERCE P.O. BOX 6340 .... MCLEAN **VA** 22106 (703) 821-3088
CANADA-ISRAEL CHAMBER OF COMMERCE & INDUSTRY
FIRST CANADIAN PLACE, P.O. BOX 31, 100 KING STREET .... TORONTO **ON** M5X 1A9 (416) 362-7424

INFORMATION BUREAUS

NATIONAL JEWISH HOSPITALITY COMMITTEE AND INFORMATION CENTER
TEMPLE AKIBA, 5249 S. SEPULVEDA BOULEVARD .... CULVER CITY **CA** 90230 (213) 398-5783
FREDA MOHR MULTISERVICE CENTER 351 FAIRFAX AVENUE .... LOS ANGELES **CA** 90036 (213) 655-5141
JEWISH FEDERATION COUNCIL OF GREATER LOS ANGELES DIRECTORY
6505 WILSHIRE BOULEVARD.. LOS ANGELES **CA** 90048 (213) 852-1234
NAT'L JEW. INFO. SERVICE FOR THE PROPAGATION OF JUDAISM, INC
5174 W. 8TH STREET.. LOS ANGELES **CA** 90036 (213) 936-6033
REFORM SYNAGOGUE INFORMATION 13107 VENTURA BLVD ..NORTH HOLLYWOOD **CA** 91606 (818) 872-3550

JEWISH COMMUNITY INFORMATION & REFERRAL
121 STEWART STREET ... SAN FRANCISCO **CA** 94105 (415) 777-0411
JEWISH ACTIVIST FRONT-ISRAEL INFORMATION CENTER
800 21ST STREET N.W., ROOM 417 ... WASHINGTON **DC** 20006 (202) 686-7574
FEDERATION INFORMATION & REFERRAL SERVICE
4200 BISCAYNE BOULEVARD ... MIAMI **FL** 33137 (305) 576-4000
RABBI RUBIN R. DOBIN, 'JEWS FOR JEWS'
17720 NORTH BAY ROAD, SUITE 8D ... N. MIAMI BEACH **FL** 33160
JEWS FOR JEWS ORGANIZATION P.O. BOX 6194 ... SURFSIDE **FL** 33154 (305) 931-0001
JEWISH INFORMATION SOCIETY 1129 THORN TREE ... HIGHLAND PARK **IL** 60035
MID-EAST INFORMATION RESOURCE 871 MARION AVENUE ... HIGHLAND PARK **IL** 60035 (312) 432-1735
JEWISH COMMUNITY INFORMATION SERVICE OF GREATER BOSTON
31 NEW CHARDON STREET ... BOSTON **MA** 02114 (617) 227-6641
JEWISH INFORMATION SERVICE 5750 PARK HEIGHTS AVENUE ... BALTIMORE **MD** 21215 (301) 466-INFO
JEWISH INFORMATION & REFERRAL SERVICE
15110 WEST TEN MILE ROAD ... OAK PARK **MI** 48237 (313) 967-4357
AMERICAN JEWISH PUBLIC RELATIONS SOCIETY 234 FIFTH AVENUE ... NEW YORK **NY** 10001 (212) 697-5895
BLACK-JEWISH INFORMATION CENTER 16 E. 85TH STREET ... NEW YORK **NY** 10028 (212) 879-4577
JEWISH INFORMATION & REFERRAL SERVICE-FEDERATION
130 E. 59TH STREET ... NEW YORK **NY** 10022 (212) 980-1000
JEWISH INFORMATION BUREAU, INC. 250 W. 57TH STREET ... NEW YORK **NY** 10019 (212) 582-5318
JEWISH INFORMATION SERVICE 2030 SOUTH TAYLOR ROAD ... CLEVELAND **OH** 44118 (216) 566-9200
JEWISH INFORMATION SERVICE 4600 BATHURST STREET, #345 ... WILLOWDALE **ON** M2R 3V2 (416) 635-5600
JEWISH INFORMATION & REFERRAL SERVICE - PHILADELPHIA
226 SOUTH 16TH STREET ... PHILADELPHIA **PA** 19102 (215) 893-5821
JEWISH INFORMATION BUREAU 234 MCKEE PLACE ... PITTSBURGH **PA** 15213 (412) 681-8000

INTERFAITH ORGANIZATIONS

ARK. COUNCIL ON BROTHERHOOD/NAT'L CONF. OF CHRISTIANS & JEWS
350 TOWER BUILDING ... LITTLE ROCK **AR** 72205 (501) 372-5129
CANADIAN COUNCIL OF CHRISTIANS AND JEWS
736 GRANVILLE STREET, #1114 ... VANCOUVER **BC** V6Z 2G3 (604) 684-6024
NATIONAL CONFERENCE OF CHRISTIANS & JEWS
6711 E. 9TH STREET ... LONG BEACH **CA** 90815
NATIONAL CONFERENCE OF CHRISTIANS & JEWS
3580 WILSHIRE BLVD ... LOS ANGELES **CA** 90010 (213) 385-0491
NATIONAL CONFERENCE OF CHRISTIANS & JEWS 326 BROADWAY ... SAN DIEGO **CA** 92101 (619) 232-6113
NATIONAL CONFERENCE OF CHRISTIANS & JEWS
703 MARKET STREET, SUITE 809 ... SAN FRANCISCO **CA** 94103 (415) 391-2850
NATIONAL CONFERENCE OF CHRISTIANS & JEWS
777 NORTH FIRST STREET, SUITE 620 ... SAN JOSE **CA** 95112 (408) 286-9663
NATIONAL CONFERENCE OF CHRISTIANS & JEWS 111 PEARL STREET ... HARTFORD **CT** 06103 (203) 522-4231
NATIONAL CONFERENCE OF CHRISTIANS & JEWS
1425 H STREET N.W. ... WASHINGTON **DC** 20005 (202) 628-9141
SECRETARIAT FOR CATHOLIC-JEWISH RELATIONS
1312 MASSACHUSETTS AVENUE N.W. ... WASHINGTON **DC** 20005 (202) 659-6857
NATIONAL CONFERENCE OF CHRISTIANS & JEWS
9300 S. DADELAND BLVD, SUITE 511 ... MIAMI **FL** 33156
NATIONAL CONFERENCE OF CHRISTIANS & JEWS
1002 FLEMING BUILDING ... DES MOINES **IA** 50309 (515) 244-7227
NATIONAL CONFERENCE OF CHRISTIANS & JEWS 203 NORTH WABASH .. CHICAGO **IL** 60601 (312) 236-9272
NATIONAL CONFERENCE OF CHRISTIANS & JEWS
1815 NORTH MERIDIAN ... INDIANAPOLIS **IN** 46260 (317) 924-5731
NATIONAL CONFERENCE OF CHRISTIANS & JEWS
512 INSURANCE BUILDING ... WICHITA **KS** 67202 (316) 264-0356
NATIONAL CONFERENCE OF CHRISTIANS & JEWS
305 WEST BROADWAY ... LOUISVILLE **KY** 40202 (502) 583-0281
NATIONAL CONFERENCE OF CHRISTIANS & JEWS
612 INTERNATIONAL BUILDING ... NEW ORLEANS **LA** 70130
NATIONAL CONFERENCE OF CHRISTIANS & JEWS
1031 DUDLEY DRIVE ... SHREVEPORT **LA** 71104
NATIONAL CONFERENCE OF CHRISTIANS & JEWS
88 TREMONT STREET, ROOM 610 ... BOSTON **MA** 02108 (617) 532-7510
NATIONAL CONFERENCE OF CHRISTIANS & JEWS
300 EQUITABLE BUILDING ... BALTIMORE **MD** 21201 (301) 539-2660
NATIONAL CONFERENCE OF CHRISTIANS & JEWS 150 W. BOSTON BLVD .. DETROIT **MI** 48202 (313) 869-6306
NATIONAL CONFERENCE OF CHRISTIANS & JEWS
18 E. ARROWHEAD ROAD ... DULUTH **MN** 55803
NATIONAL CONFERENCE OF CHRISTIANS & JEWS
84 S. 6TH STREET, SYNDICATE BUILDING-#542 ... MINNEAPOLIS **MN** 55402
NATIONAL CONFERENCE OF CHRISTIANS & JEWS 721 OLIVE STREET ... ST. LOUIS **MO** 63101
NATIONAL CONFERENCE OF CHRISTIANS & JEWS P.O. BOX 4436 ... CHARLOTTE **NC** 28204 (704) 332-4420
NATIONAL CONFERENCE OF CHRISTIANS & JEWS
515 SOUTHEASTERN BLDG ... GREENSBORO **NC** 27401 (919) 273-8800
NATIONAL CONFERENCE OF CHRISTIANS & JEWS 423 CENTER BUILDING ... OMAHA **NE** 68105 (402) 346-3357
NATIONAL CONFERENCE OF CHRISTIANS & JEWS 40 BAY STREET ... MANCHESTER **NH** 03104
NATIONAL CONFERENCE OF CHRISTIANS & JEWS 790 BROAD STREET ... NEWARK **NJ** 07102 (201) 642-6025
NATIONAL CONFERENCE OF CHRISTIANS & JEWS P.O. BOX 3165 ... ALBUQUERQUE **NM** 87110 (505) 266-4964
NATIONAL CONFERENCE OF CHRISTIANS & JEWS
4220 S. MARYLAND PARK, 304 ... LAS VEGAS **NV** 89109
BROTHERHOOD RESEARCH INSTITUTE, INC. 2879 W. 12TH STREET ... BROOKLYN **NY** 11224 (718) 372-5280
NATIONAL CONFERENCE OF CHRISTIANS & JEWS
STATLER HILTON HOTEL ... BUFFALO **NY** 14202 (716) 853-9596
NATIONAL CONFERENCE OF CHRISTIANS & JEWS 43 W. 57TH STREET ... NEW YORK **NY** 10019 (212) 688-7530
NATIONAL CONFERENCE OF CHRISTIANS & JEWS
175 MAIN STREET ... WHITE PLAINS **NY** 10601 (914) 946-1604
NATIONAL CONFERENCE OF CHRISTIANS & JEWS 617 VINE STREET ... CINCINNATI **OH** 45202 (513) 381-4660

NATIONAL CONFERENCE OF CHRISTIANS & JEWS
621 NORTH ROBINSON ... OKLAHOMA CITY **OK** 73102 (405) 232-3861
NATIONAL CONFERENCE OF CHRISTIANS & JEWS 309 CENTER BLDG ... TULSA **OK** 74127 (918) 583-1361
NATIONAL CONFERENCE OF CHRISTIANS & JEWS
141 WAYLAND AVENUE ... PROVIDENCE **RI** 02906 (401) 351-5120
NATIONAL CONFERENCE OF CHRISTIANS & JEWS
3373 POPLAR AVENUE-414 ... MEMPHIS **TN** 38111 (901) 327-0010
NATIONAL CONFERENCE OF CHRISTIANS & JEWS
1028 DALLAS ATHLETICS BLDG ... DALLAS **TX** 75201
NATIONAL CONFERENCE OF CHRISTIANS & JEWS
409 EXECUTIVE CENTER-SUITE 202 ... EL PASO **TX** 79902 (915) 532-6637
NATIONAL CONFERENCE OF CHRISTIANS & JEWS
1801 T.W.C. ELECTRIC BLDG ... FORT WORTH **TX** 76102 (817) 332-3271
NATIONAL CONFERENCE OF CHRISTIANS & JEWS
4848 GUITON-SUITE 212 ... HOUSTON **TX** 77027 (713) 960-9244
NATIONAL CONFERENCE OF CHRISTIANS & JEWS
118 BROADWAY #623 ... SAN ANTONIO **TX** 78205 (713) 960-9244
NATIONAL CONFERENCE OF CHRISTIANS & JEWS
2006 SHAW STREET ... WICHITA FALLS **TX** 76301
NATIONAL CONFERENCE OF CHRISTIANS & JEWS
4326 ZARAHEMIA DRIVE ... SALT LAKE CITY **UT** 84117
NATIONAL CONFERENCE OF CHRISTIANS & JEWS
3808 HAYNSWORTH PLACE ... FAIRFAX **VA** 22030 (703) 591-6024
NATIONAL CONFERENCE OF CHRISTIANS & JEWS
2317 WESTWOOD AVENUE ... RICHMOND **VA** 23230
NATIONAL CONFERENCE OF CHRISTIANS & JEWS 715 SEABOARD BLDG .. SEATTLE **WA** 98101

INVESTMENT - ISRAEL

ISRAEL INVESTMENT & EXPORT AUTHORITY 6404 WILSHIRE BLVD ... LOS ANGELES **CA** 90048 (213) 658-8721
ISRAEL INVESTMENT & EXPORT AUTHORITY
174 NORTH MICHIGAN AVENUE ... CHICAGO **IL** 60601 (312) 332-2160
DEVELOPMENT CORPORATION FOR ISRAEL 3803 NAUTILUS AVENUE ... BROOKLYN **NY** 11224 (718) 677-9650
AMERICAN-ISRAELI INVESTORS LTD. 345 EAST 46TH STREET ... NEW YORK **NY** 10017 (212) 599-0868
AMPAL-AMERICAN ISRAEL CORPORATION
10 ROCKEFELLER PLAZA, 8TH FLOOR ... NEW YORK **NY** 10020 (212) 586-3232
CAPITAL FOR ISRAEL 215 PARK AVENUE SOUTH ... NEW YORK **NY** 10003 (212) 673-5500
DEVELOPMENT CORPORATION FOR ISRAEL
215 PARK AVENUE SOUTH ... NEW YORK **NY** 10003 (212) 677-9650
GOVERNMENT OF ISRAEL INVESTMENT AUTHORITY
EMPIRE STATE BUILDING, 350 FIFTH AVENUE ... NEW YORK **NY** 10118
ISRAEL GOVERNMENT INVESTMENT AUTHORITY 850 THIRD AVENUE ... NEW YORK **NY** 10022 (212) 940-9400

ISRAEL INVESTORS CORP. 10 ROCKEFELLER PLAZA ... NEW YORK **NY** 10020 (212) 582-8431
ISRAEL INVESTORS REPORT, ISRAEL COMMUNICATIONS
350 FIFTH AVENUE, SUITE 1902 ... NEW YORK **NY** 10118 (212) 213-2200
LEUMI SECURITIES CORPORATION 18 EAST 48TH STREET ... NEW YORK **NY** 10017 (212) 759-1310
PEC ISRAEL ECONOMIC CORPORATION 511 FIFTH AVENUE ... NEW YORK **NY** 10017 (212) 687-2400
STATE OF ISRAEL BONDS 215 PARK AVENUE SOUTH ... NEW YORK **NY** 10003 (212) 677-9650
ISRAEL INVESTMENT & EXPORT AUTHORITY
180 BLOOR STREET, SUITE 700 ... TORONTO **ON** M5S 1M8 (416) 961-1242
ISRAEL INVESTMENT & EXPORT AUTHORITY
2085 UNION STREET, SUITE 675 ... MONTREAL **QU** H3A 1B9 (514) 288-9276
ISRAEL INVESTMENT & EXPORT AUTHORITY
1 GREENWAY PLAZA EAST, SUITE 722 ... HOUSTON **TX** 77042 (713) 840-0510

ISRAEL - CENTERED ORGANIZATIONS

COMMITTEE FOR PROGRAMS IN ISRAEL
6505 WILSHIRE BOULEVARD ... LOS ANGELES **CA** 90048 (213) 852-1234
HISTADRUT ISRAEL CAMPAIGN 8455 BEVERLY BLVD., #308 ... LOS ANGELES **CA** 90048 (213) 651-4892
INTERNS FOR PEACE 3875 WILSHIRE BOULEVARD, ROOM 407 ... LOS ANGELES **CA** 90010 (213) 381-6621
AMERICAN FRIENDS OF RELIGIOUS FREEDOM IN ISRAEL
P.O. BOX 5888 ... WASHINGTON **DC** 20014 (301) 530-1737
AMERICAN ISRAEL PUBLIC AFFAIRS COMMITTEE
444 N CAPITOL STREET N.W., SUITE 412 ... WASHINGTON **DC** 20001 (202) 638-2256
B'NAI B'RITH ISRAEL COMMISSION
1640 RHODE ISLAND AVENUE, N.W. ... WASHINGTON **DC** 20036 (202) 857-6580
ISRAEL NATIONAL FUND 111 MASSACHUSETTS AVENUE, N.W. ... WASHINGTON **DC** 20001 (202) 842-8608
NATIONAL CHRISTIAN LEADERSHIP CONFERENCE FOR ISRAEL
1629 K STREET N.W., SUITE 700 ... WASHINGTON **DC** 20006 (202) 223-4016
GOVERNMENT OF ISRAEL TRADE CENTER & ECONOMIC OFFICE
111 EAST WACKER DRIVE ... CHICAGO **IL** 60611 (312) 565-3300
AMERICAN EDUCATIONAL LEAGUE FOR A SECURE ISRAEL
101 GREYSTONE ... KANSAS CITY **KS** 66103 (913) 342-1393
MIZRACHI HAPOEL HAMIZRACHI 611 WASHINGTON STREET ... BOSTON **MA** 02111 (617) 426-9148
ISRAEL HISTADRUT COUNCIL 6810 PARK HEIGHTS AVENUE ... BALTIMORE **MD** 21215 (301) 358-1533
DISKIN ORPHAN HOME OF ISRAEL 4305 18TH AVENUE ... BROOKLYN **NY** 11218
HA'VAADA L'DOVREI IVRIT 788 EASTERN PARKWAY ... BROOKLYN **NY** 11213 (718) 774-9847
ISRAELI WAR HEROES FUND 667 EASTERN PARKWAY ... BROOKLYN **NY** 11213 (718) 773-4960
KACH INTERNATIONAL P.O. BOX 425, MIDWOOD STATION ... BROOKLYN **NY** 11230 (718) 646-7301
ISRAEL NATIONAL FUND 433 BARNARD AVENUE ... CEDARHURST **NY** 11516 (516) 295-5646
KACH - LONG ISLAND P.O. BOX 214 ... MERRICK **NY** 11566
JORDAN IS PALESTINE COMMITTEE P.O. BOX 2003 ... NEW HYDE PARK **NY** 11040
AMERICA ISRAEL FRIENDSHIP LEAGUE 136 EAST 39TH STREET ... NEW YORK **NY** 10016 (212) 679-4822
AMERICA-ISRAEL CULTURAL FOUNDATION 485 MADISON AVENUE ... NEW YORK **NY** 10022 (212) 751-2700
AMERICAN ASSOCIATES BEN-GURION UNIVERSITY OF NEGEV INC.
342 MADISON AVENUE ... NEW YORK **NY** 10017 (212) 687-7721
AMERICAN ASSOCIATION FOR BIKUR CHOLIM HOSPITAL
119 FIFTH AVENUE ... NEW YORK **NY** 10021 (212) 260-4260
AMERICAN COMM. FOR SHAARE ZEDEK HOSPITAL IN JERUSALEM, INC.
49 WEST 45TH STREET ... NEW YORK **NY** 10036 (212) 354-8801
AMERICAN COMMITTEE FOR THE ISRAEL FASHION COLLEGE INC.
855 AVENUE OF THE AMERICAS ... NEW YORK **NY** 10001 (212) 947-1597
AMERICAN COMMITTEE FOR THE WEIZMANN INST. OF SCIENCE, INC.
515 PARK AVENUE ... NEW YORK **NY** 10022 (212) 752-1300
AMERICAN FRIENDS OF ISRAEL 850 THIRD AVENUE ... NEW YORK **NY** 10022 (212) 582-8431
AMERICAN FRIENDS OF THE STATE OF ISRAEL 3 WEST 16TH STREET ... NEW YORK **NY** 10011 (212) 929-1525
AMERICAN HISTADRUT CULTURAL EXCHANGE INSTITUTE
33 E. 67TH STREET ... NEW YORK **NY** 10020 (212) 628-1000
AMERICAN ISRAEL CORPORATION-AMPAL 10 ROCKEFELLER PLAZA ... NEW YORK **NY** 10019 (212) 586-3232
AMERICAN JEWISH ALTERNATIVES TO ZIONISM, INC.
133 EAST 73RD STREET ... NEW YORK **NY** 10021 (212) 628-2727
AMERICAN JEWISH LEAGUE FOR ISRAEL 30 EAST 60TH STREET ... NEW YORK **NY** 10022 (212) 371-1583
AMERICAN MIZRACHI WOMEN 817 BROADWAY ... NEW YORK **NY** 10003 (212) 477-4720
AMERICAN NETUREI KARTA 545 FIFTH AVENUE ... NEW YORK **NY** 10017
AMERICAN PROFESSORS FOR PEACE IN THE MIDDLE EAST
330 SEVENTH AVENUE ... NEW YORK **NY** 10001 (212) 563-2580
AMERICAN RED MAGEN DAVID FOR ISRAEL 888 SEVENTH AVE. ... NEW YORK **NY** 10106 (212) 757-1627
AMERICAN TRADE UNION COUNCIL FOR HISTADRUT
33 E. 67TH STREET ... NEW YORK **NY** 10021 (212) 628-1000
AMERICAN ZIONIST FEDERATION 515 PARK AVENUE ... NEW YORK **NY** 10022 (212) 371-7750
AMERICAN ZIONIST YOUTH FOUNDATION 515 PARK AVENUE ... NEW YORK **NY** 10022 (212) 751-6070
AMERICAN-ISRAEL CHAMBER OF COMMERCE 500 FIFTH AVENUE ... NEW YORK **NY** 10017 (212) 354-6510
AMERICAN-ISRAEL CULTURAL FOUNDATION 485 MADISON AVENUE ... NEW YORK **NY** 10022 (212) 751-2700
AMERICAN-ISRAEL FRIENDSHIP HOUSE 136 EAST 39TH STREET ... NEW YORK **NY** 10016 (212) 371-1583
AMERICAN-ISRAELI TORAH CENTER 5 BEEKMAN STREET ... NEW YORK **NY** 10038 (212) 964-4851
AMERICAN-JEWISH LEAGUE FORUM: AMERICAN-ISRAEL FRIENDSHIP-HOUSE
136 EAST 39TH STREET ... NEW YORK **NY** 10016 (212) 371-1583
AMERICANS FOR PROGRESSIVE ISRAEL 150 FIFTH AVENUE ... NEW YORK **NY** 10011 (212) 255-8760
AMERICANS FOR A SAFE ISRAEL INC. 114 EAST 28TH STREET ... NEW YORK **NY** 10016 (212) 696-2611
AMPAL-AMERICAN ISRAEL CORP. 10 ROCKEFELLER PLAZA ... NEW YORK **NY** 10020 (212) 586-3232
BEIT TRUMPELDOR, BETAR 136 DUANE STREET ... NEW YORK **NY** 10013
CONFERENCE OF PRESIDENTS OF MAJOR AMERICAN JEWISH ORGS.
515 PARK AVENUE ... NEW YORK **NY** 10022 (212) 752-1616
COUNCIL FOR A BEAUTIFUL ISRAEL 350 FIFTH AVENUE ... NEW YORK **NY** 10118 (212) 947-5709
ERETZ YISRAEL MOVEMENT 15 EAST 26TH STREET, SUITE 1303 ... NEW YORK **NY** 10010 (212) 684-7370
FREELAND LEAGUE-JEWISH TERRITORIAL COLONIZATION
200 W. 72ND STREET ... NEW YORK **NY** 10023 (212) 767-7765
GARIN YARDIN-YOUNG KIBBUTZ MOVEMENT
215 PARK AVENUE SOUTH #1806 ... NEW YORK **NY** 10003 (212) 777-9388
GOVERNMENT BUREAU FOR ISRAELI PROFESSIONALS
800 SECOND AVENUE ... NEW YORK **NY** 10017 (212) 986-6360
GOVERNMENT OF ISRAEL ECONOMIC OFFICE 111 WEST 40TH STREET ... NEW YORK **NY** 10017 (212) 560-0600
GOVERNMENT OF ISRAEL TRADE CENTER & ECONOMIC OFFICE
111 WEST 40TH STREET ... NEW YORK **NY** 10017 (212) 560-0660
HABONIM DROR OF NORTH AMERICA 27 WEST 20TH STREET ... NEW YORK **NY** 10011 (212) 255-1796
HADASSAH-WOMEN'S ZIONIST ORGANIZATION OF AMERICA
50 WEST 58TH STREET ... NEW YORK **NY** 10019 (212) 355-7900
HERUT-USA 41 E. 42ND STREET ... NEW YORK **NY** 10017 (212) 687-4502
HERZL FOUNDATION 515 PARK AVENUE ... NEW YORK **NY** 10022 (212) 752-0600
HISTADRUTH IVRITH OF AMERICA 1841 BROADWAY ... NEW YORK **NY** 10023 (212) 581-5151
INSTITUTE OF STUDENTS & FACULTY ON ISRAEL 55 W. 42ND STREET ... NEW YORK **NY** 10036 (212) 997-1812
INTERNS FOR PEACE 270 WEST 89TH STREET ... NEW YORK **NY** 10024 (212) 580-0540
ISRAEL DEVELOPMENT CORP. 10 ROCKEFELLER PLAZA ... NEW YORK **NY** 10020 (212) 586-3232
ISRAEL FOUNDATION FUND (KEREN HAYESOD), INC.
515 PARK AVENUE ... NEW YORK **NY** 10022 (212) 688-0800
ISRAELI COMMITTEE OF MIZRACHI-HAPOEL HAMIZRACHI
25 WEST 26TH STREET ... NEW YORK **NY** 10001 (212) 679-2050
JEWISH AGENCY AMERICAN SECTION, INC. 515 PARK AVENUE ... NEW YORK **NY** 10022 (212) 752-0600
JEWISH AMERICAN POLITICAL ACTION COMMITTEE
220 EAST 57TH STREET ... NEW YORK **NY** 10022 (212) 980-1519
KIBBUTZ ALIYA DESK 27 WEST 20TH STREET ... NEW YORK **NY** 10011 (212) 255-1338
LABOR ZIONIST ALLIANCE 275 SEVENTH AVENUE ... NEW YORK **NY** 10001 (212) 989-0300
LEAGUE FOR LABOR ISRAEL 275 SEVENTH AVENUE ... NEW YORK **NY** 10001 (212) 989-0300
MERCAZ (THE MOVEMENT TO REAFFIRM CONSERVATIVE ZIONISM)
155 FIFTH AVENUE ... NEW YORK **NY** 10010 (212) 533-7800
NATIONAL COMMITTEE FOR LABOR ISRAEL 33 E. 67TH STREET ... NEW YORK **NY** 10021 (212) 628-1000
NEW JEWISH AGENDA 64 FULTON STREET, #1100 ... NEW YORK **NY** 10038 (212) 227-5885
PEC ISRAEL ECONOMIC CORPORATION 511 FIFTH AVENUE ... NEW YORK **NY** 10017 (212) 687-2400
PIONEER WOMEN-WOMEN'S LABOR ZIONIST ORGANIZATION
200 MADISON AVENUE ... NEW YORK **NY** 10016 (212) 725-8010
POALE AGUDATH ISRAEL OF AMERICA 156 FIFTH AVENUE ... NEW YORK **NY** 10010 (212) 924-9475
RELIGIOUS ZIONISTS OF AMERICA 25 WEST 26TH STREET ... NEW YORK **NY** 10010 (212) 689-1414
SERVIS-ERETZ YISRAEL MOVEMENT 210 WEST 91 STREET ... NEW YORK **NY** 10024 (212) 595-6890
SHERUT LA'AM 515 PARK AVENUE ... NEW YORK **NY** 10022 (212) 753-0230
UNITED ISRAEL APPEAL 515 PARK AVENUE ... NEW YORK **NY** 10022 (212) 688-0800
UNITED ISRAEL WORLD UNION 507 FIFTH AVENUE, ROOM 903 ... NEW YORK **NY** 10017 (212) 688-7557
UNITED STATES COMMITTEE SPORTS FOR ISRAEL, INC.
823 UNITED NATIONS PLAZA ... NEW YORK **NY** 10017 (212) 687-9625
WOMEN'S LEAGUE FOR ISRAEL 515 PARK AVENUE ... NEW YORK **NY** 10022 (212) 838-1997
WOMEN'S SOCIAL SERVICE FOR ISRAEL 240 W. 98TH STREET ... NEW YORK **NY** 10025 (212) 666-7880
WORLD CONFEDERATION OF UNITED ZIONISTS
595 MADISON AVENUE ... NEW YORK **NY** 10022 (212) 371-1452
WORLD ZIONIST ORGANIZATION-AMERICAN SECTION
515 PARK AVENUE ... NEW YORK **NY** 10022 (212) 752-0600
YOUTH CENTERS OF ISRAEL, INC. 51 EAST 42ND STREET ... NEW YORK **NY** 10017 (212) 490-2340
YOUTH ZIONIST ORGANIZATION-DROR 215 PARK AVENUE SOUTH ... NEW YORK **NY** 10003 (212) 751-6070
ZIONIST ORGANIZATION OF AMERICA 4 EAST 34TH STREET ... NEW YORK **NY** 10016 (212) 481-1500
JEWISH PEACE FELLOWSHIP P.O. BOX 271 ... NYACK **NY** 10960 (914) 358-4601
AMERICAN ISRAEL PUBLIC AFFAIRS COMMITTEE (AIPAC)
23700 MERCANTILE ROAD ... CLEVELAND **OH** 44122 (216) 464-2353
ASSOCIATION OF PARENTS OF AMERICAN ISRAELIS
2567 LAFAYETTE ROAD ... CLEVELAND **OH** 44118 (216) 932-5269
CLEVELAND COMMITTEE FOR ECONOMIC GROWTH IN ISRAEL
10800 BROOKPARK ROAD ... CLEVELAND **OH** 44130 (216) 267-1200
CONSUMERS FOR ISRAELI PRODUCTS 2162 SOUTH TAYLOR ROAD ... CLEVELAND **OH** 44118 (216) 371-1138
VOLUNTEERS FOR CLEVELANDERS IN ISRAEL
1414 SOUTH GREEN ROAD, #309 ... CLEVELAND **OH** 44121 (216) 291-2218
KACH INTERNATIONAL P.O. BOX 21330 ... SOUTH EUCLID **OH** 44121 (800) 247-5224
CANADIAN FOUNDATION OF PIONEERING ISRAEL
111 FINCH STREET ... DOWNSVIEW **ON** (416) 736-0977
UNITED STATES COMMITTEE SPORTS FOR ISRAEL
275 SOUTH 19TH STREET, SUITE 1203 ... PHILADELPHIA **PA** 19103 (215) 546-4700
U.S. MACCABIAH COMMITTEE
275 SOUTH 19TH STREET, SUITE 1203 ... PHILADELPHIA **PA** 19103 (215) 546-4700
CANADA-ISRAEL COMMITTEE-NATIONAL OFFICE
1310 GREENE AVENUE ... MONTREAL **QU** H3Z 2B2 (514) 934-0771
FRIENDS OF PIONEERING ISRAEL (MAPAM) 600 COTE ST. LUC ROAD ... MONTREAL **QU**
COMMITTEE FOR THE ECONOMIC GROWTH OF ISRAEL
P.O. BOX 2053, 5301 NORTH IRONWOOD ROAD ... MILWAUKEE **WI** 53201 (414) 961-1000

ISRAEL BONDS

ISRAEL BONDS CITY FEDERAL BUILDING ... BIRMINGHAM **AL** 35203 (205) 871-6161
STATE OF ISRAEL BONDS 5763 OAK STREET, #4 ... VANCOUVER **BC** V6M 2V8 (604) 266-7210
BONDS FOR ISRAEL-DEVELOPMENT CORPORATION FOR ISRAEL
6380 WILSHIRE BOULEVARD ... LOS ANGELES **CA** 90048 (213) 653-8400
STATE OF ISRAEL BONDS DEVELOPMENT CORPORATION FOR ISRAEL
47 KEARNY STREET, SUITE 705 ... SAN FRANCISCO **CA** 94108 (415) 781-3212
ISRAEL BONDS 470 S. COLORADO BOULEVARD ... DENVER **CO** 80202 (303) 321-2921
ISRAEL BONDS 740 N. MAIN STREET ... HARTFORD **CT** 06117 (203) 236-4523
ISRAEL BONDS 419 WHALLEY AVENUE ... NEW HAVEN **CT** 06511 (203) 624-9975
STATE OF ISRAEL BONDS 4601 W. KENNEDY BLVD.,SUITE 118 ... TAMPA **FL** 33609 (813) 978-8850
ISRAEL BONDS 230 N. MICHIGAN AVENUE ... CHICAGO **IL** 60601 (312) 558-9400
ISRAEL BONDS 1 INDIANA SQUARE, SUITE 3370 ... INDIANAPOLIS **IN** 46204 (317) 848-2000
BONDS FOR ISRAEL 3415 BARDSTOWN ROAD ... LOUISVILLE **KY** 40218 (502) 459-1896
ISRAEL BONDS BARONNE BUILDING, 305 BARONNE STREET ... NEW ORLEANS **LA** 70112 (504) 524-8756
ISRAEL BONDS 262 WASHINGTON STREET ... BOSTON **MA** 02108 (617) 723-2400
ISRAEL BONDS 645 CHANDLER STREET ... WORCESTER **MA** 01602 (617) 752-2864
ISRAEL BONDS 1515 REISTERSTOWN ROAD ... BALTIMORE **MD** 21208 (301) 484-6670
ISRAEL BONDS ... BETHESDA **MD** (301) 654-6575
ISRAEL BONDS 24123 GREENFIELD ROAD ... OAK PARK **MI** 48237 (313) 557-2900

Listing	City	State	ZIP	Phone
STATE OF ISRAEL BONDS 1488 NORTHWESTERN BANK BUILDING	MINNEAPOLIS	**MN**	55402	(612) 338-8475
ISRAEL BONDS 916 WALNUT STREET	KANSAS CITY	**MO**	64106	(913) 642-5800
ISRAEL BONDS 225 S. MERAMEC AVENUE	ST. LOUIS	**MO**	63105	(314) 721-7866
ISRAEL BONDS 920 CITY NATIONAL BANK, 405 S. 16TH STREET	OMAHA	**NE**	68102	(402) 341-1177
ISRAEL BONDS 701 NEWARK AVENUE	ELIZABETH	**NJ**	07201	(201) 354-5400
ISRAEL BONDS 1425 PLAZA ROAD	FAIRLAWN	**NJ**	07505	(201) 794-1050
ISRAEL BONDS 28 WEST STATE STREET	TRENTON	**NJ**	08608	(609) 882-9290
ISRAEL BONDS 28 COLVIN	ALBANY	**NY**	12206	(518) 489-2509
ISRAEL BONDS 775 MAIN STREET	BUFFALO	**NY**	14203	(716) 856-3464
ISRAEL BONDS WHOLESALERS 120 WALL STREET	NEW YORK	**NY**	10005	(212) 344-6676
LEUMI SECURITIES CORPORATION 18 EAST 48TH STREET	NEW YORK	**NY**	10017	(212) 759-1310
OSCAR GRUSS & SONS 80 PINE STREET	NEW YORK	**NY**	10005	(212) 943-6313
STATE OF ISRAEL BOND ORGANIZATION 730 BROADWAY	NEW YORK	**NY**	10003	(212) 677-9650
ISRAEL BONDS 94 N. MAIN STREET	SPRING VALLEY	**NY**	10977	(914) 352-3550
STATE OF ISRAEL BONDS 3645 WARRENSVILLE CENTER ROAD	CLEVELAND	**OH**	44122	(216) 751-3984
ISRAEL BONDS 2375 E. MAIN STREET	COLUMBUS	**OH**	43209	(614) 239-7212
STATE OF ISRAEL BONDS 3130 BATHURST STREET, SUITE 210	TORONTO	**ON**	M6A 2A1	(416) 789-3351
ISRAEL BONDS 200 S.W. MARKET	PORTLAND	**OR**	97201	(503) 228-8541
ISRAEL BONDS 801 HAMILTON STREET	ALLENTOWN	**PA**	18101	(215) 435-8095
ISRAEL BONDS 1405 LOCUST STREET	PHILADELPHIA	**PA**	19102	(215) 546-1022
ISRAEL BONDS 717 LIBERTY AVENUE	PITTSBURGH	**PA**	15222	(412) 521-6500
ISRAEL BONDS CONNELL BUILDING	SCRANTON	**PA**	18503	(717) 346-7418
ISRAEL BOND ORGANIZATION 1255 UNIVERSITY STREET #1120	MONTREAL	**QU**	H3B 3W7	(514) 878-1871
ISRAEL BONDS 6 BRAYMAN STREET	PROVIDENCE	**RI**	02903	(401) 751-6767
ISRAEL BONDS 81 MADISON BUILDING	MEMPHIS	**TN**	38103	(901) 682-7841
STATE OF ISRAEL BONDS 5118 PARK AVENUE, P.O. BOX 17008	MEMPHIS	**TN**	38117	(901) 682-7841
ISRAEL BONDS 12810 HILLCREST ROAD	DALLAS	**TX**	75231	(214) 661-9191
ISRAEL BONDS 112 MEYERLAND PLAZA MALL	HOUSTON	**TX**	77035	(713) 666-0221
ISRAEL BONDS 740 DUKE	NORFOLK	**VA**	23510	(804) 622-4631
ISRAEL BONDS 1940 THIRD AVENUE	SEATTLE	**WA**	98101	(206) 624-0910
ISRAEL BONDS 212 W. WISCONSIN AVENUE	MILWAUKEE	**WI**	53203	(414) 273-7425

ISRAEL GOVERNMENT TOURIST OFFICES

Listing	City	State	ZIP	Phone
WEST COAST 6380 WILSHIRE AVENUE	LOS ANGELES	**CA**	90048	(213) 658-7462
MIDWEST REGION 5 SOUTH WABASH AVENUE	CHICAGO	**IL**	60603	(312) 782-4306
EASTERN REGION 350 FIFTH AVENUE	NEW YORK	**NY**	10118	(212) 560-0620
HEDI SHULMAN, COMMISSIONER OF TOURISM, ISRAEL MIN. OF TOURISM 350 FIFTH AVENUE	NEW YORK	**NY**	10118	(212) 560-0621
ISRAEL GOVERNMENT TOURIST OFFICE 180 BLOOR STREET WEST, #700	TORONTO	**ON**	M5S 2V6	(416) 964-3784
SOUTHERN REGION 4151 S.W. FREEWAY	HOUSTON	**TX**	77027	(713) 850-9341

ISRAEL GOVERNMENT TRADE CENTERS

Listing	City	State	ZIP	Phone
ABRAHAM ROSENTAL 6404 WILSHIRE BLVD	LOS ANGELES	**CA**	90048	(213) 658-7924
DAN HALPERIN, ECONOMIC MINISTER, EMBASSY OF ISRAEL 3514 INTERNATIONAL DRIVE N.W.	WASHINGTON	**DC**	20009	(202) 364-5500
AMI TALMOR 174 N. MICHIGAN AVENUE	CHICAGO	**IL**	60601	(312) 332-2160
ARIE SHEER, CHIEF FISCAL OFFICER, DEP'T OF THE TREASURY 350 FIFTH AVENUE	NEW YORK	**NY**	10118	(212) 560-0640
DIRECTOR, INVESTMENT AUTHORITY, GOV'T OF ISRAEL 350 FIFTH AVENUE	NEW YORK	**NY**	10118	(212) 560-0610
ISRAEL PICKOL, ECONOMIC MINISTER, GOVERNMENT OF ISRAEL 350 FIFTH AVENUE	NEW YORK	**NY**	10118	(212) 560-0630
JOSEPH MAZUR, SUPPLY MISSION, GOVERNMENT OF ISRAEL 350 FIFTH AVENUE	NEW YORK	**NY**	10118	(212) 560-0680
SHMUEL BEN-TOVIM, CONSUL & TRADE COMMISSIONER TO THE U.S. 350 FIFTH AVENUE	NEW YORK	**NY**	10118	(212) 560-0660
AVRAHAM GOLAN 1 GREENWAY PLAZA E.	HOUSTON	**TX**	77046	(713) 840-0510

ISRAEL MISSIONS IN THE UNITED STATES

Listing	City	State	ZIP	Phone
ISRAELI EMBASSY 3514 INTERNATIONAL DRIVE, N.W.	WASHINGTON	**DC**	20008	(202) 364-5500
PERMANENT MISSION TO THE UNITED NATIONS 800 SECOND AVENUE	NEW YORK	**NY**	10017	(212) 697-5500

ISRAEL PROGRAMS

Listing	City	State	ZIP	Phone
AMPAL (ISRAEL DEVELOPMENT) 6505 WILSHIRE BLVD. #203	LOS ANGELES	**CA**	90048	(213) 653-5633
COMMITTEE FOR PROGRAMS IN ISRAEL 6505 WILSHIRE BOULEVARD	LOS ANGELES	**CA**	90048	(213) 852-1234
HISTADRUT ISRAEL CAMPAIGN 8455 BEVERLY BLVD., #308	LOS ANGELES	**CA**	90048	(213) 651-4892
ISRAEL PROGRAMS OFFICE 4200 BISCAYNE BLVD	MIAMI	**FL**	33137	(305) 576-4000
FELLOWSHIP IN ISRAEL FOR ARAB-JEWISH YOUTH 45 FRANCIS AVENUE	CAMBRIDGE	**MA**	02138	(617) 354-1198
PROGRAMS IN ISRAEL COMMITTEE MN JCC, 4330 S. CEDAR LAKE RD	MINNEAPOLIS	**MN**	55455	(612) 377-8330
AMERICAN JEWISH LEAGUE FOR ISRAEL 595 MADISON AVENUE	NEW YORK	**NY**	10022	(212) 371-1583
AZYF ISRAEL PROGRAM CENTER 515 PARK AVENUE	NEW YORK	**NY**	10022	(212) 750-7773
BETAR ISRAEL SUMMER PROGRAMS 9 EAST 38TH STREET	NEW YORK	**NY**	10016	(212) 696-0080
CENTER FOR STUDY IN ISRAEL 60 EAST 42ND STREET	NEW YORK	**NY**	10017	(212) 286-9474
GARIN YARDIN-YOUNG KIBBUTZ MOVEMENT 215 PARK AVENUE SOUTH #1806	NEW YORK	**NY**	10003	(212) 777-9388
ISRAEL PROGRAM CENTER 515 PARK AVENUE	NEW YORK	**NY**	10022	(212) 751-6070
ISRAEL SEMINARS FOUNDATION 515 PARK AVENUE	NEW YORK	**NY**	10022	(212) 371-7761
NOAM-BAR ILAN SUMMER PROGRAM 25 WEST 26TH STREET	NEW YORK	**NY**	10010	
SHERUT LA'AM COLL. GRAD. PROGRAM, AMER. ZIONIST YOUTH FOUND. 515 PARK AVENUE	NEW YORK	**NY**	10022	(212) 751-6070
USY PILGRIMAGE (YOUTH) 155 FIFTH AVENUE	NEW YORK	**NY**	10010	(212) 533-7800
UNITED SYNAGOGUE TOUR SERVICE (ADULTS) 155 FIFTH AVENUE	NEW YORK	**NY**	10010	(212) 533-7800
VOLUNTEERS FOR ISRAEL 40 WORTH STREET, ROOM 710	NEW YORK	**NY**	10013	(212) 608-4848
YOUTH & HECHALUTZ DEPARTMENT (ISRAEL PROGRAM CENTRE) 1000 FINCH AVENUE WEST, #104	DOWNSVIEW	**ON**	M3J 2E7	(416) 665-7733
YOUTH & HECHALUTZ DEPARTMENT (ISRAEL PROGRAM CENTRE) 1310 GREENE AVENUE	WESTMOUNT	**QU**	H3Z 2B2	(514) 934-0804

ISRAELI CONSULATES IN THE U.S.

Listing	City	State	ZIP	Phone
ISRAEL CONSULATE 6380 WILSHIRE BLVD	LOS ANGELES	**CA**	90048	(213) 651-5700
ISRAEL CONSULATE 693 SUTTER	SAN FRANCISCO	**CA**	94102	(415) 775-5535
ECONOMIC MINISTER, EMBASSY OF ISRAEL 3514 INTERNATIONAL DRIVE N.W.	WASHINGTON	**DC**	20008	(202) 364-5500
ISRAEL CONSULATE 805 PEACHTREE STREET, N.E.	ATLANTA	**GA**	30308	(404) 875-7851
ISRAEL CONSULATE 111 EAST WACKER DRIVE	CHICAGO	**IL**	60601	(312) 565-3300
ISRAEL CONSULATE 1020 STATLER OFFICE BUILDING	BOSTON	**MA**	02116	(617) 542-0041
ISRAEL CONSULATE 800 SECOND AVENUE	NEW YORK	**NY**	10017	(212) 697-5500
ISRAEL CONSULATE 1720 LEWIS TOWER BUILDING, 225 SOUTH 15TH STREET	PHILADELPHIA	**PA**	19102	(215) 546-2555
ISRAEL CONSULATE 1 GREENWAY PLAZA EAST	HOUSTON	**TX**	77046	(713) 627-3780

ISRAELI GOVERNMENT

Listing	City	State	ZIP	Phone
ISRAEL GOVERNMENT MINISTRY OF DEFENSE 850 THIRD AVENUE	NEW YORK	**NY**	10022	(212) 940-9400
ISRAEL GOVERNMENT TOURISM ADMINISTRATION 350 FIFTH AVENUE	NEW YORK	**NY**	10118	(212) 560-0620
ISRAEL GOVERNMENT TOURIST OFFICE 350 FIFTH AVENUE	NEW YORK	**NY**	10118	(212) 560-0650
ISRAEL GOVERNMENT-BEQUESTS & LEGACIES 350 FIFTH AVENUE	NEW YORK	**NY**	10118	(212) 560-0635
ISRAEL GOVERNMENT-COINS & MEDALS 350 FIFTH AVENUE	NEW YORK	**NY**	10118	(212) 560-0690
ISRAEL GOVERNMENT-ECONOMIC MINISTER 350 FIFTH AVENUE	NEW YORK	**NY**	10118	(212) 560-0630
ISRAEL GOVERNMENT-ECONOMIC OFFICES 350 FIFTH AVENUE	NEW YORK	**NY**	10118	(212) 560-0600
ISRAEL GOVERNMENT-INVESTMENT AUTHORITY 350 FIFTH AVENUE	NEW YORK	**NY**	10118	(212) 560-0610
ISRAEL GOVERNMENT-MINISTRY OF FINANCE 350 FIFTH AVENUE	NEW YORK	**NY**	10118	(212) 560-0640
ISRAEL GOVERNMENT-SUPPLY MISSION 350 FIFTH AVENUE	NEW YORK	**NY**	10118	(212) 560-0680
ISRAEL GOVERNMENT-TRADE CENTER 350 FIFTH AVENUE	NEW YORK	**NY**	10118	(212) 560-0660

JEWELRY

Listing	City	State	ZIP	Phone
LAOR JEWELRY 4605 13TH AVENUE	BROOKLYN	**NY**	11219	(212) 436-5055
DUMAY JEWELERS 166 ROUTE 59	MONSEY	**NY**	10952	(914) 356-2833
JEWELRY DIAMONDS & COIN EXCHANGE 94 ROUTE 59	MONSEY	**NY**	10952	(914) 356-7104
JEWELRY SHOWROOM, THE 4 COLLEGE ROAD	MONSEY	**NY**	10952	(914) 352-6622
SIMCHA SHOPPE, THE 18 HILLTOP LANE	MONSEY	**NY**	10952	(914) 352-4543
BEN ARI ARTS LTD. 11 AVENUE A	NEW YORK	**NY**	10009	(212) 677-4730
DIAMOND DEALERS ALLIANCE, INC. 580 FIFTH AVENUE	NEW YORK	**NY**	10036	(212) 757-4589
DIAMOND DEALERS INFORMATION SERVICE, INC. 22 WEST 48TH STREET	NEW YORK	**NY**	10036	(212) 997-0015
GIA GEM TRADE LABORATORY, INC 580 FIFTH AVENUE	NEW YORK	**NY**	10036	(212) 221-5858
GEM INSTRUMENTS 1180 AVENUE OF THE AMERICAS	NEW YORK	**NY**	10036	(212) 354-2970
GEMOLOGICAL INSTITUTE OF AMERICA, INC.-ED. & CLASSROOM 1180 AVENUE OF THE AMERICAS	NEW YORK	**NY**	10036	(212) 944-5900
HIZME NISSIM HEBREW JEWELRY, INC. (WORKSHOP) 80 CANAL STREET	NEW YORK	**NY**	10002	(212) 925-2922
ISRAEL CREATIONS 350 FIFTH AVENUE	NEW YORK	**NY**	10118	(212) 213-2200
ISRAELI GIFTS 575 7TH AVENUE	NEW YORK	**NY**	10018	(212) 391-4928
MICHAEL STRAUSS SILVERSMITHS, LTD. 164 EAST 68TH STREET	NEW YORK	**NY**	10021	(212) 744-8500
MORIAH ART CRAFTS INCORPORATED 699 MADISON AVENUE	NEW YORK	**NY**	10021	(212) 751-7090
WHITE HOUSE JEWELERS, THE 78 ROUTE 59	SPRING VALLEY	**NY**	10977	(914) 425-2565
SARAH'S JEWELRY ROUTE 59 & AIRMONT ROAD	SUFFERN	**NY**	10901	(914) 357-6663

JEWISH COMMUNITY CENTERS

Listing	City	State	ZIP	Phone
JEWISH COMMUNITY CENTER P.O. BOX 9157	BIRMINGHAM	**AL**	35213	(205) 879-0416
JEWISH COMMUNITY CENTER 6150 AIRPORT BLVD	MOBILE	**AL**	36608	(205) 342-1450
JEWISH FEDERATION OF LITTLE ROCK, THE 226 DONAGHEY BLDG., MAIN AT 7TH STREET	LITTLE ROCK	**AR**	72201	(501) 372-3571
JEWISH COMMUNITY CENTER - TRI-CITY BRANCH 1720 WEST SOUTHERN, SUITE C-6	MESA	**AZ**	85202	(602) 962-0441
JEWISH COMMUNITY CENTER OF GREATER PHOENIX 1718 WEST MARYLAND AVENUE	PHOENIX	**AZ**	85015	(602) 249-1832
JEWISH COMMUNITY CENTER - EAST VALLEY BRANCH 7119 EAST SHEA BLVD., SUITE 101	SCOTTSDALE	**AZ**	85253	(602) 998-9145
JEWISH COMMUNITY CENTER 3822 EAST RIVER ROAD	TUCSON	**AZ**	85715	(602) 323-7167
CALGARY JEWISH CENTRE 1607 90TH AVENUE, S.W.	CALGARY	**AT**	T2V 4V7	(403) 253-8600
JEWISH COMMUNITY CENTRE, HILLCREST FOUNDATION 7200 156TH STREET	EDMONTON	**AT**	T5R 1X3	(403) 487-0585
JEWISH COMMUNITY CENTER OF GREATER PHOENIX PHOENIX BRANCH, 1718 WEST MARYLAND AVENUE	PHOENIX	**AZ**	85015	(602) 249-1832
HA'EMEK JEWISH COMMUNITY 2543 MONTROSE AVENUE, #1	ABBOTSFORD	**BC**	V2S 3T4	(604) 853-4625
OKANAGAN JEWISH COMMUNITY 2515 GRENFELL ROAD	KELOWNA	**BC**	V1Y 3L9	(604) 763-5271
BURQEST JEWISH COMMUNITY ASSOCIATION P.O. BOX 2311	NEW WESTMINSTER	**BC**	V3L 5A7	(604) 420-9797
JEWISH COMMUNITY CENTRE 950 WEST 41ST AVENUE	VANCOUVER	**BC**	V5Z 2N7	(604) 266-9111
PENINSULA JCC 2440 CARLMONT DRIVE	BELMONT	**CA**	94002	(415) 591-4438
JEWISH COMMUNITY CENTER OF BERKELEY-RICHMOND 1414 WALNUT	BERKELEY	**CA**	94709	(415) 848-0237
MACCABEE ATHLETIC CLUB 239 E. LA CIENEGA BLVD	BEVERLY HILLS	**CA**	90211	
WEST VALLEY JCC 22622 VANOWEN	CANOGA PARK	**CA**	91307	(818) 346-3003
NORTH COUNTY JCC 2725 JEFFERSON STREET, #8-B	CARLSBAD	**CA**	92008	(619) 729-5932

Organization / Address	City	State	Zip	Phone
NORTH VALLEY JCC 16601 RINALDI STREET	GRANADA HILLS	**CA**	91324	(213) 701-7601
NORTH CITY JCC 8950 VILLA LA JOLLA DRIVE, SUITE 2131	LA JOLLA	**CA**	92037	(619) 460-9937
JEWISH COMMUNITY CENTER OF SOUTH ORANGE COUNTY 298 BROADWAY	LAGUNA BEACH	**CA**	92651	(714) 497-2070
JEWISH COMMUNITY CENTER 3801 EAST WILLOW AVENUE	LONG BEACH	**CA**	90815	(213) 426-7601
HOLLYWOOD-LOS FELIZ JCC 1110 BATES AVENUE	LOS ANGELES	**CA**	90029	(213) 663-2255
JEWISH CENTERS ASSOCIATION 5870 WEST OLYMPIC BLVD	LOS ANGELES	**CA**	90036	(213) 938-2531
WESTSIDE JCC 5870 WEST OLYMPIC BLVD	LOS ANGELES	**CA**	90036	(213) 938-2531
JEWISH COMMUNITY CENTER OF OAKLAND-PIEDMONT 3245 SHEFFIELD AVENUE	OAKLAND	**CA**	94602	(415) 533-9222
JEWISH WELFARE FEDERATION OF PALM SPRINGS - DESERT AREA 611 SOUTH PALM CANYON DRIVE	PALM SPRINGS	**CA**	92262	(619) 325-7281
SOUTH PENINSULA JCC 830 EAST MEADOW DRIVE	PALO ALTO	**CA**	94303	(415) 494-2511
JEWISH FEDERATION OF SACRAMENTO 2351 WYDA WAY, P.O. BOX 25489	SACRAMENTO	**CA**	95865	(916) 486-0906
JEWISH COMMUNITY CENTER - CENTRAL OFFICE 7510 CLAIREMONT, MESA BLVD	SAN DIEGO	**CA**	92111	(619) 565-0280
JEWISH COMMUNITY CENTER - COLLEGE AREA BRANCH 4079 54TH STREET	SAN DIEGO	**CA**	92105	(619) 583-3300
BROTHERHOOD WAY CENTER 655 BROTHERHOOD WAY	SAN FRANCISCO	**CA**	94132	(415) 334-7474
KOSHER NUTRITION PROGRAM 3200 CALIFORNIA STREET	SAN FRANCISCO	**CA**	94118	(415) 346-6040
MONTEFIORE SENIOR CENTER 3200 CALIFORNIA STREET	SAN FRANCISCO	**CA**	94118	(415) 922-3131
RETIRED SENIOR VOLUNTEER PROGRAM 3195 CALIFORNIA STREET	SAN FRANCISCO	**CA**	94115	(415) 346-1812
SAN FRANCISCO CENTER 3200 CALIFORNIA STREET	SAN FRANCISCO	**CA**	94118	(415) 346-6040
UNITED JEWISH COMMUNITY CENTERS 3272 CALIFORNIA STREET	SAN FRANCISCO	**CA**	94118	(415) 929-1986
JEWISH COMMUNITY CENTER 2300 CANOAS GARDEN ROAD	SAN JOSE	**CA**	95125	(408) 266-6317
MARIN JCC 200 NORTH SAN PEDRO ROAD	SAN RAFAEL	**CA**	94903	(415) 479-2000
BAY CITIES JCC 2601 SANTA MONICA BLVD	SANTA MONICA	**CA**	90404	(213) 870-8883
COMMUNITY SERVICES DIVISION 3848 CARSON STREET, SUITE 101	TORRANCE	**CA**	90503	(213) 540-2631
VALLEY CITIES JCC 13164 BURBANK BLVD	VAN NUYS	**CA**	91401	(818) 786-6310
ISRAEL LEVIN SENIOR ADULT CENTER 201 OCEAN FRONT WALK	VENICE	**CA**	90291	(213) 399-9584
CONTRA COSTA JEWISH COMMUNITY CENTER 1355 CREEKSIDE DRIVE	WALNUT CREEK	**CA**	94596	(415) 938-7800
JEWISH COMMUNITY CENTER P.O. BOX 6196, 4800 ALAMEDA AVENUE	DENVER	**CO**	80206	(303) 399-2660
GREATER BRIDGEPORT JEWISH COMMUNITY CENTER 4200 PARK AVENUE	BRIDGEPORT	**CT**	06604	(203) 372-6567
JEWISH COMMUNITY CENTER SHOREHAVEN ROAD, P.O. BOX 483	EAST NORWALK	**CT**	06855	(203) 838-7504
JEWISH COMMUNITY CENTER 1156 CHAPEL STREET	NEW HAVEN	**CT**	06511	(203) 865-5181
JEWISH COMMUNITY CENTER, THE P.O. BOX 3326, NEWFIELD AVENUE AT VINE ROAD	STAMFORD	**CT**	06905	(203) 322-7900
JEWISH FEDERATION OF WATERBURY 1020 COUNTRY CLUB ROAD	WATERBURY	**CT**	06708	(203) 758-2441
JEWISH COMMUNITY CENTER 335 BLOOMFIELD AVENUE	WEST HARTFORD	**CT**	06117	(203) 236-4571
D.C. OFFICE 2027 MASSACHUSETTS AVENUE N.W.	WASHINGTON	**DC**	20036	(202) 966-3236
JEWISH COMMUNITY CENTER 101 GARDEN OF EDEN ROAD	WILMINGTON	**DE**	19803	(302) 478-5660
JEWISH COMMUNITY CENTER OF GREATER FT. LAUDERDALE 6501 WEST SUNRISE BLVD	FT. LAUDERDALE	**FL**	33313	(305) 792-6700
JEWISH COMMUNITY CENTER OF SOUTH BROWARD 2838 HOLLYWOOD BLVD	HOLLYWOOD	**FL**	33020	(305) 921-6511
JACKSONVILLE JEWISH FEDERATION 5846 MOUNT CARMEL TERRACE	JACKSONVILLE	**FL**	32216	(904) 733-7613
JEWISH COMMUNITY CENTER OF CENTRAL FL 851 N. MAITLAND AVE., P.O. BOX 1508	MAITLAND	**FL**	32751	(305) 645-5933
JEWISH COMMUNITY CENTERS OF SOUTH FLORIDA, CENTRAL OFFICE 4200 BISCAYNE BLVD	MIAMI	**FL**	33137	(305) 576-1660
SOUTH DADE JCC 12401 S.W. 102 AVE	MIAMI	**FL**	33176	(305) 251-1394
MIAMI BEACH JCC 25 WASHINGTON AVENUE	MIAMI BEACH	**FL**	33139	(305) 673-6060
MICHAEL-ANN RUSSELL JCC 18900 N.E. 25TH AVENUE	NORTH MIAMI BEACH	**FL**	33180	(305) 932-4200
PENSACOLA FEDERATED JEWISH CHARITIES 1320 E. LEE STREET	PENSACOLA	**FL**	32503	(904) 438-1772
SARASOTA JEWISH FEDERATION 1900 MAIN STREET, SUITE 315	SARASOTA	**FL**	33577	(813) 365-4410
JEWISH COMMUNITY CENTER OF PINELLAS COUNTY 8167 ELBOW LANE NORTH	ST. PETERSBURG	**FL**	33710	(813) 344-5795
JEWISH COMMUNITY CENTER 2808 HORATIO STREET	TAMPA	**FL**	33609	(813) 872-4451
JEWISH COMMUNITY CENTER OF THE PALM BEACHES, INC. 2415 OKEECHOBEE BLVD	WEST PALM BEACH	**FL**	33409	(305) 689-7700
JEWISH COMMUNITY CENTER 1745 PEACHTREE ROAD N.E.	ATLANTA	**GA**	30309	(404) 875-7881
JEWISH COMMUNITY CENTER P.O. BOX 3251	AUGUSTA	**GA**	30904	(404) 736-1918
ZABAN BRANCH 5342 TILLY MILL ROAD N.E.	DUNWOODY	**GA**	30338	(404) 396-3250
MIDDLE GEORGIA FEDERATION OF JEWISH CHARITIES P.O. BOX 5276	MACON	**GA**	31208	
JEWISH EDUCATIONAL ALLIANCE 5111 ABERCORN STREET	SAVANNAH	**GA**	31405	(912) 355-8111
JEWISH FEDERATION OF HAWAII 817 COOKE STREET	HONOLULU	**HA**	96813	(808) 536-7228
BUREAU FOR JEWISH LIVING BRANCH 954 CUMMINS PARKWAY	DES MOINES	**IA**	50311	(515) 274-3467
BUREAU FOR JEWISH LIVING-EDUCATION-CULTURE-RECREATION 924 POLK BLVD	DES MOINES	**IA**	50312	(515) 277-5566
JEWISH FEDERATION 525 14TH STREET	SIOUX CITY	**IA**	51105	(712) 258-0618
JEWISH FEDERATION OF SOUTH ILLINOIS 6464 WEST MAIN, SUITE 7A	BELLEVILLE	**IL**	62223	(618) 271-2400
BERNARD HORWICH JCC 3003 WEST TOUHY AVENUE	CHICAGO	**IL**	60645	(312) 761-9100
HYDE PARK JCC 1100 EAST HYDE PARK BLVD	CHICAGO	**IL**	60615	(312) 268-4600
JEWISH COMMUNITY CENTERS 1 SOUTH FRANKLIN STREET	CHICAGO	**IL**	60606	(312) 346-6700
LINCOLN PARK-LAKEVIEW JCC 524 WEST MELROSE	CHICAGO	**IL**	60657	(312) 871-6780
ROGERS PARK JCC 7101 NORTH GREENVIEW AVENUE	CHICAGO	**IL**	60626	(312) 274-0920
SENIOR ADULT DEPARTMENT 3003 WEST TOUHY AVENUE	CHICAGO	**IL**	60645	(312) 761-9100
YOUNG MEN'S JEWISH COUNCIL 30 WEST WASHINGTON STREET	CHICAGO	**IL**	60602	(312) 726-8891
ANITA M. STONE JCC 18600 GOVERNORS HIGHWAY	FLOSSMOOR	**IL**	60422	(312) 799-7650
NORTH SUBURBAN JCC 459 CENTRAL STREET	HIGHLAND PARK	**IL**	60035	(312) 433-6424
JEWISH FEDERATION OF PEORIA 3100 NORTH KNOXVILLE, SUITE 17	PEORIA	**IL**	61603	(309) 686-0611
JEWISH FEDERATION OF THE QUAD CITIES 224-18 STREET, SUITE 511	ROCK ISLAND	**IL**	61201	(309) 793-1300
PHILIP BEHR JCC 1500 PARKVIEW AVENUE	ROCKFORD	**IL**	61107	(815) 399-5497
MAYER KAPLAN JCC 5050 CHURCH STREET	SKOKIE	**IL**	60076	(312) 675-2200

Organization / Address	City	State	Zip	Phone
SPRINGFIELD JEWISH FEDERATION 730 EAST VINE STREET, ROOM 212	SPRINGFIELD	**IL**	62704	(217) 528-3446
NORTH LAKE COUNTY FEDERATED JEWISH CHARITIES 1500 SUNSET AVENUE	WAUKEGAN	**IL**	60087	(312) 336-9110
NORTHWEST SUBURBAN JCC 3316 NORTH SCHOENBECK ROAD	WHEELING	**IL**	60090	
JEWISH COMMUNITY COUNCIL P.O. BOX 5026	EVANSVILLE	**IN**	47715	(812) 425-8222
JEWISH COMMUNITY CENTER ASSOCIATION 6701 HOOVER ROAD	INDIANAPOLIS	**IN**	46260	(317) 251-9467
JEWISH FEDERATION OF ST. JOSEPH VALLEY 804 SHERLAND BLDG	SOUTH BEND	**IN**	46601	(219) 233-1164
MID-KANSAS JEWISH WELFARE FEDERATION, INC. 400 NORTH WOODLAWN, SUITE 8	WICHITA	**KA**	67208	(316) 686-4741
CENTRAL KENTUCKY JEWISH ASSOCIATION, INC. 258 PLAZA DRIVE, #208	LEXINGTON	**KY**	40503	(606) 277-8048
JEWISH COMMUNITY CENTER 3600 DUTCHMANS LANE	LOUISVILLE	**KY**	40205	(502) 459-0660
JEWISH COMMUNITY CENTER 5342 ST. CHARLES AVENUE	NEW ORLEANS	**LA**	70175	(504) 897-0143
SHREVEPORT JEWISH FEDERATION 2030 LINE AVENUE	SHREVEPORT	**LA**	71104	(318) 221-4129
JEWISH COMMUNITY CENTER OF GREATER BOSTON 72 FRANKLIN STREET	BOSTON	**MA**	02110	(617) 542-1870
BROOKLINE-BRIGHTON-NEWTON JEWISH COMMUNITY CENTER 50 SUTHERLAND ROAD	BRIGHTON	**MA**	02146	(617) 734-0800
SOUTH AREA JEWISH COMMUNITY CENTER 71 LEGION PARKWAY	BROCKTON	**MA**	02401	(617) 586-6404
JEWISH YOUNG ADULT CENTER 1120 BEACON STREET	BROOKLINE	**MA**	02146	(617) 566-5946
CHELSEA/REVERE JEWISH COMMUNITY CENTER 19 CRESCENT AVENUE	CHELSEA	**MA**	02150	(617) 884-5672
JEWISH COMMUNITY COUNCIL 56 NORTH MAIN STREET	FALL RIVER	**MA**	02720	(617) 673-7791
JEWISH COMMUNITY CENTER 76 SALEM END ROAD	FRAMINGHAM	**MA**	01701	(617) 879-3300
TEMPLE EMANU-EL COMMUNITY CENTER 514 MAIN STREET	HAVERHILL	**MA**	01830	(617) 373-3861
JEWISH COMMUNITY CENTER 580 HAVERHILL STREET	LAWRENCE	**MA**	01841	(617) 686-4157
NORTH SHORE JEWISH COMMUNITY CENTER 4 COMMUNITY ROAD	MARBLEHEAD	**MA**	01945	(617) 631-8330
CENTRAL AREA EXTENSION 601 WINCHESTER STREET	NEWTON	**MA**	02161	(617) 969-0733
JEWISH COMMUNITY CENTER ON THE CAMPUS 333 NAHANTON STREET	NEWTON CENTRE	**MA**	02159	
JEWISH COMMUNITY CENTER 1160 DICKINSON STREET	SPRINGFIELD	**MA**	01108	(413) 739-4715
KINGS PLAZA JCC LOWELL STREET AT RUSSELL STREET	WEST PEABODY	**MA**	01960	(617) 535-2968
JEWISH COMMUNITY CENTER 633 SALISBURY STREET	WORCESTER	**MA**	01609	(617) 756-7109
YMHA JEWISH COMMUNITY CENTRE 370 HARGRAVE STREET	WINNIPEG	**MB**	R3B 2K1	(204) 947-0601
JEWISH COMMUNITY CENTER OF GREATER BALTIMORE PARK HEIGHTS BLDG., 5700 PARK HEIGHTS AVENUE	BALTIMORE	**MD**	21215	(301) 542-4900
JEWISH COMMUNITY CENTER 3506 GWYNNBROOK AVENUE, DALSHEIMER BLDG	OWINGS MILLS	**MD**	21117	(301) 356-5200
JEWISH COMMUNITY CENTER OF GREATER WASHINGTON 6125 MONTROSE ROAD	ROCKVILLE	**MD**	20852	(301) 881-0100
JEWISH COMMUNITY CENTER 28 SOMERSET STREET	BANGOR	**ME**	04401	(207) 945-5631
JEWISH COMMUNITY CENTER 57 ASHMONT STREET	PORTLAND	**ME**	04103	(207) 772-1959
JEWISH COMMUNITY FUND 1121 KENEBERRY WAY S.E.	GRAND RAPIDS	**MI**	49506	(616) 949-5238
TEN MILE BRANCH 15110 W. TEN MILE ROAD	OAK PARK	**MI**	48237	(313) 967-4030
JEWISH COMMUNITY CENTER OF METROPOLITAN DETROIT 6600 WEST MAPLE ROAD	WEST BLOOMFIELD	**MI**	48033	(313) 661-1000
JEWISH COMMUNITY CENTER OF GREATER MINNEAPOLIS 4330 SOUTH CEDAR LAKE ROAD	MINNEAPOLIS	**MN**	55416	(612) 377-8330
JEWISH COMMUNITY CENTER 1375 ST. PAUL AVENUE	ST. PAUL	**MN**	55116	(612) 698-0751
JEWISH COMMUNITY CENTER 8201 HOLMES ROAD	KANSAS CITY	**MO**	64131	(816) 361-5200
JEWISH COMMUNITY CENTERS ASSN. 2 MILLSTONE CAMPUS DRIVE	ST. LOUIS	**MO**	63146	(314) 432-5700
JEWISH COMMUNITY CENTER 236 CHARLOTTE STREET	ASHEVILLE	**NC**	28801	(704) 253-0701
JEWISH COMMUNITY CENTER 600 NORTH SHARON AMITY ROAD	CHARLOTTE	**NC**	28211	(704) 366-0357
HIGH POINT JEWISH FEDERATION 1308 LONG CREEK	HIGH POINT	**NC**	27260	(919) 431-7101
JEWISH COMMUNITY CENTER 333 SOUTH 132ND STREET	OMAHA	**NE**	68154	(402) 334-8200
JEWISH COMMUNITY CENTER 698 BEECH STREET	MANCHESTER	**NH**	03104	(603) 627-7679
JEWISH COMMUNITY CENTER 1050 KENNEDY BLVD	BAYONNE	**NJ**	07002	(201) 436-6900
JEWISH COMMUNITY CENTER OF SOUTHERN NEW JERSEY 2395 WEST MARLTON PIKE	CHERRY HILL	**NJ**	08002	(609) 662-8800
PASSAIC-CLIFTON YM-YWHA 199 SCOLES AVENUE	CLIFTON	**NJ**	07012	(201) 779-2980
JEWISH COMMUNITY CENTER OF GREATER MONMOUTH COUNTY 100 GRANT AVENUE	DEAL	**NJ**	07723	(201) 531-9100
JEWISH COMMUNITY CENTER OF MIDDLESEX COUNTY 1775 OAK TREE ROAD	EDISON	**NJ**	08820	(201) 494-3232
REGIONAL YM & YWHA OF RARITAN VALLEY 2 SOUTH ADELAIDE AVENUE	HIGHLAND PARK	**NJ**	08904	(201) 249-2221
YM-YWHA OF MORRIS-SUSSEX 500 ROUTE 10	LEDGEWOOD	**NJ**	07852	(201) 584-1851
JEWISH COMMUNITY CENTER OF ATLANTIC COUNTY 501 NORTH JEROME AVENUE	MARGATE	**NJ**	08402	(609) 822-1167
YM-YWHA OF WESTERN MONMOUTH COUNTY, MARLBORO BRANCH P.O. BOX 53, RTE. 79 & TENNENT ROAD	MORGANVILLE	**NJ**	07751	(201) 591-1777
YM-YWHA OF BERGEN COUNTY EAST 285 MIDLAND AVENUE	PARAMUS	**NJ**	07652	(201) 967-8810
YM/YWHA OF NORTH JERSEY - SCHNEIDER BRANCH 26 EAST 39TH STREET	PATERSON	**NJ**	07514	(201) 279-5528
YM-YWHA 316 MADISON AVENUE	PERTH AMBOY	**NJ**	08861	(201) 442-0365
JEWISH COMMUNITY CENTER OF SOMERSET COUNTY 2 DIVISION STREET, P.O. BOX 874	SOMERVILLE	**NJ**	08876	(201) 725-2231
JEWISH COMMUNITY CENTER ON THE PALISADES 411 EAST CLINTON AVENUE	TENAFLY	**NJ**	07670	(201) 569-7900
JCC OF THE DELAWARE VALLEY P.O. BOX 7365, 999 LOWER FERRY ROAD	TRENTON	**NJ**	08628	(609) 883-9550
EASTERN UNION COUNTY YM-YWHA GREEN LANE	UNION	**NJ**	07083	(201) 289-8112
YM & YWHA OF NORTH JERSEY 1 PIKE DRIVE	WAYNE	**NJ**	07470	(201) 595-0100
YM/YWHA OF METROPOLITAN NEW JERSEY - NORTHWEST BRANCH 1 HENDERSON DRIVE	WEST CALDWELL	**NJ**	07006	(201) 736-3200
YM-YWHA OF METROPOLITAN NEW JERSEY 760 NORTHFIELD AVENUE	WEST ORANGE	**NJ**	07052	(201) 736-3200
JEWISH COMMUNITY CENTER OF CENTRAL N.J. 922 SOUTH AVENUE, WEST	WESTFIELD	**NJ**	07090	(201) 889-8800

Name / Address	City	State	Zip	Phone
ATLANTIC JEWISH COUNCIL 5675 SPRING GARDEN ROAD	HALIFAX	NS	B3J 1H1	(902) 422-7491
JEWISH COMMUNITY CENTER 340 WHITEHALL ROAD	ALBANY	NY	12208	(518) 438-6651
ASTORIA CENTER OF ISRAEL 27-35 CRESCENT STREET	ASTORIA	NY	11102	(718) 278-2680
SOUTH SHORE YM & YWHA 806 MERRICK ROAD	BALDWIN	NY	11510	(516) 623-9393
JEWISH CENTER 203-05 32ND AVENUE	BAYSIDE	NY	11361	(718) 352-7900
YM & YWHA OF NORTHERN WESTCHESTER 129 PLAINFIELD AVENUE	BEDFORD HILLS	NY	10507	(914) 241-2064
JEWISH COMMUNITY CENTER OF BROOME COUNTY 500 CLUBHOUSE ROAD	BINGHAMTON	NY	13903	(607) 724-2417
BRONX HOUSE 990 PELHAM PARKWAY SOUTH	BRONX	NY	10461	(212) 792-1800
JACOB H. SCHIFF CENTER 2510 VALENTINE AVENUE	BRONX	NY	10458	(212) 295-2510
JEWISH CENTER OF WILLIAMSBRIDGE 2910 BARNES AVENUE	BRONX	NY	10467	(212) 655-4077
KINGSBRIDGE HEIGHTS JEWISH CENTER 124 EAMES PLACE	BRONX	NY	10468	(212) 549-4120
MOSHOLU JEWISH CENTER 3044 HULL AVENUE	BRONX	NY	10467	(212) 547-1515
MOSHOLU-MONTEFIORE COMMUNITY CENTER 3450 DEKALB AVENUE	BRONX	NY	10467	(212) 882-4000
RIVERDALE YM-YWHA 450 WEST 250TH STREET	BRONX	NY	10471	(212) 548-8200
BROOKLYN JEWISH CENTER, THE 667 EASTERN PARKWAY	BROOKLYN	NY	11213	(718) 493-8800
CONGREGATION SHEIRIS ISRAEL BAY RIDGE JEWISH CENTER 405 81ST STREET	BROOKLYN	NY	11209	(718) 836-3103
HEBREW EDUCATIONAL SOCIETY 9502 SEAVIEW AVENUE	BROOKLYN	NY	11236	(718) 241-3000
JEWISH COMMUNAL CENTER 1302 AVENUE I	BROOKLYN	NY	11210	(718) 377-9281
JEWISH COMMUNITY HOUSE OF BENSONHURST 7802 BAY PARKWAY	BROOKLYN	NY	11214	(718) 331-6800
KINGS BAY YM-YWHA 3495 NOSTRAND AVENUE	BROOKLYN	NY	11229	(718) 648-7703
RECREATION ROOMS & SETTLEMENT 715 EAST 105TH STREET	BROOKLYN	NY	11236	(718) 649-1461
SEPHARDIC COMMUNITY CENTER 1901 OCEAN PARKWAY	BROOKLYN	NY	11223	(718) 627-4300
SHOREFRONT YM-YWHA OF BRIGHTON-MANHATTAN BEACH 3300 CONEY ISLAND AVENUE	BROOKLYN	NY	11235	(718) 646-1444
YM & YWHA OF BORO PARK 4912 14TH AVENUE	BROOKLYN	NY	11219	(718) 438-5921
JEWISH CENTER OF GREATER BUFFALO, INC. 787 DELAWARE AVENUE	BUFFALO	NY	14209	(716) 886-3145
BETH EL, TEMPLE BROADWAY & LOCUST AVENUE	CEDARHURST	NY	11516	(516) 569-2700
GREATER FIVE TOWNS YM-YWHA 207 GROVE AVENUE, P.O. BOX 191	CEDARHURST	NY	11516	(516) 569-6733
YM & YWHA OF SUFFOLK 74 HAUPPAUGE ROAD	COMMACK	NY	11725	(516) 462-9800
JEWISH COMMUNITY CENTER OF SYRACUSE, INC. 5655 THOMPSON ROAD, P.O. BOX 29	DEWITT	NY	13214	(315) 445-2360
JEWISH COMMUNITY CENTER, THE P.O. BOX 3087, GRANDVIEW ROAD EXT	ELMIRA	NY	14905	(607) 734-8122
GUSTAVE HARTMAN YM & YWHA 1742 SEAGIRT BLVD	FAR ROCKAWAY	NY	11691	(718) 471-9600
GUSTAVE HARTMAN YM & YWHA 710 HARTMAN LANE	FAR ROCKAWAY	NY	11691	(718) 471-0200
HILLCREST JEWISH CENTER 183-02 UNION TURNPIKE	FLUSHING	NY	11366	(718) 380-4145
YM-YWHA OF GREATER FLUSHING 45-35 KISSENA BLVD	FLUSHING	NY	11355	(718) 461-3030
CENTRAL QUEENS YM-YWHA 67-09 108TH STREET	FOREST HILLS	NY	11375	(718) 268-5011
FOREST HILLS JEWISH CENTER 106-06 QUEENS BLVD	FOREST HILLS	NY	11375	(718) 263-7000
JEWISH CENTER OF GREATER BUFFALO 2640 NORTH FOREST ROAD	GETZVILLE	NY	14068	(716) 688-4033
JEWISH COMMUNITY CENTER 28 EAST FULTON STREET	GLOVERSVILLE	NY	12078	(518) 725-3161
HUNTINGTON HEBREW CONGREGATION 510 PARK AVENUE	HUNTINGTON	NY	11743	(516) 427-1089
JEWISH CENTER OF JACKSON HEIGHTS 35-25 82 STREET	JACKSON HEIGHTS	NY	11372	(718) 429-1150
SAMUEL FIELD YM-YWHA 58-20 LITTLE NECK PARKWAY	LITTLE NECK	NY	11362	(718) 225-6750
BEACH YM & YWHA 310 NATIONAL BLVD	LONG BEACH	NY	11561	(516) 431-2929
TEMPLE ISRAEL 305 RIVERSIDE BLVD	LONG BEACH	NY	11561	(516) 432-1410
SUNNYSIDE JEWISH CENTER 45-46 43RD STREET	LONG ISLAND CITY	NY	11104	(718) 786-3576
MERRICK JEWISH CENTER 225 FOX BLVD	MERRICK	NY	11566	(516) 379-8650
YM & YWHA OF LOWER WESTCHESTER 30 OAKLEY AVENUE	MOUNT VERNON	NY	10550	(914) 664-0500
92ND STREET YM-YWHA 1395 LEXINGTON AVENUE	NEW YORK	NY	10028	(212) 427-6000
ANCHE CHESED, TEMPLE 251 WEST 100 STREET	NEW YORK	NY	10025	(212) 865-0600
ASSOCIATED YM-YWHA'S OF GREATER NEW YORK 130 EAST 59TH STREET	NEW YORK	NY	10022	(212) 751-8880
EDUCATIONAL ALLIANCE, THE 197 EAST BROADWAY	NEW YORK	NY	10002	(212) 475-6200
EMANU-EL MIDTOWN YM-YWHA 344 EAST 14TH STREET	NEW YORK	NY	10003	(212) 674-7200
JWB 15 EAST 26TH STREET	NEW YORK	NY	10010	(212) 532-4949
YM & YWHA OF WASHINGTON HEIGHTS & INWOOD 54 NAGLE AVENUE	NEW YORK	NY	10040	(212) 569-6200
MID-ISLAND JEWISH YM & YWHA 45 MANETTO HILL ROAD	PLAINVIEW	NY	11803	(516) 822-3535
UNITED JEWISH Y'S OF LONG ISLAND 55 MANETTO HILL ROAD	PLAINVIEW	NY	11803	(516) 938-4600
JEWISH COMMUNITY CENTER 110 SOUTH GRAND AVENUE	POUGHKEEPSIE	NY	12603	(914) 471-0430
REGO PARK JEWISH CENTER 97-30 QUEENS BLVD	REGO PARK	NY	11374	(718) 459-1000
JEWISH COMMUNITY CENTER OF GREATER ROCHESTER, INC. 1200 EDGEWOOD AVENUE	ROCHESTER	NY	14618	(716) 461-2000
NORTH SHORE YM & YWHA REMSEN AVENUE, P.O. BOX 393	ROSLYN	NY	11576	(516) 484-1545
YM & YWHA OF MID WESTCHESTER 999 WILMOT ROAD	SCARSDALE	NY	10583	(914) 472-3300
JEWISH COMMUNITY CENTER 2565 BALLTOWN ROAD	SCHENECTADY	NY	12309	(518) 377-8803
JEWISH COMMUNITY CENTER 475 VICTORY BLVD	STATEN ISLAND	NY	10301	(718) 981-1500
MAILMAN MEM. CENTER OF THE JEWISH COMMUNITY CENTER ASSN. 2310 ONEIDA STREET	UTICA	NY	13501	(315) 733-2343
CONGREGATION SONS OF ISRAEL 111 IRVING PLACE	WOODMERE	NY	11598	(516) 374-0655
JEWISH COMMUNITY CENTER 122 SOUTH BROADWAY	YONKERS	NY	10701	(914) 963-8457
JEWISH CENTER 750 WHITE POND DRIVE	AKRON	OH	44320	(216) 867-7850
JEWISH COMMUNITY CENTER 2631 HARVARD AVENUE N.W.	CANTON	OH	44709	(216) 453-0132
JEWISH COMMUNITY CENTER 1580 SUMMIT ROAD	CINCINNATI	OH	45237	(513) 761-7500
JEWISH COMMUNITY CENTER 3505 MAYFIELD ROAD	CLEVELAND HEIGHTS	OH	44118	(216) 382-4000
LEO YASSENOFF JEWISH CENTER 1125 COLLEGE AVENUE	COLUMBUS	OH	43209	(614) 231-2731
DAYTON JEWISH CENTER 4501 DENLINGER ROAD	DAYTON	OH	45426	(513) 854-4014
JEWISH FEDERATION, INC. 667 STEWART LANE	MANSFIELD	OH	44907	(419) 756-7347
JEWISH COMMUNITY CENTER 6465 SYLVANIA AVENUE	SYLVANIA	OH	43560	(419) 885-4485
JEWISH COMMUNITY CTR. OF THE YOUNGSTOWN AREA-JEWISH FED. P.O. BOX 449, 505 GYPSY LANE	YOUNGSTOWN	OH	44501	(216) 746-3251
JEWISH COMMUNITY COUNCIL 3022 NORTHWEST EXPRESSWAY #116	OKLAHOMA CITY	OK	73112	(405) 755-6030
JEWISH COMMUNITY CENTER 2021 EAST 71ST STREET	TULSA	OK	74136	(918) 495-1111
JEWISH COMMUNITY CENTRE 57 DELAWARE AVENUE	HAMILTON	ON	L8M 1T6	(416) 528-8577
JEWISH COMMUNITY CENTRE 532 HURON STREET	LONDON	ON	N5Y 4J5	(519) 432-6337
JEWISH COMMUNITY CENTER 151 CHAPEL STREET	OTTAWA	ON	K1N 7Y2	(613) 232-7306
BLOOR BRANCH 750 SPADINA AVENUE	TORONTO	ON	M5S 2J2	(416) 493-8866
JEWISH COMMUNITY CENTRE 4588 BATHURST STREET	WILLOWDALE	ON	M2R 1W6	(416) 636-1880
KOFFLER CENTRE OF THE ARTS 4588 BATHURST STREET	WILLOWDALE	ON	M2R 1W6	(416) 636-1880
LEAH POSLUNS THEATRE 4588 BATHURST STREET	WILLOWDALE	ON	M2R 1W6	(416) 636-1880
NORTH EAST BRANCH 1091 FINCH AVENUE EAST	WILLOWDALE	ON	M2J 2X3	(416) 493-8866
NORTHERN BRANCH 4588 BATHURST STREET	WILLOWDALE	ON	M2R 1W6	(416) 636-1880
JEWISH COMMUNITY COUNCIL 1641 OUELLETTE AVENUE	WINDSOR	ON	N8X 1K9	(519) 254-7558
MITTLEMAN JCC 6651 SOUTHWEST CAPITOL HIGHWAY	PORTLAND	OR	97219	(503) 244-0111
JEWISH COMMUNITY CENTER 722 NORTH 22ND STREET	ALLENTOWN	PA	18104	(215) 435-3571
BRITH SHOLOM COMMUNITY CENTER BRODHEAD & PACKER AVENUES, P.O. BOX 5323	BETHLEHEM	PA	18015	(215) 866-8009
JEWISH COMMUNITY CENTER 100 VAUGHN STREET	HARRISBURG	PA	17110	(717) 236-9555
JEWISH COMMUNITY CENTER ASSOCIATION 2120 OREGON PIKE	LANCASTER	PA	17601	(717) 569-7352
JCC OF THE DELAWARE VALLEY 501 TRENTON ROAD	LANGHORNE	PA	19047	(215) 493-2900
JEWISH COMMUNITY CENTER 1541 POWELL STREET	NORRISTOWN	PA	19401	(215) 275-8797
DAVID G. NEUMAN SENIOR CENTER 6600 BUSTLETON AVENUE	PHILADELPHIA	PA	19149	(215) 338-9800
JEWISH YS AND CENTERS OF GREATER PHILADELPHIA 401 SO. BROAD STREET	PHILADELPHIA	PA	19147	(215) 545-4400
KAISERMAN BRANCH CITY LINE & HAVERFORD AVENUE	PHILADELPHIA	PA	19151	(215) 896-7770
KLEIN BRANCH RED LION ROAD & JAMISON AVENUE	PHILADELPHIA	PA	19116	(215) 698-7300
MULTI-SERVICE CENTER MARSHALL & PORTER STREETS	PHILADELPHIA	PA	19148	(215) 468-6285
SENIOR ADULT SERVICES AND RESEARCH 401 SOUTH BROAD STREET	PHILADELPHIA	PA	19147	(215) 545-4400
YM & YWHA BRANCH 401 SO. BROAD STREET	PHILADELPHIA	PA	19147	(215) 545-4400
JCC - SOUTH HILLS 1900 COCHRAN ROAD	PITTSBURGH	PA	15220	(412) 341-3323
JCC SQUIRREL HILL 5738 FORBES AVENUE	PITTSBURGH	PA	15217	(412) 521-8010
JEWISH COMMUNITY CENTER 315 SOUTH BELLEFIELD AVENUE	PITTSBURGH	PA	15213	(412) 621-6500
JEWISH COMMUNITY CENTER 1700 CITY LINE STREET	READING	PA	19604	(215) 921-0624
JEWISH COMMUNITY CENTER 601 JEFFERSON AVENUE	SCRANTON	PA	18510	(717) 346-6595
JEWISH COMMUNITY CENTER 60 SOUTH RIVER STREET	WILKES-BARRE	PA	18702	(717) 824-4646
JEWISH COMMUNITY CENTER 120 EAST MARKET STREET	YORK	PA	17401	(717) 843-0918
USO-JEWISH COMMUNITY ARMED FORCES CENTER, INC. BOX 105	BALBOA	PZ		52-5972
DAVIS YM-YWHA 5700 KELLERT AVENUE, COTE ST. LUC., P.Q.	MONTREAL	QU	H4W 1T4	(514) 482-0730
LAVAL JEWISH COMMUNITY CENTRE 755 DU SABLON, CHOMEDEY, LAVAL, P.Q.	MONTREAL	QU	H7W 4H5	(514) 688-8961
NEIGHBORHOOD HOUSE SERVICES 5480 WESTBURY AVENUE	MONTREAL	QU	H3W 3G2	(514) 735-5565
SAIDYE BRONFMAN CENTRE 5170 COTE ST. CATHERINE ROAD	MONTREAL	QU	H3W 1M7	(514) 739-2301
SNOWDON BRANCH 5500 WESTBURY AVENUE	MONTREAL	QU	H3W 2W8	(514) 737-6551
YM-YWHA & NHS 5500 WESTBURY AVENUE	MONTREAL	QU	H3W 2W8	(514) 737-6551
JEWISH COMMUNITY CENTER OF RHODE ISLAND 401 ELMGROVE AVENUE	PROVIDENCE	RI	02906	(401) 861-8800
JEWISH COMMUNITY CENTER 1645 WALLENBERG BLVD., P.O. BOX 31298	CHARLESTON	SC	29407	(803) 571-6565
JEWISH COMMUNITY CENTER 4540 TRENHOLM ROAD	COLUMBIA	SC	29206	(803) 787-2023
JEWISH COMMUNITY CENTER 5326 LYNNLAND TERRACE	CHATTANOOGA	TN	37411	(615) 894-1317
ARNSTEIN JEWISH COMMUNITY CENTER 6800 DEANE HILL DRIVE, P.O. BOX 10882	KNOXVILLE	TN	37919	(615) 690-6343
JEWISH COMMUNITY CENTER P.O. BOX 38349	MEMPHIS	TN	38138	(901) 761-0810
JEWISH COMMUNITY CENTER 3500 WEST END AVENUE	NASHVILLE	TN	37205	(615) 297-3588
JEWISH COMMUNITY COUNCIL OF AUSTIN 5758 BALCONES DRIVE	AUSTIN	TX	78731	(512) 451-6435
JEWISH COMMUNITY COUNCIL 750 EVERHART ROAD	CORPUS CHRISTI	TX	78411	(512) 855-6239
JEWISH COMMUNITY CENTER 7900 NORTHHAVEN ROAD	DALLAS	TX	75230	(214) 739-2737
JEWISH FED. & JEWISH COMMUNITY CENTER P.O. BOX 12097, 405 MARDI GRAS DRIVE	EL PASO	TX	79912	(915) 584-4438
DAN DANCIGER JCC 6801 GRANBURY ROAD	FT. WORTH	TX	76133	(817) 292-3111
JCC MEMORIAL CENTER 783 COUNTRY PLACE	HOUSTON	TX	77024	(713) 496-0283
JEWISH COMMUNITY CENTER 5601 SOUTH BRAESWOOD	HOUSTON	TX	77096	(713) 729-3200
JEWISH COMMUNITY CENTER 103 WEST RAMPART DRIVE	SAN ANTONIO	TX	78216	(512) 344-3453
FEDERATED JEWISH WELFARE FUND P.O. BOX 8601	TYLER	TX	75711	
JEWISH COMMUNITY CENTER 2416 EAST 1700 SOUTH	SALT LAKE CITY	UT	84108	(801) 581-0098
NORTHERN VIRGINIA JCC 8822 LITTLE RIVER TURNPIKE	FAIRFAX	VA	22031	(703) 323-0880
JEWISH COMMUNITY CENTER OF THE VIRGINIA PENINSULA 2700 SPRING ROAD, P.O. BOX 1680	NEWPORT NEWS	VA	23606	(804) 595-5544
JEWISH COMMUNITY CENTER OF TIDEWATER 7300 NEWPORT AVENUE	NORFOLK	VA	23505	(804) 489-1371
JEWISH COMMUNITY CENTER 5403 MONUMENT AVENUE	RICHMOND	VA	23226	(804) 288-6091
SAMUEL & ALTHEA STROUM JEWISH COMM. CTR. OF GREATER SEATTLE P.O. BOX 779, 3801 EAST MERCER WAY	MERCER ISLAND	WA	98040	(206) 232-7115
MADISON JEWISH COMMUNITY COUNCIL, INC. 310 NORTH MIDVALE BLVD., SUITE 325	MADISON	WI	53705	
JEWISH COMMUNITY CENTER 1400 NORTH PROSPECT AVENUE	MILWAUKEE	WI	53202	(414) 276-0716
FEDERATION JEWISH CHARITIES OF CHARLESTON, INC. 723 KANAWHA BLVD E	CHARLESTON	WV	25326	(304) 346-7500
ARGENTINE FEDERATION OF MACCABI COMMUNITY CENTERS 2233 SARMIENTO	BUENOS AIRES	AG		48-5880
EUROPEAN ASSOC. OF JEWISH COMMUNITY CENTERS 4 BIS RUE DE LOTA	PARIS	FR	75116	553-3126
FONDS SOCIAL JUIF UNIFIE 19 RUE DE TEHERAN	PARIS	FR	75008	563-1728
HAIM ZIPORI J.D.C. HILL	JERUSALEM	IS	91080	
ISRAEL FEDERATION OF COMMUNITY CENTERS 12 HESS STREET	JERUSALEM	IS	91080	
ASSOCIATION OF JEWISH YOUTH 50 LINDLEY STREET	LONDON	UK	E1 3AX	790-6407

JEWISH FAMILY SERVICES

Name / Address	City	State	Zip	Phone
JEWISH FAMILY AND CHILD SERVICES P.O. BOX 8353	MOBILE	AL	36608	(205) 343-0800
JEWISH FAMILY SERVICE, HOUSE OF ISRAEL BUILDING, ROOM 1 102 18TH AVENUE S.E.	CALGARY	AT		(403) 252-8136
JEWISH FAMILY SERVICES 606 MCLEOD BUILDING, 10136 100TH STREET	EDMONTON	AT	T5J 0P1	(403) 424-6346
JEWISH FAMILY & CHILDREN'S SERVICE 2003 N. SEVENTH STREET	PHOENIX	AZ	85006	(602) 257-1904
JEWISH FAMILY SERVICES OF TUCSON JEWISH COMMUNITY COUNCIL 102 NORTH PLUMER AVENUE	TUCSON	AZ	85719	(602) 792-3641

Name / Address	City	State	Zip	Phone
JEWISH FAMILY SERVICE AGENCY 2025 WEST 42ND AVENUE, #305	VANCOUVER	**BC**	V6M 2B5	(604) 266-2396
JEWISH FAMILY & CHILDREN'S SERVICES 490 EL CAMINO REAL	BELMONT	**CA**	94002	(415) 591-8991
JEWISH FAMILY SERVICE OF ORANGE COUNTY 121-81 BUARO STREET, SUITE G	GARDEN GROVE	**CA**	92640	(714) 537-4980
JEWISH FAMILY SERVICE 3801 EAST WILLOW STREET	LONG BEACH	**CA**	90815	(213) 427-7916
JEWISH FAMILY SERVICE 11646 WEST PICO BLVD	LOS ANGELES	**CA**	90064	(213) 879-0910
JEWISH FAMILY SERVICE OF LOS ANGELES 6505 WILSHIRE BLVD., SUITE 614	LOS ANGELES	**CA**	90048	(213) 852-1234
JEWISH FAMILY SERVICE, FREDA MOHR MULTISERVICE CENTER 351 NORTH FAIRFAX AVENUE	LOS ANGELES	**CA**	90036	(213) 655-5141
JEWISH FAMILY SERVICE OF THE GREATER EAST BAY 3245 SHEFFIELD AVENUE	OAKLAND	**CA**	94602	(415) 532-6314
JEWISH FAMILY AND CHILDREN'S SERVICES 299 CALIFORNIA STREET	PALO ALTO	**CA**	94306	(415) 326-6696
JEWISH FAMILY SERVICE 1860 HOWE AVENUE, #260	SACRAMENTO	**CA**	95825	(916) 921-1921
JEWISH FAMILY SERVICE 3355 4TH AVENUE	SAN DIEGO	**CA**	92103	(619) 291-0473
JEWISH FAMILY & CHILDREN'S SERVICES 160 SCOTT STREET	SAN FRANCISCO	**CA**	94115	(415) 567-8860
JEWISH FAMILY SERVICE OF SANTA CLARA COUNTY 2075 LINCOLN AVENUE, SUITE C	SAN JOSE	**CA**	95125	(408) 264-7140
JEWISH FAMILY AND CHILDREN'S SERVICES 1330 LINCOLN AVENUE, ROOM 204	SAN RAFAEL	**CA**	94901	(415) 456-7554
JEWISH FAMILY SERVICE OF SANTA MONICA 1424 4TH STREET	SANTA MONICA	**CA**	90401	(213) 393-0732
JEWISH FAMILY SERVICE OF SANTA MONICA 2811 WILSHIRE BOULEVARD	SANTA MONICA	**CA**	90401	(213) 828-9521
JEWISH FAMILY CENTER, SAN FERNANDO VALLEY 6851 LENNOX	VAN NUYS	**CA**	91405	(818) 873-1520
JEWISH FAMILY & CHILDREN'S SERVICE OF COLORADO 1375 DELAWARE STREER	DENVER	**CO**	80204	(303) 321-3115
JEWISH FAMILY SERVICES 300 S. DAHLIA STREET 101	DENVER	**CO**	80222	(303) 321-3115
JEWISH FAMILY SERVICE 144 GOLDEN HILL STREET	BRIDGEPORT	**CT**	06603	(203) 366-5438
JEWISH FAMILY SERVICE 2370 PARK AVENUE	BRIDGEPORT	**CT**	06604	(203) 366-5438
JEWISH FAMILY SERVICE 50 GILLETT STREET	HARTFORD	**CT**	06105	(203) 236-1927
JEWISH FAMILY SERVICE OF NEW HAVEN 52 TEMPLE STREET	NEW HAVEN	**CT**	06510	(203) 777-6641
JEWISH FAMILY SERVICE NEWFIELD AVENUE & VINE ROAD, P.O. BOX 3038	STAMFORD	**CT**	06905	(203) 322-6938
JEWISH FAMILY SERVICE 333 BLOOMFIELD AVENUE	WEST HARTFORD	**CT**	06117	
JEWISH FAMILY SERVICE TALLEYVILLE SHOPPING CENTER, 3617 SILVERSIDE ROAD	WILMINGTON	**DE**	19803	(302) 478-5111
JEWISH FAMILY SERVICE 101 GARDEN OF EDEN ROAD	WILMINGTON	**DE**	19803	(302) 478-9411
GULF COAST JEWISH FAMILY SERVICE, INC. 304 S. JUPITER AVENUE	CLEARWATER	**FL**	33515	(813) 446-1005
GULF COAST JEWISH FAMILY SERVICE, INC. DADE CITY HALL, 612 E. MERIDIAN AVENUE	DADE CITY	**FL**	33525	(904) 567-7657
JEWISH FAMILY SERVICE 4517 HOLLYWOOD BOULEVARD	HOLLYWOOD	**FL**	33021	(305) 966-0956
JEWISH FAMILY & CHILDRENS SERVICES 1415 LASALLE STREET	JACKSONVILLE	**FL**	32207	(904) 396-2941
JEWISH FAMILY & CHILDREN'S SERVICE 1790 S.W. 27TH AVENUE	MIAMI	**FL**	33145	(305) 445-0555
GULF COAST JEWISH FAMILY SERVICE, INC. 1718 W. KENNEDY BLVD	PORT RICHEY	**FL**	33568	(813) 848-5174
GULF COAST JEWISH FAMILY SERVICE, INC. 8167 ELBOW LANE N	ST. PETERSBURG	**FL**	33710	(813) 381-2373
GULF COAST JEWISH FAMILY SERVICE, INC. TRILBY ADULT & COMMUNITY SCHOOL, OLD TRILBY ROAD	TRILBY	**FL**	33593	(904) 583-3421
JEWISH FAMILY SERVICES 112 NORTH WYMORE ROAD	WINTER PARK	**FL**	32789	(305) 644-7593
JEWISH FAMILY & CHILDREN'S BUREAU OF THE ATLANTIC JEWISH WELFARE FEDERATION, 41 EXCHANGE PLACE S.E.	ATLANTA	**GA**	30303	(404) 881-1858
JEWISH FAMILY & CHILDRENS BUREAU 1753 PEACHTREE ROAD N.E.	ATLANTA	**GA**	30309	(404) 873-2277
JEWISH FAMILY & COMMUNITY SERVICE 1 SOUTH FRANKLIN STREET	CHICAGO	**IL**	60606	(312) 346-6700
JEWISH FAMILY & COMMUNITY SERVICE 210 SKOKIE VALLEY ROAD	HIGHLAND PARK	**IL**	60035	(312) 831-4225
JEWISH FAMILY & CHILDREN'S SERVICES 1475 WEST 86TH STREET	INDIANAPOLIS	**IN**	46260	(317) 872-6641
JEWISH FAMILY & CHILDREN'S SERVICES 4550 WEST 90TH TERRACE	SHAWNEE MISSION	**KS**	66207	(913) 649-1056
JEWISH FAMILY & VOCATIONAL SERVICE 3640 DUTCHMANS LANE	LOUISVILLE	**KY**	40205	(502) 452-6341
JEWISH FAMILY & CHILDREN'S SERVICE 107 CAMP STREET	NEW ORLEANS	**LA**	70130	(504) 524-8476
SHREVEPORT JEWISH FAMILY & CHILDREN'S SERVICES 2030 LINE AVENUE	SHREVEPORT	**LA**	71104	(318) 221-4129
JEWISH FAMILY & CHILDREN'S SERVICE 31 NEW CHARDON STREET	BOSTON	**MA**	02114	(617) 227-6641
JEWISH FAMILY SERVICE 71 LEGION PARKWAY	BROCKTON	**MA**	02401	(617) 588-7324
JEWISH FAMILY SERVICE 430 NORTH CANAL STREET	LAWRENCE	**MA**	01840	(617) 683-6711
JEWISH FAMILY SERVICE OF GREATER SPRINGFIELD 367 PINE STREET	SPRINGFIELD	**MA**	01105	(413) 737-2601
JEWISH FAMILY SERVICE 25 WEST STREET	WORCESTER	**MA**	01609	(617) 755-3101
JEWISH CHILD & FAMILY SERVICES 228 NOTRE DAME AVENUE, SUITE 1001	WINNIPEG	**MB**		(204) 943-6425
JEWISH FAMILY & CHILDREN'S SERVICES 5750 PARK HEIGHTS AVENUE	BALTIMORE	**MD**	21215	(301) 466-9200
JEWISH SOCIAL SERVICE AGENCY 6123 MONTROSE ROAD	ROCKVILLE	**MD**	20852	(301) 881-3700
JEWISH FAMILY & CHILDREN'S SERVICE 24123 GREENFIELD	SOUTHFIELD	**MI**	48075	(313) 559-1500
JEWISH FAMILY & CHILDREN'S SERVICE 404 SOUTH 8TH STREET, ROOM 244	MINNEAPOLIS	**MN**	55404	(612) 338-8771
JEWISH FAMILY SERVICE 1546 ST. CLAIR AVENUE	ST. PAUL	**MN**	55105	(612) 698-0767
JEWISH FAMILY & CHILDREN'S SERVICE 1115 EAST 65TH STREET	KANSAS CITY	**MO**	64131	(816) 333-1172
JEWISH FAMILY & CHILDREN'S SERVICE 9385 OLIVE BOULEVARD	ST. LOUIS	**MO**	63132	(314) 993-1000
FAMILY SERVICE DEPARTMENT OF THE JEWISH FEDERATION 101 NORTH 20TH STREET	OMAHA	**NE**	68102	(402) 330-2024
FEDERATION FAMILY SERVICE 31 SOUTH SURREY AVENUE	ATLANTIC CITY	**NJ**	08406	(609) 822-1108
JEWISH FAMILY & COUNSELING SERVICE OF JERSEY CITY-BAYONNE 1050 KENNEDY BLVD	BAYONNE	**NJ**	07002	(201) 436-1299
JEWISH FAMILY SERVICE 100 PARK BOULEVARD	CHERRY HILL	**NJ**	08002	(609) 662-8611
JEWISH FAMILY SERVICE 199 SCOLES AVENUE	CLIFTON	**NJ**	07012	(201) 777-7638
JEWISH FAMILY SERVICE AGENCY OF UNION COUNTY GREEN LANE	ELIZABETH	**NJ**	07083	(201) 352-8375
FAMILY SERVICE OF THE JEWISH WELFARE COUNCIL 20 BANTA PLACE	HACKENSACK	**NJ**	07601	(201) 488-8340
JEWISH COUNSELING & SERVICE AGENCY 161 MILLBURN AVENUE	JERSEY CITY	**NJ**	07041	(201) 436-1299
JEWISH FAMILY SERVICE	PATERSON	**NJ**	07501	(201) 777-7031
JEWISH FAMILY SERVICE 255 EAST HANOVER STREET	TRENTON	**NJ**	08608	(609) 822-9317
JEWISH FAMILY SERVICE OF ATLANTIC COUNTY 31 S. SURREY AVENUE	VENTNOR	**NJ**	08406	(201) 822-1108
JEWISH FAMILY SERVICE 2 E. RIVER DRIVE	WILLINGBORO	**NJ**	08046	(609) 871-1450
JEWISH FAMILY SERVICE AGENCY 1555 E. FLAMINGO ROAD, SUITE 125	LAS VEGAS	**NV**	89109	(702) 732-0304
JEWISH FAMILY SERVICES 930 MADISON AVENUE	ALBANY	**NY**	12208	(518) 482-8856
JEWISH BD. OF FAMILY & CH. SERVICES-BRIGHTWATERS GROUP HOME 556 MANATUCK BLVD	BRIGHTWATERS	**NY**	11718	(516) 665-8188
JEWISH BOARD OF FAM. & CHILDREN'S SVCS.-CO-OP CITY OUTPOST 140-26 CARVER LOOP	BRONX	**NY**	10475	(212) 379-7070
JEWISH FAMILY SERVICE 305 EAST KINGSBRIDGE ROAD	BRONX	**NY**	10458	(212) 933-2800
AMERICAN FRIENDS OF JEWISH BIRTHRIGHT 456 BROOKLYN AVENUE, 4C	BROOKLYN	**NY**	11225	(718) 778-0695
BETH DAVID COMMUNAL SERVICE 1145 45TH STREET	BROOKLYN	**NY**	11219	(718) 854-1620
BORO PARK CONSULTATION CTR.-JEWISH BD./FAM. & CHILDREN'S SVC 1276 47TH STREET	BROOKLYN	**NY**	11221	
JEWISH BOARD OF FAM. & CHILDRENS'S SVCS.-CONEY ISLAND SUPPORT SYSTEMS PROJECT 3312 SURF AVENUE	BROOKLYN	**NY**	11224	(718) 372-3300
JEWISH FAMILY SERVICE 283 ADAMS STREET	BROOKLYN	**NY**	11201	(718) 625-0806
JEWISH FAMILY SERVICE 3679 NOSTRAND AVENUE	BROOKLYN	**NY**	11229	(718) 769-3326
JEWISH FAMILY SERVICE - FAMILY COUNSELING 164 CONKLIN AVENUE	BROOKLYN	**NY**	11236	(718) 257-0002
JEWISH FAMILY SERVICE - FAMILY COUNSELING 186 MONTAGUE STREET	BROOKLYN	**NY**	11201	(718) 855-6900
JEWISH FAMILY SERVICE CONSULTATION CENTER 4917 12TH AVENUE	BROOKLYN	**NY**	11219	(718) 435-5700
MACHNE ISRAEL 770 EASTERN PARKWAY	BROOKLYN	**NY**	11213	(718) 493-9250
OHEL CHILDREN'S HOME & FAMILY SERVICES 4423 16TH AVENUE	BROOKLYN	**NY**	11204	(718) 851-6300
JEWISH FAMILY SERVICE 775 MAIN STREET	BUFFALO	**NY**	14203	(716) 853-9956
JEWISH FAMILY SERVICE OF ERIE COUNTY 70 BARKER STREET	BUFFALO	**NY**	14203	(716) 883-1914
JEWISH COMMUNITY SERVICES OF LONG ISLAND 1600 CENTRAL AVENUE	FAR ROCKAWAY	**NY**	11691	(718) 327-1600
JEWISH COMMUNITY SERVICES OF LONG ISLAND 50 CLINTON STREET	HEMPSTEAD	**NY**	11550	(516) 485-5710
JEWISH COMMUNITY SERVICES 76 NORTH BROADWAY	HICKSVILLE	**NY**	11801	(516) 931-7110
FAMILY STUDIES CENTER 161 E. MAIN STREET	HUNTINGTON	**NY**	11743	(516) 423-3377
JEWISH COMMUNITY SERVICES 9 WEST PROSPECT AVENUE	MOUNT VERNON	**NY**	10550	(914) 668-8938
WESTCHESTER JEWISH COMMUNITY SERVICES, INC. 271 NORTH AVENUE	NEW ROCHELLE	**NY**	10802	(914) 632-6433
ALTRO HEALTH & REHABILITATION SERVICES, INC. 345 MADISON AVENUE	NEW YORK	**NY**	10017	(212) 684-0600
ASSOCIATION OF JEWISH FAMILY & CHILDREN'S AGENCIES 40 WORTH STREET, ROOM 800	NEW YORK	**NY**	10013	(212) 608-6660
CONFERENCE OF JEWISH COMMUNAL SERVICES 15 EAST 26TH STREET	NEW YORK	**NY**	10010	(212) 683-8056
FAMILY LOCATION & LEGAL SERVICES OF JEW. FAMILY SERVICE INC. 33 WEST 60TH STREET	NEW YORK	**NY**	10023	(212) 586-4270
JEWISH BD. OF FAMILY & CH. SERVICES-CHILD DEVELOPMENT CENTER 120 W. 57TH STREET	NEW YORK	**NY**	10019	(212) 582-6300
JEWISH BOARD OF FAM. & CH. SERVICES-ADMINISTRATION & INFO. 120 WEST 57TH STREET	NEW YORK	**NY**	10019	(212) 582-9100
JEWISH BOARD OF FAM. & CHILDREN'S SVCS.-CHILD DEVELOPMENT CENTER 2720 BROADWAY	NEW YORK	**NY**	10025	(212) 662-1591
JEWISH BOARD OF FAM. & CHILDREN'S SVCS.-COMM. HOMEMAKER SVC 120 W. 57TH STREET	NEW YORK	**NY**	10019	(212) 582-9100
JEWISH BOARD OF FAM. & CHILDREN'S SVCS.-COURT SERVICES 120 W. 57TH STREET	NEW YORK	**NY**	10019	(212) 582-9100
JEWISH BOARD OF FAM. & CHILDREN'S SVCS.-CULT HOT-LINE & CLINIC 1651 THIRD AVENUE	NEW YORK	**NY**	10028	(212) 860-8533
JEWISH BOARD OF FAM. & CHILDREN'S SVCS.-DEPT. OF JEWISH ED. 120 W. 57TH STREET	NEW YORK	**NY**	10019	(212) 582-9100
JEWISH BOARD OF FAM. & CHILDREN'S SVCS.-ED. THERAPY DEPT. 33 W. 60TH STREET	NEW YORK	**NY**	10023	(212) 586-2900
JEWISH BOARD OF FAM. & CHILDREN'S SVCS.-EDUCATIONAL INST. 120 W. 57TH STREET	NEW YORK	**NY**	10019	(212) 582-9100
JEWISH BOARD OF FAM. & CHILDREN'S SVCS.-EMPLOYEE COUNSELING 120 W. 57TH STREET	NEW YORK	**NY**	10019	(212) 582-9100
JEWISH BOARD OF FAM. & CHILDREN'S SVCS.-INFANT CARE CENTER 201 W. 93RD STREET	NEW YORK	**NY**	10025	(212) 865-8200
JEWISH BOARD OF FAM. & CHILDREN'S SVCS.-PRE-SCHOOL COMM. PGM 120 W. 57TH STREET	NEW YORK	**NY**	10019	(212) 582-6300
JEWISH BOARD OF FAMILY & CHILDREN SERVICES-AFTERCARE UNIT 33 W. 60TH STREET	NEW YORK	**NY**	10023	(212) 586-2900
JEWISH BOARD OF FAMILY & CHILDREN'S SVCS.-APPLICATION & SVCS 120 W. 57TH STREET	NEW YORK	**NY**	10019	(212) 582-9100
JEWISH FAMILY SERVICE 120 WEST 57TH STREET	NEW YORK	**NY**	10019	(212) 592-9100
JEWISH FAMILY SERVICE 33 W. 60TH STREET	NEW YORK	**NY**	10023	(212) 586-2900
JEWISH WELFARE BOARD 15 E. 26TH STREET	NEW YORK	**NY**	10010	(212) 532-4949
JEWISH COMMUNITY SERVICE OF LONG ISLAND 97-45 QUEENS BLVD	REGO PARK	**NY**	11374	(718) 896-9090
JEWISH FAMILY SERVICE 130 EAST MAIN STREET	ROCHESTER	**NY**	14604	(716) 232-5440
JEWISH COMMUNITY SERVICES 22 LAWRENCE AVENUE	SMITHTOWN	**NY**	11787	(516) 724-6300
JEWISH BOARD OF FAM. & CHILDREN'S SVCS.-GELLER HOUSE 77 CHICAGO AVENUE	STATEN ISLAND	**NY**	10305	(718) 442-7828
JEWISH FAMILY SERVICE BUREAU 316 SOUTH WARREN STREET	SYRACUSE	**NY**	13202	(315) 445-0820
JEWISH FAMILY SERVICE BUREAU 4101 EAST GENESEE STREET	SYRACUSE	**NY**	13214	(315) 445-0820
WESTCHESTER JEWISH COMMUNITY SERVICES, INC. 475 TUCKAHOE ROAD	YONKERS	**NY**	10710	(914) 793-3565

WESTCHESTER JEWISH COMMUNITY SERVICES, INC.
20 SOUTH BROADWAY ... YONKERS **NY** 10701 (914) 423-4433

WESTCHESTER JEWISH COMMUNITY SERVICES, INC.
2000 MAPLE HILL STREET ... YORKTOWN HEIGHTS **NY** 10598 (914) 632-6433

JEWISH FAMILY SERVICE 73 EAST MILL STREET ... AKRON **OH** 44308 (216) 867-3388

JEWISH FAMILY SERVICE 750 WHITE POND DRIVE ... AKRON **OH** 44320 (216) 867-3388

JEWISH FAMILY SERVICE 1710 SECTION ROAD ... CINCINNATI **OH** 45237 (513) 351-3680

JEWISH FAMILY SERVICE ASSOCIATION 2060 SOUTH TAYLOR ROAD ... CLEVELAND **OH** 44118 (216) 371-2600

JEWISH FAMILY SERVICE 1175 COLLEGE AVENUE ... COLUMBUS **OH** 43209 (614) 231-1890

JEWISH FAMILY SERVICE-DIV. OF THE JEWISH FED. OF GTR. DAYTON
4501 DENLINGER ROAD ... DAYTON **OH** 45426 (513) 854-2944

JEWISH FAMILY SERVICE 2247 COLLINGWOOD BOULEVARD ... TOLEDO **OH** 43620 (419) 885-2561

JEWISH FAMILY SERVICE ASSOCIATION 28790 CHAGRIN BLVD ... WOODMERE **OH** 44122 (216) 292-3999

JEWISH FAMILY & CHILDREN'S SERVICE OF THE JEWISH FEDERATION
505 GYPSY LANE, PO BOX 449 ... YOUNGSTOWN **OH** 44501 (216) 746-3251

JEWISH SOCIAL SERVICES 57 DELAWARE AVENUE ... HAMILTON **ON** (416) 528-8579

JEWISH FAMILY & CHILD SERVICE 150 BEVERLY STREET ... TORONTO **ON** (416) 977-3811

JEWISH FAMILY & CHILD SERVICES 4600 BATHURST STREET ... WILLOWDALE **ON** M2R 3V2 (416) 638-7800

JEWISH FAMILY & CHILD SERVICE 316 MAISER BUILDING ... PORTLAND **OR** 97205 (503) 226-7079

JEWISH FAMILY & CHILD SERVICE 1130 S.W. MORRISON, 316 ... PORTLAND **OR** 97205 (503) 226-7090

JEWISH FAMILY SERVICE OF HARRISBURG 3332 N. 2ND STREET ... HARRISBURG **PA** 17110 (717) 233-1681

JEWISH FAMILY SERVICE OF PHILADELPHIA 1610 SPRUCE STREET ... PHILADELPHIA **PA** 19103 (215) 545-3290

JEWISH FAMILY & CHILDREN'S SERVICE OF PITTSBURGH
234 MCKEE PLACE ... PITTSBURGH **PA** 15213 (412) 683-4900

JEWISH FAMILY SERVICE OF LACKAWANNA COUNTY
615 JEFFERSON AVENUE ... SCRANTON **PA** 18510 (717) 344-1186

JEWISH WELFARE AGENCY 60 SOUTH RIVER STREET ... WILKES-BARRE **PA** 18701 (717) 782-4646

JEWISH FAMILY SERVICES OF THE BARON DE HIRSCH INSTITUTE
5151 COTE ST. CATHERINE ROAD ... MONTREAL **QU** H3W 1M6 (714) 731-3882

JEWISH FAMILY & CHILDREN'S SERVICE 229 WATERMAN ... PROVIDENCE **RI** 02906 (401) 331-1244

CHARLESTON JEWISH SOCIAL SERVICE RAOUL WALLENBERG ... CHARLESTON **SC** 29407 (803) 571-6565

JEWISH SERVICE AGENCY 6560 POPLAR AVENUE ... MEMPHIS **TN** 38183 (901) 767-5161

WEST END SYNAGOGUE-KHAL KODESH ADATH ISRAEL C
3500 WEST END AVENUE ... NASHVILLE **TN** 37205 (615) 269-4927

JEWISH FAMILY SERVICE 1416 COMMERCE, SUITE 614 ... DALLAS **TX** 75201 (214) 696-6400

JEWISH FAMILY SERVICE 11333 NORTH CENTRAL EXPY. 219 ... DALLAS **TX** 75231 (214) 369-8612

JEWISH FAMILY AND CHILDREN'S SERVICE 5831 NORTH MESA ... EL PASO **TX** 79912 (915) 581-3256

JEWISH FAMILY SERVICE 4131 SOUTH BRAESWOOD BOULEVARD ... HOUSTON **TX** 77025 (713) 667-9336

JEWISH FAMILY SERVICE, THE 8438 AHERN ... SAN ANTONIO **TX** 78216 (512) 349-5481

JEWISH FAMILY SERVICE OF TIDEWATER, INC. 7300 NEWPORT AVENUE ... NORFOLK **VA** 23505 (804) 489-3111

JEWISH FAMILY SERVICE 7027-3 CHOP ROAD ... RICHMOND **VA** 23230 (804) 282-5644

JEWISH FAMILY & CHILD SERVICE 1214 BOLSTON ... SEATTLE **WA** 98102 (206) 447-3240

JEWISH FAMILY & CHILDREN'S SERVICE 1110 HARVARD-#201 ... SEATTLE **WA** 98122 (206) 323-1421

JEWISH FAMILY & CHILDREN'S SERVICE
1360 NORTH PROSPECT AVENUE ... MILWAUKEE **WI** 53202 (414) 273-6515

JUDAICA & GIFT SHOPS

M.D.G. ISRAELI IMPORTS LTD. 51 WOODBROOK WAY S.W. ... CALGARY **AT** T2W 4E7

MIDBAR IMPORTS 7216 EAST 2ND ... SCOTTSDALE **AZ** 85251 (602) 949-0004

SHALOM BOOKS AND GIFTS GALORE 3712 OAK STREET ... VANCOUVER **BC** V6H 2M3 (604) 734-1106

JUDAICA UNLIMITED 2871 VIA MERTENS ... ANAHEIM **CA** 92806 (213) 541-1161

JUDAH L. MAGNES MEMORIAL MUSEUM-JEWISH MUSEUM OF THE WEST
2911 RUSSEL STREET ... BERKELEY **CA** 94705 (415) 849-2710

SHALOM HOUSE 19757 SHERMAN WAY ... CANOGA PARK **CA** 91303 (818) 882-7399

ARYE IMPORTS 6380 WILSHIRE BLVD ... LOS ANGELES **CA** 90048 (213) 661-3079

ATARA'S 450 N. FAIRFAX AVENUE ... LOS ANGELES **CA** 90036 (213) 655-3050

GIORA'S GIFTS 1756 SOUTH ROBERTSON BOULEVARD ... LOS ANGELES **CA** 90035 (213) 202-0024

HATAKLIT 436 NORTH FAIRFAX AVENUE ... LOS ANGELES **CA** 90036 (213) 655-1242

HERSKOVITZ BOOKS & GIFTS 428 NORTH FAIRFAX AVENUE ... LOS ANGELES **CA** 90036 (213) 852-9310

KOL-BO STAM-RABBI D. MISHULOVIN 152 1/2 N. LA BREA AVENUE ... LOS ANGELES **CA** 90036 (213) 933-8093

S. RIMMON & CO., INC. P.O. BOX 49456 ... LOS ANGELES **CA** 90049 (213) 476-4193

SKIRBALL MUSEUM GIFT GALLERY 3077 UNIVERSITY AVENUE ... LOS ANGELES **CA** 90007 (213) 749-3424

SOLOMON'S BOOKS & JEWELRY 447 NORTH FAIRFAX AVENUE ... LOS ANGELES **CA** 90036 (213) 653-9045

HOUSE OF DAVID 12826 VICTORY BOULEVARD ... NORTH HOLLYWOOD **CA** 91602 (818) 763-2070

EMBASSY IMPORTS 19365 BUSINESS CENTER DRIVE, UNIT 9 ... NORTHRIDGE **CA** 91324 (818) 349-5001

ALLCREST ENTERPRISES ... RESEDA **CA** 91335 (818) 345-5507

HELENE WILSON, SAN FRANCISCO WESTERN MERCHANDISE MART
1355 MARKET STREET ... SAN FRANCISCO **CA** 94103 (415) 552-2311

ISRAEL IMPORTS 5542 GEARY BOULEVARD ... SAN FRANCISCO **CA** 94121 (415) 752-5546

LIEBER'S BOOK STORE 3240 GEARY BOULEVARD ... SAN FRANCISCO **CA** 94115 (415) 387-3077

THE MERCAZ 2444 NORIEGA STREET ... SAN FRANCISCO **CA** 94122 (415) 665-9090

EYTAN'S JERUSALEM FAIR 14537 VENTURA BLVD ... SHERMAN OAKS **CA** 91403 (818) 995-0116

THE JEWISH DEVELOPMENT COMPANY 18331-C IRVINE BOULEVARD ... TUSTIN **CA** 92680 (714) 730-1419

YA-EL IMPORTS INC. 137 MAIN STREET ... DANBURY **CT** 06810 (203) 748-6062

ISRAEL GIFT SHOP & HEBREW BOOK SHOP
262 SOUTH WHITNEY STREET ... HARTFORD **CT** 06105 (203) 232-3984

YEHUDIT ISRAELI IMPORTS
33 CROSSROADS PLAZA, P.O. BOX 17091 ... WEST HARTFORD **CT** 06117 (203) 236-6069

GERSCHWALD PRODUCTS INC. 80 KING SPRING ROAD ... WINDSOR LOCKS **CT** 06096 (203) 627-5993

B'NAI B'RITH MUSEUM SHOP AND BOOKSTORE
1640 RHODE ISLAND AVENUE, N.W. ... WASHINGTON **DC** 20036 (202) 857-6583

THE SOURCE 110 LONGWOOD AVENUE ... ALTAMONTE SPRINGS **FL** 32701 (305) 830-1948

JUDAICA TREASURES 2325 SOUTH UNIVERSITY DRIVE ... DAVIE **FL** 33324 (305) 473-1444

CHERYL'S GIFTS & CARDS 242 HOLLYWOOD MALL ... HOLLYWOOD **FL** 33020 (305) 987-6059

THE CHOSEN GIFT 7146 S.W. 117TH AVENUE ... MIAMI **FL** 33183 (305) 596-3639

POTPOURRI OF GIFTS INC. 12356 S.W. 117 CT. ... MIAMI **FL** 33186 (305) 252-2094

AMERICAN ISRAELI RELIGIOUS STORE 1357 WASHINGTON AVENUE ... MIAMI BEACH **FL** 33139 (305) 531-7722

THE CAREFULLY CHOSEN GALLERY 826 LINCOLN ROAD ... MIAMI BEACH **FL** 33139 (305) 531-2627

JERUSALEM GALLERY 764 41ST STREET ... MIAMI BEACH **FL** 33140 (305) 538-3618

NATIONAL HEBREW-ISRAEL GIFT SHOP
1507 WASHINGTON AVENUE ... MIAMI BEACH **FL** 33139 (305) 532-2210

TORAH TREASURES - THE DEPARTMENT STORE OF JUDAICA
1309 WASHINGTON AVENUE ... MIAMI BEACH **FL** 33139 (305) 673-6095

JUDAICA ENTERPRISES 1074 N.E. 163RD STREET ... N. MIAMI BEACH **FL** 33162 (305) 945-5091

MASADA ISRAELI IMPORTS 8277 WEST SUNRISE BOULEVARD ... PLANTATION **FL** 33322 (305) 472-4736

HAMAKOR JUDAICA, INC. 6112 N. LINCOLN AVENUE ... CHICAGO **IL** 60659 (312) 463-6186

SCHWARTZ-ROSENBLUM, INC. 2906 WEST DEVON AVENUE ... CHICAGO **IL** 60659 (312) 338-3919

THE MUSEUM STORE, SPERTUS MUSEUM OF JUDAICA
618 SOUTH MICHIGAN AVENUE ... CHICAGO **IL** 60605 (312) 922-9012

NEW ENGLAND JUDAICA AND GIFT CENTER
154 CHESTNUTHILL AVENUE ... BRIGHTON **MA** 02135 (617) 783-9254

KOLBO 435 HARVARD STREET ... BROOKLINE **MA** 02146 (617) 731-8743

CHARLES GELLES AND SON ... CANTON **MA** (617) 828-1866

JANET KAPLAN 105 TACONIC AVENUE ... GREAT BARRINGTON **MA** 01230 (413) 528-1907

NORMAN GORDON 2 TAMARACK WAY ... SHARON **MA** 02067 (617) 784-5228

CAROL LEBEAUX 15 MONADNOCK DRIVE ... SHREWSBURY **MA** 01545 (617) 842-8730

CENTRAL HEBREW BOOK STORE 228 REISTERSTOWN ROAD ... BALTIMORE **MD** 21208 (301) 653-0550

PERN'S HEBREW BOOK & GIFT SHOP 7012 REISTERSTOWN ROAD ... BALTIMORE **MD** 21215 (301) 653-2450

ISRAELI ACCENTS 11641 BOILING BROOK PLACE ... ROCKVILLE **MD** 20852 (301) 231-7999

MAZEL TOV GIFTS 13837 DOWLAIS DRIVE ... ROCKVILLE **MD** 20853 (301) 460-0626

ISRAELI ACCENTS BY LESLIE KANNER IMPORTS
613 PERSHING DRIVE ... SILVER SPRING **MD** 20910 (301) 588-5481

KAR-BEN COPIES 11713 AUTH LANE ... SILVER SPRING **MD** 20902 (301) 984-8733

GOODMAN'S HEBREW BOOK & GIFT
2305 UNIVERSITY BOULEVARD WEST ... WHEATON **MD** 30902 (301) 933-1800

ORIGINAL PRINTS, ETCHINGS ETC....
C/O BERNSTEIN, 365 COLLEGE STREET ... LEWISTON **ME** 04240

BORENSTEIN'S BOOK & MUSIC STORE 25242 GREENFIELD ROAD ... OAK PARK **MI** 48237 (313) 967-3920

BROCHIN'S JEWISH BOOK & GIFT SHOP
4813 MINNETONKA BOULEVARD ... MINNEAPOLIS **MN** 55416 (612) 926-2011

OLSON'S CLOTHING STORE 617 WEST BROADWAY ... MINNEAPOLIS **MN** 55411 (612) 529-2222

MR. B'S ART & FRAMING 7919 SANTA FE ... KANSAS CITY **MO** 64106 (816) 649-3676

MIDWEST JEWISH BOOK & GIFT CENTER 8318 OLIVE STREET ROAD ... ST. LOUIS **MO** 63132 (314) 993-6300

GILAH INDIAN HILLS PLAZA, 8901 WEST DODGE ROAD ... OMAHA **NE** 68114 (402) 391-3500

THE NAGY CRAFTS COMPANY 19 MAPLE AVENUE, P.O. BOX 668 ... CLAREMONT **NH** 03743 (603) 542-2918

JUDAICA SPECIALTIES 45 BROAD STREET ... CARLSTADT **NJ** 07072 (201) 939-4522

AMERICAN JEWISH HOME... GIFTS BY MAIL 26 BROOKDALE DRIVE ... CHERRY HILL **NJ** 08034 (609) 667-8098

CNS JUDAICA 111 LAKEVIEW AVENUE ... CLIFTON **NJ** 07011 (201) 772-3141

TRIO ISRAELI GIFTS 246 RARITAN AVENUE ... HIGHLAND PARK **NJ** 08904 (201) 828-9555

A & C ISRAELI IMPORTS 1061 FAIRVIEW PLACE ... HILLSIDE **NJ** 07205 (201) 354-0885

SKY HEBREW BOOK STORE 1923 SPRINGFIELD AVENUE ... MAPLEWOOD **NJ** 07040 (201) 763-4244

EMANUEL MILSTEIN 29 WYNCREST ROAD ... MARLBORO **NJ** 07746 (201) 946-8604

MATANAH 50 SUSSEX AVENUE ... MORRISTOWN **NJ** 07960

JERUSALEM PRODUCTS CO./BAR/BAT MITZVAH SCROLLS
33 DEER RUN DRIVE ... RANDOLPH **NJ** 07869 (201) 895-3231

THE JUDAICA HOUSE, LIMITED 412 CEDAR LANE ... TEANECK **NJ** 07666 (201) 836-5264

ISRAEL CREATIONS 3404 BAILEY AVENUE ... BRONX **NY** 10463 (212) 796-9100

PELHAM PARKWAY HEBREW BOOKSTORE 781 LYDIG AVENUE ... BRONX **NY** 10462 (212) 892-2522

A GIFT OF GOLD 1753 53RD STREET ... BROOKLYN **NY** 11204 (718) 633-7842

A.J. WEISS 276 PENN STREET ... BROOKLYN **NY** 11211 (718) 387-4065

AVIV JUDAICA IMPORTS, LTD. 4726 NEW UTRECHT AVENUE ... BROOKLYN **NY** 11219 (718) 435-6201

BERGER GIFT SHOP 106 LEE AVENUE ... BROOKLYN **NY** 11211 (718) 387-2130

CHAIM O. EINHORN 114 LEE AVENUE ... BROOKLYN **NY** 11211 (718) 782-7782

COHEN'S RELIGIOUS ARTICLES 5302 16TH AVENUE ... BROOKLYN **NY** 11204 (718) 851-4877

CROWN RELIGIOUS ARTICLES 1105 57TH STREET ... BROOKLYN **NY** 11219 (718) 435-4327

DAVID SICHERMAN 68 LEE AVENUE ... BROOKLYN **NY** 11211 (718) 388-8215

EAST SIDE CHINA 5002 12TH AVENUE ... BROOKLYN **NY** 11219 (718) 633-8672

EDELWEISS CO.-GLASS STUDIO 1217 49 STREET ... BROOKLYN **NY** 11219 (718) 851-9687

EICHLER'S RELIGIOUS ARTICLES & GIFTS
1429 CONEY ISLAND AVENUE ... BROOKLYN **NY** 11230 (718) 258-7643

EICHLER'S RELIGIOUS ARTICLES AND GIFTS 5004 13 AVENUE ... BROOKLYN **NY** 11219 (718) 633-1505

ENGRAVING UNLIMITED 1533 CARROLL STREET ... BROOKLYN **NY** 11213 (718) 756-5307

FLOHR'S 4603 13TH AVENUE ... BROOKLYN **NY** 11219 (718) 854-0865

FLUSBERG'S HEBREW BOOK STORE 1276 47TH STREET ... BROOKLYN **NY** 11219 (718) 853-7302

FRANKEL'S HEBREW BOOK STORE 4904 16TH AVENUE ... BROOKLYN **NY** 11204 (718) 851-7766

SHOP - AT - HOME JUDAICA
Makes it easier to be Jewish
anywhere....
CALL OR WRITE FOR A FREE CATALOG
ZIONTALIS (212) 925-8558
48 ELDRIDGE ST. NYC 10002

HEBREW PUBLISHING COMPANY 100 WATER STREET ...... BROOKLYN **NY** 11201 (718) 858-6928
HERITAGE JUDAICA GIFTS UNLIMITED 4908 13TH AVENUE ...... BROOKLYN **NY** 11219 (718) 972-5252
KETER IMPORTERS & MFG. INC. 3624 12TH AVENUE ...... BROOKLYN **NY** 11218 (718) 436-6598
KOHN'S WATCH & GIFT CENTER 171 RODNEY STREET ...... BROOKLYN **NY** 11211 (718) 384-0920
MATANA GALLERY 4906 18 AVENUE ...... BROOKLYN **NY** 11204 (718) 851-4448
MATONO GIFT CENTER 190 LEE AVENUE ...... BROOKLYN **NY** 11211 (718) 625-9807
MERCAZ STAM 309 KINGSTON AVENUE ...... BROOKLYN **NY** 11213 (718) 773-1120
PRESENT PLACE, THE 4607 16TH AVENUE ...... BROOKLYN **NY** 11204 (718) 438-4785
R & W 1442 45TH STREET ...... BROOKLYN **NY** 11219 (718) 853-6570
RODAL'S C/O CROWN HEIGHTS JUDAICA, 329 KINGSTON AVENUE ...... BROOKLYN **NY** 11213 (718) 604-1020
ROYAL STERLING 5002 13TH AVENUE ...... BROOKLYN **NY** 11219 (718) 435-0230
SEFORIM WORLD 4401 16TH AVENUE ...... BROOKLYN **NY** 11204 (718) 633-5500
SHELBANK JEWISH GIFT SHOP 2121 BRAGG STREET ...... BROOKLYN **NY** 11229 (718) 891-8666
SHULSINGER JUDAICA 50 WASHINGTON STREET ...... BROOKLYN **NY** 11201 (718) 852-0042
SILVER TOWN 5219 13TH AVENUE ...... BROOKLYN **NY** 11219 (718) 851-5121
SISU RELIGIOUS ARTICLES 632 KINGS HIGHWAY ...... BROOKLYN **NY** 11223 (718) 645-8185
TORAH TECHNICS - "WHERE TORAH & TECHNOLOGY MEET"
1603 CARROLL STREET ...... BROOKLYN **NY** 11213 (718) 953-7028
TOV GIFT & DECORATING 5015 13TH AVENUE ...... BROOKLYN **NY** 11219 (718) 435-1451
TZIVOS HASHEM GIFT SHOP 332 KINGSTON AVENUE ...... BROOKLYN **NY** 11213 (718) 467-6630
THE WHAT NOT 4917 16TH AVENUE ...... BROOKLYN **NY** 11204 (718) 851-4156
THE CEDARHURST GLASSWORKS 96 SPRUCE STREET ...... CEDARHURST **NY** 11516 (516) 569-7101
ELBAUM JUDAICA 694 CENTRAL AVENUE ...... CEDARHURST **NY** 11516 (516) 569-4577
KI-TOV/HEBREW BOOK & GIFT CENTER 1847 MOTT AVENUE ...... FAR ROCKAWAY **NY** 11691 (718) 471-0963
NATHAN NEUMANN ISRAEL NOVELTIES 75-71 UTOPIA PARKWAY ...... FLUSHING **NY** 11366 (718) 969-7740
HOUSE OF ISRAEL 100-23 QUEENS BLVD ...... FOREST HILLS **NY** 11375 (718) 459-4556
ZION LION LTD. 212 WEST JERICHO TPKE ...... HUNTINGTON **NY** 11746 (516) 549-5155
GIFT WORLD & RELIGIOUS CENTER 72-20 MAIN STREET ...... KEW GARDENS HILLS **NY** 11367 (718) 261-0233
SAVANIA CERAMICS 42 OLIVE STREET ...... LAKE SUCCESS **NY** 11020 (516) 466-4495
SHALOM 363 E. PARK AVENUE ...... LONG BEACH **NY** 11561 (516) 889-0554
ATERES GIFT & TOY CENTER 4 RITA AVENUE ...... MONSEY **NY** 10952 (914) 425-9140
BIRNHACK, TZIREL ...... MONSEY **NY** 10952 (914) 356-5133
DAVID A FISHMAN 12 CAMEO RIDGE ROAD ...... MONSEY **NY** 10952 (914) 425-1653
SIMCHA SHOPPE, THE 18 HILLTOP LANE ...... MONSEY **NY** 10952 (914) 352-4543
THE ELEGANT TABLE 121 TRENOR DRIVE ...... NEW ROCHELLE **NY** 10804 (914) 632-5974
MAZEL TOV GIFT SHOP 4 EISENHOWER AVENUE ...... NEW SQUARE **NY** 10952 (914) 354-1183
ALEXANDER OLAND 120 WEST 44TH STREET ...... NEW YORK **NY** 10036 (212) 730-7903
BEN ARI ARTS 11 AVENUE A ...... NEW YORK **NY** 10009 (212) 677-4730
BLOCH PUBLISHING CO. 915 BROADWAY ...... NEW YORK **NY** 10010 (212) 673-7910
BLUMENTHAL, ZELIG 13 ESSEX STREET ...... NEW YORK **NY** 10002 (212) 267-8370

BONNIE SROLOVITZ DESIGNS - CONTEMPORARY JUDAICA
155 EAST 88TH STREET, SUITE GG ...... NEW YORK **NY** 10128 (212) 348-0879
CONCORDIA GIFTS 141 EAST 44TH STREET ...... NEW YORK **NY** 10017 (212) 972-1326
CRADLE GIFTS 27 WEST 38TH STREET ...... NEW YORK **NY** 10018 (212) 221-6466
EASTERN ORIGINS 510 SECOND AVENUE ...... NEW YORK **NY** 10016 (212) 684-6628
EASTERN SILVER COMPANY 54 CANAL STREET ...... NEW YORK **NY** 10002 (212) 226-5708
ELECTRO-SCULPTURE LTD. 168 FIFTH AVENUE ...... NEW YORK **NY** 10010 (212) 929-2999
FAR-N-WIDE 175 EAST 86TH STREET ...... NEW YORK **NY** 10028 (212) 369-0920
GENE SINGER ARTS 577 GRAND ST. ...... NEW YORK **NY** 10002 (212) 673-9669
GRAND STERLING COMPANY, INC. 345 GRAND STREET ...... NEW YORK **NY** 10002 (212) 674-6450
HA-ATIKOT-JUDAICA ANTIQUES 17 ESSEX STREET ...... NEW YORK **NY** 10002 (212) 254-8395
HAROLD RABINOWITZ DESIGNER SILVERSMITH
TOBE PASCHER WORKSHOP - JEWISH MUSEUM, 1109 FIFTH AVENUE .. NEW YORK **NY** 10028 (212) 534-7244
HEBREW RELIGIOUS ARTICLES 45 ESSEX STREET ...... NEW YORK **NY** 10002 (212) 674-1770
HOUSE OF DAVIAN 6 WEST 32ND STREET ...... NEW YORK **NY** 10001 (212) 868-8336
IMPORT PRODUCT SALES CO. 1140 BROADWAY ...... NEW YORK **NY** 10001 (212) 685-4115
IN THE SPIRIT 460 EAST 79TH STREET ...... NEW YORK **NY** 10021 (212) 662-6693
ISRAEL CREATIONS 350 FIFTH AVENUE ...... NEW YORK **NY** 10118 (212) 213-2200
ISRAEL GIFT & ERGO MANUFACTURING CO. 29 CANAL STREET ...... NEW YORK **NY** 10002 (212) 677-1670
ISRAEL GIFT CENTER 23 ESSEX STREET ...... NEW YORK **NY** 10002 (212) 475-6035
ISRAEL GIFTS 575 SEVENTH AVENUE ...... NEW YORK **NY** 10018 (212) 391-4928
ISRAEL RELIGIOUS ART, INC. 43 WEST 61ST STREET ...... NEW YORK **NY** 10023 (212) 582-1768
ISRAELI ART & CRAFT CENTER 485 MADISON AVENUE ...... NEW YORK **NY** 10022 (212) 757-2700
ISRAELI GIFTS 575 SEVENTH AVENUE ...... NEW YORK **NY** 10018 (212) 391-4928
ISRAELI HANDICRAFTS IMPORTING CO. 168 FIFTH AVENUE ...... NEW YORK **NY** 10010 (212) 929-2999
J. LEVINE CO. - LOWER EAST SIDE 58 ELDRIDGE STREET ...... NEW YORK **NY** 10002 (212) 966-4460
J. LEVINE CO. - MIDTOWN STORE 5 WEST 30TH STREET ...... NEW YORK **NY** 10001 (212) 695-6888
JACOB BEN-EZER LIMITED 440 PARK AVENUE SOUTH ...... NEW YORK **NY** 10016 (212) 532-7097
JERUSALEM GIFT CO. 48 CANAL STREET ...... NEW YORK **NY** 10002 (212) 966-0466
JEWISH MUSEUM BOOKSHOP 1109 FIFTH AVENUE ...... NEW YORK **NY** 10028 (212) 860-1866
JUDAICA EMPORIUM 3070 BROADWAY ...... NEW YORK **NY** 10027 (212) 864-6501
KIBBUTZ STORE, THE 856 LEXINGTON AVENUE ...... NEW YORK **NY** 10021 (212) 772-6644
LIEBERMAN'S JEWISH GIFT SHOPS 2404 BROADWAY ...... NEW YORK **NY** 10024 (212) 362-7846
MICHAEL STRAUSS SILVERSMITHS, LTD. 164 EAST 68TH STREET ...... NEW YORK **NY** 10021 (212) 744-8500
MIRIAM RELIGIOUS SUPPLIES MANUFACTURING CORPORATION
48 CANAL STREET ...... NEW YORK **NY** 10002 (212) 925-9272
ORIGINALS ONLY COMPANY 5 WHITE STREET ...... NEW YORK **NY** 10013 (212) 966-6464
SHALLER'S ISRAEL GIFT BOOK & RECORD CENTER
2555 AMSTERDAM AVENUE ...... NEW YORK **NY** 10033 (212) 928-2140
SHOVAL GALLERIE JUDAICA
915 BROADWAY, CORNER OF 21ST STREET ...... NEW YORK **NY** 10010 (212) 505-2580
STAVSKY'S BOOK STORE 147 ESSEX STREET ...... NEW YORK **NY** 10002 (212) 674-1289
SWANN GALLERIES 104 EAST 25TH STREET ...... NEW YORK **NY** 10010 (212) 254-4710
THE GIFT OF EDUCATION 10 ROCKEFELLER PLAZA ...... NEW YORK **NY** 10020 (212) 541-7568
WEST SIDE JUDAICA 2404 BROADWAY ...... NEW YORK **NY** 10024 (212) 362-7846
ZIONTALIS MANUFACTURING COMPANY 48 ELDRIDGE STREET ...... NEW YORK **NY** 10002 (212) 925-8558
ABBERBOCK RELIGIOUS SUPPLIES 3405 OCEANSIDE ROAD ...... OCEANSIDE **NY** 11572 (516) 764-2593
P. ITTELSON 9931 65TH ROAD ...... REGO PARK **NY** 11374 (718) 897-9503
ORGEL'S JEWISH RELIGIOUS ARTICLES & ISRAEL GIFTWARE
984 MONROE AVENUE ...... ROCHESTER **NY** 14609 (716) 271-2310
INSPIRATION GALLERY ...... SCARSDALE **NY** (914) 636-6776
CHAI & MAZEL GIFT SHOP 220 W. MAIN STREET ...... SMITHTOWN **NY** (516) 360-3331
GIFT GALLERY, THE 74 WEST ROUTE 59 ...... SPRING VALLEY **NY** 10977 (914) 356-4988
JUDAICA HOME & GIFT CENTER 26 S. CENTRAL AVENUE ...... SPRING VALLEY **NY** 10977 (914) 425-9399
MAZEL TOV 833 ENGLEWOOD AVENUE ...... TONAWANDA TWP **NY** 14150 (716) 838-5900
JUDAICA UNLIMITED, INC. 433 HEMPSTEAD AVENUE ...... WEST HEMPSTEAD **NY** 11552 (516) 486-3636
LONG ISLAND TEMPLE SUPPLIES 433 HEMPSTEAD AVENUE ...... WEST HEMPSTEAD **NY** 11552 (516) 486-3636
ENJOY-A-BOOK CLUB P.O. BOX 101 ...... WOODMERE **NY** 11598 (516) 569-0324
FRANK'S HEBREW BOOK STORE 1647 LEE ROAD ...... CLEVELAND **OH** 44118 (216) 321-6850
MEIR-LEVI STUDIOS 3055 ESSEX ROAD ...... CLEVELAND HEIGHTS **OH** 44118 (216) 321-6015
PAUL'S HEBREW BOOK STORE 13962 CEDAR ROAD ...... CLEVELAND **OH** 44114 (216) 321-7200
ISRAEL'S ... THE JUDAICA CENTRE 830 STEEPROCK DRIVE ...... DOWNSVIEW **ON** M3J 2X2 (416) 630-9261
ISRAEL'S ... THE JUDAICA CENTRE 243 WILMINGTON AVENUE ...... DOWNSVIEW **ON** M3H 5J9 (416) 636-0371
MASKIT 134 YORKVILLE AVENUE ...... TORONTO **ON** M5R 1C2 (416) 964-2444
MIRIAM'S GIFT GALLERY 3007 BATHURST STREET ...... TORONTO **ON** (416) 781-8261
NEGEV BOOK & GIFT STORE 3509 BATHURST STREET ...... TORONTO **ON** (416) 781-9356

Name	Address	City	State	Zip	Phone
ZUCKER JEWISH BOOKS & ART	3543 BATHURST STREET	TORONTO	ON		(416) 781-2133
PIOTRKOWSKI'S JUDAICA CENTER	289 MONTGOMERY AVENUE	BALA CYNWYD	PA	19004	(215) 664-1303
TREE OF LIFE, INC.	858 SUSSEX BLVD	BROOMALL	PA	19008	(215) 544-9900
ROSENBERG HEBREW BOOKS	409 OLD YORK ROAD	JENKINTOWN	PA	19046	(215) 884-1728
ANNA SCHACTER GIFTS	629 SOUTH FOURTH STREET	PHILADELPHIA	PA	19147	(215) 533-9250
ART ASSOCIATE	1526 NORTH AMERICAN STREET	PHILADELPHIA	PA	19122	(215) 235-5554
ERLICH ISRAEL IMPORTS	9 N. THIRD STREET	PHILADELPHIA	PA	19106	(215) 592-0404
FOR THE CHILDREN	8420 BUSTLETON AVE	PHILADELPHIA	PA	19152	(215) 745-2290
HEBREW BOOK & ART CENTER	6743 CASTOR AVENUE	PHILADELPHIA	PA	19149	(215) 742-2397
ISRAEL DESIGNS	45 NORTH SECOND STREET	PHILADELPHIA	PA	19106	(215) 925-1600
ISRAEL GIFTWARE DESIGNS	601 SPRING GARDEN STREET	PHILADELPHIA	PA	19123	(215) 627-6277
ROSENBERG HEBREW BOOKS & GIFTS	6743 CASTOR AVENUE	PHILADELPHIA	PA	19149	(215) 742-2397
DESIGNS BY BRENDA	1110 GROUSE DRIVE	PITTSBURGH	PA	15243	(412) 276-6602
ISAAC SKULL CAP COMPANY	3553 ST. LAWRENCE	MONTREAL	QU		(514) 274-8403
JUDAICA SALES REG'D	P.O. BOX 276, STATION YOUVILLE	MONTREAL	QU	H2P 2V5	(514) 687-0632
RODAL'S HEBREW BOOK STORE & GIFT SHOP	4689 VAN HORNE	MONTREAL	QU	H3W 1H8	(514) 733-1876
VICTORIA GIFT SHOP & BOOK CENTER	5865 VICTORIA AVENUE	MONTREAL	QU		(514) 738-1414
ELIJAH'S CUP	12306 MEADOW LAKE DRIVE	HOUSTON	TX	77077	(713) 497-2243
THE SHEPHERD'S FIELD	5141 ANTIONE DRIVE	HOUSTON	TX	77092	(713) 688-8830
THE SOURCE	9760 HILLCROFT	HOUSTON	TX	77096	(713) 721-4624
CREATIVE KNIT-WORKS	1477 EAST CARRIE DRIVE	FRUIT HEIGHTS	UT	84037	(801) 544-4404
EZRA BESSAROTH GIFTS	4217 SOUTH BRANDON	SEATTLE	WA	98102	(206) 722-5500
JUDAICA SHOP OF TEMPLE DE HIRSCH SINAI	1511 EAST PIKE STREET	SEATTLE	WA	98103	(206) 323-8488
GERSCHWALD PRODUCTS INC.	3000 WOLFF STREET	RACINE	WI	53404	(414) 632-2264

JUDAICA APPRAISALS

Name	Address	City	State	Zip	Phone
APPRAISAL CONSULTANTS	15 HIGHVIEW ROAD	MONSEY	NY	10952	(914) 352-9170
BELLE ROSENBAUM, A.S.A., C.F.A.A., I.S.A.	15 HIGHVIEW ROAD	MONSEY	NY	10952	(914) 352-9170
ERIC L. LOEB	50 OVERLOOK TERRACE	NEW YORK	NY	10033	(212) 568-4236

KADDISH

Name	Address	City	State	Zip	Phone
LUBAVITCH YOUTH ORGANIZATION	770 EASTERN PARKWAY	BROOKLYN	NY	11213	(718) 778-4270
KOLEL AMERICA/AMERICAN RABBI MEIR BAAL HANESS CHARITY	132 NASSAU STREET	NEW YORK	NY	10038	(212) 871-4111

KASHRUT SUPERVISION & INFORMATION

Name	Address	City	State	Zip	Phone
VANCOUVER KASHRUS	3476 OAK STREET	VANCOUVER	BC	V6H 2L8	(604) 736-7607
KOSHER OVERSEERS ASSOCIATION OF AMERICA, INC.	DR. HAROLD SCHARFMAN, P.O. BOX 1321	BEVERLY HILLS	CA	90213	(213) 870-0111
RABBINICAL COUNCIL OF CALIFORNIA	244-13 HENDRICK AVENUE	LOMITA	CA	90717	(213) 936-1022
IGUD HAKASHRUT	360 NORTH CURSON AVENUE	LOS ANGELES	CA	90036	(213) 935-2499
KEHILA DE LOS ANGELES	186 NORTH CITRUS	LOS ANGELES	CA	90030	(213) 935-8383
KOSHER HOTLINE		SAN JOSE	CA		(408) 243-6640
ORTHODOX RABBINICAL COUNCIL OF NORTHERN CALIFORNIA	1851 NORIEGA STREET	SAN FRANCISCO	CA	94122	(415) 564-5665
DENVER ASSOCIATION OF INTENSIVE TORAH EDUCATION	1560 WINONA COURT	DENVER	CO	80204	(303) 371-7752
CHICAGO RABBINICAL COUNCIL	3525 W. PETERSON AVE., SUITE 45	CHICAGO	IL	60659	(312) 588-1600
VAAD HORABONIM (VAAD HAKASHRUS) OF MASSACHUSETTS	177 TREMONT AVENUE	BOSTON	MA	02111	(617) 426-6268
KASHRUTH SUPERVISION SERVICE	7111 PARK HEIGHTS AVENUE	BALTIMORE	MD	21215	
VAAD HAKASHRUS OF BALTIMORE	7504 SEVEN MILE LANE	BALTIMORE	MD	21208	(301) 484-4110
VAAD HORABONIM OF GREATER DETROIT AND MERKAZ	17071 WEST TEN MILE ROAD	SOUTHFIELD	MI	48075	(313) 559-5005
METROPOLITAN KASHRUTH COUNCIL OF MICHIGAN	6533 POST OAK DRIVE,	WEST BLOOMFIELD	MI	48033	(313) 855-4324
KASHRUTH INSPECTION SERVICE OF THE VAAD HOEIR OF ST. LOUIS	4 MILLSTONE CAMPUS,	ST. LOUIS	MO	63146	(314) 569-2770
THE BOARD OF RABBIS,	143 BAY STREET, POB 214,	JERSEY CITY	NJ	07303	(201) 333-3700
KOF-K KOSHER SUPERVISION	1444 QUEEN ANNE ROAD	TEANECK	NJ	07666	(201) 837-0500
VAAD HAKASHRUTH OF THE CAPITAL DISTRICT	66 HACKETT BOULEVARD	ALBANY	NY	12209	
AGUDATH VAAD HAKASHRUTH	750 REMSEN AVENUE	BROOKLYN	NY	11236	(718) 629-1802
CENTRAL RABBINICAL CONGRESS (HISACHDUS HORABONIM)	85 DIVISION AVENUE	BROOKLYN	NY	11211	(718) 384-6765
CONGREGATION BETH MEDRASH HAGODOL	1350 56TH STREET,	BROOKLYN	NY	11219	
KASHRUS MAGAZINE	P.O. BOX 96	BROOKLYN	NY	11204	(718) 998-3201
KASHRUT CENTER	1649 PRESIDENT STREET	BROOKLYN	NY	11213	(718) 774-3025
LUBAVITCH HEADQUARTERS	770 EASTERN PARKWAY	BROOKLYN	NY	11213	(718) 493-9250
NATIONAL KASHRUS DATA BASE	1204 AVENUE U P.O.BOX 1179	BROOKLYN	NY	11229	(718) 376-1470
ORGANIZED KASHRUS LABORATORIES	POB 218	BROOKLYN	NY	11204	(718) 851-6428
SEPHARDIC RABBINICAL COUNCIL OF AMERICA SHAARE ZION CONGREGATION	2030 OCEAN PARKWAY	BROOKLYN	NY	11223	(718) 376-0009
THE JEWISH HOMEMAKER	PO BOX 324	BROOKLYN	NY	11204	
VAAD HAKASHRUS LE'MHADRIN OF KHAL BES MEDRASH HAGADOL OF BORO PARK	P.O. BOX 48 (BLYTHE STATION)	BROOKLYN	NY	11219	(718) 854-8047
VAAD HARABBONIM OF FLATBUSH	1618 CONEY ISLAND AVENUE	BROOKLYN	NY	11230	(718) 951-8585
QUALITY KASHRUS LABORATORY	92-15 69TH AVENUE, SUITE 205	FLUSHING	NY	11375	(718) 849-7006
RABBI SOLOMON B. SHAPIRO	73-09 136TH STREET	FLUSHING	NY	11367	(718) 263-1574
VAAD HARABONIM OF QUEENS	90-45 MYRTLE AVENUE	GLENDALE	NY	11385	(718) 847-9206
THE "TABLET K"	160-08 91ST STREET	HOWARD BEACH	NY	11414	(718) 835-3595
NATIONAL KASHRUTH	1 ROUTE 306	MONSEY	NY	10952	(914) 352-4448
UNITED KOSHER SUPERVISION	POB 122	MONSEY	NY	10952	(914) 352-0630
BETH DIN OF KHAL ADATH JESHURUN (BREUER'S)	85-93 BENNETT AVENUE	NEW YORK	NY	10033	(212) 923-3582
RABBI HARRY COHEN	165 WEST 91ST STREET	NEW YORK	NY	10024	
KASHRUTH ALLIANCE OF THE RABBINICAL ALLIANCE OF AMERICA/ IGUD HORABONIM	ROOM 805, 156 FIFTH AVENUE	NEW YORK	NY	10010	(212) 675-5803
KASHRUTH SUPERVISOR'S UNION LOCAL 621	37 UNION SQUARE	NEW YORK	NY	10003	(212) 691-9494
KOSHER FOOD PRICE WATCH, INC.	P.O. BOX 1738	NEW YORK	NY	10185	(212) 713-8463
KOSHER OVERSEERS ASSOCIATION OF AMERICA, INC.	565 FIFTH AVENUE	NEW YORK	NY	10017	(212) 697-7400
RABBI DR. JOSEPH RALBAG	225 WEST 86TH STREET	NEW YORK	NY	10024	(212) 877-1823
UNION OF ORTHODOX JEWISH CONGREGATIONS OF AMERICA	45 WEST 36TH STREET	NEW YORK	NY	10018	(212) 563-4000
THE SYRACUSE VAAD HA'IR	4905 ONONDAGA ROAD	SYRACUSE	NY	13215	(315) 492-6000
VAAD HAKASHRUS OF BUFFALO	76 N. MAPLEMERE	WILLIAMSVILLE	NY	14221	(716) 634-3990
BNAI EMUNAH KASHRUT COMMITTEE	1719 SOUTH OWASSO AVENUE	TULSA	OK	74120	(918) 584-2156
CANADIAN JEWISH CONGRESS OF TORONTO	4600 BATHURST STREET	DOWNSVIEW	ON	M2R 3V2	(416) 635-9550
KO KOSHER SERVICE	5871 DREXEL ROAD	PHILADELPHIA	PA	19131	(215) 879-1100
ORTHODOX ASSOCIATION FOR THE OBSERVANCE OF KASHRUTH	11006 AUDUBON AVENUE	PHILADELPHIA	PA	19116	(215) 698-1180
PENNSYLVANIA KASHRUS ASSOCIATION	7718 SUMMERDALE AVENUE	PHILADELPHIA	PA	19111	(215) 725-3773
RABBI DR. BERNARD POUPKO	2523 BEACHWOOD BLVD	PITTSBURGH	PA	15217	(412) 421-2442
VAAD HAKASHRUS OF DELAWARE VALLEY	400 DAVID DRIVE	TREVOSE	PA	19047	(215) 357-7130
MONTREAL VAAD HAIR	5491 VICTORY AVENUE	MONTREAL	QU	H3W 2PN	(514) 739-6363
DALLAS KASHRUTH COUNCIL	POB 30511	DALLAS	TX	75230	(214) 387-4778
RABBI SAUL A. PERL	POB 30662	DALLAS	TX	75230	
MANCHESTER BETH DIN	435 CHEETHAM HILL ROAD	MANCHESTER 8	GB		(061) 740-9711
KASHRUS DEPARTMENT OF THE BETH DIN OF JOHANNESBURG OF THE FEDERATION OF SYNAGOGUES OF S AFRICA	24 RALEIGH ST., YEOVILLE 2198	JOHANNESBURG	SA		648-9136

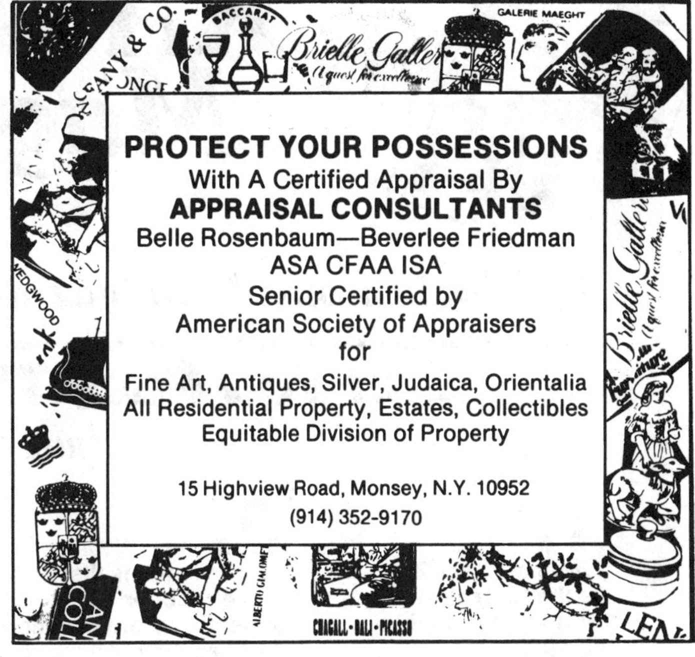

LECTURE BUREAUS

AMERICAN ISRAEL PUBLIC AFFAIRS COMMITTEE 444 NORTH CAPITAL ... WASHINGTON **DC** 20001 (202) 638-2256

B'NAI B'RITH LECTURE BUREAU 1640 RHODE ISLAND AVENUE N.W. ... WASHINGTON **DC** 20036 (213) 857-6600

B'NAI B'RITH LECTURE BUREAU - TRAVELING EXHIBIT SERVICE 1640 RHODE ISLAND AVENUE, N.W. ... WASHINGTON **DC** 20036 (202) 857-6600

TORAH TECHNICS - "WHERE TORAH & TECHNOLOGY MEET" 1603 CARROLL STREET ... BROOKLYN **NY** 11213 (718) 953-7028

ASSOCIATION OF JEWISH CLERGYMEN P.O. BOX 317 ... MONSEY **NY** 10952 (914) 352-0630

AMERICAN PROFESSORS FOR PEACE IN THE MIDDLE EAST 330 SEVENTH AVENUE ... NEW YORK **NY** 10017 (212) 563-2980

ANTI-DEFAMATION LEAGUE OF B'NAI B'RITH-LECTURE BUREAU 823 UN PLAZA ... NEW YORK **NY** 10017 (212) 490-2525

CONSULATE GENERAL OF ISRAEL SPEAKERS BUREAU 800 2ND AVENUE ... NEW YORK **NY** 10017 (212) 697-5500

ISRA-ART PRODUCTIONS, INC 157 WEST 57TH STREET ... NEW YORK **NY** 10022 (212) 724-1500

JEWISH LECTURE BUREAU (JLB) OF NORTH AMERICA G.P.O. BOX 520 ... NEW YORK **NY** 10116 (718) 268-2369

JWB LECTURE BUREAU, THE NATIONAL JEWISH WELFARE BOARD 15 EAST 26TH STREET ... NEW YORK **NY** 10010 (212) 532-4949

STATE OF ISRAEL BOND ORGANIZATION 215 PARK AVENUE SOUTH ... NEW YORK **NY** 10003 (212) 677-9650

UNITED JEWISH APPEAL SPEAKERS BUREAU 1290 6TH AVE ... NEW YORK **NY** 10019 (212) 757-1500

UNIVERSITY SERVICE DEPARTMENT 515 PARK AVENUE ... NEW YORK **NY** 10022 (212) 751-6070

ZIONIST ACADEMIC COUNCIL 330 SEVENTH AVE., SUITE 606 ... NEW YORK **NY** 10001 (212) 563-2980

LEGAL SERVICES

BET TZEDEK LEGAL SERVICES 7966 BEVERLY BOULEVARD, SUITE 210 ... LOS ANGELES **CA** 90048 (213) 658-8930

LEGAL AID SOCIETY OF LOS ANGELES 1550 WEST 8TH STREET ... LOS ANGELES **CA** 90015 (213) 487-3320

INTERNATIONAL ASSN. OF JEWISH LAWYERS AND JURISTS 600 NEW JERSEY AVENUE, N.W. ... WASHINGTON **DC** 20001 (202) 624-8083

THE ARK 3509 W. LAWRENCE AVENUE ... CHICAGO **IL** 60645 (312) 463-4545

THE ARK 2341 W. DEVON ... CHICAGO **IL** 60659 (312) 973-1000

COMMUNITY ACTION FOR LEGAL SERVICES 606 BRIGHTON BEACH ... BROOKLYN **NY** 11235 (718) 934-2989

AMERICAN JEWISH COMMITTEE 165 EAST 56TH STREET ... NEW YORK **NY** 10022 (212) 751-4000

ANTI-DEFAMATION LEAGUE OF B'NAI B'RITH 823 UNITED NATIONS PLAZA ... NEW YORK **NY** 10017 (212) 490-2525

COLPA 450 SEVENTH AVENUE ... NEW YORK **NY** 10001 (212) 563-0100

COMMISSION ON LAW & SOCIAL ACTION OF THE AM. JEWISH CONGRESS 15 EAST 84TH STREET ... NEW YORK **NY** 10028 (212) 879-4500

NATIONAL JEWISH COMMISSION ON LAW & PUBLIC AFFAIRS (COLPA) 450 SEVENTH AVENUE ... NEW YORK **NY** 10001 (212) 563-0100

LIBRARIES

I.L. PERETZ YIDDISH LIBRARY 6184 ASH STREET ... VANCOUVER **BC** V5Z 3G9 (604) 228-0044

JEWISH RESOURCE CENTRE 950 WEST 41ST AVENUE ... VANCOUVER **BC** V57 2N7 (604) 266-9111

JEWISH COMMUNITY LIBRARY 601 14TH AVENUE ... SAN FRANCISCO **CA** 94118 (415) 752-8288

ASHER LIBRARY OF SPERTUS COLLEGE 618 SOUTH MICHIGAN AVENUE ... CHICAGO **IL** 60605 (312) 922-9012

JEWISH PUBLIC LIBRARY 1725 MAIN STREET ... WINNIPEG **MB** R2V 1Z4 (204) 338-4048

SAUL BRODSKY COMMUNITY LIBRARY 12 MILLSTONE CAMPUS DRIVE ... ST. LOUIS **MO** 63146 (314) 432-0020

ASSOCIATION OF JEWISH LIBRARIES, C/O NATIONAL FOUNDATION FOR JEWISH CULTURE, 122 EAST 42ND STREET, ROOM 1512 ... NEW YORK **NY** 10168

NEW YORK PUBLIC LIBRARY, JEWISH DIVISION ROOM 84, FIFTH AVENUE AT 42ND STREET ... NEW YORK **NY** 10018 (212) 930-0601

JEWISH PUBLIC LIBRARY OF TORONTO 4600 BATHURST STREET ... WILLOWDALE **ON** M2R 3V2 (416) 635-2996

JEWISH PUBLIC LIBRARY OF MONTREAL 5151 COTE ST. CATHERINE ROAD ... MONTREAL **QU** H3W 1M6 (514) 735-6535

LOST & FOUND

LOST ... (718) 438-0592

FOUND ... (718) 436-4999

LUBAVITCH CENTERS / CHABAD

CHABAD LUBAVITCH 3348 STONERIDGE LANE ... MOUNTAINBROOK **AL** 35243 (205) 967-4417

LUBAVITCH 92 HOTHAM STREET, EAST S. KILDA 3183 ... MELBOURNE **AU**

YESHIVA GEDOLAH 67 ALEXANDRA STREET, EAST S. KILDA 3183 ... MELBOURNE **AU**

YESHIVA GEDOLAH 67A PENKIUL STREET, BONDI 2026 ... SYDNEY **AU**

CHABAD LUBAVITCH 1536 EAST MARYLAND ... PHOENIX **AZ** 85014 (602) 274-5377

LUBAVITCH CENTER 915 W. 14TH STREET ... TEMPE **AZ** 85281 (602) 966-4649

CHABAD LUBAVITCH 1301 EAST ELM ... TUCSON **AZ** 85719 (602) 881-7955

CHABAD LUBAVITCH 6200 N. ORACLE ROAD, #213 ... TUCSON **AZ** 85704 (602) 297-8150

CHABAD HOUSE 497 WEST 39TH STREET ... VANCOUVER **BC** (604) 324-2406

CHABAD HOUSE 5750 OAK STREET ... VANCOUVER **BC** V6M 2V7 (604) 266-1313

CHABAD OF ANAHEIM 518 S. BROOKHURST ST ... ANAHEIM **CA** 92804 (714) 520-0770

CHABAD HOUSE 2340 PIEDMONT AVENUE ... BERKELEY **CA** 94704 (415) 845-7791

CHABAD HOUSE 409 NORTH FOOTHILL ... BEVERLY HILLS **CA** 90210 (213) 859-3948

CHABAD OF THE VALLEY 4915 HAYVENHURST AVENUE ... ENCINO **CA** 91436 (818) 784-9985

CHABAD OF IRVINE 4872 ROYCE ROAD ... IRVINE **CA** 92715 (714) 786-5000

CHABAD HOUSE 8950 VILLA LA JOLLA DRIVE ... LA JOLLA **CA** 92037 (619) 455-1670

CHABAD HOUSE 24412 NARBONNE AVENUE ... LOMITA **CA** 90717 (213) 326-8234

CONGREGATION LUBAVITCH 3981 ATLANTIC AVENUE ... LONG BEACH **CA** 91807 (213) 434-6338

CHABAD HOUSE 741 GAYLEY AVENUE ... LOS ANGELES **CA** 90024 (213) 208-7511

CHABAD HOUSE, MID-CITY 420 NORTH FAIRFAX ... LOS ANGELES **CA** 90036 (213) 655-4739

CHABAD HOUSE, WEST COAST HEADQUARTERS 741 GAYLEY AVENUE ... LOS ANGELES **CA** 90024 (213) 272-7113

Name / Address	City	State	Zip	Phone
CONGREGATION LUBAVITCH 9017 W. PICO BLVD	LOS ANGELES	CA	90035	(213) 208-7511
LUBAVITCH 101 N. EDINBURG AVENUE	LOS ANGELES	CA	90048	(213) 931-0913
OHR ELCHONON 7215 WARING AVENUE	LOS ANGELES	CA	90046	(213) 937-3763
RUSSIAN CENTER 221 S. LA BREA AVENUE	LOS ANGELES	CA	90036	(213) 938-1837
TREATMENT CENTER 1952 ROBERTSON BLVD	LOS ANGELES	CA	90034	(213) 204-3196
CHABAD HOUSE 425 AVENIDA ORTEGA	PALM SPRINGS	CA	92262	(619) 325-0774
CHABAD HOUSE 2850 COWPER #15	PALO ALTO	CA	94306	(415) 322-4700
CHABAD HOUSE 6115 MONTEZUMA ROAD	SAN DIEGO	CA	92115	(619) 265-7700
CHABAD HOUSE 2415 VAN NESS AVENUE, #203	SAN FRANCISCO	CA	94109	(415) 928-0165
CHABAD HOUSE 4141 STATE STREET #F1	SANTA BARBARA	CA	93110	(805) 683-1544
CHABAD BAY AREA 1428 17TH STREET	SANTA MONICA	CA	90401	(213) 829-5620
CHABAD HOUSE 1247 LINCOLN BLVD	SANTA MONICA	CA	90403	(213) 395-4470
CHABAD OF LAGUNA 21452 WESLEY	SO. LAGUNA	CA	92677	(714) 786-5000
BLAUNER YOUTH CENTER 18211 BURBANK BLVD	TARZANA	CA	92356	(818) 881-2352
CHABAD HOUSE 24248 CRENSHAW	TORRANCE	CA	90506	(805) 326-8234
CHABAD HOUSE 13079 CHANDLER BOULEVARD	VAN NUYS	CA	91401	(818) 989-9539
CHABAD OF CONEJO 741 LAKEFIELD ROAD #E	WESTLAKE VILLAGE	CA	91361	(805) 497-9635
HEBREW ACADEMY 14401 WILLOW LANE	WESTMINSTER	CA	92683	(714) 895-2015
CHABAD HOUSE 85 FOREST STREET	DENVER	CO	80220	(303) 329-0211
HEBREW ACADEMY 111 ALDEN AVENUE	NEW HAVEN	CT	06511	(203) 387-8468
LUBAVITCH YOUTH ORGANIZATION 152 GOFFE TERRACE	NEW HAVEN	CT	06511	(203) 865-3649
LUBAVITCH 17 MORTON	NEW LONDON	CT	06320	(203) 444-1005
LUBAVITCH YESHIVAH 261 DERBY AVENUE	ORANGE	CT	06477	(203) 795-5261
CHABAD HOUSE 798 FARMINGTON AVENUE	WEST HARTFORD	CT	06119	(203) 233-5912
CHABAD HOUSE 1540 ALBENGA AVENUE	CORAL GABLES	FL	33146	(305) 661-7642
CHABAD LUBAVITCH 9791 SAMPLE ROAD	CORAL SPRINGS	FL	33065	(305) 344-4855
CONGREGATION LEVI YITZCHOK 1504 WILEY	HOLLYWOOD	FL	33020	(305) 923-1707
CHABAD SYNAGOGUE 13830 S.W. 73RD STREET	MIAMI	FL	33183	
CHABAD HOUSE 1401 ALTON ROAD	MIAMI BEACH	FL	33139	(305) 672-8947
CHABAD HOUSE 1835 MICHIGAN AVENUE	MIAMI BEACH	FL	33139	(305) 532-8081
MERKOS 1140 ALTON ROAD	MIAMI BEACH	FL	33139	(305) 673-5664
CHABAD OF NORTH DADE 2590 N.E. 202ND STREET	NORTH MIAMI BEACH	FL	33180	(305) 932-7770
CHABAD OF INVERRARY 7770 NORTHWEST 44TH STREET	SUNRISE	FL	33321	(305) 748-1777
CHABAD HOUSE 3645 COLLEGE PARK CIRCLE	TAMPA	FL	33612	(813) 971-6768
CHABAD HOUSE 13104 N. 50TH STREET	TAMPA	FL	33617	(813) 985-7926
CHABAD HOUSE CTR217, UC BOX 2463, UNIVERSITY OF SOUTH FLORIDA	TAMPA	FL	33617	(813) 971-6768
CHABAD HOUSE 2923 UNIVERSITY AVENUE	DES MOINES	IA	50311	(515) 277-0770
CHABAD HOUSE 2014 ORRINGTON	EVANSTON	IL	60201	(312) 869-8060
NORTH SUBURBAN CHABAD 1871 SHEAHAN COURT	HIGHLAND PARK	IL	60035	(312) 433-1567
CHABAD OF SKOKIE 3912 CHURCH	SKOKIE	IL	60076	(312) 679-1649
CHABAD LUBAVITCH 816 WEST 64TH STREET	INDIANAPOLIS	IN	46260	(317) 251-5573
CHABAD HOUSE 7037 FRERET STREET	NEW ORLEANS	LA	70118	(504) 866-5164
CHABAD HOUSE 30 N. HADLEY ROAD	AMHERST	MA	01002	(413) 253-9040
CHABAD HOUSE OF GREATER BOSTON 41 COMMONWEALTH AVENUE	BOSTON	MA	02116	(617) 254-0352
CHABAD HOUSE 491 COMMONWEALTH AVENUE	BOSTON	MA	02215	(617) 424-1190
LUBAVITCH YOUTH ORGANIZATION 42 KIRKWOOD ROAD	BRIGHTON	MA	02135	(617) 787-2667
LUBAVITCH YESHIVA 9 PRESCOTT STREET	BROOKLINE	MA	02146	(617) 731-5330
CHABAD HOUSE 74 JOSEPH ROAD	FRAMINGHAM	MA	01701	(617) 877-8888
LUBAVITCH YOUTH ORGANIZATION 74 JOSEPH ROAD	FRAMINGHAM	MA	01761	(617) 877-5313
CHABAD HOUSE 1148 CONVERSE STREET	LONG MEADOW	MA	01106	(413) 253-9040
SHALOM HOUSE 68 SMITH ROAD	MILTON	MA	02186	(617) 333-0477
CONGREGATION LUBAVITCH 100 WOODCLIFF	SOUTH BROOKLINE	MA	02167	(617) 469-9007
LUBAVITCH 15 ELWOOD DRIVE	SPRINGFIELD	MA	01108	(413) 567-8665
LUBAVITCH YOUTH ORGANIZATION 15 ELWOOD DRIVE	SPRINGFIELD	MA	01108	(413) 737-7998
LUBAVITCH YOUTH ORGANIZATION 24 CRESWELL	WORCESTER	MA	01602	(617) 752-5791
CHABAD LUBAVITCH 532 INKSTER BOULEVARD	WINNIPEG	MB	R2W 0K9	(204) 586-1867
LUBAVITCH 6711 WELLS PARKWAY	HYATTSVILLE	MD	20872	(301) 422-6200
CHABAD HOUSE 311 WEST MONTGOMERY AVENYE	ROCKVILLE	MD	20850	(301) 340-6858
CHABAD HOUSE 715 HILL STREET	ANN ARBOR	MI	48104	(313) 995-3276
CHABAD HOUSE 32276 TAREYTON	FARMINGTON HILLS	MI	48018	(313) 626-3194
CHABAD HOUSE 1549 MICHIGAN N.E.	GRAND RAPIDS	MI	49503	(616) 458-6575
CHABAD LUBAVITCH 14000 WEST NINE MILE ROAD	OAK PARK	MI	48237	(313) 548-2666
LUBAVITCH 7189 COTTONWOOD KNOLL	WEST BLOOMFIELD	MI	48033	
MERKOS L'INYONEI CHINUCH LUBAVITCH 15 MONTCALM CT.	ST. PAUL	MN	55116	(612) 698-3858
CHABAD HOUSE 8901 HOLMES STREET	KANSAS CITY	MO	64131	(816) 333-7117
CHABAD LUBAVITCH 921 GAY AVENUE	ST. LOUIS	MO	63130	(314) 863-3516
LUBAVITCH OF NORTH CAROLINA 6500 NEWHALL ROAD	CHARLOTTE	NC	28226	(704) 366-3984
CHABAD HOUSE 2801 PACIFIC AVENUE	ATLANTIC CITY	NJ	08410	(609) 345-6102
LUBAVITCH 410 NORTH 8TH AVENUE	EDISON	NJ	08817	(201) 572-3523
FRIENDS OF LUBAVITCH 409 GRAND AVENUE, #7	ENGLEWOOD	NJ	07631	(201) 568-9423
LUBAVITCH 12 BEVERLY ROAD	LIVINGSTON	NJ	07039	(201) 994-0262
LUBAVITCH 12 WELLESLEY ROAD	MAPLEWOOD	NJ	07040	(201) 762-6628
LUBAVITCH 16 IRONDALE ROAD	MORRIS PLAINS	NJ	07950	(201) 538-6321
LUBAVITCH STUDENTS ORGANIZATION 226 SUSSEX AVENUE	MORRISTOWN	NJ	07960	(201) 540-0877
RABBINICAL COLLEGE 226 SUSSEX AVENUE	MORRISTOWN	NJ	07960	(201) 267-9404
CHABAD HOUSE 8 SICARD STREET	NEW BRUNSWICK	NJ	08901	(201) 828-7374
LUBAVITCH 6 MANOR ROAD	PATERSON	NJ	07514	(201) 271-2250
LUBAVITCH 2202 SUNSET AVENUE	WANAMASSA	NJ	07712	(201) 774-5921
CHABAD HOUSE 1801 SIGMI CHI	ALBUQUERQUE	NM	87106	(505) 242-2231
CHABAD HOUSE 122 SOUTH MAIN AVENUE	ALBANY	NY	12208	(518) 482-5781
LUBAVITCH WORLD HDQ. MERKOS L'INYANEI CHINUCH MACHNE ISRAEL 770 EASTERN PARKWAY	BROOKLYN	NY	11213	(718) 493-9250
LUBAVITCH WORLD HEADQUARTERS 770 EASTERN PARKWAY	BROOKLYN	NY	11213	(718) 774-4000
SHABBOS CANDLE CAMPAIGN 603 LEFFERTS AVENUE	BROOKLYN	NY	11203	(718) 774-2060
CHABAD HOUSE 3292 MAIN STREET	BUFFALO	NY	14214	(716) 833-8334
CHABAD HOUSE 74 HAUPPAUGE ROAD	COMMACK	NY	11725	(516) 462-6640
CHABAD HOUSE 150-02 78TH ROAD	FLUSHING	NY	11385	(718) 778-0587
CHABAD HOUSE 2501 NORTH FOREST ROAD	GETZVILLE	NY	14068	(716) 688-1642
CHABAD HOUSE 4 PHYLISS TERRACE	MONSEY	NY	10952	(914) 352-7642
EDUCATION CENTER 59E HERITAGE ROAD	NEW CITY	NY	10956	(914) 638-4458
CHABAD HOUSE 550 WEST 110TH STREET	NEW YORK	NY	10025	(212) 866-3401
CONGREGATION KEHILLATH ISRAEL CHOFETZ CHAIM 310 WEST 103RD STREET	NEW YORK	NY	10025	(212) 864-5010
CHABAD LUBAVITCH 36 LATTIMORE ROAD	ROCHESTER	NY	14620	(716) 244-4324
CHABAD HOUSE 113 BERKELEY DRIVE	SYRACUSE	NY	13210	(315) 425-0363
CHABAD HOUSE 2306 15TH STREET	TROY	NY	12180	(518) 274-5572
LUBAVITCH 43 THOMPSON STREET	WELLINGTON 1	NZ		
CHABAD HOUSE 1636 SUMMIT ROAD	CINCINNATI	OH	45237	(513) 821-5100
LUBAVITCH 1542 BEAVERTON	CINCINNATI	OH	45237	(513) 761-5200
CHABAD HOUSE 2004 SOUTH GREEN ROAD	CLEVELAND	OH	44121	(216) 382-5050
CHABAD HOUSE 2057 CORNELL ROAD	CLEVELAND	OH	44106	(216) 721-5050
HOUSE OF TRADITION 57 EAST 14TH AVENUE	COLUMBUS	OH	43201	(614) 294-3296
CHABAD HOUSE 44 EDINBURGH DRIVE	DOWNSVIEW	ON	M3N 1B4	(416) 633-8020
CHABAD LUBAVITCH 87 WESTWOOD AVENUE	HAMILTON	ON	L8S 2B1	(416) 529-7458
DR. Y. BLOCK 1059 WILLIAMS STREET	LONDON	ON		(519) 439-4828
LUBAVITCH 312 ROBIN LANE	OTTAWA	ON	K1Z 7J8	(613) 820-9484
RABBI M. BERGER 690 MELBOURNE STREET	OTTAWA	ON	K2A 1XA	(613) 722-5029
CHABAD-LUBAVITCH COMMUNITY CENTRE 770 CHABAD GATE	THORNHILL	ON	L4J 3V9	(416) 731-7000
CHABAD HOUSE, RABBI Y. HECHT 1059 DOUGALL	WINDSOR	ON		(519) 258-1225
LUBAVITCH 102 THIRD AVENUE	KINGSTON	PA	18704	(717) 287-6336
LUBAVITCH CENTER 7622 CASTOR AVENUE	PHILADELPHIA	PA	19152	(215) 725-2030
CHABAD HOUSE 315 SOUTH BELLFIELD, ROOM 416	PITTSBURGH	PA	15213	(412) 681-6473
LUBAVITCH CENTER 2100 WIGHTMAN STREET	PITTSBURGH	PA	15217	(412) 422-7300
LUBAVITCH YOUTH ORGANIZATION 5819 DOUGLAS STREET	PITTSBURGH	PA	15213	(412) 521-5252
YESHIVA ACHEL TMIMIM 5717 HOBART	PITTSBURGH	PA	15217	(412) 681-2446
CHABAD HOUSE 3429 PEEL STREET	MONTREAL	QU	H3A 1W7	(514) 842-6616
CHABAD LUBAVITCH 48 SAVOY STREET	PROVIDENCE	RI	02906	(401) 273-7238
CONGREGATION SHERITH ISRAEL 3730 WHITLAND AVENUE	NASHVILLE	TN	37205	(615) 385-3730
CHABAD HOUSE 2101 NEUCES AVENUE	AUSTIN	TX	78705	(512) 472-3900
LUBAVITCH CENTER 10900 FONDREN ROAD	HOUSTON	TX	77096	(713) 777-2000
FRIENDS OF LUBAVITCH 3924 PERSIMMON DRIVE	FAIRFAX	VA	22031	(703) 323-0233
CHABAD LUBAVITCH 5311 WEST FRANKLIN STREET	RICHMOND	VA	23226	(804) 288-0588
LUBAVITCH CENTER 212 GASKINS ROAD	RICHMOND	VA	23229	(804) 740-2000
CHABAD LUBAVITCH 609 NICKLAUS	VIRGINIA BEACH	VA	23462	(804) 467-4980
CHABAD HOUSE 4541 19TH AVENUE NORTHEAST	SEATTLE	WA	98105	(206) 527-1411
CHABAD HOUSE 613 HOWARD PLACE	MADISON	WI	53703	(608) 251-6022
TZEIRE AGUDATH JABAD CORRIENTES 2470 20 '1'	BUENOS AIRES	AG	1046	47-1593
JABAD LUBAVITCH D. P. GARAT 437 (3200)	CONCORDIA, E. RIOS	AG		045-215-995
JABAD LUBAVITCH LAMADRID 752 (4000)	TUCUMAN	AG		081-225-429
LUBAVITCH YOUTH ORGANIZATION 49 PLANTIJN EN MORETUSLES 2026	ANTWERP	BE	B2000	
LUBAVITCH 1A AVENUE REINE MARIE HENRIETTE 1090	BRUSSELS	BE		345-052-2
BEIT CHABAD R. AMERICO DIAMANTINO, 78, BELLO HORIZONTE	MINAS GERAIS	BZ		221-996-6
CHABAD RUA BEUNOS AIRES 144, CURITIBA PORTO ALEGRE	PARANA	BZ		232-252-3
BEIT CHABAD R. PROF JULIO FERRIERA, DE MELO 756/401, RECIFE	PERNAMBUICO	BZ		325-370-3
YESHIVA COLEGIAL SCP 372	PETROPOLIS, R.J.	BZ		345-052-2
BEIT CHABAD F. FELIPE CAMARAO 72 # APT 22, PORTO ALEGRE	RIO GRANDE DO SUL	BZ		255-966
RABINO R. BLUMENFELD R. SANTA CLARA	RIO DE JANEIRO	BZ	ZC07	236-0249
BEIT CHABAD RUA CHABAD 60	SAO PAULO	BZ	01417	280-1819
LUBAVITCH CALLE 92 #9A-20 (405)	BOGOTA	CM		257-0436
LUBAVITCH 34 RUE DE GOULET, 93300	AUBERVILLES	FR		
YESHIVA TOMCHEI TMIMIM LUBAVITCH 2 AVENUE DU PETIT CHATEAU	BRUNOY	FR	92800	046-3146
LUBAVITCH 727 RUE JULIETTE SAVAR, 94000	CRETEIL	FR		
CHABAD 3 IMPASSE CAZENOVE	LYON, ARENOVE	FR	69003	890-832
BETH LOBAVITCH 8 RUE LAMARTINE	PARIS	FR	75009	526-8760
BUREAU EUROPEEN DE LOUBAVITCH 8 RUE MESLAY	PARIS	FR	75003	
HADAR HATORA 5 RUE DUC	PARIS	FR	75018	
BETH RIVKAH ECOLE DE FILLES 49 RUE RAYMOND POINCAIRE	YERRES	FR		948-4601
BETH RIVKAH SEMINARY FILLES 49 RUE RAYMOND POINCAIRE	YERRES	FR		948-1785
LUBAVITCH 101 OPERAWEG	AMERSFOOT	HD		033-262-04
LUBAVITCH VLASCHAARDE 59	AMSTELVEEN	HD		020-441-402
LUBAVITCH GREVELINGEN STR. 20	AMSTERDAM	HD		020-794-455
CHABAD HONG KONG HONG KONG HILTON HOTEL - 4TH FLOOR	HONG KONG	HK		5-239-770
CHABAD HOUSE VIA DAGNINI 24	BOLOGNA	IT	Y0129	051-340-936
LUBAVITCH VIA G. UHERTI 41	MILAN	IT	20129	022-720-01
CHABAD VIA GENOVA 26, LAISPOLI	ROME	IT	00055	992-6447
LUBAVITCH VIA LORENZO IL MAGNIFICO 23	ROME	IT		424-6962
CHABAD 10 WASHINGTON AVENUE	CASABLANCA	MC		222-1462
CHABAD 174 BD. ZIRAOUI	CASABLANCA	MC		(221) 2042
CHABAD 27 RUE VERLES HANUS	CASABLANCA	MC		279-218
RABBI C. SUED MOLIERE 311 P.B.		MX	5 D.F	424-6962
RABBI S. SCHABBES MOLIERE 88-301		MX	507	424-6962
LUBAVITCH FOUNDATION 31 ARTHURS ROAD, SEAPOINT, 8001	CAPETOWN	SA		443-740
LUBAVITCH FOUNDATION 33 HARLEY STREET, YEOVILLE, 2198	JOHANNESBURG	SA		648-1253
CHABAD OF SANDTON PO BOX 7861, GALLO MANOR 2052	SANDTON	SA		
LUBAVITCH CALLE GENERAL, SANJURJO, 22 APT, 5B	MADRID 3	SP		441-5430
LUBAVITCH FOUNDATION 8 ORCHARD DRIVE	GIFFNOCK, GLASGOW	ST	7NR	041-638-6116
LUBAVITCH PO BOX 565	ZURICH	SW	8018	
CHABAD 65 AV. TAIEB MEHIRI	TUNIS	TU		280-900
LUBAVITCH CENTRE, RABBI S. ARKUSH 95 WILLOWS ROAD	BIRMINGHAM	UK		021-440-5853
LEEDS LUBAVITCH, RABBI Y, ANGYALFI 594 STONEGATE ROAD	LEEDS	UK		
LUBAVITCH FOUNDATION, RABBI N. SUDAK 107-115 STAMFORD HILL	LONDON	UK		018-000-022
LUBAVITCH HOUSE, RABBI C. FARRO 62 SINGLETON ROAD	SALFORD, MANCHESTER	UK	M7OLU	
CHABAD LUBAVITCH APPARTADO 5454	CARACAS	VZ	101	

MAPS

Name / Address	City	State	Zip	Phone
ISRAEL OFFICE OF INFORMATION 800 SECOND AVENUE	NEW YORK	**NY**	10017	

MARKET RESEARCH

Name / Address	City	State	Zip	Phone
NORMARK / NORTHEAST MARKETS INC. JEWISH DIVISION 110 W. 34TH STREET	NEW YORK	**NY**	10001	(212) 714-2935
A.B. DATA LTD. 8050 NORTH PORT WASHINGTON ROAD	MILWAUKEE	**WI**	53217	(414) 352-4404

MEALS - ON - WHEELS

Name / Address	City	State	Zip	Phone
JEWISH FAMILY SERVICE AGENCY 2025 WEST 42ND AVENUE, #305	VANCOUVER	**BC**	V6M 2B5	(604) 266-2396
KOSHER MEALS FOR THE ELDERLY 7711 MELROSE AVENUE	LOS ANGELES	**CA**	90036	(213) 653-8682
THE ARK 3509 W. LAWRENCE AVENUE	CHICAGO	**IL**	60625	(312) 478-9600
JEWISH HOME OF EASTERN PENNSYLVANIA, THE 1101 VINE STREET	SCRANTON	**PA**	18510	(717) 344-6177
NATIONAL COUNCIL OF JEWISH WOMEN, MONTREAL SECTION 5775 VICTORIA	MONTREAL	**QU**		(514) 733-7589
JEWISH COMMUNITY CENTER 7300 NEWPORT AVENUE	NORFOLK	**VA**	23523	(804) 489-1371

MEAT & POULTRY - RETAIL

Name / Address	City	State	Zip	Phone
NORMAN'S KOSHER STAR MARKET 4128 NORTH 19TH AVENUE	PHOENIX	**AZ**	85015	(602) 265-3762
SEGAL'S KOSHER MARKET 2905 NORTH 16TH STREET	PHOENIX	**AZ**	85016	(602) 277-5769
FEIG'S KOSHER FOODS 5071 EAST 5TH STREET	TUCSON	**AZ**	85711	(602) 325-2255
LEON'S KOSHER KORNER/BUTCHER 3710 OAK STREET	VANCOUVER	**BC**		(604) 736-5888
ENCINO KOSHER MEATS 17942 VENTURA BOULEVARD	ENCINO	**CA**	91316	(818) 343-7900
SAM'S KOSHER MEAT MARKET 12432 LAMPTON STREET	GARDEN GROVE	**CA**	92640	(714) 534-5621
COMMUNITY KOSHER MEAT MARKET 2325 EAST ANAHEIM STREET	LONG BEACH	**CA**	90804	(213) 439-8652
AL GOLDSTEIN KOSHER MEATS 3815 SANTA ROSALIA DRIVE	LOS ANGELES	**CA**	90008	(213) 294-8067
BASTOMSKI'S KOSHER MEAT MARKET 7667 BEVERLY BOULEVARD	LOS ANGELES	**CA**	90036	(213) 933-4040
BEVERLYWOOD KOSHER MEATS 9126 WEST PICO BOULEVARD	LOS ANGELES	**CA**	90035	(213) 274-3650
CARMEL KOSHER MEATS 8914 WEST PICO BOULEVARD	LOS ANGELES	**CA**	90035	(213) 278-6347
CENTURY CITY MEATS 8973 WEST PICO BOULEVARD	LOS ANGELES	**CA**	90035	(213) 278-1754
DOHENY KOSHER MEATS 9213 WEST PICO BOULEVARD	LOS ANGELES	**CA**	90035	(213) 276-7232
EMES KOSHER MEATS 2627 SOUTH LA CIENEGA BOULEVARD	LOS ANGELES	**CA**	90034	(213) 836-0535
HAZAN 415 NORTH FAIRFAX AVENUE	LOS ANGELES	**CA**	90036	(213) 655-5554
G & K 8702 WEST PICO BOULEVARD	LOS ANGELES	**CA**	90035	(213) 652-4747
G & L KOSHER MEAT MARKET 10657 WEST PICO BOULEVARD	LOS ANGELES	**CA**	90064	(213) 475-3253
G & M 501 NORTH FAIRFAX AVENUE	LOS ANGELES	**CA**	90036	(213) 651-3034
HADAR KOSHER MEAT MARKET 440 NORTH FAIRFAX AVENUE	LOS ANGELES	**CA**	90036	(213) 655-0250
KOTLAR'S KOSHER MARKET 8622 WEST PICO BOULEVARD	LOS ANGELES	**CA**	90035	(213) 652-5355
KOTLAR'S KOSHER MARKET 456 NORTH FAIRFAX AVENUE	LOS ANGELES	**CA**	90036	(213) 655-2073
MARY & SAM KOSHER MEATS 445 NORTH FAIRFAX AVENUE	LOS ANGELES	**CA**	90036	(213) 651-2474
MAX'S KOSHER MEATS 10608 WEST PICO BOULEVARD	LOS ANGELES	**CA**	90064	(213) 837-4147
MAZEL FOODS KOSHER MEAT & POULTRY MARKETS 6151 WEST PICO BOULEVARD	LOS ANGELES	**CA**	90035	(213) 653-8244
MEHADRIN KOSHER MEAT MARKET 7613 BEVERLY BOULEVARD	LOS ANGELES	**CA**	90035	(213) 934-2196
R.K.F. 7862 SANTA MONICA BOULEVARD	LOS ANGELES	**CA**	90046	(213) 936-7119
REAL KOSHER MEAT MARKET 7965 BEVERLY BOULEVARD	LOS ANGELES	**CA**	90048	(213) 653-8355
SAM & MARTY'S 455 NORTH FAIRFAX AVENUE	LOS ANGELES	**CA**	90036	(213) 651-2474
SHALOM KOSHER MEATS 7605 BEVERLY BOULEVARD	LOS ANGELES	**CA**	90036	(213) 939-0529
SHELLY'S 345 NORTH FAIRFAX AVENUE	LOS ANGELES	**CA**	90036	(213) 655-1835
SOL'S 1458 SOUTH ROBERTSON BOULEVARD	LOS ANGELES	**CA**	90035	(213) 276-0830
SOLOMON'S KOSHER MEAT MARKET 1053 SOUTH FAIRFAX AVENUE	LOS ANGELES	**CA**	90019	(213) 935-7314
WEST L.A. KOSHER MEAT AND GROCERIES 10608 W. PICO	LOS ANGELES	**CA**	90035	(213) 837-6688
WESTERN KOSHER 426 N. FAIRFAX	LOS ANGELES	**CA**	90036	(213) 655-8870
WILSHIRE KOSHER MEAT 5407 1/2 WILSHIRE BOULEVARD	LOS ANGELES	**CA**	90036	(213) 936-6283
H. DREXLER 12519 BURBANK BOULEVARD	NORTH HOLLYWOOD	**CA**	91607	(818) 761-6405
SUPERIOR KOSHER MEATS 12820 VICTORY BOULEVARD	NORTH HOLLYWOOD	**CA**	91606	(818) 671-9500
VALLEY MARKET 9561 LAUREL CANYON BOULEVARD	NORTH HOLLYWOOD	**CA**	91607	(818) 764-0363
HENRY'S KOSHER MEAT MARKET 3256 GRAND AVENUE	OAKLAND	**CA**	94610	(415) 451-3885
ZION KOSHER MEATS 18236 SHERMAN WAY	RESEDA	**CA**	91335	(818) 881-1777
ISRAEL KOSHER MEAT MARKET 5621 GEARY BOULEVARD	SAN FRANCISCO	**CA**	94121	(415) 752-3064
JACOB'S KOSHER MEAT MARKET 2435 NORIEGA STREET	SAN FRANCISCO	**CA**	94122	(415) 564-7482
TEL AVIV KOSHER MEAT MARKET 1301 NORIEGA STREET	SAN FRANCISCO	**CA**	94122	(415) 661-7588
WILLOW GLEN 1185 LINCOLN AVENUE	SAN JOSE	**CA**	95125	(408) 297-6604
ELLIOT'S KOSHER MEATS 4609 1/2 VAN NUYS BOULEVARD	SHERMAN OAKS	**CA**	91403	(818) 783-7190
MURRAY'S KOSHER MEATS 14539 VENTURA BOULEVARD	SHERMAN OAKS	**CA**	91403	(818) 784-8722
ROZ KOSHER MEATS 12910 RIVERSIDE DRIVE	SHERMAN OAKS	**CA**	91403	(818) 984-1102
SHERMAN OAKS KOSHER MEATS 14054 VENTURA BOULEVARD	SHERMAN OAKS	**CA**	91403	(818) 784-4987
VENTURA KOSHER MEATS 18357 VENTURA BOULEVARD	TARZANA	**CA**	91356	(818) 881-3717
G & L KOSHER MEATS 10657 WEST PICO BOULEVARD	WESTWOOD	**CA**	90064	(213) 475-3253
MEYER'S KOSHER MEAT MARKET 3211 EAST COLFAX AVENUE	DENVER	**CO**	80206	(303) 377-2729
SHALOM FRESH KOSHER MEAT 7400 EAST HAMPDEN, TIFFANY PLAZA	DENVER	**CO**	80231	(303) 770-6669
WEST HILL GROCERY 3933 WEST COLFAX AVENUE	DENVER	**CO**	80204	(303) 892-1180
COPACO KOSHER MEAT DEPARTMENT COTTAGE GROVE ROAD	BLOOMFIELD	**CT**	06002	(203) 242-5521
BENNY LEVINE MEATS 1115 MADISON AVENUE	BRIDGEPORT	**CT**	06606	(203) 335-2216
STATE KOSHER MARKET 1147 MADISON AVENUE	BRIDGEPORT	**CT**	06606	(203) 579-1699
ESTRYN'S KOSHER MEAT MARKET 300 WHALLEY AVENUE	NEW HAVEN	**CT**	06511	(203) 787-5348
M & J KOSHER MEAT MARKET 418 WHALLEY AVENUE	NEW HAVEN	**CT**	06511	(203) 777-1656
TEITELMAN KOSHER MEAT MARKET 376 WHALLEY AVENUE	NEW HAVEN	**CT**	06515	(203) 387-8885
SOLTZ KOSHER MEAT MARKET 300 BANK STREET	NEW LONDON	**CT**	06320	(203) 443-4734
BLUE RIBBON PROVISION COMPANY 5646 THIRD STREET N.E.	WASHINGTON	**DC**	20011	(202) 526-4940
POSIN'S KOSHER MARKET 5756 GEORGIA AVENUE N.W.	WASHINGTON	**DC**	20011	(202) 726-4424
ROLAND FOODS 135 R STREET S.W.	WASHINGTON	**DC**	20024	(202) 488-0888
SAVAL DIRECTOR 2266 25TH PLACE N.E.	WASHINGTON	**DC**	20001	(202) 832-9400
STAR OF DAVID KOSHER BUTCHER 1806 WEST HILLSBORO BOULEVARD	DEERFIELD BEACH	**FL**	33442	(305) 427-6400
FOOD FAIR STORES 6500 NORTH ANDREWS AVENUE	FORT LAUDERDALE	**FL**	33309	(305) 371-6008
HARRISON'S KOSHER MEAT MARKET 8330 WEST OAKLAND PARK BOULEVARD	FORT LAUDERDALE	**FL**	33321	(305) 741-0855
KEZREH, INC. 1025 E. HALLANDALE BEACH BOULEVARD	HALLANDALE	**FL**	33009	(305) 454-5776
SYON KOSHER MEATS 17G-1 EAST HALLANDALE BEACH BOULEVARD	HALLANDALE	**FL**	33009	(305) 454-5659
HOLLYWOOD KOSHER MEATS 2009 HARRISON	HOLLYWOOD	**FL**	33020	(305) 922-1697
WEST HOLLYWOOD KOSHER MEATS 142 SOUTH STATE ROAD 7	HOLLYWOOD	**FL**	33020	(305) 962-5018
SUPERIOR KOSHER MEATS 677 NORTH ORLANDO	MAITLAND	**FL**	32751	(305) 645-1704
MEYERS ROYAL KOSHER MEAT MARKET 5987 SW 8TH STREET	MIAMI	**FL**	33144	(305) 264-0691
RUBINDALE KOSHER MEAT & POULTRY 10021 S.W. 72ND STREET	MIAMI	**FL**	33136	(305) 279-1568
ZION CORPORATION 1717 N.W. 7TH AVENUE	MIAMI	**FL**	33136	(305) 324-1855
ADAM'S STRICTLY KOSHER MEAT & POULTRY 1403 1/2 WASHINGTON AVENUE	MIAMI BEACH	**FL**	33139	(305) 532-0103
COMMUNITY KOSHER 525 41ST STREET, ARTHUR GODFREY ROAD	MIAMI BEACH	**FL**	33140	(305) 531-7691
FREDDY'S MEAT MARKET 1419 WASHINGTON AVENUE	MIAMI BEACH	**FL**	33139	(305) 531-1267
GOLDSTEIN & SONS PRIME MEAT 7443 COLLINS AVENUE	MIAMI BEACH	**FL**	33141	(305) 865-4981
KARL & ALLEN QUALITY MEATS 1321 WASHINGTON AVENUE	MIAMI BEACH	**FL**	33139	(305) 531-4800
M & L FOOD CENTER 7446 COLLINS AVENUE	MIAMI BEACH	**FL**	33141	(305) 865-2648
MENDELSON & SONS KOSHER MEAT MARKET 953 WASHINGTON AVENUE	MIAMI BEACH	**FL**	33139	(305) 532-2426
NORMANDY KOSHER MEAT MARKET 1112 71ST STREET	MIAMI BEACH	**FL**	33141	(305) 866-5223
S & W KOSHER MEATS 1255 WASHINGTON AVENUE	MIAMI BEACH	**FL**	33139	(305) 534-8863
SURF KOSHER MEAT & POULTRY 7432 COLLINS AVENUE	MIAMI BEACH	**FL**	33141	(305) 868-0559
NORMANDY KOSHER MEAT MARKET 1112 NORMANDY DRIVE	NORMANDY ISLAND	**FL**	33141	(305) 866-5223
KLEINMAN'S STRICTLY KOSHER MARKET 18315 N.E. 19TH AVENUE	NORTH MIAMI BEACH	**FL**	33162	(305) 932-5611
MENDELSON & SONS KOSHER MEAT MARKET 1354 N.E. 163RD STREET	NORTH MIAMI BEACH	**FL**	33162	(305) 945-6451
NEW DEAL KOSHER MEAT MARKET & POULTRY 1362 N.E. 163RD STREET	NORTH MIAMI BEACH	**FL**	33162	(305) 945-2512
SOUTH FLORIDA KOSHER MEATS 1320-24 NE 163RD STREET	NORTH MIAMI BEACH	**FL**	33162	(305) 949-6068
TOM-TOV KOSHER BUTCHER & APPETIZER 2610 NORTH UNIVERSITY DRIVE	SUNRISE	**FL**	33322	(305) 741-1995
ARTHUR'S KOSHER MEAT MARKET 2166 BRIARCLIFFE ROAD N.E.	ATLANTA	**GA**	30329	(404) 634-6881
ARTHUR'S KOSHER MEATS 215 COPELAND ROAD, NORTHEAST	ATLANTA	**GA**	30342	(404) 252-4396
BERNIE'S KOSHER MEATS 2345-3 CHESHIRE BRIDGE ROAD	ATLANTA	**GA**	30324	(404) 325-1559
DISCOUNT DELI & MEAT MARKET 2899 NORTH DRUID HILLS ROAD, NORTHEAST	ATLANTA	**GA**	31707	(404) 636-0300
QUALITY KOSHER MEATS & DELICATESSEN 2161 BRIARCLIFF ROAD, NORTHEAST	ATLANTA	**GA**	30329	(404) 636-1114
HAWAII KOSHER CO-OP BOX 23343	HONOLULU	**HI**	96822	(808) 536-0662
ARGYLE KOSHER MEAT MARKET 1009 WEST ARGYLE	CHICAGO	**IL**	60640	(312) 561-4550
COHEN & HOROWITZ KOSHER MEATS & POULTRY 3341 NORTH BROADWAY	CHICAGO	**IL**	60657	(312) 528-6565
DEVON KOSHER MEAT MARKET 2255 WEST DEVON	CHICAGO	**IL**	60659	(312) 274-6198
EBNER'S KOSHER MEAT AND POULTRY MARKET 2649 W. DEVON	CHICAGO	**IL**	60659	(312) 764-1446
FINE'S KOSHER MEAT MARKETS 3310 NORTH BROADWAY	CHICAGO	**IL**	60657	(312) 248-5599
HUNGARIAN KOSHER DELI & SAUSAGE COMPANY 2613 WEST DEVON AVENUE	CHICAGO	**IL**	60636	(312) 973-5991
J & N KOSHER MEAT MARKET 1009 WEST ARGYLE	CHICAGO	**IL**	60640	(312) 274-2220
JACOB MILLER & SONS 2727 WEST DEVON AVENUE	CHICAGO	**IL**	60636	(312) 761-4200
KOSHER KARRY OUT 2828 WEST DEVON AVENUE	CHICAGO	**IL**	60659	(312) 973-4355
KOSHER ZION 5511 NORTH KEDZIE AVENUE	CHICAGO	**IL**	60625	(312) 463-3351
LIPMAN KOSHER MEATS 2255 WEST DEVON	CHICAGO	**IL**	60659	(312) 338-6120
MILLER JACOB & SONS MEAT MARKET & POULTRY 2727 WEST DEVON	CHICAGO	**IL**	60659	(312) 761-4200
RAPOPORT KOSHER MEAT MARKET 3920 WEST LAWRENCE	CHICAGO	**IL**	60625	(312) 463-2434
ROMANIAN KOSHER SAUSAGE 7200 NORTH CLARK	CHICAGO	**IL**	60659	(312) 761-4141
SAVITZKY & MILLSTEIN KOSHER MEAT MARKET 2604 WEST DEVON	CHICAGO	**IL**	60659	(312) 274-0430
TOUHY KOSHER MARKET 2811 WEST TOUHY	CHICAGO	**IL**	60645	(312) 274-2132
TRADITION MEATS & DELI 853 SANDERS ROAD	NORTHBROOK	**IL**	60062	
HUNGARIAN KOSHER FOODS 4020 OAKTON	SKOKIE	**IL**	60076	(312) 674-8008
REISWERG'S KOSHER MEAT MARKET 6334 GUILFORD AVENUE	INDIANAPOLIS	**IN**	46220	(317) 257-0422
STRATHMOOR KEY DISTRIBUTING 2733 BARDSTOWN ROAD	LOUISVILLE	**KY**	40205	(502) 458-2276
RALPH'S KOSHER MEAT & DELICATESSEN 4518 FRERET STREET	NEW ORLEANS	**LA**	70115	(504) 891-8476
BRIGHTON KOSHER MEAT MARKET 1620 COMMONWEALTH AVENUE	BRIGHTON	**MA**	02135	(617) 277-0786
BROCKTON 217 BELMONT STREET	BROCKTON	**MA**	02401	(617) 588-6170
SAM'S 31 PLEASANT	BROCKTON	**MA**	02401	(617) 583-3748
AL'S KOSHER MEAT 415 HARVARD STREET	BROOKLINE	**MA**	02146	(617) 277-0780
ALTER BROTHERS 401 HARVARD STREET	BROOKLINE	**MA**	02146	(617) 566-9010
BEACON KOSHER 1671 BEACON STREET	BROOKLINE	**MA**	02146	(617) 277-6551
THE BUTCHERIE 428 HARVARD STREET	BROOKLINE	**MA**	02146	(617) 731-9888
NATHAN'S 400 HARVARD STREET	BROOKLINE	**MA**	02146	(617) 566-7888
PARKWAY 1004 W. ROXBURY PARKWAY	BROOKLINE	**MA**	02146	(617) 469-9100
SHAFRAN'S 423 HARVARD STREET	BROOKLINE	**MA**	02146	(617) 566-9622
THE BUTCHERIE 428 HARVARD STREET	BROOKLINE	**MA**	02146	(617) 731-9888
WARD-BEACON 1671 BEACON STREET	BROOKLINE	**MA**	02146	(617) 277-3502
SOLOMON & TUTIN 827 WASHINGTON STREET	CANTON	**MA**	02021	(617) 838-3530
TRI KOSHER MEATS 110 WASHINGTON STREET	CANTON	**MA**	02021	(617) 838-3530
ARLINGTON 139 ARLINGTON STREET	CHELSEA	**MA**	02150	(617) 884-9538
LARRY LEVINE'S KOSHER MARKET 35 CENTRAL AVENUE	CHELSEA	**MA**	02150	(617) 884-1406
SEA-LECT FOODS 5 CHARLES STREET, PO BOX 86	CHELSEA	**MA**	02150	(617) 884-7222
DELI-TIZER 147 COCHITUATE ROAD	FRAMINGHAM	**MA**	01701	(617) 875-3048
HURWITZ KOSHER MEAT MARKET 326 CONCORD STREET, ROUTE 126	FRAMINGHAM	**MA**	01701	(617) 875-0481
BENDELL'S 6 WILLOW STREET	MALDEN	**MA**	02148	(617) 324-0780
AMERICAN KOSHER 1188 BLUE HILL AVENUE	MATTAPAN	**MA**	02126	(617) 296-5605

DELI-TIZER 1657 BEACON STREET .... NEWTON **MA** 02146 (617) 566-5933
DELI-TIZER 1134 BEACON STREET .... NEWTON **MA** 02158 (617) 527-7826
FOUR CORNERS 52 COMMONWEALTH .... NEWTON **MA** 02158 (617) 527-3913
GORDON & ALPERIN 552 COMMONWEALTH .... NEWTON **MA** 02158 (617) 332-4170
SOLOMON & TUTIN'S 827 WASHINGTON STREET .... NEWTON **MA** 02158 (617) 332-7577
STAR KOSHER MEATS 1138 BEACON STREET .... NEWTON **MA** 02158 (617) 964-1177
MYER'S 412 CENTER STREET .... RANDOLPH **MA** 02368 (617) 986-6880
RANDOLPH 41 NORTH MAIN STREET .... RANDOLPH **MA** 02368 (617) 961-2931
J. KOOR MEAT MARKET 103 SHIRLEY AVENUE .... REVERE **MA** 02151 (617) 284-9766
S & M KOSHER MEAT MARKET 168 SHIRLEY AVENUE .... REVERE **MA** 02151 (617) 289-2063
SAM'S 76 SHIRLEY AVENUE .... REVERE **MA** 02151 (617) 284-1397
B. COHEN KOSHER MARKET 413 CHANDLER STREET .... WORCESTER **MA** 01602 (617) 752-2047
ACME PRODUCE 525 JARVIS .... WINNIPEG **MB** (204) 586-4709
L. OMNITSKY & SONS 1428 MAIN STREET .... WINNIPEG **MB** (204) 582-4494
NATE'S KOSHER FOODS LTD. 632 JEFFERSON AVENUE .... WINNIPEG **MB** R2V 0P2 (204) 339-8375
ZIPURSKY'S KOSHER MEAT MARKET 1836 GRANT AVENUE .... WINNIPEG **MB** (204) 489-9596
AYRDALE LIBERTY KOSHER MEAT MARKET 8122 LIBERTY ROAD .... BALTIMORE **MD** 21207 (301) 922-2030
CAPLAN BROTHERS KOSHER MEAT MARKET 6970 REISTERTOWN .... BALTIMORE **MD** 21207 (301) 358-5868
JOSEPH'S GLATT KOSHER MEATS 6719 REISTERTOWN RD. .... BALTIMORE **MD** 21215 (301) 764-1991
M & M POULTRY CO. 2703 QUANTICO AVENUE .... BALTIMORE **MD** 21215 (301) 367-5353
POSNER & SONS 6719 REISTERSTOWN ROAD .... BALTIMORE **MD** 21215 (301) 764-1991
WEINTRAUB'S KOSHER MEAT MARKET 607 REISTERSTOWN ROAD .... BALTIMORE **MD** 21208 (301) 486-2726
B. SUROSKY & SONS 106 REISTERSTOWN ROAD .... PIKESVILLE **MD** 21208 (301) 653-2000
PIKESVILLE KOSHER MEAT & FISH MARKET 1013-B REISTERSTOWN ROAD .... PIKESVILLE **MD** 21208 (301) 486-5220
SHAPIRO'S SUPERMARKET 1504 REISTERSTOWN ROAD .... PIKESVILLE **MD** 21208 (301) 484-2400
WASSERMAN & LEMBERGER 610 REISTERSTOWN ROAD .... PIKESVILLE **MD** 21208 (301) 486-4191
SHAPIRO'S SUPER MARKETS 8515 LIBERTY ROAD .... RANDALLSTOWN **MD** 21133 (301) 922-1600
KATZ KOSHER SUPERMARKET 4860 BOILING BROOK PARKWAY .... ROCKVILLE **MD** 20852 (301) 468-0400
SHALOM STRICTLY KOSHER MEATS 2307 UNIVERSITY BOULEVARD WEST .... WHEATON **MD** 20902 (301) 946-6500
SHAUL'S KOSHER MEAT MARKET 11238 GEORGIA AVENUE .... WHEATON **MD** 20902 (301) 949-8477
MORRIS KOSHER MEAT MARKET 7134 WEST SEVEN MILE ROAD .... HAZEL PARK **MI** 48221 (313) 545-7600
FRANKLIN KOSHER MEAT MARKET 32930 MIDDLEBELT RD .... FARMINGTON **MI** 48024 (313) 855-1020
CARL'S KOSHER MEAT MARKET 26020 GREENFIELD RD .... OAK PARK **MI** 48237 (313) 968-7450
DEXTER-DAVISON KOSHER MEAT MARKET 24820 COOLIDGE RD .... OAK PARK **MI** 48237 (313) 548-6800
LOUIS COHEN & SON 24721 COOLIDGE .... OAK PARK **MI** 48237 (313) 543-8860
SINGER'S MEAT MARKET 13721 WEST NINE MILE ROAD .... OAK PARK **MI** 48237 (313) 547-8111
STRICTLY KOSHER MEAT CENTER 26020 GREENFIELD ROAD .... OAK PARK **MI** 48237 (313) 967-4220
SUPERIOR KOSHER MEAT MARKET 23057 COOLIDGE .... OAK PARK **MI** 48237 (313) 547-3900
HARVARD ROW KOSHER MEAT MARKET 21780 WEST 11 MILE RD .... SOUTHFIELD **MI** 48076 (313) 356-5110
TEL AVIV FARMER JACK KOSHER MEAT MARKET 29800 SOUTHFIELD ROAD .... SOUTHFIELD **MI** 48075 (313) 559-6121
FRANKLIN KOSHER MEAT MARKET 5564 DRAKE ROAD .... WEST BLOOMFIELD **MI** 48033 (313) 661-2590
TEL AVIV FARMER JACK MARKET 6565 ORCHARD LAKE RD .... WEST BLOOMFIELD **MI** 48033 (313) 851-4175
FEINBERG DISTRIBUTING 2200 SUMMER AVENUE .... MINNEAPOLIS **MN** 55413 (612) 623-1300
L. FIDELMAN KOSHER MEAT MARKET 540 NORTH WINNETKA AVENUE .... MINNEAPOLIS **MN** 55427 (612) 544-5215
MILT'S MARKET 4000 MINNETONKA BOULEVARD .... MINNEAPOLIS **MN** 55417 (612) 926-5611
RUBIN'S KOSHER MEAT MARKET 934 SELBY AVENUE .... ST. PAUL **MN** 55104 (612) 690-5837
TEL-AVIV KOSHER MEATS 2056 MARSHALL AVENUE .... ST. PAUL **MN** 55104 (612) 690-4367
EPSTEIN KOSHER FOODS 403 WEST 79TH STREET .... KANSAS CITY **MO** 64114 (816) 361-0200
KELLER FOOD COMPANY 2917 BROADWAY .... KANSAS CITY **MO** 64108 (816) 921-3500
KOSHER CONNECTION INCORPORATION 5333 W. 94 TERRACE .... KANSAS CITY **MO** 64114 (816) 383-9533
DIAMANT'S KOSHER MEAT MARKET 618 NORTH AND SOUTH BOULEVARD .... ST. LOUIS **MO** 63130 (314) 721-9624
GALLER'S KOSHER MEAT MARKET 8502 OLIVE BOULEVARD .... ST. LOUIS **MO** 63132 (314) 993-4535
SIMON KOHN'S 10424 OLD OLIVE STREET ROAD .... ST. LOUIS **MO** 63146 (314) 569-0727
SOL'S KOSHER MEAT MARKET 8627 OLIVE STREET .... ST. LOUIS **MO** 63132 (314) 993-9977
SCHANDLER'S 50 BROADWAY .... ASHEVILLE **NC** 28802 (704) 253-5626
NEBRASKA KOSHER MEAT MARKET 4902 HAMILTON STREET .... OMAHA **NE** 68154 (402) 558-5262
K & Z KOSHER MEAT MARKET 1014 MAIN STREET .... ASBURY PARK **NJ** 07712 (201) 775-1240
REITNER & BLOCK 590 BROADWAY .... BAYONNE **NJ** 07002 (201) 437-1594
CALDWELL KOSHER MEAT MARKET 412 BLOOMFIELD AVENUE .... CALDWELL **NJ** 07006 (201) 226-0843
VILLAGE KOSHER MEATS 403 PIAGET AVENUE .... CLIFTON **NJ** 07011 (201) 772-5100
MORRIS COUNTY MEATS 303 SOUTH SALEM .... DOVER **NJ** 07801 (201) 361-1888
J & J KOSHER MEAT & POULTRY MARKET EVERGREEN ROAD .... EDISON **NJ** 08817 (201) 549-3707
ELIZABETH KOSHER MEAT & POULTRY MARKET 149 ELMORA AVENUE .... ELIZABETH **NJ** 07202 (201) 353-5448
FARKAS BROTHERS 179 ELMORA AVENUE .... ELIZABETH **NJ** 07202 (201) 352-3756
GREENSPAN'S KOSHER MEAT & LIVE POULTRY 81 WEST PALISADE AVENUE .... ENGLEWOOD **NJ** 07631 (201) 567-2868
CENTER KOSHER PRIME MEAT & POULTRY MARKET 12-76 RIVER ROAD .... FAIRLAWN **NJ** 07410 (201) 797-7928
HAROLD'S KOSHER MEATS 1911 FAIRLAWN AVENUE .... FAIRLAWN **NJ** 07410 (201) 796-0003
BLUE RIBBON SELF SERVICE KOSHER MEAT MARKET 1363 INWOOD TERRACE .... FT. LEE **NJ** 07024 (201) 224-3220
DAN'S GLATT KOSHER MEAT & POULTRY 515 RARITAN AVENUE .... HIGHLAND PARK **NJ** 08904 (201) 572-2626
SEROFF'S KOSHER MEAT MARKET 29 MILL ROAD .... IRVINGTON **NJ** 07111 (201) 399-3741
SINGER KOSHER MEAT MARKET 59 NORTH BEAVERWYCK ROAD .... LAKE HIAWATHA **NJ** 07034 (201) 263-3220
KERN Z 299 RIDGE AVENUE .... LAKEWOOD **NJ** 08201 (201) 363-0009
COUNTY KOSHER MEAT & POULTRY 1171 WEST ST. GEORGES AVENUE, LINDEN PLAZA .... LINDEN **NJ** 07036 (201) 925-4050
LIVINGSTON KOSHER MEAT MARKET 57 EAST MT. PLEASANT AVENUE .... LIVINGSTON **NJ** 07039 (201) 992-2313
MOISHAS BUTCHER & PROVISIONS 105 WILLIAM STREET .... MIDDLESEX **NJ** 08846 (201) 560-1919
E & F KOSHER MEAT 7531 BERGEN LINE .... NORTH BERGEN **NJ** 07047 (201) 869-1832
HAROLD'S KOSHER MEATS 67A EAST RIDGEWOOD AVENUE .... PARAMUS **NJ** 07652 (201) 262-0030
BROOK KOSHER MEAT MARKET 222 BROOK AVENUE .... PASSAIC **NJ** 07055 (201) 773-1910
MARTIN HERMAN 516 PARK AVENUE .... PATERSON **NJ** 07504 (201) 345-1311
COHEN LEMPERT M & M COMPANY 719 MOUNTAIN AVENUE .... SPRINGFIELD **NJ** 07081 (201) 379-6643
MARTY & HARRY'S SELF SERVICE KOSHER MEATS & DELI 205 MORRIS AVENUE .... SPRINGFIELD **NJ** 08736 (201) 376-4711
BERGEN COUNTY KOSHER MEATS 456 CEDAR LANE .... TEANECK **NJ** 07666 (201) 837-1422
CEDAR LANE KOSHER MEATS & POULTRY 445 CEDAR LANE .... TEANECK **NJ** 07666 (201) 836-6700
KURTS KOSHER MEAT 206 WEST ENGLEWOOD AVENUE .... TEANECK **NJ** 07666 (201) 386-8400
MAPLE KOSHER MEAT MARKET 2933 VAUXHALL ROAD .... VAUXHALL **NJ** 07088 (201) 688-2080
COUNTY KOSHER MEAT CENTER 1111 ST. GEORGES AVENUE .... WEST LINDEN **NJ** 07036 (201) 925-4050
FRANK GREENBERG KOSHER 500 PLEASANT VALLEY WAY .... WEST ORANGE **NJ** 07052 (201) 731-4426
NEW PLEASANTDALE KOSHER SELF SERVICE 470 PLEASANT VALLEY WAY .... WEST ORANGE **NJ** 07052 (201) 731-3216
SEGAL'S KOSHER MEATS .... LAS VEGAS **NV** (702) 734-9540
HAGELU 544 DELAWARE AVENUE .... ALBANY **NY** 12209 (518) 434-3354
KAGAN & SONS 448 MADISON .... ALBANY **NY** 12208 (518) 449-7961
SALE ON KOSHER MEATS 1044 WILLIS AVENUE .... ALBERTSON **NY** 11507 (516) 621-9615
SILVERSTEIN'S POULTRY 677 NIAGARA FALLS BOULEVARD .... AMHERST **NY** 14226 (716) 836-0762
JERRY FAYNE & MORRIS WEIDEN 3312 BROADWAY .... ASTORIA **NY** 11102
HA-MAR KOSHER MEATS 18-48 PARK STREET .... ATLANTIC BEACH **NY** 11509 (516) 371-2900
LEDERMAN & BOYER ATLANTIC BEACH 1848 PARK STREET .... ATLANTIC BEACH **NY** 11509 (516) 371-4410
MAZUR KOSHER MEATS 909 ATLANTIC AVENUE .... BALDWIN **NY** 11510 (516) 623-8252
SAHBRA PACKING COMPANY 1757 GRAND AVENUE .... BALDWIN **NY** 11510 (516) 223-3721
MERRICK PACKING CORPORATION OF BAY TERRACE 23-06 BELL BOULEVARD .... BAY TERRACE **NY** 11360 (718) 224-7577
SUSSMAN'S MEATS 47-36 BELL BOULEVARD .... BAY TERRACE **NY** 11360 (718) 223-2300
AMERICAN FEDERATION OF RETAIL KOSHER BUTCHERS 212-01A 48TH AVENUE .... BAYSIDE **NY** 11364 (718) 428-8761
BASS & SCHWEITZER 214-22 73RD AVENUE .... BAYSIDE **NY** 11364 (718) 464-8421
BAYSIDE KOSHER FOODS, INCORPORATED 47-36 BELL BOULEVARD .... BAYSIDE **NY** 11362 (718) 224-2300
D & W KOSHER MEATS 61-42 SPRINGFIELD BOULEVARD .... BAYSIDE **NY** 11364 (718) 225-1550
JOMAN, INC. 6123 SPRINGFIELD BOULEVARD .... BAYSIDE **NY** 11364 (718) 224-8149
MERRICK PACKING CORPORATION 2366 BELL BOULEVARD .... BAYSIDE **NY** 11360 (718) 224-7577
NEW BELL KOSHER CATERERS 214-22 73RD AVENUE .... BAYSIDE **NY** 11364 (718) 464-8421
STAR OF DAVID 214-22 73RD AVENUE .... BAYSIDE **NY** 11364 (718) 464-8421
AND-HOW KOSHER MEATS 450 BEACH 129TH STREET .... BELLE HARBOR **NY** 11694 (718) 474-4638
GLEN OAKS KOSHER MEAT MARKET 248-18 UNION TPKE .... BELLEROSE **NY** 11426 (718) 343-6410
BINGHAMTON KOSHER MARKETS 14-16 CONKLIN AVENUE .... BINGHAMTON **NY** 13903 (607) 723-5331
ABRAHAM COHEN 49 EAST KINGSBRIDGE ROAD .... BRONX **NY** 10468 (212) 933-3933
BEE & SEY KOSHER MEAT INC. 2100 WHITE PLAINS ROAD .... BRONX **NY** 10462 (212) 822-4658
BLUE RIBBON MEATS 101 DREISER LOOP .... BRONX **NY** 10475 (212) 379-4300
BOB & SAM 27 EAST KINGSBRIDGE ROAD .... BRONX **NY** 10468 (212) 367-6261
BRETTSCHNEIDER MEATS 246 WEST 231ST STREET .... BRONX **NY** 10463 (212) 548-0866
BRONX STAR KOSHER MEAT MARKET 132 EINSTEIN LOOP .... BRONX **NY** 10475 (212) 379-3283
BURKE KOSHER MEAT 700 BURKE AVENUE .... BRONX **NY** 10467 (212) 547-2646
CARL HOCHSTEIN 153 EAST 181ST STREET .... BRONX **NY** 10453 (212) 367-7555
DAVE & JOE KOSHER MEAT 936 SHERIDAN AVENUE .... BRONX **NY** 10451 (212) 293-2639
DAVE DAVITZ 700 BURKE AVENUE .... BRONX **NY** 10467 (212) 547-2646
DAVID GEIER 1478 WHITE PLAINS ROAD .... BRONX **NY** 10460 (212) 863-9686
FRUCHTER & STEIN 791 LYDIG AVENUE .... BRONX **NY** 10462 (212) 863-5909
G & S KOSHER 305 EAST 204TH STREET .... BRONX **NY** 10467 (212) 652-2554
GLATT SHOP OF RIVERDALE INC. 3711 RIVERDALE AVENUE .... BRONX **NY** 10463 (212) 884-1200
GLUCKSMAN BROTHERS 73 EAST KINGSBRIDGE ROAD .... BRONX **NY** 10468 (212) 933-2620
H & G KOSHER MEATS 779 LYDIG AVENUE WEST .... BRONX **NY** 10462 (212) 829-0643
HANS BROTHERS KOSHER MEAT 2232 WHITE PLAINS ROAD .... BRONX **NY** 10467 (212) 547-4998
HERBIE & LEO'S KOSHER MEAT 305 EAST 204TH STREET .... BRONX **NY** 10467 (212) 654-7993
HILLSIDE MEAT MARKET 3099 BAINBRIDGE AVENUE .... BRONX **NY** 10469 (212) 519-1580
HOCHSTEIN'S MEATS 3407 JEROME AVENUE .... BRONX **NY** 10467 (212) 367-7555
IRVING LUBIN 3478 JEROME AVENUE .... BRONX **NY** 10468 (212) 881-0448
JACK MUCHA 743 ALLERTON AVENUE .... BRONX **NY** 10467 (212) 231-1050
JOSEPH SCHULLMAN 758 LYDIG AVENUE .... BRONX **NY** 10462 (212) 863-3077
KAROUSEL 550 WEST 235TH STREET .... BRONX **NY** 10463 (212) 884-4000
KLEIN & FRUCTER MEATS 791 LYDIG AVENUE .... BRONX **NY** 10462 (212) 863-5909
KRAMES & ROSEHAM MEATS 27 EAST KINGSBRIDGE ROAD .... BRONX **NY** 10468 (212) 367-6261
L & L KOSHER MEATS 731 ALLERTON AVENUE .... BRONX **NY** 10467 (212) 231-3272
LEO BERMAN 206 EAST 198TH STREET .... BRONX **NY** 10468 (212) 365-6640
LUBIN'S OF KINGSBRIDGE ROAD 7 EAST KINGSBRIDGE ROAD .... BRONX **NY** 10468 (212) 584-1195
LYDIG MEAT 716 LYDIG AVENUE .... BRONX **NY** 10462 (212) 822-1681
MANNHEIMER'S MEATS 3711 RIVERDALE AVENUE .... BRONX **NY** 10463 (212) 884-1200
MAX KOSHER MEAT MARKET 673 ALLERTON AVENUE .... BRONX **NY** 10467 (212) 547-4197
MAYER HERBLUM 634 LYDIG AVENUE .... BRONX **NY** 10462 (212) 829-4822
MORHY & KING 2232 WHITE PLAINS ROAD .... BRONX **NY** 10467 (212) 547-4998
PELHAM KOSHER 732 LYDIG AVENUE .... BRONX **NY** 10462 (212) 838-0170
RADZIMINSKY 2037 BARTOW AVENUE .... BRONX **NY** 10475 (212) 671-0195
RIVERDALE KOSHER MEATS 246 WEST 231ST STREET .... BRONX **NY** 10463 (212) 548-2131
ROSENHEIMER & SCHWARTZ 570 WEST 235TH STREET .... BRONX **NY** 10463 (212) 548-1723
S & L MEAT MARKET INCORPORATED 116 EAST 170TH STREET .... BRONX **NY** 10452 (212) 293-2156
SSS KOSHER 131 EINSTEIN LOOP .... BRONX **NY** 10475 (212) 379-3283
SCHULMAN BROTHERS 743 ASTOR AVENUE .... BRONX **NY** 10467 (212) 654-9688
SIEGEL KOSHER MEATS 936 SHERIDAN AVENUE .... BRONX **NY** 10451 (212) 293-2639
SKYVIEW KOSHER MEATS 550 WEST 235TH STREET .... BRONX **NY** 10463 (212) 884-4000
SPECTOR & KAUFMAN 3421 JEROME AVENUE .... BRONX **NY** 10468 (212) 655-0571
STANLEY & HARVEY KOSHER MEAT 732 LYDIG AVENUE .... BRONX **NY** 10462 (212) 892-5355
STARR & ERBST 761 LYDIG AVENUE .... BRONX **NY** 10462 (212) 892-5355
VALUE PLUS KOSHER MEATS 5676 BROADWAY .... BRONX **NY** 10463 (212) 549-9602
AARON WEINSTOCK 128 LEE AVENUE .... BROOKLYN **NY** 11211
ABE NADLER & SON KOSHER MEATS 613 BRIGHTON BEACH AVENUE .... BROOKLYN **NY** 11235 (718) 648-6900
ABRAHAM JERUSALEM 5211 13TH AVENUE .... BROOKLYN **NY** 11219 (718) 436-3134
ADLER & MERMELSTEIN KOSHER MEAT 4501 14TH AVENUE .... BROOKLYN **NY** 11219 (718) 853-6115
APEX KOSHER MEATS 1817 AVENUE M .... BROOKLYN **NY** 11212 (718) 377-9081
ARUGATH HABBOSEM MEAT MARKET 67 LEE AVENUE .... BROOKLYN **NY** 11211 (718) 782-4457
BLUE CREST KOSHER MEATS 68 AVENUE O .... BROOKLYN **NY** 11204 (718) 837-4500
BOB SCHELINS KOSHER MEATS 1944 RALPH AVENUE .... BROOKLYN **NY** 11234 (718) 251-2880

Name / Address	City	State	Zip	Phone
BORO PARK GLATT KOSHER MEATS 4004 13TH AVENUE	BROOKLYN	**NY**	11218	(718) 438-9312
CHAIMOVITZ KOSHER BUTCHERS 1203 AVENUE J	BROOKLYN	**NY**	11230	(718) 377-8142
COHN & GRUNBAUM 314 MARCY AVENUE	BROOKLYN	**NY**	11211	(718) 387-8545
DANTER'S MEATS 4220 12TH AVENUE	BROOKLYN	**NY**	11219	(718) 854-3744
DAVE & JOE JOSHER MEATS 2807 NOSTRAND AVENUE	BROOKLYN	**NY**	11229	(718) 252-6302
DEBRECZINER BUTCHER CORP. 4922 FORT HAMILTON PKWY	BROOKLYN	**NY**	11219	(718) 851-2917
DORF'S MEATS 5021 AVENUE D	BROOKLYN	**NY**	11204	(718) 629-1325
E & S MEAT CORPORATION 1148 CONEY ISLAND AVENUE	BROOKLYN	**NY**	11230	(718) 859-0203
ECKHAUS BROTHERS KOSHER MEATS 497 NEPTUNE AVENUE	BROOKLYN	**NY**	11224	(718) 996-1991
EDELSTEIN, JACOB 5009 17TH AVENUE	BROOKLYN	**NY**	11204	(718) 851-0400
EMANUEL FRIED 5704 NEW UTRECHT AVENUE	BROOKLYN	**NY**	11219	(718) 633-0239
EMET MEATS 1817 AVENUE M	BROOKLYN	**NY**	11230	(718) 253-5429
FAMOUS KOSHER 1391 CONEY ISLAND AVENUE	BROOKLYN	**NY**	11230	(718) 377-3900
FELDMAN & TAUB, INC. 511 BRIGHTON BEACH AVENUE	BROOKLYN	**NY**	11235	(718) 332-2555
FREIDMAN MEATS 950 NOSTRAND AVENUE	BROOKLYN	**NY**	11225	(718) 756-0949
G & G MEATS-BENEFELD 4411 16TH AVENUE	BROOKLYN	**NY**	11204	(718) 436-2265
GANZ KOSHER MEATS 4620 AVENUE J	BROOKLYN	**NY**	11234	(718) 377-3284
GEORGETOWN KOSHER MEATS 2157 RALPH AVENUE	BROOKLYN	**NY**	11234	(718) 531-6100
GLATT BUTCHERS, INC. 539 KINGS HIGHWAY	BROOKLYN	**NY**	11223	(718) 339-4570
GLATT KOSHER MEAT MARKET 117 LEE AVENUE	BROOKLYN	**NY**	11211	(718) 387-8618
GLATT MART 1205 AVENUE M	BROOKLYN	**NY**	11230	(718) 338-4040
GLATT PACK KOSHER MEATS 4815 13TH AVENUE	BROOKLYN	**NY**	11219	(718) 633-6346
GLENWOOD KOSHER MEATS 1665 RALPH AVENUE	BROOKLYN	**NY**	11236	(718) 251-4444
GLICK BROTHERS 448 AVENUE F	BROOKLYN	**NY**	11236	(718) 376-9556
GLICK BROTHERS 2259 86TH STREET	BROOKLYN	**NY**	11214	(718) 236-9752
GLICK BROTHERS 1875 ROCKAWAY PARKWAY	BROOKLYN	**NY**	11236	(718) 444-9570
GLICK BROTHERS 3719 NOSTRAND AVENUE	BROOKLYN	**NY**	11235	(718) 769-7705
GLICK KOSHER MEATS 520 NEPTUNE AVENUE	BROOKLYN	**NY**	11224	(718) 372-9394
GOLDMAN, SHIMON 1421 CONEY ISLAND AVENUE	BROOKLYN	**NY**	11230	(718) 338-7661
GOTTESMAN'S MEAT MARKET 626 AVENUE U	BROOKLYN	**NY**	11223	(718) 375-3634
GREENBAUM BUTCHER SHOP 154 LEE AVENUE	BROOKLYN	**NY**	11211	(718) 624-7697
GRODKO KOSHER MEATS 8402 20TH AVENUE	BROOKLYN	**NY**	11214	

Name / Address	City	State	Zip	Phone
GROSSMAN'S MEAT MARKET 1919 KINGS HIGHWAY	BROOKLYN	NY	11229	(718) 375-3320
H A S KOSHER MEATS & POULTRY 421 BRIGHTON BEACH AVENUE	BROOKLYN	NY	11235	(718) 743-3900
HARRY GLAZER 8022 20TH AVENUE	BROOKLYN	NY	11214	(718) 236-1785
HARRY STEIN 2319 65TH STREET	BROOKLYN	NY	11204	(718) 645-9862
HERBST MEHADRIN MEAT MARKET 4809 18TH AVENUE	BROOKLYN	NY	11204	(718) 871-0444
HOLTZMAN & PARIS KOSHER MEATS 5513 13TH AVENUE	BROOKLYN	NY	11219	(718) 851-9270
HOUSE OF GLATT 385 KINGSTON AVENUE	BROOKLYN	NY	11213	(718) 467-9411
ISRAEL GLATT KOSHER MEATS 4907 13TH AVENUE	BROOKLYN	NY	11219	(718) 436-2948
J & L PRIME MEATS 1840 FLATBUSH AVENUE	BROOKLYN	NY	11210	(718) 338-1254
JACK & JOE'S KOSHER MEATS 621 BRIGHTON BEACH AVENUE	BROOKLYN	NY	11235	(718) 934-0809
JACK'S KOSHER MEATS 2145 KNAPP STREET	BROOKLYN	NY	11235	(718) 934-4179
JERRY LEBOWITZ KOSHER MEATS 482 AVENUE P	BROOKLYN	NY	11223	(718) 339-8555
JERUSALEM & SHAFRAN 5211 13TH AVENUE	BROOKLYN	NY	11219	(718) 436-3134
JERUSALEM GLATT 710 KINGS HIGHWAY	BROOKLYN	NY	11223	(718) 375-8879
JERUSALEM KOSHER MEAT MARKET 4516 FORT HAMILTON PKWY	BROOKLYN	NY	11219	(718) 633-5555
JOSEPH CHARATAN & SIDNEY KAPLAN, J & S 1321 AVENUE Z	BROOKLYN	NY	11235	
JOSEPH COHEN & SONS 9410 CHURCH AVENUE	BROOKLYN	NY	11212	(718) 495-1335
KASCON KOSHER MEATS 1917 AVENUE U	BROOKLYN	NY	11229	(718) 934-8948
KLENETSKY MEAT MARKET 4321 18TH AVENUE	BROOKLYN	NY	11218	(718) 854-3307
KOSHER CITY FOODS CORP. 1590 RALPH AVENUE	BROOKLYN	NY	11236	(718) 763-4992
LAMM'S MEATS 76 LEE AVENUE	BROOKLYN	NY	11211	(718) 384-6315
LANDMARK KOSHER MEATS 2104 RALPH AVENUE	BROOKLYN	NY	11234	(718) 531-7250
LEHRMAN MEAT & POULTRY 1809 SCHENECTADY AVENUE	BROOKLYN	NY	11234	(718) 353-5031
LEO MENAKER & LEIB LAKMUS 321 CHURCH AVENUE	BROOKLYN	NY	11218	(718) 435-2605
LEON HERZEK & LEONARD KRIEGER 423 CHURCH AVENUE	BROOKLYN	NY	11218	
LEON PUPKO MEAT MARKET 6914 BAY PARKWAY	BROOKLYN	NY	11204	(718) 236-2795
LIEBERMAN & RUBASHKIN GLATT KOSHER 4308 14TH AVENUE	BROOKLYN	NY	11219	(718) 436-5511
LITTMAN'S MEATS 8017 FLATBUSH AVENUE	BROOKLYN	NY	11236	(718) 763-4444
LOWY'S MEHADRIN GLATT KOSHER 502 FLUSHING AVENUE	BROOKLYN	NY	11205	(718) 625-2121
M & M KOSHER MEAT MARKET 1724 AVENUE M	BROOKLYN	NY	11230	(718) 998-7744
M & M KOSHER MEAT MARKET 1624 CORTELYOU ROAD	BROOKLYN	NY	11226	(718) 462-9144
M & M KOSHER MEATS 557 KINGS HIGHWAY	BROOKLYN	NY	11223	(718) 339-6667
M&D KOSHER MEAT MARKET 4004 13TH AVENUE	BROOKLYN	NY	11218	(718) 871-4455
MARTIN & VICTOR KOSHER MEAT MARKET 1917 AVENUE U	BROOKLYN	NY	11229	(718) 743-4927
MAX BROOKER 1624 CORTELYOU ROAD	BROOKLYN	NY	11226	
MEAL MART 54 LEE AVENUE	BROOKLYN	NY	11211	(718) 854-7800
MEAL MART 206 DIVISION AVENUE	BROOKLYN	NY	11211	(718) 963-3450
MEHADRIN GLATT KOSHER BUTCHER 1317 55TH AVENUE	BROOKLYN	NY	11219	(718) 851-7342
MENDEL WEINSTOCK 54 LEE AVENUE	BROOKLYN	NY	11211	
MENDEL'S KOSHER MEAT MARKET 4620 AVENUE J	BROOKLYN	NY	11234	(718) 252-7354
MOISHES MEAT MARKET 1706 EAST 16TH STREET	BROOKLYN	NY	11229	(718) 627-9438
MORRIS ZUHLER 1717 AVENUE M	BROOKLYN	NY	11230	
MOSES GLATT KOSHER MEAT CENTER 4602 18TH AVENUE	BROOKLYN	NY	11204	(718) 633-0493
MOSKOWITZ BUTCHER SHOP 4535 16TH AVENUE	BROOKLYN	NY	11219	(718) 853-0623
MURRAY BRAUN 771 FLATBUSH AVENUE	BROOKLYN	NY	11226	
MURRAY TEICHER KOSHER MEATS 549 KINGS HIGHWAY	BROOKLYN	NY	11223	
NADLER'S KOSHER MEAT & POULTRY 613 BRIGHTON BEACH AVENUE	BROOKLYN	NY	11235	(718) 648-6900
NETZACH ISRAEL SELF-SERVICE MEAT & POULTRY				
4924 16TH AVENUE	BROOKLYN	NY	11204	(718) 851-0051
NETZACH ISRAEL MEAT & POULTRY 5010 16TH AVENUE	BROOKLYN	NY	11204	(718) 851-0288
NETZACH ISRAEL MEAT MARKET 4310 16TH AVENUE	BROOKLYN	NY	11219	(718) 435-1128
PARKWAY KOSHER MEAT CENTER 423 CHURCH AVENUE	BROOKLYN	NY	11218	(718) 436-4321
PASTERNAK KOSHER BUTCHER 422 DITMAS AVENUE	BROOKLYN	NY	11218	(718) 438-4411
PIC-N-PAY KOSHER MEATS 1907 AVENUE M	BROOKLYN	NY	11230	(718) 377-4050
PICK-N-SAVE KOSHER MEATS 2052 ROCKAWAY PARKWAY	BROOKLYN	NY	11236	(718) 251-3420
PUPKO 6914 BAY PARKWAY	BROOKLYN	NY	11204	(718) 236-2795
R&W GLATT KOSHER BUTCHER COMPANY				
1501 CONEY ISLAND AVENUE	BROOKLYN	NY	11230	(718) 377-7391
R. GLICK MEATS 1875 ROCKAWAY PARKWAY	BROOKLYN	NY	11230	(718) 377-7391
RAN LEE KOSHER MEATS 3805 NOSTRAND AVENUE	BROOKLYN	NY	11236	(718) 444-9570
RETAIL KOSHER BUTCHER ASSOCIATION OF NEW YORK				
1907 AVENUE M	BROOKLYN	NY	11230	(718) 252-9150
REUBEN GLAZER 8022 20TH AVENUE	BROOKLYN	NY	11214	(718) 236-1785
ROSNER KOSHER MEATS 719 AVENUE U	BROOKLYN	NY	11223	(718) 645-8486
SABEN FOOD PRODUCTS 1372 39TH STREET	BROOKLYN	NY	11218	(718) 435-0200
SAM & HARRY'S KOSHER MEAT MARKET 557 KINGS HIGHWAY	BROOKLYN	NY	11223	(718) 339-6668
SAM FOX MEATS 2233 86TH STREET	BROOKLYN	NY	11214	(718) 232-3234
SAM GLICK & SONS INC. 2259 86TH STREET	BROOKLYN	NY	11214	(718) 236-9752
SAM WEISS & BROS SURKIS 1403 FOSTER AVENUE	BROOKLYN	NY	11230	
SAMUEL LITTMAN 8017 FLATLANDS AVENUE	BROOKLYN	NY	11236	(718) 436-5511
SASSON & FARRAH INCORPORATED 710 KINGS HIGHWAY	BROOKLYN	NY	11223	(718) 376-7443
SATMAR BUTCHER & MEAT MARKET 82 LEE AVENUE	BROOKLYN	NY	11211	(718) 963-1100
SATMAR MEATS 5109 NEW UTRECHT AVENUE	BROOKLYN	NY	11219	(718) 435-8200
SCHNEPS KOSHER MEATS 421 BRIGHTON BEACH AVENUE	BROOKLYN	NY	11235	
SCHNITZER'S GLATT KOSHER MEAT 4602 18TH AVENUE	BROOKLYN	NY	11204	(718) 853-2801
SPERBER'S MEATS 4535 16TH AVENUE	BROOKLYN	NY	11204	(718) 854-7335
STAR OF DAVID KOSHER MEATS 2440 NOSTRAND AVENUE	BROOKLYN	NY	11210	(718) 252-0208
SYM'S KOSHER MEATS 1913 KINGS HIGHWAY	BROOKLYN	NY	11229	(718) 375-2677
SYM'S KOSHER MEATS 2318 NOSTRAND AVENUE	BROOKLYN	NY	11210	(718) 951-7459
TAUB'S MEATS 211 CHURCH AVENUE	BROOKLYN	NY	11218	(718) 438-0422
WEISS GLATT KOSHER MEATS 5520 13TH AVENUE	BROOKLYN	NY	11219	(718) 871-5442
WERKER'S KOSHER MEATS 2802 AVENUE U	BROOKLYN	NY	11229	(718) 646-5927
ZAKEN'S KOSHER MEATS 3100 OCEAN PARKWAY	BROOKLYN	NY	11235	
COHEN'S MEAT MARKET 1258 HERTEL	BUFFALO	NY	14216	(716) 875-4690
KORNMEHL KOSHER MARKET 1440 HERTEL	BUFFALO	NY	14216	(716) 838-2429
GOURMET GLATT KOSHER MEATS 460 CENTRAL AVENUE	CEDARHURST	NY	11516	(516) 569-2662
LAWRENCE KOSHER MEAT MARKET 415 CENTRAL AVENUE	CEDARHURST	NY	11516	(516) 569-3683
COMMACK KOSHER MEATS 132 EAST JERICHO TURNPIKE	COMMACK	NY	11725	(516) 543-2300
EAST MEADOW KOSHER MEAT & POULTRY				
495 BELLMORE AVENUE	EAST MEADOW	NY	11554	(516) 481-3335
SAV-ON KOSHER MEATS 713 WHITE PLAINS ROAD	EASTCHESTER	NY	10583	(914) 725-0565
ABE LEVINE & SONS 104 CENTER STREET	ELLENVILLE	NY	12428	(914) 647-5630
KING'S MEAT-O-MART 96-23 57TH AVENUE	ELMHURST	NY	11373	(718) 271-8501
MORRIS OBERMAN'S MEATS BOX 437	FALLSBURG	NY	12733	(914) 434-4510
BERNARD BIRNBAUM 2152 MOTT AVENUE	FAR ROCKAWAY	NY	11691	
ERP'S MEATS 1813 MOTT AVENUE	FAR ROCKAWAY	NY	11691	(718) 471-3099
MENORAH POULTRY 1813 MOTT AVENUE	FAR ROCKAWAY	NY	11691	(718) 471-5166
NAGLER & SMALL MEATS 1905 MOTT AVENUE	FAR ROCKAWAY	NY	11691	(718) 327-2822
NOAM FOOD SERVICE-GLATT KOSHER BEEF & VEAL				
1216 BRUNSWICK AVENUE	FAR ROCKAWAY	NY	11691	(718) 471-3456
SMALL KOSHER MEAT MARKET 18-49 MOTT AVENUE	FAR ROCKAWAY	NY	11691	(718) 327-1972
WAVECREST KOSHER MEAT 237 BEACH 20TH STREET	FAR ROCKAWAY	NY	11691	(718) 327-9550
BLOCH & FALK FINE FOODS 73-04 37TH AVENUE	FLUSHING	NY	11367	(718) 429-2379
BRACH'S GLATT SELF SERVICE MEAT MARKET 72-49 MAIN STREET	FLUSHING	NY	11367	(718) 544-7448
EDEN KOSHER MEAT & POULTRY 79-09 MAIN STREET	FLUSHING	NY	11367	(718) 381-1386
EMMETT PACKING COMPANY INC. 7226 MAIN STREET	FLUSHING	NY	11367	(718) 544-1950
GB GLATT 71-26 MAIN STREET	FLUSHING	NY	11367	(718) 268-1279
GLICK BROTHERS 72-09 KISSENA BLVD	FLUSHING	NY	11367	(718) 658-9479
HERSHKOWITZ'S MEATS 164-08 69TH AVENUE	FLUSHING	NY	11365	(718) 591-0750
LORI KOSHER 68-24 MAIN STREET	FLUSHING	NY	11367	(718) 263-4696
MARIN'S KOSHER MEAT 184-08 HORACE HARDING EXPRESSWAY	FLUSHING	NY	11365	(718) 358-3223
MITCHELL GARDENS KOSHER MEATS 2820 UNION STREET	FLUSHING	NY	11354	(718) 463-5709
PAULINE GLASS 172-07 67TH AVENUE	FLUSHING	NY	11365	
PRIDE KOSHER MEATS 6833 FRESH MEADOW LANE	FLUSHING	NY	11365	(718) 461-9844
R. GLICK MEATS 7209 KISSENA BOULEVARD	FLUSHING	NY	11367	(718) 658-9479
REGENCY KOSHER MEATS 77-34 VLEIGH PLACE	FLUSHING	NY	11367	(718) 297-1205
RUBIN ARON 188-18 UNION TURNPIKE	FLUSHING	NY	11367	
TRU VALUE KOSHER MEATS 25-17 PARSONS BOULEVARD	FLUSHING	NY	11354	(718) 886-0444
TURNPIKE GLATT KOSHER MEATS 189-23 UNION TURNPIKE	FLUSHING	NY	11366	(718) 776-7727
YOUR KOSHER BUTCHERS, INC. 4185 MAIN STREET	FLUSHING	NY	11355	(718) 886-4464
CROFT KOSHER MEAT MARKET 65-49 99TH STREET	FOREST HILLS	NY	11374	(718) 459-8480
ABE'S GLATT KOSHER MEATS, INCORPORATED				
98-106 QUEENS BOULEVARD	FOREST HILLS	NY	11375	(718) 459-5820
CHAI KOSHER MEATS 6437 108TH STREET	FOREST HILLS	NY	11375	(718) 897-9619
CONTINENTAL MEATS 22-73 31 AUSTIN STREET	FOREST HILLS	NY	11375	(718) 721-1900
CROFT MEAT & POULTRY MARKET 65-49 99TH STREET	FOREST HILLS	NY	11374	(718) 459-8480
D & A MEATS 164-08 69TH STREET	FOREST HILLS	NY	11365	(718) 591-0750
FINEST KOSHER MEAT MARKET 6371 108TH STREET	FOREST HILLS	NY	11375	(718) 897-3053
HERMAN GLICK'S SONS 101-15 QUEENS BOULEVARD	FOREST HILLS	NY	11375	(718) 896-7736
JOE STARK 6355 108TH STREET	FOREST HILLS	NY	11375	
KISSENA KOSHER MEATS INCORPORATED				
103-35 QUEENS BOULEVARD	FOREST HILLS	NY	11375	(718) 897-8996
LAZAR'S PACKING CORP. 100-30 QUEENS BOULEVARD	FOREST HILLS	NY	11375	(718) 897-6635
PAUL & LUDWIG ZIEGLER 115-16 QUEENS BOULEVARD	FOREST HILLS	NY	11375	(718) 263-3093
SIMON'S KOSHER BUTCHER 115-06 QUEENS BOULEVARD	FOREST HILLS	NY	11375	(718) 261-7463
SIMON'S KOSHER MEAT & POULTRY 87-48 PARSONS BLVD	FOREST HILLS	NY	11375	(718) 739-6066
ZIEGLER P & L KOSHER MEAT 115-16 QUEENS BOULEVARD	FOREST HILLS	NY	11375	(718) 362-2975
GEL OF GREAT NECK 503 MIDDLE NECK ROAD	GREAT NECK	NY	11023	(516) 487-5886
GREAT NECK KOSHER MEATS 65 MIDDLE NECK ROAD	GREAT NECK	NY	11021	(516) 482-0266
JAY'S KOSHER MEAT 503 MIDDLE NECK ROAD	GREAT NECK	NY	11023	(516) 487-7353
COHEN'S KOSHER MEATS & POULTRY 1330 BROADWAY	HEWLETT	NY	11557	(516) 374-1129
FIVE TOWN KOSHER PACKING 1324 PENINSULA BOULEVARD	HEWLETT	NY	11557	(516) 791-9877
FELDWOOD KOSHER MEATS 4285 OYSTER BAY ROAD	HICKSVILLE	NY	11801	(516) 681-7766
JERUSALEM KOSHER MEATS 412 JERUSALEM AVENUE	HICKSVILLE	NY	11801	(516) 935-2238
LINDENWOOD KOSHER BUTCHER 82-09 153RD AVENUE	HOWARD BEACH	NY	11414	(718) 641-2227
R & A KOSHER MEATS INCORPORATED				
156-30 CROSS BAY BOULEVARD	HOWARD BEACH	NY	11414	(718) 641-1308
BERGER'S KOSHER MEATS 13 NEW FIFTH STREET	HUNTINGTON STATION	NY	11746	(516) 423-0960
BEACHHAVEN KOSHER MEATS & POULTRY CORPORATION				
75-11 37TH AVENUE	JACKSON HEIGHTS	NY	11372	(718) 898-0600
BRIARWOOD KOSHER MEATS 138-09 QUEENS BLVD	JAMAICA	NY	11435	(718) 237-7340
E&Z KOSHER MEAT 188-18 UNION TPKE	JAMAICA	NY	11367	(718) 465-2664
JERICHO KOSHER MEATS 441 HICKSVILLE ROAD	JERICHO	NY	11753	(516) 938-7900
H & W GLATT KOSHER MEATS 118-29A METROPOLITAN AVENUE	KEW GARDENS	NY	11415	(718) 441-1140

Listing	City	State	Postal Code	Phone
METROPOLITAN KOSHER MEAT MARKET 116-10 METROPOLITAN AVENUE	KEW GARDENS	NY	11415	(718) 441-1880
EDEN KOSHER MEAT 79-09 MAIN STREET	KEW GARDENS	NY	11367	(718) 380-1366
G&B GLATT KOSHER MEAT MARKET 71-26 MAIN STREET	KEW GARDENS HILLS	NY	11367	(718) 268-1279
SUPERSOL LTD. 330 CENTRAL AVENUE	LAWRENCE	NY	11559	(516) 295-3300
VALUE PLUS KOSHER MEATS 290 BURNSIDE AVENUE	LAWRENCE	NY	11559	(516) 239-5458
MITCHELL GARDENS KOSHER MEAT & POULTRY MARKET 28-20 UNION STREET	LINDEN HILL	NY	11354	(718) 463-5709
LITTLE NECK SELF SERVICE 254-51 HORACE HARDING BOULEVARD	LITTLE NECK	NY	11362	(718) 428-5000
GORDON MEAT MARKET 220 WEST PARK AVENUE	LONG BEACH	NY	11561	(516) 431-4540
ISRAEL KOSHER MEATS 261 WEST PARK AVENUE	LONG BEACH	NY	11561	(516) 431-4120
PICK-N-SAVE KOSHER MEATS 172 EAST PARK AVENUE	LONG BEACH	NY	11561	(516) 889-2828
BROADWAY KOSHER MEAT 33-12 BROADWAY	LONG ISLAND CITY	NY	11106	(718) 728-5658
M.F. MEAT INC. 33-15 BROADWAY	LONG ISLAND CITY	NY	11106	(718) 728-1626
MALVERNE KOSHER MEAT & POULTRY 370 HEMPSTEAD AVENUE	MALVERNE	NY	11565	(516) 599-1070
G&M KOSHER MEATS INC. 2065 MERRICK ROAD	MERRICK	NY	11566	(516) 378-6463
MENDLOWITZ'S MEATS 42 MAIN STREET	MONSEY	NY	10952	(914) 356-2376
LASHINSKY'S 338 BROADWAY	MONTICELLO	NY	12701	(914) 794-6140
LAZAR'S MEAT MONTEGO PLAZA	MONTICELLO	NY	12701	(914) 434-7300
LENK'S MEATS 380 BROADWAY	MONTICELLO	NY	12701	(914) 794-7380
LUNGEN'S MEATS 292 BROADWAY	MONTICELLO	NY	12701	(914) 794-4990
WESTCHESTER KOSHER MEAT & POULTRY MARKET 11 EAST PROSPECT AVENUE	MOUNT VERNON	NY	10552	(914) 664-4313
M.D. GLATT KOSHER MEATS 1620 MARCUS AVENUE	NEW HYDE PARK	NY	11040	(516) 488-3396
BROADWAY KOSHER MEATS 13 QUAKER RIDGE ROAD	NEW ROCHELLE	NY	10804	(914) 235-2500
EPPY'S FOOD CORPORATION 1291 NORTH AVENUE	NEW ROCHELLE	NY	10804	(914) 636-4241
ATLAS MEATS 860 WASHINGTON	NEW YORK	NY	10014	(212) 255-3030
BLOCH & FALK MEAT PRODUCTS 152 NAGLE AVENUE	NEW YORK	NY	10040	(212) 927-5010
EIGHTH AVENUE KOSHER MEAT & POULTRY, INC. 327 EIGHTH AVENUE	NEW YORK	NY	10001	(212) 929-8870
ERNST FLEISCHMAN 150 SHERMAN AVENUE	NEW YORK	NY	10040	(212) 567-2030
FISCHER BROTHERS & LESLIE 230 WEST 72ND STREET	NEW YORK	NY	10023	(212) 787-1715
GARY TURKEL 152 ESSEX STREET	NEW YORK	NY	10002	(212) 477-0146
GOLDBERG BUTCHER STORE 500 GRAND STREET	NEW YORK	NY	10002	(212) 475-6915
GRUENSPECHT & SONS 2830 BROADWAY	NEW YORK	NY	10032	(212) 568-5656
GUTMANN & MAYER MEATS 4229-4231 BROADWAY	NEW YORK	NY	10033	(212) 923-1989
H & M FELDSTEIN 2370 BROADWAY	NEW YORK	NY	10025	(212) 873-3560
HY-GRADE KOSHER MEAT 1200 MADISON AVENUE	NEW YORK	NY	10028	(212) 722-6379
I. SALZMAN 1384 SECOND AVENUE	NEW YORK	NY	10021	(212) 650-1996
INWOOD KOSHER 587 WEST 207TH STREET	NEW YORK	NY	10034	(212) 567-3088
IRVING BERGER 202 EAST 87TH STREET	NEW YORK	NY	10028	(212) 289-7234
JOE KARTIN 327 EIGHTH AVENUE	NEW YORK	NY	10001	(212) 929-8870
JONAS STERN & SONS-GLATT KOSHER 229 WEST 100TH STREET	NEW YORK	NY	10024	(212) 662-7081
MARTIN THAU 736 WEST 181ST STREET	NEW YORK	NY	10033	(212) 923-9319
MORIAH KOSHER POULTRY, INC. 407 WEST 13TH STREET	NEW YORK	NY	10014	(212) 255-6350
MURRAY SCHEIN 507 GRAND STREET	NEW YORK	NY	10002	(212) 254-0180
P. FELDSTEIN BUTCHERS 2370 BROADWAY	NEW YORK	NY	10024	(212) 873-3560
PARK EAST KOSHER 1163 MADISON AVENUE	NEW YORK	NY	10028	(212) 787-3545
PERL'S BROADWAY KOSHER MEAT MARKET 2251 BROADWAY	NEW YORK	NY	10024	(212) 877-9640
PHILIP LEVITCH 807 WEST 181ST STREET	NEW YORK	NY	10033	(212) 923-9826
RICK BROTHERS MEATS 557 GRAND STREET	NEW YORK	NY	10002	(212) 677-9230
ROSEN BROTHERS 2411 BROADWAY	NEW YORK	NY	10025	(212) 724-0220
ROSEN BROTHERS (IDEE CORP.) 2254 12TH AVENUE	NEW YORK	NY	10024	(212) 281-5750
SCHILD BROTHERS INC. 4191 BROADWAY	NEW YORK	NY	10033	(212) 927-5997
SHEDLETSKY'S MEATS 221 EAST BROADWAY	NEW YORK	NY	10002	(212) 964-1232
SIDNEY SISSUN 4230 BROADWAY	NEW YORK	NY	10033	(212) 927-8188
SMALL'S MEAT & POULTRY 221 EAST BROADWAY	NEW YORK	NY	10002	(212) 964-1232
STAHL KOSHER MEATS 62 AVENUE A	NEW YORK	NY	10009	(212) 228-2668
WARSHAYCHIK'S MEATS 181 CLINTON STREET	NEW YORK	NY	10002	(212) 982-1040
WERNER'S MEATS 4316 BROADWAY	NEW YORK	NY	10033	(212) 927-0463
PARKMERE KOSHER MEATS 951 ROSEDALE ROAD	NORTH WOODMERE	NY	11581	(516) 791-4683
D & W KOSHER MEAT & POULTRY MARKET 61-42 SPRINGFIELD BLVD	OAKLAND GARDENS	NY	11364	(718) 255-1550
COHEN'S KOSHER MEATS 351 LONG BEACH ROAD	OCEANSIDE	NY	11572	(516) 766-1714
OCEANSIDE KOSHER MEAT MARKET 18 ATLANTIC AVENUE	OCEANSIDE	NY	11572	(516) 766-5252
JOE'S MEAT MARKET 17-11 101TH AVENUE	OZONE PARK	NY		(718) 845-3060
KOSHER MEAT FARM OF PLAINVIEW 365A SOUTH OYSTER BAY ROAD	PLAINVIEW	NY	11803	(516) 931-6446
PLAINVIEW KOSHER MEATS 1113 OLD COUNTRY ROAD	PLAINVIEW	NY	11803	(516) 681-4410
STAR MARKET 73 PONINGO STREET	PORT CHESTER	NY	10573	(914) 937-8007
IDEAL KOSHER MEATS & POULTRY 97-18 63RD ROAD	REGO PARK	NY	11375	(718) 459-2815
IRVAL KOSHER MEATS 93-05 63RD DRIVE	REGO PARK	NY	11374	
LAZAR'S PACKING 110-30 QUEENS BOULEVARD	REGO PARK	NY	11375	(718) 897-6635
MID-QUEENS KOSHER MEAT CORPORATION 94-05 63RD DRIVE	REGO PARK	NY	11374	(718) 896-2927
SIDNEY REISS 6360 SAUNDERS STREET	REGO PARK	NY	11374	(718) 459-9722
GUSS' MEATS 113-17 LIBERTY AVENUE	RICHMOND HILL	NY	11419	(718) 843-1993
GLATT STOP OF RIVERDALE 3711 RIVERDALE AVENUE	RIVERDALE	NY	10471	(212) 884-1200
GORONKIN'S MEAT MARKET 1714 MONROE AVENUE	ROCHESTER	NY	14618	(716) 473-4640
LIPMAN'S KOSHER MEAT 1482 MONROE AVENUE	ROCHESTER	NY	14618	(716) 271-7886
COHEN'S KOSHER MEAT 115-06 ROCKAWAY BEACH BOULEVARD	ROCKAWAY PARK	NY	11694	(718) 634-1349
G & K MEAT MARKET 115-06 ROCKAWAY BEACH BOULEVARD	ROCKAWAY PARK	NY	11694	(718) 474-5704
GREYSTONE KOSHER MEATS 176 NORTH LONG BEACH ROAD	ROCKVILLE CENTRE	NY	11570	(516) 766-0099
S & W KOSHER MEATS 16 SOUTH PARK AVENUE	ROCKVILLE CENTRE	NY	11570	(516) 766-1771
MHADRIN 1066 WILMOT ROAD	SCARSDALE	NY	10583	(914) GR2-2240
SAVON KOSHER MEATS 713 WHITE PLAINS ROAD	SCARSDALE	NY	10709	(914) 725-0565
KING KOSHER MEATS 1087 HICKSVILLE ROAD	SEAFORD	NY	11783	(516) 735-8490
HELLMAN'S MEATS 52 NORTH MAIN STREET	SPRING VALLEY	NY	10977	(914) 356-0715
HERBIE'S KOSHER MEATS 30 SOUTH CENTRAL AVENUE	SPRING VALLEY	NY	10977	(914) 425-3113
HILLCREST KOSHER MEATS 285A NORTH MAIN STREET	SPRING VALLEY	NY	10977	(914) 352-3626
L & D 303A NORTH MAIN STREET	SPRING VALLEY	NY	10977	(914) 352-9444
M & S 94 NORTH MAIN STREET	SPRING VALLEY	NY	10977	(914) 356-1607
KOSHER ISLAND GLATT TAKE HOME 2206 VICTORY BOULEVARD	STATEN ISLAND	NY	10314	(718) 698-5800
TIKVA KOSHER MEATS & POULTRY 2845 RICHMOND AVENUE	STATEN ISLAND	NY	10314	(718) 698-2603
ADLER'S KOSHER MARKET 41 LAFAYETTE AVENUE	SUFFERN	NY	10901	(914) 357-1637
GLATT STOP 191 ROUTE 59	SUFFERN	NY	10977	(914) 357-9594
MEAL MART ROUTE 55	SWAN LAKE	NY	12783	(914) 292-9439
MARTIN TENENBAUM KOSHER MEATS 2914 EAST GENESEE	SYRACUSE	NY	13224	(315) 446-3254
PARKMERE KOSHER MEATS 951 ROSEDALE ROAD	VALLEY STREAM	NY	11581	(516) 791-3086
SHUB & NOVICK 355 NORTH CENTRAL AVENUE	VALLEY STREAM	NY	11580	(516) 825-8171
SUNRISE KOSHER MEAT MARKET 355 CENTRAL AVENUE	VALLEY STREAM	NY	11580	(516) 276-3166
KOSHER MEAT FARM #2 1172 WANTAGH AVENUE	WANTAGH	NY	11793	(516) 781-6296
NORTH NASSAU KOSHER MEATS 598 OLD COUNTRY ROAD	WESTBURY	NY	11590	(516) 333-1616
SATMAR MEATS & POULTRY C/O CONGREGATION YETEV LEV	WHITE LAKE	NY	12786	(914) 583-7020
KEN-MAR MEATS 333 MAMARONECK AVENUE	WHITE PLAINS	NY	10605	(914) 761-8046
CLEARVIEW KOSHER 160-32 WILLETS POINT BOULEVARD	WHITESTONE	NY	11357	(718) 352-2099
K & K 20-11 UTOPIA PARKWAY	WHITESTONE	NY	11357	(718) 352-2776
WOODMERE KOSHER MEATS 1017 BROADWAY	WOODMERE	NY	11598	(516) 374-4058
KESSLER'S & SONS MAIN STREET	WOODRIDGE	NY	12789	(914) 434-7550
NAT KAGEN MEATS & POULTRY GREEN AVENUE	WOODRIDGE	NY	12789	(914) 434-4334
BAKER HILL PACKING COMPANY 2558 CENTRAL PARK AVENUE	YONKERS	NY	10704	(914) 779-8100
CENTUCK 622 TUCKAHOE ROAD	YONKERS	NY	10710	(914) 779-3683
HENRY'S KOSHER MEATS 636 MCLEAN AVENUE	YONKERS	NY	10705	(914) 965-5802
SYON MEATS 2558 CENTRAL AVENUE	YONKERS	NY	10710	(914) 779-8100
VALUE PLUS MEATS OF YONKERS 1733 CENTRAL PARK AVENUE	YONKERS	NY	10710	(914) 961-2048
BONEM'S KOSHER MEAT MARKET 7377 BROOKCREST DRIVE	CINCINNATI	OH	45237	(513) 351-3144
PILDER'S KOSHER FOODS 7601 READING	CINCINNATI	OH	45237	(513) 821-7050
SIMON'S KOSHER MEAT MARKET 1436 SECTION ROAD	CINCINNATI	OH	45237	(513) 761-1864
A & W FOODS 4900 CRAYTON AVENUE	CLEVELAND	OH	44104	(216) 431-8000
ALTMAN'S KOSHER MEAT MARKET 2185 SOUTH GREEN ROAD	CLEVELAND	OH	44121	(216) 381-7615
BASCH'S KOSHER MEAT MARKET 1944 SOUTH TAYLOR ROAD	CLEVELAND	OH	44118	(216) 321-1911
BERGER'S QUALITY KOSHER MEAT MARKET BERGER'S QUALITY KOSHER MEAT MARKET	CLEVELAND	OH	44121	(216) 382-6560
BORIS' KOSHER MEAT 14406 CEDAR ROAD	CLEVELAND	OH	44118	(216) 382-5330
COVENTRY POULTRY 1825 COVENTRY ROAD	CLEVELAND	OH	44118	(216) 371-0555
IRVING'S KOSHER MEAT MARKET 13938½ CEDAR ROAD	CLEVELAND	OH	44118	(216) 321-5660
LEO'S KOSHER MEAT MARKET 1839 SOUTH TAYLOR ROAD	CLEVELAND	OH	44118	(216) 932-9212
SAM & JACK'S KOSHER MEAT MARKET 2110 SOUTH TAYLOR ROAD	CLEVELAND	OH	44118	(216) 321-7322
SILVERMAN BROTHERS KOSHER MEAT MARKETS 26301 RICHMOND ROAD	CLEVELAND	OH	44118	(216) 292-3720
MARTIN'S KOSHER FOODS 3685 EAST BROAD STREET	COLUMBUS	OH	43213	(614) 231-3653
SIEGLE'S DELICATESSEN & FOOD MART 2636 WEST CENTRAL	TOLEDO	OH	43606	(419) 473-2791
SIEGLE'S DELICATESSEN & FOOD MART 15 WEST BANCROFT	TOLEDO	OH	43620	(419) 243-6264
ABRAM'S KOSHER MEAT 7241 BATHURST STREET	TORONTO	ON	L4J 2J7	(416) 731-4112
BATHURST MEAT MARKET 3774 BATHURST STREET	TORONTO	ON		(416) 636-4440
B. GOLDSTEIN 308 WILSON AVENUE	TORONTO	ON		(416) 633-9642
HARTMAN'S KOSHER MEAT 5974 BATHURST STREET	TORONTO	ON	M2R 1Z1	(416) 663-7779
JOE KIRSHEN'S KOSHER MEAT MARKET 3544 BATHURST STREET	TORONTO	ON		(416) 781-7767
KOSHER MEATS & TREATS 2825 BATHURST STREET	TORONTO	ON	M6B 1A4	(416) 783-4231
LOBLAW'S PRIME KOSHER MART 270 WILSON AVENUE	TORONTO	ON	M3H 1S6	(416) 638-8287
MANOR KOSHER MEAT MARKET 662 SHEPPARD AVENUE WEST	TORONTO	ON		(416) 636-2000
H. PERL 3013 BATHURST STREET	TORONTO	ON		(416) 787-4234
SPRINGER'S 3393 BATHURST STREET	TORONTO	ON		(416) 787-3971
STROLI'S 3459 BATHURST STREET	TORONTO	ON		(416) 789-5333
SUNNYBROOK FOODS LTD 241 WILMINGTON AVENUE (BATHURST MANOR PLAZA)	TORONTO	ON		(416) 635-5987
YOSSI'S FINE FOODS 4117 BATHURST STREET	TORONTO	ON		(416) 635-9509
ABE'S & SONS 7410 BUSTLETON AVENUE	PHILADELPHIA	PA	19120	(215) 742-3800
BEST VALUE MEATS 8566 BUSTLETON AVENUE	PHILADELPHIA	PA	19152	(215) 342-1902
BLACK'S KOSHER MEAT & POULTRY 1601 EAST WADSWORTH	PHILADELPHIA	PA	19150	(215) 247-0215
MAIN LINE KOSHER MEATS 7562 HAVERFORD AVENUE	PHILADELPHIA	PA	19151	(215) TR7-1428
MODERN KOSHER MEAT MARKET 5948 OGONTZ AVENUE	PHILADELPHIA	PA	19141	(215) 924-8259
RHAWNHURST KOSHER PRIME MEATS 8261 BUSTLETON AVENUE	PHILADELPHIA	PA	19152	(215) 742-5287
WALLACE'S KREWSTOWN KOSHER MEATS 8919 KREWSTOWN ROAD	PHILADELPHIA	PA	19115	(215) 464-7800
KOSHER MART 2121 MURRAY AVENUE	PITTSBURGH	PA	15217	(412) 421-4450
PRIME KOSHER FOODS 1916 MURRAY AVENUE	PITTSBURGH	PA	15217	(412) 421-1015
SAUL KRONZEK MEATS 5719 BRYANT STREET	PITTSBURGH	PA	15206	(412) 661-3377
TEL AVIV KOSHER MEAT MARKET 1716 MURRAY AVENUE	PITTSBURGH	PA	15217	(412) 421-4450
GOTTESMAN'S KOSHER MEAT & POULTRY MARKET 1216 MULBERRY STREET	SCRANTON	PA	18510	(717) 342-3886
ROBINSON KOSHER MEAT MARKET 1502 VINE STREET	SCRANTON	PA	18510	(717) 961-9760
ABRAM'S KOSHER MEAT MARKET 156 ST. VIATEUR WEST	MONTREAL	QU	H2T 2L3	(514) 274-7953
BOUCHERIE SELECT 6346 VICTORIA	MONTREAL	QU		(514) 739-5042
CAPITAL UNITED 5785 VICTORIA	MONTREAL	QU	H3W 2R3	(514) 735-1744
CENTRAL KOSHER MEAT MARKET 3839 ST. LAWRENCE	MONTREAL	QU		(514) 842-8797
CONTINENTAL KOSHER MEAT POULTRY & DELICATESSEN PRODUCTS 230 FAIRMOUNT WEST	MONTREAL	QU		(514) 274-5491
COTE ST. LUC KOSHER MEAT MARKET 5636 WESTMINSTER	MONTREAL	QU	H4W 2J4	(514) 481-4094
DARLINGTON KOSHER MEAT MARKET 6530 DARLINGTON	MONTREAL	QU	H3S 2J3	(514) 733-4251
FRIENDLY KOSHER MEAT MARKET 5804 WESTMINSTER	MONTREAL	QU	H4W 2J8	(514) 484-6644
GATT'S KOSHER MEATS 7015 COTE ST LUC ROAD	MONTREAL	QU		(514) 482-6227
GLATT KOSHER MEATS 175 LAURIER WEST	MONTREAL	QU		(514) 274-9477
GLATT'S KOSHER MEATS 5897 VICTORIA	MONTREAL	QU		(514) 737-3228
J&R KOSHER MEAT MARKET 1329 VAN HORNE	MONTREAL	QU	H2V 1K7	(514) 271-6386
MARTON'S KOSHER MEAT MARKET 6270 SOMERLED	MONTREAL	QU	H3X 2B6	(514) 489-1515
MEHADRIN KOSHER MEAT MARKET 274 ST. VIATEUR WEST	MONTREAL	QU	H2V 1Y1	(514) 279-6351
OSMAN BROTHERS LTD. 55 VILLENEAUVE WEST	MONTREAL	QU	H2T 2R4	(514) 849-8693
SHALOM KOSHER MEAT MARKET 4699 VAN HORNE	MONTREAL	QU	H2W 1H8	(514) 341-5815
SHAPIRO'S KOSHER MEAT MARKET 6947 WILDERTON	MONTREAL	QU	H3S 2M4	(514) 735-3001

Name / Address	City	State	Zip	Phone
STILMAN BROS. REG'D 6460 VICTORIA	MONTREAL	**QU**	H3W 2S6	(514) 738-7079
WESTERN KOSHER MEAT MARKET 400 LEGENDRE WEST	MONTREAL	**QU**	H2N 1H7	(514) 381-8596
ST. LAURENCE STRICTLY KOSHER 2151 ST. LOUIS STREET	ST. LAURENT	**QU**	H3M 1P1	(514) 747-6531
MARTY WEISSMAN KOSHER MEAT MARKET 88½ ROLFE STREET	CRANSTON	**RI**	02910	(401) 467-8903
FRED SPIGEL'S KOSHER MEAT MARKET & DELI APPETIZER 243 RESERVOIR AVENUE	PROVIDENCE	**RI**	02907	(401) 461-0425
STONE'S HOPE STREET KOSHER MEAT MARKET 780 HOPE STREET	PROVIDENCE	**RI**	02906	(401) 421-0271
KIPPERT'S KOSHER FOODS 4965 SUMMER AVENUE	MEMPHIS	**TN**	38122	(901) 682-3801
MANNY'S KOSHER MEAT & DELICATESSEN 215 PRESTON ROYAL SHOPPING CENTER	DALLAS	**TX**	75225	(214) 943-5895
REICHMAN'S KOSHER MEAT & DELICATESSEN 215 PRESTON ROYAL SHOPPING CENTER	DALLAS	**TX**	75225	(214) 368-2847
JIM JAMAIL & SONS 3114 KIRBY DRIVE	HOUSTON	**TX**	77006	(713) 523-5535
THE KOSHER MEATING PLACE 9752 HILLCROFT, MAPLEWOOD SQUARE SHOPING CENTER	HOUSTON	**TX**	77096	(713) 721-6470
MARTIN POULTRY EGG & FROZEN FOOD COMPANY 2002 WHITE	HOUSTON	**TX**	77007	(713) 869-6191
UNITED FOODS 5901 BEVERLY HILLS	HOUSTON	**TX**	77057	(713) 789-0301
SIDNEY PERLIN'S KOSHER MEAT MARKET 619 WEST 35TH STREET	NORFOLK	**VA**	23508	(804) 622-5196
RICHMOND KOSHER MEAT MARKET 3109 WEST CARY STREET	RICHMOND	**VA**	23221	(804) 358-6905
KOSHER MEAT KLUB 4731 WEST BURLEIGH	MILWAUKEE	**WI**	53210	(414) 871-3273
KRAMER'S KOSHER CORNER 5101 WEST KEEFE	MILWAUKEE	**WI**	53216	(414) 442-2625
RABINOWITZ BROTHERS KOSHER MEAT MARKET 4622 WEST BURLEIGH	MILWAUKEE	**WI**	53210	(414) 871-3273

MEAT & POULTRY - WHOLESALE

Name / Address	City	State	Zip	Phone
EMES KOSHER MEAT PRODUCTS 2627 SOUTH LA CIENEGA BOULEVARD	LOS ANGELES	**CA**	90034	(213) 836-0535
HY-GRADE MEAT SPECIALTIES COMPANY 3462 LARIMER	DENVER	**CO**	80205	(303) 292-6328
SUPERVISED PRODUCTS 3890 ADAMS STREET, PO BOX 16432	DENVER	**CO**	80216	(303) 321-7033
ROLAND FOODS 135 R STREET S.W.	WASHINGTON	**DC**	20023	(202) 488-0888
SAVAL DIRECTOR 925 FIFTH STREET N.W.	WASHINGTON	**DC**	20023	(202) 832-9400
GOLDBERG BROTHERS SOUTH MARKET STREET	WILMINGTON	**DE**	19801	(302) 655-5301
AMERICAN KOSHER PROVISIONS 6988 N.W. 36TH AVENUE	MIAMI	**FL**	33147	(305) 653-4496
HEBREW NATIONAL KOSHER, J & J PURVEYORS 2140 N.W. 13TH AVENUE	MIAMI	**FL**	33142	(305) 592-0300
ZION CORPORATION 1717 N.W. SEVENTH AVENUE	MIAMI	**FL**	33125	(305) 324-1855
BEST KOSHER SAUSAGE COMPANY	CHICAGO	**IL**	60608	(312) 738-2100
KOSHER STAR SAUSAGE MANUFACTURING COMPANY 1000 WEST PERSHING STREET	CHICAGO	**IL**	60645	(312) 927-2810
KOSHER ZION SAUSAGE COMPANY 1455 SOUTH ABERDINE	CHICAGO	**IL**	60636	(312) 738-2208
SHELAT KOSHER FOODS 711 WEST GRAND AVENUE	CHICAGO	**IL**	60610	(312) 243-3473
SINAI KOSHER FOODS CORP. 1000 WEST PERSHING ROAD	CHICAGO	**IL**	60609	(312) 927-2810
STRATHMOOR KEY DISTRIBUTING COMPANY 2733 BARDSTOWN ROAD	LOUISVILLE	**KY**	40205	(502) 458-2276
MORRISON & SCHIFF P.O. BOX 248	BOSTON	**MA**	02135	
SNIDER'S DRESSED BEEF COMPANY 219 SUMMER STREET	WORCESTER	**MA**	01608	(617) 755-5225
EUROPEAN KOSHER PROVISION MANUFACTURING 6 SOUTH SPRING STREET	BALTIMORE	**MD**	21231	(301) 342-2002
EUROPEAN KOSHER PROVISIONS MANUFACTURING CO. 1419 EAST BALTIMORE STREET	BALTIMORE	**MD**	21231	(301) 342-2002
EMPIRE PACKING COMPANY 8648 FENKELL	DETROIT	**MI**	48221	(313) 345-6565
LANDY PACKING CO. P.O. BOX 670	ST. CLOUD	**MN**	56301	(612) 252-1331
LEVINE POULTRY 6149 PAGE	ST. LOUIS	**MO**	63133	(314) 725-7970
FEINBERG DISTRIBUTING 323 SOUTH 9TH STREET	OMAHA	**NE**	69154	(800) 247-7402
POSNOCK KOSHER FOODS 1713 ELIZABETH AVENUE	EAST LINDEN	**NJ**	07036	(201) 777-1039
SHOFAR KOSHER FOODS, INC. 219 EMMET STREET	NEWARK	**NJ**	07114	(201) 242-2434
ABELES & HEYMANN, INC. 3498 THIRD AVENUE	BRONX	**NY**	10456	(212) 589-0100
ISAAC GELLIS, INC. 968 LONGFELLOW AVENUE	BRONX	**NY**	10474	(212) 589-1770
MOGEN DAVID KOSHER MEAT PRODUCTS CORP. 968 LONGFELLOW AVENUE	BRONX	**NY**	10474	(212) 589-1770
PARKSIDE KOSHER MEATS INC. 1197 BRYANT AVENUE	BRONX	**NY**	10459	(212) 328-6999
ZION KOSHER DELICATESSEN COMPANY 968 LONGFELLOW AVENUE	BRONX	**NY**	10474	(212) 589-1770
A TO Z KOSHER PRODUCTS 123 GRAND STREET	BROOKLYN	**NY**	11211	(718) 384-7400
ALLE PROCESSING CORP. 502 FLUSHING AVENUE	BROOKLYN	**NY**	11205	(718) 855-1811
AMERICAN KOSHER PROVISIONS INC. 39 NORMAN AVENUE	BROOKLYN	**NY**	11222	(718) 963-1700
GOLDEN SIMCHA POULTRY 1602 TROY AVENUE	BROOKLYN	**NY**	11234	(718) 253-7733
HOROWITZ KOSHER PROVISIONS INC. 258 EAST 87TH STREET	BROOKLYN	**NY**	11236	(718) 629-9820
SCHMULKA BERNSTEIN & CO. INC. 1100 UTICA AVENUE	BROOKLYN	**NY**	11203	(718) 345-0050
YERUSHALAYIM KOSHER PROVISIONS INC. 502 FLUSHING AVENUE	BROOKLYN	**NY**	11205	(718) 855-4811
D. JACOBSON SONS 163 ADAMS STREET	BUFFALO	**NY**	14216	(716) 854-1150
NOAM FOOD SERVICE 1216 BRUNSWICK AVENUE	FAR ROCKAWAY	**NY**	11691	(718) 471-3456
METROPOLITAN KOSHER FOOD SERVICE HUNTS POINT COOPERATIVE MARKET	HUNTS POINT	**NY**		(212) 893-3500
FALLS POULTRY CORP. SCHOOL ROAD	LIVINGSTON MANOR	**NY**	12578	(212) 594-7826
HEBREW NATIONAL FOODS 58-80 MAURICE AVENUE	MASPETH	**NY**	11378	(718) 894-4300
HOD CARMEL KOSHER PROVISION COMPANY 58-80 MAURICE AVENUE	MASPETH	**NY**	11378	(718) 894-4300
ISRAEL FINE FOOD IMPORTS INC. P.O. BOX 76	MONSEY	**NY**	10952	(914) 352-0123
EUROPEAN KOSHER PROVISION MANUFACTURING COMPANY, INC. 15 RIVINGTON STREET	NEW YORK	**NY**	10002	(212) 254-5994
KOESTRICH BROS. 4092 BROADWAY	NEW YORK	**NY**	10032	(212) 795-1670
REAL KOSHER SAUSAGE CO., INC. 15 RIVINGTON STREET	NEW YORK	**NY**	10002	(212) 254-5994
FALLS POULTRY CORP. MAIN STREET	S. FALLSBURG	**NY**	12779	(914) 434-5000
HEBREW NATIONAL KOSHER FOODS INC. - SALES AND DISTRIBUTION 58-65 52ND ROAD	WOODSIDE	**NY**	11378	(718) 779-3600
KOSHER KING PRODUCTS 58-65 52ND ROAD	WOODSIDE	**NY**	11378	(718) 779-3600
H.J.P. WHOLESALE KOSHER MEATS, INC. 636 MCLEAN AVENUE	YONKERS	**NY**	10705	(914) 965-5802
GILDER'S KOSHER MEAT MARKET 14406 CEDAR	CLEVELAND	**OH**	44121	(216) 382-5330
SIDNEY CROSS WHOLESALE MEATS 7707 SYCAMORE AVENUE	ELKINS PARK	**PA**	19117	(215) 782-1400
EMPIRE KOSHER FOODS, INC. R.D. #3, P.O. BOX 165	MIFFLINTOWN	**PA**	17059	(717) 436-2131
LUNDY'S & SONS 934 NORTH THIRD STREET	PHILADELPHIA	**PA**	19140	(215) 627-2050
SAMUEL SANDLER MANUFACTURING COMPANY 2207 NORTH 30TH STREET	PHILADELPHIA	**PA**	19140	(215) 232-4700
ALBER & LEFF FOOD COMPANY 1505 METROPOLITAN STREET	PITTSBURGH	**PA**	15233	(412) 321-7700
WEISS PROVISION COMPANY 1114 MURIEL STREET	PITTSBURGH	**PA**	15203	(412) 431-3270
MARVID POULTRY 5671 INDUSTRIAL	MONTREAL	**QU**	H1G 3Z9	(514) 321-8376
RACHEL FARMS 5355 ST. LAWRENCE	MONTREAL	**QU**	H2T 1S5	(514) 273-5010

MEDIA

Name / Address	City	State	Zip	Phone
AISH HATORAH ON THE AIR	LOS ANGELES	**CA**		(213) 980-6934
JEWISH TELEVISION NETWORK 617 SOUTH OLIVE STREET, SUITE 515	LOS ANGELES	**CA**	90014	(213) 614-0972
ISRAEL TODAY MEDIA GROUP 10340 ROSEDA BLVD	NORTHRIDGE	**CA**	91326	(818) 786-4000
ISRAEL BROADCASTING AUTHORITY 1101 30TH STREET	WASHINGTON	**DC**	20007	(202) 338-6091
AMERICAN JEWISH RADIO NETWORK 5310 NORTH STATE ROAD 7, SUITE E	FORT LAUDERDALE	**FL**	33319	(303) 484-8900
TRADITION TIME 5310 NORTH STATE ROAD 7, SUITE E	FORT LAUDERDALE	**FL**	33319	(305) 484-8900
JEWISH RADIO HOUR 191 LOMBARD AVENUE, 12TH FLOOR	WINNIPEG	**MB**		
IDF RADIO ISRAEL GALEI ZAHAL 1110 FIDLER LANE	SILVER SPRING	**MD**	20911	(301) 565-3027
JEWISH SPECTRUM (RADIO SHOW) 621 W. MT. PLEASANT AVENUE	LIVINGSTON	**NJ**	07039	(212) 349-1111
TELE-ISRAEL CABLEVISION OF WESTCHESTER (YONKERS)-CHANNEL 25		**NY**		(212) 620-7041
TELE-ISRAEL UA COLUMBIA (BERGEN)-CHANNEL K/24		**NY**		(212) 620-7041
TELE-ISRAEL UA COLUMBIA (WESTCHESTER)-CHANNEL 23		**NY**		(212) 620-7041
TELE-ISRAEL CABLEVISION OF L.I. (NASSAU)-CHANNEL 25		**NY**		(212) 620-7041
DAILY TANYA VIA TELEPHONE	BROOKLYN	**NY**	11213	(718) 735-4377
DIAL-A-DAF, TORAH COMMUNICATIONS NETWORK 1618 43RD STREET	BROOKLYN	**NY**	11204	(718) 436-4999
DIAL-A-JEWISH STORY 770 EASTERN PARKWAY	BROOKLYN	**NY**	11213	(718) 467-7800
RAMBAM ON THE LINE 788 EASTERN PARKWAY	BROOKLYN	**NY**	11213	(718) 735-0441
JEWISH EDUCATIONAL MEDIA 784 EASTERN PARKWAY	BROOKLYN	**NY**	11213	(718) 774-6000
TORAH COMMUNICATIONS NETWORK 1618 43RD STREET	BROOKLYN	**NY**	11204	(718) 436-4999
DIAL-A-JEWISH-STORY	LONG ISLAND	**NY**		(516) 432-7811
HEBREW HOUR, THE 227 E. 45TH STREET	NEW YORK	**NY**	10017	(212) 697-8354

Name / Address	City	State	ZIP	Phone
ISRAEL BROADCASTING AUTHORITY INTERNATIONAL RELATIONS 10 ROCKEFELLER PLAZA	NEW YORK	NY	10020	(212) 489-6180
ISRAEL BROADCASTING AUTHORITY RADIO & TELEVISION 10 ROCKEFELLER PLAZA	NEW YORK	NY	10020	(212) 265-6330
ISRAEL COMMUNICATIONS, INC. 350 FIFTH AVENUE, SUITE 1902	NEW YORK	NY	10118	(212) 213-2200
JEWISH MEDIA SERVICE-J W B 15 E. 26TH STREET	NEW YORK	NY	10010	(212) 532-4949
JEWISH PEOPLE'S UNIVERSITY OF THE AIR 30 WEST 44TH STREET	NEW YORK	NY	10036	(212) 575-0190
JEWISH VIDEO WORKSHOP-TORAH VISION, INC. 576 FIFTH AVENUE	NEW YORK	NY	10036	(212) 921-2175
KAN ISRAEL - WEVD RADIO, N.Y. (HEBREW) 1700 BROADWAY	NEW YORK	NY	10019	(212) 427-1218
MESSAGE OF ISRAEL 123 EAST 55TH STREET, CENTRAL SYNAGOGUE	NEW YORK	NY	10022	
NIGHT-RAP RADIO PROGRAM CHANNEL J-MANHATTAN	NEW YORK	NY		(212) 434-1928
TELE-ISRAEL MANHATTAN CABLE-CHANNEL M	NEW YORK	NY		(212) 620-7041
TELE-ISRAEL GROUP W-CHANNEL L/25	NEW YORK	NY		(212) 620-7041
WEVD RADIO FORWARD ASSOCIATION 770 BROADWAY	NEW YORK	NY	10003	(212) 777-7900
AMERICAN-JEWISH MEDIA DIRECTORY 98-15 65TH ROAD	REGO PARK	NY	11374	(718) 275-2546
JEWISH BROADCASTING SERVICE BOX 115	REGO PARK	NY	11374	
CHIDON-CALL-IN-RADIO QUIZ - WNYM 60 WEST CASTOR PLACE	STATEN ISLAND	NY	10312	(718) 967-9696
TALKLINE COMMUNICATIONS 14 EAST CHURCH STREET	SPRING VALLEY	NY	10977	(914) 352-0630
JEWISH SCENE IN CLEVELAND - JEWISH COMMUNITY CENTER 3505 MAYFIELD ROAD	CLEVELAND	OH	44118	(216) 382-4000
JEWISH VIDEO CLEVELAND - JEWISH COMMUNITY FEDERATION 1750 EUCLID AVENUE	CLEVELAND	OH	44115	(216) 566-9200
ISRAEL RADIO BOX 204	CHELTENHAM	PA	19012	

MEMORIAL INFORMATION

Name / Address	City	State	ZIP	Phone
MEMORIAL INFORMATION SYSTEMS 21412 HILLTOP	SOUTHFIELD	MI	48034	(313) 358-1818

MEZUZOT

Name / Address	City	State	ZIP	Phone
VAAD MISHMERES STAM 4902 16TH AVENUE	BROOKLYN	NY	11204	(718) 438-4963

MIKVAOT

Name / Address	City	State	ZIP	Phone
KNESSETH ISRAEL SYNAGOGUE 3225 MONTEVALLO ROAD	BIRMINGHAM	AL	35223	(205) 879-1664
CONGREGATION AGUDATH ISRAEL 3525 CLOVERDALE ROAD	MONTGOMERY	AL	36111	(205) 281-7998
MIKVAH CHAPEL TWO, BUILDING #8-760, 8TH & J STREET, ELMENDORF AFB	ANCHORAGE	AK	99506	(907) 552-4422
CONGREGATION AGUDATH ACHIM 7901 WEST 5TH STREET	LITTLE ROCK	AR	72205	(501) 225-1683
MIKVAH (CALGARY HEBREW SCHOOL) 1415 GLENMORE TRAIL	CALGARY	AT	T2V 4Y8	(403) 455-9114
BETH ISRAEL SYNAGOGUE 10205-119TH STREET	EDMONTON	AT	T5K 1Z3	(403) 488-2840
MIKVAH SOCIETY 515 EAST BETHANY HOME ROAD	PHOENIX	AZ	85012	(602) 277-7479
YOUNG ISRAEL SYNAGOGUE 2442 EAST 4TH STREET	TUCSON	AZ	85716	(602) 881-7956
LUBAVITCH CENTRE 5750 OAK STREET	VANCOUVER	BC	V6M 2V9	(604) 266-1313
CONGREGATION SCHARA TZEDECK 3476 OAK STREET	VANCOUVER	BC	V6H 2L8	(604) 736-7607
MIKVAH TAHARAS ISRAEL 2520 WARRING STREET	BERKELEY	CA	94705	(415) 848-7221
MIKVAH YISROEL 3847 ATLANTIC AVENUE	LONG BEACH	CA	90807	(213) 427-1360
MIKVAH SOCIETY 9548 WEST PICO BOULEVARD	LOS ANGELES	CA	90035	(213) 550-4511
MOGEN ABRAHAM SYNAGOGUE 356 NORTH LA BREA AVENUE	LOS ANGELES	CA	90036	(213) 931-3792
OHEL DAVID SYNAGOGUE 7967 BEVERLY BOULEVARD	LOS ANGELES	CA	90035	(213) 939-9239
TEICHMAN MIKVAH SOCIETY 12800 CHANDLER BOULEVARD	NORTH HOLLYWOOD	CA	91607	(818) 763-2285
BETH JACOB SYNAGOGUE 3778 PARK BOULEVARD	OAKLAND	CA	94602	(415) 482-1147
MIKVAH ISRAEL 5170 LA DORNA	SAN DIEGO	CA	92115	(619) 287-6411
SAN FRANCISCO MIKVA/MIKVA ISRAEL 3355 SACRAMENTO STREET	SAN FRANCISCO	CA	94115	(415) 921-4070
MIKVAH 1404 QUITMAN	DENVER	CO	80204	(303) 893-5315
MIKVAH ISRAEL 1326 STRATFIELD ROAD	FAIRFIELD	CT	06604	(203) 374-2191
NEW HAVEN MIKVAH SOCIETY 86 HUBINGER STREET	NEW HAVEN	CT	06511	(203) 387-2184
CONGREGATION BROTHERS OF JOSEPH 2 BROAD STREET	NORWICH	CT	06360	(203) 889-7982
CONGREGATION AGUDATH SHOLOM 301 STRAWBERRY HILL AVENUE	STAMFORD	CT	06902	(203) 754-4159
CONGREGATION BNAI SHOLOM 135 ROSELAND AVENUE	WATERBURY	CT	06710	(203) 754-4159
MIKVAH BESS ISRAEL 61 NORTH MAIN STREET	WEST HARTFORD	CT	06107	(203) 521-9446
YOUNG ISRAEL OF HOLLYWOOD 3291 STIRLING ROAD	FORT LAUDERDALE	FL	33312	(305) 966-7877
MIKVEH ETZ CHAIM 5864 UNIVERSITY BOULEVARD WEST	JACKSONVILLE	FL	32216	(904) 733-0720
MIKVAH ETZ CHAIM 10167 SAN JOSE BOULEVARD	JACKSONVILLE	FL	32217	(904) 262-3565
MIKVAH (B'NAI ISRAEL GREATER MIAMI YOUTH SYN.) 16260 SOUTHWEST 288TH STREET	MIAMI	FL	33033	(305) 245-8594
DAUGHTER OF ISRAEL RITUALARIUM 151 MICHIGAN AVENUE	MIAMI BEACH	FL	33139	(305) 672-3500
MIKVAH MIAMI GARDENS DRIVE AND 10TH AVENUE	NORTH MIAMI BEACH	FL	33162	(305) 944-1334
MIKVAH ISRAEL OF TAMPA BAY 3600 E. FLETCHER AVE.	TAMPA	FL	33612	(813) 962-2375
CONGREGATION BETH JACOB 1855 LA VISTA ROAD N.E.	ATLANTA	GA	30329	(404) 633-0551
MIKVAH B'NAI TORAH 700 MT. VERNON HIGHWAY	ATLANTA	GA	30328	(404) 257-0537
CONGREGATION ADAS YESHURUN 935 JOHNS ROAD	AUGUSTA	GA	30904	(404) 733-9491
CONGREGATION BNAI BRITH JACOB 5444 ABERCORN	SAVANNAH	GA	31405	(912) 355-3406
MIKVAH OFF JEWISH CHAPEL AT MAKALAPA GATE	PEARL HARBOR	HI	96782	(718) 773-6070
BETH EL JACOB SYNAGOGUE 954 CUMMINS PARKWAY	DES MOINES	IA	50312	(515) 274-1551
JEWISH COMMUNITY CENTER 524 14TH AT NEBRASKA	SIOUX CITY	IA	55105	(712) 258-0618
MIKVAH 3110 WEST TOUHY AVENUE	CHICAGO	IL	60645	(312) 274-7425
CONGREGATION YEHUDA MOSHE 4721 WEST TOUHY AVENUE	LINCOLNWOOD	IL	60646	(312) 674-0820
CONGREGATION AGUDAS ACHIM 3616 NORTH SHERIDAN ROAD	PEORIA	IL	61604	(309) 688-4800
TRI-CITY JEWISH CENTER 2715 30TH STREET	ROCK ISLAND	IL	61201	(309) 788-3426
CONGREGATION BNAI TORAH 6510 HOOVER ROAD	INDIANAPOLIS	IN	46260	(317) 253-5253
HEBREW ORTHODOX CONGREGATION 3207 HIGH STREET	SOUTH BEND	IN	46614	(219) 291-6100
KEHILATH ISRAEL SYNAGOGUE 10501 CONSER	OVERLAND PARK	KS	66212	(913) 642-1880
AHAVATH ACHIM CONGREGATION 1850 NORTH WOODLAWN	WICHITA	KS	67208	(316) 685-1339
ANSHEI SFARD SYNAGOGUE 3700 DUTCHMANS LANE	LOUISVILLE	KY	40205	(502) 451-3122
BETH ISRAEL SYNAGOGUE 7000 CANAL BOULEVARD	NEW ORLEANS	LA	70124	(504) 283-4366

Name / Address	City	State	Postal Code	Phone
DAUGHTERS OF ISRAEL 101 WASHINGTON STREET	BRIGHTON	**MA**	02135	(617) 782-9433
BETH PINCAS 1710 BEACON STREET	BROOKLINE	**MA**	02146	(617) 566-9182
MIKVAH 146 WALNUT STREET	CHELSEA	**MA**	02150	(617) 884-5169
MIKVAH ISRAEL 1104 CONVERSE STREET	LONGMEADOW	**MA**	01106	(413) 567-1607
RITUALARIUM OF THE NORTH SHORE (CONGREGATION AHABAT SHOLOM) 151 OCEAN STREET	LYNN	**MA**	09102	(617) 595-0080
MIKVEH ORGANIZATION OF THE SOUTH SHORE, (YOUNG ISRAEL OF SHARON) 9 DUNBAR STREET	SHARON	**MA**	02067	(617) 784-7444
MIKVAH 4 HUNTLEY	WORCESTER	**MA**	01602	(617) 754-3681
CHABAD MIKVAH 455 HARTFORD AVENUE	WINNIPEG	**MB**		(204) 338-4761
MIKVAH (BAIS HAMIDRASH KHAL ARUGAS HABOSEM) 6615 PARK HEIGHTS AVE.	BALTIMORE	**MD**	21215	
MIKVAH 3500 WEST ROGERS AVENUE	BALTIMORE	**MD**	21215	(301) 664-5834
MIKVAH 8901 GEORGIA AVENUE	SILVER SPRING	**MD**	20910	(301) 565-3737
SILVER SPRING JEWISH CENTER 1401 ARCOLA AVENUE	SILVER SPRING	**MD**	20902	(301) 649-4425
BANGOR MIKVAH-C/O RABBI ISAACS	BANGOR	**ME**		(207) 945-5940
SHAARAY TEFILOH SYNAGOGUE 76 NOYES STREET	PORTLAND	**ME**	04103	(207) 773-0693
MIKVAH, CHABAD HOUSE 715 HILL STREET	ANN ARBOR	**MI**	48104	(313) 995-3276
MIKVAH (CHABAD HOUSE) 2615 MICHIGAN NORTHEAST	GRAND RAPIDS	**MI**	49506	(616) 458-6575
MIKVAH ISRAEL 15150 WEST TEN MILE ROAD	OAK PARK	**MI**	48237	(313) 968-9715
MIKVAH (BEIS CHABAD TORAH CENTER) 5075 WEST MAPLE ROAD	WEST BLOOMFIELD	**MI**	48033	(313) 626-1807
MIKVAH IN EAST GRAND FORKS	GRAND FORKS	**MN**		(218) 773-9394
KNESSETH ISRAEL SYNAGOGUE 4330 WEST 28TH STREET	MINNEAPOLIS	**MN**	55416	(612) 920-2183
CHABAD MIKVAH 15 MONTCALM COURT	ST PAUL	**MN**	55116	(612) 698-3858
MIKVAH ASSOCIATION 1516½ RANDOLPH AVENUE	ST PAUL	**MN**	55105	(612) 698-6163
KEHILATH ISRAEL SYNAGOGUE 800 EAST MEYER BOULEVARD	KANSAS CITY	**MO**	64131	(816) 333-1992
MIKVAH CHANAH 8901 HOLMES RD.	KANSAS CITY	**MO**	64131	(816) 333-7117
SYLVIA GREEN MIKVAH 4 MILLSTONE CAMPUS	ST LOUIS	**MO**	63146	(314) 569-2774
CONG. TIFERETH YISROEL 56 STEADMAN STREET	MONCTON	**NB**	E1C 4P4	(506) 854-2545
MIKVAH (LUBAVITCH OF NORTH CAROLINA) 6500 NEWHALL RD.	CHARLOTTE	**NC**	28226	(704) 366-3984
CONGREGATION SHAAREI ISRAEL 7400 FALLS OF THE NEUSE ROAD	RALEIGH	**NC**	27609	(919) 847-6286
OMAHA MIKVAH 333 SOUTH 132 STREET	OMAHA	**NE**	68154	(402) 333-5166
BETH EL SYNAGOGUE CORNER ELIZABETH & DOWNING STREET	ST JOHN'S	**NF**	A1B 1S3	(709) 726-0480
MIKVAH LEWIS HILL ROAD	BETHLEHEM	**NH**	03574	(603) 869-5737
MIKVAH SONS OF ISRAEL 720 COOPER LANDING ROAD	CHERRY HILL	**NJ**	08002	(609) 667-9700
MIKVAH 35 NORTH AVENUE	ELIZABETH	**NJ**	07208	(201) 352-5048
SHOMREI EMUNAH 89 HUGUENOT STREET	ENGLEWOOD	**NJ**	07631	(201) 568-7932
MIKVAH 112 FIRST AVENUE SOUTH	HIGHLAND PARK	**NJ**	08904	(201) 249-2411
MIKVAH 705 MADISON AVENUE	LAKEWOOD	**NJ**	08701	(201) 370-8909
LUBAVITCH OF ATLANTIC COUNTY 8223 FULTON AVENUE	MARGATE	**NJ**	08402	(609) 823-3223
MIKVAH NEAR GERSHEL AVENUE	NORMA	**NJ**	08347	(609) 691-7992
SHORE AREA MIKVAH 201 JEROME AVENUE	OAKHURST	**NJ**	07755	(201) 531-1712
MIKVAH YISROEL OF PASSAIC-CLIFTON 244 HIGH STREET	PASSAIC	**NJ**	07055	(201) 788-3596
SHAARAY TEFILOH SYNAGOGUE 15 MARKET STREET	PERTH AMBOY	**NJ**	08862	(201) 826-2977
MIKVAH ASSOCIATION 1726 WINDSOR ROAD	TEANECK	**NJ**	07666	(201) 837-8220
MIKVAH ISRAEL OF NORTH HUDSON 412 34TH STREET	UNION CITY	**NJ**	07087	(201) 866-0690
MIKVAH 717 PLEASANT VALLEY WAY	WEST ORANGE	**NJ**	07052	(201) 731-1427
BETH ISRAEL SYNAGOGUE 1480 OXFORD STREET	HALIFAX	**NS**	B3H 3Y8	(902) 422-1301
CONGREGATION SGOOLAI ISRAEL 168 WESTMORLAND STREET	FREDERICTON	**NB**	E3B 3L7	(506) 455-8425
CONGREGATION SHAAREI ZEDEK	ST JOHN	**NB**		(506) 657-1962
MIKVAH 4800 EUBANK N.E.	ALBUQUERQUE	**NM**	87111	(505) 296-6060
MIKVAH (AT THE HOME OF JOANNA KATZ), 519 FRANKLIN STREET	SANTA FE	**NM**	87501	(505) 988-4169
MIKVAH 190 ELM STREET	ALBANY	**NY**	12202	(518) 482-0603
BETH DAVID SYNAGOGUE 39 RIVERSIDE DRIVE	BINGHAMTON	**NY**	13905	(607) 722-1793
AITZ CHAIM 708 MACE AVENUE	BRONX	**NY**	10467	(212) 798-6173
AGUDAS TAHARAS HAMISHPACHAH OF CROWN HEIGHTS 1506 UNION STREET	BROOKLYN	**NY**	11213	(718) 604-8787
CANARSIE COMMUNITY MIKVAH FLATLANDS & REMSEN STREETS	BROOKLYN	**NY**	11236	(718) 251-5084
CONGREGATION ARUGAS HABOSEM 133 RODNEY STREET	BROOKLYN	**NY**	11211	(718) 782-6608
CONGREGATION KEHILAS MORIYOH-SEA GATE 3740 OCEANIC AVENUE	BROOKLYN	**NY**	11224	(718) 372-6706
KEHILAS YAAKOV 110-112 PENN STREET	BROOKLYN	**NY**	11211	(718) 625-8795
KEHILAS YAAKOV 115 RUTLEDGE	BROOKLYN	**NY**	11211	(718) 624-9262
MIKVAH 2965 OCEAN PARKWAY	BROOKLYN	**NY**	11235	(718) 891-4286
MIKVAH 1221 REMSEN AVENUE	BROOKLYN	**NY**	11236	(718) 251-5084
MIKVAH INFORMATION - FAMILY SANCTITY 780 MONTGOMERY STREET	BROOKLYN	**NY**	11213	(718) 778-1070
MIKVAH ISRAEL OF BENSONHURST 48 BAY 28 STREET	BROOKLYN	**NY**	11214	(718) 372-9563
MIKVAH ISRAEL OF BORO PARK 1351 46TH STREET	BROOKLYN	**NY**	11219	(718) 871-6866
MIKVAH ISRAEL OF BORO PARK 4623 18TH AVENUE	BROOKLYN	**NY**	11204	(718) 436-5140
MIKVAH ISRAEL OF BRIGHTON 245 NEPTUNE AVENUE	BROOKLYN	**NY**	11235	(718) 769-8599
MIKVAH OF BORO PARK 1249 52ND STREET	BROOKLYN	**NY**	11219	(718) 438-9808
MIKVAH-CONGREGATION HAMAOR 5012 18TH AVENUE	BROOKLYN	**NY**	11204	(718) 633-7724
RITUALARIUM OF EAST FLATBUSH 340 EAST 52ND STREET	BROOKLYN	**NY**	11203	(718) 385-7707
RITUALARIUM OF EASTERN PARKWAY 1506 UNION STREET	BROOKLYN	**NY**	11213	(718) 773-8826
SEPHARDIC MIKVAH ISRAEL 810 AVENUE S	BROOKLYN	**NY**	11223	(718) 339-4600
TAHARATH ISRAEL OF EAST FLATBUSH 1013 EAST 15TH STREET	BROOKLYN	**NY**	11226	(718) 377-9813
Y.I. OF BEDFORD BAY 2113 HARING STREET	BROOKLYN	**NY**	11229	(718) 332-4120
YETEV LEV D'SATMAR 212 WILLIAMSBURG STREET	BROOKLYN	**NY**	11211	(718) 387-9388
MIKVAH 1248 KENMORE	BUFFALO	**NY**	14216	(716) 875-8451
CONGREGATION EZRATH ISRAEL RABBI EISNER SQUARE	ELLENVILLE	**NY**	12428	(914) 647-4472
HEBREW COMMUNITY SERVICE 1125 BAYPORT PLACE	FAR ROCKAWAY	**NY**	11691	(718) 327-9727
FLEISCHMANNS	FLEISCHMANNS	**NY**	12430	(914) 254-4205
MIKVAH (CONG. OF GEORGIAN JEWS FROM RUSSIA) 102-58 63RD AVENUE	FOREST HILLS	**NY**	11375	(718) 897-6139
MIKVAH OF QUEENS 75-48 GRAND CENTRAL PARKWAY	FOREST HILLS	**NY**	11375	(718) 261-6380
MIKVAH ASSOCIATION OF GREAT NECK 26 OLD MILL ROAD	GREAT NECK	**NY**	11023	(516) 487-2726
MIKVAH SOUTH SHORE, CONGREGATION 1156 PENINSULA BLVD	HEWLETT	**NY**	11557	(516) 569-5514
MIKVAH 209 NORTH MEADOW STREET	ITHACA	**NY**	14850	(607) 273-8314
MIKVAH ISRAEL 71-11 VLEIGH PLACE	KEW GARDEN HILLS	**NY**	11367	(718) 268-6500
MIKVAH 37 LINCOLN PLACE	LIBERTY	**NY**	12754	(914) 292-6677
HOTEL AISHEL	LIVINGSTON MANOR	**NY**	12758	(914) 439-5161
SCHARF MANOR 274 WEST BROADWAY	LONG BEACH	**NY**	11561	(516) 431-7758
CONGREGATION YETEV LEV 20 QUICKWAY ROAD	MONROE	**NY**	10950	(914) 783-8858
MIKVAH ISRAEL 4 MAPLE LEAF ROAD	MONSEY	**NY**	10952	(914) 356-1000
MIKVAH 16 NORTH STREET	MONTICELLO	**NY**	12701	(914) 794-6757
YESHIVA FARM SETTLEMENT MIKVAH PINES BRIDGE ROAD	MOUNT KISCO	**NY**	10549	(914) 666-5321
MIKVAH	MOUNTAINDALE	**NY**	12763	(914) 434-9192
AHAVAT SHLOMO 163 EAST 69TH STREET	NEW YORK	**NY**	10021	(212) 472-3968
MIKVAH OF EAST SIDE 313 EAST BROADWAY	NEW YORK	**NY**	10002	(212) 475-8514
MIKVAH OF MID-MANHATTAN 234 WEST 78TH STREET	NEW YORK	**NY**	10024	(212) 799-1520
MIKVAH OF WASHINGTON HEIGHTS 4351 BROADWAY	NEW YORK	**NY**	10033	(212) 923-1100
MIKVAH 3397 PARK AVENUE	OCEANSIDE	**NY**	11572	(516) 766-3242
SHOMREI ISRAEL SYNAGOGUE 18 PARK AVENUE	POUGHKEEPSIE	**NY**	12603	(914) 454-4078
MIKVAH 3708 HENRY HUDSON PARKWAY	RIVERDALE	**NY**	10463	(212) 549-8336
BETH HAKNESES HACHODOSH 27 ST. REGIS DRIVE N	ROCHESTER	**NY**	14618	(716) 244-4888
Y.I. OF SCARSDALE 1313 WEAVER STREET	SCARSDALE	**NY**	10583	(914) 636-8686
MIKVAH 33 TRUMAN AVENUE	SPRING VALLEY	**NY**	10977	(914) 354-6578
COMMUNITY MIKVAH (Y.I. OF STATEN ISLAND) 835 FOREST HILL ROAD	STATEN ISLAND	**NY**	10314	(718) 494-6704
MIKVAH ISRAEL 98 RUPERT AVENUE	STATEN ISLAND	**NY**	10314	(718) 494-3359
YOUNG ISRAEL SYNAGOGUE 2200 EAST GENESEE STREET	SYRACUSE	**NY**	13210	(315) 446-6194
CONGREGATION ANSHEI HASHARON THOMPKINS STREET	TANNERSVILLE	**NY**	12485	(518) 589-5830
MIKVAH (CHABAD) 2306 15TH STREET	TROY	**NY**	12180	(518) 274-5572
MIKVAH IN UTICA 110 MEMORIAL PKWY	UTICA	**NY**	13501	(315) 724-8357
MIKVAH ASSOCIATION OF NASSAU COUNTY 775 HEMPSTEAD AVENUE	WEST HEMPSTEAD	**NY**	11552	(516) 489-9358
MIKVAH EAST POND ROAD	WOODRIDGE	**NY**	12789	(914) 434-4987
CONG. SOUTH SHORE 1156 PENINSULA BOULEVARD	WOODMERE	**NY**	11557	(516) 569-5514
MIKVAH 2479 SOUTH GREEN RD	BEECHWOOD	**OH**	44122	(216) 381-9178
MIKVAH 1546 KENOVA AVENUE	CINCINNATI	**OH**	45237	(513) 821-6679
MIKVAH 1774 LEE ROAD	CLEVELAND HEIGHTS	**OH**	44118	(216) 321-0270
CONGREGATION BETH JACOB 1223 COLLEGE AVENUE	COLUMBUS	**OH**	43209	(614) 237-1068
MIKVAH 556 KENWOOD AVENUE	DAYTON	**OH**	45406	(513) 277-6754
AITZ CHAIM SYNAGOGUE 3853 WOODLEY ROAD	TOLEDO	**OH**	43606	(419) 473-2401
CHILDREN OF ISRAEL 1702 FIFTH AVENUE	YOUNGSTOWN	**OH**	44504	(216) 744-1754
GREATER YOUNGSTOWN AREA MIKVEH ASSOCIATION 3970 LOGAN WAY	YOUNGSTOWN	**OH**	44504	(216) 759-2167
CONGREGATION BNAI EMUNAH 1719 SOUTH OWASSO	TULSA	**OK**	74120	(918) 583-7121
LUBAVITCH MIKVAH 44A EDINBURGH DRIVE	DOWNSVIEW	**ON**	M3H 1B4	(416) 633-4608
MIKVAH SOCIETY 694 SHEPPARD AVENUE WEST	DOWNSVIEW	**ON**	M3H 2S6	(416) 633-4729
ADAS ISRAEL RITUALARIUM OF HAMILTON 128 CLINE AVENUE SOUTH	HAMILTON	**ON**	L85 1X2	(416) 525-3768
BETH ISRAEL SYNAGOGUE 116 CENTRE STREET	KINGSTON	**ON**	K7L 4E6	(613) 542-5012
CONGREGATION BETH TEFILOH 1210 ADELAIDE STREET	LONDON	**ON**	N5Y 4J6	(519) 433-7081
RITUALARIUM (IN SYNAGOGUE) 151 CHAPEL STREET	OTTAWA	**ON**	K1N 7Y2	(613) 232-7306
LUBAVITCH MIKVAH 770 CHABAD GATE	THORNHILL	**ON**	L4J 3V9	(416) 731-4068
BAIS YAAKOV ELEMENTARY SCHOOL 85 STORMONT AVENUE	TORONTO	**ON**	M5N 2C3	(416) 787-5958
B'NAI TORAH CONG. 465 PATRICIA AVENUE	WILLOWDALE	**ON**	M2R 2N1	(416) 225-6620
CONGREGATION SHAAREY ZEDEK 610 GILES BLVD. EAST	WINDSOR	**ON**	N9A 4E2	(519) 252-1594
JEWISH RITUALARIUM 1425 S.W. HARRISON STREET	PORTLAND	**OR**	97201	(503) 295-0387
MIKVAH 1836 WHITEHALL STREET	ALLENTOWN	**PA**	18104	(215) 433-6089
PHILADELPHIA MIKVAH ASSN. WYNNEWOOD & ARGYLE RDS.	ARDMORE	**PA**	19003	(215) 642-8679
MIKVAH 3601 NORTH 4TH STREET	HARRISBURG	**PA**	17110	(717) 232-2023
OHEV ZEDEK 3RD AVENUE & DAVIS STREET	KINGSTON	**PA**	18704	(717) 287-5793
CONGREGATION OHEV SHOLOM 20 EAST THIRD STREET	LEWISTOWN	**PA**	17044	(717) 248-8070
CONGREGATION GEMILAS CHESED 1545 OHIO AVENUE	MCKEESPORT	**PA**	15131	(412) 678-8859
MIKVAH 4600 OLD YORK ROAD	PHILADELPHIA	**PA**	19140	(215) 455-0699
PHILADELPHIA MIKVAH ASSOCIATION (NORTHEAST BRANCH) 7525 LORETTO AVENUE	PHILADELPHIA	**PA**	19111	(215) 745-3334
JEWISH WOMEN'S LEAGUE 2336 SHADY AVENUE	PITTSBURGH	**PA**	15217	(412) 422-7110
MACHZIKEH HADAS MADISON AVENUE & VINE STREET	SCRANTON	**PA**	18510	(717) 344-5138
MIKVAH 3RD AVENUE AND INSTITUTE LANE	WILKES-BARRE	**PA**	18704	(717) 287-2032
OHEV SHALOM CHERRY & BELMONT STREETS	WILLIAMSPORT	**PA**	17701	(717) 322-7050
MIKVE KIRYAT THAS AVE. BET HALEVI	BOISBRIAND	**QU**	J7E 4H4	(514) 435-1493
Y.I. OF CHOMEDEY 1025 ELIZABETH STREET	CHOMEDEY	**QU**		(514) 681-2571
MIKVAH ISRAEL 7015 KILDARE, COTE ST. LUC	MONTREAL	**QU**	H4W 1C1	(514) 487-5581
MIKVAH MAYEN (CONGREGATION YETEV LEV) 5214 ST. URBAIN STREET	MONTREAL	**QU**	H2T 2W9	(514) 279-9443
MIKVAH TAHARATH HAMISHPACHA 5124 ST. URBAIN STREET	MONTREAL	**QU**	H2T 2W5	(514) 271-4574
MIKVAH OF MONTREAL 6235 HILLSDALE ROAD	MONTREAL	**QU**		(514) 737-2625
CONGREGATION SHAARE ZEDEK 688 BROAD STREET	PROVIDENCE	**RI**	02907	(401) 751-4936
JEWISH COMMUNITY CENTER 401 ELMGROVE AVENUE	PROVIDENCE	**RI**	02906	(401) 751-0025
BRITH SHOLOM BETH ISRAEL 182 RUTLEDGE	CHARLESTON	**SC**	29403	(803) 577-6599
MIKVAH 44 CALHOUN ROAD & NORTH KINGS HIGHWAY	MYRTLE BEACH	**SC**	29577	
CONGREGATION BETH JACOB 1640 VICTORIA AVENUE	REGINA	**SK**	S4P 0P7	(306) 757-8643
JEWISH COMMUNITY CENTER 715 MCKINNON AVENUE	SASKATOON	**SK**	S7H 2G2	(306) 343-7023
BETH SHOLOM CONGREGATION 20 PISGAH AVENUE	CHATTANOOGA	**TN**	37411	(615) 894-0801
BARON HIRSCH CONGREGATION 1740 VOLLINTINE AVENUE	MEMPHIS	**TN**	38107	(901) 683-7458
CONGREGATION SHERITH ISRAEL 3600 WEST END AVENUE	NASHVILLE	**TN**	37205	(615) 292-6614
ANSHE SPHARD-BETH EL EMETH 120 EAST YATES DRIVE	NORTH MEMPHIS	**TN**	38119	(901) 682-1611
MIKVE TAHARA 2101 NUECES	AUSTIN	**TX**	78705	(512) 478-8222
CONGREGATION TIFERETH ISRAEL 10909 HILLCREST ROAD	DALLAS	**TX**	75230	(214) 691-3611
MIKVAH (CONG. BNAI ZION) 805 CHERRY HILL LANE	EL PASO	**TX**	79912	(915) 833-2222
MIKVAH ISRAEL OF HOUSTON 10900 FONDREN	HOUSTON	**TX**	77096	(713) 777-2000
UNITED ORTHODOX SYNAGOGUE 9001 GREENWILLOW	HOUSTON	**TX**	77096	(713) 723-3850
CONGREGATION RODFEI SHOLOM 115 EAST LAUREL	SAN ANTONIO	**TX**	78212	(512) 227-0015
CONGREGATION ETZ CHAIM 720 WILSON STREET	DANVILLE	**VA**	24541	

Name / Address	City	State	Zip	Phone
CONGREGATION ADATH JESHURUN 12646 NETTLES DRIVE	NEWPORT NEWS	**VA**	23606	(804) 599-0820
CONGREGATION BNAI ISRAEL 420 SPOTSWOOD AVENUE	NORFOLK	**VA**	23517	(804) 627-7358
CONGREGATION KOL EMES 4811 PATTERSON AVENUE	RICHMOND	**VA**	23226	(804) 288-3119
MIKVAH 168 ARCHIBALD STREET	BURLINGTON	**VT**	05401	(802) 658-7612
MIKVAH 5140 SOUTH HOLLY STREET	SEATTLE	**WA**	98118	(206) 723-3644
CONGREGATION AGUDAS ACHIM 5820 WEST BURLEIGH	MILWAUKEE	**WI**	53210	(414) 442-2296
CONGREGATION BETH JEHUDA 2700 NO. 54TH STREET	MILWAUKEE	**WI**	53210	(414) 447-7727
MIKVAH (LUBAVITCH HOUSE) 3109 N. LAKE DRIVE	MILWAUKEE	**WI**	53211	(414) 962-0566
BNAI JACOB SYNAGOGUE 1599 VIRGINIA	CHARLESTON	**WV**	25311	(304) 346-4722
MT. SINAI CONGREGATION 2610 PIONEER AVENUE	CHEYENNE	**WY**	82001	(307) 634-3052
MIKVAH (IN SYNAGOGUE) JOACHIMSTALERSTRASSE 13	1 BERLIN 15			881-3031
MIKVAH AVENUE MOULAY ABDELLAH	AGADIR, MOROCCO			
MIKVAH (ASHKENAZI) HEINZSTR. 3	AMSTERDAM			020-763155
MIKVAH (SEPHARDI) J.D. MEYERPLEIN 7	AMSTERDAM			
MIKVAH (IN SYN.) VIA S. MARCELLIONO 11	ANCONA	**IT**		55-654
MIKVAH STEENBOKSTRAAT 22	ANTWERP			239-7588
MIKVAH LEVIN'S HOTEL METROPOL	AROSA	**SW**		31-10-58
MIKVAH ANTHEON & KAMELION STREETS, SUBURB OF P. PSIHICO	ATHENS			6714-598
MIKVAH (BETH ISRAEL) GREY'S AVENUE	AUCKLAND			
MIKVAH JUDISCHE KURHOTEL, FRANKFURTERSTR. 63-65	BAD NAUHEIM			81726
MIKVAH (IN SYNAGOGUE) KARLSTRASSE 34	BAD NAUHEIM			5605
MIKVAH (IN SYNAGOGUE) CALLE PORVENIR 24	BARCELONA			200-6148
MIKVAH LEIMENSTR. 24	BASEL			239850
MIKVAH, WOLFSON CENTRE 49 SOMERTON ROAD	BELFAST			716-525
MIKVAH BOURNEVILLE LANE BATHS	BIRMINGHAM			021-440-1019
MIKVAH (BLOEMFONTEIN HEBREW CONGREGATION) CORNER OF FAIRVIEW & UNION ROAD	BLOEMFONTEIN			
MIKVAH CALLE 25 N. 27A 39	BOGOTA			
MIKVAH CALLE 79N. 9-66	BOGOTA			
MIKVAH (IN SYNAGOGUE) VIA MARIO FINZI	BOLOGNA			051-340-936
MIKVAH (BOURNEMOUTH HEBREW CONGREGATION) WOOTTON GARDENS	BOURNEMOUTH			0202-27433
MACHSIKE HADASS 67A RUE DE LA CLINIQUE	BRUSSELS			521-1289
MIKVAH (IN SYNAGOGUE) STR. MAMULARI 21	BUCHAREST			123720
MIKVAH, VII KAZINCZY UTCA 16	BUDAPEST			
MIKVAH BOGOTA 3015 (FLORES)	BUENOS AIRES			612-4905
MIKVAH MOLDES 2449 (BELGRANO)	BUENOS AIRES			781-4859
MIKVAH LARREA 730-732 (ONCE)	BUENOS AIRES			
MIKVAH (HEBREW CONGREGATION) P.O. BOX 337, ABERCORN STREET	BULAWAYO			
CALGARY HEBREW SCHOOL 1415 GLENMORE TRAIL	CALGARY			(403) 253-3992
MIKVAH (BETH DIN) P.O. BOX 543	CAPETOWN			
MIKVAH (UNION ISRAELITA SYNAGOGUE) AV. MARQUES DEL TORO. SAN BERNARDINO	CARACAS			
MIKVAH WALES EMPIRE POOL BUILDING	CARDIFF			(022) 238-2296
MIKVAH (ECOLE LUBAVITCH) 174 BLVD. ZIRAOUI	CASABLANCA			
MIKVAH (EN HABANIM 14 RUE LUSITANIA	CASABLANCA			
MIKVAH (OZAR HATORAH) 59 RUE VERLET HANUS	CASABLANCA			
MIKVAH (IN SYNAGOGUE) ROONSTRASSE 50	COLOGNE			235626
JEWISH COMMUNITY CENTER 6 NY KONGENSGADE 1472 K	COPENHAGEN			128868
MIKVAH (IN SYNAGOGUE) UL. MIODOWA 24	CRACOW			62064
MIKVAH ETANIA SANATORIUM	DAVOS			55404
MIKVAH 37 ADELAIDE ROAD	DUBLIN			984865
MIKVAH (GREAT SYNAGOGUE) ESSENWOOD ROAD, BEREA	DURBAN			
MIKVAH (IN SYNAGOGUE) ZEITENSTRASSE 50	DUSSELDORF			480313
MIKVAH PRINSESTRAAT 16	ENSCHEDE			
MIKVAH 463 CRANBROOK ROAD, ILFORD	ESSEX			(01) 554-8532
MIKVAH (IN SYNAGOGUE) VIA L.C. FARINI 4	FLORENCE			210-763
MIKVAH (IN SYNAGOGUE) FREIHERR VON STEINSTRASSE 30	FRANKFURT-AM-MAIN			721-568
MIKVAH (IN SYNAGOGUE) JULIENSTRASSE 2	FUERTH			776422
MIKVAH PARTIZANSKA 907	GALANTA			
MIKVAH (IN SYNAGOGUE) 180 BEWICK ROAD	GATESHEAD			(091) 477-3047
MIKVAH (HEKHAL HANESS) 54 TER ROUTE DE MALGNOU	GENEVA			369632
MIKVAH 10 BOMB HOUSE LANE	GIBRALTAR			7831-6
MIKVAH (GIFFNOCK & NEWLANDS SYNAGOGUE) MARYVILLE AVENUE	GIFFNOCK, GLASGOW			(041) 649-3740
MIKVAH KAHN'S SILBERHORN HOTEL	GRINDELWALD			532822
MIKVAH KENAUPARK 7	HAARLEM			143-42
MIKVAH (IN SYNAGOGUE) HOHE WEIDE 34	HAMBURG			492904
MIKVAH (IN SYNAGOGUE) HAECKELSTRASSE 10	HANOVER			812782
JEWISH COMMUNITY CENTER MALMINKATU 26	HELSINKI			6491297
MIKVAH 70 ROBINSON ROAD	HONG KONG			
MIKVAH, CAGALOGLU KADINLAR HAMAMI CAGALOGLU	ISTANBUL			440-472
MIKVAH (ADATH JESHURUN SYNAGOGUE) 34 FORTESCUE ROAD, YEOVILLE	JOHANNESBURG			433-380
MIKVAH (BETH DIN) 24 RALEIGH STREET, YEOVILLE	JOHANNESBURG			432-161
MIKVAH VRIDELNI 59	KARLSBAD			
MIKVAH	KNOKKE			
MIKVAH (JEWISH COMMUNITY OF JAPAN) 66-1, KITANO-CHO, 4-CHOME. IKUTA-KU	KOBE 650			221-7236
MIKVAH (CONGREGATION SHOMREI HADASS) 368 HARROGATE ROAD	LEEDS			(532) 681-461
MIKVAH (CHILDWALL SYNAGOGUE PRECINCT) DUNBABIN ROAD	LIVERPOOL			(051) 722-2079
MIKVAH 62 FILEY AVENUE	LONDON, N. 16			(01) 806-3961
NORTH LONDON MIKVAH 40 QUEEN ELIZABETH'S WALK	LONDON, N. 16			(01) 802-2554
STAMFORD HILL MIKVAH MARGARET STREET (LAMPARD GROVE)	LONDON, N. 16			(01) 806-3880
NORTH WEST LONDON COMMUNAL MIKVAH 10 SHIREHALL LANE	LONDON, N.W.4			(01) 202-8517
MIKVAH BRUCHSTR. 51	LUCERNE			454-750
MIKVAH (IN SYNAGOGUE) 11 VIA MADERNO	LUGANO			513531
MIKVAH (IN SYNAGOGUE) CALLE BALMES 3	MADRID			445-9843

Name / Address	City	State	Zip	Phone
MIKVAH	MALAGA			214-875
MIKVAH (JEWISH COMMUNITY CENTER) KAMERGATAN 11	MALMO			118860
COMMUNITY MIKVAH BROOM HOLME, TETLOW LANE, SALFORD 7	MANCHESTER			(061) 792-3970
MANCHESTER & DISTRICT MIKVAH SEDGLEY PARK ROAD, PRESTWICH	MANCHESTER			(061) 773-1537
MIKVAH (ADAS ISRAEL SYNAGOGUE) 24 GLEN EIRA AVENUE, RIPPONLEA, ST. KILDA	MELBOURNE			523-5587
MIKVAH CAMPECHE 255, COLONIA HIPODROMO	MEXICO CITY			574-2224
MIKVAH (MOGEN DAVID SYNAGOGUE) PRESIDENTE MASARYK & BERNARD SHAW, COLONIA POLANCO	MEXICO CITY			540-3492
MIKVAH VIA SALLY MEYER 4-6	MILAN			412-1539
MIKVAH (IN SYNAGOGUE) VIA GUASTALLA 19	MILAN			791-892
MIKVAH MALDONADO 1168	MONTEVIDEO			981-405
MIKVAH MARCELINO BERTELOT 1884	MONTEVIDEO			257-09
MIKVAH (CENTRAL SYNAGOGUE) 8 ARKHIPOVA STREET	MOSCOW			
MIKVAH (IN SYNAGOGUE) REICHENBACHSTRASSE 27	MUNICH			269006
MIKVAH (IN SYNAGOGUE) POSSARTSTRASSE 15	MUNICH			476353
MIKVAH BERGSTIEN 15	OSLO			292-612
MIKVAH 55 ROOSEVELT ROAD, GLENGINNINGVALE	PORT ELIZABETH			331-332
MIKVAH RUA FRANCISCO FERRER 170	PORTO ALEGRE			
MIKVAH ZAMOCKA 13	PRESSBURG			
MIKVAH (GREAT SYNAGOGUE) 717 PRETORIUS STREET	PRETORIA			742-069
MIKVAH RUA GENERAL CANABARRA 454	RIO DE JANEIRO			
MIKVAH (IN SYNAGOGUE) VIA BALBO 33	ROME			475-9881
MIKVAH (IN SYNAGOGUE) LUNGOTEVERE CENCI 9	ROME			655-051
MIKVAH (IN SYNAGOGUE) A.B.N. DAVIDSPLEIN 4	ROTTERDAM			010-466 9765
MIKVAH LASSERSTRASSE 8	SALZBURG			
MIKVAH, NEXT TO CONGREGATION CHEVRA KADISHA	SANTIAGO			465-927
MIKVAH RUA HADDOCK LOBO 1279	SAO PAOLO			
MIKVAH BOM RETIRO, RUA TENENTE PENA 310	SAO PAOLO			
MIKVAH (CONGREGATION KHAL CHASIDIM) RUA MAMORE 597	SAO PAOLO			220-1735
MIKVAH (KHAL MACHZIKEI HADASS) RUA PADRE JOAO MANOEL 693	SAO PAOLO			282-6762
MIKVAH, SISLI SINAJONU EFE SOKATE NO. 4	SISLI-ISTANBUL			
MIKVAH (SOUTHPORT HEBREW CONGREGATION) ARNSIDE ROAD	SOUTHPORT			(704) 32964
MIKVAH HOTEL EDELWEISS	ST. MORITZ			(082) 355-33
MIKVAH (JEWISH COMMUNITY CENTER) NYBROGATAN 19	STOCKHOLM			636-566
MIKVAH (IN SYNAGOGUE) HOSPITALSTRASSE 36	STUTTGART			295-665
MIKVAH (BAIS 'AMEDRASH) MOWBRAY ROAD	SUNDERLAND			(783) 658093
MIKVAH 117 GLENAYR AVENUE, BONDI	SYDNEY			302-509
MIKVAH (IN SYNAGOGUE) WAGENSTR. 101	THE HAGUE			450-417
MIKVAH (JEWISH COMMUNITY CENTER) 8-8, HIROO 3-CHOME. SHIBUYA-KU	TOKYO 150			(400) 255-9
MIKVAH (LUBAVITCH) IN TUNIS 65 AV. TAIEB MEHIRI	TUNIS			280-900
MIKVAH SPRINGWEG 164	UTRECHT			030-314-742
MIKVAH, JEWISH REST HOME GHETTO NUOVO 2874	VENICE			201-92
MIKVAH FLEISCHMARKT 22	VIENNA I			525262
MIKVAH (AGUDAS ISRAEL) TEMPELGASSE 3	VIENNA			24 92 62
MIKVAH DOBLINGER GURTEL 11	VIENNA XIX			
MIKVAH (WELLINGTON HEBREW CONGREGATION) 80 WEBB STREET	WELLINGTON			845-081
MIKVAH 44 GENESTA ROAD	WESTCLIFF			344900
MIKVAH VALENTIN-BECKERSTRASSE 11	WURZBURG			51190
MIKVAH (IN SYNAGOGUE) FREIGUTSTRASSE 37	ZURICH			201-6746
MIKVAH, PAVILLION SALVATOR RUE DE PRESIDENT ROOSEVELT	AIX-LES-BAINS	**FR**		(42) 352-843
MIKVAH (IN SYNAGOGUE) 3 RUE JERUSALEM	AIX-EN-PROVENCE	**FR**		(42) 266-939
MIKVAH (IN SYNAGOGUE) RUE GANBETTA	ARACHON	**FR**		
MIKVAH 82 RUE CHRISTIAN GILBERT	ASNIERES	**FR**		
MIKVAH 213 RUE STE. CATHERINE	BORDEAUX	**FR**		(56) 917-939
MIKVAH 28 AVENUE DE NEWBURN	CHOISY-LE-ROI	**FR**		(48) 534-821
MIKVAH	CLERMONT-FERRAND	**FR**		(70) 984-402
MIKVAH 3 RUE DE LA SYNAGOGUE	COLMAR	**FR**		(89) 413-829
MIKVAH RUE DU 8 MAI 1945	CRETEIL	**FR**		(43) 770-170
MIKVAH 5 RUE DE LA SYNAGOGUE	DIJON	**FR**		(80) 653-578
MIKVAH 47 RUE MALLEVILLE	ENGHIEN	**FR**		(34) 124-234
MIKVAH 15 RUE COROT	GARGES-LES-GONESSE	**FR**		(39) 867-564
MIKVAH (IN SYNAGOGUE) 11 RUE MAGINOT	GRENOBLE	**FR**		(76) 870-280
MIKVAH (COMM. CENTER) 39 RUE DE VERSAILLES	LE CHESNAY	**FR**		(39) 513-742
MIKVAH RUE DE WETZ	LENS	**FR**		
MIKVAH (CHAARE TZEDEK) 18 RUE SAINT-MATHIEAU	LYON	**FR**		(78) 007-250
MIKVAH 317 RUE DUGUESCLIN	LYON	**FR**		(78) 581-874
MIKVAH 40 RUE A. BOUTIN	LYON VILLEURBANNE	**FR**		
MIKVAH (YESHIVA PINTO) 20 BIS, RUE DE MURIERS	LYON VILLEURBANNE	**FR**		(78) 038-914
MIKVAH (BETH MYRIAM) 60 CHEMIN VALLON-DU-TOULOUSE	MARSEILLES	**FR**		(91) 752-864
MIKVAH (COLLEL) 43A CHEMIN VALLON-DU-TOULOUSE	MARSEILLES	**FR**		(91) 752-864
MIKVAH (REDON) 13 BOULEVARD DU REDON	MARSEILLES	**FR**		(91) 821-889
MIKVAH 45A RUE CONSOLAT	MARSEILLES	**FR**		(91) 624-261
MIKVAH 73 RUE DE LA PALUD	MARSEILLES	**FR**		
MIKVAH 41 RUE AUX ARENES	METZ	**FR**		
MIKVAH RUE DE LA SYNAGOGUE	MEUDON-LA-FORET	**FR**		(46) 326-482
MIKVAH 19 RUE DE LA SYNAGOGUE	MULHOUSE	**FR**		(89) 458-541
MIKVAH (IN SYNAGOGUE) 5 IMPASSE COPERNIC	NANTES	**FR**		(40) 734-892
MIKVAH 1 BIS RUE BOISSY D'ANGLAS	NICE	**FR**		(93) 805-896
MIKVAH 22 RUE MICHELET	NICE	**FR**		(93) 510-812
MIKVAH 176 RUE DU TEMPLE	PARIS	**FR**	75003	(42) 718-928
MIKVAH 50 RUE DU FAUBOURG ST. MARTIN	PARIS	**FR**	75010	(42) 064-395
MIKVAH 8 RUE DES TROIS-FRERES	PAU	**FR**		(59) 623-785
MIKVAH 74 AVENUE PAUL VALERY	SARCELLES	**FR**		(39) 902-051
MIKVAH RUE GEORGE V	SARRAGUEMINES	**FR**		(87) 950-952
MIKVAH LA RUE RENE HIRSCHLER	STRASBOURG	**FR**		(88) 364-368
MIKVAH (ETS HAIM) 33 FAUBOURG DE SAVERNE	STRASBOURG	**FR**		(88) 323-541

MIKVAH (COMM. CENTER) AVENUE LAZARE-CARNOT	TOULON	**FR**	(94) 926-105
MIKVAH 15 RUE FRANCISQUE SARCEY	TOULOUSE	**FR**	(61) 488-984
MIKVAH (IN SYNAGOGUE) 5 RUE BRUNNEVAL	TROYES	**FR**	(25) 733-444
MIKVAH 2 RUE DE MARECHAL FOCH	VICHY	**FR**	(70) 598-296
MIKVAH 42/44 RUE DU FOND DE LA NOUE	VILLENEUVE-LA-GARENNE	**FR**	(47) 948-998
MIKVAH GIVAT HAMOREH, SHCHUNAT YAAR EXTENSION	AFULA	**IS**	
MIKVAH RECHOV KINAMON (OPPOSITE FOOTBALL FIELD)	AFULA	**IS**	
MIKVAH SHIKUN RASSCO	AFULA ILLIT	**IS**	
MIKVAH DERECH HAARBAAH (NEAR EGGED BUS STATION)	AKKO	**IS**	
MIKVAH SHIKUN GIMMEL	AKKO	**IS**	
MIKVAH NEAR YOUTH HOSTEL, OPPOSITE EMPLOYMENT OFFICE	ARAD	**IS**	
MIKVAH DISTRICT A, NEAR RAMBAM SCHOOL	ASHDOD	**IS**	
MIKVAH SHCHUNAT HAPOLANIM	ASHKELON	**IS**	
MIKVAH 38 HALPER STREET	BAT YAM	**IS**	
MIKVAH KIRYAT BOBOV	BAT YAM	**IS**	
MIKVAH HAVRADIM ST., RAMAT YOSEF	BAT YAM	**IS**	
MIKVAH SHCHUNA DALED, HAKNIZI CIRCLE, NEAR THE OLD CENTER	BEERSHEVA	**IS**	
MIKVAH RECHOV CHOFETZ CHAIM, CORNER MAHARSHAL	BNEI BRAK	**IS**	
MIKVAH RECHOV RAMBAM	BNEI BRAK	**IS**	
MIKVAH SHIKUN VISHNITZ	BNEI BRAK	**IS**	
MIKVAH NEXT TO THE CENTRAL SYNAGOGUE	EILAT	**IS**	
MIKVAH 55 TIBER STREET	GIVATAYIM	**IS**	
MIKVAH 2 MENORAH STREET	GIVATAYIM	**IS**	
MIKVAH RECHOV HAGIBORIM, ENTER FROM YOVEL STREET	HADERA	**IS**	
CENTRAL MIKVAH RECHOV ARLOZOROV, WOMEN'S ENTRANCE, 2 BEZALEL STREET	HAIFA	**IS**	
MIKVAH 5 RECHOV TZFAT (CORNER HANEVIIM & HERZLIA STREETS) HADAR	HAIFA	**IS**	
MIKVAH NEAR CENTRAL SYNAGOGUE, KIRYAT SHMUEL	HAIFA	**IS**	
MIKVAH (CARMEL CENTRAL SYNAGOGUE) 10 DERECH HAYAM., MT. CARMEL	HAIFA	**IS**	
MIKVAH (IN SYNAGOGUE) 16 SDEROT SINAI. ACHUZA	HAIFA	**IS**	
MIKVAH SIRKIN STREET, NEAR CENTRAL SYNAGOGUE	HERZLIA	**IS**	
MIKVAH NEAR CENTRAL SYNAGOGUE, RAMATAYIM	HOD HASHARON	**IS**	
MIKVAH RECHOV SOKOLOV, MAGDIEL	HOD HASHARON	**IS**	
MIKVAH NEAR ASHKENAZI SYNAGOGUE, GANEI ZVI	HOD HASHARON	**IS**	
MIKVAH RECHOV SHIMON HATZADIK, NEVEI NE'EMAN	HOD HASHARON	**IS**	
MIKVAH EDNA INSTITUTE, 9 RAV KOOK ST., AGROBANK	HOLON	**IS**	
MIKVAH SHCHUNAT G. COHEN, RECHOV HASANHEDRIN	HOLON	**IS**	
MIKVAH 3 RECHOV FLORENTIN. KIRYAT HAYOVEL	JERUSALEM	**IS**	
MIKVAH 1 RECHOV PANIM MEIROT. KIRYAT MATTERSDORF	JERUSALEM	**IS**	
MIKVAH 5 RECHOV HA'ARI. RECHAVIA	JERUSALEM	**IS**	
MIKVAH 7 RECHOV HAMATZOR. KATAMON	JERUSALEM	**IS**	
MIKVAH 13 RECHOV YEHUDA HANASI. KATAMON HEH	JERUSALEM	**IS**	
MIKVAH ORENSTEIN BUILDINGS. ZICHRON MOCHE	JERUSALEM	**IS**	
MIKVAH 8 RECHOV HANATZIV. SHCHUNAT BATEI RAND	JERUSALEM	**IS**	
MIKVAH 22 RECHOV HARAV BLAU, SANHEDRIA	JERUSALEM	**IS**	
MIKVAH NEAR CENTRAL SYNAGOGUE, SHCHUNAT MEKOR CHAIM	JERUSALEM	**IS**	
MIKVAH (CENTRAL HOTEL) 6 PINES STREET	JERUSALEM	**IS**	
MIKVAH (CENTRAL SHEPHARDI SYNAGOGUE) RECHOV BAYIT VEGAN 9	JERUSALEM	**IS**	
MIKVAH TAL 7 RECHOV GID'ON. SHCHUNAT BAK'A	JERUSALEM	**IS**	
MIKVAH YISROEL OFF STRAUSS STREET	JERUSALEM	**IS**	
MIKVAH 23 RECHOV HATIKVAH	KFAR SABA	**IS**	
MIKVAH RECHOV HAMEYASDIM	KIRYAT ATTA	**IS**	
MIKVAH 15 RECHOV REUVEN	KIRYAT BIALIK	**IS**	
MIKVAH RECHOV BET GURBIN- NEXT TO BET YISROEL V'DAMESEK ELIEZER	KIRYAT GAT	**IS**	
MIKVAH SHUCHUNAT NACHALAT HAR-CHABAD, NEXT TO KUPAT CHOLIM CLINI	KIRYAT MALACHI	**IS**	
MIKVAH RECHOV EILAT, NEXT TO CENTER FOR THE AGED	KIRYAT MALACHI	**IS**	
MIKVAH RAMBAM STREET, NEXT TO MAON WIZO	KIRYAT MALACHI	**IS**	
MIKVAH 1 RECHOV GRUSHKEVITZ	KIRYAT MOTZKIN	**IS**	
MIKVAH 53 RECHOV JABOTINSKY	KIRYAT ONO	**IS**	
MIKVAH RECHOV S.Y. AGNON	KIRYAT ONO	**IS**	
MIKVAH SHIKUN CHABAD, SHCHUNAT HARAKEVET	LOD	**IS**	
MIKVAH RECHOV ELPAEL, CORNER RECHOV NATAN SCHWARTZ	LOD	**IS**	
MIKVAH RECHOV AHAD HA'AM	NAHARIYA	**IS**	
MIKVAH NEAR HAGALIL CIRCLE, NEXT TO KINDERGARTEN	NAZARETH ILLIT	**IS**	
MIKVAH 29 RECHOV HA'ATZMAUT	NES ZIONA	**IS**	
CENTRAL MIKVAH 25 YEHUDA HALEVI	NETANYA	**IS**	
MIKVAH KIRYAT ZANS	NETANYA	**IS**	
MIKVAH KIRYAT NORDAU	NETANYA	**IS**	
MIKVAH RECHOV HAMACHABIM, CORNER OF ORLOV, NEXT TO CENTRAL BUS ST	PETACH TIKVAH	**IS**	
MIKVAH RECHOV HERZL, CENTER OF TOWN	RA'ANANA	**IS**	
MIKVAH 7 HAGIBORIM STREET	RAMAT GAN	**IS**	
MIKVAH 5 RECHOV UZIEL	RAMAT GAN	**IS**	
MIKVAH RECHOV AZNEL, NEXT TO SCHOOL, RAMAT HASHIKMAH	RAMAT GAN	**IS**	
MIKVAH SHCHUNAT WEIZMANN	RAMLAH	**IS**	
MIKVAH RECHOV MOTZKIN	RAMLAH	**IS**	
MIKVAH RECHOV HASHOFTIM, CENTER OF TOWN, NEAR TNUVA	RECHOVOT	**IS**	
CENTRAL MIKVAH RECHOV NECHAMA, NEAR CENTRAL SYNAGOGUE	RISHON LEZION	**IS**	
MIKVAH SHCHUNAT MIZRACH RECHOV YOSEF HANASI	RISHON LEZION	**IS**	
MIKVAH SHCHUNAT RAMAT ELIAHU, RECHOV TORAH V'AVODAH	RISHON LEZION	**IS**	
MIKVAH SHIKUN DAROM, RECHOV HERZL, OPPOSITE RASSCO	SAFED	**IS**	
MIKVAH HAMAGINIM CIRCLE	SAFED	**IS**	
MIKVAH 202 BNEI EPHRAIM STREET. HADAR YOSEF	TEL AVIV	**IS**	
MIKVAH 24 PINES STREET	TEL AVIV	**IS**	
MIKVAH 5 RECHOV HATECHIYA. YAFO	TEL AVIV	**IS**	
MIKVAH SDEROT HACHAYAL. YAD ELIAHU	TEL AVIV	**IS**	
MIKVAH 10 RECHOV YAVNE	TEL AVIV	**IS**	
MIKVAH 8 RECHOV HAKOVSHIM	TEL AVIV	**IS**	
MIKVAH (ICHUD SHAVEI ZION SYNAGOGUE) 86 RECHOV BEN YEHUDA	TEL AVIV	**IS**	
MIKVAH RECHOV HAYARKON, IN LOWER CITY	TIBERIAS	**IS**	
MIKVAH SHIKUN DALED, ON STREET OF DAN HALL	TIBERIAS	**IS**	
MIKVAH END OF RECHOV HARAV VERNER, KIRYAT SHMUEL	TIBERIAS	**IS**	
MIKVAH SHIKUN DROMI, OPPOSITE SCHOOL	ZICHRON YAAKOV	**IS**	
MIKVAH RECHOV HAMEYASDIM, CENTER OF TOWN, OPPOSITE SCHOOL	ZICHRON YAAKOV	**IS**	

MONUMENTS

ACME MEMORIAL CO. 1900 HILLSIDE BOULEVARD	COLMA	**CA**	94014	(415) 755-1117
AMERICAN MONUMENT CO. 253 EL CAMINO REAL	COLMA	**CA**	94014	(415) PL5-1141
LODGE MEMORIALS 1247 S. FAIRFAX AVENUE	LOS ANGELES	**CA**	90019	(213) 931-1081
ERNST BERLIN MONUMENTS 706 REGAL COURT	MENLO PARK	**CA**	94025	(415) 322-6398
ALPINE MONUMENTS 1240 SOUTH KALAMATH	DENVER	**CO**	80223	(303) 777-1034
LICHTENSTEIN CO. 323 WASHINGTON AVENUE	HAMDEN	**CT**	06518	(203) 287-1593
ARTCRAFT MEMORIALS 1450 MAIN STREET	HARTFORD	**CT**	06120	(203) 247-3054
GELB MONUMENTS 140 S.W. 57TH AVENUE	MIAMI	**FL**	33144	(305) 266-2888
SAM CANTOR & SONS 47 EVERETT AVENUE	CHELSEA	**MA**	02150	(617) 889-1562
S. SLOTNICK MONUMENTAL WORKS 232 FULLER STREET	EVERETT	**MA**	02149	(617) 387-3980
MILTON MONUMENT CO., INC. 1040 NORTH MAIN STREET	RANDOLPH	**MA**	02368	(617) 963-3660
THE FREEDMAN MONUMENT CO. 115 STATE STREET	SPRINGFIELD	**MA**	01108	(413) 736-2958
VENEZIAN MONUMENTAL WORKS 1587 STATE STREET	SPRINGFIELD	**MA**	01109	(413) 734-3044
EDEN MEMORIALS MAIN STREET	WINNIPEG	**MB**		(204) 586-8579
BARRE MONUMENT CO. 1630 E. BALTIMORE STREET	BALTIMORE	**MD**	21231	(301) 327-1344
FRAM MONUMENT CO., INC. 7020 REISTERSTOWN ROAD	PIKESVILLE	**MD**	21208	(301) 484-3121
UDELL'S ARLINGTON MONUMENT CO. 708 REISTERSTOWN ROAD	PIKESVILLE	**MD**	21208	(301) 653-1888
SHELDON GRANITE COMPANY 19800 WOODWARD AVENUE	DETROIT	**MI**	48203	(313) 368-3550
MONUMENT CENTER 661 EAST EIGHT MILE ROAD	FERNDALE	**MI**	48220	(313) 542-8266
BERG & URBACH MONUMENT WORKS 13405 CAPITAL	OAK PARK	**MI**	48203	(313) 544-2212
DETROIT MONUMENT WORKS 14441 WEST ELEVEN MILE ROAD	OAK PARK	**MI**	49835	(313) 399-2711
MINNEAPOLIS GRANITE & MARBLE COMPANY 4400 CHICAGO AVENUE	MINNEAPOLIS	**MN**	55407	(612) 822-3135
AARON MONUMENT COMPANY 1799 HILLCREST	ST. PAUL	**MN**	55116	(612) 698-6262
KANSAS CITY MONUMENT COMPANY 6842 TROOST	KANSAS CITY	**MO**	64100	(816) 333-0075
ROSENBLOOM MONUMENT COMPANY 7501 OLIVE	ST. LOUIS	**MO**	63130	(314) 721-5070
J.F. BLOOM MONUMENT COMPANY 4431 NORTH 20TH STREET	OMAHA	**NE**	68110	(402) 451-6000
J.F. BLOOM MONUMENT COMPANY 2701 NORTH 90TH STREET	OMAHA	**NE**	68134	(402) 393-6222
BRONZE & GRANITE MEMORIALS 45 SAMWORTH ROAD	CLIFTON	**NJ**	07012	(201) 473-3922
GOODMAN BROTHERS MONUMENTS 402 PARK STREET	HACKENSACK	**NJ**	07601	(201) 487-3810
M&K MONUMENTS 1767 SPRINGFIELD AVENUE	MAPLEWOOD	**NJ**	07040	(201) 763-8500
LIMAN'S NEWARK MEMORIALS 358 GROVE STREET	NEWARK	**NJ**	07103	(201) 373-6514
ORLOVSKY MEMORIALS 284 SOUTH 20TH STREET	NEWARK	**NJ**	07103	(201) 372-6487
SHALOM MEMORIALS 1519 STUYVESANT AVENUE	UNION	**NJ**	07083	(201) 686-5151
HAIMM GARDEN MEMORIAL CENTER U.S. HIGHWAY 1	WOODBRIDGE	**NJ**	07095	(201) 634-8500
BRONX MEMORIAL CORP. 1888 WASHINGTON AVENUE	BRONX	**NY**	10457	(212) 733-5400
HASKELL, BENJAMIN & SON 1888 WASHINGTON AVENUE	BRONX	**NY**	10457	(212) 294-3848
PARKWAY MONUMENTS 764 LYDIG AVENUE	BRONX	**NY**	10457	(212) 583-6461
TREMONT MONUMENT WORKS 1811 WASHINGTON AVENUE	BRONX	**NY**	10457	(212) 294-2626
BRENNER MONUMENTS CORP. 1572 CONEY ISLAND AVENUE	BROOKLYN	**NY**	11230	(718) 438-0500
GREENBAUM MONUMENTS 4509 14TH AVENUE	BROOKLYN	**NY**	11219	(718) 436-2411
HASKEL BROTHERS 1572 CONEY ISLAND AVENUE	BROOKLYN	**NY**	11230	(718) 258-3230
J. GOLDSTEIN & SONS 826 JAMAICA AVENUE	BROOKLYN	**NY**	11208	(718) 277-2937
KLEIN'S MONUMENTS 1640 CONEY ISLAND AVENUE	BROOKLYN	**NY**	11230	(718) 627-1115
RABBI PREMOCK	BROOKLYN	**NY**	11204	(718) 851-1314
WEISS MONUMENTS 2223 AVENUE U	BROOKLYN	**NY**	11229	(718) 646-0300
WILLIAM ROSEN MONUMENTS 1912 FLATBUSH AVENUE	BROOKLYN	**NY**	11210	(718) 951-6900
HEBREW MEMORIAL COMPANY 1640 EAST DELAVAN AVENUE	BUFFALO	**NY**	14215	(716) 893-2500
TEL-AVIV MEMORIALS 314 ELMONT ROAD	ELMONT	**NY**	11003	(516) 481-3700
GOODMAN BROTHERS MONUMENTS 130-30 HORACE HARDING BOULEVARD	FLUSHING	**NY**	11367	(718) 359-3724
WENIG MONUMENT WORKS, INC. 159-05 HORACE HARDING EXPRESSWAY	FRESH MEADOWS	**NY**	11365	(718) 445-3136
GINSBERG MEMORIAL 1285 NORTHERN BOULEVARD	MANHASSET	**NY**	11030	(516) 821-7330
ADLER'S MONUMENTS 148 EAST 57TH STREET	NEW YORK	**NY**	10022	(212) 753-6330
BLEVITZKY BROTHERS MONUMENTS 210-212 FORSYTH STREET	NEW YORK	**NY**	10002	(212) 477-9908
DUBIN & STEINBERG 245 EAST HOUSTON STREET	NEW YORK	**NY**	10002	(212) 475-7697
FORSYTH/M. GOLDFINGER MONUMENTS 172 SUFFOLK STREET	NEW YORK	**NY**	10002	(212) 473-2388
L. NEUMANN MONUMENTS 219 EAST THIRD STREET	NEW YORK	**NY**	10002	(212) 228-7530
SHASTONE MONUMENTS 217 EAST HOUSTON STREET	NEW YORK	**NY**	10002	(212) 475-0360
WEINREB BROTHERS & GROSS 172 SUFFOLK STREET	NEW YORK	**NY**	10002	(212) 254-2360
WEITZNER BROTHERS & PAPPER 25 SECOND AVENUE	NEW YORK	**NY**	10003	(212) 254-8826
GALLE MEMORIAL STUDIOS 1481 LAKE AVENUE	ROCHESTER	**NY**	14615	(716) 458-5302
JEWISH MEMORIALS OF ROCKLAND, INC. 15 STATE STREET	SPRING VALLEY	**NY**	10977	(914) 425-2256
GOLDENBERG MONUMENTS 12 YOUNG AVENUE	YONKERS	**NY**	10710	(914) 779-3717
FRIEDMAN MONUMENTS 1900 SOUTH TAYLOR ROAD	CLEVELAND	**OH**	44118	(216) 932-9122
PLYMOUTH MEMORIALS CO. 1936 SOUTH TAYLOR ROAD	CLEVELAND	**OH**	44118	(216) 321-1800
BARNETT BOOKATZ CLEVELAND TEMPLE MEMORIAL, INC. 1985 SOUTH TAYLOR ROAD	CLEVELAND HEIGHTS	**OH**	44118	(216) 421-8484
COLUMBUS ART MEMORIAL CO. 766 GREENLAWN AVE.	COLUMBUS	**OH**	43223	(216) 221-2726
GOLDBERG MONUMENTS 2687 BATHURST STREET	TORONTO	**ON**		(416) 781-6669
KILVINGTON BROTHERS 2751 BLOOR STREET WEST	TORONTO	**ON**		(416) 233-5531
SAM IZENBERG MONUMENTS 3173 BATHURST STREET	TORONTO	**ON**		(416) 787-0319

ART MONUMENT COMPANY 4709 NORTH BROAD STREET — PHILADELPHIA **PA** 19141 (215) 324-5006
NATHAN SHAPIRO MONUMENTS 7956 BUSTLETON AVENUE — PHILADELPHIA **PA** 19152 (215) 745-7220
QUALITY MONUMENT 1869 COTTMAN AVENUE — PHILADELPHIA **PA** 19111 (215) 745-3333
REIBSTEIN MEMORIALS 4709 NORTH BROAD STREET — PHILADELPHIA **PA** 19141 (215) 324-6400
WERTHEIMER MONUMENTS 6720 BUSTLETON AVENUE — PHILADELPHIA **PA** 19152 (215) 333-1222
FALEDER MONUMENTS 2414 FIFTH AVENUE — PITTSBURGH **PA** 15215 (412) 682-5500
URBACH MONUMENTAL WORKS 2635 MURRAY AVENUE — PITTSBURGH **PA** 15215 (412) 421-8655
MOUNT SINAI MEMORIAL MONUMENT COMPANY 825 HOPE STREET — PROVIDENCE **RI** 02906 (401) 331-3337
SUGARMAN MONUMENT COMPANY 458 HOPE STREET — PROVIDENCE **RI** 02906 (401) 331-8094
QUIRING MONUMENTS 9608 AURORO NORTH — SEATTLE **WA** 98103 (206) 522-8400
UNIVERSAL MONUMENT WORKS 6339 WEST APPLETON AVENUE — MILWAUKEE **WI** 53210 (414) 445-5330

MUSEUMS

TEMPLE BETH ISRAEL 3310 NORTH 10TH AVENUE — PHOENIX **AZ** 85031 (602) 264-4428
JUDAH L. MAGNES MEMORIAL MUSEUM 2911 RUSSELL STREET — BERKELEY **CA** 94705 (415) 849-2710
HEBREW UNION COLLEGE-SKIRBALL MUSEUM 3077 UNIVERSITY AVENUE — LOS ANGELES **CA** 90007 (213) 749-3424
MARTYRS MEMORIAL & MUSEUM OF THE HOLOCAUST JEWISH FEDERATION COUNCIL 6505 WILSHIRE BOULEVARD — LOS ANGELES **CA** 90048 (213) 852-1234
PRECIOUS LEGACY OF CONG. RODEF SHALOM 450 SOUTH KEARNEY — DENVER **CO** 80224 (303) 399-0035
B'NAI B'RITH KLUTZNICK EXHIBIT HALL 1640 RHODE ISLAND AVENUE N.W. — WASHINGTON **DC** 20036 (202) 857-6583
B'NAI B'RITH KLUTZNICK MUSEUM 1640 RHODE ISLAND AVENUE N.W. — WASHINGTON **DC** 20036 (202) 857-6600
JEWISH WAR VETERANS OF U.S.A NATIONAL MEMORIAL MUSEUM 1811 R STREET, N.W. — WASHINGTON **DC** 20009 (202) 265-6280
KOL AMI MUSEUM 145 EAST OHIO STREET — CHICAGO **IL** 60611
MORTON WEISS MEMORIAL MUSEUM OF JUDAICA-K.A.M. ISAIAH ISRAEL 1110 EAST HYDE PARK BOULEVARD — CHICAGO **IL** 60615 (312) 924-1234
RODFEI ZEDEK CONGREGATION MUSEUM 5200 HYDE PARK — CHICAGO **IL** 60615 (312) 752-2770
SPERTUS MUSEUM OF JUDAICA 618 SOUTH MICHIGAN AVENUE — CHICAGO **IL** 60605 (312) 922-9012
SEMITIC MUSEUM OF HARVARD UNIVERSITY 6 DIVINITY AVENUE — CAMBRIDGE **MA** 02138 (617) UN8-7600
RABBI HERMAN H. & MIGNON L. RUBENOVITZ MUSEUM & ARCHIVES C/O TEMPLE MISHKAN TEFILA 300 HAMMOND POND PARKWAY — CHESTNUT HILL **MA** 02167
AMERICAN JEWISH HISTORICAL SOCIETY 2 THORNTON ROAD — WALTHAM **MA** 02154 (617) 891-8110
JEWISH HISTORICAL SOCIETY OF WESTERN CANADA, INC. 403-322 DONALD STREET — WINNIPEG **MB** R3B 2H3 (204) 942-4822
CHIZUK AMUNO CONGREGATION 8100 STEVENSON ROAD — BALTIMORE **MD** 21208 (301) 486-6400
LLOYD STREET SYNAGOGUE MUSEUM BALTIMORE HEBREW COLLEGE, 5800 PARK HEIGHTS AVENUE — BALTIMORE **MD** 21215 (301) 588-2808
HOLOCAUST MEMORIAL CENTER 6602 WEST MAPLE ROAD — WEST BLOOMFIELD **MI** 48033 (313) 661-0840
TEMPLE-CONGREGATION B'NAI JEHUDA 712 EAST 69TH STREET — KANSAS CITY **MO** 64131 (816) 363-1050
JUDAICA MUSEUM 5961 PALISADE AVENUE — BRONX **NY** 10471 (212) 548-1006
TEMPLE BETHEL MUSEUM 5 OLD MILL ROAD — GREAT NECK **NY** 11023 (516) 487-0900
FERKAUF MUSEUM OF THE INTERNATIONAL SYNAGOGUE JFK INTERNATIONAL AIRPORT — JAMAICA **NY** 11430 (718) 656-5044
CONGREGATION EMANU-EL MUSEUM 1 EAST 65TH STREET — NEW YORK **NY** 10021 (212) 744-1400
JEWISH MUSEUM, THE 1109 FIFTH AVENUE — NEW YORK **NY** 10028 (212) 860-1888
YIVO 1048 FIFTH AVENUE — NEW YORK **NY** 10028 (212) 535-6700
YESHIVA UNIVERSITY MUSEUM 2520 AMSTERDAM AVENUE — NEW YORK **NY** 10033 (212) 920-5390
TEMPLE B'RITH KODESH MUSEUM 2131 ELMWOOD AVENUE — ROCHESTER **NY** 14618 (716) 244-7060

TEMPLE BETH SHOLOM, JUDAICA MUSEUM ROSLYN ROAD AT NORTHERN STATE PARKWAY — ROSLYN **NY** 11577 (516) 621-2288
GALLERY OF ART AND ARTIFACTS-HEBREW UNION COLLEGE 3101 CLIFTON AVENUE — CINCINNATI **OH** 42522 (513) 221-1875
TEMPLE MUSEUM OF RELIGIOUS ART, THE UNIVERSITY CIRCLE AND SILVER PARK — CLEVELAND **OH** 44106 (216) 791-7755
REBECCA AND GERSHON FENSTER GALLERY OF JEWISH ART 1223 EAST 17TH PLACE — TULSA **OK** 74120 (918) 582-3732
BETH TZEDEC MUSEUM 1700 BATHURST STREET — TORONTO **ON** M5P 3K3 (416) 781-3511
MUSEUM OF AMERICAN JEWISH HISTORY INDEPENDENCE MALL E., 55 N. 5TH STREET — PHILADELPHIA **PA** 19106 (215) 923-3811
ASSOCIATED AMERICAN JEWISH MUSEUMS, INC. 303 LEROI ROAD — PITTSBURGH **PA** 15208
TEMPLE MUSEUM OF RELIGIOUS ART/TEMPLE EMANUEL 4100 SHERBROOKE STREET WEST — MONTREAL **QU** H32 1A5 (514) 937-3575
BETH YESHURIN JEWISH MUSEUM 4525 BEECHNUT — HOUSTON **TX** 77000 (713) 666-1381

MUSIC

THE KLEZMORIM 1846 SPRUCE, 23 — BERKELEY **CA** 94709 (415) 540-5501
THE KLEZMORIM 87 EDGECROFT — KENSINGTON **CA** 94707 (415) 540-5501
AMERICAN JEWISH CHORAL SOCIETY — LOS ANGELES **CA** (213) 653-1041
BARUCH COHON, SHALOM CONCERT BUREAU PO BOX 35092 — LOS ANGELES **CA** 90035 (213) 931-6125
SHALOM CONCERT BUREAU PO BOX 35092 — LOS ANGELES **CA** 90035 (213) 931-6125
HUGHES DULCIMER COMPANY, INC. 441 WEST COLFAX AVENUE — DENVER **CO** 80204 (303) 572-3753
SHIRU SHIR CHADASH C/O TEMPLE SHEARITH ISRAEL 46 PEACEABLE STREET — RIDGEFIELD **CT** 06877 (203) 438-6589
NEW ENGLAND JEWISH MUSIC FORUM C/O MARY WOLFMAN EPSTEIN 327 ST. PAUL STREET — BROOKLINE **MA** 02146 (617) 566-4042
KADIMA C/O HAL KATZMAN 34 IRVING STREET — NEWTON CENTRE **MA** 02158 (617) 969-1926
DAVID SHNEYER 2307 FOREST GLEN ROAD — SILVER SPRING **MD** 20910 (301) 565-9422
SHANACHIE RECORDS CORPORATION DALEBROOK PARK — HO-HO-KUS **NJ** 07423 (201) 445-5561
KAPELYE C/O HENRY SAPOZNIK 2018 VOORHIES AVENUE, #B24 — BROOKLYN **NY** 11235 (718) 934-3859
MERKOS L'INYONEI CHINUCH, INC. 770 EASTERN PARKWAY — BROOKLYN **NY** 11213 (718) 493-9250
ISRAEL MUSIC FOUNDATION 109 CEDARHURST AVENUE — CEDARHURST **NY** 11516 (516) 569-1541
TARA PUBLICATIONS 29 DERBY AVENUE — CEDARHURST **NY** 11516 (516) 295-2290
MOSHE SHUR, HILLEL FOUNDATION, STUDENT SERVICES CORPORATION PO BOX 446 — FLUSHING **NY** 11367 (718) 793-2222
PAUL ZIM P.O. BOX 310 — FOREST HILLS **NY** 11375 (718) 520-0666
RAMIE & MERRI ARIAN, ETZ CHAIM CREATIVE JEWISH MUSIC 736 FOREST AVENUE — LARCHMONT **NY** 10538 (914) 834-2813
AMERICAN SOCIETY FOR JEWISH MUSIC 155 FIFTH AVENUE — NEW YORK **NY** 10010 (212) 533-2601
AMERICAN ZIONIST YOUTH FOUNDATION-EDUCATION DEPARTMENT 515 PARK AVENUE — NEW YORK **NY** 10022 (212) 308-4733
BALKAN ARTS CENTER 325 SPRING STREET — NEW YORK **NY** 10013 (212) 691-9510
BOARD OF JEWISH EDUCATION OF GREATER NEW YORK 426 WEST 58TH STREET — NEW YORK **NY** 10019 (212) 245-8200
DIASPORA YESHIVA BAND, B'NAI B'RITH LECTURE BUREAU 823 U.N. PLAZA — NEW YORK **NY** 10017 (212) 490-1170
GLORIA FELDMAN, B'NAI B'RITH LECTURE BUREAU 823 U.N. PLAZA — NEW YORK **NY** 10017 (212) 490-1170
HEBREW ARTS SCHOOL FOR MUSIC & DANCE 129 WEST 67TH STREET — NEW YORK **NY** 10023 (212) 787-0650
HERSHMAN MUSICAL INSTRUMENT CO., INC. 135 WEST 29TH STREET — NEW YORK **NY** 10001 (212) 564-0252
JEWISH MUSIC & RECORD SHOP 147 ESSEX STREET — NEW YORK **NY** 10002 (212) 674-1289
JEWISH MUSIC ALLIANCE 1 UNION SQUARE — NEW YORK **NY** 10003 (212) 924-8311
JEWISH MUSIC COUNCIL, NATIONAL JEWISH WELFARE BOARD 15 EAST 26TH STREET — NEW YORK **NY** 10010 (212) 532-4949
MERKIN CONCERT HALL-ABRAHAM GOODMAN HOUSE 129 WEST 67TH STREET — NEW YORK **NY** 10023 (212) 944-9300
NAT'L FEDERATION OF TEMPLE YOUTH-UNION OF AMER. HEBR. CONG. 838 FIFTH AVENUE — NEW YORK **NY** 10021 (212) 249-0100
NAT'L JEWISH MUSIC COUNCIL OF THE NAT'L JEWISH WELFARE BOARD 15 EAST 26TH STREET — NEW YORK **NY** 10010 (212) 532-4949
SHERWOOD GOFFIN 142 WEST END AVENUE — NEW YORK **NY** 10023 (212) 799-1393
THE JEWISH MUSIC SOCIETY 315 WEST 37TH STREET — NEW YORK **NY** 10018 (212) 594-1690
TRANSCONTINENTAL MUSIC PUBLISHING, UNION OF AMER. HEBR. CONG. 838 FIFTH AVENUE — NEW YORK **NY** 10021 (212) 249-0100
UNITED SYNAGOGUE, DEPARTMENT OF MUSIC 155 FIFTH AVENUE — NEW YORK **NY** 10010 (212) 533-7800
WORDTONE MUSIC, INC., RECORD LOFT INTERNATIONAL 230 SEVENTH AVENUE — NEW YORK **NY** 10011 (212) 691-1934
WORKMEN'S CIRCLE, EDUCATION DEPARTMENT 45 EAST 33RD STREET — NEW YORK **NY** 10016 (212) 889-6800
WORLD ZIONIST ORGANIZATION, DEPT. OF EDUCATION AND CULTURE 515 PARK AVENUE — NEW YORK **NY** 10022 (212) 752-0600
JOSEPH BACH 1432 NORTH 49TH STREET — ALLENTOWN **PA** 18104 (215) 398-2494
JAY M. BURMAN MUSIC 3 GREENWAY PLAZA EAST, SUITE B110 — HOUSTON **TX** 77024 (713) 776-8183

NEEDLEWORK

CALIFORNIA STITCHERY, ETC. 6015 SUNNYSLOPE AVENUE — VAN NUYS **CA** 91401 (818) 781-9515
BONNIE YALES 23 DANE ROAD — LEXINGTON **MA** 02173 (617) 861-8125
ALICE NUSSBAUM 2835 SALEM AVENUE SOUTH — MINNEAPOLIS **MN** 55416 (612) 922-3531
BETTY WINTER SAMUELS 390 WEST HUDSON AVENUE — ENGLEWOOD **NJ** 07631 (201) 567-8468
JANE BEARMAN 30 SPIER DRIVE — LIVINGSTON **NJ** 07039 (201) 992-3369
THE POMEGRANATE GUILD OF JUDAIC NEEDLEWORK 12 BAYVIEW AVENUE, C/O GILDA HECHT, VP MEMBERSHIP — GREAT NECK **NY** 11021
THE POMEGRANATE GUILD OF JUDAIC NEEDLEWORK 289 LINDEN PLACE — YORKTOWN HEIGHTS **NY** 10598

NEWS SERVICES & SYNDICATES

LUBAVITCH NEWS SERVICE 784 EASTERN PARKWAY .... BROOKLYN **NY** 11213 (718) 774-4000
INTERNATIONAL JEWISH PRESS BUREAU 5 BEEKMAN STREET .... NEW YORK **NY** 10038 (212) 267-5450
JEWISH NEWSPAPER AGENCY 1 PENN PLAZA .... NEW YORK **NY** 10119 (212) 760-5555
JEWISH STUDENT PRESS SERVICE 15 E. 26TH STREET .... NEW YORK **NY** 10010 (212) 679-1411
JEWISH TELEGRAPHIC AGENCY 165 WEST 46TH STREET, ROOM 511 ..... NEW YORK **NY** 10036 (212) 575-9370
UJA PRESS SERVICE
C/O UNITED JEWISH APPEAL, 99 PARK AVENUE, SUITE 300 .... NEW YORK **NY** 10016 (212) 818-9100
AMERICAN JEWISH PRESS ASSOCIATION P.O. BOX 742 .... FORT WORTH **TX** 76101 (817) 927-2831
ISRAEL NEWS SERVICE C/O ISRAEL GOVERNMENT PRESS OFFICE
BEIT AGRON, 37 HILLEL STREET .... JERUSALEM **IS** 94581 (02) 241222

NEWSPAPERS & PERIODICALS

CONTEMPORARY JEWRY (SEMI-ANNUAL)
DEPT. OF SOCIOLOGY/UNIVERSITY OF ALABAMA .... BIRMINGHAM **AL** 35294 (205) 934-4011
THE JEWISH STAR (MONTHLY) CIRC. 8,000 EST. 1976
P.O. BOX 9112 .... BIRMINGHAM **AL** 35213 (205) 956-3929
JEWISH MONITOR P.O. BOX 396 .... SHEFFIELD **AL** 35660 (205) 766-0508
JEWISH STAR - CALGARY (BI-WEEKLY) CIRC. 1,900 EST. 1980
2315 98TH AVE. SW .... CALGARY **AT** T2V 4S7 (403) 238-0010
JEWISH STAR - EDMONTON (MONTHLY) CIRC. 1,500 EST.1980
2315 98TH AVENUE SOUTHWEST .... CALGARY **AT** T2V 4S7 (403) 238-0010
GREATER PHOENIX JEWISH NEWS (WEEKLY) CIRC. 7,000 EST. 1948
7220 N. 16 STREET, SUITE G .... PHOENIX **AZ** 85020 (602) 870-9470
ARIZONA POST (FORTNIGHTLY) CIRC. 6,000 EST. 1946
102 NORTH PLUMER AVENUE .... TUCSON **AZ** 85719 (602) 791-9962
CHABAD TIMES (MONTHLY 11X) CIRCULATION 10,000 (ENGLISH) .... TUCSON **AZ**
CANADIAN JEWISH OUTLOOK (CIRC. 4,000 EST. 1962
6184 ASH STREET .... VANCOUVER **BC** V52-3G9 (604) 324-5101
JEWISH WESTERN BULLETIN 3268 HEATHER STREET .... VANCOUVER **BC** V5Z 3K5 (604) 879-6575
SHMATE (BI-MONTHLY) P.O. BOX 4228 .... BERKELEY **CA** 94704
ISRAEL TODAY - SAN DIEGO 500 FESLER STREET, SUITE 103 .... EL CAJON **CA** 92020 (619) 440-5890
CENTRAL CALIFORNIA JEWISH HERITAGE 1105 NORTH WISHON AVENUE .. FRESNO **CA** 93728 (213) 737-2122
ORANGE COUNTY JEWISH HERITAGE P.O. BOX 3120 .... GARDEN GROVE **CA** 92642 (714) 639-2121
JEWISH FEDERATION NEWS 3801 EAST WILLOW STREET .... LONG BEACH **CA** 90815 (213) 426-7601
B'NAI B'RITH MESSENGER (WEEKLY) CIRC. 67,000 EST. 1897
2510 WEST SEVENTH STREET .... LOS ANGELES **CA** 90057 (213) 380-5000
CALIFORNIA JEWISH PRESS CIRC. 37,000 EST. 1945
6399 WILSHIRE BLVD. #511 (WEEKLY) .... LOS ANGELES **CA** 90048 (213) 651-2230
HA'AM (6X YEAR) CIRC. 10,000 (ENGLISH)
112 KH/308 WESTWOOD PLAZA .... LOS ANGELES **CA** 90024
HERITAGE-SOUTHWEST (WEEKLY) CIRC. 15,000 EST. 1914
2130 SOUTH VERMONT AVENUE .... LOS ANGELES **CA** 90007 (213) 737-2122

JEWISH DAILY FORWARD 1161 N. OGDEN DRIVE .... LOS ANGELES **CA** 90046 (213) 659-0861
JEWISH JOURNAL (WEEKLY) CIRC. 58,000 EST. 1986
3660 WILSHIRE BOULEVARD, SUITE 204 .... LOS ANGELES **CA** 90010 (213) 738-7778
LIFE IN ISRAEL (6 TIMES/YR. L.A. TIMES)
CIRCULATION 198,000 (ENGLISH) .... LOS ANGELES **CA**
ULTIMATE ISSUES (QUARTERLY) EST. 1985
10573 WEST PICO BOULEVARD .... LOS ANGELES **CA** 90064 (213) 558-3958
JEWISH COMMUNITY NEWS (MONTHLY) CIRC. 5,500 EST. 1958
14855 OKA ROAD .... LOS GATOS **CA** 95030 (408) 358-3033
TIKKUN (BIMONTHLY) CIRC. 40,000 EST. 1986
5100 LEONA STREET .... OAKLAND **CA** 94619 (415) 482-0805
SAN DIEGO JEWISH PRESS-HERITAGE
3443 CAMINO DEL RIO SOUTH, SUITE 315 .... SAN DIEGO **CA** 92108 (619) 282-7177
JEWISH STAR (5X/YR) CIRC. 2,000 (ENGLISH) EST. 1956
109 MINNA, #323 .... SAN FRANCISCO **CA** 94105 (415) 421-4874
NORTH CALIFORNIA JEWISH BULLETIN (WEEKLY) CIRC. 23,000
121 STEUART ST. SUITE 302 .... SAN FRANCISCO **CA** 94105 (415) 957-9340
NORTHERN CALIFORNIA JEWISH BULLETIN (WEEKLY) CIRC. 22,900 EST. 1946
870 MARKET STREET, SUITE 954 .... SAN FRANCISCO **CA** 94102 (415) 391-9444
JEWISH COMMUNITY NEWS 1777 HAMILTON AVENUE, SUITE 210 .... SAN JOSE **CA** 95125 (408) 267-2770
JEWISH SPECTATOR (QUARTERLY) CIRC. 17,500, EST. 1935
P.O. BOX 2016, 1025 OCEAN AVENUE .... SANTA MONICA **CA** 90406 (213) 393-9063
WESTERN STATES JEWISH HISTORICAL QUARTERLY
2429 23RD STREET .... SANTA MONICA **CA** 90405 (213) 470-6033
ISRAEL TODAY (DAILY & WEEKLY) CIRC. 106,000 EST. 1963
6742 VAN NUYS BLVD. .... VAN NUYS **CA** 91405 (818) 786-4000
INTERMOUNTAIN JEWISH NEWS (WEEKLY) CIRC. 10,000
1275 SHERMAN STREET, SUITE 214, ESTABLISHED 1913 .... DENVER **CO** 80203 (303) 861-2235
JEWISH DIGEST (MONTHLY) ESTABLISHED 1955
1363 FAIRFIELD AVENUE .... BRIDGEPORT **CT** 06605 (203) 384-2284
CONNECTICUT JEWISH LEDGER (WEEKLY) CIRC. 25,000
PO BOX 1688, ESTABLISHED 1929 .... HARTFORD **CT** 06101 (203) 233-2148
ORIM - A JEWISH JOURNAL AT YALE P.O. BOX 1904A, YALE STATION ... NEW HAVEN **CT** 06520 (203) 432-6600
THE JEWISH LEADER (BIWEEKLY) CIRC. 2,300, EST. 1972
1 BUCKLEY PLACE .... NEW LONDON **CT** 06320 (203) 442-7395
ALERT, EST. 1970 1411 K STREET, N.W., SUITE 402 .... WASHINGTON **DC** 20005 (202) 775-9770
JERUSALEM POST WASHINGTON BUREAU
2233 WISCONSIN AVE., NW .... WASHINGTON **DC** 20007 (202) 338-4553
JEWISH VETERAN (5X/YR.) CIRC. 55,800 EST 1896
1811 R STREET NW .... WASHINGTON **DC** 20009 (202) 265-6280
JEWISH WEEK (WEEKLY) CIRC. 20,000 EST. 1930
1910 K STREET NORTHWEST .... WASHINGTON **DC** 20006 (202) 872-1100
MENORAH (MONTHLY) EST. 1979
1747 CONNECTICUT AVENUE, N.W. .... WASHINGTON **DC** 20009

MOMENT (MONTHLY) CIRC. 26,000 EST. 1975
3000 CONNECTICUT AVENUE, NORTHWEST, SUITE 30 .... WASHINGTON **DC** 20015 (202) 387-8888

NEAR EAST REPORT (WEEKLY) CIRC. 50,000, EST. 1957
500 NORTH CAPITOL STREET, N.W./SUITE 307 .... WASHINGTON **DC** 20001 (202) 638-1225

SHOFAR (6X/YR.) CIRC. 40,000-B'NAI B'RITH YOUTH ORG.
1640 RHODE ISLAND AVENUE, N.W. .... WASHINGTON **DC** 20036 (202) 857-6644

THE B'NAI B'RITH INTERNATIONAL JEWISH MONTHLY (10X/YEAR)
1640 RHODE ISLAND AVENUE,
NORTHWEST CIRC. 200,000, EST. 1886 .... WASHINGTON **DC** 20036 (202) 857-6645

WOMEN'S WORLD - B'NAI B'RITH WOMEN (BIMONTHLY) CIRC. 120,000 EST. 1951
1640 RHODE ISLAND AVENUE, NORTHWEST .... WASHINGTON **DC** 20036 (202) 857-4964

JEWISH VOICE (BIWEEKLY) CIRC. 3,000 EST. 1970
101 GARDEN OF EDEN ROAD .... WILMINGTON **DE** 19803 (302) 478-6200

HERITAGE FLORIDA JEWISH NEWS P.O. BOX 742 .... FERN PARK **FL** 32730 (305) 834-8277

JEWISH JOURNAL (WEEKLY) CIRC. 53,000 EST. 1977
P.O. BOX 23909 .... FORT LAUDERDALE **FL** 33307 (305) 563-3200

SOUTHERN JEWISH WEEKLY, CIRC 28,500 EST. 1924
PO BOX 3297 .... JACKSONVILLE **FL** 32206 (904) 634-1812

JEWISH FLORIDIAN NEWSPAPERS (WEEKLY) CIRC. 54,700 EST. 1926
PO BOX 012973 .... MIAMI **FL** 33101 (305) 373-4605

THE JEWISH FLORIDIAN & SHOFAR OF GR. HOLLYWOOD (26X YEAR)
JEWISH FLORIDIAN GROUP/PO BOX 012973, CIRC. 12,000 .... MIAMI **FL** 33101 (305) 373-4605

THE JEWISH FLORIDIAN OF MIAMI (WEEKLY) CIRC. 25,000
JEWISH FLORIDIAN GROUP/PO BOX 012973 .... MIAMI **FL** 33101 (305) 373-4605

THE JEWISH FLORIDIAN OF PALM BEACH COUNTY (26X YEAR)
JEWISH FLORIDIAN GROUP/PO BOX 012973, CIRC. 10,000 .... MIAMI **FL** 33101 (305) 373-4605

MIAMI JEWISH TRIBUNE, THE (WEEKLY)
3550 BISCAYNE BOULEVARD, SUITE 600 .... MIAMI **FL** 33137 (305) 576-9500

JEWISH FLORIDIAN OF GREATER FORT LAUDERDALE (BIWEEKLY) CIRC. 16,000
EST. 1971 P.O. BOX 26810 .... TAMARAC **FL** 33320 (305) 748-8400

JEWISH FLORIDIAN OF TAMPA, THE (BIWEEKLY) CIRC. 4,100 EST. 1979
2808 HORATIO .... TAMPA **FL** 33609 (813) 872-4470

PALM BEACH JEWISH WORLD (WEEKLY) CIRC. 50,000 EST. 1982
P.O. BOX 3343 .... WEST PALM BEACH **FL** 33402 (305) 833-8331

ATLANTA JEWISH TIMES (WEEKLY) CIRC. 7,200 EST. 1925
P.O. BOX 25287 .... ATLANTA **GA** 30325 (404) 355-6139

HAWAII JEWISH TIMES (MONTHLY) CIRC. 2,000 EST. 1977
817 COOKE STREET .... HONOLULU **HI** 96813 (808) 531-4634

M'GODOLIM/THE JEWISH QUARTERLY 621 HOLD .... IOWA CITY **IA** 52240

SOUTHERN ILLINOIS JEWISH NEWS (6X/YEAR) CIRC. 800 EST. 1945
6464 W. MAIN, SUITE 7A .... BELLEVILLE **IL** 62223 (618) 271-2400

JEWISH CHICAGO 1801 BYRON .... CHICAGO **IL** 60613 (312) 327-8181

JUF NEWS (MONTHLY) (CIRC. 48,000) EST. 1940
ONE SOUTH FRANKLIN, ROOM 722 .... CHICAGO **IL** 60606 (312) 444-2863

SENTINEL (WEEKLY) CIRC. 26,000 EST. 1911
323 SOUTH FRANKLIN STREET .... CHICAGO **IL** 60606 (312) 663-1101

D'VAR SHALOM P.O. BOX 554 .... HIGHLAND PARK **IL** 60035

INDIANA JEWISH POST AND OPINION (WEEKLY) EST. 1935
P.O. BOX 449097 .... INDIANAPOLIS **IN** 46202 (317) 927-7800

NATIONAL JEWISH POST AND OPINION (WEEKLY) CIRC. 103,000 EST. 1935
P.O. BOX 449097 .... INDIANAPOLIS **IN** 46202 (317) 927-7800

KANSAS CITY JEWISH CHRONICLE (WEEKLY) CIRC. 20,000 EST. 1920
7373 W 107TH STREET .... OVERLAND PARK **KS** 66212 (913) 648-4620

COMMUNITY (BI-WEEKLY) CIRC. 5,400
3620 DUTCHMANS LANE .... LOUISVILLE **KY** 40205 (502) 451-8840

KENTUCKY JEWISH POST AND OPINION (WEEKLY) CIRC. 4,500
1551 BARDSTOWN ROAD .... LOUISVILLE **KY** 40205 (502) 459-1914

JEWISH TIMES (BIWEEKLY) CIRC. 10,700 EST. 1945
1539 JACKSON STREET, SUITE 323 .... NEW ORLEANS **LA** 70130 (504) 525-0673

THE JEWISH CIVIC PRESS (BIWEEKLY) CIRC. 7,000 EST. 1965
PO BOX 15500 .... NEW ORLEANS **LA** 70175 (504) 895-8784

BOOK PEDDLER, THE
C/O NATIONAL YIDDISH BOOK CENTER, P.O. BOX 969 .... AMHERST **MA** 01004 (413) 253-9201

GENESIS 2 (6X ANNUALLY) CIRC. 15,000 EST. 1970
99 BISHOP ALLEN DRIVE .... CAMBRIDGE **MA** 02139 (617) 576-1801

JEWISH ADVOCATE (WEEKLY) CIRC. 28,000 EST. 1902
1168-70 COMMONWEALTH AVENUE .... BOSTON **MA** 02134 (617) 227-8988

JEWISH TIMES (WEEKLY) CIRC. 8,200 EST. 1948
35 WAREHAM STREET .... BOSTON **MA** 02118 (617) 357-8635

JEWISH SPORTS REVIEW 198 MT. VERNON STREET .... DEDHAM **MA** 02026 (617) 326-0938

JEWISH REPORTER (MONTHLY) CIRC. 6,300 EST. 1970
76 SALEM END ROAD .... FRAMINGHAM **MA** 01701 (617) 879-3300

THE JOURNAL OF THE NORTH SHORE JEWISH COMMUNITY CIRC. 12,500 EST. 1976
564 LORING AVENUE .... SALEM **MA** 01970 (617) 741-1558

JEWISH WEEKLY NEWS, CIRC. 2,500 EST. 1945
PO BOX 1569/99 EAST MILL STREET .... SPRINGFIELD **MA** 01101 (413) 739-4771

SHOFAR, THE 1160 DICKINSON STREET .... SPRINGFIELD **MA** 01108 (413) 737-4313

AMERICAN JEWISH HISTORY (QUARTERLY) CIRC. 3,600 EST. 1892
2 THORNTON ROAD .... WALTHAM **MA** 02154 (617) 891-8110

JEWISH CHRONICLE LEADER (SEMIMONTHLY) CIRC. 4,700 EST. 1926
167 PLEASANT STREET .... WORCESTER **MA** 01609 (617) 752-2512

JEWISH CIVIC LEADER 11 HARVARD STREET .... WORCESTER **MA** 01609 (617) 791-0953

JEWISH POST 117 HUTCHINGS STREET .... WINNIPEG **MB** R2X 2V4 (204) 694-3332

WESTERN JEWISH NEWS (WEEKLY) CIRC. 5,000 EST. 1926
P.O. BOX 87, 259 PORTAGE AVENUE .... WINNIPEG **MB** R3C 2G6 (204) 942-6361

YIDDISH PRESS 230 CATHEDRAL AVENUE .... WINNIPEG **MB**

BALTIMORE JEWISH TIMES (WEEKLY) CIRC. 19,000 EST. 1919
2104 NORTH CHARLES STREET .... BALTIMORE **MD** 21218 (301) 752-3504

KASHRUS KURRENTS/VAAD HAKASHRUS OF BALTIMORE
7504 SEVEN MILE LANE .... BALTIMORE **MD** 21208 (301) 484-4110

WASHINGTON INTERNATIONAL REPORT 5608 GREENTREE ROAD .... BETHESDA **MD** 20014 (703) 573-7192

WASHINGTON JEWISH WEEK 9030 COMPRINT COURT .... GAITHERSBURG **MD** 20877 (301) 948-4630

AMERICAN JEWISH JOURNAL (QUARTERLY) CIRC. 8,000, EST. 1944
1220 BLAIR MILL ROAD .... SILVER SPRING **MD** 20910 (301) 585-1756

JEWISH WEEK 8630 FENTON STREET, SUITE 611 .... SILVER SPRING **MD** 20910 (301) 565-9336

MICHIGAN JEWISH HISTORY (SEMI-ANNUAL) EST. 1960
24680 RENSSELAER .... OAK PARK **MI** 48237 (313) 548-9176

DETROIT JEWISH NEWS (WEEKLY) CIRC. 17,000 EST. 1942
20300 CIVIC CENTER DRIVE, SUITE 240 .... SOUTHFIELD **MI** 48076 (313) 354-6060

AMERICAN JEWISH WORLD (WEEKLY) CIRC. 7,000 EST. 1912
4509 MINNETONKA BLVD. .... MINNEAPOLIS **MN** 55416 (612) 920-7000

AMERICAN JEWISH PRESS ASSOCIATION C/O ST. LOUIS JEWISH LIGHT,
12 MILLSTONE CAMPUS DRIVE .... ST. LOUIS **MO** 63146 (314) 432-3353

MISSOURI JEWISH POST AND OPINION (WEEKLY) CIRC. 3,500
8235 OLIVE .... ST. LOUIS **MO** 63132 (314) 993-2842

ST. LOUIS JEWISH LIGHT (WEEKLY) CIRC 14,500 EST. 1947
12 MILLSTONE CAMPUS DRIVE .... ST. LOUIS **MO** 63146 (314) 432-3353

AMERICAN JEWISH TIMES OUTLOOK (MONTHLY) CIRC. 5,300 EST. 1934
PO BOX 33218 .... CHARLOTTE **NC** 28233 (704) 372-3296

FEDERATION NEWS (10X/YR) CIRC. 1,400 713-A N. GREENE ST. .... GREENSBORO **NC** 27401 (919) 272-3189

THE JEWISH PRESS (WEEKLY) CIRC. 4,000 EST.1921
333 SOUTH 132ND STREET .... OMAHA **NE** 68154 (402) 334-8200

JEWISH RECORD (WEEKLY) CIRC. 10,000 EST. 1939
1537 ATLANTIC AVENUE, ROOM 200 .... ATLANTIC CITY **NJ** 08401 (609) 344-5119

JEWISH COMMUNITY VOICE (BIWEEKLY) CIRC. 10,300 EST. 1944
2393 WEST MARLTON PIKE .... CHERRY HILL **NJ** 08002 (609) 665-6100

JEWISH COMMUNITY NEWS (MONTHLY 11X) CIRCULATION 3,700
199 SCOLES AVENUE .... CLIFTON **NJ** 07012 (201) 777-8313

JEWISH VOICE, THE (MONTHLY) CIRC. 8,000 EST. 1970
P.O. BOX 210, 100 GRANT AVENUE .... DEAL **NJ** 07723 (201) 531-6200

JEWISH NEWS (WEEKLY) CIRC. 25,900 EST. 1947
60 GLENWOOD AVENUE .... EAST ORANGE **NJ** 07017 (201) 678-3900

JEWISH STAR, THE 100 METROPLEX DRIVE .... EDISON **NJ** 08817 (201) 985-1234

JEWISH VOICE (BIWEEKLY) CIRC. 5,000 EST. 1975
100 MENLO PARK, SUITE 101-102 .... EDISON **NJ** 08837 (201) 494-3920

JEWISH STANDARD (WEEKLY) CIRC. 21,000 EST. 1931
385 PROSPECT AVENUE .... HACKENSACK **NJ** 07601 (201) 342-1115

JEWISH JOURNAL (SEMIMONTHLY) CIRC. 8,000 EST. 1956
2 SOUTH ADELAIDE AVENUE .... HIGHLAND PARK **NJ** 08904

NEW AMERICAN, THE 80 GRAND STREET .... JERSEY CITY **NJ** 07302 (201) 332-9191

JEWISH WOMEN'S OUTLOOK 690 8TH STREET .... LAKEWOOD **NJ** 08701 (201) 364-8716

JEWISH WOMEN'S OUTLOOK 690 8TH STREET .... LAKEWOOD **NJ** 08701 (201) 364-8860

THE JEWISH VOICE (24X/YEAR) CIRC. 6,500
574A SOMERSET STREET .... NORTH PLAINFIELD **NJ** 07060

BERGEN JEWISH NEWS (WEEKLY) CIRC. 24,000 EST. 1985
277 FOREST STREET, #200 .... PARAMUS **NJ** 07652 (201) 265-2800

METRO WEST JEWISH NEWS (WEEKLY) CIRC. 27,000 EST. 1983
375 STATE HIGHWAY 10 .... RANDOLPH **NJ** 07869 (201) 366-3113

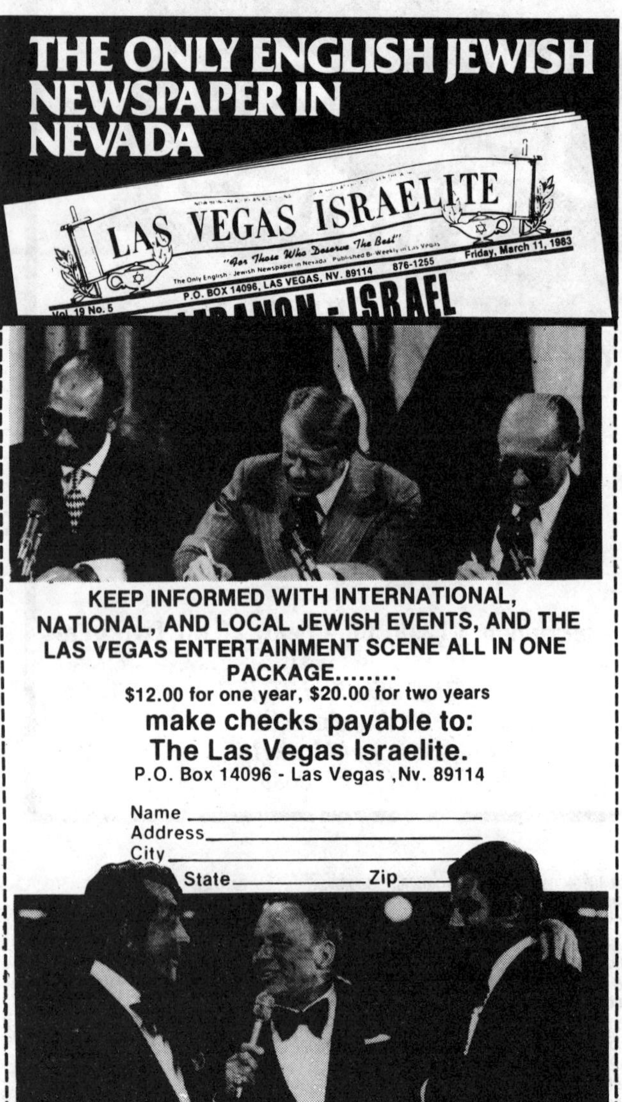

BERGEN JEWISH NEWS 111 KINDERKAMACK ROAD .... RIVER EDGE **NJ** 07661 (201) 265-2800
THE JEWISH HORIZON (WEEKLY) CIRC. 13,000 EST. 1981
1391 MARTINE AVENUE .... SCOTCH PLAINES **NJ** 07076 (201) 889-9200
JEWISH HORIZON, THE GREEN LANE .... UNION **NJ** 07083 (201) 351-1473
THE JEWISH CHRONICLE 629 WOOD ST., SUITE 204 .... VINELAND **NJ** 08360 (609) 696-4445
LINK, THE C/O JEWISH FEDERATION OF GREATER ALBUQUERQUE
12800 LOMAS BOULEVARD NORTHEAST, SUITE F .... ALBUQUERQUE **NM** 87112 (505) 292-1061
JEWISH REPORTER (MONTHLY) ESTABLISHED 1976 CIRC. 10,000
1030 EAST TWAIN AVENUE .... LAS VEGAS **NV** 89109 (702) 732-0556
LAS VEGAS ISRAELITE (BIWEEKLY) CIRC. 40,000 EST. 1965
PO BOX 14096 .... LAS VEGAS **NV** 89114 (702) 876-1255
ALBANY JEWISH WORLD CIRC. (WEEKLY) CIRC. 5,400 EST. 1965
1104 CENTRAL AVENUE .... ALBANY **NY** 12205 (518) 459-8455
THE REPORTER (WEEKLY) CIRC. 2,200
500 CLUBHOUSE ROAD .... BINGHAMTON **NY** 13903 (607) 724-2360
KINDER JOURNAL, EST. 1920 3301 BAINBRIDGE AVENUE .... BRONX **NY** 10467 (212) 881-3588
A THOUGHT FOR THE WEEK - LUBAVITCH 788 EASTERN PARKWAY .... BROOKLYN **NY** 11213 (718) 778-5436
BORO PARK VOICE (MONTHLY) CIRC. 45,000 EST. 1977
4616 13TH AVENUE .... BROOKLYN **NY** 11219 (718) 436-1800
CROWN HEIGHTS CHRONICLE, THE - KEREN PUBLICATIONS (QUARTERLY)
CIRC. 5,000 EST. 1981 G.P.O. BOX 2007 .... BROOKLYN **NY** 11202
DER YID (WEEKLY) CIRC. 33,000 (YIDDISH)
543 BEDFORD AVENUE .... BROOKLYN **NY** 11211 (718) 782-4900
DI YIDDISH HEIM (QUARTERLY) CIRC. 3,000 (ENG-YID) EST. 1958
770 EASTERN PARKWAY .... BROOKLYN **NY** 11213 (718) 778-4270
ESRA - THE WOMEN'S INTEREST GUIDE 774 E. 8TH STREET .... BROOKLYN **NY** 11230
JEWISH AMERICAN RECORD P.O. BOX 1100, 271 CAMDEN PLAZA E .... BROOKLYN **NY** 11201
JEWISH GUARDIAN CIRC. 10,000, EST. 1974
GPO BOX 2143 .... BROOKLYN **NY** 11202 (718) 384-4661
JEWISH HERALD, THE 1689 46TH STREET .... BROOKLYN **NY** 11204 (718) 435-5100
JEWISH JOURNAL (WEEKLY) CIRC. 45,000 EST. 1970
8723 THIRD AVENUE .... BROOKLYN **NY** 11209 (718) 238-6600
JEWISH PRESS (WEEKLY) CIRC. 209,000 EST. 1950
338 THIRD AVENUE .... BROOKLYN **NY** 11215 (718) 330-1100
KASHRUS - BIMONTHLY, CIRC. 10,000 EST. 1980 P.O. BOX 96 .... BROOKLYN **NY** 11204 (718) 998-3201
MOSHIACH TIMES 332 KINGSTON AVENUE .... BROOKLYN **NY** 11213 (718) 467-6630
SEPHARDIC HOME NEWS, THE 2266 CROPSEY AVENUE .... BROOKLYN **NY** 11214 (718) 266-6100
SEPHARDIC VOICE OF AMERICA, THE 2667 CONEY ISLAND AVENUE .... BROOKLYN **NY** 11223 (718) 891-8342
SHMUESSEN MIT KINDER IN YUGENT (MONTHLY) EST. 1942
770 EASTERN PARKWAY .... BROOKLYN **NY** 11213 (718) 774-4000
SVET (LIGHT)(MONTHLY) CIRC. 25,000 (RUSSIAN)
455 ALBANY AVENUE .... BROOKLYN **NY** 11213 (718) 774-0065
TALKS AND TALES (MONTHLY) EST. 1942, LUBAVITCH PUBLICATION
770 EASTERN PARKWAY .... BROOKLYN **NY** 11213 (718) 493-9250
THE JEWISH HOMEMAKER (5X/YEAR) CIRC. 43,000
PO BOX 218 .... BROOKLYN **NY** 11204 (718) 851-6428
THE UFORATZTO JOURNAL (QUARTERLY) CIRC. 20,000
770 EASTERN PARKWAY .... BROOKLYN **NY** 11213
TZIVOS HASHEM CHILDREN'S NEWSLETTER
770 EASTERN PARKWAY .... BROOKLYN **NY** 11213 (718) 467-6630
YAGDIL TORAH 770 EASTERN PARKWAY .... BROOKLYN **NY** 11213
BUFFALO JEWISH REVIEW (WEEKLY) CIRC. 3,800 EST. 1918
15 E. MOHAWK STREET .... BUFFALO **NY** 14203 (716) 854-2192
JEWISH WORLD OF LONG ISLAND AND QUEENS (BIWEEKLY)
1 OLD INDIAN HEAD ROAD CIRC. 12,500-NEWSPAPER .... COMMACK **NY** 11725 (516) 543-2427
JEWISH OBSERVER (BIWEEKLY) CIRC. 6,000 EST. 1978 P.O. BOX 510 .... DEWITT **NY** 13214 (315) 422-4104
FOUR WORLDS JOURNAL (QUARTERLY) CIRC. 1,500
P.O. BOX 540 .... EAST MEADOW **NY** 11554 (718) 496-4275
JEWISH CURRENT EVENTS (BIWEEKLY) EST. 1959 430 KELLER AVENUE .... ELMONT **NY** 11003 (516) 328-3796

America's Largest and Liveliest Independent Anglo-Jewish Newspaper · Printed in English

SPECIAL FEATURES

● Super Singles Section ● Questions and Answers by our own Inquiring Photographer ● Largest Listing of Events of the Week ● Social Register Column featuring Your Special Occasion, FREE of charge ● Exciting Women's Magazine Section ● Editorial Comments on the current Jewish scene ● Tales of the Talmud and the Sages ● Questions & Answers on Jewish Law and Customs ● Original Cartoon Strips ● Children's Page

* * *

- *Hard-hitting Exclusive On the Scene Israel Reports from our own Jerusalem Based Correspondents*
- *Exciting News Items from Israel's Top Radio and Newspaper Columnists*
- *The Inside View on Israel's Political, Religious and Judicial Systems by Experienced News analysts*

For Free Sample Copy, Advertising Rates and all other information call or write today:

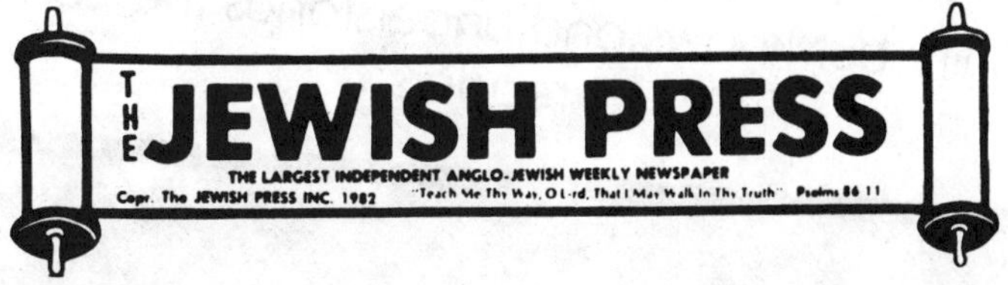

338 THIRD AVENUE, BROOKLYN, N.Y. ● Tel: (718) 330-1100

OUR TELEPHONE OPERATORS ARE WAITING FOR YOUR CALL!

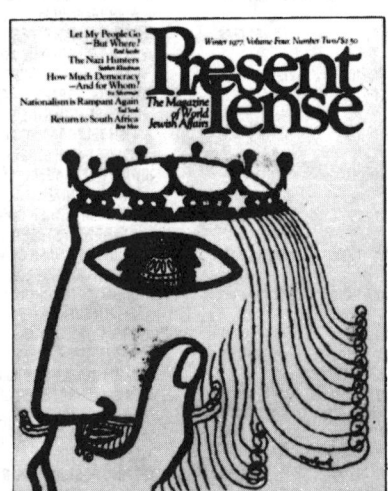

CONTEMPORARY JEWRY (SEMI-ANNUAL) EST. 1974
65-30 KISSENA BOULEVARD-QUEENS CLG, DEPT. OF SOCIOLOGY ...... FLUSHING **NY** 11367 (718) 222-3699

MODERN JEWISH STUDIES ANNUAL, QUEENS COLLEGE, EST. 1977
65-30 KISSENA BOULEVARD ...... FLUSHING **NY** 11367 (718) 520-7067

YIDDISH QUEENS COLLEGE ACADEMY (QUARTERLY) ESTABLISHED 1973
65-30 KISSENA BOULEVARD ...... FLUSHING **NY** 11367 (718) 520-7067

LONG ISLAND GREAT NECK RECORD (WEEKLY) CIRC. 11,000 EST. 1917
1 GREAT NECK ROAD ...... GREAT NECK **NY** 11021 (516) 482-4490

LONG ISLAND JEWISH WORLD (WEEKLY) CIRC. 45,000 EST. 1971
115 MIDDLE NECK ROAD ...... GREAT NECK **NY** 11021 (516) 829-4000

JEWISH VIEW - BIWEEKLY CIRC. 12,000 P.O. BOX 145 ...... ISLAND PARK **NY** 11558 (516) 431-6109

SHOFAR (MONTHLY [SCHOOL YEAR]) CIRC. 10,000 EST. 1983
43 NORTHCOTE DRIVE ...... MELVILLE **NY** 11747 (516) 643-4598

EDUCATION MEDIA EXPOSITION SOCIETY, INC. PO BOX 122 ...... MONSEY **NY** 10952 (914) 352-0630

AFN SHVEL (QUARTERLY) CIRC. 1,000 (YIDDISH) EST. 1941
200 WEST 72ND STREET ...... NEW YORK **NY** 10023 (212) 787-6675

ALGEMEINER JOURNAL (WEEKLY) CIRC. 210,000 (YIDDISH) EST. 1972
404 PARK AVENUE SOUTH ...... NEW YORK **NY** 10016 (212) 689-3390

ALIYON/THE JEWISH AGENCY (QUARTERLY) CIRC. 4,000 (ENGLISH) EST. 1968
515 PARK AVENUE ...... NEW YORK **NY** 10022 (212) 752-0600

AMERICAN JEWISH YEARBOOK (ANNUAL) EST. 1899
165 EAST 56TH STREET ...... NEW YORK **NY** 10022 (212) 751-4000

AMIT WOMEN (5X/YR.) CIRC. 30,000 EST. 1925 817 BROADWAY ...... NEW YORK **NY** 10003 (212) 477-4720

AUFBAU (BIWEEKLY) CIRC. 13,400 (GERMAN) EST. 1934
2121 BROADWAY ...... NEW YORK **NY** 10023 (212) 873-7400

B'NAI YIDDISH (BIMONTHLY) CIRC. 1,500-ENGLISH-YIDDISH
41 UNION SQUARE ...... NEW YORK **NY** 10003

B'NAI B'RITH INT'L JEWISH MONTHLY (10X/YR.) CIRC. 189,000
823 UNITED NATIONS PLAZA ...... NEW YORK **NY** 10016 (212) 490-2525

BITZARON (QUARTERLY) CIRC. 19,000 (HEBREW) EST. 1939
COOPER STATION, P.O. BOX 623 ...... NEW YORK **NY** 10003 (212) 598-3987

BOOKS IN REVIEW (BIMONTHLY) BOOK REVIEWS
15 EAST 26TH STREET ...... NEW YORK **NY** 10010 (212) 532-4949

BROTHERHOOD (3X YR.) CIRC. 70,000 REL/EDUC.
838 FIFTH AVENUE ...... NEW YORK **NY** 10021 (212) 570-0707

CALL, THE (MONTHLY) CIRC. 34,000 EST. 1940 45 EAST 33RD STREET ...... NEW YORK **NY** 10016 (212) 889-6800

COMMENTARY (MONTHLY) CIRC. 60,000 EST. 1945
165 EAST 56TH STREET ...... NEW YORK **NY** 10022 (212) 751-4000

CONGRESS MONTHLY (8X/YR.) CIRC. 31,600 EST. 1933
15 EAST 84TH STREET ...... NEW YORK **NY** 10028 (212) 879-4500

CONSERVATIVE JUDAISM (QUARTERLY) CIRC. 2,400, EST. 1945
3080 BROADWAY ...... NEW YORK **NY** 10027 (212) 678-8863

DER WECKER (BIMONTHLY) YIDDISH, EST. 1921 45 EAST 33RD STREET ...... NEW YORK **NY** 10016 (212) 686-1538

DI ZUKUNFT (MONTHLY) CIRC. 3,430, EST. 1892 25 EAST 78TH STREET ...... NEW YORK **NY** 10021

DOS YIDDISHE VORT (MONTHLY) YIDDISH, EST. 1953
84 WILLIAM STREET ...... NEW YORK **NY** 10038 (212) 797-9000

ECONOMIC HORIZONS CIRC. 3,000, EST. 1953
500 FIFTH AVENUE ...... NEW YORK **NY** 10110 (212) 354-6510

EMUNAH WOMAN (QUARTERLY) CIRC. 40,000
370 SEVENTH AVENUE ...... NEW YORK **NY** 10001

FARBAND NEWS (IRREGULAR) CIRC. 26,000 - LABOR ZIONISM
275 SEVENTH AVENUE ...... NEW YORK **NY** 10001 (212) 989-0300

HADAROM (SEMI-ANNUAL) CIRC. 1,500, EST. 1957 1250 BROADWAY ...... NEW YORK **NY** 10001

HADASSAH MAGAZINE (MONTHLY) CIRC. 370,000 EST. 1921
50 WEST 58TH STREET ...... NEW YORK **NY** 10019 (212) 355-7900

HADOAR (WEEKLY) CIRC. 5,300 (HEBREW) EST. 1921 1841 BROADWAY ...... NEW YORK **NY** 10023 (212) 581-5151

ISRA-LAMED (BIMONTHLY) RIGHTS OF THE JEWISH PEOPLE
515 PARK AVENUE ...... NEW YORK **NY** 10022 (212) 752-0600

ISRAEL HORIZONS (BIMONTHLY) CIRC. 3,000, EST. 1952
150 FIFTH AVENUE, SUITE 911 ...... NEW YORK **NY** 10011 (212) 255-8760

ISRAEL QUALITY (QUARTERLY) CIRC. 15,000, EST. 1976
500 FIFTH AVENUE ...... NEW YORK **NY** 10110 (212) 354-6510

ISRAEL SCENE (MONTHLY) CIRCULATION 9,000 (ENGLISH)
515 PARK AVENUE ...... NEW YORK **NY** 10022

ISRAEL TODAY (DAILY 5X) CIRC. 100,000
205 WEST 34TH STREET, SUITE 2306 ...... NEW YORK **NY** 10001 (212) 695-1581

JASA BROOKDALE NEWS (BIMONTHLY) CIRC. 25,000-NEWSLETTER
222 PARK AVENUE SOUTH ...... NEW YORK **NY** 10003

JDC WORLD 711 THIRD AVENUE ...... NEW YORK **NY** 10017 (212) 687-6200

JWB CIRCLE (4-6X/YR.) CIRC. 25,000 EST. 1946 15 EAST 26TH STREET ...... NEW YORK **NY** 10010 (212) 532-4949

JERUSALEM POST, THE (DAILY) CIRC. 55,000 EST. 1932
120 EAST 56TH STREET ...... NEW YORK **NY** 10022 (212) 355-4440

JEWISH ACTION (QUARTERLY) CIRC. 60,000, EST. 1950
45 WEST 36TH STREET ...... NEW YORK **NY** 10018 (212) 244-2011

JEWISH AMERICAN RECORD (MONTHLY) EST. 1973 G.P.O. BOX 317 ...... NEW YORK **NY** 10116

JEWISH BOOK ANNUAL, CIRC. 18,000, EST. 1942 15 EAST 26TH STREET ...... NEW YORK **NY** 10010 (212) 532-4949

JEWISH BOOKS IN REVIEW, EST. 1945, JEWISH BOOK COUNCIL
15 EAST 26TH STREET ...... NEW YORK **NY** 10010 (212) 532-4949

JEWISH BRAILLE INSTITUTE VOICE (10X/YR.) CIRC. 2,000 EST. 1978
110 EAST 30TH STREET ...... NEW YORK **NY** 10016 (212) 889-2525

JEWISH BRAILLE REVIEW (10X/YR.) CIRC. 2,000, EST. 1931
110 EAST 30TH STREET ...... NEW YORK **NY** 10016 (212) 889-2525

JEWISH CHRONICLE NEWS SERVICE 235 WEST 102ND STREET ...... NEW YORK **NY** 10025 (212) 866-6139

JEWISH CURRENTS (MONTHLY) CIRC. 3,800 EST. 1946
22 EAST 17TH STREET, SUITE 601 ...... NEW YORK **NY** 10003 (212) 924-5740

JEWISH DAILY FORWARD (WEEKLY) CIRC. 20,000 (YIDDISH) EST. 1897
45 EAST 33RD STREET ...... NEW YORK **NY** 10016 (212) 889-8200

JEWISH EDUCATION (QUARTERLY) CIRC. 1,000 EST. 1926
426 WEST 58TH STREET ...... NEW YORK **NY** 10019 (212) 713-0290

JEWISH EDUCATION DIRECTORY (IRREGULAR) EST. 1951
730 BROADWAY ...... NEW YORK **NY** 10003 (212) 529-2000

JEWISH EDUCATION NEWS (IRREGULAR) CIRC. 2,000, EST. 1939
27 WEST 20TH STREET ...... NEW YORK **NY** 10011 (212) 675-5656

JEWISH FRONTIER - LABOR ZIONISM (MONTHLY) CIRC. 13,500 EST. 1934
275 SEVENTH AVENUE ...... NEW YORK **NY** 10001 (212) 243-2741

JEWISH FUNERAL DIRECTOR, THE 122 EAST 42ND STREET, SUITE 1120 ...... NEW YORK **NY** 10168 (212) 370-0024

JEWISH MUSIC NOTES (SEMI-ANNUAL) CIRC. 18,000, EST. 1945
15 EAST 26TH STREET ...... NEW YORK **NY** 10010 (212) 532-4949

JEWISH OBSERVER (MONTHLY) CIRC. 13,700 EST. 1963
84 WILLIAM STREET ...... NEW YORK **NY** 10038 (212) 797-9000

JEWISH PARENT, THE 229 PARK AVENUE SOUTH ...... NEW YORK **NY** 10003

JEWISH POST OF NEW YORK (WEEKLY) CIRC. 88,000 EST. 1977
101 FIFTH AVENUE ...... NEW YORK **NY** 10003

JEWISH PRESS FEATURES (MONTHLY) EST. 1970
15 EAST 26TH STREET, SUITE 1350 ...... NEW YORK **NY** 10010 (212) 679-1411

JEWISH SINGLES NEWSLETTER (MONTHLY) EVENTS CALENDAR
130 EAST 59TH STREET ...... NEW YORK **NY** 10022

JEWISH SOCIAL STUDIES 2112 BROADWAY, #206 ...... NEW YORK **NY** 10023 (212) 724-5336

JEWISH STUDENT PRESS SERVICE 15 E. 26TH ST. SUITE 1350 ...... NEW YORK **NY** 10010 (212) 679-1411

JEWISH TELEGRAPHIC AGENCY COMMUNITY NEWS REPORTER (WEEKLY)
165 WEST 46TH STREET, ROOM 511 ...... NEW YORK **NY** 10036 (212) 575-9370

JEWISH TELEGRAPHIC AGENCY DAILY NEWS BULLETIN
165 WEST 46TH STREET, ROOM 511 ...... NEW YORK **NY** 10036 (212) 575-9370

JEWISH TELEGRAPHIC AGENCY WEEKLY NEWS DIGEST
165 WEST 46TH STREET, ROOM 511 ...... NEW YORK **NY** 10036 (212) 575-9370

JEWISH TELEGRAPHIC AGENCY, INC. (DAILY) EST. 1917
165 WEST 46TH STREET, ROOM 511 ...... NEW YORK **NY** 10036 (212) 575-9370

JEWISH WEEK (WEEKLY) CIRC. 112,000 EST 1876, REORG 1970
1 PARK AVENUE ...... NEW YORK **NY** 10016 (212) 686-2320

JOURNAL OF JEWISH COMMUNAL SERVICE (QUARTERLY) EST. 1899
15 EAST 26TH STREET ...... NEW YORK **NY** 10010

JOURNAL OF JEWISH CONSERVATIVE EDUCATION (QUARTERLY)EST. 1942
155 FIFTH AVENUE ...... NEW YORK **NY** 10010

JOURNAL OF PSYCHOLOGY-JUDAISM (QUARTERLY)
72 FIFTH AVENUE ...... NEW YORK **NY** 10011

JOURNAL OF REFORM JUDAISM (QUARTERLY) CIRC. 2,200, EST. 1953
21 EAST 40TH STREET ...... NEW YORK **NY** 10016 (212) 684-4990

JUDAICA BOOK NEWS (SPRING & FALL) 303 WEST 10 STREET ...... NEW YORK **NY** 10014 (212) 691-3817

JUDAISM (QUARTERLY) CIRC. 5,000 EST. 1952
15 EAST 84TH STREET ...... NEW YORK **NY** 10028 (212) 879-4500

KEEPING POSTED (7X/YR.) CIRC. 56,000 - ADULT EDUCATION
838 FIFTH AVENUE ...... NEW YORK **NY** 10021 (212) 249-0100

KEEPING POSTED (BIMONTHLY) CIRC. 10,000-YOUTH PUBLICATION
116 EAST 27TH STREET ...... NEW YORK **NY** 10016 (212) 725-3420

KOL HAT'NUAH (MONTHLY) HASHACHAR, EST. 1943
50 WEST 58TH STREET ...... NEW YORK **NY** 10019 (212) 355-7900

KOL YAVNEH, CIRC. 18,000, EST. 1960, (JEWISH STUDENT INT.)
25 WEST 26TH STREET ...... NEW YORK **NY** 10010 (212) 679-4574

KOSHER GOURMET, THE
K.G. PUBLICATIONS - P.O. BOX 387A, PLANETARIUM STATION ...... NEW YORK **NY** 10024 (212) 595-1714

KULTUR UN LEBN-CULTURE LIFE (5X/YR.) CIRC. 1,500 EST. 1940
45 EAST 33RD STREET ...... NEW YORK **NY** 10016 (212) 889-6800

LILITH-THE JEWISH WOMEN'S MAGAZINE (QUARTERLY) CIRC. 15,000 EST. 1975
250 WEST 57TH STREET, SUITE 2432 ...... NEW YORK **NY** 10019 (212) 757-0818

METROPOLITAN STAR (MONTHLY) COMB. FEB-MAR, NOV-DEC
823 UNITED NATIONS PLAZA, CIRC. 70,000-GENERAL NEWS ...... NEW YORK **NY** 10017 (212) 983-5800

MIDSTREAM (10X/YR.) CIRC. 10,000 EST. 1954
515 PARK AVENUE ...... NEW YORK **NY** 10022 (212) 752-0600

MORGEN FREIHEIT (WEEKLY) CIRC. 10,000 (YIDDISH) EST. 1922
43 WEST 24TH STREET ...... NEW YORK **NY** 10010 (212) 255-7661

NCJW JOURNAL (BIMONTHLY 6X) CIRC. 90,000 15 EAST 26TH STREET ...... NEW YORK **NY** 10010 (212) 532-1740

NA'AMAT WOMAN (5X/YR.) CIRC. 26,800 EST. 1926 200 MADISON AVE. ...... NEW YORK **NY** 10016 (212) 725-8010

OU INSTITUTIONAL & INDUSTRIAL KOSHER PRODUCTS DIRECTORY
45 WEST 36TH STREET ...... NEW YORK **NY** 10018 (212) 563-4000

OU KOSHER PRODUCTS DIRECTORY (IRREGULAR) EST. 1925
45 WEST 36TH STREET ...... NEW YORK **NY** 10018 (212) 563-4000

OU NEWS REPORTER (IRREGULAR) (NEW FOODS UNDER OU SUPERVISION)
45 WEST 36TH STREET ...... NEW YORK **NY** 10018 (212) 563-4000

OU PASSOVER PRODUCTS DIRECTORY (ANNUAL) EST. 1923
45 WEST 36TH STREET ...... NEW YORK **NY** 10018 (212) 563-4000

OLOMEINU-OUR WORLD (MONTHLY) CIRC. 15,000 (ENG/HEB)EST. 1945
160 BROADWAY ...... NEW YORK **NY** 10038 (212) 227-1000

OR CHADASH (2-4X/YR.) EST. 1981, JEWISH BRAILLE INST. OF AM. CIRC. 200
110 EAST 30TH STREET ...... NEW YORK **NY** 10016 (212) 889-2525

PEDAGOGIC REPORTER (QUARTERLY) CIRC. 2,000 EST. 1949, JEWISH EDUC. SVCE.
730 BROADWAY ...... NEW YORK **NY** 10003 (212) 529-2000

PRESENT TENSE (BIMONTHLY) CIRC. 25,000 EST. 1973
165 EAST 56TH STREET ...... NEW YORK **NY** 10022 (212) 751-4000

PROCEEDINGS OF THE AMERICAN ACADEMY FOR JEWISH RESEARCH (AN)
3080 BROADWAY ...... NEW YORK **NY** 10027

RABBINICAL COUNCIL RECORD (QUARTERLY) CIRC. 1,200, EST.1953
1250 BROADWAY ...... NEW YORK **NY** 10001 (212) 594-3780

RECONSTRUCTIONIST (MONTHLY) CIRC. 8,300 EST. 1935
270 WEST 89TH STREET ...... NEW YORK **NY** 10024 (212) 496-2960

REFORM JUDAISM (4X/YR) CIRC. 280,000 EST. 1972
838 FIFTH AVENUE ...... NEW YORK **NY** 10021 (212) 249-0100

RESPONSE (QUARTERLY) EST. 1967 610 WEST 113TH STREET ...... NEW YORK **NY** 10025

SAFRA: JEWISH SCHOOL MATERIALS REVIEW (SEMI-ANNUAL) EST. 1980
114 FIFTH AVENUE ...... NEW YORK **NY** 10011

SEPHARDIC CONNECTION C/O AMERICAN SEPHARDI FEDERATION
8 WEST 40TH STREET ...... NEW YORK **NY** 10018 (212) 730-1210

SHEVILEY HAHINUCH (QUARTERLY) CIRC. 900 EST. 1939
426 WEST 58TH STREET ...... NEW YORK **NY** 10019 (212) 713-0290

SHOAH (3X/YR.) CIRC. 3,500, EST. 1977
250 WEST 57TH STREET, ROOM 216 .... NEW YORK **NY** 10107 (212) 582-6116
SPECTRUM, NORTH AMERICAN JEWISH STUDENT NETWORK CIRC. 20,000
1 PARK AVENUE SUITE 418 .... NEW YORK **NY** 10016 (212) 689-0790
STAR, THE (B'NAI B'RITH) 823 UNITED NATIONS PLAZA .... NEW YORK **NY** 10017 (212) 490-2525
SYNAGOGUE LIGHT (QUARTERLY) CIRC. 19,000 EST. 1933
47 BEEKMAN STREET .... NEW YORK **NY** 10038 (212) 227-7800
TOLEDOT: THE JOURNAL OF JEWISH GENEALOGY
155 EAST 93RD STREET, SUITE 3C .... NEW YORK **NY** 10028
TORCHLIGHT (QUARTERLY) CIRC, 36,000, EST. 1929
475 RIVERSIDE DRIVE .... NEW YORK **NY** 10115 (212) 749-8100
TRADITION (QUARTERLY) CIRC. 4,000, EST. 1958
275 SEVENTH AVENUE .... NEW YORK **NY** 10001 (212) 807-7888
UNITED ISRAEL BULLETIN 1123 BROADWAY .... NEW YORK **NY** 10010 (212) 688-7557
UNITED SYNAGOGUE REVIEW (2X/YR.) CIRC. 260,000
155 FIFTH AVENUE .... NEW YORK **NY** 10010 (212) 533-7800
UNSER TSAIT (MONTHLY) ESTABLISHED 1941, (YIDDISH)
25 EAST 78TH STREET .... NEW YORK **NY** 10021 (212) 535-0850
WEST SIDE JEWISH NEWS, THE 210 WEST 91ST STREET .... NEW YORK **NY** 10024 (212) 496-0401
WOMEN'S AMERICAN ORT REPORTER (QUARTERLY) CIRC. 150,000 EST. 1966
315 PARK AVENUE SOUTH .... NEW YORK **NY** 10010 (212) 505-7700
WOMEN'S LEAGUE OUTLOOK (QUARTERLY) CIRC. 200,000, EST. 1930
48 EAST 74TH STREET .... NEW YORK **NY** 10021 (212) 628-1600
YIVO ANNUAL OF JEWISH SOCIAL SCIENCE (BI-ANNUAL)CIRC. 2,700
1048 FIFTH AVENUE .... NEW YORK **NY** 10028 (212) 535-6700
YIVO BLETER (IRREGULAR) EST. 1931 1048 FIFTH AVENUE .... NEW YORK **NY** 10028 (212) 535-6700
YAVNEH REVIEW (ANNUAL) CIRC. 5,000, EST. 1963
25 WEST 26TH STREET .... NEW YORK **NY** 10010
YEARBOOK OF THE CENTRAL CONFERENCE OF AMERICAN RABBIS
21 EAST 40TH STREET .... NEW YORK **NY** 10016 (212) 684-4990
YIDDISHE KULTUR (MONTHLY) CIRC. 3,000
1123 BROADWAY, ROOM 203 .... NEW YORK **NY** 10010 (212) 691-0708
YIDDISHE SHPRAKH CIRC. 2,500 (YIDDISH) EST. 1941
1048 FIFTH AVENUE .... NEW YORK **NY** 10028 (212) 535-6700
YIDDISHER KEMFER (WEEKLY) CIRC. 3,000 (YIDDISH) EST. 1906
275 SEVENTH AVENUE .... NEW YORK **NY** 10001 (212) 675-7808
YOUNG ISRAEL VIEWPOINT (8X/YR.) CIRC. 33,000 EST. 1952
3 WEST 16TH STREET .... NEW YORK **NY** 10011 (212) 929-1525
YOUNG JUDAEAN (6X/YR. [OCT.-JUNE]) CIRC. 5,000 EST. 1910
50 WEST 58TH STREET .... NEW YORK **NY** 10019 (212) 355-7900
JEWISH DIGEST (MONTHLY) CIRC. 15,500 3459 FREDERICK STREET .... OCEANSIDE **NY** 11572 (516) 764-6250
SH'MA (BIWEEKLY) CIRC. 9,000, EST. 1970 BOX 567 .... PORT WASHINGTON **NY** 11050 (516) 944-9791
LONG ISLAND JEWISH PRESS (MONTHLY) CIRC. 12,700, EST. 1942
95-20 63RD ROAD .... REGO PARK **NY** 11374
WESTCHESTER JEWISH TRIBUNE (MONTHLY) CIRC. 15,000, EST. 1942
95-20 63RD ROAD .... REGO PARK **NY** 11374
JEWISH LEDGER (WEEKLY) CIRC. 2,400 EST. 1924
721 MONROE AVENUE .... ROCHESTER **NY** 14607
THE SCARSDALE INQUIRER (WEEKLY) CIRC. 10,000, EST. 1901
1088 CENTRAL AVENUE .... SCARSDALE **NY** 10583 (914) 725-2500
JEWISH TRIBUNE 49 SOUTH MAIN STREET, SUITE 108 .... SPRING VALLEY **NY** 10977 (914) 578-5811
TIKKUN MAGAZINE (BIMONTHLY) EST. 1986 P.O. BOX 6406 .... SYRACUSE **NY** 13217
STARK JEWISH NEWS, INCORPORATED (10X/YR.) CIRC. 2,000
2631 HARVARD AVENUE NORTHWEST .... CANTON **OH** 44709 (216) 452-6444
AMERICAN JEWISH ARCHIVES (SEMI-ANNUAL) CIRC 5,000, EST. 1947
3101 CLIFTON AVENUE .... CINCINNATI **OH** 45220 (513) 221-1875
HEBREW UNION COLLEGE ANNUAL (ENGLISH, HEBREW, FRENCH, GERMAN)
3101 CLIFTON AVENUE .... CINCINNATI **OH** 45220 (513) 221-1875
STUDIES IN BIBLIOGRAPHY AND BOOKLORE (IRREGULAR) HUC-JIR
3101 CLIFTON AVENUE .... CINCINNATI **OH** 45220 (513) 221-1875
AMERICAN ISRAELITE, THE (WEEKLY) CIRC. 6,700 EST. 1854
906 MAIN STREET, ROOM 505 .... CINCINNATI **OH** 45202 (513) 621-3145
CHABAD TIMES, THE (MONTHLY) CIRC.20,000
1636 SUMMIT ROAD .... CINCINNATI **OH** 45237
CLEVELAND JEWISH NEWS (WEEKLY) CIRC. 18,000 EST. 1964
13910 CEDAR ROAD .... CLEVELAND **OH** 44118 (216) 371-0800
INDEX TO JEWISH PERIODICALS (SEMI-ANNUALLY) EST. 1963
PO BOX 18570 .... CLEVELAND HEIGHTS **OH** 44118 (216) 321-7296
OHIO JEWISH CHRONICLE (WEEKLY) CIRC. 3,000 EST. 1921
2831 MAIN STREET, P.O. BOX 09744 .... COLUMBUS **OH** 43209 (614) 237-4296
DAYTON JEWISH CHRONICLE (WEEKLY) CIRC. 1,550 EST. 1961
118 SALEM AVENUE .... DAYTON **OH** 45406 (513) 222-0783
TOLEDO JEWISH NEWS (MONTHLY) CIRC. 3,000 EST. 1951
5151 MONROE STREET .... TOLEDO **OH** 43604
SOUTHWEST JEWISH CHRONICLE (QUARTERLY) EST. 1929
324 NORTH ROBINSON STREET, SUITE 313 .... OKLAHOMA CITY **OK** 73102 (405) 236-4226
TULSA JEWISH REVIEW (BIMONTHLY) CIRC. 1,500 EST. 1930
2021 EAST 71ST STREET .... TULSA **OK** 74136 (918) 495-1100
CANADIAN JEWISH NEWS (WEEKLY) CIRC. 80,000
10 GATEWAY BOULEVARD, SUITE 420 .... DUNMILLS **ON** M3C 3A1 (416) 422-2331
JEWISH STANDARD 67 MOWAT AVENUE, SUITE 319 .... TORONTO **ON** M6K 3E3 (416) 363-3289
JEWISH TIMES, THE 2828 BATHURST STREET, SUITE 502 .... TORONTO **ON** M6B 3A7 (416) 789-4503
PORTLAND JEWISH REVIEW, THE P.O. BOX 40728 .... PORTLAND **OR** 97204 (503) 226-3701
JEWISH REPORTER (MONTHLY 11X) CIRC.6,700 .... DELAWARE VALLEY **PA**

If you care about ultimate issues, read . . .

ULTIMATE ISSUES

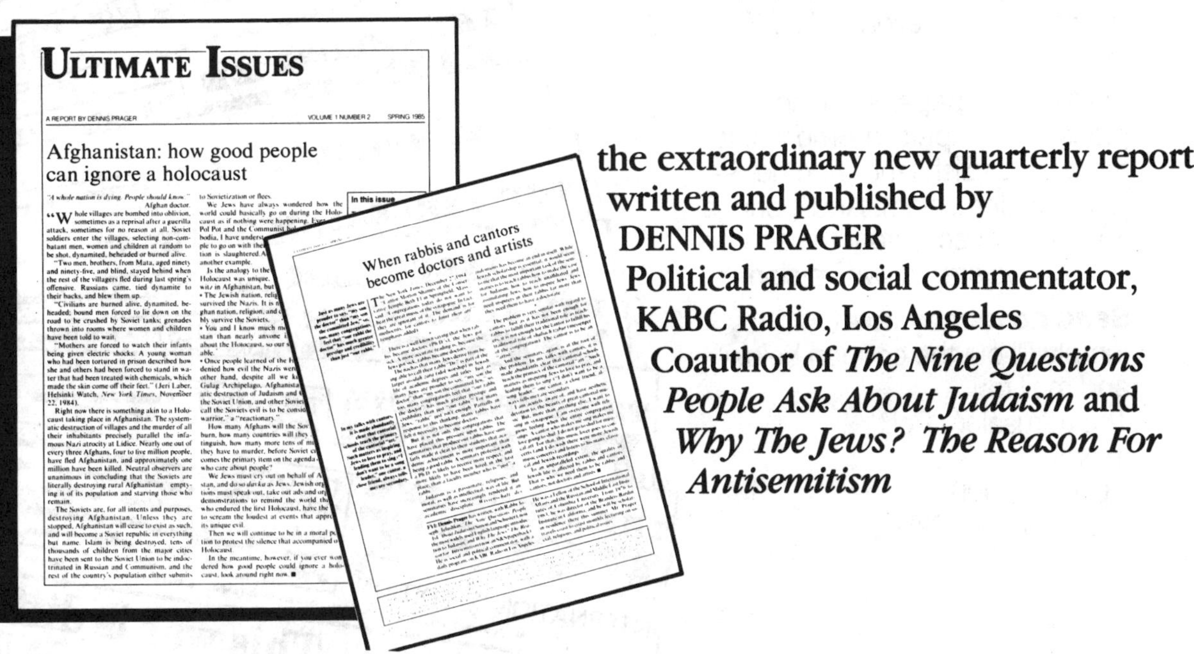

ULTIMATE ISSUES

A REPORT BY DENNIS PRAGER VOLUME 1 NUMBER 2 SPRING 1985

Afghanistan: how good people can ignore a holocaust

When rabbis and cantors become doctors and artists

the extraordinary new quarterly report
written and published by
DENNIS PRAGER
Political and social commentator,
KABC Radio, Los Angeles
Coauthor of *The Nine Questions People Ask About Judaism* and *Why The Jews? The Reason For Antisemitism*

Editor's Note: I am so impressed with *Ultimate Issues* that I have featured two of Dennis Prager's *Ultimate Issues* articles in *The Jewish Almanac: "Bitburg Revisited: What is the Jewish Role in the World?"* (see page 25) and *"The Relevance of Judaism"* (see page 100). I believe that *Ultimate Issues* may be the most important publication of its type in the Jewish world today.

Ivan Tillem

The *Los Angeles Times,* in a feature article on Dennis Prager, described him as an "amazingly gifted man and charismatic moralist . . . whose mission in life already has been crystalized . . . to get people obsessed with what's right and wrong."

For a year's subscription send fifteen dollars to:

Ultimate Issues
10573 W. Pico Boulevard
Los Angeles, CA 90064
213 558-3958

Mention *The Jewish Almanac,* and you will receive at no additional cost the entire issue containing "The Greatest Jewish Problem." (Or you may obtain this issue separately by sending three dollars to *Ultimate Issues.*)

INTRODUCING THE NATION'S FIRST DAILY JEWISH NEWSPAPER.

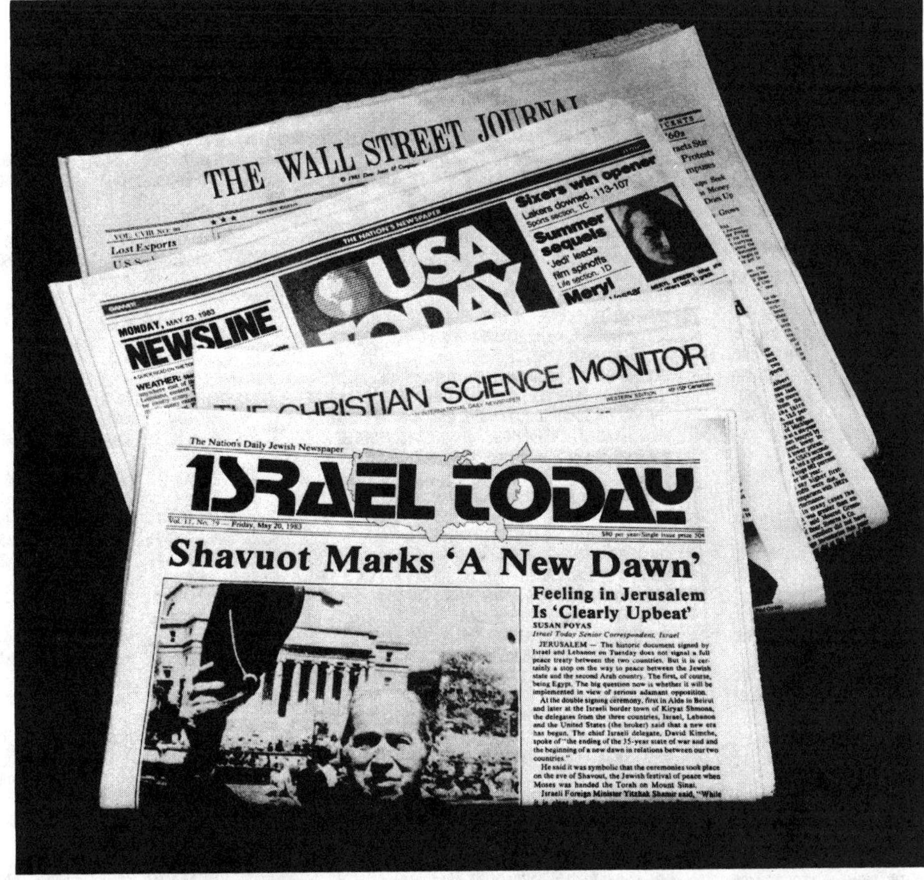

MAZEL TOV.

Congratulations indeed. At last there is a national daily that not only reports on national and international news, but focuses primarily on matters of Jewish importance. It is called Israel Today, and that means world Jewry. That's why we have one hundred correspondents from Miami to Moscow. Twelve of them in Israel alone.

Israel Today is one of the four national daily newspapers in America. We cover everything from Business to Books. Medicine to Music. Education to Entertainment. And Sports to Stamps. So congratulations are in order because now the Jewish people in America have a national daily they can call their own.

RYE HUMOR.

Israel Today is built for speed. You can read it in about thirty minutes. That's not funny, but it sure is fast.

CHICKEN SOUP FOR THE MIND.

Once Israel Today is digested it does for your mind what chicken soup does for your body. It makes you feel good. It's good to know that the publisher of Israel Today fought for you in Skokie during the Nazi uprising there. It's good to know what is happening to Jewish people everywhere in the world. It's good to keep in touch with one's roots. And anything that brings the Jewish people together is like chicken soup for the mind.

THE 11TH COMMANDMENT.

As with all commandments, what is right must be preserved. At Israel Today we're dedicated to journalism that gives both sides of the story. To always be fair, unbiased, and truthful. So if thou shalt read us, thou shalt get that.

PRO-SEMITIC.

Israel Today is a Jewish newspaper, yet we've reported pro and con sides of important issues which has given us credibility. Israel Today is for the Jewish people, but you don't have to be Jewish to read it. You just have to be a concerned individual.

READ IT OR FEEL GUILTY.

You don't have to read Israel Today. You don't have to know what is happening to the 14 million Jews in the world. You don't have to really know both sides of the story. You don't have to know about world events that effect Jewish people everywhere. You don't have to be informed. You don't have to be effective.

But if you do like chicken soup and rye humor, then please subscribe to Israel Today. For yourself, for a relative, or for a friend. Israel Today is the nation's first daily Jewish newspaper. And the bottom line is, what's not to like?

I want Chicken Soup For The Mind
☐ for myself ☐ for a gift.
☐ 1 year for $80 (Normally $120)
☐ 2 years for $140 (Normally $240)
☐ 3 years for $190 (Normally $360)
☐ I enclose $______. ☐ Please charge my subscription to ☐ Visa ☐ MasterCard.
Exp. Date ______
Acct. # ______
SIGNATURE ______
NAME ______
ADDRESS ______
CITY ______ STATE ______ ZIP ______
GIFT FOR:
NAME ______
ADDRESS ______
CITY ______ STATE ______ ZIP ______
We will send a gift card for you.

ISRAEL TODAY

6742 Van Nuys Boulevard Van Nuys, California 91405
(818) 786-4000 Toll Free Outside California (800) 992-9000

AMERICAN JEWISH PRESS ASSOCIATION 226 S. 16TH STREET .... PHILADELPHIA **PA** 19102 (215) 893-5700
INSIDE MAGAZINE (QUARTERLY) CIRC. 65,000 EST. 1979
226 SOUTH 16TH STREET .... PHILADELPHIA **PA** 19102 (215) 893-5700
JEWISH NEWSPAPER GROUP OF GREATER PHILADELPHIA (WEEKLIES)
2417 WELSH ROAD CIRC. 150,000 (ENGLISH) .... PHILADELPHIA **PA** 19114 (215) 464-3900
JEWISH QUARTERLY REVIEW (QUARTERLY) CIRC. 1,000, EST. 1910
BROAD & YORK STREETS .... PHILADELPHIA **PA** 19132 (215) 229-0110
JEWISH TIMES (WEEKLY) CIRC. 40,000 EST. 1925
2417 WELSH ROAD .... PHILADELPHIA **PA** 19114 (215) 464-3900
THE JEWISH EXPONENT (WEEKLY) CIRC. 72,000 EST. 1887
226 SOUTH 16TH STREET .... PHILADELPHIA **PA** 19102 (215) 893-5700
JEWISH CHRONICLE (WEEKLY) CIRC. 14,250 EST. 1962
5600 BAUM BOULEVARD .... PITTSBURGH **PA** 15206 (412) 687-1000
JEWISH LIFE MAGAZINE (QUARTERLY) CIRC. 10,000 EST. 1977
BOX 573 .... READING **PA** 19602
RAAYONOT, RECONSTRUCTIONIST RABBINICAL ASSN. (QUARTERLY)
CHURCH ROAD & GREENWOOD AVENUE .... WYNCOTE **PA** 19095 (215) 576-0800
CANADIAN JEWISH NEWS (WEEKLY) CIRC. 76,000
DECARIE SQUARE, SUITE 157/6900 DECARIE BOULEVARD .... MONTREAL **QU** H3X 2T8 (514) 735-2612
CANADIAN JEWISH HERALD EST. 1977
17 ANSELME LAVIGNE BOULEVARD .... DOLLARD DES ORMEAUX **QU** H9A 1N3 (514) 684-7667
FEDERATION VOICE (MONTHLY) CIRC. 7,000
C/O JEWISH FEDERATION OF RHODE ISLAND, 130 SESSIONS ST .... PROVIDENCE **RI** 02906 (401) 421-4111
RHODE ISLAND JEWISH HERALD EST. 1923 P.O. BOX 6063 .... PROVIDENCE **RI** 02940 (401) 724-0200
RHODE ISLAND JEWISH HISTORICAL NOTES (ANNUAL) EST. 1954
130 SESSIONS STREET .... PROVIDENCE **RI** 02906
CHARLESTON JEWISH JOURNAL (MONTHLY) CIRC. 2,000 EST. 1946
P.O. BOX 31298 .... CHARLESTON **SC** 29417 (803) 571-6565
HEBREW WATCHMAN, THE (WEEKLY) CIRC. 2,400 EST. 1925
P.O. BOX 241183 .... MEMPHIS **TN** 38124 (901) 763-2215
OBSERVER (BIWEEKLY) 801 PERCY WARNER BOULEVARD .... NASHVILLE **TN** 37205 (615) 356-3242
B'NAI B'RITH VOICE 11300 NORTH CENTRAL EXPRESSWAY, #607 .... DALLAS **TX** 75243 (214) 691-6190
TEXAS JEWISH POST (F) 11333 N. CENTRAL EXPRESSWAY .... DALLAS **TX** 75231 (214) 692-7283
TEXAS JEWISH POST (WEEKLY) CIRC. 4,400 EST. 1947 PO BOX 742 .... FORT WORTH **TX** 76101 (817) 927-2831
JEWISH CIVIC PRESS (MONTHLY) CIRC. 4,800, EST. 1971 P.O. BOX 35656 .... HOUSTON **TX** 77035 (713) 721-8901
JEWISH HERALD-VOICE (WEEKLY) CIRC. 7,500 EST. 1908 P.O. BOX 153 .... HOUSTON **TX** 77001 (713) 630-0391
NOAH'S ARK & NEWSPAPER FOR JEWISH CHILDREN (MONTHLY) CIRC. 450,000
EST. 1978 7726 PORTAL .... HOUSTON **TX** 77071 (713) 771-7143
THE JEWISH JOURNAL OF SAN ANTONIO (MONTHLY) CIRC. 2,500 ENG.
8434 AHERN DRIVE .... SAN ANTONIO **TX** 78216 (512) 341-8234
UJF NEWS CIRC. 4,900 (ENGLISH) EST. 1973
7300 NEWPORT AVENUE, P.O. BOX 9776 .... NORFOLK **VA** 23505 (804) 489-8040
THE JEWISH NEWS (WEEKLY) CIRC. 3,900 - GENERAL NEWS (ENGLISH)
PO BOX 29917 .... RICHMOND **VA** 23233
THE JEWISH TRANSCRIPT (BIMONTHLY) CIRC. 4,000 EST. 1924
SECURITIES BUILDING, 510 .... SEATTLE **WA** 98101 (206) 624-0136
WISCONSIN JEWISH CHRONICLE (WEEKLY) CIRC. 7,500 EST. 1921
1360 NORTH PROSPECT AVENUE .... MILWAUKEE **WI** 53202 (414) 271-2992
JEWISH CHRONICLE 25 FURNIVAL STREET .... LONDON **GB** EC4A 1JT (01) 405-9252
JEWISH TRIBUNE 97 STAMFORD HILL .... LONDON **GB**
SEPHARDIC WORLD, THE (ENGLISH)
WZO-SEPHARDIC DEPARTMENT, P.O. BOX 92 .... JERUSALEM **IS**

NEWSPAPERS - HEBREW & ISRAELI

DAVAR 913 NATIONAL PRESS BUILDING .... WASHINGTON **DC** 20054
JERUSALEM POST & AL HAMISHMAR
615 NATIONAL PRESS BUILDING .... WASHINGTON **DC** 20045 (202) 783-1161
MA'ARIV 2939 VAN NESS STREET, N.W. .... WASHINGTON **DC** 20008 (202) 362-8526
HA'ARETZ 4515 S. WILLARD AVENUE .... CHEVY CHASE **MD** 20015 (301) 951-0182
YEDIOT AHRONOTH 4824 DERUSSEY PARKWAY .... CHEVY CHASE **MD** 20015 (301) 652-3230
HA'ARETZ-INDEPENDENT MORNING DAILY 24 TEHAMA STREET .... BROOKLYN **NY** 11218 (718) 581-5151
HAZOFE-NEWSPAPER OF ISRAEL'S NATIONAL RELIGIOUS PARTY
785 E. SECOND STREET .... BROOKLYN **NY** 11218 (718) 436-9153
ISRAEL SHELANU - WEEKLY (HEBREW) 933 E. 17TH STREET .... BROOKLYN **NY** 11230 (718) 258-8696
YEDIOT AHRONOTH 2367 EAST 16TH STREET .... BROOKLYN **NY** 11229 (718) 934-3887
AL HAMISHMAR 301 W. 108TH STREET .... NEW YORK **NY** 10025 (212) 758-5125
HA'ARETZ 350 FIFTH AVENUE, 19TH FL .... NEW YORK **NY** 10118 (212) 695-2998
HADOAR HEBREW WEEKLY 1841 BROADWAY .... NEW YORK **NY** 10023 (212) 581-5151
JERUSALEM POST, THE 120 EAST 56TH STREET .... NEW YORK **NY** 10022 (212) 355-4440
JEWISH TELEGRAPHIC AGENCY, GLOBAL NEWS 165 W. 46TH STREET .... NEW YORK **NY** 10036 (212) 575-9370
LAMISHPAHA ILLUSTRATED HEBREW MONTHLY 1841 BROADWAY .... NEW YORK **NY** 10023 (212) 581-5151
M. DWORKIN AND CO. 150 FIFTH AVENUE .... NEW YORK **NY** 10011 (212) 924-5788
MA'ARIV-INDEPENDENT EVENING DAILY 130 W. 67TH STREET .... NEW YORK **NY** 10023 (212) 580-8099
MAARIV ISRAEL NEWSPAPER 350 FIFTH AVENUE .... NEW YORK **NY** 10001 (212) 695-2998
OMER-DAVER ISRAEL NEWSPAPERS 150 FIFTH AVENUE .... NEW YORK **NY** 10010 (212) 564-5165
YEDIOT AHRONOTH - INDEPENDENT EVENING DAILY
230 E. 44TH STREET .... NEW YORK **NY** 10017 (212) 687-6086
YEDIOT AHRONOTH C/O M. DWORKIN & COMPANY 350 FIFTH AVENUE .... NEW YORK **NY** 10001 (212) 564-5165
ISRAEL PHILATELIC MONTHLY P.O. BOX 21224 .... TEL AVIV **IS** 61211

NEWSPAPERS - YIDDISH & FOREIGN LANGUAGE

JEWISH FORWARD 1161 NORTH OGDEN DRIVE .... LOS ANGELES **CA** 90046 (213) 659-0861
JEWISH MORNING FREIHEIT 163 SOUTH FAIRFAX AVENUE #4 .... LOS ANGELES **CA** 90036 (213) 937-5017
DE YIDDISH HEIM/THE JEWISH HOME 770 EASTERN PARKWAY .... BROOKLYN **NY** 11213 (718) 493-0571
DER YID 543 BEDFORD AVENUE .... BROOKLYN **NY** 11211 (718) 782-4900
SHMUESSEN MIT KINDER UN YUGENT 770 EASTERN PARKWAY .... BROOKLYN **NY** 11213 (718) 774-4000
YID: VOICE OF AMERICAN ORTHODOX JEWRY YID PUB ASSOCIATION
260 BROADWAY .... BROOKLYN **NY** 11211
ALGEMEINER JOURNAL 404 PARK AVE. SOUTH .... NEW YORK **NY** 10016 (212) 689-3390
AUFBAU 2121 BROADWAY .... NEW YORK **NY** 10023 (212) 873-7400
JEWISH FORWARD, THE 45 EAST 33RD STREET .... NEW YORK **NY** 10016 (212) 889-8200
JEWISH FORWARD, THE-CLASSIFIED ADVERTISEMENT DEPT.
45 EAST 33RD STREET .... NEW YORK **NY** 10016 (212) 689-5505
JEWISH MORNING FREIHEIT 22 WEST 21ST STREET .... NEW YORK **NY** 10010 (212) 255-7661
THE JEWISH EAGLE (EST. 1907) 4180 DE COURTRAI, SUITE 218 .... MONTREAL **QU** H3S 1C3 (514) 735-6577
YISROEL SHTIMME 4 ITAMAR BEN AVI STREET .... TEL AVIV **IS**
MISMAR—ROMANIAN WEEKLY 4 ITAMAR BEN AVI STREET .... TEL AVIV **IS**
DOS YIDDISHE FOLK (WEEKLY) 151 ANSON ROAD .... LONDON **GB** NW2 (01) 452-8673

NURSING HOMES, REST HOMES & OLD AGE HOMES

KIVEL NURSING HOME 3020 NORTH 36 STREET .... PHOENIX **AZ** 85018 (602) 956-3110
HANDMAKER JEWISH GERIATRIC CENTER 2221 NO. ROSEMONT BLVD .... TUCSON **AZ** 85712 (602) 881-2323
JEWISH HOME FOR THE AGED OF B.C. (LOUIS BRIER HOME & HOSPITAL)
1055 WEST 41ST AVENUE .... VANCOUVER **BC** V6M 1W9 (604) 261-9376
HOME FOR JEWISH PARENTS 2780 26TH AVENUE .... OAKLAND **CA** 94601 (415) 536-4604
JEWISH HOMES FOR THE AGING OF GREATER L.A.
18855 VICTORY BOULEVARD .... RESEDA **CA** 91335 (818) 881-4411
SAN DIEGO HEBREW HOME FOR THE AGED 4075 54TH STREET .... SAN DIEGO **CA** 92105 (619) 582-5168
JEWISH HOME FOR THE AGED 302 SILVER AVENUE .... SAN FRANCISCO **CA** 94112 (415) 334-2500
MENORAH PARK 3365 SACRAMENTO STREET .... SAN FRANCISCO **CA** 94118 (415) 929-7912
PINECREST 320 SILVER AVENUE .... SAN FRANCISCO **CA** 94112 (415) 587-4666
BETH ISRAEL 1620 MEADA WAY .... DENVER **CO** 80209 (303) 825-2190
JEWISH HOME FOR THE ELDERLY OF FAIRFIELD COUNTY
175 JEFFERSON STREET .... FAIRFIELD **CT** 06432 (203) 347-9461
HEBREW HOME & HOSPITAL 615 TOWER AVENUE .... HARTFORD **CT** 06112 (203) 242-6207
JEWISH HOME FOR THE AGED, INC. 169 DAVENPORT AVENUE .... NEW HAVEN **CT** 06519 (203) 788-1650
THE MILTON & HATTIE KUTZ HOME, INC. 704 RIVER ROAD .... WILMINGTON **DE** 19809 (302) 764-7000
RIVER GARDEN HEBREW HOME 1800 STOCKTON STREET .... JACKSONVILLE **FL** 32204 (904) 389-3665
MIAMI JEWISH HOME AND HOSPITAL FOR THE AGED
151 N.E. 52ND STREET .... MIAMI **FL** 33137 (305) 751-8626
HEBREW HOME FOR THE AGED OF MIAMI BEACH
320 COLLINS AVENUE .... MIAMI BEACH **FL** 33139 (305) 672-6464
KINNERET, INC. 515-517 S. DELANEY AVENUE .... ORLANDO **FL** 32801 (305) 425-4537
THE JEWISH HOME TOWER INC. 3160 HOWELL MILL ROAD N.W. .... ORLANDO **FL** 32801 (305) 425-4537
JEWISH HOME FOR AGED 501 S. FLAGLER DRIVE, SUITE 305 .... WEST PALM BEACH **FL** 33401
THE JEWISH HOME 3150 HOWELL MILL ROAD, N.W. .... ATLANTA **GA** 30327 (404) 351-8410
IOWA JEWISH HOME 1620 PLEASANT .... DES MOINES **IA** 50312 (515) 288-1001
NORTHWEST HOME FOR AGED 6300 N. CALIFORNIA .... CHICAGO **IL** 60645 (312) 973-1900
GEORGE J. GOLDMAN MEMORIAL HOME FOR THE AGED 6601 W. TOUHY .... NILES **IL** 60648 (312) 647-9875
JACOB & MARCELLE LIEBERMAN GERIATRIC CENTRE
9700 GROSS POINT ROAD .... SKOKIE **IL** 60076 (312) 674-7210
INDIANAPOLIS JEWISH HOME, INC. (HOOVERWOOD)
7001 HOOVER ROAD .... INDIANAPOLIS **IN** 46260 (317) 251-2261
JEWISH WELFARE FED. HOUSING CORP.-PARK REGENCY
8851 COLBY BLVD .... INDIANAPOLIS **IN** 46268 (317) 875-5763
FOUR COURTS (THE LOUISVILLE HEBREW HOME)
2100 MILLVALE ROAD .... LOUISVILLE **KY** 40205 (502) 451-0990
WILLOW WOOD HOME FOR JEWISH AGED 3701 BEHRMAN PLACE .... NEW ORLEANS **LA** 70114 (504) 367-5640
COOLIDGE CORNER CONVALESCENT HOME 30 WEBSTER STREET .... BROOKLINE **MA** 02146 (617) 734-2300
CHELSEA JEWISH NURSING HOME 17 LAFAYETTE AVENUE .... CHELSEA **MA** 02150 (617) 884-6766
FALL RIVER JEWISH HOME 201 HANOVER STREET .... FALL RIVER **MA** 02720 (617) 672-1214
SPRINGFIELD JEWISH HOME FOR THE AGED
770 CONVERSE STREET .... LONGMEADOW **MA** 01106 (413) 567-6211
WILLOW MANOR RETIREMENT & NURSING HOME
30 PRINCETON BOULEVARD .... LOWELL **MA** 01851 (617) 454-8086
NEW BEDFORD JEWISH CONVALESCENT HOME, INC.
200 HAWTHORN STREET .... NEW BEDFORD **MA** 02740 (617) 997-9314
H.R.C.A. HOUSING FOR ELDERLY - REVERE HOUSE
420 REVERE BEACH BLVD .... REVERE **MA** 01108 (617) 289-4505
HEBREW REHABILITATION CENTER FOR AGED
1200 CENTRE STREET .... ROSLINDALE **MA** 02131 (617) 325-8000
RECUPERATIVE CENTER, THE 1245 CENTRE STREET .... ROSLINDALE **MA** 02131 (617) 325-5400
NEW ENGLAND SINAI HOSPITAL 150 YORK STREET (BOX 647) .... STOUGHTON **MA** 02072
JEWISH REHABILITATION CENTER FOR AGED OF THE NORTH SHORE
330 PARADISE ROAD .... SWAMPSCOTT **MA** 01907 (617) 598-5310
JEWISH HOME FOR AGED OF WORCESTER COUNTY
629 SALISBURY STREET .... WORCESTER **MA** 01609 (617) 798-8653
SHARON HOME 146 MAGNUS AVENUE .... WINNIPEG **MB** R2W 2B4 (204) 586-9781
CONCORD HOUSE 2500 WEST BELVEDERE AVENUE .... BALTIMORE **MD** 21215 (301) 542-4111
HURWITZ HOUSE 133 SLADE AVENUE .... BALTIMORE **MD** 21208 (301) 466-8700
JEWISH CONVALESCENT & NURSING HOME
7920 SCOTTS LEVEL ROAD .... BALTIMORE **MD** 21208 (301) 521-3600
JEWISH CONVALESCENT & NURSING HOME 4601 PALL MALL ROAD .... BALTIMORE **MD** 21208 (301) 521-3600
LEVENDALE HEBREW HOME & INFIRMARY
BELVEDERE AND GREENSPRING .... BALTIMORE **MD** 21215 (301) 466-8700
HEBREW HOME OF GREATER WASHINGTON 6121 MONTROSE ROAD .... ROCKVILLE **MD** 20852 (301) 881-0300
JEWISH HOME FOR THE AGED P.O. BOX 446 DTS .... PORTLAND **ME** 04112
JEWISH HOME FOR AGED 19100 WEST SEVEN MILE ROAD .... DETROIT **MI** 48219 (313) 532-7112
JEWISH FEDERATION APARTMENTS, INC. 15100 WEST TEN MILE .... OAK PARK **MI** 48237 (313) 967-4240
COMMUNITY HOUSING & SERVICE CORP. - MENORAH PLAZA APARTMENTS
4925 MINNETONKA BLVD .... ST. LOUIS PARK **MN** 55416 (612) 927-0460
SHOLOM HOME, INC. 1554 MIDWAY PARKWAY .... ST. PAUL **MN** 55108 (612) 646-6311

Name / Address	City	State	Zip	Phone
JEWISH CENTER FOR AGED 13190 SOUTH OUTER 40 ROAD	CHESTERFIELD	MO	63017	(314) 434-3330
JEWISH GERIATRIC & CONVALESCENT CENTER 7801 HOLMES	KANSAS CITY	MO	64131	(816) 333-7800
BLUMENTHAL JEWISH HOME FOR THE AGED, INC. P.O. BOX 38	CLEMONS	NC	27012	(919) 766-6401
DR. PHILIP SHER JEWISH HOME 4801 NORTH 52ND STREET	OMAHA	NE	68104	
SEASHORE GARDENS/HEBREW OLD AGE CENTER 3850 ATLANTIC AVENUE	ATLANTIC CITY	NJ	08401	(609) 345-5941
JEWISH GERIATRIC HOME 3025 WEST CHAPEL AVENUE	CHERRY HILL	NJ	08034	(609) 667-3100
DAUGHTERS OF MIRIAM CENTER FOR THE AGED 155 HAZEL STREET	CLIFTON	NJ	07015	(201) 772-3700
WORKMEN'S CIRCLE HOME FOR AGED & INFIRM OF NJ, BRANCHES INC. 225 WEST JERSEY STREET	ELIZABETH	NJ	07202	(201) 353-1220
JEWISH HOSPITAL & REHABILITATION CENTER OF N.J. 198 STEVENS AVENUE	JERSEY CITY	NJ	07305	(201) 451-9000
CHARLES BIERMAN HOME FOR AGED 10 MADISON AVENUE	MONTCLAIR	NJ	07042	(201) 744-6333
JEWISH HOME FOR THE AGED 380 DE MOTT LANE	SOMERSET	NJ	08873	(201) 873-2000
GREENWOOD HOUSE, HOME FOR JEWISH AGED 53 WALTER STREET	TRENTON	NJ	08628	(609) 883-5391
DAUGHTERS OF ISRAEL GERIATRIC CENTER 1155 PLEASANT VALLEY WAY	WEST ORANGE	NJ	07052	(201) 731-5100
DAUGHTERS OF SARAH HOME WASHINGTON AVENUE & RAPP ROAD	ALBANY	NY	12203	(518) 456-7831
BETH ABRAHAM HOSPITAL 612 ALLERTON AVENUE	BRONX	NY	10467	(212) 920-6001
DAUGHTERS OF JACOB NURSING HOME 1160 TELLER AVENUE	BRONX	NY	10456	(212) 293-1500
HEBREW HOME FOR THE AGED AT RIVERDALE, THE 5901 PALISADE AVENUE	BRONX	NY	10471	(212) 549-8700
HEBREW HOSPITAL FOR CHRONIC SICK 2200 GIVAN AVENUE	BRONX	NY	10475	(212) 379-5020
HOME & HOSPITAL OF THE DAUGHTERS OF JACOB 321 E 167TH STREET	BRONX	NY	10456	(212) 293-1500
JEWISH HOME & HOSPITAL FOR AGED, THE (KINGSBRIDGE CENTER) 100 W KINGSBRIDGE ROAD	BRONX	NY	10468	(212) 579-0500
UNITED ODDFELLOW AND REBEKAH HOME 1072 HAVEMEYER AVENUE	BRONX	NY	10462	(212) 863-6200
WORKMAN'S CIRCLE HOME 3155 GRACE AVENUE	BRONX	NY	10469	(212) 379-8100
AISHEL AVRAHAM RHF INC. 40 HEYWARD STREET	BROOKLYN	NY	11211	(718) 858-6200
DAVID MINKIN REHABILITATION INSTITUTE (RUTLAND NURSING HOME) 585 SCHENECTADY AVENUE	BROOKLYN	NY	11203	(718) 756-9700
JHMCB CENTER FOR NURSING & REHABILITATION 520 PROSPECT PLACE	BROOKLYN	NY	11238	(718) 636-1000
JEWISH GERIATRIC CENTER WEST 29TH STREET & BOARDWALK	BROOKLYN	NY	11224	
LEMBERG HOME & GERIATRIC INSTITUTE, INC. 8629 BAY PARKWAY	BROOKLYN	NY	11214	(718) 606-0901
MENORAH HOME 871 BUSHWICK AVENUE	BROOKLYN	NY	11221	(718) 443-3000
METROPOLITAN JEWISH GERIATRIC CENTER 4915 TENTH AVENUE	BROOKLYN	NY	11219	(718) 853-2800
SEPHARDIC HOME 2266 CROPSEY AVENUE	BROOKLYN	NY	11214	(718) 266-6100
ROSA COPLON JEWISH HOME AND INFIRMARY 10 SYMPHONY CIRCLE	BUFFALO	NY	14201	(716) 885-3311
BEZALEL HEALTH RELATED FACILITY 29-38 FAR ROCKAWAY BLVD.	FAR ROCKAWAY	NY	11691	(718) 471-2600
MARGARET TIETZ CENTER FOR NURSING CARE 164-11 CHAPIN PARKWAY	JAMAICA	NY	11432	(718) 523-6400
CHARLES T SITRIN NURSING HOME CO., INC RD 1 BOX 318 TILDEN AVENUE	NEW HARTFORD	NY	13413	(315) 797-3114
JIGC NURSING HOME CO., INC 271-11 76TH AVENUE	NEW HYDE PARK	NY	11042	(718) 343-2100
UNITED HOME FOR AGED HEBREWS 60 WILLOW DRIVE	NEW ROCHELLE	NY	10805	(914) 632-2804
BIALYSTOKER HOME FOR AGED 228 EAST BROADWAY	NEW YORK	NY	10002	(212) 475-7755
CENTRAL BUREAU FOR JEWISH AGED 80 FIFTH AVENUE	NEW YORK	NY	10011	(212) 929-3999
HOME OF THE SAGES OF ISRAEL 25 WILLETT STREET	NEW YORK	NY	10002	(212) 673-8500
JEWISH ASSOCIATION FOR SERVICES 40 WEST 68TH STREET	NEW YORK	NY	10023	
JEWISH HOME & HOSPITAL FOR AGED, THE (ZEMAN CENTER) 120 W. 106TH STREET	NEW YORK	NY	10025	(212) 870-5000
FAIRFIELD DIVISION-HEBREW HOME 3220 HENRY HUDSON PARKWAY EAST	RIVERDALE	NY	10463	(212) 549-9400
HEBREW HOME HOUSING DEV. FUND CO., INC. - RIVER HOUSE WEST 5961 PALISADE AVENUE	RIVERDALE	NY	10471	(212) 543-9600
JEWISH HOME OF ROCHESTER 201 SOUTH WINTON ROAD	ROCHESTER	NY	14618	(716) 427-7760
JEWISH HOME OF CENTRAL NEW YORK 4101 EAST GENESEE STREET	SYRACUSE	NY	13214	(315) 446-9111
JEWISH FED. HOUSING DEV. FUND CO., INC.-JEWISH FED. HOUSING 275 ESSJAY ROAD	WILLIAMSVILLE	NY	14221	(716) 631-8471
HOME FOR AGED BLIND 5 STRATTON STREET	YONKERS	NY	10701	(204) 582-5583
MENORAH PARK-JEWISH HOME FOR THE AGED 27100 CEDAR ROAD	BEACHWOOD	OH	44122	(216) 831-6500
R.H. MEYERS APARTMENTS 27200 CEDAR ROAD	BEACHWOOD	OH	44122	(216) 831-6515
GLEN MANOR HOME FOR JEWISH AGED 6969 GLEN MEADOW LANE	CINCINNATI	OH	45222	(513) 351-7007
ORTHODOX JEWISH HOME FOR THE AGED 1171 TOWNE STREET	CINCINNATI	OH	45216	(513) 242-1360
MENORAH PARK - JEWISH HOME FOR AGED 27100 CEDAR ROAD	CLEVELAND	OH	44122	(216) 831-6500
COUNCIL GARDENS 2501 N. TAYLOR ROAD	CLEVELAND HEIGHTS	OH	44118	(216) 382-8625
THE MONTEFIORE HOME, INC. 3151 MAYFIELD ROAD	CLEVELAND HEIGHTS	OH	44118	(216) 371-5500
HERITAGE TOWER - JEWISH COMM. SR. CITIZENS HOUSING CORP. 1145 COLLEGE AVENUE	COLUMBUS	OH	43209	(614) 237-2521
HERITAGE VILLAGE 1151 COLLEGE AVENUE	COLUMBUS	OH	43209	(614) 237-7417
COVENANT HOUSE 4911 COVENANT HOUSE DRIVE	DAYTON	OH	45426	(513) 837-2651
DARLINGTON HOUSE, TOLEDO JEWISH HOME FOR AGED 2735 DARLINGTON ROAD	TOLEDO	OH	43606	(419) 531-4465
TOLEDO JEWISH HOME FOR THE AGED - PELHAM MANOR 2700 PELHAM ROAD	TOLEDO	OH	43606	(419) 537-1515
HERITAGE MANOR 517 GYPSY LANE, P.O. BOX 449	YOUNGSTOWN	OH	44501	(216) 746-1076
HILLEL LODGE 125 WURTEMBURG STREET	OTTAWA	ON	K1N 8L9	
BAYCREST CENTER, JEWISH HOME FOR THE AGED 3560 BATHURST	TORONTO	ON	M6A 2E1	(416) 789-5131
JEWISH HOME FOR THE AGED 3560 BATHURST STREET	TORONTO	ON	M6A 2E1	(416) 789-5131
LINCOLN PLACE NURSING HOME 429 WALMER ROAD	TORONTO	ON	M1P 2X7	(416) 967-6949
ROBINSON JEWISH HOME FOR AGED 6125 S.W. BOUNDARY STREET	PORTLAND	OR	97221	
JEWISH HOME OF GREATER HARRISBURG 4000 LINGLESTOWN ROAD	HARRISBURG	PA	17112	(717) 657-0700
FEDERATION HOUSING, INC. 8900 ROOSEVELT BLVD	PHILADELPHIA	PA	19115	(215) 673-6446
PHILADELPHIA GERIATRIC CENTER 5301 OLD YORK ROAD	PHILADELPHIA	PA	19141	(215) 455-6100
UPTOWN HOME FOR THE AGED 7800 BUSTLETON AVENUE	PHILADELPHIA	PA	19152	(215) 722-2300
YORK HOUSE INC. - YORK HOUSE NORTH AND SOUTH 5325 OLD YORK ROAD	PHILADELPHIA	PA	19141	(215) 455-6100
BICKUR CHOLIM CONVALESCENT & NURSING HOME 234 MCKEE PLACE	PITTSBURGH	PA	15213	(412) 683-4900
JEWISH HOME & HOSPITAL FOR AGED 4724 BROWN'S HILL ROAD	PITTSBURGH	PA	15217	(412) 521-5900
THE JEWISH HOME OF EASTERN PENNSYLVANIA 1101 VINE STREET	SCRANTON	PA	18510	(717) 344-6177
JEWISH NURSING HOME 3939 CURATTEAU STREET	MONTREAL	QU	H1K 4A6	
MAIMONIDES HOSPITAL GERIATRIC CENTER 5795 CALDWELL AVENUE	MONTREAL	QU	H4W 1W3	(514) 483-2121
JEWISH HOME FOR THE AGED OF RHODE ISLAND 99 HILLSIDE AVENUE	PROVIDENCE	RI	02906	(401) 351-4750
B'NAI B'RITH HOME FOR AGED 131 N. TUCKER STREET	MEMPHIS	TN	38104	(504) 367-5640
DALLAS HOME FOR JEWISH AGED (GOLDEN ACRES) 2525 CENTERVILLE ROAD	DALLAS	TX	75228	(214) 327-4503
ECHAD, INC. - ECHAD APARTMENTS 2620 RUIDOSA	DALLAS	TX	75228	(214) 321-2130
NORTH AMERICAN ASSOC. OF JEWISH HOMES & HOUSING FOR THE AGED 2525 CENTERVILLE ROAD	DALLAS	TX	75228	(214) 327-4503
B'NAI B'RITH SEN. CITIZENS HOUSING COMM. OF HOUSTON, INC. 10909 FONDREN ROAD	HOUSTON	TX	77096	(713) 771-2417
JEWISH HOME FOR THE AGED - 'SEVEN ACRES' 6200 NORTH BRAESWOOD	HOUSTON	TX	77074	(713) 771-4111
GOLDEN MANOR 130 SPENCER LANE	SAN ANTONIO	TX	78201	(512) 736-4544
BETH SHOLOM HOME OF CENTRAL VIRGINIA 5700 FITZHUGH AVENUE	RICHMOND	VA	23226	(804) 282-5471
BETH SHOLOM HOUSING CORP. - BETH SHOLOM WOODS 2027 LAUDERDALE ROAD	RICHMOND	VA	23233	(804) 741-4691
BETH SHOLOM HOME OF EASTERN VIRGINIA 6401 AUBURN DRIVE	VIRGINIA BEACH	VA	23464	(804) 420-2512
THE CAROLINE KLINE GALLAND HOME 7500 STEWARD PARK AVENUE SOUTH	SEATTLE	WA	98118	(206) 725-8800
MILWAUKEE JEWISH CONVALESCENT CENTER 5555 N. 51ST BLVD	MILWAUKEE	WI	53218	(414) 464-2300
MILWAUKEE JEWISH HOME 1414 N. PROSPECT AVENUE	MILWAUKEE	WI	53202	(414) 276-2627

NUTRITION & HEALTH

Name / Address	City	State	Zip	Phone
KOSHER NUTRITION - BETH SHOLOM 320 15TH AVENUE	SAN FRANCISCO	CA	94118	(415) 221-1025
JEWISH VOCATIONAL SERVICE NUTRITIONAL PROJECT 920 ALTON ROAD	MIAMI BEACH	FL	33139	(305) 672-6263
ADWE BEAUTY & HEALTH AIDS (INC. KOSHER FOR PASSOVER) 141 20TH STREET	BROOKLYN	NY	11232	(718) 788-6838
PRECISION VITAMINS 1524 47TH ST.	BROOKLYN	NY	11219	(718) 435-4333
START FRESH - UNIQUE KOSHER WEIGHT CONTROL PROGRAM 1173 50TH STREET	BROOKLYN	NY	11219	(718) 851-0081
ZAHLER'S NUTRITION CENTER 4724 NEW UTRECHT AVENUE	BROOKLYN	NY	11219	(718) 438-5336
FAR ROCKAWAY HEALTH FOOD CENTER 1815 MOTT AVENUE	FAR ROCKAWAY	NY	11691	(718) 327-9087
FREEDA (OU) VITAMINS (INC. KOSHER FOR PASSOVER) 36 EAST 41ST STREET	NEW YORK	NY	10017	(212) 685-8980
LOIS LANE'S NINTH & NATURAL 580 NINTH AVENUE CORNER 42ND ST.	NEW YORK	NY	10036	(212) 695-5055
NEWLIFE CENTER BOX 248	WOODBOURNE	NY	12788	(800) LESS WGT

ORCHESTRAS

CINDY PALEY ABOODY	LOS ANGELES	CA	(213) 785-8273
DAVE & GILA BELL	LOS ANGELES	CA	(213) 931-6125
DAVID KAMENIR ORCHESTRA	LOS ANGELES	CA	(213) 990-7802
EVERETT COVIN ORCHESTRAS	LOS ANGELES	CA	(213) 822-8404
HAL BREGMAN ORCHESTRAS	LOS ANGELES	CA	(213) 393-4813
HAL SANDACK ORCHESTRAS	LOS ANGELES	CA	(213) 934-3610
HERB SILVER ORCHESTRAS	LOS ANGELES	CA	(213) 981-9293
JAY SAUNDERS MUSIC	LOS ANGELES	CA	(213) 347-5600
JERRY ROSEN ORCHESTRAS	LOS ANGELES	CA	(213) 939-2027
JOEY SHARPE ORCHESTRAS	LOS ANGELES	CA	(213) 987-3249
KOL ECHAD CHORALE 1620 CORNING STREET	LOS ANGELES	CA	(213) 859-1057
LIONEL AMES ORCHESTRAS	LOS ANGELES	CA	(213) 985-0010
LOS ANGELES MANDOLIN ORCHESTRA	LOS ANGELES	CA	(213) 731-2353
LUDDY DREYFUSS	LOS ANGELES	CA	(213) 931-6125
MANNY HARMON ORCHESTRAS	LOS ANGELES	CA	(213) 656-8720
MERRILL LISH ORCHESTRAS	LOS ANGELES	CA	(213) 992-6330
MICKEY KATZ & HIS CAPITOL RECORDING ORCHESTRA	LOS ANGELES	CA	(213) 271-0256
MURRAY KORDA STRINGS & ORCHESTRAS	LOS ANGELES	CA	(213) 274-3404
NEIL SEIDEL	LOS ANGELES	CA	(213) 852-1035
NEW YORK SOUND	LOS ANGELES	CA	(213) 931-0346
QUABAL BAND	LOS ANGELES	CA	(213) 876-3285
SHALOM SHERMAN	LOS ANGELES	CA	(213) 931-6125
SIMCHA ORCHESTRA	LOS ANGELES	CA	(213) 271-6909
THE NAMA ORCHESTRA AND SINGERS	LOS ANGELES	CA	(213) 475-6262
THE SABRAS BAND	LOS ANGELES	CA	(213) 999-4193
ANAT & YEHOSHUA - THE 'DUO BAND'		MA	(617) 592-6981
KOLI		MA	(617) 527-8946
KOL CHAYIM ORCHESTRA	BALTIMORE	MD	(301) 764-8676
EILAT ORCHESTRAS		NJ	(201) 471-9179
RONNIE BARAS ORCHESTRA		NJ	(201) 572-9493
ALBERT WARMAN & HIS CORDOVOX		NY	(718) 531-9767
BEN SIMCHA - ONE MAN BAND		NY	(718) 633-4290
DAVID NULMAN ORCHESTRAS		NY	(718) 252-0308
ED MEYERS ENTERTAINMENT		NY	(516) 781-0383
ELI LIPSKER ORCHESTRA		NY	(718) 774-5174
EZRA INTERNATIONAL ENTERTAINER		NY	(718) 268-8707
FOR WOMEN ONLY		NY	(718) 377-4154
FREILACH ORCHESTRA		NY	(718) 436-3106
HAROLD DAVIS MUSIC		NY	(516) 764-7876

ISRA ART PRODUCTIONS		NY	(212) 246-4500
JERRY MARKOWITZ ORCHESTRA		NY	(718) 698-9380
JERUSALEM ORCHESTRA		NY	(718) 438-0406
JERRY KING ORCHESTRAS		NY	(718) 217-0326
JOEL BERNARD - ONE MAN BAND		NY	(914) 794-7069
JOSH GOLDBERG		NY	
KESHER		NY	(718) 327-3292
KOL CHODOSH ORCHESTRA		NY	(718) 851-4620
KOL ZAHAV ORCHESTRA		NY	(718) 896-2606
LEIB GILDIN ORCHESTRA		NY	(718) 251-4213
MARVIN B'SIMCHA		NY	(718) 633-4298
MESSENGERS ORCHESTRA, THE		NY	(718) 471-2801
MEYER DAVIS ORCHESTRA		NY	(212) 247-6161
MIZMOR SHIR ORCHESTRA		NY	(718) 339-2218
NAT EPSTEIN MUSIC		NY	(718) 229-4343
NAT SAMBERG DISCO PRODUCTIONS		NY	(212) 379-6572
NEGINAH ORCHESTRA		NY	(718) 854-2911
NESHOMA ORCHESTRAS		NY	(718) 376-6122
NOBLEMEN ORCHESTRAS		NY	(516) 731-9810
PAUL GLASSER ORCHESTRA, THE		NY	(718) 544-2361
PAUL ZAHN ORCHESTRA		NY	(516) 484-0077
PIAMENTA ORCHESTRA, THE		NY	(718) 756-6086
RAYA MEHEMNA ORCHESTRA		NY	(718) 467-4947
RUACH		NY	(718) 339-9009
RUACH ORCHESTRA & SINGERS		NY	(718) 435-3285
RUACH REVIVAL ORCHESTRA		NY	(516) 374-6444
RUDY TEPEL		NY	(718) 377-0655
SHELLEY LANG ORCHESTRA		NY	(718) 438-3402
SHEMA YISRAEL ORCHESTRA		NY	(718) 575-1635
SHEMESH ORCHESTRA, THE		NY	(718) 263-9431
SHIRIM ORCHESTRAS		NY	(914) 356-4366
SHLOMO RABINOWITZ ORCHESTRA		NY	(718) 641-5150
SHMA ECHAD - ONE MAN BAND		NY	(718) 859-0019
SHMUEL BEIM ORCHESTRAS		NY	(718) 436-9255
SHMUEL GOLDMAN ORCHESTRA		NY	(718) 604-1234
SIMCHA SOUND ORCHESTRA		NY	(516) 489-0880
SIMCHATONE ORCHESTRAS		NY	(718) 853-5284
SMALL SIMCHAS		NY	(718) 435-4207
STANLEY MILLER BAND, THE		NY	(516) 569-2374
STONE & STUART 'DUO' OR 'TRIO'		NY	(718) 763-0394
SY MANDEL ORCHESTRA		NY	(718) 268-6400
TZAHALAH ORCHESTRA		NY	(718) 438-3014
YOEL HECHT		NY	(718) 435-2453
YOSSI SOIBELMAN		NY	(718) 436-2145
ZIMRIAH ORCHESTRAS		NY	(718) 327-3291
KEN JAMES ORCHESTRAS		NY	(516) 829-6480
SIMCHA ORCHESTRA	TORONTO	ON	(416) 781-8286
KOL ECHAD	PHILADELPHIA	PA	(215) 742-4284
SHIR HADASH	PHILADELPHIA	PA	(215) 750-1158

OVERSEAS AID

Name / Address	City	State	Zip	Phone
AMERICAN ASSOCIATION OF ETHIOPIAN JEWS 304 ROBIN HOOD LANE	COSTA MESA	CA	92627	(714) 642-8613
AMERICAN ASSOCIATION FOR ETHIOPIAN JEWS, NAT'L MATERIALS CTR. 6505 WILSHIRE BLVD., ROOM 802	LOS ANGELES	CA	90048	(213) 852-1234
THE SINO-JUDAIC INSTITUTE 3197 LOUIS ROAD	PALO ALTO	CA	94303	(415) 493-4096
NORTH AMERICAN CONFERENCE ON ETHIOPIAN JEWRY 1816 KALORAMA ROAD, NORTHWEST, ROOM 301	WASHINGTON	DC	20009	(202) 387-1502
AMERICAN ASSOCIATION FOR ETHIOPIAN JEWS 2789 OAK STREET	HIGHLAND PARK	IL	60035	(312) 433-8150
AMERICAN JEWISH WORLD SERVICE 29 COMMONWEALTH AVENUE, SUITE 101	BOSTON	MA	02116	(617) 267-6656
HATZILU RESCUE ORGANIZATION 1770 PITKIN AVENUE	BROOKLYN	NY	11212	(718) 389-5538
ARIF - ASSOCIATION POUR LA RETABLISSEMENT DES INSTITUTIONS ET OEUVRES ISRAELITES EN FRANCE, 119 EAST 95TH STREET	NEW YORK	NY	10028	
ALLIANCE ISRAELITE UNIVERSELLE, AMERICAN FRIENDS OF 61 BROADWAY	NEW YORK	NY	10006	(212) 349-0537
AMERICAN COMMITTEE FOR RESCUE & RESETTLEMENT OF IRAQI JEWS 1200 FIFTH AVENUE	NEW YORK	NY	10029	(212) 427-1246
AMERICAN COUNCIL FOR JEWISH PHILANTHROPIC FUND 386 PARK AVENUE SOUTH	NEW YORK	NY	10016	(212) 684-1525
AMERICAN FRIENDS OF THE ALLIANCE ISRAELITE UNIVERSELLE 135 WILLIAM STREET	NEW YORK	NY	10038	(212) 349-0537
AMERICAN JEWISH JOINT DISTRIBUTION COMMITTEE, INC. 60 E. 42ND STREET	NEW YORK	NY	10017	(212) 687-6200
AMERICAN ORT FEDERATION-ORG. FOR REHABIL. THROUGH TRAINING 817 BROADWAY	NEW YORK	NY	10003	(212) 677-4400
AMERICAN PRO-FALASHA COMMITTEE 507 FIFTH AVENUE	NEW YORK	NY	10017	(212) 697-5895
CONFERENCE ON JEWISH MATERIAL CLAIMS AGAINST GERMANY 15 EAST 26TH STREET	NEW YORK	NY	10010	(212) 696-4944
FREELAND LEAGUE FOR JEWISH TERRITORIAL COLONIZATION 200 WEST 72ND STREET	NEW YORK	NY	10023	
INTERNATIONAL LEAGUE FOR REPATRIATION OF RUSSIAN JEWS 315 CHURCH STREET	NEW YORK	NY	10013	(212) 431-6789
JEWISH RESTITUTION SUCCESSOR ORGANIZATION 15-19 EAST 26TH STREET	NEW YORK	NY	10010	
JOINT DISTRIBUTION COMMITTEE 60 EAST 42ND STREET	NEW YORK	NY	10165	(212) 687-6200
NORTH AMERICAN CONFERENCE ON ETHIOPIAN JEWRY 165 EAST 56TH STREET	NEW YORK	NY	10022	(212) 752-6340
RELIEF COMMITTEE OF GENERAL JEWISH WORKERS - POLAND 25 EAST 78TH STREET	NEW YORK	NY	10021	
UNITED HIAS SERVICE 200 PARK AVENUE SOUTH	NEW YORK	NY	10003	(212) 674-6800
UNITED JEWISH APPEAL 1290 AVENUE OF THE AMERICAS	NEW YORK	NY	10019	(212) 757-1500
WOMEN'S SOCIAL SERVICE FOR ISRAEL 240 WEST 98TH STREET	NEW YORK	NY	10025	(212) 666-7880
AMERICAN ASSOCIATION FOR ETHIOPIAN JEWS 340 CORLIES AVENUE	PELHAM	NY	10803	(914) 738-0956

PASSOVER PRODUCTS

Name / Address	City	State	Zip	Phone
SCHWARTZ PASSOVER BAKERY 431 NORTH FAIRFAX AVENUE	LOS ANGELES	CA	90036	(213) 653-2106
B. MANISCHEWITZ CO. 9 CLINTON STREET	JERSEY CITY	NJ	07302	(201) 333-3700
ADWE LABS 141 20TH STREET	BROOKLYN	NY	11232	(718) 788-6838
BELZER SHMURA MATZOH BAKERY 4312 NEW UTRECHT AVENUE	BROOKLYN	NY	11219	(718) 854-0597
CONGREGATION YETEV LEV MATZOH BAKERY 152 RODNEY	BROOKLYN	NY	11230	(718) 384-7449
GOLDBERG'S GROCERY/THE PESACH STORE 5021 18TH AVENUE	BROOKLYN	NY	11204	(718) 435-7177
PUPOVER MATZAH BAKERY 658 BEDFORD AVENUE	BROOKLYN	NY	11211	
SATMAR MATZOH BAKERY 427 BROADWAY	BROOKLYN	NY	11211	
SCHICK'S BAKERY 4710 16TH AVENUE	BROOKLYN	NY	11219	(718) 436-8020
SHATZER MATZOS 210 CORTELYOU ROAD	BROOKLYN	NY	11230	(718) 435-2873
HOROWITZ MARGARETEN COMPANY 29-00 REVIEW AVENUE	LONG ISLAND CITY	NY	11101	(718) 729-5420
FREEDA VITAMINS 36 EAST 41ST STREET	NEW YORK	NY	10017	(212) 685-8980
GERTEL'S BAKERY 53 HESTER STREET	NEW YORK	NY	10002	(212) 982-3250
JOINT PASSOVER ASSOCIATION 197 EAST BROADWAY	NEW YORK	NY	10002	(212) 260-6360
JOINT PASSOVER ASSOCIATION OF THE CITY OF NEW YORK 235 PARK AVENUE SOUTH	NEW YORK	NY	10003	(212) 586-2900
STREIT MATZO COMPANY 150 RIVINGTON STREET	NEW YORK	NY	10002	(212) 475-7000
FOODTOWN PASSOVER STORE 123 FROST STREET	WESTBURY	NY	11590	(516) 334-9730
JEWISH RELIEF SOCIETY 1775 SOUTH TAYLOR ROAD	CLEVELAND	OH	44118	(216) 321-3650

PEN PALS

Name / Address	City	State	Zip	Phone
INTERNATIONAL JEWISH CORRESPONDENCE/CORRESPONDANCE JUIVE INTERNATIONALE 1590 AVE. DR. PENFIELD	MONTREAL	QU	H3G 1C5	

PERIODICALS - HISTORICAL & SCHOLARLY

Name / Address	City	State	Zip	Phone
SHIRIM-A JEWISH POETRY JOURNAL C/O HILLEL EXTENSION 900 HILGARD AVE.	LOS ANGELES	CA	90024	
SIMON WIESENTHAL CENTER ANNUAL 9760 W. PICO BLVD.	LOS ANGELES	CA	90035	(213) 553-9036
WESTERN STATES JEWISH HISTORICAL QUARTERLY 2429 23RD STREET	SANTA MONICA	CA	90405	
AMERICAN JEWISH HISTORICAL QUARTERLY 2 THORNTON ROAD	WALTHAM	MA	02154	(617) 891-8110
MICHIGAN JEWISH HISTORY 1036 WHITNEY BUILDING	DETROIT	MI	48226	
LIKKUTEI SICHOT (SCHOLARLY-LUBAVITCH) 784 EASTERN PARKWAY	BROOKLYN	NY	11213	(718) 774-7200
SICHOS IN ENGLISH 784 EASTERN PARKWAY	BROOKLYN	NY	11213	(718) 778-5436
JEWISH SOCIAL STUDIES 2112 BROADWAY	NEW YORK	NY	10025	(212) 724-5336
PROCEEDINGS OF THE AMERICAN ACADEMY OF JEWISH RESEARCH 3080 BROADWAY	NEW YORK	NY	10027	
YIVO ANNUAL OF JEWISH SOCIAL SCIENCE 1048 FIFTH AVENUE	NEW YORK	NY	10028	(212) 535-6700
AMERICAN JEWISH ARCHIVES 3101 CLIFTON AVENUE	CINCINNATI	OH	45220	(513) 221-1875
STUDIES IN BIBLIOGRAPHY & BOOKLORE 3101 CLIFTON AVENUE	CINCINNATI	OH	45220	(513) 221-1875
CANADIAN JEWISH HISTORICAL SOCIETY JOURNAL 150 BEVERLY STREET	TORONTO	ON	M5T 1Y6	
JEWISH QUARTERLY REVIEW BROAD AND YORK STREETS	PHILADELPHIA	PA	19132	(215) 229-0110
RHODE ISLAND JEWISH HISTORICAL NOTES 209 ANGELL STREET	PROVIDENCE	RI	02906	(401) 331-0956

PERIODICALS - ISRAELI & ISRAEL-CENTERED

Name / Address	City	State	Zip	Phone
ISRAEL TODAY 16661 VENTURA BOULEVARD	ENCINO	CA	91396	(818) 786-4000
NEAR EAST REPORT 444 NORTH CAPITOL	WASHINGTON	DC	20005	(202) 638-1225
AMERICAN ZIONIST 515 PARK AVENUE	NEW YORK	NY	10016	(212) 371-7750
HADOAR 220 PARK AVENUE SOUTH	NEW YORK	NY	10003	(212) 581-5151
HISTADRUT 33 EAST 67TH STREET	NEW YORK	NY	10021	(212) 628-1000
ISRAEL HORIZONS 150 FIFTH AVENUE	NEW YORK	NY	10011	(212) 255-8760
ISRAEL JOURNAL OF MEDICAL SCIENCES 114 EAST 32ND STREET	NEW YORK	NY	10018	(212) 889-8040

PERIODICALS - YIDDISH & FOREIGN LANGUAGE

Name / Address	City	State	Zip	Phone
MACCABEE PUBLISHING 14 WEST FOREST AVENUE	ENGLEWOOD	NJ	07631	(201) 569-8700
DE YIDDISH HEIM / THE JEWISH HOME 770 EASTERN PARKWAY	BROOKLYN	NY	11213	(718) 493-0571
DER YID 543 BEDFORD AVENUE	BROOKLYN	NY	11211	(718) 782-4900
MESORAH PUBLICATIONS 1969 CONEY ISLAND AVENUE	BROOKLYN	NY	11223	(718) 339-1700
SHMUESSEN MIT KINDER UN YUGENT 770 EASTERN PARKWAY	BROOKLYN	NY	11213	(718) 774-4000
ASSOCIATION OF JEWISH ANTI-POVERTY WORKERS 141 EAST 44TH STREET, ROOM 802	NEW YORK	NY	10017	(212) 686-2777
BNAI YIDDISH 22 EAST 17TH STREET	NEW YORK	NY	10003	
DER WECKER 175 EAST BROADWAY	NEW YORK	NY	10002	
DOS YIDDISHE VORT 84 WILLIAM STREET	NEW YORK	NY	10038	(212) 797-9000
KINDER ZEITUNG 41 UNION SQUARE WEST	NEW YORK	NY	10003	
KULTURE UN LEBN 175 EAST BROADWAY	NEW YORK	NY	10002	
NCSY/ORTHODOX UNION 45 WEST 36TH STREET	NEW YORK	NY	10018	(212) 563-4000
OYFN SHVEL 200 WEST 72ND STREET	NEW YORK	NY	10023	
UNSER TSAIT 25 EAST 21 STREET	NEW YORK	NY	10010	(212) 505-8040
VISTA CORE, JEWISH ASSOCIATION FOR COLLEGE YOUTH 30 WEST 60TH STREET	NEW YORK	NY	10023	
YIVO BLETER 1048 FIFTH AVENUE	NEW YORK	NY	10028	(212) 535-6700
YIDDISHE KULTUR 1123 BROADWAY	NEW YORK	NY	10011	(212) 691-0708
YIDISHE SHPRAKH 1048 FIFTH AVENUE	NEW YORK	NY	10028	(212) 535-6700
ZUKUNFT 25 EAST 21 STREET	NEW YORK	NY	10010	(212) 505-8040
UNDZER VEG 272 CODSELL AVENUE	TORONTO	ON		

PHOTOGRAPHERS

Name / Address	City	State	ZIP	Phone
BILL ARON PHOTOGRAPHY 1227 SOUTH HI POINT	LOS ANGELES	**CA**	90035	(213) 934-0426
STEVE GOLDBERG P.O. BOX 493	HALLANDALE	**FL**	33009	(305) 940-6629
ROBERT CUMINS 140 HEPBURN STREET, SUITE 14A	CLIFTON	**NJ**	07012	(201) 778-9279
SUE STEMBER 8 HONEY BROOK DRIVE	PRINCETON	**NJ**	08540	(609) 737-2380
AKSELRUD STUDIOS 1160 EAST 24TH STREET	BROOKLYN	**NY**	11210	(718) 338-6536
AURA STUDIOS LTD. 819 KINGS HIGHWAY	BROOKLYN	**NY**	11223	(718) 627-6969
ELITE PHOTOGRAPHERS LTD. 516 KINGS HIGHWAY	BROOKLYN	**NY**	11223	(718) 627-0499
FOCUS STUDIO (ABRAHAM HOLD) 4419 13TH AVENUE	BROOKLYN	**NY**	11219	
LIONEL STUDIO 1723 AVENUE M	BROOKLYN	**NY**	11230	(718) 252-0702
MORGEN STUDIOS (SHLOMO STROH) 4411 16TH AVENUE	BROOKLYN	**NY**	11204	(718) 435-0323
NISSEN STUDIO & RECORDING (SHLOMO NISSEN) 200 ROSS STREET	BROOKLYN	**NY**	11211	(718) 384-0205
ONLY WEDDINGS (SID PERRIS) 1716 EAST 7TH STREET	BROOKLYN	**NY**	11223	(718) 627-8956
OSCAR ISRAELOWITZ P.O. BOX 228	BROOKLYN	**NY**	11229	(718) 951-7072
PHOTO CREATIONS 4702 18TH AVENUE	BROOKLYN	**NY**	11204	(718) 851-5077
PHOTOGRAPHIC ELEGANCE BY SHALOM NEUMANN 5521 13TH AVENUE	BROOKLYN	**NY**	11219	(718) 633-6403
ROYAL PHOTOGRAPHY - YISROEL FERBER 5513 12TH AVENUE	BROOKLYN	**NY**	11219	(718) 436-3823
SILVIO BUCHRIS: PHOTOGRAPHER 3021 AVENUE I	BROOKLYN	**NY**	11210	(718) 377-4518
TRAINER STUDIO 5321 13TH AVENUE	BROOKLYN	**NY**	11219	(718) 851-0600
ZELMAN STUDIOS 623 CORTELYOU ROAD	BROOKLYN	**NY**	11218	(718) 941-5500
JERRY MEYERS STUDIOS 147-53 77TH ROAD	FLUSHING	**NY**	11367	(718) 591-7079
FIRST ROW VIDEO (MARK HERSLY) 99-15 66TH AVENUE	FOREST HILLS	**NY**	11374	(718) 275-0768
BATYA AND ROCHEL	MONSEY	**NY**	10952	(914) 356-3540
LENI SONNENFELD 552 RIVERSIDE DRIVE	NEW YORK	**NY**	10027	(212) 222-0445
THREE STAR PHOTOGRAPHERS LTD.	STATEN ISLAND	**NY**		(718) 494-3249
VILLAGE STUDIO 1 DUTCH COURT	WEST NYACK	**NY**	10994	(914) 353-0412

PLAQUES

Name / Address	City	State	ZIP	Phone
ARCHITECTURAL BRONZE & ALUMINUM CORPORATION 3638 OAKTON STREET	SKOKIE	**IL**	60076	(312) 674-3638
EMANUEL MILSTEIN 29 WYNCREST ROAD	MARLBORO	**NJ**	07746	(201) 946-8604
BRONZE ARTS & CRAFTS CO. 1135 36TH STREET	BROOKLYN	**NY**	11218	(718) 853-5010
W. & E. BAUM BRONZE TABLET CORP. 200 60TH STREET	BROOKLYN	**NY**	11220	(800) 922-7377
W. & E. BAUM BRONZE TABLET CORP. 200 60TH STREET	BROOKLYN	**NY**	11220	(718) 439-3311
BEN ARI ARTS LTD. 11 AVENUE A	NEW YORK	**NY**	10009	(212) 677-4730
GENE SINGER ARTS 577 GRAND ST	NEW YORK	**NY**	10002	(212) 673-9669
IN THE SPIRIT 460 EAST 79TH STREET	NEW YORK	**NY**	10021	(212) 662-6693
MICHAEL STRAUSS SILVERSMITHS, LTD. 164 EAST 68TH STREET	NEW YORK	**NY**	10021	(212) 744-8500
UNITED STATES BRONZE SIGN COMPANY 101 WEST 31ST STREET	NEW YORK	**NY**	10001	(212) 563-5670
EMES EDITIONS LIMITED 2001 LEVICK STREET	PHILADELPHIA	**PA**	19149	(215) 288-8787

POLITICAL ORGANIZATIONS

Name / Address	City	State	ZIP	Phone
AMERICAN ISRAEL PUBLIC AFFAIRS COMMITTEE (AIPAC) 500 NORTH CAPITOL STREET NORTHWEST, SUITE 300	WASHINGTON	**DC**	20001	(202) 638-2256
NATIONAL JEWISH COALITION 415 SECOND STREET NORTHEAST, SUITE 100	WASHINGTON	**DC**	20002	(202) 547-7701
MIPAC 303 CHARAL LANE	HIGHLAND PARK	**IL**	60035	(312) 433-4685
AIPAC NEW YORK REGIONAL OFFICE 370 LEXINGTON AVENUE	NEW YORK	**NY**	10017	(212) 557-2408
CONFERENCE OF PRESIDENTS OF MAJOR AMERICAN JEWISH ORGANIZATIONS 515 PARK AVENUE	NEW YORK	**NY**	10022	(212) 752-1616

POOR & ELDERLY, AID FOR THE

Name / Address	City	State	ZIP	Phone
FREDA MOHR CENTER 330 NORTH FAIRFAX	LOS ANGELES	**CA**	90024	(213) 937-5901
COUNCIL FOR JEWISH ELDERLY 1415 WEST MORSE	CHICAGO	**IL**	60645	(312) 973-6065
COUNCIL FOR THE JEWISH ELDERLY 1 SOUTH FRANKLIN STREET	CHICAGO	**IL**	60606	(312) 973-6065
THE ARK 2341 W. DEVON	CHICAGO	**IL**	60659	(312) 973-1000
COUNCIL FOR JEWISH ELDERLY 1015 W. HOWARD STREET	EVANSTON	**IL**	60202	(312) 973-4105
JEWISH COUNCIL FOR THE AGING 6111 MONTROSE ROAD	ROCKVILLE	**MD**	20852	
JEWISH ASSOCIATION FOR SERVICES FOR THE AGED 3450 DEKALB AVENUE	BRONX	**NY**	10467	(212) 231-1234
JEWISH ASSOCIATION FOR SERVICES FOR THE AGED 2488 GRAND CONCOURSE	BRONX	**NY**	10458	(212) 365-4044
BOARD FOR LEGAL ASSISTANCE - JEWISH POOR 130 CLINTON STREET	BROOKLYN	**NY**	11201	
COLEL TIFERES ZKEINIM - LEVI YITZCHAK 779 EASTERN PARKWAY	BROOKLYN	**NY**	11213	(718) 778-4270
JEWISH ASSOCIATION FOR SERVICES FOR THE AGED 575 BEDFORD AVENUE	BROOKLYN	**NY**	11211	(718) 387-6695
JEWISH ASSOCIATION FOR SERVICES FOR THE AGED 555 REMSEN AVENUE	BROOKLYN	**NY**	11236	(718) 385-0010
JEWISH ASSOCIATION FOR SERVICES FOR THE AGED 2410 SURF AVENUE	BROOKLYN	**NY**	11224	(718) 449-9600
JEWISH ASSOCIATION FOR SERVICES FOR THE AGED 242 GRAHAM AVENUE	BROOKLYN	**NY**	11206	(718) 384-3354
JEWISH ASSOCIATION FOR SERVICES FOR THE AGED 202 GRAHAM AVENUE	BROOKLYN	**NY**	11206	(718) 388-6865
JEWISH ASSOCIATION FOR SERVICES FOR THE AGED 2211 CHURCH AVENUE	BROOKLYN	**NY**	11226	(718) 693-7606
JEWISH ASSOCIATION FOR SERVICES FOR THE AGED 158 3RD STREET	MINEOLA	**NY**	11501	(516) 742-2050
CENTRAL BUREAU FOR THE JEWISH AGED 130 EAST 59TH STREET	NEW YORK	**NY**	10022	(212) 308-7316
COUNCIL FOR THE JEWISH POOR 141 E. 44 SUITE 802	NEW YORK	**NY**	10017	
DOROT 251 WEST 100TH STREET	NEW YORK	**NY**	10025	(212) 864-7410
JEWISH ASSOCIATION FOR SERVICES FOR THE AGED 40 WEST 68TH STREET	NEW YORK	**NY**	10023	(212) 724-3200
JEWISH ASSOCIATION FOR SERVICES FOR THE AGED 222 PARK AVENUE S	NEW YORK	**NY**	10003	(212) 677-2530

Name / Address	City	State	ZIP	Phone
JEWISH POVERTY COORDINATING COUNCIL 15 PARK ROW	NEW YORK	**NY**	10038	(212) 267-9500
METROPOLITAN N.Y. COORDINATING COUNCIL OF JEWISH POVERTY 9 MURRAY STREET	NEW YORK	**NY**	10007	(212) 267-9500
PROJECT EZRA 197 EAST BROADWAY	NEW YORK	**NY**	10002	(212) 982-3700

POSTERS

Name / Address	City	State	ZIP	Phone
HEINLE & HEINLE ENTERPRISES 29 LEXINGTON ROAD	CONCORD	**MA**	01742	(617) 369-7525
JEWISH COMMUNITY CENTER 633 SALISBURY STREET	WORCESTER	**MA**	01609	(617) 756-7109
THE EXHUMATION PO BOX 2057	PRINCETON	**NJ**	08540	(609) 921-2339
GOLDEN GRAPHICS INC. 35 BRIDLE PATH	GREAT NECK	**NY**	11021	(516) 482-4282
CENTRAL CONFERENCE OF AMERICAN RABBIS 21 EAST 40TH STREET	NEW YORK	**NY**	10021	(212) 684-4990
EL AL ISRAEL AIRLINES 850 THIRD AVENUE	NEW YORK	**NY**	10022	(212) 940-0708
ISRAEL GOVERNMENT TOURIST OFFICE 350 FIFTH AVENUE, 19TH FLOOR	NEW YORK	**NY**	10118	(212) 560-0650
ISRAEL OFFICE OF INFORMATION, JEWISH AGENCY 515 PARK AVENUE	NEW YORK	**NY**	10022	(212) 752-0600
NATIONAL CONFERENCE ON SOVIET JEWRY 10 EAST 40TH STREET	NEW YORK	**NY**	10016	(212) 679-6122
ROLNICK PUBLISHERS 295 MADISON AVENUE, SUITE 1001	NEW YORK	**NY**	10017	(212) 557-5637
YIVO INSTITUTE FOR JEWISH RESEARCH 1048 FIFTH AVENUE	NEW YORK	**NY**	10028	(212) 535-6700

PREPARED FOODS

Name / Address	City	State	ZIP	Phone
LOMA LINDA FOODS 11503 PIERCE STREET	RIVERSIDE	**CA**	92515	(714) 687-7800
HEBREW NATIONAL KOSHER FOOD 625 SOUTH SANTA FE	SANTA ANA	**CA**	92705	(714) 558-8651
SUPERVISED PRODUCTS 3890 ADAMS STREET, PO BOX 16432	DENVER	**CO**	80216	(303) 321-7033
POSINS 5756 GEORGIA AVENUE, N.W.	WASHINGTON	**DC**	20011	(202) 726-4424
EVERYTHING'S KOSHER 1344 WASHINGTON AVENUE	MIAMI BEACH	**FL**	33139	(305) 672-4154
PARAMOUNT BAKERY 1407 WASHINGTON AVENUE	MIAMI BEACH	**FL**	33139	(305) 534-2683
KOSHER TREATS 1678 N.E. 164TH STREET	NORTH MIAMI BEACH	**FL**	33162	(305) 947-1800
SPECIALTY FOOD SALES 2619 23RD AVENUE NORTH	ST. PETERSBURG	**FL**	33713	(813) 321-3847
HUNGARIAN KOSHER SAUSAGE COMPANY 2613 WEST DEVON AVENUE	CHICAGO	**IL**	60659	(312) 973-5991
NEW YORK KOSHER SAUSAGE 2900 W. DEVON AVENUE	CHICAGO	**IL**	60659	(312) 743-1664
SINAI KOSHER SAUSAGE CORP. 1000 WEST PERSHING ROAD	CHICAGO	**IL**	60601	(312) 927-2810
KOSHER GOURMET 3552 W. DEMPSTER	SKOKIE	**IL**	60076	(312) 679-0432
SIMCHA'S SIMCHAS 3552 W. DEMPSTER	SKOKIE	**IL**	60076	(312) 679-0432
MYER'S KOSHER KITCHEN 168 SHIRLEY AVENUE	REVERE	**MA**	02151	(617) 289-2063
THE KNISH SHOP 508 REISTERSTOWN ROAD	BALTIMORE	**MD**	21208	(301) 484-5850
BLUEFELD'S BUTLER'S PANTRY 401 REISTERSTOWN ROAD	PIKESVILLE	**MD**	21208	(301) 486-2100
SCHLEIDER CATERERS OF GREATER WASHINGTON	ROCKVILLE	**MD**		(301) 881-3787
EPSTEIN KOSHER FOODS 403 WEST 79TH STREET	KANSAS CITY	**MO**	64114	(816) 361-0200
SCHANDLER'S PICKLE BARREL 50 BROADWAY	ASHEVILLE	**NC**	28801	(704) 253-5626
GOODWILL PANTRY CATERING 815 BROADWAY	BAYONNE	**NJ**	07002	(201) 339-2392
INTERMILO, INC. 185 LINDEN STREET	HACKENSACK	**NJ**	07601	(201) 488-4242
DEER PARK BAKING COMPANY	HAMMONTON	**NJ**	08037	(609) 561-2900
LEGUME INC. 170 CHANGE BRIDGE ROAD	MONTVILLE	**NJ**	07045	(201) 882-9190
TABATCHNICK SOUPS 2951 VAUXHALL ROAD	VAUXHALL	**NJ**	07088	(201) 687-6447
ZANIO'S EGG MARKET 308 MENAUL ROAD	ALBUQUERQUE	**NM**	87107	(505) 843-9292

MAUZONE HOME KOSHER PRODUCTS 61-36 SPRINGFIELD BOULEVARD... BAYSIDE **NY** 11361 (212) 225-1188
KINGSBRIDGE KOSHER KITCHEN, INC. 58 W. KINGSBRIDGE ROAD .... BRONX **NY** 10468 (212) 584-5688
MRS. WEINBERG'S FOOD PRODUCTS CORP. 1303 HERSCHELL .... BRONX **NY** 10461 (212) 824-6940
ZION KOSHER DELICATESSEN & RESTAURANT 750 LYDIG AVENUE .... BRONX **NY** 10469 (212) 597-6360
APPETIZING KING 4924 13TH AVENUE .... BROOKLYN **NY** 11219 (718) 854-5075
ERBA FOOD PRODUCTS 624 COURT STREET .... BROOKLYN **NY** 11231 (718) 522-1800
ISRAEL'S TAKE HOME FOODS 409 BRIGHTON BEACH AVENUE .... BROOKLYN **NY** 11235
KENERETH GLATT KOSHER CATERERS 1920 AVENUE D .... BROOKLYN **NY** 11226 (718) 743-2473
LEON & MARK TAKE HOME FOODS 1877 ROCKAWAY PARKWAY .... BROOKLYN **NY** 11236
MATZLIACH GOURMET 1922 CONEY ISLAND AVENUE .... BROOKLYN **NY** 11230 (718) 375-8666
MEAL MART 206 DIVISION AVENUE .... BROOKLYN **NY** 11211 (718) 963-3450
MEAL MART 510 BRIGHTON BEACH AVENUE .... BROOKLYN **NY** 11235 (718) 769-6800
MEAL MART 4621 13TH AVENUE .... BROOKLYN **NY** 11219 (718) 854-7800
MEAL MART 54 LEE AVENUE .... BROOKLYN **NY** 11211 (718) 387-1445
MEAL MART 128 LEE AVENUE .... BROOKLYN **NY** 11211 (718) 855-9368
MEAL MART 4410 FT. HAMILTON PARKWAY .... BROOKLYN **NY** 11219 (718) 853-3900
MEAL MART 1101 BRIGHTON BEACH AVENUE .... BROOKLYN **NY** 11235 (718) 769-6800
MEAL MART 1920 AVENUE M .... BROOKLYN **NY** 11230 (718) 998-0800
MEAL MART 5417 NEW UTRECHT AVENUE .... BROOKLYN **NY** 11219 (718) 851-8800
MEAL MART 502 FLUSHING AVENUE .... BROOKLYN **NY** 11211 (718) 855-9600
MEAL MART 1412 AVENUE J .... BROOKLYN **NY** 11230 (718) 338-8100
MEAL MART 4722 16TH AVENUE .... BROOKLYN **NY** 11219 (718) 871-5335
MELROSE TAKE HOME FOODS 924 KINGS HIGHWAY .... BROOKLYN **NY** 11223 (718) 336-7500
MELROSE TAKE HOME FOODS 407 BRIGHTON BEACH AVENUE .... BROOKLYN **NY** 11235
MRS. ADLER'S FOOD CORPORATION 902 ESSEX STREET .... BROOKLYN **NY** 11208 (718) 649-9121
NEGEV KOSHER HOMEMADE FOOD 1211 AVENUE J .... BROOKLYN **NY** 11230 (718) 258-8440
NOAM GOURMET, INC. 392 CLASSON AVENUE .... BROOKLYN **NY** 11238 (718) 230-3371
OLD FASHIONED KITCHENS FOODS 401 MARCY AVENUE .... BROOKLYN **NY** 11211 (718) 388-1132
ONEG TAKE HOME FOODS 4911 12TH AVENUE .... BROOKLYN **NY** 11219 (718) 438-3388
SAY CHICKEN 1681 EAST 16TH STREET .... BROOKLYN **NY** 11229 (718) 627-1615
SCHECHTER'S TAKE HOME FOODS 509 BRIGHTON BEACH AVENUE ..... BROOKLYN **NY** 11235 (718) 743-5900
SCHREIBER CATERERS 9024 FOSTER AVENUE .... BROOKLYN **NY** 11236 (718) 272-9184
SEUDA FOODS 705 KINGS HIGHWAY .... BROOKLYN **NY** 11223 (718) 375-1500
TAAM KOSHER PRODUCTS 344 AVENUE Y .... BROOKLYN **NY** 11235 (718) 376-5400
TAM-GAN EDEN 1780 RALPH AVENUE .... BROOKLYN **NY** 11236 (718) 241-6102
TOV UMAITIV - GLATT ORIENTAL & AMERICAN 401 AVENUE M .... BROOKLYN **NY** 11230 (718) 377-1900
TUVIA'S TAKE OUT 1813 KINGS HIGHWAY .... BROOKLYN **NY** 11229 (718) 627-8626
MAZEL TAKE HOME FOODS 119 CEDARHURST AVENUE .... CEDARHURST **NY** 11516 (516) 569-1666
KING DAVID KNISHES 67-07 MAIN STREET .... FLUSHING **NY** 11367 (718) 268-1734
MAUZONE HOME KOSHER PRODUCTS 69-60 MAIN STREET .... FLUSHING **NY** 11367 (718) 261-7723
MEAL MART 72-10 MAIN STREET .... FLUSHING **NY** 11367 (718) 261-3300
NEW FOREST TAKE HOME FOODS 64-20 108TH STREET .... FOREST HILLS **NY** 11375 (718) 275-9793
KOSHER KONSULTANTS 64 HALSTEAD AVENUE .... HARRISON **NY** 10528 (914) 835-4700

HOROWITZ BROTHERS & MARGARETEN
29-00 REVIEW AVENUE .... LONG ISLAND CITY **NY** 11106 (718) 729-5420
KOSHER KONNECTION 1284 NORTH AVENUE .... NEW ROCHELLE **NY** 10804 (914) 636-5636
KOSHER DESSERTS, INC. 8 W. 28TH STREET .... NEW YORK **NY** 10001 (212) 685-4672
LEIBEL BISTRITZKY 27-1/2 ESSEX STREET .... NEW YORK **NY** 10002 (212) 254-0335
MEAL MART 2180 BROADWAY .... NEW YORK **NY** 10024 (212) 787-4720
MEAL MART 4403 BROADWAY .... NEW YORK **NY** 10033 (212) 568-7401
YONAH SCHIMMEL'S KNISHES BAKERY 137 E. HOUSTON STREET .... NEW YORK **NY** 10002 (212) 477-2858
MEAL MART MAIN STREET .... SOUTH FALLSBURG **NY** 12779 (914) 434-3689
WILTON FOODS INC./WILTON CATERERS, INC.
710 SOUTH MAIN STREET .... SPRING VALLEY **NY** 10977 (914) 352-4800
KOSHER ISLAND TAKE HOME FOODS 2206 VICTORY BLVD. .... STATEN ISLAND **NY** 10314 (718) 698-5800
MEAL MART .... SWAN LAKE **NY** 12783 (914) 292-9439
PERL'S 3013 BATHURST STREET .... TORONTO **ON** (416) 787-4234
STROLI'S 3459 BATHURST STREET .... TORONTO **ON** (416) 789-5333
RHAWNHURST 8261 BUSTLETON AVENUE .... PHILADELPHIA **PA** 19152 (215) 742-5287
ALBER & LEFF FOOD COMPANY 405 COLLEGE AVENUE .... PITTSBURGH **PA** 15237 (412) 321-7700
CANTON & SMOLAR COMPANY 1816 BEDFORD AVENUE .... PITTSBURGH **PA** 15212 (412) 261-4777
MILLER'S DELICATESSEN 776 HOPE STREET .... PROVIDENCE **RI** 02906 (401) 521-0368

PRINTERS & PRINT SERVICES

SWEN COMMUNICATIONS, INC. 214 WEST FIRST STREET .... SYLACAUGA **AL** 35150 (205) 245-3236
LETTER PERFECT 396 NEW BRIDGE ROAD .... BERGENFIELD **NJ** 07621 (201) 387-2006
GOTTLIEB TORAH GRAPHICS 406 YESHIVA PLAZA .... LAKEWOOD **NJ** 08701 (201) 363-8025
BEEHIVE PRESS 3609 BOSTON ROAD .... BRONX **NY** 10466 (212) 654-1200
DAVE'S PRINTING 1279 44TH STREET .... BROOKLYN **NY** 11219 (718) 853-1919
FINK GRAPHICS 1406 45TH STREET .... BROOKLYN **NY** 11219 (718) 438-4148
GOLDSTEIN PRESS 4602 16TH AVENUE .... BROOKLYN **NY** 11204 (718) 853-7444
HADDAR PRINTING 195 LEE AVENUE .... BROOKLYN **NY** 11211 (718) 384-4249
M&M PRINTING LTD. 170 MARCY AVENUE .... BROOKLYN **NY** 11211 (718) 338-3942
MASH PRINTING 1305 43RD STREET .... BROOKLYN **NY** 11219 (718) 436-1543
MODERN LINOTYPE COMPANY 371 EAST 98TH STREET .... BROOKLYN **NY** 11212 (718) 498-7580
NATIONAL PRINTING & STATIONERY 5314 13TH AVENUE .... BROOKLYN **NY** 11219 (718) 438-7200
SHALLER PRINTERS .... BROOKLYN **NY** 11230 (718) 859-0281
TOVA PRESS INC. 945 39TH STREET .... BROOKLYN **NY** 11219 (718) 438-8877
TOWER TYPE 1319 58TH STREET .... BROOKLYN **NY** 11219 (718) 438-1102
JUDAH H. KLEIN ASSOCIATES, COMMUNICATIONS
433 BARNARD AVENUE, SUITE 100 .... CEDARHURST **NY** 11516 (516) 295-5646
KLASS PUBLICATIONS, INC. 112 BROADWAY .... MALVERNE **NY** 11565 (516) 887-7878
ARTSCROLL STUDIOS .... MONSEY **NY** 10952 (914) 352-2207
ALILEAH PRESS C/O ALPERT, 60 EAST 12TH STREET .... NEW YORK **NY** 10003 (212) 777-0163
ENQUIRE PRINTING & PUBLISHING CO. 601 WEST 54TH STREET .... NEW YORK **NY** 10019 (212) 581-5050
GOLDMARK GROUP, THE 137 WEST 25TH STREET .... NEW YORK **NY** 10001 (212) 691-7111
KETER INC. 475 FIFTH AVENUE .... NEW YORK **NY** 10017 (212) 889-7750
KING TYPOGRAPHIC SERVICE 300 PARK AVENUE SOUTH, 3RD FLOOR ... NEW YORK **NY** 10010 (212) 254-7421
MENORAH PRINTING COMPANY 51 WEST 21ST STREET .... NEW YORK **NY** 10010 (212) 691-2050
OLIVESTONE PUBLISHING SERVICES 137 WEST 25TH STREET .... NEW YORK **NY** 10001 (212) 691-8420
SOLOGRAPHIC PHOTOCOMPOSITION SERVICE
137 WEST 25TH STREET .... NEW YORK **NY** 10001 (212) 924-9300
INVITATIONS PLUS 600 WEST 246TH STREET .... RIVERDALE **NY** 10471 (212) 548-3900
INVITATIONS PLUS 600 WEST 246TH STREET .... RIVERDALE **NY** 10471 (800) INV-PLUS

PRISONERS ASSISTANCE

COMMITTEE FOR JEWISH PRISONERS PO BOX 31265 .... SAN FRANCISCO **CA** 94131
BNAI BRITH COMMISSION ON COMMUNITY AND VETERANS SERVICE
1640 RHODE ISLAND AVENUE N.W. .... WASHINGTON **DC** 20036 (202) 857-6600
THE ALEPH INSTITUTE 420 LINCOLN ROAD, SUITE 335 .... MIAMI BEACH **FL** 33139 (305) 674-8794
NORTH SHORE JEWISH COMMUNITY CENTER C/O ROBERTA KALECHOFSKY
2 COMMUNITY ROAD .... MARBLEHEAD **MA** 01945 (617) 631-8338
AMERICAN JEWISH CORRECTIONAL CHAPLAINS ASSOCIATION
10 E. 73RD STREET .... NEW YORK **NY** 10021 (212) 879-8415
JEWISH BOARD OF GUARDIANS, VOLUNTEER SERVICES DEPARTMENT
120 WEST 57TH STREET .... NEW YORK **NY** 10019 (212) 582-9100
JEWISH IDENTITY CENTER-UNION OF JEWISH PRISONERS
1133 BROADWAY, SUITE 302 .... NEW YORK **NY** 10010
NAT'L COUNCIL OF JEWISH WOMEN-JUSTICE FOR CHILDREN TASK FORCE
1 WEST 47TH STREET .... NEW YORK **NY** 10036 (212) 532-1740
ALLENWOOD JEWISH CONGREGATION PO BOX 1000 .... MONTGOMERY **PA** 17752

PROFESSIONAL ORGANIZATIONS

HEBREW TEACHERS FEDERATION PO BOX 824 .... VAN NUYS **CA** 91408 (818) 980-2191
INTERNATIONAL ASSOCIATION OF HILLEL DIRECTORS
5715 SOUTH WOODLAWN AVENUE .... CHICAGO **IL** 60637 (312) 752-1127
JEWISH FUNERAL DIRECTORS OF AMERICA 1170 ROCKVILLE PIKE ...... ROCKVILLE **MD** 20852 (301) 340-1400
NAT'L ASSOC. OF JEWISH FAMILY, CHILDREN'S & HEALTH PROF.
24123 GREENFIELD .... SOUTHFIELD **MI** 48075 (313) 559-1500
ASSOCIATION OF ORTHODOX JEWISH TEACHERS
1577 CONEY ISLAND AVENUE .... BROOKLYN **NY** 11230 (718) 258-3586
ASSOCIATION OF ORTHODOX JEWS IN COMMUNICATIONS
973 EAST 10TH STREET .... BROOKLYN **NY** 11230 (718) 258-4268
NATIONAL JEWISH CIVIL SERVICE EMPLOYEES P.O. BOX 525 .... BROOKLYN **NY** 11202 (718) 646-8366
AMERICAN ASSOCIATION OF PROFESSORS OF YIDDISH
A1309 QUEENS COLLEGE .... FLUSHING **NY** 11367 (718) 520-7067
JEWISH ALLIANCE OF BUSINESSMEN 10-25 44TH AVENUE .... LONG ISLAND CITY **NY** 11101 (718) 937-9813
ASSOCIATION OF JEWISH CLERGYMEN P.O. BOX 317 .... MONSEY **NY** 10952 (914) 352-0630

AMERICAN ACADEMIC ASSOCIATION FOR PEACE IN THE MIDDLE EAST
9 EAST 40TH STREET ... NEW YORK **NY** 10016 (212) 532-5085
AMERICAN JEWISH CORRECTIONAL CHAPLAINS ASSOCIATION
10 EAST 73RD STREET ... NEW YORK **NY** 10021 (212) 879-8415
AMERICAN JEWISH PUBLIC RELATIONS SOCIETY 234 FIFTH AVENUE ... NEW YORK **NY** 10001 (212) 697-5895
ASSOCIATION OF JEWISH ANTI-POVERTY WORKERS
18 E. 41ST STREET, ROOM 806 ... NEW YORK **NY** 10017 (212) 686-2777
ASSOCIATION OF JEWISH BOOK PUBLISHERS 1646 FIRST AVENUE ... NEW YORK **NY** 10028 (212) 799-6517
ASSOCIATION OF JEWISH BOOK PUBLISHERS 838 FIFTH AVENUE ... NEW YORK **NY** 10021 (212) 249-0100
ASSOCIATION OF JEWISH CENTER WORKERS 15 E. 26TH STREET ... NEW YORK **NY** 10010 (212) 532-4949
ASSOCIATION OF JEWISH CHAPLAINS OF THE ARMED FORCES - JWB
15 EAST 26TH STREET ... NEW YORK **NY** 10010 (212) 532-4949
ASSOCIATION OF JEWISH COMMUNITY RELATIONS WORKERS
155 FIFTH AVENUE ... NEW YORK **NY** 10010 (212) 533-7800
ASSOCIATION OF ORTHODOX JEWISH NURSES 116 E. 27TH STREET ... NEW YORK **NY** 10016 (212) 889-1364
ASSOCIATION OF ORTHODOX JEWISH SCIENTISTS
45 WEST 36TH STREET ... NEW YORK **NY** 10018 (212) 695-7525
ASSOCIATION OF ORTHODOX JEWISH TEACHERS 3 W. 16TH STREET ... NEW YORK **NY** 10011 (212) 436-0440
DIAMOND DEALERS ALLIANCE, INC. 580 FIFTH AVENUE ... NEW YORK **NY** 10036 (212) 757-4589
DIAMOND DEALERS CLUB, INC. 11 WEST 47TH STREET ... NEW YORK **NY** 10036 (212) 869-9555
EDUCATORS COUNCIL OF AMERICA 500 WEST 185TH STREET ... NEW YORK **NY** 10033 (212) 940-5262
GOVERNMENT BUREAU FOR ISRAELI PROFESSIONALS
800 SECOND AVENUE ... NEW YORK **NY** 10017 (212) 986-6360
HEBREW ACTORS UNION 31 E. SEVENTH STREET ... NEW YORK **NY** 10003 (212) 674-1923
HEBREW BUTCHERS UNION - LOCAL 50 27 UNION SQUARE ... NEW YORK **NY** 10003 (212) 255-3400
JEWISH FUNERAL DIRECTORS OF AMERICA 122 E. 42ND STREET ... NEW YORK **NY** 10168 (212) 370-0024
JEWISH OCCUPATIONAL COUNCIL 114 FIFTH AVENUE ... NEW YORK **NY** 10011
JEWISH POSTAL WORKERS WELFARE LEAGUE 363 7TH AVENUE ... NEW YORK **NY** 10001 (212) 594-1488
JEWISH TEACHER'S ASSOCIATION 45 E. 33RD STREET ... NEW YORK **NY** 10016 (212) 684-0556
JEWISH THEATRICAL GUILD 1501 BROADWAY ... NEW YORK **NY** 10036 (212) 221-1848
KASHRUTH SUPERVISOR'S UNION LOCAL 621 37 UNION SQUARE ... NEW YORK **NY** 10003 (212) 691-9494
NATIONAL ASSOCIATION OF JEWISH CENTER WORKERS
15 E. 26TH STREET ... NEW YORK **NY** 10010 (212) 532-4949
NATIONAL ASSOCIATION OF JEWISH VOCATIONAL SERVICES
386 PARK AVENUE ... NEW YORK **NY** 10022 (212) 685-8355
NATIONAL CONFERENCE OF JEWISH COMMUNAL SERVICE
15 EAST 26TH STREET ... NEW YORK **NY** 10010
NATIONAL CONFERENCE OF YESHIVA PRINCIPALS 160 BROADWAY ... NEW YORK **NY** 10038 (212) 406-4190
YESHIVA ENGLISH PRINCIPALS ASSOCIATION 426 WEST 58TH STREET .. NEW YORK **NY** 10019 (212) 245-8200
NATIONAL ASSOCIATION OF JEWISH LEGISLATORS
45 THORNDALE ROAD ... SLINGERLANDS **NY** 12159 (518) 439-9597
INTERNATIONAL ASSOCIATION OF HILLEL DIRECTORS
611 LANGDON STREET ... MADISON **WI** 53703 (608) 256-8361
WORLD FEDERATION OF JEWISH JOURNALISTS
SOKOLOV HOUSE, 4 KAPLAN STREET, P.O. BOX 7009 ... TEL AVIV **IS** (03) 255588

PUBLISHERS

UNIVERSITY OF ALABAMA PRESS BOX 2877 ... UNIVERSITY **AL** 35486 (205) 348-6010
UNIVERSITY OF ARIZONA PRESS 1615 EAST SPEEDWAY BOULEVARD ... TUCSON **AZ** 85719 (602) 621-1441
BEN MIR BOOKS 570 VISTAMONT AVE ... BERKELEY **CA** 94708 (415) 527-0282
HAMOROH PRESS P.O. BOX 48862 ... LOS ANGELES **CA** 90048
TZE ULMAD PRESS 10573 WEST PICO BOULEVARD ... LOS ANGELES **CA** 90064 (213) 558-3958
JOSEPH SIMON/PANGLOSS PRESS P.O. BOX 4071 ... MALIBU **CA** 90265 (213) 457-3293
EKS PUBLISHING CO. 5336 COLLEGE AVENUE ... OAKLAND **CA** 94618 (415) 653-5183
UNIVERSITY OF CALIFORNIA PRESS 1428 HARBOUR WAY SOUTH ... RICHMOND **CA** 94804 (415) 231-9400
ALTERNATIVES IN RELIGIOUS EDUCATION, INC.
3945 SOUTH ONEIDA STREET ... DENVER **CO** 80237 (303) 363-7779
PRAYER BOOK PRESS, THE 1363 FAIRFIELD AVENUE ... BRIDGEPORT **CT** 06605 (203) 384-2284
YALE UNIVERSITY PRESS 92A YALE STATION ... NEW HAVEN **CT** 06520 (203) 436-8926
B'NAI B'RITH YOUTH ORGANIZATION
1640 RHODE ISLAND AVENUE N.W. ... WASHINGTON **DC** 20036 (202) 857-6633
UNIVERSITY OF IOWA PRESS GRAPHIC SERVICES BUILDING ... IOWA CITY **IA** 52242 (319) 353-2121
UNIVERSITY OF ILLINOIS PRESS
54 EAST GREGORY DRIVE, BOX 5081 - STATION A ... CHAMPAIGN **IL** 61820 (217) 333-0950
FLYING FISH RECORDS ... CHICAGO **IL** (312) 528-5455
UNIVERSITY OF CHICAGO PRESS 5801 SOUTH ELLIS AVENUE ... CHICAGO **IL** 60637 (312) 962-7700
INDIANA UNIVERSITY PRESS 10TH AND MORTON STREETS ... BLOOMINGTON **IN** 47405 (812) 335-4203
DAVID R. GODINE 306 DARTMOUTH ST ... BOSTON **MA** 02116 (617) 536-0761
MICAH PUBLICATIONS 255 HUMPHREY STREET ... MARBLEHEAD **MA** 01945 (617) 631-7601
THE BEATE KLARSFELD FOUNDATION BOX 157 ... SOUTH DEERFIELD **MA** 01373 (617) 948-8733
WOODBINE HOUSE 10400 CONNECTICUT AVENUE, SUITE 512 ... KENSINGTON **MD** 20895 (301) 949-3590
KAR-BEN COPIES 6800 TILDENWOOD LANE ... ROCKVILLE **MD** 20852 (301) 984-8733
UNIVERSITY OF NORTH CAROLINA PRESS PO BOX 2288 ... CHAPEL HILL **NC** 27514 (919) 966-3561
ASHLEY PUBLICATIONS 263 VETERANS ROAD ... CARLSTADT **NJ** 07072 (201) 935-1113
MACCABEE PUBLISHING HOUSE 14 WEST FOREST AVENUE ... ENGLEWOOD **NJ** 07631 (201) 569-8700
KTAV PUBLISHING HOUSE 900 JEFFERSON ST. PO BOX 6249 ... HOBOKEN **NJ** 07030 (201) 963-9524
M.P. PRESS 317 ST. PAULS AVENUE ... JERSEY CITY **NJ** 07306 (201) 656-9173
CIS COMMUNICATIONS, INC. 674 8TH STREET ... LAKEWOOD **NJ** 08701 (201) 367-7858
CIS COMMUNICATIONS, INC. 674 8TH STREET ... LAKEWOOD **NJ** 08701 (201) 364-1629
SHIMON EIDER PUBLICATIONS 418 TWELFTH STREET ... LAKEWOOD **NJ** 08701 (201) 363-3965
FAIRLEIGH DICKINSON UNIVERSITY PRESS 285 MADISON AVENUE ... MADISON **NJ** 07940 (201) 377-4700
PAULIST PRESS 997 MACARTHUR BOULEVARD ... MAHWAH **NJ** 07430 (201) 825-7300
JASON ARONSON INC. 230 LIVINGSTON STREET ... NORTHVALE **NJ** 07647 (201) 767-4093
BRISTOL, RHEIN & ENGLANDER 301 NORTH HARRISON STREET ... PRINCETON **NJ** 08540 (201) 364-1629
BRISTOL, RHEIN & ENGLANDER 301 NORTH HARRISON STREET ... PRINCETON **NJ** 08540 (201) 367-7858
OPTIONS PUBLISHING BOX 311 ... WAYNE **NJ** 07470 (201) 694-2327
M.P. PRESS 231 HACKENSACK PLANK RD. ... WEEHAWKEN **NJ** 07087 (201) 867-4700
BEHRMAN HOUSE 235 WATCHUNG AVENUE ... WEST ORANGE **NJ** 07052 (201) 669-0447

AURA PUBLISHING COMPANY (JEWISH JUVENILE)
1549 57TH STREET ... BROOKLYN **NY** 11219 (718) 435-9103
CENTER FOR HOLOCAUST STUDIES 1609 AVENUE J ... BROOKLYN **NY** 11230 (718) 338-6494
CHEMED BOOKS & CO., INC. 915 EAST 17TH STREET, APT. 111 ... BROOKLYN **NY** 11230 (718) 253-2112
HEBREW PUBLISHING COMPANY 100 WATER STREET ... BROOKLYN **NY** 11201 (718) 858-6902
JEP (JEWISH EDUCATION PROGRAM) PUBLICATIONS
425 EAST 9TH STREET ... BROOKLYN **NY** 11218 (718) 941-2600
JEWISH COMBATANTS PUBLISHERS HOUSE P. O. BOX 323 ... BROOKLYN **NY** 11236
KEHOT PUBLICATIONS SOCIETY 770 EASTERN PARKWAY ... BROOKLYN **NY** 11213 (718) 774-4000
MERKOS L'INYONEI CHINUCH 770 EASTERN PARKWAY ... BROOKLYN **NY** 11213 (718) 774-4000
MESORAH PUBLICATIONS 1969 CONEY ISLAND AVENUE ... BROOKLYN **NY** 11223 (718) 339-1700
MOZNAIM PUBLISHING CORPORATION 4304 TWELFTH AVENUE ... BROOKLYN **NY** 11219 (718) 438-7680
OTZAR HACHASSIDIM 770 EASTERN PARKWAY ... BROOKLYN **NY** 11213 (718) 774-4000
SEPHER-HERMON PRESS 1265 46TH STREET ... BROOKLYN **NY** 11219 (718) 972-9010
TRADITIONAL PRESS, INC. 1306 40TH STREET ... BROOKLYN **NY** 11218 (718) 435-4411
ZUNDEL BERMAN BOOKS 4520 17TH AVENUE ... BROOKLYN **NY** 11204
TARA PUBLICATIONS 29 DERBY AVENUE ... CEDARHURST **NY** 11516 (516) 295-2290
BOOK NOOK PUBLICATIONS 1525 CENTRAL AVENUE ... FAR ROCKAWAY **NY** 11691 (718) 327-0163
HASHKAFAH PUBLICATIONS 68-61 SELFRIDGE STREET ... FOREST HILLS **NY** 11375 (718) 261-6076
BIBLIO PRESS P.O. BOX 22 ... FRESH MEADOWS **NY** 11365
ORBIS BOOKS ... MARYKNOLL **NY** 10545 (914) 941-7590
DECALOGUE BOOKS 7 NORTH MACQUESTEN PARKWAY ... MOUNT VERNON **NY** 10550 (914) 664-7944
THE BIBLIOPHILE LIBRARY 145 SUSSEX ROAD ... NEW ROCHELLE **NY** 10801 (914) 633-0501
ADAMA BOOKS 306 W. 38TH ST. ... NEW YORK **NY** 10018 (212) 594-5770
ALFRED A. KNOPF, INC. 201 EAST 50TH STREET ... NEW YORK **NY** 10022 (212) 751-2600
AMERICAN JEWISH COMMITTEE-INST. OF HUMAN RELATIONS PRESS
165 E. 56TH STREET ... NEW YORK **NY** 10022 (212) 751-4000
AMERICAN MIZRACHI WOMEN 817 BROADWAY ... NEW YORK **NY** 10016
ANTI-DEFAMATION LEAGUE OF B'NAI B'RITH
823 UNITED NATIONS PLAZA ... NEW YORK **NY** 10017 (212) 490-2525
ASSOCIATION OF JEWISH BOOK PUBLISHERS 838 FIFTH AVENUE ... NEW YORK **NY** 10021 (212) 249-0100
ASSOCIATION OF JEWISH BOOK PUBLISHERS 1646 FIRST AVENUE ... NEW YORK **NY** 10028 (212) 799-6517
BANTAM BOOKS 666 FIFTH AVENUE ... NEW YORK **NY** 10019 (212) 765-6500
BASIC BOOKS, INC. 10 EAST 53RD STREET ... NEW YORK **NY** 10022 (212) 207-7057
BLOCH PUBLISHING COMPANY 19 WEST 21ST STREET ... NEW YORK **NY** 10010 (212) 989-9104
CENTRAL CONFERENCE OF AMERICAN RABBIS 21 E. 40TH STREET ... NEW YORK **NY** 10010 (212) 684-4990
CLARION BOOKS 52 VANDERBILT AVENUE ... NEW YORK **NY** 10017 (212) 972-1192
COLUMBIA UNIVERSITY PRESS 562 W. 113TH ST. ... NEW YORK **NY** 10025 (212) 316-7130
CONGRESS FOR JEWISH CULTURE & CYCO PUBLISHERS
25 E. 78TH STREET ... NEW YORK **NY** 10021 (212) 879-2232
DODD, MEAD & COMPANY 79 MADISON AVENUE ... NEW YORK **NY** 10016 (212) 685-6464
DOUBLEDAY & COMPANY, INC. 245 PARK AVENUE ... NEW YORK **NY** 10167 (212) 984-7561
E.P. DUTTON 2 PARK AVENUE ... NEW YORK **NY** 10016 (212) 725-1818
EMET-RABBI HERZOG WORLD ACADEMY 122 W. 76TH STREET ... NEW YORK **NY** 10023 (212) 435-0115
FARRAR, STRAUS & GIROUX 19 UNION SQ. WEST ... NEW YORK **NY** 10003 (212) 741-6900
GARLAND PUBLISHING 136 MADISON AVENUE ... NEW YORK **NY** 10016 (212) 686-7492
GREENWILLOW BOOKS 105 MADISON AVENUE ... NEW YORK **NY** 10016 (212) 889-3050
HARPER & ROW 10 E. 53RD STREET ... NEW YORK **NY** 10010 (212) 593-7000
HERZL PRESS 515 PARK AVENUE ... NEW YORK **NY** 10022 (212) 752-0600
HIPPOCRENE BOOKS, INC. 171 MADISON AVENUE ... NEW YORK **NY** 10016 (212) 685-4371
HOLIDAY HOUSE 18 EAST 53RD STREET ... NEW YORK **NY** 10022 (218) 688-0085
HOLMES & MEIER PUBLISHING INC. IUB BUILDING, 30 IRVING PLACE ... NEW YORK **NY** 10003 (212) 254-4100

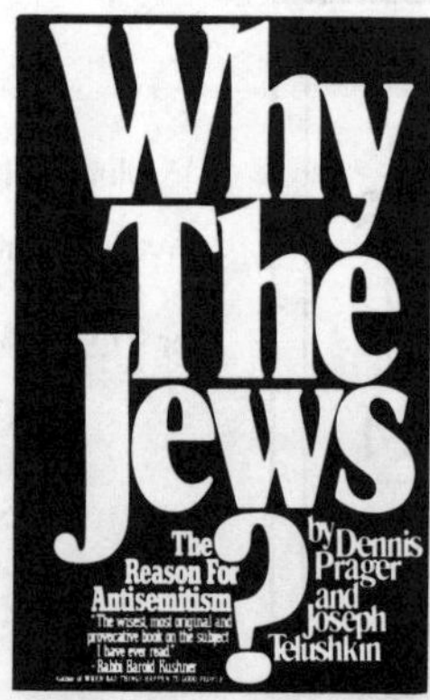
Why
The
Jews
?
The
Reason For
Antisemitism
by Dennis
Prager
and
Joseph
Telushkin

Name / Address	City	State	Zip	Phone
HOLOCAUST LIBRARY 216 WEST 18TH STREET	NEW YORK	NY	10011	(212) 691-9220
HOLOCAUST PUBLICATIONS, INC. 216 WEST 18TH STREET	NEW YORK	NY	10011	(212) 691-9220
JWB JEWISH BOOK COUNCIL 15 EAST 26TH STREET	NEW YORK	NY	10010	(212) 532-4949
JEWISH EDUCATION OF GREATER NEW YORK 426 WEST 58TH STREET	NEW YORK	NY	10019	(212) 245-8200
JEWISH MUSEUM 1109 FIFTH AVENUE	NEW YORK	NY	10028	(212) 860-1888
JEWISH PUBLICATION SOCIETY OF AMERICA 60 EAST 42ND STREET	NEW YORK	NY	10017	(212) 687-0809
JEWISH RADIO THEATER 175 FIFTH AVENUE	NEW YORK	NY	10010	
JEWISH THEOLOGICAL SEMINARY 3080 BROADWAY	NEW YORK	NY	10020	(212) 678-8074
JUDAICA PRESS INC. 521 FIFTH AVENUE	NEW YORK	NY	10175	(212) 260-0520
JUDAICA PRESS INC. 5 ESSEX STREET	NEW YORK	NY	10002	(212) 505-8900
KETER PUBLICATIONS, INC. 475 FIFTH AVENUE	NEW YORK	NY	10017	(212) 889-7750
KINDERBUCH PUBLICATIONS 1133 BROADWAY, ROOM 1023	NEW YORK	NY	10010	
LEO BAECK INSTITUTE, INC. 129 EAST 73RD STREET	NEW YORK	NY	10021	(212) 744-6400
MCGRAW-HILL INC. 1221 AVENUE OF THE AMERICAS	NEW YORK	NY	10020	(212) 512-2000
MENDY PUBLICATIONS 450 SEVENTH AVENUE	NEW YORK	NY	10001	(212) 410-1155
MENORAH RECORD DISTRIBUTORS 36 ELDRIDGE STREET	NEW YORK	NY	10002	(212) 925-7573
NCSY/OU PUBLICATIONS 45 WEST 36TH STREET	NEW YORK	NY	10018	(212) 563-4000
NEW AMERICAN LIBRARY, INC. 1633 BROADWAY	NEW YORK	NY	10019	(212) 397-8000
NEW YORK UNIVERSITY PRESS 70 WASHINGTON SQ. SOUTH	NEW YORK	NY	10012	(212) 598-2886
NEWMARKET PRESS 18 EAST 48TH STREET	NEW YORK	NY	10017	(212) 832-3575
PACIFIC PRESS 295 MADISON AVENUE, SUITE 1228	NEW YORK	NY	10017	(212) 687-0500
PANTHEON BOOKS 201 E. 50TH ST.	NEW YORK	NY	10022	(212) 751-2600
PHILLIP FELDHEIM, INC. 96 EAST BROADWAY	NEW YORK	NY	10002	(212) 925-3180
PHILOSOPHICAL LIBRARY 200 W. 57TH ST.	NEW YORK	NY	10019	(212) 265-6050
PILGRIM PRESS 132 WEST 31ST ST	NEW YORK	NY	10018	(212) 594-8555
POCKET BOOKS SIMON & SCHUSTER BUILDING-1230 AVENUE OF THE AMERICAS	NEW YORK	NY	10020	(212) 246-2121
REBECCA BENNET PUBLICATIONS, INC. 5409 18TH AVENUE	NEW YORK	NY	11204	(212) 256-1954
RECONSTRUCTIONIST PRESS 270 WEST 89TH STREET	NEW YORK	NY	10024	(212) 496-2960
SACRED MUSIC PRESS, HUC-JIR 1 W. 4TH STREET	NEW YORK	NY	10012	(212) 873-0388
ST. MARTIN'S PRESS 175 FIFTH AVENUE	NEW YORK	NY	10010	(212) 674-5151
SCARF PRESS 58 EAST 83RD STREET	NEW YORK	NY	10028	(212) 744-3901
SCHOCKEN BOOKS, INC. 200 MADISON AVENUE	NEW YORK	NY	10016	(212) 685-6500
SHAPOLSKY PUBLISHERS, INC. 56 EAST 11TH STREET	NEW YORK	NY	10003	(212) 505-2505
SHENGOLD PUBLISHERS, INC. 23 W. 45TH STREET	NEW YORK	NY	10036	(212) 944-2555
SIMON & SCHUSTER 1230 AVENUE OF THE AMERICAS	NEW YORK	NY	10020	(212) 245-6400
SONCINO 5 ESSEX STREET	NEW YORK	NY	10002	(212) 505-8900
SUMMIT BOOKS 1230 AVE. OF THE AMERICAS	NEW YORK	NY	10020	(212) 246-2471
TIMES BOOKS 201 EAST 50TH STREET	NEW YORK	NY	10022	(212) 751-2600
UNION OF AMERICAN HEBREW CONGREGATIONS 838 FIFTH AVENUE	NEW YORK	NY	10021	(212) 249-0100
UNITED SYNAGOGUE BOOK SERVICE 155 FIFTH AVENUE	NEW YORK	NY	10010	(212) 533-7800
VIKING PENGUIN, INC. 40 W. 23RD ST.	NEW YORK	NY	10010	(212) 807-7300
WOMEN'S LEAGUE FOR CONSERVATIVE JUDAISM 48 EAST 74TH STREET	NEW YORK	NY	10021	(212) 628-1600
WORKMEN'S CIRCLE PUBLICATIONS 45 EAST 33RD STREET	NEW YORK	NY	10016	(212) 889-6800
YIVO INSTITUTE FOR JEWISH RESEARCH 1048 FIFTH AVENUE	NEW YORK	NY	10028	(212) 535-6700
YESHIVA UNIVERSITY PRESS 500 WEST 185TH STREET	NEW YORK	NY	10033	(212) 960-5400
ZIONTALIS/BOOK DIVISION 48 ELDRIDGE STREET	NEW YORK	NY	10002	(212) 925-8558
PHILIPP FELDHEIM INC. 200 AIRPORT EXECUTIVE PARK	SPRING VALLEY	NY	10977	(914) 356-2282
SYRACUSE UNIVERSITY PRESS 1600 JAMESVILLE AVENUE	SYRACUSE	NY	13210	(315) 423-1870
SIMCHA PUBLISHING COMPANY, INC. 1 COVE DRIVE	WOODMERE	NY	11598	(516) 569-0830
WRITERS DIGEST BOOKS 9933 ALLIANCE ROAD	CINCINNATI	OH	45242	(513) 984-0717
HEBREW ACADEMY OF CLEVELAND PUBLISHING HOUSE 1860 SOUTH TAYLOR ROAD	CLEVELAND HEIGHTS	OH	44118	
SETH PRESS 221 ARGYLE ROAD	ARDMORE	PA	19003	(215) 642-8633
INSTITUTE FOR THE STUDY OF HUMAN ISSUES 3401 MARKET STREET, SUITE 252	PHILADELPHIA	PA	19104	(215) 387-9002
JEWISH PUBLICATION SOCIETY OF AMERICA 1930 CHESTNUT STREET	PHILADELPHIA	PA	19103	(215) 564-5925
SINISTER WISDOM BOOKS P.O. BOX 1308M	MONTPELIER	VT	05602	(802) 229-9104
UNIVERSITY OF WISCONSIN PRESS 114 NORTH MURRAY STREET	MADISON	WI	53715	(608) 262-4928

PUBLISHERS - ISRAEL

MASSADA PUBLISHERS, LTD/PELI PRINTING WORKS, LTD. 11-15 TFUTSOT ISRAEL	GIVATAYIM	IS	53583	(03) 740-811
ARTSCROLL JERUSALEM BINYAN HACLAL ROOM 346	JERUSALEM	IS		(02) 244-032
BIALIK INSTITUTE, THE PO BOX 92	JERUSALEM	IS	91920	(02) 227-189
CARTA, THE ISRAEL MAP AND PUBLISHING COMPANY 4/6 YAD HARUTZIM ST, INDUSTRIAL ZONE, TALPIOT, POB 2500	JERUSALEM	IS	92014	(02) 713536
DOMINO PRESS, LTD., THE P.O. BOX 4143	JERUSALEM	IS	94041	(02) 660-868
HARRY FISCHEL INSTITUTE FOR RESEARCH IN JEWISH LAW ISRAEL AHARON FISCHEL STREET, P.O. BOX 16002	JERUSALEM	IS		(02) 286-453
ISRAEL ACADEMY OF SCIENCES & HUMANITIES P.O. BOX 4040	JERUSALEM	IS	91040	(02) 636-211
ISRAEL EXPLORATION SOCIETY 3 SHMUEL HANAGID STREET, P.O. BOX 7041	JERUSALEM	IS	91070	(02) 227-991
JERUSALEM PUBLISHING HOUSE, LTD., THE 39 TCHERNICHOVSKY STREET, P.O. BOX 7147	JERUSALEM	IS	91071	(02) 667-744

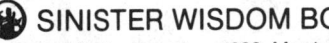

KETER PUBLISHING HOUSE JERUSALEM, LTD.
INDUSTRIAL ZONE, GIVAT SHAUL B, P.O. BOX 7145 .... JERUSALEM **IS** 91071 (02) 521-201
LA SEMANA PUBLISHING CO. LTD. P.O. BOX 2427 .... JERUSALEM **IS** 91023 (02) 636-765
MAGNES PRESS, THE THE HEBREW UNIVERSITY .... JERUSALEM **IS** 91904 (02) 660-341
MASSADA PRESS, LTD. 46 BETHLEHEM ROAD, P.O. BOX 1232 .... JERUSALEM **IS** 91012
SHIKMONA PUBLISHING COMPANY, LTD.
33 HERZOG STREET, P.O. BOX 4044 .... JERUSALEM **IS** 91040 (02) 660-188
VAN LEER JERUSALEM FOUNDATION, THE P.O. BOX 4070 .... JERUSALEM **IS** 91040
WEIZMANN SCIENCE PRESS OF ISRAEL, THE
8A HORKANIA, P.O. BOX 801 .... JERUSALEM **IS** 91007 (02) 663-203
ZALMAN SHAZAR CENTRE 22 RASHBA STREET, P.O. BOX 4179 .... JERUSALEM **IS** 91041 (02) 637-171
MASSADA PRESS, LTD. 21 JABOTINSKY ROAD, P.O. BOX 3154 .... RAMAT GAN **IS** 52131 (03) 734-203
SETTLEMENT STUDY CENTER (SSC) P.O. BOX 2355 .... REHOVOT **IS** 76120 (05) 474-111
BOOK PUBLISHERS ASSOCIATION OF ISRAEL, THE
29 CARLEBACH STREET, P.O. BOX 20123 .... TEL AVIV **IS** 61201
BOOK AND PRINTING CENTER OF THE ISRAEL EXPORT INSTITUTE
29 HAMERED STREET, P.O. BOX 50084 .... TEL AVIV **IS** 68125 (03) 630-858
GAALYAH CORNFELD PUBLISHERS 185 HAYARKON STREET .... TEL AVIV **IS** 63453 (03) 221-737
I.L. PERETZ PUBLISHING 14 BRENNER ST. .... TEL AVIV **IS** 65246 (03) 281-751
INSTITUTE FOR THE TRANSLATION OF HEBREW LITERATURE, LTD., THE
66 SHLOMO HAMELECH STREET .... TEL AVIV **IS** 64511 (03) 244-879
ISRAEL MUSIC INSTITUTE 6 CHEN BLVD., P.O. BOX 11253 .... TEL AVIV **IS** 61112 (03) 284-397
MINISTRY OF DEFENCE PUBLISHING HOUSE
27 DAVID ELAZAR STREET, HAKIRYA, P.O. BOX 7103 .... TEL AVIV **IS** 67673 (03) 217-940
MOSADOT PUBLICATIONS, INC. 6 BEN ZION BLVD .... TEL AVIV **IS** 64285 (03) 295-479
R. SIRKIS PUBLISHERS 131 BIALIK STREET, RAMAT GAN, P.O. BOX 22027 .. TEL AVIV **IS** 61220 (03) 731-796
SADAN PUBLISHING HOUSE, LTD. 1 DAVID HAMELECH STREET .... TEL AVIV **IS** 64953 (03) 267-543
SHILOAH CENTER FOR MIDDLE EASTERN & AFRICAN STUDIES
TEL AVIV UNIVERSITY, RAMAT AVIV, PO BOX 39012 .... TEL AVIV **IS** 69978 (03) 420-646
SIFRIAT POALIM 2 HOMA U'MIGDAL .... TEL AVIV **IS** (03) 623-622
SINAI PUBLISHING 72 ALLENBY ROAD .... TEL AVIV **IS** (03) 623-622
STEIMATZKY, LTD. P.O. BOX 628 .... TEL AVIV **IS** 61006 (03) 612-060
TAMMUZ PUBLISHING HOUSE, LTD
3 TCHERNICHOVSKY STREET, PO BOX 23029 .... TEL AVIV **IS** 63291 (03) 657-868
TERRA SANCTA ARTS, LTD. 522 DIZENGOFF CENTER, P.O. BOX 10009 .... TEL AVIV **IS** 61100 (03) 289-630
YACHDAV UNITED PUBLISHERS COMPANY 29 CARLEBACH STREET .... TEL AVIV **IS** 67132 (03) 284-191

PUPPETRY

RED RUG PUPPET THEATRE, BETH KATZ, PUPPETEER
434 BUTTERFIELD DRIVE .... EAST LANSING **MI** 48823 (517) 332-8442
ROBERT BINDER, B'YAD HAYOTZER 24 WARWICK AVENUE .... TORONTO **ON** M6C 1T6 (416) 979-3393

RABBINICAL ORGANIZATIONS

RABBINICAL COUNCIL OF CALIFORNIA 24413 HENDRICKS AVENUE .... LOMITA **CA** 90717 (213) 326-8234
BOARD OF RABBIS 6505 WILSHIRE BLVD .... LOS ANGELES **CA** 90048 (213) 852-1234
BOARD OF RABBIS OF NORTHERN CALIFORNIA
121 STUART, ROOM 403 .... SAN FRANCISCO **CA** 94105 (415) 788-3630
DENVER RABBINICAL COUNCIL 3614 SOUTH IVORY COURT .... AURORA **CO** 80013 (303) 690-4108
BRIDGEPORT BOARD OF RABBIS 85 ARLINGTON STREET .... BRIDGEPORT **CT** 06606
BRIDGEPORT BOARD OF RABBIS 1200 FAIRFIELD WOODS ROAD .... FAIRFIELD **CT** 06430
RABBINICAL COUNCIL 7826 EASTERN AVENUE N.W. .... WASHINGTON **DC** 20036 (202) 291-6052
BRIT AMERICA - ASSOCIATION OF CERTIFIED MOHALIM .... DELRAY BEACH **FL** (800) 367-2748
RABBINICAL ASSOCIATION OF MIAMI 4200 BISCAYNE BLVD .... MIAMI **FL** 33137 (305) 576-4000
CHICAGO BOARD OF RABBIS ONE SOUTH FRANKLIN .... CHICAGO **IL** 60606 (312) 444-2896

ORTHODOX UNION MEMBERSHIP IS YOUR INVESTMENT IN:

30,000 youth served by NCSY in **400** Regional Youth Events and Seminars ☐ **4** Jerusalem Experiences ☐ **50,000** visitors in the Jerusalem Israel Center ☐ **7** Free Torah High Schools ☐ **1,000** participants in *Yachad* for the developmentally disabled and *Our Way* for the Jewish deaf ☐ **100** adult Shabbatons, Retreats, Lectures, Yarchei Kallah ☐ **20,000** products Ⓤ certified ☐ **9** national publications reaching **500,000** families including Jewish Action Magazine and Kashruth Directories ☐ **12** new synagogues ☐ **4,000** participants in Singles Programs ☐ **30,000** books distributed ☐ **280** Israel Summer Seminar, Cross Country Torah Tour, Jewish Overseas Leadership and Camp NCSY participants ☐ Public Affairs, Political Action and a central voice for **1,200** synagogues ☐ **13** full time regional offices

ALL IMPACTING ON HUNDREDS OF THOUSANDS OF LIVES

Yes . . . I wish to be a partner in the Ⓤ by joining in the membership category I have checked:

☐ $36 BASIC MEMBERSHIP
includes:

- ***Jewish Action Magazine,*** published quarterly, containing articles on Jewish living and contemporary issues and the latest Kashruth and public affairs information.
- ***Two Kosher Directories,*** *Kosher Directory* listing by food category over 20,000 products supervised by the Orthodox Union and the annual *Passover Directory.*
- ***Pocket Calendar Diary,*** bound in leatherette, containing an expanded prayer section and other vital information.

☐ $50 SUPPORTING MEMBER
includes:

- Jewish Action • Kosher Directories
- Pocket Calendar Diary

AND

- *Jerusalem The Eye of the Universe*

by Rabbi Aryeh Kaplan explaining the significance of Jerusalem, and the source of its holiness.

☐ $72 SUBSCRIBING MEMBER
(includes):

- Jewish Action • Kosher Directories
- Pocket Calendar Diary • *Jerusalem The Eye of the Universe* AND
- Luach Limud Torah Diary

A one year enrollment in one of the largest Torah Home Study Programs of its kind. The Diary, published monthly, offers a program of day-to-day Mishnah Study and a full day-by-day guide to Jewish practices and observances.

Please consider enrolling in one of the special categories below, which in addition to the above benefits gives you the extra satisfaction of further strengthening the activities of the Orthodox Union.

☐ $100 DONOR MEMBER

☐ $180 PATRON MEMBER

☐ $250 ENDOWING MEMBER

☐ $500 CONTRIBUTING MEMBER

☐ $1,000 UNION ASSOCIATE

As a member you will be invited to National Convention and other events such as National or Regional Dinners, Retreats, Shabbatons, Lectures or Congressional Breakfasts.

CHICAGO RABBINICAL COUNCIL 3525 W. PETERSON AVENUE ... CHICAGO **IL** 60659 (312) 588-1600
MERKAZ HARABONIM 6500 N. CALIFORNIA AVENUE ... CHICAGO **IL** 60645 (312) 761-3800
AMERICAN ASSOCIATION OF RABBIS 705 W. WILDWOOD AVENUE ... FORT WAYNE **IN** 46807
JEWISH CHAPLAINCY COUNCIL 177 TREMONT STREET ... BOSTON **MA** 02111 (617) 426-1832
MASSACHUSETTS BOARD OF RABBIS 177 TREMONT STREET ... BOSTON **MA** 02115 (617) 426-2139
MASSACHUSETTS COUNCIL OF RABBIS 611 WASHINGTON STREET ... BOSTON **MA** 02111 (617) 426-9148
ORTHODOX RABBINICAL COUNCIL OF GREATER BOSTON 611 WASHINGTON STREET, ROOM 507 ... BOSTON **MA** 02111 (617) 426-9148
RABBINICAL COUNCIL OF MASSACHUSETTS (VAAD HARABONIM) 177 TREMONT STREET ... BOSTON **MA** 02111 (617) 426-2139
COUNCIL OF ORTHODOX RABBIS OF DETROIT 17071 W. TEN MILE ROAD ... SOUTHFIELD **MI** 48075 (313) 559-5005
MINNESOTA RABBINICAL ASSOCIATION; TEMPLE OF AARON CONG. 616 S. MISSISSIPPI RIVER BLVD ... ST. PAUL **MN** 55116 (612) 698-8874
ST. LOUIS RABBINICAL ASSOCIATION 1251 GUELBRETH LANE ... ST. LOUIS **MO** 63146 (314) 432-2103
ST. LOUIS RABBINICAL COUNCIL 4 MILLSTONE CAMPUS DRIVE ... ST. LOUIS **MO** 63146 (314) 569-2770
VAAD HOEIR OF ST. LOUIS 4 MILLSTONE CAMPUS DRIVE ... ST. LOUIS **MO** 63146 (314) 569-2770
CENTRAL RABBINICAL CONGRESS OF U.S. AND CANADA 85 DIVISION AVENUE ... BROOKLYN **NY** 11211 (718) 384-6765
INTERNATIONAL RABBINICAL COUNCIL 4000 MANHATTAN AVENUE ... BROOKLYN **NY** 11224 (718) 372-4863
KNESSET HORABONIM RABBINICAL SOCIETY 1537 41ST STREET ... BROOKLYN **NY** 11218 (718) 871-1754
LIKUTEI HALACHOS 537 EAST 4TH STREET ... BROOKLYN **NY** 11218 (718) 633-3521
NATIONAL ASSOCIATION OF RABBIS P.O. BOX 111 ... BROOKLYN **NY** 11219 (718) 853-3273
NATIONAL COMMITTEE ORTHODOX JEWISH COMMUNITIES 260 BROADWAY ... BROOKLYN **NY** 11211 (718) 936-1911
RABBINICAL BOARD OF BAY RIDGE 4723 SEVENTH AVENUE ... BROOKLYN **NY** 11220 (718) 633-6378
RABBINICAL BOARD OF FLATBUSH 1575 CONEY ISLAND AVENUE ... BROOKLYN **NY** 11230 (718) 951-8585
VAAD HARABONIM OF FLATBUSH 1575 CONEY ISLAND AVENUE ... BROOKLYN **NY** 11230 (718) 951-8585
VAAD RABONEI LUBAVITCH 333A KINGSTON AVENUE ... BROOKLYN **NY** 11213 (718) 493-4061
ATID-UNITED SYNAGOGUE OF AMERICA 155 FIFTH AVENUE ... NEW YORK **NY** 10010 (212) 533-7800
AGUDATH HORABONIM-UNION OF ORTHODOX RABBIS OF U.S. & CANADA 235 EAST BROADWAY ... NEW YORK **NY** 10002 (212) 964-6337
AMERICAN ASSOCIATION OF RABBIS 350 FIFTH AVENUE ... NEW YORK **NY** 10001 (212) 244-3350
AMERICAN JEWISH CORRECTIONAL CHAPLAINS ASSOCIATION 10 E. 73RD STREET ... NEW YORK **NY** 10021 (212) 879-8415
ASSOCIATION OF JEWISH CHAPLAINS OF THE ARMED FORCES 15 E. 26TH STREET ... NEW YORK **NY** 10010 (212) 532-4949
CENTRAL CONFERENCE OF AMERICAN RABBIS 21 E. 40TH STREET ... NEW YORK **NY** 10016 (212) 684-4990
COMMISSION ON JEWISH CHAPLAINCY 15 E. 26TH STREET ... NEW YORK **NY** 10010 (212) 532-4949
COUNCIL OF YOUNG ISRAEL RABBIS 3 W. 16TH STREET ... NEW YORK **NY** 10011 (212) 929-1525
JEWISH MINISTERS CANTORS ASSOCIATION OF AMERICA 3 W. 16TH STREET ... NEW YORK **NY** 10011 (212) 675-6601
JEWISH WELFARE BOARD COMMISSION ON JEWISH CHAPLAINCY 15 E. 26TH STREET ... NEW YORK **NY** 10010 (212) 532-4949
NEW YORK BOARD OF RABBIS 10 EAST 73RD STREET ... NEW YORK **NY** 10021 (212) 879-8415
RABBINICAL ALLIANCE OF AMERICA-IGUD HARABONIM 156 FIFTH AVENUE, SUITE 807 ... NEW YORK **NY** 10010 (212) 242-6420
RABBINICAL ASSEMBLY 3080 BROADWAY ... NEW YORK **NY** 10027 (212) 749-8000
RABBINICAL COUNCIL OF AMERICA, INC. 1250 BROADWAY ... NEW YORK **NY** 10001 (212) 594-3780
UNION OF CHASIDIC RABBIS OF AMERICA 47 BEEKMAN STREET ... NEW YORK **NY** 10038
UNION OF ORTHODOX RABBIS OF THE U.S. & CANADA, INC. 235 EAST BROADWAY ... NEW YORK **NY** 10002 (212) 964-6337
CLEVELAND BOARD OF RABBIS 3557 WASHINGTON BLVD ... CLEVELAND **OH** 44118 (216) 321-1000
ORTHODOX RABBINICAL COUNCIL 1970 SOUTH TAYLOR ROAD ... CLEVELAND **OH** 44118 (216) 321-4875
COLUMBUS BOARD OF RABBIS 1226 COLLEGE AVENUE ... COLUMBUS **OH** 43209
BOARD OF RABBIS OF GREATER PHILADELPHIA 117 S. 17TH STREET, ROOM 903 ... PHILADELPHIA **PA** 19103 (215) 563-1463
JEWISH CHAPLAINCY OF BUCKS COUNTY 800 DAVID DRIVE ... TREVOSE **PA** 19047 (215) 357-7131
RECONSTRUCTIONIST RABBINICAL ASSOCIATION CHURCH ROAD & GREENWOOD AVENUE ... WYNCOTE **PA** 19095 (215) 576-0800
HOUSTON RABBINICAL ASSOCIATION 4610 BELLAIRE BLVD ... BELLAIRE **TX** 77401 (713) 667-9201

REAL ESTATE

AMBASSADOR REAL ESTATE & INVESTMENTS COMPANY 23 REHOV RAMBAN ... JERUSALEM **IS** 92422 (02) 639164
ISRAEL HOMES & REAL ESTATE CORP. LTD. 800 SECOND AVENUE ... NEW YORK **NY** 10017 (212) 684-2219
ISRALOM-ISRAEL HOMES & REAL ESTATE CORP., LTD. 440 PARK AVENUE SOUTH ... NEW YORK **NY** 10016 (212) 684-2219
ISRALOM-ISRAEL HOMES & REAL ESTATE CORP., LTD. 440 PARK AVENUE SOUTH ... NEW YORK **NY** 10016 (212) 582-0844
HERITAGE INVESTMENTS 13 S. RIGAUD ROAD ... SPRING VALLEY **NY** 10977 (914) 356-6432

RECORDS, SHEET MUSIC & TAPES

LYRON MUSIC ENTERPRISES PO BOX 6103 ... BEVERLY HILLS **CA** 90212
HATAKLIT 436 NORTH FAIRFAX ... LOS ANGELES **CA** 90036 (213) 655-1242
NAMA RECORDS 2367 GLENDON AVENUE ... WESTWOOD **CA** 90064 (213) 475-6262
HEBREW PUBLISHING COMPANY 100 WATER STREET ... BROOKLYN **NY** 11201 (718) 858-6928
KEHOT MUSIC DEPARTMENT 770 EASTERN PARKWAY ... BROOKLYN **NY** 11213 (718) 774-4000
TORAH TAPES 1814 50 STREET ... BROOKLYN **NY** 11204 (718) 438-3904
TARA PUBLICATIONS 29 DERBY AVENUE ... CEDARHURST **NY** 11516 (516) 295-2290
NEFESH AMI P.O. BOX 651 ... HICKSVILLE **NY** 11801 (516) 933-2660
BLOCH PUBLISHING 19 WEST 21ST STREET ... NEW YORK **NY** 10010 (212) 989-9104
HOUSE OF MENORAH, INC. 36 ELDRIDGE STREET ... NEW YORK **NY** 10002 (212) 925-7573
ISRAELI PRODUCTIONS 322 WEST 57TH STREET ... NEW YORK **NY** 10019 (212) 245-3463
J. LEVINE CO. - LOWER EAST SIDE 58 ELDRIDGE STREET ... NEW YORK **NY** 10002 (212) 966-4460
J. LEVINE CO. - MIDTOWN STORE 5 WEST 30TH STREET ... NEW YORK **NY** 10001 (212) 695-6888
MUSIC MASTERS UPTOWN 25 WEST 43RD STREET ... NEW YORK **NY** 10036 (212) 840-1958
RABBINICAL ALLIANCE OF AMERICA 156 FIFTH AVENUE, SUITE 807 ... NEW YORK **NY** 10010 (212) 242-6420
SUKI & DING/UNCLE MOISHY 225 WEST 86TH STREET ... NEW YORK **NY** 10024 (212) 724-9351
WORKMEN'S CIRCLE, EDUCATIONAL DEPARTMENT 45 EAST 33RD STREET ... NEW YORK **NY** 10016 (212) 889-6800
YESHIVA UNIVERSITY, RABBINIC ALUMNI OFFICE 500 WEST 185TH STREET ... NEW YORK **NY** 10033 (212) 960-5400
ELITE RECORDS 214-18 WHITEHALL TERRACE ... QUEENS VILLAGE **NY** 11427
HEBRAICA RECORD DISTRIBUTORS 50 ANDOVER ROAD ... ROSLYN HEIGHTS **NY** 11577 (516) 484-4006

RELIGIOUS ORGANIZATIONS

ORTHODOX UNION/NCSY 9030 W. OLYMPIC BLVD ... BEVERLY HILLS **CA** 90211 (213) 859-8944
UNITED SYNAGOGUE OF AMERICA-PACIFIC SOUTHWEST REGION 15600 MULHOLLAND DRIVE ... LOS ANGELES **CA** 90024 (213) 879-4114
UNION OF AMERICAN HEBREW CONGREGATIONS-PACIFIC SOUTHWEST 13197 VENTURA BOULEVARD ... NORTH HOLLYWOOD **CA** 91604
UNITED SYNAGOGUE OF AMERICA-NORTHERN CALIFORNIA REGION 1419 BROADWAY SUITE 612 ... OAKLAND **CA** 94612 (415) 839-6333
UNITED SYNAGOGUE OF AMERICA-PACIFIC NORTHWEST REGION 1419 BROADWAY ... OAKLAND **CA** 94612 (415) 839-6333
UNION OF AMERICAN-HEBREW CONGREGATIONS-N. CAL. & PACIFIC NW 703 MARKET STREET, SUITE 705 ... SAN FRANCISCO **CA** 94103 (415) 392-7080
SYNAGOGUE COUNCIL OF AMERICA 1776 MASSACHUSETTS AVENUE, N W ... WASHINGTON **DC** 20036
UNION OF AMERICAN HEBREW CONGREGATIONS-MID ATLANTIC COUNCIL 2027 MASSACHUSETTS AVENUE, N.W. ... WASHINGTON **DC** 20036 (202) 387-2800
UNION OF AMERICAN HEBREW CONGREGATIONS-SOUTHEAST COUNCIL 3785 NW 82ND AVENUE #210 ... MIAMI **FL** 33166 (305) 592-4792
UNITED SYNAGOGUE OF AMERICA-SOUTHEAST REGION 282 S. UNIVERSITY DRIVE, SUITE 216 ... PLANTATION **FL** 33324 (305) 947-6094
JEWS FOR JEWS ORGANIZATION P.O. BOX 6194 ... SURFSIDE **FL** 33154 (305) 931-0001
UNITED SYNAGOGUE OF AMERICA-CENTRAL STATES & PROVINCES REG. 525 14TH STREET ... SIOUX CITY **IA** 51105 (712) 258-6007
UNION OF AMERICAN HEBREW CONGREGATIONS-GREAT LAKES COUNCIL 100 WEST MONROE STREET ROOM 312 ... CHICAGO **IL** 60603 (312) 782-1477
UNITED SYNAGOGUE OF AMERICA-MIDWEST REGION 180 N. MICHIGAN AVENUE ... CHICAGO **IL** 60605 (312) 726-1802
ASSOCIATED SYNAGOGUES OF MASSACHUSETTS 177 TREMONT STREET ... BOSTON **MA** 02111 (617) 426-1832
MIZRACHI-HAPOEL HAMIZRACHI OF NEW ENGLAND 611 WASHINGTON STREET ... BOSTON **MA** 02111 (617) 426-9148
ASSOCIATED SYNAGOGUES OF MASSACHUSETTS 177 TREMONT STREET ... BROOKLINE **MA** 02111 (617) 426-1832
UNION OF AMERICAN HEBREW CONGREGATIONS-NORTHEAST COUNCIL 1330 BEACON STREET ... BROOKLINE **MA** 02146 (617) 277-1655
UNITED SYNAGOGUE OF AMERICA-NEW ENGLAND REGION 180 BLUE HILL AVENUE ... MILTON **MA** 02186 (617) 698-0085
COUNCIL OF ORTHODOX SYNAGOGUES OF GREATER WASHINGTON 801 WHITTINGTON TERRACE ... SILVER SPRING **MD** 20901
UNITED SYNAGOGUE OF AMERICA-SEABOARD REGION 420 UNIVERSITY BOULEVARD, E ... SILVER SPRING **MD** 20901 (301) 434-6650
THE SOCIETY FOR HUMANISTIC JUDAISM 28611 WEST TWELVE MILE ROAD ... FARMINGTON HILLS **MI** 48018 (313) 478-7610
UNITED SYNAGOGUE OF AMERICA-MICHIGAN REGION 29901 MIDDLEBELT ROAD ... FARMINGTON HILLS **MI** 48018 (313) 855-5950
UNION OF AMERICAN HEBREW CONGREGATIONS-MIDWEST COUNCIL 8420 DELMAR, SUITE 304 ... ST. LOUIS **MO** 63124 (314) 997-7566
UNITED SYNAGOGUE OF AMERICA-NEW JERSEY REGION 910 SALEM AVENUE ... HILLSIDE **NJ** 07205 (201) 353-8844
UNITED ORTHODOX SYNAGOGUES 75 SOMERSET STREET ... NORTH PLAINFIELD **NJ** 07060
UNITED SYNAGOGUE OF AMERICA-EMPIRE REGION 18 PINE STREET ... AMSTERDAM **NY** 12010 (518) 842-2829
AGUDATH ISRAEL OF AMERICA 813 AVENUE H ... BROOKLYN **NY** 11230 (718) 434-8670
BETH SHIFRA INSTITUTIONS 3044 CONEY ISLAND AVENUE ... BROOKLYN **NY** 11235 (718) 449-1397
CENTRAL RABBINICAL CONGRESS 85 DIVISION ... BROOKLYN **NY** 11211 (718) 384-6766
COMMITTEE FOR THE FURTHERANCE OF TORAH OBSERVANCE 1430 57TH STREET ... BROOKLYN **NY** 11219 (718) 851-6428
COUNCIL FOR SABBATH OBSERVANCE 1688 EAST 18TH STREET ... BROOKLYN **NY** 11229
MACHNE ISRAEL 770 EASTERN PARKWAY ... BROOKLYN **NY** 11213 (718) 493-9250
MITZVAH CAMPAIGN-LUBAVITCH 770 EASTERN PARKWAY ... BROOKLYN **NY** 11213 (718) 493-9250
ORGANIZATION FOR TORAH ETHICS, THE 928 46TH STREET ... BROOKLYN **NY** 11219 (718) 438-1574
PHYSICIANS FOR TORAH OBSERVANCE 4718 12TH AVENUE ... BROOKLYN **NY** 11219 (718) 438-3090
POALE AGUDATH ISRAEL OF AMERICA, INC. 3190 BEDFORD AVENUE ... BROOKLYN **NY** 11210 (718) 377-4111
SIMAN UMESORAH INSTITUTE 1448 50TH STREET ... BROOKLYN **NY** 11219 (718) 435-8171
TZIVOS HASHEM 770 EASTERN PARKWAY ... BROOKLYN **NY** 11213 (718) 467-6630
VAAD LEHAROMAS KEREN HATORAH COMMITTEE TO STRENGTHEN TORAH JUDAISM 970 42ND STREET, APT. 2B ... BROOKLYN **NY** 11219
AMERICAN TORAH SHELEMAH COMMITTEE 24 W. MAPLE AVENUE ... MONSEY **NY** 10952 (914) 352-4609
ACADEMY FOR JEWISH RELIGION 112 E. 88TH STREET ... NEW YORK **NY** 10028 (212) 722-5811
AGUDAS ISRAEL WORLD ORGANIZATION 471 WEST END AVENUE ... NEW YORK **NY** 10024 (212) 874-7979
AGUDATH ISRAEL OF AMERICA 84 WILLIAM STREET ... NEW YORK **NY** 10038 (212) 797-9000
FEDERATION OF RECONSTRUCTIONIST CONGREGATIONS AND HAVUROT 270 WEST 89TH STREET ... NEW YORK **NY** 10024 (212) 496-2960
JEWISH RECONSTRUCTIONIST FOUNDATION 2521 BROADWAY ... NEW YORK **NY** 10025 (212) 316-3011
LEAGUE FOR SAFEGUARDING THE FIXITY OF THE SABBATH 122 W. 76TH STREET ... NEW YORK **NY** 10023 (212) 877-7652
NATIONAL ASSOCIATION FOR THE ADVANCEMENT OF ORTHODOX JUDAISM 132 NASSAU STREET ... NEW YORK **NY** 10038 (212) 964-7829
NATIONAL COUNCIL OF YOUNG ISRAEL 3 WEST 16TH STREET ... NEW YORK **NY** 10011 (212) 929-1525
NATIONAL HAVURAH COMMITTEE 270 WEST 89TH STREET ... NEW YORK **NY** 10024 (212) 496-0055

NEW YORK FEDERATION OF REFORM SYNAGOGUES
838 FIFTH AVENUE NEW YORK **NY** 10021 (212) 249-0100
OZAR HATORAH, INC. 411 FIFTH AVENUE NEW YORK **NY** 10016 (212) 684-4733
RABBINICAL COUNCIL OF AMERICA 1250 BROADWAY NEW YORK **NY** 10001 (212) 594-3780
RECONSTRUCTIONIST FEDERATION OF CONGREGATIONS & FELLOWSHIPS
270 WEST 89TH STREET NEW YORK **NY** 10024 (212) 496-2960
SHOFAR ASSOCIATION OF AMERICA, INC. 234 FIFTH AVENUE NEW YORK **NY** 10001 (212) 687-2570
SOCIETY FOR THE ADVANCEMENT OF JUDAISM
15 WEST 86TH STREET NEW YORK **NY** 10024 (212) 724-7000
SYNAGOGUE COUNCIL OF AMERICA 327 LEXINGTON AVENUE NEW YORK **NY** 10016 (212) 686-8670
UNION OF AMERICAN HEBREW CONGREGATIONS 838 FIFTH AVENUE NEW YORK **NY** 10021 (212) 249-0100
UNION OF AMERICAN HEBREW CONGREGATIONS-NJ-W. HUDSON COUNCIL
838 FIFTH AVENUE NEW YORK **NY** 10021 (212) 249-0100
UNION OF AMERICAN HEBREW CONGREGATIONS-NY FEDERATION
838 FIFTH AVENUE NEW YORK **NY** 10021 (212) 249-0100
UNION OF ORTHODOX JEWISH CONGREGATIONS OF AMERICA
45 WEST 36TH STREET NEW YORK **NY** 10018 (212) 563-4000
UNION OF SEPHARDIC CONGREGATIONS 8 WEST 70TH STREET NEW YORK **NY** 10023 (212) 873-0300
UNITED SYNAGOGUE OF AMERICA 155 FIFTH AVENUE NEW YORK **NY** 10010 (212) 533-7800
UNITED SYNAGOGUE OF AMERICA-CONNECTICUT VALLEY REGION
155 FIFTH AVENUE NEW YORK **NY** 10010 (212) 533-7800
UNITED SYNAGOGUE OF AMERICA-NEW YORK METROPOLITAN REGION
155 FIFTH AVENUE NEW YORK **NY** 10010 (212) 533-7800
UNITED SYNAGOGUE OF AMERICA-OHIO REGION 155 FIFTH AVENUE NEW YORK **NY** 10010 (212) 533-7800
UNITED SYNAGOGUE OF AMERICA-WESTERN PENNSYLVANIA REGION
155 FIFTH AVENUE NEW YORK **NY** 10010 (212) 533-7800
WORLD COUNCIL OF SYNAGOGUES 155 FIFTH AVENUE NEW YORK **NY** 10010 (212) 533-7800
WORLD UNION FOR PROGRESSIVE JUDAISM 838 FIFTH AVENUE NEW YORK **NY** 10021 (212) 249-0100
UNIVERSAL TORAH REGISTRY, INC. 1320 STONY BROOK ROAD STONY BROOK **NY** 11790
UNION OF AMERICAN HEBREW CONGREGATIONS-DETROIT & NORTHEAST
25550 CHAGRIN ROAD BEACHWOOD **OH** 44122 (216) 831-6722
ORTHODOX UNION/NCSY 3600 BATHURST STREET TORONTO **ON** M6A 2C9 (416) 782-3117
UNION OF AMERICAN HEBREW CONGREGATIONS-CANADIAN COUNCIL
534 LAWRENCE AVENUE W TORONTO **ON** M6A 1A2 (416) 787-9838
UNITED SYNAGOGUE OF AMERICA-ONTARIO-CANADA REGION
3199 BATHURST STREET, SUITE 200 TORONTO **ON** M6A 2B2 (416) 781-6908
UNION OF AMERICAN HEBREW CONGREGATIONS-PA COUNCIL
117 SOUTH 17TH STREET PHILADELPHIA **PA** 19103 (215) 563-8726
UNITED SYNAGOGUE OF AMERICA-E. PA. & DEL. VALLEY REGION
1701 WALNUT STREET PHILADELPHIA **PA** 19103 (215) 563-8809
UNITED SYNAGOGUE OF AMERICA-EASTERN CANADA REGION
875 MARLBORO DRIVE MONTREAL **QU** H4P 1B7 (514) 733-7217
UNION OF AMERICAN HEBREW CONGREGATIONS-SOUTHWEST COUNCIL
13773 N. CENTRAL EXPRESSWAY DALLAS **TX** 75243 (214) 699-0656
UNITED SYNAGOGUE OF AMERICA-SOUTHWEST REGION
8525 STELLA LINK ROAD HOUSTON **TX** 77025 (713) 661-4520

RESTAURANTS & DELICATESSENS

SEGAL'S NEW PLACE 4818 N. 7TH STREET PHOENIX **AZ** 85012 (602) 285-1515
SOL'S FISHERY KOSHER DELI 7021 NORTH 19TH AVENUE PHOENIX **AZ** 85021 (602) 995-0112
FEIG KOSHER FOODS 5071 EAST 5TH STREET TUCSON **AZ** 85711 (602) 325-2255
THE ANGLER SMOKE HOUSE 8030 GRANVILLE STREET VANCOUVER **BC** V6P 4Z4 (604) 266-9019
BEAUMONT KOSHER KETTLE 17614 VENTURA BOULEVARD ENCINO **CA** 91316 (818) 995-1484
MASADA GLATT KOSHER RESTAURANT
12181 BUARO (NEAR DISNEYLAND) GARDEN GROVE **CA** 92640 (714) 956-0544
CHICK-A-DELI 7170 BEVERLY BOULEVARD LOS ANGELES **CA** 90036 (213) 930-0966
ELITE CUISINE 9303 WEST PICO BOULEVARD LOS ANGELES **CA** 90035 (213) 859-7633
ELITE CUISINE 10614 WEST PICO BOULEVARD LOS ANGELES **CA** 90064 (213) 836-2619
FAIRFAX KOSHER PIZZA 453 NORTH FAIRFAX LOS ANGELES **CA** 90036 (213) 653-7200
HANCOCK PARK GOURMET 129 NORTH LA BREA AVENUE LOS ANGELES **CA** 90036 (213) 936-1551
I'M A DELI & RESTAURANT 8930 WEST PICO BOULEVARD LOS ANGELES **CA** 90035 (213) 274-2452
JUDY'S GRILL 129 SOUTH LABREA AVENUE LOS ANGELES **CA** 90036 (213) 934-7667
JUDY'S LA PETITE 7257 BEVERLY BOULEVARD LOS ANGELES **CA** 90036 (213) 936-7372
KOSHER CUTTING BOARD 6505 WILSHIRE BOULEVARD LOS ANGELES **CA** 90048 (213) 852-1234
KOSHER EXPRESS 363 S. FAIRFAX AVENUE LOS ANGELES **CA** 90036 (213) 651-0147
KOSHER KOLONEL 9301 WEST PICO BOULEVARD LOS ANGELES **CA** 90035 (213) 858-0111
KOSHER NOSTRA 365 SOUTH FAIRFAX AVENUE LOS ANGELES **CA** 90036 (213) 655-1994
KOSHER PIZZA NOSH 8844 WEST PICO BOULEVARD LOS ANGELES **CA** 90035 (213) 276-8708
LA GLATT 446 NORTH FAIRFAX AVENUE LOS ANGELES **CA** 90036 (213) 651-0242
L'ORIENT 7257 BEVERLY BLVD. LOS ANGELES **CA** 90036 (213) 932-9029
MARCELLE'S CUISINE 448 N. FAIRFAX LOS ANGELES **CA** 90036 (213) 653-2090
MICHELINE'S 8965 WEST PICO BOULEVARD LOS ANGELES **CA** 90035 (213) 274-6534
MILKY WAY 9108 WEST PICO BOULEVARD LOS ANGELES **CA** 90035 (213) 859-0004
PICO KOSHER DELI 8826 WEST PICO BOULEVARD LOS ANGELES **CA** 90035 (213) 273-9381
PIZZA MAYVEN 140 NORTH LA BREA AVENUE LOS ANGELES **CA** 90036 (213) 857-6353
RAPHY'S 9307 WEST PICO BOULEVARD LOS ANGELES **CA** 90035 (213) 275-6256
TWO WORLDS HEALTH FOOD RESTAURANT
8022 WEST THIRD STREET LOS ANGELES **CA** 90048 (213) 653-4212
UNIVERSITY OF JUDAISM 15600 MULHOLLAND DRIVE LOS ANGELES **CA** 90077 (213) 476-9777
WESTERN KOSHER 426 NORTH FAIRFAX AVE. LOS ANGELES **CA** 90036 (213) 655-8870
YESHIVA UNIVERSITY OF LOS ANGELES
9760 WEST PICO BOULEVARD LOS ANGELES **CA** 90035 (213) 277-9924
DREXLER'S 12519 1/2 BURBANK BOULEVARD NORTH HOLLYWOOD **CA** 91607 (818) 761-6405
KOSHER EXPRESS 5200 CLAREMONT AVENUE OAKLAND **CA** 94618 (415) 652-5880
NOAH'S ARK 5157 COLLEGE AVENUE SAN DIEGO **CA** 92115 (213) 265-9335
ISRAEL'S DELI 5621 GEARY BOULEVARD SAN FRANCISCO **CA** 94121 (415) 752-3064
SHANGRI LA CAFE 2026 IRVING STREET SAN FRANCISCO **CA** 94122 (415) 753-9494
LA PIZZA RISTORANTE 4454 VAN NUYS BOULEVARD SHERMAN OAKS **CA** 91403 (818) 986-0581
EAST SIDE KOSHER DELI 5600 EAST CEDAR AVENUE DENVER **CO** 80224 (303) 322-9862
STEINBERG'S GROCERY 4017 EAST COLFAX AVENUE DENVER **CO** 80220 (303) 534-0314
UTICA DELI 4500 WEST COLFAX AVENUE DENVER **CO** 80204 (303) 534-2253
MOISHE'S KOSHER DELICATESSEN BAKERY
2081 BLACK ROCK TURNPIKE FAIRFIELD **CT** 06430 (203) 333-3059
ABEL'S DELICATESSEN & RESTAURANT 2100 DIXWELL AVENUE HAMDEN **CT** 06514 (203) 281-3434
HARTFORD KOSHER CATERERS FORD AND PEARL HARTFORD **CT** 06111 (203) 527-7770
M & T APPETIZERS & DELICATESSEN 1150 WHALLEY AVENUE NEW HAVEN **CT** 06515 (203) 389-5603
BEE BEE DAIRY RESTAURANT TOWN STREET NORWICH **CT** 06360 (203) 887-4101
DELI-LAND KOSHER DELICATESSEN 850 HIGH RIDGE ROAD STAMFORD **CT** 06905 (203) 322-3649
POSINS' BAKERY-DELI 5756 GEORGIA AVENUE N.W. WASHINGTON **DC** 20008 (202) 726-4424
SARA'S DAIRY RESTAURANT
1898 WEST HILLSBORO BOULEVARD DEERFIELD BEACH **FL** 33441 (305) 427-2272
EMBASSY NORTH 1025 E. HALLANDALE BEACH BLVD HALLANDALE **FL** 33009 (305) 949-1317
KEZREH GLATT KOSHER DELI
1025 EAST HALLANDALE BEACH BOULEVARD HALLANDALE **FL** 33009 (305) 454-5776
SAGE BAGEL & APPETIZER SHOP
800 EAST HALLANDALE BEACH BOULEVARD HALLANDALE **FL** 33009 (305) 456-7499
ARNEE'S GLATT KOSHER DELI 1814 HARRISON STREET HOLLYWOOD **FL** 33020 (305) 921-2564
WORMAN'S BAKERY & DELICATESSEN
1712 SAN MARCO BOULEVARD JACKSONVILLE **FL** 32207 (904) 396-0393
WORMAN'S BAKERY & DELICATESSEN 204 BROAD STREET JACKSONVILLE **FL** 32202 (904) 354-5702
STAGECOACH RESORT INN 4311 W. VINE STREET KISSIMMEE **FL** 32741 (305) 396-4213
SUPERIOR DELI 677 NORTH ORLANDO AVENUE MAITLAND **FL** 32751 (305) 645-1704
ROYAL HUNGARIAN OF BROWARD 342 SOUTH STATE ROAD 7 MARGATE **FL** 33068 (305) 975-5327
BERNARD WACHTEL'S TOWER SUITE 4101 PINE TREE DRIVE MIAMI BEACH **FL** 33140 (305) 673-8308
DAIRY PATCH 534 41ST STREET MIAMI BEACH **FL** 33140 (305) 531-1511
DINE OR NOSH 420 ARTHUR GODFREY ROAD, 41ST STREET MIAMI BEACH **FL** 33140 (305) 538-9104
EMBASSY 41 534 41ST STREET MIAMI BEACH **FL** 33140 (305) 534-7550
KOSHER KORNER 2701 COLLINS AVENUE MIAMI BEACH **FL** 33140 (305) 674-9222
H & M STEIN DELI 1141 WASHINGTON AVENUE MIAMI BEACH **FL** 33139 (305) 534-2557
KING DAVID DELICATESSEN 1339 WASHINGTON AVENUE MIAMI BEACH **FL** 33139 (305) 534-0197
THE PEKING EMBASSY 1417 WASHINGTON AVENUE MIAMI BEACH **FL** 33139 (305) 538-7550
ROYAL HUNGARIAN SASSON HOTEL-OCEAN AT 20TH STREET MIAMI BEACH **FL** 33139
SARA'S RESTAURANT 534 41ST STREET MIAMI BEACH **FL** 33140 (305) 531-1511
SEA GULL KOSHER STEAK HOUSE
ON THE OCEAN AT 21ST STREET MIAMI BEACH **FL** 33139 (305) 531-4114
SHLOMI'S FAMOUS VEGETARIAN RESTAURANT 753 41ST STREET MIAMI BEACH **FL** 33140 (305) 538-7333
TOTTIE'S RESTAURANT 6345 COLLINS AVENUE MIAMI BEACH **FL** 33141 (305) 865-7932
TOWER SUITE 4101 PINE TREE DRIVE MIAMI BEACH **FL** 33140 (305) 673-8308
WEBERMAN'S TRADITIONAL FOODS 6345 COLLINS AVENUE MIAMI BEACH **FL** 33141 (305) 865-1931
DAIRY PATCH 9802 N.E. 2ND AVENUE MIAMI SHORES **FL** 33138 (305) 758-4821
SARAH'S PIZZA 2214 NE. 123RD ST. NORTH MIAMI **FL** 33161 (305) 891-3312
AVI'S STEAK HOUSE 175 SUNNY ISLES BLVD NORTH MIAMI BEACH **FL** 33160 (305) 947-4781
ISAAC'S KOSHER KITCHEN & CATERING
16460 NORTHEAST 16TH AVENUE NORTH MIAMI BEACH **FL** 33162 (305) 944-5222
JERUSALEM KOSHER PIZZA & FALAFEL
761 NORTHEAST 167TH STREET NORTH MIAMI BEACH **FL** 33162 (305) 653-6662
LA DIFFERENCE 1344 N.E. 163 STREET NORTH MIAMI BEACH **FL** 33162 (305) 949-4552
MAMMA'S ESSEN 1330 NORTHEAST 163RD STREET NORTH MIAMI BEACH **FL** 33162 (305) 948-6031
SHIPUDAY AHUVA ISRAELI RESTAURANT
133024 N.E. 163RD STREET NORTH MIAMI BEACH **FL** 33162
PALM TERRACE HYATT ORLANDO HOTEL ORLANDO **FL** (305) 396-1234
KATZ'S DELICATESSEN 2205 CHESHIRE BRIDGE ROAD N.E. ATLANTA **GA** 30324 (404) 321-7444
CAFE HANEGEV 6407 N. CALIFORNIA CHICAGO **IL** 60645 (312) 761-8222
JERUSALEM 3014 W. DEVON CHICAGO **IL** 60659 (312) 262-0515
KOSHER KARRY AND RESTAURANT 2828 WEST DEVON CHICAGO **IL** 60659 (312) 973-4355
L'CHAYIM 3104 W. DEVON CHICAGO **IL** 60659 (312) 274-5544
RACHEL'S PLACE 3144 WEST DEVON AVENUE CHICAGO **IL** 60659 (312) 465-3325
SABRA 2712 WEST PRATT CHICAGO **IL** 60645 (312) 764-3563
TEL AVIV KOSHER PIZZA & DAIRY RESTAURANT
6349 WEST CALIFORNIA CHICAGO **IL** 60659 (312) 764-3776
SELIG'S KOSHER DELICATESSEN 309 SKOKIE VALLEY ROAD HIGHLAND PARK **IL** 60035 (312) 831-5560
FALAFEL KING 4507 WEST OAKTON SKOKIE **IL** 60076 (312) 677-6020
KOSHER GOURMENT 3552 DEMPSTER SKOKIE **IL** 60076 (312) 679-0432
ZIGGY'S 4120 W. DEMPSTER SKOKIE **IL** 60076 (312) 673-5500
SHAPIRO'S DELICATESSEN 808 SOUTH MERIDIAN INDIANAPOLIS **IN** 46225 (317) 631-4041
EPSTEIN'S 403 WEST 79TH STREET KANSAS CITY **KS** 66102 (816) 361-0200
MILK STREET CAFE 50 MILK STREET BOSTON **MA** 02109 (617) 546-2433
ESS, ESS 30 WALLINGFORD ROAD BRIGHTON **MA** 02135 (617) 254-3965
CAFE SHALOM 404 HARVARD STREET BROOKLINE **MA** 02146 (617) 277-0698
RUBIN'S KOSHER DELICATESSEN & RESTAURANT
500 HARVARD STREET BROOKLINE **MA** 02146 (617) 731-8787
YESHIVA ACADEMY CAFETERIA 22 NEWTON AVENUE WORCESTER **MA** 01602 (617) 752-0904
O'FISHEL CATERING 3615 SEVEN MILE LANE BALTIMORE **MD** 21208 (301) 358-8969
THE KNISH SHOP 508 REISTERSTOWN ROAD BALTIMORE **MD** 21208 (301) 484-5850
ROYAL RESTAURANT 1630 REISTERSTOWN ROAD BALTIMORE **MD** 21208 (301) 484-3544
TOV PIZZA 6313 REISTERSTOWN ROAD BALTIMORE **MD** 21215 (301) 358-5338
THE GARDEN 7723 WISCONSIN AVENUE BETHESDA **MD** 20814 (301) 654-3511
MARION'S CUSTOM CATERING 2702 NAVARE DRIVE CHEVY CHASE **MD** 20815 (301) 587-5820
LIEBES KOSHER DELI 607 REISTERSTOWN ROAD PIKESVILLE **MD** 21208 (301) 653-1977
THE JAFFA GATE 2420 BLUERIDGE AVENUE SILVER SPRING **MD** 20902 (301) 933-9331
SHALOM TAKE-OUT 2307 UNIVERSITY BOULEVARD WEST SILVER SPRING **MD** 20902 (301) 946-6500
WORLD'S GREATEST PIZZA 11419 GEORGIA AVENUE WHEATON **MD** 20902 (301) 942-5900
THE BAGEL SHOP 8 SECOND STREET BANGOR **ME** 04401 (207) 947-1654
BLOOM'S KARRY OUT 24711 COOLIDGE ROAD OAK PARK **MI** 48237 (313) 546-5444
MERTZ "CAFE KATON" 23005 COOLIDGE OAK PARK **MI** 48237 (313) 547-3581
PIZZA MAVEN 25226 GREENFIELD OAK PARK **MI** 48237 (313) 968-5777
SARA'S DELI & RESTAURANT 24980 COOLIDGE OAK PARK **MI** 48237 (313) 545-6320
SPERBER'S "KARRY-OUT" 25250 GREENFIELD OAK PARK **MI** 48237 (313) 967-1161

SPERBER NORTH - JCC 6600 WEST MAPLE ROAD ... WEST BLOOMFIELD **MI** 48033 (313) 661-5151
CECIL'S KOSHER DELICATESSEN RESTAURANT & BAKERY
651 CLEVELAND AVENUE SOUTH ... ST. PAUL **MN** 55416 (612) 698-6276
EPSTEIN'S KOSHER FOOD 403 WEST 79TH ... KANSAS CITY **MO** 64114 (816) 361-0200
M & M BAKERY & DELICATESSEN 1721 EAST 31ST STREET ... KANSAS CITY **MO** 64109 (816) 924-9172
SIMON KOHN'S 10424 OLIVE STREET ROAD ... ST. LOUIS **MO** 63146 (314) 569-0727
WORLD TOWER DELI 109 S. NORTH CAROLINA AVENUE ... ATLANTIC CITY **NJ** 08401 (609) 347-8000
GOODWILL KOSHER DELICATESSEN & APPETIZERS 815 BROADWAY ... BAYONNE **NJ** 07002 (201) 339-2392
KOSHER KITCHEN 5901 BROADWAY ... BAYONNE **NJ** 07002 (201) 437-1594
FOSTER VILLAGE KOSHER DELICATESSEN 469 S. WASHINGTON ... BERGENFIELD **NJ** 07621 (201) 384-7100
BRADLEY KOSHER DELICATESSEN 401 MAIN STREET ... BRADLEY BEACH **NJ** 07720 (201) 775-1081
NEW JERSEY PIZZA FALAFEL 105 NORWOOD AVENUE ... DEAL **NJ** 07723 (201) 531-9800
KOSHER IRISHMAN DELI 392 CENTRAL AVENUE ... EAST ORANGE **NJ** 07011 (201) 673-2407
SUPERIOR DELI & APPETIZER CO. 150 ELMORA AVENUE ... ELIZABETH **NJ** 07202 (201) 352-0355
ENGLEWOOD KOSHER DELI 95 WEST PALISADE AVENUE ... ENGLEWOOD **NJ** 07632 (201) 567-0732
PIZZA & STUFF 14-20 PLAZA ROAD ... FAIR LAWN **NJ** 07410 (201) 796-1494
JERUSALEM MEATING PLACE 229 RARITAN AVENUE ... HIGHLAND PARK **NJ** 08904 (201) 846-3444
JERUSALEM RESTAURANT 231 RARITAN AVENUE ... HIGHLAND PARK **NJ** 08904 (201) 249-0070
LAKEWOOD KOSHER PIZZA & FALAFEL
GREBOW'S SHOPPING PLAZA (ROUTE 9) ... HOWELL **NJ** 07731 (201) 363-5684
THE KOSHER EXPERIENCE DELI/RESTAURANT
ROUTE 9 & KENNEDY BOULEVARD ... LAKEWOOD **NJ** 08701 (201) 370-0707
MIDDLEBROOK KOSHER DELICATESSEN 1594 STATE HIGHWAY 35 ... OAKHURST **NJ** 07755 (201) 493-8300
LARRY'S KOSHER DELI RESTAURANT - APPETIZERS & CATERERS
1353 SOUTH AVENUE ... PLAINFIELD **NJ** 07062 (201) 755-8013
JERUSALEM RESTAURANT 496 CEDAR LANE ... TEANECK **NJ** 07666 (201) 836-2120
DELI KING 628 ST. GEORGES AVENUE ... WEST LINDEN **NJ** 07036 (201) 925-3909
CAFE DEVORAH 760 NORTHFIELD AVENUE ... WEST ORANGE **NJ** 07052 (201) 267-9404
TABATCHNIK WESTWOOD DELI & APPETIZERS
226 FAIRVIEW AVENUE ... WESTWOOD **NJ** 07675 (201) 666-1051
WESTERN KOSHER FLAMINGO & MOJAVE ROADS ... LAS VEGAS **NV** (702) 451-DELI
SAMMY'S KOSHER PIZZA AND FELAFEL 2492 MERRICK ROAD ... BELLMORE **NY** 11710 (516) 783-8193
THE KOSHER PIZZA HOUSE 483 WASHINGTON AVENUE ... ALBANY **NY** 12210 (518) 465-5638
SAM'S FAMOUS KNISHES (DAIRY)
504 BRIGHTON BEACH AVENUE ... BRIGHTON BEACH **NY** 11235 (718) 646-5450
DEXTER'S RESTAURANT (FRENCH CUISINE) 5652 MOSHOLU AVENUE ... BRONX **NY** 10471 (212) 548-0440
FLASH KOSHER PIZZA 3702 RIVERDALE AVENUE ... BRONX **NY** 10463 (212) 543-1811
K & G KOSHER DELICATESSEN 772 ALLERTON AVENUE ... BRONX **NY** 10467 (212) 655-9424
LEVINE'S KOSHER DELICATESSEN RESTAURANT
2144 WHITE PLAINS ROAD ... BRONX **NY** 10462 (212) 409-9600
LIEBMAN'S KOSHER DELICATESSEN & CATERING
552 WEST 235TH STREET ... BRONX **NY** 10463 (212) 548-4534
LOESSER'S KOSHER DELICATESSEN & CATERER 214 WEST 231ST STREET ... BRONX **NY** 10463 (212) 548-9735
NATURE'S EXCHANGE
2131 WILLIAMSBRIDGE ROAD AND PELHAM PARKWAY SOUTH ... BRONX **NY** 10461 (212) 822-7892
OTHER'S KOSHER DELI GRAND CONCOURSE AT EAST 188TH STREET ... BRONX **NY**
PALACE KOSHER DELICATESSEN 122 EAST 188TH STREET ... BRONX **NY** 10468 (212) 933-0043
PIZZA & STUFF #1 782 LYDIG AVENUE ... BRONX **NY** 10462 (212) 822-8926
S & O KOSHER DELICATESSEN 1596 WESTCHESTER AVENUE ... BRONX **NY** 10472 (212) 842-2214
SCHWELLER'S KOSHER CATERERS 3411 JEROME AVENUE ... BRONX **NY** 10467 (212) 655-8649
SIMON'S KOSHER TAKE HOME FOODS 3532 JOHNSON AVENUE ... BRONX **NY** 10463 (212) 796-7530
SKYVIEW KOSHER DELICATESSEN & CATERERS 5665 RIVERDALE AVENUE ... BRONX **NY** 10471 (212) 796-8596
ZION KOSHER DELICATESSEN 968 LONGFELLOW AVENUE ... BRONX **NY** 10462 (212) 589-1770
ZION KOSHER DELICATESSEN & RESTAURANT 750 LYDIG AVENUE ... BRONX **NY** 10462 (212) 597-6360
18TH AVENUE KOSHER PIZZA 4418 18TH AVENUE ... BROOKLYN **NY** 11204
A-1 EILAT RESTAURANT 4823 18TH AVENUE ... BROOKLYN **NY** 11204 (718) 853-9501
ACH TOV KOSHER DAIRY RESTAURANT 5001 13TH AVENUE ... BROOKLYN **NY** 11219 (718) 438-8494
ADELMAN'S DELI 1906 KINGS HIGHWAY ... BROOKLYN **NY** 11229 (718) 336-4915
ALTERNATIVE HEALING CENTER—(MACROBIOTIC)
1767 52ND STREET ... BROOKLYN **NY** 11204 (718) 871-3100
ATIRA RESTAURANT/SUPPER NIGHT CLUB 1925 FLATBUSH AVENUE ... BROOKLYN **NY** 11229 (718) 338-2438
AVENUE M PIZZA 228 AVENUE M ... BROOKLYN **NY** 11223 (718) 376-5801
AVENUE U KOSHER PIZZA 2117 AVENUE U ... BROOKLYN **NY** 11229 (718) 646-9740
BERNAT BERKOWITZ RESTAURANT 1427 CONEY ISLAND AVENUE ... BROOKLYN **NY** 11229 (718) 252-5308
BERWIE'S BAR-B-Q 123 CHURCH AVENUE ... BROOKLYN **NY** 11218 (718) 854-3340
THE BIG HEART RESTAURANT 702 KINGS HIGHWAY ... BROOKLYN **NY** 11223 (718) 627-9039

BOROUGH PARK KOSHER PIZZA 4303 19TH AVENUE ... BROOKLYN **NY** 11204 (718) 436-1064
BOROUGH PARK KOSHER PIZZA 4923 18TH AVENUE ... BROOKLYN **NY** 11204 (718) 438-8542
BRIGHTON BEACH DAIRY RESTAURANT
410 BRIGHTON BEACH AVENUE ... BROOKLYN **NY** 11235 (718) 646-7421
B'TEYAVON RESTAURANT & DELI 1427 CONEY ISLAND AVENUE ... BROOKLYN **NY** 11230 (718) 252-5308
CAN TAAM 4813-13TH AVENUE ... BROOKLYN **NY** 11219 (718) 436-0400
CARMEL RESTAURANT (ISRAELI) 523 KINGS HIGHWAY ... BROOKLYN **NY** 11223 (718) 339-0172
CHAP-A-NOSH 1426 ELM AVENUE ... BROOKLYN **NY** 11230 (718) 627-0072
CHEF'S DELIGHT 4704-18TH AVENUE ... BROOKLYN **NY** 11204 (718) 871-1515
CLARA'S KOSHER RESTAURANT 1348 CONEY ISLAND AVENUE ... BROOKLYN **NY** 11230 (718) 377-9899
COURT GARDEN 187 STATE STREET ... BROOKLYN **NY** 11201 (718) 875-9746
COUSIN'S KOSHER DELI 5014 AVENUE D ... BROOKLYN **NY** 11203 (718) 451-9811
CROWN GLATT KOSHER CATERERS & RESTAURANT
4909-13TH AVENUE ... BROOKLYN **NY** 11219 (718) 853-9000
DAGAN PIZZA 1560 RALPH AVENUE ... BROOKLYN **NY** 11236 (718) 209-0636
DAVID'S SYRIAN & ISRAELI RESTAURANT 547 KINGS HIGHWAY ... BROOKLYN **NY** 11223 (718) 998-8600
EDNA'S GLATT KOSHER DELICATESSEN & RESTAURANT
125 CHURCH AVENUE ... BROOKLYN **NY** 11218 (718) 438-8207
EILAT RESTAURANT 4823 18TH AVENUE ... BROOKLYN **NY** 11204 (718) 853-9501
EL MOROCCO 502 AVENUE M ... BROOKLYN **NY** 11230 (718) 376-4197
ELI ISRAELI GLATT KOSHER RESTAURANT 1622 EAST 16TH STREET ... BROOKLYN **NY** 11229 (718) 376-9862
ELI'S RESTAURANT 5908 AVENUE N ... BROOKLYN **NY** 11234 (718) 531-1783
EMIL FRIEDMAN 1555 48TH STREET ... BROOKLYN **NY** 11219 (718) 854-3596
EMPRESS KOSHER DELI 2210 86TH STREET ... BROOKLYN **NY** 11214 (718) 266-7679
ESS & BENCH 299 KINGSTON AVENUE ... BROOKLYN **NY** 11213
FAMOUS DAIRY RESTAURANT 4818-13TH AVENUE ... BROOKLYN **NY** 11219 (718) 435-4201
FRANKEL'S 5301 NEW UTRECHT AVENUE ... BROOKLYN **NY** 11219 (718) 972-0300
GLATT CHINA RESTAURANT 923 KINGS HIGHWAY ... BROOKLYN **NY** 11223 (718) 336-2500
GLATT CHOW 1204 AVENUE J ... BROOKLYN **NY** 11230 (718) 692-0001
GOLDEN PALATE, THE 492 AVENUE P ... BROOKLYN **NY** 11223 (718) 998-4445
GOTTLIEB'S GLATT KOSHER DELICATESSEN 352 ROEBLING STREET ... BROOKLYN **NY** 11211 (718) 384-9037
GOURMET CAFE 1622 CONEY ISLAND AVENUE ... BROOKLYN **NY** 11230 (718) 338-5825
GRABSTEIN BROS. 1845 ROCKAWAY PARKWAY ... BROOKLYN **NY** 11236 (718) 251-2280
GUTTMAN'S RESTAURANT 5120-13TH AVENUE ... BROOKLYN **NY** 11219 (718) 436-4830
H & S KOSHER DELI 1654 SHEEPSHEAD BAY ROAD ... BROOKLYN **NY** 11235 (718) 646-9032
HIGHWAY ISRAELI GREEK RESTAURANT, THE 1811 KINGS HIGHWAY ... BROOKLYN **NY** 11229 (718) 627-9516
IMPERIAL 4910 13TH AVENUE ... BROOKLYN **NY** 11219 (718) 851-7550
IRVINGS KNISHERY & KOSHER PIZZA 7922 FLATLANDS AVENUE ... BROOKLYN **NY** 11236 (718) 451-1645
IRWIN JAY'S DELI 1121 AVENUE J ... BROOKLYN **NY** 11230 (718) 258-9363
ISRAEL KOSHER PIZZA & FALAFEL 4810 13TH AVENUE ... BROOKLYN **NY** 11219 (718) 438-9872
ITZU'S DAIRY RESTAURANT 45 LEE AVENUE ... BROOKLYN **NY** 11211
JACK'S KOSHER DELI 116 COURT STREET ... BROOKLYN **NY** 11201 (718) 875-0225
JACK'S KOSHER PIZZA 709 KINGS HIGHWAY ... BROOKLYN **NY** 11223
JAY'S KOSHER DELI 1416 AVENUE J ... BROOKLYN **NY** 11230 (718) 253-7440
JERUSALEM KOSHER PIZZA 1312 AVENUE J ... BROOKLYN **NY** 11230 (718) 338-8156
JERUSALEM II PIZZA 1424 AVENUE M ... BROOKLYN **NY** 11230 (718) 645-4753
JERUSALEM RESTAURANT 5209 13TH AVENUE ... BROOKLYN **NY** 11219
JOE'S KOSHER DELI 545 KINGS HIGHWAY ... BROOKLYN **NY** 11223 (718) 336-4040
KING ARTHUR'S KOSHER DELI 9732 SEAVIEW AVENUE ... BROOKLYN **NY** 11236 (718) 763-2233
KINGS DELI & TAKE HOME FOODS 924 KINGS HIGHWAY ... BROOKLYN **NY** 11223 (718) 336-7500
KOSHER CASTLE 5006 13TH AVENUE ... BROOKLYN **NY** 11219 (718) 871-2100
KOSHER CHEF 1906 AVENUE M ... BROOKLYN **NY** 11230 (718) 339-3579
KOSHER COUNTRY-BROOKLYN COLLEGE
AVENUE H & BEDFORD AVENUE ... BROOKLYN **NY** 11210 (718) 434-9798
KOSHER DELIGHT 1223 AVENUE J ... BROOKLYN **NY** 11230 (718) 377-6873
KOSHER DELIGHT 13TH AVENUE AT 46TH STREET ... BROOKLYN **NY** 11219 (718) 435-8500
KOSHER HUT 709 KINGS HIGHWAY ... BROOKLYN **NY** 11223 (718) 376-8996
KOSHER PIZZA 5114 13TH AVENUE ... BROOKLYN **NY** 11219
KOSHER PRIDE 4924 13TH AVENUE ... BROOKLYN **NY** 11219
LA GVINA PIZZARIA 379 KINGSTON AVENUE ... BROOKLYN **NY** 11213 (718) 778-9500
LANDAU'S GLATT KOSHER DELICATESSEN 65 LEE AVENUE ... BROOKLYN **NY** 11211 (718) 782-3700
LAVYAN - DAIRY FRENCH CUISINE 1619 AVENUE M ... BROOKLYN **NY** 11230 (718) 627-2600
LE GOURMET - GLATT KOSHER 1210 KINGS HIGHWAY ... BROOKLYN **NY** 11229 (718) 376-8600
LE PALAIS ISRAELI - GREEK RESTAURANT 923 KINGS HIGHWAY ... BROOKLYN **NY** 11223 (718) 336-2500
LEE KOSHER PIZZA 108 LEE AVENUE ... BROOKLYN **NY** 11211 (718) 384-9380
LEE VELACH RESTAURANT 487 KINGS HIGHWAY ... BROOKLYN **NY** 11223 (718) 336-6658
LEVY'S KOSHER PIZZA 4810 13TH AVENUE ... BROOKLYN **NY** 11219 (718) 438-9872
LITTLE BUDAPEST 1776 OCEAN AVENUE ... BROOKLYN **NY** 11230 (718) 377-9230
LITTLE JERUSALEM 502 AVENUE M ... BROOKLYN **NY** 11230 (718) 376-9831
LOU'S KOSHER DELI 514 KINGS HIGHWAY ... BROOKLYN **NY** 11223 (718) 339-9353
LULU'S KOSHER DELI 107 BRIGHTON BEACH AVENUE ... BROOKLYN **NY** 11235
M & D KOSHER PIZZA 380 KINGSTON AVENUE ... BROOKLYN **NY** 11225
MASADA RESTAURANT 2178 NOSTRAND AVENUE ... BROOKLYN **NY** 11210 (718) 434-9835
MAZAL CHOLOV YISROEL KOSHER PIZZA
4807 NEW UTRECHT AVENUE ... BROOKLYN **NY** 11219 (718) 854-3753
MCDANIEL'S KOSHER PIZZA 555 KINGS HIGHWAY ... BROOKLYN **NY** 11223 (718) 627-9668
MENDELES & ABRAHAM 942 MCDONALD AVENUE ... BROOKLYN **NY** 11218 (718) 436-1702
ME "V" ME 1521 KINGS HIGHWAY ... BROOKLYN **NY** 11229
MILL BASIN KOSHER DELI 5823 AVENUE T ... BROOKLYN **NY** 11234 (718) 241-4910
MUCHKIES 228 AVENUE M ... BROOKLYN **NY** 11230 (718) 376-5801
NATANYA PIZZA 1506 AVENUE J ... BROOKLYN **NY** 11230 (718) 258-5160
NATANYA PIZZA 1383 CONEY ISLAND AVENUE ... BROOKLYN **NY** 11230
NEW PALACE KOSHER DELI 1906 AVENUE M ... BROOKLYN **NY** 11230 (718) 339-2650
NOSHERIA FAST FOOD, INC. 4813-13TH AVENUE ... BROOKLYN **NY** 11219 (718) 436-0400
NOSHIN' GOOD DONUTS 1217 AVENUE J ... BROOKLYN **NY** 11230 (718) 252-3731
P & K KOSHER DELI 2001 AVENUE U ... BROOKLYN **NY** 11229 (718) 646-9700
PALACE, THE 4910-13TH AVENUE ... BROOKLYN **NY** 11219 (718) 871-7660
PIZZA COURT, THE 52 COURT STREET ... BROOKLYN **NY** 11201 (718) 237-0226
RACHEL'S KOSHER LUNCHEONETTE 4926 NEW UTRECHT AVENUE ... BROOKLYN **NY** 11219
REGENCY 4910 13 AVENUE ... BROOKLYN **NY** 11219 (718) 851-7550

Name / Address	City	State	Zip	Phone
REICH'S KOSHER DAIRY RESTAURANT 702 KINGS HIGHWAY	BROOKLYN	NY	11223	
RUTHIE'S RESTAURANT 1427 CONEY ISLAND AVENUE	BROOKLYN	NY	11230	(718) 252-5308
SAM'S KNISHES 504 BRIGHTON BEACH AVENUE	BROOKLYN	NY	11235	(718) 646-5450
SAM'S FAMOUS KNISHES & PIZZA 5006 13TH AVENUE	BROOKLYN	NY	11219	(718) 871-2100
SAMSON'S PIZZA 1922 AVENUE U	BROOKLYN	NY	11229	(718) 934-4009
SAMUEL'S RESTAURANT 5508-16TH AVENUE	BROOKLYN	NY	11204	(718) 438-8927
SCHICK'S RESTAURANT 4901-12TH AVENUE	BROOKLYN	NY	11219	(718) 853-6329
SHALOM ISRAELI ORIENTAL FOODS 538 KINGS HIGHWAY	BROOKLYN	NY	11223	(718) 339-8085
SHANG CHAI RESTAURANT 2189 FLATBUSH AVENUE	BROOKLYN	NY	11234	(718) 377-6100
SHARONE KOSHER PIZZA 4916 13TH AVENUE	BROOKLYN	NY	11219	(718) 438-8800
SHAY'S RESTAURANT 4819 16TH AVENUE	BROOKLYN	NY	11204	
SHELANU ISRAELI & SYRIAN RESTAURANT 521 KINGS HIGHWAY	BROOKLYN	NY	11223	(718) 339-0612
SAMSON'S PIZZA 1922 AVENUE U	BROOKLYN	NY	11229	(718) 934-4009
SHEM TOV KOSHER DAIRY 1040 46TH STREET	BROOKLYN	NY	11219	(718) 438-9366
SHMUEL'S KOSHER PIZZA & FALAFEL 1621 KINGS HIGHWAY	BROOKLYN	NY	11229	(718) 339-7884
SIMMY'S PIZZA 1383 CONEY ISLAND AVENUE	BROOKLYN	NY	11230	(718) 377-9435
SPARKLING NIGHT 1416 AVENUE J	BROOKLYN	NY	11230	(718) 253-7440
TACOS OLE (MEXICAN) 1932 KINGS HIGHWAY	BROOKLYN	NY	11229	(718) 339-1116
TEL AVIV AK'TANA 1121 AVENUE J	BROOKLYN	NY	11230	(718) 258-9583
TOV RESTAURANT & PIZZA SHOP 4001 13TH AVENUE	BROOKLYN	NY	11218	(718) 871-4221
WEISS KOSHER DAIRY RESTAURANT 1146 CONEY ISLAND AVENUE	BROOKLYN	NY	11230	(718) 421-0184
WILLIAMSBURG KOSHER PIZZA 216 WILLIAMSBURG STREET W	BROOKLYN	NY	11211	(718) 384-2540
WILLIAMSBURG RESTAURANT 214 ROSS STREET	BROOKLYN	NY	11211	(718) 384-2540
WINDSOR KOSHER DELI 2281 NOSTRAND AVENUE	BROOKLYN	NY	11210	(718) 377-1476
YUN KEE 1424 ELM AVENUE	BROOKLYN	NY	11230	(718) 627-0072
ZEL-MAR KOSHER DELI 509 BRIGHTON BEACH AVENUE	BROOKLYN	NY	11235	(718) 646-9751
MASTMAN'S KORNER DELICATESSEN 1322 HERTEL AVENUE	BUFFALO	NY	14216	(716) 877-9446
PRESERVATION HALL 752 ELMWOOD	BUFFALO	NY	14222	(716) 884-4242
BURGER NOSH 530 CENTRAL AVENUE	CEDARHURST	NY	11559	(516) 569-6183
DELICIOUS KOSHER DAIRY RESTAURANT 698 CENTRAL AVENUE	CEDARHURST	NY	11559	(516) 569-6725
JACOB'S LADDER 83 SPRUCE STREET	CEDARHURST	NY	11559	(516) 569-3373
KING DAVID RESTAURANT & CATERERS 550 CENTRAL AVENUE	CEDARHURST	NY	11516	(516) 569-2920
KOSHER WOK 592 CENTRAL AVENUE	CEDARHURST	NY	11516	(516) 374-1401
SABRA KOSHER PIZZA 560 CENTRAL AVENUE	CEDARHURST	NY	11516	(516) 569-1563
P & C FOOD MARKETS (DELI SECTION) 4410 EAST GENESEE STREET	DEWITT	NY	13214	(315) 446-6421
BENJY'S KOSHER PIZZA 72-72 MAIN STREET	FLUSHING	NY	11367	(718) 268-0791
DAVID'S KNISHES 67-11 MAIN STREET	FLUSHING	NY	11367	(718) 520-8892
KOSHER HEAVEN 65-30 KISSENA BOULEVARD	FLUSHING	NY	11367	(718) 261-0149
LEVY'S KOSHER PIZZA 68-28 MAIN STREET	FLUSHING	NY	11367	
LINDEN HILLS KOSHER DELI 29-20 UNION STREET	FLUSHING	NY	11354	(718) 762-1515
ND KOSHERIA (QUEENS COLLEGE) 142-45 MELBOURNE AVENUE	FLUSHING	NY	11367	(718) 463-9508
NAOMI LEVY'S KOSHER PIZZA 68-28 MAIN STREET	FLUSHING	NY	11367	
NATURE'S NOSH 67-03 MAIN STREET	FLUSHING	NY	11367	(718) 268-4010
SHALOM JAPAN 67-05 MAIN STREET	FLUSHING	NY	11367	(718) 575-1375
SURREY KOSHER DELICATESSEN & RESTAURANT 179-08 UNION TURNPIKE	FLUSHING	NY	11366	(718) 658-9243
BERSO 64-20 108 STREET	FOREST HILLS	NY	11375	(718) 275-9793
BOULEVARD KOSHER DELI 98-02 QUEENS BLVD	FOREST HILLS	NY	11374	(718) 896-0900
GOURMET EXPRESS 72-42 AUSTIN STREET	FOREST HILLS	NY	11375	(718) 830-5851
JOMAN KOSHER DELI 97-20 QUEENS BLVD	FOREST HILLS	NY	11374	
KATZ'S KOSHER DELI 98-102 QUEENS BLVD	FOREST HILLS	NY	11374	(718) 896-0900
KNISH NOSH 101-02 QUEENS BLVD	FOREST HILLS	NY	11374	(718) 897-5554
LEVY'S KOSHER PIZZA 93-01 63RD DRIVE	FOREST HILLS	NY	11374	
SAM'S ZION KOSHER PIZZA 63-45 108TH STREET	FOREST HILLS	NY	11375	(718) 897-0907
SHALOM TZVI 64-19 108TH STREET	FOREST HILLS	NY	11375	(718) 997-6363
STARK'S KOSHER RESTAURANT 63-55 108TH STREET	FOREST HILLS	NY	11375	
ZION PIZZA CORP 63-46 108TH STREET	FOREST HILLS	NY	11375	(718) 897-0907
GILARI CATERING 710 DOGWOOD AVENUE	FRANKLIN SQUARE	NY	11010	(516) 481-2060
CAFE SHALOM 188-02 UNION TURNPIKE	FRESH MEADOWS	NY	11366	(718) 479-2600
PRESERVATION CAFE C/O JEWISH CENTER, 2640 NORTH FOREST	GETZVILLE	NY	14068	(716) 688-1223
MENORAH RESTAURANT 178 MIDDLE NECK ROAD	GREAT NECK	NY	11023	(516) 466-8181
EPSTEIN'S KOSHER DELICATESSEN & RESTAURANT 389 CENTRAL AVENUE	HARTSDALE	NY	10530	(914) 428-5320
HAPPY'S KOSHER DELI & APPETIZING 82-41 153RD AVENUE	HOWARD BEACH	NY	11433	(718) 641-4007
PATIO KOSHER DELICATESSEN & RESTAURANT 78-16A LINDEN BLVD	HOWARD BEACH	NY	11433	(718) 296-3064
MURRAY'S KOSHER DELI 75-16 37TH AVENUE	JACKSON HEIGHTS	NY	11377	(718) 639-8016
SUTPHIN KOSHER DELICATESSEN 87-71 SUTPHIN BLVD	JAMAICA	NY	11435	(718) 526-9591
KOSHER KETTLE 81-70 LEFFERTS BOULEVARD	KEW GARDENS	NY	11415	(718) 441-9129
BURGER NOSH 69-74 MAIN STREET	KEW GARDENS HILLS	NY	11367	(718) 793-6927
NOT JUST DONUTS 72-04A MAIN STREET	KEW GARDENS HILLS	NY	11367	(718) 268-7830
PINAT SHALOM 69-26 MAIN STREET	KEW GARDENS HILLS	NY	11367	(718) 268-8552
SHALOM JAPAN QUEENS 67-05 MAIN STREET	KEW GARDENS HILLS	NY	11367	(718) 575-1375
SHIMON'S KOSHER PIZZA FALAFEL 71-24 MAIN STREET	KEW GARDENS HILLS	NY	11367	(718) 793-1491
TAIN LEE CHOW 72-24 MAIN STREET	KEW GARDENS HILLS	NY	11367	(718) 268-0960
MAZUR'S MARKET PLACE & RESTAURANT OF LITTLE NECK 254-51 HORACE HARDING BOULEVARD	LITTLE NECK	NY	11362	(718) 428-5000
NOAH'S ARK RESTAURANT 66 WEST PARK AVENUE	LONG BEACH	NY	11561	(516) 536-5630
B & H KOSHER DELI 4811 43RD AVENUE	LONG ISLAND CITY	NY	11377	(718) 457-9052
EUROPEAN HOMEMADE FOODS 82 ROUTE 59	MONSEY	NY	10952	(914) 356-9555
KOSHER DELIGHT 82 ROUTE 59	MONSEY	NY	10952	(914) 356-9555
TOV TAAM DAIRY RESTAURANT 32 MAIN STREET	MONSEY	NY	10952	(914) 352-0207
FIALKOFF'S PIZZA MAIN STREET	MONTICELLO	NY	12701	(914) 794-2663
MT. KISCO KOSHER DELICATESSEN 41 SOUTH MOGER AVENUE	MT. KISCO	NY	10549	(914) 666-6600
THE PELHAMS 675 EAST LINCOLN AVENUE	MT. VERNON	NY	10552	(914) 667-1116
KOSHER KONNECTION TOO 1282 NORTH AVENUE - (WYKAGYL SHOPPING CENTER)	NEW ROCHELLE	NY	10804	(914) 633-3910
LIPSON'S KOSHER DELICATESSEN & RESTAURANT 1291 NORTH AVENUE	NEW ROCHELLE	NY	10804	(914) 636-4241
A&O DIAMOND DAIRY LUNCHEONETTE 4 WEST 47TH STREET	NEW YORK	NY	10036	(212) 719-2694
AVI'S GLATT KOSHER RESTAURANT 150 EAST 39TH STREET	NEW YORK	NY	10016	(212) 557-3088

Name / Address	City	State	Zip	Phone
A YIDDISHE MAMA 562 AMSTERDAM AVENUE	NEW YORK	NY	10024	(212) 769-8940
B'TEAVON LUNCHEONETTE, INC. 2549 AMSTERDAM AVENUE	NEW YORK	NY	10033	
BENJAMIN OF TUDELA 307 AMSTERDAM AVENUE	NEW YORK	NY	10023	(212) 496-5018
BERNSTEIN'S ON ESSEX STREET 135 ESSEX STREET	NEW YORK	NY	10002	(212) 473-3900
BOYCHIK'S 19 WEST 45TH STREET	NEW YORK	NY	10036	(212) 719-5999
BROWNIE'S CREATIVE COOKERY 21 EAST 16TH STREET	NEW YORK	NY	10003	(212) 255-2838
BURGER SPOT 25 ESSEX STREET	NEW YORK	NY	10002	
CAFFE MASADA 1239 FIRST AVENUE AT 67 ST	NEW YORK	NY	10021	(212) 988-0950
CAFE MISADAH 49 WHITE STREET	NEW YORK	NY	10013	(212) 966-7141
CHANDRA GARDENS VEGETARIAN RESTAURANT 310 E. 86TH STREET (BTWN. 1ST & 2ND AVENUE)	NEW YORK	NY	10028	(212) 628-2642
CHEERS RESTAURANT (ITALIAN) 120 WEST 41ST STREET	NEW YORK	NY	10036	(212) 840-8810
CHEZ DAVID - CHOLOV ISRAEL 494 AMSTERDAM AVENUE	NEW YORK	NY	10024	(212) 874-4974
CHOPSIE'S PIZZA 2500 AMSTERDAM AVENUE	NEW YORK	NY	10033	(212) 568-1637
CONTINENTAL KOSHER DELICATESSEN & RESTAURANT 732 WEST 181ST STREET	NEW YORK	NY	10033	(212) 928-9661
CORNUCOPIA KOSHER DELICATESSEN & APPETIZERS 1651 SECOND AVENUE	NEW YORK	NY	10028	(212) 879-0733
DAIRY PLANET 182 BROADWAY (CORNER JOHN STREET)	NEW YORK	NY	10038	(212) 227-8252
DELI CITY 7 WEST 47TH STREET	NEW YORK	NY	10036	(212) 819-0202
DELI GLATT SANDWICH SHOP 150 FULTON STREET	NEW YORK	NY	10038	(212) 349-3622
DELI-ART KOSHER DELICATESSEN 333 SEVENTH AVENUE	NEW YORK	NY	10001	(212) 564-5994

Name / Address	City	State	Zip	Phone
DIVA (ITALIAN CUISINE) 306 EAST 81ST STREET	NEW YORK	**NY**	10028	(212) 650-1928
EDIBLE PURSUITS—(DAIRY) 325 FIFTH AVENUE	NEW YORK	**NY**	10016	(212) 686-5330
EDNA'S RESTAURANT & DELI 401 GRAND STREET	NEW YORK	**NY**	10002	(212) 473-7630
EL AVRAM 80 GROVE STREET	NEW YORK	**NY**	10014	(212) 243-9661
ELI'S GLATT KOSHER DELI & BAKERY 1026 AVENUE OF THE AMERICAS	NEW YORK	**NY**	10018	(212) 382-2494
FAMOUS RESTAURANT (DAIRY) 222 WEST 72ND STREET	NEW YORK	**NY**	10023	(212) 595-8487
FINE & SHAPIRO 138 WEST 72ND STREET	NEW YORK	**NY**	10023	(212) 877-2874
FRIEDMAN'S KOSHER DAIRY RESTAURANT 43 CANAL STREET	NEW YORK	**NY**	10002	(212) 226-9444
GEFEN KOSHER DAIRY RESTAURANT 297 7TH AVENUE	NEW YORK	**NY**	10001	(212) 929-6476
GIRLCHIK'S 155 W. 47TH STREET	NEW YORK	**NY**	10036	(212) 391-2033
GLATT NOSH 884 AVENUE OF THE AMERICAS	NEW YORK	**NY**	10001	(212) 684-0530
GOLDIE'S 211 EAST 46TH STREET	NEW YORK	**NY**	10017	(212) 421-5905
GRANDMA'S COOKIE JAR 2543 AMSTERDAM AVENUE	NEW YORK	**NY**	10033	(212) 568-4855
GREAT AMERICAN HEALTH BAR 55 JOHN ST. (BET. NASSAU & WILLIAM)	NEW YORK	**NY**	10038	(212) 227-6100
GREAT AMERICAN HEALTH BAR 2 PARK AVENUE (BET. 32ND & 33RD STREETS)	NEW YORK	**NY**	10016	(212) 685-7117
GREAT AMERICAN HEALTH BAR 11 PARK PLACE	NEW YORK	**NY**	10007	(212) 962-4444
GREAT AMERICAN HEALTH BAR 15 E. 40TH ST.	NEW YORK	**NY**	10017	(212) 532-3232
GREAT AMERICAN HEALTH BAR 30 WEST 48TH STREET	NEW YORK	**NY**	10036	(212) 719-4520
GREAT AMERICAN HEALTH BAR 35 W. 57TH ST.	NEW YORK	**NY**	10019	(212) 355-5177
GREENER PASTURES 117 EAST 60TH STREET	NEW YORK	**NY**	10022	(212) 832-3212
GROSS' DAIRY RESTAURANT 1372 BROADWAY	NEW YORK	**NY**	10018	(212) 921-1969
HENRY'S KOSHER DELICATESSEN & RESTAURANT 195 EAST HOUSTON STREET	NEW YORK	**NY**	10002	(212) 674-2200
INTERNATIONAL GLATT KOSHER 142 FULTON STREET	NEW YORK	**NY**	10038	(212) 406-4620
JERUSALEM PIZZA 1275 LEXINGTON AVENUE	NEW YORK	**NY**	10028	(212) 534-8541
JERUSALEM II 1375 BROADWAY	NEW YORK	**NY**	10018	(212) 398-1475
JERUSALEM II 112 FULTON STREET	NEW YORK	**NY**	10038	(212) 732-6523
JEWISH THEOLOGICAL SEMINARY 3080 BROADWAY	NEW YORK	**NY**	10027	(212) 678-8000
JUST-A-BITE 106 GREENWICH STREET	NEW YORK	**NY**	10006	(212) 425-5470
KING DAVID KOSHER PIZZA 2549 AMSTERDAM AVENUE	NEW YORK	**NY**	10033	(212) 923-9470
KOSHER DELIGHT 1365 BROADWAY	NEW YORK	**NY**	10018	(212) 563-3366
KOSHER HUT 866 6TH AVENUE	NEW YORK	**NY**	10001	(212) 686-8319
KOSHER INN #2, INC. 2500 AMSTERDAM AVENUE	NEW YORK	**NY**	10033	(212) 927-5858
LA FRELLA 121 UNIVERSITY PLACE	NEW YORK	**NY**	10003	(212) 420-1300
LA KASBAH (MOROCCAN & MEDITERRANEAN) 79 WEST 71ST STREET	NEW YORK	**NY**	10023	(212) 769-1690
LEVANA'S CAFE (FISH & VEGETARIAN) 141 WEST 69TH STREET	NEW YORK	**NY**	10023	(212) 877-8457
LEVY'S KOSHER PIZZA 330 SEVENTH AVENUE	NEW YORK	**NY**	10001	(212) 594-4613
LOIS LANE'S NINTH & NATURAL 580 9TH AVENUE AT 42 ST.	NEW YORK	**NY**	10036	(212) 695-5055
LOU G. SIEGEL'S 209 WEST 38TH STREET	NEW YORK	**NY**	10018	(212) 921-4433
MACCABEEM RESTAURANT 147 WEST 47TH STREET	NEW YORK	**NY**	10036	(212) 575-0226
MADRAS PALACE—(SOUTH INDIAN CUISINE) 104 LEXINGTON AVENUE	NEW YORK	**NY**	10016	(212) 532-3314
MAGEN PIZZA & DAIRY RESTAURANT 25 CANAL STREET	NEW YORK	**NY**	10002	(212) 598-4178
MARCY KOSHER DELICATESSEN 2511 BROADWAY	NEW YORK	**NY**	10025	(212) 222-0700
MARRAKESH WEST 149 BLEEKER STREET	NEW YORK	**NY**	10012	(212) 777-8911
MCDOVID'S 2502 AMSTERDAM AVENUE	NEW YORK	**NY**	10033	(212) 928-4497
MEAL MART 2189 BROADWAY	NEW YORK	**NY**	10024	(212) 787-4720
MOSHE PEKING 40 WEST 37TH STREET	NEW YORK	**NY**	10018	(212) 594-6500
MY MOST FAVORITE DESSERT COMPANY CAFE 1165 MADISON AVENUE	NEW YORK	**NY**	10028	(212) 517-5222
MY PLACE 2553 AMSTERDAM AVENUE	NEW YORK	**NY**	10033	(212) 568-4600
N.Y. PITA DEPOT 267 AMSTERDAM AVENUE	NEW YORK	**NY**	10023	(212) 724-6000
NOGA - MEDITERRANEAN CABARET 40 WEST 8TH STREET	NEW YORK	**NY**	10011	(212) 473-3361
RATNER'S DAIRY RESTAURANT 138 DELANCEY STREET	NEW YORK	**NY**	10002	(212) 677-5588
SAM'S KOSHER DELICATESSEN 37 ESSEX STREET	NEW YORK	**NY**	10002	(212) 674-0980
SHALOM KOSHER PIZZA 1000 SIXTH AVENUE	NEW YORK	**NY**	10018	(212) 730-0008
SOMEPLACE SPECIAL DELI-RESTAURANT 401 GRAND STREET	NEW YORK	**NY**	10002	(212) 674-0980
STEINBERG'S DAIRY RESTAURANT 21 ESSEX STREET	NEW YORK	**NY**	10002	(212) 254-7787
STERN COLLEGE CAFETERIA 245 LEXINGTON AVENUE	NEW YORK	**NY**	10016	(212) 340-7712
TEVA NATURAL FOODS 122 EAST 42ND STREET	NEW YORK	**NY**	10017	(212) 599-1265
TSABAR PIZZA 218 WEST 35TH STREET	NEW YORK	**NY**	10001	(212) 947-2167
VERVE NATURELLE (VEGETARIAN) 157 WEST 57TH STREET	NEW YORK	**NY**	10019	(212) 265-2255
WEST 35TH ST. DAIRY 218 W. 35 STREET	NEW YORK	**NY**	10001	(212) 947-2167
YESHIVA UNIVERSITY CAFETERIA 2501 AMSTERDAM AVENUE	NEW YORK	**NY**	10033	(212) 960-5248
EVERYTHING IN A PITA 2882 LONG BEACH ROAD	OCEANSIDE	**NY**	11572	(516) 536-5630
HUNKI'S KOSHER PIZZA & FALAFEL 3300 LONG BEACH ROAD	OCEANSIDE	**NY**	11572	(516) 766-3666
PELHAM KOSHER RESTAURANT 91 WOLF LANE	PELHAM	**NY**	10803	(914) 738-1617
BEN'S KOSHER DELICATESSEN & RESTAURANT 96-40 QUEENS BLVD.	REGO PARK	**NY**	11374	(718) 897-1700
CAFE BABA OF ISRAEL 91-33 63RD DRIVE	REGO PARK	**NY**	11374	(718) 275-2660
FLAME-LAPID, THE 97-04 QUEENS BLVD	REGO PARK	**NY**	11374	(718) 275-1403
GOLAN RESTAURANT 97-28 63RD ROAD	REGO PARK	**NY**	11374	(718) 897-7522
PIZZA FALAFEL OF QUEENS 93-01 63RD DRIVE	REGO PARK	**NY**	11374	(718) 897-5111
FLASH KOSHER PIZZA 3602 RIVERDALE AVENUE	RIVERDALE	**NY**	10463	(212) 543-1811
JASON'S PLACE C/O JCC, 1200 EDGEWOOD AVENUE	ROCHESTER	**NY**	14618	(716) 461-2020
CHOLOV YISROEL PIZZA MAIN STREET	SOUTH FALLSBURG	**NY**	12779	(914) 434-5845
FINE-ESS ICE CREAM ROUTE 42, MAIN STREET	SOUTH FALLSBURG	**NY**	12779	(914) 434-1565
GOURMET GLATT MAIN STREET	SOUTH FALLSBURG	**NY**	12779	
NOSH-A-BAGEL ROUTE 42, MAIN STREET	SOUTH FALLSBURG	**NY**	12779	(914) 434-0440
ROADSIDE DAIRY RESTAURANT ROUTE 42	SOUTH FALLSBURG	**NY**	12779	(914) 434-6064
THE CREST HILL DELI MAIN STREET & ECKERSON ROAD	SPRING VALLEY	**NY**	10977	(914) 352-3696
GARTNER'S INN HUNGRY HOLLOW ROAD	SPRING VALLEY	**NY**	10977	(914) 356-0875
HERSHEY'S KOSHER RESTAURANT 33 MAPLE AVENUE	SPRING VALLEY	**NY**	10977	(914) 352-9720
DAIRY PALACE 2210 VICTORY BOULEVARD	STATEN ISLAND	**NY**	10314	(718) 761-5200
CAFE NETANYA 2811 RICHMOND AVENUE	STATEN ISLAND	**NY**	10314	(718) 494-4484
PICKLES UNLIMITED 4469 EAST GENESEE	SYRACUSE	**NY**	13214	(315) 445-1294
BAGEL CRAFT OF HEMPSTEAD 118 HEMPSTEAD TPKE	WEST HEMPSTEAD	**NY**	11552	(516) 485-2314
HUNKI'S 338 HEMPSTEAD AVENUE	WEST HEMPSTEAD	**NY**	11552	(516) 538-6655
KOSHER COTTAGE 338 HEMPSTEAD AVENUE	WEST HEMPSTEAD	**NY**	11552	(516) 486-8362
DELI COUNTRY MAIN STREET	WOODBOURNE	**NY**	12788	(914) 434-2298
WOODBOURNE KOSHER PIZZA 398 MAIN STREET	WOODBOURNE	**NY**	12788	(914) 434-4790
PIZZA PIOUS 1063 BROADWAY	WOODMERE	**NY**	11598	(516) 295-2050
PILDER'S KOSHER FOODS 7601 READING STREET	CINCINNATI	**OH**	45215	(513) 821-7050
DELI CELLAR 11291 EUCLID AVENUE, HILLEL BUILDING - CWRU	CLEVELAND	**OH**	44106	(216) 231-0040
KINNERET KOSHER RESTAURANT 1869 SOUTH TAYLOR ROAD	CLEVELAND	**OH**	44118	(216) 321-1404
KOSHER KORNER 1026 SOUTH TAYLOR ROAD	CLEVELAND	**OH**	44118	(216) 321-6308
THE DELI 1805 SOUTH TAYLOR ROAD	CLEVELAND	**OH**	44118	(216) 321-9545
THE DINING ROOM 1805 SOUTH TAYLOR ROAD	CLEVELAND	**OH**	44118	(216) 321-9545
VEGETARIA 2057 CORNELL ROAD	CLEVELAND	**OH**	44118	(216) 791-9914
HARRY'S APPETIZER & DELICATESSEN 2072 SOUTH TAYLOR ROAD	CLEVELAND HEIGHTS	**OH**	44118	(216) 932-5000
SIEGLER'S DELICATESSEN & FOOD MARKET 15 WEST BANCROFT	TOLEDO	**OH**	43603	(419) 243-6264
SIEGLER'S DELICATESSEN & FOOD MARKET 2636 WEST CENTRAL	TOLEDO	**OH**	43603	(419) 473-2791
KRAVITZ'S DELICATESSEN 3135 BELMONT	YOUNGSTOWN	**OH**	44505	(216) 544-3842
NEWPORT DELICATESSEN & SANDWICH SHOP 4609 HILLMAN WAY	YOUNGSTOWN	**OH**	44512	(216) 782-4213
SPIEGLE'S DELICATESSEN & GOURMET SHOP UNION SQUARE	YOUNGSTOWN	**OH**		(216) 746-1993
MARKY'S DELI 280 WILSON STREET	DOWNSVIEW	**ON**	M3H 1S8	(416) 638-1081
BAGELS GALORE FIRST CANADIAN PLACE	TORONTO	**ON**		(416) 363-4233
BAYCREST JEWISH CENTRE HOME FOR THE AGED 3560 BATHURST STREET	TORONTO	**ON**		(416) 789-5131
HERSCHEL'S 4630 DUFFERIN STREET	TORONTO	**ON**		(416) 661-3600
KIVA'S BAGEL BAKERY & RESTAURANT 1027 STEELES AVENUE WEST	TORONTO	**ON**	M2R 2S9	(416) 663-9933
THE LOWER EAST SIDE CAFE 604 SPADINA AVENUE	TORONTO	**ON**		(416) 923-9861
MARKY'S DELICATESSEN 280 WILSON	TORONTO	**ON**		(416) 638-1081
MATI'S FALAFEL HOUSE 3430 BATHURST STREET	TORONTO	**ON**		(416) 783-9505
NEW YORK, NEW YORK (MALKAT PEKING ROOM) 3426 BATHURST	TORONTO	**ON**		(416) 783-6622
PERL'S MEAT & DELICATESSEN PRODUCTS 3013 BATHURST STREET	TORONTO	**ON**		(416) 787-4234
YITZ'S RESTAURANT & CATERING 346 ENGLINTON AVENUE WEST	TORONTO	**ON**	M5N 1A2	(416) 487-4506
DRAGON INN (CHINESE) 7628 CASTOR AVENUE	PHILADELPHIA	**PA**	19152	(215) 742-2575
GOLD CUTS 245 S. 17TH STREET	PHILADELPHIA	**PA**	19103	(212) 735-4762
ABE'S DELICATESSEN & RESTAURANT 325 PENN AVENUE	SCRANTON	**PA**	18503	(717) 342-4517
Y.M.H.A. THE EATERY 775 DU SABLON	CHOMEDEY	**QU**	H7W 4H5	(514) 688-8961
Y.M.H.A. SNACK BAR 5700 KELLERT AVENUE	COTE ST. LUC	**QU**	H4W 1T4	(514) 482-0730
Y.M.H.A. THE EATERY 5700 KELLERT AVENUE	COTE ST. LUC	**QU**	H4W 1T4	(514) 482-0730
BBQ MCDAVID 5611 COTE DES NEIGES	MONTREAL	**QU**	H3T 1Y8	(514) 341-1633
CASSE CROUTE EILAT 6459 VICTORIA AVENUE	MONTREAL	**QU**	H3W 2S9	(514) 731-3310
CHABAD HOUSE 3429 PEEL STREET	MONTREAL	**QU**	H3A 1W7	(514) 842-6616
DELI PEKING 6900 DECARIE BLVD	MONTREAL	**QU**	H3T 2T8	(514) 738-2844
EL MOROCCO 3450 DRUMMOND	MONTREAL	**QU**	H3G 1Y1	(514) 844-6888
FOXY'S 5987-A VICTORIA AVENUE	MONTREAL	**QU**	H3W 2R9	(514) 739-8777
GOLDEN SPOON 5217 DECARIE BOULEVARD	MONTREAL	**QU**	H3W 3C2	(514) 481-3431
HILLEL HOUSE - MCGILL 3460 STANLEY STREET	MONTREAL	**QU**	H3A 1R8	(514) 845-9171
JONATHAN RESTAURANT 4699 VAN HORNE AVENUE	MONTREAL	**QU**	H3W 1H8	(514) 341-4434
MILK & HONEY 4950 QUEEN MARY ROAD	MONTREAL	**QU**	H3W 1X3	(514) 733-7823
ODELIA 5897-A VICTORIA AVENUE	MONTREAL	**QU**	H3W 2R6	(514) 733-0984
OLD MONTREAL KOSHER DELI 768 ST. PIERRE STREET	MONTREAL	**QU**	H2Y 2N5	(514) 849-0283
Y.M.H.A. CAFETERIA 5500 WESTBURY AVENUE	MONTREAL	**QU**	H3W 2W8	(514) 737-8704
DAVIS' DAIRY PRODUCTS COMPANY 721 HOPE STREET	PROVIDENCE	**RI**	02906	(401) 331-4239
TEVYE'S 1131 BABCOCK ROAD	SAN ANTONIO	**TX**	78201	(512) 735-5109
KOSHER DELIGHT 1509 1ST AVENUE	SEATTLE	**WA**	98101	(206) 624-4555
JEWISH COMMUNITY CENTER KOSHER RESTAURANT 1400 WEST PROSPECT AVENUE	MILWAUKEE	**WI**	53202	(414) 276-0716

RETIREMENT HOMES

Name / Address	City	State	Zip	Phone
KIVEL MANOR 3040 NORTH 36TH STREET	PHOENIX	**AZ**	85018	(602) 956-0150
PREMIER MANOR 655 SOUTH MOLLISON AVENUE	EL CAJON	**CA**	92020	(619) 444-3181
BETH AVOT 7721 BEVERLY BOULEVARD	LOS ANGELES	**CA**	90048	(213) 932-8889
BEVERLY HILLS CARMEL RETIREMENT HOTEL 8750 BURTON WAY	LOS ANGELES	**CA**	90048	(213) 278-9720
BEVERLY HILLS GARDENS 1470 SOUTH ROBERTSON BOULEVARD	LOS ANGELES	**CA**	90035	(213) 273-3668
BEVERLY SINAI TOWERS 8435 BEVERLY BOULEVARD	LOS ANGELES	**CA**	90048	(213) 852-9237
FLORA TERRACE RETIREMENT HOTEL 6070 WEST PICO BOULEVARD	LOS ANGELES	**CA**	90035	(213) 653-5565
GOLDEN STATE RETIREMENT HOTEL 4340 LOCKWOOD	LOS ANGELES	**CA**	90036	(213) 663-2153
HANCOCK PARK RETIREMENT HOTEL 515 NORTH LA BREA AVENUE	LOS ANGELES	**CA**	90036	(213) 938-2131
NEW GARDEN OF ROSES 960 NORTH MARTEL AVENUE	LOS ANGELES	**CA**	90046	(213) 876-0373
SHALOM KOSHER HOTEL 330 NORTH HAYWORTH	LOS ANGELES	**CA**	90036	(213) 655-1500
MARGO'S MANOR 5527 LAUREL CANYON BOULEVARD	NORTH HOLLYWOOD	**CA**	90046	(818) 760-9940
ROYAL BELLINGHAM 12229 CHANDLER BOULEVARD	NORTH HOLLYWOOD	**CA**	91607	(818) 980-2997
BEACH FRONT GUEST HOME 20 OZONE AVENUE	VENICE	**CA**	90291	(213) 396-0206
MOUNT CARMEL GARDENS 5846 MT. CARMEL TERRACE	JACKSONVILLE	**FL**	33216	(904) 733-6696
THE RENAISSANCE 1690 COLLINS AVENUE	MIAMI BEACH	**FL**	33139	(305) 538-4222
ORANGE BLOSSOM MANOR 3535 SOUTHWEST 52ND AVENUE	PEMBROKE PARK	**FL**	33023	(305) 961-8111
WILTON HOUSE 1039 WEST LAWRENCE	CHICAGO	**IL**	60640	(312) 561-1133
MONASH MANOR 865 SINCLAIR STREET	WINNIPEG	**MB**	R2V 3H3	(204) 334-4537
DELCREST 8350 DELCREST DRIVE	ST. LOUIS	**MO**	63124	(314) 991-2055
MIRIAM APARTMENTS 127 HAZEL STREET	CLIFTON	**NJ**	07011	(201) 772-9383
B'NAI B'RITH PARKVIEW APARTMENTS 400 HUDSON AVENUE	ALBANY	**NY**	12203	(518) 465-2293
OHAV SHALOM SENIOR CITIZEN HOUSING PROJECT 115 NEW KRUMKILL ROAD	ALBANY	**NY**	12208	(518) 489-5531
QUEEN ESTHER HOME FOR ADULTS 124-05 ROCKAWAY BEACH BOULEVARD	BELLE HARBOR	**NY**	11694	(718) 474-0400
HARBOR VIEW HOTEL 3900 SHORE PARKWAY	BROOKLYN	**NY**	11235	(718) 769-9700
OCEAN BREEZE HOTEL 3811 SURF AVENUE	BROOKLYN	**NY**	11235	(718) 266-1456
PARK SHORE MANOR 1555 ROCKAWAY PARKWAY	BROOKLYN	**NY**	11236	(718) 498-6400
SCHAROME MANOR 631 FOSTER AVENUE	BROOKLYN	**NY**	11230	(718) 859-2400
SCHARF MANOR HOME FOR ADULTS 112-14 CORONA AVENUE	CORONA	**NY**	11368	(718) 699-4100
ROCKAWAY MANOR HOME 145 BEACH 8TH STREET	FAR ROCKAWAY	**NY**	11691	(718) 327-6300
HOMESTEAD HOME 82-45 GRENFELL STREET	KEW GARDENS	**NY**	11415	(718) 441-2000

AMBASSADOR MANOR 351 WEST BROADWAY ... LONG BEACH NY 11561 (516) 431-2200
ATLANTIC HOME FOR ADULTS 125 EAST BROADWAY ... LONG BEACH NY 11561 (516) 432-6300
BRIGHTON MANOR HOME 403 EAST BROADWAY ... LONG BEACH NY 11561 (516) 431-0200
BROADWAY MANOR 165 EAST BROADWAY ... LONG BEACH NY 11561 (516) 431-5400
CROWN HOME FOR ADULTS 172 WEST BROADWAY ... LONG BEACH NY 11561 (516) 889-8900
KING DAVID MANOR 80 WEST BROADWAY ... LONG BEACH NY 11561 (516) 889-1300
LINCOLN HOME FOR ADULTS 405 EAST BROADWAY ... LONG BEACH NY 11561 (516) 889-7100
PALACE HOTEL 275 EAST BROADWAY ... LONG BEACH NY 11561 (516) 432-9000
PROMENADE HOME FOR ADULTS 102 WEST BROADWAY ... LONG BEACH NY 11561 (516) 431-0100
SCHARF MANOR 274 WEST BROADWAY ... LONG BEACH NY 11561 (516) 431-1400
PHILADA APARTMENTS 7732 GREENLAND PLACE ... CINCINNATI OH 45237 (513) 761-5544
COUNCIL GARDENS 2501 TAYLOR ROAD ... CLEVELAND OH 44118 (216) 382-8625
MIGDAL DAVID 3705 BATHURST ... TORONTO ON (416) 636-3030
YORK HOUSE YORK ROAD AND SOMERVILLE AVENUE ... PHILADELPHIA PA 19141 (215) 456-2906
FORWARD-SHADY APARTMENTS 5841 FORWARD AVENUE ... PITTSBURGH PA 15217 (412) 521-3065
RIVERVIEW APARTMENTS 52 GARETTA STREET ... PITTSBURGH PA 15217 (412) 521-7876
ROSE GARDEN SENIOR CITIZENS HOME 4387 BURRET ... MONTREAL QU (514) 733-6625
JEWISH COMMUNITY COUNCIL
5601 SOUTH BRAESWOOD BOULEVARD ... HOUSTON TX 77035 (713) 729-3200

RETREAT CENTER & SITES

BOB RUSSELL COMMUNITY RETREAT CENTER
4200 BISCAYNE BOULEVARD ... MIAMI FL 33137 (305) 576-1660
CLAL 421 SEVENTH AVENUE ... NEW YORK NY 10001 (212) 714-9500
DR. ELLIOT UDELL (PROFESSIONAL SINGLES) ... PLAINVIEW NY (516) 349-7125
ASCENT INSTITUTE - INNER DIMENSIONS OF JEWISH LIFE
6 RIDBAZ STREET, P.O. BOX 296 ... SAFED IS (06) 971407

RUBBER STAMPS

COMMERCIAL STAMP COMPANY 106 DEKALB AVENUE ... BROOKLYN NY 11215 (718) 858-3880

SAFES - ISRAELI

ACME SAFE COMPANY 150 LAFAYETTE STREET ... NEW YORK NY 10013 (212) 226-2500
I. S. M. (MAXIMUM SECURITY SAFES FROM ISRAEL)
103 GRAND STREET ... NEW YORK NY 10002 (212) 226-1969
ISRAEL SAFES MANUFACTURING CO.,LTD. 103 GRAND STREET ... NEW YORK NY 10002 (212) 226-1969

SCHOOLS - ART

BEZALEL SCHOOL OF ART, JERUSALEM 3938 WEST 13TH AVENUE ... VANCOUVER BC V6R 2T2 (604) 224-0380
HEBREW ARTS SCHOOL 129 WEST 67TH STREET ... NEW YORK NY 10023 (212) 362-8060
SAIDYE BRONFMAN CENTRE 5170 COTE ST. CATHERINE ... MONTREAL QU H3W 1M7 (514) 739-2301

SCHOOLS - SPECIAL EDUCATION & LEARNING DISABILITY

GATEWAYS HOSPITAL & COMMUNITY MENTAL HEALTH CENTER
1891 EFFIE STREET ... LOS ANGELES CA 90026 (213) 666-0171
HOPE CENTER FOR THE RETARDED 3601 EAST 32ND AVENUE ... DENVER CO 80205 (303) 388-4308
JEWISH CHILDREN'S BUREAU 1 SOUTH FRANKLIN STREET ... CHICAGO IL 60606 (312) 346-6700
MICHAEL REESE HOSPITAL & MEDICAL CENTER
29TH STREET AND ELLIS AVENUE ... CHICAGO IL 60616 (312) 791-2000
TEMPLE KEHILATH ISRAEL D. CARE/EDUC. SVCS. FOR RETARDED CHILDREN
384 HARVARD STREET ... BROOKLINE MA 02146 (617) 277-9155
SHALOM RESIDENCE 175 CATHEDRAL AVENUE ... WINNIPEG MB R2W 0X1 (204) 586-4310
P'TACH SCHOOL OF BALTIMORE 6307 PIMLICO ROAD ... BALTIMORE MD 21209 (301) 358-5713
P'TACH 25311 RONALD COURT ... OAK PARK MI 48237 (313) 399-6281
TORAH WORKSHOP DAY CARE/EDUC. SERVICE FOR RETARDED CHILDREN
1 HENDERSON ... WEST CALDWELL NJ 07006 (201) 575-6050
SHIELD INSTITUTE FOR RETARDED CHILDREN 1800 ANDREWS AVENUE ... BRONX NY 10453 (212) 731-0481
BROOKLYN HEBREW SCHOOL FOR SPECIAL CHILDREN
376 BAY 44TH STREET ... BROOKLYN NY 11214 (718) 946-9700
CAMP HUNTINGTON C/O DR. KURTZER 1017 EAST 80TH STREET ... BROOKLYN NY 11236 (718) 633-1591
COMMUNITY SCHOOL BETH MOSHE 913 49TH STREET ... BROOKLYN NY 11219
HEBREW ACADEMY FOR SPECIAL CHILDREN 1311 55TH STREET ... BROOKLYN NY 11219 (718) 851-6100
HEBREW INSTITUTE FOR THE DEAF 2025 67TH STREET ... BROOKLYN NY 11204 (718) 259-2626
ORTHODOX TORAH SERVICES & ADVOCACY FOR THE RETARDED
1717 15TH STREET ... BROOKLYN NY 11229 (718) 376-0557
P'TACH 1363 49TH STREET ... BROOKLYN NY 11219 (718) 854-8600
PESHA SOLOVEICHIK DAY SCHOOL - SPECIAL CHILDREN
376 BAY 44TH STREET ... BROOKLYN NY 11214
PRIDE OF JUDEA CHILDREN'S SERVICES 1000 DUMONT AVENUE ... BROOKLYN NY 11208
THE JEWISH CENTER FOR SPECIAL EDUCATION 430 KENT AVENUE ... BROOKLYN NY 11211 (718) 782-0064
YESHIVA BAIS SHALOM ALTERNATIVE SCHOOL 555 REMSEN AVENUE ... BROOKLYN NY 11236 (718) 495-2100
YESHIVA CHESED YISROEL 2422 AVENUE K ... BROOKLYN NY 11230 (718) 338-8300
MAIMONIDES SCHOOL FOR EXCEPTIONAL CHILDREN
3401 MOTT AVENUE ... FAR ROCKAWAY NY 11691 (718) 471-0100
SUMMIT INSTITUTE IN ISRAEL, LTD. 71-11 112TH STREET ... FOREST HILLS NY 11375 (718) 268-0020
MAIMONIDES DAY SCHOOL & RESIDENTIAL CENTER
FOR SPECIAL CHILDREN ... MONTICELLO NY 12701
NATIONAL COMMISSION ON TORAH EDUCATION
500 WEST 185TH STREET ... NEW YORK NY 10033 (212) 960-5400
P'TACH PROGRAM, MARSHA STERN TALMUDICAL ACADEMY, YU HIGH SCHOOL
AMSTERDAM AVENUE & 186TH STREET ... NEW YORK NY 10033 (212) 960-5337
SHALAYIM, UNITED SYNAGOGUE DEPARTMENT OF EDUCATION
155 FIFTH AVENUE ... NEW YORK NY 10010 (212) 553-7800
TIKVAH PROGRAM, NATIONAL RAMAH COMMISSION 3080 BROADWAY ... NEW YORK NY 10027
HEBREW ACADEMY FOR SPECIAL CHILDREN ... PARKSVILLE NY 12768
SUBURBAN EAST SCHOOL OF PVA 3031 MONTICELLO BOULEVARD ... CLEVELAND OH 44118
EZRA LEARNING CENTER 200 WILMINGTON AVENUE ... DOWNSVIEW ON (416) 633-8247
WOODS SCHOOLS, THE ROUTE 213 ... LANGHORNE PA 19047 (215) 757-3731
HAR ZION RELIGIOUS SCHOOL HAGYS FORK AT HOLLOW ROAD ... PENN VALLEY PA 19072 (215) 667-5002
ADATH ZION BRANCH OF THE UNITED HEBREW SCHOOLS
PENNWAY & FRIENDSHIP STREETS ... PHILADELPHIA PA 19111 (215) 742-8500
BETH T'FILLAH BRANCH OF THE UNITED HEBREW SCHOOLS
7630 WOODBINE AVENUE ... PHILADELPHIA PA 19151 (215) 477-9146
PENNSYLVANIA SCHOOL FOR THE DEAF
7500 GERMANTOWN AVENUE ... PHILADELPHIA PA 19119 (215) 247-9700
PHILADELPHIA PSYCHIATRIC CENTER
FORD ROAD AND MONUMENT AVENUE ... PHILADELPHIA PA 19131
SCHOOL OF OBSERVATION & PRACTICE 701 BYBERRY ROAD ... PHILADELPHIA PA 19116 (215) 677-7261
CAMP WOODEN ACRES C/O JEWISH COMMUNITY CAMPS
5151 COTE STE. CATHERINE ROAD #203 ... MONTREAL QU
MIRIAM HOME FOR THE EXCEPTIONAL CHILD 4321 GUIMONT ... MONTREAL QU

SCHOOLS - TECHNICAL

COPE INSTITUTE 4419 18TH AVENUE ... BROOKLYN NY 11204 (718) 436-1700
SHEVET Y'HUDAH RESNICK INSTITUTE OF TECHNOLOGY
670 ROCKAWAY PARKWAY ... BROOKLYN NY 11236 (718) 342-6878
SYRIT COMPUTER SCHOOL 5220 13TH AVENUE ... BROOKLYN NY 11219 (718) 853-1212
BRAMSON ORT 304 PARK AVENUE SOUTH ... NEW YORK NY 10010 (212) 677-7420

SCIENTIFIC ORGANIZATIONS

TORAH TECHNICS - "WHERE TORAH & TECHNOLOGY MEET"
1603 CARROLL STREET ... BROOKLYN NY 11213 (718) 953-7028
ASSOCIATION OF ORTHODOX JEWISH SCIENTISTS
45 WEST 36TH STREET ... NEW YORK NY 10018 (212) 695-7525
SOCIETY OF JEWISH SCIENCE
P.O. BOX 114, 825 ROUND SWAMP ROAD ... OLD BETHPAGE NY 11804 (516) 249-6262

SCOUTING

NATIONAL JEWISH COMMITTEE ON SCOUTING-BOY SCOUTS OF AMERICA
... NEW BRUNSWICK NJ 08902 (201) 249-6000
BOY SCOUTS OF AMERICA, NATIONAL DIRECTOR OF JEWISH RELATIONS
... NEW BRUNSWICK NJ 08902 (201) 821-6500
JEWISH COMM. ON SCOUTING-BERGEN COUNCIL, BOY SCOUTS OF AMER.
1060 MAIN STREET ... RIVER EDGE NJ 07661
JEWISH COMMITTEE ON SCOUTING 4314 SILSBY ROAD ... CLEVELAND OH 44118 (216) 381-6788
NATIONAL JEWISH COMMITTEE ON SCOUTING
P.O. BOX 61030 ... DALLAS-FT WORTH AIRPORT TX 75261 (214) 659-2000

SCULPTORS

EMANUEL MILSTEIN 29 WYNCREST ROAD ... MARLBORO NJ 07746 (201) 946-8604
JANE TELLER 200 PROSPECT AVENUE ... PRINCETON NJ 08540 (619) 924-6371
PHIL KUZNEZOFF 773 TOBIA ROAD ... SOMERVILLE NJ 08876 (201) 725-1333
ERNA WEILL 886 ALPINE DRIVE ... TEANECK NJ 07666 (201) 837-1627
EDELWEISS CO. - GLASS STUDIO 1217 49TH STREET ... BROOKLYN NY 11219 (718) 851-9687
SAMPSON SEYMOUR ENGOREN 11 HOLMES PLACE ... LYNBROOK NY 11563 (516) 599-3173
EFREM WEITZMAN - SYNAGOGUE ART 334 WEST 86TH STREET ... NEW YORK NY 10024 (212) 877-6590
SHAMIR STUDIO 609 KAPPOCK STREET ... RIVERDALE NY 10463 (212) 695-5378

SEA TRAVEL

ADRIATICA 437 MADISON AVENUE ... NEW YORK NY 10017 (212) 838-2113
CHANDRIS CRUISES 666 FIFTH AVENUE ... NEW YORK NY 10022 (212) 586-8370
EPIROTIKI LINES 551 FIFTH AVENUE ... NEW YORK NY 10017 (212) 599-1750
HELLENIC MEDITERRANEAN LINES 200 PARK AVENUE ... NEW YORK NY 10017 (212) 697-4220
PRUDENTIAL LINES 1 WORLD TRADE CENTER ... NEW YORK NY 10005 (212) 775-0550
ZIM PASSENGER LINES 1 WORLD TRADE CENTER ... NEW YORK NY 10047 (212) 432-0300

SECURITIES

AMPAL-AMERICAN ISRAEL CORPORATION
6501 WILSHIRE BOULEVARD ... LOS ANGELES CA 90048 (213) 653-5633
AMPAL SECURITIES CORPORATION 10 ROCKEFELLER PLAZA ... NEW YORK NY 10020 (212) 586-3232
AMPAL-AMERICAN ISRAEL CORPORATION 10 ROCKEFELLER PLAZA ... NEW YORK NY 10020 (212) 586-3232
DATEK SECURITIES 1 WHITEHALL STREET ... NEW YORK NY 10004 (212) 797-9700
H.L.WOLF & COMPANY 120 WALL STREET, SUITE 1044 ... NEW YORK NY 10005 (212) 425-2315
ISRAEL BOND DISCOUNTERS 120 WALL STREET ... NEW YORK NY 10005 (212) 344-6676
ISRAEL SECURITIES 10 ROCKEFELLER PLAZA ... NEW YORK NY 10020 (212) 541-7568
LEUMI SECURITIES CORPORATION 342 MADISON AVENUE ... NEW YORK NY 10173 (212) 867-7600
TRANSMITTAL SECURITIES CORP. 82 WALL STREET ... NEW YORK NY 10005 (212) 344-8245

SEMINARIES

BAIS CHANA WOMEN'S INSTITUTE 15 MONTCALM COURT ... ST. PAUL MN 55116 (612) 698-3858
BETH JACOB HEBREW TEACHERS COLLEGE 1213 ELM AVENUE ... BROOKLYN NY 11230 (718) 339-4747
BETH JACOB TEACHERS SEMINARY OF AMERICA 132 S. 8TH STREET ... BROOKLYN NY 11211 (718) 388-2701
MACHON CHANA WOMAN'S COLLEGE 825 EASTERN PARKWAY ... BROOKLYN NY 11213 (718) 735-0217
MAIMONIDES HEBREW TEACHER'S COLLEGE 701 48TH STREET ... BROOKLYN NY 11220 (718) 871-0913

Organization / Address	City	State	ZIP	Phone
SARA SCHENIRER HIGH SCHOOL & TEACHERS SEMINARY 4622 14TH AVENUE	BROOKLYN	NY	11219	(718) 633-8557
AYELET HASHACHAR TEACHERS SEMINARY 1284 CENTRAL AVENUE	FAR ROCKAWAY	NY	11691	(718) 471-2182
LONG ISLAND SEMINARY OF JEWISH STUDIES FOR WOMEN 540 JARVIS AVENUE	FAR ROCKAWAY	NY	11691	(718) 471-8444
RIKA BREUER TEACHERS SEMINARY 91 BENNETT AVENUE	NEW YORK	NY	10033	(212) 675-9260
RIKA BREUER TEACHERS SEMINARY 85-93 BENNETT AVENUE	NEW YORK	NY	10033	(212) 568-6200
MIDRASHA L'MORIM/TORONTO JEWISH TEACHERS SEMINARY 4600 BATHURST STREET, SUITE 232	WILLOWDALE	ON	M2R 3V3	(416) 633-7770
BETH JACOB TEACHER'S SEMINARY OF MONTREAL 1750 GLENDALE AVENUE	MONTREAL	QU	H2V 1B3	(514) 739-3614
UNITED JEWISH TEACHERS' SEMINARY 5237 CLANRANALD AVENUE	MONTREAL	QU	H3X 2S5	(514) 489-4401

SENIOR CITIZENS

Organization / Address	City	State	ZIP	Phone
GOLDEN AGE CLUB 950 WEST 41ST AVENUE	VANCOUVER	BC	V5Z 2N7	(604) 266-9111
FREDA-MOHR CENTER 446 NORTH FAIRFAX AVENUE	LOS ANGELES	CA	90004	(213) 937-5901
JEWISH FAMILY SERVICE DROP-IN CENTER 4451 30TH STREET	SAN DIEGO	CA	92116	(619) 291-0473
SOUTHEAST SENIOR DAY CARE CENTER OF THE JEWISH COMMUNITY CENTERS OF SOUTH BROWARD 1201 JOHNSON STREET	HOLLYWOOD	FL	33020	(305) 922-5048
KOSHER NUTRITION PROGRAM 5846 MOUNT CARMEL TERRACE	JACKSONVILLE	FL	32216	(904) 737-9075
AGED SERVICE CENTER 1751 EAST 55TH STREET	CHICAGO	IL	60615	(312) 939-1399
AGED SERVICE CENTER 1345 WEST JARVIS	CHICAGO	IL	60626	(312) 939-1399
AGED SERVICE CENTER 6400 WEST DEVON AVENUE	CHICAGO	IL	60626	(312) 939-1399
AGED SERVICE CENTER 1415 WEST MORSE	CHICAGO	IL	60626	(312) 939-1399
COUNCIL FOR JEWISH ELDERLY 1 SOUTH FRANKLIN STREET	CHICAGO	IL	60606	(312) 346-6700
JEWISH FAMILY & CHILDREN'S SERVICE 31 NEW CHARDON STREET	BOSTON	MA	02114	(617) 227-6641
JEWISH SERVICE CENTER FOR OLDER ADULTS 1030 PLEASANT STREET	WORCESTER	MA	01602	(617) 756-4363
JEWISH COUNCIL FOR THE AGING 6111 MONTROSE ROAD	ROCKVILLE	MD	20852	(301) 881-8782
MULTI-SERVICE SENIOR CENTER - MSSC 8656 KINGSBRIDGE DRIVE	ST. LOUIS	MO	63132	(314) 997-6772
CO-OP CITY OUTREACH CENTER 1356 EINSTEIN LOOP	BRONX	NY	10467	(212) 671-4959
EAST CONCOURSE LUNCHEON CLUB 236 EAST TREMONT AVENUE	BRONX	NY	10467	(212) 731-6300
JASA-BRONX BOROUGH SERVICE CENTER 2488 GRAND CONCOURSE	BRONX	NY	10458	(212) 365-4044
JASA-BRONX HOME CARE PROGRAM 2166 MATTHEWS AVENUE	BRONX	NY	10462	(212) 823-2121
JASA-CO-OP CITY OUTREACH CENTER 135 EINSTEIN LOOP	BRONX	NY	10475	(212) 671-4959
JASA-EAST CONCOURSE LUNCHEON CLUB 236 E TREMONT AVENUE	BRONX	NY	10457	(212) 731-6300
JASA-MOSHOLU SERVICE CENTER 3450 DEKALB AVENUE	BRONX	NY	10467	(212) 231-1234
JASA-PELHAM SERVICE CENTER 2166 MATTHEWS AVENUE	BRONX	NY	10462	(212) 829-7150
JASA-THROGS NECK LUNCHEON CLUB 2705 SCHLEY AVENUE	BRONX	NY	10465	(212) 823-1623
AGUDATH ISRAEL OF AMERICA 803 KINGS HIGHWAY	BROOKLYN	NY	11223	(718) 627-3500
BROOKLYN BOROUGH SERVICE CENTER 44 COURT	BROOKLYN	NY	11201	(718) 852-0880
FLATBUSH YM/YWHA 1401 FLATBUSH AVENUE	BROOKLYN	NY	11210	(718) 469-8100
HABER HOUSES SERVICE CENTER 2410 SURF AVENUE	BROOKLYN	NY	11235	(718) 449-9600
JASA - BRIGHTON BEACH SERVICE CENTER 2915 BRIGHTON 6 STREET	BROOKLYN	NY	11235	(718) 769-5669
JASA-ASSOCIATION FOR SERVICES FOR THE AGED 2211 CHURCH AVENUE	BROOKLYN	NY	11226	(718) 941-2200
JASA-BOROUGH PARK SERVICE CENTER 4116 14TH AVENUE	BROOKLYN	NY	11219	(718) 854-3535
JASA-BROOKLYN BORO SERVICE CENTER 44 COURT STREET	BROOKLYN	NY	11201	(718) 852-0880
JASA-CONEY ISLAND MEALS ON WHEELS 3601 SURF AVENUE	BROOKLYN	NY	11224	(718) 996-4874
JASA-EAST FLATBUSH COMMUNITY SERVICES FOR THE ELDERLY 666 REMSEN AVENUE	BROOKLYN	NY	11236	(718) 342-5454
JASA-HARBER HOUSES SERVICES CENTER 2410 SURF AVENUE	BROOKLYN	NY	11224	(718) 449-9600
JASA-SCHEUER HOUSE GROUP CENTER & SCHEUER HOUSE COMMISSARY 1360 SURF AVENUE	BROOKLYN	NY	11224	(718) 373-3954
JASA-SHOREFRONT SERVICE CENTER 3212 CONEY ISLAND AVENUE	BROOKLYN	NY	11235	(718) 769-3100
JASA-STARRETT CITY CENTER 11325 SEAVIEW AVENUE	BROOKLYN	NY	11239	(718) 642-1300
JASA-STARRETT CITY GROUP CENTER 1540 VAN SICLEN AVENUE	BROOKLYN	NY	11239	(718) 642-1010
JASA-WILLIAMSBURG GROUP CENTER 202 GRAHAM AVENUE	BROOKLYN	NY	11206	(718) 388-6865
KINGS BAY YM/YWHA SENIOR CITIZEN CENTER 3643 NOSTRAND AVENUE	BROOKLYN	NY	11226	(718) 648-2053
SEPHARDIC MULTI-SERVICE CITIZENS CENTER 2165 71ST STREET	BROOKLYN	NY	11204	(718) 259-0100
WILLIAMSBURG GROUP CENTER 202 GRAHAM AVENUE	BROOKLYN	NY	11211	(718) 388-6805
WILLIAMSBURG YM/YWHA SERVICE CENTER 575 BEDFORD AVENUE	BROOKLYN	NY	11211	(718) 782-2315
THE LONG ISLAND HEBREW LIVING CENTER 431 BEACH 20TH STREET	FAR ROCKAWAY	NY	11691	(718) 327-2700
JASA-BROOKDALE VILLAGE SENIOR CENTER 131 BEACH 19 STREET	FAR ROCKAWAY	NY	11691	(718) 471-3200
JASA-QUEENS BORO SERVICE CENTER 97-45 QUEENS BLVD	FOREST HILLS	NY	11375	(718) 263-4700
JASA-ROCHDALE VILLAGE LUNCHEON CLUB 169-65 137 AVENUE	JAMAICA	NY	11434	(718) 525-2800
JASA-BROOKDALE CENTER OF LONG BEACH-TEMPLE BETH EL 570 W. WALNUT	LONG BEACH	NY	11561	(516) 432-5555
JASA-LONG BEACH SERVICE CENTER 72 W. PARK AVENUE	LONG BEACH	NY	11561	(516) 432-0570
JASA-NASSAU DISTRICT SERVICE CENTER 158 3RD STREET	MINEOLA	NY	11501	(516) 742-2050
NASSAU DISTRICT SERVICE CENTER 158 THIRD STREET	MINEOLA	NY	11501	(516) 742-2050
JEWISH INSTITUTE OF GERIATRIC CARE 271-11 76TH AVENUE	NEW HYDE PARK	NY	11040	(516) 437-0090
CENTRAL BUREAU FOR THE JEWISH AGED 130 EAST 59TH STREET	NEW YORK	NY	10022	(212) 308-7316
DOROT 251 WEST 100TH STREET	NEW YORK	NY	10025	(212) 864-7410
FEDERATION JOINT SERVICES OF THE LOWER EAST SIDE 197 EAST BROADWAY	NEW YORK	NY	10002	(212) 475-6200
JASA-CENTRAL ADMINISTRATION 40 W. 68 STREET	NEW YORK	NY	10023	(212) 724-3200
JASA-FEDERATION JOINT SERVICES OF THE EAST SIDE ED. ALLIANCE 197 E. BROADWAY	NEW YORK	NY	10002	(212) 475-6200
JASA-MANHATTAN BOROUGH SERVICES CENTER 40 W. 68 STREET	NEW YORK	NY	10023	(212) 724-3200
JASA-MARSEILLES SENIOR CENTER 230 W. 103 STREET	NEW YORK	NY	10025	(212) 663-6000
JASA-WASHINGTON HEIGHTS SERVICE 711 W. 179TH STREET	NEW YORK	NY	10033	(212) 928-0100
JASA-WEST SIDE SENIOR CITIZEN CENTER 40 W. 68 STREET	NEW YORK	NY	10023	(212) 724-3200
JEWISH ASSOCIATION FOR SERVICES FOR THE AGED 40 WEST 68TH STREET	NEW YORK	NY	10023	(212) 724-3200
MANHATTAN BOROUGH SERVICE CENTER 40 WEST 68TH STREET	NEW YORK	NY	10023	(212) 724-3200
PROJECT EZRA 197 EAST BROADWAY	NEW YORK	NY	10002	(212) 982-3700
WASHINGTON HEIGHTS SERVICE CENTER C/O SELF HELP 717 WEST 177TH STREET	NEW YORK	NY	10033	(212) 928-0010
JASA-QUEENS LEGAL SERVICE FOR THE ELDERLY 97-45 QUEENS BLVD	REGO PARK	NY	11374	(718) 897-2515
RIVERVIEW CENTER FOR JEWISH SENIORS 4724 BROWN'S HILL ROAD	PITTSBURGH	PA	15217	(412) 521-5900
JEWISH INFORMATION SERVICE FOR THE AGING 5418 WEST BURLEIGH	MILWAUKEE	WI	53210	(414) 445-4014

SEPHARDIC ORGANIZATIONS

Organization / Address	City	State	ZIP	Phone
IRANIAN JEWISH FEDERATION 6505 WILSHIRE BOULEVARD, SUITE 101	LOS ANGELES	CA	90048	(213) 655-7730
KAHAL JOSEPH CONGREGATION 10505 SANTA MONICA BOULEVARD	LOS ANGELES	CA	90025	(213) 474-0559
MIDRASH OD YOSEF HAI 420 NORTH FAIRFAX AVENUE	LOS ANGELES	CA	90036	(213) 653-5163
SEPHARDIC ASSOC. MAX NORDAU, C/O AMERICAN SEPHARDI FED. 6505 WILSHIRE BOULEVARD, SUITE 208	LOS ANGELES	CA	90048	(213) 653-8177
SEPHARDIC CONGREGATION KAHAL YOSEPH 10505 SANTA MONICA BLVD	LOS ANGELES	CA	90056	(213) 474-0559
SEPHARDIC EDUCATIONAL CENTER IN JERUSALEM 6505 WILSHIRE BOULEVARD, SUITE 208	LOS ANGELES	CA	90048	(213) 653-7365
SEPHARDIC HEBREW ACADEMY 310 NORTH HUNTLEY DRIVE	LOS ANGELES	CA	90048	(213) 659-2456
SEPHARDIC HEBREW CENTER 4911 WEST 59TH STREET	LOS ANGELES	CA	90056	(213) 295-5541
SEPHARDIC MAGEN DAVID CONGREGATION 7454 MELROSE AVENUE	LOS ANGELES	CA	90046	(213) 655-3441
SEPHARDIC TEMPLE TIFERETH ISRAEL 10500 WILSHIRE BOULEVARD	LOS ANGELES	CA	90024	(213) 475-7311
SEPHARDIC WOMEN'S DIVISION-UJWF 6505 WILSHIRE BOULEVARD, SUITE 1002	LOS ANGELES	CA	90048	(213) 852-1234
SEPHARDIC YOUTH AND YOUNG ADULTS 6505 WILSHIRE BOULEVARD, SUITE 208	LOS ANGELES	CA	90048	(213) 653-8177
TIFARET TEIMAN, CONGREGATION OF YEMENITE JEWS 1940 LINDA FLORA DRIVE	LOS ANGELES	CA	90024	(213) 479-4114
ADATH YESHURUN VALLEY SEPHARDIC CONGREGATION 6348 WHITSETT AVENUE	NORTH HOLLYWOOD	CA	91606	(818) 766-4682
CONGREGATION EM HABANIM 12052 CALIFA STREET	NORTH HOLLYWOOD	CA	91607	(818) 762-7779
SEPHARDIC CONGREGATION OF GREATER HARTFORD 31 LYMAN ROAD	WEST HARTFORD	CT	06117	(203) 233-1888
SEPHARDIC CONGREGATION OF FLORIDA 1200 NORMANDY DRIVE	MIAMI BEACH	FL	33141	(305) 861-6308
SEPHARDIC JEWISH CENTER OF GREATER MIAMI 645 COLLINS AVENUE	MIAMI BEACH	FL	33139	(305) 534-4092
SEPHARDIC JEWISH CENTER OF NORTH MIAMI BEACH 571 NORTHEAST 171ST STREET	NORTH MIAMI BEACH	FL	33162	(305) 652-2099
SEPHARDIC CONGREGATION OF THE PORTUGUESE ISRAELITE FRATERNITY 1819 WEST HOWARD STREET	EVANSTON	IL	60202	(312) 475-9287
TOURO 1501 GENERAL PERSHING AVENUE	NEW ORLEANS	LA	70115	(504) 895-4843
SEPHARDIC COMMUNITY OF GREATER BOSTON C/O YOUNG ISRAEL OF BROOKLINE, 62 GREEN STREET	BROOKLINE	MA	02147	(617) 734-0276
SEPHARDIC COMMUNITY OF GREATER DETROIT 21830 BEVERLY	OAK PARK	MI	48237	(313) 968-8393
SEPHARDIC COMMUNITY OF GREATER DETROIT 17030 NEW JERSEY	SOUTHFIELD	MI	48075	(313) 557-8551
SEPHARDIC JEWISH BROTHERHOOD 116 EAST 169TH STREET	BRONX	NY	10452	
SEPHARDIC JEWISH CENTER OF THE BRONX, INC. 116 EAST 169TH STREET	BRONX	NY	10452	
SEPHARDIC SHAARE RAHAMIM OF EAST BRONX, INC. 100 CO-OP CITY BLVD	BRONX	NY	10475	(212) 671-8882
ADELANTRE-JUDEZMO SOCIETY 4594 BEDFORD AVENUE	BROOKLYN	NY	11235	
ATERET TORAH 1750 EAST 4TH STREET	BROOKLYN	NY	11223	(718) 627-9494
COMMITTEE FOR RESCUE OF SYRIAN JEWRY 1616 OCEAN PARKWAY	BROOKLYN	NY	11223	
PERSIAN JEWISH CENTER OF BROOKLYN 828 EASTERN PARKWAY	BROOKLYN	NY	11213	
SEPHARDIC BETH MIDRASH KINGS HIGHWAY & EAST 5TH	BROOKLYN	NY	11223	
SEPHARDIC CENTER OF CONEY ISLAND 2911 WEST 16TH STREET	BROOKLYN	NY	11224	
SEPHARDIC CENTER OF MAPLETON 2143-45 65TH STREET	BROOKLYN	NY	11204	(718) 239-9451
SEPHARDIC COMMUNITY CENTER 1901 OCEAN PARKWAY	BROOKLYN	NY	11223	(718) 627-4300
SEPHARDIC HOME, THE 2266 CROPSEY AVENUE	BROOKLYN	NY	11214	(718) 266-6100
SEPHARDIC INSTITUTE 511 AVENUE R	BROOKLYN	NY	11223	(718) 998-8171
SEPHARDIC JEWISH CENTER OF CANARSIE 9320 FLATLANDS AVENUE	BROOKLYN	NY	11236	(718) 257-0400
SEPHARDIC MIKVEH ISRAEL 810 AVENUE S	BROOKLYN	NY	11223	(718) 339-4600
SEPHARDIC TEMPLE TORAH 60 BRIGHTON 11 STREET	BROOKLYN	NY	11235	(718) 743-4616
RHODES LEAGUE OF BROTHERS AID SOCIETY 118-84 223RD STREET	CAMBRIA HEIGHTS	NY	11411	
THE SEPHARDIC TEMPLE BRANCH BOULEVARD	CEDARHURST	NY	11516	(516) 295-4644
ISRAELI JEWISH COMMUNITY CENTER 106-16 70TH AVENUE	FOREST HILLS	NY	11375	
MOROCCAN JEWISH ORGANIZATION 112-21 22ND AVENUE	FOREST HILLS	NY	11375	
SEPHARDIC JEWISH CENTER OF FOREST HILLS 67-67 108TH STREET	FOREST HILLS	NY	11375	(718) 520-1989
SEPHARDIC JEWISH CONGREGATION & CENTER OF QUEENS 101-17 67TH DRIVE	FOREST HILLS	NY	11375	(718) 520-1537
SEPHARDIC CONGREGATION OF LONG BEACH 161 LAFAYETTE BLVD., P.O. BOX 779	LONG BEACH	NY	11561	(516) 432-9224
AMERICAN SEPHARDI FEDERATION 8 WEST 40TH STREET	NEW YORK	NY	10018	(212) 730-1210
AMERICAN SOCIETY OF SEPHARDIC STUDIES 500 W. 185TH STREET	NEW YORK	NY	10033	(212) 960-5236
ASSOCIATION OF YUGOSLAVIAN JEWS 247 WEST 99TH STREET	NEW YORK	NY	10025	(212) 865-2211
CENTRAL SEPHARDIC JEWISH COMMUNITY OF AMERICA 8 W. 70TH STREET	NEW YORK	NY	10023	(212) 787-2850

Organization	City	State	Zip	Phone
FOUND. FOR ADVANCEMENT OF SEPHARDIC STUDIES & CULTURE, INC. 599-601 BROADWAY	NEW YORK	NY	10012	
INTERNATIONAL SEPHARDIC EDUCATION FOUNDATION 1345 AVENUE OF THE AMERICAS (45TH FLOOR)	NEW YORK	NY	10105	(212) 841-6073
KEHILA KEDOSHA JANINA 280 BROOME STREET	NEW YORK	NY	10002	(212) 673-4441
SEPHARDIC HOUSE AT THE CONG. SHEARITH ISRAEL 2 W. 70TH STREET	NEW YORK	NY	10023	(212) 873-0300
SEPHARDIC STUDIES PROGRAM - YESHIVA UNIVERSITY 500 WEST 185 STREET	NEW YORK	NY	10033	(212) 960-5235
SPANISH & PORTUGUESE SYNAGOGUE 8 WEST 70TH STREET	NEW YORK	NY	10023	(212) 873-0300
UNION OF SEPHARDIC CONGREGATIONS, INC. 2 WEST 70TH STREET	NEW YORK	NY	10023	(212) 873-0300
WORLD INSTITUTE FOR SEPHARDIC STUDIES 310 WEST 72ND STREET	NEW YORK	NY	10023	
YESHIVA UNIVERSITY SEPHARDIC STUDIES PROGRAM 500 WEST 185TH STREET	NEW YORK	NY	10033	(212) 960-5235
PARNAS JEWISH ORGANIZATION 97-30 QUEENS BOULEVARD	REGO PARK	NY	11374	(718) 459-4645
SEPHARDIC JEWISH BROTHERHOOD OF AMERICA, INC. 97-29 64TH ROAD	REGO PARK	NY	11374	(718) 459-1600
SEPHARDIC COMMUNITY OF NEW ROCHELLE-SCARSDALE, THE C/O YOUNG ISRAEL OF SCARSDALE, 1313 DAISY FARMS ROAD	SCARSDALE	NY	10583	(914) 636-8686
SEPHARDIC GROUP OF SYRACUSE C/O MR. HABIB, 119 DOLL PARKWAY	SYRACUSE	NY	13214	(315) 446-0760
SEPHARDIC BETH SHALOM CONGREGATION P.O. BOX 37431	CINCINNATI	OH	45222	(513) 793-6936
SEPHARDIC CONGREGATION AHAVAT ACHIM 3225 S.W. BARVUR BLVD.	PORTLAND	OR	97215	(503) 227-0010
MEYSOS ISRAEL 521 LOMBARD STREET	PHILADELPHIA	PA	19147	
CANADIAN SEPHARDI FEDERATION 1310 GREENE AVENUE	MONTREAL	QU	H3Z 2B2	(514) 934-0804
TOURO SYNAGOGUE - JESHUAT ISRAEL 85 TOURO STREET	NEWPORT	RI	02840	(401) 847-4794
MAGEN DAVID SEPHARDIC CONGREGATION 9112 BOLLER DRIVE	FAIRFAX	VA	22031	(703) 251-0766
SEPHARDIC BIKUR HOLIM CONGREGATION 6500 52ND AVENUE SOUTH	SEATTLE	WA	98118	(206) 723-9661

SHATNES TESTING

Organization	City	State	Zip	Phone
SHATNES LABORATORY OF TORAH AND MITZVOTH, J. ROSENBERG-FOUNDER 203 LEE AVENUE	BROOKLYN	NY	11206	(718) 387-8520
SHATNES TESTING	CLEVELAND	OH		(216) 932-4313

SHIPPING

Organization	City	State	Zip	Phone
ZIM CONTAINER SERVICE 3450 WILSHIRE BOULEVARD	LOS ANGELES	CA	90010	(213) 385-2400
ZIM CONTAINER SERVICE 100 CALIFORNIA STREET	SAN FRANCISCO	CA	94111	(415) 986-5717
T.D.Y. FREIGHT SERVICES, LTD. P.O. BOX 630132	MIAMI	FL	33163	(305) 653-8338
ZIM CONTAINER SERVICE 1644 TULLIE CIRCLE, SUITE 111	ATLANTA	GA	30329	(404) 325-4100
ZIM CONTAINER SERVICE 124 WEST BAY STREET, SUITE E	SAVANNAH	GA	31402	(912) 236-4263
ZIM - AMERICAN-ISRAELI SHIPPING COMPANY, INC. 10600 WEST HIGGINS ROAD, SUITE 410	ROSEMONT	IL	60018	(312) 298-9700
ZIM - AMERICAN-ISRAELI SHIPPING CO. HIBERNIA NATIONAL BANK BUILDING 812 GRAVIER STREET, SUITE 1106	NEW ORLEANS	LA	70112	(504) 524-1184
FARRELL LINES, INC. ONE WHITEHALL STREET	NEW YORK	NY	10004	(212) 440-4200
FLEET LINES 440 PARK AVENUE SOUTH	NEW YORK	NY	10016	(212) 696-5210
MARITIME OVERSEAS CORPORATION 511 FIFTH AVENUE	NEW YORK	NY	10017	(212) 953-4100
P.E.C. 511 FIFTH AVENUE	NEW YORK	NY	10017	(212) 687-2400
YORK SHIPPING CORPORATION 342 MADISON AVENUE	NEW YORK	NY	10017	(212) 697-9510
ZIM - AMERICAN-ISRAELI SHIPPING COMPANY, INC. 1 WORLD TRADE CENTER, SUITE 2969	NEW YORK	NY	10048	(212) 432-0300
BURLINGTON NORTHERN AIR FREIGHT 145 HOOK CREEK BOULEVARD	ROSEDALE	NY	11422	(718) 889-7750
E. ROSEMAN COMPANY 829 N. SECOND ST.	PHILADELPHIA	PA	19123	(215) 627-0539
ZIM CONTAINER SERVICE 201 COTTON EXCHANGE	DALLAS	TX	75201	(214) 742-1693
ZIM - AMERICAN-ISRAELI SHIPPING COMPANY, INC. 1314 TEXAS AVENUE, SUITE 812	HOUSTON	TX	77002	(713) 224-9461

SINGLES

Organization	City	State	Zip	Phone
HEART-TO-HEART	LOS ANGELES	CA		(213) 463-5590
NEW JEWISH SINGLES - ORANGE COUNTY P.O. BOX 631	ARTESIA	CA	90701	(714) 761-1870
NORTH PENINSULA JCC SINGLES (25-37)	BELMONT	CA		(415) 591-4438
BERKELEY/RICHMOND JCC SINGLES & SINGLES PARENTS	BERKELEY	CA		(415) 848-0237
NEW SHUL SINGLES 9454 WILSHIRE BLVD	BEVERLY HILLS	CA	90212	(213) 276-9338
T.O.Y.A. C/O BETH JACOB CONGREGATION 9030 W. OLYMPIC BLVD.	BEVERLY HILLS	CA	90211	(213) 935-8233
BRANDEIS - BARDIN YOUNG ADULTS (AGE 25-35)	BRANDEIS	CA	93064	(213) 348-7201
BETH AM 30 PLUS	CUPERTINO	CA		(408) 886-5350
SHALOM SINGLES 15739 VENTURA BOULEVARD	ENCINO	CA	91436	(818) 988-1253
LONG BEACH JEWISH CONNECTION 3801 EAST WILLOW	LONG BEACH	CA	90815	(213) 426-7601
30'S PLUS SINGLES, CONGREGATION BETH AM	LOS ALTOS	CA		(415) 592-7759
DEPARTMENT OF SINGLE ADULTS, JEWISH FEDERATION COUNCIL 6505 WILSHIRE BOULEVARD	LOS ANGELES	CA	90048	(213) 852-1234
JASS-JEWISH ASSOCIATION OF SINGLES SERVICES 6505 WILSHIRE BOULEVARD	LOS ANGELES	CA	90048	(213) 852-1234
JASSLINE (AGES 21-35) 6505 WILSHIRE BOULEVARD	LOS ANGELES	CA	90048	(213) 852-0909
JASSLINE (AGES 35 UP) 6505 WILSHIRE BOULEVARD	LOS ANGELES	CA	90048	(213) 651-4420
JEWISH SINGLES COMPUTER SERVICE 15600 MULHOLLAND DRIVE	LOS ANGELES	CA	90077	(213) 471-3055
JEWISH SINGLES CONNECTION, JEWISH CENTERS ASSOC., JCC 5870 WEST OLYMPIC BOULEVARD	LOS ANGELES	CA	90036	(213) 272-1073
LA JEWISH SINGLES INDEX P.O. BOX 49330	LOS ANGELES	CA	90049	(213) 207-0058
MARINA DEL REY YOUNG SINGLES 6505 WILSHIRE BLVD	LOS ANGELES	CA	90048	(213) 651-4602
NEW BEGINNINGS BOX 241622	LOS ANGELES	CA	90024	(213) 458-1101
THE JEWISH SINGLES GUIDE TO LOS ANGELES, DEPT/SINGLE ADULTS 6505 WILSHIRE BOULEVARD	LOS ANGELES	CA	90048	(213) 852-1234
VIP CLUB 9831 WEST PICO BOULEVARD #12A	LOS ANGELES	CA	90035	(213) 553-6642

Organization	City	State	Zip	Phone
MALIBU SINGLES HAVURAH P.O. BOX 4063	MALIBU	CA	90265	(213) 457-2979
TEMPLE BETH ABRAHAM SINGLES	OAKLAND	CA		(415) 832-0936
JASSLINE ORANGE COUNTY (AGE 21=)	ORANGE COUNTY	CA		(714) 537-JASS
YOUNG JEWISH SINGLES OF BETH AM (21-29)	PALO ALTO	CA		(415) 325-6405
JEWISH DATING 1742 UNION STREET	SAN FRANCISCO	CA	94123	(415) 346-6229
L'CHAIM & MID-PENINSULA JEWISH SINGLES	SAN FRANCISCO	CA		(415) 341-2462
MARIN JEWISH SINGLES	SAN FRANCISCO	CA		(415) 479-2000
SAN FRANCISCO JCC ADULT GROUP PROGRAMS	SAN FRANCISCO	CA		(415) 346-6040
YOUNG ADULT DIVISION, JEWISH COMMUNITY FEDERATION OF SAN FR.	SAN FRANCISCO	CA		(415) 781-3082
EMET JEWISH YOUNG PROFESSIONALS 6467 VAN NUYS BLVD. #300	VAN NUYS	CA	91401	(818) 988-7278
AMERIDATE SINGLES, INC.		FL		(305) 667-5757
THE JEWISH MATCHMAKERS		FL		(305) 891-1246
JEWISH INTRODUCTIONS, INC.	DADE, BROWARD	FL		(305) 923-0777
JEWISH DATING NETWORK	ATLANTA	GA		(404) 252-0251
THE MATCHMAKERS 6857 NORTH FRANCISCO AVENUE	CHICAGO	IL	60645	(312) 743-8421
JEWISH-SINGLES INFORMATION LINE		MD		(301) 654-5397
JEWISH SINGLES MATCHING SOCIETY 2010 JONES ROAD	FORT LEE	NJ	07024	(201) 947-5151
JEWISH COMPUTER DATING SERVICE 1314 AVENUE P	BROOKLYN	NY	11229	(718) 336-7911
JEWISH SINGLES REGISTRY 4911 16TH AVENUE	BROOKLYN	NY	11204	(718) 851-1314
YOUNG ADULTS, YOUNG ISRAEL OF FLATBUSH 1012 AVENUE I	BROOKLYN	NY	11230	
DATING FOR DISABLED, INC. P.O. BOX 452	KATONAH	NY	10536	(914) 232-8881
COMPATIMATES—EDUCATIONAL ALLIANCE WEST 51 EAST 10TH STREET	NEW YORK	NY	10003	(212) 982-8196
FEDERATION OF JEWISH PHILANTHROPIES 130 EAST 59TH STREET	NEW YORK	NY	10022	(212) 980-1000
FIELDS MATRIMONIAL BROKER SERVICE 41 EAST 42ND STREET	NEW YORK	NY	10017	(212) 391-2233
JEWISH PROFESSIONAL SINGLES	NEW YORK	NY		(212) 734-5566
JEWISH COMPUTERMATES		NY		(212) 533-0400
JEWISH SINGLES CONNECTION 160 BROADWAY	NEW YORK	NY	10038	(212) 962-0155
JEWISH SINGLES DATE PHONE 301 E. 49TH STREET	NEW YORK	NY	10017	(212) 755-3008
JEWISH SINGLES HOT LINE 301 E. 49TH STREET	NEW YORK	NY	10017	(212) 753-7282
JEWISH SINGLES INTRODUCTION SERVICE UNITED SYNAGOGUE OF AMERICA, 155 FIFTH AVENUE	NEW YORK	NY	10010	(212) 533-7800
LE JUDA (TAPE RECORDING OF CURRENT PARTY INFO.)	NEW YORK	NY		(212) 753-7282
MAIMONIDES TEMPLE - SYNAGOGUE FOR SINGLES P.O. BOX 20374	NEW YORK	NY	10017	(212) 722-6984
TASK FORCE ON JEWISH SINGLES, FED. OF JEWISH PHILANTHROPIES 130 EAST 59TH STREET	NEW YORK	NY	10022	(212) 980-1000
TZEMED-HELENA, INC. 400 MADISON AVENUE	NEW YORK	NY	10017	(212) 759-9009
YOUNG ISRAEL SINGLES—YOUNG ADULTS 3 WEST 16TH STREET	NEW YORK	NY	10011	(212) 929-1525
DR. ELLIOT UDELL—SINGLES RETREATS	PLAINVIEW	NY		(516) 349-7125
MITZVAH MAKERS OF UPSTATE N.Y. 30 EDGEMORE ROAD	ROCHESTER	NY	14618	(716) 461-5176
T.A.N.D.U. BOX 184H	SCARSDALE	NY	10883	
MARRIAGE ENCOUNTER JEWISH EXPRESSION 365 WOODMERE BOULEVARD	WOODMERE	NY	11598	(516) 374-6430
SINGLES CENTER OF THE GREATER FIVE TOWNS 207 GROVE STREET	WOODMERE	NY	11598	(516) 569-6733
FAIRMOUNT TEMPLE SINGLES 3666 TOWNLEY ROAD	CLEVELAND	OH	44122	(216) 491-9275
FAIRMOUNT TEMPLE SINGLES 24650 S. WOODLAND ROAD	CLEVELAND	OH	44122	(216) 464-2583
HATIKVAH YOUNG ISRAEL ADULT GROUP 13817 CEDAR ROAD	CLEVELAND	OH	44118	(216) 371-2244
PARK SINGLES	CLEVELAND	OH		(216) 371-2244
RAVAKIM 1369 FORD ROAD	CLEVELAND	OH	44124	(216) 449-3797
JEWISH DATING SERVICE P.O.BOX 14393	PHILADELPHIA	PA	19115	(215) 342-9951

SOCIAL, COMMUNAL & FRATERNAL ORGANIZATIONS

Organization	City	State	Zip	Phone
ROYAL CANADIAN LEGION - SHALOM BRANCH 2020 WEST 6TH AVENUE	VANCOUVER	BC	V6J 1R9	(604) 273-6350
B'NAI B'RITH—DISTRICT 4 6300 WILSHIRE BOULEVARD, SUITE 1717	LOS ANGELES	CA	90048	(213) 655-8994
JEWISH WAR VETERANS OF THE U.S.A.—CALIFORNIA 6505 WILSHIRE BOULEVARD, ROOM 401	LOS ANGELES	CA	90048	(213) 635-4752
LABOR ZIONIST ALLIANCE (YIDDISHER NAZIONALER ARBETER FARBAND) 8339 WEST THIRD STREET	LOS ANGELES	CA	90048	(213) 655-2842
MACCABEE ATHLETIC CLUB, INC. 6399 WILSHIRE BOULEVARD	LOS ANGELES	CA	90048	(213) 651-3182
WORKMEN'S CIRCLE (ARBEITER RING) 1525 SOUTH ROBERTSON BOULEVARD	LOS ANGELES	CA	90035	(213) 522-2007

B'NAI B'RITH 1640 RHODE ISLAND AVENUE, N.W. .... WASHINGTON **DC** 20036 (202) 857-6600
B'NAI B'RITH INTERNATIONAL 1640 RHODE ISLAND AVENUE, N.W. .... WASHINGTON **DC** 20036 (202) 857-6600
JEWISH WAR VETERANS OF THE UNITED STATES OF AMERICA
1811 R STREET NORTHWEST .... WASHINGTON **DC** 20009 (202) 265-6280
LEADERSHIP CONFERENCE ON CIVIL RIGHTS
2027 MASSACHUSETTS AVENUE N.W. .... WASHINGTON **DC** 20036 (202) 667-1780
WORKMEN'S CIRCLE 311 LINCOLN ROAD, ROOM 217 .... MIAMI BEACH **FL** 33139
NATIONAL JEWISH CIVIL SERVICE EMPLOYEES
1451 N.E. 169TH STREET .... NORTH MIAMI BEACH **FL** 33162
B'NAI B'RITH—DISTRICT 5
P.O. BOX 54386, 3379 PEACHTREE ROAD, N.E. .... ATLANTA **GA** 30308 (404) 876-3681
BUREAU FOR JEWISH LIVING 924 POLK BLVD .... DES MOINES **IA** 50312 (515) 277-5566
ARK, THE 3509 W. LAWRENCE AVENUE .... CHICAGO **IL** 60625 (312) 478-9600
FREE SONS OF ISRAEL 6335 NORTH CALIFORNIA .... CHICAGO **IL** 60659 (312) 338-9810
JEWISH CIVIL SERVICE EMPLOYEES IN CHICAGO
7064 N. SHERIDAN ROAD .... CHICAGO **IL** 60626 (312) 973-4558
JEWISH DEFENSE LEAGUE 22 WEST MADISON, SUITE 900 .... CHICAGO **IL** 60626 (312) 973-4558
JEWISH DEFENSE LEAGUE 22 WEST MADISON, SUITE 900 .... CHICAGO **IL** 60602 (312) 338-3800
JEWISH WAR VETERANS 536 S. CLARK STREET, SUITE 484 .... CHICAGO **IL** 60605 (312) 353-2872
MACCABI SPORT CLUB 6237 NORTH SACRAMENTO .... CHICAGO **IL** 60659 (312) 338-7597
NATIONAL JEWISH CIVIL SERVICE EMPLOYEES
7075 N. PAULINA STREET .... CHICAGO **IL** 60626 (312) 973-6125
YOUNG MEN'S JEWISH COUNCIL 30 W. WASHINGTON STREET .... CHICAGO **IL** 60602 (312) 726-8891
NATIONAL FEDERATION OF JEWISH MEN'S CLUBS
9129 WAUKEGAN .... MORTON GROVE **IL** 60053 (312) 965-7202
B'NAI B'RITH—DISTRICT 6 9933 LAWLER STREET, SUITE 100 .... SKOKIE **IL** 60077 (312) 676-0011
SHALOM ORGANIZATION OF CHICAGO 4050 TOWER CIRCLE .... SKOKIE **IL** 60076 (312) OR6-9408
JEWISH WAR VETERANS OF THE U.S.A.—MASSACHUSETTS
JFK FEDERAL BUILDING, GOVERNMENT CENTER, ROOM E314A .... BOSTON **MA** 02203 (617) 223-4580
COUNCIL OF CONCERNED JEWISH CITIZENS
113 WASHINGTON STREET .... BRIGHTON **MA** 02135 (617) 254-1334
NEW ENGLAND CHASSIDIC CENTER 2720 BEACON STREET .... BROOKLINE **MA** 02146 (617) 566-9182
ROFEH 1710 BEACON STREET .... BROOKLINE **MA** 02146 (617) 566-9182
CONCORD AREA JEWISH GROUP P.O. BOX 1339 .... CONCORD **MA** 01742
JEWISH SURVIVAL LEGION 388 N. MAIN STREET .... SHARON **MA** 02067
JEWISH ARMED SERVICES COMM. 5750 PARK HEIGHTS AVENUE .... BALTIMORE **MD** 21215 (301) 466-4242
JEWISH WAR VETERANS OF THE U.S.A.-MARYLAND
31 HOPKINS PLAZA .... BALTIMORE **MD** 21201 (301) 752-3526
JEWISH ATHLETIC & CULTURAL ASSOCIATION
1118 CHICKASAW DRIVE .... SILVER SPRING **MD** 20903 (301) 431-1077
WORKMEN'S CIRCLE 5790 CLEVELAND AVENUE, SUITE 225 .... ST. PAUL **MN** 55116 (612) 699-5146
JEWISH WAR VETERANS MEMORIAL CENTER OF GREATER ST. LOUIS
7091 OLIVE .... ST. LOUIS **MO** 63130 (314) 727-3490
NORTH CAROLINA ASSOCIATION OF JEWISH MEN P.O. BOX 10628 .... CHARLOTTE **NC** 28201
PAULSBORO JEWISH COMMUNITY CLUB 39 W. BROAD .... PAULSBORO **NJ** 08066
VAN CORTLANDT WORKMEN'S CIRCLE COMMUNITY HOUSE
3990 HILLMAN AVENUE .... BRONX **NY** 10463
JEWISH ATHLETIC CLUB OF BROOKLYN
P.O. BOX 190, GRAVESEND STATION .... BROOKLYN **NY** 11223 (718) 376-9683
VOICE OF JEWISH ACTIVISM P.O. BOX 391 .... FLUSHING **NY** 11367 (718) 232-2583
AMERICAN VETERANS OF ISRAEL
C/O SIDNEY RABINOVICH, 110-23 63RD AVENUE .... FOREST HILLS **NY** 11375
AMERICAN VETERANS OF ISRAEL 548 E. WALNUT STREET .... LONG BEACH **NY** 11561 (516) 431-8316
LIFE - LABOR AND INDUSTRY FOR EDUCATION 261 WILLIS AVENUE .... MINEOLA **NY** 11501 (516) 374-6465
ABRAHAM GOODMAN HOUSE 129 WEST 67TH STREET .... NEW YORK **NY** 10023 (212) 362-8060
ADATH ISRAEL OF NEW YORK, UNITED HEBREW COMMUNITY OF NEW YORK
201 EAST BROADWAY .... NEW YORK **NY** 10002 (212) 674-3580
AGUDAS ISRAEL WORLD ORGANIZATION 471 WEST END AVENUE .... NEW YORK **NY** 10024 (212) 874-7979
AGUDATH ISRAEL OF AMERICA 84 WILLIAM .... NEW YORK **NY** 10038 (212) 797-9000
AM. FED. OF JEWISH FIGHTERS, CAMP INMATES & NAZI VICTIMS, INC
823 UNITED NATIONS PLAZA .... NEW YORK **NY** 10017 (212) 490-2525
AM. VETERANS OF THE JEWISH LEGION-HAGDUD HAIVRI LEAGUE, INC.
C/O DR. JUDAH LAPSON, 1776 BROADWAY .... NEW YORK **NY** 10019 (212) 245-8200
AMERICAN CONGREGATION OF JEWS FROM AUSTRIA
188 W. 95TH STREET .... NEW YORK **NY** 10025 (212) 663-1920
AMERICAN COUNCIL FOR JUDAISM 307 FIFTH AVENUE .... NEW YORK **NY** 10016 (212) 889-1313
AMERICAN FAR EASTERN SOCIETY 259 W. 30TH STREET .... NEW YORK **NY** 10001 (212) 244-6225
AMERICAN FEDERATION OF JEWS FROM CENTRAL EUROPE, INC.
570 SEVENTH AVENUE .... NEW YORK **NY** 10018 (212) 921-3871
AMERICAN FRIENDS OF THE ALLIANCE ISRAELITE UNIVERSELLE
61 BROADWAY, ROOM 811 .... NEW YORK **NY** 10006 (212) 425-5171
AMERICAN JEWISH LEAGUE AGAINST COMMUNISM, INC.
39 EAST 68TH STREET .... NEW YORK **NY** 10021 (212) 472-1400
AMERICAN JEWISH SOCIETY FOR SERVICE 15 E. 26TH STREET .... NEW YORK **NY** 10010 (212) 683-6178
AMERICAN VETERANS OF ISRAEL 15 E. 26TH STREET .... NEW YORK **NY** 10010 (212) 532-4949
ASSOCIATION OF YUGOSLAV JEWS IN THE U.S.A. 247 W. 99TH STREET .... NEW YORK **NY** 10025 (212) 865-2211
B'NAI B'RITH-DISTRICT 1 823 UNITED NATIONS PLAZA .... NEW YORK **NY** 10017 (212) 490-2525
B'NAI ZION 136 EAST 39TH STREET .... NEW YORK **NY** 10016 (212) 725-1211
COMMISSION ON STATUS OF JEWISH WAR ORPHANS IN EUROPE-AM.
47 BEEKMAN STREET .... NEW YORK **NY** 10038 (212) 227-7800
EDUCATIONAL ALLIANCE, INC., THE 197 EAST BROADWAY .... NEW YORK **NY** 10002 (212) 475-6200
FEDERATION OF POLISH JEWS, INC. 342 MADISON AVENUE .... NEW YORK **NY** 10017 (212) 986-3693
FREE SONS OF ISRAEL 932 BROADWAY .... NEW YORK **NY** 10010 (212) 260-4222
FREE SONS OF ISRAEL-CREDIT UNION 932 BROADWAY .... NEW YORK **NY** 10010 (212) 475-2200
FREE SONS OF ISRAEL-FOUNDATION FUND 932 BROADWAY .... NEW YORK **NY** 10010 (212) 475-2150
FREE SONS OF ISRAEL-INSURANCE DEPARTMENT 932 BROADWAY .... NEW YORK **NY** 10010 (212) 228-1070
FRIENDS OF BELLEVUE HOSPITAL SYNAGOGUE
FIRST AVENUE & 27TH STREET .... NEW YORK **NY** 10016 (212) 685-1376
HIAS, INC. 200 PARK AVENUE S .... NEW YORK **NY** 10003 (212) 674-6800
HINENI 155 E. 38TH STREET .... NEW YORK **NY** 10016 (212) 557-1190
HISTADRUTH IVRITH OF AMERICA 1841 BROADWAY .... NEW YORK **NY** 10023 (212) 581-5151
ISRAELI COMMUNITY OF MIZRACHI-HAPOEL HAMIZRACHI
25 W. 26TH STREET .... NEW YORK **NY** 10010 (212) 679-2050
JEWISH ASSOCIATION FOR SERVICES FOR THE AGED
40 W. 68TH STREET .... NEW YORK **NY** 10023 (212) 724-3200
JEWISH DEFENSE LEAGUE 76 MADISON AVENUE .... NEW YORK **NY** 10016 (212) 686-3041
JEWISH DEFENSE ORGANIZATION 134 WEST 32ND STREET, ROOM 602 .... NEW YORK **NY** 10001 (212) 239-0447
JEWISH LABOR BUND 25 E. 78TH STREET, SUITE 501 .... NEW YORK **NY** 10021 (212) 535-0850
JEWISH LABOR COMMISSION 25 E. 78TH STREET .... NEW YORK **NY** 10021 (212) 535-3700
JEWISH POSTAL EMPLOYEES WELFARE LEAGUE OF MANHATTAN & BRONX, INC.
45 E. 33RD STREET .... NEW YORK **NY** 10016 (212) 689-1629
JEWISH RESTITUTION SUCCESSOR ORGANIZATION
15 E. 26TH STREET .... NEW YORK **NY** 10010 (212) 679-4074
JEWISH SOCIALIST VERBAND OF AMERICA 45 EAST 33RD STREET .... NEW YORK **NY** 10016 (212) 686-1536
JEWISH WAR VETERANS OF THE U.S.A.-COMMUNITY RELATIONS OFFICE
1457 BROADWAY .... NEW YORK **NY** 10036 (212) 234-3000
JEWISH WAR VETERANS OF THE U.S.A.-DEPT.OF NEW YORK JWV
51 CHAMBERS STREET, ROOM 1411 .... NEW YORK **NY** 10007 (212) 349-6640
JEWISH WAR VETERANS OF THE U.S.A.-NEW YORK
VETERANS ADMINISTRATION 252 SEVENTH AVENUE .... NEW YORK **NY** 10001 (212) 924-7590
JEWISH WAR VETERANS OF THE USA - DEPT. OF N.Y. - SHOW DIV.
51 CHAMBERS STREET .... NEW YORK **NY** 10007 (212) 349-6420
JEWISH WAR VETERANS OF THE USA-DEPT. OF N.Y.-COUNTY COUNCIL
346 BROADWAY .... NEW YORK **NY** 10013 (212) 962-2176
JEWISH WELFARE BOARD 15 E. 26TH STREET .... NEW YORK **NY** 10010 (212) 532-4949
MEDEM JEWISH SOCIALISTS GROUP 25 E. 78TH STREET .... NEW YORK **NY** 10021 (212) 535-0850
NATIONAL COUNCIL OF YOUNG ISRAEL 3 W. 16TH STREET .... NEW YORK **NY** 10011 (212) 929-1525
NATIONAL FEDERATION OF JEWISH MENS CLUBS, INC.
475 RIVERSIDE DRIVE, SUITE 244 .... NEW YORK **NY** 10115 (212) 749-8100
NATIONAL FEDERATION OF TEMPLE BROTHERHOODS-CHAUTAUQUA SOC.
838 FIFTH AVENUE .... NEW YORK **NY** 10021 (212) 249-0100
NATIONAL JEWISH WELFARE BOARD 15 EAST 26TH STREET .... NEW YORK **NY** 10010 (212) 532-4949
NEW JEWISH AGENDA 149 CHURCH STREET, #2N .... NEW YORK **NY** 10007 (212) 227-5885
NEW WORLD CLUB 2121 BROADWAY .... NEW YORK **NY** 10023 (212) 873-7400
RABBI ISAAC ELCHANAN THEOLOGICAL SEMINARY-DIV./COMMUNAL SVS.
2540 AMSTERDAM AVENUE .... NEW YORK **NY** 10033 (212) 960-5265
ROUMANIAN JEWISH FEDERATION OF AMERICA, INC.
210 W. 101 STREET .... NEW YORK **NY** 10025 (212) 866-2214
SELFHELP COMMUNITY SERVICES 44 E. 23RD STREET .... NEW YORK **NY** 10010 (212) 533-7100
UNITED HEBREW COMMUNITY OF NEW YORK, ADATH ISRAEL OF NEW YORK
201 EAST BROADWAY .... NEW YORK **NY** 10002 (212) 674-3580
UNITED HEBREW TRADES OF THE STATE OF NEW YORK
853 BROADWAY .... NEW YORK **NY** 10003 (212) 674-2573
UNITED ORDER TRUE SISTERS, INC. 150 W. 85TH STREET .... NEW YORK **NY** 10024 (212) 362-2520
UNITED PARENT-TEACHERS ASSOCIATION OF JEWISH SCHOOLS
426 W. 58TH STREET .... NEW YORK **NY** 10019 (212) 245-8200
UNITED ROUMANIAN JEWS OF AMERICA 485 FIFTH AVENUE .... NEW YORK **NY** 10017 (212) 867-9696
UNITED SONS OF ISRAEL 41 UNION SQUARE .... NEW YORK **NY** 10003 (212) 255-6648
WORKMEN'S CIRCLE 45 EAST 33RD STREET .... NEW YORK **NY** 10016 (212) 889-6800
WORLD FEDERATION OF BERGEN-BELSEN ASSOCIATES P.O. BOX 333 .... NEW YORK **NY** 10021 (212) 752-0600
WORLD FEDERATION OF HUNGARIAN JEWS 136 E. 39TH STREET .... NEW YORK **NY** 10016 (212) 683-5377
WORLD JEWISH CONGRESS 15 EAST 84TH STREET .... NEW YORK **NY** 10028 (212) 879-4500
WORLD ORG. FOR JEWS FROM ARAB COUNTRIES, INC. (EXEC. OFFICE)
165 E. 56TH STREET .... NEW YORK **NY** 10022 (212) 751-4000
WORLD ORGANIZATION FOR JEWS FROM ARAB COUNTRIES, INC.
1200 FIFTH AVENUE .... NEW YORK **NY** 10022 (212) 427-1246
JEWISH PEACE FELLOWSHIP P.O. BOX 271 .... NYACK **NY** 10960 (914) 358-4601
WESTCHESTER JEWISH COMMUNITY SERVICES, INC.
475 TUCKAHOE ROAD .... YONKERS **NY** 10710 (914) 793-3565
WESTCHESTER JEWISH COMMUNITY SERVICES, INC.
20 SOUTH BROADWAY .... YONKERS **NY** 10701 (914) 423-4433
B'NAI B'RITH-DISTRICT 2 7750 MONTGOMERY ROAD .... CINCINNATI **OH** 45236 (513) 891-2880
WORKMEN'S CIRCLE 1980 S. GREEN ROAD .... CLEVELAND **OH** 44121 (216) 381-4515
B'NAI B'RITH-DISTRICT 22 15 HOVE STREET, SUITE 200 .... DOWNSVIEW **ON** M3H 4YS (416) 633-6224
B'NAI B'RITH-DISTRICT 3 230 SOUTH 15TH STREET .... PHILADELPHIA **PA** 19102 (215) 732-6400
BRITH SHOLOM 3939 CONSHOHOCKEN AVENUE .... PHILADELPHIA **PA** 19131 (215) 878-5696
JWB ARMED SERVICES COMMITTEE 401 S. BROAD STREET .... PHILADELPHIA **PA** 19147 (215) 545-4400
MULTI-SERVICE CENTER MARSHALL & PORTER STREETS .... PHILADELPHIA **PA** 19148 (215) 468-6285
JEWISH WAR VETERANS OF THE U.S.A.-PENNSYLVANIA
1000 LIBERTY AVENUE FEDERAL BUILDING .... PITTSBURGH **PA** 15222 (412) 644-6797
THE SHALOM CENTER CHURCH ROAD AND GREENWOOD AVENUE .... WYNCOTE **PA** 19095 (215) 886-1510
CANADIAN MACCABIAH ASSOCIATION 1225 HODGE STREET .... MONTREAL **QU** (514) 748-7711
JEWISH WAR VETERANS OF THE U.S.A-RHODE ISLAND
VETERANS ADMINISTRATION 321 SOUTH MAIN STREET .... PROVIDENCE **RI** 02903 (401) 528-4416
B'NAI B'RITH-DISTRICT 7
ROYAL CENTER TOWER, 11300 N CENTRAL EXPRESSWAY, #604 .... DALLAS **TX** 75243 (214) 691-6190

SOFRIM

BERGER, RABBI D. 1319 GEORGIAN TERRACE .... LAKEWOOD **NJ** 08701 (201) 363-5725
PINCUS, RABBI Z. 602 5TH STREET .... LAKEWOOD **NJ** 08701 (201) 998-2053
ROTHSCHILD, RABBI Z. 230 PRIVATE WAY .... LAKEWOOD **NJ** 08701 (201) 370-8052
BEN DOVID, RABBI Y. 3326 PALISADES AVENUE, #B6 .... UNION CITY **NJ** 07087 (201) 866-1269
BERKOWITZ, RABBI AVROHOM Y. 1470 CONEY ISLAND AVENUE .... BROOKLYN **NY** 11230 (718) 377-3664
BERLINGER, RABBI M. .... BROOKLYN **NY** (718) 972-5184
BETH HASOFRIM 1406 45TH STREET .... BROOKLYN **NY** 11219 (718) 851-1637
BIXENSPAN, RABBI YITZCHOK 185 RODNEY STREET .... BROOKLYN **NY** 11211 (718) 384-6755
BODNER, RABBI S. 1620 45TH STREET .... BROOKLYN **NY** 11204 (718) 438-7036
BRITZ, RABBI SHAYA 1364 58TH STREET .... BROOKLYN **NY** 11219 (718) 435-7788
COHEN, AMRAM 238 KEAP STREET .... BROOKLYN **NY** 11211 (718) 384-7173
ECKSTEIN, YEHOSHUA 190 WILSON STREET .... BROOKLYN **NY** 11211 (718) 388-0091

Name / Address	City	State	Zip	Phone
FELDMAN, RABBI N. 711 AVENUE S	BROOKLYN	**NY**	11223	(718) 375-1576
FINKEL, RABBI Y. 1444 50TH STREET	BROOKLYN	**NY**	11219	(718) 851-0815
FRIED, MORDECHAI 1554 39TH STREET	BROOKLYN	**NY**	11210	(718) 853-2182
FRIEDMAN, RABBI LIPOT 1311 43RD STREET	BROOKLYN	**NY**	11219	(718) 853-8432
FRIEDMAN, RABBI Y. 4519 16TH AVENUE	BROOKLYN	**NY**	11204	(718) 633-1884
GRUNFELD, RABBI E. 80 ROSS STREET	BROOKLYN	**NY**	11211	(718) 384-2317
GRUNHUT, RABBI S. 104 ROSS STREET	BROOKLYN	**NY**	11211	(718) 387-7030
HABERFELD, RABBI N. 1673 55TH STREET	BROOKLYN	**NY**	11204	(718) 851-0352
HALBERSTAM, RABBI MOSHE SHEA 1519 52ND STREET	BROOKLYN	**NY**	11219	(718) 633-0069
HIRSCHFELD, RABBI DOVID 94 ROSS STREET	BROOKLYN	**NY**	11211	(718) 387-7066
HOROWITZ, RABBI Y. 5324 12TH AVENUE	BROOKLYN	**NY**	11219	(718) 853-0621
KASNETT, RABBI B. 4904 16TH AVENUE	BROOKLYN	**NY**	11204	(718) 436-0543
KATZ, RABBI EZRA 1336 53RD STREET	BROOKLYN	**NY**	11219	(718) 851-9683
KATZ, RABBI YITZCHOK 217 ROSS STREET	BROOKLYN	**NY**	11211	(718) 388-6719
KATZ, YESOSHUA 1349 53RD STREET	BROOKLYN	**NY**	11219	(718) 436-8885
KLEIN BROTHERS 4104 16TH AVENUE	BROOKLYN	**NY**	11204	(718) 633-4490
KLEIN, AKIVA 135 HEYWARD STREET	BROOKLYN	**NY**	11206	(718) 875-6096
KREIMAN, RABBI P. 1158 53RD STREET	BROOKLYN	**NY**	11219	(718) 435-7708
LAUFER, YITZCHOK 112 DIVISION STREET	BROOKLYN	**NY**	11211	(718) 388-6570
LENCHEVSKY, RABBI NATHAN 1122 45TH STREET	BROOKLYN	**NY**	11219	(718) 851-6508
LIPOT FRIEDMAN 5501 15TH AVENUE	BROOKLYN	**NY**	11219	(718) 436-0901
MAKOR STAM/EPHRAIM GOTTLIEB 4807 18TH AVENUE	BROOKLYN	**NY**	11204	(718) 436-7826
MATKOFF, RABBI YEHUDA 1663 47TH STREET	BROOKLYN	**NY**	11204	(718) 633-5537
MAYBLOOM, RABBI A. 1819 AVENUE O	BROOKLYN	**NY**	11230	(718) 336-5604
PINCUS, RABBI ZVI CHAIM 1664 CONEY ISLAND AVENUE	BROOKLYN	**NY**	11230	(718) 336-6866
POLLACK, RABBI ARON 220 HOOPER STREET	BROOKLYN	**NY**	11211	(718) 384-5248
POLLACK, RABBI Y. 258 KEAP STREET	BROOKLYN	**NY**	11211	(718) 388-3012
RABBI Y. MISHULOVIN 309 KINGSTON AVENUE	BROOKLYN	**NY**	11213	(718) 773-1120
ROSENBERG, RABBI MENACHEM 1118 55TH STREET	BROOKLYN	**NY**	11219	(718) 851-0966
SCHECHTER, RABBI A. 1553 41ST STREET	BROOKLYN	**NY**	11218	(718) 871-5477
SCHERTZER, RABBI DAVID 924 EAST 13TH STREET	BROOKLYN	**NY**	11215	(718) 258-2595
SHARABI, RABBI M. 1736 EAST 4TH STREET	BROOKLYN	**NY**	11223	(718) 645-2974
SHUSHAN, RABBI A. 1435 40TH STREET	BROOKLYN	**NY**	11218	(718) 438-3207
SIFREI KODESH STAM 1525 55TH STREET	BROOKLYN	**NY**	11219	(718) 436-1697
TEITELBAUM, RABBI L. 547 BEDFORD AVENUE	BROOKLYN	**NY**	11211	(718) 963-0497
TEITELBAUM, RABBI M. 140 WILSON STREET	BROOKLYN	**NY**	11211	(718) 387-0290
TIFERES STAM 1664 CONEY ISLAND AVENUE	BROOKLYN	**NY**	11230	(718) 336-6866
TWERSKY, RABBI NACHUM 5721 13TH AVENUE	BROOKLYN	**NY**	11218	
TZVI BARNETT 802 MONTGOMERY STREET	BROOKLYN	**NY**	11213	(718) 493-1243
WALKENFELD, RABBI S. 1651 42ND STREET	BROOKLYN	**NY**	11204	(718) 871-2585
WEIDER, RABBI P. 74 ROSS STREET	BROOKLYN	**NY**	11211	(718) 388-8393
YEHUDAH CLAPMAN 719 MONTGOMERY STREET	BROOKLYN	**NY**	11213	(718) 774-9313
ZOLDAN, RABBI S. 210 ROSS STREET	BROOKLYN	**NY**	11211	(718) 782-6178
FULD, RABBI MICHAEL 141-21 77TH AVENUE	KEW GARDENS HILLS	**NY**	11367	(718) 793-7411
BRAUNSDORFER, RABBI C. 5 WALTER DRIVE	MONSEY	**NY**	10952	(914) 352-2855
EIDENSOHN, RABBI DAVID 2 PHYLLIS TERRACE	MONSEY	**NY**	10952	(914) 352-7267
FEIG, RABBI YITZCHOK 28 RITA AVENUE	MONSEY	**NY**	10952	(914) 352-0825
FREIDUS, KALMAN 28 CARLTON ROAD	MONSEY	**NY**	10952	(914) 352-7363
FRIEDMAN, RABBI N. 4 ELYON ROAD	MONSEY	**NY**	10952	(914) 356-7572
GALANDER, ISSAMAR TUVIA 18 RITA AVENUE	MONSEY	**NY**	10952	(914) 352-1647
LEITNER, M. 18 RITA AVENUE	MONSEY	**NY**	10952	(914) 356-7807
MORRIS, RABBI MENDEL 9 ORCHARD	MONSEY	**NY**	10952	(914) 352-6876
TEICHER, AVROHOM S. 12 EDWIN LANE	MONSEY	**NY**	10952	(914) 425-8242
VICENTOWSKY, RABBI D. 37 MAIN STREET	MONSEY	**NY**	10952	(914) 356-1390
WUDOWSKY, RABBI SHMUEL 25 ORCHARD STREET	MONSEY	**NY**	10952	(914) 356-6124
YAKTER, RABBI CHAIM 134 WEST CENTRAL AVENUE	MONSEY	**NY**	10952	(914) 352-6561
FISHER, YITZCHOK 38 LINCOLN AVENUE	NEW SQUARE	**NY**	10952	(914) 354-6467
A&Y SOFREI STAM 47 ESSEX STREET	NEW YORK	**NY**	10002	(212) 254-1400
BLUMENTHAL, ZELIG 13 ESSEX STREET	NEW YORK	**NY**	10002	(212) 267-8370
BODENHEIM, RABBI S. 121 BENNETT AVENUE	NEW YORK	**NY**	10033	(212) 781-5385
EISENBACH, RABBI MOSHE 49 ESSEX STREET	NEW YORK	**NY**	10002	(212) 674-8840
LASDUN, RABBI Y. 80 BENNETT AVENUE	NEW YORK	**NY**	10033	(212) 927-1655
LUBART, RABBI M. 50 CANAL STREET	NEW YORK	**NY**	10002	(212) 966-0526
UNGER, RABBI MOSHE 20 JACKSON AVENUE	SPRING VALLEY	**NY**	10977	(914) 354-5542
SOFER 3320 DESOTO AVENUE	CLEVELAND	**OH**	44118	(216) 932-6186

SOLDIERS & SAILORS

Name / Address	City	State	Zip	Phone
ASSOCIATION OF JEWISH CHAPLAINS OF ARMED FORCES 15 E. 26TH STREET	NEW YORK	**NY**	10010	(212) 532-4949
JEWISH WELFARE BOARD-ASSOC. WELFARE SOLDIERS IN ISRAEL 15 E. 26TH STREET	NEW YORK	**NY**	10010	(212) 532-4949
JWB ARMED SERVICES COMMITTEE 401 S. BROAD STREET	PHILADELPHIA	**PA**	19147	(215) 545-4400

SOVIET JEWRY

Name / Address	City	State	Zip	Phone
ALABAMA COUNCIL TO SAVE SOVIET JEWS 3113 JASMINE RD	MONTGOMERY	**AL**	36111	(205) 264-3101
ARIZONA COUNCIL ON SOVIET JEWS 421 EAST LA MAR RD	PHOENIX	**AZ**	85012	(602) 264-2325
VANCOUVER SOVIET JEWRY ACTION COMMITTEE 950 WEST 41ST AVENUE	VANCOUVER	**BC**	V5Z 2N7	(604) 261-8101
SOUTHERN CALIFORNIA COUNCIL FOR SOVIET JEWS P.O. BOX 113, 8621 WILSHIRE BLVD	BEVERLY HILLS	**CA**	90211	(213) 556-2598
SAN DIEGO COUNCIL FOR SOVIET JEWRY 1770 AVENUE, DEL MUNDO 902	CORONADO	**CA**	92118	(619) 435-5519
CALIFORNIA STUDENTS FOR SOVIET JEWS 900 HIGARD AVENUE	LOS ANGELES	**CA**	90026	
SAN DIEGO COUNCIL FOR SOVIET JEWS 4079 54TH STREET	SAN DIEGO	**CA**	92105	
BAY AREA COUNCIL ON SOVIET JEWRY 106 BADEN STREET	SAN FRANCISCO	**CA**	94131	(415) 585-1400
SOVIET EMBASSY 2790 GREEN STREET	SAN FRANCISCO	**CA**	94123	(415) 922-6642
COLORADO COMMITTEE OF CONCERN FOR SOVIET JEWRY 22 S. JERSEY ST	DENVER	**CO**	80224	(303) 377-7859

Name / Address	City	State	Zip	Phone
CONNECTICUT COMMITTEE FOR SOVIET JEWS 502 FOUNTAIN ST., #3A	NEW HAVEN	**CT**	06515	(203) 387-4526
NATIONAL CONFERENCE ON SOVIET JEWRY 2027 MASSACHUSETTS AVENUE N.W.	WASHINGTON	**DC**	20036	(202) 265-8114
SOVIET EMBASSY 1511 K STREET N.W.	WASHINGTON	**DC**	20005	(202) 628-9693
UNION OF COUNCILS FOR SOVIET JEWS 1411 K STREET N.W. SUITE 402	WASHINGTON	**DC**	20005	(202) 393-4117
WASHINGTON COMMITTEE FOR SOVIET JEWRY 2129 F STREET	WASHINGTON	**DC**	20037	
JEWISH FEDERATION OF SOUTH BROWARD 2719 HOLLYWOOD BOULEVARD	HOLLYWOOD	**FL**	33020	(305) 921-8810
SOUTH FLORIDA CONFERENCE ON SOVIET JEWRY 4200 BISCAYNE BLVD	MIAMI	**FL**	33161	(305) 576-4000
SARASOTA COUNCIL ON SOVIET JEWRY PO BOX 2778	SARASOTA	**FL**	33578	(813) 349-5725
WEST PALM BEACH-JEWISH FEDERATION OF PALM BEACH COUNTY 120 SOUTH OLIVE STREET	WEST PALM BEACH	**FL**	33401	(305) 832-2120
DES MOINES ACTION COMMITTEE FOR SOVIET JEWRY 705 41ST ST	WEST DES MOINES	**IA**	50265	(515) 223-1247
NATIONAL INTERRELIGIOUS TASK FORCE ON SOVIET JEWRY 1307 SOUTH WABASH	CHICAGO	**IL**	60605	(312) 922-1983
CHICAGO ACTION FOR SOVIET JEWRY 1724 FIRST STREET	HIGHLAND PARK	**IL**	60035	(312) 433-0144
SOVIET JEWRY COMMITTEE, JEWISH FEDERATION OF SOUTH BEND 1105 N. IRONWOOD DR	SOUTH BEND	**IN**	46615	(219) 234-3829
KANSAS CITY COUNCIL FOR SOVIET JEWRY 5812 W. 100TH ST	OVERLAND PARK	**KS**	66207	(913) 649-0290
NEW ENGLAND STUDENT STRUGGLE FOR SOVIET JEWRY 233 BAY STATE ROAD	BOSTON	**MA**	02215	(617) 267-8250
PITTSFIELD COUNCIL FOR SOVIET JEWRY 22 MARLBORO DR	PITTSFIELD	**MA**	01201	(413) 448-8043
SOVIET JEWRY COMMITTEE OF THE NORTH SHORE 1000 LORING AVENUE, #C91	SALEM	**MA**	01970	(617) 745-5453
BOSTON ACTION FOR SOVIET JEWRY 24 CRESCENT STREET, SUITE 3B	WALTHAM	**MA**	02154	(617) 893-2331
MEDICAL MOBILIZATION FOR SOVIET JEWRY 24 CRESCENT STREET	WALTHAM	**MA**	02154	(617) 893-2331
SOVIET JEWRY LEGAL ADVOCACY CENTER 24 CRESCENT STREET, #2G	WALTHAM	**MA**	02154	(617) 893-2331
BALTIMORE COUNCIL FOR SOVIET JEWRY 6503 PARK HEIGHTS AVE., APT 1-C	BALTIMORE	**MD**	21215	(301) 764-7242
MEDICAL MOBILIZATION FOR SOVIET JEWRY 8402 FREYMAN DRIVE	CHEVY CHASE	**MD**	20015	
WASHINGTON COMMITTEE FOR SOVIET JEWRY 8402 FREYMAN DR	CHEVY CHASE	**MD**	20015	(301) 587-4455
DETROIT SOVIET JEWRY COMMITTEE OF THE JCC 163 MADISON AVENUE	DETROIT	**MI**	58226	(313) 962-1880
FRIENDS OF THE SOVIET JEWRY EDUCATION & INFORMATION CENTER 5600 WEST MAPLE ROAD, SUITE C-301	WEST BLOOMFIELD	**MI**	48033	(313) 626-4998
MINNESOTA-DAKOTAS ACTION COMM. FOR SOVIET JEWRY 15 SOUTH 9TH ST	MINNEAPOLIS	**MN**	55402	(612) 338-7816
GREENSBORO ACTION FOR SOVIET JEWRY 222 MISTLETOE DRIVE	GREENSBORO	**NC**	27403	(919) 282-1710
OMAHA COMMITTEE FOR SOVIET JEWRY 11217 WOOLWORTH PLAZA	OMAHA	**NE**	68144	(402) 334-1055

COMMITTEE FOR THE ABSORPTION OF SOVIET EMIGREES (CASE)
80 GRAND STREET .... JERSEY CITY **NJ** 07302 (201) 332-7962
LOS ALAMOS COMMITTEE ON SOVIET ANTI-SEMITISM
9 VILLAGE PL.; WHITE ROCK VILLAGE .... LOS ALAMOS **NM** 87544 (505) 672-3783
ASSOCIATION OF SOVIET JEWS IN AMERICA 1050 OCEAN AVENUE .... BROOKLYN **NY** 11226 (718) 434-4518
FREE FRIENDS OF REFUGEES OF EASTERN EUROPE
1383 PRESIDENT STREET .... BROOKLYN **NY** 11213 (718) 467-0860
OCEANFRONT COUNCIL FOR SOVIET JEWRY 4089 OCEAN AVENUE .... BROOKLYN **NY** 11235 (718) 891-9685
STUDENT STRUGGLE FOR SOVIET JEWRY 1118 AVENUE J .... BROOKLYN **NY** 11230 (718) 253-3800
LONG ISLAND COMMITTEE FOR SOVIET JEWRY
ONE OLD COUNTRY ROAD, SUITE 393 .... CARLE PLACE **NY** 11514 (516) 294-8181
SOVIET JEWRY HOT LINE 98 CUTTER MILL ROAD .... GREAT NECK **NY** 11021 (516) 466-4699
LONG ISLAND COMMITTEE FOR SOVIET JEWRY
134 JACKSON STREET .... HEMPSTEAD **NY** 11550 (516) 538-5454
LONG ISLAND MEDICAL/DENTAL/HEALTH COMMITTEE FOR SOVIET JEWRY
91 NORTH FRANKLIN .... HEMPSTEAD **NY** 11550 (516) 538-5454
ACADEMIC COMMITTEE ON SOVIET JEWRY 345 E 46TH STREET .... NEW YORK **NY** 10017 (212) 557-9013
CENTER FOR RUSSIAN JEWRY 210 W 91ST STREET .... NEW YORK **NY** 10024 (212) 799-8900
COMMITTEE FOR DEFENSE OF SOVIET POLITICAL PRISONERS
254 WEST 31ST STREET .... NEW YORK **NY** 10001 (212) 695-3895
CTR FOR RUSSIAN JEWRY-STUDENT STRUGGLE FOR SOVIET JEWRY, THE
210 W 91ST STREET .... NEW YORK **NY** 10024 (212) 799-8900
COALITION TO FREE SOVIET JEWS 8 WEST 40TH STREET, SUITE 602 .... NEW YORK **NY** 10018 (212) 354-1316
24 HOUR SOVIET JEWRY ACTIONLINE .... NEW YORK **NY** (212) 391-0954
JACOB BIRNBAUM-CENTER FOR RUSSIAN AND EAST EUROPEAN JEWRY
240 CABRINI BLVD .... NEW YORK **NY** 10033 (212) 928-7451
INTERNATIONAL LEAGUE FOR REPATRIATION OF RUSSIAN JEWS
315 CHURCH STREET .... NEW YORK **NY** 10013 (212) 431-6789
INTERNATIONAL LEAGUE FOR REPATRIATION OF RUSSIAN JEWS
41 E 42ND STREET, SUITE 515 .... NEW YORK **NY** 10017 (212) 682-7865
INTERNATIONAL LEAGUE FOR THE REPATRIATION OF RUSSIAN JEWS
315 CHURCH STREET .... NEW YORK **NY** 10013 (212) 431-6866
JOINT COMM. ON SOC. ACTION/COMM. ON JEW. COMMUNITY & PUB. POL
155 FIFTH AVENUE .... NEW YORK **NY** 10010 (212) 533-7800
NATIONAL CONFERENCE ON SOVIET JEWRY
10 E. 40TH STREET, SUITE 907 .... NEW YORK **NY** 10016 (212) 679-6122
NATIONAL CONFERENCE ON SOVIET JEWRY 10 W. 40TH STREET .... NEW YORK **NY** 10016 (212) 679-6122
PROJECT RISE-RUSSIAN IMMIGRANT SERVICES & EDUCATION
84 WILLIAM STREET .... NEW YORK **NY** 10038 (212) 797-9000
PROJECT RISE-A DIVISION OF AGUDATH ISRAEL 84 WILLIAM STREET .... NEW YORK **NY** 10038 (212) 797-9000
THE RAOUL WALLENBERG COMMITTEE OF THE UNITED STATES
127 EAST 73RD STREET .... NEW YORK **NY** 10021 (212) 737-7790
RUSSIAN IMMIGRANT RESCUE FUND 84 WILLIAM STREET .... NEW YORK **NY** 10038 (212) 964-8262
SOVIET JEWRY RESEARCH BUREAU-NAT'L CONF. ON SOVIET JEWRY
10 E. 40TH STREET, SUITE 907 .... NEW YORK **NY** 10016 (212) 679-6122
SOVIET UN MISSION 136 EAST 67TH STREET .... NEW YORK **NY** 10021 (212) 861-4900
STUDENT STRUGGLE FOR SOVIET JEWRY 210 WEST 91ST STREET .... NEW YORK **NY** 10024 (212) 799-8900
TASS NEWS AGENCY 50 ROCKEFELLER PLAZA .... NEW YORK **NY** 10020 (212) 245-4250
CINCINNATI COUNCIL FOR SOVIET JEWRY 2615 CLIFTON AVE .... CINCINNATI **OH** 45220 (513) 221-7134
CLEVELAND COUNCIL ON SOVIET ANTI-SEMITISM (CCSA, INC.)
6325 ALDENHAM DRIVE .... CLEVELAND **OH** 44143 (216) 449-3662
OKLAHOMA COMMISSION FOR SOVIET JEWRY 5633 SOUTH GARY .... TULSA **OK** 74105 (918) 747-6390
GREATER PHILADELPHIA COUNCIL FOR SOVIET JEWS PO BOX 83 ... BALA CYNWYD **PA** 19004
SOVIET JEWRY ACTION COUNCIL OF HARRISBURG
3560 GREEN STREET .... HARRISBURG **PA** 17110 (717) 238-5673
SOVIET JEWRY COUNCIL OF THE JCRC 1520 LOCUST ST .... PHILADELPHIA **PA** 19102 (215) 545-8430
PITTSBURGH VOICE ON SOVIET JEWRY 234 MCKEE PLACE .... PITTSBURGH **PA** 15213 (412) 681-8000
CANADIAN 35'S 118 ABERDEEN AVENUE .... WESTMONT **QU** (518) 891-3319
KNOXVILLE-OAK RIDGE COUNCIL FOR SOVIET JEWS
7113 CHESHIRE DR .... KNOXVILLE **TN** 37919 (615) 584-6042
HOUSTON ACTION FOR SOVIET JEWRY 9107 TIMBERSIDE DRIVE .... HOUSTON **TX** 77025 (713) 665-6753
WACO COUNCIL OF CONCERN ON SOVIET JEWRY 5501 FAIRVIEW DR .... WACO **TX** 76710 (817) 772-8929
NEWPORT NEWS SOVIET JEWRY COMMITTEE UNITED JEWISH FEDERATION
317 LYNCHBURG DRIVE .... NEWPORT NEWS **VA** 23606 (804) 599-5546
SEATTLE ACTION FOR SOVIET JEWRY 5229 S. MORGAN .... SEATTLE **WA** 98118 (206) 723-6897
LONDON 35'S (WOMEN'S CAMPAIGN FOR SOVIET JEWRY)
564 FINCHLEY ROAD .... LONDON **GB**
COMITE DES QUINZE 14 RUE DE LONGCHAMP .... 9200 NEUILLY **FR**
ASSOC. FOR DISSEMINATION OF THE HEBREW LANGUAGE IN THE USSR
PO BOX 3897 .... JERUSALEM **IS** 91037
SHVUT AMI CENTER FOR SOVIET JEWS
10 BELILIUS STREET, P.O. BOX 6141 .... JERUSALEM **IS** 91061 02-232414

SPORTS

INTERNATIONAL JEWISH SPORTS HALL OF FAME-USA
9200 SUNSET BOULEVARD, SUITE 1010 .... LOS ANGELES **CA** 90069 (213) 276-1014
MACCABEE ATHLETIC CLUB, INC 6399 WILSHIRE BOULEVARD .... LOS ANGELES **CA** 90048 (213) 651-3182
ISRAEL TENNIS CENTER COMMITTEE 350 FIFTH AVENUE .... NEW YORK **NY** 10118 (212) 594-5250
UNITED STATES COMMITTEE SPORTS FOR ISRAEL, INC
275 SOUTH 19TH STREET, SUITE 1203 .... PHILADELPHIA **PA** 19103 (215) 546-4700
U.S. MACCABIAH COMMITTEE
275 SOUTH 19TH STREET, SUITE 1203 .... PHILADELPHIA **PA** 19103 (215) 546-4700

STAINED GLASS

STAINED GLASS ASSOCIATES P.O. BOX 1531 .... RALEIGH **NC** 27602 (919) 266-2493
ASCALON STUDIOS 115 ATLANTIC AVENUE .... BERLIN **NJ** 08009 (609) 768-3779
EDELWEISS CO - GLASS STUDIO 1217 49 STREET .... BROOKLYN **NY** 11219 (718) 851-9687
THE CEDARHURST GLASSWORKS 96 SPRUCE STREET .... CEDARHURST **NY** 11516 (516) 569-7101

STAMPS

SHARON HOLY LAND INC. P.O. BOX 3364 .... BEVERLY HILLS **CA** 90212 (213) 278-7260
JNF SPECIALTIES P.O. BOX 255 .... LA CANADA **CA** 91011
SOCIETY OF ISRAEL PHILATELISTS 1125 EAST CARSON STREET #2 .... LONG BEACH **CA** 90807 (213) 595-9224
SOCIETY OF ISRAEL PHILATELISTS .... LOS ANGELES **CA** 90025 (213) 345-7645
HOUSE OF ZION P.O. BOX 5502-S .... REDWOOD CITY **CA** 94063 (415) 367-0814
BICK INTERNATIONAL PO BOX 854 .... VAN NUYS **CA** 91408 (818) 997-6496
ISRAEL STAMP COLLECTORS SOCIETY PO BOX 854 .... VAN NUYS **CA** 91408 (818) 997-6496
B'NAI B'RITH PHILATELIC SERVICE
1640 RHODE ISLAND AVENUE N.W. .... WASHINGTON **DC** 20036 (202) 857-6600
KLUTZNICK EXHIBIT HALL 1640 RHODE ISLAND AVENUE N.W. .... WASHINGTON **DC** 20036 (202) 857-6600
TOWER OF DAVID P.O. BOX 2620 .... SARATOGA **FL** 33578
ISRAEL NUMISMATIC SOCIETY PO BOX 427 .... SKOKIE **IL** 60035
THEO VAN DAM P.O. BOX 26 .... BREWSTER **NY** 10509
MARTEN STAMPS/COINS 156 B MIDDLE NECK ROAD .... GREAT NECK **NY** 11021 (516) 482-8404
GAREL COMPANY PO BOX 374 .... HEWLETT **NY** 11557 (516) 374-2909
MOSDEN TRADING CO. 145 JERICHO TURNPIKE .... MINEOLA **NY** 11501 (516) 741-0993
AMERICAN ZIONIST YOUTH FOUNDATION 515 PARK AVENUE .... NEW YORK **NY** 10022 (212) 751-6070
ATLAS STAMP CO. 48 WEST 48TH STREET, DEPARTMENT Y .... NEW YORK **NY** 10036 (212) 869-5545
COLLECTOR'S CLUB 22 EAST 35TH STREET .... NEW YORK **NY** 10016 (212) 683-0559
ISRAEL PHILATELIC AGENCY IN AMERICA, INC.
116 WEST 32ND STREET .... NEW YORK **NY** 10001 (212) 695-0008
ISRAEL PHILATELIC AGENCY IN AMERICA 41 WEST 25TH STREET .... NEW YORK **NY** 10001 (212) 807-6044
MOSDEN STAMP COMPANY 232 EAST 54TH STREET .... NEW YORK **NY** 10022 (212) 758-7818
SAM MALAMUD, IDEAL STAMP COMPANY 48 WEST 48TH STREET .... NEW YORK **NY** 10036 (212) 869-5545
JAYLEE CO. DRAWER 160 .... OLD BETHPAGE **NY** 11804
JUDAICA HISTORICAL PHILATELIC SOCIETY 80 BRUCE AVENUE .... YONKERS **NY** 10705
CLEVELAND CHAPTER OF THE SOCIETY OF ISRAEL PHILATELISTS
24355 TUNBRIDGE LANE .... CLEVELAND **OH** 44122 (216) 292-3843
ISRAEL NUMISMATIC SOCIETY OF CLEVELAND
614 W. SUPERIOR ROAD, #600 .... CLEVELAND **OH** 44113 (216) 241-2258
CANADIAN ASSOC. FOR ISRAEL PHILATELY
3877 BATHURST STREET, APARTMENT 2 .... DOWNSVIEW **ON** M3H 3N4 (416) 781-9779
CAFIP - CANADIAN ASSOCIATION FOR ISRAEL PHILATELY
159 WILLOWDALE AVENUE .... WILLOWDALE **ON** M2N 4Y7 (416) 222-9900
JUDAICA SALES REG'D P.O. BOX 276, YOUVILLE STATION .... MONTREAL **QU** H2P 2V5 (514) 687-0632
AMERICAN TOPICAL ASSOCIATION 5014 WEST CENTER .... MILWAUKEE **WI** 53216
ISRAEL STAMP AGENCY IN NORTH AMERICA 1 UNICOVER CENTER .... CHEYENNE **WY** 82008 (800) 443-3232
CAPITAL STAMPS P.O. BOX 3769, 23 BEN YEHUDA STREET .... JERUSALEM **IS** 94624 (02) 245623
ISRAEL PHILATELIC FOUNDATION P.O. BOX 10175 .... JERUSALEM **IS** 91101
SOCIETY OF THE POSTAL HISTORY OF ERETZ-ISRAEL
P.O. BOX 10175 .... JERUSALEM **IS** 91101
MARVIN SIEGEL P.O. BOX 196 .... RAMAT GAN **IS** (03) 721619
DR. JOSEF WALLACH P.O. BOX 1414 .... REHOVOT **IS** 76113 (08) 457274
GEVA STAMP AUCTION DIZENGOFF CENTRE .... TEL AVIV **IS** 64332 (03) 287486
INTERNATIONAL STAMP AUCTIONS P.O. BOX 29154 .... TEL AVIV **IS** 61291 (03) 283650
MATSA CO. LTD. P.O. BOX 46099, 5 DROYANOV STREET (BEIT CLAL) .... TEL AVIV **IS** 63143
UNISTAMPS LTD. P.O. BOX 32120 .... TEL AVIV **IS** (03) 299758
ZODIAC STAMPS LTD. P.O. BOX 4895, 11 HESS STREET .... TEL AVIV **IS** 63324 (03) 291395
F.I.B. - FREUNDE DER ISRAELISCHEN BRIEFMARKE
RECHTE WIENZEILE 37 .... WIEN **AU** A 1040
AMICALE PHILATEIQUE FRANCE - ISRAEL 45 AV. DE LA REPUBLIQUE .... PARIS **FR** 75011
BRITISH ASSOCIATION OF PALESTINE - ISRAEL PHILATELISTS
21 TORRINGTON DRIVE .... THINGSWALL **GB** L6I 7U2
CENTRAL STAMP GALLERY 48 PORTLAND PLACE .... LONDON **GB** W1N 3DG (01) 636-4193
JUDAICA PHILATELIC SOCIETY
HAROLD POSTER HOUSE, KINGSBERY CIRCLE .... LONDON **GB** NW9 9PJ
NEGEV HOLYLAND STAMPS LTD. P.O. BOX 1 .... ILFRACOMBE DEVON **GB** Ex34 9BR
VERENIGING NEDERLAND - ISRAEL PHILATELIE
OVERMEER-SEWEG 90, 1394 BG .... NEDERHORSTDENBERG **HD**
TERRA SANTA SOCIETY VIA DOGANA 3 .... MILANO **IT** 20123
CAPE SOCIETY FOR PALESTINE - ISRAEL PHILATELY P.O. BOX 6160 ... ROGGEBAAL **SA** 8012
SCHWEIZERISHER VEREIN DER ISRAEL - PHILATELISTEN 32 SIBERGASSE .... BIEL **SW** 2503
ARBEITSGEMEINSCHAFT ISRAEL IM BUND DEUTSCHER PHILATELISTEN
MOOR DAMM 72 .... ELLERBECK **WG** 2081

STREIMELS

EINHORN MOSHE 50-18 14TH AVENUE .... BROOKLYN **NY** 11219 (718) 853-5599
KESER SHTREIMLICH (M. HERZL) 1769 50TH STREET .... BROOKLYN **NY** 11204 (718) 633-3563
KRAUSS, SHMUEL 202 KEAP STREET .... BROOKLYN **NY** 11211 (718) 387-7832
ONE-HA-STREIMEL 193 LEE AVENUE .... BROOKLYN **NY** 11211
ONEG SHTREIMLICH (GESTETNER) 110 LEE AVENUE .... BROOKLYN **NY** 11211 (718) 387-0218
SCHWARTZ, YISROEL NECHEMIA 190 ROSS STREET .... BROOKLYN **NY** 11211 (718) 387-4491
SELCO HATTERS 228 BROADWAY .... BROOKLYN **NY** 11211 (718) 388-6848
SHMUEL KRAUSS 167 PENN STREET .... BROOKLYN **NY** 11211
KLEIN, CHAIM YEHUDA 24 RALPH BOULEVARD .... MONSEY **NY** 10952 (914) 425-1068

STUDENT, YOUNG ADULT & YOUTH ORGANIZATIONS

NATIONAL CONFERENCE OF SYNAGOGUE YOUTH
3476 OAK STREET .... VANCOUVER **BC** V6H 2L8 (604) 736-7607
TEMPLE SHOLOM YOUTH (NIFTY) 4426 WEST 10TH AVENUE .... VANCOUVER **BC** V6R 2H9 (604) 224-1381
UNITED SYNAGOGUE YOUTH (USY) 4350 OAK STREET .... VANCOUVER **BC** V6H 2N4 (604) 736-4161
VANCOUVER JEWISH YOUTH COUNCIL 950 WEST 41ST AVENUE .... VANCOUVER **BC** V5Z 2N7 (604) 266-9111

YOUNG JUDEA 950 WEST 41ST AVENUE — VANCOUVER **BC** V5Z 2N7 (604) 266-9111
BRANDEIS-BARDIN YOUNG ADULTS 1101 PEPPERTREE LANE — BRANDEIS **CA** 93064 (213) 348-7201
JEWISH COMMUNITY CENTER OF LONG BEACH, COLLEGE STUDENT SERV.
3801 EAST WILLOW — LONG BEACH **CA** 90815 (213) 426-7601
HA'AM 112 E KERCKHOFF HALL, 308 WESTWOOD PLAZA — LOS ANGELES **CA** 90024
JEWISH YOUTH DEPT. 6505 WILSHIRE BLVD — LOS ANGELES **CA** 90048 (213) 852-1234
NITZAN CHAPTER FOR YOUNG CAREER WOMEN
1494 S ROBERTSON BLVD — LOS ANGELES **CA** 90035 (213) 275-5345
NORTHERN PACIFIC COAST, HASHACHAR-YOUNG JUDEA
1419 BROADWAY, SUITE 308 — OAKLAND **CA** 94612 (415) 832-8448
THE BAYIT PROJECT
5311 TOPANGA CANYON BOULEVARD, #300 — WOODLAND HILLS **CA** 91364 (818) 888-0355
LUBAVITCH YOUTH ORGANIZATION 152 GOFFE TERR — NEW HAVEN **CT** 06511 (203) 865-3649
B'NAI B'RITH YOUTH ORGANIZATION
1640 RHODE ISLAND AVENUE N.W. — WASHINGTON **DC** 20036 (202) 857-6600
FLORIDA UNION OF JEWISH STUDENTS C/O MIAMI HILLEL
100 MILLER DRIVE — CORAL GABLES **FL** 33146 (305) 661-8549
BNEI AKIVA OF CHICAGO 6500 NORTH CALIFORNIA — CHICAGO **IL** 60645 (312) 338-6569
CHICAGO JEWISH YOUTH COUNCIL 3003 W. TOUHY AVENUE — CHICAGO **IL** 60645 (312) 961-9100
DEBORAH BOYS CLUB 3201 W. AINSLIE STREET — CHICAGO **IL** 60625 (312) 539-5907
FEDERATION OF TEMPLE YOUTH 100 WEST MONROE — CHICAGO **IL** 60603 (312) 782-1477
YOUNG MEN'S JEWISH COUNCIL 30 WEST WASHINGTON — CHICAGO **IL** 60602 (312) 726-8891
LUBAVITCH YOUTH ORGANIZATION 42 KIRKWOOD ROAD — BRIGHTON **MA** 02135 (617) 787-2667
FELLOWSHIP IN ISRAEL FOR ARAB-JEWISH YOUTH
45 FRANCIS AVENUE — CAMBRIDGE **MA** 02138 (617) 354-1198
LUBAVITCH YOUTH ORGANIZATION 74 JOSEPH ROAD — FRAMINGHAM **MA** 01761 (617) 877-5313
NANTASKET YOUTH CENTER 7 WILSON STREET — HULL **MA** 02045 (413) 925-4445
LUBAVITCH YOUTH ORGANIZATION 15 ELWOOD DRIVE — SPRINGFIELD **MA** 01108 (413) 737-7998
EMANUEL, TEMPLE R 280 MAY STREET — WORCESTER **MA** 01602 (617) 755-1257
LUBAVITCH YOUTH ORGANIZATION 24 CRESWELL — WORCESTER **MA** 01602 (617) 752-5791
NAT'L CONFERENCE OF SYNAGOGUE YOUTH-ATLANTIC SEABOARD REGION
4001 CLARKS LANE — BALTIMORE **MD** 21215 (301) 358-6279
NAT'L CONFERENCE OF SYNAGOGUE YOUTH-DISTRICT OFFICE
11710 HUNTERS LANE — ROCKVILLE **MD** 20852 (301) 231-5300
JEWISH STUDENTS OF CARLETON CARLETON COLLEGE — NORTHFIELD **MN** 55057 (507) 645-4431
NATIONAL CONFERENCE OF SYNAGOGUE YOUTH - MIDWEST REGION
8147 DELMAR, SUITE 211 — ST. LOUIS **MO** 63130 (314) 725-2483
LUBAVITCH STUDENTS ORGANIZATION 226 SUSSEX AVENUE — MORRISTOWN **NJ** 07960 (201) 540-0877
YUGNTRUF 3328 BAINBRIDGE AVENUE — BRONX **NY** 10467 (212) 654-8540
AKIVA JEWISH CULTURE CLUBS OF THE N.Y.C. PUBLIC HIGH SCHOOLS
1577 CONEY ISLAND AVENUE — BROOKLYN **NY** 11230 (718) 258-3585
JEWISH ORTHODOX YOUTH, INC. 563 BEDFORD AVENUE — BROOKLYN **NY** 11211 (718) 384-0461
JEWISH STUDENT UNION OF BROOKLYN LAW SCHOOL
250 JORALEMON STREET — BROOKLYN **NY** 11201 (718) 625-2200
LUBAVITCH YOUTH ORGANIZATION 770 EASTERN PARKWAY — BROOKLYN **NY** 11213 (718) 778-6000
TZIVOS HASHEM 770 EASTERN PARKWAY — BROOKLYN **NY** 11213 (718) 467-6630
LUBAVITCH OF LONG ISLAND 74 HAPPAUGE ROAD — COMMACK **NY** 11725 (516) 462-6640
QUEENS COLLEGE UNION B-42 COUNCIL OF JEWISH ORGANIZATIONS
65-30 KISSENA BLVD BOX 24 — FLUSHING **NY** 11367 (718) 591-8978
AMERICAN JEWISH SOCIETY FOR SERVICE 15 E 26TH STREET — NEW YORK **NY** 10010 (212) 683-6178
AMERICAN ZIONIST YOUTH FOUNDATION 515 PARK AVENUE — NEW YORK **NY** 10022 (212) 751-6070
BETAR 9 EAST 38TH STREET — NEW YORK **NY** 10016 (212) 696-0080
BNEI AKIVA OF NEW YORK 25 W. 26TH STREET — NEW YORK **NY** 10010 (212) 889-5992
BNEI AKIVA OF NORTH AMERICA 25 WEST 26TH STREET — NEW YORK **NY** 10010 (212) 889-5260
BNOS AGUDATH ISRAEL 84 WILLIAM STREET — NEW YORK **NY** 10038 (212) 797-9000
COLLEGE YOUTH FOR TORAH 116 E. 27TH STREET — NEW YORK **NY** 10016 (212) 725-3420
DEPT. OF YOUTH ACTIVITIES/USY, KADIMA 155 FIFTH AVENUE — NEW YORK **NY** 10010 (212) 533-7800
DROR YOUNG KIBBUTZ MOVEMENT 27 WEST 20TH STREET — NEW YORK **NY** 10011 (212) 675-1168
HABONIM LABOR ZIONIST YOUTH 27 WEST 20TH STREET — NEW YORK **NY** 10011 (212) 255-1796
HAMAGSHIMIM 50 WEST 58TH STREET — NEW YORK **NY** 10019 (212) 355-7900
HASHACHAR 50 W. 58TH STREET — NEW YORK **NY** 10019 (212) 355-7900
HASHOMER HATZAIR SOCIALIST ZIONIST YOUTH MOVEMENT
150 FIFTH AVENUE, SUITE 911 — NEW YORK **NY** 10011 (212) 929-4955
ICHUD HABONIM LABOR ZIONIST YOUTH 27 W. 20 STREET — NEW YORK **NY** 10011 (212) 255-1796
ISRAEL SUMMER SEMINAR 1776 BROADWAY — NEW YORK **NY** 10019 (212) 247-0741
ISRAELI STUDENTS' ORGANIZATION IN THE U.S. & CANADA
515 PARK AVENUE — NEW YORK **NY** 10022 (212) 688-6796
JEWISH ASSOCIATION FOR COLLEGE YOUTH 130 EAST 59TH STREET — NEW YORK **NY** 10022 (212) 688-0808
JEWISH MEDIA SERVICE 15 EAST 26TH STREET — NEW YORK **NY** 10010 (212) 532-4949
JEWISH STUDENT APPEAL 15 EAST 26TH STREET — NEW YORK **NY** 10010 (212) 679-2293
JEWISH STUDENT PRESS SERVICE 15 E. 26TH STREET, SUITE 1350 — NEW YORK **NY** 10010 (212) 679-1411
LUBAVITCH YOUTH ORGANIZATION 770 EASTERN PARKWAY — NEW YORK **NY** 11213 (212) 493-0571
MESORAH 45 W 36TH STREET — NEW YORK **NY** 10018 (212) 563-4000
METROPOLITAN UNION OF JEWISH STUDENTS 515 PARK AVENUE — NEW YORK **NY** 10022
NATIONAL CONFERENCE OF SYNAGOGUE YOUTH (NCSY)
45 WEST 36TH STREET — NEW YORK **NY** 10018 (212) 563-4000
NATIONAL FEDERATION OF TEMPLE YOUTH 838 FIFTH AVENUE — NEW YORK **NY** 10021 (212) 249-0100
NETWORK 36 WEST 37TH STREET — NEW YORK **NY** 10018
NEW JEWISH MEDIA PROJECT 36 WEST 37TH STREET — NEW YORK **NY** 10018
NOAR MIZRACHI 25 WEST 26TH STREET — NEW YORK **NY** 10010 (212) 684-6091
NORTH AMERICAN FEDERATION OF TEMPLE YOUTH
838 FIFTH AVENUE — NEW YORK **NY** 10021 (212) 249-0100
NORTH AMERICAN JEWISH STUDENT APPEAL 15 EAST 26TH STREET — NEW YORK **NY** 10010 (212) 679-2293
NORTH AMERICAN JEWISH STUDENTS NETWORK, INC.
1 PARK AVENUE — NEW YORK **NY** 10016 (212) 689-0790
NORTH AMERICAN JEWISH YOUTH COUNCIL 515 PARK AVENUE — NEW YORK **NY** 10022 (212) 751-6070
ORT YOUTH FELLOWSHIP 315 PARK AVENUE SOUTH — NEW YORK **NY** 10010 (212) 505-7700
ORT YOUTH FELLOWSHIP 1250 BROADWAY — NEW YORK **NY** 10001
P'EYLIM-AMERICAN YESHIVA STUDENT UNION 3 W. 16TH STREET — NEW YORK **NY** 10011 (212) 989-2500
PIRCHEI AGUDATH ISRAEL 84 WILLIAM STREET — NEW YORK **NY** 10038 (212) 797-9000
SEIXAS-MENORAH SOCIETY OF COLUMBIA & BARNARD
102 EARL HALL-COLUMBIA UNIVERSITY — NEW YORK **NY** 10027
STUDENT STRUGGLE FOR SOVIET JEWRY 210 WEST 91ST STREET — NEW YORK **NY** 10024 (212) 799-8900
STUDENTS ON SCHOLARSHIP/NAT'L. COUNCIL OF YOUNG ISRAEL
3 WEST 16TH STREET — NEW YORK **NY** 10011 (212) 929-1525
TAGAR 9 EAST 38TH STREET — NEW YORK **NY** 10016 (212) 696-0080
UNITED SYNAGOGUE YOUTH 155 FIFTH AVENUE — NEW YORK **NY** 10010 (212) 533-7800
YAVNEH - NATIONAL RELIGIOUS STUDENTS ASSOCIATION
156 FIFTH AVENUE — NEW YORK **NY** 10010 (212) 929-5434
YAVNEH-NATIONAL RELIGIOUS JEWISH STUDENTS ASSOCIATION
25 W. 26TH STREET — NEW YORK **NY** 10010 (212) 679-4574
YISRAEL HATZAIR-YOUNG ISRAEL SYNAGOGUE YOUTH
3 WEST 16TH STREET — NEW YORK **NY** 10011 (212) 929-1525
YOUNG ISRAEL MASSORAH COLLEGIATE COUNCIL
3 WEST 16TH STREET — NEW YORK **NY** 10011 (212) 929-1525
ZEIREI AGUDATH ISRAEL OF AMERICA 84 WILLIAM STREET — NEW YORK **NY** 10038 (212) 797-9000
HEBREW UNION COLLEGE STUDENT ASSOCIATION
3101 CLIFTON AVENUE — CINCINNATI **OH** 45220 (513) 221-1875
ETHIC, THE 3246 DESOTA AVENUE — CLEVELAND **OH** 44118 (216) 932-0206
NEW OHIO UNION OF JEWISH STUDENTS 11291 EUCLID AVENUE — CLEVELAND **OH** 44106
ISRAEL YOUTH PROGRAM CENTRE 1000 FINCH AVENUE WEST — DOWNSVIEW **ON** (416) 665-7733
CANADIAN YOUNG JUDEA ZIONIST YOUTH MOVEMENT
788 MARLEE AVENUE — TORONTO **ON** M6B 3K1 (416) 787-5350
YOUNG HERUT 3417 BATHURST STREET — TORONTO **ON**
HASHACHAR YOUNG JUDAEA 1825 SPRUCE STREET — PHILADELPHIA **PA** 19103 (215) 545-6270
PENNSYLVANIA FED. OF TEMPLE YOUTH, PA COUNCIL UAHC
2111 ARCHITECTS BLDG., 117 S. 17TH STREET — PHILADELPHIA **PA** 19103 (215) 563-8183
WESTERN PENNSYLVANIA HASHACHAR-YOUNG JUDEA
6328 FORBES AVENUE — PITTSBURGH **PA** 15217 (412) 521-4877
B'NAI ISRAEL, CONGREGATION O 7 EAST SUNBURY STREET — SHAMOKIN **PA** 17872 (717) 648-2281
BNEI AKIVA OF MONTREAL 5497A VICTORIA AVENUE, SUITE 103 — MONTREAL **QU** H3W 2R1 (514) 739-1119
BRITH TRUMPELDOR BETAR OF AMERICA
5234 CLANRANALD AVENUE — MONTREAL **QU** (514) 486-8926
CANADIAN YOUNG JUDEA 5319 DECARIE BOULEVARD — MONTREAL **QU** (514) 481-8910
YOUNG HERUT 5234 CLANRANALD AVENUE — MONTREAL **QU** H3X 2S4
SHERUT LA'AM 1310 GREENE AVENUE — WESTMOUNT **QU** H3Z 2B2 (514) 934-0804
STUDENT ZIONIST ORGANIZATIONS 1310 GREENE AVENUE — WESTMOUNT **QU** H3Z 2B2 (514) 934-0804
YOUTH & HECHALUTZ DEPARTMENT (ISRAEL PROGRAM CENTRE)
1310 GREENE AVENUE — WESTMOUNT **QU** H3Z 2B2 (514) 934-0804

SUKKOT SUPPLIES

ATARAH — LOS ANGELES **CA** 90036 (213) 655-3050
TORAH TREASURES 1202 WASHINGTON AVENUE — MIAMI BEACH **FL** 33139 (305) 673-6095
JUDAICA ENTERPRISES 1074 NE 163RD STREET — NORTH MIAMI BEACH **FL** 33162 (305) 945-5091
CRAFTWOOD LUMBER COMPANY 1590 OLD DEERFIELD ROAD — HIGHLAND PARK **IL** 60035 (312) 831-2800
R. KROCHMAL 71 MONASTERY RD. — BRIGHTON **MA** 02135 (617) 254-1760
GOODMAN'S HEBREW BOOK SHOP — BALTIMORE **MD** (301) 933-1800
CUSTOM SUKKAHS — BERGEN COUNTY **NJ** (201) 568-9423
8TH AVENUE LUMBER 5002 8TH AVENUE — BROOKLYN **NY** 11220 (718) 854-0401
BORO PARK LUMBER & HOME CENTER 4601 NEW UTRECHT AVENUE — BROOKLYN **NY** 11219 (718) 853-3100
CERTIFIED LUMBER COMPANY 470 KENT AVENUE — BROOKLYN **NY** 11211 (718) 387-1233
CUSTOM SUKKAHS 1605 45TH STREET — BROOKLYN **NY** 11204 (718) 436-6333
SUKKAH HOTLINE — BROOKLYN **NY** (800) 382-5252
EICHLER'S 1429 CONEY ISLAND AVENUE — BROOKLYN **NY** 11230 (718) 258-7643
F & F SUKKAH FACTORY & SHOWROOM 32 LYNCH STREET — BROOKLYN **NY** 11206 (718) 596-0597
F & F SUKKAH FACTORY & SHOWROOM 1271 56TH STREET — BROOKLYN **NY** 11219 (718) 435-5433
LEITER'S, THE SOURCE 4301 14TH AVENUE — BROOKLYN **NY** 11219 (718) 436-0303
RABBI LEIB PURETZ 1571 CONEY ISLAND AVENUE — BROOKLYN **NY** 11230 (718) 252-7532
SUKKAS SHOLOM 196 LEE AVENUE — BROOKLYN **NY** 11211 (718) 855-1163
FRANK SUPPLY COMPANY 21-07 CORNAGA AVENUE — FAR ROCKAWAY **NY** 11691 (718) 471-2663
GIFT WORLD 72-20 MAIN STREET — FLUSHING **NY** 11367 (718) 261-0233
PRI ETROG COMPANY, THE 69-66 MAIN STREET — FLUSHING **NY** 11367 (718) 263-6040
HECKER SILVERSMITHS 605 FIFTH AVENUE (49TH STREET) — NEW YORK **NY** 10017 (212) 593-2424
ISRAEL ETROG CENTER 38 CANAL STREET — NEW YORK **NY** 10002 (212) 431-4140
J. LEVINE CO. - LOWER EAST SIDE 58 ELDRIDGE STREET — NEW YORK **NY** 10002 (212) 966-4460
J. LEVINE CO. - MIDTOWN STORE 5 WEST 30TH STREET — NEW YORK **NY** 10001 (212) 695-6888
MOSHE TARLOW 45 CANAL STREET — NEW YORK **NY** 10002 (212) 226-8115
S. GOLDMAN OTZAR HASEFARIM, JACOB D. GOLDMAN
38 CANAL STREET — NEW YORK **NY** 10002 (212) 674-1707
ROSENBERG BOOKS 413 YORK ROAD — JENKINTOWN **PA** 19046 (215) 884-1728
ROSENBERG BOOKS 6408 CASTOR AVENUE — PHILADELPHIA **PA** 19149 (215) 744-5205

SUPERMARKETS

E & S GROCERY MARKET 370 N. FAIRFAX AVENUE — LOS ANGELES **CA** 90036 (213) 938-1512
FAIRFAX KOSHER MARKET 439 NORTH FAIRFAX AVENUE — LOS ANGELES **CA** 90036 (213) 653-2530
KOSHER BASKET 8664 WEST PICO BOULEVARD — LOS ANGELES **CA** 90035 (213) 854-0447
KOTLAR'S KOSHER MARKET 8622 WEST PICO BOULEVARD — LOS ANGELES **CA** 90036 (213) 652-5355
LA BREA MARKET 320 N. LA BREA — LOS ANGELES **CA** 90036 (213) 931-1221
LITTLE JERUSALEM 8971 WEST PICO BOULEVARD — LOS ANGELES **CA** 90035 (213) 858-8361
DREXLER'S 12519½ BURBANK BOULEVARD — NORTH HOLLYWOOD **CA** 91607 (818) 761-6405
CROWN SUPERMARKETS 2471 ALBANY AVENUE — WEST HARTFORD **CT** 06117 (203) 236-1965
EVERYTHING'S KOSHER 1344 WASHINGTON AVENUE — MIAMI BEACH **FL** 33139 (305) 672-4154
SOUTH FLORIDA KOSHER MEATS 1320-24 NE 163RD STREET — N MIAMI BEACH **FL** 33162 (305) 949-6068
HUNGARIAN KOSHER DELICATESSEN & FRESH MEAT CO.
2613 W DEVON — CHICAGO **IL** 60659 (313) 973-5991
ELIYOHU'S FOOD MART 686 MCGREGOR STREET — WINNIPEG **MB** R2V 3E5 (204) 586-4514

JACK'S GROCERY & DELICATESSEN 6311 REISTERSTOWN ROAD	PIKESVILLE	**MD**	21208	(301) 764-1616
SHAPIRO'S FOOD MART 1504 REISTERSTOWN ROAD	PIKESVILLE	**MD**	21208	(301) 484-2400
KATZ KOSHER SUPERMARKET 4860 BOILING BROOK PARKWAY	ROCKVILLE	**MD**	20852	(301) 468-0400
SHALOM KOSHER SUPERMARKET 2307 WEST UNIVERSITY BOULEVARD	WEST SILVER SPRING	**MD**	20902	(301) 946-6500
SIMON NUNBERG'S STRICTLY KOSHER SUPERMARKET & DELI 11238 GEORGIA	WHEATON	**MD**	20902	(301) 949-8477
BAT YAM 525 KINGS HIGHWAY	BROOKLYN	**NY**	11223	(718) 998-8200
BORO PARK CASH & CARRY 1325 39TH STREET	BROOKLYN	**NY**	11218	(718) 438-3191
E&S FOSTER AVENUE GROCERY 506 FOSTER AVENUE	BROOKLYN	**NY**	11230	(718) 438-8516
FOOD BASKET 5023 13TH AVENUE	BROOKLYN	**NY**	11219	(718) 435-8759
FOOD CAROUSEL 2319 AVENUE U	BROOKLYN	**NY**	11229	(718) 332-5191
GEFEN FINE FOODS 1350 CONEY ISLAND AVENUE	BROOKLYN	**NY**	11230	(718) 252-4963
GLATT MART 1205 AVENUE M	BROOKLYN	**NY**	11230	(718) 338-4040
GOLDBERG'S GROCERY/THE PESACH STORE 5021 18TH AVENUE	BROOKLYN	**NY**	11204	(718) 435-7177
GOLDSTEIN BROTHERS 5201 13TH AVENUE	BROOKLYN	**NY**	11219	(718) 851-9100
KOLBO KOSHER 712 KINGS HIGHWAY	BROOKLYN	**NY**	11223	(718) 375-9152
KOSHER CITY 1590 RALPH AVENUE (BTWN.FARRAGUT & FOSTER)	BROOKLYN	**NY**	11236	(718) 763-4992
KOSHER CORNER 573 KINGS HIGHWAY	BROOKLYN	**NY**	11223	(718) 375-3442
LANDAU'S 4510 18TH AVENUE	BROOKLYN	**NY**	11204	(718) 633-0633
MITTLEMAN'S FOOD CENTER 5024 16TH AVENUE	BROOKLYN	**NY**	11204	(718) 851-1205
SAY CHEESE 1218 AVENUE M	BROOKLYN	**NY**	11230	(718) 998-7819
SAY CHEESE 1220 AVENUE M	BROOKLYN	**NY**	11230	(718) 998-8778
SEMEL'S FOOD INC. 5013 13TH AVENUE	BROOKLYN	**NY**	11219	(718) 438-9038
SETTON'S MIDDLE EASTERN & AMERICAN FOODS 509 KINGS HIGHWAY	BROOKLYN	**NY**	11223	(718) 375-2558
SHEHOA ZABO 702 AVENUE U	BROOKLYN	**NY**	11223	(718) 376-0984
SUPER "K" 3910 13TH AVENUE	BROOKLYN	**NY**	11219	(718) 853-0337
COUNTRY KOSHER	FERNDALE	**NY**	12734	(914) 292-8485
SUPERSOL 330 CENTRAL AVENUE	LAWRENCE	**NY**	11559	(516) 295-3300
B&H SUPERETTE 65-47 99TH STREET	REGO PARK	**NY**	11374	(718) 459-5090
MHADRIN KOSHER FOOD SHOP 1066 WILMOT ROAD	SCARSDALE	**NY**	10583	(914) 472-2240
SEMEL'S OF WOODBOURNE MAIN STREET	WOODBOURNE	**NY**	12788	(914) 434-2402
MARTIN'S FOODS 3685 EAST BROAD STREET	COLUMBUS	**OH**	43213	(614) 231-3653
AKIVA'S KOSHER FOODS 3858 BATHURST STREET, LAWRENCE PLAZA	TORONTO	**ON**		(416) 635-0470
YOSSI'S FINE FOODS 4117 BATHURST STREET	TORONTO	**ON**		(416) 635-9509

SYNAGOGUE INTERIORS

JUDSON STUDIES 200 SOUTH AVENUE 66	LOS ANGELES	**CA**	90042	(213) 255-0130
EDWARD GOLDMAN 50 ELM STREET	SAXONVILLE	**MA**	01701	(617) 877-2188
STAINED GLASS ASSOCIATES PO BOX 1531	RALEIGH	**NC**	27602	(919) 266-2493
ASCALON STUDIOS 115 ATLANTIC AVENUE	BERLIN	**NJ**	08009	(609) 768-3779
EMANUEL MILSTEIN 29 WYNCREST ROAD	MARLBORO	**NJ**	07746	(201) 946-8604
ATELIER D'ART DONA ARK CURTAINS, TORAH COVERS, DECORATIVE FABRIC/FIBER 927 RED ROAD	TEANECK	**NJ**	07666	(201) 692-9513
THE SPECIALTY BULB CO. INC. 345A CENTRAL AVENUE	BOHEMIA	**NY**	11716	(516) 589-3393
THE SPECIALTY BULB CO. INC. 345A CENTRAL AVENUE	BOHEMIA	**NY**	11716	(800) 331-BULB
CARVED GLASS & SIGNS 697 EAST 132ND STREET	BRONX	**NY**	10456	(212) 665-6240
EDELWEISS CO.- GLASS STUDIO 1217 49 STREET	BROOKLYN	**NY**	11219	(718) 851-9687
FULL LINE CO. 4903 16TH AVENUE	BROOKLYN	**NY**	11204	(718) 851-1106
SANCTUARY DESIGNS 11 HOLMES PLACE	LYNBROOK	**NY**	11565	(516) 599-3173
EFREM WEITZMAN 334 WEST 86TH STREET	NEW YORK	**NY**	10024	(212) 877-6590
ELVAIGH CARMEN & AHRONN 463 WEST STREET	NEW YORK	**NY**	10014	(212) 691-0099
HAROLD RABINOWITZ DESIGNER SILVERSMITH/TOBE PASCHER WORKSHOP - JEWISH MUSEUM 1109 FIFTH AVENUE	NEW YORK	**NY**	10028	(212) 534-7244

J. LEVINE CO. - LOWER EAST SIDE 58 ELDRIDGE STREET	NEW YORK	**NY**	10002	(212) 966-4460
J. LEVINE CO. - MIDTOWN STORE 5 WEST 30TH STREET	NEW YORK	**NY**	10001	(212) 695-6888
ALBERT WOOD & FIVE SONS INC. ONE PLEASANT AVENUE	PORT WASHINGTON	**NY**	11050	(516) 767-0794
BETTY GOLDSTEIN 35 BENEDICT ROAD	SCARSDALE	**NY**	10583	(914) 723-9552
ART & DESIGN STUDIO OF SARA SHAPIRO 13 DR. FRANK ROAD	SPRING VALLEY	**NY**	10977	(914) 352-3988
WILLET STAINED GLASS COMPANY 10 EAST MORELAND AVENUE	PHILADELPHIA	**PA**	19118	(215) 247-5721

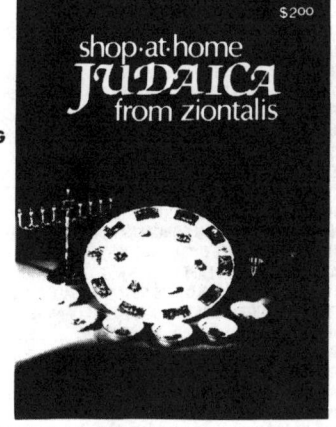

SYNAGOGUES

Synagogue / Address	City	State	Zip	Phone
BETH EL, TEMPLE R P.O.BOX 1364	ANNISTON	AL	36202	(205) 236-9249
BETH EL, TEMPLE C 2179 HIGHLAND AVENUE	BIRMINGHAM	AL	35256	(205) 933-2740
EMANU-EL, TEMPLE R 2100 HIGHLAND AVENUE P.O.BOX 3303-A	BIRMINGHAM	AL	35205	(205) 933-8037
KNESSETH ISRAEL CONGREGATION O 3225 MONTEVALLO ROAD	BIRMINGHAM	AL	35223	(205) 879-1664
B'NAI JESHURUN, CONGREGATION R 406 NORTH MAIN STREET	DEMOPOLIS	AL	36732	(205) 289-2378
EMANU-EL, TEMPLE R 110 NORTH PARK AVENUE	DOTHAN	AL	36303	(205) 792-5001
B'NAI ISRAEL, TEMPLE R 210 HAWTHORNE STREET	FLORENCE	AL	35630	(205) 764-9242
BETH ISRAEL, CONGREGATION R 761 CHESTNUT STREET	GADSDEN	AL	35902	(205) 546-3223
B'NAI SHOLOM, TEMPLE R 103 LINCOLN STREET S.E.	HUNTSVILLE	AL	35801	(205) 536-4771
ETZ CHAYIM - HUNTSVILLE CONSERVATIVE SYNAGOGUE C 7705 BAILEY COVE ROAD S.E.	HUNTSVILLE	AL	35802	(205) 881-6260
EMANUEL, TEMPLE R 1501 FIFTH AVENUE, P.O.BOX 1627	JASPER	AL	35501	(205) 221-4000
AHAVAS CHESED CONGREGATION - DAUPHIN STREET SYNAGOGUE C 1717 DAUPHIN STREET	MOBILE	AL	36604	(205) 476-6010
SPRING HILL AVENUE TEMPLE, CONGREGATION SHA'ARAI SHOMAYIM R 1769 SPRING HILL AVENUE	MOBILE	AL	36607	(205) 478-0415
AGUDATH ISRAEL SYNAGOGUE C 3525 CLOVERDALE ROAD	MONTGOMERY	AL	36111	(205) 281-7394
BETH OR, TEMPLE R P.O.BOX 6180, 2246 NARROW LANE ROAD	MONTGOMERY	AL	36106	(205) 262-3314
CHABAD-LUBAVITCH O P.O. BOX 230212	MONTGOMERY	AL	36123	
ETZ AHAYEM SYNAGOGUE C 725 AUGUSTA STREET	MONTGOMERY	AL	36111	(205) 281-9819
MISHKAN ISRAEL CONGREGATION R C/O SEYMOUR COHN, HOUSTON PARK	SELMA	AL	36701	(205) 874-9811
EMANUEL, TEMPLE R P.O.BOX 5607	TUSCALOOSA	AL	35405	(205) 553-3286
BETH SHALOM, CONGREGATION 1000 W. 20TH AVENUE	ANCHORAGE	AK	99510	(907) 272-8874
ISRAEL, TEMPLE R 1500 WEST CHICKASAWBA	BLYTHEVILLE	AR	72315	(501) 763-4148
BETH ISRAEL, TEMPLE R P.O.BOX 570	EL DORADO	AR	71730	
SHALOM, TEMPLE R 607 STORER STREET	FAYETTEVILLE	AR	72701	(501) 521-8447
UNITED HEBREW CONGREGATION O 126 NORTH 47TH STREET	FORT SMITH	AR	72315	(501) 452-1468
BETH EL, TEMPLE R 406 PERRY STREET	HELENA	AR	72342	(501) 338-6654
BETH JACOB, CONGREGATION O 200 QAPAW AVENUE	HOT SPRINGS	AR	71901	(501) 623-9335
HOUSE OF ISRAEL, CONGREGATION R 300 QUAPAW AVENUE	HOT SPRINGS	AR	71901	(501) 623-5821
ISRAEL, TEMPLE R 203 W. OAK, P.O.BOX 293	JONESBORO	AR	72401	(501) 932-9333
AGUDATH ACHIM, CONGREGATION O 7901 W. 5TH STREET	LITTLE ROCK	AR	72205	(501) 225-1683
B'NAI ISRAEL, CONGREGATION R 3700 RODNEY PARHAM ROAD	LITTLE ROCK	AR	72212	(501) 225-9700
MEIR CHAYIM, TEMPLE R 210 N. 4TH	MCGEHEE	AR	71654	(501) 222-3546
ANSHE EMETH, TEMPLE R 40TH & HICKORY	PINE BLUFF	AR	71611	(501) 534-3853
B'NAI TIKVAH, TEMPLE R 7211 11TH STREET S.W.	CALGARY	AT	T2V IN2	(403) 252-1654
BETH ISRAEL CONGREGATION C 1325 GLENMORE TERRACE S.W.	CALGARY	AT	T2V 4Y8	(403) 255-6868
HOUSE OF JACOB - MIKVEH ISRAEL CONG. O 1613-92ND AVENUE SOUTHWEST	CALGARY	AT	T2V 4N4	(403) 259-3230
BETH ISRAEL SYNAGOGUE O 10219 119TH STREET	EDMONTON	AT	T5K IZ3	(403) 482-2470
BETH ORA CONGREGATION, TEMPLE R 7200 156TH STREET	EDMONTON	AT	TSR IX3	(403) 456-9616
BETH SHALOM SYNAGOGUE C 10219 119TH STREET	EDMONTON	AT	T5K IZ3	(403) 482-2470
EDMONTON BETH SHALOM CONGREGATION 11916 JASPER AVENUE	EDMONTON	AT	T5K OM9	(403) 488-6333
BETH SHOLOM, TEMPLE C 104 WEST FIRST STREET	MESA	AZ	85201	(602) 964-1981
AHAVAT TORAH C 6816 EAST CACTUS ROAD	PHOENIX	AZ	85214	(602) 991-5645
BETH EL, CONGREGATION C 1118 WEST GLENDALE AVENUE	PHOENIX	AZ	85021	(602) 944-3359
BETH HEBREW CONGREGATION C 4003 EAST ORANGEWOOD	PHOENIX	AZ	85021	(602) 934-0124
BETH ISRAEL, TEMPLE R 3310 N. 10TH AVENUE	PHOENIX	AZ	85013	(602) 264-4428
BETH JOSEPH CONG O 515 EAST BETHANY HOME	PHOENIX	AZ	85012	(602) 277-8858
CHABAD-LUBAVITCH O 1536 EAST MARYLAND	PHOENIX	AZ	85014	(604) 274-5377
CHAI, TEMPLE R 16026 N. 32ND STREET	PHOENIX	AZ	85032	(602) 971-1234
TIPHERETH CONGREGATION, ISRAEL O 1536 EAST MARYLAND AVENUE	PHOENIX	AZ	85014	(602) 274-5377
TORAT MOSHE MINYAN, CONGREGATION O 337 E. BETHANY HOME ROAD	PHOENIX	AZ	85012	(602) 277-8858
BETH EMETH, TEMPLE C 6110 NORTH SCOTTSDALE ROAD	SCOTTSDALE	AZ	85253	(602) 947-4604
HAR ZION CONGREGATION C 5929 EAST LINCOLN DRIVE	SCOTTSDALE	AK	85258	(602) 991-0720
SOLEL, TEMPLE R 6805 EAST MCDONALD DRIVE	SCOTTSDALE	AZ	85253	(602) 991-7414
KOL HAMIDBAR, TEMPLE 1204 CAMELOT DRIVE	SIERRA VISTA	AZ	85635	(602) 458-5263
BETH EMETH CONGREGATION C 10810 EL DORADO DRIVE	SUN CITY	AZ	85351	(602) 977-1786
BETH SHALOM, TEMPLE R 12202 101ST AVENUE	SUN CITY	AZ	85351	(602) 977-3240
CHABAD-LUBAVITCH O 23 WEST 9TH STREET	TEMPE	AZ	85281	
TEMPLE EMANUEL OF TEMPE R 5801 S. RURAL ROAD	TEMPE	AZ	85283	(602) 838-1414
ANSHEI ISRAEL CONGREGATION C 5550 E. 5TH STREET	TUCSON	AZ	85711	(602) 745-5550
BET SHALOM, CONG. C 8276 EAST CAMINO HERADURA	TUCSON	AZ	85715	(602) 296-9104
BETH SHALOM C 2915 INDIAN RUINS ROAD	TUCSON	AZ	85715	(602) 296-2735
CHABAD LUBAVITCH, CONG. O 1301 EAST ELM	TUCSON	AZ	85719	(602) 881-7955
CHAVERIM, CONG. R 9932 EAST 5TH STREET	TUCSON	AZ	85748	(602) 886-1592
CHOFETZ CHAIM O 5150 EAST 5TH STREET	TUCSON	AZ	85711	(602) 747-7780
EMANU-EL, TEMPLE R 225 NORTH COUNTRY CLUB ROAD,	TUCSON	AZ	85716	(602) 327-4501
YOUNG ISRAEL OF TUCSON O 2443 EAST 4TH STREET	TUCSON	AZ	85716	(602) 326-8326
BETH TIKVAH CONGREGATION & CENTRE ASSOCIATION C P.O.BOX 94374	RICHMOND	BC	V6Y 2A8	(604) 271-6262
BETH TIKVAH SYNAGOGUE OF RICHMOND C 9711 GEAL ROAD	RICHMOND	BC	V7E 1R4	(604) 271-6262
EITZ CHAIM O 9211 BLUNDELL ROAD	RICHMOND	BC	V6Y 1K5	(604) 274-3107
BETH HAMIDRASH, CONGREGATION O 3231 HEATHER STREET	VANCOUVER	BC	V5Z 3K4	(604) 872-4222
BETH ISRAEL, CONGREGATION C 4350 OAK STREET	VANCOUVER	BC	V6H 2N4	(604) 731-4161
CHABAD HOUSE O 5750 OAK STREET	VANCOUVER	BC	N5Y 2T2	(604) 266-1313
LOUIS BRIER CHAPEL 1055 WEST 41ST AVENUE	VANCOUVER	BC	V6M 1W9	(604) 261-9376
SCHARA TZEDECK CONG. O 3476 OAK STREET	VANCOUVER	BC	V6H 2L8	(604) 736-7607
SHOLOM, TEMPLE R 4426 WEST TENTH AVENUE	VANCOUVER	BC	V6R 2H9	(604) 224-1381
CONG. EMANU-EL C 1461 BLANCHARD STREET	VICTORIA	BC	V8W 2J3	(604) 382-0615
CHABAD-LUBAVITCH O 29039 CATHERWOOD COURT	AGOURA HILLS	CA	91301	
ISRAEL, TEMPLE C 3183 MCCARTNEY ROAD	ALAMEDA	CA	94501	(415) 522-9355
BETH TORAH, TEMPLE C 225 S. ATLANTIC BLVD	ALHAMBRA	CA	91801	(818) 284-0296
BETH EMET, TEMPLE C 1770 W. CERRITOS AVENUE	ANAHEIM	CA	92804	(714) 772-4720
CHABAD OF ANAHEIM O 518 SOUTH BROOKHURST	ANAHEIM	CA	92804	(714) 520-0770
FOOTHILL JEWISH TEMPLE-CENTER C 550 S. 2ND AVENUE	ARCADIA	CA	91006	(818) 445-0810
SHAAREI TIKVAH, TEMPLE C 550 S. SECOND AVENUE	ARCADIA	CA	91006	(818) 445-0810
BETH SOLOMON OF THE DEAF, TEMPLE R 13580 OSBORNE STREET	ARLETA	CA	91331	(213) 889-2202
B'NAI JACOB, CONGREGATION C 600 17TH STREET	BAKERSFIELD	CA	93301	(805) 325-8017
BETH EL, TEMPLE R 2906 LOMA LINDA DRIVE	BAKERSFIELD	CA	93305	(805) 322-7607
BETH ISRAEL, CONGREGATION R 2009 BARCELONA AVENUE	BARSTOW	CA	92311	(619) 256-7693
BETH EL, CONGREGATION R 2301 VINE STREET	BERKELEY	CA	94708	(415) 848-3988
BETH ISRAEL, CONGREGATION O 1630 BANCROFT WAY	BERKELEY	CA	94703	(415) 843-5246
B'NAI B'RITH HILLEL 2736 BANCROFT WAY	BERKELEY	CA	94704	(415) 845-7793
CHABAD HOUSE O 2340 PIEDMONT AVENUE	BERKELEY	CA	94704	(415) 540-5824
BETH JACOB, CONGREGATION O 9030 W. OLYMPIC BLVD	BEVERLY HILLS	CA	90211	(213) 278-1911
CHABAD OF NORTH BEVERLY HILLS O 409 FOOTHILL ROAD	BEVERLY HILLS	CA	90210	(213) 859-3948
EMANUEL OF BEVERLY HILLS, TEMPLE R 8844 BURTON WAY	BEVERLY HILLS	CA	90211	(213) 274-6388
TANYA, TEMPLE 133 S. ALMOUNT DRIVE	BEVERLY HILLS	CA	90211	
YOUNG ISRAEL OF BEVERLY HILLS 8701 W. PICO BOULEVARD	BEVERLY HILLS	CA	90035	(213) 275-3020
B'NAI EMUNAH, CONGREGATION O 4001 W. MAGNOLIA BLVD	BURBANK	CA	91505	(408) 843-9248
BURBANK TEMPLE EMANU-EL C 1302 N. GLENOAKS BLVD	BURBANK	CA	91504	(408) 845-1734
PENINSULA TEMPLE SHOLOM R 1655 SEBASTIAN DRIVE	BURLINGAME	CA	94010	(415) 697-2266
BETH KODESH, CONGREGATION C 7401 SHOUP AVENUE	CANOGA PARK	CA	91307	(818) 346-0811
SOLAEL, TEMPLE R 6601 VALLEY CIRCLE BLVD	CANOGA PARK	CA	91307	(818) 348-3885
SHIR AMI, CONGREGATION R 4529 MALABAR AVENUE	CASTRO VALLEY	CA	94546	(415) 537-1787
BETH ISRAEL, CONGREGATION R 1336 HEMLOCK STREET, P.O.BOX 3266	CHIO	CA	95927	(916) 342-6146
ALL-FAITH CHAPEL, HEBREW CONGREGATION R NAVAL WEAPONS CENTER	CHINA LAKE	CA	93555	(619) 939-3506
BETH SHOLOM, TEMPLE C 208 MADRONA STREET	CHULA VISTA	CA	92010	(619) 420-6040
BETH TORAH CONG. O 380 TELEGRAPH CANYON ROAD	CHULA VISTA	CA	92011	(619) 427-9820
BETH SHOLOM, TEMPLE C 823 SOUTH SHERIDAN	CORONA	CA	91720	(714) 737-9322
ISAIAH OF NEWPORT BEACH/IRVINE, TEMPLE C P.O.BOX 10414, 2401 IRVINE AVENUE	COSTA MESA	CA	92627	(714) 540-1310
TEMPLE SHARON C 617 W. HAMILTON	COSTA MESA	CA	92627	(714) 631-3262
AKIBA, TEMPLE R 5249 S. SEPULVEDA BLVD	CULVER CITY	CA	90230	(213) 870-6575
B'NAI ISRAEL, CONGREGATION C 1575 ANNIE STREET	DALY CITY	CA	94015	(415) 756-5430
TEMPLE NE'VE SHALOM 66-777 E. PIERSON BLVD	DESERT HOT SPRINGS	CA	92240	(619) 329-5168
NER TAMID, TEMPLE R 10629 LAKEWOOD BLVD	DOWNEY	CA	90241	(213) 861-9276
EILAT, TEMPLE C 24432 MUIRLANDS BLVD	EL TORO	CA	92630	(714) 770-9606
HEBREW CONGREGATION, THE O P.O.BOX 245	ELSINORE	CA	92330	(714) 674-3046
SINAI, TEMPLE C 677 SANTA FE DRIVE	ENCINITAS	CA	92024	
SOLEL, TEMPLE R 552 SOUTH EL CAMINO REAL	ENCINITAS	CA	92024	(619) 436-0654
CHABAD OF THE VALLEY O 4915 HAYVENHURST AVENUE	ENCINO	CA	91436	(818) 784-9985
MAAREV, TEMPLE C 5180 YARMOUTH AVENUE	ENCINO	CA	91436	(818) 345-7833
VALLEY BETH SHALOM C 15739 VENTURA BLVD	ENCINO	CA	91436	(818) 788-6000
BETH EL, TEMPLE R P. O.BOX 442	EUREKA	CA	95501	(707) 442-9686
ISRAEL, TEMPLE C 14795 MERRILL	FONTANA	CA	92335	
PENINSULA SINAI CONGREGATION 499 BOOTH BAY	FOSTER CITY	CA	94404	(415) 349-2816
CONGREGATION B'NAI TZEDEK R 9669 TALBERT AVENUE	FOUNTAIN VALLEY	CA	92708	(714) 963-4611
BETH TORAH, TEMPLE R 42000 PASEO PADRE PARKWAY, P.O.BOX 6017	FREMONT	CA	94538	(415) 656-7141
BETH ISRAEL, TEMPLE R 2336 CALAVERAS STREET	FRESNO	CA	93721	(209) 264-2929
BETH JACOB, CONGREGATION C 406 WEST SHIELDS AVENUE, P.O.BOX 6017	FRESNO	CA	93705	(209) 222-0664
BETH TIKVAH OF NORTH ORANGE COUNTY, TEMPLE R 1600 NORTH ACACIA AVENUE	FULLERTON	CA	92631	(714) 871-3535
SOUTHWEST TEMPLE BETH TORAH C 14725 SOUTH GRAMERCY PLACE	GARDENA	CA	90249	(213) 327-8734
SINAI, TEMPLE R 1212 PACIFIC AVENUE	GLENDALE	CA	91202	(818) 246-8101
HUNTINGTON PARK HEBREW CONGREGATION C 2877 EAST FLORENCE AVENUE	HUNTINGTON PARK	CA	90255	(213) 585-4436
CHABAD OF IRVINE O 4872 ROYCE ROAD	IRVINE	CA	92715	(714) 786-5000
IRVINE JEWISH COMMUNITY R P.O.BOX 4420	IRVINE	CA	92716	(714) 786-0823
BETH AM, CONG. C 525 STEVENS AVENUE	LA JOLLA	CA	92037	(619) 481-8454
BETH EL, CONGREGATION C 8660 GILMAN	LA JOLLA	CA	92037	(619) 452-1734
TIFERETH ISRAEL SYNAGOGUE 9019-A PARK PLAZA DRIVE	LA MESA	CA	92041	(619) 697-0181
BETH OHR, TEMPLE R 15721 ROSECRANS BLVD	LA MIRADA	CA	90638	(714) 521-6765
ISAIAH, TEMPLE R 3800 MT. DIABLO BLVD	LAFAYETTE	CA	94549	(415) 283-8575
CHABAD OF LAGUNA O 21452 WESLEY DRIVE	LAGUNA BEACH	CA	92677	(714) 786-5000
TEMPLE JUDEA 24512 MOULTON PARKWAY	LAGUNA HILLS	CA	92653	(714) 830-0470
BETH ZION-SINAI, TEMPLE C 6440 DEL AMO BLVD	LAKEWOOD	CA	90713	(213) 429-1014
BETH KNESSET BAMIDBAR R P.O.BOX 1008, 1611 EAST AVENUE J	LANCASTER	CA	93534	(805) 942-4415
LANCASTER HEBREW CONGREGATION 1611 AVENUE J	LANCASTER	CA	93535	
KOL SHOFAR C 20 MAGNOLIA AVENUE	LARKSPUR	CA	94939	(415) 924-6081
BETH EMEK, CONGREGATION R 1886 COLLEGE AVENUE, P.O.BOX 722	LIVERMORE	CA	94550	(415) 443-1689
CHABAD OF SOUTH BAY O 24412 NARBONNE AVENUE	LOMITA	CA	90717	(213) 326-8234
BETH EL, TEMPLE C 853 LINDEN AVENUE	LONG BEACH	CA	90813	(213) 447-4430
BETH SHALOM, TEMPLE C 3635 ELM AVENUE	LONG BEACH	CA	90807	(213) 426-6413
BETH ZION - TEMPLE SINAI C 6440 DEL AMO BLVD	LONG BEACH	CA	90713	(213) 429-0715
ISRAEL, TEMPLE R 3538 E. 3RD STREET, P.O.BOX 14406	LONG BEACH	CA	90814	(213) 434-0996
LUBAVITCH, CONGREGATION O 3981 ATLANTIC AVENUE	LONG BEACH	CA	90807	(213) 434-6338
YOUNG ISRAEL OF LONG BEACH O 4134 ATLANTIC AVENUE	LONG BEACH	CA	90807	(213) 428-1200
BETH AM, CONGREGATION R 26790 ARASTRADERO ROAD	LOS ALTOS HILLS	CA	94022	(415) 493-4661
AATZEI CHAIM, CONGREGATION O 8018 W. 3RD STREET	LOS ANGELES	CA	90048	(213) 852-9104
ADAS CHASAM SOFER, CONGREGATION O 8013 MELROSE AVENUE	LOS ANGELES	CA	90046	(213) 852-9463
ADAT MOSHE, CONGREGATION 110 SOUTH VISTA	LOS ANGELES	CA	90036	
ADAT SHALOM C 3030 WESTWOOD BLVD	LOS ANGELES	CA	90034	(213) 475-4985
AGUDATH ISRAEL OF LOS ANGELES O 501 SOUTH FAIRFAX AVENUE	LOS ANGELES	CA	90036	
AHAVATH ISRAEL, CONGREGATION O 5454 VIRGINIA AVENUE	LOS ANGELES	CA	90029	(213) 464-3885
ANSHE-EMET SYNAGOGUE O 1490 S. ROBERTSON BLVD	LOS ANGELES	CA	90035	(213) 275-5640
B'NAI DAVID-JUDEA, CONGREGATION O 8906 WEST PICO BLVD	LOS ANGELES	CA	90035	(213) 272-7223
B'NAI TIKVAH, CONGREGATION C 5820 W. MANCHESTER BLVD	LOS ANGELES	CA	90045	(213) 776-5933
BAIS HACHASIDIM D-GUR, CONGREGATION O 7575 MELROSE AVENUE	LOS ANGELES	CA	90046	(213) 653-3237
BETH AM, TEMPLE C 1039 S LA CIENEGA BLVD	LOS ANGELES	CA	90035	(213) 652-7353
BETH CHAYIM CHADASHIM, TEMPLE R 6000 W. PICO BLVD	LOS ANGELES	CA	90035	(213) 931-7023

Congregation / Address	City	State	Zip	Phone
BETH HATIKVA-CITY OF HOPE MEDICAL CENTER, CONGREGATION 208 W. 8TH STREET	LOS ANGELES	CA	90014	(213) 656-4611
BETH ISRAEL OF HIGHLAND PARK-EAGLE ROCK, TEMPLE C 5711 MONTE VISTA STREET	LOS ANGELES	CA	90042	(213) 255-5416
BETH ISRAEL, CONGREGATION O 8056 BEVERLY BLVD	LOS ANGELES	CA	90048	(213) 651-4022
BETH TORAH, TEMPLE C 11827 VENICE BLVD	LOS ANGELES	CA	90066	(213) 398-4536
BETH ZION, TEMPLE C 5555 W. OLYMPIC BLVD	LOS ANGELES	CA	90036	(213) 933-9136
BEVERLY ISRAEL SYNAGOGUE C 447 N. FAIRFAX AVENUE	LOS ANGELES	CA	90036	(213) 651-2227
BNAI JACOB, CONGREGATION O 2833 FAIRMOUNT STREET	LOS ANGELES	CA	90033	(213) 261-2788
CHABAD HOUSE O 741 GAYLEY AVENUE	LOS ANGELES	CA	90024	(213) 208-7511
CHABAD-LUBAVITCH O 9017 WEST PICO BOULEVARD	LOS ANGELES	CA	90035	
CHABAD-LUBAVITCH O 7215 WARING	LOS ANGELES	CA	90046	
CHABAD-LUBAVITCH O 221 SOUTH LA BREA AVENUE	LOS ANGELES	CA	90036	
CHABAD-LUBAVITCH O 420 NORTH FAIRFAX AVENUE	LOS ANGELES	CA	90036	
CHABAD-LUBAVITCH O 1952 ROBERTSON BOULEVARD	LOS ANGELES	CA	90034	
CHABAD-LUBAVITCH O 7414 S. MONICA	LOS ANGELES	CA	90046	
CHABAD-LUBAVITCH O 1101 S. ROBERTSON BOULEVARD-206	LOS ANGELES	CA	90035	
ETZ JACOB, CONGREGATION O 7659 BEVERLY BLVD	LOS ANGELES	CA	90036	(213) 938-2619
HOLLYWOOD TEMPLE BETH EL C 1317 N. CRESCENT HEIGHTS BLVD	LOS ANGELES	CA	90046	(213) 474-1518
ISAIAH, TEMPLE R 10345 W. PICO BLVD	LOS ANGELES	CA	90064	(213) 277-2772
ISRAEL, TEMPLE R 7300 HOLLYWOOD BLVD	LOS ANGELES	CA	90046	(213) 876-8330
JEREMIAH, TEMPLE R 8333 AIRPORT BLVD	LOS ANGELES	CA	90045	(213) 776-4074
KEHILATH YITZCHOK, CONGREGATION O 7711 BEVERLY BLVD	LOS ANGELES	CA	90036	(213) 936-4232
KNESSET ISRAEL OF HOLLYWOOD 1260 N. VERMONT AVENUE	LOS ANGELES	CA	90029	(213) 665-5171
LEO BAECK, TEMPLE R 1300 N. SEPULVEDA BLVD	LOS ANGELES	CA	90049	(213) 476-2861
MAGEN DAVID, CONGREGATION O 9717 WEST PICO BLVD	LOS ANGELES	CA	90035	(213) 879-3681
MISHKAN YICHESKE, CONGREGATION O 8344 MELROSE AVENUE	LOS ANGELES	CA	90069	(213) 938-9292
MOGEN ABRAHAM, CONGREGATION O 354 N. ORANGE DRIVE	LOS ANGELES	CA	90036	(213) 937-9690
NER ISRAEL, CONGREGATION O 5822 W. 3RD STREET	LOS ANGELES	CA	90036	(213) 933-3405
NETZACH ISRAEL, CONGREGATION O 4117 BEVERLY BLVD	LOS ANGELES	CA	90004	(213) 663-2383
OHEL DAVID, CONGREGATION O 7967 BEVERLY BLVD	LOS ANGELES	CA	90048	(213) 655-0973
OHEV SHALOM CONGREGATION O 525 SOUTH FAIRFAX AVENUE	LOS ANGELES	CA	90036	(213) 653-7190
SEPHARDIC CONGREGATION KEHAL YOSEPH O 10505 SANTA MONICA BLVD	LOS ANGELES	CA	90056	(213) 474-0559
SEPHARDIC MAGEN DAVID, CONGREGATION O 7454 MELROSE AVENUE	LOS ANGELES	CA	90046	(213) 655-3441
SEPHARDIC TEMPLE TIFERETH ISRAEL O 10500 WILSHIRE BLVD	LOS ANGELES	CA	90024	(213) 475-7311
SHAAREI TEFILA, CONGREGATION O 7269 BEVERLY BLVD	LOS ANGELES	CA	90028	(213) 938-7147
SHAAREY ELIMELECH, CONGREGATION 6111 W. OLYMPIC BLVD	LOS ANGELES	CA	90048	
SHYERIT SHAARE TORAH, CONGREGATION O 220 W. 8TH STREET	LOS ANGELES	CA	90057	(213) 389-3181
SINAI, TEMPLE C 10400 WILSHIRE BLVD	LOS ANGELES	CA	90024	(213) 474-1518
STEPHEN S. WISE TEMPLE R 15500 STEPHEN WISE DRIVE	LOS ANGELES	CA	90077	(213) 476-8561
TALMUD TORAH, CONGREGATION O 247 N. BREED STREET	LOS ANGELES	CA	90033	(213) 262-3922
TIFERETH ZVI, CONGREGATION O 7561 BEVERLY BLVD	LOS ANGELES	CA	90048	(213) 931-3252
UNIVERSITY SYNAGOGUE R 11960 SUNSET BLVD	LOS ANGELES	CA	90049	(213) 472-1255
VISTA DEL MAR TEMPLE 3200 MOTOR AVENUE	LOS ANGELES	CA	90034	(213) 836-1223
WESTWOOD KEHILA O C/O RABBI DOV OSINA, 10655 WILSHIRE BOULEVARD, #402	LOS ANGELES	CA	90024	
WILSHIRE BOULEVARD TEMPLE R 3663 WILSHIRE BLVD	LOS ANGELES	CA	90010	(213) 388-2401
YOUNG ISRAEL OF BEVERLY HILLS 8701 WEST PICO BLVD.	LOS ANGELES	CA	90035	(213) 275-3020
YOUNG ISRAEL OF CENTURY CITY 9315 W. PICO BLVD.	LOS ANGELES	CA	90035	(213) 273-6954
YOUNG ISRAEL OF HANCOCK PARK 225 SOUTH LA BREA AVENUE	LOS ANGELES	CA	90036	(213) 931-4030
YOUNG ISRAEL OF LOS ANGELES 660 NORTH SPAULDING AVENUE	LOS ANGELES	CA	90036	(213) 655-0300
SHIR HADASH, CONGREGATION R P.O.BOX 1635	LOS GATOS	CA	95030	(408) 227-8880
MALIBU JEWISH CENTER & SYNAGOGUE RE POB 4063	MALIBU	CA	90265	(213) 457-2979
CHABAD-LUBAVITCH O 13221-D ADMIRAL AVENUE	MARINA DEL RAY	CA	90292	
JEWISH COMMUNITY CENTER OF MERCED CO., R P.O.BOX 2531	MERCED	CA	95344	(209) 722-0530
SHABBOS, SHUL 220 REDWOOD HIGHWAY	MILL VALLEY	CA	94941	
EILAT, TEMPLE C P.O.BOX 2004	MISSION VIEJO	CA	92675	(714) 830-1001
TEMPLE BETH EL R 28261 MARGUERITE PARKWAY	MISSION VIEJO	CA	92692	(714) 495-2332
TEMPLE OHAVEI SHALOM 27276 VIA AVILA	MISSION VIEJO	CA	92675	(714) 855-4823
BETH SHOLOM OF MODESTO, CONGREGATION 1705 SHERWOOD AVENUE, P.O.BOX 4082	MODESTO	CA	94941	(209) 522-5613
B'NAI EMET, TEMPLE C 482 NORTH GARFIELD AVENUE	MONTEBELLO	CA	90640	(213) 721-7064
BETH ISRAEL, CONGREGATION R 151 PARK AVENUE	MONTEREY	CA	93940	(408) 675-2759
BETH SHOLOM, CONGREGATION C 1455 ELM STREET	NAPA	CA	94558	
BETH SHALOM OF THE SANTA CLARITA VALLEY, CONGREGATION P.O.BOX 39	NEWHALL	CA	91321	(805) 259-4975
BAT YAHM, TEMPLE R 1011 CAMELBACK STREET	NEWPORT BEACH	CA	92660	(714) 644-1999
SHIR HAMA'ALOT R 2100 A MAR VISTA	NEWPORT BEACH	CA	92660	(714) 644-7203
TEMPLE ISAIAH OF NEWPORT BEACH C 2401 IRVINE AVENUE	NEWPORT BEACH	CA	92660	(714) 548-6900
ADAT ARI EL C 5540 LAUREL CANYON BLVD	NORTH HOLLYWOOD	CA	91607	(818) 766-9426
ADATH YESHURUN VALLEY SEPHARDIC CONGREGATION 6348 WHITSETT AVENUE	NORTH HOLLYWOOD	CA	91606	(818) 766-4682
BETH HILLEL, TEMPLE R 12326 RIVERSIDE ROAD, SAN FERNANDO VALLEY	NORTH HOLLYWOOD	CA	91607	(818) 763-9148
EM HABANIM, CONGREGATION 12052 CALIFA STREET	NORTH HOLLYWOOD	CA	91607	(818) 762-7779
MISHKAN ISRAEL, CONGREGATION O 6450 BELLINGHAM	NORTH HOLLYWOOD	CA	91606	(818) 769-8043
SHAAREY ZEDEK, CONGREGATION O 12800 CHANDLER BLVD	NORTH HOLLYWOOD	CA	91607	(818) 984-3878
VALLEY JEWISH COMMUNITY CENTER & TEMPLE C 5540 LAUREL CANYON BLVD	NORTH HOLLYWOOD	CA	91607	(818) 877-0666
AHAVAT SHALOM, TEMPLE R 18200 RINALDI PLACE	NORTHRIDGE	CA	91326	(818) 360-2258
RAMAT ZION, TEMPLE C 17655 DEVONSHIRE STREET	NORTHRIDGE	CA	91325	(818) 360-1881
YOUNG ISRAEL NORTHRIDGE 17332 DEARBORNE	NORTHRIDGE	CA	91325	
BETH ABRAHAM, TEMPLE C 327 MACARTHUR BLVD	OAKLAND	CA	94610	(415) 832-0936
BETH JACOB CONGREGATION O 3778 PARK BLVD	OAKLAND	CA	94610	(415) 482-1147
SINAI, TEMPLE R 2808 SUMMIT STREET	OAKLAND	CA	94609	(415) 451-3263
SHOLOM OF ONTARIO, TEMPLE C 936 W. 6TH STREET	ONTARIO	CA	91762	(714) 983-9661
JEWISH CONGREGATION OF PACIFIC PALISADES RE 16019 SUNSET BLVD	PACIFIC PALISADES	CA	90272	(213) 459-2328
KEHILLATH ISRAEL 16019 SUNSET BLVD	PACIFIC PALISADES	CA	90272	(213) 454-9130
BETH AMI, CONGREGATION 2015 TACHEVAH	PALM SPRINGS	CA	92262	
CHABAD OF PALM SPRINGS O 425 AVIENDA ORTEGA	PALM SPRINGS	CA	92262	(619) 265-7700
ISAIAH, TEMPLE R PALM SPRINGS JEWISH COMMUNITY CENTER, 332 WEST ALEJO RD	PALM SPRINGS	CA	92662	(619) 325-2281
ORTHODOX MINYAN OF PALM SPRINGS O 332 WEST ALEJO ROAD	PALM SPRINGS	CA	92262	
CHABAD OF THE PENINSULA O 3070 LOUIS ROAD	PALO ALTO	CA	94303	(415) 424-9800
KOL EMETH, CONGREGATION C 4175 MANUELA AVENUE	PALO ALTO	CA	94306	(415) 948-7498
PALO ALTO ORTHODOX MINYAN O C/O DR. SUSSMAN, 739 JOSINA AVENUE	PALO ALTO	CA	94306	(415) 326-5001
NER TAMID OF SOUTH BAY, CONGREGATION 5721 CRESTRIDGE ROAD	PALOS VERDES	CA	90274	(213) 377-4482
PASADENA JEWISH TEMPLE C 1434 NORTH ALTADENA DRIVE	PASADENA	CA	91107	(818) 798-1161
B'NAI ISRAEL 740 WESTERN AVENUE	PETALUMA	CA	94952	(707) 762-0340
BETH ISRAEL, TEMPLE R 3033 N. TOWNE AVENUE	POMONA	CA	91767	(714) 626-1277
ADAT SHALOM, TEMPLE R 15847 POMERDO ROAD	POWAY	CA	92046	(619) 489-1918
NER TAMID OF SOUTH BAY, CONGREGATION C 5721 CRESTRIDGE ROAD	RANCHO PALOS VERDES	CA	90274	(213) 377-6986
BETH ISRAEL, CONGREGATION R P.O.BOX 201	REDDING	CA	96001	(916) 243-4159
MENORA, TEMPLE R 1101 CAMINO REAL	REDONDO BEACH	CA	90277	(213) 316-8444
BETH JACOB, TEMPLE C 1550 ALAMEDA DE LAS PULGAS	REDWOOD CITY	CA	94061	(415) 366-8481
BETH AMI, TEMPLE C 18449 KITTRIDGE STREET	RESEDA	CA	91335	(818) 343-4624
BETH HILLEL, TEMPLE R 801 PARK CENTRAL	RICHMOND	CA	94803	(415) 223-2560
BETH EL, TEMPLE R 2675 CENTRAL AVENUE	RIVERSIDE	CA	92506	(714) 684-4511
SONOMA COUNTY SYNAGOGUE CENTER RE POB 1066	ROHNERT PARK	CA	94928	(707) 763-7508
B'NAI ISRAEL, TEMPLE R 3600 RIVERSIDE BLVD	SACRAMENTO	CA	95818	(916) 446-4861
BETH SHALOM, CONGREGATION 525 FULTON AVENUE	SACRAMENTO	CA	95825	
KENESSET ISRAEL TORAH CENTER O 1024 MORSE AVENUE	SACRAMENTO	CA	95864	(916) 481-1159
MOSAIC LAW CONGREGATION C 1300 SIERRA BLVD	SACRAMENTO	CA	95825	(916) 488-1122
BETH EL, TEMPLE R 1212 RIKER STREET	SALINAS	CA	93901	(408) 424-9151
EMANU-EL, CONGREGATION R 3512 NORTH 'E' STREET	SAN BERNARDINO	CA	92405	(714) 886-4818
BETH ISRAEL, TEMPLE R 2512 THIRD AVENUE AT LAUREL STREET	SAN DIEGO	CA	92103	(619) 239-0149
BETH JACOB, CONGREGATION O 4855 COLLEGE AVENUE	SAN DIEGO	CA	92115	(619) 287-9890
BETH TEFILAH, CONGREGATION 4967 69TH STREET	SAN DIEGO	CA	92115	(619) 463-0391
CHABAD HOUSE O 6115 MONTEZUMA ROAD	SAN DIEGO	CA	92115	(619) 265-7700
DOR HADASH RE 2504 QUIDDE AVENUE	SAN DIEGO	CA	92127	(619) 450-9588
EMANU-EL, TEMPLE R 6299 CAPRI DRIVE	SAN DIEGO	CA	92120	(619) 286-2555
TIFERETH ISRAEL SYNAGOGUE 6660 COWLES MOUNTAIN BLVD	SAN DIEGO	CA	92119	(619) 697-6001
ADATH ISRAEL 1851 NORIEGA STREET	SAN FRANCISCO	CA	94122	(415) 564-5665
AHAVAT SHALOM P.O. BOX 421464	SAN FRANCISCO	CA	94142	(415) 621-1020
ANSHEY SFARD, CONGREGATION O 1500 CLEMENT STREET	SAN FRANCISCO	CA	94118	(415) 752-4979
B'NAI DAVID, CONGREGATION 3535 19TH STREET	SAN FRANCISCO	CA	94110	(415) 826-2595
B'NAI EMUNAH, CONGREGATION C 3595 TARAVEL STREET	SAN FRANCISCO	CA	94116	(415) 664-7373
B'NAI ISRAEL, CONGREGATION 590 WASHINGTON	SAN FRANCISCO	CA	94111	(415) 756-5430
BETH ISRAEL, CONGREGATION C 625 BROTHERHOOD WAY	SAN FRANCISCO	CA	94132	(415) 586-8833
BETH SHOLOM C 14TH AVENUE & CLEMENT STREET	SAN FRANCISCO	CA	94118	(415) 221-8736
CHABAD - SAN FRANCISCO 3036 OCTAVIA	SAN FRANCISCO	CA	94123	
CHEVRA THILIM, CONGREGATION O 751 25TH AVENUE	SAN FRANCISCO	CA	94121	(415) 752-2866
EMANU-EL, CONGREGATION R P.O.BOX 18247, ARQUELLO BLVD. & LAKE STREET	SAN FRANCISCO	CA	94118	(415) 751-2535
JEWISH HOME FOR THE AGED 302 SILVER AVENUE	SAN FRANCISCO	CA	94112	(415) 334-2500
KEHILATH JACOB HOUSE OF LOVE & PRAYER, CONGREGATION O 1456 9TH AVENUE	SAN FRANCISCO	CA	94122	(415) 731-9507
KENESETH ISRAEL, CONGREGATION O 1255 POST	SAN FRANCISCO	CA	94109	(415) 771-3420
MAGAIN DAVID SEPHARDIM, CONGREGATION O 351 4TH AVENUE	SAN FRANCISCO	CA	94118	(415) 752-9095
NER TAMID, CONGREGATION C 1250 QUINTARA STREET	SAN FRANCISCO	CA	94116	(415) 661-3383
SAN FRANCISCO BAY AREA RECONSTRUCTIONIST HAVURAH C/O SHANA WINOKUR	SAN FRANCISCO	CA		(415) 655-7776
SHAAR ZAHAV, CONGREGATION R 201 CASSELI AVENUE	SAN FRANCISCO	CA	94101	
SHERITH ISRAEL, CONGREGATION R 2266 CALIFORNIA STREET	SAN FRANCISCO	CA	94115	(415) 346-1720
TORAT EMETH, CONG. O 768 27TH AVENUE	SAN FRANCISCO	CA	94121	(415) 387-1447
UNITED TALMUD TORAH CONGREGATION O 1822 26TH AVENUE	SAN FRANCISCO	CA	94107	(415) 564-5672
YOUNG ISRAEL - O 1806A NORIEGA STREET	SAN FRANCISCO	CA	94122	(415) 387-1744
AM ECHAD, CONGREGATION O 1537 A MERIDIAN AVENUE	SAN JOSE	CA	95125	(408) 267-2591
BETH SHOLOM, TEMPLE R 325 CHEYNOWETH AVENUE	SAN JOSE	CA	95136	(408) 224-1009
EMANU-EL, TEMPLE R 1010 UNIVERSITY AVENUE	SAN JOSE	CA	95126	(408) 292-0939
SHIR HADASH, CONGREGATION R 13500 QUITO ROAD	SAN JOSE	CA	95130	(408) 379-7522
SINAI, CONGREGATION T 1532 WILLOWBRAE AVENUE	SAN JOSE	CA	95125	(408) 264-8542
YOUNG ISRAEL SAN JOSE 1975 HAMILTON AVE., SUITE #5	SAN JOSE	CA	95125	(408) 265-9255
BETH SHOLOM, TEMPLE C 642 DOLORES AVENUE	SAN LEANDRO	CA	94577	(415) 357-8505
BETH DAVID, CONGREGATION R 2932 AUGUSTA STREET	SAN LUIS OBISPO	CA	93401	(805) 544-0760
PENINSULA TEMPLE BETH EL R 1700 ALAMEDA DE LAS PULGAS	SAN MATEO	CA	94403	(415) 341-7701
BETH EL & CENTER, TEMPLE R 1435 W. 7TH STREET	SAN PEDRO	CA	90732	(213) 833-2467
CHABAD OF MARIN O 7 MT. LASSEN DRIVE, P.O. BOX 13871	SAN RAFAEL	CA	94913	(415) 492-1666
KOL SHOFAR, CONGREGATION C P.O.BOX 1235	SAN RAFAEL	CA	94902	(415) 456-1515
RODEF SHOLOM 170 NORTH SAN PEDRO ROAD	SAN RAFAEL	CA	94903	(415) 479-3441
BETH SHOLOM, TEMPLE - ORANGE COUNTY R 13031 TUSTIN AVENUE	SANTA ANA	CA	92705	(714) 532-6724
B'NAI B'RITH, CONGREGATION R 900 SAN ANTONIO CREEK ROAD	SANTA BARBARA	CA	93111	(805) 964-7869
CHABAD OF SANTA BARBARA O 5020 SAN SIMEON DRIVE, #14	SANTA BARBARA	CA	93111	(805) 683-1544
YOUNG ISRAEL OF SANTA BARBARA O 1826 C CLIFF DRIVE	SANTA BARBARA	CA	93109	(805) 965-8990
YESHIVAT & MIDRASHA KEREM 250 HOWARD DRIVE	SANTA CLARA	CA	95051	(408) 247-1722
BETH EL, TEMPLE R 920 BAY STREET	SANTA CRUZ	CA	95060	(408) 423-3012
BETH EL, TEMPLE R 1501 E. ALVIN	SANTA MARIA	CA	93454	(805) 925-9028
BETH SHOLOM, TEMPLE R 1827 CALIFORNIA AVENUE	SANTA MONICA	CA	90403	(213) 453-3361
CHABAD OF BAY AREA O 1428 17TH STREET	SANTA MONICA	CA	90401	(213) 829-5620
PACIFIC JEWISH CENTER O 3115 6TH STREET	SANTA MONICA	CA	90405	(213) 392-8512

Name / Address	City	State	Zip	Phone
YOUNG ISRAEL OF SANTA MONICA 216 MARINE STREET	SANTA MONICA	CA	90405	(213) 452-0488
BETH AMI, CONGREGATION C 4676 MAYETTE AVENUE	SANTA ROSA	CA	95405	(707) 545-4334
SHOMREI TORAH, CONGREGATION R 1717 YULUPA AVENUE	SANTA ROSA	CA	95405	(707) 539-6127
BETH DAVID, CONGREGATION C 19700 PROSPECT AVENUE	SARATOGA	CA	95070	(408) 257-3333
SHOLOM OF LEISURE WORLD, CONGREGATION C 13044 DEL MONTE DRIVE #34A	SEAL BEACH	CA	90740	(213) 596-3188
BETH TORAH, TEMPLE 8936 LANGDON AVENUE	SEPULVEDA	CA	91343	
BETH TORAH, TEMPLE R 8756 WOODLEY AVENUE	SEPULVEDA	CA	91343	(213) 893-3756
B'NAI HAYIM, TEMPLE C 4302 VAN NUYS BLVD	SHERMAN OAKS	CA	91403	(818) 788-4664
BETH DALIAH, TEMPLE C 13754 VENTURA BLVD	SHERMAN OAKS	CA	91403	(818) 784-3914
B'NAI EMET, CONGREGATION R P.O.BOX 878	SIMI VALLEY	CA	93065	(805) 581-3723
NER TAMID, TEMPLE C 3050 LOS ANGELES AVENUE	SIMI VALLEY	CA	93065	(805) 522-4747
ADAS YESHURUN, CONGREGATION O 427 E. FREMONT STREET	STOCKTON	CA	95202	
ISRAEL, TEMPLE R 5105 NORTH EL DORADO STREET	STOCKTON	CA	95207	(209) 477-9306
BETH MEIRER, CONGREGATION C 11725 MOORPARK STREET	STUDIO CITY	CA	91604	(818) 769-0515
BETH OHR, CONGREGATION RE 12355 MOORPARK STREET	STUDIO CITY	CA	91604	(818) 766-3826
VALLEY BETH ISRAEL C 13060 ROSCOE BLVD	SUN VALLEY	CA	91352	(818) 782-2281
BETH AMI, TEMPLE C 19258 BERNETTA PLACE	TARZANA	CA	91356	(818) 343-4624
CHABAD OF TARZANA O 18211 BURBANK BOULEVARD	TARZANA	CA	92356	(213) 881-2352
JUDEA, TEMPLE R 5429 LINDLEY AVENUE	TARZANA	CA	91356	(213) 987-2616
BETH DAVID OF THE SAN GABRIEL VALLEY, TEMPLE R 9677 E. LONGDEN AVENUE	TEMPLE CITY	CA	91780	(818) 287-9994
ADAT ELOHIM, TEMPLE R 2420 E. HILLCREST DRIVE	THOUSAND OAKS	CA	91360	(805) 497-7101
ETZ CHAIM, TEMPLE C 1080 E. JANSS ROAD	THOUSAND OAKS	CA	91360	(805) 497-6891
VERDUGO HILLS HEBREW CENTER C 10275 TUJUNGA CANYON BLVD	TUJUNGA	CA	91040	(818) 352-3171
B'NAI ISRAEL, CONGREGATION C 13112 NEWPORT AVENUE, SUITE H	TUSTIN	CA	92680	(714) 730-9693
BNAI ISRAEL, CONGREGATION C 1256 NEBRASKA STREET	VALLEJO	CA	94590	(707) 642-6526
BETH DAVID, TEMPLE C 7452 HAZELTINE AVENUE	VAN NUYS	CA	91405	(818) 780-4141
CHABAD OF NORTH HOLLYWOOD O 13079 CHANDLER BOULEVARD	VAN NUYS	CA	91401	(818) 989-9539
NER TAMID, TEMPLE C 15339 SATICOY STREET	VAN NUYS	CA	91406	(818) 782-9010
BAY CITIES SYNAGOGUE O 505 OCEAN FRONT WALK	VENICE	CA	90291	(213) 390-8868
MISHKON TEPHILO, TEMPLE C 206 MAIN STREET	VENICE	CA	90291	(213) 828-2445
PACIFIC JEWISH CENTER/BAY CITY SYNAGOGUE O 720 ROSE AVENUE	VENICE	CA	90291	(213) 452-2790
BETH TORAH, TEMPLE R VENTURA CITY JEWISH COUNCIL, 7620 FOOTHILL ROAD	VENTURA	CA	93004	(805) 647-4181
B'NAI DAVID, CONGREGATION R P.O.BOX 3822	VISALIA	CA	93278	(209) 732-7196
JUDEA, TEMPLE C 1930 SUNSET DRIVE	VISTA	CA	92083	(619) 724-8318
B'NAI SHOLOM, CONGREGATION C 74 ECKLEY LANE	WALNUT CREEK	CA	94598	(415) 934-9446
B'NAI TIKVAH, CONGREGATION 25 HILLCROFT WAY	WALNUT CREEK	CA	94596	(415) 933-5397
BETH AMI, TEMPLE C 3508 E. TEMPLE WAY	WEST COVINA	CA	91791	(818) 331-0515
SHALOM, TEMPLE R 1912 W. MERCED AVENUE	WEST COVINA	CA	91790	(818) 337-6500
CHABAD OF CONEJO O 741 LAKEFIELD ROAD, #E	WESTLAKE VILLAGE	CA	91361	(805) 497-9635
BETH DAVID OF ORANGE COUNTY, TEMPLE R 6100 HEFLEY STREET	WESTMINSTER	CA	92683	(714) 892-6623
CHABAD OF WEST ORANGE COUNTY O 14401 WILLOW LANE	WESTMINSTER	CA	92683	(213) 596-1681
BETH SHALOM OF WHITTIER C 14564 E. HAWES STREET	WHITTIER	CA	90604	(213) 941-8744
WHITTIER RECONSTRUCTIONIST HAVURAH C/O LEONARD HALE	WHITTIER	CA		(714) 694-1123
ALIYAH, TEMPLE C 6025 VALLEY CIRCLE BLVD	WOODLAND HILLS	CA	91367	(818) 346-3545
EMET, TEMPLE R 20400 VENTURA BLVD	WOODLAND HILLS	CA	91364	(818) 348-0670
BONAI SHALOM 1520 EUCLID AVENUE	BOULDER	CO	80302	(303) 494-2112
HAR HASHEM, CONGREGATION 3950 BASELINE ROAD	BOULDER	CO	80303	(303) 499-7077
CHABAD-LUBAVITCH O 3465 NONCHALANT CIRCLE EAST	COLORADO SPRINGS	CO	80917	
SHALOM, TEMPLE C & R 1523 E. MONUMENT	COLORADO SPRINGS	CO	80909	(303) 634-5311
BETH HAMEDROSH HAGODOL, CONGREGATION O 560 S. MONACO PARKWAY	DENVER	CO	80222	(303) 388-4203
CHABAD HOUSE O 85 FOREST STREET	DENVER	CO	80220	(303) 329-0211
CHABAD-LUBAVITCH O 362 SOUTH JASMINE	DENVER	CO	80224	
BETH JOSEPH CONGREGATION 825 IVANHOE STREET	DENVER	CO	80220	(303) 355-7321
COLORADO JEWISH RECONSTRUCTIONIST FEDERATION 6565 EAST EVANS, SUITE 104	DENVER	CO	80222	(303) 753-1610
EAST DENVER ORTHODOX CONGREGATION O 198 SOUTH HOLLY	DENVER	CO	80222	(303) 322-7943
EMANUEL, CONGREGATION R 51 GRAPE STREET	DENVER	CO	80220	(303) 388-4013
HEBREW EDUCATIONAL ALLIANCE, CONGREGATION O 1555 STUART STREET	DENVER	CO	80204	(303) 629-0410
MICAH, TEMPLE R 2600 LEYDEN STREET	DENVER	CO	80207	(303) 388-4239
MICAH, TEMPLE 195 S. MONACO PARKWAY	DENVER	CO	80222	
OSTROVER SYNAGOGUE OF BETH ISRAEL O 1620 MEADE STREET	DENVER	CO	80204	(303) 825-2190
RODEPH SHALOM, CONGREGATION C 450 S. KEARNEY STREET	DENVER	CO	80224	(303) 399-0035
SINAI, TEMPLE R 8050 E. DARTMOUTH AVENUE	DENVER	CO	80231	(303) 750-3006
TALMUDIC RESEARCH INSTITUTE O 295 SOUTH LOCUST STREET	DENVER	CO	80224	(303) 623-8467
ZERA ABRAHAM, CONGREGATION O 1560 WINONA COURT	DENVER	CO	80204	(303) 825-7517
ZERA ISRAEL, CONGREGATION O 3934 W. 14TH AVENUE	DENVER	CO	80204	(303) 571-0166
HAR SHALOM P.O. BOX 12	FT. COLLINS	CO	80522	(303) 223-5191
JEWISH COMMUNITY CENTER OF GRAND JUNCTION P.O. BOX 1311	GRAND JUNCTION	CO	81502	(303) 242-0943
BETH SHALOM, CONGREGATION C 2280 E. NOBLE PLACE	LITTLETON	CO	80120	(303) 794-6643
EMANUEL, TEMPLE R 1325 N. GRAND AVENUE	PUEBLO	CO	81003	(303) 544-6448
UNITED HEBREW CENTER C 106 W. 15TH STREET	PUEBLO	CO	81003	(303) 544-9897
AARON, CONGREGATION R THIRD & MAPLE	TRINIDAD	CO	81082	(303) 846-3193
UNITED BRETHREN SYNAGOGUE	AMSTON	CT	06231	
BETH HILLEL SYNAGOGUE C 160 WINTONBURY AVENUE	BLOOMFIELD	CT	04002	(203) 242-5561
TEFERES ISRAEL, CONGREGATION O 27 BROWN STREET	BLOOMFIELD	CT	06002	(203) 243-1719
TIKVOH CHADOSHOH, CONGREGATION C 180 STILL ROAD	BLOOMFIELD	CT	06002	(203) 236-2010
BETH TIKVAH, TEMPLE R 64 MEADOW WOOD ROAD	BRAMFORD	CT	06405	
ADATH ISRAEL, CONGREGATION O 540 E. WASHINGTON AVENUE	BRIDGEPORT	CT	06608	(203) 336-3929
ADATH YESHURAN, CONGREGATION O 246 LENOX AVENUE	BRIDGEPORT	CT	06605	(203) 336-3929
AGUDAS ACHIM, CONGREGATION O 85 ARLINGTON STREET	BRIDGEPORT	CT	06606	(203) 335-6353
B'NAI ISRAEL, CONGREGATION R 2710 PARK AVENUE	BRIDGEPORT	CT	06604	(203) 336-1858
BIKUR CHOLIM, CONGREGATION O P.O.BOX 3462	BRIDGEPORT	CT	06605	(203) 336-2272
RODEPH SHOLOM, CONGREGATION C PARK & CAPITOL AVENUES	BRIDGEPORT	CT	06604	(203) 334-0159
SHAARE TORAH, CONGREGATION O 3050 MAIN STREET	BRIDGEPORT	CT	06606	(203) 372-6513
BETH ISRAEL SYNAGOGUE C 339 W STREET	BRISTOL	CT	06010	(203) 583-6293
BETH DAVID, TEMPLE R 3 MAIN STREET, P.O.BOX 274	CHESHIRE	CT	06410	(203) 272-0037
AHAVATH ACHIM SYNAGOGUE C LEBANON AVENUE	COLCHESTER	CT	06415	(203) 537-2809
AGUDATH ACHIM, CONGREGATION O	COLUMBIA	CT	06237	
CLAPBOARD RIDGE SYNAGOGUE-CONGREGATION B'NAI ISRAEL C 193 CLAPBOARD RIDGE ROAD	DANBURY	CT	06810	(203) 792-6161
UNITED JEWISH CENTER R 141 DEER HILL AVENUE	DANBURY	CT	06810	(203) 748-3355
BETH ISRAEL, TEMPLE C KILLINGLY DRIVE	DANIELSON	CT	06239	(203) 774-9874
BETH ISRAEL SYNAGOGUE CENTER C 300 ELIZABETH STREET	DERBY	CT	06418	(203) 734-3361
SONS OF ISRAEL, CONGREGATION C 6 ANSON STREET	DERBY	CT	06418	(203) 734-9821
RODFE ZEDEK, CONGREGATION C ORCHARD ROAD	EAST HADDAM	CT	06423	(203) 873-8061
BETH TEFILAH, TEMPLE C 465 OAK STREET	EAST HARTFORD	CT	06118	(203) 569-0670
KENESSETH ISRAEL, CONGREGATION O PINNEY STREET	ELLINGTON	CT	06029	(203) 875-3623
AHAVATH ACHIM, CONGREGATION O 1571 STRATFIELD ROAD	FAIRFIELD	CT	06432	(203) 372-6529
BETH EL, CONGREGATION C 1200 FAIRFIELD WOODS ROAD	FAIRFIELD	CT	06430	(203) 374-5544
SHOLOM, TEMPLE C 300 E. PUTNAM AVENUE	GREENWICH	CT	06830	(203) 869-7191
EMANU-EL, TEMPLE R 16 FORT STREET	GROTON	CT	06340	(203) 442-4955
BETH SHOLOM, TEMPLE C 1809 WHITNEY AVENUE	HAMDEN	CT	06517	(203) 288-7748
MISHKAN ISRAEL, CONGREGATION R 785 RIDGE ROAD	HAMDEN	CT	06517	(203) 288-3877
ADOS ISRAEL, CONGREGATION O 215 PEARL	HARTFORD	CT	06103	(203) 525-3590
AGUDAS ACHIM, CONGREGATION O 1244 N. MAIN STREET	HARTFORD	CT	06117	(203) 233-6241
ANSHE SHOLOM, TEMPLE 130 W. RIDGE DRIVE	HARTFORD	CT	06117	
BETH EL, TEMPLE C 2626 ALBANY AVENUE	HARTFORD	CT	06117	
BETH ISRAEL, CONGREGATION R 701 FARMINGTON AVENUE	HARTFORD	CT	06119	(203) 233-8215
HEBREW HOME CONGREGATION O 615 TOWER AVENUE	HARTFORD	CT	06112	(203) 247-3418
UNITED SYNAGOGUES OF GREATER HARTFORD O 840 N. MAIN STREET	HARTFORD	CT	06117	(203) 236-3338
JEWISH CONGREGATION	LEBANON	CT	06249	
BETH TIKVAH, TEMPLE R 196 DURHAM ROAD, P.O.BOX 523	MADISON	CT	06443	(203) 245-7028
BETH SHOLOM, TEMPLE C 400 E. MIDDLE TURNPIKE	MANCHESTER	CT	06040	(203) 643-9563
B'NAI ABRAHAM, TEMPLE C 127 E. MAIN STREET	MERIDEN	CT	06450	(203) 235-2581
ADATH ISRAEL, CONGREGATION C P.O.BOX 337	MIDDLETOWN	CT	06457	(203) 346-8780
B'NAI SHALOM, TEMPLE C 88 NOBLE AVENUE	MILFORD	CT	06460	(203) 874-5910
RODFE ZEDEK, CONGREGATION C P.O.BOX 38A, SILLIMANVILLE ROAD	MOODUS	CT	06469	(203) 873-8061
B'NAI ISRAEL, TEMPLE C 265 W. MAIN STREET	NEW BRITAIN	CT	06052	(203) 224-0479
TIPHERETH ISRAEL, CONGREGATION O P.O.BOX 490, 76 WINTER STREET	NEW BRITAIN	CT	06052	(203) 229-1485
B'NAI JACOB, CONGREGATION C RIMMON ROAD	NEW HAVEN	CT	06525	(203) 389-2111
BETH EL, CONGREGATION - KESER ISRAEL C 85 HARRISON STREET	NEW HAVEN	CT	06515	(203) 389-2108
BETH HAMEDROSH HAGODOL B'NAI ISRAEL-WESTVILLE SYNAGOGUE O 74 W. PROSPECT STREET	NEW HAVEN	CT	06515	(203) 389-9513
BETH ISRAEL, CONGREGATION O 232 ORCHARD STREET	NEW HAVEN	CT	06511	(203) 776-1468
BIKUR CHOLIM SHEVET ACHIM, CONGREGATION O 279 WINTHROP AVENUE	NEW HAVEN	CT	06510	(203) 776-4997
LUBAVITCH YOUTH ORGANIZATION OF CONNECTICUT O 300 NORTON STREET	NEW HAVEN	CT	06511	(203) 789-9879
YOUNG ISRAEL OF NEW HAVEN 292 NORTON STREET	NEW HAVEN	CT	06511	(203) 776-4212
AHAVATH CHESED, CONGREGATION 590 MONTAUK AVENUE	NEW LONDON	CT	06320	(203) 442-3234
BETH EL C 660 OCEAN AVENUE	NEW LONDON	CT	06320	(203) 442-0418
OHAVE SHALOM, CONGREGATION 109 BLINMAN STREET	NEW LONDON	CT	06230	
SHOLOM, TEMPLE R P.O.BOX 509	NEW MILFORD	CT	06776	(203) 354-0273
B'NAI SHOLOM R 26 CHURCH STREET	NEWINGTON	CT	06111	(203) 667-0826
SINAI, TEMPLE R 41 W. HARTFORD ROAD	NEWINGTON	CT	06111	(203) 561-1055
ADATH ISRAEL, CONGREGATION C HUNTINGTON ROAD	NEWTOWN	CT	06470	(203) 426-6309
BETH EL, CONGREGATION C 109 E AVENUE	NORWALK	CT	06851	(203) 838-2710
BETH ISRAEL SYNAGOGUE O 40 KING STREET	NORWALK	CT	06851	(203) 866-0534
SHALOM, TEMPLE R 259 RICHARDS AVENUE	NORWALK	CT	06850	(203) 866-0148
BETH JACOB SYNAGOGUE C 400 NEW LONDON TURNPIKE	NORWICH	CT	06360	(203) 886-2459
BETH JACOB, CONGREGATION C 63 CHURCH STREET	NORWICH	CT	06360	(203) 887-8331
BROTHERS OF JOSEPH, CONGREGATION O 2 BROAD STREET	NORWICH	CT	06360	(203) 887-3777
B'NAI SHALOM, TEMPLE - ORANGE SYNAGOGUE CENTER C 205 OLD GRASSY HILL ROAD	ORANGE	CT	06477	(203) 795-2341
CHABAD-LUBAVITCH O 261 DERBY AVENUE	ORANGE	CT	06477	
EMANUEL, TEMPLE R P.O.BOX 897, 150 DERBY AVENUE	ORANGE	CT	06477	(203) 397-3000
SONS OF ZION, CONGREGATION C CHURCH STREET	PUTNAM	CT	06260	(203) 928-4496
SHEARITH ISRAEL, TEMPLE R 46 PEACEABLE STREET	RIDGEFIELD	CT	06877	(203) 438-6589
B'NAI ISRAEL C 54 TALCOTT AVENUE	ROCKVILLE	CT	06066	(203) 875-5685
FARMINGTON VALLEY JEWISH CONGREGATION R 55 BUSHY HILL ROAD, P.O.BOX 261	SIMSBURY	CT	06070	(203) 658-1075
BETH HILLEL, TEMPLE R P.O.BOX 403, 1001 FOSTER STREET	SOUTH WINDSOR	CT	06074	(203) 644-8466
AGUDATH SHOLOM, CONGREGATION O 301 STRAWBERRY HILL AVENUE	STAMFORD	CT	06902	(203) 325-3501
BETH EL, TEMPLE C 350 ROXBURY ROAD	STAMFORD	CT	06902	(203) 322-6901
SINAI, TEMPLE R LAKESIDE DRIVE	STAMFORD	CT	06903	(203) 322-1649
STAMFORD RECONSTRUCTIONIST HAVURAH	STAMFORD	CT		(203) 322-5042
YOUNG ISRAEL OF STAMFORD P.O.BOX 2124	STAMFORD	CT	06906	(203) 323-3390
BETH SHOLOM, TEMPLE C 275 HUNTINGTON ROAD	STRATFORD	CT	06497	(203) 378-6175
BETH EL SYNAGOGUE C 124 LITCHFIELD STREET	TORRINGTON	CT	06790	(203) 482-8263
B'NAI TORAH, CONGREGATION C 5700 MAIN STREET	TRUMBULL	CT	06611	(203) 268-6940
SOUTHERN NEW ENGLAND LUBAVITCH-CHABAD O 77 MT. PLEASANT DRIVE	TRUMBULL	CT	06611	(203) 266-7700
BETH ISRAEL, CONGREGATION C 22 N. ORCHARD STREET	WALLINGFORD	CT	06492	(203) 269-5983
B'NAI SHALOM SYNAGOGUE O 135 ROSELAND AVENUE	WATERBURY	CT	06710	(203) 754-4159
BETH EL SYNAGOGUE C 359 COOKE STREET	WATERBURY	CT	06710	(203) 749-4659
ISRAEL, TEMPLE R 100 WILLIAMSON DRIVE	WATERBURY	CT	06710	(203) 754-0187
SHARES ISRAEL, CONGREGATION 94 RANDOLPH AVENUE	WATERBURY	CT	06710	
EMANU-EL, TEMPLE 29 DAYTON ROAD, P.O.BOX 288	WATERFORD	CT	06835	(203) 443-3069
AGUDAS ACHIM CONGREGATION O 1244 NORTH MAIN STREET	WEST HARTFORD	CT	06117	(203) 233-6241
BETH DAVID SYNAGOGUE O 20 DOVER ROAD	WEST HARTFORD	CT	06119	(203) 236-1241

Name / Address	City	State	Zip	Phone
BETH EL TEMPLE OF WEST HARTFORD C 2626 ALBANY AVENUE	WEST HARTFORD	**CT**	06117	(203) 233-9696
BETH ISRAEL, TEMPLE R 701 FARMINGTON AVENUE	WEST HARTFORD	**CT**	06119	(203) 233-8215
CHABAD HOUSE O 798 FARMINGTON AVENUE	WEST HARTFORD	**CT**	06119	(203) 233-5912
EMANUEL SYNAGOGUE C 160 MOHEGAN DRIVE	WEST HARTFORD	**CT**	06117	(203) 236-1275
SEPHARDIC CONGREGATION OF GREATER HARTFORD 31 LYMAN ROAD	WEST HARTFORD	**CT**	06117	(203) 233-1888
UNITED SYNAGOGUES O 840 NORTH MAIN STREET	WEST HARTFORD	**CT**	06117	(203) 236-3388
YOUNG ISRAEL OF HARTFORD 1137 TROUT BROOK DRIVE	WEST HARTFORD	**CT**	06107	(203) 523-7804
YOUNG ISRAEL OF WEST HARTFORD 2240 ALBANY AVENUE	WEST HARTFORD	**CT**	06117	(203) 523-8670
ISRAEL, TEMPLE R 14 COLEYTOWN ROAD	WESTPORT	**CT**	06880	(203) 227-1293
BETH TORAH, TEMPLE C 130 MAIN STREET	WETHERSFIELD	**CT**	06109	(203) 529-2410
B'NAI ISRAEL, TEMPLE C 345 JACKSON STREET	WILLIMANTIC	**CT**	06226	(203) 423-3743
B'NAI CHAIM, TEMPLE R P.O.BOX 764	WILTON	**CT**	06897	(203) 762-8852
BETH AHM, CONGREGATION C 362 PALISADO AVENUE	WINDSOR	**CT**	06095	(203) 688-9989
BETH ISRAEL, TEMPLE C 74 PARK PLACE	WINSTED	**CT**	06098	
B'NAI JACOB, CONGREGATION C 75 RIMMON ROAD	WOODBRIDGE	**CT**	06525	(203) 389-2111
ADAS ISRAEL HEBREW CONGREGATION C 2850 QUEBEC STREET NW	WASHINGTON	**DC**	20008	(202) 362-4433
AGUDATH ACHIM, CONGREGATION T 6343 13TH STREET N.W.	WASHINGTON	**DC**	20011	(202) 338-4816
BETH EL CONGREGATION & TALMUD TORAH C/O LEVINSON, 6101 16TH STREET	WASHINGTON	**DC**	20011	
BETH JOSHUA, CONGREGATION O 6045 16TH STREET N.W.	WASHINGTON	**DC**	20012	
BETH SHOLOM CONGREGATION O 7930 EASTERN AVENUE N.W.	WASHINGTON	**DC**	20012	(202) 726-3869
GALLAUDET COLLEGE HILLEL CLUB, THE C/O OFF OF CAMPUS MINISTRIES, GALLAUDET COLLEGE	WASHINGTON	**DC**	20002	(202) 651-5106
KESHER ISRAEL, CONGREGATION O 2801 N. STREET N.W.	WASHINGTON	**DC**	20007	(202) 333-2337
MICAH, TEMPLE R 600 M STREET S.W.	WASHINGTON	**DC**	20024	(202) 554-3099
OHEV SHOLOM TALMUD TORAH CONGREGATION O 1600 JONQUIL STREET N.W.	WASHINGTON	**DC**	20012	(202) 882-7225
RECONSTRUCTIONIST FELLOWSHIP OF GREATER WASHINGTON C/O HARRIET OSTROFF	WASHINGTON	**DC**		(301) 770-3591
SINAI, TEMPLE R 3100 MILITARY ROAD N W	WASHINGTON	**DC**	20015	(202) 363-6394
TIFERETH ISRAEL CONGREGATION C 7701 26TH STREET N.W.	WASHINGTON	**DC**	20012	(202) 882-1605
WASHINGTON HEBREW CONGREGATION R 3935 MACOMB STREET N.W.	WASHINGTON	**DC**	20016	(202) 362-7100
BETH SHOLOM, CONGREGATION C NORTH QUEEN & CLARA STREETS, BOX 223	DOVER	**DE**	19901	(302) 734-5578
BETH-EL, TEMPLE 70 AMSTEL AVENUE	NEWARK	**DE**	19711	(302) 366-8330
BETH EMETH, CONGREGATION R 300 W. LEA BLVD	WILMINGTON	**DE**	19802	(302) 764-2393
BETH SHALOM C 18TH & BAYNARD BLVD	WILMINGTON	**DE**	19802	(302) 654-4462
CHABAD-LUBAVITCH O 9701 COLLINS AVENUE	BAL HARBOUR	**FL**	33154	
SHUL OF BAL HARBOR 9955 COLLINS AVENUE	BAL HARBOR	**FL**	33154	(305) 868-1411
B'NAI ISRAEL, CONG. - R 22445 BOCA RIO ROAD	BOCA RATON	**FL**	33433	(305) 483-9982
B'NAI TORAH CONGREGATION C 1401 N.W. 4TH AVENUE	BOCA RATON	**FL**	33432	(305) 392-8566
BETH AMI CONGREGATION C 2134 NORTHWEST 19TH WAY	BOCA RATON	**FL**	33431	(305) 994-8693
BETH EL, TEMPLE R 333 S.W. 4TH AVENUE	BOCA RATON	**FL**	33432	(305) 391-8900
BETH SHALOM, TEMPLE - C P.O. BOX 340015	BOCA RATON	**FL**	33434	(305) 483-5557
BOCA RATON SYNAGOGUE O P.O. BOX 2262, 7900 MONIAYA CIRCLE	BOCA RATON	**FL**	33427	(305) 394-5732
ETERNAL LIGHT, TEMPLE 499 N.W. 13TH STREET, P.O. BOX 3	BOCA RATON	**FL**	33432	(305) 391-1111
FREE SYNAGOGUE CENTER, THE 499 N.W. 13TH STREET, P.O. BOX 3	BOCA RATON	**FL**	33432	(305) 368-1600
BETH EL, TEMPLE C 2209 75TH STREET W	BRADENTON	**FL**	33529	(813) 792-0870
BETH-EL, TEMPLE R 2721 DEL PRADO BLVD	CAPE CORAL	**FL**	33904	(305) 574-5115
B'NAI ISRAEL, TEMPLE R 1685 S. BELCHER ROAD	CLEARWATER	**FL**	33516	(813) 531-5829
BETH SHALOM C 1325 S. BELCHER ROAD	CLEARWATER	**FL**	33516	(813) 531-1418
BETH ORR, TEMPLE R P.O. BOX 8242, 2151 RIVERSIDE DRIVE	CORAL GABLES	**FL**	33065	(305) 753-3232
JUDEA, TEMPLE R 5500 GRANADA BLVD	CORAL GABLES	**FL**	33146	(305) 667-5657
ZAMORA, TEMPLE C 44 ZAMORA AVENUE	CORAL GABLES	**FL**	33134	(305) 448-7132
BETH ORR, TEMPLE R 2151 RIVERSIDE DRIVE	CORAL SPRINGS	**FL**	33065	(305) 753-3232
CHABAD-LUBAVITCH O 10503 NORTHWEST 45TH STREET	CORAL SPRINGS	**FL**	33065	
CORAL SPRINGS HEBREW CONGREGATION R P.O. BOX 8242	CORAL SPRINGS	**FL**	33060	
BETH EL, TEMPLE R 507 FIFTH AVENUE	DAYTONA BEACH	**FL**	32018	(904) 252-1248
ISRAEL OF DAYTONA BEACH, TEMPLE C 1400 S. PENINSULA DRIVE	DAYTONA BEACH	**FL**	32018	(904) 252-3097
BETH ISRAEL, TEMPLE C 200 SOUTH CENTURY BOULEVARD	DEERFIELD BEACH	**FL**	33441	(305) 421-7060
B'NAI SHALOM OF DEERFIELD BEACH, TEMPLE R 2305 WEST HILLSBORO BOULEVARD	DEERFIELD BEACH	**FL**	33441	(305) 426-2532
YOUNG ISRAEL OF DEERFIELD BEACH 1880 WEST HILLSBORO BOULEVARD	DEERFIELD BEACH	**FL**	33441	(305) 421-1367
ANSHEI EMUNA O 16189 CARTER ROAD	DELRAY BEACH	**FL**	33480	(305) 499-9229
ANSHEI SHALOM T 7099 WEST ATLANTIC	DELRAY BEACH	**FL**	33446	(305) 495-1300
EMETH, TEMPLE C 5780 W. ATLANTIC AVENUE	DELRAY BEACH	**FL**	33445	(305) 498-3536
SINAI, TEMPLE R P.O. BOX 1901	DELRAY BEACH	**FL**	33446	(305) 276-6161
SHALOM, TEMPLE R P.O. BOX 132, 1785 ELCAM BLVD	DELTONA	**FL**	32725	(904) 789-2202
AHAVAT SHOLOM, TEMPLE R 2000 MAIN STREET	DUNEDIN	**FL**	33528	(813) 734-9428
BETH ISRAEL, TEMPLE 7100 W. OAKLAND PARK BLVD	FORT LAUDERDALE	**FL**	33313	(305) 742-4040
EMANU-EL, TEMPLE R 3245 W. OAKLAND PARK BLVD	FORT LAUDERDALE	**FL**	33311	(305) 731-2310
OHEL B'NAI RAPHAEL, TEMPLE 4351 W. OAKLAND PARK BLVD	FORT LAUDERDALE	**FL**	33313	(305) 733-7684
YOUNG ISRAEL OF HOLLYWOOD 3291 STIRLING ROAD	FORT LAUDERDALE	**FL**	33312	(305) 966-7877
BETH EL, TEMPLE R 4600 OLEANDER AVENUE	FORT PIERCE	**FL**	33450	(305) 461-7428
B'NAI ISRAEL C 3830 N.W. 16TH BLVD	GAINESVILLE	**FL**	32605	(904) 376-1508
BETH SHOLOM OF GULFPORT, CONGREGATION C 1844 54TH STREET S.	GULFPORT	**FL**	33707	(305) 345-7232
CONGREGATION LEVI YITZCHOK O 1295 EAST HALLANDALE BEACH BOULEVARD	HALLANDALE	**FL**	33009	(305) 458-1877
HALLANDALE JEWISH CENTER C 416 N.E. 8TH AVENUE	HALLANDALE	**FL**	33009	(305) 454-9100
TIFERETH JACOB, TEMPLE C 951 E. 4TH AVENUE	HIALEAH	**FL**	33010	(305) 887-9595
BETH AHM, TEMPLE 9730 STIRLING ROAD	HOLLYWOOD	**FL**	33024	(305) 431-4959
BETH EL, TEMPLE R 1351 S. 14TH AVENUE	HOLLYWOOD	**FL**	33020	(305) 920-8225
BETH SHALOM, TEMPLE C 1400 N. 46TH AVENUE	HOLLYWOOD	**FL**	33021	(305) 981-6111
SINAI, TEMPLE C 1201 JOHNSON STREET	HOLLYWOOD	**FL**	33019	(305) 920-1577
SOLEL, TEMPLE R 5100 SHERIDAN STREET	HOLLYWOOD	**FL**	33021	(305) 989-0205
HOMESTEAD JEWISH CENTER 183 N.E. 8TH STREET	HOMESTEAD	**FL**	33023	(305) 248-5724
AHAVATH CHESED, CONGREGATION R 8727 SAN JOSE BLVD	JACKSONVILLE	**FL**	32217	(904) 733-7078
BETH SHALOM C 4072 SUNBEAM ROAD	JACKSONVILLE	**FL**	32217	(904) 268-0404
ETZ CHAIM SYNAGOGUE O 5864 UNIVERSITY BLVD. W.	JACKSONVILLE	**FL**	32216	(904) 733-0720
ETZ CHAIM SYNAGOGUE - SAN JOSE BRANCH O 10167 SAN JOSE BLVD.	JACKSONVILLE	**FL**	32217	(904) 262-3565
JACKSONVILLE JEWISH CENTER C 3662 CROWN POINT ROAD	JACKSONVILLE	**FL**	32217	(904) 268-6736
CHABAD-LUBAVITCH O 4311 WEST VINE	KISSIMEE	**FL**	32741	
BETH SHOLOM, TEMPLE 315 NORTH A STREET, P.O. BOX 1209	LAKE WORTH	**FL**	33460	(305) 585-5020
EMANUEL, TEMPLE C 730 LAKE HOLLINGSWORTH DRIVE	LAKELAND	**FL**	33803	(813) 682-8616
CHABAD LUBAVITCH OF PINNELLAS COUNTY O P.O. BOX 1426	LARGO	**FL**	34294	(813) 584-7756
OHEL B'NAI RAPHAEL, TEMPLE O 4351 WEST OAKLAND PARK BOULEVARD	LAUDERDALE LAKES	**FL**	33313	(305) 733-7684
CHABAD OF INVERRARY O 4561 NORTH UNIVERSITY DRIVE	LAUDERHILL	**FL**	33321	(305) 748-1777
HEBREW CONGREGATION OF LAUDERHILL C 2048 NORTHWEST 49TH AVENUE	LAUDERHILL	**FL**	33313	(305) 733-9560
CHABAD-LUBAVITCH O 2021 MOHAWK TRAIL	MAITLAND	**FL**	32751	(305) 273-3280
BETH AM, TEMPLE C 7205 ROYAL PALM BLVD	MARGATE	**FL**	33063	(305) 974-8650
BETH HILLEL, CONGREGATION C 7640 MARGATE BLVD	MARGATE	**FL**	33063	(305) 974-3090
NER TAMID, CONGREGATION C 820 E. STRAWBRIDGE AVENUE	MELBOURNE	**FL**	32901	(305) 723-9112
ISRAEL, TEMPLE R P.O. BOX 592	MERRITT ISLAND	**FL**	32952	(305) 636-4920
AHAVAT SHALOM, CONGREGATION O 985 S.W. 67TH AVENUE	MIAMI	**FL**	33144	(305) 261-5479
ANSHEI EMES, CONGREGATION C 2533 S.W. 19TH AVENUE	MIAMI	**FL**	33133	(305) 854-7623
AVENTURA JEWISH CENTER C 2972 AVENTURA BLVD.	MIAMI	**FL**	33180	(305) 932-0666
B'NAI ISRAEL & GREATER MIAMI YOUTH SYNAGOGUE 1425 SOUTHWEST 85TH AVENUE	MIAMI	**FL**	33144	(305) 595-9336
BET BREIRA, CONGREGATION R 9400 S.W. 87TH AVENUE	MIAMI	**FL**	33176	(305) 595-1500
BET SHIRA CONGREGATION 7500 SOUTHWEST 120TH STREET	MIAMI	**FL**	33156	(305) 238-2601
BETH AM, TEMPLE R 5950 N. KENDALL DRIVE	MIAMI	**FL**	33156	(305) 667-6667
BETH DAVID CONGREGATION C 2625 S.W. THIRD AVENUE	MIAMI	**FL**	33129	(305) 854-3911
BETH KODESH, CONGREGATION C 1101 S.W. 12TH AVENUE	MIAMI	**FL**	33129	(305) 858-6334
BETH MOSHE, CONGREGATION C 2225 N.E. 121 STREET	MIAMI	**FL**	33181	(305) 801-5508
BETH TOV, TEMPLE C 6438 S.W. 8TH STREET	MIAMI	**FL**	33144	(305) 261-9821
CONGREGATION SHAARE TEFILLAH OF KENDALL O 15410 S.W. 75TH CIRCLE LANE	MIAMI	**FL**	33193	(305) 382-3343
HAVURAH OF SOUTH FLORIDA 9315 SOUTHWEST 61ST COURT	MIAMI	**FL**	33156	(305) 666-7349
ISRAEL OF GREATER MIAMI, TEMPLE R 137 N.E. 19TH STREET	MIAMI	**FL**	33132	(305) 573-5900
ISRAELITE CENTER TEMPLE, THE C 3175 S.W. 25TH STREET	MIAMI	**FL**	33133	(305) 445-1529
KENDALL LAKES, SYNAGOGUE OF - CHABAD O 14456 KENDALL LAKES BLVD	MIAMI	**FL**	33183	(305) 271-8277
OR OLAM, TEMPLE C 8755 S.W. 16TH STREET	MIAMI	**FL**	33165	(305) 221-9131
SAMU-EL, TEMPLE C 9353 S.W. 152ND AVENUE	MIAMI	**FL**	33196	(305) 382-3668
SHAARE TEFILLAH OF KENDALL O C/O BECKER-8475 SOUTHWEST 156TH COURT-310	MIAMI	**FL**	33193	
TEMPLE BETH OR RE POB 160081	MIAMI	**FL**	33116	(305) 596-4523
TEMPLE ISRAEL OF GREATER MIAMI 137 NORTHEAST 19TH STREET	MIAMI	**FL**	33132	(305) 573-5900
TEMPLE ISRAEL OF GREATER MIAMI 9990 NORTH KENDALL DRIVE	MIAMI	**FL**	33176	(305) 595-5055
TIFERETH ISRAEL, TEMPLE C 6500 N. MIAMI AVENUE	MIAMI	**FL**	33150	(305) 947-1435
ZION, TEMPLE C 8000 MILLER ROAD	MIAMI	**FL**	33155	(305) 271-2311
AGUDATH ISRAEL HEBREW INSTITUTE 7801 CARLYLE AVE	MIAMI BEACH	**FL**	33141	(305) 866-5226
AHAVAS ISRAEL, CONGREGATION 525 78TH STREET	MIAMI BEACH	**FL**	33141	
ALL PEOPLES REFORM SYNAGOGUE 7455 COLLINS AVENUE	MIAMI BEACH	**FL**	33141	(305) 861-5554
BEIS HAMEDRASH LEVI YITZCHAK, CONGREGATION O 1140 ALTON ROAD	MIAMI BEACH	**FL**	33139	(305) 673-5664
BETH EL, TEMPLE O 2400 PINE TREE DRIVE	MIAMI BEACH	**FL**	33140	(305) 532-6421
BETH ISRAEL CONGREGATION O 770 40TH STREET	MIAMI BEACH	**FL**	33140	(305) 534-1461
BETH JACOB, CONGREGATION O 311 WASHINGTON AVENUE	MIAMI BEACH	**FL**	33139	(305) 672-6150
BETH RAPHAEL, TEMPLE C 1545 JEFFERSON AVENUE	MIAMI BEACH	**FL**	33139	(305) 538-4112
BETH SHOLOM, TEMPLE R 4144 CHASE AVENUE	MIAMI BEACH	**FL**	33140	(305) 538-7231
BETH TFILAH, CONGREGATION O 935 EUCLID AVENUE	MIAMI BEACH	**FL**	33139	(305) 538-1521
CHABAD-LUBAVITCH O 4545 NORTH JEFFERSON AVENUE	MIAMI BEACH	**FL**	33140	
CHABAD-LUBAVITCH O 4130 COLLINS AVENUE	MIAMI BEACH	**FL**	33140	
CONGREGATION OHR CHAIM 317 W. 47 ST	MIAMI BEACH	**FL**	33140	(305) 674-1326
CUBAN HEBREW CONGREGATION 1700 MICHIGAN AVENUE	MIAMI BEACH	**FL**	33139	(305) 534-7213
CUBAN SEPHARDIC HEBREW CONGREGATION O 1200 NORMANDY DRIVE	MIAMI BEACH	**FL**	33141	(305) 531-4732
EMANU-EL, TEMPLE C 1701 WASHINGTON AVENUE	MIAMI BEACH	**FL**	33139	(305) 538-2503
ETZ CHAIM, CONGREGATION 1544 WASHINGTON AVENUE	MIAMI BEACH	**FL**	33139	(305) 674-1326
JACOB J. COHEN COMMUNITY CONGREGATION O 1532 WASHINGTON AVENUE	MIAMI BEACH	**FL**	33139	(305) 534-0271
JEWISH CULTURAL CENTER 429 LENOX AVENUE	MIAMI BEACH	**FL**	33139	(305) 672-7784
KING SOLOMON TEMPLE C 910 LINCOLN ROAD	MIAMI BEACH	**FL**	33139	(305) 534-9776
KNESETH ISRAEL, CONGREGATION O 1415 EUCLID AVENUE	MIAMI BEACH	**FL**	33139	(305) 538-2741
LUBAVITCH, CONGREGATION O 1220 OCEAN AVENUE	MIAMI BEACH	**FL**	33139	(305) 673-1800
LUBAVITCH, CONGREGATION O 1120 COLLINS AVENUE	MIAMI BEACH	**FL**	33139	(305) 673-1800
MENORAH, TEMPLE C 620 75TH STREET	MIAMI BEACH	**FL**	33141	(305) 866-0221
MERKOS CHABAD O 1140 ALTON ROAD	MIAMI BEACH	**FL**	33139	(305) 673-5664
MOGAN DAVID OF SURFSIDE, CONGREGATION O 9348 HARDING AVENUE (SURFSIDE)	MIAMI BEACH	**FL**	33154	(305) 865-9714
NER TAMID, TEMPLE C 7902 CARLYLE STREET	MIAMI BEACH	**FL**	33141	(305) 866-9833
NORTH BAY VILLAGE JEWISH CENTER C 1720 79TH STREET CAUSEWAY	MIAMI BEACH	**FL**	33141	(305) 861-4005
OHEV SHALOM CONGREGATION O 7055 BONITA DRIVE	MIAMI BEACH	**FL**	33141	(305) 865-9851
OHR HACHAIM CONGREGATION O 317 47TH STREET	MIAMI BEACH	**FL**	33140	(305) 674-1326
SEPHARDIC JEWISH CENTER OF GREATER MIAMI 645 COLLINS AVENUE	MIAMI BEACH	**FL**	33139	(305) 534-4092
TALMUDIC UNIVERSITY OF FLORIDA O 1910 ALTON ROAD	MIAMI BEACH	**FL**	33139	(305) 534-7050
TEMPLE HATIKVAH ISRAEL 800 71 STREET	MIAMI BEACH	**FL**	33141	(305) 865-0479

Synagogue / Address	City	State	ZIP	Phone
TEMPLE MOSES/SEPHARDIC CONGREGATION OF FLORIDA O 1200 NORMANDY DRIVE	MIAMI BEACH	FL	33141	(305) 861-6308
YAD V KIDUSH HASHEM O 4200 SHERIDAN AVENUE	MIAMI BEACH	FL	33140	(305) 532-0363
YOUNG ISRAEL OF SUNNY ISLES, O 17274 COLLINS AVENUE	MIAMI BEACH	FL	33160	(305) 931-0001
ISRAEL OF MIRAMAR, TEMPLE C 6920 S.W. 35TH STREET	MIRAMAR	FL	33023	(305) 961-1700
BETH MOSHE, TEMPLE C 2225 N.E. 121ST STREET	NORTH MIAMI	FL	33181	(305) 891-5508
ADATH YESHURUN, TEMPLE C 1025 N.E. MIAMI GARDENS	NORTH MIAMI BEACH	FL	33162	(305) 947-1435
AGUDATH ACHIM, CONGREGATION 19255 NORTHEAST 3RD AVENUE	NORTH MIAMI BEACH	FL	33179	(305) 652-5947
AVENTURA JEWISH CENTER 2972 AVENTURA BOULEVARD	NORTH MIAMI BEACH	FL	33180	(305) 935-0666
B'NAI RAPHAEL, CONGREGATION C 1401 N.W. 183RD STREET	NORTH MIAMI BEACH	FL	33169	
BETH TORAH CONGREGATION C 1051 N. MIAMI BEACH BLVD	NORTH MIAMI BEACH	FL	33162	(305) 947-7528
CHABAD OF NORTH DADE O 2590 NORTHEAST 202ND STREET	NORTH MIAMI BEACH	FL	33180	(305) 923-7770
ETZ CHAIM, CONG. - METRO COMMUNITY SYN. OF GREATER MIAMI R 19094 W. DIXIE HIGHWAY	NORTH MIAMI BEACH	FL	33180	(305) 931-9318
KOL YISRAEL CHAVERIM, CONGREGATION 17720 N. BAY ROAD, SUITE 8D	NORTH MIAMI BEACH	FL	33160	(305) 931-0001
MAGEN DAVID OF THE SEPHARDIC JEWISH CENTER, CONGREGATION 17100 NORTHEAST 6TH AVENUE	NORTH MIAMI BEACH	FL	33162	(305) 652-2099
METROPOLITAN COMM. SYN./GREATER MIAMI, CONG. ETZ CHAIM, 19094 W. DIXIE HIGHWAY	NORTH MIAMI BEACH	FL	33180	(305) 931-9318
SHAARAY TEFILAH, CONGREGATION 971 NORTHEAST 172ND STREET	NORTH MIAMI BEACH	FL	33162	(305) 651-1562
SINAI OF NORTH DADE, TEMPLE R 18801 N.E. 22ND AVENUE	NORTH MIAMI BEACH	FL	33180	(305) 932-9010
SKY LAKE SYNAGOGUE O 18151 N.E. 19TH AVENUE	NORTH MIAMI BEACH	FL	33162	(305) 945-8712
YOUNG ISRAEL OF GREATER MIAMI 990 N.E. 171ST STREET	NORTH MIAMI BEACH	FL	33162	(305) 651-3591
YOUNG ISRAEL OF SKY LAKE 1850 N.E. 183RD STREET	NORTH MIAMI BEACH	FL	33179	(305) 945-8712
BETH DAVID OF NORTHERN PALM BEACH COUNTY, TEMPLE C 321 NORTHLAKE BLVD	NORTH PALM BEACH	FL	33408	(305) 845-1134
ISRAEL, TEMPLE C 4917 ELI STREET	ORLANDO	FL	32804	(305) 647-3055
LIBERAL JUDAISM CONGREGATION R 928 MALONE DRIVE	ORLANDO	FL	32810	(305) 645-0444
OHEV SHALOM C 5015 GODDARD AVENUE	ORLANDO	FL	32810	(305) 298-4650
WILLIAMSBURG CONGREGATION 5121 GATEWAY AVENUE	ORLANDO	FL	32821	(305) 351-1745
EMANU-EL OF PALM BEACH, TEMPLE C 190 N. CITY ROAD	PALM BEACH	FL	33480	(305) 832-0804
BETH EMET, TEMPLE R P.O. BOX 8842	PEMBROKE PINES	FL	33024	(305) 431-3638
IN THE PINES, TEMPLE C 9730 STIRLING ROAD	PEMBROKE PINES	FL	33024	(305) 431-5100
B'NAI ISRAEL SYNAGOGUE C P.O. BOX 9002, 1909 N. 9TH AVENUE	PENSACOLA	FL	32503	(904) 433-7311
BETH EL, TEMPLE R 800 N. PALAFOX STREET	PENSACOLA	FL	32501	(904) 438-3321
KOL AMI, TEMPLE - PLANTATION JEWISH CONGREGATION 8200 PETERS ROAD	PLANTATION	FL	33324	(305) 472-1988
RAMAT SHALOM RECONSTRUCTIONIST SYNAGOGUE 11301 W. BROWARD BLVD.	PLANTATION	FL	33325	(305) 472-3600
B'NAI MOSHE, TEMPLE C 1434 SOUTHEAST 3RD STREET	POMPANO BEACH	FL	33060	(305) 942-5380
SHOLOM, TEMPLE C 132 S.E. 11TH AVENUE	POMPANO BEACH	FL	33060	(305) 942-6410
BETH SHOLOM, TEMPLE C 1050 S. TUTTLE AVENUE	SARASOTA	FL	33577	(813) 955-8121
CHABAD-LUBAVITCH O 2886 RINGLING BOULEVARD, #C	SARASOTA	FL	33577	
EMANU-EL, TEMPLE R 151 S. MCINTOSH ROAD	SARASOTA	FL	33582	(813) 371-2788
BETH SHOLOM, TEMPLE C P.O. BOX 2253 (N.E. THIRD STREET)	SATELLITE BEACH	FL	32937	(305) 773-3039
BETH CHAI C P.O. BOX 3235	SEMINOLE	FL	33542	(813) 393-5525
B'NAI ISRAEL C 301 59TH STREET N	ST. PETERSBURG	FL	33710	(813) 381-4900
BETH EL, TEMPLE R 400 S. PASADENA AVENUE	ST. PETERSBURG	FL	33707	(813) 347-6136
BETH ISRAEL, TEMPLE C 7100 W. OAKLAND PARK BLVD	SUNRISE	FL	33313	(305) 742-4040
SHA'ARAY TZEDEK, TEMPLE C 4099 PINE ISLAND ROAD	SUNRISE	FL	33321	(305) 741-0295
SYNAGOGUE OF INVERRARY CHABAD O 7770 NORTHWEST 44TH STREET	SUNRISE	FL	33321	(305) 748-1777
MOGAN DAVID CONGREGATION OF SURFSIDE 9348 HARDING AVENUE	SURFSIDE	FL	33154	(305) 865-9714
ISRAEL, TEMPLE R 2215 MAHAN DRIVE	TALLAHASSEE	FL	32308	(904) 877-3517
BETH TORAH, TEMPLE - TAMARAC JEWISH CENTER C 9101-15 N.W. 57TH STREET	TAMARAC	FL	33321	(305) 721-7660
MIGDAL DAVID, CONGREGATION O 8575 WEST MCNAB ROAD	TAMARAC	FL	33321	(305) 726-3583
NORTH LAUDERDALE HEBREW CONGREGATION C 6050 BAILEY ROAD	TAMARAC	FL	33319	(305) 722-7607
BAIS TEFILLAH - CHABAD HOUSE O P.O. BOX 271157	TAMPA	FL	33624	(813) 962-2375
BETH ISRAEL, CONGREGATION C 2111 SWANN AVENUE	TAMPA	FL	33606	
BETH ISRAEL O 530 LUCERNE AVENUE	TAMPA	FL	33606	(813) 251-2552
CHABAD-LUBAVITCH O 13801 NORTH 37TH STREET, 1114	TAMPA	FL	33613	
CHABAD-LUBAVITCH O 3418 HANDY ROAD, #103	TAMPA	FL	33618	
DAVID, TEMPLE C 2001 SWANN AVENUE	TAMPA	FL	33609	(813) 251-4215
KOL AMI, CONGREGATION C P.O. BOX 270444	TAMPA	FL	33688	(813) 885-3356
RODEPH SHOLOM, CONGREGATION C 2713 BAYSHORE	TAMPA	FL	33609	(813) 837-1911
SHAARAI ZEDEK, TEMPLE R 3303 SWANN AVENUE	TAMPA	FL	33609	(813) 876-2377
BETH SHALOM, TEMPLE R P.O. BOX 2113	VERO BEACH	FL	32960	(305) 569-1082
BETH EL, TEMPLE C 2815 N. FLAGLER DRIVE	WEST PALM BEACH	FL	33407	(305) 833-0339
BETH TORAH, TEMPLE R 1125 JACKPINE STREET	WEST PALM BEACH	FL	33411	(305) 793-2700
ISRAEL, TEMPLE R 1901 N. FLAGLER DRIVE	WEST PALM BEACH	FL	33407	(305) 833-8421
ALBANY HEBREW CONGREGATION R P.O. BOX 3288	ALBANY	GA	31706	(912) 432-6536
CHILDREN OF ISRAEL R DUDLEY DRIVE, P.O. BOX 5694	ALBANY	GA	30604	(912) 549-4192
AHAVATH ACHIM SYNAGOGUE C 600 PEACHTREE BATTLE AVENUE N.W.	ATLANTA	GA	30327	(404) 355-5222
ANSHEI SFARD, CONGREGATION O 1324 N. HIGHLAND AVENUE N.E.	ATLANTA	GA	30312	
ATLANTA HILLEL 1531 CLIFTON ROAD NORTHEAST	ATLANTA	GA	30329	(404) 329-6490
BETH JACOB, CONGREGATION O 1855 LA VISTA ROAD, N.E.	ATLANTA	GA	30329	(404) 633-0551
BETH SHALOM, CONGREGATION C 3147 CHAMBLEE-TUCKER ROAD	ATLANTA	GA	30341	(404) 458-0489
B'NAI TORAH T 300 JOHNSON FERRY ROAD, P.O. BOX 76564	ATLANTA	GA	30358	(404) 257-0537
CHABAD HOUSE O 6600 ROSEWELL ROAD, SUITE G	ATLANTA	GA	30328	(404) 843-2464
CHABAD-LUBAVITCH O 5065 HIGH POINT ROAD	ATLANTA	GA	30342	
EMANU-EL, TEMPLE R 120 COPELAND ROAD, SUITE 254	ATLANTA	GA	30342	(404) 257-0633
HEBREW BENEVOLENT CONGREGATION; THE TEMPLE 1589 N.E. PEACHTREE ROAD	ATLANTA	GA	30367	(404) 873-1731
ISRAEL, TEMPLE OF 891 MAYSON TURNER AVENUE N.W.	ATLANTA	GA	30309	(404) 524-7952
KEHILLAT CHAIM R 141 W. WIEUCA ROAD, N.W.	ATLANTA	GA	30342	(404) 252-4441
OR VESHALOM, CONGREGATION O 1681 N. DRUID HILLS ROAD N.E.	ATLANTA	GA	30319	(404) 633-1737
SHEARITH ISRAEL, CONGREGATION C 1180 UNIVERSITY DRIVE N.E.	ATLANTA	GA	30306	(404) 873-1743
SINAI, TEMPLE R 5645 N.W. DUPREE DRIVE	ATLANTA	GA	30327	(404) 252-3073
CHILDREN OF ISRAEL, CONGREGATION - WALTON WAY TEMPLE R 3005 WALTON WAY	AUGUSTA	GA	30909	(404) 736-3140
BETH EL, TEMPLE R P.O. BOX 476	BAINBRIDGE	GA	31717	(912) 432-6536
BETH TEFILLOT, TEMPLE R P.O. BOX 602	BRUNSWICK	GA	31521	(912) 265-7575
ISRAEL, TEMPLE R P.O. BOX 5086	COLUMBUS	GA	31906	(404) 323-1617
SHEARITH ISRAEL CONGREGATION C 2550 WYNNTON ROAD, P.O. BOX 5515	COLUMBUS	GA	31906	(404) 323-1443
BETH EL, TEMPLE C VALLEY DRIVE	DALTON	GA	30720	(404) 278-6798
EMANU-EL, TEMPLE R 1580 SPALDING DRIVE	DUNWOODY	GA	30338	(404) 395-1340
FITZGERALD HEBREW CONGREGATION C ROUTE 4 BOX 520	FITZGERALD	GA	31750	
BETH-EL, CONGREGATION C C/O ISAAC STRULETZ, 200 SPRINGDALE DRIVE	LA GRANGE	GA	30240	(404) 884-7708
BETH ISRAEL, TEMPLE R 892 CHERRY STREET	MACON	GA	31201	(912) 745-6727
SHERAH ISRAEL C 611 FIRST STREET	MACON	GA	31201	(912) 745-4571
ETZ CHAIM, CONGREGATION C 1190 INDIAN HILLS PARKWAY	MARIETTA	GA	30067	(404) 973-0137
TEMPLE KOL EMETH R P.O. BOX 71031	MARIETTA	GA	30067	(404) 973-3533
B'NAI ISRAEL R P.O. BOX 383	RIVERDALE	GA	30274	
RODEPH SHOLOM, TEMPLE R 406 E. FIRST STREET	ROME	GA	30161	(404) 291-6315
AGUDATH ACHIM C P.O. BOX 14317, 9 LEE BLVD	SAVANNAH	GA	31406	(912) 352-4737
B'NAI B'RITH JACOB, CONGREGATION O 5444 ABERCORN STREET, P.O. BOX 6326	SAVANNAH	GA	31405	(912) 354-7721
MIKVE ISRAEL, TEMPLE R 20 E. GORDON STREET	SAVANNAH	GA	31401	(912) 233-1547
TEMPLE BETH DAVID R P.O. BOX 865	SNELLVILLE	GA	30278	(404) 662-4373
ISRAEL, TEMPLE C 511 BAYTREE ROAD	VALDOSTA	GA	31601	(912) 244-1813
VALDOSTA HEBREW CONGREGATION-TEMPLE ISRAEL C 600 WEST PARK	VALDOSTA	GA	31601	(912) 242-2590
EMANU-EL, TEMPLE R 2550 PALI HIGHWAY	HONOLULU	HI	96817	(808) 595-7521
SHAAREI GAN EDEN O 54-41 KIRKWOOD PLACE	HONOLULU	HI	96821	(808) 377-5545
SOF MA'ARAV, CONGREGATION C P.O. BOX 11154	HONOLULU	HI	96828	(808) 923-5563
ALOHA JEWISH CHAPEL C NAVAL STATION, BOX 47	PEARL HARBOR	HI	96860	(808) 471-0050
BETH ALOHA HILO, TEMPLE 229 AINAKAHELE	ST. HILO	HI	96720	(808) 959-4437
KONA BETH SHALOM P.O. BOX 3122	WAIKALOA	HI	96743	(808) 883-9514
AMES JEWISH CONGREGATION R 6712 CALHOUN	AMES	IA	50010	(515) 233-1347
ISRAEL, TEMPLE R 830 DIVISION	BURLINGTON	IA	52601	(319) 752-1138
JUDAH, TEMPLE R 3221 S.E. LINDSAY LANE	CEDAR RAPIDS	IA	52403	(319) 362-1261
B'NAI ISRAEL SYNAGOGUE C 618 MYNSTER STREET	COUNCIL BLUFFS	IA	51501	(712) 322-4705
EMANUEL, TEMPLE R 1115 MISSISSIPPI AVENUE	DAVENPORT	IA	52803	(319) 326-4419
B'NAI JESHURUN, TEMPLE R 5101 GRAND AVENUE	DES MOINES	IA	50312	(515) 274-4679
BETH EL JACOB, CONGREGATION O 954 CUMMINS PARKWAY	DES MOINES	IA	50312	(515) 274-1551
CHABAD HOUSE O 2932 UNIVERSITY AVENUE	DES MOINES	IA	50311	(515) 277-0770
CHILDREN OF ISRAEL, CONGREGATION 1816 61ST STREET	DES MOINES	IA	50322	
TIFERETH ISRAEL C 924 POLK BLVD	DES MOINES	IA	50312	(515) 255-1137
BETH EL, CONGREGATION R 475 W. LOCUST STREET, P.O. BOX 185	DUBUQUE	IA	52001	(319) 583-3473
BETH EL, CONGREGATION C 507 N. 12TH STREET	FORT DODGE	IA	50501	(515) 576-2024
AGUDAS ACHIM C 602 E. WASHINGTON STREET	IOWA CITY	IA	52240	(319) 337-3813
B'NEI ISRAEL, CONGREGATION 302 EAST WASHINGTON	IOWA CITY	IA	52240	
ADAS ISRAEL, CONGREGATION C 396 WILLOWBROOK DRIVE	MASON CITY	IA	50401	
B'NAI JACOB C 529 E. MAIN STREET	OTTUMWA	IA	52501	(515) 684-7465
MOUNT SINAI TEMPLE R P.O. BOX 2128 NS STATION	SIOUX CITY	IA	51104	(712) 252-4265
SHAARE ZION SYNAGOGUE C 1522 DOUGLAS STREET	SIOUX CITY	IA	51105	(712) 252-4057
SONS OF JACOB SYNAGOGUE C 411 MITCHELL AVENUE	WATERLOO	IA	50702	(319) 233-9448
CHABAD-LUBAVITCH O 217 WEST 35TH STREET	WEST DES MOINES	IA	50265	
AHAVATH ISRAEL SYNAGOGUE C 2620 BANNOCK STREET	BOISE	ID	83702	(208) 343-6601
BETH ISRAEL, CONGREGATION R P.O. BOX 353	BOISE	ID	83701	(208) 343-6601
ADAT YISRAEL CONGREGATION C 2550 N. ARLINGTON HEIGHTS RD.	ARLINGTON HEIGHTS	IL	60004	(312) 885-1569
B'NAI ISRAEL, TEMPLE C 400 NORTH EDGELAWN	AURORA	IL	60506	(312) 892-2450
BETH ISRAEL, TEMPLE 225 N. HIGH STREET	BELLEVILLE	IL	62220	(618) 233-3602
UNITED HEBREW TEMPLE C P.O. BOX 160	BENTON	IL	62812	(618) 439-9090
MOSES MONTEFIORE R 102 ROBIN HOOD LANE	BLOOMINGTON	IL	61701	(309) 662-3182
BETH JUDEA, CONGREGATION C P.O. BOX 763	BUFFALO GROVE	IL	60090	(312) 634-0777
MISHPAHA-OUR FAMILY C 760 CHECKER DRIVE	BUFFALO GROVE	IL	60090	(312) 459-3279
MONTEFIORE TEMPLE C 3014 ELM STREET	CAIRO	IL	62914	
BETH JACOB, CONGREGATION C P.O. BOX 1042	CARBONDALE	IL	62901	(618) 529-1409
SOLOMON, TEMPLE R C/O MR. LINKON, ROUTE 161 E	CENTRALIA	IL	62801	(618) 532-8749
SINAI CONGREGATION R 3104 W. WINDSOR ROAD	CHAMPAIGN	IL	61820	(217) 352-8140
A.G. BETH ISRAEL T 3635 WEST DEVON	CHICAGO	IL	60659	(312) 539-9060
ADAS BNAI ISRAEL O 6200 NORTH KIMBALL	CHICAGO	IL	60659	(312) 583-8141
ADAS YESCHURUN O 2949 W. TOUHY	CHICAGO	IL	60645	(312) 465-2288
ADATH HATIKVAH CONGREGATION C 6327 N. WASHTENAW AVENUE, P.O. BOX 59056	CHICAGO	IL	60659	(312) 761-8872
AGUDAS ACHIM NORTH SHORE, CONGREGATION T 5029 N. KENMORE AVENUE	CHICAGO	IL	60640	(312) 561-0435
AGUDAS ANSHEI LUBAVITCH, CONGREGATION O 7424 NORTH PAULINA	CHICAGO	IL	60626	(312) 274-0623
AGUDATH ACHIM - BIKUR CHOLIM O 8927 S. HOUSTON	CHICAGO	IL	60617	(312) 768-7685
AGUDAH ISRAEL OF CHICAGO O 3540 WEST PETERSON	CHICAGO	IL	60659	(312) 588-5085
ALBANY PARK HEBREW CONGREGATION C 4601 N. LAWNDALE AVENUE	CHICAGO	IL	60625	
ANSHE EMET SYNAGOGUE C 3760 PINE GROVE AVENUE	CHICAGO	IL	60613	(312) 281-1423
ANSHE KNESSESS ISRAEL, CONGREGATION O 2357 E. 75TH STREET	CHICAGO	IL	60649	
ANSHE MIZRACH, CONGREGATION O 627 W. PATTERSON AVENUE	CHICAGO	IL	60613	(312) 525-4034
ANSHE MOTELE O 6520 N. CALIFORNIA AVENUE	CHICAGO	IL	60645	(312) 743-2420

Synagogue / Address	City	State	ZIP	Phone
ANSHE SHOLOM BNAI ISRAEL CONGREGATION O				
540 W. MELROSE STREET	CHICAGO	IL	60657	(312) 248-9200
ANSHIE LUBAVITCH, CONGREGATION O 4928 RIDGEWAY AVENUE	CHICAGO	IL	60625	
ATERES YEHOSHUA CONGREGATION O 2819 W. TOUHY	CHICAGO	IL	60645	(312) 764-1382
AUSTRIAN GALICIAN BETH ISRAEL CONGREGATION T				
3635 WEST DEVON	CHICAGO	IL	60645	
B'NAI DAVID-SHAARE ZEDEK, CONGREGATION C				
2508 W. FITCH AVENUE	CHICAGO	IL	60625	(312) 764-8825
B'NAI JACOB, CONGREGATION C 6200 N. ARTESIAN AVENUE	CHICAGO	IL	60659	(312) 274-1586
B'NAI YAKOV, CONGREGATION O 2700 W. HADDON AVENUE	CHICAGO	IL	60622	
B'NAI ZION, CONGREGATION C 6759 N. GREENVIEW AVENUE	CHICAGO	IL	60626	(312) 465-2161
BETH AM, THE PEOPLE'S SYNAGOGUE R 3480 N. LAKE SHORE	CHICAGO	IL	60657	
BETH DAVID O 6307 NORTH MOZART	CHICAGO	IL	60635	(312) 274-3752
BETH DAVID O 4830 NORTH ST. LOUIS AVENUE	CHICAGO	IL	60625	
BETH EL OF CHICAGO, TEMPLE R 3050 W. TOUHY STREET	CHICAGO	IL	60645	(312) 274-0341
BETH EL OF ROGERS PARK, CONGREGATION O				
7612 N. ROGERS AVENUE	CHICAGO	IL	60626	
BETH HAKNESSETH, CONGREGATION O 5000 NORTH LAWNDALE	CHICAGO	IL	60625	
BETH HAMEDROSH HAGODOL KESSER MAARIV, CONGREGATION				
6418 N. GREENVIEW AVENUE	CHICAGO	IL	60626	(312) 764-5370
BETH ISRAEL ANSHE YANOVA, CONGREGATION O				
1328 W. MORSE AVENUE	CHICAGO	IL	60626	(312) 248-9200
BETH ISRAEL, TEMPLE R 4850 N. BERNARD STREET	CHICAGO	IL	60625	(312) 677-0915
BETH ITZCHOK OF ALBANY PARK, CONGREGATION O				
4645 NORTH DRAKE	CHICAGO	IL	60625	(312) 478-6416
BETH ITZCHOK OF WEST ROGERS PARK, CONGREGATION O				
6716 NORTH WHIPPLE	CHICAGO	IL	60645	(312) 973-2522
BETH JACOB OF ALBANY PARK, CONGREGATION O				
4926 N. KIMBALL AVENUE	CHICAGO	IL	60625	
BETH SHOLOM AHAVAS ACHIM, CONGREGATION O				
5665 N. JERSEY AVENUE	CHICAGO	IL	60659	(312) 267-9055
BETH SHOLOM OF ROGERS PARK, CONGREGATION T				
1233 W. PRATT BLVD	CHICAGO	IL	60626	(312) 743-4160
BNAI DAVID, CONGREGATION C 2626 W. FOSTER AVENUE	CHICAGO	IL	60625	
BNAI ISRAEL, CONGREGATION O 1814 FARWELL AVENUE	CHICAGO	IL	60626	
BNEI RUVEN, CONGREGATION O 6350 N. WHIPPLE STREET	CHICAGO	IL	60659	(312) 743-5434
CENTRAL SYNAGOGUE OF THE SOUTH SIDE HEBREW CONGREGATION C				
30 E. CEDAR STREET	CHICAGO	IL	60611	(312) 787-0450
CHESSED L'AVROHOM NACHLAS DAVID, CONGREGATION O				
6342 N. TROY STREET	CHICAGO	IL	60659	(312) 743-2156
CHEVRA KADISHO MACHZIKAI HADAS O 2040 W. DEVON AVENUE	CHICAGO	IL	60645	(312) 764-8760
CHICAGO COMMUNITY KOLLEL O 6506 N. CALIFORNIA	CHICAGO	IL	60645	(312) 262-4160
CHICAGO LOOP SYNAGOGUE T 16 S. CLARK STREET	CHICAGO	IL	60603	(312) 346-7370
CHICAGO SINAI CONGREGATION R 5350 S. SHORE DRIVE	CHICAGO	IL	60615	(312) 288-1600
CONGREGATION HAKAFA R	CHICAGO	IL		(312) 441-6020
DREXEL HOME TEMPLE R 6140 S. DREXEL AVENUE	CHICAGO	IL	60637	(312) 643-2384
EMANUEL CONGREGATION R 5959 N. SHERIDAN ROAD	CHICAGO	IL	60660	(312) 561-5173
ETHIOPIAN HEBREWS, CONGREGATION OF 6734 SOUTH ABERDEEN	CHICAGO	IL	60621	(312) 874-5332
EZRA-HABONIM, CONGREGATION C 2620 W. TOUHY AVENUE	CHICAGO	IL	60645	(312) 743-0154
EZRAS ISRAEL, CONGREGATION T 7001 N. CALIFORNIA AVENUE	CHICAGO	IL	60645	(312) 764-8320
FREE FRIENDS OF REFUGEES OF EASTERN EUROPE				
6418 N. GREENVIEW	CHICAGO	IL	60626	(312) 274-5123
GARFIELD RIDGE HEBREW CONGREGATION T				
6524 W. ARCHER AVENUE	CHICAGO	IL	60638	(312) 586-7108
K.I.N.S. OF WEST ROGERS PARK, CONGREGATION T				
2800 W. NORTH SHORE AVENUE	CHICAGO	IL	60645	(312) 761-4000
KAM ISAIAH ISRAEL CONGREGATION R 1100 E. HYDE PARK BLVD	CHICAGO	IL	60615	(312) 924-1234
KEHILAT JESHURUN, CONGREGATION C 3707 W. AINSLIE STREET	CHICAGO	IL	60625	(312) 539-7776
KEHILATH JACOB BETH SAMUEL CONGREGATION O				
3701 W. DEVON AVENUE	CHICAGO	IL	60659	(312) 539-7779
KOL-AMI, CONGREGATION R 233 E. ERIE STREET	CHICAGO	IL	60611	(312) 644-6900
KOLLEL TORAS CHESED O 2938 W. ARTHUR	CHICAGO	IL	60645	(312) 262-0666
LAKE SHORE DRIVE SYNAGOGUE T 70 EAST ELM	CHICAGO	IL	60611	(312) 337-6811
LAKEVIEW ANSHE SHOLOM BNAI ISRAEL O 540 W. MELROSE AVENUE	CHICAGO	IL	60613	(312) 248-9200
LAWN MANOR HEBREW CONGREGATION C 6601 S. KEDZIE AVENUE	CHICAGO	IL	60629	(312) 476-2924
LEV SOMEACH, CONGREGATION O 5555 N. BERNARD STREET	CHICAGO	IL	60625	(312) 267-4390
MENORAH TEMPLE R 2800 W. SHERWIN AVENUE	CHICAGO	IL	60645	(312) 761-5700
MEYER & ANNIE HANDELSMAN SYNAGOGUE 2828 PRATT BLVD	CHICAGO	IL	60645	
MIKRO KODESH ANSHE TIKTIN, CONGREGATION O				
2832 W. FOSTER AVENUE	CHICAGO	IL	60625	(312) 784-1010
MISHNA UGMORO, CONGREGATION O 6045 N. CALIFORNIA AVENUE	CHICAGO	IL	60659	(312) 465-1433
MOUNT SINAI, CONGREGATION O 4710 N. KEDZIE AVENUE	CHICAGO	IL	60625	(312) 478-8545
NACHLAS DOVID, CONGREGATION O 3135 W. DEVON AVENUE	CHICAGO	IL	60659	(312) 465-3616
NER TAMID CONGREGATION C 2754 W. ROSEMONT AVENUE	CHICAGO	IL	60659	(312) 465-6090
NORTH SHERIDAN HEBREW CONGREGATION ADATH ISRAEL				
6301 N. SHERIDAN ROAD	CHICAGO	IL	60660	(312) 262-0330
NUSACH ARIE, CONGREGATION O 4706 N. MONTICELLO AVENUE	CHICAGO	IL	60625	(312) 588-9520
OIR ISRAEL, CONGREGATION O 4610 N. KEDZIE AVENUE	CHICAGO	IL	60625	(312) 463-9325
PARK SYNAGOGUE OF CHICAGO, THE O 505 N. MICHIGAN AVENUE	CHICAGO	IL	60611	(312) 467-5928
PARK VIEW HOME C 1401 S. CALIFORNIA AVENUE	CHICAGO	IL	60622	(312) 278-6420
POALIE ZEDECK, CONGREGATION O 2801 WEST ALBION	CHICAGO	IL	60645	(312) 764-5680
RODFEI ZEDEK, CONGREGATION C 5200 HYDE PARK BLVD	CHICAGO	IL	60615	(312) 752-2770
SHAARE TIKVAH, CONGREGATION C 5800 N. KIMBALL AVENUE	CHICAGO	IL	60659	(312) 539-2202
SHAAREI TORAH ANSHEI MAARIV, CONGREGATION O				
2756 W. MORSE AVENUE	CHICAGO	IL	60645	(312) 262-6819
SHEARITH ISRAEL O 2938 W. ARTHUR	CHICAGO	IL	60645	
SHEVET ACHIM, CONGREGATION O 730 W. WAVELAND AVENUE	CHICAGO	IL	60613	
SHOLOM, TEMPLE R 3480 LAKE SHORE DRIVE	CHICAGO	IL	60657	(312) 525-4707
SINAI OF ROGERS PARK, CONGREGATION O 6905 N. SHERIDAN ROAD	CHICAGO	IL	60626	(312) 764-0042
SOUTHSIDE SENIOR ADULT JEWISH CENTER 1642 E. 56TH STREET	CHICAGO	IL	60637	(312) 667-7373
SOUTHTOWN ANSHE EMET CONGREGATION O 8100 S. LOOMIS BLVD	CHICAGO	IL	60605	
SOVEREIGN SYNAGOGUE CONGREGATION KESER TORAH O				
6159 N. KENMORE AVENUE	CHICAGO	IL	60626	(312) 761-9050
SYNAGOGUE OF THE NORTHWEST/HOME FOR AGED O				
6300 NORTH CALIFORNIA AVENUE	CHICAGO	IL	60659	(312) 973-1900
TIFERETH MOSHE, CONGREGATION O 6308 N. FRANCISCO AVENUE	CHICAGO	IL	60659	(312) 764-5322
WARSAW BICKUR CHOLxIM O 3541 WEST PETERSON	CHICAGO	IL	60659	(312) 588-0021
YOUNG ISRAEL OF CHICAGO 4931 KIMBALL STREET	CHICAGO	IL	60659	(312) 478-8650
ISRAEL SYNAGOGUE, CONGREGATION C 949 N. WALNUT STREET	DANVILLE	IL	61832	(217) 442-6643
B'NAI ABRAHAM, TEMPLE R 1326 W. ELDORADO STREET	DECATUR	IL	62522	(217) 429-5740
B'NAI TIKVAH, CONGREGATION C 795 WILMOT ROAD	DEERFIELD	IL	60015	(312) 945-0470
BETH OR, CONGREGATION R 2075 DEERFIELD ROAD BOX 234	DEERFIELD	IL	60015	(312) 945-0477
MORIAH CONGREGATION C 200 HYACINTH LANE	DEERFIELD	IL	60015	(312) 948-5340
INDEPENDENT TEMPLE O 355 BELLAIRE DR	DES PLAINES	IL	60016	(312) 296-5641
MAINE TOWNSHIP JEWISH CONGREGATION C 8800 BALLARD ROAD	DES PLAINES	IL	60016	(312) 297-2006
AGUDAS ACHIM, CONGREGATION 425 N. 88 STREET	EAST ST. LOUIS	IL	62201	
KNESETH ISRAEL, CONGREGATION C 330 DIVISION STREET	ELGIN	IL	60120	(312) 741-5656
AGUDATH JACOB, CONGREGATION T 633 W. HOWARD	EVANSTON	IL	60202	(312) 475-9317
BETH EMETH, THE FREE SYNAGOGUE R 1224 DEMPSTER	EVANSTON	IL	60202	(312) 869-4230
CHABAD HOUSE O 2014 ORRINGTON	EVANSTON	IL	60201	(312) 869-8060
JEWISH RECONSTRUCTIONIST CONGREGATION RE				
2525 HARTREY AVENUE	EVANSTON	IL	60201	(312) 328-7678
MIKDOSH EL HAGRO HEBREW CENTER C 303 DODGE AVENUE	EVANSTON	IL	60202	(312) 328-9677
SEPHARDIC CONGREGATION O 1819 W. HOWARD	EVANSTON	IL	60202	(312) 475-9287
ANSHE SHOLOM, TEMPLE 707 ELM STREET	FLOSSMOOR	IL	60422	
SHOLOM, TEMPLE R				
CORNER NORTH & MONROE STREETS, P.O. BOX 501	GALESBURG	IL	61401	(309) 343-3323
AM SHALOM R 614 SHERIDAN ROAD	GLENCOE	IL	61401	(312) 835-4800
NORTH SHORE CONGREGATION ISRAEL R 1185 SHERIDAN ROAD	GLENCOE	IL	60022	(312) 835-4800
AM CHAI, CONGREGATION C 292 NORTH BRANDON	GLENDALE HEIGHTS	IL	60137	(312) 980-6699
B'NAI JEHOSHUA BETH ELOHIM R 901 MILWAUKEE AVENUE	GLENVIEW	IL	60025	(312) 729-7575
ISRAEL, TEMPLE R 1414 WEST DELMAR	GODFREY	IL	62035	(618) 466-4641
UNITED HEBREW CONGREGATION				
C/O LOUIS COHEN 2300 ILLINOIS AVENUE	GRANITE CITY	IL	62040	
UNITED HEBREW TEMPLE OF BENTON R 120 N. PARK AVENUE	HERRIN	IL	62948	(618) 439-3521
B'NAI TORAH, CONGREGATION R 2789 OAK STREET	HIGHLAND PARK	IL	60035	(312) 433-7100
LAKESIDE CONGREGATION FOR REFORM JUDAISM R				
1221 CITY LINE ROAD	HIGHLAND PARK	IL	60035	(312) 432-7950
NORTH SUBURBAN CHABAD O 1871 SHEAHEN COURT	HIGHLAND PARK	IL	60035	(312) 433-1567
NORTH SUBURBAN SYNAGOGUE BETH EL C				
1175 SHERIDAN ROAD	HIGHLAND PARK	IL	60035	(312) 432-8900
SOLEL, CONGREGATION R 1301 CLAVEY ROAD	HIGHLAND PARK	IL	60035	(312) 433-3555
BETH TIKVA CONGREGATION R 300 HILLCREST BLVD	HOFFMAN ESTATES	IL	60195	(312) 885-4545
B'NAI YEHUDA, TEMPLE R 1424 W. 183RD STREET	HOMEWOOD	IL	60430	(312) 799-4110
JOLIET JEWISH CONGREGATION C 250 N. MIDLAND	JOLIET	IL	60435	(815) 725-7078
B'NAI ISRAEL, TEMPLE C 600 S. HARRISON AVENUE	KANKAKEE	IL	60901	(815) 933-7814
OR SHALOM R P.O. BOX 773	LIBERTYVILLE	IL	60048	(312) 680-9696
BETH TORAH O 4721 WEST TOUHY	LINCOLNWOOD	IL	60646	
LINCOLNWOOD JEWISH CONGREGATION O				
7117 N. CRAWFORD AVENUE	LINCOLNWOOD	IL	60646	(312) 676-0491
YEHUDAH MOSHE, CONGREGATION O 4721 W. TOUHY AVENUE	LINCOLNWOOD	IL	60646	(312) 673-5870
ETZ CHAIM, CONGREGATION R 1710 S. HIGHLAND AVENUE	LOMBARD	IL	60148	(312) 627-3912
BETH JUDEA, CONGREGATION BOX 5304 RFD	LONG GROVE	IL	60047	(312) 634-0777
CHAI, TEMPLE R ROUTE 6, P.O. BOX 423	LONG GROVE	IL	60047	(312) 537-1771
MATTOON JEWISH CENTER R P.O. BOX 881	MATTOON	IL	61938	(312) 537-1771
ADAS SHALOM CONGREGATION T 6945 DEMPSTER	MORTON GROVE	IL	60053	(312) 965-1880
NORTHWEST SUBURBAN JEWISH CONGREGATION C				
7800 WEST LYONS	MORTON GROVE	IL	60053	(312) 965-0900
BETH AM R 2005 KIOWA LANE	MT. PROSPECT	IL	60056	(312) 827-7599
CONGREGATION BETH SHALOM RE 21 EAST FRANKLIN AVENUE	NAPERVILLE	IL	60540	(312) 961-1818
BETH SHALOM C 3433 WALTERS AVENUE	NORTHBROOK	IL	60062	(312) 498-4100
B'NAI ISRAEL 601 SKOKIE BLVD.	NORTHBROOK	IL	60062	(312) 480-0092
EZRA HABONIM OF NORTHBROOK C 2095 LANDWEHR RD.	NORTHBROOK	IL	60062	(312) 480-1690
AM YISROEL CONSERVATIVE CONGREGATION OF THE NORTH SHORE				
4 HAPP ROAD	NORTHFIELD	IL	60093	(312) 446-7215
JEREMIAH TEMPLE R P.O. BOX N 193, 937 HAPP ROAD	NORTHFIELD	IL	60093	(312) 441-5760
CONGREGATION SHIR AMI C P.O. BOX 1094	OAK PARK	IL	60304	(312) 386-4408
OAK PARK TEMPLE R 1235 N. HARLEM AVENUE	OAK PARK	IL	60302	(312) 386-3937
ANSHE SHOLOM, TEMPLE - BETH TORAH R				
20820 WESTERN AVENUE	OLYMPIA FIELDS	IL	60461	(312) 748-6010
AM ECHAD, CONGREGATION C 160 WESTWOOD	PARK FOREST	IL	60466	(312) 747-9513
BETH SHOLOM, CONGREGATION R 1 DOGWOOD	PARK FOREST	IL	60466	(312) 747-3040
AGUDAS ACHIM, CONGREGATION C 3616 N. SHERIDAN ROAD	PEORIA	IL	61604	(309) 688-5720
ANSHAI EMETH, CONGREGATION R 5614 N. UNIVERSITY STREET	PEORIA	IL	61614	(309) 691-3323
B'NAI SHOLOM TEMPLE C 427 NORTH 9TH	QUINCY	IL	62301	(217) 222-8532
WEST SUBURBAN TEMPLE HAR ZION C 1040 N. HARLEM AVENUE	RIVER FOREST	IL	60305	(312) 366-9000
TRI-CITY JEWISH CENTER C 2715 30TH STREET	ROCK ISLAND	IL	61201	(309) 788-3426
BETH EL, TEMPLE R 1203 COMANCHE DRIVE	ROCKFORD	IL	61107	(815) 398-5020
OHAVE SHOLOM SYNAGOGUE C 3730 GUILFORD ROAD	ROCKFORD	IL	61107	(815) 226-4900
OR CHADASH TRADITIONAL CONGREGATION T				
664 S. ROSELLE RD.	SCHAUMBERG	IL	60172	(312) 529-6390
B'NAI EMUNAH, CONGREGATION C				
9131 NILES CENTER ROAD, P.O. BOX 272	SKOKIE	IL	60076	(312) 674-9292
BENE SHALOM, CONGREGATION - HEBREW ASSN. FOR THE DEAF R				
4435 OAKTON	SKOKIE	IL	60076	(312) 677-3330
BETH ISRAEL, TEMPLE R 3939 W. HOWARD STREET	SKOKIE	IL	60076	(312) 675-0951
CHABAD OF SKOKIE/LUBAVITCH - ILLINOIS O 4043 DEMPSTER	SKOKIE	IL	60076	(312) 677-1770
HEBREW THEOLOGICAL COLLEGE O 7135 CARPENTER ROAD	SKOKIE	IL	60077	(312) 267-9800
HYDE PARK HEBREW CENTER T 3661 DAVIS STREET	SKOKIE	IL	60076	
IRAN HEBREW CONGREGATION O 3820 MAIN STREET	SKOKIE	IL	60076	(312) 674-5444
JUDEA MIZPAH, TEMPLE R 8610 NILES CENTER ROAD	SKOKIE	IL	60077	(312) 676-1566
KOL EMETH C 5130 W. TOUHY AVENUE	SKOKIE	IL	60077	(312) 673-3370

Congregation / Address	City	State	ZIP	Phone
MIZPAH, TEMPLE R 8610 NILES CENTER ROAD	SKOKIE	**IL**	60077	(312) 676-1566
NILES TOWNSHIP JEWISH CONGREGATION, THE C/RE 4500 DEMPSTER STREET	SKOKIE	**IL**	60076	(312) 675-4141
OR TORAH, CONGREGATION O 3740 WEST DEMPSTER	SKOKIE	**IL**	60076	(312) 674-3695
SKOKIE CENTRAL TRADITIONAL CONGREGATION T 4040 MAIN STREET	SKOKIE	**IL**	60076	(312) 674-4117
SKOKIE VALLEY TRADITIONAL SYNAGOGUE 8825 E. PRAIRIE ROAD	SKOKIE	**IL**	60076	(312) 674-3473
B'RITH SHALOM, TEMPLE R 1004 S. 4TH STREET	SPRINGFIELD	**IL**	62703	(217) 525-1360
ISRAEL, TEMPLE C 1140 WEST GOVERNOR	SPRINGFIELD	**IL**	62704	(217) 546-2481
SHOLOM, TEMPLE R 21956 RIDGE ROAD, ROUTE #2	STERLING	**IL**	61081	(815) 625-2599
AM ECHOD C 1500 SUNSET AVENUE	WAUKEGAN	**IL**	60085	(312) 336-9110
B'NAI ISRAEL OF PROVISO, CONGREGATION O 10216 KITCHENER	WESTCHESTER	**IL**	60153	(312) 343-0288
B'NAI SHALOM TRADITIONAL P.O. BOX 173	WHEELING	**IL**	60090	(312) 541-1460
BETH HILLEL CONGREGATION C 3220 BIG TREE LANE	WILMETTE	**IL**	60091	(312) 256-1213
B'NAI SHOLOM CONGREGATION C 4508 BARING AVENUE	EAST CHICAGO	**IN**	46312	(219) 397-3106
ADATH B'NAI ISRAEL R 3600 WASHINGTON AVENUE	EVANSVILLE	**IN**	47715	(812) 425-8222
ADATH ISRAEL, TEMPLE C 3600 WASHINGTON AVENUE	EVANSVILLE	**IN**	47715	(812) 477-1577
WASHINGTON AVENUE TEMPLE R 100 WASHINGTON AVENUE	EVANSVILLE	**IN**	47713	
ACHDUTH VESHOLOM, CONGREGATION R 5200 OLD MILL ROAD	FORT WAYNE	**IN**	46807	(219) 744-4245
B'NAI JACOB, CONGREGATION C 2340 FAIRFIELD AVENUE	FORT WAYNE	**IN**	46807	(219) 744-2183
ISRAEL, TEMPLE R 601 N. MONTGOMERY STREET	GARY	**IN**	46403	(219) 938-5232
BETH EL, TEMPLE R 6947 HOHMAN AVENUE	HAMMOND	**IN**	46324	(219) 932-3754
BETH ISRAEL, CONGREGATION C 7105 HOHMAN AVENUE	HAMMOND	**IN**	46324	(219) 931-1312
KNESETH ISRAEL, CONGREGATION C 7105 HOHMAN AVENUE	HAMMOND	**IN**	46324	(219) 931-1312
B'NAI TORAH, CONGREGATION O 6510 HOOVER ROAD	INDIANAPOLIS	**IN**	46260	(317) 253-5253
BETH EL ZEDEK, CONGREGATION C/RE 600 W. 70TH STREET	INDIANAPOLIS	**IN**	46260	(317) 253-3441
CHABAD LUBAVITCH O 1037 GOLF LANE	INDIANAPOLIS	**IN**	46260	(317) 251-5573
INDIANAPOLIS HEBREW CONGREGATION R 6501 N. MERIDIAN STREET	INDIANAPOLIS	**IN**	46260	(317) 255-6647
UNITED ORTHODOX HEBREW CONGREGATION O 5879 CENTRAL AVENUE	INDIANAPOLIS	**IN**	46220	(317) 253-4591
B'NAI ISRAEL, TEMPLE R 618 W. SUPERIOR STREET, P.O. BOX 1290	KOKOMO	**IN**	46901	(317) 452-0383
ISRAEL, TEMPLE R 620 CUMBERLAND AVENUE	LAFAYETTE	**IN**	47906	(317) 463-3455
SONS OF ABRAHAM, CONGREGATION T 661 N. 7TH STREET	LAFAYETTE	**IN**	47901	(317) 742-2113
SINAI TEMPLE R 1001 EUCLID AVENUE	MARION	**IN**	46952	(317) 664-4453
SINAI TEMPLE R 2800 FRANKLIN STREET	MICHIGAN CITY	**IN**	46360	(219) 874-4477
BETH EL TEMPLE R P.O. BOX 2395, 525 W. JACKSON STREET	MUNCIE	**IN**	47302	(317) 288-4662
BETH BORUK TEMPLE R 3040 PARKWOOD DRIVE	RICHMOND	**IN**	47374	(317) 962-6501
BETH EL, TEMPLE R 305 W. MADISON STREET	SOUTH BEND	**IN**	46601	(219) 234-4402
B'NAI ISRAEL CONGREGATION RE POB 1091	SOUTH BEND	**IN**	46624	(219) 289-5636
HEBREW ORTHODOX CONGREGATION O 3207 SOUTH HIGH STREET	SOUTH BEND	**IN**	46614	(219) 291-4239
SINAI SYNAGOGUE O 1102 E. LASALLE AVENUE	SOUTH BEND	**IN**	46617	(219) 234-8584
SONS OF ISRAEL, CONGREGATION O 420 S. WILLIAM STREET	SOUTH BEND	**IN**	46601	(219) 289-5636
UNITED HEBREW CONGREGATIONS R 540 S. 6TH STREET	TERRE HAUTE	**IN**	47807	(812) 232-5988
ISRAEL, TEMPLE C 1405 EAST EVANS	VALPARAISO	**IN**	46383	(219) 464-0159
ISRAEL, TEMPLE R 620 CUMBERLAND	WEST LAFAYETTE	**IN**	47906	(317) 463-3455
B'NAI JUDAH, CONGREGATION C P.O. BOX 233, 1549 DAVIS AVENUE	WHITTING	**IN**	46394	(317) 659-0797
MANHATTAN JEWISH CONGREGATION R 1509 WREATH	MANHATTAN	**KS**	66502	(913) 539-8462
BETH EL, TEMPLE R 9400 NALL AVENUE	OVERLAND PARK	**KS**	66207	(913) 642-8707
YOUNG ISRAEL OF OVERLAND PARK 8716 WOODWARD	OVERLAND PARK	**KS**	66212	(913) 341-1597
OHEV SHOLOM, CONGREGATION O 5311 W. 75TH STREET	PRAIRIE VILLAGE	**KS**	66208	(913) 642-6460
BETH SHOLOM, TEMPLE R 4200 MUNSON	TOPEKA	**KS**	66604	(913) 272-6040
EMANU-EL, TEMPLE R 7011 EAST CENTRAL	WICHITA	**KS**	67206	(316) 684-5148
HEBREW CONGREGATION O 1850 WOODLAWN	WICHITA	**KS**	67208	(316) 685-1339
ADATH ISRAEL, TEMPLE R 124 N. ASHLAND AVENUE	LEXINGTON	**KY**	40502	(606) 266-3251
LEXINGTON HAVURAH C 3379 SUTHERLAND DRIVE	LEXINGTON	**KY**	40502	(606) 272-1459
OHAVAY ZION, CONGREGATION T 120 W. MAXWELL STREET	LEXINGTON	**KY**	40508	
ADATH ISRAEL, CONGREGATION R 834 S. THIRD STREET	LOUISVILLE	**KY**	40203	
ADATH JESHURUN, CONGREGATION C 2401 WOODBOURNE AVENUE	LOUISVILLE	**KY**	40205	(502) 458-5359
ANSHEI SFARD, CONGREGATION O 3700 DUTCHMANS LANE	LOUISVILLE	**KY**	40205	(502) 451-3122
CHABAD LUBAVITCH O 2607 LANDOR AVENUE	LOUISVILLE	**KY**	40205	(502) 459-1770
KENESETH ISRAEL CONGREGATION O P.O. BOX 5295	LOUISVILLE	**KY**	40205	(502) 459-2780
SHALOM, TEMPLE R 4220 TAYLORSVILLE ROAD	LOUISVILLE	**KY**	40220	(502) 458-4739
TEMPLE, THE R 5101 BROWNSBORD ROAD	LOUISVILLE	**KY**	40222	(502) 423-1818
B'NAI ISRAEL SYNAGOGUE C P.O. BOX 5086, VANCE & HICKORY STREETS	ALEXANDRIA	**LA**	71301	(318) 445-4586
GEMILUTH CHASSODIM R P.O. BOX 863, 2021 TURNER STREET	ALEXANDRIA	**LA**	71301	(318) 445-3655
B'NAI ISRAEL, TEMPLE R 3354 KLEINERT AVENUE	BATON ROUGE	**LA**	70806	(504) 343-0111
LIBERAL SYNAGOGUE R 9111 JEFFERSON HIGHWAY	BATON ROUGE	**LA**	70800	(504) 924-6773
BETH EL JEWISH CENTER, CONGREGATION P.O. BOX 1207	BOGALUSA	**LA**	70427	
RODEPH SHOLOM, TEMPLE R 603 LEE AVENUE, P.O. BOX 2564	LAFAYETTE	**LA**	70501	(318) 234-3760
YESHURUN SYNAGOGUE R P.O. BOX 53711 OCS, 1520 KALISTE SALOOM ROAD	LAFAYETTE	**LA**	70505	(318) 984-1775
SINAI, TEMPLE R 713 HODGES STREET	LAKE CHARLES	**LA**	70601	(318) 439-2866
GATES OF PRAYER R 4000 W. ESPLANADE AVENUE	METAIRIE	**LA**	70002	(504) 885-2600
TIKVAT SHALOM CONSERVATIVE CONGREGATION C 3737 W. ESPLANADE AVENUE	METAIRIE	**LA**	70002	(504) 899-1144
YOUNG ISRAEL OF METAIRIE 4428 COURTLAND DRIVE	METAIRIE	**LA**	70002	(504) 887-6997
B'NAI ISRAEL, CONGREGATION R 2400 ORELL PLACE	MONROE	**LA**	71201	(318) 387-0730
SHAARE ZEDEK, TEMPLE R P.O. BOX 329	MORGAN CITY	**LA**	70380	(318) 385-2552
GATES OF PRAYER, CONGREGATION R P.O. BOX 488	NEW IBERIA	**LA**	70560	(318) 364-1218
A.A. ANSHE SFARD, CONGREGATION O 2230 CARONDELET STREET	NEW ORLEANS	**LA**	70130	(504) 522-4714
BETH ISRAEL, CONGREGATION O 7000 CANAL BLVD	NEW ORLEANS	**LA**	70124	(504) 283-4366
CHABAD HOUSE O 7037 FRERET STREET	NEW ORLEANS	**LA**	70018	(504) 866-5164
CHEVRA THILIM, CONGREGATION O 4429 S. CLAIBORNE AVENUE	NEW ORLEANS	**LA**	70125	(504) 895-7987
GATES OF PRAYER, CONGREGATION R 4000 W. ESPLANADE AVENUE	NEW ORLEANS	**LA**	70119	(504) 885-2600
SINAI, TEMPLE R 6227 ST. CHARLES AVENUE	NEW ORLEANS	**LA**	70118	(504) 861-3693
TIKVAT SHALOM CONGREGATION C 923 NAPOLEON AVENUE	NEW ORLEANS	**LA**	70115	(504) 889-1144
TOURO SYNAGOGUE R ST. CHARLES AT GENERAL PERSHING	NEW ORLEANS	**LA**	70115	(504) 895-4843
AGUDATH ACHIM, CONGREGATION C 9401 VILLAGE GREEN DRIVE	SHREVEPORT	**LA**	71115	(318) 797-6401
B'NAI ZION CONGREGATION R 175 SOUTHFIELD ROAD	SHREVEPORT	**LA**	71105	(318) 861-2122
SHAARAY SHALOM, CONGREGATION R P.O. BOX 15	ACCORD	**MA**	02018	(617) 749-8103
CHABAD HOUSE O 30 NORTH HADLEY ROAD	AMHERST	**MA**	01002	(413) 253-9040
EMANUEL, TEMPLE R 7 HAGGETTS POND ROAD	ANDOVER	**MA**	01810	(617) 470-1356
ISRAEL, TEMPLE C 107 WALNUT STREET	ATHOL	**MA**	01331	(617) 249-9481
AGUDAS ACHIM, CONGREGATION C TONER & KELLEY BLVDS	ATTLEBORO	**MA**	02703	(617) 222-2243
ANSHE SHOLOM, CONGREGATION	AYER	**MA**	01432	
BETH CHAVERIM, CONGREGATION 16 YVONNE ROAD	BELLINGHAM	**MA**	02019	
BETH EL TEMPLE CENTER R 2 CONCORD AVENUE	BELMONT	**MA**	02178	(617) 484-6668
B'NAI ABRAHAM, TEMPLE C 200 E. LOTHROP STREET	BEVERLY	**MA**	01915	(617) 927-3211
OHAV SHOLOM, CONGREGATION O 3 BECKFORD STREET	BEVERLY	**MA**	01915	
ASSOCIATED SYNAGOGUES CHAPEL 177 TREMONT STREET	BOSTON	**MA**	02111	(617) 742-3412
B'NAI JACOB, CONGREGATION 100 BLUE HILLS PARKWAY	BOSTON	**MA**	02187	(617) 731-5290
CHABAD HOUSE O 491 COMMONWEALTH AVENUE	BOSTON	**MA**	02215	(617) 424-1190
CHARLES RIVER PARK SYNAGOGUE O 55 MARTHA ROAD (AMY CT)	BOSTON	**MA**	02114	(617) 523-0453
ISRAEL, TEMPLE R LONGWOOD AVENUE AT PLYMOUTH STREET	BOSTON	**MA**	02215	(617) 566-3960
B'NAI SHALOM, TEMPLE C 41 STORES AVENUE	BRAINTREE	**MA**	02184	(617) 843-3687
AGUDATH ISRAEL OF BOSTON 81 WALLINGFORD ROAD	BRIGHTON	**MA**	02135	(617) 254-0260
ANSHE LUBAVITCH, CONGREGATION O 241 CHESTNUT HILL ROAD	BRIGHTON	**MA**	02135	(617) 782-8340
B'NAI MOSHE, TEMPLE C 1845 COMMONWEALTH AVENUE	BRIGHTON	**MA**	02135	(617) 254-3620
BETH DAVID, CONGREGATION O 64 COREY ROAD	BRIGHTON	**MA**	02460	
KADIMAH-TORAS MOSHE, CONGREGATION O 113 WASHINGTON STREET	BRIGHTON	**MA**	02135	(617) 254-1333
AGUDAS ACHIM, CONGREGATION O 144 BELMONT AVENUE	BROCKTON	**MA**	02401	(617) 583-0717
BETH EMUNAH, TEMPLE C TORREY & PEARL STREETS	BROCKTON	**MA**	02401	(617) 583-5810
ISRAEL, TEMPLE R 184 W. ELM STREET	BROCKTON	**MA**	02401	(617) 587-4130
BETH ISRAEL, CONGREGATION 114 WILLARD ROAD	BROOKLINE	**MA**	02146	
BETH PINCHAS, CONGREGATION O 1710 BEACON STREET	BROOKLINE	**MA**	02146	(617) 566-9182
BETH ZION, TEMPLE C 1566 BEACON STREET	BROOKLINE	**MA**	02146	(617) 566-8171
CHABAD-LUBAVITCH O 9 PRESCOTT STREET	BROOKLINE	**MA**	02146	
CHAI ODOM, CONGREGATION O 77 ENGLEWOOD AVENUE	BROOKLINE	**MA**	02146	(617) 277-8794
EMETH, TEMPLE 194 GROVE	BROOKLINE	**MA**	02146	
GREATER BOSTON RECONSTRUCTIONIST HAVURAH POB 1197	BROOKLINE	**MA**	02146	(617) 964-2791
KADDISHA OF BOSTON, CONGREGATION 156 LONGWOOD AVENUE	BROOKLINE	**MA**	02146	
KEHILLATH ISRAEL, CONGREGATION C 384 HARVARD STREET	BROOKLINE	**MA**	02146	(617) 277-9155
OHABEI SHALOM, TEMPLE R 1187 BEACON STREET	BROOKLINE	**MA**	02146	(617) 277-6610
SEPHARDIC CONGREGATION OF GREATER BOSTON O C/O Y.I. BROOKLINE, 62 GREEN STREET	BROOKLINE	**MA**	02147	(617) 734-0276
SINAI, TEMPLE R 50 SEWALL AVENUE	BROOKLINE	**MA**	02146	(617) 277-5888
YOUNG ISRAEL OF BROOKLINE 62 GREEN STREET	BROOKLINE	**MA**	02146	(617) 734-0276
SHALOM EMETH, TEMPLE R P.O. BOX 216	BURLINGTON	**MA**	01803	(617) 272-7454
ASHKENAZ, TEMPLE C 8 TREMONT STREET	CAMBRIDGE	**MA**	02139	
BETH SHALOM, TEMPLE 8 TREMONT STREET	CAMBRIDGE	**MA**	02139	
BETH ABRAHAM, TEMPLE C 1301 WASHINGTON STREET	CANTON	**MA**	02021	
BETH DAVID OF SOUTH SHORE, TEMPLE R 250 RANDOLPH	CANTON	**MA**	02021	
SHALOM, CONGREGATION RICHARDSON ROAD	CHELMSFORD	**MA**	01824	
AGUDAS SHALOM, CONGREGATION 145 WALNUT STREET #265	CHELSEA	**MA**	02150	(617) 884-8668
AHAVAS ACHIM ANSHE SFARD, CONGREGATION O 48 WASHINGTON AVENUE	CHELSEA	**MA**	02150	(617) 884-7945
ELM STREET SYNAGOGUE 48 WASHINGTON AVENUE	CHELSEA	**MA**	02150	
EMANUEL, TEMPLE C 16 CARY AVENUE	CHELSEA	**MA**	02150	
SHAARE ZION, CONGREGATION O 76 ORANGE STREET	CHELSEA	**MA**	02150	
SHOMREI LINATH HAZEDEK, CONGREGATION O 140 SHURTLEFF STREET	CHELSEA	**MA**	02150	(617) 884-9443
YOUNG ISRAEL OF CHELSEA 40 CRESCENT AVENUE	CHELSEA	**MA**	02150	(617) 889-2992
EMETH, TEMPLE C 194 GROVE STREET	CHESTNUT HILL	**MA**	02167	(617) 738-5344
MISHKAN TEFILA, CONGREGATION C 300 HAMMOND POND PARKWAY	CHESTNUT HILL	**MA**	02167	(617) 332-7770
SHAARI ZEDECK, CONGREGATION C WATER STREET	CLINTON	**MA**	01510	
SONS OF ISRAEL, CONGREGATION O 43 W. MAIN STREET	DUDLEY	**MA**	01570	
TIFERETH ISRAEL COMMUNITY CENTRE, CONGREGATION O 34 MALDEN STREET	EVERETT	**MA**	02149	
ADAS ISRAEL, CONGREGATION O 1647 ROBESON	FALL RIVER	**MA**	02720	(617) 674-9761
AGUDAS MACHZIKAY HORAV, CONGREGATION O 470 MADISON STREET	FALL RIVER	**MA**	02720	
AMERICAN BROTHERS OF ISRAEL, CONGREGATION O P.O. BOX 1215	FALL RIVER	**MA**	02722	
BETH EL, TEMPLE C 385 HIGH STREET	FALL RIVER	**MA**	02720	(617) 674-3529
FALMOUTH JEWISH CONGREGATION, THE P.O. BOX 9	FALMOUTH	**MA**	02541	
AGUDATH ACHIM, CONGREGATION C 122 LINCOLN STREET	FITCHBURG	**MA**	01420	
BAIS CHABAD, CONGREGATION O 74 JOSEPH ROAD	FRAMINGHAM	**MA**	01761	(617) 877-8888
BETH AM, TEMPLE R 300 PLEASANT STREET	FRAMINGHAM	**MA**	01701	(617) 872-8300
BETH SHOLOM, TEMPLE C PAMELA ROAD	FRAMINGHAM	**MA**	01701	(617) 877-2540
OHAVE SHOLOM, CONGREGATION C 152 PLEASANT STREET	GARDNER	**MA**	01440	(617) 632-2779
AHAVATH ACHIM, TEMPLE C 86 MIDDLE STREET	GLOUCESTER	**MA**	01930	(617) 281-0739
LOVE OF PEACE, CONGREGATION R 29 NORTH STREET	GREAT BARRINGTON	**MA**	01230	
GREENFIELD HEBREW CONGREGATION C 89 BURNHAM ROAD	GREENFIELD	**MA**	01301	
ISRAEL OF GREENFIELD, INC., TEMPLE C 27 PIERCE STREET	GREENFIELD	**MA**	01301	(413) 773-5884
EMANU-EL, TEMPLE R 514 MAIN STREET	HAVERHILL	**MA**	01830	(617) 373-3861
SHA'ARAY SHALOM, CONGREGATION 1112 MAIN STREET	HINGHAM	**MA**	02043	
BETH TORAH, TEMPLE R WASHINGTON STREET	HOLLISTON	**MA**	01746	
RODPHEY SHOLOM, CONGREGATION O 1800 NORTHAMPTON STREET	HOLYOKE	**MA**	01040	(413) 533-6556
SONS OF ZION, CONGREGATION C 378 MAPLE STREET	HOLYOKE	**MA**	01040	(413) 534-3369
BETH SHOLOM, TEMPLE C 600 NANTASKET AVENUE	HULL	**MA**	02045	(617) 925-0091
ISRAEL OF NANTASKET, TEMPLE SAMOSET AVENUE & WILSON STREET	HULL	**MA**	02045	
CAPE COD SYNAGOGUE R 145 WINTER STREET, P.O. BOX 61	HYANNIS	**MA**	02601	(617) 775-2988
ADAS HADRATH ISRAEL, TEMPLE C 28 ARLINGTON STREET	HYDE PARK	**MA**	02136	(617) 364-2661
GEORGETOWN, CONGREGATION O 412 GEORGETOWN DRIVE	HYDE PARK	**MA**	02136	
ANSHAI SFARD AND SONS OF ISRAEL, CONGREGATION C 492 LOWELL STREET	LAWRENCE	**MA**	01841	(617) 686-0391

ANSHAI SHOLOM, CONGREGATION O 411 HAMPSHIRE STREET.......... LAWRENCE **MA** 01841 (617) 683-4544
EMANUEL, TEMPLE R 483 LOWELL STREET .... LAWRENCE **MA** 01841 (413) 682-8443
SONS OF ISRAEL, CONGREGATION 380 ELM STREET .... LAWRENCE **MA** 01841
AGUDAT ACHIM C 268 WASHINGTON STREET .... LEOMINSTER **MA** 01453 (617) 534-6121
CHABAD-LUBAVITCH O 9 BURLINGTON STREET.......... LEXINGTON **MA** 02173 (617) 863-8656
EMUNAH, TEMPLE C 9 PIPER ROAD .... LEXINGTON **MA** 02139 (617) 861-0300
ISAIAH, TEMPLE R 55 LINCOLN STREET.......... LEXINGTON **MA** 02173 (617) 862-7160
B'NAI JACOB C 2 EUNICE DRIVE .... LONGMEADOW **MA** 01106 (413) 567-0058
BETH ISRAEL, CONGREGATION 1280 WILLIAMS STREET .... LONGMEADOW **MA** 01106 (413) 567-3210
CHABAD-LUBAVITCH O 1148 CONVERSE STREET .... LONGMEADOW **MA** 01106
JEWISH NURSING HOME OF WESTERN MASSACHUSETTS O
770 CONVERSE STREET .... LONGMEADOW **MA** 01106 (413) 567-6211
BETH EL, TEMPLE C 105 PRINCETON BLVD .... LOWELL **MA** 01851 (617) 453-0073
EMANUEL, TEMPLE R 101 W. FOREST STREET.......... LOWELL **MA** 01851 (617) 454-1372
MONTEFIORE SYNAGOGUE O 460 WESTFORD AVENUE .... LOWELL **MA** 01851 (617) 455-5264
AHABAT SHOLOM, CONGREGATION O 151 OCEAN STREET.......... LYNN **MA** 01902 (617) 595-9492
ANSHE SFARD, CONGREGATION O 150 S. COMMON STREET.......... LYNN **MA** 01905
CHEVRA TEHILLEM, CONGREGATION O 12 BREED STREET .... LYNN **MA** 01902 (617) 598-2964
AGUDAS ACHIM, CONGREGATION T 160 HARVARD STREET .... MALDEN **MA** 01248
BETH ISRAEL, CONGREGATION O 10 DEXTER STREET .... MALDEN **MA** 02148 (617) 322-5686
EZRATH ISRAEL, TEMPLE C 245 BRYANT STREET .... MALDEN **MA** 02148 (617)322-7205
TEFERETH ISRAEL, TEMPLE R 3539 SALEM STREET .... MALDEN **MA** 02148 (617) 322-2794
YOUNG ISRAEL OF MALDEN 45 HOLYOKE AVENUE .... MALDEN **MA** 02148 (617) 322-9438
EMANU-EL, TEMPLE R 393 ATLANTIC AVENUE .... MARBLEHEAD **MA** 01945 (617) 631-9300
SINAI, TEMPLE C 1 COMMUNITY ROAD .... MARBLEHEAD **MA** 01945 (617) 631-7539
EMANUEL, TEMPLE C 150 BERLIN ROAD, P.O. BOX 596 .... MARLBOROUGH **MA** 01752 (617) 485-7565
OHEL TORAH, CONGREGATION O 149 GREENFIELD ROAD.......... MATTAPAN **MA** 02126
SHALOM, TEMPLE - MEDFORD JEWISH COMMUNITY CENTER C
475 WINTHROP STREET .... MEDFORD **MA** 02155 (617) 396-3262
AGUDATH ACHIM, CONGREGATION C 13 HOLLISTON STREET.......... MEDWAY **MA** 02053
MELROSE JEWISH CENTER R 21 E. FOSTER STREET .... MELROSE **MA** 02176 (617) 665-4520
BETH SHALOM-MILFORD HEBREW ASSOCIATION, CONGREGATION O
P.O. BOX 30 PINE STREET .... MILFORD **MA** 01757
HOUSE OF JACOB, CONGREGATION O VILLAGE STREET .... MILLIS **MA** 02054
B'NAI JACOB, CONGREGATION O 159 TOURO LANE .... MILTON **MA** 02186 (617) 698-9649
CHABAD-LUBAVITCH O 68 SMITH ROAD .... MILTON **MA** 02186
SHALOM HOUSE 68 SMITH ROAD .... MILTON **MA** 02186 (617) 333-0477
SHALOM OF MILTON, TEMPLE C 180 BLUE HILL AVENUE.......... MILTON **MA** 02186 (617) 698-3394
ISRAEL OF NATICK, TEMPLE C 145 HARTFORD STREET .... NATICK **MA** 01760 (617) 653-8591
ALIYAH, TEMPLE C 1664 CENTRAL AVENUE .... NEEDHAM **MA** 01292 (617) 444-8522
BETH SHALOM, TEMPLE R HIGHLAND AVENUE AT WEBSTER STREET.......... NEEDHAM **MA** 02194 (617) 444-0077
AHAVATH ACHIM, CONGREGATION O 385 COUNTY STREET .... NEW BEDFORD **MA** 02740 (617) 994-1760
TIFERETH ISRAEL CONGREGATION C 145 BROWNELL AVENUE .... NEW BEDFORD **MA** 02740 (617) 997-3171
AHAVAS ACHIM, CONGREGATION O
OLIVE & WASHINGTON STREETS.......... NEWBURYPORT **MA** 01950
BETH EL-ATERETH ISRAEL, CONGREGATION 561 WARD .... NEWTON **MA** 02159 (617) 244-7233
CHEVRA SHA'AS, CONGREGATION O 35 MORSELAND AVENUE .... NEWTON **MA** 02159
REYIM, TEMPLE C 1860 WASHINGTON STREET.......... NEWTON **MA** 02166 (617) 527-2410
SHALOM, TEMPLE R 175 TEMPLE STREET.......... NEWTON **MA** 02165 (617) 332-9550
BETH AVODAH, TEMPLE R 45 PUDDING STONE LANE .... NEWTON CENTER **MA** 02159 (617) 527-0045
BETH EL - ATERETH ISRAEL O 561 WARD STREET.......... NEWTON CENTER **MA** 02159 (617) 244-7233
EMANUEL, TEMPLE C 385 WARD STREET.......... NEWTON CENTER **MA** 02159 (617) 332-5770
SHAAREI TEFILLAH CONGREGATION O
35 MORSELAND AVENUE .... NEWTON CENTER **MA** 02159 (617) 527-7637
BETH ISRAEL, CONGREGATION C 265 CHURCH STREET .... NORTH ADAMS **MA** 01247 (413) 663-5830
SHALOM, CONGREGATION R RICHARDSON ROAD.......... NORTH CHELMSFORD **MA** 01863 (617) 251-8091
SINAI, TEMPLE R P.O. BOX 188 .... NORTH DARTMOUTH **MA** 02747
B'NAI ISRAEL, CONGREGATION C 253 PROSPECT STREET .... NORTHAMPTON **MA** 01060 (413) 584-3593
SHAARE TEFILAH, TEMPLE C 556 NICHOLS STREET.......... NORWOOD **MA** 02602 (617) 762-8670
BETH ISRAEL OF ONSET, CONGREGATION O .... ONSET **MA** 02558
BETH SHALOM, TEMPLE R 489 LOWELL STREET .... PEABODY **MA** 01960 (617) 535-2100
NER TAMID, TEMPLE C 368 LOWELL STREET .... PEABODY **MA** 01960 (617) 532-1293
TIFERETH ISRAEL, CONGREGATION PIERPONT STREET .... PEABODY **MA** 01960
AHAVATH SHOLEM CONGREGATION O P.O. BOX 1061 .... PITTSFIELD **MA** 01201 (413) 442-2885
ANSHE AMUNIM, TEMPLE R 26 BROAD STREET, P.O. BOX 544 .... PITTSFIELD **MA** 01202 (413) 443-9400
KNESSET ISRAEL, CONGREGATION C 16 COLT ROAD.......... PITTSFIELD **MA** 01960 (413) 445-4872
BETH JACOB, CONGREGATION R P.O. BOX 3284 .... PLYMOUTH **MA** 02361 (617) 746-1575
ADAS SHALOM C 435 ADAMS STREET.......... QUINCY **MA** 02169 (617) 471-1818
BETH EL, TEMPLE C 1001 HANCOCK STREET .... QUINCY **MA** 02169 (617) 479-4309
BETH ISRAEL SYNAGOGUE O 33 GRAFTON STREET .... QUINCY **MA** 02169 (617) 472-6796
BETH AM, TEMPLE C 871 N. MAIN STREET.......... RANDOLPH **MA** 02368 (617) 963-0440
BETH DAVID OF THE SOUTH SHORE, TEMPLE R P.O. BOX 284 .... RANDOLPH **MA** 02368 (617) 828-2275
YOUNG ISRAEL OF MATTAPAN-RANDOLPH 374 NORTH MAIN STREET .... RANDOLPH **MA** 02368 (617) 961-9817
AHAVAS ACHIM, CONGREGATION O 89 WALNUT AVENUE .... REVERE **MA** 02151 (617) 289-1026
B'NAI ISRAEL, TEMPLE C 1 WAVE AVENUE .... REVERE **MA** 02151
TIFERETH ISRAEL, CONGREGATION O P.O. BOX 81 .... REVERE **MA** 02151
SHALOM, TEMPLE C 287 LAFAYETTE STREET .... SALEM **MA** 01970 (617) 744-9709
AHAVAS SHOLOM, CONGREGATION C 36 HURD AVENUE .... SAUGUS **MA** 01906
ADATH SHARON, TEMPLE C 18 HARDING STREET .... SHARON **MA** 02067 (617) 784-2517
ISRAEL, TEMPLE C 125 POND STREET.......... SHARON **MA** 02067 (617) 784-3986
SINAI, TEMPLE R 100 AMES STREET, P.O. BOX 414.......... SHARON **MA** 02067 (617) 784-6081
TIKVAS ISRAEL, CONGREGATION 7 SUNSET DRIVE .... SHARON **MA** 02067
YOUNG ISRAEL OF SHARON 9 DUNBAR STREET .... SHARON **MA** 02067 (617) 784-6112
B'NAI BRITH, TEMPLE C 201 CENTRAL STREET.......... SOMERVILLE **MA** 02145
HAVURAT SHALOM CONGREGATION 113 COLLEGE AVENUE .... SOMERVILLE **MA** 02144 (617) 623-3376
LUBAVITCH CONGREGATION O 100 WOODCLIFF ROAD.......... SOUTH BROOKLINE **MA** 02167 (617) 469-9007
BETH EL, TEMPLE C 979 DICKINSON STREET .... SPRINGFIELD **MA** 01108 (413) 733-4149
BETH ISRAEL, CONGREGATION O
565 CHESTNUT STREET, P.O. BOX 874 .... SPRINGFIELD **MA** 01107
CHABAD LUBAVITCH O 782 DICKINSON .... SPRINGFIELD **MA** 01108 (413) 253-9040

KESSER ISRAEL SYNAGOGUE O 19 OAKLAND STREET .... SPRINGFIELD **MA** 01108 (413) 732-8492
KODIMOH, CONGREGATION O 124 SUMNER AVENUE .... SPRINGFIELD **MA** 01108 (413) 781-0171
SINAI TEMPLE R 1100 DICKINSON STREET .... SPRINGFIELD **MA** 01108 (413) 736-3619
JUDEA, TEMPLE C 188 FRANKLIN STREET.......... STONEHAM **MA** 02180 (617) 665-5752
AHAVATH TORAH CONGREGATION C 1179 CENTRAL AVENUE .... STOUGHTON **MA** 02072 (617) 344-8733
B'NAI TORAH, CONGREGATION P.O. BOX 195 .... SUDBURY **MA** 01776
BETH EL, CONGREGATION R HUDSON ROAD .... SUDBURY **MA** 01176 (617) 443-9622
BETH EL, TEMPLE C 55 ATLANTIC AVENUE .... SWAMPSCOTT **MA** 01907 (617) 599-8005
ISRAEL OF SWAMPSCOTT & MARBLEHEAD, TEMPLE C
837 HUMPHREY STREET .... SWAMPSCOTT **MA** 01907 (617) 595-6636
AGUDATH ACHIM, CONGREGATION C 36 WINTHROP STREET .... TAUNTON **MA** 02780 (617) 822-3230
MARTHAS VINEYARD HEBREW CENTER C CENTER STREET.......... VINEYARD HAVEN **MA** 02568 (617) 693-0745
EMANUEL, TEMPLE C 120 CHESTNUT STREET .... WAKEFIELD **MA** 01880 (617) 245-1886
BETH ISRAEL, TEMPLE R 25 HARVARD STREET .... WALTHAM **MA** 02154
WARE HEBREW CONGREGATION C 89 MAIN STREET .... WARE **MA** 01082
SHIR TIKVA, TEMPLE R P.O. BOX 265 .... WAYLAND **MA** 01778 (617) 358-7719
SONS OF ISRAEL, CONGREGATION 281 MAIN STREET .... WEBSTER **MA** 01570
BETH ELOHIM, TEMPLE R 10 BETHEL ROAD.......... WELLESLEY HILLS **MA** 02181 (617) 235-8419
AGUDATH ACHIM, CONGREGATION 40 MILO STREET.......... WEST NEWTON **MA** 02165
SHALOM OF NEWTON, TEMPLE 175 TEMPLE STREET.......... WEST NEWTON **MA** 02165 (617) 332-9550
ADATH JESHURUN, CONGREGATION O
5230 WASHINGTON STREET .... WEST ROXBURY **MA** 02132
B'NAI TORAH HILLEL C 120 COREY STREET .... WEST ROXBURY **MA** 02132 (617) 323-0486
B'NAI SHALOM, CONGREGATION R 9 CHARLES STREET .... WESTBOROUGH **MA** 01581 (617) 366-7191
BETH DAVID OF DEDHAM, TEMPLE - EAST WESTWOOD R
40 POND STREET, P.O. BOX 459.......... WESTWOOD **MA** 02090 (617) 329-1938
TIFERETH ABRAHAM, CONGREGATION 283 SHIRLEY STREET .... WINTHROP **MA** 02152
TIFERETH ISRAEL, TEMPLE O 93 VETERANS ROAD.......... WINTHROP **MA** 02152 (617) 846-1390
SHALOM EMETH, TEMPLE R 14 GREEN STREET .... WOBURN **MA** 01801
AGUDAS SONS OF JACOB, CONGREGATION O
14 WOODFORD STREET .... WORCESTER **MA** 01604
B'NAI ZION, CONGREGATION 56 GRANITE STREET .... WORCESTER **MA** 01604
BETH ISRAEL, CONGREGATION C
JAMESBURY DRIVE & KINNICUTT ROAD.......... WORCESTER **MA** 01609 (617) 756-6204
BETH JUDAH, CONGREGATION O 889 PLEASANT STREET .... WORCESTER **MA** 01602 (617) 754-3681
CHABAD-LUBAVITCH O 9 MIDLAND STREET .... WORCESTER **MA** 01602
CHABAD-LUBAVITCH O 340 MAIN STREET .... WORCESTER **MA** 01608
CHABAD-LUBAVITCH O 22 NEWTON AVENUE .... WORCESTER **MA** 01602
LUBAVITCH O 24 CRESSWELL .... WORCESTER **MA** 01602 (617) 752-0904
MOGEN DAVID, CONGREGATION O 1029 PLEASANT STREET.......... WORCESTER **MA** 01602
SHAARAI TORAH, CONGREGATION O 123 DORCHESTER STREET .... WORCESTER **MA** 01604
SHAAREI TORAH EAST O 155 PROVIDENCE STREET .... WORCESTER **MA** 01604 (617) 756-3276
SHAAREI TORAH WEST CONGREGATION O 835 PLEASANT STREET.......... WORCESTER **MA** 01602 (617) 791-0013
SINAI, TEMPLE R 661 SALISBURY STREET.......... WORCESTER **MA** 01609 (617) 755-2519
TIFERETH ISRAEL, CONGREGATION O 22 NEWTON AVENUE .... WORCESTER **MA** 01602 (617) 755-0718
ASHKENAZI O 297 BURROWS AVENUE .... WINNIPEG **MB** (204) 589-1517
BETH ISRAEL CONGREGATION C 1007 SINCLAIR STREET.......... WINNIPEG **MB** R2V 3J5 (204) 582-2353
B'NAI ABRAHAM O 235 ENNISKILLEN AVENUE .... WINNIPEG **MB** (204) 339-9297
CHABAD HOUSE O 532 INKSTER BOULEVARD .... WINNIPEG **MB** R2W 0K9 (204) 586-1867
CHAVURAT TEFILLAH O 459 HARTFORD .... WINNIPEG **MB** (204) 338-9451
CHEVRA MISHNAYES SYNAGOGUE 700 JEFFERSON AVENUE .... WINNIPEG **MB** (204) 338-8503
HERZLIA-ADAS YESHURUN CONGREGATION O 620 BROCK STREET .... WINNIPEG **MB** R3N OZ4 (204) 489-6262
ROSH PINA CONGREGATION C
P.O. BOX 3586, STATION B, 123 MATHESON AVENUE.......... WINNIPEG **MB** R2W 3R4 (204) 589-6306
SHAAREY ZEDEK, CONGREGATION C 561 WELLINGTON CRESCENT .... WINNIPEG **MB** R3M OA6 (204) 452-3711
HARFORD JEWISH CENTER R 402 PARADISE ROAD .... ABERDEEN **MD** 21001 (301) 272-8316
KNESETH ISRAEL, CONGREGATION O
P.O. BOX 626, HILLTOP LANE & SPA ROAD.......... ANNAPOLIS **MD** 21403 (301) 269-0740
KOL AMI, CONGREGATION C 1909 HIDDEN MEADOW LANE .... ANNAPOLIS **MD** 21401 (301) 266-6006
BETH SHOLOM, TEMPLE R P.O. BOX 1461, OLD ANNAPOLIS ROAD .... ARNOLD **MD** 21012 (301) 974-0900
ADATH YESHURIN CONGREGATION O
OLD COURT ROAD & MARRIOTS LANE .... BALTIMORE **MD** 21208 (301) 655-7818
AGUDATH ISRAEL O 6202 PARK HEIGHTS AVENUE.......... BALTIMORE **MD** 21215 (301) 764-7778
AGUDATH ISRAEL OF BALTIMORE 5719 NARCISSUS AVENUE .... BALTIMORE **MD** 21215 (301) 358-4985
AGUDATH ISRAEL OF GREENSPRING O 6504 GREENSPRING AVENUE.......... BALTIMORE **MD** 21209 (301) 484-4943
ARUGAT HABOSEM O 6615 PARK HEIGHTS AVENUE .... BALTIMORE **MD** 21215 (301) 358-4340
B'NAI JACOB O 3610 SEVEN MILE LANE .... BALTIMORE **MD** 21208 (301) 358-5164
B'NAI REUBEN SYNAGOGUE O 3725 MILFORD MILL ROAD .... BALTIMORE **MD** 21207 (301) 922-7990
BAIS LUBAVITCH O 5721 PARK HEIGHTS AVENUE.......... BALTIMORE **MD** 21215 (301) 358-0659
BALTIMORE HEBREW CONGREGATION R
7401 PARK HEIGHTS AVENUE.......... BALTIMORE **MD** 21208 (301) 764-1587
BEIT TIKVAH RE 8600 LOCH RAVEN BOULEVARD.......... BALTIMORE **MD** 21204 (301) 335-2159
BETH ABRAHAM ANSHEI SEFARD, CONGREGATION O
6210 WALLIS AVENUE .... BALTIMORE **MD** 21215 (301) 358-7456
BETH AM SYNAGOGUE 2501 EUTAW PLACE.......... BALTIMORE **MD** 21217 (301) 523-2446
BETH EL C 8101 PARK HEIGHTS AVENUE.......... BALTIMORE **MD** 21208 (301) 484-0411
BETH ISAAC ADATH ISRAEL, CONGREGATION
4398 CREST HEIGHTS ROAD.......... BALTIMORE **MD** 21215 (301) 486-8338
BETH JACOB WISHEER, CONGREGATION O 1016 HILLEN STREET.......... BALTIMORE **MD** 21202
BETH JACOB, CONGREGATION O 5713 PARK HEIGHTS AVENUE .... BALTIMORE **MD** 21215 (301) 466-1266
BETH TFILOH CONGREGATION O 3330 OLD COURT ROAD .... BALTIMORE **MD** 21208 (301) 486-1900
BNAI ISRAEL CONGREGATION O 3701 SOUTHERN AVENUE .... BALTIMORE **MD** 21206 (301) 426-3534
BNAI JACOB CONGREGATION O 3615 SEVEN MILE LANE .... BALTIMORE **MD** 21208 (301) 358-8308
CHABAD-LUBAVITCH O 5721 PARK HEIGHTS AVENUE .... BALTIMORE **MD** 21215
CHIZUK AMUNO CONGREGATION C 8100 STEVENSON ROAD .... BALTIMORE **MD** 21208 (301) 486-6400
CHOFETZ CHAIM ADATH BNEI ISRAEL, CONGREGATION O
3702 W. ROGERS AVENUE .... BALTIMORE **MD** 21215 (301) 578-0774
DARCHEI TZEDEK O 7307 SEVEN MILE LANE .... BALTIMORE **MD** 21208
EMANUEL, TEMPLE R 3301 MILFORD MILL ROAD .... BALTIMORE **MD** 21207 (301) 922-3642
HAR SINAI CONGREGATION R 6300 PARK HEIGHTS AVENUE.......... BALTIMORE **MD** 21215 (301) 764-2882

Name and Address	City	State	ZIP	Phone
LLOYD STREET SYNAGOGUE S LLOYD & WATSON STREETS	BALTIMORE	MD	21215	(301) 358-9417
MACHZIKEI TORAH, CONGREGATION O 6216 BILTMORE AVENUE	BALTIMORE	MD	21215	(301) 358-4630
MOGEN ABRAHAM, CONGREGATION O 3114C PARKINGTON AVENUE	BALTIMORE	MD	21215	
MOSES MONTEFIORE EMUNATH ISRAEL WOODMOOR HEBREW CONG. O				
3605 CORONADO ROAD	BALTIMORE	MD	21207	(301) 655-4484
NER TAMID GREENSPRING VALLEY SYNAGOGUE & CENTER O				
6214 PIMLICO ROAD	BALTIMORE	MD	21209	(301) 358-6500
OHEB SHALOM, TEMPLE R 7310 PARK HEIGHTS AVENUE	BALTIMORE	MD	21208	(301) 358-0105
OHEL YAKOV, CONGREGATION O 3200 GLEN AVENUE	BALTIMORE	MD	21215	(301) 578-9336
OHR KNESSETH ISRAEL ANSHE SPHARD, CONGREGATION O				
3910 W. ROGERS AVENUE	BALTIMORE	MD	21215	(301) 466-8800
PICKWICK JEWISH CENTER-HAR ZION PETACH TIKVAH O				
6221 GREENSPRING AVENUE	BALTIMORE	MD	21209	(301) 358-9660
SHAAREI TFILAH CONGREGATION O 2001 LIBERTY HEIGHTS AVENUE	BALTIMORE	MD	21217	
SHAAREI ZION CONGREGATION O 6602 PARK HEIGHTS AVENUE	BALTIMORE	MD	21215	(301) 764-6810
SHEARITH ISRAEL O PARK HEIGHTS AVENUE & GLEN AVENUE	BALTIMORE	MD	21215	(301) 466-3060
SHOMREI EMUNAH O 6213 GREENSPRING AVENUE	BALTIMORE	MD	21209	(301) 764-6186
SUBURBAN ORTHODOX CONGREGATION O 7504 SEVEN MILE LANE	BALTIMORE	MD	21208	(301) 486-6114
SYNAGOGUE CENTER O 7124 PARK HEIGHTS AVENUE	BALTIMORE	MD	21215	(301) 764-0262
TZEMACH ZEDEK V'SHOMREI HADAS, CONGREGATION O				
7037 SURREY DRIVE	BALTIMORE	MD	21215	(301) 764-8213
BETH EL OF MONTGOMERY COUNTY, CONGREGATION C				
8215 OLD GEORGETOWN ROAD	BETHESDA	MD	20014	(301) 652-2606
BETHESDA JEWISH CONGREGATION R 6601 BRADLEY BLVD	BETHESDA	MD	20817	(301) 469-8636
MAGEN DAVID SEPHARDIC CONGREGATION P.O. BOX 41019	BETHESDA	MD	20014	(301) 588-0446
NEVEY SHALOM C 12218 TORAH LANE	BOWIE	MD	20715	(301) 262-9020
OHR KODESH CONGREGATION C 8402 FREYMAN DRIVE	CHEVY CHASE	MD	20815	(301) 589-3880
SHALOM, TEMPLE R 8401 GRUBB ROAD	CHEVY CHASE	MD	20815	(301) 587-2273
BETH SHOLOM C P.O. BOX 2878	COLUMBIA	MD	21045	(301) 997-0669
CHABAD-LUBAVITCH O 10409 MAYWIND COURT	COLUMBIA	MD	21044	
ISAIAH, TEMPLE R 5885 ROBERT OLIVER PLACE	COLUMBIA	MD	21045	(301) 730-8277
MEETING HOUSE, THE - TEMPLE BETH SHALOM C				
5885 ROBERT OLIVER PLACE	COLUMBIA	MD	21045	(301) 730-4090
BER CHAYIM CONGREGATION R 107 UNION STREET	CUMBERLAND	MD	21502	(301) 722-5688
BETH JACOB C 11 COLUMBIA STREET	CUMBERLAND	MD	21502	(301) 722-6570
B'NAI ISRAEL, TEMPLE C ADKINS AVENUE	EASTON	MD	21601	
BETH SHOLOM C 925 STREAKER ROAD	ELDERSBURG	MD	21784	
BETH SHOLOM, CONGREGATION C 20 W. 2ND STREET	FREDERICK	MD	21701	
GAITHERSBURG HEBREW CONGREGATION C				
9915 APPLE RIDGE ROAD	GAITHERSBURG	MD	20760	(301) 869-7699
MISHKAN TORAH CONGREGATION C/RE RIDGE & WESTWAY ROADS	GREENBELT	MD	20770	(301) 474-4223
B'NAI ABRAHAM R 53 E. BALTIMORE STREET	HAGERSTOWN	MD	21740	(301) 733-5039
ADAS SHOLOM R ROUTE 155 & EARLTON ROAD	HAVRE DE GRACE	MD	21078	(301) 939-3170
HARTFORD JEWISH CENTER R 8 N. EARLTON ROAD	HAVRE DE GRACE	MD	21078	(301) 939-9673
RABBI B. CHANOWITZ O 6711 WELLS PARKWAY	HYATTSVILLE	MD	29872	(301) 422-6200
EMANUEL, TEMPLE R 10101 CONNECTICUT AVENUE	KENSINGTON	MD	20895	(301) 942-2000
CONGREGATION OSEH SHALOM RE POB 387	LAUREL	MD	20810	(301) 725-9795
BETH ISRAEL, CONGREGATION C 335 MIDWAY DRIVE	LEXINGTON PARK	MD	20653	(301) 863-8886
B'NAI SHALOM OF OLNEY C 3701 OLNEY-LAYTONSVILLE ROAD	OLNEY	MD	20832	(301) 774-0879
ADAT CHAIM C P.O. BOX 10	OWINGS MILLS	MD	21117	(301) 356-5511
BETH KNESETH O 2 TAHOE CIRCLE	OWINGS MILLS	MD	21117	(301) 363-4718
ISRAEL, CONGREGATION OF C THIRD STREET	POCOMOKE CITY	MD	21851	
BETH SHOLOM OF POTOMAC O 11825 SEVEN LOCKS ROAD	POTOMAC	MD	20854	(301) 882-5666
HAR SHALOM, CONGREGATION C 11510 FALLS ROAD	POTOMAC	MD	20854	(301) 299-7087
ANSHE AMUNAH-AITZ CHAIM-LIBERTY JEWISH CENTER O				
8615 CHURCH LANE	RANDALLSTOWN	MD	21133	
BETH ISRAEL MIKRO KODESH CONGREGATION C				
9411 LIBERTY ROAD	RANDALLSTOWN	MD	21133	(301) 922-6565
BETH YEHUDA ANSHE KURLAND/WINANDS ROAD O				
8701 WINANDS ROAD	RANDALLSTOWN	MD	21133	(301) 655-1353
LIBERTY JEWISH CENTER O 8615 CHURCH LANE	RANDALLSTOWN	MD	21133	(301) 922-1333
MOGEN ABRAHAM, CONGREGATION O 3800 PIKESWOOD DRIVE	RANDALLSTOWN	MD	21133	
RANDALLSTOWN SYN. CTR; AHAVAS SHOLOM-AGUDAS ACHIM-SEPHARDIC O				
8729 CHURCH LANE	RANDALLSTOWN	MD	21133	(301) 655-6665
WINANDS ROAD SYNAGOGUE CENTER O 8701 WINANDS ROAD	RANDALLSTOWN	MD	21133	(301) 655-1353
B'NAI ISRAEL CONGREGATION C 6301 MONTROSE ROAD	ROCKVILLE	MD	20852	(301) 649-3440
BETH AMI, TEMPLE R 800 HURLEY AVENUE	ROCKVILLE	MD	20850	(301) 340-6818
BETH TIKVAH C 2200 BALTIMORE ROAD	ROCKVILLE	MD	20853	(301) 762-7338
BETHESDA-CHEVY CHASE JEWISH COMMUNITY GROUP				
6125 MONTROSE ROAD	ROCKVILLE	MD	20858	
CHABAD HOUSE O 311 WEST MONTGOMERY AVENUE	ROCKVILLE	MD	20850	(301) 340-6858
BETH ISRAEL CONGREGATION C				
CAMDEN AVENUE & WICOMICO STREET	SALISBURY	MD	21801	(301) 742-2564
AHAVATH TORAH/WOODSIDE SYNAGOGUE O				
9001 GEORGIA AVENUE	SILVER SPRING	MD	20910	(301) 587-8252
B'NAI ISRAEL C 10500 GEORGIA AVENUE	SILVER SPRING	MD	20902	
HAR TZEON AGUDATH ACHIM, CONGREGATION C				
1840 UNIVERSITY BLVD. W	SILVER SPRING	MD	20902	(301) 649-3800
ISRAEL, TEMPLE C 420 UNIVERSITY BLVD E	SILVER SPRING	MD	20901	(301) 439-3600
OHAVEI ZEDEK CONGREGATION O 1100 EAST-WEST HIGHWAY	SILVER SPRING	MD	20910	
SHAARE TEFILA CONGREGATION C 11120 LOCKWOOD DRIVE	SILVER SPRING	MD	20901	(301) 593-3410
SILVER SPRING JEWISH CENTER; SILVER SPRING HEBREW DAY INST. O				
1401 ARCOLA AVENUE	SILVER SPRING	MD	20902	(301) 649-4425
SOUTHEAST HEBREW CONGREGATION 10900 LOCKWOOD DRIVE	SILVER SPRING	MD	20901	(301) 593-2120
SUMMIT HILL CONGREGATION O 8512 16TH STREET	SILVER SPRING	MD	20910	
YOUNG ISRAEL SHOMREI EMUNAH 1132 ARCOLA BLVD.	SILVER SPRING	MD	20902	(301) 593-4465
BETH SHALOM C 2020 LIBERTY ROAD	TARFSVILLE	MD	21107	(301) 795-7766
SHAARE TIKVAH, CONGREGATION C				
5404 OLD TEMPLE HILLS ROAD	TEMPLE HILLS	MD	20031	(301) 894-4303
BETH ABRAHAM C MAIN STREET & LAUREL AVENUE	AUBURN	ME	04210	(207) 783-1302
BETH ABRAHAM, CONGREGATION O 145 YORK STREET	BANGOR	ME	04401	(207) 947-0876
BETH ISRAEL, CONGREGATION T 144 YORK STREET	BANGOR	ME	04401	(207) 945-3433
TOLDOS ITZCHOK, CONGREGATION O 142 YORK STREET	BANGOR	ME	04401	
BETH ISRAEL CONGREGATION C WASHINGTON STREET	BATH	ME	04530	(207) 443-5181
ETZ CHAIM, CONGREGATION C P.O. BOX 473	BIDDEFORD	ME	04005	
BETH JACOB, CONGREGATION O SHAWMUT & SABBATUS STREETS	LEWISTON	ME	04240	
BETH ISRAEL, CONGREGATION O				
49 EAST GRAND AVENUE	OLD ORCHARD BEACH	ME	04064	(207) 934-2973
BET HA'AM R 267 CONGRESS STREET	PORTLAND	ME	04112	(207) 879-0028
BETH EL, TEMPLE C 400 DEERING AVENUE	PORTLAND	ME	04103	(207) 774-2649
SHAAREY TPHILOH, CONGREGATION O 76 NOYES STREET	PORTLAND	ME	04103	(207) 773-0693
BETH ISRAEL SYNAGOGUE C 291 MAIN STREET	WATERVILLE	ME	04901	(207) 773-4453
BETH EL, TEMPLE R 610 S. 3RD STREET	ALPENA	MI	49707	(517) 354-5106
BETH EMETH, TEMPLE R 2309 PACKARD ROAD	ANN ARBOR	MI	48104	(313) 665-4744
BETH ISRAEL CONGREGATION C 2000 WASHTENAW	ANN ARBOR	MI	48104	(313) 663-5543
CHABAD HOUSE O 715 HILL STREET	ANN ARBOR	MI	48104	(313) 769-3078
BETH EL, TEMPLE R 306 CAPITAL AVENUE N.E.	BATTLE CREEK	MI	49107	(616) 963-4921
ISRAEL, TEMPLE C 2300 CENTER AVENUE	BAY CITY	MI	48706	(517) 893-7811
B'NAI SHALOM, TEMPLE C 2050 BROADWAY	BENTON HARBOR	MI	49022	(616) 925-8021
BETH EL, TEMPLE R 7400 TELEGRAPH ROAD	BIRMINGHAM	MI	48010	(313) 851-1100
BETH ABRAHAM HILLEL MOSES, CONGREGATION T				
5075 W. MAPLE ROAD	BLOOMFIELD	MI	48033	(616) 851-6880
SOLEL, CONGREGATION R 304 W. WASHINGTON STREET	BRIGHTON	MI	48843	(517) 546-2527
CONGREGATION T'CHIYA 1035 ST. ANTOINE	DETROIT	MI	48226	(313) 353-1569
DOWNTOWN SYNAGOGUE C 1457 GRISWOLD	DETROIT	MI	48226	(313) 961-9328
ISRAEL, TEMPLE R 17400 MANDERSON ROAD	DETROIT	MI	48235	(313) 863-7769
KEHILLAT ISRAEL C 855 GROVE STREET	EAST LANSING	MI	48823	(517) 315-3221
SHAAREY ZEDEK, CONGREGATION C 1924 COOLIDGE ROAD	EAST LANSING	MI	48823	(517) 351-3570
ADAT SHALOM SYNAGOGUE C 29901 MIDDLEBELT	FARMINGTON HILLS	MI	48018	(313) 851-5100
BIRMINGHAM TEMPLE, THE R 28611 W. TWELVE MILE ROAD	FARMINGTON HILLS	MI	48018	(313) 477-1410
CHABAD HOUSE O 32000 MIDDLEBELT ROAD	FARMINGTON HILLS	MI	48018	(313) 626-3194
CHABAD-LUBAVITCH O 28555 MIDDLEBELT ROAD	FARMINGTON HILLS	MI	48018	
BETH EL, TEMPLE R 501 S. BALLENGER HIGHWAY	FLINT	MI	48504	(313) 232-3138
BETH ISRAEL, CONGREGATION C 5240 CALKINS ROAD	FLINT	MI	48504	(313) 732-6310
AHAVAS ISRAEL, CONGREGATION C 2727 MICHIGAN NORTHEAST	GRAND RAPIDS	MI	49506	(616) 949-2840
CHABAD HOUSE O 1910 MICHIGAN NORTHEAST	GRAND RAPIDS	MI	49503	(616) 458-6575
EMANUEL, TEMPLE R 1715 E. FULTON STREET	GRAND RAPIDS	MI	49503	(616) 459-5976
FIRST ISRAEL CONGREGATION C 113 W. HOUGHTON AVENUE	HOUGHTON	MI	49931	
ANSHE KNESSETH ISRAEL, CONGREGATION C				
P.O. BOX 218, KIMBERLY & A STREET	IRON MOUNTAIN	MI	49801	
BETH SHOLOM, TEMPLE R				
C/O DR. DANIEL ARNOLD, 80 EDGEWOOD DRIVE	ISHPEMING	MI	49855	(906) 486-6246
BETH ISRAEL, TEMPLE R 801 W. MICHIGAN AVENUE	JACKSON	MI	49202	(517) 784-3862
B'NAI ISRAEL, CONGREGATION R 2232 CROSSWIND DRIVE	KALAMAZOO	MI	49008	(616) 344-9762
MOSES, CONGREGATION OF C 2501 STADIUM DRIVE	KALAMAZOO	MI	49008	(616) 312-5463
LIVONIA JEWISH CONGREGATION C 31840 W. SEVEN MILE ROAD	LIVONIA	MI	48152	(313) 477-8974
BETH EL, TEMPLE C 2505 BAY CITY ROAD	MIDLAND	MI	48640	(517) 496-3720
BETH TEPHILATH MOSES, CONGREGATION O				
53 S. AVENUE, P.O. BOX 842	MOUNT CLEMENS	MI	48043	(313) 465-0641
BENJAMIN, TEMPLE C 502 N. BROWN STREET, P.O. BOX 246	MOUNT PLEASANT	MI	48858	
B'NAI ISRAEL, CONGREGATION R 391 WEST WEBSTER	MUSKEGON	MI	49441	(616) 722-2702
B'NAI ISRAEL BETH YEHUDA O 15400 W. TEN MILE ROAD	OAK PARK	MI	48237	(313) 967-3969
B'NAI MOSHE, CONGREGATION C 14390 W. TEN MILE ROAD	OAK PARK	MI	48237	(313) 548-9000
B'NAI ZION O 15250 W. NINE MILE ROAD	OAK PARK	MI	48237	(313) 968-2414
BETH SHALOM, CONGREGATION C 14601 W. LINCOLN ROAD	OAK PARK	MI	48237	(313) 547-7970
CHABAD LUBAVITCH O 14000 WEST 9 MILE ROAD	OAK PARK	MI	48237	(313) 548-2666
DOVID BEN NUCHIM, CONGREGATION O 14800 LINCOLN ROAD	OAK PARK	MI	48237	(313) 398-1017
EMANU-EL, TEMPLE R 14450 W. TEN MILE ROAD	OAK PARK	MI	48237	(313) 967-4020
MISHKAN ISRAEL LUBAVITCHER CENTER, CONGREGATION O				
14000 W. NINE MILE ROAD	OAK PARK	MI	48237	(313) 548-2666
SEPHARDIC COMMUNITY OF DETROIT O 24021 MARLOW	OAK PARK	MI	48237	(313) 967-4414
SHAAREY SHOMAIM, CONGREGATION O 14131 VICTORIA	OAK PARK	MI	48237	(313) 542-4444
YOUNG ISRAEL OF GREENFIELD PARK O 15140 W. TEN MILE ROAD	OAK PARK	MI	48237	(313) 967-3655
YOUNG ISRAEL OF OAK WOODS O 24061 COOLIDGE	OAK PARK	MI	48237	(313) 398-1177
B'NAI ISRAEL CONGREGATION R CORNER WAVKAZOO & MICHIGAN	PETOSKEY	MI	49770	
B'NAI ISRAEL, CONGREGATION C 143 ONEIDA ROAD	PONTIAC	MI	48053	
BETH JACOB, TEMPLE R 79 ELIZABETH LAKE ROAD	PONTIAC	MI	48053	(313) 332-3212
MOUNT SINAI, CONGREGATION O P.O. BOX 794	PORT HURON	MI	48060	
B'NAI ISRAEL, TEMPLE C 1424 S. WASHINGTON AVENUE	SAGINAW	MI	48601	(517) 753-5230
BETH EL, TEMPLE R C/O MR. LEO A. KAHAN, 100 S. WASHINGTON	SAGINAW	MI	48607	(517) 754-5171
FIRST HEBREW CONGREGATION O 249 BROADWAY	SOUTH HAVEN	MI	49090	
B'NAI DAVID, CONGREGATION O 24350 SOUTHFIELD ROAD	SOUTHFIELD	MI	48075	(313) 557-8210
BETH ACHIM, CONGREGATION C 21100 W. TWELVE MILE ROAD	SOUTHFIELD	MI	48076	(313) 352-8670
BETH TEFILAH, CONGREGATION O 24225 GREENFIELD ROAD	SOUTHFIELD	MI	48075	(313) 557-6828
BNEI ISRAEL, CONGREGATION O 15751 W. 10½ MILE ROAD	SOUTHFIELD	MI	48075	(313) 559-6354
KOLLEL INSTITUTE O 15230 W. LINCOLN BLVD.	SOUTHFIELD	MI	48076	(313) 645-2585
MOGEN ABRAHAM, CONGREGATION O 15751 W. TEN½ MILE ROAD	SOUTHFIELD	MI	48075	(313) 557-6750
SHAAREY ZEDEK, CONGREGATION C 27375 BELL ROAD	SOUTHFIELD	MI	48034	(313) 357-5544
SHOMREY EMUNAH, CONGREGATION O 25451 SOUTHFIELD ROAD	SOUTHFIELD	MI	48075	(313) 559-1533
YOUNG ISRAEL OF DETROIT 15894 HARDEN CIRCLE	SOUTHFIELD	MI	48075	(313) 557-4047
YOUNG ISRAEL OF SOUTHFIELD 27705 LAHSER ROAD	SOUTHFIELD	MI	48034	(313) 358-0154
ZIONIST CULTURAL CENTER 18451 WEST 10 MILE ROAD	SOUTHFIELD	MI	48237	(313) 569-1515
BETH EL, CONGREGATION R 3545 ORCHARD VIEW	TRAVERSE CITY	MI	49685	(616) 946-9586
BETH EL, TEMPLE 311 S. PARK STREET	TRAVERSE CITY	MI	49684	(313) 946-1913
BETH ISAAC, CONGREGATION C 2730 EDSEL DRIVE	TRENTON	MI	48183	(313) 675-0355
B'NAI ISRAEL C 4200 WALNUT LAKE ROAD	WEST BLOOMFIELD	MI	48033	(313) 681-5353
BAIS CHABAD OF WEST BLOOMFIELD O				
5595 WEST MAPLE ROAD	WEST BLOOMFIELD	MI	48033	(313) 855-6170
BETH ABRAHAM-HILLEL-MOSES, CONGREGATION				
5075 W. MAPLE ROAD	WEST BLOOMFIELD	MI	48033	(313) 851-6880

Synagogue / Address	City	State	ZIP	Phone
ISRAEL, TEMPLE R 5725 WALNUT LAKE ROAD	WEST BLOOMFIELD	MI	48033	(313) 661-5700
KOL AMI, TEMPLE R 5085 WALNUT LAKE ROAD	WEST BLOOMFIELD	MI	48033	(313) 661-0040
ADAS ISRAEL CONGREGATION O 302 E. 3RD STREET	DULUTH	MN	55805	(218) 722-6459
ISRAEL, TEMPLE R 1602 E. 2ND STREET	DULUTH	MN	55812	(218) 724-2956
AGUDATH ACHIM SYNAGOGUE C 2320 SECOND AVENUE W	HIBBING	MN	55746	(218) 263-9237
ADATH JESHURUN CONGREGATION C 3400 DUPONT AVENUE	MINNEAPOLIS	MN	55408	(612) 824-2685
B'NAI ABRAHAM-MIKRO TIFERETH SYNAGOGUE C OTTAWA AVENUE SOUTH & HIGHWAY 7	MINNEAPOLIS	MN	55416	
B'NAI EMET SYNAGOGUE C 1804 NEVADA SOUTH	MINNEAPOLIS	MN	55416	(612) 545-8131
BET SHALOM, CONGREGATION R 1559 PENNSYLVANIA AVENUE N	MINNEAPOLIS	MN	55427	(612) 336-4391
BETH EL SYNAGOGUE C 5224 W. 26TH STREET	MINNEAPOLIS	MN	55416	(612) 920-3512
HILLEL, CONGREGATION 1521 UNIVERSITY AVENUE S.E.	MINNEAPOLIS	MN	55414	
ISRAEL, TEMPLE R 2324 EMERSON AVENUE S	MINNEAPOLIS	MN	55405	(612) 377-8680
KENESSETH ISRAEL CONGREGATION O 4330 W. 28TH STREET	MINNEAPOLIS	MN	55416	(612) 920-2183
MIKRO KODESH TIFERETH B'NAI JACOB, CONGREGATION C OTTAWA AVENUE SOUTH & HIGHWAY 7	MINNEAPOLIS	MN	55416	
MINNESOTA RECONSTRUCTIONIST HAVURAH C/O HOWARD BRIN	MINNEAPOLIS	MN		(612) 377-3887
SHAREI-CHESED CONGREGATION O 2734 RHODE ISLAND AVENUE S	MINNEAPOLIS	MN	55426	(612) 929-2734
B'NAI ISRAEL SYNAGOGUE R 621 2ND STREET S.W.	ROCHESTER	MN	55901	(507) 288-5825
BET SHALOM CONG. 5001 CEDAR LAKE ROAD	ST. LOUIS PARK	MN	55416	(612) 929-2900
B'NAI EMET SYNAGOGUE C 3115 OTTAWA AVENUE S	ST. LOUIS PARK	MN	55416	(612) 927-7309
SHAARE SHALOM CONGREGATION C 2524 AQUILA AVENUE S	ST. LOUIS PARK	MN	55426	(612) 546-4022
AARON, TEMPLE OF C 616 S. MISSISSIPPI RIVER BLVD	ST. PAUL	MN	55116	(612) 698-8874
ADATH ISRAEL ORTHODOX SYNAGOGUE O 2337 EDGCUMBE ROAD	ST. PAUL	MN	55116	(612) 698-8300
BETH JACOB CONGREGATION C 1133 RANKIN	ST. PAUL	MN	55116	(612) 699-9003
LUBAVITCH HOUSE O 15 MONTCALM COURT	ST. PAUL	MN	55116	(612) 698-3858
MOUNT ZION HEBREW CONGREGATION R 1300 SUMMIT AVENUE	ST. PAUL	MN	55105	(612) 698-3881
SHAARE SHALOM CONGREGATION C 1922 SARGENT	ST. PAUL	MN	55105	(612) 699-1014
UNITED ORTHODOX SERVICES 1530 HARTFORD AVENUE	ST. PAUL	MN	55116	(612) 699-0592
B'NAI ABRAHAM, CONGREGATION O P.O. BOX 1174	VIRGINIA	MN	55792	
TPHERIS ISRAEL CHEVRA KADISHA CONGREGATION O 14550 LADUE ROAD	CHESTERFIELD	MO	63017	(314) 469-7060
TRADITIONAL CONGREGATION OF MISSOURI T 12437 LADUE ROAD	CREVE COEUR	MO	63141	(314) 576-5230
BETH EL, TEMPLE R 1005 ADAMS STREET	JEFFERSON CITY	MO	65101	(314) 636-3821
UNITED HEBREW CONGREGATION R 702 SERGEANT STREET	JOPLIN	MO	64801	(417) 624-1181
BETH ISRAEL, CONGREGATION O ABRAHAM & VOLINER, 8310 HOLMES	KANSAS CITY	MO	64131	(816) 444-5747
BETH SHALOM CONGREGATION C 9400 WORNALL ROAD	KANSAS CITY	MO	64114	(816) 361-2990
CHABAD HOUSE O 8901 HOLMES STREET	KANSAS CITY	MO	64131	(816) 333-7117
CONGREGATION B'NAI JEHUDAH, THE TEMPLE R 712 E. 69TH STREET	KANSAS CITY	MO	64131	(816) 363-1050
KEHILATH ISRAEL SYNAGOGUE T 800 E. MEYER BLVD	KANSAS CITY	MO	64131	(816) 333-1992
NEW REFORM TEMPLE, THE R 7100 MAIN STREET AT GREGORY	KANSAS CITY	MO	64114	(816) 523-7809
GENESIS OF ST. LOUIS R 14 HIGH ACRES	OLIVETTE	MO	63132	(314) 725-0494
BETH EL, TEMPLE R 232 S. DUNDEE STREET	SEDALIA	MO	65301	(816) 826-3392
UNITED HEBREW CONGREGATION R 931 S. KICKAPOO	SPRINGFIELD	MO	65804	(417) 866-4760
B'NAI TORAH 24 VICKSBURG STATION ROAD	ST. CHARLES	MO	63303	(314) 441-4432
ADATH JOSEPH, TEMPLE R 17TH & FELIX STREETS	ST. JOSEPH	MO	64501	(816) 279-3179
B'NAI SHOLOM C 615 N. 10TH STREET	ST. JOSEPH	MO	64501	
AGUDAS YISROEL 602 OLD BONHOMME	ST. LOUIS	MO	63130	(314) 727-4395
B'NAI AMOONA, CONGREGATION C 324 S. MASON ROAD	ST. LOUIS	MO	63141	(314) 576-9990
B'NAI EL TEMPLE R 11411 HIGHWAY 40	ST. LOUIS	MO	63131	(314) 432-6393
BAIS ABRAHAM CONGREGATION O 6910 DELMAR	ST. LOUIS	MO	63130	(314) 721-3030
BETH HAMEDROSH HAGODOL, CONGREGATION O 1227 NORTH & SOUTH ROAD	ST. LOUIS	MO	63130	(314) 721-1037
BRITH SHOLOM KNESETH ISRAEL CONGREGATION 1107 LINDEN AVENUE	ST. LOUIS	MO	63117	(314) 725-6230
CENTRAL REFORM CONGREGATION 4425 LACLEDE	ST. LOUIS	MO	63108	(314) 652-3135
CHABAD LUBAVITCH O 921 GAY AVENUE	ST. LOUIS	MO	63130	(314) 863-3516
CHESED SHEL EMETH, CONGREGATION O 700 NORTH & SOUTH ROAD	ST. LOUIS	MO	63130	(314) 727-7585
EMANUEL, TEMPLE R 12166 CONWAY ROAD	ST. LOUIS	MO	63141	(314) 432-5877
ISRAEL, TEMPLE R 10675 LADUE ROAD	ST. LOUIS	MO	63141	(314) 432-8050
KOL AM, CONGREGATION R 11155 CLAYTON ROAD	ST. LOUIS	MO	63131	(314) 569-0797
MISHKAN ISRAEL, CONGREGATION O 7205 DORSET STREET	ST. LOUIS	MO	63130	(314) 863-7753
SHAARE EMETH, TEMPLE R 11645 LADUE ROAD	ST. LOUIS	MO	63141	(314) 569-0010
UNITED HEBREW CONGREGATION R 225 S. SKINNER BLVD	ST. LOUIS	MO	63105	(314) 726-4666
YOUNG ISRAEL OF ST. LOUIS 7800 GROBY ROAD	ST. LOUIS	MO	63130	(314) 727-1880
BETH HAMEDROSH HAGODOL CONGREGATION O 1227 NORTH & SOUTH ROAD	UNIVERSITY CITY	MO	63130	(314) 721-1037
NUSACH HARI-B'NAI ZION CONGREGATION O 8630 OLIVE BLVD	UNIVERSITY CITY	MO	63132	(314) 991-2100
SHAARE ZEDEK C 829 N. HANLEY ROAD	UNIVERSITY CITY	MO	63130	(314) 727-1747
BETH ISRAEL, CONGREGATION C CAMILLIA & SOUTHERN AVENUE, P.O. BOX 851	BILOXI	MS	39533	(601) 388-5574
B'NAI SHOLOM, TEMPLE R P.O. BOX 622	BROOKHAVEN	MS	39601	
B'NAI ISRAEL, CONGREGATION R P.O. BOX 284	CANTON	MS	39046	
BETH ISRAEL, CONGREGATION R P.O. BOX 165, 401 CATALPA STREET	CLARKSDALE	MS	38614	(601) 624-5862
ADATH ISRAEL R 201 S. BOLIVAR AVENUE	CLEVELAND	MS	38732	(601) 843-2005
B'NAI ISRAEL R 717 SECOND AVENUE NORTH	COLUMBUS	MS	39701	(601) 328-8355
HEBREW UNION CONGREGATION R P.O. BOX 212, 504 MAIN STREET	GREENVILLE	MS	38701	(601) 332-4153
AHAVATH RAYIM, CONGREGATION O P.O. BOX 1235	GREENWOOD	MS	38930	(601) 453-7537
BETH ISRAEL, CONGREGATION R 506 E. HARDING STREET	GREENWOOD	MS	38930	(601) 453-5749
B'NAI ISRAEL, CONGREGATION R P.O. BOX 1753	HATTIESBURG	MS	39401	(601) 583-0375
BETH ISRAEL CONGREGATION R P.O. BOX 12329	JACKSON	MS	39211	(601) 956-6215
BETH EL, TEMPLE R 224 COURT STREET S	LEXINGTON	MS	39095	
BETH ISRAEL, CONGREGATION R P.O. BOX 3456	MERIDIAN	MS	39301	(601) 483-3193
OHEL JACOB, CONGREGATION O P.O. BOX 766	MERIDIAN	MS	39302	
B'NAI ISRAEL, CONGREGATION R P.O. BOX 1003	NATCHEZ	MS	39120	(601) 445-5407
GEMILUTH CHASADIM, CONGREGATION R	PORT GIBSON	MS	39150	
B'NAI ISRAEL, TEMPLE C MARSHALL & HAMLIN STREETS, P.O. BOX 515	TUPELO	MS	38801	(601) 842-9169
ANSHE CHESED, TEMPLE R 2414 GROVE STREET	VICKSBURG	MS	39280	(601) 636-1126
BETH AARON R 1148 NORTH BROADWAY	BILLINGS	MT	59101	(406) 248-6412
B'NAI ISRAEL CONGREGATION C 327 W. GALENA STREET	BUTTE	MT	59701	(406) 792-9330
SGOOLAI ISRAEL SYNAGOGUE WESTMORLAND STREET	FREDERICTON	NB	E3B 2V5	
TIFERES ISRAEL SYNAGOGUE 50 STEADMAN STREET	MONCTON	NB	E1C 8L9	(506) 382-8324
SHAAREI ZEDEK, CONGREGATION C P.O. BOX 2041, 76 CARLETON STREET	ST. JOHN	NB	E2L 3T5	(506) 657-4790
B'NAI JESHURUN, CONGREGATION R 20TH & SOUTH STREETS	LINCOLN	NE	68502	(402) 435-8004
TIFERETH ISRAEL, CONGREGATION C 3219 SHERIDAN BLVD	LINCOLN	NE	68502	(402) 423-8569
B'NAI JACOB ADASS YESURIN, CONGREGATION O 3028 CUMING STREET	OMAHA	NE	68102	
BETH EL SYNAGOGUE C 210 S. 49TH STREET	OMAHA	NE	68132	(402) 553-3221
BETH ISRAEL, CONGREGATION O 1502 N. 59TH STREET	OMAHA	NE	68132	
ISRAEL, CONGREGATION OF 1802 N. 56TH STREET	OMAHA	NE	68104	
ISRAEL, TEMPLE R 7023 CASS STREET	OMAHA	NE	68132	(402) 556-6536
BETH ISRAEL, CONGREGATION 141 CHURCH STREET	BERLIN	NH	03570	
BETH ISRAEL, CONGREGATION EXCHANGE STREET	BERLIN	NH	03570	
BETHLEHEM HEBREW CONGREGATION C P.O. BOX 167 STRAWBERRY HILL STREET	BETHLEHEM	NH	03574	(603) 869-5747
MEYER DAVID, TEMPLE C HIGH STREET	CLAREMONT	NH	03843	(603) 542-6773
BETH JACOB, TEMPLE R 67 BROADWAY	CONCORD	NH	03301	(603) 228-8581
ISRAEL, TEMPLE C 4 & GROVE STREETS	DOVER	NH	03820	(603) 742-3976
B'NAI ISRAEL, TEMPLE R 208 COURT STREET	LACONIA	NH	03246	(603) 524-1276
ADATH YESHURUN, TEMPLE R 152 PROSPECT STREET	MANCHESTER	NH	03104	(603) 669-5650
ISRAEL, TEMPLE C 678 PINE STREET	MANCHESTER	NH	03104	(603) 622-6171
BETH ABRAHAM, TEMPLE C 4 RAYMOND STREET	NASHUA	NH	03060	(603) 883-8184
ISRAEL, TEMPLE C 200 STATE STREET	PORTSMOUTH	NH	03801	(603) 436-5301
BETH AHM, TEMPLE C 550 LLOYD ROAD	ABERDEEN	NJ	07747	(201) 583-1700
SHALOM, TEMPLE R 5 AYRMONT LANE	ABERDEEN	NJ	07747	(201) 566-2621
SONS OF ISRAEL, CONGREGATION O 412 ASBURY AVENUE	ASBURY PARK	NJ	07712	(201) 775-1964
BETH JACOB AMUNATH ISRAEL, CONGREGATION O 506 PACIFIC AVENUE	ATLANTIC CITY	NJ	08401	
CHABAD-LUBAVITCH O 9 BAYSHORE COURT	ATLANTIC CITY	NJ	08402	
CHELSEA HEBREW CONGREGATION C 4001 ATLANTIC AVENUE	ATLANTIC CITY	NJ	08401	
COMMUNITY SYNAGOGUE C 901-903 PACIFIC AVENUE	ATLANTIC CITY	NJ	08401	(609) 345-3282
RODEF SHOLOM, CONGREGATION O 2016 PACIFIC AVENUE	ATLANTIC CITY	NJ	08401	
SONS OF JACOB, CONGREGATION LORD STREET	AVENEL	NJ	07001	
BETH ABRAHAM, CONGREGATION O 42 W. 21ST STREET	BAYONNE	NJ	07002	
BETH AM, TEMPLE R 111 AVENUE B	BAYONNE	NJ	07002	(201) 858-2020
EMANU-EL OF BAYONNE, TEMPLE C 735 KENNEDY BLVD	BAYONNE	NJ	07002	(201) 436-4499
OHAB SHOLOM, CONGREGATION O 1016-22 AVENUE C	BAYONNE	NJ	07002	
OHAV ZEDEK, CONGREGATION O 912 AVENUE C	BAYONNE	NJ	07002	(201) 437-1488
OHAVE SHOLOM ANSHE SFARD, CONGREGATION O 190 AVENUE B	BAYONNE	NJ	07002	
TALMUD TORAH, CONGREGATION O 489 KENNEDY BLVD	BAYONNE	NJ	07002	
UPTOWN SYNAGOGUE O 49TH STREET & AVENUE C	BAYONNE	NJ	07002	
AHAVATH ACHIM C 125 ACADEMY STREET	BELLEVILLE	NJ	07109	(201) 759-9731
SONS OF ISRAEL, CONGREGATION O P.O. BOX 298, 505 11TH AVENUE	BELMAR	NJ	07719	(201) 681-3200
BERGENFIELD-DUMONT JEWISH CENTER C 169 N. WASHINGTON AVENUE	BERGENFIELD	NJ	07621	(201) 384-3911
BETH ABRAHAM CONGREGATION O 338 SOUTH PROSPECT AVENUE	BERGENFIELD	NJ	07621	
MENORAH, TEMPLE R 936 BROAD STREET	BLOOMFIELD	NJ	07003	(201) 338-6482
NER TAMID, TEMPLE C & R 936 BROAD STREET	BLOOMFIELD	NJ	07003	(201) 338-6482
BETH SHOLOM, TEMPLE C HARRISON STREET	BOONTON	NJ	07005	(201) 334-2714
B'NAI ABRAHAM, CONGREGATION C 58 CROSSWICK STREET	BORDENTOWN	NJ	08505	
KNESSETH ISRAEL, CONGREGATION C 229 MOUNTAIN AVENUE	BOUND BROOK	NJ	08805	(201) 356-1634
AGUDATH ACHIM, CONGREGATION O 301 MCCABE AVENUE	BRADLEY BEACH	NJ	07720	(201) 774-2495
MAGEN DAVID CONGREGATION O 101 5TH AVENUE	BRADLEY BEACH	NJ	07720	
BETH OR, TEMPLE C 200 VAN ZILE ROAD	BRICKTOWN	NJ	08723	(201) 458-4700
BETH ABRAHAM, CONGREGATION C FAYETTE STREET & BELMONT AVENUE	BRIDGETON	NJ	08302	(609) 451-7652
SHOLOM, TEMPLE C P.O. BOX 6007, N. BRIDGE STREET	BRIDGEWATER	NJ	08807	
AGUDATH ISRAEL OF WEST ESSEX, CONGREGATION C 20 ACADEMY ROAD	CALDWELL	NJ	07006	(201) 226-3600
SHALOM OF WEST ESSEX, TEMPLE R 760 POMPTON AVENUE	CEDAR GROVE	NJ	07009	(201) 239-1321
BETH EL, CONGREGATION C P.O. BOX 481, 2901 W. CHAPEL AVENUE	CHERRY HILL	NJ	08003	(609) 677-1300
EMANUEL, TEMPLE R COOPER RIVER PARKWAY & DONAHUE	CHERRY HILL	NJ	08002	(609) 665-0888
SONS OF ISRAEL, CONGREGATION O 720 COOPER LANDING ROAD	CHERRY HILL	NJ	08034	(609) 667-9700
SINAI, TEMPLE C NEW ALBANY ROAD & ROUTE 130	CINNAMINSON	NJ	08077	(609) 829-0658
BETH OR, TEMPLE C 111 VALLEY ROAD	CLARK	NJ	07066	(201) 381-8403
SONS OF ISRAEL, CONGREGATION C EAST CENTER STREET	CLAYTON	NJ	08312	
ISRAEL COMMUNITY CENTER, TEMPLE C 207 EDGEWATER ROAD	CLIFFSIDE PARK	NJ	07010	(201) 945-7310
BETH SHOLOM REFORM TEMPLE R 733 PASSAIC AVENUE	CLIFTON	NJ	07012	(201) 773-0355
CLIFTON JEWISH CENTER C 18 DELAWARE STREET	CLIFTON	NJ	07011	(201) 772-3131
BETH EL, TEMPLE R 211 SCHRAALENBURGH ROAD	CLOSTER	NJ	07624	(201) 768-5112
BETH AM, TEMPLE C 220 TEMPLE WAY	COLONIA	NJ	07067	
OHEV SHALOM, TEMPLE C 220 TEMPLE WAY	COLONIA	NJ	07067	(201) 388-7222
BETH EL, TEMPLE C 338 WALNUT AVENUE	CRANFORD	NJ	07016	(201) 276-9231
SYNAGOGUE OF DEAL O 128 NORWOOD AVENUE	DEAL	NJ	07723	(201) 531-3200
ADATH ISRAEL-DOVER JEWISH CENTER C 18 THOMPSON AVENUE	DOVER	NJ	07801	(201) 366-0179
EAST BRUNSWICK JEWISH CENTER C 511 RYDERS LANE	EAST BRUNSWICK	NJ	08816	(201) 257-7070
EAST BRUNSWICK REFORM TEMPLE R P.O. BOX 337	EAST BRUNSWICK	NJ	08816	(201) 251-4300
YOUNG ISRAEL OF EAST BRUNSWICK 5 NEW DOVER ROAD	EAST BRUNSWICK	NJ	08816	(201) 254-1860
SHAREY TEFILO, TEMPLE R 57 PROSPECT STREET	EAST ORANGE	NJ	07017	(201) 678-0005
BETH EL SYNAGOGUE C 50 MAPLE STREAM ROAD	EAST WINDSOR	NJ	08520	(609) 443-4454
TORAS EMES/TWIN RIVERS COMMUNITY SYNAGOGUE O 639 ABBINGTON DRIVE	EAST WINDSOR	NJ	08520	(609) 443-4877

Name & Address	City	State	ZIP	Phone
EDISON JEWISH COMMUNITY CENTER-CONGREGATION BETH EL C 91 JEFFERSON BLVD	EDISON	NJ	08817	(201) 985-7272
EMANU-EL, TEMPLE R 100 JAMES STREET	EDISON	NJ	08817	(201) 549-4442
OHR TORAH O 2 HARRISON STREET	EDISON	NJ	08817	(201) 572-7181
BETH MIRIAM, TEMPLE R P.O. BOX 2097	ELBERON	NJ	07740	(201) 222-3754
ADATH JESHURUN, CONGREGATION O 200 MURRAY STREET	ELIZABETH	NJ	07202	(201) 355-6723
B'NAI ISRAEL, CONGREGATION C 1005 E. JERSEY STREET	ELIZABETH	NJ	07201	(201) 354-0400
BAIS YITZCHOK CHEVRA THILLIM, CONGREGATION O 153 BELLEVUE STREET	ELIZABETH	NJ	07202	(201) 354-4789
BETH EL, TEMPLE R 737 NORTH BROAD STREET	ELIZABETH	NJ	07208	(201) 354-3021
ELMORA HEBREW CENTER O 420 WEST END AVENUE	ELIZABETH	NJ	07202	(201) 353-1740
JEWISH EDUCATIONAL CENTER SYNAGOGUE O 330 ELMORA AVENUE	ELIZABETH	NJ	07208	(201) 353-4446
JEWISH EDUCATIONAL CENTER SYNAGOGUE C 1391 NORTH AVENUE	ELIZABETH	NJ	07208	(201) 354-6058
ELMWOOD PARK JEWISH CENTER C 100 GILBERT AVENUE	ELMWOOD PARK	NJ	07407	(201) 797-7320
EMERSON JEWISH CENTER C P.O. BOX 591, 53 PALISADE AVENUE	EMERSON	NJ	07630	(201) 261-9692
AHAVATH TORAH OF ENGLEWOOD, CONGREGATION O 240 BROAD AVENUE	ENGLEWOOD	NJ	07631	(201) 569-1315
EMANU-EL, TEMPLE C 147 TENAFLY ROAD	ENGLEWOOD	NJ	07631	(201) 567-1300
FRIENDS OF LUBAVITCH O 409 GRAND AVENUE, #7	ENGLEWOOD	NJ	07631	(201) 568-9423
SHOMEREI EMUNAH, CONGREGATION O 273 VAN NOSTRAND AVENUE	ENGLEWOOD	NJ	07631	(201) 568-7932
SHAARI EMETH, TEMPLE R P.O. BOX 393	ENGLISHTOWN	NJ	07726	(201) 462-7744
SONS OF ISRAEL, CONGREGATION O 4 PARK AVENUE, P.O. BOX 306 GORDON'S CORNER ROAD	ENGLISHTOWN	NJ	07726	(201) 446-3000
AHAVAT ACHIM O 18-19 SADDLE RIVER ROAD	FAIR LAWN	NJ	07410	(201) 797-0502
AVODA, TEMPLE R 10-10 PLAZA ROAD	FAIR LAWN	NJ	07410	(201) 797-9716
B'NAI ISRAEL, CONGREGATION C PINE AVENUE & 30TH STREET	FAIR LAWN	NJ	07410	(201) 797-9735
BETH SHOLOM, TEMPLE C 40-25 FAIR LAWN AVENUE	FAIR LAWN	NJ	07410	(201) 797-9321
EMANUEL, TEMPLE C 151 E. 33RD STREET	FAIR LAWN	NJ	07514	(201) 684-5565
FAIR LAWN JEWISH CENTER C 10-10 NORMA AVENUE	FAIR LAWN	NJ	07410	(201) 796-5040
ORTHODOX CONGREGATION OF FAIR LAWN-SHOMREI TORAH O 19-09 MORLOT AVENUE	FAIR LAWN	NJ	07410	(201) 791-7910
MOUNT OLIVE JEWISH CENTER C P.O. BOX 152, PLEASANT HILL ROAD	FLANDERS	NJ	07836	(201) 584-0212
FLEMINGTON JEWISH COMMUNITY CENTER C P.O. BOX 567	FLEMINGTON	NJ	08822	(201) 782-6410
JEWISH COMMUNITY CENTER OF FORT LEE C 1449 ANDERSON AVENUE	FORT LEE	NJ	07024	(201) 947-1735
YOUNG ISRAEL OF FORT LEE 1610 PARKER AVE	FORT LEE	NJ	07024	(201) 592-1518
SONS OF ISRAEL, CONGREGATION OAK STREET	FRANKLIN	NJ	07416	
AGUDATH ACHIM, CONGREGATION O BROAD & STOKES STREETS	FREEHOLD	NJ	07728	(201) 462-0254
JEWISH COMMUNITY CENTER C 537 HARRISON AVENUE	GARFIELD	NJ	07026	
GLEN ROCK JEWISH CENTER C 682 HARRISTOWN ROAD	GLEN ROCK	NJ	07452	(201) 652-6624
BETH EL, TEMPLE C 280 SUMMIT AVENUE	HACKENSACK	NJ	07601	(201) 342-2045
BETH SHOLOM, TEMPLE C WHITE HORSE PIKE & GREEN STREET	HADDON HEIGHTS	NJ	08035	(609) 593-6113
SHOLOM, TEMPLE GREEN STREET & WHITE HORSE PIKE	HADDON HEIGHTS	NJ	08035	(201) 547-6113
BETH EL, TEMPLE C BELLEVUE AVENUE	HAMMONTON	NJ	08037	
ETZ CHAIM, CONGREGATION O 230 DENNISON STREET	HIGHLAND PARK	NJ	08904	(201) 247-3839
HIGHLAND PARK CONSERVATIVE TEMPLE & CENTER C 201 S. 3RD AVENUE	HIGHLAND PARK	NJ	08904	(201) 545-6482
OHAV EMETH, CONGREGATION O 415 RARITAN AVENUE	HIGHLAND PARK	NJ	08904	(201) 247-3038
BETH CHAIM, CONGREGATION R P.O. BOX 128	HIGHTSTOWN	NJ	08520	(609) 799-9401
HILLSIDE JEWISH CENTER O 1550 SUMMIT AVENUE	HILLSIDE	NJ	07205	(201) 923-6191
SHOMREI TORAH, TEMPLE C 910 SALEM AVENUE	HILLSIDE	NJ	07205	(201) 351-1945
SINAI TORATH CHAIM, CONGREGATION O 1531 MAPLE AVENUE	HILLSIDE	NJ	07205	(201) 923-9500
UNITED SYNAGOGUE OF HOBOKEN T 830 HUDSON STREET	HOBOKEN	NJ	07030	(201) 659-2614
LAKE HOPATCONG JEWISH COMMUNITY CENTER C P.O. BOX 333	HOPATCONG	NJ	07843	(201) 398-8700
JEWISH COMMUNITY CENTER-CONGREGATION AHAVAT ACHIM C P.O. BOX 344	HOWELL	NJ	07731	(201) 367-1677
AGUDATH ISRAEL, CONGREGATION O 1125 STUYVESANT AVENUE	IRVINGTON	NJ	07111	(201) 372-1780
AHAVATH ACHIM BIKUR CHOLIM, CONGREGATION O 644 CHANCELLOR AVENUE	IRVINGTON	NJ	07111	
B'NAI ISRAEL, TEMPLE C 706 NYE AVENUE	IRVINGTON	NJ	07111	(201) 327-9656
CHEVRA ANSHE LUBOWITZ, CONGREGATION O 74 MILL ROAD	IRVINGTON	NJ	07111	(201) 399-1199
CHEVRA THILIM TIFERETH ISRAEL, CONGREGATION O 745 CHANCELLOR AVENUE	IRVINGTON	NJ	07111	(201) 371-6699
BETH SHOLOM C 90 COOPER AVENUE	ISELIN	NJ	08830	(201) 283-0239
AGUDATH SHOLOM, CONGREGATION O 472 BERGEN AVENUE	JERSEY CITY	NJ	07304	(201) 432-8379
B'NAI JACOB C 176 WEST SIDE AVENUE	JERSEY CITY	NJ	07305	(201) 435-5725
BERGEN HEBREW INSTITUTE-TALMUD TORAH AGUDATH SHOLEM 2-8 OXFORD AVENUE	JERSEY CITY	NJ	07304	(201) 432-9022
BETH EL, TEMPLE R 2419 KENNEDY BLVD	JERSEY CITY	NJ	07304	(201) 333-4229
EMANU-EL, CONGREGATION C 633 BERGEN AVENUE	JERSEY CITY	NJ	07304	
FREEDOM SYNAGOGUE/KEHILATH AHAVATH ISRAEL O 80 GRAND STREET	JERSEY CITY	NJ	07302	
MOUNT SINAI, CONGREGATION O 128 SHERMAN AVENUE	JERSEY CITY	NJ	07307	(201) 659-4267
MOUNT ZION, CONGREGATION O 233 WEBSTER AVENUE	JERSEY CITY	NJ	07307	
OHAB SHALOM, CONGREGATION O 225 CLAREMONT AVENUE	JERSEY CITY	NJ	07305	
SONS OF ISRAEL, CONGREGATION O 35 COTTAGE	JERSEY CITY	NJ	07306	(201) 798-0172
SONS OF ISRAEL, CONGREGATION O 294 GROVE STREET	JERSEY CITY	NJ	07302	(201) 332-3212
B'NAI ISRAEL OF KEARNY & NORTH ARLINGTON C 780 KEARNY AVENUE	KEARNY	NJ	07032	(201) 998-3813
BETH SHALOM, TEMPLE C 9 STANWOOD ROAD	KENDALL PARK	NJ	08824	
LAKE HIAWATHA JEWISH CENTER C LINCOLN AVENUE	LAKE HIAWATHA	NJ	07034	(201) 334-0959
LAKE HOPATCONG JEWISH COMMUNITY CENTER C P.O. BOX 333	LAKE HOPATCONG	NJ	07834	(201) 398-8700
AHAVAT SHALOM, CONGREGATION C FOREST AVENUE & 11TH STREET	LAKEWOOD	NJ	08701	(201) 363-5190
ANSHEI SEFARD, CONGREGATION O MADISON AVENUE	LAKEWOOD	NJ	08701	(201) 364-9309
BETH AM, TEMPLE R MADISON AT CAREY	LAKEWOOD	NJ	08701	(201) 363-2800
BEZALAL HEBREW DAY SCHOOL O 419 5TH STREET	LAKEWOOD	NJ	08701	(201) 363-1768
CHEVRA LOMDEI TORAH O 617 5TH STREET	LAKEWOOD	NJ	08701	(201) 367-6393
SONS OF ISRAEL, CONGREGATION O MADISON AVENUE & 6TH STREET	LAKEWOOD	NJ	08701	(201) 364-2230
TALMUD TORAH-CONGREGATION SONS OF ISRAEL 6TH STREET & MADISON AVENUE	LAKEWOOD	NJ	08701	(201) 364-2230
YOUNG ISRAEL OF LAWRENCEVILLE 25 TEXAS AVENUE	LAWRENCEVILLE	NJ	08648	(609) 883-8833
ADAS EMUNO, CONGREGATION R 254 BROAD AVENUE	LEONIA	NJ	07605	(201) 461-4045
SONS OF ISRAEL, CONGREGATION C 150 GRAND AVENUE	LEONIA	NJ	07605	(201) 592-9700
ANSHE CHESED, CONGREGATION O ORCHARD TERRACE AT ST. GEORGE AVENUE	LINDEN	NJ	07036	(201) 486-8616
BETH DAVID, CONGREGATION O P.O. BOX 185	LINDEN	NJ	07036	
SUBURBAN JEWISH CENTER-TEMPLE MEKOR CHAYIM C DEERFIELD ROAD & ACADEMY TERRACE	LINDEN	NJ	07036	(201) 925-2283
B'NAI ABRAHAM, TEMPLE C 300 E. NORTHFIELD ROAD	LIVINGSTON	NJ	07039	(201) 994-2290
BETH SHALOM, TEMPLE C 193 MT. PLEASANT AVENUE	LIVINGSTON	NJ	07039	(201) 992-3600
CHABAD-LUBAVITCH O 85 WEST MOUNT PLEASANT AVENUE	LIVINGSTON	NJ	07039	
EMANU-EL, TEMPLE R 264 W. NORTHFIELD ROAD	LIVINGSTON	NJ	07039	(201) 992-5560
SUBURBAN TORAH CENTER, SYNAGOGUE OF THE O 85 W. MT. PLEASANT AVENUE	LIVINGSTON	NJ	07039	(201) 994-0122
BROTHERS OF ISRAEL, CONGREGATION O 85 2ND AVENUE	LONG BRANCH	NJ	07740	(201) 222-6666
LYNDHURST HEBREW CENTER C 333 VALLEY BROOK AVENUE	LYNDHURST	NJ	07071	(201) 438-9582
BETH HAVERIM R P.O. BOX 332, 59 MASONICUS ROAD	MAHWAH	NJ	07430	(201) 327-4333
TEMPLE BETH SHALOM 108 FREEHOLD ROAD	MANALAPAN	NJ	07726	(201) 446-1200
AHAVATH ZION, CONGREGATION O 421 BOYDEN AVENUE	MAPLEWOOD	NJ	07040	(201) 761-5444
ANSHE RUSSIA, CONGREGATION O 14 HAUSEMAN COURT	MAPLEWOOD	NJ	07040	
BETH EPHRAIM-MAPLEWOOD JEWISH CENTER O 520 PROSPECT STREET, P.O. BOX 279	MAPLEWOOD	NJ	07040	(201) 762-5722
CHABAD-LUBAVITCH O 421 BOYDEN AVENUE	MAPLEWOOD	NJ	07040	
CHABAD-LUBAVITCH O 39 BURROWS WAY	MAPLEWOOD	NJ	07040	
ATERES TZVI, CONGREGATION O 419 N. ESSEX AVENUE	MARGATE	NJ	08402	
BETH EL, TEMPLE C 500 N. JEROME AVENUE	MARGATE	NJ	08402	(609) 823-2725
BETH ISRAEL, CONGREGATION R 8401 VENTNOR AVENUE, P.O. BOX 1	MARGATE	NJ	08402	(609) 823-4116
CHABAD LUBAVITCH O 703 NORTH JEROME AVENUE	MARGATE	NJ	08402	(609) 823-3223
EMETH SHALOM, TEMPLE R 8501 VENTNOR AVENUE	MARGATE	NJ	08402	(609) 822-4343
OHAV SHALOM C P.O. BOX 98	MARLBORO	NJ	07746	(609) 536-2300
BETH TIKVAH-MT. LAUREL C EVESBORO-MEDFORD ROAD	MARLTON	NJ	08053	(609) 983-8090
BET TEFILAH, CONGREGATION O 110 DEERFIELD LANE	MATAWAN	NJ	07747	(201) 583-6262
BETH AHM, TEMPLE C 550 LLOYD ROAD (ABERDEEN)	MATAWAN	NJ	07747	(201) 583-1700
SHALOM OF MATAWAN, TEMPLE R 5 AYRMONT LANE	MATAWAN	NJ	07747	(201) 566-2621
UNITED HEBREW CONGREGATION - TEMPLE BETH AHM 550 LLOYD ROAD	MATAWAN	NJ	07747	
BETH ISRAEL, TEMPLE C 34 W. MAGNOLIA AVENUE	MAYWOOD	NJ	07607	(201) 845-7550
SHALOM, TEMPLE R P.O. BOX 93	MCAFEE	NJ	07428	(201) 827-5655
BETH JACOB, CONGREGATION C 109 E. MAPLE AVENUE	MERCHANTVILLE	NJ	08109	(609) 662-4509
NEVE SHALOM, TEMPLE - JCC C 250 GROVE AVENUE	METUCHEN	NJ	08840	(201) 548-2238
B'NAI ISRAEL, CONGREGATION C 160 MILLBURN AVENUE	MILLBURN	NJ	07041	(201) 379-3811
BETH HILLEL, TEMPLE C 3RD & OAK STREETS	MILLVILLE	NJ	08332	
CONGREGATION B'NAI KESHET RE 87-89 VALLEY ROAD	MONTCLAIR	NJ	07043	(201) 746-4489
SHOMREI EMUNAH, CONGREGATION C 67 PARK STREET	MONTCLAIR	NJ	07042	(201) 746-5031
RODEPH TORAH, TEMPLE R P.O. BOX 23	MORGANVILLE	NJ	07751	(201) 536-2417
AHAVATH YISRAEL O 9 CUTLER STREET	MORRISTOWN	NJ	07960	(201) 267-4184
B'NAI OR, TEMPLE R OVERLOOK ROAD	MORRISTOWN	NJ	07960	(201) 539-4539
MORRISTOWN JEWISH COMMUNITY CENTER C 177 SPEEDWELL AVENUE	MORRISTOWN	NJ	07960	(201) 538-9292
RABBINICAL COLLEGE OF AMERICA O 226 SUSSEX AVENUE	MORRISTOWN	NJ	07960	(201) 267-9404
MOUNT FREEDOM JEWISH CENTER O SUSSEX TURNPIKE	MOUNT FREEDOM	NJ	07970	
HAR-ZION, TEMPLE C HIGH & RIDGWAY STREETS	MT. HOLLY	NJ	08060	(609) 267-0660
M'KOR SHALOM, CONGREGATION R CHURCH & FELLOWSHIP ROADS	MT. LAUREL	NJ	08054	(609) 235-0590
AHAVAS ACHIM O 35 RICHMOND STREET	NEW BRUNSWICK	NJ	08901	(201) 247-0532
ANSHE EMETH MEMORIAL TEMPLE R 222 LIVINGSTON AVENUE	NEW BRUNSWICK	NJ	08901	(201) 545-6484
CHABAD HOUSE O 8 SICARD STREET	NEW BRUNSWICK	NJ	08901	(201) 828-7374
POALE ZEDEK, CONGREGATION T 145 NEILSON STREET, P.O. BOX 166	NEW BRUNSWICK	NJ	08901	
BETH TIKVA-NEW MILFORD JEWISH CENTER C 435 RIVER ROAD	NEW MILFORD	NJ	07646	(201) 261-4847
B'NAI MOSHE, CONGREGATION O 19-29 ROSS STREET	NEWARK	NJ	07114	
B'NAI ZION, CONGREGATION O 215 CHANCELLOR AVENUE	NEWARK	NJ	07112	
BETH DAVID JEWISH CENTER C 828 SANFORD AVENUE	NEWARK	NJ	07106	(201) 372-9360
CHEBRA ANSHE LUBAWITZ, CONGREGATION O P.O. BOX 416	NEWARK	NJ	07101	
MOUNT SINAI CONGREGATION OF IVY HILL O 250 MT. VERNON PLACE (IVY HILL)	NEWARK	NJ	07106	(201) 372-3551
JEWISH CENTER OF SUSSEX COUNTY C 13 WASHINGTON STREET, P.O. BOX 334	NEWTON	NJ	07860	(201) 383-4570
NORMA BROTHERHOOD CONGREGATION O P.O. BOX 56	NORMA	NJ	08347	(201) 691-4740
BETH ABRAHAM, TEMPLE O 8410 FOURTH AVENUE	NORTH BERGEN	NJ	07047	(201) 869-2425
BETH-EL, TEMPLE O 7501 HUDSON AVENUE	NORTH BERGEN	NJ	07047	
ZEMACH DAVID, CONGREGATION O 8402 FIRST AVENUE	NORTH BERGEN	NJ	07047	(201) 869-2480
B'NAI TIKVAH, CONGREGATION C BOX 3028	NORTH BRUNSWICK	NJ	08902	(201) 297-0696
SHARRI SHOLOM, CONGREGATION C R.F.D. #4-BOX 454E, GEORGES ROAD	NORTH BRUNSWICK	NJ	08902	
B'NAI ISRAEL, TEMPLE C 192 CENTRE STREET	NUTLEY	NJ	07110	(201) 667-3713
BETH EL, TEMPLE C 301 MONMOUTH ROAD	OAKHURST	NJ	07755	(201) 531-0300
BETH TORAH, TEMPLE C 1200 ROSELD AVENUE	OCEAN	NJ	07712	(201) 531-4410
MAGEN DAVID CONGREGATION OF BRADLEY BEACH O 395 DEAL ROAD	OCEAN	NJ	07712	(201) 531-3220
BETH OHR C 300 ROUTE 516	OLD BRIDGE	NJ	08857	(201) 257-9867
BETH TORAH, CONGREGATION C 270 REYNOLDS TERRACE	ORANGE	NJ	07050	(201) 678-1269
SONS OF ISRAEL, CONGREGATION BROAD & EDSALL AVENUES, P.O. BOX 2	PALISADES PARK	NJ	07650	
BETH TEFILLAH, CONGREGATION O 241 E.MIDLAND AVENUE	PARAMUS	NJ	07652	(201) 265-4100
JEWISH COMMUNITY CENTER OF PARAMUS C 304 E. MIDLAND AVENUE	PARAMUS	NJ	07652	(201) 262-7691
K'HAL ADATH JESHURUN OF PARAMUS O 140 ARNOT PLACE	PARAMUS	NJ	07652	(201) 967-9898
BETH SHOLOM, TEMPLE C P.O. BOX 104, 32 PARK AVENUE	PARK RIDGE	NJ	07656	

OHAV SHALOM, TEMPLE - SAYREVILLE JEWISH CENTER C P.O. BOX 341 ..... PARLIN **NJ** 08859 (201) 727-4334
AHAVAT TORAH OF PARSIPPANY, CONGREGATION O
1180 HIGHWAY 46 ..... PARSIPPANY **NJ** 07054 (201) 335-3636
BETH AM, TEMPLE R P.O. BOX 50, 879 S. BEVERWYCK ROAD ..... PARSIPPANY **NJ** 07504 (201) 887-0046
ADAS ISRAEL, CONGREGATION O 565 BROADWAY ..... PASSAIC **NJ** 07055 (201) 773-7272
AHAVAS ISRAEL, CONG.-PASSAIC PARK JEWISH COMMUNITY CTR. T
181 VAN HOUTEN AVENUE ..... PASSAIC **NJ** 07055 (201) 777-5929
B'NAI JACOB, CONGREGATION O P.O. BOX 293 ..... PASSAIC **NJ** 07055 (201) 473-2164
BIKUR CHOLIM, CONGREGATION O 22 MARKET STREET ..... PASSAIC **NJ** 07055
CHEVRAH THILIM, CONGREGATION O 132 SPRING STREET ..... PASSAIC **NJ** 07055 (201) 473-0263
EMANUEL, TEMPLE C 181 LAFAYETTE AVENUE ..... PASSAIC **NJ** 07055
HUNGARIAN HEBREW MEN, CONGREGATION C 71 DAYTON AVENUE ..... PASSAIC **NJ** 07055
TIFERETH ISRAEL, CONGREGATION O 180 PASSAIC AVENUE ..... PASSAIC **NJ** 07055 (201) 773-2552
YOUNG ISRAEL OF PASSAIC-CLIFTON 200 BROOK AVENUE ..... PASSAIC **NJ** 07055 (201) 778-7117
ANSHAI LUBAVITZ, CONGREGATION O 427 11TH AVENUE ..... PATERSON **NJ** 07514
B'NAI ISRAEL AHAVATH JOSEPH, CONGREGATION O
561 PARK AVENUE ..... PATERSON **NJ** 07504 (201) 742-5566
B'NAI JESHURUN, CONGREGATION R 152 DERROM AVENUE ..... PATERSON **NJ** 07504 (201) 279-2111
BETH HAMEDROSH HAGODOL, CONGREGATION O
115 VREELAND AVENUE ..... PATERSON **NJ** 07504
CHABAD-LUBAVITCH O 6 MANOR ROAD ..... PATERSON **NJ** 07514
COMMUNITY SYNAGOGUE C 660 14TH AVENUE ..... PATERSON **NJ** 07504 (201) 742-9345
EASTSIDE HEBREW CENTER O 467 E. 37TH STREET ..... PATERSON
EMANUEL OF NORTH JERSEY, TEMPLE C 151 E. 33RD STREET ..... PATERSON **NJ** 07514 (201) 684-5564
ISRAEL CENTER O 115 VREELAND AVENUE ..... PATERSON **NJ** 07504
UNITED BROTHERHOOD HENRY RAMER O 100 HAMILTON PLACE ..... PATERSON **NJ** 07505
YAVNEH ACADEMY SYNAGOGUE O 413 12TH AVENUE ..... PATERSON **NJ** 07514
SHARI TZADEK, CONGREGATION C N. BROAD STREET ..... PENNS GROVE **NJ** 08069
BETH ISRAEL, CONGREGATION O 166 JEFFERSON STREET ..... PERTH AMBOY **NJ** 08861
BETH MORDECAI, CONGREGATION C 224 HIGH STREET ..... PERTH AMBOY **NJ** 08862 (201) 442-2431
SHAAREY TEFILOH, CONGREGATION O
15 MARKET STREET, P.O. BOX 633 ..... PERTH AMBOY **NJ** 08862 (201) 826-2977
PINE BROOK JEWISH CENTER C CHANGEBRIDGE ROAD ..... PINE BROOK **NJ** 07058 (201) 227-3520
CONGREGATION B'NAI ISRAEL PISCATAWAY JEWISH COMMUNITY
CONGREGATION RE POB 965 ..... PISCATAWAY **NJ** 08854 (201) 981-1096
BET CHAVURAH OF GREATER PLAINFIELD O 105 EAST 7TH STREET ..... PLAINFIELD **NJ** 07060 (201) 755-8233
BETH EL, TEMPLE C 225 E. 7TH STREET ..... PLAINFIELD **NJ** 07060 (201) 756-2333
SHOLOM, TEMPLE R 815 W. 7TH STREET ..... PLAINFIELD **NJ** 07063 (201) 756-6447
UNITED ORTHODOX SYNAGOGUE O 526 WEST 7TH STREET ..... PLAINFIELD **NJ** 07060 (201) 755-0043
B'NAI ISRAEL, CONGREGATION C
W. JERSEY AVENUE & FRANKLIN BLVD ..... PLEASANTVILLE **NJ** 08232
BETH SHALOM, CONGREGATION C 21 PASSAIC AVENUE ..... POMPTON LAKES **NJ** 07442 (201) 835-9785
POMPTON LAKES JEWISH CENTER 525 WANAQUE AVENUE ..... POMPTON LAKES **NJ** 07442
JEWISH CENTER, THE C 457 NASSAU STREET ..... PRINCETON **NJ** 08540 (609) 921-0100
YAVNEH HOUSE 83 PROSPECT AVENUE ..... PRINCETON **NJ** 08540 (609) 452-3610
BETH TORAH, TEMPLE - RAHWAY HEBREW CONGREGATION C
1365 BRYANT STREET ..... RAHWAY **NJ** 07065 (201) 388-1913
BETH SHOLOM C MAPLE STREET & PLAZA LANE ..... RAMSEY **NJ** 07446 (201) 327-7759
B'NAI ISRAEL, CONGREGATION P.O. BOX 252 ..... RED BANK **NJ** 07701 (201) 842-1800
BETH SHALOM, CONGREGATION O 186 MAPLE AVENUE ..... RED BANK **NJ** 07701 (201) 741-1657
EMANUEL, TEMPLE C 120 PARK STREET ..... RIDGEFIELD PARK **NJ** 07660 (201) 440-9464
ISRAEL OF RIDGEWOOD, TEMPLE C 475 GROVE STREET ..... RIDGEWOOD **NJ** 07450 (201) 444-9320
LAKELAND HILLS JEWISH CENTER C P.O. BOX 115 ..... RINGWOOD **NJ** 07456 (201) 835-4786
SHOLOM, TEMPLE R 385 HOWLAND AVENUE ..... RIVER EDGE **NJ** 07661 (201) 489-2463
UNITED JEWISH COMMUNITY OF BERGEN COUNTY
111 KINDERKAMACK ROAD, P.O. BOX 176, N. HACKENSACK STA. ..... RIVER EDGE **NJ** 07661 (201) 488-6800
OHAV SHALOM, CONGREGATION C 385 W. PASSAIC STREET ..... ROCHELLE PARK **NJ** 07662 (201) 845-6882
B'NAI TORAH OF WHITE MEADOW LAKE O 103 WHITE MEADOW ROAD ..... ROCKAWAY **NJ** 07866
WHITE MEADOW TEMPLE C 153 WHITE MEADOW ROAD ..... ROCKAWAY **NJ** 07866 (201) 627-4500
ANSHEI ROOSEVELT, CONGREGATION O 20 HOMESTEAD LANE ..... ROOSEVELT **NJ** 08555 (201) 448-2526
B'NAI ISRAEL, CONGREGATION C HANCE & RIDGE ROADS ..... RUMSON **NJ** 07760 (201) 842-1800
BETH EL, TEMPLE C 185 MONTROSS AVENUE ..... RUTHERFORD **NJ** 07070 (201) 438-4931
OHEB SHOLOM SYNAGOGUE C 240 GRANT STREET ..... SALEM **NJ** 08079
ISRAEL OF SCOTCH PLAINS & FANWOOD, TEMPLE C
1920 CLIFFWOOD STREET ..... SCOTCH PLAINS **NJ** 07076 (201) 889-1830
B'NAI JESHURUN, CONGREGATION R 1025 S. ORANGE AVENUE ..... SHORT HILLS **NJ** 07078 (201) 379-1555
BETH EL, TEMPLE C 1495 AMWELL ROAD ..... SOMERSET **NJ** 08873 (201) 873-2225
BETH EL, TEMPLE R 67 RTE. 206 SOUTH ..... SOMERVILLE **NJ** 08876 (201) 722-0674
BETH EL OF THE ORANGES & MAPLEWOOD C
222 IRVINGTON AVENUE ..... SOUTH ORANGE **NJ** 07079 (201) 763-0111
ISRAEL OF THE ORANGES & MAPLEWOOD, TEMPLE R
432 SCOTLAND ROAD ..... SOUTH ORANGE **NJ** 07079 (201) 763-4116
MONROE TOWNSHIP JEWISH CENTER R P.O. BOX 71 ..... SOUTH ORANGE **NJ** 08884 (201) 251-0594
OHEB SHALOM, CONGREGATION C 170 SCOTLAND ROAD ..... SOUTH ORANGE **NJ** 07079 (201) 762-7067
ANSHE EMETH & JEWISH COMMUNITY CENTER O 88 MAIN STREET ..... SOUTH RIVER **NJ** 08882 (201) 257-4190
BETH AHM, TEMPLE C 60 BALTUSROL WAY & TEMPLE DRIVE ..... SPRINGFIELD **NJ** 07081 (201) 376-0539
ISRAEL OF SPRINGFIELD, CONGREGATION O
339 MOUNTAIN AVENUE ..... SPRINGFIELD **NJ** 07081 (201) 467-9666
SHA-AREY SHALOM, TEMPLE R 78 S. SPRINGFIELD AVENUE ..... SPRINGFIELD **NJ** 07081 (201) 379-5387
SHALOM, TEMPLE R 215 S. HILLSIDE AVENUE ..... SUCCASUNNA **NJ** 07876 (201) 584-5666
SINAI, TEMPLE R 208 SUMMIT AVENUE ..... SUMMIT **NJ** 07901 (201) 273-4921
SUMMIT JEWISH COMMUNITY CENTER C 67 KENT PLACE BLVD ..... SUMMIT **NJ** 07901 (201) 273-8130
BETH AARON CONGREGATION O 950 QUEEN ANNE ROAD ..... TEANECK **NJ** 07666 (201) 836-4655
B'NAI YESHURUN, CONGREGATION O 641 W. ENGLEWOOD AVENUE ..... TEANECK **NJ** 07666 (201) 836-8916
BETH AM, CONGREGATION R 510 CLAREMONT AVENUE ..... TEANECK **NJ** 07666 (201) 836-5752
BETH SHOLOM, CONGREGATION C RUGBY ROAD & RUTLAND AVENUE ..... TEANECK **NJ** 07666 (201) 833-2620
EMETH, TEMPLE R 1666 WINDSOR ROAD ..... TEANECK **NJ** 07666 (201) 833-1322
JEWISH CENTER OF TEANECK C 70 STERLING PLACE ..... TEANECK **NJ** 07666 (201) 833-0515
RINAT YISRAEL, CONGREGATION 361 WEST ENGLEWOOD AVENUE ..... TEANECK **NJ** 07666 (201) 837-2795
BETH CHAVAIRUTH, CONGREGATION R 49 LEONARD AVENUE ..... TENAFLY **NJ** 07670 (201) 569-8323
SINAI OF BERGEN COUNTY, TEMPLE R 1 ENGLE STREET ..... TENAFLY **NJ** 07670 (201) 568-3035
MONMOUTH REFORM TEMPLE R 332 HANCE AVENUE ..... TINTON FALLS **NJ** 07724 (201) 747-9365
B'NAI ISRAEL, CONGREGATION C 1488 OLD FREEHOLD ROAD ..... TOMS RIVER **NJ** 08753 (201) 349-1244
ADATH ISRAEL CONGREGATION C 715 BELLEVUE AVENUE ..... TRENTON **NJ** 08618 (609) 599-2591
AHAVATH ISRAEL, CONGREGATION C 1130 LOWER FERRY ROAD ..... TRENTON **NJ** 08618 (201) 882-3092
ANSHE EMES O 1201 WEST STATE STREET ..... TRENTON **NJ** 08618 (609) 396-4343
BROTHERS OF ISRAEL, CONGREGATION C 499 GREENWOOD AVENUE ..... TRENTON **NJ** 08609 (609) 695-3479
HAR SINAI HEBREW CONGREGATION R 491 BELLEVUE AVENUE ..... TRENTON **NJ** 08618 (609) 392-7143
PEOPLE OF TRUTH CONGREGATION JESHURUN O
1201 W. STATE STREET ..... TRENTON **NJ** 08618
BETH SHALOM, CONGREGATION C VAUXHALL ROAD & PLANE STREET ..... UNION **NJ** 07083 (201) 686-6773
ISRAEL OF UNION, TEMPLE C 2372 MORRIS AVENUE ..... UNION **NJ** 07083 (201) 687-2120
BETH JACOB, CONGREGATION O 325 4TH STREET ..... UNION CITY **NJ** 07087 (201) 863-3114
ISRAEL EMANUEL, TEMPLE O 33 STREET & NEW YORK AVENUE ..... UNION CITY **NJ** 07087 (201) 866-6656
MESIVTA SANZ O 3400 NEW YORK AVENUE ..... UNION CITY **NJ** 07087 (201) 867-6890
BETH JUDAH, CONGREGATION C 6725 VENTNOR AVENUE ..... VENTNOR **NJ** 08406 (609) 822-7116
JEWISH COMMUNITY CENTER OF VERONA C 56 GROVE AVENUE ..... VERONA **NJ** 07044 (201) 239-0754
AHAVAS ACHIM, CONGREGATION O 618 PLUM STREET ..... VINELAND **NJ** 08360 (609) 691-2118
BETH ISRAEL CONGREGATION C 1015 PARK AVENUE, P.O. BOX 465 ..... VINELAND **NJ** 08360 (609) 691-0852
SONS OF JACOB, CONGREGATION O 321 GRAPE STREET ..... VINELAND **NJ** 08360
MOUNTAIN JEWISH CENTER 104 MT. HOREB ROAD ..... WARREN **NJ** 07060 (201) 356-8777
BETH OR, TEMPLE R 56 RIDGEWOOD ROAD ..... WASHINGTON TOWNSHIP **NJ** 07675 (201) 664-7422
BETH TIKVAH, TEMPLE R P.O. BOX 3182, 950 PREAKNESS AVENUE ..... WAYNE **NJ** 07470 (201) 595-6565
EMANUEL, TEMPLE 1412 ALPS ROAD ..... WAYNE **NJ** 07470
WAYNE CONSERVATIVE CONGREGATION C 8 MAYFAIR DRIVE ..... WAYNE **NJ** 07470 (201) 696-2500
YOUNG ISRAEL METROPOLITAN NEW JERSEY
1 HENDERSON DRIVE ..... WEST CALDWELL **NJ** 07006 (201) 575-1194
B'NAI SHOLOM, CONGREGATION C 213 LENOX AVENUE ..... WEST END **NJ** 07740 (201) 229-2700
SHAARE ZEDEK SYNAGOGUE O 5308 PALISADE AVENUE ..... WEST NEW YORK **NJ** 07093 (201) 867-6859
TALMUD TORAH, CONGREGATION O 5308 PALISADE AVENUE ..... WEST NEW YORK **NJ** 07093
AHAVAS ACHIM, B'NAI JACOB & DAVID, CONGREGATION O
700 PLEASANT VALLEY WAY ..... WEST ORANGE **NJ** 07052 (201) 736-1407
DAUGHTERS OF ISRAEL/PLEASANT VALLEY HOME
1155 PLEASANT VALLEY WAY ..... WEST ORANGE **NJ** 07052 (201) 731-5100
JEWISH CENTER OF WEST ORANGE C 300 PLEASANT VALLEY WAY ..... WEST ORANGE **NJ** 07052 (201) 731-0160
YOUNG ISRAEL OF WEST ORANGE 567 PLEASANT VALLEY WAY ..... WEST ORANGE **NJ** 07052 (201) 731-3383
EMANU-EL OF WESTFIELD, TEMPLE R 756 E. BROAD STREET ..... WESTFIELD **NJ** 07090 (201) 232-6770
RABBINIC CENTER SYNAGOGUE 128 E. DUDLEY AVENUE ..... WESTFIELD **NJ** 07090 (201) 233-0419
BETH OR, TEMPLE R 56 RIDGEWOOD ROAD ..... WESTWOOD **NJ** 07675 (201) 644-7422
EMANUEL, TEMPLE 111 WASHINGTON AVENUE ..... WESTWOOD **NJ** 07675 (201) 664-2880
BETH JUDAH SYNAGOGUE C SPENCER & PACIFIC AVENUE ..... WILDWOOD **NJ** 08260 (201) 522-7541
BETH TORAH, CONGREGATION C BEVERLY-RANCOCAS ROAD ..... WILLINGBORO **NJ** 08046 (609) 877-4214
EMANU-EL, TEMPLE R JOHN F. KENNEDY WAY ..... WILLINGBORO **NJ** 08046 (609) 871-1736
WOODBINE BROTHERHOOD, CONGREGATION O
614 WASHINGTON AVENUE ..... WOODBINE **NJ** 08270
ADATH ISRAEL, CONGREGATION C
424 AMBOY AVENUE & S. PARK DRIVE ..... WOODBRIDGE **NJ** 07095 (201) 634-9601
BETH ISRAEL C P.O. BOX 143, HIGH & WARNER STREETS ..... WOODBURY **NJ** 08096 (609) 848-7272
EMANUEL, TEMPLE - PASACK VALLEY C 87 OVERLOOK DRIVE ..... WOODCLIFF LAKE **NJ** 07675 (201) 664-2880
BETH RISHON, TEMPLE 585 RUSSELL AVENUE BOX 345 ..... WYCKOFF **NJ** 07481 (201) 891-4466
ALBERT, CONGREGATION R 1006 LEAD AVENUE S.E. ..... ALBUQUERQUE **NM** 87106 (505) 243-3533
B'NAI ISRAEL, CONGREGATION C 4401 INDIAN SCHOOL RD., N.E. ..... ALBUQUERQUE **NM** 87110 (505) 266-0155
BETH EL, TEMPLE P.O. BOX 1029 ..... LAS CRUCES **NM** 88003 (505) 524-3380
LOS ALAMOS JEWISH CENTER 2400 CANYON ROAD ..... LOS ALAMOS **NM** 87544 (505) 662-2140
B'NAI ISRAEL, CONGREGATION C 8TH & WASHINGTON STREETS ..... ROSWELL **NM** 88201
BETH SHALOM 205 EAST BARCELONA ROAD ..... SANTA FE **NM** 87501 (505) 982-1376
SONS OF ISRAEL, CONGREGATION PRINCE STREET ..... GLACE BAY **NS** B1A 2J6
SHAAR SHALOM CONGREGATION C 1981 OXFORD STREET ..... HALIFAX **NS** B3H 4A4 (902) 422-2580
BETH SHOLOM, TEMPLE C 1600 E. OAKEY BLVD ..... LAS VEGAS **NV** 89104 (702) 384-5070
EMANU-EL, TEMPLE C 4241 WEST CHARLESTON BOULEVARD ..... LAS VEGAS **NV** 89102 (702) 870-1217
NER TAMID, CONGREGATION R 2761 EMERSON AVENUE ..... LAS VEGAS **NV** 89121 (702) 733-6292
SHAAREI TEFILLA, CONGREGATION O
1331 SOUTH MARYLAND PARKWAY ..... LAS VEGAS **NV** 89104 (702) 384-3565
EMANU-EL, TEMPLE C
1031 MANZANITA LANE, AT THE CORNER OF LAKESIDE DRIVE ..... RENO **NV** 89509 (702) 825-5600
SINAI, TEMPLE R P.O. BOX 3114 ..... RENO **NV** 89505 (702) 747-9927
B'NAI SHOLOM, THE NEW REFORM CONGREGATION R
420 WHITEHALL ROAD ..... ALBANY **NY** 12208 (518) 482-5283
BETH ABRAHAM-JACOB, CONGREGATION O 66 HACKETT BLVD ..... ALBANY **NY** 12209 (518) 449-7813
BETH EMETH, TEMPLE R 100 ACADEMY ROAD ..... ALBANY **NY** 12208 (518) 436-9761
CHABAD LUBAVITCH O 122 S. MAIN STREET ..... ALBANY **NY** 12208 (518) 482-5781
ISRAEL, TEMPLE C 600 NEW SCOTLAND AVENUE ..... ALBANY **NY** 12208 (518) 438-7858
OHEV SHOLOM, CONGREGATION C NEW KRUMKILL ROAD ..... ALBANY **NY** 12208 (518) 489-4706
RECONSTRUCTIONIST HAVURAH OF THE CAPITAL DISTRICT
C/O PAUL GREENBERG ..... ALBANY **NY** (518) 439-5870
BETH DAVID CONGREGATION R P.O. BOX 76 ..... AMENIA **NY** 12501 (914) 373-8264
SINAI, TEMPLE R/RE 50 ALBERTA DRIVE ..... AMHERST **NY** 14226 (716) 834-0708
BETH SHOLOM CENTER OF AMITYVILLE & THE MASSAPEQUAS C
79 CITY LINE ROAD ..... AMITYVILLE **NY** 11701 (516) 264-2891
ISRAEL, TEMPLE OF R 166 LOCUST AVENUE ..... AMSTERDAM **NY** 12010
SONS OF ISRAEL 355 GUY PARK AVENUE ..... AMSTERDAM **NY** 12010 (518) 842-8691
B'NAI YISRAEL, CONGREGATION R
485 BEDFORD ROAD, BOX 766 LOCUST AVENUE ..... ARMONK **NY** 10504 (914) 273-2220
ANSHE SFARD, CONGREGATION O 208-10 BEACH 75TH STREET ..... ARVERNE **NY** 11692
DERECH EMUNOH, CONGREGATION O 199 BEACH 67TH STREET ..... ARVERNE **NY** 11692 (718) 634-2288
BETH EL OF ASTORIA, CONGREGATION O 30-85 35TH STREET ..... ASTORIA **NY** 11103 (718) 278-8930
BETH JACOB OF ASTORIA, CONGREGATION O 22-51 29TH STREET ..... ASTORIA **NY** 11105 (718) 278-4170
MISHKAN ISRAEL, CONGREGATION O 27-31 CRESCENT STREET ..... ASTORIA **NY** 11102
JEWISH CENTER OF ATLANTIC BEACH O
PARK STREET & NASSAU AVENUE ..... ATLANTIC BEACH **NY** 11509 (516) 371-0972
B'NAI ISRAEL, CONGREGATION C P.O. BOX 101, 8 JOHN SMITH AVENUE ..... AUBURN **NY** 13021 (315) 253-6675
BETH SHOLOM, CONGREGATION C 441 DEER PARK AVENUE ..... BABYLON **NY** 11702 (516) 587-5650

BALDWIN JEWISH CENTER C 885 E. SEAMAN AVENUE BALDWIN NY 11510 (516) 223-5599
SOUTH BALDWIN JEWISH CENTER-CONGREGATION SHAAREI SHALOM C
2959 GRAND AVENUE BALDWIN NY 11510 (516) 223-8688
EMANU-EL, TEMPLE C 124 BANK STREET BATAVIA NY 14020 (716) 343-7027
AGUDAS ISRAEL OF RIDGEWOOD, CONGREGATION O
52 PINE BROOK PLACE BAY SHORE NY 11706
JEWISH CENTRE OF BAY SHORE C 34 N. CLINTON AVENUE BAY SHORE NY 11706 (516) 665-1140
SINAI REFORM TEMPLE R 39 BRENTWOOD ROAD BAY SHORE NY 11706 (516) 665-5755
BAY TERRACE JEWISH CENTER C
209 STREET & CROSS ISLAND PARKWAY BAYSIDE NY 11360 (718) 428-6363
BAYSIDE JEWISH CENTER C 203-05 32ND AVENUE BAYSIDE NY 11361 (718) 352-7900
BAYSIDE-OAKS JEWISH CENTER C 50-35 CLOVERDALE BLVD BAYSIDE NY 11364 (718) 631-0100
JEWISH CENTER OF BAYSIDE HILLS C 48TH AVENUE & 212TH STREET BAYSIDE NY 11364 (718) 225-5301
OAKLAND JEWISH CENTER 61-35 220TH STREET BAYSIDE NY 11364 (718) 225-7800
YOUNG ISRAEL OF BAYSIDE 209-34 26TH AVENUE BAYSIDE NY 11360 (718) 423-3720
YOUNG ISRAEL OF WINDSOR PARK 67-45 215TH STREET BAYSIDE NY 11364 (718) 224-2100
BEACON HEBREW ALLIANCE C 55 FISHKILL AVENUE BEACON NY 12508 (914) 831-2012
OHEL SHMUEL, YESHIVAH O HAINES ROAD BEDFORD NY 10507 (914) 241-2700
SHAARAY TEFILA, TEMPLE R P.O. BOX 416 BEDFORD NY 10506 (914) 666-3133
B'NAI DAVID, CONGREGATION 567 BEACH 130TH STREET BELLE HARBOR NY 11694
BETH EL OF ROCKAWAY PARK, TEMPLE C
445 BEACH 135TH STREET BELLE HARBOR NY 11694 (718) 634-8100
CONGREGATION SHAARE TEFILA OF BELLE HARBOR
214 BEACH 120TH STREET BELLE HARBOR NY 11694 (718) 945-2298
OHAB ZEDEK, CONGREGATION O
134-01 ROCKAWAY BEACH BLVD BELLE HARBOR NY 11694 (718) 474-3300
YOUNG ISRAEL OF BELLE HARBOR 505 BEACH 129TH STREET BELLE HARBOR NY 11694 (718) 474-9223
SHOLOM, TEMPLE 80-63 249TH STREET BELLEROSE NY 11426
BELLMORE JEWISH CENTER C 2550 CENTRE AVENUE BELLMORE NY 11710 (516) 781-3072
BETH EL, TEMPLE C 1373 BELLMORE ROAD BELLMORE NY 11710 (516) 781-2650
SHAAREI SHALOM, THE EAST BAY REFORM TEMPLE R
2569 MERRICK ROAD BELLMORE NY 11710 (516) 781-5599
BETHPAGE JEWISH COMMUNITY CENTER C 600 BROADWAY BETHPAGE NY 11714 (516) 938-7909
BETH DAVID, CONGREGATION O 39 RIVERSIDE DRIVE BINGHAMTON NY 13905 (607) 722-1793
CONCORD, TEMPLE R 9 RIVERSIDE DRIVE BINGHAMTON NY 13905 (607) 723-7355
ISRAEL, TEMPLE C DEERFIELD PLACE BINGHAMTON NY 13903 (607) 723-7461
LUBAVITCH OF BINGHAMTON O 435 PLAZA DRIVE 2-14 BINGHAMTON NY 13903 (607) 797-0015
BETH ELOHIM, TEMPLE R ROUTE 22 BREWSTER NY 10509 (914) 279-4585
CHAVURAH BETH CHAI (MAHOPAC) R RFD 6 BREWSTER HILL ROAD BREWSTER NY 10509 (914) 279-8307
PUTNAM COUNTY TEMPLE, JEWISH CENTER R ROUTE 22 BREWSTER NY 10509 (914) 279-4585
CONGREGATION SONS OF ISRAEL C
1666 PLEASANTVILLE ROAD BRIARCLIFF MANOR NY 10510 (914) 762-2700
AHAV TSEDEK OF KINGSBRIDGE C 3425 KINGSBRIDGE AVENUE BRONX NY 10463 (212) 543-6969
AHAVATH ACHIM OF WESTCHESTER, CONGREGATION O
1524 PARKER STREET BRONX NY 10462 (212) 829-4570
ANSHE AMAS, CONGREGATION O 713 EAST 222 STREET BRONX NY 10467 (212) 231-5036
ANSHE SFARD OF PELHAM PARKWAY CONGREGATION O
2163 MULINER AVENUE BRONX NY 10462
B'NAI ISRAEL OF EDENWALD, CONGREGATION 1014 E. 227TH STREET BRONX NY 10466 (212) 881-4921
BETH EL OF CITY ISLAND, TEMPLE 480 CITY ISLAND AVENUE BRONX NY 10464 (212) 885-9865
BETH EL CO-OP CITY, TEMPLE R 920-1 BAYCHESTER AVENUE BRONX NY 10475 (212) 671-9719
BETH EL, THE HOUSE OF YAH 1231 FRANKLIN AVENUE BRONX NY 10465 (212) 681-4912
BETH JACOB, CONGREGATION O 1461 LELAND AVENUE BRONX NY 10460 (212) 892-1339
BETH SHRAGA INSTITUTE O 2757 MORRIS AVENUE BRONX NY 10468 (212) 295-3160
BRONX PARK EAST CHOTINER JEWISH CENTER O 2256 BRONX PARK E. BRONX NY 10451 (212) 655-9934
CASTLE HILL JEWISH COMMUNITY CENTER O 486 HOWE AVENUE BRONX NY 10473 (212) 892-2372
CHEVRA MACHZIKEI HORAV O 3417 KNOX PLACE BRONX NY 10467
CHOTINER JEWISH CENTER O 2256 BRONX PARK EAST BRONX NY 10467 (212) 655-9934
CO-OP CITY JEWISH CENTER C 900 CO-OP CITY BLVD BRONX NY 10475 (212) 671-4579
COMMUNITY CENTER OF ISRAEL C 2440 ESPLANADE BRONX NY 10469 (212) 882-2400
CONCOURSE CENTER OF ISRAEL O 2323 GRAND CONCOURSE BRONX NY 10468
CONSERVATIVE SYNAGOGUE ADATH ISRAEL OF RIVERDALE C
250TH STREET & HENRY HUDSON PARKWAY BRONX NY 10471 (212) 543-8400
EDUCATIONAL JEWISH CENTER O 805 ASTOR AVENUE BRONX NY 10467 (212) 655-9865
EMANUEL AT PARKCHESTER, TEMPLE C 2000 BENEDICT AVENUE BRONX NY 10462 (212) 828-3400
FIRST VAN NEST HEBREW CONGREGATION O 1712 GARFIELD STREET BRONX NY 10460
GHETTO LITZMANNSTADT (LODZ) MEMORIAL SYNAGOGUE O
2435 KINGSLAND AVENUE BRONX NY 10469
GUN HILL JEWISH CENTER O 3380 RESERVOIR OVAL E BRONX NY 10467 (212) 652-6700
HEBREW CENTER OF EAST BRONX O 1276 COMMONWEALTH AVENUE BRONX NY 10472 (212) 829-1772
HEBREW INSTITUTE OF RIVERDALE
3700 HENRY HUDSON PARKWAY BRONX NY 10463 (212) 796-4730
HEBREW TABERNACLE O 2150 HOLLAND AVENUE BRONX NY 10462 (212) 822-8756
HOPE OF ISRAEL, CONGREGATION O 843 WALTON AVENUE BRONX NY 10451 (212) 292-6667
INTERVALE JEWISH CENTER OF THE BRONX O 1024 INTERVALE AVENUE BRONX NY 10459 (212) 842-5238
JACOB H. SCHIFF CENTER C 2510 VALENTINE AVENUE BRONX NY 10457 (212) 295-2510
JEWISH CENTER OF PELHAM BAY O 1807 MAHAN AVENUE BRONX NY 10461 (212) 892-8171
JEWISH CENTER OF UNIONPORT O 2137 ELLIS AVENUE BRONX NY 10462 (212) 822-8601
JEWISH CENTER OF VIOLET PARK O 3356 SEYMOUR AVENUE BRONX NY 10469 (212) 654-2712
JEWISH CENTER OF WAKEFIELD & EDENWALD O 641 EAST 233 STREET BRONX NY 10466
JEWISH CENTER OF WILLIAMSBRIDGE O 2910 BARNES AVENUE BRONX NY 10467 (212) 655-4077
JOSEPH BEN MAYER, CONGREGATION O 80 WEST KINGSBRIDGE ROAD BRONX NY 10468
JUDEA, TEMPLE R 615 REISS PLACE BRONX NY 10467 (212) 881-5118
KHAL ADATH YESHURUN, CONGREGATION O 2222 CRUGER AVENUE BRONX NY 10467 (212) 653-4698
KINGSBRIDGE CENTER OF ISRAEL O 3115 CORLEAR AVENUE BRONX NY 10463 (212) 548-1678
KINGSBRIDGE HEIGHTS JEWISH CENTER O 124 EAMES PLACE BRONX NY 10468 (212) 549-4120
LANZUTER BETH DAVID, CONGREGATION R 2364 WOODHULL AVENUE BRONX NY 10469
LOMDAI TORAH CONGREGATION O 2507 TENBROECK AVENUE BRONX NY 10469 (212) 653-3918
LUBAVITCH OF THE BRONX, CONGREGATION 2731 KRUGER AVENUE BRONX NY 10467 (212) 654-5318
MERCAZ HARAV, CONGREGATION O 2832 VALENTINE AVENUE BRONX NY 10458
MORRIS PARK HEBREW CENTER O 1812 PAULDING AVENUE BRONX NY 10461 (212) 822-8669
MOSHOLU JEWISH CENTER O 3044 HULL AVENUE BRONX NY 10467 (212) 547-1515
MOUNT HOREB, CONGREGATION O 1042 STEBBINS AVENUE BRONX NY 10459 (212) 589-2651
NATHAN STRAUS JEWISH CENTER O 3512 DEKALB AVENUE BRONX NY 10467 (212) 547-1616
OHEL MOSHE B'NAI JOSEPH, CONGREGATION O 2144 MULINER AVENUE BRONX NY 10462
OHEL MOSHE CONGREGATION 2149 WALLACE AVENUE BRONX NY 10462 (212) 792-8544
OHEL TORAH SYNAGOGUE 629 W. 239TH STREET BRONX NY 10463
PELHAM PARKWAY JEWISH CENTER C 900 PELHAM PARKWAY S BRONX NY 10462 (212) 792-6450
RIVERDALE JEWISH CENTER O 3700 INDEPENDENCE AVENUE BRONX NY 10463 (212) 548-1850
RIVERDALE TEMPLE R 4545 INDEPENDENCE AVENUE BRONX NY 10471 (212) 548-3800
SEPHARDIC SHAARE RAHAMIM CONGREGATION, INC. O
100 CO-OP CITY BLVD BRONX NY 10475 (212) 671-8882
SHIELD OF DAVID INSTITUTE C 1800 ANDREWS AVENUE BRONX NY 10453 (212) 731-0481
SONS OF ISRAEL, CONGREGATION O 2521 CRUGER AVENUE BRONX NY 10467 (212) 231-6213
TALMUD CLUB/EINSTEIN MEDICAL SCHOOL MINYAN
1925 EASTCHESTER ROAD, #3C BRONX NY 10461 (212) 822-2120
THROGGS NECK JEWISH CENTER 2918 LAFAYETTE AVENUE BRONX NY 10465 (212) 822-9829
TORAS CHAIM 620A BAYCHESTER AVENUE BRONX NY 10475 (212) 671-0310
TORAS CHAIM OF CO-OP CITY, CONGREGATION
620 BAYCHESTER AVENUE BRONX NY 10475 (212) 671-0310
TRADITIONAL SYNAGOGUE OF CO-OP CITY T 115 EINSTEIN LOOP BRONX NY 10475 (212) 379-6920
UNITED ODD FELLOW & REBEKAH HOME SYNAGOGUE
1072 HAVEMEYER AVENUE BRONX NY 10462
VAN CORTLANDT JEWISH CENTER O 3880 SEDGEWICK AVENUE BRONX NY 10463 (212) 884-6105
YOUNG ISRAEL OF ASTOR GARDENS 1328 ALLERTON AVENUE BRONX NY 10469 (212) 653-1363
YOUNG ISRAEL OF BAYCHESTER 115 EINSTEIN LOOP BRONX NY 10475 (212) 379-6920
YOUNG ISRAEL OF CO-OP CITY 147 DREISER LOOP BRONX NY 10475 (212) 671-2300
YOUNG ISRAEL OF MOSHOLU PARKWAY 100 EAST 208TH STREET BRONX NY 10467 (212) 882-8181
YOUNG ISRAEL OF PARKCHESTER 1375 VIRGINIA AVENUE BRONX NY 10462 (212) 822-9576
YOUNG ISRAEL OF PELHAM PARKWAY 2126 BARNES AVENUE BRONX NY 10462 (212) 824-0630
YOUNG ISRAEL OF RIVERDALE 4502 HENRY HUDSON PARKWAY BRONX NY 10471 (212) 548-4765
ZICHRON MOSHE CONGREGATION O 1925 GRAND CONCOURSE BRONX NY 10453
ZION, TEMPLE 1925 GRAND CONCOURSE BRONX NY 10453 (212) 588-5800
ADAS YEREIM, CONGREGATION O LEE AVENUE & ROEBLING BROOKLYN NY 11211
ADAS YEREIM OF BORO PARK O 5402 14TH AVENUE BROOKLYN NY 11219 (718) 851-7800
ADATH ISRAEL, CONGREGATION O 672 LEFFERTS AVENUE BROOKLYN NY 11203
ADATH JACOB, CONGREGATION O 1569 47TH STREET BROOKLYN NY 11219 (718) 436-1133
ADATH YESHURUN OF FLATBUSH, CONGREGATION O
3418 AVENUE N. BROOKLYN NY 11234 (718) 258-0241
ADUDATH ISRAEL OF FLATBUSH 1302 OCEAN PARKWAY BROOKLYN NY 11236 (718) 375-2706
AGUDAS ACHIM ANSHEI MEREDITZ & KLOIZ, CONGREGATION O
45 RANDALLS PARK N.W. BROOKLYN NY 11205
AGUDAS ACHIM OF EAST FLATBUSH, CONGREGATION O
902 LENOX ROAD BROOKLYN NY 11203
AGUDAS ACHIM OF MIDWOOD O 1564 CONEY ISLAND AVENUE BROOKLYN NY 11230
AGUDATH ACHIM TALMUD TORAH, CONGREGATION O
1048 54TH STREET BROOKLYN NY 11219 (718) 438-8718
AGUDATH CHASIDEI SPINKA, CONGREGATION O 1460 56TH STREET BROOKLYN NY 11219
AGUDATH ISRAEL BRANCH CHOFETZ CHAIM, CONGREGATION O
5413 18TH AVENUE BROOKLYN NY 11218
AGUDATH ISRAEL BROOKLYN COMMUNITY CENTER O
803 KINGS HIGHWAY BROOKLYN NY 11223
AGUDATH ISRAEL OF 18TH AVENUE O 5413 18TH AVENUE BROOKLYN NY 11204 (718) 236-9578
AGUDATH ISRAEL OF BORO PARK O 4511 14TH AVENUE BROOKLYN NY 11219 (718) 438-6508
AGUDATH ISRAEL OF BORO PARK WEST O 867 50TH STREET BROOKLYN NY 11220 (718) 438-8718
AGUDATH ISRAEL OF BORO PARK, CONGREGATION O
4909 16TH AVENUE BROOKLYN NY 11204
AGUDATH ISRAEL OF CROWN HEIGHTS O 456 CROWN STREET BROOKLYN NY 11225 (718) 778-7195
AGUDATH ISRAEL OF EAST MIDWOOD O 3120 BEDFORD BROOKLYN NY 11210
AGUDATH ISRAEL OF EIGHTEENTH AVENUE O 5413 18TH AVENUE BROOKLYN NY 11204 (718) 236-9578
AGUDATH ISRAEL OF FLATBUSH O 1032 OCEAN PARKWAY BROOKLYN NY 11230
AGUDATH ISRAEL OF FLATBUSH/SOUTH O 803 KINGS HIGHWAY BROOKLYN NY 11223
AGUDATH ISRAEL OF KINGS HIGHWAY O 1796 EAST 7TH STREET BROOKLYN NY 11223 (718) 375-1630
AGUDATH ISRAEL OF MIDWOOD O 817 AVENUE H BROOKLYN NY 11230
AGUDATH ISRAEL OF SIXTEENTH AVENUE O 4906 16TH AVENUE BROOKLYN NY 11204
AGUDATH ISRAEL OF WILLIAMSBURG O 616 BEDFORD AVENUE BROOKLYN NY 11211
AGUDATH SHOLOM OF FLATBUSH, CONGREGATION O
3714 18TH AVENUE BROOKLYN NY 11218 (718) 854-2226
AHABA VE AHVA, CONGREGATION O 2022 66TH STREET BROOKLYN NY 11204
AHAVAS ACHIM ANSHEI SFARD, CONGREGATION O
1385 E. 94TH STREET (NEAR AVENUE L) BROOKLYN NY 11236 (718) 272-6933
AHAVAS ACHIM (EMPIRE SHTEEBLE), CONGREGATION O
489 EMPIRE BOULEVARD BROOKLYN NY 11213 (718) 388-8062
AHAVAS MOISCHE, CONGREGATION O 612 MAPLE STREET BROOKLYN NY 11203 (718) 771-7365
AHAVATH ACHIM ANSHEI CANARSIE, CONGREGATION O
9420 GLENWOOD ROAD BROOKLYN NY 11236 (718) 257-9586
AHAVATH ACHIM OF FLATBUSH, CONGREGATION O
549 EAST 2 STREET BROOKLYN NY 11218 (718) 853-1959
AHAVATH ACHIM, CONGREGATION C 151 WOODRUFF AVENUE BROOKLYN NY 11226
AHAVATH ACHIM, CONGREGATION O 1750 E. 4TH STREET BROOKLYN NY 11223 (718) 375-3895
AHAVATH ISRAEL OF GREENPOINT SYNAGOGUE, CONGREGATION O
108 NOBLE STREET BROOKLYN NY 11222 (718) 383-8475
AHAVATH ISRAEL, CONGREGATION O 2818 AVENUE K BROOKLYN NY 11210 (718) 258-6666
AHAVATH SHALOM, CONGREGATION O
1495 CONEY ISLAND AVENUE BROOKLYN NY 11230 (718) 338-0648
AHAVATH SHOLOM, TEMPLE R 1906 AVENUE B BROOKLYN NY 11229 (718) 769-5350
AHAVATH TORAH 1655 EAST 24TH STREET BROOKLYN NY 11229 (718) 338-0500
AHAVATH TORAH, INC. 1630 50TH STREET BROOKLYN NY 11204
AHI EZER CONGREGATION O 1885 OCEAN PARKWAY BROOKLYN NY 11223 (718) 376-4088
AHI EZER YESHIVA O 2433 OCEAN PARKWAY BROOKLYN NY 11223 (718) 648-6100

Listing	City	State	ZIP	Phone
ANSHE SHOLOM, CONGREGATION - AVENUE U EDUCATIONAL CENTER O 2066 EAST 9TH STREET	BROOKLYN	NY	11223	(718) 339-8844
ANSHEI LUBAWITZ, CONGREGATION O 4204 12TH AVENUE	BROOKLYN	NY	11218	(718) 436-2200
ANSHEI SEFARD, CONGREGATION O 8214 21ST AVENUE	BROOKLYN	NY	11214	(718) 837-2145
ANSHEI SFARD OF BORO PARK O 4502 14TH AVENUE	BROOKLYN	NY	11219	(718) 436-2691
ANSHEI UYHELY O 1346 45TH STREET	BROOKLYN	NY	11219	
ANSHEI ZEDEK OF BENSONHURST CONGREGATION O 6720 19TH AVENUE	BROOKLYN	NY	11204	(718) 837-0478
ARUGATH HABOSEM, CONGREGATION O 559 BEDFORD AVENUE	BROOKLYN	NY	11211	
ATERES ISRAEL CONG/ISRAEL CENTER OF CANARSIE O 1234 EAST 87TH STREET	BROOKLYN	NY	11236	(718) 763-6777
ATERES YESHUA O 1555 51ST STREET	BROOKLYN	NY	11219	(718) 438-9133
ATERETH ZVI-LISKER KOLLEL, CONGREGATION O 1449 50TH STREET	BROOKLYN	NY	11219	(718) 854-5555
ATZEI CHAIM SIGET, CONGREGATION 4915 15TH AVENUE	BROOKLYN	NY	11219	(718) 438-9126
ATZEI CHAIM SIGET O 1511 50TH STREET	BROOKLYN	NY	11219	(718) 851-9370
ATZEI CHAIM, CONGREGATION O 152 HEWES STREET	BROOKLYN	NY	11211	(718) 624-6392
AVENUE M JEWISH CENTER O 1898 BAY AVENUE	BROOKLYN	NY	11230	(718) 339-7747
AVENUE N JEWISH COMMUNITY CENTER 321 AVENUE N	BROOKLYN	NY	11230	(718) 339-7747
AVENUE U EDUCATIONAL CENTER O 2080 EAST 9TH STREET	BROOKLYN	NY	11223	
AVENUE Z JEWISH CENTER O 875 AVENUE Z	BROOKLYN	NY	11235	(718) 646-9874
AVRECHEL GUR, CONGREGATION O 1573 51ST STREET	BROOKLYN	NY	11219	(718) 435-2070
AVREICHEI GUR, CONGREGATION O 4622 16TH AVENUE	BROOKLYN	NY	11204	(718) 871-8683
B'NAI ABRAHAM, CONGREGATION 409 E. 53RD STREET	BROOKLYN	NY	11203	(718) 495-2660
B'NAI ABRAHAM, CONGREGATION O 1415 55TH STREET	BROOKLYN	NY	11219	(718) 851-9849
B'NAI ADATH KOL BETH ISRAEL, CONGREGATION O 1006 GREENE AVENUE	BROOKLYN	NY	11221	
B'NAI AHARON O 913 48TH STREET	BROOKLYN	NY	11219	(718) 435-7671
B'NAI ISAAC, CONGREGATION O 54 AVENUE O	BROOKLYN	NY	11204	(718) 232-3466
B'NAI ISRAEL O 4304 15TH AVENUE	BROOKLYN	NY	11219	(718) 871-2312
B'NAI ISRAEL CONGREGATION O 1540 VAN SICLEN AVENUE (ROOM 8A)	BROOKLYN	NY	11239	(718) 642-8804
B'NAI ISRAEL JEWISH CENTER 3192 BEDFORD AVENUE	BROOKLYN	NY	11210	(718) 258-2784
B'NAI ISRAEL JEWISH CENTER O 357 REMSEN AVENUE	BROOKLYN	NY	11212	(718) 342-4554
B'NAI ISRAEL OF LINDEN HEIGHTS, CONGREGATION O 4502 9TH AVENUE	BROOKLYN	NY	11220	
B'NAI ISRAEL OF LINDEN HEIGHTS O C/O JACOB GROSSMAN - 865 46TH STREET	BROOKLYN	NY	11220	(718) 435-7290
B'NAI ISRAEL OF MIDWOOD, CONGREGATION O 1800 UTICA AVENUE	BROOKLYN	NY	11234	(718) 763-5500
B'NAI ISRAEL OF MIDWOOD, CONGREGATION O 4815 AVENUE I	BROOKLYN	NY	11234	(718) 763-5500
B'NAI ISRAEL, CONGREGATION 859 HENDRIX STREET	BROOKLYN	NY	11207	(718) 649-1144
B'NAI ISRAEL, CONGREGATION 1455 GENEVA LOOP	BROOKLYN	NY	11239	(718) 642-8804
B'NAI ISRAEL, CONGREGATION O 3007 OCEAN AVENUE	BROOKLYN	NY	11235	(718) 332-6231
B'NAI JACOB OF FLATBUSH, CONGREGATION O 3017 GLENWOOD ROAD	BROOKLYN	NY	11210	(718) 434-8855
B'NAI JONAH, CONGREGATION O 858 STANLEY AVENUE	BROOKLYN	NY	11208	
B'NAI JOSEF, CONGREGATION O 1616 OCEAN PARKWAY	BROOKLYN	NY	11223	(718) 627-9861
B'NAI MOSHE CONGREGATION O 1250 46TH STREET	BROOKLYN	NY	11219	(718) 633-4402
B'NAI TORAH INSTITUTE CONGREGATION O 4722 18TH AVENUE	BROOKLYN	NY	11204	
B'NAI USHER CONGREGATION O 4706 12TH AVENUE	BROOKLYN	NY	11219	(718) 438-8520
B'NAI YESOCHOR CONGREGATION O 5402 16TH AVENUE	BROOKLYN	NY	11204	(718) 851-7338
B'NEI MATISYAHU CONGREGATION O 5510 11TH AVENUE	BROOKLYN	NY	11219	(718) 854-5029
B'NEI MOISHE CONGREGATION O 1547 55TH STREET	BROOKLYN	NY	11219	(718) 851-6111
BAIS AHARON O 1466 57TH STREET	BROOKLYN	NY	11219	(718) 851-8087
BAIS AVROHAM, CONGREGATION O 1719 AVENUE P	BROOKLYN	NY	11229	
BAIS CHAIM YOSHUA O 4911 17TH AVENUE	BROOKLYN	NY	11204	(718) 438-9031
BAIS CHASIDIM D'GUR-YAGDIL O 5110 18TH AVENUE	BROOKLYN	NY	11204	(718) 633-6809
BAIS EPHRAIM, CONGREGATION O 2802 AVENUE J	BROOKLYN	NY	11210	
BAIS HAMEDRASH AVREICHEI T.V. O 1580 53RD STREET	BROOKLYN	NY	11219	(718) 633-9459
BAIS HAMEDRASH YESHIAS ISRAEL, CONGREGATION O 1315 54TH STREET	BROOKLYN	NY	11219	
BAIS HATFILA FOLTICHAN O 1437 49TH STREET	BROOKLYN	NY	11219	(718) 438-5461
BAIS HAYOTZER CONGREGATION O 628 BEDFORD AVENUE	BROOKLYN	NY	11211	(718) 852-0619
BAIS HENOCH O 4401 14TH AVENUE	BROOKLYN	NY	11219	(718) 438-5025
BAIS HILLEL O 1105 54TH STREET	BROOKLYN	NY	11219	(718) 436-9419
BAIS ISAAC ZVI O 1019 46TH STREET	BROOKLYN	NY	11219	
BAIS SHLOMIE O 1451 46TH STREET	BROOKLYN	NY	11219	(718) 853-4313
BAIS YISROEL O 5518 14TH AVENUE	BROOKLYN	NY	11219	(718) 851-6646
BAIS YISROEL MUOR VESUMES KHAL CLEVE O 882 56TH STREET	BROOKLYN	NY	11220	(718) 436-1654
BAIS YISROEL OF RUGBY, CONGREGATION 1821 OCEAN PARKWAY	BROOKLYN	NY	11223	(718) 376-9689
BAIS YOSEF O 1454 49TH STREET	BROOKLYN	NY	11219	(718) 633-3262
BAITH ISRAEL ANSHEI EMES, CONGREGATION C 236 KANE STREET	BROOKLYN	NY	11231	(718) 875-1550
BAY RIDGE JEWISH CENTER - CONGREGATION SHEIRIS ISRAEL C 405-81ST STREET	BROOKLYN	NY	11209	(718) 835-3103
BAYONER KLOYS, CONGREGATION O 260 MARCY AVENUE	BROOKLYN	NY	11211	
BE'ER MOSHE OF GROSSWARDEIN, CONGREGATION O 4617 10TH AVENUE	BROOKLYN	NY	11219	
BE'ER SHMUEL CONGREGATION O 1363 50TH STREET	BROOKLYN	NY	11219	(718) 436-6100
BEACH HAVEN JEWISH CENTER O 723 AVENUE Z	BROOKLYN	NY	11223	(718) 375-5200
BEIS MEDRASH TELSE ALUMNI O 5218 16TH AVENUE	BROOKLYN	NY	11204	(718) 438-8937
BEIS CHASIDEI AMSINOV CONGREGATION O 4404 15TH AVENUE	BROOKLYN	NY	11219	(718) 436-3938
BEIS MEDRASH BAIS SHMUEL CHUSTER O 1360 55TH STREET	BROOKLYN	NY	11219	(718) 851-0034
BEIS MEDRASH CHAIM SIMCHA O 1650 56TH STREET	BROOKLYN	NY	11204	(718) 851-4735
BEIS MEDRASH CHEMED - NITRAH O 1462 50TH STREET	BROOKLYN	NY	11219	(718) 851-7800
BEIS MEDRASH KOSEVER O 1112 52ND STREET	BROOKLYN	NY	11219	(718) 853-5244
BEIS MEDRASH RADZINER O 1344 54TH STREET	BROOKLYN	NY	11219	(718) 851-1025
BEIS MEDRASH SANZ O 1643 45TH STREET	BROOKLYN	NY	11204	(718) 435-0500
BEIS MEDRASH SHEMDISHOVER SHOTZER O 1846 50TH STREET	BROOKLYN	NY	11204	(718) 438-0728
BEIS MEDRASH SHINIVER O 1563 42ND STREET	BROOKLYN	NY	11219	(718) 438-8615
BEIS MEDRASH VAJDOSLOVER O 1546 47TH STREET	BROOKLYN	NY	11219	(718) 854-1863
BEIS MEDRASH YESHIAS YISROEL O 1315 54TH STREET	BROOKLYN	NY	11219	(718) 851-5050
BEIS SHARIM MACHNE CHAIM O 5223 17TH AVENUE	BROOKLYN	NY	11204	(718) 435-2551
BEIS YITZCHOCK O 1335 48TH STREET	BROOKLYN	NY	11219	(718) 854-6661
BEITCHER CONGREGATION O 4424 12TH AVENUE	BROOKLYN	NY	11219	(718) 436-3118
BELZ, CONGREGATION O 186 ROSS STREET	BROOKLYN	NY	11211	(718) 384-8193
BELZ YESHIVA AND KOLLEL, CONGREGATION O 662 EASTERN PARKWAY	BROOKLYN	NY	11213	
BELZER BETH MEDRASH O 1411 45TH STREET	BROOKLYN	NY	11219	(718) 438-2890
BER MOISHE O 1569 48TH STREET	BROOKLYN	NY	11219	(718) 435-9178
BERLINER CONGREGATION KAHAL KENESETH ISRAEL O 1340 EAST 9TH STREET	BROOKLYN	NY	11230	(718) 375-3955
BETH AARON V'ISRAEL CHASIDEI STOLIN, CONGREGATION O 4609 16TH AVENUE	BROOKLYN	NY	11204	(718) 438-8190
BETH AARON OF FLATBUSH CONGREGATION O 1670 OCEAN AVENUE	BROOKLYN	NY	11230	(718) 338-6064
BETH AARON, CONGREGATION O 2261 BRAGG STREET	BROOKLYN	NY	11229	
BETH AARON, CONGREGATION O 18TH AVENUE & 49TH STREET	BROOKLYN	NY	11204	(718) 435-2087
BETH ABRAHAM OF FLATBUSH, CONGREGATION 1089 CONEY ISLAND AVENUE	BROOKLYN	NY	11230	
BETH ABRAHAM OF FLATLANDS, CONGREGATION O 720 EAST 91ST STREET	BROOKLYN	NY	11235	(718) 495-4900
BETH ABRAHAM, CONGREGATION O 2997 OCEAN PARKWAY	BROOKLYN	NY	11235	(718) 373-4533
BETH ABRAHAM, TEMPLE C 301 SEA BREEZE AVENUE	BROOKLYN	NY	11224	(718) 266-6544
BETH AHARON, CONGREGATION O 649 BEDFORD AVENUE	BROOKLYN	NY	11211	
BETH AM CENTER C 1182 BRIGHTON BEACH AVENUE	BROOKLYN	NY	11235	(718) 743-4442
BETH AM JEWISH CENTER C 3574 NOSTRAND AVENUE	BROOKLYN	NY	11229	(718) 646-5467
BETH ASHUR O 5019 10TH AVENUE	BROOKLYN	NY	11219	(718) 438-1397
BETH CHANOCH - K'HAL MACHZIKEI HADASS O 1636 49TH STREET	BROOKLYN	NY	11204	(718) 851-0005
BETH DAVID GERSHON TALMUD TORAH O 450 NEW YORK AVENUE	BROOKLYN	NY	11225	
BETH DAVID OF CROWN HEIGHTS, CONGREGATION O 442 CROWN STREET	BROOKLYN	NY	11225	(718) 774-2699
BETH DAVID, INC., CONGREGATION 802 44TH STREET	BROOKLYN	NY	11220	(718) 851-8829
BETH DOVID, CONGREGATION O 1248 49TH STREET	BROOKLYN	NY	11219	
BETH EL JEWISH CENTER OF FLATBUSH C 1981 HOMECREST AVENUE	BROOKLYN	NY	11229	(718) 375-0120
BETH EL OF BENSONHURST, TEMPLE C 1656 W. 10TH STREET	BROOKLYN	NY	11223	(718) 232-0019
BETH EL OF BOROUGH PARK, CONGREGATION O 4802 15TH AVENUE	BROOKLYN	NY	11219	(718) 435-9020
BETH EL OF FLATBUSH, CONGREGATION O 2181 E. 3RD STREET	BROOKLYN	NY	11223	(718) 336-1926
BETH EL OF MANHATTAN BEACH, TEMPLE C 111 WEST END AVENUE	BROOKLYN	NY	11235	(718) 891-3500
BETH ELIYOHU, CONGREGATION 111 RUTLEDGE STREET	BROOKLYN	NY	11211	(718) 855-0091
BETH ELOCHIM, CONGREGATION R 8TH AVENUE & GARFIELD PLACE	BROOKLYN	NY	11215	(718) 768-3814
BETH EMETH, TEMPLE R 83 MARLBOROUGH ROAD	BROOKLYN	NY	11226	(718) 282-1596
BETH GERSHON RABENU, CONGREGATION O 1537 41ST STREET	BROOKLYN	NY	11218	
BETH HALEVI CONGREGATION O 1777 49TH STREET	BROOKLYN	NY	11204	(718) 892-2805
BETH HAMEDRESH HAGODOL O 3120 BEDFORD AVENUE	BROOKLYN	NY	11210	(718) 377-7774
BETH HAMEDRASH OHOLEI TORAH, CONGREGATION O 1267-71 EASTERN PARKWAY	BROOKLYN	NY	11213	
BETH HAMEDRASH SHOMREI HADATH BIKUR CHOLIM O 1327 41ST STREET	BROOKLYN	NY	11219	
BETH HAMEDROSH HAGODOL OF EAST FLATBUSH, CONGREGATION O 777 SCHENECTADY AVENUE	BROOKLYN	NY	11203	
BETH HATALMUD O 2127 82ND STREET	BROOKLYN	NY	11214	
BETH ISAAC, CONGREGATION O 1719 AVENUE P	BROOKLYN	NY	11229	(718) 336-7655
BETH ISRAEL CONGREGATION OF EAST FLATBUSH O 660 REMSEN AVENUE	BROOKLYN	NY	11236	(718) 495-4900
BETH ISRAEL V'DAMESEK ELIEZER O 179 TAYLOR STREET	BROOKLYN	NY	11211	
BETH ISRAEL OF BORO PARK, CONGREGATION O 5602 11TH AVENUE	BROOKLYN	NY	11219	(718) 853-1720
BETH ISRAEL, CONGREGATION 1424 51ST STREET	BROOKLYN	NY	11219	(718) 438-9087
BETH JACOB O C/O BUCHBINDER - 2069 82ND STREET	BROOKLYN	NY	11214	(718) 236-8436
BETH JACOB OHEV SHOLOM, CONGREGATION O 284 RODNEY STREET	BROOKLYN	NY	11211	(718) 384-8715
BETH JESHAYE, CONGREGATION O 711 EASTERN PARKWAY	BROOKLYN	NY	11213	(718) 744-2068
BETH JUDAH, CONGREGATION 1960 SCHENECTADY AVENUE	BROOKLYN	NY	11234	(718) 338-3968
BETH JUDAH TALMUD TORAH O 1350 EAST 54TH STREET	BROOKLYN	NY	11234	(718) 338-3969
BETH MEDRASH ASHKENAZE O 605 OCEAN PARKWAY	BROOKLYN	NY	11218	
BETH MEDRASH CHEMED OF NITRA, CONGREGATION O 2 LEE AVENUE	BROOKLYN	NY	11211	(718) 384-9546
BETH MEDRASH GOVOHA MINYAN O 5113 16TH AVENUE	BROOKLYN	NY	11204	(718) 853-9209
BETH MEDRASH HAGADOL OF BORO PARK O P.O. BOX 48 (BLYTHE STATION)	BROOKLYN	NY	11219	(718) 854-8047
BETH MOSES, CONGREGATION 124 WEST END AVENUE	BROOKLYN	NY	11235	(718) 769-9794
BETH SAMUEL, CONGREGATION O 5216 13TH AVENUE	BROOKLYN	NY	11219	(718) 633-5742
BETH SHALOM OF KINGS BAY, CONGREGATION C 2710 AVENUE X	BROOKLYN	NY	11235	(718) 891-4500
BETH SHALOM, CONGREGATION O 730 WILLOUGHBY AVENUE	BROOKLYN	NY	11206	
BETH SHOLOM PEOPLES TEMPLE R BAY PARKWAY & BENSON AVENUE	BROOKLYN	NY	11214	(718) 372-7164
BETH TALMUD TORAH, CONGREGATION O 25 BOERUM STREET, APT. 9R	BROOKLYN	NY	11206	
BETH TIKVAH, INC., CONGREGATION O 8800 SEA VIEW AVENUE	BROOKLYN	NY	11236	(718) 763-5577
BETH TORAH, CONGREGATION O 1061 OCEAN PARKWAY	BROOKLYN	NY	11230	(718) 252-9840
BETH TORAH, CONGREGATION O 3574 NOSTRAND AVENUE	BROOKLYN	NY	11229	(718) 646-5467
BETH TORAH DAMESEK ELIEZER O 403 AVENUE I	BROOKLYN	NY	11230	(718) 338-2271
BETH YASHAYA CONGREGATION (KERESTURER) O 711 EASTERN PARKWAY	BROOKLYN	NY	11213	(718) 774-2068
BETH YEHUDA, INC., CONGREGATION O 62 KEAP STREET	BROOKLYN	NY	11211	(718) 625-8732
BETH-EL TEMPLE 470 LAFAYETTE AVENUE	BROOKLYN	NY	11205	
BIKUR CHOLIM ANSHEI LUBASHOW, CONGREGATION O 72 EAST 89TH STREET	BROOKLYN	NY	11236	
BIKUR CHOLIM HYMAN JOSEPH, CONGREGATION O 255 PENN STREET	BROOKLYN	NY	11211	
BNEI YEHUDAH, CONGREGATION O 5311 16TH AVENUE	BROOKLYN	NY	11204	(718) 851-9199
BORO PARK PROGRESSIVE SYNAGOGUE CONGREGATION B'NAI SHOLOM R 1515 46TH STREET	BROOKLYN	NY	11219	(718) 436-5082

BOSTONER BETH MEDRASH-NETZACH ISRAEL O 1535 49TH STREET .... BROOKLYN NY 11219 (718) 853-6570
BOULEVARD JEWISH CENTER O 1380 LINDEN BLVD .... BROOKLYN NY 11212
BOYANER BETH MEDRASH O 4405 14TH AVENUE .... BROOKLYN NY 11219
BROOKLYN HEIGHTS SYNAGOGUE R 117 REMSEN STREET .... BROOKLYN NY 11201 (718) 522-2070
BROOKLYN JEWISH CENTER, THE C 667 EASTERN PARKWAY .... BROOKLYN NY 11213 (718) 493-8800
CANARSIE JEWISH CENTER 965 E. 107TH STREET .... BROOKLYN NY 11236 (718) 272-2484
CHAMDATH TORAH V'CHESSED, CONGREGATION O
1640 50TH STREET .... BROOKLYN NY 11204
CHASAN SOFER CONGREGATION O 1876 50TH STREET .... BROOKLYN NY 11204 (718) 236-1171
CHASIDEI BELZ O 1169 48TH STREET .... BROOKLYN NY 11219
CHASIDEI BELZ OF BOROUGH PARK, CONGREGATION O
4814 16TH AVENUE .... BROOKLYN NY 11204 (718) 851-5345
CHASIDEI BELZ, CONGREGATION O 662 EASTERN PARKWAY .... BROOKLYN NY 11213 (718) 773-8561
CHASIDEI BELZ, CONGREGATION O 4814 16TH AVENUE .... BROOKLYN NY 11204 (718) 851-9890
CHASIDEI BRESILOV O 5504 16TH AVENUE .... BROOKLYN NY 11204
CHASIDEI GER CONGREGATION O 5104 18TH AVENUE .... BROOKLYN NY 11204 (718) 871-8160
CHASIDEI GUR, CONGREGATION O 5104 18TH AVENUE .... BROOKLYN NY 11204 (718) 438-8818
CHASIDEI GUR, CONGREGATION O 1317 49TH STREET .... BROOKLYN NY 11219 (718) 438-8199
CHASIDEI SOTZ OF BORO PARK CONGREGATION O
4814 16TH AVENUE .... BROOKLYN NY 11204 (718) 851-5345
CHEISHEK SHLOMO OF YOKA, CONGREGATION O
1243 55TH STREET .... BROOKLYN NY 11219 (718) 853-0070
CHEVRA AHAVATH ACHIM ANSHEI SFARD, CONGREGATION O
489 EMPIRE BLVD .... BROOKLYN NY 11225
CHEVRA B'NEI ISRAEL OF BORO PARK, CONGREGATION O
4304 15TH AVENUE .... BROOKLYN NY 11219
CHEVRA BIKUR CHOLIM O 2953 WEST 31ST STREET .... BROOKLYN NY 11224
CHEVRA GEMILUTH CHESED, CONGREGATION
771 MCDONALD AVENUE .... BROOKLYN NY 11218 (718) 435-4218
CHEVRA LIADY O 5302 16TH AVENUE .... BROOKLYN NY 11204 (718) 851-0084
CHEVRA SHAAS, CONGREGATION O 1564 EAST 7TH STREET .... BROOKLYN NY 11230 (718) 376-8783
CHEVRA SHAAS, CONGREGATION O 398 KINGSTON AVENUE .... BROOKLYN NY 11213
CHEVRA SHAAS & MISHNAYOTH OF FLATBUSH, CONGREGATION O
1706 MCDONALD AVENUE .... BROOKLYN NY 11230
CHEVRA SHOMREI EMUNEI ANSHE LOMZA O 474 E. 96TH STREET .... BROOKLYN NY 11212 (718) 343-8401
CHEVRA SHOMREI SHABBOS 4404 14TH AVENUE .... BROOKLYN NY 11219 (718) 871-8118
CHEVRA THILIM OHEL MOSHE LUBAVITCH, CONGREGATION O
841 OCEAN PARKWAY .... BROOKLYN NY 11230 (718) 859-7600
CHEVRA TORAH ANSHE CHESED V'ANSHEI RADISHKOW O
731 MONTAUK STREET .... BROOKLYN NY 11235 (718) 934-8116
CHIZUK HADAS O 1421 AVENUE O .... BROOKLYN NY 11230
CHOVEVEI TORAH CONGREGATION O 875 EASTERN PARKWAY .... BROOKLYN NY 11213
CHOVEVEI TORAH, CONGREGATION O 329 KINGSTON AVENUE .... BROOKLYN NY 11213
CHUNE DAVID CONGREGATION & YESHIVA O 1538 OCEAN PARKWAY .... BROOKLYN NY 11230 (718) 627-9057
COMMUNITY TEMPLE BETH OHR R 1010 OCEAN AVENUE .... BROOKLYN NY 11226 (718) 284-5760
CONGREGATION CHASIDEI RADOMSK O 14 AVENUE & 42 STREET .... BROOKLYN NY 11219
CONGREGATION KEREN ORAH O 592 DITMAS AVENUE .... BROOKLYN NY 11218 (718) 436-5715
CONGREGATION YEREIM OF SEA GATE, INC. 3868 POPLAR AVENUE .... BROOKLYN NY 11224 (718) 372-9385
CONGREGATION YETEV LEV BIKUR CHOLIM 152 RODNEY STREET .... BROOKLYN NY 11211 (718) 387-0546
CROWN HEIGHTS OF ISRAEL 310 CROWN STREET .... BROOKLYN NY 11225 (718) 773-6520
CROWN OF ISRAEL TALMUD TORAH O 1769 56TH STREET .... BROOKLYN NY 11204 (718) 232-4827
DARCHEI TESHUVA CONGREGATION O 574 EAST 9TH STREET .... BROOKLYN NY 11218
DERECH EMMUNAH CONGREGATION D'VIEN O 2305 OLEAN STREET .... BROOKLYN NY 11210
EAST FLATBUSH JEWISH COMMUNITY CENTER O 661 LINDEN BLVD .... BROOKLYN NY 11203
EAST MIDWOOD JEWISH CENTER C 1625 OCEAN AVENUE .... BROOKLYN NY 11230 (718) 338-3800
EAST NEW YORK JEWISH CENTER O 965 EAST 107TH STREET .... BROOKLYN NY 11236
EIGHTEENTH AVENUE JEWISH CENTER 3714 18TH AVENUE .... BROOKLYN NY 11218 (718) 438-9131
ELIEZER OF EAST NEW YORK, CONGREGATION O
133 HINSDALE STREET .... BROOKLYN NY 11207
EMANU-EL OF BORO PARK, TEMPLE C 1362 49TH STREET .... BROOKLYN NY 11219 (718) 871-4200
EMANU-EL OF CANARSIE, TEMPLE R 1880 ROCKAWAY PARKWAY .... BROOKLYN NY 11236 (718) 251-0450
EMREI NOAM CONGREGATION O 1447 52ND STREET .... BROOKLYN NY 11219 (718) 854-2948
EMUNAS YISROEL, CONGREGATION O 4420 14TH AVENUE .... BROOKLYN NY 11219 (718) 853-9249
ETZ CHAIM CONGREGATION O 971 47TH STREET .... BROOKLYN NY 11219 (718) 854-2617
ETZ CHAIM OF BORO PARK, CONGREGATION O 5000 13TH AVENUE .... BROOKLYN NY 11219
ETZ CHAIM OF FLATBUSH, CONGREGATION O 1649 E. 13TH STREET .... BROOKLYN NY 11229 (718) 339-4886
FIRST CONGREGATION ANSHE SFARD OF BOROUGH PARK O
4502 14TH AVENUE .... BROOKLYN NY 11219 (718) 436-2691
FLATBUSH & SHAARE TORAH JEWISH CENTER C
500 CHURCH AVENUE .... BROOKLYN NY 11218 (718) 871-5200
FLATBUSH JEWISH CENTER 222 OCEAN PARKWAY .... BROOKLYN NY 11218
FLATBUSH MINYAN O 1049 EAST 13TH STREET .... BROOKLYN NY 11230 (718) 338-8442
FLATBUSH PARK JEWISH CENTER O 6363 AVENUE U .... BROOKLYN NY 11234 (718) 444-6868
GIVATH SHAUL CONGREGATION O 5102 11TH AVENUE .... BROOKLYN NY 11219 (718) 435-2702
GLENWOOD JEWISH CENTER O 888 EAST 56TH STREET .... BROOKLYN NY 11234 (718) 251-5335
GVODZITZ-SADAGURA BETH MEDRASH O 1254 49TH STREET .... BROOKLYN NY 11219 (718) 854-2075
G'VUL YA'AVETZ O 1518 EAST 7TH STREET .... BROOKLYN NY 11230
HARBOTZAS TORAH CONGREGATION O
1274 49TH STREET, SUITE 131A .... BROOKLYN NY 11219 (718) 438-8544
HAYM SALOMON COMMUNITY CONGREGATION O
2300 CROPSEY AVENUE .... BROOKLYN NY 11214 (718) 373-1700
HAYOSHOR V'HATOV, CONGREGATION O 1345 46TH STREET .... BROOKLYN NY 11219
HEBREW ALLIANCE OF BRIGHTON BY THE SEA O
2901 BRIGHTON 6 STREET .... BROOKLYN NY 11235 (718) 648-1820
HILLEL OF FLATLANDS, TEMPLE C 2164 RALPH AVENUE .... BROOKLYN NY 11234 (718) 763-2400
HYDE PARK JEWISH CENTER O 85-15 AVENUE J .... BROOKLYN NY 11210 (718) 629-4800
INSTITUTE OF ADAS ISRAEL, INC. O 1454 OCEAN PARKWAY .... BROOKLYN NY 11230 (718) 375-9292
ISAAC TEMPLE O 1419 DORCHESTER BOULEVARD .... BROOKLYN NY 11226 (718) 284-8032
ISRAEL CENTER OF CANARSIE O 1234 EAST 87TH STREET .... BROOKLYN NY 11236 (718) 251-9891
ISRAEL OF KINGS BAY, CONGREGATION O 3903 NOSTRAND AVENUE .... BROOKLYN NY 11235 (718) 934-5176
JEWISH CENTER NACHLATH ZION O 2201 EAST 23RD STREET .... BROOKLYN NY 11229 (718) 648-4865
JEWISH CENTER OF BRIGHTON BEACH O 2915 OCEAN PARKWAY .... BROOKLYN NY 11235 (718) 769-7400
JEWISH CENTER OF FORT GREENE O 209 CLERMONT AVENUE .... BROOKLYN NY 11205
JEWISH CENTER OF HYDE PARK O 779 EAST 49TH STREET .... BROOKLYN NY 11203 (718) 629-1040
JEWISH CENTER OF KINGS HIGHWAY C 1202 AVENUE P .... BROOKLYN NY 11229 (718) 645-9000
JEWISH CENTER OF MAPLETON PARK, CONG. BETH HAMEDRASH HAGODOL
1477 W. 8TH STREET .... BROOKLYN NY 11204 (718) 837-8875
JEWISH COMMUNAL CENTER OF FLATBUSH C 1302 AVENUE I .... BROOKLYN NY 11230 (718) 258-2411
JEWISH COMMUNITY CENTRE OF BENSONHURST O
6222 23RD AVENUE .... BROOKLYN NY 11204 (718) 236-4767
JEWISH COMMUNITY HOUSE SYNAGOGUE O 7802 BAY PARKWAY .... BROOKLYN NY 11214 (718) 331-6800
JEWISH FRIENDS CONGREGATION 1410 CONEY ISLAND AVENUE .... BROOKLYN NY 11230 (718) 253-0974
JEWISH RECONSTRUCTIONIST SOCIETY 2701 NECK ROAD .... BROOKLYN NY 11229 (718) 332-5700
JUDEA CENTER SYNAGOGUE O 2059 BEDFORD AVENUE .... BROOKLYN NY 11226
K'HAL CHASSIDIM, CONGREGATION O 4820 15TH AVENUE .... BROOKLYN NY 11219 (718) 871-0110
K'HAL NACHLAT YAAKOV O 1402 AVENUE N .... BROOKLYN NY 11230
K'HAL YERAIM O 51 ROSS STREET, APARTMENT 3C .... BROOKLYN NY 11211
K'HAL YESODEL HATORAH O 4918 16TH AVENUE .... BROOKLYN NY 11204 (718) 851-5193
K'HALL BNEI EMUNIM, CONGREGATION O 215 HEWES STREET .... BROOKLYN NY 11211
KAHAL ADATH KRASA, CONGREGATION O 1654 43RD STREET .... BROOKLYN NY 11204 (718) 438-8880
KAHAL ADATH YEREYIM O 672 LEFFERTS AVENUE .... BROOKLYN NY 11203
KAHAL YERAIM OF BOROUGH PARK, CONGREGATION O
1184 53RD STREET .... BROOKLYN NY 11219 (718) 438-9499
KAHAL YESODE HATORAH, CONGREGATION O 4914 16TH AVENUE .... BROOKLYN NY 11204 (718) 851-9858
KAHAL YITZCHOK O 1462 50TH STREET .... BROOKLYN NY 11219 (718) 851-1600
KAPITSHNITZER KLOIZ, CONGREGATION O 1415 55TH STREET .... BROOKLYN NY 11219
KAV CHAIM, CONGREGATION O 1642 54TH STREET .... BROOKLYN NY 11204 (718) 851-7442
KEHAL RAATZFERT, CONGREGATION O 182 DIVISION AVENUE .... BROOKLYN NY 11211 (718) 387-2217
KEHILATH KODESH D'KOHANIM O 2879 WEST 12TH STREET .... BROOKLYN NY 11224 (718) 372-5280
KEHILATH YAKOV, CONGREGATION O 1137 53RD STREET .... BROOKLYN NY 11219 (718) 871-0149
KEHILATH YAKOV, CONGREGATION O 654 BEDFORD AVENUE .... BROOKLYN NY 11211
KESSER ISRAEL, CONGREGATION O 1769 56TH STREET .... BROOKLYN NY 11204
KESSER TORAH, CONGREGATION O 2310 CORTELYOU ROAD .... BROOKLYN NY 11226 (718) 282-3958
KHAL ADAS KRASNA CONGREGATION O 1654 43RD STREET .... BROOKLYN NY 11204 (718) 438-8880
KHAL ADAS YISROEL, CONGREGATION 4712 14TH AVENUE .... BROOKLYN NY 11219 (718) 633-2305
KHAL BAIS HALEVI O 953 46TH STREET .... BROOKLYN NY 11219 (718) 438-2180
KHAL BEER MOISHE D'GROSSWARDEN O 4617 10TH AVENUE .... BROOKLYN NY 11219 (718) 438-8567
KHAL CHASIDEI SKWERE, CONGREGATION O 1334 47TH STREET .... BROOKLYN NY 11219
KHAL CHASIDIM OF BROOKLYN, CONGREGATION O
4820 15TH AVENUE .... BROOKLYN NY 11219 (718) 871-0110
KHAL SHEYA OF KERISZTER O 1455 48TH STREET .... BROOKLYN NY 11219 (718) 853-4894
KHAL TORATH CHAIM, CONGREGATION O 6 LEE AVENUE .... BROOKLYN NY 11211
KHAL UNGVAR, CONGREGATION O 5306 16TH AVENUE .... BROOKLYN NY 11204 (718) 252-0005
KHAL YERAIM HALLEN O 1047 50TH STREET .... BROOKLYN NY 11219 (718) 853-5578
KHALL MACHENKA HADAS O 1631 50TH STREET .... BROOKLYN NY 11204
KINGSWAY JEWISH CENTER O 2810 NOSTRAND AVENUE .... BROOKLYN NY 11229 (718) 258-3344
KLAUZENBERG B.M. CHATZOR HAKODESH O 1420 50TH STREET .... BROOKLYN NY 11219 (718) 435-2626
KNESES ISRAEL OF SEAGATE, CONGREGATION O
3803 NAUTILUS AVENUE .... BROOKLYN NY 11224 (718) 372-1668
KNESETH ISRAEL KLAUS, CONGREGATION O 95 DIVISION AVENUE .... BROOKLYN NY 11211
KNESSET HORABONIM, CONGREGATION O 701 48TH STREET .... BROOKLYN NY 11220 (718) 633-6378
KOL ISRAEL CONGREGATION 3211 BEDFORD AVENUE .... BROOKLYN NY 11210 (718) 377-9809
KOL ISRAEL, CONGREGATION O 603 ST. JOHNS PLACE .... BROOKLYN NY 11238 (718) 638-6583
KOLEL BNEI YAAKOV O 1546 47TH STREET .... BROOKLYN NY 11219
KOLEL TIFERETH MENACHEM O 241 MARCY AVENUE .... BROOKLYN NY 11211
KOLLEL TIFERETH ZVI, CONGREGATION O 4122 14TH AVENUE .... BROOKLYN NY 11219
KRULER MIKVA, CONGREGATION O 5102 11TH AVENUE .... BROOKLYN NY 11219
LANZUT, CONGREGATION OF O 159 RODNEY STREET .... BROOKLYN NY 11211 (718) 384-3132
LOMDAI TORAH, CONGREGATION O 2209 63RD STREET .... BROOKLYN NY 11204
MACHNAH LOMDAI TORAH O 239 HAVEMEYER STREET .... BROOKLYN NY 11211
MACHNE ISRAEL, CONGREGATION O 2413 EAST 23RD STREET .... BROOKLYN NY 11235 (718) 332-8788
MACHNE ISRAEL, INC. O 770 EASTERN PARKWAY .... BROOKLYN NY 11213 (718) 493-9250
MACHNE TORAH O 1375 57TH STREET .... BROOKLYN NY 11219
MACHZIKEI HADAS, CONGREGATION O 150 OCEAN PARKWAY .... BROOKLYN NY 11218
MACHZIKEI HADAS, CONGREGATION O 1636 49TH STREET .... BROOKLYN NY 11204 (718) 871-5986
MACHZIKEI HADAS OF BORO PARK CONGREGATION O
972 45TH STREET .... BROOKLYN NY 11219 (718) 438-4486
MACHZIKEI TALMUD TORAH, CONGREGATION O 4622 14TH AVENUE .... BROOKLYN NY 11219 (718) 436-8690
MACHZIKEI TORAH, CONGREGATION O 1016 BEVERLY ROAD .... BROOKLYN NY 11218 (718) 284-5607
MADISON JEWISH CENTER C 2989 NOSTRAND AVENUE .... BROOKLYN NY 11229 (718) 375-2271
MAGEN DAVID CONGREGATION O 2104 EAST 2ND STREET .... BROOKLYN NY 11223
MAGEN DAVID OF OCEAN PARKWAY, CONGREGATION O
1616 OCEAN PARKWAY .... BROOKLYN NY 11233
MANHATTAN BEACH JEWISH CENTER O 60 WEST END AVENUE .... BROOKLYN NY 11235 (718) 891-8700
MAPLETON PARK HEBREW INSTITUTE O 2022 66TH STREET .... BROOKLYN NY 11204 (718) 236-5551
MARAH YECHESKAL CONGREGATION O 1016 EAST 15TH STREET .... BROOKLYN NY 11230 (718) 252-2521
MARINE PARK JEWISH CENTER O 3311 AVENUE S .... BROOKLYN NY 11234 (718) 376-5200
MARLBORO JEWISH CENTER O 2324 WEST 13TH STREET .... BROOKLYN NY 11223 (718) 996-5558
MASEI ROCKEACH O 5423 12TH AVENUE .... BROOKLYN NY 11219 (718) 436-8727
MEAH SHEARIM, CONGREGATION O 1061 OCEAN PARKWAY .... BROOKLYN NY 11230
MENORAH SYNAGOGUE OF MENORAH HOME & HOSPITAL O
871 BUSHWICK AVENUE .... BROOKLYN NY 11221 (718) 443-3000
MENUCHAT USHER, CONGREGATION O 582 MONTGOMERY STREET .... BROOKLYN NY 11225
MESIFTA HEICHAL HAKODESH 851 47TH STREET .... BROOKLYN NY 11220 (718) 438-9097
MESIVTA BAIS YISROEL (GUR) O 5407 16TH AVENUE .... BROOKLYN NY 11204 (718) 633-2472
MESIVTA EITZ CHAIM OF BOBOV O 1533 48TH STREET .... BROOKLYN NY 11219 (718) 854-2444
MESIVTA HAICHAL HATORAH O 2449 OCEAN AVENUE .... BROOKLYN NY 11229 (718) 646-8900
MESIVTA TORAH VODAATH O 425 EAST 9TH STREET .... BROOKLYN NY 11218 (718) 941-8000
MIFAL TORAH VODAATH, CONGREGATION O 4116 16TH AVENUE .... BROOKLYN NY 11204 (718) 438-2206
MIKVAH ISRAEL OF BORO PARK, CONGREGATION O
1351 46TH STREET .... BROOKLYN NY 11219

Name	Address	City	State	ZIP	Phone
MINCHA CHADOSHA O	1243 48TH STREET	BROOKLYN	NY	11219	(718) 438-8805
MINCHAS ELUZER MINKATSCH, CONGREGATION O	5202 13TH AVENUE	BROOKLYN	NY	11219	(718) 438-9253
MINCHAS YEHUDA O	1266 50TH STREET	BROOKLYN	NY	11219	(718) 854-3104
MINYAN BE'ER SHMUEL O	203 AVENUE F, #4C	BROOKLYN	NY	11218	
MINYAN MIR O	5401 16TH AVENUE	BROOKLYN	NY	11204	(718) 438-9173
MINYAN SFARD OF BORO PARK, CONGREGATION O	803 46TH STREET	BROOKLYN	NY	11220	
MIRRER YESHIVA SYNAGOGUE O	1791 OCEAN PARKWAY	BROOKLYN	NY	11223	(718) 645-0536
MIZRACHI HAPOEL HAMIZRACHI, CONGREGATION O	378 KINGSTON AVENUE	BROOKLYN	NY	11225	
MOUNT SINAI, CONGREGATION C	305 SCHERMERHORN STREET	BROOKLYN	NY	11217	(718) 875-9124
NACHLAS ISRAEL, CONGREGATION O	745 CROWN STREET	BROOKLYN	NY	11213	(718) 756-4593
NACHLAS MOSHE O	1227 50TH STREET	BROOKLYN	NY	11219	(718) 853-5331
NACHLATH ZION JEWISH CENTER O	2201 EAST 23RD STREET	BROOKLYN	NY	11229	(718) 648-4865
NER BARUCH CONGREGATION O	4306 15TH AVENUE	BROOKLYN	NY	11219	(718) 435-3498
NETZACH YISROEL BOSTON O	1535 49TH STREET	BROOKLYN	NY	11219	(718) 851-5379
NEW BRIGHTON JEWISH CENTER O	184 BRIGHTON 11 STREET	BROOKLYN	NY	11235	(718) 332-9689
NEW LOTS, CONGREGATION O	4320 16TH AVENUE	BROOKLYN	NY	11204	
NOVOMINSKER BETH MEDRASH O	1569 47TH STREET	BROOKLYN	NY	11204	(718) 633-4861
OCEAN AVENUE JEWISH CENTER-CONGREGATION PRI ETZ CHAIM O	2600 OCEAN AVENUE	BROOKLYN	NY	11229	(718) 743-5533
OCEAN AVENUE SYNAGOGUE O	1057 EAST 28TH STREET	BROOKLYN	NY	11210	
OCEAN PARKWAY JEWISH CENTER C	550 OCEAN PARKWAY	BROOKLYN	NY	11218	(718) 436-4900
OCEANVIEW JEWISH CENTER	3100 BRIGHTON STREET	BROOKLYN	NY	11235	(718) 646-9639
OHEIV YISROEL D'CHASIDEI ZIDITSHOV O	4801 11TH AVENUE	BROOKLYN	NY	11219	(718) 871-2681
OHEL AVROHOM, CONGREGATION O	4907 18TH AVENUE	BROOKLYN	NY	11204	
OHEL ELIMELECH O	BROOKLYN AVENUE BETWEEN MONTGOMERY & EMPIRE	BROOKLYN	NY	11213	
OHEL ELIMELECH, CONGREGATION O	5120 FT. HAMILTON PARKWAY	BROOKLYN	NY	11219	(718) 871-5226
OHEL SHALOM, CONGREGATION OF O	4419 12TH AVENUE	BROOKLYN	NY	11219	(718) 854-7240
OHELEY SHEM, CONGREGATION O	5206 12TH AVENUE	BROOKLYN	NY	11219	(718) 435-1639
OHEV SHEM YESHIVA CONGREGATION	5206 12TH AVENUE	BROOKLYN	NY	11219	(718) 435-1639
OHEV SHOLOM ANSHEI MARMOROSH, CONGREGATION O	1266 47TH STREET	BROOKLYN	NY	11219	
OHR TORAH, CONGREGATION O	1520 48TH STREET	BROOKLYN	NY	11219	
PARK SLOPE JEWISH CENTER O	8TH AVENUE & 14TH STREET	BROOKLYN	NY	11215	(718) 508-4153
PETACH TIKVAH, CONGREGATION O	971 E. 10TH STREET	BROOKLYN	NY	11230	
POALEI AGUDATH ISRAEL O	4820 16TH AVENUE	BROOKLYN	NY	11204	(718) 436-6556
PORTUGAL CRETIENBERGER, CONGREGATION O	4924 16TH AVENUE	BROOKLYN	NY	11204	
PRIDE OF ISRAEL ANSHE BRISK, CONGREGATION O	274 KEAP STREET	BROOKLYN	NY	11211	(718) 384-6283
PROGRESSIVE SHAARI ZEDEK SYNAGOGUE R	1395 OCEAN AVENUE	BROOKLYN	NY	11230	(718) 377-1818
PROSPECT PARK JEWISH CENTER O	1604 AVENUE R	BROOKLYN	NY	11229	(718) 376-4400
PROSPECT PARK TEMPLE ISAAC	1419 DORCHESTER ROAD	BROOKLYN	NY	11226	(718) 248-8032
RABBI ARIA LEIB TEITELBAUM - AITZ CHAIM CONGREGATION O	4822 11TH AVENUE	BROOKLYN	NY	11219	
RABBI HOROWITZ, CONGREGATION O	1706 47TH STREET	BROOKLYN	NY	11204	
RABBI MOSHE BICK, CONGREGATION O	1545 55TH STREET	BROOKLYN	NY	11219	
RACHMISTRIVKER BETH MEDRASH O	1223 45TH STREET	BROOKLYN	NY	11219	(718) 435-7802
RAMBAM YESHIVA O	3300 KINGS HIGHWAY	BROOKLYN	NY	11234	(718) 338-6918
REFUGEES DEB'AY D'MIZRACH EUROPE, CONGREGATION O	711 EASTERN PARKWAY	BROOKLYN	NY	11213	
REMSEN HEIGHTS JEWISH CENTER C	8700 AVENUE K	BROOKLYN	NY	11236	(718) 763-2244
RODFEH ZEDEK, CONGREGATION	2080 77TH STREET	BROOKLYN	NY	11214	
ROZENOYER ADAS KODEISHEM, CONGREGATION	1510 OCEAN PARKWAY	BROOKLYN	NY	11230	(718) 336-1195
SANZ KLAUZENBURG, CONGREGATION	1420 50TH STREET	BROOKLYN	NY	11219	(718) 438-9611
SARATOGA JEWISH CENTER & TALMUD TORAH O	163 PARKVILLE AVENUE	BROOKLYN	NY	11230	(718) 435-6550
SEA BREEZE JEWISH CENTER O	311 SEA BREEZE AVENUE	BROOKLYN	NY	11224	(718) 372-9749
SEAVIEW JEWISH CENTER O	1440 EAST 99TH STREET	BROOKLYN	NY	11236	(718) 251-1900
SEFARD ANSHEI POLEN, CONGREGATION O	216 KEAP STREET	BROOKLYN	NY	11211	
SEFAS EMES, CONGREGATION O	1337 42ND STREET	BROOKLYN	NY	11219	(718) 853-5371
SEPHARDIC CENTER OF MAPLETON O	7216 BAY PARKWAY	BROOKLYN	NY	11204	(718) 236-9451
SEPHARDIC INSTITUTE O	511 AVENUE R	BROOKLYN	NY	11223	(718) 998-8171
SEPHARDIC JEWISH CENTER OF CANARSIE O	9320 FLATLANDS AVENUE	BROOKLYN	NY	11236	(718) 257-0400
SEPHARDIC TEMPLE TORAH ISRAEL CONGREGATION O	60 BRIGHTON 11TH STREET	BROOKLYN	NY	11235	(718) 743-4616
SHAARE EMETH ANNEX, TEMPLE	6012 FARRAGUT ROAD	BROOKLYN	NY	11226	(718) 444-9519
SHAARE EMETH, CONGREGATION C	6012 FARRAGUT ROAD	BROOKLYN	NY	11236	(718) 444-3223
SHAARE SHALOM O	472 AVENUE P	BROOKLYN	NY	11223	(718) 339-2796
SHAARE TEFILO OF KINGS HIGHWAY O	1679 WEST 1ST STREET	BROOKLYN	NY	11223	(718) 375-3095
SHAARE TORAH OF FLATBUSH, CONGREGATION C	305 EAST 21ST STREET	BROOKLYN	NY	11226	(718) 496-5300
SHAARE TORAH, CONGREGATION O	1061 OCEAN PARKWAY	BROOKLYN	NY	11230	
SHAARE ZION CONGREGATION O	2030 OCEAN PARKWAY	BROOKLYN	NY	11223	(718) 376-0009
SHAARI ISRAEL, CONGREGATION C	810 E. 49TH STREET	BROOKLYN	NY	11203	(718) 629-0476
SHAR MESHAMAYIM CONGREGATION O	5012 17TH AVENUE	BROOKLYN	NY	11204	(718) 851-0394
SHAREI ZEDEK, CONGREGATION O	3701 SURF AVENUE	BROOKLYN	NY	11224	
SHAREI ZEDEK-SEA GATE SISTERHOOD & T.T.O	2301 MERMAID AVENUE	BROOKLYN	NY	11224	(718) 372-2731
SHAREI ZION, CONGREGATION O	1533 48TH STREET	BROOKLYN	NY	11219	
SHEARITH ISRAEL O	5224 15TH AVENUE	BROOKLYN	NY	11219	(718) 851-1560
SHELLBANK JEWISH CENTER C	2121 BRAGG STREET	BROOKLYN	NY	11229	(718) 891-8666
SHEVES ACHIM, CONGREGATION O	1184 EAST 14TH STREET	BROOKLYN	NY	11230	(718) 252-1998
SHMUEL TOVA V'OHR MOLAH, KASONZ CONGREGATION O	906 50TH STREET	BROOKLYN	NY	11219	(718) 435-5786
SHOLOM OF FLATBUSH, TEMPLE C	2075 E. 68TH STREET	BROOKLYN	NY	11234	(718) 251-0370
SHOMREI EMUNAH, CONGREGATION O	5202 14TH AVENUE	BROOKLYN	NY	11219	(718) 851-8586
SHOMREI HADATH OF BORO PARK, CONGREGATION O	1327 41ST STREET	BROOKLYN	NY	11218	(718) 438-0066
SHOMREI SHABOS ANSHEI SFARD, CONGREGATION O	1280 53RD STREET	BROOKLYN	NY	11219	
SHORE PARK JEWISH CENTER C	2959 AVENUE Y	BROOKLYN	NY	11235	(718) 648-2900
SHORE PARKWAY JEWISH CENTER C	8885 26TH AVENUE	BROOKLYN	NY	11214	(718) 449-6530
SHOTZER SASSOWER CONGREGATION O	143 RODNEY STREET	BROOKLYN	NY	11211	
SINAI OF BROOKLYN, TEMPLE C	24 ARLINGTON AVENUE	BROOKLYN	NY	11207	(718) 827-8695
SKVARER BETH MEDRASH O	12TH AVENUE & 54TH STREET	BROOKLYN	NY	11219	
SKVERER BAIS MEDROSH O	1657 OCEAN PARKWAY	BROOKLYN	NY	11223	
SONS OF ISRAEL, CONGREGATION O	2115 BENSON AVENUE	BROOKLYN	NY	11214	(718) 372-4830
SONS OF JUDAH, CONGREGATION O	5311 16TH AVENUE	BROOKLYN	NY	11204	(718) 851-9828
SQUER, CONGREGATION O	394 KINGSTON AVENUE	BROOKLYN	NY	11213	
STARRETT CITY JEWISH CENTER	1540 VAN SICLEN AVENUE	BROOKLYN	NY	11239	(718) 642-8804
TABERNACLE BETH EL	85 FOUNTAIN AVENUE	BROOKLYN	NY	11208	(718) 277-8035
TALMUD TORAH AHAVATH ACHIM, CONGREGATION O	1750 E. 4TH STREET	BROOKLYN	NY	11223	(718) 375-3895
TALMUD TORAH BETH JUDAH COMMUNITY CENTER O	1960 SCHENECTADY AVENUE	BROOKLYN	NY	11234	
TALMUD TORAH B'NAI ABRAHAM, CONGREGATION O	407 EAST 53RD STREET	BROOKLYN	NY	11203	
TALMUD TORAH OHEV SHALOM, CONGREGATION O	1387 E. 96TH STREET	BROOKLYN	NY	11236	(718) 251-1430
TALMUD TORAH SONS OF ISRAEL, CONGREGATION O	2115 BENSON AVENUE	BROOKLYN	NY	11214	(718) 372-4830
TALMUD TORAH TIFERES BUNIM O	1377 42ND STREET	BROOKLYN	NY	11219	(718) 436-6868
TALMUD TORAH TIFERETH ELCHANAN O	5311 16TH AVENUE	BROOKLYN	NY	11204	(718) 851-9828
TALMUD TORAH TIFERETH ISRAEL O	1915 WEST 7TH STREET	BROOKLYN	NY	11223	(718) 339-1927
TALMUD TORAH TOLDOIS YAAKOV YOSEF O	105 HEYWARD	BROOKLYN	NY	11206	(718) 852-0502
TALMUD TORAH TOMCHAI TORAH O	1320 SUTTER AVENUE	BROOKLYN	NY	11208	
TALMUD TORAH TOMCHAI TORAH O	8807 AVENUE A	BROOKLYN	NY	11236	
TALMUD TORAH ZICHRON MENACHEM LEVI, CONGREGATION O	1424 58TH STREET	BROOKLYN	NY	11219	
TALMUD TORAH OF FLATBUSH O	1305 CONEY ISLAND AVENUE	BROOKLYN	NY	11230	(718) 377-2528
TALMUD TORAH, CONGREGATION O	64 TEHAMA STREET	BROOKLYN	NY	11218	
TEFERETH TZVI, CONGREGATION O	2174 85TH STREET	BROOKLYN	NY	11214	(718) 266-3878
TELSHE ALUMNI BAIS HAMEDRASH, INC. O	5218 16TH AVENUE	BROOKLYN	NY	11204	(718) 438-8937
TFILA LEMOSHE, CONGREGATION O	1319 50TH STREET	BROOKLYN	NY	11219	(718) 633-6221
TIFERES MORDECHAI SHLOMIE O	4405 14TH AVENUE	BROOKLYN	NY	11219	
TIFERETH ISRAEL OF BENSONHURST, CONGREGATION O	1835 BAY RIDGE PARKWAY	BROOKLYN	NY	11204	(718) 236-8283
TIFERETH ISRAEL OF MAPLETON PARK, CONGREGATION O	2025 64TH STREET	BROOKLYN	NY	11204	
TIFERETH ISRAEL OF WILLIAMSBURG, CONGREGATION O	491 BEDFORD AVENUE	BROOKLYN	NY	11211	(718) 384-8145
TIFERETH ISRAEL, CONGREGATION O	2025 64TH STREET	BROOKLYN	NY	11204	(718) 236-9884
TIFERETH TORAH OF BENSONHURST, CONGREGATION O	23 AVENUE & 83RD STREET	BROOKLYN	NY	11214	(718) 236-6646
TIFERETH YEHUDAH, CONGREGATION O	347 EAST 49TH STREET	BROOKLYN	NY	11203	
TOLDAS YAKOV, CONGREGATION O	551 BEDFORD AVENUE	BROOKLYN	NY	11211	
TOLDOS YAKOV YOSEF	1223 53RD STREET	BROOKLYN	NY	11219	(718) 438-8312
TOMCHE TMIMIM LUBAVICH O	841 OCEAN PARKWAY	BROOKLYN	NY	11230	(718) 434-0784
TORAH ISRAEL, TEMPLE O	60 BRIGHTON 11 STREET	BROOKLYN	NY	11235	(718) 743-4616
TORAH TEMIMAH, CONGREGATION O	1575 50TH STREET	BROOKLYN	NY	11219	
TORAS CHAIM VIZNITZ, CONGREGATION O	5228 NEW UTRECHT AVENUE	BROOKLYN	NY	11219	(718) 853-6010
TORAS EMES SYNAGOGUE O	1650 56TH STREET	BROOKLYN	NY	11204	
TORAS YISROEL, CONGREGATION O	5311 NEW UTRECHT AVENUE	BROOKLYN	NY	11219	
TORATH MOSHE JEWISH CENTER O	4314 10TH AVENUE	BROOKLYN	NY	11219	(718) 438-9578
UNION TEMPLE R	17 EASTERN PARKWAY	BROOKLYN	NY	11238	(718) 638-7600
VISNITZ, CONGREGATION O	680 MONTGOMERY STREET	BROOKLYN	NY	11213	
WALLERSTEIN INSTITUTE	750 REMSEN AVENUE	BROOKLYN	NY	11236	
WALTON AVENUE SYNAGOGUE O	1486 OCEAN PARKWAY	BROOKLYN	NY	11230	(718) 627-3777
YAGDIL TORAH, CONGREGATION O	5110 18TH AVENUE	BROOKLYN	NY	11204	
YESHIVA ATERES YISROEL O	8101 AVENUE K	BROOKLYN	NY	11236	(718) 763-6777
YESHIVA BETH SHEARIM CONGREGATION O	5306 16TH AVENUE	BROOKLYN	NY	11204	(718) 851-9809
YESHIVA BIRKAS REUVEN O	4911 16TH AVENUE	BROOKLYN	NY	11204	(718) 998-3201
YESHIVA JACOB ISAAC REINES, CONGREGATION O	417 TROY AVENUE	BROOKLYN	NY	11213	
YESHIVA KETANA OF OCEAN AVENUE O	2449 OCEAN AVENUE	BROOKLYN	NY	11229	(718) 648-1150
YESHIVA LEV SOMEACH, INC., CONGREGATION O	674 E. 2ND STREET	BROOKLYN	NY	11218	(718) 438-4800
YESHIVA MEOR HATORAH CONGREGATION O	2221 OCEAN AVENUE	BROOKLYN	NY	11229	(718) 998-7663
YESHIVA RABBI DAVID LEIBOWITZ, SYNAGOGUE OF O	9102 CHURCH AVENUE	BROOKLYN	NY	11236	
YESHIVA RABBI MEYER SIMCHE HACOHEN, CONGREGATION O	289 EAST 53RD STREET	BROOKLYN	NY	11203	(718) 385-7100
YESHIVA TORAH TEMIMAH O	555 OCEAN PARKWAY	BROOKLYN	NY	11218	(718) 853-8500
YESHIVA YESHURIN OF FLATBUSH, CONGREGATION	1454 OCEAN PARKWAY	BROOKLYN	NY	11230	(718) 375-9292
YESHIVAT ERETZ ISRAEL CONGREGATION O	1666 EAST 7TH STREET	BROOKLYN	NY	11230	
YESHIVATH YAVNE, CONGREGATION O	510 DAHILL ROAD	BROOKLYN	NY	11218	
YESHURIM-ADAS ISRAEL, CONGREGATION O	1454 OCEAN PARKWAY	BROOKLYN	NY	11230	(718) 375-9292
YETEV LEV, CONGREGATION	4507 10TH AVENUE	BROOKLYN	NY	11219	(718) 438-8144
YETEV LEV, CONGREGATION O	4514 15TH AVENUE	BROOKLYN	NY	11219	(718) 438-9638
YETEV LEV D'SATMAR O	1346 53RD STREET	BROOKLYN	NY	11219	(718) 438-9328
YETEV LEV D'SATMAR CONGREGATION O	150 RODNEY STREET	BROOKLYN	NY	11211	
YISMACH MOISHE O	5021 16TH AVENUE	BROOKLYN	NY	11204	(718) 851-1668
YITAV LEV D'SATMAR, CONGREGATION O	390 KINGSTON AVENUE	BROOKLYN	NY	11213	
YOUNG ISRAEL OF AVENUE J	1721 AVENUE J	BROOKLYN	NY	11230	(718) 338-2056
YOUNG ISRAEL OF AVENUE K	2818 AVENUE K	BROOKLYN	NY	11210	(718) 258-6666

YOUNG ISRAEL OF AVENUE U 2119 HOMECREST AVENUE — BROOKLYN NY 11229 (718) 375-6942
YOUNG ISRAEL OF BEDFORD BAY 2114 BROWN STREET — BROOKLYN NY 11229 (718) 332-4120
YOUNG ISRAEL OF BENSONHURST 48 BAY 28TH STREET — BROOKLYN NY 11214 (718) 372-5610
YOUNG ISRAEL OF BORO PARK 1349 50TH STREET — BROOKLYN NY 11219 (718) 438-1464
YOUNG ISRAEL OF BRIGHTON BEACH 293 NEPTUNE AVENUE — BROOKLYN NY 11235 (718) 332-7000
YOUNG ISRAEL OF BROOKLYN 563 BEDFORD AVENUE — BROOKLYN NY 11211 (718) 384-0461
YOUNG ISRAEL OF CANARSIE 1265 EAST 108TH STREET — BROOKLYN NY 11236 (718) 251-2600
YOUNG ISRAEL OF CONEY ISLAND 2801 SURF AVENUE — BROOKLYN NY 11224 (718) 449-1949
YOUNG ISRAEL OF EAST FLATBUSH 66 EAST 89TH STREET — BROOKLYN NY 11236 (718) 495-2600
YOUNG ISRAEL OF EASTERN PARKWAY 937 EASTERN PARKWAY — BROOKLYN NY 11213 (718) 774-6555
YOUNG ISRAEL OF FLATBUSH 1012 AVENUE I — BROOKLYN NY 11230 (718) 377-4400
YOUNG ISRAEL OF KENSINGTON 305 CHURCH AVENUE — BROOKLYN NY 11218 (718) 871-4543
YOUNG ISRAEL OF KINGS BAY O 1038 EAST 28TH STREET — BROOKLYN NY 11210
YOUNG ISRAEL OF MAPLETON PARK 1400 WEST 6TH STREET — BROOKLYN NY 11204 (718) 256-1060
YOUNG ISRAEL OF MIDWOOD 1694 OCEAN AVENUE — BROOKLYN NY 11230 (718) 253-6266
YOUNG ISRAEL OF MILL BASIN 2082 EAST 58TH STREET — BROOKLYN NY 11234 (718) 253-1016
YOUNG ISRAEL OF OCEAN PARKWAY 1781 OCEAN PARKWAY — BROOKLYN NY 11223 (718) 376-6305
YOUNG ISRAEL OF PROSPECT PARK 2170 BEDFORD AVENUE — BROOKLYN NY 11226 (718) 287-9432
YOUNG ISRAEL OF REDWOOD 619 E. 76TH STREET — BROOKLYN NY 11236 (718) 763-8040
YOUNG ISRAEL OF REMSEN 9302 AVENUE B — BROOKLYN NY 11236 (718) 345-7810
YOUNG ISRAEL OF SHEEPSHEAD BAY 2546 EAST 7TH STREET — BROOKLYN NY 11235 (718) 891-6767
YOUNG ISRAEL OF VANDERVEER PARK 2811-15 FARRAGUT ROAD — BROOKLYN NY 11210 (718) 434-2910
ZEMACH DAVID CHASIDEI SQUARE, CONGREGATION O
571 BEDFORD AVENUE — BROOKLYN NY 11211
ZEMACH SADAH CONGREGATION O 1318 55TH STREET — BROOKLYN NY 11219
ZEMACH ZEDEK OF BORO PARK CONGREGATION O
1546 46TH STREET — BROOKLYN NY 11219 (718) 438-7047
ZICHRON YEHUDAH O 158 HEWES STREET — BROOKLYN NY 11211
ZICHRON YOSEF CONGREGATION O 1371 46TH STREET — BROOKLYN NY 11219
ZIV YISROEL D'GUR, CONGREGATION O 4904 16TH AVENUE — BROOKLYN NY 11204 (718) 436-8515
ZVI LEZADIK (BLUSHEV), CONGREGATION O 1431 58TH STREET — BROOKLYN NY 11219 (718) 851-1361
ACHAI TMIMIM SARANAC SYNAGOGUE 85 SARANAC AVENUE — BUFFALO NY 14216 (716) 833-7881
AHAVAS ACHIM LUBAVITZ SYNAGOGUE O 345 TACOMA AVENUE — BUFFALO NY 14216 (716) 877-5790
AMHERST SYNAGOGUE, THE O 504 FRANKHAUSER ROAD — BUFFALO NY 14221 (716) 634-5255
BETH ABRAHAM, CONGREGATION O 1073 ELMWOOD AVENUE — BUFFALO NY 14222
BETH AM TEMPLE R 4660 SHERIDAN DRIVE — BUFFALO NY 14221 (716) 633-8877
BETH EL OF GREATER BUFFALO, TEMPLE C 2368 EGGERT ROAD — BUFFALO NY 14150 (716) 836-3762
BETH ZION TEMPLE R 805 DELAWARE AVENUE — BUFFALO NY 14209 (716) 886-7150
BRITH ISRAEL ANSHE EMES, CONGREGATION O 1237 HERTEL AVENUE — BUFFALO NY 14126 (716) 877-4601
BRITH SHOLEM, CONGREGATION O 787 DELAWARE AVENUE — BUFFALO NY 14209 (716) 885-7848
CHABAD-LUBAVITCH O 500 STARIN AVENUE — BUFFALO NY 14216
CHABAD-LUBAVITCH O 3292 MAIN STREET — BUFFALO NY 14214
CHAVURAH CONGREGATION R 11 HUXLEY DRIVE — BUFFALO NY 14226
SHAAREY ZEDEK, TEMPLE C 621 GETZVILLE ROAD — BUFFALO NY 14226 (716) 838-3232
SINAI, TEMPLE R 50 ALBERTA DRIVE — BUFFALO NY 14226 (716) 834-0708
ISRAEL, TEMPLE R SPRING STREET — CATSKILL NY 12414 (518) 943-5758
CHABAD LUBAVITCH O 902 TRIPHAMMER ROAD — CAYUGA HT-ITHACA NY 14850 (607) 273-8314
BAIS MEDRASH CONGREGATION O 504 WEST BROADWAY — CEDARHURST NY 11516 (516) 569-1971
BETH EL, TEMPLE C BROADWAY & LOCUST AVENUE — CEDARHURST NY 11516 (516) 569-2700
SEPHARDIC TEMPLE BRANCH BLVD. AT HALEY DRIVE — CEDARHURST NY 11516 (516) 295-4644
YOUNG ISRAEL OF LAWRENCE-CEDARHURST
26 COLUMBIA STREET — CEDARHURST NY 11516 (516) 569-3324
JEWISH CENTER OF THE MORICHES P.O. BOX 127 — CENTER MORICHES NY 11934 (516) 878-0388
ETZ HAYYIM, TEMPLE O P.O. BOX 90 — CENTRAL ISLIP NY 11722
BETH EL, TEMPLE R 220 BEDFORD ROAD — CHAPPAQUA NY 10514 (914) 238-3928
BETH SHALOM, CONGREGATION C
P.O. BOX 82, CLIFTON PARK CENTER — CLIFTON PARK NY 12065 (518) 371-0608
KEHILLATH SHALOM, CONGREGATION
58 GOOSE HILL ROAD — COLD SPRING HARBOR NY 11724 (516) 234-0548
BETH DAVID, TEMPLE R 100 HAUPPAUGE ROAD — COMMACK NY 11725 (516) 499-0915
CHABAD HOUSE O 74 HAUPPAGUE ROAD — COMMACK NY 11725 (516) 462-6640
COMMACK JEWISH CENTER C 83 SHIRLEY COURT — COMMACK NY 11725 (516) 543-3311
YOUNG ISRAEL OF COMMACK 40 KINGS PARK RD. — COMMACK NY 11725 (516) 543-1441
CORAM JEWISH CENTER O 981 OLD TOWN ROAD, P.O. BOX 116 — CORAM NY 11727 (516) 698-3939
TIFERETH ISRAEL ANSHEI-CORONA O 109-18 54TH AVENUE — CORONA NY 11368 (718) 592-6254
CONGREGATION ANSHE DORSHE EMES RE POB 626 — CROTON NY 10562 (914) 941-9687
ISRAEL OF NORTHERN WESTCHESTER, TEMPLE R
GLENGARY ROAD — CROTON-ON-HUDSON NY 10520 (914) 271-4705
SUFFOLK JEWISH CENTER C 330 CENTRAL AVENUE — DEER PARK NY 11729 (516) 667-7695
BETH SHOLOM, CONGREGATION C 5205 JAMESVILLE ROAD — DEWITT NY 13214 (315) 446-9570
YOUNG ISRAEL/SHAAREI TORAH O 4313 EAST GENESEE — DEWITT NY 13214 (315) 446-6194
BETH TORAH, TEMPLE R 35 BAGATELLE ROAD — DIX HILLS NY 11746 (516) 643-1200
DIX HILLS JEWISH CENTER C
VANDERBILT PARKWAY & DEFOREST ROAD — DIX HILLS NY 11746 (516) 499-6644
GREENBURGH HEBREW CENTER C 515 BROADWAY — DOBBS FERRY NY 10522 (914) 693-4260
MARATHON JEWISH COMMUNITY CENTER C 245-37 60TH AVENUE — DOUGLASTON NY 11362 (718) 428-1580
BETH EL, TEMPLE C 507 WASHINGTON AVENUE — DUNKIRK NY 14048 (716) 366-6646
TIFERETH ISRAEL OF JACKSON HEIGHTS, CONGREGATION O
88TH STREET & 32ND AVENUE — EAST ELMHURST NY 11369 (718) 429-4100
JEWISH CENTER OF THE HAMPTONS R
44 WOODS LANE, P.O. BOX 871 — EAST HAMPTON NY 11937 (516) 324-9858
EAST MEADOW JEWISH CENTER C 1400 PROSPECT AVENUE — EAST MEADOW NY 11554 (516) 483-4205
EMANU-EL OF EAST MEADOW, TEMPLE R 123 MERRICK AVENUE — EAST MEADOW NY 11554 (516) 794-8911
SUBURBAN PARK JEWISH CENTER C 400 OLD WESTBURY ROAD — EAST MEADOW NY 11554 (516) 796-2626
EAST NORTHPORT JEWISH CENTER C 328 ELWOOD ROAD — EAST NORTHPORT NY 11731 (516) 368-6474
YOUNG ISRAEL OF EAST NORTHPORT 547 LARKFIELD RD. — EAST NORTHPORT NY 11731 (516) 368-5880
HEWLETT-EAST ROCKAWAY JEWISH CENTER, CONGREGATION ETZ CHAIM
295 MAIN STREET — EAST ROCKAWAY NY 11518 (516) 599-2634
SHAARE ZEDEK CONGREGATION O 321 BEACH 30TH STREET — EDGEMERE NY 11691 (718) 327-0830
CONGREGATION ANSHE TZAYDIK 186 CANAL — ELLENVILLE NY 12428 (914) 647-9207
CONGREGATION KNESSET ISRAEL OF ULSTER HEIGHTS — ELLENVILLE NY 12428 (914) 647-7329
EZRATH ISRAEL, CONGREGATION O 31 CENTER STREET — ELLENVILLE NY 12428 (914) 647-4450
EMANU-EL OF QUEENS R 91-15 CORONA AVENUE — ELMHURST NY 11373 (718) 592-1343
B'NAI ISRAEL, TEMPLE R 900 W. WATER STREET — ELMIRA NY 14905 (607) 734-7735
SHOMRAY HADATH, CONGREGATION C COBBLES PARK — ELMIRA NY 14905 (607) 732-7410
B'NAI ISRAEL, TEMPLE R ELMONT ROAD, BAYLIS AVENUE — ELMONT NY 11003 (516) 354-1156
ELMONT JEWISH CENTER O 500 ELMONT ROAD — ELMONT NY 11003 (516) 488-1616
BETH EL-ENDICOTT JEWISH COMMUNITY CENTER C
119 JEFFERSON AVENUE — ENDICOTT NY 13760 (914) 785-3840
AGUDATH ISRAEL OF LONG ISLAND O 1121 SAGE STREET — FAR ROCKAWAY NY 11691 (718) 471-4861
BAIS MEDRASH ATERES YISROEL 827 CORNAGA AVENUE — FAR ROCKAWAY NY 11691 (718) 471-5346
BAIS TEFILAH - JASA/BROOKDALE O 131 BEACH 19TH STREET — FAR ROCKAWAY NY 11691 (718) 471-3200
BAYSWATER JEWISH CENTER-CONGREGATION DARCHAY NOAM C
2355 HEALY AVENUE — FAR ROCKAWAY NY 11691 (718) 471-7771
KEHILAS JAKOB CONGREGATION O 612 BEACH 9TH STREET — FAR ROCKAWAY NY 11691 (718) 327-8007
KNESETH ISRAEL, CONGREGATION O 728 EMPIRE AVENUE — FAR ROCKAWAY NY 11691 (718) 327-7545
KNESSETH MEIR CONGREGATION O 711 SEAGIRT AVENUE — FAR ROCKAWAY NY 11691 (718) 327-0951
SHAARE ZEDEK OF EDGEMERE, CONGREGATION O
315 BEACH 30TH STREET — FAR ROCKAWAY NY 11691 (718) 327-0830
SH'OR YOSHUV INSTITUTE O 1526 CENTRAL AVE. — FAR ROCKAWAY NY 11691 (718) 327-2048
TIFERETH CHAIM, CONGREGATION O
29-04 FAR ROCKAWAY BLVD. — FAR ROCKAWAY NY 11691 (718) 337-5685
YESHIVA DARCHEI TORAH CONGREGATION
257 BEACH 17TH STREET — FAR ROCKAWAY NY 11691 (718) 337-5880
YOUNG ISRAEL OF FAR ROCKAWAY O 716 BEACH 9TH STREET — FAR ROCKAWAY NY 11691 (718) 471-6724
YOUNG ISRAEL OF WAVECREST & BAYSWATER
2360 BROOKHAVEN AVENUE — FAR ROCKAWAY NY 11691 (718) 327-8606
FARMINGDALE JEWISH CENTER C 425 FULTON STREET — FARMINGDALE NY 11735 (516) 694-2343
BNAI ISRAEL, CONGREGATION C — FLEISHMANNS NY 12430 (914) 254-9837
BELLEROSE JEWISH CENTER C 254-04 UNION TURNPIKE — FLORAL PARK NY 11004 (718) 343-9001
FLORAL PARK JEWISH CENTER C 26 NORTH TYSON AVENUE — FLORAL PARK NY 11001 (718) 354-6980
SHOLOM, TEMPLE R 263-10 UNION TURNPIKE — FLORAL PARK NY 11004 (718) 343-8660
BETH SHALOM, TEMPLE - HEBREW COMMUNITY CENTER R
ROOSEVELT AVENUE — FLORIDA NY 10921 (914) 651-7817
AGUDAS ISRAEL CONGREGATION O 147-37 70TH ROAD — FLUSHING NY 11367
B'NAI ABRAHAM O 33-02 UNION STREET — FLUSHING NY 11354 (718) 359-0137
B'NAI ABRAHAM, CONGREGATION O 75-09 MAIN STREET — FLUSHING NY 11367
BEIS DOVID CONGREGATION O 144-55 77TH AVENUE — FLUSHING NY 11367
BEIS YOSEF CONGREGATION O 139-19 72ND ROAD — FLUSHING NY 11367
BETH HILLEL OF JACKSON HEIGHTS, CONGREGATION R
23-38 81ST STREET — FLUSHING NY 11373 (718) 899-6666
BETH OR OF THE DEAF, TEMPLE R 171-39 NORTHERN BLVD — FLUSHING NY 11358 (718) 776-4400
BETH SHOLOM OF REGO PARK, CONGREGATION O
55-36 97TH STREET — FLUSHING NY 11368 (718) 699-4510
BETH SHOLOM, TEMPLE R 171-39 NORTHERN BLVD — FLUSHING NY 11358 (718) 463-4143
DEGEL ISRAEL CONGREGATION O 144-02 68TH DRIVE — FLUSHING NY 11367
DEGEL MORDECAI, CONGREGATION O 73-09 136TH STREET — FLUSHING NY 11367 (718) 263-1575
EITZ CHAIM, CONGREGATION 54-96 KISSENA BLVD — FLUSHING NY 11355 (718) 762-2323
ELECTCHESTER JEWISH CENTER, INC. C 65-15 164TH STREET — FLUSHING NY 11365 (718) 886-4454
EMUNA SHLEIMA, CONGREGATION O 69-69 MAIN STREET — FLUSHING NY 11367
ETZ CHAIM CONGREGATION O P.O. BOX 34, STATION C — FLUSHING NY 11367 (718) 263-0525
FLUSHING JEWISH CENTER T 43-00 171 STREET — FLUSHING NY 11358 (718) 358-7071
FREE SYNAGOGUE OF FLUSHING R 41-60 KISSENA BLVD — FLUSHING NY 11355 (718) 961-0030
HILLCREST JEWISH CENTER, THE C 183-02 UNION TURNPIKE — FLUSHING NY 11366 (718) 380-4145
HILLCREST JEWISH CENTER, THE C 210-10 UNION TURNPIKE — FLUSHING NY 11364 (718) 776-3500
ISRAEL CENTER OF HILLCREST MANOR C 167-11 73RD AVENUE — FLUSHING NY 11366 (718) 969-8085
JEWISH CENTER OF KEW GARDENS HILLS, THE C 71-25 MAIN STREET — FLUSHING NY 11367 (718) 263-6500
JEWISH CENTER OF TORAH EMETH O 78-15 PARSONS BLVD — FLUSHING NY 11366 (718) 591-4240
KHAL ADAS YEREIM O 173-20 73RD AVENUE — FLUSHING NY 11366
KISSENA JEWISH CENTER O 43-43 BOWNE STREET — FLUSHING NY 11355 (718) 461-1871
MACHZEKEI HADATH, CONGREGATION O 147-30 73RD AVENUE — FLUSHING NY 11367
OHEL YITZCHOK CONGREGATION O 137-58 70TH AVENUE — FLUSHING NY 11367
OHR YITZCHAK CONGREGATION O 165-14 69TH AVENUE — FLUSHING NY 11365 (718) 591-4726
QUEENSBORO HILL JEWISH CENTER C
156-03 HORACE HARDING BLVD — FLUSHING NY 11367 (718) 445-4141
SHAARAI TEFILA-TEMPLE GATES OF PRAYER, CONGREGATION C
38-20 PARSONS BLVD — FLUSHING NY 11354 (718) 359-1160
TIFERETH ISRAEL OF CORONA, CONGREGATION O
109-18 54TH AVENUE — FLUSHING NY 11368
TIKVAS YISROEL SHALOM CONGREGATION O 141-25 70TH AVENUE — FLUSHING NY 11367
TORAH CENTER OF HILLCREST O 171-05 JEWEL AVENUE — FLUSHING NY 11365
UTOPIA JEWISH CENTER C 64-41 UTOPIA PARKWAY — FLUSHING NY 11365 (718) 461-8347
YOUNG ISRAEL OF HILLCREST 169-07 JEWEL AVENUE — FLUSHING NY 11365 (718) 969-2990
YOUNG ISRAEL OF QUEENS VALLEY 141-55 77TH AVENUE — FLUSHING NY 11367 (718) 263-3921
AHAVATH ACHIM, CONGREGATION O 67-62 BURNS STREET — FOREST HILLS NY 11375
AHAVATH REIM, CONGREGATION O 67-62 BURNS STREET — FOREST HILLS NY 11375 (718) 261-1191
AHAVATH SHOLOM, CONGREGATION O 75-02 113TH STREET — FOREST HILLS NY 11375 (718) 263-1949
BETH SHOLOM, CONGREGATION O 103-11 68TH DRIVE — FOREST HILLS NY 11375
CHOFETZ CHAIM, CONGREGATION O 92-15 69TH AVENUE — FOREST HILLS NY 11375 (718) 544-4662
DOV REVEL SYNAGOGUE O 71-02 113TH STREET — FOREST HILLS NY 11375 (718) 263-8687
FOREST HILLS JEWISH CENTER, THE C 106-06 QUEENS BLVD — FOREST HILLS NY 11375 (718) 263-7000
ISAIAH, TEMPLE R 75-24 GRAND CENTRAL PARKWAY — FOREST HILLS NY 11375 (718) 544-2800
HAVURAT YISRAEL CONGREGATION O 106-20 70TH AVENUE — FOREST HILLS NY 11375 (718) 261-5500
JEWISH EDUCATIONAL CENTER 102-35 63RD ROAD — FOREST HILLS NY 11375 (718) 896-4444
MACHNE CHODOSH, CONGREGATION O 67-29 108TH STREET — FOREST HILLS NY 11375 (718) 793-5656
MISHKAN ISRAEL, CONGREGATION O 108-11 69TH ROAD — FOREST HILLS NY 11375 (718) 263-9889
QUEENS JEWISH CENTER & TALMUD TORAH O
66-05 108TH STREET — FOREST HILLS NY 11375 (718) 459-8432
SEPHARDIC JEWISH CONGREGATION & CENTER OF QUEENS O
101-17 67TH DRIVE — FOREST HILLS NY 11375 (718) 544-6932

Synagogue / Address	City	State	Zip	Phone
SINAI, TEMPLE R 71-11 112TH STREET	FOREST HILLS	NY	11375	(718) 261-2900
YOUNG ISRAEL OF FOREST HILLS 7100 YELLOWSTONE BLVD.,	FOREST HILLS	NY	11375	(718) 268-7100
FRANKLIN SQUARE JEWISH CENTER C PACIFIC & LLOYD STREETS	FRANKLIN SQUARE	NY	11010	(516) 354-2322
B'NAI ISRAEL OF FREEPORT, CONGREGATION C 91 N. BAYVIEW AVENUE	FREEPORT	NY	11520	(516) 623-4200
UNION REFORM TEMPLE R 475 N. BROOKSIDE AVENUE	FREEPORT	NY	11520	(516) 623-1810
FRESH MEADOWS JEWISH CENTER C 193-10 PECK AVENUE	FRESH MEADOWS	NY	11365	(718) 357-5100
GARDEN CITY JEWISH CENTER R 168 NASSAU BLVD	GARDEN CITY	NY	11530	(516) 248-9180
BETH EL, TEMPLE R 755 S. MAIN STREET	GENEVA	NY	14456	(315) 789-9710
CHABAD HOUSE OF BUFFALO O 2501 NORTH FOREST ROAD	GETZVILLE	NY	14068	(716) 688-1642
NORTH COUNTRY REFORM TEMPLE R CRESCENT BEACH ROAD	GLEN COVE	NY	11542	(516) 671-4760
TIFERETH ISRAEL, CONGREGATION C HILL STREET & LANDING ROAD	GLEN COVE	NY	11542	(516) 676-5080
BETH EL, TEMPLE R 3 MARION AVENUE	GLEN FALLS	NY	12801	(518) 792-4364
SHAAREY TEFILA C 68 BAY STREET	GLEN FALLS	NY	12801	(518) 792-4945
GLEN WILD JEWISH SYNAGOGUE	GLEN WILD	NY	12738	
FOREST PARK JEWISH CENTER O 90-45 MYRTLE AVENUE	GLENDALE	NY	11385	(718) 847-6273
KNESSETH ISRAEL SYNAGOGUE C 34 E. FULTON STREET	GLOVERSVILLE	NY	12078	(518) 725-0649
BETH EL, TEMPLE R 5 OLD MILL ROAD	GREAT NECK	NY	11023	(516) 487-0900
BETH JOSEPH, TEMPLE 1 LINDEN PLACE	GREAT NECK	NY	11021	
EMANUEL, TEMPLE R 150 HICKS LANE	GREAT NECK	NY	11024	(516) 482-5701
GREAT NECK SYNAGOGUE O 26 OLD MILL ROAD	GREAT NECK	NY	11023	(516) 487-6100
ISAIAH OF GREAT NECK, TEMPLE R P.O. BOX 229	GREAT NECK	NY	11022	(516) 487-8709
ISRAEL OF GREAT NECK, TEMPLE C 108 OLD MILL ROAD	GREAT NECK	NY	11023	(516) 582-7800
LONG ISLAND RECONSTRUCTIONIST HAVURAH POB 2023	GREAT NECK	NY	11022	(516) 482-6532
NORTH SHORE SEPHARDIC SYNAGOGUE O 26 OLD MILL ROAD	GREAT NECK	NY	11023	(516) 487-6100
YOUNG ISRAEL OF GREAT NECK 236 MIDDLE NECK ROAD	GREAT NECK	NY	11023	(516) 829-6040
TIFERETH ISRAEL, TEMPLE C 4TH STREET	GREENPORT	NY	11944	
YOUNG ISRAEL OF HARRISON O 46 CRAWFORD ROAD	HARRISON	NY	10528	(914) 967-6215
BETH SHALOM, TEMPLE R 740 NORTH BROADWAY	HASTINGS-ON-HUDSON	NY	10706	(914) 478-3833
BETH CHAI, TEMPLE C 870 TOWNLINE ROAD	HAUPPAUGE	NY	11787	
CONGREGATION SONS OF JACOB 30 CLOVE AVENUE	HAVERSTRAW	NY	10927	(914) 429-4644
BETH ISRAEL, CONGREGATION C 141 HILTON AVENUE	HEMPSTEAD	NY	11550	(516) 489-1818
NASSAU COMMUNITY TEMPLE R 240 HEMPSTEAD AVENUE	HEMPSTEAD	NY	11552	(516) 485-1811
BETH AM, TEMPLE C 3249 E. HENRIETTA ROAD, P.O. BOX 177	HENRIETTA	NY	14467	(716) 334-4855
BETH JOSEPH, TEMPLE C 327 N. PROSPECT STREET	HERKIMER	NY	13350	(315) 866-4270
BETH EMETH, CONGREGATION C 36 FRANKLIN AVENUE	HEWLETT	NY	11557	(516) 374-9220
HICKSVILLE JEWISH CENTER C 6 MAGLIE DRIVE	HICKSVILLE	NY	11801	(516) 931-9323
SHAARI ZEDEK, CONGREGATION O OLD COUNTRY & NEW SOUTH ROAD	HICKSVILLE	NY	11801	(516) 938-0420
YOUNG ISRAEL OF HILLCREST O 169-07 JEWEL AVENUE	HILLCREST	NY	11365	(718) 461-8347
ISRAEL OF JAMAICA, TEMPLE R 188-15 MCLAUGHLIN AVENUE	HOLLIS	NY	11423	(718) 776-4400
MISHKAN ISRAEL 153-14 90TH AVENUE	HOLLIS	NY	11423	
BETH EL, TEMPLE C 12 CHURCH STREET	HORNELL	NY	14843	(607) 324-2236
HOWARD BEACH JEWISH CENTER C 162-05 90TH STREET	HOWARD BEACH	NY	11414	(718) 845-9443
JUDEA, TEMPLE R 151-44 80TH STREET	HOWARD BEACH	NY	11414	(718) 848-0999
ROCKWOOD PARK JEWISH CENTER O 156-45 84TH STREET	HOWARD BEACH	NY	11414	(718) 641-5822
ANSHE KOL ISRAEL, CONGREGATION O	HUNTER	NY	12442	
BETH EL OF HUNTINGTON, TEMPLE R 660 PARK AVENUE	HUNTINGTON	NY	11743	(516) 421-5835
HUNTINGTON HEBREW CONGREGATION C 510 PARK AVENUE	HUNTINGTON	NY	11743	(516) 427-1089
SOUTH HUNTINGTON JEWISH CENTER C 2600 NEW YORK AVENUE	HUNTINGTON STATION	NY	11747	(516) 421-3224
ANSHEI HURLEYVILLE, CONGREGATION O	HURLEYVILLE	NY	12747	(914) 434-9766
JEWISH COMMUNITY CENTER O BAYSWATER BLVD & ELM ROAD	INWOOD	NY	11696	
BETH EMETH JEWISH CENTER, CONGREGATION C 191 LONG BEACH ROAD	ISLAND PARK	NY	11558	(516) 432-6706
BETH EL, TEMPLE COURT & TIOGA STREETS	ITHACA	NY	14850	(607) 273-5775
YOUNG ISRAEL OF CORNELL 106 WEST AVENUE	ITHACA	NY	14850	(607) 272-5810
BETH HILLEL CONGREGATION R 23-38 81ST STREET	JACKSON HEIGHTS	NY	11370	(718) 899-6666
ELMHURST JEWISH CENTER O 37-53 90TH STREET	JACKSON HEIGHTS	NY	11372	(718) 426-5642
JEWISH CENTER OF JACKSON HEIGHTS C 34-25 82ND STREET	JACKSON HEIGHTS	NY	11372	(718) 429-1150
NORTHSIDE HEBREW CONGREGATION C 90-11 35TH AVENUE	JACKSON HEIGHTS	NY	11372	
TIFERETH ISRAEL OF JACKSON HEIGHTS, CONGREGATION O 88TH STREET & 32ND AVENUE	JACKSON HEIGHTS	NY	11369	(718) 429-4100
YOUNG ISRAEL OF JACKSON HEIGHTS 86-15 37TH AVENUE	JACKSON HEIGHTS	NY	11372	(718) 639-8888
BRIARWOOD JEWISH CENTER C 139-06 86TH AVENUE	JAMAICA	NY	11435	(718) 657-5151
CONSERVATIVE SYNAGOGUE OF JAMAICA C 182-69 WEXFORD TERRACE	JAMAICA	NY	11432	(718) 739-7500
FIRST HEBREW CONGREGATION O 90-21 160TH STREET	JAMAICA	NY	11432	
INTERNATIONAL SYNAGOGUE OF JOHN F. KENNEDY AIRPORT, THE JFK AIRPORT	JAMAICA	NY	11430	(718) 656-5044
ROCHDALE VILLAGE JEWISH CENTER C 167-10 137TH AVENUE	JAMAICA	NY	11434	(718) 528-0200
SANHEDRIN JEWISH COMMUNITY CENTER O 103-06 131ST STREET	JAMAICA	NY	11419	
TALMUD TORAH OF RICHMOND HILL O 109-25 114TH STREET	JAMAICA	NY	11420	(718) 843-5481
YOUNG ISRAEL OF BRIARWOOD 84-75 DANIELS STREET	JAMAICA	NY	11435	(718) 657-2880
YOUNG ISRAEL OF JAMAICA ESTATES 83-10 188 STREET	JAMAICA	NY	11423	(718) 454-1152
YM/YWHA MISHKAN ISRAEL-LINAS HAZEDEK O 153-14 90TH AVENUE	JAMAICA	NY	11432	(718) 739-0412
HESED ABRAHAM, TEMPLE R 215 HALL AVENUE	JAMESTOWN	NY	14701	(716) 484-1800
JERICHO JEWISH CENTER C NORTH BROADWAY	JERICHO	NY	11753	(516) 933-2540
OR ELOKIM, TEMPLE R 18 TOBIE LANE	JERICHO	NY	11753	(516) 433-9888
BETH TORAH, TEMPLE C 243 CONTIAGUE ROCK ROAD	JERICHO GARDENS	NY	11590	(516) 334-7979
BETH EL, TEMPLE C P.O. BOX 682	KAUNEONGA	NY	12749	(914) 583-4442
TIFERETH YEHUDA YISROEL, CONGREGATION O P.O. BOX 295	KERHONKSON	NY	12446	
ADAS YEREIM, CONGREGATION O 122-25 METROPOLITAN AVENUE	KEW GARDENS	NY	11415	
KEW GARDENS ANSHE SHOLOM JEWISH CENTER C 82-52 ABINGDON ROAD	KEW GARDENS	NY	11415	(718) 441-2470
KEW GARDENS SYNAGOGUE ADATH YESHURUN O 82-17 LEFFERTS BLVD	KEW GARDENS	NY	11415	(718) 846-7541

Synagogue / Address	City	State	Zip	Phone
SHAAR HATORAH O 83-96 117TH STREET	KEW GARDENS	NY	11418	(718) 849-8579
SHAARE TOVA CONGREGATION O 84-24 ABINGDON ROAD	KEW GARDENS	NY	11415	(718) 849-7988
TIFERETH AL-OZER V'YESHIVA DEGEL-HATORAH, CONGREGATION O 82-61 BEVERLY ROAD	KEW GARDENS	NY	11415	(718) 441-3862
TIFERETH MOSHE CONGREGATION O 82-33 GREENFELL STREET	KEW GARDENS	NY	11415	(718) 441-2110
AGUDATH ISRAEL OF KEW GARDENS O 147-37 70TH ROAD	KEW GARDENS HILLS	NY	11367	
AHAVAT YISRAEL O 75-09 MAIN STREET	KEW GARDENS HILLS	NY	11367	(718) 422-0903
BAIS MEDRASH REM O 144-55 77TH AVENUE	KEW GARDENS HILLS	NY	11367	
B'NAI ABRAHAM, CONGREGATION C 75-09 MAIN STREET	KEW GARDENS HILLS	NY	11367	(718) 261-4580
JEWISH CENTER OF KEW GARDENS HILLS O 71-25 MAIN STREET	KEW GARDENS HILLS	NY	11367	
NACHLAS YITZCHOK CONGREGATION O 141-43 73RD AVENUE	KEW GARDENS HILLS	NY	11367	
YOUNG ISRAEL OF KEW GARDENS HILLS 70-11 150TH STREET	KEW GARDENS HILLS	NY	11367	(718) 261-9723
ETZ CHAIM OF KINGS PARK, CONGREGATION O 44 MEADOW ROAD	KINGS PARK	NY	11754	(516) 269-9666
KINGS PARK JEWISH CENTER, INC. C ROUTE 25A, P.O. BOX 301	KINGS PARK	NY	11754	(516) 269-1133
AGUDAS ACHIM, CONGREGATION O 254 LUCAS AVENUE, P.O. BOX 3573	KINGSTON	NY	12401	(914) 331-1176
AHAVATH ISRAEL, CONGREGATION C 100 LUCAS AVENUE	KINGSTON	NY	12401	(914) 338-4409
EMANUEL, TEMPLE R 243 ALBANY AVENUE, P.O. BOX 1421	KINGSTON	NY	12401	(914) 338-4271
TALMUD TORAH OF KINGSTON 100 LUCAS AVENUE	KINGSTON	NY	12401	
LAKE GROVE JEWISH CENTER 821 HAWKINS AVENUE	LAKE GROVE	NY	11755	(516) 585-9710
RONKONKOMA JEWISH CENTER C P.O. BOX 20	LAKE GROVE	NY	11755	(516) 585-0521
LAKE PLACID SYNAGOGUE T 30 SARANAC AVENUE	LAKE PLACID	NY	12946	(518) 523-3876
LAKE SUCCESS JEWISH CENTER C 354 LAKEVILLE ROAD	LAKE SUCCESS	NY	11020	(516) 466-0569
NORTH SHORE JEWISH CENTER C 354 LAKEVILLE ROAD	LAKE SUCCESS	NY	11020	
BETH EMETH SYNAGOGUE C 2111 BOSTON POST ROAD	LARCHMONT	NY	10538	(914) 834-1093
LARCHMONT TEMPLE R 75 LARCHMONT AVENUE	LARCHMONT	NY	10538	(914) 834-6120
BETH EL OF LAURELTON, TEMPLE R 133-21 232ND STREET	LAURELTON	NY	11413	(718) 528-6378
LAURELTON JEWISH CENTER C 139-49 228TH STREET	LAURELTON	NY	11413	(718) 527-0400
BETH SHOLOM, CONGREGATION O 390 BROADWAY	LAWRENCE	NY	11559	(516) 569-3600
ISRAEL, TEMPLE R 140 CENTRAL AVENUE	LAWRENCE	NY	11559	(516) 239-1140
KOL YISROEL CHAVERIM, CONGREGATION O 124 RICHMOND PLACE	LAWRENCE	NY	11559	(516) 239-1033
SHAARAY TEFILA, CONGREGATION O CENTRAL & LORD AVENUE	LAWRENCE	NY	11559	(516) 239-2444
SINAI OF LONG ISLAND, TEMPLE R 131 WASHINGTON AVENUE	LAWRENCE	NY	11559	(516) 569-0267
ISRAEL COMMUNITY CENTER OF LEVITTOWN C 3235 HEMPSTEAD TURNPIKE	LEVITTOWN	NY	11756	(516) 731-2580
AHAVATH ISRAEL, CONGREGATION O 39 CHESTNUT STREET	LIBERTY	NY	12754	(914) 292-8843
FERNDALE SYNAGOGUE O LIBERTY GARDENS, A-3	LIBERTY	NY	12754	(914) 292-3690
LIDO BEACH JEWISH CENTER O ONE FAIRWAY ROAD	LIDO BEACH	NY	11561	(516) 889-9650
BNEI ABRAHAM, CONGREGATION O 33-01 UNION STREET	LINDEN HILL	NY	11354	(718) 539-7742
LINDENHURST HEBREW CONGREGATION 225 NORTH FOURTH STREET	LINDENHURST	NY	11757	(516) 226-2022
LITTLE NECK JEWISH CENTER C 49-10 LITTLE NECK PARKWAY	LITTLE NECK	NY	11362	(718) 224-0404
MARATHON JEWISH COMMUNITY CENTER C 245-37 60TH AVENUE	LITTLE NECK	NY	11362	(718) 428-1580
MENORAH OF LITTLE NECK, TEMPLE R 252-00 H. HARDING EXPRESSWAY	LITTLE NECK	NY	11362	(718) 321-1920
TORAH OF LITTLE NECK, TEMPLE C 54-27 LITTLE NECK PARKWAY	LITTLE NECK	NY	11362	(718) 423-2100
AGUDAS ACHIM, CONGREGATION	LIVINGSTON MANOR	NY	12758	
BACHUREI CHEMED CONGREGATION O 210 EDWARDS BOULEVARD	LONG BEACH	NY	11561	(516) 431-3434
BETH EL OF LONG BEACH, TEMPLE O 570 W. WALNUT STREET	LONG BEACH	NY	11561	(516) 432-1678
BETH SHOLOM OF LONG BEACH & LIDO, CONGREGATION C 700 E. PARK AVENUE	LONG BEACH	NY	11561	(516) 432-7464
EAST END SYNAGOGUE EAST PARK AVENUE AT ROOSEVELT BLVD	LONG BEACH	NY	11561	
EMANU-EL, TEMPLE R 455 NEPTUNE BLVD	LONG BEACH	NY	11561	(516) 431-4060
ISRAEL OF LONG BEACH, TEMPLE T 305 RIVERSIDE BLVD	LONG BEACH	NY	11561	(516) 432-1410
MUSMACH YESHUAH SYNAGOGUE O 369 EAST BEECH STREET	LONG BEACH	NY	11561	(516) 432-6841
SEPHARDIC CONGREGATION OF LONG BEACH O 161 LAFAYETTE BLVD, P.O. BOX 779	LONG BEACH	NY	11561	(516) 432-9224
TIFERETH ELIYAHU O 161 WEST BEECH STREET	LONG BEACH	NY	11561	
YOUNG ISRAEL OF LONG BEACH 158 LONG BEACH BLVD	LONG BEACH	NY	11561	(516) 431-2404
ZION, TEMPLE O 62 MARYLAND AVENUE, P.O. BOX 389	LONG BEACH	NY	11561	(516) 432-5657
ADATH ISRAEL, CONGREGATION O 36-02 14TH STREET	LONG ISLAND CITY	NY	11106	
ASTORIA CENTER OF ISRAEL C 27-35 CRESCENT STREET	LONG ISLAND CITY	NY	11102	(718) 278-2680
ASTORIA HEIGHTS JEWISH CENTER 32-49 49TH STREET	LONG ISLAND CITY	NY	11103	(718) 728-1012
BNEY ISRAEL, CONGREGATION O P.O. BOX 1215, 45-11 21ST STREET	LONG ISLAND CITY	NY	11101	
SONS OF ISRAEL, CONGREGATION O 33-21 CRESCENT STREET	LONG ISLAND CITY	NY	11106	(718) 274-2125
SUNNYSIDE JEWISH CENTER C 45-46 43RD STREET	LONG ISLAND CITY	NY	11104	(718) 729-9176
YOUNG ISRAEL OF SUNNYSIDE 41-12 45TH STREET	LONG ISLAND CITY	NY	11104	(718) 786-4103
BETH DAVID CONGREGATION C 188 VINCENT AVENUE	LYNBROOK	NY	11563	(516) 599-9464
EMANU-EL, TEMPLE R SAPERSTEIN PLAZA	LYNBROOK	NY	11563	(516) 593-4004
JEWISH CENTER OF THE MAHOPACS-TEMPLE BETH SHALOM C ROAD 10, P.O. BOX 245	MAHOPAC	NY	10541	(914) 628-6133
MALVERNE JEWISH CENTER C 1 NORWOOD AVENUE	MALVERNE	NY	11564	(516) 593-6364
WESTCHESTER JEWISH CENTER C ROCKLAND & PALMER AVENUE	MAMARONECK	NY	10543	(914) 698-2960
JUDEA, TEMPLE R 333 SEARINGTOWN ROAD	MANHASSET	NY	11030	(516) 621-8049
MASPETH JEWISH CENTER O 66-64 GRAND AVENUE	MASPETH	NY	11378	(718) 639-7559
BETH EL, CONGREGATION C 99 JERUSALEM AVENUE	MASSAPEQUA	NY	11758	(516) 541-0740
HILLEL HEBREW CONGREGATION C 1066 HICKSVILLE ROAD, P.O. BOX 244	MASSAPEQUA	NY	11758	(516) 799-0616
JUDEA, TEMPLE R JERUSALEM & CENTRAL AVENUE	MASSAPEQUA	NY	11758	(516) 798-5444
SINAI, TEMPLE R 270 CLOCK BLVD	MASSAPEQUA	NY	11758	(516) 795-5015
ADATH ISRAEL CONGREGATION C P.O. BOX 196	MASSENA	NY	13662	(315) 769-6878
MASTIC BEACH HEBREW CENTER NEIGHBORHOOD ROAD	MASTIC BEACH	NY	11951	
SOUTH HUNTINGTON JEWISH CENTER C 2600 NEW YORK AVENUE	MELVILLE	NY	11747	(516) 421-3224
BETH AM, TEMPLE R MERRICK & KIRKWOOD AVENUE	MERRICK	NY	11566	(516) 378-3477

ISRAEL OF SOUTH MERRICK, TEMPLE C 2655 CLUBHOUSE ROAD ... MERRICK **NY** 11566 (516) 378-1963
MERRICK JEWISH CENTER-CONGREGATION OHR TORAH C 225 FOX BLVD ... MERRICK **NY** 11566 (516) 379-8650
OHAV SHOLOM, CONGREGATION O 145 SOUTH MERRICK AVENUE ... MERRICK **NY** 11566 (516) 378-1988
REFORM JEWISH CONGREGATION OF MERRICK R MERRICK & KIRKWOOD AVENUES ... MERRICK **NY** 11566
JEWISH CENTER OF FOREST HILLS C 63-25 DRY HARBOR ROAD ... MIDDLE VILLAGE **NY** 11379 (718) 639-2110
SONS OF ISRAEL AHAVATH ACHIM O 75-27 67TH DRIVE ... MIDDLE VILLAGE **NY** 11379 (718) 326-7240
SINAI, TEMPLE C (MIDDLETOWN HEBREW ASSOCIATION) 75 HIGHLAND AVENUE ... MIDDLETOWN **NY** 10940 (914) 343-1861
BETH SHOLOM, CONGREGATION C 261 WILLIS AVENUE ... MINEOLA **NY** 11501 (516) 756-3211
BAIS NAFTULY, CONGREGATION O 5 KENNEDY COURT ... MONROE **NY** 10950 (914) 782-6192
BETH EL-MONROE TEMPLE OF LIBERAL JUDAISM, TEMPLE R 314 N. MAIN STREET ... MONROE **NY** 10950 (914) 783-2626
BETH ROPSHITZ & CONGREGATION KAHAL KDUSHAS YOM TOV O 4 RAYWOOD DRIVE ... MONROE **NY** 10950 (914) 782-5494
EITZ CHAIM, CONGREGATION C 251 SPRING STREET ... MONROE **NY** 10950 (914) 783-7424
KEDDUSHAS YOM TOV, CONGREGATION O 4 RAYWOOD DRIVE ... MONROE **NY** 10950 (914) 782-5494
MHARY ASHKENAZY, CONGREGATION O ROAD 5, P.O. BOX 157 4-A FOREST ROAD ... MONROE **NY** 10950 (914) 783-9033
MONROE-WOODBURY JEWISH COMMUNITY CENTER & CONG. EITZ CHAIM 251 SPRING STREET ... MONROE **NY** 10950 (914) 783-7424
YETEV LEV MONROE DIVISION, CONGREGATION P.O. BOX 566 ... MONROE **NY** 10950 (914) 782-5149
YETEV LEV, CONGREGATION O P.O. BOX 420 ... MONROE **NY** 10950 (914) 782-7546
AGUDATH ISRAEL OF MONSEY O ... MONSEY **NY** 10952
BAIS MEIR CHEVRA SHAS O 3 SMOLLEY DRIVE ... MONSEY **NY** 10952 (914) 356-8162
BETH ISRAEL MAPLE AND MAIN ... MONSEY **NY** 10952 (914) 356-1000
BETH MEDROSH ELYON 73 MAIN STREET ... MONSEY **NY** 10952 (914) 356-9711
AYSHEL AVRAHAM, CONGREGATION O P.O. BOX 317 ... MONSEY **NY** 10952 (914) 352-0630
B'NAI JESHURUN SYNAGOGUE OF MONSEY N.Y. O PARK LANE, P.O. BOX 423 ... MONSEY **NY** 10952 (914) 352-3239
CHABAD-LUBAVITCH O 4 PHYLLIS TERRACE ... MONSEY **NY** 10952
COMMUNITY SYNAGOGUE OF MONSEY O 1½ CLOVERDALE LANE ... MONSEY **NY** 10952 (914) 356-2720
CONGREGATION BETH MIKROH 23 W. MAPLE AVENUE ... MONSEY **NY** 10952 (914) 356-1239
CONGREGATION BETH TEFILA MAPLEWOOD LANE ... MONSEY **NY** 10952 (914) 356-5089
CONGREGATION OHAIV YISROEL 30 BLUEBERRY HILL ROAD ... MONSEY **NY** 10952 (914) 356-5728
CONGREGATION TOLDOTH YAKOV YOSEF 12 ROMAN BLVD. ... MONSEY **NY** 10952 (914) 352-9809
HADAR, CONGREGATION O 70 HIGHVIEW ROAD ... MONSEY **NY** 10952 (914) 357-1515
K'HAL TORATH CHAIM, CONGREGATION O P.O. BOX 446, PHYLLIS TERRACE ... MONSEY **NY** 10952 (914) 356-6666
MACHZIKEI TORAH, CONGREGATION O 3 RALPH BLVD ... MONSEY **NY** 10952
MONSEY JEWISH CENTER C 101 ROUTE 306 ... MONSEY **NY** 10952 (914) 352-6444
OHAIV YISROEL CONGREGATION O 30 BLUEBERRY HILL ROAD ... MONSEY **NY** 10952 (914) 356-5728
SHAAREI TORAH OF ROCKLAND 1 SCHOOL TERRACE ... MONSEY **NY** 10952 (914) 356-9773
TORAS CHAIM, CONGREGATION O PHYLLIS TERRACE ... MONSEY **NY** 10952
VAJOEL MOSHE, CONGREGATION O 214 MAPLE AVENUE ... MONSEY **NY** 10952 (914) 356-9807
YOUNG ISRAEL OF MONSEY 58 PARKER BOULEVARD ... MONSEY **NY** 10952 (914) 354-3665
SHOLOM, TEMPLE R PORT JERVIS & E. DILLON ROADS, P.O. BOX 664 ... MONTICELLO **NY** 12701 (914) 794-8731
TIFERETH ISRAEL, CONGREGATION O 18 LANDFIELD AVENUE ... MONTICELLO **NY** 12701 (914) 794-8470
BET TORAH C 60 SMITH AVENUE ... MOUNT KISCO **NY** 10549 (914) 241-0608
BETH MEDRASH CHEMED, CONGREGATION O PINES BRIDGE ROAD ... MOUNT KISCO **NY** 10549
SHAARAY TEFILA, TEMPLE R ROUTE 172 ... MOUNT KISCO **NY** 10549 (914) 666-3133
BROTHERS OF ISRAEL, CONGREGATION O 116 CRARY AVENUE ... MOUNT VERNON **NY** 10550 (914) 667-1302
EMANU-EL JEWISH CENTER C 261 E. LINCOLN AVENUE ... MOUNT VERNON **NY** 10552 (914) 667-0161
FLEETWOOD SYNAGOGUE O 11 EAST BROAD STREET ... MOUNT VERNON **NY** 10552 (914) 664-7643
FREE SYNAGOGUE OF WESTCHESTER R 500 N. COLUMBUS AVENUE ... MOUNT VERNON **NY** 10552 (914) 664-1727
JEWISH CENTER C 261 EAST LINCOLN AVENUE ... MOUNT VERNON **NY** 10552 (914) 667-0161
SINAI TEMPLE R 132 CRARY AVENUE ... MOUNT VERNON **NY** 10550 (914) 668-9471
HEBREW CONGREGATION OF MOUNTAINDALE O P.O. BOX 297 ... MOUNTAINDALE **NY** 12763 (914) 434-9306
NANUET HEBREW CENTER C 34 S. MIDDLETOWN ROAD ... NANUET **NY** 10954 (914) 623-3735
WEST END TEMPLE-CONGREGATION SINAI R 147-02 NEWPORT AVENUE ... NEPONSIT **NY** 11694 (718) 634-0301
BETH SHOLOM, TEMPLE R 228 NEW HEMPSTEAD ROAD ... NEW CITY **NY** 10956 (914) 638-0770
CHABAD EDUCATIONAL CENTER O 216 CONGERS ROAD ... NEW CITY **NY** 10956 (914) 634-9051
NEW CITY JEWISH CENTER C OLD SCHOOLHOUSE ROAD ... NEW CITY **NY** 10956 (914) 634-3619
EMANUEL, TEMPLE R 3315 HILLSIDE AVENUE ... NEW HYDE PARK **NY** 11040 (516) 746-1120
NEW HYDE PARK JEWISH COMMUNITY CENTER C 100 LAKEVILLE ROAD ... NEW HYDE PARK **NY** 11040 (516) 354-7583
YOUNG ISRAEL OF NEW HYDE PARK 264-15 77TH AVENUE ... NEW HYDE PARK **NY** 11040 (718) 343-0496
AHAVATH ACHIM C CHURCH STREET ... NEW PALTZ **NY** 12561 (914) 255-9817
ANSHE SHOLOM, CONGREGATION O 50 NORTH AVENUE ... NEW ROCHELLE **NY** 10805 (914) 632-9220
BETH EL SYNAGOGUE OF NEW ROCHELLE, INC. C NORTHFIELD ROAD AT N AVENUE ... NEW ROCHELLE **NY** 10804 (914) 235-2700
ISRAEL, TEMPLE R 1000 PINEBROOK BLVD ... NEW ROCHELLE **NY** 10804 (914) 235-1800
YOUNG ISRAEL OF NEW ROCHELLE 1228 NORTH AVENUE ... NEW ROCHELLE **NY** 10804 (914) 636-2215
ADAS BNEI ISRAEL, CONGREGATION - THE HEBREW LEAGUE O 257 EAST BROADWAY ... NEW YORK **NY** 10002
ADATH ISRAEL OF NEW YORK, UNITED HEBREW COMMUNITY OF NEW YORK O 201 EAST BROADWAY ... NEW YORK **NY** 10002 (212) 674-3580
AGUDAS CHAVERIM ANSHEI MARMAROS, CONGREGATION O 215 EAST BROADWAY ... NEW YORK **NY** 10002
AGUDATH ANSHEI MAMOD HOUSE OF SAGES, INC., CONGREGATION O 283 EAST BROADWAY ... NEW YORK **NY** 10002 (212) 732-3131
AGUDATH ANSHEI MAMOD, CONGREGATION 152 HENRY STREET ... NEW YORK **NY** 10002
AGUDATH ISRAEL OF EAST SIDE O 233 EAST BROADWAY ... NEW YORK **NY** 10002
AGUDATH ISRAEL OF WASHINGTON HEIGHTS O 617 W. 179TH STREET ... NEW YORK **NY** 10033 (212) 927-5404
AGUDATH TAHARAS MISHPACHAM OF EAST SIDE 311 EAST BROADWAY ... NEW YORK **NY** 10002
AHAVATH CHESED, CONGREGATION O 309 W. 89TH STREET ... NEW YORK **NY** 10024 (212) 724-8065
AHAVATH ISRAEL, CONGREGATION O 502 W. 157TH STREET ... NEW YORK **NY** 10032 (212) 927-5696
AMERICAN CONGREGATION OF JEWS FROM AUSTRIA 118 WEST 95TH STREET ... NEW YORK **NY** 10025 (212) 663-1920
ANSCHE CHESED, CONGREGATION C 251 WEST 100TH STREET ... NEW YORK **NY** 10025 (212) 864-6637
ANSHE TASHKANVEH, CONGREGATION O 241 EAST BROADWAY ... NEW YORK **NY** 10002
ANSHEI LEBEDOWE-RADZILOWE MANSE, CONGREGATION O 266 EAST BROADWAY ... NEW YORK **NY** 10002 (212) 254-2384
ANSHEI LIBOVNEH VILLIN-SHOMER SHABBOS, CONGREGATION O 237 EAST BROADWAY ... NEW YORK **NY** 10002
ANSHEI VEISKAW, CONGREGATION O 257 EAST BROADWAY ... NEW YORK **NY** 10002
AUSTRIA HUNGARY ANSCHE SFARD, CONGREGATION O 239 EAST BROADWAY ... NEW YORK **NY** 10002 (212) 227-6145
B'NAI ISRAEL CHAIM, CONGREGATION O 353 W. 84TH STREET ... NEW YORK **NY** 10024 (212) 874-0644
B'NAI ISRAEL SHEARITH JUDAH, TEMPLE O 610 W. 149TH STREET ... NEW YORK **NY** 10031
B'NAI ISRAEL, CONGREGATION 335 E. 77TH STREET ... NEW YORK **NY** 10021 (212) 570-6650
B'NAI JESHURUN C 257 WEST 88TH STREET ... NEW YORK **NY** 10024 (212) 787-7600
B'NAI YITZHUK (BOJANER SHTIEBL) O 441 WEST END AVENUE ... NEW YORK **NY** 10024 (212) 873-2064
BAYONER KLOYS, CONGREGATION O 247 EAST BROADWAY ... NEW YORK **NY** 10002
BETH AM, THE PEOPLE'S TEMPLE R 178 BENNETT AVENUE ... NEW YORK **NY** 10040 (212) 927-2230
BETH HACHASSIDIM DE POLEN, CONGREGATION O 233 EAST BROADWAY ... NEW YORK **NY** 10002 (212) 673-5191
BETH HACHNESES MOGEN ABRAHAM O 87 ATTORNEY STREET ... NEW YORK **NY** 10002 (212) 475-7253
BETH HAMEDRASH HAGODOL OF WASHINGTON HEIGHTS, CONGREGATION O 610 W. 175TH STREET ... NEW YORK **NY** 10033 (212) 927-6000
BETH HAMEDRASH HAGODOL, CONGREGATION O 60 NORFOLK STREET ... NEW YORK **NY** 10002 (212) 674-3330
BETH HAMEDRASH OF INWOOD, CONGREGATION 1781 RIVERSIDE DRIVE ... NEW YORK **NY** 10034 (212) 567-9776
BETH HILLEL & BETH ISRAEL, INC., CONGREGATION C 571 W. 182ND STREET ... NEW YORK **NY** 10033 (212) 568-3933
BETH ISRAEL CENTER O 646 WEST END AVENUE ... NEW YORK **NY** 10025 (212) 874-6135
BETH ISRAEL, CONGREGATION O 347 WEST 34TH STREET ... NEW YORK **NY** 10001 (212) 279-0016
BETH SHOLOM OF WASHINGTON HEIGHTS, TEMPLE C PINEHURST AVENUE & 179TH STREET ... NEW YORK **NY** 10033
BETH TILLEM O 7 EAST 14TH STREET, #215 ... NEW YORK **NY** 10003 (212) 242-6450
BETH TOMCHEI TORAH V'ZIKNEI YISROEL-HOME/SAGES ISRAEL CONG O 25 WILLETT STREET ... NEW YORK **NY** 10002 (212) 673-8500
BIALYSTOKER SYNAGOGUE O 7-11 WILLETT STREET ... NEW YORK **NY** 10002 (212) 475-0165
BNAI ISAAC ANSHEI LECHOWITZ, CONGREGATION O 217 HENRY STREET ... NEW YORK **NY** 10002
BNAI ISRAEL, CONGREGATION 335 EAST 77TH STREET ... NEW YORK **NY** 10021 (212) 570-6650
BNAI MOSES JOSEPH, CONGREGATION 317 E. 8TH STREET ... NEW YORK **NY** 10009
BNAI SHOLOM, TEMPLE R 4580 BROADWAY ... NEW YORK **NY** 10040
B'NEI JACOB AND ANSHE BRZEZAN CONGREGATION O 180 STANTON STREET ... NEW YORK **NY** 10002 (212) 533-4122
BROTHERHOOD SYNAGOGUE, THE C 28 GRAMERCY PARK S ... NEW YORK **NY** 10003 (212) 674-5750
CENTRAL SYNAGOGUE R 123 E. 55TH STREET ... NEW YORK **NY** 10022 (212) 838-5122
CHABAD HOUSE - UPPER WEST SIDE O 310 WEST 103RD STREET ... NEW YORK **NY** 10025 (212) 864-5010
CHAI ODOM MINSKI, CONGREGATION O 145 EAST BROADWAY ... NEW YORK **NY** 10002 (212) 964-2830
CHASAM SOPHER, CONGREGATION O 8 CLINTON STREET ... NEW YORK **NY** 10002 (212) 777-5140
CHASIDEI GER O 215 WEST 90TH STREET, #1D ... NEW YORK **NY** 10024 (212) 799-0075
CHASSIDEI BELZ CONGREGATION O 255 EAST BROADWAY ... NEW YORK **NY** 10002
CHATHAM JEWISH CENTER-CONGREGATION BETH SHOLOM C 217 PARK ROW ... NEW YORK **NY** 10038 (212) 233-0428
CHEVRA ANSHI STUZINER VEI-ANSHI GREIVER O 257 EAST BROADWAY ... NEW YORK **NY** 10002
CHEVRA BECHURIM B'NAI MENASHE AHAVAS ACHIM O 225 EAST BROADWAY ... NEW YORK **NY** 10002 (212) 349-0089
CHEVRA B'NEI YITZCHOK CHASSEDI BOYON O 247 EAST BROADWAY ... NEW YORK **NY** 10002 (212) 674-1817
CHEVRA MISHKAN ISRAEL ANSHEI ZETEL O 135 HENRY STREET ... NEW YORK **NY** 10002 (212) 677-0728
CHEVRA SFARD, CONGREGATION 490 WEST 187TH STREET, 4G ... NEW YORK **NY** 10033 (212) 928-3423
CHEVRA TALMUD TORAH/OLD BROADWAY SYNAGOGUE O 15 OLD BROADWAY ... NEW YORK **NY** 10027 (212) 662-8086
CIVIC CENTER SYNAGOGUE CONGREGATION SHAARE ZEDEK O 49 WHITE STREET ... NEW YORK **NY** 10013 (212) 966-7141
COMMUNITY SYNAGOGUE CENTER O 325 E. 6TH STREET ... NEW YORK **NY** 10003 (212) 473-3665
CONGREGATION BINA O 600 WEST END AVENUE ... NEW YORK **NY** 10024 (212) 873-4261
CONSERVATIVE SYNAGOGUE OF FIFTH AVENUE C 11 EAST 11TH STREET ... NEW YORK **NY** 10003 (212) 929-6954
COVENANT, TEMPLE OF THE R 612 W. 180TH STREET ... NEW YORK **NY** 10033
DARECH AMUNO, CONGREGATION O 53 CHARLES STREET ... NEW YORK **NY** 10014 (212) 242-6425
DOMBROV WEST O 714 WEST 187TH STREET ... NEW YORK **NY** 10033
DOWNTOWN TALMUD TORAH SYNAGOGUE O 142 BROOME STREET ... NEW YORK **NY** 10002 (212) 473-4500
EAST 55TH STREET CONSERVATIVE SYNAGOGUE C 308 E. 55TH STREET ... NEW YORK **NY** 10022 (212) 752-1200
EAST END TEMPLE R 398 SECOND AVENUE ... NEW YORK **NY** 10010 (212) 254-8518
EAST SIDE TORAH CENTER O 313 HENRY STREET ... NEW YORK **NY** 10002 (212) 473-1000
EDATH LEI ISRAEL ANSHEI MESARITZ, CONGREGATION O P.O. BOX 124 ... NEW YORK **NY** 10002
EITZ CHAIM ANSHEI WOLOZIN, CONGREGATION O 209 MADISON STREET ... NEW YORK **NY** 10002 (212) 254-6674
ELDRIDGE STREET SYNAGOGUE O 12 ELDRIDGE STREET ... NEW YORK **NY** 10002 (212) 219-0888
EMANU-EL OF THE CITY OF NEW YORK, CONGREGATION R 1 E. 65TH STREET ... NEW YORK **NY** 10021 (212) 744-1400
EMES WOZEDEK, INC., CONGREGATION O 560 W. 166TH STREET ... NEW YORK **NY** 10032 (212) 928-9785
EMUNATH ISRAEL, CONGREGATION O 236 WEST 23RD STREET ... NEW YORK **NY** 10011 (212) 675-2819
ERSTE LUTOWISKA MACHZIKA HADAS, CONGREGATION 262 DELANCEY STREET ... NEW YORK **NY** 10002 (212) 982-0007
EZRATH ISRAEL, CONGREGATION-THE ACTOR'S TEMPLE C 339 WEST 47TH STREET ... NEW YORK **NY** 10036 (212) 245-6975

Name / Address	City	State	Zip	Phone
FIFTH AVENUE SYNAGOGUE O 5 E. 62ND STREET	NEW YORK	NY	10021	(212) 838-2122
FIRST ROUMANIAN-AMERICAN CONGREGATION O 89 RIVINGTON STREET	NEW YORK	NY	10002	(212) 673-2835
FIRST STREET SYNAGOGUE - ANSHE PODAETZA SOCIETY SHUL 108 EAST 1ST STREET	NEW YORK	NY	10009	
FORT TRYON JEWISH CENTRE C 524 FORT WASHINGTON AVENUE	NEW YORK	NY	10033	(212) 795-1391
FORT WASHINGTON SYNAGOGUE R 555 W. 182ND STREET	NEW YORK	NY	10033	
FREE SYNAGOGUE R 30 WEST 68TH STREET	NEW YORK	NY	10023	(212) 877-4050
FRIENDS OF BELLEVUE HOSPITAL SYNAGOGUE FIRST AVENUE & 27TH STREET	NEW YORK	NY	10016	(212) 685-1376
FUR CENTER SYNAGOGUE O 230 WEST 29TH STREET	NEW YORK	NY	10001	(212) 594-9480
GARMENT CENTER CONGREGATION O 205 W. 40TH STREET	NEW YORK	NY	10018	(212) 391-6966
GATES OF ISRAEL, CONGREGATION O 560 WEST 185TH STREET	NEW YORK	NY	10033	(212) 923-2900
HABONIM, CONGREGATION R 44 W. 66TH STREET	NEW YORK	NY	10023	(212) 787-5347
HAVURAH HADASHAH RE	NEW YORK	NY		(212) 646-9009
HEBREW TABERNACLE CONGREGATION R 551 FORT WASHINGTON AVENUE	NEW YORK	NY	10033	(212) 568-8304
HECHAL MOSHE CONGREGATION O 303 WEST 91ST STREET	NEW YORK	NY	10024	(212) 362-1091
HOME OF THE SAGES O 25 WILLETT STREET	NEW YORK	NY	10002	(212) 673-8500
HOUSE OF SAGES, INC. O 283 E. BROADWAY	NEW YORK	NY	10002	(212) 732-3131
INWOOD HEBREW CONGREGATION C 111 VERMILYEA AVENUE	NEW YORK	NY	10034	(212) 569-4010
INWOOD JEWISH CENTER & TALMUD TORAH, INC. 12 ELLWOOD STREET	NEW YORK	NY	10040	(212) 569-4311
ISRAEL OF THE CITY OF NEW YORK, TEMPLE R 112 E. 75TH STREET	NEW YORK	NY	10021	(212) 249-5000
JEWISH BOARD OF GUARDIANS RESIDENCE 74 ST. MARKS PLACE	NEW YORK	NY	10003	(212) 582-9100
JEWISH CENTER, THE O 131 W. 86TH STREET	NEW YORK	NY	10024	(212) 724-2700
JEWISH THEOLOGICAL SEMINARY, SYNAGOGUE OF THE C 3080 BROADWAY	NEW YORK	NY	10027	(212) 678-8000
JOSHUA JACOB ANSHEI HORODETZ, CONGREGATION O 253 EAST BROADWAY	NEW YORK	NY	10002	(212) 233-3949
K'HAL ADATH JESHURUN, CONGREGATION O 90 BENNETT AVENUE	NEW YORK	NY	10033	(212) 923-8984
K'HAL ADATH JESHURUN, CONGREGATION O 85 BENNETT AVENUE	NEW YORK	NY	10033	(212) 923-3582
K'HAL YERAIM (SASSOVER SHTIEBL) O 254 WEST 103RD STREET	NEW YORK	NY	10025	(212) 663-4038
KAHAL MINCHAS CHINUCH, CONGREGATION O 321 W. 100TH STREET	NEW YORK	NY	10025	
KEHILA KEDOSHA JANINA O 280 BROOME STREET	NEW YORK	NY	10002	(212) 226-5823
KEHILATH ISRAEL CHOFETZ CHAIM, CONGREGATION O 310 W. 103RD STREET	NEW YORK	NY	10025	(212) 864-5010
KEHILATH JACOB, CONGREGATION C 150 WEST 72ND STREET	NEW YORK	NY	10023	(212) 787-8680
KEHILATH JACOB, CONGREGATION O 305 W. 79TH STREET	NEW YORK	NY	10024	(212) 580-2391
KEHILATH JESHURUN, CONGREGATION O 125 EAST 85TH STREET	NEW YORK	NY	10028	(212) 427-1000
KEHILLAS YAACOV O 390 FORT WASHINGTON AVENUE	NEW YORK	NY	10033	
KIPITZNITZER SYNAGOGUE O 233 EAST BROADWAY	NEW YORK	NY	10002	
KOL ISRAEL, CONGREGATION 865 WEST END AVENUE	NEW YORK	NY	10025	
LEBEDONE RADZILOWE, CONGREGATION O 225 EAST BROADWAY	NEW YORK	NY	10002	
LINCOLN SQUARE SYNAGOGUE O 200 AMSTERDAM AVENUE	NEW YORK	NY	10023	(212) 874-6100
LISKER CONGREGATION O 163 EAST 69TH STREET, P.O. BOX 519	NEW YORK	NY	10021	(212) 472-1445
LITOWISKER CHEVRA O 262 DELANCEY STREET	NEW YORK	NY	10002	(212) 982-0007
LOMETZ GOTCH CONGREGATION O 313 HENRY STREET	NEW YORK	NY	10002	
MACHZEH ABRAHAM, CONGREGATION O 2581 BROADWAY	NEW YORK	NY	10025	
MACHZIKEI TORAH, CONGREGATION 851 W. 181ST STREET	NEW YORK	NY	10033	(212) 927-6740
MAIMONIDES TEMPLE/SYNAGOGUE FOR SINGLES O P.O. BOX 20374	NEW YORK	NY	10017	(212) 722-6984
MANHATTAN RECONSTRUCTIONIST HAVURAH C/O ETHEL EPSTEIN/FRITZI JACOBS	NEW YORK	NY		(212) 362-5819
MASSAS BENJAMIN ANSHEI PODHAJCE, CONGREGATION O 108 E. 1ST STREET	NEW YORK	NY	10009	
MESIVTA TIFERETH JERUSALEM 145 EAST BROADWAY	NEW YORK	NY	10002	(212) 964-2830
METROPOLITAN SYNAGOGUE OF NEW YORK R 10 PARK AVENUE	NEW YORK	NY	10016	(212) 679-8580
MILLINERY CENTER SYNAGOGUE C 1025 SIXTH AVENUE	NEW YORK	NY	10018	(212) 921-1580
MINCHAS CHINUCH (BABAD SHTEIBL) O 321 WEST 100TH STREET	NEW YORK	NY	10025	
MIZRACHI HAPOEL HAMIZRACHI, CONGREGATION O 249 EAST BROADWAY	NEW YORK	NY	10002	(212) 964-6111
MORYA, CONGREGATION O 2228 BROADWAY	NEW YORK	NY	10024	(212) 724-6909
MOUNT NEBOH, CONGREGATION R 130 W. 79TH STREET	NEW YORK	NY	10024	
MOUNT SINAI JEWISH CENTER O 135 BENNETT AVENUE	NEW YORK	NY	10040	(212) 568-9090
MT. SINAI ANSHE EMETH, CONGREGATION 135 BENNETT AVENUE	NEW YORK	NY	10040	(212) 928-9870
NODAH B'YEHUDA, CONGREGATION O 392 FORT WASHINGTON AVENUE	NEW YORK	NY	10033	(212) 795-1552
OHAB ZEDEK, CONGREGATION O 118 WEST 95TH STREET	NEW YORK	NY	10025	(212) 749-5150
OHAV SHOLOM, CONGREGATION 270 W. 84TH STREET	NEW YORK	NY	10024	(212) 877-5850
OHAV SHALOM, CONGREGATION O 4624 BROADWAY	NEW YORK	NY	10040	(212) 567-0900
OLD BROADWAY SYNAGOGUE O 15 OLD BROADWAY	NEW YORK	NY	10027	(212) 662-8086
ORACH CHAIM, CONGREGATION O 1459 LEXINGTON AVENUE	NEW YORK	NY	10028	(212) 722-6566
PARK AVENUE SYNAGOGUE C 50 E. 87TH STREET	NEW YORK	NY	10028	(212) 369-2600
PARK EAST SYNAGOGUE O 163 E. 67TH STREET	NEW YORK	NY	10021	(212) 737-6900
PORT WASHINGTON SYNAGOGUE R C/O MR. BAKER-25C, 1751 SECOND AVENUE	NEW YORK	NY	10028	
RADIO CITY SYNAGOGUE O 30 WEST 47TH STREET	NEW YORK	NY	10036	(212) 819-0839
RAMATH ORAH, CONGREGATION O 550 W. 110TH STREET	NEW YORK	NY	10025	(212) 222-2470
RODEPH SHOLOM CONGREGATION R 7 W. 83RD STREET	NEW YORK	NY	10024	(212) 362-8800
SHAARAY TEFILA, CONGREGATION R 250 E. 79TH STREET	NEW YORK	NY	10021	(212) 535-8008
SHAARE HATIKVAH AHAVATH TORAH V'TIKVOH CHADOSHOH, INC., CONG. 711 W. 179TH STREET	NEW YORK	NY	10033	(212) 927-2720
SHAARE TORAH, CONGREGATION O 15 W. 73RD STREET	NEW YORK	NY	10023	(212) 874-6322
SHAARE ZEDEK, CONGREGATION C 212 W. 93RD STREET	NEW YORK	NY	10025	(212) 874-7005
SHAARY TEFILA, CONGREGATION 250 EAST 79TH STREET	NEW YORK	NY	10021	(212) 535-8008
SHEARITH ADAS ISRAEL MINHAG SFARD, CONGREGATION O 237 EAST BROADWAY	NEW YORK	NY	10002	
SHEARITH ISRAEL, CONGREGATION O 8 W. 70TH STREET	NEW YORK	NY	10023	(212) 873-0300
SHEVETH ACHIM ANSHEI SLONIM, CONGREGATION O 172 NORFOLK STREET	NEW YORK	NY	10002	

SHMUEL JOSEF VCHAYAH, CONGREGATION
587B FORT WASHINGTON AVENUE ... NEW YORK **NY** 10033 (212) 927-9012
SIEINIAWE AND ANSHIE SFARD CONGREGATION O
237 EAST BROADWAY ... NEW YORK **NY** 10002
SIENEWER CHEVRAH O 217 HENRY STREET ... NEW YORK **NY** 10002
SMUEL JOSEF VCHAYAH, CONGREGATION
587-B FORT WASHINGTON AVENUE ... NEW YORK **NY** 10033 (212) 927-9012
SOCIETY FOR THE ADVANCEMENT OF JUDAISM RE
15 W. 86TH STREET ... NEW YORK **NY** 10024 (212) 724-7000
SONS OF ISRAEL KALWARIA, CONGREGATION O 13 PIKE STREET ... NEW YORK **NY** 10002
SONS OF MOSES ANSHEI ANDRZIEVO CONGREGATION O
135 HENRY STREET ... NEW YORK **NY** 10002 (212) 677-0728
SPANISH-PORTUGUESE SYNAGOGUE 8 W. 70TH STREET ... NEW YORK **NY** 10023 (212) 873-0300
STEPHEN WISE FREE SYNAGOGUE R 30 W. 68TH STREET ... NEW YORK **NY** 10023 (212) 877-4050
SUTTON PLACE SYNAGOGUE C 225 E. 51ST STREET ... NEW YORK **NY** 10022 (212) 593-3300
SYNAGOGUE COUNCIL OF AMERICA 327 LEXINGTON AVENUE ... NEW YORK **NY** 10016 (212) 686-8670
TALMUD TORAH ADERETH EL, CONGREGATION O 135 E. 29TH STREET .. NEW YORK **NY** 10016 (212) 685-0241
TEL AVIV, CONGREGATION 27 EAST 20TH STREET ... NEW YORK **NY** 10003 (212) 475-7081
TIKVATH ISRAEL OF HARLEM, CONGREGATION O
160 E. 112TH STREET ... NEW YORK **NY** 10029 (212) 289-9677
TORAH VA'AVODAH INSTITUTE O 25 W. 26TH STREET ... NEW YORK **NY** 10010 (212) 683-4484
TORATH CHAIM, CONGREGATION 489 WEST END AVENUE ... NEW YORK **NY** 10024 (212) 874-3823
TOWN & VILLAGE SYNAGOGUE-TEMPLE TIFERETH ISRAEL C
334 E. 14TH STREET ... NEW YORK **NY** 10003 (212) 677-8090
UNION OF SEPHARDIC CONGREGATIONS 8 W. 70TH STREET ... NEW YORK **NY** 10023 (212) 873-0300
UNITED HEBREW COMMUNITY OF NEW YORK, ADATH ISRAEL OF NEW YORK O
201 EAST BROADWAY ... NEW YORK **NY** 10002 (212) 674-3580
UNIVERSAL JUDAISM, TEMPLE-CONGREGATION DAAT ELOHIM R
1010 PARK AVENUE ... NEW YORK **NY** 10028 (212) 673-1810
UNIVERSAL JUDAISM, TEMPLE OF 15 RUTHERFORD PLACE ... NEW YORK **NY** 10003 (212) 673-1810
VILLAGE TEMPLE R 33 E. 12TH STREET ... NEW YORK **NY** 10003 (212) 674-2340
WALL STREET SYNAGOGUE O 47 BEEKMAN STREET ... NEW YORK **NY** 10038 (212) 227-7800
WASHINGTON HEIGHTS CONGREGATION O 815 W. 179TH STREET ... NEW YORK **NY** 10033 (212) 923-4407
WASHINGTON MARKET SYNAGOGUE O 410 W. 14TH STREET ... NEW YORK **NY** 10014 (212) 243-2507
WEST END SYNAGOGUE 270 WEST 89TH STREET ... NEW YORK **NY** 10024 (212) 769-3100
WEST SIDE INSTITUTIONAL SYNAGOGUE O 120-138 W. 76TH STREET ... NEW YORK **NY** 10023 (212) 877-7652
WEST SIDE JEWISH CENTER O 347-49 WEST 34TH STREET ... NEW YORK **NY** 10001 (212) 502-5291
YANOVER CHEVRA O 249 EAST BROADWAY ... NEW YORK **NY** 10002
YESHIVA CHOFETZ CHAIM O 346 WEST 89TH STREET ... NEW YORK **NY** 10025 (212) 362-1435
YESHIVA OF THE WEST SIDE 305 WEST 79TH STREET ... NEW YORK **NY** 10024 (212) 799-6235
YORKVILLE SYNAGOGUE B'NAI JEHUDA O 352 E. 78TH STREET ... NEW YORK **NY** 10021 (212) 249-0766
YOUNG ISRAEL OF FIFTH AVENUE 3 WEST 16TH STREET ... NEW YORK **NY** 10011 (212) 929-1525
YOUNG ISRAEL OF MANHATTAN 225 EAST BROADWAY ... NEW YORK **NY** 10002 (212) 732-0966
YOUNG ISRAEL OF WEST SIDE 210 WEST 91ST STREET ... NEW YORK **NY** 10024 (212) 787-7513
ZEMACH TZEDEK, CONGREGATION O 241 EAST BROADWAY ... NEW YORK **NY** 10002
ZICHRON EPHRAIM, CONGREGATION 163 E. 67TH STREET ... NEW YORK **NY** 10021 (212) 737-6900
ZICHRON MOSHE, CONGREGATION O 342 E. 20TH STREET ... NEW YORK **NY** 10003 (212) 475-9330
AGUDAS ISRAEL, CONGREGATION O 290 NORTH STREET ... NEWBURGH **NY** 12550 (914) 562-5604
BETH JACOB, TEMPLE R 344 GIDNEY AVENUE ... NEWBURGH **NY** 12550 (914) 562-5516
BETH EL, TEMPLE R 720 ASHLAND AVENUE ... NIAGARA FALLS **NY** 14302 (716) 282-2717
BETH ISRAEL, TEMPLE C COLLEGE & MADISON AVENUE ... NIAGARA FALLS **NY** 14305 (716) 285-9894
BETH EL OF BELLMORE, TEMPLE C 1373 BELLMORE ROAD ... NORTH BELLMORE **NY** 11710 (516) 781-2650
YOUNG ISRAEL OF NORTH BELLMORE 2428 HAMILTON ROAD ... NORTH BELLMORE **NY** 11710 (516) 826-0048
YOUNG ISRAEL OF MASSAPEQUA 314 BANBURY ROAD ... NORTH MASSAPEQUA **NY** 11758 (516) 798-8391
NER TAMID, CONGREGATION C
P.O. BOX 126 5061 WEST TAFT ROAD ... NORTH SYRACUSE **NY** 13212 (315) 458-2022
OHR TORAH O 410 HUNGRY HARBOR ROAD ... NORTH WOODMERE **NY** 11581 (516) 791-2130
YOUNG ISRAEL OF NORTH WOODMERE-LAURELTON
785 GOLF DRIVE ... NORTH WOODMERE **NY** 11581 (516) 791-5099
NORWICH JEWISH CENTER R 72 SOUTH BROAD ... NORWICH **NY** 13815 (607) 334-2691
SONS OF ISRAEL, CONGREGATION C 300 NORTH BROADWAY ... NYACK **NY** 10960 (914) 358-3767
B'NAI ISRAEL REFORM TEMPLE R 96 BILTMORE AVENUE ... OAKDALE **NY** 11769 (516) 589-8948
JEWISH CENTER OF BAYSIDE OAKS C
50-35 CLOVERDALE BLVD ... OAKLAND GARDENS **NY** 11364 (718) 321-0300
OAKLAND JEWISH CENTER C 61-35 220TH STREET ... OAKLAND GARDENS **NY** 11364 (718) 225-7800
AVODAH, TEMPLE R 3050 OCEANSIDE ROAD ... OCEANSIDE **NY** 11572 (516) 766-6809
DARCHAI NOAM O WAUKENA AND SKILLMAN STREETS ... OCEANSIDE **NY** 11572
JEWISH CENTER OF OCEAN HARBOR C ROYAL & WEIDNER AVENUES .. OCEANSIDE **NY** 11572 (516) 536-6481
OCEANSIDE JEWISH CENTER C 2860 BROWER AVENUE ... OCEANSIDE **NY** 11572 (516) 764-4213
SHAAR HASHAMAYIM, CONGREGATION O 3309 SKILLMAN AVENUE ... OCEANSIDE **NY** 11572 (516) 764-6888
YOUNG ISRAEL OF OCEANSIDE 150 WAUKENA AVENUE ... OCEANSIDE **NY** 11572 (516) 764-1099
ANSHE ZOPHEN, CONGREGATION C 416 GREENE STREET ... OGDENSBURG **NY** 13669 (315) 393-3787
BETH ELOHIM, TEMPLE R 926 ROUND SWAMP ROAD ... OLD BETHPAGE **NY** 11804 (516) 694-4544
SOCIETY OF JEWISH SCIENCE & SYNAGOGUE
825 ROUND SWAMP ROAD ... OLD BETHPAGE **NY** 11804 (516) 249-6262
OLD WESTBURY HEBREW CONGREGATION C
21 OLD WESTBURY ROAD ... OLD WESTBURY **NY** 11590 (516) 333-7977
B'NAI ISRAEL, CONGREGATION R 127 S. BARRY STREET ... OLEAN **NY** 14760 (716) 372-3431
BETH EL C 83 CHESTNUT STREET ... ONEONTA **NY** 13802 (607) 432-5522
ORANGETOWN JEWISH CENTER C INDEPENDENCE AVENUE ... ORANGEBURG **NY** 10962 (914) 359-5920
ORTHODOX CONGREGATION OF ORANGEBURG/SHAARE TORA
14 EDGEWOOD COURT ... ORANGEBURG **NY** 10962
ANSHE DORSHE EMES, CONGREGATION RE 100 S. HIGHLAND AVENUE ... OSSINING **NY** 10562
ADATH ISRAEL, CONGREGATION C EAST THIRD & ONEIDA AVENUE ... OSWEGO **NY** 13126 (315) 342-0371
OYSTER BAY JEWISH CENTER C BERRY HILL ROAD ... OYSTER BAY **NY** 11771 (516) 922-6650
OZONE PARK JEWISH CENTER O 107-01 CROSS BAY BLVD ... OZONE PARK **NY** 11417 (718) 848-4096
SONS OF JACOB, TEMPLE C 97-44 75TH STREET ... OZONE PARK **NY** 11416 (718) 296-8334
GEMILUTH CHESSED, CONGREGATION OAK TREE ROAD ... PALISADES **NY** 10964
TIFERETH ISRAEL, CONGREGATION - ANSHE PARKSVILLE ... PARKSVILLE **NY** 12768
BETH EL OF PATCHOGUE, TEMPLE C 45 OAK STREET ... PATCHOGUE **NY** 11772 (516) 475-1882
YOUNG ISRAEL OF PATCHOGUE 28 MOWBRAY STREET ... PATCHOGUE **NY** 11772 (516) 654-0882

BETH AM TEMPLE R 60 E. MADISON AVENUE, P.O. BOX 236 ... PEARL RIVER **NY** 10965 (914) 735-5858
FIRST HEBREW CONGREGATION C 1821 E. MAIN STREET, P.O. BOX 590 .. PEEKSKILL **NY** 10566 (914) 739-0500
ISRAEL, TEMPLE LAKE DRIVE ... PEEKSKILL **NY** 10537 (914) 528-2305
PELHAM JEWISH CENTER C 451 ESPLANADE ... PELHAM **NY** 10803 (914) 738-0870
BETH ELOHIM, TEMPLE R 926 ROUND SWAMP ROAD ... PLAINVIEW **NY** 11803 (516) 694-4544
MANETTO HILL JEWISH CENTER C 244 MANETTO HILL ROAD ... PLAINVIEW **NY** 11803 (516) 935-5454
PLAINVIEW JEWISH CENTER C 95 FLORAL DRIVE ... PLAINVIEW **NY** 11803 (516) 938-9610
YOUNG ISRAEL OF PLAINVIEW 132 SOUTHERN PARKWAY ... PLAINVIEW **NY** 11803 (516) 433-4811
BETH ISRAEL, TEMPLE R BOWMAN & MARCY LANE ... PLATTSBURGH **NY** 12901 (518) 563-3343
POMONA JEWISH CENTER C 106 POMONA ROAD ... POMONA **NY** 10970 (914) 354-2226
KNESSET TIFERETH ISRAEL, CONGREGATION C
575 KING STREET ... PORT CHESTER **NY** 10573 (914) 939-1004
NORTH SHORE JEWISH CENTER C 385 OLD TOWN ROAD ... PORT JEFFERSON **NY** 11776 (516) 928-3737
BETH EL C 88 E. MAIN STREET ... PORT JERVIS **NY** 12271 (914) 856-1722
BETH ISRAEL, TEMPLE C TEMPLE DRIVE ... PORT WASHINGTON **NY** 11050 (516) 767-1708
COMMUNITY SYNAGOGUE R 150 MIDDLE NECK ROAD ... PORT WASHINGTON **NY** 11050 (516) 883-3144
PORT JEWISH CENTER R P.O. BOX 852 ... PORT WASHINGTON **NY** 11050 (516) 883-5117
BETH EL, CONGREGATION C 81 MARKET STREET ... POTSDAM **NY** 13676
BETH EL, TEMPLE C 118 GRAND AVENUE ... POUGHKEEPSIE **NY** 12603 (914) 454-0570
BRETHREN OF ISRAEL, CONGREGATION - VASSAR TEMPLE R
140 HOOKER AVENUE ... POUGHKEEPSIE **NY** 12601 (914) 454-2570
SHOMRE ISRAEL, CONGREGATION O 18 PARK AVENUE ... POUGHKEEPSIE **NY** 12603 (914) 454-2890
VASSAR TEMPLE R 140 HOOKER AVENUE ... POUGHKEEPSIE **NY** 12601 (914) 454-2570
REFORM TEMPLE OF PUTNAM VALLEY R
P.O. BOX 232, CHURCH ROAD ... PUTNAM VALLEY **NY** 10579 (914) 528-9721
AHAVATH ISRAEL, CONGREGATION O P.O. BOX 25 ... QUEENS VILLAGE **NY** 11429
BELL PARK JEWISH CENTER C 231-10 HILLSIDE AVENUE ... QUEENS VILLAGE **NY** 11427 (718) 464-9144
HOLLISWOOD JEWISH CENTER O 86-25 FRANCIS LEWIS BLVD ... QUEENS VILLAGE **NY** 11427 (718) 776-8500
QUEENS JEWISH CENTER C 94-34 HOLLIS COURT BLVD ... QUEENS VILLAGE **NY** 11428 (718) 465-4993
ATERES ZVI, CONGREGATION O 63-34 99TH STREET ... REGO PARK **NY** 11374
BETH ISRAEL, CONGREGATION O 90-14 63RD DRIVE ... REGO PARK **NY** 11374
BETH JACOB, CONGREGATION O 6602 SAUNDERS STREET ... REGO PARK **NY** 11374 (718) 897-8331
JEWISH COMMUNITY CENTER OF QUEENS O 99-07 66TH AVENUE ... REGO PARK **NY** 11374 (718) 896-6695
KEHAL YESMACH MOSHE OF LAPUSH O 90-14 63RD DRIVE ... REGO PARK **NY** 11374 (718) 459-2632
LEFRAK CITY JEWISH CENTER
98-54 HORACE HARDING EXPRESSWAY ... REGO PARK **NY** 11374 (718) 699-7752
PARAS JEWISH ORGANIZATION O 97-30 QUEENS BOULEVARD ... REGO PARK **NY** 11374 (718) 459-4645
PLAZA TORAH CENTER O 98-54 HORACE HARDING EXPRESSWAY ... REGO PARK **NY** 11374 (718) 699-7752
REGO PARK JEWISH CENTER C 97-30 QUEENS BLVD ... REGO PARK **NY** 11374 (718) 459-1000
AGUDATH ISRAEL OF KEW GARDENS 117-01 PARK LANE SO ... RICHMOND HILL **NY** 11418
BETH ISRAEL, CONGREGATION C 88-01 102ND STREET ... RICHMOND HILL **NY** 11418 (718) 847-9688
JEWISH CENTER OF RICHMOND HILL O 101-54 117TH STREET ... RICHMOND HILL **NY** 11419 (718) 849-2507
RICHMOND HILL JEWISH CENTER O 101-54 117TH STREET ... RICHMOND HILL **NY** 11418 (718) 849-8217
AGUDAS ISRAEL OF RIDGEWOOD O
1618 CORNELIA STREET, P.O. BOX 165 ... RIDGEWOOD **NY** 11385 (718) 417-0709
HEBREW INSTITUTE AT RIVERDALE 3700 HENRY HUDSON PARKWAY ... RIVERDALE **NY** 10463 (212) 796-4730
OHEL TORAH SYNAGOGUE O 629 WEST 239TH STREET ... RIVERDALE **NY** 10463 (212) 543-5618
RIVERDALE JEWISH CENTER O 3700 INDEPENDENCE AVENUE ... RIVERDALE **NY** 10463 (212) 548-1850
RIVERDALE TEMPLE R 246TH STREET & INDEPENDENCE AVENUE ... RIVERDALE **NY** 10471 (212) 548-3800
ISRAEL OF RIVERHEAD, TEMPLE C 490 NORTHVILLE TURNPIKE ... RIVERHEAD **NY** 11901 (516) 727-3191
TRADITIONAL SYNAGOGUE OF ROCHDALE VILLAGE O
165-27 BAISLEY BLVD ... ROCHDALE VILLAGE **NY** 11434 (718) 525-3610
B'NAI ISRAEL, CONGREGATION O 692 JOSEPH AVENUE ... ROCHESTER **NY** 14621 (716) 544-9261
B'RITH KODESH, TEMPLE R 2131 ELMWOOD AVENUE ... ROCHESTER **NY** 14618 (716) 244-7060
BETH DAVID, TEMPLE C 3200 ST. PAUL BLVD ... ROCHESTER **NY** 14617 (716) 266-3223
BETH EL, TEMPLE C 139 WINTON ROAD S ... ROCHESTER **NY** 14610 (716) 473-1770
BETH HAKNESSES HACHODOSH O 33 ST. REGIS DRIVE N. ... ROCHESTER **NY** 14618 (716) 271-5390
BETH HAMEDRESH BETH ISRAEL C 1369 EAST AVENUE ... ROCHESTER **NY** 14610 (716) 244-2060
BETH JOSEPH CENTER O 1150 ST. PAUL STREET ... ROCHESTER **NY** 14621 (716) 266-1331
BETH SHALOM, CONGREGATION O 1161 MONROE AVENUE ... ROCHESTER **NY** 14620 (716) 473-1625
CHABAD LUBAVITCH O 36 LATTIMORE ROAD ... ROCHESTER **NY** 14620 (716) 244-4324
EMANU-EL OF IRONDEQUOIT, TEMPLE R 2956 ST. PAUL BLVD ... ROCHESTER **NY** 14617 (716) 266-1978
LIGHT OF ISRAEL, CONGREGATION O 206 NORTON STREET ... ROCHESTER **NY** 14621 (716) 544-1381
SINAI, TEMPLE R 363 PENFIELD ROAD ... ROCHESTER **NY** 14625 (716) 381-6890
VAAD HAKOLEL, CONGREGATION O P.O. BOX 362 ... ROCHESTER **NY** 14602
DERECH EMUNAH, CONGREGATION
199 BEACH 67TH STREET ... ROCKAWAY BEACH **NY** 11692 (718) 634-2288
ISRAEL, TEMPLE OF C 188 BEACH 84TH STREET ... ROCKAWAY BEACH **NY** 11693 (718) 327-6420
B'NAI SHOLOM, TEMPLE C 100 HEMPSTEAD AVENUE ... ROCKVILLE CENTRE **NY** 11570 (516) 764-4100
CENTRAL SYNAGOGUE R 430 DEMOTT AVENUE ... ROCKVILLE CENTRE **NY** 11570 (516) 766-4300
ADAS ISRAEL C 705 HICKORY STREET ... ROME **NY** 13440 (315) 337-3170
YOUNG ISRAEL OF ROOSEVELT ISLAND 560-1 MAIN STREET ... ROOSEVELT ISLAND **NY** 10044 (212) 826-6390
ROSEDALE JEWISH CENTER C 247-11 FRANCIS LEWIS BLVD ... ROSEDALE **NY** 11422 (718) 528-3988
BETH SHOLOM, TEMPLE C
ROSLYN ROAD & N. STATE PARKWAY ... ROSLYN HEIGHTS **NY** 11577 (516) 621-2288
RECONSTRUCTIONIST SYNAGOGUE 1 WILLOW STREET ... ROSLYN HEIGHTS **NY** 11577 (516) 621-5540
ROSLYN SYNAGOGUE, THE O 274 GARDEN STREET ... ROSLYN HEIGHTS **NY** 11577 (516) 484-9138
SHELTER ROCK JEWISH CENTER C
SEARINGTON & SHELTER ROCK ROADS ... ROSLYN HEIGHTS **NY** 11577 (516) 741-4305
SINAI OF ROSLYN, TEMPLE R 425 ROSLYN ROAD ... ROSLYN HEIGHTS **NY** 11577 (516) 621-6800
COMMUNITY SYNAGOGUE R 200 FOREST AVENUE ... RYE **NY** 10550 (914) 967-6262
EMANU-EL OF WESTCHESTER, CONGREGATION R
WESTCHESTER AVENUE & KENILWORTH ROAD ... RYE **NY** 10580 (914) 967-4382
SONS OF ISRAEL, CONGREGATION O 127 STREET & FOCH BLVD ... S. OZONE PARK **NY** 11420
TALMUD TORAH OF RICHMOND HILL O 109-25 114TH STREET ... S. OZONE PARK **NY** 11420
ADAS ISRAEL, TEMPLE R ELIZABETH STREET & ATLANTIC AVENUE ... SAG HARBOR **NY** 11963 (516) 725-0054
COMMUNITY SYNAGOGUE, THE 150 MIDDLE NECK ROAD ... SANDS POINT **NY** 11021 (516) 883-3144
SHA'AREI TEFILAH CONGREGATION O
260 BROADWAY, P.O. BOX 128 ... SARATOGA SPRINGS **NY** 12866 (518) 584-2370
SINAI, TEMPLE R 509 BROADWAY, P.O. BOX 224 ... SARATOGA SPRINGS **NY** 12866 (518) 584-8730
SHALOM, TEMPLE C 225 GREELEY AVENUE ... SAYVILLE **NY** 11782 (516) 567-3207
MAGEN DAVID SEPHARDIC CONGREGATION O
P.O. BOX 242H/1225 WEAVER STREET ... SCARSDALE **NY** 10583 (914) 633-3728

Name / Address	City	State	Zip	Phone
SCARSDALE SYNAGOGUE-TREMONT TEMPLE R 2 OGDEN ROAD	SCARSDALE	NY	10583	(914) 725-5175
SCARSDALE, YOUNG ISRAEL OF O 1313 DAISY FARMS ROAD	SCARSDALE	NY	10583	(914) 723-6273
SEPHARDIC COMMUNITY OF NEW ROCHELLE-SCARSDALE, THE O C/O YOUNG ISRAEL OF SCARSDALE, 1313 DAISY FARMS ROAD	SCARSDALE	NY	10583	(914) 636-8686
WESTCHESTER REFORM TEMPLE R 255 MAMARONECK ROAD	SCARSDALE	NY	10583	(914) 723-7727
YOUNG ISRAEL OF SCARSDALE 1313 WEAVER STREET P.O.B. 103H	SCARSDALE	NY	10583	(914) 636-8686
ADATH ISRAEL, CONGREGATION 872 ALBANY STREET	SCHENECTADY	NY	12307	
AGUDAT ACHIM, CONGREGATION C 2117 UNION STREET	SCHENECTADY	NY	12309	
BETH ISRAEL, CONGREGATION O 2195 EASTERN PARKWAY	SCHENECTADY	NY	12309	(518) 377-3700
GATES OF HEAVEN, CONGREGATION R 852 ASHMORE AVENUE	SCHENECTADY	NY	12309	(518) 374-8173
HEBREW CONGREGATION OF SOMERS, INC. C MERVYN DRIVE & CYPRESS LANE	SHENOROCK	NY	10587	(914) 248-5166
BETH SHOLOM OF SMITHTOWN, TEMPLE C P.O. BOX 764, EDGEWOOD AVENUE & RIVER ROAD	SMITHTOWN	NY	11787	(516) 724-0424
SOUTH FALLSBURG HEBREW ASSOCIATION P.O. BOX 457	SOUTH FALLSBURG	NY	12279	(914) 434-9675
SOUTH SHORE LONG ISLAND HAVURAH RE C/O FLATOW	SOUTH SHORE	NY		(516) 766-7390
AYSHEL AVRAHAM, CONGREGATION O 14 EAST CHURCH STREET	SPRING VALLEY	NY	10977	(914) 352-0630
B'NAI YECHIEL, CONGREGATION 80 WASHINGTON AVENUE	SPRING VALLEY	NY	10977	
BETH EL, TEMPLE R 415 VIOLA ROAD	SPRING VALLEY	NY	10977	(914) 356-2000
JEWISH COMMUNITY CENTER OF SPRING VALLEY C 250 N. MAIN STREET	SPRING VALLEY	NY	10977	(914) 356-3710
NEW SQUARE, YESHIVA OF 766 NORTH MAIN STREET	SPRING VALLEY	NY	10977	(914) 354-2237
OHEV SHOLOM, CONGREGATION O 14 LINDEN AVENUE	SPRING VALLEY	NY	10977	
RAMAT SHALOM LOMOND AVENUE	SPRING VALLEY	NY	10977	(914) 623-7604
SHAAREY TFILOH, CONGREGATION C 972 S. MAIN STREET	SPRING VALLEY	NY	10977	(914) 356-2225
SONS OF ISRAEL, CONGREGATION C 80 WILLIAMS AVENUE	SPRING VALLEY	NY	10977	(914) 352-6767
WEST CLARKSTOWN JEWISH CENTER 277 W. CLARKSTOWN ROAD	SPRING VALLEY	NY	10977	(914) 352-0017
YOUNG ISRAEL OF CLARKSTOWN 11 ELLEN STREET	SPRING VALLEY	NY	10977	(914) 352-8654
YOUNG ISRAEL OF SPRING VALLEY 23 UNION ROAD	SPRING VALLEY	NY	10977	(914) 356-3363
ZEMACH DAVID OF NEW SQUARE, CONGREGATION O 13 TRUMAN AVENUE	SPRING VALLEY	NY	10977	(914) 354-9736
RAMAT TORAH JEWISH COMMUNITY HOUSE, CONGREGATION C 221-03 137TH AVENUE	SPRINGFIELD GARDENS	NY	11413	
CAMBRIA HEIGHTS JEWISH CENTER 222-05 116TH AVENUE	ST. ALBANS	NY	11412	
AGUDAS SHOMREI HADAS O 98 RUPERT AVENUE	STATEN ISLAND	NY	10314	(718) 698-4066
AGUDATH ACHIM ANSHE CHESED, CONGREGATION O 641 DELAFIELD AVENUE, P.O. BOX 400	STATEN ISLAND	NY	10310	(718) 442-9445
AGUDATH ISRAEL OF STATEN ISLAND O 207 WARWICK AVENUE	STATEN ISLAND	NY	10314	
AHAVATH ISRAEL, CONGREGATION C 7630 AMBOY ROAD	STATEN ISLAND	NY	10307	(718) 984-2113
AHAVATH SHALOM, CONGREGATION C 2044 RICHMOND AVENUE	STATEN ISLAND	NY	10314	(718) 761-8446
ARDEN HEIGHTS BOULEVARD JEWISH CENTER 1766 ARTHUR KILL ROAD	STATEN ISLAND	NY	10312	(718) 948-6782
B'NAI ISRAEL, CONGREGATION C 45 TWOMBLY AVENUE	STATEN ISLAND	NY	10306	(718) 987-8188
B'NAI JESHURUN CONGREGATION C 275 MARTLING AVENUE	STATEN ISLAND	NY	10314	(718) 981-5550
BETH SHLOIME OF STATEN ISLAND, CONGREGATION O 84 OAKVILLE STREET	STATEN ISLAND	NY	10314	(718) 761-5559
BETH YEHUDA O 240 WOODWARD AVENUE	STATEN ISLAND	NY	10314	
EMANU-EL OF STATEN ISLAND, TEMPLE C 984 POST AVENUE	STATEN ISLAND	NY	10302	(718) 942-5966
ISRAEL, TEMPLE R 315 FOREST AVENUE	STATEN ISLAND	NY	10301	(718) 727-2231
NEW BRIGHTON JEWISH CONGREGATION O 199 VICTORY BOULEVARD, P.O. BOX 194	STATEN ISLAND	NY	10301	
NEW SPRINGVILLE JEWISH CENTER O 120 SAXON AVENUE	STATEN ISLAND	NY	10314	(718) 983-8063
TIFERETH ISRAEL, TEMPLE C 119 WRIGHT STREET	STATEN ISLAND	NY	10304	
TORAS EMES CONGREGATION O 3151 HYLAN BOULEVARD	STATEN ISLAND	NY	10306	(718) 987-0032
YOUNG ISRAEL OF ELTINGVILLE 374 RIDGEWOOD AVENUE	STATEN ISLAND	NY	10312	(718) 948-1993
YOUNG ISRAEL OF STATEN ISLAND 835 FOREST HILL ROAD	STATEN ISLAND	NY	10314	(718) 494-6700
ISAIAH, TEMPLE R 1404 STONYBROOK ROAD	STONY BROOK	NY	11790	(516) 751-8518
STONYBROOOK HEBREW CONGREGATION O C/O REZAK, P.O. BOX 660	STONYBROOK	NY	11790	
BAIS TORAH CONGREGATION O 36 CARLTON ROAD	SUFFERN	NY	10901	(914) 585-9515
REFORM TEMPLE OF SUFFERN R 70 HAVERSTRAW ROAD, P.O. BOX 472	SUFFERN	NY	10901	(914) 357-5872
SONS OF ISRAEL, CONGREGATION C SUFFERN PLACE	SUFFERN	NY	10901	(914) 357-9827
AHAVAS SHULEM, CONGREGATION O	SWAN LAKE	NY	12783	
AHAVATH ACHIM, CONGREGATION 1207 ALMOND STREET	SWAN LAKE	NY	13210	
EAST NASSAU HEBREW CONGREGATION O 310-A SOUTH OYSTER BAY ROAD	SYOSSET	NY	11791	(516) 921-1800
MIDWAY JEWISH CENTER C 330 S. OYSTER BAY ROAD	SYOSSET	NY	11791	(516) 938-8390
NORTH SHORE CONGREGATION R 83 MUTTONTOWN ROAD	SYOSSET	NY	11791	(516) 921-2282
ADATH YESHURUN, TEMPLE C 450 KIMBER ROAD	SYRACUSE	NY	13224	(315) 445-0002
BETH SHOLOM-CHEVRA SHAS, CONGREGATION C 5205 JAMESVILLE ROAD	SYRACUSE	NY	13214	(315) 446-9570
CHABAD LUBAVITCH O 113 BERKELEY DRIVE	SYRACUSE	NY	13210	(315) 424-0363
SEPHARDIC GROUP OF SYRACUSE O 119 DOLL PARKWAY	SYRACUSE	NY	13214	(315) 446-0760
SHAAREI TORAH 2200 EAST GENESSEE	SYRACUSE	NY	13210	(315) 472-8411
SOCIETY OF CONCORD, TEMPLE R 910 MADISON STREET	SYRACUSE	NY	13210	(315) 475-9952
CONGREGATION BAIS TORAH 36 CARLTON ROAD	TALLMAN	NY	10982	(914) 578-9515
BETH ABRAHAM, TEMPLE R 25 LEROY AVENUE	TARRYTOWN	NY	10591	(914) 631-1770
BETH EL OF GREATER BUFFALO, TEMPLE C 2368 EGGERT ROAD	TONAWANDA	NY	14150	(716) 836-3762
BERITH SHOLOM, CONGREGATION R 167 THIRD STREET	TROY	NY	12180	(518) 272-8872
BETH EL, TEMPLE C 409 HOOSICK STREET	TROY	NY	12180	(518) 272-6113
BETH ISRAEL BIKUR CHOLIM, CONGREGATION 27 CENTERVIEW DRIVE	TROY	NY	12181	
BETH TEPHILA, CONGREGATION O 82 RIVER STREET	TROY	NY	12181	(518) 272-3182
TROY CHABAD CENTER O 2306 15TH STREET	TROY	NY	12180	(518) 274-5572
GENESIS-AGUDAS ACHIM C 25 OAKLAND AVENUE	TUCKAHOE	NY	10707	(914) 961-3766
UNIONDALE JEWISH CENTER C 760 JERUSALEM AVENUE	UNIONDALE	NY	11553	(516) 486-8788
BETH TORAH, TEMPLE R ROUTE 9W	UPPER NYACK	NY	10960	(914) 358-2248
SONS OF ISRAEL, CONGREGATION C 300 NORTH BROADWAY	UPPER NYACK	NY	10960	(914) 358-3767
BETH EL, TEMPLE C 1607 GENESEE STREET	UTICA	NY	13501	(315) 724-4751
EMANU-EL, TEMPLE R 2710 GENESEE STREET	UTICA	NY	13502	(315) 724-4177
ZVI JACOB CONGREGATION O 110 MEMORIAL PARKWAY	UTICA	NY	13501	(315) 724-8357
BETH SHOLOM, CONGREGATION - SUNRISE JEWISH CENTER O 550 ROCKAWAY AVENUE	VALLEY STREAM	NY	11581	(516) 561-9245
GATES OF ZION, TEMPLE C 322 N. CORONA AVENUE	VALLEY STREAM	NY	11580	(516) 561-2308
HILLEL, TEMPLE - SOUTHSIDE JEWISH CENTER C 1000 ROSEDALE ROAD	VALLEY STREAM	NY	11581	(516) 791-6344
TREE OF LIFE, CONGREGATION C 502 NORTH CENTRAL AVENUE	VALLEY STREAM	NY	11580	(516) 825-2090
BETH HILLEL, CONGREGATION O 20 PINE STREET	WALDEN	NY	12586	
SUBURBAN TEMPLE, THE R 2900 JERUSALEM AVENUE	WANTAGH	NY	11793	(516) 221-2370
WANTAGH JEWISH CENTER C 3710 WOODBINE AVENUE	WANTAGH	NY	11793	(516) 785-2445
DEGEL ISRAEL, CONGREGATION C 557 THOMPSON BLVD	WATERTOWN	NY	13601	(315) 782-2860
BETH ISRAEL, CONGREGATION C 339 BROAD STREET	WAVERLY	NY	14892	
WOODSTOCK RECONSTRUCTIONIST HAVURAH C/O STEWART MAURER	WEST HARLEY	NY	12491	(914) 331-0319
ANSHEI SHALOM O 453 HEMPSTEAD AVENUE	WEST HEMPSTEAD	NY	11552	(516) 489-8112
JEWISH COMMUNITY CENTER OF WEST HEMPSTEAD C 711 DOGWOOD AVENUE	WEST HEMPSTEAD	NY	11552	(516) 481-7448
NASSAU COMMUNITY TEMPLE R 240 HEMPSTEAD AVENUE	WEST HEMPSTEAD	NY	11552	(516) 485-1811
YOUNG ISRAEL OF WEST HEMPSTEAD 630 HEMPSTEAD AVENUE	WEST HEMPSTEAD	NY	11552	(516) 481-7429
AGUDATH ISRAEL OF FAR ROCKAWAY 1 BALSAM COURT	WEST LAWRENCE	NY	11691	(718) 471-4861
BETH TORAH, CONGREGATION C 243 CANTIAGUE ROAD	WESTBURY	NY	11590	(516) 334-7979
COMMUNITY REFORM TEMPLE R 712 THE PLAIN ROAD	WESTBURY	NY	11590	(516) 333-1839
SHOLOM, TEMPLE C 675 BROOKSIDE COURT	WESTBURY	NY	11590	(516) 334-2800
WESTBURY HEBREW CONGREGATION C P.O. BOX B, 21 OLD WESTBURY ROAD	WESTBURY	NY	11590	
BETH AM SHALOM, CONGREGATION RE 295 SOUNDVIEW AVENUE	WHITE PLAINS	NY	10606	
CHABAD-LUBAVITCH O 26 WEST STREET	WHITE PLAINS	NY	10605	(914) 681-6064
HEBREW INSTITUTE OF WHITE PLAINS O 20 GREENRIDGE AVENUE	WHITE PLAINS	NY	10605	(914) 948-3095
ISRAEL CENTER OF WHITE PLAINS, TEMPLE C 280 OLD MAMARONECK ROAD	WHITE PLAINS	NY	10605	(914) 948-2800
JEWISH COMMUNITY CENTER OF WHITE PLAINS R 252 SOUNDVIEW AVENUE	WHITE PLAINS	NY	10606	(914) 949-4717
LUBAVITCH OF WESTCHESTER O 26 WEST STREET	WHITE PLAINS	NY	10605	(914) 681-6064
WOODLANDS COMMUNITY TEMPLE R 50 WORTHINGTON ROAD	WHITE PLAINS	NY	10607	(914) 592-7070
YOUNG ISRAEL OF WHITE PLAINS P.O. 275, GEDNEY STATION	WHITE PLAINS	NY	10605	(914) 997-7097
AGUDAS ACHIM, CONGREGATION 21-08 UTOPIA PARKWAY	WHITESTONE	NY	11377	
CLEARVIEW JEWISH CENTER C 16-50 UTOPIA PARKWAY	WHITESTONE	NY	11357	(718) 352-6670
GARDEN JEWISH CENTER T 24-20 PARSONS BLVD	WHITESTONE	NY	11357	
WHITESTONE HEBREW CENTER C 12-45 CLINTONVILLE STREET	WHITESTONE	NY	11357	(718) 767-1500
HAVURAH, CONGREGATION R 6320 MAIN STREET	WILLIAMSVILLE	NY	14221	(716) 634-3010
YOUNG ISRAEL OF GREATER BUFFALO 105 MAPLE ROAD	WILLIAMSVILLE	NY	14221	(716) 634-0212
B'NAI ISRAEL, CONGREGATION O MAIN STREET	WOODBOURNE	NY	12788	(914) 434-7436
BNAI ISRAEL OF WOODHAVEN JEWISH CENTER O 89-07 ATLANTIC AVENUE	WOODHAVEN	NY	11421	
WOODSIDE JEWISH CENTER O 89-07 ATLANTIC AVENUE	WOODHAVEN	NY	11421	
SONS OF ISRAEL, CONGREGATION O 111 IRVING PLACE	WOODMERE	NY	11598	(516) 374-0655
YOUNG ISRAEL OF WOODMERE 859 PENINSULA BOULEVARD	WOODMERE	NY	11598	(516) 295-0150
OHAVE SHALOM, CONGREGATION O MAURICE ROSE STREET	WOODRIDGE	NY	12789	(914) 434-4987
BNEI ISRAEL, CONGREGATION 48-53 44TH STREET	WOODSIDE	NY	11377	
WOODSIDE JEWISH CENTER O 37-20 61ST STREET	WOODSIDE	NY	11377	(718) 424-6762
EMANU-EL, TEMPLE R 306 RUMSEY ROAD ON THE PARKWAY	YONKERS	NY	10705	(914) 963-0575
GREYSTONE JEWISH CENTER O 600 NORTH BROADWAY	YONKERS	NY	10701	(914) 963-8888
LINCOLN PARK JEWISH CENTER C 311 CENTRAL PARK AVENUE	YONKERS	NY	10704	(914) 965-7119
MIDCHESTER JEWISH CENTER C 236 GRANDVIEW BLVD	YONKERS	NY	10710	(914) 779-3660
NORTHEAST JEWISH CENTER C 11 SALISBURY ROAD	YONKERS	NY	10710	(914) 337-0268
OHEB ZEDEK OF YONKERS N.Y., CONGREGATION O 63 HAMILTON AVENUE	YONKERS	NY	10705	(914) 963-1951
ROSH PINAH CONGREGATION O P.O. BOX 269	YONKERS	NY	10705	(914) 968-9186
SONS OF ISRAEL, CONGREGATION O 105 RADFORD STREET	YONKERS	NY	10705	(914) 969-4453
YOUNG ISRAEL OF NORTH RIVERDALE 25 CLIFTON AVENUE	YONKERS	NY	10705	(914) 963-9448
BETH AM, TEMPLE R CHURCH STREET, P.O. BOX 433	YORKTOWN HEIGHTS	NY	10598	(914) 962-7500
YORKTOWN JEWISH CENTER C 2966 CROMPOND ROAD	YORKTOWN HEIGHTS	NY	10598	(914) 245-2324
BETH HA-TEPHILA, CONGREGATION R 43 N. LIBERTY STREET	ASHEVILLE	NC	28801	(704) 253-4911
BETH ISRAEL SYNAGOGUE C 229 MURDOCK AVENUE	ASHEVILLE	NC	28804	(704) 252-8431
BETH EL, TEMPLE R 1727 PROVIDENCE ROAD	CHARLOTTE	NC	28207	(704) 366-1948
BETH SHALOM, TEMPLE 1727 PROVIDENCE ROAD	CHARLOTTE	NC	28207	(704) 366-1948
CHABAD LUBAVITCH O 6500 NEW HALL ROAD	CHARLOTTE	NC	28226	(704) 366-3984
ISRAEL, TEMPLE C 1014 DILWORTH ROAD	CHARLOTTE	NC	28203	(704) 376-2796
BETH EL CONGREGATION C P.O. BOX 1762, WATTS & MARKHAM AVENUE	DURHAM	NC	27702	(919) 682-1238
DURHAM ORTHODOX KEHILAH O 1004 WATTS STREET	DURHAM	NC	27701	(919) 682-1238
JUDEA REFORM CONGREGATION R 2115 CORNWALLIS ROAD	DURHAM	NC	27705	(919) 489-7062
RECONSTRUCTIONIST HAVURAH IN DURHAM, NC 1004 WATTS STREET	DURHAM	NC	27701	(919) 682-1238
BETH ISRAEL, CONGREGATION C 2204 MORGANTON ROAD	FAYETTEVILLE	NC	28303	(919) 484-6462
EMANUEL, TEMPLE R 320 SOUTH STREET	GASTONIA	NC	28052	(704) 865-1541
OHEB SHOLOM, TEMPLE R P.O. BOX 2063	GOLDSBORO	NC	27530	(919) 867-9975
B'NAI ISRAEL SYNAGOGUE 804 WINVIEW DRIVE, P.O.BOX 10214	GREENSBORO	NC	27404	(919) 855-5091
B'NAI ISRAEL SYNAGOGUE C 713 NORTH GREEN STREET, P.O. BOX 5426	GREENSBORO	NC	27403	
B'NAI SHOLOM SYNAGOGUE C P.O. BOX 10214	GREENSBORO	NC	27408	(919) 855-5091
BETH DAVID SYNAGOGUE C 804 WINEVIEW DRIVE	GREENSBORO	NC	27410	(919) 297-0007
EMANUEL, TEMPLE R 713 N. GREENE STREET	GREENSBORO	NC	27401	(919) 275-6316
AGUDAS ISRAEL, CONGREGATION C P.O. BOX 668, 328 N. KING STREET	HENDERSONVILLE	NC	28793	(704) 693-9838
HICKORY JEWISH CENTER C P.O. BOX 1032, 4 STREET DRIVE & 11TH AVENUE N.W.	HICKORY	NC	28601	(704) 327-4081

Synagogue / Address	City	State	Zip	Phone
HIGH POINT B'NAI ISRAEL SYNAGOGUE C 1207 KENSINGTON DRIVE	HIGH POINT	NC	27260	(919) 883-1966
JACKSONVILLE HEBREW CONGREGATION C P.O. BOX 430	JACKSONVILLE	NC	28540	
ISRAEL, TEMPLE R P.O. BOX 903	KINSTON	NC	28501	(919) 523-2057
BETH EL, TEMPLE C P.O. BOX 16	LUMBERTON	NC	28358	(919) 739-6576
B'NAI SHOLEM CONGREGATION R 505 MIDDLE STREET	NEW BERN	NC	28560	(919) 637-5663
BETH MEYER SYNAGOGUE C P.O. BOX 2045, 806 W. JOHNSON STREET	RALEIGH	NC	27602	(919) 832-6498
BETH OR, TEMPLE R 5315 CREEDMOOR ROAD	RALEIGH	NC	27612	(919) 781-4895
SH'AREI ISRAEL CONGREGATION O 7400 FALLS OF NEWS ROAD	RALEIGH	NC	27609	(919) 847-8986
BETH EL, TEMPLE R SUNSET AVENUE AT PINE, P.O. BOX 291	ROCKY MOUNT	NC	27801	(919) 446-7675
ISRAEL, TEMPLE C P.O. BOX 815, 1600 BRENNER AVENUE	SALISBURY	NC	28144	(704) 633-1152
EMANUEL, CONGREGATION C P.O. BOX 5171, KELLY STREET & WEST END AVENUE	STATESVILLE	NC	28677	(704) 873-7611
EMANU-EL, TEMPLE R EIGHTH & SYCAMORE STREETS	WELDON	NC	27890	
BETH ISRAEL, CONGREGATION C P.O. BOX 911	WHITEVILLE	NC	28472	(919) 642-4039
B'NAI ISRAEL, CONGREGATION C 2601 CHESTNUT STREET, P.O. BOX 3752	WILMINGTON	NC	28401	(919) 762-4117
ISRAEL, TEMPLE OF R 1 S. 4TH STREET	WILMINGTON	NC	28401	(919) 762-0000
BETH JACOB CONGREGATION C 1833 ACADEMY STREET	WINSTON-SALEM	NC	27103	(919) 725-3880
EMANUEL, TEMPLE R 201 OAKWOOD DRIVE	WINSTON-SALEM	NC	27103	(919) 722-6640
BISMARCK HEBREW CONGREGATION N. 5TH STREET	BISMARCK	ND	58501	(701) 223-1768
BETH EL, TEMPLE R 809 S. 11TH AVENUE	FARGO	ND	58103	(701) 232-0441
B'NAI ISRAEL SYNAGOGUE 601 COTTONWOOD AVENUE	GRAND FORKS	ND	58201	(701) 775-5124
BETH ISRAEL, TEMPLE 6TH STREET & FIRST AVENUE S.E.	MINOT	ND	58701	(701) 838-8798
MINOT HEBREW CONGREGATION C 205 8TH STREET	MINOT	ND	58701	
AHAVAS ZEDEK, CONGREGATION 189 OWASSO	AKRON	OH	44313	
ANSHE SFARD, CONGREGATION O 646 NORTH REVERE ROAD	AKRON	OH	44313	
BETH EL CONGREGATION C 464 S. HAWKINS AVENUE	AKRON	OH	44320	(216) 864-2105
ISRAEL, TEMPLE R 133 MERRIMAN ROAD	AKRON	OH	44303	(216) 762-8617
NEW HEBREW CONGREGATION O 1500 ROWLES DRIVE	AKRON	OH	44313	(216) 867-3407
REVERE ROAD SYNAGOGUE O 646 NORTH REVERE ROAD	AKRON	OH	44313	(216) 867-7292
TIFERETH ISRAEL CONGREGATION R 713 PROSPECT AVENUE, P.O. BOX 739	ASHTABULA	OH	44004	
BETH AYNU, CONGREGATION C 25400 FAIRMOUNT BLVD	BEACHWOOD	OH	44122	
GREEN ROAD SYNAGOGUE O 2437 SOUTH GREEN ROAD	BEACHWOOD	OH	44122	(216) 381-4751
SUBURBAN TEMPLE, THE R 22401 CHAGRIN BLVD	BEACHWOOD	OH	44122	(216) 991-0700
AGUDAS ACHIM, CONGREGATION 34TH STREET & NORTH BELMONT	BELLAIRE	OH	43906	
AGUDAS ACHIM SYNAGOGUE 2767 EAST BROAD STREET	BEXLEY	OH	43209	(614) 237-2747
AHAVAS SHOLOM, CONGREGATION O 2568 EAST BROAD STREET	BEXLEY	OH	43209	(614) 252-4815
AGUDAS ACHIM, CONGREGATION O 929 CHERRY AVENUE N.E.	CANTON	OH	44704	(216) 456-8781
ISRAEL, TEMPLE R 333 25TH STREET N.W.	CANTON	OH	44709	(216) 455-5179
SHAARAY TORAH SYNAGOGUE, THE C 432 30TH STREET N.W.	CANTON	OH	44709	(216) 492-0310
YOUNG ISRAEL OF CANTON 2508 N. MARKET STREET	CANTON	OH	44714	(216) 456-8781
ADATH ISRAEL CONGREGATION C 3201 E. GALBRAITH ROAD	CINCINNATI	OH	45236	(513) 793-1800
AGUDAS ISRAEL, CONGREGATION O 6442 STOVER AVENUE	CINCINNATI	OH	45237	(513) 531-6654
AGUDATH ACHIM ROSELAWN SYNAGOGUE O 7600 READING ROAD	CINCINNATI	OH	45237	(513) 761-7755
B'NAI TZEDEK, CONGREGATION C 1580 SUMMIT ROAD	CINCINNATI	OH	45237	(513) 821-0941
BETH HAMEDRASH HAGODOL, BOND HILL SYNAGOGUE O 4906 READING	CINCINNATI	OH	45237	
BETH JACOB SYNAGOGUE 3770 ST. LAWRENCE AVENUE	CINCINNATI	OH	45205	
CHABAD HOUSE O 1636 SUMMIT ROAD	CINCINNATI	OH	45237	(513) 821-5100
DOWNTOWN SYNAGOGUE ENQUIRER BUILDING, 617 VINE	CINCINNATI	OH	45202	(513) 241-3576
ISAAC M. WISE TEMPLE R 8329 RIDGE ROAD	CINCINNATI	OH	45236	(513) 793-2556
K.K. BENE ISRAEL-ROCKDALE TEMPLE R 8501 RIDGE ROAD	CINCINNATI	OH	45236	(513) 891-9900
KNESETH ISRAEL, CONGREGATION O 1515 SECTION ROAD	CINCINNATI	OH	45237	(513) 948-2209
NEW HOPE CONGREGATION O 1625 CREST HILL AVENUE	CINCINNATI	OH	45237	(513) 821-6274
NORTH AVONDALE SYNAGOGUE 3870 READING	CINCINNATI	OH	45229	(513) 281-3243
NORTHERN HILLS SYNAGOGUE-CONGREGATION B'NAI AVRAHAM C 715 FLEMING ROAD	CINCINNATI	OH	45231	(513) 931-6038
OHAV SHALOM, CONGREGATION O 1834 SECTION ROAD	CINCINNATI	OH	45237	(513) 531-4676
PRICE HILL BETH JACOB, CONGREGATION R ST. LAWRENCE & RAPIDS AVENUES	CINCINNATI	OH	45205	
ROCKDALE TEMPLE, K. K. BENE ISRAEL R 8501 RIDGE ROAD	CINCINNATI	OH	45236	(513) 891-9900
ROSELAWN SYNAGOGUE 7600 READING ROAD	CINCINNATI	OH	45237	(513) 761-7755
SEPHARDIC BETH SHALOM CONGREGATION P.O. BOX 37431	CINCINNATI	OH	45222	(513) 793-6936
SHOLOM, TEMPLE R 3100 LONGMEADOW LANE	CINCINNATI	OH	45236	(513) 791-1330
SYNAGOGUE/MIKVAH O 1546 KENOVA AVENUE	CINCINNATI	OH	45237	(513) 821-6679
VALLEY TEMPLE, THE R 145 SPRINGFIELD PIKE	CINCINNATI	OH	45215	(513) 761-3555
YAD CHARUTZIM-TIFERES ISRAEL CONGREGATION O 3870 READING	CINCINNATI	OH	45229	(513) 281-3243
AGUDATH ISRAEL OF CLEVELAND O 3840 SEVERN ROAD	CLEVELAND	OH	44118	(216) 321-9718
AHAVATH ISRAEL O 3448 EUCLID HEIGHTS BLVD	CLEVELAND	OH	44118	(216) 371-3665
B'NAI JESHURUN (TEMPLE ON THE HEIGHTS) C 27501 FAIRMOUNT BLVD	CLEVELAND	OH	44124	(216) 831-6555
BETH AM, CONGREGATION C 3557 WASHINGTON BLVD	CLEVELAND	OH	44118	(216) 321-1000
BETH EL O 15808 CHAGRIN BLVD	CLEVELAND	OH	44120	(216) 991-6044
BETH ISRAEL-THE WEST TEMPLE R 14308 TRISKETT ROAD	CLEVELAND	OH	44111	(216) 941-8882
BETHAYNU C 25400 FAIRMOUNT BLVD	CLEVELAND	OH	44122	(216) 292-2931
BRITH EMETH R 27575 SHAKER BLVD	CLEVELAND	OH	44124	(216) 831-5363
CHABAD LUBAVITCH O 3392 DESOTA	CLEVELAND	OH	44118	
CONGREGATIONAL PLENUM OF GREATER CLEVELAND 26000 SHAKER BLVD	CLEVELAND	OH	44122	(216) 831-3233
EMANU-EL, TEMPLE R 2200 S. GREEN ROAD	CLEVELAND	OH	44121	(216) 381-6600
ETZ CHAYIM (TREE OF LIFE CONGREGATION) C MAYFIELD HEIGHTS COMMUNITY CENTER, 6803 MARSOL ROAD	CLEVELAND	OH	44124	(216) 382-8925
FAIRMOUNT TEMPLE R 23737 FAIRMOUNT BLVD	CLEVELAND	OH	44122	(216) 464-1330
GREEN ROAD SYNAGOGUE O 2437 GREEN ROAD	CLEVELAND	OH	44122	(216) 381-4757
HEIGHTS JEWISH CENTER O 14270 CEDAR ROAD	CLEVELAND	OH	44121	(216) 382-1958
HEIGHTS JEWISH CENTER O 14274 SUPERIOR ROAD	CLEVELAND	OH	44118	(216) 932-7424
K'HAL YEREIM O 1771 SOUTH TAYLOR ROAD	CLEVELAND	OH	44118	(216) 321-9554
K'HAL YEREIM O 2203 S. GREEN	CLEVELAND	OH	44121	
MAYFIELD HILLCREST SYNAGOGUE C 1732 LANDER ROAD	CLEVELAND	OH	44124	(216) 449-6200
NER TAMID, TEMPLE (EUCLID JEWISH CENTER) R 24950 LAKE SHORE BLVD	CLEVELAND	OH	44132	(216) 261-2280
OER-CHODOSH ANSHE SFARD O 3466 WASHINGTON BLVD	CLEVELAND	OH	44118	(216) 932-7739
OHEB ZEDEK - THE TAYLOR ROAD SYNAGOGUE O 1970 S. TAYLOR ROAD	CLEVELAND	OH	44118	(216) 321-4875
SHAAREI TORAH, CONGREGATION 2436 BEECHWOOD AVENUE	CLEVELAND	OH	44118	
SHOMRE SHABOTH O 1801 SOUTH TAYLOR ROAD	CLEVELAND	OH	44118	(216) 932-2619
SINAI SYNAGOGUE O 3246 DESOTA AVENUE	CLEVELAND	OH	44118	(216) 932-0206
SUBURBAN TEMPLE, THE R 22401 CHAGRIN BLVD	CLEVELAND	OH	44122	(216) 991-0700
TAYLOR ROAD SYNAGOGUE O 1970 SOUTH TAYLOR ROAD	CLEVELAND	OH	44118	(216) 321-4875
TEMPLE ON THE HEIGHTS C 27501 FAIRMOUNT BLVD	CLEVELAND	OH	44124	(216) 831-6555
TEMPLE, THE R UNIVERSITY CIRCLE & SILVER PARK	CLEVELAND	OH	44106	(216) 791-7755
TIFERETH ISRAEL - THE TEMPLE R UNIVERSITY CIRCLE AT SILVER PARK	CLEVELAND	OH	44106	(216) 791-7755
TORAH U'TEFILAH O 1970 SOUTH TAYLOR ROAD	CLEVELAND	OH	44118	(216) 371-5872
UNITED JEWISH RELIGIOUS SCHOOLS 25400 FAIRMOUNT BLVD	CLEVELAND	OH	44122	(216) 464-8050
YESHIVATH ADATH B'NAI ISRAEL SYNAGOGUE O 2308 WARRENSVILLE CENTER	CLEVELAND	OH	44118	(216) 932-7664
ZEMACH ZEDEK O 1922 LEE ROAD	CLEVELAND	OH	44118	(216) 321-5169
PARK SYNAGOGUE 3300 MAYFIELD ROAD	CLEVELAND HEIGHTS	OH	44118	(216) 371-2244
TAYLOR ROAD SYNAGOGUE/OHEB ZEDEK O 1970 SOUTH TAYLOR ROAD	CLEVELAND HEIGHTS	OH	44118	(216) 321-4875
WARRENSVILLE CENTER SYNAGOGUE O 1508 WARRENSVILLE CENTER ROAD	CLEVELAND HEIGHTS	OH	44121	(216) 382-6566
AGUDAS ACHIM, CONGREGATION O 2767 EAST BROAD STREET	COLUMBUS	OH	43209	(614) 237-2747
AHAVAS SHOLOM, CONGREGATION 2568 E. BROAD STREET	COLUMBUS	OH	43209	(614) 258-4815
BETH JACOB, CONGREGATION O 1223 COLLEGE AVENUE	COLUMBUS	OH	43209	(614) 237-8641
BETH SHALOM, TEMPLE R 3100 E. BROAD STREET	COLUMBUS	OH	43209	(614) 231-4598
BETH TIKVAH, CONGREGATION R 6121 OLENTANGY RIVER ROAD	COLUMBUS	OH	43214	(614) 885-6286
HOUSE OF TRADITION O 57 EAST 14TH AVENUE	COLUMBUS	OH	43201	(614) 294-3296
ISRAEL, TEMPLE R 5419 E. BROAD STREET	COLUMBUS	OH	43213	(614) 866-0010
TIFERETH ISRAEL, CONGREGATION C 1354 E. BROAD STREET	COLUMBUS	OH	43205	(614) 253-8523
BETH ABRAHAM SYNAGOGUE C 1306 SALEM AVENUE	DAYTON	OH	45406	(513) 275-7403
BETH JACOB SYNAGOGUE 7020 N. MAIN STREET	DAYTON	OH	45415	(513) 274-2149
ISRAEL, TEMPLE R 1821 EMERSON AVENUE	DAYTON	OH	45406	(513) 278-9621
ISRAEL, TEMPLE - SOUTH BRANCH R 1136 W. CENTERVILLE ROAD	DAYTON	OH	45959	(513) 434-9067
SHOMREI EMUNAH YOUNG ISRAEL O 1706 SALEM AVENUE	DAYTON	OH	45406	(513) 274-6941
YOUNG ISRAEL OF DAYTON 1706 SALEM AVENUE	DAYTON	OH	45406	(513) 274-6941
BETH SHALOM, CONGREGATION R P.O. BOX 309	EAST LIVERPOOL	OH	43920	(216) 386-6820
BNAI ISRAEL, CONGREGATION P.O. BOX 309	EAST LIVERPOOL	OH	43920	
B'NAI ABRAHAM, TEMPLE C P.O. BOX 530, GULF ROAD	ELYRIA	OH	44036	(216) 366-1177
NER TAMID, TEMPLE R 24950 LAKE SHORE DRIVE	EUCLID	OH	44132	(216) 261-2280
BETH ISRAEL, TEMPLE C 514 BIRCHARD AVENUE	FREMONT	OH	43420	(419) 332-6302
OHEV ISRAEL TEMPLE R 324 MT. PARNASSUS	GRANVILLE	OH	43023	(614) 326-4501
ETZ CHAYIM, CONGREGATION P.O. BOX 2882	KENWOOD	OH	43606	
BETH ISRAEL, TEMPLE R LAKEWOOD AVENUE AT GLENWOOD	LIMA	OH	45805	(419) 223-9616
AGUDATH B'NAI ISRAEL C 1715 MEISTER ROAD AT POLE AVENUE	LORAIN	OH	44053	(216) 282-3307
B'NAI JACOB CONGREGATION R 973 LARCHWOOD ROAD	MANSFIELD	OH	44907	(419) 756-7355
EMANUEL, TEMPLE R COOK ROAD AT LARCHWOOD, P.O. BOX 1665	MANSFIELD	OH	44901	(419) 756-7266
BNEI ISRAEL, CONGREGATION O 522 4TH STREET	MARIETTA	OH	45750	
ISRAEL, TEMPLE R 730 HARDING ROAD	MARION	OH	43302	(614) 382-3629
B'NAI JESHURUN CONGREGATION C 1732 LANDER ROAD	MAYFIELD HEIGHTS	OH	44124	(216) 449-6200
MAYFIELD HILLCREST CONGREGATION C 1732 LANDER ROAD	MAYFIELD HEIGHTS	OH	44124	(216) 449-6200
NER TAMID, TEMPLE - EUCLID JEWISH CENTER EAST 250TH & LAKE SHORE BLVD	MAYFIELD HEIGHTS	OH	44132	(216) 261-2280
AM SHALOM (LAKE COUNTY JEWISH CENTER) R P.O. BOX 454	MENTOR	OH	44060	(216) 953-1315
BETH SHOLOM, TEMPLE R 610 GLADYS DRIVE	MIDDLETOWN	OH	45042	(513) 422-8313
B'NAI JESHURUN CONGREGATION-THE TEMPLE ON THE HEIGHTS C 27501 FAIRMOUNT BLVD	PEPPER PIKE	OH	44124	(216) 831-6555
BRITH EMETH TEMPLE R 27575 SHAKER BLVD	PEPPER PIKE	OH	44124	
ANSHE EMETH CONGREGATION R C/O MR. HERMAN BARR, 1409 NICKLIN	PIQUA	OH	45356	(513) 773-4253
B'NAI ABRAHAM, CONGREGATION R 325 MASONIC BLDG	PORTSMOUTH	OH	45662	(614) 354-1671
OHEB SHALOM CONGREGATION R 1521 E. PERKINS AVENUE	SANDUSKY	OH	44870	(419) 433-6051
CHABAD HOUSE O 2004 SOUTH GREEN ROAD	SOUTH EUCLID	OH	44121	(216) 382-5050
YOUNG ISRAEL OF CLEVELAND 14141 CEDAR ROAD	SOUTH EUCLID	OH	44121	(216) 382-5740
BETH EL SYNAGOGUE C 2424 N. LIMESTONE STREET	SPRINGFIELD	OH	45505	(513) 399-7512
SHOLOM, TEMPLE R 2424 N. LIMESTONE STREET	SPRINGFIELD	OH	45503	(513) 399-1231
BETH ISRAEL, TEMPLE R 300 LOVERS LANE	STEUBENVILLE	OH	43952	(614) 264-5514
BNAI ISRAEL, CONGREGATION C 128 S. 5TH STREET	STEUBENVILLE	OH	43952	
CONGREGATION SHOMER EMUNIM, THE TEMPLE R 6453 SYLVANIA AVENUE	SYLVANIA	OH	43560	(419) 885-3341
B'NAI ISRAEL, TEMPLE C 2727 KENWOOD BLVD	TOLEDO	OH	43606	(419) 531-1677
BNAI JACOB-SHAREI ZEDECK O P.O. BOX 2882	TOLEDO	OH	43606	
ETZ CHAYIM, CONGREGATION O 3853 WOODLEY ROAD	TOLEDO	OH	43606	(419) 473-2401
BETH SHALOM, TEMPLE R P.O. BOX 315	TWINSBURG	OH	44087	
BETH HAMIDROSH HAGADOL CONGREGATION O 14270 CEDAR ROAD	UNIVERSITY HEIGHTS	OH	44121	(216) 382-1958
OER CHODOSH ANSHE SFARD O 3466 WASHINGTON BOULEVARD	UNIVERSITY HEIGHTS	OH	44118	(216) 932-7880
BETH ISRAEL TEMPLE CENTER C 2138 E. MARKET STREET	WARREN	OH	44483	(216) 395-3877
AGUDATH ISRAEL OF WICKLIFFE O 2606 BISHOP ROAD	WICKLIFFE	OH	44092	(216) 913-4162
KNESSETH ISRAEL, TEMPLE C 1670 CLEVELAND ROAD	WOOSTER	OH	44691	(216) 262-3516
BETH TIKVA, CONGREGATION R 6121 OLENTANGY RIVER ROAD	WORTHINGTON	OH	43085	(614) 885-6286
ANSHE EMETH, TEMPLE C FIFTH & FAIRGREEN	YOUNGSTOWN	OH	44504	
CHILDREN OF ISRAEL, CONGREGATION O 3970½ LOGAN WAY	YOUNGSTOWN	OH	44505	(216) 759-2167
EL EMETH, TEMPLE C FIFTH & FAIRGREEN	YOUNGSTOWN	OH	44515	(216) 744-5055
OHEV TZEDEK-SHAAREI TORAH C 5245 GLENWOOD AVENUE	YOUNGSTOWN	OH	44512	(216) 758-2321
RODEF SHOLOM, CONGREGATION R ELM & WOODBINE STREETS	YOUNGSTOWN	OH	44505	(216) 744-5001
BETH ABRAHAM, CONGREGATION C 1740 BLUE AVENUE	ZANESVILLE	OH	43701	(614) 453-5391
KNESETH ISRAEL, CONGREGATION 522 WEST HIGHLAND	ZANESVILLE	OH	43701	

EMETH, TEMPLE R	421 STANLEY	ARDMORE	**OK**	73401	(405) 223-3064
BETH AHABA, TEMPLE R	4131 SOUTH ROBB	MUSKOGEE	**OK**	74401	(918) 682-1432
B'NAI ISRAEL, TEMPLE R	4901 N. PENNSYLVANIA AVENUE	OKLAHOMA CITY	**OK**	73112	(405) 848-0965
EMANUEL SYNAGOGUE C	900 N.W. 47TH STREET	OKLAHOMA CITY	**OK**	73118	(405) 528-2113
EMANUEL, TEMPLE R	P.O. BOX 1081	PONCA CITY	**OK**	74601	(405) 765-5898
B'NAI EMUNAH, CONGREGATION C	1719 S. OWASSO AVENUE, P.O. BOX 52430	TULSA	**OK**	74152	(918) 583-7121
ISRAEL, TEMPLE R	2004 E. 22ND PLACE	TULSA	**OK**	74114	(918) 747-1309
BETH DAVID, CONGREGATION O	50 WATERLOO STREET	BRANTFORD	**ON**	N3T 3R8	(519) 752-8950
ADATH ISRAEL CONGREGATION C	37 SOUTHBOURNE AVENUE	DOWNSVIEW	**ON**	M3H 1A4	(416) 635-5340
ADATH SHOLOM SYNAGOGUE O	864 SHEPPARD AVENUE WEST	DOWNSVIEW	**ON**		(416) 635-0131
BETH DAVID B'NAI ISRAEL, BETH AM SYNAGOGUE C	55 YEOMANS ROAD	DOWNSVIEW	**ON**	M3H 3J7	(416) 633-5500
BETH EMETH BAIS YEHUDA SYNAGOGUE C	100 ELDER STREET	DOWNSVIEW	**ON**	M3H 5G7	(416) 633-3838
BETH JACOB V'ANSHE DRILDZ SYNAGOGUE O	147 OVERBROOK PLACE	DOWNSVIEW	**ON**	M3H 4R1	(416) 638-5955
BETH RADOM SYNAGOGUE	18 REINER ROAD	DOWNSVIEW	**ON**		(416) 636-3451
CLANTON PARK SYNAGOGUE O	11 LOWESMOORE AVENUE	DOWNSVIEW	**ON**	M3H 2B5	(416) 633-4193
CONGREGATION DARCHEI NOAM, RECONSTRUCTIONIST SYNAGOGUE OF TORONTO	15 HOVE STREET	DOWNSVIEW	**ON**	M3H 4Y8	(416) 633-3526
PETAH TIKVA ANSHE CASTILLA CONGREGATION O	20 DANBY AVENUE	DOWNSVIEW	**ON**	M3H 2J3	(416) 636-4725
ADAS ISRAEL CONGREGATION OF HAMILTON O	125 CLINE AVENUE SOUTH	HAMILTON	**ON**	L8S 1X2	(416) 528-0039
ANSHE SHOLOM, TEMPLE R	215 CLINE AVENUE N	HAMILTON	**ON**	L85 4A1	(416) 528-0121
BETH JACOB SYNAGOGUE C	375 ABERDEEN AVENUE	HAMILTON	**ON**	L8P 2R7	(416) 522-1351
CHABAD LUBAVITCH O	87 WESTWOOD AVENUE	HAMILTON	**ON**	L8S 2B1	(416) 529-7458
OHEV ZEDEK OF HAMILTON, CONGREGATION O	HESS & PETER STREETS	HAMILTON	**ON**	L8S 0O0	(416) 529-7097
BETH ISRAEL O	116 CENTRE STREET	KINGSTON	**ON**	K7L 4E6	(613) 542-5012
IYR HA-MELECH R	842 MILFORD DRIVE	KINGSTON	**ON**	K7P 1AB	(613) 544-3088
SHALOM, TEMPLE R	1284 OTTAWA STREET S	KITCHENER	**ON**	N2E 1M1	(519) 743-0401
BETH TEFILAH, CONGREGATION O	1210 ADELAIDE STREET N	LONDON	**ON**	N5Y 4T6	(519) 433-7081
DR. Y. BLOCK O	1059 WILLIAM STREET	LONDON	**ON**	N5Y 2T2	(519) 439-4828
OR SHALOM, CONGREGATION C	534 HURON STREET	LONDON	**ON**	N5Y 4J5	(519) 438-3081
SOLEL CONGREGATION R	2399 FOLKWAY DRIVE	MISSISSAUGA	**ON**	L5L 2M6	(416) 828-5915
B'NAI JACOB, CONGREGATION C	5328 FERRY STREET	NIAGARA FALLS	**ON**		(416) 354-3934
BETH EL CONGREGATION	186 MORRISON ROAD	OAKVILLE	**ON**	L6J 4J4	(416) 845-0837
ADATH SHALOM CONGREGATION C	P.O. BOX 106, POSTAL STATION B	OSHAWA	**ON**	K1P 6C3	(613) 225-7081
BETH ZION CONGREGATION OF OSHAWA C	144 KING STREET EAST	OSHAWA	**ON**	L1H 1C2	
AGUDATH ISRAEL CONGREGATION C	1400 COLDREY AVENUE	OTTAWA	**ON**	K1Z 7P9	(613) 728-3501
BETH SHALOM, CONGREGATION O	151 CHAPEL STREET	OTTAWA	**ON**	K1N 7Y2	(613) 232-3501
ISRAEL, TEMPLE R	1301 PRINCE OF WALES DRIVE	OTTAWA	**ON**	K2C 1N2	(613) 224-1802
MACHZIKEI HADAS, CONGREGATION O	2310 VIRGINIA DRIVE	OTTAWA	**ON**	K1H 6S2	(613) 521-9700
YOUNG ISRAEL OF OTTAWA	627 KIRKWOOD AVENUE	OTTAWA	**ON**	K2U 5X5	(613) 722-8394
BETH ISRAEL CONGREGATION C	WELLER STREET	PETERBOROUGH	**ON**		(705) 745-7483
B'NAI ISRAEL C	190 CHURCH STREET	SAINT CATHERINES	**ON**	L2R 4C4	(416) 685-6767
TIKVAH, TEMPLE R	83 CHURCH STREET, P.O. BOX 484	SAINT CATHERINES	**ON**	L2R 6Y9	(416) 682-4191
AHAVAS ISAAC SYNAGOGUE C	202 COBDEN STREET	SARNIA	**ON**		
BETH ABRAHAM YAAKOV - TORONTO O	51 BEVSHIRE CIRCLE	THORNHILL	**ON**	L4J 3E3	(416) 886-3810
CHABAD LUBAVITCH COMMUNITY CENTER O	770 CHABAD GATE	THORNHILL	**ON**	L4J 3V9	(416) 731-7000
HAR ZION, TEMPLE R	7360 BAYVIEW AVENUE	THORNHILL	**ON**	L3T 2R7	(416) 889-2252
SHAAR SHALOM SYNAGOGUE	2 SIMONSTON BOULEVARD	THORNHILL	**ON**		(416) 889-4975
AGUDATH ISRAEL OF TORONTO O	129 MCGILLIVRAY	TORONTO	**ON**		
BAYCREST TERRACE REFORM CONGREGATION R	3560 BATHURST	TORONTO	**ON**	M6A 2E1	(416) 789-5131
BETH SHOLOM SYNAGOGUE C	1445 EGLINTON AVENUE W	TORONTO	**ON**	M6C 2E6	(416) 783-6103
BETH TORAH CONGREGATION C	47 GLENBROOK AVENUE	TORONTO	**ON**	M6B 2L7	(416) 782-3561
BETH TZEDEC CONGREGATION C	1700 BATHURST STREET	TORONTO	**ON**	M5P 3K3	(416) 781-3511
HABONIM	3101 BATHURST STREET, SUITE 305	TORONTO	**ON**		
HOLY BLOSSOM TEMPLE R	1950 BATHURST STREET	TORONTO	**ON**	M5P 3K9	(416) 781-9185
SHAAREI SHOMAYIM CONGREGATION O	470 GLENCAIRN AVENUE	TORONTO	**ON**	M5N 1V8	(416) 789-3213
SHAAREI TEFILLAH, CONGREGATION O	3600 BATHURST STREET	TORONTO	**ON**	M6A 2C9	(416) 787-1631
SHOMRAI SHABOTH, CONGREGATION O	583-585 GLENGROVE AVENUE	TORONTO	**ON**	M6B 2H5	(416) 782-8849
SINAI, TEMPLE R	210 WILSON AVENUE	TORONTO	**ON**	M5M 3B1	(416) 487-4161
TORATH EMETH JEWISH CENTER O	1 VIEWMOUNT AVENUE	TORONTO	**ON**	M6B 1R3	
B'NAI TORAH, CONGREGATION O	465 PATRICIA AVENUE	WILLOWDALE	**ON**	M2R 2N1	(416) 226-3700
BETH TIKVAH C	3080 BAYVIEW AVENUE	WILLOWDALE	**ON**	M2N 5L3	(416) 221-3433
EMANU-EL, TEMPLE R	120 OLD COLONY ROAD	WILLOWDALE	**ON**	M2L 2K2	(416) 449-3880
KEHILLAT SHAAREI TORAH OF TORONTO O	2640 BAYVIEW AVENUE	WILLOWDALE	**ON**	M2L 1V7	(416) 444-5444
PRIDE OF ISRAEL SYNAGOGUE	59 LISSOM CRESCENT	WILLOWDALE	**ON**	M2R 2P2	(416) 226-0111
SHAAREI ZION/YI OF TORONTO/ASSOCIATION HEBREW O	6100 LESLIE STREET	WILLOWDALE	**ON**	M2H 3J1	(416) 225-0536
YOUNG ISRAEL SHAAREI ZION OF TORONTO	325 GOLDENWOOD ROAD	WILLOWDALE	**ON**		
BETH EL, CONGREGATION R	2525 MARK AVENUE	WINDSOR	**ON**	N9E 2W2	(519) 969-2422
SHAAR HASHAMAYIM, CONGREGATION O	115 GILES BOULEVARD EAST	WINDSOR	**ON**	N9A 4C1	(519) 256-3123
SHAAREY ZEDEK, CONGREGATION O	610 GILES BOULEVARD EAST	WINDSOR	**ON**	N9A 4C1	(591) 252-1594
BETH ISRAEL, TEMPLE C	2550 PORTLAND STREET	EUGENE	**OR**	97401	(503) 485-7218
ROGUE VALLEY JEWISH COMMUNITY CONGREGATION R	P.O. BOX 1094	MEDFORD	**OR**	97501	(503) 779-7648
AHAVATH ACHIM, CONGREGATION	3225 S.W. BARBUR BLVD	PORTLAND	**OR**	97215	(503) 227-0010
BETH ISRAEL, TEMPLE R	1931 N.W. FLANDERS STREET	PORTLAND	**OR**	97209	(503) 222-1069
CHABAD-LUBAVITCH O	136 SOUTHWEST MEADE	PORTLAND	**OR**	97201	(503) 277-5999
HAVURAH SHALOM	6201 SOUTHWEST CAPITOL HIGHWAY	PORTLAND	**OR**	97201	(503) 292-4462
NEVEH SHALOM, CONGREGATION C	2900 S.W. PEACEFUL LANE	PORTLAND	**OR**	97201	(503) 246-8831
SHAARIE TORAH, CONGREGATION O	920 N.W. 25TH AVENUE	PORTLAND	**OR**	97210	(503) 226-6131
TIFERETH ISRAEL, CONGREGATION C	4744 N.E. 15TH AVENUE	PORTLAND	**OR**	97211	(503) 288-1659
SALEM JEWISH CONGREGATION-TEMPLE BETH SHOLOM C	1795 BROADWAY N.E.	SALEM	**OR**	97308	
OLD YORK ROAD TEMPLE BETH AM R	971 OLD YORK ROAD	ABINGTON	**PA**	19001	(215) 886-8000
BETH EL, TEMPLE C	17TH & HAMILTON STREETS	ALLENTOWN	**PA**	18104	(215) 435-3521
CONGREGATION AM HASKALAH RE	903 NORTH 18TH STREET	ALLENTOWN	**PA**	18104	(215) 435-3775
KENESETH ISRAEL, CONGREGATION R	2227 CHEW STREET	ALLENTOWN	**PA**	18104	(215) 435-9074
SONS OF ISRAEL, CONGREGATION O	2715 TILGHMAN STREET	ALLENTOWN	**PA**	18104	(215) 433-6089
AGUDATH ACHIM SYNAGOGUE C	1306 17TH STREET	ALTOONA	**PA**	16601	(814) 944-5317
BETH ISRAEL, TEMPLE R	3004 UNION AVENUE	ALTOONA	**PA**	16602	(814) 942-0057
BETH SAMUEL JEWISH CENTER C	P.O. BOX 219, 810 KENNEDY DRIVE	AMBRIDGE	**PA**	15003	(412) 266-9871
LOWER MERION SYNAGOGUE O	123 OLD LANCASTER ROAD	BALA CYNWYD	**PA**	19004	(215) 664-5626
BNAI ISRAEL, CONGREGATION		BARNESBORO	**PA**	15714	
AGUDATH ACHIM CONGREGATION C	P.O. BOX 293	BEAVER FALLS	**PA**	15010	(412) 846-5696
BETH SHOLOM CONGREGATION R	1409 EIGHTH AVENUE	BEAVER FALLS	**PA**	15010	(412) 846-0068
NES AMI PENN VALLEY CONGREGATION C	50 ASHLAND AVENUE	BELMONT HILLS	**PA**	19127	
TIFERETH ISRAEL OF LOWER BUCKS COUNTY, CONGREGATION C	2909 BRISTOL ROAD	BENSALEM	**PA**	19020	(215) 752-3468
OHEV SHOLOM, CONGREGATION C	1401 HOLLY DRIVE	BERWICK	**PA**	18603	
AGUDATH ACHIM, CONGREGATION O	1555 LINWOOD STREET	BETHLEHEM	**PA**	18016	(215) 866-8891
BRITH SHOLOM COMMUNITY CENTER C	P.O. BOX 5323, BRODHEAD & PACKER AVENUE	BETHLEHEM	**PA**	18015	(215) 866-8000
BETH ISRAEL CONGREGATION C	144 E. 4TH STREET	BLOOMSBURG	**PA**	17815	(717) 784-5778
BETH EL, TEMPLE R	P.O. BOX 538, 111 JACKSON AVENUE	BRADFORD	**PA**	16701	(814) 368-8204
BRISTOL JEWISH CENTER C	216 POND STREET	BRISTOL	**PA**	19007	(215) 788-4995
BETH EL SUBURBAN, CONGREGATION C	715 PAXON HOLLOW ROAD	BROOMALL	**PA**	19008	(215) 246-8700
SHOLOM, TEMPLE R	55 N. CHURCH ROAD	BROOMALL	**PA**	19008	(215) 356-5165
B'NAI ABRAHAM C	519 N. MAIN STREET	BUTLER	**PA**	16001	(412) 287-5806
AGUDATH SHOLOM, CONGREGATION O	51 1/2 PIKE STREET	CARBONDALE	**PA**	18407	
AHAVATH ACHIM C	LYDIA & CHESTNUT STREETS	CARNEGIE	**PA**	15106	(412) 276-9777
SONS OF ISRAEL, CONGREGATION C	KING & SECOND STREETS	CHAMBERSBURG	**PA**	17201	(717) 264-2915
MELROSE B'NAI ISRAEL, CONGREGATION C	2ND STREET AT CHELTENHAM AVENUE	CHELTENHAM	**PA**	19012	
BETH ISRAEL CONGREGATION C	FIFTH AVENUE & HARMONY STREETS	COATESVILLE	**PA**	19320	(215) 384-1978
AHAVATH SHOLOM TEMPLE R	FLEMING STREET & VANCE AVENUE	CORAOPOLIS	**PA**	15108	(412) 264-4100
OHAV SHOLOM, CONGREGATION O	THOMPSON AVENUE	DONORA	**PA**	15033	(412) 379-9943
JUDEA OF BUCKS COUNTY, TEMPLE R	SWAMP ROAD, P.O. BOX 215	DOYLESTOWN	**PA**	18901	(215) 348-5022
SINAI, TEMPLE C	LIMEKILN PIKE & DILLON ROAD	DRESHER	**PA**	19025	(215) 643-6510
BETH JACOB, CONGREGATION O	431 CATHERINE STREET	DUQUESNE	**PA**	15110	
OHAB ZEDEK, CONGREGATION C	ELECTRIC AVENUE	EAST PITTSBURGH	**PA**	15112	
ISRAEL, TEMPLE C	P.O. BOX 368, 660 WALLACE STREET	EAST STROUDSBURG	**PA**	18360	(717) 421-8781
BNAI ABRAHAM SYNAGOGUE C	16TH & BUSHKILL STREETS	EASTON	**PA**	18042	(215) 258-5343
COVENANT OF PEACE, TEMPLE R	1451 NORTHAMPTON STREET	EASTON	**PA**	18042	(215) 253-2031
ADATH JESHURUN, CONGREGATION C	YORK & ASHBOURNE ROADS	ELKINS PARK	**PA**	19117	(215) 635-6611
BETH SHOLOM CONGREGATION C	OLD YORK & FOXCROFT ROADS	ELKINS PARK	**PA**	19117	(215) 887-3625
KENESETH ISRAEL, CONGREGATION R	YORK ROAD & TOWNSHIP LINE	ELKINS PARK	**PA**	19117	(215) 887-8700
RODEPH SHALOM R	8201 HIGH SCHOOL ROAD	ELKINS PARK	**PA**	19117	(215) 324-1010
TREE OF LIFE CONGREGATION C	BEATTY STREET	ELLWOOD CITY	**PA**	16617	(412) 758-7329
BETH TIKVAH-B'NAI JESHURUN C	1001 PAPER MILL ROAD	ERDENHEIM	**PA**	19118	(215) 836-5677
ANSHE HESED, TEMPLE R	10TH & LIBERTY STREETS	ERIE	**PA**	16502	(814) 454-2426
BRITH SHOLOM, CONGREGATION C	3207 STATE STREET	ERIE	**PA**	16508	(814) 454-2431
BETH CHAIM, CONGREGATION C	350 EAST STREET	FEASTERVILLE	**PA**	19047	(215) 355-3626
KNESSETH ISRAEL CONGREGATION	416 FORD STREET	FORD CITY	**PA**	16226	(412) 762-2621
B'NAI ISRAEL, CONGREGATION C	WEST FRACK STREET	FRACKVILLE	**PA**	17931	
EMANU-EL ISRAEL, CONGREGATION R	222 N. MAIN STREET	GREENSBURG	**PA**	15601	(412) 834-0560
HANOVER HEBREW CONGREGATION C	179 SECOND AVENUE	HANOVER	**PA**	17331	
BETH EL C	2637 N. FRONT STREET	HARRISBURG	**PA**	17110	(717) 232-0556
CHISUK EMUNA CONGREGATION C	FIFTH & DIVISION STREETS	HARRISBURG	**PA**	17110	(717) 232-4851
KESHER ISRAEL, CONGREGATION O	2500 NORTH 3RD STREET	HARRISBURG	**PA**	17110	(717) 238-0736
REFORM TEMPLE OHEV SHOLOM R	2345 N. FRONT STREET	HARRISBURG	**PA**	17110	(717) 233-6459
UNITED JEWISH COMMUNITY OF GREATER HARRISBURG	100 VAUGHN STREET	HARRISBURG	**PA**	17110	(717) 236-9555
SUBURBAN JEWISH COMMUNITY CENTER, B'NAI AARON C	560 MILL ROAD	HAVERTOWN	**PA**	19083	(215) 528-5011
AGUDAS ISRAEL CONGREGATION C	PINE & OAK STREETS	HAZELTON	**PA**	18201	(717) 454-9294
BETH ISRAEL CONGREGATION R	98 N. CHURCH STREET	HAZELTON	**PA**	18201	(717) 455-3971
HOMESTEAD HEBREW CONGREGATION RODEF SHALOM O	331 10TH AVENUE	HOMESTEAD	**PA**	15120	(412) 461-9251
BETH ISRAEL, CONGREGATION R	P.O. BOX 311	HONESDALE	**PA**	18431	(717) 253-2222
AGUDATH ACHIM, CONGREGATION C	1009 WASHINGTON STREET	HUNTINGTON	**PA**	16652	
BETH ISRAEL CONGREGATION C	5TH & WASHINGTON STREETS	INDIANA	**PA**	15701	(412) 465-6721
BETH SHOLOM CONGREGATION	FOXCROFT & OLD YORK STREETS	JENKINTOWN	**PA**	19117	(215) 924-2223
BETH SHOLOM CONGREGATION R	700 INDIANA AVENUE	JOHNSTOWN	**PA**	15905	(814) 536-0647
RODEF SHOLOM, CONGREGATION C	100 DARTMOUTH AVENUE	JOHNSTOWN	**PA**	15905	
BETH JACOB, CONGREGATION		KANE	**PA**	16735	
BRITH ACHIM, TEMPLE R	481 S. GULPH ROAD, P.O. BOX I68	KING OF PRUSSIA	**PA**	19406	(215) 337-2222
B'NAI B'RITH OF WILKES BARRE, TEMPLE R	408 WYOMING AVENUE	KINGSTON	**PA**	18704	(717) 287-9606
RABBI ZVI PERLMAN O	102 3RD AVENUE	KINGSTON	**PA**	18704	(717) 287-6336
OR AMI, CONGREGATION R	P.O. BOX 156, 708 RIDGE PIKE	LAFAYETTE HILL	**PA**	19444	(215) 828-9066
BETH EL, TEMPLE C	25 N. LINE STREET	LANCASTER	**PA**	17602	(717) 392-1379
DEGEL ISRAEL SYNAGOGUE O	1120 COLUMBIA AVENUE	LANCASTER	**PA**	17603	(717) 397-0183
SHAARAI SHOMAYIM, TEMPLE R	508 N. DUKE STREET	LANCASTER	**PA**	17602	(717) 397-5575
BETH ISRAEL, CONGREGATION C	1080 SUMNEYTOWN PIKE	LANSDALE	**PA**	19446	(215) 855-8328
BETH ISRAEL C	414 WELDON STREET	LATROBE	**PA**	15650	(412) 539-1450
BETH ISRAEL, CONGREGATION C	411 S. 8TH STREET	LEBANON	**PA**	17042	(717) 273-6669
ISRAEL, TEMPLE C	BANKWAY STREET	LEHIGHTON	**PA**	18235	(215) 377-0400
BETH EL, CONGREGATION C	21 PENN VALLEY ROAD	LEVITTOWN	**PA**	19055	(215) 945-1172
SHALOM, TEMPLE R	EDGELY ROAD OFF MILL CREEK PARKWAY	LEVITTOWN	**PA**	19057	(215) 945-4154
BETH YEHUDA SYNAGOGUE R	320 W. CHURCH STREET	LOCK HAVEN	**PA**	17745	(717) 748-3908

B'NAI ISRAEL, TEMPLE R 536 SHAW AVENUE .... MCKEESPORT **PA** 15132 (412) 678-6181
GEMILAS CHESED, CONGREGATION O 1400 SUMMIT STREET........ MCKEESPORT **PA** 15131 (412) 678-8859
TEMPLE BETH SHALOM RE 913 ALLENDALE ROAD........ MECHANICSBURG **PA** 17055 (717) 697-2662
BETH ISRAEL, CONGREGATION RE GAYLEY TERRACE........ MEDIA **PA** 19063 (215) 566-4645
ADATH ISRAEL OF THE MAIN LINE, TEMPLE C OLD LANCASTER ROAD & HIGHLAND AVENUE .... MERION STATION **PA** 19066 (215) 664-5150
BETH AM, TEMPLE R 1000 WATKINS AVENUE........ MONESSEN **PA** 15062 (412) 684-8290
BETH AM, TEMPLE R C/O MR. SIDNEY ACKERMAN, ROUTE 1, P.O. BOX 615........ MONONGAHELA **PA** 15063 (412) 379-5312
DAVID, TEMPLE R 4415 NORTHERN PIKE .... MONROEVILLE **PA** 15146 (412) 372-1200
TIFERETH ISRAEL, CONGREGATION O 135 SOUTH MAPLE STREET........ MOUNT CARMEL **PA** 17851
TREE OF LIFE, CONGREGATION O CHURCH STREET........ MOUNT PLEASANT **PA** 15666
BETH AM ISRAEL C 1301 HAGYS FORK ROAD .... NARBERTH **PA** 19072 (215) 667-1651
ISRAEL, TEMPLE R 908 HIGHLAND AVENUE .... NEW CASTLE **PA** 16101 (412) 652-7551
TIFERETH ISRAEL, CONGREGATION C 403 EAST MOODY AVENUE, P.O. BOX 1432 .... NEW CASTLE **PA** 16101 (412) 658-3321
BETH JACOB CONGREGATION C 1040 KENNETH AVENUE .... NEW KENSINGTON **PA** 15068 (412) 335-8525
SHIR AMI, BUCKS COUNTY JEWISH CONGREGATION R 101 RICHBORO ROAD .... NEWTOWN **PA** 18940 (215) 968-3400
TIFERES ISRAEL CONGREGATION-JEWISH COMMUNITY CENTER C 1541 POWELL STREET .... NORRISTOWN **PA** 19401 (215) 275-8797
TREE OF LIFE, CONGREGATION C 316 W. 1ST STREET .... OIL CITY **PA** 16301
BICKOR CHOILIM, CONGREGATION O 302 LACKAWANNA AVENUE .... OLYPHANT **PA** 18447 (717) 489-1955
BETH AM ISRAEL C 1301 HAGYSFORD ROAD........ PENN VALLEY **PA** 19072 (215) 667-1651
HAR ZION TEMPLE C HAGYS FORK ROAD AT HOLLOW ROAD........ PENN VALLEY **PA** 19072 (215) 667-1651
ADATH SHALOM C MARSHALL & RITNER STREETS .... PHILADELPHIA **PA** 19148 (215) 463-2224
ADATH TIKVAH MONTEFIORE CONGREGATION C HOFFNAGLE STREET & SUMMERDALE AVENUE .... PHILADELPHIA **PA** 19152 (215) 752-9191
AGUDATH ISRAEL OF PHILADELPHIA O 2401 N. 59TH STREET........ PHILADELPHIA **PA** 19131 (215) 473-4397
AHAVAS TORAH - RHAWNHURST TORAH CENTER O 7525 LORETTO AVENUE .... PHILADELPHIA **PA** 19111 (215) 725-3610
AHAVATH ISRAEL OF OAK LANE C 6735 N. 16TH STREET........ PHILADELPHIA **PA** 19126 (215) 924-7675
AHAVATH ISRAEL, CONGREGATION O 2302 NORTH MASCHER STREET .... PHILADELPHIA **PA** 19133
AITZ CHAIM SYNAGOGUE CENTER O 7600 SUMMERDALE AVENUE... PHILADELPHIA **PA** 19111 (215) 742-4870
ANSHEI VILNA, CONGREGATION O 509 PINE STREET .... PHILADELPHIA **PA** 19106
B'NAI ABRAHAM JEWISH CENTER C 9037 EASTVIEW ROAD........ PHILADELPHIA **PA** 19152
B'NAI ISRAEL OHAVE ZEDEK, CONGREGATION O 8201 CASTOR AVENUE .... PHILADELPHIA **PA** 19152 (215) 742-0400
B'NAI JESHURUN AHAVAS CHESED, CONGREGATION C 1001 PAPER MILL ROAD .... PHILADELPHIA **PA** 19118
B'NAI JESHURUN, CONGREGATION C 6826 ROOSEVELT BLVD .... PHILADELPHIA **PA** 19149
B'NAI JESHURUN, CONGREGATION O 2029 N. 33RD STREET .... PHILADELPHIA **PA** 19121 (215) 763-9616
B'NAI TORAH, CONGREGATION C 11082 KNIGHTS ROAD........ PHILADELPHIA **PA** 19154
B'NAI YITZHOK, CONGREGATION O B & ROOSEVELT BLVD .... PHILADELPHIA **PA** 19120 (215) 329-3712
BETH AHAVAH, CONGREGATION P.O. BOX 7566 .... PHILADELPHIA **PA** 19101 (215) 922-3872
BETH AMI, TEMPLE C 9201 BUSTLETON AVENUE........ PHILADELPHIA **PA** 19115 (215) 673-2511
BETH EMETH CONGREGATION C BUSTLETON & UNRUH AVENUE ... PHILADELPHIA **PA** 19149 (215) 338-1533
BETH HAMEDROSH OF OVERBROOK PARK O 7505 BROOKHAVEN ROAD........ PHILADELPHIA **PA** 19151 (215) 473-9671
BETH JACOB, CONGREGATION O 6018 LARCHWOOD AVENUE........ PHILADELPHIA **PA** 19143 (215) 747-3116
BETH MIDRASH HARAV, CONGREGATION O 7926 ALGON AVENUE ... PHILADELPHIA **PA** 19111 (215) 722-6161
BETH SOLOMON SUBURBAN OF SOMERTON O 11006 AUDUBON AVENUE .... PHILADELPHIA **PA** 19116 (215) 698-1180
BETH T'FILLAH OF OVERBROOK PARK, CONGREGATION C 7630 WOODBINE AVENUE .... PHILADELPHIA **PA** 19151 (215) 477-2415
BETH TEFILATH ISRAEL OF PENNYPACK PARK C 2605 WELSH ROAD .... PHILADELPHIA **PA** 19114 (215) 464-1242
BETH TIKVAH, CONGREGATION C 1001 PAPER MILL ROAD .... PHILADELPHIA **PA** 19118
BETH TORAH, TEMPLE R 608 WELSH ROAD .... PHILADELPHIA **PA** 19115 (215) 677-1555
BETH TOVIM, CONGREGATION O 5871 DREXEL ROAD .... PHILADELPHIA **PA** 19131 (215) 879-1100
BETH UZIEL, CONGREGATION C ROBAT STREET & WYOMING AVENUE .... PHILADELPHIA **PA** 19120 (215) 329-0250
BETH ZION BETH ISRAEL, TEMPLE C S.W. CORNER 18TH & SPRUCE STREETS........ PHILADELPHIA **PA** 19103 (215) 735-5148
BNAI ABRAHAM, CONGREGATION O 527 LOMBARD STREET .... PHILADELPHIA **PA** 19147 (215) 627-3123
BNAI ISRAEL OHEV ZEDEK O 8573 BUSTLETON AVENUE........ PHILADELPHIA **PA** 19152 (215) 742-0400
BNAI JACOB CONGREGATION - DERSHU TOV O 1147-45 GILHAM STREET .... PHILADELPHIA **PA** 19111 (215) 725-5181
BNAI YAACOV BELLS CORNER O 8574 BUSTLETON AVENUE .... PHILADELPHIA **PA** 19152
BNAI YOSHIA, CONGREGATION O 5000 WYNNEFIELD, KENWYN APARTMENTS 17-C .... PHILADELPHIA **PA** 19131
BRITH ISRAEL, CONGREGATION C ROOSEVELT BLVD. & D STREETS........ PHILADELPHIA **PA** 19120 (215) 329-2230
BUSTLETON SOMERTON SYNAGOGUE C TOMLINSON ROAD & FERNDALE STREET........ PHILADELPHIA **PA** 19116 (215) 677-6886
EMANU-EL, CONGREGATION C OLD YORK ROAD & STENTON AVENUE .... PHILADELPHIA **PA** 19141 (215) 548-1658
FAR NORTHEAST CONGREGATION O 11001 BUSTLETON AVENUE ... PHILADELPHIA **PA** 19116 (215) 464-6206
FOX CHASE JEWISH COMMUNITY CENTER C 7816 HALSTEAD........ PHILADELPHIA **PA** 19111 (215) 342-4722
GERMANTOWN JEWISH CENTER C LINCOLN DRIVE & ELLET STREET .... PHILADELPHIA **PA** 19119 (215) 814-1507
ISRAEL, TEMPLE - WYNNEFIELD C 901 WOODBINE AVENUE........ PHILADELPHIA **PA** 19131 (215) 877-3200
KESHER ISRAEL, CONGREGATION O 412 LOMBARD STREET........ PHILADELPHIA **PA** 19147
KNESES ISRAEL, CONGREGATION C 2101 FRIENDSHIP .... PHILADELPHIA **PA** 19144
LENAS HAZEDEK, CONGREGATION O WOODSIDE JEWISH CENTER, 2749 CRANSTON ROAD .... PHILADELPHIA **PA** 19131
LUBAVITCH HOUSE O 4032 SPRUCE STREET........ PHILADELPHIA **PA** 19104 (215) 222-3130
LUBAVITCHER CENTRE O 7622 CASTOR AVENUE .... PHILADELPHIA **PA** 19152 (215) 725-2030
MENORAH OF THE NORTHEAST JEWISH COMMUNITY CENTER, TEMPLE C ALGARD & TYSON AVENUE........ PHILADELPHIA **PA** 19135 (215) 624-9600
MENORAH, TEMPLE C 4301 TYSON AVENUE........ PHILADELPHIA **PA** 19149 (215) 624-9600
MIKVEH ISRAEL, CONGREGATION C 44 N. 4TH STREET .... PHILADELPHIA **PA** 19106 (215) 922-5446
NER ZEDEK-EZRATH ISRAEL C BUSTLETON & OAKMONT STREETS.. PHILADELPHIA **PA** 19152 (215) 728-1155
OHEL JACOB, CONGREGATION O CASTOR & LONGSHORE AVENUES .... PHILADELPHIA **PA** 19152 (215) 728-9488
OXFORD CIRCLE JEWISH COMMUNITY CENTER C 1009 UNRUH AVENUE........ PHILADELPHIA **PA** 19111 (215) 352-2400
PHILADELPHIA RECONSTRUCTIONIST HAVURAH C/O FRED HOFKIN........ PHILADELPHIA **PA** (215) 886-4780
RAIM AHUVIM, CONGREGATION O 5854 DREXEL ROAD .... PHILADELPHIA **PA** 19131 (215) 473-3634
RHAWNHURST JEWISH CENTER C SUMMERDALE AVENUE & HOFFNABLE .... PHILADELPHIA **PA** 19152
RODEPH SHALOM SUBURBAN CENTER R 8201 HIGH SCHOOL ROAD........ PHILADELPHIA **PA** 19117 (215) 635-2500
RODEPH SHALOM, CONGREGATION R 615 N. BROAD STREET .... PHILADELPHIA **PA** 19123 (215) 627-6747
RODEPH ZEDEK, TEMPLE O 10TH & RUSCOMB STREETS........ PHILADELPHIA **PA** 19141 (215) 329-1114
SHAARE SHAMAYIM, CONGREGATION C 9768 VERREE ROAD .... PHILADELPHIA **PA** 19115
SHAREI ELI, CONGREGATION O 8 & PORTER STREETS........ PHILADELPHIA **PA** 19148
SHOLOM, TEMPLE C LARGE STREET & ROOSEVELT BLVD .... PHILADELPHIA **PA** 19149 (215) 288-7600
SOCIETY HILL SYNAGOGUE-AGUDATH AHIM/OHR HADASH C 418 SPRUCE STREET .... PHILADELPHIA **PA** 19106 (215) 922-6590
SONS OF ISRAEL, CONGREGATION O SPRUCE & 6TH STREETS .... PHILADELPHIA **PA**
SYNAGOGUE OF THE TALMUDICAL YESHIVA O 6063 DREXEL ROAD .... PHILADELPHIA **PA** 19131
TIKVOH CHADOSHOH C 5364 W. CHECO AVENUE........ PHILADELPHIA **PA** 19138 (215) 438-1508
YM/YMHA BRANCH, CONGREGATION OF THE C 401 SOUTH BROAD STREET .... PHILADELPHIA **PA** 19147 (215) 545-4400
YAGDIL TORAH OF OAK LANE, CONGREGATION O 5701 NORTH 13 STREET .... PHILADELPHIA **PA** 19141
YOUNG ISRAEL OF OXFORD CIRCLE 6427 LARGE STREET .... PHILADELPHIA **PA** 19149 (215) 535-9328
YOUNG ISRAEL OF WYNNEFIELD 5300 WYNNEFIELD AVENUE .... PHILADELPHIA **PA** 19131 (215) 473-3511
YOUNG PEOPLES CONGREGATION SHARI ELI C 728 W. MOYAMENSING AVENUE WEST........ PHILADELPHIA **PA** 19148 (215) 339-9897
ZEMACH DAVID, CONGREGATION O 4900 NORTH 8TH STREET .... PHILADELPHIA **PA** 19120
ZION, TEMPLE R 1620 PINE ROAD .... PHILADELPHIA **PA** 19115
B'NAI JACOB, CONGREGATION C STARR & MANAVON STREETS........ PHOENIXVILLE **PA** 19460 (215) 933-5550
ADATH ISRAEL, CONGREGATION O 3257 WARD STREET .... PITTSBURGH **PA** 15213 (412) 682-6020
ADATH JESHURUN, CONG. - CONGREGATION KNESSETH ISRAEL O 5643 E. LIBERTY BLVD .... PITTSBURGH **PA** 15206 (412) 361-0173
B'NAI EMUNOH, CONGREGATION O 4315 MURRAY AVENUE........ PITTSBURGH **PA** 15217 (412) 521-1477
B'NAI ISRAEL, CONGREGATION C 327 N. NEGLEY AVENUE........ PITTSBURGH **PA** 15206 (412) 661-0252
BAIS YOSEF CONGREGATION O 6225 NICHOLSON STREET .... PITTSBURGH **PA** 15217 (412) 422-7437
BETH EL, CONGREGATION C 1900 COCHRAN ROAD .... PITTSBURGH **PA** 15220 (412) 561-1168
BETH HAMEDRASH HAGODOL-BETH JACOB CONGREGATION O 1230 COLWELL STREET........ PITTSBURGH **PA** 15219
BETH ISRAEL CENTER C P.O. BOX 10873, GILL HALL ROAD........ PITTSBURGH **PA** 15236 (412) 655-9253
BETH ISRAEL, CONGREGATION C 1023 REBECCA AVENUE........ PITTSBURGH **PA** 15221
BETH JACOB, CONGREGATION 1512 MURRAY AVENUE .... PITTSBURGH **PA** 15217
BETH SHALOM, CONGREGATION C 5915 BEACON STREET AT SHADY AVENUE .... PITTSBURGH **PA** 15217 (412) 421-2288
CHABAD HOUSE O 5867 MARLBOROUGH AVENUE .... PITTSBURGH **PA** 15217 (412) 422-4619
CHABAD-LUBAVITCH O 2100 WIGHTMAN .... PITTSBURGH **PA** 15217
CHABAD-LUBAVITCH O 5819 DOUGLAS STREET .... PITTSBURGH **PA** 15217
CHABAD-LUBAVITCH O 2410 5TH AVENUE .... PITTSBURGH **PA** 15213
CHOFETZ CHAIM, CONGREGATION O 5807 BEACON STREET .... PITTSBURGH **PA** 15217
DOR HADASH RE P.O. BOX 8223........ PITTSBURGH **PA** 15217 (412) 421-9594
EMANUEL, TEMPLE R 1520 BOWER HILL ROAD........ PITTSBURGH **PA** 15243 (412) 279-7600
INSTITUTE FOR TORAH STUDIES O 5706 BARTLETT STREET........ PITTSBURGH **PA** 15217 (412) 521-9514
KETHER TORAH, CONGREGATION O 5706 BARTLETT STREET .... PITTSBURGH **PA** 15217 (412) 521-9992
MACHSIKEI HADAS, CONGREGATION O 814 NORTH NEGLEY AVENUE........ PITTSBURGH **PA** 15206
NEW LIGHT CONGREGATION C 1700 BEECHWOOD BLVD .... PITTSBURGH **PA** 15217 (412) 421-1017
OHAVE ZEDECK OF OAKLAND, CONGREGATION O 356 CRAFT AVENUE .... PITTSBURGH **PA** 15213
PARKWAY JEWISH CENTER C 300 PRINCETON DRIVE .... PITTSBURGH **PA** 15235 (412) 823-4338
POALE ZEDECK, CONGREGATION O PHILLIPS & SHADY AVENUES........ PITTSBURGH **PA** 15217 (412) 421-9786
RODEF SHALOM CONGREGATION R FIFTH & MOREWOOD AVENUE........ PITTSBURGH **PA** 15213 (412) 621-6566
SHAARAY TEFILLAH, CONGREGATION O 5741 BARTLETT .... PITTSBURGH **PA** 15217 (412) 521-9911
SHAARE TORAH, CONGREGATION O 2319 MURRAY AVENUE........ PITTSBURGH **PA** 15217 (412) 421-8855
SHAARE ZEDEK, CONGREGATION O 5751 BARTLETT .... PITTSBURGH **PA** 15217
SINAI, TEMPLE R 5505 FORBES AVENUE........ PITTSBURGH **PA** 15217 (412) 421-9715
TORATH CHAIM, CONGREGATION O 729 NORTH NEGLEY AVENUE .... PITTSBURGH **PA** 15206
TREE OF LIFE C WILKINS & SHADY AVENUE........ PITTSBURGH **PA** 15217 (412) 521-6788
YOUNG ISRAEL OF GREATER PITTSBURGH 5751 BARTLETT STREET... PITTSBURGH **PA** 15217 (412) 421-9757
YOUNG PEOPLES SYNAGOGUE OF PITTSBURGH O 6401 FORBES AVENUE........ PITTSBURGH **PA** 15217
MERCY & TRUTH, CONGREGATION C 575 N. KEIM STREET........ POTTSTOWN **PA** 19464 (215) 326-1717
OHEB ZEDEK SYNAGOGUE CENTER C 2300 MAHANTONGO STREET .... POTTSVILLE **PA** 17901 (717) 622-4320
CHEVRA AGUDATH ACHIM O CHURCH STREET........ PUNXSUTAWNEY **PA** 15767
HAR ZION TEMPLE C 639 COUNTY LINE ROAD .... RADNOR **PA** 19087
BETH JACOB, CONGREGATION 955 NORTH 10TH STREET .... READING **PA** 19604 (215) 372-8508
KESHER ZION SYNAGOGUE C 1245 ECKERT & PERKIOMEN AVENUE .... READING **PA** 19602 (215) 372-3818
MORRIS HASSEL RELIGIOUS SCHOOL C 1245 PERKIOMEN AVENUE........ READING **PA** 19602 (215) 372-3818
OHEB SHOLOM, CONGREGATION R 13TH STREET & PERKIOMEN AVENUE .... READING **PA** 19602 (215) 373-4623
SHOMREI HABRITH CONGREGATION O P.O. BOX 1394, 2320 HAMPDEN BOULEVARD .... READING **PA** 19603 (215) 921-0881
OHEV SHALOM OF BUCKS COUNTY C 944 2ND STREET PIKE........ RICHBORO **PA** 18954 (215) 322-9595

BETH ISRAEL, TEMPLE 202 LINCOLN STREET — SAYRE PA 18840
BETH SHALOM, CONGREGATION O CLAY AVENUE & VINE STREET — SCRANTON PA 18510 (717) 346-0502
HARRIS CHAPEL-JEWISH HOME OF EAST PENNSYLVANIA T 1101 VINE STREET — SCRANTON PA 18510 (717) 344-6177
HESED, TEMPLE R LAKE SCRANTON ROAD & KNOX STREET — SCRANTON PA 18505 (717) 344-7201
ISRAEL, TEMPLE C GIBBON STREET & MONROE AVENUE — SCRANTON PA 18510 (717) 342-0350
MACHZIKEI HADAS, CONGREGATION 501 MADISON AVENUE — SCRANTON PA 18510 (717) 342-6271
MADISON AVENUE TEMPLE R LAKE SCRANTON ROAD & KNOX STREET — SCRANTON PA 18505
OHEV ZEDEK, CONGREGATION O 1432 MULBERRY STREET — SCRANTON PA 18510
PENN MONROE SYNAGOGUE 901 OLIVE STREET — SCRANTON PA 18510 (412) 347-3704
YOUNG ISRAEL OF SCRANTON 501 MADISON AVENUE — SCRANTON PA 18510 (717) 342-6271
BETH ISRAEL, TEMPLE R 840 HIGHLAND ROAD — SHARON PA 16146 (412) 346-4754
KEHILAT ISRAEL, CONGREGATION O 35 SOUTH JARDIN STREET — SHENANDOAH PA 17976
BETH OR R PENLLYN PIKE & DAGER ROAD — SPRING HOUSE PA 19477 (215) 646-5806
DELAWARE COUNTY JCC-CONGREGATION NER TAMID C 300 W. WOODLAND AVENUE, P.O. BOX 266 — SPRINGFIELD PA 19064 (215) 543-4241
ISRAEL, TEMPLE C WALLACE STREET — STROUDSBURG PA 18360 (717) 421-8781
BETH EL, CONGREGATION C 249 ARCH STREET — SUNBURY PA 17801 (717) 286-9197
B'NAI YOSHIA, CONGREGATION O DAVID DRIVE & JEROME ROAD — TREVOSE PA 19047 (215) 357-7131
ISRAEL, TEMPLE R 119 E. FAYETTE STREET — UNIONTOWN PA 15401 (412) 437-6431
TREE OF LIFE, CONGREGATION C P.O. BOX 264, PENNSYLVANIA AVENUE — UNIONTOWN PA 15401 (412) 437-6431
ISRAEL OF UPPER DARBY, TEMPLE C BYWOOD AVENUE & WALNUT STREET — UPPER DARBY PA 19082 (215) 352-2125
OHEV SHALOM, CONGREGATION C 2 CHESTER ROAD, P.O. BOX 157 — WALLINGFORD PA 19086 (215) 874-1465
WARREN HEBREW CONGREGATION O 112 CONEWANGO AVENUE, P.O. BOX 365 — WARREN PA 16365 (814) 723-7122
BETH ISRAEL, CONGREGATION C 265 NORTH AVENUE — WASHINGTON PA 15301 (215) 225-7080
OR SHALOM, THE CONSERVATIVE SYNAGOGUE OF THE MAIN LINE C P.O. BOX 476 — WAYNE PA 19087 (215) 296-3041
KESHER ISRAEL SYNAGOGUE C 206 NORTH CHURCH STREET, P.O. BOX 170 — WEST CHESTER PA 19380 (215) 696-7210
AGUDATH ACHIM, TEMPLE C — WEST PITTSTON PA 18643
TREE OF LIFE SFARD CONGREGATION C 2025 CYPRESS DRIVE — WHITE OAK PA 15131 (215) 673-0938
ANSHEI EMES, CONGREGATION O 13 SOUTH WELLES STREET — WILKES-BARRE PA 18702
ANSHEI SFARD, CONGREGATION 53 SOUTH WELLES STREET — WILKES-BARRE PA 18702
ISRAEL, TEMPLE C 236 RIVER STREET — WILKES-BARRE PA 18702 (717) 824-8927
OHAV ZEDEK SYNAGOGUE O 242 S. FRANKLIN STREET — WILKES-BARRE PA 18702 (717) 825-6619
BETH HA-SHOLOM R 425 CENTER STREET — WILLIAMSPORT PA 17701 (717) 323-7751
OHEV SHALOM CONGREGATION C CHERRY & BELMONT — WILLIAMSPORT PA 17701 (717) 322-4209
CONGREGATION OF THE RECONSTRUCTIONIST RABBINICAL COLLEGE CHURCH ROAD & GREENWOOD AVENUE — WYNCOTE PA 19095 (215) 576-0800
EAST LANE TEMPLE C 501 CEDARBROOK HILL — WYNCOTE PA 19095 (717) 884-4555
BETH HILLEL-BETH EL, TEMPLE C REMINGTON ROAD & LANCASTER AVENUE — WYNNEWOOD PA 19096 (215) 649-5300
MAIN LINE REFORM TEMPLE, BETH ELOHIM R 410 MONTGOMERY AVENUE — WYNNEWOOD PA 19096 (215) 649-7800
BETH TEFILAH-YEADON JEWISH COMMUNITY CENTER C WHITBY AVENUE & WEST COBBS CORK — YEADON PA 19050 (215) 625-2156
BETH ISRAEL, TEMPLE R 2090 HOLLYWOOD DRIVE — YORK PA 17403 (717) 843-2676
OHEV SHOLOM SYNAGOGUE C 2251 EASTERN BLVD — YORK PA 17402 (717) 755-2714
BETH SHALOM, TEMPLE R 900 PONCE DE LEON AVENUE — SANTURCE PR 00907
SHAAR SHALOM, CONGREGATION C 4880 NOTRE DAME BOULEVARD — CHOMEDAY QU H7W 1V4 (418) 688-8100
YOUNG ISRAEL OF CHOMEDY 1025 ELIZABETH BOULEVARD — CHOMEDY QU H7W 3J7 (514) 681-2571
BETH ZION CONGREGATION O 5740 HUDSON AVENUE — COTE ST. LUC QU H4W 2K5 (514) 489-8411
BETH ISRAEL CONGREGATION OF COTE ST. LUC O 6800 MACKLE ROAD — COTE ST. LUC QU H4W 1A4 (514) 487-1323
RINAT YISRAEL, CONGREGATION O 5775 AVENUE HUDSON — COTE ST. LUC QU H4W 2K7
TIFERETH BETH DAVID JERUSALEM SYNAGOGUE 6519 BAILY ROAD — COTE ST. LUC QU H4V 1A1 (514) 484-3841
BETH TIKVAH, CONGREGATION O 136 WESTPARK BOULEVARD — DOLLARD DES ORMEAUX QU H9A 2K2 (514) 683-5610
RODEPH SHALOM, TEMPLE R 96 FREDMIR BOULEVARD — DOLLARD DES ORMEAUX QU H9A 2R3 (514) 626-2173
ADATH ISRAEL CONGREGATION O 223 HARROW CRESCENT — HAMPSTEAD QU H3X 3X7 (514) 482-4252
YOUNG ISRAEL OF CHOMEDEY 1025 ELIZABETH BOULEVARD — LAVAL QU H7W 3J7 (514) 681-2571
ADATH ISRAEL, CONGREGATION O 223 HARROW CRESCENT — MONTREAL QU H3X 3X7 (514) 482-4252
BETH HAMEDRASH TIFERET ISRAEL O 4605 MACKENZIE STREET — MONTREAL QU H3W 1B2 (514) 733-5356
BETH HILLEL O 6230 COOLBROOKE AVENUE — MONTREAL QU H3X 2M8 (514) 487-1323
CHABAD HOUSE/LUBAVITCH YOUTH ORGANIZATION O 3429 PEEL STREET — MONTREAL QU H3A 1W7 (514) 842-6616
CHEVRA KADISHA BNAI JACOB, CONGREGATION O 5237 CLANRANALD AVENUE — MONTREAL QU H3X 2S5 (514) 482-3366
CHEVRA SHAAS ADATH JESHURUN O 5855 LAVOIE AVENUE — MONTREAL QU H3W 2K1 (514) 739-2448
CHEVRA THILIM PINSKER SYNAGOGUE O 1904 VAN HORNE AVENUE — MONTREAL QU H3S 2X3
CONGREGATION DORSHEI EMET, RECONSTRUCTIONIST SYNAGOGUE OF MONTREAL 18 CLEVE ROAD — MONTREAL QU H3X 1A6 (514) 486-9400
EMANU-EL BETH SHOLOM, TEMPLE R 4100 SHERBROOKE STREET WEST — MONTREAL QU H3Z 1A5 (514) 937-3575
SHAARE ZEDEK CONGREGATION C 5305 ROSEDALE AVENUE — MONTREAL QU H4V 2H7 (514) 484-1122
SHAARE ZION CONGREGATION C 5575 COTE ST. LUC ROAD — MONTREAL QU H3X 2C9 (514) 481-7727
SHEVET ACHIM CHAVERIM KOL YISRAEL O 5329 COTE DE NEIGES — MONTREAL QU H3S 1Z2
SHOMRIM LABOKER-BETH YEHUDAH-SHAARE O 5150 PLAMONDON AVENUE — MONTREAL QU H3W 1G1 (514) 731-6831
SPANISH & PORTUGUESE/SHEARITH ISRAEL O 4894 ST. KEVIN AVENUE — MONTREAL QU H3W 1P2 (514) 737-3695
YOUNG ISRAEL OF MONTREAL 6235 HILLSDALE ROAD — MONTREAL QU H3S 2M8 (514) 737-6589
YOUNG ISRAEL OF VAL ROYAL 2855 VICTOR DORE — MONTREAL QU H3M 1T1 (514) 334-4610
ZICHRON KODOSHIM, CONGREGATION O 5215 WESTBURY AVENUE — MONTREAL QU H3W 2W4 (514) 735-2113
BETH EL, CONGREGATION C 1000 LUCERNE ROAD — MOUNT ROYAL QU H3R 2H9 (418) 738-4766
AGUDATH ISRAEL OF MONTREAL O 1819 GLENDALE AVENUE, #3 — OUTREMOND QU H2V 1B3
BETH ORA, CONGREGATION O 2600 BADEAUX STREET — VILLE ST. LAURENT QU H4M 1M5 (514) 748-6559
YOUNG ISRAEL OF VAL ROYAL O 2855 VICTOR DORE STREET — VILLE ST. LAURENT QU H3M 1T1 (514) 334-4610
SHAAR HASHOMAYIM C 450 KENSINGTON AVENUE — WESTMOUNT QU H3Y 3A2 (514) 937-9471
BARRINGTON JEWISH CENTER R 147 COUNTY ROAD — BARRINGTON RI 02806
HABONIM, TEMPLE R 165 MEADOW ROAD — BARRINGTON RI 02806 (401) 245-6536
BETH TORAH, TEMPLE C 330 PARK AVENUE — CRANSTON RI 02905 (401) 785-1800
SINAI, TEMPLE R 30 HAGEN STREET — CRANSTON RI 02920 (401) 942-8350
TORAT YISRAEL, TEMPLE C 330 PARK AVENUE — CRANSTON RI 02905
SHALOM, TEMPLE C 221 VALLEY ROAD, P.O. BOX 372 — MIDDLETOWN RI 02840 (401) 846-9002
AHAVAS ACHIM, CONGREGATION O 136 KAY STREET — NEWPORT RI 02840
JESHUAT ISRAEL - TOURO SYNAGOGUE O 85 TOURO STREET — NEWPORT RI 02840 (401) 847-4794
OHAVE SHALOM, CONGREGATION O EAST AVENUE — PAWTUCKET RI 02860 (401) 722-3146
AHAVATH SHOLOM - SONS ZION - BETH SHOLOM O 275 CAMP STREET/ROCHAMBEAU AVENUE — PROVIDENCE RI 02906 (401) 331-9393
BETH DAVID ANSHE KOVNO, TEMPLE C 145 OAKLAND AVENUE — PROVIDENCE RI 02908
BETH EL, TEMPLE R 70 ORCHARD AVENUE — PROVIDENCE RI 02906 (401) 331-6070
BETH ISRAEL, TEMPLE C 155 NIAGARA STREET — PROVIDENCE RI 02907
BETH SHOLOM, TEMPLE C 275 CAMP STREET — PROVIDENCE RI 02906
CHABAD LUBAVITCH O 48 SAVOY STREET — PROVIDENCE RI 02906 (401) 273-7238
CHABAD-LUBAVITCH O 360 HOPE STREET — PROVIDENCE RI 02906
EMANU-EL, TEMPLE C 99 TAFT AVENUE — PROVIDENCE RI 02906 (401) 331-1616
MISHKON TFILOH, CONGREGATION O 203 SUMMIT AVENUE, P.O. BOX 9592 — PROVIDENCE RI 02906 (401) 521-1616
PROVIDENCE HEBREW DAY SCHOOL MINYAN O 450 ELMGROVE AVENUE — PROVIDENCE RI 02906 (401) 331-5327
SHAARE ZEDEK-SONS OF ABRAHAM, CONGREGATION O 688 BROAD STREET — PROVIDENCE RI 02907 (401) 751-4936
SONS OF JACOB, CONGREGATION O 24 DOUGLAS AVENUE — PROVIDENCE RI 02908 (401) 274-5260
BETH AM-BETH DAVID, TEMPLE C 40 GARDINER STREET — WARWICK RI 02888 (401) 463-7944
SHARAH ZEDEK, CONGREGATION C UNION STREET — WESTERLY RI 02891
B'NAI ISRAEL, CONGREGATION C 224 PROSPECT STREET — WOONSOCKET RI 02895 (401) 765-3651
ADATH JESHURUN CONGREGATION C GREENVILLE STREET N.W., P.O. BOX 398 — AIKEN SC 29801
B'NAI ISRAEL, TEMPLE R OAKLAND AVENUE, P.O. BOX 491 — ANDERSON SC 29622 (803) 226-0310
BETH ISRAEL C P.O. BOX 387 — BEAUFORT SC 29003
BETH EL, CONGREGATION R P.O. BOX 496 — CAMDEN SC 29020
BRITH SHOLOM-BETH ISRAEL O 182 RUTLEDGE AVENUE, P.O. BOX 2248 — CHARLESTON SC 29401 (803) 577-6599
EMANU-EL, SYNAGOGUE C 5 WINDSOR DRIVE — CHARLESTON SC 29407 (803) 571-3264
KAHAL KADOSH BETH ELOHIM R 90 HASELL STREET — CHARLESTON SC 29401 (803) 723-1090
BETH SHALOM, CONGREGATION C P.O. BOX 11482 — COLUMBIA SC 29211 (803) 782-2500
BETH SHOLOM, SYNAGOGUE C 5827 TRENHOLM ROAD — COLUMBIA SC 29206 (803) 782-2500
TREE OF LIFE CONGREGATION R 2701 HEYWARD STREET — COLUMBIA SC 29205 (803) 799-2485
OHAV SHALOM, CONGREGATION C CALHOUN STREET — DILLON SC 29536
BETH ISRAEL, TEMPLE R 316 PARK AVENUE, P.O. BOX 3008 — FLORENCE SC 29502 (803) 669-9724
BETH ELOHIM, TEMPLE R C/O SYLVAN ROSEN, ATTY. AT LAW, SCREVEN STREET — GEORGETOWN SC 29440 (803) 546-7925
BETH ISRAEL, CONGREGATION C 425 SUMMIT DRIVE, P.O. BOX 83 — GREENVILLE SC 29602 (803) 232-9031
ISRAEL, TEMPLE R 115 BUIST AVENUE — GREENVILLE SC 29609 (803) 233-2421
BETH OR C 107 HIRSCH STREET — KINGSTREE SC 29556 (803) 354-6425
EMANU-EL, TEMPLE C P.O. BOX 1171 — MYRTLE BEACH SC 29577 (803) 449-5552
B'NAI ISRAEL, CONGREGATION C 145 HEYWOOD AVENUE — SPARTANBURG SC 29302 (803) 582-7087
SINAI, TEMPLE R 11 CHURCH STREET, P.O. BOX 1673 — SUMTER SC 29150 (803) 773-2122
MOUNT SINAI, TEMPLE C P.O. BOX 506 — WALTERBORO SC 29488 (803) 549-5770
B'NAI ISAAC, CONGREGATION C P.O. BOX 91, 202 NORTH KLINE — ABERDEEN SD 57401 (605) 225-3404
HILLS, SYNAGOGUE OF THE R P.O. BOX 391 — RAPID CITY SD 57709 (605) 342-3875
MOUNTAIN ZION CONGREGATION R 523 W. 14TH STREET — SIOUX FALLS SD 57104 (605) 338-5454
SONS OF ISRAEL, CONGREGATION C 1207 SOUTH PHILLIPS AVENUE — SIOUX FALLS SD 57105
BETH JACOB, CONGREGATION 1640 VICTORIA AVENUE — REGINA SK S4P 0P7 (306) 527-8643
AGUDAS ISRAEL 715 MCKINNON AVENUE — SASKATOON SK S7H 2G2 (306) 527-8643
JEWISH COMMUNITY CENTRE, CONGREGATION AGUDAS ISRAEL C 715 MCKINNON AVENUE — SASKATOON SK S7H 2G2 (306) 343-7023
B'NAI SHOLOM, CONGREGATION R MT. TUCKER ADDITION, RT. 6 — BLOUNTVILLE TN 37617 (615) 323-7596
B'NAI SHOLOM, CONGREGATION C — BRISTOL TN 37620 (615) 669-9199
ADAS ISRAEL CONGREGATION R N. WASHINGTON STREET — BROWNSVILLE TN 38012
B'NAI ZION SYNAGOGUE C 114 MCBRIEN ROAD — CHATTANOOGA TN 37411 (615) 894-8900
BETH SHALOM CONGREGATION O 20 PISGAH AVENUE — CHATTANOOGA TN 37411 (615) 894-0801
MIZPAH CONGREGATION R 923 MCCALLIE AVENUE — CHATTANOOGA TN 37403 (615) 267-9771
B'NAI ISRAEL, CONGREGATION R P.O. BOX 278, 401 W. GRAND STREET — JACKSON TN 38301 (901) 427-6141
BETH EL, TEMPLE R P.O. BOX 3037, KINGSTON PIKE — KNOXVILLE TN 37919 (615) 524-3521
HESKA AMUNA SYNAGOGUE C 3811 KINGSTON PIKE — KNOXVILLE TN 37919 (615) 522-0701
ANSHEI SPHARD BETH EL EMETH CONGREGATION O 120 E. YATES ROAD N — MEMPHIS TN 38117 (901) 682-1611
BARON HIRSCH CONGREGATION O 5631 SHADY GROVE ROAD — MEMPHIS TN 38117 (901) 683-4767
BARON HIRSCH CONGREGATION O 1740 VOLLINTINE AVENUE — MEMPHIS TN 38107 (901) 274-3525
BETH SHALOM SYNAGOGUE C 482 S. MENDENHALL ROAD — MEMPHIS TN 38117 (901) 683-3591
ISRAEL, TEMPLE R 1376 EAST MASSEY ROAD — MEMPHIS TN 38119 (901) 761-3130
CHABAD-LUBAVITCH O 3600 WEST END AVENUE — NASHVILLE TN 37205
OHABAI SHOLOM, CONGREGATION R 5015 HARDING ROAD — NASHVILLE TN 37205 (615) 352-7620
RABBI ZALMAN POSNER O 3730 WHITLAND AVENUE — NASHVILLE TN 37205 (615) 385-3730
SHERITH ISRAEL, CONGREGATION O 3600 WEST END AVENUE — NASHVILLE TN 37205 (615) 292-6614
WEST END SYNAGOGUE, KHAL KODESH ADATH ISRAEL C 3814 WEST END AVENUE — NASHVILLE TN 37205 (615) 269-4592
BETH EL, CONGREGATION C W. MADISON LANE — OAK RIDGE TN 37830 (615) 483-4284
JEWISH CONGREGATION OF OAK RIDGE C P.O. BOX 3248, 101 WEST MADISON — OAK RIDGE TN 37830 (615) 483-3581

Congregation / Address	City	State	ZIP	Phone
MIZPAH, TEMPLE R 849 CHESTNUT, P.O. BOX 1283	ABILENE	**TX**	79604	(915) 672-8225
B'NAI ISRAEL, TEMPLE R 4316 ALBERT	AMARILLO	**TX**	79106	(806) 352-7191
BETH SHALOM OF ARLINGTON, CONGREGATION 1211 THANNISCH DRIVE	ARLINGTON	**TX**	76011	(817) 860-5448
AGUDAS ACHIM, CONGREGATION C 4300 BULL CREEK ROAD	AUSTIN	**TX**	78758	(512) 459-3287
BETH ISRAEL, TEMPLE R 3901 SHOAL CREEK BLVD	AUSTIN	**TX**	78756	(512) 454-6806
CHABAD HOUSE O 2101 NUECES AVENUE	AUSTIN	**TX**	78705	(512) 472-3900
EMANUEL, TEMPLE R P.O. BOX 423, 1120 BROADWAY	BEAUMONT	**TX**	77704	(713) 832-6131
KOL ISRAEL, CONGREGATION C P.O. BOX 423	BEAUMONT	**TX**	77704	
BRITH SHALOM, CONGREGATION C 4610 BELLAIRE BLVD	BELLAIRE	**TX**	77401	(713) 667-9201
BETH ISRAEL, TEMPLE 1317 CYPRESS STREET	BRECKENRIDGE	**TX**	76024	
BETH EL, TEMPLE R P.O. BOX 3851	BROWNSVILLE	**TX**	78520	(512) 542-5263
BETH SHALOM, CONGREGATION R P.O. BOX 3523	BRYAN	**TX**	77801	(817) 846-7313
B'NAI ISRAEL SYNAGOGUE C 3434 FORT WORTH STREET	CORPUS CHRISTI	**TX**	78411	(512) 855-7308
BETH EL, TEMPLE R 1315 CRAIG STREET, P.O. BOX 3214	CORPUS CHRISTI	**TX**	78404	(512) 883-0831
AGUDAS ACHIM, CONGREGATION O PARK AVENUE & 19TH STREET	CORSICANA	**TX**	75110	(214) 874-3045
BETH-EL, TEMPLE R 208 SOUTH 15TH STREET	CORSICANA	**TX**	75110	
AGUDAS ACHIM, CONGREGATION 5810 FOREST LANE	DALLAS	**TX**	75230	
ANSHAI EMET, CONGREGATION C/O JCC, 7900 NORTHAVEN ROAD	DALLAS	**TX**	75230	(214) 739-2737
BETH TORAH, CONGREGATION 720 LOOKOUT DRIVE	DALLAS	**TX**		(214) 234-1542
CHABAD-LUBAVITCH O 5175 PLACID WAY PLACE	DALLAS	**TX**	75234	(214) 991-5031
EMANU-EL, TEMPLE R 8500 HILLCREST ROAD	DALLAS	**TX**	75225	(214) 368-3613
SHALOM, TEMPLE R 6930 ALPHA ROAD	DALLAS	**TX**	75240	(214) 661-1810
SHEARITH ISRAEL, CONGREGATION C 9401 DOUGLAS AVENUE	DALLAS	**TX**	75225	(214) 361-6606
TIFERET ISRAEL CONGREGATION O 10909 HILLCREST ROAD	DALLAS	**TX**	75230	(214) 691-3611
YOUNG ISRAEL OF DALLAS 1450 PRESTON FOREST SQUARE SUITE 218	DALLAS	**TX**	75230	(214) 934-1263
B'NAI ZION, CONGREGATION C 210-220 E. CLIFF DRIVE	EL PASO	**TX**	79902	(915) 532-3137
MOUNT SINAI, TEMPLE R 4408 NORTH STANTON	EL PASO	**TX**	79902	(915) 532-5959
AHAVATH SHOLOM C 1600 WEST MYRTLE	FORT WORTH	**TX**	76401	
AHAVATH SHOLOM, CONGREGATION T 4050 SOUTH HULEN	FORT WORTH	**TX**	76109	(817) 923-7379
BETH EL, CONGREGATION R 207 WEST BROADWAY	FORT WORTH	**TX**	76104	(817) 332-7141
B'NAI ISRAEL, CONGREGATION R 3008 AVENUE O	GALVESTON	**TX**	77550	(713) 765-5796
BETH JACOB, CONGREGATION C 2401 AVENUE K	GALVESTON	**TX**	77550	(713) 762-7267
ISRAEL OF SCHULENBURG, TEMPLE R C/O MR. ARMAND G. SCHWARTZ, P.O. BOX 385	HALLETSVILLE	**TX**	77964	(713) 743-3864
BETH ISRAEL, TEMPLE R 1702 EAST JACKSON, P.O. BOX 611	HARLINGEN	**TX**	78550	
BETH AM, CONGREGATION C 1431 BRITTMOORE ROAD	HOUSTON	**TX**	77043	(713) 461-7725
BETH ISRAEL, CONGREGATION R 5600 N. BRAESWOOD BLVD	HOUSTON	**TX**	77906	(713) 771-6221
BETH RAMBAM O 11333 BRAESRIDGE DRIVE	HOUSTON	**TX**	77071	(713) 723-3030
BETH YESHURUN, CONGREGATION C 4525 BEECHNUT	HOUSTON	**TX**	77906	(713) 666-1881
CHABAD-LUBAVITCH CENTER O 10900 FONDREN ROAD	HOUSTON	**TX**	77096	(713) 777-2000
CHABAD HOUSE OF TEXAS MEDICAL CENTER O 1955 UNIVERSITY BOULEVARD	HOUSTON	**TX**	77030	(713) 522-2004
EMANU-EL, CONGREGATION R 1500 SUNSET BLVD	HOUSTON	**TX**	77005	(713) 529-5771
HOUSTON CONGREGATION FOR REFORM JUDAISM R P.O. BOX 27151	HOUSTON	**TX**	77027	(713) 782-4162
JEWISH COMMUNITY NORTH P.O. BOX 90448	HOUSTON	**TX**	77090	(713) 376-0016
SHAAR HASHALOM, CONGREGATION C 16020 EL CAMINO REAL	HOUSTON	**TX**	77062	(713) 488-5861
SINAI, TEMPLE R P.O. BOX 42888, SUITE 111	HOUSTON	**TX**	77042	(713) 496-5950
UNITED ORTHODOX SYNAGOGUES OF HOUSTON O 9001 GREENWILLOW	HOUSTON	**TX**	77096	(713) 723-3850
YOUNG ISRAEL OF HOUSTON 11523 BOB WHITE	HOUSTON	**TX**	77056	(713) 728-2316
AGUDAS ACHIM C LAREDO & MALINCHE STREETS	LAREDO	**TX**	78040	(713) 723-4435
B'NAI ISRAEL, TEMPLE R C/O MRS DEAN SANDITEN, 2120 MUSSER STREET	LAREDO	**TX**	78040	
EMANU-EL TEMPLE R 1205 EDEN DRIVE, P.O. BOX 423	LONGVIEW	**TX**	75601	(214) 753-6512
SHAARETH ISRAEL, CONGREGATION R P.O. BOX 6192, 1706 23RD STREET	LUBBOCK	**TX**	79413	(806) 744-6084
MOSES MONTEFIORE, TEMPLE R P.O. BOX 1146	MARSHALL	**TX**	75670	
EMANUEL, TEMPLE R 1410 REDWOOD, P.O. BOX 896	MCALLEN	**TX**	78501	(512) 686-9432
RODEF SHALOM, CONGREGATION R 3984 PROCTER STREET	PORT ARTHUR	**TX**	77640	(713) 985-7616
BETH TORAH, CONGREGATION C 810 LOOKOUT DRIVE	RICHARDSON	**TX**	75080	(214) 234-1541
BETH TSIYON, CONGREGATION 401 CANYON CREEK	RICHARDSON	**TX**	75080	
AGUDAS ACHIM, CONGREGATION C 1201 DONALDSON AVENUE	SAN ANTONIO	**TX**	78228	(512) 736-4216
BETH EL, TEMPLE R 211 BELKNAP PLACE	SAN ANTONIO	**TX**	78212	(512) 733-9135
CHABAD-LUBAVITCH O 201 WEST CRAIG PLACE, UNIT 6	SAN ANTONIO	**TX**	78212	(512) 735-4656
NEW JEWISH CONGREGATION OF SAN ANTONIO R C/O DR. D. SHAPIRO, 9214 OLD HOMESTEAD	SAN ANTONIO	**TX**	78320	
RODFEI SHOLOM, CONGREGATION O 115 EAST LAUREL STREET	SAN ANTONIO	**TX**	78212	(512) 227-3603
ISRAEL, TEMPLE R 508 BAUMGARTEN STREET	SCHULENBURG	**TX**	78956	
BETH EMETH, TEMPLE R 304 NORTH RUSK STREET	SHERMAN	**TX**	75090	(214) 892-9326
MOUNT SINAI CONGREGATION R 1310 WALNUT STREET	TEXARKANA	**TX**	75501	(214) 792-2394
AHAVATH ACHIM C 1014 WEST HOUSTON STREET	TYLER	**TX**	75702	(214) 597-4284
BETH EL, TEMPLE R 1102 SOUTH AUGUSTA	TYLER	**TX**	75701	(214) 597-2917
B'NAI ISRAEL, TEMPLE R P.O. BOX 2088	VICTORIA	**TX**	77901	(512) 578-5140
AGUDATH JACOB C 4925 HILLCREST DRIVE	WACO	**TX**	76710	(817) 772-1451
RODEF SHOLOM, TEMPLE R 1717 NORTH 41ST STREET	WACO	**TX**	76707	(817) 754-3703
SHEARITH ISRAEL, CONGREGATION C 219 HOLLIS STREET	WHARTON	**TX**	77488	
HOUSE OF JACOB, CONGREGATION C 2624 AMHERST	WICHITA FALLS	**TX**	76308	(817) 692-2326
ISRAEL, TEMPLE R P.O. BOX 952	WICHITA FALLS	**TX**	76307	
KOL AMI, CONGREGATION C & R 2425 EAST HERITAGE WAY	SALT LAKE CITY	**UT**	84109	(801) 484-1501
AGUDAS ACHIM CONGREGATION C 2908 VALLEY DRIVE	ALEXANDRIA	**VA**	22302	(703) 548-4122
BETH EL HEBREW CONGREGATION R 3830 SEMINARY ROAD	ALEXANDRIA	**VA**	22304	(703) 370-9400
ARLINGTON-FAIRFAX JEWISH CONGREGATION C 2920 ARLINGTON BOULEVARD	ARLINGTON	**VA**	22204	(703) 979-4466
BETH ISRAEL, CONGREGATION R THIRD & JEFFERSON STREETS	CHARLOTTESVILLE	**VA**	22902	(804) 295-6382
AITZ CHAYIM, CONGREGATION O 168 STATFORD PLACE	DANVILLE	**VA**	24541	
BETH SHOLOM, TEMPLE R 127 SUTHERLIN AVENUE	DANVILLE	**VA**	24541	(804) 792-3489
FRIENDS OF LUBAVITCH O 3924 PERSIMMON DRIVE	FAIRFAX	**VA**	22031	(703) 323-0233
MAGEN DAVID, CONGREGATION 9112 BOLLER AVENUE	FAIRFAX	**VA**	22031	
OLAM TIKVAH, CONGREGATION C 3800 GLENBROOK ROAD	FAIRFAX	**VA**	22030	(703) 978-3333
RODEF SHALOM, TEMPLE R 2100 WESTMORELAND STREET	FALLS CHURCH	**VA**	22043	(703) 532-2217
FORT BELVOIR JEWISH CONGREGATION	FORT BELVOIR	**VA**	22060	(703) 664-1218
BETH SHOLOM, TEMPLE R P.O. BOX 481	FREDERICKSBURG	**VA**	22404	(703) 373-4834
B'NAI ISRAEL SYNAGOGUE O 3116 KECOUGHTAN ROAD	HAMPTON	**VA**	23661	
RODEF SHOLOM, CONGREGATION C 318 WHEALTON ROAD	HAMPTON	**VA**	23666	(804) 826-5894
BETH EL, CONGREGATION R P.O. BOX 845	HARRISONBURG	**VA**	22801	(703) 434-2744
AGUDATH SHOLOM, CONGREGATION R P.O. BOX 2262	LYNCHBURG	**VA**	24501	(804) 846-0739
OHEV ZION CONGREGATION R 801 PARKVIEW AVENUE	MARTINSVILLE	**VA**	24112	(703) 632-2828
ADATH JESHURUN SYNAGOGUE O 1815 CHESTNUT AVENUE	NEWPORT NEWS	**VA**	23607	(804) 245-7485
RODEF SHOLOM, TEMPLE C P.O. BOX 5726	NEWPORT NEWS	**VA**	23605	(804) 826-5894
SINAI, TEMPLE R 11620 WARWICK BOULEVARD	NEWPORT NEWS	**VA**	23601	(804) 596-8352
B'NAI ISRAEL, CONGREGATION O 420 SPOTSWOOD AVENUE	NORFOLK	**VA**	23517	(804) 627-7358
BETH EL C 422 SHIRLEY AVENUE, P.O. BOX 11206	NORFOLK	**VA**	23517	(804) 625-7821
ISRAEL, TEMPLE C 7255 GRANBY STREET	NORFOLK	**VA**	23505	(804) 489-4550
MIKVE KODESH CONGREGATION O P.O. BOX 1035	NORFOLK	**VA**	23501	
OHEV SHOLOM, TEMPLE R 530 RALEIGH AVENUE, STOCKLEY GARDENS	NORFOLK	**VA**	23507	(804) 625-4295
BRITH ACHIM, CONGREGATION C 314 SOUTH BOULEVARD	PETERSBURG	**VA**	23805	(804) 732-3968
GOMLEY CHESED CONGREGATION C 3110 STERLING POINT DRIVE	PORTSMOUTH	**VA**	23703	(804) 484-1019
SINAI, TEMPLE R 4401 HATTON POINT ROAD	PORTSMOUTH	**VA**	23703	(804) 484-1730
NORTH VIRGINIA HEBREW CONGREGATION R 1441 WIEHLE AVENUE, P.O. BOX 2758	RESTON	**VA**	22090	(703) 437-7733
B'NAI SHALOM CONGREGATION C 6007 WEST CLUB LANE	RICHMOND	**VA**	23226	(804) 270-7011
BETH AHABAH, CONGREGATION R 1111 WEST FRANKLIN STREET	RICHMOND	**VA**	23220	(804) 358-6757
BETH EL, TEMPLE C 3330 GROVE AVENUE	RICHMOND	**VA**	23221	(804) 355-3564
BETH SHOLOM, CONGREGATION R 5100 MONUMENT AVENUE	RICHMOND	**VA**	23223	
KENESETH BETH ISRAEL CONGREGATION O 6300 PATTERSON AVENUE	RICHMOND	**VA**	23226	(804) 288-7953
KOL EMES, CONGREGATION O 4811 PATTERSON AVENUE	RICHMOND	**VA**	23226	(804) 353-5831
LUBAVITCH CENTER O 212 GASKINS ROAD	RICHMOND	**VA**	23233	(804) 740-2000
OR AMI, CONGREGATION R 3406 NORTH HUGUENOT ROAD	RICHMOND	**VA**	23226	(804) 272-0017
BETH ISRAEL SYNAGOGUE C 920 FRANKLIN ROAD SW	ROANOKE	**VA**	24016	(703) 343-0289
EMANUEL, TEMPLE R 1163 PERSINGER ROAD SW	ROANOKE	**VA**	24015	(703) 342-3378
HOUSE OF ISRAEL, TEMPLE R MOUNTAINSIDE FARMS, RT. 1 BOX 1896	STAUNTON	**VA**	24401	(703) 885-6878
CHABAD LUBAVITCH O 372 SOUTH INDEPENDENCE BOULEVARD	VIRGINIA BEACH	**VA**	23452	(804) 490-9699
EMANUEL, TEMPLE C 25TH STREET & BALTIC AVENUE	VIRGINIA BEACH	**VA**	23451	(804) 428-2591
KEHILLAT BET HAMIDRASH C 740 ARTHUR AVENUE	VIRGINIA BEACH	**VA**	23452	(804) 424-9715
BETH EL CONGREGATION R 528 FAIRMONT AVENUE, P.O. BOX 1041	WINCHESTER	**VA**	22601	(703) 667-1043
NER TAMID, CONGREGATION R P.O. BOX 54	WOODBRIDGE	**VA**	22194	(703) 494-3251
HEBREW CONGREGATION O CHARLOTTE AMALIE	ST. THOMAS	**VI**	00801	
HEBREW CONGREGATION OF ST. THOMAS R P.O. BOX 266	ST. THOMAS	**VI**	00801	(809) 774-4312
BETH EL, TEMPLE C 151 NORTH STREET	BENNINGTON	**VT**	05201	
CHABAD-LUBAVITCH O 158 NORTH WILLARD STREET	BURLINGTON	**VT**	05401	(902) 658-7612
OHAVI ZEDEK SYNAGOGUE 188 NORTH PROSPECT STREET	BURLINGTON	**VT**	05401	(802) 864-0128
RUTLAND JEWISH CENTER C 96 GROVE STREET	RUTLAND	**VT**	05701	(802) 773-3455
SINAI, TEMPLE R 899 DORSET STREET	SOUTH BURLINGTON	**VT**	05401	(802) 862-5125
JEWISH CONGREGATION 55 HIGH STREET	ST. ALBANS	**VT**	05478	
BETH EL, CONGREGATION 76 RAILROAD STREET	ST. JOHNSBURY	**VT**	05819	
BETH ISRAEL, TEMPLE R 1801 SHERWOOD LANE	ABERDEEN	**WA**	98520	(206) 532-7485
DE HIRSCH SINAI, TEMPLE R 556 124TH NORTHEAST	BELLEVUE	**WA**	98005	(206) 454-5085
BETH ISRAEL, CONGREGATION C 1320 LAKEWAY DRIVE, APARTMENT 127	BELLINGHAM	**WA**	98225	
B'NAI TORAH, TEMPLE R 6195 92ND AVENUE SE	MERCER ISLAND	**WA**	98040	(206) 232-7243
HERZL-NER TAMID CONSERVATIVE CONGREGATION C P.O. BOX 574, 3700 EAST MERCER WAY	MERCER ISLAND	**WA**	98040	(206) 232-8555
BETH HATFILOH, TEMPLE C/R 802 SOUTH JEFFERSON	OLYMPIA	**WA**	98501	(206) 753-9986
BETH SHOLOM, CONGREGATION P.O. BOX 761	RICHLAND	**WA**	99352	(509) 943-9457
BETH AM, TEMPLE R 8015 27TH AVENUE NORTHEAST	SEATTLE	**WA**	98115	(206) 525-0915
BETH SHALOM, CONGREGATION C 6800 35TH AVENUE NORTHEAST	SEATTLE	**WA**	98115	(206) 524-0075
BIKUR CHOLIM MACHZIKAY HADATH CONGREGATION O 5145 SOUTH MORGAN STREET	SEATTLE	**WA**	98118	(206) 723-0970
CHABAD HOUSE O 4541 19TH AVENUE NORTHEAST	SEATTLE	**WA**	98105	(206) 527-1411
CHABAD-LUBAVITCH O 5220 20TH AVENUE	SEATTLE	**WA**	98105	
DE HIRSCH SINAI, TEMPLE R 1511 EAST PIKE STREET	SEATTLE	**WA**	98122	(206) 323-8486
EMANUEL CONGREGATION O 3412 NE 65TH STREET	SEATTLE	**WA**	98115	(206) 525-1055
EZRA BESSAROTH, CONGREGATION O 5217 SOUTH BRANDON STREET	SEATTLE	**WA**	98118	(206) 722-5500
SEPHARDIC BIKUR HOLIM CONGREGATION O 6500 52ND AVENUE SOUTH	SEATTLE	**WA**	98118	(206) 723-3028
YESHIVA GEDOLAH T 5220 20TH AVENUE NORTHEAST	SEATTLE	**WA**	98105	(206) 527-1100
BETH SHALOM, TEMPLE C P.O. BOX 8013, EAST 1322 30TH AVENUE	SPOKANE	**WA**	99203	(509) 747-3304
BETH EL, TEMPLE R 5975 SOUTH 12TH STREET	TACOMA	**WA**	98465	(206) 564-7101
MOSES MONTEFIORE SYNAGOGUE C 3131 NORTH MEADE STREET	APPLETON	**WI**	54911	(414) 733-1848
ZION, CONGREGATION R 1751 NORTH DIVISION	APPLETON	**WI**	54911	
B'NAI ABRAHAM R P.O. BOX 964	BELOIT	**WI**	53511	(608) 364-4916
SHOLOM, TEMPLE C 1223 EMERY STREET	EAU CLAIRE	**WI**	54701	(715) 834-4667
BETH ISRAEL, TEMPLE C	FOND DU LAC	**WI**	54935	
CHABAD - NORTH SHORE O 7811 NORTH FAIRCHILD ROAD	FOX POINT	**WI**	53217	(414) 351-4119
CNESSES ISRAEL, CONGREGATION C P.O. BOX 1252, 222 SOUTH BAIRD STREET	GREEN BAY	**WI**	54301	(414) 437-4841
B'NAI ZEDEK, CONGREGATION C 1600 56TH STREET	KENOSHA	**WI**	53140	
BETH HILLEL TEMPLE R LIBRARY SQUARE	KENOSHA	**WI**	53140	(414) 654-2716
SONS OF ABRAHAM, CONGREGATION O 1820 MAIN STREET	LA CROSSE	**WI**	54601	(608) 784-2708
BETH EL, TEMPLE R 2702 ARBOR DRIVE	MADISON	**WI**	53711	(608) 238-3123
BETH ISRAEL CENTER C 1406 MOUND STREET	MADISON	**WI**	53711	(608) 256-7763
CHABAD HOUSE O 613 HOWARD PLACE	MADISON	**WI**	53703	(608) 251-6022
ANSHE POALE ZEDEK, CONGREGATION O 1422 WASHINGTON STREET	MANITOWOC	**WI**	54220	
MONTEFIORE & SONS OF JACOB, CONGREGATION O P.O. BOX 224	MARINETTE	**WI**	54143	
AGUDAS ACHIM, CONGREGATION O 5820 WEST BURLEIGH STREET	MILWAUKEE	**WI**	53210	(414) 447-9239

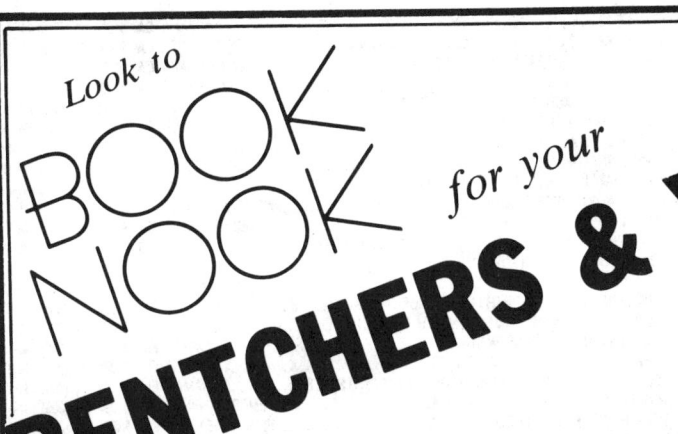

Name / Address	City	State	Zip	Phone
ANSHAI LEBOWITZ, CONGREGATION O 3100 NORTH 52ND STREET	MILWAUKEE	**WI**	53216	
ANSHE EMETH, CONGREGATION C 8057 WEST APPLETON AVENUE	MILWAUKEE	**WI**	53218	(414) 463-7680
ANSHE SFARD, CONGREGATION T 3447 NORTH 51ST BOULEVARD	MILWAUKEE	**WI**	53216	(414) 444-9640
BETH EL NER TAMID SYNAGOGUE C 4650 NORTH PORT WASHINGTON	MILWAUKEE	**WI**	53212	(414) 332-8602
BETH ISRAEL, CONGREGATION C 6880 NORTH GREEN BAY AVENUE	MILWAUKEE	**WI**	53209	(414) 352-7310
BETH JEHUDAH, CONGREGATION O 2700 NORTH 54TH STREET	MILWAUKEE	**WI**	53210	
BNAI JACOB, CONGREGATION O 3056 NORTH 55TH STREET	MILWAUKEE	**WI**	53210	
CHABAD HOUSE O 3109 NORTH LAKE DRIVE	MILWAUKEE	**WI**	53211	(414) 962-0566
EMANU-EL B'NE JESHURUN, CONGREGATION R 2419 EAST KENWOOD BOULEVARD, P.O. BOX 11698	MILWAUKEE	**WI**	53211	(414) 964-4100
LAKE PARK SYNAGOGUE O C/O SHEFFEY - 2905 NORTH SUMMIT	MILWAUKEE	**WI**	53211	(414) 332-4970
MENORAH, TEMPLE C 9363 NORTH 76TH STREET	MILWAUKEE	**WI**	53223	(414) 355-1120
SHALOM, CONGREGATION R 7630 NORTH SANTA MONICA BOULEVARD	MILWAUKEE	**WI**	53217	(414) 352-9288
SINAI, CONGREGATION R 8223 NORTH PORT WASHINGTON ROAD	MILWAUKEE	**WI**	53217	(414) 352-2970
B'NAI ISRAEL, TEMPLE R 1121 ALGOMA BOULEVARD	OSHKOSH	**WI**	54901	(414) 235-4270
BETH ISRAEL SINAI CONGREGATION C 944 SOUTH MAIN STREET	RACINE	**WI**	53403	(414) 633-7093
BETH EL, CONGREGATION C 1007 NORTH AVENUE	SHEBOYGAN	**WI**	53081	(414) 452-5828
BETH EL OF SUPERIOR HEBREW CONGREGATION, TEMPLE C 603 FAXON AVENUE	SUPERIOR	**WI**	54880	(715) 392-4279
EMANUEL, CONGREGATION R 830 WEST MORELAND BOULEVARD	WAUKESHA	**WI**	53186	
MOUNT SINAI CONGREGATION R 622 4TH STREET	WAUSAU	**WI**	54401	(715) 845-7461
BETH EL, TEMPLE R BELLVIEW LANE, P.O. BOX 1363	BECKLEY	**WV**	25801	(304) 253-9421
AHAVATH SHOLOM, CONGREGATION R 632 ALBEMARLE STREET	BLUEFIELD	**WV**	24701	(304) 325-9372
B'NAI JACOB, CONGREGATION O VIRGINIA & ELIZABETH STREETS	CHARLESTON	**WV**	25311	
TREE OF LIFE SYNAGOGUE C 5TH & WEST PIKE STREETS	CLARKSBURG	**WV**	26301	(304) 622-3453
FAIRMONT JEWISH COMMUNITY CENTER R 216 BROADVIEW AVENUE	FAIRMONT	**WV**	26554	(304) 363-5630
B'NAI ISRAEL, CONGREGATION C 900 9TH STREET, P.O. BOX 847	HUNTINGTON	**WV**	25712	
B'NAI SHOLOM CONGREGATION C & R P.O. BOX 2004, 10TH AVENUE & 10TH STREET	HUNTINGTON	**WV**	25720	(304) 522-2980
OHEV SHOLOM, TEMPLE R P.O. BOX 2004	HUNTINGTON	**WV**	25720	
B'NAI EL, CONGREGATION R P.O. BOX 899	LOGAN	**WV**	25601	(304) 752-2275
BETH JACOB, CONGREGATION R 126 WEST MARTIN STREET, P.O. BOX 1147	MARTINSBURG	**WV**	25401	(304) 267-4347
TREE OF LIFE, TEMPLE R P.O. BOX 791	MORGANTOWN	**WV**	26505	
B'NAI ISRAEL, CONGREGATION R 1703 20TH STREET	PARKERSBURG	**WV**	26101	(304) 428-1192
BETH ISRAEL, CONGREGATION O 500 BROOKLINE DRIVE	WEIRTON	**WV**	26062	
EMANUEL CONGREGATION R	WELCH	**WV**	24801	(304) 436-4768
ISRAEL, SYNAGOGUE OF C 115 1/2 EDGINTON LANE	WHEELING	**WV**	26003	
SHALOM, TEMPLE-CONGREGATION LESHEM SHOMAYIM R 23 BETHANY PIKE	WHEELING	**WV**	26003	(304) 233-4870
B'NAI ISRAEL R P.O. BOX 21	WILLIAMSON	**WV**	25661	(304) 235-2947
TEMPLE BETH EL 4105 SOUTH POPLAR	CASPER	**WY**	82601	(307) 237-2330
MT. SINAI CONGREGATION 2610 PIONEER AVENUE	CHEYENNE	**WY**	82001	(307) 634-3052

TALLITOT & KIPPOT

Name / Address	City	State	Zip	Phone
ROSA FISCHER MISRACH 1709 SHATTUCK AVENUE	BERKELEY	**CA**	94709	(415) 849-2089
DEBORAH PESSA OLES 3649 JAMINE AVENUE	LOS ANGELES	**CA**	90034	(213) 837-9898
IRENE TABATSKY 231 PARKER STREET	MANCHESTER	**CT**	06040	(203) 647-9578
JUDY TSUKROFF, SUN PORCH WEAVING STUDIO	NORFOLK	**CT**	06058	
MR. E. E.HOISINGTON 1227 S.E. 12TH STERRACE	DEERFIELD BEACH	**FL**	33441	(305) 421-6704
ATELIER D'ART DONA - HANDWOVEN, CUSTOM DESIGNED 927 RED ROAD	TEANECK	**NJ**	07666	(201) 692-9513
ALTMAN. S. 193 BROADWAY	BROOKLYN	**NY**	11211	(718) 384-7528
BORO PARK JUDAICA 5413 NEW UTRECHT AVENUE	BROOKLYN	**NY**	11219	(718) 435-4465
CHUSTER TALIS MANUFACTURING CO. 141 DIVISION STREET	BROOKLYN	**NY**	11211	(718) 384-3146
MAZEL SKULL CAPS 3823 13TH AVENUE	BROOKLYN	**NY**	11218	(718) 435-3288
WEISS'S TALIS & TEFILIN BAGS 541 WYTHE AVENUE	BROOKLYN	**NY**	11211	(718) 387-7742
BOOK NOOK PUBLICATIONS 1525 CENTRAL AVENUE	FAR ROCKAWAY	**NY**	11691	(718) 327-0163
TIRTZAH, TALITOT FOR WOMEN BOX 220-M	GUILDERLAND	**NY**	12084	
KIPPAH ART 141-46 PERSHING CRESCENT	JAMAICA	**NY**	11435	(718) 657-0929
RIKMAH	LONG BEACH	**NY**	11561	(718) 377-2466
SIMCHA SHOPPE, THE 18 HILLTOP LANE	MONSEY	**NY**	10952	(914) 352-4543
CHARISMA, MANUFACTURER OF SKULL CAPS 3 BURROWS COURT	NEW CITY	**NY**	10956	(914) 354-3103
BEN ARI ARTS LTD. 11 AVENUE A	NEW YORK	**NY**	10009	(212) 677-4730
H & M SKULL CAP (OFFICE) 61 HESTER STREET	NEW YORK	**NY**	10002	(212) 777-2280
H & M SKULL CAP MANUFACTURING CO. 46 HESTER STREET	NEW YORK	**NY**	10002	(212) 475-1910
J. LEVINE CO. - LOWER EAST SIDE 58 ELDRIDGE STREET	NEW YORK	**NY**	10002	(212) 966-4460
J. LEVINE CO. - MIDTOWN STORE 5 WEST 30TH STREET	NEW YORK	**NY**	10001	(212) 695-6888
MIRIAM MANUFACTURING COMPANY 48 CANAL STREET	NEW YORK	**NY**	10002	(212) 925-9272
MUNKACZER TALIS MANUFACTURING 87 EAST BROADWAY	NEW YORK	**NY**	10002	(212) 267-0540
RONA RONES - THE LOOM ROOM 607 WEST END AVENUE	NEW YORK	**NY**	10024	(212) 873-5276

Name / Address	City	State	Zip	Phone
S & W SKULL CAP COMPANY 45 ESSEX STREET	NEW YORK	NY	10002	(212) 673-3330
TALITNIA DISTRIBUTORS 48 CANAL STREET	NEW YORK	NY	10002	(212) 966-5060
ZIONTALIS MANUFACTURING COMPANY, INC. 48 ELDRIDGE STREET	NEW YORK	NY	10002	(212) 925-8558
INVITATIONS PLUS 600 WEST 246TH STREET	RIVERDALE	NY	10471	(212) 548-3900
INVITATIONS PLUS 600 WEST 246TH STREET	RIVERDALE	NY	10471	(800) INV-PLUS
ANITA FREIMARK 7054 ROUNDELAY ROAD, NORTH	REYNOLDSBURG	OH	43068	(614) 864-7784
PHYLLIS KANTOR 250 EAST 38TH STREET	EUGENE	OR	97405	(503) 421-6704
RABBI PIOTRKOWSKI'S JUDAICA CENTER 289 MONTGOMERY AVENUE	BALA CYNWYD	PA	19004	(215) 887-0343
DORETTE BOEHM 411 NORTH STERLING ROAD	ELKINS PARK	PA	19117	(215) 635-2442
ZALMAN SCHACTER C/O RELIGION DEPT., TEMPLE UNIVERSITY	PHILADELPHIA	PA	19121	(215) 849-5385
ROSE S. BANK 3 ROSELAWN TERRACE	PITTSBURGH	PA	15213	(412) 681-2863
ELSA WACHS 2 SOUTH PROVIDENCE ROAD	WALLINGFORD	PA	19086	(215) 566-5693
ISAAC SKULL CAP COMPANY 170 JEAN TALON WEST, #409	MONTREAL	QU	H2R 2X4	(514) 274-8403

TALMUD TORAH & SUPPLEMENTARY SCHOOLS

Name / Address	City	State	Zip	Phone
NORTH SHORE JEWISH CENTRE 1735 INGLEWOOD	WEST VANCOUVER	BC		(604) 922-8245
TEMPLE BETH TORAH 225 SOUTH ATLANTIC BOULEVARD	ALHAMBRA	CA	91801	(818) 723-2978
TEMPLE SHAAREI TIKVAH 550 SOUTH SECOND AVENUE	ARCADIA	CA	91006	(818) 445-0810
MIDRASHA, EAST BAY COMMUNITY HIGH SCHOOL 2301 VINE STREET	BERKELEY	CA	94708	(415) 848-3988
TEMPLE EMANUEL 8844 BURTON WAY	BEVERLY HILLS	CA	90211	(213) 274-6388
TEMPLE BETH EMET 600 NORTH BUENA VISTA	BURBANK	CA	91505	(818) 843-9444
CONGREGATION BETH KODESH 7401 SHOUP AVENUE	CANOGA PARK	CA	91307	(818) 346-0811
TEMPLE SOLAEL 6600 VALLEY CIRCLE BOULEVARD	CANOGA PARK	CA	91340	(818) 348-3885
TEMPLE NER TAMID, BRANCH SCHOOL 10824 TOPANGA CANYON BOULEVARD	CHATSWORTH	CA	91311	(818) 341-1270
TEMPLE AKIBA 5249 SEPULVEDA BOULEVARD	CULVER CITY	CA	90230	(213) 398-5783
TEMPLE NER TAMID 10629 LAKEWOOD BOULEVARD	DOWNEY	CA	90241	(213) 861-9276
MAAREV TEMPLE 5180 YARMOUTH AVENUE	ENCINO	CA	91316	(818) 345-7833
VALLEY BETH SHALOM 15739 VENTURA BOULEVARD	ENCINO	CA	91436	(818) 788-6000
TEMPLE SINAI OF GLENDALE 1212 NORTH PACIFIC AVENUE	GLENDALE	CA	91202	(818) 246-8101
TEMPLE BETH OHR 15721 EAST ROSECRANS AVENUE	LA MIRADA	CA	90638	(714) 521-6765
BETH KNESSEL BAMIDBAR 1611 EAST AVENUE J, PO BOX 1008	LANCASTER	CA	93534	(805) 942-4415
CHABAD OF SOUTH BAY 24412 NARBONNE AVENUE	LOMITA	CA	90717	(213) 326-8234
ADAT SHALOM 3030 WESTWOOD BOULEVARD	LOS ANGELES	CA	90034	(213) 475-4985
B'NAI DAVID-JUDEA CONGREGATION 8906 WEST PICO BOULEVARD	LOS ANGELES	CA	90035	(213) 272-7223
B'NAI TIKVAH CONGREGATION 5820 MANCHESTER AVENUE	LOS ANGELES	CA	90045	(213) 645-6262
CHABAD COMMUNITY TALMUD TORAH 7215 WARING AVENUE	LOS ANGELES	CA	90048	(213) 937-3763
CONGREGATION MOGEN DAVID 9717 WEST PICO BOULEVARD	LOS ANGELES	CA	90035	(213) 879-3861
ETZ JACOB CONGREGATION 7659 BEVERLY BOULEVARD	LOS ANGELES	CA	90036	(213) 938-2619
HOLLYWOOD TEMPLE BETH EL 1317 NORTH CRESCENT HEIGHTS BOULEVARD	LOS ANGELES	CA	90046	(213) 656-3150
INSTITUTE OF JEWISH EDUCATION 3889 WEST THIRD STREET	LOS ANGELES	CA	90048	(213) 655-1341
JEWISH ACADEMY OF LOS ANGELES - LA HEBREW HIGH SCHOOL 1317 NORTH CRESCENT HEIGHTS BOULEVARD	LOS ANGELES	CA	90046	(213) 656-3060
LEO BAECK TEMPLE 1300 NORTH SEPULVEDA BOULEVARD	LOS ANGELES	CA	90049	(213) 879-0368
SEPHARDIC TALMUD TORAH OF LOS ANGELES 420 NORTH FAIRFAX AVENUE	LOS ANGELES	CA	90036	
SEPHARDIC TEMPLE TIFERETH ISRAEL 10500 WILSHIRE BOULEVARD	LOS ANGELES	CA	90024	(213) 475-7311
SHIR SHALOM PO BOX 67487	LOS ANGELES	CA	90067	(213) 471-1643
SINAI TEMPLE 10400 WILSHIRE BOULEVARD	LOS ANGELES	CA	90024	(213) 474-1518
STEPHEN S. WISE TEMPLE 15500 STEPHEN S. WISE DRIVE	LOS ANGELES	CA	90077	(213) 788-7554
TEMPLE BETH AM 1039 SOUTH LA CIENEGA BOULEVARD	LOS ANGELES	CA	90035	(213) 655-6401
TEMPLE BETH TORAH 11827 VENICE BOULEVARD	LOS ANGELES	CA	90066	(213) 398-4536
TEMPLE ISAIAH 10345 WEST PICO BOULEVARD	LOS ANGELES	CA	90064	(213) 879-2191
TEMPLE ISRAEL OF HOLLYWOOD 7300 HOLLYWOOD BOULEVARD	LOS ANGELES	CA	90046	(213) 876-8330
UNIVERSITY SYNAGOGUE 11960 SUNSET BOULEVARD	LOS ANGELES	CA	90049	(213) 272-3650
WILSHIRE BOULEVARD TEMPLE 3663 WILSHIRE BOULEVARD	LOS ANGELES	CA	90010	(213) 388-2401
MALIBU JEWISH CENTER 28925 PACIFIC COAST HIGHWAY #6	MALIBU	CA	90265	(213) 457-2979
CONGREGATION TIFERETH JACOB 1613 SIXTH STREET	MANHATTAN BEACH	CA	90266	(213) 644-6900
TEMPLE B'NAI EMET 482 NORTH GARFIELD AVENUE	MONTEBELLO	CA	90640	(213) 723-2978
CONGREGATION BETH SHALOM PO BOX 39	NEWHALL	CA	91321	(805) 259-4975
ADAT ARI EL 5440 LAUREL CANYON BOULEVARD	NORTH HOLLYWOOD	CA	91607	(818) 877-4881
SHAAREY ZEDEK CONGREGATION 12800 CHANDLER BOULEVARD	NORTH HOLLYWOOD	CA	91607	(818) 763-0560
SOUTH BAY HEBREW HIGH SCHOOL, UNION HEBREW HIGH SCHOOL 13107 VENTURA BOULEVARD	NORTH HOLLYWOOD	CA	91604	(818) 872-3550
TEMPLE BETH HILLEL 12326 RIVERSIDE DRIVE	NORTH HOLLYWOOD	CA	91607	(818) 877-3431
TEMPLE AHAVAT SHALOM 18200 RINALDI PLACE	NORTHRIDGE	CA	91324	(818) 360-6349
TEMPLE RAMAT ZION 17655 DEVONSHIRE STREET	NORTHRIDGE	CA	91324	(818) 360-1881
TEMPLE SHOLOM 963 EAST SIXTH STREET	ONTARIO	CA	91764	(714) 983-9661
KEHILLATH ISRAEL 16019 SUNSET BOULEVARD	PACIFIC PALISADES	CA	90272	(213) 459-2328
PALO ALTO SCHOOL FOR JEWISH EDUCATION 830 E. MEADOW	PALO ALTO	CA	94303	(415) 494-2511
PASADENA JEWISH TEMPLE-CENTER 1434 NORTH ALTADENA DRIVE	PASADENA	CA	91107	(818) 798-1164
TEMPLE BETH ISRAEL 333 NORTH TOWNE AVENUE	POMONA	CA	91767	(714) 521-6765
CONGREGATION NER TAMID OF SOUTH BAY 5721 CRESTRIDGE ROAD	RANCHO PALOS VERDES	CA	90274	(213) 377-6986
TEMPLE MENORAH 1101 CAMINO REAL	REDONDO BEACH	CA	90277	(213) 316-8444
TEMPLE BETH AMI 18449 KITTRIDGE STREET	RESEDA	CA	91335	(818) 343-4624
TEMPLE BETH EL 1435 WEST SEVENTH STREET	SAN PEDRO	CA	90732	(213) 833-2467
BETH SHOLOM TEMPLE 1827 CALIFORNIA AVENUE	SANTA MONICA	CA	90403	(213) 451-1361
KEHILLAT MA'ARAV 2210 WILSHIRE BOULEVARD, PO BOX 287	SANTA MONICA	CA	90403	(213) 393-4507
TEMPLE BETH TORAH 8756 WOODLEY AVENUE	SEPULVEDA	CA	91343	(213) 893-3756
TEMPLE B'NAI HAYIM 4302 VAN NUYS BOULEVARD	SHERMAN OAKS	CA	91403	(818) 788-4664
TEMPLE NER TAMID 3050 LOS ANGELES AVENUE	SIMI VALLEY	CA	93065	(805) 522-4747
VALLEY BETH ISRAEL 12060 ROSCOE BOULEVARD	SUN VALLEY	CA	91352	(818) 782-2281
TEMPLE JUDEA 5429 LINDLEY AVENUE	TARZANA	CA	91356	(213) 342-3177
TEMPLE BETH DAVID 9677 EAST LONGDEN AVENUE	TEMPLE CITY	CA	91780	(818) 287-9994
ADAT ELOHIM 2420 EAST HILLCREST DRIVE	THOUSAND OAKS	CA	91360	(805) 497-7101
TEMPLE ETZ CHAIM 1080 JANSS ROAD	THOUSAND OAKS	CA	91360	(805) 497-6891
TEMPLE NER TAMID 15339 SATICOY STREET	VAN NUYS	CA	91406	(818) 782-9010
CONGREGATION MISHKON TEPHILO 206 MAIN STREET	VENICE	CA	90291	(213) 399-1432
TEMPLE BETH AMI 3508 EAST TEMPLE WAY	WEST COVINA	CA	91791	(818) 331-0515
TEMPLE SHALOM 1921 WEST MERCED AVENUE	WEST COVINA	CA	91790	(818) 337-6500
BETH SHALOM 14564 EAST HAWES STREET	WHITTIER	CA	90604	(213) 941-8744
TEMPLE ALIYAH 6025 VALLEY CIRCLE BOULEVARD	WOODLAND HILLS	CA	91367	(818) 346-3545
TEMPLE EMET 20400 VENTURA BOULEVARD	WOODLAND HILLS	CA	91364	(818) 348-0670
BMH-BJ HEBREW SCHOOL 560 SOUTH MONACO PARKWAY	DENVER	CO	80220	(303) 388-4203
CONGREGATION LEVI YITZHAK 1295 EAST HALLANDALE BEACH BOULEVARD	HALLANDALE	FL	33009	(305) 458-1877
TEMPLE BETH EL 1351 SOUTH 14TH AVENUE	HOLLYWOOD	FL	33020	(305) 920-8225
TEMPLE BETH SHALOM 1400 NORTH 46TH AVENUE	HOLLYWOOD	FL	33021	(305) 966-2200
TEMPLE SINAI 1201 JOHNSON STREET	HOLLYWOOD	FL	33019	(305) 920-1577
TEMPLE SOLEL 5100 SHERIDAN STREET	HOLLYWOOD	FL	33021	(305) 989-0205
TEMPLE ISRAEL OF MIRAMAR 6920 SOUTHWEST 35TH STREET	MIRAMAR	FL	33023	(305) 961-1700
TEMPLE BETH AHM 9730 STIRLING ROAD	PEMBROKE PINES	FL	33024	(305) 431-5100
TEMPLE BETH EMET P.O. BOX 8842	PEMBROKE PINES	FL	33024	(305) 431-3638
HEBREW COMMUNITY SCHOOL OF SAVANNAH, THE 5111 ABECORN STREET	SAVANNAH	GA	31405	(912) 355-8111
TEMPLE EMANU-EL SCHOOL OF JEWISH STUDIES 2550 PALI HIGHWAY	HONOLULU	HI	96817	(808) 595-7521
ALOHA JEWISH CHAPEL RELIGIOUS SCHOOL 1514 MAKALAPA DRIVE, MAKALAPA GATE	PEARL HARBOR	HI	96818	(808) 471-0050
LOUISVILLE HEBREW SCHOOL 3600 DUTCHMANS LANE	LOUISVILLE	KY	40205	(502) 459-0799
COMMISSION OF JEWISH EDUCATION-COMMUNAL HEBREW SCHOOL 1631 CALHOUN STREET	NEW ORLEANS	LA	70118	(504) 861-7508
TIFERETH ISRAEL RELIGIOUS SCHOOL, TEMPLE R 3539 SALEM STREET	MALDEN	MA	02148	(617) 322-2794
BETH EL COMMUNITY HEBREW SCHOOL OF NEWTON WARD STREET & MORSELAND AVENUE	NEWTON	MA	02159	(617) 244-7233
ROSH PINA EVENING SCHOOL 123 MATHESON AVENUE	WINNIPEG	MB	R2W 0C3	(204) 589-6306
SHAAREY ZEDEK RAMAH EVENING SCHOOL 705 LANARK	WINNIPEG	MB	R3N 1M4	(204) 453-4136
TEMPLE SHALOM SUNDAY SCHOOL 215 STAFFORD STREET	WINNIPEG	MB		(204) 477-1488
THE JEWISH FAMILY SCHOOL C/O ETARAE WEINSTEIN, PRINCIPAL, 6964 SUNFLECK ROW	COLUMBIA	MD	21045	(301) 730-5261
MIDRASHA COMMUNITY HEBREW HIGH SCHOOL OF GREATER WASHINGTON 9325 BROOKVILLE ROAD	SILVER SPRING	MD	20910	(301) 589-3180
BETH ISRAEL HEBREW SCHOOL 862 WASHINGTON STREET	BATH	ME	04530	(207) 443-5181
UNITED HEBREW SCHOOLS 21550 W. TWELVE MILE ROAD	SOUTHFIELD	MI	48076	(313) 354-1050
TALMUD TORAH LOF MINNEAPOLIS, THE 8200 W. 33RD STREET	MINNEAPOLIS	MN	55426	(612) 935-0316
TALMUD TORAH OF ST. PAUL, THE 636 S. MISSISSIPPI RIVER BLVD	ST PAUL	MN	55116	(612) 698-8807
COMMUNITY JEWISH SCHOOL PO BOX 961	NEW BRUNSWICK	NJ	08903	(201) 545-6484
BETH SHALOM CENTER 79 COUNTY LINE ROAD	AMITYVILLE	NY	11701	(516) 264-2891
JEWISH CENTER OF ATLANTIC BEACH PARK STREET & NASSAU AVENUE	ATLANTIC BEACH	NY	11509	(516) 371-0972
BETH SHALOM, CONGREGATION 441 DEER PARK AVENUE	BABYLON	NY	11702	(516) 587-5650
JEWISH CENTER OF BALDWIN 885 EAST SEAMAN AVENUE	BALDWIN	NY	11510	(516) 223-5599
SHOLOM ALEICHEM FOLKSHULE #32 C/O SOUTH SHORE YMHA-806 MERRICK ROAD	BALDWIN	NY	11510	(516) 678-5092
SOUTH BALDWIN JEWISH CENTER 2959 GRAND AVENUE	BALDWIN	NY	11510	(516) 223-8688
BAY SHORE JEWISH CENTER-MARY SELEY MEMORIAL SCHOOL 26 NORTH CLINTON AVENUE	BAY SHORE	NY	11706	(516) 665-1140
SINAI REFORM TEMPLE/HARRIET S. LEVIN RELIGIOUS SCHOOL 39 BRENTWOOD ROAD	BAY SHORE	NY	11706	(516) 665-5755
BAY TERRACE JEWISH CENTER 209TH STREET & WILLETS POINT BOULEVARD	BAYSIDE	NY	11360	(718) 428-6363
BAYSIDE HILLS JEWISH CENTER 212-22 48TH AVENUE	BAYSIDE	NY	11364	(718) 229-2372
BAYSIDE JEWISH CENTER 203-05 32ND AVENUE	BAYSIDE	NY	11361	(718) 352-7900
OAKLAND JEWISH CENTER 61-35 220TH STREET	BAYSIDE	NY	11364	(718) 225-7800
SHAARAY TEFILA OF NORTH WESTCHESTER ROUTE 172	BEDFORD	NY	10549	(914) 666-3133
BETH EL OF ROCKAWAY PARK, TEMPLE 445 B. 135TH STREET	BELLE HARBOR	NY	11694	(718) 634-8110
OHAV ZEDEK, CONGREGATION 134-01 ROCKAWAY BEACH BOULEVARD	BELLE HARBOR	NY	11694	(718) 474-3300
SHAAREI SHALOM, TEMPLE 2579 MERRICK ROAD	BELLMORE	NY	11710	(516) 781-5599
BETHPAGE JEWISH COMMUNITY CENTER 600 BROADWAY	BETHPAGE	NY	11714	(516) 938-7909
SONS OF ISRAEL, CONGREGATION 1666 PLEASANTVILLE ROAD	BRIARCLIFF	NY	10510	(914) 762-2700
BRONX HOUSE NURSERY 2222 WALLACE AVENUE	BRONX	NY	10467	(212) 792-1800
CO-OP CITY JEWISH CENTER 900 CO-OP CITY BOULEVARD	BRONX	NY	10475	(212) 671-4579
COMMUNITY CENTER OF ISRAEL 2440 ESPLANADE AVENUE	BRONX	NY	10469	(212) 882-2400
CONSERVATIVE SYNAGOGUE ADATH ISRAEL OF RIVERDALE 250TH STREET-HENRY HUDSON PARKWAY	BRONX	NY	10471	(212) 543-8400
JACOB H. SCHIFF CENTER-EVA BECKER HEBREW SCHOOL 2510 VALENTINE AVENUE	BRONX	NY	10458	(212) 295-2510
KINGSBRIDGE CENTER OF ISRAEL 3115 CORLEAR AVENUE	BRONX	NY	10463	(212) 548-1678
KINGSBRIDGE HEIGHTS JEWISH CENTER 124 EAMES PLACE	BRONX	NY	10468	(212) 549-4120
MOSHOLU MONTEFIORE NURSERY 3450 DEKALB AVENUE	BRONX	NY	10467	(212) 882-4000
NATHAN STRAUSS JEWISH CENTER 3512 DEKALB AVENUE	BRONX	NY	10467	(212) 547-1617
PELHAM PARKWAY JEWISH CENTER 900 PELHAM PARKWAY SOUTH	BRONX	NY	10462	(212) 792-6458
RIVERDALE JEWISH CENTER 3700 INDEPENDENCE AVENUE	BRONX	NY	10463	(212) 548-2922
RIVERDALE TEMPLE 4545 INDEPENDENCE AVENUE	BRONX	NY	10471	(212) 548-3800
TEMPLE BETH EL OF CO-OP CITY 920-1 BAYCHESTER AVENUE	BRONX	NY	10475	(212) 671-9719
TRADITIONAL SYNAGOGUE OF CO-OP CITY 115 EINSTEIN LOOP NORTH	BRONX	NY	10475	(212) 379-6920
VAN CORTLANDT JEWISH CENTER 3880 SEDGWICK AVENUE	BRONX	NY	10463	(212) 844-6105
WORKMEN'S CIRCLE AMALGAMATED NURSERY SCHOOL 3980 ORLOFF AVENUE	BRONX	NY	10463	(212) 543-8688
WORKMEN'S CIRCLE SCHOOL #3 3990 HILLMAN AVENUE	BRONX	NY	10463	(212) 548-2217
YM-YWHA RIVERDALE NURSERY 450 WEST 250 STREET	BRONX	NY	10471	(212) 548-8200
YOUNG ISRAEL OF PARKCHESTER 1375 VIRGINIA AVENUE	BRONX	NY	10462	(212) 822-9576
YOUNG ISRAEL OF PELHAM PARKWAY 2126 BARNES AVENUE	BRONX	NY	10462	(212) 824-0630

AHAVATH SHOLOM, TEMPLE 1609 AVENUE R ... BROOKLYN **NY** 11229 (718) 375-4500
ATERES YISROEL TALMUD TORAH 8101 AVENUE K ... BROOKLYN **NY** 11229 (718) 763-6777
AVENUE Z JEWISH CENTER 875 AVENUE Z ... BROOKLYN **NY** 11235 (718) 646-9874
B'NAI ISRAEL CONGREGATION 1540 VAN SICLEN AVENUE ... BROOKLYN **NY** 11239 (718) 642-8804
B'NAI ISRAEL OF MIDWOOD-BERNICE FISHKIND HEBREW SCHOOL
1800 UTICA AVENUE ... BROOKLYN **NY** 11234 (718) 763-5500
BAY RIDGE JEWISH CENTER-SHEARITH ISRAEL 405 81ST STREET ... BROOKLYN **NY** 11209 (718) 745-4366
BEACH HAVEN JEWISH CENTER 723 AVENUE Z ... BROOKLYN **NY** 11223 (718) 375-5200
BETH ABRAHAM, TEMPLE 301 SEA BREEZE AVENUE ... BROOKLYN **NY** 11224 (718) 266-6544
BETH EL OF MANHATTAN BEACH 111 WEST END AVENUE ... BROOKLYN **NY** 11235 (718) 891-3500
BETH ELOHIM, CONGREGATION 8 AVENUE & GARFIELD PLACE ... BROOKLYN **NY** 11215 (718) 768-3814
BETH EMETH, TEMPLE 83 MARLBORO ROAD ... BROOKLYN **NY** 11226 (718) 282-1596
BETH OHR COMMUNITY TEMPLE 1010 OCEAN AVENUE ... BROOKLYN **NY** 11226 (718) 284-5760
BETH SHALOM HEBREW SCHOOL 2710 AVENUE X ... BROOKLYN **NY** 11235 (718) 891-4500
BETH SHALOM PEOPLE'S TEMPLE BAY PARKWAY & BENSON AVENUE ... BROOKLYN **NY** 11214 (718) 372-0933
BETH TIKVA TALMUD TORAH 8800 SEAVIEW AVENUE ... BROOKLYN **NY** 11236 (718) 763-5577
BETH TORAH OF SHEEPSHEAD BAY 3574 NOSTRAND AVENUE ... BROOKLYN **NY** 11229 (718) 646-5467
BRIGHTON BEACH JEWISH CENTER 2915 OCEAN PARKWAY ... BROOKLYN **NY** 11235 (718) 769-7400
BROOKLYN HEIGHTS SYNAGOGUE 117 REMSEN STREET ... BROOKLYN **NY** 11201 (718) 522-2070
CANARSIE JEWISH CENTER 965 EAST 107TH STREET ... BROOKLYN **NY** 11236 (718) 272-2848
CENTRAL TALMUD TORAH 1305 CONEY ISLAND AVENUE ... BROOKLYN **NY** 11230 (718) 377-4400
COMMUNITY TALMUD TORAH 2115 BENSON AVENUE ... BROOKLYN **NY** 11214 (718) 372-4830
EAST MIDWOOD JEWISH CENTER 1625 OCEAN AVENUE ... BROOKLYN **NY** 11230 (718) 338-3800
EMANU-EL OF CANARSIE, TEMPLE 1880 ROCKAWAY PARKWAY ... BROOKLYN **NY** 11236 (718) 251-0450
FLATBUSH JEWISH CENTER - HILLEL SCHOOL 500 CHURCH AVENUE ... BROOKLYN **NY** 11218 (718) 871-5200
FLATBUSH PARK JEWISH CENTER 6363 AVENUE U ... BROOKLYN **NY** 11234 (718) 444-6868
HEBREW EDUCATIONAL SOCIETY NURSERY 9502 SEAVIEW AVENUE ... BROOKLYN **NY** 11236 (718) 241-3000
HILLEL OF FLATLANDS, TEMPLE 2164 RALPH AVENUE ... BROOKLYN **NY** 11234 (718) 763-2400
JEWISH COMMUNITY HOUSE OF BENSONHURST 7802 BAY PARKWAY ... BROOKLYN **NY** 11214 (718) 331-6800
KINGS HIGHWAY JEWISH CENTER 1202 AVENUE P ... BROOKLYN **NY** 11229 (718) 645-9000
MADISON JEWISH CENTER 2989 NOSTRAND AVENUE ... BROOKLYN **NY** 11234 (718) 339-7755
MANHATTAN BEACH JEWISH CENTER 60 WEST END AVENUE ... BROOKLYN **NY** 11235 (718) 891-8700
MARINE PARK JEWISH CENTER 3311 AVENUE S ... BROOKLYN **NY** 11234 (718) 376-5200
OCEAN AVENUE JEWISH CENTER 2600 OCEAN AVENUE ... BROOKLYN **NY** 11229 (718) 743-5534
OCEAN PARKWAY JEWISH CENTER 550 OCEAN PARKWAY ... BROOKLYN **NY** 11218 (718) 436-4900
OCEANVIEW JEWISH CENTER 3100 BRIGHTON 4 STREET ... BROOKLYN **NY** 11235 (718) 648-6662
OHEV SHOLOM TALMUD TORAH 1387 EAST 96TH STREET ... BROOKLYN **NY** 11236 (718) 251-1430
PROGRESSIVE SYNAGOGUE 1395 OCEAN AVENUE ... BROOKLYN **NY** 11230 (718) 377-1818
REMSEN HEIGHTS JEWISH CENTER 8700 AVENUE K ... BROOKLYN **NY** 11236 (718) 763-2244
SEAVIEW JEWISH CENTER 1440 EAST 99TH STREET ... BROOKLYN **NY** 11236 (718) 251-1900
SEPHARDIC JEWISH CENTER OF CANARSIE 9320 FLATLANDS AVENUE ... BROOKLYN **NY** 11236 (718) 257-0400
SHAARE EMETH, TEMPLE 6012 FARRAGUT ROAD ... BROOKLYN **NY** 11236 (718) 444-3222
SHELLBANK JEWISH CENTER 2121 BRAGG STREET ... BROOKLYN **NY** 11229 (718) 891-8666
SHOLOM OF FLATBUSH, TEMPLE 2075 EAST 68TH STREET ... BROOKLYN **NY** 11234 (718) 251-0370
SHORE PARK JEWISH CENTER 2959 AVENUE Y ... BROOKLYN **NY** 11235 (718) 648-2900
SHORE PARKWAY JEWISH CENTER 8885 26TH AVENUE ... BROOKLYN **NY** 11214 (718) 449-6530
TALMUD TORAH AHAVATH ACHIM, CONGREGATION O
1750 E. 4TH STREET ... BROOKLYN **NY** 11223 (718) 375-3895
UNION TEMPLE 17 EASTERN PARKWAY ... BROOKLYN **NY** 11238 (718) 638-7600
YM-YWHA-SHOREFRONT 3300 CONEY ISLAND AVENUE ... BROOKLYN **NY** 11235 (718) 646-1444
YM-YWHA NURSERY OF KINGS BAY 3643 NOSTRAND AVENUE ... BROOKLYN **NY** 11229 (718) 648-7703
YM-YWHA OF CONEY ISLAND 3312-30 SURF AVENUE ... BROOKLYN **NY** 11224 (718) 449-1000
YESHIVA INSTITUTE 6414 BAY PARKWAY ... BROOKLYN **NY** 11204 (718) 259-1432
YOUNG ISRAEL OF BEDFORD BAY 21-14 BROWN STREET ... BROOKLYN **NY** 11229 (718) 332-4120
YOUNG ISRAEL OF SHEEPSHEAD BAY 2546 EAST 7TH STREET ... BROOKLYN **NY** 11225 (718) 449-1397
BETH EL, TEMPLE BROADWAY & LOCUST AVENUE ... CEDARHURST **NY** 11516 (516) 569-2700
SEPHARDIC TEMPLE, THE BRANCH BOULEVARD ... CEDARHURST **NY** 11516 (516) 295-4644
MORICHES, JEWISH CENTER OF THE PO BOX 127 ... CENTER MORICHES **NY** 11934 (516) 878-0388
BETH EL, TEMPLE 220 SOUTH BEDFORD ROAD ... CHAPPAQUA **NY** 10514 (914) 238-3928
KEHILAT SHALOM RELIGIOUS SCHOOL
58 GOOSE HILL ROAD ... COLD SPRING HARBOR **NY** 11724 (516) 595-3347
BETH DAVID, TEMPLE 100 HAUPPAUGE ROAD ... COMMACK **NY** 11725 (516) 499-0915
COMMACK JEWISH CENTER 83 SHIRLEY COURT ... COMMACK **NY** 11725 (516) 543-3311
ISRAEL, TEMPLE GLENGARY ROAD ... CROTON-ON-HUDSON **NY** 10520 (914) 271-8006
SUFFOLK JEWISH CENTER-SAMUEL BERKOWITZ RELIGIOUS SCHOOL
330 CENTRAL AVENUE ... DEER PARK **NY** 11729 (516) 667-7695
BETH TORAH, TEMPLE 35 BAGATELLE ROAD ... DIX HILLS **NY** 11746 (516) 271-1657
DIX HILLS JEWISH CENTER DEFOREST ROAD & VANDERBILT PARKWAY ... DIX HILLS **NY** 11746 (516) 499-6644
SHOLOM ALEICHEM SCHOOL #41
C/O MS. ROSEMAN-83 MCCULLOCH DRIVE ... DIX HILLS **NY** 11746 (516) 864-2367
GREENBURGH HEBREW CENTER 515 NORTH BROADWAY ... DOBBS FERRY **NY** 10522 (914) 693-4260
MARATHON JEWISH COMMUNITY CENTER 245-37 60TH STREET ... DOUGLASTON **NY** 11362 (718) 428-1580
HAMPTONS, JEWISH CENTER OF THE 44 WOODS LANE ... EAST HAMPTON **NY** 11937 (516) 324-9858
EAST MEADOW JEWISH CENTER 1400 PROSPECT AVENUE ... EAST MEADOW **NY** 11554 (516) 483-4205
EMANUEL, TEMPLE 123 MERRICK AVENUE ... EAST MEADOW **NY** 11554 (516) 794-8937
SUBURBAN PARK JEWISH CENTER 400 OLD WESTBURY ROAD ... EAST MEADOW **NY** 11554 (516) 796-2626
WORKMEN'S CIRCLE SCHOOL-I.L. PERETZ SCHOOL OF NASSAU
574 NEWBRIDGE AVENUE ... EAST MEADOW **NY** 11554 (516) 542-9640
EAST NORTHPORT JEWISH CENTER 328 ELWOOD ROAD ... EAST NORTHPORT **NY** 11731 (516) 368-6474
HEWLETT-EAST ROCKAWAY JEWISH CENTER 295 MAIN STREET ... EAST ROCKAWAY **NY** 11518 (516) 599-0424
EMANU-EL, TEMPLE 91-15 CORONA AVENUE ... ELMHURST **NY** 11373 (718) 592-4343
B'NAI ISRAEL, TEMPLE ELMONT ROAD & BAYLIS AVENUE ... ELMONT **NY** 11003 (516) 354-1156
ELMONT JEWISH CENTER 500 ELMONT ROAD ... ELMONT **NY** 11003 (516) 437-3937
BAYSWATER JEWISH CENTER 2355 HEALY AVENUE ... FAR ROCKAWAY **NY** 11691 (718) 471-7771
YM-YWHA, GUSTAV HARTMAN 710 HARTMAN LANE ... FAR ROCKAWAY **NY** 11691 (718) 471-0200
FARMINGDALE JEWISH CENTER 425 FULTON STREET ... FARMINGDALE **NY** 11735 (516) 694-2343
BELLEROSE JEWISH CENTER 254-04 UNION TPKE ... FLORAL PARK **NY** 11004 (718) 343-9001
SHOLOM, TEMPLE 263-10 UNION TURNPIKE ... FLORAL PARK **NY** 11004 (718) 343-8660
BAYSIDE OAKS, JEWISH CENTER OF 50-35 CLOVERDALE BOULEVARD ... FLUSHING **NY** 11364 (718) 631-0100
BETH SHOLOM, TEMPLE 171-39 NORTHERN BOULEVARD ... FLUSHING **NY** 11358 (718) 463-4143
ELECTCHESTER JEWISH CTR.-HENRY F. FISCHBAUM RELIGIOUS SCHOOL
65-15 164TH STREET ... FLUSHING **NY** 11365 (718) 886-4454
FLUSHING JEWISH CENTER 43-00 171ST STREET ... FLUSHING **NY** 11358 (718) 358-7071
FREE SYNAGOGUE OF FLUSHING 41-60 KISSENA BOULEVARD ... FLUSHING **NY** 11355 (718) 961-0030
FRESH MEADOWS - UTOPIA JEWISH CENTER 193-10 PECK AVENUE ... FLUSHING **NY** 11365 (718) 357-5100
GARDEN JEWISH CENTER 24-20 PARSONS BOULEVARD ... FLUSHING **NY** 11357 (718) 445-1317
GATES OF PRAYER, TEMPLE 38-20 PARSONS BOULEVARD ... FLUSHING **NY** 11354 (718) 359-7641
HILLCREST JEWISH CENTER 183-02 UNION TPKE ... FLUSHING **NY** 11366 (718) 380-4145
HOLLIS HILLS JEWISH CENTER 210-10 UNION TPKE ... FLUSHING **NY** 11364 (718) 776-3500
ISRAEL CENTER OF HILLCREST MANOR 167-11 73RD AVENUE ... FLUSHING **NY** 11366 (718) 591-5353
JEWISH CENTER OF TORATH EMETH 78-15 PARSONS BOULEVARD ... FLUSHING **NY** 11366 (718) 591-4240
KEW GARDENS HILLS, JEWISH CENTER OF 71-25 MAIN STREET ... FLUSHING **NY** 11367 (718) 263-6500
WORKMEN'S CIRCLE SCHOOL-FLUSHING 45-25 KISSENA BOULEVARD ... FLUSHING **NY** 11355
YM-YMHA OF GREATER FLUSHING 45-35 KISSENA BOULEVARD ... FLUSHING **NY** 11355 (718) 461-3030
FOREST HILLS JEWISH CENTER 106-06 QUEENS BOULEVARD ... FOREST HILLS **NY** 11375 (718) 263-7000
ISAIAH, TEMPLE 75-24 GRAND CENTRAL PARKWAY ... FOREST HILLS **NY** 11375 (718) 544-2800
QUEENS JEWISH CENTER 66-05 108 STREET ... FOREST HILLS **NY** 11375 (718) 459-8432
SINAI, TEMPLE-HORTENSE LIEBMAN SCHOOL 71-11 112 STREET ... FOREST HILLS **NY** 11375 (718) 261-2900
YM-YWHA OF CENTRAL QUEENS 108-05 68 ROAD ... FOREST HILLS **NY** 11375 (718) 268-5011
YOUNG ISRAEL OF FOREST HILLS
7100 YELLOWSTONE BOULEVARD ... FOREST HILLS **NY** 11375 (718) 268-7100
B'NAI ISRAEL, CONGREGATION 91 NORTH BAYVIEW AVENUE ... FREEPORT **NY** 11520 (516) 623-4200
UNION REFORM TEMPLE 475 NORTH BROOKSIDE AVENUE ... FREEPORT **NY** 11520 (516) 623-1810
GARDEN CITY JEWISH CENTER 168 NASSAU BOULEVARD ... GARDEN CITY **NY** 11530 (516) 248-9180
NORTH COUNTY REFORM TEMPLE CRESCENT BEACH ROAD ... GLEN COVE **NY** 11542 (516) 671-4760
TIFERETH ISRAEL, CONGREGATION HILL STREET & LANDING ... GLEN COVE **NY** 11542 (516) 676-5080
BETH EL OF GREAT NECK, TEMPLE 5 OLD MILL ROAD ... GREAT NECK **NY** 11023 (516) 487-0900
BETH HAGAN NURSERY
C/O TEMPLE ISRAEL, TEMPLE COURT & OLD MILL ROAD ... GREAT NECK **NY** 11023 (516) 482-7821
EMANUEL, TEMPLE 150 HICKS LANE ... GREAT NECK **NY** 11024 (516) 482-5701
GREAT NECK SYNAGOGUE 26 OLD MILL ROAD ... GREAT NECK **NY** 11023 (516) 487-6100
HEBREW HIGH SCHOOL OF TEMPLE ISRAEL 108 OLD MILL ROAD ... GREAT NECK **NY** 11023 (516) 482-4399
ISAIAH, TEMPLE PO BOX 229-OLD VILLAGE STATION ... GREAT NECK **NY** 11023 (516) 487-8709
ISRAEL, TEMPLE 108 OLD MILL ROAD ... GREAT NECK **NY** 11023 (516) 482-7800
JEWISH COMMUNITY CENTER 349 UNION AVENUE ... HARRISON **NY** 10528 (914) 835-2860
BETH SHALOM, TEMPLE 740 NORTH BROADWAY ... HASTINGS-ON-HUDSON **NY** 10706 (914) 478-3833
BETH CHAI, TEMPLE PO BOX 74 ... HAUPPAUGE **NY** 11787 (516) 724-5807
BETH EMETH, TEMPLE 36 FRANKLIN AVENUE ... HEWLETT **NY** 11557 (516) 374-9220
HICKSVILLE JEWISH CENTER JERUSALEM AVENUE & MAGLIE DRIVE ... HICKSVILLE **NY** 11801 (516) 374-9220
SHARREI ZEDEK, CONGREGATION
NEW SOUTH & OLD COUNTRY ROADS ... HICKSVILLE **NY** 11801 (516) 938-0420
ISRAEL OF JAMAICA, TEMPLE 188-15 MCLAUGHLIN AVENUE ... HOLLISWOOD **NY** 11423 (718) 776-4400
HOWARD BEACH JEWISH CENTER 162-05 90TH STREET ... HOWARD BEACH **NY** 11414 (718) 845-9444
ROCKWOOD PARK JEWISH CENTER 156-45 84 STREET ... HOWARD BEACH **NY** 11414 (718) 641-5822
WORKMEN'S CIRCLE SCHOOL-SUFFOLK COUNTY
C/O KAPLAN-19 LARKIN STREET ... HUNGTINGTON STATION **NY** 11746 (516) 421-3049
BETH EL, TEMPLE 660 PARK AVENUE ... HUNTINGTON **NY** 11743 (516) 421-5836
HUNTINGTON JEWISH CENTER 510 PARK AVENUE ... HUNTINGTON **NY** 11743 (516) 427-1089
SOUTH HUNTINGTON JEWISH CENTER
2600 NEW YORK AVENUE ... HUNTINGTON STATION **NY** 11746 (516) 421-3244
ISLAND PARK, JEWISH CENTER OF 191 LONG BEACH ROAD ... ISLAND PARK **NY** 11558 (516) 432-6706
JACKSON HEIGHTS, JEWISH CENTER OF 34-25 82ND STREET ... JACKSON HEIGHTS **NY** 11372 (718) 429-1150
BRIARWOOD JEWISH CENTER 139-06 86TH AVENUE ... JAMAICA **NY** 11435 (718) 657-5151
HOLLISWOOD JEWISH CENTER 86-25 FRANCIS LEWIS BOULEVARD ... JAMAICA **NY** 11427 (718) 776-8500
ROCHDALE VILLAGE JEWISH CENTER 167-10 137 AVENUE ... JAMAICA **NY** 11434 (718) 528-0200
CONSERVATIVE SYNAGOGUE OF JAMAICA
182-69 WEXFORD TERRACE ... JAMAICA ESTATES **NY** 11432 (718) 526-6275
JERICHO JEWISH CENTER NORTH BROADWAY ... JERICHO **NY** 11753 (516) 938-2540
OR ELOHIM, TEMPLE-IRVING WEINER RELIGIOUS SCHOOL
18 TOBIE LANE ... JERICHO **NY** 11753 (516) 433-9888
KEW GARDENS ANSHE SHOLOM JEWISH CENTER
82-52 ABINGDON ROAD, BOX 21 ... KEW GARDENS **NY** 11415 (718) 441-2470
KEW GARDENS SYNAGOGUE ADATH JESHURUN
82-17 LEFFERTS BOULEVARD ... KEW GARDENS **NY** 11415 (718) 849-7988
COMMUNITY TALMUD TORAH AT YOUNG ISRAEL OF KEW GARDENS HILLS
151-01 70TH ROAD ... KEW GARDENS **NY** 11367 (718) 261-9723
QUEENSBORO HILLS JEWISH CENTER
156-03 HORACE HARDING BOULEVARD ... KEW GARDENS **NY** 11367 (718) 445-4141
ETZ CHAIM, CONGREGATION 44 MEADOW ROAD ... KINGS PARK **NY** 11754 (516) 269-9666
KINGS PARK JEWISH CENTER ROUTE 25-A ... KINGS PARK **NY** 11754 (516) 269-1133
LAKE GROVE JEWISH CENTER 821 HAWKINS AVENUE ... LAKE GROVE **NY** 11755 (516) 585-0521
RONKONKOMA JEWISH CENTER 821 HAWKINS AVENUE, PO BOX 20 ... LAKE GROVE **NY** 11755 (516) 585-0521
LAKE SUCCESS JEWISH CENTER 354 LAKEVILLE ROAD ... LAKE SUCCESS **NY** 11020 (516) 466-0569
BETH EMETH, CONGREGATION 2111 BOSTON POST ROAD ... LARCHMONT **NY** 10543 (914) 834-2543
LARCHMONT TEMPLE 75 LARCHMONT AVENUE ... LARCHMONT **NY** 10538 (914) 834-6121
WORKMEN'S CIRCLE SCHOOL-WESTCHESTER
C/O MIRIAM CREEMER-1 CREST AVENUE ... LARCHMONT **NY** 10538 (914) 834-6041
BETH SHOLOM CONGREGATION 390 BROADWAY ... LAWRENCE **NY** 11559 (516) 569-3600
HEBREW HIGH SCHOOL OF FIVE TOWNS 25 FROST LANE ... LAWRENCE **NY** 11559 (516) 239-1116
ISRAEL, TEMPLE 140 CENTRAL AVENUE ... LAWRENCE **NY** 11559 (516) 239-9213
SINAI, TEMPLE 131 WASHINGTON AVENUE ... LAWRENCE **NY** 11559 (516) 569-0267
ISRAEL COMMUNITY CENTER 3235 HEMPSTEAD TURNPIKE ... LEVITTOWN **NY** 11756 (516) 731-2580
CHAVURAT BETH CHAI LINCOLN HALL ... LINCOLNDALE **NY** 10540 (914) 628-5848
LINDENHURST HEBREW CONGREGATION
224 NORTH FOURTH STREET, PO BOX 100 ... LINDENHURST **NY** 11757 (516) 226-2022
LITTLE NECK JEWISH CENTER 49-10 LITTLE NECK PARKWAY ... LITTLE NECK **NY** 11362 (718) 225-9699
TORAH, TEMPLE 54-27 LITTLE NECK PARKWAY ... LITTLE NECK **NY** 11362 (718) 423-1235
BETH SHOLOM OF LONG BEACH & LIDO, CONGREGATION
700 EAST PARK AVENUE, BOX 599 ... LONG BEACH **NY** 11561 (516) 432-7464
COMMUNITY HEBREW SCHOOL OF LONG BEACH & LIDO
570 WEST WALNUT STREET/75 EAST WALNUT STREET ... LONG BEACH **NY** 11561 (516) 432-1678
EMANUEL, TEMPLE 455 NEPTUNE BOULEVARD ... LONG BEACH **NY** 11561 (516) 431-4060
SEPHARDIC CONGREGATION OF LONG BEACH
161 LAFAYETTE BOULEVARD ... LONG BEACH **NY** 11561 (516) 432-9224

ASTORIA CENTER OF ISRAEL 27-35 CRESCENT STREET .... LONG ISLAND CITY **NY** 11102 (718) 278-2680
SUNNYSIDE JEWISH CENTER 45-46 43 STREET .... LONG ISLAND CITY **NY** 11104 (718) 729-9716
BETH DAVID, CONGREGATION 188 VINCENT AVENUE .... LYNBROOK **NY** 11563 (516) 599-9464
EMANU-EL, TEMPLE ROSS PLAZA .... LYNBROOK **NY** 11563 (516) 593-4004
MALVERNE-WEST HEMPSTEAD RELIGIOUS SCHOOL
1 NORWOOD AVENUE .... MALVERNE **NY** 11565 (516) 593-6364
WESTCHESTER JEWISH CENTER ROCKLAND & PALMER AVENUES .. MAMARONECK **NY** 10543 (914) 698-2966
JUDEA, TEMPLE 333 SEARINGTON ROAD .... MANHASSET **NY** 11030 (516) 621-8049
MASPETH JEWISH CENTER 66-64 GRAND AVENUE .... MASPETH **NY** 11378 (718) 639-7559
BETH EL, CONGREGATION 99 JERUSALEM AVENUE .... MASSAPEQUA **NY** 11758 (516) 541-0740
JUDEA, TEMPLE JERUSALEM & CENTRAL AVENUES .... MASSAPEQUA **NY** 11758 (516) 798-5444
BETH AM, TEMPLE KIRKWOOD & MERRICK AVENUES .... MERRICK **NY** 11566 (516) 378-3477
ISRAEL OF SOUTH MERRICK, TEMPLE 2655 CLUBHOUSE ROAD .... MERRICK **NY** 11566 (516) 378-1963
MERRICK JEWISH CENTER-RABBI SOLOMON LIPMAN RELIGIOUS SCHOOL
225 FOX BOULEVARD .... MERRICK **NY** 11566 (516) 378-8384
MERRICK-BELLMORE SYNAGOGUE, OHAV SHOLOM OF MERRICK
145 SOUTH MERRICK AVENUE .... MERRICK **NY** 11566 (516) 378-1988
FOREST HILLS W., JEWISH CENTER OF
63-25 DRY HARBOR ROAD .... MIDDLE VILLAGE **NY** 11379 (718) 639-2110
BETH SHOLOM, CONGREGATION 261 WILLIS AVENUE .... MINEOLA **NY** 11501 (516) 746-3211
BET TORAH 60 SMITH AVENUE .... MOUNT KISCO **NY** 10549 (914) 666-7595
EMANUEL-FLEETWOOD RELIGIOUS SCHOOL
261 EAST LINCOLN AVENUE .... MT VERNON **NY** 10552 (914) 664-4587
FREE SYNAGOGUE OF WESTCHESTER
500 NORTH COLUMBUS AVENUE .... MT VERNON **NY** 10552 (914) 664-1727
SINAI TEMPLE 132 CRARY AVENUE .... MT VERNON **NY** 10550 (914) 668-9471
YM-YWHA, MT VERNON 30 OAKLEY AVENUE .... MT VERNON **NY** 10550 (914) 664-0500
WEST END TEMPLE 147-02 NEWPORT AVENUE .... NEPONSIT **NY** 11694 (718) 634-0301
EMANUEL, TEMPLE 3315 HILLSIDE AVENUE .... NEW HYDE PARK **NY** 11580 (516) 746-1120
NEW HYDE PARK JEWISH CENTER 100 LAKEVILLE ROAD .... NEW HYDE PARK **NY** 11040 (516) 354-7583
YOUNG ISRAEL OF NEW HYDE PARK 264-15 77 AVENUE .... NEW HYDE PARK **NY** 11040 (516) 343-0496
ANSHE SHOLOM, CONGREGATION 50 NORTH AVENUE .... NEW ROCHELLE **NY** 10805 (914) 632-9220
BETH EL SYNAGOGUE NORTH AVENUE & NORTHFIELD ROAD ...... NEW ROCHELLE **NY** 10804 (914) 235-2700
COMMUNITY HEBREW HIGH SCHOOL OF NEW ROCHELLE
NORTH AVENUE & NORTHFIELD ROAD .... NEW ROCHELLE **NY** 10804 (914) 235-2700
ISRAEL, TEMPLE 1000 PINEBROOK BOULEVARD .... NEW ROCHELLE **NY** 10804 (914) 235-1800
BROTHERHOOD SYNAGOGUE 28 GRAMERCY PARK S .... NEW YORK **NY** 10003 (212) 674-5750
CENTRAL SYNAGOGUE 123 EAST 55TH STREET .... NEW YORK **NY** 10022 (212) 838-5122
COMM. HEBREW SCHOOL-FT TYRON J.C./HEBREW TABERNACLE CONG.
524 FORT WASHINGTON AVENUE .... NEW YORK **NY** 10033 (212) 795-1391
CONSERVATIVE SYNAGOGUE OF FIFTH AVENUE
11 EAST 11TH STREET .... NEW YORK **NY** 10003 (212) 929-6954
DARCHEI SHOLOM 344 EAST 14TH STREET .... NEW YORK **NY** 10003 (212) 677-8090
EAST END TEMPLE 398 SECOND AVENUE .... NEW YORK **NY** 10010 (212) 254-8518
EDUCATIONAL ALLIANCE 197 EAST BROADWAY .... NEW YORK **NY** 10002 (212) 475-6200
EMANU-EL, CONGREGATION 1 EAST 65TH STREET .... NEW YORK **NY** 10021 (212) 744-1400
FIFTH AVENUE SYNAGOGUE 5 EAST 62ND STREET .... NEW YORK **NY** 10021 (212) 838-2122
HABONIM, CONGREGATION 44 WEST 66TH STREET .... NEW YORK **NY** 10023 (212) 787-5347
HAVURAH SCHOOL 251 WEST 100TH STREET .... NEW YORK **NY** 10025 (212) 662-3436
ISRAEL, TEMPLE 112 EAST 75TH STREET .... NEW YORK **NY** 10021 (212) 249-5000
LINCOLN SQUARE SYNAGOGUE & GUSTAV STERN HEBREW HIGH SCHOOL
200 AMSTERDAM AVENUE .... NEW YORK **NY** 10023 (212) 874-6100
PARK AVENUE SYNAGOGUE 50 EAST 87TH STREET .... NEW YORK **NY** 10028 (212) 369-2600
PARK EAST SYNAGOGUE 164 EAST 68TH STREET .... NEW YORK **NY** 10021 (212) 737-6900
PROZDOR OF THE JEWISH THEOLOGICAL SEMINARY
3080 BROADWAY .... NEW YORK **NY** 10027 (212) 678-8825
RODEPH SHOLOM, CONGREGATION 7 WEST 83RD STREET .... NEW YORK **NY** 10023 (212) 362-8800
SHAARAY TEFILA, TEMPLE 250 EAST 79TH STREET .... NEW YORK **NY** 10021 (212) 535-8008
SHEARITH ISRAEL 8 WEST 70TH STREET .... NEW YORK **NY** 10023 (212) 873-0300
SOCIETY FOR THE ADVANCEMENT OF JUDAISM
15 WEST 86TH STREET .... NEW YORK **NY** 10024 (212) 724-7000
STEPHEN WISE FREE SYNAGOGUE 30 WEST 68TH STREET .... NEW YORK **NY** 10023 (212) 877-4050
VILLAGE TEMPLE 33 EAST 12TH STREET .... NEW YORK **NY** 10003 (212) 674-2340
YM-YWHA NINETY-SECOND STREET 1395 LEXINGTON AVENUE .... NEW YORK **NY** 10028 (212) 427-6000
YM-YWHA OF INWOOD & WASHINGTON HEIGHTS 54 NAGLE AVENUE .... NEW YORK **NY** 10040 (212) 569-6200
AGUDAS ISRAEL 290 NORTH STREET .... NEWBURGH **NY** 12550 (914) 562-5604
BETH-EL, TEMPLE 1373 BELLMORE ROAD .... NORTH BELLMORE **NY** 11710 (516) 781-6923
OHR TORA, NORTH WOODMERE JEWISH CENTER
410 HUNGRY HARBOR ROAD .... NORTH WOODMERE **NY** 11581 (516) 791-2346
BNAI ISRAEL REFORM TEMPLE
PO BOX 158-IDLE HOUR BOULEVARD & BILTMORE AVENUE .... OAKDALE **NY** 11769 (516) 589-8948
AVODAH, TEMPLE 3050 OCEANSIDE ROAD .... OCEANSIDE **NY** 11572 (516) 766-6835
CENTRAL HEBREW HIGH SCHOOL 2860 BROWER AVENUE .... OCEANSIDE **NY** 11572 (516) 766-3412
OCEAN HARBOR, JEWISH CENTER OF ROYAL & WEIDNER AVENUES .... OCEANSIDE **NY** 11572 (516) 536-6144
OCEANSIDE JEWISH CENTER 2860 BROWER AVENUE .... OCEANSIDE **NY** 11572 (516) 764-4213
SHAARY HASHOMAIM 3309 SKILLMAN .... OCEANSIDE **NY** 11572 (516) 764-9379
SOUTH SHORE HEBREW SCHOOL FOR SPECIAL CHILDREN
3369 PARK AVENUE .... OCEANSIDE **NY** 11572 (516) 764-2529
YOUNG ISRAEL OF OCEANSIDE 150 WAUKENA AVENUE .... OCEANSIDE **NY** 11572 (516) 764-1099
BETH ELOHIM, TEMPLE 926 ROUND SWAMP ROAD .... OLD BETHPAGE **NY** 11804 (516) 694-4544
SOCIETY OF JEWISH SCIENCE 825 ROUND SWAMP ROAD .... OLD BETHPAGE **NY** 11804 (516) 249-6262
WESTBURY HEBREW CONGREGATION 21 OLD WESTBURY ROAD ... OLD WESTBURY **NY** 11568 (516) 333-7977
OYSTER BAY JEWISH CENTER BERRY HILL ROAD .... OYSTER BAY **NY** 11771 (516) 922-6650
BNAI JACOB RELIGIOUS SCHOOL 80-05 101ST AVENUE .... OZONE PARK **NY** 11416 (718) 296-8334
OZONE PARK JEWISH CENTER 107-01 CROSS BAY BOULEVARD .... OZONE PARK **NY** 11417 (718) 848-4096
BETH EL OF PATCHOGUE, TEMPLE 45 OAK STREET .... PATCHOGUE **NY** 11772 (516) 475-1882
FIRST HEBREW CONGREGATION 1821 EAST MAIN STREET .... PEEKSKILL **NY** 10566 (914) 739-0500
PELHAM JEWISH CENTER 451 ESPLANADE .... PELHAM MANOR **NY** 10803 (914) 738-9765
MANETTO HILL JEWISH CENTER 244 MANETTO HILL ROAD .... PLAINVIEW **NY** 11803 (516) 935-5454
PLAINVIEW JEWISH CENTER 95 FLORAL DRIVE .... PLAINVIEW **NY** 11803 (516) 938-8610
KNESES TIFERETH ISRAEL 575 KING STREET .... PORT CHESTER **NY** 10573 (914) 939-1004
SUFFOLK COUNTY INSTITUTE FOR JEWISH STUDIES
BOX 363, HUNTINGTON STATION 7 .... PORT JEFFERSON **NY** 11776 (516) 462-9839
NORTH SHORE JEWISH CENTER 385 OLD TOWN ROAD ...... PORT JEFFERSON STA. **NY** 11776 (516) 928-3737
BETH ISRAEL, CONGREGATION TEMPLE DRIVE .... PORT WASHINGTON **NY** 11050 (516) 767-1708
COMMUNITY SYNAGOGUE 150 MIDDLE NECK ROAD .... PORT WASHINGTON **NY** 11050 (516) 883-3144
PORT JEWISH CENTER PO BOX 852 .... PORT WASHINGTON **NY** 11050 (516) 883-5174
HABONIM, CONGREGATION 63-44 WETHEROLE STREET .... REGO PARK **NY** 11374 (718) 897-0693
RANANAH NURSERY SCHOOL 90-14 63RD DRIVE .... REGO PARK **NY** 11374 (718) 275-5668
REGO PARK JEWISH CENTER 97-30 QUEENS BOULEVARD .... REGO PARK **NY** 11374 (718) 459-1000
ISRAEL, TEMPLE 490 NORTHVILLE TURNPIKE .... RIVERHEAD **NY** 11901 (516) 727-3191
B'NAI SHOLOM, TEMPLE 100 HEMPSTEAD AVENUE .... ROCKVILLE CENTRE **NY** 11570 (516) 764-4100
CENTRAL SYNAGOGUE OF NASSAU COUNTY
430 DEMOTT AVENUE .... ROCKVILLE CENTRE **NY** 11570 (516) 766-4300
ROOSEVELT ISLAND, JEWISH CONGREGATION OF
555 MAIN STREET .... ROOSEVELT ISLAND **NY** 10044
ROSEDALE JEWISH CENTER 247-11 FRANCIS LEWIS BOULEVARD .... ROSEDALE **NY** 11422 (718) 528-3988
SHELTER ROCK JEWISH CENTER
SHELTER ROCK & SEARINGTON ROADS .... ROSLYN **NY** 11576 (516) 741-4305
BETH SHOLOM, TEMPLE
ROSLYN ROAD AT NORTHERN STATE PARKWAY .... ROSLYN HEIGHTS **NY** 11577 (516) 484-4980
RECONSTRUCTIONIST SYNAGOGUE 1 WILLOW STREET .... ROSLYN HEIGHTS **NY** 11577 (516) 621-5540
SINAI, TEMPLE 425 ROSLYN ROAD .... ROSLYN HEIGHTS **NY** 11577 (516) 621-6800
COMMUNITY SYNAGOGUE 200 FOREST AVENUE .... RYE **NY** 10580 (914) 967-6262
EMANU-EL, CONGREGATION
WESTCHESTER AVENUE AND KENILWORTH ROAD .... RYE **NY** 10580 (914) 967-7977
SAYVILLE JEWISH CENTER 225 GREENLEY AVENUE .... SAYVILLE **NY** 11782 (516) 589-9722
SCARSDALE SYNAGOGUE 2 OGDEN ROAD .... SCARSDALE **NY** 10583 (914) 725-5175
WESTCHESTER REFORM TEMPLE 255 MAMARONECK ROAD .... SCARSDALE **NY** 10583 (914) 723-7727
YM-YWHA, MID-WESTCHESTER 999 WILMOT ROAD .... SCARSDALE **NY** 10583 (914) 472-3300
YOUNG ISRAEL OF SCARSDALE 1313 WEAVER ROAD-PO BOX 103H ..... SCARSDALE **NY** 10583 (914) 636-8686
SEAFORD JEWISH CENTER 2343 SOUTH SEAMANS NECK ROAD, BOX 81 ... SEAFORD **NY** 11783 (516) 785-4570
BETH SHOLOM, TEMPLE-LAWRENCE KARP RELIGIOUS SCHOOL
PO BOX 764 .... SMITHTOWN **NY** 11787 (516) 724-0424
JEWISH CENTER OF BELLMORE 25-50 CENTER AVENUE .... SOUTH BELLMORE **NY** 11710 (516) 781-3072
AGUDAS ACHIM ANSHE CHESED, CONGREGATION
641 DELAFIELD AVENUE .... STATEN ISLAND **NY** 10310 (718) 727-5920
B'NAI ISRAEL, CONGREGATION 45 TROMBLEY AVENUE .... STATEN ISLAND **NY** 10306 (718) 987-8188
B'NAI JESHURUN, CONGREGATION 275 MARTLING AVENUE .... STATEN ISLAND **NY** 10314 (718) 981-5550
EMANUEL OF STATEN ISLAND, TEMPLE 984 POST AVENUE .... STATEN ISLAND **NY** 10302 (718) 442-5966
ISRAEL, TEMPLE 315 FOREST AVENUE .... STATEN ISLAND **NY** 10301 (718) 727-2231
JEWISH COMMUNITY CENTER 475 VICTORY BOULEVARD .... STATEN ISLAND **NY** 10301 (718) 981-1500
YOUNG ISRAEL OF ELTINGVILLE, INCORPORATED
374 RIDGEWOOD AVENUE .... STATEN ISLAND **NY** 10308 (718) 984-8393
YOUNG ISRAEL OF STATEN ISLAND 835 FOREST HILL ROAD .... STATEN ISLAND **NY** 10314 (718) 698-7041
ISAIAH, TEMPLE 1404 STONY BROOK ROAD .... STONY BROOK **NY** 11790 (516) 751-8518
EAST NASSAU HEBREW CONGREGATION
310A SOUTH OYSTER BAY ROAD .... SYOSSET **NY** 11791 (516) 921-1800
MIDWAY HEBREW HIGH SCHOOL #18 330 SOUTH OYSTER BAY ROAD ...... SYOSSET **NY** 11791 (516) 822-3639
MIDWAY JEWISH CENTER - DR. FELIX BERGER SCHOOL
330 SOUTH OYSTER BAY ROAD .... SYOSSET **NY** 11791 (516) 938-8390
NORTH SHORE SYNAGOGUE 83 MUTTONTOWN ROAD .... SYOSSET **NY** 11791 (516) 921-2282
BETH ABRAHAM, TEMPLE 25 LEROY AVENUE .... TARRYTOWN **NY** 10591 (914) 631-1770
GENESIS HEBREW CENTER 25 OAKLAND AVENUE .... TUCKAHOE **NY** 10707 (914) 961-3766
UNIONDALE JEWISH CENTER 760 JERUSALEM AVENUE .... UNIONDALE **NY** 11553 (516) 486-8788
BETH SHOLOM CONGREGATION-SUNRISE JEWISH CENTER
550 ROCKAWAY AVENUE .... VALLEY STREAM **NY** 11581 (516) 561-9245
GATES OF ZION, TEMPLE 322 NORTH CORONA AVENUE .... VALLEY STREAM **NY** 11580 (516) 262-6193
HILLEL, TEMPLE 1000 ROSEDALE ROAD .... VALLEY STREAM **NY** 11581 (516) 791-6344
SUBURBAN TEMPLE 2900 JERUSALEM AVENUE .... WANTAGH **NY** 11793 (516) 221-2370
WANTAGH JEWISH CENTER 3710 WOODBINE AVENUE .... WANTAGH **NY** 11973 (516) 221-1650
NASSAU COMMUNITY TEMPLE-BETH EL
240 HEMPSTEAD AVENUE .... WEST HEMPSTEAD **NY** 11552 (516) 485-1811
WEST HEMPSTEAD JEWISH CENTER 711 DOGWOOD AVENUE .... WEST HEMPSTEAD **NY** 11552 (516) 481-7448
BETH TORAH, TEMPLE 243 CANTIAGUE ROAD .... WESTBURY **NY** 11590 (516) 334-7979
COMMUNITY REFORM TEMPLE 712 THE PLAIN ROAD .... WESTBURY **NY** 11590 (516) 333-1839
SHOLOM, TEMPLE 675 BROOKSIDE CENTER .... WESTBURY **NY** 11590 (516) 334-2800
BET AM SHALOM SYNAGOGUE 295 SOUNDVIEW AVENUE .... WHITE PLAINS **NY** 10606 (914) 946-8851
HEBREW INSTITUTE OF WHITE PLAINS 20 GREENRIDGE AVENUE ..... WHITE PLAINS **NY** 10605 (914) 948-3095
ISRAEL CENTER, TEMPLE 280 OLD MAMARONECK ROAD .... WHITE PLAINS **NY** 10605 (914) 779-3782
JEWISH COMMUNITY CENTER-LAWRENCE W. SCHWARTZ SCHOOL
252 SOUNDVIEW AVENUE .... WHITE PLAINS **NY** 10606 (914) 949-4717
WOODLANDS COMMUNITY TEMPLE 50 WORTHINGTON ROAD .... WHITE PLAINS **NY** 10607 (914) 592-7070
CLEARVIEW JEWISH CENTER 1650 UTOPIA PARKWAY .... WHITESTONE **NY** 11357 (718) 352-6670
WHITESTONE HEBREW CENTER 12-45 CLINTONVILLE STREET .... WHITESTONE **NY** 11357 (718) 767-7852
SONS OF ISRAEL, CONGREGATION 111 IRVING PLACE .... WOODMERE **NY** 11598 (516) 374-0805
EMANU-EL, TEMPLE 306 RUMSEY ROAD .... YONKERS **NY** 10705 (914) 963-0575
LINCOLN PARK JEWISH CENTER-NORTHEAST JEWISH CENTER
311 CENTRAL PARK AVENUE .... YONKERS **NY** 10704 (914) 965-7119
MIDCHESTER JEWISH CENTER 236 GRANDVIEW BOULEVARD .... YONKERS **NY** 10710 (914) 779-3660
NORTHEAST JEWISH CENTER 11 SALISBURY ROAD .... YONKERS **NY** 10710 (914) 337-0268
SONS OF ISRAEL 105 RADFORD STREET .... YONKERS **NY** 10705 (914) 423-2070
YORKTOWN JEWISH CENTER 2966 CROMPOND ROAD .... YORKTOWN **NY** 10598 (914) 245-2324
BETH AM TEMPLE CHURCH & SUMMIT STREETS .... YORKTOWN HEIGHTS **NY** 10598 (914) 962-7500
ANSHE CHESED (FAIRMOUNT TEMPLE) 23737 FAIRMOUNT BLVD .... CLEVELAND **OH** 44122 (216) 464-5890
B'NAI JESHURUN (TEMPLE ON THE HEIGHTS)
27501 FAIRMOUNT BLVD .... CLEVELAND **OH** 44124 (216) 831-6555
BETH AM (COMMUNITY TEMPLE) 3557 WASHINGTON BLVD .... CLEVELAND **OH** 44118 (216) 321-1247
BETH ISRAEL (THE WEST TEMPLE) 14308 TRISKETT ROAD .... CLEVELAND **OH** 44111 (216) 941-8882
BETH TORAH - BETH AM CONGREGATION 3557 WASHINGTON BLVD ... CLEVELAND **OH** 44124 (216) 371-9313

BETHAYNU 25400 FAIRMOUNT BLVD .... CLEVELAND **OH** 44122 (216) 292-2931
BRITH EMETH 27575 SHAKER BLVD .... CLEVELAND **OH** 44124 (216) 831-5363
EMANU-EL, TEMPLE 2200 SOUTH GREEN ROAD .... CLEVELAND **OH** 44121 (216) 381-6600
MAYFIELD HILLCREST SYNAGOGUE 1732 LANDERS ROAD .... CLEVELAND **OH** 44124 (216) 449-6200
PARK SYNAGOGUE 3300 MAYFIELD ROAD .... CLEVELAND **OH** 44118 (216) 371-2244
SUBURBAN TEMPLE 22401 CHAGRIN BLVD .... CLEVELAND **OH** 44122 (216) 991-0700
TAYLOR ROAD SYNAGOGUE 1970 SOUTH TAYLOR ROAD .... CLEVELAND **OH** 44118 (216) 321-5875
WARRENSVILLE CENTER SYNAGOGUE
1508 WARRENSVILLE CENTER ROAD .... CLEVELAND **OH** 44121 (216) 382-6566
COLUMBUS HEBREW SCHOOL 1125 COLLEGE AVENUE .... COLUMBUS **OH** 43209 (614) 231-7764
COMMUNITY HEBREW SCHOOL 4501 DENLINGER ROAD .... DAYTON **OH** 45426 (513) 854-2021
AM SHALOM (LAKE COUNTY JEWISH CENTER) R P.O. BOX 454 .... MENTOR **OH** 44060 (216) 953-1315
BETH SHALOM, TEMPLE P.O. BOX 315 .... TWINSBURG **OH** 44087 (216) 266-3161
ADATH ISRAEL SCHOOL 37 SOUTHBOURNE AVENUE .... DOWNSVIEW **ON** M3H 1A4 (416) 635-5340
BETH DAVID - B'NAI ISRAEL - BETH AM 55 YEOMANS ROAD .... DOWNSVIEW **ON** (416) 633-1338
BETH EMETH - BAIS YEHUDA 100 ELDER STREET .... DOWNSVIEW **ON** (416) 636-3096
OR SHALOM TALMUD TORAH 534 HURON STREET .... LONDON **ON** N5Y 4J5 (519) 438-3081
OTTAWA TALMUD TORAH AFTERNOON SCHOOL 453 RIDEAU STREET ..... OTTAWA **ON** K1N 5Z3
SHAAREH HAIM HEBREW SCHOOL 422 CARRVILLE ROAD .... RICHMOND HILL **ON** (416) 884-8400
BETH TZEDEC ELEMENTARY AND HEBREW HIGH SCHOOL
1700 BATHURST STREET .... TORONTO **ON** M5P 3K3 (416) 787-0381
CONGREGATION HABONIM OF TORONTO RELIGIOUS SCHOOL
12 HOLLAMAN ROAD .... TORONTO **ON** M6B 3B8 (416) 881-6952
MILDRED ARNOFF MEMORIAL SCHOOL - BETH SHOLOM
1445 EGLINTON AVENUE WEST .... TORONTO **ON** M6C 2E6 (416) 781-9161
MORRIS WINCHEVSKY SUNDAY SCHOOLS 585 CRANBROOK AVENUE .... TORONTO **ON** M6A 2X9 (416) 789-5502
WORKMEN'S CIRCLE I.L. PERETZ SCHOOLS
471 LAWRENCE AVENUE WEST .... TORONTO **ON** M5M 1C6 (416) 787-2081
BETH TIKVAH CONGREGATIONAL SCHOOL 3080 BAYVIEW AVENUE .. WILLOWDALE **ON** M2N 5L3 (416) 221-5083
HEBREW SUNDAY SCHOOL SOCIETY OF GREATER PHILADELPHIA, THE
1729 PINE STREET .... PHILADELPHIA **PA** 19103 (215) 735-7972
HEBREW INSTITUTE 6401 FORBES AVENUE .... PITTSBURGH **PA** 15217 (412) 521-1100
SCHOOL OF ADVANCED JEWISH STUDIES
1824 MURRAY AVENUE, SUITE 303, P.O. BOX 81800 .... PITTSBURGH **PA** 15217 (412) 421-6110

TEACHERS ASSOCIATIONS

JEWISH TEACHERS ASSOCIATION 45 E. 33RD STREET .... NEW YORK **NY** 10016 (212) 684-0556
YESHIVA ENGLISH PRINCIPALS ASSOCIATION 426 WEST 58TH STREET .. NEW YORK **NY** 10019 (212) 245-8200

THEATRE

A TRAVELING JEWISH THEATRE, COREY FISCHER .... LOS ANGELES **CA** (213) 650-7063
SHALOM CONCERT BUREAU BOX 35092 .... LOS ANGELES **CA** 90035 (213) 931-6125
THE NEW ARTEF PLAYERS PO BOX 345 .... LOS ANGELES **CA** 90048 (213) 655-1697
NORMAN J. FEDDER, THEATER PROGRAM, SPEECH DEPARTMENT
KANSAS STATE UNIVERSITY .... MANHATTAN **KS** 66506 (913) 532-6011
FOLKSBIENE THEATER 123 EAST 55TH STREET .... NEW YORK **NY** 10022 (212) 755-2231
HEBREW ACTORS' UNION 31 EAST 7TH STREET .... NEW YORK **NY** 10003 (212) 674-1923
JEWISH REPERTORY THEATRE 344 E. 14TH STREET .... NEW YORK **NY** 10003 (212) 674-7200
JEWISH THEATRE ASSOCIATION 122 E. 44TH STREET .... NEW YORK **NY** 10017 (212) 490-2280
JEWISH THEATRE FOR CHILDREN 426 W. 58TH STREET .... NEW YORK **NY** 10019 (212) 245-8200
LIVELY & YIDDISH CO., INC. (PRODUCER OF YIDDISH SHOWS)
45 EAST 33RD STREET .... NEW YORK **NY** 10016 (212) 686-3535
SASHA NANUS C/O LECTURE BUREAU J.W.B. 15 EAST 26TH STREET ..... NEW YORK **NY** 10010 (212) 532-4949
YESHIVA COLLEGE DRAMATICS SOCIETY 2475 AMSTERDAM AVENUE ... NEW YORK **NY** 10033 (212) 928-0181
SALLY FOX, JEWISH INVOLVEMENT THEATRE
PO BOX 3309, OSU STATION .... COLUMBUS **OH** 43210

TORAH TECHNOLOGY

TORAH TECHNICS - "WHERE TORAH & TECHNOLOGY MEET"
1603 CARROLL STREET .... BROOKLYN **NY** 11213 (718) 953-7028
ZOMET ALON SHVUT .... GUSH ETZION **IS** 90940 (02) 931442
INSTITUTE FOR SCIENCE AND HALACHA 1 HAPISGA STREET .... JERUSALEM **IS** 96465 (02) 416505

TOURS & TRAVEL PROGRAMS

FOREIGN/SHARON TOURS 9300 WILSHIRE BOULEVARD .... BEVERLY HILLS **CA** 90212 (213) 273-8872
TRAVEL CENTER OF BEVERLY HILLS - LEVY SPITZER
291 S. LA CIENEGA BLVD. SUITE 101 .... BEVERLY HILLS **CA** 90211 (213) 652-3434
BESTWAY TRAVEL SERVICE 334 NO. FAIRFAX AVENUE .... LOS ANGELES **CA** 90036 (213) 937-1565
ISRAEL GOVERNMENT TOURIST OFFICE
6380 WILSHIRE BOULEVARD .... LOS ANGELES **CA** 90048 (213) 658-7462
L&R TRAVEL 442½ NORTH FAIRFAX AVENUE .... LOS ANGELES **CA** 90036 (213) 653-4233
MADAN TRAVEL SERVICE 7970 BEVERLY BOULEVARD .... LOS ANGELES **CA** 90048 (213) 651-3155
B'NAI B'RITH TOURS 1640 RHODE ISLAND AVENUE .... WASHINGTON **DC** 20036 (202) 857-6600
HERITAGE TOURS 3305 MACOMB STREET, N.W. .... WASHINGTON **DC** 20008 (202) 362-4367
ISRAEL GOVERNMENT TOURIST OFFICE 795 PEACHTREE STREET N.E. .... ATLANTA **GA** 30308 (404) 875-7851
IDEAL TOURS OF CHICAGO 6600 NORTH LINCOLN AVENUE .... CHICAGO **IL** 60645 (312) 982-0444
ISRAEL GOVERNMENT TOURIST OFFICE 5 SOUTH WABASH AVENUE ..... CHICAGO **IL** 60603 (312) 782-4306
AKIVA TOURS 5009 16TH AVENUE .... BROOKLYN **NY** 11219 (718) 851-1121
ARIEL TOURS, INC. 4311 18TH AVENUE .... BROOKLYN **NY** 11218 (718) 633-7900
BEDFORD GLATT RESORTS 4211 AVENUE K .... BROOKLYN **NY** 11210 (718) 258-9072
CERTIFIED TRAVEL 4311 18TH AVENUE .... BROOKLYN **NY** 11204 (718) 633-1707
EXECUTIVE MOTOR TOURS 81 BROOKFIELD .... BROOKLYN **NY** 11204 (718) 436-1385
HARIM KOSHER TOURS 1736 E. 4TH ST. .... BROOKLYN **NY** 11223 (718) 645-2974
SWEET SIXTEEN TRAVEL 1706 E. 16TH STREET .... BROOKLYN **NY** 11229 (718) 627-0097
J.T.A. TOURS 527 CHESTNUT STREET .... CEDARHURST **NY** 11516 (718) 476-0900

Name / Address	City	State	Zip	Phone
EZRA TOURS 144-35 69TH AVENUE	FLUSHING	NY	11367	(718) 544-5341
TULI TRAVEL 69-54 MAIN STREET	FLUSHING	NY	11367	(718) 544-2000
AMIT TRAVEL 817 BROADWAY	NEW YORK	NY	10003	(212) 477-4720
AGUDATH ISRAEL TRAVEL DEPARTMENT 84 WILLIAM STREET	NEW YORK	NY	10038	(212) 797-9000
AMERICAN FRIENDS OF HAIFA UNIVERSITY 206 FIFTH AVENUE	NEW YORK	NY	10010	(212) 696-4022
AMERICAN FRIENDS OF HEBREW UNIVERSITY 11 EAST 69TH STREET	NEW YORK	NY	10021	(212) 472-9E00
AMERICAN FRIENDS OF TEL AVIV UNIVERSITY 342 MADISON AVENUE	NEW YORK	NY	10017	(212) 687-5651
AMERICAN JEWISH CONGRESS, OVERSEAS TRAVEL DEPARTMENT 15 EAST 84TH STREET	NEW YORK	NY	10028	(212) 879-4588
ARCHAEOLOGICAL TOURS OF ISRAEL 1560 BROADWAY	NEW YORK	NY	10019	(212) 719-5500
ATLAS AMBASSADOR KOSHER TOURS 25 WEST 43RD STREET	NEW YORK	NY	10036	(212) 575-8840
BAR/BAT MITZVAH PILGRIMAGE - WORLD ZIONIST ORGANIZATION 515 PARK AVENUE	NEW YORK	NY	10022	(212) 752-0600
B'NAI B'RITH TOURS 823 U.N. PLAZA	NEW YORK	NY	10017	(212) 490-2525
COMPASS TRAVEL BUREAU, INC. 70 WEST 40TH STREET	NEW YORK	NY	10018	(212) 354-6868
DAPHNA TRAVEL BUREAU, INC. 444 MADISON AVENUE	NEW YORK	NY	10022	(800) 223-6874
E.T.S. TOURS 5 PENN PLAZA (8TH AVENUE & 34TH STREET)	NEW YORK	NY	10001	(212) 563-0780
EASTOURS, INC. 461 EIGHTH AVENUE	NEW YORK	NY	10001	(212) 947-9595
EMUNAH TOURS/EMUNAH WOMEN OF AMERICA 370 SEVENTH AVENUE	NEW YORK	NY	10001	(212) 947-5454
FOREIGN/SHARON TOURS 461 EIGHTH AVENUE	NEW YORK	NY	10001	(212) 947-9595
GELLER-HOWARD TRAVEL 630 THIRD AVENUE	NEW YORK	NY	10017	(212) 599-0888
HABONIM LABOR ZIONIST YOUTH 27 WEST 20TH STREET	NEW YORK	NY	10011	(212) 255-1796
HADASSAH 50 WEST 58TH STREET	NEW YORK	NY	10022	(212) 355-7900
HADASSAH ZIONIST YOUTH COMMISSION 50 WEST 58TH STREET	NEW YORK	NY	10022	(212) 355-7900
HAPOEL-MIZRACHI WOMEN'S ORGANIZATION 370 7TH AVENUE	NEW YORK	NY	10001	(212) 564-9045
HASHOMER HATZAIR ZIONIST YOUTH ORGANIZATION 150 FIFTH AVENUE	NEW YORK	NY	10011	(212) 242-0532
HISTADRUT FOUNDATION FOR EDUCATIONAL TRAVEL 630 THIRD AVENUE	NEW YORK	NY	10017	(212) 697-6822
HISTADRUT TOURS 630 THIRD AVENUE	NEW YORK	NY	10017	(212) 697-6822
ISRAEL AIR GROUP TRAVEL INFORMATION 20 EAST 49TH STREET	NEW YORK	NY	10017	(212) 688-5170
ISRAEL GOVERNMENT TOURIST OFFICE 350 FIFTH AVENUE	NEW YORK	NY	10001	(212) 560-0560
ISRAEL HOTEL REPRESENTATIVES 120 EAST 56TH STREET	NEW YORK	NY	10022	(212) 752-6120
ISRAEL TRAVEL CENTER FOR STUDENTS 1140 BROADWAY	NEW YORK	NY	10001	(212) 691-2200
ISRAM WHOLESALE TOURS & TRAVEL, LTD. 630 THIRD AVENUE	NEW YORK	NY	10017	(212) 661-1193
JEWISH EDUCATIONAL VENTURES, INC. ONE PARK AVENUE/SUITE 1900	NEW YORK	NY	10016	(212) 684-2010
KESHER KOSHER TOURS 1501 BROADWAY	NEW YORK	NY	10036	(212) 921-7740
KIBBUTZ ALIYA DESK 27 WEST 20TH STREET	NEW YORK	NY	10011	(212) 255-1338
KO-TOURS 183 MADISON AVENUE, SUITE 716	NEW YORK	NY	10016	(212) 725-4800
KOPEL TOURS, LTD. 40 EAST 49TH STREET	NEW YORK	NY	10017	(212) 838-0500
LABOR ZIONIST ALLIANCE, KIBBUTZ ALIYAH DESK 275 SEVENTH AVENUE	NEW YORK	NY	10001	(212) 989-0300
MIZRACHI TOURS 200 PARK AVENUE SOUTH	NEW YORK	NY	10003	(212) 673-6610
NATIONAL HEBREW CULTURE COUNCIL 1776 BROADWAY	NEW YORK	NY	10019	(212) 247-0741
NATIONAL JEWISH WELFARE BOARD 15 EAST 26TH STREET	NEW YORK	NY	10010	(212) 532-4949
NOAM - HAMISHMERET 25 WEST 26TH STREET	NEW YORK	NY	10010	(212) 684-6091
ORIENT FLEXI-PAX TOURS 630 THIRD AVENUE	NEW YORK	NY	10017	(212) 692-9550
ORIENT FLEXI-PAX TOURS 630 THIRD AVENUE	NEW YORK	NY	10017	(800) 545-5540
TEK TRAVEL 45 EAST 17TH STREET	NEW YORK	NY	10003	(212) 673-6610
USY ON WHEELS, USY PILGRIMAGE (YOUTH) 155 FIFTH AVENUE	NEW YORK	NY	10010	(212) 533-7800
UNION OF AMERICAN HEBREW CONGREGATIONS 838 FIFTH AVENUE	NEW YORK	NY	10021	(212) 249-0100
WOMEN'S AMERICAN ORT 162 WEST 56TH STREET	NEW YORK	NY	10019	(212) 247-4640
WORLD ZIONIST ORGANIZATION 515 PARK AVENUE	NEW YORK	NY	10022	(212) 752-0600
YOUNG ISRAEL TOURS 3 WEST 16TH STREET	NEW YORK	NY	10011	(212) 929-1525
ZIONIST ORGANIZATION OF AMERICA - ISRAEL SUMMER PROGRAMS 4 EAST 34TH STREET	NEW YORK	NY	10016	(212) 481-1500
AMERICAN ORGANIZATION OF TOUR OPERATORS TO ISRAEL 145-98 GUY BREWER BOULEVARD	QUEENS	NY	11434	(718) 528-0700
LEISURE TIME TOURS 145-98 GUY BREWER BLVD	QUEENS	NY	11434	(718) 528-0700
HANS WEINBERG SYNAGOGUE TRAVEL INC. 640 HOWARD AVENUE	WEST HEMPSTEAD	NY	11552	(516) 489-6586
CANADIAN FRIENDS OF HEBREW UNIVERSITY 1506 MCGREGOR AVENUE	MONTREAL	QU		(514) 932-2133

TRANSLATIONS

Name / Address	City	State	Zip	Phone
BARON WRITING ENTERPRISES P.O. BOX 23741	PHOENIX	AZ	85063	(602) 269-8327
"TARGEM" TRANSLATION SERVICE 1731 51ST STREET	BROOKLYN	NY	11204	(718) 854-2848
'A' CERTIFIED TRANSLATIONS 21-07 CORNAGA AVENUE	FAR ROCKAWAY	NY	11691	(718) 471-2711
HEBREW TRANSLATIONS SERVICE 22 CORNELIA STREET	NEW YORK	NY	10014	(212) 242-2469
"TARGEM" TRANSLATION SERVICE P.O. BOX 173	SPRING VALLEY	NY	10977	(914) 354-8176

TRAVEL TO THE SOVIET UNION

Name / Address	City	State	Zip	Phone
AMERICAN JEWISH CONGRESS 15 EAST 84TH STREET	NEW YORK	NY	10028	(212) 879-4500
INTOURIST 630 FIFTH AVENUE	NEW YORK	NY	10111	(212) 757-3884
NATIONAL CONFERENCE ON SOVIET JEWRY 10 EAST 40TH STREET	NEW YORK	NY	10036	(212) 679-6122
STUDENT STRUGGLE FOR SOVIET JEWRY 210 WEST 91ST STREET	NEW YORK	NY	10024	(212) 799-8900

ULPAN

Name / Address	City	State	Zip	Phone
HEBREW ULPAN CENTER 515 PARK AVENUE	NEW YORK	NY	10022	(212) 752-0600
KEREN HATARBUT INSTITUTE 788 MARLEE AVENUE	TORONTO	ON	M6B 3K1	(416) 787-0197

VEGETARIANS

Name / Address	City	State	Zip	Phone
JEWISH VEGETARIAN SOCIETY P.O. BOX 5722	BALTIMORE	MD	21208	(301) 521-3061
THE JEWISH VEGETARIAN SOCIETY-AMERICAN SECRETARIAT 68-38 YELLOWSTONE BOULEVARD, C/O SAMUEL JUDAH GROSSBERG	FOREST HILLS	NY	11375	(718) 459-1014
JEWISH VEGETARIAN SOCIETY C/O MR. J. WOLF, 210 RIVERSIDE DRIVE	NEW YORK	NY	10025	(212) 666-6216

VITAMINS

Name / Address	City	State	Zip	Phone
PRECISION VITAMINS 1524 47TH ST	BROOKLYN	NY	11219	(718) 435-4333
ZAHLER'S NUTRITION CENTER 4724 NEW UTRECHT AVENUE	BROOKLYN	NY	11219	(718) 438-5336
FREEDA (OU) VITAMINS 36 EAST 41ST STREET	NEW YORK	NY	10017	(212) 685-4980
LOIS LANE'S NINTH & NATURAL 580 NINTH AVENUE AT 42ND ST	NEW YORK	NY	10036	(212) 695-5055

VOCATIONAL SERVICES

Name / Address	City	State	Zip	Phone
JEWISH VOCATIONAL SERVICE 22634 VANOWEN STREET	CANOGA PARK	CA	93107	(818) 710-8891
JEWISH VOCATIONAL SERVICE 6505 WILSHIRE BLVD	LOS ANGELES	CA	90048	(213) 655-8910
JEWISH VOCATIONAL SERVICE 6505 WILSHIRE BOULEVARD	LOS ANGELES	CA	90048	(213) 852-1234
JEWISH VOCATIONAL & CAREER COUNSELING SERVICE 870 MARKET STREET, ROOM 872	SAN FRANCISCO	CA	94102	(415) 391-3595
JEWISH FAMILY & CHILDREN'S SERVICE 300 SOUTH DAHLIA STREET	DENVER	CO	80222	(303) 321-3115
JEWISH VOCATIONAL SERVICE 318 N.W. 25TH STREET	MIAMI	FL	33137	(305) 576-3220
JEWISH VOCATIONAL SERVICE OF THE ATLANTA JEWISH FEDERATION 1745 PEACHTREE ROAD N.E.	ATLANTA	GA	30309	(404) 876-5872
JEWISH VOCATIONAL SERVICE 1 S. FRANKLIN STREET	CHICAGO	IL	60606	(312) 346-6700
JEWISH FAMILY VOCATIONAL SERVICE 3640 DUTCHMANS LANE	LOUISVILLE	KY	40205	(502) 452-6341
JEWISH VOCATIONAL SERVICE 31 NEW CHARDON STREET	BOSTON	MA	02114	(617) 723-2846
ASSOCIATED PLACEMENT & GUIDANCE SERVICE 5750 PARK HEIGHTS AVENUE	BALTIMORE	MD	21215	(301) 466-9200
JEWISH VOCATIONAL SERVICE 5750 PARK HEIGHTS AVENUE	BALTIMORE	MD	21215	(301) 466-9200
JEWISH VOCATIONAL SERVICE 4250 WOODWARD	DETROIT	MI	48201	(313) 833-8100
JEWISH VOCATIONAL OFFICE LOWER CONCOURSE-811 LASALLE COURT BUILDING	MINNEAPOLIS	MN	55402	(612) 338-8771
JEWISH VOCATIONAL SERVICES 1821 UNIVERSITY AVENUE	ST. PAUL	MN	55104	(612) 645-9377
JEWISH VOCATIONAL SERVICE 1516 GRAND AVENUE	KANSAS CITY	MO	64108	(816) 471-2808
JEWISH EMPLOYMENT & VOCATIONAL SERVICE 1727 LOCUST STREET	ST. LOUIS	MO	63103	(314) 241-3464
WORK EXPERIENCE CENTER OF JEWISH EMPLOYMENT VOCATIONAL SERV. 2545 SOUTH HANLEY	ST. LOUIS	MO	63144	
JEWISH VOCATIONAL SERVICE 67 N. CLINTON STREET	EAST ORANGE	NJ	07017	(201) 674-2415
JEWISH VOCATIONAL SERVICE 454 WILLIAM STREET	EAST ORANGE	NJ	07017	(201) 674-2415
JEWISH VOCATIONAL SERVICE OF METROPOLITAN NEW JERSEY 111 PROSPECT	EAST ORANGE	NJ	07017	(201) 674-6330
ALTRO WORK SHOPS 3600 JEROME AVENUE	BRONX	NY	10467	(212) 881-7600
CHABAD TRADE SCHOOL 770 EASTERN PARKWAY	BROOKLYN	NY	11213	(718) 774-5531
OHEL CHILDREN'S HOME & FAMILY SERVICES 4423 16TH AVENUE	BROOKLYN	NY	11204	(718) 851-6300
SHEVET Y'HUDAH RESNICK INSTITUTE OF TECHNOLOGY 670 ROCKAWAY PARKWAY	BROOKLYN	NY	11236	(718) 342-6878
BRAMSON ORT TECHNICAL INSTITUTE 44 EAST 23RD STREET	NEW YORK	NY	10010	(212) 677-7420
BRAMSON ORT TRADE SCHOOL 817 BROADWAY	NEW YORK	NY	10003	(212) 228-9560
COPE VOCATIONAL INSTITUTE: BUSINESS SKILLS DIVISION 84 WILLIAM STREET	NEW YORK	NY	10038	(212) 797-9000
COPE VOCATIONAL INSTITUTE: VOCATIONAL SKILLS DIVISION 84 WILLIAM STREET	NEW YORK	NY	10038	(212) 797-9000
COUNCIL JEWISH MANPOWER ASSOCIATES 299 BROADWAY	NEW YORK	NY	10007	(212) 233-8448
FEDERATION EMPLOYMENT & GUIDANCE SERVICE 114 FIFTH AVENUE	NEW YORK	NY	10011	(212) 741-7110
HEBREW TECHNICAL INSTITUTE 235 PARK AVENUE S	NEW YORK	NY	10003	
JEWISH OCCUPATIONAL COUNCIL 114 FIFTH AVENUE	NEW YORK	NY	10011	(212) 741-7110
NATIONAL ASSOCIATION OF JEWISH VOCATIONAL SERVICES 386 PARK AVENUE SOUTH, SUITE 301	NEW YORK	NY	10016	(212) 685-8355
NEW YORK ASSOCIATES FOR NEW AMERICANS 225 PARK AVENUE S	NEW YORK	NY	10003	(212) 674-7400
PROJECT COPE-DIVISION OF AGUDATH ISRAEL 84 WILLIAM STREET	NEW YORK	NY	10038	(212) 797-9000
VOCATIONAL INSTITUTE & PROJECT COPE 84 WILLIAM STREET	NEW YORK	NY	10038	(212) 797-9000
PROJECT COPE OF AGUDATH ISRAEL OF AMERICA 98-12 66TH AVENUE, SUITE 4	REGO PARK	NY	±1374	
JEWISH VOCATIONAL SERVICE 13878 CEDAR ROAD	UNIVERSITY HEIGHTS	OH	44118	(216) 321-1381
JEWISH VOCATIONAL SERVICE 74 TYCOS DRIVE	TORONTO	ON		(416) 787-1151
JEWISH EMPLOYMENT & VOCATIONAL SERVICE, THE 1624 LOCUST STREET	PHILADELPHIA	PA	19103	(215) 893-5900
JEWISH VOCATIONAL SERVICE 5151 COTE STE. CATHERINE ROAD	MONTREAL	QU		(514) 735-3541
JEWISH VOCATIONAL COUNSELING SERVICES 11300 NORTH CRESCENT EXWY., SUITE 402	DALLAS	TX	75231	
JEWISH VOCATIONAL SERVICES 7800 NORTHHAVEN ROAD-#C	DALLAS	TX	75230	(214) 369-4211
VOCATIONAL GUIDANCE SERVICE 2529 SAN JACINTO	HOUSTON	TX	77002	(713) 225-0053
JEWISH VOCATIONAL SERVICE 1339 NORTH MILWAUKEE STREET	MILWAUKEE	WI	53202	(414) 272-1344

WINES & SPIRITS

Name / Address	City	State	Zip	Phone
HAGAFEN CELLARS PO BOX 3035	NAPA	CA	94558	(707) 252-0781
BEST BRANDS 10700 EAST 40TH AVENUE	DENVER	CO	80239	(303) 371-2750
SKYVIEW DISCOUNT KOSHER WINE 5681 RIVERDALE AVENUE	BRONX	NY	10471	(212) 549-1229
KEDEM ROYAL WINE CORP. 420 KENT AVENUE	BROOKLYN	NY	11211	(718) 384-2400
MANISCHEWITZ WINE COMPANY 4500 SECOND AVENUE	BROOKLYN	NY	11232	(212) 421-3900
MONARCH WINE COMPANY, INC. 4500 SECOND AVENUE	BROOKLYN	NY	11232	(212) 421-3900
ORLANDER LIQUORS 4812 13TH AVENUE	BROOKLYN	NY	11219	(718) 436-1031
PEERLESS IMPORTERS 16 BRIDGEWATER STREET	BROOKLYN	NY	11222	(718) 383-5500
ROYAL WINE CORP. 420 KENT AVENUE	BROOKLYN	NY	11211	(718) 384-2400

Name / Address	City	State	Zip	Phone
J&J WINES & LIQUORS 71-43 KISSENA BOULEVARD	FLUSHING	NY	11367	(718) 591-1900
TIROSH WINE CO. 3349 MULBERRY STREET	MIDDLETOWN	NY	10940	(914) 344-0090
KEDEM ROYAL WINERY DOCK ROAD	MILTON	NY	12547	(914) 795-2240
ARIEL IMPORTERS INC. 120 WEST 44TH STREET, SUITE 308	NEW YORK	NY	10036	(212) 302-9152
CARMEL WINE COMPANY 271 MADISON AVENUE	NEW YORK	NY	10016	(212) 532-4016
EIN GUEDI IMPORT COMPANY 271 MADISON AVENUE	NEW YORK	NY	10016	(212) 532-4016
GANELES KOSHER WINE COMPANY 107 NORFOLK STREET	NEW YORK	NY	10002	(212) 477-5797
GENERAL WINE & SPIRITS COMPANY 375 PARK AVENUE	NEW YORK	NY	10022	(212) 572-7000
GROSS WINES & LIQUORS 204 WEST END AVENUE	NEW YORK	NY	10023	(212) 724-3007
JOSEPH E. SEAGRAMS, INC. CLASSIC WINES 375 PARK AVENUE	NEW YORK	NY	10152	(212) 572-7000
KEDEM KOSHER WINES 107 NORFOLK STREET	NEW YORK	NY	10002	(212) 673-2780
PARK AVENUE IMPORTS 375 PARK AVENUE	NEW YORK	NY	10022	(212) 572-7642
SCHAPIRO WINE CO. 126 RIVINGTON STREET	NEW YORK	NY	10002	(212) 674-4404
YORKVILLE WINE & LIQUOR 1392 THIRD AVENUE	NEW YORK	NY	10021	(212) 263-6780
MARGULIS 719 S. 4TH STREET	PHILADELPHIA	PA	19147	(215) 925-3118
REISER KOSHER WINE CO. 4834 NORTH BROAD STREET	PHILADELPHIA	PA	19141	(215) 329-3350

WOMEN'S ORGANIZATIONS

Name / Address	City	State	Zip	Phone
DEBORAH, THE JEWISH WOMEN'S GROUP C/O WIZO, DWARSLAAN 18, 126 B.B.BLARICUM	AMSTERDAM			
LONDON JEWISH FEMINIST GROUP C/O MARGARET GREEN, FLAT 7, CALLCOTT COURT, CALLCOTT RD	LONDON			
PIONEER WOMEN-NA'AMAT 1-703 56TH AVENUE S.W.	CALGARY	AT	T2V 0G9	(403) 253-9060
HADASSAH - WIZO COUNCIL OF VANCOUVER 950 WEST 41ST AVENUE	VANCOUVER	BC	V5Z 2N7	(604) 263-2778
MIZRACHI WOMEN 3530 CAMBIE STREET, #203	VANCOUVER	BC		(604) 875-1976
NATIONAL COUNCIL OF JEWISH WOMEN OF CANADA 950 WEST 41ST AVENUE, ROOM H	VANCOUVER	BV	V5Z 2N7	(604) 261-5413
PIONEER WOMEN - NA'AMAT 950 WEST 41ST AVENUE	VANCOUVER	BC	V5Z 2N7	(604) 263-1012
HADASSAH - WIZO COUNCIL OF VANCOUVER 142 CAMBRIDGE	VICTORIA	BC	V8V 4B3	(604) 382-0780
NATIONAL COUNCIL OF JEWISH WOMEN, INC.-WESTERN DISTRICT 2734 A. COLLEGE AVENUE	BERKELEY	CA	94705	(415) 549-0788
B'NAI B'RITH WOMEN 48 PARK PLAZA DRIVE, #201	DALY CITY	CA	94015	(415) 994-3400
WOMEN'S AMERICAN ORT,INC.-PACIFIC NORTHWEST 75 SOUTHGATE AVENUE, SUITE 10	DALY CITY	CA	94015	(415) 994-2002
AIDES TO GATEWAYS HOSPITAL 1891 EFFIE STREET	LOS ANGELES	CA	90026	(213) 666-0171
AMERICAN MIZRACHI WOMEN 6505 WILSHIRE BOULEVARD, SUITE 405	LOS ANGELES	CA	90048	(213) 653-6606
AMERICAN SOCIETY FOR TECHNION-WOMEN'S DIVISION 8170 BEVERLY BOULEVARD, SUITE 108	LOS ANGELES	CA	90048	(213) 651-3321
B'NAI B'RITH WOMEN 6399 WILSHIRE BOULEVARD, SUITE 706	LOS ANGELES	CA	90048	(213) 651-4924
BRANDEIS UNIV. NAT'L WOMEN'S CMTEE.C/O JFC WOMEN'S CONF. 6505 WILSHIRE BOULEVARD, SUITE 1002	LOS ANGELES	CA	90048	(213) 852-1234
BUILDERS OF SCOPUS 8665 WILSHIRE BOULEVARD	LOS ANGELES	CA	90211	(213) 657-6511
CEDARS-SINAI MEDICAL CENTER 8700 BEVERLY BOULEVARD	LOS ANGELES	CA	90048	(213) 855-3674
EMMA LAZARUS JEWISH WOMEN'S CLUBS 7213 BEVERLY BOULEVARD	LOS ANGELES	CA	90036	(213) 934-4866
GATEWAYS ASSOCIATES 1891 EFFIE STREET	LOS ANGELES	CA	90026	(213) 666-0171
HADASSAH 6505 WILSHIRE BOULEVARD	LOS ANGELES	CA	90048	(213) 653-9727
IDA MAYER CUMMINGS AUXILIARY-LA JEWISH HOMES FOR THE AGING 6505 WILSHIRE BOULEVARD	LOS ANGELES	CA	90048	(213) 658-7145
JEWISH CENTERS ASSOCIATES 5870 WEST OLYMPIC BOULEVARD	LOS ANGELES	CA	90036	(213) 938-2531
JEWISH PROFESSIONAL WOMEN'S CLUB, C/O WOMEN'S CONF. OF JFC 6505 WILSHIRE BOULEVARD, SUITE 1002	LOS ANGELES	CA	90048	(213) 852-1234
JEWISH WAR VETERAN'S WOMEN'S AUXILIARY 6505 WILSHIRE BOULEVARD, SUITE 401	LOS ANGELES	CA	90048	(213) 655-4752
LOS ANGELES LADIES BIKUR CHOLIM SOCIETY	LOS ANGELES	CA		(213) 655-7891
LOS ANGELES MIKVAH SOCIETY 9548 WEST PICO BOULEVARD	LOS ANGELES	CA	90035	(213) 550-9124
NASHEI CHABAD 741 GAYLEY AVENUE	LOS ANGELES	CA	90024	(213) 208-7511
NATIONAL COUNCIL OF JEWISH WOMEN 543 NORTH FAIRFAX AVENUE	LOS ANGELES	CA	90036	(213) 651-2930
NITZAN CHAPTER FOR YOUNG CAREER WOMEN 1494 S. ROBERTSON BLVD	LOS ANGELES	CA	90035	(213) 275-5345
ON GUARD 6505 WILSHIRE BOULEVARD, SUITE 315	LOS ANGELES	CA	90048	(213) 655-7071
PIONEER WOMEN-NA'AMAT 5820 WILSHIRE BLVD	LOS ANGELES	CA	90036	(213) 275-5345
PIONEER WOMEN-NA'AMAT 1494 S. ROBERTSON BLVD	LOS ANGELES	CA	90035	(213) 275-5345
THE WOMEN OF BRANDEIS-BARDIN PO BOX 24B89	LOS ANGELES	CA	90024	(213) 348-7201
UNION OF ORTHODOX HEBREW CONGREGATIONS OF AMERICA-WOMEN'S BR 7269 BEVERLY BOULEVARD	LOS ANGELES	CA	90036	(213) 857-1206
UNITED ORDER OF TRUE SISTERS 977 SOUTH WESTERN AVENUE	LOS ANGELES	CA	90029	(213) 737-9854
UNIVERSITY WOMEN 15600 MULHOLLAND DRIVE	LOS ANGELES	CA	90077	(213) 476-9777
VISTA DEL MAR ASSOCIATES/JUNIOR ASSOCIATES 3200 MOTOR AVENUE	LOS ANGELES	CA	90034	(213) 826-1223
WOMEN FOR BAR ILAN 6505 WILSHIRE BOULEVARD, SUITE 402	LOS ANGELES	CA	90048	(213) 658-6668
WOMEN'S AMERICAN ORT, INC.-PACIFIC SOUTHWEST 6505 WILSHIRE BOULEVARD, SUITE 512	LOS ANGELES	CA	90036	(213) 655-2911
WOMEN'S CONFERENCE OF JFC 6505 WILSHIRE BOULEVARD, SUITE 1002	LOS ANGELES	CA	90048	(213) 852-1234
WOMEN'S DIVISION OF AMERICAN JEWISH CONGRESS 6505 WILSHIRE BOULEVARD, SUITE 1102	LOS ANGELES	CA	90048	(213) 651-4601
WOMEN'S DIVISION-UNITED JEWISH WELFARE FUND 6505 WILSHIRE BOULEVARD, SUITE 1002	LOS ANGELES	CA	90048	(213) 852-1234
WOMEN'S LEAGUE FOR CONSERVATIVE JUDAISM 15600 MULHOLLAND DRIVE	LOS ANGELES	CA	90024	(213) 476-9777
NATIONAL FEDERATION OF TEMPLE SISTERHOODS 13107 VENTURA BOULEVARD	NORTH HOLLYWOOD	CA	91604	(818) 986-5720
VALLEY MIKVAH SOCIETY 12800 CHANDLER BOULEVARD	NORTH HOLLYWOOD	CA	91607	(818) 506-0996
WESTERN FEDERATION OF TEMPLE SISTERHOODS 13107 VENTURA BLVD	NORTH HOLLYWOOD	CA	91604	(818) 872-3550
WOMEN'S INSTITUTE FOR CONTINUING JEWISH EDUCATION 4079 54TH STREET	SAN DIEGO	CA	92105	
AMERICAN MIZRACHI WOMEN 2237 JUDAH STREET	SAN FRANCISCO	CA	94122	(415) 664-6309
HADASSAH 2215 JUDAH STREET	SAN FRANCISCO	CA	94122	(415) 665-1505
NATIONAL COUNCIL OF JEWISH WOMEN 1825 DIVISADERO STREET	SAN FRANCISCO	CA	94115	(415) 346-4600
PIONEER WOMEN BRACHA CLUB 3240 GEARY BLVD	SAN FRANCISCO	CA	94118	(415) 387-3077
WOMEN'S CAMPAIGN FOR SOVIET JEWRY-35'S 111 SANTA MONICA BOULEVARD	SANTA MONICA	CA	90401	(213) 393-6751
PIONEER WOMEN-NA'AMAT 13609 VICTORY BLVD	VAN NUYS	CA	91401	(818) 780-4165
B'NAI B'RITH WOMEN 1640 RHODE ISLAND AVENUE N.W.	WASHINGTON	DC	20036	(202) 857-6600
NAT'L LADIES AUXILIARY JEWISH WAR VETERANS OF THE USA, INC. 1712 NEW HAMPSHIRE AVENUE N.W.	WASHINGTON	DC	20009	(202) 667-9061
NATIONAL COUNCIL OF JEWISH WOMEN, INC.-EA.PA.-DE-MD-VA-NC-DC 1346 CONNECTICUT AVENUE, NW	WASHINGTON	DC	20036	(202) 785-0222
WOMEN'S AMERICAN ORT, INC.-DISTRICT 6/SOUTHEAST FLORIDA 2101 E. HALLANDALE BEACH BOULEVARD, SUITE 301	HALLANDALE	FL	33009	(305) 458-1557
PIONEER WOMEN-NA'AMAT 1303 N. STATE ROAD 7	MARGATE	FL	33063	(305) 979-3311
NATIONAL COUNCIL OF JEWISH WOMEN, INC.-SOUTHERN DISTRICT 5220 BISCAYNE BOULEVARD, #202	MIAMI	FL	33137	(305) 757-1305
MIZRACHI WOMEN'S ORGANIZATION 420 LINCOLN ROAD, SUITE 402	MIAMI BEACH	FL	33139	(305) 531-7996
PIONEER WOMEN-NA'AMAT 605 LINCOLN ROAD	MIAMI BEACH	FL	33139	(305) 538-6213
B'NAI B'RITH WOMEN 1350 NORTHEAST 172ND STREET	NORTH MIAMI BEACH	FL	33162	(305) 653-0838
WOMEN'S LEAGUE FOR ISRAEL, INC 5975 W. SUNRISE BLVD	SUNRISE	FL	33313	(305) 791-4840
AMERICAN MIZRACHI WOMEN 3018 W. DEVON AVENUE	CHICAGO	IL	60659	(312) 973-0688
CONFERENCE OF JEWISH WOMEN'S ORGANIZATIONS 2840 WEST COYLE	CHICAGO	IL	60645	(312) 764-5636
EMMA LAZARUS JEWISH WOMEN'S CLUBS 1673 W. PRATT BLVD	CHICAGO	IL	60626	(312) 761-1336
NATIONAL COUNCIL OF JEWISH WOMEN, INC.-CENTRAL DIST.-MIDWEST 53 WEST JACKSON, SUITE 724	CHICAGO	IL	60604	(312) 965-5156
PIONEER WOMEN-NA'AMAT 220 S. STATE STREET	CHICAGO	IL	60604	(312) 922-3736
WOMEN'S AMERICAN ORT,INC.-DISTRICT 8/MIDWEST 111 N. WABASH-GARLAND BUILDING, SUITE 1205	CHICAGO	IL	60602	(312) 726-6466
PIONEER WOMEN-NA'AMAT 466 CENTRAL AVENUE	NORTHFIELD	IL	60093	(312) 446-7275
NATIONAL COUNCIL OF JEWISH WOMEN 3650 DUTCHMANS LANE	LOUISVILLE	KY	40205	(502) 458-5566
PIONEER WOMEN-NA'AMAT 294 WASHINGTON STREET	BOSTON	MA	02108	(617) 426-1059
WOMEN'S AMERICAN ORT, INC.- DISTRICT 1/NEW ENGLAND 990 WASHINGTON STREET	DEDHAM	MA	02026	(617) 329-6693
NATIONAL COUNCIL OF JEWISH WOMEN, INC.-UPSTATE NY & N. ENG. 950 BOYLSTON STREET	NEWTON HIGHLANDS	MA	02161	(617) 244-8000
BRANDEIS UNIVERSITY NATIONAL WOMEN'S COMMITTEE BRANDEIS UNIVERSITY	WALTHAM	MA	02254	(617) 647-2194
HADASSAH - WIZO 309 HARGRAVE STREET, #205	WINNIPEG	MB	R3B 2J8	(204) 942-8201
PIONEER WOMEN-NA'AMAT 1727 MAIN STREET	WINNIPEG	MB	R2V 1Z4	(204) 334-3637
HADASSAH 4000 GLENGYLE AVENUE	BALTIMORE	MD	21215	(301) 358-2524
MIZRACHI WOMEN'S ORGANIZATION 8415 ALLENSWOOD ROAD	BALTIMORE	MD	21133	(301) 655-4141
NATIONAL COUNCIL OF WOMEN 7241 PARK HEIGHTS AVENUE	BALTIMORE	MD	21208	(301) 358-0707
PIONEER WOMEN - NA'AMAT, BALTIMORE COUNCIL 3612 FORDS LANE	BALTIMORE	MD	21215	(301) 358-3337
PIONEER WOMEN-NA'AMAT OHR KODESH SYNAGOGUE, 8402 FREYMAN DRIVE	CHEVY CHASE	MD	20815	(301) 565-3130
PIONEER WOMEN-NA'AMAT 25900 GREENFIELD, ROOM 205D	OAK PARK	MI	48237	(313) 967-4750
BAIS CHANA WOMEN'S INSTITUTE 15 MONTCALM COURT	ST. PAUL	MN	55116	(612) 698-3858
HADASSAH 6820 DELMAR	ST. LOUIS	MO	63130	(314) 863-5866
NATIONAL COUNCIL OF JEWISH WOMEN 8420 DELMAR, SUITE 203	ST. LOUIS	MO	63124	(314) 993-5181
PIONEER WOMEN-NA'AMAT 8123 DELMAR BLVD	ST. LOUIS	MO	63130	(314) 721-5856
WOMEN'S AMERICAN ORT 1722 STUDT AVENUE, ROOM 105	ST. LOUIS	MO	63141	(314) 567-4343
MIZRACHI WOMEN'S ORGANIZATION OF AMERICA 615 NYE AVENUE	IRVINGTON	NJ	07111	(201) 399-1127
WOMEN'S AMERICAN ORT, INC.-DISTRICT 3/NEW JERSEY 1767 MORRIS AVENUE	UNION	NJ	07083	(201) 686-4660
HADASSAH-THE WOMEN'S ZIONIST ORG. OF AMERICA: BRONX CHAPTER 2534 MARION AVENUE	BRONX	NY	10458	(212) 654-8800
AGUDAS NSHEI UB'NOS CHABAD 770 EASTERN PARKWAY	BROOKLYN	NY	11213	(718) 493-9250
LADIES HEBREW BENEVOLENT SOCIETY 285 SCHERMERHORN STREET	BROOKLYN	NY	11217	(718) 875-7753
LUBAVITCH WOMEN'S COOKBOOK 852 EASTERN PARKWAY	BROOKLYN	NY	11213	(718) 604-2785
LUBAVITCH WOMEN'S ORGANIZATION 398 KINGSTON AVENUE	BROOKLYN	NY	11213	(718) 493-9650
N'SHEI AHAVAS CHESED 1680 47TH STREET	BROOKLYN	NY	11204	(718) 438-0211
PIONEER WOMEN-NA'AMAT 3858 NOSTRAND AVENUE	BROOKLYN	NY	11229	(718) 769-9604
KAYAMA P.O. BOX 4007	COLLEGE POINT	NY	11356	(718) 544-0357
PIONEER WOMEN-NA'AMAT 1931 MOTT AVENUE	FAR ROCKAWAY	NY	11691	(718) 471-8453
PIONEER WOMEN-NA'AMAT 45 CONKLIN STREET	FARMINGDALE	NY	11735	(516) 735-2675
U.S./ISRAEL WOMEN-TO-WOMEN AND COALITION FOR WOMEN IN ISRAEL 35-24 78TH STREET, APT. B-39	JACKSON HEIGHTS	NY	11372	
AGUDAH WOMEN OF AMERICA 84 WILLIAM STREET	NEW YORK	NY	10038	(212) 363-8940
AMIT WOMEN 817 BROADWAY	NEW YORK	NY	10003	(212) 477-4720
AMERICAN MIZRACHI WOMEN - AMIT 817 BROADWAY	NEW YORK	NY	10003	(212) 477-4720
B'NAI B'RITH - WOMEN EMPIRE REGION 823 U.N. PLAZA	NEW YORK	NY	10017	(212) 599-2123
BRANDEIS UNIVERSITY NATIONAL WOMEN'S COMMITTEE 215 EAST 68TH STREET	NEW YORK	NY	10021	(212) 249-4827
EMUNAH WOMEN OF AMERICA 370 SEVENTH AVENUE, SUITE 11N	NEW YORK	NY	10001	(212) 564-9045
FEDERATION OF JEWISH WOMEN'S ORGANIZATIONS, INC. 415 LEXINGTON AVENUE	NEW YORK	NY	10017	(212) 661-8090
HADASSAH 50 WEST 58TH STREET	NEW YORK	NY	10022	(212) 355-7900
HADASSAH-THE WOMEN'S ZIONIST ORG. OF AMERICA: N.Y.CHAPTER 250 W. 57TH STREET	NEW YORK	NY	10107	(212) 765-7050
HAPOEL HAMIZRACHI WOMEN'S ZIONIST ORGANIZATION 370 SEVENTH AVENUE	NEW YORK	NY	10001	(212) 564-9045
INTERNATIONAL COUNCIL OF JEWISH WOMEN 15 E. 26TH STREET	NEW YORK	NY	10010	(212) 532-1740

Organization / Address	City	State	Zip	Phone
JEWISH FOUNDATION FOR EDUCATION OF WOMEN				
120 W. 57TH STREET	NEW YORK	**NY**	10019	(212) 265-2565
JEWISH WOMEN'S CLUB 234 W. 78TH STREET	NEW YORK	**NY**	10024	(212) 799-1520
JEWISH WOMEN'S RESOURCE CENTER, 92ND STREET YM/YWHA LIBRARY				
1395 LEXINGTON AVENUE	NEW YORK	**NY**	10028	
JEWISH WOMENS SOCIAL SERVICE FOR ISRAEL 265 RIVERSIDE DRIVE	NEW YORK	**NY**	10025	(212) 666-7880
LEADERSHIP CONFERENCE OF NAT'L JEWISH WOMEN'S ORGANIZATIONS				
838 FIFTH AVENUE	NEW YORK	**NY**	10021	(212) 249-0100
LEADERSHIP CONFERENCE-JEWISH WOMEN'S ORGANIZATIONS				
15 E. 84TH STREET	NEW YORK	**NY**	10028	
LILITH MAGAZINE 250 W. 57TH STREET	NEW YORK	**NY**	10019	(212) 757-0818
MIZRACHI WOMEN'S ORGANIZATION 817 BROADWAY	NEW YORK	**NY**	10003	(212) 477-4720
NAT'L COUNCIL OF JEWISH WOMEN, INC. 15 E. 26TH STREET	NEW YORK	**NY**	10010	(212) 532-1740
NAT'L COUNCIL OF JEWISH WOMEN-COUNCIL THRIFT SHOP				
842 9TH AVENUE	NEW YORK	**NY**	10019	(212) 535-5900
NAT'L COUNCIL OF JEWISH WOMEN-COUNCIL WKSHOP/SENIOR CITIZENS				
915 BROADWAY	NEW YORK	**NY**	10010	(212) 674-8010
NAT'L COUNCIL OF JEWISH WOMEN-KATHERINE ENGEL CENTER				
241 WEST 72ND STREET	NEW YORK	**NY**	10023	(212) 799-7205
NAT'L COUNCIL OF JEWISH WOMEN-N.Y.SECTION				
241 WEST 72ND STREET	NEW YORK	**NY**	10023	(212) 535-5900
NATIONAL BUREAU OF FEDERATED JEWISH WOMEN'S ORGANIZATIONS				
55 W. 42ND STREET	NEW YORK	**NY**	10036	(212) 736-0240
NATIONAL COUNCIL OF JEWISH WOMEN 15 EAST 26TH STREET	NEW YORK	**NY**	10010	(212) 532-1740
NATIONAL COUNCIL OF JEWISH WOMEN, INC.-MIDDLE ATLANTIC, NJ				
15 EAST 26TH STREET	NEW YORK	**NY**	10010	(212) 532-1740
NATIONAL COUNCIL OF JEWISH WOMEN, INC.-NORTHERN DISTRICT				
15 EAST 26TH STREET	NEW YORK	**NY**	10010	(212) 532-1740
NATIONAL FEDERATION OF TEMPLE SISTERHOODS				
838 FIFTH AVENUE	NEW YORK	**NY**	10021	(212) 249-0100
NATIONAL JEWISH WELFARE BOARD-WOMEN'S ORGANIZATIONAL SVCS.				
15 E. 26TH STREET	NEW YORK	**NY**	10010	(212) 539-4949
NEW YORK STATE FOUNDATION OF TEMPLE SISTERHOODS				
838 FIFTH AVENUE	NEW YORK	**NY**	10010	(212) 249-0100
PIONEER WOMEN-NA'AMAT 200 MADISON AVENUE	NEW YORK	**NY**	10016	(212) 725-8010
POALE AGUDATH ISRAEL OF AMERICA 156 FIFTH AVENUE	NEW YORK	**NY**	10010	(212) 924-9475
U.S./ISRAEL WOMEN-TO-WOMEN				
4 SNIFFEN COURT, 156 E. 36TH STREET	NEW YORK	**NY**	10016	
UNION OF ORTHODOX JEWISH CONGREGATIONS-WOMEN'S BRANCH				
45 W. 36TH STREET	NEW YORK	**NY**	10018	(212) 563-4000
UNITED ORDER OF TRUE SISTERS 150 WEST 85TH STREET	NEW YORK	**NY**	10024	(212) 362-2502
WOMEN'S AMERICAN ORT, INC. 315 PARK AVENUE SOUTH	NEW YORK	**NY**	10010	(212) 505-7700
WOMEN'S AMERICAN ORT, INC.-DISTRICT 2/NY STATE				
254 WEST 31ST STREET 10TH FLOOR	NEW YORK	**NY**	10001	(212) 695-1772
WOMEN'S DIVISION OF AMERICAN JEWISH CONGRESS				
15 EAST 84TH STREET	NEW YORK	**NY**	10028	(212) 879-4500
WOMEN'S DIVISION OF JEWISH LABOR COMMITTEE				
25 EAST 78TH STREET	NEW YORK	**NY**	10021	(212) 535-3700
WOMEN'S DIVISION OF UNITED JEWISH APPEAL				
130 EAST 59TH STREET	NEW YORK	**NY**	10022	(212) 980-1000
WOMEN'S DIVISION, COUNCIL OF JEWISH FED. & WELFARE FUNDS				
575 LEXINGTON AVENUE	NEW YORK	**NY**	10022	(212) 751-1311
WOMEN'S DIVISION, UNITED JEWISH APPEAL				
1290 AVENUE OF THE AMERICAS	NEW YORK	**NY**	10019	(212) 757-1500
WOMEN'S LEAGUE FOR CONSERVATIVE JUDAISM 48 E. 74TH STREET	NEW YORK	**NY**	10021	(212) 628-1600
WOMEN'S LEAGUE FOR ISRAEL 515 PARK AVENUE	NEW YORK	**NY**	10022	(212) 838-1997
WOMEN'S LEAGUE FOR ISRAEL, INC. 1860 BROADWAY	NEW YORK	**NY**	10023	(212) 245-8742
WOMEN'S ORGANIZATION OF HAPOEL HAMIZRACHI				
370 SEVENTH AVENUE	NEW YORK	**NY**	10001	(212) 564-9045
WOMEN'S ORGANIZATION OF YESHIVA UNIVERSITY				
500 WEST 185TH STREET, SH 713	NEW YORK	**NY**	10033	(212) 960-0855
WOMEN'S SOCIAL SERVICE FOR ISRAEL 240 W. 98TH STREET	NEW YORK	**NY**	10025	(212) 666-7880
AMERICAN MIZRACHI WOMEN 2260 WARRENSVILLE CENTER ROAD	CLEVELAND	**OH**	44118	(216) 932-8656
DAUGHTERS BIKUR CHOLIM 1585 MALLARD DRIVE	CLEVELAND	**OH**	44124	(216) 449-6301
MIZRACHI WOMEN'S ORGANIZATIONS 4170 BAYARD ROAD	CLEVELAND	**OH**	44121	(216) 291-3108
NATIONAL COUNCIL OF JEWISH WOMEN - CLEVELAND SECTION				
3535 LEE ROAD	CLEVELAND	**OH**	44120	(216) 283-1500
PIONEER WOMEN-NA'AMAT 13969 CEDAR ROAD, ROOM 208	CLEVELAND	**OH**	44418	(216) 321-2002
WOMEN'S AMERICAN ORT, INC.-DISTRICT 7/MI, OH, W.PA., NW NY				
SHAKER BLDG. 3645 WARRENSVILLE CENTER ROAD	SHAKER HEIGHTS	**OH**	44122	(216) 921-0228
PIONEER WOMEN-NA'AMAT 272 CODSELL AVENUE	DOWNSVIEW	**ON**	M3H3X2	(416) 636-5425
HERUT WOMEN 3417 BATHURST STREET	TORONTO	**ON**		
AMERICAN MIZRACHI WOMEN 1015 CHESTNUT STREET	PHILADELPHIA	**PA**	19107	(215) 925-8550
PIONEER WOMEN-NA'AMAT 1405 LOCUST STREET, ROOM 1117	PHILADELPHIA	**PA**	19102	(215) 545-1328
WOMEN'S AMERICAN ORT, INC.-DISTRICT 4/PA, VA, DC, MD, DE				
1405 LOCUST STREET, SUITE 300	PHILADELPHIA	**PA**	19102	(215) 546-8888
PIONEER WOMEN-NA'AMAT 6328 FORBES AVENUE	PITTSBURGH	**PA**	15217	(412) 521-5253
HERUT WOMEN 5234 CLANRANALD AVENUE	MONTREAL	**QU**	H3X 2S4	
PIONEER WOMEN-NA'AMAT 4770 KENT AVENUE, SUITE 304	MONTREAL	**QU**	H3W 1H2	(514) 735-6253
WOMEN'S AMERICAN ORT, INC.-DISTRICT 9				
4740 INGERSOLL SE GEN. BUILDING, SUITE 100	HOUSTON	**TX**	77027	(713) 961-3759
HEBREW LADIES CHARITY SOCIETY 1321 NOBLE STREET	NORFOLK	**VA**	23518	
PHILANTHROPIC FOCUS, INC.-CONSULTANTS IN CHARITABLE GIVING				
10701 WEST NORTH AVENUE	MILWAUKEE	**WI**	53226	(414) 453-8282
SECOND SEX PUBLISHING COMPANY, THE 55 RECHOV SHENKIN	GIVATAYIM	**IS**	53298	
KOL HAISHAH - THE WOMAN'S VOICE 4 HAHISTADRUT STREET	JERUSALEM	**IS**	94320	(02) 243-971
NATIONAL COUNCIL OF JEWISH WOMEN, INC.-ISRAEL OFFICE				
NJCW RESEARCH INSTITUTE HEBREW UNIVERSITY-MT. SCOPUS	JERUSALEM	**IS**		
NOGA P.O. BOX 21376	TEL AVIV	**IS**		

YESHIVOT

Organization / Address	City	State	Zip	Phone
JEWISH LEARNING EXCHANGE				
5322 WILSHIRE BLVD., SUITE 230 P.O. BOX 36B05	LOS ANGELES	**CA**	90036	(213) 857-0923
KOLLEL OF LOS ANGELES 314 N. GARDNER STREET	LOS ANGELES	**CA**	90036	(213) 655-2631
OHR SOMAYACH 7466 BEVERLY BOULEVARD	LOS ANGELES	**CA**	90036	(213) 857-0923
WEST COAST TALMUDICAL SEMINARY (YESHIVA OHR ELCHONON CHABAD)				
7215 WARING AVENUE	LOS ANGELES	**CA**	90046	(213) 937-3763
YESHIVA GEDOLAH OF LOS ANGELES 5822 WEST THIRD	LOS ANGELES	**CA**	90036	(213) 938-2071
YESHIVA UNIVERSITY OF LOS ANGELES 9760 W. PICO BLVD.	LOS ANGELES	**CA**	90035	(213) 553-4478
BETH MIDRASH KETER TORAH 1898 MERIDIAN AVENUE, APT 42	SAN JOSE	**CA**	95125	
YESHIVAT & MIDRASHA KEREM 250 HOWARD DRIVE	SANTA CLARA	**CA**	95051	(408) 247-1722
TALMUDIC RESEARCH INSTITUTE 4634 W. 14TH AVENUE	DENVER	**CO**	80204	(303) 623-8466
YESHIVA TORAS CHAIM 1400 QUITMAN STREET	DENVER	**CO**	80204	(303) 629-9746
GIBORIM RABBINICAL SEMINARY 29 FAIRFIELD BOARD	ENFIELD	**CT**	06082	
TALMUDIC UNIVERSITY OF FLORIDA 4014 CHASE AVENUE	MIAMI BEACH	**FL**	33140	(305) 534-7050
YESHIVAS BRISK 9000 FORESTVIEW ROAD	SKOKIE	**IL**	60203	(312) 674-4652
LUBAVITCH YESHIVA 9 PRESCOT STREET	BROOKLINE	**MA**	02146	(617) 731-5330
TORAH INSTITUTE OF NEW ENGLAND 1710 BEACON STREET	BROOKLINE	**MA**	02146	(617) 734-5100
YESHIVAT OHR YISROEL 1730 BEACON STREET	BROOKLINE	**MA**	02146	(617) 731-5720
NER ISRAEL RABBINICAL COLLEGE 400 MT. WILSON LANE	BALTIMORE	**MD**	21208	(301) 484-7200
TALMUDICAL ACADEMY OF BALTIMORE, THE				
4445 OLD COURT ROAD	BALTIMORE	**MD**	21208	(301) 484-6600
YESHIVAH KOLLEL 17266 HILTON	SOUTHFIELD	**MI**	48075	
ST. LOUIS RABBINICAL COLLEGE 7400 OLIVE	ST. LOUIS	**MO**	63130	
BETH MEDRASH GOVOHA OF AMERICA 617 6TH STREET	LAKEWOOD	**NJ**	08701	(201) 367-1060
RABBINICAL COLLEGE OF AMERICA 226 SUSSEX AVENUE	MORRISTOWN	**NJ**	07960	(201) 267-9404
RABBINICAL COLLEGE OF QUEENS				
141-20 GRAND CENTRAL PARKWAY	BRIARWOOD	**NY**	11435	(718) 291-1336
BEER SHMUEL TALMUDICAL ACADEMY 1363 59TH STREET	BROOKLYN	**NY**	11219	
BELZER YESHIVA MACHZIKEI TORAH SEMINARY				
632 BEDFORD AVENUE	BROOKLYN	**NY**	11211	
BETH HAMEDRASH SHAAREI YOSHER INSTITUTE				
4102-10 16TH AVENUE	BROOKLYN	**NY**	11204	
BETH HAMEDRASH TORAS CHEMED NITRA 1462 50TH STREET	BROOKLYN	**NY**	11219	(718) 871-9847
BETH HAMEDRASH YAAKOV MOSHE MOSAD BNEI TORAH				
4722 18TH AVENUE	BROOKLYN	**NY**	11204	
BETH HATALMUD 2127 82ND STREET	BROOKLYN	**NY**	11214	(718) 259-2525
BETH MEDRASH & YESHIVA EMEK HALACHA 1763 63RD STREET	BROOKLYN	**NY**	11204	(718) 232-1600
BETH MEDRASH GOVOHA 314 MCDONALD AVENUE	BROOKLYN	**NY**	11218	(718) 638-8300
BNAI TORAH INSTITUTE 4722 18TH AVENUE	BROOKLYN	**NY**	11204	
CENTRAL YESHIVA BETH JOSEPH RABBINICAL SEMINARY				
1427 49TH STREET	BROOKLYN	**NY**	11219	(718) 436-7591
CENTRAL YESHIVA TOMCHEI TMIMIM LUBAVITCH				
841-53 OCEAN PARKWAY	BROOKLYN	**NY**	11230	(718) 859-7600
CENTRAL YESHIVA TOMCHEI TMIMIM LUBAVITCH				
770 EASTERN PARKWAY	BROOKLYN	**NY**	11213	(718) 773-9778
EDUCATION INSTITUTE OHOLEI TORAH 667 EASTERN PARKWAY	BROOKLYN	**NY**	11213	(718) 778-3340
HADAR HATORAH RABBINICAL SEMINARY 824 EASTERN PARKWAY	BROOKLYN	**NY**	11213	(718) 735-0250
ISRAEL TORAH RESEARCH INSTITUTE 1712 43RD STREET	BROOKLYN	**NY**	11204	
KEHILATH YAKOV RABBINICAL SEMINARY 638 BEDFORD AVENUE	BROOKLYN	**NY**	11211	
KOL ARYEH RESEARCH INSTITUTE 1642 54TH STREET	BROOKLYN	**NY**	11204	(718) 871-7442
KOLEL MAREI YECHESKEL & YESHIVA MAGLEI ZEDEK				
1223 45TH STREET	BROOKLYN	**NY**	11219	(718) 436-0239
KOLLEL BAIS TORAH 1636 49TH STREET	BROOKLYN	**NY**	11204	
KOLLEL NACHLAS YISROEL MOSHE 25 CHURCH AVENUE	BROOKLYN	**NY**	11218	
MECHON HAHOYROA 4533 16 AVENUE	BROOKLYN	**NY**	11204	(718) 438-2100
MESIVTA EASTERN PARKWAY RABBINICAL SEMINARY				
418 EAST 45TH STREET	BROOKLYN	**NY**	11203	
MESIVTA TORAH VODAATH SEMINARY 425 EAST 9TH STREET	BROOKLYN	**NY**	11218	(718) 941-8000
MESIVTA-YESHIVA RABBI CHAIM BERLIN RABBINICAL ACADEMY				
1571 CONEY ISLAND AVENUE	BROOKLYN	**NY**	11230	(718) 377-0777
MIRRER YESHIVA CENTRAL INSTITUTE 1791-5 OCEAN PARKWAY	BROOKLYN	**NY**	11223	(718) 645-0536
OHR TORAH 239 HAVEMEYER STREET	BROOKLYN	**NY**	11211	(718) 387-9749
RABBINICAL ASSEMBLY COLLEGE, THE				
48TH STREET AT SEVENTH AVENUE	BROOKLYN	**NY**	11220	(718) 633-6378
RABBINICAL COLLEGE CHSAN SOFER NEW YORK 1876 50TH STREET	BROOKLYN	**NY**	11204	
RABBINICAL COLLEGE OF KAMENITZ YESHIVA 1315 43RD STREET	BROOKLYN	**NY**	11219	
RABBINICAL SEMINARY ADAS YEREIM 185 WILSON STREET	BROOKLYN	**NY**	11211	
RABBINICAL SEMINARY MIKOR CHAIM 1571 55TH STREET	BROOKLYN	**NY**	11219	
RABBINICAL SEMINARY NETZACH ISRAEL				
3044 CONEY ISLAND AVENUE	BROOKLYN	**NY**	11235	(718) 656-1997
RABBINICAL SEMINARY OF MUNKACS 1377 42ND STREET	BROOKLYN	**NY**	11219	(718) 438-5246
SHA'AREI ORAH INSTITUTE 39 WEBSTER AVENUE	BROOKLYN	**NY**	11230	(718) 436-6758
UNITED LUBAVITCHER YESHIVOS 841 OCEAN PARKWAY	BROOKLYN	**NY**	11213	(718) 859-7600
UNITED TALMUDICAL ACADEMY 500 BEDFORD AVENUE	BROOKLYN	**NY**	11211	(718) 384-9034
YAVNE HEBREW THEOLOGICAL SEMINARY 510 DAHILL ROAD	BROOKLYN	**NY**	11218	(718) 436-5610
YESHIVA BETH SHEARIM MISHNE HALACHOTH GEDOLOTH RABBIN. INST.				
5306 16TH AVENUE	BROOKLYN	**NY**	11204	(718) 851-9809
YESHIVA BIRKAS REUVEN 1221 AVENUE S	BROOKLYN	**NY**	11204	(718) 375-8611
YESHIVA D'VAR YESHORIM 1776 EAST 12TH STREET	BROOKLYN	**NY**	11229	(718) 627-4005
YESHIVA GEDOLA OF BORO PARK 1456 46TH STREET	BROOKLYN	**NY**	11219	
YESHIVA OHR SHRAGA D'VERETZSKY AVENUE L & EAST 9TH STREET	BROOKLYN	**NY**	11230	(718) 377-4335
YESHIVA TORAH VODAATH OF FLATBUSH 425 E. 9TH STREET	BROOKLYN	**NY**	11219	(718) 941-8000
YESHIVA TORAS YISROEL & RABBINICAL SEMINARY				
5311 NEW UTRECHT AVENUE	BROOKLYN	**NY**	11219	(718) 633-5306
YESHIVA YAGDIL TORAH 5110 18TH AVENUE	BROOKLYN	**NY**	11219	(718) 871-9100
YESHIVA OF NITRA RABBINICAL COLLEGE 194 DIVISION AVENUE	BROOKLYN	**NY**	11211	(718) 384-5460
YESHIVAH SHAAREI TORAH RABBINICAL INSTITUTE				
1164 E. 12TH STREET	BROOKLYN	**NY**	11230	(718) 377-9005

Name / Address	City	State	Zip	Phone
YESHIVAS HAMATMONIM 4320 16TH AVENUE	BROOKLYN	NY	11204	(718) 252-5524
YESHIVAT TORAH VODAATH & MESIVTA RABBINICAL SEMINARY 425 E. 9TH STREET	BROOKLYN	NY	11218	(718) 941-8000
DERECH AYSON RABBINICAL SEMINARY - YESHIVA OF FAR ROCKAWAY 802 HICKSVILLE ROAD	FAR ROCKAWAY	NY	11691	(718) 327-7600
SH'OR YOSHUV RABBINICAL COLLEGE-INSTITUTE FOR JEWISH STUDIES 1526 CENTRAL AVENUE	FAR ROCKAWAY	NY	11691	(718) 327-2048
YESHIAV B'NEI TORAH 737 ELVIRA AVENUE	FAR ROCKAWAY	NY	11691	(718) 337-6419
PNIMIM TEACHERS COLLEGE	FERNDALE	NY	12734	
OHR TORAH INSTITUTE 66-35 108 STREET	FOREST HILLS	NY	11375	(718) 268-3444
RABBINICAL SEMINARY OF AMERICA 92-15 69TH AVENUE	FOREST HILLS	NY	11375	(718) 268-4700
YESHIVA CHOFETZ CHAIM 68-54 KESSEL STREET	FOREST HILLS	NY	11375	(718) 263-1445
MESIVTA ATERES YAAKOV 411 SERENA ROAD	HEWLETT	NY	11557	(516) 374-7634
RABBINICAL COLLEGE OF QUEENS 141-20 GRAND CENTRAL PARKWAY	JAMAICA	NY	11435	(718) 291-1335
BETH MEDRASH EEYON HATALMUD 216 VIOLA ROAD	MONSEY	NY	10952	(914) 352-9837
BETH MEDROSH ELYON 73 MAIN STREET	MONSEY	NY	10952	(914) 356-9711
JEWISH LEARNING EXCHANGE 142 ROUTE 306, PO BOX 462	MONSEY	NY	10952	(914) 352-7600
OHR SOMAYACH/CENTRAL CAMPUS 142 ROUTE 306, PO BOX 344	MONSEY	NY	10952	(914) 425-1370
RABBINICAL COLLEGE BETH SHRAGA 30 SADDLE RIVER ROAD	MONSEY	NY	10952	(914) 578-9623
YESHIVA GEDOLA TORAS CHESED SEVEN CAMEO RIDGE ROAD	MONSEY	NY	10952	(914) 352-6214
YESHIVA FARM SETTLEMENT - NITRA YESHIVA PINES BRIDGE ROAD	MOUNT KISCO	NY	10549	(914) 666-9705
OHR HAMEIR THEOLOGICAL SEMINARY 3 BOULEVARD	NEW ROCHELLE	NY	10801	(914) 633-9655
ASSOCIATION OF ADVANCED RABBINICAL & TALMUDICAL SCHOOLS 175 FIFTH AVENUE	NEW YORK	NY	10003	(212) 477-0950
BEIT MIDRASH L'TORAH, JERUSALEM TORAH COLLEGE FOR MEN TORAH DEPT., WORLD ZIONIST ORGANIZATION, 515 PARK AVENUE	NEW YORK	NY	10022	(212) 752-0600
MESIVTA TIFERETH JERUSALEM OF AMERICA 145 EAST BROADWAY	NEW YORK	NY	10002	(212) 964-2830
RABBI ISAAC ELCHANAN THEOLOGICAL SEMINARY 2540 AMSTERDAM AVENUE	NEW YORK	NY	10033	(212) 960-5346
YESHIVA CHOFETZ CHAIM 346 WEST 89TH STREET	NEW YORK	NY	10024	(212) 362-1435
YESHIVA HAICHAL HATORAH 630 RIVERSIDE DRIVE	NEW YORK	NY	10031	(212) 283-6000
YESHIVA RABBI SAMSON RAPHAEL HIRSCH 85-93 BENNETT AVENUE	NEW YORK	NY	10033	(212) 568-6200
YESHIVA TIFERETH ISRAEL OF RIZHIN 247 EAST BROADWAY	NEW YORK	NY	10002	(212) 732-3660
YESHIVAT RADIN 314 WEST 100TH STREET	NEW YORK	NY	10025	(212) 222-4141
YESHIVA GEDOLAH ZICHRON MOSHE LAUREL PARK ROAD	SOUTH FALLSBURG	NY	12779	(914) 434-5240
RABBINICAL SEMINARY OF NEW SQUARE 766 N. MAIN	SPRING VALLEY	NY	10977	(914) 354-2237
YESHIVAH CHOFETZ CHAIM OF RADIN 24 HIGHVIEW ROAD	SUFFERN	NY	10901	(914) 368-0154
RABBINICAL COLLEGE OF TELSHE, INC. 28400 EUCLID AVENUE	WICKLIFFE	OH	44092	(216) 943-5300
NER ISRAEL YESHIVA COLLEGE 8950 BATHURST STREET, P.O. BOX 5002	THORNHILL	ON	I3T 6R1	(416) 731-1224
KOLLEL AVREICHIM 515 COLDSTREAM	TORONTO	ON	M6B 2K7	(416) 789-1853
OHR SOMAYACH 2939 BATHURST STREET	TORONTO	ON	M6B 2B2	(416) 785-5899
TALMUDICAL YESHIVA OF PHILADELPHIA 6063 DREXEL ROAD	PHILADELPHIA	PA	19131	(215) 477-1000
SCHOOL OF ADVANCED JEWISH STUDIES 315 SOUTH BELLEFIELD AVENUE	PITTSBURGH	PA	15213	(412) 681-1630
YESHIVAH ACHAI TMIMIM 2410 FIFTH AVENUE	PITTSBURGH	PA	15213	(412) 681-2446

YIDDISH ORGANIZATIONS

Name / Address	City	State	Zip	Phone
VANCOUVER PERETZ SCHOOL 6184 ASH STREET	VANCOUVER	BC	V5Z 3G9	(604) 325-1812
LOS ANGELES FRIENDS OF YIVO 1311 NORTH KENTER AVENUE	LOS ANGELES	CA	90049	(213) 472-6111
LOS ANGELES YIDDISH CULTURE CLUB 8339 WEST THIRD STREET	LOS ANGELES	CA	90048	(213) 934-9195
SHOLOM ALEICHEM YIDDISH CLUB LOS ANGELES VALLEY COLLEGE	LOS ANGELES	CA		(213) 454-4081
NORTHRIDGE YIDDISH CULTURE CLUB	NORTHRIDGE	CA		(818) 886-7657
NATIONAL YIDDISH BOOK CENTER OLD E. ST. SCHOOL, P.O. BOX 969	AMHERST	MA	01004	(413) 253-9201
SHOLEM ALEICHEM FOLK INSTITUTE, INC. 3301 BAINBRIDGE AVENUE	BRONX	NY	10467	(212) 881-6555
YUGNTRUF 3328 BAINBRIDGE AVENUE	BRONX	NY	10467	(212) 654-8540
ADELANTRE! - THE JUDEZMO SOCIETY 4594 BEDFORD AVENUE	BROOKLYN	NY	11235	
AMERICAN ASSOCIATION OF PROFESSORS OF YIDDISH QUEENS COLLEGE KILEY 802	FLUSHING	NY	11367	(718) 520-7067
B'NAI YIDDISH SOCIETY 41 UNION SQUARE	NEW YORK	NY	10003	(212) 989-3162
CENTRAL YIDDISH CULTURE ORGANIZATION (CYCO) 25 EAST 78TH STREET	NEW YORK	NY	10021	(212) 535-4320
COMM. FOR THE IMPLEMENTATION/STANDARDIZED YIDD. ORTHOGRAPHY PHILOSOPHY HALL, COLUMBIA UNIV., ROOM 406	NEW YORK	NY	10027	
CONGRESS FOR JEWISH CULTURE 25 EAST 21 STREET	NEW YORK	NY	10010	(212) 505-8040
LEAGUE FOR YIDDISH, INC. 200 W. 72ND STREET, SUITE 40	NEW YORK	NY	10023	(212) 787-6675
MAX WEINREICH CENTER FOR ADVANCED STUDIES - YIVO 1048 FIFTH AVENUE	NEW YORK	NY	10028	(212) 535-6700
WORKMEN'S CIRCLE 45 EAST 33RD STREET	NEW YORK	NY	10016	(212) 889-6800
YIVO INSTITUTE FOR JEWISH RESEARCH 1048 FIFTH AVENUE	NEW YORK	NY	10028	(212) 535-6700
YIDDISHE SHPRAKH 1048 FIFTH AVENUE	NEW YORK	NY	10028	(212) 535-6700
YIDDISHER KULTUR FARBAND 853 BROADWAY, #2121	NEW YORK	NY	10003	(212) 673-4631
YIDDISHER KULTUR FARBAND 853 BROADWAY	NEW YORK	NY	10003	(212) 228-1955
YIDDISHER KULTUR FARBAND-YKUF 1123 BROADWAY	NEW YORK	NY	10010	(212) 691-0708
YIVO INSTITUTE FOR JEWISH RESEARCH 1048 FIFTH AVENUE	NEW YORK	NY	10028	(212) 535-6700

ZIONIST ORGANIZATIONS

Name / Address	City	State	Zip	Phone
PIONEER WOMEN-NA'AMAT 1-703 56TH AVENUE S.W.	CALGARY	AT	T2V 0G9	(403) 253-9060
CANADIAN ZIONIST FEDERATION-WESTERN, THE 7200-156TH STREET	EDMONTON	AT	T5N 3R4	(403) 487-0901
CANADIAN ZIONIST FEDERATION-PACIFIC, THE 950 WEST 41ST AVENUE	VANCOUVER	BC	V5Z 2N7	(604) 266-5366
PIONEER WOMEN-NA'AMAT 950 WEST 41ST STREET, ROOM G	VANCOUVER	BC	V5Z 2N7	(604) 266-8308
WORKERS FOR ZION 5850 BALSAM, #312	VANCOUVER	BC	V6M 4B9	(604) 261-6629
AMERICAN ZIONIST FEDERATION 6505 WILSHIRE BOULEVARD	LOS ANGELES	CA	90048	(213) 655-4636

Organization	Address	City	State	Zip	Phone
AMERICAN ZIONIST YOUTH FOUNDATION	6505 WILSHIRE BOULEVARD	LOS ANGELES	**CA**	90048	(213) 655-9828
AMERICAN ZIONIST YOUTH FOUNDATION - WEST COAST REGION	6505 WILSHIRE BOULEVARD	LOS ANGELES	**CA**	90048	(213) 655-4636
AMERICANS FOR PROGRESSIVE ISRAEL	319 NORTH ORANGE DRIVE	LOS ANGELES	**CA**	90036	(213) 933-5358
ASSOCIATION OF PARENTS OF AMERICAN ISRAELIS	1706 GARTH AVENUE	LOS ANGELES	**CA**	90035	(213) 870-8435
BETAR	1204 SOUTH STEARNS DRIVE	LOS ANGELES	**CA**	90035	(213) 934-0032
B'NAI ZION	6351 WILSHIRE BOULEVARD, SUITE 211	LOS ANGELES	**CA**	90048	(213) 655-9128
DROR CHAPTER	6351 WILSHIRE BLVD, SUITE 211	LOS ANGELES	**CA**	90048	(213) 655-9128
JEWISH PEACE ALLIANCE	3208 CAHUENGA BOULEVARD WEST	LOS ANGELES	**CA**	90068	(213) 828-6589
LABOR ZIONIST ALLIANCE	8339 WEST THIRD STREET	LOS ANGELES	**CA**	90048	(213) 655-2842
PIONEER WOMEN-NA'AMAT	5820 WILSHIRE BLVD	LOS ANGELES	**CA**	90036	(213) 938-9149
PIONEER WOMEN-NA'AMAT	1494 S. ROBERTSON BLVD	LOS ANGELES	**CA**	90035	(213) 275-5345
TAGAR	1204 SOUTH STEARNS DRIVE	LOS ANGELES	**CA**	90035	(213) 934-0032
TELEM	6505 WILSHIRE BOULEVARD, SUITE 811	LOS ANGELES	**CA**	90048	(213) 658-5021
ZIONIST ORGANIZATION OF AMERICA	5225 WILSHIRE BOULEVARD, SUITE 717	LOS ANGELES	**CA**	90036	(213) 938-9183
PIONEER WOMEN-NA'AMAT	5511 EL CAJON BLVD., UJF BUILDING	SAN DIEGO	**CA**	92115	(619) 265-1325
AZF AMERICAN ZIONIST ORGANIZATION, NORTHERN CALIFORNIA REGION	2266 GEARY BOULEVARD	SAN FRANCISCO	**CA**	94118	(415) 931-5155
ZIONIST ORGANIZATION OF AMERICA	46 KEARNY STREET	SAN FRANCISCO	**CA**	94108	(415) 391-7741
GRASP	PO BOX 5433	SHERMAN OAKS	**CA**	91403	
ASSOC. OF REFORM ZIONISTS OF AMERICA - UAHC	13107 VENTURA BOULEVARD	STUDIO CITY	**CA**	91604	(213) 986-5720
PIONEER WOMEN-NA'AMAT	13609 VICTORY BLVD	VAN NUYS	**CA**	91401	(818) 780-4165
AMERICAN ISRAEL PUBLIC AFFAIRS COMMITTEE (AIPAC)	500 NORTH CAPITOL STREET, NORTHWEST, SUITE 300	WASHINGTON	**DC**	20001	(202) 638-2256
JEWISH ACTIVIST FRONT-ISRAEL INFORMATION CENTER	800 21ST STREET N.W. ROOM 417	WASHINGTON	**DC**	20006	(202) 686-7574
PIONEER WOMEN-NA'AMAT	1303 N. STATE ROAD 7	MARGATE	**FL**	33063	(305) 979-3311
FARBAND LABOR ZIONIST ALLIANCE	1 LINCOLN ROAD, SUITE 320	MIAMI BEACH	**FL**	33139	(305) 532-1887
PIONEER WOMEN-NA'AMAT	605 LINCOLN ROAD	MIAMI BEACH	**FL**	33139	(305) 538-6213
BETAR EDUCATIONAL YOUTH ORGANIZATION	C/O JCC, 2808 HORATIO STREET	TAMPA	**FL**	33609	(813) 872-4451
TAGAR	C/O JCC, 2808 HORATIO STREET	TAMPA	**FL**	33609	(813) 872-4451
CHICAGO ZIONIST FEDERATION	220 S. STATE STREET	CHICAGO	**IL**	60604	(312) 922-5282
PIONEER WOMEN-NA'AMAT	220 S. STATE STREET	CHICAGO	**IL**	60604	(312) 922-3736
ZIONIST ORGANIZATION OF CHICAGO	6328 N. CALIFORNIA AVENUE	CHICAGO	**IL**	60659	(312) 973-3232
PIONEER WOMEN-NA'AMAT	466 CENTRAL AVENUE	NORTHFIELD	**IL**	60093	(312) 446-7275
MIZRACHI-HAPOEL HAMIZRACHI OF NEW ENGLAND	611 WASHINGTON STREET	BOSTON	**MA**	02111	(617) 426-9148
NEW ENGLAND ZIONIST FEDERATION	17 COMMONWEALTH AVENUE	BOSTON	**MA**	02116	(617) 267-2235
PIONEER WOMEN-NA'AMAT	294 WASHINGTON STREET	BOSTON	**MA**	02108	(617) 426-1059
RELIGIOUS ZIONISTS OF AMERICA-N.E. REGION	611 WASHINGTON STREET, ROOM 507	BOSTON	**MA**	02110	(617) 426-9148
ZIONIST HOUSE-ISRAEL CULTURAL CENTER	17 COMMONWEALTH AVENUE	BOSTON	**MA**	02116	(617) 267-3600
ZIONIST ORGANIZATION OF AMERICA-NEW ENGLAND REGION	17 COMMONWEALTH AVENUE	BOSTON	**MA**	02116	(617) 437-1647
HERUT-UNITED ZIONIST REVISIONISTS OF AMERICA	388 N. MAIN STREET	SHARON	**MA**	02067	
CANADIAN ZIONIST FEDERATION-MIDWEST, THE	365 HARGRAVE STREET	WINNIPEG	**MB**	R3B 2K3	(204) 943-6494
PIONEER WOMEN-NA'AMAT	1727 MAIN STREET	WINNIPEG	**MB**	R2V 1Z4	(204) 334-3637
AMERICAN MIZRACHI WOMEN-SARAH RIBAKOW CHAPTER	8415 ALLENSWOOD ROAD	BALTIMORE	**MD**	21133	(301) 655-4141
PIONEER WOMEN - NA'AMAT, BALTIMORE COUNCIL	3612 FORDS LANE	BALTIMORE	**MD**	21215	(301) 358-3337
RELIGIOUS ZIONISTS OF AMERICA	3911 EMMART AVENUE	BALTIMORE	**MD**	21215	(301) 466-5255
ZIONIST ORGANIZATION OF AMERICA	6503 PARK HEIGHTS AVENUE	BALTIMORE	**MD**	21215	(301) 358-2000
PIONEER WOMEN-NA'AMAT	OHR KODESH SYNAGOGUE, 8402 FREYMAN DRIVE	CHEVY CHASE	**MD**	20815	(301) 565-3130
PIONEER WOMEN-NA'AMAT	25900 GREENFIELD, ROOM 205D	OAK PARK	**MI**	48237	(313) 967-4750
DETROIT ZIONIST FEDERATION, THE	6600 W. MAPLE ROAD	WEST BLOOMFIELD	**MI**	48033	(313) 661-1000
HISTADRUT ISRAEL LABOR CAMPAIGN	4517 MINNETONKA BLVD	MINNEAPOLIS	**MN**	55416	(612) 927-4927
ZIONIST ORGANIZATION OF AMERICA	1595 HIGHLAND PARKWAY	ST. PAUL	**MN**	55116	(612) 698-3234
PIONEER WOMEN-NA'AMAT	8123 DELMAR BLVD	ST. LOUIS	**MO**	63130	(314) 721-5856
ZIONIST ORGANIZATION OF AMERICA	2816 MORRIS AVENUE	UNION CITY	**NJ**	07083	(201) 964-0100
CANADIAN ZIONIST FEDERATION-ATLANTIC, THE	5675 SPRING GARDEN ROAD	HALIFAX	**NS**	B3J 1H1	(902) 422-7491
BRIT TRUMPELDOR BETAR OF AMERICA, INC.	85-40 149TH STREET	BRIARWOOD MANOR	**NY**	11435	(718) 526-3310
BETH AM-LABOR ZIONIST CENTER	1182 BRIGHTON BEACH AVENUE	BROOKLYN	**NY**	11235	(718) 646-9409
PIONEER WOMEN-NA'AMAT	3858 NOSTRAND AVENUE	BROOKLYN	**NY**	11229	(718) 769-9604
PIONEER WOMEN-NA'AMAT	1931 MOTT AVENUE	FAR ROCKAWAY	**NY**	11691	(718) 471-8453
PIONEER WOMEN-NA'AMAT	45 CONKLIN STREET	FARMINGDALE	**NY**	11735	(516) 735-2675
ARZA-ASSOCIATION OF REFORM ZIONISTS OF AMERICA	838 FIFTH AVENUE	NEW YORK	**NY**	10021	(212) 249-0100
AMERICA ISRAEL FRIENDSHIP HOUSE OF BNAI ZION	136 EAST 39TH STREET	NEW YORK	**NY**	10016	(212) 725-1211
AMERICAN FRIENDS OF BEIT HALOCHEM	136 EAST 39TH STREET	NEW YORK	**NY**	10016	(212) 725-1211
AMERICAN JEWISH ALTERNATIVES TO ZIONISM	133 E. 73RD STREET, SUITE 404	NEW YORK	**NY**	10021	(212) 628-2727
AMERICAN JEWISH LEAGUE FOR ISRAEL	595 MADISON AVENUE	NEW YORK	**NY**	10022	(212) 371-1583
AMERICAN ZIONIST FEDERATION	515 PARK AVENUE	NEW YORK	**NY**	10022	(212) 371-7750
AMERICAN ZIONIST YOUTH COUNCIL	515 PARK AVENUE	NEW YORK	**NY**	10022	(212) 751-6070
AMERICAN ZIONIST YOUTH FOUNDATION RESOURCE CENTER	515 PARK AVENUE	NEW YORK	**NY**	10022	(212) 751-6070
AMERICANS FOR PROGRESSIVE ISRAEL-HASHOMER HATZAIR	150 FIFTH AVENUE	NEW YORK	**NY**	10010	(212) 255-8760
ASSOCIATION OF REFORM ZIONISTS OF AMERICA	838 FIFTH AVENUE	NEW YORK	**NY**	10021	(212) 249-0100
B'NAI ZION	136 E. 39TH STREET	NEW YORK	**NY**	10016	(212) 725-1211
BAR/BAT MITZVAH PILGRIMAGE - WORLD ZIONIST ORGANIZATION	515 PARK AVENUE	NEW YORK	**NY**	10022	(212) 752-0600
BETAR	9 EAST 38TH STREET	NEW YORK	**NY**	10016	(212) 696-0080
BNAI ZION-AMERICAN FRATERNAL ZIONIST ORGANIZATION	136 EAST 39TH STREET	NEW YORK	**NY**	10016	(202) 725-1211
BNEI AKIVA OF NORTH AMERICA	25 W. 26TH STREET	NEW YORK	**NY**	10010	(212) 889-5260
CONTINUING SEMINAR ON ZIONIST THOUGHT	9 EAST 40TH STREET	NEW YORK	**NY**	10016	(212) 532-5615
DOR HEMSHECH, UNITED STATES	515 PARK AVENUE	NEW YORK	**NY**	10022	(212) 752-0600
DROR YOUNG ZIONIST ORGANIZATIONS	215 PARK AVENUE S	NEW YORK	**NY**	10003	(212) 777-9388
FARBAND LABOR ZIONIST ORDER	575 6TH AVENUE	NEW YORK	**NY**	10011	(212) 989-0300
HAPOEL HAMIZRACHI WOMEN'S ZIONIST ORGANIZATION	370 SEVENTH AVENUE	NEW YORK	**NY**	10001	(212) 564-9045
HASHACHAR	50 W. 58TH STREET	NEW YORK	**NY**	10019	(212) 355-7900
HASHOMER HATZAIR SOCIALIST ZIONIST YOUTH MOVEMENT	150 FIFTH AVENUE, #710	NEW YORK	**NY**	10010	(212) 929-4955
HERUT-U.S.A. (UNITED REVISIONISTS OF AMERICA)	41 EAST 42ND STREET	NEW YORK	**NY**	10017	(212) 687-4502
HERUT ZIONISTS OF AMERICA, INC.	9 EAST 38TH STREET, SUITE 1000	NEW YORK	**NY**	10016	(212) 696-0900
ICHUD HABONIM LABOR ZIONIST YOUTH	575 SIXTH AVENUE	NEW YORK	**NY**	10011	(212) 255-1796
ICHUD HABONIM LABOR ZIONIST YOUTH	27 W. 20 STREET	NEW YORK	**NY**	10011	(212) 255-1796
JABOTINSKY FOUNDATION, INC., THE	261 FIFTH AVENUE	NEW YORK	**NY**	10016	(212) 679-6868
LABOR ZIONIST ALLIANCE	114 FIFTH AVENUE	NEW YORK	**NY**	10011	(212) 989-0300
LABOR ZIONIST ORGANIZATION OF AMERICA - POALE ZION	575 6TH AVENUE	NEW YORK	**NY**	10011	
LEAGUE FOR THE NATIONAL LABOR IN ISRAEL	60 EAST 42ND STREET	NEW YORK	**NY**	10165	(212) 599-3670
LEAGUE OF FRIENDS OF LABOR ISRAEL	114 FIFTH AVENUE	NEW YORK	**NY**	10011	(212) 675-7192
LEAGUE OF RELIGIOUS SETTLEMENTS, INC.	156 FIFTH AVENUE	NEW YORK	**NY**	10010	(212) 924-9475
NATIONAL COUNCIL FOR TORAH EDUCATION	C/O RELIGIOUS ZIONISTS OF AMERICA, 25 W. 26TH STREET	NEW YORK	**NY**	10010	(212) 289-1414
NOAM - MIZRACHI NEW LEADERSHIP COUNCIL	25 WEST 26TH STREET	NEW YORK	**NY**	10010	(212) 684-6091
PIONEER WOMEN-NA'AMAT	200 MADISON AVENUE	NEW YORK	**NY**	10016	(212) 725-8010
RELIGIOUS ZIONISTS OF AMERICA (MIZRACHI-HAPOEL HAMIZRACHI)	25 WEST 26TH STREET	NEW YORK	**NY**	10010	(212) 689-1414
TAGAR	9 EAST 38TH STREET	NEW YORK	**NY**	10016	(212) 696-0080
THEODOR HERZL FOUNDATION	515 PARK AVENUE	NEW YORK	**NY**	10022	(212) 752-0600
THEODOR HERZL INSTITUTE	515 PARK AVENUE	NEW YORK	**NY**	10022	(212) 752-0600
UNITED LABOR ZIONIST PARTY	305 BROADWAY	NEW YORK	**NY**	10007	
UNITED ZIONIST REVISIONISTS OF AMERICA-HERUT, U.S.A.	41 EAST 42ND STREET	NEW YORK	**NY**	10017	(212) 687-4502
WORLD CONFEDERATION OF UNITED ZIONISTS-HEAD OFFICE	595 MADISON AVENUE, ROOM 1004	NEW YORK	**NY**	10022	(212) 371-1452
WORLD UNION OF GENERAL ZIONISTS	ZOA HOUSE, 4 E. 34TH STREET	NEW YORK	**NY**	10016	(212) 481-1500
WORLD ZIONIST ORGANIZATION-AMERICAN SECTION	515 PARK AVENUE	NEW YORK	**NY**	10022	(212) 752-0600
ZIONIST ARCHIVES & LIBRARY/WORLD ZIONIST ORG.-AMER. SECTION	515 PARK AVENUE	NEW YORK	**NY**	10022	(212) 753-2167
ZIONIST ORGANIZATION OF AMERICA - ZOA HOUSE	4 EAST 34TH STREET	NEW YORK	**NY**	10016	(212) 481-1500
ASSOCIATION OF REFORM ZIONISTS OF AMERICA - ARZA	19425 VAN AKEN BLVD	CLEVELAND	**OH**	44122	(216) 283-1276
LABOR ZIONIST ALLIANCE	1708 BEACONWOOD DRIVE	CLEVELAND	**OH**	44121	(216) 241-2258
LABOR ZIONIST ALLIANCE	3715 WARRENSVILLE CENTER ROAD	CLEVELAND	**OH**	44122	(216) 752-2907
PIONEER WOMEN-NA'AMAT	13969 CEDAR ROAD, ROOM 208	CLEVELAND	**OH**	44418	(216) 321-2002
UNITED ZIONIST REVISIONISTS OF CLEVELAND	23759 WENDOVER DRIVE	CLEVELAND	**OH**	44122	(216) 381-3967
ZIONIST ORGANIZATION OF AMERICA	25400 FAIRMOUNT BLVD	CLEVELAND	**OH**	44122	(216) 321-6131
BETAR	P.O. BOX 21086	SOUTH EUCLID	**OH**	44121	(216) 932-1811
TAGAR	P.O. BOX 21086	SOUTH EUCLID	**OH**	44121	(216) 932-1811
ACHDUT HAAVODA-POALE ZION OF CANADA	272 CODSELL AVENUE	DOWNSVIEW	**ON**	M3H 3X2	(416) 636-4021
PIONEER WOMEN-NA'AMAT	272 CODSELL AVENUE	DOWNSVIEW	**ON**	M3H 3X2	(416) 636-5425
CANADIAN ZIONIST FEDERATION-CENTRAL, THE	788 MARLEE AVENUE	TORONTO	**ON**	M6B 3K1	(416) 787-6171
LABOR ZIONIST ALLIANCE	14 VIEWMOUNT AVENUE	TORONTO	**ON**	M6B 1T3	(416) 787-0339
LABOR ZIONIST MOVEMENT OF CANADA	3101 BATHURST STREET, SUITE 305	TORONTO	**ON**	M6A 2A6	(416) 783-8440
ZIONIST ORGANIZATION OF CANADA	788 MARLEE AVENUE	TORONTO	**ON**	M6B 3K1	(416) 781-3571
ZIONIST REVISIONIST ORGANIZATION OF CANADA	3417 BATHURST STREET	TORONTO	**ON**		
PIONEER WOMEN-NA'AMAT	1405 LOCUST STREET, ROOM 1117	PHILADELPHIA	**PA**	19102	(215) 545-1328
PIONEER WOMEN-NA'AMAT	6328 FORBES AVENUE	PITTSBURGH	**PA**	15217	(412) 521-5253
CANADIAN ZIONIST FEDERATION, THE	1310 GREENE AVENUE	MONTREAL	**QU**	H3Z 2B2	(514) 934-0804
HASHOMER HATZAIR	5234 CLANRANALD AVENUE	MONTREAL	**QU**	H3X 2S4	
JEWISH COLONISATION ASSOCIATION OF CANADA	5151 COTE ST. CATHERINE ROAD	MONTREAL	**QU**	H3W 1M6	
LABOR ZIONIST MOVEMENT OF CANADA	4770 KENT AVENUE	MONTREAL	**QU**	H3W 1H2	(514) 735-1593
MIZRACHI-HAPOEL HAMIZRACHI ORGANIZATION OF CANADA	5497A VICTORIA AVENUE, SUITE 101	MONTREAL	**QU**	H3W 2R1	(514) 739-4748
PIONEER WOMEN-NA'AMAT	4770 KENT AVENUE, SUITE 304	MONTREAL	**QU**	H3W 1H2	(514) 735-6253
ZIONIST REVISIONIST ORGANIZATIONS OF CANADA	5234 CLANRANALD AVENUE	MONTREAL	**QU**	H3X 2S4	
STUDENT ZIONIST ORGANIZATIONS	1310 GREENE AVENUE	WESTMOUNT	**QU**	H3Z 2B2	(514) 934-0804